The first book of its kind, the **Handbook of Research on Sport Psychology** contains an extensive array of chapters on theories, research, and applications authored by a host of international experts.

This valuable resource not only covers what is presently known in sport psychology, but extends to the frontiers of investigation, where conclusions have yet to be drawn. The authors emphasize a comprehensive treatment of each research area cited and link findings and methods throughout the **Handbook**'s entire research collection.

Ultimately, this book provides its readers with useful theoretical explanations for current findings in sport psychology and guides them to new areas of research activity.

The **Handbook**'s forty-four chapters begin with a general orientation on research in sport psychology. The book goes on to cover a variety of specialized areas of research and influence in the field. The second section deals with assessment of skill acquisition, followed by a section on psychological characteristics and high-level performance. Another section deals with social-cognitive dimensions of motivation, leading to a discussion of research on popular psychological techniques that may enhance athletic performance.

Social factors such as socialization, moral psychology, and the impact of spectators on athletic performance are addressed, followed by a specific consideration of group structure, leadership, and group psychology. Also assessed are the connections between sport and life-span development, including age, gender, and enhancement of the quality of life. The coverage of specific research topics concludes with discussions on exercise and health psychology.

The **Handbook** goes on to explore research methodology in a stimulating section on psychometrics. Analyses of research paradigms and protocols typically used in sport psychology are provided, as well as suggestions on how to improve current research methods.

(Continued on back flap)

HANDBOOK OF RESEARCH
ON SPORT PSYCHOLOGY

Errata

Page	For	Read
6, line 38	fifteenth of December	sixteenth of December
21, line 12	December 15	December 16
53, line 25	assistant director, William White	assistant executive secretary, Walter White

HANDBOOK OF RESEARCH ON SPORT PSYCHOLOGY

Sponsored by The International Society of Sport Psychology

EDITED BY:

Robert N. Singer

Milledge Murphey

L. Keith Tennant

MACMILLAN PUBLISHING COMPANY
New York

Collier Macmillan Canada
Toronto

Maxwell Macmillan International
New York   Oxford   Singapore   Sydney

Macmillan Publishing Company   Maxwell Macmillan Canada, Inc.
866 Third Avenue   1200 Eglinton Avenue East, Suite 200
New York, NY 10022   Don Mills, Ontario M3C 3N1

Macmillan Publishing Company is part of the Maxwell Communication Group

Library of Congress Catalog Card Number: 92-13400

Printed in the United States of America

printing number
1 2 3 4 5 6 7 8 9 10

Library of Congress Cataloging-in-Publication Data
Handbook of research on sport psychology / sponsored by The
   International Society of Sport Psychology ; edited by Robert N.
   Singer, Milledge Murphey, L. Keith Tennant.
      p. cm.
   Includes indexes.
   ISBN 0-02-897195-7 (alk. paper)
   1. Sports—Psychological aspects. 2. Sports—Research.
I. Singer, Robert N. II. Murphey, Milledge. III. Tennant, L.
Keith. IV. International Society of Sport Psychology.
GV706.4.H37 1993
796'.01—dc20   92-13400
                                CIP

CONTENTS

Section I

OVERVIEW OF SPORT PSYCHOLOGY

Section II

SKILL ACQUISITION

Section III

PSYCHOLOGICAL CHARACTERISTICS AND HIGH-LEVEL PERFORMANCE

Section IV

SOCIAL-COGNITIVE DIMENSIONS OF MOTIVATIONS

Section V

PSYCHOLOGICAL TECHNIQUES FOR INDIVIDUAL PERFORMANCE

Section VI

SOCIAL INFLUENCES

Section X

PSYCHOMETRICS

Section XI

PROFESSIONAL ETHICS IN SPORT PSYCHOLOGY

PREFACE

A volume of this magnitude is indeed an ambitious project. As the first comprehensive overview of contemporary research associated with the many dimensions of sport psychology, it required a great deal of risk taking in determining, to begin with, the topics to be included. How should they be treated? Sequenced? Who should be invited to author chapters? How could we maximize a representation of research activities throughout the world, considering language barriers and difficulties in having access to published research in different countries, written in native languages?

Then there were mechanical considerations. We, the editors, decided on a limited time frame of objectives that would, in sequence, lead to the completion of the entire manuscript within one year from its conception to the time it would be submitted to Macmillan. The process included the formation of an international advisory board of experts to review our proposed book outline and to provide helpful comments for its refinement. Potential authors were identified and asked to write the chapters. Replacements were necessary on occasion, when commitments could not be honored. Chapters were written, edited preliminarily by the editors, and mailed to reviewers who had agreed to be involved in this stage of the project. Our comments and those of reviewers were forwarded to the authors. Chapters were revised and returned to us.

We then reviewed every chapter again and contacted authors for missing information or clarification of ideas as needed. Chapters were cross-referenced as to where supplementary material on certain topics could be located in other chapters in the *Handbook*. Then all the text material was forwarded to Macmillan, in slightly less than a year from the time we began the project! Macmillan took it from there. The editing, revising, and production process took 8 months to bring the book to fruition. We are extremely pleased that this project could be completed that quickly, considering the many chapters (44), the number of authors responsible for different parts of each chapter, and the international scope of the book (with numerous authors from other countries), which made lapses in communication, understandings, and delays unavoidable.

And here it is.

The *Handbook* is truly comprehensive and contemporary. We attempted to include as many sport psychology-related topics as could be conceived. In different parts of the world, some areas are emphasized much more than others. Also there are difficulties and ambiguities in the use of such terms as *sport psychology, motor behavior, motor learning, motor control,* and *motor development.* In certain countries, distinct meanings are attached to these terms and separate bodies of knowledge are generated. However, in other countries such terms are used interchangeably and within the framework of the major title: Sport Psychology. We opted for the latter approach. That is, we attempted to include more rather than less, to provide the most encompassing picture possible concerning the nature of sport psychology.

The Table of Contents speaks for itself. However, it does not indicate chapters we would have liked to include but for various reasons were not able to. These chapters were: (1) "Risk-Taking Behavior"; (2) "The Motivation to Achieve"; (3) "The Aging Process and Achievement Potential"; (4) "Sport-Specific Tests and Non-Sport-Specific Tests"; (5) "Special Populations and Exercise Benefits"; and (6) "Future Directions in Research."

We would be remiss not to mention that Dorothy Harris had agreed to write the chapter "Individual Differences." Unfortunately Dorothy died of cancer on January 4, 1991, while in the process of developing her ideas. As one of the all-time leaders in sport psychology, as well as a person with endless energies, extreme dedication, and unparalleled compassion, she will be missed by the many friends and colleagues she amassed from all areas of the world.

This volume is intended as a source book for scholars interested in sport psychology everywhere. Serious students should also find the book valuable. Our major mission was to produce a comprehensive scholarly overview of research developments on the diverse contemporary themes that could be associated with the umbrella term *sport psychology.*

The book should be informative. It should provide a clear picture of what we know, as well as of what we don't know. The text has material that amplifies the body of knowledge as well as provides implications for practical approaches (e.g., psychological intervention strategies) that might be defensible in view of available research. Thus different perspectives can be experienced as one progresses through the contents. In addition, we would expect that the book will stimulate substantial awareness of research that has been done and what would appear to be undertaken, acknowledging conceptual and methodological considerations that might be improved based on shortcomings pointed out throughout various chapters.

This book would not have been realized without the contributions of many people. Lloyd Chilton, former series editor for Macmillan (and a close personal friend for over two decades), was the prime mover. He convinced us that the project, as immense as it would be (and was), would produce an invaluable sourcebook worldwide. More importantly he showed us that it was "do-able." Because of our (the editors) comprehensive understanding of research directions in sport psychology and our collaborative, efficient working style, he convinced us that we could manage the many tasks associated with the development and completion of the project.

Our Advisory Board made pertinent suggestions for the refinement of our proposed outline of the book. Most important, of course, were the contributions of the authors themselves, especially considering the tight time constraints the editors established in order to complete the operations. We wanted all text material to be timely when the book was published. Also, these authors are among the most prolific scholars in the world. They had to budget their time for their respective chapters in the context of all of their other responsibilities. Their considerate and considerable efforts to produce quality manuscripts, and to revise them according to comments made by reviewers, are greatly appreciated. And of course, the constructive suggestions of the reviewers for each chapter strengthened the text even more.

Our secretarial staff, including June Masters, Diane Williams, Susie Weldon, and Jo Lynn Drake, provided the necessary technical assistance. From producing extensive correspondence to helping with the editing and retyping process, they kept things moving, and moving effectively.

Furthermore, only a book company with the reputation of Macmillan could produce a book of this magnitude with such quality, such cooperation, and in a reasonable time period. We are forever indebted to the editorial and production services provided by Macmillan. We are also proud to have the *Handbook of Research on Sport Psychology* published by such a prestigious company. Many people at Macmillan helped to bring this book to fruition—namely, publisher Phil Friedman, managing editor Michael Sander, project editor Scott Kurtz, copy editor Joan Zseleczky, production director Terri Dieli, and production assistant Ben Barros.

The International Society of Sport Psychology (ISSP) is honored to have the opportunity to officially endorse the book. Formed in 1965, the ISSP has been the major influence on the development and advancement of sport psychology societies and activities in all parts of the globe. Proceeds from book sales will go to the ISSP, to enable it to further its valuable contributions in supporting professional sport psychology activities in their many and diverse forms.

Finally we would like to express our gratitude to the University of Florida, and particularly the Department of Exercise and Sport Sciences, for the encouragement and support continually given throughout the duration of the project.

As can be seen, the *Handbook* is the result of the efforts of many individuals, collaborating in a harmonious manner, within a series of rigid time frames for the fulfillment of each facet of the production. To say that this was merely a team effort would be an understatement. The work represents the highest level of cooperative interaction.

We look forward to the publication of the next *Handbook of Research on Sport Psychology*, perhaps 5 to 10 years from now. It should be even better, as research efforts will be continually expanding and becoming more sophisticated through the subsequent years. We hope that our *Handbook* will provide an impetus for research that will lead to future major breakthroughs in the many important areas associated with sport psychology. Such research will help make the next *Handbook* even more comprehensive, insightful, and valuable in providing the relevant knowledge base in sport psychology. In turn, sport psychology will receive even greater attention and recognition for its many real and potential contributions to the high-level athlete and highly competitive teams, as well as to the average/recreational athlete/exerciser interested in some form of engagement and fulfillment.

Robert N. Singer
Milledge Murphey
L. Keith Tennant

ADDRESSES OF CONTRIBUTING AUTHORS

Abernethy, Bruce
Department of Human Movement Studies
The University of Queensland
Brisbane, Queensland
Australia

Anshel, Mark H.
Department of Human Movement Science
University of Wollongong
Wollongong, New South Wales
Australia

Bar-Eli, Michael
Department of Research & Sports Medicine
Wingate Institute
Netanya
Israel

Bahrke, Michael S.
Department of Physical Education and Dance
University of Wisconsin–Madison
Madison, Wisconsin

Berger, Bonnie G.
Department of Physical Education
Brooklyn College
Brooklyn, New York

Biddle, Stuart J. H.
School of Education Saint Lukes
University of Exeter
Exeter
England

Boutcher, Steve
Department of Human Movement Science
University of Wollongong
Wollongong, New South Wales
Australia

Brawley, Lawrence R.
Department of Kinesiology
University of Waterloo
Waterloo, Ontario
Canada

Bredemeier, Brenda J. Light
Department of Physical Education
University of California
Berkeley, California

Brustad, Robert J.
School of Kinesiology and Physical Education
University of Northern Colorado
Greeley, Colorado

Burton, Damon
Division of HPERD
University of Idaho
Moscow, Idaho

Carron, Albert V.
Faculty of Kinseiology
The University of Western Ontario
London, Ontario
Canada

Chamberlin, Craig
Department of Kinesiology and Physical Education
University College of the Fraser Valley
Abbotsford, British Columbia
Canada

Chelladurai, P.
School of HPER
The Ohio State University
Columbus, Ohio

Coakley, Jay
Center for the Study of Sport and Leisure
University of Colorado at Colorado Springs
Colorado Springs, Colorado

Cox, Richard H.
Department of Health and Physical Education
University of Missouri–Columbia
Columbia, Missouri

Crews, Debra J.
University of North Carolina–Greensboro
Department of Exercise and Sport Science
Greensboro, North Carolina

De Cuyper, Bert
Katholieke Vlaamse Hogeschool
St. Andriesstraat 2
Antwerpen
Belgium

Dishman, Rod K.
Department of Exercise Science
University of Georgia
Athens, Georgia

Duda, Joan L.
Department of Physical Education, Health, and
    Recreation Studies
West Lafayette, Indiana

Fujita, Atsushi H.
College of Humanities and Sciences
Nihon University
Tokyo
Japan

Gallagher, Jere D.
Department of Health, Physical and Recreation Education
University of Pittsburgh
Pittsburgh, Pennsylvania

Gallois, Cynthia
Department of Psychology
The University of Queensland
Queensland
Australia

Gauvin, Lise
Department of Exercise Science
Concordia University
Montreal, Quebec
Canada

Gessaroli, M.E.
Department of Education
University of Ottawa
Ottawa, Ontario
Canada

Gill, Diane L.
Department of Exercise and Sport Science
University of North Carolina at Greensboro
Greensboro, North Carolina

Glencross, Denis
School of Psychology
Curtin University of Technology
Perth, Western Australia
Australia

Hackfort, Dieter
Institut für Sportwissenschaft und Sport
Universität der Bundeswehr München
Neuberg
Germany

Hanrahan, Stephanie
Department of Human Movement Studies
The University of Queensland
Brisbane, Queensland
Australia

Hill, Karen L.
Department of Exercise and Sport Science
Pennsylvania State University
University Park, Pennsylvania

Ichimura, Soichi
Institute of Health and Sport Sciences
University of Tsukuba
Tsukuba, P.C.
Japan

Kantor, Elena
Laboratory of Psychology
Central Scientific Research Institute of Sports
    and Physical Culture
Moscow
Russia

Lee, Timothy D.
School of Physical Education and Athletics
McMaster University
Hamilton, Ontario
Canada

Lerner, J. Dana
Department of Human Services
University of Virginia
Charlottesville, Virginia

Liu, Zhan
Department of Human Performance and Sport Studies
University of Tennessee
Knoxville, Tennessee

Magill, Richard
Department of Kinesiology
Louisiana State University
Baton Rouge, Louisiana

McCullagh, Penny
Department of Kinesiology
University of Colorado
Boulder, Colorado

McInman, Adrian
Department of Human Movement and Recreation Studies
University of West Australia
Nedlands, Western Australia
Australia

Nideffer, Robert N.
1320 Dexter Place
Escondido, California

Ogilvie, Bruce
P.O. Box 194
Los Gatos, California

Oglesby, Carole A.
Department of Physical Education
Temple University
Philadelphia, Pennsylvania

Pargman, David
Department of Educational Research
Florida State University
Tallahassee, Florida

Paulus, Paul B.
Department of Psychology
University of Texas at Arlington
Arlington, Texas

Qiu, Yijun
Department of Sport Psychology
Wuhan Institute of Physical Education
Wuchang, Wuhan
China

Qiu, Zhuo-Ying
Department of Sport Psychology
Wuhan Institute of Physical Education
Wuchang, Wuhan
China

Raglin, John S.
Department of Kinesiology
Indiana University
Bloomington, Indiana

Régnier, Guy
Régie De LaSécurité Dans Les Sports Du Québec
100, Rue Laviolette, Bureau 114
Trois-Rivières, Québec
Canada

Ripoll, Hubert
U.F.R. d'Activités Physiques et Sportives
Université de Poitiers
Poitiers
France

Roberts, Glyn
Department of Kinesiology
University of Illinois
Urbana, Illinois

Roepke, Nancy
Department of Psychology
University of Arizona
Tucson, Arizona

Rotella, Robert
Department of Human Services
University of Virginia
Charlottesville, Virginia

Russell, Storm J.
Canadian Fitness and Lifestyle
  Research Institute
Gloucester, Ontario
Canada

Ryzonkin, Juri
Laboratory of Psychology
Central Scientific Research Institute of Sports
  and Physical Culture
Moscow
Russia

Rzewnicki, Randy
Katholieke Universiteit Leuven
Instituut voor Lichamelijke Opleiding
Leuven
Belgium

Sachs, Michael L.
Department of Physical Education
Temple University
Philadelphia, Pennsylvania

Salmela, John
School of Human Kinetics
University of Ottawa
Ottawa Ontario
Canada

Schutz, Robert W.
School of Physical Education
University of British Columbia
Vancouver, British Columbia
Canada

Schwenkmezger, Peter
Fachbereich I–Psychologie
Universität Trier
Trier
Germany

Shields, David L. Light
Peace and Conflict Studies
University of California at Berkeley
Berkeley, California

Suinn, Richard
Department of Psychology
Colorado State University
Ft. Collins, Colorado

Takenaka, Koji
Department of Lifelong Education
Okayama University School of Education
Okayama
Japan

Taylor, Jim
Center for Psychological Studies
Nova University
Ft. Lauderdale, Florida

Tenenbaum, Gershon
Department of Research and Sports Medicine
Wingate Institute
Netanya
Israel

Thill, Edgar
U.F.R. de Psychologie
Université Blaise Pascal
Clermont-Ferrand
France

Thirer, Joel
Division of Physical Education,
Recreation and Athletics
State University of New York at Binghamton
Binghamton, New York

Thomas, Jerry R.
Department of Exercise Science and Physical Education
Arizona State University
Tempe, Arizona

Thomas, Katherine T.
Department of Exercise Science and Physical Education
Arizona State University
Tempe, Arizona

Van Mele, Veerle
Instituut voor Lichamelijke Opleiding
Katholieke Universiteit Leuven
Leuven
Belgium

Vanden Auweele, Yves
Instituut voor Lichamelijke Opleiding
Katholieke Universiteit Leuven
Leuven
Belgium

Widmeyer, W. Neil
Department of Kinesiology
University of Waterloo
Waterloo, Ontario
Canada

Williams, Jean
School of Health Related Professions
University of Arizona
Tucson, Arizona

Wrisberg, Craig A.
Department of Human Performance and Sport Studies
University of Tennessee
Knoxville, Tennessee

Yesalis, III, Charles E.
Departments of Health Policy and Administration and
   Exercise and Sport Science
Pennsylvania State University
University Park, Pennsylvania

Zaichkowsky, Leonard
Department of Developmental Studies and Counseling
Boston University
Boston, Massachusettes

Zillmann, Dolf
Department of Psychology
University of Alabama
Tuscaloosa, Alabama

LIST OF REVIEWERS

The editors would like to acknowledge the important contribution made by those individuals listed below. These reviewers were responsible for ensuring that chapter authors emphasized a conceptual orientation for their areas and provided a comprehensive, integrated discussion of the research. Each chapter was reviewed by two or three reviewers. Specifically, reviewers were to consider whether the manuscripts (1) were comprehensive and complete, (2) included relevant research, (3) posed significant questions about future directions for research, and (4) read smoothly. We appreciate the involvement of the following reviewers:

Bruce Abernethy
Fran Allard
Gloria Balague
David R. Brown
James H. Cauraugh
Robert Christina
Jay Coakley
Peter R. E. Crocker
Henry Davis
Janice M. Deakin
Rod K. Dishman
Jacques Douchamps
Mary Duquin
Craig Fisher
Karen E. French
Jeffery H. Goldstein
Sandy Gordon
Susan L. Greendorfer
J. Robert Grove
Craig R. Hall
Charles J. Hardy
Cynthia A. Hasbrook

Kate F. Hays
John Heil
Don Hellison
Keith Henschen
Steve Houseworth
Don R. Kirkendall
Karla A. Kubitz
Timothy D. Lee
Arnold LeUnes
Edward McAuley
Andrew Meyers
Shane M. Murphy
Mimi Murray
Jack Nations
Robert N. Nideffer
Vincent Nougier
Patrick J. O'Connor
Andrew C. Ostrow
David Pargman
Cynthia L. Pemberton
Linda M. Petlichkoff
Jack Rejeski

Hubert Ripoll
Glyn Roberts
Mary E. Rudisill
Brent Rushall
Michael Sachs
Charles H. Shea
John M. Silva
Daniel Smith
Frank L. Smoll
Kevin S. Spink
Janet Starkes
Stephan Swinnen
Jim Taylor
Gershon Tenenbaum
Jerry R. Thomas
Michael G. Wade
Leonard M. Wankel
Maureen R. Weiss
Klaus Willimczik
Carolee J. Winstein
Leonard Zaichkowsky

PROLOGUE

The topics covered in this *Handbook* and their order of appearance received much consideration from the editors. Our intent was to address those contemporary areas, issues, and research thrusts that were considered viable and of potential interest to sport psychologists throughout the world and to weave these topics into a logically presented format. The content and sequence of the *Handbook* reached fruition in the following structure.

The *Handbook* has been divided into 11 different sections that include 44 chapters. These sections include a wide range of topics and are designed to view sport psychology from.a broad and comprehensive perspective. The initial part, Section I, consists of two chapters that attempt to provide a general orientation about research in sport psychology. Chapter 1 presents an overview that addresses sport psychology from primarily a North American orientation and sets the tone for the remainder of the *Handbook*. Chapter 2 highlights contemporary areas of research in six arbitrarily selected countries.

Section II includes a number of topics that pertain to the acquisition of skill. Typically many of these areas, such as levels of skill performance, children's capabilities, attention, modeling, decision making, feedback, practice conditions, and conceptual directions are found in standard motor learning texts. The editors felt that discussions on these topics were relevant to sport psychology since a basic understanding of the nature of skill and how it is acquired is a necessary prerequisite for many of the subsequent sections, especially the use of intervention strategies.

Following this part, Section III introduces a variety of psychological considerations and how they relate to high-level performance. Research that has been of particular interest to sport psychologists and is discussed in this section includes personality testing and athletic performance, the prediction of success and talent detection, the nature of competitiveness, anxiety, aggression, and individual difference considerations.

The fourth section of the *Handbook* examines contemporary perspectives of motivation. Motivational factors have attracted considerable research interest, particularly the social-cognitive dimensions. Emphasized in this section are such topics as attributions and perceived ability. Motivation is also addressed in other chapters in this volume from different perspectives, in chapters on youth in sport, goal setting, and exercise adherence.

Section V offers six chapters that provide opportunities for reviewing research pertaining to popular psychological techniques that may help to enhance athletic performance. Such intervention strategies enable applied sport psychologists to help an individual athlete to compete more effectively. Topics in this section cover a broad spectrum of areas of interest, including considerations in goal setting, self-regulation strategies, attention control, coping with competitive stress, imaging for performance, and optimizing arousal level.

Social factors are discussed next in Section VI of the *Handbook*. This unit begins with an examination of sport and socialization factors and concludes with a review of the research literature on spectators and their impact on the athlete in performance. This unit naturally leads to the following section, which includes perspectives on group dynamics. This area, Section VII, specifically addresses the nature of formal group structure and group psychology, with special emphasis on personal interactions, leadership styles, and the nature of small groups.

In the life-span development section, Section VIII, special groups or topics have been targeted for discussion because they are generating increasing interest in sport psychology. These include unique considerations for youth in sport, gender, and athletes who have ended their careers. Also described is research on exercise for all-age groups and psychological benefits.

Sport psychology encompasses psychological factors associated with involvement in sport as well as regular programs of exercise. Readers may be familiar with exercise and its relationship to sport. However, a growing area of interest and literature has evolved in exercise/health psychology. Section IX begins by examining aspects of exercise adherence as well as aerobic exercise and emotions. In the latter part of this unit, topics related to psychological responses to special circumstances are addressed. They include the psychology of recovery from injury, psychological and behavioral variables associated with drug use, and an analysis of overtraining and staleness.

Section X deals with psychometrics. Analyses are made of research paradigms and protocols that are typically used in sport psychology research. Suggestions are made as to how to improve research methodology and the use of statistics. In another chapter, psychological testing and problems associated with tests are described.

The final section of the *Handbook* goes beyond science and research to address philosophical professional issues. The one chapter in Section XI takes a look at the ethical questions facing sport psychologists and how they are being resolved today. The viewpoint expressed in this section is from a U.S./Canadian orientation but may be of interest to sport psychologists in other parts of the world.

As mentioned earlier, our attempt was to provide a comprehensive, systematic overview of research associated with sport psychology. Some topics may have been inadvertently omitted. However, we hope that the *Handbook* will be an invaluable source as to the scope of scholarly activity currently being demonstrated by sport psychologists, and that all interested scholars will benefit from reviewing the following chapters.

HANDBOOK OF RESEARCH
ON SPORT PSYCHOLOGY

·1·

OVERVIEW OF SPORT PSYCHOLOGY

·1·

OVERVIEW OF SPORT PSYCHOLOGY

Richard H. Cox

Yijun Qiu

Zhan Liu

The purpose of this introductory chapter is to provide an overview of research in sport psychology from a historical as well as an intuitive perspective. The chapter has three main parts. Part one provides a brief introduction and history of sport psychology as an emerging scientific discipline. Part two is the core of the chapter and addresses the topic of research in sport psychology. In this part, research is discussed in terms of past and current trends, important questions that need to be addressed, and future directions. Finally, in part three, the authors will provide a summary and synthesis of sport psychology research from a historical perspective.

HISTORICAL PERSPECTIVE OF SPORT PSYCHOLOGY

Sport psychology is the science of applying psychology to sport. Psychology as a discipline has existed as long as man has been interested in studying the mind and its influence on the body and human behavior. As sport psychology has emerged as a discipline, the delineation of what a sport psychologist does has also developed. Presently, various individuals who are referred to as sport psychologists can be doing very different kinds of things. If someone is considered to be a *research* sport psychologist, then he or she is interested in the discovery and development of new knowledge associated with the discipline of sport psychology. For example, the research sport psychologist is concerned with testing theory and various conceptual models that purport to predict sport behavior. If, on the other hand, someone indicates that (s)he is an *educational* sport psychologist,

then (s)he is primarily involved in the dissemination of sport psychology knowledge. University and college professors are typically some combination of educational and research sport psychologists. A third category of sport psychologist is the *clinical,* or *counseling,* sport psychologist. The clinical/counseling sport psychologist is professionally prepared to help athletes who experience severe emotional problems associated with such things as depression, anxiety, drug dependency, and interpersonal conflict. The three categories of sport psychology have been clearly differentiated by the United States Olympic Committee (USOC, 1983; May, 1986).

From a worldwide perspective, sport psychology has experienced its greatest growth in North America and in Eastern Europe. In this historical review, we will touch briefly on these two geopolitical areas. The emphasis in this chapter is on North America and current historical perspectives. The next chapter will focus on other geographic areas in the world.

North America

It is likely that applied sport psychology took place long before the term *sport psychology* was ever used. For example, it is reasonable to assume that the ancient Greeks must have placed some emphasis on the mental preparation needed for Olympic competition. Indeed, the early Greek philosophers speculated about the mind-body relationship (Zeigler, 1964).

Perhaps the first clear example of research being conducted in the area of sport psychology was reported by Norman Triplett (1897). Triplett studied the performance of cyclists in various conditions of social interaction and concluded that the presence of other competitors facilitated or enhanced cycling performance. This initial research laid the foundation for what is currently referred to as social facilitation research. Although Triplett provided one of the first examples of sport psychology research, he was not the first individual to systematically conduct research in this area (Wiggins, 1984). According to Kroll and Lewis (1970), this distinction belongs to Coleman Roberts Griffith, often referred to as the father of sport psychology in America. Coleman Griffith is credited with establishing the first sport psychology laboratory at the University of Illinois. The laboratory was established in 1925 and focused upon such issues as the enhancement of psychomotor skill development and the relationship between personality and performance. Griffith wrote two books on the topic of sport psychology during the 1920s and consulted with the Chicago White Sox professional baseball team on sport psychology topics (Singer, 1989).

During the 1960s in the United States, sport psychology began to differentiate itself from psychomotor learning as a separate and distinct discipline. Such historical figures as Franklin M. Henry (University of California-Berkeley), John Lawther (Pennsylvania State University) and Arthur Slater-Hammel (University of Indiana) began to develop and offer courses in sport psychology at their respective universities. Also in the 1960s in the United States, Bruce Ogilvie and Thomas Tutko (1966) wrote their historic book entitled *Problem Athletes and How to Handle Them*. This book became very popular with coaches and players alike. As a result of this work and others, Ogilvie has been referred to as the father of *applied* sport psychology in America (Williams & Straub, 1986).

Since the early 1960s, a number of professional sport psychology organizations have emerged. The first of these, organized in Rome in 1965, was the International Society of Sport Psychology (ISSP). The first president of the ISSP was Ferruccio Antonelli of Italy (Antonelli, 1989). The stated purpose of the ISSP is to promote and disseminate information about sport psychology throughout the world. Hence, the ISSP sponsors worldwide meetings on the topic of sport psychology and publishes the *International Journal of Sport Psychology,* and *The Sport Psychologist*. Shortly after the organization of the ISSP, the North American Society for the Psychology of Sport (NASPSPA) was organized. On being recognized by the ISSP, the NASPSPA officially came into existence in 1966. An organizational meeting, however, took place in 1965 in Dallas, Texas. The first official meeting of NASPSPA took place just prior to the 1967 American Association of Health, Physical Education, and Recreation (AAHPER) convention of that year, which was held in Las Vegas. According to Salmela (1981), NASPSPA has evolved into the world's most influential academic sport psychology society. Since its inception, the primary goal of NASPSPA has been to advance the knowledge base of sport psychology through experimental research (Williams & Straub, 1986). This goal has been reflected in the types of articles published in the *Journal of Sport and Exercise Psychology*.

Shortly after the emergence of NASPSPA in the United States, the Canadian Society for Psychomotor Learning and Sport Psychology (CSPLSP) was organized in 1969. The CSPLSP was initially organized as a subsidiary of the Canadian Association for Health, Physical Education, and Recreation, but became an independent society in 1977. Many of the members of the CSPLSP are also prominent members in NASPSPA.

Of recent origin is the emergence of two different approaches to the way in which sport psychology is practiced (Martens, 1987). The first is referred to as *academic* sport psychology, while the second approach focuses on *applied* sport psychology. Traditional or academic sport psychology continues to focus on research and the expansion of knowledge on which the discipline is based. Conversely, applied sport psychology seeks to apply the knowledge base in real-life situations.

Because NASPSPA was traditionally academic in nature, promoters of the new field of applied sport psychology felt compelled to form an independent organization. Consequently, in fall 1985 the Association for the Advancement of Applied Sport Psychology (AAASP) was formed. A new applied sport psychology journal, the *Journal of Applied Sport Psychology,* was published in March 1989 and became the official publication of the AAASP. The first issue featured historical articles on the development of applied sport psychology in Australia, Britain, Canada, Italy, Sweden, and the United States. As each of the individual articles attest, the historical roots of applied sport psychology in each of these countries were similar. Each country has their own recent historical development, but early beginnings can be traced to the United States as well as the inception of the ISSP in Europe.

Perhaps one of the most critical issues facing applied sport psychology today and in the near future is the issue of who is ethically and technically qualified to practice the science of applied sport psychology. It would appear that the vast number of university-prepared sport psychologists are able to function as educational and research sport psychologists. However, the question of who may legitimately function as a counseling and/or clinical sport psychologist still needs to be resolved. With the inception of Division 47 in 1986 in the American Psychological Association (APA), it is likely that stricter ethical and legal guidelines will emerge relative to who is qualified to provide clinical and counseling services to athletes in the United States. Division 47 was formed by the APA to deal specifically with issues related directly to applied sport psychology. Concurrently, physical education (sport science)–trained sport psychology consultants have also recognized the need for certification. This development is evidenced by the certification requirements that have been adopted by AAASP (Staff, 1991).

Although it is clear that two sport psychologies (academic and applied) have emerged in recent years, it should be evident that both approaches to sport psychology are necessary. Without basic research as a building block to draw on, applied sport psychology would eventually dwindle and die. Applied science cannot endure without new knowledge to keep it alive and vibrant. Where would modern medicine (an applied science) be without basic medical research to provide answers to previously unanswered questions? Conversely, what good is a body of scientific knowledge that is not being applied? Academic and applied sport psychologists must never lose sight of the fact that working together will be more effective than working separately.

Eastern Europe

Whereas the history of sport psychology in Western Europe, England, Australia, and North America has been well documented in English (Singer, 1989; Wiggins, 1984), the same is not true for Eastern Europe and much of Asia. Nonetheless, a brief history of the development of sport psychology in Eastern Europe has been presented by Williams and Straub (1986).

Most of what North Americans know about sport psychology in the former Soviet Union and Eastern European countries comes from the writings of Salmela (1981, 1984, 1991), Vanek and Cratty (1970), and Garfield and Bennett (1984). Sport psychology in these countries has tended to emphasize the enhancement of elite athletes' performance through applied sport psychology. Because international sport in the Soviet Union and in many of the Eastern European countries has been valued highly, it has received considerable government financial support. Consequently, the application of sport psychology for athlete enhancement purposes has received considerable official government backing.

Much of the research in the former Soviet Union and in what was formerly East Germany can be traced to the Institutes for Physical Culture in Moscow and Leningrad and the Leipzig Institute of Sports in what was formerly East Germany (Garfield & Bennett, 1984; Vanek & Cratty, 1970). While difficult to document, Vanek and Cratty (1970) traced the early beginnings of sport psychology in the Soviet Union to P. F. Lesgaft. Reportedly, Lesgaft described the possible benefits of psychological interventions for sport performance as early as 1901. In Czechoslovakia, the first glimmering of interest in sport psychology research was manifested through a doctoral dissertation completed in 1928 by Augustin Pechlat of Charles University (Vanek & Cratty, 1970). Pechlat's dissertation linked physical exercise with possible psychological development of individuals participating in sport and games.

According to Salmela (1984, 1991), the scope of research in Eastern Europe has been limited due to government control. Government has set the goals of research projects and has carefully monitored whether or not the specific goals were achieved. Because the goals of government have tended to be narrowly defined, it is no wonder that most research has focused on the elite athlete. To sup-

port this contention, Salmela (1984) reports statistics indicating that North American research sport psychologists devote approximately 53% of their time testing nonathletes, and only 39% testing the elite athlete. The remaining 8% is devoted to other categories of research. Conversely, past research in Eastern Europe indicates a reverse pattern. According to Salmela, Eastern European sport psychologists have traditionally spent only 28% of their research effort on nonathlete populations, while approximately 55% is devoted to the elite athlete. It will be interesting to see how recent political changes taking place in Eastern Europe will affect research efforts in sport psychology and other sport sciences. Will it become more broad and less focused, as in North America, or will it continue to be closely aligned with government goals and purposes? Time and history will tell.

INTRODUCTION TO RESEARCH IN SPORT PSYCHOLOGY

In this part, areas of past and present research as well as important research questions and future directions are discussed relative to eight historically significant sport psychology topics. The sport psychology topics to be previewed include sport personality, activation and arousal, anxiety and performance, intervention strategies, development of self-confidence, causal attribution theory, psychology of aggression, and team cohesion. Each of these topics will be developed further in subsequent chapters.

Research in Sport and the Personality of the Athlete

Early research in sport personality revolved around the concept that great athletes exhibit personality profiles that would be uniquely different from those of less successful athletes. This approach to the study of personality and the athlete paralleled the study of great leaders and personality. The "great man" concept of leadership held that great leaders possess personality traits that distinguish them from lesser individuals (Behling & Schriesheim, 1976). Similarly it was believed that great athletes would possess personality traits that would distinguish them from lesser athletes. The myth that great leaders, or great athletes for that matter, could be easily distinguished from less successful individuals was exposed by Stoghill (1948) and Sage (1975). Their reviews and general conclusions made it clear that the relationship between personality and performance was very weak, at best. This was not to say that statistically significant trends and relationships could not be observed, but rather that they were invariably weak.

Interest in sport personality research was at its height in the United States between 1960 and 1980. During that time, Ruffer (1975, 1976a, 1976b) cited 572 sources of original research on the relationship between personality and athletic performance. It was near the end of this period of time that the "great debate" between those who took a credulous (credible) stance and those who were more skeptical on this topic was at its peak. Regarding this controversy, Morgan (1980a) published an article entitled "Sport personology: The credulous-skeptical argument in perspective." Morgan (1980b) further suggested that if all research design flaws were removed from sport personality research studies, a significant but slight relationship could be observed between athletic performance and personality testing.

Perhaps the single best study conducted and published on the relationship between personality and athletic performance was carried out by Schurr, Ashley, and Joy (1977). In this investigation, all of the methodological concerns identified by Morgan (1980a, 1980b) were addressed. The study involved 1,596 college students who completed the Cattell 16 PF Questionnaire as entering freshen during a five-year period of time. The investigation involved nonathletes and athletes from several different sports. The results of the investigation indicated significant relationships could be observed between athletes and nonathletes, and between athletes of individual and team sports. Although relationships were observed, the predictive power of relationships were low.

Interactional Approach. In recent years, researchers have adopted a research model that considers the interaction between an athlete's personality and the environment in which the athlete is involved (Bowers, 1973; Carron, 1980; Fisher & Zwart, 1982). The impact of the environment on an athlete is potentially far more powerful than a particular personality disposition. That is, an individual athlete may have a personality disposition to be anxious, but who wouldn't be anxious if placed in a high-anxiety–provoking sport situation? Pinch hitting in American baseball in the ninth inning with the score tied and bases loaded, for example, would be an anxiety-provoking situation. Another might be kicking a penalty kick in World Cup soccer with the score tied and only a few seconds remaining in the game.

Concern for the interaction between the environment and the personality of the athlete has caused most sport psychology researchers to abandon a pure personality model for an interactional model. In other words, it is not how an athlete generally feels and responds that is of critical importance, but how (s)he feels and responds at a particular moment in time. Consequently, researchers such as Morgan lead the way in the utilization of mood state inventories as a means of studying the relationship between psychological variables and athletic performance. The most prominent mood state instrument used by Morgan and other sport psychologists is the Profile of Mood States (POMS) (McNair, Lorr, & Droppleman, 1971).

Using the interactional model and the POMS, Morgan and associates identified what has come to be called the "iceberg" profile of the elite world-class athlete (Morgan, 1979). According to the iceberg profile, the elite world-class athlete displays mood-state scores that are low in tension, depression, anger, fatigue, and confusion, but high in vigor. The iceberg profile is essentially the profile of a psy-chologically healthy individual (mental health model). Using the "mental health model" for predictive purposes, Morgan (1979) and Silva, Shultz, Haslam, and Murray (1981) demonstrated that they could accurately categorize between 70 and 80% of the athletes selected for elite competition by their coaches.

Types of Sports and Activities. Many important descriptive and predictive research questions remain to be answered relative to sports personology. For example, the question of whether a relationship exists between personality and the types of sports and activities individuals select has not yet been adequately addressed. Early research with bodybuilders suggests that male bodybuilders suffer from masculine inadequacy and are overly concerned with body build and manliness (Harlow, 1951; Henry, 1941; Thune, 1949). Yet more recent research by Thirer and Greer (1981) suggests that bodybuilders are high in motivation, tend to resist change, but are quite normal in terms of other traits measured. Inconsistencies such as this one need to be clarified.

In another study involving the sports of football, wrestling, gymnastics, and karate, Kroll and Crenshaw (1970) demonstrated that participants in these sports often differ in personality characteristics. While football players and wrestlers displayed similar personality profiles, both differed from the gymnasts and martial arts participants. Similarly, Singer (1969) demonstrated that the personality profile of collegiate tennis players differs from that of baseball players. Utilizing Chinese athletes, Qiu (1986) reported that elite sprinters differ from elite marksmen on various personality variables. In this regard Qiu (1990) outlined procedures for selection of athletes through psycho-diagnosis. More generally Schurr, Ashley, and Joy (1977) reported that athletes who participate in team sports can be differentiated from individual sport athletes. Future research in this area should focus on the development of a model that could be tested and modified as data dictate. At the present time the research literature associated with personality and sport performance is inconsistent and sometimes contradictory.

Another question that has not been adequately addressed focuses on the relationship between an athlete's playing position on a team and that athlete's personality profile. Intuitively, one would expect some personality differences to exist between athletes who excel in different team-sport playing positions. For example, goalies in soccer or ice hockey should be of a different personality type from players who are responsible for scoring. In studying the personality profiles of offensive and defensive players in volleyball, rugby, and handball, Kirkcaldy (1982) observed that attacking players were more emotionally unstable and extrovert than defensive players. Cox (1987) reported that setters in volleyball displayed different attentional focus characteristics from middle blockers and outside attackers. Setters had a broad-internal focus and were able to keep track of several things at one time. In a study involving American football, Schurr, Ruble, Nisbet, and Wallace (1984) reported that linemen differed significantly from backfield players in terms of the trait of judging and perceiving. Additionally linemen tend toward being more organized and practical, whereas backfield players were more flexible and adaptable. These studies suggest a relationship exists between playing position and personality variables, yet no overall theory or paradigm was proposed to guide the research on this topic.

Research Directions. Recently, Vealey (1989) reported a content analysis study in which she reviewed 463 investigations conducted on the topic of sport personology between 1974 and 1987. The investigation categorized the published research under the headings of trait, trait-state (interactive), and cognitive. The cognitive category included a whole range of cognitive topics that are not traditionally categorized under the heading of personality research. Thus the investigation included studies dealing with such topics as causal attribution, achievement motivation, self-concept, and self-confidence. In a review of the literature from 1950 to 1973, Martens (1975) indicated that 89% of the investigations were correlational. Conversely Vealey reported that between 1974 to 1987 only 68% of them were correlational in nature. Vealey's data showed a decided shift toward more experimental studies since 1974. In 1974–1975, over 80% of the investigations conducted were purely trait or personality related. In 1986–1987 the percent of trait studies had declined to 30%, which is approximately the same as the interactive (state-trait) and cognitive percentages.

Since 1974 the percentage of field studies increased from 25% to over 60%, whereas the percentage of survey and laboratory studies declined. During this same period of time, the percentages of studies categorized by research objective also changed. In 1974–1975, there were no studies documenting the effect of intervention strategies on personality variables, whereas in 1986–1987, 20% of the investigation focused on intervention. The percentage of studies focusing on description and prediction declined slightly in 1974–1975, from approximately 50% each to approximately 40% each in 1986–1987.

Vealey's (1989) content analysis illustrates that future personality research will emphasize field studies more, with a trend toward intervention effects as a research goal. Clearly there is a need for future research to focus more on how various interventions can positively impact on personality variables. A study conducted by Tattersfield (1971) provides an example of the kind of research that is needed. Tattersfield monitored the personality profiles of boys participating in an age-group swimming program across a five-year training period. Significant changes were observed in the boys during the training period toward greater extroversion, stability, and dependence. With so much emphasis being placed on youth sports in recent years, it is critical that sport psychologists investigate the positive and negative psychological effects of these experiences. Sport experiences that developmentally enhance personality and the psychological well-being of participants need to be identified and fostered.

Research on the Effects of Arousal on Athletic Performance

The primary focus of research on arousal and athletic performance has centered on testing two major theories of human behavior. The first is *inverted-U theory* and the second is *drive theory.* Both of these traditional theories of arousal are discussed in some detail in the following paragraphs.

Inverted-U Theory. Very early research by Yerkes and Dodson (1908) established the Yerkes-Dodson Law as the best predictor of the relationship between performance and activation or arousal. The law simply states that the relationship between performance and arousal is quadratic as opposed to linear, and takes the form of an inverted U. Using dancing mice as subjects, Yerkes and Dodson demonstrated that the relationship between arousal (electrical shock) and performance was curvilinear in nature. When arousal was low or high, performance was low. Performance was at its highest when arousal was at an ideal or moderate level. Performance was measured in terms of the number of trials it took for the mice to select the brighter of two compartments.

The inverted-U relationship between performance (motor or verbal) has been demonstrated many times since Yerkes and Dodson first published their classic research (Duffy, 1957; Malmo, 1959). The quadratic relationship between motor performance and arousal is well documented in the literature for such tasks as reaction time (Lansing, Schwartz, & Lindsley, 1956), auditory tracking (Stennet, 1957), and hand steadiness (Martens & Landers, 1970). More recently evidence supporting the quadratic relationship between athletic performance and arousal has been reported.

Klavora (1978) demonstrated that the relationship between precompetitive arousal and basketball performance took the form of an inverted U. In this research Klavora obtained precompetition arousal scores for 145 male high school basketball players throughout the second half of a competitive season. After each game, the coach assessed the performance of each player using a three-point scale (poor, average, outstanding). By plotting each boy's game performance against his arousal score for the game, Klavora came up with a bell-shaped curve that was very close to the expected hypothetical U-shaped curve. Using similar research design procedures, other investigators have also documented the inverted-U relationship between athletic performance and arousal (Burton, 1988; Gould, Petlichkoff, Simons & Vevera, 1987; Sonstroem & Bernardo, 1982).

It is clear from sport psychology research that the expected relationship between athletic performance and activation of the sympathetic nervous system is curvilinear or quadratic in nature. Moreover, in addition to being supported by research, the inverted-U relationship between athletic performance and arousal has logical and intuitive appeal. It makes sense that performance would be low when arousal is very low (drowsy) or very high (frenzy). Although it is not clear why this occurs, a number of theories have been proposed to explain the inverted-U relationship between athletic performance and arousal.

According to information-processing theory (Welford, 1962), brain cells become active with increased levels of arousal, and they begin to fire. With increased firing, the information-processing system becomes noisy and its channel capacity is reduced. At low levels of arousal, the system is relatively inactive, and performance is low. At high levels of arousal, a performance decrement occurs because of the reduced information-processing capacity of the channels. At some ideal or moderate level of arousal, the information-processing capacity of the system is at its optimum and performance is at its best.

Another theory that is intuitively appealing but has not been adequately tested in the sports domain is signal detection theory. According to Welford (1973), when arousal levels are very low, individuals suffer errors associated with the failure to detect a signal or an event. Consequently at very low levels of arousal, performance would be expected to be low. When arousal levels are very high, however, the individual becomes overly sensitive and declares the existence of signals and events that do not exist. At a moderate or optimal level of arousal, errors are balanced between errors of commission and errors of omission, and performance is at its highest.

The theory that has been most widely accepted by sport psychologists for explaining the inverted-U relationship between athletic performance and arousal is Easterbrook's (1959) cue utilization theory. The basic premise of cue utilization or attentional narrowing theory is that as arousal increases, attention narrows. Relevant and irrelevant task-related cues are always available to the performer. While relevant cues enhance performance, irrelevant cues detract from performance. At a low level of arousal, when attentional focus is broad, performance will be low due to the presence of irrelevant cues. When attentional focus is very narrow (i.e., at a high level of arousal) a performance decrement will occur because many relevant as well as irrelevant cues will be gated out. At some moderate or optimum level of arousal, irrelevant but not relevant task-related cues will be gated out. Thus as predicted by inverted-U theory, performance is expected to be poor at high and low levels of arousal, and highest at a moderate or optimal level of arousal.

Unlike the signal detection and information-processing theories, cue utilization theory has received considerable empirical laboratory support. The basic paradigm used in most of the research was to monitor the performance of some peripheral task while performing a central task under conditions of increased arousal. The general observation was that as arousal increased, the performer attended to the central task at the expense of the peripheral task. Investigations by Bahrick, Fitts, and Rankin (1952), Bursill (1958), Weltman and Egstrom (1966), Weltman, Smith, and Egstrom (1971) and Bacon (1974) have all reported results that are supportive of Easterbrook's cue utilization theory. Most recently Landers, Qi, and Courtet (1985) reported a

sports-related study in which cue utilization theory was supported. In this field experiment, rifle shooters were required to respond to a peripheral auditory reaction time task while at the same time attending to a primary shooting task. The results of the experiment demonstrated that increased arousal caused a narrowing of attention for the primary task to the detriment of the secondary reaction time task.

The results of this investigation and others support Easterbrook's general thesis that as arousal increases, attention narrows. When arousal is low and attentional focus is broad, relevant and irrelevant cues are readily available. The presence of the irrelevant cues will tend to be distracting and result in a decrement in the performance of the primary task. Conversely, when arousal is very high, performance will suffer because attentional focus is too narrow. When attentional focus is too narrow, even relevant cues will be excluded. At very high levels of arousal, the phenomenon of distractibility occurs in which the athlete's ability to focus on anything is affected. When this occurs, the person's attention begins to jump randomly from one cue to another without focusing on any specific cue (Schmidt, 1988).

Drive Theory. At the present time, the inverted-U theory as explained by Easterbrook's cue utilization theory is the most commonly accepted approach to explain the relationship between arousal and performance. However, another theory that has tremendous intuitive appeal and research support is the drive theory. Drive theory, as developed by Hull (1943, 1951) and Spence (1956), is a complex stimulus-response theory of motivation and learning. The great appeal of drive theory is that it helps to explain the relationship between learning and increased arousal, not just performance and increased arousal. Many writers have suggested that drive theory is inferior to the inverted-U theory because it predicts a linear as opposed to a curvilinear relationship between performance and arousal (Gill, 1986). Unfortunately this is not an entirely fair or accurate assessment. Early drive theorists were aware of the quadratic relationship between arousal and performance, and made adjustments in the drive theory to account for this notion (Broen & Storms, 1961).

According to drive theory, performance is a function of habit times drive. In applying drive theory to the whole area of sport and motor performance, habit is equivalent to skill and drive is equivalent to arousal. In the early stages of learning or when a task is very complex, many competing responses exist for any particular stimulus. Although most of these competing responses are incorrect, only one of them is correct. A basic premise of drive theory is that increased drive or arousal will illicit the execution of the dominant or best-learned drive or skill. Early in learning, the dominant response is likely to be the incorrect response, whereas late in learning the dominant response is likely to be the correct response. Drive theory is best conceptualized as a theory of competing responses. For the beginner, an environment of high arousal will result in error and the execution of a dominant but incorrect response. When a beginner first learns how to swing a tennis racquet, most of the possible movements in response to the ball (the stimulus) are likely to be incorrect. Yet after a year or two of practice, the correct response will have emerged as the dominant response.

Support for drive theory in the motor domain has come from investigations by Castaneda and Lipsitt (1950), Ryan (1961, 1962), and Griffiths, Steel, and Vaccaro (1979). In the Griffiths et al. investigation, it was observed that arousal correlated significantly with performance of complex scuba-diving tasks. Specifically, 62 beginning scuba-diving students were asked to perform four increasingly difficult underwater tasks. Results from the study indicated that the subjects with the highest levels of arousal performed the worst on difficult tasks. It was concluded that the results were in general agreement with the drive theory, because high levels of drive should inhibit performance of unlearned or complex tasks.

Research Directions. Many fundamental questions remain to be answered relative to the relationship between arousal and athletic performance. Perhaps the single most significant unanswered question has to do with the nature of arousal itself. In almost every case in the literature, when the nature of the relationship between arousal and performance has been tested, arousal has been defined as being synonymous with state anxiety, or what Hans Selye (1975) has preferred to call distress. Although it is true that an increase in distress or state anxiety is associated with an increase in arousal (Cox, 1990), it is also true that an increase in eustress is associated with an increase in arousal. Distress or state anxiety, however, is clearly associated with negative affect, while eustress is associated with joy, exhilaration, and happiness. Clearly, only one aspect of arousal has been investigated by sport psychologists, this being the negative aspect. We know very little about the effect of eustress upon athletic performance. This is an area of investigation that research sport psychologists need to address.

Inverted-U theory has been very useful to sport psychologists in terms of explaining behavior and predicting future behavior; however, like drive theory, it has its limitations. One of the major limitations of the inverted-U theory is that it assumes the relationship between performance and increased arousal is symmetrical and orderly. With every increase in arousal, a measured increase or decrease in performance is expected. In other words, the inverted U is conceived as being smooth and gradual. On the front end of the quadratic curve, performance is thought to increase gradually as arousal increases. At some optimal level of arousal, performance levels off and then gradually declines as arousal continues to increase. This view of human behavior is overly simplistic, however. In the sport environment, performance decrements rarely occur in an orderly and measured manner. Recently several alternatives to the inverted-U hypothesis have been proposed. One of them, the catastrophe theory, proposes that changes in performance associated with increases in arousal may be drastic and

catastrophic in nature rather than gradual and orderly. According to catastrophe theory, when an athlete "goes over the top" in terms of arousal, there will be a large and dramatic decline in performance (Gould & Krane, 1992). Catastrophe theory was originally derived by Thom (1972/1975) as a mathematical model to explain physical world phenomena but was later adopted by Zeeman (1976) for application in the social sciences. In the future, research on the effects of arousal on performance will focus on theories and models such as catastrophe theory that take into consideration drastic fluctuations in behavior.

Research on Anxiety and Its Effect on Athletic Performance

The effects of anxiety on athletic performance is one of the major components of the discipline of sport psychology. In the paragraphs that follow, anxiety is discussed in terms of its measurement as well as its manifestation prior to, during, and following athletic competition.

Anxiety Inventories. Much of the sport psychology research on anxiety has been devoted to establishing an operational definition and developing ways to measure anxiety. Perhaps the most significant development in our understanding of anxiety can be attributed to the work of Charles Spielberger. Spielberger (1971) introduced the terms *trait anxiety* and *state anxiety* to sport psychology. Spielberger defined state anxiety as an immediate emotional state that is characterized by apprehension, fear, and tension in a specific context. State anxiety involves acute feelings of apprehension and fear accompanied by physiological arousal. Spielberger defined trait anxiety as a personality predisposition to be anxious. It is defined as a predisposition to perceive many environmental situations in general as threatening, and to respond to these situations with increased state anxiety. In addition, Spielberger, Gorsuch, and Lushene (1970) and Spielberger (1983) developed the Trait Anxiety Inventory (TAI) and State Anxiety Inventory (SAI), both of which have been widely utilized by sport psychologists in research designed to assess anxiety.

Martens (1977, 1982) hypothesized that a situation-specific measure of trait anxiety would more accurately predict sports performance than a general measure of trait anxiety. Consequently Martens developed the Sport Competition Anxiety Test (SCAT) as a situation-specific inventory for ascertaining an athlete's competitive trait anxiety. Since its development in 1977, SCAT has been the subject of numerous research investigations designed to establish the reliability and predictive power of the test (Gerson & Deshaies, 1978; Martens & Gill, 1976; Martens & Simon, 1976; Rupnow & Ludwig, 1981; Weinberg & Genuchi, 1980). Studies have generally shown that competitive trait anxiety, measured via SCAT, is a better predictor of competitive state anxiety than Spielberger's TAI or coaches' ratings (Martens & Simon, 1976).

In addition to developing SCAT, Martens (1977, 1982)

reasoned that a shorter, more concise instrument for measuring competitive state anxiety could also be developed. Based on Spielberger's observation that as few as 5 items from the 20-item SAI inventory could be used as a subscale, Martens developed and tested the Competitive State Anxiety Inventory (CSAI). The CSAI is composed of 10 items from the parent SAI inventory. Shortly after developing the CSAI, Martens and colleagues developed the Competitive State Anxiety Inventory-2 (CSAI-2) (Martens, Vealey, & Burton, 1990). The CSAI-2 was developed to ascertain the multidimensional nature of competitive anxiety. Karteroliotis and Gill (1987), reported that the multidimensional nature of the competitive state anxiety construct and the independence of cognitive and somatic anxiety were confirmed.

The current view of anxiety is that it is multidimensional in nature. The development of the CSAI-2 and the Cognitive Somatic Anxiety Questionnaire (CSAQ) (Schwartz, Davidson, & Goleman, 1978) is evidence of this line of thinking. The multidimensional nature of anxiety was also studied and confirmed by Fisher and Zwart (1982) and by Gould, Horn, and Spreeman (1983a). Among other things, these researchers identified ego threat, positive anticipation, and negative-outcome certainty as three independent factors associated with the measurement of anxiety.

Precompetitive Anxiety Research. In studying precompetitive anxiety, researchers have made two important observations. First, experienced and nonexperienced athletes often differ markedly in their pattern of precompetitive anxiety. Experienced athletes tend to reach their acme, in terms of precompetitive state anxiety, at a different time than do inexperienced athletes. A second important finding is that precompetitive anxiety seems to take the form of an inverted V, which is not to be confused with the inverted U. As competition nears, precompetitive anxiety begins to build, and it continues to build until just before the athletic event begins. The athlete experiences a gradual increase in precompetitive anxiety as the event gets nearer, and a sudden drop in anxiety immediately prior to the beginning of the event.

The inverted-V pattern has been observed by researchers studying skydivers (Fenz, 1975, 1988) and wrestlers (Gould, Horn, & Spreeman, 1983b). Gould, Petlichkoff, and Weinberg (1984) clarified that the inverted-V pattern is primarily a function of somatic as opposed to cognitive state anxiety. Additionally, Huband and McKelvie (1986) observed that the inverted-V pattern is flatter or less pronounced for low-as opposed to high-trait anxious subjects. The inverted-V pattern has been observed also and documented by Karolezak-Biernacka (1986). The presence of the precompetitive inverted-V pattern suggests that anxiety prior to competition may be worse than during competition. Moreover, research has verified that the more important an impending contest is, the higher the precompetitive state anxiety is likely to be (Dowthwaite & Armstrong, 1984).

Several competitive situations have been shown to differentially affect an individual's state anxiety. Research has shown, for example, that state anxiety increases as the percentage of losses a team suffers increases (Scanlan, 1977, 1978; Scanlan & Passer, 1978; Scanlan & Ragan, 1978). Furthermore, the nature of the sport or the activity differentially influences the state anxiety response. A study by Simon and Martens (1979) revealed that precompetitive anxiety is higher for individual-sport athletes than for team-sport athletes. Furthermore the investigation revealed that the highest levels of state anxiety were experienced by children playing a musical instrument in solo passages as opposed to participating in sporting events.

In a previous section the effects of arousal on athletic performance were discussed. The discussion focused on the notion that a quadratic relationship exists between arousal and performance. It was also mentioned, however, that the inverted-U theory may not adequately explain the complexities of the relationship between arousal and performance. Recent research on the relationship between athletic performance and multidimensional measures of competitive state anxiety have provided sport psychologists with important new information. Burton (1988) and Gould, Petlichkoff, Simons, and Vevera (1987) demonstrated that the nature of the relationship between anxiety and performance depends on the dimension of anxiety being measured. Using the CSAI-2, these researchers observed a quadratic or inverted-U relationship between performance and somatic competitive state anxiety, but a negative linear relationship between performance and cognitive competitive state anxiety. An increase in somatic or bodily indicators of anxiety tends to be associated with an increase in performance up to a certain optimum level. After reaching an optimum level, if somatic state anxiety continues to increase, there will be a decline in performance. Conversely, an increase in cognitive competitive state anxiety is associated with a constant decrease in athletic performance. The finding that different dimensions of competitive state anxiety differentially affect performance represents a major breakthrough in anxiety research.

Research Directions. Catastrophe theory, as introduced in a previous part, hypothesizes that the relationship between anxiety and performance is predictable but often associated with dramatic changes in performance. Interestingly, the theory proposes that the relationship between arousal and performance is based on an interaction between increased arousal and cognitive anxiety. As arousal increases, the theory predicts that performance will increase gradually and, then, decrease gradually (the inverted-U), as long as cognitive state anxiety remains constant and low. If arousal (somatic state anxiety) and cognitive state anxiety both increase at a constant rate, performance will suffer a rather striking and dramatic turn for the worse, from which the athlete is unlikely to soon recover.

With the discovery that somatic and cognitive state anxiety differentially affect performance, it is expected that future anxiety research will focus on models such as the catastrophe theory. More appropriate models are more likely to explain the rather complex relationship between anxiety and performance. The notion that different aspects of state anxiety differentially influence athletic performance must be clarified through well-controlled research designs.

Research on Controlling the Debilitating Effects of Anxiety and Activation Through Intervention Strategies

Uncontrolled competitive state anxiety is a factor that is known to have a debilitating effect on athletic performance and mental well-being. In many cases, an increase in competitive state anxiety leads to a decrease in performance. This results in even greater anxiety, leading to the so-called anxiety-stress spiral (Cox, 1990). A great deal of research in sport psychology has focused on the effectiveness of reducing state anxiety through various intervention and stress-management procedures. Numerous studies have supported the observation that stress-management procedures can effectively be used to reduce anxiety and tension.

To a lesser degree, research has supported the proposition that intervention strategies directly facilitate improved athletic performance. Intervention relaxation strategies that have been studied relative to anxiety reduction include progressive relaxation, autogenic training, transcendental meditation, hypnosis, and biofeedback. Each of these relaxation techniques rely heavily on attentional focus and control of the sympathetic nervous system to bring about the desired effect.

Relaxation Strategies. Progressive relaxation procedures and techniques used by sport psychologists are all variations of those outlined by Edmond Jacobson (1929, 1976). It was Jacobson's basic hypothesis that if the muscles of the body are relaxed, then anxiety and tension will be dissipated. From an athletic performance perspective, it is believed that a relaxation of tension in the muscles of the body will result in more efficient and smooth contraction of the muscles involved in a voluntary movement. Jacobson's full progressive relaxation procedure involves systematically tensing and relaxing specific muscle groups in a predetermined order. After several months of progressive relaxation training, it should be possible for the athlete to evoke the relaxation response in a matter of minutes (Nideffer, 1981).

Research has consistently shown that relaxation techniques effectively reduce oxygen consumption, respiration rate, blood pressure, and muscle tension (Beary, Benson, & Klemchuk, 1974; Deabler, Fidel, Dillenkoffer, & Elder, 1973; Jacobson, 1938). Recently, Long and Haney (1988) reported that an eight-week progressive relaxation program is as effective as an eight-week walk/jog program in reducing trait anxiety levels of nonclinical working women.

Reported research that has indicated that relaxation training enhances athletic performance has generally been of the case study variety. Nideffer and Deckner (1970) reported an increase in shot-putting ability as a result of relaxation training. Similarly, Winter (1982) indicated that San Jose State sprinters (USA) have broken 37 world records in track by learning progressive relaxation techniques. Griffiths, Steel, Vaccaro, Allen, and Karpman (1985) used an experimental design to demonstrate that scuba divers can improve performance and decrease anxiety through learning how to relax. Finally, Berger, Friedmann, and Eaton (1988) reported that regular practice is needed to maintain the benefits of progressive relaxation procedures.

Autogenic Training. Autogenic training is another strategy designed to elicit the relaxation response and to reverse the negative effects of anxiety and tension. Autogenic training technique was developed by Johannes Schultz, a German physician (Schultz & Luthe, 1959). It is based on progressive relaxation procedures, attention to breathing, perceived warmth and heaviness of limbs, and self-talk statements. According to Vanek and Cratty (1970), autogenic training techniques have enjoyed widespread use in Europe. They have been shown to elicit the relaxation response and to influence respiration and heart rate, brain waves, skin resistance, and muscle tension (Luthe, 1969). Research has not been reported, however, demonstrating improved athletic performance as a result of autogenic training.

Hypnosis. Another technique studied by sport psychologists has been hypnosis. The primary goal of this research has been to determine its effectiveness in reducing anxiety and enhancing athletic performance. The initial stages of hypnosis are identical to progressive relaxation, autogenic training, and transcendental meditation in eliciting the relaxation response (Cox, 1990). Once the athlete is in the hypnotic trance, however, suggestions may be given that may cause an increase in the subject's arousal level. Clearly the initial stages of inducing the hypnotic trance have the effect of reducing oxygen consumption, respiratory rate, and heart rate, while increasing skin resistance (Barber, 1971; Dudley, Holmes, Martin, & Ripley, 1963; Davis & Kantor, 1935).

Numerous investigations have been conducted and reported on the effect of hypnosis upon motor performance. Since 1933 several important reviews have been published on this topic (Gorton, 1949: Hull, 1933; Johnson, 1961; Morgan, 1972; Morgan & Brown, 1983; Weitzenhoffer, 1963). None of these reviews resulted in clear-cut conclusions about the effectiveness of hypnosis on facilitating motor performance. However, the reviews by Johnson (1961), Morgan (1972), and Morgan and Brown (1983) were remarkably consistent in their basic conclusions. These conclusions are very important, and remain valid even today. They are as follows:

1. The deeper the hypnotic trance, the more likely it is that suggestions will work.
2. General arousal techniques are more useful in enhanc-

ing muscular strength and endurance than hypnotic suggestions.

3. Negative suggestions invariably work to the detriment of the performer.
4. Hypnosis can help a successful athlete, but it cannot make a good performer out of a poor one.
5. Hypnotizing athletes may do more harm than good, underscoring the importance of a trained psychotherapist.
6. To avoid the problems associated with dependency on a psychotherapist, autohypnosis as opposed to heterohypnosis is recommended.

Recently a case study was reported by Heyman (1987) in which hypnosis was used to help an amateur boxer. In this illustration a single-case experimental design was presented in which hypnosis was systematically used as an intervention strategy. Prior to the intervention the boxer was described as suffering a performance decrement due to anxiety caused by crowd behavior and noise. As a result of the intervention, the boxer was reported to exhibit increased performance characteristics.

Mental Imagery. Stress management and intervention programs are based primarily on some sort of relaxation strategy, as described above, and the application of imagery skills. The use of mental imagery, in conjunction with relaxation procedures, has been shown to be effective in reducing anxiety. Hecker and Kaczor (1988) had college athletes imagine four different scenes while their heart rates were being monitored. Subjects showed increased heart rates when imagining scenes for which they have had personal experience, and for which an increase in heart rate would be expected in real life. Wrisberg and Anshel (1989) demonstrated that a preshot cognitive strategy that involved imagery and arousal adjustment (eliciting the relaxation response) was effective in enhancing basketball free-throw shooting performance. Effective imagery in sport is linked with the ability to relax and to reduce anxiety and arousal (Suedfeld & Bruno, 1990).

Mental practice and imagery is also linked to increased athletic performance. Clark (1960) compared the effect of mental practice with that of physical practice when learning the Pacific Coast one-hand foul shot in basketball. Results showed that mental practice was almost as effective as physical practice for the more advanced athletes but less effective for the beginners. Corbin (1967) and Landers, Boutcher, and Wang (1986) observed similar results using a wand-juggling task and archery, respectively. In a meta-analysis conducted by Feltz and Landers (1983), it was concluded that mental practice is clearly superior to no practice at all but not necessarily better than physical practice. Hall, Rodgers, and Barr (1990) reported that the frequency of imagery use is related to the level of competition. The higher the level of competition and the more skilled the athletes are, the more imagery is practiced.

It has been demonstrated also that athletes engage in one of two different types of imagery (Mahoney & Avener, 1977). Internal imagery is kinesthetic in nature and in-

volves imagining yourself practicing a skill as if you are within your own body. Some researchers feel that internal imagery is most effective because it involves subliminal contractions of muscles (Harris & Robinson, 1986). External imagery is visual in nature and involves watching yourself (through imagery) perform a task.

According to Smith (1987), the effective application of imagery to sport is contingent upon four basic principles: (a) it must be recognized that imagery as a psychological skill can be developed; (b) the athlete must have a positive attitude about its effectiveness; (c) imagery is most effective when practiced by skilled performers; and (d) effective imagery is contingent upon effective relaxation skills.

Cognitive Intervention Programs. Numerous stress management and cognitive intervention programs have been utilized by sport psychologists to control anxiety and to enhance athletic performance. All of the reported intervention programs utilize the skills of relaxation training and imagery to some degree. One of the first reported and easiest to apply is called Visuo-Motor Behavior Rehearsal (VMBR). The VMBR program was developed and reported by Suinn (1972). The program consisted of (a) relaxing the athlete's body through progressive relaxation, (b) practicing imagery in sport-related situations, and (c) using imagery and relaxation to practice a stressful, gamelike situation. Other stress management programs have been developed and applied in sport settings by Meichenbaum (1977) and by Smith (1980b). More recently Boutcher and Rotella (1987) developed the comprehensive Psychological Skills Education Program (PSEP). The PSEP program is composed of four specific phases. In phase one (sport analysis), the sport psychologist takes the time to become completely familiar with the mechanics involved in the sport or sport skill that the athlete is competing. In phase two, the sport psychologist assesses the psychological strengths and weaknesses of the athlete through psychological testing. In phase three, the athlete is asked to make commitment for excellence. In the final phase the sport psychologist assists the athlete in the development of psychological skills necessary for peak performance. Research has supported the position that athletic performance can be enhanced through psychological skills training (Kolonay, 1977; Mace & Carroll, 1985; Noel, 1980; Weinberg, Seabourne, & Jackson, 1981). More recently Kendall, Hrycaiko, Martin, and Kendall (1990) reported a single-subject design in which imagery, relaxation training, and self-talk were observed to be effective in enhancing basketball performance and skill during actual competition. Indeed, in a review reported by Greenspan and Feltz (1989), in which 19 published studies involving 23 interventions were summarized, it was concluded that educationally based intervention programs were generally effective in enhancing athletic performance.

Research Directions. An important development in sport psychology has been the development of the Psychological Skills Inventory for Sports (PSIS) by Mahoney, Gabriel, and

Perkins (1987). The PSIS allows the sport psychologist to assess an athlete's knowledge, understanding, and application of various cognitive skills believed to be important in athletic performance. The psychological skills measured by the PSIS include anxiety control, concentration, confidence, mental preparation, motivation, and emphasis on team goals. Future research in sport psychology will likely involve the incorporation of psychological skill measurement with the application of intervention programs. A before-and-after assessment of psychological skills would allow the sport psychologist to determine if a particular intervention program effectively enhances mental as well as physical skill.

Vealey (1988) conducted a content analysis of psychological skills training approaches from 1980 to 1988 and identified six important future directions. These six areas can also be identified in terms of areas for future research. Research and practice must focus more on young athletes who are developing psychologically as well as physically. Research and practice must do more than educate athletes about intervention and stress management, it must implement psychological skill development into their training programs. Athletes must learn how to differentiate between psychological skill (i.e., confidence, focused attention, arousal) and methods used to obtain these skills (i.e., goal setting, imagery, thought control). Sport psychologists must embrace a holistic approach to psychological skills training and not dwell only on a performance enhancement model. The athlete can be understood and assisted only by taking into consideration all aspects of the environment and the inner self. The fifth need or future direction is to define sport psychology and psychological services in terms of a personal development model and not merely as a performance enhancement model. The final need identified through Vealy's research on psychological skills training is to nurture a continued balance between theory, research, and practice. Psychological skills training practices must be consistent with theory as well as research.

Research on Achievement Motivation and the Enhancement of Self-Confidence in Young Athletes

Motivation is more than experiencing a high state of arousal. Just as a car engine that is running at full throttle can go nowhere until the transmission is engaged, a highly aroused athlete can accomplish little without a goal and a purpose. Sport psychologists and coaches have long recognized that an inner desire and drive is necessary before an athlete can be fully successful. Numerous theories and models have been proposed that explain what motivation is and how it can be nurtured and developed. As with psychology, in general, these theories can be broken down into behavioral models and cognitive models.

Behavioral Models. The most influential and thoroughly tested behavioral model was developed by McClelland and Atkinson and is referred to as the McClelland-Atkinson

Achievement Motivation Model (Arkes & Garske, 1982; McClelland, Atkinson, Clark, & Lowell, 1953). The model was composed of a number of mathematical constructs that when added together predicted whether or not an individual would enter into an achievement situation (e.g., athletic competition). The two major constructs were the motive to achieve success (MAS) and the motive to avoid failure (MAF). The constructs are measured using one of several different psychological inventories. The motive to achieve success could be reduced down to self-confidence and an inner drive, while the motive to avoid failure was essentially the fear of failure or anxiety. In the final analysis, if the motive to achieve success was greater than the motive to avoid failure, then the individual could be expected to enter into an achievement situation.

Another important component of the McClelland-Atkinson Model was that of risk-taking behavior. Athletes take into consideration when they enter into competition the probability of achieving success and the incentive value of success. If the probability of success is very high or very low, then little risk is involved in entering into competition. However, if the probability of success is about 50%, only highly motivated athletes would enter into the competition. Numerous studies were reported in which the risk-taking hypothesis was supported using male subjects (Atkinson & Litwin, 1960; Brody, 1963; Feather, 1961; Isaacson, 1964; Roberts, 1974).

The predictions of the McClelland-Atkinson Model have been tested on motor as well as nonmotor tasks. Many of the studies in which nonmotor tasks were utilized resulted in superior performance of individuals scoring high in achievement motivation as measured by the McClelland-Atkinson Model (Atkinson, 1958; Atkinson & Raphelson, 1956; Cox, 1962). When a motor or athletic task was used, however, the results were much less clear. Several studies indicated, for example, that highly motivated individuals tended to do better on motor tasks during early trials than individuals low in motivation (Fodero, 1980; Healey & Landers, 1973; Roberts, 1972). The research seems to indicate that the real value of achievement motivation is in terms of predicting and achieving long-term success as opposed to a single isolated manifestation of success (DeCharms & Carpenter, 1968).

During the period of time the McClelland-Atkinson Model was popular, a number of elaborations, improvements, or additions were proposed. One such elaboration was the notion that intrinsic motivation (MAS) was not always enough to predict success, so it was necessary to hypothesize the presence of some sort of extrinsic reward or motivation such as money, praise, or acclaim (Atkinson, 1964). Another elaboration was that of perceived contingency. The perceived contingency construct took into account that motivation is often contingent on future goals and aspirations. For example, if an individual is driven to become a major league baseball player, then the motivational value of being a successful little league and high school baseball player is significantly elevated. Research by Raynor (1968, 1969, 1970), Raynor and Rubin (1971), and

Weinberg (1977) has provided support for the perceived contingency construct.

A third hypothesized elaboration to the McClelland-Atkinson Model was that of fear of success (FOS). The fear of success construct hypothesized that some individuals (especially girls and women) avoid competition and achievement motivation situations out of a fear of being successful. While the construct was initially embraced by many sport psychologists wishing to predict achievement motivation in women, the vast majority of the research has not been supportive of this construct (McElroy & Willis, 1979; Tresemer, 1974, 1976). Although women do not avoid success to a greater degree than men, they do tend to avoid physical activities they perceive to be inappropriate to their sex role. Young women, for example, may tend to avoid competing in such male-dominated sports as boxing, football, and wrestling, yet feel very comfortable competing in such neutral sports as tennis and volleyball (Peplau, 1976; Sanguinetti, Lee & Nelson, 1985). Lenny (1977), for example, has pointed out that men and women enjoy equal levels of self-confidence as long as the tasks are not male sex-typed, are not ambiguous, and do not involve social comparison.

The way in which men and women view themselves in a competitive situation is related to their perceived sex roles. At least two psychological inventories have been developed that allow psychologists to categorize men and women in terms of their perceived sex roles. The first, the Personal Attributes Questionnaire (PAQ), was developed by Helmreich and Spence (1977). The second, called the Bem Sex-Role Inventory (BSRI), was developed by Bem (1974). Both the PAQ and BSRI measure an individual's masculine and feminine attributes and characteristics, regardless of biological gender. Masculine attributes are those characteristics considered to be socially desirable in both sexes, but found in greater abundance in males. Feminine attributes are those characteristics considered to be socially desirable to both sexes, but found in greater abundance in females.

In a study designed to investigate the relationship between gender role and competitive trait anxiety, Anderson and Williams (1987) classified male and female subjects as a function of their biological gender and their male and female attributes. Thus subjects were classified as being feminine-females, feminine-males, androgynous-females, androgynous-males, masculine-females, and masculine-males. Androgynous persons are those individuals who endorse both feminine and masculine gender roles. The results of the investigation revealed that the highest anxiety scores were displayed by the feminine-females and the lowest by the masculine-males. Consistent with the predictions of the Mclelland-Atkinson need achievement model, feminine-females would be the most likely to avoid a competitive situation.

Cognitive Models. Although the foregoing discussion has emphasized the behavioral mathematical model as proposed by McClelland and Atkinson, the following discussion focuses upon cognitive models of self-confidence that have become popular in recent years. As observed by Arkes and Garske (1982), the broad notion of self-confidence is consistent with McClelland and Atkinson's notion of need achievement. Athletes who are high in achievement motivation are individuals who also display high levels of self-confidence.

Perhaps the most documented and theoretically sound theory of self-confidence was proposed by Bandura (1977). Bandura, however, uses the phrase self-efficacy to describe an individual's personal perception of self-confidence or competence. According to Bandura, self-efficacy is enhanced through successful performance, vicarious experience, verbal persuasion, and emotional arousal. Of these four factors, the most important for the development of self-efficacy to occur is successful performance. When athletes repeatedly experience success, they begin to expect to be successful and thereby develop feelings of self-efficacy. Bandura has demonstrated the most effective way of helping individuals develop self-efficacy is through participatory modeling. In participatory modeling, the teacher or model shows the subject how to perform a task and then assists the subject in successfully performing the task. The subject is not allowed to experience failure. Through repeated experiences with successful task performance, the subject begins to develop an optimistic attitude and comes to feel confident in his or her ability to perform the task. Sport psychology researchers such as Feltz and Mugno (1983), Kavanagh and Hausfeld (1986), and Weinberg (1985) have successfully demonstrated the effectiveness of participatory modeling in sports-related situations. Gould, Hodge, Peterson, and Giannini (1989) provided support for Bandura's model by demonstrating that performance-based techniques were considered to be most successful in enhancing self-efficacy in athletes. Research with gymnasts has demonstrated also that athletes exhibiting higher self-efficacy expectations are more successful than those with lower expectations (Weiss, Wiese & Klint, 1989).

Somewhat similar to Bandura's self-efficacy approach, Harter (1978) proposed a theory of motivation based on concept of perceived competence. A young athlete is innately motivated to achieve success and to be competent in sports-related tasks. In order to develop feelings of perceived competence, the athlete must make mastery attempts. For example, in football (soccer), the athlete tries to be successful by dribbling the ball by or around an opponent. Success at the mastery attempt results in feelings of perceived competence, positive affect, and a desire to try the task again (McAuley & Duncan, 1989). Unfortunately, unsuccessful performance results in negative affect and feelings of low self-confidence. Numerous sport-related studies have supported Harter's concept of self-competence (Klint & Weiss, 1987; Ulrich, 1987). Clearly it is important for teachers to give young people the chance to learn sport skills and to experience repeated success.

Another approach to studying the relationship between athletic performance and self-confidence was proposed by Vealey (1986). Vealey's model suggests that sport confidence is a function of an athlete's personality trait of confidence, the situation, and the competitive orientation. These three factors interact to produce the psychological state of sport confidence. State sport confidence in turn influences the quality of an athlete's behavioral response or athletic performance. Successful athletic performance results in feelings of self-confidence and satisfaction.

Research Directions. Past research and theory development have been effective in demonstrating that self-confidence is a result of successful experiences and that athletes high in self-confidence are more likely to experience success (McAuley & Tammen, 1989). Several important research questions must be addressed relative to the study of motivation and sport. The first and most critical question focuses on whether or not sport and athletic involvement is the most desirable avenue for developing self-confidence in young people. A second area of needed investigation is related to the question of transfer of self-confidence. Can self-confidence, developed in a sport environment, be transferred to a nonsport environment? If so, then future research must focus on identifying the best and most efficient ways of developing self-confidence through sport for all sport participants. Sport psychologists must build upon the work of Miller and McAuley (1987) and Richman and Heather (1986) to demonstrate the effectiveness of sport in developing increased self-confidence and the motive to achieve success.

Research on Causal Attribution Theory and Prediction of Behavior

Causal attribution is a cognitive theory of motivation that attempts to attach meaning to an individual's perception of why an outcome occurred. Athletes generally have explanations as to why they won or lost a contest or why they played good or bad. The kinds of attributions athletes give can provide a great deal of information about the athlete's self-confidence and source of motivation.

The basic model of attribution was proposed by Fritz Heider (1944, 1958). According to Heider, outcomes are attributed either to the person or to the environment (internal versus external control of events). Basing his theorizing on Heider's writings, Bernard Weiner (1972) restructured factors associated with attribution into two causal dimensions. Weiner labeled the two dimensions *stability* and *locus of control.* Locus of control was defined as being internal or external in nature, while stability was viewed as being either stable or unstable. Weiner's model resulted in a two-by-two matrix in which Heider's four basic attributions were categorized. Ability was categorized as an internal but stable attribution, effort as an internal but unstable attribution, task difficulty as an external but stable dimension, and luck as an external but unstable attribution.

Problems in Attribution Research. The main shortcoming of Weiner's attribution model was that only 45% of the attri-

butions children typically cite for outcomes can easily be categorized in terms of ability, effort, task difficulty, or luck (Roberts & Pascuzzi, 1979). Yet the use of an open-ended system in which the athlete identifies causes is often ambiguous (Ross, 1977)—that is, the researcher was in danger of misclassifying an athlete's open-ended attribution. Thus the development of the Causal Dimension Scale (CDS) by Russell (1982) represented a major breakthrough in research involving causal attributions. The scale is composed of several questions that, in effect, allows the subject to categorize his/her own attribution in terms of the dimensions of locus of causality, stability, and controllability. Recently the scale was revised and expanded to four dimensions (McAuley, Duncan, & Russell, 1989). In the CDS-2, the four dimensions are locus of causality, stability, personal control, and external control.

Although the development of the CDS and CDS-2 resulted in a significant improvement in the accuracy of categorizing and quantifying attributions, several related measurement problems persist. Because attributions are based on perceptions, it is clear that culture could play an important role in the kind of attributions that people make. Attributions depend on what we learn to value. Ability, for example, is very important for Iranian children. Consequently ability becomes a very important attribution, regardless of whether a child succeeds or fails. American children, on the other hand, tend to value effort and intent over innate ability (Salili, Maehr, & Gillmore, 1976). Therefore, when studying causal attribution, it is important to take into consideration cultural and sociological differences.

A second problem that may affect attribution research is the inadvertent subject bias by the experimenter. It often seems clear to the researcher that an athlete either failed or succeeded at a task. However, this may not be the same perception the subject has for success or failure. A subject may feel very good about an outcome, until the researcher asks him/her to suggest an attribution for his/her failure or poor performance. Clearly this kind of biasing could have a tremendous impact on results and conclusions. Spink and Roberts (1980) studied this problem in a sport setting and demonstrated that a person's causal attributions are affected by the ambiguity of the outcome. Clearly perceived wins or losses are attributed to internal factors, such as ability or effort, whereas ambiguous results are attributed to external factors, such as task difficulty and luck. An ambiguous outcome was defined as one in which the athlete's perception of success or failure differed from the objective outcome.

Attribution and Motivation. It is useful to discuss attribution theory in conjunction with motivation theory. Causal attributions are very instructive relative to understanding the motivation of athletes and young children. In terms of internal and external attributions, several lines of research have been conducted. One line of research has focused on locus of control, or the extent that people believe they are in control of their own behavior. The individual most responsible for the conceptual framework associated with locus of control was Julian B. Rotter (1966, 1971), who developed an inventory for measuring locus of control. Some interesting findings have been reported on the subject of locus of control in a sport setting. For example, American female softball players tend to be more internally oriented than their Dutch counterparts, suggesting a cultural relationship (Finn & Straub, 1977). Of even greater interest is the observation that children are able to experience a shift from external to internal control as a function of participation in an eight-week sport fitness camp (Duke, Johnson, & Nowicki, 1977). This finding is particularly important considering the observation that an internal locus of control is considered a more mature and more desirable state (Chalip, 1980). Consequently it would appear that sport camps, athletic experiences, and other physical activity–related planned experiences can have a positive effect on the psychological makeup of participants.

Affect and Causal Attributions. Another interesting line of research, associated with internal and external attributions, is the relationship between affect and the kind of causal attribution statements made by athletes. Indeed, it is possible to predict, with a high degree of certainty, if an athlete believes he or she was a success or a failure simply by recording his/her emotional response or affect relative to an outcome. Furthermore it is possible to determine an athlete's locus of control attribution (internal or external) as a function of affect (McAuley, Russell, & Gross, 1983; Weiner, 1981, 1985; Weiner, Russell & Lerman, 1979).

Athletes who internalize success exhibit emotional responses associated with pride, confidence, competence, and satisfaction. Conversely, athletes who externalize success exhibit emotional responses associated with gratitude, thankfulness, and luck. Athletes who internalize failure (blame themselves) exhibit emotional affect associated with guilt, shame, incompetence, and depression. Conversely athletes who externalize failure exhibit emotional responses associated with anger, surprise, and astonishment. These are highly predictable responses and provide the observant coach, teacher, or parent with valuable information about an athlete's motivation.

Generally, internal attributions are associated with greater emotional affect than external attributions (Weiner, 1985). In addition, emotional affect associated with success tends to be positive, whereas affect associated with failure tends to be negative and subdued. This is one critical reason why it is important that children perceive that they are experiencing success, because children who continually experience feelings of shame, guilt, and incompetence are likely to be sports dropouts (Roberts, 1980).

Stability and Causal Attribution. In terms of the stability dimension of Weiner's attribution model, several important lines of research inquiry have been developed. One such line of inquiry is the observation that a relationship exists between attribution and expectancy. When athletes perform, they do so with certain outcome expectancies based on past history. Athletes who have built a long record of success do not expect to lose. Conversely athletes who lose a lot do not necessarily expect to win. When an athlete's outcome differs from his/her expectation of what should have happened, he or she is shocked and tends to ascribe the outcome to an unstable outcome such as effort or luck. However, if the outcome of a contest is consistent with expectations, then a stable attribution is generally selected. The attribution and expectancy relationship is supported by research reported by Frieze and Weiner (1971), Iso-Ahola (1977), Roberts (1977), and Spink (1978).

Considering the above generalizations, it is reasonable to predict that an athlete's expected future performance will be related to the kinds of attributions he or she gives for current performance. For example, if an athlete loses in tennis but responds with an unstable attribution such as "I didn't try hard enough," we can assume that the athlete expects to win in the future, when he or she tries harder. This line of reasoning is supported by research reported by Duquin (1978), Roberts (1980), and Ryan (1981).

Learned Helplessness and Attribution. Given the link between attribution and expectation, it should be possible to utilize this principle to develop self-esteem in young athletes. Children who habitually experience failure often adopt a syndrome referred to as "learned helplessness." Learned helplessness is defined as a psychological state in which people feel that events are out of their control. Invariably learned helpless children attribute their failures to stable attributions such as low ability. These children feel they failed because they aren't any good and never will be (stable unchanging attribution). Of interest, however, is the observation that children can be encouraged to select an unstable attribution that would imply future performance is not etched in stone (Dweck, 1980; Valle & Frieze, 1976; Weiner, 1985). With this in mind, children who suffer from feelings of helplessness should be encouraged by adult leaders to select unstable attributions for their failures and stable attributions for their successes. In this way they will come to view future performance as being linked to their attributions associated with past performance. This is a way to enhance feelings of self-confidence and hope in the minds of young sport performers (Grove & Pargman, 1986).

Self-Serving Attributions. Oftentimes individuals select causal attributions that appear to be very logical. For example, if an athlete fails at a task everyone else succeeds at, it would seem logical the athlete would select an internal attribution such as ability to explain the outcome. Certainly it would be illogical to blame the outcome on some external cause such as luck or task difficulty. Evidence suggests, however, that people are not always logical in selecting causal attributions to explain their behavior. Instead of choosing a logical attribution, people often select blatantly self-serving attributions. For example, an athlete who has just lost a tennis match to a vastly superior opponent might attribute the loss to an external cause such as bad luck. This is considered to be an ego-protecting strategy on the part of the losing player. Conversely an athlete who has just won a match against a weaker opponent might attribute the success to his/her superior ability. This is considered to be an ego-enhancing strategy. Both of these strategies are self-serving in nature and are considered to fit an illogical as opposed to a logical model of attribution (Fontaine, 1975).

Perhaps the first serious review of the self-serving hypothesis was reported by Miller and Ross (1975). They argued that in order for the self-serving hypothesis to be true, it must be shown that people habitually indulge in both ego-enhancing and ego-protecting strategies. Consequently they pointed out that the self-serving hypothesis could not be unequivocally supported. The literature provided strong evidence that individuals tend to make ego-enhancing attributions under conditions of success, but no consistent pattern could be identified under conditions of failure. A review of 14 articles conducted since 1975 also failed to reveal unequivocal support for the self-serving or illogical model (Cox, 1990). People experiencing success typically attribute their success to an internal attribution, but individuals experiencing failure attribute their outcomes to either internal or external outcomes.

It would appear that attributions to failure are often qualified in terms of some situational factor. For example, some data indicate that athletes will attribute clear success and failure to an internal cause, but ambiguous outcomes to an external cause (Spink & Roberts, 1980). However, Iso-Ahola (1977) and Spink (1978) observed that athletes attribute successful outcomes (clear and ambiguous) to an internal attribution, while attributing unsuccessful outcomes to either an internal or external outcome. Bradley (1978) summarized the situation by concluding that the attributional process is probably neither purely logical nor illogical (self-serving). The disposition to use a self-serving attribution is within each individual to some degree. In fact, in some cases it might be recommended that an individual select a certain kind of attribution in order to protect a delicate self-concept (Dweck, 1980).

Attribution Theory and Rewards. Attribution theory has also been linked to intrinsic and external rewards. It was argued by Atkinson (1964) that an extrinsic reward such as money or a trophy would add to an athlete's motivation to achieve. Lepper and Greene (1976), however, argued that the athlete's intrinsic motivation toward an activity might be reduced as a result of receiving an external reward. The reason for this concern is based upon attribution theory, and the athlete's perception of the reward. According to Lepper and Greene's concept of the "overjustification hypothesis," if the athlete receives an external reward for doing something that is intrinsically appealing, he or she may discount the value of the activity. In other words, the athlete may perceive that he or she is participating in the activity for external rather than internal reasons. This has the effect of reducing the athlete's intrinsic motivation for the activity (Lepper & Greene, 1975, 1976).

An important contribution to our understanding of the relationship between intrinsic motivation and extrinsic rewards comes from the work of Deci and associates (Deci, 1971, 1978, 1980; Deci, Cascio, & Krusell, 1975). Deci's Cognitive Evaluation Theory explains that extrinsic motivation can affect intrinsic motivation in one of two ways. A decrement in intrinsic motivation will occur if the athlete perceives an intrinsic-to-extrinsic shift in locus of control. An increase in intrinsic motivation will occur if the athlete views the external reward as being informational in nature relative to his/her performance. In the first case the external reward is viewed as being controlling in nature, causing a shift in the perceived reason for the athlete's participation. When an athlete perceives that the primary cause or reason for his/her participation in an otherwise desirable activity is external in nature, intrinsic motivation declines. If the athlete perceives the external reward is not the primary cause for participation, but merely provides valuable information about the quality of performance, the external reward has no debilitating effect on intrinsic motivation.

Research Directions. From a future-directions perspective, it is important that research focus on the utilization of the attribution model for enhancing and maintaining self-confidence and achievement motivation. Previous research involving attribution and sport has focused on the identification of typical attributions and the development of accurate tools for correctly categorizing responses. For example, the recent work by Russell (1982) and McAuley et al. (1989) in developing the Causal Dimension Scale has greatly improved the measurement and categorization of causal attributions.

Research in achievement motivation has provided a great deal of information relative to how self-confidence (i.e., self-esteem, competence motivation, self-efficacy, etc.) is developed from a theoretical perspective. Theoretical testing of Bandura's (1977) theory of self-efficacy and Harter's (1978) competence motivation theory has resulted in a great deal of data to support the position that self-confidence can be developed and maintained through successful experiences. Similarly researchers must build on Dweck (1980) and Weiner's (1985) observation that self-confidence can be developed and protected through the judicious application of attribution theory. The proposition that self-confidence can be maintained and nurtured by encouraging children to select certain kinds of attributions is promising. The groundwork laid by Dweck and Weiner must be built on within the context of sport. Hopefully the application of attribution theory to the enhancement of sport confidence will be a prime focus of researchers for the future. It is not enough to leave it to the practitioner to make applications. The researcher must provide tested models and clear guidelines for application. Related to this is the recent finding that children exhibiting high and low levels of self-esteem can be differentiated as a function of attribution (Weiss, McAuley, Ebbeck, & Wiese, 1990). When compared to children who are low in self-esteem, high self-esteem children tend to select attributions that are more internal, stable, and personally controllable.

Another area that needs to be addressed more aggressively in the future is the effect that extrinsic motivation and rewards have upon intrinsic motivation. The research by Lepper and Green (1976) and Deci (1980) makes it quite clear that the indiscriminant use of extrinsic rewards may severely damage intrinsic motivation. Because professional sport in the United States and in many other nations throughout the world is based on monetary rewards, it would seem that a careful investigation of the benefits of extrinsic rewards would be of critical importance. These same kinds of investigations would be of use to youth sport programs as well. Does the receiving of extrinsic rewards undermine the intrinsic motivation of young athletes? If the answer to this question is yes, serious reevaluation of the use of extrinsic rewards in youth sport programs should be considered. Decisions relative to the giving and receiving of rewards should be based on research data.

Research on the Psychology of Aggression in Sport

Aggression in sport is a phenomenon that has tarnished sport throughout the world. Examples of player and fan aggression can be cited in international competitions such as the Olympic Games, as well as amateur and professional competition within various countries. In 1978 a crushing blow by Jack Tatum of the Oakland Raiders (professional American football) left Darryl Stingley a quadriplegic (Noverr & Ziewaez, 1981). Aggression by soccer fans has become a national embarrassment for Great Britain (Gammon, 1985), and aggression among athletes is commonplace in American professional baseball and basketball.

Idealists have argued eloquently and optimistically that organized sport provides young athletes with the ideal environment to learn how to control their aggression and emotions (Scott, 1970). Fisher (1976), however, has argued that the many examples of sport aggression actually provide evidence of an alternate hypothesis: i.e., sport teaches and promotes aggression as opposed to controlling it. In an effort to understand the phenomenon of aggression, sport psychologists and sociologists have attempted to study acts of aggression in various laboratory and field settings. A fundamental problem arises in defining exactly what aggression is. In many cases, research results appear to be contradictory owing to different definitions of what is being studied.

Cox (1990) has specified that three factors must be present in order for a behavior to be labeled as aggression. First the act must be directed against another human being. Beating up on a water cooler or wall does not constitute an act of aggression. Second, for an act to be labeled aggression, there must be a clear attempt on the part of the aggressor to harm another human being. Screaming, hollering, and threatening another person while being restrained by another person, does not qualify as an act of aggression. Finally, there must be a reasonable expectation that the act of aggression will be successful. By adhering to a standardized definition of what aggression is, researchers will not fall into the trap of studying something that is not aggression and calling it aggression.

In studying the phenomenon of aggression, researchers have generally identified two types of aggression (Baron, 1977). The first type is called *hostile aggression* and is characterized by the presence of the intent to harm, the goal to harm, and increased arousal manifested in the form of anger and hostility. The second type of aggression is called *instrumental aggression* and is characterized by the presence of the intent to harm, the goal to win, and the absence of hostility. The main difference in the two types of aggression rests with the goal of the behavior. In hostile aggression the goal is to inflict pain and suffering, whereas in instrumental aggression the goal is to win an athletic contest. Neither form of aggression is acceptable, and in many ways instrumental aggression is the more repugnant because it is planned and calculated. A third category of behavior that is often confused with hostile and instrumental aggression is *assertive behavior*. Assertive behavior is characterized by legitimate force, unusual effort, and high arousal, but no intent or goal to harm is present (Silva, 1980a).

Theories of Aggression. Several theories have been proposed to explain the phenomenon of aggression. They are instinct theory (Lorenz, 1966), frustration-aggression theory (Dollard, Miller, Doob, Mourer, & Sears, 1939), and social learning theory (Bandura, 1973). Instinct theory is based on the notion that aggression is an inborn drive similar to sex, hunger, or thirst. Because aggression is proposed to be the natural state of humanity, it is important that society provide positive outlets for it. These positive outlets, generally in the form of sport, would allow hostility to be released through a process of catharsis, thus reducing the need or drive to aggress. The single greatest flaw in this theory is the failure of researchers to show a reduction in aggression as a result of engaging in aggressive behavior. Rather, research demonstrates that acts of aggression increase rather than decrease the possibility of future acts of aggression (Berkowitz, 1972; Goranson, 1970; Leith, 1977; Russell, 1981).

The frustration-aggression hypothesis is similar to instinct theory in that the act of aggression should result in a reduction of future acts of aggression. The theory states that frustration results in the need to be aggressive. For example, if we are frustrated in our attempts to score a winning goal in football (soccer), we are likely to resort to aggressive behavior. Aggressive behavior acts as a catharsis for the venting of pent-up frustrations, which results in a reduction in the need for further aggression. As with instinct theory, however, research fails to support the frustration-aggression hypothesis. This is because acts of aggression increase rather than decrease the probability of future acts of aggression. Hence aggression does not serve as a catharsis. Rather it serves as a precursor to future acts of aggression.

Social learning theory, as proposed by Bandura (1973) and Mischel (1986), argues that aggressive behavior is learned. Therefore, an act of aggression only reinforces the probability of future acts of aggression as learned behavior. That people can learn aggression is well documented in the experimental literature. Studies have shown children's play behavior will change as a result of watching models display acts of aggression and hostility (Bandura, Ross, & Ross, 1961). Bandura has argued that aggression has a circular effect on future acts of aggression. That is, aggression merely perpetuates further acts of aggression through the process of learned behavior. Smith (1980a) used professional ice hockey as an example of the circular effect of aggression. Children watch their role models carry out acts of aggression on the ice against other ice hockey players. Through modeling, the children adopt this behavior, believing it to be acceptable. As the children learn to aggress, these acts are reinforced and learned. Therefore, to the social learning theorist, aggression is nothing more than a learned behavior.

Perhaps the leading theorist in the area of aggression, in general, is Leonard Berkowitz (1962). Berkowitz formulated a theory of aggression that was somewhat eclectic in nature. He recognized the viability of the frustration-aggression hypothesis, but also took into consideration the powerful effect of learning. The theory Berkowitz espoused has come to be referred to as Berkowitz's reformulation of the frustration-aggression hypothesis (Berkowitz, 1958). Berkowitz argued that aggression can act as a catharsis to further acts of aggression as long as one of three factors do not occur. They are: (1) the frustration that caused the aggression persists, (2) the aggressive behavior becomes a learned response, and (3) aggression leads to anxiety, which is frustrating and will lead to further aggression.

According to Berkowitz and Alioto (1973), frustration does not necessarily result in aggression, but it does lead to a readiness for aggression. Readiness for aggression can be triggered by stimuli that are associated with aggression. Berkowitz and Le Page (1967), for example, observed that frustrated and angry subjects are further angered when placed in the presence of a weapon as opposed to a badminton racket. Berkowitz's reformulation of the frustration-aggression (F-A) hypothesis states that frustration does not necessarily lead to aggression, but it heightens the predisposition for aggression. Aggression would serve as a stimulus for further aggression (Cox, 1990).

Theoretical Constructs. The literature in sport aggression identifies a number of theoretical constructs related to the phenomenon of aggression. Physiological or undifferentiated arousal, for example, has been observed to be a necessary precursor to hostile aggression (Lefebvre, Leith & Bredemeier, 1980). Consistent with Berkowitz's (1958) reformulation of the frustration-aggression hypothesis, arousal represents a readying mechanism for aggression.

Moral reasoning is another psychological construct that has been demonstrated to be related to aggression. Consistent with Jean Piaget's theory of cognitive development (Ginsburg & Opper, 1969), athletes are viewed as progressing in moral reasoning and moral judgment. Individuals at a low level of moral reasoning have a difficult time making correct decisions regarding aggression, because they do not perceive it as being immoral. At a high level of moral reasoning, athletes are capable of making moral decisions about aggression. Research by Bredemeier and associates (Bredemeier & Shields, 1986; Bredemeier, Weiss, Shields, & Cooper, 1987) has demonstrated that contact sports may actually retard moral development by legitimizing acts of aggression on the athletic field. Bredemeier refers to this suspension of ethical morality as bracketed morality, because normal ethical behavior is suspended for an athletic contest.

Consistent with Bredemeier's research on aggression and moral reasoning, Silva (1979) has observed that feelings of guilt are not particularly effective in retarding acts of aggression in sport. Athletes come to feel an act of aggression that is unacceptable in society is acceptable during competition. The explanation for this notion is that violence in sport is often viewed as legitimate and expected (Silva, 1983). A study reported by Ryan, Williams, and Wimer (1990) observed a significant relationship between a basketball player's preseason rating of legitimate aggressive acts and actual acts of aggression carried out during the season.

Situational Factors. Research in sport aggression has identified also a number of situational factors that are associated with aggression. For example, Harrell (1980) observed that an athlete is much more likely to carry out an act of aggression against an opponent if he or she perceives the opponent has aggression on his/her mind.

Expected retaliation is another situational factor that is related to the phenomenon of aggression. Initially it was believed that fear of retaliation serves as a retardant to aggression (Baron, 1971). It has also been demonstrated, however, that attack-escalating aggressive behavior tends to result in more aggression rather than less (Knott & Drost, 1972). Initial aggression can be inhibited by fear of retaliation, but once aggression and counteraggression begins, it tends to escalate rapidly.

Research associated with game variables and aggression have revealed several interesting findings (Cullen & Cullen, 1975; Lefebvre & Passer, 1974; Martin, 1976; Russell, & Drewery, 1976; Volkamer, 1972; Wankel, 1972). Acts of aggression often occur when the point differential between teams is large. When this is so, players may engage in aggression without seriously affecting the game outcome. Consistent with the frustration-aggression hypothesis, losing teams are more likely to engage in acts of aggression than winning teams. This is because losing is a frustrating experience. Finally, as a general rule, acts of aggression tend to increase in number as an athletic contest progresses from beginning to end.

Silva (1980b) has argued that a negative relationship should exist between player aggression and athletic performance. He based this argument on the notion that aggression diverts attention from the performance goal; and that aggression is associated often with high levels of arousal, which may have a debilitating effect upon performance. Russell (1974) and McCarthy and Kelly (1978a, 1978b), however, reported data suggesting a modest positive relationship between aggression and performance, especially in the case of ice hockey. There are two plausible explanations for this apparent conflict. First, high levels of aggressive behavior and associated arousal may be ideal for a very physical sport such as ice hockey. Second, it is very likely that many of the behaviors categorized by Russell, McCarthy, and Kelly were examples of assertive behavior (no intent to harm) and not aggression (intent to harm). In these investigations, aggression was defined in terms of penalty shots awarded and challenge to authority. As suggested by Silva (1980b), if the truly aggressive acts were separated from the assertive acts, performance may have been negatively instead of positively related to aggression.

Research Directions. Although past research has focused on defining and explaining aggression, future research must focus upon research models designed to eliminate sport aggression. From the perspective of the athlete, research initiatives pioneered by Bredemeier and associates are most promising. Once it can be clearly demonstrated that aggressive behavior is associated with moral development, then athletes can be taught that aggression is morally wrong. However, as long as the belief exists that bracketed morality is acceptable, then little progress can be made with athletes. It would seem that with the assistance of good research, necessary rule changes, and training for athletes, coaches, and officials, the problem of athlete aggression could be minimized.

Future researchers in sport aggression must identify and develop better ways of measuring and identifying acts of aggression. Past field research, in sport aggression, has been plagued by inadequate and ambiguous selection of dependent variables. This situation is due primarily to the use of archival data (historical records) in defining and measuring the dependent variable of interest. Data based on archival records are suspect because acts of true aggression and assertiveness are confounded. There is simply no way a researcher can tell from looking at an official scorer's record whether a violation was due to an act of aggression (intent to harm) or merely assertive behavior. Many penalties in basketball, soccer, American football, and ice hockey are a direct result of assertive behavior, not aggression. In order for researchers to identify true acts of aggression, recorders must be highly trained observers and be physically present when the acts occur.

Another measurement approach utilized by Ryan, Williams, and Wimer (1990) is to ask athletes to keep track of their own acts of aggression throughout a season and to record them. Although this approach is better than the archival approach, it is difficult to know if the athletes all used the same criterian for identifying a behavior as aggression. On the other hand, the athlete is probably the best person to determine if an act was intentional and calculated to harm the opponent.

Problems associated with fan violence and aggression are more difficult to resolve. In this respect, aggression be-

comes a social issue and must be addressed by society as a whole. For example, it has been documented that fan violence is associated with the availability of alcoholic beverages at sporting events (Valzelli, 1981). Other factors that are known to facilitate fan violence include irresponsible media coverage, the dehumanization of competitors, and the failure to promote attendance at sporting events as a family affair (Bryant & Zillman, 1983; Cox, 1991).

If the promoters of sporting were truly interested in limiting fan violence, they would restrict the availability of alcoholic beverages and administer severe penalties for acts of spectator aggression. In respect to spectator violence, continued research is needed to determine the effectiveness of various strategies in curtailing violence. Data are needed, for example, to demonstrate that encouraging family attendance at sports events actually results in a reduction in spectator violence.

Research on Team Cohesion and Its Relationship to Athletic Performance

It is a well-documented observation that a positive relationship exists between athletic performance and team cohesion (Martens & Peterson, 1971). What is not well established is the direction of causality between the two variables as well as the nature of the interaction between performance and various multidimensional measures of cohesion. Much of the research conducted on team cohesion has focused upon defining cohesion, establishing its nature, and studying its relationship with performance. In a very real sense, a great deal of progress has been made over the past 20 years relative to our understanding of group or team cohesion and athletic performance.

As indicated by Fisher (1982), the key to understanding team cohesion is group dynamics. From a social-psychological perspective, it is clear that the behavior of a group is vastly different from the sum total of the individual behaviors that make up the group (Wittig & Belkin, 1990). When teams work together as a single unified whole and toward a common goal, they are often able to realize success. Examples from two American professional baseball teams serve to highlight this observation. In 1979 the Pittsburgh Pirate professional baseball franchise won the World Series of baseball. Their theme throughout the season and the playoffs was that "we are family," suggesting that members of the team liked each other and worked together to accomplish team goals. Conversely the 1988 Cincinnati Reds professional baseball team never developed this kind of feeling. They were picked by the experts to be the best team in their division and were favored to win their division, yet they never lived up to their expectations. Rob Murphy, a relief pitcher on the team, made the following observation about the 1988 Cincinnati Reds (Kay, 1988):

We've got a funny chemistry here. It's a strange mixture of guys. They're all good guys: I don't have any personal problems with any of them. They are guys who have great talent and good dispositions, but the mix—something's not there. I can't really explain it other than it's a strange chemistry (p. 15).

The basic model for studying group cohesion, or what shall be referred to as team cohesion, comes from the writings of Cartwright (1968) and Carron (1982). Cartwright explained and demonstrated that certain factors determine whether or not cohesion will develop among members of a group, and that certain outcomes or consequences will result if cohesion does develop. A number of definitions of cohesion have been proposed by Cartwright (1968) and Festinger, Schachter, and Back (1950). However, the most appealing definition, from the perspective of many sport psychologists, is one proposed by Carron (1982), a Canadian sport scientist. According to Carron, team cohesion is best defined as "a dynamic process which is reflected in the tendency for a group to stick together and remain united in the pursuit of goals and objectives" (p. 124).

Measuring Team Cohesion. An early obstacle to studying team cohesion effectively was the difficulty in measuring the phenomenon. Not only are there different approaches to measuring team cohesion, but there are different aspects of cohesion to be measured. The two different approaches to the measurement of team cohesion are the direct and indirect methods. In the direct approach, the athlete is simply asked about his/her attraction to the team in general. In the indirect approach, athletes are asked about their attraction to individual members of the group. Research in which the direct approach was utilized yielded very different results from research in which the indirect approach was used (Carron, 1980; Cox, 1990; Gill, 1978). For example, Lenk (1969) reported a negative relationship between team cohesion and Olympic rowing performance when an indirect measure of cohesion was used. Conversely Klein and Christensen (1969) reported a positive relationship between three-on-three basketball-playing performance and team cohesion when a direct measure of cohesion was used.

The different aspects of team cohesion include social and task cohesion, which have been clearly differentiated by Mikalachki (1969). Groups that are high in social cohesion tend to be composed of individuals who are personally attracted to each other, who enjoy being together, and who enjoy socializing as a group. Teams that score high in social team cohesion tend not to be dedicated to team goals. Their motivation for staying together as a group lies in the social pleasures they receive and not the attainment of team goals such as winning ball games. This is not to say that a team high in social cohesion cannot be successful, but it does mean that the focus is on the social benefits derived from group membership. Teams who score high in task cohesion tend to identify closely with team goals. A case in point might be the 1978 New York Yankees professional baseball team, which was the best team in baseball that year as evidenced by its performance on the field. The Yankees were the best in terms of advancing baserunners, turning double plays, and generally working together to achieve team goals. Yet as a team, they were very low in terms of social co-

hesion. Members of this team did not like each other. They fought with each other, cliques were formed, and angry words were exchanged.

Much of the early research on the topic of team cohesion failed to take into consideration the different approaches to measuring cohesion (direct vs. indirect), and to differentiate between the different aspects or dimensions of cohesion. Consequently it is easy to understand why various research investigations yielded conflicting results and conclusions. Carron, Widmeyer, and Brawley (1985) addressed this problem by developing a conceptual model of team cohesion. The Carron et al. model of team cohesion is based upon two dimensions. The first dimension is labeled *athlete's perception of team,* whereas the second dimension is labeled *group orientation.* An athlete's perception of a team is further classified in terms of group integration (how the team functions as a whole) and individual attraction (factors that personally attract an athlete to a team). Group orientation is further classified in terms of task cohesion and social cohesion.

Consistent with the Conceptual Model of Team Cohesion, the Group Environment Questionnaire (GEQ) was developed for the purpose of measuring the multidimensional construct of team cohesion (Widmeyer, Brawley, & Carron, 1985). The GEQ allows the researcher to identify four distinct aspects of team cohesion. As explained by the authors, the GEQ measures the following, somewhat independent dimensions of team cohesion:

1. Bonding to the team as a whole to satisfy social needs.
2. Bonding to the team as a whole to satisfy task completion needs.
3. Attraction to team and team members to satisfy social needs.
4. Attraction to team and team members to satisfy task completion needs.

Determinants of Team Cohesion. Some of the determinants of team cohesion investigated by sport psychology researchers include member cooperation, team stability, team homogeneity, and team size. Cooperation of team members to attain a goal is an example of task cohesion. A large body of experimental literature has been developed comparing the desirable benefits of cooperation and competition among members of a group. Of particular interest to the sport psychologist is the relative effect that cooperation and competition have on performance. In an important meta-analysis reported by Johnson, Maruyama, Johnson, Nelson, and Skon (1981), the results of 60 years of research were summarized (122 studies).

The meta-analysis reinforced the general conclusion that intragroup cooperation is superior to intragroup competition in terms of productivity and cooperation. Team members who learn to cooperate for the attainment of team goals are much more likely to enjoy success than are team members who seek individual goals at the expense of team goals. The superiority of cooperative as opposed to competitive behavior on the part of team members is related also to the nature of the task. The more teammate interaction required for success, the more important cooperation becomes.

High interaction sports such as football, volleyball, and basketball require greater cooperation among members than do low interaction sports such as golf and bowling (Goldman, Stockbauer, & McAuliffe, 1977; Miller & Hamblin, 1963). Not withstanding the predicted importance of cooperation in interactive team sports, evidence is available also that points to the importance of cooperative behavior in low-interaction individual sports. Johnson, Bjorkland, and Krotee (1984), for example, demonstrated that cooperative behavior among members of a golf team enhances putting behavior.

Team stability is another determinant of team cohesion. Teams with a high turnover rate do not have sufficient time to develop team cohesion. Conversely it appears that if teams remain together too long, they will also suffer in terms of team cohesion and team performance. The notion that there is an optimal length of time to keep a team together was investigated and documented by Donnelly, Carron, and Chelladurai (1978). Utilizing major league baseball teams and players as subjects, these researchers demonstrated the optimum amount of time to keep a team together was approximately five years. Teams suffered a decline in league standings when they remained together for a longer or shorter period of time than five years.

Eitzen (1973) reported empirical evidence to support the proposition that team homogeneity is another factor that determines team cohesion. Team homogeneity has to do with how similar teammates are in terms of such factors as cultural background, ethnic background, socioeconomic status, and religion. Eitzen's data indicated clique formation was lower in homogeneous teams than in teams that were more heterogeneous. Additionally, homogeneity was also observed to be related to team success.

Another variable that is thought to be a determinant of team cohesion is group size. The larger a team is, the harder it is to develop cohesion among its members. For this reason, Davis (1969) recommended that team pride and team cohesion should be fostered among members of subunits, when dealing with large groups as in American football. A recent study reported by Widmeyer, Brawley, and Carron (1990) documents the importance of team size in fostering and developing cohesion among members of sports teams. The development of team cohesion among members of three-on-three basketball teams was studied. As predicted, team cohesion and enjoyment was observed to increase as the size of the team rosters decreased.

Consequences of Team Cohesion. There are many potential consequences of team cohesion (Cartwright, 1968). Two consequences of critical importance to the sport psychologist are feelings of satisfaction and team success. Successful teams tend to enjoy high levels of team cohesion and member satisfaction (Davids, Nutter, 1988; Gruber & Gray, 1982; Martens & Peterson, 1971; Spink, 1990; Williams & Hacker, 1982). It is an oversimplification, however, to assume that this relationship is caused by team cohesion. Most coaches assume that a high degree of team cohesion will naturally lead to team success as well as member satisfaction. The evidence suggests, however, that the direction of causality may lead primarily in the other direction. That is, the direction of causality may be from team success to team cohesion rather than from team cohesion to team success (Bakeman & Helmreich, 1975; Carron & Ball, 1977; Ruder & Gill, 1982; Williams & Hacker, 1982).

Research Directions. Although past research has answered some questions about the relationship between team performance and team cohesion, many questions remain unanswered. In a sense, the cause-and-effect relationship between cohesion and performance/success remains an unanswered question. Most of the reported cause-and-effect research was conducted using a measurement tool that may not have adequately distinguished between social and task cohesion, or between individual attraction and attraction to the group (Carron, 1980). Studies, such as those reported by Carron and Ball (1977) and Williams and Hacker (1982), should be repeated using the Group Environment Questionnaire (Widmeyer, Brawley, & Carron, 1985). In addition, future research on the topic of team cohesion should focus also on the development and testing of models designed to enhance social and task cohesion among team members.

THE FUTURE OF RESEARCH IN SPORT PSYCHOLOGY

In the parts of this chapter that follow, sport psychology is addressed relative to the trend toward specialization, trends in academic preparation, and future research directions. Relative to research directions, four specific research needs and directions are identified and explained.

Trend Toward Specialization

Sport psychology has experienced rapid growth and development over the past 25 years. This growth, however, will seem small when compared to the knowledge explosion that will take place in the next 25 years. Sport psychology emerged, and is emerging, from the broader disciplines of psychology and motor behavior. In North America, sport psychology is currently viewed as a discipline that is separate and distinct from the psychology of motor learning, as well as from motor control. In Asia and many other parts of the world, however, this is not necessarily true. A case in point would be Qiu's sport psychology laboratory at the Wuhan Institute of Physical Education in Wuhan, China (PRC). Qiu's research includes topics such as psychological selection, personality assessment, reaction time, and psychomotor learning. In the future, the trend will be for sport psychology research to become more specialized, similar to what has taken place in North America.

Trends in Academic Preparation

During the 1970s and 1980s, research in sport psychology was primarily conducted by faculty and graduate students associated with physical education and sport science departments. During this period, individuals interested in pursuing careers in sport psychology did so by taking their advanced degrees in physical education with support work in psychology. This method of professional preparation will likely continue for those prospective doctoral candidates seeking to become research and/or educational sport psychologists. A trend is emerging, however, for students interested in becoming clinical/counseling sport psychologists to pursue a different approach to professional training.

This approach, as recommended by the United States Olympic Committee, calls for licensure or certification in clinical or counseling psychology (USOC, 1983; May, 1986). Consequently it is expected that future clinical/counseling sport psychologists, at least in the United States, will receive primary or secondary training in clinical or counseling psychology. Training in clinical or counseling psychology should be merged with preparation in the sport sciences (i.e., academic training as an educational or research sport psychologist). It is expected that this trend will continue, not withstanding that the Association for the Advancement of Applied Sport Psychology (AAASP) has adopted provisions for certification that do not necessarily require the recipient to have an academic degree in clinical or counseling psychology (Gould, 1990).

Future Research Directions

In recent years, a great deal of momentum has developed for greater emphasis on an applied as opposed to a discipline or basic research approach to the practice of sport psychology. The emergence of the Association for the Advancement of Applied Sport Psychology (AAASP) as a society separate and distinct from the North American Society for the Psychology of Sport and Physical Activity (NASPSPA) is evidence of this development. The viability of sport psychology as a discipline, however, is contingent on an uninterrupted flow of research and new knowledge. Therefore, it is critical that research and the discovery of new knowledge remain the cornerstone of the discipline of sport psychology. In the following part, several sport psychology research directions and needs are identified.

Psychological Skills Training. With the emergence of applied sport psychology, there has been a great deal of interest in psychological skills training (PST) programs for performance enhancement. The effectiveness, however, of various PST programs for enhancing athletic performance remains an open question. Additional data and critical research is needed to demonstrate the effectiveness of PST in various sports and changing environmental conditions. Research involving psychological skills training programs typ-

ically provides evidence for anxiety and mood control, but not necessarily for enhanced performance.

Youth Sport Research. While performance enhancement is an important and exciting area of research investigation, it is critical that research in the area of youth sport continues to be emphasized. With greater and greater numbers of unqualified individuals coaching youth sport and interscholastic teams, the potential for a form of sport-related child abuse remains a concern (Cox & Noble, 1989). Professionals are concerned that the lack of adequate knowledge and training in the psychosociological aspects of coaching increases the likelihood of unsafe procedures in the conduct of youth sport programs (Sisley & Wiese, 1987). Consequently research is needed to document the effects of various sport programs and practices on children.

Methodological Concerns. A long-standing goal of the sport psychologist is to establish and maintain high standards relative to research methods. There is a need for methodologically sound sport-specific measurement tools and for well-defined dependent and independent variables. Dependent and independent variables must be operationally defined and remain consistent across research investigations. Psychological measurement tools should not be published until the reliability and validity of such tools are clearly documented and verified. Premature dissemination of psychological measurement tools only encourages their use in ways that are counterproductive to the advancement of sport psychology.

Need for Cross-Cultural Research. Future research in sport psychology should emphasize more cross-cultural investigations (Duda & Allison, 1990). Research that focuses only on the mainstream of North America, Asia, Europe, or any other part of the world, fails to take into consideration cultural diversity and behavioral interaction.

As outlined by Duda and Allison (1990), there are several reasons why there is a need for cross-cultural investigations. First, research that focuses only on the mainstream ethnic group fails to identify sport ethnic-group behavioral interactions. Second, sport in general cannot be understood if it is only observed in isolated ethnic environments. Third, restricting the study of sport to a single ethnic group is in fundamental conflict with the nature and goal of scientific inquiry. Fourth, cross-cultural research has the effect of shedding greater light on the effect of sport on the mainstream culture. Fifth, sport participants from different ethnic backgrounds tend to perceive accomplishments and outcomes in different ways. For example, winning is perceived as a primary goal of Anglo-white males, whereas personal mastery of a task is perceived as more important to Navajo males (Duda, 1980). Finally, awareness of different ethnic backgrounds may alter the manner in which an applied sport psychologist works with an athlete. Individuals with different racial backgrounds often hold distinctly different views regarding the need for counseling and other psychological interventions (Markides & Coreil, 1986).

References

Anderson, M. B., & Williams, J. M. (1987). Gender role and sport competition anxiety: A re-examination. *Research Quarterly for Exercise and Sport, 58,* 52–56.

Antonelli, F. (1989). Applied sport psychology in Italy. *Journal of Applied Sport Psychology, 1,* 45–51.

Arkes, H. R., & Garske, J. P. (1982). *Psychological theories of motivation* (2nd ed.). Monterey, CA: Brooks/Cole.

Atkinson, J. W. (1958). *Motives in fantasy, action, and society.* New York: D. Van Nostrand.

Atkinson, J. W. (1964). *An introduction to motivation.* New York: D. Van Nostrand.

Atkinson, J. W., & Litwin, G. H. (1960). Achievement motivation and test anxiety conceived as motive to approach success and motive to avoid failure. *Journal of Abnormal and Social Psychology, 60,* 52–63.

Atkinson, J. W., & Raphelson, A. C. (1956). Individual differences in motivation and behavior in particular situations. *Journal of Personality, 24,* 349–363.

Bahrick, H. P., Fitts, P. M., & Rankin, R. E. (1952). Effect of incentives upon reactions to peripheral stimuli. *Journal of Experimental Psychology, 44,* 400–446.

Bacon, S. J. (1974). Arousal and the range of cue utilization. *Journal of Experimental Psychology, 102,* 81–87.

Bakeman, R., & Helmreich, R. (1975). Cohesiveness and performance: Covariation and causality in an undersea environment. *Journal of Experimental Social Psychology, 11,* 478–489.

Bandura, A. (1973). *Aggression: A social learning analysis.* Englewood Cliffs, NJ: Prentice-Hall.

Bandura, A. (1977). Self-efficacy: Toward a unifying theory of behavioral change. *Psychological Review, 84,* 191–215.

Bandura, A., Ross, D., & Ross, S. (1961). Transmission of aggression through imitation of aggressive models. *Journal of Abnormal and Social Psychology, 63,* 575–582.

Barber, T. X. (1971). Physiologic effects of hypnosis and suggestion. In T. X. Barber et al. (Eds.), *Biofeedback and self-control (1971): An Aldine reader on the regulation of bodily process and consciousness.* New York: Aldine-Atherton.

Baron, R. A. (1971). Exposure to an aggressive model and apparent probability of retaliation from the victim as determinants of adult aggressive behavior. *Journal of Experimental Social Psychology, 7,* 343–355.

Baron, R. A. (1977). *Human aggression.* New York: Plenum Press.

Beary, J. F., Benson, H., & Klemchuk, H. P. (1974). A simple psychophysiologic technique which elicits the hypometabolic changes of the relaxation response. *Psychosomatic Medicine, 36,* 115–120.

Behling, O., & Schriesheim, C. (1976). *Organizational behavior: Theory, research and application.* Boston: Allyn and Bacon.

Bem, S. L. (1974). The measurement of psychological androgyny. *Journal of Consulting and Clinical Psychology, 42,* 155–162.

Berger, B. G., Friedmann, E., & Eaton, M. (1988). Comparison of jogging, the relaxation response, and group interaction for stress reduction. *Journal of Sport & Exercise Psychology, 10,* 431–447.

Berkowitz, L. (1958). The expression and reduction of hostility. *Psychological Bulletin, 55,* 257–283.

Berkowitz, L. (1962). *Aggression: A social psychological analysis.* New York: McGraw-Hill.

Berkowitz, L. (1972). Sports, competition, and aggression. In I. D. Williams & L. M. Wankel (Eds.), *Proceedings of the Fourth Canadian Psychomotor Learning and Sport Psychology Symposium* (pp. 321–326). Waterloo, Ontario: University of Waterloo.

Berkowitz, L., & Alioto, J. T. (1973). The meaning of an observed event as a determinant of its aggressive consequences. *Journal of Personality and Social Psychology, 28,* 206–217.

Berkowitz, L., & LePage, A. (1967). Weapons as aggression-eliciting stimuli. *Journal of Personality and Social Psychology, 7,* 202–207.

Boutcher, S. H., & Rotella, R. J. (1987). A psychological skills education program for closed-skill performance enhancement. *The Sport Psychologist, 1,* 127–137.

Bowers, K. S. (1973). Situationalism in psychology: An analysis and a critique. *Psychological Review, 80,* 307–336.

Bradley, G. W. (1978). Self-serving biases in the attribution process: Reexamination of the fact or fiction question. *Journal of Personality and Social Psychology, 36,* 56–71.

Bredemeier, B. J., & Shields, D. L. (1986). Athletic aggression: An issue of contextual morality. *Sociology of Sport Journal, 3,* 15–28.

Bredemeier, B. J., Weiss, M. R., Shields, D. L., & Cooper, B. A. B. (1987). The relationship between children's legitimacy judgements and their moral reasoning, aggression tendencies, and sport involvement. *Sociology of Sport Journal, 4,* 48–60.

Brody, N. N. (1963). Achievement, test anxiety, and subjective probability of success in risk-taking behavior. *Journal of Abnormal and Social Psychology, 66,* 413–418.

Broen, W. F., Jr., & Storms, L. H. (1961). A reactive potential ceiling and response decrements in complex situations. *Psychological Review, 68,* 405–415.

Bryant, J., & Zillman, D. (1983). Sports violence and media. In J. H. Goldstein (Ed.), *Sports violence.* New York: Springer-Verlag.

Bursill, A. E. (1958). The restriction of peripheral vision during exposure to hot and humid conditions. *Quarterly Journal of Experimental Psychology, 10,* 113–129.

Burton, D. (1988). Do anxious swimmers swim slower?: Reexamining the elusive anxiety-performance relationship. *Journal of Sport and Exercise Psychology, 10,* 45–61.

Carron, A. V. (1980). *Social psychology of sport.* Ithaca, NY: Mouvement Publications.

Carron, A. V. (1982). Cohesiveness in sport groups: Interpretations and considerations. *Journal of Sport Psychology, 4,* 123–138.

Carron, A. V., & Ball, J. R. (1977). An analysis of the cause-effect characteristics of cohesiveness and participation motivation in intercollegiate hockey. *International Review of Sport Sociology, 12,* 49–69.

Carron, A. V., Widmeyer, W. N., & Brawley, L. R. (1985). The development of an instrument to assess cohesion in sport teams: The group environment questionnaire. *Journal of Sport Psychology, 7,* 244–266.

Cartwright, D. (1968). The nature of group cohesiveness. In D. Cartwright & A. Zander (Eds.), *Group dynamics: Research and theory* (3rd ed.) (pp. 91–109). New York: Harper & Row.

Castaneda, A., & Lipsitt, L. P. (1950). Relation of stress and differential position habits to performance in motor learning. *Journal of Experimental Psychology, 57,* 25–30.

Chalip, L. (1980). Social learning theory and sport success: Evidence and implications. *Journal of Sport Behavior, 3,* 76–85.

Clark, L. V. (1960). Effect of mental practice on the development of a certain motor skill. *Research Quarterly, 31,* 560–569.

Corbin, C. B. (1967). Effects of mental practice on skill development after controlled practice. *Research Quarterly, 38,* 534–538.

Cox, F. N. (1962). An assessment of the achievement behavior system in children. *Child Development, 33,* 907–916.

Cox, R. H. (1987). *Relationship between psychological variables with player position and experience in women's volleyball.* Unpublished manuscript.

Cox, R. H. (1990). *Sport psychology: Concepts and applications.* Dubuque, IA: Wm. C. Brown.

Cox, R. H., & Noble, L. (1989). Preparation and attitudes of Kansas high school head coaches. *Journal of Teaching in Physical Education, 8,* 329–341.

Criteria for AAASP certification. (1991, Winter 1). *AAASP Newsletter, 6,* 4.

Cullen, J. B., & Cullen, F. T. (1975). The structure and contextual conditions of group norm violations: Some implications from the game of ice hockey. *International Review of Sport Sociology, 10,* 69–77.

Davids, K., & Nutter, A. (1988). The cohesion-performance relationship of English national league volleyball teams. *Journal of Human Movement Studies, 15,* 205–213.

Davis, J. H. (1969). *Group performance.* Reading, MA: Addison-Wesley.

Davis, R. C., & Kantor, J. R. (1935). Skin resistance during hypnotic states. *Journal of General Psychology, 13,* 62–81.

Deabler, H. L., Fidel, E., Dillenkoffer, R. L., & Elder, S. (1973). The use of relaxation and hypnosis in lowering high blood pressure. *American Journal of Clinical Hypnosis, 16,* 75–83.

DeCharms, R. C., & Carpenter, V. (1968). Measuring motivation in culturally disadvantaged school children. *Journal of Experimental Education, 37,* 31–41.

Deci, E. L. (1971). Effects of externally mediated rewards on intrinsic motivation. *Journal of Personality and Social Psychology, 18,* 105–115.

Deci, E. L. (1978). Intrinsic motivation: Theory and application. In D. M. Landers & R. W. Christina (Eds.), *Psychology of motor behavior and sport, 1977* (pp. 388–396). Champaign, IL: Human Kinetics.

Deci, E. L. (1980). *The psychology of self-determination.* Lexington, MA: Lexington Books.

Deci, E. L., Cascio, W. F., & Krusell, J. (1975). Cognitive evaluation theory and some comments on the Calder and Straw critique. *Journal of Personality and Social Psychology, 31,* 81–85.

Dollard, J., Miller, N., Doob, L., Mourer, O. H., & Sears, R. R. (1939). *Frustration and aggression,* New Haven, CT: Yale University Press.

Donnelly, P., Carron, A. V., & Chelladurai, P. (1978). *Group cohesion and sport.* Ottawa, Ontario: Canadian Association for Health, Physical Education and Recreation.

Dowthwaite, P. K., & Armstrong, M. R. (1984). An investigation into the anxiety levels of soccer players. *International Journal of Sport Psychology, 15,* 149–159.

Duda, J. L. (1980). Achievement motivation among Navajo students: A conceptual analysis with preliminary data. *Ethos, 8,* 131–155.

Duda, J. L., & Allison, M. T. (1990). Cross-cultural analysis in exercise and sport psychology: A void in the field. *Journal of Sport & Exercise Psychology, 12,* 114–131.

Dudley, D. L., Holmes, T. H., Martin, C. J., & Ripley, H. S. (1963). Changes in respiration associated with hypnotically induced emotion, pain, and exercise. *Psychosomatic Medicine, 26,* 46–57.

Duffy, E. (1957). The psychological significance of the concept of arousal or activation. *Psychological Review, 64,* 265–275.

Duke, M., Johnson, T. C., & Nowicki, S., Jr. (1977). Effects of sports fitness campus experience on locus of control orientation in children, ages 6 to 14. *Research Quarterly, 48,* 280–283.

Duquin, M. E. (1978). Attributions made by children in co-educational sport settings. In D. M. Landers & R. W. Christina (Eds.). *Psychology of motor behavior and sport, 1977* (pp. 462–469). Champaign, IL: Human Kinetics.

Dweck, C. S. (1980). Learned helplessness in sport. In C. H. Nadeau, W. R. Halliwell, K. M. Newell, & G. C. Roberts (Eds.), *Psychology of motor behavior and sport, 1979* (pp. 1–11). Champaign, IL: Human Kinetics.

Easterbrook, J. A. (1959). The effect of emotion on cue utilization and the organization of behavior. *Psychological Review, 66,* 183–201.

Eitzen, D. S. (1973). The effects of group structure on the success of athletic teams. *International Review of Sport Sociology, 8,* 7–17.

Feather, N. P. (1961). The relationship of persistence at a task to expectation of success and achievement-related motives. *Journal of Abnormal and Social Psychology, 63,* 552–561.

Feltz, D. L., & Landers, D. M. (1983). The effects of mental practice on motor skill learning and performance: A meta-analysis. *Journal of Sport Psychology, 5,* 25–57.

Feltz, D. L., & Mugno, D. A. (1983). A replication of the path analysis of the causal elements in Bandura's theory of self-efficacy and the influence of autonomic perception. *Journal of Sport Psychology, 5,* 263–277.

Fenz, W. D. (1975). Coping mechanisms and performance under stress. In D. M. Landers (Ed.), *Psychology of sport and motor behavior II* (pp. 3–24). Penn State HPER Series, No. 10. University Park: Pennsylvania State University Press.

Fenz, W. D. (1988). Learning to anticipate stressful events. *Journal of Sport and Exercise Psychology, 10,* 223–228.

Festinger, L., Schachter, S., & Back, K. (1950). *Social pressures in informed groups: A study of a housing project.* New York: Harper.

Finn, J. A., & Straub, W. F. (1977). Locus of control among Dutch and American women softball players. *Research Quarterly, 48,* 56–60.

Fisher, A. C. (1976). *Psychology of sport.* Palo Alto, CA: Mayfield.

Fisher, A. C., & Zwart, E. F. (1982). Psychological analysis of athletes' anxiety responses. *Journal of Sport Psychology, 4,* 139–158.

Fisher, R. J. (1982). *Social psychology of an applied approach.* New York: St. Martin's Press.

Fodero, J. M. (1980). An analysis of achievement motivation and motivational tendencies among men and women collegiate gymnasts. *International Journal of Sport Psychology, 11,* 100–112.

Fontaine, C. (1975). Causal attribution on simulated versus real situations: When are people logical, when are they not? *Journal of Personality and Social Psychology, 32,* 1021–1029.

Frieze, I. H., & Weiner, B. (1971). Cue utilization and attributional judgements for success and failure. *Journal of Personality, 39,* 591–605.

Gammon, C. (1985, June 10). A day of horror and shame. *Sports Illustrated, 62,* 20–35.

Garfield, C. A., & Bennett, H. Z. (1984). *Peak performance.* Los Angeles: Tarcher.

Gerson, R., & Deshaies, P. (1978). Competitive trait anxiety and performance as predictors of pre-competitive state anxiety. *International Journal of Sport Psychology, 9,* 16–26.

Gill, D. L. (1978). Cohesiveness and performance in sport groups. In R. S. Hutton (Ed.), *Exercise and Sport Science Reviews, 5,* 131–155.

Gill, D. L. (1986). *Psychological dynamics of sport.* Champaign, IL: Human Kinetics.

Ginsburg, H., & Opper, S. (1969). *Piaget's theory of intellectual development.* Englewood Cliffs, NJ: Prentice-Hall.

Goldman, M., Stockbauer, J. W., & McAuliffe, T. G. (1977). Intergroup and intragroup competition and cooperation. *Journal of Experimental Social Psychology, 13,* 81–88.

Goranson, R. E. (1970). Media violence and aggressive behavior: A review of experimental research. In L. Berkowitz (Ed.), *Advances in experimental social psychology,* Vol. 5, (pp. 1–31). New York: Academic Press.

Gorton, B. E. (1949). The physiology of hypnosis. *Psychiatric Quarterly, 23,* 457–485.

Gould, D. (1990, Summer). President's message. *AAASP Newsletter, 5.*

Gould, D., Hodge, K., Peterson, K., & Giannini, J. (1989). An exploratory examination of strategies used by elite coaches to enhance self-efficacy in athletes. *Journal of Sport & Exercise Psychology, 11,* 128–140.

Gould, D., Horn, T., & Spreeman, J. (1983a). Sources of stress in junior elite wrestlers. *Journal of Sport Psychology, 5,* 159–171.

Gould, D., Horn, T., & Spreeman, J. (1983b). Competitive anxiety in junior elite wrestlers. *Journal of Sport Psychology, 5,* 58–71.

Gould, D., & Krane, V. (1992). The arousal-athletic performance relationship: Current status and future directions. In T. Horn (Ed.), *Advances in sport psychology.* Champaign, IL: Human Kinetics (pp. 119–141).

Gould, D., Petlichkoff, L., Simons, J., & Vevera, M. (1987). Relationship between competitive state anxiety inventory-2 subscales scores and pistol shooting performance. *Journal of Sport Psychology, 9,* 33–42.

Gould, D., Petlichkoff, L., & Weinberg, R. S. (1984). Antecedents of temporal changes in, and relationships between CSAI-2 subcomponents. *Journal of Sport Psychology, 6,* 289–304.

Greenspan, M. J., & Feltz, D. L. (1989). Psychological Interventions with athletes in competitive situations: A review. *The Sport Psychologist, 3,* 219–236.

Griffiths, T. J., Steel, D. H., & Vaccaro, P. (1979). Relationship between anxiety and performance in SCUBA diving. *Perceptual and Motor Skills, 48,* 1009–1010.

Griffiths, T. J., Steel, D. H., Vaccaro, P., Allen, R., & Karpman, M. (1985). The effects of relaxation and cognitive rehearsal on the anxiety levels and performance of scuba students. *International Journal of Sport Psychology, 16,* 113–119.

Grove, J. R., & Pargman, D. (1986). Attributions and performance during competition. *Journal of Sport Psychology, 8,* 129–134.

Gruber, J. J., & Gray, G. R. (1982). Responses to forces influencing cohesion as a function of player status and level of male varsity basketball competition. *Research Quarterly for Exercise and Sport, 53,* 27–36.

Hall, C. R., Rodgers, W. M., & Barr, K. A. (1990). The use of imagery by athletes in selected sports. *The Sport Psychologist, 4,* 1–10.

Harlow, R. G. (1951). Masculine inadequacy and compensatory development of physique. *Journal of Personality, 19,* 312–323.

Harrell, W. A. (1980). Aggression by high school basketball players: An observational study of the effects of opponents' aggression and frustration-inducing factors. *International Journal of Sport Psychology, 11,* 290–298.

Harris, D. V., & Robinson, W. J. (1986). The effects of skill level on EMG activity during internal and external imagery. *Journal of Sport Psychology, 8,* 105–111.

Harter, S. (1978). Effectance motivation reconsidered: Towards a developmental model. *Human Development, 21,* 34–64.

Healey, T. R., & Landers, D. M. (1973). Effect of need achievement and task difficulty on competitive and noncompetitive motor performance. *Journal of Motor Behavior, 5,* 121–128.

Hecker, J. E., & Kaczor, L. M. (1988). Application of imagery theory to sport psychology: Some preliminary findings. *Journal of Sport & Exercise Psychology, 10,* 363–373.

Heider, F. (1944). Social perception and phenomenal causality. *Psychological Review, 51,* 358–374.

Heider, F. (1958). *The psychology of interpersonal relations.* New York: John Wiley.

Helmreich, R., & Spence, J. T. (1977). Sex roles and achievement. In R. W. Christina & D. M. Landers (Eds.), *Psychology of motor behavior and sport, 1976* (Vol. 2). Champaign, IL: Human Kinetics.

Henry, F. M. (1941). Personality differences in athletes, physical education, and aviation students. *Psychological Bulletin, 38,* 745.

Heyman, S. R. (1987). Research and intervention in sport psychology: Issues encountered in working with an amateur boxer. *The Sport Psychologist, 1,* 208–223.

Huband, E. D., & McKelvie, J. S. (1986). Pre-and post-game state anxiety in team athletes high and low in competitive trait anxiety. *International Journal of Sport Psychology, 17,* 191–198.

Hull, C. L. (1933). *Hypnosis and suggestibility.* New York: Appleton.

Hull, C. L. (1943). *Principles of behavior.* New York: Appleton-Century-Crofts.

Hull, C. L. (1951). *Essentials of behavior.* New Haven, CT. Yale University Press.

Isaacson, R. L. (1964). Relation between achievement test anxiety and curricular choices. *Journal of Abnormal and Social Psychology, 68,* 447–452.

Iso-Ahola, S. E. (1977). A test of the attributional theory of success and failure with Little League baseball players. In J. H. Salmela (Ed.), *Canadian Symposium for Psychomotor Learning and Sport Psychology, 1975* (pp. 323–337). Ithaca, NY: Mouvement Publications.

Jacobson, E. (1929). *Progressive relaxation* (1st ed.). Chicago: University of Chicago Press.

Jacobson, E. (1938). *Progressive relaxation* (2nd ed.). Chicago: University of Chicago Press.

Jacobson, E. (1976). *You must relax.* New York: McGraw-Hill.

Johnson, D. W., Maruyama, G., Johnson, R. T., Nelson, D., & Skon, L. (1981). Effects of cooperative, competitive, and individualistic goal structures on achievement: A meta-analysis. *Psychological Bulletin, 89,* 47–62.

Johnson, R. T., Bjorkland, R., & Krotee, M. L. (1984). The effects of cooperation, competitive, and individualistic student interaction patterns on the achievement and attitudes of students learning the golf skill of putting. *Research Quarterly for Exercise and Sport, 55,* 129–134.

Johnson, W. R. (1961). Hypnosis and muscular performance. *Journal of Sports Medicine and Physical Fitness, 1,* 71–79.

Karolezak-Biernacka, B. (1986). Anxiety and stress in sport: A tentative theoretical reflection. *International Journal of Sport Psychology, 17,* 398–410.

Karteroliotis, C., & Gill, D. L. (1987). Temporal changes in psychological and physiological components of state anxiety. *Journal of Sport Psychology, 9,* 261–274.

Kay, J. (1988, June 30). Trouble in river city: Players can't cite reason for Reds' poor play. *Muncie Evening Press,* 15.

Kavanagh, D., & Hausfeld, S. (1986). Physical performance and self-efficacy under happy and sad moods. *Journal of Sport Psychology, 8,* 112–123.

Kendall, G., Hrycaiko, D., Martin, G. L., & Kendall, T. (1990). The effects of an imagery rehearsal, relaxation, and self-talk package on basketball game performance. *Journal of Sport & Exercise Psychology, 12,* 157–166.

Kirkcaldy, B. D. (1982). Personality and sex differences related to positions in team sports. *International Journal of Sport Psychology, 13,* 141–153.

Klavora, P. (1978). An attempt to derive inverted-U curves based on the relationship between anxiety and athletic performance. In D. M. Landers & R. W. Christina (Eds.), *Psychology of motor behavior and sport* (pp. 369–377). Champaign, IL: Human Kinetics.

Klein, M., & Christensen, G. (1969). Group composition, group structure, and group effectiveness of basketball teams. In J. W. Loy & G. S. Kenyon (Eds.), *Sport, culture, and society.* London: Macmillan.

Klint, K. A., & Weiss, M. R. (1987). Perceived competence and motives for participating in youth sports: A test of Harter's competence motivation theory. *Journal of Sport Psychology, 9,* 55–65.

Knott, P. D., & Drost, B. A. (1972). Effects of varying intensity of attack and fear arousal on the intensity of counteraggression. *Journal of Personality, 4,* 27–37.

Kolonay, B. J. (1977). *The effects of visuo-motor behavior rehearsal on athletic performance.* Unpublished master's thesis, Hunter College, New York.

Kroll, W., & Crenshaw, W. (1970). Multivariate personality profile analysis of four athletic groups. In G. S. Kenyon (Ed.), *Contemporary psychology of sport: Second International Congress of Sport Psychology* (pp. 97–106). Chicago: The Athletic Institute.

Kroll, W., & Lewis, G. (1970). America's first sport psychologist. *Quest, 13,* 1–4.

Landers, D. M., Boutcher, S. H., & Wang, M. Q. (1986). A psychobiological study of archery performance. *Research Quarterly for Exercise and Sport, 57,* 236–244.

Landers, D. M., Qi, W. M., & Courtet, P. (1985). Peripheral narrowing among experienced rifle shooters under low and high stress conditions. *Research Quarterly for Exercise and Sport, 56,* 122–130.

Lansing, R. W., Schwartz, E., & Lindsley, D. B. (1956). Reaction time and EEG activation. *American Psychologist, 11,* 433.

Leith, L.M. (1977). *An experimental analysis of the effect of direct and vicarious participation in physical activity on subject aggressiveness.* Unpublished doctoral dissertation, University of Alberta, Edmonton.

Lefebvre, L. M., Leith, L. L., & Bredemeier, B. B. (1980). Modes for aggression assessment and control. *International Journal of Sport Psychology, 11,* 11–21.

Lefebvre, L. M., & Passer, M. W. (1974). The effects of game location and importance on aggression in team sport. *International Journal of Sport Psychology, 5,* 102–110.

Lenk, H. (1969). Top performance despite internal conflict: An antithesis to a functional proposition. In J. W. Loy & G. S. Kenyon (Eds.), *Sport, culture, and society* (pp. 393–396). New York: Macmillan.

Lenney, E. (1977). Women's self-confidence in achievement situations. *Psychological Bulletin, 84,* 1–13.

Lepper, M. R., & Greene, D. (1975). Turning play into work: Effects of adult surveillance and extrinsic rewards on children's intrinsic motivation. *Journal of Personality and Social Psychology, 31,* 479–486.

Lepper, M. R., & Greene, D. (1976). On understanding overjustification: A reply to Reiss and Sushinsky. *Journal of Personality and Social Psychology, 33,* 25–35.

Long, B. C., & Haney, C. J. (1988). Long-term follow-up of stressed working women: A comparison of aerobic exercise and progressive relaxation. *Journal of Sport and Exercise Psychology, 10,* 461–470.

Lorenz, K. (1966). *On aggression.* New York: Harcourt Brace and World.

Luthe, W. (Ed.). (1969). *Autogenic therapy* (Vol. 15). New York: Grune and Stratton.

Mace, R. D., & Carroll, D. (1985). The control of anxiety in sport: Stress inoculation training prior to abseiling. *International Journal of Sport Psychology, 16,* 165–175.

Mahoney, M. J., & Avener, M. (1977). Psychology of the elite athlete: An exploratory study. *Cognitive Therapy and Research, 1,* 135–141.

Mahoney, M. J., Gabriel, T. J., & Perkins, T. S. (1987). Psychological skills and exceptional athletic performance. *The Sport Psychologist, 1,* 181–199.

Malmo, R. B. (1959). Activation: A neuropsychological dimension. *Psychological Review, 66,* 367–386.

Markides, K. S., & Coreil, J. (1986). The health of Hispanics in the southwestern United States: An epidemiologic paradox. *Public Health Reports, 101,* 253–265.

Martens, R. (1975). The paradigmatic crisis in American sport personology. *Sportwissenschaft, 1,* 9–24.

Martens, R. (1977). *Sport competition anxiety test.* Champaign, IL: Human Kinetics.

Martens, R. (1982). *Sport competition anxiety test.* Champaign, IL: Human Kinetics.

Martens, R. (1987). Science, knowledge, and sport psychology. *The Sport Psychologist, 1,* 29–55.

Martens, R., & Gill, D. L. (1976). State anxiety among successful competitors who differ in competitive trait anxiety. *Research Quarterly, 47,* 698–708.

Martens, R., & Landers, D. M. (1970). Motor performance under stress: A test of the inverted-U hypothesis. *Journal of Personality and Social Research, 16,* 29–37.

Martens, R., & Peterson, J. A. (1971). Group cohesiveness as a determinant of success and member satisfaction in team performance. *International Review of Sport Sociology, 6,* 49–61.

Martens, R., & Simon, J. A. (1976). Comparison of three predictors of state anxiety in competitive situations. *Research Quarterly, 47,* 381–387.

Martens, R., Vealey, R. S., & Burton, D. (1990). *Competitive anxiety in sport.* Champaign, IL: Human Kinetics.

Martin, L. A. (1976). Effects of competition upon the aggressive responses of college basketball players and wrestlers. *Research Quarterly, 47,* 388–393.

May, J. R. (1986). Sport psychology: Should psychologists become involved? *The Clinical Psychologist,* Summer, 77–81.

McAuley, E., & Duncan, T. E. (1989). Causal attributions and affective reactions to disconfirming outcomes in motor performance. *Journal of Sport & Exercise Psychology, 11,* 187–200.

McAuley, E., Duncan, T., & Russell, D. (1989). *The revised causal dimension scale (CDS II): Multi-group construct validity.* Unpublished manuscript.

McAuley, E., Russell, D., & Gross, J. B. (1983). Affective consequences of winning and losing: An attributional analysis. *Journal of Sport Psychology, 5,* 278–287.

McAuley, E., & Tammen, V. V. (1989). The effects of subjective and objective competitive outcomes on intrinsic motivation. *Journal of Sport & Exercise Psychology, 11,* 84–93.

McCarthy, J. F., & Kelly, B. R. (1987a). Aggression, performance variables, and anger self-report in ice hockey players. *Journal of Psychology, 99,* 97–101.

McCarthy, J. F., & Kelly, B. R. (1987b). Aggressive behavior and its effect on performance over time in ice hockey athletes: An archival study. *International Journal of Sport Psychology, 9,* 90–96.

McClelland, D. C., Atkinson, J. W., Clark, R. W., & Lowell, E. L. (1953). *The achievement motive.* New York: Appleton-Century-Crofts.

McElroy, M. A., & Willis, J. D. (1979). Women and the achievement conflict in sport: A preliminary study. *Journal of Sport Psychology, 1,* 241–247.

McNair, D. M., Lorr, M., & Droppleman, L. F. (1971). *Profile of mood states manual.* San Diego, CA: Educational and Industrial Testing Service.

Meichenbaum, D. (1977). *Cognitive behavior modification.* New York: Plenum Press.

Mikalachki, A. (1969). *Group cohesion reconsidered.* London, Ontario: School of Business Administration, University of Western Ontario.

Miller, D. T., & Ross, M. (1975). Self-serving biases in the attribution of causality: Fiction or fact? *Psychological Bulletin, 82,* 213–225.

Miller, J. T., & McAuley, E. (1987). Effects of a goalsetting training program on basketball free-throw self-efficacy and performance. *The Sport Psychologist, 1,* 103–113.

Miller, L. K., & Hamblin, R. L. (1963). Interdependence, differential rewarding, and productivity. *American Sociological Review, 28,* 768–777.

Mischel, W. (1986). *Introduction to personality.* New York: Holt, Rinehart and Winston.

Morgan, W. P. (1972). Hypnosis and muscular performance. In W. P. Morgan (Ed.), *Ergogenic aids in muscular performance* (pp. 193–233). New York: Academic Press.

Morgan, W. P. (1979). Prediction of performance in athletics. In P. Klavora & J. V. Daniel (Eds.) *Coach, athlete, and the sport psychologist* (pp. 172–186). Champaign, IL: Human Kinetics.

Morgan, W. P. (1980a). Sport personology: The credulous-skeptical argument in perspective. In W. F. Straub (Ed.), *Sport psychology: An analysis of athlete behavior* (2nd ed.) (pp. 330–339). Ithaca, NY: Mouvement Publications.

Morgan, W. P. (1980b). The trait psychology controversy. *Research Quarterly for Exercise and Sport, 51,* 50–76.

Morgan, W. P., & Brown, D. R. (1983). Hypnosis. In M. H. Williams (Ed.), *Ergogenic aids in sport* (pp. 223–252). Champaign, IL: Human Kinetics.

Nideffer, R. M. (1981). *The ethics and practice of applied sport psychology.* Ithaca, NY: Mouvement Publications.

Nideffer, R. M., & Deckner, C. W. (1970). A case study of improved athletic performance following use of relaxation procedures. *Perceptual and Motor Skills, 30,* 821–822.

Noel, R. C. (1980). The effect of visuo-motor behavior rehearsal on tennis performance. *Journal of Sport Psychology, 2,* 221–226.

Noverr, D. A., & Ziewaez, L. E. (1981). Violence in American Sports. In W. J. Baker & J. M. Carroll (Eds.), *Sports in modern America* (pp. 129–145). St. Louis: River City Publishers.

Ogilvie, B. C., & Tutko, T. A. (1966). *Problem athletes and how to handle them.* London: Pelham Books.

Peplau, L. A. (1976). Impact of fear of success and sex-role attitudes on women's competitive achievement. *Journal of Personality and Social Psychology, 34,* 561–568.

Qiu, Y. J. (1986). Research on personality of Chinese elite athletes. *Sport Science, 3,* 41–45.

Qiu, Y. J. (1990). *Psychodiagnosis in sport.* Wuhan, P.R. China: China Geology Publishing House.

Raynor, J. O. (1968). *The relationship between distant future goals and achievement motivation.* Unpublished doctoral dissertation, University of Michigan, Ann Arbor.

Raynor, J. O. (1969). Future orientation and motivation of immediate activity: An elaboration of the theory of achievement motivation. *Psychological Review. 76,* 606–610.

Raynor, J. O. (1970). Relationship between achievement-related motives, future orientation, and academic performance. *Journal of Personality and Social Psychology, 15,* 28–33.

Raynor, J. O., & Rubin, I. S. (1971). Effects of achievement and future orientation on level of performance. *Journal of Personality and Social Psychology, 17,* 36–41.

Richman, C. L., & Heather, R. (1986). The development of self-esteem through the martial arts. *International Journal of Sport Psychology, 17,* 234–239.

Roberts, G. C. (1972). Effects of achievement motivation and social environment motivation on performance of a motor task. *Journal of Motor Behavior, 4,* 37–46.

Roberts, G. C. (1974). Effect of achievement motivation and social environment on risk taking. *Research Quarterly, 45,* 42–55.

Roberts, G. C. (1977). Win-loss causal attributions of Little League players. In J. Salmela (Ed.), *Canadian symposium for psychomotor learning an sport psychology, 1975* (pp. 315–322). Ithaca, NY: Mouvement Publications.

Roberts, G. C. (1980). Children in competition: A theoretical perspective and recommendation for practice. *Motor Skills: Theory into Practice, 4,* 37–50.

Roberts, G. C., & Pascuzzi, D. (1979). Causal attributions in sport: Some theoretical implications. *Journal of Sport Psychology, 1,* 203–211.

Ross, L. (1977). The intuitive psychologist and his shortcomings: Distortions in the attribution process. In L. Berkowitz (Ed.), *Advances in experimental social psychology* (Vol. 10) (pp. 121–141). New York: Academic Press.

Rotter, J. B. (1966). Generalized expectancies for internal versus external control of reinforcement. *Psychological Monographs: General and Applied, 80,* (1, Whole No. 609).

Rotter, J. B. (1971, June). External control and internal control. *Psychology Today, 5*(1), 37–42, 58–59.

Ruder, M. K., & Gill, D. L. (1982). Immediate effects of win-loss on perceptions of cohesion in intramural and intercollegiate volleyball teams. *Journal of Sport Psychology, 4,* 227–234.

Ruffer, W. A. (1975). Personality traits of athletes. *The Physical Educator, 32,* 105–109.

Ruffer, W. A. (1976a). Personality traits of athletes. *The Physical Educator. 33,* 50–55.

Ruffer, W. A. (1976b). Personality traits of athletes. *The Physical Educator. 33,* 211–214.

Rupnow, A., & Ludwig, D. A. (1981). Psychometric note on the reliability of the sport competition anxiety test: Form C. *Research Quarterly for Exercise and Sport, 52,* 35–37.

Russell, D. (1982). The causal dimension scale: A measure of how individuals perceive causes. *Journal of Personality and Social Psychology, 42,* 1137–1145.

Russell, G. W. (1974). Machiavellianism, locus of control, aggression, performance and precautionary behavior in ice hockey. *Human Relations, 27,* 825–837.

Russell, G. W. (1981). Spectator moods at an aggressive sporting event. *Journal of Sport Psychology, 3,* 217–227.

Russell, G. W., & Drewery, B. P. (1976). Crowd size and competitive aspects of aggression in ice hockey: An archival study. *Human Relations, 29,* 723–735.

Ryan, E. D. (1961). Motor performance under stress as a function of the amount of practice. *Perceptual and Motor Skills, 13,* 103–106.

Ryan, E. D. (1962). Effects of stress on motor performance and learning. *Research Quarterly, 33,* 111–119.

Ryan, E. D. (1981). Attribution and affect. In G. C. Roberts & D. M. Landers (Eds.), *Psychology of motor behavior and sport-1980* (pp. 49–59). Champaign, IL: Human Kinetics.

Ryan, M. K., Williams, J. M., & Wimer, B. (1990). Athletic aggression: perceived legitimacy and behavioral intentions in girls' high school basketball. *Journal of Sport and Exercise Psychology, 12,* 48–55.

Sage, G. H. (1975). An occupational analysis of the college coach. In D. W. Ball & J. W. Loy (Eds.), *Sport and social order* (pp. 408–455). Reading, MA: Addison-Wesley.

Salili, F., Maehr, M. L., & Gillmore, G. (1976). Achievement and morality: A cross-cultural analysis of causal attribution and evaluation. *Journal of Personality and Social Psychology, 33,* 327–337.

Salmela, J. H. (1981). *The world sport psychology sourcebook.* Ithaca, NY: Mouvement Publications.

Salmela, J. H. (1984). Comparative sport psychology. In J. M. Silva, III & R. A. Weinberg (Eds.), *Psychological foundations of sport* (pp. 23–24). Champaign, IL: Human Kinetics.

Salmela, J. H. (1991). *The world sport psychology sourcebook* (2nd ed.). Champaign, IL: Human Kinetics.

Sanguinetti, C., Lee, A. M., & Nelson, J. (1985). Reliability estimates and age and gender comparisons of expectations of success in sex-typed activities. *Journal of Sport Psychology, 7,* 379–388.

Scanlan, T. K. (1977). The effects of success-failure on the perception of threat in a competitive situation. *Research Quarterly, 48,* 144–153.

Scanlan, T. K. (1978). Perception and responses of high and low competitive trait-anxious males to competition. *Research Quarterly, 49,* 520–527.

Scanlan, T. K., & Passer, M. W. (1978). Factors related to competitive stress among male youth sport participants. *Medicine and Science in Sports, 10,* 103–108.

Scanlan, T. K., & Ragan, J. T. (1978). Achievement motivation and competition: Perceptions and responses. *Medicine and Science in Sports, 10,* 276–281.

Schmidt, R. A. (1988). *Motor control and learning.* Champaign, IL: Human Kinetics.

Schultz, J. H., & Luthe, W. (1959). *Autogenic training: A psychophysiological approach to psychotherapy.* New York: Grune and Stratton.

Schurr, K. T., Ashley, M. A., & Joy, K. L. (1977). A multivariate analysis of male athlete characteristics: Sport type and success. *Multivariate Experimental Clinical Research, 3,* 53–68.

Schurr, K. T., Ruble, V. E., Nisbet, J., & Wallace, D. (1984). Myers-Briggs type inventory characteristics of more and less successful players on an American football team. *Journal of Sport Behavior, 7,* 47–57.

Schwartz, G. E., Davidson, R. J., & Goleman, D. J. (1978). Patterning of cognitive and somatic processes in the self-regulation of anxiety: Effects of meditation versus exercise. *Psychosomatic Medicine, 40,* 321–328.

Scott, J. P. (1970). Sport and aggression. In G. S. Kenyon (Ed.), *Contemporary psychology of sport* (pp. 11–34). Chicago: The Athletic Institute.

Selye, H. (1975). *Stress without distress.* New York: New American Library.

Silva, J. M., III. (1979). Changes in the affective state of guilt as a function of exhibiting proactive assertion on hostile aggression. In G. C. Roberts & K. M. Newell (Eds.), *Psychology of motor behavior and sport, 1978* (pp. 98–108). Champaign, IL: Human Kinetics.

Silva, J. M., III. (1980a). Assertive and aggressive behavior in Psychology: a definitional clarification. In C. H. Nadeau (Ed.), *Psychology of motor behavior and sport, 1979* (pp. 199–208). Champaign, IL: Human Kinetics.

Silva, J. M., III. (1980b). Understanding aggressive behavior and its effects upon athletic performance. In W. F. Straub (Ed.), *Sport psychology: An analysis of athlete behavior* (2nd ed.) (pp. 177–186). Ithaca, NY: Mouvement publications.

Silva, J. M., III. (1983). The perceived legitimacy of rule violating behavior in sport. *Journal of Sport Psychology, 5,* 438–448.

Silva, J. M., III, Shultz, B. B., Haslam, R. W., & Murray, D. (1981). A psychological assessment of elite wrestlers. *Research Quarterly for Exercise and Sport, 52,* 348–358.

Simon, J. A., & Martens, R. (1979). Children's anxiety in sport and nonsport evaluative activities. *Journal of Sport Psychology, 1,* 160–169.

Singer, R. N. (1969). Personality differences between and within baseball and tennis players. *Research Quarterly, 40,* 582–587.

Singer, R. N. (1989). Applied sport psychology in the United States. *Journal of Applied Sport Psychology, 1,* 61–80.

Sisley, B. L., & Wiese, D. M. (1987). Current status: Requirements for interscholastic coaches. *Journal of Physical Education, Recreation and Dance, 58,* 329–341.

Smith, D. (1987). Conditions that facilitate the development of sport imagery training. *The Sport Psychologist, 1,* 237–247.

Smith, M. D. (1980a). Hockey violence: Interring some myths. In W. F. Straub (Ed.) *Sport psychology: An analysis of athlete behavior* (pp. 187–192). Ithaca, NY: Mouvement Publications.

Smith, M. D. (1980b). A cognitive-affective approach to stress management training for athletes. In C. H. Nadeau (Ed.), *Psychology of motor behavior and sport, 1979* (pp. 54–72). Champaign, IL: Human Kinetics.

Sonstroem, R. J., & Bernardo, P. (1982). Intraindividual pregame state anxiety and basketball performance: A reexamination of the inverted-U cure. *Journal of Sport Psychology, 4,* 235–245.

Spence, K. W. (1956). *Behavior theory and conditioning.* New Haven, CT: Yale University Press.

Spielberger, C. D. (1971). Trait-state anxiety and motor behavior. *Journal of Motor Behavior, 3,* 265–279.

Spielberger, C. D., Gorsuch, R. L., & Lushene, R. F. (1970). *Manual for the state-trait anxiety inventory.* Palo Alto, CA: Consulting Psychologists Press.

Spielberger, C. D. (1983). *Manual for the state-trait anxiety inventory* (Form Y). Palo Alto, CA: Consulting Psychologists Press.

Spink, K. S. (1978). Win-loss causal attributions of high school basketball players. *Canadian Journal of Applied Sport Sciences, 3,* 195–201.

Spink, K. S. (1990). Group cohesion and collective efficacy of volleyball teams. *Journal of Sport & Exercise Psychology, 12,* 301–311.

Spink, K. S., & Roberts, G. C. (1980). Ambiguity of outcome and causal attributions. *Journal of Sport Psychology, 2,* 237–244.

Stennet, R. C. (1957). The relationship of performance level to level of arousal. *Journal of Experimental Psychology, 54,* 54–61.

Stoghill,, R. M. (1948). Personal factors associated with leadership: Survey of literature. *Journal of Psychology, 25,* 35–71.

Suedfeld, P., & Bruno, T. (1990). Flotation REST and imagery in the improvement of athletic performance. *Journal of Sport & Exercise Psychology, 12,* 82–85.

Suinn, R. M. (1972). Removing emotional obstacles to learning and performance by visuo-motor behavior rehearsal. *Behavioral Therapy. 31,* 308–310.

Tattersfield, C. R. (1971). *Competitive sport and personality development.* Unpublished doctoral dissertation, University of Durham, NC.

Thirer, J., & Greer, D. L. (1981). Personality characteristics associated with beginning, intermediate, and competitive bodybuilders. *Journal of Sport Behavior, 4,* 3–11.

Thom, R. (1975). *Structural stability and morphogenesis.* (D. H. Fowler, Trans.) New York: Benjamin-Addison Wesley (Originally published in 1972).

Thune, A. R. (1949). Personality of weight lifters. *Research Quarterly,. 20,* 296–306.

Tresemer, D. (1974). Fear of success: Popular but unproven. *Psychology Today, 7,* 82–85.

Tresemer, D. (1976). The cumulative record of research on "fear of success." *Sex Roles, 2,* 217–236.

Triplett, N. (1897). The dynamogenic factors in pacemaking and competition. *American Journal of Psychology, 9,* 507–553.

Ulrich, B. D. (1987). Perceptions of physical competence, motor competence and participation in organized sport: Their interrelationships in young children. *Research Quarterly for Exercise and Sport, 58,* 57–67.

United States Olympic Committee. (1983). US Olympic committee establishes guidelines for sport psychology services. *Journal of Sport Psychology, 5,* 4–7.

Valle, V. A., & Frieze, I. H. (1976). The stability of causal attributions as a mediator in changing expectations for success. *Journal of Personality and Social Psychology, 33,* 579–587.

Valzelli, L. (1981). *Psychobiology of aggression and violence.* New York: Raven Press.

Vanek, M., & Cratty, B. J. (1970). *Psychology and the superior athlete.* London: Macmillan.

Vealey, R. S. (1986). Conceptualization of sport-confidence and competitive orientation: Preliminary investigation and instrument development. *Journal of Sport Psychology, 8,* 221–246.

Vealey, R. S. (1988). Future directions in psychological skills training. *The Sport Psychologist, 2,* 318–336.

Vealey, R. S. (1989). Sport personology: A paradigmatic and methodological analysis. *Journal of Sport & Exercise Psychology, 11,* 216–235.

Volkamer, N. (1972). Investigations into the aggressiveness in competitive social systems. *Sportwissenschaft, 1,* 33–64.

Wankel, L. M. (1972). An examination of illegal aggression in intercollegiate hockey. In I. D. Williams & L. M. Wankel (Eds.), *Proceedings of the Fourth Canadian Psychomotor Learning and Sport Psychology Symposium* (pp. 531–542). Waterloo, Ontario: University of Waterloo.

Weinberg, R. S. (1985). Relationship between self-efficacy and cognitive strategies in enhancing endurance performance. *International Journal of Sport Psychology, 17,* 135–155.

Weinberg, R. S., & Genuchi, M. (1980). Relationship between competitive trait anxiety, state anxiety, and golf performance: A field study. *Journal of Sport Psychology, 2,* 148–154.

Weinberg, R. S., Seabourne, T. G., & Jackson, A. (1981). Effects of visuomotor behavior rehearsal, relaxation, and imagery on karate performance. *Journal of Sport Psychology, 3,* 228–238.

Weinberg, W. T. (1977). Future orientation and competence motivation: New perspectives in achievement motivation research. In R. W. Christina & D. M. Landers (Eds.), *Psychology of motor behavior and sport, 1976* (Vol. 2) (pp. 123–131). Champaign, IL: Human Kinetics.

Weiner, B. (1972). *Theories of motivation: From mechanism to cognition.* Chicago: Rand McNally.

Weiner, B. (1979). A theory of motivation for some classroom experiences. *Journal of Educational Psychology, 71,* 3–25.

Weiner, B. (1981). The role of affect in sports psychology. In G. C. Roberts & D. M. Landers (Eds.), *Psychology of motor behavior and sport, 1980* (pp. 37–48). Champaign, IL: Human Kinetics.

Weiner, B. (1985). An attributional theory of achievement motivation and emotion. *Psychological Review, 92,* 548–573.

Weiner, B., Russell, D., & Lerman, D. (1979). The cognition-emotion process in achievement-related contexts. *Journal of Personality and Social Psychology, 37,* 1211–1220.

Weiss, M. R., McAuley, E., Ebbeck, V., & Wiese, D. M. (1990). Self-esteem and causal attributions for children's physical and social competence in sport. *Journal of Sport & Exercise Psychology, 12,* 21–36.

Weiss, M. R., Wiese, D. M., & Klint K. A. (1989). Head over heels with success: The relationship between self-efficacy and performance in competitive youth gymnastics. *Journal of Sport & Exercise Psychology, 11,* 444–451.

Weitzenhoffer, A. M. (1963). *Hypnotism: An objective study in suggestibility.* New York: John Wiley.

Welford, A. T. (1962). Arousal, channel-capacity, and decision. *Nature, 194,* 365–366.

Welford, A. T. (1973). Stress and performance. *Ergonomics, 16,* 567–580.

Weltman, G., & Egstrom, G. H. (1966). Perceptual narrowing in novice divers. *Human Factors, 8,* 499–905.

Weltman, G., Smith, J. E., & Egstrom, G. H. (1971). Perceptual narrowing during simulated pressure-chamber exposure. *Human Factors, 13,* 99–107.

Widmeyer, W. N., Brawley, L. R., & Carron, A. V. (1985). *The measurement of cohesion in sport teams: The group environment questionnaire.* London, Ontario: Sports Dynamics.

Widmeyer, W. N., Brawley, L. R., & Carron, A. V. (1990). The effects of group size in sport. *Journal of Sport & Exercise Psychology, 12,* 177–190.

Wiggins, D. K. (1984). The history of sport psychology in North America. In J. M. Silva & R. S. Weinberg (Eds.), *Psychological foundations of sport* (pp. 9–22). Champaign, IL: Human Kinetics.

Williams, J. M., Hacker, C. M. (1982). Causal relationships among cohesion, satisfaction, and performance in women's intercollegiate field hockey teams. *Journal of Sport Psychology, 4,* 324–337.

Williams, J. M., & Straub, W. F. (1986). Sport psychology: Past, present, future. In J. M. Williams (Ed.), *Applied sport psychology* (pp. 1–13). Palo Alto, CA: Mayfield Company.

Winter, B. (1982, May). Relax and win. *Sports and Athlete.* 72–78.

Wittig, A. F., & Belkin, G. (1990). *Introduction to psychology.* New York: McGraw-Hill.

Wrisberg, C. A., & Anshel, M. H. (1989). The effect of cognitive strategies on the free throw shooting performance of young athletes. *The Sport Psychologist, 3,* 95–104.

Yerkes, R. M., & Dodson, J. D. (1908). The relationship of strength of stimulus to rapidity of habit formation. *Journal of Comparative Neurology and Psychology, 18,* 459–482.

Zeeman, E. C. (1976). Catastrophe theory. *Scientific American, 234,* 65–83.

Zeigler, E. F. (1964). *Philosophical foundation for physical, health and recreation education.* Englewood Cliffs, NJ: Prentice-Hall.

·2·

CONTEMPORARY AREAS OF RESEARCH IN SPORT PSYCHOLOGY IN SELECTED COUNTRIES

Hubert Ripoll, FRANCE
Edgar Thill

Dieter Hackfort, GERMANY

Denis Glencross, AUSTRALIA

Elena Kantor, THE FORMER U.S.S.R.
Juri Ryzonkin

Yijun Qiu, P.R. CHINA
Zhuo-ying Qiu

Atsushi H. Fujita, JAPAN
Soichi Ichimura

Chapter 1 presented a general overview of historical perspectives on contemporary research topics in sport psychology as a lead-in to the material that will be covered in depth in this book. However, the orientation in Chapter 1 was, to a substantial degree, North American. It is obviously difficult to describe research directions in one chapter that would truly depict the primary scholarly interests of focus from country to country.

Therefore, the purpose of Chapter 2 is to provide material indicating contemporary thrusts in sport psychology in selected countries around the world, other than in North America. The determination of country was arbitrary. It would be impossible here to include all countries in which research is being generated. For the most part, however, those selected to appear in this chapter are noteworthy because of the quality of research associated with scholars working in these countries. Furthermore, an attempt has been made to represent different cultures in all parts of the world.

Primary research interests in a country depend, of course, on many factors. These include the professional backgrounds and interests of the most productive scholars, their influence on others, opportunities for and support of research, and, of course, unique considerations from culture to culture that might suggest priorities in research activity. Nonetheless, there are more and more opportunities in contemporary times for the exchange of ideas among sport psychologists from different countries. International conferences and publishing opportunities are increasing considerably. Language and political barriers are being diminished. Consequently, commonalities among research interests as well as unique approaches may be found as we analyze what is happening around the world.

The following countries are presented in this chapter: France, China, Germany, the former Soviet Union, Australia, and Japan. The scholars contacted were asked to provide an overview of the contemporary research thrusts in their countries. They undertook their assignments in varying ways, from being highly specific to general in approach. Nevertheless a global picture of primary research interests in sport psychology emerges, especially when considered in addition to the perspectives provided in Chapter 1.

CONTEMPORARY AREAS OF RESEARCH IN SPORT PSYCHOLOGY IN FRANCE: OVERVIEW AND PERSPECTIVES

Hubert Ripoll

Edgar Thill

Until the early 1980s French research in sport psychology had been particularly modest. Two events occurred which initiated operational sport psychology research. One was the creation of a research department, including a Laboratory of Sport Psychology at the Institut National du Sport et de l'Education Physique of Paris (INSEP). The other was the creation of a specialization in Science and Technique in Physical and Sport Activities at the university upper graduate levels, including the development of doctoral programs.

Sport psychology has traditionally involved the use of applied psychology in order to provide assistance to athletes and coaches. Sport federations have been concerned with the detection of talent and the training of young people in sport-specialized schools. Such psychological interventions, which apply methods from experimental and clinical psychology, are in current use, and most research today emphasizes possibilities suggested by the use of these applications. The later development of research in different universities has led psychologists to develop academic research projects including and beyond applications from the field of sport.

Therefore, as earlier research was concerned with the study of overt behavior and factors leading to performance, we can now see that researchers appear to have placed more emphasis on the processes underlying factors involved in performance. This research is expanding in several laboratories at the universities of Aix-Marseille, Clermont-Ferrand, Dijon, Grenoble, Montpellier, Paris, and Reims, and at INSEP in psychology and cognitive neuroscience laboratories. Researchers are represented by the Societé Française de Psychologie du Sport (SFPS), which is associated with the European Federation of Sport Psychology (FEPSAC) and the International Society of Sport Psychol-

ogy (ISSP). Representative perspectives of research developments in France follow.

PERSONALITY AND MOTIVATION

If the purpose of some sport psychology researchers in the past was to identify an "ideal athletic personality" (Morgan, 1980) in a perspective of theoretical traits, the aim of the Questionnaire de Personnalité pour Sportifs (Q.P.S.) constructed by Thill and Brenot (1982) was, in contrast, to assess psychological factors affecting athletic performance. Another aim was to develop scientific research documenting relationships between psychological factors and athletic performance. Several studies (Thill, 1988; Thill & Brenot, 1982, 1985) have provided considerable psychometric evidence for internal consistency, content validity, construct validity, predictive validity, and concurrent validity of the Q.P.S. In particular, concurrent validity was demonstrated by the comparison of psychological assessments and various external criteria: (a) the level of practice and the possible differentiation between experts, novices, and nonsportsmen (Missoum, 1982), (b) the behavioral assessments of coaches (Thill & Brenot, 1985), and (c) the results of other questionnaires (Thill & Brenot, 1985).

The use of the questionnaire in further research allowed the identification of psychological traits in relation to: (a) sport specialties such as cycling (Vanhaverbeke, 1987), fencing (Pardo, 1985), and handball (Bléou Tokou, 1987), (b) the type of specialization in soccer (Michel, 1984), fencing (Rosnet, 1989), shooting (Joly, 1985), swimming

(Dubois, 1988), and (c) playing styles adopted in table tennis (Croiziers de Lactivier, 1987). A longitudinal study that included several groups of sportsmen provided the possibility of specifying the direction of the causal relationship existing between personality traits and sport practice (Thill, 1988). Three tests with athletes over a 27-month period showed an increase in extrinsic motivation, competitiveness, dominance, aggressiveness, emotional control, psychological resistance, and a decrease in acquiescence and social desirability. More specifically, particular psychological changes were associated with the type of sport in which the athletes were involved. For example, swimming short distances was associated with the development of speed and intensity of reactions, and swimming long distances was related to a rise in psychological endurance.

Sport situations may, therefore, be considered with regard to causal factors and individual psychological traits. Important remaining questions include: Why is the athlete involved in sport and why is he or she engaged in a specific way? Further, what is the effect of particular cognitive factors (e.g., expectations or goals) and/or motivational factors? According to the cognitive evaluation theory (Deci, 1975; Deci & Ryan, 1985), experiments conducted by Thill and Mouanda (1990) including both informational (i.e., performance-contingent) individual vs. collective financial rewards, and informational positive vs. negative feedback, confirmed that informational reinforcers led to significantly higher levels of intrinsic motivation than controlling reinforcers in natural settings. Additionally, the effects of feedback on motivation interacted, in the short term, with efficiency expectations, and in the long term, with possibilities of choice and positive verbalization. Moreover, the effects of controlling (i.e., task-contingent) feedback on attitudes and performances in a sport context seemed to be affected by other individual differences, such as the causality orientations or the capacities for imagery (Thill & Mouanda, 1991).

Consequently the meaning of external events, and thus its effect on intrinsic motivation and related variables, appears jointly influenced by characteristics of the subject and of the events in a dynamic interaction. It seems that future research should also be more concerned with: (a) understanding how thoughts (i.e., declarative or procedural knowledge) about such causality perceptions (first-order cognitions) affect motivation and (b) exploring relations between motivational variables and the use of different kinds of processing strategies and the subsequent performance.

PSYCHOLOGICAL EVALUATION OF AND INTERVENTIONS WITH THE ELITE ATHLETE

The aim of the Sport Psychology Laboratory of the National Institute of Sport and Physical Education (INSEP) and of the Applied Psychology Laboratory of Reims University is a psychological approach to stress in sport and in im-

provement in the mental control demonstrated by high-level athletes. Research which concerns two main types of evaluations and mental training involves techniques carried out in working situations which present similar characteristics with sport situations—living in space (Rivolier & Bachelard, 1988), in Antarctic stations (Rivolier et al., 1991), and working in a hostile environment (Rivolier & Cazes, 1987). The main idea is that stress sensitivity is specific in each subject, making it necessary to individually evaluate the subject's capacity for coping with stress (Rivolier & Veron, 1989). Also considered is how he/she handles a situation and his/her conscious or subconscious evaluation of stress in terms of self-success or failure perception related to past experiences. Results clarify the role played by social learning and the effects of mental training in the acquisition of positive and adaptative behaviors (Thomas et al., 1987).

Research consists of identifying each subject's individual characteristics according to his/her stress resistance at different levels: cognitive, emotional, neuropsychological, and psychobiological. Different techniques of evaluation are used, either those classically associated with psychology (evaluation of attention, anxiety, emotional stability) or more innovatively in sport psychology evaluation (cognitive styles, decision and risk taking, social behavior in groups, defense mechanisms). These are combined with psychophysiological (RED, EMG, ECG) and biochemical examinations (Rivolier et al., 1983). Results provided by these methods are used at the psychology laboratory of INSEP in the mental training and psychological monitoring of athletes (Le Scanff, 1990). Studied is stress management—i.e., strategies for coping with aggressive conditions—and the improvement of performance using specific mental imagery.

Different methods of mental imagery, such as suggestion and auto-suggestion, concentration, imagery, relaxation, breathing, stopping of thinking, and increase of tension (Rivolier, 1989) are combined. Studies conducted in different sports (tennis, golf, basketball, archery, fencing, judo) show that each method must respect certain principles to be efficient (Le Scanff, 1990): the adaptation to individual psychological characteristics, the adaptation to the task, a sufficient duration of learning and amount of practice, and the evaluation of its efficiency over an extended time.

Another example concerns the interventions carried out with the French sailing team at first by the Laboratory of Sport Psychology of INSEP (Paris) and now pursued by Levêque at the Université de Dijon. Since 1977, each member of the French crews have completed tests (e.g., Thill's Q.P.S.) in order to: (a) establish statistical criteria allowing differentiation between helmsmen and crewmen, (b) select reliable crews based on complementary and compatible personalities, (c) provide team members' psychological characteristics to the complete crew, and (d) direct and optimize pedagogical interventions of coaches (Thill, 1981). Further, exchanges on board between crew members were systematically recorded in order to eliminate conflicts and stimulate communication based on a common code.

After 1985 and until the Seoul Olympic Games, competitors were also encouraged to follow a meticulous preparation of regatta race procedures as a means to reduce precompetitive anxiety and eliminate internal or external distractors (Levêque, 1987). At the same time, role-play simulations were systematically implemented in order to strengthen the athletes' cohesion. These interventions, and some others (e.g., mental visualization) were then carried out at varying levels, ranging from interpersonal development to interpersonal behavior and interactive functioning of group systems.

MOTOR LEARNING AND PEDAGOGY IN CHILDREN

Research on motor learning in children began during 1981 with Famose and his colleagues at the Laboratory of Psychopedagogy of INSEP. Such research is now conducted by other researchers (Durand at the University of Montpellier and Bertsch at the University of Caen). The rationale of this research is that understanding the learning process should take into account the characteristics of the tasks which children encounter. These characteristics concern, first, the specificity of each task mainly related to event complexity and, second, the characteristics of the pedagogical intervention itself. Two main areas of research have been identified. The first consists of the elaboration of task characteristics by applying a methodology classically used in work psychology: Tasks are classified in relation to a certain number of descriptors and a grid of analysis, based on an ordinal rating scale as suggested by Famose (1985). The second concerns the subject's modifications of behavior related to systematic variations of the task characteristics. For instance, Famose, Durand, and Berstch (1986) have shown that the level of performance in a complex coincidence-anticipation task is highly correlated with the level of spatio-temporal uncertainty. This study of different methods of learning related to different types of pedagogical intervention consists of reducing the task constraints in the early stages of learning, and then gradually increasing the difficulty.

Durand and Barna (1987) have studied the evolution of motor performance according to the amount of spatiotemporal uncertainty, the number of response alternatives, and the required accuracy from a developmental point of view. They have shown that children's performances are lower than adults only when tasks involved uncertainty. In a stable environment, children's performances are comparable to those of adults. Famose et al. (1991) indicated that it is possible to predict the performances of a group of subjects accurately in a series of ballistic adjustment tasks. They used a multiple regression analysis of average performances according to the level of the main descriptors of the tasks as evaluated on ordinal rating scales.

COGNITIVE NEUROSCIENCE

The aim of the research teams involved in cognitive and behavioral neuroscience is to study the interrelations between mental operations and neural mechanisms, and their consequences on behavior. This approach considers the functioning of a system to be dependent on an underlying logic which corresponds to "software," and its structural organization, which corresponds to "hardware." It is influenced by different models from psychology, neuropsychology, neurophysiology, neurolinguistics, cybernetics, artificial intelligence, and information theory. It is assumed that the behavior involved in complex sport depends on the structural organization of the central nervous system and on the modes (or strategies) of information processing used by the person. The role played by each of these components is generally analyzed by comparing athletes with differing levels of expertise.

The approach developed at INSEP by Ripoll concerns the study of visual information processing in complex sport skills directly analyzed in the field. Examples are basketball shooting (Ripoll et al., 1986), pistol shooting (Ripoll, 1986; Ripoll et al., 1985); show jumping (Laurent et al., 1989), table tennis (Ripoll, 1989; Ripoll & Fleurance, 1988), and climbing (Dupuy & Ripoll, 1989), as well as problem solving in a task simulation (Ripoll, 1988a, 1988b). Results show that expert athletes use specific strategies which are frequently subconsciously activated. More unusual is the attempt to describe the mental processes, from the observation of the operations involved at the input (visual) side and at the output (motor) side of the human information-processing system. The aim of this research is to analyze the relationship between sensorimotor and semantic visual functions and to consider how understanding and acting cooperate.

Some sport skills (table tennis, climbing) are characterized by a high degree of uncertainty, stress, and movement complexity. The research procedure consists of comparing visual factors (with the video-oculographic method using the Nac Eye Mark Recorder) and motor behavior (with bi- or tridimensional video or cinematographic analysis) in situations where either the sensory-motor or the semantic complexity varies. The behavioral variations corresponding to the degree of complexity of each situation are used to isolate each component in order to describe the relationship between the cognitive and the sensorimotor behavior, and to reveal the relationships between understanding and acting. The main results show that expert athletes use heuristic rules to marry their limited processing capacities, the multidimensional characteristics of the situation (semantic and sensorimotor), and temporal stress.

From the study of two characteristically "open" situations, a general model of information processing has been proposed. In externally paced situations (such as table tennis, tennis, and fencing), time pressure leads to a specific relationship between the identification stage, which involves the semantic process, and the execution stage, which involves the sensorimotor process. Semantic and sensorimotor operations occur within a closed relationship, so that the semantic/sensorimotor trade-off forces athletes to use the time necessary to process the semantic information, thereby shortening the time needed to initiate the response or to prepare for the more probable event. In self-paced situations (such as rock climbing, skiing, and canoeing), the level of uncertainty is determined by the physical characteristics of the environment. The earlier the athlete selects the relevant information, the quicker he or she can carry out the movement. However, motor behavior is little affected by temporal stress, meaning that semantic and sensorimotor operations are likely to be processed more independently than in externally paced situations (see Ripoll, 1989c; 1991, for an overview).

At Marseille (Université Aix-Marseille 2), Laurent has analyzed the visuomotor mechanisms underlying complex motor skills in the perspective of Gibson's (1966, 1979) ecological approach. This approach is based on the principle that visual and motor systems should be viewed as a unitary system, making their study as separate systems, as conceived in classical psychophysiology, illogical. Questions concern the role played by vision in the planning and anticipatory control of the action, the nature of the parameters that are manipulated in such control, the visual information that corresponds to these parameters, and the nature of the link between vision and action. Laurent has analyzed various situations in which the subject must make a time-to-contact estimate (see Laurent & Thomson, 1991, for an overview). The activities studied involve locomotion (Laurent, 1991), long jumping (Laurent, 1981), obstacle jumping (Laurent et al., 1989), and automobile driving (Bardy & Laurent, 1989; Cavallo & Laurent, 1988).

A new aspect suggested by these results is the central notion that the control of complex skills, like intercepting an object, braking, or reaching a target, involves one or two higher order parameters used by the subject. This is in opposition to the notion that the processing of a large number of parameters is individually controlled, as described by the classical psychophysiological multidimensional model. The originality of Laurent's approach is his attempt at combining the ecological approach with methodologies used in classical psychophysiology in order to identify the different components of visual information, such as correlating the visual and locomotor maps (Laurent et al., 1988) or restricting visual information (Bardy & Laurent, 1989; Laurent et al., 1989). Another original development concerns the analysis of the possible use of original strategies related to

the athletes' skill level. This perspective, which is not taken into account by the classical ecological approach, suggests that the development of skill involves the progressive selection of alternative strategies so that the most economical and effective are eventually adopted.

The approach developed by Nougier, at Grenoble University, and Stein, at INSEP (for an overview, see Nougier, et al., 1991), concerns the study of attentional processes. It is based on mental chronometry in which reaction time is supposed to reflect the nature and the length of the cognitive processes intervening in successive stages of information processing between the presentation of a stimulus and the initiation of the response. Using different methodologies, they study the attentional characteristics of subjects related to their age (Nougier et al., in press), level of expertise and the nature of practice (Nougier et al., 1989), and their neuropsychological organization (Bisiacchi et al., 1985). In the costs and benefits methodology (Posner & Snyder, 1975), the subject is cued to expect a stimulus to occur with high probability at a specific location in space and with much lower probability at another location. Dependent variables are evaluated in terms of attentional costs to detect an uncued stimulus and in terms of attentional benefits to detect a cued stimulus which is related to a neutral condition in which no information is given before the stimulus appears.

Another methodology is based on the signal detection theory paradigm (Green & Sweets, 1966). It can be used to separate the subject's ability to discriminate the signal from the "noise" (which is a measure of the sensibility of the system), and the decision criterion, which is chosen by the subject to accept information such as a noise or a signal, according to *a priori* probabilities and payoffs (which is a measure of the subject's strategy). Particularly interesting is the study of the effect of the orientation of attention on different types of motor responses of variable complexity used to identify the mechanisms at different stages of information processing. The concept of "ideal athletes" suggested by Nougier et al. (1991) considers that expert athletes may have both the qualities of a powerful computer—i.e., highly automatized—and those of a very efficient decider—i.e., mobilizing powerful attentional resources when necessary. This enables them to minimize the perturbations induced by environmental "noise." They show attentional flexibility, which is the ability to quickly switch to the appropriate mode of processing, automatic vs. controlled, adapted to the physical and semantic characteristics of the situation.

References

Bardy, B. G., & Laurent, M. (1989). Use of peripheral vision in the decision to brake. *Perceptual and Motor Skills, 69,* 163–166.

Bisiacchi, P., Ripoll, H., Stein, P., Simonet, P., & Azemar, G. (1985). Left-handedness in fencers: An attentional advantage? *Perceptual and Motor Skills, 61,* 507–513.

Bléou Tokou, J. L. (1987). *Contribution à l'évaluation des caractéristiques psychologiques de hand-balleurs.* Paris: INSEP.

Cavallo, V., & Laurent, M. (1988). Visual information and skill level in time-to-collision estimation. *Perception, 17,* 623–632.

Croziers de Lactivier, P. (1987). *Etude prospective de tennis de table. Psychologie et styles de jeu.* Paris: INSEP.

Deci, E. L. (1975). *Intrinsic motivation.* New York: Plenum Press.

Deci, E. L., & Ryan, R. M. (1985). *Intrinsic motivation and self-determination in human behavior.* New York: Plenum Press.

Dubois, C., (1988). *Spécialité en natation et traits de personnalité.* Paris: INSEP.

Dupuy, C., & Ripoll, H. (1989). Analyse des stratégies visuo-motrices en escalade sportive. *Science et Motricité, 7,* 19-26.

Durand, M., & Barna, R. (1987). Motor performance in a complex situation according to age and task requirements. *Cahier de Psychologie Cognitive, 6,* 573-590.

Durand, M., Famose, J. P., & Bertsch, J. (1986). *Motor skill acquisition and complexity of the task: Trends and development in physical education.* London: E & F. Spon.

Famose, J. P. (1985). L'habileté motrice: Analyse et enseignement. *Sciences et Techniques des Activités Physiques et Sportives, 12,* 31-48.

Famose, J. P., Genty, J., & Durand, M. (1991). Tâches motrices et prédiction de la performance. *Science et Motricité, 15,* 7-12.

Gibson, J. J. (1966). *The senses considered as perceptual systems.* Boston: Houghton Mifflin.

Gibson, J. J. (1979). *The ecological approach to visual perception.* Boston: Houghton Mifflin.

Green, D., & Sweets, J. (1966). *Signal detection theory and psychophysics.* New York: Wiley.

Joly, A. (1985). *Appréciation du controle émotionnel, de la résistance psychologique et du désir de réussite aux différents niveaux techniques des tireurs français.* Paris: INSEP.

Laurent, M. (1981). Problèmes posés par l'étude du pointage locomoteur d'une cible visuelle. *Cahiers de Psychologie Cognitive, 1,* 173-197.

Laurent, M. (1991). Visual cues and processes involved in goal-directed locomotion. In A. E. Plata (Ed.), *Adaptability of human gait: Implications for the control of locomotion. Advances in psychologies series* (pp. 99-123). North-Holland: Elsevier Science Publisher.

Laurent, M., Dinh-Phung, R., & Ripoll, H. (1989). What visual information is used by riders in jumping. *Human Movement Sciences, 8,* 481-501.

Laurent, M., Paul, P., & Cavallo, V. (1988). How gait is visually regulated when the head goes faster than the legs? *Journal of Motor Behavior, 20,* 301-316.

Laurent, M., & Thomson, J. A. (1991). Anticipation and control in visually-guided locomotion. *International Journal of Sport Psychology, 22,* 3/4, 251-270.

Le Scanff, C. (1990). *Approche théorique et expérimentale de la sophrologie et des états modifiés de conscience.* Thèse pour le Doctorat S.T.A.P.S. (option sciences humaines). Université de Paris V.

Levêque M. (1987). Les tribulations de l'entraîneur: Analyse psychologique et mesures d'accompagnement. *Education Physique et Sport, 207,* 8-11.

Michel, H. (1984). *Contribution à l'évaluation psychologique du joueur de football de haut niveau.* Paris: INSEP.

Missoum, G. (1982). *Optimisation de l'entraînement physique: Analyse systématique des facteurs psychologiques.* Paris: INSEP.

Morgan, W. P. (1980). Personality dynamics and sport. In R. M. Suinn (Ed.), *Psychology in sports* (pp. 145-155). Minneapolis, MN: Burgess.

Nougier, V., Azemar, G., Stein, J. F., & Ripoll, H. (1991). *Covert orienting to central cues and sport practice relations in the development of visual attention.* Manuscript submitted for publication.

Nougier, V., Ripoll, H., & Stein, G. F. (1989). Orienting of attention with highly skilled athletes. *International Journal of Sport Psychology, 20,* 305-223.

Nougier, V., Stein, J. F., & Bonnel, A. M. (1991). Information processing in sport and orienting of attention. *International Journal of Sport Psychology, 22,* 3/4, 307-327.

Pardo, A. (1985). *Contribution a l'évaluation psychologique de l'escrimeur de haut niveau.* Paris: INSEP.

Posner, M. I., & Snyder, C. (1975). Facilitation and inhibition in the processing of signals. In P. Rabbit & S. Dornic (Eds.), *Attention and Performance V.* (pp. 669-682). London: Academic Press.

Ripoll, H. (1986). The study of visuo-manual coordination in rapid fire pistol. In D. Landers (Ed.). *Sport and elite performers* (pp. 153-162). Champaign, IL: Human Kinetics.

Ripoll, H. (1988a). Analysis of visual scanning patterns of volley-ball players in a problem solving task. *International Journal of Sport Psychology. 19,* 9-25.

Ripoll, H. (1988b). Stratégies de prises d'informations visuelles dans la résolution de problèmes tactiques en sport. In H. Ripoll & G. Azemar (Eds.), *Traitement des informations visuelles, prises de décision et réalisation de l'action en sport* (pp. 329-353). Paris: INSEP.

Ripoll, H. (1988c). La résolution du conflit sémantique sensorimoteur en sport. In H. Ripoll & G. Azemar (Eds.). *Traitement des informations visuelles, prises de decision et réalisation de l'action en sport* (pp. 127-159). Paris: INSEP.

Ripoll H. (1989). Uncertainty and visual strategy in table tennis. *Perceptual and Motor Skills, 68,* 507-512.

Ripoll, H. (1991). The understanding-acting process in sport. The relationship between the semantic and the sensorimotor visual function. *International Journal of Sport Psychology, 22,* 3/4, 221-243.

Ripoll, H., Bard, C., & Paillard, J. (1986). Stabilization of head and eyes on target as a factor in successful basketball shooting. *Human Movement Sciences, 5,* 47-58.

Ripoll, H., & Fleurance, P. (1988). What does keeping one's eye on the ball mean? *Ergonomics, 31,* 1647-1654.

Ripoll, H., Papin, J. P., Guezennec, J. Y., Verdy, J. P., & Philip, M. (1985). Analysis of visual scanning patterns of pistol shooters: Speed shooting in duelling pistol. *Journal of Sport Sciences, 3,* 93-103.

Rivolier, J. (1989). *L'homme stressé.* Paris: PUF.

Rivolier, J., & Bachelard, C. (1988). *Study of analogies between living conditions at an Antarctic scientific base and on a space station.* Paris: European Space Agency.

Rivolier, J., & Cazes, G. (1987). *Sélection et préparation psychologiques des sujets ayant à vivre et travailler en environnements inhabituels et hostiles. Proceedings of the Conference on Space and Sea* (pp. 87-89). Paris: European Space Agency.

Rivolier, J., & Veron, G. (1989). Prévention et situations extrêmes. *Neuro-Psychologie, 4,* 84-92.

Rivolier, J., Bachelard, C., & Cazes, G. (in press). Crew selection for an Antarctic base space simulation. In A. Harrison (Ed.), *The experience of Antarctica: Application to space.* New York: Springer-Verlag.

Rosnet, E. (1989). *Description comparée de la personnalité de jeunes escrimeurs.* Paris: Fédération Française d'Escrime, unpublished manuscript.

Rowe, D. C. (1987). Resolving the person-situation debate. *American Psychologist, 42,* 218-227.

Thill, E. (1981). La constitution d'équipages en voile. Définition des profils des barreurs et des équipiers. *Cinesiologie, 80,* 193–200.

Thill, E. (1986). Études des caractéristiques psychologiques de la personnalité dans une perspective interactionniste. In A. Vom Hofe & R. Simonet (Eds.), *Recherches en psychologie du sport* (pp. 290–302). Paris: EAP.

Thill, E. (1988). Validité concourante et conceptuelle du Questionnaire de Personnalité pour sportifs: Des procédures symétriques. *Proceedings of the VIIth Congress of the European Federation of Sport Psychology.* (pp. 158–167). Leipzig, DDR: Wissenschaftlicher Rat beim Staatssekreteriat für Köpperkultur und Sport des DDR.

Thill, E., & Brenot, G. (1982). Procédures d'analyse de la consistance interne d'un Questionnaire de personnalité. *Le Travail Humain, 45* (2), 267–283.

Thill, E., & Brenot, J. (1985). Le modèle de mesure des traits reconsidére. Validité des interprétations descriptives et prédictives d'un questionnaire de personnalite. *Revue de Psychologie Appliquée, 35,* 175–200.

Thill, E., Chauvier, R., Levêque, M., Missoum, G., & Thomas, R. (1982). Validité de pronostic de la réussite sportive à partir de critères psychologiques. In T. Orlick, J. T. Partington, & J. Salmela (Eds.). *Proceeding of the Fifth World Sport Psychology Congress: Mental Training for Coaches and Athletes* (pp. 102–104). Ottawa: Coaching Association of Canada.

Thill, E., & Mouanda, J. (1990). Autonomie ou contrôle en contexte sportif. Validité de la théorie de l'évaluation cognitive. *International Journal of Sport Psychology, 21,* 1–20.

Thill, E., & Mouanda, J. (1991). *Effects of causality orientations, imagery, and feedbacks on attitudes and performance in handball.* Manuscript submitted for publication.

Thomas, R., Missoum, G., & Rivolier, J. (1987). *La psychologie du sport de haut niveau.* Paris: PUF.

Vanhaverbeke, J.P. (1987). *Contribution à la connaissance de la personnalité du cycliste.* Paris: INSEP.

CONTEMPORARY AREAS OF RESEARCH IN SPORT PSYCHOLOGY IN GERMANY

Dieter Hackfort

Since 1990 sport psychologists in Germany have been unified in the German Association for Sport Psychology (ASP). At the last annual meeting, in September 1991 at Cologne, there were more than 220 members. Most of them (75%) are working at universities and colleges, and many of them are engaged in research. Different personal interests and specializations have led to a variety of investigations, including different theoretical and methodological approaches.

Overviews about topics and problems in sport psychological research in Germany have been prepared recently by Hahn (1989) as well as by Schwenkmezger and Rieder (1991), with lengthy contributions describing the past 20 years. This chapter will provide a brief overview and will focus on empirical research as well as fundamental concepts and contributions as they are representative of contemporary sport psychology in Germany.

There are two main German publications that specialize in sport psychology. The series of edited volumes and monographs in sport psychology *Betrifft: Psychologie und Sport* is published by Nitsch and Hackfort. The journal *Sportpsychologie (Sport Psychology)* is the official organ of the ASP. In this journal, reports on basic problems and applied contributions are included. In addition proceedings of the annual meeting of the ASP are published, providing an overview of contemporary areas of sport psychological research in Germany.

Although a distinction should be made between predominantly fundamental and applied research, it should be understood that in Germany today sport psychology is vitally concerned with basic research as well as application. A main characteristic and perhaps a peculiarity of sport psychology research in Germany is its holistic orientation. A substantial contribution to theory is associated with the elaboration of action theory, especially focusing on an integration of psychobiological and psychosocial factors, cognition, emotion, and kinetics. This perspective is essential in analyzing psychomotor or sensorimotor processes, the functional meaning of cognitions, emotions, and motivation and volition in action regulation (the organization of goal-directed behavior). The roots of this approach can be traced to the socialist countries of Eastern Europe (e.g., Rubinstein, Leontjew) as well as to the West (Miller, Galanter, and Pribram), and it may be regarded as an important common link between research in the eastern and western parts of the now-united Germany.

From this perspective and in recognition of the necessity of situation- and task-specific instruments, much work has been directed to methodological considerations and the development of sport-specific measurements. This area was discussed at the annual meeting of the ASP in 1990 (Singer, 1991).

Applied research has been especially designated for elite sports by the Federal Institute of Sport Science (Bundesinstitut für Sportwissenschaft). A project supported by this institution concerns the training of technique. This is an interdisciplinary project, including sport psychology considerations. Research on coping strategies, psychoregulation, regeneration from a psychological perspective, motivation strategies, and the ways that coaches and athletic programs can help athletes are topics of investigations supported recently by this institution. Also funded is research on children in top-level sports, career counseling, and the participation of old people in high-level sports.

Research in top-level sports is of great interest to the public but certainly not the only area in which German sport psychologists are engaged. With regard to the curriculum developed by the ASP for postgraduate students, three other foci for sport psychology should be pointed out: sport in different areas of education, leisure time and health sports, and sport in rehabilitation and therapy.

Currently in the framework of basic research there are conceptual and methodological developments in Germany drawing from an action-theory perspective (Hackfort & Nitsch, 1989; Hackfort & Schlattmann, 1992; Nitsch, 1986). Specific research efforts relate to motor memory, especially short-term storage of force time parameters (Janssen, Stoll, & Volkens, 1987), and the effects on motor memory performance of defects in mental training (Rockmann-Rüger,

1989). Recent contributions on the attentional demands of sport have been made by Maxeiner (1989). In addition, the influence of anxiety and anger on attentional processes (Schwenkmezger, 1990; Schwenkmezger & Laux, 1986) and the influence of exercise on emotions (Hackfort, 1991a, 1991b) are major topics of empirical sport psychological research.

Examples of methodological developments are represented by the sport-specific instrument to measure flow experiences (Strang & Schwenkmezger, 1989) and the sport anxiety diagnosis (SAD) developed by Hackfort and Nitsch (1989; also see Hackfort, 1987).

There is a broad scope of applied research in competitive top-level sport. Coping strategies in table tennis (Hindel, 1989), the development of problem-solving strategies in team sports, especially by reframing (Grau, Möller, & Rohweder, 1990), and investigations on the application of mental training programs (Eberspächer, 1990) are still main topics in this area. Also cognitive processes, perception, tactical decisions, anticipation (Sonnenschein, 1987; Widmaier, 1987), and the analysis of strategies of mental and physical regeneration (Renzland & Eberspächer, 1987) are central concerns. Beckmann (1989) is analyzing strategies of coaching, especially in basketball. Applied psychoregulative programs in various sports are being developed (see Frester, 1991; Kratzer, 1988; Schuck, 1991).

The phenomenon of contralateral transfer is being theoretically studied by Kuhn (1987). The significance of visual representations in motor learning (Daugs, Blischke, Olivier, & Marschall, 1989) is of interest. Also, investigations about the manifestations of personality traits of an athlete or other physically active person (Mummendey & Mielke, 1989) are based on a long tradition of research, and are being put into a new conceptual frame. Teipel (1988) carried out a series of investigations comparing fine and gross motor movements in young and old trained and untrained subjects. On the basis of a specific motivational concept, Heckhausen and Strang (1988) have analyzed the effects of strain on the cognitive processes of athletes in team sports.

In rehabilitative sport and sport therapy, researchers are analyzing the effects on depressive patients of exercise in sports (Golz, Erkelenz, & Sack, 1990; Huber, 1990). Motivational analyses for initiation and adherence in therapeutic sport programs are being made by Pölzer (1990). Klein (1988) regards sport therapy as an integrated component of a psychoanalytically oriented, long-term treatment of alcohol-or drug-addicted patients.

In leisure time sport, the effects of leisure time sport activities on subjective well-being are being measured by Abele, Brehm, and Gall (1991). Baumann (1989) and Hackfort (1991c) are engaged in research on the meaning of exercise and physical activity in the elderly. Gabler and Kempf (1987) are analyzing the psychological effects of long-distance running.

Sport psychological research related to physical education is focusing on programs to improve the motivation of students (Wessling-Lünnemann, 1986) and possibilities for intervention based on the analysis of social behavior of students (see Ungerer-Röhrich, 1988). Allmer (1991) is studying teacher behavior and emotions of students, and Alfermann (see Bierhoff-Alfermann, 1986) is concerned with the process and effects of coeducation.

More and more sport psychologists in Germany are engaged in multidisciplinary projects (e.g., the analysis of the risks and costs of doping, see Sehling, Pollert, & Hackfort, 1989). But there still is a considerable gap between frequently proclaimed interdisciplinary research and appropriate concepts and methodological strategies.

We (ASP in cooperation with the association of psychologists in Germany) are deliberating about ethical guidelines for research and application (Nitsch, 1988) and have just finished a revision of our curriculum in sport psychology to improve the application and scientific distinctiveness of sport psychological practice. To put this into practice we also need more methodological control in the development of applied programs and evaluative studies to direct our practical procedures. Progress in sport psychology is largely dependent on what Nitsch (1989, p. 203) summarizes as follows: "(1) We must intensify basic research, if we want to progress in application. . . . (2) We must consider the whole to really understand the details. . . . (3) We have to go into details, if we don't want to provide nothing but trivial things."

References

Abele, A., Brehm, W., & Grall, T. (1991). Sportliche Aktivität und Wohlbefinden (Sports activity and well-being). In A. Abele & P. Becker (Eds.), *Wohlbefinden* (*Well-being*) (pp. 279–296). Weinheim: Beltz.

Allmer, H. (1991). Emotions in sport lessons: What pupils feel joy about. In D. Hackfort (Ed.), *Research on emotions in sport* (pp. 57–66). Cologne: Sport and Book Strauss.

Baumann, H. (1989). Motorische Lernfähigkeit –altersbedingte limitierende Faktoren (Motor learning—limiting factors of aging). In H. Eberspächer & D. Hackfort (Eds.), *Entwicklungs-*

felder der Sportpsychologie (*Areas of development in sport psychology*) (pp. 265–270). Cologne: bps.

Beckmann, J. (1989). Psychologische Betreuung einer Basketball-Bundesligamannschaft (Psychological coaching of a basketball team). *Sportpsychologie, 3,* 5–9.

Bierhoff-Alfermann, D. (1986). *Sportpsychologie* (*Sport psychology*). Stuttgart: Kohlhammer.

Daugs, R., Blischke, K., Olivier, N., & Marschall, F. (1989). *Beiträge zum visuomotorischen Lernen im Sport* (*Contributions to visuomotor learning in sports*). Schorndorf: Hofmann.

Eberspächer, H. (1990). Mentales Fertigkeitstraining (Mental skill training). *Sportpsychologie, 4,* 5–13.

Frester, R. (1991). Psychologisches Voraussetzungstraining bei der Vervollkommnung der sportlichen Technik. (Optimizing motor skills by psychological training). Paper presented at the VIII FEPSAC Congress 1991, Cologne.

Gabler, H., & Kempf, W. (1987). Psychologische Aspekte des Langlaufs (Psychological aspects of long-distance running). *Sportwissenschaft, 17,* 171–183.

Golz, N., Erkelenz, M., & Sack, H. G. (1990). Ein erlebnis-orientiertes Sportprogramm zur Behandlung von Depressionen. Theoretische Grundlagen und empirische Ergebnisse (An experience-oriented program of physical exercise for the treatment of depression: Theoretical foundations and empirical evidence). *Report Psychologie, 4,* 12–19.

Grau, U., Möller, J., & Rohweder, N. (1990). *Erfolgreiche Strategien zur Problemlösung im Sport (Successful strategies of problem solving in sports).* Münster: Philippka.

Hackfort, D. (1987). *Theorie und Analyse sportbezogener Ängstlichkeit (Theory and diagnosis of sport-related trait anxiety).* Schorndorf: Hofmann.

Hackfort, D. (Ed.). (1991a). *Funktionen von Emotionen im Sport (Functions of emotions in sports).* Schorndorf: Hofmann.

Hackfort, D. (Ed.). (1991b). *Research on emotions in sport.* Cologne: Sport and Book Strauss.

Hackfort, D. (1991c). Sportliche Aktivität in ihrer Bedeutung für die Lebensgestaltung und den Lebensstil im Alter (The meaning of sports activity for the organization of life and lifestyle in the elderly). In H. Baumann (Ed.), *Altern und körperliches Training (Aging and physical exercise).* Bern, Switzerland: Huber.

Hackfort, D., & Nitsch, J. R. (1989). *Das Sportangst-Deutungsverfahren SAD. Grundlagen und Handanweisung (The Sport-Anxiety Diagnosis SAD: Theoretical bases and instruction).* Schorndorf: Hofmann.

Hackfort, D., & Schlattmann, A. (1992). Qualitative und quantitative Analysen im Verfahrensverbund –Das Beispiel der Video(selbst)kommentierung (VSK) (A strategy to combine qualitative and quantitative analyses—The example of the video (self) commentary). In H. Haag & B. G. Strauss (Eds.), *Forschungsmethoden-Untersuchungspläne-Techniken der Datenerhebung in der Sportwissenschaft (Research methods, designs, techniques of data collection in sport science).* Schorndorf: Hofmann.

Hahn, E. (1989). Emotions in sports. In D. Hackfort & C. D. Spielberger (Eds.), *Anxiety in sports* (pp. 153–162). Washington, DC: Hemisphere.

Heckhausen, H., & Strang, H. (1988). Efficiency under record performance demands. Exertion control—An individual difference variable? *Journal of Personality and Social Psychology, 55,* 489–498.

Hindel, C. (1989). Die Bewältigung kritischer Situationen im Tischtennis (Coping in critical situations in table tennis). *Sportpsychologie, 3,* 18–25.

Huber, G. (1990). *Sport und Depression. Ein bewegungstherapeutisches Modell (Sport and depression. A movement-therapy model).* Frankfurt: Deutsch.

Janssen, J. P., Stoll, H., & Volkens, K. (1987). Zur Kurzzeitspeicherung von Kraft-Zeit-Parametern: Untersuchungen mit dem Ruder- und Fahrradergometer zur motorischen Kodierung (Short-term storage of power-time parameters: Studies with the rowing and bicycle ergometer for motor coding). *Psychologische Beiträge, 29,* 494–523.

Klein, T. (1988). *Sporttherapie* und *Körperarbeit als integrierter Bestandteil einer psychoanalytisch orientierten Langzeitbehandlung alkohol-und medikamentenabhängiger Frauen und Männer (Sporttherapy and body work as integrated components in a psychoanalytically oriented long-term treatment of alcohol-and drug-addicted women and men).* Unpublished dissertation, Universität Giessen.

Kratzer, H. (1988). Die psychoregulative Einheit (The psychoregulative entity). *Visier, 14*(10), 7–9 and 14 (11), 11–13.

Kuhn, W. (1987). *Zum Phänomen des kontralateralen Transfers (The phenomenon of contralateral transfer).* Cologne: bps.

Maxeiner, J. (1989). *Wahrnehmung, Gedächtnis und Aufmerksamkeit im Sport (Perception, memory, and attention in sports).* Schorndorf: Hofmann.

Mummendey, H.D., & Mielke, R. (1989). Die Selbstdarstellung von Sportlern als Persönlichkeit (The self-presentation of athletes as personality). *Sportwissenschaft, 19,* 52–69.

Nitsch, J.R. (1986). Zur handlungstheoretischen Grundlegung der Sportpsychologie (Action theory foundation of sport psychology). In H. Gabler, J. R. Nitsch, & R. Singer (Eds.), *Einführung in die Sport psychologie, Teil 1: Grundthemen (Introduction to sportpsychology, Vol. 1: Basic topics)* (pp. 188–270). Schorndorf: Hofmann.

Nitsch, J.R. (1988). Verantwortbarkeit des Machbaren –auf dem Wege zu einer Berufsethik (Responsibility for what can be done—On the way to a professional ethic). In P. Schwenkmezger (Ed.), *Sportpsychologische Diagnostik, Intervention und Verantwortung (Sport psychological diagnosis, intervention, and responsibility)* (pp. 66–84). Cologne: bps.

Nitsch, J. R. (1989). Future trends in sport psychology and sport sciences. In C.K. Criam, U.K. Chook, & K.C. The (Eds.), *Proceedings of the 7th world congress in sport psychology.* Singapore: ISSP.

Pölzer, V. H. (1990). Sporttreiben, weil es gesund ist (Practicing sports because it is healthy). *Sportpsychologie, 4,* 24–28.

Renzland, J., & Eberspächer, H. (1987). *Regeneration im Sport (Regeneration in sports).* Cologne: bps.

Rockmann-Rüger, U. (1989). Zur Bedeutung von mentalem Training für motorische Vergessensprozesse im Sport (The meaning of mental training for processes of motoric forgetting in sports). In H. Eberspächer & D. Hackfort (Eds.), *Entwicklungsfelder der Sportpsychologie (Areas of development in sport psychology)* (pp. 141–146). Cologne: bps.

Schuck, H. (1991). Psychologisches Starttraining im Schwimmsport (Psychological training of starting in swimming). *Sportpsychologie, 5,* 17–20.

Schwenkmezger, P. (1990). Ärger, Ärgerausdruck und Gesundheit (Anger, anger expression, and health). In R. Schwarzer (Ed.), *Gesundheitpsychologie (Health psychology)* (pp. 295–310). Göttingen: Hogrefe.

Schwenkmezger, P., & Laux, L. (1986). Trait anxiety, worry and emotionality in athletic competition. In C. D. Spielberger & R. Diaz-Guerrero (Eds.), *Cross-cultural anxiety* (Vol. 3, pp. 65–77). Washington, DC: Hemisphere.

Schwenkmezger, P., & Rieder, H. (1991). *Sport psychology: Examples of current research.* Unpublished paper.

Sehling, M., Pollert, R., & Hackfort, D. (1989). Doping im Sport (Doping in sports). Munich: blv.

Singer, R. (Ed.). (1991). *Sportpsychologische Forschungsmethodik (Methodology for research in sport psychology).* Cologne: bps.

Sonnenschein, I. (1987). *Wahrnehmung und taktisches Handeln im Sport* (*Perception and tactical behavior in sports*). Cologne: bps.

Strang, H., & Schwenkmezger, P. (1989). Grenzerlebnisse im Sport: Der Fragebogen zur Grenzleistung und Grenzerfahrung (Marginal experiences in sport: The questionnaire on marginal performance and marginal experience). *Sportwissenschaft, 19,* 194–203.

Teipel, D. (1988). *Diagnostik koordinativer Fähigkeiten. Eine Studie zur Struktur und querschnittlich betrachteten Entwicklung fein-und grobmotorischer Leistungen* (*Diagnostics of coordinative abilities: A study on the structure and cross-sectional development of fine and gross motor performances*). Munich: Profil.

Ungerer-Röhrich, U. (1988). Zur Evaluation der sozialen Kompetenz und des (pro-)sozialen Verhaltens im Sport (-unterricht) (Evaluation of social competency and [pro-]social behavior in physical education classes). In P. Schwenkmezger (Ed.), *Sportpsychologische Diagnostik, Intervention und Verantwortung* (*Sport psychological diagnosis, intervention, and responsibility*) (pp. 130–136). Cologne: bps.

Wessling-Lünnemann, G. (1986). Förderung der Leistungsmotivation und des sozialisierten Einflussstrebens (Enhancement of achievement motivation and socialized power motivation). In J. R. Nitsch (Ed.), *Anwendungsfelder der Sportpsychologie* (*Applied areas for sport psychology*) (pp. 75–88). Cologne: bps.

Widmaier, H. (1987). *Situative Antizipation im Sportspiel* (*Situational anticipation in sport games*). Frankfurt: Deutsch.

SPORT PSYCHOLOGY IN AUSTRALIA:

CURRENT RESEARCH

Denis Glencross

Research in sport psychology in Australia is maintained by three overlapping groups. First, there is research in universities within departments of Psychology, Human Movement Studies, and Sport Science. Second, research is conducted through the Institute of Sport, particularly the Australian Institute of Sport in Canberra and to a lesser extent by state-based Institutes of Sport. Third there is a limited research effort by individuals working closely with sporting bodies and individual athletes.

In recent years the major impetus and encouragement for research has come via the research funding agencies, primarily the Australian Sports Commission Applied Research Grant's Scheme and secondarily the Australian Research Council (ARC).

Sport psychology research in Australian universities is well established and represents a broad spectrum of both "pure" and applied interests. All departments of human movement studies, sport science, and physical education incorporate sport psychology within their programs, and most have sport psychology staff involved in research. Australian universities are currently undergoing a major reorganization involving what were formerly known as Institutes of Technology and Colleges of Advanced Education. As a consequence readers will recognize some new designations for older institutions.

The Australian Sports Commission is the major source of research funds for sport psychology, through the National Sports Research Program. For example, in 1987–1988 the total value of grants allocated (to all sport sciences) was $106,600. Nearly $600,000 had been allocated since 1983. Sport psychology received proportionately less than other areas, being designated $46,000 of the total allocated.

In recent years, however, we have seen a substantial increase in the monies available for sport research. In 1989–1990, the allocation was $294,800, of which $89,200 was allocated to sport psychology projects. For 1990–1991 the allocations were $253,000 and $45,000, respectively.

Limited research monies are available through each university's research budget and to a lesser extent, through the federal government's allocation to research via the Austra-lian Research Council (ARC). However, under this agency, research areas are more restricted and support is typically given to more fundamental areas such as motor control and motor learning, for example. Most universities have independent research budgets for which staff can compete for research monies.

The Australian Institute of Sport (AIS), based in Canberra, has played a major part in the development and application of sport psychology at both the elite and general performance levels. The Sport Psychology Unit has provided the impetus for much research in the areas of assessment and profiling; sport psychology protocols and procedures; stress management; and relaxation and flotation R.E.S.T. Much of this research at the AIS and elsewhere in Australia is reviewed in a recent book by Bond and Gross (1990), *Sport Psychology in Australia: Current Research.*

Similarly in South Australia at the South Australian Sports Institute (SASI), areas of interest have included mental skills training schedules, psychological factors, and the incidence of injuries. In other states, new institutes or academies are appointing sport psychology staff, all of whom no doubt will contribute to the ground swell of research in applied sport psychology.

In the Australian and State Institutes of Sport, there is usually a close collaboration between psychologists there and colleagues in universities in that state.

Extensive research is conducted within university departments of psychology, human movement, sport sciences, and physical education. It is difficult to review all of this, particularly in light of the recent amalgamation of tertiary institutions into fewer, but larger universities. It is also difficult to identify coherent research themes. Instead I will present a survey of some of the ongoing research.

• *University of Western Australia,* Department of Human Movement and Recreation Studies. Primary areas of research include individual performance, team strategies, and team behavior in predicting team performance in baseball; psychological aspects of sports injuries; and applied programs in cricket and tennis.

- *University of Queensland,* Department of Human Movement Studies. Research efforts are directed toward cues and expert perception in anticipation in squash; and perceptual-motor characteristics and talent in target sports.
- *University of Melbourne,* Department of Psychology. Timing and motor programming; and psychological factors in distance runners are of primary interest.
- *Curtin University,* School of Psychology. Research topics include talent identification in field hockey; expert perception in field hockey; and human skill, learning, and coaching.
- *University of Wollongong,* Department of Human Movement Studies. Studied are models for coping with acute stress in sport; and coaching, player, and team relationships.
- *University of Newcastle,* Department of Psychology. Self-regulation in athletics is a primary research direction.
- *University of Adelaide,* Department of Psychology. Behavioral persistence and self-regulation; and exercise adherence, exercise interventions, and health represent the research thrusts of most interest.

- *University of South Australia,* Department of Physical Education and Recreation. "Dropout" and the motivation of young athletes; skill and coaching procedures are being researched.
- *University of Western Sydney,* Department of Physical Education. Imagery and performance represents the major research direction.
- *University of Canberra,* Department of Sport Studies. Of interest are talent identification in basketball; coaching behavior and performance; and success, failure, and motivation.
- *Deakin University,* School of Education. Studied are youth sport and psychological strategies in coaching.
- *University of Tasmania.* Relaxation, self-hypnosis, and performance; and motivation and performance are recent research themes.
- *Victoria University of Technology,* Department of Physical Education and Recreation. Research involves visual cues in batting in cricket; and modified rules approaches to mini-football.
- *Victoria College,* Department of Physical Education. Mental training and coaching elite athletes are of interest.

References

Australian Sports Commission. (1987–1991). *Annual reports applied sports research programs.* Canberra: A.I.S. Press.

Bond, J., & Gross, J. (1990). *Australian sport psychology: The eighties.* Canberra: A.I.S. Press.

SPORT PSYCHOLOGY IN THE FORMER U.S.S.R.

Elena Kantor

Juri Ryzonkin

Contemporary sport psychology in the former U.S.S.R., like that in many other countries, has two major areas of concentration. The first deals with the solution of theoretical and applied issues in high-performance sport. It encompasses the following aspects: the psychological assessment of an athlete's state and the means to influence this state; the personality and psychological traits of the coach; and the psychological problems of children involved in youth sport. The second area of concentration deals with psychological issues of group involvement in recreational sport activities.

HIGH-PERFORMANCE SPORT PSYCHOLOGY

The major effort of research in this field is focused on the psychological preparation of individual athletes and of teams for competition. The first report on the subject, "The Problem of Psychological Preparation of Athletes for Competition," was made by Lalayan 36 years ago in 1956 at the All-Union Convention of Sport Psychologists. In this report psychological preparation was viewed as a process of developing determination to achieve the highest possible results despite the various unexpected circumstances that may occur during competition. Emphasized was the need for mutual efforts by the coach, the team, and each individual athlete in psychologically preparing for competition. Considerable time has passed since this report appeared, but the problem remains important at present.

Accumulated information on various aspects of the psychological preparation of the athlete has not ameliorated the problem, but, on the contrary, has emphasized it, especially in the following areas: goals of psychological preparation; the subject, structure, and forms of psychological preparation; principles of organizing research and practical activity in the field of psychological preparation; and the like. Besides these traditional considerations, new ones have emerged. These include problems of differences in psychic readiness during specific periods of time, starting from the point when an athlete learns about his/her participation in a competition until the competition is over, as well as problems of regulating an athlete's competitive performance during the event itself. Scholars working in these areas include Bril, Dvali, Gorbunov, Grigolava, Jermolayeva, Lashkhi, Lazitsky, and Savenkov, among others.

A special area of research deals with the study of factors enhancing more reliable competitive performance, with Gaparov, Ivanova, Jampolsky, Khudadov, Mclnikov, Plakhtienko, Shklyaruk, Turetsky, and others making important contributions. Moreover, the psychological preparation of an athlete is considered as an integral part of a standard system of control, consisting of comprehensive, recurrent, and routine checkups, as well as checkups during competition. Psychological control as a system of organizational, scientific, and pedagogical means of diagnosis and intervention is developing at present into an independent sphere of sport psychology. It plays a particularly important role in the process of psychological support for sport activity, as shown by Eidman, Gorskaya, Kalinin, Kantor, Khudadov, Rodionova, Romanina, Tishin, and Tsirgiladze, among others.

The elicitation of competitive motivation and effective anxiety management had been considered for a long time as central aspects of preparing for competition in the former Soviet Union. The peculiarity of competitive activity is known to consist of the unique circumstances of competition, on the one hand, and the individual personality of the athlete, on the other hand. Psychological preparation is focused on psychic readiness, which in turn is related to individual personality traits and psychic processes, where the former constitute the background for the latter. Most studies in the field are thus devoted to peculiarities of the psychic state of athletes in training and competitive activity, as well as methods and criteria for the diagnosis of this state. Alekseev, Badalyan, Baturin, Belyaev, Dubenuk, Grigoryants, Kantor, Paliy, Solntseva, Stavitsky, Voronova, and others have made contributions in this area.

Although there is the traditional division of psychological preparation considerations into general and specific focus, more studies are now emerging that have expanded the scope of this traditional approach, thus changing the goals and practices of preparation. For instance, several scholars, such as Kiselev and Rodionova believe that psychological preparation is the only way to reduce emotional and psychic strain during coaching and competition. The general goal of preparation for competition is to evoke a particular psychic state. This could enhance the realization of functional and special skills to achieve the highest possible result, on the one hand, and could help to cope with pre-event and during-event destabilizing factors on the other hand. This goal is achieved by teaching an athlete special techniques that may provide psychic readiness for activity in extreme conditions. These techniques include various means of self-regulation of emotional state, activity level, selective and distributive attention, persistence motivation, and mobilization of physical effort. Mental rehearsal of competition through verbalization, visualization, or actual imitation is also taught to athletes, as indicated by Alekseev, Gorbunov, Mkrtumayan, Stavitsky, and others. The decisive factor for psychic readiness is the psychic state of an athlete providing the most efficient self-regulation of that athlete's behavior and performance. This state is predetermined by the athlete's achievement motivation and level of emotional arousal.

Some researchers, such as Kalinin and Kantor, believe that the most efficient self-regulation of an athlete's behavior and performance is achieved due to a particular structure of motivation: the predominance of achievement motivation over fear of failure, urge for challenge, and self-perfection, as well as a specific combination of personality traits. The state of readiness for a pending event is created by regulating the level of achievement motivation, forming an efficacy-oriented structure of motivation, and evaluating the individual psychological characteristics of the athlete's personality. Major contributors on this topic include Blumentstein, Chikova, Danilina, Dashkevich, Ganyushkin, Grigolava, Merlinkin, Nepopalov, Paliy, Pospelov, Rodionova, Sanaya, Savchenko, Sopov, Vasukova, and others.

A separate area of theoretical and practical research deals with provision of psychological services to teams. Psychologists working in this sphere solve a wide range of real-world problems: selection of candidates and team formation, creation and upkeep of a healthy psychological atmosphere and the state of the team as a unit, and tactical preparation. Psychological backup for teams is provided by the scientifically based use of techniques and methods of control and intervention. Major contributions to the development of psychological backup systems for teams have been made by Chichanadze, Gorskaya, Kalinin, Rodionova, Ryzonkin, and Travina.

Finally, the personality of the coach is also taken into consideration in this context with regard to his/her major goals, ambitions, and personality traits. The activity of a coach also has specific characteristics, as follows: the probability of meeting the established goals, specific regime of work, and the coach's personal efforts. The coach's performance is to some degree dependent on an athlete's performance. Success or failure of a coach's activity is also predetermined by his/her personality traits. The problems of individual psychological and personality traits of the coach and specificity of a coach's activity are at present being studied by Arabatyan, Kazakova, Pavlova, Pristavkin, Rachkauskayte, Ruybite, and Stanislavskaya.

CHILDREN AND YOUTH SPORT PSYCHOLOGY

Youth sport psychology has been a rather new area of sport psychology in the former U.S.S.R. It was mostly brought about due to a modern shift in top-level sport toward younger ages (and considerations are given to specialization, what age to start training, and dropout in sports at an earlier age).

Some studies in this area appeared during the 1950s and '60s. These studies were initiated by Puni, who believed in the importance and future of the development of children and applications from psychology, since it is impossible to expect good results in adult sport without the proper development of young athletes. Puni believed that a basic, humane approach should prevail for youth. The problems of combining harmonious development with early specialization, maximum physical loads with intensive intellectual loads, and maintaining children's physical health have remained acute up to the present time. The program of research in youth sport psychology focuses on these issues.

A survey of studies, conducted by Stambulova, outlines the following issues as most developed among the wide range of problems considered in youth sport psychology:

1. The influence of involvement in sport on the psychological development of children of different age groups (with contributions by Danilina, Gorbunov, Kolman, Matova, Oya, Puni, Solntseva, Stambulova, and others).
2. Psychological aspects of sport selection (with contributions by Abolin, Bafgulov, Bril, Groshenkov, Ozerov, Rodionova, Romanin, Uyin, and others).
3. Psychological aspects of technical and tactical preparation of young adults (Belkin, Menshikov, Omyrzakova, Puni, Salmanov, Shennikov, Shlemin, Surkov, Tolochek, Zolotukhin, and others).
4. Development of willpower in young athletes (Agafonov, Makarova, Movigovich, Palaima, Puni, Smirnov, Voitov, and others).
5. Psychological preparation of young athletes for competition (Belov, Dashkevich, Ganushkin, Kapustin, Kiselev, Lalayan, Livmane, Puni, and others).
6. Personality characteristics of young athletes and psychological aspects of individual development (Dikunov, Enin, Gissen, Jampolsky, Kofman, Melnikov, Mikheev, Stambulova, and Vyatkin, and others).
7. Social and psychological considerations for preparing youth sport teams (Bogdanova, Khanin, Kolomeitsev, Malchikov, Prokorova, Ryzonkin, Volkov, and others).

Some of the key problems in these areas are just emerging at present. Several of the most acute issues had never been considered for study until recently, the problem of young athletes abandoning sport being one of them. Numerous recent articles in sport journals concerned with the psychological difficulties confronting well-known athletes, after they retire from participation in a sport emphasize the importance of this problem. This particularly concerns early-specialization and early-dropout sports (examples are swimming and gymnastics).

However, the success of these studies and the possibility of utilizing the results depends very much on the correct research methodology. Puni has paid special attention to this issue in his writing.

A group of Puni's research associates for a number of years have developed the concept of forming psychological skills in younger athletes that are important for sport. They selected functional, motivational, operative, and behavioral mechanisms of psychological skills important in sport and outlined four stages of their development. In each of these stages these mechanisms undergo logical and interfacing changes. They distinguished three stages of forming skills important in sport, determined goals, means and methods, and developed criteria for evaluating these skills. They determined the mode of a coach's and psychologist's psychological and pedagogical activities for developing important sport psychological skills in young athletes. The results of this research brought about a new approach to the general and specialized development of willpower, and led to the conclusion that the formation of appropriate psychological skills should begin at the same time as specialization in sport, thereby accelerating the process and allowing these skills to be applied to other kinds of activities typical of young athletes.

Contemporary youth sport psychology has undergone extensive development with the ongoing accumulation of scientific data. Numerous studies in this area have been published, but articles, monographs and textbooks, summing up the general body of knowledge, have not yet appeared in the Soviet Union.

RECREATIONAL, EXERCISE, AND HEALTH SPORT PSYCHOLOGY

Noncompetitive sport psychology is the least developed area of contemporary sport psychology in the former U.S.S.R.; however, now there is greater interest in this specialty. Accumulated knowledge in this area illustrates the positive influence of noncompetitive sport activity on such psychological factors as stress, depression, and psychological work capability. It enhances such factors as confidence, self-control, and stress resistance. Thus noncompetitive sport psychology should be treated as a basic concept of psychological health, and its structural components are rooted in social, psychological, personal, and psychophysiological factors. In addition, Kantor, Ryzonkin, and

Slobunov have made contributions in the area of psychomotor and cognitive processes.

Recreational sport psychology does not focus on overcoming the negative consequences of insufficient physical activity or its complete absence. Instead it is associated with selecting different kinds of physical activity according to personal psychological characteristics that maintain and enhance the psychological health of different types of people in society: children of school and preschool age, older students, intellectuals, military personnel involved in low physical activity, and many other groups. Recreational sport psychology can serve to rehabilitate survivors of earthquakes in Armenia and catastrophes in Chernobyl, postsurgical patients, patients recovering from myocardial infarction, and the like. Carefully portioned and specified physical loads for these special groups are sure to play a rehabilitative role in returning people to normal life functions. People can be stimulated to carry out physical exercise only by psychological means—motivation, conviction, and the introduction of play elements. The major focus of research in the field of recreational sport psychology is associated with motivation problems in exercise (with major contributions by Mironova, Pimonova, Pytenko, Skrebets, and others).

For example, during exercise a nonmotivated person may, at a certain point, discontinue training and in the long run drop out of physical activity. Information accumulated in elite-level sport research on the psychological regulation of an athlete's state, autotraining, and appropriate motivations can be applied to recreational athletes as well. These topics are now being studied by a number of researchers, such as Budyka, Efimova, Ivannikov, Kupriyanov, Nikiforov, Niyazbekova, Novikov, Shuvalov, Titova, and Voronin.

Researchers are also interested in the influence of regular noncompetitive physical exercise on the psychic development of various processes, and on personality evolution as a part of the global process of the development of self-image. (Alexandrova, Dashkevich, Dubova, Garalis, Gasmov, Glazov, Khodjaev, Kupriyanov, Lidskaya, Udini, Zubkov, and others have contributed to this literature.)

The success of mass involvement in exercise and fitness programs depends to a great extent on the personality of a coach or teacher at a school, a university, or sports club. These specialists are prepared by sports educational institutions at the university or secondary education level. There are far fewer studies concerning the personality of the coach and his/her individual personality traits in the field of recreational sport psychology as compared to the field of high-level-athlete sport psychology. However, such studies do exist. For example, Krichevsky and Marzhinya have singled out most of the important personal traits of a coach for enhancing a team's efficacy: emotional openness in communication, a developed sense of responsibility, social courage, flexibility in personal relationships, low anxiety, and high emotional tension.

Only the most positive of all possible attitudes maximally promotes physical activity, while neutral or obviously negative functional and situational attitudes create negative results. Research on the coach's personality has been undertaken by Chernov, Khachaturyan, Torpchin, and others.

Finally, a separate area of sport psychology that develops methods of psychodiagnostics and computational diagnostics is pursuing several additional goals to the ones associated with the research described so far. These goals include the creation of a bank of data and knowledge, the automation of psychological research, and the creation of an expert psychological system for both high-performance and recreational sport. Interesting studies in this area have been undertaken by Kalinin, Nilopets, Ryzonkin, and Turetsky.

CONTEMPORARY AREAS OF RESEARCH IN SPORT PSYCHOLOGY IN THE PEOPLE'S REPUBLIC OF CHINA

Yi-jun Qiu

Zhuo-ying Qiu

OVERVIEW AND PERSPECTIVES

Research on sport psychology emerged from the needs determined in physical education and sports. Considering sport practice and the development of specialities in sport science, we have established our research system.

Since 1978, six nationwide projects on the following topics have been completed: (1) the psychological selection of athletes (1980–1982); (2) the personality characteristics of elite athletes (1983–1984); (3) the formulation of a psychomotor ability test for youngsters (1985–1986); (4) the investigation of the psychological traits of elite athletes, including consultation with them (1987–1990); (5) the psychological diagnosis and selection of athletes (1987–1990); (6) the psychological counseling and training of Chinese elite fencing athletes (1990). All these projects were supported by the China Physical Education and Sport Commission, and they have had a great impact on the development of sport psychology and the practice of sports.

In China there are three types of researchers involved in sport psychology: (1) teachers/researchers majoring in applied psychology; (2) teachers/researchers majoring in physical education and sport science; (3) coaches/practical workers. Up to now, the research areas are associated with: fundamental theories, cognitive psychology, emotion and affection, personality, the teaching of physical education, sports training, sports competition, mental training, psychological characteristics of teachers and coaches, the psychology of gymnastics, track and field, ball sports, swimming, shooting, the social psychology of sport, and managerial psychology in physical education and sport.

The Sport Psychology Research Division and Sport Psychology Department of the Wuhan Institute of Physical Education, the center of sport psychology in P.R. China, plays a key role in scientific research, professional training, and academic exchanges. An outstanding educational and scientific research system has been established headed by professor Qiu Yi-jun. Master's degree and bachelor's degree programs are provided for sport psychology majors. More than 20 books and 100 articles have been published, and formal academic exchange programs with some institutions in the U.S., Canada, and Germany have been established.

MOST SIGNIFICANT THEMES

During the past decade, sport psychology research in China has focused on theoretical and applied areas. A series of projects have been undertaken, the most significant ones being: (1) the psychological selection of athletes and (2) the psychological diagnosis of athletes.

The psychological selection of athletes is associated with identifying talent in the young and predicting their future successes in terms of psychological demands. The screening of elite athletes has gradually drawn great attention in China. In fact, the development of modern science, especially the advancement of brain science, has contributed to the necessary conditions for organizing the psychological selection of athletes. For example, research on heredity has made it possible to predict psychological abilities. Furthermore, the law of mental ages has made it possible to evaluate psychological abilities. In addition, an understanding of the variability and stability of mental development has made it possible to diagnose psychological abilities.

Psychological selection is based on the concept of heredity, superiority, and the starting point of training. The primary contents of the psychological selection of athletes include the measurement and evaluation of athletes' cognitive processes, emotional process, willpower, psychological dynamics, personality, and the like. The major steps in psychological selection include choosing parameters, selecting instrumentation, working out detailed rules of measurement, pretesting, testing, data processing, establishing models of prediction, and having follow-up studies. Research methods relate to experimental psychology, psychometrics, physiopsychology, and social psychology. The process of selection is characterized by its long duration, which involves a variety of athletic levels, including primary election, semiselection, and precise selection.

In research on the psychological characteristics of the elite, we tested athletes involved in sprinting, gymnastics, swimming, and volleyball events on their reactions, senses, perceptions, memory, mental load, ability, will, emotional change pattern, etc. Models of elite athletes were formulated for different events.

In research on the personality characteristics of elite athletes, personality inventories such as the 16PF, EPQ, MMPI, the U-K, the 808 Neurotype, and field dependence-field independence were administered. We found that there were differences among athletes in different events, as well as typical personality profiles and characteristic neurotypes.

The testing of the psychological abilities and aptitudes of the young athletes involved more than 20 types of ability tests administered in China and abroad. More than 1,000 subjects were involved. We selected 7 criteria for testing athletes' psychological abilities and establishing standards of evaluation. Since 1980, 2,719 athletes (including short-distance runners, swimmers, gymnasts, and volleyball players) have been tested according to 53 cognitive testing criteria and 39 derived criteria. Forty-three research papers have been completed in this area. A series of referential criteria for the psychological selection of athletes, together with the methods and equipment used for the selection, have been developed and applied.

The *psychological diagnosis of athletes* is a comprehensive program. Since 1986, we used various methods and criteria to measure psychomotor abilities, intelligence, personality, anxiety, emotional state changes, psychological load, and so on. Now the psychological diagnosis system has been established and applied to sports training, sports psychological consultation, and sport talent selection.

The system includes the following aspects:

1. The theories, principles, contents, procedures, indices, and methods for the psychological diagnosis of athletes.
2. A system of criteria for the psychological diagnosis of different events.
3. Criteria, methods, and evaluation procedures associated with the diagnosis of cognitive processes (such as reactions, stability, time and space perception, senses, attention, memory, and operational thinking).
4. The psychological diagnosis of psychomotor ability and aptitude.
5. Sociometry and its applications to sports.
6. Diagnosis of the personality of athletes.
7. Psychological diagnosis of attitudes toward sport, sport motivation, and causal attribution.
8. Diagnosis of anxiety.
9. Diagnosis of the cohesion of sports teams.
10. Diagnosis of coaches' behaviors.
11. Methods of athletes' self-evaluation of psychological states.

PROSPECTS FOR FUTURE DEVELOPMENT

Although we have made great research progress in sport psychology, there are still some problems to be solved. On the one hand, we have to summarize our achievements. On the other hand, we need to improve our research theoretically and practically according to the characteristics of sport situations and the science of psychology.

The following areas will probably be of increasing interest in the future: (1) methods of evaluation, diagnosis and training of psychological characteristics, (2) the selection of athletes, and (3) psychological consultation and training. We have completed research in one of these areas, which includes a determination of the psychological traits of Chinese elite athletes, mental training, and psychological consultation with elite athletes. However, research methods need to be improved and programs need to be developed to meet the needs of athletes. Other research areas of increasing future interest include the social psychology of sport, and the training of professional personnel.

Qualified researchers are basic to the development of sport psychology, and China has a great need for professionally trained sport psychologists. We also need to establish regulations with regard to sport psychology services in order to ensure their quality and effectiveness.

CONTEMPORARY AREAS OF RESEARCH IN SPORT PSYCHOLOGY IN JAPAN

Atsushi H. Fujita

Soichi Ichimura

OVERVIEW

As reported by Fujita (1987), research on sport psychology in Japan has developed through physical education in colleges and universities. Today in Japan, 6 colleges and nearly 30 universities have undergraduate programs, and 2 colleges and over 14 universities have postgraduate programs in their departments of physical education. In most of these institutions, the psychology of physical education, or sport psychology, is a compulsory subject. Indeed, the psychology of physical education or sport psychology is so popular that many students write their theses on the psychology of physical education or sport psychology in both undergraduate and postgraduate courses. Most of these institutions publish research bulletins of their own, which are important sources of information for sport psychology.

The Japanese Society of Physical Education (JSPE) was formed with the purpose of promoting research activities in these institutions in 1950. By 1960, 11 different research areas had been developed, one of which was the Division of Psychology of Physical Education. This provided a forum for the delivery and discussion of papers dealing with the psychology of physical education and with sport psychology. The JSPE has a membership of nearly 6,000 at present and meets annually. As one of 13 divisions in the JSPE, the Division of Psychology of Physical Education, with a membership of 500, holds symposia and research sections at these annual meetings. The JSPE publishes the *Japan Journal of Physical Education (JJPE)* quarterly which was the *Japanese Journal of Physical Education* before 1989. The *JJPE* is important as a source of information for research in sport psychology.

In the early 1960s, there emerged a prevailing recognition in western countries that sport is an interesting social and cultural phenomenon in its own right. This resulted in the formation of the International Society of Sport Psychology (ISSP) in 1965 in Rome. In parallel with the development of sport in western countries, elite sport has blossomed in Japan since 1960. After the Olympic Games in Tokyo in 1964, research in sport began to develop as a science independent of physical education. Thus widespread interest in sport psychology, already evident in Japan, led in 1973 to the formation of the Japanese Society of Sport Psychology (JSSP), a separate society from JSPE, to oversee the direction and promotion of sport psychology in Japan. The JSSP has a membership of nearly 350 at present, most of whom are also members of the Division of Psychology of Physical Education in the JSPE. It meets annually to provide a forum for the delivery and discussion of papers at symposia, workshops, and research sections. Most of the papers presented at the annual meetings have been published in the *Japanese Journal of Sport Psychology (JJSP)* annually since its formation in 1973. This journal provides an important source about research information in sport psychology.

In addition to the above-mentioned sources of information, published in both English and Japanese (with an English summary), there are several papers contributed to international publications. These also provide an important source of information. Ichimura (1988) compiled research in sport psychology from 1980 to 1987 based on the sources just described. In this section, the contents of the most significant research are summarized under six headings and supplemented with additional research findings from 1988 to 1990.

We thank Christine Le Scanff (INSEP) and Marc Durand (University of Montpellier) for their help in preparing this manuscript.

MOST SIGNIFICANT RESEARCH

Developmental Studies

For developmental studies in sport psychology in Japan in recent years, multivariate statistical procedures are prevalent. Ichimura (1981) and Matsuura (1982) developed new mathematical methods to compare factor structures from different populations. Ichimura (1981) found that the strength of the general factor increased from the developmental stage of primary school (grades 4–6) to junior high school (grades 7–9). Matsuura and Aoyagi (1985) investigated the increase of balance ability of 3.5-year-old through 6.5-year-old children. They obtained the developmental curves of six factor scores, and found that the components of balance ability did not coincide with their growth curves. Dynamic balance tasks in jumping and rolling were better performed by older children, while static balance tasks were performed by 4-year-old children as well as by 5-year-old children. Niwa (1981, 1982) investigated the developmental relationship between motor ability and verbal understanding. Although he confirmed a close relationship between the ability to transform verbal instructions into motor behavior and regulative motor ability, coordination, and rhythmical movement, no close relationship between verbal ability and muscle strength was found.

Sugihara (1985) studied the relationship between the perceived motor competence of kindergarten children and their personality traits, as evaluated by their teachers and mothers. The findings showed that those children who were confident in their own motor ability were regarded as confident, active, and cooperative by teachers, and were considered vivid, active, obedient, and less timid by their mothers. Kim and Matsuura (1988) examined both quantitative and qualitative developmental changes of fundamental movement skills through 3.0-and 7.5-year-old male and female children, and clarified the relationship between these two changes. As for the running, jumping, and throwing movement skills, both quantitative and qualitative changes showed an almost linear developmental trend in both boys and girls, although the trend was less pronounced for the girls. These findings led to the inference that nearly 28.8–35.2% of boys and 11.3–12.9% of girls aged 7.5 would show matured fundamental movement patterns, the sole exception being the throwing movements of girls. As for the relationship between the quantitative and qualitative changes in running, jumping, and throwing movements, a close relationship was found in both boys and girls, again except for the girls' throwing movement skill.

Achievement Motivation

Nishida and Inomata (1981) used factor analysis to examine an Achievement Motive Test in Sport. Seven factors were extracted from the test, namely: unique accomplishment, mental toughness, overcoming obstacles, instrumen-

tal activity, endurance, the desire to achieve success, and the desire to develop motor skills. Nishida (1984) explored the facilitating effect of achievement motivation on motor learning and found that the high motivation group showed constantly better performance than the low motivation group. Nishida (1989) developed the Achievement Motivation in Physical Education Test (AMPET), which consisted of eight scales. They included learning strategy, overcoming obstacles, diligence, seriousness, competence of motor ability, value of learning, anxiety about stress-causing situations, and failure anxiety. The test was administered to 10,055 elementary, junior, and senior high school pupils, and correlations were examined between external variables (scores on the motor ability test, scores in physical education classes, participation in sporting activities, and the like). All external variables were successful in validating the AMPET, and split-half and test-retest reliability estimates for AMPET were sufficiently high. The author concluded that AMPET was valid and reliable as a standardized test for assessing achievement motivation in physical activities and sport for boys and girls.

Perceptual Motor Behaviors

Memory and Imagery in Motor Control. Ito and Sanjo published studies on transforming short-term memory information into muscle contractions (M. Ito, 1982, 1983, 1986; M. Ito & Sanjo, 1984). In these studies, mental rehearsal techniques and symbolic coding strategies were applied to diminish the error in recalling the short-term memory of muscle force, and response set characteristics and sex differences in recalling the short-term memory of muscle force were investigated. Tanaka (1990) examined the changes and the developmental differences of representation (of imagery) in the learning process of children's motor proficiency. It was found that the frequency of motor representation increased in accordance with the advancement of motor proficiency, especially in older children, while visual representation showed none of the changes, regardless of the advancement of motor proficiency in the children.

Timing, Anticipation, and Cognition. Kudo (1984) analyzed the error in reaction time and found that negative (delayed) error to the signal occurred more often than the positive (anticipatory) error, and delay in response time increased as the duration of the response movement increased. Shinoda and Yoshida (1987) investigated EEG (CNV) during the timing task and found that the number of probable patterns of stimuli and the time lag between the last distinct point and motor response could affect the slow brain waves. Some cognitive factors, such as strategies for reacting to the target stimulus, anticipation, and simple reaction seemed to have a certain effect on evoking slow waves. Araki and Nishihira (1983, 1984) also have been active in research on CNV during reactive timing tasks. Kaino and Sugihara (1989) conducted an experiment in a simulated condition on a tennis net-player's anticipation. The findings showed that the learning of pattern recognition with the film was significantly effective in improving the anticipation, speed, and accuracy of motor responses to the filmed stimulus of the opponent's striking of the ball.

Suzuki et al. (1989) investigated the mechanism of the serve return in tennis, using the "Cyclic Pre-Stimulus" with both preparatory and discriminating stimuli. It was found that practice under simulated conditions was effective in improving the response, presumably by reinforcing the memory processes in the central nervous system. They recommended the use of simulated practice conditions in tennis practice. Nakagawa (1982) conducted a field experiment on cue recognition in rugby football and found that skilled players had a better cognitive ability regarding game situations. Sugihara and Yoshida (1989) constructed a tennis-specific version (T-TAIS) of Nideffer's Test of Attentional and Interpersonal Style (TAIS). Analysis showed a significant main effect for skill on the T-TAIS subscales but not on the TAIS subscales. High correlation coefficients were not found between corresponding subscales of the T-TAIS and TAIS. Based on this, the authors concluded that T-TAIS was a more accurate indicator of the attentional style of tennis players than was the TAIS subscales.

Reaction Time. Fujita (1984) and Fujita et al. (1982) investigated selective jump reaction time accompanied with eye-head coordination. They classified reaction time into four time phases—(1) latency of eye movement; (2) eye movement time; (3) decision time; and (4) contraction time—and examined the effects of development and athletic training. Results showed that development and athletic training caused marked shortening of jump reaction time depending on the shortening of the latency of eye movement and decision time. Significant high correlations were found between reaction time as a whole and latency of eye movement as well as eye movement time. Based on these results, the authors recommended utilizing the selective eye-head coordination reaction time, which consisted of latency of eye movement and eye movement time, for predicting achievement in open skills. Kasai (1982, 1983, 1985) conducted a series of experiments on the dependency of reaction time upon movement patterns. In 1982, he confirmed the difference in reaction time of supination (S) and flexion (F) of a forearm muscle group based on EMG reaction potential. Reaction time in supination was shorter than flexion. In 1983 he found that the EMG-RT difference between S and F were also different between preferred and nonpreferred hands and among sporting events, presumably due to learning effects. Therefore, in 1985, he had subjects practice the swing of a tennis racquet 100 times to alter the EMG-RT difference. As a result of practice, the EMG-RT difference was altered to some extent in the trained hand, but the effects of training disappeared within 3 or 4 months, supposedly a result of the lack of long-term training.

Biofeedback for Motor Control

The application of biofeedback to sport is a rather new area of interest in Japan. Araki and Sakuma (1982, 1983) were forerunners in the application of EMG feedback to motor learning. Subjects were instructed to exert a certain degree of tension in the forearm. The difference between the assigned degree and exerted degree of tension was given by visual, auditory, and EMG feedback. Results showed that EMG feedback was most effective in regenerating the assigned tension. In their studies, physiopsychological characteristics of EMG feedback among other feedback methods were not demonstrated. However, these pilot studies were soon followed by more sophisticated experimental studies. Takenaka (1984a, 1984b, 1986) subsequently published research in which EMG feedback from the biceps and triceps at elbow flexion was applied to improve the self-awareness of muscle tension. After EMG feedback training, subjects improved the sensitivity to the tension of their own arm muscle group. Sakuma and Nagata (1983) successfully applied this technique to improve motor skills for a compensatory tracking task. Sakuma and Nagata (1984) and Sakuma (1985) also studied EMG feedback to control the microvibration of muscles (physiological tremor) for clinical applications.

The application of biofeedback is a promising field, not only with regard to motor learning but also for relaxation and stress management purposes. However, there are several problems in its use in sporting situations. Takenaka (1990) has pointed out these problems in a comprehensive review of the biofeedback literature related to motor control.

Personality Studies of Athletes

A comparison of the personality characteristics of athletes with nonathletes using personality tests based on trait theory can no longer be regarded as important in Japan. Interests have shifted to the field of personal and social identity development through sporting activities (Nakagomi, 1987; Nakagomi, Kisi, & Ino, 1986; Nakagomi & Suzuki, 1985). They studied Rorschach's Test (Nakagomi, Ino, Ichimura, & Sekioka, 1984), the Tree-Drawing Test (Tsuda & Moriwaki, 1981), and other projective tests. Nakagomi (1987) raised the theoretical issue that an athlete who devoted himself or herself solely to a competitive sporting activity developed an identity only as an athlete. It was conceptualized that there was little development of any real identity following an athlete's retirement from competitive sport because of a failure to form human relationships during the former sporting life.

Anxiety and Anxiety Control in Sport

Studies on anxiety in sport cover a wide range of interests, from a taxonomy of emotional states before and during the competition to clinical studies for alleviating stress and its harmful effects on performance in sport. As for a taxonomy of the psychophysiological states of competitive anxiety, factor analysis was predominantly applied to reported responses. Tokunaga et al. (1986) analyzed two sets of inventories based on Spielberger's state-trait-anxiety theory. Ichimura (1986) carried out factor analysis on psychologically induced physiological responses to competitive situations. The results revealed that sympathetic and parasympathetic groups of items formed a constellation in a measurably clear-cut way on a plane spanned by two axes, contrary to his assumption that two groups of items would be allocated to both ends of a one-dimensional sympathetic and parasympathetic factor axis, indicating that each system could be antagonistic. The reaction of the autonomic nervous system among athletes appeared to be two-dimensional and independent of each other. He inferred that there might exist two types of athletes. One was apt to feel arousal of the sympathetic system, and the other was more likely to be aware of parasympathetic tension. The former arousal was more closely related to feelings of fear and apprehension, while the latter was more closely related to awareness of motor disorder. Indicated is the importance of applying a specific stress-control strategy in accordance with individual differences.

Nakagomi and Suzuki (1983) investigated the characteristics of the ego function of athletes who displayed strong competitive anxiety in Ichimura's stage fright questionnaire and Klopfer's Rorschach Prognostic Rating Scale. The athletes who showed emotional stability and toughness had greater (a) susceptibility to follow their own inner impulse, (b) ability in reality testing, and (c) capability of self-realization. Besides these characteristics, they had an active and exuberant inner world in which they managed to deal with competitive anxiety and to adjust to the demands of the external world. These results suggested the necessity of examining the cause of excessive and unreasonable anxiety in sport in order to improve the performance and personality development of young athletes.

Along with the six headings and relevant research just described, there are several important research studies on causal attributions conducted by T. Ito (1982, 1985, 1987). Regarding contemporary issues, Kisi and Nakagomi (1989) have analyzed the burnout syndrome. In addition, Takenaka (1989) also has described and analyzed the psychological background of drug-related problems with particular emphasis on American athletes.

ACCEPTANCE OF SPORT PSYCHOLOGY RESEARCH FINDINGS AND FUTURE TRENDS

In 1961, the Sport Sciences Committee of distinguished researchers was formed within the Japan Olympic Committee (JOC) as a part of the Japan Amateur Sports Association (JASA), to apply sport sciences to elite male and female athletes. A subcommittee representing sport psychology was formed within it, and this was the first time that an attempt was made to apply sport psychology to a sporting situation. Although the subcommittee became smaller following the 1964 Olympics in Tokyo, it continued to conduct research on topics related to sport psychology.

From 1980 to 1982, the subcommittee conducted research on the psychological aptitude of athletes, and designed an achievement motivation inventory for athletes called the Taikyo Sport Motivation Inventory (TSMI). The inventory is widely being applied to the national teams representing every sport. The subcommittee also conducted research on mental management for athletes from 1985 to 1988 and designed mental management programs for each sport event. These mental management programs were applied effectively to the national teams active in the 1986 Asian Games and the 1988 Olympic Games in Seoul. Since 1989 the subcommittee has been conducting research on talent identification and promotion in sport. These efforts are described in the annual *Reports on Sport Sciences* of the Japan Amateur Sports Association.

Today the application of sport psychology to sporting situations is a promising area in Japan. However, there are two major problems to be solved. One of them is the problem of training counselors who can bridge the gap and apply psychological knowledge in both elite competitive and recreational sporting settings. Another problem concerns the lack of social-psychological research in sport. Although there are many considerations in group dynamics in team sport, only a few research studies have been conducted from a psychological viewpoint. The subcommittee of sport psychology in the Sport Sciences Committee in JOC is now initiating a research project called "Mental Management for Team Sport." This is expected to be a forerunner of psychological research in team sport.

At the annual meetings of the JSSP, these and other problems have been discussed and it has been confirmed that the JSSP should be responsible for promoting future efforts to resolve them.

References

Araki, H., & Nishihira, Y. (1983). Relationship between the change of EEG based on intra-subject analysis and that of reaction time and CNV during reaction movement. *Japanese Journal of Sport Psychology, 10,* 4–11.

Araki, H., & Nishihira, Y. (1984). Changes of alpha-blocking and component of CNV under the condition of reaction movement with regular and irregular foreperiod. *Japanese Journal of Sport Psychology, 11,* 4–11.

Araki, M., & Sakuma, H. (1982). A study on the application of EMG biofeedback technique in motor learning. *Japanese Journal of Physical Education, 27*, 207–215.

Araki, M., & Sakuma, H. (1983). The effect of EMG biofeedback training in the motor learning. *Japanese Journal of Sport Psychology, 10*, 12–17.

Fujita, A. (1984). The training effect on eye-head coordination. In H. Rieder (Ed.), *Sport psychology—international* (pp. 241–261). Cologne: bps-Verlag.

Fujita, A. (1987). The development of sport psychology in Japan. *The Sport Psychologist, 1*, 69–73.

Fujita, A., Yoshimoto, T., & Fukami, K. (1982). A proposal for utilizing selective eye-head coordination reaction time in predicting so called "open skill." *International Journal of Sport Psychology, 13*, 71–84.

Ichimura, S. (1981). Developmental psychological approach to factor structures of physical fitness. *Bulletin of the Institute of Health and Sport Sciences,* University of Tsukuba, *4*, 11–18.

Ichimura, S. (1986). Two dimensional structure model of psychophysiological syndrome of anxiety in sport competition. *Bulletin of the Institute of Health and Sport Sciences,* University of Tsukuba, *9*, 15–20.

Ichimura, S. (1988). Contemporary research work in sport psychology in Japan. In J. Nitsch & D. Hackfort (Eds.), *Sportpsychologische Diagnostik, Intervention und Verantwortung* (pp. 97–108). Cologne: bps-Verlag.

Ito, M. (1982). The effects of symbolic coding strategy and covert rehearsal in short term retention of force information. *Japanese Journal of Physical Education, 27*, 187–195.

Ito, M. (1983). The effects of coding strategies and the number of reinforcements in short-term retention of force information. *Japanese Journal of Physical Education, 28*, 237–250.

Ito, M. (1986). The functional equivalence of kinesthetic imagery and movement in short-term memory of force information. *Japanese Journal of Physical Education, 31*, 113–121.

Ito, M., & Sanjo, T. (1984). The response set characteristics of immediate recall errors in short-term memory of force information. *Japanese Journal of Physical Education, 29*, 143–151.

Ito, T. (1982). A study on causal attributions for win and loss in sport setting. *Japanese Journal of Sport Psychology, 9*, 21–26.

Ito, T. (1985). Factorial structure of attribution styles in sport situations and its characteristics. *Japanese Journal of Physical Education, 30*, 153–160.

Ito, T. (1987). Effects of attributional style and perceived physical competence on sport behavior. *Japanese Journal of Physical Education, 31*, 263–272.

Kaino, T., & Sugihara, T. (1989). The learning effect of pattern recognition on a tennis net-player's anticipation. *Japan Journal of Physical Education, 34*, 117–132.

Kasai, T. (1982). Variable amount of reaction time on different movement patterns. *Japanese Journal of Physical Education, 27*, 97–109.

Kasai, T. (1983). Analysis of movement specialities of upper limbs in twelve sporting events by means of reaction times and EMG. *Japanese Journal of Physical Education, 28*, 227–236.

Kasai, T. (1985). Dependence of reaction times on movement patterns. *Japanese Journal of Physical Education, 30*, 13–24.

Kim, S., & Matsuura, Y. (1988). A study on quantitative change and qualitative change of fundamental movement skills in children. *Japanese Journal of Physical Education, 33*, 27–38.

Kishi, J., & Nakagomi, S. (1989). An approach to clear the definition of athletes' burnout syndrome. *Japan Journal of Physical Education, 34*, 235–243.

Kudo, K. (1984). Analysis of timing delay. *Japanese Journal of Physical Education, 29*, 195–206.

Matsuura, Y. (1982). A study on changes in the factorial structure of motor ability along with the physical growth and development with longitudinal data. *Bulletin of the Institute of Health and Sport Sciences,* University of Tsukuba, *5*, 79–94.

Matsuura, Y., & Aoyagi, O. (1985). A study on the classification of growth and development curves with metrical procedure. *Bulletin of the Institute of Health and Sport Sciences,* University of Tsukuba, *8*, 193–203.

Nakagawa, A. (1982). A field experiment on recognition of game situation in ball games. *Japanese Journal of Physical Education, 27*, 17–26.

Nakagomi, S. (1987). On the sports experience and the athlete's search for ego identity, 5th report. *Bulletin of the Institute of Health and Sport Sciences,* University of Tsukuba, *10*, 43–51.

Nakagomi, S., Ino, T., Ichimura, S., & Sekioka, Y. (1984). Rorschach responses of high performers in sport. *Bulletin of the Institute of Health and Sport Sciences,* University of Tsukuba, *7*, 263–270.

Nakagomi, S., Kishii, J., & Ino, T. (1986). On the search for ego identity of the athlete and the sport experience, 4th report. *Bulletin of the Institute of Health and Sport Sciences,* University of Tsukuba, *9*, 21–29.

Nakagomi, S., & Suzuki, M. (1983). Differences in ego function between high and low stage fright in sport. *Japanese Journal of Physical Education, 28*, 113–128.

Nakagomi, S., & Suzuki, M. (1985). On the search for ego identity of the athlete and the sport experience, 1st report. *Japanese Journal of Physical Education, 30*, 249–260.

Nishida, T. (1984). The effect of achievement motivation on motor skill learning. *Japanese Journal of Physical Education, 29*, 15–24.

Nishida, T. (1989). A study on standardization of the Achievement Motivation in Physical Education Test. *Japan Journal of Physical Education, 34*, 45–65.

Nishida, T., & Inomata, K. (1981). A factor analytical study on achievement motives in sport. *Japanese Journal of Physical Education, 26*, 101–110.

Niwa, T. (1981). The relationship between coordination and verbal understanding in pre-school children. *Japanese Journal of Sport Psychology, 8*, 1–9.

Niwa, T. (1982). The relationship between motor coordination and verbal aspect of intellectual faculties in pre-school children. *Japanese Journal of Sport Psychology, 9*, 13–20.

Sakuma, H. (1985). EEG alpha wave biofeedback effect on microvibration control. *Journal of Sport Science of Tokyo Metropolitan University, 10*, 31–39.

Sakuma, H., & Nagata, A. (1983). The effect of EMG biofeedback on improving motor performance. *Journal of Sport Science of Tokyo Metropolitan University, 4*, 15–27.

Sakuma, H., & Nagata, A. (1984). Biofeedback effect on microvibration control. *Biofeedback Kenkyu, 11*, 10–15.

Shinoda, N., & Yoshida, S. (1987). The changes of scalp-recorded slow potential in the discrimination task of the temporal patterns. *Bulletin of the Institute of Health and Sport Sciences,* University of Tsukuba, *10*, 85–90.

Sugihara, T. (1985). The relationship between perceived motor competence and personality characteristics in pre-school children. *Japanese Journal of Physical Education, 30*, 25–36.

Sugihara, T., & Yoshida, T. (1989). Attentional style of tennis players in varying skills. *Japanese Journal of Sport Psychology, 16*, 20–27.

Suzuki, T., Fujita, A., Kawahara, M., Yoshimoto, T., Fukami, K.,

Kondoh, A., Satoh, M., Mizuochi, F., & Ishii, M. (1989). Trial manufacture of simulator for service in tennis and practice in returning the serve under a simulated condition. *Japanese Journal of Sport Psychology, 16,* 28–36.

Takenaka, K. (1984a). A study on the application of EMG biofeedback training to muscle control. *Japanese Journal of Physical Education, 29,* 89–98.

Takenaka, K. (1984b). Effect of feedback from the muscle biceps brachii, the muscle triceps brachii, or the both of the two muscles on muscle-control. *Japanese Journal of Sport Psychology, 11,* 12–18.

Takenaka, K. (1986). A study on the application of EMG biofeedback training to muscle control. *Japanese Journal of Physical Education, 31,* 133–142.

Takenaka, K. (1989). Drug problem in American athletes. *Japan Journal of Physical Education, 34,* 1–13.

Takenaka, K. (1990). Application of EMG biofeedback to motor control. *Japan Journal of Physical Education, 35,* 1–17.

Tanaka, M. (1990). The changes and developmental differences of representation in the process of motor proficiency. *Japan Journal of Physical Education, 34,* 293–303.

Tokunaga, M., Kanezaki, R., Tatano, H., Hashimoto, K., & Umeda, Y. (1986). A study on the process of development and change of anxiety in sport and application of biofeedback to alleviate anxiety. *Research Report of Health Science Center, Special Issue,* Kyushu University.

Tsuda, T., & Moriwaki, T. (1981). A clinical-psychological study of athletes by means of the material of "Tree-Drawing." *Japanese Journal of Sport Psychology, 8,* 10–20.

SKILL ACQUISITION

·3·

LEVELS OF PERFORMANCE SKILL

Craig A. Wrisberg

Even the most casual observations of elite athletic performance prompt speculation as to the possible factors that distinguish the movements of experts from those of average or novice performers. For years the prevailing opinion of coaches has been that the best athletes possess certain physical traits or perceptual-motor abilities that allow them to achieve extraordinary performance levels. Not surprisingly, tests (e.g., McDavid, 1977) or profiles (e.g., Rodionov, 1978) for predicting athletic superiority have emphasized the "hardware" attributes of individuals (e.g., eye-hand coordination, movement speed, etc.) that presumably contribute to their success in sport. Persons scoring higher on such tests or demonstrating more of the abilities associated with the "ideal" profile are expected to be the better performers.

In addition to the possibility that superior athletes possess more elegant neuromuscular systems (i.e., "hardware"), there is reason to believe that at least some of the performance advantage these individuals enjoy is due to sophisticated functional knowledge (i.e., "software") developed over their years of sporting experience (see Allard & Burnett, 1985, and Starkes, 1987, for more detailed discussions of this issue). Such software might include superior strategies or more efficient information-processing capabilities (see Abernethy, 1987, for an example).

In this chapter, literature is reviewed that addresses possible explanations for differences in the skill levels of performers. The chapter is divided into parts devoted to (a) a brief description of the stages of practice notion, (b) experimental approaches that have been used to explain or examine differences in the skill level of individuals, (c) a synthesis of the research findings emanating from such studies, and (d) implications of the available evidence for the sport psychology consultant.

THE STAGES OF PRACTICE NOTION

The contribution of practice to the development of high-level skill is well recognized. Therefore, one approach to the examination of differences in the skill levels of individuals has been to compare the characteristics of performers at various stages of practice. The notion of practice stages is not a new one. In fact, anyone who has ever attempted to learn a sport can probably recall the different kinds of experiences they had over the course of practice.

Theoretical discussions of this concept have typically centered on two (Adams, 1971; Gentile, 1972) or three (Anderson, 1982; Fitts & Posner, 1967) relatively distinct stages of practice. All viewpoints seem to be in agreement that the initial stage is characterized by attempts to get a general idea of the task. Many strategies are implemented and retained, modified, or discarded; errors are frequent; and the consistency of responding is quite low. However, once a rough notion of performance requirements has been achieved, practice advances to a second stage during which skill refinement occurs. In this stage, movements are performed with more precision and consistency and environmental cues appropriate to successful performance are processed more effectively and efficiently (Gentile, 1972). Many individuals never progress beyond this stage. However, a few advance to yet another level of practice in which performance is characterized by seemingly effortless execution of the correct response. In fact, movements appear to be made almost automatically (Anderson, 1982; Fitts & Posner, 1967). Since very little conscious thought is required to produce appropriate movements, the performer is able to focus attention on other aspects of the competitive environment (e.g., actions of the opponent, speed and trajectory of the approaching ball, etc.).

The stages-of-practice notion offers a useful framework for differentiating performance characteristics of individuals. That is, beginning, intermediate, and advanced performers would generally be expected to exhibit characteristics associated with the cognitive, associative, and autonomous stages of practice, respectively (Fitts & Posner, 1967). However, it should be noted that the *stability* of performance achieved by expert athletes who have had years of experience in their sport is likely different from that of subjects in experiments who have been given no more than a few hundred trials of practice on a novel laboratory task. Therefore, parallels between the findings of studies with general population subjects and those with athletes should only be drawn with proper caution.

EXPERIMENTAL APPROACHES

For the most part, three experimental approaches have been employed by researchers to identify factors contributing to skilled performance. One approach has been used to explore the relationship of relatively permanent abilities (such as eye-hand coordination, reaction time, and movement speed) to perceptual-motor performance. This approach has usually been adopted by individual differences researchers (e.g., Fleishman, 1978, 1982; Fleishman & Hempel, 1955). A second strategy attempts to isolate the processes used by individuals in dealing with sundry types of information found in the performance environment (e.g., Kerr, 1973; Marteniuk, 1976). These two approaches have produced considerable data on a variety of populations that offer insights into the kinds of factors that might distinguish the performance level of individuals on novel laboratory tasks at various stages of practice. More recently, a third approach has been devised to directly explore differences in the characteristics of expert and novice performers on tasks (e.g., chess, badminton, etc.) with which they have had considerable (i.e., years of) personal experience (e.g., Chase & Simon, 1973; Housner, 1981). Taken together, the results of investigations incorporating these three approaches provide a rather comprehensive picture of a number of factors associated with various levels of performance skill. However, as mentioned previously, comparisons between the performance of subjects from a general population on novel tasks (as has generally been the case with the first two approaches) and that of athletes who have practiced a specific skill for several thousand hours (as in the expert-novice approach) may often be inappropriate. Therefore, rather than emphasizing possible linkages between the three lines of investigation, the focus of the present chapter will be on what each has contributed to our understanding of skilled performance.

The Individual Differences Approach

Since the advent of the scientific method, investigators have typically employed an approach to experimentation that isolates factors in order to determine their influence on the performance of groups of subjects. However, a few researchers have deviated from this method in an attempt to identify abilities or traits that distinguish the performance of individuals in various situations or on a variety of tasks (see Schmidt, 1988, for a more detailed discussion of differences in the experimental and differential approaches to scientific inquiry). Most prominent have been the efforts of

Fleishman and colleagues (e.g., Fleishman, 1972, 1978; Fleishman & Bartlett, 1969; Fleishman & Hempel, 1955; Fleishman & Rich, 1963) and, more recently, Keele and his associates (Keele & Hawkins, 1982; Keele, Ivry, & Pokorny, 1987; Keele, Pokorny, Corcos, & Ivry, 1985).

Abilities are typically considered to be *relatively stable* characteristics of individuals, the levels of which change little over time or practice. Thus it is assumed that persons possessing high levels of certain abilities important to the performance of a particular task will have a greater probability of success or, in light of the present discussion, demonstrate greater skill. The approach that has generally been adopted to identify abilities underlying task performance involves the testing of many subjects on many tasks. Statistical correlations are then calculated between the various possible pairs of scores or occasionally among larger groups of scores to determine which tasks are highly related. Those tasks producing higher correlations are presumed to depend on similar underlying abilities.

Following the development of test batteries, relationships between performance on those tests and on some new task may be determined. For example, scores on a test measuring an ability called "eye-foot coordination" might be expected to correlate highly with the performance of certain tasks required of a soccer goalie (e.g., receiving a pass from a teammate, making a kick save, etc.). If this were to be the case, elite soccer goalies would be predicted to score higher on tests of eye-foot coordination than would novice or nonelite athletes. If the notion of groupings of abilities underlying the performance of different tasks is a valid one, then it should be possible to assess the potential of aspiring athletes for success in their chosen sport or activity by determining the level of task-relevant abilities possessed by each individual.

The Information-Processing Approach

In addition to the fact that performers may differ with respect to the abilities (i.e., hardware characteristics) they bring to a task situation, there is also a likelihood that individuals respond differently to information contained in the skill context. Clearly the most important contributions to our understanding of how humans handle information have come from studies adopting an information-processing approach. An important assumption of this approach is that nonoverlapping processing stages exist between a stimulus and a response. Research supporting this assumption has often employed a reaction-time paradigm in which increased decision time is linked to delays in various information processes (see Marteniuk, 1976, or Schmidt, 1988, for more complete discussions of the information-processing approach in motor behavior research).

The results of many laboratory studies have suggested the existence of at least three stages (not to be confused with stages of practice) that comprise the interval between a stimulus and response. The first stage, termed *stimulus identification*, involves the activation of *perceptual processes* such as stimulus detection and pattern recognition.

In this stage the performer's task is to make sense of the stimulus. Not surprisingly, variables that have been shown to influence the duration of this stage are the intensity, clarity, and familiarity of the stimulus (e.g., Posner, 1964; Swets, 1964). In the second stage, *response selection* takes place and *decision processes* are activated. At this point the performer has presumably identified the important features of the stimulus and now must decide on an appropriate response. Factors that have been shown to influence the duration of this stage include the number of stimulus-response alternatives and the compatibility of the stimulus and response (e.g., Fitts & Seeger, 1963; Hick, 1952). In the third stage, *effector processes* are used to determine the correct spatial-temporal pattern of the movement that has been selected. The primary task of the performer in this stage is to decide which motor commands should be issued in order to assure accurate *response execution.* Two factors that have most often been demonstrated to influence the duration of this stage are response complexity and response duration (e.g., Henry & Rogers, 1960; Klapp & Erwin, 1976). Generally more complex movements and those of longer duration take longer to initiate than do those that are simpler or of shorter duration.

Later in this paper, research findings will be presented that illustrate how the efficiency of the three stages of information processing may be improved with practice and how elite performers may be able to perform more quickly and accurately by bypassing and/or expediting the activities of certain stages.

The Expert-Novice Approach

The most direct approach to assessing differences in the performance of elite and nonelite performers has been to compare various measures of skill on tasks individuals are highly familiar with. Pioneered originally by Chase and Simon (1973) with chess players, this paradigm has more recently been adopted by investigators interested in expert-novice differences in the perceptual-cognitive characteristics of sport performers.

Studies have typically involved comparisons of the perceptual processing or recall/retention characteristics of elite athletes with those of nonelite athletes or general populations. The results of these investigations have indicated that skilled athletes encode/retrieve game structure information differently and/or more quickly (e.g., Allard, Graham, & Paarsalu, 1980), structure their visual search of the environment differently (e.g., Bard & Fleury, 1981), and selectively attend to different kinds of information in the game environment (e.g., Allard & Starkes, 1980) than do less skilled athletes or the general population.

SYNTHESIS OF RESEARCH FINDINGS

Research in this area has been quite extensive, as the bibliography concluding this chapter attests. We will attempt to summarize what has so far been determined.

The Role of General Abilities

The notion of general abilities falls somewhere between the older view of a *single* general ability that was presumed to distinguish the performance of subjects on all types of motor tasks (i.e., "he/she sure has a lot of *ability*") and the hypothesis that every task has a constellation of abilities that are unique to the performance of that task and totally unlike those required for any other task (Henry, 1968). According to the general motor ability view, correlations between the performance of a large group of people on any two motor tasks should be quite high, with those individuals possessing more "ability" doing better on both tasks and those with less doing worse. By way of contrast, a strict specificity interpretation would postulate intertask correlations to be extremely low since performance on one task is expected to require an entirely different set of abilities than those needed for performance on any other task.

The available evidence from studies using general populations of subjects and novel laboratory tasks has provided consistent support for the specificity notion (Bachman, 1961; Henry, 1961; Lotter, 1960; Parker & Fleishman, 1960). However, it should be pointed out that while most intertask correlations have been found to be uniformly low and statistically nonsignificant, they have *not* been zero, suggesting that subjects' performance on any two tasks is, to varying degrees, attributable to at least *some* similar underlying ability or abilities. Perhaps the best illustration of this fact was demonstrated by Parker and Fleishman (1960) in a study comparing the performance of subjects on 50 different novel motor tasks. Not surprisingly, tasks that were more similar in nature (e.g., balance tasks) correlated more highly than those that were not. Thus it might be presumed that tasks containing similar requirements have at least some common underlying abilities. If such a proposal is correct (i.e., it could be shown that certain abilities are important to the performance of particular types of tasks), then individuals possessing high levels of the "right" abilities might be predicted to achieve greater success in a given task or sport than would those possessing lower levels of the abilities.

The results of a recent series of studies appear to offer more promising support for the notion of general abilities. Keele and his associates (Keele & Hawkins, 1982; Keele, Ivry, & Pokorny, 1987; Keele, Pokorny, Corcos, & Ivry, 1985) speculated that at least part of the reason lower intertask correlations were found in earlier studies may have been due to the fact that scores from complete tasks were correlated with each other. More specifically they reasoned that since entire tasks typically share some processes but not others, the contribution of a shared process (e.g., attention switching) to the performance of two different tasks may have been masked by the fact that the tasks did not share a variety of other processes. Thus Keele's group adopted an information-processing approach that allowed them to derive scores that reflected *only* the process presumed to be shared by two tasks. Correlations resulting from their investigations have proven to be uniformly higher than those reported in earlier studies, suggesting the existence of general abilities such as maximum rate of repetitive movements (Keele & Hawkins, 1982), timing control (Keele, Pokorny, Corcos, & Ivry, 1985), and force control (Keele, Ivry, & Pokorny, 1987). While further work in this area is needed, this research offers an encouraging new direction for investigators interested in identifying abilities important to the performance of various classes of motor tasks (i.e., those sharing certain processes).

While the majority of studies exploring the notion of general abilities have used novel tasks and general populations, there is a modest literature, some of it quite old, outlining attempts by sport scientists to identify general abilities possessed by elite athletes that might distinguish their performance from that of average performers. Generally the approach taken in these studies has been to catalogue the abilities of athletes, either for comparison with those of the general population or in order to relate them to some measure of athletic proficiency.

Extensive investigation of the relationship of specific abilities of athletes to their own performance probably originated with Soviet researchers (see Vanek & Cratty, 1970, for a more detailed historical perspective). Studies of this nature often included attempts to identify traits such as will power, concentration, and the feeling of the water by swimmers. For example, during the National Championship in Leningrad in 1963, an effort was made to determine the relationship of concentration time (i.e., the time prior to a performance attempt) and the performance of the world-class high jumper Valeri Brumel. Summarizing the findings of this experiment, Vanek and Cratty (1970) reported that "concentration time, when coupled with performance scores [i.e., height-jumped], purportedly reveals important relationships between preperformance activation and optimum effort" (p. 18). A significant outgrowth of such research has been the development of models of the "ideal" athlete for a variety of sport disciplines (Rodionov, 1978). In addition, psychobiological profiles called "sportprofessiograms" have been constructed by Russian sport psychologists that detail the important traits required for optimum performance of any particular sporting activity (Schneidman, 1979).

Sport scientists in Europe and North America have not been as successful in demonstrating a strong relationship between general abilities and athletic prowess. The bulk of this research seems to have involved the investigation of visual perceptual factors that might be important to performance. For example, depth perception (i.e., the ability to judge the relative distance of objects) was for some time assumed to be keener for elite athletes than for their lesser skilled counterparts or for nonathletes. In one early study, Bannister and Blackburn (1931) found that the interpupillary distance of rugby players was greater than that of nonplayers and concluded that the more advantageous angle of visual convergence of the players promoted superior depth perception, which enhanced their athletic prowess. Similar studies reported higher-caliber athletes to be superior to average athletes or nonathletes on visual attributes such as depth perception (Graybiel, Jokl, & Trapp, 1955; Miller, 1960; Montebello, 1953; Olsen, 1956), distance estimation (Cockerill, 1981), dynamic visual acuity (Morris & Kreighbaum, 1977), and peripheral vision (Olsen, 1956; Williams & Thirer, 1975), as well as on other abilities like velocity judgments (Parker, 1981), reaction time (Olsen, 1956; Wilkinson, 1958), movement time (Keller, 1940; Pierson, 1956), spatial perception (Meek & Skubic, 1971), and kinesthetic sensitivity (Wiebe, 1954). However, the results of most correlational analyses examining the relationship between such attributes and sport performance have been nonsignificant (Dickson, 1953; Montebello, 1953; Olsen, 1956; Ridini, 1968; Winograd, 1942).

Not surprisingly, very little of this type of research has been conducted in North America for the past 30 years. A promising exception is the recent work of Landers, Boutcher, and Wang (1986), in which certain physical, perceptual-motor, and psychological characteristics were found to be accurate predictors of archery performance. Perhaps this and the recent work of Keele and his associates using an information-processing approach will revive scientific efforts to identify important general abilities underlying athletic performance.

Information-Processing Characteristics of Performers at Various Stages of Practice

While the contribution of general abilities to performance skill remains somewhat equivocal, there are a number of information-processing capabilities and cognitive processes that have been found to be associated with skill level (Starkes & Deakin, 1984). Most likely, superior skill is attributable to the functioning of a variety of processes. For example, the elite performer might excel because she/he (1) recognizes the stimulus sooner (perceptual processing), (2) has a variety of appropriate responses ready to be executed (decision processing), and/or (3) initiates movement commands more rapidly (effector processing). The expert may also be able to respond more efficiently by "speeding up" certain aspects/stages of information processing. For example, the baseball batter who has learned that a particular mannerism displayed by a pitcher is a signal that a fastball is coming would have a reduced perceptual-processing demand associated with the differentiation of pitch speed. Thus an appropriate swing could be prepared in advance, with adjustments made according to the spatial flightpath of the pitch.

In this section, discussion will be devoted to research that has demonstrated that the elite performer selects, processes, and retrieves information more effectively and efficiently than the average performer or the novice. Separate attention will be given to those aspects of perceptual, decision, and effector processing that have been shown to differentiate levels of performance skill.

Perceptual Processing

This aspect of information processing deals with the reception and interpretation of environmental or movement-related cues. Most of the laboratory research conducted in this area has focused on two subprocesses, stimulus detection and pattern recognition. The former pertains to the picking up of environmental information while the latter concerns the recognition of performance-relevant aspects of selected cues.

The two variables that have most often been shown to exert the greatest influence on the stimulus detection subprocess are stimulus intensity and stimulus clarity (e.g., Posner, 1964; Swets, 1964). Specifically the more intense and clearly presented the stimulus, the more rapidly it is detected (see Schmidt, 1988, for a more complete discussion). Since intensity and clarity in a given sport situation is theoretically the same for performers regardless of their skill level, it might be predicted that the existence of superior stimulus detection capability in expert performers is due to the *way* they search the performance environment for relevant sources of information.

Exactly what aspects of the environment experts direct their attention to has been the focus of several studies. For example, Allard and Starkes (1980) found that skilled volleyball players were able to detect the presence of the ball in slides of briefly presented volleyball situations faster than were nonplayers. Years earlier, Hubbard and Seng (1954) photographed the eye movements of professional baseball players and speculated that elite batters linked their vision of the moment of ball release from the pitcher's hand with stride initiation and used perception of the speed of the pitch to determine stride duration. Employing a more sophisticated eye movement apparatus, Bard and Fleury (1981) found that a greater proportion of the ocular fixations of expert ice hockey goaltenders were on the stick of the shooter, presumably allowing them to anticipate the type of shot that was about to be taken and to initiate their blocking movements more rapidly than novice goalies, who were found to fixate more on the puck.

Interestingly the visual search patterns of experts and novices have not been found to be that different (Bard & Fleury, 1976; Abernethy & Russell, 1984, Experiment 1; 1987b; Tyldesley, Bootsma, & Bomhoff, 1982). However, as Adams (1966) has suggested, "the principal difficulty in using eye movements for inferring observing responses is that they measure looking, not seeing. Thus they fail as a primary measure of an observing response which functions to provide the discriminating stimuli for the criterion response" (p. 177). In spite of this point, it might be argued that the *product* of the advanced performer's attentional focus (i.e., the extraction of task-relevant information) is more crucial than the attention-directing process.

Another technique for determining the types of cues experts attend to is the visual occlusion paradigm. In studies adopting this approach, vision of the movements of a videotaped or filmed performer is blocked at various points in the sequence and the observer is asked to make certain pre-dictions about the outcome of the movement. Jones and Miles (1978) reported that expert tennis players were better than novices at predicting the position of the ball landing for a tennis serve even when their vision of the serve was occluded prior to ball impact. A similar result was obtained by Starkes and Deakin (1984) in a study comparing the shot prediction accuracy of national team, varsity, and control field hockey players. Subjects viewed (from the perspective of a goalie) a videotape of an approaching offensive player who variously shot or passed the ball high or low to the right, left, or straight ahead. Vision of the player was occluded for 1/20 sec prior to impact on half of the trials and for 1/6 sec after impact on the other half. The results revealed that national team players predicted shot placement more accurately than the other groups under both occlusion conditions and were the only group that performed better than chance would allow when they were forced to rely on advance visual cues (i.e., when occlusion occurred 1/20 sec prior to impact). Taking a slightly different approach, Salmela and Fiorito (1979) found that predictions about the horizontal direction of an approaching shot were facilitated for young ice hockey goaltenders when preshot information about the shooter's movements was *not* occluded. Thus it was deduced that the goalies must have been using preshot cues to enhance their predictions of shot direction.

Work by Abernethy and Russell (1984, Experiment 2) has revealed that skilled cricket batsmen extract advance information from the movements of bowlers more than lesser skilled batsmen do. In a subsequent study they (Abernethy & Russell, 1987a, Experiment 1) demonstrated that expert badminton players were superior to novices in predicting the depth of approaching badminton shots, even when occlusion of the shot occurred 83 ms prior to racquet-shuttle contact. A second experiment in this study revealed that experts attended to the arm action of an opponent more than novice performers did. Work by Howarth, Walsh, Abernethy, and Snyder (1984) similarly indicated that advanced squash players made their initial anticipatory movements to return a shot *prior* to ball contact, suggesting the usage of preshot cues from their opponent. In that study, average players were not found to begin such movements until after ball contact. In summary, then, it appears that while the visual search patterns of elite athletes may be similar to those of average or novice performers, the meaningfulness of the information that is being attended to is different.

The foregoing discussion suggests that the most important aspect differentiating the perceptual processing of expert and average or novice performers is their *interpretation* of selected information. Rapid recognition of relevant environmental cues would appear to be particularly advantageous for sport performers who must respond quickly to their opponents' movements. That elite performers are able to accurately recognize the important aspects of a game environment has perhaps best been illustrated in studies comparing the ability of chess experts and novices in reconstructing game situations from briefly presented configurations (e.g., Chase & Simon, 1973). Of more relevance to sport situations are experiments that have demonstrated superior recall of game-structure information by advanced basketball (Allard, Graham, & Paarsalu, 1980), rugby (Nakagawa, 1982), volleyball (Borgeaud & Abernethy, 1987), and field hockey (Starkes, 1987) players.

Of particular significance is the Starkes (1987) study in which a multiple regression technique was used to determine which of a number of factors differentiated three groups of field hockey players of varying expertise. Of the nine possible predictor variables (simple reaction time, coincident anticipation, ball detection speed and accuracy, shoot/dribble/dodge decision accuracy and speed, accuracy of shot prediction before and after the view of ball impact, and recall accuracy of structured game positions) the only significant predictors were recall of game-structured information and shot prediction accuracy following the view of ball impact. In light of this finding, Starkes concluded that advanced "tuning" of the stimulus search process is an important factor differentiating the performance of highly skilled and average performers. She further suggested that the tuning of search is characterized by three processes: "generalization" (i.e., broadening of the applicability of rules), "discrimination" (i.e., narrowing of rules), and "strengthening" (i.e., fortifying of better rules and weakening of poorer ones).

With practice, performers also become more in tune with the sensory consequences of their movements, which represents a slightly different form of perceptual processing. Using a simple-movement time task and a general college student population, Schmidt and White (1972) found that with practice the error-detection capabilities of subjects improved along with improvements in movement production. That elite athletic performers are also more adept than average or novice performers at evaluating the quality of their movements has been implied in the results of a study by Henderson (1975) in which skilled darts throwers were found to be more accurate than unskilled throwers in estimating the location of dart landing in the absence of visual feedback. This finding suggests that the skill level of advanced performers may be distinguished from that of average or novice performers in terms of the degree to which integration of effector and perceptual processing has been achieved (i.e., the capability to effectively construct the motor commands necessary to produce a movement as well as to evaluate the sensory consequences and response outcomes associated with that movement).

In summary, the available research indicates that the perceptual processing of information, particularly that dealing with attention to and recognition of salient cues, is an important factor that differentiates highly skilled and less skilled performers. Such processing would be particularly advantageous for athletes who must perform in situations requiring the continual monitoring of environmental cues. By knowing what to look for, experts are able to extract meaningful information from the environment and quickly prepare appropriate responses (Adams, 1966).

Decision Processing

Once the performer has completed perceptual processing of the environment, it is necessary to decide on an appropriate response. That response selection is associated with levels of performance skill has recently been suggested in a study by Abernethy and Russell (1984) in which skilled cricket batsmen were found to be more accurate in their response selection decisions than were less skilled batsmen. In this experiment, subjects were asked to watch a filmed presentation of a bowler's run-up and make a keypress response as soon as they decided what stroke they would play. In all cases the response selected by expert batsmen was a general movement designed to place their body in the best position to complete a successful response. Such generalized preparation might be likened to that of elite baseball batters who initiate the stride phase of their batting response when the ball is released from the pitcher's hand but do not begin the swing until an estimate of ball speed is made (Hubbard & Seng, 1954).

Two factors that have been demonstrated to influence the response selection process in laboratory studies with general student populations are the number of stimulus response choices and the compatibility of stimuli and responses. Generally speaking, the results of these experiments have indicated that the greater the number of stimulus-response choices and the less compatible the stimulus and response, the longer it takes to select the appropriate response (Fitts & Peterson, 1964; Hick, 1952; Hyman, 1953). Although these principles might be expected to hold for athletes, it must be pointed out that an elite sport performer may sometimes select a response that is, in her/his view, the most appropriate, even though it may not be the most "compatible." For example, a setter in volleyball may attempt to hit the ball directly over the net (less compatible) rather than set up the outside hitter for a spike (more compatible) if she/he suddenly sees that the opposition has left an area of the floor uncovered. Thus it should be remembered that the decision processing of athletes is often contingent on factors other than those dealing with the number of stimulus-response choices and stimulus-response compatibility.

Another important issue concerning the response selection process of athletes is that both the number and the compatibility of stimulus-response combinations may differ for different sports activities. For example, badminton players may have a larger number of possible responses in their repertoire and deal with more levels of stimulus-response compatibility than do racquetball players. In one study, Housner (1981) obtained verbal reports from expert and novice badminton players and observed their play in competitive situations. He found that experts not only had more strategies than novices but applied them more appropriately and with greater flexibility. Thus differences in levels of performance skill for this sport appear to be associated with the rapid selection of the most appropriate (i.e., compatible) of a number of possible responses in the face of a variety of possible shots (i.e., S-R choices) by an opponent.

By way of contrast, racquetball players probably have fewer possible responses and employ them more predictably than do badminton players. In support of this proposition, Alain and Girardin (1978) found no difference in the amount of uncertainty conveyed by the shots of expert and novice racquetball players, suggesting that successful execution (i.e., effector processing) of the shot was more crucial than response selection, which, in racquetball, is generally predictable (e.g., kill shots are usually hit from the front court area while ceiling or passing shots are typically made from the rear court area).

While the results of laboratory studies using novel tasks have repeatedly shown that extensive practice with difficult stimulus-response arrangements reduces decision time (e.g., Mowbray & Rhoades, 1959), it is likely that the increased skill of athletes in the form of more rapid reactions is due more to a learning of event probabilities, which allows the advance preparation of appropriate movements (Alain & Proteau, 1980; Rosenbaum, 1980). In an investigation of the preparatory responses of racquet sport players (badminton, racquetball, squash, tennis), Alain and Proteau (1978) found that the greater the perceived probability of an anticipated event (i.e., the certainty of the player as to what he thought an opponent's shot was going to be), the higher the proportion of anticipatory movements.

An enhanced appreciation of event probabilities with increased task experience has also been demonstrated in a number of laboratory studies. For example, Larish and Stelmach (1982) found that the reactions of subjects to highly probable stimuli became faster with practice while those to less probable stimuli became slower. For elite athletes, faster reactions to highly probable events are occasionally "paid for" by an increased susceptibility to false information presented by an opponent in the form of fakes or infrequent variations of a familiar play. I recall a Super Bowl game a number of years ago in which an important touchdown was scored when a defensive player vacated a zone he was assigned to protect. This happened because he falsely assumed the movements of an opponent indicated that the offensive play would be going in the same direction as it had on every previous situation in which those types of movements were made. The point, of course, is that early response selection may have costs as well as benefits associated with it.

In summary, it might be concluded that the response selection capabilities of expert performers are another factor that contributes to their exceptional demonstrations of skill. Early response selection may be one reason the movements of elite athletes rarely appear to be hurried or rushed. Knowing which responses are likely to be needed in a particular situation and having them primed for subsequent execution undoubtedly contributes to rapid responses (Tyldesley, 1981). As in the case of perceptual processing, this capability would be particularly advantageous to the open skill performer who must adapt responses to changing environmental conditions.

Once response selection has taken place, the remaining information-processing demand, response programming, must be satisfactorily met. How this process is carried out by individuals differing in skill level is the focus of the next section.

Effector Processing

Over practice both the quality and consistency of movement production improves. Moreover, an increased automatization of response execution occurs that enables the performer to produce movements with very little cognitive involvement. Or, as elite athletes sometimes say, to "let it happen." An excellent illustration of the way performers increasingly automate their movements in order to diminish the demands of effector processing may be found in a laboratory study by Pew (1966). In this experiment, subjects attempted to keep a constantly moving dot of light centered on an oscilloscope screen by alternately depressing two keys with their index fingers. Depression of the right key accelerated the movement of the dot to the right, and depression of the left key caused the dot to accelerate to the left. Early in practice, subjects appeared to control the dot by intermittently observing the direction it was moving and then depressing the key required to reverse its direction before it left the screen. After several weeks of practice, however, subjects adopted a control style that involved a rapid succession of alternating right and left key presses to keep the dot centered. This more automated response mode was only interrupted if the dot began to drift off center. On such occasions one of two correction strategies was implemented. Subjects either stopped their movements to institute a single correction with one of the keys and then resumed the pattern of alternate depression, or they continued in the rapid mode but slowly returned the dot to the center by depressing one of the keys for a slightly longer time than the other. A major point of this study is that by shifting to a more automated form of control over practice, subjects required the use of vision only to make periodic corrections of the response rather than to monitor each individual movement. While an advanced performer in a task such as that employed by Pew can hardly be equated to an athlete who has achieved performance stability over hundreds of hours of practice, it is likely that elite athletes often shift the control of their movements to an "automatic" mode in order to devote attention to important environmental information (e.g., the speed and spin of an approaching shot in tennis or the moves of an opponent in wrestling).

The results of several laboratory studies indicate that while the attention demands of effector processing diminish over practice (Wrisberg & Shea, 1978), movements are never performed attention-free (Stelmach & Hughes, 1983). Whether this is true for elite athletes performing highly familiar movements remains to be determined. However, it is probably safe to say that differences in the effector processing of advanced and average or novice performers lies in the *degree* to which automation has been achieved. Obviously the more performers are able to program a to-be-performed movement, the more their attention can be devoted to other aspects of the competitive environment (Allport, Antonis, & Reynolds, 1972). This capability would be especially crucial for athletes who must be able to process environmental cues during the course of movement execution (e.g., a point guard in basketball who must break a full-court press while dribbling). However, it is possible that closed-skill performers may also enjoy the benefits of automated movements (e.g., the figure skater who can express spontaneous creativity during the execution of a programmed routine).

The majority of findings from laboratory studies using novel tasks suggests that automation is particularly difficult when movements are more complex (Christina, Fischman, Vercruyssen, & Anson, 1982; Henry & Rogers, 1960; Klapp, 1977) or of longer duration (Klapp & Erwin, 1976; Quinn, Schmidt, Zelaznik, Hawkins, & McFarquhar, 1980). These factors have not been systematically explored in investigations with athletes. It might be expected, however, that the duration factor would be of little consequence in many sporting movements that are executed in relatively brief (i.e., <500 ms) periods of time (e.g., jumping, kicking, striking, throwing) and are likely controlled in an open-loop fashion (i.e., in the absence of feedback-based corrections). As an example, Hubbard and Seng (1954) reported that movement time during the swing phase (i.e., duration) of the standard batting response was extremely short and tended to vary little with the speed of the pitch.

If it may be assumed that response duration is not a crucial factor in the effector processing of most sport movements, it follows that differences in the skill levels of athletes may be associated more with the way individuals deal with the response complexity factor. One way skilled performers appear to reduce the complexity of movements over practice is to progressively "chunk" (i.e., cluster or subjectively organize) multiple components of an action, as in the case of concert pianists who are able to run off long sequences of notes in rapid fashion (Shaffer, 1981). Another strategy involves the programming of individual components of larger responses, as elite batters seem to do with the swing phase of the total hitting movement (Hubbard & Seng, 1954). Recent motor control theorists have proposed that practice leads to the development of coordinative structures that constrain the numerous muscles and limbs involved in a complex movement to act as a single unit (Fitch, Tuller, & Turvey, 1982; Turvey, 1977). While this notion has not been examined with sport populations, it is not unreasonable to assume that some of the efficiency evident in the movements of elite athletes is due to the development of such structures. And, of course, any increase in the automation of motor acts means that higher centers are freed up to attend to the more global aspects of performance (see Greene, 1972, for a more detailed discussion of the concept of hierarchical control).

In summary, it would appear that another important contributor to differences in the skill levels of advanced and average or novice performers is a capability to efficiently produce movements that are appropriate to situational demands. With practice, effector processing is probably improved by an enhanced organization of movement components and an increased automatization of motor commands. This in turn is reflected in a variety of changes in the quality of resulting movements, such as increased accuracy and consistency of kinematics (Marteniuk & Romanow, 1983), mechanical and energy efficiency (Sparrow & Irizarry-Lopez, 1987), and coordination (Moore & Marteniuk, 1986; Southard & Higgins, 1987; Vorro, Wilson, & Dainis, 1978).

In combination with a more accurate interpretation of environmental cues (i.e., perceptual processing) and a more rapid selection of an appropriate response (i.e., decision processing), the advanced performer is able to execute a smooth and efficient movement (i.e., effector processing) that usually accomplishes the intended goal of the action. Allard and Starkes (in press) have recently suggested that a distinguishing feature of experts is their adeptness at *both* "knowing" what to do (i.e., perceptual and decision processing) *and* "doing" it (i.e., effector processing). While lesser skilled persons may achieve a degree of success with one or the other of these capabilities, they are unable to "link" the two (e.g., the experienced reserve player who completely understands the nuances of a sport but is unable to produce the appropriate movements skillfully or the athlete who demonstrates skillful movements in practice but produces them at inappropriate moments in actual competition). Allard and Starkes propose that one way automaticity or expertise might be assessed is to determine the degree to which a performer has achieved a "linkage" between knowing and doing. These investigators have obtained preliminary support for their notion in experiments using videogame players, an oral surgeon, and baseball batters, all of whom had considerable experience in their respective activities. The results of these studies also suggested that it is the *appropriate* linking of doing to the present state of knowing (i.e., *flexibility* in linking rather than the establishment of stable condition-action links) that is crucial to successful performance. Such flexibility might be exemplified by the elite figure skater who knows how and when to modify a routine while it is in progress in order to maximize his/her chances for success. The nonelite skater, on the other hand, may "stick to the program" regardless of present circumstances. In any case, the concept of linkage development is an appealing one that deserves the attention of future investigators of motor expertise.

IMPLICATIONS FOR THE SPORT PSYCHOLOGY CONSULTANT

In this chapter, research literature addressing factors that might contribute to differences in the skill levels of advanced, average, and novice performers has been summarized. Particular attention has been devoted to the role of general abilities (i.e., hardware characteristics) and information-processing capabilities (i.e., software characteristics) in demonstrations of skilled performance. As a result of this discussion, two implications of possible relevance to the sport psychology consultant are offered. The first deals with the issue of whether factors contributing to differences in skill level can be reliably assessed; and if so, how? The second concerns a possible approach consultants might use to identify the role of various information processes in the performance of athletes in different sports.

The prediction of behavior in any context is usually an extremely difficult task because performance is based on a large constellation of variables. Indeed, a prevalent theme suggested by the literature reviewed in this chapter is that no *single* factor, ability, or behavioral characteristic is likely to account for all of the differences observed in the performance skill of individuals. Therefore, it behooves the practitioner to consider as many sources of variance as possible in order to locate the particular grouping of factors that contributes most to skillful behavior. Perhaps Fisher (1984) put it best when he contended that "to seriously begin understanding athletes' behavior, and to improve or predict performance outcomes, the reciprocal interaction between the athlete as a person and the specific sport environment must be considered" (p. 73). Key terms for anyone interested in maximizing predictions of skill would appear to be *interactionism* and *multidimensional*. This means that more sport psychology research must incorporate multivariate approaches. Investigations like that of Starkes (1987) are needed to determine which of a variety of predictor variables differentiate the performance skill of athletes. In addition to psychological/behavioral factors like general abilities and information-processing capabilities, assessments should probably include physical and physiological parameters. An excellent example of this type of research has been offered by Landers, Christina, Hatfield, Daniels, Wilkinson, Doyle, and Feltz (1981). In an extensive project examining the characteristics of competitive shooters, these investigators administered a variety of physical, psychological, and psychophysiological tests in order to determine which types of factors most clearly differentiated groups of elite and subelite performers.

While approaches such as this have obvious utility for the assessment of differences between individuals, the consultant may also want to consider using such methods to determine the sources of variance *within* an individual across situations and tasks. For example, it might be discovered that certain traits, characteristics, or abilities are important to the performance of a number of tasks/situations while others are essential for only one or two. In tennis, accurate visual tracking of the ball is probably more critical for producing effective service returns, volleys, and groundstrokes than it is for executing a service. While it is acknowledged that a player must always keep her/his eyes on the ball while serving, inferior performance of this shot is more likely due to other factors (e.g., inconsistent ball toss, deficiency of interlimb coordination, excessive muscle tension levels, etc.). By determining those tasks (and components) that pose consistent difficulty for the athlete, a consultant

may be able to identify the possible factors most in need of attention/improvement.

A second implication for the consultant deals with the issue of how information processes most crucial to performance skill in different sports might be determined. An excellent theoretical discussion of information-processing considerations in the learning and performance of motor skills has been provided by Marteniuk (1976). In this book, particular attention is given to the mechanisms of perceptual, decision, and effector processing that must be considered by practitioners in determining the types of information-processing demands associated with motor performance. Fundamental to an information-processing approach is an identification of the types of demands inherent in the task. For example, one important consideration in the determination of task demands is whether the performer must deal with environmental uncertainty or not. A performance environment that is "open" or less predictable would impose a greater demand on perceptual and decision processing than would one that is "closed" or stable (Poulton, 1957). For example, an option quarterback in football must deal with more stimulus-response pairs and less stimulus-response compatibility than a sprinter in track. Therefore, the practice experiences of the quarterback should include opportunities to view the various types of circumstances he can expect to see when running the option play and to learn which types of responses are most appropriate for each situation. With sufficient experience of this type, the time it will take the quarterback to recognize defensive patterns and select the most appropriate response should be decreased, thereby elevating his skill level. Similarly levels of volleyball skill should improve as the performer becomes more adept at handling the spatial, temporal, and event uncertainties inherent in the competitive environment. On the other hand, the skill of a gymnast performing in a relatively stable environment would be primarily determined by her/his ability to produce a consistent movement.

Preliminary analysis of the demands of various tasks should allow the consultant to determine the types of processing requirements performers must deal with and perhaps ascertain those that are limiting their skill levels. A useful method for assessing the demands of a task has been suggested by Salmela (1974; 1976). Fundamental to this approach is the identification of important task components, the assessment of athlete aptitude, and the provision of training experiences that target components most in need of attention by the performer. It is assumed that performance deficiencies may be due to the ineffectual functioning of one or more information processes. For example, inconsistent spiking performance of a volleyball player may be caused by a misreading of the spatial-temporal path of the ball from the setter (perceptual processing), uncertainty about where to direct the spike, given the type of set and configuration of the opponent's block (decision processing), and/or improper mechanics (effector processing). In order to determine which of these various processes may be impairing task performance, a process of component isolation is used. For example, isolation of the player's mechanics (reflecting the quality of effector processing) could be achieved by requiring her/him to spike a volleyball that is suspended in a fixed position. If she/he is able to execute mechanically correct spikes toward a variety of target locations, then it may be presumed that the problem is due more to difficulties associated with perceptual and/or decision processing than to those of effector processing. Progressive isolation of the other components would allow determination of the source of the difficulty. Once the problem is identified, appropriate drills or practice experiences could be suggested to enable the athlete to develop those processing skills that will contribute the most to improved performance.

Since skill refinement is an ongoing challenge for all athletes, it is important to identify as many factors as possible that are important to performance improvement. Once this is done, opportunities may be presented for the individual to sharpen those skills that will produce the biggest gains in performance. In the future we may be better able to determine which constellation of factors contributes the most to high levels of performance skill. However, this alone will not be enough. The consultant or coach-practitioner must also be able to assist performers with the improvement of requisite capabilities. Only then will athletes find themselves in a position to completely realize their performance potential.

References

Abernethy, B. (1987). Anticipation in sport: A review. *Physical Education Review, 10,* 5–16.

Abernethy, B., & Russell, D. G. (1984). Advance cue utilisation by skilled cricket batsmen. *Australian Journal of Science and Medicine in Sport, 16,* 2–10.

Abernethy, B., & Russell, D. G. (1987a). Expert-novice differences in an applied selective attention task. *Journal of Sport Psychology, 9,* 326–345.

Abernethy, B., & Russell, D. G. (1987b). The relationship between expertise and visual search strategy in a racquet sport. *Human Movement Science, 6,* 283–319.

Adams, J. A. (1966). Some mechanisms of motor responding: An examination of attention. In E. A. Bilodeau (Ed.), *Acquisition of skill* (pp. 169–200). New York: Academic Press.

Adams, J. A. (1971). A closed-loop theory of motor learning. *Journal of Motor Behavior, 3,* 111–150.

Alain, C., & Girardin, Y. (1978). The use of uncertainty in racquetball competition. *Canadian Journal of Applied Sport Sciences, 3,* 240–243.

Alain, C., & Proteau, L. (1978). Étude des variables relatives au traitement de l'information en sports de raquette. *Journal Canadien des Sciences Appliqués aux Sports, 3,* 27–35.

Alain, C., & Proteau, L. (1980). Decision making in sport. In C. H. Nadeau, W. R. Halliwell, K. M. Newell, & G. C. Roberts (Eds.), *Psychology of motor behavior and sport* (pp. 465–477). Champaign, IL: Human Kinetics.

Allard, F., & Burnett, N. (1985). Skill in sport. *Canadian Journal of Psychology, 39,* 294–312.

Allard, F., Graham, S., & Paarsalu, M. E. (1980). Perception in sport: Basketball. *Journal of Sport Psychology, 2,* 14–21.

Allard, F., & Starkes, J. L. (1980). Perception in sport: Volleyball. *Journal of Sport Psychology, 2,* 22–33.

Allard, F., & Starkes, J. L. (in press). Motor skill experts. In A. Ericsson & J. Smith (Eds.), *The study of expertise: Prospects and limits.* Wellesley, MA: Cambridge Press.

Allport, D. A., Antonis, B., & Reynolds, P. (1972). On the division of attention: A disproof of the single channel hypothesis. *Quarterly Journal of Experimental Psychology, 24,* 225–235.

Anderson, J. R. (1982). Acquisition of cognitive skill. *Psychological Review, 89,* 369–406.

Bachman, J. C. (1961). Specificity vs. generality in learning and performing two large muscle motor tasks. *Research Quarterly, 32,* 3–11.

Bannister, H., & Blackburn, J. H. (1931). An eye factor affecting proficiency at ball games. *British Journal of Psychology, 21,* 382–384.

Bard, C., & Fleury, M. (1976). Analysis of visual search activity during sport problem situations. *Journal of Human Movement Studies, 3,* 214–222.

Bard, C., & Fleury, M. (1981). Considering eye movement as a predictor of attainment. In I. M. Cockerill & W. W. MacGillivary (Eds.), *Vision and sport* (pp. 28–41). Cheltenham, U.K.: Stanley Thornes.

Borgeaud, P., & Abernethy, B. (1987). Skilled perception in volleyball defense. *Journal of Sport Psychology, 9,* 400–406.

Chase, W. G., & Simon, H. A. (1973). Perception in chess. *Cognitive Psychology, 4,* 55–81.

Christina, R. W., Fischman, M. G., Vercruyssen, M. J. P., & Anson J. G. (1982). Simple reaction time as a function of response complexity: Memory drum theory revisited. *Journal of Motor Behavior, 14,* 301–321.

Cockerill, I. M. (1981). Peripheral vision and hockey. In I. M. Cockerill & W. W. MacGillivary (Eds.), *Vision and sport* (pp. 54–63). Cheltenham, U.K.: Stanley Thornes.

Dickson, J. F. (1953). *The relationship of depth perception to goal shooting in basketball.* Unpublished doctoral dissertation, University of Iowa, Iowa City, IA.

Fisher, A. C. (1984). New directions in sport personality research. In J. M. Silva & R. S. Weinberg (Eds.), *Psychological foundations of sport* (pp. 70–80). Champaign, IL: Human Kinetics.

Fitch, H. L., Tuller, B., & Turvey, M. T. (1982). The Bernstein perspective: III. Tuning of coordinative structures with special reference to perception. In J. A. S. Kelso (Ed.), *Human motor behavior: An introduction* (pp. 271–281). Hillsdale, NJ: Erlbaum.

Fitts, P. M., & Peterson, J. R. (1964). Information capacity of discrete motor responses. *Journal of Experimental Psychology, 67,* 103–112.

Fitts, P. M., & Posner, M. I. (1967). *Human performance.* Belmont, CA: Brooks/Cole.

Fitts, P. M., & Seeger, C. M. (1953). S-R compatibility: Spatial characteristics of stimulus and response codes. *Journal of Experimental Psychology, 46,* 199–210.

Fleishman, E. A. (1972). On the relationship between abilities, learning, and human performance. *American Psychologist, 27,* 1017–1032.

Fleishman, E. A. (1978). Relating individual differences to the dimensions of human tasks. *Ergonomics, 21,* 1007–1019.

Fleishman, E. A. (1982). Systems for describing human tasks. *American Psychologist, 37,* 821–834.

Fleishman, E. A., & Bartlett, C. J. (1969). Human abilities. *Annual Review of Psychology, 20,* 349–380.

Fleishman, E. A., & Hempel, W. E. (1955). The relationship between abilities and improvement with practice in a visual discrimination reaction task. *Journal of Experimental Psychology, 49,* 301–311.

Fleishman, E. A., & Rich, S. (1963). Role of kinesthetic and spatial-visual abilities in perceptual motor learning. *Journal of Experimental Psychology, 66,* 6–11.

Gentile, A. M. (1972). A working model of skill acquisition with application to teaching. *Quest, 17,* 3–23.

Graybiel, A., Jokl, E., & Trapp, C. (1955). Russian studies of vision in relation to physical activity and sports. *Research Quarterly, 26,* 212–223.

Greene, P. H. (1972). Problems of organization of motor systems. In R. Rosen & F. M. Snell (Eds.), *Progress in theoretical biology* (Vol. 2, pp. 303–338). New York: Academic Press.

Henderson, S. E. (1975). Predicting the accuracy of a throw without visual feedback. *Journal of Human Movement Studies, 1,* 183–189.

Henry, F. M. (1961). Reaction time–movement time correlations. *Perceptual and Motor Skills, 12,* 63–66.

Henry, F. M. (1968). Specificity vs. generality in learning motor skill. In R. C. Brown & G. S. Kenyon (Eds.), *Classical studies on physical activity* (pp. 331–340). Englewood Cliffs, NJ: Prentice-Hall.

Henry, F. M., & Rogers, D. E. (1960). Increased response latency for complicated movements and the "memory drum" theory of neuromotor reaction. *Research Quarterly, 31,* 448–458.

Hick, W. E. (1952). On the rate of gain of information. *Quarterly Journal of Experimental Psychology, 4,* 11–26.

Housner, L. D. (1981). Expert-novice knowledge structure and cognitive processing differences in badminton. (Abstract.) *Psychology of motor behavior and sport—1981* (p. 1). Proceedings of the annual meeting of the North American Society for the Psychology of Sport and Physical Activity, Asilomar, CA.

Howarth, C., Walsh, W. D., Abernethy, B., & Snyder, C. W. (1984). A field examination of anticipation in squash: Some preliminary data. *Australian Journal of Science and Medicine in Sport, 16,* 7–11.

Hubbard, A. W., & Seng, C. N. (1954). Visual movements of batters. *Research Quarterly, 25,* 42–57.

Hyman, R. (1953). Stimulus information as a determinant of reaction time. *Journal of Experimental Psychology, 45,* 188–196.

Jones, C. M., & Miles, T. R. (1978). Use of advance cues in predicting the flight of a lawn tennis ball. *Journal of Human Movement Studies, 4,* 231–235.

Keele, S. W., & Hawkins, H. L. (1982). Explorations of individual differences relevant to high level skill. *Journal of Motor Behavior, 14,* 3–23.

Keele, S. W., Ivry, R. I., & Pokorny, R. A. (1987). Force control and its relation to timing. *Journal of Motor Behavior, 19,* 96–114.

Keele, S. W., Pokorny, R. A., Corcos, D. M., & Ivry, R. I. (1985). Do perception and motor production share common timing mechanisms: A correlational analysis. *Acta Psychologica, 60,* 173–191.

Keller, L. P. (1940). *The relation of quickness of bodily movement to success in athletics.* Unpublished doctoral dissertation, New York University.

Kerr, B. (1973). Processing demands during mental operations. *Memory and Cognition, 1,* 401–412.

Klapp, S. T. (1977). Reaction time analysis of programmed control. *Exercise and Sport Sciences Reviews, 5,* 231–253.

Klapp, S. T., & Erwin, C. I. (1976). Relation between programming time and duration of the response being programmed. *Journal of Experimental Psychology: Human Perception and Performance, 2,* 591–598.

Landers, D. M., Boutcher, S. H., & Wang, M. Q. (1986). A psychobiological study of archery performance. *Research Quarterly for Exercise and Sport, 57,* 236–244.

Landers, D. M., Christina, R. W., Hatfield, B. D., Daniels, F. S., Wilkinson, M. O., Doyle, L. A., & Feltz, D. L. (1981). A comparison of elite and subelite competitive shooters on selected physical, psychological, and psychophysiological tests. In G. C. Roberts & D. M. Landers (Eds.), *Psychology of motor behavior and sport—1980* (p. 93). Champaign, IL: Human Kinetics.

Larish, D. D., & Stelmach, G. E. (1982). Preprogramming, programming, and reprogramming of aimed hand movements as a function of age. *Journal of Motor Behavior, 14,* 322–340.

Lotter, W. S. (1960). Interrelationships among reaction times and speeds of movement in different limbs. *Research Quarterly, 31,* 147–155.

Marteniuk, R. G. (1976). *Information processing in motor skills.* New York: Holt, Rinehart, & Winston.

Marteniuk, R. G., & Romanow, S. K. E. (1983). Human movement organization and learning as revealed by variability of movement, use of kinematic information and Fourier analysis. In R. A. Magill (Ed.), *Memory and control of action* (pp. 167–197). Amsterdam: North-Holland.

McDavid, R. F. (1977). Predicting potential in football players. *Research Quarterly, 48,* 98–104.

Meek, F., & Skubic, V. (1971). Spatial perception of highly skilled and poorly skilled females. *Perceptual and Motor Skills, 33,* 1309–1310.

Miller, D. M. (1960). *The relationships between some visual-perceptual factors and the degree of success realized by sports performers.* Unpublished doctoral dissertation, University of Southern California, Los Angeles.

Montebello, R. A. (1953). *The role of stereoscopic vision in some aspects of baseball playing ability.* Unpublished master's thesis, Ohio State University, Columbus.

Moore, S. P., & Marteniuk, R. G. (1986). Kinematic and electromyographic changes that occur as a function of learning a time-constrained aiming task. *Journal of Motor Behavior, 18,* 397–426.

Morris, G. S. D., & Kreighbaum, E. (1977). Dynamic visual acuity of varsity women volleyball and basketball players. *Research Quarterly, 48,* 480–483.

Mowbray, G. H., & Rhoades, M. U. (1959). On the reduction of choice reaction times with practice. *Quarterly Journal of Experimental Psychology, 11,* 16–23.

Nakagawa, A. (1982). A field experiment on recognition of game situations in ball games—in the case of static situations in rugby football. *Japanese Journal of Physical Education, 27,* 17–26.

Olsen, E. A. (1956). Relationship between psychological capacities and success in college athletics. *Research Quarterly, 27,* 79–89.

Parker, H. E. (1981). Visual detection and perception in netball. In

I. M. Cockerill & W. W. MacGillivary (Eds.), *Vision and sport* (pp. 42–53). Cheltenham, U.K.: Stanley Thornes.

Parker, J. F., & Fleishman, E. A. (1960). Ability factors and component performance measures as predictors of complex tracking behavior. *Psychological Monographs, 74* (Whole No. 503).

Pew, R. W. (1966). Acquisition of hierarchical control over the temporal organization of a skill. *Journal of Experimental Psychology, 71,* 764–771.

Pierson, W. R. (1956). Comparison of fencers and nonfencers by psychomotor, space perception and anthropometric measures. *Research Quarterly, 27,* 90–96.

Posner, M. I. (1964). Uncertainty as a predictor of similarity in the study of generalization. *Journal of Experimental Psychology, 63,* 113–118.

Poulton, E. C. (1957). On prediction in skilled movements. *Psychological Bulletin, 54,* 467–478.

Quinn, J. T., Schmidt, R. A., Zelaznik, H. N., Hawkins, B., & McFarquhar, R. (1980). Target-size influences on reaction time with movement time controlled. *Journal of Motor Behavior, 12,* 239–261.

Ridini, L. M. (1968). Relationships between psychological functions tests and selected sport skills of boys in junior high school. *Research Quarterly, 39,* 674–683.

Rodionov, A. V. (1978). *Psikhologiia sportivnoi deiatel'nosti (The psychology of sport activity).* Moscow: Government Press.

Rosenbaum, D. A. (1980). Human movement initiation: Specification of arm, direction, and extent. *Journal of Experimental Psychology: General, 109,* 444–474.

Salmela, J. H. (1974). An information processing approach to volleyball. *CVA Volleyball Technical Journal, 1,* 49–62.

Salmela, J. H. (1976). Application of a psychological taxonomy to sport performance. *Canadian Journal of Applied Sport Sciences, 1,* (23–32).

Salmela, J. H., & Fiorito, P. (1979). Visual cues in ice hockey goaltending. *Canadian Journal of Applied Sport Sciences, 4,* 56–59.

Schmidt, R. A. (1988). *Motor control and learning: A behavioral emphasis* (2nd ed.). Champaign, IL: Human Kinetics.

Schmidt, R. A., & White, J. L. (1972). Evidence for an error detection mechanism in motor skills: A test of Adams' closed-loop theory. *Journal of Motor Behavior, 4,* 143–153.

Schneidman, N. N. (1979). Soviet sport psychology in the 1970s and the superior athlete. In P. Klavora & J. V. Daniel (Eds.), *Coach, athlete, and the sport psychologist* (pp. 230–247). Champaign, IL: Human Kinetics.

Shaffer, L. H. (1981). Performances of Chopin, Bach, and Beethoven: Studies in motor programming. *Cognitive Psychology, 13,* 326–376.

Southard, D., & Higgins, T. (1987). Changing movement patterns:

Effects of demonstration and practice. *Research Quarterly for Exercise and Sport, 58,* 77–80.

Sparrow, W. A., & Irizarry-Lopez, V. M. (1987). Mechanical efficiency and metabolic cost as measures of learning a novel gross motor task. *Journal of Motor Behavior, 19,* 240–264.

Starkes, J. L. (1987). Skill in field hockey: The nature of the cognitive advantage. *Journal of Sport Psychology, 9,* 146–160.

Starkes, J. L., & Deakin, J. (1984). Perception in sport: A cognitive approach to skilled performance. In W. F. Straub & J. M. Williams (Eds.), *Cognitive sport psychology* (pp. 115–128). Lansing, NY: Sport Science Associates.

Stelmach, G. E., & Hughes, B. G. (1983). Does motor skill automation require a theory of attention? In R. A. Magill (Ed.), *Memory and control of action* (pp. 67–92). Amsterdam: North-Holland.

Swets, J. A. (1964). *Signal detection and recognition by human observers.* New York: Wiley.

Turvey, M. T. (1977). Preliminaries to a theory of action with reference to vision. In R. Shaw & J. Bransford (Eds.), *Perceiving, acting, and knowing* (pp. 211–265). Hillsdale, NJ: Erlbaum.

Tyldesley, D. A. (1981). Motion perception and movement control in fast ball games. In I. M. Cockerill & W. W. MacGillivary (Eds.), *Vision and sport* (pp. 91–115). Cheltenham, U.K.: Stanley Thornes.

Tyldesley, D. A., Bootsma, R. J., & Bomhoff, G. T. (1982). Skill level and eye-movement patterns in a sport oriented reaction time task. In H. Rieder, K. Bös, H. Mechling, & K. Reischle (Eds.), *Motor learning and movement behavior: Contribution to learning in sport* (pp. 290–296). Cologne: Hofmann.

Vanek, M., & Cratty, B. J. (1970). *Psychology and the superior athlete.* Toronto: Macmillan.

Vorro, J., Wilson, F. R., & Dainis, A. (1978). Multivariate analysis of biomechanical profiles for the coracobrachialis and biceps brachii (caput breve) muscles in humans. *Ergonomics, 21,* 407–418.

Wiebe, V. R. (1954). A study of tests of kinesthesis. *Research Quarterly, 25,* 222–230.

Wilkinson, J. J. (1958). *A study of reaction-time measures to a kinesthetic and a visual stimulus for selected groups of athletes and nonathletes.* Unpublished doctoral dissertation, Indiana University, Bloomington, IN.

Williams, J. M., & Thirer, J. (1975). Vertical and horizontal peripheral vision in male and female athletes and nonathletes. *Research Quarterly, 46,* 200–205.

Winograd, S. (1942). The relationship of timing and vision to baseball performance. *Research Quarterly, 13,* 481–493.

Wrisberg, C. A., & Shea, C. H. (1978). Shifts in attention demands and motor program utilization during motor learning. *Journal of Motor Behavior, 10,* 149–158.

·4·

DEVELOPMENTAL CONSIDERATIONS IN SKILL ACQUISITION

Jerry R. Thomas

Katherine T. Thomas

Jere D. Gallagher

Human motor performance changes significantly during a life span. Across childhood and adolescence, performance generally improves; it remains relatively stable during the early adult years and gradually deteriorates with aging. This phenomenon appears to be generally true from the most simple reaction time task to complex forms of movement such as sport skills. To truly grasp the role of movement, sport, and exercise among humans, one must understand both the development, maintenance, and deterioration of skill across the life span.

Elsewhere in this volume, life span development of skill and exercise (Section VIII) is discussed. However, in this chapter we will focus specifically on descriptions of and explanations for changes in motor performance that occur across childhood and adolescence. During this time rapid changes occur and are attributable to several sources: *biological* factors such as genetics, growth, changes in body composition, puberty, and maturation; *environmental* factors such as practice, opportunity, and encouragement; and, of course, the *interaction* of biological and environmental factors such as skill practice during optimal periods of development.

Our developmental perspective comes from the theoretical framework from which we view skill acquisition. The question we ask is, "How do children/adolescents acquire/control skillful movements, and what roles do factors such as cognitive development, growth, heredity, and environmental characteristics play?" For example:

1. Motor skills generally improve across childhood and adolescence. Yet younger children who have an expert level knowledge and skills in a sport (e.g., baseball) can perform considerably better in this sport than older children (and even adults) who are more novice in their knowledge and skills. Thus expertise (given both ability and practice) appears to override the normal developmental processes associated with changes in cognition, skill, and growth.

2. Growth occurs across childhood and adolescence, producing associated changes in size and strength. How do children and adolescents maintain/increase/control skillful movements when their body continues to get larger and stronger (e.g., arms and legs become longer, center of gravity changes, weight increases)?

3. Hereditary advantages/disadvantages obviously are important in skillful performance. The old adage "If you want to be a good athlete, choose your parents wisely" applies. But more importantly how do inherited skill advantages interact with environment and growth in developing expertise in sport?

4. Environment plays an obvious role in the development of skillful movement. Opportunities, encouragement, and practice are essential features in skill development. Yet clearly environment is not the only factor; it interacts with ability, growth factors, and cognitive development in producing expert performers.

Our developmental perspective examines the role of cognitive development in movement and sport performance. In particular we are interested in how sport and movement expertise develops across childhood and adolescence (for overviews, see Thomas, French, & Humphries, 1986; Thomas, French, Thomas, & Gallagher, 1988; Thomas & Thomas, in press). However, other perspectives exist for viewing development and motor performance. For example, action systems (dynamical systems) place much more emphasis on the direct perception-movement connections and less on cognitive factors that influence skill development (for a developmental overview, see Thelen, 1987). A nice presentation of this perspective is contained in the book *Development of Posture and Gait Across the Life Span* (edited by Woollacott & Shumway-Cook, 1989; see Chapter 1 by Reed, chapter 2 by Thelen, Ulrich, & Jensen, Chapter 4 by Woollacott, Shumway-Cook, & Williams, and Chapter 6 by Clark & Whitall).

While these two views are different (and some would argue not compatible), we believe they are both useful ways to study the development of expertise. Literal views of central motor programs as ways to select, plan, execute, and control movements are probably not accurate representations of skilled behavior. The dynamical perspective has clearly focused on two of the major weaknesses of motor programs (and hierarchical theories in general): How does the system reduce the degrees-of-freedom problem associated with complex movements? If the degrees of freedom are constrained for a particular skill, how does the system maintain the flexibility to deal with changing environmental demands found in sports (particularly more open, skilled sports like basketball and tennis)?

Yet complex sport performance obviously involves cognitive function, and a dynamical view which downplays this influence is unlikely to be an accurate representation of behavior. Because of these different perspectives on the development of skilled behavior, the proponents of each have tended to choose movement tasks compatible with their perspective. For example, in our research we look at sport skills as they are contained in the sport environment (basketball, French & Thomas, 1987; tennis, McPherson & Thomas, 1989). This selection of motor activities allows us to examine the complex cognitive components. Successful action in a complex sport environment cannot happen without cognitive activity. Dynamical systems theorists often choose phylogenetic skills such as locomotion (e.g., see Woollacott & Shumway-Cook, 1989; but for an interesting view of coordination and control in locomotion, see Whitall, 1991) or underlying motor characteristics such as eye-hand coordination (e.g., see Bard, Fleury, & Hay, 1990). These types of actions may require minimal cognitive activity by the subjects. The complete solution to studying complex movement skills as they are used in sport is likely to require both perspectives and some merging of their approaches.

In this chapter we will present a view of skill development (particularly the development of expertise) that involves cognitive function, growth, and environmental characteristics. We do this for two reasons. First, that is our area of expertise. Second, this approach is probably most appropriate for this book and is why the editors selected us to prepare a chapter.

MODELS FOR STUDYING SKILL DEVELOPMENT

Three of the most common frameworks for studying motor skill development are stage models, expertise models, and readiness models. Each of these makes an important contribution to the understanding of development, and more specifically the influence of development on motor skill acquisition. A brief description of each of these paradigms is appropriate before discussing the results of research using these paradigms.

Stage Models

Stage models use specific behaviors or clusters of behaviors to describe typical patterns which progress in an orderly, linear, and invariant manner. Stage theories vary greatly but have appeal for both application and research. Being able to classify students and/or subjects into groups based on common performance characteristics or stages is an approach that is associated with many research paradigms and has intuitive appeal for teachers. Accuracy of classification is clearly an issue, as is the difficulty of dealing with individuals in transition between stages. The breadth of a stage is also an issue. While it is easier to classify accurately when a stage is very specific and narrow in scope, having to identify a stage for each different skill or class of skills is less than pleasing. Piaget (1952) devised a theory of cognitive development that has relatively broad stages; conversely information processing demands identification of stages within each component of the processing system (Kail & Hagen, 1977; Thomas, 1980). Each has inherent advantages and disadvantages.

Piagetian. Piaget described the development of cognition after observing his two daughters (Piaget, 1952). The resulting theory of cognitive development was comprised of four stages: sensorimotor, preoperational, concrete operations, and formal operations. Each stage was identified by the ability or inability to solve certain tasks. The tasks focused on several skills that Piaget related to cognitive operations. The solution to the task then became both the definition of the stage and the criteria for the stage. Preoperational children were characterized by the ability to sort on one characteristic, but not to conserve or sort by two characteristics (Flavell, 1977). Concrete operators were characterized by their need to adhere to a strict set of rules and to rely on these rules for decision making. Concrete operators solve a conservation task. These children understand that when water is poured from a short fat beaker to a tall thin beaker, the amount of water is constant, while pre-operational children feel there is more water in the taller container. Formal operators are able to make exceptions yet still apply general rules when appropriate; also, they can solve problems that require dealing with things they have never experienced.

The limitation of Piaget's theory for research purposes is twofold: First, the inability to quantify the cognitive abilities necessary to do the tasks. The tasks, therefore the stages, were identified by a few tasks that were either pass/ fail or had levels of solutions. Piaget believed that maturation was the cause of transition from stage to stage, and that little if anything could (and perhaps should) be done to manipulate the cognitive system. This is the essence of the second limitation. The explanation for variations between children was maturation, a variable which is virtually impossible to manipulate (or even measure). This explanation proved frustrating to some individuals studying human development—perhaps human nature rejects Piaget's notion to "leave well enough alone." While Piaget's theory is eloquent and describes cognitive development in a simple, straightforward manner, another problem exists with the theory.

Exact changes in cognitive processing were difficult to assess. For instance, when a child was moving from one stage to another, neither stage adequately identified the child's cognitive functioning, and the theory was not precise enough to clearly identify these levels. Intuitively one can see that an 11-year-old child has cognitive abilities that were not present in that child at 7 years of age, yet those changes may not be great enough to move that child from concrete to formal operations.

Pascual-Leone and Smith (1969) devised a solution for this problem, called the Neo-Piagetian Theory. They proposed a numerical formula to identify the amount of capacity demanded by each task. The more levels of each task that a child could solve, the higher the child's level of functioning. This system allowed researchers to show differences between children within a single stage and to better study the differences between children in different stages. The problem was, and is, that the mathematical description of the tasks was complex. Few researchers were able to master or implement the system effectively. What has resulted, at least for motor skill acquisition research, is a theoretical solution for using Piaget's theory, but not a practical solution. The ultimate result of both the Piagetian and neo-Piagetian models is little published research testing the models and ultimately explaining the impact of development on motor skill acquisition. Perhaps a more important issue with neo-Piagetian research was noted with Piaget's theory—the age-related changes in cognitive behavior were attributed to structural rather than functional changes in the system (Thomas, 1984). However, researchers still use both Piaget and resulting stage research to describe specific changes in motor skills: Roberton's (1984) work is an example of the application and extension of stage theory to motor development.

Information Processing

During the 1970s with the growth in computer literacy and usage came an explanation of cognitive behavior that used a computer model. Shiffrin and Schneider (1977) and Atkinson and Shiffrin (1968) developed detailed models that simulated computer hardware and software to explain human thinking. Following this, Ornstein and Naus (1984, 1985), Chi (1976, 1978, 1982) and Kail (1979) sought to explain development in a similar way—they tried to "build" an adult processing system by studying children's processing of information. The paradigm was similar to those created by Atkinson and Shiffrin, and Shiffrin and Schneider. This model worked quite well and focused on memory span, speed of processing, short-term memory processes (encoding, rehearsal, retrieval, organization), and metacognition (knowing about knowing and strategies). Considerable research on motor skill acquisition has been done using these paradigms (see Thomas, 1980, 1984 for summaries). The overall result is that as children get older, they get better. However, these studies also used experimental manipulations from which two unique concepts resulted. First, when given a specific solution to a task, younger children could often use the solution effectively and perform like older children (Gallagher & Thomas, 1984, 1986; Thomas, Lee, Thomas, & Testerman, 1983; Winther & Thomas, 1981). The second result was that some younger children performed better than older children when the task related to one specific content area. This notion resulted in the expertise models to be described in the next section.

The typical information processing experiment would use three or four ages of children, with two or more years between age groups. A novel task would be presented to the child, and the child's accuracy of recall would be the dependent variable. Most studies would include an experimental condition that gave one group of children at each age a good way to remember the target information. The expected results would be for older children to remember more accurately, but younger children who were given the memory strategy to do better than children their age in the control group. Research using memory of movement was often more sensitive to age-related performance differences than research using purely cognitive tasks because the data in motor research paradigms is usually continuous, while cognitive tasks often use discrete data. The dependent variables for developmental motor skill acquisition research using the information processing paradigms were time, distance, direction, location, acceleration, and force.

Expertise Models. The information processing literature indicated that long-term memory, or knowledge, increased linearly with age. The older a child, the more information they have stored in a permanent memory bank. This results from experience and learning. The research on information processing also produced another knowledge phenomenon that was considerably more surprising than the linear increase in knowledge. Certain individuals could perform specific memory tasks much better than would be predicted by either chronological age or performance on the same memory task with different content. This discovery led to the study of expertise (Chase & Simon, 1973; Chi, 1978; Chiesi, Spilich, & Voss, 1979). Both child and adult experts were studied using a variety of content areas from fighter pilots, computer programmers, and teachers to dinosaur connoisseurs and basketball players (see Thomas, French, Thomas, & Gallagher, 1988, for review). Case studies were used, as well as quasi-experimental designs to study expertise. Sport has employed two perspectives, the perceptual model and the knowledge model to explore expertise. Both often use levels of expertise and levels of age and measure performance on one or more aspects of performance. The perceptual experiments (e.g., Abernethy, 1988) focus on speed and/or accuracy of perceptual processing. The knowledge models typically use skill tests, game play, knowledge tests, and situation interviews to ascertain differences related to age and expertise in sport performance (e.g., McPherson & Thomas, 1989).

Readiness Models

Readiness implies that the learner is in a position to acquire new skills (Seefeldt, 1988). Two components are implied in readiness. One relates to the skill itself, the other to the performer of the skill. First, the identification of prerequisite behaviors or skills that are precursors for performing other skills is necessary in the readiness model. Second, the ability to recognize behaviors which indicate that the performer has the necessary prerequisites. A third component of the readiness model is suggested by some—the spontaneous attempt to perform the skill by the learner. Researchers now agree that readiness is a result of environmental and genetic factors.

The readiness model has shown consistently that children progress in an invariant manner through a sequence of motor skills, but that children differ greatly in their rate of progression (Branta, Haubenstricker, & Seefeldt, 1984). These models are not concerned with manipulating events so much as identifying the relationships between events and describing the progressions.

DESCRIBING AGE-RELATED CHANGES IN SKILLED PERFORMANCE

To undertake the task of describing age-related changes in skilled performance in less than a complete book (or at least several chapters of a book) is impossible. In fact motor development books (e.g., Eckert, 1987; Gallahue, 1989; Haywood, 1986; Payne & Isaacs, 1987; Thomas, 1984; Williams, 1983) use significant sections and chapters to accomplish this purpose. Other books devote their total focus to specific aspects of motor development: e.g., posture and gait (Woollacott & Shumway-Cook, 1989) or eye-hand coordination (Bard, Fleury, & Hay, 1990). This section represents an attempt to tie together through theory and illustration the developmental nature of motor performance as it is influenced by specific factors such as gender, cognitive development, expertise, and growth. The purpose is to assist the reader in understanding the developmental process. Reference will be made frequently to more complete reports and explanations for the phenomenon being described.

PERFORMANCE DATA

Chapters in the previously listed textbooks as well as in more general books on performance have addressed the developmental nature of skilled performance (e.g., Branta, Haubenstricker, & Seefeldt, 1984; Haubenstricker & Seefeldt, 1986; Seefeldt & Haubenstricker, 1982). In this section an attempt is made to provide descriptive data about the outcome measures of motor performance (e.g., time, distance) as they change across childhood and adolescence. These are followed by a discussion of qualitative descriptions of the movements themselves (e.g., throwing patterns). Figure 4–1 is an overview of how the skill process develops during childhood and adolescence. The idea represented by the triangle is that later phases of movement development are built on earlier phases. Gallahue's (1982) conception of this is a good one that provides a nice

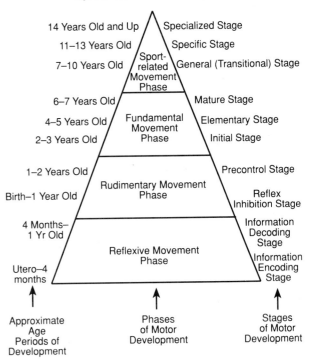

FIGURE 4–1. The phases of motor development.
(Reprinted with the permission of Macmillan, from Gallahue, D. L. (1982). *Understanding motor development* (p. 45).

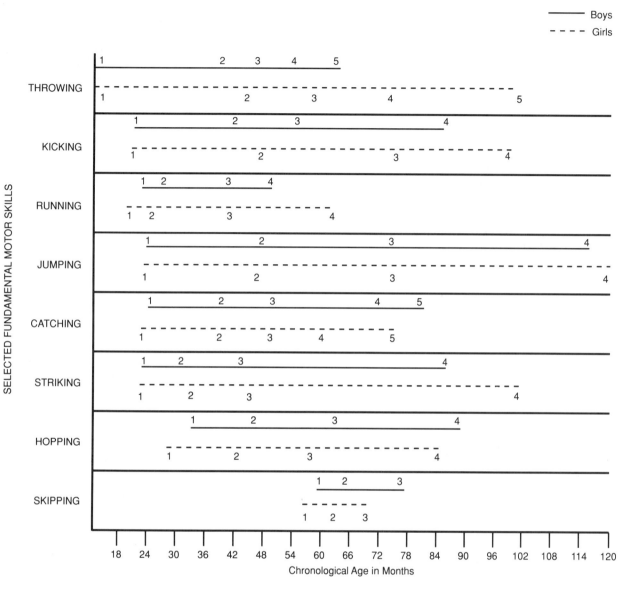

FIGURE 4–2. The age at which 60% of the boys and girls were able to perform at a specific developmental level for selected fundamental motor skills.

(Reprinted with permission of John Wiley & Sons, from Seefeldt, V. & Haubenstricker, J. (1982). Patterns, phases, or stages: An analytical model for the study of developmental movement. In J. A. S. Kelso & J. E. Clark (Eds.), *The development of movement control and co-ordination* (p. 314).

pictorial view of this process. However, we must recognize that the evidence available to support this orderly sequence is limited—not that the evidence collected refutes it, just that limited research data are available.

A few representative skills on which substantial data are available have been selected for discussion here. Figure 4–2 (from Seefeldt & Haubenstricker, 1982) provides an overview of the age (in months) that 60% of boys and girls are able to perform eight fundamental motor skills at a

specific level. As an example, most boys can throw overhand with a fairly mature pattern (the number "5" above the solid line represents the accomplishment of the mature pattern) at about 60 months of age (5 years), but most girls are 102 months (8.5 years) of age before they exhibit a mature pattern. Similar interpretations can be made for the other skills listed.

In the following sections, two of the fundamental skills, running and throwing, are selected from Figure 4–2

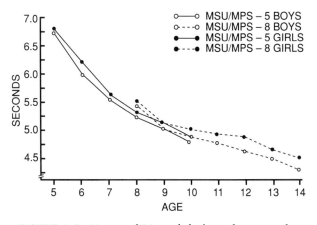

FIGURE 4–3. Means of 30-yard dash performance for four groups of children, measured longitudinally from 5 to 10 or 8 to 14 years of age.

(Reprinted with permission of D. C. Heath, from Branta, C., Haubenstricker, J., & Seefeldt, V. (1984). Age changes in motor skills during childhood and adolescence. In R. L. Terjung (Ed.), *Exercise and sport sciences reviews* (Vol. 12, p. 485).

on which we supply more data. These are skills that have substantial importance in the sports and physical activities of many cultures as well as in human evolution. We present performance data at various age levels on the two skills and then provide information about the qualitative analysis of the movements themselves.

Qualitative Descriptions of Skill

Qualitative descriptions of skilled movement have a long history (e.g., overhand throwing, Wild, 1938). Wickstrom's book *Fundamental Motor Patterns* (editions in 1970, 1977, 1983) provides a description of the qualitative development of fundamental movement patterns—walking, running, jumping, throwing, catching, striking, and kicking. Numerous studies have provided the data on the developmental nature of fundamental skills that have been summarized and explained by Wickstrom and in numerous other motor development books (e.g., Eckert, 1987; Gallahue, 1989; Haywood, 1986; Payne & Isaacs, 1987; Thomas, 1984; Williams, 1983).

Considerable discussion has occurred concerning the level and nature of these qualitative analyses. Seefeldt and Haubenstricker (1982) have argued for whole body descriptions of the levels or stages of qualitative skill analysis, while Roberton (1982) presents a case for the need to analyze the components of the movement (e.g., arm action, trunk action, and leg action in throwing). Either approach is certainly useful for teachers and coaches because movement analysis is done at a level the eye can observe (or at least can be recorded and observed on a video-camera). However, if the purpose is to truly understand the nature of the movement and how it is influenced by other characteristics such as growth, gender, implements (e.g., ball size/weight), practice, fatigue, or any number of other characteristics, a more detailed and quantitative biomechanical

analysis is needed (e.g., high-speed video or film from several cameras). Additionally, if the purpose of the analysis is understanding skill and characteristics that influence it rather than providing a basis for visual skill analysis, related measures such as muscle EMG and ground reaction forces must be considered.

Running

Figure 4–3 depicts the developmental nature of running speed for boys and girls. This plot (from a Michigan State study; see Branta, Haubenstricker, & Seefeldt, 1984) reflects two sets of longitudinal data, one set for boys and girls from 5 to 10 years of age, and a second set for boys and girls from 8 to 14 years of age. Two characteristics of these data are obvious: Girls and boys steadily increase in running speed over the age ranges reported; and boys run slightly faster (on the average) at each age. A less obvious characteristic is that the differences in running speed between boys and girls becomes slightly greater beginning at about 11–12 years of age (gender differences are discussed in greater detail in a subsequent part of this chapter).

While the mean running speed of boys is faster than girls at every age level, there is considerable overlap in the distributions. In fact it is very common in an elementary physical education class or on a young coeducational age group sport team to observe that the fastest person is a girl. As children reach and pass puberty, less overlap in the distributions of running speeds between boys and girls is seen. However, it is still fairly common to find a girl, particularly one on a sport team where speed is important, who is faster than many boys.

Much of the change in running speed across childhood and adolescence is a result of increased leg length. As children grow taller, the legs increase in length and make up a proportionately greater percentage of total statue (Malina, 1975). This probably accounts for the stride length data seen in Figure 4–4. Observe that the stride rate per second

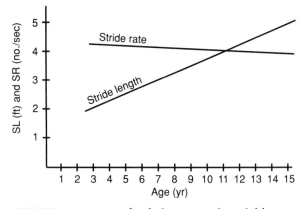

FIGURE 4–4. Longitudinal changes in five children in stride length (SL) and stride rate (SR).

From Smith, S. (1977). *Longitudinal changes in stride length and stride rate during sprint running.* Unpublished master's thesis, University of Wisconsin–Madison.

TABLE 4–1. Developmental Sequences for Running*†

Leg Action Component	
Level 1	Run is flat-footed, with minimal flight. Swing leg is slightly abducted as it comes forward. When seen from overhead, path of swing leg curves out to side during movement forward (Wickstrom, 1977). Foot eversion gives toeing-out appearance to swinging leg (Wickstrom, 1977). Angle of knee of swing leg is greater than 90 degrees during forward motion.
Level 2	Swing thigh moves forward with greater acceleration, causing 90 degrees of maximal flexion in knee. Viewed from rear, foot is no longer toed out nor is thigh abducted. Sideward swing of thigh continues, however, causing foot to cross body midline when viewed from rear (Wickstrom 1977). Flight time increases. After contact, which may still be flat-footed, support knee flexes more as child's weight rides over his foot (Seefeldt, Reuschlein, and Vogel, 1972).
Level 3	Foot contact is with heel or ball of foot. Forward movement of swing leg is primarily in sagittal plane. Flexion of thigh at hip carries knee higher at end of forward swing. Support leg moves from flexion to complete extension by takeoff.

Arm Action Component	
Level 1	Arms are held in high to middle guard position, as described in development of walking (Seefeldt, Reuschlein, and Vogel, 1972).
Level 2	Spinal rotation swings arms bilaterally to counterbalance rotation of pelvis and swing leg. Frequently oblique plane of motion plus continual balancing adjustments give flailing appearance to arm action.
Level 3	Spinal rotation continues to be prime mover of arms. Now elbow of arm swinging forward begins to flex, then extend, during backward swing. Combination of rotation and elbow flexion causes arm rotating forward to cross body midline and arm rotating back to abduct, swinging obliquely outward from body.
Level 4	Humerus (upper arm) begins to drive forward and back in sagittal plane, independent of spinal rotation. Movement is in opposition to other arm and to leg on same side. Elbow flexion is maintained, oscillating through approximately 90-degree angle during forward and backward arm swings.

*These sequences have not been validated.

†Used with permission from Roberton, M. A. (1984). Changing motor patterns during childhood. In J. R. Thomas (Ed.), *Motor development during childhood and adolescence*. Minneapolis, MN: Burgess.

during running remains fairly constant across the age ranges; however, stride length increases as age increases, probably reflecting changes in leg length.

Not all of the change in running speed as age advances is due to increased leg length. Improved running form also accounts for increases in running speed. We have chosen to present the component view (Roberton, 1982) of qualitative analysis, although we have found the Seefeldt and Haubenstricker (1982) approach equally useful. Table 4–1 provides a description of the changes in running form that occur across childhood. This work by Roberton (1984) is divided into the levels of development for leg action and arm action (note that these are based on analyses that have not gone through the complete sequence of examination that Roberton uses—they are invalidated). Increasingly higher levels represent more mature patterns that are likely to be present in older and more skillful children.

Throwing

Figure 4–5 is a sample of data depicting throwing performance for boys and girls across childhood and adolescence. These data (from Espenschade, 1960) are typical, showing steady increases in performance across childhood. Boys throw farther than girls, and the differences become larger with each passing year, particularly after puberty.

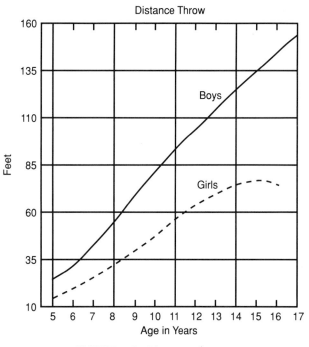

FIGURE 4–5. Distance throw.

(Used with permission of Harper & Row, from Espenschade, A. S. (1960). Motor development. In W. R. Johnson (Ed.), *Science and medicine of exercise and sports* (pp. 419–439).

TABLE 4–2. Developmental Sequences for the Overarm Throw for Force[ad]

	Preparatory Arm Backswing Component[b]
Level 1	No backswing. Ball in hand moves directly forward to release from its position when hand first grasped ball.
Level 2	Elbow and humeral flexion. Ball moves away from intended line of flight to position behind or alongside head by upward flexion of humerus and concomitant elbow flexion.
Level 3	Circular, upward backswing. Ball moves away from intended line of flight to position behind head via circular overhead movement with elbow extended, or oblique swing back, or vertical lift from hip.
Level 4	Circular, downward backswing. Ball moves away from intended line of flight to position behind head via circular, down, and back motion that carries hand below waist.

	Humerus (Upper Arm) Action Component
Level 1	Humerus oblique. Humerus moves forward for ball's release in plane that intersects trunk obliquely above or below horizontal line of shoulders. Occasionally during backswing, humerus is placed at right angle to trunk, with elbow pointing toward target. It maintains this fixed position during throw.
Level 2	Humerus aligned but independent. Humerus moves forward for ball's release in plane horizontally aligned with shoulder, forming right angle between humerus and trunk. By time shoulders (upper spine) reach front facing, humerus (elbow) has moved independently ahead of outline of body (as seen from side) via horizontal adduction at shoulder.
Level 3	Humerus lags. Humerus moves forward for ball's release and is horizontally aligned, but at moment shoulders (upper spine) reach front facing, humerus remains within outline of body (as seen from side). No horizontal adduction of humerus occurs before front facing.

	Forearm Action Component
Level 1	No forearm lag. Forearm and ball move steadily forward to release throughout throwing action.
Level 2	Forearm lag. Forearm and ball appear to lag (i.e., to remain stationary behind the child or to move downward or backward in relation to his body). Lagging forearm reaches its farthest point back, deepest point down, or last stationary point before shoulders (upper spine) reach front facing.
Level 3	Delayed forearm lag. Lagging forearm delays reaching its final point of lag until moment of front facing.

	Trunk (Pelvis-Spine) Action Component
Level 1	No trunk action or forward-backward movements. Only arm is active in throw. Sometimes forward thrust of arm pulls trunk into passive left rotation (assuming a right-handed throw), but no twist-up precedes that action. If trunk action occurs, it accompanies forward thrust of arm by flexing forward at hips. Preparatory extension sometimes precedes forward hip flexion.
Level 2	Upper trunk rotation or total trunk block rotation. Spine and pelvis both rotate away from intended line of flight and then simultaneously begin forward rotation, acting as unit or block. Occasionally, only upper spine twists away and then twists toward direction of force. Pelvis then remains fixed, facing line of flight, or joins rotary movement after forward spinal rotation has begun.
Level 3	Differentiated rotation of trunk. Pelvis precedes upper spine in initiating forward rotation. Child twists away from intended line of ball flight and then begins forward rotation with pelvis while upper spine is still twisting away.

	Foot Action Component[c]
Level 1	No movement. Child throws from whatever position feet happen to be in.
Level 2	Child steps with foot on same side as throwing hand.
Level 3	Child steps with foot on opposite side from throwing hand.
Level 4	Child steps with opposite foot a distance of over half his standing height.

[a]Validation studies (Roberton 1977, 1978; Roberton and Langendorfer 1980; Roberton and DiRocco 1981; Halverson et al. 1982) support these sequences with the exception of notes b and c.

[b]Preparatory arm backswing sequence hypothesized from work of Langendorfer (1980).

[c]Foot action sequence hypothesized from work of Leme and Shambes (1978), Seefeldt et al. (1972), and Wild (1938).

[d]Used with permission from Roberton, M. A. (1984). Changing motor patterns during childhood. In J. R. Thomas (Ed.), *Motor development during childhood and adolescence*. Minneapolis, MN: Burgess.

The overlap between the distributions of girls and boys is less than in running (and most other fundamental skills). At postpuberty, little overlap in the throwing distributions exist if athletes are excluded from the data. That is, excluding baseball and softball athletes, less skilled male performers exceed higher skilled female performers when throwing for distance. Of course greater size, longer arms and legs, and greater strength in males accounts for a substantial part of this difference, as does the fact that males are likely to receive more encouragement and practice in throwing. These factors will be discussed, as will other potential reasons for the differences, in a subsequent part on gender differences in motor performance.

Overhand throwing patterns have been one of the more researched areas of fundamental movements (e.g., Roberton, 1984, as well as Branta, Haubenstricker, & Seefeldt, 1984). However, as mentioned previously, these studies have mainly involved a qualitative form of analysis designed for the use of teachers and coaches rather than bio-mechanical analyses resulting in the ability to quantify the nature and changes in the movement pattern. As with most fundamental skills, the two approaches of total body analysis and component analysis have been used.

Table 4–2 is from Roberton's work and uses the component model of preparatory arm backswing, upper arm action, forearm action, trunk action, and foot action to describe the overhand throwing movement as it develops across levels of performance (this sequence has been validated using Roberton's standards). The movement sequence goes from the very crude one seen in young children—using the same hand and foot with little trunk rotation—to the smooth and coordinated action seen in more expert performers (see Figure 4–6).

Seefeldt and Haubenstricker (1982) and Roberton (1984) suggest that girls simply lag behind boys in the development of a quality overhand throwing pattern. However, we have already indicated that making these types of claims is tenuous from qualitative analyses where the observational categories are rather crude and only one camera is used (e.g., rotational components cannot be estimated accurately; variables such as step length and ball velocity cannot be estimated accurately unless they are absolutely perpendicular to the camera lens). In fact *we believe that expert male and female throwing patterns are different;* thus the patterns developed by young females are not just lagging behind the patterns used by young males, but are developing toward a different pattern (see the next part on gender differences).

GENDER DIFFERENCES

The development of gender differences in motor performance, motor activity, and physical fitness across childhood and adolescence is a common topic in motor development books (Eckert, 1987; Gallahue, 1989; Haywood, 1986; Payne & Isaacs, 1987; Thomas, 1984; Williams, 1983). Many studies have been conducted examining the development of gender differences in motor performance, motor activity, and physical fitness. Summaries of these studies have been reported in qualitative reviews (e.g., Eaton, 1989; Thomas & Thomas, 1988). However, three particularly interesting quantitative evaluations of the developmental nature of this literature have been done: A meta-analysis of gender differences in motor performance (Thomas & French, 1985); a meta-analysis of sex differences in motor activity (Eaton & Enns, 1986); and a secondary analysis of gender differences (Thomas, Nelson, & Church, 1991) based on the data from the large normative study (National Children and Youth Fitness Study—Ross & Gilbert, 1985; Ross & Pate, 1987) on the physical fitness of U.S. children. We will use the results of the three large-scale analyses to discuss this topic and some individual papers to focus on possible explanations.

FIGURE 4–6. Key changes in the development of throwing.
Used with permission of Macmillan, Roberton, M. A. (1984). Changing motor patterns during childhood. In J. R. Thomas (Ed.), *Motor development during childhood and adolescence* (p. 75). Minneapolis, MN: Burgess.

Motor Performance

Thomas and French (1985) conducted a meta-analysis of gender differences across age for 20 motor performance tasks. This analysis was based on 64 previous studies yielding 702 effect sizes (the standardized difference between males and females on a given motor performance task) from

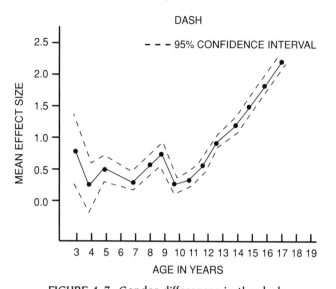

FIGURE 4–7. Gender differences in the dash.

Used with permission, from Thomas, J. R., & French, K. E., (1985). Gender differences across age in motor performance: A meta-analysis. *Psychological Bulletin*, 98, 260–282.

31,444 subjects. The development of gender differences was found to be related to age in 12 of the 20 tasks: balance, catching, dash, grip strength, long jump, pursuit rotor tracking, shuttle run, sit-ups, tapping speed, distance throw, throwing velocity, and vertical jump. Five of the tasks (dash, sit-ups, long jump, grip strength, and shuttle run) have a similar profile across age. Figure 4–7 shows this for the dash (we are continuing the use of running speed here since we used it in the previous discussion). In Figure 4–7 from Thomas and French (1985) the solid line represents the standardized performance difference between girls and boys where 0 is no difference, plus values represent better performance for boys, and minus values represent better performance for girls. Dotted lines are the confidence intervals for each data point. Thus running speed (as measured across many studies using the dash) shows an effect size of about 0.5 (standard deviation units) from 3 to 9 or 10 years of age. Then boys' performance becomes increasingly better than girls' during the adolescent years.

Thomas and French suggested that differences following this pattern type are likely caused by environmental factors (encouragement, practice, parental/peer norms) prior to puberty, but after puberty the biological factors previously suggested (e.g., boys now have longer legs and greater muscle mass than girls) interact with the same environmental characteristics to produce the rapid increase in performance differences. However, Smoll and Schutz (1990) reported a large study (2,142 students, ages 9, 13, and 17 years) in which they found the degree of body fatness to be a significant factor in physical performance (including running) at pre-and postpuberty. While the degree of fatness is a biological variable, Smoll and Schutz (1990) readily acknowledge that it is influenced by environmental characteristics (e.g., amount of exercise,

type of diet); thus some confounding of data seem likely. Regardless, the gender differences in running prior to puberty are relatively small but become greater postpuberty. Differences this small are probably produced by differing environmental demands placed on children. Of course we do not believe the large differences postpuberty are produced completely by growth/biological variables. Clearly environment plays a major role and in its interaction with biology.

Another way to consider how a fundamental task varies across age is to consider the stability of the same children's performance as they become older (e.g., year to year). Branta, Haubenstricker, and Seefeldt (1984) summarize stability data from several studies (including their own) and find that the year-to-year correlations for running speed become smaller with a greater number of intervening years. For example, the values with 1 intervening year range from the high .5s to .8, but are similar for boys and girls. Correlations decrease as more years intervene, but particularly for girls (at least in Branta et al., 1984); thus correlations decrease to the .4s and .5s for boys and .2s to .4s for girls. Tasks with correlations of .5 or higher across 1 year have been called stable (Bloom, 1964). Thus running would be considered a stable task. Stable tasks might be considered as having a stronger hereditary component.

Of the 7 remaining tasks that Thomas and French (1985) reported as related to gender differences across age, 5 (balance, catching, pursuit rotor tracking, tapping, and vertical jump) have patterns like the dash, except that the differences begin at about 0.0 (no difference), show an

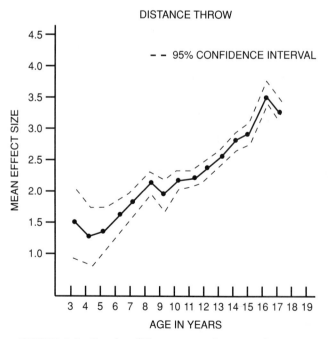

FIGURE 4–8. Gender differences in throwing distance.

Used with permission, from Thomas, J. R., & French, K. E., (1985). Gender differences across age in motor performance: A meta-analysis. *Psychological Bulletin*, 98, 260–282.

increasing effect size up to about 0.5 across childhood, followed by the rapid rise in gender differences typically associated with puberty (up to 1.0–1.5 standard deviation units). As with the first 5 tasks discussed, we believe the explanations are similar: mostly environmental effects prior to puberty with an environmental-biological interaction following puberty.

Throwing (distance and velocity) was a task very different from the others. Figure 4–8 depicts the throwing distance data from Thomas and French (1985). The gender differences are as large as 1.5 standard deviation units at ages 3 to 5 years and show a nearly linear increase up to 3.0 to 3.5 standard deviation units by 16 to 18 years of age. These data reflect minimal overlaps in the female-male distribution prior to puberty and practically no overlap after puberty (at 3.0 to 3.5 standard deviation units, just the extreme tails of the distributions overlap; or, to put it another way, the average boy's distance throw is greater than the 99th percentile for girls).

Because the gender differences in throwing for distance are so much larger than those for other motor tasks, Thomas and colleagues (Nelson, Thomas, Nelson, & Abraham, 1986; Nelson, Thomas, & Nelson, 1991) have done two follow-up studies attempting to identify explanations. In the first (Nelson et al., 1986) 5-year-old girls threw only 57% as far as 5-year-old boys (4.8 vs. 8.4 m). However, when these differences were corrected taking into account a series of biological variables (joint diameters, shoulder/hip ratio, and sum of skinfolds), girls' corrected performance was 69% of boys' (5.4 vs. 7.8 m).

In a longitudinal follow-up, Nelson, Thomas, and Nelson (1991) tested the same children when they were 9 years of age. The girls now only threw 47% of the distance thrown by boys (8.8 vs. 18.7 m). Boys increased the distance thrown by 11 m (143%) over the 3+ years while girls increased by 4.6 m (109%). The correlations between throwing performance over the time period was .43 for girls and .44 for boys. Roberton, Halverson, Langendorfer, and Williams (1979) found the year-to-year correlations for throwing velocity to be higher, .65 to .78, suggesting that throwing is also a stable task. When considering throwing form, Nelson, Thomas, and Nelson (1991) indicated that by age 9, boys had reached the ceiling on the scale for rating form, but girls showed minimal improvements. This is somewhat different from the data reported in Figure 4–2, where Branta, Haubenstricker, and Seefeldt (1984) suggested that 60% of the girls reach mature form between 8 and 9 years of age. Practically none of the 9-year-old girls in the Nelson, Thomas, and Nelson (1991) study demonstrated mature form.

Why are gender differences in throwing performance so much greater than those for any of the other tasks reviewed by Thomas and French (1985)? Very little data are directly available to explain this. For example, are there differences in the mechanics and forces used by females and males to throw? The traditional view has been that girls simply lag behind boys in developing good throwing mechanics (Roberton, 1982; see Figure 4–2, based on Branta,

Haubenstricker, & Seefeldt, 1984). Previously we suggested that making inferences about gender differences (and other characteristics) from qualitative movement analyses was hazardous. That applies particularly to this instance. Actually, no evidence has been published to suggest that the throwing kinematics, ground-reaction forces, or muscle EMGs of expert males and females are either similar or different.

A vital question is "Do expert females and males use the same movement pattern resulting from the same sequence of muscle contractions to generate force in throwing?" Some preliminary evidence (Thomas, Thomas, Hinrichs, Martin, & Marzke, 1990) suggests that the answer

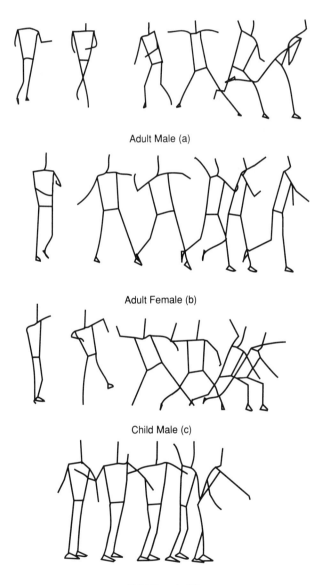

Adult Male (a)

Adult Female (b)

Child Male (c)

Child Female (d)

FIGURE 4–9. Stick figures of throwing: (a) adult male, (b) adult female, (c) child male, (d) child female.

to that question is *no!* Look carefully at the stick drawings of overhand throwing sequences (all are throwing a tennis ball with maximum force) in Figure 4–9: Panel a is an expert male baseball player; panel b is an expert female softball player; panel c is a 5-year-old boy; and panel d is a 5-year-old girl. Two observations seem relevant: (1) The patterns are dissimilar for the two experts; and (2) the movement pattern for the 5-year-old boy resembles the expert male's pattern more than the expert female's pattern resembles the expert male's pattern.

In Figure 4–10 are the data on the angle of twist (angle in degrees between the shoulders and hips) from the two experts (male and female). Note three characteristics about these data:

1. Timing in maximum angle of twist—200 msec before ball release for the male, 300 msec before ball release for the female;
2. Slope (angular velocity) of the twist just before ball release—the male's slope is nearly twice as large as the female's;
3. Continuation of the twist following release—the male continued counterclockwise rotation after ball release, the female maintained a constant twist after release (100 msec) and then begin to rotate back.

Figure 4–11 shows the internal/external rotational angular velocity (the rate of rotation of the humerus about its long axis at the shoulder) for the same expert male and female. Again note that the male had nearly twice the throwing angular velocity of the female (2,100 deg/s vs. 1,100 deg/s) at or immediately following the ball release.

Is the development of the overhand throwing pattern for males and females across age moving toward a different final pattern? Of course this is only a high-speed qualitative analysis from four subjects (Figure 4–9), plus a small amount of the quantitative data from the two experts (Figures 4–10 and 4–11). We have data on several additional expert males and females and other young children. We are currently conducting quantitative analyses of the high-speed video, ground reaction forces, and EMGs of these subjects. But the thought is provocative.

Data from the field of human evolution provide some support for this idea. Numerous authors have reported that bipedal locomotion (McHenry, 1982; Washburn & Moore, 1980) and the use of sharp-edged tools (Tobias, 1968; Washburn & Moore, 1980) may have played significant roles in human evolution. Isaac (1987) suggest that "... skilled overarm throwing of missiles deserves a similar scrutiny, since it is possible that it developed into a behavior of adaptive importance with repercussions far beyond the simple scoring of a hit" (pp. 3–4). Calvin (1982, 1983) and Darlington (1975) have indicated that overhand throwing is a prime candidate in evolution to explain rapid increases in brain size, redundancy, and lateralization because the task involves a three-factor problem: the location of the person throwing, whether moving or stationary; the location of the

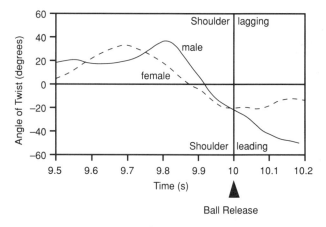

FIGURE 4–10. Twist angle (shoulders relative to hips) in overhand throwing for an expert male and female.

Our thanks to Tim Joganich, M. S. student at Arizona State University, for developing these plots of our data.

target, moving or stationary; and the trajectory-velocity of the object being thrown.

Even if throwing is important in human evolution, why should males have developed greater throwing skill than females? Were males more likely to be the hunters and warriors, resulting in greater reproductive selection for those who threw effectively? If women provided more child care such as carrying a young child rather than leaving him/her unattended, did that inhibit their throwing action (e.g., there was minimal differentiated trunk rotation)? After a substantial review of the anthropological and historical records on throwing, Isaac (1987) concluded, "It will have been noted by the reader that all historical instances so far quoted related to throwing by males . . . The implications of this will not be pursued here, but they are not unimportant" (p. 15).

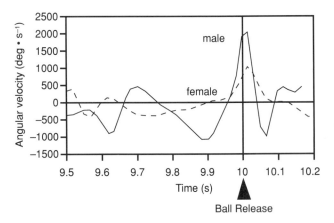

FIGURE 4–11. Internal/external angular velocity (of the humerus) in overhand throwing for an expert male and female.

Motor Activity Level

Eaton and Enns (1986) have provided an extensive meta-analysis of sex differences in human motor activity level. Their data are based on 90 citations. Motor activity level reflects energy expenditure through movement using instruments designed to measure motor activity, ratings, and observations. Included are very specific measures such as arm movements and global measures such as how many different marked areas the child entered. They reported that males were more active than females (effect size of 0.49 standard deviation units), but greater differences were found in studies with older samples (citations were limited for ages beyond late adolescence, restricting these findings to an upper age of about 15 years). This finding suggests that social influence enlarges the sex differences across age.

However, significant sex differences were present in infants (under 12 months), with males being more active than females (effect size = 0.29). In addition males were more active than females (effect size = 0.33) in 6 prenatal studies, although this difference was not significant or conclusive because of the small number of studies conducted. These findings at least suggest that the social differences hypothesis may only serve to magnify those sex differences in level of motor activity that are already present (perhaps because of genetics?). As an aside, Schachar, Rutter, and Smith (1981) reported in a large sample of British children, the rate of hyperactivity for boys to girls was 2 to 1.

Even though Eaton and Enns (1986) found sex differences in motor activity to increase with age, the absolute amount of motor activity decreases with age (e.g., Eaton & Yu, 1989). Since girls are known to be relatively more mature than boys at every age (Tanner, 1978), Eaton and Yu (1989) attempted to determine if sex differences in motor activity were a function of sex differences in maturation rate. Using relative maturity (percent of estimated adult height) as a potential moderator variable, differences in motor activity were determined for 5- to 8-year-old boys and girls ($N = 83$). While the sex differences were reduced by relative maturity, girls were still less active than boys.

Thus while absolute amount of motor activity tends to decrease with increasing age, sex differences become larger in motor activity across age. This effect is found as early as infancy (with some evidence of it prenatally), suggesting a genetic component, and is partially moderated by maturation rate. However, the steady increase across childhood and adolescence suggests a social/environmental explanation.

Health-Related Physical Fitness

In the previous section the finding that girls show a lower motor activity level than boys at every age suggests that they might maintain lower levels of health-related physical fitness. Evidence from a secondary analysis (Thomas, Nelson, & Church, 1991) of the National Children and Youth Fitness Study (Ross & Gilbert, 1985; Ross & Pate, 1987) indicate that this hypothesis is correct (for additional support of this statement see Smoll & Schutz, 1990). The National Children and Youth Fitness Study reported a nationwide (U.S.) sample from 6,800 boys and 6,523 girls where sampling and testing were carefully controlled.

Figure 4–12 is a plot from this data converted to effect sizes for the mile (half-mile for children under 8 years of age), chin-ups (modified pull-ups for children under 10 years of age), and sit-ups. The open squares in the figure are unadjusted differences while the solid markings have been adjusted for biological and environmental characteristics. All of the health-related measures in Figure 4–12 show a linear increase in the differences between boys and girls across age. The increase in differences is greatest for the chin-ups and least for the sit-ups. This might be anticipated, since chin-ups are most likely to be influenced by the increased strength and muscle mass associated with puberty in boys and the increased level of fat in girls. However, adjusting for the degree of fatness before puberty and for the degree of fatness and amount of exercise outside the school setting following puberty generally reduced the differences at each age.

These findings are consistent with those reported in other large-scale studies for similar tasks: motor activity level (Eaton & Enns, 1986), motor performance (Thomas & French, 1985), and physical performance (Smoll & Schutz, 1989). Environmental characteristics (e.g., social situations, amount of exercise, peers, parents, teachers, opportunities, encouragement, practice) are the major factors in producing gender differences. However, biological variables (e.g., maturation, fatness) seem to mediate this difference. In a few instances (e.g., motor activity, throwing) there is some circumstantial evidence of the influence of heredity in producing some part of the differences observed. But even in those instances, environmental characteristics enhance and amplify these initial differences.

GROWTH

The studies of growth that are of interest here, fall into three categories, general body development (e.g., height, weight or mass, fatness), gender and cultural differences, and the influence of physical parameters on motor skill performance. While many of the components of growth (e.g., height, breadths, location of fat, ratios) are susceptible to relatively little environmental influence, and others (fat, body circumferences, muscle) are relatively difficult to change, even though they are at least partially influenced by environment, physical characteristics must be considered when studying skilled performance (Malina, 1975). This point will be made clear in the discussion of the influence of growth on performance.

General Body Development

While growth and development are continuous and orderly, the systems of the body do not grow at equal rates—

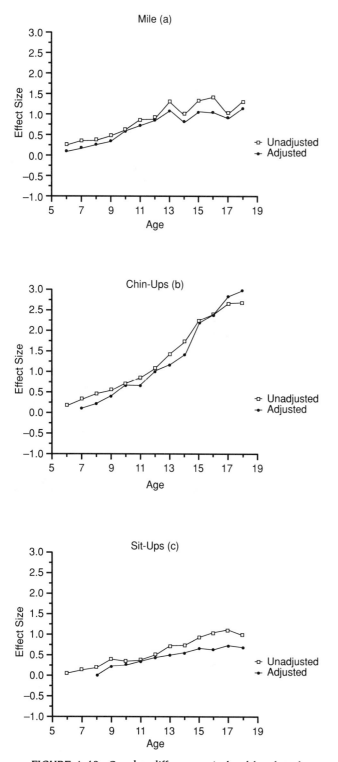

FIGURE 4–12. Gender differences in health-related physical fitness: (a) mile (or half-mile) run, (b) chin-ups, (c) sit-ups.

Used with permission, from Thomas, J. R., Nelson, J. K., & Church, G. (1991). A developmental analysis of gender differences in health related physical fitness. *Pediatric Exercise Science*, 3, 28–42.

in fact, the rate of growth varies within each system. This point was graphically brought to everyone's attention by Scammon (1930), who indicated the very different developmental patterns for the reproductive, endocrine, neural, and general body systems. The body gains the most length (height) and weight from birth to 2 years of age; then the rate slows, but the child continues to gain both height and weight during childhood (Malina, 1975). The rate increases dramatically at puberty; then both rate and actual growth slow until the child stops growing at adulthood (see Figure 4–13).

Body proportions change as a result of the differences in rates of growth for different body parts (Malina, 1984). The torso and head grow relatively slowly, while the extremities grow at a faster rate. This means that the center of gravity moves downward, the head accounts for less of the body mass, and the greater the length of time the body grows the more these relationships are influenced. The body gains lean tissue faster than fat tissue. In addition, breadths and circumferences increase across childhood.

From birth to school age the nervous system develops rapidly in three ways (Williams, 1983): The neurons grow to match the physical lengthening of the body; myelin becomes thicker (and longer) to protect the speed and fidelity of the neural transmissions; and the synapses increase, allowing better communication between neurons. Both myelinization and synapses continue to develop during the maturational process but in fewer areas of the body and at a slower rate.

The maturation of the reproductive system influences anthropometric factors such as height, weight, proportions, fatness, and growth rate. This influence is seen in robust gender differences and in cultural differences in anthropometric data.

Gender Differences. While the means for height and weight favor males from birth through the lifespan, the differences during childhood are small, and the overlap between males and females is great (Malina, 1975). Thus most of the boys and girls are similar in height and weight prior to puberty. Since girls usually enter puberty between 11 and 12 years of age and boys follow at 13 to 14 years of age, girls have their prepubescent growth spurt before boys. Girls also stop growing before boys stop growing. The only time when the average height and weight for girls is greater than for boys is during the girls' growth spurt. There is great variation within each gender for height and weight, which is reflected in the considerable overlap of male and females in both height and weight.

The fact that males grow for a greater length of time, combined with the fact that their legs grow at a faster rate during childhood, means that males have relatively longer legs than females (Malina, 1984). Males also gain more shoulder breadth than hip breadth as well as more shoulder breadth than females gain. This means that the shoulder-hip ratio is greater for males. Males also gain less fat and more lean tissue than females. While females gain both

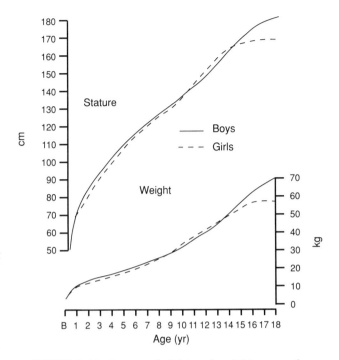

FIGURE 4–13. Average height and weight curves for American boys and girls.

Used with permission of Macmillan, from Malina, R. M. (1984). Physical growth and maturation. In J. R. Thomas (Ed.), *Motor development during childhood and adolescence* (p. 7). Minneapolis: Burgess.

fat and lean tissue, they gain less lean tissue and more fat than males.

Today children are maturing at an earlier age, and are taller and heavier than preceding generations (Malina, 1975). Children in different cultures mature at varying rates, with extremes such as Norway (late maturing) and the United States (early maturing). Clearly varying maturation influences growth, as does genetics. Gender differences are similar across cultures, and growth trends are similar within cultures.

Relationship of Growth to Movement

This relationship can be viewed from either perspective —how growth influences performance and how activity influences growth. Clearly greater size is an advantage in many motor skills. Greater height, weight, muscle mass, or shoulder-hip ratio positively impacts on performance in many skills—especially those where lever length or strength is important. Some of the improvement observed across age in motor skill performance is undoubtedly due to greater size and accompanying strength. In addition, the change in body proportions (e.g., sitting height/standing height ratio) also has an impact on motor performance. Consider a static balance task—the infant has a head which is 25% of body height, while the adult's head is only one eighth of body height. Imagine trying to maintain your balance with two heads above your shoulders if your head was

25% of your height! The moment of inertia and the amount of resistance to acceleration of a body part also change with growth. Jensen (1981) tracked growth and moment of inertia in boys. The findings indicated that over a 12-month time period the growth-related constraint on the boy's ability to accelerate increased by 27.7%, which far exceeded their increase in actual size. The problem observed in children is maintaining increases in strength to generate the increasing force necessary to move larger body parts. The amount of force needed is disproportionately greater than the actual physical increase in size.

Related to this is the notion that children often practice particular skills during a related sport season, then continue to grow in the off-season. When the season begins again, whatever information was learned and stored about the movement pertained to a very different body—with different ratios and moments of inertia. The idea of motor programs—especially invariant characteristics like relative force and timing—helps us to understand part of the performance decrement noted during growth.

Clearly, physical parameters which change during the growth process influence performance more at the extremes—i.e., very fat performers are adversely affected; but within the average range of fatness, having more or less probably does not correlate to performance (Malina, 1975). While certain body types tend to be associated with excellent sport performance, those relationships are less clear than was once believed (Malina, 1984). Taller children tend to be stronger, which is usually an advantage, while heavier children show no consistent pattern for performance. Heavier children do better at throwing, but worse at running and jumping. Physical parameters also tend to have less influence as age increases (Espenschade, 1963). Body size (height and weight) has even less impact on performance for girls.

The amount of performance which is accounted for by physical parameters is a unique way to look at gender differences in performance. Using overarm throwing as the task, Nelson, Thomas, Nelson, and Abraham (1986) found that physical parameters (joint diameters, shoulder-hip ratios, and sums of skinfolds) accounted for 12% of the differences between 5-year-old boys and girls in throwing distance. Since those parameters are relatively similar at age 5, 12% is a meaningful contribution—however, the differences not accounted for by growth factors are equally meaningful.

Considering the impact of exercise and/or activity on growth is a very interesting proposition. While there is apparently some minimal amount of exercise necessary for "normal" growth, the definition of minimal is elusive (Broekoff, 1985). To describe optimal exercise for growth is even more difficult. Early studies of the relationship have been criticized for lack of experimental control—specifically, the failure to match the exercise and non-exercise groups before the exercise programs. Other studies have failed to quantify exercise. The results of more recent, less controversial research indicates that regular exercise and intensive training does not increase stature. While lack of activity may result in decreased bone density, intense training may increase skeletal thickness and bone density. Activity is an important factor in regulating body weight, muscle hypertrophy, and bone growth, density, and mineralization (Malina, 1986).

A major question has been whether later-maturing individuals select certain sports (gymnastics, ballet, track and field) or whether participation in those sports causes the later maturing (Broekoff, 1975; Malina, 1983). In either case, the relationship between maturation and performance is evident at the extremes of both performance and maturation. This means that in world-class athletes, later maturing is observed in certain sports, but could be a result of or caused by participation.

COGNITIVE ASPECTS OF MOTOR SKILLS PERFORMANCE

Previously, age- and gender-related changes in children's performance were described across childhood and adolescence. Of course cognitive factors influence how children learn and perform motor skills. This general area, called the development of cognitive processing, can be subdivided into strategic, declarative, and procedural knowledge and how they influence motor and sport performance. In this section general information will be presented about the development of cognitive function as well as ways in which cognitive functioning relates to motor and sport skill performance. In particular, strategic knowledge will be emphasized in this section, and declarative and procedural knowledge in subsequent sections. This topic is important because children use cognitive processes as they perform, learn, and control motor and sport skills.

In many ways these cognitive processes operate in movement as they do for any type of skill or knowledge to be acquired or performed. But movements are clearly different in at least one way: knowing and doing are not necessarily perfectly correlated. If a child knows how to solve a math problem, the solution is nearly always correct. However, knowing how to solve a movement problem (e.g., fielding a ground ball in baseball and throwing the runner out at first) is often unrelated to the skill necessary to execute the solution. So while we will talk about cognition and motor performance, it should be realized that knowing and executing are not the same thing.

In the following sections cognitive features of processing will be discussed as if they were relatively independent functions. Of course they are not, but they are presented in this way as a means of dealing with the large volume of literature on this topic. Focus will be on the movement and sport-related literature in these sections. However, by necessity, research on the development of cognitive processes from more generic sources such as developmental psychology and child development will be incorporated in the discussion. Our presentation will be organized around age-related issues involving such topics as speed of processing, perceptual development, memory, and learning.

Speed of Processing

A well-documented research finding is that as children age, they are able to process the same information more quickly or process more information in the same amount of time. Consistent results have been found with tasks such as simple reaction time (Thomas, Gallagher, & Purvis, 1981), the processing of feedback (Gallagher & Thomas, 1980; Thomas, Mitchell, & Solmon, 1979), anticipation timing (Dunham & Reid, 1987), the Fitts tapping task (Burton, 1987; Kerr, 1985; Salmoni & Pascoe, 1979), and decision making (Newell & Kennedy, 1978). Thus if the processing interval is reduced, children's motor performance will be hindered, not because they cannot perform the task, but because they have not been given enough time to "think" about what they need to do (Gallagher & Thomas, 1980).

Since it is clear that children process information less efficiently than adults, subsequent research has focused on whether the speed of processing differences is due to structural or functional components. Information-processing theorists have attributed the cause to functional differences such as memory strategy usage (Chi, 1977; Lindberg, 1980) and more recently knowledge base differences (Chi, 1982), while researchers adopting Piagetian theory have attributed differences to increases in memory capacity (Pascual-Leone, 1970; Tudor, 1979).

Dempster (1988) indicated four problems with a capacity-increase hypothesis. First, there has not been a satisfactory method of measuring capacity. The size of the capacity has ranged from 3 to 7 items, depending upon the task, criteria used, and definition of a chunk (Chi, 1976). Second, task memory span is generally considered the best estimate of capacity, but the data reported has suggested that it is a relatively insensitive measure of short-term memory, one that is confounded by production factors such as chunking. Since the size of a chunk is indeterminate (Anderson, 1980), not much is known about what 7 ± 2 chunks are. Additionally, Case, Kurland, and Goldberg (1982) found that by eliminating speed-of-recognition differences, adult-child differences were reduced, suggesting that the speed of processing causes span differences. Third, preconscious representations or sensory memory representations influence capacity. This would facilitate perception and recall. Finally, the recent development of more than one pool of capacity (i.e., attention, effort) makes measuring a single capacity difficult.

Although an increase in the physical aspects of memory (myelinization, brain size) cannot be completely eliminated from causing the developmental increase in memory performance, the contributions appear to be minimal with the amount of information in long-term memory and mnemonic strategies playing a greater role. Gallagher (1980, Experiment 1; Gallagher & Fisher, 1983) demonstrated the importance of memory strategy use for remembering movements. When asked to recall simple linear movements of varying amplitudes, children performed as accurately as adults; however, their performance was impaired when the complexity of the task increased.

Chi and Gallagher (1982) reviewed the developmental literature to determine the source of speed-of-processing differences. After separating the information-processing interval into four components—encoding, manipulation, response selection, and motor response—they determined differences between adults and children in manipulation and response selection. Children used different movement strategies to perform the tasks (McCracken, 1983; Sugden, 1980). In addition, they appeared to use different muscle groups and/or increased EMG activity to accomplish the tasks. This quite possibly caused a time delay in responding. Thus movement-time differences do not appear to be caused by a developmental change in the capacity of the motor system (Burton, 1987; Chi & Gallagher, 1982; Kerr, 1985; Salmoni & Pascoe, 1978).

More recent research on speed-of-processing differences has focused on the relative contribution of two hypotheses that can explain processing-speed differences (Kail, 1986, 1988, 1991). One hypothesis relates to previous research in that it reviews changes that are specific to a particular process, task, or domain (Kail, 1988). This would be the acquisition of more efficient strategies, additions to the knowledge base, and accessibility of information in long-term memory. Dempster (1988) adopts the hypothesis that speed-of-processing differences stem from additions to the knowledge base and from changes in the accessibility of information in long-term memory.

A second explanation of the speed of processing differences is that age differences are due to a more general developmental change (Kail, 1988). An example of this would be the efficient allocation of processing resources or attention, and mental effort. By increasing resources and/or mental effort, increases in speed of processing would be evident.

The remainder of this part addresses specific factors that elucidate age-related changes in speed of processing. Changes in perception, memory strategy use, and knowledge base are discussed.

Perceptual Development

The use and interpretation of the information in sensory store is termed *perception*. Some researchers have suggested that a developmental shift occurs in the hierarchy of the dominant sensory systems, with intrasensory discrimination increasing (Thomas & Thomas, 1987) and intersensory integration improving (Williams, 1983).

A shift from initial reliance on kinesthetic information to the more reliable visual information has been suggested (Williams, 1973). Williams has noted that the 4-year-old is quite dependent on tactile-kinesthetic (bodily) cues in performing motor acts and, therefore, cannot fully and effectively use specific visual cues to regulate behavior successfully. Visual information predominates by 7 or 8 years of age. On the basis of such findings, she has suggested that sensory-perceptual development in the young child is characterized by a shift in reliance on tactile kinesthetic or

somatosensory information to information from the visual system as a basis for regulating or modifying motor behavior. This transition to visual dominance represents a shift from the use of input from sensory systems with relatively crude information-processing capacities to the use of input from a much more refined sensory system (Williams, 1983). Jones (1981) argues that little evidence exists for the view that touch is dominant early in life. His review, however, focused on the tactile-kinesthetic mode for shape identification (Bryant & Raz, 1975) and not for use in movement control. Whether or not a developmental transition from tactile to visual dependence actually occurs awaits further research.

An increase in intrasensory discrimination has been documented. With age, children are more accurate with positioning a limb (Williams, Temple, & Bateman, 1979; Thomas & Thomas, 1987), tactile point discrimination (Van Dyne, 1973), and anticipation timing (Dunham & Reid, 1987; Thomas, Gallagher, & Purvis, 1981). Improved discrimination within a sensory system gives the individual higher quality information on which to make decisions for motor program selection, parameterization of the program, or detection and correction of errors.

Thomas and Thomas (1987) found that children's movement performance improved with age, due not only to memory factors but also to perception. Young children (5-year-olds) needed nearly 3 times the distance of adults to differentiate a well-learned movement from a foil. Thomas and Thomas concluded that children should not be assumed to perceive the same level of information as an adult. The result is that a child may think the movement has been effectively reproduced, when in fact it has not.

An improvement in intersensory integration occurs at one of three levels (Williams, 1983): automatic integration of basic sensory information, cognitive integration of stimulus information, and the application of concepts across different systems. Millar (1974) suggests that intersensory development is related to the development of better processing strategies, whereas Bryant (1968) has proposed that improvement results from intrasensory functioning. Certainly both factors appear important.

After the information has been perceived, the individual must then manipulate that information, select a response, and attempt to move. Manipulation of the information occurs as an interaction of short- and long-term memory. Short-term memory processes are covered next.

Memory

The concept of *short-term memory* (STM) is controversial. The need for a separate STM system has been raised (Dempster, 1988). STM has historically been defined as a passive rehearsal buffer for information (Atkinson & Shiffrin, 1968). Dempster views STM as the active portion of long-term memory. Thus the term *short-term memory* has been replaced by the term *working memory* in order to convey the idea of more that just a warehouse of information. Long-term memory is the one aspect of the unitary memory concept.

Several memory strategies have been researched. The strategies reviewed in this paper include attention, labeling, rehearsal, and organization.

Attention is a global term that has been used to address a variety of processes including attention span, attentional capacity, and selective attention. Attention span refers to the amount of time that the individual focuses on a task. Attentional capacity and memory capacity have been used interchangeably.

Typically older children and adults have longer attention spans than younger children. However, when motivated, younger children can attend for long periods of time. Who quits first when an adult pitches a ball for a child to bat? Certainly not the children related to any of us!

Selective Attention. Selective attention serves in the perceptual encoding of task-appropriate cues and as a control process to continually maintain relevant information in working memory. The development of selective attention has been reviewed by Ross (1976) and includes three levels: overexclusive, overinclusive, and selective attention. The overexclusive child (up to 5–6 years of age) attends to limited cues regardless of task appropriateness. Being unaware of the majority of information available in the environment causes low recall of incidental information. The overexclusive child (between 6–7 years and 11–12 years) directs attention to the entire display without focusing on task-appropriate cues. The child constantly attends to irrelevant information that serves as a distractor from task performance (incidental memory recall is high). At approximately 11 years of age, the child develops the ability to selectively attend to task-appropriate cues and ignore irrelevant information.

Stratton (1978) reviewed basic research on selective attention to conclude that teachers/coaches should evaluate task requirements, environmental demands, and teacher input. This will allow the teacher/coach to assist the child in developing a strategy to deal with the wealth of information. During the performance of most motor skills, a wealth of task-irrelevant cues are available. When cued, younger children are capable of acquiring strategies of selective attention when higher levels of interference are imposed early in the learning situation. This enables the child to develop a plan to deal with the irrelevant information. Note, however, that the irrelevant information cannot reach a level that prevents learning of the primary task (as opposed to learning the strategy).

Although Ross and Stratton have described how and to what children typically attend, they do not describe what changes allow the child to attend selectively. Recent research has moved from a description of the development of selective attention to determining the mechanisms of selective attention. The mechanisms of selective attention are covered next, followed by the relationship between perception and attention.

Kahneman (1973) developed a model that explained allocation of cognitive resources. Enduring dispositions and momentary intentions are used to explain how incoming stimuli are selected for further processing. Enduring dispositions are similar to Shiffrin and Schneider's (1977) concept of automation; attention is allocated to certain types of information without conscious awareness. An example of an enduring disposition would be the "cocktail party phenomenon," where our attention is automatically drawn to conversation in which our name has been mentioned. Other processes that automatically dictate attention are loud noises, sudden motion, and bright colors. Momentary intentions are current decisions to allocate cognitive resources to a particular source of information.

Tipper, MacQueen, and Brehaut (1988) have proposed a model in which the environment is initially screened for familiar items regardless of task appropriateness. Two mechanisms of selective attention are used: an excitatory process, where the representations of the selected object receive further analysis, and an inhibitory process where the responses are actively inhibited.

A further mechanism of attention has been proposed by Lorch and Horn (1986); Lorch, Anderson, and Well (1984); and Reisberg, Barron, and Kemler (1980). They include a habituation response; once the environment is familiar, the inhibitory process does not have to be invoked and attention is not distracted by irrelevant stimuli (Tipper, Bourque, Anderson, & Brehaur, 1989).

Not only does attention to task-appropriate cues improve with age, but perceptual development and the development of attention are also related. During the past 10 years, the joint development of perceptual organization and attention has been researched (Barret & Shepp, 1988). One finding that has been dominant is that young children perceive objects as integral wholes, whereas older children and adults perceive the same objects as aggregates of features (whole-part perception). Secondly, younger children are regarded as less capable of controlling their attentional resources than older children and adults are.

An implication from the interaction of perception and attention is that questions about the development of attention must also address the issue of perceived structure. If aspects of the stimuli are perceptually independent, the development of attention can be assessed. If, however, a child perceives an object as a whole, the failure to attend to a feature of the object cannot be attributed to an inability to attend but must be attributed to the nature of the perceived structure. Recent research has supported this linkage of perceptual and attentional development. Most stimuli are integral for young children but become increasingly separate with increasing age. A series of studies by Shepp, Barrett, and Kolbet (1987) concluded that the development of perceived structure increases the flexibility of perception. Thus the young child attends primarily to holistic properties; however, with increasing age and experience, the child becomes increasingly proficient in extracting either featural or holistic properties.

Memory Strategies. Of concern to contemporary researchers are developmental questions relating to the effectiveness of a particular strategy and conditions under which a strategy will be used and generalized. The difficulty with the research is that there is not a single, agreed-upon definition for what a strategy is (Bjorklund & Buchanan, 1989), and the factors responsible for emergence of memory strategies in early childhood have not been identified (Ornstein, Baker-Ward, & Naus, 1988).

Ornstein et al. view development of children's memory strategies as a process analogous to the development of skill. With increases in age and experience, the various cognitive operations that are involved in strategy production and execution may become increasingly routinized and thus less demanding of attentional capacity. Three points are suggested for the development of mnemonic skill. First, children develop an understanding that special behaviors are required but a mediation deficiency exists (if the strategy is used, it does not benefit performance). Secondly, children use strategies, but the use varies as a function of the organizational salience of the stimulus materials. Next, children routinely apply strategies but must use a greater degree of effort than is the case with older subjects. After the strategy has been automated, the individual can allocate greater resources to the incoming information. Development of the memory strategies of labeling, rehearsal, and organization are discussed next.

Labeling is a memory strategy that facilitates perception and memory. Performance improves when the meaningfulness of the label increases. Winther and Thomas (1981) investigated the development of a labeling strategy. The performance of young children (5-year-olds) improved when they were forced to label a movement meaningfully. Adult performance was hindered when adults were forced to use an irrelevant label. Weiss (1983) expanded this to a more ecologically valid paradigm to find that younger children (5-year-olds) benefitted more from a model when verbal labels were given by the model. As a follow-up, Weiss and Klint (1987) found that 6-and 9-year-olds who were forced to use a verbal label and rehearse were superior in performance when compared to a control group. Miller (1990) found that learning-disabled (LD) 7-year-olds' performance was improved when they were forced to label whereas their age-related non-LD peers and both LD and non-LD 9-year-olds' performance was not affected when they were forced to label.

Rehearsal is an important strategy needed to maintain information in memory. The importance of active rehearsal was demonstrated in a study by Gallagher and Thomas (1984). Given a series of eight movements, 5-and 7-year-old children chose to rehearse on an instance-by-instance basis, while 11-and 19-year-old subjects grouped the movements for recall. When forced to rehearse in an adult fashion, the performance of 5- and 7-year-olds improved. Reid (1980) found similar results for mentally retarded children in the IQ range of 43–83, while Schroeder's (1981) findings were for severely mentally retarded subjects.

Organization is a strategy used to combine information

in a meaningful way in order to reduce cognitive demands. Instead of thinking of separate pieces of information, the individual groups and recodes the information into one unit. Using a series of eight movements, and manipulating the degree of organization in the material, Gallagher and Thomas (1986) found that 5-year-old children were unable to increase performance regardless of organization strategy or input of information. The 7-year-old children were able to use organized input to facilitate recall, but the strategy failed to transfer to a new task. The 11-year-old children used organized input and showed some transfer of strategy. However, they could not restructure the information or provide self-generated organization. The 19-year-old subjects organized the information regardless of input.

Integrating the studies on rehearsal and organization of input, Gallagher and Thomas (1986) indicated that forcing the use of the strategies was of greater importance to younger children, but it had less effect on older children and adults (See Figure 4–14). The older children and adults were using the strategies when not forced to do so, whereas the younger children were not. Even though the 5-year-old children were given organizational cues, they failed to recall the movements in order (from short to long). Forcing rehearsal, on the other hand, aided recall of the 5-year-old children. The 7-year-old children used the organizational strategy to recall 8 movements. The older

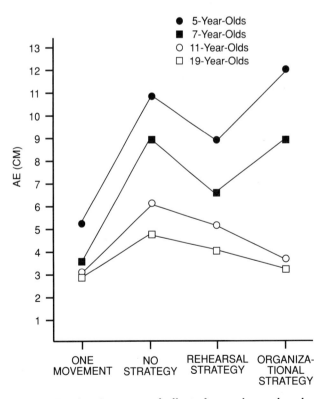

FIGURE 4–14. Summary of effects from rehearsal and organization of movement performance.

Used with permission from Gallagher, J. D., & Thomas, J. R. (1986). Developmental effects of grouping and recoding on learning a movement series. *Research Quarterly for Exercise and Sport*, 57, 117–127.

children and adults in the self-determined strategy group were similar in recall to the organizational strategy group. They rehearsed spatially similar groups of movement.

In sum, there is evidence that even 4-year-olds behave strategically when asked to remember, but the younger children do not spontaneously use memory strategies. As Chi (1982) has suggested, this could be due to an inefficient knowledge base. Children's earliest successful memory strategies begin with highly familiar information as does successful training efforts. The automation of these strategies occurs as a result of practice and experience, and it leads to a functional increase of the space available in working memory for the handling of information-processing operations. Limited research has been concerned with the changing effort requirements associated with the automation of mnemonic skill (Ornstein et al., 1988; Ornstein & Naus, 1985). Future research needs to be longitudinal to investigate within-subject skill development (Ornstein et al., 1988). Secondly, individual variation needs to be related to varying task demands. Finally, the mental effort required of the various strategies needs to be determined.

Knowledge Base. As stated previously, memory is no longer viewed as compartmentalized into short-term and long-term memory but rather in terms of activation. A more appropriate term for long-term memory is *knowledge base*. In most situations, young children, because of their limited experiences with a wide variety of domains, can be considered universal novices (Brown, 1975).

Age-related changes in both the contents and familiarity of the knowledge base have significant implications for the deployment of strategies (Bjorklund, 1985; Ornstein & Naus, 1985). Knowledge base theorists postulate that knowledge is represented more elaborately with increased practice. Children who possess a greater amount of knowledge in a given domain have shown that knowledge plays a salient role in the performance of domain-related tasks. Chi and Koesky (1983) documented that a 4-year-old child used a sophisticated organizational strategy to recall well-learned dinosaurs. The strategy to recall unfamiliar dinosaurs was childlike. Other research has suggested that domain-specific knowledge may reduce the capacity limitations of working memory (Chase & Simon, 1973), reduce the attentional demands of certain tasks (Leavitt, 1979), and facilitate the effective use of memory strategies (Ornstein & Naus, 1985). Thus information is accessed with less mental effort, leaving more of their mental resources available for the execution of strategies. Chi (1985) suggests that the relationship between strategy and knowledge is interdependent.

Knowledge can be represented as one of three types: declarative, procedural, and strategic. Declarative knowledge is the knowledge of factual information while procedural knowledge is the knowledge of how to do something. Both declarative knowledge and procedural knowledge are task-specific within a given knowledge domain. Strategic knowledge is knowledge of general rules (i.e., memory strategies

such as rehearsal) that may be generalized across all knowledge domains.

The next issue is to determine whether children know what they are doing. Recently research has returned to metamemory, to determine if a child understands the workings of the memory system, and if memory strategy use is facilitated. Currently the role of metamemory in memory performance is unclear.

Metamemory. Schneider and Sodian (1988) have documented that very young children's performance on memory tasks was accompanied by some degree of conscious awareness of the usefulness of these behaviors. With increasing age, the children's ability to spontaneously establish meaningful relationships between cues and targets that were not highly associated increased.

Fabricius and Cavalier (1989) attempted to determine whether conceptions of how memory strategies work were important aspects of children's memory knowledge. They concluded that children's understanding of how and why labeling worked determined whether their labeling became more self-initiated. The results suggest that the effects of increasing accessibility and increasing strategy effectiveness on strategy acquisition were mediated through children's causal theories of memory.

Explaining the lack of strategy generalization, Rao and Moely (1989) suggested that children tend to abandon a trained strategy in novel situations if they do not understand the benefits of the strategy used. To improve strategy transfer, the training procedures focused on developing children's metamemory. Results demonstrated strong effects of training even on a trial that involved a different recall task. Also, training is more apt to occur when training is performed on sets of highly familiar materials (Bjorklund & Buchanan, 1989; Rabinowitz, 1988).

To this point, the various aspects of memory have been discussed with adult/child differences highlighted. The next section focuses on how the learning environment can be structured to facilitate strategy usage of young children.

Learning

The goal of learning is to automate the skill. While performance is how a task is executed at a given point in time, learning is a relatively permanent change in the level of performance. When in the process of learning, the individual moves from the cognitive phase through the associative phase to the autonomous phase. For example, when in the cognitive phase of learning a tennis serve, the learner is concerned with solving the problem of contacting the ball with the racquet to successfully get the ball over the net. The learner thinks of such factors as how high does the ball need to be tossed or is the racquet back too far or not far enough. Moving to the associative phase, the learner is concerned with determining the links between action and outcome. During this phase, consistency in getting the ball over the net is no longer a problem; the learner now attempts to refine the skill by focusing on getting the ball into the service box. During the autonomous phase, the player has automated the serve pattern and is very successful with the first serve. However, under the pressure of the second serve, consistency is not high; therefore, the player now needs to work on his/her serve under more stressful conditions.

An example of the three stages of learning for game play would be that the cognitive-level player is concerned with keeping the ball in play (limited shot selection) while the associative-level player focuses on directing the ball within the court (offensive play). This level of player would also be more consistent because of the integration of a combination of skills but would be concerned with not making errors. The autonomous player would concentrate on detecting the weaknesses of the other player and consistently use shots with which the opponent has difficulty. Thus at the autonomous phase, the player is trying to force errors instead of focusing on trying to keep from making errors. Automation is important in learning a motor skill because it can reduce the attention demanded by the various decisions that an individual makes. Eberts and Schneider (1980) note that the benefits of automatic processing are that fewer resources are required, processing is faster, the task is less susceptible to distractions, performance becomes more accurate, and the internal structure associated with the movement becomes more economical and efficient.

When learning a skill, feedback is critically important. Young children tend to ignore feedback, but when forced to use feedback they can use it to facilitate task performance (Gallagher & Thomas, 1980; Thomas, Solmon, & Mitchell, 1979). Research on feedback has typically investigated knowledge of results (KR), which is outcome information. Traditionally it has been hypothesized that the "more feedback the better." However, in a review of the literature on KR, Salmoni, Schmidt, and Walters (1984) discussed the guidance nature of KR. If KR is provided on every trial, the individual relies on KR for guiding performance, resulting in a failure to develop an internal error detection and correction mechanism. Therefore, after a retention interval, performance without KR deteriorates. On the other hand, individuals given summary KR maintain or increase performance after the retention interval.

The majority of research has been conducted with KR instead of knowledge of performance (KP). Newell and Barclay (1982) have identified two factors a person learns and remembers about their actions: the association between the movement and its consequences, and a knowledge of variables or factors that affect outcome. Young children who lack experience and knowledge in a skill are not likely to understand movement outcome relationships and probably lack an appropriate frame of reference for evaluating their movements. In this instance KP takes on critical importance. During early learning it appears that the learner is developing "content knowledge," a generalized knowledge base upon which more specific procedural knowledge can be developed. Adams (1984) has

suggested that the learner may have difficulty evaluating the mechanics of the movement during the early stages of learning (an apparently critical operation for the development of the production systems). Thus novice learners benefit from KP in the early stages of skill learning. Future research needs to focus on the ability of children to process descriptive information regarding their movements or to relate that information to movements planned for the preceding trial. In addition, little is known regarding the meaning children attach to common descriptors of movement, even such common terms as *throw harder* and *jump higher*. If you ask young children to jump as high as they can, they move their feet as high off the ground as they can. Children, when asked by the teacher to look at the ball, put their chin on their chest in order to align their head with the oncoming ball, yet they still focus their eyes on the teacher. Thus the effectiveness of knowledge of performance for children will ultimately depend on the experimenter/coach/teacher's understanding of each child's lexicon of movement terminology.

Another factor that is related to the role of KR in performance and learning is contextual interference and practice variability. Sequencing of multiple tasks is a current question in the contextual interference and variability of practice research. Similar tasks or a task with varying environmental conditions can be presented under blocked or random conditions. The same task or conditions present on every trial is termed *blocked practice*. If several tasks or conditions are interchanged across trials, the practice is random. Polkis (1990) found that under closed-skill conditions, young children were able to use random practice, but for an open environment when task complexity was increased, young children's performance was hindered under random practice schedules. Many tasks require continual adjustments from one performance to the next. In order to adjust to a changing environment, the learner must practice under a variety of circumstances and detect the relationship between the parameters selected and performance outcome.

Another factor that influences learning is the presence or absence of a model (see Chapter 5). For the information the model provides to be of value in learning, the individual must be attentive to the modeled behavior and retain the modeled sequence. The major focus, developmentally, is on whether children are able to attend to and remember the task-appropriate cues. Here we need to determine whether learners merely try to copy the model, or if they match their performance to the models to detect errors. In the first situation, the model performs more of a guidance function similar to KR and performance should deteriorate rapidly with the withdrawal of the model.

The effectiveness of a model for performance improvement has been investigated developmentally. Thomas, Pierce, and Rídsdale (1977) examined the effects of giving 7-and 9-year-old girls a model either at the beginning of the learning session, after they had already attempted the task, or without a model. Conclusions were that 9-year-olds could effectively use modeled cues regardless of when the model was given. The 7-year-olds did benefit from the model's performance only when the model was given before the practice.

Supporting and extending the work of Thomas et al. (1977), Weiss (1983) found that the effectiveness of a model depended on differences in cognitive development evident in children of different ages. The major factors in her study were a model vs. no-model condition and verbal vs. no-verbal label groups for 5- and 7-year-old children. Results indicated that several cognitive developmental factors (attention span, memory capacity, coding capabilities, and physical abilities) were necessary for a model to be effective in skill learning.

The modeling literature has used simple tasks and the learners were in the cognitive phases of learning (developing the general strategy to approach the task). For the Thomas et al. study, the learner used the model to determine which of the two strategies to use to balance on the stabilometer. The children in Weiss's study used the model to determine sequencing of skills that they could already perform individually. A future area of investigation should be later stages of learning and how a model can be used to refine parameter selection and error detection and correction.

EXPERTISE AND SKILLED PERFORMANCE

The development of expertise is studied in many areas and for various reasons. Sometimes the focus is on the cognitive processes that form the basis for expertise while at others the focus is on more applied and context-specific aspects of expertise (see Abernethy, 1988b, for a review of visual search and selective attention; Abernethy, in this volume; or Thomas & Thomas, in press, for a review of decision making and expertise). Since coverage of this topic from an attentional (particularly a visual) basis is provided by Abernethy (in this volume), we will focus our attention (excuse the pun) on the development of knowledge structures (declarative, procedural, strategic) and sport performance. The study of the development of expertise in sport is particularly appropriate because:

1. The knowledge base, skills, and game performance are context-specific and can be circumscribed (Thomas, French, & Humphries, 1986).
2. Sport often stresses the cognitive processing system because time constraints on decisions are encountered (Abernethy, 1990; Thomas & Thomas, in press).
3. In sport knowing when and how to execute a skill are not synonymous with executing the skill (McPherson & Thomas, 1989; Thomas & Thomas, in press).

Exactly where the focus on expertise originated is hard to determine, but the work by Chase and Simon (1973) on the memory of expert chess players sparked substantial interest. In the area of children's memory development, there were arguments about whether or not stages existed (e.g.,

see Chi, 1976, for an overview and likely the most influential paper at that time). One of the papers which directed the developmental area toward expertise was Chi's (1978) work in which she demonstrated that after a brief visual exposure to pieces arranged on a chessboard, child experts recalled the standard positioning of pieces better than adult novices, but the adult novices recalled numbers on a backward digit span test better (as would be expected). Subsequent work by Chi and colleagues on physics problems (Chi, Feltovich, & Glaser, 1981) and dinosaur knowledge (Chi & Koeske, 1983) played a significant role in explaining the developmental nature of expertise (for reviews see Chi & Ceci, 1987; Chi & Reese, 1983; or Gobbo & Chi, 1986).

Often models of cognition (knowledge, memory, and learning) are conceptualized as declarative (factual information), procedural (how to do things), and strategic (cognitive processes) knowledge (Thomas & Thomas, in press). Sometimes declarative knowledge is said to develop in advance of procedural knowledge (e.g., Chi & Rees, 1983) but evidence for that is mixed and the order of development could vary by context (McPherson & Thomas, 1989). How knowledge is represented and differs between experts and novices has been investigated in various areas: badminton (Abernethy, 1988a), baseball (Chiesi, Spilich, & Voss, 1979; Spilich, Vesonder, Chiesi, & Voss, 1979), basketball (Allard, Graham, & Paarsalu, 1980; Bard & Fleury, 1976; French & Thomas, 1987), bridge (Charness, 1979), chess (Chase & Simon, 1973; Chi, 1978), dinosaurs (Chi & Koeske, 1983), field hockey (Starkes & Deakin, 1984; Starkes, 1987), figure skaters (Deakin & Allard, 1991), Go (Reitman, 1976), squash (Abernethy, 1990), and tennis (McPherson & Thomas, 1989). In the following sections we will focus on two aspects of expertise: its development across childhood and adolescence; and the relations among decision making, skills, and performance (a more theoretical basis for this discussion can be found in Thomas, French, & Humphries, 1986; Thomas, French, Thomas, & Gallagher, 1988; or Thomas & Thomas, in press).

Development of Sport Knowledge, Skill, and Performance

The fact that older children perform better than younger children in sport skills is not new information. This was clearly documented in the previous section on motor performance. In a previous part as well, substantial evidence demonstrated that part of this difference can be accounted for by the use of cognitive strategies (e.g., rehearsal, grouping, labeling). However, here we show that expertise changes the developmental nature of this finding.

French and Thomas (1987) and McPherson and Thomas (1989) showed that for basketball and tennis knowledge (declarative and procedural), skills, and game performance (decisions and executions), younger experts (8 to 11 years of age) not only perform better than the same-age novices, but better than older novices (11 to 13 years of age). These findings were consistent across knowledge tests (declarative), interviews (procedural), skills tests (e.g., basketball—shooting, dribbling; tennis—serve, forehand, backhand), and coding of game performance (see Figure 4–15).

Figure 4–15 is an example from McPherson and Thomas (1989) showing how game performance in tennis was coded. Subjects were videotaped as they played tennis. Then the sequence of actions was coded into the categories of control (were they in position to hit a return?), decisions (did they make a good decision about the shot to hit?), and executions (were they able to execute the decision that was made?). On the far right of the decision tree are examples

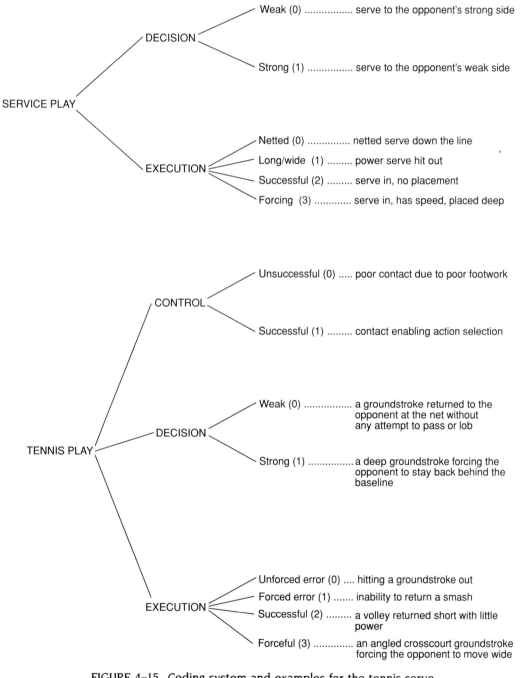

FIGURE 4–15. Coding system and examples for the tennis serve and tennis play following the serve.

Used with permission from McPherson, S. L., & Thomas, J. R. (1989). Relation of knowledge and performance in boys' tennis: Age and expertise. *Journal of Experimental Child Psychology*, 48, 190–211.

of actions that would result in certain categories being coded (this same idea was used for basketball in French & Thomas, 1987).

Relations Among Sport Knowledge, Skill, and Performance

Both French and Thomas (1987) and McPherson and Thomas (1989) found significant multivariate relationships between knowledge and skill as one component and game performance as the other. In both instances the canonical correlation was above .70. For basketball, knowledge and skills (shooting and dribbling) related significantly to game performance (decisions and execution). For tennis, knowledge and ground strokes related significantly to game performance (decisions and execution). Thus, the relations between knowledge, skill, and game performance were consistent across the two sports for children ages 8 to 13 years.

French and Thomas (1987) followed the younger children (both experts and novices) over the course of a basketball season and measured knowledge, skill, and game performance at the end of the season. Only basketball knowledge improved over the season; skill did not. The only game-performance measure to improve over the season was decisions (more good ones). At the end of the season knowledge and decisions were the only variables that remained significantly correlated. Thus the cognitive components of performance (knowledge about basketball and decisions during the game) appear to be improving in advance of skill components (dribbling, shooting, execution). French and Thomas (1987) suggest that this result may well be caused by what the coaches emphasized in practice (cognitive aspects of the game rather than skill), as indicated by coaches' and children's self-reports.

Children in both studies (French & Thomas, 1987; McPherson & Thomas, 1989) were interviewed to assess their procedural knowledge about basketball and tennis. Tapes of these interviews were coded according to specific criteria for analysis (see Table 4–3 for an example from McPherson & Thomas, 1989). Results from these interviews can be summarized as follows:

1. Basketball (situations 1, 2, and 3—list all possible options for a fast break, offensive 2-on-1, offensive 3-on-2, defensive 3-on-2; situation 4—list all possible out-of-bounds plays; situation 5—list all possible ways to score a goal)
   a. Situations 1, 2, and 3—older players produced more correct answers than younger players; experts gave more correct answers than novices; experts were more likely to qualify answers by saying actions were dependent on the other team/players (IF-THEN statements).
   b. Situations 4 and 5—experts generated more possible out-of-bounds plays and more ways to score a goal than novices; experts had more and better organized knowledge than novices.

2. Tennis—Situation Interview (what would you do under specific situations that were shown to you?)
   a. Experts generated more concepts and a greater variety of concepts about conditions and actions (IF-THEN statements) than did novices.
   b. Experts' conditions and actions were of higher quality than those of novices.
   c. Experts had more double and triple linkages between concepts and actions than did novices (reflecting a more complex and well-organized knowledge base).

These results suggest that experts have a larger, more complex, and better organized knowledge base than novices in basketball and tennis. The concept that procedural knowledge is more developed in experts is supported by their greater and more varied use of IF-THEN statements in both sports and the lack of their use by novices. In addition McPherson and Thomas (1989) provided support for the idea that sport experts develop IF-THEN-DO productions. They show that level of expertise is what matters in the relation between THEN and DO. Younger experts had more disagreements between their ability to select an action (THEN) and execute it (DO) than did novices. This was because experts selected more complex and difficult actions to execute. Older experts had fewer disagreement between actions selected and executed than did younger experts demonstrating that skill level was continuing to increase

TABLE 4–3. The Decision Rules for Coding the Quality of Each Concept for the Point and Situation Interviews

Concept quality: Each concept will be coded according to the quality of the concept in the context of the interview situation or point situation.

Category	Code	Decision Rule
Condition concept:	0 =	Inappropriate condition
	1 =	Appropriate only regarding himself
	2 =	Appropriate and forceful—regarding himself and one other condition
	3 =	Appropriate and very forceful—regarding himself and two other conditions
Action concept:	0 =	Inappropriate action
	1 =	Appropriate action but weak—no forceful qualities only execution mentioned
	2 =	Appropriate and forceful—one forceful quality
	3 =	Appropriate and very forceful—two or more forceful qualities
Goal concept:	0 =	Skill and himself—execution, getting it in, keeping the ball in play
	1 =	Himself and opponent—keeping the ball away, preventing opponent's aggressive shots
	2 =	Winning the point, game, match

with practice and experience. We might speculate that the successful incorporation of the DO part into a single unit IF-THEN-DO loop is the real mark of expertise. That is, greater expertise results in a greater number of agreements between the "condition/action selection" and "execution" phases of performance. In this instance automaticity (Logan, 1990) might well mean a "bonded" IF-THEN-DO loop.

METHODOLOGICAL ISSUES IN STUDYING MOTOR SKILL ACQUISITION

When measuring motor skill performance, movement characteristics or movement outcome are typically assessed. Traditionally, movement outcome has been the favored type of measurement since it determines achievement of the goal of the task. Describing movement kinematics requires the child coming to the laboratory setting, whereas measuring movement outcome can be done in the child's school. The type of measurement is dependent on the research question.

Movement Outcome

When measuring movement outcome, three types of measurement (Schmidt, 1988) are generally recorded: error, speed, and response magnitude. Error measurement describes deviations from the desired goal. Several error scores have been used in the literature: absolute error (AE), constant error (CE), absolute constant error (|CE|), variable error (VE), and total error (the combination of deviation and variability called E or root mean square). The type of error score calculated is dependent upon the research question. If consistency of performance is important, then VE should be selected. However if response biasing is important then CE or |CE| should be used. For overall accuracy E should be used. Historically, AE has been used for overall accuracy, but AE has been demonstrated to be a combination of CE and VE. However, difficulty exists in determining the relative contribution of each. Since E is $\sqrt{VE^2 + CE^2}$, the weighing of both scores is known. Schmidt (1988) provides a comprehensive review of error scores.

A second type of outcome measure is time and speed. Reaction time and movement time have been the traditional measures. Additionally, reaction time has been fractionated into premotor and motor time. Premotor time is an indicator of information processing while motor time can indicate neuromotor maturation.

The last category of movement outcome measurement is response magnitude, a traditional measure of outcome that has been used in motor development research. Examples of this outcome measure would be how far the ball is thrown, or how many sit-ups an individual can complete.

Movement Characteristics

Measurement of movement characteristics provides information about the quality of the movement. This type of measurement is beneficial when the researcher wants to know how the child moves, whether there is a change in the process of the action between trials, days, or years. Those researchers who have described fundamental motor pattern development have assessed movement characteristics (e.g., Halverson & Williams, 1985; Roberton, 1984; Seefeldt & Haubenstricker, 1982; Wickstrom, 1983).

When describing movement characteristics, three types of measurement are generally made: kinematic, electromyographic (EMG), and ground reaction forces. Kinematic measurement describes the movement of the limbs and/or entire body. The various ways to describe movement kinematics are recordings of locations, velocities, and acceleration. Traditionally, the recording of locations has been determined by cinematographical analysis. Anatomical landmarks were determined and the children were filmed with a high-speed camera (video or film). A frame-by-frame analysis was completed to determine the changes in the locations of the landmarks. With recent technological advances, computer analysis systems have been developed (e.g., Peak Performance, WatSmart) where a tape marker or light-emitting diode is placed on the anatomical landmarks. Multiple cameras record the markings and a frame-by-frame analysis is computer-generated.

In a recent developmental study, Thomas, Thomas, Hinrichs, Martin, and Marzke (1990) analyzed children's one-hand overhand throw for velocity. Data can be generated as previously shown in Figures 4–9, 4–10, and 4–11. Comparisons between adult/child, expert/novice, male/female patterns can then be evaluated to detect pattern differences.

From the cinematographical analysis, velocity and acceleration of specific limbs can be generated. The velocity information (speed of the limb/body across positions) can be used to determine the timing of the movement, and to locate pauses or hesitation in the action. Acceleration refers to the change in velocity at each position. This gives an indication as to whether the body/limb has a change in force generation.

Electromyographic (EMG) recordings measure the involvement of a muscle in the movement by recording the electrical activity associated with contraction. The common method of measurement with children is by attaching surface electrodes to the agonist and antagonist muscles of interest. After recording the electrical potential of the muscle, the EMGs have to be rectified. Additionally, to determine the pattern of action, the EMGs are averaged for a number of responses to remove trial-to-trial variation. The EMG tracing provides records of the temporal patterning of the movement segments and the intensity of the action.

Another kinematic measure of force production is ground reaction force, as determined by use of a force platform. Fortney (1983) determined that, when running, young children produced peak and impact forces three times greater than their body weight, an extremely high value when compared to adults.

Using a combination of kinematics and EMG technology, Whitney (1991) investigated postural response differences between children who have had experience with balance in a variety of movements (5-year-old gymnasts) and children who have not had extensive experience with balance (5-year-old swimmers). Electrodes were attached to the tibialis anterior, medial quadriceps, rectus abdominous, medial gastrocnemius, biceps femoris, and the lumbar paraspinal muscles. A peak-performance system was used to determine motion on a moving posture platform. Both measurements were integrated to determine sequencing of the muscular contractions with overt movement.

Training Studies

An important consideration in motor skill performance is the effects of training over time. The first question would be whether motor performance can be changed through intervention, or whether it can be controlled by maturational forces. Secondly, is the benefit to performance retained across time. The evidence seems to indicate that given appropriate instruction and practice, motor skill learning can be enhanced (see Haubenstricker & Seefeldt, 1986, for a review). To determine if benefits to performance last over time, longitudinal investigations must be completed. To date, the run, jump, and throw skills (Glassow & Kruse, 1960; Halverson, Roberton & Langendorfer, 1982; Rarick & Smoll, 1967) have been investigated longitudinally to determine skill ranking across time. Stability of group ranking has not been high. Clark (1967) reported data from the coaches of boys when they were in elementary and junior high school. Forty-four percent of the boys were stars during elementary school and not junior high school, while 30% were stars during junior high school but not elementary school. Only 25% were stars at both levels. Data were not collected during the high school years, but one would expect a significant change in who the "stars" would be. With the onset of adolescence, the early-maturing boys no longer have a size advantage.

Measurement Issues

Since children are inherently variable and are not miniature adults, several methodological issues must be addressed (see Table 4-4). First, a knowledge of the variability of the subject population is important in any research. Research on young children is difficult due to the fact that they are not consistent in their performance. Thus when planning any research project investigating children, the researcher must be sure that the child understands what is required and has given his or her best performance.

Selection of age groups for a developmental study should be determined by the theoretical basis for the research project. Weiss and Bredemeier (1983) highlighted a problem with much of the sport psychology research in that

subjects were selected with wide age bands. They indicated, as did Thomas (1980), that this can significantly interfere with the conclusions from the study in that the 6-year-olds are responding much differently from 12-year-olds, but when the groups are averaged together, the data do not fit any age group.

Age differences in processing speed and difference limens must be also be considered. Not only does speed of processing affect memory and learning studies for children, but if researchers do not understand that young children think differently from adults, the instructions will not be modified for comprehension. Therefore, the children's performance can be hindered before experimental manipulation. Additionally, when results are interpreted, maturational differences or difference limens need to be reviewed. Thomas and Thomas (1987) found that young children needed as much as three times the difference between movements as older children to determine that the movements were different. Thus adult/child movement differences must be greater than the difference limen to indicate experimental differences.

Another factor to be considered is the measurement constraints of the task (e.g., floor and ceiling effects). When wide age ranges are selected, such as 5-year-olds and 19-year-olds, task selection becomes critical. A task could easily be selected where the 5-year-olds were unable to successfully complete the task (floor effect) while all the 19-year-olds were able to complete the task (ceiling effect). This would be an example of an artificial developmental difference. In this case, the developmental differences are still unknown. Both minimum and maximum performance levels tend to increase across childhood and the difference between minimum and maximum performance seems to become greater with age.

A final problem relates to performance versus learning. As reviewed by Schmidt (1988), in order to determine learning effects, a retention interval needs to be included such that the subjects are required to perform the task without the experimental variable present. Gallagher and Thomas (1980) manipulated the processing interval, and gave subjects 3, 6, or 12 seconds to process the knowledge of results. At the end of 36 trials, they concluded that the

---

TABLE 4–4. Developmental Methodological Issues*

1. Is there theoretical reasoning behind the selection of age groups?

2. Is age level variability of between- and within-subject-age groups accounted for?

3. When planning developmental studies, are important variables considered, such as age differences in processing speed, difference limens, or both?

4. Does the experimenter really understand children, and is this reflected in all aspects of the planning of the research?

*Adapted from Thomas & Thomas (1984). Planning "kiddie" research: Little "kids" but big problems. In J. R. Thomas (Ed.). *Motor development during childhood and adolescence* (pp. 260–273). Minneapolis, MN: Burgess.

young subjects, when given 12 seconds to process the information, were able to perform similarly to adults. However, Gallagher and Thomas did not include a retention interval, and they were unable to determine whether these effects were temporary or lasting.

DO WE KNOW ANYTHING BESIDES "AS CHILDREN GET OLDER, THEY GET BETTER"?

The improvements, both qualitative and quantitative, during childhood are so robust that developmental research hypotheses are relatively easy and accurate to formulate. In fact, this improvement is so linear in nature, regardless of the task, that sometimes we wonder why we need to study motor skill acquisition during childhood. Three factors drive research: First, the idiosyncrasies must be studied and explained; second, something which is so obvious, orderly, and robust as the developmental process must not be merely accepted—it must be explained; and third, we feel an overwhelming desire to manipulate the critical interaction between nature and nurture!

If one looked at the curves for stature, development of cognitive processes, and motor performance, the curves look remarkably similar. In fact, French and Thomas (1992) have shown that effect size curves (created across age levels) for several motor performance tasks closely resemble velocity curves across age, a finding suggesting a close association with growth. There is a steady increase through childhood, often a sharper increase at puberty, and then a gradual leveling off. While on the one hand, this seems very neat and tidy, the underlying causes clearly must be different. As we have pointed out in earlier discussions, physical growth is dramatically impacted by the hormones associated with sexual maturity. Intuitively we reason that it is unlikely that those hormones are responsible for the mature use of rehearsal strategies. So while the change on all fronts—physical growth, motor patterns and performance, cognitive processing—is toward the same end, and that end is in a similar chronological location, the routes are quite different. The effect of age is robust, but the interactions are perhaps more interesting.

Beyond the effect of age, we know that environment—specifically practice and training—dramatically influences performance. This has been shown in cross-sectional studies (e.g., Gallagher & Thomas, 1984, 1986; Winther & Thomas, 1981) that manipulated the practice and in studies that followed children after extensive practice (McPherson & Thomas, 1989) or more longitudinally (French & Thomas, 1987). So while children get better with age, they can perform well beyond their age peers (and our age-related expectations) with interventions or extensive practice.

Gender differences have also brought forth questions and explanations resulting from different improvements associated with increasing age. While the gender differences in overhand throwing are large and continue to in-

crease after puberty, differences in fitness are relatively small, but increase after puberty. Note, however, that during childhood males and females are more similar than different in performance! Some differences are of interest because they are rare and large. Unfortunately, many cultures have expectations and biases which create or increase differences between the genders where there should be none. With few exceptions (e.g., throwing), the differences between the genders are of more interest and importance in theory than in everyday life, where gender similarities are probably of more importance. Nevertheless, the presence of gender differences where none should logically exist does have implications for cultural changes and training programs.

Research also indicates that all children do not develop at the same rate, and the rates vary across characteristics (e.g., growth, cognition) and within children. Mean performances show trends that are smooth and linear. Within individuals, there is day-to-day variation and times when change is rapid or slow. Some of the underlying causes of individual differences and of age-related increases are beginning to be understood. Early research in motor development focused on description, while recent research has often used experimental or quasi-experimental designs to allow some manipulation of characteristics. While being able to influence development by manipulation is desirable, much can be learned by careful description and observation. As McCall (1977) suggested:

Developmental psychologists should accord description the esteem other disciplines do because much has been learned at its hand: Consider the theory of evolution, the plate theory of continental drift, and our knowledge of the early evolution of *Homo sapiens*. Paleontology, geology, and and astronomy seem to be alive and well without manipulating fossils, continents, or heavenly bodies. (p. 337)

In addition, there is a complex interaction of factors that influence performance during childhood—growth, cognition, motor patterns, and practice. While development can be described within those factors, it cannot be understood without looking across them. Individuals vary greatly, and the causes of those variations are of critical interest. As with gender, even though there are individual differences and each child is unique, children are more alike than different. All children move in a linear manner toward maturity through childhood, but all children exhibit variability in rate between and across factors of development.

Future Research

Where should research on the developmental nature of skill acquisition go from here? We believe that the challenge—but also the essence—of developmental research will be a more interdisciplinary approach to studying the questions of motor development. While the questions may seem old, grandiose, and theoretical, they will ultimately lead to better theories, applications, and understandings. Among the important questions are:

- What are the limitations of genetics?
- What are the critical nurturing aspects of environment?
- What are the limits of performance?
- How is skill/performance enhanced?
- How do fitness and skill interact during development?
- What factors facilitate exercise and sport adherence?

Clearly these are not new ideas, but to provide new information and insight, new research paradigms are needed. A move should be made away from typical descriptive and cross-sectional studies. Multiple studies, with factors from across several areas, will be needed to answer these questions. Studies of experts as well as the use of technology and dependent variables from across several areas (e.g., biomechanics, neurophysiology) indicate the benefits from novel approaches to studying developmental issues. Theories and explanations from a dynamical systems perspective may help explain the perception, cognition, action relationship.

Cross-cultural and gender studies can contribute to the understanding of the roles of genetics and environment. Studies of parents and siblings may help us to understand those factors that limit performance. Studies following the same children across childhood and measuring the many contributors to performance may be informative as to how performance is enhanced (or limited) and how participation is encouraged. All of these efforts are costly, time-consuming, and ambitious. Progress can be made through smaller projects that study varying combinations of fewer factors. In addition, a shift from descriptive research to experimental research or to the kind of descriptive research that uses multiple dependent variables is desirable. Behavior is complex, and this complexity must be captured within appropriate research designs.

Applications

While scholars in the ivory tower may see a limited need for their work to have application, governments and the general public believe that meaningful products should be evolved. Somehow the need to know is simply not enough. Fortunately there is considerable (perhaps post-hoc) use for research in developmental skill acquisition. Much of the information resulting from this research, for example, has been used to develop or modify youth sport programs, which is gratifying to those who did the research. Seeing children benefit from one's scholarly efforts is often as rewarding as "knowing just to know"!

Norms from performance data have been used by physicians, therapists, and educators to prescribe treatments or to diagnose problems in children. These data have also been used for selecting and grouping children for activity. Normative data have been used to improve curricula and instruction. Parents and educators are informed of "normal" performance as a guide for understanding (and judging) their children. Norms have been used and misused to denote gender differences. These are perhaps the most common applications of motor development research.

There are other uses for motor development research beyond the "knowing to know" and normative data functions. As noted, research that can help to determine factors that enhance performance is helpful in developing programs and for training personnel. Understanding the typical progression also allows the teacher/coach to predict (and perhaps facilitate) what should be accomplished next. It is hoped that as the view becomes more acceptable that girls' and boys' performance during childhood should be similar, higher quality performance from both boys and girls will be encouraged rather than accepting less simply because the performer is a girl.

The work with experts, cognition, and learning suggests ways to enhance performance—especially at the extremes of performance (the expert and the klutz). Factors that are identified as precursors to better performance or necessary for skilled performance may be the focus of programs for young performers. While growth must be accommodated, understanding growth may help children and adults select appropriate activities. Children who are late maturers will not be small forever, and sports that require greater size may be appropriate for these children, even though they are small during childhood. Likewise, early maturers may be large in elementary school but too small in secondary school for the sport in which their size gave them an advantage earlier. Understanding the growth/maturation relationship has a clear application in children's sport.

Understanding expertise and performance in sport and exercise may help identify factors that encourage lifelong participation. Regular exercise in adults is linked to a healthy life, yet we know little about when those patterns are established. Although it has not been clearly established (Simons-Morton, O'Hara, Simons-Morton, & Parcel, 1987), one would guess that a foundation of skill, fitness, and positive experiences might encourage a healthy lifestyle.

References

Abernethy, B. (1990). Expertise, visual search, and information pick-up in squash. *Perception, 18,* 63–77.

Abernethy, B. (1988a). The effects of age and expertise upon perceptual skill development in a racquet sport. *Research Quarterly for Exercise and Sport, 59,* 210–221.

Abernethy, B. (1988b). Visual search in sport and ergonomics: Its relationship to selective attention and performer expertise. *Human Performance, 1,* 205–235.

Adams, J. A. (1984). Learning of movement sequences. *Psychological Bulletin, 96,* 3–28.

Allard, F., Graham, S., & Paarsalu, M.E. (1980). Perception in sport: Basketball. *Journal of Sport Psychology, 2,* 14–21.

Anderson, J. R. (1980). *Cognitive psychology and its implications.* San Francisco: Freeman.

Atkinson, R. C., & Shiffrin, R. M. (1968). Human memory: A proposed system and its control process. In K. W. Spence & J. T. Spence (Eds.), *The psychology of learning and motivation* (Vol. 2, pp. 90–197). New York: Academic Press.

Barclay, C., & Newell, K. (1980). Children's processing of information in motor skill acquisition. *Journal of Experimental Child Psychology, 30,* 98–108.

Bard, C., & Fleury, M. (1976). Analysis of visual search activity during sport problem situations. *Journal of Human Movement Studies, 3,* 214–222.

Bard, C., Fleury, M., & Hay, L. (Eds.). (1990). *Development of eye-hand coordination across the life span.* Columbia, SC: University of South Carolina Press.

Barrett, S. E., & Shepp, B. E. (1988). Developmental changes in attentional skills: The effect of irrelevant variations on encoding and response selection. *Journal of Experimental Child Psychology, 45,* 382–399.

Bjorklund, D. F. (1985). The role of conceptual knowledge in the development of organization in children's memory. In C. J. Brainerd & M. Pressley (Eds.), *Basic processes in memory development: Progress in cognitive development research* (pp. 103–142). New York: Springer-Verlag.

Bjorklund, D. F., & Buchanan, J. J. (1989). Developmental and knowledge base differences in the acquisition and extension of a memory strategy. *Journal of Experimental Child Psychology, 48,* 451–471.

Bloom, B. S. (1964). *Stability and change in human characteristics.* New York: Wiley.

Branta, C., Haubenstricker, J., & Seefeldt, V. (1984). Age changes in motor skills during childhood and adolescence. In R. L. Terjung (Ed.), *Exercise and sport sciences reviews* (Vol. 12, pp. 467–520). Lexington, MA: D. C. Heath (Collamore Press).

Broekoff, J. (1985). The effects of physical activity on physical growth and development. In G. A. Stull & H. M Eckert (Eds.), *The Academy papers: Effects of physical activity on children* (No. 19, pp. 75–87), Champaign, IL: Human Kinetics.

Brown, A. L. (1975). The development of memory: Knowing, knowing how to know and knowing about knowing. In H. W. Reese (Ed.). *Advances in child development and behavior* (Vol. 10, pp. 104–153). New York: Academic Press.

Bryant, P. E. (1968). Comments on the design of developmental studies of cross-modal matching and cross-modal transfer. *Cortex, 4,* 127–137.

Bryant, P. E., & Raz, I. (1975). Visual and tactile perception of shape by young children. *Developmental Psychology, 11,* 525–526.

Burton, A. W. (1987). The effect of number of movement components on response time. *Journal of Human Movement Studies, 13,* 231–247.

Calvin, W. H. (1983). A stone's throw and its launch window: Timing precision and its implications for language and hominid brains. *Journal of Theoretical Biology, 104,* 121–135.

Calvin, W. H. (1982). Did throwing stones shape hominid brain evolution? *Ethology and Sociobiology, 3,* 115–124.

Case, R., Kurland, D. M., & Goldberg, J. (1982). Operational effi-

ciency and the growth of short-term memory span. *Journal of Experimental Child Psychology, 33,* 386–404.

Charness, N. (1979). Components of skill in bridge. *Canadian Journal of Psychology, 33,* 1–16.

Chase, W. G., & Simon, H. A. (1973). Perception in chess. *Cognitive Psychology, 4,* 55–81.

Chi, M. T. H. (1976). Short-term memory limitations in children: Capacity of processing deficits? *Memory and Cognition, 4,* 559–572.

Chi, M. T. H. (1977). Age differences in memory span. *Journal of Experimental Child Psychology, 23,* 266–281.

Chi, M. T. H. (1978). Knowledge structures and memory development. In R. S. Siegler (Ed.), *Children's thinking: What develops?* (pp. 73–105), Hillsdale, NJ: Erlbaum.

Chi, M. T. H. (1982). Knowledge development and memory performance. In M. Friedman, J. P. Das, & N. O'Connor (Eds.), *Intelligence and learning* (pp. 221–230). New York: Plenum Press.

Chi, M. T. H. (1985). Interactive roles of knowledge and strategies in the development of organized sorting and recall. In S. F. Chipman, J. W. Segal, & R. Glaser (Eds.). *Thinking and learning skills: Vol. 2. Research and open questions* (pp. 457–483). Hillsdale, NJ: Erlbaum.

Chi, M. T. H., & Ceci, S. J. (1987). Content knowledge: Its role, representation, and restructuring in memory development. *Advances in Child Development and Behavior, 20,* 91–142.

Chi, M. T. H., Feltovich, P. J., & Glaser, R. (1981). Categorization and representation of physics problems by experts and novices. *Cognitive Science, 5,* 121–152.

Chi, M. T. H., & Gallagher, J. D. (1982). Speed of processing: A developmental source of limitation. *Topics of Learning and Learning Disabilities, 2,* 23–32.

Chi, M. T. H., & Koeske, R. D. (1983). Network representation of a child's dinosaur knowledge. *Developmental Psychology, 19,* 29–39.

Chi, M. T. H., & Rees, E. T. (1983). A learning framework for development. In M. T. H. Chi (Ed.), *Contributions in human development* (Vol. 9, pp. 71–107). Basel, Switzerland: S. Karger.

Chiesi, H. L., Spilich, G. J., & Voss, J. F. (1979). Acquisition of domain related information in relation to high and low domain knowledge. *Journal of Verbal Learning and Verbal Behavior, 18,* 257–273.

Clarke, H. (1967). Characteristics of the young athlete: A longitudinal look. In *AMA Proceedings of the Eighth Annual Conference on the Medical Aspects of Sports—1966* (pp. 49–57). Chicago: American Medical Association.

Darlington, P. J., Jr. (1975). Group selection, altruism, reinforcement, and throwing in human evolution. *Proceedings of the National Academy of Science, U.S.A., 72,* 3748–3752.

Deakin, J. M., & Allard, F. (1991). Skilled memory in expert figure skaters. *Memory and Cognition, 19,* 79–86.

Dempster, F. N. (1988). Short-term memory development in childhood and adolescence. In C. J. Brainerd & M. Pressley (Eds.), *Basic processes in memory development: Progress in cognitive development research* (pp. 209–248). New York: Springer-Verlag.

Dunham, P., & Reid, D. (1987). Information processing: Effect of stimulus speed variation on coincidence-anticipation of children. *Journal of Human Movement Studies, 13,* 151–156.

Eaton, W. O. (1989). Childhood sex differences in motor performance and activity level: Findings and implications. In B. Kirkcaldy (Ed.), *Normalities and abnormalities in human movement* (pp. 58–75). Basel, Switzerland: S. Karger.

Eaton, W. O., & Enns, L. R. (1986). Sex differences in human motor activity level. *Psychological Bulletin, 100,* 19–28.

Eaton, W. O., & Yu, A. P. (1989). Are sex differences in child motor activity level a function of sex differences in maturational status? *Child Development, 60,* 1005–1011.

Eberts, R., & Schneider, W. (1980). *The automatic and controlled processing of temporal and spatial patterns* (Report No. 8003). Arlington, VA: Office of Naval Research.

Eckert, H. M. (1987). *Motor development* (3rd. ed.). Indianapolis, IN: Benchmark Press.

Espenschade, A. S. (1963). Motor development. In W. R. Johnson (Ed.), *Science and medicine of exercise and sports* (pp. 419–439). New York: Harper & Row.

Espenschade, A. S. (1963). Restudy of relationships between physical performances of school children and age, height, and weight. *Research Quarterly, 34,* 144–153.

Espenschade, A. S. (1960). Motor development. In W. R. Johnson (Ed.), *Science and medicine of exercise and sports* (pp. 419–439). New York: Harper & Row.

Fabricius, W. V., & Cavalier, L. (1989). The role of causal theories about memory in young children's memory strategy choice. *Child Development, 60,* 298–308.

Flavell, J. H. (1977). *Cognitive development.* Englewood Cliffs, NJ: Prentice-Hall.

Fortney, V. L. (1983). The kinematics and kinetics of the running pattern of 2-, 4-, and 6-year-old children. *Research Quarterly for Exercise and Sport, 54,* 126–135.

French, K. E., & Thomas, J. R. (1987). The relation of knowledge development to children's basketball performance. *Journal of Sport Psychology, 9,* 15–32.

French, K. E., & Thomas, J. R. (1992). How is performance constrained by growth? Unpublished paper. University of South Carolina, Columbia.

Gallagher, J. D. (1980). *Adult-child motor performance differences: A developmental perspective of control processing deficits.* Doctoral dissertation, Louisiana State University.

Gallagher, J., & Fisher, J. (1983). A developmental investigation of the effects of grouping on memory capacity. In C. Branta & D. Feltz (Eds.), *Psychology of motor behavior and sport* (Abstracts from NASPSPA and CSPSLP, p. 160). East Lansing, MI: Michigan State University.

Gallagher, J. D., & Thomas, J. R. (1980). Effects of varying post-KR intervals upon children's motor performance. *Journal of Motor Behavior, 12,* 41–46.

Gallagher, J. D., & Thomas, J. R. (1984). Rehearsal strategy effects on developmental differences for recall of a movement series. *Research Quarterly for Exercise and Sport, 55,* 123–128.

Gallagher, J. D., & Thomas, J. R. (1986). Developmental effects of grouping and recoding on learning a movement series. *Research Quarterly for Exercise and Sport, 57,* 117–127.

Gallahue, D. L. (1989). *Understanding motor development: Infants, children, adolescence* (2nd. ed.). Indianapolis, IN: Benchmark Press.

Glassow, R., & Kruse, P. (1960). Motor performance of girls age 6 to 14 years. *Research Quarterly, 31,* 426–433.

Gobbo, C., & Chi, M. T. H. (1986). How knowledge is structured and used by expert and novice children. *Cognitive Development, 1,* 221–237.

Halverson, L., Roberton, M. A., & Langendorfer, S. (1982). Development of the overarm throw: Movement and ball velocity changes by seventh grade. *Research Quarterly for Exercise and Sport, 53,* 198–205.

Halverson, L. E., & Williams, K. (1985). Developmental sequences for hopping over distance: A prelongitudinal screening. *Research Quarterly for Exercise and Sport, 56,* 37–44.

Haubenstricker, J., & Seefeldt, V. (1986). Acquisition of motor skills during childhood. In V. Seefeldt (Ed.), *Physical activity and well-being* (pp. 41–102). Reston, VA: AAHPERD.

Haywood, K. M. (1986). *Life span motor development.* Champaign, IL: Human Kinetics.

Isaac, B. (1987). Throwing and human evolution. *The African Archaeological Review, 5,* 3–17.

Jensen, R. K. (1981). The effect of a 12-month growth period on the body movements of inertia of children. *Medicine and Science in Sport and Exercise, 13,* 238–242.

Jones, B. (1981). The developmental significance of cross-modal matching. In R. D. Walk & H. L. Pick (Eds.), *Intersensory perception and sensory integration* (pp. 109–135). New York: Plenum Press.

Kahneman, D. (1973). *Attention and effort.* Englewood Cliffs, NJ: Prentice-Hall.

Kail, R. (1986). Sources of age differences in speed of processing. *Child Development, 57,* 969–987.

Kail, R. (1988). Developmental functions for speeds of cognitive processes. *Journal of Experimental Child Psychology, 45,* 339–364.

Kail, R. (1991). Processing time declines exponentially during childhood and adolescence. *Developmental Psychology, 27,* 259–266.

Kail, R. V. (1979). *The development of memory in children.* San Francisco: Freeman.

Kail, R. V., & Hagen, J. W. (1977). *Perspectives on the development of memory and cognition.* Hillsdale, NJ: Erlbaum.

Kerr, R. (1985). Fitts' law and motor control in children. In J. Clark & H. H. Humphrey (Eds.), *Motor development: Current selected research* (pp. 45–53). Princeton, NJ: Princeton Book Co.

Leavitt, J. (1979). Cognitive demands of skating and stick handling in ice hockey. *Canadian Journal of Applied Sport Science, 4,* 46–55.

Lindberg, M. A. (1980). Is the knowledge base development a necessary and sufficient condition for memory development? *Journal of Experimental Child Psychology, 30,* 401–410.

Logan, G. D. (1990). Repetition priming and automaticity: Common underlying mechanisms? *Cognitive Psychology, 22,* 1–35.

Lorch, E. P., Anderson, D. R., & Well, A. D. (1984). Effects of irrelevant information on speeded classification tasks: Interference is reduced by habituation. *Journal of Experimental Psychology: Human Perception and Performance, 10,* 850–864.

Lorch, E. P., & Horn, D. G. (1986). Habituation of attention to irrelevant stimuli in elementary school children. *Journal of Experimental Child Psychology, 41,* 184–197.

Malina, R. M. (1975). *Growth and development: The first twenty years in man.* Minneapolis: Burgess.

Malina, R. M. (1984). Physical growth and maturation. In J. R. Thomas (Ed.), *Motor development during childhood and adolescence* (pp. 1–26), Minneapolis: Burgess.

Malina, R. M. (1986). Physical growth and maturation. In V. Seefeldt (Ed.), *Physical activity and well-being* (pp. 3–38), Reston, VA: AAHPERD.

McCall, R. B. (1977). Challenges to a science of developmental psychology. *Child Development, 48,* 333–344.

McCracken, H. D. (1983). Movement control in a reciprocal tapping task: A developmental study. *Journal of Motor Behavior, 15,* 262–279.

McHenry, H. M. (1982). The pattern of human evolution: Studies in bipedalism, mastication and encephalization. *American Review of Anthropology, 11,* 151–173.

McPherson, S. L., & Thomas, J. R. (1989). Relation of knowledge and performance in boys' tennis: Age and expertise. *Journal of Experimental Child Psychology, 48,* 190–211.

Millar, S. (1974). Tactile short-term memory by blind and sighted children. *British Journal of Psychology, 65,* 253–263.

Miller, M. B. (1990). *The use of labeling to improve movement recall involving learning disabled children.* Doctoral dissertation, University of Pittsburgh.

Nelson, J. K., Thomas, J. R., Nelson, K. R., & Abraham, P. C. (1986). Gender differences in children's throwing performance: Biology and environment. *Research Quarterly for Exercise and Sport, 57,* 280–287.

Nelson, K. R., Thomas, J. R., & Nelson, J. K. (1991). Longitudinal changes in throwing performance: Gender differences. *Research Quarterly for Exercise and Sport, 62,* 105–108.

Newell, K. M., & Barclay, C. R. (1982). Developing knowledge about action. In J. A. S. Kelso & J. E. Clark (Eds.), *The development of movement control and co-ordination* (pp. 175–212). New York: John Wiley.

Newell, K. M., & Kennedy, J. A. (1978). Knowledge of results and children's motor learning. *Developmental Psychology, 14,* 531–536.

Ornstein, P. A., Baker-Ward, L., & Naus, M. J. (1988). The development of mnemonic skill. In F. E. Weinert & M. Perlmutter (Eds.), *Memory development: Universal changes and individual differences* (pp. 31–50). Hillsdale, NJ: Erlbaum.

Ornstein, P. A., & Naus, M. J. (1984). *Effects of knowledge base on children's processing of information.* Unpublished manuscript, University of North Carolina, Chapel Hill.

Ornstein, P. A., & Naus, M. J. (1985). Effects of knowledge base on children's memory strategies. In H. W. Reese (Ed.), *Advances in child development and behavior* (pp. 113–148). New York: Academic Press.

Pascual-Leone, J., & Smith, J. (1969). The encoding and decoding of symbols by children: A new paradigm and neo-Piagetian model. *Journal of Experimental Child Psychology, 8,* 328–353.

Pascual-Leone, J. (1970). A mathematical model for the transition rule in Piaget's developmental stages. *Acta Psychologica, 32,* 301–345.

Payne, G. V., & Isaacs, L. D. (1987). *Human motor development: A lifespan approach.* Mountain View, CA: Mayfield.

Perlmutter, M. (1988). Research on memory and its development: Past, present, and future. In F. E. Weinert & M. Perlmutter (Eds.), *Memory development: Universal changes and individual differences* (pp. 353–380). Hillsdale, NJ: Erlbaum.

Piaget, J. (1952). *The origins of intelligence in children.* New York: International Universities Press.

Polkis, G. A. (1990). *The effects of environmental context and contextual interference on the learning of motor skills: A developmental perspective.* Doctoral dissertation, University of Pittsburgh.

Rabinowitz, M. (1988). On teaching cognitive strategies: The influence of accessibility of conceptual knowledge. *Contemporary Educational Psychology, 13,* 229–235.

Rao, N., & Moely, B. E. (1989). Producing memory strategy maintenance and generalization by explicit or implicit training of memory knowledge. *Journal of Experimental Child Psychology, 48,* 335–352.

Rarick, G. L., & Smoll, F. (1967). Stability of growth in strength and motor performance from childhood to adolescence. *Human Biology, 39,* 295–306.

Reid, G. (1980). The effects of motor strategy instruction in the short-term memory of the mentally retarded. *Journal of Motor Behavior, 12,* 221–227.

Reisberg, D., Barron, J., & Kemler, D. C. (1980). Overcoming Stroop interference: The effects of practice on distractor potency. *Journal of Experimental Psychology: Human Perception and Performance, 6,* 140–150.

Reitman, J. (1976). Skilled perception in Go: Deducing memory structures from inter-response times. *Cognitive Psychology, 8,* 336–356.

Roberton, M. A. (1982). Describing "stages" within and across motor tasks. In J. A. S. Kelso & J. E. Clark (Eds.), *The development of movement control and co-ordination* (pp. 294–307). New York: Wiley.

Roberton, M. A. (1984). Changing motor patterns during childhood. In J. R. Thomas (Ed.), *Motor development during childhood and adolescence* (pp. 48–90). Minneapolis: Burgess.

Roberton, M. A., Halverson, L. E., Langendorfer, S., & Williams, K. (1979). Longitudinal changes in children's overarm throw ball velocities. *Research Quarterly, 50,* 256–264.

Ross, A. (1976). *Psychological aspects of learning disabilities and reading disorders.* New York: McGraw-Hill.

Ross, J. G., & Gilbert, G. G. (1985). The national children and youth fitness study: A summary of findings. *Journal of Physical Education, Recreation and Dance, 56*(1), 45–50.

Ross, J. G., & Pate, R. R. (1987). The national children and youth fitness study II: A summary of findings. *Journal of Physical Education, Recreation and Dance, 58*(9), 51–56.

Salmoni, A. W., & Pascoe, C. (1979). Fitts reciprocal tapping task: A developmental study. In G. C. Roberts & K. M. Newell (Eds.), *Psychology of motor behavior and sport—1978* (pp. 355–386). Champaign, IL: Human Kinetics.

Salmoni, A. W., Schmidt, R. A., & Walter, C. B. (1984). Knowledge of results and motor learning: A review and critical reappraisal. *Psychological Bulletin, 95,* 355–386.

Scammon, R. E. (1930). The measurement of the body in childhood. In J. A. Harris, C. M. Jackson, D. G. Jackson, & R. E. Scammon, *The measurement of man* (pp. 171–215). Minneapolis: University of Minnesota Press.

Schachar, R., Rutter, M., & Smith, A. (1981). The characteristics of situationally and pervasively hyperactive children: Implications for syndrome definition. *Journal of Child Psychology and Psychiatry, 22,* 375–392.

Schmidt, R. A. (1988). *Motor control and learning: A behavioral emphasis.* Champaign, IL: Human Kinetics.

Schneider, W., & Sodian, B. (1988). Metamemory—memory behavior relationships in young children: Evidence from a memory-for-location task. *Journal of Experimental Child Psychology, 45,* 209–233.

Schroeder, R. K. (1981). *The effects of rehearsal on information processing efficiency of severely/profoundly retarded normal individuals.* Unpublished doctoral dissertation, Louisiana State University, Baton Rouge, LA.

Seefeldt, V. (1988). The concept of readiness applied to motor skill acquisition. In F. L. Smoll, R. A. Magill, & M. J. Ash (Eds.), *Children in sport* (pp. 45–52). Champaign, IL: Human Kinetics.

Seefeldt, V., & Haubenstricker, J. (1982). Patterns, phases, or stages: An analytical model for the study of developmental movement. In J. A. S. Kelso & J. E. Clark (Eds.), *The development of movement control and co-ordination* (pp. 309–318). New York: Wiley.

Shepp, B. E., Barrett, S. E., & Kolbet, L. K. (1987). The development of selective attention: Holistic perception versus resource allocation. *Journal of Experimental Child Psychology, 43,* 159–180.

Shiffrin, R. M., & Schneider, W. (1977). Controlled and automatic human information processing: II. Perceptual learning, automatic attending, and a general theory. *Psychological Review, 84,* 127–190.

Simons-Morton, B. G., O'Hara, N. M., Simons-Morton, D. G., & Parcel, G. S. (1987). Children and fitness: A public health perspective. *Research Quarterly for Exercise and Sport, 58,* 295–302.

Smoll, F. L., & Schutz, R. W. (1990). Quantifying gender differences in physical performance: A developmental perspective. *Developmental Psychology, 26,* 360–369.

Starkes, J. L. (1987). Skill in field hockey: The nature of the cognitive advantage. *Journal of Sport Psychology, 9,* 146–160.

Starkes, J. L., & Deakin, J. (1984). Perception in sport: A cognitive approach to skilled performance. In W. F. Straub & J. M. Williams (Eds.), *Cognitive sport psychology* (pp. 115–128). Lansing, NY: Sport Science Associates.

Stigler, J. W., Nusbaum, H. C., & Chalip, L. (1988). Developmental changes in speed of processing: Central limiting mechanism or skill transfer? *Child Development, 59,* 1144–1153.

Stratton, R. (1978). Information processing deficits in children's motor performance: Implications for instruction. *Motor Skills: Theory into Practice, 3,* 49–55.

Sugden, D. A. (1980). Movement speed in children. *Journal of Motor Behavior, 12,* 125–132.

Tanner, J. M. (1978). *Foetus into man: Physical growth from conception to maturity.* Cambridge, MA: Harvard University Press.

Thelen, E. (1987). The role of motor development in developmental psychology: A view of the past and agenda for the future. In N. Eisenberg (Ed.), *Contemporary topics in developmental psychology* (pp. 3–33). New York: Wiley.

Thomas, J. R. (1980). Acquisition of motor skills: Information processing differences between children and adults. *Research Quarterly, 50,* 158–173.

Thomas, J. R. (1982). Planning "Kiddie" research: Little "Kids" but big problems. In J. R. Thomas (Ed.), *Motor development during childhood and adolescence* (pp. 260–273). Minneapolis: Burgess.

Thomas, J. R. (1984). *Motor development during childhood and adolescence.* Minneapolis: Burgess.

Thomas, J. R. (1984). Children's motor skill development. In J.R. Thomas (Ed.), *Motor development during childhood and adolescence* (pp. 91–104). Minneapolis, MN: Burgess.

Thomas, J. R., & French, K. E. (1985). Gender differences across age in motor performance: A meta-analysis. *Psychological Bulletin, 98,* 260–282.

Thomas, J. R., French, K. E., & Humphries, C. A. (1986). Knowledge development and sport skill performance: Directions for motor behavior research. *Journal of Sport Psychology, 8,* 259–272.

Thomas, J. R., French, K. E., Thomas, K. T., & Gallagher, J. D. (1988). Children's knowledge development and sport performance. In F. L. Smoll, R. A. Magill, & M. J. Ash (Eds.), *Children in sport* (3rd ed.) (pp. 179–202). Champaign, IL: Human Kinetics.

Thomas, J. R., Gallagher, J. D., & Purvis, G. (1981). Reaction time and anticipation time: Effects of development. *Research Quarterly for Exercise and Sport, 52,* 359–367.

Thomas, J. R., Mitchell, B., & Solmon, M. A. (1979). Precision knowledge of results and motor performance: Relationship to age. *Research Quarterly for Exercise and Sport, 50,* 687–698.

Thomas, J. R., Nelson, J. K., & Church, G. (1991). A developmental analysis of gender differences in health related physical fitness. *Pediatric Exercise Science, 3,* 28–42.

Thomas, J. R., Pierce, C., & Ridsdale, S. (1977). Age differences in children's ability to model motor behavior. *Research Quarterly, 48,* 592–597.

Thomas, J. R., & Thomas, K. T. (1988). Development of gender differences in physical activity. *Quest, 40,* 219–229.

Thomas, J. R., Thomas, K. T., Hinrichs, R., Mayin, P., & Marzke, M. (1990). Development of kinematics in throwing: Gender differences. Unpublished paper, Arizona State University, Tempe, AZ.

Thomas, J. R., Thomas, K. T., Lee, A. M., & Testerman, E. (1983). Age differences in use of strategy for recall of movement in a large scale environment. *Research Quarterly for Exercise and Sport, 3,* 264–272.

Thomas, K. T., & Thomas, J. R. (in press). Developing expertise in sport: The relation of knowledge and performance. *International Journal of Sport Psychology.*

Thomas, K. T., & Thomas, J. R. (1987). Perceptual development and its differential influence on limb positioning under two movement conditions in children. In J. E. Clark (Ed.), *Advances in motor development research* (pp. 83–96). Baltimore: AMS Press.

Tipper, S. P., Bourque, T. A., Anderson, S. H., & Brehaur, J. C. (1989). Mechanisms of attention: A developmental study. *Journal of Experimental Child Psychology, 48,* 353–378.

Tipper, S. P., MacQueen, G. M., & Brehaut, J. C. (1988). Negative priming between response modalities: Evidence for the central locus of inhibition in selective attention. *Perception & Psychophysics, 43,* 42–52.

Tobias, P. V. (1968). Cultural hominization among the earliest African Pleistocene hominids. *Proceedings of the Prehistoric Society, 33,* 367–376.

Tudor, J. (1979). Developmental differences in motor task integration: A test of Pascual-Leone's Theory of constructive operators. *Journal of Experimental Child Psychology, 28,* 314–322.

VanDyne, H. J. (1973). Foundations of tactical perception in three to seven year olds. *Journal of the Association of Perception, 8,* 1–9.

Washburn, S. L., & Moore, R. (1980). *Ape into human.* Boston: Little, Brown.

Weiss, M. R. (1983). Modeling and motor performance: A developmental perspective. *Research Quarterly for Exercise and Sport, 54,* 190–197.

Weiss, M. R., & Bredemeier, B. J. (1983). Developmental sport psychology: A theoretical perspective for studying children in sport. *Journal of Sport Psychology, 5,* 216–230.

Weiss, M. R., & Klint, K. A. (1987). "Show and tell" in the gymnasium: An investigation of developmental differences in modeling and verbal rehearsal of motor skills. *Research Quarterly for Exercise and Sport, 58,* 234–241.

Whitall, J. (1991). The developmental effects of concurrent cognitive and locomotor skills: Time-sharing from a dynamical perspective. *Journal of Experimental Child Psychology, 51,* 245–266.

Whitney, S. (1991). *Development of postural control in young children.* Unpublished doctoral dissertation, University of Pittsburgh, Pittsburgh, PA.

Wickstrom, R. L. (1983). *Fundamental motor patterns* (3rd. ed.). Philadelphia: Lea & Febiger.

Wild, M. R. (1938). The behavior pattern of throwing and some observations concerning its course of development in children. *Research Quarterly, 9,* 20–24.

Williams, H., Temple, J., & Bateman, J. (1979). A test battery to assess intrasensory and intersensory development of young children. *Perceptual and Motor Skills, 48,* 643–659.

Williams, H. G. (1983). *Perceptual and motor development.* Englewood Cliffs, NJ: Prentice-Hall.

Winther, K. T., & Thomas, J. R. (1981). Developmental differences in children's labeling of movement. *Journal of Motor Behavior, 13,* 77–90.

Woollacott, M. H., & Shumway-Cook, A. (Eds.) (1989). *Development of gait across the life span.* Columbia, SC: University of South Carolina Press.

· 5 ·

MODELING: LEARNING, DEVELOPMENTAL, AND SOCIAL PSYCHOLOGICAL CONSIDERATIONS

Penny McCullagh

Providing demonstrations to learners has long been recognized as an important method of augmenting information. The adage "a picture is worth a thousand words" is reflective of our notion that action portrays information more efficiently than verbal instructions. Beyond the provision of information for skill learning, social psychologists have acknowledged modeling "to be one of the most powerful means of transmitting values, attitudes and patterns of thought and behaviors" (Bandura, 1986, p. 47). Thus modeling is a pervasive topic that encompasses a variety of disciplines. It is an especially appropriate topic for the *Handbook of Research on Sport Psychology* since it spans learning, developmental, and social psychological issues related to movement and sport skills (see McCullagh, Weiss, & Ross, 1989, for a review).

MODELING ISSUES RELATED TO THE ACQUISITION AND RETENTION OF MOTOR SKILLS

The purpose of this chapter is to present the current status of modeling research from learning, developmental, and social psychological perspectives by reviewing theoretical considerations and empirical research in each area starting with motor skills.

THEORETICAL CONSIDERATIONS

Theoretical Explanations of Modeling

Over the last century a variety of explanations have been proposed to account for imitative behavior, and these have typically concurred with the psychological orientation of the era. In fact, as early as 1896 (Morgan, 1896) it was believed that many common behaviors were achieved by copying the behaviors of others. Based mostly on speculation, rather than empirical data, Morgan presumed that intelligent imitation was dependent on conscious guidance as well as innate satisfaction. McDougall (1908) refused to accept an instinctual approach and instead proposed that imitative behavior could be classified according to the types of mental processes that mediated the outcome. Thus he differentiated between a variety of imitative responses. Sympathetic imitation (e.g., responding to a smile with a smile) was presumed to occur in all gregarious animals. (You have perhaps attempted to solicit such responses on your last visit to the primate section at

Much of the initial research for this chapter was conducted while preparing an earlier review 1:1 McCullagh, P., Weiss, M. R., & Ross, D. (1989), Modeling considerations in motor skill acquisition and performance: An integrated approach. In K. B. Pandolf (Ed.), *Exercise and sport sciences reviews,* Vol. 17 (pp. 475–513). Baltimore: Williams & Wilkins. The author would like to thank Janice Deakin and Tim Lee for their comments on an earlier draft of this manuscript.

the zoo). Imitation of ideomotor actions seemed to require higher mental processes and was thought to be at least partially under voluntary control. For example, observing the movements of another (e.g., a dancer) supposedly evoked a similar movement representation in the observer. McDougall was not explicit in the exact nature of this representation but suggested that the representation realized itself in overt action. A third type of imitation was voluntary and self-conscious and was assigned to later stages of development. The final type of imitation was presumed to be an innately organized disposition that was instinctual. Thus McDougall provided us with the concept of a movement representation that both rejected and accepted an instinctual interpretation.

Although instinctual explanations of behavior predominated the late 1800s and early 1900s, by the mid-1920s psychologists (e.g., Allport, 1924; Holt, 1931) turned to associative principles to explain the imitation process. For example, Allport negated the instinctive interpretation by suggesting that imitation was not really common in young children but appeared to occur because individuals responded similarly to the same stimulus. He further concluded that many presumed imitative responses were actually a result of circular conditioning. Unfortunately, this explanation could only explain the occurrence of responses already in the observer's repertoire and not the acquisition of novel responses.

As reinforcement approaches to learned behavior developed, it was suggested that reinforcement was a necessary component for imitative behavior. Miller and Dollard (1942), forerunners in the reinforcement approach, suggested four necessary components of imitative behavior. The imitator (observer) must be motivated, cues for the requisite behavior must be provided, matching responses must be performed, and reinforcement must be provided. Such an analysis is not dissimilar to approaches later proposed in the 1960s (e.g., Bandura, 1969).

Gerwitz and Stingle (1968) employed instrumental conditioning principles to explain imitative behavior. It was their contention that an imitative response must occur by choice and be extrinsically reinforced. With continual repetition, imitative behavior becomes more generalized and extrinsic reinforcement may be reduced to an intermittent schedule. Thus generalized imitation occurs when "many different responses of a model are copied in diverse situations" (Gerwitz & Stingle, p. 375, 1968).

All of the above attempts at theoretical explanations seem to have some shortcomings. The early instinctual (Morgan, 1896) and pseudo-instinctual (e.g., McDougall, 1908) approaches stifled empirical investigations. If imitative responses could not be modified, they were not of great scientific interest. Later researchers advocated circular conditioning procedures (e.g., Allport, 1924; Holt, 1931), whereby imitation could occur only if the responses were already existent in the observer's behavioral repertoire. Miller and Dollard (1941) systematically studied imitative behavior, suggesting that the observer responds to cues produced by the model, and Gerwitz and Stingle (1968) extended these reinforcement principles to include more generalized forms of imitation. For the most part, these early approaches were helpful in explaining how responses already existent in the observer's repertoire were elicited, yet little attention was directed to the acquisition and retention of new responses.

Sheffield (1961) was one of the first investigators to undertake an extensive research program concerned with observational learning. He developed a contiguity-mediational theory to explain the relationship between filmed demonstrations and the learning of complex serial motor skills. According to his interpretation, an observer formed a symbolic representation of the observed skill, and it was this "blueprint" or perceptual code that subsequently guided the individual's overt reproduction of the task. Sheffield and his associates found that observation of skilled behavior was not sufficient to produce completely accurate performance. Rather, subjects required overt practice. Little empirical work stemmed from Sheffield's research until Bandura (1965) incorporated and extended his viewpoints.

In agreement with Sheffield, Bandura (1969) advocated that modeled behavior is stored by the observer in representational form. These verbal or imaginal representations that are covert in nature mediate the observers' responses and allow the learner to acquire a behavior before it is actually enacted. Thus in contrast to Sheffield's position, Bandura asserted that response acquisition can be attained without overt practice and has been labeled "no trial learning" (Bandura, 1965). Through his progressive reformulations (1965, 1969, 1971, 1986) of observational learning processes, Bandura has held to the notion that overt action is not necessary for the acquisition of responses, especially behaviors that are social or cognitive in nature. In fact, Bandura has recently stated that "most human behavior is learned by observation through modeling" (1986, p. 47). According to Bandura's (1969, 1971, 1986) progressive theoretical reformulations, observational learning is primarily an information-processing activity that is governed by four subprocesses: attention, retention, production, and motivation.

Attention is the first component of the observational learning process and is influenced by both characteristics of the modeled event and observer characteristics. Thus the complexity, discriminability, and saliency of the modeled event will influence the observer's attentional level. If the behavior to be modeled is extremely complex, then attention-directing aids may need to accompany the demonstration so the observer can extract "generative rules." According to Bandura, absorption of the sensory events provided by a demonstration is not the sole determinant of the attentional phase. Rather cognitive attributes such as cognitive capabilities, arousal level, and expectations influence the perceptual process. Bandura has suggested that a number of variables can be employed to enhance the attentional phase of observational learning. Emphasizing salient features of the performance, providing verbal cues or alternating good and poor performances are all mechanisms that may help the learner to distinguish important performance cues. Alternating practice with demonstrations or providing feedback are also hypothesized to influence selective attention. Thus attentional processes "regulate exploration and perception of modeled activities" (Bandura, 1986, p. 51).

The second phase in the observational learning process is retention. The basic premise of the retention phase is that once a behavior is demonstrated, it must be retained in representational form in memory in order for the behavior to be enacted without continual reinforcement or repetition from the model. The representation is presumed to be either imaginal or verbal in nature. Additionally, it need not contain all aspects of the demonstration, but rather may be a representation or abstraction of relevant features. Imaginal or visual memory is especially important in early developmental stages when verbal skills are not fully developed or for movement behaviors that require spatial and temporal coordination, since such skills may be difficult to represent verbally. Thus "a golf swing is much better visualized than should be described." (Bandura, 1986, p. 58). The second representation system that can be used to retain modeled acts is verbal in nature. Certain types of information may be more amenable to verbal than imaginal coding. For example, the sequencing of right and left turns to follow a specified route may be better retained in verbal as opposed to imaginal form. This issue was addressed in a recent experiment using a five-component skill (McCullagh, Stiehl, & Weiss, 1990). Children were provided with either verbal instructions or a visual demonstration and assessed their recall of the correct sequence of movements as well as the quality of their reproductions. Visual demonstration aided children more than verbal instructions if quality of movement was assessed, but verbal instructions were more beneficial than demonstrations if the sequence of skills was the dependent measure.

In addition to the cognitive organization of modeled acts, it is postulated that both cognitive rehearsal and enactment rehearsal (practice) influence the retention phase of observational learning (Carroll & Bandura, 1985). The use of cognitive rehearsal or mental practice has been advocated for situations when behavioral enactment is impractical. While Bandura recognized the potency of cognitive rehearsal for enhancing motor skills (Feltz & Landers, 1983), he questioned whether it primarily influenced cognitive set, attentional mechanisms, or perceived self-efficacy. Interestingly Bandura (1986) suggested that the symbolic representations derived from modeled behaviors "serve as the internal models for response production and standards for response correction" (p. 51). This is a point I will return to after discussion of traditional motor skill learning theories.

The third phase in Bandura's formulation of observational learning consists of production processes. This phase was not well developed for the acquisition of motor

responses in Bandura's original writings, since he was interested primarily in the acquisition of social responses that could be dichotomous in nature (i.e., the behavior was either exhibited or not). However, when assessing motor skills we are not only interested in exhibition of the behavior, but in the movement quality as well. It is important to note that if we truly want to measure qualitative motor performance, both the spatial and temporal aspects of movements need to be assessed. Indeed, numerous experiments have shown that spatial aspects of movements can be modified through demonstrations (e.g., Carroll & Bandura, 1982, 1985, 1987, 1990). Limited evidence has also suggested that the timing of movement sequences may be amenable to modification from demonstrations (Adams, 1986; McCullagh & Caird, 1990), although the role of visual demonstrations in the absence of auditory cues seems weak in this acquisition process (McCullagh & Little, 1989). An issue that has clearly evaded researchers to this point is whether subjects can learn complex movement skills when both spatial and temporal aspects need to be coordinated to produce a desired outcome.

According to Bandura, the behavioral production of modeled acts involves a conception-matching process wherein the feedback from the response is compared to the cognitive representation. Based on the comparison process, modifications to the performance are made. While we typically infer the correctness of this process from overt performance, Bandura suggests alternative means for assessing the degree of observational learning. Multiple behavioral measures such as verbal production tests, recognition tests, comprehensive tests, and maximizing enactment tests are suggested as possible measures for assessing the amount learned through demonstrations, suggesting the necessity for multiple behavioral measures. The role of visual observation of one's own movements and feedback have been addressed in a recent series of experiments by Carroll and Bandura (1982, 1985, 1987, 1990). Essentially this research has shown that visual monitoring of one's own movements aids performance as long as subjects have sufficient practice to form a reasonably accurate cognitive representation. The importance of auditory and verbal feedback in the conception-matching process is also noted, as well as the necessity for requisite physical skills to execute the desired behavior.

The final subprocess in observational learning is motivational in nature and has received the most focused attention in the psychological literature. Simply expressed, we may attend to and remember the modeled behavior and have the physical skills to execute the skill, but if we are not sufficiently motivated, behavioral enactment will not occur. Thus Bandura recognized the role of external, vicarious, and self-incentives in the observational learning process.

The influence of external incentives has been clearly demonstrated in a number of research experiments (e.g., Bandura & Barab, 1973), suggesting that individuals are more likely to model behavior that is rewarded than behavior that is punished. The same principle applies to the vicarious reinforcement of others. Finally, self-incentives such as tangible rewards or self-evaluation of one's own behavior can serve as strong motivational determinants of behavior.

A final consideration within Bandura's formulation is the influence of these four subprocesses on differential aspects of observational learning. It is hypothesized that attention and retention affect the learning of responses whereas motor reproduction and motivation affect the performance of responses. Such a learning-versus-performance distinction has been clearly examined by Bandura in the social psychological literature but has received only limited attention in the sport psychology literature (e.g., McCullagh, 1986, 1987).

Theoretical Explanations of Motor Skill Acquisition

The two most prominent theories that have been proposed to explain motor skill acquisition and retention were published in the 1970s and held the attention of motor learning researchers for quite some time. The first theory was proposed by Adams (1971) and was based on empirical data that had been generated primarily from slow-positioning responses. It was Adams's contention that the principles generated from these data could be generalized to other types of motor skill responses. Labeled *closed-loop theory,* it was Adams's hypothesis that feedback obtained during movement execution is compared to an internal reference labeled the *perceptual trace.* The perceptual trace, which develops from practice and the corresponding proprioceptive feedback, serves as the reference for correctness, and the ability of the learner to perform is dependent on the strength of the perceptual trace. To establish if the perceptual trace is correct, it is expected that the subjects receive sensory feedback and knowledge of results, and thus experiencing correct practice is optimal. If either source of feedback is less than optimal, then the perceptual trace will not be as accurate and learning will be impaired. Once the movement is completed, subjects compare the sensory feedback to the perceptual trace and the discrepancy, termed *subjective reinforcement,* could later help maintain performance without knowledge of results. In addition to the memory mechanism that evaluated the correctness of movements (i.e., the perceptual trace), Adams suggested that a second memory mechanism was essential to initiate the movement. The rationale here for two memory mechanisms was an important contribution by Adams, since it was recognized that the same memory state could not both produce and evaluate the correctness of a response.

Adams's notions generated a great deal of research, but they were countered by Schmidt (1975), who proposed schema theory as an alternative. Although Schmidt agreed with Adams's proposal of two memory states and the notion of subjective reinforcement, he argued for more open-loop control of movements. Thus according to schema theory, when individuals make a response, they store in memory a number of items: (1) the initial conditions of the movements, (2) the characteristics of the generalized motor program, (3) the result of the movement and accompanying knowledge of results, and (4) the sensory consequences of the movement. Rather than specifically storing these four sources indefinitely, the learner abstracts the information into two generalized schemas. The recall schema is concerned with response production and the recognition schema is concerned with response evaluation. According to Schmidt, if any of these four sources of information are missing the schemas will be degraded and less learning will occur.

A primary difference between the two theories relates to the variability of practice a learner receives. According to Adams's theory, practice should be correct in order to develop a strong perceptual trace. According to Schmidt, both correct and incorrect responses can aid learning since they contribute to the development of a schema. Although Schmidt believes his theory can explain more about learning motor skills than Adams's theory, he also recognizes a number of limitations in his own theory (see Schmidt, 1988).

A Comparison of Motor Skill Learning and Observational Learning Theories

While observational learning theory (Bandura, 1986) and traditional motor learning theories (Adams, 1971, Schmidt, 1975) have not been intertwined, it seems reasonable to draw from both theoretical camps to explain how we acquire skills. Essentially, observational learning theory suggests that from observing others perform, we form a cognitive representation that both initiates our subsequent responses and serves as a reference to determine the correctness of these responses. In opposition to this notion, motor learning theories suggest that error information after action (knowledge of results) is the primary variable affecting learning and suggests that two memory mechanisms are essential in the learning process. Thus a primary difference in these two approaches to learning is the distinction between recall memory (initiation of action) and recognition memory (standard of correctness) in motor learning theories and no differentiation of these memory states in observational learning theory. The lack of such a theoretical distinction is indeed surprising, considering that Bandura, in some of his own work (e.g., Carroll & Bandura, 1982, 1985, 1987, 1990), has empirically attempted to distinguish these two processes. From a theoretical and practical standpoint, it is important to determine if individuals can indeed develop recognition memory from demonstrations. Adams's (1971) original notions suggest that proprioceptive feedback would be necessary to develop the perceptual trace, an information source that is obviously missing if we merely observe another individual. However, we can cite many practical examples of individuals who can clearly distinguish errors in other individuals, even though their own level of performance may be quite minimal. Application of this idea to industrial as well as educational and sport settings suggests that supervisors of manual skills, teachers, or any individuals who evaluate the movement patterns of other individuals such as judges and referees need to be able to detect appropriate responses in others, whether or not they are actually required to execute those responses themselves. Thus an issue that could add theoretically to Bandura's notions would be the separation of recall and recognition within the observational learning paradigm.

A general approach for examining the recall recognition issue within the observational learning paradigm would be to vary the strength of the cognitive representation induced by modeling. This could be done, for example, by systematically varying the number of demonstrations. Recall memory could be assessed by measuring spatial and temporal errors during acquisition, immediate, and delayed retention periods. Recognition could also be assessed during these same experimental periods but appropriate recognition measures would need to be developed. Carroll and Bandura (1990) assessed recognition memory for spatial components of movements by showing subjects a series of still photographs and asking them to place these in the correct order as previously demonstrated. While this type of recognition does provide some information, it does not reveal anything about recognition for temporal aspects of movements. An analogy could be the comparison of photographs of identical twins. While it may be difficult to differentiate these individuals from still photographs, the comparison might become easier if the subjects were asked to walk or run. Thus an important development in this area is the creation of appropriate measures to assess recognition and recall.

Variables That Influence the Acquisition and Retention of Motor Skills Within the Observational Learning Paradigm

When subjects are provided with a demonstration, there are numerous variables that may influence the subsequent performance levels of observers. The presentation of auditory or visual cues in the demonstration, the skill level of the demonstrator, the type of task, and the rehearsal strategies are all variables that can influence the acquisition and retention of motor skills.

Augmented Information

Augmented information, although typically thought of as feedback, can be any source that provides information to the learner (Newell, Morris & Scully, 1985). Thus a logical question is what information in addition to the visual stimulus of a demonstration may be useful for skill acquisition and performance. For example, what is the role of other mo-

dalities such as audition in modeling, and does the provision of verbal cues along with demonstrations enhance skill learning?

Although use of the visual modality when presenting demonstrations is typically presumed, it may also be possible to learn from the auditory modality. This notion was clearly documented in an experiment by Newell (1976) that examined subjects' ability to develop recognition memory for auditory demonstrations in the absence of movement practice. Increasing the number of auditory demonstrations led to development of better recognition memory for auditorily presented ballistic movements despite the absence of physical practice. This notion is one in need of replication as well as extension to more complex movement skills.

Doody, Bird, and Ross (1985) examined the role of two demonstration modalities by studying the effect of auditory, visual, and auditory-plus-visual modeling on the acquisition and retention of a timing skill. Examination of acquisition data indicated that the combination of auditory and visual demonstrations produced better performance than either visual demonstrations or control conditions without demonstrations. The superior performance by all groups during retention led the authors to conclude that demonstrations were more effective for learning than physical practice with knowledge of results. Caution must, however, accompany such an interpretation. All subjects in the experiment received knowledge of results during the acquisition phase. Thus the superior performance of the demonstrations groups was due to a combination of modeling and physical practice with knowledge of results, not modeling alone. In addition, the physical-practice-with-KR control group had only 10 task exposures during the acquisition phase, whereas the modeling groups had a total of 63 task exposures.

A subsequent experiment in our laboratory (McCullagh & Little, 1989) addressed the same issue but attempted to determine the potency of demonstrations in the absence of knowledge of results. Subjects practiced a timing skill interspersed with either visual, auditory, or visual-plus-auditory demonstrations. The control group received the same number of task exposures but received knowledge of results on half their trials. In opposition to the Doody et al. experiment, we found knowledge of results to be superior to modeling during immediate transfer. The contradiction in these two studies points to the necessity of assessing modeling effects independent of other potent performance modifiers.

Both of these experiments, as well as the one previously discussed by Newell, point to the strong role of auditory models in skill learning. At least for the types of timing tasks employed, visual demonstrations, although inherently favored, may not be the optimum model for all tasks. Perhaps the modality of presentation interacts with the type of task to be learned. Perhaps visual information is superior to auditory information if the task requires positional or spatial components (Newell, 1976, Experiment 4), whereas audition may be a more important modality for timing tasks.

These issues have not yet been clearly addressed in the modeling literature.

Besides providing demonstrations in different modalities, it may be possible to augment a demonstration with verbal information. A number of sources immediately come to mind. In addition to the visual demonstration, verbal cues could be provided to accentuate important task elements. Instead of providing attention-directing cues during the demonstration, the verbal information could be provided after the demonstration and could be in the form of knowledge of results about the demonstrator's performance. Finally, verbal information could relate to what the models should do to modify their performance as opposed to telling them what they did in their previous performance attempt. While Bandura (1986) has noted the potential importance of the verbal directing cues during demonstrations, only limited research has examined these issues.

In examining the role of verbal directing cues, Roach and Burwitz (1986) assessed both the form and accuracy of cricket batting and found that verbal cues in conjunction with modeling led to better performance than either modeling alone or a control condition. This experiment was not reported in sufficient detail to determine the exact nature of the verbal directing cues, and subsequent research is needed to determine the potency and importance of this variable. Determination of relevant cues is an important issue to be addressed here and a great deal of research will need to be generated to determine exactly what observers derive from moving demonstrations.

An initial experiment examining the role of KR in the observational learning paradigm was conducted by Adams (1986), who through his closed-loop theory was responsible for generating copious amounts of research on knowledge of results. He recognized, however, that learning theories had emphasized knowledge of results at the expense of other paradigms and combined observational learning and knowledge of results within one paradigm. Adams proposed that observational learning could be enhanced if subjects viewing a model also received the model's KR. It was his contention that subjects would become actively, instead of passively, involved in the learning process, and this would lead to higher performance levels. To empirically test this notion, subjects either viewed a model learning a skill and received that model's KR or viewed a model learning the skill but did not receive the model's KR, or physically practiced the skill themselves and received their own KR. The results produced slight advantages for some of the movement sequences of subjects who viewed a model and also received the model's KR over the other two groups.

While Adams's research posed some interesting questions, it also left many issues unanswered. It may have been interesting to examine retention of the skill over a longer period of time to determine whether the effects were relatively stable. Moreover, the lack of a correct model condition in the experiment did not allow the determination of whether correct displays by a skilled model would pro-

duce a better cognitive representation and thus enhanced performance to a greater degree than a learning model condition.

We tested this notion (McCullagh & Caird, 1990) and additionally were concerned about the ability of demonstration subjects to learn without ever receiving knowledge of results about their own movements. Therefore, demonstration subjects either viewed a correct model, a learning model along with the model's KR, or a learning model with no model KR. The control group practiced and received KR about their own movements. Superior performance by any of the demonstration groups would call into question the long-held view that knowledge of results is the most potent variable for learning, since only the practice control group received KR about their own movements. The experiment indicated that subjects who viewed a learning model and were privy to the model's knowledge of results performed as well as subjects who physically practiced and received KR. This finding generalized across acquisition, immediate and delayed retention, as well as transfer to a new task. Therefore, the view that KR about one's own movements is the most critical variable for learning could be called into question by this finding, since subjects in the modeling conditions never received KR about their own movements! The generalizability of these findings beyond timing components to more complex movements and spatial components awaits empirical test.

Further examination of the use of a model's KR by an observer was conducted by Weir and Leavitt (1990). Using a dart-throwing task, they combined presence or absence of model KR with either a high- or low-skilled model. They found no main effects on performance for either variable. First trial analyses produced a significant interaction of these variables, indicating that subjects viewing a skilled model also needed to receive the model's KR to ensure good performance. Unfortunately there were no reported increases in performance over the 60 practice trials with KR. Thus one could argue that the task employed or the dependent variable assessed (accuracy) were rather insensitive to any changes for the time period assessed. If a task is impervious to the rather strong impact of KR and practice, then examining other variables may be futile.

While research has begun to answer issues related to the role of augmented information in modeling, there are numerous issues still in need of research, including:

1. Does the modality of demonstration (e.g., visual versus auditory) interact with the type of task to be learned (e.g., timing versus spatial)?
2. What is the role of verbal directing cues and toward what movement aspects should a learner's attention be directed?
3. If the importance of KR within the observational learning paradigm can be clearly established, will the laws of KR that have already been derived in the motor skill literature be applicable to vicariously experiencing the KR?

Model Skill Level

A primary concern when providing demonstrations is the skill level of the model. While it may be intuitively appealing to assume that a skilled demonstrator who provides a correct demonstration would help to develop the most accurate cognitive representation, an examination of the literature does not necessarily validate this notion.

Martens, Burwitz, and Zuckerman (1976) tested the idea that subjects would learn more by watching someone learn a skill than by observing either a correct or incorrect model. It was hypothesized that observers would be better able to discriminate pertinent information in the learning condition as opposed to identical repetitions by a correct model. Results from three experiments failed to clearly support this hypothesis. Observing a correct or learning model produced initial performance increments over incorrect or control conditions on a skill with rather low cognitive demands, but these effects were relatively short-lived. On a more cognitive task, it was clear that subjects were adapting the strategies displayed by correct models, suggesting that it is best to show learners a model demonstrating the correct movement form or strategy if this is an important component to be learned.

An early experiment by Landers and Landers (1973) examined the role of skilled and unskilled model outcomes in combination with model type. This commonly cited experiment found a rather dramatic interaction between the model's skill level and model type. Subjects performed well after viewing a skilled teacher but rather poorly after viewing an unskilled teacher. The exact opposite results were found for peer models. Performance was superior in the unskilled as opposed to skilled peer condition. Recently, Lirgg and Feltz (1991) questioned the generalizability of these findings, suggesting that "using familiar models may have created idiosyncratic results." They, therefore, replicated the teacher/peer and skilled/unskilled conditions but used unfamiliar models. Additionally they assessed form and not merely outcome performance. Contrary to the Landers and Landers experiment, Lirgg and Feltz found a significant main effect for model skill level but no skill by model type of interaction. The effects for outcome paralleled the effects found for form. Viewing a skilled model led to better performance than did viewing an unskilled model, regardless of whether the model was a teacher or a peer. A primary difference in this replication attempt was the familiarity of the model. Whereas Landers and Landers used live familiar models, the present experiment involved unfamiliar filmed models. Thus the stability of either finding requires additional research that clearly examines the familiarity issue as well as the issue of filmed versus live models.

While intuitively it may seem better to use a skilled model over an unskilled model, the results from the Adams (1986) as well as the McCullagh and Caird (1990) papers reported in the previous discussion question this notion. In both these latter experiments, however, the unskilled models were individuals who were attempting to learn the skill and thus improved their own performance over time. In the Landers and Landers experiment, the model demonstrated the same poor performance repeatedly. Recently Lee and White (1990) developed the notion of learning models further, arguing on two counts as to why observing an unskilled model may be an appropriate learning technique. First, agreeing with Adams (1986), they suggested that if the subject views an unskilled model and also receives that subject's KR, the subject can become actively involved in the problem-solving process, which should lead to better learning. Second, while some might argue that learning is impaired if errors are made during acquisitions, others suggest that this is not the case (Schmidt, 1975).

Thus Lee and White attempted to replicate Adams's findings using a different task. In addition, they wanted to examine contextual interference effects within the observational learning paradigm. Contextual interference deals with performance and learning differences attributable to blocked and random practice schedules. Although observational learning effects were achieved, the model's practice schedule did not impact on the observer's performance levels. The authors concluded that observational learning was robust enough to overcome the deficiencies typically attributable to blocked practice and additionally concluded that acquisition was facilitated by observing a model. This last conclusion perhaps needs some additional consideration beyond that provided by the authors. Perhaps the observers performed well because the KR provided a goal to be achieved. Since only outcome was measured and not movement form, it may be that observers were motivated to outperform the models. Of course, an additional control group that just received outcome information would be needed to assess this motivational component of modeling, and a retention test should also be included to examine if differential learning occurred.

In a subsequent experiment, Pollock and Lee (1992) further pursued the influence of model skill level on motor performance. Observers watched either a skilled or unskilled model perform a computer game. Results indicated no effect for the type of model observed, although both conditions produced better performance than learning the task with knowledge of results. It should be noted that modeling groups received demonstrations as well as KR about their own performances and perhaps the same motivational argument expressed earlier could apply here as well.

In examining model skill level, Weir and Leavitt (1990) made some interesting arguments about different information conveyed by skilled and unskilled models. While they note that previous studies had purportedly manipulated the model's skill level (e.g., Landers & Landers, 1973; Martens, Burwitz, & Zuckerman, 1976), they argue that all models were really skilled at the task but feigned low skill levels in the appropriate experimental conditions. Weir and Leavitt proposed that demonstrators were possibly executing the same movement patterns in both skilled and unskilled conditions and only altered the movement outcome. While this is indeed a valid criticism, it would seem essential that movement patterns would somehow need to be assessed to validate this concern empirically. Thus form scores of both the model and the learner would need to be compared. Unfortunately Weir and Leavitt made no attempt to do this. They did, however, make some improvements on previous research by incorporating additional control groups to balance for task exposures and also examined initial trial performance to eliminate the confound of experimental conditions on practice. Subjects either viewed a skilled or unskilled model and either received or did not receive the model's KR. Analysis of first trial performance indicated that model skill level interacted with model KR. For viewing an unskilled model, receiving the model's KR did not affect performance. However, subjects viewing a skilled model needed the model's KR to perform as accurately as the unskilled model groups. Analysis of the first block of trials upheld the skill level but not the model KR effect. Subjects performed better after viewing an unskilled model than after viewing a skilled model. Although this experiment points out some interesting issues, its primary limitation seems to be the lack of improvement for any groups with practice. This may point either to the rather easy nature of the task, which allowed individuals to reach a high level of performance immediately, or perhaps to the difficult nature of the task, which precluded individuals from gaining rapid improvements. Also, since form was not assessed, one of the major purposes of the study, relating to movement patterns exhibited by skilled and unskilled models, could not be addressed. Some issues that need to be addressed relative to model skill level include:

1. Model skill level warrants further investigation as an important modeling variable as well as in terms of its interaction with feedback to the model.
2. In examining model skill level, it may be important to actually employ skilled and unskilled models so movement patterns can be allowed to vary. However, it would thus seem important to attempt to assess these patterns in the observer's subsequent movements.

Cognitive Task Elements

What do we learn from watching a demonstration? An experiment cited in the previous part of this chapter (Martens et al., 1976) suggests that strategies or cognitive task components are learned, as opposed to motor task components. This cognitive-versus-motor-component distinction is one that has been made in the mental imagery literature (Feltz & Landers, 1983; Ryan & Simons, 1981, 1983). The research clearly suggests that imagery is best suited for tasks that are high in cognitive as opposed to motor demands. Although to date researchers have not empirically verified a correspondence between imagery and modeling, suggestions have been made that the processes may be similar (Druckman & Swets, 1988; Feltz & Landers, 1983; Housner, 1984; Ryan & Simons, 1983). Within the observational learning paradigm, one receives a demonstration, encodes

and rehearses this information, and then produces a response. Within the imagery paradigm, one thinks about what is to be performed, rehearses the encoded information, and then produces a response. If modeling can be viewed as a form of covert rehearsal that primarily influences performance due to symbolical coding and subsequent rehearsal, and these internal representations serve as the internal standard for response production, then it may seem reasonable that both modeling and imagery are similar.

Housner (1984a, 1984b) has provided some data that speak to the role of imagery in conjunction with modeling. He hypothesized that imaginal coding strategies induced by modeling were similar to imagery-coding strategies and thus suggested that individuals with high imaging ability should benefit more from modeling than people with low imaging ability. Results suggested that free-recall performance was affected by imaging ability, whereas serial recall was not. Housner relied on Paivio's (1971) work to interpret these findings, suggesting that visual imagery may be important for recognition or free recall whereas verbal processes may be more important for tasks that require temporal ordering. Preliminary evidence from one of our experiments examining developmental issues (McCullagh, Stiehl, & Weiss, 1990) lends credibility to this interpretation.

Modeling has been combined with the imagery paradigm on a limited basis. Hall and Erffmyer (1983) compared an imagery and relaxation group to a group that received imagery, relaxation, and modeling. For basketball foul shooting they observed pronounced performance improvements for the group that received modeling in addition to other treatments.

To date, the cognitive-motor distinction has not received direct empirical testing in the literature. At least two approaches could be viable research directions:

1. A direct test of the cognitive motor hypothesis within the observational learning paradigm is needed.
2. If indeed modeling is beneficial for cognitive task components, then it may be that task strategies are learned from demonstrations (Feltz, 1982; McCullagh, 1987). Thus more than outcome needs to be assessed if these subtleties are to be observed.

Encoding and Rehearsal Strategies

Once learners have observed a demonstration, they must maintain this information in memory if they desire to approximate the same response. Both how the information is coded initially, as well as how the information is rehearsed, will affect memory representation. In this section, four strategies will be discussed.

Verbalizing. Bandura and Jeffrey (1973) attempted to assess the role of symbolic coding and rehearsal processes by assigning either numeric or letter codes to movements. They found that allowing subjects to verbally rehearse these codes led to better retention than when rehearsal was not allowed.

Weiss (1983) examined the role of verbal guidance in observational learning by either prompting or not allowing children to verbalize concurrently a series of motor skills during execution after watching demonstrations or receiving verbal instructions. She found no performance effects for this procedure but found that it did interact with the type of modeling that children received. Verbally guiding movements seemed only to help performance if children had received verbal instructions while watching the demonstrations. If no verbal cues were provided during observation, then asking children to verbalize did not aid performance.

In a subsequent experiment, Weiss and Klint (1987) further investigated the role of modeling and verbal rehearsal in children's motor skill performance. Subjects either viewed a demonstration with concurrent verbal labels or received verbalizations with no demonstrations. After this initial task exposure, subjects either verbally rehearsed the task sequence or did not. Results indicated that verbal rehearsal led to better reproduction than no verbal rehearsal.

Both of the Weiss studies focused on whether subjects could reproduce movements in the same order or sequence as the model. However, another important aspect of movements is the quality or form of movement. The experiment by Weiss and Klint (1987) found that serial recall of movements was facilitated by verbal rehearsal. McCullagh, Stiehl, and Weiss (1990) extended this finding by assessing the importance of verbal rehearsal on both sequencing and form. In this experiment no verbal rehearsal effects were found. However, the type of information presented prior to action did impact on form and sequencing differentially. Children who viewed a model along with verbal cues reproduced the qualitative or formal aspects of movement better than children who received verbal explanations only. In contrast, verbal instructions without the advantage of visual demonstrations were superior for sequencing or serial reproduction of movements. These results suggest that differential coding and rehearsal mechanisms may be in operation for the quantitative and qualitative aspects of performance.

Imaging. If observing motor skills results in some cognitive representation, then it should be possible to rehearse the skill through imagery without physical practice. Within the imagery literature, subjects are typically required to rehearse without the advantage of an external stimulus. As previously mentioned, only a limited number of studies have used a demonstration before imagery (e.g., Hall & Erffmeyer 1983). It may be that the benefits of modeling can be enhanced by inducing imaginal rehearsal. Hall and Erffmeyer examined this issue with basketball players. Although they labeled their experimental manipulations VMBR (Visuo-Motor Behavior Rehearsal) and relaxation, they really had two visualization groups. One received an external modeling stimulus to induce the imagery process, whereas the other group visualized without the modeling stimulus. The results clearly indicated an improvement for the group that received modeling over the group that merely visualized.

Theoretical approaches to imagery have suggested various ways in which information is stored in memory. Lang (1979) suggests that we store propositional networks that contain abstract forms of relationships among concepts. For motor skills, it is not clear exactly what these relationships are. Paivio (1971) and Finke (1986) suggest alternatively that information is stored in either verbal or visual codes. Verbal codes are thought to represent auditory information and the visual codes store spatial information. This idea parallels Bandura's (1986) notions that information from demonstrations is symbolically transferred into images or verbal symbols that guide action, and these representations are especially important during the early stages of learning. However, Bandura also seems to be in agreement with Lange's notions, since he contends that "imaginal representations are abstractions of events, rather than simply mental pictures of past observances" (p. 56). Since the motor skill imagery literature clearly indicates that cognitive as opposed to motor skills benefit from the imagery process (Feltz & Lander, 1983; Ryan & Simons, 1981; 1983), then it may be profitable to use modeling in situations where cognitive components of the skill can be emphasized.

Organizational Strategies. How the demonstration is initially presented to subjects may have an important impact on how they encode and subsequently rehearse the information. For example, how often a demonstration should be given and when in the learning sequence it should be introduced have received scant attention, either empirically or theoretically. A number of issues could be addressed here. For example, it may be best to view a demonstration before attempting to learn a new skill, or it may be best to physically practice the skill and then provide demonstrations. By employing such a sequence, it could be argued that the learner would have a better idea of what aspects of the skill are important. Landers (1975) examined this question by providing learners with demonstrations before, or midway, or both before and midway (interspersed) through a series of physical practice trials. Results indicated that the two groups receiving demonstrations before they physically executed trials initially performed better than the group receiving demonstrations midway through practice. The interspersed group also maintained its superiority over the midway-only group on the trial block immediately following midway demonstrations. An interesting addition to this experiment would have been a retention phase to determine whether the temporal spacing of demonstrations had any long-term performance effects, and replication of the experiment using a variety of tasks is warranted before generalizations regarding spacing can be made.

Another way to organize the scheduling of demonstrations is to provide a variety of demonstrations as opposed to repeating the same demonstration. The hypothesis that variability of practice will lead to better performance than constant practice stems from Schmidt's (1975) schema theory.

Bird and Rikli (1983) extended this notion to the observational learning paradigm by comparing variable and constant modeling and physical practice. Surprisingly they found that subjects performed as well under variable demonstration as under constant physical practice, despite the fact that they had not overtly practiced the skill.

Physical Practice. A final and extensively used method for rehearsing information after demonstrations is through the use of physical practice, which Bandura (1986) has recognized as an important and perhaps necessary procedure, especially in the case of difficult skills. A few research studies have attempted to determine the potency of demonstrations and physical practice.

Bird, Ross, and Laguna (1983) systematically manipulated the ratio of demonstrations and physical practice during the acquisition phase for subjects learning a timing response. Seven experimental groups were formed, and subjects received either 100% physical practice, 100% demonstrations, or a combination of physical practice and demonstrations. Skill retention was superior for those subjects who spent a greater proportion of their time observing as opposed to physically practicing with KR. Performance, however, was poor for subjects who spent all of their time observing. Thus some amount of practice with KR was needed to form an accurate cognitive representation. Future research will need to determine the importance of relative and absolute numbers of demonstrations in combination with KR and without KR to determine the strength of demonstrations in the learning process.

Carroll and Bandura (1982) examined the importance of physical practice or motor rehearsal on both the development of a cognitive representation and reproduction accuracy of subjects learning a sequence of hand movements. They found that motor rehearsal enhanced subjects' cognitive representation as measured by a recognition test, and also enhanced the subjects' ability to reproduce the response pattern accurately. Of course most experiments have subjects physically execute demonstrated movements over a series of trials. Thus subjects are actually physically practicing and it is difficult to determine the potency of demonstrations. In the absence of physical practice, it is thus necessary to assess performance through nonovert means such as recognition tests or to assess performance on the first physical execution trial if the concern is to determine how much can be learned from demonstrations in the absence of physical practice.

This section has highlighted a number of important issues to be considered in the encoding and rehearsal of movements after demonstrations. Research questions in need of further investigation include:

1. Do verbally induced coding and rehearsal strategies differentially affect the qualitative and quantitative aspects of movements?
2. How effective is mental imagery in reinforcing the cognitive representations induced by modeling?

3. What organizational strategies can enhance the scheduling of demonstrations?
4. Is there some optimum relative or absolute ratio of demonstrations that can enhance their effectiveness?

The Assessment of Performance

Within Bandura's original formulation of modeling, very little consideration was given to motor reproduction or the actual assessment of the skill. Since the theory was primarily designed for the acquisition of social behaviors, many of the response categories that were assessed were dichotomous (i.e., the behavior was either exhibited or it was not). However, when assessing motor performance, we are not only interested in whether an attempt at enactment was made, we are also interested in the quality of the movements. Three different response issues will be discussed.

Outcome Versus Process or Quality. When providing learners with a demonstration, at least two important aspects of the skill to be learned can be conveyed. First, the observer can view the outcome of the skill or the end goal that is to be achieved. Second, the observer can learn the movement pattern or process that can be used to achieve the desired outcome. Most investigations have determined the potency of modeling effects by assessing the movement outcome as opposed to measuring whether the learner exhibits the same movement form as the model. Recently, however, a few studies have attempted to assess movement form components as well (Carroll & Bandura, 1982; 1985; 1987; 1990; Feltz, 1982; Little & McCullagh, 1989; McCullagh, 1987).

In examining age differences in modeling, Feltz (1982) assessed movement form (as rated by judges) and movement outcome for subjects learning a balance task. Her findings indicated that form was a better indication of modeling effects than movement outcome. McCullagh (1987), using the same task and assessing both performance measures, found that no demonstration-control-group subjects could reach the same level of performance outcome as demonstration-group subjects, without exhibiting the desired form. Early evidence by Martens et al. (1976) supported this same notion. These studies point to the importance of assessing both movement outcome and movement form, since modeling may have differential effects on these performance components. While judging how closely a learner approximates a model's form is one way to assess form, it is also possible to assess numerous movement parameters through the use of a two-or three-dimensional kinematic analysis (i.e., displacement velocity and acceleration profiles). Relatively few studies have used such an approach.

Southard and Higgins (1987) investigated the role of demonstrations and physical practice in altering the form of a racquetball serve. They found that subjects receiving physical practice or subjects receiving a combination of demonstrations and practice changed their limb configurations from the first to fifth test day, whereas subjects receiving demonstrations without the benefit of practice were no better than control subjects in successfully altering their movements. The authors concluded that providing a demonstration was not sufficient for changing constrained movement patterns, whereas practice allowed subjects to adopt the appropriate kinematic characteristics. An interesting addition to this experiment would have been the assessment of outcome or accuracy. Contrary to this finding, Whiting, Bijard, and denBrinker (1987) found enhanced performance on a ski simulation task for subjects that viewed demonstrations over no-demonstration physical practice subjects. The model's performance was videotaped, and the frequency, amplitude, and fluency of the movements were recorded using a Selspot motion analysis system. The results indicated that none of the subjects reached the same performance level as the model but that demonstration-group subjects were significantly more fluent and produced more consistent movements than the physical practice subjects. The limited findings generated thus far indicate the need to assess both outcome and form when assessing modeling effects.

Recall and Recognition. Earlier in this chapter a comparison was made between motor learning theories (Adams, 1971; Schmidt, 1975) and Bandura's notions. As discussed earlier, one obvious difference in the approaches is the distinction between recall and recognition. Both Adams and Schmidt posit two separate memory states: one that produces the movement (recall) and one that evaluates the outcome (recognition). Bandura (1986), on the other hand, suggests that the cognitive representation generated by observing a model "provides the internal model for response production and the standard for response correction" (p. 64). Thus it appears that Bandura assumes a common mechanism for recall and recognition. While motor learning researchers have for years attempted experimentally to differentiate recall and recognition, observational learning researchers have not pursued this issue fervently, although a review of the literature suggests that modeling may differentially affect these processes. Surprisingly, in a series of experiments, Carroll and Bandura (1982; 1985; 1987; 1990) have consistently assessed the effects of modeling on recall and recognition, although they have not theoretically proclaimed a need to differentiate these memory mechanisms.

In their 1987 study, Carroll and Bandura examined the role of visual guidance in the reproduction of a motor skill sequence. They assessed recall through reproduction accuracy of a nine-component wrist-arm paddle motion. Recognition was assessed by showing subjects photographs of correct and incorrect components of the movement and requiring them to select the correct components. In addition, subjects were asked to arrange the components in order. The experimental manipulation of whether subjects concurrently or separately matched their movements with the model and also whether they could visually monitor their own movements did have an effect on reproduction accu-

racy but not on recognition measures. Also, the correlations between recognition measures and reproduction, although significant ($r = .34$ to $.64$), were not extremely high, suggesting that perhaps recall and recognition did not develop at the same rate.

In a subsequent experiment using the same task, Carroll and Bandura (1990) examined the role of repetitions and verbal coding on both recognition and recall, and found an interaction between verbal coding and repetitions. Simultaneously providing verbal cues to subjects while they watched a demonstration was beneficial for subjects who received eight demonstrations but was not beneficial for subjects who only received two demonstrations. In this experiment the modeling manipulations seemed to have a similar effect on recall and recognition.

An early experiment by Newell (1976) was primarily interested in determining the independence of recall and recognition but used an observational learning paradigm utilizing an auditory stimulus to test whether the two states developed independently. The results indicated that increasing the number of auditory demonstrations increased recognition memory, but since demonstration subjects were also accurate in their first movement reproduction, it was concluded that providing demonstration also enhanced recall. With direct empirical testing of the effects of demonstrations on recall and recognition, it may become necessary to modify Bandura's original notions, if independence of these mechanisms within the observational learning setting can be shown.

If it can be clearly documented that demonstrations can enhance recognition memory, even though recall or reproduction does not improve, the finding would have clear implications for practitioners as well. Following from this argument, perhaps demonstrations could serve a useful function for motor skill teachers who must be able to recognize correct and incorrect performances in learners. Furthermore, by providing learners with correct demonstrations and then with videotapes of their own performances as opposed to the performances of others, perhaps recognition of one's own errors could be enhanced (McCullagh, Burch, & Siegel, 1990). Within the observational learning paradigm, subjects are typically required to perform this conception-matching process based on their memory of the correct demonstration as well as memory for the movements they have performed. Through enhanced technology of split-screen techniques, this conception-matching process can be explored.

Learning Versus Performance. Although Bandura made a distinction between learning and performance in his early writings, few motor behavior studies have attempted to empirically separate the effects of demonstrations on learning and performance, and in fact many studies use the terms interchangeably and therefore incorrectly.

This is especially true in studies examining social-psychological effects of modeling wherein performance is almost exclusively measured and the long-term effects of variables are not assessed. Schmidt (1988) has clearly outlined the procedures for using transfer designs to assess whether the effects of variables are relatively transient (performance variables) or more permanent (learning variables). To make this distinction empirically, it is necessary to manipulate the independent variables during an initial acquisition phase, followed by performance under a common level of the independent variable (usually the absence of the manipulation during the transfer phase). The transfer phase, which should occur after the independent variable has had time to dissipate, occurs anywhere from a few minutes to days after the acquisition phase.

A few studies have attempted to make this learning-versus-performance distinction. McCullagh (1986; 1987) examined the influence of model status and model similarity on both performance and learning. Supporting previous investigations (Gould & Weiss, 1981; Landers & Landers, 1973), model characteristics were found to influence performance. However, both experiments found the effects of modeling to be rather short-lived, since group differences did not maintain themselves through the transfer phase.

Ross, Bird, Doody, and Zoeller (1985) assessed both immediate and delayed retention using a transfer design after manipulating physical practice and modeling with videotape feedback during acquisition. While all experimental groups performed similarly during acquisition, differential group effects were found during the transfer phase suggesting differential learning. In a subsequent experiment Doody, Bird, and Ross (1985) found learning differences to be a function of modeling.

Concerns for future research include:

1. It is important that both form and accuracy or outcome of movements be assessed, since various modeling manipulations may differentially affect those two performance measures.
2. It is important to determine empirically if recall and recognition are differentially affected by modeling.
3. Learning, in addition to performance, needs to be assessed in modeling studies, regardless of whether learning, developmental, or social psychological variables are being studied. It must be determined whether modeling is indeed a potent performance modifier that has a relatively lasting effect on behavior.

Feedback

Research has clearly documented the potent role of feedback in motor skill learning. In fact, knowledge of results (KR) or error information after movement has been claimed to be the "most potent variable in learning" (Newell, 1981, p. 212). However, another way to provide subjects with error information in lieu of verbally announcing errors is to provide subjects with a videotape of their own performance. An early review by Rothstein and Arnold (1976) attempted to bridge the gap between research and practice and analyzed a rather extensive literature base that had examined the role of videotape feedback in motor skill learning. These authors concluded that certain variables (age, gender, type of skill, performance measure assessment) did not differentially affect what was learned from videotape feedback. However, they did find that the skill level of the learner, whether verbal cues were provided along with the videotape, and whether the study was of short or long duration did have an impact on the effectiveness of videotape.

In a series of experiments, Carroll and Bandura examined the role of visual monitoring of one's own movements on subsequent ability to reproduce accurately a nine-component sequence of hand movements with a paddle. In their first experiment (1982) they manipulated the time in the practice sequence when subjects would visually monitor their movements while performing. They found that visually monitoring movements that lay outside the learner's field of vision enhanced physical performance, but only after subjects had sufficient task exposures to develop an accurate cognitive representation. In a subsequent experiment (1985) they wanted to determine whether the timing of this visual feedback was important. They hypothesized that the conception-matching process would be enhanced if subjects could monitor their movements as they produced them as opposed to seeing a videotape replay shortly after movement completion or no visual feedback whatsoever. Half the subjects in each group physically practiced the skill during a short interval whereas half the subjects did not. Reproduction accuracy was clearly affected by both the timing of the feedback and whether or not subjects physically practiced the movements. Concurrent visual monitoring of movements and motor rehearsal (practice) clearly aided reproduction accuracy, and if subjects received delayed feedback, they were no more accurate than if no visual feedback was provided. In this experiment subjects in the delayed–visual feedback condition were not allowed to rehearse their movements cognitively or imaginally during the retention interval. The addition of such a rehearsal group could test the potency of imaginal rehearsal after demonstrations. An interesting finding was that the visual feedback or monitoring conditions did not differentially affect the development of the cognitive representation, at least as assessed by the recognition test, which required subjects to arrange still photographs that depicted the sequence of the movements. The authors interpreted this finding to suggest that the visual feedback may help subjects correct reproduction errors but is not helpful in detecting errors.

Carroll and Bandura (1987) further pursued the role of visual monitoring in a third experiment. The question of concern was whether performance was better if subjects watched a model and then performed, or whether subjects concurrently performed the skill with the model and whether they did or did not visually monitor their own movements. Reproduction accuracy results indicated that if subjects performed movements concurrently with the model (mirrored the model's actions) or visually monitored their own movements during reproduction, they could perform better than if they performed in the absence of either of those treatments. The experimental manipulations did not, however, affect recognition, since no group differences emerged on either of the recognition tests. Based on their experiments, the authors (Carroll & Bandura, 1990) argued that visual monitoring of movements is helpful, but only if subjects have received sufficient demonstrations to develop a reasonable cognitive presentation.

Recent research from our laboratory has attempted to examine the role of two types of feedback within the observational learning paradigm (McCullagh, Burch, & Siegel, 1990). In two experiments we manipulated whether subjects saw correct demonstrations, correct demonstrations alternated with videotape feedback of the subjects' previous performances, or only videotapes of the subjects' own previous performances. Additionally, we either gave subjects verbal cues highlighting important aspects of performance or we did not provide such prescriptive information. We found a strong role for the verbally presented information. Subjects who received this verbal information performed better than subjects who did not. We found that this variable interacted with our modeling conditions during an immediate retention phase. All subjects benefited from the verbal prescriptive information except those who received a combination of correct demonstrations and self-videos. Perhaps subjects who receive both demonstrations and video feedback focus attention on these two information sources and the additional verbal information is disregarded. Future research will need to address the role of these information sources in skill learning.

DEVELOPMENTAL ISSUES RELATED TO MODELING

THEORETICAL CONSIDERATIONS

Historically motor behavior researchers interested in developmental issues did not focus much of their attention on observational learning. While it is not immediately evident why there was a paucity of interest, the lack of developmental concerns in Bandura's original writings could have contributed to this complacency. In 1978, Yando, Seitz, and Zigler addressed the role of developmental issues in their two-factor theory of imitation. They incorporated issues discussed by both Piaget and Bandura to explain how children acquire behaviors from demonstrations. From their in-depth examination of children, 4, 7, 10, and 13 year of age, they found that the period from 4 to 7 years was a transitional phase characterized by marked increases in cognitive, perceptual, and motor organization. For example, they found that verbal control of motor functions became increasingly important during this stage, which would well influence the encoding of information within the observational learning paradigm.

Within Yando et al.'s two-factor theory, the cognitive-developmental factor addresses attention, memory, and coding capabilities, the use of rehearsal strategies, as well as the physical capabilities of the learner. The first factor addresses many of the issues within Bandura's attention, retention, and motor reproduction phases. The second factor of motivational orientation addresses the role of intrinsic and extrinsic incentives in the modeling process and thus parallels Bandura's fourth subprocess of motivation. In Bandura's most recent analysis of observational learning (Bandura, 1986), he has placed considerable emphasis on developmental factors. He argues that researchers can either adopt an age-based or a competency-based approach when examining modeling. He suggests that an age-based approach is useful if individuals within a given age group do not vary much on the variable of interest. However, he suggests that for many tasks, the variability within an age group may be so great that comparison with other age groups is only helpful if the comparison group is extremely discrepant in age. In lieu of this age-based approach, Bandura favors a competency-based approach, wherein the level of the desired skill is initially assessed and then subsequent changes are noted. This approach has not been used in the motor skill modeling literature, although such an approach could provide insight into the potency of modeling. For example, one could ask: Given the initial skill level or patterning of movement by an individual, how resistant to change is the established movement pattern by modeling manipulations? Consideration of this issue may prove a fruitful avenue for motor behavior researchers, if their objective is modification of skill through modeling procedures.

DEVELOPMENTAL FACTORS INFLUENCING MODELING

Cognitive and Memory Development

Gallagher and her associates (Gallagher, 1982, 1984; Gallagher & Hoffman, 1987; Gallagher & Thomas, 1984, 1986) have continually focused their research on cognitive and memory development, and have demonstrated age-related differences on a number of information-processing skills that are important for observational learning. For example, selective attention varies developmentally. Very young children progress from being overexclusive, thus using only a limited number of features from a display, to being overinclusive, wherein many features, including irrelevant ones, are attended to. One way to help children attend to relevant cues is through the use of verbal labels. However, in dealing with very young children, these verbal labels may need to be externally supplied since the children themselves do not generate these labels until approximately seven years of age.

Gallagher (1984) also discusses numerous developmental issues as they relate to rehearsal and organization. For example, very young children rehearse a series of items individually as opposed to chunking the information for rehearsal purposes. However, if instructed, young children can use the more sophisticated strategy to improve their recall. Testing this notion in the motor domain, Gallagher and Thomas (1984) found that 5- to 7-year-olds could perform as well as 11-year-olds who were forced to use the less sophisticated strategy. Extending this finding to the modeling domain would suggest that external rehearsal strategies imposed after demonstrations may be helpful, especially for young children, or that chunking components of a complicated skill during the demonstration phase may be useful.

A limited number of motor behavior researchers have examined age-related differences in modeling (Feltz, 1982; Thomas, Pierce & Ridsdale, 1977), and more recently some researchers have studied developmentally based differences in observational learning. Based on Yando et al.'s theory and on the verbal self-regulation literature (i.e., Zivin, 1979), Weiss (1983) assigned children of two age groups (4 years to 5 years 11 months and 7 years to 8 years 11 months) to a silent model (visual demonstration only) or verbal model (visual plus verbal explanation) with the task being a six-part motor skill obstacle course. Children were also asked or not asked to use verbal self-instruction to guide their motor performance through the skill sequence. Results revealed that older children performed equally well with either a verbal or silent model, and this was significantly better than the no-model group. The younger children, however, performed better with a verbal model than with silent or no models. Thus the verbal cues provided with the model demonstration appeared to facilitate the younger children's performance, perhaps by focusing their attention to task-relevant cues or helping them to remember the order of skills.

A subsequent study by Weiss and Klint (1987) further investigated the role of modeling and verbal rehearsal on motor skill performance. The task was a six-part motor skill sequence. Children comprising two age groups (5 years to 6 years 11 months and 8 years to 9 years 11 months) received additional instructions based on their random assignment to model type and verbal rehearsal conditions. In the verbal model condition, children viewed a model demonstrating the skill sequence while concurrently verbalizing a label for each skill component. In the no-model condition, subjects only received the aforementioned verbal explanation of the order in which the skills were to be executed. In the verbal rehearsal condition, subjects first repeated the names of the skills to be executed, then recited the sequence on their own before reproducing the task. In the no-verbal-rehearsal condition, children merely reproduced the task. Results revealed that children who comprised the two conditions that included verbal rehearsal performed better than those who did not practice verbal rehearsal. This was the case for both age groups leading the authors to conclude that "a visual model may not be a sufficient means of instruction" (Weiss & Klint, 1987, p. 240), at least for motor skill tasks or a sequence like the one used in that study. An interpretation of this finding is that the verbal rehearsal of the sequence prior to performance was critical for being able to reproduce the sequence of already learned skills in a predetermined order.

The two studies by Weiss focused on performance outcome measures or the sequencing of skills in a predetermined order. If one considers the quality-of-movement reproduction, however, interest is focused primarily on particular movement mechanics, strategies, or form. As discussed earlier, modeling may have a more profound impact on imparting information about movement form rather than outcome, and thus both movement components should be assessed.

A subsequent experiment by McCullagh, Stiehl, and Weiss (1990) extended previous findings by assessing both quantitative and qualitative aspects of movement. During acquisition trials, subjects received the model type and rehearsal manipulations as well as a feedback cue. During immediate transfer, these cues were removed. Thus children of two age groups (5 years to 6 years 6 months and 7 years 6 months to 9 years) received a model with concurrent verbal cues or verbal instructions only, and then either verbally rehearsed or did not. The results indicated that the model-type effectiveness depended on whether the quantitative or qualitative aspects of performance were considered. That is, subjects who observed a model, regardless of whether they practiced verbal rehearsal, had significantly higher form or quality scores than no-model groups. However, for recalling the sequencing of the skills, the no-model groups that received verbal explanations only were better than model groups that received concurrent verbal cues, regardless of verbal rehearsal. Thus the hypothesis that modeling groups would produce better qualitative performance than no-model groups was supported. Verbal explanations, however, were sufficient for reproducing the correct order of skills. These results suggest that differential coding or rehearsal mechanisms may be in operation for quantitative and qualitative aspects of performance and point to the importance of identifying the critical qualities of task requirements in order to ensure maximal motor performance.

Physical Characteristics

One of the major subprocesses in Bandura's formulation of modeling was motor reproduction. As previously mentioned, this phase was not very well developed in his earlier writings, at least in terms of application to qualitative movement behaviors. However, when discussing movement skills we are interested in physical reproduction, which will necessarily be related to the physical characteristics of the learner. Bandura (1986) illustrated this point nicely when he discussed the example of a young child who can adequately execute the individual components for driving a car but is too short to reach the controls. Bandura thus recognizes the importance of physical characteristics such as height, weight, and agility in learning physical skills.

Ulrich (1987) recently reviewed the developmental literature on motor skill development and highlighted two different approaches to assessing motor skills. The total body approach (Seefeldt & Haubenstricker, 1982) assumes that the relationship among body segments can be described by characterizing the total movement. The alternative approach (Halverson, 1983; Roberton, 1983) uses a component approach wherein each separate component (e.g., arm, leg, trunk) is described. The argument for using this approach rests on the notion that each segment does not necessarily develop or change in parallel. Depending on which approach is used, the description of children's motor skill behavior can be quite different. For example, using the total body approach, Seefeldt and Haubenstricker determined that 60% of 6-year-old boys and girls were able to perform 2 out of 8 skills with a mature pattern. Many boys and girls demonstrated mature running patterns, whereas girls demonstrated mature skipping and boys mature overhand throwing ability. Using the component approach led to markedly different results (Halverson, Roberton, & Langendorfer, 1982). Assessing a number of different skills, it was found that by age 13 only a few males and no females reached an advanced level of performance on all the components.

This contrast in findings provides us with important consideration for modeling research. If we are interested in assessing qualitative performance, we need to determine whether a total body approach, a component approach or perhaps some combination of both is best for describing the acquired action patterns of learners. As noted earlier, interest is often focused on the qualitative aspects of motor skill performance, but researchers are frequently at a loss as to the best means for behaviorally describing the temporal and spatial aspects of movement.

Another consideration illustrated by the above comparison is gender differences in motor skills. According to Ulrich (1987), the issue of gender differences has been addressed for over 50 years, with little resolve. Two meta-analyses have been conducted on gender difference in motor skills (Clark & Ewing, 1985; Thomas & French, 1985), indicating that in general males outperform females. The arguments continue as to whether these differences can be primarily attributed to anatomical or social influences. Although there is considerable overlap in skill ability between boys and girls during the childhood years, researchers examining developmental modeling effects should be sensitive to the physical characteristics of their learners.

Motivational Orientation

Yando et al. (1978) also discussed developmental issues as they relate to motivation. They noted the importance of both extrinsic and intrinsic motives in the modeling process. While neither aspect has received much attention in the modeling motor behavior literature, the idea that the need to demonstrate competency is a prime intrinsic motivator has been discussed at length (Harter, 1978; White, 1959). Weiss and Bredemeir (1983) demonstrated the potential for applying the competence-motivation idea to sport psychology and discussed developmental and gender difference in specific competence domains.

To date, the blending of competence motivation notions with developmental modeling issues has not occurred, although one previously discussed experiment has examined modeling issues in conjunction with motivational orientation (Little & McCullagh, 1989). A primary issue that could be addressed here is how modeling might impact on cognitive, social, and physical perceived competencies and in turn influence performance.

Knowledge Development

Differences in the ability to remember between children and adults has been attributed to a number of factors, and recently Chi (1981) has suggested that domain-related knowledge can significantly improve children's performance on a variety of memory tasks. Thomas, French, and Humphries (1986) have called for the application of this literature to motor behavior, and there may be logical extensions to the modeling literature as well. The work of Chi (1981) suggests that individuals develop three different types of knowledge. Declarative knowledge is factual knowledge. In a sport situation this knowledge is the number of players, their position, and the size of the field/court, for example. Procedural knowledge reveals the workings of the particular game or how to do things. Finally, strategic knowledge, which is more general in nature, can provide, for example, information on how to rehearse information in memory so it can be readily recalled.

The development of knowledge structures has been used to analyze expert/novice differences in a number of cognitive tasks, and the importance of cognitive abilities has recently been used to examine expert/novice differences in sport performance (Abernethy, 1989; Allard, Graham, & Paarsalu, 1980; Allard & Starkes, 1980; Deakin & Allard, 1991; Starkes & Deakin, 1984). To date, the application of knowledge structures to sport performance has received only limited attention (French & Thomas, 1987; McPherson & Thomas, 1989). It has been hypothesized that it is necessary to develop declarative knowledge before procedural knowledge (Chi & Rees, 1983). We are fully aware, however, that children often enter a sport environment with minimal factual knowledge about the game, and many of their errors can be attributed to this lack of knowledge. Thus French and Thomas (1987) attempted to determine the relationship between knowledge development, physical skill development, and expertise in 8- to 10-year-old and 11- to 12-year-old children. They found that both cognitive and motor skills were contributing factors in the development of basketball skills in children. However, these two skill components did not develop at the same rate. Children were able to acquire the cognitive components of skill and thus knew "what to do" before they acquired the motor reproduction skills to execute the appropriate movements. We already discussed the notion that modeling may be a potent information source for developing appropriate task strategies (e.g., Marten et al., 1976) and could perhaps be used as a training technique for acquiring the appropriate cognitive components of a task. This idea can be combined with the earlier discussion of recall and recognition. If learners can acquire information from demonstrations that can accurately be assessed through recognition, modeling could become a useful training technique in a number of practical sport situations. For example, judges, referees, and coaches must make instantaneous judgments about skills that have been executed by other individuals. Modeling techniques might be used to enhance their skills in this observational process.

SOCIAL PSYCHOLOGICAL ISSUES RELATED TO MODELING

THEORETICAL CONSIDERATIONS

One of the most prominent psychological theories in the literature to date is Bandura's (1977) theory of self-efficacy. According to Bandura, self-efficacy is situation-specific self-confidence and is related to a person's convictions that he or she can produce a desired outcome. According to this powerful theory of behavior change, self-efficacy will determine choice, effort, and persistence in an activity. Efficacy expectations are influenced by four sources of information: performance accomplishments, vicarious experiences, verbal persuasion, and emotional arousal. While one source (vicarious experience) is obviously related to modeling, the other sources could be enhanced through modeling techniques and will, therefore, be discussed briefly.

The most dependable source for increasing efficacy expectations is through performance accomplishments. The hypothesis here is that mastery attempts that are perceived as successful will raise efficacy, whereas attempts perceived as failures will lower efficacy. One variable that has received attention in the modeling literature and is related to performance accomplishments is participant modeling. Feltz, Landers, and Raeder (1979) compared modeling techniques to determine their influence on self-efficacy and performance. Subjects received either live demonstrations, video demonstrations, or participant-modeling techniques during the learning of a high-avoidance back dive task. The participant modeling condition involved a demonstration plus guided practice with the assistance of the model. The results revealed that the participant modeling condition led to higher efficacy and better performance than was achieved with the other conditions. Thus receiving physical guidance that allowed the subjects to accomplish the task led to higher efficacy than merely viewing another individual perform. It has been documented that in practical situations, coaches try to ensure that their athletes receive plenty of performance accomplishments through repeated drilling in order to ensure maximum efficacy (Gould, Hodge, Petersen, & Giannini, 1989). Another technique that has not received much attention in the motor performance literature is that of self-modeling, wherein individuals are shown videotapes of themselves approximat-

ing the skill in question. This technique has been referred to as self-modeling by Dowrick (1983), who uses the term to refer to situations in which subjects are shown performance attempts that approximate successes and incorrect responses are removed from the videotape through editing. Perhaps this term will need additional clarification in the motor skill literature if self-modeling is used to provide subjects with videotape feedback that shows correct as well as incorrect performance.

The second way to enhance efficacy is through vicarious experience of either watching or imagining another individual achieve the task. Thus observational learning or modeling is presumed to serve as a behavioral change strategy through its influence on efficacy and subsequently performance. Although not all modeling studies assess efficacy, it has been shown that various modeling techniques have led to increased efficacy and better performance and persistence at muscular endurance tasks (Gould & Weiss, 1981; Weinberg, Gould, Yukelson, & Jackson, 1981), gymnastic skills (McAuley, 1985), and diving performances (Feltz et al., 1979). It is hypothesized that vicarious experiences are not as strong a mediator of efficacy as performance accomplishments. However, if subjects are unfamiliar with the task and view a model who is similar to themselves or view multiple models of varying skill levels, then efficacy should be enhanced through vicarious experiences. Thus in situations in which physical practice is difficult, it may be appropriate to provide learners with vicarious experiences through modeling.

The third major source of efficacy expectations is verbal persuasion. Although we would typically think of this source as consisting of attempts by an individual such as a teacher or coach to convince another that they can accomplish a certain feat (Gould et al., 1989), verbal persuasion can also be combined with modeling techniques. For example, Gould and Weiss (1981) combined modeling and model talk procedures to examine the performance of subjects on a muscular endurance task. When performance was assessed, they found an interaction between model talk and model similarity. Subjects who perceived the model to be similar to themselves performed better if the model exhibited positive self-talk or no self-talk as opposed to negative or irrelevant self-talk. Future research may need to further define the limits of this variable by examining both what models do and say (Gould & Weiss, 1981).

The final source of efficacy in Bandura's theory is the influence of physiological states on efficacy. Bandura suggests that the individual's cognitive appraisal of their arousal states, for example, will lead to efficacy expectations. If an increase in arousal state is cognitively interpreted as readiness for performance, then efficacy expectations will increase. On the other hand, if an individual interprets these arousal increases as fear or anxiety, then efficacy will decrease. Few research studies (e.g., Feltz, Landers, & Raeder, 1979; McAuley, 1985) have attempted to determine the effects of differential modeling techniques on efficacy, anxiety, and performance.

While not all the sources of efficacy expectations in

Bandura's theory were designed to be modeling techniques, all could be combined with various modeling manipulations within the observational learning paradigm. The strong empirical evidence across numerous domains supporting the strength of efficacy as a behavioral change strategy warrants its measurement in modeling studies whether they are learning, developmental, or social-psychological in nature.

SOCIAL-PSYCHOLOGICAL CONSIDERATIONS IN MODELING

Motivational Orientation

Not a great deal of research has examined subject's pre-existing motivational orientation and then assessed the effects of differential modeling techniques. In 1985, Weiss, Bredemeier, and Shewchuk evaluated a motivation scale designed for the youth sport setting. From the previous work of Harter (1981), they developed an intrinsic/extrinsic scale with six subdomains for use in the youth sport setting. One of the subscales, mastery, differentiated children who prefer to figure out skill on their own (intrinsic) from those who prefer guidance from external sources (extrinsic). The importance of this dichotomy lies not only in the task the child may choose to attempt, but also in the manner the child may be best primed for instruction. Extending this idea to the modeling domain, Little and McCullagh (1989) reasoned that intrinsically motivated children would focus on their own movement performances while extrinsically motivated children would depend on external sources of information to judge their own performance. In teaching someone a new skill it could be hypothesized that focusing on knowledge of performance (form or process variables) would be best for children who are intrinsically motivated whereas focusing on knowledge of results (outcome) would be best for externally motivated children. To test this notion, children who were high in intrinsic or extrinsic motivation received observational learning training that was either form- or outcome-focused. The results provided limited support for these hypotheses but pointed to the importance of motivational orientation when considering modeling instructional techniques.

Model Characteristics

Within Bandura's theory, model characteristics were hypothesized to influence the attentional phase of observational learning. Thus it was presumed that a model of high status would command more attention than a low-status model and thus lead to greater learning. Although there have been few direct tests of this hypothesis, numerous studies have found performance differences dependent on model characteristics such as competence (Baron, 1970), prestige (Mausner, 1953), status level (Landers & Landers, 1973; McCullagh 1986), age (Bandura & Kapers, 1964), social power (Mischel & Grusec, 1966), similarity (Gould & Weiss, 1981; McCullagh, 1987), and skill level that was dis-

cussed earlier. In line with Bandura's predictions, an early study by Yussen and Levy (1975) attempted to directly measure visual attention after observing either a warm or neutral model and found that children paid more attention to a warm model than to a neutral one. Within the motor skill domain, McCullagh (1986, 1987) conducted two studies to examine the attention-model characteristic relationship. In the first experiment, subjects viewed a filmed model that was construed to be of either high or low status. However, half of the subjects were pre-cued regarding the status variable, whereas half viewed the demonstration and were then informed of model status (post-cued). The assumption was that subjects in the pre-cued condition could differentially focus their attention dependent on model status whereas the attentional phase would be over by the time post-cued subjects become aware of model status. The hypothesis based on Bandura's notions was that there should only be performance differences in the pre-cued conditions if model status exerts its prime influence on attention. The results indicated that subjects performed better after viewing a high- as opposed to low-status model, irrespective of the cueing manipulations, thus suggesting a lack of differential attention. The results of an incentive transfer phase further contradicted Bandura because no learning differences emerged.

A second experiment (McCullagh, 1987) attempted to extend this finding by manipulating model similarity and assessing both performance outcome and strategy. Initial performance differences were found to be dependent on model characteristics and performance strategy was influenced more by the modeling manipulation than performance outcome. These experiments thus question the influence of model characteristics on attention and further reinforce the importance of assessing more than outcome scores as well as learning in the modeling paradigm.

Coping Models

Coping models can be likened to the learning models discussed earlier, in that they are models who do not repeatedly display exemplary behaviors. Rather, coping models demonstrate the negative cognitions that may initially accompany performance and through repeated trials move toward demonstrating more positive thoughts and efficacy. Thus these models show a psychological progression of ability to cope with the demands of the task at hand. Schunk, Hanson, and Cox (1987) employed single or multiple coping models or mastery models to assist in the learning of mathematics. The mastery models demonstrated exemplary or errorless performance, while the coping models verbalized their fears but gradually improved over trials. Observers rated themselves as more similar to the coping models and also exhibited greater efficacy and performance than subjects who observed a mastery model. This finding provides support for the psychological aspects of modeling and parallels previously discussed findings on model skill level (e.g., McCullagh & Caird, 1990).

Although coping models have been used fairly extensively within a clinical or therapeutic setting (e.g., Kulik & Mahler, 1987; Thelan et al., 1979), the idea of employing coping modeling in sport, exercise, or athletic rehabilitation settings has received only limited attention (Weiss & Troxal, 1986; Wiese & Weiss, 1987; Flint, 1991). The logical extension of this work to the sport or motor skill domain suggests that coping models may be especially useful in high-fear situations or when the task to be learned is extremely difficult. Additional research will need to address this important variable.

Self-Modeling.

Dowrick and a number of other researchers (see Dowrick & Biggs, 1983; Dowrick, 1991) have been conducting research in the area of self-modeling for a number of years. Dowrick has defined self-modeling as "the behavioral change that results from the repeated observation of oneself on videotapes that show only desired target behavior" (Dowrick & Dove, 1980). Using such a definition would create different experimental conditions than were previously discussed in the "Feedback" part of this chapter. In those experiments that have used videotape of one's own movements, all, not just desirable actions, were shown to subjects (e.g., Carroll & Bandura, 1990; McCullagh, Burch, & Siegel, 1990). Dowrick would refer to this type of manipulation as unstructured video replay. Thus the primary difference between self-modeling and video replay is that errors are eliminated in self-modeling. The basis of using such a technique is that correct approximations will enhance self-esteem and subsequently lead to enhanced performance. Most of the research examining self-modeling issues has been done with small sample sizes in therapeutic settings dealing with various psychological treatments. In his review on self-modeling, Dowrick (1983) also makes some extension to the realm of physical skills, although empirical verification of the effectiveness of this technique is minimal. Theoretically it would seem important to determine whether or not individuals can learn from their own mistakes. Earlier discussion of motor learning theories suggests that there is some discrepancy on this issue. With the advent of less expensive video-editing technology, it is highly likely that the area of self-modeling will receive increased research interest in the future.

CONCLUDING REMARKS

The purpose of this chapter was to review research relevant to modeling and motor skills. While numerous issues were addressed and discussed, many received only brief attention or were overlooked and will require our dedication in the future. A couple of concerns that were only briefly addressed related to perception and practical issues. One topic that is of critical importance is what is perceived from a demonstration, especially since motor skill researchers are interested in how perception is translated to action. Newell, Morris, and Scully (1985) were highly critical of the observational learning literature, suggesting that researchers need to determine what information is conveyed through demonstrations. Future research is needed to approach this issue.

Another issue of concern extends into the practical domain. At the present time there are numerous commercial videotapes on the market that display high-level athletes repeatedly demonstrating sport skills designed to enhance the observer's athletic prowess. While there is no immediate reason to believe that these modeling films should not work, a review of the literature indicates that there is no published evidence to support their validity (Druckman & Swets, 1988). Applied research examining their effectiveness is definitely warranted. If they are shown to contribute to learning in their present configuration, it may be that many of the variables discussed in this chapter could be used to improve their quality.

The topic of modeling has only begun to receive the attention it deserves in the literature. It should have wide appeal to sport psychology researchers interested in learning, social psychological, and developmental issues, since it clearly spans all these concerns. However, a recent conversation with a colleague who was beginning to investigate modeling issues illustrates that many individuals have not yet realized the diversity of this topic. The individual was questioned on why a motor learning researcher would investigate modeling when it was clearly only a social phenomenon. Hopefully the literature reviewed here will dispel this notion. Only if this topic is approached from a multidisciplinary perspective will we begin to gain a clear understanding of how movement skills are acquired and modified through observation.

References

Abernethy, B. (1989). Expert-novice differences in perception: How expert does the expert have to be? *Canadian Journal of Sport Science, 14*(1), 27–30.

Adams, J. A. (1971). A closed-loop theory of motor learning. *Journal of Motor Behavior, 3,* 111–150.

Adams, J. A. (1986). Use of the model's knowledge of results to increase the observer's performance. *Journal of Human Movement Studies, 12,* 89–98.

Allard, F., & Starkes, J. L. (1980). Perception in sport: Volleyball. *Journal of Sport Psychology, 2,* 22–33.

Allard, F., Graham, S., & Paarsalu, E. (1980). Perception in sport: Basketball. *Journal of Sport Psychology, 2,* 14–21.

Allport, F. H. (1924). *Social psychology.* Cambridge, MA: Riverside Press.

Bandura, A. (1965). Vicarious processes: A case of no-trial learning. In L. Berkowitz (Ed.), *Advances in experimental social psychology, Vol II* (pp. 1–55). New York: Academic Press.

Bandura, A. (1969). *Principles of behavior modification.* New York: Holt, Rinehart and Winston.

Bandura, A. (1971). Analysis of modeling processes. In A. Bandura (Ed.), *Psychological modeling conflicting theories* (105–124). New York: Adline-Atherton.

Bandura, A. (1977). Social learning theory. Englewood Cliffs, NJ: Prentice Hall.

Bandura, A. (1986). *Social foundations of thought and action: A social cognitive theory.* Englewood Cliffs, NJ: Prentice-Hall.

Bandura, A., & Barab, P. G. (1973). Processes governing disinhibitory effects through symbolic modeling. *Journal of Abnormal Psychology, 82,* 1–9.

Bandura, A., & Jeffery, R. W. (1973). Role of symbolic coding and rehearsal processes in observational learning. *Journal of Personality and Social Psychology, 26:*122–130.

Bandura, A., & Kapers, C. J. (1964). Transmission of patterns of self-reinforcement through modeling. *Journal of Abnormal and Social Psychology, 69,* 1–9.

Baron, R. A. (1970). Attraction toward the model and model's competence as determinants of adult imitative behavior. *Journal of Personality and Social Psychology, 14,* 345–351.

Bird, A. M., & Rikli, R. (1983). Observational learning and practice variability. *Research Quarterly for Exercise and Sport, 54,* 1–4.

Bird, A. M., Ross, D., & Laguna, P. (1983). The observational learning of a timing task. ERIC # ED 269 370.

Carroll, W. R., & Bandura, A. (1982). The role of visual monitoring in observational learning of action patterns: Making the unobservable observable. *Journal of Motor Behavior, 14,* 153–167.

Carroll, W. R., & Bandura, A. (1985). A role of timing of visual monitoring and motor rehearsal in observational learning of action patterns. *Journal of Motor Behavior, 17,* 269–281.

Carroll, W. R., & Bandura, A. (1987). Translating cognition into action: The role of visual guidance in observational learning. *Journal of Motor Behavior, 19,* 385–398.

Carroll, W. R., & Bandura, A. (1990). Representation guidance of action production in observational learning: A causal analysis. *Journal of Motor Behavior, 22,* 85–97.

Chi, M. T. H. (1981). Knowledge development and memory performance. In M. P. Friedman, J. P. Dos & N. O. O'Connor (Eds.). *Intelligence and learning* (pp. 221–229). New York: Plenum Press.

Chi, M. T. H., & Rees, E. T. (1983). A learning framework for development. In M. T. H. Chi (Ed.), *Contributions to human development* (pp. 71–107). Basel, Switzerland: Karger.

Clark, J., & Ewing, M. (1985). A meta-analysis of gender differences and similarities in the gross motor skill performances of prepubescent children. Paper presented at the annual meeting of the North American Society for the Psychology of Sport and Physical Activity, Gulf Park, MS.

Deakin, J. M., & Allard, F. (1991). Skilled memory in expert figure skaters. *Memory & Cognition, 19,* 79–86.

Doody, S. G., Bird, A. M., & Ross, D. (1985). The effect of auditory and visual models on acquisition of a timing task. *Human Movement Science, 4,* 271–281.

Dowrick, P. W. (1983). Self-modeling. In P. W. Dowrick & S. J. Biggs (Eds.). *Using video: Psychological and social applications.* (pp. 105–124). New York: Wiley.

Dowrick, P. W. (1991). *Practical guide to using videos in the behavioral sciences.* New York: Wiley.

Dowrick, P. W., & Biggs, S. J. (1983). *Using video: Psychological and social applications.* New York: Wiley.

Dowrick, P. W., & Dove, C. (1980). The use of self-modeling to improve the swimming performance of spina bifada children. *Journal of Applied Behavior Analysis, 13,* 51–55.

Druckman, D., & Swets, J. A. (1988). *Enhancing human performance: Issues, theories and techniques.* Washington, DC: Academy Press.

Feltz, D. L. (1982). The effect of age and number of demonstrations on modeling of form and performance. *Research Quarterly for Exercise and Sport, 53,* 291–296.

Feltz, D. L., & Landers, D. M. (1983). The effects of mental practice on motor skill learning and performance: A meta-analysis. *Journal of Sport Psychology, 5,* 25–57.

Feltz, D. L., Landers, D. M., & Raeder, U. (1979). Enhancing self-efficacy in high avoidance motor tasks: A comparison of modeling techniques. *Journal of Sport Psychology, 1:*112–122..

Finke, R. A. (1986). Mental imagery and the visual system. *Scientific American, 254,* 88–95.

Flint, F. A. (1991). *The psychological effects of modeling in athletic injury rehabilitation.* Unpublished doctoral dissertation, University of Oregon, Eugene.

French, K. E., & Thomas, J. R. (1987). The relation of knowledge development to children's basketball performance. *Journal of Sport Psychology, 9,* 15–32.

Gallagher, J. D. (1982). The effects of developmental memory differences on learning motor skills. *Journal of Physical Education, Recreation and Dance, 52,* 36–37.

Gallagher, J. D. (1984). Influence of developmental information processing abilities on children's motor performance. In W. Straub & J. Williams (Eds.), *Cognitive sport psychology* (pp. 153–167). Lansing, NY: Sport Science Associates.

Gallagher, J. D., & Hoffman, S. (1987). Memory development and children's sport skill acquisition. In D. Gould & M. R. Weiss (Eds.), *Advances in pediatric sport sciences* (pp. 187–210). Champaign, IL: Human Kinetics.

Gallagher, J. D., & Thomas, J. R. (1984). Rehearsal strategy effects on developmental differences for recall of a movement series. *Research Quarterly for Exercise and Sport, 55,* 123–128.

Gallagher, J. D., & Thomas, J. R. (1986). Developmental effects of grouping and recording on learning a movement series. *Research Quarterly for Exercise and Sport, 57,* 117–127.

Gerwitz, J. L., & Stingle, K. C. (1968). The learning of generalized imitation as the basis for identification. *Psychological Review, 75,* 374–397.

Gould, D., Hodge, K., Peterson, K., & Giannini, J. (1989). An exploratory examination of strategies used by elite coaches to enhance self-efficacy in athletes. *Journal of Sport and Exercise Psychology, 11,* 128–140.

Gould, D., & Weiss, M. R. (1981). The effects of model similarity and model talk on self-efficacy and muscular endurance. *Journal of Sport Psychology, 3,* 17–29.

Hall, E. G., & Erffmeyer, E. S. (1983). The effect of visuo-motor behavior rehearsal with videotaped modeling on free throw accuracy of intercollegiate female basketball players. *Journal of Sport Psychology, 5,* 343–346.

Halverson, L. (1983). Observing children's motor development in action. Eugene, OR: Microform Publications.

Halverson, L., Roberton, M. A., & Langendorfer, S. (1982). Development of the overarm throw: Movement and ball velocity changes by seventh grade children. *Research Quarterly for Exercise and Sport, 53,* 198–205.

Harter, S. (1978). Effectance motivation reconsidered. *Human Development, 21,* 34–64.

Harter, S. (1981). A model of intrinsic mastery motivation in children: Individual differences and developmental change. In W. A. Collines (Ed.), *Minnesota symposium on child psychology* (pp. 215–255). Hillsdale, NJ: Erlbaum.

Holt, E. B. (1931). *Animal drive and the learning process.* New York: Holt.

Housner, L. D. (1984a). The role of imaginal processing in the retention of visually presented sequential motoric stimuli. *Research Quarterly for Exercise and Sport, 55,* 24–31.

Housner, L. D. (1984b). The role of visual imagery in recall of modeled motoric stimuli. *Journal of Sport Psychology, 6,* 148–158.

Kulik, J. A., & Mahler, H. I. (1987). Effects of preoperative roommate assignment on preoperative anxiety and recovery from coronary bypass surgery. *Health Psychology, 6,* 525–543.

Landers, D. M. (1975). Observational learning of a motor skill: Temporal spacing of demonstrations and audience presence. *Journal of Motor Behavior, 7,* 281–287.

Landers, D. M., & Landers, D. M. (1973). Teacher versus peer models: Effects of model's presence and performance level on motor behavior. *Journal of Motor Behavior, 5,* 129–139.

Lang, P. J. (1979). A bio-informational theory of emotional imagery. *Psychophysiology, 16,* 495–512.

Lee, T. D., & White, M. A. (1990). Influence of an unskilled model's practice schedule on observational motor learning. *Human Movement Science, 9,* 349–367.

Lirgg, C. D., & Feltz, D. L. (1991). Teacher versus peer models revisited: Effects on motor performance and self-efficacy. *Research Quarterly for Exercise and Sport, 62,* 217–224.

Little, W. S., & McCullagh. P. (1989). Motivational orientation and modeled instructional strategies: The effects on form and accuracy. *Journal of Sport & Exercise Psychology, 11,* 41–53.

Martens, R., Burwitz, L., & Zuckerman, J. (1976). Modeling effects on motor performance. *Research Quarterly, 47,* 277–291.

Mausner, B. (1953). Studies in social interaction. III: Effect of variation in one partner's prestige on the interaction of observer pairs. *Journal of Applied Psychology, 37,* 391–393.

McAuley, E. (1985). Modeling and self-efficacy: A test of Bandura's model. *Journal of Sport Psychology, 7,* 283–295.

McCullagh, P. (1986). Model status as a determinant of attention in observational learning and performance. *Journal of Sport Psychology, 8,* 319–331.

McCullagh, P. (1987). Model similarity effects on motor performance. *Journal of Sport Psychology, 9,* 249–260.

McCullagh, P., Burch, C. D., & Siegel, D. I. (1990). *Correct and self-modeling and the role of feedback in motor skill acquisition.* Paper presented at the annual meeting of the North American Society for the Psychology of Sport and Physical Activity. Houston, TX.

McCullagh, P., & Caird, J. K. (1990). Correct and learning models and the use of model knowledge of results in the acquisition and retention of a motor skill. *Journal of Human Movement Studies, 18,* 107–116.

McCullagh, P., & Little, W. S. (1989). A comparison of modalities in modeling. *Human Performance, 2,* 101–111.

McCullagh, P., Stiehl, J., & Weiss, M. R. (1990). Developmental modeling effects on the quantitative and qualitative aspects of motor performance acquisition. *Research Quarterly for Exercise and Sport, 61,* 344–350.

McCullagh, P., Weiss, M. R., & Ross, D. (1989). Modeling considera-tion in motor skill acquisition and performance: An integrated approach. In K. B. Pandolf (Ed.), *Exercise and sport science reviews* (pp. 475–513), Baltimore: Williams & Wilkins.

McDougall, W. (1908). *An introduction to social psychology.* London: Methuen.

McPherson, S. L., & Thomas, J. R. (1989). Relation of knowledge and performance in boy's tennis: Age and expertise. *Journal of Experimental Child Psychology, 48,* 190–211.

Miller, N. E., & Dollard, J. (1941). *Social learning and imitation.* New Haven: Yale University Press.

Mischel, W., & Grusec, J. (1966). Determinants of the rehearsal and transmission of neutral and aversive behaviors. *Journal of Personality and Social Psychology, 3,* 197–205.

Morgan, C. L. (1896). *Habit and instinct.* London: E. Arnold.

Newell, K. M. (1976). Motor learning without knowledge of results through the development of a response recognition mechanism. *Journal of Motor Behavior, 8,* 209–217.

Newell, K. M. (1981). Skill learning. In D. Holding (Ed.), *Human skills* (pp. 203–226). New York: Wiley.

Newell, K. M., Morris, L. R., & Scully, D. M. (1985). Augmented information and the acquisition of skills in physical activity. In R. L. Terjung (Ed.). *Exercise and sport science reviews* (pp. 235–261). New York: Macmillan.

Paivio, A. (1971). *Imagery and verbal processes.* New York: Holt, Rinehart & Winston.

Pollock, B. J., & Lee, T. D. (1992). Effects of the model's skill level on observational motor learning. *Research Quarterly for Exercise and Sport, 63,* 25–29.

Roach, N. K., & Burwitz, L. (1986). Observational learning in motor skill acquisition: The effect of verbal directing cues. In J. Watkins, T. Reilly, & L. Burwitz (Eds.), *Sports science: Proceedings of the VIII Commonwealth and International conference on sport, physical education, dance, recreation and health* (pp. 349–354). London: E. & F. N. Spon.

Roberton, M. A. (1983). Changing motor patterns during childhood. In J. R. Thomas (Ed.), *Motor development during childhood and adolescence* (pp. 48–90). Minneapolis, MN: Burgess.

Ross, D., Bird, A. M., Doody, S. G., & Zoeller, M. (1985). Effect of modeling and videotape feedback with knowledge of results on motor performance. *Human Movement Science, 4,* 149–157.

Rothstein, A. L., & Arnold, R. K. (1976). Bridging the gap: Application of research on videotape feedback and bowling. *Motor Skills: Theory Into Practice, 1,* 35–62.

Ryan, E. D., & Simons, J. (1981). Cognitive demand, imagery, and frequency of mental rehearsal as factors influencing acquisition of motor skills. *Journal of Sport Psychology, 3,* 35–45.

Ryan, E. D., & Simons, J. (1983). What is learned in mental practice of motor skills: A test of the cognitive-motor hypothesis. *Journal of Sport Psychology, 5,* 419–426.

Schmidt, R. A. (1975). A schema theory of discrete motor skill learning. *Psychological Review, 82,* 225–260.

Schmidt, R. A. (1988). *Motor control and learning: A behavioral emphasis.* Champaign, IL: Human Kinetics.

Schunk. D. H., Hanson, R. A., & Cox, P. D. (1987). Peer-model attributes and children's achievement behaviors. *Journal of Educational Psychology, 79,* 54–61.

Seefeldt, V., & Haubenstricker, J. (1982). Patterns, phases, or stages: An analytical model for the study of developmental movement. In J. A. S. Kelso & J. E. Clark (Eds.), *The development of movement control and co-ordination* (pp. 309–318). New York: Wiley.

Sheffield, F. N. (1961). Theoretical considerations in the learning of complex sequential tasks from demonstrations and practice.

In A. A. Lumsdaine (Ed.), *Student response in programmed instruction* (pp. 13–32). Washington, DC: National Academy of Sciences, National Research Council.

Southard, D., & Higgins, T. (1987). Changing movement patterns: Effects of demonstration and practice. *Research Quarterly for Exercise and Sport, 58,* 77–80.

Starkes, J. L. & Deakin, J. M. (1984). Perception in sport: A cognitive approach to skilled performance. In W. F. Straub & J. M. Williams (Eds.), *Cognitive sport psychology* (pp. 115–128). Lansing, NY: Sport Science Associates.

Thelen, M. H., Fry, R. A., & Gehrenbach, P. A. (1979). Therapeutic videotape and film modeling: A review. *Psychological Bulletin, 86,* 701–720.

Thomas, J. R., & French, K. E. (1985). Gender differences in motor performance: A meta-analysis. *Psychological Bulletin, 98,* 260–282.

Thomas, J. R., French, K. E., & Humphries, C. A. (1986). Knowledge developmental and sport skill performance: Directions for motor behavior research. *Journal of Sport Psychology, 8,* 259–272.

Thomas, J. R., Pierce, C., & Ridsdale, S. (1977). Age differences in children's ability to model motor behavior. *Research Quarterly, 48,* 592–597.

Ulrich, B. D. (1987). Developmental perspectives of motor skill performance in children. In D. Gould & M. R. Weiss (Eds.), *Advances in pediatric sport sciences* (pp. 167–186). Champaign, IL: Human Kinetics.

Weinberg, R. S., Gould, D., Yukelson, D., & Jackson, A. (1981). The effect of preexisting and manipulated self-efficacy on a competitive muscular endurance task. *Journal of Sport Psychology, 4,* 345–354.

Weir, P. L., & Leavitt, J. L. (1990). Effects of model's skill level and model's knowledge of results on the performance of a dart throwing task. *Human Movement Science, 9,* 369–383.

Weiss, M. R. (1983). Modeling and motor performance: A developmental perspective. *Research Quarterly for Exercise and Sport, 54,* 190–197.

Weiss, M. R., & Bredemeier, B. J. (1983). Developmental sport psychology: A theoretical perspective for studying children in sport. *Journal of Sport Psychology, 5,* 216–230.

Weiss, M. R., Bredemeier, B. J., & Shewchuk, R. M. (1985). An intrinsic/extrinsic motivation scale for the youth sport setting: A confirmatory factor analysis. *Journal of Sport Psychology, 1,* 75–91.

Weiss, M. R., & Klint, K. A. (1987). "Show and tell" in the gymnasium: An investigation of developmental differences in modeling and verbal rehearsal of motor skills. *Research Quarterly for Exercise and Sport, 58,* 234–241.

Weiss, M. R., & Troxel, R. K. (1986). Psychology of the injured athlete. *Athletic Training, 21,* 104–109, 154.

Wiese, D. M., & Weiss, M. R. (1987). Psychological rehabilitation and physical injury: Implication for the sports medicine team. *The Sport Psychologist, 1,* 318–330.

White, R. (1959). Motivation reconsidered: The concept of competence. *Psychological Review, 66,* 297–333.

Whiting, H. T. A., Bijlard, M. J., & den Brinker, B. P. L. M. (1987). The effect of the availability of a dynamic model on the acquisition of a complex cyclical action. *Quarterly Journal of Experimental Psychology, 39A,* 43–59.

Wrisberb, C. A., & Ragsdale, M. R. (1979). Cognitive demand and practice level: Factors in the mental rehearsal of motor skills. *Journal of Human Movement Studies, 5,* 201–208.

Yando, R., Seitz, V., & Zigler, E. (1979). *Imitation: A developmental perspective.* New York: Wiley.

Yussen, S. R., & Levy, N. M. (1975). Effects of warm and neutral models on the attention of observational learners. *Journal of Experimental Child Psychology, 20,* 66–72.

Zivin, S. (1979). *The development of self-regulation through private speech.* New York: Wiley.

· 6 ·

ATTENTION

Bruce Abernethy

INTRODUCTION

The Importance of Attention in Sport Performance

It is difficult to imagine that there can be anything more important to the learning and performance of sport skills than paying attention to the task at hand. The anecdotal reports of athletes who have performed poorly because they were not quite prepared (e.g., the 100-meter sprinter who "missed" the gun), because they lost concentration (e.g., the pistol shooter whose thoughts wandered away from the target to internal thoughts of hunger and fatigue), because they were distracted (e.g., the basketballer who was disturbed at the free-throw line by crowd noise), or because they became confused (e.g., the defensive player in football who was disoriented by the sheer complexity of the opposition's offensive pattern), all bear testimony to the importance of the optimal, selective, and sustained allocation of attention. At a superficial level the notion of paying attention (or concentrating) would appear to be a rather straightforward one, yet cognitive psychologists, and more recently motor learning and control theorists, have long grappled with the intricacies and complexities of this intuitive notion.

The Long History of Research Interest in the Concept of Attention

Interest in the concept of attention is at least as old as the field of experimental psychology itself (see Boring, 1970, for a review), with the early works having their origins in phenomenology. Hamilton (1859), James (1890), Jastrow (1891), Wundt (1905), Pillsbury (1908), and Titchener (1908) all wrote on the concept of attention from introspective perspectives, although such essentially philosophical works were supplemented by some, now classical, empirical examinations of divided attention by Binet (1890), Bliss (1892–1893), Solomons and Stein (1896), and Welch (1898). (We shall refer to a number of these works at various points later in this chapter.) Discovery of the concept of attention did not, in itself, prove particularly illuminating and, as Titchener (1908) noted, actually unearthed more problems than it solved:

The discovery of attention did not result in any immediate triumph of the experimental method. It was something like the discovery of a hornet's nest: the first touch brought out a whole swarm of instant problems.

However, the early work did, if nothing else, alert psychologists to the complexity underlying the phenomenological experience of attention.

Interest in the concept of attention waned dramatically in the first half of the twentieth century during the reign of behaviorism as the dominant paradigm in experimental psychology. Behaviorism's inherent distrust of internal processes placed issues of attention out of favor with experimenters of the time. Interest in the concept of attention was renewed in the late 1950s, fuelled specifically by the work of English psychologists such as Cherry (1953), Broadbent (1958), and Moray (1959) on the problems posed by selective attention, and more generally by the advent and acceptance of the information-processing model (originating from the works of Craik, 1947, 1948; Wiener, 1948; and later Welford, 1952). For the reader interested further in the historical development of research on attention, Eysenck (1984) and Stelmach and Hughes (1983) provide more detailed reviews.

Appreciation is extended to an anonymous reviewer for helpful comments on an earlier version of this chapter.

The Historical Linkage of the Concept of Attention to Consciousness

Of the early works by the phenomenologists, the most enduringly influential is undoubtedly the work of William James. His famous definition of attention is among the most cited quotes in psychology. In reading any contemporary piece on attention one is inevitably presented with James's (1890) quote:

Everyone knows what attention is. It is the taking possession by the mind, in clear and vivid form, of one out of what seem several simultaneously possible objects or trains of thought. Focalization, concentration, of consciousness are of its essence. It implies withdrawal from some things in order to deal effectively with others. (pp. 403–404)

Given that James's insight into the phenomenon of attention was gained through introspection, it is perhaps not surprising to see his close linkage of the concept of attention to notions of consciousness. Indeed, our own naive impressions are that our consciousness determines our thoughts and our choices of action (see also Schmidt, 1988, p. 100).

There are, however, at least two major problems with defining attention in terms of consciousness. First, our attention may be equally the product of apparently automatic processes which selectively direct our thinking and behavior without our conscious awareness (e.g., see Underwood, 1982). As we will see later in this chapter, the contemporary study of attention is equally directed at understanding these so-called automatic processes, which operate below the level of consciousness, as it is at understanding attentional control processes that are voluntary and within the realm of our awareness (e.g., Shiffrin & Schneider, 1977). Given our specific interest in attention as it applies to skilled sports performance, the understanding of automatic processes is necessarily a principal focus of this chapter.

Second, introspections about consciousness are notoriously inaccurate and sufficiently prone to situational bias to make the relationship between self-reported consciousness and behavior an unreliable one (e.g., Nisbett & Wilson, 1977; Posner, 1973, 1978). Such observations cast doubts on the credibility of consciousness as a basis upon which to ground a scientific theory of attention, although some authors (e.g., Stelmach & Hughes, 1983) still argue that consciousness should be the centerpiece of any definition of attention. It does remain possible that our experience of consciousness is reliable but that the inaccuracies that are observed arise in the reporting of this experience to others (White, 1980, 1982). Nevertheless the problem remains that if consciousness cannot be reliably and unambiguously linked to attention, an operational definition of attention in terms of consciousness is likely to be fraught with many kinds of measurement problems.

The Multidimensional Nature of Attention

It should be clear from the preceding discussion that, despite James's assertion, we do *not* know what attention is

(see also Stelmach & Hughes, 1983). Certainly scientists working in the field cannot reach unanimous agreement on how to define attention. In the modern study of perception, cognition, and action, attention has become a ubiquitous concept that is used in a range of diverse and only loosely related ways. Moray (1969, 1970) has noted at least six different meanings and uses of the term *attention* in the psychology literature, including its synonymous use for terms such as *selectivity, concentration, mental set, visual search, information processing,* and *arousal.* Although all of these terms relate to legitimate areas of study for experimental psychology (and legitimate areas of focus for sport psychology as well), the danger of a concept so broad is that it may have little or no explanatory power (Eysenck, 1984, p. 49). There is a clear need for a more focused treatment of the concept of attention than contemporary experimental psychology appears to provide.

A useful means of categorizing attention into principal areas of focus was provided some time ago by Posner and Boies (1971), who identified three major uses of the term *attention* in contemporary psychology.

1. Attention as *alertness,* including concerns with the development and both short- and long-term maintenance of optimal sensitivity and readiness (or preparedness) for responding.
2. Attention as a *limited capacity or resource,* as examined in studies of divided attention aimed at isolating capacity and/or resource limitations in information processing.
3. Attention as *selectivity,* as examined in studies of selective attention requiring the reporting of information from a particular modality, spatial location, or context in the face of competition from other items and sources of distraction.

This categorization provides a useful organizational framework for reviewing the mass of literature on the topic of attention although it will become apparent in the forthcoming discussions, as indeed it was in the empirical work of Posner and Boies (1971), that these three attentional contexts are interrelated in a number of ways.

The Organization of This Chapter

In this chapter we use Posner and Boies's (1971) categorization to examine attention in its different contexts, giving particular reference throughout the chapter to the relevance and application of attention to the learning and performance of sport skills. The concept of attention as alertness is subdivided to give separate treatment to the issues of momentary versus long-term preparedness, giving, in all, four major attentional contexts. Each of these contexts is then examined in some detail by considering, under separate subsections:

1. The definition of attention in its specific context and its importance, in that context, to sports performance and instruction.

2. Major paradigms of study and principal measures of the key concepts, including the use of measures derived from a number of different levels of analysis.
3. Performance limitations imposed by attention in its specific context (primarily through a review of pivotal research).
4. Theoretical explanations and the evidence supporting and refuting given theories.
5. Changes in attention that accompany skill acquisition (through consideration of the available research from training studies and expert-novice comparisons).
6. Practical implications of the available research for skill acquisition, instruction, and the design of practice for sport.

ATTENTION AS ALERTNESS OR PREPAREDNESS

One popular use of the term *attention* in experimental psychology literature relates to the act of attending as a means of increasing the alertness of the performer for processing incoming information. A heightened state of preparedness may be needed either short-term (such as the momentary alertness a diver needs to develop for the performance of a single dive or a baseball batter needs to develop for receiving a single pitch) or long-term (such as the alertness that must be maintained by a golfer over the four-hour duration of a round or by a tennis player over the duration of a five-set match). We will consider these two types of situations and the demands they place on the athlete's alertness separately.

ALERTNESS FOR A SINGLE ACTION (MOMENTARY ALERTNESS)

Defining Alertness and Its Importance

The necessity of optimal mental *preparation* and appropriate marshaling of resources for the performance of specific discrete responses is well documented (e.g., Singer, 1988). The personal experiences of all of us provide unique insights into how alertness is variable (on a continuum from deep sleep through to hyperactivity) and how, phenomenologically, alertness appears to be related to performance. Athletes' attributions for poor performance of a particular action (e.g., returning service in volleyball, handball, or any of the racquet sports) to "not being ready" are supported by controlled laboratory studies of reaction time (RT) (e.g., Bertelson, 1967; Bertelson & Tisseyre, 1968; Woodrow, 1914), which demonstrate that prior warning of an impending stimulus can enhance performance. Clearly alertness can be altered, and in some ways optimized, although our ability to sustain optimal alertness appears to be quite limited. It has been shown using RT paradigms, for example, that RT slows when the foreperiod (the time between the presentation of a warning signal and the presentation of the stimulus) exceeds about 4 seconds (Botwinick

& Thompson, 1966; Woodrow, 1914). Because alertness is variable, a useful way of thinking about alertness is in terms of an alterable setting or activation that provides variable access to our limited information-processing capacity or resources. (This notion will be explored fully in a later section of this chapter.) Capacity (or resource) that is not activated cannot be used, although high levels of activation do not guarantee that all processing will be directed at the task at hand (Kahneman, 1973). Thought of in this way, alertness (or preparedness) is clearly dependent on, and perhaps synonymous with, the concept of *arousal.*

Arousal is a physiological state that reflects the energy level or degree of activation of the performer at any particular instant. It is mediated through a number of brain mechanisms but most specifically the reticular formation (a neuronal network within the brain stem extending from the medulla to the posterior hypothalamus) and the hypothalamus. Stimulation of these areas gives rise to behavioral properties of excitement and high activity and cortically recorded electroencephalographic (EEG) patterns consistent with high activation. Lesions to these areas reverse both the behavioral and EEG patterns to those consistent with drowsiness and low activation (Lindsley, Schreiner, Knowles, & Magoun, 1950; Ranson, 1939; Thompson, 1967). The term *anxiety* is often used essentially interchangeably with arousal (e.g., Landers, 1980; Magill, 1989), although distinction should be drawn between the two (Cox, 1985). Whereas arousal is a physiological state (and therefore best measured from physiological variables), anxiety is primarily a cognitive manifestation of high arousal in the form of apprehension or fear (Levitt, 1980). Therefore, although arousal is essentially a neutral term, anxiety clearly has negative connotations (Cox, 1985; Martens, 1982). The two are further disassociable in the sense that although low arousal and low anxiety typically coexist, high arousal need not necessarily be associated with high anxiety.

Major Paradigms and Principal Measure of Alertness, Arousal, and Related Concepts

Methods of Studying and Measuring Arousal. Arousal and, to some extent, anxiety may be measured at a number of different levels of analysis. The measurement of the overt behaviors of sports performers, their cognitions (or thoughts), and their underlying physiological states may all be enlightening, although it should be clear from our preceding discussion that the most direct measurement of arousal/activation will involve the use of physiological variables, whereas the most direct assessment of anxiety will require cognitive measures.

BEHAVIORAL MEASURES
Behavioral measures of arousal and anxiety may include the categorization of overt behaviors by an observer (using some form of checklist or behavioral observation instrument, e.g., Rushall, 1977) and, from there, the use of infer-

ence on the observer's part to link the overt behaviors to the underlying activation constructs. At a gross level, observations of high levels of performer activity or of avoidance behaviors (such as opting not to compete) may be broadly indicative of high arousal and high anxiety respectively, but the measurement grain is necessarily imprecise. More precise behavioral techniques (in particular the dual-task technique) exist for determining the allocation of limited processing resources to different aspects of a given task, but since these measures impact more on attention in contexts other than those related to arousal/alertness, they will be discussed elsewhere in the chapter.

COGNITIVE MEASURES

The favored cognitive measures of activation are typically those which require performers to self-report their own level of activation, usually within the context of anxiety. The subject's self-report may be continuous throughout the duration of the activity and unprompted by the experimenter although, typically, structured questionnaires with known psychometric properties are used and are administered either immediately before or immediately after the event of interest. Such pencil-and-paper attempts to measure anxiety typically draw distinctions between temporary, situationally determined anxiety (so-called *state anxiety*), and enduring anxiety, which is a general cross-situational characteristic of the particular individual under examination (so-called *trait anxiety*) (Spielberger, 1966, 1971).

Of the trait anxiety measures available, the general purpose Taylor Manifest Anxiety Scale (TMAS) (Taylor, 1953) and Spielberger Trait Anxiety Inventory (STAI) (Spielberger, Gorsuch, & Lushene, 1970) and the sport-specific Sport Competition Anxiety Test (SCAT) (Martens, 1982) are the most frequently used. Of the state anxiety instruments, the general purpose Autonomic Perception Questionnaire (APQ) (Mandler, Mandler, & Urviller, 1958), Affective Adjective Check List (AACL) (Zuckerman, 1960), Activation-Deactivation Checklist (AD-CL) (Thayer, 1967) and especially Spielberger's State Anxiety Inventory (SSAI) (Spielberger et al., 1970) are popular. The Competitive State Anxiety Inventories of Martens (1982) (CSAI) and Martens, Vealey, and Burton (1990) (CSAI-2) are attractive to sport psychologists because of the sport-specific nature of the component items. Cox (1985) and Anshel (1987) provide more detailed discussion of these and other anxiety-measurement instruments. The interested reader is directed to these sources for comparative information and to the original sources for details of the psychometrics of the individual tests.

These tests of anxiety, like all self-report measures, suffer from potential difficulties associated with the subjects' abilities or inabilities to report reliably on their own cognitive processes (Le Plat & Hoc, 1981; Nisbett & Wilson, 1977) and hence concerns associated with response distortion and with the possible intent of subjects to make responses that are in line with those expected of an ideal performance. The latter is a particular concern if the athlete being measured suspects any linkage between test perform-

ance and his/her subsequent treatment by coaches, selectors, or fellow athletes. The noncontinuous nature of the measurements of anxiety provided through cognitive tests and the potential contamination of data arising from repeat administration of such tests present substantial constraints to the investigation of athlete activation.

PHYSIOLOGICAL MEASURES

Because arousal is a physiological state it follows that the measurement of physiological parameters is most likely to provide the most reliable and valid indicators of an athlete's level of activation. The autonomic nervous system is responsible for spreading the level of arousal, dictated centrally by the ascending reticular formation and especially the hypothalamus, to the peripheral organs and it does so by controlling the relative levels of sympathetic and parasympathetic neural activity. Sympathetic activation results in increased arousal and manifests itself in a number of measurable peripheral changes, including pupil dilation, tachycardia (increased heart rate), blood pressure and respiratory rate elevation, and increased sweating. Parasympathetic stimulation reverses these effects, acting to restrict arousal to its homeostatic level. Measurement of the state of cortical activity, blood levels of sympathetic neurotransmitters, or the state of effected systems and organs, including the cardiorespiratory system and the muscular system, therefore provide potential indicators of an individual's level of arousal.

Electroencephalographic recordings over the scalp reveal spontaneous patterns of electrical activity containing wave forms of a number of different frequencies, some of which are reliably linked to arousal. Each frequency range (delta $<3.5H_z$; theta $4-7H_z$; alpha $8-13H_z$; beta $14-25H_z$) is associated with different behavioral states, with delta waveforms predominating in deep sleep and beta II waves during high activation or tension (Guyton, 1981). Suppression of EEG alpha-wave activity appears to be the most reliable indicator of increased activation, however, and is frequently used as an indicator of the relative activation of the left and right cerebral hemispheres in a given task (Collins, Powell, & Davies, 1990; Hatfield, Landers, & Ray, 1984; Landers, 1980).

The catecholamines (adrenaline and noradrenaline), which are released into the bloodstream by the adrenal medulla as a means of enacting increased arousal at various peripheral sites and organs within the body, can also be directly measured as an indicator of arousal level. The accurate measurement of circulating catecholamines is made difficult, however, by the rapid perfusion of these neurotransmitters into active tissue, and this, along with the invasive and noncontinuous nature of the recordings, limits their utility as measures of activation during the performance of specific sports skills. Measurements of changes in the target organs affected by the action of the catecholamines provide a less invasive, more continuous, and more convenient means of assessing the activation state of the performer.

As sympathetic innervation causes dilation of the pupils,

measurement of pupil diameter (via a pupillometer) provides a useful and apparently quite sensitive measure of the time course of activation on a particular task. Pupil dilation varies quite linearly with task difficulty (e.g., Beatty & Wagoner, 1978; Hess & Polt, 1964; Kahneman & Beatty, 1967) and therefore also provides, as we will see later, a useful measure of the information-processing load. Increased arousal also manifests itself in terms of increased heart rate, blood pressure, and respiratory rate. The cardiovascular measures are, nevertheless, somewhat restricted in utility; *absolute* heart rate is subject to influence from a range of factors in addition to arousal and blood pressure, is difficult to measure without interfering with the athlete's normal activities, and provides only a discontinuous measure. Heart rate *changes,* however, may be enlightening, especially with respect to the direction of attentional focus (Lacey, 1967). Respiratory rate can be reliably and easily measured but is subject to more conscious, nonautonomic control than a number of other potential measures of arousal.

One of the more obvious effects of sympathetic stimulation is copious sweating, with secretion from the sweat glands of the palm being selectively affected more by anxiety than by environmental temperature (Harrison & MacKinnon, 1966). Counting palmar sweat gland activation, therefore, provides one potential means of assessing an individual's level of arousal (e.g., Dabbes, Johnson, & Leventhal, 1968), although recording of the decreased skin resistance associated with increased palmar sweating, the so-called galvanic response (Montagu & Coles, 1966), provides a more convenient alternative.

An additional effect of sympathetic stimulation is increased activity in skeletal muscle, believed to result in increased muscle tension, a factor that, in turn, is frequently linked to anxiety (e.g., Jacobson, 1929, 1931). Electromyographic (EMG) recordings of electrical activity in muscle have been used as indirect measures of arousal level (e.g., Weinberg & Hunt, 1976), although this measure is fraught with potential difficulties. EMG amplitude and muscle tension are far from linearly related (Vredenbregt & Rau, 1973), and the potential stabilizing and synergistic roles of muscle during given actions need to be carefully assessed before choosing a particular muscle as a site for arousal measurement.

SELECTING THE MOST APPROPRIATE MEASURE(S)

There are clearly a number of potential means of assessing activation/arousal available to the researcher at a number of different levels of analysis. The selection of the most appropriate single measure in any given circumstance is complicated by the poor relationship between the different measures—the pattern of activation across the behavioral, cognitive, and physiological levels (Borkovec, 1976; Landers, 1980), and even within the different physiological measures (Lacey & Lacey, 1958), being very specific to the individual subject. Two similar individuals may show heightened arousal on different physiological variables with one displaying overt behavioral changes in the absence of self-reported cognitive anxiety and the other heightening anxiety but no behavioral or performance changes. The low concordance within and between levels of analysis is obviously a constraint in terms of isolating a single, universally acceptable measure of activation and highlights the necessity of using a range of measures from different levels to adequately assess the level of activation of a given athlete. The advantage of using an ensemble of measures is the capacity to develop useful and insightful profiles of individual differences (Landers, 1980).

Methods of Studying the Time Course of Alertness Changes in Discrete Actions. In addition to gaining overall measures of the arousal level of individual subjects, researchers in experimental psychology in general, and sport psychology in particular, have been interested in deriving measures that provide insight into the pattern of activation changes accompanying the performance of discrete actions. Given that peak activation only appears to be maintainable for a relatively short period of time, probably in the order of 1–4 seconds, (Woodrow, 1914), finding reliable markers of the development of response preparedness is obviously important. Such markers will clearly need to come from continuous measures that are easily and unobtrusively derived. These criteria dismiss the cognitive, self-report measures as a means of assessing alertness changes and limit potential markers to behavioral and physiological measures.

A potential behavioral means of plotting the increased allocation of available information-processing resources to the task at hand is to assess the extent to which athletes remain capable of responding to stimuli peripheral to the main task as the time for responding in the main task approaches. Dual-task techniques have been used to demonstrate increased peripheral narrowing as concentration on the immediate task is maximized. As alertness to the task increases (generally as the time for responding approaches), subjects become both slower in their response to peripheral stimuli and less accurate, frequently in the visual modality missing peripherally presented stimuli altogether (e.g., Landers, Wang, & Courtet, 1985). We will discuss the relationship between this peripheral narrowing and arousal and performance in more detail later in this part.

The dual-task technique provides the opportunity for discrete and fairly rapid measurement of alertness within a given skill, but nevertheless data need to be collected over a number of repetitions of the skill of interest before patterns of alertness begin to emerge. Likewise the data logging available with physiological variables allows temporal patterns of alertness to be revealed but again only over a number of repetitions of the skill of interest, although the continuous nature of the collected data results in a more extensive record of activation development than can be gained from dual-task measures. Patterns of heart rate changes and EEG changes are being used by a growing number of sport scientists to describe the attentional changes that accompany preparation for action in discrete skills such as rifle shooting (e.g., Hatfield, Landers, & Ray,

1984, 1987), archery (e.g., Salazar, Landers, Petruzzello, Crews, & Kubitz, 1988; Salazar, Landers, Petruzzello, Crews, Kubitz, & Han, 1990) and golf putting (e.g., Boutcher & Zinsser, 1990; Crews, 1989; Crews & Landers, 1991; Molander & Backman, 1989). Analysis to date has been restricted to these activities because of the necessity for actions in which the athlete is essentially steady, allowing good baseline recordings of physiological parameters to be achieved without contamination of these measures by physical exertion or movement artefacts.

One measure that appears to be sensitive to the subject's preparation for responding is heart rate (HR). Lacey and Lacey (1964, 1970), using an RT paradigm with a fixed foreperiod duration, were the first to document the presence of a systematic HR deceleration 3 to 4 seconds prior to stimulus onset, and to demonstrate that this deceleration was unrelated to the respiratory patterns of the subjects. Similar cardiac deceleration patterns have since been documented within the few seconds prior to response execution in a number of sport tasks. Stern (1976) observed cardiac deceleration in the final second prior to the GO signal in a simulated GET SET-GO paradigm (with a 5-second foreperiod) in which subjects were preparing for either a sprint up a flight of stairs or sprint on a bicycle. Boutcher and Zinsser (1990), Molander and Backman (1989), and Crews and Landers (1991) have all observed cardiac decelerations of the order of 4–11 beats per minute in the last 3–7 seconds prior to initiation of a self-paced golf putt. Hatfield et al. (1987) noted a trend, albeit a nonsignificant one, for HR deceleration in the 2–5 seconds leading up to trigger release in their sample of elite marksmen. A reverse trend was reported by Salazar et al. (1990) for elite archers, but in this case the HR acceleration that was apparent may reflect the imposition of the physiological demands of overcoming the inertia of a 14–22-kg bow tension on top of the relatively small attentional influences on HR. The Salazar et al. (1990) observation is important, *inter alia,* in demonstrating the limited range of sport tasks from which cardiac measures of preparedness may be realistically obtained. In the final section of this chapter, we return to the question of the mechanisms underlying HR deceleration as a possible tool for discriminating internal versus external focuses of attention.

Given that cardiovascular changes may differentially affect the left and right sides of the brain (Walker & Sandman, 1979, 1982), it is perhaps not surprising to note that hemispheric asymmetries have been observed in the EEG patterns collected over the final seconds prior to response execution in a number of sport tasks. Using suppressed alpha activity in the spontaneous EEG as an indication of increased activation, Hatfield et al. (1984, 1987), in their studies of rifle shooters, demonstrated reduced cortical activity in the left hemisphere as the time of pulling the trigger approached. These findings were interpreted in terms of a transition from a verbal-based left hemisphere control to a predominant visual-spatial right hemisphere control as alertness was maximized for response execution. The time course of these changes matched the time course of the car-

diac changes, suggesting that both were reflecting a common attentional mechanism. Subsequent studies of other discrete actions (e.g., Crews, 1989; Salazar et al., 1988, 1990) have revealed a similar pattern of EEG changes, with left hemisphere activity decreasing and right hemisphere activity remaining essentially unchanged as the moment of response execution approaches.

In addition to the use of spontaneous EEG changes to draw implications regarding the relative involvement of different regions of the brain in the development of alertness for a specific action, there may also be value in examining the EEG for electrical potential changes that are specifically coupled to the occurrence of discrete events (Donchin, 1979; Regan, 1972). Event-related potentials (ERPs) are small in amplitude compared to the spontaneous brain activity and need the use of averaging procedures to reveal their presence and form. ERPs typically consist of a systematically ordered set of negative and positive waves with the interest being in isolating wave components whose amplitude or latency appears systematically related to task variables (Donchin, Ritter, & McCallum, 1978). A number of movement-related brain potentials have been identified that emerge in the 1–1.5-second period prior to EMG onset in simple ballistic movements, most notably the readiness or *Bereitschafts* potential (N1), the premotion positivity (P1), and the negative motor potential (N2) (Gilden, Vaughan, & Costa, 1966; Kornhuber & Deecke, 1965). To date, however, the attentional significance of each of these components has not been reliably determined and the dearth of data on these potentials from tasks involving gross body movements makes it premature to try and draw applications or implications to sport tasks. Excellent reviews of the existing state of knowledge on ERPs associated with simple movements are provided by Brunia (1987, 1988) and Ritter, Kelso, Kutas, and Shiffrin (1984). (We will discuss a well-documented cognitive ERP, the P300, in a later section of this chapter as a potential measure of mental workload.)

Of the other measures of arousal/activation that offer potential as indicators of the time-varying allocation of alertness in discrete motor tasks, pupillometry appears to offer the greatest potential. As yet, however, pupillometry has not attracted the research interest of sport psychologists, and as such the possible utility and limitations of the method remain unknown.

Performance Limitations Imposed by Variations in Alertness/Arousal

The Arousal-Performance Relationship. The relationship between arousal and performance is undoubtedly the best known one in the whole sport psychology field (Figure 6–1). Performance follows an inverted-U function as arousal increases—the relationship being thus frequently described as the *inverted-U hypothesis* (Duffy, 1962) or as the *Yerkes-Dodson Law,* after its initial discoverers (Yerkes & Dodson, 1908), who described the brightness discrimi-

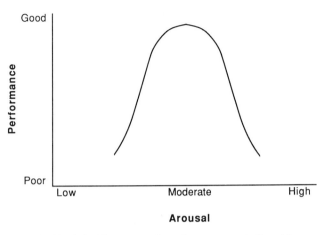

FIGURE 6-1. The arousal-performance relationship.

nation performance of mice subjected to varying levels of electrical shock. Demonstrations of the inverted-U relationship between arousal and human motor performance have been provided on simple laboratory tasks requiring hand steadiness (Martens & Landers, 1970) and RT (Lansing, Schwartz, & Lindsley, 1956), and, more recently, on more gross movement skills, such as throwing, where arousal is manipulated through evaluative feedback regarding the performance of the subjects relative to their peers (e.g., Weinberg & Ragan, 1978). The same relationship has also been shown, more generally, to adequately describe the relationship between precompetitive state anxiety in basketball players and the players' performances throughout a portion of a competitive season (Klavora, 1978; Sonstroem & Bernardo, 1982), arguing that the activation-performance relationship is a generic and robust one.

The essence of the Yerkes-Dodson Law is that there exists for each and every activity a specific level of activation at which performance is maximal. Above and below this optimal level of arousal, performance is submaximal, presumably because effective information processing is in some way impaired. Attaining the optimal level of arousal is obviously, therefore, an important precondition for expert performance in sport.

Factors Influencing the Arousal Level for Optimum Performance. A number of factors will influence the absolute level of arousal that will be optimal for a given athlete on a given sport task. In particular, optimal arousal level will be heavily dependent on the nature of the task—a fact clearly demonstrated in Yerkes and Dodson's original study. Sports tasks that emphasize precision and the recruitment of fine motor skills (e.g., the shooting and aiming sports, putting in golf) are performed best under relatively low levels of arousal, while activities in which the emphasis is upon power and which require a greater recruitment of total muscle mass (e.g., weight lifting, wrestling, shot-putting) require higher levels of arousal for optimal performance (Figure 6–2). In sports where athletes must combine a

range of skills varying in their relative power/precision requirements (e.g., the biathlon; basketball shooting and rebounding), being able to adjust activation levels rapidly is obviously essential for high-level performance.

Individual differences in trait anxiety are also known to systematically influence the level of arousal that supports optimal performance on a given task. As a general rule, individuals who show high levels of trait anxiety are more prone to suffer performance decrements due to overarousal than are individuals with lower levels of trait anxiety (Spielberger, 1966). Likewise, Welford (1968) has argued that individual differences in introversion-extroversion on Eysenck's (1967, 1976) Personality Inventory (EPI) relate closely to the level of activation, with introverts having a higher basal level of arousal than extroverts. Extroverts, by this logic, would therefore require a higher level of task-related arousal in order to perform maximally. Welford further contends that the neuroticism-stability dimension within the EPI relates to tolerance of nonoptimal arousal, neurotic individuals having less tolerance for changes in arousal than stable individuals whose level of performance remains relatively unaffected by substantial changes in activation level (Figure 6–3). The effect of arousal on performance is, therefore, equally a function of the personality of the individual athlete as it is of the nature of the task.

Theoretical Explanations of the Alertness-Performance Relationship

Explanations of the inverted-U relationship between arousal and performance have proceeded on two levels. Welford (1968) has attempted to explain the arousal-performance relationship in general information-processing terms, using an analogy between the brain and nervous system and a communications channel. Welford has argued that at low levels of arousal the channel is largely "inert" and input signals are frequently lost in the various

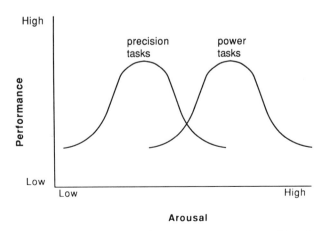

FIGURE 6-2. Task-dependent variations in optimal levels of arousal.

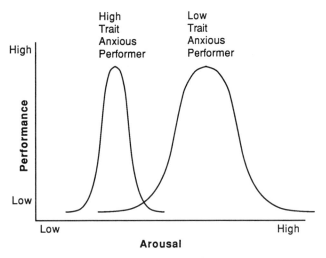

FIGURE 6–3. Variations in optimal arousal levels for performers differing in trait anxiety.

information-processing stages preceding action, whereas at high arousal levels the "noise" arising from the random firing of nerve cells is such as to interfere with, and confuse, the processing of relevant information. At intermediate (optimal) arousal levels neural cells are seen to be readily activated by relevant stimuli, but there is insufficient background neural activity to cause information processing to be inefficient.

A not unrelated, but more specific explanation of the inverted-U relationship between arousal and performance is provided by Easterbrook's (1959) *cue-utilization hypothesis* and the related notion of peripheral narrowing (Kahneman, 1973). Easterbrook argues that performers constantly pick up information from a range of environmental cues, some of which are relevant to the task at hand (e.g., the position of teammates in ball sports) and others of which are not (e.g., the color of the referee's shirt; the movement of the crowd). At low levels of arousal a wide range of cues are picked up and processed, including cues that are irrelevant to the task at hand, and this lack of selectivity results in relatively poor performance (Figure 6–4). As arousal is increased to moderate levels, the range of cues that the performer can process is reduced, irrelevant cues, or cues which initially attracted little interest (Bacon, 1974), are no longer processed, and performance is subsequently maximized. Continued narrowing of the range of cues the performer can process at high levels of arousal eventually leads to the exclusion of some essential task-relevant cues, and this, in turn, manifests itself in less than maximal performance. The explanation is a convincing one, given the presence of a strong body of literature (e.g., Bacon, 1974; Bahrick, Fitts, & Rankin, 1952; Hockey, 1970; Weltman & Egstrom, 1966), including some recent sport-specific evidence (Landers et al., 1985), demonstrating perceptual narrowing under conditions of high stress. (See Cox, 1985, pp. 97–98; Landers, 1982, or Wickens, 1984, pp. 269–270, for reviews of this literature.)

Changes in Alertness/Preparedness That Accompany Skill Acquisition

Arousal Optimization and Increased Resistance to Over-Arousal. Given that performance improves substantially with practice it would be reasonable to suspect that one of the by-products of practice may be a greater ability to control arousal to optimal levels and an increased resistance to the effects of nonoptimal arousal upon performance (i.e., an improved ability to produce high-level performance across a broad bandwidth of arousal levels). Superior self-monitoring, which has been advanced as a characteristic of expertise across a range of cognitive and motor tasks (Glaser & Chi, 1988), may also manifest itself in superior arousal control by experts. Although a number of authors have hypothesized the existence of practice effects on arousal control (e.g., Cox, 1985, p. 95; Schmidt, 1988, p. 137) (see Figure 6–5), documented evidence of these effects is lacking.

Superior reduction of anxiety by qualifiers as opposed to nonqualifiers at an Olympic trial in gymnastics (Mahoney & Avener, 1977) is one of the few pieces of reported evidence consistent with the practice effects typically hypothesized in the textbooks. It is worth noting in passing that the development of greater tolerance to variations in arousal with practice (as shown by a broadened inverted-U function; Figure 6–5) may provide a mechanism through which athletes who are required to combine precision and power

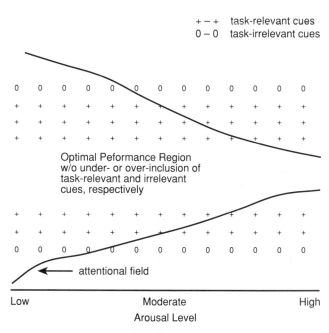

FIGURE 6–4. Peripheral narrowing as a potential explanation of the arousal-performance relationship.

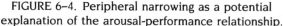

From "The Arousal-Performance Relationship Revisited" by D. M. Landers, 1980, *Research Quarterly for Exercise and Sport, 51*, p. 82. Copyright 1980 by the American Alliance for Health, Physical Education, Recreation and Dance. Reprinted by permission.

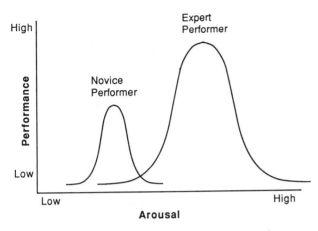

FIGURE 6–5. The effects of expertise on the arousal-performance relationship.

components in their sports performance (such as the biathletes and basketballers referred to earlier) can preserve high performance without repeated, and necessarily rapid, adjustments of arousal level.

Optimization and Improved Consistency in the Temporal Pattern of Alertness Development. We have noted previously evidence for systematic changes in HR and the hemispheric distribution of EEG activity as performers in a number of closed-skill sports prepare to optimize their alertness for response initiation. An important concern with respect to the significance of the observed HR deceleration and the observed shift in information processing from the left to the right hemisphere in the final seconds prior to response initiation is whether or not these physiological changes in alertness are in any way systematically related to skilled performance. Although the available studies have focused primarily on elite athletes and have not used control groups of untrained subjects, comparisons within the elite performers' best and worst trial performances prove enlightening. In particular the presence and extent of cardiac deceleration appears to be directly linked to the level of performance; greater cardiac deceleration immediately prior to initiation of the putt in golf being observed on the best trials of performance (Boutcher & Zinsser, 1990; Crews & Landers, 1991) and the poorest trials frequently showing HR acceleration rather than deceleration (Crews & Landers, 1991; Molander & Backman, 1989). Moreover, the best trials of performance also tend to be those in which the pattern of cardiac deceleration is most consistent (Crews & Landers, 1991), clearly pointing to the potential performance benefits of teaching performers, in this sport at least, consistent preparatory patterns based on HR deceleration.

Available research on hemispheric EEG differences between trials of best and poorest performances is quite limited, but what is available (e.g., Salazer et al., 1990) points promisingly toward a relationship between left hemisphere activity and performance in archery. Perhaps more important is recent evidence (Landers et al., in press) that HR de-

celeration and hemispheric asymmetries in EEG activity are learned patterns, such that after 14 weeks of practice novice archers come to demonstrate temporal patterns of alertness on these measures similar to those observed in elite archers. At initial testing the novice archers showed no evidence of hemispheric EEG differences or of cardiac deceleration. Clearly much more remains to be learned about the significance of these and other physiological markers of the development of alertness, but the implications for practice from the initial works are very promising.

Implications for Skill Acquisition, Instruction, and the Design of Practice

Methods for Optimizing Arousal. Means of optimizing the arousal level of particular athletes for the performance of specific sport tasks are clearly vital for performance enhancement, and warrant separate treatment. Psychological techniques for optimizing arousal level are examined in detail elsewhere in this *Handbook.* It is sufficient to note at this point that methods are presently in use that attack each level of the manifestation of attention and arousal, viz., behavior modification techniques (at the behavioral level), cognitive therapy and mental preparation strategies (at the cognitive level), and biofeedback techniques (at the physiological level).

Methods for Developing Consistent and Appropriate Patterns of Preparation for Responding. There appear to be considerable benefits in developing a highly regimented and consistent pattern of preparation for performance in discrete, self-paced motor skills (see Singer, 1988, for a five-step cognitive strategy for optimizing performance in such tasks and Boutcher & Crews, 1987, for empirical evidence of the performance benefits of routine preparations). Given that psychophysiological variables known to be associated with successful performance in sport skills such as shooting, archery, and golf putting are able to be learned there would appear to be considerable potential for the use of biofeedback on these variables as an aid to learning. Preliminary work by Landers et al. (1991) on pre-elite archers given correct, incorrect, or no feedback on the hemispheric distribution of their EEG activity has shown the expected performance benefits for the correct feedback group alone, suggesting that biofeedback training offers potentially great benefits to athletes in these self-paced aiming tasks. It remains to be seen to what extent these psychophysiological methodologies for enhancing alertness can be eventually applied to other, less constrained types of sporting activities.

SUSTAINING ALERTNESS (THE STUDY OF VIGILANCE)

Defining Vigilance and Its Importance

Many sport events have durations that are of the order of hours or days rather than seconds and require the athletes to sustain a high level of alertness or preparedness over an extended period of time. Outfielders in cricket or softball, for example, need to maintain alertness over a long period of time, as do sports officials such as line or net cord judges in tennis. The difficulty for these athletes and officials is that they are only rarely required to respond, and the alertness problem becomes one of responding quickly and accurately to stimuli that occur infrequently and irregularly over an extended period of time. In the experimental psychology literature, tasks of this nature are referred to as *vigilance* tasks.

A related set of problems in sustaining alertness is confronted by performers who are required to make regular and frequent responses but over a long period of time (e.g., the squash player involved in a long match, the golfer playing a 72-hole tournament, the central referee in a soccer match). Given that maximal alertness appears to be only sustainable over short time periods (of the order of 1–4 seconds in RT paradigms; Woodrow, 1914), constantly and repetitively developing maximal alertness over a number of hours is clearly a taxing undertaking, one that inevitably results in some errors and submaximal performances. Such difficulties may well be exacerbated in situations where substantial physical fatigue accompanies the extended duration of the sport task. Competitive road cyclists, marathon runners, or track and field athletes competing in events such as the decathlon appear more prone to attentional errors as they become fatigued in the later rather than the early stages of their respective events.

The questions of concern in this section are therefore (1) what are the limits to sustaining alertness? (2) how are these limits affected by physical fatigue? and (3) what strategies do successful athletes use to counteract these limits? These problems of sustaining alertness are related to areas of performance that coaches and athletes would generally equate with poor concentration. There is a significant body of literature on vigilance tasks to aid our understanding of alertness in situations where stimuli are infrequent; there is less empirical evidence to guide our understanding of the limits of alertness in repetitive activities.

Paradigms for Studying Vigilance

The study of vigilance owes its origins to the practical problems encountered in World War II by radar operators who were required to sustain alertness for detecting rarely occurring signals over a number of hours at a time. It is not surprising, given these origins, that the paradigms which have been developed to study vigilance are essentially analogues of the radar operator's task. A prototypic example is the early work by Mackworth (1948, 1956) in which subjects watched a clock face over a 2-hour period in order to detect the infrequent occasions (usually about 24 per hour) where the sweep hand jumped 2 seconds at a time rather than the usual 1-second jump. Although the specific tasks have changed slightly over the years the basic vigilance task still typically remains that of de-

tecting and reporting the occurrence of infrequent target events.

Two basic variations in the vigilance paradigm can be identified (Wickens, 1984). In the *free response* paradigm, target events may occur at any time throughout the duration of the experiment and there is no inherent temporal regularity in the display. This is a situation analogous to that facing the road cyclist who must remain vigilant at every second throughout the full duration of the race for potential "break-away" moves by other riders. In the *inspection* paradigm events occur at fairly regular intervals and the task is one of detecting the few *targets* from within a large number of *nontargets*. This paradigm is, therefore, analogous to the task of the softball outfielder or the baseline judge in tennis, where infrequently occurring events (the ball being hit in the outfielder's direction or the ball landing over the baseline) must be detected within a regular pattern of events (each pitch in softball or each stroke hit in tennis). In the laboratory setting the vigilance paradigm is frequently accompanied by concurrent measurement of arousal/alertness using one or more of the range of measures described in the section on momentary alertness.

The favored means of analyzing the performance of subjects on these vigilance tasks is to apply analysis techniques developed as part of Tanner and Swets's *signal-detection theory* (e.g., Swets, 1964; Swets, Tanner, & Birdsall, 1961; Tanner & Swets, 1954). Signal-detection theory grew out of a need to explain the variable capabilities of humans to detect target stimuli (the *signals*) from within an array of nontarget items (the *noise*); precisely the kind of capabilities that are measured in vigilance experiments. The theory is based on the assumption that the extent of background activity within the nervous system unrelated to the processing of signal information ("noise") is normally distributed and the effect of adding a signal that has to be processed (by recruiting more neural activity) is to displace the activation curve to the right. This effectively gives rise to another, normally distributed, "signal plus noise" distribution (Figure 6–6). Because intermediate levels of neural activity may be caused by either the "noise" or "signal plus noise" distributions, it is not surprising that detection errors and errors of judgment, in general, are made.

The frequency of errors a subject will make in these tasks will depend on their sensitivity (d'), which is effectively the mean displacement between the two distributions, while the type of errors they make will depend on the response criterion or cut-off point (β) they adopt. Lenient cut-off points (to the left on the activation continuum) result in more correct detections of target stimuli but at the cost of a large number of false alarms, whereas stringent criteria (β values to the right of the activation continuum) minimize false alarms but at the cost of failing to detect some target stimuli. High arousal has the effect of displacing both distributions to the right, and, if the β criterion is not adjusted, this results in a higher number of both correct detections and false alarms. The model, therefore, predicts that the overaroused or anxious athlete is likely to make responses when they are not required

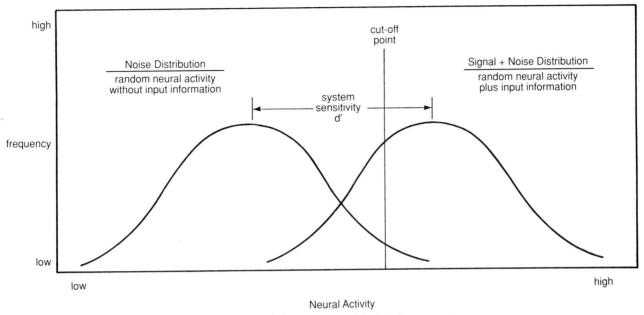

FIGURE 6–6. The signal-detection model of vigilance performance.

(e.g., a baseball batter swinging at a ball outside the strike zone). Conversely under low-arousal conditions, both false alarms and correct detections are predicted to be increased, the error in this case being more probably the failure to respond when a response is called for. Within this view optimal arousal may be meaningfully conceived of as the situation where errors associated with false alarms and missed detections are perfectly balanced (Welford, 1973). Calculation of individual differences in sensitivity (d'), response criterion (β), and the relative false alarm–correct detection rates (usually plotted as Receiver-Operating-Characteristic [ROC] curves) may therefore provide useful measures of vigilance performance.

Signal-detection methodology has outgrown simple applications to vigilance problems and is frequently used to investigate other processes, including comparison (Cox & Hawkins, 1976), recognition (Swensson, 1980), response selection (Jagacinski, Isaac, & Burke, 1977; Newell, 1974), and response execution (Jagacinski, Newell, & Isaac, 1979). Newell (1974) provides an excellent example of the applications of signal-detection methods to the decision processes of baseball batters. It needs to be recognized, however, that signal-detection theory is based on a number of assumptions that may prove tenuous in some instances. Aside from the statistical assumptions about the normality and equal variances of the two component distributions (Pastore & Scheirer, 1974), some of which may be difficult to assess in dynamic settings (Edwards, 1962), and analytical difficulties that arise if the false alarm rate is low (Long & Waag, 1981), the major concern is the extent to which human attentional processes adhere to strict statistical principles (Cohen & Christensen, 1970). In particular, the subjective probabilities subjects use to determine their response criterion may differ from the actual (objective) stimulus probabilities (e.g., see Taylor, 1967; Whiting, 1979), and the response criterion may be multidimensional rather than unidimensional as the theory assumes (Broadbent, 1971).

Performance Limitations Imposed by Vigilance

From the mass of vigilance research conducted since Mackworth's (1948) original work (see Davies & Parasuraman, 1980, or Mackie, 1977, for comprehensive reviews), two principal findings emerge (Wickens, 1984), both of which have practical significance for performers in a number of sport tasks. First, it is apparent that humans have difficulty in sustaining alertness over an extended period of time with high miss rates and/or slow detection latencies being the norm. Second, performance in detecting signals deteriorates very rapidly, with substantial vigilance decrements being evident even with the first 30 minutes of performance. Stressors such as fatigue and sleep loss (e.g., Wilkinson, 1963) exacerbate the vigilance decrements, suggesting that a high level of training and regular sleep patterns may be beneficial in offsetting some of the inevitable lapses in concentration that accompany prolonged physical activity. Although there is a clear dearth of sport-specific research (and indeed any "real-world" data; see Wickens, 1984) to verify the laboratory-based findings, if one assumes any kind of similarity between the laboratory findings and alertness decrements in sport performance, it is clear that human performance limitations on the sustainment of alertness are likely to be a major constraint to performance in many sport tasks.

Theories of the Vigilance Decrements

The decrements in signal-detection performance that occur over extended periods of vigilance appear to be of two types. Vigilance decrements may arise due to a reduction in sensitivity (i.e., a diminished d') or due to the adoption of a more conservative response criterion (a β displacement to the right) (cf. Figure 6–6). The major theories of vigilance decrement address these causes independently. Broadbent (1971) and Parasuraman (1979) argue for reduced sensitivity as the cause of vigilance decrements; the former using visual fatigue as the causal mechanism and the latter arguing that it is the memory load imposed by constant comparison of current stimuli with the memorized template of the target stimulus that creates d' reductions. Welford (1968) maintains that because both correct detections and false alarms decrease over time (e.g., Broadbent & Gregory, 1965), vigilance decrement is simply a consequence of an effective shift in β toward a more conservative level. He postulates that the low frequency of signals in vigilance tasks results in low arousal, and this in turn causes both the "noise" and "signal plus noise" distributions to shrink in magnitude, placing the β level farther into the "signal plus noise" distribution than it was at the commencement of the task. Baker (1961) also attributes vigilance decrement to an effective β criterion shift, but views the adjustment as an active one in response to the expectancy of a lower target stimulus frequency than is encountered in training situations. Wickens (1984) provides a more detailed discussion of the respective merits of these different theories and a sensible caution that each theory may be correct under specific combinations of task conditions and constraints.

Changes in Vigilance Performance That Accompany Skill Acquisition

Although there is a dearth of sport-specific evidence on expert-novice differences on vigilance tasks, simple observations and anecdotes of successful performers suggest the presence of great capabilities for preserving alertness (concentration) over long periods of time. Resistance to the vigilance decrements through the minimizing of fatigue levels (due to superior physical conditioning, technique efficiency, and task strategies) and through the sensitive control of activation at an optimal level may contribute to expert performance. In signal-detection terms it appears, at least from studies of experts in ergonomic tasks (e.g., Blignaut, 1979), that experts are characterized by superior sensitivity (as determined from the area under the correct detection-false alarm rate curve; see Figure 6–7). A superior ability to recognize the attributes of relevant (target) stimuli may contribute to this greater sensitivity of expert performers. We will explore this possibility in more detail later in considering expert-novice differences in selective attention.

Implications for Skill Acquisition, Instruction, and the Design of Practice

From our foregoing discussions on mechanisms of vigilance decrement, it is apparent that improving performance in tasks that require vigilance to be preserved will necessitate developing means of either (a) combatting the reductions in sensitivity (d decreases), (b) preventing conservative shifts in the response criterion, or preferably (c) both. The following strategies may be useful.

Strategies for Combatting Sensitivity Losses. If fatigue is the principal source of sensitivity losses, as Broadbent (1971) has hypothesized, then strategies for offsetting fatigue are obviously to be valued. In this regard improvements in the physical conditioning of athletes and improvements in the efficiency of their technique may assist in reducing or at least delaying vigilance decrements. An alternative means of offsetting vigilance decrements (grounded in Parasuraman's 1979 theory of vigilance) is through enhancing the athlete's capability to recognize relevant stimuli. Learning the distinctive properties of the relevant stimuli for a particular sport and therefore improving attentional selectivity through stimulus enhancement may prove beneficial. (Some strategies for improving selective attention to relevant cues in a sport task will be considered later in this chapter.) Repeated exposure of subjects to the target stimuli may also be a useful training approach, with the putative development of automatic processing having potential benefits in reducing fatigue effects due to mental workload (Fisk & Schneider, 1981).

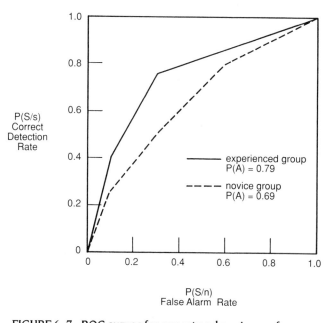

FIGURE 6–7. ROC curves for expert and novice performers. Data are from "The Perception of Hazard: II: The Contribution of Signal-Detection to Hazard" by C. J. M. Blignaut, 1979, *Ergonomics, 22*, p. 1179. Copyright 1979 by Taylor and Francis, Inc. Reprinted by permission.

Strategies for Preventing Conservative Shifts in Response Criterion. If Welford's (1968) arousal theory view of vigilance decrements is correct, then means of increasing subjects' arousal should be beneficial in counteracting vigilance decrements. Biofeedback training aimed at teaching subjects to suppress EEG theta waves (waves typically associated with low arousal) has been reported as helpful in some laboratory settings (Beatty, Greenberg, Deibler, & O'Hanlon, 1974). For the sports performer or coach a more practical means of avoiding lowered arousal is to break up the task as much as possible in order to avoid monotony and boredom at all costs. For athletes involved in repetitive tasks over a long period of time it is vital that natural breaks in the peak attentional requirements of the sport (e.g., the time when the golfer walks from one shot to the next; the breaks between points and between games for the tennis player and umpire) be used for relaxation rather than attempts to maintain peak concentration—a state that we have seen earlier can usually only be retained for a few seconds. Practicing consistent routines that include relaxation or use cognitive strategies such as self-talk to avoid monotony may, therefore, be potentially beneficial to athletes in many sports. For athletes in team sports who are involved only infrequently in plays during a game, such as hockey or soccer goalkeepers, provision of periodic instructions, encouragement, or feedback of any form may be beneficial in avoiding vigilance decrements associated with low arousal (Magill, 1988) and with the automatic adjustment of their response criterion to match the low frequency of relevant stimuli (cf. Baker, 1961).

ATTENTION AS A LIMITED CAPACITY OR RESOURCE

Defining Limited Attentional Capacity and Its Importance

It has long been known that humans have some very real limitations in their ability to perform two or more tasks simultaneously. In the late nineteenth century, Binet (1890) was able to demonstrate that performing a mental arithmetic task interfered with subjects' capability to squeeze a rubber ball at a regular rate (see Keele, 1973), while Welch (1898) showed that hand-grip strength deteriorated during the performance of concurrent mental tasks, including arithmetic. Two tasks performed simultaneously may cause selective decrements in the performance of either one of the two tasks or general decrements in both of the tasks, although in some cases apparently no interference exists. The nature of the observed interference, if any, appears to depend on a number of factors, but as a general rule, newly acquired or difficult tasks appear less able to be performed in parallel with other tasks than well-learned or simple tasks. Adults (with some notable exceptions) have little difficulty walking and chewing gum at the same time, whereas the slightest imposition of a second task to toddlers is gen-

erally sufficient to cause them to either stop walking or, in most cases, to lose balance. Skilled basketball players are able to carefully monitor the position of all teammates and opponents while dribbling the ball, whereas a novice trying to do the same thing will inevitably either lose control of the ball or be forced to switch *attention* rapidly between the two tasks.

Attention in this context, therefore, is equated with notions of limited information-processing space (after Keele, 1973), capacity (after Moray, 1967), or resources (Wickens, 1984), such that difficult tasks performed together are conceived to have cumulative processing requirements that may exceed the available space, capacity, or resources. In such instances the processing of information relevant to one or both of the tasks will be either incomplete or delayed, and this, in turn, causes the observed performance decrements. The limited capacity or space perspective of attention draws an analogy between attention and the fixed capacity of storage devices such as the available memory in a general purpose computer (Moray, 1967). The available processing capacity is fixed but may be partitioned to different tasks in any way the performer decides. When demand exceeds supply, performance in one or both tasks must suffer. The resource analogy is similarly grounded but adds a second constraint that different tasks and processes may require access to different types of resources. The importance of this constraint will be discussed in greater detail later in this section when contrasting theories of attention are examined. At this point it is sufficient to note that the pattern of interference that is observed between different tasks provides vital clues for understanding the nature of the underlying control processes and the capacity or resources available to different individuals, and this information can be useful both practically and theoretically.

Because the performance of many sports (especially team ball games like soccer, water polo, field and ice hockey, and football) frequently require the concurrent performance of two or more skills (e.g., carrying the ball while visually scanning for teammates to pass to), understanding more about attention in this particular context is important for the sport psychologist, coach, and athlete alike. In this section we attempt to determine, among other things, to what extent our information-processing capacities and resources are limited and how skilled performers manage to alleviate some of the attentional constraints that are apparent in the performance of novices. Our discussions take us into considerations of the *attention demands* of different tasks and component processes and into examination of the possibility of *automatic* processes that require apparently none of our capacity or resources.

Paradigms for Studying Capacity/Resource Limitations and Divided Attention

The assessment of the mental workload of particular tasks requires access to measures displaying *sensitivity* to alterations in capacity/resource demand, *selective* influence only to factors affecting resource demand, *diagnosticity* in terms of identifying which capacities or resources are being taxed, *unobtrusiveness* in the sense of not interfering with the performance of the task of interest, and *reliability* (Sheridan & Stassen, 1979; Wickens, 1984). The available behavioral, cognitive, and physiological measures of mental workload vary in the extent to which they satisfy each of these occasionally competing criteria (Wickens, 1979).

The Dual-Task Paradigm.

BASIC LOGIC AND ASSUMPTIONS

It follows logically from the preceding discussion of attention in the context of capacity/resource limitations that the best means of detailing the extent and the nature of the limitations imposed by different tasks and component processes on different individuals may be to have these people perform two (or more) tasks concurrently and measure how successfully they manage to divide attention between the competing tasks. The dual-task paradigm is therefore based on having subjects perform two tasks simultaneously. The task, for which an assessment of attention demand is sought, is termed the *primary task,* while the *secondary task* provides the principal performance-measure changes from which the implications regarding primary task demand are derived. A large range of secondary tasks have been described in the literature (Ogden, Levine, & Eisner, 1979; Rolfe, 1973), but the most popular are simple RT tasks (usually referred to in the dual-task configuration as probe reaction time—PRT).

Different instructional sets may be used to alter the priorities subjects are required to assign to the two tasks. In the simplest case subjects are required to give attentional priority to the primary task (so that primary task performance remains at a level in the dual situation comparable to that when the task is performed in isolation), and changes in secondary task performance in this instance can be directly linked to attentional fluctuations in the demands of the primary task. Such an instructional set is most likely to be used if the interest is principally in understanding more about the primary task. Careful monitoring of primary task performance levels throughout the course of such experiments is clearly needed to ensure that the required priorities are indeed followed by the subjects. An alternative instructional set, which might be employed if interest is in understanding the capability of subjects to switch attention and time share between concurrent tasks rather than the attentional demands of the primary task per se, involves simply instructing subjects to perform both tasks to the best of their capability. Ogden et al. (1979) have suggested that the term *secondary-task paradigm* be used to describe the first of these instructional sets and the term *dual-task paradigm* be reserved for use with the latter, but in the majority of the published literature the terms have been used interchangeably.

If one assumes (1) an instructional set that places priority on the primary task and (2) the preexistence of a finite information-processing capacity (Figure 6–8), then it seems reasonable to posit that secondary task performance will be a direct reflection of the residual processing capacity that remains after the demands of the primary task have been met. Poor secondary task performance would be expected to accompany difficult primary tasks (for which the demands on processing capacity are substantial), whereas secondary task performance with response latencies or error rates essentially unchanged from those evident when the secondary task is performed in isolation would be expected to accompany primary tasks that are simple and that tap little of the performer's limited processing capacity. Secondary task performance (relative to control levels) therefore reflects the attention demand of the primary task and its component processes. The total absence of secondary task decrements for secondary tasks known to be sensitive to primary task demands may indicate that the primary task is performed automatically, requiring none of the

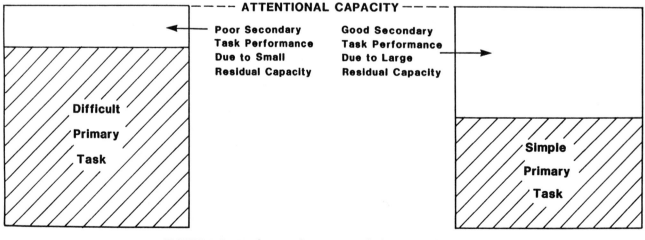

FIGURE 6–8. Fundamental notions underlying the dual-task measure of attention.

available processing capacity. The notion of automaticity is a fundamental one for attention in this context (e.g., Shiffrin & Schneider, 1977), and the evidence to support such a mode of processing will be critically evaluated later in this section. The tenability of the basic assumptions within the dual-task paradigm varies somewhat, depending on whether one adopts a theory of attention based on a single, common capacity or one based on a number of resource pools, each with its own unique capacities and limitations. We shall also examine these various theoretical propositions in greater detail later in this discussion. At this point it is sufficient to note that there are a number of important methodological concerns that need to be met if the dual-task paradigm is to be provide data of value.

METHODOLOGICAL CONCERNS AND CONSTRAINTS

There are at least four major methodological concerns to be addressed by the researcher using the dual-task paradigm. The first of these concerns relates to the question of task selection. When the dual-task method is applied to understanding the attentional demands of sport tasks, the sport task of interest automatically becomes the primary task. The vexing methodological question then becomes what secondary task from the enormous range of possible secondary tasks (Ogden et al., 1979; Wickens, 1984) should be coupled with the primary task. Issues to be considered in secondary task selection include deciding between continuous and discrete measures and deciding between tasks that create or apparently avoid structural interference. *Structural interference* is interference caused by the simultaneous use of common input or output processes by both tasks, whereas *capacity interference* is interference that arises when the cumulative attentional demands of the two tasks exceeds the available central-processing capacity (Kahneman, 1973).

Continuous or temporarily coextensive secondary tasks (Heuer & Wing, 1984) have the advantage of keeping the cumulative (primary plus secondary) demands relatively constant throughout the task but are limited in terms of how much they can help the researcher equate attentional fluctuations with specific phases in the primary task (secondary task errors may accumulate with continuous secondary tasks). For this reason discrete secondary tasks like PRT are greatly favored if the precise localization of attentional demands is sought.

The decision of whether or not to seek secondary tasks that may cause structural rather than capacity interference depends largely on the purpose of the study. If the principal interest is in seeing how well performers can cope with specific resource overloads of the type normally encountered in the natural setting (e.g., the visual overloads existing in many ball sports, where visual resources are needed for the two concurrent tasks, such as in catching a ball while scanning ahead for unmarked teammates), then simulation of the precise structural interference of the "real world" setting is obviously desirable. If the interest is rather to develop a general measure of the residual attention remaining after the attentional needs of a particular primary task are

met, then care should be taken to ensure that the secondary task utilizes different sensory and response modalities from those used by the primary task. The difficulty here is that structural interference may arise in subtle and unexpected manners, as in the case of tasks requiring bimanual responses (McLeod, 1977) or tasks sharing a common timing structure (e.g., Kelso, Tuller, & Harris, 1983; McLeod, 1978). Perhaps more alarming is the possibility that a single, common, general-purpose central-processing capacity may not exist (or even if it does exist, its total capacity may be variable; Kahneman, 1973) and that rather a finite number of special-purpose resource pools exist that make the search for general measures of spare attention fruitless endeavors (Allport, 1980; Navon & Gopher, 1979).

A second methodological problem relates to the control of temporal uncertainty in the presentation of the secondary task. If discrete secondary tasks such as PRT are used, care needs to be taken to ensure that the probability of the probe stimulus occurrence remains consistent throughout the duration of the primary task. Random presentations of the secondary task stimuli result in increased stimulus probability across the primary task extent. The longer the primary task proceeds without the probe stimulus occurring, the more probable it becomes, and this probability change can influence PRT independent of the concurrent primary task attentional demands. The inclusion of frequent "catch trials" (primary task trials without secondary stimuli) within the dual testing conditions provides one potential means of alleviating this problem (Salmoni, Sullivan, & Starkes, 1976). (Also see McLeod, 1980, for an alternative based on a constant rate of probe stimulus presentations.)

Generating appropriate baseline measures for the primary and secondary task presents a third major methodological concern. Dual-task data are only interpretable through comparison of the performance of both the primary and secondary task when they are completed together with their level of performance in isolation. Single-to-dual comparisons of primary task performance provide an indication of the extent to which the subjects adhere to the imposed instructional set or attempt to time-share between the two tasks, whereas the single-to-dual comparisons of secondary task performance provide a measure of the attentional demand of the primary task. Given the uses to which the secondary task data in particular are put, it is essential that the baseline (single) conditions match exactly the dual conditions with respect not only to the stimulus-response configurations used but also with respect to the spacing and relative frequency of stimuli. Measurement of baseline levels of the secondary task under conditions with a higher relative frequency of stimuli than in the dual setting may result in artificially low control values of PRT and, in turn, an inflated estimate of the attention demands of the primary task.

Finally it should be noted that there are problems within the dual-task paradigm in precisely localizing attentional demands. A common practice in many studies concerned with plotting the time course of attentional fluctuations in specific primary tasks and concerned with precisely locating attentional peaks and troughs in given tasks (e.g., Ells, 1973; Posner & Keele, 1969) is to plot PRT as a function of the time of probe stimulus presentation during the primary task and then to equate attention levels directly with events and processes occurring at the time of stimulus presentation. The inaccuracy in this approach is that attention may remain elevated from the time of probe presentation until the time at which the response to the probe is actually completed. Plotting attention demand relative to stimulus presentation may therefore place peak attentional demands systematically too early in the primary task, a bias that can be eliminated by also plotting PRT relative to the point of response completion (McLeod, 1980). When such plotting procedures are used, more conservative but nevertheless more accurate estimates of the location of attentional peaks in the primary task can be derived (Girouard, Laurencelle, & Proteau, 1984). (More detailed considerations of these and other methodological concerns and constraints with the use of the dual-task paradigm may be found in Bainbridge, 1974; Brown, 1978; McLeod, 1980; and Abernethy, 1988a.)

APPLICATIONS AND POTENTIAL APPLICATIONS OF THE DUAL TASK TECHNIQUE

The dual-task technique offers potential for insight into attention-demand differences within and between different movement tasks and between different individuals performing the same movement tasks.

A relatively common application of the dual-task technique has been to use PRT measurements to determine attention-demand fluctuations within particular motor tasks, especially simple limb movements. The results from such studies have been somewhat mixed, although high attention demands are typically observed at the start of the movement and attributed to preprogramming (e.g., Ells, 1973; Glencross, 1980; Glencross & Gould, 1979) and at the end of movement and attributed to error correction (e.g., Kerr, 1975; Posner & Keele, 1969; Zelaznik, Shapiro, & McClosky, 1981). The middle, ballistic phase of simple positioning movements appears to place relatively low demands on available processing capacity/resources (Posner & Keele, 1969), although these conclusions now appear at least partially dependent on the modality used for stimulus presentation or response initiation (Girouard et al., 1984; McLeod, 1980). Schmidt (1988), in reviewing the available evidence, argues for increasing attention demands as information processing moves beyond stimulus identification and approaches the response programming stage.

There has been a pleasing recent increase in applications of the dual-task paradigm to study the time course of attentional changes in sport tasks. Studies by Nettleton (1979, 1984) that aim to assess the attention demand of ball-tracking skills in sports like soccer and hockey by examining PRT changes throughout the performance of a laboratory coincidence-timing task suggest a time course of attentional changes similar to those revealed in the control of simple linear aiming movements (cf. Posner & Keele, 1969). Attention demands appear greatest during the initial and final stages of observation of the approaching motion with monitoring in the middle, essentially redundant phase being relatively attention-free. Studies of simple catching tasks indicate that attention demands are greatest in the later stages of ball flight as the initiation of the grasping response is being undertaken (Populin, Rose, & Heath, 1990; Starkes, 1986). Recent comparisons of the attention demands of a diverse range of sport tasks (volleyball, tennis, 100-m sprinting, and hurdling) by Castiello and Umilta (1988) demonstrate the presence of a high degree of specificity in the demands different athletic events place upon human attentional capacities and resources, indicating, among other things, the need for an expanded database on the patterns of attention within specific sport tasks (see also Tenenbaum, Benedick, & Bar-Eli, 1988). The limited evidence currently available from the above studies and studies of the tasks of rifle shooting (Landers et al., 1985; Rose & Christina, 1990), badminton (Abernethy, 1988a), and high jumping (Girouard, Perreault, Vachon, & Black, 1978) do not permit categorization of sport tasks on the basis of patterns of attentional demands.

Although comparisons between different tasks are commonplace in the ergonomics field as a means of assessing relative workloads (Wickens, 1984), systematic comparisons between the attention demands of different sport tasks do not appear to have been undertaken to date. Two particular applications appear worthy of pursuit, however: (1) the use of dual-task comparisons between "real world" tasks and laboratory simulations as a means of assessing the extent to which simulations are successful in replicating the processing demands of the natural setting; and (2) the use of dual-task comparisons of different lead-up activities for particular sport skills as a means of objectively ordering the presentation of the activities in terms of ascending complexity/attentional demand. With this information a more suitable matching of training activities to learner capability may be achieved than when this matching is done purely on the basis of performance scores on the (primary task) activities. (See Abernethy, 1988a, for a more detailed consideration of these two potential applications.)

One of the most powerful applications of the dual-task technique, and the one particularly relevant to sport coaches, involves the use of dual-task techniques to determine the relative workloads given tasks impose on different individuals. The technique offers an objective means of determining attentional effort and the extent of spare (residual) attentional capacity, and provides an avenue for isolating differences in untapped performance potential between two individuals, even when their performance levels on the primary task may be indistinguishable. We will consider the existing evidence on expert-novice differences in attentional loads later in this section of this chapter when the links between attentional capacities, resources, and skill acquisition are discussed.

Other Measures of Divided Attention and Mental Workload.

SUBJECTIVE, SELF-REPORT MEASURES

One simple means of estimating the mental workload imposed by any particular task or combination of tasks is to have the individual performing the task self-report or rate the mental load he or she experiences (Moray, 1982; Sheridan, 1980). A number of scales for the subjective rating of mental workload have been developed for use in ergonomic settings, among the most popular being Reid, Shingledecker, and Eggemeier's (1981) Subjective Workload Assessment Technique (e.g., Eggemeier, Crabtree, & Pointe, 1983), the Cooper-Harper Scale (Cooper & Harper, 1969) and its modifications (e.g., Casali & Wierwille, 1983), Sheridan's (1980) dimensional scale, and multidimensional scaling approaches such as those provided by Derrick (1981) and Miller and Hart (1984). (See Meshkati & Loewenthal, 1988, and Wickens, 1984, for comprehensive reviews.) Although such measures are convenient in the sense that they can be easily administered and derived without disrupting primary task performance, the ever present concern is that the performer's verbal estimates may not accurately reflect the demand placed on available processing resources. Because subjective workload assessments have been demonstrated, at least in some tasks, to be insensitive to changes in secondary task performance (Vidulich, 1988), such methods for assessing task demands have not, as yet, become popular in the sport psychology literature.

PHYSIOLOGICAL MEASURES

The dual-task technique may actively alter the nature of primary task performance and may, in most cases, provide only a discontinuous measure of attentional fluctuations on a task. However, physiological measures of the information-processing load have the advantage of being generally continuous and nonintrusive, although it can be argued that the inconvenience and constraints imposed by the presence of recording electrodes and other equipment may, in fact, affect the nature of primary task performance. The collective disadvantage of the many different physiological measures of information-processing load that are available are that they are at a different level of analysis and hence, in effect, are one step farther removed from dual-task measures and from the phenomenon of capacity or resource limitations that we seek to understand (Wickens, 1984). Pupil diameter, cardiac acceleration/deceleration and variability, and EEG event-related potentials have all been used at various times to provide markers of information-processing load.

Small changes in pupil diameter appear to provide a reasonable indication of the resource demands of particular cognitive tasks (Beatty, 1982). Pupil dilations occur systematically with the imposition of arithmetic, memory, or problem-solving tasks (e.g., Beatty & Kahneman, 1966; Beatty & Wagoner, 1978; Kahneman, Beatty, & Pollack, 1967), although the changes themselves provide little illumination as to the nature/location of the underlying resource limitations. As we have seen previously, pupil diameter also reflects arousal levels, and therefore arousal level changes between tasks or between individuals may act to confound and limit the types of comparisons justifiable from pupillometry.

Although absolute HR levels do not appear to be reliable indicators of task workload across a range of tasks (Wierwille & Connor, 1983; Wierwille, Rhami, & Casali, 1985), at least two other HR measures may be related to the attentional demands of tasks. Jennings, Lawrence, and Kasper (1978), building on Kahneman's (1973) theory of attention, have argued that cardiac acceleration/deceleration (as assessed from relative changes in interbeat interval) may be systematically related to available processing capacity. These authors have demonstrated that while absolute HR is affected more by the overall response requirements of the task (an RT task in their case), the relative acceleration/deceleration patterns in HR relate closely to PRT measures. HR deceleration appears to accompany and index the presence of spare capacity or attentional reserves, whereas HR acceleration is more prevalent in conditions of processing overload. To date investigation of the utility of this measure in the sport context is only in its infancy (Crews & Landers, 1991), although clearly this, like other potential cardiac measures of attention, will be of use only in those activities where the performer remains essentially stationary.

An increasingly popular measure of mental workload within the ergonomics literature is HR *variability*. Across a range of different methods of calculating variability, including, most recently, spectral analyses (e.g., Meshkati, 1988; Opmeer, 1973), heart rate variability appears to decrease as the attentional demands of a task are increased (Mulder & Mulder, 1980, 1981; Vincente, Thornton, & Moray, 1987), making it one of the more promising physiological indicators of attentional workload or effort. This measure, like pupil diameter, however, appears to reflect more the total demand on all available processing resources than the specific competition between processing resources (Wickens & Derrick, 1981) and, therefore, may have limitations as a diagnostic device (Wickens, 1984). Heart rate variability has not, as yet, been used in assessing the attentional demands of different sport tasks, probably because the cardiac changes associated with any form of physical activity would confound and "swamp" the relatively small effects due to cognitive processing. The measure may be useful in sports (such as the aiming sports), where the maintenance of body stability during preparation is important to performance.

We noted previously in discussing measures of the time course of alertness that event-related (or evoked) potentials (ERPs) within the EEG may also provide valuable measures of attention. The typical ERP is composed of two types of components: *exogenous components* that are always present, regardless of how the particular evoking stimulus is to be processed, and *endogenous components* that vary according to the type of information processing that is required. A number of endogenous ERP components appear to be related to the demands placed by tasks on available processing capacity and resources. The N200 component (components are typically named with respect to their polarity and time of appearance relative to stimulus presentation) appears to reflect modality-specific processes, but the later P300, which is recorded maximally over the parietal scalp at a minimum peak latency of 300 milliseconds post-stimulus (Sutton, Braren, Zubin, & John, 1965), appears to be non–modality-specific (Simson, Vaughan, & Ritter, 1977; Snyder, Hillyard, & Galambos, 1980) and, therefore, a potentially promising general marker of attention. The P300 *latency* appears to be sensitive to the memory load imposed by the primary task (Kramer & Strayer, 1988), although reported correlations between P300 latency and RT vary considerably in their strength (Donchin, 1984; Donchin, Ritter, & McCallum, 1978). More importantly the *amplitude* of the P300 component appears sensitive to the resource demands of different processes, with the P300 amplitude decreasing as secondary task demands are increased (e.g., Israel, Chesney, Wickens, & Donchin, 1980; Israel, Wickens, Chesney, & Donchin, 1980; Kramer, Wickens, & Donchin, 1983). (See Kramer & Strayer, 1988, Wilson & O'Donnell, 1988, Hillyard, 1984, and Donchin, 1984, for detailed reviews of the P300 component.) The P300 measure has an important advantage over other physiological measures of attentional demand in that it provides a measure that is graded to perceptual/cognitive load, and therefore may have some diagnostic value in isolating specific resource limitations (Wickens, 1984). The downside for sport psychologists is the relative inaccessibility and expense of the required recording technology, the task constraints that are imposed by the recording electrodes, and the necessity for subject stillness to avoid movement artifacts in the recordings.

Relating and Combining Task Measures

As was noted previously in examining behavioral, cognitive, and physiological measures of arousal, concordance between different measures of attention is not always high. For this reason the question of finding the best single measure of attention demand is one that clearly depends on the use to which the collected measures are to be put and, to a lesser extent, the nature of the task(s) and individual(s) under examination. The use of multiple measures from a number of different levels of analysis appears as a logical strategy for assessing attentional workload (Wickens, 1984; Wilson & O'Donnell, 1988), the physiological and cognitive measures in particular complementing well the strengths and weaknesses of the other measure.

Performance Limitations Imposed by Limited Processing Capacity and Resources

Substantial research on cognition and some on action using the dual-task technique (e.g., see Eysenck, 1984, for a review) makes it clear, as coaches of young athletes will well recognize, that human information-processing resources do indeed have finite limits and these limits can be sufficiently restrictive in some situations to make errors and performance decrements inevitable. A *complementarity principle* (Norman & Bobrow, 1975) appears to be in effect wherein resource (or capacity) availability determines performance and increases in the allocation of resources to one task produces a commensurate reduction in the availability of resources to other tasks or processes being performed at the same time. The resource allocation–performance relationship need not necessarily be a linear one, however, as measurement artifacts, such as ceiling effects (Heuer & Wing, 1984), and performance limiting factors other than resources (Norman & Bobrow, 1975) may be present. The magnitude of the errors observed on secondary tasks depends on a number of factors, with performance decrements being generally greatest for anxious, untrained subjects performing two or more complex tasks simultaneously and least for experienced subjects performing two apparently simple tasks together (e.g., an experienced motor racer driving a civilian vehicle in light traffic while conducting a conversation with a passenger). If we assume for the moment that available attention exists in the form of a general, undifferentiated capacity (cf. Kahneman, 1978), then there are at least three major factors that will determine our capability to perform a secondary task. These factors are depicted schematically in Figure 6–9 and described in more detail below.

The Total Available Capacity as a Limiting Factor. The total available attentional capacity may depend on the alertness/arousal of the individual subject or athlete with greatest information-processing capacity being available when the performer is optimally aroused (cf. Figure 6–1). All the factors we noted previously that may affect alertness, including individual differences in personality, may therefore affect available processing capacity and, in turn, secondary task performance.

The Primary Task Demand as a Limiting Factor. Secondary task performance depends strongly on the proportion of the available capacity that is consumed by the primary task, and this in turn depends on the extent to which the primary task (or processes within it) can be performed automatically. Influential work, inspired by earlier research on visual search by Neisser (1964), Schneider and Shiffrin (1977), and Shiffrin and Schneider (1977), drew a distinction between two fundamentally and qualitatively different forms of information processing. The term *controlled processing* was used to describe processing that was (1) attention demanding or effortful (in the sense of causing and experiencing interference with other concurrent tasks), (2) serial in nature, (3) slow, and (4) volitional, in the sense of being able to be consciously altered or prevented. Such processing was expected (and observed) in situations where the nature of the task and the type of processing required is constantly changing (what Shiffrin and Schneider operationalized through *variable stimulus-response mapping* conditions). In contrast, what Shiffrin

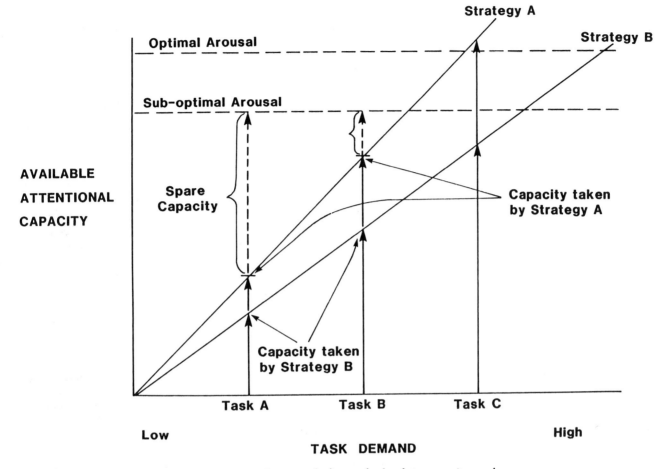

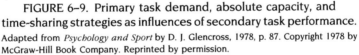

FIGURE 6–9. Primary task demand, absolute capacity, and
time-sharing strategies as influences of secondary task performance.
Adapted from *Psychology and Sport* by D. J. Glencross, 1978, p. 87. Copyright 1978 by
McGraw-Hill Book Company. Reprinted by permission.

and Schneider (1977) termed *automatic processing,* and
what has been variously described elsewhere as "involuntary" (Kimble & Perlmutter, 1970), "obligatory" (LaBerge,
1975), "mindless" (Norman, 1976), "nonstrategic" (Klein,
1978), and "mandatory" (Navon & Gopher, 1979), appears
to be (1) largely without attention demand or effort (in the
sense that other concurrent processes do not interfere with
it, (2) parallel in nature, (3) fast, and (4) inevitable, in the
sense that processing of this type does not appear to be consciously alterable or preventable. Shiffrin and Schneider
(1977) maintain that such processing develops with practice when subjects repetitively experience the same
stimulus-and-response patterns (e.g., *consistent mapping*
conditions).

The notion of automatic processing is a particularly
appealing one in terms of explaining the apparent release
from effortful processing that accompanies skill acquisition
and in explaining errors made in daily activities (Norman,
1981; Reason, 1979), but its operationalization as a theoretical concept is confused by the range of different features
and dimensions used to distinguish it from controlled proc-

essing. The difficulty is that there is a lack of internal consistency between the various features used to distinguish
controlled and automatic processing (Phillips & Hughes,
1988) such that some processes that are considered to be
beyond the voluntary control of subjects, for example, may
still be slow or elicit interference. The lack of consistent
distinction between controlled and automatic processing
has been the principal source of challenge to dichotomous
views of processing, such as those posited by Shiffrin and
Schneider (1977) (e.g., Broadbent, 1982; Cheng, 1985;
Heuer, 1984; Neumann, 1984; and Ryan, 1983). We consider
the evidence for automaticity in more detail later in this
section in evaluating changes in capacity and resource allocation that accompany skill acquisition.

***Strategies for Attentional Switching and Time Sharing as
a Limiting Factor.*** A third factor influencing secondary
task performance is the strategy individual subjects use in
order to share resources and switch attention between the
primary and secondary tasks (Figure 6–9). Clear evidence
exists that subjects can apportion the allocation of at-

tentional capacity and resources between two or more tasks in a flexible manner (e.g., Gopher & Navon, 1980; Schneider & Fisk, 1982a; Wickens & Gopher, 1977), and an improved capability to share attentional resources and time between the concurrent tasks is an important component of skill acquisition in multitask situations (Adams, 1966; Klein, 1976). Damos and Wickens (1980), for example, have clearly demonstrated improvements in multiple-task performance that are a function of improved time sharing rather than decreasing attention demands (improved automation) of the primary task. The strategies adopted by subjects are apparently not always fixed ones and may vary as the demands of the primary task alter (Sperandio, 1978).

If our limiting attention consists not of a single capacity but rather a multiple set of relatively specific resources, each with its own unique capacity limits (e.g., Navon & Gopher, 1979; Wickens, 1980), then consideration of a fourth factor, the specific resources demanded by given combinations of tasks, also needs to be made in order to understand secondary task performance. Such a view also challenges some of the more fundamental assumptions on which the dual-task method in particular is based. These contrasting capacity and resource views of attention (terms that we have used somewhat synonymously to date) are considered in more detail in the next subsection.

Theories of Attentional Capacity and Resources

Attention as a Fixed Capacity with Structural Constraints: The Single-Channel Theory and Related Views. The earliest fixed-capacity theory of attention was the *single-channel theory* in which the processing of information from sensation all the way through to the production of action was conceived as occurring through a single processing channel limited to the sequential handling of either one signal at a time (Welford, 1952, 1967) or a finite number of bits of information per second (Broadbent, 1958). The principal support for the single-channel theory came from RT studies using a double-stimulation paradigm in which subjects were required to respond to two stimuli presented in rapid succession (each stimulus having its own unique response requirement). Of interest within this paradigm was the extent to which the RT to the second stimulus was elevated beyond normal control levels—the extent of any delay being known as the psychological refractory period (PRP). PRP effects are well known to sports performers; offensive players in a number of sports use fakes in an attempt to fool their opponents into processing incorrect information that, if successful, delays their opponent's response to their imperative move. (See Schmidt, 1988, p. 114, for a fuller discussion of this problem.)

Early PRP studies revealed (1) an essentially linear relationship between the extent of the PRP delay and the length of the interstimulus interval (ISI) for ISIs less than the duration of the first RT, with the PRP delay disappearing when the length of the ISI exceeded the duration of the RT to the first stimulus (e.g., Davis, 1959; Welford, 1967), and (2) re-

duced PRP delays when the RT to the first stimulus was fast rather than slow (e.g., Broadbent & Gregory, 1967). (See Figure 6–10.) Such evidence was consistent with the view that the processing of the second signal could not be commenced until the channel had been cleared of the demands imposed by the first signal. Unfortunately the supportive evidence was gathered primarily from studies in which both stimuli were presented to the same modality, therefore potentially creating structural interference by overloading specific processors (Allport, Antonis, & Reynolds, 1972; Kahneman, 1973). When different stimulus and response modes were used for the two RT tasks, consistent violations of the expected 45° slope between PRP and ISI were obtained (e.g., Greenwald & Schulman, 1973), RT to the second stimulus was frequently found to remain elevated after the channel in theory should have been cleared (e.g., Karlin & Kestenbaum, 1968), and the nature and difficulty of the second task was found to unexpectedly influence the RT to the first stimulus (Barber, 1989; Way & Gottsdanker, 1968). The presence of these contradictory data, along with evidence from dual-task paradigms for parallel processing in the early stages of visual search and memory retrieval (e.g., Keele, 1972, 1973; LaBerge, 1981), resulted in general abandonment of a global single-channel view and the search rather for those specific processes within the information-processing chain that appeared to be limited to serial, single-channel kinds of processing.

Attempts to locate the so-called "bottlenecks" in human information processing (i.e., the points at which processing alters from a parallel mode to a serial mode and signals are forced to queue) also proved far from fruitful. Different bottlenecks appeared to exist, dependent on the task combinations and on the attention- and time-sharing strategies used by the subjects, arguing against the presence of fixed structural constraints to processing capacity. (See Allport, 1980a, Glencross, 1978, Schmidt, 1988, and Barber, 1989, for reviews of this literature and a later portion of this chapter for examples of this work in the selective attention field.)

Attention as a General, Flexible Capacity. On the basis of these inconsistent data concerning the location of the limited processing channel within the information-processing chain, Moray (1967) and later Kahneman (1973) proposed that attention be more appropriately viewed as a flexible commodity that while having finite overall limitations, can be flexibly allocated between concurrent tasks in any manner the subject chooses. Flexible allocation of a limited resource provides a reasonable explanation of why different processing limitations (and hence conclusions about bottlenecks) emerge from different subjects and from different task combinations. As Allport (1980a) observes, the natural analogue for this type of capacity is not a passive, structurally fixed container but rather a limited power supply. Once the task demands fully load the system, additional "power consumption" at any point in the system can only be offset by reductions somewhere else, regardless of the use to which the power is to be put. Within this model ". . . inter-

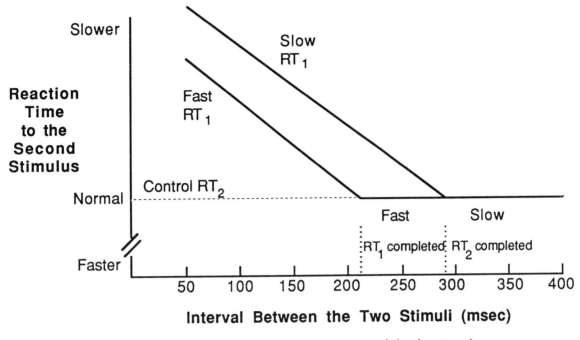

FIGURE 6-10. Relationships between RT_2, ISI, and the duration of RT_1 as predicted by single-channel theory.

ference is non-specific, and depends only on the (combined) demands of both the tasks" (Kahneman, 1973, p. 11). Although the available power supply (capacity) is limited, Kahneman suggests that the total available power may vary somewhat, dependent on the arousal level of the performer.

Like its predecessors, the fixed-capacity theories, the variable allocation theory of attention has also proven to be flawed, although it nevertheless retains a number of influential supporters (e.g., Kantowitz, 1985). The most damning evidence against the theories of Kahneman and others comes from observations of inconsistent interference when different secondary tasks are coupled with the same primary task. This ironically turns out not to be a new finding but something that has been evident since the early studies of the late 1800s (see Keele, 1973, p. 4). If attention really exists in the form of a large, undifferentiated general capacity, then different secondary tasks performed in conjunction with a common primary task should reveal consistent conclusions regarding the attention demand of the primary task, yet such does not appear to be the case (e.g., Navon & Gopher, 1979; Wakelin, 1967).

Attention as Multiple-Resource Pools. The difficulties with viewing attention as a general-purpose, limited-capacity central processor were clearly articulated by Navon and Gopher (1979) and Allport (1980a) and a major theoretical reformulation was set in place in the early 1980s. The contemporary view of attention is as a series of resource pools (Gopher & Sanders, 1984; Navon & Gopher, 1979; Wickens, 1980, 1984) or multiprocessors (Allport, 1980b;

Allport et al., 1972; McLeod, 1977), each with their own unique capacities and resource-performance relationships. Within such a theory of attention, capacity is seen not to be centralized but rather *distributed* throughout the nervous system, and the interest therefore becomes not that of measuring the limits of central-processing capacity but rather isolating the specific, special-purpose ("dedicated" or "informationally encapsulated"; Fodor, 1983) modular subsystems that collectively comprise the resource pool. Autonomous visual mechanisms for the pickup of time-to-contact information, for example, have been proposed as examples of such modules (McLeod, McLaughlin, & Nimmo-Smith, 1985). The implications of such a view for dual-task performance are important, viz., (1) primary tasks (such as the movement skills basic to many sports) do not carry any absolute attention demand that is measurable from a set of standardized secondary tasks and (2) the level of dual-task performance observed is a consequence of the unique resource requirements and competition for resources that exists between the two tasks. Perhaps more radically the resource view causes one to question whether indeed there is any finite capacity limitation at all within human performance (Neumann,1987).

Evidence in support of the resource model of attention comes from a number of sources (Stelmach & Hughes, 1983), including (1) mutual interference increases when tasks share common sensory or output modalities (e.g., Allport et al., 1972; Mcleod, 1977), (2) absence of secondary task decrements under some unique conditions of dissimilarity between the two tasks (e.g., Allport et al., 1972; Shiffrin & Gardner, 1972), and (3) minimal commonality in time-sharing strategies across altered task combinations (e.g., Wickens, Mountford, & Schreiner, 1981). More detailed reviews of the evidence favoring resource models of attention are provided by Wickens (1984) and Barber (1989).

A number of propositions have already been advanced as to the composition of some of the many processing resources. Wickens (1984) has proposed that resources may be defined in terms of the subcells formed by the combination of a number of simple dichotomous dimensions, including stage of processing (e.g., early versus late processes), input and output modalities (e.g., visual versus auditory input; manual versus vocal output), and processing codes (e.g., spatial versus visual). (See Figure 6–11.) Interference can then be explained in terms of the extent to which the two tasks tap common resource features (or cells). An alternative means of identifying resources is in terms of the capabilities of each of the cerebral hemispheres (e.g., Friedman & Polson, 1981; Kinsbourne & Hicks, 1978; McFarland & Ashton, 1978), the advantage in this case being that manual and vocal control asymmetries can be used as markers of resource usage.

There remain acknowledged difficulties with the resource theories as currently formulated, especially with respect to the persistence of some minimal interference effects when tasks apparently share no specific resource demands in common (Barber, 1989; Broadbent, 1982; Wickens, 1984), but clearly the greatest difficulty and future challenge lies in the specific identification of the different resource pools and the testing of their concordance with known patterns of interference from dual-task studies (Neumann, 1987). The fact that alternative models of attention—especially those of Neumann (1984, 1987), which argue for dual-task interference as a consequence of active (and functional) suppression of competing responses rather than a consequence of capacity or resource limitations—are attracting increasing interest indicates that we are still far from a satisfactory, universally accepted theory of attention. The testing of resource theories is complicated by the possibility that performance, in all cases, may be limited by factors other than resources (e.g., see Norman & Bobrow, 1975, for a useful distinction of *resource-limited* and *data-limited* processing).

Changes in Capacity and Resource Allocation That Accompany Skill Acquisition

Evidence and Mechanisms for Improved Dual-Task Performance with Practice. Both training studies and expert-novice comparisons clearly indicate that the performance of two or more concurrent tasks can be improved with practice and that a capacity for handling concurrent task demands is an important ingredient of expert performance in many activities. It has been known that dual-task performance can be improved with practice since the time of Solomons and Stein's (1896) introspections on concurrent reading and writing, although the most widely cited empirical demonstration of the extent of improvement that is possible is a latter-day replication and extension of the Solomons and Stein work by Spelke, Hirst, and Neisser

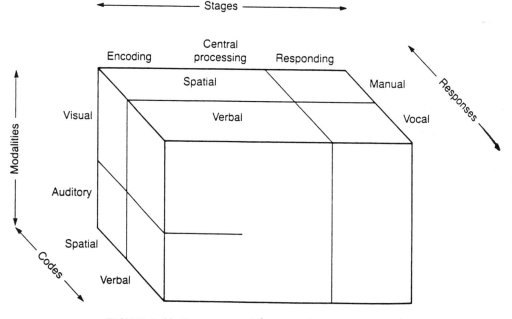

FIGURE 6–11. Some potential processing resources and their structure.

From *Engineering Psychology and Human Performance* by C. D. Wickens, 1984, p. 302. Copyright 1984 by Charles E. Merrill Publishing Company. Reprinted by permission.

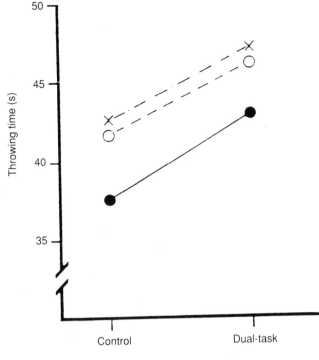

FIGURE 6–12. Primary task performance on a throwing and catching task by A, B, and C grade netball players.
From "Visual Detection and Perception in Netball." In I. M. Cockerill and W. W. MacGillivary (Eds.), *Vision and Sport,* 1981, p. 49. Copyright 1981 by Stanley Thornes Publishers. Reprinted by permission.

tasks selected for inclusion in this study mimicked fairly closely the demands of the actual game situation, where players are required to perform basic skills like passing and catching under severe time constraints while simultaneously monitoring, primarily through peripheral vision, the movements of teammates and opponents.

The primary task required the players to complete as many passes to a designated target and return as many catches as possible in a 30-second period. Analysis of primary task performance (Figure 6–12) revealed (1) no significant differences in the number of passes and catches successfully completed between the A, B, and C grade players; and (2) some decrements in task performance for all the groups of subjects when they were required to perform the passing and catching task in conjunction with a secondary task. Secondary task performance, as assessed by the number of errors in detecting the illumination of peripherally located lights during the performance of the primary task, was, however, sensitive to the skill level of the players with the higher skilled (A grade) players making fewer detection errors than the lesser skilled (B and C grade) players (Figure 6–13). The expert players apparently have more "spare" capacity or resources to allocate to the secondary task (or, stated alternatively, need less capacity or resource to perform the primary task) than the lesser skilled players.

(1976). Spelke et al. gave 2 subjects 5 hours of training a week for 4 months on a range of tasks, including concurrent reading for comprehension and written dictation. After initially experiencing great difficulty with the concurrent tasks, the 2 subjects acquired the combined skill to the point where the reading-for-comprehension task showed no single-to-dual task decrement, although their memory for the dictation task remained poorer in the dual condition than it was when performed alone. These findings, demonstrating comprehensively that interference between tasks is not fixed but is readily modifiable with practice, are supported by a host of more recent studies (e.g., Damos, Bittner, Kennedy, & Harbeson, 1981).

Comparisons of the dual-task performance of experts and novices in a range of ergonomic tasks (e.g., Brown, 1962; Crosby & Parkinson, 1979; Damos, 1978; North & Gopher, 1976) and, more recently, in some selected sports tasks (e.g., Leavitt, 1979; Parker, 1981; Vankersschaver, 1984) have clearly revealed systematic secondary task performance superiority for expert performers even in instances where expert-novice differences are not apparent on the primary task. Parker's (1981) study of the concurrent performance of a ball-catching and -throwing task (the primary task) and a peripheral visual detection task (the secondary task) by netball players of different skill levels provides a good example of such a study from sport. The

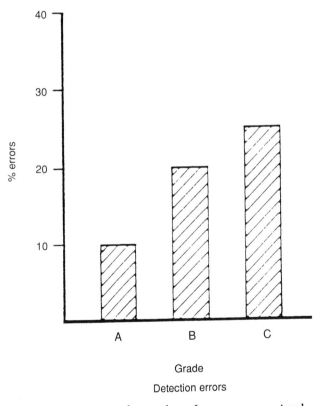

FIGURE 6–13. Secondary task performance on a visual detection task by A, B, and C grade netball players.
From "Visual Detection and Perception in Netball." In I. M. Cockerill and W. W. MacGillivary (Eds.), *Vision and Sport,* 1981, p. 49. Copyright 1981 by Stanley Thornes Publishers. Reprinted by permission.

These data also provide an important demonstration of one of the great advantages of the dual-task paradigm, viz., the capability of the technique to isolate differences in attention demand between individuals, even when primary task capabilities *appear* equivalent (cf. Glencross, 1978; Wickens, 1984). Players who require relatively large amounts of their limited attentional capacity or resources to be allocated to the performance of basic game skills are those more likely to display "tunnel vision" during game situations, missing opportunities to pass to free teammates and to "read" the developing patterns of play.

Eysenck (1984, p. 63) suggests that there are at least three potential mechanisms through which dual-task performance may be improved. These are:

1. The attentional demands of one or both tasks may be reduced (presumably through a complete or partial transition from controlled processing to automatic processing; cf. Shiffrin & Schneider, 1977);
2. The subjects may develop new time-sharing and attentional-switching strategies that allow intertask interference to be reduced;
3. A more economical mode of functioning may be established that either decreases the number of processing resources required (Norman & Bobrow, 1975) or spreads the processing requirements so that both tasks avoid using resources that are required by the other (Allport, 1980a).

Consideration of Figure 6–9 also suggests a fourth potential mechanism through which dual-task performance may be improved, namely, increased availability of capacity or resources through optimization of arousal. The possibility of automaticity will be considered in further detail here because of the extent of attention it has attracted in the research literature and because empirical investigations (e.g., Brown & Carr, 1989) argue that increased intratask automaticity, rather than improved deployment of resources through attentional switching strategies, is the principal mechanism through which dual-task performance is enhanced with practice.

Evidence and Mechanisms for Increased Automaticity with Practice. As noted earlier the most influential arguments for an automatic mode of processing have been advanced by Shiffrin and Schneider (1977). Shiffrin and Schneider's arguments for automaticity have been based on evidence that, with extensive practice under conditions of consistent stimulus-response mapping, RT becomes essentially independent of the number of items within the memory set that needs to be scanned (Figure 6–14). (See also Schneider & Fisk, 1982b, 1983.) Nevertheless, when RT is plotted against memory set size, small positive slopes remain, suggesting that the memory-scanning process is still not completely automatic (Logan, 1979). Similar effects can be seen in older studies on choice RT (Mowbray & Rhoades, 1959), where the slope of the RT–number of choices plot decreases with practice but never quite

reaches a zero value. Likewise, although the single-to-dual differences in secondary task performance decrease with practice, secondary task decrements of zero, as a strict notion of automaticity requires, are rarely, if ever, found in dual-task experiments (e.g., Hoffman, Nelson, & Houck, 1983; Schneider & Fisk, 1982b). Spelke et al.'s (1976) subjects, for example, still showed poorer performance in the dictation test when performed in tandem with the reading task than when performed alone and Parker's (1981) A-grade netballers made errors in the secondary detection task that they would not have committed had the detection task been performed alone (Figure 6–13).

These data, which appear to indicate that there are some inevitable costs associated with performing two tasks together (Navon & Gopher, 1979), argue against the existence of automaticity in its strictest sense as defined by Shiffrin and Schneider (1977) (Näätänen, 1988; Stelmach & Hughes, 1983) and suggest that a more sensible way to conceive of controlled-automatic processing may be as a continuum rather than as a dichotomy (Logan, 1985). In line with this kind of view, Navon and Gopher (1979) and Kahneman and Treisman (1984) have made arguments for the recognition of different levels of automaticity, the latter authors suggesting that a meaningful distinction can be drawn between *strong automaticity* (in which processing is neither facilitated by volition or impaired by distraction), *partial automaticity* (in which processing is normally nonvolitional but can be facilitated by volition) and *occasional automaticity* (in which processing generally demands attention but can sometimes be completed without it). It is important to recognize that some component

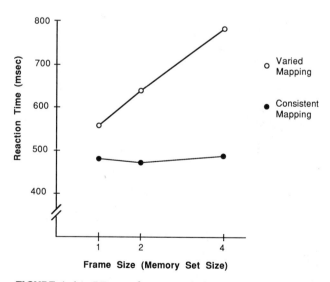

FIGURE 6–14. RT as a function of memory set size over consistent and varied practice.

Adapted from "Controlled and Automatic Human Information Processing: I: Detection, search, and attention" by W. Schneider and R. M. Shiffrin, 1977, *Psychological Review, 84*, p. 20. Copyright 1977 by American Psychological Association. Reprinted by permission.

processes within a given task may be strongly automated and others only occasionally automated (Jonides, Naveh-Benjamin, & Palmer, 1985; Logan, 1979), although the general transition with practice appears to be away from controlled processing toward strongly automated processing (Schneider, 1985). Even with these modifications to Shiffrin and Schneider's (1977) original notion of automatic processing, the concept of increased automaticity with practice remains an appealing one with particular relevance to sport. One particularly interesting by-product of increased automaticity is a decreased ability of performers to self-report on the control processes they use, and this frequently presents particular problems to expert sports performers who find themselves in the position of attempting to coach or instruct learners.

It is not quite clear what mechanisms are responsible for the emergence of automaticity with practice, but a number of propositions appear feasible. Improved recognition and utilization of redundancies available in the perception of stimulus patterns and in the production of stereotyped movement responses may facilitate automation of processing through reducing the information-processing load imposed on the performer. On the perceptual side, improved recognition of task-relevant sources of information (to be discussed in further detail in the next section) and, on the response side, the feedback redundancy that supports the transition from closed-loop to open-loop movement control (Schmidt & McCabe, 1976; Wrisberg & Shea, 1978) provide mechanisms for decreasing the processing demands of tasks, presumably allowing attentional resources to be freed up. The more efficient self-organizational strategies (Fowler & Turvey, 1978) subjects discover for resource sharing between tasks also undoubtedly lays an important foundation for automaticity. Indeed, some authors (e.g., Heuer, 1984) have argued that what we observe and label as automaticity may simply be the result of a displacement in resource demands. The transition from primarily visual to primarily kinesthetic control, which occurs with skill acquisition on some tasks (e.g., Fleishman & Rich, 1963), may provide a case in point here. Some claims have been made for attention switching between tasks being a generalizable ability (Keele, 1982; Keele & Hawkins, 1982; Lane, 1982), and therefore a potentially useful advance predictor of success on tasks requiring divided attention, but this generalizability seems limited (Wickens, 1984) and perhaps a methodological artifact (Ackerman, Schneider, & Wickens, 1984).

Evidence and Mechanisms for Reduced PRP Delays with Practice. We noted in discussing the single-channel theory earlier that human performers experience considerable delays in responding to two signals presented in rapid succession and that this has potentially devastating effects on the performance of defensive players in some sports. How might the potential problem of PRP delays be overcome by skilled performers? Practice in laboratory tasks reduces but does not eliminate PRP delays (Gottsdanker & Stelmach, 1971), suggesting that the benefits of practice may be primarily due to faster processing of the first stimulus. The only sure way to eliminate the PRP delays confronted in sport tasks is not to respond to the first (false) stimulus, and one of the distinguishing attributes of skilled performers appears to be this general ability to selectively attend to only relevant sources of information. (We will discuss this capability more fully in the next section.)

Implications for Skill Acquisition, Instruction, and the Design of Practice

The preceding discussions of theories of divided attention and of mechanisms of skilled performance suggest the following practical implications:

1. Given that interference effects appear very task-specific and that the development of strategies for attentional sharing between tasks is an integral part of skill acquisition, it follows that training situations must afford the opportunity for the performer to practice the specific attention-switching and resource-sharing strategies required in the natural skill. Practice is only likely to be effective if it is *content-specific* (Allport, 1980a). Schneider (1985) and Ackerman and Schneider (1985), on the basis of their visual search experiments, argue for consistent rather than varied practice as a means of invoking automaticity (see again Figure 6–14), although care needs to be exercised in extending this conclusion to all types of tasks. Schmidt (1983), on the basis of a range of motor control studies, argues rather for variability as an important requirement in practice, especially if training is for sport skills that require the performer to be adaptable. Empirical attempts to replicate the Shiffrin and Schneider (1977) findings of consistent practice superiority with sport-specific stimuli (e.g., Schilling, 1987) have not always been successful, and psychophysiological studies using the P300 measure have been inconsistent in demonstrating differences between variable and consistent mapping conditions (e.g., compare Kramer & Strayer, 1988, and Hoffman, Simons, & Houck, 1983). The issue of how practice should be structured for maximal learning is considered in detail elsewhere in this *Handbook.*

2. Evidence of long-term improvements in dual-task performance (e.g., Spelke et al., 1976) suggests that there may be value in using progressively more difficult dual-task combinations as a continued stimulus for primary task automation in performers at all skill levels (see also Schneider, 1985). Since there appears to be little evidence to suggest that skill development ever ceases, even after millions of trials of practice (e.g., Crossman, 1959), continued attentional overload in practice (either through the addition of a more demanding secondary task or the addition of a third concurrent task) may be a useful method for maintaining skill improvements, even in expert performers. To date there appear to have been

few attempts to systematically apply this type of strategy to elite coaching.

3. Dual-task measures appear to offer particular benefits as measures of skill learning, and consideration should be given by teachers and coaches to the inclusion of measures of this type in skill assessment and talent identification. The real advantage of dual-task measures, as we have seen in Figures 6–12 and 6–13, is that they allow differences in skill acquisition to be uncovered when such differences are not apparent from observation of the primary task alone. In using dual-task measures in this way, however, it must be remembered that performance is determined by a range of factors in addition to resource allocation and availability (e.g., see Ackerman & Schneider, 1985).

4. Knowledge of the attentional demands of different phases and types of movement also has important implications for how instruction might best proceed in sport skills. Magill (1989, pp. 210–211) provides a range of examples from the learning of sport skills illustrating how instruction and practice should focus selectively on those aspects of the skill that are initially attention demanding but that ultimately need to be executed with little or no attention demand.

ATTENTION IN THE CONTEXT OF SELECTIVITY

Defining Selective Attention and Its Importance

The previous section has demonstrated that there exist substantial limitations in our available attentional capacity or resources. Given the enormous amount of information that bombards the human performer every second (from both external and internal sources), it becomes essential for performance efficiency that only the most relevant (or pertinent) information actually gets processed. *Selective attention* is the general term used to describe the process by which certain information is preferentially selected for detailed processing while other information is ignored.

In fast ball sports, where the time constraints are such that response selection decisions must frequently be made on the basis of information available either prior to ball flight or, at least, very early ball flight (Abernethy, 1987a; Glencross & Cibich, 1977), selective attention to only the most relevant sources of information is clearly fundamental to successful performance. The success of the boxer trying to anticipate his opponent's punches, the baseball batter trying to predict the forthcoming pitch, the pole-vaulter or golfer trying to avoid distractions from crowd noise, or the fullback in rugby trying to field a high kick while being stormed by opposing tacklers all depend on the extent to which they can attend to only relevant information and exclude attending to irrelevant or distracting events. Distracting information may come not only from external sources (e.g., crowd noise, the fakes of an opponent) but also from within (e.g., subjective feelings of fatigue or excessive thinking about past successes or failures).

The important issues to address in furthering our understanding of selective attention, especially as it applies to sport tasks, are, therefore:

1. What stimulus events are sufficiently informative (and hence relevant) to warrant detailed processing and, equally, what stimuli (both internal and external) should be ignored? (Identifying relevant sources of information for particular sport skills is vital as a means of providing a principled basis for instruction in these activities.)

2. Through what mechanism(s) are processing resources selectively allocated to relevant rather than irrelevant stimuli?

3. Given this knowledge, how might attentional allocation to only relevant sources of information be improved with practice?

Paradigms for Studying Selective Attention

Paradigms for Examining Fundamental Theories of Selective Attention.

AN AUDITORY PARADIGM: THE DICHOTIC LISTENING TASK

Early investigations into selective attention (e.g., Cherry, 1953; Moray, 1959) utilized a dichotic listening paradigm that, in essence, was a laboratory analogue for the selective listening that occurs at many social gatherings (the so-called "cocktail party phenomenon"; Cherry, 1953). In this paradigm subjects were presented with separate messages at the left and right ears, and were required to repeat verbally or *shadow* the message presented to one of the ears. The shadowing task was assumed to cause subjects to allocate attention preferentially to the message that was to be repeated, and the interest was in determining to what extent selective attention to only the shadowed message was complete. These experimenters, therefore, measured how much and what features of the message presented to the other ear could be reported. (Reporting on features of the unshadowed message was taken as evidence that those features had received additional processing.) Studies of this kind (e.g., Cherry, 1953; Mowbray, 1953) consistently indicated that subjects processed very little of the information from the unshadowed message, apparently being able to selectively process only the information that was relevant to the task at hand, although some particular physical characteristics of the unshadowed message (such as a change from a male to a female voice or the insertion of a high-frequency tone) were regularly detected, suggesting preferential (arguably automatic) processing of this kind of information. Work by Spieth, Curtis, and Weber (1954), for example, suggests that the frequency characteristics of different voices may aid selective attention to one speaker over another in natural situations.

VISUAL ANALOGUES TO DICHOTIC LISTENING

Since many more of the selective attention problems encountered in sport involve selecting between competing

FIGURE 6–15. Sample single (A and B) and combined (C) video images from a selective looking experiment.
From "Selective looking: Attending to visually specified events" by U. Neisser and R. Becklen, 1975, *Cognitive Psychology, 9,* p. 485. Copyright 1975 by Academic Press. Reprinted by permission.

visual signals rather than auditory signals, selective-looking rather than selective-listening paradigms may be more appropriate. Neisser and Becklen (1975) have presented one such paradigm by superimposing videotapes of separate games on the same television monitor (Figure 6–15). In this case the subject's task is to follow one of the games only and to detect the occurrence of a particular event—e.g., a ball being thrown or caught. Despite changes in the stimulus modalities used, the same basic conclusions emerge regarding selective attention from studies using this visual analogue—i.e., subjects can selectively attend to only one of the images with relative ease and effectiveness, even when the competing displays are quite similar (Neisser, 1979), and even unusual events in the other display are only rarely noticed.

Methods for Determining the Direction and Breadth of Selective Attention.

SELF-REPORT MEASURES

A popular psychological inventory for assessing individual attentional strengths and weaknesses in a range of performance settings, including sport, is the Test of Attentional and Interpersonal Style (TAIS) (Nideffer, 1976). The TAIS (see the chapter by Nideffer elsewhere in this *Handbook* for more detail) is a 144-item pencil-and-paper test structured on two basic theoretical premises. The first, derived from the work of Silverman (1964) and Wachtel (1967), is that the attentional requirement of tasks can be adequately represented along two independent dimensions—a width dimension, which refers to the number of concurrent stimuli that can be effectively attended to, and a direction dimension, which refers to the extent to which attention is directed externally to environmental stimuli or internally to cognitions and emotions. Collectively these dimensions allow the attentional requirements of different tasks to be positioned in one of four possible quadrants (e.g., see

Nideffer, 1979, for examples). The second premise is that individuals, like tasks, can be classified with respect to some enduring attentional styles, and measurement of these styles is sought primarily through six attentional scales within the TAIS, three measuring elements of effective attention, and three complementary aspects of ineffective attention.

Despite its persistent use by sport psychologists, both the construct and predictive validity of the TAIS have been queried by a number of researchers. Factor analyses of data collected from the TAIS on sport groups do not appear to reveal the two-dimensional structure of attention on which the TAIS was developed, the attentional breadth (or bandwidth) dimension in particular appearing to be multidimensional rather than unidimensional (e.g., Summers & Ford, 1990; Van Schoyck & Grasha, 1981). Further, although some gains in predictive validity may be achieved through the use of sport-specific rather than general test items (Albrecht & Feltz, 1987; Van Schoyck & Grasha, 1981), the TAIS has been generally shown to be a poor discriminator of experts and novices in sports in which selective attention is known to be important (e.g., Aronson, 1982; Landers, Boutcher, & Wang, 1986; Zaichkowsky, Jackson, & Aronson, 1982).

When expert-novice differences have been observed, they have often been on subscales other than those presupposed to be important for the particular activity (Jackson, 1981; Landers, Furst, & Daniels, 1981). Moreover, the expected relationships between given subscales and specific behavioral tests of different aspects of attention (e.g., dual-task and visual search tests) are also rarely observed (e.g., Dewey, Brawley, & Allard, 1989; Reis & Bird, 1982; Turner & Gilliland, 1977; Vallerand, 1983), casting further doubt on the validity of the measure. Although refutation of much of this contradictory evidence has been attempted (e.g., see Nideffer, 1990), the empirical evidence indicates that the test must be interpreted with caution. Concerns of the type outlined above have lead a number of researchers (e.g., Landers, 1982) to seek more objective behavioral and physiological measures or selective attention.

BEHAVIORAL MEASURES

The dual-task methods described elsewhere in this paper for assessing peripheral/attentional narrowing provide a potential objective means of assessing attentional breadth but not direction (e.g., see Landers et al., 1985). Decreased awareness or slowed responses to peripheral stimuli while performing a demanding task utilizing central vision may be directly indicative of a transition in attentional focus from broad to narrow. The reduced awareness of fatigued athletes to events occurring around them is a practical example of the kind of attentional breadth changes quantifiable by dual-task methods in which the secondary task taps peripheral awareness.

PHYSIOLOGICAL MEASURES

One of the most influential hypotheses in psychophysiology is Lacey's (1967) *intake-rejection hypothesis,* which posits a direct relationship between HR changes and attentional direction. Lacey proposes that HR deceleration accompanies the intake of environmental information (i.e., an external focus of attention), whereas in situations where environmental information is rejected in order to focus on internal processes HR acceleration is predicted. The intake-rejection hypothesis has received considerable empirical support (see Martin & Venables, 1980, and Graham & Clifton, 1966), especially from visual RT tasks showing cardiac deceleration (e.g., Lacey & Lacey, 1970) and mental arithmetic tasks showing HR increases (e.g., Dahl & Spence, 1971; Sharit, Salvendy, & Deisenroth, 1982). Although Lacey's (1967) hypothesis is consistent with the HR deceleration that occurs immediately prior to response initiation in a number of sport tasks, other explanations of this phenomenon, which do not involve an attentional direction notion, are also possible (e.g., Jennings et al., 1978; van der Molen, Somsen, & Orlebeke, 1985). Recent work on golf putting by Crews and Landers (1991), for example, suggests that an explanation of cardiac changes based on an attentional direction notion is at least partially viable. Crews and Landers argue that sensory awareness creates the cardiac deceleration pattern while cognitive elaboration acts to inhibit this effect. These suggestions, like those of Ray and Cole (1985), which suggest that spontaneous EEG alpha activity is sensitive to the internality-externality of attentional focus, clearly need further empirical verification, especially from examinations conducted in sport-specific settings.

Methods for Determining the Relevance of Specific Cues/Information Sources.

VERBALIZATION/SELF-REPORT METHODS

One obvious means of attempting to find out what cues are important in a particular sport task is to simply ask expert performers what information they look for or place pri-

ority on. The difficulty with this self-report approach, as we have noted at a number of points throughout this chapter, is that performers may not have direct verbal access to their control processes (Nisbett & Wilson, 1977), especially if these processes are automated ones, and as a consequence athletes may tend to report the usage of cues that they expect to be important (or have been told are important), rather than the ones they actually use. For example, many tennis players and baseball batters report that they watch the ball right up to the point of contact with the racquet or bat and report on seeing the ball actually hit the racquet or bat, yet objective measures of their visual tracking behavior make it clear that visual fixation on the ball is discontinued well before actual contact (Bahill & La Ritz, 1984; Stein & Slatt, 1981). The great difficulty with the study of selective attention is that improvements occur through recognition of stimulus patterns which the subjects are themselves not consciously aware of (e.g., Nissen & Bullemer, 1987; Pew, 1974). As Sharp (1978) notes,

> The fact that top-level performers sometimes cannot recount and describe how it is they perform so skilfully . . . suggests that they may be operating at a pre-attentive level of processing having predicted the situation through contextual information and expectations derived from experience (p. 5).

If self-report techniques are to be used to determine the relevance of different cue sources, they should clearly be used cautiously and preferably in tandem with other, more objective measures.

CUE OCCLUSION TECHNIQUES

Selectively occluding visibility to specific information sources in the display, through either temporal or spatial masking procedures, provides a viable and sensitive means of determining the importance of different environmental cues for sports performance. In the occlusion techniques the visual display (often the action of an opposing player in sports such as tennis, soccer, and ice hockey) is typically simulated by filming from the performer's normal viewing position, and then this film is selectively edited to either mask out visibility to specific time periods of environmental information (temporal occlusion) or specific spatial regions of the display (spatial occlusion). The subject's task in these instances may be to make either a perceptual decision (e.g., "where will the ball land?") or a response-selection decision (e.g., "what stroke should be played?") on the basis of the information available.

In the temporal occlusion technique the emphasis is upon discovering those time periods (or time windows) in which response accuracy is rapidly improved, indicating the pickup of information from the display. By scanning the display for principal events occurring during these time windows implications can be drawn as to probable cue usage. The technique has been used quite extensively to demonstrate the value of advance cues for anticipating the action of an opponent in many ball sports. Film simulations have generally been used (see Abernethy, 1987a, for a review), but "real-world" analogues using occluding visors (e.g., Day, 1980) and electronically controlled glasses (e.g., Milgram, 1987) are also possible.

In the spatial occlusion technique, cue importance can be assessed directly from the response decrements that occur when visibility of a given cue is occluded. Provided that realistic display simulations can be developed, both of these occlusion techniques are very useful ones for determining patterns of selective information pickup by different subjects, especially when both procedures are applied to the same activity to provide confirmatory checks (see Abernethy, 1985, for a more detailed discussion of the strengths and limitations of the occlusion techniques and Abernethy & Russell, 1987a, for a sample application). We will discuss data collected from studies using these methods in examining selective attention changes that accompany skill acquisition.

EYE MOVEMENT RECORDING TECHNIQUES

An increasingly popular means of attempting to ascertain patterns of information pickup or cue usage in sport tasks is to monitor where performers look through the use of sophisticated eye movement–recording devices (e.g., see Bard & Fleury, 1976, 1981; Ripoli, Papin, Guezennec, Verdy, & Philip, 1985; Tyldesley, Bootsma, & Bomhoff, 1982). As performers constantly move their eyes in order to maintain high visual clarity on features of interest and as information is, as a rule, only actively picked up during fixations (periods when the eye remains relatively stationary), information about the location, duration, and order of fixations in a given performer's visual search pattern *may* be insightful with respect to their selective attention. Although at a global level visual search-pattern analyses may be revealing, there are limitations in the eye movement approach that need to be recognized and differences between visual search and selective attention that need to be highlighted (Abernethy, 1988b). The major limitations with the eye movement–recording approach are:

1. Because attention can be moved around the visual field without making eye movements, visual fixation and attention are therefore not one and the same (e.g., Littman & Becklan, 1976; Posner, 1980; Remington, 1980; Shulman, Remington, & McLean, 1979).
2. Visual orientation (as shown through fixations) does not necessarily guarantee information pickup (e.g., Stager & Angus, 1978), i.e., "looking" does not equate with "seeing" (Adams, 1966);
3. Eye movement recording techniques are only informative with respect to central vision; they reveal nothing about the important pickup of information for orienting, locating stimuli, and judging speed of motion and orientation, much of which occurs through peripheral vision (e.g., Leibowitz & Post, 1982);
4. The substantial trial-to-trial variability (Noton & Stark, 1971) and task specificity (Peterson, 1969; Yarbus, 1967) of eye movement patterns makes it difficult to reach reli-

able conclusions about the relevance/importance of different display features.
5. The data collection technique is in itself difficult, and the recording devices are potentially disruptive to subjects' normal allocation of attention and information pickup (e.g., Megaw & Richardson, 1979).

More detailed consideration of these constraints and the general value of eye movement–recording approaches in sport are provided elsewhere (Abernethy, 1985, 1988b). Like the verbalization procedures, eye movement–recording approaches to determining cue usage in sport may be most effective when used in combination with other methods.

Performance Limitations Imposed by Selective Attention

Selective attention is something of a double-edged phenomenon—it is a blessing in terms of helping the performer overcome potential distractions but a curse in situations where attention needs to be simultaneously divided between more information sources than the performer is able to concurrently process. A useful metaphor for describing these strengths and limitations of selective attention is in terms of a searchlight (Watchel, 1967). The intent in using a searchlight is to focus the light only on that which is important (as everything within the beam of light comes under attention regardless of whether it is important or not). The breadth of the beam in this sense has to be adjusted according to the range of information we want to pick up, and the position of the beam may need to be constantly adjusted if important information exists at a number of different spatial locations. Further, just as the searchlight is only a guide to its user, varied visual attention may only be a guide to the human brain—the brain interpreting the information available with regard to particular past experiences, contexts, and plans.

The searchlight metaphor is useful in describing the three main types of error associated with attentional selectivity, viz.,

1. Failure to focus all attention on the limited essential elements for task success ("having the searchlight too broad").
2. Being distracted from relevant information by irrelevant information ("having the searchlight pointed in the wrong direction").
3. Being unable to divide our attention between all the stimuli we need to process concurrently ("having the searchlight beam too narrow or being unable to move the searchlight rapidly enough from one spot to the next").

The archer who performs poorly through directing attention in only the general direction of the target rather than concentrating intently on the precise point on the target he or she wishes to hit provides an example of the first type of error, while the basketball player who falls for an opponent's head fake rather than watching his or her trunk for cues, or the golfer who is distracted from the task at hand by thoughts about previous shots commit errors of the second type outlined above. Errors of the third type arise in situations where there is simply too much relevant information to process in too short a time. The beginning soccer player may have concurrent processing demands for relevant visual information (regarding the position of teammates, opponents, the sidelines, and goalposts), kinesthetic information (to help in the control of the dribbled ball), and auditory information (verbal instructions from the coach, captain, and teammates), but some of this information will not be able to be processed in the time available, and errors such as losing possession of the ball will inevitably arise. Switching attention between different stimulus modalities appears to be a time-consuming process, and delays in processing of the order of 100 ms may occur if this switching is unanticipated (La Berge, van Gelder, & Yellott, 1971; Moray & Fitter, 1973).

In sport situations, therefore, a number of factors will influence the efficiency of the selective attention process. In addition to limitations posed by the amount of irrelevant information (and its discernibility from relevant information sources) and by the extent of attentional switching required by the task, the three principal factors influencing the effectiveness of the selective attention process will be (1) the total amount of information in the display, (2) the time required to pick up and process the essential information, and (3) the ability of the player (Jones, 1972). We will examine expert-novice differences in selective attention later in this section. Before considering the theoretical explanations of selective attention that have been posited, it is worth noting that attentional selectivity is not an insular concept nor one completely removed from the notions of attention as alertness and as a limited processing resource examined previously. The peripheral narrowing effects of heightened arousal, for instance, impact on the breadth of cue processing the player can partake in, while processing resource limitations ultimately constrain the extent to which simultaneous attention to different information sources is possible.

Theories and Models of Selective Attention

The older formal theories of selective attention, which still tend to dominate the selective attention literature, have been largely theories that have assumed the existence of fixed structural limitations to the parallel processing of input information (an assumption that we noted in the previous section on resources may be unjustifiable). These older theories have varied mainly in terms of where they assume the selection process to take place, and hence where they assume the bottleneck between parallel and serial processing to be located (Shiffrin, Craig, & Cohen, 1973). (See Figure 6–16.)

Filter Models of Selective Attention. Broadbent (1958) attempted to explain the findings from the dichotic listening

experiments of Cherry (1953) and others by proposing the existence of an early filter mechanism that selects incoming signals for further processing on the basis of some physical characteristics. Selected information was assumed to receive further detailed (resource-intensive) processing while the nonselected information was assumed, in the absence of further processing, to be subject to rapid decay and loss. The difficulty for the Broadbent theory was in demonstrating that some apparently irrelevant information nevertheless appears to receive further, detailed processing. Some aspects of the nonshadowed message in dichotic listening tasks, for example, manage to gain access to the limited processing resource(s) and to our consciousness (e.g., Moray, 1959), while in the visual domain the Stroop phenomenon (Stroop, 1935) provides a powerful demonstration of the interference effects of irrelevant stimulus features on RT (e.g., Keele, 1972). To account for these effects, Deutsch and Deutsch (1963) proposed that the selective filter was located much later in the information-processing chain, at the completion of the perceptual analysis stage rather than at the completion of the stimulus encoding stage. The question of early versus late selection remains a persistently interesting one to cognitive psychologists (e.g., see Broadbent, 1982) and increasingly to phys-

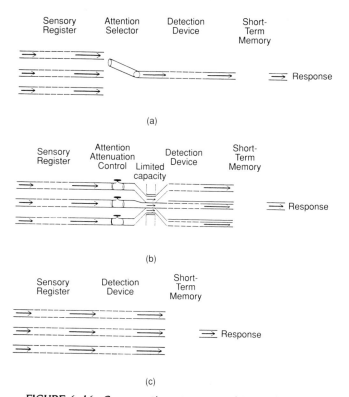

(a)

(b)

(c)

FIGURE 6–16. Comparative structure of (a) early filter models, (b) attentuation models, and (c) late selection models of selective attention.

From "On the degree of attention and capacity limitations in tactile processing" by R. M. Shiffrin, J. C. Craig, & E. Cohen, 1973, *Perception and Psychophysics, 13,* p. 329. Copyright 1973 by The Psychonomics Society, Inc. Reprinted by permission.

iological psychologists (e.g., Hansen & Hillyard, 1983; Naatanen, 1988), with considerable evidence to support both positions (see Broadbent, 1982, and Wickens, 1984, pp. 282–284, for summaries). The presence of such conflicting evidence is perhaps not surprising, given the notions discussed previously about the flexible allocation of attentional capacity (e.g., Kahneman, 1973) and resources (e.g., Navon & Gopher, 1979).

The Attenuation Model of Selective Attention. An alternative way of explaining how some, apparently irrelevant stimuli manage to gain access to our limited processing resources without necessitating a late-selection filter, as Deutsch and Deutsch (1963) proposed, is to assume that all incoming stimuli are subject to a series of increasingly complex signal analysis tests. The attenuation model of Treisman (1964, 1969) proposed a series of tests (the first based on the physical properties of the stimuli, the second based on collective stimulus patterns, and the third based on semantics) with irrelevant information being progressively attenuated at each of these levels of analysis. The attenuation model, therefore, differs from the filter model in two principal ways, viz., (1) it proposes that selection is based on elements in addition to the simple physical properties of the incoming stimuli; and (2) it proposes that the analyses that guide the selection of stimuli for further processing (the so-called *preattentive analyses;* Neisser, 1967) occur in an essentially continuous rather than discrete fashion. The advantage of the attenuation model conceptually is that it provides a mechanism for reducing the inefficiency that would occur if all signals were to be processed through a full perceptual analysis (as a late selection model requires); its apparent disadvantage is its complexity (e.g., Wessells, 1982), although this in itself should not be a reason for discarding the theory. Empirical evidence that is available to compare the two approaches (e.g., Johnston & Heinz, 1979; Johnston & Wilson, 1980; Treisman & Geffen, 1967) appears more consistent with the attenuation model than a filter model of late selection (Eysenck, 1984).

Pertinence-Based Models of Selective Attention. An attractive model in terms of explaining selective attention in "real-world" settings is the pertinence-based model presented by Norman (1968, 1969). In keeping with Deutsch and Deutsch's (1963) approach, Norman's model assumes that late selection takes place, with short-term memory rather than the stimulus-encoding process being the effective locus of selectivity. Signal pertinence, derived largely from the performer's past experiences and contextual knowledge of similar situations, is assumed to be the foundation on which the discrimination between those signals for further processing and those to be ignored is based (see Figure 6–17).

Signals arriving at the sensory receptors are believed to be initially subjected to feature analysis, the result of which is automatic representation in short-term memory. In many cases representations for given signals preexist through ac-

tivation based on expectations of importance (pertinence) derived from past experience. Selection for further, attention-demanding processing is conceived to be determined on the basis of the overall level of memory activation arising from the joint inputs from the current sensory analysis and the expectancies arising from prior, remembered experiences. The input signals most likely to be selected for continued processing within this model are therefore those that are both preconceived as being of high pertinence and that are also revealed by the sensory analyses as being physically present. The selection in this context is, therefore, conceived of as being both *data-driven* (by the current sensory information) and *conceptually driven* (by the experiential input), or, in other words, to be the product of both *bottom-up* and *top-down* processes. The model is limited in terms of its use of fixed-capacity assumptions (cf. Kahneman, 1973, or Wickens, 1980, 1984) and its failure to provide any explicit statement about how the control of action proceeds (Allport, 1980a), but nevertheless it provides a very useful framework from within which to consider the changes in selective attention that accompany skill acquisition (Abernethy, 1987b).

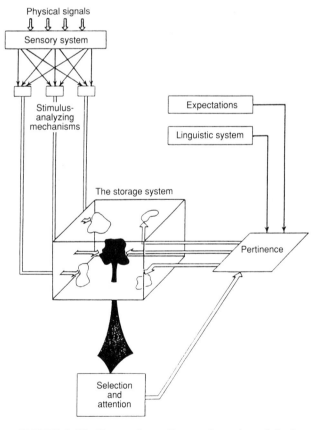

FIGURE 6–17. Norman's pertinence-based model of selective attention.

From "Memory and Attention" by D. A. Norman, 1976, 2nd ed., p. 31. Copyright 1976 by John Wiley and Sons. Reprinted by permission.

Changes in Selective Attention That Accompany Skill Acquisition

Selective attention can apparently be improved considerably with practice, even in simple motor tasks (e.g., Vadhan & Smothergill, 1977), although, as noted previously, much of this improvement appears to occur below the level of consciousness. In the motor skills literature, persistent claims have been made regarding differences in the selective-attention capabilities of expert and novice sports performers, Knapp (1963), for example, suggesting that:

> The unskilled performer may notice a number of stimuli, but he will be unable to perceive which are the important ones or what the responses should be. He will tend not to perceive any pattern to the stimuli and since the capacity to take in information is limited the number of stimuli to which he can pay attention will be relatively few. The skilled person on the other hand possesses a mental framework which takes into account a large number of the stimuli that have occurred before. He notices small changes from the expected display and is therefore able to react to them quickly. (p. 160)

Norman's (1968, 1969) selective attention model suggests at least two potential avenues for improvements in selective attention with practice (and hence expert-novice differences in selective attention), viz.,

1. There may be changes in the manner in which the available current perceptual analysis is conducted.
2. There may be changes in the assignment of pertinence arising as a consequence of the learner's expanding experiential base.

In the subsections that follow we briefly examine the existing evidence (primarily from within the visual modality) for differences between expert and novice sports performers on these two aspects of the selective attention process. (See Abernethy, 1987c, for a more detailed review.)

Expert-Novice Differences in Performing the Current Perceptual Analysis. A useful distinction, in considering expert-novice differences in performing perceptual analyses, can be drawn between visual "hardware" and "software" (Starkes & Deakin, 1984). This distinction, which has obvious origins in the information-processing model of human performance, is between physical characteristics of the performer's visual systems (as determined from generalized optometric measures, for example) and specific information-processing capabilities (as determined from sport-specific tests). Although there have been some reports of differences between expert and novice sports performers on some optometric parameters (e.g., Graybiel, Jokl, & Trapp, 1955; Williams & Thirer, 1975) and measures such as simple reaction time (e.g., Bhanot & Sidhu, 1979; Rotella & Bunker, 1978), the evidence is largely equivocal. While there appears to be little evidence to indicate that

the visual "hardware" of the highly skilled players is systematically superior to that of the general population, there are increasingly clear demonstrations of expert-novice differences in the ability to perform selective attention tasks in which the opportunity for using acquired situation-specific strategies (or "software") is present (Abernethy, 1987c; Starkes, 1987; Starkes & Deakin, 1984). The following expert-novice differences in tasks requiring sport-specific selective attention have been empirically verified:

DIFFERENCES IN ANTICIPATORY CAPABILITY

Evidence exists, primarily through the use of the temporal occlusion paradigm, to demonstrate in a range of fast ball sports that (1) information available prior to ball flight (often referred to as advance cues) is of use in predicting the direction and speed of forthcoming ball flight (predictions made on the basis of advance information are in excess of chance levels, usually for novices as well as experts), and (2) that experts are superior to novices in their ability to pick up this early information from the action of the opponent or opposing team (see Abernethy, 1987a, for a review of this literature). More recently, through the use of both temporal and spatial occlusion paradigms in conjunction with eye movement recordings in the racquet sports of badminton and squash, it has been demonstrated that these observable differences in anticipatory performance are related to differences in selective attention. Expert players in these activities attend more to earlier occurring, more proximal sources of advance information (viz., arm and racquet cues) than do novices (who use racquet cues alone) (Abernethy & Russell, 1987a), with a transition to using these earlier cues systematically accompanying skill development through practice (Abernethy, 1988c). Expert-novice differences in visual search patterns occur less systematically, being observed in some sport activities (e.g., Bard & Fleury, 1976, 1981) but not in others (e.g., Abernethy, 1990; Abernethy & Russell, 1987b). The latter observations of search pattern similarities in the face of expertise-related differences in cue usage highlight the potential difficulties of using eye movement recording alone as an indicator of individual differences in selective attention. It should be noted, however, that there is some evidence to suggest that differences in visual search rate in sports tasks *may* exist, with experts making fewer fixations, each of longer duration. This effect, if it indeed exists, may be explicable either in terms of the experts' lower total processing load (the *variable processing rate hypothesis* of Teichner & Krebs, 1974) or their need for fewer perceptual cues in order to construct the whole event (the *perceptual automatizing hypothesis* of Furst, 1971) (Abernethy, 1988b).

The obvious advantage of selectively attending to advance cues that are useful in anticipating the action of an opponent or opposing team is that not only does it allow responses to be initiated earlier, hence allowing experts to give the impression of "... having all the time in the world ..." (Bartlett, 1947, p. 836), but the recognition of redundancy in the display also decreases the information-processing load. The reduced processing load frees up processing resources and, therefore, may also contribute to the apparent ease that characterizes skilled sports performance (Kay, 1957). The transition to attending to different (earlier) information sources, which occurs with experience as the distinctive features of the display are learned and the relationship between display features is acquired, is typical of most types of perceptual learning (Gibson, 1969), and may provide an applied example of the kind of progression in cue usage with training proposed by Fuchs (1962).

DIFFERENCES IN THE RECOGNITION AND ENCODING OF COMPLEX DISPLAY STRUCTURE

Allied with the expert-novice differences in selective attention to different advance cues is a large body of evidence indicating expert superiority in the pickup of complex structure of the type that exists in the stimulus patterns provided by many team sports. Using a paradigm initially developed by de Groot (1965) and Chase and Simon (1973) for examining chess skill, Allard and Starkes (Allard & Burnett, 1985; Allard, Graham, & Paarsalu, 1980; Starkes, 1987; Starkes & Allard, 1983) have been able to demonstrate that expert basketball and field hockey players, for example, have superior recall for the position of the players within briefly presented slides of structured game situations (such as an offensive pattern in basketball) than do novices. These differences disappear, however, if the slides fail to depict structured events (e.g., a time-out in basketball), indicating that experts do not have larger general memory capacities than novices (a "hardware" difference) but rather have a superiority that relates to the ability to selectively attend to structure that is inherent within their particular sports (a "software" difference). Consequently there appears to be objective evidence that skilled players have a superior ability to "read" patterns of play, and this is, in all probability, a result of selective attention differences between skilled players and novices.

DIFFERENCES IN EXTRACTING BALL FLIGHT INFORMATION

Because accurate processing of information from the flight of an approaching ball or its equivalent is obviously a crucial part of successful performance in many sports, it may be reasonable to expect expert-novice differences in selective attention to key visual variables that inform about the position and time-of-arrival of the ball. Although coincidence-timing tasks that use apparent motion rather than real ball flight generally do not discriminate expert from novice performers (e.g., Del Rey, Whitehurst, Wughalter, & Barnwell, 1983), the timing of interceptive tasks such as hitting and catching performed in response to real ball flight indicate significant proficiency-related differences (e.g., Savelsbergh & Bootsma, in press; Williams, 1969). Selective attention differences to critical optical control variables, such as Lee's (1976) *tau* for determining the time-to-contact of the approaching ball, may well account for the observed differences between experts and novices in timing accuracy (Savelsbergh & Bootsma, in press).

DIFFERENCES IN SUSCEPTIBILITY TO DISTRACTION

For selective attention to operate effectively in sports situations it is imperative that, just as processing resources be allocated to relevant cues, distracting sources of information receive no detailed processing. To date there appear to have been few studies attempting to assess this using behavioral measures, although pencil-and-paper tests such as Witkin et al.'s (1962) field dependence/independence (or perceptual style) test have been used for some time, albeit with limited success. The field dependence/independence, or perceptual style, test examines the capabilities of performers to locate a particular figure (usually a regular geometric shape) within a background field full of distractions of different kinds, the assumption being that those individuals who can ignore the irrelevant background information in order to focus only on the characteristics of the target item (classified as field-independent individuals) will also be better equipped to avoid distractions in natural tasks of the type that exist in sport. Although there are some studies demonstrating the expected greater prevalence of field independence among elite athletes (e.g., Pargman, Schreiber, & Stein, 1974; Rotella & Bunker, 1978), the majority of studies have been unable to find proficiency differences on this measure (e.g., Petrakis, 1979; MacGillivary, 1981). The absence of sport-specific stimuli and the attendant losses of ecological validity from within tests of this type have undoubtedly contributed to the failure to demonstrate clear expert-novice differences. This is a problem that we have already seen limits other potential tests of distracted processing of information, such as Nideffer's (1976) TAIS.

Expert-Novice Differences in the Assignment of Pertinence to Different Events and Sources of Information. In laboratory selective attention tasks, the sampling of different information sources by subjects becomes more optimal as the subjects gain sufficient experience to generate an accurate statistical model of the environment (Senders, 1964). Knowledge of the probabilities of different events occurring in sport settings may be advantageous, both in the reduction of RT (e.g., Alain & Proteau, 1980) and in the optimization of available attentional resources. In sport tasks the nonequiprobability of different events provides a basis for facilitating RT to the more probable event (Alain & Girardin, 1978; Alain & Proteau, 1980), although in laboratory simulations large deviations from equiprobability for two events, of the order of 9:1, are needed before RT to the more probable stimulus is significantly decreased (e.g., Dillon, Crassini, & Abernethy, 1989; Proteau & Dugas, 1982). There is some limited evidence to suggest that the subjective estimates of event probabilities developed by experts in sport may more closely approximate actual event probabilities than the estimates novices use as a basis for their selective attention and decision making (e.g., see Cohen & Dearnaley, 1962; Whiting, 1979), but advancement of knowledge in this area seems to be restricted substantially by the absence of a suitable investigative paradigm (Abernethy, 1987c). Indications that the P300 component of ERPs may reflect updating of subjective probabilities (Donchin, 1984) perhaps offers hope for a fruitful psychophysiological approach to this issue.

Implications for Skill Acquisition, Instruction, and the Design of Practice

It is clear from the preceding discussions that isolation of the relevant cues used by performers in specific sports tasks is an essential element for improved and informed practice and instruction. Until the relevant cues for expert performance in a given activity are known, the effectiveness of instruction and of practice drills aimed at enhancing performance will be necessarily limited.

In sports where the relevant cues for expert performance have been isolated, skill acquisition may be enhanced by highlighting these cues in practice (e.g., if the wrist is a crucial cue source, highlight this by having the practice opponent wear a bright wristband; if a particular opposing team's formation is informative as to the offense they intend to run, then the players should attempt to focus on this during videotape viewings of the opposing team and should prepare appropriate responses in advance). (See Abernethy & Wollstein, 1989; Christina, Barresi, & Shaffner, 1990; and Maschette, 1980, for possible practice strategies for improving anticipation skills.) Psychological skills training (such as the Attentional Control Training by Nideffer in this *Handbook*) and biofeedback training (e.g., Landers et al., 1991) may prove effective in enhancing selective attention, although clearly the chances of these programs being effective will increase substantially if the optimal pattern of cue usage needed for maximal performance in the particular sport is known. Although there is little empirical evidence available to date to determine the effectiveness of these types of training programs (Singer et al., 1991), what is available indicates that multicomponent attentional training that provides athletes with skills in relaxation, visualization, and focusing and refocusing is helpful in maintaining performance in the face of external and unexpected distractors (Singer, Cauraugh, Murphey, Chen, & Lidor, 1991).

Given that specific tests of selective attention are easily generated for most sports, it makes considerable sense to assess individual athletes regularly on their selective attention skills in the same way that other elements of skill and physical fitness development are monitored throughout the course of a competitive season. Such tests may have diagnostic utility where an athlete attends to cues that are irrelevant and/or fails to attend to cues that are known to be informative and essential for expert performance. As with all types of practice, the more specific the practice of selective attention skills can be, the more likely it is that benefits to sport performance will accrue. Considerations in the design of practice should, therefore, include not only the presentation of sport-specific stimuli but also the regular presentation of a range of potentially distracting stimuli, including those associated with performance under fatigue conditions.

PROSPECTIVE DIRECTIONS IN THE STUDY OF ATTENTION IN SPORT

Attention is clearly a broad and multifaceted psychological construct that impacts on sport performance and learning in a large number of quite diverse ways. In its various contexts of momentary alertness, vigilance, information-processing resources, and selectivity, attention imposes constraints on human performance that can only be partially offset by strategic planning. Knowing more about the sport-specific constraints imposed on performance by attention and knowing more about how these constraints are either alleviated or exploited by skilled performers is fundamental to the development of principled approaches to coaching and instruction of all types and at all levels.

Given the long history of research interest in the topic of attention, the limited nature of existing knowledge about attention in "real world" tasks like sport is somewhat disappointing. The limited emergence of knowledge about attention that is of direct practical significance to the sport psychologist is, however, a reflection of a general failure of cognitive psychology to resolve satisfactorily two fundamental issues in the study of attention, viz., (1) the clear delineation of the *function(s) of attention,* and (2) the development of *plausible, global theories of attention.*

Failure to satisfactorily delineate the function(s) of attention has been largely a consequence of the historical preoccupation with the determination of capacity limitations and the discovery of processing bottlenecks, endeavors that have turned out to be largely fruitless. Coupled with this structural mindset has been an almost exclusive use of simple laboratory tasks—tasks that place demands on attention that are far removed from the kinds of demands that exist in the natural tasks for which explanation is ultimately sought. A particular concern—given that (one of) the prime function(s) of attention may be in selectivity of perceptual-motor control (selection-for-action) (Allport, 1989)—is the decoupling, in experimental settings, of the normal functional links between perception and action. The importance of studying perception and action (and hence also attention) in natural tasks is a fundamental premise of the growing ecological psychology movement, which takes its roots from the writings of Gibson (1979) on perception and Bernstein (1967) on action. (See Turvey and Carello, 1986, 1988, and Turvey, Carello, & Kim, 1990, for syntheses.) Only by studying action in such settings may the true functional importance of attention be revealed.

Such a perspective suggests a prospective focus on a different set of research questions. As Allport (1989) suggests:

These questions are not about the processing limitations, or "bottlenecks," but about the mechanisms of attentional control: questions about the—multiform—computational mechanisms by which attentional engagement is established, coordinated, maintained, interrupted, and redirected, both in spatial and nonspatial terms, in the preparation and control of action. (pp. 662–663)

The reductionist philosophy that has historically underridden much of the experimental work has also dominated much of the contemporary theorizing on attention. There is a disturbing trend in many of the modern theories away from global explanations of attention to more microlevel treatments, where the explanatory power is restricted to attention to simple visual forms. Such "local" theories are linked more closely to visual neurophysiology than they are to human performance.

Fortunately there are two emerging, albeit contrasting, theoretical viewpoints that appear to offer some hope toward a more satisfactory global perspective on attention. The development in cognitive science of parallel distributed processing models (or connectionist models) (e.g., Rumelhart & McClelland, 1986) offers a computational viewpoint based on the complex and plastic networking of simple processing units rather than fixed structures with known capacities and limits. Such a model sees attention (and knowledge) not as address-specific and describable in terms of the properties of individual units, structures, or resources, as the traditional models do, but rather as an integral property of performance that is understandable and definable only by considering the whole operation of the network. (See Rumelhart, Hinton, & McClelland, 1986, for further details.) This view is attractive not only because of its compatibility with neurophysiological evidence but also because of its potential for explaining learning effects—effects that are of prime interest to the sport psychologist. A second, as yet less developed, view is of intentionality as an ecological dynamic (Kugler, Shaw, Vicente, & Kinsella-Shaw, 1990; Shaw & Kinsella-Shaw, 1988) in which an explanation of goal-directed behavior is sought in the laws of physics. It remains to be seen how effective both these approaches will prove in furthering our currently rudimentary knowledge of attentional processes as they operate in the sport context.

References

Abernethy, B. (1985). Cue usage in "open" motor skills: A review of the available procedures. In D. G. Russell & B. Abernethy (Eds.), *Motor memory and control: The Otago symposium* (pp. 110–122). Dunedin, New Zealand: Human Performance Associates.

Abernethy, B. (1987a). Anticipation in sport: A review. *Physical Education Review, 10,* 5–16.

Abernethy, B. (1987b). Selective attention in fast ball sports. I: General principles. *Australian Journal of Science and Medicine in Sport, 19*(4), 3–6.

Abernethy, B. (1987c). Selective attention in fast ball sports. II: Expert-novice differences. *Australian Journal of Science and Medicine in Sport, 19*(4), 7–16.

Abernethy, B. (1988a). Dual-task methodology and motor skills research: Some applications and methodological constraints. *Journal of Human Movement Studies, 14,* 101–132.

Abernethy, B. (1988b). Visual search in sport and ergonomics: Its relationship to selective attention and performer expertise. *Human Performance, 1,* 205–235.

Abernethy, B. (1988c). The effects of age and expertise upon perceptual skill development in a racquet sport. *Research Quarterly for Exercise and Sport, 59,* 210–221.

Abernethy, B. (1990). Expertise, visual search, and information pick-up in squash. *Perception, 19,* 63–77.

Abernethy, B., & Russell, D. G. (1987a). Expert-novice differences in an applied selective attention task. *Journal of Sport Psychology, 9,* 326–345.

Abernethy, B., & Russell, D. G. (1987b). The relationship between expertise and visual search strategy in a racquet sport. *Human Movement Science, 6,* 283–319.

Abernethy, B., & Wollstein, J. R. (1989). Improving anticipation in racquet sports. *Sports Coach, 12,* 15–18.

Ackerman, P. L., & Schneider, W. (1985). Individual differences in automatic and controlled processing. In R. F. Dillon (Ed.), *Individual differences in cognition. Vol. 2* (pp. 35–66). New York: Academic Press.

Ackerman, P. L., Schneider, W., & Wickens, C. D. (1984). Deciding the existence of a time-sharing ability: A combined methodological and theoretical approach. *Human Factors, 26,* 71–82.

Adams, J. A. (1966). Some mechanisms of motor responding: An examination of attention. In E. A. Bilodeau (Ed.), *Acquisition of skill* (pp. 169–200). New York: Academic Press.

Alain, C., & Girardin, Y. (1978). The use of uncertainty in racquetball competition. *Canadian Journal of Applied Sport Sciences, 3,* 240–243.

Alain, C., & Proteau, L. (1980). Decision making in sport. In C. H. Nadeau, W. R. Halliwell, K. M. Newell, & G. C. Roberts (Eds.), *Psychology of motor behavior and sport, 1979* (pp. 465–477). Champaign, IL: Human Kinetics.

Albrecht, R. R., & Feltz, D. L. (1987). Generality and specificity of attention related to competitive anxiety and sport performance. *Journal of Sport Psychology, 9,* 231–248.

Allard, F., & Burnett, N. (1985). Skill in sport. *Canadian Journal of Psychology, 39,* 294–312.

Allard, F., Graham, S., & Paarsalu, M. L. (1980). Perception in sport: Basketball. *Journal of Sport Psychology, 2,* 14–21.

Allport, D. A. (1980a). Attention and performance. In G. Claxton (Ed.), *New directions in cognitive psychology* (pp. 112–153). London: Routledge & Kegan Paul.

Allport, D. A. (1980b). Patterns and actions: Cognitive mechanisms are content-specific. In G. Claxton (Ed.), *New directions in cognitive psychology* (pp. 26–64). London: Routledge & Kegan Paul.

Allport, D. A. (1989). Visual attention. In M. I. Posner (Ed.), *Foundations of cognitive science* (pp. 631–682). Cambridge, MA: MIT Press.

Allport, D. A., Antonis, B., & Reynolds, P. (1972). On the division of attention: A disproof of the single channel hypothesis. *Quarterly Journal of Experimental Psychology, 24,* 225–235.

Anshel, M. H. (1987). Psychological inventories used in sport psychology research. *The Sport Psychologist, 1,* 331–349.

Aronson, R. M. (1982). Attentional and interpersonal factors as discriminators of elite and non-elite gymnasts. (Doctoral dissertation, Boston University, 1981.) *Dissertations Abstracts International, 43,* 106-A.

Bacon, S. J. (1974). Arousal and the range of cue utilization. *Journal of Experimental Psychology, 102,* 81–87.

Bahill, A. T., & LaRitz, T. (1984). Why can't batters keep their eyes on the ball? *American Scientist, 72,* 249–253.

Bahrick, H. P., Fitts, P. M., & Rankin, R. E. (1952). Effect of incentives upon reactions to peripheral stimuli. *Journal of Experimental Psychology, 44,* 400–446.

Bainbridge, L. (1974). Problems in the assessment of mental load. *Le Travail Humain, 37,* 279–302.

Baker, C. H. (1961). Maintaining the level of vigilance by means of knowledge of results upon a secondary vigilance task. *Ergonomics, 4,* 311–316.

Barber, P. J. (1989). Executing two tasks at once. In A. M. Colley & J. R. Beech (Eds.), *Acquisition and performance of cognitive skills* (pp. 217–245). Chichester: Wiley.

Bard, C., & Fleury, M. (1976). Analysis of visual search activity in sport problem situations. *Journal of Human Movement Studies, 3,* 214–222.

Bard, C., & Fleury, M. (1981). Considering eye movement as a predictor of attainment. In I. M. Cockerill & W. W. MacGillivary (Eds.), *Vision and sport* (pp. 28–41). Cheltenham: Stanley Thornes.

Bartlett, F. C. (1947). The measurement of human skill. *British Medical Journal,* June 14, 835–838, 877–880.

Beatty, J. (1982). Task-evoked pupillary reponses, processing load, and the structure of processing resources. *Psychological Bulletin, 91,* 276–292.

Beatty, J., Greenberg, A., Deibler, W. P., & O'Hanlon, J. P. (1974). Operator control of occipital theta rhythm affects performance in a radar monitoring task. *Science, 183,* 871–873.

Beatty, J., & Kahneman, D. (1966). Pupillary changes in two memory tasks. *Psychonomic Science, 5,* 371–372.

Beatty, J., & Wagoner, B. L. (1978). Pupillometric signs of brain activation vary with level of cognitive processing. *Science, 199,* 1216–1218.

Bernstein, N. (1967). *The co-ordination and regulation of movements.* Oxford: Pergamon.

Bertelson, P. (1967). The time course of preparation. *Quarterly Journal of Experimental Psychology, 19,* 272–279.

Bertelson, P., & Tisseyre, F. (1968). The time-course of preparation with regular and irregular foreperiods. *Quarterly Journal of Experimental Psychology, 20,* 297–300.

Bhanot, J. L., & Sidhu, L. S. (1979). Reaction time of Indian hockey players with reference to three levels of participation. *Journal of Sports Medicine and Physical Fitness, 19,* 199–204.

Binet, A. (1890). La concurrence des états psychologiques. *Revue philosophique de la France et de l'étranger, 24,* 138–155.

Blignaut, C. J. H. (1979). The perception of hazard. II. The contribution of signal detection to hazard perception. *Ergonomics, 22,* 1177–1185.

Bliss, C. B. (1892–1893). Investigations in reaction time and attention. *Studies of the Yale Psychological Laboratory, 1,* 1–55.

Boring, E. G. (1970). Attention: Research and beliefs concerning the concept in scientific psychology before 1930. In D. I. Mostofsky (Ed.), *Attention: Contemporary theory and analysis.* New York: Appleton-Century-Crofts.

Borkovec, T. D. (1976). Physiological and cognitive processes in the regulation of anxiety. In G. E. Schwartz & D. Shapiro (Eds.), *Consciousness and self-regulation: Advances in research* (Vol. 1). New York: Plenum Press.

Botwinick, J., & Thompson, L. W. (1966). Premotor and motor components of reaction time. *Journal of Experimental Psychology, 71,* 9–15.

Boutcher, S. H., & Crews, D. J. (1987). The effect of a preshot attentional routine on a well-learned skill. *International Journal of Sport Psychology, 18,* 30–39.

Boutcher, S. H., & Zinsser, N. W. (1990). Cardiac deceleration of elite and beginning golfers during putting. *Journal of Sport and Exercise Psychology, 12,* 37–47.

Broadbent, D. E. (1958). *Perception and communication.* New York: Pergamon.

Broadbent, D. E. (1971). *Decision and stress.* London: Academic Press.

Broadbent, D. E. (1982). Task combination and selective intake of information. *Acta Psychologica, 50,* 253–290.

Broadbent, D. E. & Gregory, M. (1965). Effects of noise and of signal rate upon vigilance as analyzed by means of decision theory. *Human Factors, 7,* 155–162.

Broadbent, D. E. & Gregory, M. (1967). Psychological refractory period and the length of time required to make a decision. *Proceedings of the Royal Society, 168B,* 181–193.

Brown, I. D. Measuring the spare "mental capacity" of car drivers by a subsidiary auditory task. *Ergonomics, 5,* 247–250.

Brown, I. D. (1978). Dual task methods of assessing work-load. *Ergonomics, 21,* 221–224.

Brown, T. L., & Carr, T. H. (1989). Automaticity in skill acquisition: Mechanisms for reducing interference in concurrent performance. *Journal of Experimental Psychology: Human Perception and Performance, 15,* 686–700.

Brunia, C. H. M. (1987). Brain potentials related to preparation and action. In H. Heuer & A. F. Sanders (Eds.), *Perspectives on perception and action* (pp. 105–130). Hillsdale, NJ: Erlbaum.

Brunia, C. H. M. (1988). Movement and stimulus preceding negativity. *Biological Psychology, 26,* 165–178.

Casali, J. G., & Wierwille, W. W. (1983). A comparison of rating scale, secondary task, physiological, and primary task workload estimation techniques in a simulated flight task emphasizing communications load. *Human Factors, 25,* 623–641.

Castiello, U., & Umilta, C. (1988). Temporal dimensions of mental effort in different sports. *International Journal of Sport Psychology, 19,* 199–210.

Chase, W. G., & Simon, H. A. (1973). Perception in chess. *Cognitive Psychology, 4,* 55–81.

Cheng, P. W. (1985). Restructuring versus automaticity: Alternative accounts of skill acquisition. *Psychological Review, 92,* 414–423.

Cherry, E. C. (1953). Some experiments on the recognition of speech, with one and with two ears. *Journal of the Acoustical Society of America, 25,* 975–979.

Christina, R. W., Barresi, J. V., & Shaffner, P. (1990). The development of response selection accuracy in a football linebacker using video training. *The Sport Psychologist, 4,* 11–17.

Cohen, J., & Dearnaley, E. J. (1962). Skill and judgement of footballers in attempting to score goals. *British Journal of Psychology, 53,* 71–88.

Cohen, J., & Christensen, I. (1970). *Information and choice.* Edinburgh: Oliver & Boyd.

Collins, D., Powell, G., & Davies, I. (1990). An electroencephalographic study of hemispheric processing patterns during karate performance. *Journal of Sport and Exercise Psychology, 12,* 223–234.

Cooper, G. E., & Harper, R. P. (1969, April). *The use of pilot ratings in the evaluation of aircraft handling qualities* (NASA Ames Technical Report NASA TN-D-5153). Moffett Field, CA: NASA Ames Research Center.

Cox, R. H. (1985). *Sport psychology: Concepts and applications.* Dubuque, IA: Brown.

Cox, R. H., & Hawkins, H. L. (1976). Application of the theory of signal detectability to kinesthetic discrimination tasks. *Journal of Motor Behavior, 8,* 225–232.

Craik, K. J. W. (1947). Theory of the human operator in control systems I. The operator as an engineering system. *British Journal of Psychology, 38,* 56–61.

Craik, K. J. W. (1948). Theory of the human operator in control systems II. Man as an element in a control system. *British Journal of Psychology, 38,* 142–148.

Crews, D. L. (1989). *The influence of attentive states on golf putting as indicated by cardiac and electrocortical activity.* Unpublished doctoral dissertation, Arizona State University, Tempe, AZ.

Crews, D. L., & Landers, D. M. (1991). *Cardiac pattern as an indicator of attention: A test of two hypotheses.* Manuscript submitted for publication.

Crosby, J. V., & Parkinson, J. R. (1979). A dual task investigation of pilots' skill level. *Ergonomics, 22,* 1301–1313.

Crossman, E. R. F. W. (1959). A theory of the acquisition of speed skill. *Ergonomics, 2,* 153–166.

Dabbs, J. M., Jr., Johnson, J. E., & Leventhal, H. (1968). Palmar sweating: A quick and simple measure. *Journal of Experimental Psychology, 78,* 347–350.

Dahl, H., & Spence, D. P. (1971). Mean heart rate predicted by task demand characteristics. *Psychophysiology, 7,* 369–376.

Damos, D. L. (1978). Residual attention as a predictor of pilot performance. *Human Factors, 20,* 435–440.

Damos, D. L., Bittner, A. C., Kennedy, R. S., & Harbeson, M. M. (1981). Effects of extended practice on dual-task tracking performance. *Human Factors, 23,* 627–632.

Damos, D. L., & Wickens, C. D. (1980). The identification and transfer of timesharing skills. *Acta Psychologica, 46,* 15–39.

Davies, D. R., & Parasuraman, R. (1980). *The psychology of vigilance.* London: Academic Press.

Davis, R. (1959). The role of "attention" in the psychological refractory period. *Quarterly Journal of Experimental Psychology, 11,* 211–220.

Day, L. J. (1980). Anticipation in junior tennis players. In J. Groppel & R. Sears (Eds.), *Proceedings of the International Symposium on the Effective Teaching of Racquet Sports* (pp. 107–116). Urbana-Champaign, IL: University of Illinois.

De Groot, A. D. (1965). *Thought and choice in chess.* The Hague: Mouton.

Del Rey, P., Whitehurst, M., Wughalter, E., & Barnwell, J. (1983). Contextual interference and experience in acquisition and transfer. *Perceptual and Motor Skills, 57,* 241–242.

Derrick, W. L. (1981). The relationship between processing resources and subjective dimensions of operator workload. In R. Sugarman (Ed.), *Proceedings of the 25th Annual Meeting of the Human Factors Society.* Santa Monica, CA: Human Factors Society.

Deutsch, J. A., & Deutsch, D. (1963). Attention: Some theoretical considerations. *Psychological Review, 70,* 80–90.

Dewey, D., Brawley, L. R., & Allard, F. (1989). Do the TAIS attentional-style scales predict how visual information is processed? *Journal of Sport and Exercise Psychology, 11,* 171–186.

Dillon, J. M., Crassini, B., & Abernethy, B. (1989). Stimulus uncertainty and response time in a simulated racquet-sport task. *Journal of Human Movement Studies, 17,* 115–132.

Donchin, E. (1979). Event-related brain potentials: A tool in the study of human information-processing. In H. Begleiter (Ed.), *Evoked potentials and behavior* (pp. 13–75). New York: Plenum Press.

Donchin, E. (1984). Dissociation between electrophysiology and behavior—A disaster or a challenge? In E. Donchin (Ed.), *Cognitive psychophysiology: Event-related potentials and the study of cognition* (pp. 107–118). Hillsdale, NJ: Erlbaum.

Donchin, E., Ritter, W., & McCallum, C. (1978). Cognitive psychophysiology: The endogenous components of the ERP. In E. Callaway, P. Tueting, & S. Koslow (Eds.), *Brain event-related potentials in man* (pp. 349–441). New York: Academic Press.

Duffy, E. (1962). *Activation and behavior.* New York: Wiley.

Easterbrook, J. A. (1959). The effect of emotion on cue utilization and the organization of behavior. *Psychological Review, 66,* 183–201.

Edwards, W. (1962). Dynamic decision theory and probabilistic information processing. *Human Factors, 4,* 59–74.

Eggemeier, F. T., Crabtree, M. S., & La Pointe, P. A. (1983). The effect of delayed effort on subjective ratings of mental workload. *Proceedings of the Human Factors Society, 27,* 139–143.

Ells, J. G. (1973). Analysis of temporal and attentional aspects of movement control. *Journal of Experimental Psychology, 99,* 10–21.

Eysenck, H. J. (1967). *The biological basis of personality.* Springfield, IL: Thomas.

Eysenck, H. J. (1976). *The measurement of personality.* London: MTP Press.

Eysenck, M. W. (1984). *A handbook of cognitive psychology.* London: Erlbaum.

Fisk, A. D., & Schneider, W. (1981). Controlled and automatic processing during tasks requiring sustained attention. *Human Factors, 23,* 737–750.

Fleishman, E. A., & Rich, S. (1963). Role of kinesthetic and spatial-visual abilities in perceptual motor learning. *Journal of Experimental Psychology, 66,* 6–11.

Fodor, J. (1983). *The modularity of mind: An essay on faculty psychology.* Cambridge, MA: MIT Press.

Fowler, C. A., & Turvey, M. T. (1978). Skill acquisition: An event approach with special reference to searching for the optimum of a function of several variables. In G. E. Stelmach (Ed.), *Information processing in motor control and learning* (pp. 1–40). New York: Academic Press.

Friedman, A., & Polson, C. M. (1981). Hemispheres as independent resource systems: Limited-capacity processing and cerebral specialization. *Journal of Experimental Psychology: Human Perception and Performance, 7,* 1031–1058.

Fuchs, A. H. (1962). The progression-regression hypothesis in perceptual-motor skill learning. *Journal of Experimental Psychology, 63,* 177–182.

Furst, C. J. (1971). Automatizing of visual attention. *Perception and Psychophysics, 10,* 65–70.

Gibson, E. J. (1969). *Principles of perceptual learning and development.* New York: Appleton-Century-Crofts.

Gibson, J. J. (1979). *An ecological approach to visual perception.* Boston, MA: Houghton-Mifflin.

Gilden, L., Vaughan, H. G., Jr., & Costa, L. D. (1966). Summated human EEG potentials with voluntary movement. *Electroencephalography and Clinical Neurophysiology, 20,* 433–438.

Girouard, Y., Laurencelle, L., & Proteau, L. (1984). On the nature of the probe reaction-time to uncover the attentional demands of movement. *Journal of Motor Behavior, 16,* 442–459.

Girouard, Y., Perreault, R., Vachon, L., & Black, P. (1978). Attention demands of high jumping (abstract). *Canadian Journal of Applied Sport Sciences, 3,* 193.

Glencross, D. J. (1978). Control and capacity in the study of skill. In D. J. Glencross (Ed.), *Psychology and sport* (pp. 72–96). Sydney: McGraw-Hill.

Glencross, D. J. (1980). Response planning and the organization of speed movements. In R. S. Nickerson (Eds.), *Attention and performance VIII* (pp. 107–125). Hillsdale, NJ: Erlbaum.

Glencross, D. J., & Cibich, B. J. (1977). A decision analysis of games skills. *Australian Journal of Sports Medicine, 9,* 72–75.

Glencross, D. J., & Gould, J. H. (1979). The planning of precision movements. *Journal of Motor Behavior, 11,* 1–9.

Gopher, D., & Navon, D. (1980). How is performance limited: Testing the notion of central capacity. *Acta Psychologica, 46,* 161–180.

Gopher, D., & Sanders, A. F. (1984). S-Oh-R: Oh stages! Oh resources! In W. Prinz & A. F. Sanders (Eds.), *Cognition and motor processes* (pp.231–253). Berlin-Heidelberg: Springer-Verlag.

Gottsdanker, R., & Stelmach, G. E. (1971). The persistence of psychological refractoriness. *Journal of Motor Behavior, 3,* 301–312.

Graham, F. K., & Clifton, R. K. (1966). Heart-rate change as a component of orienting response. *Psychology Bulletin, 65,* 305–320.

Graybiel, A., Jokl, E., & Trapp, C. (1955). Russian studies of vision in relation to physical activity. *Research Quarterly, 26,* 480–485.

Greenwald, A. G., & Shulman, H. G. (1973). On doing two things at once. II. Elimination of the psychological refractory period. *Journal of Experimental Psychology, 101,* 70–76.

Guyton, A. C. (1981). *Textbook of medical physiology* (6th. ed.). Philadelphia: Saunders.

Hamilton, W. (1859). *Lectures on metaphysics and logic.* Edinburgh: Blackwood.

Hansen, J. C., & Hillyard, S. A. (1983). Selective attention to multidimensional stimuli. *Journal of Experimental Psychology: Human Perception and Performance, 9,* 1–19.

Harrison, J., & MacKinnon, P. C. B. (1966). Physiological role of the adrenal medulla in the palmar anhidrotic response in stress. *Journal of Applied Physiology, 21,* 88–92.

Hatfield, B. D., Landers, D. M., & Ray, W. J. (1984). Cognitive processes during self-paced motor performance: An electroencephalographic profile of skilled marksmen. *Journal of Sport Psychology, 6,* 42–59.

Hatfield, B. D., Landers, D. M., & Ray, W. J. (1987). Cardiovascular-CNS interactions during a self-paced, intentional state: Elite marksmanship performance. *Psychophysiology, 24,* 542–549.

Hess, E. H., & Polt, J. M. (1964). Pupil size in relation to mental activity during simple problem-solving. *Science, 143,* 1190–1192.

Heuer, H. (1984). Motor learning as a process of structural constriction and displacement. In W. Prinz & A. F. Sanders (Eds.), *Cognition and motor processes* (pp. 295–305). Berlin-Heidelberg: Springer-Verlag.

Heuer, H., & Wing, A. M. (1984). Doing two things at once: Process limitations and interactions. In M. M. Smyth & A. M. Wing (Eds.), *The psychology of human movement* (pp. 183–213). London: Academic Press.

Hillyard, S. A. (1984). Event-related potentials and selective attention. In E. Donchin (Ed.), *Cognitive psychophysiology: Event-related potentials and the study of cognition* (pp. 51–72). Hillsdale, NJ: Erlbaum.

Hockey, G. R. (1970). Signal probability and spatial location as possible bases for increased selectivity in noise. *Quarterly Journal of Experimental Psychology, 22,* 37–42.

Hoffman, J. E., Nelson, B., & Houck, M. R. (1983). The role of attentional resources in automatic detection. *Cognitive Psychology, 15,* 379–410.

Hoffman, J. E., Simons, R. F., & Houck, M. R. (1983). Event-related potentials during controlled and automatic target detection. *Psychophysiology, 20,* 625–632.

Israel, J. B., Chesney, G. L., Wickens, C. D., & Donchin, E. (1980). P300 and tracking difficulty: Evidence for multiple resources in dual-task performance. *Psychophysiology, 17,* 259–273.

Israel, J. B., Wickens, C. D., Chesney, G. L., & Donchin, E. (1980). The event-related brain potential as an index of display monitoring workload. *Human Factors, 22,* 211–224.

Jackson, C. W. (1981). The relationship of swimming performance to measures of attentional and interpersonal style (doctor dissertation, Boston University, 1980). *Dissertations Abstracts International, 41,* 3353-A.

Jacobson, E. (1929). *Progressive relaxation.* Chicago: University of Chicago Press.

Jacobson, E. (1931). Electrical measurements of neuromuscular states during mental activities. *American Journal of Physiology, 96,* 115–121.

Jagacinski, R. J., Isaac, P. D., & Burke, M. W. (1977). Application of signal detection theory to perceptual motor skills: Decision processes in basketball shooting. *Journal of Motor Behavior, 9,* 225–234.

Jagacinski, R. J., Newell, K. M., & Isaac, P. D. (1979). Predicting the success of a basketball shot at various stages of execution. *Journal of Sport Psychology, 1,* 301–310.

James, W. (1890). *Principles of psychology.* New York: Holt.

Jastrow, O. (1891). The interference of mental processes. *American Journal of Psychology, 4,* 219–223.

Jennings, J. R., Lawrence, B. E., & Kasper, P. (1978). Changes in alertness and processing capacity in a serial learning task. *Memory and Cognition, 6,* 43–53.

Johnston, W. A., & Heinz, S. P. (1979). Depth of non-target processing in an attention task. *Journal of Experimental Psychology, 5,* 168–175.

Johnston, W. A., & Wilson, J. (1980). Perceptual processing of non-targets in an attention task. *Memory & Cognition, 8,* 372–277.

Jones, M. G. (1972). Perceptual characteristics and athletic performance. In H. T. A. Whiting (Ed.), *Readings in sports psychology* (pp. 96–115). London: Henry Kimpton.

Jonides, J., Naveh-Benjamin, M., & Palmer, J. (1985). Assessing automaticity. *Acta Psychologica, 60,* 157–171.

Kahneman, D. (1973). *Attention and effort.* Englewood Cliffs, NJ: Prentice-Hall.

Kahneman, D., & Beatty, J. (1967). Pupillary response in a pitch-discrimination task. *Perception and Psychophysics, 2,* 101–105.

Kahneman, D., Beatty, J., & Pollack, I. (1967). Perceptual deficits during a mental task. *Science, 157,* 218–219.

Kahneman, D., & Treisman, A. (1984). Changing views of attention and automaticity. In R. Parasuraman & D. R. Davies (Eds.), *Varieties of attention* (pp. 29–61). London: Academic Press.

Kantowitz, B. H. (1985). Channels and stages in human information processing: A limited analysis of theory and methodology. *Journal of Mathematical Psychology, 29,* 135–174.

Karlin, L., & Kestenbaum, R. (1968). Effects of number of alternatives on psychological refractory period. *Quarterly Journal of Experimental Psychology, 20,* 167–178.

Kay, H. (1957). Information theory in the understanding of skills. *Occupational Psychology, 31,* 218–224.

Keele, S. W. (1972). Attention demands of memory retrieval. *Journal of Experimental Psychology, 93,* 245–248.

Keele, S. W. (1973). *Attention and human performance.* Pacific Palisades, CA: Goodyear Publishing.

Keele, S. W. (1982). Component analysis and conception of skill. In J. A. S. Kelso (Ed.), *Human motor behavior: An introduction* (pp. 143–159). Hillsdale, NJ: Erlbaum.

Keele, S. W., & Hawkins, H. L. (1982). Explorations of individual differences relevant to high level skill. *Journal of Motor Behavior, 14,* 3–23.

Kelso, J. A. S., Tuller, B. H., & Harris, K. S. (1983). A "dynamic pattern" perspective on the control and coordination of movement. In P. MacNeilage (Ed.), *The production of speech* (pp. 137–173). New York: Springer-Verlag.

Kerr, B. (1975). Processing demands during movement. *Journal of Motor Behavior, 7,* 15–27.

Kimble, G. A., & Perlmutter, L. C. (1970). The problem of volition. *Psychological Review, 77,* 361–383.

Kinsbourne, M., & Hicks, R. E. (1978). Functional cerebral space: A model of overflow, transfer and interference effects in human performance: A tutorial review. In J. Requin (Ed.), *Attention and performance VII* (pp. 345–362). Hillsdale, NJ: Erlbaum.

Klavora, P. (1978). Customary arousal for peak athletic performance. In P. Klavora & J. V. Daniel (Eds.), *Coach, athlete, and the sport psychologist* (pp. 155–163). Champaign, IL: Human Kinetics.

Klein, R. M. (1976). Attention and movement. In G. E. Stelmach (Ed.), *Motor control: Issues and trends* (pp. 143–173). New York: Academic Press.

Klein, R. M. (1978). Automatic and strategic processes in skilled performance. In G. C. Roberts & K. M. Newell (Eds.), *Psychology of motor behavior and sport, 1977* (pp. 270–287). Champaign, IL: Human Kinetics.

Knapp, B. N. (1963). *Skill in sport.* London: Routledge & Kegan Paul.

Kornhuber, H. H., & Deecke, L. (1965). Hirnpotentialänderungen bei Willkürbewegungen und passiven Bewegungen des Menschen: Bereitschaftspotential und reafferente Potentiale. *Pflügers Archiv für die gesammte Physiologie, 248,* 1–17.

Kramer, A. F., & Strayer, D. L. (1988). Assessing the development of automatic processing: An application of dual-task and event-related brain potential methodologies. *Biological Psychology, 26,* 231–267.

Kramer, A. F., Wickens, C. D., & Donchin, E. (1983). An analysis of the processing demands of a complex perceptual-motor task. *Human Factors, 25,* 597–622.

Kugler, P. N., Shaw, R. E., Vicente, K. J., & Kinsella-Shaw, J. (1990). Inquiry into intentional systems. I: Issues in ecological physics. *Report No. 30/1990, Research Group on Mind and Brain, Perspectives in Theoretical Physics and the Philosophy of Mind,* University of Bielefeld.

LaBerge, D. (1975). Acquisition of automatic processing in perceptual and associative learning. In P. M. A. Rabbitt & S. Dornic (Eds.), *Attention and performance V* (pp. 50–64). London: Academic Press.

LaBerge, D. (1981). Automatic information processing—A review. In J. Long & A. Baddeley (Eds.), *Attention and performance IX* (pp. 173–186). Hillsdale, NJ: Erlbaum.

LaBerge, D., Van Gelder, P., & Yellott, S. (1971). A cueing technique in choice reaction time. *Journal of Experimental Psychology, 87,* 225–228.

Lacey, B. C., & Lacey, J. I. (1964, October). *Cardiac deceleration and simple visual reaction time in a fixed foreperiod experiment.* Paper presented at the meeting of the Society of Psychophysiological Research, Washington, DC.

Lacey, B. C., & Lacey, J. I. (1970). Some autonomic-central nervous system interrelationships. In P. Block (Ed.), *Physiological correlates of emotion* (pp. 50–83). New York: Academic Press.

Lacey, J. I. (1967). Somatic response patterning and stress: Some revision of activation theory. In M. H. Appley & R. Trumbull (Eds.), *Psychological stress: Issues in research* (pp. 170–179). New York: Appleton-Century-Crofts.

Lacey, J. I., & Lacey, B. C. (1958). Verification and extension of the principle of autonomic response-stereotypy. *American Journal of Psychology, 71,* 50–73.

Landers, D. M. (1980). The arousal-performance relationship revisited. *Research Quarterly for Exercise and Sport, 51,* 77–90.

Landers, D. M. (1982). Arousal, attention, and skilled performance: Further considerations. *Quest, 33,* 271–283.

Landers, D. M., Boutcher, S. H., & Wang, M. Q. (1986). A psychobiological study of archery performance. *Research Quarterly for Exercise and Sport, 57,* 236–244.

Landers, D. M., Furst, D. M., & Daniels, F. S. (1981, June). *Anxiety/attention and shooting ability: Testing the predictive validity of the test of attentional and interpersonal style (TAIS).* Paper presented at the Annual Conference of the North American Society for the Psychology of Sport and Physical Activity.

Landers, D. M., Han, N., Salazar, W., Petruzzello, S. J., Kubitz, K. A., & Gannon, T. L. (in press). Effects of learning on electroencephalographic patterns in novice archers. *International Journal of Sport Psychology.*

Landers, D. M., Petruzzello, S. J., Salazar, W., Crews, D. J., Kubitz, K. A., Gannon, T. L., & Han, M. (1991). *The influence of electrocortical biofeedback on performance in pre-elite archers.* Manuscript submitted for publication.

Landers, D. M., Wang, M. Q., & Courtet, P. (1985). Peripheral narrowing among experienced and inexperienced rifle shooters under low-and high-time stress conditions. *Research Quarterly for Exercise and Sport, 56,* 122–130.

Lane, D. M. (1982). Limited capacity, attentional allocation, and productivity. In W. C. Howell & E. A. Fleishman (Eds.), *Human performance and productivity. Vol. 2. Information processing and decision making* (pp. 121–156). Hillsdale, NJ: Erlbaum.

Lansing, R. W., Schwartz, E., & Lindsley, D. B. (1956). Reaction time and EEG activation. *American Psychologist, 11,* 433.

Leavitt, J. L. (1979). Cognitive demands of skating and stick handling in ice hockey. *Canadian Journal of Applied Sport Sciences, 4,* 46–55.

Lee, D. N. (1976). A theory of visual control of braking based on information about time-to-collision. *Perception, 5,* 437–459.

Leibowitz, H. W., & Post, R. B. (1982). The two modes of processing concept and some implications. In J. Beck (Ed.), *Organization and representation in perception* (pp. 343–363). Hillsdale, NJ: Erlbaum.

Le Plat, J., & Hoc, J-M. (1981). Subsequent verbalization in the study of cognitive processes. *Ergonomics, 24,* 743–756.

Levitt, E. E. (1980). *The psychology of anxiety.* Hillsdale, NJ: Erlbaum.

Lindsley, D. B., Schreiner, L. H., Knowles, W. B., & Magoun, H. W. (1950). Behavioral and EEG changes following chronic brain stem lesions in the cat. *Electroencephalography and Clinical Neurophysiology, 2,* 483–498.

Littman, D., & Becklan, R. (1976). Selective looking with minimal eye movements. *Perception and Psychophysics, 20,* 77–79.

Logan, G. D. (1979). On the use of a concurrent memory load to measure attention and automaticity. *Journal of Experimental Psychology: Human Perception and Performance, 5,* 189–297.

Logan, G. D. (1985). Skill and automaticity: Relations, implications, and future directions. *Canadian Journal of Psychology, 39,* 367–386.

Long, C. M., & Waag, W. L. (1981). Limitations and practical applicability of d and β as measures. *Human Factors, 23,* 283–290.

MacGillivary, W. W. (1981). The contribution of perceptual style to human performance. In I. M. Cockerill & W. W. MacGillivary (Eds.), *Vision and sport* (pp. 8–16). Cheltenham: Stanley Thornes.

Mackie, R. R. (1977). *Vigilance: Relationships among theories, physiological correlates, and operational performance.* New York: Plenum Press.

Mackworth, N. H. (1948). The breakdown of vigilance during prolonged visual search. *Quarterly Journal of Experimental Psychology, 1,* 5–61.

Mackworth, N. H. (1956). Vigilance. *Nature, 178,* 1375–1377.

Magill, R. A. (1989). *Motor learning: Concepts and applications* (3rd ed.). Dubuque, IA: Wm. C. Brown.

Mahoney, M. J., & Avener, M. (1977). Psychology of the elite athlete: An exploratory study. *Cognitive Therapy and Research, 1,* 135–141.

Mandler, G., Mandler, J. M., & Urviller, E. T. (1958). Autonomic feedback: The perception of autonomic activity. *Journal of Abnormal and Social Psychology, 56,* 367–373.

Martens, R. (1982). *Sport competition anxiety test.* Champaign, IL: Human Kinetics.

Martens, R., & Landers, D. M. (1970). Motor performance under stress: A test of the inverted-U hypothesis. *Journal of Personality and Social Research, 16,* 29–37.

Martens, R., Vealey, R. S., & Burton, D. (1990). *Competitive anxiety in sport.* Champaign, IL: Human Kinetics.

Martin, I., & Venables, P. H. (1980). *Techniques in psychophysiology.* London: Wiley.

Maschette, W. (1980). The use of advance cues during high-speed skilled performance. *Sports Coach, 4*(1), 10–12.

McFarland, K., & Ashton, R. (1978). The lateralized effects of concurrent cognitive and motor performance. *Perception and Psychophysics, 23,* 344–349.

McLeod, P. (1977). A dual-task response modality effect: Support for multiprocessor models of attention. *Quarterly Journal of Experimental Psychology, 29,* 651–667.

McLeod, P. (1978). Does probe RT measure central processing demand? *Quarterly Journal of Experimental Psychology, 30,* 83–89.

McLeod, P. (1980). What can probe RT tell us about the attentional demands of movement? In G. E. Stelmach & J. Requin (Eds.), *Tutorials in motor behavior* (pp. 579–589). Amsterdam: North-Holland.

McLeod, P., McLaughlin, C., & Nimmo-Smith, I. (1985). Information encapsulation and automaticity: Evidence from the visual control of finely timed actions. In M. I. Posner & O. Marin (Eds.), *Attention and performance XI* (pp. 391–406). Hillsdale, NJ: Erlbaum.

Megaw, E. D., & Richardson, J. (1979). Eye movements and industrial inspection. *Applied Ergonomics, 10,* 145–154.

Meshkati, N. (1988). Heart rate variability and mental workload assessment. In P. A. Hancock & N. Meshkati (Eds.), *Human mental workload* (pp. 101–115). Amsterdam: North-Holland.

Meshkati, N., & Loewenthal, A. (1988). An eclectic and critical review of four primary mental workload assessment methods: A guide for developing a comprehensive model. In P. A. Hancock & N. Meshkati (Eds.), *Human mental workload* (pp. 251–267). Amsterdam: North-Holland.

Milgram, P. (1987). A spectacle-mounted liquid-crystal tachistoscope. *Behavior Research Methods, Instruments, & Computers, 19,* 449–456.

Miller, R. C., & Hart, S. G. (1984, June). Assessing the subjective workload of directional orientation tasks. *Proceedings of the 20th Annual Conference on Manual Control.*

Molander, B., & Backman, L. (1989). Age differences in heart rate patterns during concentration in a precision sport: Implications for attentional functioning. *Journal of Gerontology: Psychological Sciences, 44,* 80–87.

Montagu, J. D., & Coles, E. M. (1966). Mechanism and measurement of the galvanic skin response. *Psychological Bulletin, 65,* 261–279.

Moray, N. (1959). Attention in dichotic listening: Affective cues and the influence of instructions. *Quarterly Journal of Experimental Psychology, 11,* 59–60.

Moray, N. (1967). Where is attention limited? A survey and a model. *Acta Psychologica, 27,* 84–92.

Moray, N. (1969). *Listening and attention.* Baltimore: Penguin.

Moray, N. (1970). *Attention: Selective processes in vision and hearing.* New York: Academic Press.

Moray, N. (1982). Subjective mental workload. *Human Factors, 23,* 25–40.

Moray, N., & Fitter, M. (1973). A theory and the measurement of attention: Tutorial review. In S. Kornblum (Ed.), *Attention and performance IV* (pp. 3–19). New York: Academic Press.

Mowbray, G. H. (1953). Simultaneous vision and audition: The comprehension of prose passages with varying levels of difficulty. *Journal of Experimental Psychology, 46,* 365–372.

Mowbray, G. H., & Rhoades, M. U. (1959). On the reduction of choice reaction times with practice. *Quarterly Journal of Experimental Psychology, 11,* 16–23.

Mulder, G., & Mulder, L. J. M. (1980). Coping with mental workload. In S. Levine & H. Ursine (Eds.), *Coping and health.* New York: Plenum.

Mulder, G., & Mulder, L. J. M. (1981). Information processing and cardiovascular control. *Psychophysiology, 18,* 392–401.

Näätänen, R. (1988). Implications of ERP data for psychological theories of attention. *Biological Psychology, 26,* 117–163.

Navon, D., & Gopher, D. (1979). On the economy of the human processing system. *Psychological Review, 86,* 214–255.

Neisser, U. (1964). Visual search. *Scientific American, 210,* 94–102.

Neisser, U. (1967). *Cognitive psychology.* New York: Appleton-Century-Crofts.

Neisser, U. (1979). The control of information pick-up in selective looking. In A. D. Pick (Ed.), *Perception and its development: A tribute to Eleanor J. Gibson.* Hillsdale, NJ: Erlbaum.

Neisser, U., & Becklen, R. (1975). Selective looking: Attending to visually specified events. *Cognitive Psychology, 7,* 480–494.

Nettleton, B. (1979). Attention demands of ball-tracking skills. *Perceptual and Motor Skills, 49,* 531–534.

Nettleton, B. (1984). Coincident anticipation and fast ball games. In M. L. Howell & B. D. Wilson (Eds.), *Proceedings of the VIIth Commonwealth and International Conference on Sport, Physical Education, Recreation and Dance. Vol. 7: Kinesiological Sciences* (pp. 67–73). Brisbane: University of Queensland.

Neumann, O. (1984). Automatic processing: A review of recent findings and a plea for an old theory. In W. Prinz & A. F. Sanders (Eds.), *Cognition and motor processes* (pp. 256–293). Berlin: Springer-Verlag.

Neumann, O. (1987). Beyond capacity: A functional view of attention. In H. Heuer & A. F. Sanders (Eds.), *Perspectives on perception and action* (pp. 361–394). Hillsdale, NJ: Erlbaum.

Newell, K. M. (1974). Decision processes of baseball batters. *Human Factors, 16,* 520–527.

Nideffer, R. M. (1976). The test of attentional and interpersonal style. *Journal of Personality and Social Psychology, 34,* 394–404.

Nideffer, R. M. (1979). The role of attention in optimal athletic performance. In P. Klavora & J. V. Daniel (Eds.), *Coach, athlete and the sport psychologist* (pp. 99–112). Toronto, Ontario: University of Toronto.

Nideffer, R. M. (1990). Use of the Test of Attentional and Interpersonal Style (TAIS) in sport. *The Sport Psychologist, 4,* 285–300.

Nideffer, R. M., & Sharpe, R. (1987). *A.C.T.: Attention control training.* New York: Wyden Books.

Nisbett, R. E., & Wilson, T. D. (1977). Telling more than we can know: Verbal reports on mental processes. *Psychological Review, 84,* 231–259.

Nissen, M. J., & Bullemer, P. (1987). Attentional requirements of learning: Evidence from performance measures. *Cognitive Psychology, 19,* 1–32.

Norman, D. A. (1968). Toward a theory of memory and attention. *Psychological Review, 75,* 522–536.

Norman, D. A. (1969). *Memory and attention.* New York: Wiley.

Norman, D. A. (1976). *Memory and attention.* (2nd. ed.). New York: Wiley.

Norman, D. A. (1981). Categorization of action slips. *Psychological Review, 88,* 1–15.

Norman, D. A., & Bobrow, D. (1975). On data-limited and resource-limited processing. *Cognitive Psychology, 7,* 44–60.

North, R. A., & Gopher, D. (1976). Measures of attention as predictors of flight performance. *Human Factors, 18,* 1–13.

Noton, D., & Stark, L. (1971). Eye movements and visual perception. *Scientific American, 224,* 34–43.

Ogden, G. D., Levine, J. M., & Eisner, E. J. (1979). Measurement of workload by secondary tasks. *Human Factors, 21,* 529–548.

Opmeer, C. H. J. M. (1973). The information content of successive RR interval times in the ECG: Preliminary results using factor analysis and frequency analyses. *Ergonomics, 16,* 105–112.

Parasuraman, R. (1979). Memory load and event rate control sensitivity decrements in sustained attention. *Science, 205,* 924–927.

Pargman, D., Schreiber, L. E., & Stein, F. (1974). Field dependence of selected athletic sub-groups. *Medicine and Science in Sports, 6,* 283–286.

Parker, H. (1981). Visual detection and perception in netball. In I. M. Cockerill & W. W. MacGillivary (Eds.), *Vision and sport* (pp. 42–53). London: Stanley Thornes.

Pastore, R. E., & Scheirer, C. J. (1974). Signal detection theory: Considerations for general application. *Psychological Review, 81,* 945–958.

Peterson, R. P. (1969). Patterns of eye movements in rapid symbol identification and their relation to reading achievement. *Perceptual and Motor Skills, 28,* 307–310.

Petrakis, E. (1979). Perceptual style of varsity tennis players. *Perceptual and Motor Skills, 48,* 266.

Pew, R. W. (1974). Levels of analysis in motor control. *Brain Research, 71,* 393–400.

Phillips, J. G., & Hughes, B. G. (1988). Internal consistency of the concept of automaticity. In A. M. Colley & J. R. Beech (Eds.), *Cognition and action in skilled behavior* (pp. 317–331). Amsterdam: North-Holland.

Pillsbury, W. B. (1908). *Attention.* New York: Macmillan.

Populin, L., Rose, D. J., & Heath, K. (1990). The role of attention in one-handed catching. *Journal of Motor Behavior, 22,* 149–158.

Posner, M. I. (1973). *Cognition: An introduction.* Glenview, IL: Scott, Foresman.

Posner, M. I. (1978). *Chronometric explorations of mind.* Hillsdale, NJ: Erlbaum.

Posner, M. I. (1980). Orienting of attention. *Quarterly Journal of Experimental Psychology, 32,* 3–25.

Posner, M. I., & Boies, S. J. (1971). Components of attention. *Psychological Review, 78,* 391–408.

Posner, M. I., & Keele, S. W. (1969). Attention demands of movements. *Proceedings of the 17th International Congress of Applied Psychology.* Amsterdam: Swets & Zeitlinger.

Proteau, L., & Dugas, C. (1982). Stratégie de décision d'un groupe de jouers de basketballe Inter-Universitaire. *Canadian Journal of Applied Sport Sciences, 7,* 127–133.

Ranson, S. W. (1939). Somnolence caused by hypothalamic lesions in the monkey. *Archives of Neurological Psychiatry, 41,* 1–23.

Ray, W. J., & Cole, H. W. (1985). EEG alpha activity reflects attentional demands, and beta activity reflects emotional and cognitive processes. *Science, 228,* 750–752.

Reason, J. T. (1979). Actions not as planned: The price of automatization. In G. Underwood & R. Stevens (Eds.), *Aspects of consciousness. Vol. 1, Psychological issues* (pp. 67–89). London: Academic Press.

Regan, D. (1972). *Evoked potentials in psychology, sensory physiology and clinical medicine.* London: Chapman & Hall.

Reis, J., & Bird, A. M. (1982). Cue processing as a function of breadth of attention. *Journal of Sport Psychology, 4,* 64–72.

Remington, R. W. (1980). Attention and saccadic eye movements. *Journal of Experimental Psychology:Human Perception and Performance, 6,* 726–744.

Ripoll, H., Papin, J-P., Guezennec, J-Y., Verdy, J-P., & Philip, M. (1985). Analysis of visual scanning patterns of pistol shooters. *Journal of Sport Sciences, 3,* 93–101.

Ritter, W., Kelso, J. A. S., Kutas, M., & Shiffrin, R. (1984). Report of panel III: Preparatory processes. In E. Donchin (Ed.), *Cognitive psychophysiology: Event-related potentials and the study of cognition* (pp. 179–219). Hillsdale, NJ: Erlbaum.

Rolfe, J. M. (1971). The secondary task as a measure of mental workload. In W. T. Singleton, J. G. Fox, & D. Whitfield (Eds.), *Measurement of man at work* (pp. 135–148). London: Taylor & Francis.

Rose, D. J., & Christina, R. W. (1990). Attention demands of precision pistol-shooting as a function of skill level. *Research Quarterly for Exercise and Sport, 61,* 111–113.

Rotella, R. J., & Bunker, L. K. (1978). Field dependence and reaction time in senior tennis players (65 and over). *Perceptual and Motor Skills, 46,* 585–586.

Rumelhart, D. E., Hinton, G. E., & McClelland, J. L. (1986). A general framework for Parallel Distributed Processing. In D. E. Rumelhart & J. L. McClelland (Eds.), *Parallel distributed processing.* Cambridge, MA: MIT Press.

Rumelhart, D. E., & McClelland, J. L. (Eds.) (1986). *Parallel distributed processing.* Cambridge, MA: MIT Press.

Rushall, B. S. (1977). Two observation schedules for sporting and physical education environments. *Canadian Journal of Applied Sport Sciences, 2,* 15–21.

Ryan, C. (1983). Reassessing the automaticity-control distinction: Item recognition as a paradigm case. *Psychological Review, 90,* 171–178.

Salazar, W., Landers, D. M., Petruzzello, S. J., Crews, D. J., & Kubitz, K. (1988). The effects of physical/cognitive load on electrocortical patterns preceding response execution in archery. *Psychophysiology, 25,* 478–479.

Salazar, W., Landers, D. M., Petruzzello, S. J., Crews, D. J., Kubitz, K., & Han, M. W. (1990). Hemispheric asymmetry, cardiac response, and performance in elite archers. *Research Quarterly for Exercise and Sport, 61,* 351–359.

Salmoni, A. W., Sullivan, J. J., & Starkes, J. L. (1976). The attentional demands of movement: A critique of the probe technique. *Journal of Motor Behavior, 8,* 161–169.

Savelsbergh, G. J. P., & Bootsma, R. J. (in press). Perception-action coupling in hitting and catching. *International Journal of Sport Psychology.*

Schilling, R. F. (1987). *Automaticity and skill development for pistol marksmanship.* Unpublished doctoral dissertation, Florida State University.

Schmidt, R. A. (1983). On the underlying structure of well-learned motor responses: A discussion of Namikas and Schneider and Fisk. In R. A. Magill (Ed.), *Memory and control of action* (pp. 145–165). Amsterdam: North-Holland.

Schmidt, R. A. (1988). *Motor control and learning: A behavioral emphasis* (2nd. ed). Champaign, IL: Human Kinetics.

Schmidt, R. A., & McCabe, J. F. (1976). Motor program utilization over extended practice. *Journal of Human Movement Studies, 2,* 239–247.

Schneider, W. (1985). Towards a model of attention and the development of automatic processing. In M. I. Posner & O. Marin (Eds.), *Attention and performance XI* (pp. 475–492). Hillsdale, NJ: Erlbaum.

Schneider, W., & Fisk, A. D. (1982a). Concurrent automatic and controlled visual search: Can processing occur without cost? *Journal of Experimental Psychology: Learning, Memory, and Cognition, 8,* 261–278.

Schneider, W., & Fisk, A. D. (1982b). Degree of consistent training: Improvements in search performance and automatic process development. *Perception and Psychophysics, 31,* 160–168.

Schneider, W., & Fisk, A. D. (1983). Attention theory and mechanisms for skilled performance. In R. A. Magill (Ed.), *Memory and control of action* (pp. 119–143). Amsterdam: North-Holland.

Schneider, W., & Shiffrin, R. M. (1977). Controlled and automatic human information processing. I. Detection, search, and attention. *Psychological Review, 84,* 1–66.

Senders, J. (1964). The human operator as a monitor and controller of multidegree of freedom system. *IEEE Transactions on Human Factors in Electronics, HFE-5,* 2–6.

Sharit, J., Salvendy, G., & Deisenroth, M. P. (1982). External and internal attentional environments. I. The utilization of cardiac deceleratory and acceleratory response data for evaluating differences in mental workload between machine-paced and self-paced work. *Ergonomics, 25,* 107–120.

Sharp, R. H. (1978). Visual information-processing in ball games: Some input considerations. In F. Landry & W. A. R. Orban (Eds.), *Motor learning, sport psychology, pedagogy and didactics of physical activity* (pp. 3–12). Quebec: Symposia Specialists.

Shaw, R., & Kinsella-Shaw, J. (1988). Ecological mechanics: A physical geometry for intentional constraints. *Human Movement Science, 7,* 155–200.

Sheridan, T., (1980). Mental workload: What is it? Why bother with it? *Human Factors Society Bulletin, 23,* 1–2.

Sheridan, T., & Stassen, H. (1979). Definitions, models and measures of human workload. In N. Moray (Ed.), *Mental workload: Its theory and measurement* (pp. 219–233). New York: Plenum Press.

Shiffrin., R. M., Craig, J. C., & Cohen, E. (1973). On the degree of attention and capacity limitation in tactile processing. *Perception and Psychophysics, 13,* 328–336.

Shiffrin, R. M., & Gardner, G. T. (1972). Visual processing capacity and attentional control. *Journal of Experimental Psychology, 93,* 72–82.

Shiffrin, R. M., & Schneider, W. (1977). Controlled and automatic human information processing: II. Perceptual learning, automatic attending, and a general theory. *Psychological Review, 84,* 127–190.

Shulman, G. L., Remington, R. W., & McLean, J. P. (1979). Moving attention through visual space. *Journal of Experimental Psychology: Human Perception and Performance, 5,* 522–526.

Silverman, J. (1964). The problem of attention in research and theory in schizophrenia. *Psychological Review, 71,* 352–379.

Simson, R., Vaughan, H. G., & Ritter, W. (1977). The scalp topography of potentials in auditory and visual Go/No Go tasks. *Electroencephalography and Clinical Neurophysiology, 43,* 864–875.

Singer, R. N. (1988). Strategies and metastrategies in learning and performing self-paced athletic skills. *The Sport Psychologist, 2,* 49–68.

Singer, R. N., Cauraugh, J. H., Murphey, M., Chen, D., & Lidor, R. (1991). Attentional control, distractors, and motor performance. *Human Performance, 4,* 55–69.

Singer, R. N., Cauraugh, J. H., Tennant, L. K., Murphey, M., Chen, D., & Lidor, R. (1991). Attention and distractors: Considerations for enhancing sport performances. *International Journal of Sport Psychology, 22,* 95–114.

Snyder, E., Hillyard, S. A., & Galambos, R. (1980). Similarities and differences in P3 waves to detected signals in three modalities. *Psychophysiology, 17,* 112–122.

Solomons, L., & Stein, G. (1896). Normal motor automatism. *Psychological Review, 3,* 492–512.

Sonstroem, R. J., & Bernardo, P. (1982). Intraindividual pregame state anxiety and basketball performance: A reexamination of the inverted-U curve. *Journal of Sport Psychology, 4,* 235–245.

Spelke, E., Hirst, W., & Neisser, U. (1976). Skills of divided attention. *Cognition, 4,* 215–230.

Sperandio, J. C. (1978). The regulation of working methods as a function of workload among air traffic controllers. *Ergonomics, 21,* 193–202.

Spielberger, C. D. (1966). Theory and research on anxiety. In C. D. Spielberger (Ed.), *Anxiety and behavior* (pp. 3–20). New York: Academic Press.

Spielberger, C. D. (1971). Trait-state anxiety and motor behavior. *Journal of Motor Behavior, 3,* 265–279.

Spielberger, C. D., Gorsuch, R. L., & Luschene, R. F. (1970). *Manual of the state-trait anxiety inventory.* Palo Alto, CA: Consulting Psychologists Press.

Spieth, W., Curtis, J. F., & Webster, J. C. (1954). Responding to one of two simultaneous messages. *Journal of the Acoustical Society of America, 26,* 391–396.

Stager, P., & Angus, R. (1978). Locating crash sites in simulated air-to-ground visual search. *Human Factors, 20,* 453–466.

Starkes, J. L. (1986). Attention demands of spatially locating the position of a ball in flight. *Perceptual and Motor Skills, 63,* 1327–1335.

Starkes, J. L. (1987). Skill in field hockey: The nature of the cognitive advantage. *Journal of Sport Psychology, 9,* 146–160.

Starkes, J. L., & Allard, F. (1983). Perception in volleyball: The effects of competitive stress. *Journal of Sport Psychology, 5,* 189–196.

Starkes, J. L., & Deakin, J. (1984). Perception in sport: A cognitive approach to skilled performance. In W. F. Straub & J. M. Williams (Eds.), *Cognitive sport psychology* (pp. 115–128). Lansing, NY: Sport Science Associates.

Stein, H., & Slatt, B. (1981). *Hitting blind: The new visual approach to winning tennis.* Ontario: Mussen.

Stelmach, G. E., & Hughes, B. (1983). Does motor skill automation require a theory of attention? In R. A. Magill (Ed.), *Memory and control of action* (pp. 67–92). Amsterdam: North-Holland.

Stern, R. M. (1976). Reaction time and heart rate between the GET SET and GO of simulated races. *Psychophysiology, 13,* 149–154.

Stroop, J. R. (1935). Studies of interference in serial verbal reactions. *Journal of Experimental Psychology, 18,* 643–662.

Summers, J. J., & Ford, S. K. (1990). The test of attentional and interpersonal style: An evaluation. *International Journal of Sport Psychology, 21,* 102–111.

Sutton, S., Braren, M., Zubin, J., & John, E. R. (1965). Evoked-potential correlates of stimulus uncertainty. *Science, 150,* 1187–1188.

Swensson, R. G. (1980). A two-stage detection model applied to skilled visual search by radiologists. *Perception and Psychophysics, 2,* 88–96.

Swets, J. A. (1964). *Signal detection and recognition by human observers.* New York: Wiley.

Swets, J. A., Tanner, W. P., & Birdsall, T. G. (1961). Decision processes on perception. *Psychological Review, 68,* 301–340.

Tanner, W. P., & Swets, J. A. (1954). A decision-making theory of visual detection. *Psychological Review, 61,* 401–409.

Taylor, J. A. (1953). A personality scale of manifest anxiety. *Journal of Abnormal and Social Psychology, 48,* 285–290.

Taylor, M. M. (1967). Detectability theory and the interpretation of vigilance data. *Acta Psychologica, 27,* 390–399.

Teichner, W. H., & Krebs, M. J. (1974). Visual search for simple targets. *Psychological Bulletin, 81,* 15–28.

Tenenbaum, G., Benedick, A. A., & Bar-Eli, M. (1988). Quantity, consistency, and error-rate of athletes' mental concentration. *International Journal of Sport Psychology, 19,* 311–319.

Thayer, R. E. (1967). Measurement of activation through self report. *Psychological Reports, 20,* 663–678.

Thompson, R. F. (1967). *Foundations of physiological psychology.* New York: Harper & Row.

Titchener, E. B. (1908). *Lectures on the elementary psychology of feeling and attention.* New York: Macmillan.

Treisman, A. (1964). Selective attention in man. *British Medical Bulletin, 20,* 12–16.

Treisman, A. (1969). Strategies and models of selective attention. *Psychological Review, 76,* 282–299.

Treisman, A., & Geffen, G. (1967). Selective attention: Perception or response? *Quarterly Journal of Experimental Psychology, 19,* 1–18.

Turner, R. G., & Gilliland, L. (1977). Comparision of self-report and performance measures of attention. *Perceptual and Motor Skills, 45,* 409–410.

Turvey, M. T., & Carello, C. (1986). The ecological approach to perceiving-acting: A pictorial essay. *Acta Psychologica, 63,* 133–155.

Turvey, M. T., & Carello, C. (1988). Exploring a law-based, ecological approach to skilled action. In A. M. Colley & J. R. Beech (Eds.), *Cognition and action in skilled behaviour* (pp. 191–203). Amsterdam: North-Holland.

Turvey, M. T., Carello, C., & Kim, N-G. (1990). Links between active perception and action. In H. Haken & M. Stadler (Eds.), *Synergetics of cognition* (pp. 269–295). Berlin: Springer Verlag.

Tyldesley, D. A., Bootsma, R. J., & Bomhoff, G. T. (1982). Skill level

and eye-movement patterns in a sport-oriented reaction time task. In H. Reider, K. Bös, H. Mechling, & K. Reischle (Eds.), *Motor learning and movement behavior: Contribution to learning and knowledge* (pp. 290–296). Cologne: Hofmann.

Underwood, G. (1982). Attention and awareness in cognitive and motor skills. In G. Underwood (Ed.), *Aspects of consciousness. Vol. 3: Awareness and self-awareness* (pp. 111–145). London: Academic Press.

Vadhan, V. P., & Smothergill, D. W. (1977). Attention and cognition. *Cognition, 5,* 251–263.

Vallerand, R. J. (1983). Attention and decision-making: A test of the predictive validity of the Test of Attentional and Interpersonal Style (TAIS) in a sport setting. *Journal of Sport Psychology, 5,* 449–459.

Van der Molen, M. W., Somsen, R. J. M., & Orlebeke, J. F. (1985). The rhythm of the heart beat in information processing. In P. K. Ackles, J. R. Jennings & M. G. H. Coles (Eds.), *Advances in psychophysiology* (pp. 1–88). Greenwich, CT: JAI Press.

Vankersschaver, J. (1984). Capacités de traitement des informations dans une habileté sensori-motrice: L'exemple d'une habilete sportive. (Information processing capacities in a sensory-motor skill: A sport skill example). *Le Travail Humain, 47,* 281–286.

Van Schyock, S. R., & Grasha, A. F. (1981). Attentional style variations and athletic ability: The advantages of a sport-specific test. *Journal of Sport Psychology, 3,* 149–165.

Vidulich, M. A. (1988). The cognitive psychology of subjective mental workload. In P. A. Hancock, & N. Meshkati (Eds.), *Human mental workload* (pp. 219–229). Amsterdam: North-Holland.

Vincente, K. J., Thornton, D. C., & Moray, N. (1987). Spectral analyses of sinus arrhythmia: A measure of mental effort. *Human Factors, 29,* 171–182.

Vredenbregt, J., & Rau, G. (1973). Surface electromyography in relation to force, muscle length and endurance. In J. E. Desmedt (Ed.), *New developments in electromyography and clinical neurophysiology, Vol. 1* (pp. 607–622). Karger: Basel.

Wakelin, D. R. (1967). The role of the response in psychological refractoriness. *Acta Psychologica, 40,* 163–175.

Walker, B. B., & Sandman, C. A. (1979). Human visual evoked responses are related to heart rate. *Journal of Comparative and Physiological Psychology, 4,* 717–729.

Walker, B. B., & Sandman, C. A. (1982). Visual evoked potentials change as heart rate and carotid pressure change. *Psychophysiology, 5,* 520–527.

Watchel, P. (1967). Conceptions of broad and narrow attention. *Psychological Bulletin, 68,* 417–429.

Way, T. C., & Gottsdanker, R. (1968). Psychological refractoriness with varying differences between tasks. *Journal of Experimental Psychology, 78,* 38–45.

Weinberg, R. S., & Hunt, U. V. (1976). The interrelationship between anxiety, motor performance and electromyography. *Journal of Motor Behavior, 8,* 219–224.

Weinberg, R. S., & Ragan, J. (1978). Motor performance under three levels of trait anxiety and stress. *Journal of Motor Behavior, 10,* 169–176.

Welch, J. C. (1898). On the measurement of mental activity through muscular activity and the determination of a constant of attention. *American Journal of Physiology, 1,* 253–306.

Welford, A. T. (1952). The psychological refractory period and the timing of high-speed performance—A review and a theory. *British Journal of Psychology, 43,* 2–19.

Welford, A. T. (1967). Single channel operation in the brain. *Acta Psychologica, 27,* 5–22.

Welford, A. T. (1968). *Fundamentals of skill.* London: Methuen.

Welford, A. T. (1973). Stress and performance. *Ergonomics, 16,* 567–580.

Weltman, G., & Egstrom, G. H. (1966). Perceptual narrowing in novice divers. *Human Factors, 8,* 499–505.

Wessells, M. G. (1982). *Cognitive psychology.* New York: Harper & Row.

White, P. A. (1980). Limitations on verbal reports of internal events: A refutation of Nisbett and Wilson and of Bem. *Psychological Review, 87,* 105–112.

White, P. A. (1982). Beliefs about conscious experience. In G. Underwood (Ed.), *Aspects of consciousness. Vol. 3: Awareness and self-awareness* (pp. 1–25). London: Academic Press.

Whiting, H. T. A. (1979). Subjective probability in sport. In G. C. Roberts & K. M. Newell (Eds.), *Psychology of motor behavior and sport, 1978* (pp. 3–25). Champaign, IL: Human Kinetics.

Wickens, C. D. (1979). Measures of workload, stress, and secondary tasks. In N. Moray (Ed.), *Mental workload: Its theory and measurement* (pp. 79–99). New York: Plenum Press.

Wickens, C. D. (1980). The structure of attentional resources. In R. Nickerson & R. Pew (Eds.), *Attention and performance VIII* (pp. 239–257). Hillsdale, NJ: Erlbaum.

Wickens, C. D. (1984). *Engineering psychology and human performance.* Columbus, OH: Charles E. Merrill.

Wickens, C. D., & Derrick, W. (1981). Workload measurement and multiple resources. *Proceedings of the IEEE Conference on Cybernetics and Society.* New York: Institute of Electrical and Electronics Engineers.

Wickens, C. D., & Gopher, D. (1977). Control theory measures of tracking as indices of attention allocation strategies. *Human Factors, 19,* 349–365.

Wickens, C. D., Mountford, S. J., & Schreiner, W. (1981). Multiple resources, task-hemispheric integrity, and individual differences in time-sharing. *Human Factors, 23,* 211–229.

Wiener, N. (1948). *Cybernetics.* New York: Wiley.

Wierwille, W. W., & Connor, S. A. (1983). Evaluation of 20 workload measures using a psychomotor task in a moving-base aircraft simulator. *Human Factors, 25,* 1–16.

Wierwille, W. W., Rahimi, M., & Casali, J. G. (1985). Evaluation of 16 measures of mental workload using a simulated flight task emphasizing mediational activity. *Human Factors, 27,* 489–502.

Wilkinson, R. T. (1963). Interaction of noise with knowledge of results and sleep deprivation. *Journal of Experimental Psychology, 66,* 332–337.

Williams, H. G. (1969). The effects of systematic variations of speed and direction of object flight and skill and age classifications upon visuo-perceptual judgements of moving objects in three-dimensional space. *Dissertations Abstracts International, 29,* 2555-A.

Williams, J. M., & Thirer, J. (1975). Vertical and horizontal peripheral vision in male and female athletes and non-athletes. *Research Quarterly, 46,* 200–205.

Wilson, G. F., & O'Donnell, R. D. (1988). Measurement of operator workload with the neuropsychological workload test battery. In P. A. Hancock, & N. Meshkati (Eds.), *Human mental workload* (pp. 63–100). Amsterdam: North-Holland.

Witkin, H. A., Dyk, R., Faterson, H. F., Goodenough, D. R., & Karp, S. A. (1962). *Psychological differentiation.* New York: Wiley.

Woodrow, H. (1914). The measurement of attention. *Psychological Monographs* (No. 76).

Wrisberg, C. A., & Shea, C. H. (1978). Shifts in attention demands and motor program utilization during motor learning. *Journal of Motor Behavior, 10,* 149–158.

Wundt, W. (1905). *Grundriss der psychologie.* Leipzig: Engelmann.

Yarbus, A. L. (1967). *Eye movement and vision.* New York: Plenum Press.

Yerkes, R. M., & Dodson, J. D. (1908). The relationship of strength of stimulus to rapidity of habit formation. *Journal of Comparative Neurology and Psychology, 18,* 459–482.

Zaichkowsky, L. D., Jackson, C., & Aronson, R. (1982). Attentional and interpersonal factors as predictors of elite athletic performance. In T. Orlick, J. T. Partington, J. H. Salmela (Eds.), *Mental training for coaches and athletes* (pp. 103–104). Ottawa, Ontario: Coaching Association of Canada.

Zelaznik, H. N., Shapiro, D. C., & McClosky, D. (1981). Effects of secondary task on the accuracy of single aiming movements. *Journal of Experimental Psychology: Human Perception and Performance, 7,* 1007–1018.

Zuckerman, M. (1960). The development of an affect adjective checklist for the measurement of anxiety. *Journal of Consulting Psychology, 24,* 457–462.

DECISION MAKING IN SPORT: A COGNITIVE PERSPECTIVE

Gershon Tenenbaum
Michael Bar-Eli

INTRODUCTION TO THE CONCEPT OF DECISION MAKING

Historical Background

The current state of research on decision making (DM) represents a blend of approaches. Since the late 1940s, DM has been studied by investigators from a diverse array of disciplines, including such fields as mathematics, economics, medicine, sociology, education, political science, geography, engineering, marketing, management science, and psychology (Slovic, Fischhoff, & Lichtenstein, 1977). From a historical perspective, three main independent directions of development may be identified within the DM domain (Langenheder, 1975):

1. Decision-and game-theoretical approaches, which have a close relationship to economics and applied mathematics.
2. Psychological approaches, which focus on individual motivational and learning processes.
3. Social-psychological and sociological approaches, which attempt to explain human DM behavior in social situations.

The various approaches to DM have two interrelated facets: normative and descriptive. The origin of normative theory is economics (Edwards, 1954). Central to normative theories is the concept of optimality, associated with rationality. Normative theories are concerned with prescribing courses of action, which are based on a series of rational postulates expressed in order to optimally maximize gain and minimize loss, and which most closely conform to an actor's beliefs and values. However, Simon (1955, 1957, 1976) has argued for "bounded" rationality, distinguishing between the narrow economic meaning of optimizing/maximizing behavior and a more general definition of being sensible, agreeable to reason, and intelligent. Accordingly the acceptability of the fundamental axioms of the normative-rational DM approach has been seriously challenged.

Consequently DM has been heavily "psychologized" (Einhorn & Hogarth, 1981; Slovic, Fischhoff, & Lichtenstein, 1977). Thus the descriptive approach comes from psychology. Whereas economists continue trying to model rational behavior (e.g., Binmore, 1988), psychologists (starting with major contributions of Meehl, 1954) have demonstrated that human decisions depart significantly from the prescriptions of formal decision theory (Kahneman, Slovic, & Tversky, 1982; Slovic, Fischhoff, & Lichtenstein, 1977). Descriptive approaches investigate the gaps between normative ("ideal") and real DM behavior, and identify the causes of such gaps, in terms of actors' beliefs, expectations, and preferences. Along with this line, DM is currently viewed as a central facet of human information processing and part of the larger fields of cognitive and social psychology (Pitz & Sachs, 1984), with cognitive and social psychologists' increasing interest in the study of human DM behavior (Hogarth, 1980; Kahneman, Slovic, & Tversky, 1982; Nisbett & Ross, 1980).

A unique approach has been introduced by several decision theorists (e.g., Coombs, Dawes, & Tversky, 1970; Tanner & Sweets, 1954) who have suggested signal-detection theory as an alternative to the concept of perceptual thresholds. These theorists have proposed statistical techniques of data treatment to provide precise and independent estimates of perceivers' sensitivity and willingness to guess. The theory presents hypothetical frequency distributions of excitation as a function of whether an event originated from noise alone or from a signal embedded in noise. These distributions, which are based on four possible outcomes (hit, miss, false alarm, correct rejection), are used to analyze the perceiver's sensitivity and, independently, his cautiousness or willingness to take risks. Thus this theory offers a means of providing information about the perceiver's sensitivity without its being confounded with his level of confidence. In this way the basic concept of threshold, which is a major dependent variable to perception research, is discarded as being misleading.

Decision Making in Sport: Central Orientations

Gilovich (1984) states that the world of sport is most appropriate for DM research. For example, sport is viewed as a milieu in which observations of behavioral deviations involved in operative DM can be conducted. Furthermore how people think, judge, and analyze in the sport setting is a subject for research free of the limitations existing under laboratory conditions. Thus the sport setting can be used as a live laboratory for the study of cognitive processes (Gilovich, 1984; Gilovich, Vallone, & Tversky, 1985).

According to Pitz and Sachs (1984), a DM task is characterized either by uncertainty of information or outcome, or by a concern for a person's preferences, or both. Unlike other tasks (e.g., problem solving), there may exist no criterion for determining whether a single choice or judgment is correct, since the response is based in part on personal opinions or preferences. It is possible, however, to impose a logical (e.g., mathematical) structure on the task that defines the consistency of a set of responses. Pitz and Sachs (1984) assume the existence of a sequential process that passes through separate stages, with possible subsidiary decisions that can be made at each stage.

Accordingly they identify several basic cognitive mechanisms involved in the recursive activity of performing DM tasks. Specifically, when a problem is presented, salient features are identified, other information is retrieved from memory, and a meaningful organization of this information is created. The various sources of information are evaluated and integrated, and a decision is made. Thus a study of cognitive processes related to an athlete's DM performance refers to factors such as sensation, perception, memory, concentration, general intellectual ability, and problem solving. The reference to cognition relates to two basic assumptions: First, every athletic activity involves cognitive processes that influence the athlete's quality of DM performance, and second, it is possible to identify, assess, and, to a certain extent, influence these processes.

Athletic tasks may be characterized as being dynamic, complex, and, up to a point, as involving risk. They are usually performed in an uncertain environment, with the athlete being expected to cope with tasks like problem solving under psychological stress. Accordingly the study of human

exercise and sport performance has been substantially influenced by the rapid development that has taken place in the cognitive sciences in general, and in the computer sciences and artificial intelligence in particular. Within this framework of research, five foci can be identified: memory (long-and short-term), cognitive styles, intellectual ability, attention and concentration, and, finally, experience. The core of this chapter includes a detailed review of the literature on these cognitive constructs and their influence on DM in exercise and sport.

When a sequential, multistage recursive process of actively making decisions is taking place (Pitz & Sachs, 1984), DM researchers often discuss dynamic DM tasks. In such tasks, "decisions are made sequentially in time; the task specifications may change over time, either independently or as a result of previous decisions; information available for later decisions may be contingent upon the outcomes of earlier decisions; and implications of any decision may reach into the future" (Rapoport, 1975, p. 345). According to our previous description, athletic tasks are typically characterized by a dynamic nature, which requires this type of DM. For example, a coach is often required to continually assess athletes' motor behavior during competition, in order to induce and encourage optimal sport performance (Kaminski, 1975). Performance of this task may be hindered by cognitive as well as emotional difficulties (Zakay, 1982).

Sport skills consist of much information that should be processed in a short time. Thus, according to Ripoll (in press), the athlete is confronted with critical relevant signals and noise signals that, in a state of uncertainty, their ratio imposes a complex DM situation. During a competitive situation the athlete is required to distinguish between feints and the meaningful environmental information. DM and the athlete's subsequent action is therefore dependent on the signal/noise ratio, which determines the uncertainty (Coombs, Dawes, & Tversky, 1970).

Relating to Poulton's (1957) classification of sport actions into open and closed skills, Ripoll (in press) argues that in ball games the semantic function is to identify and interpret the situation. So far, separate studies were devoted to the semantic processes and to the sensorimotor processes. Future research should investigate these two processes integratively. This approach will contribute to better understanding of the "perceiving-acting" relationship, as well as the "perceiving-understanding" relationship. The first is directed toward exploring how the neurological organization interacts with the environmental structure, and the stages in which information is processed and delivered to the motor system. The second is concerned with the visual cues involved in identifying situations, and the operations involved in DM.

This line of research, according to Ripoll (in press), should be further developed in situations where time pressure is externally paced and uncertainty is "manipulated" by the opponent, as well as in situations where uncertainty is "conveyed" by the physical characteristics of the environment and action is self-paced. The fact that cognitive skills are operated unconsciously by athletes raises the questions of the substance of these operations, the neurological level in which these operations are processed, the role of attention and intention, and the degree of attainability of motor-perceptual skills. These directions raise important challenges to sport psychology research.

Cognitive social psychologists (McGuire, 1976; Ross, 1977) have repeatedly demonstrated people's resistance to attitude change, caused by strong perseverence mechanisms that contribute to the formation of change-resistant self-perceptions and social inferences. Furthermore, erroneous impressions, judgments, and data-processing strategies are hardly changed through mere exposure to new evidence. Accordingly, when a diagnosis is conceptualized as the process of revising the subjective probabilities of events on the basis of new data, people will tend to suffer from cognitive strain, which typically results in "conservatism" (Rapoport & Wallsten, 1972; Slovic & Lichtenstein, 1971). Upon receipt of new information, attitudes are usually revised in the same direction as an optimal model would allow, but the revision is too small. Thus when a continuous revision is needed, cognitive overload may cause nonoptimal "conservative" decisions, as was demonstrated with elite basketball coaches in competition (Eberstadt, 1980).

In addition, a coach in competition is frequently under pressure to make decisions for which he or she is perceived as having exclusive responsibility. However, he/she may often experience competitive events as uncontrollable (as when players do not follow the coach's instructions). As a result, not only increased emotional distress and anxiety may be experienced, but also problem-solving and decision-making efficiency may be impaired (Baum & Singer, 1980; Garber & Seligman, 1980; Miller, 1979; Minecka & Hendersen, 1985). Similar cognitive and emotional difficulties may negatively influence an athlete's decision-making process.

In this chapter, cognitive and emotional aspects that distort and disturb the making of optimal decisions will be reviewed. Using the Bayesian model (Slovic & Lichtenstein, 1971), a decision aid will be offered for the coach in order to enhance his or her coping ability with inefficient decisions regarding a specific task, namely, the diagnosis of an athlete's psychological state in competition. Finally, an integrative view of future directions will be presented for investigating decision making in sport.

It should be noted that the study of leadership is viewed by several sport psychologists as critical to the understanding of athletic performance (e.g., Chelladurai, 1984). Within this framework, social sport psychologists have also shown a great deal of interest in DM. The investigations along this line of research focus mainly on the concept of decision styles. Decision styles are defined as learned methods of processing information and making decisions (Hunsaker & Alessandra, 1980), and are viewed as habits acquired through a person's past experiences, similar to people's characteristic methods of learning from and relating to others (Gordon, 1988). Decision styles were usually investigated in sport within the framework of theoretical models adapted from business and industrial settings, with researchers attempting to relate a leader's (e.g., coach's) decision style to leadership effectiveness. However, this chapter will not review the literature on decision styles as cognitive-social processes in sport.

COGNITIVE PROCESSES IN DECISION MAKING

Introduction

The study of human behavior has been influenced in the last generation by the rapid development that has taken place in the cognitive sciences, computer sciences, and artificial intelligence in particular. The psychology of information processing suggests cognitive models describing the flow of information perceived by receptors, and stages through which this information passes until a decision is made.

Neisser (1982) maintains that there is no justification for relying on independent cognitive models, since their ecological validity is questionable. Neisser's ecological approach relies on the natural environment as the ethnologists did in the study of animal behavior in their natural environment (the area of interest did not focus on the principles of learning, but rather on the behavior itself in a natural environment). The approaches of Hull (1951), Spence (1956), and Skinner (1938) on the one hand, and of Neisser (1967) on the other, together with Piaget's (1952) cognitive development psychology, constitute a comprehensive construct for the understanding of man's intelligent behavior.

The perceptual-motor process is defined as the performance of a voluntary movement that requires the continual processing of information coming from either the body or environment (Arnheim & Sinclair, 1979; Cratty, 1979; Gallahue, 1982; Williams & Deoreo, 1980). Information-processing models constitute a representation, description, or analogy of processes which cannot be observed or investigated directly (Keogh & Sugden, 1985). In a stage between perceiving the information through the various senses (INPUT) and the implementation of a motor response (OUTPUT), there exists a cognitive-perceptual process through which the individual analyzes and organizes the information for the purposes of making decisions (Singer, 1980).

The perceptual-motor process relies on the past experiences of the individual. The information, flowing in through the sensory systems, undergoes a process of identification, analysis, and diagnosis before it is processed in the central nervous system. One of the significant components in processing is the feedback that supplies information about the performance and appears in the form of internal and external feedback. Internal feedback supplies information related to a movement's range, speed, and the like, while the external feedback supplies information related to the environment. The processed information is integrated with and compared to information that was previously stored and can be used in the present and/or future. The retention mechanism is one of the most basic and important in information processing.

The athlete perceives information from two sources: (1) external sources of stimuli such as a ball, a goal, an umpire, spectators, and players, and (2) internal sources or sensory stimuli related to muscle tension, range of movement, and the like. According to Singer (1980), every stimulus must pass through a certain threshold for the athlete to pay attention to it. The peripheral sensation systems transfer the stimuli in the form of neural codes to the sensory memory mechanism. Information below the stimulus threshold does not pass through the next stage and is forgotten. The function of the sensory memory is to collect the information, filter it, and transfer it to the perceptual mechanism.

The function of the perceptual mechanism is to identify and give meaning to the environmental information. After identifying the information, the perceptual mechanism controls most of the information perceived by paying selective attention to the information relevant to the immediate performance, and ignoring irrelevant information. The more experienced the actor is, the faster and more efficient is the process described (Marteniuk, 1976).

According to Singer (1980), information is essential for DM only following the integration between stimuli sensation and long-term memory mechanism. This mechanism gives meaning to the environmental stimuli and enables the application of selective attention.

Alderson (1972) believes that personal perceptual abilities and skills are related to the central nervous system, and are mediators between the variables related to the environment and those related to the performance (the acquisition of motor skills). Their quality is what determines the athlete's skill level in a task.

Sensation and Memory

McNamara (1986) maintained that we navigate in a three-dimensional world and are guided by perception and memory of spatial relations. Shepard (1975, 1981, 1984) argued that physical constraints, unique to our spatial environment, were internalized during the evolution of our perception system. These constraints were internalized in structure and in the mental processing of language. An understanding of the imparting, storing, and organizing of spatial knowledge is the basis of understanding complex mental functioning.

The sensory mechanism makes it possible to distinguish stimuli, to identify them according to color and shape without any labeling (names) whatsoever. This process takes place before naming the stimulus. The sensory mechanism is capable of storing much information for the shortest possible times. Sensory storage was investigated mainly in the visual iconic memory and the auditory echonic memory. The length of the visual iconic memory in adults is estimated to be 250 msec (Crowder, 1976) and 10 seconds for the auditory echonic memory when a certain auditory iden-

tification was required (Eriksen & Johnson, 1973). The sensory store is important for selection and interpretation of information stored in memory. Crowder (1976) maintained that visual constructs (models) appear at the same time, scattered in space, while auditory structures appear scattered in the time dimension. The necessity of the kinesthetic sensory store is important for the perception of information such as auditory and visual data for the purpose of processing it at a later stage.

Following Atkinson and Shiffrin (1968, 1971), the concepts of "input," "thinking," and "decision making" are based on sensory store, short-term store (STS), and long-term store (LTS). Sensory store is an almost perfect replica of physical stimuli containing perceptual/kinesthetic data before processing. Any information that is not processed within a given time limitation disappears from the system. Attention to correct cues in the sensory store enables the encoding of environmental information, and, through processing, allows it to be transferred from the STS to the LTS. STS is basically a limited processor, while LTS has no defined or clear limits. The STS mechanism operates during a temporary action as a location of storage for important information before it is transferred for *processing, reaction selection,* and *reaction planning.* Control mechanisms such as *rehearsal* and *organization* serve to transfer information from STS to LTS.

In recent years working memory has become a dominant field of cognitive research. Working memory was perceived as functional analysis of temporary storage manipulation during information processing in situations where control process and complex decisions were involved (Logie, 1986). Two subsystems associated with working memory were termed the "articulatory loop" and the "visual-spatial scratch pad" (VSSP). The first was investigated quite intensively as a subvocal rehearsal buffer (Baddeley, Thomson, & Buchanan, 1975; Salame & Baddeley, 1982; Vallar & Baddeley, 1982).

The articulatory loop was investigated through several techniques aimed at the articulatory suppression of attention (repeating irrelevant speech sounds or counting numbers simultaneously while performing other tasks). Articulatory suppression was found to significantly affect tasks such as digit span, suggesting that the task shares cognitive resources (Baddeley & Hitch, 1974). This was not found with verbal reasoning, which involves the central executive component of working memory (Hitch & Baddeley, 1976).

Research has indicated that material that contains spatial coding was recalled less well when paired with a concurrent tracking task (Baddeley, Grant, Wright, & Thomson, 1975), while memory for equivalent verbally encoded material was not affected by tracking. This suggests that spatial material may involve the VSSP, which is also involved in tracking. In an additional study, Baddeley and Lieberman (1980) found that tracking during encoding was shown to interfere with recall of spatially coded material when a nonvisual tracking task was performed with the eyes blindfolded, receiving auditory feedback rather than visual. Additional studies (Phillips & Christie, 1977a, 1977b) concluded that short-term visual processing uses general-purpose resources rather than a system specializing in process and storage of visual-spatial material.

The studies by Baddeley et al. suggest that general-purpose resources are used in spatial coding where VSSP may be involved. The advantage of concrete over abstract nouns was probably due to the richer semantic coding of the concrete material, not due to the use of a visual-spatial system (Logie, 1986).

The two subsystems of "articulatory loop" and "VSSP" were not investigated in the sport domain, where the athletes are required to recall complex situations while dribbling a ball, searching for cues in the environment, and being substantially interfered with by the opponent, and sometimes vocally by the audience and referees. The visual-spatial working memory investigated so far in sport is limited to recall of structured and unstructured game situations. Therefore, a methodology should be developed to examine this construct within the motor domain.

Short-Term Store in Sport

The recall paradigm is of value in the presentation of interrelations between skills and information about the stimuli (Chase & Simon, 1973b). Chess experts were allowed to observe a chessboard for 5 seconds with pieces set out, as if for a game. Afterward they were asked to reconstruct this arrangement on another board. Top chess experts performed the task better than Class A players. The latter succeeded more in a task than did new players. When the same players were asked to reconstruct the organization of the chess pieces that had been placed randomly on the board, all the players did so in a similar way. Since the memory capacity is a constant variable beyond all skill levels, the game construct is coded differently in very skilled players.

Allard, Graham, and Paarsalu (1980) also presented the interrelations between skill and stimulus (SXS) by comparing basketball players with nonbasketball players. Both groups were presented with a succession of slides describing structured offense situations next to the board, and unstructured transitional situations (passing the ball, returning a ball, etc.). The slides were taken from actual games and were screened for 4 seconds. The subjects were asked to reconstruct the situations immediately on a board that contained magnetic surfaces representing players and a field. Players were more accurate in recalling structured game situations. The two groups recalled defense better than offense situations.

Starkes and Deakin (1984) examined female field hockey players in the recall of structured game situations that were screened for 8 seconds. Again, female players recalled structured situations better than female nonathletes did. National League female players were better than local players at recalling structured situations. Although the differences between skilled players and others lie mainly in the recall of structured situations in a specific sport, differ-

ences must be found in actual game settings in simulated situations.

Allard and Starkes (1980) applied a detection paradigm to examine perceptual skill in volleyball. One strategy in research of this type is to avoid a number of visual cues and to concentrate on information related to the ball. Volleyball players and nonplayers were asked to detect whether or not a ball was present in the slide. Fifty percent of the slides included volleyball game situations and 50% were nongame situations (time-out, warm-up, etc.). The design was aimed at examining whether skilled players are more sensitive to information related to the structure of the game, as was proven in the past, through the use of the recall paradigm. The slides were projected for 16 msec, and the subjects responded "yes" or "no" as quickly and accurately as possible into a microphone (in half of the slides a ball was present and in the other half, the ball was absent).

Irrespective of the five series of experiments, it seemed that volleyball players were faster (but not more accurate) than nonplayers in indicating the presence of the ball in the situations presented. It seems that the recall strategy of the players consists of a very fast search of the ball location, while more or less ignoring the game situation. It is assumed that in sports related to hitting or standing at the goal, detecting skill is required, whereas in sports such as football (American and European) and field hockey, grouping strategy is required (Allard, 1982). In field hockey and volleyball, perceptual accuracy did not distinguish skilled athletes from unskilled ones, but voice RT was faster in National League players. It thus seems that perceptual accuracy is a skill component related to the recall paradigm, whereas perceptual speed depends more on the detection paradigm.

Starkes and Allard (1983) added a further condition to their research-competition. Under competitive pressure, volleyball players and nonplayers used completely different strategies related to a tradeoff between perceptual accuracy and speed of decision making. The results showed that stress is interrelated with perceptual skills in various directions depending on the particular sport investigated.

Visual Search in Athletes

Visual search is an applied perceptual process for locating objects in the visible display. This process is necessary for eliminating spatial uncertainty (Prinz, 1977). A number of researchers adopted the visual search paradigm in sport (Allard, 1984; Allard, Graham, & Paarsalu, 1980; Allard & Starkes, 1980; Bard & Fleury, 1976; Bard, Fleury, Carrière, & Halle, 1980; Starkes & Deaken, 1984). In these studies, athletes were asked to scan slides or films in order to detect, recognize, or recall targets, involving structured and unstructured situations in sport settings. The results of these studies showed that (1) visual scanning is useful for assessing athletes' cognitive ability in a game; (2) the carrying out of a visual scan by experienced athletes is different in nature from that of nonathletes; and (3) visual scanning is a perceptual process of substantial importance for athletic performance.

Allard and Starkes (1980) and Starkes and Allard (1983) found that experienced female volleyball players were also skilled at visual scan, detection, and recognition of the ball in a game, but this process was not found in game situations of sports other than volleyball. Recognizing the ball as fast as possible is a learned process that should be emphasized during practice. In basketball and field hockey it was found that female players recalled game situations with greater accuracy than female nonplayers (Allard & Burnett, 1985; Allard, Graham, & Paarsalu, 1980; Starkes & Deaken, 1984). The researchers assumed that game structure interacts with the degree of experience (seniority) of the player.

Bard and Fleury (1976) found that the visual search pattern used by (men) basketball players differs from that of nonplayers, and similarly it differs according to the position of the player in a game. In their study they presented offense situations and the subjects were asked to decide whether to shoot, pass, bounce the ball, or remain in position. Eye fixation was measured by using a corneal reflection recorder. The results showed that senior (experienced) basketball players made fewer fixations for identifying details when looking for a solution. Similar findings were also reported by Bard, Fleury, Carrière, and Halle (1980) for female judges of competitive gymnastics with different levels of experience.

Extensive research has been conducted to examine how a person controls the visual search process. Neisser (1967) suggested two theories that account for visual search: the target control theory and the context control theory. The target control theory states that visual search to discover a target is executed by controlling the memory representation of the target. When the stimulus representation and memory representation are compatible, a person discovers the target. Contrary to this theory, the context control theory states that visual search is carried out under the control of memory representation, which contains presentations not sensitive to individual objects, but rather to a greater number of items in the display. According to this theory, the observer is under situational control when the stimulus is compatible with the representational memory of the context.

Research showed that control of the visual search differs in the course of skill development (Neisser, 1967; Prinz, 1977, 1979a; Prinz & Atalan, 1973; Prinz, Tweer, & Roffeige, 1974). Without practice, a person functions under target control, since the context is unfamiliar. With practice (training), a person develops memory representations sensitive to objects that together make up a considerable part of the display. Practice improves context control (i.e., control of memory search alters target control to situation control). Gentile, Higgins, Miller, and Rosen (1975) and also Beitel (1980) recognize this change, which begins with training, and maintain that sport and motor skills necessitate a separation of perceptual search strategies, both in the environmental demands of the task and in the learning stages of the individual.

The "hurdle technique" is a useful experimental paradigm in studies dealing with visual search for determining under which control situation the observer scans the visual display. According to this technique, an object that is not related in any way to the formal target is displayed in space. It is hypothesized that (1) the discovery of the hurdle occurs when the observer is able to recall the hurdle, and (2) the speed of the search decreases when a hurdle is present compared to the speed when a hurdle is absent in the context (environment). If the observer discovers the hurdle, it is a sign that the visual search has been carried out under context control (Prinz, 1977, 1979b; Prinz & Atalan, 1973; Prinz, Tweer & Roffeige, 1974). Bard, Fleury, Carrière, and Halle (1980) and Bard and Fleury (1976) suggested that the visual search strategies of experienced and inexperienced basketball players, as well as those of gymnastics judges, were different in keeping with the demands and characteristics made by each respective sport. Allard (1984) hypothesizes that volleyball players focus attention on the ball and ignore the environmental information, whereas experienced basketball players focus attention on all the details in the environment. The athlete, in the course of training, develops the ability to scan the visual display in order to perform successfully. It may thus be assumed that the inexperienced athlete performs under target control while the experienced athlete performs under context and target control together.

Millslagle (1988) found that RT in experienced women basketball players in a task that involved recalling the presence of the ball in structured game situations and transitional situations was faster than RT in inexperienced women players. Inexperienced players recalled the ball in unstructured situations better than experienced ones in structured situations. Inexperienced players recalled the presence of the ball in structured situations better than experienced players in the same situations.

There were similar findings in unstructured situations. All the players recalled structured situations better than unstructured ones. The hurdle in the slides did not change RT, in new female basketball players and in experienced ones, However, a number of significant interactions were found. The average RT was faster when both the ball and the hurdle were in the slides rather than when they were omitted. RT was faster when the ball was present in the slides and the hurdle was taken out, as opposed to when both were in the slides. RT was faster when the hurdle was present and the ball was not, as opposed to when both were lacking. RT was faster when the ball but not the hurdle was present, as opposed to when the hurdle but not the ball was present. Interactions of the two with experience were not found to be significant—RT was similar in new and experienced female players when the ball, the hurdle, or both, were present/absent.

The research on visual search in sport (Allard & Burnett, 1985; Allard & Starkes, 1980; Bard & Fleury, 1976) points to a number of differences between well-trained athletes and untrained ones in the following variables: (1) speed of recognition, (2) accuracy of recognition, and (3) recall.

Millslagle (1988) indeed found that the greater the experience, the faster the RT, but this was not so for accuracy. These findings were also supported by other studies (Allard & Starkes, 1980; Starkes & Allard, 1983) involving experienced and inexperienced female volleyball players. In structured situations, recall was better than in unstructured ones, but no difference in the speed of identification was found between structured and unstructured situations. In many studies, it was reported that the recall ability of experienced players was much better than that of inexperienced players (Allard & Burnett, 1985; Bard & Fleury, 1976; Bard, Fleury, Carrière, & Halle, 1980; Starkes & Deaken, 1984). Bard and Fleury (1976) reported that the cognition and perception of game organization in experienced women basketball players is much more refined than that in inexperienced women players. Millslagle's (1988) research did not support Prinz's (1977, 1979b) theory regarding context control and target control measured by the inclusion of a hurdle in slides—neither the RT nor the recall changed as a result of the inclusion of the hurdle. The researcher hypothesizes that experienced and inexperienced female players operated under target control. When the ball and hurdle were present, RT was faster than in a situation where both were absent.

Examination of visual search patterns used in preparing serve returns in squash, badminton, and tennis indicated that eye fixation depends on the search sequence (Abernethy & Russell, 1987; Derrider, 1985; Goulet, Bard, & Fleury, 1989). Fixation on large features occurs early in the sequence, while later the gaze is transferred to the racquet. This changing direction of eye gaze is a strategy that probably decreases the situational uncertainty (Ripoll, in press). Ripoll further argues that the difference between experts and novice athletes is that experts direct the gaze to a position in which many events can be seen integratively during one single eye fixation (i.e., synthetic analysis), while novices gaze at events according to their chronological order (i.e., analytic analysis). Bard and Fleury (1976) confirmed this phenomenon in basketball. Later, investigating volleyball players, Ripoll (1988) termed the visual search "inter-event fixation."

Ripoll (1979), in examining table tennis players, showed that in a situation of lack of information or uncertainty, the player's gaze was not directed toward the opponent. Later on, the gaze was directed to different points on the ball's flight path. In situations of uncertainty, expert players employed strategies that optimally adopt the sensorimotor system to the extremely high constraint of the situation.

ATTENTION AND CONCENTRATION

Introduction

In William James's book *Principles of Psychology* (1890) reference is made to the concept of attention. According to his definition, attention is a cerebral state in which "pure" images and shapes, free of other environmental stimuli and interfering thoughts, are perceived. This is in fact a state of focalization and concentration of the consciousness. This state necessitates a withdrawal of certain stimuli, with a view to making the perception of the other stimuli more efficient. This cerebral state is the opposite of a cerebral state that reflects confusion and vagueness. Neisser (1967), in his book *Cognitive Psychology,* described man making intelligent decisions as a result of his ability to focus attention on what he perceives, to recall and to use language.

In selective processes, Jones (1972) states that environmental stimuli depend on three factors: (1) the ability to be conscious and select the information sources that are most essential (2) the quantity of stimuli, and (3) the time at the athlete's disposal. No athlete is capable of perceiving all the potential information from the field in the limited time available. Thus he/she has to be selective in order to process essential information and to direct attention to the most essential cues (stimuli) within the limits (cognitive and motor) of ability, the information accumulated, and time. It may be hypothesized that a skilled athlete perceives essential stimuli for an optimal performance better than a less skilled athlete, and that experience makes a considerable contribution to this ability. A selective diagnostic ability is necessary for performing open skills, since the stimulus range and attention focus constitute an information transfer and processing (Jones, 1972). Relying on laboratory and field research, Jones (1972) concluded that selective attention is influenced by, among other things, variables such as arousal level, habits, inner and external disturbances, tension, and personal differences.

Discovering an object in the environment depends on two factors: (1) the number of objects (stimuli) in the field, and (2) the extent to which the target object shares properties with the nontargets around it. In most of the studies, the greater the number of nontargets, the longer the visual scan lasts (Carter, 1982; Drury & Clement, 1978; Farmer & Taylor, 1980; Green & Anderson, 1956; Jonides & Gleitman, 1972; Schneider & Shiffrin, 1977; Teichner & Krebs, 1974). When the space includes expected targets that are familiar, well known, and conspicuous, the search time remains almost constant (Egeth, Jonides, & Wall, 1972; Gleitman & Jonides, 1978; Jonides & Gleitman, 1972). Posner and Boies (1971) made this function dependent on the quantity of attention sources within the central storage needed for the performance of the task. In a number of studies, this function has been used as proof of capacity-free processing during visual scanning and, simultaneously, a rising linear function as proof of capacity-limited processing (Neisser, 1967).

Sport psychologists distinguish between focal and diffuse (i.e., expanded) attention. Focal attention is determined by a small extent of the attentional field with enhanced details (operates more systematically, exploring efficiently a given area of the informational field). Diffuse attention is determined by a wider size of attentional span, but a lower extent for details about the objects within the field of view (more efficient to explore the visual field globally and quickly in order to detect any significant signals).

In sports such as fencing, tennis, and boxing, which require much information processing, a diffuse distribution of attention to analyze the information is needed. The athlete is supposed to orient attention to an intermediate location of the visual field (Ripoll, 1988a, 1988b). Visual scanning strategies of expert athletes show that they conduct an "inter-event" analysis, by gazing at an intermediate location of the stimuli that are to occur. On the contrary, for sport skills such as archery or shooting, it might be more useful to focus attention on the target (Nougier, Azemar, & Stein, 1990; Nougier, Ripoll, & Stein, 1987).

Automatization of processing and acting enables athletes to control attention in complex tasks, particularly in situations involving high uncertainty. It allows the simultaneous processing of two or more tasks. Attentional flexibility enables the athlete to detect peripheral signals and to face various situations more homogeneously. Attentional flexibility may induce an efficient ability to switch quickly from automatic processes to controlled ones.

A discussion exists between defenders of early and defenders of late selection of attention. Kahneman and Treisman (1984) have proposed an intermediate model of dual mechanism. The first aspect of this mechanism consists of filtering and selecting perceptual information on the basis of elementary features of the signal by reference to early selection models. The second one controls the access of the information to the processes of producing the response by reference to the late selection models. Attention, then, is used to recognize objects on the basis of the object's features. Correct identification is made when the object is localized. Motor preparation is a functional and optimal process that intervenes specifically at each stage of information processing (Keele & Hawkins, 1982; Keele & Neill, 1979). In a series of studies, Nougier, Stein, and Bonnel (in press) concluded that expert-novice differences of information processing are due to experts' optimization of the processes implied in the late stages of information processing.

Perceptual Anticipation and Sport

Poulton (1957) maintained that in a number of cases, motor performance is partly dependent on partial information or effective utilization of environmental cues. In fact, very little is known about the use of environmental information and its application for the effective performance of a motor task.

Jones and Miles (1978) examined top tennis players and beginners in predicting a ball's landing location after an opening stroke. The film was shown to athletes at time intervals of 1/24 second, 1/8 second, and 1/3 second after the racquet had made contact with the ball. All the examinees performed at all the time intervals. At a time of 1/3 second, all the examinees performed the task similarly. In the shortest time, and even at a time of 1/8 second after contact, the

experienced tennis players predicted the ball's final location better than the beginners.

Salmela and Fiorito (1979) investigated perceptual anticipation among ice hockey goalies by using a film sequence. The goalkeepers watched the film in which there was a player approaching the goal and aiming to shoot. The film sequences were cut at one of three times before the stick-puck contact—1/12 second, 1/6 second, and 1/3 second. The predicted performance and level of confidence in the reaction, horizontally and vertically, were examined for a wrist shot and a slap shot. Accurate prediction of the puck's final location depended on a number of environmental cues in the visual field. A wrist shot provided many more environmental cues to the goalies than a slap shot. The players succeeded in predicting which side the puck would go (its direction) better than in predicting its height. Even at 1/3 second before puck contact there were more successful predictions than chance guesses. Thus the enrichment of environmental visual cues is an important component of skill, especially when the average speed of the shot performed from the blue line, by a professional player, is roughly 10 times faster than the ordinary reaction time of a less skilled player (Drouin & Salmela, 1975).

Bard and Fleury (1981) examined ice hockey goalies using a special corneal reflection eye-tracking instrument. The goalies looked at a number of offensive situations on the ice rink or in a laboratory situation where there was an offensive player on an artificial surface. Despite the fact that the top goalies and the beginners showed a similar ocular fixation on the stick and puck, the novice goalies had more fixations on the puck than the outstanding experienced goalies, whether the shots were slap or sweep.

The expert goalies were also faster than the novices in initiating blocking movements. The researchers hypothesized, therefore, that excellent, experienced goalies predict the path of the puck by perceiving cues from the stick and not from cues related to the puck. The novice goalies made decisions related to the path of the puck only when it was hit by a stick.

In another perceptual anticipation study, Starkes and Deakin (1984) found that in National League field hockey, the players were able to predict the location of the shot in a sequence, before or after the shot, more precisely than Regular League players or a control group. All the participants (irrespective of their level) improved their ability (their accuracy in predicting the path of the ball) when there was contact between the stick and the ball. In sequences where observation was cut 1/20 second before contact, regular players and control group examinees predicted the direction of the ball similarly to that in ordinary guessing (16.7%—with reference to 6 possible ball placements). Only the top National League players predicted more accurately rather than simply guessing, when they were forced to rely on advanced visual cues.

In studies of a variety of sports, in which temporal and spatial occlusion conditions were manipulated for expert and novice athletes, differences in predicting forthcoming actions were observed (Abernethy & Russell, 1987; Bard &

Fleury, 1976; Barras, 1987; Derrider, 1985; Goulet, Bard, & Fleury, 1989; Kerlirzin, 1990; Neumaier, 1982; Ripoll, 1988b). Ripoll (in press) summarized that quality differences between experts and novices occur only under time pressure, occluded events, and forced choices. Experts needed less information to solve problems appropriately.

From these studies, it was concluded that skilled athletes are capable of using environmental information (cues) in order to improve their perceptual anticipation.

Attentional Styles

Nideffer (1976a) defined various attentional styles that enable people to cope successfully or unsuccessfully with environmental information. His ideas have made a special contribution to the sport setting as well (Nideffer, 1976b).

Relying on the theories of Easterbrook (1959), Heilbrun (1972), and Wachtel (1967), Nideffer suggested that attention has two dimensions: breadth of focus and direction. Space is based on a continuum from narrow to broad, and the direction is from internal to external. Breadth refers to the number of elements one can focus on in a stimulus field, whereas direction refers to whether an individual's attentional focus is directed to internal or to external stimuli. People are different from one another in their attentional styles, and every style has its weaknesses and advantages. A person's capacity for moving from one attention style to another depends on the arousal level.

According to Nideffer (1976a), in all kinds of sport, individual or team, a different dimensional integration is required for optimal performance. In general, when the situations are more complex and change rapidly, an exceptionally focused attention is required of the athlete. When the level of decision making necessitates analyzing or planning, the need for a reflective internal attention style rises. As a result of an incompatible attention style, athletes make mistakes. Thus, for example, players do not adapt to changes in the situation during a competition, in keeping with changes taking place among the opposition teams (tactical changes). They develop one type of action and remain so without taking into consideration the environmental conditions. This kind of athlete represents a fairly external and narrow attention style.

In the majority of sports, the athlete is expected to change attentional styles, both in terms of breadth and direction, and occasionally fairly rapidly. It would seem, therefore, that the ability to change attentional style, voluntarily and controlled, is an extremely important component in an athlete's performance. On the other hand, lack of control and/or the inability to change attention style are likely to be associated with a deterioration in performance. Nideffer (1976a) supported this concept when he obtained a positive correlation between cognitive confusion and attention scales.

Additionally Nideffer (1979) stated that attention was closely related to the level of anxiety and arousal. He maintained that a rise in the anxiety and arousal levels limits the capacity for passing from one attentional style to another and limits the attention level. The narrowing of attention was determined in studies in which the examinees were presented with tasks based on a dual-task paradigm. The examinee was asked to focus on one task and to listen simultaneously to an additional task under conditions of pressure. The pressure factors were: drugs, exercises, electric shock, lack of sleep, hypoxia, and threat (Landers, 1980). Subjects systematically reported a narrowing of attention as the arousal level rose. The reason for the narrowing of attention under pressure is not sufficiently clear. Bacon (1974) argued that the arousal level influences performance by lowering the level of sensitivity to environmental stimuli, and in doing so, the processing of information is limited.

Easterbrook (1959) related anxiety and attention through the "cue-utilization theory," which maintains that in a high state of arousal, the range of perceived stimuli is narrowed and the perception of the stimuli relevant for the performance of the task is limited. In the course of a competitive game, it is possible to hypothesize that most of the time the level of anxiety is low. Thus it can be assumed that physical fatigue, on the one hand, and intellectual ability (the ability to counteract irrelevant stimuli and to focus on relevant ones), on the other, are the factors influencing the quality of the performance. Nideffer (1976a) reported that inconsistent swimmers, who tended to be under an extremely high internal and external stimulus load, were unable to integrate thoughts and ideas, or to focus their attention level. Richards and Landers (1981) showed that inexperienced shooters were under an extremely high external stimulus load. The researchers reported that shooters, in general, are not overloaded with external stimuli and do not commit mistakes as a result of narrowing attention. Kirschenbaum and Bale (1980) found that experienced golf players are more sensitive to external stimuli that disturb and tend to intensely focus their level of attention.

In a team of swimmers, Jackson (1980) found that the ability to limit attention distinguished skilled and fairly good swimmers from weak ones. Divers were categorized successfully in 70% of the cases for excellence or inferior skills based on the overload scale scores. Mahoney and Avener (1977) reported that skilled gymnasts indicated their confidence in their ability to focus attention during a competition.

A specific attentional style is necessary for every task (Fisher, 1984). For an open task such as field hockey, an athlete requires a broad-external focus in order to capture all the essential stimuli from teammates and opposing players. Field hockey players also require a broad-internal focus in order to store the actions that they have to perform in varying game situations. For these wide foci, a narrow focus is needed in order to perform a movement. In the event that a nonessential stimulus is distinguished from an essential one, movements are likely to be performed precisely. In Fisher's opinion, an appropriate attention focus enriches intelligent behavior, whereas an inappropriate focus blocks intelligent behavior. Flexibility of attention and the ability to make the demands of the task appropriate to the attention style are the keys to optimal performance. An inappropriate attentional style constitutes a threat to intelligent behavior.

COGNITIVE STYLE: FIELD DEPENDENCE/INDEPENDENCE

Introduction

Field independence is defined as the capacity to perceive details of information within the set of general information (Witkin, Dyk, Faterson, Goodenough, & Karp, 1962). The capacity to "perceive" and remain with an object is independent of the field or the background. An athlete who competes is expected to distinguish the movement of the ball, the players of his or her team as well as those of the opponent, the field boundaries, and other stimuli, to make it possible to cope with the tasks in the game. The athlete who is able to move from dependence to independence of the field has a clear advantage in finding the optimal solutions to problems in the game over the athlete who is limited in this respect.

The cognitive styles, as defined by Swinnen, Vandenberghe, and Van Assche (1986), have an important influence on personal cognitive functioning in a wide variety of behaviors, such as perception, memory, thinking, and problem solving. From among more than 20 cognitive styles, field dependence has been the most widely studied. Field dependence was at first derived from laboratory research on the perception of verticality (Witkin, Moore, Goodenough, & Cox, 1977) and afterward, it also encompassed perceptual tasks that require the examinee to distinguish between the item and the field. The main factor separating the examinees' performances is analytical, or the extent to which the examinee perceives part of a given field as separate from its environment.

Cognitive Style and Motor Performance

Witkin (1959, 1967) reported on the relationship between learning and motor performance and that of the field-dependence cognitive-perceptual style. A number of studies (Barrell & Trippe, 1975; Kane, 1972; McLeod, 1985; Pargman, Schreiber, & Stein, 1974) examining the relationship between field dependence of athletes and the kind of sport in which they participated, supported the claim that athletes who took part in team sports, in which they are required to perform open skills, are more field dependent than athletes who are involved in individual sports, in which they are required to perform closed skills. As Knapp (1964) and Jones (1972) stated, closed skills are based almost entirely on physical components such as strength, force, and technique, while open skills require, in addition to these resources, the coordination of movement in a changing environment.

The performer assesses a situation and subsequently chooses the appropriate movement. Both Jones (1972, 1973) and Loader, Edwards, and Henschen (1982) maintain that the perceptual style of field independence is an advantage in team sports, since field-independent athletes are able to demonstrate the cognitive styles as required.

Macgillivary (1980a, b) investigated perception under various environmental conditions. He found a significant relationship between the level of learning of the perceptual task, the duration in which the ball was observed, and the cognitive style of the examinee. Field-independent examinees learned the perceptual task better than those who were field dependent. Swinnen and Vandenberghe (1983) and Swinnen (1982) examined the learning of skill in gymnastics and found that field-independent examinees performed better than field-dependent ones in learning the skill. Swinnen, Vandenberghe, & Van Assche (1986) hypothesized in their research that field-dependent examinees would be less successful in a nonstructured learning environment, since their information-processing methods were not dependent on analyzing and constructing. On the other hand, field-independent subjects use the capacity for organizing when the environment being learned is not clear, and thus they will be more successful than those who are field dependent. Subjects in the study were students of age 13 who were examined in visual-perception tests and in the performance of physical training exercises. The hypothesis of the research was verified only for boys. From this result and others, Swinnen, Vandenberghe, and Van Assche (1986) concluded that field-independent subjects who also had the capacity for analyzing and reorganizing were more advantaged in learning gymnastics skills (and possibly also similar other skills) than field-dependent examinees.

According to Jones (1972), people with a field-dependent cognitive style are influenced more by external disturbances, while those with a field-independent cognitive style are capable of counteracting nonessential stimuli for the performance of the task and focusing their attention on essential information. Poulton (1957) distinguished between "closed skills" and "open skills." In open skills the perceptual component is of the utmost importance for the efficient performance of a task. In order to construct the motor skill appropriate to the environmental data, a selective attention level is necessary that will allow the perception and processing of all the significant stimuli for the purpose of finding the optimal solution.

INTELLECTUAL APTITUDE: INTELLIGENCE AND PROBLEM-SOLVING

Definition

Intelligence is the ability to acquire and apply information. People are thought to be intelligent when they are capable of coping with demands created by new situations and new problems, and applying what has been learned through experience. They use the power of thinking and analogy (to make inferences), which influences the direction of behavior. Intelligence represents appropriate behavior based on the capacity for problem solving. The effectiveness of this behavior is regulated through rational (cognitive) processes and operations (Combs, 1952; Estes, 1982a). Thus intelligence depends on the richness and variety of perceptions processed in a given moment, and the capacity of the brain to code (to store and display) and to retrieve (access) essential information for the solution or performance of the task.

Although it has been agreed for a long time that attention and perception are part of what is termed "intelligence" (Spearman, 1927; Thurstone, 1938), today this agreement is no longer unequivocal. Sigler and Richards (1982) maintained that the skill of perceptual and motor identification is important in the early assessment of intelligence, and that this skill had not been analyzed in the sport setting. The most essential variable for sport is perceptual intelligence. Coding and accessing are mechanisms with a close relationship to perception and attention. Behavior is an external representation of neural competence. Behavior may be no more intelligent than the way in which events are perceived in the brain. Categorization and organization are the most important mechanisms for the collection of information. It is more important to be able to utilize the knowledge stored in the memory than to contain a great amount of knowledge (Sternberg & Salter, 1982). Most people usually have more than enough knowledge to cope with tasks in particular situations, but few are capable of accessing the appropriate knowledge stored in the memory so that it is specific and successful for coping with particular situations.

Therefore, perceptual style is directly responsible for the quality and quantity of the behaviors presented. This mechanism is characterized by a number of features: (1) coding and transforming of environmental stimuli, (2) paying attention to a number of stimuli and ignoring others, (3) using stimuli for creating an internal representation of the external world, (4) creating a representation of the events in time and space, and (5) organizing, initiating, and controlling those same movements (Marteniuk, 1976).

The neural mechanism that unites environmental contingencies and past experiences controls one's activities through the elicitation of an image of achievement that creates a spatial-temporal reenactment of the action (what an action looks like, sensation, feeling, the sounds of each action, etc.) (Pribram, 1971). This image of achievement, in fact, precedes the action and biases the servomechanism (an electrical mechanism performing controlled actions through feedback) that operates the motor neurons. The image decays every 5 seconds and is replaced by another one; each image contains all the input and output necessary for the next action of the plan. Current perceptual stimuli are screened and filtered by the representative image of the previous experience. When an external image appears quickly and constitutes a challenge to the neural competence, as a result of a complex addition of information pro-

cessing, the intelligent individual becomes more alert and makes efforts to observe the situation more thoroughly. Here there exists a "rapid relationship" between the motor cortex and the muscle spindles. When the course of action looks good, the last image of achievement serves to guide (to lead to) the final step of the performance of the action.

Athletic Intelligence

According to Fisher (1984), intelligence is an interactive construct that relies on the capacity to cope with specific environmental demands. Intelligence depends on perception and memory (coding and perceiving). These are essential for the performance of skilled movements of athletes. There is clear proof that motor proficiency, in its basic sense, is an intelligent action. The characteristics of the task are related to athletic intelligence in that tasks are performed successfully when cues are oriented and processed in such a way that appropriate actions are performed at the end of the process (Robb, 1972). According to Fisher (1984), the athletic tasks with which the athlete should cope are:

1. Locating, finding, and perceiving the characteristics of the environment (important cues).
2. Searching for and finding essential cues for the task (distinguishing essential from nonessential stimuli).
3. Identifying cue patterns (identifying passive internal situations as opposed to external ones).
4. Using short-term memory to plan the game, for time-out strategy, and for previous defense tactics (these are examples of the strategies that exist in memory and precede given response patterns).
5. Using long-term memory (movement patterns can improve if warning signs are coded and identified in the brain).
6. Decision making.

There is not much time for information processing and reacting. The need for excellence creates a potential for failure accompanied by thoughts of disaster. Despite this, extraordinary performances are executed by athletes according to the process described. Starkes and Deakin (1984) maintain that the best basketball player is not necessarily the best dribbler, the fastest runner, or the most accurate shooter. He or she also does not necessarily have the best spatial visualization or information-processing characteristics. In spite of this, it is possible to determine the nature of the cognitive dimensions (software) of athletes, and how they differ from sport to sport. The skilled athlete *selects, processes,* and *retrieves* construct information of the situation differently from the inexperienced player.

An analysis of the actions that athletes perform in their specific kind of sport makes it possible to understand their actions better. Using a specific paradigm, it is possible to examine the cognitive actions the skilled athlete undergoes and to hypothesize that he/she has an appropriate visualization and neurological ability, since otherwise such actions would not be successful.

The content metaphor raises questions such as "Do skilled athletes encode and retrieve information related to the environmental construct differently, and at different speeds from lesser skilled athletes?", "Do skilled athletes understand visual search of the environmental stimuli differently from nonathletes?", "Do skilled athletes have a different diagnostic attention for details of information in the environment than others?", "How are speed and accuracy in decision making in games demonstrated differently in skilled athletes and in lesser skilled athletes?", or "What is the nature of perceptual anticipation in game situations?" At the same time there remains the basic question: "Is intelligence in a game (i.e., the ability to solve problems) related to general intelligence, or is intelligence in a game one specific characteristic of the range of characteristics that is typical of general intelligence (G)?"

Problem Solving in the Sport Setting

A number of laboratory simulation tests were developed in order to examine athletes' ability to solve problems in real volleyball situations (Macak, 1955). The tests of the athletes consisted of exposure to a game situation for a given period of time. Each player was asked to respond in the way he/she would behave in this situation. Psychologists in countries such as Czechoslovakia, the former East Germany, and Poland developed an array of more than 20 visual situations in various sports, such as volleyball, football, ice hockey, and others (Vanek & Hosek, 1967). In each situation, more than one player, ball, and movement were shown. The situations were exposed to athletes for the shortest possible time (0.1 second to 1 second). Each athlete was asked to react to questions such as: what did he/she see, the number of players in a situation, the direction of their movements, the location of the ball, what the stages were that preceded what was shown, where the player came from, who passed the ball, what the next move would be, and, above all, which defense or attack moves would he/she have performed if he/she had participated in the game? This method of evaluation was found to be effective in predicting athletic performance (Macak, 1963).

Vanek and Cratty (1970) concluded that abstract pictures are not sufficient in distinguishing between various levels of athletes. For this purpose, real and concrete game situations are required in each type of sport. In an attempt to apply similar examinations to the laboratory setting, Vanek and Cratty (1970) relied on many previous studies. It was found that the more complex the tasks given to athletes (in a laboratory) were, the higher the probability was of predicting precisely the athletes' performances in the field (in a competition).

The research findings in sports, while they are similar to those in other fields (in terms of the integration of shapes and words in time and space) give rise to the hypothesis that senior and experienced athletes perform more qualitatively in complex problem solving, in situations that demand fast reactions to a brief exposure to complex situations. They also exhibit superiority at choosing a strategy in such complex situations, since their integrative cognitive ability is superior to that of younger, less skilled athletes.

EXPERIENCE

Expert-Novice Differences

For the most part, there are clear differences in the performance of motor skills between those with experience (the experts) and those without (the novices). These differences are not sufficiently understood. Many studies have focused on motor behavior and cognitive-psychological behavior in order to assess the motor-perceptual factors that distinguish experts from novices. One of the conclusions derived from information-processing models of focused attention is that the experts are more aware of the data presented to them, than are the novices, and that experts use such data more efficiently. This attention ability may explain how experts, as opposed to novices, analyze only necessary information related to performing skills, in which time constitutes a determining factor such as, for example, the skills required in fast ball games (Abernethy & Russell, 1987). When relating to a regular sequence of events, Annett and Kay (1956) maintain that skilled people examine all the essential information in the early stages, while the unskilled expect information to arrive in the course of the events. It follows that skilled athletes have more time to decide and to act. A number of studies provide evidence for the claim made. Expert ball players use early cues better than do the novices (Abernethy & Russell, 1984; Jones & Miles, 1978; Starkes & Deakin, 1984) and likewise succeeded better in coding and recalling situations of ball games that were screened (Allard & Burnett, 1985; Allard, Graham & Paarsalu, 1980). Abernethy and Russell (1987) examined expert and novice tennis players in a task in which they were asked to predict the location of a landing ball following a tennis stroke they were watching. It was found that the experts, in comparison with the novices, succeeded in collecting a greater amount of essential information from cues that preceded the stroke itself, and this was a result of their ability to use early information drawn from the movements of the arm and racquet together. Additionally, Rothstein (1985) reports that skilled athletes can perceive more information in one glance, because they tend to recognize patterns and not individual stimuli.

In a summary of research, Ripoll (in press) concludes that expert athletes use heuristic rules (Kahneman, 1973; Norman, 1976) to cope with the multidimensionality of the situation (semantic and sensorimotor) and the pressure conditions. The rules consist of synthetic visual behavior, processing relevant information, and, finally, eliminating the nonrelevant cues, concentrating only on the relevant ones. Abernethy and Russell (1987) maintained that experts are more aware of, and probably use more efficiently, display redundancy than do novices. This was supported by evidence of better use of advanced cues (Abernethy & Russell, 1984; Jones & Miles, 1978; Starkes & Deakin, 1984), and more capability to check, encode, and retrieve structural aspects of ball-sport displays (Allard & Burnett, 1985; Allard, Graham, & Paarsalu, 1980).

Studies that analyzed the visual field in sport (Bard & Fleury, 1976; Bard, Fleury, Carrière, & Halle, 1980; Vickers, 1985) and ergometrics (Kundel & Follette, 1972; Mourant & Rockwell, 1972) indicate the possible differences between experts and novices in the utilization of given spatial cues. The important separation that exists between visual orientation and visual attention (Shulman, Remington, & McLean, 1979) is quite limited to conclude with certainty (from an analysis of the visual field only) that the existing differences between experts and beginners in the division of the visual field is attributed to the differences in selective attention.

Testing the visual information perceived by athletes is carried out by photographing the event from the athlete's point of view and recording the location where the player directed his/her eye gaze using a special technique. Ripoll, Papin, and Simonet (1983) maintain that the nature of the task and the athlete's experience are the significant factors in the visual functioning context in sport. The researchers point out that there are several common denominators among the various sports, but at the same time there is also a specific characteristic style. Eye movement was examined in basketball (Bard, 1982; Bard & Fleury, 1976; Ripoll, 1979), fencing (Bard, Guezennec, & Papin, 1981), ice hockey (Bard, 1982), and shooting at a target (Ripoll, Papin, & Simonet, 1983). The findings showed that unskilled athletes focus their gaze firmly for longer periods of time and more unsystematically in comparison to skilled players.

Bard and Carrière (1975) showed that skilled players tend to fix their gaze in the space around them, while the novices do not. A possible explanation for this is that novice players are at a stage where they are able to perceive only one stimulus at a time, in comparison to skilled athletes, who perceive groups of stimuli. This explanation is also compatible with the existing difference between beginners and skilled athletes in the time required for information processing, which was shorter among skilled athletes. Konorski (1967) reported that expert athletes organize early cues into information units, which allows them to predict quickly the next move or moves in a game.

Experimental studies indicate that the perception of visual stimuli becomes weaker at great speed (Bryden, 1986; Hellige, Jonsson, & Corwin, 1984; Kirsner & Schwartz, 1986). It is reasonable to hypothesize that when examining skilled athletes through short exposure to game situations, when the central vision is focused on a single player (fixation point) who has to perform an action, the peripheral visual scan performed (perception of the stimuli in the environment) will be more effective, the higher the skill level, and obviously the problem solving will be more effective.

Experience and Decision Making in Sport

Two studies conducted by Thiffault (1974, 1980) demonstrated the influence of practice on specific decision making in sport. In 1974, young ice hockey players were shown slides of actual tactical game situations. The players watched the slides for a defined time period and were asked to make decisions as quickly as possible regarding the move that the player had to make with the puck. The possible responses (the decisions) were determined by 10 experts, and the answers were closed and not open. Voice reaction time (VRT) was the dependent variable. One experimental group was exposed afterward to practice with similar slides when the screening time was gradually reduced to 10 msec. After a review of the initial differences, it was found that practice had a significant influence. Trained players were characterized after the practice by quicker VRTs.

In the 1980 research, 5 groups of hockey players were examined according to age, experience, and playing caliber. The players were tested in tactical decisions involving real-game situations. After a short screening, the players were asked to choose from among the possibilities: shooting, passing, and sliding. As was mentioned, VRT was measured. The correlation between the laboratory situations and game situations was 0.75. Overall, these studies indicated that the time for making complex decisions is likely to be quicker through appropriate practice, while experience and skill are likely to influence the speed of tactical decision making.

It seems that in sports actions, both kinds of knowledge, declarative (factual knowledge) and procedural (know-how), are important for performing motor moves. Skilled athletes in baseball and field hockey recalled more information in structured situations (declarative knowledge). The hypothesis is that procedural knowledge enhances the acquisition and retention of declarative knowledge.

Chase and Ericsson (1981) found that after 250 hours of practice in the laboratory, first-degree students selectively increased their digit span from 7 to roughly 80. They stated that the memory of unskilled examinees derives from a hierarchical system of encoding and retrieving information. As a result of this organization, the retrieval speed increases. Through practicing the perception processes, the relation between mnemonic codes and the construct expressed is more direct, reliable, and quickly retrieved.

It is thus not surprising that skilled athletes make decisions more quickly when they are exposed to game situations. The more complex the situations in a game, and the more difficult the decisions, the more significant the difference between skilled and unskilled players will become. In situations involving complex decisions, skilled players perceive game situations quicker and retrieve the correct reaction with greater speed. Skilled volleyball and field hockey players were faster than others by 10% to 23%, respectively. In extremely complex situations of decision making, the skill and experience raised this gap to about 111%. In situations of this kind, declarative knowledge is not only more elaborated, but also more accessible in the skilled athlete.

The question that remains unsolved at this point is whether experience and skill are expressed in the *quality of decision making,* and not only in the time required to carry it out or solve it.

COPING WITH INEFFICIENT DECISION PROCESSES IN COMPETITION

Distortions and Disturbances in Competitive Decision Making

Athletic tasks are typically characterized by a dynamic nature—that is, they demand a sequential, multistage recursive process of actively making decisions (Pitz & Sachs, 1984). In dynamic tasks, "decisions are made sequentially in time; the task specifications may change over time, either independently or as a result of previous decisions; information available for later decisions may be contingent on the outcomes of earlier decisions, and implications of any decision may reach into the future" (Rapoport, 1975, p. 345). For example, a coach is often required to continually diagnose athletes' motor behavior during competition to induce and encourage optimal sport performance (Kaminski, 1975). Performance of this task may be hindered by cognitive as well as emotional difficulties (Zakay, 1982).

Cognitive social psychologists (e.g., McGuire, 1976; Ross, 1977) have repeatedly demonstrated people's resistance to attitude changes, caused by strong perseverance mechanisms that contribute to the formation of change-resistant self-perceptions and social inferences. Furthermore, erroneous impressions, judgments, and data-processing strategies are hardly changed through mere exposure to new evidence. Accordingly, when a diagnosis is conceptualized as the process of revising the subjective probabilities of events on the basis of new data, people will tend to suffer from cognitive strain, which typically results in "conservatism" (Rapoport & Wallsten, 1972; Slovic & Lichtenstein, 1971). Upon receipt of new information, attitudes are usually revised in the same direction as an optimal model would allow, but the revision is minor. Thus when a continuous revision is needed (e.g., as in the case of the coach), cognitive overload may cause nonoptimal, "conservative" decisions, as was demonstrated with elite basketball coaches in competition (Eberstadt, 1980).

Cognitive distortions and disturbances in the process of decision making have been a central subject for research, particularly in the 1970s. Several heuristics were identified that people use when they make judgments and decisions in uncertain environments (Kahneman, Slovic, & Tversky, 1982; Kahneman & Tversky, 1972, 1973; Tversky & Kahneman, 1971, 1973, 1974). These heuristics serve as rules of thumb by reducing complex judgments to simple ones, with regard to individual probability estimations.

Among the most important heuristics, Tversky and Kahneman (1974) describe: (1) representativeness, which is usually employed when people are asked to judge the probability that a certain object or event belongs to a certain class or process; (2) availability of instances or scenarios, which is often employed when people are asked to assess the frequency of a class or the plausibility of a particular development, and (3) adjustment from an anchor, which is usually employed in numerical prediction when a relevant value is available. Heuristics are highly economical and usually effective, but they lead to systematic and predictable errors. For example, when the heuristic of representativeness is used (Kahneman & Tversky, 1972, 1973; Tversky & Kahneman, 1971), people reveal insensitivity to prior probability of outcomes, insensitivity to sample size, misconception of chance, insensitivity to predictability, illusion of validity, and misconception of regression. When the heuristic of availability is used (Tversky & Kahneman, 1973), biases due to the retrievability of instances, biases due to the effectiveness of a search set, biases of imaginability, and illusory correlations are revealed. Finally, the heuristic of adjustment and anchoring (Tversky & Kahneman, 1974) causes insufficient adjustment, biases in the evaluation of conjunctive and disjunctive events, and anchoring in the assessment of subjective probability distributions.

Concepts such as causal schemes may explain these heuristics (e.g., Tversky & Kahneman, 1980). Heuristics are related to short-term and long-term memory, which makes problem solving and decision making possible and has an effect on decisions, but does not necessarily lead to the prevention of systematic errors. A variety of heuristics for deciding have been formulated, investigated, and applied in different settings (Aschenbrenner, 1981; Bettman, 1979; Fischhoff, 1976; Huber, 1982, Mischel, 1979; Nisbett & Ross, 1980; Ross, 1977; Slovic, Fischhoff, & Lichtenstein, 1977; Svenson, 1979), with psychological decision theory dealing mainly with identifying the cognitive sources that lead an individual to disregard rational postulates. For example, Ross (1977) outlined instances, causes, and consequences of attributional biases, partly governed by the above-mentioned heuristics. He further described in detail several distortions in the attribution process, such as the (1) fundamental attribution error (i.e., the general human tendency to overestimate the importance of personal or dispositional factors relative to environmental influences), (2) "false consensus" or "egocentric attribution" bias (i.e., humans' tendency to see their own behavioral choices and judgments as relatively common and appropriate to existing circumstances while viewing alternative responses as uncommon, deviant, and inappropriate), and (3) the inadequate allowances for the role-biased nature of social data, and the human tendency to overlook the informational value of nonoccurence. Such biases are quite difficult to overcome, mainly because they result from "logical" schemata leading to "nonlogical" biases, with people tending to be highly overconfident in their faulty judgments (Ross, 1977; Slovic, Fischhoff, & Lichtenstein, 1977).

In fact, psychologists have indeed described a long list

of human judgmental biases, deficiencies, and cognitive illusions, characterized by extensive violations of normative rationality models (Kahneman, Slovic, & Tversky, 1982; Nisbett & Ross, 1980; Ross, 1977). Moreover, human judgments seem to depart significantly from the prescriptions of formal decision theory also in sport (Gilovich, 1984). According to some critics, normative criteria cannot be taken to constitute a part of natural science, nor can they be established by metamathematical proof, and therefore rationality must be ascribed to ordinary people (Cohen, 1981, 1982, 1986). Although the question of human rationality still remains unresolved and open to debate, it may be concluded that in an athletic environment, in which dynamic revision of information is continually required, decision makers (e.g., coaches) will suffer from substantial cognitive overload and strain, which will often result in less-than-optimal decisions.

In addition to the cognitive difficulties just illustrated, a coach in competition is frequently under pressure to make decisions for which he or she is perceived as having exclusive responsibility. However, he or she may often experience competitive events as uncontrollable (because players do not follow his/her instructions). As a result, not only increased emotional distress and anxiety may be experienced, but also problem-solving and decision-making efficiency may be impaired (Baum & Singer, 1980; Garber & Seligman, 1980; Miller, 1979; Minecka & Hendersen, 1985). Such phenomena were indeed demonstrated with sports coaches (Gazes, Sovell, & Dellastatious, 1969; Holland, 1979; Husman, Hanson, & Walker, 1970; McCafferty, Gliner, & Horvath, 1978; Porter & Allsen, 1978; Ryan, 1981), having the potential to cause coaching burnout in the long run (Caccese & Mayerberg, 1984; Capel, Sisley, & Desertrain, 1987; Dale & Weinberg, 1989; Haggerty, 1982; Pate, Rotella, & McClenaghan, 1984; Smith, 1986). Hence cognitive and emotional variables interact to distort and disturb the making of optimal decisions in competitive sport, at least as far as coaches are concerned. However, other participants (athletes, referees, etc.) undergo similar processes (Bar-Eli, 1984; Cox, 1985; LeUnes & Nation, 1989).

A Crisis-Related Decision Aid for Competition

Decision makers in the applied setting of sport (e.g., coaches) may, in principle, substantially benefit from being aided in using information more optimally. Such a decision aid system could relieve them of cognitive difficulties related to the process of judgment and decision making. For example, people have great difficulty in aggregating information, and thus it could facilitate the aggregation of various pieces of information required to produce each single response (Slovic & Lichtenstein, 1971; Slovic, Fischhoff, & Lichtenstein, 1977).

Often a coach faces the problem of diagnosing an athlete's psychological state in competition. Athletes in competition frequently experience psychological stress and, as a result, their arousal levels may increase and negatively af-

fect their performance. Under extreme levels of arousal, an athlete may enter a "psychological performance crisis," a state in which the ability to cope adequately with the competitive requirements substantially deteriorates. According to Bar-Eli and Tenenbaum (1989a), a crisis develops when a system (athlete) is no longer characterized by stability (Phase A), but is accumulatedly under-or overcharged and thus is characterized by lability (Phase B). In case of extreme lability, the failure of coping and defense mechanisms may lead to crisis (Phase C). If we define events C ("crisis") and $\bar{C}$ ("no crisis") as mutually exclusive and exhaustive, then $P(C) + P(\bar{C}) = 1$. In Phase A, $P(C) << P(\bar{C})$; in Phase B, $P(C) < P(\bar{C})$ or $P(C) \approx P(\bar{C})$ or $P(C) >) P(\bar{C})$; and in Phase C, $P(C) >> P(\bar{C})$. Finally, $P(A) + P(B) + P(C) = 1$ (for a detailed explanation, see Bar-Eli & Tenenbaum, 1989a).

This model can be used in order to diagnose the development of an athlete's psychological performance crisis in competition. The probabilistic measure of diagnostic value used here for this purpose is based on the Bayesian approach, comprehensively reviewed by Slovic and Lichtenstein (1971), Edwards, Lindman, and Savage (1963), and Rapoport and Wallsten (1972). Bayes's theorem in its ratio form with respect to two mutually exclusive and exhaustive hypotheses, H_i and H_j, and a (new) datum D, is presented as:

$$\frac{P(H_i/D)}{P(H_j/D)} = \frac{P(D/H_i)}{P(D/H_j)} \times \frac{P(H_i)}{P(H_j)} \qquad (1)$$

where $P(D/H_i)$ and $P(D/H_j)$ represent the impact of datum D on each of the hypotheses respectively. Therefore, $P(D/H_i)/P(D/H_j)$, which is the likelihood ratio (LR) for this specific datum, reflects its diagnosticity with respect to these two hypotheses. In general, then, the likelihood ratio is an index of data diagnosticity (Slovic & Lichtenstein, 1971).

Replacing H_i and H_j in equation (1) by the two following mutually exclusive and exhaustive hypotheses:

C—The athlete is in a psychological performance crisis during the competition.
$\bar{C}$—The athlete is not in a psychological performance crisis during the competition.

equation (I) takes the form of:

$$\frac{P(C/D)}{P(\bar{C}/D)} = \frac{P(D/C)}{P(D/\bar{C})} \times \frac{P(C)}{P(\bar{C})} \qquad (2)$$

As mentioned before, people do have substantial difficulties in weighing and combining information as a result of their limited information-processing and DM capability. Accordingly, most decision aids rely on the old Roman principle of "divide and conquer," that is, on the "decomposition" approach. According to this principle, the decision aid fractionates the total problem into a series of structurally related parts, and the decision maker is asked to make subjective assessments for only the smaller components. Such assessments are presumably simpler and more manageable than assessing more global entities (Slovic, Fischhoff, & Lichtenstein, 1977), and thus decomposition usually improves judgment and decision making (Armstrong, Denniston, & Gordon, 1975; Gettys, Michel, Steiger, Kelly, & Peterson, 1973; Slovic & Lichtenstein, 1971). Since cognitive aggregation processes are faulty, judgment tasks have often been decomposed into a number of presumably simpler estimation tasks, using "probabilistic information processing" (PIP) systems. Edwards (1962), introducing these systems, attempted to circumvent aggregation difficulties by having people estimate $P(D/H)$ values and letting a computer combine them. In case of only two hypotheses, H_i and H_j, people estimate $P(D/H_i)$ and $P(D/H_j)$ values, which are integrated across data and across hypotheses by means of Bayes's theorem. After all the relevant data have been processed, the resulting output is a ratio of posterior probabilities, $P(H_i/D) / P(H_j/D)$. In this way, a probabilistic diagnosis may be substantially facilitated (Edwards, 1962; Slovic & Lichtenstein, 1971).

In order to carry out a diagnosis of crisis development in the individual athlete during competition, what is needed is the identification of factors that are diagnostic in this respect. Through these factors, the problem of diagnosing an athlete's psychological state in competition (e.g., crisis) can be decomposed. Each such factor includes several components (i.e., Bayesian data) that can be separately assessed by experts with regard to their probability of occurrence when a crisis $[P(D/C)]$ or a noncrisis $[P(D/\bar{C})]$ is given. Later on, the ratio of $P(C/D) / P(\bar{C}/D)$ can be computed via Bayes's rule (equation 2).

Several such factors have been identified thus far:

1. Pre-start susceptibility to psychological crises in competitive sport, into which the athlete enters competition. Bar-Eli, Tenenbaum, and Elbaz (1989) considered the athlete's ability to cope with psychological stress and his/her competitive motivation as affecting motor performance and psychological crisis.
2. During competition, the following factors were investigated:
   a. A competition (e.g., in basketball and team handball) can be structured temporally into six psychologically meaningful phases: a beginning, main and end phase within each half. These phases do have a considerable crisis-related diagnostic relevance (Bar-Eli & Tenenbaum, 1988a, b; Bar-Eli, Tenenbaum, & Elbaz, 1990b).
   b. Athletes perceive team performance in competition in terms of "event expectancy" (expected or unexpected), "direction of lead" (one's own team or the opposing team) and "momentum" or "game tendency" (positive or negative). These three variables determine "game standings," which were found to have a considerable diagnostic relevance for an athlete's crisis development in basketball and team handball competitions (Bar-Eli & Tenenbaum, 1989b; Bar-Eli, Tenenbaum, & Elbaz, 1991).

   c. Task-related behavior (performance) and rule-and norm-related behavior ("fairness" and "sanctions by officials") are highly relevant to an athlete's psychological crisis vulnerability during competitive situations in basketball, team handball, and tennis (Bar-Eli & Tenenbaum, 1988c; Bar-Eli, Tenenbaum, & Elbaz, 1990a; Bar-Eli, Taoz, Levy-Kolker, & Tenenbaum, 1990).

Experts' probability assessments of the Bayesian likelihood ratio components, $P(D/C)$ and $P(D/\bar{C})$, for each one of the diagnostic factors' components outlined above, enable a diagnosis of the athlete's chances of being in a psychological performance crisis in each and every moment of a competition. For this purpose, the Bayesian model can be used, as previously presented with regard to hypotheses C and $\bar{C}$ (see equation 2). Upon exposure to information about the existence of a certain datum (i.e., a particular component of one of the diagnostic factors), the ratio of probabilities concerning the occurrence of the two events, C and $\bar{C}$, is revised, *all previous data taken into account*.

It is, of course, quite difficult to predict the combination of conditional probabilities corresponding to the events occurring in any specific game. However, this model provides coaches with a decision aid to improve and optimize their decisions in competition, using the principle of decomposition. For example, when a particular combination of events is observed during a basketball game, empirical data on $P(D/C)$ and $P(D/\bar{C})$ from investigations with basketball experts (Bar-Eli & Tenenbaum, 1988a, b, c; 1989b; Bar-Eli, Tenenbaum, & Elbaz, 1989) can be used in order to diagnose the player's psychological state in this very moment of competition. The same principle can be easily applied to team handball (using data from Bar-Eli, Tenenbaum, & Elbaz, 1989, 1990a, b; 1991). For this purpose, however, the technical hurdle associated with computerization of such a diagnostic process must be overcome. Furthermore, posterior probabilities should preferably be associated with practical measures aimed at coping with players' psychoregulative problems at each phase of crisis development during competition (Bar-Eli & Tenenbaum, 1989a).

The model presented here needs validation at other behavioral levels beyond experts' estimations (i.e., the observational and psychophysiological levels). Thus far, observations of behavioral violations as crisis indicators in basketball competitions have been encouraging in supporting the model (Bar-Eli & Tenenbaum, 1989c). Such investigations should be continued, including additional factors (e.g., social-psychological variables such as teammates and spectators), as well as additional sport disciplines. In this way, sport psychologists can proceed more effectively in consulting with coaches to minimize the difference in their utility concepts and enhance mutual collaboration (Bar-Eli & Tenenbaum, 1989d). This could be achieved when decision aids such as the PIP system could be used for diagnosing athletes' psychological performance crises in competition. Moreover, to solve other complex problems that require fast information processing, diagnosis, aggregation of information, and DM under high cognitive uncertainty and extreme emotional pressure could also effectively use such decision aids.

INTEGRATIVE VIEW OF FUTURE DIRECTIONS

The subject matter of DM applied to sport presented in this review gives evidence and support to the view that decision making is comprised of perceptual-cognitive, emotional, social, and developmental properties. Therefore, future research should apply designs that will account for their integrative-interactive impact on the nature of DM in competitive situations.

From a cognitive perspective, it was demonstrated that decision making depends on strategical aspects, such as visual search and attentional styles of locating objects in a multistimulus environment. It also depends on the short- and long-term stores, attentional and cognitive style, concentration, and other intellectual (deductive and inductive) properties. However, an athlete usually encounters situations in which he or she should make decisions that are not static. Both individual and environment are dynamic in nature. Individuals take risks, possess self- and social expectations, and experience somatic and cognitive arousal, as well as react to environmental disturbances. As a result of continuous alterations, decisions for one particular moment may not necessarily be appropriate for the next moment. Accordingly, athletes often make decisions under risk or uncertainty, as well as under physical and emotional constraints. Future research should investigate these conditions in a transactional manner, in which all properties of the individual and the environment are studied (Bar-Eli, 1985; Dewey & Bentley, 1949; Pervin, 1968). This is undoubtedly a challenge that requires control over variables that characterize the individual (personality, experience, etc.), and the environment (sport-specific rules, spectators, competition, etc.).

Research findings also provide evidence that the encoding process of the environment is quite similar for experienced and inexperienced athletes. What makes the difference are the strategies of search and the neural pathways to the LTS that characterize the expert in comparison to the novice. Thus it is also recommended to apply the transactional paradigm longitudinally to account for age independently from experience.

This review presented several studies conducted in the sport domain, which investigated perceptual processes in sport environments. In addition, the concept of psychological performance crisis in competition was presented to illustrate the PIP system. It can be concluded that environmental as well as individual components influence athletes' perceptions as well as psychological performance crises. This undoubtedly necessitates the design of studies in which environmental and individual conditions interact with perceptual components to determine decision-making behavior.

This line of research will yield more ecological validity to theoretically derived models. Moreover, previous studies in the psychological domain have too often taken a deterministic approach, despite the fact that human behavior is probabilistic in nature. For example, the same athlete may make different decisions in the same situation on different occasions. Accordingly, decision research should consider factors such as risk and uncertainty, and thus it should be probabilistic. The different decisions may be attributed to the nature of the transactions between several conditions (e.g., cognitive, emotional, task-related, and situational) in each single moment. Thus the integrative approach presented here, which takes developmental together with probabilistic perspectives into account, may substantially enlighten the process of decision-making behavior in sport.

References

Abernethy, B., & Russell, D. G. (1984). Advance cue utilisation by skilled cricket batsmen. *Australian Journal of Science and Medicine in Sport, 16*, 2–10.

Abernethy, B., & Russell, D. G. (1987). Expert-novice differences in an applied selective attention task. *Journal of Sport and Exercise Psychology, 9*, 326–345.

Alderson, G. J. (1972). Variables affecting the perception of velocity in sports situations. In H. T. A. Whiting (Ed.), *Readings in sport psychology* (pp. 116–155). London: Henry Kimpton.

Allard, F. (1982). Cognition, expert performance and sport. In J. H. Salmela, J. T. Partington, & T. Orlick (Eds.), *New paths of sport rearing and excellence* (pp. 22–26). Ottawa: Coaching Association of Canada.

Allard, F. (1984). Cognition, expert performance, and sport. In M. Whiting (Ed.), *New paths to sport learning* (pp. 22–26). Ontario: Coaching Association of Canada.

Allard, F., & Burnett, N. (1985). Skill in sport. *Canadian Journal of Sport Psychology, 39*, 294–312.

Allard, F., Graham, S., & Paarsalu, M. E. (1980). Perception in sport: Basketball. *Journal of Sport Psychology, 2*, 14–21.

Allard, F., & Starkes, J. L. (1980). Perception in sport: Volleyball. *Journal of Sport Psychology, 2*, 22–23.

Annett, J., & Kay, H. (1956). Skilled performance. *Occupational Psychology, 30*, 112–117.

Armstrong, J. S., Denniston, W. B., & Gordon, M. M. (1975). The use of the decomposition principle in making judgments. *Organizational Behavior and Human Performance, 14*, 257–263.

Arnheim, D. D., & Sinclair, W. A. (1979). *The clumsy child. A program of motor therapy*. St. Louis: C. V. Mosby.

Aschenbrenner, K. M. (1981). Efficient sets, decision heuristics, and single-peaked preferences. *Journal of Mathematical Psychology, 23*, 227–256.

Atkinson, R. C., & Shiffrin, R. M. (1968). Human memory: A proposed system and its control processes. In K. W. Spence & J. T. Spence (Eds.), *The psychology of learning and motivation* (Vol. 2, pp. 89–197). New York: Academic Press.

Atkinson, R. C., & Shiffrin, R. M. (1971). The control of short-term memory. *Scientific American, 225,* 82–90.

Bacon, S. J. (1974). Arousal and the range of cue utilization. *Journal of Experimental Psychology, 102,* 81–87.

Baddeley, A. D., Grant, S., Wight, E., & Thomson, N. (1975). Imagery and visual working memory. In P. M. A. Rabbitt and S. Dornic (Eds.), *Attention and performance V* (pp. 205–217). London: Academic Press.

Baddeley, A. D., & Hitch, G. (1974). Working memory. In G. Bower (Ed.), *The psychology of learning and motivation* (pp. 47–89), Vol. VIII. New York: Academic Press.

Baddeley, A. D., & Lieberman, K. (1980). Spatial working memory. In R. S. Nickerson (Ed.), *Proceedings of the Pittsburgh Conference on Interactive Processes in Reading* Sept. 1979 (pp. 107–129). Hillsdale, NJ: Erlbaum.

Baddeley, A. D., Thomson, N., & Buchanan, M. (1975). Word length and the structure of long term memory. *Journal of Verbal Learning and Verbal Behavior, 14,* 575–589.

Bard, C. (1982). La prise d'information visuelle et la preparation de l'action. In G. Azemar & H. Ripoll (Eds.), *Neurobiologie des comportements moteurs* (pp. 181–194). Paris: INSEP.

Bard, C., & Fleury, M. (1976). Analysis of visual search activity during sport problem situation. *Journal of Human Movement Studies, 3,* 214–222.

Bard, C., & Fleury, M. (1981). Considering eye movement as a predictor of attainment. In I. M. Cockerill & W. W. MacGillivary (Eds.), *Vision and sport* (pp. 28–41). Cheltenham, England: Stanley Thornes.

Bard, C., Fleury, M., Carrière, L., & Halle, M. (1980). Analysis of gymnastics judges' visual search. *Research Quarterly for Exercise and Sport, 51,* 267–273.

Bard, C., Guezennec, Y., & Papin, J. P. (1981). Analyse de l'exploration visuelle en escrime. *Academie d'Armes, 13,* 7–26.

Bar-Eli, M. (1984). *Zur Diagnostik individueller psychischer Krisen im sportlichen Wettkampf. Eine wahrscheinlichkeitsorientierte, theoretische und empirische Studie unter besonderer Berücksichtigung des Basketballspiels* (Diagnosis of individual psychological crises in sports competition. A probabilistically oriented, theoretical, and empirical study giving special attention to the game of basketball). Unpublished doctoral dissertation, Deutsche Sporthochschule, Cologne.

Bar-Eli, M. (1985). Arousal-performance relationship: A transactional view on performance jags. *International Journal of Sport Psychology, 16,* 193–209.

Bar-Eli, M., Taoz, E., Levy-Kolker, N., & Tenenbaum, G. (1990). *Performance quality and behavioral violations as crisis indicators in competition.* Unpublished manuscript.

Bar-Eli, M., & Tenenbaum, G. (1988a). Time phases and the individual psychological crisis in sports competition: Theory and research findings. *Journal of Sports Sciences, 6,* 141–149.

Bar-Eli, M., & Tenenbaum, G. (1988b). The interaction of individual psychological crisis and time phases in basketball. *Perceptual and Motor Skills, 66,* 523–530.

Bar-Eli, M., & Tenenbaum, G. (1988c). Rule-and norm-related behavior and the individual psychological crisis in competitive situations: Theory and research findings. *Social Behavior and Personality, 16,* 187–195.

Bar-Eli, M., & Tenenbaum, G. (1989a). A theory of individual psychological crisis in competitive sport. *Applied Psychology, 38,* 107–120.

Bar-Eli, M., & Tenenbaum, G. (1989b). Game standings and psychological crisis in sport: Theory and research. *Canadian Journal of Sport Sciences, 14,* 31–37.

Bar-Eli, M., & Tenenbaum, G. (1989c). Observations of behavioral violations as crisis indicators in competition. *The Sport Psychologist, 3,* 237–244.

Bar-Eli, M., & Tenenbaum, G. (1989d). Coach-psychologist relations in competitive sport. *Journal of Applied Research in Coaching and Athletics, 4,* 150–156.

Bar-Eli, M., & Tenenbaum, G., & Elbaz, G. (1989). Pre-start susceptibility to psychological crises in competitive sport: Theory and research. *International Journal of Sport Psychology, 20,* 13–30.

Bar-Eli, M., Tenenbaum, G., & Elbaz, G. (1990). Psychological performance crisis in high arousal situations—Diagnosticity of rule violations and performance in competitive team-handball. *Anxiety Research, 2,* 281–292.

Bar-Eli, M., Tenenbaum, G., & Elbaz, G. (1990b). Psychological strain in competition: The role of time phases. *Sportwissenschaft, 20,* 182–191.

Bar-Eli, M., Tenenbaum, G., & Elbaz, G. (1991). A three-dimensional crisis-related analysis of perceived team performance. *Journal of Applied Sport Psychology, 3,* 160–175.

Barras, N. (1987). *Vision and batting in cricket.* Report to the Australian Sports Commission National Sports Research Program. Belconen, A.C.T. 2616.

Barrell, G. V., & Trippe, H. R. (1975). Field dependence and physical ability. *Perceptual and Motor Skills, 41,* 216–218.

Baum, A., & Singer, J. E. (Eds.) (1980). *Advances in environmental psychology. Vol. 2: Applications of personal control.* Hillsdale, NJ: Erlbaum.

Beitel, P. A. (1980). Multivariate relationship among visual-perceptual attributes and gross-motor tasks with different environmental demands. *Journal of Motor Behavior, 12,* 29–40.

Bettman, J. R. (1979). *An information processing theory of consumer choice.* Reading, MA: Addison-Wesley.

Binmore, K. (1988). Modeling rational players. *Economics and Philosophy, 4,* 9–55.

Bryden, M. P. (1986). On the possible dangers of using horizontal word displays in visual field studies. *Brain and Cognition, 5,* 362–368.

Caccese, T., & Mayerberg, C. (1984). Gender differences in perceived burnout of college coaches. *Journal of Sport Psychology, 6,* 279–288.

Capel, S. A., Sisley, B. L., & Desertrain, G. S. (1987). The relationship of role conflict and role ambiguity to burnout in high school basketball coaches. *Journal of Sport Psychology, 9,* 106–117.

Carter, R. C. (1982). Visual search with color. *Journal of Experimental Psychology: Human Perception and Human Performance, 8,* 127–136.

Chase, W. G., & Ericsson, K. A. (1981). Skilled memory. In J. R. Anderson (Ed.), *Cognitive skills and their acquisition* (pp. 141–189). Hillsdale, NJ: Erlbaum.

Chase, W. G., & Simon, H. A. (1973b). Perception in chess. *Cognitive Psychology, 4,* 55–81.

Chelladurai, P. (1984). Leadership in sports. In J. M. Silva & R. S. Weinberg (Eds.), *Psychological foundations of sport* (pp. 329–339). Champaign, IL: Human Kinetics.

Cohen, L. J. (1981). Can human irrationality be experimentally demonstrated? *Behavioral and Brain Sciences, 4,* 317–370.

Cohen, L. J. (1982). Are people programmed to commit fallacies? Further thoughts about the interpretation of experimental data on probability judgment. *Journal for the Theory of Social Behavior, 12,* 251–274.

Cohen, L. J. (1986). *The dialogue of reason.* London, U.K.: Clarendon Press.

Combs, A. W. (1952). Intelligence from a perceptual point of view. *Journal of Abnormal and Social Psychology, 47*, 662–673.

Coombs, C. H., Dawes, R. M., & Tversky, A. (1970). *Mathematical psychology.* Englewood Cliffs, NJ: Prentice-Hall.

Cox, R. H. (1985). *Sport psychology: Concepts and applications.* Dubuque, IA: Brown.

Cratty, B. J. (1979). *Perceptual and motor development in infants and children* (2nd ed.). Englewood Cliffs, NJ: Prentice-Hall.

Crowder, R. G. (1976). *Principles of learning and memory.* Hillsdale, NJ: Erlbaum.

Dale, J., & Weinberg, R. S. (1989). The relationship between coaches' leadership style and burnout. *The Sport Psychologist, 3*, 1–13.

Derrider, M. (1985). Enrigistrement et analyze des comportements exploratoires visuels de gardien de but en situation de penalty. In: M. Laurent and P. Therme (Eds). *Recherches en activites physiques et sportives* (259–272).

Dewey, J., & Bentley, A. F. (1949). *Knowing and the known.* Boston: Beacon.

Drouin, D., & Salmela, J. H. (1975). La tache de gardien de but et le temps de reaction classique: Un test du concept de "reflexes." Actes du 7eme Symposium Canadien en apprentissage psycho-moteur et psychologies du sport, *Mouvement* (pp. 49–54). Quebec: De l'Association des professionels de l'activite physique du Quebec.

Drury, C. G., & Clement, M. R. (1978). The effect of area, density and number of background characters on visual search. *Human Factors, 20*, 597–602.

Easterbrook, J. A. (1959). The effect of emotion on cue utilization and the organization of behavior. *Psychological Review, 64*, 183–201.

Eberstadt, G. (1980). Untersuchungen zu Spielerwechsel-strategien von Basketballtrainern (Investigation of coaches' strategies for players' substitution in basketball). Cologne: Deutsche Sporthochschule (Diplomarbeit).

Edwards, W. (1954). The theory of decision making. *Psychological Bulletin, 51*, 380–417.

Edwards, W. (1962). Dynamic decision theory and probabilistic information processing. *Human Factors, 4*, 59–73.

Edwards, W., Lindman, H., & Savage, L. J. (1963). Bayesian statistical inference for psychological research. *Psychological Review, 70*, 193–242.

Einhorn, H. J., & Hogarth, R. M. (1981). Behavioral decision theory: Processes of judgment and choice. *Annual Review of Psychology, 32*, 53–88.

Egeth, H., Jonides, J., & Wall, W. (1972). Parallel processing of multielement displays. *Cognitive Psychology, 3*, 674–689.

Eriksen, C. W., & Johnson, H. J. (1973). Storage and decal characteristics of nonattended auditory practice items. *Memory and Cognition, 1*, 77–79.

Estes, W. K. (1982a). Learning, memory, and intelligence. In R. J. Sternberg (Ed.), *Handbook of human intelligence* (pp. 170–224). New York: Cambridge University Press.

Estes, W. K. (1982b). Similarity-related channel interactions in visual processing. *Journal of Experimental Psychology: Human Perception and Performance, 8*, 353–382.

Farmer, E. W., & Taylor, R. M. (1980). Visual search through color displays: Effects of target-background similarity and background uniformity. *Perception and Psychophysics, 27*, 267–272.

Fisher, A. C. (1984). Sport intelligence. In W. F. Straub & J. M. Williams (Eds.), *Cognitive sport psychology* (pp. 42–50). Lansing, NY: Sport Science Associates.

Fischhoff, B. (1976). Attribution theory and judgment under un-certainty. In J. H. Harvey, W. J. Ickes, & R. F. Kidd (Eds.), *New directions in attribution research, Vol. 1* (pp. 421–452). Hillsdale, NJ: Erlbaum.

Gallahue, D. L. (1982). *Understanding motor development in children.* New York: Wiley.

Garber, J., & Seligman, M. E. P. (1980). *Human helplessness: Theory and application.* New York: Academic Press.

Gazes, P., Sovell, B., & Dellastatious, J. (1969). Continuous radio-electrocardiographic monitoring of football and basketball coaches during games. *American Heart Journal, 78*, 509–512.

Gentile, A. M., Higgins, J. R., Miller, E. A., & Rosen, B. M. (1975). The structure of motor tasks. In C. Bard, M. Fluery, & J. H. Salmela (Eds.), *Movement: Actes du 7 Canadien en appretissage psychomoteur et psychologie du sport* (pp. 11–28). Quebec: Association of Professionals in Physical Education of Quebec.

Gettys, C. F., Michel, C., Steiger, J. H., Kelly, C. W., & Peterson, C. R. (1973). Multiple-stage probabilistic information processing. *Organizational Behavior and Human Performance, 10*, 374–387.

Gilovich, T. (1984). Judgmental biases in the world of sport. In W. F. Straub & J. M. Williams (Eds.), *Cognitive sport psychology* (pp. 31–41). New York: Sport Science Associates.

Gilovich, T., Vallone, R., & Tversky, A. (1985). The hot hand in basketball: On the misperception of random sequences. *Cognitive Psychology, 17*, 295–314.

Gordon, S. (1988). Decision styles and coaching effectiveness in university soccer. *Canadian Journal of Sport Sciences, 13*, 56–65.

Goulet, C., Bard, C., & Fleury, M. (1989). Expertise differences in preparing to return a tennis serve: A visual information processing approach. *Journal of Sport and Exercise Psychology, 11*, 382–398.

Green, B. F., & Anderson, L. K. (1956). Color coding in a visual search task. *Journal of Experimental Psychology, 51*, 19–24.

Haggerty, T. (1982). *An assessment of the degree of burnout in Canadian university coaches.* Unpublished master's thesis, York University, Toronto, Ontario.

Heilbrun, A. B. (1972). Style of adaptation to perceived aversive maternal control and scanning behavior. *Journal of Consulting & Clinical Psychology, 29*, 15–21.

Hellige, J. B., Jonsson, J. E., & Corwin, W. H. (1984). Effects of perceptual quality on the processing of human faces presented to the left and right cerebral hemispheres. *Journal of Experimental Psychology: Human Perception and Performance, 19*, 90–107.

Hitch, G., & Baddeley, A. D. (1976). Verbal reasoning and working memory. *Quarterly Journal of Experimental Psychology, 29*, 603–621.

Holland, J. C. (1979). Heart rate response of high school basketball officials. *The Physician and Sports Medicine, 7*, 78–87.

Hogarth, R. M. (1980). *Judgment and choice.* New York: Wiley.

Huber, O. (1982). Entscheiden als Problemlosen (Deciding as problem solving). Bern, Switzerland: Hans Huber.

Hull, C. (1951). *Essentials of behavior.* New Haven: Yale University Press.

Hunsaker, P. L., & Alessandra, A. L. (1980). *The art of managing people.* Englewood Cliffs, NJ: Prentice-Hall.

Husman, B. F., Hanson, D., & Walker, R. (1970). The effect of coaching basketball and swimming upon emotion as measured by telemetry. In G. S. Kenyon (Ed.), *Contemporary psychology of sport* (pp. 410–415). Chicago: Athletic Institute.

Jackson, C. W. (1980). *The relationship of swimming performance to measures of attentional and interpersonal style.* Unpublished doctoral dissertation, Boston University.

James, W. (1890). *Principles of psychology.* Vol. 1. London: Macmillan.

Jones, C. M., & Miles, T. R. (1978). Use of advance cues in predicting the flight of a lawn tennis ball. *Journal of Human Movement Studies, 4,* 231–235.

Jones, M. G. (1972). Perceptual characteristics and athletic performance. In H. T. A. Whiting (Ed.), *Readings in Sport Psychology* (pp. 96–115). London: Kimpton.

Jones, M. G. (1973). Personality and perceptual characteristics. In H. T. A. Whiting (Ed.), *Personality and performance in physical education and sport* (pp. 11–42). London: Kimpton.

Jonides, J., & Gleitman, H. (1972). A conceptual category-effect in visual search: O as letter or as digit. *Perception & Psychophysics, 12,* 457–460.

Kahneman, D., Slovic, P., & Tversky, A. (Eds.) (1982). *Judgment under uncertainty: Heuristics and biases.* New York: Cambridge University Press.

Kahneman, D., & Treisman, A. (1984). Changing views of attention and automaticity. In R. Parasuraman & D. R. Davies (Eds.), *Varieties of Attention* (pp. 29–61). New York: Academic Press.

Kahneman, D., & Tversky, A. (1972). Subjective probability: A judgment of representativeness. *Cognitive Psychology, 3,* 430–454, 1972.

Kahneman, D., & Tversky, A. (1973). On the psychology of prediction. *Psychological Review, 80,* 237–251.

Kaminski, G. (1975). Einige Probleme der Beobachtung sportmotorischen Verhaltens (Several problems of observing motor behavior in sport). In H. Rieder, H. Eberspächer, K. Feige, & E. Hahn (Eds.), *Empirische Methoden in der Sportpsychologie* (pp. 43–65). Schorndorf: Hofmann.

Kane, J. E. (1972). Personality, body concept and performance. In J. E. Kane (Ed.), *Psychological aspects of physical education and sport* (pp. 91–127). London: Western Printing Services.

Keele, S., & Hawkins, H. (1982). Exploration of individual differences relevant to high level skill. *Journal of Motor Behavior, 14,* 3–23.

Keele, S., & Neill, T. (1979). Mechanisms of attention. In E. Carterette & M. Friedman (Eds.), *Handbook of Perception* (Vol. 9) (pp. 3–47). New York: Academic Press.

Keogh, J., & Sugden, D. (1985). *Movement skill development.* New York: Macmillan.

Kerlirzin, Y. (1990). Traitement des informations visuelles et prises de decision en boxe française. *Memoire pour le Diplome de l'I.N.S.E.P.* Paris: I.N.S.E.P.

Kirschenbaum, D. S., & Bale, R. M. (1980). Cognitive-behavioral skills in golf: Brain power golf. In R. M. Suinn (Ed.), *Psychology in sports: Methods and applications* (pp. 334–343). Minneapolis: Burgess.

Kirsner, K. M., & Schwartz, S. (1986). Words and hemifields: Do the hemispheres enjoy equal opportunity? *Brain and Cognition, 5.* 354–361.

Knapp, B. (1964). *Skill in sport.* London: Routledge & Kegan Paul.

Konorski, J. (1967). *Integrative activity of the brain.* Chicago: University of Chicago Press.

Kundel, H. L., & La Follette, P. S. (1972). Visual search patterns and experience with radiological images. *Radiology, 103,* 523–528.

Landers, D. M. (1980). The arousal-performance relationship revised. *Research Quarterly for Exercise and Sport, 51,* 77–90.

Langenheder, W. (1975). *Theorie menschlicher Entscheidungshandlungen (A theory of human decisions).* Stuttgart: Enke.

LeUnes, A. D., & Nation, J. R. (1989). *Sport psychology.* Chicago: Nelson-Hall.

Loader, E. C., Edwards, S. W., & Henschen, K. P. (1982). field-dependent/field-independent characteristics of male and female basketball players. *Perceptual and Motor Skills, 55,* 883–890.

Logie, R. H. (1986). Visuo-spatial processing in working memory. *The Quarterly Journal of Experimental Psychology, 38A,* 229–247.

Mačák, I. (1955). Výchova Pozornosti ve Volejbole (The education of attention in volleyball games). *Teorie a Praxe Telesné* Výchovy, Prague, *3,* 8.

Mačák, I. (1963). O Koncetraci Pozornosti Hrača na Výkon vo Futbalovom Stretnutí (About the concentration of attention of the player on the performance in a soccer game). *Tréner a Učitel* (Trainer and Physical Education Instructor), (Bratislava), *7,* 11.

Macgillivary, W. (1980a). Perceptual style, critical viewing time, and catching skill. *International Journal of Sport Psychology, 11,* 22–33.

Macgillivary, W. (1980b). The contribution of perceptual style to human performance. *International Journal of Sport Psychology, 11,* 132–141.

Mahoney, M. J., & Avener, M. (1977). Psychology of the elite athlete: An exploratory study. *Cognitive Therapy and Research, 1,* 135–141.

Marteniuk, R. G. (1976). *Information processing in motor skills.* New York: Holt, Rinehart & Winston.

McCafferty, W., Gliner, J., & Horvath, S. (1978). The stress of coaching. *Physician and Sports Medicine, 6,* 67–71.

McGuire, W. J. (1976). Attitude change and the information processing paradigm. In E. P. Hollander & R. G. Hunt (Eds.): *Current perspectives in social psychology* (pp. 305–316). New York: Oxford University Press.

McLeod, B. (1985) Field dependence as a factor in sports with preponderance of open or closed skills. *Perceptual and Motor Skills, 60,* 369–370.

McNamara, T. P. (1986). Mental representations of spatial relations. *Cognitive Psychology, 18,* 87–121.

Meehl, P. E. (1954). *Clinical versus statistical prediction: A theoretical analysis and review of the evidence.* Minneapolis: University of Minnesota Press.

Miller, S. M. (1979). Controllability and human stress: Method, evidence and theory. *Behavior Research and Therapy, 17,* 287–304.

Millslagle, D. G. (1988). Visual perception, recognition, recall and mode visual search control in basketball involving novice and experienced basketball players. *Journal of Sport Behavior, 11,* 32–44.

Minecka, S., & Hendersen, R. W. (1985). Controllability and predictability in acquired motivation. *Annual Review of Psychology, 36,* 495–529.

Mischel, W. (1979). On the interface of cognition and personality: Beyond the person-situation debate. *American Psychologist, 34,* 740–754.

Mourant, R. R., & Rockwell, T. H. (1972). Strategies of visual search by novice and experienced drivers. *Human Factors, 14,* 325–335.

Neisser, U. (1967). *Cognitive psychology.* New York: Appleton-Century-Crofts.

Neisser, U. (1982, December). *Cognitive science: External validity.* Paper presented at SUNY-Cortland, New York.

Neumaier, A. (1982). Untersuchung zur Funktion des Bliskverhaltens bei Visuellen Wahrnehmungsprozessen im Sport. *Sportswissenschaft, 12,* 78–91.

Nideffer, R. M. (1976a). Test of attentional and interpersonal style. *Journal of Personality and Social Psychology, 34.* 394–404.

Nideffer, R. M. (1976b). *The inner athlete: Mind plus muscle for winning.* New York: Crowell.

Nideffer, R. M. (1979). The role of attention in optimal athletic performance. In P. Klavora & J. V. Daniel (Eds.), *Coach, athlete and the sport psychologist* (pp. 99–112). Toronto: University of Toronto.

Nisbett, R., & Ross, L. (1980). *Human inference: Strategies and shortcomings of social judgment.* Englewood Cliffs, NJ: Prentice Hall.

Norman, D. A. (1976). *Memory and attention: An introduction to human information processing.* New York: Academic Press.

Nougier, V., Azemar, G., & Stein, J. R. (1990). Attention et controle du mouvement dans l'execution de gestes de precision en escrime. In V. Nougier & J. P. Blanchi (Eds.), *Pratiques sportives et modelisation du Gests* (pp. 107–129). Grenoble: Grenoble Sciences.

Nougier, V., Ripoll, H., & Stein, J. F. (1987). Processus attentionnels et practique sportive de haut niveau. In M. Laurent & P. Therme (Eds.), *Recherches en APS II* (pp. 209–221). Aix-Marseille II: Centre de Recherche de l'UEREPS.

Nougier, V., Stein, J. F., & Bonnel, A. M. (in press). Information processing in sport. *International Journal of Sport Psychology.*

Pargman, D., Schreiber, L. E., & Stein, F. (1974). Field dependence of selected athletic subgroups. *Medicine and Science in Sports, 6,* 283–286.

Pate, R., Rotella, R., & McClenaghan, B. (1984). *Scientific foundations of coaching.* Philadelphia, PA: Saunders.

Pervin, L. A. (1968). Performance and satisfaction as a function of individual-environment fit. *Psychological Bulletin, 69,* 56–68.

Phillips, W. A., & Christie, D. F. M. (1977a). Components of visual memory. *Quarterly Journal of Experimental Psychology, 29,* 117–133.

Phillips, W. A., & Christie, D. F. M. (1977b). Interference with visualization. *Quarterly Journal of Experimental Psychology, 29,* 637–650.

Piaget, J. (1952). *The origins of intelligence in children.* New York: International Universities Press.

Pitz, G. F., & Sachs, N. J. (1984). Judgment and decision: Theory and application. *Annual Review of Psychology, 35,* 139–163.

Porter, D. T., & Allsen, P. E. (1978). Heart rates of basketball coaches. *The Physician and Sports Medicine, 6,* 84–90.

Posner, M. I., & Boies, S. J. (1971). Components of attention. *Psychological Review, 78,* 391–408.

Poulton, E. C. (1957). On prediction in skilled movements. *Psychological Bulletin, 54,* 467–478.

Pribram, K. H. (1971). *Languages of the brain.* Monterey, CA: Brooks/Cole.

Prinz, W. (1977). Memory control of visual search. In S. Dornic (Ed.), *Attention and performance VI* (pp. 441–462). Hillsdale, NJ: Erlbaum.

Prinz, W. (1979a). Searching as a theme of experimental psychology. *Psychologische Rundschau, 30,* 198–218.

Prinz, W. (1979b). Integration of information visual search. The Experimental Psychology Society. *Psychological Beitrage, 25,* 57–70.

Prinz, W., & Atalan, D. (1973). Two components and two stages in search performance: A case study in visual search. *Acta Psychologica, 37,* 218–242.

Prinz, W., Tweer, R., & Roffeige, R. (1974). Context control of

search behavior: Evidence from a hurdling technique. *Acta Psychologica, 38,* 73–80.

Rapoport, A. (1975). Research paradigms for studying dynamic decision behavior. In D. Wendt & C. A. J. Vlek (Eds.), *Utility, probability, and human decision making* (pp. 345–369). Dordrecht: Reidel.

Rapoport, A., & Wallsten, T. S. (1972). Individual decision behavior. *Annual Review of Psychology, 23,* 131–176.

Richards, D. E., & Landers, D. M. (1981). *Test of attentional and interpersonal style scores of shooters.* Unpublished manuscript, Pennsylvania State University, University Park, PA.

Ripoll, H. (1979). Le traitement de l'information de donnes visuelles dans les situations tactiques en sport. L'exemple du basketball. *Travaux et Recherches en ESP, 4,* 99–104.

Ripoll, H. (1988a). Analysis of visual scanning patterns of volley ball players in a problem solving task. *International Journal of Sport Psychology, 19,* 9–25.

Ripoll, H. (1988b). Utilisation d'un dispositif videooculographique d'enregistrement de la direction du regard en situation sportive. *Science et Motricite, 4,* 25–31.

Ripoll, H. (in press). The understanding-acting process in sport: The relationship between the semantic and the sensorimotor visual function. *International Journal of Sport Psychology.*

Ripoll, H., Papin, J. P., & Simonet, P. (1983). Approche de la fonction visuelle en sport. *Le Travail Humain, 46,* 163–173.

Robb, M. D. (1972). *The dynamics of motor-skill acquisition.* Englewood Cliffs, NJ: Prentice-Hall.

Ross, L. (1977). The intuitive psychologist and his shortcomings: Distortions in the attribution process. In L. Berkowitz (Ed.), *Advances in experimental social psychology, Vol. 10* (pp. 173–220). New York: Academic Press.

Rothstein, A. L. (1985). Visual perception and motor skills. In Z. Fooks, D. Ben Sira, & L. Jacovski (Eds.), *Selected subjects in motor learning, 8,* 29–48.

Ryan, E. D. (1981). Attribution and affect. In G. C. Roberts & D. M. Landers (Eds.), *Psychology of motor behavior and sport* (pp. 78–86). Champaign, IL: Human Kinetics.

Salame, P., & Baddeley, A. D. (1982). Disruption of short-term memory by unattended speech: Implications for the structure of working memory. *Journal of Verbal Learning and Verbal Behavior, 21.* 150–164.

Salmela, J. H., & Fiorito, P. (1979). Visual cues in ice hockey goaltending. *Canadian Journal of Applied Sport Science, 4,* 56–59.

Schneider, W., & Shiffrin, R. M. (1977). Controlled and automatic human information processing: I. Detection, search, and attention. *Psychological Review, 84,* 1–66.

Shepard, R. N. (1975). Form, formation, and transformation of internal representations. In R. Solso (Ed.), *Information processing and cognition: The Loyola Symposium* (pp. 122–141). Hillsdale, NJ: Erlbaum.

Shepard, R. N. (1981). Psychophysical complementarity. In M. Kubovy & J. Pomerantz (Eds.), *Perceptual organization.* Hillsdale, NJ: Erlbaum.

Shepard, R. N. (1984). Ecological constraints on internal representation: Resonant kinematics or perceiving, imagining, thinking, and dreaming. *Psychological Review, 91,* 417–447.

Shulman, G. L., Remington, R. W., & McLean, J. P. (1979). Moving attention through visual space. *Journal of Experimental Psychology: Human Perception and Performance, 5,* 522–526.

Sigler, R. S., & Richards, D. D. (1982). The development of intelligence. In R. J. Sternberg (Ed.), *Handbook of human intelligence* (pp. 897–971). New York: Cambridge University Press.

Simon, H. (1955). A behavioral model of rational choice. *Quarterly Journal of Economics, 69,* 99–118.

Simon, H. (1957). *Models of man: Social and rational.* New York: Wiley.

Simon, H. (1976). From substantive to procedural rationality. In S. Latsis (Ed.), *Method and appraisal in economics* (pp. 129–148). Cambridge, UK: Cambridge University Press.

Singer, R. N. (1980). *Motor learning and human performance: An application to motor skills and movement behaviors.* New York: Macmillan.

Skinner, B. F. (1938). *The behavior of organisms.* New York: Appleton-Century-Crofts.

Slovic, P., Fischhoff, B., & Lichtenstein, S. (1977). Behavioral decision theory. *Annual Review of Psychology, 28,* 1–39.

Slovic, P., & Lichtenstein, S. (1971). Comparison of Bayesian and regression approaches to the study of information processing in judgment. *Organizational Behavior and Human Performance, 6,* 649–744.

Smith, R. E. (1986). Toward a cognitive-affective model of athletic burnout. *Journal of Sport Psychology, 8,* 36–50.

Spearman, C. (1927). *The abilities of man.* New York: Macmillan.

Spence, K. W. (1956). *Behavior theory and conditioning.* New Haven: Yale University Press.

Starkes, J. L., & Allard, F. (1983). Perception in volleyball: The effects of competitive stress. *Journal of Sport Psychology, 5,* 189–196.

Starkes, J. L., & Deakin, J. M. (1984). Perception in sport: A cognitive approach to skilled performance. In W. F. Straub & J. M. Williams (Eds.), *Cognitive Sport Psychology* (pp. 115–128). Lansing, NY: Sport Science Associates.

Sternberg, R. J., & Salter, W. (1982). Conceptions of intelligence. In R. J. Sternberg (Ed.), *Handbook of human intelligence* (pp. 3–28). New York: Cambridge University Press.

Svenson, O. (1979). Process description of decision making. *Organizational Behavior and Human Performance, 23,* 86–112.

Swinnen, S. (1982). *Global or analytic orientation in learning gymnastic skills.* Paper presented at the International Symposium on Motor Learning and Movement Behavior, Heidelberg.

Swinnen, S., & Vandenberghe, J. (1983). Are cognitive styles and verbal reports means to identify learning strategies in the acquisition of gymnastic skills? In H. Rieder, K. Bos, H. Mechling, & K. Reischle (Eds.), *Motorik und Bewegungsforschung. Ein Beitrag zum Lernen im Sport* (Movement and movement research. A contribution to learning in sport) (pp. 234–239). Schorndorf: Karl Hofmann.

Swinnen, S., Vandenberghe, J., & Van Assche, E. (1986). Role of cognitive style constructs, field dependence-independence, and reflection-impulsivity in skill acquisition. *Journal of Sport Psychology, 8,* 51–69.

Tanner, W. P. J., & Swets, J. A. (1954). A decision making theory of visual detection. *Psychological Review, 61,* 401–409.

Teichner, W. H., & Krebs, M. J. (1974). Visual search for simple targets. *Psychological Review, 81,* 15–28.

Thiffault, C. (1974). Tachistoscopic training and its effect upon visual perceptual speed of ice hockey players. *Proceedings of the Canadian Association of Sport Sciences,* Edmonton, Alberta.

Thiffault, C. (1980). Construction et validation d'une measure de la rapidité de la pansee tactique des joueurs de hockey sur glace. In C. H. Nadeau, W. R. Halliwell, K. M. Newell, & G. C. Roberts (Eds.), *Psychology of motor behavior and sports* (pp. 643–649). Champaign, IL: Human Kinetics.

Thurstone, L. L. (1938). Primary mental abilities. *Psychometric Monographs, I.*

Tversky, A., & Kahneman, D. (1971). The belief in the "law of small numbers." *Psychological Bulletin, 76,* 105–110.

Tversky, A., & Kahneman, D. (1973). Availability: A heuristic for judging frequency and probability. *Cognitive Psychology, 5,* 207–232.

Tversky, A., & Kahneman, D. (1974). Judgment under uncertainty: Heuristics and biases. *Science, 185,* 1124–1131.

Tversky, A., & Kahneman, D. (1980). Causal schemas in judgments under uncertainty. In M. Fishbein (Ed.), *Progress in social psychology,* Vol. 1 (pp. 49–72). Hillsdale, NJ: Erlbaum.

Vallar, G., & Baddeley, A. D. (1982). Short term forgetting and the Articulatory Loop. *Quarterly Journal of Experimental Psychology, 34A,* 53–60.

Vanek, M., & Cratty, B. J. (1970). *Psychology and the superior athlete.* London: Macmillan.

Vanek, M., & Hosek, V. (1967). Tachistoskopické Vyšetrení Hráčú Jako Ukozatel kvality rozhodování (Tachistoscopic investigations of players as indicators of the quality of their judgment). Paper read at the Meeting of Sports Psychologists in Hrachov, Czechoslovakia.

Vickers, J. N. (1985). *Expert-novice differences in knowledge structure of action* (Doctoral dissertation, University of British Columbia, 1984). DAI, 46, 384-A.

Wachtel, P. L. (1967). Conceptions of broad and narrow attention. *Psychological Bulletin, 68,* 417–429.

Williams, H., & Deoreo, K. (1980). Perceptual-motor development: A theoretical overview. In: C. Corbin (Ed.). *A textbook of motor development* (pp. 136–147). Dubuque, IA: Brown.

Witkin, H. A. (1959). The perception of the upright. *Scientific American, 20,* 50–56.

Witkin, H. A. (1967). A cognitive style approach to cross-cultural research. *International Journal of Psychology, 2,* 233–250.

Witkin, H. A., Dyk, R. B., Faterson, H. F., Goodenough, D. R., & Karp, S. (1962). *Psychological differentiation.* New York: Wiley.

Witkin, H. A., Morre, C. A., Goodenough, D. R., & Cox, P. W. (1977). Field-dependent and field-independent cognitive styles and their educational implications. *Review of Educational Research, 47,* 1–64.

Zakay, D. (1982). Decision-making processes and thought shortcomings in sports competition. In E. Geron & A. Mashiach (Eds.). *Proceedings of the first national conference on psychology and sociology of sports and physical education* (pp. 93–96). Netanya, Israel: Wingate Institute (Hebrew).

· 8 ·

AUGMENTED FEEDBACK IN
SKILL ACQUISITION

Richard Magill

While there are many variables that influence motor skill acquisition, probably none has been investigated or discussed more than augmented feedback. This long history of research has established a large number of issues about augmented feedback and its relationship to skill acquisition. Unfortunately, the knowledge gained from this research has not led to a well-defined list of principles that can be applied to skill-learning situations. As a result, a discussion of the status of research on augmented feedback must consider the various issues related to augmented feedback and determine what consensus can be derived so that appropriate direction is provided for future research and application to learning settings. In this chapter, selected examples of research are discussed that appear to best establish the present state of affairs of the role of this variable in skill acquisition.

DEFINING AUGMENTED FEEDBACK

The first task in any review of augmented feedback research is to define the term *augmented feedback*. Performing this task is not without its problems, however, as this term has been used in a variety of ways, and several different terms have been used synonymously with it. To simplify matters, the term *augmented feedback* will be used in this chapter to refer to *any* form of augmented external feedback that is provided to an individual or group of individuals. As used here, augmented feedback should be distinguished from internal, or sensory, feedback, which is sensory information that is available during and after a movement and involves information inherent in the environment and/or the movement response itself. Augmented feedback, on the other hand, is feedback provided by a source external to the person's own sensory system. While

sensory feedback can be augmented and provided to a person by some external means, as will be discussed later, this form of feedback will be considered as a specific type of augmented feedback.

The term *augmented feedback* is used in a general way in this chapter to include several different types of augmented feedback, each of which has been referred to by different terms in the research literature. Specifically three different types will be considered in this discussion. One type is *knowledge of results (KR)*. KR is externally presented information about the outcome of a response. An example of KR occurs when a person shoots an arrow at a target and a person or machine indicates the score of that shot. Also, the information may be error-related, such as telling the archer, "the shot was in the blue at nine o'clock." The second type of augmented feedback is commonly referred to as *knowledge of performance (KP)*. KP is information about the movement characteristics that led to the outcome of a response. KP can be presented in several different forms. The most common is verbal KP, such as in the archery situation just described, the archer could be told that he or she pulled the bow to the left at the release of the arrow. KP can also be provided by showing the person a videotape of his or her performance. And KP can be presented graphically, such as when a golfer is shown the movement kinematics of his or her golf swing. The third type is *augmented sensory feedback,* where an external device is used to augment sensory feedback that is already available. In the archery example, sensory feedback would be augmented if a sound device indicated to the archer when the arrow was correctly aimed or when the bow was being held in a steady position. Typically, KR and KP are presented after a response is made (i.e., terminally) while augmented sensory feedback is provided while the movement is in progress (i.e., concurrently). However, it is possible to give KP concurrently and augmented sensory feedback terminally.

It is important to note that in this chapter, when a specific type of augmented feedback is being discussed, the term appropriate to that type of feedback will be used. However, in general, it will be assumed that research on any one type of augmented feedback can be generalized to the other types (see a discussion of this issue by Schmidt, 1988, pp. 427–428). The degree to which this generalization is valid is clearly a point that needs to be addressed in future research.

THE ROLES OF AUGMENTED FEEDBACK IN SKILL ACQUISITION

It seems clear from the research literature that augmented feedback plays two roles in the learning process. One role is to provide the learner with performance information about the success of the movement in progress or just completed and/or what must be done on a succeeding performance attempt. This information may be very general and indicate that the movement was or was not successful. Or this information may be quite specific and indicate precisely what movement errors were made or what movement corrections need to be made. In this form, augmented feedback is high in prescriptive information value and enables the learner to plan an upcoming performance attempt.

The second role played by augmented feedback is to motivate the learner to continue striving toward a goal. Although the feedback here is also informational, it is a different type of information and is used in a different way than for planning an upcoming response. Here the feedback indicates how well the learner is doing in comparison to a performance goal that the person has established. As such, the feedback is used to engage in evaluation decisions related to continuing to strive toward that goal or to stop and either change goals or stop performing the activity.

In early research concerning augmented feedback, this motivation role was considered to be an important function in skill learning and performance. For example, Elwell and Grindley (1938) had subjects learn a two-hand coordination task that involved keeping a spot of light on a moving target. The subjects improved their performance with practice, but after 200 trials, the light was taken away, which removed the augmented feedback. Performance dropped immediately, which the experimenters attributed to subjects losing interest in the task, since they could no longer see how they were performing. This loss of interest was supported by subjects' complaints and beginning to arrive late for experimental sessions.

An interesting different approach to investigating the motivational aspects of augmented feedback on skill learning was presented by Little and McCullagh (1989). They considered motivation from the perspective of the learner's goal orientation as related to learning a particular skill. Some people, referred to as intrinsic mastery motivated, prefer to figure out how to perform a skill on their own and as a result tend to focus on their own practice attempts and movement performance. Others, on the other hand, are extrinsic mastery motivated and seem to prefer guidance from an expert, such as a teacher or coach. During practice, these people tend to focus on external sources of information to judge their performance. Little and McCullagh reasoned that the type of augmented feedback received may be related to the type of goal orientation of the learner. They hypothesized that intrinsic mastery learners would more likely be influenced by KP, since it provides information about movement performance characteristics, while extrinsic mastery learners would more likely be influenced by KR, since it provides information about movement outcome. The experiment developed to test this hypothesis involved 12- to 15-year-old female novice tennis players who practiced the forehand ground stroke for 3 days. Four groups were formed on the basis of their intrinsic or extrinsic mastery orientation and whether they received KP or KR after each practice trial. While the results only partially supported the hypothesis, they provided sufficient evidence to suggest that the relationship between goal orientation and the type of augmented feedback received is an issue worthy of further research efforts.

While the motivational role of augmented feedback is not to be taken lightly, the focus of this chapter is on augmented feedback as a source of information to help the learner acquire the skill by providing information that can be used to evaluate an ongoing or just completed movement or to plan an upcoming response. This delimitation will help keep this review within reasonable limits for a review chapter (for more complete discussions of the motivational role of augmented feedback in skill performance, see Little & McCullagh, 1989; Locke, Cartledge, & Koeppel, 1968; and Adams, 1978, 1987). It is also important to point out that in many cases, it is difficult to know where one role ends and another begins. While this is an important issue to be addressed to develop appropriate theory related to augmented feedback and skill acquisition, it will not be an issue of concern in this chapter.

HOW ESSENTIAL IS AUGMENTED FEEDBACK FOR SKILL ACQUISITION?

When a learner performs a skill during practice, is it essential that augmented external information be provided to that person to enable him or her to learn the skill successfully? A review of the augmented feedback literature indicates that the only appropriate answer to this question is that it depends on the skill being performed. While this view is not consistent with traditional theories of motor learning (e.g., Adams, 1971; Schmidt, 1975), it is becoming increasingly apparent from the research literature that the need for augmented feedback depends on the skill being learned. That is, there are skills that appear to be learned only when augmented feedback is provided, there are other skills that do not appear to require augmented feedback to be learned, there are some skills that actually are learned more poorly with augmented feedback, and there are still other skills that will be learned more quickly and at a higher performance level if augmented feedback is available. In this section, each of these four situations will be discussed by considering the skill characteristics that appear to be related to each situation and some research examples supporting the effect of augmented feedback in each situation.

It is important to keep in mind here that an important part of learning any skill is comparing the outcome of a just-performed movement with the goal of that movement. To make this comparison, the learner must detect and use certain sensory information detected in the environment or from the movement itself. Thus an important feature for distinguishing situations related to the need for augmented feedback appears to be the degree to which critical environmental information can be detected and used for making this comparison. If the environmental information is adequate to make such a comparison, then it is likely that augmenting available sensory feedback is not necessary for learning the skill. However, if the environmental information is impoverished or not adequate, then augmenting external feedback will be necessary either for learning the skill or for enhancing learning. These characteristics will be discussed more completely in the following sections.

Augmented Feedback Can Be Essential for Skill Acquisition

For certain skills, it appears that the information needed to determine the appropriateness of a movement cannot adequately be detected or used by a learner and therefore must be augmented in some way. For example, if a person is learning to throw a ball at a target as accurately as possible but cannot see the target, then important information that is needed to determine the appropriateness of a throw is not directly available to that person. In this situation, some form of augmented feedback would be necessary for learning this skill. Or if a person is learning to throw a ball at a certain rate of speed and, due to lack of experience, was not able to determine the rate of speed of a throw, then feedback would need to be augmented to learn this skill. For skills or skill-learning situations such as these, augmented feedback appears to be critical for skill acquisition to occur.

Examples of research evidence supporting the need for augmented feedback in these situations can be seen throughout the motor learning literature. Consider first the situation where the learner does not have critical sensory feedback information available. If movements cannot be seen, such as while trying to draw a line of a certain length (e.g., Trowbridge & Cason, 1932), or while trying to move a lever to a criterion location (e.g., Bilodeau, Bilodeau, & Schumsky, 1959), then augmented feedback in the form of KR has been shown to be essential for learning. In the two research examples cited, KR was verbal information about

the accuracy of the response. In these situations, KR served to augment visual feedback that was not available to the subjects and thereby provided a means for making the response outcome versus task goal comparison needed to plan and perform succeeding responses during practice. If KR were not available in these situations, such a comparison would be difficult if not impossible, and learning would not occur.

A different type of situation occurs when all the sensory feedback systems are available to the learner, but the learner is not capable of using the environmental information to determine the adequacy of a response. Such a situation is typically characteristic of beginning learners. An example in the research literature that involves this situation was reported by Newell (1974). Subjects learned to make a 24-cm lever movement in 150 msec. Although they could see their arms, the lever, and the target, the subjects did not have a referent for comparing the actual speed of their own movement response with the 150-msec goal. In this situation, subjects who received KR about the accuracy of their responses for 52 or 75 trials learned the skill very well, while those who received KR for only 2 trials showed no improvement and actually performed worse with practice. Thus augmented feedback was necessary to help the learner establish a referent for 150 msec that could be used to compare the appropriateness of any practice attempt. After that referent was established, which occurred between 32 and 52 trials of practice with KR, the subjects no longer needed KR and effectively used the available sensory information to make the comparison between the outcome of the movement and the goal of the task.

An intriguing feature appears to exist in the relationship between augmented feedback and skills, where the information needed to determine the appropriateness of a movement cannot adequately be detected or used by a learner. While augmented feedback is needed to learn these skills, there are certain conditions in which a dependency on the augmented feedback may develop that can actually hinder learning. These conditions, which tend to relate to the type, timing, and frequency of the augmented feedback that is presented, will be considered more specifically in later portions of this chapter.

Augmented Feedback May Not Be Needed for Skill Acquisition

Some motor skills inherently provide sufficient sensory feedback so that augmenting this feedback for the learner is not necessary. For these skills, the learner can obtain the information needed to determine the appropriateness of his or her movement and compare the outcome and/or movements of the just-performed response with the goal of the task. Augmented feedback for these skills becomes information that is redundant with information available in the environment and is therefore not needed to learn the skill.

A research example of this augmented feedback redundancy situation was reported recently for KR by

Magill, Chamberlin, and Hall (1991). Subjects learned a coincidence-anticipation skill that simulated striking a moving object, such as batting a pitched baseball or hitting a moving tennis ball. Ball movement was simulated as a series of sequentially lighting LEDs on a 281-cm-long trackway. The subject faced the trackway at eye level with the LEDs lighting from the subject's left to right. Directly in front of the subject's eyes was the target LED. There was a small wooden barrier directly under the target that the subject was to knock down with a hand-held bat coincident with the lighting of the target. KR was given as the number of msec the barrier was knocked down before or after the target lighted. Four experiments were completed in which subjects made the striking response to either one or three trackway speeds during the practice sessions. Results of these experiments indicated that all subjects significantly improved their anticipation performance during practice, regardless of the feedback condition. More importantly, receiving KR during the practice trials did not lead to better learning than practice without KR, which was determined by evaluating retention performance of the practiced speeds one day later and transfer performance for new trackway speeds.

Similar redundancy results have been found for augmented sensory feedback. Most of the research investigating this type of feedback was reported in the 1950s and 1960s (see Armstrong, 1970, for a review of this research). A good example of this work can be seen in an experiment by Goldstein and Rittenhouse (1954) in which both augmented sensory feedback and KR were investigated. Subjects learned to use a Pedestal Sight Manipulation Test (PSMT), which requires a person to manipulate a joystick to track a target aircraft with a cursor dot and to make "ranging adjustments" by framing the wingtips of the aircraft by adjusting the diameter of a ring of small diamonds that are visible around the target cursor. There is good visual feedback for the tracking part of this task but little for the ranging-adjustment part of the task. Three different augmented feedback situations were used in this experiment. One involved a buzzer that sounded when both tracking and ranging were being done accurately. Another involved telling the subject the proportion of time he was on-target and how that compared to other trials. The third condition combined the augmented feedback characteristics of the first two. Results of both retention tests and transfer tests showed no benefit of augmented feedback compared to practice without augmented feedback.

Motor skills that do not need augmented feedback during practice to learn them have at least one important identifiable characteristic. There is some detectable external referent in the environment that a learner can use to determine the correctness of a movement response, either while the response is in progress, such as in the tracking task, or at the completion of the response, as in the anticipation timing task. This feature was clearly characteristic for the tasks in the two research examples just described. For the anticipation timing task, the target and other LEDs were the external referents. The learner could see when the barrier was

contacted in comparison to when the target lighted. For the PSMT task, the aircraft wings and the ring that the subject adjusted was the external referent for the ranging task, while the aircraft and the target cursor were the referent for the tracking task. For each task, the subject could see the relationship between his own movements and the goal of those movements. It is important to note here that the learner may *not* consciously be aware of this relationship. The sensory system and the motor control system appear to operate in these situations in a way that does not demand the person's awareness of the environmental characteristics. Thus to enhance these characteristics by providing augmented sensory feedback or KR does nothing to influence learning the skill.

It is worth noting here that several studies investigating the use of feedback from teachers in physical education classes have found consistently low correlations for the relationship between teacher feedback and student achievement (e.g., Eghan, 1988; Pieron, 1982; Silverman, Tyson, & Krampitz, 1991; Silverman, Tyson, & Morford, 1988). This finding suggests that the amount and quality of teacher feedback is not essential for improving skill by beginners in sport skills in class settings. Whether this is a phenomenon limited to teaching in class settings, to the specific skills being taught, or to other instructional variables, such as the amount of practice or teacher demonstration, awaits further research. However, these results do open to question the traditional view that motor skills cannot be learned without augmented feedback (see Magill, 1991, for further discussion of this issue).

Augmented Feedback Can Be a Hindrance to Skill Acquisition

Augmenting feedback for certain motor skills during practice appears to have the effect of making the learner become dependent on the availability of that feedback. As a result, when the augmented information is removed, performance deteriorates. In fact, there is research evidence showing that not only does performance deteriorate when augmented feedback is withdrawn, the transfer performance is no better than that for subjects who practiced without augmented feedback. This effect seems to be prevalent in situations where augmented sensory feedback is concurrently presented with performance. For example, Annett (1959) had subjects learn to produce a specified amount of force by either depressing a movable plunger or pressing against a fixed metal bar. Concurrent augmented feedback was provided in different ways. One way was to show the force produced graphically on an oscilloscope. Another was to have a neon indicator illuminate when the force being exerted was within a certain range of the criterion force. Terminal augmented feedback was provided either verbally as the amount of force exerted or by allowing the subject to see the oscilloscope reading after the subject indicated that he had made his response. In both the concurrent and terminal augmented feedback conditions, when transfer performance required subjects to produce the force without augmented feedback available, performance deteriorated. Interestingly, transfer performance for the group trained with concurrent augmented feedback deteriorated immediately and the error became very large while the group trained with terminal augmented feedback showed a gradual decrement in performance without augmented feedback available.

The most prevalent hypothesis proposed to explain the deterioration effect found in these types of situations is that when sensory feedback intrinsic to the task itself is minimal or difficult to interpret, learners will substitute concurrently provided augmented feedback for task-intrinsic feedback and therefore become dependent on the augmented feedback to perform the skill. They do not learn the sensory feedback characteristics associated with performing the skill because they have learned to perform the skill on the basis of the augmented feedback (e.g., Adams, 1964; Lintern, Roscoe, & Sivier, 1990).

Instances of performance deterioration during transfer have also been found in studies investigating the question of the optimal frequency for providing terminal KR. For example, Winstein and Schmidt (1990) had subjects practice for two days (almost 200 trials) a single-limb lever movement to produce a complex wave-form pattern. They reported results indicating that subjects who received KR after every practice trial performed the practiced skill without KR at a level that was essentially the same as when they had performed the skill during the first 24 trials of practice. They accounted for these results by proposing that subjects became dependent on KR when it was available after every trial. This dependence led subjects to need the KR information to perform the skill successfully. When KR was not available during the transfer trials, performance deteriorated. Proteau and his colleagues (Proteau & Cournoyer, 1990; Proteau, Marteniuk, Girouard, & Dugas, 1987) have taken this notion of dependence one step further and have argued that the KR becomes a part of the memory representation that develops during practice. Thus when subjects are required to perform the skill in a situation where KR is not provided, the memory representation is not adequate to enable successful performance.

Augmented Feedback Can Enhance Skill Acquisition

There appear to be some motor skills that can be learned without augmented feedback being provided during practice but that will be learned more quickly or at a higher level if augmented feedback is provided during practice. Thus the augmented feedback is neither essential nor redundant but *enhances* learning. An example of a skill where augmented feedback operates in this way can be seen in an experiment reported by Stelmach (1970). Subjects learned a 3-segment arm movement that required them to move their hand 28 cm forward from a response key to hit a piece of rubber tubing, then back to the response key near the start position, and finally forward again to hit a

response key. The goal of this movement was to do it as quickly as possible. KR was provided as the movement time for the entire 3-segment movement. Results showed that a group who did not receive KR improved during the practice trials, indicating that learning was occurring. However, the group that received KR improved more rapidly and reached a higher level of performance than was reached by the group that did not get KR. Similar results were reported by Newell, Quinn, Sparrow, and Walter (1983) for a task having the same move-as-fast-as-you-can goal. Without KR, subjects showed improvement only to a certain level and then showed no further improvement, while subjects who received KR continued to show improvement during practice.

An interesting experiment using a sport skill that demonstrated the enhancement benefit of augmented feedback was reported by Wallace and Hagman (1979). Beginners in basketball learned to make a one-hand set-shot with the nondominant hand while they were 3.03 m from the basket and 45 degrees to the left side of the basket. One group of subjects received KP by being told performance-error information about their stance and limb movement during each shot. Another group did not receive this information but were given verbal encouragement statements after each shot, such as "Good shot," "You can do it," "Try harder next time," and so on. The results showed that after 25 practice attempts, both groups were performing similarly. However, beyond that point, the verbal encouragement group showed no further improvement while the group receiving KP continued to improve. This trend continued for an additional 25 trials on which no KP or verbal encouragement was given.

To perform the type of task used in the experiments just described, subjects seemed to be able to determine to a limited degree the amount of success they had in achieving the task goal on a previous trial. Thus improvement during practice could occur without KR about the movement times, in the Stelmach (1970) and Newell et al. (1983) experiments, and without KP about shooting stance and limb movements in the Wallace and Hagler (1979) experiment. However, KR and KP seems to have added sufficient information to the available sensory feedback to enable subjects to compare present and past movements more specifically so they could more effectively plan an upcoming movement and therefore move faster than they would have without KR or KP.

Summary

Conclusions about the need for augmented feedback must be considered incorrect when they state that motor skill learning cannot occur without some form of augmented feedback (e.g., Adams, 1971; Bilodeau, 1969; Schmidt, 1975). Research evidence has been considered in this section that demonstrated four different effects of the presence of augmented feedback during motor skill training. This evidence has shown that for learning motor skills, the effect varies according to the skill being learned. Augmented feedback can be essential, not essential, detrimental, or an enhancement for learning skills. Given these different effects, it seems clear that research needs to establish the skill characteristics or skill-learning conditions that relate specifically to each of these four effects. Some hypotheses concerning these characteristics and conditions have been proposed. It appears that when the performance of the skill provides the performer with sensory feedback that can effectively be interpreted by the performer so that the performance can be evaluated, then augmenting that feedback is not necessary. This sensory feedback can be from the environmental characteristics of the performance context or from the movements involved in the skill itself. However, when this type of interpretable sensory feedback is not available, then some form of augmented feedback is beneficial. The exact type that is needed and how or when it should be provided appears to be related to the skill being performed. Situations exist in which the learner can become dependent on augmented feedback such that learning will be hindered because of the augmented feedback.

THE INFORMATION PROVIDED BY AUGMENTED FEEDBACK

The discussion in the preceeding section indicated that augmented feedback can be several different types of information. KR was discussed as information that indicates the outcome of a particular movement response while KP indicates what movement characteristics were associated with that outcome. Augmented sensory feedback can provide similar information, although it is usually limited to indicating if a response is correct, not correct, or within or outside a certain performance range. An important question for both motor learning theory and motor skill instruction concerns the information provided by augmented feedback and how characteristics of that information influence skill learning. In this section, this question will be considered by discussing research that has focused on several issues related to these information characteristics.

Qualitative vs. Quantitative Information

Because augmented feedback can be either qualitative or quantitative, the influence of these two levels of information on skill learning is a relevant issue. The difference between qualitative and quantitative augmented feedback relates to how specific, or precise, the information is that is conveyed by the feedback to the learner. For example, a person learning a serve in tennis could be told that a particular serve is "good", or "long," or "you made contact with the ball too far in front of you," or a bell could ring when the serve is good. In each of these situations, the augmented feedback conveys information about the quality of the serve just performed. On the other hand, the person could be told "the serve was 6 cm too long," or "you made contact with the ball 10 cm too far in front of you," or the person

could be presented with precise kinematic displays of his or her serving motion. In each of these latter situations, more quantitatively precise information is conveyed than in the qualitative feedback situations. An important question that has been investigated is, how do these two levels of precision of augmented feedback influence skill learning? While the research investigating this question typically has been directed toward KR, it seems reasonable that the results can be generalized to other forms of augmented feedback as well.

The investigation of the question concerning the precision of KR and its effect on skill learning has a very long history in motor learning research. For example, the research by Trowbridge and Cason (1932), described earlier in this chapter, addressed this issue as a means of demonstrating the informational value of KR and distinguishing it from simple reinforcement. Blindfolded subjects practiced drawing a line of a specified length. One group of subjects received qualitative information after each trial (e.g., "too long"), another group received quantitative information that indicated the exact amount of error they had made, another group received nonsense syllables as KR, and a fourth group received no KR. Results revealed that the more precise quantitative KR was superior to the other conditions.

The result of the superiority of quantitative over qualitative KR for skill learning has typified investigations of the KR precision issue not only for learning laboratory tasks but for learning sport skills as well. For example, Smoll (1972) had subjects learn to roll a duckpin bowling ball at 70% of each person's maximum velocity. KR was provided after each practice attempt in one of three ways. One group received qualitative KR in the form of statements indicating that a roll was "too fast," "too slow," or "correct." One of two quantitative KR groups was told how many tenths of a second that the roll was in error of the goal velocity, while the other quantitative KR group was told this error information in hundredths of a second. Results showed that the two quantitative groups performed better during practice than the qualitative group, and that there was no difference between the two quantitative groups. Thus while quantitative information was more beneficial, the more precise hundredth-of-a-second level KR was not more beneficial than the less precise tenth-of-a-second level KR.

A problem that has typified most of the research investigating the KR precision issue was pointed out in an excellent review of the KR literature by Salmoni, Schmidt, and Walter (1984). That is, the conclusion that quantitative KR is better for learning must be considered as tentative because retention or transfer tests are not provided to determine the influence of qualitative vs. quantitative KR on learning as opposed to immediate performance in the presence of the respective types of KR. Two experiments that included no-KR retention tests were reported by Reeve and Magill (1981) and by Magill and Wood (1986). Although both investigations found results favoring quantitative over qualitative KR, they also supported a view of the precision effect that previously had not been considered. That is, the question of KR precision should not be viewed simply as qualitative vs. quantitative. It is important to include the stage of learning or the amount of practice of the learner. The experiment by Magill and Wood (1986) illustrates this point.

Magill and Wood (1986) had subjects learn to move an arm through a series of wooden barriers to produce a specific six-segment movement pattern. Each segment had its own criterion movement time that had to be learned. Following each of 120 practice trails, subjects were given either qualitative KR for each segment (i.e., "too fast," "too slow," or "correct") or quantitative KR for each segment (i.e., the number of msec too fast or too slow). The results indicated that during the first 60 trials, there was no difference between these two levels of KR precision. However, during the final 60 trials and on the 20 no-KR retention trials, the quantitative KR condition yielded better performance.

There appears to be sufficient evidence to conclude that a certain degree of quantitatively precise augmented feedback is beneficial only after a sufficient amount of practice has been experienced so that the learner can effectively use this information. Prior to that time, it appears that the learner needs less precise, i.e., more general, information about their performance errors. In the Magill and Wood (1986) experiment, it seemed that subjects needed to establish what was meant in movement terms by "too fast" or "too slow." Only after that meaning was established could the subjects use the specific information provided by quantities indicating how many msec too fast or too slow.

In a similar way, a beginner in a sport skill will receive limited benefit from augmented feedback that provides information that is more specific than he or she is capable of using. Thus to tell beginners in tennis that they "contacted the ball 10 cm too far in front" of them, while quantitatively more specific, is probably communicating no more than the qualitative information that they "contacted the ball too far in front." This point seems particularly pertinent in terms of providing highly sophisticated movement-analysis information as augmented feedback to beginners. The benefit of providing such precise information must be evaluated in terms of each individual's capability of translating that information into action terms that will enable each person to make needed corrections in the future. This capability appears to be one of the important characteristics that develops as a person moves from being a beginner, or novice, to being a skilled performer.

Augmented Feedback Based on Errors vs. Correct Performance

An important concern for determining what information to present as augmented feedback is whether the information should be related to the errors being made during the performance or to aspects of the performance that have been done correctly. Unfortunately this question has not been investigated very intensely. The few studies that have addressed this question were done in the 1950s and 1960s using tracking types of tasks. However, the results of these studies are reasonably consistent and have implications for learning theory and skill instruction.

The most informative studies investigating this question have used the rotary pursuit task where subjects must maintain stylus contact on a target on a rotating disk for as long as possible. Augmented feedback can be provided in a variety of ways for this task. Both error and correct-performance information can be given either concurrently or terminally. Error information can be provided as concurrent augmented sensory feedback by providing an auditory signal indicating when the stylus is off-target, or it can be provided as terminal KR by telling the subject by how much time he or she was off-target. Correct performance information can be provided in similar ways by making the augmented sensory feedback or the terminal KR relate to on-target rather than off-target performance.

A representative example of an experiment investigating the on-target vs. off-target feedback issue for learning the rotary pursuit task was reported by Gordon and Gottlieb (1967). Subjects practiced for 33 trials with one of three augmented feedback conditions. One group received visual augmented sensory feedback in the form of a yellow light illuminating the entire rotary-pursuit apparatus when they were on-target, while a second group saw this light when they were off-target. The third group was a control group that received no augmented feedback. Results for both the practice trials and 9 transfer trials without augmented feedback showed that the two augmented feedback groups performed better than the no-augmented feedback group. Also, the off-target feedback condition led to slightly better learning than occurred with the on-target feedback condition.

Similar off-target augmented feedback benefits were reported by Williams and Briggs (1962) for a compensatory tracking task, while Annett (1959) found that augmented feedback based on error was better than augmented feedback based on correct performance for the force production task described earlier. These few experiments are consistent in demonstrating that error-based augmented feedback is beneficial and typically leads to better learning than augmented feedback that indicates when a movement is being done correctly. Thus the research evidence supports the hypothesis proposed by Annett (1959) that repeating a precise response is not sufficient to produce learning but that the addition of experience with error-based feedback is needed for skill acquisition in tasks that benefit from augmented feedback. And, as Lintern and Roscoe (1980) argued, on-target augmented feedback, when it relates to sensory feedback from the task itself that is relatively obscure, can create a strong dependency on the on-target augmented information that will lead to poor performance when the augmented feedback is withdrawn.

It is clear that more research needs to be conducted to investigate the question of whether error or correct-performance augmented feedback is better for skill learning. Given the typical skill-dependent characteristics of most of the augmented feedback research, the need exists to address this question in experiments using a variety of skills, especially sport skills. In addition to determining if one or the other of these two types of augmented feedback is better for learning, it would also be useful to investigate the question of whether developing certain combinations of error and correct-performance feedback during practice sessions would be more beneficial than providing feedback that provides information only about one or the other. Although sport pedagogy texts give indications that such combinations are desirable (e.g., Siedentop, 1983), there is no published empirical evidence supporting such conclusions.

Augmented Feedback Based on a Performance-Based Bandwidth

Closely related to the question of whether to provide augmented feedback that indicates correct performance or the errors in a performance is the question of how much of an error should be made before augmented feedback is given. This question has distinct practical appeal because it undoubtedly reflects what occurs in actual teaching or coaching situations, especially when large groups are involved. Because augmented feedback cannot be given about every error made by students, it seems reasonable to provide feedback only about those errors that are large enough to warrant attention. This practice suggests that the instructor establishes a performance-based bandwidth that provides a criterion for when augmented feedback will be given or not given. If the student is performing within the tolerance limits of that bandwidth, then augmented feedback will not be given. But if an error is made that is outside that performance bandwidth, the feedback will be given.

Probably the earliest experimental example of using this performance-based bandwidth basis for giving augmented feedback was seen in the experiment described earlier as reported by Thorndike (1927). Subjects who were in the qualitative KR condition were actually in a performance-based bandwidth condition. These blindfolded subjects were told that their line-drawing attempts were "right" when they were within 0.25 in. of the line-length goal and "wrong" if they drew lines that erred with distances greater than this limit. When compared to a group that received no KR, the performance-based bandwidth KR group improved considerably. However, since these were the only two groups compared, it is not possible to determine how the bandwidth KR would compare to more precise KR for learning the skill.

A more recent experiment that is a better illustration of the effectiveness of basing augmented feedback on a performance-based bandwidth criterion is one reported by Sherwood (1988). He had subjects practice a rapid elbow-flexion task, where the goal was to make the movement in 200 msec. One group received KR about their movement time error after every trial, regardless of the amount of error, i.e., a 0% bandwidth. Two other groups received KR only when their error exceeded bandwidths of 5% and 10% of the 200 msec goal movement time. The results of a no-KR retention test showed that the 10% bandwidth condition resulted in the least amount of variable movement times (i.e., variable error), while the 0% condition resulted in the most variable error. These results, which were replicated by Lee, White, and Carnahan (1990), support the point discussed earlier in this chapter that error information is not always needed to learn a skill and can in fact negatively influence learning. And, as will be discussed later, providing augmented feedback based on performance bandwidths appears to be an effective means of determining an appropriate frequency for providing augmented feedback to individuals in practice settings. The use of performance-based bandwidths for providing augmented feedback needs to be investigated more by researchers interested in motor skill acquisition, since there are significant theoretical and practical implications associated with it.

Erroneous Augmented Feedback When Augmented Feedback Is Not Needed

In an earlier section of this chapter, situations were described where motor skill learning could occur without augmented feedback. In these situations, augmented feedback was redundant information with available sensory feedback and did not lead to better learning than that resulting from no-augmented feedback situations. But in these redundancy situations, a question arises concerning whether the augmented feedback is ignored or used in some way by the learner. One way to address this question is to consider the influence of erroneous augmented feedback. The idea here is that if augmented feedback is ignored, because it is not needed to learn the skill, then erroneous information should be ignored and sensory feedback would be the information source. This approach to studying this question was described recently by Buekers, Magill, and Hall (1992). They reported two experiments in which subjects practiced an anticipation timing task similar to the one described earlier in the experiments by Magill, Chamberlin, and Hall (1991). Experiment 2 will serve as an example of addressing this issue.

Subjects practiced the anticipation timing skill for 75 trials. For three groups, KR was given after every trial. KR was the correct direction and amount of timing error for one group, while it was not the correct error information for another group. For this incorrect KR group, KR indicated that the subjects were 100 msec later than they actually were. A third group received correct KR for the first 50 trials and then received the incorrect KR for the last 25 trials. A fourth group did not receive KR during practice. Following the practice trials, all subjects performed 25 trials without KR one day later and then 25 more no-KR trials one week later. The results of this experiment showed two things. First, support was found for the results of the Magill, Chamberlin, and Hall (1991) experiments, discussed earlier in this chapter, which showed that KR was not needed to learn this skill as the correct-KR and the no-KR groups did not differ during the practice or the retention trials. Second, the results indicated that KR is used by subjects when it is available to them, since the erroneous KR information led subjects to perform according to the KR rather than according to the feedback intrinsic to the task itself. This effect was seen even for the group that had received correct KR for the first 50 trials and then was switched to the erroneous information. After the switch, this group began performing similarly to the group that had received the incorrect KR for all the practice trials. This erroneous information not only influenced performance when the incorrect KR was provided, it also influenced retention performance one day and one week later, when no KR was provided.

When augmented feedback is presented to beginning learners and it is not needed for learning the skill, the role played by this information appears to depend on whether the augmented feedback agrees or is in conflict with the information the person has derived intrinsically through the sensory system. If there is conflict, the conflict is resolved in favor of the augmented feedback. However, if the augmented feedback agrees with the person's intrinsically derived information, then two possibilities exist: (1) The augmented feedback may be ignored after this agreement is determined. (2) The augmented feedback is used to interpret, or calibrate, the sensory feedback they received. Recent evidence reported by Buekers, Magill, and Sneyers (1991) argues for this latter use of augmented feedback. Because beginners are not certain how to use or interpret their own sensory feedback, the externally presented augmented feedback becomes a critical source of information for making movement adjustments on future trials.

From a learning theory perspective, this use of augmented feedback by novices suggests that the motor control system does not "automatically" use sensory feedback in an appropriate way. There seems to be a need to calibrate the motor control system so that the sensory feedback can be appropriately used. If augmented feedback is available, then the learner can use this information to carry out this calibration process. If augmented feedback is not available, and if the task is one where augmented information is not necessary for learning the skill, then this calibration process appears to occur by means of trial-and-error experience occurring during practice. From an applied perspective, this use of augmented feedback suggests that instructors need to be certain that the information they provide as augmented feedback is correct and establishes a means of interpreting sensory feedback so that performance can eventually be carried out without the need for this augmented feedback being provided by the instructor. Beginning learners are of particular concern here because they will ignore what their own sensory feedback is telling them, even though it is correct, and will adjust movements on the basis of what the instructor tells them, even though it may be incorrect.

Videotape as Augmented Feedback

Research evidence relating to teaching and coaching sport skills indicates that the most common means of providing augmented feedback to students is verbal (e.g., Eghan, 1988; Fischman & Tobey, 1978). This is undoubtedly due to the convenience of providing verbal feedback

as well as to the limited availability of alternative means for providing feedback. However, there is an increasing use of videotape as a means of presenting augmented feedback as videotape equipment becomes less expensive and more readily available. Unfortunately, we know very little about the use of videotape as a means of providing augmented feedback. In fact, the only extensive review of the research literature was published in 1976 by Rothstein and Arnold.

In the Rothstein and Arnold review, over 50 studies were considered that involved 18 different sport activities, including archery, badminton, bowling, gymnastics, skiing, swimming, and volleyball. In most of these studies, the students were beginners, although there were a few studies that included intermediate and advanced level performers. Although there were generally mixed results concerning the effectiveness of videotape as a method of providing augmented feedback, two points were clear. First, while the type of activity was not a critical factor in determining the effectiveness of videotape, the skill level of the student was a critical factor. Beginners need the aid of an instructor to point out information from the videotape replay. Advanced or intermediate performers did not appear to need instructor aid as much as did beginners. Second, videotape replays were most effective when used for at least five weeks. In those studies in which videotape was used less than this amount of time, they typically found replays to be an ineffective form of augmented feedback to aid learning.

It is also apparent that certain types of information related to skill performance are transmitted to the learner better than other types. An example of this was reported in a study by Selder and Del Rolan (1979) in which 12- and 13-year-old girls were learning to perform a balance beam routine. A control group received only verbal feedback about their performance on each trial. Each girl was given a checklist to use for critically analyzing her own performance on the basis of the verbal feedback they received. Another group of girls observed videotape replays of their performances. These girls were told to use the checklist as a means of determining what to observe on the videotape and for evaluating their own performances. At the end of four weeks of practice, the overall results indicated that there were no differences between the two groups' performances of the practiced routine. However, at the end of six weeks of practice, the videotape group scored significantly higher than the verbal feedback group. What was more revealing, however, was that the videotape group scored significantly higher on only four of the eight factors making up the total score. These factors were precision, execution, amplitude, and orientation and direction. The other four factors—rhythm, elegance, coordination, and lightness of jumping and tumbling—did not show any differences between the two feedback groups. Thus it appears that the use of videotape will benefit those aspects of a performance that can be readily observed and corrected on the basis of visual information. Other factors, not as readily discernible, appear to be difficult to translate from the visual input to the motor output modes and may need to be augmented by verbal information.

Graphic Kinematic Representations as Augmented Feedback

With the advent of personal computers and software capable of doing sophisticated kinematic analysis of movement, it has become increasingly more common to find instructors who provide students with graphic kinematic representations about their performances as a form of feedback. As with videotape, it is important to determine the effectiveness of this means of providing augmented feedback and to establish guidelines for implementing its use. Unfortunately there is very little empirical evidence that provides definitive answers to these concerns. In this section we will consider two reported experiments that may provide some insight. (For additional information about graphic kinematic representations used as augmented feedback in motor skill learning, see Schmidt & Young, 1991.)

In a study by Lindahl (1945), evidence was provided that kinematic representations of movement can be effective for enhancing the training of machine operators in industry. Workers in this study had to be trained to precisely and quickly cut thin disks of tungsten with a machine that required fast, accurate, and rhythmic coordination of the hands and feet. Typical training for this job was by trial and error. Lindahl developed an alternative training method in which workers were presented with a paper tracing of the pattern made by the foot during the cutting of the tungsten disks. The foot movement was used for this feedback because it had been identified as the most critical component of this complex task. Results of using this feedback method showed that the trainees achieved production performance levels in 11 weeks that had taken other trainees 5 months to achieve. Additionally, the trainees reduced their percentage of broken cutting wheels to almost zero in 12 weeks, a level not achieved by those trained with the traditional method in less than 9 months. Thus the use of a graphic kinematic representation as feedback was not only effective in helping workers to achieve desired performance levels, it helped them achieve these levels in significantly less time.

Additional support for the effectiveness of this method of providing augmented feedback was provided in a laboratory setting by Newell, Quinn, Sparrow, and Walter (1983), which was an extension of an earlier experiment by Hatze (1976). In the second experiment of this study, subjects practiced moving a lever as fast as possible to a target. Three types of KR conditions were used. One group of subjects was verbally given their movement time as KR. A second group was shown a graphic display on the computer monitor of their movement velocity-time trace as KR, while a third group received no KR. Results indicated that the graphic kinematic representation form of KR led to the best performance, followed by the verbal-KR condition, and then the no-KR condition. It is interesting to note here that the no-KR condition showed improvement for the first 25 trials, but then performance reached a steady state without further improvement while the two KR conditions continued to show improvement. For this skill, the graphic presentation of movement velocity led to better overall performance than verbal KR. The difference between these types of KR became more pronounced as practice continued.

The study of the use and benefit of kinematic representations as a means of providing augmented feedback needs more attention (see Schmidt & Young, 1991, for a discussion concerning this issue). As the use of computers and movement analysis systems becomes more commonplace, the possibility of using information derived from these systems will increase. Accordingly there will be a continuing increase in the need to know how to use these systems more effectively to enhance skill learning and performance. Initial attempts at providing theory-based guidelines for effective feedback use have been made by Newell and his colleagues (e.g., Newell & McGinnis, 1985; Newell, Morris, & Scully, 1985) and by Fowler and Turvey (1978). However, it is clear that both theoretical and empirical work are needed to develop guidelines that will lead to the most effective use of the various methods available for providing augmented feedback.

FREQUENCY OF PRESENTING AUGMENTED FEEDBACK

Closely related to the issue of the content of augmented feedback is the question of how frequently augmented feedback should be given to a person. This frequency question has been investigated in the research literature primarily as it relates to KR. In this section, three issues will be discussed. The first concerns whether absolute or relative frequency is important, and if so, what frequency would be optimal for learning. The next two issues relate to integrating the frequency and content of KR as the second part of this discussion considers the relationship between KR frequency and providing KR on the basis of performance bandwidths and the last section addresses the question of whether KR can be given in summary form and be effective for learning.

Absolute vs. Relative KR Frequency

The term *absolute frequency* refers to giving KR a specific number of trials during practice, whereas the term *relative frequency* refers to the percentage of trials on which KR is given. For example, if a person were to practice a skill for 80 trials, and a person received KR on 20 of them, the absolute frequency would be 20 while the relative frequency would be 25%. The traditional conclusion in motor learning has been that the more frequently a person receives KR, the better will be the learning that results. Bilodeau and Bilodeau (1958a), for example, held absolute frequency constant while allowing relative frequency to vary among four groups learning a simple lever-pulling task. Since the results found no differences among the relative frequencies, they argued that the critical variable for learning motor skills is the absolute frequency of KR. That is, learning will increase as a function of the number of exposures a learner has to KR. This view argues that receiving KR is essential for learning and that the learner will not benefit from practice trials where KR is not provided.

However, in experiments where absolute frequency has been permitted to vary, and where a learning test was included in the experiment (which was not done in the Bilodeau and Bilodeau experiment), results have argued against the conclusion that absolute frequency of KR is the critical factor for learning. In these experiments (e.g., Annett, 1959; Ho & Shea, 1978; Winstein & Schmidt, 1990, Experiment 1), reduced KR frequency did not produce detrimental or beneficial learning effects. Since relative and absolute frequency covaried in these experiments, as all conditions had the same number of practice trials, support for an absolute-KR-frequency view could not be established.

Additionally, the results of experiments such as these provided evidence that 100% frequency of KR is not necessary to establish an optimal learning condition. However, since these experiments reported no differences among the different frequencies, they do not provide insight into the question of how frequently KR must be provided to optimize learning. To address this question, Winstein and Schmidt (1990, Experiments 2 & 3) applied an experimental procedure that was found by Landauer and Bjork (1978) to optimize learning word lists. The approach taken by Winstein and Schmidt was to systematically expand the number of trials on which KR was *not* provided during practice. To consider this procedure another way, they systematically reduced the frequency of KR during practice from 100% to 25%, which yielded an average KR frequency of 50% for the practice sessions.

A brief description of Experiment 2 by Winstein and Schmidt (1990) will illustrate the procedure and results. Subjects practiced producing a complex movement pattern by moving a lever on a table top to manipulate a cursor on a computer monitor. During the 192 practice trials (96 trials for each of 2 days), subjects received KR after either 100% or 50% of the trials. For the 50% condition, a "fading" technique was used where the KR was systematically reduced in frequency by providing KR after each of the first 22 trials of each day, then 8 trials of no KR, then KR for 8, 7, 4, 3, 2, and 2 trials for each of the remaining 8-trial blocks each day. The results showed that on a retention test given 1 day later, on which no KR was given, the "faded" 50% KR frequency condition led to better performance than the 100% condition. In fact, subjects in the 100% condition performed their retention test trials at a level resembling their performance early on the first day of practice.

It seems clear that optimal learning of motor skills does not depend on receiving KR after every practice trial. Research has been consistent in demonstrating that when KR is provided on fewer than 100% of the practice trials, learning is as good as or better than when KR was provided on 100% of the practice trials. What remains to be determined is whether or not there exists an optimal KR frequency to optimize skill learning. Research is needed to address this question, which obviously is complicated by the complex

array of skills that exist. It is doubtful that one frequency would be found to be "best" for learning all skills. However, empirical evidence must be provided before even this speculative generalization can be supported.

The finding that learning does not depend on 100% frequency, and, in fact, can actually be hindered in some cases when KR is given after every practice trial, has important theoretical and practical implications for skill learning. The theoretical importance here is that motor learning theory needs to accommodate the findings that the learner is actively involved in solving the problem of performing the skill correctly on trials where KR is not given. One such view, which has been promoted by Schmidt and his colleagues (e.g., Salmoni, Schmidt, & Walter, 1984; Schmidt, 1988; Winstein & Schmidt, 1990) is the *guidance hypothesis.* According to this view, KR frequency can be related to the learner being involved in fundamentally different learning processes. If the learner receives KR on every trial—i.e., 100% frequency—then the KR will be used as an effective "guide" that enables the learner to perform the movement correctly. The negative part of this process is that by using KR in this way, the learner develops a dependency on the availability of KR such that when the skill must be performed without KR, performance will be poorer than if KR were provided. In effect, to provide KR on every trial is to provide a crutch for the learner that becomes essential for performing the skill. If KR is removed, it is like removing the crutch and performance suffers. On the other hand, when KR is provided less frequently during practice, the learner engages in more beneficial learning processes during practice such as problem-solving activities on the trials where no KR is given. Under these conditions, the learner does not become dependent on the availability of KR and can therefore perform the skill well, even in the absence of KR. Whether the guidance hypothesis describes the relationship between skill-learning processes and the frequency of KR depends on much needed empirical tests of the hypothesis.

An important practical implication of the finding that less than 100% frequency leads to learning as good as 100% frequency, or even better in some cases, is that it reduces the demand on the instructor to provide feedback all the time. It is comforting to the instructor to realize that he or she will not be causing the athlete harm by failing to provide feedback after every practice attempt. In fact, if Schmidt's guidance hypothesis is correct, then the coach could actually be doing harm by giving feedback after every practice attempt. It is interesting in this regard that sport pedagogy research has shown that teachers and coaches of sport skills do not provide feedback with 100% frequency. In fact, in group practice situations, feedback typically is provided about one or two times per minute with the same student rarely receiving more than a few feedback statements throughout a class session or practice period (e.g., see Eghan, 1988; Fishman & Tobey, 1978; Silverman, Tyson, & Krampitz, 1991). If a coach is working with an athlete individually, however, it is much easier to give feedback after every trial. But it appears that this is not an optimal strategy and that less frequent feedback would be preferable.

Frequency of Augmented Feedback and Performance-Based Bandwidths

In an earlier section, the question of providing augmented feedback on the basis of a performance-based bandwidth criterion was considered. That discussion indicated that research evidence shows that learning can be enhanced by providing KR only when performance is not within a preestablished tolerance limit, or bandwidth. If the bandwidth issue is considered together with the frequency-of-giving-augmented-feedback issue, it is possible to see an interesting relationship between them. That is, if augmented feedback is based on a performance bandwidth, then feedback will be provided with less frequency than when feedback is given, regardless of the magnitude of the performance error. This relationship was initially addressed by Lee, White, and Carnahan (1990) and directly investigated in a follow-up experiment by Lee and Carnahan (1990).

To address the possible relationship between the size of the bandwidth for giving KR and the frequency of giving KR, Lee and Carnahan yoked subjects in the 5% and 10% bandwidth conditions with subjects who would receive KR according to the trials on which the bandwidth subjects received KR. Thus the yoked subjects controlled for frequency of KR since they received KR on a frequency basis rather than on a performance-criterion basis. If the bandwidth effect is essentially a frequency effect, then subjects should perform similarly in the yoked bandwidth and frequency conditions. Subjects practiced for 60 trials a two-segment limb movement task that had a goal movement time of 500 msec. Results showed that the bandwidth-based KR conditions led to better retention performance than the yoked frequency KR conditions. Thus the effect of performance-based bandwidth criterion for giving KR appears to be the result of more than simple frequency effects. Lee and Carnahan proposed that the bandwidth effect is due to combining KR with what the motor control system is capable of doing. That is, early in practice, the system is not capable of correcting errors with the precision required if errors must be corrected within a 5% or 10% tolerance limit. Thus the bandwidth-based KR delivery allows the control system to adapt to the demands of the task and develop appropriate error-correction processes needed to perform the skill correctly and to stabilize performance from one trial to the next. From an applied perspective, the bandwidth procedure provides an interesting means of individualizing the systematic reduction of the frequency of augmented feedback for students. If, as suggested by the results discussed earlier of Winstein and Schmidt (1990), weaning individuals from the need for augmented feedback is beneficial for learning, then providing augmented feedback on the basis of performance-based bandwidths naturally reduces the frequency with which augmented feedback is given. Because the bandwidth is related to individual performance, the "weaning" process becomes one that is specific to the performance of each individual.

Summary KR

Another way to reduce the frequency of KR while providing the same amount of information as if KR were given after every trial is to provide a summary of KR after a certain number of trials during practice. For example, suppose that a person is practicing a shooting skill where he or she cannot see the target because of the distance involved. Efficiency of practice could be increased if that person did not have to receive KR after each shot but could receive KR about each shot after every 10 shots. The question here, however, is how would this influence learning? Since the frequency of KR research has been reasonably consistent in showing that reduced KR frequency does not hinder learning, could learning actually be enhanced by reducing frequency while at the same time providing the same amount of information as if it were given 100% of the time during practice?

An experiment by Schmidt, Young, Swinnen, and Shapiro (1989) effectively demonstrates a current view about providing KR in summary form during practice. In this experiment, which was a replication and extension of an earlier study by Lavery (1962), subjects practiced moving a lever along a trackway to achieve a goal-movement time. During the 90 trials of practice, KR was presented to subjects as a graphical representation on a piece of paper. One group received this KR after every trial; the other three groups received a summary of their performances after 5, 10, or 15 trials. Results showed little differences among the groups during practice or on a retention test given 10 minutes after practice. However, on a retention test given 2 days later, the group that had received KR after every trial performed the worst, while the group who had summary KR every 15 trials performed the best.

The summary KR benefit has been considered to be related to factors similar to the frequency of KR benefit. That is, during the no-KR practice trials, subjects engage in beneficial cognitive processing that is not characteristic of subjects who receive KR after every trial. This processing is speculated to involve working-memory effort related to comparing sensory feedback information with KR, which results in developing a memory representation that does not depend on the presence of KR for retrieval. Thus in both summary and frequency of KR experimental situations, subjects may in effect operate on KR in a similar way. KR is used by subjects simply to compare their own sensory feedback–based performance and to update their developing memory representation of the skill being learned. If this is so, then in the summary conditions, where more trials are summarized than can be effectively stored in working memory, subjects are probably not attending to the complete summary but either to the general trend of their performance over the summarized trials or only to the most recent trials provided. If the latter is what occurs, then the summary condition becomes essentially the same as the frequency-of-KR experimental condition. Some support for this contention has been provided recently by Sidaway, Moore, and Schoenfelder-Zohdi (1991).

THE TIMING OF AUGMENTED FEEDBACK

Several issues relate to the timing aspects of augmented feedback. The first concerns whether it is better to give augmented feedback while the person is practicing, which is known as *concurrent feedback,* or to give it at the end of a practice attempt, which is known as *terminal feedback.* The other issues relate to when augmented feedback is given terminally and concern the two intervals of time between the end of one practice attempt and the beginning of the next. The interval of time between the end of a practice attempt and the giving of augmented feedback is typically referred to as the *KR-delay interval.* The interval that follows giving augmented feedback and the beginning of the next practice trial is the *post-KR interval.* It is clear from the terminology used to describe these two intervals that the research investigating issues related to these intervals has focused on the use of KR as augmented feedback.

Concurrent and Terminal Augmented Feedback

Concurrent Augmented Feedback. When augmented feedback is given concurrently with performing a skill, it is usually in the form of augmented sensory feedback. Two types seem to be the most common. One type involves enhancing the feedback available in the environment. Examples of this type include having a buzzer sound when a target is hit or having a light be on while a response is off-target. The other type is popularly known as biofeedback, which involves providing information about physiological processes through the use of instrumentation. Thus sensory feedback can be augmented by providing an external source of information. Two examples of biofeedback that relates to motor skill learning are having a buzzer sound added to an electromyographic (EMG) signal from a muscle group or augmenting the heartbeat so the person can hear each beat.

For the first type of augmented sensory feedback, there is evidence for two types of effects. One is that the concurrent application of this type of augmented feedback can show initial performance that is very good, but then performance asymptotes and can actually decline on transfer trials where the augmented feedback is removed (e.g., Annett, 1959, 1970; Fox & Levy, 1969; Patrick & Mutlusoy, 1982). In these situations, it appears that learners direct their attention away from the critical sensory feedback related to the movement being made and direct it toward the augmented feedback so that this information becomes a crutch and therefore necessary for future performance (e.g., Karlin & Mortimer, 1963; Lintern & Roscoe, 1980).

The other effect is that the concurrent use of augmented sensory feedback can be an effective training device. Examples of this effect have been reported by Lintern and his colleagues in work related to the training of flight skills for airplane pilots (e.g., Lintern, 1980; Lintern, Roscoe, Koonce, & Segal, 1990; Lintern, Roscoe, & Sivier, 1990). In these experiments, augmented sensory feedback is provided by instrumentation on the control panel of the aircraft. Specific benefits of visual augmentation of feedback have been reported for training pilots in landing and bombing skills. It is worth noting that in these studies, Lintern and his colleagues also have found situations where augmenting feedback is no benefit and where it actually hinders performance. They argue (Lintern, Roscoe, & Sivier, 1990) that learning with augmented feedback will benefit to the extent that the feedback sensitizes the learner to properties or relationships in the task that specify how the system being learned can be controlled.

Another perspective on the type of effect to expect from using concurrent augmented sensory feedback has been provided by Annett (1959, 1969, 1970). He hypothesized that there is probably a maximum usefulness in information value for augmented feedback, which can be related to the informativeness of feedback instrinsic to the task itself. If the task-intrinsic feedback is high, such that the skill could actually be learned without augmented feedback, then to augment this feedback and provide it concurrently while performing can lead to improved learning and does not establish dependence on the augmented feedback. On the other hand, when the task-intrinsic feedback is low, providing augmented sensory feedback concurrently appears to develop a dependency on the augmented feedback. In this latter case, there appears to be a tendency for people to become dependent on the augmented feedback and not to try to discover the critical feedback that their own sensory system is receiving while performing the task.

When EMG biofeedback has been provided concurrently to aid skill learning in rehabilitation settings, beneficial effects typically have been reported (for examples and reviews of research on biofeedback related to motor skill rehabilitation, see Inglis, Campbell, & Donald, 1976; Leiper, Miller, Lang, & Herman, 1981; Sandweiss & Wolf, 1985; Wolf, 1983). A further example can be seen in the work of Mulder and Hulstijn (1984, 1985). In one of their experiments (Mulder & Hulstijn, 1985), subjects practiced a movement that required the abduction of the big toe while keeping the other toes of the foot from moving. While this may seem to be a strange task, the authors argued that the task required subjects to control a specific muscle group to enable the action to occur, a requirement that was common to many of the motor skills that people must learn. Five different feedback conditions were compared. One condition allowed normal proprioceptive feedback, but subjects could not see their foot and received no verbal feedback about their performance. Another condition involved proprioceptive and visual feedback where subjects could see their foot but received no verbal feedback. The third condition provided subjects with proprioceptive, visual, and tactile feedback, where they could see their foot and received tactile feedback from a force meter but received no verbal feedback. Two additional groups received augmented sensory feedback in the form of biofeedback. These groups saw either an EMG signal or a force meter display in addition to normal proprioceptive and visual feedback. Results showed that the two augmented biofeedback groups performed better than the nonaugmented groups on each of the two days of training. However, it is important to note here that, as in many other biofeedback studies, tests of learning were not provided. As a result, we can only speculate concerning the effects on learning—that is, whether the observed effects were temporary performance or were long-lasting learning effects.

Another use of biofeedback as a learning aid was reported by Daniels and Landers (1981) in an experiment involving rifle-shooting training. Concurrently presented augmented heartbeat information was auditorially provided to subjects to assist them in learning to squeeze the rifle trigger between heartbeats, which had been established as characteristic of elite shooters. Results indicated that the use of this form of biofeedback facilitated the acquisition of this important shooting skill and led to improved shooting scores.

Concurrent Versus Terminal Augmented Feedback. While an earlier section of this chapter considered the various effects of using terminal augmented feedback, it will be instructive to consider how concurrent and terminal augmented feedback compare when considered together in an experimental setting. Research in which this comparison has been made has typically considered augmented sensory feedback of the first type described earlier. That is, environmental feedback was augmented by using a mechanical device to signify some performance characteristic, such as being on- or off-target. Some examples of these types of experiments were discussed earlier in this chapter. Experiments by Goldstein and Rittenhouse (1954) and by Annett (1959) described in the section on how essential augmented feedback is to skill learning, provided evidence that terminal feedback for two different types of tasks led to better learning than did concurrent feedback. This result appears to typify most of the research in which these two feedback presentation times were compared (see Armstrong, 1970, for an extensive review of this research).

There is clearly a lack of information available to make an appropriate conclusion about the comparison of concurrently and terminally presented augmented sensory feedback. Unfortunately, research investigating this comparison became virtually nonexistent after the 1960s. This may in part have been due to an increased interest in motor learning on the influence of KR on skill learning, which is terminally presented. This increased interest in KR can be attributed in large measure to the influence of Adams's (1971) theory on motor learning research. However, it is clear that the determination of whether concurrently or terminally presented feedback is better for skill learning depends on the skill being learned. What future research

needs to establish are those task characteristics that will determine, a priori, when concurrently presented augmented feedback works best and when terminally presented feedback works best.

The KR-Delay Interval

The interval of time between the completion of a movement and the presentation of augmented feedback traditionally has been termed the *KR-delay interval,* although Bilodeau (1969) called it the information feedback (IF) delay interval. Because the vast majority of research addressing this interval of time has investigated KR, the term *KR-delay interval* will be used in the present discussion. This time interval has led to much confusion with regard to its relationship to learning. For example, Ammons (1958) proposed that lengthening this interval would lead to poorer learning because the information value of the KR would diminish over time. On the other hand, Adams (1971) concluded that the delay of KR has little or no effect on skill learning. Since the time of these two conclusions, researchers have provided a clearer picture of the actual influence of various manipulations that can be associated with this interval.

To discuss this interval appropriately, it will be best to consider two variables that are commonly manipulated in investigations of the role of the KR-delay interval on skill learning. These two variables are time, or variations in the length of the interval, and activity, which involves investigating cognitive and motor activity during the interval.

The Length of the KR-Delay Interval. One of the early outcomes of studying the KR-delay interval was that distinct contrasts were evident between human and animal learning (see Adams, 1987). Human research established that KR was more than a reward, as KR had informational value that humans used to solve problems, such as to learn a skill. And it became evident that the effect of delaying KR in human skill learning led to different results than what occurred when rewards were delayed in animal learning. Whereas animal learning studies showed that delaying reward led to decreased learning (e.g., Roberts, 1930), human skill-learning studies showed that delaying KR did not influence learning. Perhaps the most striking example of this latter finding is a study by Bilodeau and Bilodeau (1958b). They reported five experiments in which they used tasks such as lever positioning and micrometer dial turning. The KR-delay interval was varied from a few seconds to seven days. The consistent results in all of these experiments was that KR delays, even of up to one week, did not affect learning these skills.

While delaying the presentation of KR does not appear to affect skill learning, there does seem to be a minimum amount of time that must pass before KR is given. In a recent study by Swinnen, Schmidt, Nicholson, and Shapiro (1990), they reported evidence that giving KR too soon after a movement was completed had a negative effect on learning. Two experiments involved learning a task in which subjects moved a lever through a two-reversal movement to achieve a specific movement-time goal (Experiment 1), and learning a coincident timing task where subjects had to make a lever movement that was coincident in time with a target light appearing and that passed by the light with the appropriate rate of speed (Experiment 2). In each experiment, KR was given "instantaneously," which meant that the subjects saw their score immediately upon the completion of the required movement, or KR was delayed for 8 seconds after completing the movement in Experiment 1 or for 3.2 seconds in Experiment 2. In each experiment, the two KR-delay conditions were not different from each other at the end of the practice trials but were significantly different from each other on retention tests given 10 minutes and 2 days later (Experiment 1) and at 10 minutes, 2 days, and 4 months (Experiment 2). The authors proposed that the degrading of learning resulting from providing KR too soon after the completion of a movement was due to the need for learners to engage in the subjective analysis of response-produced feedback, which is essential for developing appropriate error-detection capabilities. This poorly developed capability was not evident until retention tests were given where subjects had to respond without KR and therefore had to rely on their own error-detection capabilities to respond. Delaying KR by only a few seconds appeared to be sufficient to enable subjects to develop this capability while providing KR immediately after completing a movement hindered the development of this capability.

Activity During the KR-Delay Interval. The evidence that has accumulated from the research investigating the effects of activity during the KR-delay interval has provided a variety of results. In some cases, activity has no effect on skill learning, while in other cases, activity has been shown to hinder learning or to benefit learning. Rather than establish a confusing state of affairs, these different results have provided insights into the learning processes in which a learner engages during the KR-delay interval, and they have provided distinct implications for developing effective teaching strategies.

The most common effect of activity during the KR-delay interval on skill learning is that it has *no influence on learning.* Experiments investigating the activity effect have demonstrated this result for over 20 years (e.g., Bilodeau, 1969; Boulter, 1964; Marteniuk, 1986). The experiment by Marteniuk will serve as an appropriate example of the research yielding this conclusion. Subjects practiced a complex lever movement that required them to move a lever to produce a specific sine-wave–like pattern that had both spatial and temporal goals. A control group received KR within a few seconds after completing the movement and engaged in no activity during the KR-delay interval. Another group had a 40-second KR-delay interval but did not engage in any activity during the interval. The third group also had a 40-second KR-delay interval but engaged in a lever movement task in which the subjects attempted to reproduce a move-

ment pattern that the experimenter had just performed. The results of this experiment indicated that during acquisition trials and on a no-KR retention test given 10 minutes later, there were no differences among the groups.

An example of an experiment in which activity during the KR-delay interval *hinders learning* is one that was a part of the study by Marteniuk (1986) referred to in the preceding paragraph. Marteniuk reasoned that the activity of reproducing a movement pattern during the KR-delay interval did not interfere with learning because this activity did not demand the same type of learning processes as did learning the lever movement task. He hypothesized that if the KR-delay interval activity were to interfere with learning, it would have to interfere with the same learning processes as those required by the primary task being learned. Therefore, in two follow-up experiments to the one described above, he added a condition in which subjects had to learn another skill during the KR-delay interval. In one experiment, this skill was another lever-movement skill, while in the other experiment, this skill was a cognitive skill that was a number-guessing task. In both experiments the results indicated that learning another skill during the KR-delay interval interfered with learning the primary skill. This interference effect has also been reported by Shea and Upton (1976), in which subjects engaged in short-term memory tasks during the KR-delay interval, and by Swinnen (1990) in two experiments in which subjects were required to estimate the movement-time error of the experimenter's lever movement performed during the KR-delay interval.

Finally, there have been experiments reported indicating that certain activities during the KR-delay interval can actually *benefit learning.* The first evidence of this beneficial effect of activity was reported by Hogan and Yanowitz (1978). Subjects practiced a task where the goal was to move a handle along a trackway a specified distance of 47 cm in 200 msec. One group did not engage in any activity before receiving KR, while a second group was required to give a verbal estimate of their own error for each trial before receiving KR for that trial. The results showed that while there were no differences between groups at the end of the 50 trials of practice, the group that had engaged in the error-estimation activity during the KR-delay interval performed significantly better on retention trials where no KR was provided. These same error-estimation benefits have been reported in two experiments by Swinnen (1990).

What do these different effects of activity in the KR-delay interval reveal about learning processes that occur during the interval of time? Swinnen (1990; Swinnen et al., 1990) has argued that the learner is actively engaged in processing movement information and detecting errors during the KR-delay interval. During this period of time, learners are involved in self-generated error-estimation activities that may benefit future performance. If the evidence described earlier is viewed from this perspective, then the three different effects of activity during the KR-delay interval would be expected. When learners are encouraged to engage in this type of error-detection activity, as occurred in the experiments by Hogan and Yanowitz (1976) and Swinnen (1990), then learning benefits due to the enhancement of the learner's error-detection capability. However, if learners are engaged in activity that does not permit such self-generation of error estimation, as would appear to have occurred in the experiments by Marteniuk (1986), Shea and Upton (1976), and Swinnen, et al. (1990), where attention-demanding activity was required during the KR-delay interval, then learning is hindered. Finally, if the activity engaged in during this interval is not attention demanding to the degree that the learner can still engage in appropriate error-estimation processing, then learning will not be influenced by the KR-delay interval activity, which was demonstrated in the experiments by Marteniuk (1986) and others.

For instructional purposes, the most significant implication of these results is that students can be engaged in activity following the completion of a movement and before they receive augmented feedback from a teacher or coach that will benefit them. This activity should require them to attempt actively to determine what they did wrong on that particular trial. They should try to answer the question "What do you think you did wrong?" before being told what they did wrong. Based on the research evidence, this type of activity will have a positive influence on skill learning, since it forces the learner to subjectively evaluate his or her own sensory feedback in relation to the response that was just made.

The Post-KR Interval

The interval of time between the presentation of augmented feedback and the beginning of the next trial, or practice attempt, is commonly called the *post-KR interval.* This interval of time became the focus of research interest following research and comments by the Bilodeaus (e.g., Bilodeau & Bilodeau, 1958b; Bilodeau, 1969) and Adams (1971) that this interval may be the most important interval of time during skill acquisition. The basis for this view was that the post-KR interval represents the period of time during which the learner has both his or her own sensory feedback and the externally provided augmented feedback about the response just made, and he or she must use this information to develop a plan of action for the next trial. Accordingly, the amount of time available for this processing and the activity that may occur concurrently with it became the variables of interest for research about the post-KR interval.

The Length of the Post-KR Interval. The expectations of how the length of the post-KR interval would influence skill learning are similar to those discussed earlier for the KR-delay interval. That is, there would appear to be an optimal range of time during which the next trial should occur after KR is given. If the next trial occurs too soon after KR, then the important processing activities would not have sufficient time to be carried out. Or if the next trial is delayed for too long after KR is given, then some forgetting will

occur and the next response will not be as good as it would have been otherwise. This reasoning seems logical and indeed has been stated before by others (e.g., Adams, 1971).

What is interesting here is that the only empirical support for these expectations relates to the "too early" end of the time continuum just described. This evidence was reported by Weinberg, Guy, and Tupper (1964) as they demonstrated that for learning a limb-positioning movement, a 1-second post-KR interval led to poorer acquisition than did a 5-, 10-, or 20-second interval. None of these latter three interval lengths revealed any differences. A similar finding indicating the need for a minimum post-KR interval length was reported by Rogers (1974). What is particularly noteworthy in this study is that the variable of primary interest was the degree of precision of KR. In the first experiment, evidence was found that when micrometer settings were given as direction and quantity of error to the nearest thousandth of a unit, a post-KR interval of 7 seconds led to acquisition as poor as when only direction of error was given. Subjects who received direction and quantity of error to the nearest tenth or one-hundredth of a unit performed better. However, when a 14-second post-KR interval was used in the second experiment, subjects learned the skill with this precise information better than those who had received the qualitative KR. Gallagher and Thomas (1980) reported similar results for children. Thus, similar to the KR-delay interval, there appears to be some minimum amount of time needed to engage in the learning processes required during the KR-delay interval if optimal learning is to be achieved. What is not known, and will await further research, is how this minimum amount of time changes as a function of the skill being learned or as a function of the stage of learning of the learner.

With respect to the other end of the optimum range of time for the next trial to begin following KR being given, there is no evidence indicating that too long a delay will hinder learning. An example of the type of research addressing this question was reported by Magill (1977), who compared post-KR interval lengths of 10 and 60 seconds for subjects learning three limb positions on a curvilinear positioning device. Results showed no differences between these two interval lengths.

Activity During the Post-KR Interval. Here again the effect of engaging in activity is similar to what was seen for the KR-delay interval. Depending on the kind of activity, the effect can be to interfere with learning, to benefit learning, or to have no influence on learning. The interesting feature of these different effects is that these are not in line with traditional predictions of the effect of activity during the post-KR interval. Earlier views of KR (e.g., Adams, 1971; Bilodeau, 1969; Newell, 1976) typically suggested that because so many important information-processing activities occurred during this interval, engaging in other activity during this time would interfere with learning. But more recent evidence has shown that this is only one of three effects that can occur.

That activity during the post-KR interval has *no effect* on skill learning has clearly been the most common finding. An example of this result is seen in an experiment reported by Lee and Magill (1983). Subjects practiced making an arm movement through a series of three small wooden barriers in 1,050 msec. During the post-KR interval, one group engaged in a motor activity of learning the same movement in 1,350 msec, one group engaged in a cognitive activity involving number guessing, and a third group did not do any activity. At the end of the practice trials, the two activity groups showed poorer performance than the nonactivity group. However, on a no-KR retention test, the three groups did not differ from each other.

Results indicating *detrimental effects* of activity during the post-KR interval have been reported by several researchers (e.g., Benedetti & McCullagh, 1987; Boucher 1974; Hardy, 1983; Swinnen, 1990, Experiment 3). Of these experiments, only those by Benedetti and McCullagh (1987) and Swinnen (1990) included an appropriate test for learning. In both of these experiments, the interfering activity was a cognitive activity. Subjects in the experiment by Benedetti and McCullagh engaged in a mathematics problem–solving task while subjects in the experiment by Swinnen were involved in guessing the movement-time error of the experimenter's lever movement made during the post-KR interval.

Only one experiment has reported *beneficial learning* effects for activity in the post-KR interval. An experiment reported by Magill (1988) involved subjects in learning to perform a two-component movement in which each component had its own criterion movement time. One group was required to learn two additional two-component movements during the post-KR interval and one group was required to learn a mirror-tracing task. A third group did not engage in activity during the post-KR interval. Results showed different effects for retention and transfer. When subjects were asked to perform the skill on a no-KR retention test given one day after practice, there were no group differences. However, on a transfer test where subjects had to perform a new two-component task, similar to the one they had learned, the two post-KR interval activity groups performed better than the no-activity group. These beneficial transfer effects were proposed to be due to the increased problem-solving activity experience during practice by the post-KR interval activity groups, which enabled them to transfer more successfully to a situation that required new problem-solving activity of a kind similar to that experienced in practice.

Research is critically needed to further explore the post-KR interval. At present, only logical argument exists to support the nature of the processing activity that occurs during this interval. While different effects on learning have been reported for different types of activity during this interval, it is not yet clear what produces these different effects nor what the implications are of these different effects for determining the processing activity characterizing the post-KR interval. In terms of instructional implications, the evidence related to this interval suggest that it is not an interval that needs to be given much direct concern in teach-

ing settings. Although there appears to be a minimum post-KR interval length, this minimum does not seem problematic when applied to the typical teaching situation. And although some activities have been found to be both detrimental and beneficial to skill learning, it is clear that more evidence is needed to address these effects before instruction applications can be made with confidence.

Summary

One of the benefits of investigating issues related to the timing of providing augmented feedback is that it provides a means of addressing questions concerning learning processes involved between trials during practice. It seems clear from the evidence discussed in this section that attention to processing of sensory feedback critical to performing the skill is important for effective skill learning. Evidence for this was provided in studies showing the problems that can result from providing augmented feedback concurrently with performing the skill. The typical finding seems to be that this form of presentation of augmented feedback establishes a dependence on the availability of this external information by shifting the learner's attention away from sensory feedback related to task performance to the augmented feedback itself. Also, the processing of the sensory feedback seems critical, as both the KR-delay and post-KR intervals can be too short to allow optimal learning. Further support for this need for processing sensory feedback was seen in experiments where subjects who estimated their own error prior to receiving KR learned the skill better than those who did not.

CONCLUSION

In this chapter, diverse issues related to augmented feedback and skill learning and performance have been discussed. One of the common messages that characterized the discussion of each of these issues was that more research is needed. One of the reasons for this need can be related to the resurgence in interest in augmented feedback that resulted in large part to the review and reassessment of the KR literature by Salmoni, Schmidt, and Walter (1984) and to current controversies existing concerning the role of cognition in motor skill learning and performance (see Meijer & Roth, 1988, for an example of a current controversy here). The Salmoni et al. review established the need to distinguish between the effect of various manipulations of KR on learning from the effect on performance. Learning, they argued, as have others (e.g., Magill, 1989; Schmidt, 1988) should only be inferred when appropriate tests of learning have been administered following a practice period. These tests can be retention tests given at some later time after a period of no practice, or they can be transfer tests, where people must perform the practiced skill in a new context or under new conditions, or where people must perform a novel variation of the practiced skill. The reason for the need for such tests is that performance during practice, when augmented feedback is available, may be different when that feedback is not available. This effect has been shown in the investigation of several different issues related to augmented feedback, such as the frequency of KR and the KR-delay interval. Performance at the end of practice with KR available may not be indicative of performance at some time in the future when KR will not be available.

The controversy over the role of cognition in skill learning and performance is a relevant concern for the investigation of augmented feedback, especially if that feedback is verbal information. KR, for example, represents cognitive information provided to a person who is learning a skill. The degree to which cognitive processes are involved in skill learning can in many ways be reflected by the degree to which interventions with variables such as KR influence the course of skill learning. As this controversy continues, it would seem that interest in the study of augmented feedback will continue to expand. Effects related to augmented feedback manipulations must be accounted for in theories of motor skill learning.

Finally a very practical reason to increase the study of augmented feedback relates to its popular use as an instructional strategy. If teachers and coaches are convinced that providing augmented feedback is important for skill learning and performance, then research is needed to determine if this conviction is valid. If it is, then research is also needed to establish how to most effectively implement the provision of augmented feedback. There is evidence developing, for example, that suggests that the role given verbal feedback by teachers of motor skills is an exaggerated one (see Magill, 1991) and may not be the critical variable many textbooks and teacher-behavior assessment instruments assume. As doubts such as this arise, it becomes increasingly important that an appropriate knowledge base be developed about the role of augmented feedback in skill acquisition and performance.

References

Adams, J. A. (1964). Motor skills. In P. R. Farnsworth (Ed.), *Annual review of psychology* (pp. 181–202). Palo Alto, CA: Annual Reviews.

Adams, J. A. (1971). A closed-loop theory of motor learning. *Journal of Motor Behavior, 3,* 111–149.

Adams, J. A. (1978). Theoretical issues for knowledge of results. In G. E. Stelmach (Ed.), *Information processing in motor control and learning* (pp. 229–240). New York: Academic Press.

Adams, J. A. (1987). Historical review and appraisal of research on learning, retention, and transfer of human motor skills. *Psychological Bulletin, 101,* 41–74.

Annett, J. (1959). Learning a pressure under conditions of immediate and delayed knowledge of results. *Quarterly Journal of Experimental Psychology, 11,* 3–15.

Annett, J. (1969). *Feedback and human behavior.* Baltimore: Penguin.

Annett, J. (1970). The role of action feedback in the acquisition of simple motor responses. *Journal of Motor Behavior, 11,* 217–221.

Armstrong, T. R. (1970). *Feedback and perceptual-motor skill learning: A review of information feedback and manual guidance training techniques.* Technical Report No. 25, Human Performance Center, University of Michigan.

Benedetti, C., & McCullagh, P. M. (1987). Post-knowledge of results delay: Effects of interpolated activity on learning and performance. *Research Quarterly for Exercise and Sport, 58,* 375–381.

Bilodeau, E. A., & Bilodeau, I. M. (1958a). Variable frequency of knowledge of results and the learning of a simple skill. *Journal of Experimental Psychology, 55,* 379–383.

Bilodeau, E. A., & Bilodeau, I. M. (1958b). Variation of temporal intervals among critical events in five studies of knowledge of results. *Journal of Experimental Psychology, 55,* 603–612.

Bilodeau, E. A., Bilodeau, I. M., & Schumsky, D. A. (1959). Some effects of introducing and withdrawing knowledge of results early and late in practice. *Journal of Experimental Psychology, 58,* 142–144.

Bilodeau, I. M. (1969). Information feedback. In E. A. Bilodeau (Ed.), *Principles of skill acquisition* (pp. 225–285). New York: Academic Press.

Boucher, J. L. (1974). Higher processes in motor learning. *Journal of Motor Behavior, 6,* 131–137.

Boulter, L. R. (1964). Evaluations of mechanisms in delay of knowledge of results. *Canadian Journal of Psychology, 18,* 281–291.

Buekers, M. J. A., Magill, R. A., & Hall, K. G. (1992). The effect of erroneous knowledge of results on skill acquisition when augmented information is redundant. *Quarterly Journal of Experimental Psychology, 44A,* 105–117.

Buekers, M. J. A., Magill, R. A., & Sneyers, K. M. (1991). *Resolving a conflict between sensory feedback and knowledge of results while learning a motor skill.* Manuscript submitted for publication.

Daniels, F. S., & Landers, D. M. (1981). Biofeedback and shooting performance: A test of disregulation and systems theory. *Journal of Sport Psychology, 3,* 271–282.

Eghan, T. (1988). *The relation of teacher feedback to student achievement in learning selected tennis skills.* Unpublished doctoral dissertation, Louisiana State University, Baton Rouge.

Elwell, J. L., & Grindley, G. C. (1938). The effect of knowledge of results on learning and performance. I. A co-ordinated movement of both hands. *British Journal of Psychology, 29,* 39–54.

Fishman, S., & Tobey, C. (1978). Augmented feedback. In W. G. Anderson & G. Barrette (Eds.), *What's going on in gym: Descriptive studies of physical education classes. Motor Skills: Theory into Practice, Monograph 1,* 51–62.

Fox, P. W., & Levy, C. M. (1969). Acquisition of a simple motor response as influenced by the presence or absence of action visual feedback. *Journal of Motor Behavior, 1,* 169–180.

Gallagher, J. D., & Thomas, J. R. (1980). Effects of varying post-KR intervals upon children's motor performance. *Journal of Motor Behavior, 12,* 41–46.

Goldstein, M., & Rittenhouse, C. H. (1954). Knowledge of results in the acquisition and transfer of a gunnery skill. *Journal of Experimental Psychology, 48,* 187–196.

Gordon, N. B., & Gottlieb, M. J. (1967). Effect of supplemental visual cues on rotary pursuit. *Journal of Experimental Psychology, 75,* 566–568.

Hardy, C. J. (1983). The post-knowledge of results interval: Effects of interpolated activity on cognitive information processing. *Research Quarterly for Exercise and Sport, 54,* 144–148.

Hatze, H. (1976). Biomechanical aspects of a successful motion organization. In P. Komi (Ed.), *Biomechanics V–B* (pp. 5–12). Baltimore: University Press.

Ho, L., & Shea, J. B. (1978). Effects of relative frequency of knowledge of results on retention of a motor skill. *Perceptual and Motor Skills, 46,* 859–866.

Hogan, J., & Yanowitz, B. (1978). The role of verbal estimates of movement error in ballistic skill acquisition. *Journal of Motor Behavior, 10,* 133–138.

Inglis, J., Campbell, D., & Donald, M.W. (1976). Electromyographic biofeedback and neuromuscular rehabilitation. *Canadian Journal of Behavioral Science, 8,* 299–323.

Karlin, L., & Mortimer, R. G. (1963). Effect of verbal, visual, and auditory augmenting cues on learning a complex motor skill. *Journal of Experimental Psychology, 65,* 75–79.

Landauer, T. K., & Bjork, R. A. (1978). Optimal rehearsal patterns and name learning. In M. M. Gruneberg, P. E. Morris, & R. N. Sykes (Eds.), *Practical aspects of memory* (pp. 625–632). New York: Academic Press.

Lavery, J. J. (1962). Retention of simple motor skills as a function of type of knowledge of results. *Canadian Journal of Psychology, 16,* 300–311.

Lee, T. D., & Carnahan, H. (1990). Bandwidth knowledge of results and motor learning: More than just a relative frequency effect. *Quarterly Journal of Experimental Psychology, 42A,* 777–789.

Lee, T. D., & Magill, R. A. (1983). Activity during the post-KR interval: Effects upon performance or learning. *Research Quarterly for Exercise and Sport, 54,* 340–345.

Lee, T. D., White, M. A., & Carnahan, H. (1990). On the role of knowledge of results in motor learning: Exploring the guidance hypothesis. *Journal of Motor Behavior, 22,* 191–208.

Leiper, C. I., Miller, A., Lang, L., & Herman, R. (1981). Sensory feedback for head control in cerebral palsy. *Physical Therapy, 61,* 512–518.

Lewthwaite, R. (1990). Motivational considerations in physical activity involvement. *Physical Therapy, 70,* 808–819.

Lindahl, L. G. (1945). Movement analysis as an industrial training method. *Journal of Applied Psychology, 29,* 420–436.

Lintern, G. (1980). Transfer of landing skill after training with supplementary visual cues. *Human Factors, 22,* 81–88.

Lintern, G., & Roscoe, S. N. (1980). Visual cue augmentation in contact flight simulation. In S. N. Roscoe (Ed.), *Aviation psychology* (pp. 227–238). Ames, IA: Iowa State University Press.

Lintern, G., Roscoe, S. N., Koonce, J. M., & Segal, L. D. (1990). Transfer of landing skills in beginning flight training. *Human Factors, 32,* 319–327.

Lintern, G., Roscoe, S. N., & Sivier (1990). Display principles, control dynamics, and environmental factors in pilot training and transfer. *Human Factors, 32,* 299–317.

Little, W. S., & McCullagh, P. (1989). Motivation orientation and modeled instruction strategies: The effects on form and accuracy. *Journal of Sport and Exercise Psychology, 11,* 41–53.

Locke, E. A., Cartledge, N., & Koeppel, J. (1968). Motivational effects of knowledge of results: A goal-setting phenomenon. *Psychological Bulletin, 70,* 474–485.

Lorge, I., & Thorndike, E. L. (1935). The influence of the delay in the aftereffect of a connection. *Journal of Experimental Psychology, 18,* 186–194.

Magill, R. A. (1988). Activity during the post-knowledge of results interval can benefit motor skill learning. In O. G. Meijer & K. Roth (Eds.), *Complex motor behaviour: "The" motor-action controversy* (pp. 231–246). Amsterdam: North-Holland.

Magill, R. A. (1989). *Motor learning: Concepts and applications* (3rd ed.). Dubuque, IA: Brown.

Magill, R. A. (1991). *The exaggerated role of verbal feedback in motor skill learning.* Manuscript submitted for publication.

Magill, R. A., Chamberlin, C. J., & Hall, K. G. (1991). Verbal knowledge of results as redundant information for learning an anticipation timing skill. *Human Movement Science, 10,* 485–507.

Magill, R. A., & Wood, C. A. (1986). Knowledge of results as a learning variable in motor skill acquisition. *Research Quarterly for Exercise and Sport, 57,* 170–173.

Marteniuk, R. G. (1986). Information processes in movement learning: Capacity and structural interference. *Journal of Motor Behavior, 18,* 249–259.

Meijer, O.G., & Roth, K. (Eds.) (1988). *Complex motor behaviour: "The" motor-action controversy.* Amsterdam: North-Holland.

Mulder, T., & Hulstijn, W. (1984). Sensory feedback therapy and theoretical knowledge of motor control and learning. *American Journal of Physical Medicine, 63,* 226–244.

Mulder, T., & Hulstijn, W. (1985). Sensory feedback in the learning of a novel motor task. *Journal of Motor Behavior, 17,* 110–128.

Newell, K. M. (1974). Knowledge of results and motor learning. *Journal of Motor Behavior, 6,* 235–244.

Newell, K. M. (1976). Knowlege of results and motor learning. In J. Keogh & R. S. Hutton (Eds.), *Exercise and sport sciences reviews* (Vol. 4, pp. 196–228). Santa Barbara, CA: Journal Publishing Affiliates.

Newell, K. M., & McGinnis, P. M. (1985). Kinematic information feedback for skilled performance. *Human Learning, 4,* 39–56.

Newell, K. M., Morris, L. R., & Scully, D. M. (1985). Augmented information and the acquisition of skill in physical activity. In R. J. Terjung (Ed.), *Exercise and sport sciences reviews* (Vol. 13, pp 235–261). New York: Macmillan.

Newell, K. M., Quinn, J. T., Jr., Sparrow, W. A., & Walter, C. B. (1983). Kinematic information feedback for learning a rapid arm movement. *Human Movement Science, 2,* 255–269.

Patrick, J., & Mutlusoy, F. (1982). The relationship between types of feedback, gain of a display and feedback precision in acquisition of a simple motor task. *Quarterly Journal of Experimental Psychology, 34A,* 171–182.

Pieron, M. (1982). Effectiveness of teaching a psychomotor task: Study in a micro-teaching setting. In M. Pieron & J. Cheffers (Eds.), *Studying the teaching of physical education* (pp. 79–89). Liège, Belgium: Association Internationale des Écoles Superieures d'Education Physique.

Proteau, L., & Cournoyer, J. (1990). Vision of the stylus in a manual aiming task: The effects of practice. *Quarterly Journal of Experimental Psychology, 42B,* 811–828.

Proteau, L., Marteniuk, R.G., Girouard, Y., & Dugas, C. (1987). On the type of information used to control and learn an aiming movement after moderate and extensive training. *Human Movement Science, 6,* 181–199.

Reeve, T. G., & Magill, R. A. (1981). Role of components of knowledge of results information in error correction. *Research Quarterly for Exercise and Sport, 52,* 80–85.

Roberts, W. H. (1930). The effect of delayed feeding on white rats in a problem cage. *Journal of Genetic Psychology, 37,* 35–38.

Salmoni, A. W., Schmidt, R. A., & Walter, C. B. (1984). Knowledge of results and motor learning: A review and reappraisal. *Psychological Bulletin, 95*, 355–386.

Sandweiss, J. H., & Wolf, S. L. (Eds.) (1985). *Biofeedback and sports science.* New York: Plenum.

Schmidt, R. A. (1975). A schema theory of discrete motor skill learning. *Psychological Review, 82*, 225–260.

Schmidt, R. A. (1988). *Motor control and learning: A behavioral emphasis* (2nd ed.). Champaign, IL: Human Kinetics.

Schmidt, R. A., & Young, D. E. (1991). Methodology for motor learning: A paradigm for kinematic feedback. *Journal of Motor Behavior, 23*, 13–24.

Schmidt, R. A., Young, D. E., Swinnen, S., & Shapiro, D. C. (1989). Summary knowledge of results for skill acquisition: Support for the guidance hypothesis. *Journal of Experimental Psychology: Learning, Memory, and Cognition, 15*, 352–359.

Selder, D. J., & Del Rolan, N. (1979). Knowledge of performance, skill level and performance on a balance beam. *Canadian Journal of Applied Sport Sciences, 4*, 226–229.

Shea, J. B., & Upton, G. (1976). The effects on skill acquisition of an interpolated motor short-term memory task during the KR-delay interval. *Journal of Motor Behavior, 8*, 277–281.

Sherwood, D. E. (1988). Effect of bandwidth knowledge of results on movement consistency. *Perceptual and Motor Skills, 66*, 535–542.

Sidaway, B., Moore, B., & Schoenfelder-Zohdi, B. (1991). Summary and frequency of KR presentation effects on retention of a motor skill. *Research Quarterly for Exercise and Sport, 62*, 27–32.

Siedentop, D. (1983). *Developing teaching skills in physical education* (2nd ed.). Palo Alto, CA: Mayfield.

Silverman, S., Tyson, L. A., & Morford, L. M. (1988). Relationships of organization, time, and student achievement in physical education. *Teaching and Teacher Education, 4*, 247–257.

Silverman, S., Tyson, L. A., & Krampitz, J. (1991, April). *Teacher feedback and achievement in physical education: Interaction with student practice.* Paper presented at the annual meeting of the American Educational Research Association, Chicago.

Smoll, F. L. (1972). Effects of precision of information feedback upon acquisition of a motor skill. *Research Quarterly, 43*, 489–493.

Stelmach, G. E. (1970). Learning and response consistency with augmented feedback. *Ergonomics, 13*, 421–425.

Swinnen, S. P. (1990). Interpolated activities during the knowledge-of-results delay and post–knowledge-of-results interval: Effects on performance and learning. *Journal of Experimental Psychology: Learning, Memory, and Cognition, 16*, 692–705.

Swinnen, S. P., Schmidt, R. A., Nicholson, D. E., & Shapiro, D. C. (1990). Information feedback for skill acquisition: Instantaneous knowledge of results degrades learning. *Journal of Experimental Psychology: Learning, Memory, and Cognition, 16*, 706–716.

Thorndike, E. L. (1927). The law of effect. *American Journal of Psychology, 39*, 212–222.

Wallace, S. A., & Hagler, R. W. (1979). Knowledge of performance and the learning of a closed motor skill. *Research Quarterly, 50*, 265–271.

Williams, A. C., & Briggs, G. E. (1962). On-target versus off-target information and the acquisition of tracking skill. *Journal of Experimental Psychology, 64*, 519–525.

Winstein, C. J., & Schmidt, R. A. (1990). Reduced frequency of knowledge of results enhances motor skill learning. *Journal of Experimental Psychology: Learning, Memory, and Cognition, 16*, 677–691.

Wolf, S. L. (1983). Electromyographic biofeedback applications to stroke patients: A critical review. *Physical Therapy, 63*, 1448–1455.

9

ARRANGING PRACTICE CONDITIONS AND DESIGNING INSTRUCTION

Craig Chamberlin

Timothy Lee

The main intent in writing this chapter is to identify a number of factors that influence the arrangement of practice conditions and the design of instruction. The overriding theme will be to determine how these factors influence the performance and learning of motor skills, and in particular, their impact on retention and transfer. Before beginning this undertaking, however, a few words of caution must be offered.

The practice environment is exceedingly complex, and the impact of practice on the learning and performance of a motor skill is the result of a dynamic interaction of a large number of variables. Absolute statements regarding the effectiveness of a particular practice condition are not possible. Rather, we hope to examine various areas of research that have received concentrated attention with the goal of highlighting the empirical parameters that characterize the literature. Where appropriate, an attempt will be made to provide tentative emergent principles that have some justification based on the relevant body of literature. Perhaps due to the complex nature of the practice environment, it became apparent, after reviewing the literature, that few substantive principles could be identified. Thus, as is indicated throughout this chapter, few issues regarding our topic of interest have reached a stage of closure, and the need for further research is evident.

Finally, due to the nature of the practice condition arrangement topic and the relevant literature, a number of factors will be considered as relatively independent entities. That is, each section of this chapter could be considered a "small whole" rather than a part. The central theme that runs throughout each section, however, is the impact of that particular factor (or practice consideration) on the

learning and performance of motor skills. More specifically of interest is how the manipulation of each factor might affect the transfer of learning from the acquisition stage (practice) to test an evaluation condition (context). The somewhat bewildering array of potential factors that can be considered by an instructor is indicative of how complex it is to provide learners with the optimal conditions for learning and performance in the practice environment.

This chapter is comprised of five parts. The first one provides historical perspective on the investigation of practice conditions and identifies a number of general concerns that are relevant to interpreting the related literature. The second part outlines the current status regarding theories underlying the transfer of learning effect. Instructional concerns, particularly the provision of information to an individual prior to performance of a motor skill, are discussed in the third part. The fourth part will deal with the arrangement of practice conditions. A summary is presented in the fifth part.

HISTORICAL AND GENERAL CONCERNS

A HISTORICAL PERSPECTIVE

The study of practice conditions has its experimental roots in the work of Ebbinghaus (1885/1964), whose research interest was the learning and retention of verbal materials. Ebbinghaus investigated a variety of experimental conditions that are still a concern over a century later (Gorfein & Hoffman, 1987). Research on practice conditions using motor skills began after Ebbinghaus and, by the late 1920s, there was a large body of empirical data regarding the effects of various types of practice conditions on the learning and performance of a variety of tasks (see McGeoch, 1927, 1929, 1931, for reviews).

"MOTOR" LEARNING?

Discussion of the empirical work on practice conditions in the early part of the century shifted freely between verbal and motor tasks. Indeed, "motor" tasks might better be considered in terms of one or more continua. Consider a verbal/motor continuum, for example. A task such as card sorting, where the subject's goal is to sort a deck of cards by placing them in specific spatial locations as rapidly as possible, might be considered well toward the verbal end of the continuum. Learning the task is primarily a verbal/spatial problem. Various types of finger mazes might also be considered primarily verbal. Learning a sequential, two-choice (left or right) maze can be accomplished by learning the sequence "LLRLRRRLRLRR". In contrast, a blindfolded line-drawing task may be considered as more motor on this continuum, since often the movements are ballistic in nature and performed in the absence of visual feedback (e.g., Thorndike, 1927).

Deciding what types of tasks to review when considering the effects of practice conditions on "motor" learning is rather arbitrary. Although we consider a wide range of simple tasks in this chapter, we have limited our discussion to those tasks in which the motor component serves more than just a perfunctory role (such as writing as many words as possible in a free-recall experiment).

THE LEARNING VS. PERFORMANCE DISTINCTION.

The need to distinguish between effects of practice variables on *performance,* versus their effect on *learning,* evolved from the animal-conditioning literature. Two paradigms for animal conditioning dominated the research in this area, and a common underlying distinction between performance and learning existed. The classical conditioning paradigm was popularized by Pavlov. It showed how a previously nonassociated relation between a stimulus and a response could become associated if the (to-be-conditioned) stimulus was presented together with another (unconditioned) stimulus, one that normally elicited the response. The effect on learning was examined by removing the unconditioned stimulus. The degree to which the relation between the conditioned stimulus and the response had been learned was evaluated in terms of how often the presentation of the conditioned stimulus could reliably elicit the response during this "extinction" period. In essence, there was a need to make an assessment of the learning effect that was independent of the conditions under which the learning had occurred.

The instrumental learning paradigm used reward (or re-inforcement) as the key variable in learning. Under this paradigm, a behavior was selectively reinforced, often with positive reinforcement (such as food), or sometimes with negative reinforcement (such as shock). Of particular interest here were experiments investigating a variety of reinforcement schedules. In studies of this type, reinforcement was provided every time a behavior occurred, or only on a proportion of the responses. If proportional, they could be provided according to a fixed schedule (such as every fifth response), or a variable schedule (such that the average was every five responses). Learning under these schedules of practice conditions was assessed by removing the reinforcement and examining how long (or often) the learned response continued to be given. (Often factors that resulted in faster acquisition of the response, such as continued reinforcement, also resulted in faster extinction of the response, relative to a condition such as a variable-ratio schedule.)

Results from the research using these animal-conditioning paradigms made us aware of the distinction between learning and performance. In many cases, the schedule that led to better performance during the acquisition of a task was not necessarily the schedule that resulted in the best performance when subjects were later tested under common conditions. Thus, it can be seen that research on conditions of practice in motor skills acquisition has some of its roots in animal conditioning.

MEASURES OF LEARNING

The literature on conditions of practice will be reviewed by referring to how *performance* is affected during the trials under which the conditions are manipulated, and by referring to how *learning* is affected by performance on a retention or transfer test. Although the evaluation of performance effects is relatively straightforward, the assessment of learning effects is not that simple. Performance is directly observable and measurable. Learning must be inferred from performance. Schmidt (1971, 1972, 1988) has provided an extensive evaluation of various measures of motor learning, and these have recently been applied to the specific evaluation of distribution-of-practice effects (Lee & Genovese, 1988). In their review, Lee and Genovese (1988) referred to a study by Bourne and Archer (1956) to illustrate how the various measures of learning could lead to widely disparate interpretations of the effects on learning of rest between practice trials. Separate groups of subjects practiced for 21 trials on a pursuit rotor-tracking task. The groups differed in terms of the amount of rest between 30-second trials: 0, 15, 30, 45, or 60 seconds of rest. Following this practice period, all groups were given a 5-minute rest, and then performed 9 transfer trials under a common, massed-practice condition (i.e., all groups performed with 0 seconds between trials). The results of the Bourne and Archer experiment are reprinted in Figure 9–1.

Four measures of learning may be contrasted that exemplify how conditions of practice have previously been com-

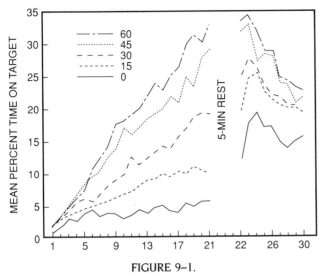

FIGURE 9–1.

From "Time continuously on target as a function of distribution of practice" by L. E. Bourne Jr. & E. J. Archer, 1956, *Journal of Experimental Psychology*, 51, 27. Copyright 1956 by the APA. Reprinted by permission.

pared. One measure that is readily discounted is the comparison of groups over practice trials. This analysis involves a comparison of *learning curves*. Under this analysis, the *amount* of improvement over practice and the *rate* at which improvement occurs are used as the basis for discussing learning effects. As noted in the previous discussion, however, the use of learning curves (which might be more appropriately called practice curves or acquisition curves) ignores the effectiveness of practice as measured by retention or transfer tests. Learning curves also may give a false impression of the relative permanence of changes in performance. The remaining measures use retention trials as the basis for the evaluation of learning.

One method of using the retention data is to express learning in terms of comparing the performance at the end of practice trials with the performance on retention trials. For example, the transfer performance of the most massed group (0 seconds between trials) in the Bourne and Archer study improved by about 6.8 seconds, compared to the tracking performance at the end of the acquisition trials. The most distributed group (60 seconds between acquisition trials), however, improved by only 1.0 second of tracking time-on-target. This measure of learning is termed *relative* retention, since the retention performance is considered relative to the level of performance that had been attained at the end of practice. For this measure, the relative savings (or improvement, in this case) of the final level in performance achieved as a function of practice is the measure of the amount learned.

A similar method is to express the relative retention measure in terms of the amount of improvement that had occurred during practice. Such a method uses the relative retention score as the numerator, divided by the amount of improvement from the beginning to the end of acquisition. This measure may be termed the *percent relative retention*. Expressed in this way, the 0-second group demonstrated a

142.7% relative improvement, whereas the 60-second group had only a 3.2% relative improvement. The percent of relative retention expresses the amount learned in terms of the savings (or improvement) relative to the amount of original improvement.

A measure of learning that is different from the above two methods incorporates only the retention scores as the basis for comparison. Performance during the acquisition trials is ignored for the purposes of examining the effects on learning. One method of calculating this *absolute* measure of retention is to compare the groups on the first trial of retention. Another method would be to average one or more scores over a number of retention trials. In both cases, the group that had maximum distributed practice in the Bourne and Archer study resulted in the best retention scores (an absolute retention score of 34.0 seconds on trial 22, and an average retention score of 28.2 seconds over the 9 massed-retention trials. In contrast, the most massed condition had an absolute retention score on trial 22 of 12.3 seconds, and an average retention score of 15.9 seconds. The absolute retention measure of learning makes no conclusion about "how much" or "how rapidly" a motor task was learned. Rather, it provides a measure upon which the effectiveness of various practice conditions can be compared when all groups perform on a common test.

Data from the Bourne and Archer groups are expressed in Table 9–1 in terms of these measures of learning. This analysis presents a clear dichotomy of interpretations. When retention is expressed relative to practice performance, both measures (relative retention and percent of relative retention) may be used to argue that learning is better as a function of *decreasing* the time between acquisition trials. However, when retention is expressed in absolute terms, whether it be the first trial or averaged over retention trials, the interpretation supported is that learning is better as a function of *increasing* the time between trials.

Deciding which interpretation is correct depends, to some extent, on theoretical presumptions (Christina & Shea, 1988; Newell, Antoniou, & Carlton, 1988). However, Schmidt makes a very strong case that relative retention and percent of relative retention are contaminated measures of learning. Since performance during acquisition trials is not always a reliable indication of learning, the use of a performance score in the calculation of these relative retention

TABLE 9–1. A comparison of various measures of learning using the Bourne and Archer (1956) practice distribution results

Group*	Relative Retention	% Relative Retention	Absolute Retention	Avg. Abs. Retention
0	6.8	142.7	12.3	15.9
15	9.4	102.2	19.6	21.5
30	5.5	29.7	25.0	23.3
45	2.8	10.1	32.0	26.1
60	1.0	3.2	34.0	28.2

*Defined in terms of the length of the intertrial rest periods (in seconds).

measures contaminates the assessment of learning, especially when the research question deals with practice variables that *are designed to affect practice performance*. However, we do not imply that relative measures of retention performance are not useful in other areas of motor learning. For example, these measures are very useful and valuable measures of individual differences in the amount and rate of learning. Our contention is that when groups of subjects are performing in conditions of practice that affect performance, by their very nature, then, any measure of retention that uses a practice performance score biases that assessment of learning.)

The absolute retention score, though limited in that it only measures learning following one practice condition *relative* to another condition, provides the most objective and uncontaminated measure of learning. The decision as to whether to use the first retention score or an average of retention scores is problematic. Undoubtedly, the first score provides the best single trial score. However, single trials are not as statistically reliable as an average over trials (Henry, 1967; Whitley & Smith, 1963). But averaging over retention trials brings with it the possible confound that subjects of different groups are improving during these trials at different rates. The research reported in this chapter generally has made use of a one-trial measure or an average.

THE RELATIONSHIP BETWEEN PRACTICE AND RETENTION/TRANSFER

The theoretical concerns that stimulated research on practice condition arrangements are not given a prominent role in this chapter. Nevertheless, it is important to consider briefly the theoretical issues that precipitated much of the empirical work in this area. These issues revolve around the relationship between practice and retention/transfer. In particular, the concern is with the relation between conditions of practice and conditions of retention and transfer.

GENERALITY

The doctrine of formal discipline was popularized by educational psychologists late in the 19th century (e.g., Angell, 1908; Pillsbury, 1908). The doctrine suggested that the mind was comprised of a number of faculties, or general intellectual abilities. Improvement of these abilities required that the mind engage in the process of thought. It mattered less *what* was thought than the *effort* with which the thought was undertaken. As reiterated by Singley and Anderson (1989), the doctrine treated the mind as something to be exercised, just as one would exercise a set of muscles. The intensity of the "exercise" was the factor of greatest importance to the growth of intellectual capability. Further, the capability for transfer was considered to be very general.

In motor skills, a common view of generality is the layperson's explanation of the "all-around athlete." Although supported by very little experimental evidence, a common version of this view is that a child possesses an overall capability to perform motor skills. This capability may be considered on a continuum from clumsiness to exceptionally skilled in all aspects of motor skill. That there are children who can be classified as such is not the issue. The issue is whether there is an underlying, overall predisposition that determines a person's capacity to learn and perform motor skills. This view continues to be popularized in spite of the overwhelming evidence against it that has been generated.

SPECIFICITY

In contrast to the doctrine of formal discipline were the theoretical arguments of Thorndike. Over a period of years, Thorndike promoted the view that transfer was very specific to what had been learned (e.g., Thorndike, 1903, 1906; Thorndike & Woodworth, 1901). In his Identical Elements Theory, Thorndike argued that the capability for transfer depended on the similarity of the elements involved in each task. Maximum transfer would be expected when the tasks were exactly identical, and minimum transfer would be expected when two tasks shared no common elements.

Thorndike's ideas were met with severe criticism from educational psychologists. For instance, Meiklejohn (1908) suggested, "Think of learning to drive a nail with a yellow hammer, and then realize your helplessness if, in time of need, you should borrow your neighbour's hammer and find it painted red. Nay, further think of learning to use a hammer at all if at each other stroke the nail has gone further into the wood, and the sun has gone lower in the sky, and the temperature of the body has risen from the exercise, and in fact, everything on earth and under the earth has changed so far as to give each new stroke a new particularity all of its own" (p. 126).

Despite these criticisms, other learning theorists (especially behaviorists such as Guthrie and Skinner) espoused the view that transfer was very specific to the conditions under which training had occurred (Hilgard & Bower, 1966). Retention was also viewed like transfer. The similarity of the encoding and retrieval context was considered important for good memory performance (e.g., Robinson, 1927; Semon, 1923).

Theories of motor skill specificity have also been popular. Early research on the issue was initiated by Perl, Seashore, Woodrow, and others (Adams, 1987). Later research was conducted mostly in Henry's laboratory (Schmidt, 1988). In general, this research examined the correlations obtained from various skills performed by the same individuals. Correlations were found to be quite low, even among skills that shared many common features (such as speed or balance). If there is an overall, underlying predisposition to perform and learn motor skills, the correlations among various skills should have been quite high. The results of this research do not support this generality view. Rather, the capacity to perform, learn, and possibly *transfer* to other skills appears to be highly specific to each skill.

A MODERATE VIEW

Recent ideas on "transfer-appropriate processing" (e.g., Bransford, Franks, Morris, & Stein, 1979) may be considered as a position that is more intermediate than the extremes of the continuum defined by theories of specificity and generality. By this view, transfer performance should be maximized when the processing undertaken during practice is appropriate for the processing that is required by the transfer test. In this theory, the nature of the material is less important (cf. the doctrine of formal discipline) than is the appropriateness of the processing during training and transfer. Although not put to a stringent test in the acquisition and transfer of motor skills, there is support for further investigation of this view (Lee, 1988; Schmidt, 1988).

These views on retention and transfer should be kept in mind when reading the following sections. Learning is best viewed in terms of how an individual performs on a retention or transfer test that follows a period of acquisition trials. However, one must also be sensitive to the similarity of the conditions of practice relative to the conditions of the retention or transfer test. In each of the following sections the relation between practice and retention/transfer will be an important factor in interpreting learning effects.

DESIGNING INSTRUCTION— PREPRACTICE ISSUES

PROVIDING INFORMATION

Information can be provided to the performer during any of the three phases of performance; i.e., prior to, during, or following the completion of an action. This section will be concerned with the provision and structuring of information by an instructor for a learner prior to performance. From a cognitive perspective, this should be a critical time for considering the nature of the information presented for the learning and performance of a motor skill. Rather than being a post-hoc reinforcer of skilled actions, as suggested by behaviorism, the cognitive view prescribes an information flow that results in maximizing the learning and performance potential of the student. Understanding the important nature of providing information at this point in time gives rise to a number of questions. Unfortunately, as Holding (1965), Newell (1981), and Schmidt (1988) have pointed out, there has been little empirical investigation of a systematic nature conducted into the influence of information provided a priori on the performance and learning of a motor skill.

Most teachers and coaches instinctively provide information prior to performance, either through verbal instructions, modeling, or both. The impact of modeling on skill learning and performance is discussed by McCullagh elsewhere in this *Handbook*. The concern here will be with the provision of verbal instructions. Of the studies identified that have investigated this question, the majority have been directed toward understanding the nature of information provided to the performer. Three areas have been explored: (1) developing a priori knowledge of the kinesthetic sense of correct performance; (2) provision of knowledge concerning general principles or rules that underlie performance; and (3) the effect of providing information regarding the nature of the stimuli that will be encountered during performance (verbal pretraining).

Knowledge of Kinesthesis

Both Adams (1971) and Schmidt (1975) theorized that a necessary ingredient for successful performance of skilled actions is an error-detection mechanism. At the heart of the error-detection mechanism is a reference of correctness, a representation of the kinesthesis arising from the correct performance of that particular skill. Kinesthesis is defined here as both a sense of movement and static limb position (Winstein & Schmidt, 1989).

Can an individual's development of an error-detection mechanism be enhanced by the provision of a reference of correctness prior to skill performance and will this influence skill learning and performance in a positive way? The research that has been reported is very similar in that the auditory consequences of moving have been used in an attempt to establish a sense of the correct movement pattern in the subjects.

Keele (1986) suggested that a template for the correct performance facilitates the acquisition of a motor program to control the performance. In other words, we need to know what to do before we learn how to do it. He cites data from an unpublished doctoral dissertation by Stenius (1976) in which subjects were auditorially preexposed to the accelerative patterns for a lever-turning task. Initial performance of the task for these subjects was better than for subjects who did not receive this preexposure. However, the effect was eliminated after 60 trials of practice.

In a study similar to the one by Stenius, Zelaznik and Spring (1976) used a yoked-subjects design in which one subject actively performed a rapid timing task while a second subject listened to the sound of that performance. The physically active subject performed 72 trials of the task with both subjects being provided knowledge of results (KR) concerning the efficacy of each physically performed trial for the first 24 trials. Following their experience of listening to the performance, the yoked subjects performed 5 trials of the timing task. A comparison of this performance to the performance of the physical practice group's first 5 trials revealed a large advantage for the yoked subjects on the first trial, but this difference had disappeared by the fifth trial.

It seems, then, that providing a reference of correctness through audition enhances initial performance levels. However, it is not possible to conclude if this will result in increased learning. It is also not possible to conclude if providing information regarding a reference of correctness through other sensory-perceptual systems can also be effective in promoting higher levels of performance. More research is required on this question before a practical generalization can be drawn for the teaching of motor skills. It should be pointed out, however, that providing a reference of correctness through audition forms the basis for the Suzuki method of violin playing, which appears to be a successful program in enhancing the learning of that particular skill (Suzuki, 1969).

Knowledge of General Principles

Another question that has been addressed concerns the provision of knowledge about general principles or rules that govern performance and the impact that this information has on the learning and performance of motor skills. Judd (1908) had subjects throwing darts at submerged targets. One group was provided with knowledge about the principle of light refraction, while a second group was not. Although no data were presented, Judd reported an advantage for the group receiving light-refraction instruction, but only when transferred to a target at a different water depth. Initial performance at the original target depth was similar for both groups. These findings were replicated later by Hendrickson and Schroeder (1941) but contrast sharply with the nonexperimental description by Polanyi (1958) of the highly skilled cyclist who was unaware of the mechanical principle involved in maintaining equilibrium on the bicycle.

One other example of the knowledge of general principles or rules that underlie performance not being useful in enhancing skill learning and performance can be found. Pew (1974) had subjects perform 60-second trials of a sine-wave tracking task. On all trials, the middle 20-second segment was kept constant. Subjects demonstrated considerable improvement on this segment as opposed to the first or third 20-second segments, yet were completely unaware of the constant nature of the stimulus. Although it might be interesting to contrast the performance of the uninformed group to a second group that was provided with knowledge of the repetitiveness of the middle segment, this study does demonstrate that a lack of this knowledge does not prevent skill improvement. These findings have recently been replicated in work done by Magill and Green (1989).

Considerable research needs to be conducted before a clear understanding of how the knowledge of general principles or rules that govern performance of a skill influences the achievement of proficiency at that task. The best conclusion that can be drawn currently has been expressed by Holding (1965), who stated that knowledge of general principles is effective only if the principle is one that is simple and is directly applicable to the skill being performed. Schneider (1985) offered a similar view in concluding that conceptual knowledge does not necessarily equal operational proficiency. There is a need to experience the general principle in operation before this knowledge will impact on skill performance.

Verbal Pretraining

Considerably more research concerning the nature and effect of a priori instructions given to a performer has been generated to study verbal pretraining. The essential idea here is to provide the individual with knowledge concerning the stimuli that will be experienced during the performance of the task. As Schmidt (1988) has pointed out, the label *verbal pretraining* is somewhat of a misnomer because not all of the pretraining investigated has been verbal. However, much of the research has been directed at the impact of identifying and attaching a verbal label to the stimuli that will be experienced on the learning and performance of a motor skill.

Adams and Creamer (1962) had subjects performing continuous or discrete tracking tasks in which anticipation of changes in the target being tracked was essential for successful performance. One group received pretraining on the stimulus pattern. This pretraining consisted of watching the stimulus pattern and either verbalizing or pushing a button in anticipation of a directional change in the track. When transferred to the actual tracking task, the group that received pretraining demonstrated superior levels of performance. Adams and Creamer (1962) concluded that pretraining was an effective mediator of performance, although for the discrete tracking task, feedback during the pretraining stage was necessary to elicit this effect. These findings were supported in a study done by Trumbo, Ulrich, and Noble (1965) in which subjects in the pretraining group learned to name stimuli positions in a regular stimulus series. These subjects demonstrated greater performance levels on a tracking task that involved the same pattern of stimuli.

Neither of these studies were able to provide a locus for the effectiveness of verbal pretraining. Adams and Creamer (1962) concluded that either the establishment of a proprioceptive trace or cognitive learning could account for their findings. A more recent investigation by Ban and Minke (1984) sheds some light on this question. In their experiment, subjects were presented with a projected line that was at a 60° angle. Subjects in the experimental group were provided with a verbal label that was either high or low in imagery value. The control group did not receive verbal labels. Both groups were then asked to respond either "same" or "different" to other projected lines that ranged from 40° to 60°. The results indicated that the control group incorrectly identified lines at the 50° angle as being the same more often than did the experimental group. Thus Ban and Minke (1984) concluded that the verbal labels maintained the distinctive nature of the stimuli and prevented a stimulus generalization effect. There was no influence on the data for the imagery value of the verbal label. This would seem to indicate that the effectiveness of verbal pretraining is a result of cognitive learning.

It seems safe to conclude that verbal pretraining is effective for enhancing skill performance and that the effect lies in the cognitive learning of the regularity of stimulus occurrence, which allows for effective use of anticipatory responses. However, as with the other areas of prepractice instruction, more work is required before definitive conclusions can be reached. This would appear to be a useful area of empirical endeavor as many athletes, particularly those involved in the performance of continuous skills (e.g., downhill skiers and race car drivers), make use of preperformance rehearsal techniques that are analogous to verbal pretraining.

SUMMARY

There are more questions than answers regarding the provision of information to an individual prior to performance of a motor skill. The lack of empirical evidence is particularly troublesome when learning and performance is placed within a cognitive framework. Providing information to the performer prior to attempting a skill is an important component of a teacher or coach's role. This information should contain movement goals and patterns of actions to achieve these goals, as well as knowledge concerning conditions that surround performance of the movement skills. Establishing an awareness of the kinestheses for a correct movement pattern and providing knowledge about the expected occurrence of stimuli patterns can be effective in enhancing performance of a motor skill. Also, knowledge of the general principles that underlie skill performance can be effective in enhancing performance if that principle can be presented simply and within the context of the skill being performed.

STRUCTURING PRACTICE

In this section we will consider a number of factors concerning practice condition arrangements. Although many more factors can be identified, our focus will be on eight particular ones that have received empirical attention. These are: (1) distribution of practice, (2) fatigue, (3) variability of practice, (4) contextual interference, (5) part versus whole practice, (6) simulation, (7) bilateral transfer, and (8) amount of practice. As mentioned at the beginning of the chapter, our treatment of each of these factors can be considered as "small wholes" rather than integrated parts. The underlying theme is the impact that these practice-condition-arrangement factors have on the learning and performance of motor skills in general, and more specifically on the transfer of learning.

DISTRIBUTION OF PRACTICE

Historical Notes

One of the earliest and most often studied practice variables in motor learning is the distribution of practice effect (e.g., Bilodeau & Bilodeau, 1961; Lee & Genovese, 1988; McGeoch & Irion, 1952). This research issue was first stud-

ied in the verbal domain (Ebbinghaus, 1885/1964) and received attention with respect to the learning of motor skills in a card-sorting experiment by Browning, Brown, and Washburn (1913). In this study, a trial consisted of sorting a deck of cards as rapidly as possible. Distribution of practice was defined by the amount of time elapsed between the completion of one trial and start of the next trial (either 0 or 60 seconds). Performance was measured during acquisition trials, but not on a retention test. The results showed that practice with 60 seconds of rest between trials resulted in faster acquisition of the performance criterion than with 0 seconds of rest. This study was the first of over 100 published articles to appear on the effects of practice distribution on motor learning and performance.

Parameters of Study

Of the wide assortment of motor tasks employed in the study of distribution of practice effects, the overwhelming majority involved tracking performance, often with the pursuit rotor apparatus. The objective of this task is to keep a hinged stylus in contact with a rotating disk. Performance is normally measured in terms of time in contact with the disk (time-on-target). Although numerous other tasks have been used to investigate distribution of practice effects, the pursuit rotor task is popular since a variety of task variables can be manipulated (Ammons, 1988).

The most common variable manipulated in distribution of practice research is the length of rest between trials, given a constant trial length. For example, in the Bourne and Archer (1956) study discussed earlier, trial lengths for all groups were kept constant (30 seconds) and the distribution variable was defined along an empirical, massed to distributed continuum: 0, 15, 30, 45, or 60 seconds of rest between trials. Many researchers have manipulated more than 2 periods of rest, rendering absolute definitions of "massed" and "distributed" practice *across* studies as meaningless. Various other manipulations of practice distribution have also been investigated, and these will be considered after we review the effects of the length between trials.

Effects of Distribution of Practice Variables

Varied Intertrial Intervals Given Constant Trial Lengths. By far the most common distribution of practice manipulation is the effect of the length of the intertrial rest interval. At the massed end of the continuum are studies in which performance is continuous—no rest at all between trials (e.g., Ammons, 1950; Bourne & Archer, 1956). A common method in defining the distributed end of the continuum is when the length of the rest between trials is equal to or slightly longer than the trial length—such as 30 or 60 seconds of rest between 30-second trials. Toward the extreme distributed end of this continuum are some studies where individual trials are separated by rests of an entire day (e.g., Ammons, 1950; Bunch, 1944; Ericksen, 1942). As stated earlier, it is not possible to make absolute conclusions regarding this literature. Variables such as the nature of the task, the length of trials, the length of rest intervals, the number of trials practiced, the length of the retention interval, and the manner by which retention trials were conducted all have an important impact on the outcome of those studies that defined distribution variables in terms of the length of the intertrial interval.

A meta-analysis was undertaken by Lee and Genovese (1988) to examine this literature. From the studies that provided the relevant statistics needed for the meta-analysis (which was about half of the studies reviewed), effect sizes were calculated by comparing each experiment's "most massed" condition (shortest intertrial interval group) versus the "most distributed" condition (longest intertrial interval group). These two conditions were compared at the end of practice and at the beginning of the retention interval. The meta-analysis revealed two important findings. As expected, distributed practice resulted in superior performance as indicated by the levels of performance at the end of the practice period. Following the rest period, the magnitude of the difference between the massed and distributed practice conditions was reduced, but was still relatively large compared to what would have been expected had there been no learning effect.

The results of the meta-analysis by Lee and Genovese (1988) provided a rather narrow view of the entire distribution of practice literature. The method of comparing each study's most massed condition against its most distributed condition only offered one answer regarding the potential effect of intertrial rest. In studies that examined a variety of intertrial rest conditions, there appears to be a limited benefit to the length of the rest interval. For example, the data from the Bourne & Archer (1956) experiment reprinted in Figure 9–1 suggest little benefit for retention when the rest period was extended from 45 to 60 seconds. Indeed, some experiments have revealed that there may be an optimal rest period between practice trials. For example, Ammons (1960, Experiment 1) tested subjects learning the Tsai-Partington Numbers Test, with 60-second trial durations and rests of either 0, 60, 150, or 300 seconds. The retention test was performed best by the 60-second rest group (although both of the other distributed groups also outperformed the 0-second group).

Again, it is emphasized here that there can be no absolute conclusions on the influence of lengthening intertrial rest intervals. That *relatively* long intertrial rest intervals facilitate the learning of motor skills, as compared to no or very brief rest intervals, is well supported by the literature. Other definitions and factors related to the distribution of practice literature are also of interest.

Varied Trial Lengths Given Constant Intertrial Intervals. The focus of these investigations is the period of time under which the subject is performing, with intertrial interval rest periods held constant. Kimble and Bilodeau (1949) compared groups of subjects that learned the Minnesota Rate of Manipulation Task. Two groups had 30 trials of practice, each of 10 seconds duration, while another two groups had 10 trials of practice, each of 30 seconds duration (thereby keeping the total amount of practice on the task constant). Each trial-length condition was also divided into groups with intertrial rests of 10 or 30 seconds. As expected, the groups with longer intertrial rest performed better by the end of the practice period. However, given constant intertrial interval lengths, the group that received the shorter trial durations also performed better at the end of the acquisition period. Unfortunately, the Kimble and Bilodeau study, a replication by Barch (1959), and other studies by Conwell and Ammons (1951) and by Hagan, Wilkerson, and Noble (1980) using the pursuit rotor, failed to include a retention test. Thus the effects on learning are unknown (cf. Kimble, 1949).

Covaried Trial and Intertrial Interval Lengths. A few investigators have held constant the ratio between the trial length and intertrial rest intervals. Plutchik and Petti (1964) gave five groups of subjects 20 minutes of total practice time on a pursuit rotor tracking task, with each group receiving trial-length to intertrial-rest-interval ratios of 2:1 (40 seconds:20 seconds, 60:30, 120:60, 240:120, or 300:150). Under these conditions, the effect on performance of increased rest between trials was countered by the increased trial length, and all groups performed equally at the end of practice. Noble, Salazar, Skelley, and Wilkerson (1979) held the trial-length to intertrial-interval ratio constant at 1:1 and found a small advantage for a 60-second:60-second condition over a 20:20 condition. However, two other groups, practicing at tracking cycles of 90:90 and 120:120, produced intermediate results. Both of these findings must be considered as only performance effects, since neither study included a retention test.

Altered Schedules of Rest. Following the lead of Snoddy (1935), several investigators explored the effect of increasing or decreasing the length of the rest period during the practice session. In one study, two groups of subjects performed five blocks of seven trials each on a tracking task (Renshaw & Schwarzbek, 1938). After each block of trials, the length of the rest period was systematically altered. One group was given increased rest periods between trials on each successive block, while the other group received decreased rest periods. The decreasing group (which received long intertrial rests initially) performed better than the increasing group (which received short rests early in practice) during the initial stages of acquisition. However, by the end of practice, the increasing group (which was now receiving long rests) was performing better than the decreasing rest group, although the magnitude of the difference was smaller than had been found early in practice. This finding, however, was not replicated by Dore and Hilgard (1938), who found a larger advantage at the end of practice for the increasing rest group than the advantage held by the decreasing rest group early in practice. These disparate findings are further clouded by the absence of retention tests in both studies.

Distribution of Practice Effects Between Sessions. A number of early investigations involved the learning of nonlaboratory skills over much longer periods of acquisition and retention than in the studies reported so far, with practice distributions varied according to the length of time between practice *sessions* (e.g., Lashley, 1915; Murphy, 1916; Pyle, 1914; Webb, 1933). In the Murphy (1916) study, right-handed subjects practiced throwing a javelin at a target with their left hand. Each subject made 5 throws on each of 34 days of practice. A massed group practiced on each of 5 days per week (over 7 weeks), while the distributed group practiced 3 times a week (Monday-Wednesday-Friday) over 12 weeks. Accuracy at hitting the target was compared on the last 10 sessions of practice, and was found to favor the distributed group. Interestingly, Murphy also included retention tests 3 months later. All subjects made 10 throws per day on each of 5 consecutive days. Again, target-accuracy performance was better for the distributed group than the massed group on the mean of these retention tests.

A considerable number of studies were later conducted in which practice was distributed across many sessions. Much of this work can be found in reviews by Knapp (1963) and Mohr (1960). A more recent study, however, deserves attention. Baddeley and Longman (1978) trained adult postal workers to type alphanumeric code material using a conventional typewriter keyboard. Subjects were divided into four groups, which differed both in the length of each practice session (1 or 2 hours) and the number of sessions per day (1 or 2). Groups that practiced for 2 sessions per day received at least 2 hours of rest between sessions. All groups received practice for 5 days per week until 80 hours of practice had been accumulated (with the exception of the one-hour session/once-a-day group, which discontinued practice after 60 total hours). In addition, Baddeley and Longman included retention tests after 1, 3, and 9 months of no practice on the typing test. The most massed of these practice conditions (2 sessions per day of 2 hours each in duration) led to both the poorest acquisition and retention performance of the four groups.

Effects of Work During the Rest Interval. An interesting experiment by Boswell (1971) suggested that the period of time between trials may benefit performance merely due to a change in work conditions. Subjects practiced the pursuit rotor tracking task under typical massed (no rest) or distributed (30-second rest) conditions between 30-second trials. In addition, another group of subjects practiced the task under distributed conditions, with the intertrial interval "filled" with practice on the task using the opposite hand. The performance of this group was intermediate: much better than the performance of the massed group but much poorer than the distributed group. Unfortunately, the effects on retention of this filled intertrial interval group were not assessed. The detrimental effect due to practice on an alternate task, compared to rest, was also found by Norrie and Henry (1978) in learning the Bachman ladder task (using pursuit rotor practice as the intertrial interval task).

However, a massed control group was not included in the study.

Final Notes

Research on the distribution of practice effects began early in the 20th century, became the focus of furious empirical investigation during the 1940s and 1950s, then gradually dissipated to the point where very little attention was given to the topic. Without question, studies on distribution of practice diminished with the fall of the theoretical issues that spawned their research. Research on practice effects in motor learning has since shifted to alternate areas, with different underlying theoretical foci.

FATIGUE

Parameters of Study

For the sake of efficiency, most coaches or trainers would like to maximize the amount of work performed by an athlete in a given period of time. However, the cost of maximizing the amount of work performed is the level of fatigue induced. Of critical interest in determining the work rate of the athlete is the impact that the level of fatigue induced has on the learning and performance of sport skills. This question has been pursued with a great deal of vigor in the literature, although as Poulton (1988) pointed out, the frequency of published studies has declined in recent years. This trend can be interpreted as a belief either that closure is being reached on this issue or that it no longer holds any contemporary significance or interest. In reviewing the literature, it appears that despite a great deal of information being gathered regarding the impact of fatigue on the learning and performance of motor skills, a number of issues still remain unresolved.

Early research on fatigue was concerned mainly with the impact of repetitive performance of a motor skill over a discrete unit of time. The standard finding was that this type of fatigue resulted in performance decrements but had little impact on learning (Caplan, 1969; Stelmach, 1969). It was believed that the type of fatigue induced in this situation was analogous to reactive inhibition and was central in nature; continuously repeating an action leads to a decreased desire to perform that task. Therefore, level of performance diminishes as the individual becomes, in effect, "bored" with the task. The impairment is at the level of central processing, not in the periphery (i.e., the musculature). Since this early work, investigators have been more concerned with the impact of fatigue induced by interpolated activities on the learning and performance of motor skills. This type of fatigue is considered more peripheral in nature in that the impairment to performance is within the working muscles.

A number of difficulties have plagued the research attempts at investigating fatigue, such as the lack of a consistently applied research paradigm and insufficient experimental controls. For example, in a number of studies only a single application of a fatiguing condition has been used (e.g., Alderman, 1965; Carron, 1969; Dwyer, 1984). Other researchers have applied a fatiguing condition between each trial of the criterion task (e.g., Carron, 1972; Cotten, Thomas, Spieth, & Biasiotto, 1972; Godwin & Schmidt, 1971). In another study, the subjects engaged in the fatiguing task while, at the same time, performing the criterion task (Spano & Burke, 1976). The fatiguing tasks have ranged from step-ups, to bicycle and arm ergometers, to treadmills. The level of fatigue induced by these tasks has, for the most part, not been adequately controlled, although a few researchers have attempted to make use of heart rate data for this purpose (Carron, 1972; Nunney, 1963; Spano & Burke, 1976; Thomas, Cotten, Spieth, & Abraham, 1975). Many investigators have simply assumed that a certain level of fatigue was induced by the amount of work that the subjects were asked to undertake. This, however, does not take into account the fitness level of each subject and her or his capability for withstanding the amount of work produced in any study. Dwyer (1984) has identified a potentially fruitful approach with regard to this problem by measuring the decline in work rate over the bout of fatiguing exercise. In addition to these problems, the criterion tasks have varied considerably in the research, with both discrete and continuous tasks being used, although the most common tasks have been the pursuit rotor and the Bachman ladder climb. Despite these methodological and paradigmatic difficulties, a number of consistencies emerge.

As with the investigation of all the other variables that can influence the arranging of practice conditions, it is necessary to distinguish the impact of fatigue on the performance of a motor skill from the learning of a motor skill. Those researchers who have pursued this question have shown a high level of sensitivity to this consideration, although there has been some debate over the measurement of learning (see Cotten et al., 1972). We will consider the effects on performance and learning in separate sections.

The Impact of Fatigue on the Performance of a Motor Skill

The impact of fatigue on the performance of motor skills is dependent on the amount of fatigue that is induced. The most robust finding is that high levels of induced fatigue result in significant decrements in performance. A few studies in which an attempt was made to regulate the severity of fatigue have demonstrated that low to moderate levels of fatigue may have an enhancing effect on skill performance (Carron, 1972; Pack, Cotten, & Biasiotto, 1974; Richards, 1968; Thomas et al., 1975; Williams & Singer, 1975). The result is the proposal of an inverted-U (Carron, 1972; Richards, 1968) or inverted-J hypothesis (Thomas et al., 1975). Despite the alphabetic discrepancy, both of these hypotheses basically present the same view and borrow from the Yerkes-Dodson inverted-U hypothesis relating arousal to performance.

The general idea of the inverted-U and -J hypotheses is that a low to moderate amount of fatigue provides a warm-up effect that results in enhanced performance levels as compared to no-fatigue conditions. This performance-enhancement artifact is maximized at some optimal level-of-fatigue state. Increasing fatigue beyond this level would result in performance decrements up to a theoretical point where fatigue would be so great that physical functioning would no longer be possible. This point is well below the level of performance that can be attained under no-fatigue conditions; thus the designation by Thomas et al. (1975) that the relationship should be hypothesized as an inverted J rather than an inverted U.

The decrements in performance that are noted for high levels of fatigue likely occur for two reasons. One is that the biochemical products of fatigue act in some way to cause decreased levels of performance (Carron, 1972; Phillips, 1963; Richards, 1968). The other is that fatigue reduces the efficacy of information processing, perhaps in the response selection and movement programming stages, thus resulting in a decreased quality of the control elements for neuromotor coordination (Caplan, 1969; Carron, 1969; Dwyer, 1984). If these hypotheses are veridical, it would seem that fitness and skill level should play a mediating role in the impact of fatigue on motor skill performance. Unfortunately, these factors have not been systematically investigated. Some insight into skill level as a mediating influence can be seen in studies that introduced the fatiguing task at varying points during the acquisition session (e.g., Dwyer, 1984; Schmidt, 1969). It seems that generally, fatigue introduced early in practice has a greater decremental effect on performance than fatigue introduced later in practice. Since novel tasks were used in these experiments, we can assume that subjects were less skilled at the beginning of acquisition than at some point later in time.

There is some indication in the literature that the impact of fatigue on the performance of a motor skill is localized. In a study by Welch (1969), fatiguing the legs did not impair the performance of an arm task. On the other hand, for most investigations in which performance decrements have been observed with high levels of fatigue, the fatigue-inducing task was normally performed with the limbs that were involved in the criterion task performance. For example, when the Bachman ladder has been the criterion task, researchers have used either a bicycle ergometer or a step-up as the fatiguing task (e.g., Caplan, 1969; Carron, 1972; Schmidt, 1969). When the pursuit rotor has been the criterion task, researchers have used an arm ergometer as the fatiguing task (Alderman, 1965; Carron, 1969; Williams & Singer, 1975). As mentioned, all of these studies have indicated performance decrements with high levels of fatigue.

There are some exceptions to this localized effect of fatigue, however. Cotten et al. (1972) employed a step-up as the fatiguing task and a mirror toss as the criterion task. Spano and Burke (1976) used a bicycle ergometer as the fatiguing task and the pursuit rotor as the criterion task, but had the subjects performing both tasks simultaneously.

Nunney (1963) fatigued subjects on a treadmill and bicycle ergometer while performing a mirror trace and the pursuit rotor as criterion tasks. In all of these studies, it was found that the fatigue produced did have a decremental effect on performance. Although it is generally believed that the impact of fatigue on performance is localized, there appears to be enough evidence to the contrary to warrant further investigation of this question.

The Impact of Fatigue on the Learning of a Motor Skill

Investigations into the effect fatigue has on the learning of a motor skill have produced contradictory results. A number of studies have indicated that fatigue has no effect on learning (e.g., Alderman, 1965; Carron, 1969; Cotten et al., 1972; Schmidt, 1969), while other studies have indicated that fatigue does have a decremental effect on learning (e.g., Caplan, 1969; Carron, 1972; Dwyer, 1984; Godwin & Schmidt, 1971; Thomas et al, 1975). The key to understanding these divergent results appears to be the level of fatigue induced, the maintenance of fatigue over the duration of the acquisition session, and the point during acquisition at which fatigue was induced.

As mentioned previously, one of the shortcomings of the typical research that has been designed to investigate fatigue is the lack of control over the degree of fatigue induced. In many cases, no attempt was made to monitor the cardiorespiratory response to the exercise used, nor has there been an attempt to relate the fitness level of the subject to the amount of work being performed. It appears that researchers who failed to observe a learning effect for fatigue have not induced adequate levels of fatigue, or have allowed sufficient time for recovery from the fatiguing task during the acquisition session (e.g., Alderman, 1965; Carron, 1969). Researchers who have induced high levels of fatigue in their subjects, and have maintained these levels by using bouts of fatiguing exercise between trials of the criterion task, have noted decrements in learning (e.g., Carron, 1972, Thomas et al., 1975).

When low to moderate levels of fatigue have been generated during the acquisition session, there is an indication that low levels of fatigue may actually have an enhancing effect on the learning of motor skills (Pack et al., 1974; Williams & Singer, 1975). In particular, Williams and Singer (1975) reported a trend for the group that received low levels of fatiguing exercise not only to perform better during the initial acquisition session than no-fatigue, medium-fatigue, and high-fatigue groups, but also to maintain and extend this advantage on a 48-hour retention test. The trend, however, was not statistically significant. These data do suggest that the inverted-J hypothesis outlined in the previous discussion may be applicable to the fatigue/learning relationship as well as the fatigue/performance relationship. A more systematic investigation of this model would appear to be warranted.

The time during the acquisition session at which the fatiguing task is introduced also seems to have a significant effect on the fatigue/learning relationship. When decrements in learning have been demonstrated under fatiguing conditions, the fatiguing exercise has been provided either prior to any trials of the criterion task, or very early in the acquisition session. Researchers that introduced the fatiguing task later in the acquisition session did not demonstrate a significant decrement in learning (Alderman, 1965; Carron, 1969; Dwyer, 1984; Schmidt, 1969). Most of the tasks that have been used in these investigations were quite simple in nature, and it could be assumed that a great deal of the learning would take place rather early in the acquisition session. These findings would imply that fatigue is a more powerful learning variable during the early, rather than later, stages of learning.

Other findings have also indicated that the impact of fatigue on learning may be task-dependent. Benson (1968) had subjects learn two tasks: a complex jumping task in which both speed and accuracy in performance were measured, and a juggling task. High levels of fatigue were induced initially using a bicycle ergometer and were maintained throughout the course of the acquisition phase of the experiment. The data indicated that the fatigue had no detrimental effect on the learning and performance of the juggling task. This could be expected, given the localized nature of fatiguing effects. However, the data indicated that fatigue actually enhanced the learning of the juggling task. With the jumping task, fatigue had a decremental effect on learning when speed was the dependent measure but a beneficial effect on learning when accuracy was the dependent measure. These results indicate that the enhancement of learning caused by practicing in a fatigued state may be due to processes occurring at a higher (cognitive) level. However, an organized program of research investigating the impact of task classification on fatigue and learning is lacking, so any conclusions at this point in time would be presumptuous, at best.

As just mentioned, it is not possible to provide a definitive hypothesis underlying the facilitating effect of fatigue on the learning of motor skills. For the debilitating effects, it is generally hypothesized that the fatigued subject performs a motor skill differently than when in a nonfatigued state. Therefore, if the subject is fatigued during the acquisition session, performance may be achieved using a modified, or even different, version of the desired skill. When tested for degree of learning in a nonfatigued state, the version of the skill acquired during acquisition may not be most effective for optimal performance (for more discussion of this hypotheses, see Caplan, 1969; Carron, 1969; Dwyer, 1984).

This hypothesis brings up an interesting methodological issue. Researchers investigating the effect of fatigue on the learning and performance of motor skills have made use of performance in a nonfatigued state to assess relative amounts of learning. Given that many sport skills are often performed under fatiguing conditions, it would seem that there is a need to assess learning using a transfer or retention test performed under a fatigued state. If transfer was specific, it could be predicted that acquisition of a motor skill while fatigued would result in higher levels of performance when the skill is used during a game in a fatigued state. This type of research, in which subjects acquire a skill in a fatigued or nonfatigued state and are transferred to fatigued or nonfatigued conditions, would appear to be a valuable undertaking, not only for understanding the mechanism underlying the impact of fatigue on the learning of motor skills, but also for the practical applications of this information to sport performance.

VARIABILITY OF PRACTICE

Conceptual Framework

The most investigated prediction arising from schema theory (Schmidt, 1975) is the variability of practice hypothesis. This hypothesis contends that experiencing a greater degree of variability within a movement class (all movements controlled by the same motor program) during a practice session will lead to superior acquisition of that movement class, especially if measured by transfer to a novel variation of the movement class (novel task transfer). The basis for this prediction is that experiencing a wider range of movement experiences during acquisition should result in the development of stronger recall and recognition schemata (the cognitive structures responsible for movement production and evaluation). For example, the stronger recall schema would allow for greater accuracy in predicting the correct response parameters required for a particular movement outcome, even if the movement had not been previously experienced (Schmidt, 1988).

Variability of practice has stimulated a great deal of empirical investigation. Given the apparent simplicity of the hypothesis, it would be logical to assume that closure would be reached quite rapidly on this issue. However, this is not the case. A number of confounding factors, particularly methodological ones, have served to muddy research endeavors, inhibiting the possibility of a clear conclusion.

A great deal of empirical investigation of the variability hypothesis has been undertaken, and several reviews of the literature are available (Lee, Magill, & Weeks, 1985; Shapiro & Schmidt, 1982; van Rossum, 1987). The reader is referred to one of these reviews for a more in-depth treatment of this topic. It is our intent to provide an overview of the issues that have been debated regarding the variability of practice hypothesis. These include issues concerning the design of experiments to test the variability of practice hypothesis, such as the age and gender of the subjects, type of tasks employed, and organization of the variable practice session, as well as assumptions about underlying memory representation.

Experimental Design Issues

Age and Gender of Subjects. Support for the variability hypothesis has been somewhat equivocal. The most often cited argument for this ambivalence in the literature is the disparate nature of the age and gender of the subjects tested. Shapiro and Schmidt (1982) contend that the majority of research that has not supported the variability hypothesis made use of adult subjects and, in particular, male adult subjects. They argue that adult subjects could be expected to have previously established schemata for the tasks being used in the experiments, especially given the rather simple tasks commonly found in laboratory-based research. Because the intent of the research is to promote the acquisition of cognitive structures (i.e., recall and recognition schemata or generalized motor programs) that would allow for skilled performance, reliance on adult subjects would result in a confound as these subjects could be expected to have the cognitive structures that mediate skilled performance already in place. Therefore, the experimental manipulations to test the variability hypothesis would not be effective since subjects in all groups learning the task may already have developed schemata to mediate performance.

Children, on the other hand, would be less likely to have existing schemata to influence skilled performance. Therefore, exploring the variability hypothesis with younger subjects would be a much cleaner test, as the experimental manipulations could actually be expected to impact on the development of the cognitive structures that are formed during skill acquisition. Shapiro and Schmidt (1982) conclude that support for the variability hypothesis is stronger when children have been used as subjects. This, they believe, indicates the efficacy of the hypothesis for motor skill acquisition. They also conclude that the evidence for the variability hypothesis is stronger for female subjects. The logic here is that females can be considered, on average, to have fewer and less motoric experiences at a given age than males. Thus females should be more susceptible to experimental manipulations of the learning environment, such as variability of practice (Schmidt, 1988).

The conclusion that "motoric" age (either by comparing children to adults, or females to males) is a confounding factor in findings of the research on the variability of practice hypothesis has been questioned by van Rossum (1987). In a rather extensive treatment of the variability of practice hypothesis, he challenges the process that led to Shapiro and Schmidt's (1982) conclusion. In particular, von Rossum concludes that Shapiro and Schmidt included articles in their review of literature that could not be applied to the topic under investigation. Specifically his concern was with the inclusion of articles that did not demonstrate "learning over practice." In other words, van Rossum suggested that any studies that did not have a significant trial-block main effect for acquisition should not be considered. This eliminated approximately half of the articles that are normally included in the body of literature used to explain the variability of practice hypothesis. From this reduced subset of the literature, van Rossum (1987) concluded that, contrary to the contention of Shapiro and Schmidt (1982), more support could be found for the variability hypothesis using adult subjects than child subjects. Overall, however, van Rossum contends that minimal support for the variability hypothesis exists and as much, if not more, disconfirming findings can be located within the literature. To provide more evidence for his position, van Rossum reports an experiment to test the variability hypothesis in which ball weight was used as the variable being manipulated with skilled versus nonskilled child subjects. Neither group provided any support for the variability hypothesis, and only the nonskilled group met the "learning over practice" criterion that he had established.

Although van Rossum's (1987) review of the literature does raise some doubts regarding the veracity of Shapiro and Schmidt's (1982) conclusions, his article-selection methodology can also be subjected to criticism. Particularly troubling is the elimination of all articles that did not demonstrate a significant trial-block main effect during acquisition. The blanket application of this criterion ignores the basic performance versus learning distinction that was discussed earlier in this chapter. It is possible that some variable (the most likely candidate being the amount of variability provided during acquisition) would have a temporary depressing effect on performance during acquisition but would not hinder the learning process. In other words, increased amounts of variability might result in slower rates of performance gains across acquisition. Because the subject's performance did not improve during the acquisition session does not necessarily mean that the task was not learned.

It is apparent that there is divergent opinions about the degree of support for the variability hypothesis when the age of the subjects is taken into consideration. Shapiro and Schmidt (1982) and van Rossum (1987) provided conclusions based on distinct subsets of the literature. In both cases, questions have been raised regarding the article selection process. As with much of the research conducted on practice condition arrangement factors, an absolute statement regarding the impact of the variability of practice on the learning and performance of a motor skill is not possible. However, given the overly conservative nature of van Rossum's selection method, it would appear that the weight of evidence would side with Shapiro and Schmidt.

Type of Task. Schmidt's (1975) schema theory was developed to explain the acquisition of discrete motor tasks. It would be logical to assume that testing the various predictions from schema theory should make use of these types of motor skills. But this has not always been the case (van Rossum, 1987). Van Rossum argues that selecting a task for a variability of practice experiment should not be arbitrary, and he suggests a specific set of criteria for task selection. He suggests that tasks should be discrete, novel, and self-paced. As schema theory is concerned with the acquisition of discrete tasks, little argument can be raised with the first two criteria. However, the need for self-paced tasks does not seem justified. In fact, externally paced tasks might result in more sensitive tests of the variability of practice hypothesis. Many real-world performances of discrete sport skills are externally paced. That is, the athlete is performing in a time-restricted situation where the initiation of the movement is determined by variables outside the control of the performer. According to schema theory, success in these sit-

uations would be partially dependent on the rapidity with which an individual can produce the movement parameters required for performance. A stronger recall schema would seem to allow for a more efficient retrieval of movement parameters.

Thus the logical conclusion from this discussion would be that an investigation into the variability of practice hypothesis should be conducted using novel, externally paced, discrete motor skills. Two findings support this conclusion. First, stronger evidence for the variability hypothesis has been found with open (externally paced) motor skills. Second, a related phenomenon, the contextual interference effect, is stronger when tested using a reaction time (externally paced) paradigm. In fact, it can be argued that van Rossum's (1987) contrary findings to the variability of practice hypothesis noted previously may be due to the use of a self-paced throw for accuracy task. It would be interesting to contrast his findings to a situation in which an externally paced throw for accuracy task was the criterion activity.

Organization of Variability. In their review of the literature, Lee, Magill, and Weeks (1985) contend that some of the equivocality in findings assessing the variability hypothesis may be due to the way that variable practice has been structured. Citing work done on the contextual interference effect, they argue that scheduling of practice variability has a significant impact on the acquisition of motor skills. That is, presenting the variations of the motor task to subjects in a random order (changing the variation practiced from trial to trial) leads to greater levels of acquisition than presenting the variations of the motor task in a blocked order (each variation practiced for a specified number of trials). We provide greater treatment of the contextual interference effect in the following section of this chapter. However, the point is that researchers investigating the variability of practice hypothesis have not accounted for the scheduling of variability. It would seem that analysis of the variability hypothesis should involve a random practice schedule.

Memory Representation Assumption

The last issue that may provide a confound in the research directed at understanding the variability of practice hypothesis is the hypothesized memory representation assumed to underlie skill acquisition. Schmidt's argument for a schema-based memory representation is somewhat circular. That is, successful novel task transfer is indicative of schema formation and a stronger schema formation leads to successful novel task transfer. In a recent review of the literature on form of memory representation, Chamberlin and Magill (1992a) found minimal evidence for an abstract schema form of representation for motor skills. In fact, based on a parallel debate on the representation of category information in the allied field of cognitive psychology, support for a schema-based system of memory representation seems to be tenuous, at best. From this particular debate, it appears that a hybrid model of representation involving both abstracted and specifically experienced information is more tenable. The current direction is to identify what conditions of performance lead to the use of the abstracted or specifically experienced information for classification of novel items into categories.

If a similar hybrid model of memory representation is found to exist for motor skills, then understanding the conditions under which variable practice was performed may provide some insight into the equivocal nature of the empirical data. That is, if specific conditions of practice invoke an abstract form of memory representation, then the variability hypothesis will be supported. However, if the specific conditions of practice invoke a more instantiated, specifically experienced form of memory representation, then success on novel task transfer will be due to the relationship between the practice and transfer variations of the task, not the degree of variability experienced during practice.

The need, then, is to identify the specific form that a motor skill memory representation will take. Preliminary work on this question has provided some evidence for the schema abstraction model (Chamberlin & Magill, 1992b). However, since the specific conditions under which motor tasks are acquired seem to be a critical factor, more substantiated research is necessary before any concrete evidence will be available

CONTEXTUAL INTERFERENCE

Battig's Influence

We now turn our attention to one of the most actively investigated topics in the motor behavior literature. The recent interest in the contextual interference effect can be attributed directly to the influence of Battig (1966, 1972, 1979). His research was primarily on the learning of verbal material, although he retained a fondness for motor skills investigations throughout his career (Battig, 1956, 1966, 1977; Battig & Shea, 1980). Battig's initial theoretical contribution to contextual interference research was his 1966 paper, in which he summarized efforts to examine the effects of within-task and between-task interference on learning lists of words. His proposal that "intertask facilitation is produced by intratask interference" (Battig, 1966, p. 227) was in direct contradiction to the predominant ways of conceptualizing the role of interference in learning and memory at that time. Although Battig made impressive arguments in support of his proposal (Battig, 1966, 1972), it was given little attention (Battig, 1979).

Battig's concept of "contextual" interference, which was an extension of the intratask interference hypothesis (Battig, 1979), was used to explain a motor learning study by Shea and Morgan (1979). Although the term *contextual interference* and the methodology of Shea and Morgan have become virtually synonymous, we specifically refer to contextual interference here in terms of a research method-

ology and a set of effects, since the original conceptualization of the term included a theoretical position that not all researchers have embraced (e.g., Lee & Magill, 1983b, 1985).

The Shea and Morgan (1979) Study

Shea and Morgan's experimental methodology and the set of effects that resulted became the prototype against which later contextual interference research was compared. In their study, 2 groups of university-age subjects practiced 3 variations of a rapid arm reversal task. The task required subjects, upon seeing a stimulus light, to pick up a tennis ball, knock over 3 of 6 wooden barriers, and put the tennis ball into a final rest position. Three sets of movement patterns (the spatial direction of the movements) were defined in terms of the order of the 3 barriers to be knocked over. Each pattern was illustrated in full view of the subject during the acquisition trials and was paired with a specific colored stimulus light. The goal was to complete the movement pattern as fast as possible while maintaining spatial accuracy. All subjects performed 18 practice trials on each of the 3 movement patterns, for a total of 54 acquisition trials.

The 2 groups of subjects were defined in terms of the order by which their practice trials were arranged. The *blocked* group performed their first 18 acquisition trials on one of the movement patterns. Another movement pattern was practiced next for 18 trials; then the remaining pattern was practiced for the final set of 18 trials. Thus the entire period of practice on any one movement pattern was considered a "block." The *random* group was equivalent to the blocked group in terms of the number of practice trials conducted on each of the movement patterns. However, the random group's acquisition period proceeded such that after every set of 18 trials, each pattern had been practiced 6 times, and no one pattern had been practiced for more than 2 consecutive trials. Thus the practice order was "random" within certain restrictions.

Ten minutes after the acquisition trials, half of the subjects in each of the groups completed retention and transfer tests. The remaining subjects returned to perform these retention and transfer trials 10 days later. Subjects undertook 18 retention trials on the practiced patterns. Nine total trials (3 trials per pattern) were performed in a blocked order, and 9 trials were performed in a random order. Following retention, each subject then completed 3 trials on each of 2 new (transfer) patterns. One pattern was made up of 3 barriers and the other pattern was made up of 5 barriers.

The results of the Shea and Morgan (1979) study are illustrated in Figure 9–2 (note that the retention and transfer data are averaged over the 10-minute and 10-day retention tests). There are a number of findings illustrated in this figure that collectively have been referred to as the *contextual interference effect*. (It is curious to note that the contextual interference effect actually refers to several differences between groups. We argue that the most important effect

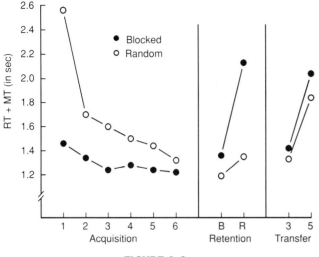

FIGURE 9–2.

Redrawn from "Contextual interference effects on the acquisition, retention, and transfer of a motor skill" by J. B. Shea & R. L. Morgan, 1979, *Journal of Experimental Psychology: Human Learning and Memory*, 5, 179–187.

is the absolute difference between groups on measures of learning—i.e., retention and transfer). During acquisition, the performance of the blocked group was better than the performance of the random group. However, during retention, the random group performed better than the blocked group. Two additional features of the retention data are worth noting. The performance of the random group was maintained at about the same level as that achieved by the end of acquisition. However, the performance of the blocked group was not maintained and, in fact, reverted to a very poor standard of performance during the randomly ordered retention trials. The other important feature of these data is that the advantage of the random group occurred on both the random and blocked-ordered retention trials. For transfer, the random group again performed better than the blocked group, the difference being greater for the five-barrier than the three-barrier transfer test.

Historical Note

As we mentioned earlier, the research methodology used by Shea and Morgan has become closely linked with the term *contextual interference*. However, research along similar lines but not under the contextual interference rubric can be found prior to 1979. A study by Pyle (1919), for example, illustrates a related effect on acquisition. The task was to sort cards into random compartments of a box, two of which were used in the experiment. Subjects sorted the cards into one of the boxes on each of 30 days of practice. One group of subjects used the same box for 15 days, then switched to the other box. The other group alternated boxes daily. As anticipated, the blocked practice group quickly attained a performance advantage that was maintained throughout the practice period. Unfortunately no re-

tention or transfer was given, so the effects on learning were not determined.

Dunham (1977, 1978) investigated the effects of scheduling practice of the two arms during practice on a pursuit rotor tracking task. One group of subjects practiced with one arm exclusively until a performance criterion was reached, then practiced with the other arm to the same criterion level (similar to blocked practice). The other group of subjects alternated arms on each trial until the criteria for both arms were attained. As expected, performance on each arm in the blocked group reached the criterion level sooner than did the alternating arm group (Dunham, 1977, 1978). Unfortunately, a retention test was not performed, so the effects on learning, and the similarity of these data to the results obtained by Shea and Morgan (1979) is not known. Dunham (1978) did include a "relearning" test one month after original practice. However, a common comparison of groups was not made, since these relearning trials were ordered identically to the original trials, with both groups performing under the same practice schedule as in the first section.

Perhaps the recent interest in contextual interference can be illustrated by reflecting on Dunham's conclusion about his data. That a blocked method of practice would promote better skill acquisition than an alternating method "would agree with inferences to be drawn from an interference theory of forgetting: that is, the holding of conflicting events to a minimum will maximize the strength of recall" (Dunham, 1977, p. 287). Most theoretical approaches at that time viewed interference as a hindrance to learning and memory, to be avoided when possible. Dunham's conclusions were both consistent with his data and many theoretical views at that time. Perhaps it was in reaction to contentment with theoretical parsimony that the Shea and Morgan (1979) findings and the theoretical views of Battig (1979) attracted research attention to the contextual interference effect.

Factors That Influence Contextual Interference

A recent review of the literature by Magill and Hall (1990) cited over 40 empirical investigations of contextual interference since the Shea and Morgan (1979) study. By far the most common feature of these studies was a comparison of random and blocked practice schedules during periods of practice, retention, and transfer. Important differences among this research were the impact of various factors on the contextual interference effect. These factors include, but are not limited to, variations in scheduling of practice, variations in scheduling retention, subject variations, and task variations.

Variations in Scheduling Practice. Random and blocked orders of practice may represent the opposite ends of a scheduling continuum. The primary characteristic of Shea and Morgan's blocked practice method was that all practice trials on one task variation were performed consecutively, without any intervening practice on other task variations. A random order maximized the amount of task-to-task variations encountered during practice. Variations of these practice orders, however, have produced mixed results.

Shea, Ho, and Morgan (cited by Shea & Zimny, 1983) combined one or more periods of random and blocked practice orders within the same acquisition period, and compared retention and performance of these mixed schedules to completely random and completely blocked schedules. Using a task similar to the one used by Shea and Morgan (1979), they found that learning was facilitated relative to an entirely blocked practice schedule, regardless of how the mixed periods of random and blocked practice were alternated. A related finding was reported by Gabriele, Hall, and Lee (1989). Random and blocked physical practice trials were interspersed with imagery trials on either the other task variations (random imagery) or on the same task (blocked imagery). The effects on retention were additive: both blocked and random physical practice was enhanced more by random imagery than by blocked imagery.

Lee and Magill (1983b) devised a serial practice order by rotating the task variations in an orderly manner on every trial (e.g., a serial order of three task variations might be ABCABCABC ...). In an experiment similar to Shea and Morgan (1979), both the acquisition and retention performance of the serial group were identical to the performance of the random group (Lee & Magill, 1983b, Experiment 2). However, the results of serial practice on a timing task (Lee & Magill, 1983b, Experiment 3) and on learning three badminton serves (Goode & Magill, 1986) were no better than blocked practice.

A modified form of blocked practice was used recently by Shea, Kohl, and Indermill (1990). Their goal was to assess the effects of 50, 200, or 400 trials of blocked or random practice on learning 5 target forces. The blocked practice groups, however, were defined in terms of repeating sets of 50 trials (10 trials of practice for each force). Thus the blocked groups that practiced for 200 or 400 trials practiced each target force for 4 or 8 sets of 10 trial blocks. Under this method, blocked practice for the 200- and 400-trial groups should have benefited by renewed practice on the task variations. However, the results of this study suggested just the opposite. The retention benefit following random practice became larger with increasing amounts of acquisition performance. The cause of this benefit could have been due either to the unconventional blocked practice method, or to benefits accrued to increasing practice trials under a random order.

Variations in Scheduling Retention. Shea and Morgan (1979) found that the random retention advantage was larger under randomly ordered retention trials than under blocked retention trials. This finding has been replicated several times (e.g., Del Rey, 1989; Shea et al., 1990). One of the interesting implications of this finding is that it appears to violate a rather long-standing principle regarding the specificity of learning: that performance will be optimized

when the conditions of retention or transfer are identical to the conditions of practice (e.g., Proteau, Marteniuk, Girouard, & Dugas, 1987; Schmidt, 1988; see also the earlier discussion on the practice/transfer relationship). The key finding in this respect is the advantage of random practice under blocked retention orders. Although not all studies of contextual interference have found a random advantage under blocked retention conditions, a significant number of such findings (e.g., Gabriele, Hall, & Buckolz, 1987; Gabriele, Hall, & Lee, 1989) have caused some to reconsider theories of practice specificity (e.g., Del Rey, 1989; Lee, 1988; Schmidt, 1988).

Subject Variations. Most studies of contextual interference have involved university-aged subjects, with no particular inclusion or exclusion criteria. However, Magill and Hall (1990) suggest that variations in the contextual interference effect may be seen when different subject samples are considered. A mixed pattern of results appears to emerge when children serve as subjects. Del Rey, Whitehurst, and Wood (1983) examined the acquisition and retention performance of 6- to 10-year-olds under either a random or a blocked practice schedule. Unlike the performance of adults, the performance of the blocked group of children was better than the random group during both acquisition and retention. Pigott and Shapiro (1984) found no differences during acquisition and transfer between the blocked and random groups. However, they did observe that a group of subjects that received random blocks of trials outperformed all others during acquisition and transfer. On the other hand, clear benefits following random practice have been demonstrated in seven-year-old children on retention (Pollock & Lee, 1990), and in six-year-old children on transfer (Edwards, Elliott, & Lee, 1986). In neither of these latter two studies, however, were there acquisition differences between the random and blocked groups of children.

Contextual interference effects have also been observed in mentally handicapped subjects. Both Down's syndrome (Edwards et al., 1986) and nondifferentiated mentally handicapped adolescents (Heitman & Gilley, 1989) appear to show some retention and transfer benefits due to random practice.

Contextual interference effects have also been analyzed in older adults. Similar to university-age subjects, the typical contextual interference effects during acquisition and retention were found for older adults, ranging from 65 to 92 years of age (Chamberlin, Torrence, & Sexton, 1990). However, Del Rey (1982) found that these effects were more pronounced for active than less active older adults. Interestingly Del Rey has also found an interaction between involvement in physical activity and contextual interference in college-age females (Del Rey, Wughalter, & Whitehurst, 1982), although no interaction was found for college-age males (Del Rey, Whitehurst, Wughalter, & Barnwell, 1983).

Finally there is some evidence that the magnitude of the contextual interference effect may interact with an individual's cognitive style. Jelsma and Van Merrienboer (1989) administered a test battery to their subjects in order to identify cognitive style. Subjects who scored high on reflectivity were considered to work slowly on problems but to make few errors. Subjects who scored high on the opposite end of the continuum, impulsivity, were considered to be quick with solutions for problems, at the expense of making more errors. Jelsma and Van Merrienboer correctly predicted that cognitive style would interact with conditions of contextual interference, since blocked practice appears to encourage impulsive behavior, whereas random practice encourages reflective behavior. The results of their study were clear: the blocked/random differences during acquisition and retention were largest for subjects measured with the highest degree of impulsivity and smallest for subjects determined to be most reflective.

Task Variations. When considering the large body of literature that has evolved since Shea and Morgan's (1979) original work, the one parameter of study that has varied considerably is the type of task. The acquisition of laboratory tasks has been the primary focus, although their nature and requisite skills have varied considerably. Examples of the tasks that have been used include Shea and Morgan's (1979) rapid response task as well as other laboratory tasks that involved movement timing, anticipation timing, force production, linear positioning, and tracking (see Magill & Hall, 1990, for a review). Even among investigations that have used the same task, a wide selection of parameters within the task have been manipulated. Also employed in the research have been more real-world tasks, such as shooting in basketball (Chamberlin, Rimer, & Skaggs, 1990; Crumpton, Abendroth-Smith, & Chamberlin, 1990) and serving in badminton (Goode & Magill, 1986).

Based on their review of the literature, Magill and Hall (1990) stated that no one task, either laboratory or real-world, consistently failed to demonstrate the contextual interference effect. However, two possible exceptions have been proposed. Magill and Hall (1990) hypothesized that contextual interference effects may interact with motor control mechanisms underlying the set of task variations that were practiced. If the tasks to be learned are all variations of the same generalized motor program (Schmidt, 1988), then contextual interference effects were predicted to be small, or nonexistent. However, if the task variations are each under the control of a different generalized motor program, then contextual interference effects were predicted to be large. Although there is some evidence to support this suggestion (e.g., Chamberlin, Rimer, Skaggs, Crumpton, & Abendroth-Smith, 1991; Hall & Magill, 1991; Lee, Wulf, & Schmidt, in press; Wood & Ging, 1991), the hypothesis has been criticized (see comments by Shea, in Shea & Wright, 1991).

An alternate proposal regarding the effect of task type in the contextual interference paradigm has been made by Lee and White (1990). Random practice appears to engender more effort by subjects than blocked practice, especially for tasks that are quite simple or tedious. Lee and White suggested that contextual interference effects might be reduced or eliminated for tasks that are intrinsically motivating (such as computer games). A motivational consideration of the task might help to explain, for example, why random/blocked retention differences were higher following 400 trials of practice than following 50 trials of practice in the study by Shea et al. (1990). Presumably, blocked practice would become more tedious with increased trials, and may account for the enhancement of the retention effect.

Final Notes

The contextual interference effect demonstrated by Shea and Morgan (1979) has sparked considerable research interest for several reasons. Perhaps foremost, the set of findings posed a paradox: how could a variable have such a potent effect on acquisition performance, and an equally potent but opposite effect on retention and transfer? Some research has been driven by this theoretical question. Another area of research has been to extend the findings of Shea and Morgan by considering various factors that might interact with these results (e.g., subject and task characteristics). Pedagogical interest in the contextual interference effect has also generated some research activity.

PART VERSUS WHOLE TASK PRACTICE

Whether a complex motor skill should be presented to, and practiced by, a learner as a whole or in parts is a basic question that a teacher or coach must answer. Most of the research that has been performed on whole versus part practice has been based on the principle of effective transfer to the whole skill. In essence, the question is whether substantial levels of positive transfer in performing the whole skill can be achieved from separate practice on each of the skill's parts. Wightman and Lintern (1985) claim a weakness in this approach is a rather limited amount of useful knowledge regarding the principles and theories underlying transfer. Despite this shortcoming, however, a number of empirically supported principles seem to be emerging from the literature. Basically, the effectiveness of practicing a motor skill as a whole, or in parts, seems to be dependent on the nature of the skill, the capatibility of the learner, and the organization of the part practice.

Nature of the Skill

The types of skills used in this research have ranged from mostly cognitive tasks, such as predictive skills (Naylor & Briggs, 1963), to tracking tasks, such as simulated carrier landings (Wightman & Sistrunk, 1987), and video games (Newell, Carlton, Fisher, & Rutter, 1989). Generally it seems that the degree of interdependence of the parts, both spatially and temporally, are critical in determining the extent to which training on a part of the skill will transfer to performing the whole skill. As the degree of interdependence of the parts increases, the effectiveness of part training decreases. The interdependence of the parts within a skill has been referred to as the organization of a task (Magill, 1989; Naylor & Briggs, 1963).

Naylor and Briggs (1963) had subjects predict the appearance of objects on a video screen. Three characteristics of the objects' appearance were utilized—type, number, and location. The investigators manipulated the degree of interdependence among the three characteristics. When the three characteristics were highly interdependent, the subjects learned the task best through a whole practice schedule. When the degree of interdependence was decreased, part training produced the best results. Other studies in which the degree of interdependence among the parts can be determined have produced similar results (e.g., Briggs & Waters, 1958; Stammers, 1980). One criticism that has been made of these studies, however, is the arbitrary and unsystematic method by which skills are formed into parts. As Wightman and Lintern (1985) point out, the only study in which there appears to be an interdependence between the parts and a systematic partitioning procedure is the one reported by Mane (1984). In this study, subjects practiced on a space fortress video game. The results indicated a strong advantage for the part practice group. In a follow-up study using the same task, Newell et al. (1989) also demonstrated superiority for part practice.

The apparent discrepancy in the preceding conclusions might be due to the interpretation of interdependence among the parts of the skill. We speculate that highly interdependent parts in which the interdependence is invariant (i.e., must always be accounted for) will not be conducive to learning the skill in parts. An example of this would be the pitch and roll components of aircraft piloting. Since pitch and roll components constantly interact to allow for level flight, then practicing each component in isolation would be less effective than practicing both components as a whole (Briggs & Waters, 1958). However, when the interdependence among the parts of the skill is variant (i.e., may or may not need to be accounted for), part practice is effective for learning the whole task. In the space fortress game used in the study by Newell et al. (1989), a number of parts can be identified, such as maneuvering the spaceship in a linear or curvilinear fashion, firing on the fortress, avoiding the fortress's fire, and destroying mines. Although performance of some, or all, of these parts may occur in a highly interdependent fashion, there may also be a requirement to perform each part separately. Therefore, the degree of interdependence of the parts varies during the performance of the task. This variant interdependence allows for the effectiveness of part practice.

Capability of the Learner

Another principle that can be identified that mediates the effectiveness of part versus whole practice is the capability of the learner. It seems that if the demands of the task exceed the capability of the learner to process the neces-sary information and consequently hinder the acquisition of the correct pattern of responding, then part practice becomes a necessary requirement for learning. Therefore, we can conclude that part practice is more effective for beginning or low-aptitude learners.

This hypothesis has been supported by an empirical study in which subjects practiced simulated carrier landings on an airplane simulator. The authors investigated several part practice techniques and found an interaction between treatment and subject aptitude. This interaction indicated that part practice was most effective for low-aptitude subjects (Wightman & Sistrunk, 1987).

Organization of Part Practice

Part practice can be organized in a number of ways. Wightman and Lintern (1985) identified three basic categories of part practice that can be used. These categories are fractionation, simplification, and segmentation. Fractionation is a method by which two or more parts that are performed simultaneously are separated into independent units for practice. Research evidence has indicated that this type of part practice is ineffective for the learning of the whole skill, probably due to the high degree of invariant interdependence that would be characteristic of a task with simultaneously performed parts.

Simplification is an approach to part practice by which the whole task is simplified by adjusting the characteristics of task performance. In their review of the literature, Wightman and Lintern (1985) conclude that this method of part practice organization results in positive transfer but is not superior to whole skill practice. Therefore, this technique is not recommended unless there is a cost-effectiveness rationale for using the simplified version of the skill. The use of lead-up and scaled-down games in developing sport-specific performances might reflect a specific example for its use, due to available resources.

Segmentation seems to be the most useful of the part practice techniques. In this procedure, the whole skill is partitioned into parts along spatial or temporal dimensions. These parts can then be presented to the learners in a number of ways. Each part can be practiced to a criterion level separately and then combined for performing the whole skill (pure part), or one part can be acquired first, then a second part added to the first part and both parts practiced together, and so on, until the entire skill is being performed (the progressive part). The progressive part can be achieved by using either a forward (beginning with the initial segment) or backward (beginning with the final segment) chaining technique. Other variants include whole-part or part-whole practice (Magill, 1989). Research seems to indicate that progressive part practice is the most effective. Wightman and Lintern (1985) note that of four studies reviewed that investigated segmentation, the three studies that demonstrated the strongest effect for part practice all used backward chaining (but see Ash & Holding, 1990). However, a limitation to this conclusion is that in the studies reviewed, all tasks required a high degree of spatial accuracy in the end component. It would be interesting to compare forward to backward chaining of tasks that did, and did not, have a spatial accuracy requirement for the end segment.

A caveat to the use of part practice is that the learner needs to be aware of the relationship of the part being practiced to the whole skill. Newell et al. (1989, Experiment 3) compared subjects who received part practice and an overall strategy for game performance to subjects who only received part practice. Subjects who performed part practice within the context of an overall game strategy (which we can assume conveyed the nature and goal of the game to the subjects) learned the task better than the subjects who only received part practice. This procedural knowledge would most likely enhance the meaningfulness of the parts being practiced. It would seem safe to conclude that the overall goals and objectives of the whole skill need to be communicated to the learners prior to engaging in part practice. For example, in learning to play basketball, time should be spent initially in providing the students with knowledge concerning the nature of the game before instruction begins on the individual skills of which basketball is composed, such as dribbling, shooting, and passing. It would also follow that if individual skills are decomposed into component parts for practice, time should be dedicated to providing the goals and objectives of performing that skill.

Why Is Part Practice Effective?

Although a great deal of research has been directed toward identifying the conditions under which part practice is, or is not, effective, and in developing guiding principles for the use of part practice, much less effort has been expended in identifying the theoretical basis that underlies the effectiveness of part practice. A notable exception is found in the article by Wightman and Lintern (1985). Several hypotheses can be suggested to explain the enhanced learning that occurs with part practice under the conditions in which part practice has been found to be effective (i.e., complex segmental tasks with low or variant interdependence among the parts).

From an information-processing perspective, part practice could be hypothesized to be effective because of the reduced information load placed on the learner. Most attention theorists have proposed that humans have a limited capacity for attending to information (e.g., Broadbent, 1958; Kahneman, 1973; Welford, 1968). It would not be difficult to envision the attentional demands of the whole skill exceeding the learner's capacity to process this information. This situation of information overload would lead to an impoverished processing of the information that, in all likelihood, would cause a poor assimilation of the correct response dynamics. The net result would probably be errorful performance and decreased motivation for learning. By practicing a part of the whole skill, the information demands are most likely reduced to a level that is within the capability of the learner to process that information, in-

creasing the probability of acquiring the correct response dynamics and maintaining a suitable level of motivation for learning. Evidence for this hypothesis can be seen in Wightman and Sistrunk's (1987) study in which low-aptitude subjects gained more from part practice than did high-aptitude subjects.

A second hypothesis for the effectiveness of part practice is that there appears to be an analogy between the technique of providing part practice within the context of the overall procedural strategy being employed (Newell et al., 1989) and effective goal-setting behavior (Martens, 1987). In effective goal setting, challenging yet obtainable short-term goals that lead to an overall objective are established. This procedure has been demonstrated to lead to superior levels of skill acquisition and performance (Martens, 1987). It could be that having to learn the whole skill may present the learner with a goal that they perceive as unobtainable. For example, a beginning gymnast presented with the task of learning a tumbling run as part of a floor exercise sequence may be overwhelmed by the complexity of the entire performance. However, breaking the skill into parts and presenting one part initially to the learner may result in a perceived goal that is obtainable. Initially learning a round-off may be a challenging, yet obtainable goal. However, once the round-off is acquired, putting that skill together with a back handspring may now seem to be obtainable, and so on, until the entire tumbling run is successfully acquired.

Two other hypotheses have been suggested by Wightman and Lintern (1985). In one hypothesis, they suggest that part practice allows for more intensive practice on the critical, or more difficult, elements of the task. In whole practice, the learner will perform all segments of the movement, even those parts that may be easier or previously learned. In part practice, more of the practice time can be spent engaged in practice on the more difficult, or novel, parts of the skill. Therefore, larger gains in performance can be made on the more difficult or unlearned parts of the task by allowing more trials on these segments. This should result in an overall learning benefit through part practice. However, they do acknowledge that simply isolating the critical elements of the skill for extended practice does not seem to be the only reason, or even the most important reason, for part practice superiority.

Because of this, Wightman and Lintern (1985) propose a second hypothesis. They have derived this hypothesis based on the temporal relationship between performance of a skill and the provision of knowledge of results (KR). They suggest that since KR is normally provided at the conclusion of a performance, earlier performed segments of the movement are more removed temporally from the source of KR than later performed segments. In fact, the later performed segments act as a source of interfering activity during the time interval from the initial segment's performance and the KR, an interval commonly referred to as the KR delay interval (Magill, 1989). Research has indicated that activity during the KR delay interval can be detrimental to learning (e.g., Shea & Upton, 1976). Thus in attempting to learn the whole task, acquisition of the earlier segments of the task may be impaired, resulting in an inefficient movement which would limit potential performance levels on the whole task. By learning the skill in parts, activity during the KR delay interval is eliminated. Wightman and Lintern (1985) believe that this is most likely the mechanism that results in the apparent superiority of the backward chaining technique with aiming tasks. Since the accuracy of the termination of the movement provides a powerful source of feedback, the segment most likely to receive benefit from this source of information is the terminal segment. Once acquired, accuracy in performing this segment can become the source of feedback information for the immediately preceding segment. By successively adding each segment in a reverse order, the entire skill can be acquired most effectively.

Wightman and Lintern (1985) go on to hypothesize that performance of the initial segments of a skill may act as interfering activity during the post-KR delay interval, the interval of time between the receipt of KR and the next performance of the task. In whole skill practice, if the KR received at the end of performance relates most strongly to the final segment, then performance of the initial segments must occur before the next performance of the final segment can take place. They propose that this interference may degrade learning of the later segments. The difficulty with this argument is that recent investigations into activity during the post-KR delay interval have indicated that this activity has either no effect or perhaps a beneficial effect, on the acquisition of a motor skill (e.g., Lee & Magill, 1983a). It would seem that Wightman and Lintern's (1985) hypothesis relating the effectiveness of part practice to the KR delay and post-KR delay paradigms could be empirically investigated by observing the acquisition patterns of each part of the movement, rather than looking at an overall performance score.

SIMULATION

Many training techniques applied to motor skills involve simulations of the perceived context to which the learner will be transferring her or his acquired knowledge. In sport, competitive conditions are simulated by the practice environment. Included in this simulation is the potential use of various training devices and simulators. A large number of these devices to aid in simulation exist in the sports world. Golf seems to be a particularly viable sport for the development of simulators and training devices. Viewers of late-night television are likely well aware of advertisements for devices that are "guaranteed" to lower one's handicap by several strokes. Video golf is becoming quite popular, especially in areas with harsh winter climates, where an individual can "play" various golf courses indoors by using videographic simulations of the real courses. Examples from other sports include the use of blocking and tackling dummies in football, rebound machines in basketball, and pitching machines in baseball.

With the widespread use of simulators and simulation in sport, it would seem logical to assume that the development of these devices has been founded on sound theoretical principles based on empirical data. Actually, minimal research has been undertaken about the applicability of these devices in sport contexts. Although a substantial body of data exists from the investigation of the use of simulators, the majority of this work has been done in industrial settings and, in particular, in the training of pilots. It is relatively safe to conclude that the most advanced development of simulators has occurred in flight simulation, although considerable development has also occurred with driver's education.

Despite the lack of research on the use of simulation in sport contexts, a number of principles can be derived from the literature and applied in a speculative manner to sport environments. The typical approach in the research has been to determine the impact of simulators, and their characteristics, on the transfer of learning between the simulated and "real" performance. The program of research has been somewhat plagued by a number of problems, including the lack of a definitive theoretical basis to the transfer of learning phenomena.

Reflecting a general belief that transfer increases as the similarity between the learning and transfer contexts increase, such as is seen in the law of encoding specificity (Tulving & Thomson, 1973) or the identical elements theory (Osgood, 1949; Thorndike, 1914), simulator engineering has often been directed toward developing increased realism in simulator performance. In general, the degree of similarity between the simulator and the actual performance is termed "fidelity." When training to fly an airplane, for example, piloting an actual airplane would be very high in fidelity whereas practicing on flight simulators would have decreasing levels of fidelity, depending on the degree of realism built into the flight simulators. The attempt, then, has been to develop simulators that are high in fidelity, based on the belief that increasing fidelity will increase transfer of learning (see Alessi, 1988, for a review of simulation fidelity). We note a similar belief in the sport environment as a guiding principle that is often used is to simulate the competitive context as realistically as possible in the practice environment. Some empirical evidence exists, however, that casts doubt on this assumption. It appears that the relationship between fidelity and transfer is mediated by a number of intervening variables. These variables include the type of fidelity manipulated, the information to be learned, and the capability of the learner.

Type of Fidelity

Fidelity is not a unitary construct. For instance, Allen, Hays, and Buffardi (1986) differentiate physical from functional fidelity. They define physical fidelity as the degree to which a simulator *looks like* the actual device. Functional fidelity refers to the degree to which a simulator *feels like* the actual device. Lintern, Sheppard, Parker, Yates, and Nolan (1989) discuss physical fidelity versus functional equivalence and psychological fidelity. Physical fidelity and functional equivalence are similar to the concepts proposed by Allen et al. (1986). Psychological fidelity is the degree to which the learner perceives the simulator to be realistic. From these studies, it appears that each type of fidelity differentially impacts on the transfer of learning process.

Physical fidelity has been studied in the majority of investigations. Data have indicated that decreasing physical fidelity can lead to greater transfer of learning, contrary to transfer theory expectations. Boreham (1985) demonstrated this effect in a hypothesis generation task. Povenmire and Roscoe (1973) and Roscoe (1971) found initial training on a flight simulator to be more effective for learning than initial training with the actual airplane that the pilots were learning to fly. (The assumption is that the actual device—in this case, an airplane—will always have a higher fidelity than a simulator.) Investigations into the impact of functional and psychological fidelity still remain to be done (see Lintern et al., 1989). The speculation that we can draw from this research is that increasing the fidelity of the practice context by physically simulating the game context as exactly as possible (e.g., using intrasquad games with referees, scorers, etc.) may not result in a greater transfer of learning to the game environment. In fact, decreasing some aspects of physical similarity of the practice to the game context may actually enhance transfer of learning. However, this conclusion is tempered by a consideration of other factors, such as the nature of the information that is to be learned.

Type of Knowledge

One of the factors that mitigates the fidelity/transfer of learning relationship is the information to be learned. Early flight simulation was concerned with helping the learner to acquire the neuromuscular coordination for the skilled act of flying. (Although considerable debate exists over the definition of procedural versus declarative knowledge, for our purposes we will define this type of knowledge as being declarative.) Flight simulation currently is almost completely dedicated to providing knowledge about the process of flying. That is, the interest appears to be more with the acquisition of procedures to follow in response to specific stimulus events (see Whiteside, 1983). This type of knowledge may be defined as procedural knowledge. We can only speculate that this change in target knowledge may have been prompted by the fact that as flight simulators increased in fidelity, the effectiveness in developing declarative knowledge may have decreased. Alessi (1988) suggests that the research done on simulators and fidelity has indicated that increasing the similarity of the practice environment to the test environment through higher fidelity enhances the transfer of procedural knowledge. However, transfer of declarative knowledge would be enhanced by providing variation, which would result in decreased fidelity. Although the variability of practice hypothesis (Schmidt, 1988; see also earlier in this chapter) has not been discussed in terms of a procedural/declarative knowl-

edge dichotomy, Alessi's (1988) reasoning allows for some interesting speculation.

We conclude, then, that high fidelity simulation results in high positive transfer of procedural information. Schmidt (1988) echoes this finding when he states that "Simulation devices are usually excellent for teaching procedural details" (p. 413). However, in acquiring more declarative-type knowledge, such as the neuromotor details of the movement, high fidelity simulation is not as useful. Here, variability of practice, which tends to decrease fidelity, provides for greater positive transfer.

Capability of the Learner

A second factor that mitigates the transfer/fidelity relationship is the capability of the learner. Of particular concern here is the stage of learning. In his review of the literature, Alessi (1988) concludes that higher fidelity simulations are more effective for enhancing positive transfer of learning in advanced performers as compared to novices. In fact, he proposes that low to moderate fidelity is superior for transfer of learning in novices as compared to high fidelity. This idea has been supported in two recent articles. Lintern et al. (1989) found that advanced individuals, in terms of stage of learning, gained more from high fidelity simulation than did beginners. Andrews (1988) concluded that high fidelity simulation may overwhelm the beginner and, as such, not be effective for enhancing the positive transfer of learning.

It appears that high fidelity simulation should not be used with beginners. However, this conclusion leaves a number of questions unanswered. For example, if decreased fidelity is effective with beginners, how low should the fidelity be? Eventually, decreasing fidelity would reach a point where the practice environment is so dissimilar to the "real" environment that no transfer of learning will occur. Also, as a learner gains proficiency with a skill, how and when should fidelity be increased? There is a need for a comprehensive principle that provides an understanding of the relationship between simulation fidelity and stage of learning.

What Should Be Simulated?

As mentioned at the beginning of this section, simulation and simulators enjoy a widespread usage in sport settings. The evidence that has been cited indicates that simulation can be effective in enhancing positive transfer of learning as long as the impact of specific intervening variables is taken into consideration. Although a comprehensive principle on which to base the application of simulation in sport settings has not been formulated, we do know that simply basing a simulation on a principle of increased similarity (fidelity) between the practice and game context is not the most effective approach for optimizing transfer of learning. Before establishing the proper level of fidelity for the simulation, consideration must be given to the knowledge to be learned and to the stage of learning of the performer. Lower fidelity appears to be more effective in enhancing transfer of learning for novices and in acquiring the patterns of action for a specific movement. As the performer gains proficiency with the task, fidelity should be increased. High fidelity would seem to be effective for the acquisition of procedural knowledge.

Given the previous conclusions, we can begin to develop principles that govern the use of simulation. One important question is "What aspects of the transfer context should be simulated in the practice environment?" Coaches have chosen to simulate a number of interesting aspects of the game context in practice. For instance, crowd noise is frequently simulated. Coaches have used stereophonic equipment to "pipe in" crowd noise during the practice session in an attempt to simulate the environment that will be encountered in a particular opponent's gymnasium or stadium. Is this an important element of the stimulus display that needs to be simulated for optimal transfer of learning?

A number of articles can be identified that provide some indication of what the answer to this question would be. Andrews (1988) argues that the need is to identify the critical elements in the stimulus display that are needed for optimizing transfer of learning. He states that we need to conduct task analyses for the purpose of determining these critical elements. Lintern and his colleagues (Lintern, Roscoe, Koonce, & Segal, 1990; Lintern, Roscoe, & Sivier, 1990) have conducted a series of studies that follow up on the ideas expressed by Andrews. In these studies, elements of the visual display that is provided to pilots working on flight simulators were manipulated. They found that moderately detailed, realistic displays in which critical elements were enhanced through adaptive visual augmentation led to greater transfer of learning. They also noted that symbolic renderings of the actual visual display were not effective for transfer of learning.

Extending these findings to a sport setting, we can conclude that coaches should identify those elements of the stimulus display that are critical for the learning and performance of a particular movement, and present these elements in an enhanced fashion within the context of a moderately detailed, realistic background. Simulating these elements in a symbolic manner, however, would not appear to be useful for the transfer of learning. Given these conclusions, then, would the use of piped-in crowd noise be helpful? The answer, when considering enhancement of an individual's level of performance, would appear to be "no" as we propose that providing crowd noise through an amplified, stereophonic system is mostly a symbolic rendering of "real" crowd noise.

BILATERAL TRANSFER

A number of sport skills, such as dribbling a ball in soccer or basketball, are bilateral in nature; i.e., the requirements of the sport are such that the skill must be performed with either limb. The basic question that confronts a coach is how should the practice environment be arranged to optimize the acquisition of these skills? The usual approach is to provide equal training with each limb. In this section, we will attempt to provide evidence that can be applied to discerning the veracity of this approach to the acquisition of bilateral motor tasks by investigating the phenomenon of bilateral transfer.

Investigations have demonstrated that transfer of training does occur between limbs. That is, training one limb to perform a particular motor skill will result in an increase in performance of that skill in the nontrained limb. This transfer of training for skilled performance from a practiced to a nonpracticed limb is known as bilateral transfer, although terms such as cross-education (e.g., Cook, 1936) and bimanual skill transfer (e.g., Hicks, Frank, & Kinsbourne, 1982) have been used. The occurrence of bilateral transfer has been demonstrated frequently, and this particular effect seems to be robust across a variety of motor tasks, such as the pursuit rotor (e.g., Kohl & Roenker, 1980), one-hand typing (e.g., Hicks et al., 1982), and finger tapping (e.g., Taylor & Heilman, 1980).

Most researchers have typically used normal, college-age males and females, although others have demonstrated the bilateral transfer effect in children (Byrd, Gibson, & Gleason, 1986), and mentally retarded subjects (Elliott, 1985). The only recently published article in which a bilateral transfer of training effect was not found was by Byrd and Gibson (1988) in which mentally retarded subjects ranging in chronological age from 7 to 17 years were studied. Nevertheless, the existence of the bilateral transfer effect does not seem to be in question, and the more recent investigations have been concerned with understanding why bilateral transfer occurs and how the effect can best be utilized in the acquisition of bilateral tasks.

Theoretical Bases for Bilateral Transfer

Investigations into the cause of bilateral transfer have been generated by two hypotheses. The earliest investigated hypothesis can be termed a neuromuscular activation hypothesis and is quite similar in nature to the bilateral transfer of physical training that has been noted across limbs. The second hypothesis has been labeled a cognitive hypothesis (Magill, 1989). Each will be considered separately here.

Neuromuscular Activation Hypothesis. A phenomenon that has been noted when performing a task with one limb is that EMG activity can be recorded in the nonperforming limbs and this EMG activity is strongest between contralateral, as opposed to ipsilateral or diagonal, limbs (Davis, 1942). This "motor overflow at a submotor level" (Hicks et al., 1982, p. 280) provides the nonpracticing limb with the kinesthetic sensation of moving without any overt movement. Within the framework of schema theory (Schmidt, 1975), this information can be used for error detection and correction, and can be integrated into the development of a generalized motor program for control of the movement. In effect, the neural activity that is evidenced by EMG readings in the nonpracticing limb facilitates the transfer of task-specific motor components between limbs and is covertly promoting the development of a motor program to control the performance of the nonpracticing limb (Hicks, Gualtieri, & Schroeder, 1983).

Two predictions can be drawn from this hypothesis. The first prediction is that blocking the motor overflow into the nonpracticing limb should eliminate the bilateral transfer effect. This prediction was upheld in a study by Hicks et al. (1982). Subjects learned to perform a one-hand typing task. The nonpracticing hand was either free or gripped the leg of a table. The logic was that gripping the table leg would block the motor overflow from the practicing hand. Bilateral transfer was evident when the hand was left free, but not when the table leg was gripped, supporting the neuromuscular activation hypothesis.

The second prediction is that after sufficient practice with one limb, bilateral transfer to the nonpracticing limb should be greatest if the nonpracticing limb performs the task as a mirror image of that performed with the practicing limb. The logic is that the mirror-image performance would have an identical pattern of neural functioning to the original task. Thus the covertly acquired motor program would be more directly applicable to the control of the nonpracticing limb's performance. Hicks et al. (1983) had subjects practice the pursuit rotor task with their preferred limb. After either 5 or 25 trials of practice, they were required to perform the task with their nonpreferred limb in either the same direction as original practice, or as a mirror-image performance. After 25 acquisition trials, the greatest amount of bilateral transfer was achieved for the mirror-image performance, supporting the prediction.

Cognitive Hypothesis. An alternative explanation is that bilateral transfer is a result of central information processing and does not entail peripheral neuromuscular transmissions (Kohl & Roenker, 1980, 1983). In their experiments, they noted that the amount of bilateral transfer was the same whether the subjects physically or mentally practiced a motor task. Since other research had demonstrated that mental rehearsal only causes neuromuscular activation in the limb being mentally rehearsed, the explanation that bilateral transfer is due to motor overflow into the nonpracticing limb could not account for their data. It should be noted, however, that Kohl and Roenker do not discount the neuromuscular activation explanation; rather, they propose that it is an interaction between the cognitive and neuromuscular explanations that provide for the bilateral transfer effect (Kohl & Roenker, 1983).

One interesting finding of the Kohl and Roenker (1980, 1983) studies is that the amount of bilateral transfer is roughly equal between groups that physically practice the task and groups that mentally practice the task. This seems to raise the question of whether bilateral transfer would be maximized by allowing physical and mental practice on the task (similar to what has been done in the mental practice

literature, e.g., McBride & Rothstein, 1979). To our knowledge, this particular experimental manipulation has not been undertaken.

Training Bilateral Motor Skills

Given that the evidence seems quite conclusive that bilateral transfer does occur and that both neuromuscular activation and cognitive explanations seem to underlie the effect, we now return to our original question. That is, how should practice be structured to optimize the acquisition of bilateral tasks? The notion is that the bilateral transfer effect can be used to optimize bilateral skill acquisition. Several characteristics that influence the bilateral transfer effect have been noted and would seem to offer insight into the optimal practice schedule, including asymmetry of bilateral transfer, the age of the learner, and the cognitive capacity of the learner.

Asymmetry of Bilateral Transfer. The most significant finding with regard to practice scheduling is that bilateral transfer is asymmetrical. That is, the amount of bilateral transfer is not equal between limbs. The problem with this conclusion, however, is that there does not seem to be conclusive evidence as to whether bilateral transfer is greatest from the preferred to the nonpreferred limb, or vice versa. Ammons (1958), in an extensive review of the literature on bilateral transfer, concluded that the greatest amount of bilateral transfer will take place from the preferred to the nonpreferred limb. This conclusion was supported in a more recent work by Byrd et al. (1986). However, Taylor and Heilman (1980), using finger key–pressing sequences as the experimental task, found that for right-handed subjects the greatest amount of bilateral transfer occurred from the left (nonpreferred) to the right (preferred) hand. Their finding was supported in a subsequent follow-up study by Elliott (1985). Taylor and Heilman (1980) argue that, due to motor control being in the left hemisphere of the brain and the need for contralateral activation to occur, right-handed practice would only activate the left hemisphere whereas left-handed practice would activate both hemispheres, causing greater activation and enhancing bilateral transfer. This seems to indicate that bilateral transfer would be asymmetrical, with the greatest amount of transfer occurring from the nonpreferred to preferred hand (for right-handed subjects).

The impact of this finding from a practice scheduling perspective would be that initial practice with the bilateral task should be implemented with the limb from which the greatest amount of bilateral transfer could be expected. This would allow for more efficiency in practice. Although eventual levels of skill performance may not be affected by this scheduling manipulation, the number of trials required to reach criterion performance level may be. Therefore, serially organized equal practice with both limbs may not limit ultimate skill level, but may increase the time needed in practice, decreasing practice efficiency.

This hypothesis has been investigated by Dunham (1977, 1978). Subjects practiced a pursuit rotor task until a criterion level of performance was reached. One group of subjects performed under a practice schedule that had them alternating hands on each trial until reaching the criterion performance level (the serial group). The second group of subjects practiced the task with their preferred hand until reaching the criterion performance level and then practiced with the opposite hand to the same criterion level (the sequential group). The sequential group took fewer trials overall to reach the criterion. This finding indicates that practicing with one limb until reaching a particular level of performance before practicing with the opposite limb would be the desirable practice schedule for the acquisition of a bilateral task. However, as noted earlier, the problem with the Dunham (1977) study is that learning was not assessed.

Therefore, conclusive evidence concerning this sequencing manipulation for the acquisition of a bilateral task remains to be provided. However, as Magill (1989) has pointed out, this may be more of a theoretical, as opposed to practical, problem. It is possible that factors such as motivation to perform a task will outweigh the sequencing effect. Most individuals have a higher degree of motor control with their preferred limbs. Because of this, it is most likely that initial attempts with a task would be more successful when done with the preferred limb. Initial success may lead to a greater desire to learn that task and increased motivation for performance. Forced initial practice with the non-preferred limb may lead to greater errors, less motivation to learn, and decreased effort toward skill acquisition.

Age of Learner. Another factor that may be associated with the use of bilateral transfer is the age of the learner. An interesting finding of the Byrd et al. (1986) study is that the amount of bilateral transfer noted was directly related to the age of the subject. Subjects ranged in age from 7 to 17 years, and they performed a typical bilateral transfer experiment using a pursuit rotor task. Greater bilateral transfer was noted as a function of age, with the older groups demonstrating more bilateral transfer than did the younger groups. The reason that bilateral transfer may be an age-related phenomenon might be related to the maturity of the neuromuscular system, or to the deficient knowledge base of the younger subjects. However, there is a need for replication.

Cognitive Capacity of Learner. Finally, related to the age-dependent finding just cited, level of cognitive capability may be a factor influencing the amount of bilateral transfer. A bilateral transfer paradigm with cognitively deficient subjects has been used in two studies. Byrd and Gibson (1988) found no evidence of bilateral transfer in 7- to 17-year-old mentally retarded children. Elliott (1985), however, did find evidence for bilateral transfer in both adolescents and adults with Down's syndrome. It is clear that more research is required before a definitive conclusion can be made on this question. However, based on the two explanations expounded on previously regarding the bilateral transfer effect, it would seem logical that diminished cognitive capacity should have at least an attenuating effect, even if it does not eliminate bilateral transfer completely.

Amount of Practice

What is the optimal amount of practice required to influence positively the greatest gains in learning and performance of a motor skill? This basic question that every coach faces does not seem to have a clear and consistent answer. Two prominent textbooks on motor learning and control provide what appears to be contradictory responses to this question. Schmidt (1988) states, "In structuring the practice session, the number of practice attempts should be maximized" and ". . . usually, more practice leads to more learning" (p. 384). However, Magill (1989) argues that increasing the amount of practice may eventually lead to a point of "diminishing returns," in that although more practice beyond a certain optimal point will not be harmful to learning, it will not provide any benefits that will justify the amount of time spent in practice (pp. 420–425). Which of these interpretations is correct?

Most of the research on the amount of practice issue has been associated with the heading of "overlearning" or "overtraining." These terms can be defined as "the amount of time spent in practice after reaching a criterion level of performance in a particular skill" (Magill, 1989, p. 421). The largest single body of work has been done from the behaviorist perspective investigating the overtraining of of a stimulus-response pairing with animals. Most of the studies concerned with human subjects have examined the acquisition of cognitive material, with only a few studies being concerned with the learning of motor skills.

In one of the motor skill studies, Schendel and Hagman (1982) trained subjects to be able to disassemble and reassemble a machine gun. They called this type of task a procedural task, and it resembles the serial learning that occurs in many sport-specific skills. Three groups of subjects learned the task to a criterion performance level, defined as one errorless disassemble/reassemble trial. One group then received 100% more trials at this point (overtraining trials equal to the number of trials required to reach criterion performance levels). A second group received the 100% overtraining trials four weeks after the original acquisition session. The third group did not receive any extra trials of practice. Eight weeks following the original acquisition session, all groups were tested for their retention of the skill and the number of trials required to be retrained to the criterion performance level. The group that received the overtraining trials immediately after the original acquisition trials exhibited less forgetting over the eight-week retention interval than did the second overtraining group, which received the trials at the four-week overtraining session. Also, both overtraining groups performed better on retention and retraining than the group that did not receive any overtraining trials.

These results indicate an effectiveness of overtraining in

promoting the learning and performance of a motor skill (Schendel & Hagman, 1982). However, their study cannot provide us with any information regarding our central question of concern, i.e, how much practice is needed? We know there is a beneficial effect of practicing a skill after reaching a level of proficiency, but not how much overtraining is desirable.

Melnick (1971) provides some insight into this question. In this study, subjects learned to perform a dynamic balance task. Using a stabilometer, subjects were required to learn to be on balance for 28 seconds of a 50-second trial. Once reaching this criterion performance level, subjects either received no extra trials, 50%, 100%, or 200% overtraining trials. Administration of one-week and one-month retention tests indicated that all three of the overtraining groups performed at higher levels than the group that did not receive overtraining, but that none of the overtraining groups outperformed any of the other overtraining groups. Thus it must be concluded that the 50% overtraining group learned the balancing task as well as did the 100% and 200% overtraining groups. Therefore, from an efficiency perspective, the 50% overtraining trials would be the more desirable schedule as additional practice beyond this point did not seem to be beneficial for learning.

Because of the limited amount of available evidence, making conclusions regarding the amount of practice required for the acquisition of a motor skill would be a tenuous undertaking, at best. Several issues remain to be clarified before determining the number of trials at a particular task that would be most effective to optimize learning. First, in overtraining experiments, a subjectively determined criterion level of performance is used to provide the point at which overtraining begins. In the real world, how do we decide on this criterion performance level? Second, would it not be reasonable to assume that the amount of practice required would be dependent on the level of performance to which the learner aspires? Third, it seems that the amount of practice alone is insufficient to ensure skill acquisition. Effective practice must also combine a number of other important variables, such as knowledge of results and the motivation to achieve.

The principle of overtraining appears to be valid for optimizing motor skill learning in diverse skills such as gun assembly, dynamic balancing, and two-point-touch cane technique in the blind (Croce & Jacobson, 1986). How much training constitutes overtraining would appear to be dependent on a number of other factors. Crossman's (1959) classical study of cigar rolling indicates that many repetitions of a skill are required before high levels of proficiency can be reached. Furthermore, Kottke, Halpern, Easton, Ozel, and Burrill (1978) estimated from a number of sources that 3 million steps are required before proficiency at walking is achieved, that 1 million shots are required before proficiency at shooting in basketball is achieved, that 800,000 punts are required before proficiency at punting is achieved, and that 1.6 million throws are required before proficiency at baseball pitching is achieved. Given the predicted magnitude of repetitions of these motor skills, it seems that Schmidt's (1988) advice to "maximize the number of practice attempts" is the best principle to follow.

SUMMARY

Providing a summary statement regarding the arrangement of practice conditions and the designing of instruction is a somewhat daunting task, considering the complexity and relative independence of factors that interact during a typical practice session. However, two observations seem rather clear. First, the research that has been directed toward investigating the arrangement of practice conditions and the designing of instruction is incomplete. A substantial array of variables, specifically task and subject variables, mitigate the influence of particular factors in optimizing the transfer of learning. Therefore, few principles can be identified that will generalize beyond a very narrow range of independent variables. Second, continued research into questions of practice conditions arrangement will be limited until a clear understanding of the theoretical basis for the transfer of learning is established. Although substantial progress has been made regarding an understanding of the optimal practice environment, it is apparent that considerably more research energy must be expended in this direction.

References

Adams, J. A. (1971). A closed-loop theory of motor learning. *Journal of Motor Behavior, 3,* 111–150.

Adams, J. A. (1987). Historical review and appraisal of research on the learning, retention and transfer of human motor skills. *Psychological Review, 101,* 41–74.

Adams, J. A., & Creamer, L. R. (1962). Anticipatory timing of continuous and discrete responses. *Journal of Experimental Psychology, 63,* 84–90.

Alderman, R. (1965). Influence of local fatigue on speed and accuracy in motor learning. *Research Quarterly, 36,* 131–140.

Alessi, S. M. (1988). Fidelity in the design of instructional simulators. *Journal of Computer-Based Instruction, 15,* 40–47.

Allen, J. A., Hays, R. T., & Buffardi, L. C. (1986). Maintenance training simulator fidelity and individual differences in transfer of training. *Human Factors, 28,* 497–509.

Ammons, C. H. (1960). Temporary and permanent inhibitory effects associated with the acquisition of a simple perceptual-motor skill. *Journal of General Psychology, 62,* 223–245.

Ammons, R. B. (1950). Acquisition of motor skills: III. Effects of initially distributed practice on rotary pursuit performance. *Journal of Experimental Psychology, 40,* 777–787.

Ammons, R. B. (1958). Le mouvement. In G. H. Steward & J. P. Steward (Eds.), *Current psychological issues* (pp. 146–183). New York: Holt.

Ammons, R. B. (1988). Distribution of practice in motor skill acquisition: A few questions and comments. *Research Quarterly for Exercise and Sport, 59,* 288–290.

Andrews, D. H. (1988). Relationship among simulators, training devices, and learning: A behavioral view. *Educational Technology, 28* (1), 48–54,

Angell, J. R. (1908). The doctrine of formal discipline in the light of the principles of general psychology. *Educational Review, 36,* 1–14.

Ash, D. W., & Holding, D. H. (1990). Backward versus forward chaining in the acquisition of a keyboard skill. *Human Factors, 32,* 139–146.

Baddeley, A. D., & Longman, D. J. A. (1978). The influence of length and frequency of training session on the rate of learning to type. *Ergonomics, 21,* 627–635.

Ban, D. K., & Minke, K. A. (1984). The use of generalization gradients for the study of mediational processes. *Journal of General Psychology, 110,* 115–128.

Barch, A. M. (1959). Replication report: Work and rest variables in cyclical motor performance. *Journal of Experimental Psychology, 58,* 415–416.

Battig, W. F. (1956). Transfer from verbal pretraining to motor performance as a function of motor task complexity. *Journal of Experimental Psychology, 51,* 371–378.

Battig, W. F. (1966). Facilitation and interference. In E. A. Bilodeau (Ed.), *Acquisition of skill* (pp. 215–244). New York: Academic Press.

Battig, W. F. (1972). Intratask interference as a source of facilitation in transfer and retention. In R. F. Thompson & J. F. Voss (Eds.), *Topics in learning and performance* (pp. 131–159). New York: Academic Press.

Battig, W. F. (1977). Reaction to Schutz. In D. Mood (Ed.), *The measurement of change in physical education* (pp. 101–104). Boulder, CO: University of Colorado Press.

Battig, W. F. (1979). The flexibility of human memory. In L. S. Cermak & F. I. M. Craik (Eds.), *Levels of processing in human memory* (pp. 23–44). Hillsdale, NJ: Erlbaum.

Battig, W. F., & Shea, J. B. (1980). Levels of processing of verbal materials: An overview. In P. Klavora & J. Flowers (Ed.), *Motor learning and biomechanical factors in sport* (pp. 24–33). Toronto: University of Toronto.

Benson, D. W. (1968). Influence of imposed fatigue on learning a jumping task and a juggling task. *Research Quarterly, 39,* 251–257.

Bilodeau, E. A., & Bilodeau, I. M. (1961). Motor-skills learning. *Annual Review of Psychology, 12,* 243–280.

Boreham, N. C. (1985). Transfer of training in the generation of diagnostic hypotheses: The effect of lowering fidelity of stimulation. *British Journal of Educational Psychology, 55,* 213–223.

Boswell, J. J. (1971). Effects of three levels of interpolated activity on the acquisition of a simple motor skill. *Perceptual and Motor Skills, 32,* 35–42.

Bourne, L. E. Jr., & Archer, E. J. (1956). Time continuously on target as a function of distribution of practice. *Journal of Experimental Psychology, 51,* 25–32.

Bransford, J. D., Franks, J. J., Morris, C. D., & Stein, B. S. (1979). Some general constraints on learning and memory research. In L. S. Cermak & F. I. M. Craik (Eds.), *Levels of processing in human memory* (pp. 331–355). Hillsdale, NJ: Erlbaum.

Briggs, G. E., & Waters, L. K. (1958). Training and transfer as a function of component interaction. *Journal of Experimental Psychology, 56,* 492–500.

Broadbent, D. E. (1958). *Perception and communication.* Oxford: Pergamon Press.

Browning, M., Brown, D. E., & Washburn, M. F. (1913). The effect of the interval between repetitions on the speed of learning a series of movements. *American Journal of Psychology, 24,* 580–583.

Bunch, M. E. (1944). Cumulative transfer of training under different temporal conditions. *Journal of Comparative Psychology, 37,* 265–272.

Byrd, R., & Gibson, M. (1988). Bilateral transfer in mentally retarded children of ages 7 to 17 years. *Perceptual and Motor Skills, 66,* 115–119.

Byrd, R., Gibson, M., & Gleason, M. H. (1986). Bilateral transfer across ages 7 to 17 years. *Perceptual and Motor Skills, 62,* 87–90.

Caplan, C. S. (1969). *The influence of physical fatigue on massed versus distributed motor learning.* Unpublished doctoral dissertation, University of California, Berkeley.

Carron, A. V. (1969). Performance and learning in a discrete motor task under massed vs. distributed practice. *Research Quarterly, 4,* 481–489.

Carron, A. V. (1972). Motor performance and learning under physical fatigue. *Medicine and Science in Sport, 4,* 101–106.

Chamberlin, C. J., & Magill, R. A. (1992a). A note on schema and exemplar approaches to motor skill representation in memory. *Journal of Motor Behavior.*

Chamberlin, C. J., & Magill, R. A. (1992b). The memory representation of motor skills: A test of schema theory. *Journal of Motor Behavior.*

Chamberlin, C. J., Rimer, T. N., & Skaggs, D. J. (1990, May). *The ecological validity of the contextual interference effect: A practical application to learning the jump shot in basketball.* Paper presented at the annual meeting of the North American Society for the Psychology of Sport and Physical Activity, Houston, TX.

Chamberlin, C. J., Rimer, T. N., & Skaggs, D. J., Crumpton, R. L., & Abendroth-Smith, J. (1991). *Laboratory based principles in the real world: Contextual interference effects applied in the classroom.* Unpublished manuscript.

Chamberlin, C. J., Torrence, B., & Sexton, J. (1990). [Age-dependent effects of contextual interference]. Unpublished raw data.

Christina, R. W., & Shea, J. B. (1988). The limitations of generalization based on restricted information. *Research Quarterly for Exercise and Sport, 59,* 291–297.

Conwell, H. R., & Ammons, R. B. (1951). Joint effects of cyclical practice and rest in rotary pursuit. *Journal of Psychology, 31,* 137–146.

Cook, T. W. (1936). Studies in cross-education. V. Theoretical. *Psychological Review, 43,* 149–178.

Cotten, D. J., Thomas, J. R., Spieth, W. R., & Biasiotto, J. (1972). Temporary fatigue effects in a gross motor skill. *Journal of Motor Behavior, 4,* 217–222.

Croce, R. V., & Jacobson, W. H. (1986). The application of two-point touch cane technique to theories of motor control and learning: Implications for orientation and mobility training. *Journal of Visual Impairment and Blindness, 80,* 790–793.

Crossman, E. R. F. W. (1959). A theory of the acquisition of speed skill. *Ergonomics, 2,* 153–166.

Crumpton, R. L., Abendroth-Smith, J., & Chamberlin, C. J. (1990, May). *Contextual interference and the acquisition of motor skills in a field setting.* Paper presented at the annual meeting of the North American Society for the Psychology of Sport and Physical Activity, Houston, TX.

Davis, R. C. (1942). The pattern of muscular action in simple voluntary movements. *Journal of Experimental Psychology, 31,* 437–466.

Del Rey, P. (1982). Effects of contextual interference on the memory of older females differing in levels of physical activity. *Perceptual and Motor Skills, 55,* 171–180.

Del Rey, P. (1989). Training and contextual interference effects on memory and transfer. *Research Quarterly for Exercise and Sport, 60,* 342–347.

Del Rey, P., Whitehurst, M., & Wood, J. M. (1983). Effects of experience and contextual interference on learning and transfer by boys and girls. *Perceptual and Motor Skills, 56,* 581–582.

Del Rey, P., Whitehurst, M., & Wughalter, E., & Barnwell, J. (1983). Contextual interference and experience in acquisition and transfer. *Perceptual and Motor Skills, 57,* 241–242.

Del Rey, P., Wughalter, E. H., & Whitehurst, M. (1982). The effects of contextual interference on females with varied experience in open sport skills. *Research Quarterly for Exercise and Sport, 53,* 108–115.

Dore, L. R., & Hilgard, E. R. (1938). Spaced practice as a test of Snoddy's two processes in mental growth. *Journal of Experimental Psychology, 23,* 359–374.

Dunham, P., Jr. (1977). Effect of practice order on the efficiency of bilateral skill acquisition. *Research Quarterly, 48,* 284–287.

Dunham, P., Jr. (1978). Retention of bilateral performance as a function of practice order. *Perceptual and Motor Skills, 46,* 43–46.

Dwyer, J. (1984). Influences of physical fatigue on motor performance and learning. *Physical Educator, 41,* 130–136.

Ebbinghaus, H. (1964). *Memory: A contribution to experimental psychology.* New York: Dover. (Original work published 1885).

Edwards, J. M., Elliott, D., & Lee, T. D. (1986). Contextual interference effects during skill acquisition and transfer in Down's Syndrome adolescents. *Adapted Physical Activity Quarterly, 3,* 250–258.

Elliott, D. (1985). Manual asymmetries in the performance of sequential movements by adolescents and adults with Down's Syndrome. *American Journal of Mental Deficiency, 90,* 90–97.

Ericksen, S. C. (1942). Variability of attack in massed and distributed practice. *Journal of Experimental Psychology, 31,* 339–345.

Gabriele, T., Hall, C. R., & Buckolz, E. E. (1987). Practice schedule effects on the acquisition and retention of a motor skill. *Human Movement Science, 6,* 1–16.

Gabriele, T., Hall, C. R., & Lee, T. D. (1989). Cognition in motor learning: Imagery effects in contextual interference. *Human Movement Science, 8,* 227–245.

Godwin, M. A., & Schmidt, R. A. (1971). Muscular fatigue and learning a discrete motor skill. *Research Quarterly, 42,* 374–382.

Goode, S., & Magill, R. A. (1986). Contextual interference effects in learning three badminton serves. *Research Quarterly for Exercise and Sport, 57,* 308–314.

Gorfein, D., & Hoffman, R. R. (1987). *Memory and cognitive processes: The Ebbinghaus centennial conference.* Hillsdale; NJ: Erlbaum.

Hagan, S. J., Wilkerson, H. R., & Noble, C. E. (1980). Pursuit tracking skill as a joint function of work and rest intervals. *Perceptual and Motor Skills, 50,* 683–697.

Hall, K. G., & Magill, R. A. (1991). Variability of practice and contextual interference in motor skill learning. Manuscript under review.

Heitman, R. J., & Gilley, W. F. (1989). Effects of blocked versus random practice by mentally retarded subjects on learning a novel skill. *Perceptual and Motor Skills, 69,* 443–447.

Henry, F. M. (1967). "Best" versus "average" individual scores. *Research Quarterly, 38,* 317–320.

Henry, F. M. (1968). Specificity vs. generality in learning motor skill. In R. C. Brown & G. S. Kenyon (Eds.), *Classical studies on physical activity* (pp. 331–340). Englewood Cliffs, NJ: Prentice-Hall.

Hendrickson, G., & Schroeder, W. H. (1941). Transfer of training in learning to hit a submerged target. *Journal of Educational Psychology, 32,* 205–213.

Hicks, R. E., Frank, J. M., & Kinsbourne, M. (1982). The locus of bimanual skill transfer. *Journal of General Psychology, 107,* 277–281.

Hicks, R. E., Gualtieri, C. T., & Schroeder, S. R. (1983). Cognitive and motor components of bilateral transfer. *American Journal of Psychology, 96,* 223–228.

Hilgard, E. R., & Bower, G. H. (1966). *Theories of learning* (3rd ed). New York: Appleton-Century-Crofts.

Holding, D. H. (1965). *Principles of training.* London: Pergamon.

Jelsma, O., & Van Merrienboer, J. J. G. (1989). Contextual interference interactions with reflection-impulsivity. *Perceptual and Motor Skills, 68,* 1055–1064.

Judd, C. H. (1908). The relation of special training to general intelligence. *Educational Review, 36,* 28–42.

Kahneman, D. (1973). *Attention and effort.* Englewood Cliffs, NJ: Prentice-Hall.

Keele, S. W. (1986). Motor control. In K. R. Boff, L. Kaufman, & J. P. Thomas (Eds.), *Handbook of perception and human performances: Volume II* (pp. 30.1–30.60). New York: Wiley.

Kimble, G. A. (1949). A further analysis of the variables in cyclical motor learning. *Journal of Experimental Psychology, 39,* 332–337.

Kimble, G. A., & Bilodeau, E. A. (1949). Work and rest as variables in cyclical motor learning. *Journal of Experimental Psychology, 39,* 150–157.

Knapp, B. (1963). *Skill in sport.* London: Routledge & Kegan Paul.

Kohl, R. M., & Roenker, D. L. (1980). Bilateral transfer as a function of mental imagery. *Journal of Motor Behavior, 12,* 197–206.

Kohl, R. M., & Roenker, D. L. (1983). Mechanism involvement during skill imagery. *Journal of Motor Behavior, 15,* 179–190.

Kottke, F. H., Halpern, D., Easton, J. K. M., Ozel, A. T., & Burrill, C. A. (1978). The training of coordination, *Archives of Physical Medicine and Rehabilitation, 59,* 567–572.

Lashley, K. S. (1915). The acquisition of skill in archery. Papers from the Department of Marine Biology of the Carnegie Institution of Washington, vol. VII, pp. 107–128.

Lee, T. D. (1988). Transfer-appropriate processing: A framework for conceptualizing practice effects in motor learning. In K. Roth & O. Meijer (Eds.), *Human movement behaviour: The "motor-action" controversy* (pp. 201–215). Amsterdam: North Holland.

Lee, T. D., & Genovese, E. D. (1988). Distribution of practice in motor skill acquisition: Learning and performance effects reconsidered. *Research Quarterly for Exercise and Sport, 59,* 277–287.

Lee, T. D., & Magill, R. A. (1983a). Activity during the post-KR interval: Effects upon performance or learning? *Research Quarterly for Exercise and Sport, 54,* 340–345.

Lee, T. D., & Magill, R. A. (1983b). The locus of contextual interference in motor-skill acquisition. *Journal of Experimental Psychology: Learning, Memory and Cognition, 9,* 730–746.

Lee, T. D., & Magill, R. A. (1985). Can forgetting facilitate skill acquisition? In D. Goodman, R. B. Wilberg & I. M. Franks (Eds.),

Differing perspectives on motor memory, learning and control (pp. 3–22). Amsterdam: North Holland.

Lee, T. D., Magill, R. A., & Weeks, D. J. (1985). Influence of practice schedule on testing schema theory predictions in adults. *Journal of Motor Behavior, 17,* 283–299.

Lee, T. D., & White, M. A. (1990). Influence of an unskilled model's practice schedule on observational motor learning. *Human Movement Science, 9,* 349–367.

Lee, T. D., Wulf, G., & Schmidt, R. A. (in press). Action plan reconstruction and the contextual interference effect in motor learning. *Quarterly Journal of Experimental Psychology.*

Lintern, G., Roscoe, S. N., Koonce, J. M., & Segal, L. D. (1990). Transfer of landing skills in beginning flight training. *Human Factors, 32,* 319–327.

Lintern, G., Roscoe, S. N., & Sivier, L. D. (1990). Display principles, control dynamics, and environmental factors in pilot training and transfer. *Human Factors, 32,* 299–317.

Lintern, G., Sheppard, D. J., Parker, D. L., Yates, K. E., & Nolan, M. D. (1989). Simulator design and instructional features for air-to-ground-attack: A transfer study. *Human Factors, 31,* 87–99.

Magill, R. A. (1989). *Motor learning: Concepts and applications.* Dubuque, IA: Brown.

Magill, R. A., & Green, K. J. (1989, November). *Implicit learning in a complex tracking skill.* Paper presented at the annual meeting of the Psychonomics Society, Atlanta, GA.

Magill, R. A., & Hall, K. G. (1990). A review of the contextual interference effect in motor skill acquisition. *Human Movement Science, 9,* 241–289.

Mane, A. M. (1984). Acquisition of perceptual motor skill: Adaptive and part-whole training. *Proceedings of the Human Factors Society, 28th Annual Meeting* (pp. 522–526). Santa Monica, CA: Human Factors Society.

Martens, R. (1987). *Coaches' guide to sport psychology.* Champaign, IL: Human Kinetics.

McBride, E., & Rothstein, A. (1979). Mental and physical practice and the learning and retention of open and closed skills. *Perceptual and Motor Skills, 49,* 359–365.

McGeoch, J. A. (1927). The acquisition of skill. *Psychological Bulletin, 24,* 437–466.

McGeoch, J. A. (1929). The acquisition of skill. *Psychological Bulletin, 26,* 457–498.

McGeoch, J. A. (1931). The acquisition of skill. *Psychological Bulletin, 28,* 413–466.

McGeoch, J. A., & Irion, A. L. (1952). *The psychology of human learning.* New York: Longmans.

Meikeljohn, A. (1908). Is mental training a myth? *Educational Review, 37,* 126–141.

Melnick, M. J. (1971). Effects of overlearning on the retention of a gross motor skill. *Research Quarterly, 42,* 60–69.

Mohr, D. R. (1960). The contributions of physical activity to skill learning. *Research Quarterly, 31,* 321–350.

Murphy, H. H. (1916). Distribution of practice periods in learning. *Journal of Educational Psychology, 7,* 150–162.

Naylor, J., & Briggs, G. (1963). Effects of task complexity and task organization on the relative efficiency of part and whole training methods. *Journal of Experimental Psychology, 65,* 217–244.

Newell, K. M. (1981). Skill learning. In D. H. Holding (Ed.), *Human Skills* (pp. 203–226). New York: Wiley.

Newell, K. M., Antoniou, A., & Carlton, L. G. (1988). Massed and distributed practice effects: Phenomena in search of a theory? *Research Quarterly for Exercise and Sport, 59,* 308–313.

Newell, K. M., Carlton, M. J., Fisher, A. T., & Rutter, B. G. (1989). Whole-part training strategies for learning the response dynam-

ics of microprocessor driven simulators. *Acta Psychologica, 71,* 197–210.

Noble, C. E., Salazar, O. G., Skelley, C. S., & Wilkerson, H. R. (1979). Work and rest variables in the acquisition of psychomotor tracking skill. *Journal of Motor Behavior, 11,* 233–246.

Norrie, M. L., & Henry, F. M. (1978). Influence of an interpolated nonrelated motor task on short- and long-term memory, learning and retention of a gross motor skill. *Perceptual and Motor Skills, 46,* 987–994.

Nunney, D. N. (1963). Fatigue, impairment, and psycho-motor learning. *Perceptual and Motor Skills, 16,* 369–375.

Osgood, C. E. (1949). The similarity paradox in human learning: A resolution. *Psychological Review, 56,* 132–143.

Pack, M., Cotten, D. J., & Biasiotto, J. (1974). Effect of four fatigue levels on performance and learning of a novel dynamic balance skill. *Journal of Motor Behavior, 6,* 191–198.

Pew, R. W. (1974). Levels of analysis in motor control. *Brain Research, 71,* 393–400.

Phillips, W. H. (1963). Influence of fatiguing warm-up exercises on speed of movement and reaction latency. *Research Quarterly, 34,* 370–378.

Pigott, R. E., & Shapiro, D. C. (1984). Motor schema: The structure of the variability session. *Research Quarterly for Exercise and Sport, 55,* 41–45.

Pillsbury, W. B. (1908). The effects of training on memory. *Educational Review, 36,* 15–27.

Plutchik, R., & Petti, R. D. (1964). Rate of learning on a pursuit rotor task at a constant work-rest ratio with varying work and rest periods. *Perceptual and Motor Skills, 19,* 227–231.

Polanyi, M. (1958). *Personal knowledge: Towards a post-critical philosophy.* London: Routledge and Kegan Paul.

Pollock, B. J., & Lee, T. D. (1990). *Contextual interference in motor learning: Dissociated effects due to age.* Manuscript under review.

Poulton, E. C. (1988). The Journal of Motor Behavior in the 1960s and the 1980s. *Journal of Motor Behavior, 20,* 75–78.

Povenmire, H. K., & Roscoe, S. N. (1973). Incremental transfer effectiveness of a ground-based general aviation trainer. *Human Factors, 15,* 534–542.

Proteau, L., Marteniuk, R. G., Girouard, Y., & Dugas, C. (1987). On the type of information used to control and learn an aiming movement after moderate and extensive training. *Human Movement Science, 6,* 181–199.

Pyle, W. H. (1914). Concentrated versus distributed practice. *Journal of Educational Psychology, 5,* 247–258.

Pyle, W. H. (1919). Transfer and interference in card-distributing. *Journal of Experimental Psychology, 10,* 107–110.

Renshaw, S., & Schwarzbek, W. C. (1938). The dependence of the form of the pursuit-meter learning function on the length of the inter-practice rests: I. Experimental. *Journal of General Psychology, 18,* 3–16.

Richards, D. K. (1968). A two factor theory of the warm-up effect in jumping performance. *Research Quarterly, 39,* 668–673.

Robinson, E. S. (1932). *Association theory today.* New York: Appleton-Century-Crofts.

Roscoe, S. N. (1971). Incremental transfer effectiveness. *Human Factors, 13,* 561–567.

Schendel, J. D., & Hagman, J. D. (1982). On sustaining procedural skill over a prolonged retention interval. *Journal of Applied Psychology, 67,* 605–610.

Schmidt, R. A. (1969). Performance and learning a gross muscular skill under conditions of artificially induced fatigue. *Research Quarterly, 40,* 185–191.

Schmidt, R. A. (1971). Retroactive interference and amount of original learning in verbal and motor tasks. *Research Quarterly, 42,* 314–326.

Schmidt, R. A. (1972). The case against learning and forgetting scores. *Journal of Motor Behavior, 4,* 79–88.

Schmidt, R. A. (1975). A schema theory of discrete motor skill learning. *Psychological Review, 82,* 225–260.

Schmidt, R. A. (1988). *Motor control and learning: A behavioral emphasis.* (2nd ed.). Champaign, IL: Human Kinetics.

Schneider, W. (1985). Training high performance skills: Fallacies and guidelines. *Human Factors, 27,* 285–300.

Shapiro, D. C., & Schmidt, R. A. (1982). The schema theory: Recent evidence and developmental implications. In J. A. S. Kelso & J. E. Clark (Eds.), *The development of movement control and coordination* (pp. 113–150). New York: Wiley.

Shea, C. H., & Kohl, R. M. (1990). Specificity and variability of practice. *Research Quarterly for Exercise and Sport, 61,* 169–177.

Shea, C. H., Kohl, R., & Indermill, C. (1990). Contextual interference: Contributions of practice. *Acta Psychologica, 73,* 145–157.

Shea, C. H., & Wright, D. L. (1991). *Factors affecting motor skill acquisition: Report on the contextual interference symposium.* Unpublished manuscript.

Shea, J. B., & Morgan, R. L. (1979). Contextual interference effects on the acquisition, retention, and transfer of a motor skill. *Journal of Experimental Psychology: Human Learning and Memory, 5,* 179–187.

Shea, J. B., & Upton, G. (1976). The effects of skill acquisition of an interpolated motor short-term memory task during the KR-delay interval. *Journal of Motor Behavior, 8,* 277–282.

Shea, J. B., & Zimny, S. T. (1983). Context effects in memory and learning movement information. In R. A. Magill (Ed.), *Memory and control of action* (pp. 345–366). Amsterdam: North-Holland.

Singley, M. K., & Anderson, J. R. (1989). *The transfer of cognitive skill.* Cambridge, MA: Harvard University Press.

Snoddy, G. S. (1935). *Evidence for two opposed processes in mental growth.* Lancaster, PA: Science Press.

Spano, J. F., & Burke, E. J. (1976). Effect of three levels of work intensity on performance of a fine motor skill. *Perceptual and Motor Skills, 42,* 63–66.

Stammers, R. B. (1980). Part and whole practice for a tracking task: Effects of task variables and amount of practice. *Perceptual and Motor Skills, 50,* 203–210.

Stelmach, G. E. (1969). Efficiency of motor learning as a function of inter-trial rest. *Research Quarterly, 40,* 198–202.

Suzuki, S. (1969). *Nurtured by love: A new approach to education.* New York: Exposition Press.

Taylor, H. G., & Heilman, K. M. (1980). Left-hemisphere motor dominance in righthanders. *Cortex, 16,* 587–603.

Thomas, J. R., Cotten, D. J., Spieth, W. R., & Abraham, N. L. (1975).

Effects of fatigue on stabilometer performance and learning of males and females. *Medicine and Science in Sports, 7,* 203–206.

Thorndike, E. L. (1903). *Educational psychology.* New York: Lemke & Buechner.

Thorndike, E. L. (1906). *Principles of teaching.* New York: Seiler.

Thorndike, E. L. (1914). *Educational psychology.* New York: Columbia University.

Thorndike, E. L. (1927). The law of effect. *American Journal of Psychology, 39,* 212–222.

Thorndike, E. L. & Woodworth, R. S. (1901). The influence of improvement of one mental function upon the efficiency of other functions. *Psychological Review, 8,* 247–261.

Trumbo, D., Ulrich, L., & Noble, M. (1965). Verbal coding and display coding in the acquisition and retention of tracking skill. *Journal of Applied Psychology, 49,* 368–375.

Tulving, E., & Thomson, D. M. (1973). Encoding specificity and retrieval processes in episodic memory. *Psychological Review, 80,* 352–373.

Van Rossum, J. H. A. (1987). *Motor development and practice: The variability of practice hypothesis in perspective.* Amsterdam: Free University Press.

Webb, W. W. (1933). Massed versus distributed practice in pursuitmeter learning. *Journal of General Psychology, 8,* 272–278.

Welch, M. (1969). Specificity of heavy work fatigue: Absence of transfer from heavy leg work to coordination tasks using the arms. *Research Quarterly, 40,* 401–406.

Welford, A. T. (1968). *Fundamentals of skill.* London: Methuen.

Whiteside, T. C. D. (1983). Simulators and realism. *Quarterly Journal of Experimental Psychology, 35A,* 3–15.

Whitley, J. D., & Smith, L. E. (1963). Larger correlations obtained by using average rather than "best" strength scores. *Research Quarterly, 34,* 248–249.

Williams, J., & Singer, R. N. (1975). Muscular fatigue and the learning and performance of a motor control task. *Journal of Motor Behavior, 7,* 265–270.

Wightman, D. C., & Lintern, G. (1985). Part-task training for tracking and manual control. *Human Factors, 27,* 267–283.

Wightman, D. C., & Sistrunk, F. (1987). Part-task training strategies in simulated carrier landing final-approach training. *Human Factors, 29,* 245–254.

Winstein, C. J., & Schmidt, R. A. (1989). Sensorimotor feedback. In D. H. Holding (Ed.), *Human Skills* (2nd ed., pp. 17–47). New York: Wiley.

Wood, C. A., & Ging, C. A. (1991). The role of interference and task similarity on the acquisition, retention and transfer of simple motor skills. *Research Quarterly for Exercise and Sport, 62,* 18–26.

Zelaznik, H., & Springs, J. (1976). Feedback in response recognition and production. *Journal of Motor Behavior, 8,* 309–312.

10

HUMAN SKILLS: IDEAS, CONCEPTS AND MODELS

Denis Glencross

INTRODUCTION: HISTORICAL PERSPECTIVES

The center point in the study of sport psychology is human skill, and in particular skilled performance. It is to the "vagaries" of such performance, the variability and inconsistency of athletes (and others) at all levels, that sport psychologists initially directed their attention. As the scientific study of human performance intensified, it soon became clear that we needed a better understanding of the nature of human skill. This meant not only an understanding of how skills are performed, but also how they are learned and acquired, how they can be effectively practised, and how this practice may be facilitated in training, teaching, and coaching programs.

In the present chapter, it is proposed that sport psychologists should be more directly concerned with understanding the nature of human skill, both from a theoretical and a practical point of view. Sport psychologists should attempt to understand and facilitate the skill-learning process at all levels. However, to do this more needs to be understood about the acquisition of skill. With this perspective, major ideas and concepts that have influenced research on human skill are reviewed in this chapter. This is done deliberately, so that we might evaluate and appreciate the major theoretical issues facing any researcher interested in this area. This historical perspective leads to a review of the controversy between the so-called computational or prescriptive approach and the emergent properties, dynamic systems approach. Sport psychologists, it is argued, must become more involved in this debate, because of the important implications that an understanding of, for example, knowledge structures has in the coaching and teaching of human skills. The chapter concludes with a discussion of some of these implications and applications.

Human skill, not only because it is at the center of all human behavior, but also because skilled performance is readily observable and thus to some extent measurable, has been featured in theories and models of human behavior almost since the formal study of behavior began.

Historically the pioneering work of Bryan and Harter (1897, 1899) and Woodworth (1899) introduced two fundamental concepts that have been influential on all subsequent modeling of human skill. Bryan and Harter systematically studied the acquisition of "the telegraphic language," the skill of sending and receiving Morse code. They reported that as the skill was practiced, larger and larger "habits" seemed to operate as a whole and seemed to be organized or controlled at a higher level, in a "hierarchy of habits," to use their terminology. This enabled larger and larger chunks of the Morse code to be sent (and received) in a single burst of activity, at a faster rate, and with fewer errors.

We will see later that what Bryan and Harter were suggesting was the important concept of "levels of control" and the development of automaticities, both of which are key concepts in information theory. Similarly, Woodworth (1899), studying rapid, repetitive aiming movements, introduced the notion of two phases of control, which he called the "initial impulse" phase followed by the "current-control" phase. We will see that these concepts parallel the notions of "automatic" and "controlled" information processing, respectively, which are central to cognitive psychology today.

Bartlett (1932, 1947) made a further important contribution in the conceptualization of human skill, rejecting the earlier notion of skill as an acquired habit and the notion that complex skills were merely the melding of combinations of habits.

Bartlett (1932) introduced the concept of a schema, which is central to our understanding of memory systems and human skill. Following the early speculations of Sir

Henry Head, the eminent neurologist, Bartlett proposed that a schema refers to an active organization of previous reactions or experiences, which must be operating in any well-adapted response. He went on to say that when there is consistency of behavior, a particular skilled response is possible because it is related to other similar past responses. "How I make the stroke depends on the relating of certain new experiences, most of them visual, to other immediately preceding visual experiences and to my posture. . . . When I make the stroke I do not, as a matter of fact, produce something absolutely new, and I never repeat something old. The stroke is literally manufactured out of the living visual and postural schemata of the moment and their interrelations" (Bartlett, 1932, pp. 201–202).

Two aspects of Bartlett's contribution need to be emphasized. Firstly, schema represent some kind of generalized model or standard of the performance about to be made. Secondly, a comparison is involved between the produced response and the schema representing that skill. You will see that these two concepts, the schema and some comparison process, are at the center of modern models of human skill, which are discussed later in this chapter.

At about the same time as Bartlett's work, the Russian scientist Nicholai Bernstein (1947, published in English in 1967) directed the interests of researchers toward the control and regulation of human movement. Indeed, so influential was Bernstein's work that many researchers oriented their efforts to the more fundamental issues of motor control and away from skill and motor learning. Bernstein (1967) identified as the crucial control issue what he called "the degrees of freedom" problem. That is, how does the brain control and organize the enormous number of possible outcomes of action? Whether we are talking about motor units, muscles, movements, or forces, there are too many of these free variables to be systematically regulated, controlled, and organized into effective patterns of action. There cannot be a direct or one-to-one correspondence between the units or elements of action and their representation in the brain.

This control issue emphasized the limitations of ongoing control and monitoring by feedback-based explanations, and drew attention to the need for organized units of action, acting as whole units and not as separate elements. Such a perspective drew into conflict traditional cognitive approaches, based on prescriptive planning and programming, and the emergent properties approach, based on self-organization and task dynamics (Glencross, Whiting, & Abernethy, in press).

COMMUNICATION AND INFORMATION THEORY

A major conceptual development in the understanding of human skill occurred as a consequence of the developments and close relationship between experimental psychology, engineering, and the communication sciences during World War II. In particular it was the developments in communication theory and cybernetics that were most influential. Wiener (1948), in *Cybernetics,* proposed the formal study of self-regulation in biological as well as physical systems, and Shannon and Weaver (1949), in *The Mathematical Theory of Communication,* presented the bases for the information theory approach to human behavior. Information theory provided a formal framework for the manner in which information is abstracted and processed by the brain.

It was Kenneth Craik (1947, 1948) who helped forge the link between communication theory, cybernetics, and human behavior. In two important papers, collectively entitled *Theory of the Human Operator in Control Systems,* Craik elaborated two fundamental concepts: firstly, that of an error-actuated servomechanism or comparator; and secondly, the notion of intermittency. These two concepts have been central in human skills research and an integral feature of models of human skill for the quarter of a century following Craik's publications. In biological systems, body temperature and posture are maintained according to comparator or closed-loop servo principles. The feedback information occurring in such systems is an important concept that challenged the traditional use of reinforcement as the primary consequence of behavior, influencing learning.

Intermittency or discontinuity refers to the observation that in many tracking tasks and other skills, adjustments do not appear to be made continuously, but discontinuously, at reasonably regular intervals of 300–500 milliseconds. The implication of this evidence is that the use of feedback information for controlling behavior is discontinuous or intermittent. As a consequence, under some circumstances, this discontinuity places serious limitations on both the speed and the capacity of the operating system.

Welford (1952, 1959) formalized the intermittency concept in his "single channel" model, which proposed that between an input mechanism and an output or effector mechanism was a single-channel decision mechanism, of limited capacity, which takes a finite time to process information and can deal with only a limited amount of information in a given time (Welford, 1959). Information theory was now well established as the major theoretical framework within cognitive psychology, and this perspective was consolidated by the advances in computer technology, the computer being adopted as the primary analogue for describing human behavior, including, of course, human skill.

Let us now turn our attention to the models of human skill that flourished as a consequence of the demise of behaviorism and the emergence of communication and information theory, and the growth of cognitive psychology.

MILLER, GALANTER AND PRIBRAM'S TOTE MODEL

In an influential book, *Plans and the Structure of Behavior,* Miller, Galanter, and Pribram (1960) elaborated, for the first time, not only the conceptual structure, but also the possible operation of plans and programs for a wide range of human behaviors, including human skills. The starting point for Miller et al.'s (1960) conceptualization was Bartlett's (1932) schema, which we have discussed earlier, but they talked in terms of a "Plan": A Plan is any hierarchical process in the organism that can control the order in which a sequence of operations is to be performed" (Miller et al., 1960, p. 16). Furthermore, not only did the Plan attempt to address the content, instructions, or information contained, but it also described a possible operational mechanism. That is, both the crucial issues of structure and function were addressed.

The functional or operational mechanism elaborated followed closely the cybernetic principles outlined by Wiener (1948) and Shannon and Weaver's (1949) communication and information theory. We will see that what is described is essentially a "closed-loop" control operation. A further important development was that as skill is acquired, the control changed from a "closed-loop" to an "open-loop" form, and what Miller et al. (1960) proposed was that larger sections of the Plan operated automatically and this was related to changes in how feedback was used. In review, then, Miller et al. addressed the three issues central to our understanding of complex human behavior, including human skill—namely, structure, function, and change over time. They further proposed that all human skills (and behaviors) were based on common structures and functions and a common set of principles.

Returning to the question of operation, it was proposed that the functional unit was the "TOTE" unit, a feedback-controlled servomechanism. TOTE is an acronym for "TEST-OPERATE-TEST-EXIT." It is interesting that for their description of the operation of the TOTE unit, Miller et al. (1960) used a simple human skill, that of the repetitive hammering of a nail into a piece of wood. Let me elaborate briefly on the operational features of the TOTE unit: TEST, the current status of the nail (projecting) and the hammer (raised above the nail); OPERATE, striking the nail head with the hammer; TEST, the projection of the nail, and if it is still protruding, the raising of the hammer for the next strike or operation. This sequence of TEST and OPERATE will continue until the goal or desired outcome is achieved; then an EXIT from this specific plan will take place. We should recognize that the specific TOTE unit may be only one such unit within a more complex TOTE unit, to build a wooden cabinet, which may itself be a smaller unit within a larger TOTE unit, to earn one's living as a carpenter and cabinetmaker. All of these TOTE units are hierarchically organized within a hierarchical PLAN.

One of the potential difficulties in the description of the TOTE unit, whereby each operation is initiated and monitored by a feedback test or evaluation, is that such a process is too slow for the ongoing serial organization of rapid, complex skills such as typing, playing the piano, and speech, for example (Lashley, 1951). "The problem for most theories of the neural bases of skilled movements is that the skilled movements run off so very rapidly that there is little time for proprioceptive (or other) feedback

from one movement before another must occur. Any simple conception in terms of feedback, or error correcting, circuits must cope with the relatively slow transmission rates that are possible over neural paths" (Miller et al., p. 91). The conception of the Plan, with feedback loops being used to control progressively larger and larger segments of behavior, provides a meaningful description of one possible control process for the serial organization of complex skills.

The simple example of a carpenter, described above, incorporates another aspect of human skill that is often overlooked in such modeling, and this aspect is the question of values and intentions or motivations. This is the issue of determining *which* of several competing or possible alternative Plans is to be executed. This issue is separate from but related to the question of *how* and *why* such Plans are executed.

Let us now turn briefly to the specific discussion of human skills: ". . . skills are Plans that were originally voluntary but that have become relatively inflexible, involuntary, automatic" (Miller et al., 1960, p. 82). It is in their description of human skills that Miller et al. attempt to elaborate both the information content of the Plan as well as the operational details. Interestingly, they also grappled with the interaction between coach (teacher) and athlete (student), and the sharing of a communicable plan.

One of the central issues that Miller et al. (1960) discuss is the distinction between information and reinforcement. Information comprises the instructions within the Plan and reinforcement, which is recognized as an inadequate concept for control purposes. This is best seen in the elaboration of Plans for human skills. However, of course, there is a dilemma here, for as we know it is possible to acquire skills without verbalizing the details. Remember, however, that much of this verbalization has been forgotten (and in adults is no longer necessary) since infancy and childhood. Even so, the nature of the verbal instructions for new skills, the availability of other nonverbal information, and the form such information must take if it is to be useful to the learner are not clearly understood.

This very issue, the nature of information or knowledge structures, has most recently been readdressed by Anderson (1982, 1987) and Mackay (1987), for example. However, Miller et al. in 1960 did not take the elaboration of knowledge structures very far. Even so, an exception to this was in the domain of problem solving, where, influenced by Newell, Shaw, and Simon (1958), some attempts were made to describe knowledge structures in the specification of heuristic problem-solving Plans.

In retrospect, it is very apparent that the work of Miller, Galanter, and Pribram (1960) was most influential in cognitive psychology. Their contribution to human skills research is often not fully acknowledged, but there is little doubt that their syntheses of concepts from cybernetics and communication theory provided a coherent framework for many of the conceptual developments that followed.

FITTS'S THREE-STAGE MODEL OF SKILL LEARNING

Fitts (1964), influenced by developments in information theory, presented a model specifically developed to explain skill learning. The starting point of Fitts's model was that all skills are basically the same and that a common set of principles or processes can be used to describe the whole range of skilled behavior (a view shared also by Bartlett (1932, 1947). The development of the model was also influenced by the increasing emphasis on research into verbal learning, at the time of Fitts's study.

The three-stage or three-phase model for skill learning incorporated an early (cognitive) phase, an intermediate (associative) phase, and a late (autonomous) phase. Fitts did not elaborate each stage with precise operational details, based on empirical evidence, but rather relied largely on descriptive evidence to formulate the model. Even though the model was presented as a three-stage process, Fitts was clear that these were not distinct or separate phases, but rather represented different aspects along a continuum.

The Early (Cognitive) Phase

During the early phase the learner attempts to understand the task: What are the perceptual or input features? What actions have to be made? What are the rules, constraints, and conditions? What is the form of the feedback and knowledge of results that can be used during subsequent practice? This search by the learner to understand the parameters of the task led Fitts to identify the involvement of cognitive processes, particularly at this early stage. Fitts (1964) indicated that this phase may be very short for simple tasks and longer as the tasks become more and more complex, as in the case of what Poulton (1957) called "open skills." Another aspect of this early stage is what Fitts referred to as response integration, such as attempting to integrate the two hands in playing the piano, or trying to coordinate the breathing with the arm and leg strokes in swimming.

The Intermediate (Associative) Phase

The early phase merges into the intermediate or associative phase. Fitts's important contribution was to propose the learning of cognitive "sets" rather than the more direct connections or association of a stimulus and a response. Here the close link between verbal learning and skill learning becomes apparent, but it must be emphasized that the notion of a cognitive set is an important conceptual step. "The point of emphasis here is not so much that people develop cognitive or learning sets ... but that they can develop many different cognitive sets, can switch from one to another readily, and can include the same stimulus or response elements as members of many different cognitive

sets" (Fitts, 1964, p. 269). A further feature of cognitive sets is that they operate in a probabilistic fashion, depending on the contingencies of the particular situation.

Recall that during the early stage the learner comes to identify the perceptual and response components of the task. The transition to the intermediate phase occurs when perception and action (viz. stimuli and responses) are somehow linked or associated. This phase is thus identified by cognitive set learning, when common sets of stimuli are associated with common sets of responses in a probabilistic (or stochastic) fashion. "Cognitive set refers to preparation in advance for the probabilities or contingencies characterizing a given situation. This meaning of the term set is similar to what Miller, Galanter, and Pribram (1960) call a Plan" (Fitts, 1964, p. 270).

Cognitive set learning has been systematically investigated, primarily in terms of the time taken to process information by manipulating the compatibility of the array, the number of alternative stimuli and responses, the probability of occurrence of particular stimuli and responses, the familiarity and meaningfulness of the material, and the redundancy of the material (see Welford, 1968, for a comprehensive review). In all this work the continued influence of the verbal learning paradigm was highly apparent, with Fitts (1964) himself continually cross-referencing to the studies on skill and studies on verbal learning.

The Late (Autonomous) Phase

Human skilled performance continues to improve over millions of trials and years of repetition and practice. Data collected from diverse tasks in industry, commerce, and sport indicate that the learning curve for human skills is a constant, logarithmic improvement in speed and a concomitant increase in accuracy (Crossman, 1959). The implication of the evidence, according to Fitts (1964) and later Anderson (1982, 1987), is that we are dealing with a single learning process.

The effect of extensive practice is that information processing, at all levels, becomes more automatic, requiring less attention to detail by the performer. The automatic stage is still not well understood, but it appears that larger and larger chunks of both perception and action can be processed and controlled without direct monitoring or sensory control. Longer, more complex sequences can be planned in advance and merely triggered into action, and such motor programs, as they have been called, can be run off without any further need for attention. However, Fitts (1964) did not elaborate this final stage in any detail, only emphasizing that "It is very rare for peak performance in any of these activities to be reached short of several years of intensive, daily practice. And the fact that performance even levels off at all appears to be due as much to the effects of physiological aging and/or loss of motivation as to the reaching of a true learning asymptote or limit in capacity for further improvement" (Fitts, 1964, p. 268).

In spite of the generally descriptive nature of Fitts's

three-stage model, it has influenced subsequent modeling and has provided a basic framework for the understanding of human skill.

ADAMS'S CLOSED-LOOP MODEL OF MOTOR LEARNING

In 1971 Adams, influenced by developments in information theory, presented a comparator-based model of human skill, specifically called "a closed-loop model of motor learning." Although the model related to the learning of simple (relatively slow) movements, Adams suggested that it had much wider implications, and indeed both researchers and practitioners quickly extended its application to the broader domain of learning skills. A further important feature of Adams's model was that it was operational, in that specific hypotheses could be objectively and systematically tested.

We have already introduced the notion of a closed-loop comparator or servosystem in our analogy of the thermostatically controlled oven. Recall that the current state is compared to some desired or set "standard" by using feedback information. The state of the system is adjusted until the standard is matched—that is, until there is no mismatch between intention and action, to use Miller, Galanter, and Pribram's (1960) expression. Briefly, one of the key features of Adams's model is the concept of the *perceptual trace,* which provides a kind of image or standard of the required movement. This perceptual trace is based on memory of past experiences and over time (with practice) becomes more and more precise.

Another key conceptual feature is the *memory trace,* which enables the selection of an appropriate movement response, including the initiation and direction of the movement. The selection is based on previous movement experiences or motor memory traces of a similar kind.

Further, it is proposed that *response-produced feedback* is sensory information arising from the movement response itself, about the position of the limb relative to the target (via both vision and proprioception).

Finally, it is conjectured that the *comparator process* involves the comparison of the difference between the response-produced feedback and the perceptual trace of the desired standard or outcome. In effect, it is this ongoing comparison between the error or discrepancy feedback and the perceptual trace that guides or directs the movement to the target or goal.

Adams maintained that movements and actions are achieved by a direct comparison of the feedback arising during movement with the perceptual trace, which is a learned representation of the appropriate movement to be made. Adams's introduction of some central referent—in this case, the perceptual trace—is an important conceptual development. This trace is laid down as a trace of the movement just completed, perhaps an afterimage of that movement. The whole learning (and performance) process

hinges around the quality of the perceptual trace. Repetition consolidates or strengthens the perceptual trace and also enables the trace itself to be specified more and more accurately.

Knowledge of results about the success or outcome of each trial serves to strengthen the perceptual trace. This is the next important conceptual development of the model —that is, it is the information content of the knowledge of results (rather than the reinforcement value) that is crucial to learning. Here the association between verbal learning, cognition, and learning skills is most apparent. Clearly, according to Adams, the learner is a problem solver, using information and rules, observing constraints and conditions, in which verbal (and other) information is crucial to the learning process.

Adams (1971) makes reference to a second memory state, the memory trace, which is responsible for the actual production of the movement and specifying the details or program of action. It is argued by Adams that for a comparison process to occur, a trace of the intended or correct action (the perceptual trace) must be available and different from the memory that actually produces the movement (the memory trace). Otherwise, he says, the movement outcome would be compared with the movement program, and assumedly there would never be a mismatch.

Although Adams's model is a significant contribution to the human skills and motor learning literature, it is not without some shortcomings. Its applicability to rapid movements and complex, serially organized sequences of action is open to question. In particular, the dependence on feedback arising during the movement for ongoing control is an unlikely mechanism, because such feedback loops are too slow (see Glencross, 1977, for a review of this evidence). There is also a substantial body of evidence, both in animals and man, which shows that quite complex movement sequences can be effectively performed in the absence of any apparent sensory information and feedback (Keele, 1968).

SCHMIDT'S SCHEMA MODEL

Largely as a result of the limitations of Adams's (1971) model and its applicability primarily to slow positioning movements, Schmidt (1975) formulated a more comprehensive model to address a wider range of skilled movements. Schema theory, as it was called, retained some of the more general features of Adams's model, notably the two memory states, one concerned with movement production (recall schema) and another concerned with the comparator function (recognition schema). The concept of a schema is an elaboration of that used by Bartlett (1932) as a general abstract representative of knowledge about a particular domain.

How is the movement or action produced? According to Schmidt, a memory state, which he calls the recall schema, is responsible for the production of both rapid and slow movement and presumably for complex sequential movements. This is similar to Adams's (1971) memory trace, but in fact, Schmidt's proposal is quite different in concept and principle, and this is perhaps Schmidt's major conceptual contribution. He suggests that the recall memory is a form of generalized motor program, and only the specific details and parameters need to be mapped in for each specific context. This permits adaptation to account for contextual variability, an essential aspect of skilled performance in changing environments. For rapid and complex sequences, motor program control (viz. recall memory) is heavily implicated. However, for slow movements, recall memory may be only minimally involved with response specification and initiation. In most cases, response-produced feedback is used to guide the movement, although this may also be achieved by dynamic means as well.

Although Schmidt does not address the important question of the origins of the generalized motor program, he does go further than any other theorist in specifying the details that gives the program its idiosyncratic form, namely: the starting conditions, body postures, weight of the implement; the parameters of force, time, speed, and direction; the knowledge of results available or presented; the sensory feedback or outcome in terms of proprioception, vision, and even audition if available. The performer extracts from this wealth of information details that can be used for the next practice or learning trial—that is, to map the parameters onto the generalized motor program, prior to execution.

Schmidt's (1975) second memory state, the recognition schema, is implicated in comparison and evaluation. It is a sensory-based system that enables a judgment to be made of the "correctness" of the response on the basis of an assessment or evaluation of the response-produced feedback. In a manner similar to Adams's perceptual trace, the learner establishes the expected sensory consequences that would be "expected" from the now parametized motor program. When the movement is executed, the actual sensory feedback occurring from the movement can then be compared with the temporarily stored expected sensory consequences (the recognition schema).

A strong feature of Schmidt's model is that it is operational and presents a number of testable hypotheses. For example, strengthening or consolidation of the schema is dependent on the availability of knowledge of results about the movement outcome. Again, learning is facilitated if variation in practice is permitted, because a wider range of parameters will result and the subsequent norm or rule will be more robust.

A final aspect of Schmidt's model should be noted, because it has implications for the emerging interest in what are now called cognitive skills. Schmidt's proposal is essentially a rule-based, problem-solving approach to skilled behavior. Indeed, the concept of the generalized motor program is that of a hierarchically organized abstract knowledge structure, on to which parametric details are mapped, according to rules established over a period of successive trials and repetitions. Successive approximations are made by the learner to solve the problem (e.g., to reach the tar-

get). A comparator process is used to evaluate each effort on the basis of a wide range of available information; this is then used to modify the schema of each subsequent repetition or trial. Future attempts by researchers will take this lead and tackle directly the detailed nature of memory and knowledge (information) structures. We now turn our attention to these initiatives.

During the 1980s a renewed interest in human skill took the form of research into a wide variety of so-called cognitive skills, such as speech, problem solving in physics, handwriting, keyboard skills, and the like. Further, there was interest in the acquisition of skill and the changes over time. Although much of this work has been relatively specific, as for example, with models of handwriting (Van Galen, 1991), two approaches in particular have attempted to represent the broader spectrum of human skills, namely, Anderson's (1976, 1982, 1987) *ACT model* and Mackay's (1982, 1987) *node structure model*. These two models will be briefly elaborated in order to indicate the conceptual thrust of research into the cognitive skills domain.

ANDERSON'S ACT MODEL

Anderson's ACT production system model was first presented in 1976, and was subsequently developed and refined in 1982 and 1987. The model was developed directly from the three-stage framework proposed by Fitts (1964), and it addresses the issue of how structured cognition emerges. Anderson suggests that all skills involve general problem solving based on the information available about the task. The development of skill is the development of a solution to a problem (i.e., given this information, these rules, and constraints, how do I type, how do I write, how do I play chess, how do I catch the ball?).

Anderson's model is a further development of the notion of information, and its conceptual contribution is that the different types of information are elaborated as forms of knowledge, abstractly represented, in hierarchically organized knowledge structures. This is an elaboration of the concept of information well beyond the specifications attempt by Miller et al. (1960), Adams (1971), and Schmidt (1975). It is beyond the scope of the present chapter to outline in detail the ACT model. However, a brief discussion of the main concepts will suffice to realize its contribution to our understanding of human skills.

Anderson's first stage, the declarative stage (similar to Fitts's cognitive phase), involves using facts or information about the task, usually in working memory, in the form of declarative knowledge organized as a propositional network. A proposition is the smallest unit of knowledge that can stand alone and be judged as true, false, or meaningful.

The second stage involves the gradual change from the use of declarative knowledge to the organization of procedures (procedural knowledge) by a process called knowledge compilation. This is similar to Fitts's associative phase. As the name implies, procedural knowledge involves an organized, orderly sequence of instructions or procedures that achieve a specific outcome. Thus, for example, the declarative knowledge about the gear stick of a car, with practice, becomes organized into a procedure that determines the responses for changing from first gear to top gear, given the appropriate environmental conditions.

The third stage involves the representation of procedural knowledge into a set of productions. "Productions are condition-action pairs that specify that if a certain state occurs in working memory, then particular mental (and possibly physical) actions should take place" (Anderson, 1987, p. 193). This step is the outcome of extensive practice. You will recognize the probabilistic nature of condition-action pairs as being similar to Fitts's use of the concept of "cognitive set" to explain the flexible or plastic association between stimulus-response pairs.

Anderson's model is perhaps the most sophisticated and systematically detailed model developed to this date. It is beyond the scope of the present chapter to elaborate these details. However, it is of value to present a number of the salient concepts, for many of these are consistent with earlier theoretical notions. For example, the cognitive system is hierarchically organized and operations are serially or sequentially ordered. Only one active goal (or subgoal) can be pursued at a time (viz. there exists a serial-capacity limitation). Anderson elaborates three other principles: refractoriness, specificity, and strengthening. Refractoriness dictates that the same production cannot apply to the same data in working memory. According to the specificity principle, the more specific or relevant production takes priority over other competing productions. A production is strengthened by its success and frequency of usage. A final feature of the model, similar to the notions of parameters, are local variables or free values that can be assigned to a more general production to make it specific to changing circumstances.

The significance of the ACT model is that, firstly, it takes the information concept and looks in detail at the qualitative nature of the information or knowledge. Secondly, it is concerned with the organization or structure of this knowledge. Of all the descriptions of the concepts that have been introduced earlier in this chapter—e.g., schema, plans, and programs—Anderson (1982, 1987) has provided the most detailed account of the "contents," i.e., the knowledge and knowledge structures. Thus, according to Anderson (1982), skill acquisition "starts out as the interpretative application of declarative knowledge; this becomes compiled into a procedural form, and this procedural form undergoes a process of continual refinement of conditions and raw increase in speed" (Anderson, 1982, p. 403).

The ACT model also emphasizes that the control architecture is goal-subgoal structured, hierarchically organized, and directed toward problem solving. Looking specifically at the major conceptual developments of ACT theory, there are two that Anderson (1982) suggests are the most essential: (1) the detailed specification and distinction between declarative knowledge and procedural knowledge, and (2) the production system architecture.

Anderson's claim that ACT represents the whole domain of skill learning needs to be looked at critically in relation to these two (and the other) concepts proposed. There has been little application of the model in the perceptual-motor skills domain, beyond the example that Anderson (1990) provides of changing gears in an automobile. What of other, more complex open and closed skills such as playing tennis and basketball on the one hand and pole vaulting and high diving on the other? Of course, part of the difficulty with these types of skills is that it is not clear as to the nature or form of information that is needed to learn, refine, and improve such skills, for clearly the use of the information changes dramatically over time.

What of nonsymbolic information, used for the control of movement and actions (Kelso, 1982)? Can one specify the declarative knowledge and establish the propositional network of abstract "facts" for complex skills such as typing, playing the piano, playing tennis, or golf? Do we see primitive attempts at this in teaching and coaching manuals? The transition from declarative knowledge to procedural knowledge and the development and organization of subsequent production systems is at the heart of the learning process. As these productions are developed, declarative facts, important during the initial stages of learning, are combined and replaced by larger procedures, the basis for larger units of action. It seems useful to understand these "larger units of action" in terms of procedural knowledge. Is this the same transition, as from "controlled" to "automatic" processing (Schneider and Schiffrin, 1977), and hence the development of automatic programs of action?

Anderson's (1982) integration of the production system architecture with the goal subgoal structure, is also a significant initiative, because it provides a basis for accommodating the varying and changing contexts in which the skill may occur. "ACT productions have the virtue of stimulus-response bonds with respect to their simplicity but also have considerable computational power." (Anderson, 1982, p. 404) Despite the elegance of Anderson's model, it does not address, in any systematic way, the organization and control of complex motor sequences, the time scale of rapid updating and amendment of action with changes in context, nor the part played by nonverbal and implicit (tacit) knowledge in skill learning.

MACKAY'S NODE STRUCTURE MODEL

Mackay (1982, 1987) presents a comprehensive theory of cognitive skill that integrates findings and concepts from psycholinguistics, motor control, neuropsychology, and cybernetics, in an ambitious attempt to present a unified theory of skill. Mackay (1982, 1987) addresses a central issue and controversy—that is, whether there exist separate or common mechanisms or processes for perception and action (or production). He makes the assumption that there are some common or shared component processes for perception and production. "If there are shared perception-production components, how do they function in a theory of (speech) production? What processes involving these common components give rise to perception rather than production? And how do these processes involving shared components account for the basic facts of perception such as the regularities in perceptual errors?" (Mackay, 1987, p. 302). However, even though there are common and shared perception-production components, how do they account for asymmetries, such as the observation that perception can proceed at a much faster pace than production?

Mackay (1987) also highlights the distinction between structural features and functional, real-time processes. First, the common structural components underlying perception and production are *nodes*. Nodes are processing units that have the same structural and processing features and respond to repetition and practice in the same way. Second, there are nodes that cannot be shared. For example, the sensory analysis nodes (vision and audition) do not contribute to the production of action, and likewise the muscle/movement nodes do not contribute directly to perception. Mackay proposes a third system of nodes that is at a higher "abstract" level and represents common abstract features of perception and action, as when we perceive a word or sentence and when we produce the appropriate speech. "... this mental node hypothesis is not limited to speech but applies more broadly to all systems for everyday action and perception" (Mackay, 1987, p. 303). Conceptually, these higher order mental nodes are an elaboration of some of the earlier notions of schemas and plans (see, for example, Bartlett, 1932; Miller et al., 1960; Schmidt, 1975). One final concept needs to be elaborated, and that is, according to Mackay (1987), the three types of nodes (mental, motor, sensory) all communicate with one another in the same way and all use the same processing language.

If we take basketball as a sporting example, the sensory analysis nodes analyze the visual, auditory, and proprioceptive sensory array of players, court, and ball; the muscle/movement or motor nodes control the sequence of running, dribbling, catching, and throwing movements; the mental nodes interpret the ongoing sequence of movements of the players and ball, within the constraints of the rules and court parameters and predict the likely outcome(s) and plan an appropriate short-term strategy, which, in turn, is effected via the motor nodes in a "top-down" fashion.

Mackay elaborated three functional classes of mental nodes: content nodes, sequence nodes, and timing nodes. Content nodes represent the substance or the knowledge about the specific skill (e.g., speech, chess, or basketball). For example, in speech there exists a hierarchy of propositional nodes and lexical nodes at the top, with syllable nodes and phonological nodes at a lower level.

Content nodes are linked in a hierarchical fashion. At the highest level, content nodes represent meanings, intentions, desired outcomes. At lower levels more specific content knowledge is represented at a conceptual level (concepts of throwing, catching, swimming, or in speech, the concepts of nouns and verbs). Again, lower down in the hierarchy, more specific content nodes represent specific means to achieve ends. Thus in speech, phonological nodes represent syllables and consonants, for example. In sports, specific content nodes represent general throwing actions differentiated as bowling actions, pitching actions, and so on. Little is known about the nodal structure and connections of movement content nodes.

Sequence nodes specify the order of "activation" and hence determine the sequence of the component or content nodes. This activation of the mental nodes in the correct sequence is preceded by the preparation or "priming" of all of the connected or related nodes, at all levels down to the motor node level. Which primed nodes become activated and how is the order or sequence determined? According to Mackay, the content node with the greatest degree of priming achieves activation first, and this is the "most-primed-wins" principle. Such priming and activation can occur top-down via a superordinate node or bottom-up via sensory perception. Finally, connections between sequence nodes represent the serial order rules that determine the order of activation—these serial order rules (e.g., rules of syntax) are learned and eventually operate automatically in the specific skill context. That is, the activation occurs in the correct sequence according to the "rules."

Timing nodes are concerned with the actual or real-time activation of the components. The timing nodes are connected with sequence nodes in the same way that sequence nodes are connected with content nodes (Mackay, 1987); thus the timing nodes determine the temporal organization of the movement sequence. In addition, the rate of production (e.g., walking, tapping, or speech) is controlled by the timing nodes by adjusting the periodicity of these nodes. Mackay (1987) goes on to elaborate four properties of mental nodes that are fundamental to the understanding of the functional characteristics of the node structure system. These features, two of which we have briefly discussed, are priming, activation, self-inhibition, and linkage strength.

Priming represents low levels of activity, the subthreshold activity of a node. Different levels of priming or preparatory activity occur in all related or connected nodes. That is, priming spreads and also summates across all simultaneously active connections (Mackay, 1987). Priming is thus a necessary condition and precursor to activation.

Activation is an all-or-none period of activity that occurs when a particular node is eventually primed beyond its threshold level. Behavior will result only if the muscle/movement node at the "bottom" of the hierarchy becomes activated. Further, during this period of activation, all nodes linked to the activated node are simultaneously primed.

Self-inhibition follows the period of activation of a node, and during this short phase, the level of priming falls below resting levels before returning to normal resting levels. During this period the node is less responsive to priming, and this is accentuated by continued activation whereby a state of "fatigue" occurs in that node.

Linkage strength refers to the slope and hence the rate of onset of the priming condition, and this is a function of repetition (practice). Following periods of practice, the increases in linkage strength are characterized by more rapid priming of the node and an increase in the speed with which priming is transmitted across connections.

As we can see, Mackay's model attempts to represent the broad spectrum of human skills, although the model is elaborated for speech. It does address the issues of serial organization, sequencing, and timing, and the integration of perception and action. However, at this stage in its development, it has not elaborated in any detail the specifications for movement production, monitoring, and amendment, a necessary requirement for many complex human skills. However, Mackay (1987) asserts that "... speech is not fundamentally special in the theory because similar node structures and degrees of practice can in principle be achieved for other perceptual and motor systems" (p. 330). A strength of the model is its attempt to draw upon converging evidence from a variety of disciplines, including motor control, cognitive science, and psycholinguistics. It has the potential to present a unified theory of human skill.

At about the same time as the interest in cognitive skills was occurring, a parallel but completely different approach was emerging, which was a reaction, in part at least, to the computational burden and complexity of the prescriptive models.

THE EMERGENT PROPERTIES AND DYNAMIC SYSTEMS APPROACH

The emergent properties view rejects the prescriptive or computational approach as being computationally too burdensome and proposes that movement and skill are largely consequences of the underlying system dynamics. Earlier in this chapter, I made brief reference to the contribution by Bernstein (1967), who emphasized the self-organizing, emergent properties of the motor system to explain two basic problems: (1) contextual specificity and (2) the large number of degrees of freedom that need to be controlled in the skilled act.

A central feature of the dynamic systems approach is that groups of muscles "become" constrained to act as a single functional unit and that this is an essential feature of the skill-learning process. Muscles are functionally linked together to form an autonomously acting, coordinative structure. In this way, the skilled performer has reduced the number of degrees of freedom that need to be constrained and controlled. It is proposed that coordinative structures exhibit several self-organizing principles, to facilitate the skill acquisition process. First, separate coordinative structures will integrate and appear to act in unison as a single unit. Second, the system can automatically change from one level of organization (or phase) to another, as with the changes in gait during locomotion. Third, the coordinative structure is self-correcting in that it will automatically adjust to achieve its final desired state (e.g., analogous to a mass-spring system). Fourth, the system is not context-specific and can achieve the desired outcome even though

the initial, starting conditions and contexts may vary. (Tuller, Turvey, & Fitch, 1982). In summary, what these dynamic, self-organizing properties of the system do is to reduce the computational burden of a prescriptive, executive system. Let me briefly summarize two specific models of motor control that exemplify this approach.

When making a rapid movement to a target, how do we achieve end-point accuracy? For relatively slow movements, we can use visual information to guide the finger to the tip of the nose. However, for rapid movements and for movements made without vision, the muscles must be "told" the end-point location. One possible mechanism, which has been proposed by Fel'dman (1986), is that the muscles behave as though they were coiled springs—viz., a mass-spring system. One feature of such a model is that, like a spring, the muscle tends to find its own equilibrium point. That is, the muscle will move, because of its mechanical properties, to a specified location or specific equilibrium point. Essentially the desired end-point location is specified in terms of the length-tension function for the flexors and extensors about the joint. The target or equilibrium point is achieved when there is no difference in torque between the two groups of muscles. Thus you can imagine that every point in space about a joint can be specified as an equilibrium point, in terms of a torque ratio between the flexors and extensors moving the limb.

According to Fel'dman (1986), the mass-spring operation is dependent on the closed-loop muscle-spindle mechanisms within each of the muscles, to bring the limb to the final equilibrium point.

One alternative explanation of this mechanism, is that proposed by Polit and Bizzi (1978, 1979), who suggested that sensory feedback was not needed to achieve the equilibrium point. They based this conclusion on a number of deafferentation studies using monkeys. No matter how the experimenters varied the starting conditions of the limb movement (e.g., increasing the mass of the lever arm, applying a small force to assist or restrain the movement, passively moving the starting position of the limb), the limb always achieved the specified end point, with reasonable accuracy. That is, once specified, the end-point equilibrium is attained irrespective of the intervening perturbations, because of the mechanical properties of the "spring."

From the point of view of our understanding of human skill, the mass-spring model has important implications. In particular it potentially reduces the computational burden for specifying target accuracy and at the same time reduces the need for the sensory monitoring of some amendments and end-point corrections. However, we are still confronted with the enormous problem of "knowing" the environment, that is, of being able to specify all possible end-point locations with a high degree of accuracy. However, assumedly, once learned, these specifications are largely automatic.

One other model addressing the same questions as the mass-spring model, is the impulse-timing model. In essence the impulse-timing model proposes that the trajectory of a limb is a function of the forces (impulses) generated and the timing or phasing of these periods of muscle activity, their onset, duration, and offset. According to Schmidt, Zelaznik, Hawkins, Frank, & Quinn (1979), the motor program specifies in advance the timing and duration of the forces that are produced in the agonist, antagonist, and assumedly fixator muscles involved in the limb trajectory. As we know from physics, it is the combination of force generated over time that produces an impulse, which determines (in conjunction with the impulses from other muscles) the final trajectory of the limb. From this description, one can appreciate the complexity of this computational process—the specification of which muscles are involved, the onset firing times, the amounts of (activity) force in each muscle, the durations of the offset times. Unlike the mass-spring model, the impulse-timing model is much more complex in that the starting point (the initial limb location) must be known by the system, and furthermore the specific level of muscle activation and the duration (from onset to offset) for each muscle must be specified in advance. In addition, consistent with the impulse-timing model, if the trajectory misses the target, corrections must then be computed. Overall this seems a very cumbersome and unlikely mechanism.

An extension of the original impulse-timing model is the impulse-variability hypothesis (Schmidt & Sherwood, 1982). Essentially this hypothesis proposes that in rapid ballistic types of movement, the end-point error or variability is directly related to the variability of the impulse (force per time) in each of the muscles involved. We can conceive of this as being a combination of the variability in the force (activation level) and/or the variability of the duration of muscle activation. This model has had some success in predicting a reduction in variability (or spatial error) as movement time is increased or as the mass to be moved increases. However, the model seems to have little application to the speed-accuracy features of aiming tasks in general, and it seems only to apply to the class of single-impulse, ballistic movements.

In our study of human skill, however, we must not forget that motor control and the organization of action needs to be integrated with a complex and rapidly changing perceptual display. Motor control theorists often ignore this fact. How do we achieve the integration of perception and action in the production of the skilled act?

Fortunately, one of the outcomes of the emergent properties perspective has been to emphasize the integration of perception and action. How does action influence perception and how does perception influence action? Foremost in this research has been J. J. Gibson's (1979) ecological approach to perception, which proposes that under certain circumstances perception maps directly onto action (without any intervening computational process).

Let me cite just one example. Lee (1976) has shown that the time to contact a remote object is directly related to the rate of change of the size of the object's image on the retina. This can be expressed as a mathematical variable that Lee called *tau*. This optic variable interacts directly with a response parameter, influencing the time that the response parameter is initiated or modified. Direct perception theorists propose that this type of integration between perception and action is the essential basis of skill learning and highly skilled performance.

The dynamic systems approach will have a major influence on how we study and investigate human skills and perhaps eventually on teaching and coaching methodologies. Researchers, as a consequence, are asking different questions than were asked with the more conventional approaches: How do we constrain the large number of degrees of freedom, in learning a new skill? How do we learn to release some specific degrees of freedom, to maximize force production, without losing control over other degrees of freedom? How do we recognize and develop the invariant properties of coordinative structures? Can we learn to maximize the precision of free variables or parameters? How can we facilitate direct perception and recognize the appropriate perceptual-response variables? These, and many other interesting questions, signal a new direction in the study of human skill that will have a major impact on psychology and education in general, including of course sport psychology.

CONCLUSIONS AND IMPLICATIONS

In this chapter I have suggested that the understanding of human skill is central to the study of sport psychology. Sport psychologists should, both at the theoretical and practical level, endeavor to understand and to influence the skill-acquisition process as well as to facilitate the process of attaining skilled performance. The historical development of ideas and concepts has been deliberately plotted in this chapter to show the integrity of the early research and how much of it is still influential today. Furthermore, this review will serve to remind us of some of the theoretical conundrums that tend to be ignored or overlooked as new models emerge.

Currently researchers of human skill are faced with what appears on the surface to be two conflicting theoretical approaches, namely the prescriptive, computational view of cognitive psychology compared with the dynamic emergent properties approach. It is true that on some issues these two approaches are in conflict. However, out of this healthy conflict an understanding of human skill will probably emerge, based on an integration of the principles derived from both fields. Viewed simply, what this may mean is that the dynamic approach offers a partial solution to the computational burden of the prescriptive information-processing system.

The most recent developments in cognitive psychology and in particular in cognitive skill have emphasized the need for a greater understanding of knowledge structures and the associated knowledge architecture. In the study of sport skills, this is a particular challenge, because much of the knowledge must be nonsymbolic and implicit. The study of the skill acquisition process in young children may be particularly revealing, as has been the comparison of expert and novice performers.

Clearly we will have to grapple with such issues as: what knowledge is needed (and what knowledge is not needed) at each stage of the learning process, and how this knowledge can be best presented or delivered to the learner. Knowledge used in one form, at an earlier stage in the learning process, is not used or is used differently at a later stage in the learning process. We know little about knowledge delivery—i.e., knowledge in a form or a language that is easily understood or "coded" by the learner. Other, more specific issues relate to: how we use knowledge to establish the initial "model," or "schema," what language is used in the comparator process, and how such a comparison discrepancy is interpreted by the performer to change the knowledge structure for subsequent action.

One of the important implications of the knowledge structures approach is a realization of the levels of representation, and of the fact that knowledge, particularly at the highest level, is represented in an abstract form. Images and imagery are important but little understood concepts. In sport and sport psychology, mental practice, mental rehearsal, visualization, and the like have been extensively used, even if poorly understood. We may be on the threshold of unraveling some of these mysteries about images and imagery, now that we have theoretical frameworks to direct research. Sport psychologists would do well to undertake research into the nature of imagery and how it influences learning and performance. Can such a process be facilitated by using, for example, a knowledge structures approach?

One further comment should be made, and this relates to the inadequacies of all the models reviewed in addressing issues of motivation and the impact that personality and affective factors can have upon performance. Indeed, the sport psychologist usually sees these factors as his or her major concern, the single major issue in an applied setting. It is timely that models of human skill and performance address these affective factors as an integral part of skill learning and performance, not as separate factors, too often ignored or assumed not to be relevant by those interested in studying human skill.

Sport psychologists frequently argue that sport psychology is an applied discipline, and indeed at one level this is the case, as long as there is something substantial to apply. Sport psychology must be more than the mere application of intervention procedures and mental skills training. It would be short-sighted and indeed naive to presume that any applied discipline is not strengthened by having a sound, empirically based theoretical framework. The intent in this chapter, has been to outline the extent of such a theoretical framework, and examples have been given of a number of models that have contributed to our understanding of human skill and human performance. Eventually this approach will provide a sound, coherent base from which the discipline can extend and expand its applied contribution, not only in sport but in the broader domain of human skill and human performance.

Sport psychologists should be more directly involved in the investigation of skill learning and performance. First, sport psychology is primarily concerned with facilitating sports performance; indeed, this was the basis for the emergence of sport psychology as a discipline and professional study in its own right. Second, to facilitate performance the underlying basis of that skilled performance must be known—that is, the nature of human skill. Third, performance is known to be facilitated by a number of factors in addition to physical practice, including, for example, training in concentration, focusing, visualization, relaxation, mental rehearsal, confidence, and so on. But it is not clearly understood how these mechanisms operate, partly because they are not studied in the context of the skill-learning process.

Fourth, skill learning and performance is a consequence of a biological control system subject to variations in a person's affective or emotional state. In the formal study of skill, the researcher attempts to control or eliminate such "nuisance" factors, yet in the sporting context, performance invariably occurs in an "affective environment." Sport psychologists would do well to understand the interaction of the learning, performance, and affective domains.

Fifth, following the previous point, sport psychologists typically have little understanding of the "tools" they use and why indeed they work to facilitate performance. Let us use one example: visualization. How and why does it facilitate performance? Does visualization facilitate attentional processes? Does this mean the athlete is better able to attend to a limited set of specific knowledge (information) structures? Does it mean that the athlete is better able to ignore irrelevant or distracting information? Does it mean that the athlete can actually prime some specific neural or cognitive structure? Or does visualization achieve nothing more than a heightened level of general physiological arousal. Research is needed that will differentiate between these alternative explanations.

Finally let me conclude by suggesting that sport psychologists should be more directly involved in skills practice sessions as well as coaching and training programs. Almost without exception sports practice sessions for athletes are appallingly inefficient and ineffective as a learning experience. Sport psychologists should endeavor to influence and facilitate both the quantity and quality of skill practice. An understanding of the nature of human skill, the study of the acquisition of skill, and an appreciation of the factors that facilitate skilled performance should be objectives for all sport psychologists.

References

Adams, J. A. (1971). A closed-loop theory of motor learning. *Journal of Motor Behavior, 3,* 111–149.

Anderson, J. R. (1976). *Language, memory and thought.* Hillsdale, NJ: Erlbaum.

Anderson, J. R. (1982). Acquisition of cognitive skill. *Psychological Review, 89,* 369–406.

Anderson, J. R. (1987). Skill acquisition: Compilation of weak-method problem solving. *Psychological Review, 94,* 192–210.

Anderson, J. R. (1990). *Cognitive psychology and its implications.* New York: W. H. Freeman.

Bartlett, F. C. (1932). Remembering. A study in experimental and social psychology. Cambridge, U.K.: Cambridge University Press.

Bartlett, F. C. (1947). The measurement of human skill. *British Medical Journal, 116,* 835–838, 877–880.

Bernstein, N. (1967). *The coordination and regulation of movement.* London: Pergamon Press.

Bryan, W. L., & Harter, N. (1897). Studies in the physiology and psychology of the telegraphic language. *Psychological Review, 4,* 27–53.

Bryan, W. L. & Harter, N. (1899). Studies on the telegraphic language. The acquisition of a hierarchy of habits. *The Psychological Review, 7,* 345–375.

Craik, K. J. W. (1947). Theory of the human operator in control systems. I. The operator as an engineering system. *British Journal of Psychology, 38,* 56–61.

Craik, K. J. W. (1948). Theory of the human operator in control systems. II. Man as an element in a control system. *British Journal of Psychology, 38,* 142–148.

Crossman, E. R. F. W. (1959). A theory of the acquisition of speed-skill. *Ergonomics, 2,* 153–166.

Fel'dman, A. G. (1986), Once more on the equilibrium point hypothesis (model) for motor control. *Journal of Motor Behavior, 18,* 17–54.

Fitts, P. M. (1964). Perceptual-motor skill learning. In A. W. Melton (Ed.), *Categories of human learning* (pp. 243–285). New York: Academic Press.

Gibson, J. J. (1979). *The senses considered as perceptual systems.* Boston: Houghton Mifflin.

Glencross, D. J. (1977). Control of skilled movement. *Psychological Bulletin, 84,* 14–29.

Glencross, D. J., Whiting, H. T. A., & Abernethy, B., (in press). Motor control, motor learning and the acquisition of skill: Historical trends and future directions. *International Journal of Sport Psychology.*

Keele, S. W. (1968). Movement control in skilled motor performance. *Psychological Bulletin, 70,* 387–403.

Kelso, J. A. S. (1982). *Human Motor Behavior: An Introduction,* Hillsdale, NJ: Erlbaum.

Lashley, K. S. (1951). The problem of serial order in behavior. In L. A. Jeffress (Ed.), *Cerebral mechanisms in behavior* (pp. 112–136). New York: Wiley.

Lee, D. N. (1976). A theory of visual control of braking based on time-to-collision. *Perception, 5,* 437–459.

Mackay, D. G. (1982). The problem of flexibility, fluency, and speed-accuracy trade-off in skilled behavior. *Psychological Review, 89,* 483–506.

Mackay D. G. (1987). Asymmetries in the relationship between speech perception and production. In H. Heuer & A. F. Sanders (Eds.), *Perspectives on perception and action* (pp. 301–333). Hillsdale, NJ: Erlbaum.

Miller, G. A., Galanter, E., & Pribram, K. H. (1960). *Plans and the structure of behavior.* New York: Holt, Rinehart & Winston.

Newell, A., Shaw, I. C., & Simon, H. A. (1958). Elements of a theory of human problem solving. *Psychological Review, 65,* 151–166.

Polit, A., & Bizzi, E. (1978). Processes controlling arm movements in monkeys. *Science, 201,* 1235–1237.

Polit, A., & Bizzi, E. (1979). Characteristics of motor programs underlying arm movements in monkeys. *Journal of Neurophysiology. 42,* 183–194.

Poulton, E. C. (1957). In prediction in skilled movements. *Psychological Bulletin. 54,* 467–78.

Schmidt, R. A. (1975). A schema theory of discrete motor skill learning. *Psychological Review, 82,* 225–260.

Schmidt, R. A., & Sherwood, D. E., (1982). An inverted-U relation between spatial error and force requirements in rapid limb movements: Further evidence for the impulse-variability model. *Journal of Experimental Psychology: Human Perception and Performance, 8,* 158–170.

Schmidt, R. A., Zelaznik, H. N., Hawkins, B., Frank, J. S., & Quinn, J. T. (1979). Motor-output variability: A theory for the accuracy of rapid motor acts. *Psychological Review, 86,* 415–451.

Schneider, W., & Shiffrin, R. M. (1977). Controlled and automatic human information processing: 1. Detecting, search and attention. *Psychological Review, 84,* 1–66.

Shannon, C. E., & Weaver, W. (1949). *The mathematical theory of communication,* Urbana-Champaign, IL: University of Illinois Press.

Tuller, B., Turvey, M. T., & Fitch, H. L. (1982). The Bernstein perspective: II. The concept of muscle linkage or coordinative structure. In J. A. S. Kelso (Ed.), *Human motor behavior: An introduction,* (pp. 253–270). Hillsdale, NJ: Erlbaum.

Van Galen, G. P. (1991). Handwriting: Issues for a psychological theory. *Human Movement Science, 10* (2–3), 165–191.

Welford, A. T. (1952). The "psychological refractory period" and the timing of high-speed performance: as a review and a theory. *British Journal of Psychology, 43,* 2–19.

Welford, A. T. (1959). Evidence of a single-channel decision mechanism limiting performance in a serial reaction task. *The Quarterly Journal of Experimental Psychology, 11,* 193–208.

Welford, A. T. (1968). *Fundamentals of skill.* London: Methuen.

Wiener, N. (1948). *Cybernetics.* New York: Technological Press of M.I.T. and John Wiley.

Woodworth, R. S. (1899). The accuracy of voluntary movements. *Psychological Review, 3,* 1–114.

PSYCHOLOGICAL CHARACTERISTICS AND HIGH-LEVEL PERFORMANCE

·11·

ELITE PERFORMANCE AND PERSONALITY: FROM DESCRIPTION AND PREDICTION TO DIAGNOSIS AND INTERVENTION

Yves Vanden Auweele

Bert De Cuyper

Veerle Van Mele

Randy Rzewnicki

This chapter deals with research on the personality characteristics elite athletes have (or are assumed to have) in a higher amount or of a higher quality than lower level or lesser skilled athletes. It is also concerned with research on the psychological characteristics (unique patterns) elite performers show when they are performing optimally (which is known as "peak performance").

The identification of relationships between personality or psychological characteristics and some criterion of success and the identification of the nature of such characteristics, whether determined by genetic or environmental factors, could lead subsequently to diagnosis and prediction. Potential implications can be drawn for appropriate interventions to improve performance, i.e., counseling, selection, classification, psychological skills training, and behavioral modification.

Because the criteria used to define an elite performer have been under discussion (Highlen & Bennett, 1983), the definition of elite that has been selected is "athletes who are eligible for competition at the national, international, or Olympic level, or who are professional sportspersons" (e.g., rodeo cowboys). This interpretation includes athletes who may not actually compete at this level, but who are described as eligible for such competitions (e.g., Johnson, 1972). Candidates for Olympic teams, even those not selected for team membership, are included in this definition of elite. This definition excludes alternative competitions for older or disabled groups (e.g., the Masters as studied by Ungerleider, Golding, & Porter, 1989; and blind competitors at the Special Olympics, reported in Mastro, Sherrill, Gench, & French, 1987). This definition also excludes noncompetitive athletic endeavors, such as rock climbing and alpine mountain climbing (Magni, Rupolo, Simini, De Leo, & Rampazzo, 1985; Robinson, 1985).

Most research reported in the sport-psychological literature concerning the psychological attributes of the elite performer relates to sport personology. However, recently, important theories, concepts, methodologies, and data related to other psychological research areas have been introduced in the study of the elite athlete. Examples are achievement motivation, causal attribution, self-efficacy, imagery, attentional styles, and intrinsic motivation, among others. This development has had implications for the elaboration of the present chapter. Obviously, a very broad definition of personality must be used, including concepts and terms such as traits, states, qualities, attributes, changes, and constancies in behavior. References have to be made to different personality theories and operationalizations. However, only a few of these concepts have been considered, and then only briefly, because they are covered in other chapters.

The search for articles about elite athletes and personality relied mainly on two types of sources: Literature data bases, PSYCLIT (Psychological Abstracts), SPORT (a.k.a. SIRC), and educational literature, and the references listed in the articles we examined. The expectation was that the use of data bases would reduce the possibility of bias (see Morgan, 1985, for a discussion of this problem). The electronic literature searches were restricted by the terms *sport* or *athlete* and *personality.*

There is a large accumulation of research and even of reviews on the topic of sport personology. The study of personality is, in fact, the oldest line of systematic attention in sport psychology (Landers, 1983; Silva, 1984; Vealy, 1989). Research of this nature dominated the field of sport psychology from the 1950s to the 1970s and is still important (Aguerri, 1986). Within the topic of sport personology, a significant number of articles deal with the elite performer. With some lag of time, the same paradigmatic and methodological fluctuations as in academic psychology can be seen in sport personology (Morgan, 1980).

The most recent review, covering sport personology research from 1974, was authored by Vealy in 1989. The question is what can be added to this and other excellent reviews (e.g., Carron, 1980; Fisher, 1984; Martens, 1975; Morgan, 1980) without repeating comments and evaluations, and risking Landers (1983) losing his patience again:

I am losing patience with reviews that show some studies statistically supporting a given group difference, then reporting other studies that don't support such a difference, and concluding that the research is contradictory and more research (usually of a methodological nature) is needed. (p. 138)

In attempts to overcome this reasonable criticism, three purposes were established. The first is to present an overview of the paradigmatic and methodological trends and evolutions in both academic and sport personology from the 1950s to the present. Second, an attempt is made to reevaluate the research in light of the more sophisticated research integration tools now available (see the discussion of meta-analysis in this chapter). Reevaluation is considered also in light of the more differentiated view that has been worked out concerning the underlying trait paradigms on which the mostly atheoretical research has been implicitly based. Further still, the objectives of earlier personality research i.e., the type of questions that have been asked, are identified. They are evaluated in light of the current developments in sport-psychological research and practice described by Singer (1988).

Justification for this reevaluation is derived from the belief that the mere listing and correction of errors in methodology and interpretation does not improve the quality of personology research very much (although corrections must be noted). Second, this type of work has previously been done, and very well at that (e.g., Carron, 1980; Martens, 1975). Finally there is the possibility that the criticisms of personology research may be somewhat exaggerated. There is a risk in throwing out the baby with the bathwater (Landers, 1983; Martens, 1987).

The third purpose, concurrent with Martens' (1987) suggestion, is to identify and to operationalize some new research strategies in academic personality research that can be integrated in the primary sport-psychological objectives. We want to explore the possibility of reaching specific sport-psychological objectives better than has been the case with the traditional approaches. In this perspective, interesting conceptual and methodological developments in sport personology were examined, both in academic personality research and in other relevant areas of psychology dealing with the measurement of psychological attributes.

Attempts were made to go beyond the mere description of these interesting paradigms and research techniques by operationalizing and concretizing most of them in a sport-psychological context. More than a prologue for future research is offered here by reviewing the research in which some of these new strategies are being used in sport psychology. In addition, one example of a new technique used in an elite sport setting is elaborated on more extensively.

OVERVIEW OF MAJOR PARADIGMATIC AND METHODOLOGICAL TRENDS IN ACADEMIC AND SPORT PERSONOLOGY SINCE 1950

Like psychology, the emerging field of sport psychology has gone through various stages of inquiry into personality, and the person/situation debate has raged (there) as well . . . That is, sport psychologists debated which personality paradigm is the most efficacious to understand and predict behaviors in sport. (Vealy, 1989, p. 217)

PERSONOLOGY

The prediction of behavior is of course a major concern of psychologists in general. For personality psychologists, the trait concept has been a central within-person construct intended to predict future behavior. Traits have been defined as "stable internal structures that served as predispositions to behavior and could therefore be used as adequate predictors of behavior" (Sherman & Fazio, 1983, p. 310).

Individual differences can be subdivided into competencies (e.g., some technical sports talent), affective-dynamic traits (e.g., sensation-seeking tendency), cognitive traits (beliefs), and formal traits, referring to formal aspects of human behavior (e.g., aggressiveness).

According to traditional formal trait theories as conceptualized by the likes of Cattell, Eysenck, and Guilford, each individual can be characterized by his or her position in a number of so-called "common traits": universal personality dimensions on which all individuals can be situated (e.g., introversion-extroversion). Many personality questionnaires have been constructed in order to detect the position of individuals on those dimensions, with the intent "to learn how a person might be expected to react and to behave in various situations" (Singer, 1988, p. 89). The prototypical questionnaire is a self-report instrument, consisting of a number of personality adjectives (e.g., I am accurate, or adventurous, or sentimental . . .), whereby the respondent has to make a judgment on the degree to which each item is applicable to him- or herself.

The traditional nomothetic trait psychologies share three assumptions: (1) people are cross-situationally consistent; (2) our behavior displays a temporal stability; and (3) there is a co-occurrence of behavioral manifestations referring to the same underlying trait. It is noteworthy to emphasize that temporal and cross-situational stability were seen as a relative matter. The ranking between individuals would or should remain stable across situations (A is more anxious than B at an oral examination, driving a car, in his armchair . . .), and over time (If A is more anxious than B at the examination this year, the same would be true at next year's examination). However, these are not measures of the absolute degree of anxiety, aggressiveness, or some other behavior across situations.

In other words, trait psychologists do not pretend that people will behave the same way in all situations. The importance of situational factors is undisputed among major trait theorists (Pervin, 1985). Empirical evidence concerning the basic assumptions of the common trait theories has been reviewed by Mischel. His book *Personality and Assessment* (1968) is widely accepted as the onset of a period of serious questioning of the utility of the trait concept. Many personality psychologists, convinced that traits could not serve as predictors of future behavior, abandoned trait research and turned to research on the predictability of behavior from situational variables.

In the 1970s, several research approaches also appeared with the common message that they could present a way out of the crisis without abandoning trait psychology. They specified the conditions under which the trait concept remains useful. This research is summarized by Sherman and Fazio (1983). Some of those conditions and different research approaches will be briefly described here.

A first approach suggests that the behavior of only some people is predictable from measures of traits. Only individuals low in self-monitoring (Snyder, 1979, 1983) or with a high degree of private self-consciousness (Fenigstein, Scheier, & Buss, 1975) should show consistency between self-reports of traits and actual overt behavior. For those stable "trait people," the trait theory seems valid since assessment of their position on the traditional trait dimensions remains worthwhile. A second defense of trait theory emphasizes that only some traits are useful for describing and predicting people. One can differentiate between two versions of this position. Some authors suggest the existence of stable versus unstable traits. People should show high

trait-behavior consistency, but only for the stable traits, e.g., punctuality (McGowan & Gormly, 1976). Others argue that the behavior of individuals will be predictable only for those traits that are relevant for the particular individual. A substantial trait-behavior consistency may exist only for traits that are identified by the person as important or as personally characteristic (Kenrick & Stringfield, 1980; Markus, 1977).

Also in defense of trait theory is a research direction that stresses that trait-behavior consistency will vary as a function of the kind of situation. To the extent that there are strong situational pressures and/or that situations are norm regulated, individual differences will be minimized, and the correlation between a trait and the corresponding behavior will be small. The suggestion is that trait measurements could serve as predictors of future behavior only in situations low in constraint (Price & Bouffard, 1974) or weak in pressure to conform (Monson, Hesley, & Chernik, 1982).

The lack of empirical support for cross-situational stability, which is a basic assumption of the traditional trait theory, has promoted the adoption by most contemporary psychologists of a so-called "interactionistic position." It has to be stressed (e.g., Claeys, 1980) that the concept of interactionism has different meanings. In some publications, the person-situation interactionism seems nothing more than a statement that the person and the situation are codeterminers of behavior. This is a trivial statement: no psychologist (and no trait theorist) has ever doubted that behavior is a function of environmental as well as of person variables. Or, as Fisher (1977a) stated: "Trait theorists really are not so naive as to discount environmental influences" (p. 190). According to Claeys, analysis of the publications of modern interactionists reveals the existence of three interpretations of a person-situation interaction. The variants of organismic interaction, of statistical interaction, and of dynamic interaction are successively described here.

The organismic interactionism stresses the reciprocal causal interaction between personality factors and situational characteristics. On the one hand, the actual behavior is a function of the situation as perceived and interpreted by the individual. This perception and interpretation is influenced by preexisting cognitive-dynamic person variables (i.e., attitudes, traits, etc.). On the other hand, those personality characteristics are seen as the result of the exposure to situations in the past, an adoption of a social learning view on personality.

The variant of a statistical interaction implies that the effect of person and situational variables is not merely additive. A statistical interaction effect means that the effect of a certain level of one independent variable on the behavioral variable is a function of the level of the other independent variable. Such a significant person-situation interaction effect usually is hypothesized on the basis of some theoretical consideration.

Proponents of a dynamic interactionism argue that the exposure of the individual to certain situations is a function of the personality characteristics of that individual. By his or her overt behavior, the person can create a situation that, in combination with personality traits, elicits ensuing behavior. Snyder is convinced that except for artificial settings (as in laboratory studies) and for other unique cases, individuals have a good deal of latitude in choosing the kinds of situations they will enter and in altering situations once they have entered them. His experiments (e.g., Snyder & Gangestad, 1982) support the position that individuals may choose settings and will try to alter situations in ways that reflect their traits.

Sport Personology

Turning to the personality research in sport psychology, it is not surprising that one can find in this domain the same controversies and evolutions seen in academic psychology.

As in academic psychology, there was a cry for abandoning research on person factors, or at least for throwing away the trait concept (Martens, 1970, cited in Landers, 1983; Rushall, 1970, cited in Morgan, 1978). Landers described an almost irrational overreaction. The criticism was followed by more constructive responses: the development of new types of measurements; the selection of particular, relevant traits to examine; a plea for an interactionistic approach.

The early research was characterized by a tradition of between-groups comparisons: Athletes were compared with nonathletes, successful athletes with less successful ones, and comparisons were made among athletes representing different sport disciplines. These comparison studies were presented as serving prediction and selection goals in sport psychology. By comparing the personality profile of an individual athlete with the profile of an elite performer in a particular sport, one ought to be able to answer questions such as: Is this youngster a good investment who merits placement in an intensive program? Will this individual excel in high-level competitions, as elite performers do?

The tests typically used for those purposes were traditional nomothetic trait inventories, such as the 16PF (Institute for Personality and Ability Testing, 1986) and the EPI (Eysenck & Eysenck, 1964, 1975). According to Fisher (1984), more than 1000 sport personality studies were published in the heyday of this research in the 1960s and 1970s. The evaluation of the results of this research explosion is far from consistent. Aside from moderate points of view, as made in Singer's (1988) report that conclusive evidence is lacking, or in Browne and Mahoney's conclusion, "A few hints garnered from this research were interesting, though they held no great surprises" (1984, p. 610), remarkable contrasting evaluations can be observed.

Some reviewers of sport personality research such as Martens (1975) and Rushall (1975b) came to the conclusion that general trait measures are worthless for the purpose of predicting relevant sport behavior. A contrasting viewpoint has been defended by Morgan (1980). He argues that existing research favorable to the hypothesis that traits are useful was excluded from those pessimistic reviews,

and he presents optimistic evidence that elite athletes display unique personality characteristics. Morgan has reported that his mental health model is effective in predicting success in athletics. According to him there is substantial empirical support for this model. "An athlete who is neurotic, depressed, anxious, schizoid, introverted, confused, fatigued, and scores low on psychic vigor will tend to be unsuccessful in comparison to an athlete who is characterized by the absence of such traits" (Morgan, 1980, p. 62).

In several publications, successful athletes are characterized by such traits as emotional stability, high need for achievement, assertion, and dominance (Cooper, 1969; Kane, 1964; Ogilvie, 1976; Tutko, Lyon, & Ogilvie, 1969, cited in Alderman, 1974). Concerning the logic behind such findings, Fisher speaks of the "survival of the fittest" (1977b, p. 92).

Those discrepancies in evaluation can be explained (at least in part) by difficulties in interpreting the research data, since, as Martens (1981) notes, "Perhaps the most fundamental reason for the inconclusive findings is that the trait approach has not been based on any conceptual or theoretical framework . . . ," and as Singer (1988, p. 92) notes, "so many and varied psychological tests are available and have been used, with varied groups of subjects . . ."

Unanimous is the negative appreciation of the atheoretical use of the personality measurements in the studies on the characteristics of athletes, as illustrated by the words of Ryan:

> The research in this area has been the "shotgun" variety. By that I mean the investigators grabbed the nearest and most convenient personality test, and the closest sport group, and with little or no theoretical basis for their selection fired into the air to see what they could bring down. It isn't surprising that firing into the air at different times and at different places, and using different ammunition, should result in different findings. In fact it would be surprising if the results weren't contradictory and somewhat confusing. (Cited in Straub, 1977, p. 177.)

Although the atheoretical character or the lack of any conceptual framework in the early sport personology research can be considered as its most fundamental deficiency, other serious methodological shortcomings have been listed by several reviewers (Carron, 1980; Hardman, 1973; Heyman, 1982; Martens, 1975; Morgan, 1980; Silva, 1984). The problems most commonly mentioned include:

1. There is little or no concern for clear definitions and/or operationalizations. Crucial variables such as elite and non-nonelite athletes should be carefully defined. Several inventories include, for example, a so-called "anxiety scale." This does not mean that those operationalizations are equivalent, or that they refer to the same construct.
2. Poor sampling techniques are employed. For convenience, intact teams of athletes are used, with considerable heterogeneity of skill level and homogeneity of

environmental influences. This makes generalizations of the conclusions to other teams a very risky business.

3. Inappropriate statistical analyses are used. Critics mention the reliance on univariate statistical analyses when multivariate procedures are appropriate, and the reliance on average scores representing no individual athlete in the sample because the mean is often affected by extreme scores.

4. The misuse of personality measurements. Tests were selected without regard for their origin or for the rationale of their development. The MMPI, for example, was not developed for measuring the normal person's personality. The inappropriate use of that test for analyzing the personality of normal athletes invalidates conclusions of the research.

5. Where the data of between-group comparisons are relational, some have assumed them to be causal.

It is impossible to assess the extent to which sport psychology researchers reacted to the pessimism about the early sport personality investigations by initiating situationist research. Research was begun on the influence of situational variables on sport performance. Such research is very important, of course. No one will doubt the relevance of research, for example, in social facilitation within a motor learning and performance context. It seems to be a very good thing that the great interest in internal dispositions (personality factors) as determinants of sport behavior has lessened among sport psychologists. Attention for external determinants was needed. But when this research starts from a situationist stance, when behavior is exclusively seen as the product of environmental variables, there is consequently no belief in the utility of personality characteristics. As Martens notes (1975, p. 18): "The central assumption of situationism is that individuals behave differently across situations and that behavior across subjects is minimally different within similar situations." In other words, situationists renounce the whole concept of personality.

It is evident that the studies using a situational approach were not included in Vealy's content analysis (1989) of the sport personality research between 1974 and 1987. Several quotations, however, suggest that pure situationism, with its total neglect of interindividual differences and its exclusive reliance on external variables, has not received much success in sport psychology. Situationism is seen as "an overreaction to trait psychology" (Martens, 1975, p. 19), or as "an antithesis of personologism, . . . going too far to the other extreme" (Horsfall, Fisher, & Morris, 1975, p. 61).

It seems reasonable to believe that the nonacceptance of the situationist paradigm among sport psychologists was influenced by the rejection of the central assumption of situationism in academic psychology. The influence of the negative evaluation of the situationist model by personality researchers in academic psychology is illustrated in the theoretical viewpoint of Rushall (1978):

The reactionary approach away from general, trans-situational theories of personality to pure situational considerations was also

found to be deficient. The proposal that behavior was controlled solely by circumstantial contingencies was shown to be limited in its accountability for behavior predictions (pp. 98–99)

It is not surprising that Rushall refers for those reflections to Endler and Hunt (1969), two well-known promoters of interactionism in contemporary personality psychology. Undoubtedly, it is interactionism that has been recommended by the leading sport psychologists to replace the trait paradigm, as is illustrated by the following quotations: "Interactionism provides the best paradigm for research in personality of sport" (Straub, 1977, p. 184). Furthermore, "the conclusion of this essay for sport personology should be obvious by now: The interactional paradigm is the direction that sport personality research, indeed all personality research, should take" (Martens, 1975, p. 21).

To summarize, noteworthy attempts were made to defend trait psychology by specifying the conditions under which the trait concept remains useful. Sports personology has shifted paradigmatically from a trait approach, through a flirtation with the situationist approach, to some kind of interactionism. The most fundamental deficiency of the past sport personology research has been its atheoretical character.

REEVALUATION OF TRADITIONAL RESEARCH ON THE PERSONALITY OF ELITE PERFORMERS AND THE PREDICTION OF SUCCESS

The review discussed here is consistent with the ideas presented in the introduction of this chapter regarding efforts to use the past constructively. In the following four sections, four ways some sport psychologists have suggested to do so are elaborated. Proceeding this way covers, at the same time, most of the traditional sport personology literature on the elite performer. After reviewing the suggestions, we have undertaken some original research along those lines.

First, one of Carron's suggestions was followed. Carron (1980) recommended a continuation of the type of work Hardman (1973) had begun: comparing studies which have used the same test on comparable (elite) samples with the appropriate norms. Studies using the POMS (Profile of Mood States, McNair, Lorr, & Droppleman, 1971) on elite athletes between 1974 and 1989 are reviewed subsequently.

Second, Landers (1983) suggestion to go beyond a mere inspection of comparable data and to come forward with more statistically integrated results on the topic of personality and performance was accepted. In order to test the hypothesis concerning the existence of extroversion trait differences between elite and nonelite athletes, a meta-analysis was conducted.

Third, a review of the research is presented which recognized the complex nature of human functioning and performance prediction. Therefore, more global multidimensional designs and corresponding multivariate analysis techniques were used.

Finally, the paradigmatic reactions in the sport psychology field to the crisis in personology are commented on. Specifically, the sport personality research in the 1970s and 1980s was inspected for the presence of ideas and methodologies that emerged originally in academic personality research.

RESEARCH ON ELITE ATHLETES USING THE PROFILE OF MOOD STATES: THE ICEBERG PROFILE

The Profile of Mood States, or POMS, was developed to detect transient, fluctuating states, in order to measure changes resulting from psychotherapies and psychotropic medications. The manual recommends its use "primarily for psychiatric outpatients" (McNair et al., 1971, p. 6). This notwithstanding, the POMS has been widely used by researchers with a large variety of nonpsychiatric samples. LeUnes and Hayward reported in 1988 that many athletes had been tested with the POMS, and they summarized 56 sport-related publications in which it had been cited. More than a dozen published studies have been identified in which the POMS was administered to wrestlers, runners, rowers, divers, skaters, and cyclists, the skill levels of whom meet the definition of elite mentioned earlier.

Discussion of the POMS is included here because it has been noted that although the POMS was not designed to measure personality, "the resulting score appears to resemble a traitlike concept" (Morgan, 1988, p. 250). Morgan went on to state that POMS scores were significantly correlated with MMPI subscales (Morgan, 1986, cited in Morgan, 1988). Another reason for discussing the POMS is because it has been reported to be effective in predicting success of high level athletes (Morgan, 1978, 1988; Morgan & Johnson, 1978). "The POMS is widely used as a predictor of athletic success" (Mastro et al., 1987, p. 39).

The main proponent of the use of the POMS in sport has been Morgan. His many research articles and his identification of an "iceberg profile" of POMS scores (Morgan, 1974, 1980, 1985; Morgan et al., 1987, 1988; Morgan & Johnson, 1978; Nagle et al., 1975, among other publications) stimulated much discourse on the topic. The iceberg profile refers to a description of a visual display of an athlete's data from the POMS where the mood states labeled tension, depression, anger, fatigue, and confusion are below the 50th percentile and vigor is above the 50th percentile of the published norms (McNair et al., 1971).

With the large numbers of studies in which the POMS has been used with athletes, it was inevitable that there would be a wide variety of results. A variety of research methodologies have been reported. Athletes of different skill levels and ages have been studied. Unfortunately, many researchers have not reported relevant information,

such as the skill level, education, or ages of the athletes tested. Important methodological information has often been missing, the most important for the POMS being the response set. Because the POMS is a test of mood states, it is important to know the details of the testing environment and the relationship between the time of testing and significant athletic events for the athletes (the subjects). Some researchers have indicated when the POMS was given in relation to athlete competitions and other team selection procedures, but many have not.

For this review it is assumed that there is reasonable commonality among the populations represented and methodologies used in various studies, and that those investigators who have not reported complete methods have followed standard acceptable guidelines. In most cases this can be considered more than reasonable. For example, although Morgan has not reported the POMS response set used in every study, consistently the standard set ("last week including today") was reported in many studies.

But there were quite a few reasons to weed out other studies that cannot be considered comparable. Investigations with elite athletes which discussed POMS data and iceberg profiles, but which did not include all the POMS data points, were not included in this review section (e.g., Daus, Wilson, & Freeman, 1986; Durtschi & Weiss, 1986; Joesting, 1981).

Two good investigations in which the POMS was used with their elite samples cannot be compared with the larger body of POMS/elite athlete research because differing instruction sets were administered. The majority of researchers who reported the nature of the response set typically followed the "one-week" set. The two studies (Silva et al., 1981, 1985) in which the "right now" response set was implemented were not included in the present analysis, primarily because of the caution offered in the POMS manual:

Obviously different rating periods may yield different item and scale means and variances. Most of the data reported in this manual are based on a one-week rating period and, unless specified, *should not* be considered applicable for shorter or longer rating periods. (McNair et al., 1971, p. 5)

In another pair of investigations of elite athletes excluded from this review, athletes from another country were compared to American norms (cf. the discussion in this chapter on meta-analysis). Hardman (1973) warned about the cautious interpretations necessary when making such cross-cultural comparisons. The Miller and Miller (1985) sample of Australian netballers and the Power (1986) data on British jumpers were excluded to avoid causing further cautions in interpreting the data presented in our review.

It is worth noting, however, that variable results were reported in those four excluded studies. Miller and Miller (1985) indicated that one group of elite athletes displayed the iceberg profile but that the other did not. Seven international-level British athletes' POMS scores were above the norms for all six mood states (Power, 1986). The successful Olympic team wrestling candidates who took a "right now" POMS just before selection (Silva et al., 1985) showed a strong iceberg profile, but the unsuccessful candidates in that study did not. Neither the selected team members nor the rejected group showed any semblance of an iceberg profile in the Silva et al. (1981) study. The significant cross-cultural differences reported by Cattell and Warburton (1961) may be responsible for such discrepant results in the first two cases.

Some researchers administered the POMS repeatedly to their elite subjects (Gutmann, Knapp et al., 1984; Gutmann, Pollock et al., 1984). For comparison to the other POMS research, the time periods selected in our review were chosen to coincide with the most common methodologies, namely, during a special training phase, and usually at a special facility (Morgan & Johnson, 1978; Morgan et al., 1987, 1988).

Table 11-1 and related Figure 11-1 show all the reviewed studies that reported POMS data from elite athletes. The groups summarized in Table 11-1 are, except as noted, the entire samples indicated by the authors, not subgroupings.

Of the 18 groups totaling 308 elite athletes from 11 published articles, only one group (Morgan & Johnson, 1978), 16 lightweight wrestlers, had scores entirely not consistent with Morgan's iceberg profile. Eleven groups yielded scores completely consistent with the definition of the iceberg profile, and six groups generated one mean score for one mood state marring the profile. Thus there is more than a little conformity of the data with the iceberg profile.

On closer inspection, four of the six groups with some data that is inconsistent with the profile are cases in which the POMS was administered at times and in places differing from the other studies. Most researchers who reported their administration schedules noted that the POMS was completed well before any important competitive events that could influence POMS responses (Gutmann, Knapp et al., 1984; Gutmann, Pollock et al., 1984; Morgan, 1974; Morgan et al., 1987, 1988; Morgan & Johnson, 1978, heavyweight group).

In four reports, a temporal relationship was mentioned between POMS administration and stressful events. DeMers (1983) asked divers to answer the POMS following a warmup on the day of their national championships. Hagberg et al. (1979) reported that the cyclists had just completed 10 days of racing a total of 460 miles, before completing the POMS. And in two of Morgan's studies, wrestlers completed the POMS a short time before stressful competition (Morgan, 1974) or final Olympic team selection (Morgan & Johnson, 1978, lightweight group). Since the response set asked about mood states "during the last week including today," such events are most likely to have affected responses.

Figure 11-2 displays the data which are a subgroup of data from Figure 11-1. It contains data only from those seven studies in which there was no report of administering the POMS under stressful conditions. The mean scores from the nine groups representing 170 elite athletes show almost complete conformity to the iceberg profile.

DISCUSSION

The studies we have examined in which the POMS was administered to elite athletes have confirmed Morgan's (1980) initial findings of reduced scores on the scales labeled Tension, Anger, Depression, Fatigue, and Confusion, and elevated scores on Vigor.

Two of the reports in Figure 11-2 included more data than could be included there. An inspection of the additional data from the two Gutmann et al. (1984) studies reveals that while iceberg profiles predominate the repeated administrations, the pattern is not universal. Elite skaters under 21 years of age ($N = 18$) displayed the iceberg profile only during the training phase at the Olympic training center, while the older skaters' scores ($N = 14$) reflected the iceberg profile at each of the four administrations (Gutmann, Knapp et al., 1984). The skaters in the Gutmann, Pollock et al. (1984) study showed the iceberg profile at each of the three time periods before Olympic trials. Immediately after the trials, Fatigue scores were above the norm, and Vigor scores were equivalent to the norm. There would appear to be some consistency to this collection of mood states.

The strongest research results from this literature come from those samples which are indeed comparable with the age and education level of the norm groups of U.S. college students. Unfortunately, the education history is rarely reported. More data on ages of the populations reviewed here were available, but they were not broken down sufficiently to fit into Table 11-1. The available data show that most of the elite athletes are older than college age, although this age difference is not great. Therefore it is reasonable that these samples have been compared to the original, tentative norms.

It is important to note that this is a collection of studies on elite American athletes. With exceptions, the athletes are males. Generalizations to other populations have yet to be made. Further caution comes from the POMS manual (McNair et al., 1971, p. 19): "The norms should be considered as very tentative," since these norms are the basis of the iceberg profile. One of the particularities of this review is that Morgan is listed as an author on seven of the eleven studies we examined. It is understandable that a renowned researcher has and can create more opportunities for access to elite athletes. However, this "majority ownership" should not be overlooked when considering these results.

In conclusion, a review of these studies of groups of elite athletes supports the notion that elite American athletes typically display the iceberg profile, especially during training periods some time before competition. The few studies reporting data that are not consistent can be explained in terms of either procedural or normative variations. None of the reports examined in which the POMS was used with elite samples contained irrefutable results contradicting the existence of an iceberg profile for elite athletes.

TABLE 11-1. POMS Raw Mean Scores for Elite Athletes, Expressed as
Deviations from the Norm

NR.	SOURCE	AGE MEAN (RANGE)	POPULATION	SPORT DISCIPLINE	N	TENSION	DEPRES-SION	ANGER	VIGOR	FATIGUE	CONFU-SION
							(All POMS figures expressed as deviation scores.)				
1.	Morgan (1974) (d)	NA	U.S. males, Olympic team members	Wrestling	10	−5.4	7.1	+0.4	+8.6	−6.4	−6.2
2.	Nagle et al. (1975)	24.29 SD = 1.8	U.S. males, selected as Olympic team members	Wrestling	40	−3.1	−8.2	0	+7.3	−4.1	−6.3
3.	Morgan & Pollack (1977) (b)	NR	U.S. males, world class	Running	27	−2.4	−6.3	−2.2	+5.4	−3.5	−2.8
4.	Morgan & Johnson (1978)	NR	U.S. males, national team candidates	Heavyweight rowing	57	−3.8	−7.1	−3.4	+4.5	−3.0	−5.2
5.	Morgan & Johnson (1978)	NR	U.S. male national team candidates	Lightweight rowing	16	+0.9	−6.4	−0.4	+0.5	+2.9	−2.9
6.	Morgan (1979) (c)	NA	U.S. male Olympic team candidates	Wrestling	16	−2.3	−5.9	−3.5	+4.1	−0.5	−4.4
7.	Hagberg et al. (1979)	25.1 (20–33)	U.S. male world team candidates	Bicycling	9	−4.3*	−8.5*	−5.2*	+3.3*	+0.2	−3.4*
8. 9. 10.	DeMers (1983) (d)	NR	56 females (e) U.S. national championships	Diving 1m 3m 10m	NR NR NR	−0.9 −1.9 −1.4	−6.3 −8.3 −8.3	−1.3 −1.3 +0.9	+3.9 +4.9 +6.9	−4.7 −3.4 3.9	−5.2 −4.7 −5.7
11. 12. 13.	DeMers (1983)(d)	NR	45 males at U.S. national championships	Diving 1m 3m 10m	NR NR NR	−0.9 −0.4 −2.6	−7.1 −7.6 −8.1	−0.8 −1.1 −1.6	+4.9 +4.9 +5.9	−3.6 −2.9 −4.9	−4.2 −4.2 −5.2
14.	Gutmann, Pollack et al. (1984)	20.1 (15–27)	U.S. male Olympic team candidates	Speed skating	11	−2.8	−7.5	−3.6	+1.7	−0.1	−4.7
15.	Gutman, Knapp et al. (1984)	up to 20	8 male, 10 female candidates, U.S. Olympic team	Speed skating	18	−5.9	−7.1	−5.2	+0.3	−0.9	−5.4
16.	Gutman, Knapp et al. (1984)	over 20	9 male, 5 female candidates, U.S. Olympic team	Speed skating	14	−5.4	−9.1	−5.2	+4.3	−2.0	−6.8
17.	Morgan et al. (1987)	NR	Elite females (e)	Distance running	15	−3.5	−10.4	−4.5	+6.1	−3.7	−6.2
18.	Morgan et al. (1988)	26.4 (±2.1)	U.S. male Olympic trainees	Distance running	14	−2.7	−5.6	−1.7	+3.9	−2.1	−3.9

*p < 0.5. Note: Only Hagberg analyzed this comparison statistically.

a: norms for college males (McNair et al., 1971)

b: data obtained from Fuchs & Zaichkowsky (1983)

c: Data from Morgan (1985)

d: Data estimated from graphs

e: Compared to norms for U.S. college females, N = 516

NA: Not available

NR: Not reported

	Tension	Depression	Anger	Vigor	Fatigue	Confusion	
+10							+10
+9				1,			+9
+8							+8
+7				2,			+7
+6				13, 17			+6
+5				3, 4, 9, 10, 11, 12			+5
+4				6, 8, 16, 18			+4
+3				7†	5		+3
+2				14			+2
+1	5						+1
Norm	12		1, 2, 5	5, 15	7, 14		Norm
−1	8, 10, 11		8, 9, 10, 11, 12		6, 15		−1
−2	3, 6, 9		3, 13, 18		16, 18	3	−2
−3	2, 13, 14, 18		4		4, 13	5, 7†	−3
−4	4, 7*, 17		6, 14		2, 3, 10, 11, 17	11, 12, 18	−4
−5	1, 16		7*, 15, 16, 17		8, 9, 13	4, 6, 8, 13, 14, 15	−5
−6	15	3, 5, 6, 8, 18			1	1, 2, 9, 10, 17	−6
−7		1, 4, 11, 15				16	−7
−8		2, 8, 10, 12, 13, 14					−8
−9		7*, 16					−9
−10		17					−10

*Norms for college females and males (McNair et al., 1971).

†$p < 0.5$. Only Hagberg (1979) analyzed this comparison statistically.

FIGURE 11–1. POMS raw mean scores for elite athletes expressed
as deviations from the norm. The numbered data points refer to
the studies listed in Table 11–1.

A REEXAMINATION OF THE SPORT PERSONOLOGY LITERATURE ON EXTROVERSION WITH META-ANALYSIS

In the previous section, conclusions were merely based on a visual inspection of the differences between the results of the studies and the population norms. The use of other techniques, such as meta-analysis, allows an overall trend in the results from many studies dealing with the same topic to be founded on a statistical basis. The purpose of a meta-analysis is the quantitative integration of research findings taken from different studies in the absence of the original data. Consequently, the homogeneity or heterogeneity in results regarding a similar underlying question can be examined (Cook & Leviton, 1980; Glass, 1977; Halliwell & Gauvin, 1982; Landers, 1983; Wolf, 1986).

An important problem when considering a meta-analysis on personality data from elite athletes is the variety of research designs, reflecting divergent goals and hypotheses.

In the literature, for example, successful elite athletes are typically compared (1) with nonsuccessful athletes or athletes at a lower performance level, (2) with a control group or with nonathletes, (3) with test norms of the general population, (4) across sport disciplines, or (5) by gender. One way of overcoming this problem is to compare the mean scores from each sample with the test norms for a similar population, which is what has been done here.

The meta-analysis was conducted on a single trait: extroversion/introversion. This trait was selected because it has been argued that extroversion is a trait for which elite sportsmen score higher than is expected (Eysenck, Nias, & Cox, 1982; Hardman, 1973), as compared with normative data.

The data collected for the present analysis covers a range of sports. Since this meta-analysis focused on elite performers, only data from this high-level population were analyzed. The literature search described earlier yielded 25

	Tension	Depression	Anger	Vigor	Fatigue	Confusion	
+10							+10
+9							+9
+8							+8
+7				2			+7
+6				17			+6
+5				3, 4			+5
+4				6, 16, 18			+4
+3							+3
+2				14			+2
+1							+1
Norm			2	15	14		Norm
−1					6, 15		−1
−2	3, 6		3, 18		16, 18	3	−2
−3	2, 14, 18		4		4		−3
−4	4, 17		6, 14		2, 3, 17	18	−4
−5	16		15, 16, 17			4, 6, 14, 15	−5
−6	15	3, 6, 18				2, 17	−6
−7		4, 15				16	−7
−8		2, 14					−8
−9		16					−9
−10		17					−10

*Norms for college females and males (McNair et al., 1971).

†p < 0.5. Only Hagberg (1979) analyzed this comparison statistically.

FIGURE 11–2. POMS raw mean deviation scores for elite athletes
not tested under stressful conditions. The numbered data points
refer to the studies listed in Table 11–1.

different studies which measure elite athletes on extroversion, using the 16PF (Institute for Personality and Ability Testing, 1986), the EPI, and the more recent EPQ (Eysenck & Eysenck, 1964, 1975). The total sample consisted of 1,042 elite athletes as defined earlier. In some cases the data had to be derived from profiles drawn in the article. In other instances only first order scores on the 16PF were given, so that the extroversion score had to be computed.

Each sample yielded only one effect size, which means that the effect sizes were obtained independently. The elite data were compared with a norm group as similar as possible to the athletes (Eysenck & Eysenck, 1964, 1975; Fuchs & Zaichkowsky, 1983; Hagberg et al., 1979; Institute for Personality and Ability Testing, 1986). However, since only English norms were available for the EPQ, there was some possibility that cross-cultural differences would contaminate these results (Cattell & Warburton, 1961). Four studies (Morgan et al., 1987, 1988, on Americans; Vanek & Hosek,

1974, on Czechs; Kumar & Varma, 1989, on Indians) thus could not be compared with culturally appropriate norms and were excluded.

The null hypothesis was that there would be no difference between athletes and the normal population on the extroversion personality trait. To determine if this hypothesis would be confirmed, an average effect size was computed according to Wolf's approach of group differences (1986), based on the formula of standardized differences between means:

$$d = \frac{M_1 - M_2}{SD} \quad \begin{array}{l} (M_1, M_2 = \text{mean scores}) \\ (SD = \text{standard deviation}) \end{array}$$

This resulted in an average overall effect size of d(av) = −0.100 with a standard deviation of 0.239 for the 40 effect sizes together (see Table 11–2). This means that no significant difference was found between the samples of elite

TABLE 11–2. Effect Sizes and Weighted Effect Sizes of Studies Used in the Meta-analysis on Extroversion in Elite Athletes

Reference	Effect Size	Weighted Effect Size (d × n/N)	Reference	Effect Size	Weighted Effect Size (d × n/N)
Heusner (1952) in Hardman (1973) (athletes)	0.61	0.61 × 41 = 25.01	Morgan & Johnson (1978) (rowing) (heavyweight crew) (lightweight crew)	−0.30 −0.498	−0.30 × 57 = −17.1 −0.498 × 16 = −7.961
Kane (1964) in Hardman (1973) (athletes) (swimming)	−0.115 −0.175	−0.115 × 23 = −2.645 −0.175 × 11 = −1.925	Hagberg et al. (1979) (cycling)	−0.805	−0.805 × 9 = −7.244
Kane (1966) in Hardman (1973) (soccer: professionals young prof. amateur internat.)	0.17 0.18 −0.16	0.17 × 18 = 3.06* 0.18 × 18 = 3.24* −0.16 × 18 = −2.88*	Coleman (1980) (shooting) (prone rifle) (air rifle) (3P rifle) (free pistol) (rapid-fire pistol) (running boar) (clay pigeon skeet) (clay pigeon trap	−0.833 −0.245 −0.451 −0.533 0.808 0.03 0.167 −0.336	−0.833 × 21 = −17.493 −0.245 × 11 = −2.695 −0.451 × 15 = −6.765 −0.533 × 19 = −10.127 0.808 × 15 = 12.12 0.03 × 5 = 0.15 0.167 × 14 = 2.338 −0.336 × 13 = −4.368
Kane (1966) in Kane (1978) (swimming) (track athletes)	0.125 0.71	0.125 × 18 = 2.25* 0.71 × 18 = 12.78*			
Peterson et al. (1967) (individ.) (team)	−0.011 −0.075	−0.011 × 38 = −0.418 −0.075 × 59 = −4.425	Williams & Parkin (1980) (hockey)	−0.37	−0.37 × 18 = −6.66
Hardman (1968) in Hardman (1973) (swimming) (shooting)	−0.225 −0.32	−0.225 × 10 = −2.25 −0.32 × 10 = −3.2	Eysenck et al. (1982) (athletes)	0.184	0.184 × 192 = 35.273
			Franke (1985) (sailing)	0.395	0.395 × 14 = 5.53
Morgan (1968) (wrestling)	0.6	0.6 × 23 = 13.8	Morgan (1985) (wrestling) (successful) (unsuccessful)	−0.451 −1.334	−0.451 × 8 = −3.61 −1.334 × 8 = −10.673
Sinclair (1968) in Kane (1978) (rugby)	0.36	0.36 × 32 = 11.52	Silva et al. (1985) (wrestling)	0.055	0.055 × 64 = 3.52
Whiting & Hendry (1969) in Hardman (1973) (table tennis)	−0.03	−0.03 × 7 = −0.21	McGill et al. (1986) (rodeo)	−0.185	−0.185 × 52 = −9.62
Williams et al. (1970) (fencing)	−0.30	−0.30 × 30 = −9	Power (1986) (field)	0.26	0.26 × 7 = 1.82
Morgan & Pollack (1977) in Fuchs & Zaichkowsky (1983) (running)	0.073	0.073 × 27 = 1.976	Frazier (1987) (running)	−0.358	−0.358 × 26 × −9.322
			Nieman & George (1987) (running)	−0.243	−0.243 × 26 = −6.318
Vanek & Hosek (1977) in Franke (1985) (sailing)	−0.34	−0.34 × 21 = −7.14	Overall mean effect size Mean positive effect size Mean negative effect size	d(av) = −0.1 d(av+) = 0.315 d(av) = −0.35	d(av) = − 0.019 d(av+) = 0.266 d(av−) = −0.288
Bushan & Agarwal (1978) (table-tennis and badminton)	−0.05	−0.05 × 10 = −0.5			

American college norms for EPI are obtained from Fuchs & Zaichkowsky (1983) and Hagberg et al. (1979), based on the American version of the EPI manual, edited in 1968.

* = if the sample size was unknown, the median of the sample sizes was used (n = 18).

d × n/N, where d = effect size, n = sample size, N = total sample size.

athletes and the norm population. A closer look at the original data, however, revealed that the small value was obtained by combining 15 positive and 25 negative effect sizes of greater absolute value. The average effect size of the studies yielding a positive effect was d(av+) = 0.315, and that of the negative studies d(av−) = −0.350. In no case was the requisite criterion reached for any discussion about effect sizes significantly differing from zero. Thus the elite athletes in this sample do not differ from the normal population on extroversion, as measured by 16PF, EPI, or EPQ.

Since the formula, however, does not take into account the number of subjects in each sample, each effect size was assigned a weighting according to the number of subjects. In this case the average effect sizes were also of the same order of magnitude: d(av) = −0.019 (N = 1402); d(av+) = 0.266 (N = 506); d(av−) = −0.288 (N = 536). Using this procedure, no differences emerge between the sample populations and the norm groups.

Therefore, we can conclude that there are no significant differences between the groups examined and the norm population. To explain these results, diverse moderator variables could be checked to identify the origins of such heterogeneous data, like sex, sport discipline, and level.

Highlen and Bennett (1983), for example, suggested that the open-and closed-skill typology could be useful in differentiating elite from lesser skilled athletes. In a continuation of the above meta-analysis, the open/closed distinction was examined. The results show that neither of the two groups differ significantly from the population means. Elite athletes in the open-skill group, including table tennis, wrestling, fencing, hockey, soccer, rugby, and sailing, did not differ from nonathletes: d(av) = −0.059; N = 341. Nor did elite closed-skill athletes (running, swimming, cycling, shooting, and rowing) show any such difference from the population norms: d(ow) = −0.157, N = 348.

Eysenck et al. (1982) stated that differences could be expected between sport disciplines, between team and individual sports, and even within the same sport. However, a visual inspection of the collected data showed that sport discipline did not seem to account for the different results. Positive difference scores were obtained from research on distance running, rowing, shooting, wrestling, rugby, swimming, track and field, sailing, and athletes representing different specializations. Negative scores came from distance running, table-tennis and badminton, wrestling, fencing, hockey, rodeo, cycling, shooting, sailing, and athletes from different specializations.

Likewise, other ways of combining results are possible, when looking for differences between men and women, team and individual sports, or contact and noncontact sports, using other norm groups, or other weighting coefficients. In any case, combining results meta-analytically implies a loss of differentiation, and yet it offers the possibility to look at the totality of research outcomes. The same method of analysis could be followed for other traits, resulting in a profile of scores showing the difference between elite athletes and the normal population.

The computation of an effect size for extroversion found here indicates that:

1. Meta-analysis in sport personality research is possible and can be useful, when primary data can be fitted into such an analysis and raw scores are available.
2. Single research data have to be interpreted very carefully.
3. The high extroversion score for sportsmen, predicted by Eysenck et al. (1982), does not appear in this analysis of elite athletes. There was no overall difference between elite athletes and the population norms.

This finding concurs with Hardman's (1973) examination of reports on 42 elite athletic populations dated 1952–1968. The present meta-analysis, which included data from Hardman's report, adds weight to his conclusion. "Such results should rebut any sweeping claims that extraversion is, ipso facto, an essential element of the games players' personality" (Hardman, 1973, p. 118).

The Use of Multivariate and Multidimensional Models in Research on the Elite Athlete

Paradigmatic and Methodological Considerations

Of the numerous researchers examining the psychological characteristics of elite athletes, most have utilized univariate techniques of analysis within a unidimensional approach, i.e., examining only psychological variables. The use of both multivariate techniques and multidimensional designs has been recommended to enhance the possibilities of performance prediction, whether performance has been operationalized in terms of differences between successful/qualifier–nonsuccessful/nonqualifier or in terms of some direct measurement of ability.

The use of such multivariate statistical techniques as multiple regression, discriminant analysis, factor and cluster analysis, and recently, path analysis, has been recommended to deal with the interrelations between predictor variables (Carron, 1980; Morgan, 1973; Reeds, 1985). Predictors which are correlated with the performance criterion, but not with each other, will account for more of the variance. Second, since the early 1970s some authors have strongly advocated the use of so-called "psychobiological" and even broader multidimensional models. Such models include, in addition to psychological variables, physiological (e.g., heart rate, blood lactate), morphological (e.g., weight, body fat), and skill variables (e.g., skating speed, stick handling). The use of these models has been suggested in order to deal more adequately with the complex nature of human functioning and the multifactorial determination of performance (Deshaies et al., 1979; Landers et al., 1986; Morgan, 1973; Silva et al., 1981; Singer, 1988; Williams, 1978).

Some psychologists, although aware of the limited predictive value of the psychological factor, see no need to be masochistic. "Any variable that accounts for 20–45% of the variance should theoretically be useful in predicting behavior of utilized in concert with other dependent variables" (Morgan, 1980, p. 72).

Some (Reeds, 1985; Silva, 1984) even argue that in research on elite athletes, the psychological factor might be the most important one. The rationale might be that top-level athletes in a specific sporting discipline are, to a great extent, homogeneous on physiological, technical, and tactical parameters. Therefore, differentiation in performance might be attributed mostly to psychological factors.

Although some studies have empirically demonstrated the superiority of the psychobiological approach by producing greater overall prediction accuracy than either a physiological or a psychological model (Deshaies et al., 1979; Landers et al., 1986; Morgan, 1973; Silva et al., 1981), there is still a paucity of research using multidimensional models.

In 1984, Silva wondered why, a decade after Morgan's (1973) suggestion to use psychobiological models, the further refinement and development of sport-specific multidimensional models had not been pursued to a larger extent. As of this writing, we can ask the same question. The most important studies using multivariate models between 1973 and 1988 give an overall impression that first, multivariate research remains rare, and second, most of the recent multivariate research is solely of a unidimensional psychological nature. The fact is that there is a trend toward specialization, not toward multidisciplinary research. We see exercise physiologists attempting to explain performance in biological terms, whereas sport psychologists rely upon psychological constructs.

Another reason may lie in the actual move from the goal of prediction toward the goal of intervention in sport psychological research. That means that multivariate models, which in addition to psychological measures also include physiological and anthropometric measures, have been mostly descriptive or predictive (Williams, 1978). On the other hand, it is not recommended one use multivariate models including only psychological measures as the basis for determining membership to a team. But they are useful in the effort to gain a better understanding of the athlete and to establish appropriate strategies to enhance performance within a counseling and intervention context (Reeds, 1985; Singer, 1988).

The existence of disparate findings in multivariate research on elite athletes (Highlen & Bennett, 1983), as well as the fact that the reported overall prediction accuracy is perhaps too impressive in some studies (e.g., Silva et al., 1981, found a classification accuracy of 93.33% in wrestlers) might advise caution in generalizing the results, as well as careful evaluation of the conclusiveness of the studies. In addition to the methodological shortcomings mentioned earlier in this chapter (e.g., the criteria used to distinguish elite athletes), Landers et al. (1986) and Highlen and Bennett (1983) have identified two other methodological issues which may be partly responsible for these impressive yet disparate findings.

First, the small sample size relative to the number of variables examined is questioned in some studies. An inadequate subject-to-variable ratio is associated with instability of the data, poor statistical power, and an overestimation of the amount of explained variance.

Second, the existence of a unique set of characteristics for elite athletes across all sports is questioned. Arguing that the converse assumption that each sport requires its own unique set of characteristics seems equally untenable, Highlen and Bennett suggest a typological hypothesis. In order to explain disparate findings between elite wrestlers and gymnasts, they conducted some original research on open-and closed-skill athletes. They suggested similar research on contact versus noncontact sports and on sports requiring different types of motor activity, such as skating and golf.

Toward an Integrated Multivariate Model for Enhanced Performance Prediction

We are convinced of the value of multidimensional models in performance prediction as well as the need for more theoretically conceived research. Therefore, the purpose here is to describe briefly Reeds's (1985) study as a prototype of multivariate research able to integrate the methodological assumptions of other studies in one model for performance prediction. Although Reeds included only psychological variables and did not describe the performance criterion, what is impressive is: (1) that a theoretical model has been developed based upon previous research, (2) from this model a set of causal relationships between selected variables are drawn to test (with path analysis) whether the model adequately fits a set of empirical data, and (3) these causal relationships are presented as a sequence of temporally ordered events.

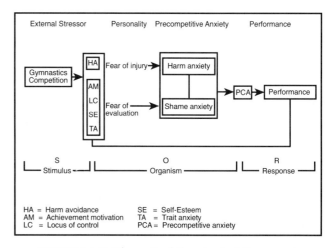

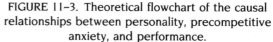

FIGURE 11–3. Theoretical flowchart of the causal relationships between personality, precompetitive anxiety, and performance.

From Reeds, 1985, p. 6.

It is useful to expand on these three points. Reeds hypothesized that performance in gymnastics would be influenced by high levels of competitive anxiety (see Figure 11–3). Competitive anxiety is defined as the emotional reaction of the individual to the subjective appraisal of the competitive situation. This appraisal is hypothesized to be influenced by the objective characteristics of the situation and by specific personality factors. Four sets of relationships were examined involving (1) each personality variable and state anxiety, (2) state anxiety and performance, (3) each personality trait and performance, and (4) the personality traits themselves.

The path analysis describes the sequence of events starting with the external stressor (the competition), which triggers interpersonal factors, hypothesized to influence anxiety reactions and consequently the performance (see Figure 11–4). It is our belief that this model might constitute a guiding perspective for predicting performance.

Characteristics of Elite Athletes

With so many definitions of elite, such a diversity of variables and instrumentation, so many sports disciplines, and such disparate findings, some reluctance to come up with conclusive results is understandable. Nevertheless, it was our purpose to identify at least some characteristics that have been found and, somewhat cautiously, reported to distinguish elite and nonelite athletes.

Consistent with the plea for an integrated multidimensional model, the results of 11 multidimensional, multivariate studies, selected according to the stringent criteria mentioned earlier, have been presented in a style echoing Reeds's (1985) model (see Figure 11–5). The objective of the reviewed multivariate studies is in testing relationships between some general and/or sport specific psychological, physiological, and anthropometric skill variables on the one hand and some criterion of performance on the other,

or to test mutual relationships between these variables. Given that, the step toward one integrated multidimensional model including all these relationships, theoretically underpinned, does not seem dramatic.

All the variables included in the selected multivariate analyses have been presented in Figure 11–5 in a format that suggests a similar path analytical design. The numbers following each variable identify the authors, and the letters indicate the sport sample examined. A star indicates that the variable has shown a significant contribution to discriminate between elite and nonelite groups or that it correlated significantly with a performance criterion. Arrows indicate the relationships to be tested.

The following list consists of the nonpsychological variables which yielded significant contributions toward discriminating between elite and nonelite athletes. Some variables were significant discriminators across sports, and some within a particular sport:

- *General*
  Lifestyle (wrestlers)
  Hours in training (wrestlers)
- *Anthropomorphic variables*
  Body type (archers)
- *Physiological variables*
  Aerobic and anaerobic capacity (rowers and wrestlers)
  Leg strength (rowers and archers)
  Back strength (rowers)
  Grip (wrestlers)
- *Visuomotor skills*
  Reaction time (archers)
  Depth perception (archers)

In Figure 11–6, only psychological variables yielding a significant contribution to the performance prediction are reported. Because there are few studies, it could be cautiously interpreted that three studies using the same measurement and revealing the same discriminant attributes may be an indication of some confirmatory evidence of the importance of that particular attribute.

In summary, sport-specific variables are better predictors than trait variables. The strongest findings seem to be that across sports, relative to their nonelite counterparts, elite athletes tend to report: (1) more self-confidence; (2) less anxiety, both prior and during competition; (3) more effective anxiety-coping strategies; (4) greatest concentration on task-specific goals and movements; (5) other coping strategies for dealing with poor performances or mistakes; and (6) more positive thoughts.

Conclusions Based on Comments from Multivariate Researchers

Some authors of these multivariate studies have made comments that can help integrate points made elsewhere in this chapter:

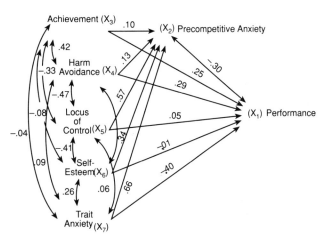

FIGURE 11–4. Recursive PATH model with beta (PATH) coefficients and Pearson correlation coefficients.
From Reeds, 1985, p. 7.

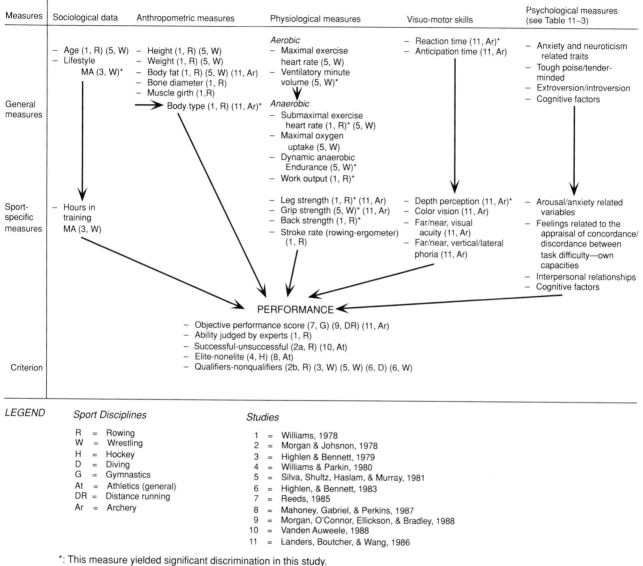

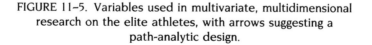

FIGURE 11-5. Variables used in multivariate, multidimensional
research on the elite athletes, with arrows suggesting a
path-analytic design.

1. The trait position is not abandoned, although researchers have become progressively more selective in measuring some traits according to their assumed relationship to performance in a specific sport (Landers et al., 1986; Morgan, 1978; Reeds, 1985; Silva, Shultz, et al., 1981).

2. The construction of more sport-specific instrumentation (cf. Mahoney's Psychological Skills Inventory for Sports, Mahoney, Gabriel & Perkins, 1987) and the grouping of sports according to their physical, psychomotor, and psychological demands, including open-versus closed-skill sports, can be considered as an expression of the orga-

nismic interactionist position (Highlen & Bennett, 1983; Mahoney et al., 1987).

3. There is interest in longitudinal and sequential aspects of psychological variables, including measurement of anxiety variations prior and during the competition (Highlen & Bennett, 1983). This will be discussed in the section of this chapter concerning new directions in sport personology.

4. The limitations of self-report measures in psychological assessment are acknowledged, but it is argued that such measures, refined, and when possible, simplified, main-

Trait Measures[a]	Sport-specific/State Measures[a]
Anxiety & neuroticism-related traits (high-low anxiety) • Emotional stability: 16PF-C (1, R) (4, H) • Trait anxiety: STAI-DY2 (9, DR) • Hypochondriasis: MMPI-Hs (2a, R) • Lie scale: MMPI (2a, R) • F-scale (frequency): MMPI (2a, R) • Confident-apprehensive: 16PF-0 (4, H) • Trusting-suspicious: 16PF-L (4, H)	*Arousal/anxiety-related variables* • Tension: POMS-t (5, W) • Anger: POMS-a (5, W) • Global mood: POMS (9, DR) • Specific state anxiety patterns: STAI-DY1 (10, At) : MA (6, D) • Sport-specific anxiety: MA (6, W)(6, D)(8, At) • Motivation: MA (8, At) • Mental preparation/psych-up: MA (3, W)(8, At) • Self-talk: MA (3, W) (6, W)(6, D) • Load-carrying capacity: (10, At)
Tough-poise/tender-minded • Tough-minded/tender-minded: 16PF-I (1, R) (4, H) • Sober-enthusiastic: 16PF-F (4, H) • Psychopathic deviate: MMPI-Pd (2a, R)	*Feelings related to the appraisal of concordance/discordance between task difficulty and own capacity* • Self-confidence: MA (3, W)(8, At)(11, Ar) • Role performance: MA (3, W) • Feeling close to maximum potential: MA (3, W)
Extraversion/introversion • (Social) Introversion-extroversion: MMPI-Si (2a, R) : EPI (2b, R) • Group-dependent/self-sufficient:16PF-Q2 (1, R) • Shy-bold: 16PF-H (4, H)	*Interpersonal relationships* • Relation athlete-parents: (10, At) • Relation athlete-trainer: (10, At)
Cognitive factors • Intelligence: 16PF-B (4, H)	*Cognitive factors* • Thoughts: MA (3, W)(6, W)(6, D) • Performance attributions: MA (6, W)(6, D)(11, Ar) • Concentration: MA (3, W)(6, W)(8, At) • Dreams: MA (3, W) • Distraction: MA (3, W) • Cognitive coping: MA (3, W)(6, D) • Blocking: MA (3, W)

[a] The trait variables are categorized according to the second-order factors (16PF). Sport-specific and state variables are categorized according to their similarity in denotation.

FIGURE 11–6. Psychological variables used in multivariate, multidimensional research with elite athletes. Only significant measures are reported here. The titles of the tests are indicated behind each item. For identification of sport disciplines and studies, see legend, Figure 11–5.

tain relevance and practical priority (Mahoney, Gabriel, & Perkins, 1987). That position will be commented on in our discussion of behavioral assessment procedures.

THE PARADIGMATIC SOLUTIONS TO THE CRISIS IN SPORT PERSONOLOGY RECONSIDERED

Sport personality research from the 1970s and 1980s is interpreted here for the presence of ideas that emerged in the academic personality research after the challenge made to the trait approach. Apparently, the plea for acceptance of the interactionism model has been followed to a great extent by researchers in sport psychology. The results of Vealy's analysis of the sport personality research published between 1974 and 1987 indicate that interactionism has in fact replaced the trait paradigm in sport personology (Vealy, 1989).

It is obvious, too, that interactionism has many faces. According to Vealy (p. 227), "the cognitive approach has over-

shadowed the trait-state approach to interactionism." However, the concept of interactionism seems to be loosely defined by many researchers, as expressed by Fisher's warning (1984, p. 75): "Just combining a number of trait and state measures in an additive sense, as in regression analysis, for instance, does not necessarily satisfy the demands of the interactional model."

There are sufficient reasons to take a closer look at the so-called "interactionism approach" in sport personology, and to inspect publications for interpretations of interactionism. A reference to dynamic interactionism, as defined earlier, has been made by Martens (1975). He stated that interactionism recognizes that the person creates and shapes his or her environment. However, the idea of a dynamic interaction does not appear in research articles. Maybe the view of the individual as an active participant in life does not fit in research from a differential psychological perspective, i.e., focused on inter-individual differences. The idiographic approach of the study of personality is more adapted to the study of a dynamic person-situation interaction. The ideas of circularity and reciprocity call for appropriate statistical techniques for interaction sequences and will be addressed shortly.

In Vealy's review (1989) of the sport personology research literature, the cognitive interactional approach and the trait-state interactional approach are considered as two different approaches. The cognitive approach emphasizes that "how one perceives the situation is what really counts" (Fisher, 1977a, p. 202). "The emphasis is on the individual's perceptions and interpretations of the environment and the way these perceptions and interpretations influence subsequent behavior" (Vealy, 1989, p. 220).

In the trait-state approach, a state is seen as the result of the interaction of personality variables (e.g., traits) and situational variables. Vealy indicates: "It may be argued that the trait-state and cognitive approaches are not distinctive paradigms, but different approaches within the interactional paradigm" (p. 220). In our opinion, both approaches can be subsumed under organismic interaction as explained earlier. Both approaches underline the same direction in the reciprocal interaction between personality characteristics and situational variables. That is, the influence of the personality is made in the transformation of objective external variables into a subjective, phenomenological situation. The cognitive approach emphasizes the cognitive processing of the situation, whereas the trait-state approach stresses the affective-emotional coping with the situation.

Obviously there is a difference between perceptions and feelings. Both perceptions and feelings, however, turn the objective situational variables into a phenomenological situation on which the person (re)acts. Vealy (1989) concludes that the cognitive approach has overshadowed the trait-state approach. She refers (1989) to a *Zeitgeist* of cognitivism in psychology as an explanation for the success of the cognitive approach.

Articles by Fisher (1977a, 1984) and Morgan (1980) suggest that the cognitive approach might be the most fruitful for sport personality research. According to Kane (1981, p. 61), the interactional model "centers on the cognitive perceptions and interpretations of the person in a given situation." Some of the cognitive variables should have a special relevance for sports performers. Kane gives a brief commentary on the significance of causal attributions and attentional styles. Fisher (1979, 1984) recommended the use of an individual differences scaling analysis (INDSCAL), saying it "allows one to see inside another's head and understand that person's cognitive schema . . ." (1984, p. 77).

However, an uncritical borrowing by sport psychologists of cognitive variables from academic personality psychology seems undesirable. It is not because locus of control is "the single most popular topic in current personality research" (cf. Fisher, 1977a, p. 201) that it is a useful variable in sport personality research. In light of Rotter's Social Learning Theory, from which locus of control originated, Straub (1977) argues that the concept is not useful in sport environments, because sport environments, not being highly ambiguous, nor loosely structured, do not offer the

required conditions to all attribution processes. This example points again to the need to develop a sport-specific theoretical basis before beginning to gather data. Very disappointing is Vealy's conclusion that "although theoretical research increased from the early to mid-1970s, still only half of our research utilizes a conceptual basis" (1989, p. 229).

The lack of a conceptual basis and the absence of a theoretical model is obvious in trait-state research. It seems to be a normal practice to change the instructions a bit, to obtain a state-measure from trait items, to add the state score to the trait score, and to see if the predictive power is enhanced by the addition of the state measure. Of course there are exceptions. For instance, one investigation by Vealy (1986) was based on a conceptual model of self-confidence in sport, from a trait-state interactional paradigm.

Unfortunately much sport personology research still is atheoretical. Interactionism seems to be nothing more than a necessary fashionable label that allows researchers to continue on in the same way: collecting paper-and-pencil data (including state scores) and correlating them with some criterion of sport performance.

Sometimes the label of "interactionism" seems to be (inappropriately) used to justify the employment of trait measurements for behavioral prediction. Dwyer and Carron (1986) refer to Martens in stating that the interactional paradigm, considered as a compromise between the trait and situational position, regards traits as dispositions or tendencies to behave in certain ways in certain classes of situations. Obviously such a definition of traits is not new, but it is consistent with a traditional Cattellian trait theory (Straub, 1977).

It is unnecessary to take a loosely defined interactionistic position to motivate the development of sport-specific or situation-specific trait measures. The use of such situation-specific inventories as the Sport Competition Anxiety Test (SCAT, Martens, 1982), the tennis-specific form of Nideffer's Test of Attentional Style (Van Schoyck & Grasha, 1981), and the wrestling-specific version of the Jackson Personality Inventory (JPI-W, Dwyer & Carron, 1986) can be done from within the traditional trait paradigm. The development of sport-specific scales is merely one option for enhancing of the predictive power of personality measures. There are other possibilities, as implied by the responses seen in the academic personality literature after the period of criticism of the trait model.

The idea that only some traits are useful for predicting an athlete's behavior seems to have advocates in contemporary sport personology, although in a specific variant. The relevance of a trait for any particular sport situation seems to be the criterion for selection, not the relevance of the trait for a particular individual (as is the case in academic personality psychology).

Highlen and Bennett (1983) hypothesized that the use of imagery (as a psychological characteristic) would differentiate successful closed-skill athletes from their less successful counterparts, but that no such differences would be found in the open-skilled sports.

The plea to stop using holistic personality inventories as the only assessment tool in personology research is clear (Fisher, 1977a, 1984; Morgan, 1980; Singer, 1988). Fisher (1977a) speaks of a fallacy of salience and argues that global personality inventories have little, if any, value to the sport scene. They presumably do not restrict themselves to areas of behavior which are salient to that specific environ. Despite the calls for the use of selected traits, an inspection of the research in the 1970s and in the '80s shows that global inventories such as MMPI, CPI, and 16PF are still used, without selection of specific scales.

To summarize, optimism as well as pessimism seem to be justifiable reactions after our reevaluation of the research literature. Pessimism is justified, because of the persistent lack of concern with theory development as revealed in the analysis of the paradigmatic shifts in sport personology. There is optimism because there are some consistent findings. Whether or not one agrees that the variable is considered personality-related, there is consistency in finding a typical pattern of mood states in elite athletes, e.g., the Iceberg profile.

And, unless one assumes that all of the differences between elite and nonelite athletes reported in the multivariate literature are due to methodological shortcomings, one has to accept that the strongest results probably reflect some truth. Relative to nonelite athletes, elite athletes report higher self-confidence, lower anxiety and more effective coping strategies, greater task-oriented concentration, increased positive thoughts, and more self-enhancing attributions. The one-shot, atheoretical, univariate studies are not entirely wasted time, insofar as their data can be analyzed with meta-analytic procedures. Optimism is also in order because there are some promising evolutions directed at enhancing prediction of success, built on theoretical bases (cf. multidimensional research).

However, as noted by Vealy (1989), the evolution of prediction studies tends to be overshadowed by the increase in intervention studies. We agree with Landers (1983) that the decrease in predictive studies is another manifestation of too little attention to theory development. On the other hand, the increase of intervention studies can be situated within a broader movement toward intervention directed testing and the diagnosis of the individual, stimulated by clinical and personality research, psychotherapeutic schools, and behavioral therapy. The incorporation and integration of recently developed diagnostic methods in sport psychology is the main objective of the last sections of this chapter.

NEW DIRECTIONS IN PERSONOLOGY AND SPORT PERSONOLOGY RELEVANT IN THE CONTEXT OF MENTAL TRAINING AND COUNSELING

With the advent of an important trend in sport psychological activity toward dealing with diagnosis and interven-

tions for the elite performer (Landers, 1983; Rushall, 1989; Silva, 1984; Singer, 1988; Williams, 1986), there is a growing need for instruments that are sensitive enough to record idiosyncratic elements and minute changes in athletic behavior.

Important problems such as the athlete's evolution toward a peak performance, the measurement of interaction processes between athletes and coaches, or the evaluation of an intervention technique all require the recording of changes. Similarly, when a mental skill training is planned, the importance of intra-individual personality diagnosis can be made clear. The sport psychologist has to know the strengths and limitations of an athlete before implementing a performance enhancement strategy. Only in this way can the logical and chronological order of diagnosis and intervention be respected. Some authors clearly call for an individualized approach to the elite athlete in the context of an interventional objective:

. . . coaches should have a big picture of each athlete's capabilities. Such information can be useful in understanding each athlete and his/her potential strengths and limitations." (Singer, 1988, p. 101)

Practicing sport psychology is characterized by its concern with helping athletes and coaches, and with the need to focus on the whole person in order to do so. (Martens, 1987, p. 31)

. . . other assessments made of the same individual . . . , clearly needed in sport personality research . . . ." (Vealy, 1989, p. 230)

These shifts in objectives and subsequent shifts in information needs towards recording changes, idiosyncracies, and focusing on the person as a whole, converge with similar developments in personology, as Pervin's directive definition of personality exemplifies most clearly. According to Pervin (1984), personality refers:

1. To similarities between people as well as to regularities within the person.
2. To stable aspects of a person's functioning (structure) as well as to fluid, changing aspects (process).
3. To cognitions, affects, and overt behaviors as well as to the complex relationships among these aspects.
4. To processes that occur in relation to stimuli and situations, created by the environment or by the person.

In 1987, Verstraeten reviewed the paradigmatic and methodological developments in personology that could be of interest for clinical psychology. In contrast with the classical emphasis on constancies in personality, according to her, recent developments seem to emphasize variations and changes as a function of time and/or the situation.

This section will describe some recent developments in general and sport personology along three different critical shifts in emphasis that share common interest in the measurement of changes. Perhaps together they would constitute a guiding theoretical perspective that can direct the efforts in the study of the elite performer.

A description of the three critical shifts in emphasis will

be given and their relevance for the primary sport psychological objectives will be indicated. Finally, some of the attempts to apply these new concepts and methods in sport psychology will be reviewed.

THREE CRITICAL SHIFTS IN EMPHASIS

The first area of development stresses behavioral assessment rather than self-description techniques such as questionnaires and projective techniques (Barlow & Hersen, 1984; Hartmann et al., 1979). Second, there is a shift from interindividual to intraindividual research or from nomothetic to idiographic research (Barlow & Hersen, 1984; Killpatrick & Cantrill, 1960; Runyan, 1983). Personologists are interested in the psychological structure within the individual, such as in the interaction between different behavioral components, i.e., cognitions, emotions, and overt behavior. They are also interested in the life history of the individual, that is, in the unique process of changes in that individual over time.

Finally, in a third development, the deterministic model has been abandoned for a probabilistic model. The deterministic model assumes that each behavior (e.g., an excellent performance) is perfectly predictable if only all relevant antecedents can be identified. With the probabilistic or stochastic model a more flexible concept of causality is used. The rationale of that model is that in a specific situation an individual can react in different ways, and only the probability of each of these reactions can be predicted (Schlicht, 1988). For example, it should be possible to predict the probability that a series of behaviors that belongs to an athlete's repertoire is likely to occur in a specific situation.

Shifting From Traditional Personality Assessment to Behavioral Assessment

In academic personality research there has been an important evolution toward the construction of behavioral assessment techniques in reaction to Mischel's (1968) arguments against traditional approaches to personality assessment. In 1979, an edition of the *Journal of Behavioral Assessment* emphasized the importance of that evolution. Because the behavioral assessment approach stresses behavior itself instead of underlying hypothetical constructs, which in sport has great face value, it has attracted researchers in sport psychology. Presumably, research focusing on behavior rather than on self-descriptions may contribute answers of more immediate application value to coaches, to resolve their main concerns and questions more than the traditional personality research (Donahue et al., 1980).

In the argument against personality as a reflection of underlying traits, it is crucial that traits are inferred from questionnaires and that questionnaires are essentially based on self-descriptions. That limitation should presumably be responsible for the low predictive value of questionnaires. For example, an individual's self-description that he or she is a punctual person seems to be only to a small degree related to actual behavioral punctuality. A lack of self-knowledge and/or a measure of self-defensiveness may be the most obvious reasons for that inappropriate self-analysis (Kenrick & Dantchik, 1983; Verstraeten, 1987).

An interesting corroboration of the interpretation of low correlations between self-descriptions and behaviors may be that, in the measurement of intelligence, high correlations have been found between test and criterion only as long as there has been a great similarity between test items and criterion items. For instance, intelligence tests usually consist of a number of items very similar to the criterion application situation. If self-descriptions are used to measure cognitive functions and abilities lacking in this similarity with some behavioral criterion of intelligence, a correlation of .30 has been obtained, as is the case with different personality characteristics (Mabe & West, 1982, cited in Verstraeten, 1987).

Hartmann et al. (1979) have formulated an outline of the main differences between behavioral and traditional approaches of assessment (see Table 11–3). Although most of these differences are well known, some deserve special attention because they have specific relevance to the psychologist working with the elite athlete. They are also of importance to the other shifts in emphasis in personality research being described here. We mention especially the emphasis on intra-individual or idiographic studies, on direct methods (behavioral observation on natural environment and field studies, on the sequential aspect of assessment, on sport-specific measures and variables, and on the use of the data in a way that fits more with the actual concerns with the elite athlete: mental training and counseling to enhance performance instead of classification and prediction).

Of special interest to the psychologist working with elite athletes is an alternative technique suggested by Hartmann et al. (1979) for the evaluation of test scores. A persistent problem in psychological measurement of elite performers is the ambiguous meaning of test scores due to the lack of concrete referents for the assessment scales from which the scores were derived. With the psychometric or norm-referenced approach, scores are interpreted by comparison with a standard or norm that is based on the performance of a suitable reference group. This method is illustrated by scores that express an individual's performance in relation to the performance of other individuals on the same measuring device. Norm-referenced assessment thus implies inter-individual research.

Because it is by definition difficult to find a suitable reference group for an elite athlete, the alternative method of criterion-referenced testing is very inspiring and perhaps more in keeping with the actual performance-enhancement-focused approach of the elite performer. This technique of evaluation is illustrated by the use of percent

TABLE 11–3. Differences Between Behavioral and Traditional
Approaches to Assessment

Parameters	Behavioral	Traditional
A. Assumptions		
1. Conception of personality	Personality constructs mainly employed to summarize specific behavior patterns, if at all	Personality as a reflection of enduring underlying states or traits
2. Causes of behavior	Maintaining conditions sought in current environment	Intrapsychic or within the individual
B. Implications		
1. Role of behavior	Important as sample of person's repertoire in specific situation	Behavior assumes importance only insofar as it indexes underlying causes
2. Role of history	Relatively unimportant, except, for example, to provide a retrospective baseline	Crucial seen as a product of the past
3. Consistency of behavior	Behavior thought to be specific to the situation	Behavior expected to be consistent across time and settings
C. Uses of Data	To describe target behaviors and maintaining conditions To select the appropriate treatment To evaluate and revise treatment	To describe personality functioning and etiology To diagnose or classify To make prognosis; to predict
D. Other Characteristics		
1. Level of inferences	Low	Medium to high
2. Comparisons	More emphasis on intraindividual or idiographic	More emphasis on interindividual or nomothetic
3. Methods of assessment	More emphasis on direct methods (e.g., observations of behavior in natural environment)	More emphasis on indirect methods (e.g., interviews and and self-reporting)
4. Timing	More ongoing: prior, during and after treatment	Pre- and perhaps posttreatment, or strictly to diagnose
5. Scope of assessment	Specific measures and of more variables (e.g., of target behaviors in various situations, of side effects, context, strengths, as well as deficiencies)	More global measures (e.g., of cure, or improvement), but only of the individual

(From Hartmann, Roper, and Bradford, 1979, p. 4. Reprinted with permission.

correct scores on well-defined performance objectives (target behaviors). Hartmann et al. (1979) summarize:

In comparison to norm-oriented assessment, criterion referenced assessment yields interpretations that are direct rather than comparative; emphasizes intra-individual change rather than interindividual differences; and gauges the level of attainment of relatively narrow, rather than broad, performance objectives. (p. 9)

Sport psychologists working with elite performers are, after all, typically interested in knowing whether their athlete-clients can execute a narrowly defined skill at a particular moment in time, or have changed in their ability to perform a specific class of behaviors as a result of an intervention.

Behavioral procedures have been used to assess sport-specific target behaviors (e.g., behavioral assessment of athletes as well as of coaches), to modify (e.g., behavioral modification, behavioral coaching), and to measure the effects of applied behavioral techniques (e.g., outcome research) on these target behaviors (Allison & Ayllon, 1980; Donahue, Gillis, & King, 1980; Martin & Hrycaiko, 1983; Rushall, 1975c; Rushall & Smith, 1979; Smith, Smoll, & Hunt, 1977; Williams, 1982).

Until now, only a few researchers, limiting their studies to very few sports (i.e., basketball, football, volleyball, and swimming), have conducted studies in this area. Of that research we have chosen to describe perhaps not the most orthodox prototype but nevertheless a popular exponent, i.e., Rushall's personal approach (1975a, 1978) in the use of behavioral assessment/modification principles in sport.

Rushall developed sets of sport-specific inventories to describe and evaluate units of behavioral information. Subjects indicate the presence, absence, or varied occurrence of specific behaviors. Those questions which are not considered pertinent by the athlete him- or herself are not considered in the interpretation. In this way, only a subset of all the questions is considered when interpreting test responses for a particular individual. Thus, neither scale scores nor total test scores is meaningful. Each response in itself yields valuable information about an athlete and is interpreted separately (Rushall, 1975a, 1978).

From a comparison of Rushall's approach with Hartmann's criteria (see Table 11–3) for the characteristics of behavioral and traditional assessment, it appears that Rushall has selected from both approaches what he considers to be most valuable. He employs the concept of personality (A) in connection with behavior patterns. Consistencies are caused by the specific sporting situation, so that behavior can be assessed and predicted not across, but within, defined activities or disciplines.

As an implication of this assumption (B), behavior is important in itself, as a sample of a person's behavioral repertoire in the specific situation and not as an index of underlying dispositions. History is not explicitly considered. Behavior is thought to be specific to the (sport discipline) environment, although individuals are not expected to behave identically. Only a unique subset of the universe of behaviors is applicable to each individual. In this way inter-individual differences are not only due to differences in situations, as would be expected by behaviorists (Hartmann et al., 1979), but also to the individuals themselves.

In the use of his data (C), Rushall (1975a) pursues the traditional goals of description/diagnosis and prediction/prognosis. He also suggests that the data can be used as a baseline measurement of behavior, thereby useful for a possible modification.

As far as other characteristics (D) are concerned, Rushall does not infer anything from the individual's answers. He refers specifically and only to the behavioral information contained in the item. Rushall's (1978, cited in Morgan, 1978) suggestion about the use of a nonparametric (cluster) analysis, however, may indirectly introduce the use of underlying constructs. The emphasis lies on intra-individual or idiographic conclusions, but Rushall's method of assessment does not follow the behavioral trend of direct, behavior observations in a natural environment. He employs indirect self-report inventories, while staying as close as possible to a direct description of behavior. Assessment is mainly done at one moment in time, the diagnostical moment, and is not ongoing, as is usual in behavioral assessment research. Behavior is assessed very specifically and in many aspects or situations within the sporting discipline, which is characteristic of the behavioral approach.

To analyze Rushall's approach in detail: in comparison with the general characteristics of behavioral and traditional assessment, he joins the behavioral approach in his theoretical views and starting points, but seems to lean toward a more traditional approach in the practical application of the assessment methodology and in the further use of the data. This is the natural result of a comparison with

the behavioral assessment and traditional approach as described by Hartmann, Roper, and Bradford (1979). Rushall defined his alternative view on sport personality assessment as situation- (or activity-) specific, taking into account individual differences and response modes. He called his approach "environment-specific behavior analysis" (Rushall 1975a, 1978, 1987).

To conclude, although Martens (1975) suggested avoiding the Skinnerian application of situationism, as he called it, sport psychologists must not overlook the behavioral assessment approach. Some assumptions and characteristics associated with behaviorism undoubtedly are of importance for sport psychologists working with elite athletes in a mental training or counseling context.

Shift in Emphasis from Inter-individual Toward Intra-individual Research

The heading of this section could just as well be "From Nomothetic Toward Idiographic Research" or, alternately, "From Research on Groups Toward Single-Subject Research," since each of these ideas are developed herein.

The nomothetic-idiographic debate in psychology is very old (Allport, 1937). Idiography means the description of the unique characteristics of an individual. It is important to note that single case research is not necessarily idiographic. Besides unique features, each individual has, some characteristics in common with at least some others. Therefore he or she can be described and compared with these others (nomothetic research). Allport defined idiography as research on the psychological structure within an individual in a moment in time as well as in the life history of that particular individual. He introduced, with the historical characteristic, both the aspect of consistency and the aspect of change as a research topic (Runyan, 1983).

One of the main criticisms of the idiographic approach is that there is no such thing as a unique trait or element; a unique trait cannot be the object of study at all unless it is compared with something or someone else. In fact, when a characteristic of an individual can be defined, that individual can be essentially compared with others on that characteristic (Runyan, 1983). The purpose here is to discuss neither questions related to the philosophy of science nor mere terminological questions. However, it is necessary to stress that since the study of the elite performer is the study of a small number of individuals, and moreover, since it is the study of performance fluctuations of these high achievers (e.g., bad versus peak performances), the possibility of stringent idiographic research is highly relevant.

Requests from elite performers to help them overcome a less-than-ideal presence of a particular psychological characteristic (e.g., high anxiety) at a particular moment in reference to competition, or to help them cope with some general or sport-specific problems that could have damaging effects on their performance, show the compelling need to understand each individual's unique organization of characteristics as well as his or her unique process of change (Browne and Mahoney, 1984; Butt, 1987; Martens, 1987; Ravizza, 1984).

To meet this goal, inter-individual nomothetic research has severe limitations which justifies the use of single-case designs. Learning what is true of groups of athletes often has limitations when applied to understanding and predicting the behavior of an elite performer. An enumeration of these limitations follows.

First, when working with elite performers, one is confronted with a small number of athletes. It is extremely difficult to find subjects with the same background, and the same performance deficiencies.

Second, the statistical handling of group data can obscure relevant changes. In group comparisons, results are usually averaged and within-group variability is interpreted as an error term. This way of looking at data reflects not individual performance nor individual fluctuations, but a nonexistent average person and error variance. Moreover, in many experimental studies, much emphasis is placed on significance level, sample size, etc. Unfortunately, there is often little relationship between what is statistically significant and what is practically significant. In single case studies, on the contrary, one stresses clinical significance or relevance, although data analysis is becoming more and more statistically sophisticated (Bryan, 1987; Martens, 1987; Runyan 1983; Zaichkowsky, 1980).

Third, in any experiment using a control group (as with much nomothetic outcome research with pre-post designs), some ethical considerations can be made about withholding an intervention from a control group. In single-case experiments, subjects serve as their own controls. Problems can arise about withdrawing the intervention only if this occurs in a later phase of the experiment.

Finally, since nomothetic research is more appropriate for recording constancies, idiographic research seems to be more sensitive to record change (cf. time-series analysis in single case research, Schlicht, 1988; Verstraeten, 1987).

In spite of these convincing arguments and some cautious suggestions in that direction from leading sport psychologists, one cannot deny that there is some reluctance to use idiographic methods in sport psychology (Martens, 1987; Williams, 1987). "Since this information is presented in a more casual style . . . we must recognize the limitations in our ability to draw strong conclusions," states Singer (1988, pp. 93–94). Seeing single-case methodology becoming more and more sophisticated and allowing for the testing of idiographic hypotheses could conceivably change that cautious attitude (Bar-Eli, 1984).

In the psychological literature, many models of idiographic research have been described. A brief overview of the methodologies, possibly relevant to sport personology, is presented in Table 11–4. Not all of these methods have been used in sport psychology until now. The intent here is only to describe the models that have some applications or have been suggested as potentially useful in sport psychology. In this way an impression of the kind of idiographic research that has previously been conducted in sport psychology can be given without any intent to be exhaustive.

Qualitative Intra-Individual Research in Sport Psychology

Content Analysis of Verbal Material; Interviews. Content analyses of statements made by athletes, coaches, and scouts can lead to a description of the ideal characteristics for sport persons. Topics appropriate for content analyses could include, but are not limited to: athletes' descriptions of their best performance, or of a peak experience; or descriptions of coaches, athletes, or scouts of the necessary conditions to "become" a good performer. Once aware of the desirability of certain characteristics of outstanding performances, athletes can try to improve behavioral tendencies where limitations exist (Singer, 1988).

Several authors have tried to identify the essence of the ideal internal psychological and physical state during peak performance through interviews (Ravizza, 1984; Singer, 1988; Williams, 1986). The mental and physical attributes they mentioned have been listed and categorized according to Csikszentmihaly's flow characteristics. In Table 11–5, one can see that the individual's energy is directed toward a small part of the present. He or she is centered on a limited stimulus field (item 2), i.e., there is no thought about the past or future, nor about irrelevant environmental stimuli. There is only consciousness of what the athlete is doing at this moment. The characteristic loss of ego (item 3), a general state of transcendency, is described by sport psychologists writing about peak performance in various terms: *absorption, harmony, oneness,* or being *in the cocoon.*

While having a peak experience, the individual is presumably in control of his or her actions and of the environment (item 4). There is no worry about a possible lack of control. Everything goes on automatically, effortlessly, and perfectly. This results in mental and physical relaxation, low anxiety, and confidence.

The peak-performing athlete has a clear knowledge of the task demands and the goals (item 5), which can be related to a certain determination to fulfill the task. The motive of the action is the performance itself (e.g., it is autotelic; see item 6), which enhances commitment and produces positive attitudes and feelings (e.g., enjoyment, pride). Some of the descriptors of peak experiences did not correspond well with Csikszentmihaly's flow characteristics. For example, Orlick's (1980) terms *mature, reacting well to mistakes,* and *able to accept criticism* and Singer's (1988) term *coping ability* were, however, comparable with Morgan's mental health model (1980, 1985).

Singer (1988) urged recognition of the limitations of the peak-performance information, since it has been gathered mostly with informal interview techniques. Even so, the convincing nature of the information cannot be ignored.

Case Studies. Case studies can also be useful in the applied field of sport psychology. Bull (1989), for example, reported a case of an ultra-distance runner. Mace, Eastman, and Carroll (1986) studied a young female gymnast, whereas Mace and Carroll (1986) undertook a case study of

TABLE 11-4. Idiographic Methodologies Potentially Relevant for Sport
Psychological Research*

A. QUALITATIVE METHODS
- Content analysis
- Case study

B. QUANTITATIVE METHODS
1. Noncorrelational designs
- Individualized questionnaire (Shapiro, 1961, cited in Runyan, 1983)
- Self-Anchoring Scale (Kilpatrick & Cantril, 1960, cited in Runyan, 1983)
- Q-sort method (Stephenson, 1953, cited in Runyan, 1983)

2. Correlational Designs
- Selection of particular traits for certain individuals (Bem & Allen, 1974)
- Role Construct Repertory Test (Kelly, 1955)
- Idiothetic approach (Lamiell, 1981)
- Self-confrontation method (Hermans, 1976)
- Semantic differential (Osgood & Luria, 1954; Osgood, 1962)
- Self-experience approach (Rosenberg, 1977)
- Hierarchical analysis of goals (Pervin, 1983)
- Hierarchical analysis of goals and behaviors (De Boeck, 1988)
- Situation-related, individual personality analysis (Pervin, 1976)
- Sequential analysis of affective scripts (Tomkins, 1979, cited in De Boeck, 1988)
- Sequential analysis of affects and behaviors (Horowitz, 1979: configurational analysis, cited in De Boeck, 1988)

Data analysis of correlational designs can be done by means of:
- Correlations
- Factor analysis (Cattell, 1946, cited in Runyan, 1983)
- Multiple regression analysis
- Cluster analysis (Rosenberg & Jones, 1972)
- Multidimensional scaling (Rosenberg & Jones, 1972)
- Hierarchical class analysis (De Boeck & Rosenberg, 1985)
- Item tree analysis (Van Leeuwe, 1974, cited in De Boeck, 1988)
- Lag sequential analysis (Sackett, 1979, cited in De Boeck, 1988)
- Markov models (Wickens, 1982, cited in De Boeck, 1988)

3. Experimental Designs
- A-B, A-B-A, A-B-A-B, and related designs (Barlow & Hersen, 1984)
- Multiple baseline designs (Barlow & Hersen, 1984)

Data-analysis of experimental designs can be done by means of:
- No statistical tests, but graphics, tables, descriptive statistics, etc.
- Time series analysis (McCleary & Hay, 1980, cited in De Boeck, 1988)
- Randomization tests (Edgington, 1980, cited in De Boeck, 1988)

*Based on Runyan, 1983, De Boeck, 1988.

two squash players. These researchers reported the diagnosis, intervention, and evaluation of their work with the athletes. Smith (1988) has offered several suggestions to improve the validity, reliability, data-analysis, planning, and reporting of case studies, which should make them more valuable to sport psychologists.

Quantitative Intra-Individual Research in Sport Psychology

In addition to qualitative ways of conducting research, many methods focus on studying the individual more restrictively. In quantitative research programs, information is collected systematically, according to a plan set up in advance. In correlational methods, this information is analyzed by relating variables within the individual. Since general laws are sought, although within one individual, the research becomes, in fact, nomothetic in the strict sense of the word (*nomos* = law) (De Boeck, 1988). These intra-individual generalities can contribute to determine strong and weak spots, and also problematical events in a behavioral pattern of an athlete. Besides the personal value for the individual athlete or coach, these quantitative methods can also be very useful in developing new hypotheses about athletes' emotions and behaviors in general. If, for example, a certain pattern is discovered in several athletes, for example the sequence "anxious—uncontrollable actions—bad performance—depressed," a hypothesis can be formulated about these specific relationships and an interindividual research design can be suggested.

Some quantitative methods have already been applied in sport psychology although many others have not, despite their possible value for working with elite athletes. Next, some examples of quantitative idiographic research in sport psychology are presented.

TABLE 11-5. Comparing Descriptions Elite Athletes' Peak Experiences

Several researchers' descriptions are compared to Czikzentmihaly's flow characteristics.

Csikzentmihaly (1977)	Orlick (1980) in Williams (1986)	Garfield (1984) in Williams (1986)	Loehr (1984) in Singer (1988)	Ravizza (1984)	Williams (1986)	Mideffer (1987)	Singer (1988)
(1) Merging of action and awareness		(1) Highly energized	(1) Energized		(1) Positive preoccupation with sport		
(2) Centering of attention on a limited stimulus field		(2) Focused on the present	(2) Alert, mentally focused	(2) Centered present focus, narrow focus of attention		(2) Optimal, effortless concentration	
(3) Loss of ego		(3) "In the co-coon," extraordinary awareness		(3) Complete absorption, harmony, and oneness		(3) Selfless observation	
(4) In control of actions and environment	(4)	(4) In control	(4) In control, automatic effortless	(4) Perfection, noncritical, and effortless	(4) In control, but not forcing it	(4) In total control, no attempt to control	(4) Self-control
	Maintaining composure, not afraid to fail, staying cool	Mentally relaxed, physically relaxed	Mentally calm, physically relaxed, low anxiety	Loss of fear	Self-regulation of arousal		
	Confident	Confident, optimistic	Self-confident, optimistic		Higher self-confidence		Confidence
(5) Coherent, noncontradictory demands for action and clear feedback	(5) Determination				(5) Determination		(5) Mastery-orientation, goal-direction
(6) Autotelic	(6) Self-motivation, desire, attitude, heart		(6) Enjoyment, pride		(6) Commitment		(6) Positive attitudes, self-orientation, commitment

Individualized Questionnaires. The idea of individualizing questionnaires (Shapiro, 1961, cited in Runyan, 1983) is reminiscent of Rushall's approach in administering inventories. Rushall (1975a, 1978) used standardized questionnaires as a starting point, but the athletes had only to answer those items that were appropriate to them. In this way Rushall individualized the assessments in the direction suggested by Shapiro.

Selection of Traits. The selection of particular traits for certain individuals, proposed by Bem and Allen (1974), can be seen as an extension of the selection of traits for certain sport disciplines. This was suggested earlier in the chapter.

Situation Related, Individual Personality Diagnosis. Vanden Auweele (1988) investigated an athlete's personality by means of a situation-related individual diagnosis, using a hierarchical class analysis to analyze the data. This example will be described extensively later.

Experimental Designs. Examples of single-case experimental designs have appeared in sport psychology since the 1980s. Suggestions for the use of this kind of research were based on developments in academic psychology and made by Callahan and Ziegler (1980), Zaichkowsky (1980), and Bryan (1987). Some applications have been described, although mostly as illustrative examples in the discussion of other research and not in separate articles: Swimming (Ziegler, 1979, cited in Callahan & Ziegler, 1980), football (Komaki & Barnett, 1977, cited in Callahan & Ziegler, 1980), tennis (Ziegler, 1980, cited in Callahan & Ziegler, 1980), boxing (Heyman, 1987), and coaching behavior (Allison & Ayllon, 1980), among other disciplines and situations. Recently, however, Schlicht (1988) published a book in which he analyzed thoroughly two single cases of hurdlers. This may be indicative of an evolution toward greater acceptance of these new methodologies in sport psychology.

Shifting from Deterministic to Probabilistic Models

Another line of research within the common trend toward a better measurement of changes can be seen in the shift from deterministic to probabilistic models. Maddi's (1984) suggestion to move psychology research from actuality to possibility can be understood as an initiation in this direction. Probabilistic or stochastic models seem more flexible and therefore better for describing psychological processes than deterministic approaches.

Well-known statistical techniques, like analysis of variance or regression analysis, are based on a linear model. The effect of an experimental treatment is evaluated with regard to a supposed constancy (e.g., linear relation between predictor and criterion). This deterministic background differs considerably from the probabilistic or stochastic starting points. In this new research direction, one tries to predict a certain probability structure, instead of assuming the total predictability of an event (Verstraeten, 1987). Changes can be thus incorporated more easily in a model, where there is a certain possibility (probability) of variables having changing values (Schlicht, 1988).

Although small in scale, the application of a probabilistic diagnostic model attempted in a sport psychological context by Bar-Eli (1988a, 1988b, 1989) is an example of the growing interest in probabilistic rather than deterministic research. He investigated the probability of an individual psychological crisis during a basketball game. A crisis was defined as the moment at which the athlete's internal equilibrium is disturbed so much by psychological stress that he or she can no longer optimally control personal behaviors. Bar-Eli studied the effect of game standings on the vulnerability of a basketball player. Experts rated probabilistically the relevance of the game standing with regard to the development of an individual psychological crisis. The Bayesian likelihood ratio was applied to these estimates. For each single moment along the time axis of the competition, a specific position on the athlete's momentary inverse U-function can be plotted, reflecting vulnerability to psychological crisis at each moment (1989).

In some methods of data analysis, the element of probability is integrated in the results. In hierarchical class analysis, as used in the study of Ingrid's case, to be described shortly, a goodness-of-fit index is computed. This index indicates to what degree an item is a good example of a class of feelings or behaviors, and how well it fits into the pattern of the class. In predictions, it can reflect the probability of the appearance of a feeling or behavior, given a certain situation.

These examples show that in addition to traditional deterministic models, more flexible stochastic ways of behavior prediction are being employed in sport psychology in order to study fluctuations in athletes' behavior. Next, some original research conducted by the senior author of this chapter (Y. Vanden Auweele) is presented to exemplify one of those new techniques which can be used in an elite sports setting.

SITUATION-RELATED INTRA-INDIVIDUAL PERSONALITY DIAGNOSIS: THE CASE OF INGRID

Ingrid is a 20-year-old female athlete. Several times she has been a Belgian age-group champion middle-distance runner. In this study of a single elite athlete, most of the important new concepts and methodologies described in the last section are operationalized: the intra-individual approach, dynamic-interactionism, a stress on behavior, and the use of a probabilistic model within the goals of intervention and counseling. Idiographic data are structured according to a grid technique elaborated by Pervin (1976) and modified by De Boeck (1988). An appropriate statistical analysis (hierarchical class analysis) has been developed by De Boeck and Rosenberg (1988).

DATA COLLECTION

The first step is to compile this athlete's repertoire of emotional and behavioral reactions in competitive situations relevant to her. In an interview, Ingrid was asked to list a number of situations, incidents, and events that had occurred during her career. These situations had to be described as concretely as possible (see Table 11–6). For every situation, the athlete had to specify how she perceived it and which emotions she experienced at the time. These emotional reactions are called "emotional characteristics." Then, the athlete had to describe her actual overt behavior in each situation. These reactions are called "behavioral characteristics."

In the second step, two grids are constructed on the basis of the information collected during the interview. The upper grid in Table 11–6 represents the relevant situations versus the emotional characteristics, while the lower grid represents the same situations versus the behavioral characteristics.

In the third step, the athlete had to rate each of the situations, saying whether or not the emotional and behavioral characteristics listed were expressed in each situation. Ingrid's scores appear in Table 11–6.

DATA ANALYSES BY MEANS OF HIERARCHICAL CLASS ANALYSES

Hierarchical class analysis (De Boeck & Rosenberg, 1988) was selected as the most appropriate statistical procedure. Other methods of analysis, such as factor or cluster analysis and multiple regression analysis (cf. Vanden Auweele, 1988), could be used. Hierarchical class analysis was chosen because it simultaneously yields a hierarchical structure of situations and the emotional characteristics as well as a hierarchical structure of situations and behavioral characteristics. These structures are exemplified by the results of the hierarchical class analysis completed on data about Ingrid and shown in Figures 11–7 and 11–8.

TABLE 11–6. Grid Used to Represent Ingrid's Rating of the Applicability of Emotions and Behaviors to Each Situation

	1. before first competition	2. improvement of personal record	3. injured during training	4. fall during the B.C.	5. preparation for B.C.	6. success in the B.C.	7. problems with preparation for E.C. selection	8. scored minimum E.C.	9. no selection E.C.	10. poor performances	11. fight with coach	12. fight with club board	13. defeat of competitor	14. selection for important competition
Emotions														
1. pleased	0*	1	0	0	0	1	0	1	0	0	0	0	1	1
2. nervous	1*	0	0	0	1	0	1	1	0	0	0	0	0	0
3. hopeful	1	1	0	0	1	1	0	1	0	0	0	0	1	1
4. discouraged	0	0	1	1	0	0	0	0	1	1	1	1	0	0
5. angry	0	0	0	1	0	0	0	0	1	0	1	1	0	0
6. curious	1	0	0	0	1	0	0	1	0	0	0	0	0	1
7. relieved	0	1	0	0	0	1	0	1	0	0	0	0	1	1
8. uncertain	1	0	1	1	1	0	1	1	1	1	1	1	0	0
9. stimulated	1	1	0	0	1	1	0	1	0	1	0	0	1	1
10. sad	0	0	1	1	0	0	0	0	1	1	1	1	0	0
Behaviors														
1. contacted my coach	1	1	0	0	1	1	1	0	0	0	0	0	1	0
2. refused to do something against my will	0	0	0	0	0	0	0	0	0	0	1	1	0	0
3. did my best	1	1	1	0	1	1	1	0	1	1	0	0	1	1
4. contacted friends	1	0	0	1	1	0	0	0	0	0	0	0	0	0
5. persevered	0	0	1	0	0	0	1	0	1	1	0	0	0	0
6. stopped training	0	0	0	0	0	0	0	0	0	0	1	1	0	0
7. no longer participated in competitions	0	0	0	0	0	0	0	0	0	0	1	1	0	0
8. did not give up	0	0	1	0	0	0	1	0	1	1	0	0	0	0
9. prepared with others	1	1	1	0	1	0	1	0	1	1	0	0	1	1
10. trained harder	0	1	0	0	1	1	1	0	0	0	0	0	1	1
11. trained intensively	0	1	1	0	1	1	1	1	1	1	0	0	1	1

*0 = No; 1 = Yes.

These figures are the results of one part of the analysis. Such a display reveals classes of situations characterized by a similar pattern of reactions as well as for classes of emotional and behavioral characteristics with a similar pattern of situations. The search for these relationships makes up the basis of this form of analysis. The degree of correspondence of characteristics to a similar pattern is called equivalence within the class. Equivalence scores (range .58–1.00) appear as decimal numbers to the right of each emotion and behavior in Figures 11–7 and 11–8. These equivalence scores could also be considered goodness-of-fit scores. The element with the highest equivalence index is the best prototype of its class (see earlier discussion of "goodness-of-fit index").

Equivalence within a class, and the hierarchy between classes are the bases of hierarchical class analysis. If a class of situations is hierarchically in a higher position than another class (e.g., in Figure 11–7, class D is in a higher position than class A), it means that all the characteristics pertaining to the lower class (e.g., A) also pertain to the higher class (e.g., D). But this higher class has even more characteristics, because it is also connected hierarchically to other lower classes (e.g., B and C). The relationships between the classes of emotional and behavioral characteristics can thus be interpreted as follows: if the emotions or behaviors of a lower class (e.g., 1) are present in a certain class of situations (e.g., A), then the emotions or behaviors of the hierarchically higher class are also present (e.g., 4).

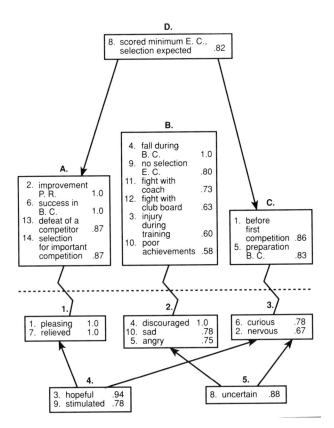

FIGURE 11–7. Hierarchical class analysis of situations and emotions with equivalence-indexes. Hierarchical relationships indicated by arrows, associative connections by zigzag lines. This chart is derived from Ingrid's scores in Table 11–7.

This hierarchy is always indicated with an arrow from the higher to the lower class.

The associative connection between the bottom classes of situations (i.e., the hierarchically lowest classes, e.g., A, B, C) and the bottom classes of emotional or behavioral characteristics (1, 2, 3) is represented with a zigzagged line. Both of these aspects, classification and hierarchy, represent important features of the structural organization of an athlete's personality. This approach is consistent with and covers all the elements of Pervin's (1984) definition of personality (cf. *Introduction to New Directions in Personology*).

RESULTS

Figure 11–7 is a representation of the results of the hierarchical class analysis for the data in the upper half of Table 11–6 (emotional matrix). In the upper half of Figure 11–7, the four classes of situations are rendered with their mutual relations. Bottom class A comprises a number of success or achievement situations of which the best prototype is: "A considerable improvement of my personal record." The emotional pattern that corresponds to this class of situa-

tions includes all classes of emotional reactions connected with it downwards, i.e., class 1 ("pleased; relieved,") and class 4 ("hopeful; stimulated"). One can also observe the relationship between bottom classes 2 and 3 and the associated emotions.

There is one hierarchically higher class of situations, class D, which includes "scored the minimum for the European Championship (E.C.); selection expected." D combines the emotional patterns of bottom classes A and C and is consequently associated with the emotions "pleased; relieved" (class 1), "curious; nervous" (class 3), "hopeful; stimulated" (class 4), and "uncertain" (class 5).

The lower half of Figure 11–7 represents the structure of the set of emotional characteristics. This structure consists of three basic classes (1, 2, and 3) and two hierarchically higher classes (4 and 5). Class 4 is associated with all situations related to classes 1 and 3. When the athlete feels pleasant and relieved as well as curious and nervous, she is also hopeful and stimulated. Class 5 is associated with the classes of situations associated with the classes 2 and 3 in the same manner.

Tension and stress are felt in the precompetitive situations used in classes C and D: "before my first official competition," "preparation for the B.C.," "scored the minimum for the E.C., selection expected." Consequently, especially in these emotionally straining situations, it is important to observe the athlete's overt behavioral reactions.

The results of the hierarchical class analysis for the data in Table 11–6 (behavioral matrix) are rendered in Figure 11–8. In the upper half, five classes of situations are rendered in their mutual structure. Basic class A in the behavioral analysis includes three success situations as well as the situation "preparation for the B.C." The behavioral pattern associated with class A contains exclusively functional behavioral reactions: "trained harder; contacted my coach" (class 1), "trained intensively" (class 5), and "did my best; preparation with others" (class 6). In all success situations with the emotional pattern "pleased, hopeful," these behavioral reactions occur.

We notice that in a number of situations, although they evoke very negative emotions (discouraged, sad, angry, uncertain), the athlete does show some very functional behavioral reactions. In these situations the athlete is able to cope positively with this stress.

There is one hierarchically higher class of situations, class E, combining the behavioral patterns of classes A and B. The only element in class E is "problems with the preparation for the E.C. selection," with the corresponding behavioral pattern "trained harder; contacted my coach" (class 1), "persevered; did not give up" (class 2), "trained intensively" (class 5), and "did my best; preparation with others" (class 6).

DISCUSSION AND CONCLUSIONS

When the athlete is involved in interpersonal conflicts, very negative emotional reactions occur, followed by a

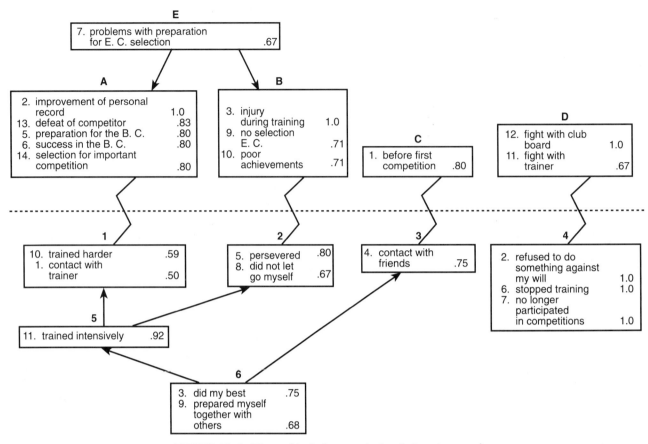

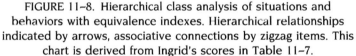

FIGURE 11-8. Hierarchical class analysis of situations and
behaviors with equivalence indexes. Hierarchical relationships
indicated by arrows, associative connections by zigzag items. This
chart is derived from Ingrid's scores in Table 11-7.

dysfunctional behavioral reaction. In order to prepare her
for successful career development, the coach's first priority
is to avoid and/or tackle relational problems. The athlete's
behavior is functional in all other situations. Yet it deserves
to be mentioned at this point that a number of other situations are also experienced as very stressful: injuries, not
being selected, and poor performances (see Fig. 11-8,
bottom class B). Although the athlete is discouraged and
uncertain in these situations (see Fig. 11-8, classes 2, 5, and
6), she does manage to cope with them in a positive way. It
should be clear how this type of information lends itself to
generating advice for the athlete.

When these data and related suggestions were presented
to the athlete and her coach, their reactions were positive.
The athlete felt her uniqueness was well understood. She
endorsed the conclusions about her way of reacting and
said she had gained some self-knowledge. The coach was
surprised because many things were revealed which he had
not previously understood, both with reference to the competition situations that had impressed the athlete and with
reference to her way of coping with them.

By combining different relevant aspects of Ingrid's functioning as an athlete (i.e., situations, emotions, behaviors),

underlying constancies and changes in idiosyncratic information could be obtained quickly and objectively. The situations mentioned were all important to her so that no time
was wasted answering questions about irrelevant events.
What also has been avoided was drawing hypothetical conclusions from situations and responses of limited relevance
to the elite athlete.

Furthermore, detailed and subtle information was obtained that could not have been gotten through questionnaires. Most important, this information has led to an
approach to advising this athlete which would not have
been possible following an evaluation with, for example, an
anxiety questionnaire. In fact, Ingrid's SCAT anxiety score
was very high. This probably would have indicated the need
for an anxiety-reducing strategy. On the contrary, intra-
individual data show that Ingrid can cope with her anxiety
most of the time. But she does not have adequate coping behavior in some very specific interpersonal situations. Relaxation may be, therefore, less necessary than some communication skill training or some other intervention related to
her interpersonal relationships.

Most of the important new directions described earlier
have been concretized in this case study. The interactional

approach has been illustrated. The cognitive and affective-emotional processing of the situation is stressed. The intra-individual coherence between the different behavioral components (cognitions, emotions, and overt behavior) has been operationalized, and the interaction between the individual and her situation as well as the changes and the constancies in this interaction have been also attended to. The example clearly emphasizes the intra-individual approach, as only one athlete has been investigated, without comparisons to others. The hierarchical class model provides a fit index, which can be used as a probabilistic value in predictions toward future feelings and behaviors. The behavioral assessment approach is incorporated as the athlete is asked for her overt behavioral reactions in relevant situations. Finally, the analysis yielded such concrete opportunities for specific guidance of that elite performer that a further exploration of these and comparable techniques is planned.

CONCLUSIONS

The major reason for studying the personality of top-level athletes has been the possibility of predicting future success in sport more accurately when personality characteristics are taken into account. According to this supposition, successful performers display a specific personality profile which differs from that of less successful performers. The successful personality profile includes sociability, emotional stability, ambition, dominance, responsibility, leadership, self-confidence, persistence, and a low level of trait anxiety.

On the other hand, the relevance of personality information in predicting future success in sport has been minimized by some skeptical sport psychologists. According to them, no incontestable scientific evidence has been produced to support the existence of a substantial relation between any personality profile or characteristic and success in sport. (See Chapter 12 for other perspectives.)

In fact, the majority of research published on this topic suffers serious deficiencies in important procedural aspects including research design, sampling and testing procedures, analyses, and interpretation. Moreover, the question remains whether scientifically sound personality research could possibly predict more than a trivial amount of the relevant variance in competition. In any case, even based on a solid research methodology, the trait approach of personality has failed to provide the conclusions that were expected in other areas of psychology. Personality psychologists have not had much success in predicting behavior in complex situations. Utilizing questionnaire data that are considered as indicators of some underlying personality traits, the maximal validity coefficients obtained were about .30. That accounts for only 10% of the relevant behavioral variance.

These serious doubts concerning the predictive power of psychological variables, based on both empirical evidence and conceptual considerations, do not have to lead to the pessimistic conclusion that personality diagnosis is useless in sports. On the contrary, they helped precipitate a critical reexamination of the field out of which emerged a more cautious and precise approach to the prediction of behavior and performance. In summary, these include the specification of the conditions under which the trait concept remains useful (when people are predictable; when traits are useful; when situations are low in constraints or pressures); a more accurate definition of the variants of interactionism (e.g., organismic, dynamic, statistical interaction); the use of new and sophisticated techniques as meta-analysis and path-analysis; and finally, the combination of psychological, physiological, anthropometric, and visuo-motor skill data in large multidimensional designs in an attempt to explain more behavioral variance.

Although caution is a scientifically sound approach, there is no need to be overly critical when attempting to generate some conclusions in this area. There is evidence that, when compared to the average athlete, the elite athlete displays a specific pattern of mood states and differs on self-confidence and some specific anxiety, motivation, and cognitive variables.

More important and promising than the attempts to enhance the predictive power of psychological variables or to increase the proportion of explained behavioral variance is the shift toward the study of relevant sport psychological phenomena and the shift toward the study of the concrete questions elite performers and coaches ask. The new questions are: What are the ideal psychological processes associated with peak performance in sport? How can athletes change less-than-adequate behavior? How can they reach the ideal convergence of physical, technical, and mental capacities at a particular moment in time?

The study of personality has regained considerable vitality due to this shift in goals from prediction to mental training and counseling, and in the starting point of research (e.g., from the validation of personality constructs in a sports setting to the testing of sport-psychological models in their multivariate complexity). With a greater focus on these new goals, more need has been expressed for a methodology and an instrumentation which is sensitive enough to register fluctuations and changes in emotions, behaviors, and performance. New methodologies have emerged that enable researchers to capture these changes. Some of them have already been used in sport-psychological contexts. Such techniques include idiographic techniques, stochastic models, and behavioral assessment and modification procedures.

Keeping in mind Landers's (1983) plea for a healthy scientific field and a sound balance between theoretical and applied research, we can conclude that, far from being a moribund field, as some critics still maintain, personality research has emerged as a phoenix from its crisis period to become one of the most exciting areas in sport psychology again.

Personality research in sport psychology is very much alive.

References

Aguerri, P. (1986). The developments of sports psychology as seen through the analysis of the first fifteen years of the "journal." *International Journal of Sport Psychology, 17,* 87–99.

Alderman, R. B. (1974). *Psychological behavior in sport.* Philadelphia: Saunders.

Allison, M. G., & Ayllon, T. (1980). Behavioral coaching in the development of skills in football, gymnastics, and tennis. *Journal of Applied Behavior Analysis, 13,* 297–314.

Allport, G. W. (1937). *Personality: A psychological interpretation.* New York: Holt, Rinehart & Winston.

Bar-Eli, M., & Tenenbaum, G. (1988a). Time phases and the individual psychological crisis in sports competition: Theory and research findings. *Journal of Sports Sciences, 6,* 141–149.

Bar-Eli, M., & Tenenbaum, G. (1988b). The interaction of individual psychological crisis and time phases in basketball. *Perceptual and Motor Skills, 66,* 523–530.

Bar-Eli, M., & Tenenbaum, G. (1989). Game standings and psychological crisis in sport: Theory and research. *Canadian Journal of Sports Science, 4,* 31–37.

Barlow, D. H., & Hersen, M. (1984). *Single case experimental designs: Strategies for studying behavior change.* New York: Pergamon Press.

Bem, D. J., & Allen, A. (1974). On predicting some of the people some of the time: The search for cross-situational consistencies on behavior. *Psychological Review, 81,* 506–520.

Browne, M. A., & Mahoney, M. J. (1984). Sport psychology. *Annual Review of Psychology, 35,* 605–625.

Bryan, A. J. (1987). Single-subject designs for evaluation of sport psychological interventions. *The Sport Psychologist, 1,* 283–292.

Bull, S. J. (1989). The role of the sport psychology consultant: A case study of ultra-distance running. *The Sport Psychologist, 3,* 254–264.

Bushan, S., & Agarwal, V. (1978). Personality characteristics of high and low achieving Indian sports persons. *International Journal of Sport Psychology, 9,* 191–198.

Butt, D. S. (1987). *Psychology of sport: The behavior, motivation, personality, and performance of athletes.* New York: Van Nostrand Reinhold.

Callahan, E. J., & Ziegler, S. G. (1980). The application of within-subject design methodology to sports psychology. *Journal of Sport Behavior, 3,* 174–183.

Carron, A. V. (1980). *Social psychology of sport and physical activity.* London: Mouvement Publications.

Cattell, R. B., & Warburton, F. W. (1961). A cross-cultural comparison of patterns of extraversion and anxiety. *The British Journal of Psychology, 52,* 3–15.

Claeys, W. (1980). Het modern interactionisme in de persoonlijkheids-psychologie (Modern interactionism in personality psychology). In J. R. Nuttin (Ed.), *Gedrag, dynamische relatie en betekeniswereld* (pp. 221–237). Leuven: Universitaire Pers.

Coleman, J. A. (1980). Personality and stress in the shooting sports. *Journal of Psychosomatic Research, 24,* 287–296.

Cook, T. D., & Leviton, L. C. (1980). Reviewing the literature: A comparison of traditional methods with meta-analysis. *Journal of Personality, 48,* 449–472.

Cooper, L. (1969). Athletics, activity and personality: Review of the literature. *The Research Quarterly, 40,* 17–22.

Csikszentmihaly, M. (1977). *Beyond boredom and anxiety: The experience of play in work and games.* San Francisco: Jossey-Bass.

Daus, A. T., Wilson, J., & Freeman, W. M. (1986). Psychological testing as an auxiliary means of selecting successful college and professional football players. *Journal of Sport Medicine and Physical Fitness, 26,* 274–278.

De Boeck, P. (1988) *Psychologie van het individu [Psychology of the individual].* Leuven: Universitaire Pers.

De Boeck, P., & Rosenberg, S. (1988). Hierarchical classes: Model and data analysis. *Psychometrika, 53,* 361–381.

DeMers, G. E. (1983). Emotional states of high-caliber divers. *Swimming Technique, 20,* 33–35.

Deshaies, P., Pargman, D., & Thiffault, C. (1979). A psychobiological profile of individual performance in junior hockey players. In G. C. Roberts & K. M. Newell (Eds.), *Psychology of motor behavior and sport—1978* (pp. 36–50). Champaign, IL: Human Kinetics.

Donahue, J. A., Gillis, J. H., & King, K. (1980). Behavior modification in sport and physical education: A review. *Journal of Sport Psychology, 2,* 311–328.

Durtschi, S. H., & Weiss, M. R. (1986) Psychological characteristics of elite and non-elite marathon runners. In D. K. Landers (Ed.), *Sport and elite performers* (pp. 73–80). Champaign, IL: Human Kinetics.

Dwyer, J. J., & Carron, A. V. (1986). Personality status of wrestlers of varying abilities as measured by a sport specific version of a personality inventory. *Canadian Journal of Applied Sport Sciences, 11,* 19–30.

Endler, N. S., & Hunt, J. M. (1969). Generalizability of contributions from sources of variance in the S-R Inventories of Anxiousness. *Journal of Personality, 37,* 1–24.

Eysenck, H. J., & Eysenck, S. B. G. (1964). *Manual of the Eysenck Personality Inventory.* London: University of London Press.

Eysenck, H. J., & Eysenck, S. B. G. (1975). *Manual of the Eysenck Personality Questionnaire.* Kent: Hodder and Stoughton.

Eysenck, H. J., Nias, D. K. B., & Cox, D. N. (1982). Sport and personality. *Advances in Behavior Research and Therapy, 1,* 1–56.

Fenigstein, A., Scheier, M. F., & Buss, A. H. (1975). Public and private self-consciousness: Assessment and theory. *Journal of Consulting and Clinical Psychology, 43,* 522–527.

Fisher, A. C. (1977a). Sport personality assessment: Fact, fiction, and methodological re-examination. In R. E. Stadulis & C. O. Dotson (Eds.), *Research and practice in physical education* (pp. 188–204). Champaign, IL: Human Kinetics.

Fisher, A. C. (1977b). Sport personality assessment: Facts, fallacies and perspectives. *Motor Skills: Theory into Practice, 1,* 87–97.

Fisher, A. C. (1979). Multidimensional scaling of sport personality data: An individual differences approach, *Journal of Sport Psychology, 1,* 76–86.

Fisher, A. C. (1984). New directions in sport personality research. In J. M. Silva & R. S. Weinberg (Eds.), *Psychological foundations of sport* (pp. 70–80). Champaign, IL: Human Kinetics.

Franke, R. (1985). Psychological counselling and personality testing of top level sportsmen. *International Journal of Sport Psychology, 16,* 20–27.

Frazier, S. E. (1987). Introversion-extraversion measures in elite and nonelite distance runners. *Perceptual and Motor Skills, 64,* 867–872.

Fuchs, C. Z., & Zaichkowsky, L. D. (1983). Psychological characteristics of male and female bodybuilders: The iceberg profile. *Journal of Sport Behavior, 6,* 136–146.

Glass, G. V. (1977). Integrating findings: The meta-analysis of research. *Review of Research in Education, 5,* 351–379.

Gutmann, M. C., Knapp, D. K., Foster, C., Pollock, M. L., & Rogowski, B. L. (1984). Age, experience and gender as predictors of psychological response to training in Olympic speed skaters. In D. M. Landers (Ed.), *Sport and elite performers* (pp. 97–102). Champaign, IL: Human Kinetics.

Gutmann, M. C., Pollock, M. L., Foster, C., & Schmidt, D. (1984). Training stress in Olympic speed skaters: A psychological perspective. *The Physician and Sports Medicine, 12*, 12, 45–47.

Hagberg, J. M., Mullin, J. P., Bahrke, M., & Limburg, J. (1979). Physiological profiles and selected psychological characteristics of national class American cyclists. *Journal of Sports Medicine, 19*, 341–346.

Halliwell, W. L., & Gauvin, L. (1982). Integrating and interpreting research findings: A challenge to sport psychologists. In J. T. Partington, T. Orlick, & J. H. Salmela (Eds.), *Sport in perspective* (pp. 94–97). Ottawa: Coaches' Association of Canada.

Hardman, K. (1973). A dual approach to the study of personality and performance in sport. In H. T. A. Whiting, K. Hardman, L. B. Hendry, & M. G. Jones, *Personality and physical education in Sport* (pp. 77–122). London: Kimpton.

Hartmann, D. P., Roper, B. L., & Bradford, D. C. (1979). Some relationships between behavioral and traditional assessment. *Journal of Behavioral Assessment, 1*, 3–21.

Hermans, H. J. M. (1976). *Value areas and their development: Theory and method of self-confrontation.* Amsterdam: Swets & Zeitlinger.

Heyman, S. R. (1982). Comparisons of successful and unsuccessful competitors: A reconsideration of methodological questions and data. *Journal of Sport Psychology, 4*, 295–300.

Heyman, S. R. (1987). Research interventions in sport psychology: Issues encountered in working with an amateur boxer. *The Sport Psychologist, 1*, 208–223.

Highlen, P. S., & Bennett, B. B. (1979). Psychological characteristics of successful and nonsuccessful elite wrestlers: An exploratory study. *Journal of Sport Psychology, 1*, 123–137.

Highlen, P. S., & Bennett, B. B. (1983). Elite divers and wrestlers: A comparison between open- and closed-skill athletes. *Journal of Sport Psychology, 5*, 390–409.

Horsfall, J. S., Fisher, A. C., & Morris, H. H. (1975). Sport personality assessment: a methodological re-examination. In D. M. Landers (Ed.), *Psychology of sport and motor behavior* (pp. 61–69). College of HPER Pennsylvania.

Institute for Personality and Ability Testing. (1986). *Administrators manual for the 16 personality factor questionnaire.* Champaign, IL: Institute for Personality and Ability Testing.

Joesting, J. (1981). Comparison of personalities of those who sail with those who run. *Perceptual and Motor Skills, 52*, 514.

Johnson, P. A. (1972). A comparison of personality traits of superior skilled women athletes in basketball, bowling, field hockey, and golf. *The Research Quarterly, 43*, 409–415.

Kane, J. E. (1964). Personality and physical ability. In K. Kato (Ed.), *Proceedings of international congress of sport sciences* (pp. 201–208). Tokyo: The Japanese Union of Sport Sciences.

Kane, J. E. (1978). Persons, situations and performance. In D. J. Glencross (Ed.), *Psychology and sport* (pp. 120–143). Sydney: McGraw-Hill.

Kane, J. E. (1981). Biosocial aspects of sport: Sport and personality. *Journal of Biosocial Sciences,* Suppl. 7, 55–68.

Kelly, G. A. (1955). *The psychology of personal constructs 1: A theory of personality.* New York: Norton.

Kenrick, D. T., & Dantschick, A. (1983). Interactionism, idiographics and the social psychological invasion of personality. *Journal of Personality, 51*, 286–307.

Kenrick, D. T., & Stringfield, D. O. (1980). Personality traits and the eye of the beholder: Crossing some traditional philosophical boundaries in the search for consistency in all of the people. *Psychological Review, 1*, 88–104.

Killpatrick, F. P., & Cantrill, H. (1960). Self-anchoring scale: A measure of the individual's unique reality world. *Journal of Individual Psychology, 16*, 158–170.

Kumar, A., & Varma, K. B. (1989). Personality correlates of high and low achieving Indian female athletes. In C. K. Giam, K. K. Chook, & K. C. Teh (Eds.), *Sport Psychology and Human Performance (World Congress in Sport Psychology 7)* (pp. 177–179). Singapore: Singapore Sports Council.

Lamiell, J. T. (1981). Toward an idiothetic psychology of personality. *The American Psychologist, 36*, 276–289.

Landers, D. M. (1983). Whatever happened to theory testing in sport psychology? *Journal of Sport Psychology, 5*, 135–151.

Landers, D. M., Boutcher, S. H., & Wang, M. Q. (1986). A psychobiological study of archery performance. *Research Quarterly for Exercise and Sport, 57*, 236–244.

LeUnes, A., & Hayward, S. A. (1988). Annotated bibliography on the Profile of Mood States in sport, 1975–1988. *Journal of Sport Behavior, 11*(3), 213–239.

Mace, R., & Carroll, D. (1986). Stress inoculation training to control anxiety in sport: Two case studies in squash. *British Journal of Sports Medicine, 20*, 115–117.

Mace, R., Eastman, C., & Carroll, D. (1986). Stress inoculation training: A case study in gymnastics. *British Journal of Sports Medicine, 20*, 139–141.

Maddi, S. R. (1984). Personology for the 1980's. In R. A. Zucker, J. Aronoff, & A. I. Rabin (Eds.), *Personality and the prediction of behaviour* (pp. 7–41). Orlando, FL: Academic Press.

Magni, G., Rupolo, R., Simini, G., De Leo, D., & Rampazzo, M. (1985). Aspects of the psychology and personality of high altitude mountain climbers. *International Journal of Sport Psychology, 16*, 12–19.

Mahoney, M. J., & Avener, M. (1977). Psychology of the elite athlete: An exploratory study. *Cognitive Therapy and Research, 1*, 135–141.

Mahoney, M. J., Gabriel, T. J., & Perkins, T. S. (1987). Psychological skills and exceptional athletic performance. *The Sport Psychologist, 1*, 181–199.

Markus, H. (1977). Self-schemata and processing information about the self. *Journal of Personality and Social Psychology, 35*, 63–78.

Martens, R. (1975). The paradigmatic crisis in American sport personology. *Sportwissenschaft, 5*, 9–24.

Martens, R. (1981). Sport personology. In G. R. F. Lüschen & G. H. Sage (Eds.), *Handbook of social science of sport* (pp. 492–508). Champaign, IL: Stipes.

Martens, R. (1982). *Sport Competition Anxiety Test.* Champaign, IL: Human Kinetics.

Martens, R. (1987). Science, knowledge, and sport psychology. *The Sport Psychologist, 1*, 29–55.

Martin, G., & Hrycaiko, D. (1983). Effective behavioral coaching: What's it all about? *Journal of Sport Psychology, 5*, 8–20.

Mastro, J. V., Sherrill, C., Gench, B., & French, R. (1987). Psychological characteristics of elite visually impaired athletes: The iceberg profile. *Journal of Sport Behavior, 10*, 39–46.

McGill, J. C., Hall, J. R., Ratliff, W. R., & Moss, R. F. (1986). Personality characteristics of professional rodeo cowboys. *Journal of Sport Behavior, 9*, 143–151.

McGowan, J., & Gormly, J. (1976). Validation of personality traits: A multicriteria approach. *Journal of Personality and Social Psychology, 34,* 791–795.

McNair, D. M., Lorr, M., & Droppleman, L. F. (1971). *Profile of Mood States Manual.* San Diego, CA: Educational and Industrial Testing Services.

Mischel, W. (1968). *Personality and assessment.* New York: Wiley.

Miller, B. P. & Miller, A. J. (1985). Psychological correlates of success in elite sportswomen. *International Journal of Sport Psychology, 16,* 289–295.

Monson, T. C., Hesley, J. W., & Chernick, L. (1982). Specifying when personality traits can and cannot predict behavior: An alternative to abandoning the attempt to predict single-act criteria. *Journal of Personality and Social Psychology, 43,* 385–399.

Morgan, W. P. (1968). Personality characteristics of wrestlers participating in the world championships. *Journal of Sports Medicine and Physical Fitness, 8,* 212–216.

Morgan, W. P. (1973). Efficacy of psychobiologic inquiry in the exercise and sport sciences. *Quest, 20,* 39–47.

Morgan, W. P. (1974). Selected psychological considerations in sport. *The Research Quarterly, 45,* 374–390.

Morgan, W. P. (1978). Sport personology: The credulous-skeptical argument in perspective. In W. F. Straub (Ed.), *Sport psychology: An analysis of athlete behavior* (pp. 330–339). Ithaca, NY: Mouvement Publications.

Morgan, W. P. (1980). The trait psychology controversy. *Research Quarterly for Exercise and Sport, 51,* 50–76.

Morgan, W. P. (1985). Selected psychological factors limiting performance: a mental health model. In D. H. Clarke & H. M. Eckert (Eds.), *Limits of human performance* (pp. 70–80). Champaign, IL: Human Kinetics.

Morgan, W. P., & Johnson, R. W. (1978). Personality characteristics of successful and unsuccessful oarsmen. *International Journal of Sport Psychology, 9,* 119–133.

Morgan, W. P., O'Connor, P. J., Ellickson, A. E., & Bradley, P. W. (1988). Personality structure, mood states, and performance in elite male distance runners. *International Journal of Sport Psychology, 19,* 247–263.

Morgan, W. P., O'Connor, P. J., Sparling, P. B., & Pate, R. R. (1987). Psychological characterization of the elite female distance runner. *International Journal of Sports Medicine, 8* (Suppl.), 124–131.

Nagle, F. J., Morgan, W. P., Hellickson, R. O., Serfass, R. C., & Alexander, J. F. (1975). Spotting success traits in Olympic contenders. *The Physician and Sports Medicine, 3,* 31–34.

Nideffer, R. M. (1987). Psychological preparation of the highly competitive athlete, *The Physician and Sports Medicine, 18,* 85–92.

Nieman, D. C., & George, D. M. (1987). Personality traits that correlate with success in distance running. *Journal of Sports Medicine and Physical Fitness, 27,* 345–356.

Ogilvie, B. (1976). Psychological consistencies within the personality of high-level competitors. In A. C. Fisher (Ed.), *Psychology of sport: Issues and insights* (pp. 335–358). Palo Alto, CA: Mayfield.

Osgood, C. E. (1962). Studies on the generality of affective meaning systems. *The American Psychologist, 17,* 10–28.

Osgood, C. E., Luria, Z. (1954). A blind analysis of a case of multiple personality using the semantic differential. *Journal of Abnormal and Social Psychology, 49,* 579–591.

Pervin, L. A. (1976). A free-response description approach to the analysis of person-situation interaction. *Journal of Personality and Social Psychology, 43,* 465–474.

Pervin, L. A. (1983). The stasis and flow of behavior: Toward a the-

ory of goals. In M. M. Page (Ed.), *Nebraska symposium on motivation—1982* (pp. 1–53). Lincoln, NE: University of Nebraska Press.

Pervin, L. A. (1984). *Personality: Theory and research,* New York: Wiley.

Pervin, L. A. (1985). Personality: Current controversies, issues, and directions. *Annual Review of Psychology, 36,* 83–114.

Peterson, S. L., Weber, J. C., & Trousdale W. W. (1967). Personality traits of women in team sports vs. women in individual sports. *The Research Quarterly, 38,* 686–690.

Power, S. (1986). Psychological assessment procedures of a track and field national event squad training weekend. In J. Watkins, T. Reilly, & L. Burwitz (Eds.), *Sports science* (pp. 181–187). New York: E. & F. N. Spon.

Price, R. H., & Bouffard, D. L. (1974). Behavioral appropriateness and situational constraint as dimensions of social behavior. *Journal of Personality and Social Psychology, 30,* 579–586.

Ravizza, K. (1984). Qualities of the peak experience in sport. In J. M. Silva & R. S. Weinberg (Eds.), *Psychological foundations of sport* (pp. 452–461). Champaign, IL: Human Kinetics.

Reeds, G. K. (1985). The relationship of personality and anxiety to performance among elite male and female gymnasts. *Canadian Association Health and Physical Education Record Journal, 51,* 5–7.

Robinson, D. W. (1985). Stress seeking: Selected behavioral characteristics of elite rock climbers. *Journal of Sport Psychology, 7,* 400–404.

Rosenberg, S. (1977). New approaches to the analysis of personal constructs in person perception. In J. K. Cole (Ed.), *Nebraska symposium on motivation—1976* (pp. 179–242). Lincoln, NE: University of Nebraska Press.

Rosenberg, S., & Jones, R. (1972). A method for investigating and representing a person's implicit theory of personality: Theodore Dreiser's view of people. *Journal of Personality and Social Psychology, 22,* 372–386.

Runyan, W. M. (1983). Idiographic goals and methods in the study of lives. *Journal of Personality, 51,* 413–437.

Rushall, B. S. (1975a). Alternative dependent variables for the study of behavior in sport. In D. M. Landers, D. V. Harris, & R. W. Christina (Eds.), *Psychology of sport and motor behavior 2* (pp. 49–55). State College, PA: Pennsylvania State University.

Rushall, B. S. (1975b). Psychodynamics and personality in sport: Status and values. In H. T. A. Whiting (Ed.), *Readings in sport psychology 2* (pp. 72–84). London: Lepus.

Rushall, B. S. (1975c). Applied behavior analysis for sports and physical education. *International Journal of Sport Psychology, 6,* 75–88.

Rushall, B. S. (1978). Environment specific behavior inventories: Developmental procedures. *International Journal of Sport Psychology, 9,* 97–110.

Rushall, B. S. (1987). *Behavior characteristics of champions.* Paper presented at the Medicine and Sport Congress, Barcelona, Spain.

Rushall, B. S. (1989). Sport psychology: The key to sporting excellence. *International Journal of Sport Psychology, 20,* 165–190.

Rushall, B. S. & Smith, K. C. (1979). The modification of the quality and quantity of behavior categories in a swimming coach. *Journal of Sport Psychology, 1,* 138–150.

Schlicht, W. (1988). Einzelfallanalysen im Hochleistungssport: zum Verlauf und zur Wirkung selbstbezogener Aufmerksamkeit im 400-Meter-Hürdenlauf (Single-case analysis in elite sport: About the process of paying attention to oneself in a 400m hurdles) (Schriftenreihe des Bundesinstituts für Sportwissen-schaft; Band 64). Schorndorf: Verlag Karl Hofmann.

Sherman, S. J. & Fazio, R. H. (1983). Parallels between attitudes and traits as predictors of behavior. *Journal of Personality, 51,* 308–339.

Silva, J. M. (1984). Personality and sport performance: Controversy and challenge. In J. M. Silva & R. S. Weinberg (Eds.), *Psychological foundations of sport* (pp. 59–69). Champaign, IL: Human Kinetics.

Silva, J. M., Shultz, B. B., Haslam, R. W., & Murray, D. (1981). A psychophysiological assessment of elite wrestlers. *Research Quarterly for Exercise and Sport, 52,* 348–358.

Silva, J. M., Shultz, B. B., Haslam, R. W., Martin, T. P., & Murray, D. F. (1985). Discriminating characteristics of contestants at the United States Olympic wrestling trials. *International Journal of Sports Psychology, 16,* 79–102.

Singer, R. N. (1988). Psychological testing: What value to coaches and athletes? *International Journal of Sport Psychology, 19,* 87–106.

Smith, R. E. (1988). The logic and design of case study research. *The Sport Psychologist, 2,* 1–12.

Smith, R. E., Smoll, F. L., & Hunt, E. (1977). A system for the behavioral assessment of athletic coaches. *The Research Quarterly, 48,* 401–407.

Snyder, M. (1979). Self-monitoring processes. *Advances in Experimental Social Psychology, 12,* 85–128.

Snyder, M. (1983). Choosing friends as activity partners: The role of self-monitoring. *Journal of Personality and Social Psychology, 45,* 1061–1072.

Snyder, M., & Gangestad, S. (1982). Choosing social situations: Two investigations of self-monitoring processes. *Journal of Personality and Social Psychology, 43,* 123–135.

Straub, W. F. (1977). Approaches to personality assessment of athletes: Personologism, situationism and interactionism. In R. E. Stadulis & C. O. Dotson (Eds.), *Research and practice in physical education* (pp. 176–187). Champaign, IL: Human Kinetics.

Ungerleider, S., Golding, J. M., & Porter, K. (1989). Mood profiles of masters track and field athletes. *Perceptual and Motor Skills, 68,* 607–617.

Van Schoyck, S. R. & Grasha, A. F. (1981). Attentional style variations and athletic ability: The advantages of a sport-specific test. *Journal of Sport Psychology, 3,* 149–165.

Vanden Auweele, Y. (1988). Personality diagnosis in young top level athletes. In FEPSAC (Ed.), *Proceedings of the 7th Congress of the European Association of Sport Psychology* (pp. 506–525). Bad Blankenburg: Wissenschaftlicher Rat beim Staatssekretariat für Körperkultur und Sport der DDR.

Vanek, M. & Hosek, V. (1974). Zur Persönlichkeit des Spitzensportlers [About the personality of top level performers]. *Leistungssport, 4,* 205–214.

Vealey, R. S. (1986). Conceptualization of sport confidence and competitive orientation: Preliminary investigation and instrument development. *Journal of Sport Psychology, 8,* 221–246.

Vealey, R. S. (1989). Sport personology: A paradigmatic and methodological analysis. *Journal of Sport and Exercise Psychology, 11,* 216–235.

Verstraeten, D. (1987). Persoonlijkheidsonderzoek en meten van verandering: Een terugblik over twintig jaar [Personality research and the measurement of change: A review over twenty years]. *Tijdschrift voor Klinische Psychologie, 17,* 232–253.

Williams, J. M. (1986). Psychological characteristics of peak performance. In J. M. Williams (Ed.), *Applied sport psychology: Personal growth to peak performance* (pp. 123–132). Palo Alto, CA: Mayfield.

Williams J. M., Hoepner, B. J., Moody, D. L., & Ogilvie, B. C. (1970). Personality traits of champion level female fencers. *The Research Quarterly, 41,* 446–453.

Williams, L. R. T. (1978). Prediction of high-level rowing ability. *Journal of Sports Medicine, 18,* 11–17.

Williams, L. R. T. (1982). Innovations in behavioural research: Implications for elite performance. *New Zealand Journal of Health, Physical Education and Recreation, 15,* 19–26.

Williams, L. R. T., & Parkin, W. A. (1980). Personality factor profiles of three hockey groups. *International Journal of Sport Psychology, 11,* 113–120.

Wolf, F. M. (1986). *Meta-analysis: Quantitative methods for research Synthesis (Series: Quantitative applications in the social sciences).* Beverly Hills, CA: Sage.

Zaichkowsky, L. D. (1980). Single-case experimental designs and sport psychology research. In C. H. Nadeau, W. R. Halliwell, K. M. Newell, & G. C. Roberts (Eds.), *Psychology of motor behavior and sport—1979* (pp. 171–179). Champaign, IL: Human Kinetics.

·12·

TALENT DETECTION AND DEVELOPMENT IN SPORT

Guy Régnier

John Salmela

Storm J. Russell

The primary concern in this chapter is to provide a better understanding of the process by which one achieves greatness in sport. For this purpose, we attempt to outline the extant research in sport psychology and the methodological processes that deal with the prediction of performance over various periods of time by use of measures of psychological aptitudes, alone or in combination with other physical, physiological, or technical abilities. The entire process can be called "sport talent detection." It fundamentally refers to the attempt to match a variety of performer characteristics, which may be innate or subject to the effect of learning or training, to the task demands of a given sport activity to ensure the highest probability of maximum performance outcome.

In that the degree of trainability of psychological skills such as mental toughness, agility, focusing, and planning varies within and between individuals over time in a manner analogous to how physiological training of strength, flexibility, and maximum aerobic power can be fostered and improved to different degrees over time, the concept of *talent development* is also central to this conceptualization. Talent detection and talent development have to be seen as interrelated and ongoing processes.

Within the context of talent detection is also the task of *talent selection,* which takes place over a shorter period and is focused upon choosing the appropriate individual who can best carry out the task within a specific situational context, such as the Olympic Games. Talent selection can be viewed as "very short-term talent detection" which ad-

dresses the question of who are the athletes who will perform best 2 months, or sometimes even 2 weeks, from now. It is not so much a process as it is a punctual task within the integrative approach of talent detection and development. Because of its particular and specific nature within the more global processes of talent detection and talent development, talent selection will not be covered in this chapter.

At the outset, it is essential to agree with the tenet that specific psychological variables must be used in conjunction with other measures in a variety of fields if predictions in complex disciplines such as sport are indeed viable.

However, the application of psychological variables within the sport context, while potentially beneficial, is not immediately self-evident in actual practice (Singer, 1988). For as the scientific method specifies, the step of *prediction* is first based upon accurate *description* and *explanation.* As Heilbrun (1966) points out, in defining human potentiality, we refer to "that which exists in possibility, not actuality" (p. 287). However, because of the necessity of validating testing instruments on what is observable in real life, the psychological testing procedure actually evaluates "that what exists in actuality, not in possibility" (p. 288).

Though the early years of modern international sport psychology were dominated by research on the personality of sports participants (Salmela, 1991), in the 1970s, noted researchers found that descriptive and explanatory features of personality testing were flawed. This led Rushall (1970) to state that "... personality is not a significant factor in sport performance" (p. 164). It might be that personality is a significant factor in sport performance but that the problem lies in its accurate measurement in the context of sport. In a more nuanced statement implying such obstacles, Martens (1975) reported, "Unfortunately, after years of study we know very little about personality as related to sport" (p. 14). Morgan (1978) later argued that these skeptical arguments on personality testing and sport could be countered if response distortion was controlled for and if the results were used with other biological measures.

In further support of the importance of psychological variables to athletic performance, Orlick and Partington (1988) showed that in terms of physical, technical, and mental preparation of Canadian Olympians, only the latter variable could significantly predict actual Olympic placings. More recently, Nideffer (1990) demonstrated that the appropriate use of the Test of Attentional and Interpersonal Style (TAIS) could be used as a means for classifying and perhaps selecting performers in open and closed skills and team sports. This latter topic of psychological testing for the purposes of selection or placement also falls within the context of this discussion. Finally, Rushall (1989), after an extensive review of the literature, made a convincing argument for the importance of psychosocial variables in contributing to sport success.

Within the context of this somewhat unsettled field of inquiry, the relevant research on talent detection in sport will be reviewed. A number of varying theoretical notions will be outlined with their supporting research as well as the presentation of certain methodological procedures currently being applied within sport settings.

WHAT UNDERLIES ATHLETIC PERFORMANCE? "TOP-DOWN" AND "BOTTOM-UP" PERSPECTIVES ON PERFORMANCE DETERMINANTS

It has already been stated that talent detection is based on the prediction of performance. The unveiling of underlying performance determinants is a particularly relevant endeavor for anyone interested in sport talent detection or selection. This paradigm is based on the assumption that underlying factors prerequisite for sporting excellence really do exist. This is the most popular, although not the only, hypothesis relating individual differences to sport excellence (Kroll, 1970).

Many authors, working under the assumption that such measurable underlying factors do exist, have tried to uncover the structures, abilities, and traits that might explain performance in a given sport or group of sports.

One of the characteristics of the studies described in the first part of this section is that they follow the precepts of orthodox science and are based upon the gathering of empirical evidence using established methods, accumulated results, hunches, and best guesses of the investigators. This approach may be considered a "top-down" approach in talent detection, where a priori hypotheses and possible solu-

tions are imposed from above, i.e., from accumulated scientific evidence. This is in contrast to "bottom-up" approaches, where elements of the solution come from the collective wisdom, the rich anecdotal evidence, and the language of the sport performers themselves.

The process by which information is elicited from expert performers is called *knowledge acquisition* (Boose & Gaines, 1988; Gaines & Boose, 1988) and may include techniques such as text analysis, protocol analysis, structured interviewing, stimulated recall, and analogical deviations (Vickers, 1990). Martens's (1987) questioning of the assumptions of the orthodox scientific approach in the general area of the social sciences such as sport psychology forms the basis for an alternative approach to the question of talent detection in the second part of this section.

"Top-down" Approaches for Performance Prediction

Univariate Studies. The first efforts to identify underlying sports performance determinants go back to the postwar period. The research design then in vogue compared a group of elite athletes with a group of nonathletes on one specific variable. A significant difference between the two groups on the variable of interest was interpreted as an indication that this variable was a performance determinant in that sport. For a review of such studies in the fields of physiology, anthropometry, psychology, and perceptual and motor skills, see, respectively, Astrand and Rodahl (1986), Carter (1970), Carron (1975), and Singer (1980).

Recently and more specifically, Abernethy (1987) extensively reviewed the potential variables related to selective attention which permitted the differentiation of expert and novice performers in fast ball sports. (See Chapters 6 and 7 for further discussion on this topic by Abernethy and by Tenenbaum and Bar-Eli.) For example, Starkes and Deakin (1984) suggested that such research could be considered from either a "hardware" or a "software" perspective. The former compared experts and novices on variables related to the "physical differences in the mechanical and optometric properties of the visual systems" while the latter to the information processing that occurred within the physical constraints of the visual system.

Abernethy reviewed a large number of studies on single "hardware" variables as related to actual performance or individual differences. For the most part they revealed that there is no relation at all between physical abilities and actual performance, or that results are equivocal. The physical variables which failed to differentiate between experts and novices included static and dynamic visual acuity, depth perception, stereoptic vision, spatial and distance perception, peripheral visual range, and even eye color.

Abernethy was, however, able to show that experts were more able than novices in using information-processing strategies reflecting their abilities to extract appropriate information from the environment, recognize and encode the display structure, resist distraction, and assign pertinence to possible game events. It was clear that experts and novices used markedly different information-processing strategies while not differing in their physical capacities to receive the information. In fact, Abernethy reports that some expert performers had uncorrected visual impairments which placed them below population norms.

Those studies were limited by the use of univariate statistical analysis as only one variable at a time was measured. Even though this design might be useful for investigating in depth one specific aspect of sport performance, it lacks the global perspective one needs to uncover the complex network of factors underlying sport performance. Even when studies included more than one variable, each was analyzed independently, and possible interactions could not be accounted for. Their predictive power was limited.

Unidisciplinary Multivariate Studies. With multivariate statistical analysis, the influence of a number of variables on performance can be considered while taking into account relationships between variables. The approach calls for the measurement of a series of attributes of a sample of athletes in one sport, the selection of a criterion of performance, and the use of a regression analysis to determine the predictive power of the selected variables. Another version of this design is to select two groups of athletes with marked differences in performance, measure them on a series of variables, and use a discriminant analysis to determine if the selected variables allow one to discriminate between the members of each group.

These two designs have been used extensively with different combinations of *physical measures* such as strength, muscular power, flexibility, and body composition to try to discriminate athletes. Applications can be found, for example, in rowing (Hay, 1969), gymnastics (Grabiner & McKelvain, 1987), and tennis (Ackland, Bloomfield, Elliott, & Blanksby, 1990). Ackland et al. conclude that "these studies highlight the limited value of physical and physiological parameters when used in isolation to identify talented athletes, especially during early adolescence. It would appear that technique may play a dominant role in competitive success, especially in team sports" (p. 162). They do not allude, however, to the potential that psychological variables might have for improving predictions.

Psychological variables which were multidimensional in nature in the form of personality inventories were quite prevalent in the early years of sport psychology. American psychologists Ogilvie and Tutko (1965) were most prominent during this formative period when they applied their sport-specific instrument the Athletic Motivation Inventory (AMI) to athletic populations. It was their intent to use the AMI to help select athletes based upon their psychological profiles. Martens (1975) later pointed that ". . . this dubious enterprise is unsubstantiated by any reported data by Ogilvie and Tutko" (p. 16).

While Martens was the most vocal opponent of psychological profiling of athletes using personality traits, he was not alone (Fisher, 1977; Rushall, 1970). The critiques were fundamentally against the use of measures of personality traits or states in isolation and suggested the adoption of an

interactionist approach as was convincingly proposed by Mischel (1973) during that same era.

At the time when personality research was coming under criticism, Nideffer (1976) published the Test of Attentional and Interpersonal Style (TAIS), which purported to assess how the attention styles of athletes matched the environmental demands of their selected sport tasks. (See Nideffer, Chapter 24 in this book.) More recently, the TAIS came under attack concerning the predictive validity of the instrument as well as the statistical independence of the subscales (Dewey, Brawley, & Allard, 1989; Summers & Ford, 1990; Vallerand, 1983; Van Schoyck & Grasha, 1981).

However, Nideffer (1990) has recently reported that the scales could correctly discriminate 1799 athletes into closed-sport skills, open-sport skills, and team games in a manner that was coherent with the theoretical nature of the TAIS subscales. Aronson (1981), using the TAIS, explained 18% of the variance between a group of elite gymnasts and a group of nonelite gymnasts.

Lufi, Porat, and Tenenbaum (1986) administered 11 different psychological tests to 202 young male athletes, ages 7 to 11, from different sports. The series of variables accounted for 58% of the variance in competition performance. Two measures of concentration explained 41% of the variance. Porat, Lufi, and Tenenbaum (1989) accounted for 49% of the performance variance of 7-to 9-year-old female gymnasts with measures of self-concept, locus of control, and trait anxiety.

Spink (1990) reviewed studies that were able to differentiate successful from less successful athletes based on their psychological characteristics in gymnastics (Mahoney & Avener, 1977), wrestling (Gould, Weiss, & Weinberg, 1981; Highlen & Bennett, 1979), and racquetball (Meyers, Schleser, Cooke, & Cuvillier, 1979). Spink (1990) himself was able to successfully distinguish gymnasts competing at different levels on the basis of two psychological factors, psychological recovery and self-confidence.

Rushall and Leet (1979) tested the predictive value of a series of *behavioral variables* for swimming performance. For Olympic-level swimmers, 88% of performance variance between the group of swimmers selected for the Olympic games and the group of nonselected performers was explained by 26 of the 264 observed behaviors. But in a follow-up study using a different group of swimmers with similar performance level, Rushall and Jamieson (1979) could not replicate the results of the first study. They concluded that relevant determinants of performance for Canadian Olympic swimmers were not likely to be found among behavioral profiles.

There is even one prominent example of using a projective test, a modified Thematic Apperception Test (TAT), to differentiate between expert and novice skydivers. Fenz and Epstein (1962) report that experienced skydivers become increasingly externally task oriented before the jump, while the novice "ruminates on his own fears or expends much of his energy defending against them" (p. 331).

The predictive power of *perceptual variables* has also been studied. For example, Nielsen and McGown (1985) found that only 12% of hitting performance in baseball was accounted for by a regression model made up of simple and multiple reaction-time measures. In the same line as Abernethy (1987) but in a multivariate perspective, Goulet (1990) and Bard, Fleury, and Goulet (in press) suggest that information-processing expertise could best be predicted by the use of a "perceptual efficiency index" combining factors such as filtering power, retrieval capacity, rapidity of detection, and processing.

Biomechanical variables were tested to predict performance in certain sports. For example, Hudson (1985) reports that five cinematographic movement analyses accounted for 64% of the variance in free-throw performance among three groups of women basketball players. Finally, *technical skills* alone have been used to try to predict sports performance. For instance, Hopkins (1979), using scores from six skill tests and a discriminant analysis, correctly classified 74% of the players according to their level of performance. The percentage of variance explained by the discriminant function was not reported.

Multidisciplinary Multivariate Studies. None of these studies incorporating variables from only one sport science was able to account for 100% of performance variance. Such results prompted sports scientists, in the 1970s, to turn to multidisciplinary multivariate models to study sports performance.

Morgan (1973) states that "Insofar as prediction is a central function of any scientific enterprise, the case for the superiority of psychobiologic models is unambiguous and uncontestable" (p. 40). It is a statistical axiom, as pointed out by Guilford (1956), that variables not related to each other but strongly related to performance will explain more variance than variables all related to each other. Bouchard, Brunelle, and Godbout (1973) published a model of sports performance that took into consideration psychological, organic, perceptual, morphological, and demographic factors. Later, many authors demonstrated the superiority of a multidisciplinary model of performance over a unidisciplinary one.

For example, Deshaies, Pargman, and Thiffault (1979) measured 116 hockey players on 6 biophysical variables, 4 specific hockey skills, and 4 psychological variables. Expert evaluations of players were used as the performance criterion. Regression analysis yielded a predictive model that included 4 variables: anaerobic power, forward skating speed, visual perception speed, and motivation. Each of the three groups of variables was represented. The model explained 55% of the performance criterion variance, with biophysical variables alone explaining 17%, psychological variables 20%, and hockey skills 33% of the performance variance, respectively.

In another effort to demonstrate the strength of a multidisciplinary approach, Williams (1978) administered a series of 62 psychological, physiological, and technical tests to 33 oarsmen from New Zealand. Using expert evaluations of the athletes as the performance criterion, a predictive model was generated. None of the 62 variables, taken individually, correlated significantly with the performance criterion. But a predictive model made up of 8 variables (strength, heartbeat, and workload during the last 30 seconds of a test on an ergocycle, and 5 personality factors) accounted for 70% of the performance variance.

Nagle, Morgan, Hellickson, Serfass, and Alexander (1975) measured 42 wrestlers trying out for the U.S. team of the 1972 Olympic Games on 12 psychological and 9 biophysical variables. A discriminant analysis between both groups of wrestlers (selected and nonselected) yielded a multiple correlation coefficient of .67 for the physiological variables, .73 for the psychological variables, and .92 when both series were combined. The authors did not specify which specific variables were kept in the final discriminant function.

Silva, Shultz, Haslam, Martin, and Murray (1985) replicated the study of Nagle et al. (1975) with American wrestlers trying out for the 1980 Olympic team. A first discriminant function using only psychological variables explained 30% of the variance between the selected and the nonselected group with 7 variables. A second discriminant function using only the physiological variables explained 21% of the variance with 3 variables. The discriminant function combining all variables explained 75% of the variance but needed a cumbersome 19 variables to do so. By reducing that number to the first 6 variables, the multidisciplinary model still accounted for 71% of the variance.

Other scholars, without directly comparing the multidisciplinary model to the unidisciplinary model, have demonstrated the strength of relying on more than merely one sports science to predict performance in different sports such as football (McDavid, 1977), women's basketball (Riezebos, Patterson, Hall, & Yuhasz, 1983), archery (Landers, Qi, Daniels, & Boutcher, 1984), women's gymnastics (Sol, 1987), diving (Kerr, Dainty, Booth, Gaboriault, & McGavern, 1979), baseball (Friend & LeUnes, 1990), and alpine skiing (Willimczik, 1986).

Knowledge-Based "Bottom-up" Approaches for Talent Development

If we turn our attention from talent detection to the area of talent development in sport, we find an intuitively seductive area, when considered from a psychological perspective. However, the early promise of achieving quick results through the application of traditional psychometric methods from sport psychology to select athletes has been shown to be short-lived, since the predictive validity of psychological inventories that assess personality, levels of anxiety, or competitive readiness have shown to be less than successful (Salmela & Russell, 1988).

One reason that sport psychology has been relatively unsuccessful in predicting how athletes will perform at a given moment in their careers is that there does not yet exist a robust model that explains how athletes learn sport skills. Much has been written about performance enhancement, while there is little on learning enhancement, and even less from a developmental perspective. There have been a number of recent paradigmatic shifts which could prove useful to understanding the sport-specific knowledge that is necessary for the success of developing athletes.

Martens (1987) has critically analyzed the various sources of knowledge in sport psychology and has made some persuasive arguments regarding the benefits of *not* subscribing strictly to the precepts of orthodox science. Martens contends that the field of experiential knowledge is rich in useful information and might be best approached nontraditionally, using the idiographic approach, introspective methods, and field studies to complement the methods of orthodox science.

In a similar vein, Wall (1986) makes a strong case for a knowledge-based approach to motor skill acquisition and development with an emphasis upon procedural knowledge about doing; declarative knowledge about concrete thinking; affective knowledge about feeling; and metacognitive knowledge about "knowing about knowing." Wall indicates that it is important to assess integrally each knowledge base in order to understand the developmental nature of learning skills and ultimately about predicting high-level performance in sport. However, Wall does not make it evident which relevant dimensions must be tapped, and more important, how to measure them.

One starting point within such a conceptual or paradigmatic shift is to use a "bottom-up" approach to studying talent, that is, by trying to find out what reported features talented performers cite in any specific domain to explain their exceptional performances. The use of an expert systems approach appears to be applicable to sport as it has been done in a number of other specific domains of human endeavor with expert and novice performers.

Expert and Novice Differences. In recent years, while there has been little research which has attempted to examine directly athletes' domain-related knowledge in sport, there have been many studies conducted with experts and novices in sport and in other areas. This work indicates that there are systematic, replicable differences in the way high- and low-skilled performers perceive and respond to different stimuli in the task environment. Expertise is by definition "the possession of large body of knowledge and procedural skill" (Chi, Glaser, & Rees, 1982, p. 2). The study of the role of expert knowledge in performance began during the mid-1960s with the work of de Groot (1966) and Chase and Simon (1973a, 1973b) on chess skill. Chi et al. concluded that "expert-novice differences may be related to poorly formed, qualitatively different, or nonexistent categories in the novice representation" (p. 122). These results suggest, along with the "perceptual chunking" hypothesis, "that much of expert power lies in the expert's ability to quickly establish correspondence between externally presented events and internal models for these events" (p. 123).

In reviewing their extensive work on physics expertise, Chi and her associates (1982) also concluded that differences in the knowledge bases of experts and novices were of crucial importance and that novice physicists responded to the surface features of a problem, while the experts responded to its deep structure and considered the underlying principles required for its resolution.

From this and other research it is becoming increasingly evident that experts across a wide range of disciplines appear to share fundamental similarities in the way their respective knowledge is both organized and utilized. Furthermore, the characteristics of expert knowledge organization and utilization appear to differ from those of novices and less skilled individuals in important and systematic ways, and these differences appear to be intrinsically related to the quality of performance. Whether one adopts the schema model proposed by Rumelhart and his colleagues (Rumelhart, 1980, 1981; Rumelhart & Ortony, 1977) or the chunking hypothesis originally put forward by Chase and Simon (1973a, b), or simply considers units of information that become systematically "packaged" with practice and utilized by the skilled individual during task performance, the process is similar. It is apparent that as individuals become more proficient at any given activity, they develop a large store of domain-related knowledge and context-related skills.

This knowledge seems to be organized and structured categorically into problem or task types, most likely in a hierarchical or heterarchical perceptual and retrieval processing system, and on the basis of the particular goals and subgoals each individual associates with those categories or types. Thus it becomes essential that appropriate attention be given to examining the knowledge base of the performer in the study of sport, motor skill, and expertise in any domain (French & Thomas, 1987; Wall, 1986).

Qualitative Data Methods in Sport Psychology Research. Scanlan and colleagues (Scanlan, Stein, & Ravizza, 1989; Scanlan, Ravizza, & Stein, 1989), while not directly concerned with studying the athlete's knowledge base, have adopted structured interviewing techniques to examine sources of stress experienced by former elite figure skaters during their competitive careers. Using this method in conjunction with inductive content analysis (Patton, 1980), five major sources of stress were identified, including (1) negative aspects of competition; (2) negative significant-other relations; (3) demands/costs of skating; (4) personal struggles; and (5) traumatic experiences. The authors concluded that the open-ended interview technique generated a rich and valuable sources of qualitative data on sources of stress which they as researchers would not have been otherwise able to identify. A broader application of qualitative data analysis methods was called for in sport psychology research. The complex cognitive perspectives from which athletes are operating in the ongoing development and performance of high-level sport skills was particularly emphasized.

Research which uses qualitative data methods such as structured interviewing and inductive content analysis, however, has always been open to the criticism that the results derived are subject to the coders' own interpretation. The results may differ if different coders are used. Furthermore, it becomes difficult to replicate the results of such work when the procedures are subject to individual variation in their application. The problem, then, is finding appropriate methods which will enable researchers to measure and model knowledge structures of different individuals in a reliable, valid, and replicable fashion.

In this respect, certain data collection procedures and multivariate methods used by social psychologists working in social cognition would seem particularly appropriate for the study of knowledge structures among sport performers.

Research in Social Psychology. Forgas (1979a) has been involved for a number of years in a program of research concerned with examining the nature of social interaction, which is construed as comprising innumerable recurring well-rehearsed social routines or episodes. It is argued that it is the "routine, predictable nature of these interactions . . . which makes social contact possible" and that "shared knowledge about such episodes is . . . what holds individuals, groups, and societies together" (p. 165). Social episodes are, by Forgas's definition (1979b), "internal, cognitive representations about common recurring interaction routines within a defined subcultural milieu" (p. 253) and he likens their structure and operation to that of schema. This research has been particularly concerned with identifying the knowledge structures and cognitive dimensions underlying interaction routines or episodes, and which are thought to subsequently define behavior within them.

In many respects, Forgas's conceptualization of social interaction and skilled social behavior in terms of routines and episodes can be applied to sporting activities and sport skills. That is, any given sport can be conceptualized as comprising a large number of recurring, relatively predictable interactions between the performer and particular kinds of performance environments in which that performer is trying to achieve certain goals. These goal-oriented interactions involve a related set of subgoals and require the application of certain specifically developed cognitive and motor skills.

In discussing theoretical and research concerns in the area of social knowledge and social skill, Forgas (1979a) argues that "the necessary first task in understanding how people think about social events is to be able to describe and quantify that knowledge empirically" (p. 170). This argument is equally pertinent for the study of an athlete's knowledge about sport, including the many episodes, tasks, and skills that it comprises.

Following the work of Magnusson and his colleagues on individuals' perceptions of various kinds of social situations (Magnusson, 1971; Magnusson & Ekehammer, 1973), Forgas has employed qualitative data collection techniques such as the structured interview, and quantitative statistical procedures such as multidimensional scaling (MDS). They have been used to examine and quantify the social episode domains of a wide variety of subcultural groups, including

students, housewives, academic departments, and rugby teams. With these methods, individuals' knowledge of their most common social episodes can be represented as points in a geometrical space in terms of their common features.

This kind of methodology has been applied successfully by a number of researchers in cognitive social psychology in investigating various aspects of knowledge and beliefs about different domains. These have included studies examining perceptions of contraceptive methods (Callan & Gallois, 1984) and alcoholics' self-evaluations (Partington, 1970).

The recent work of Russell (1990, 1991) has extended the work from the field of social cognition to that of the development of expertise in sport. The primary questions addressed were how highly skilled athletes viewed their sport experience and structured their domain-related knowledge, in terms of the different situations and sets of circumstances that athletes identify as discrete units or sport task situations (STSs). From these STSs, the primary cognitive demands and strategies were identified and comparisons were made as to how these demands and strategies varied with performers of different skill levels and across a variety of sports.

Using a methodology which combined qualitative data collection methods, such as the structured interview and repertory grid procedures (Kelly, 1955), with MDS statistical techniques, it was possible to identify important aspects of the knowledge bases of elite athletes from different sports and represent these in geometric space.

Briefly, Russell's (1990, 1991) initial research involved a series of extensive interviews with 10 highly skilled athletes from judo, powerlifting, cycling, and triathlon in order to identify the wide range of STSs which they encountered as performers. The athletes then sorted the STSs into categories based on the perceived similarities among the described situations. Similarities were defined in terms of the athletes' intentions and goals in various reported sport situations, and in terms of the habitual responses and strategies they found to be effective in achieving these goals. A repertory grid procedure was then used to relate the athletes' reported task demands and response strategies to the various sport situations they had described during the interviews and the categorization task. This procedure involved having athletes rate their STSs in terms of the different task demands and responses associated with each. The resultant data matrices were then analyzed using MDS procedures, thus producing a detailed geometric representation for each athlete in the study which illustrated their perceptions of their sporting experiences, and the knowledge they brought to the different kinds of sport and performance situations they encountered.

Figure 12–1 illustrates the kind of information that can be derived using this approach. Using these methods, individuals' knowledge of their sport experiences can be represented as points in a geometric space, where the distances between those points indicate the semantic and cognitive distances subjects perceive as existing among the various episodes they experience, and a series of orthogonal

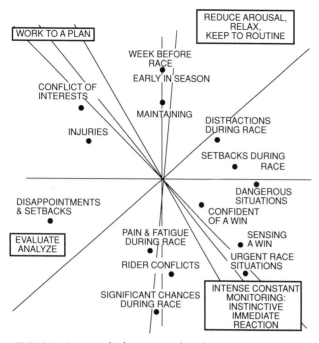

FIGURE 12-1. Multidimensional scaling representation of a cyclist's sport task situations regressed against habitually effective strategies.

From Russell, 1991.

dimensions summarizes and describes these episodes in terms of their common salient features. As can be seen from this figure, such methods offer exciting new opportunities for gaining important insights into athletes' knowledge and the way it is utilized in the sporting context.

The possibilities of opening up new vistas of research are numerous as methodologies from the literature about social cognitions are applied to sport talent development, especially if considered across the developmental spectrum. These new possibilities for research and understanding of the knowledge base in sport may permit the transformation of these methodological and paradigmatic changes from thought into action in this sphere of application.

Bloom's (1985) Perspectives on Talent Development. Another recent, innovative study by Bloom (1985) on talent development in youth also involves structured interviews for a look at the career development of Olympic swimmers and world-class tennis players, as well as outstanding neurosurgeons, concert pianists, sculptors, and mathematicians. This study is particularly revealing because it considers three career phases: initiation, development, and perfection of athletic talents. The fact that Bloom has provided some broad generalizations on talented performers, whether they be athletes, artists, or scientists, is particularly significant. It shows that there appears to be some consistency in the pattern of expertise development that transcends the field under study. Table 12–1 shows the gen-

eralized characteristics that Bloom found during the three career stages of these performers.

It is of interest that the holistic study of talent must include both the role of significant others and a developmental dimension. Bloom (1985) reports that parents and teachers notice a "specialness or giftedness" in general about the child, as well as some specific qualities in his or her talent area. These "markers," or "... attributions of uniqueness of special qualities to the individual" (p. 519), affected both the expectations for the child and the methods used in teaching the child.

At the earliest stage, the mentor was not necessarily technically advanced, but was able to kindle the love of the child, providing rewards for the effort rather than for the achievement. The parents helped the child to learn the responsibility of the activity in positive ways and shared the excitement of the child's progress. When the child became "hooked" on the activity and realized, for example, that he or she was a "gymnast," rather than merely a "kid who did gymnastics," this marked the transition to the second phase.

During this initial period, the performer probably acquired much positive affective knowledge resulting from the intrinsic joy of progressively learning, as well as from the enthusiastic support of both the family and the mentor. In Wall's (1986) terms, he or she was acquiring the procedural and resultant affective knowledge base of skill acquisition.

During the second phase of skill acquisition, the performer began careful practice with a higher level of technical precision, usually because of a new mentor with superior technical knowledge. The performer then became achievement-oriented and welcomed knowledgeable criticism. Competition became the yardstick for the measurement of progress, and higher levels of dedication to achievement were witnessed. The mentor took on a strong personal interest in the performer, and the precious, loving

TABLE 12-1. Characteristics of Talented Performers (and Their Mentors and Parents) at Various Stages of Their Careers (Bloom, 1985)

Individual	Career Phase		
	Initiation	Development	Perfection
Performer	joyful, playful, excited, "special"	"hooked," committed	obsessed, responsible
Mentor	kind, cheerful, caring, process-centered	strong, respecting, skilled, demanding	successful, respected/ feared, emotionally bonded
Parents	shared excitement, supportive, sought mentors, positive	made sacrifices, restricted activity	

relationship was often replaced by one of respect. The high level of technical or declarative knowledge, as well as skill, or procedural knowledge, provided a source of strong guidance and discipline in the performer. Quality results were expected. In order for such a high-level relationship to be maintained, moral and financial support were required of the parents. Parents also helped in restricting outside activity, while still showing concern for the total development of the performer.

When performers moved on to the final stages of performance refinement or perfection, they were obsessed by this activity, which dominated their lives. There was a shift in the initiation of ideas from the mentor to the performer. The performers began to know about their own knowledge base, or what Wall (1986) calls *metacognitive knowledge*, and to take the necessary personal responsibility for its development. The stress was now upon very high-level skill, and performers were willing to put in whatever time or effort was required to achieve the highest performance goals. The respect for the mentor often changed from respect to fear as higher and higher standards were demanded and the effort required to achieve these levels of excellence increased. Often very strong emotional love/hate ties were created. The parents played a lesser role during this phase, during which performers took personal responsibility for their progress. The main actors in the development of the talent in sport have now evolved full cycle across the athlete's career. An additional sport-specific phase might now be added to Bloom's model as the athlete begins to ease into the retirement mode, through the processes of gradual detraining and readjustment to normal life. Whereas other subjects in Bloom's study can perform their skills throughout a lifetime, an athlete's career is often terminated in midlife.

It is within such a framework that a coherent start can take place for talent development in sport. The career structure outlined by Bloom is essential for a heuristic model of talent development in sport. The broad knowledge-based approach advanced by Wall is parsimonious and compatible with this holistic view of the developing athlete. What are the knowledge-based features that differentiate between skilled and less skilled athletes, and how might they be assessed?

In that the "top-down" approach to talent detection has held a position of prominence, let us return and examine a variety of conceptual frameworks that have been applied to the actual process of talent detection.

PRINCIPLES UNDERLYING TALENT DETECTION IN SPORT

Going one step further in the study of talent detection in sport brings us to the development of conceptual models designed to identify the presumed underlying performance determinants and to search for those determinants within a population of potential athletes.

Following is a review of sport talent detection models. The proposer of each model is quick to point out the importance of relying on a multidisciplinary approach which covers the main families of possible performance determinants, including psychological variables, to achieve any success in correctly detecting potential athletes. Some of the models include a built-in short-term training period to better assess the importance of such psychological variables as emotional reactions to training demands. The major difficulties associated with a scientific approach to the question of talent detection will also be discussed. The importance of relying on factors strongly determined by heredity will be discussed further by looking at twin, sibling, parent-child, and longitudinal studies. Finally, six general guiding principles for sport talent detection will be set from the analysis of the reviewed models. A conceptual model developed by Régnier (1987) based on all six guiding principles will then be presented in the next part of the chapter.

Sport Talent Detection Models

Harre's Model. The detection model proposed by Harre (1982), a German researcher, is based on the assumption that only through training can it be determined if a youngster possesses the required attributes to succeed. The first step in talent detection, according to Harre, is putting as many kids as possible through training programs. Training orients the developmental process of young athletes and makes the emergence of their talent possible.

This does not mean that certain qualities cannot be recognized outside a training environment. Some can, particularly among the physical attributes. Besides the training environment, Harre considers the athlete's social environment as an important factor for talent detection and development. Athletic talent must be nurtured by the positive influence from parents and peers, which echoes the earlier results found by Bloom (1985) in a variety of talent domains. Having set down those two basic conditions, Harre goes on to define specific rules and principles for talent detection.

Rule 1: Talent detection is done in two stages—a first general stage, where all children showing good all-around athletic ability are identified, and a second, more specific stage, where individuals are classified according to skills associated with certain classes of sports. This classification is based on objective testing of children's abilities as well as on their potential for improvement, as measured by their reaction to training programs.

Rule 2: Talent detection must rest on critical factors playing a decisive role in top-level performance. Those factors must be chosen from among the ones highly determined by heredity.

Rule 3: Characteristics and abilities of each individual have to be evaluated in relation to their level of biological development.

Rule 4: Talent detection can not rely exclusively on physical attributes. Some psychological and social variables can help an athlete succeed. Harre mentions, among other factors, the attitude toward sports in school, participation in extra-curricular sports activities, and the personality development of the ideal "young socialist."

Those four rules, added to the two preliminary conditions, are the basis for Harre's talent detection model. The model is carried out in two stages.

The first stage consists of general detection from important performance factors. Testing would occur with all children on sports performance variables that are easy to measure. Main determinants of sports performance are height, running speed, endurance, coordination, ability in game situations, and "athletic versatility." If necessary, those data are completed with observations taken from school competitions.

The second stage is the confirmation of sports aptitudes during a junior training program. To determine a child's disposition for a given sport, the following four indicators are used: level of performance reached in the program; rate of performance improvement; performance stability under changing conditions; and reaction to training demands.

Those four factors are measured while the young athlete is taking part in a sport-specific training program. At the end of the training program, a prognostic is made on his or her chances of success at superior levels of performance. This procedure is a perfect example of the close relationship between talent detection and talent development. In Harre's model, talent is continuously "redetected" or "repetitively selected" as it is being developed.

Harre's model (1982) is probably one of the most complete sport talent detection models found in the literature to date. It raises many concepts essential to sport talent detection that are used in other models. Among such concepts are the importance of confirming the child's predicted potential in a training program and the importance of relying on more than just physical attributes to predict sports performance. Harre also insists that sport talent detection should be based on those critical performance factors that play a decisive role in achieving top-level performances, but it is not explained how those factors can be discovered. This is an important drawback of the model, since the identification of those factors is certainly a key element to any talent-detection strategy.

Harre limits those critical factors in the model to factors highly dependent upon heredity. The rationale behind such a choice is that performance can be predicted only if one relies on "predictable" variables, that is, variables not influenced by environmental situations. The limit of such an approach is that it does not consider variables also strongly related to top-level performance which depend as much on environment as on heredity. Those factors also represent a more than negligible predictive value, even though they are not as reliable as more stable factors. Finally, while Harre rightly insists on accounting for variable biological development rates before making sports performance predictions, he proposes no precise way of doing so.

Havlicek, Komadel, Komarik, and Simkova's Model. This 1982 model from Czechoslovakia presents an approach similar to that of Harre (1982) in which the authors suggest 10 principles to rely on for talent detection. These principles can be summarized as follows:

1. The objective of a talent detection system is to make sure that individuals who are talented in a sport will be training for that sport.
2. The following steps are essential: (a) identification of gifted children in physical education classes; (b) specialization in one "sports family," depending on abilities and attributes; (c) specialization in one sport; and (d) determination as to the probability of reaching top-level performance.
3. Children must not be made to specialize in one sport too early, and an approach by "sports families" should first be adopted.
4. Detection criteria must rely on predictors that have strong genetic influence, high developmental stability, and a demonstrated predictive value. However, since individuals can produce adaptations through better life conditions and training techniques, it would be a mistake to rely *only* on genetic factors to predict performance.
5. Since sports performance is multidimensional, all sports sciences must contribute to talent detection.
6. There is a hierarchy of predictive factors, with stable and noncompensatory factors (e.g., height) of greatest concern. Second are more stable and compensatory factors, such as speed. Finally, unstable and compensatory factors, such as motivation, are considered.
7. The largest possible pool population of potential athletes must be used.
8. Talent detection has to be done in a democratic and humanitarian fashion.
9. Talent detection has to be planned and managed carefully with all the related information and control activities.
10. Talent detection has to be done within the larger context of talent development.

Like Harre (1982), Havlicek et al. (1982) recognize the multidimensional nature of sport performance, which takes them to a multisciences approach to talent detection. They also underscore the importance of heredity-dependent and performance-related factors in talent detection. But contrary to Harre, they state that it would be a mistake to rely *only* on such factors. The proposed hierarchy takes into consideration the *degree* of heredity of each factor related to performance. This strategy is more realistic and less limiting than Harre's. The concept of "priorizing" the predictive contribution of each factor based on its respective stability is an original way of dealing with the heredity question.

Gimbel's Model. German scientist B. Gimbel (1976) sets the assumption that talent has to be analyzed from three angles: (1) physiological and morphological variables, (2) trainability, and (3) motivation. Moreover, talent is divided into internal factors (genetics) and external factors (environment). According to Gimbel, genetic factors are essential but they will be stifled if environmental conditions are not favorable. It is pointed out that in most sports, top-level performances are reached by the time an athlete is between 18 and 20, and that 8 to 10 years are needed to develop a champion. Promising athletes have to be identified at 8 to 9 years of age, before their growth spurt has begun. To prevent excluding late bloomers too quickly, Gimbel proposes a "recovery period" for uncertain cases.

Gimbel (1976) also addresses the question of "false positives," i.e., individuals identified as talented who never fulfill their predicted potential. Three explanations are suggested: (1) tests used to predict performance are not sufficiently valid, reliable, and objective; (2) it is impossible to accurately predict performance from such tests because of biological age differences between children; and (3) contributions from psychological variables are neglected in predictive models.

As for environmental factors, Gimbel states that sports talent detection and development are not only a question of genetics and motor skills, but also a social, ethical, and pedagogical matter. From those considerations, Gimbel proposes the following approach:

1. Identify morphological, physical, and psychological factors underlying performance for as many sports as possible.
2. Test children in schools on these variables, and, based on their results, guide them into the sports instructional program which best fit their dispositions.
3. During a 12-to 24-month instructional program, test children regularly to monitor their individual progress. Dropouts are to be considered as a "natural selection effect" in the face of psychological demands of training.
4. At the end of the instructional program, a prediction is made for each child on the probability of success in his or her respective sport. Depending on a positive or negative prognostic, the young athlete will be oriented toward an intensive training program or toward recreational sports. Another group, for which results are not conclusive, undergoes one more year of training at the end of which a final decision is made.

Gimbel introduces the important concept of a "catching-up period" for possible late-blooming athletes. This solution is one way to deal with variable development rates among individuals (the other is the introduction of developmental indices within the predictions themselves). The option proposed by Gimbel to support a group of uncertain cases for one year, if mathematically simpler, is logistically much more cumbersome.

Montpetit and Cazorla's Model. Canadian and French scientists R. Montpetit and G. Cazorla (1982) developed an improved version of Gimbel's model and applied it to talent detection in swimming. They added details on how to identify the morphological and physiological variables on which predictions must rest. The authors suggest a first step where a "top-level swimmer profile" is drawn for each event, based upon conventional physiological testing procedures. The second step is to verify the stability of the variables in the profile through longitudinal studies. Using stability indices and development rates of variables best describing swimming champions, Montpetit and Cazorla suggest that the evolution of underlying performance factors, and thus performance itself, can be predicted. The authors, as suggested by Gimbel, also provide for uncertain cases with a "catch-up" route.

Dreke's Model. In a similar vein, Dreke (1982) suggests a three-step approach for sports talent detection. Step one is called "pre-selection" and includes (1) general health status, (2) academic achievements, (3) sociability, (4) somatotype, and (5) agility. In the second step of "verification," somatotypes are compared with somatotype characteristics of different sports, and general (non-sport-specific) physical ability tests are administered. Step three is the detection per se by which children undergo a short training program during which their performance and psychological adaptation to training are evaluated.

No new concepts are introduced by Dreke when his model is compared to the three previous models. However, Dreke shows a constant preoccupation with talent detection models used in Eastern European countries, and it is worth noting the assignment of youngsters to short training programs to evaluate their reaction to the psychological demands of training. Talent detection is definitely conducted within a global approach to the athlete's development. "Raw talent" will be of very little use if it cannot be actualized within the typical environment of top-level competition. It is probably from a lack of such an ecologic and holistic approach that past and current North American efforts for sports talent detection suffer the most. Those efforts have so far been mostly characterized by an "experimental" vision of the problem, often limited to the identification of factors that characterize top-level performers.

Bompa's Model. Bompa (1985) observes the extensive and successful use of talent detection in Eastern European countries since the 1960s. He describes the advantages of talent detection: less time is needed to reach top-level performance, coaches can work with better athletes, more athletes have a chance to reach the international level, higher homogeneity of athletes in a given sport is achieved, and athletes become more confident if they are chosen. Bompa's model assumes that sports performance is determined by three types of factors: (1) motor capacities (perceptual and motor skills, endurance, strength, and power), (2) physiological capacities, and (3) morphological attributes. Bompa's model is the one exception where psychological variables are never mentioned.

Relative contributions of each group of factors to performance in a given sport are estimated from task analysis based on scientific research and expert opinions. The contribution to performance of each factor within its own group is also estimated. Factors kept from the task analysis are measured in the largest possible group of children. Results are weighted by the relative contributions expressed in percentages proposed in the theoretical model. This theoretical model of performance can then be verified experimentally through the use of multiple regression analysis. Finally, Bompa suggests that the detection of potential champions can be made by directly comparing their physiological and morphological profiles to the ones of elite athletes.

Geron's Model. According to Geron (1978), such elite athlete profiles, or "sportograms," as they are called, are not enough to detect talent. Geron underlines the difference between simply enumerating factors influencing performance in a given sport and finding out the constituent elements of talent in a given sport. There is a difference between finding out what *characterizes* a champion and the qualities required for an athlete to *become* a champion. To Geron, talent detection also has to rely on genetically determined factors.

Geron's strategy to develop a system of talent detection is very similar to the one proposed by Gimbel (1976) and refined by Montpetit and Cazorla (1982), that is: (1) determination of an elite athlete profile in the given sport, (2) identification of variables strongly related to success and highly dependent on heredity through longitudinal studies, and (3) determination of age periods when the genetic dimension of selected factors is the highest.

Bar-Or's Model. Bar-Or (1975) proposes a detailed operational procedure for sport talent detection in a five-step approach: (1) evaluate children on a series of morphological, physiological, psychological, and performance variables, (2) weigh results with a "development index" to account for biological age, (3) test reaction to training with exposure to a short training program, (4) evaluate family history (height, sport activities), and (5) use a multiple regression analysis model to predict performance from results on the first four steps.

Bar-Or does not specify what should be used as performance criteria, nor is task analysis mentioned as an important step in the model. There is also a lack of explanation as to what to do with the results. Once the predictors have been identified, how are they used to detect talented individuals?

Jones and Watson's Model. Jones and Watson (1977) propose a procedure to predict performance from psychological variables. But the same approach could be used with variables from other fields as well. Even though they do not present a talent detection model as such, their work is valuable inasmuch as any detection talent effort rests on performance prediction. The steps to performance prediction are: (1) determine target performance, (2) select a criterion to represent target performance, (3) select potential per-

formance predictors and verify their predictive power, and (4) apply the results. Verification of the predictive power of variables thought to explain performance is done with a multiple regression analysis model.

In an extension of this model, Blahus (1975) adds one more step to validate performance predictors. It is suggested that one test the stability of the precision model found with the regression analysis by cross-validating it on other samples of athletes taken from the same population on which it was originally developed.

Problems Associated with a Scientific Approach to Talent Detection

As suggested by the review of the models presented so far, talent detection based on a scientific approach is a difficult process. The issues involved are so complex that more and more questions are being raised concerning its very feasibility in general and from a psychological viewpoint (Salmela, 1990). For example, many presentations delivered at a recent symposium on talent detection reported by Bartmus, Neumann, and de Marées (1987) expressed such skepticism. In his introduction, H. de Marées, the chairman of the symposium, emphasized that "many questions are still unanswered despite numerous investigations during the second half of the seventies" (p. 415).

The Compensation Phenomenon. Among the problems discussed at the symposium was the "compensation" phenomenon, which suggests that mastery of a sport can be achieved in individual or unique ways through different combinations of skills, attributes, and capacities (Feldman, 1986). For example, conventional wisdom and research (Calderone, Berlutti, Leglise, Giastella, & Mularoni, 1987; Pettenburg, Erich, Bernink, Zonderland, & Huisveld, 1984) indicate that gymnasts who are small in stature have marked advantages over taller competitors. Yet there are a number of exceptions. Germany's Eberhard Gienger is one, as he has compensated for his height "disadvantage" by using the added stature in the performance of slower and more graceful long, levered movements not feasible for shorter gymnasts.

Bartmus et al. (1987) reported the results of a longitudinal study on 100 tennis players. The conclusion was that "no uniform tennis performance ability exists: Deficiencies in one area of performance can be compensated for by a high level in others" (p. 415). These results imply that talent detection cannot be based on only one set of supposed prerequisites of excellence. The compensation phenomenon is one of the factors that makes one-shot long-term performance predictions difficult. Use of multilayered task analysis that incorporates a variety of sport science variables, ranging from "hard" morphological measures to "softer" psychological ones, can provide flexible tools to control the phenomenon. For example, Régnier and Salmela (1987) have shown that with a population of gymnasts, measures of speed, power, and strength are adequate for the total prediction of performance results in athletes younger than 12 years of age. However, factors such as perceptual awareness and body orientation, and psychological variables such as anxiety, must also be factored in in order to differentiate between 20-year-old gymnasts at the upper levels of performance. The necessity, however, of multivariate statistics for these monitoring procedures must be emphasized.

Talent Detection or Surveillance? A second major current issue raised at the "Symposium on Talent Problems in Sport" (Bartmus et al., 1987), was the suggestion that, in view of the difficulty of the process, research efforts should be shifted from talent detection to talent guidance and development, or what could be called "talent surveillance." Willimczik, concluding a 5-year longitudinal study with alpine skiers, said that ". . . talent search with respect to individual sports discipline hardly seems possible; only scientifically based support of already identified athletes appears to be indicated" (Bartmus et al., 1987, p. 415).

Mocker took a similar stance by stating that "In the field of talent search, scientifically valid methods do not exist; the judgment of qualified coaches is preferred" (Bartmus et al., 1987, p. 415). He goes on to describe the system of sport schools for children and young people favored by the former East German regime in which a fixed set of norms are to be achieved for a student to progress toward higher levels of training and support. A similar view was taken by Ulmer, who stated that "As a scientifically based talent search is still problematic (. . .), a selection based on success in competition and especially the eye of the coach are most important" (Bartmus et al., 1987, p. 415). Those comments suggest that comprehensive talent detection based on objective scientific criteria is but a utopian viewpoint.

The alternative strategy proposed is a closer surveillance of the development of athletes previously identified as talented by experts in the field such as coaches. Ironically, while German scientists suggest one rely more on coaches and less on unproved scientific testing to detect talent (Bartmus et al, 1987, p. 415), North American coaches and federation officials prefer to have more access to scientific expertise to help them identify talented athletes (Gowan, Botterill, & Blimkie, 1979). This conclusion outlines the importance of combining both resources.

The Interaction Between Heredity and Environment. A third and most important issue in the scientific approach to talent detection is the interaction between the genetic endowment of the athlete and the environmental conditions to realize this potential. "Athletes are obviously products of their genes and their environments, in addition to possessing some characteristics that covary with performance" (Malina & Bouchard, 1986, p. xiii). This interaction, coupled with the fact that part of the athlete's physiological *reaction* to training is also genetically determined (Bouchard, 1986), is at the root of many problems in talent detection endeavors. It is also at the basis of the compensation phenomenon discussed earlier.

The relative contribution of heredity and environment to sports performance is still not well known (Malina & Bouchard, 1986). We do know, however, that both affect the level of performance attained by an athlete.

For example, it has been recognized that performance in marathon races can be predicted by such environmental variables as training intensity and quality (Bale, Bradbury, & Volley, 1986; Campbell, 1985; Foster & Daniels, 1975; McKelvie, Valliant, & Marjatta, 1985). The same has been found for cyclists (Krebs, Zinkgraph, & Virgilio, 1986) and weight lifters (Tonyan & Grigorenko, 1984). The experience of marathon runners has also been used successfully to predict race times (Celestino, Tapp, & Brumet, 1979; Ungerleider, Golding, & Porter, 1989). In-depth interviews done with elite tennis players and swimmers by Bloom (1985) demonstrated convincingly the significant influence on performance of the "environment," which is meant to include the training regimen and the kind of support received from family and coaches.

Although some environmental variables are definitely related to top-level performance, it has been suggested by many scholars that performance predictions can be made only by relying on "stable" variables related to sport success, that is, variables strongly determined genetically and less influenced by the environment (Bulgakova & Voroncov, 1978; Geron, 1978; Gimbel, 1976; Harre, 1982; Havlicek et al., 1982). The genetic component, or "heritability coefficient," of potential performance predictors can be estimated through "twin studies," "sibling studies," and "parent-child studies" (Malina, 1986). Longitudinal studies can also demonstrate the portion of variance accounted for by heredity (Kovar, 1981). Because the hereditary aspect of performance predictors is so much at the heart of the talent detection process, a brief overview of that field of study is warranted.

Twin Studies. Twin studies are done with pairs of monozygotic (MZ) and dizygotic (DZ) twins where both members of each pair are raised in the same environement. If the variable under study is determined mainly by heredity, MZ twins should be more alike on that variable than DZ twins. But if the variable is determined mainly by the environment, within-pair differences (or similarities) should be the same for MZ and DZ twins. Those comparisons are used to compute a "heredity index." Bouchard and Malina (1983), in a comprehensive review of methodological concerns in evaluating the genetics of performance determinants, found that the twin model has some limitations, such as inequality of environmental covariance of MZ and DZ twins, small sample sizes, differential effects of age and sex according to twin types, and differences in means and variances between twin samples. This is why it has been suggested that alternate models, such as the sibling model and the parent-child model, also be used to better estimate the contribution of genetics to sport performance.

So far, research on sport and genetics has been focused mainly on the heritability of morphological, physiological, and motor factors. Few studies have tried to look into the genetic component of psychological factors such as motivation or personality as they relate to sport performance (Malina & Bouchard, 1986). Yet there is evidence, for example, that part of the variation in temperament has a genetic component (Buss & Plomin, 1975, 1984).

It would be beyond the scope of this chapter to look at all the research done on the genetics of performance determinants. The reader is referred to a series of reviews published in the mid-eighties by Canadian scientist Claude Bouchard and his colleagues in which were examined the question of genetics methods in sport studies (Bouchard & Malina, 1983); the genetics of physiological fitness and motor performance (Bouchard & Malina, 1984); the importance of heredity in endurance performance (Bouchard & Lortie, 1984); the general topic of inheritance and the Olympic athletes (Bouchard & Malina, 1984); the role of the genotype in body fat and fat cell metabolism (Després & Bouchard, 1984); and the influences of biological inheritance on maximal aerobic power and capacity (Bouchard, 1986). Kovar (1981) has also reviewed numerous twin studies as well as sibling and parent-offspring studies done in Eastern Europe.

Another valuable review more relevant to the present chapter was done by Malina (1986), who examined the results of studies that deal with estimates of the genotypic contribution to motor development and performance. Twin studies, sibling studies, and parent-child studies looking at the genetics of muscular strength, running, jumping, throwing, balance, speed of limb movement, manual dexterity, coordination, and perceptual characteristics such as spatial abilities, perceptual integration, and reaction time were reviewed extensively. Malina drew the following conclusion:

Estimates of the genotypic component of variance in motor development and performance vary among studies, tasks, and types of genetically related individuals considered. Most of the data are derived from twins, but the results are unequal in quantitative value. Many studies are limited to males or females, while others combine the sexes. Some data from twins also suggest higher heritabilities for males than females. The more limited sibling data suggest a similar trend (. . .) As is the case for most biological traits, the evidence indicates a moderate heritability for many motor tasks with an unknown environmental effect. (p. 53)

On a larger perspective, concluding what was learned from the Eugene Symposium on Human Genetics held at the Olympic Scientific Congress in 1984, Bouchard and Malina (1986) state that:

1. It has been reasserted that the genotype is clearly a major force operating on physiological fitness and health-related conditions.
2. It has been demonstrated that under normal conditions, children's physical growth is largely determined by genetic factors in terms of both the level of growth achieved and the speed of that growth.
3. It has been shown that motor performance tasks are generally influenced by a moderate but significant genetic

effect, with perhaps a higher heritability in males than in females.
4. It has been confirmed that one of the most striking genetic effects is not the average genetic effect measured in the population, but rather the role of the genotype in determining the rate and the amplitude of the response to a chronic stimulation such as exercise training. (p. 184)

Longitudinal Studies. The stability of a specific variable can also be studied through the follow-up, across time, of a group of individuals (Kovar, 1981). By measuring the selected variable periodically and over a long period of time (from 3 to 10 years), and by computing correlation coefficients between measurements taken at different intervals, it is possible to determine if the variable evolves in a constant and predictable manner. Stability measured by such longitudinal studies gives an indirect assessment of the genetic determination of the variable. Variables with a low hereditary influence will have a tendency to behave unstably in longitudinal studies as external stimuli differentially influence the "performance" of each member of the group. The ranking of each member on an unstable variable will fluctuate significantly across time. Even if that variable were strongly related to sports performance, its predictive value would be low, if not negligible.

From the point of view of individual development, it can be presumed that an individual has a certain tendency to stay in a certain development zone the limits of which are determined by genetic norm of reaction. The probability of deviation from the zone increases with the decrease in stability of the given trait (property, ability) and with an extreme environment conditions influence. (p. 132)

Guiding Principles for Sports Talent Detection

After reviewing the talent detection models found in the literature and having looked more closely at some of the problems associated with the process, the following guiding principles for sport talent detection can now be proposed:

- Principle 1: Sport talent detection has to be viewed as a process within the larger context of sport talent development.
- Principle 2: It rests on a long-term prediction of the individual's performance.
- Principle 3: It must take into account each sport's specific demands.
- Principle 4: Since sport performance is multifaceted, sport talent detection must rely on a multidisciplinary approach.
- Principle 5: Sport talent detection must assign a significant role to performance determinants that are strongly determined by heredity.
- Principle 6: It must take into account the dynamic as-

pects of performance, that is, (a) the relative contribution of performance determinants changes with age, and (b) some performance determinants can improve through training and development.

A conceptual model for research in sport talent detection was developed recently by Régnier (1987) based on these six principles. The model will be presented in detail in the next part of this chapter.

CONCEPTUAL MODEL FOR TALENT DETECTION: A FRAMEWORK FOR RESEARCH.

Régnier (1987) proposed a conceptual model for sport talent detection based on orthodox science and the five guiding principles set previously. The model provides a general framework around which research and professional efforts in sport talent detection can be organized to develop detection instruments for any sport setting. It has already been used to support talent detection research in gymnastics (Jancarik & Salmela, 1987; Régnier & Salmela, 1987; Salmela, Régnier, & Proteau, 1987), and baseball (Régnier, 1987). Its broad, multidisciplinary, and multivariate nature can reach all sport scientists as well as experts from all sports discipline. The main concepts of this model are presented here.

Basis for a Sport Talent Detection Instrument

According to the proposed model, there are two basic sets of information essential to the elaboration of a reliable detection instrument for any given sport:

1. a criterion, or a list of criteria, allowing the measurement of the abstract concept of performance
2. an exhaustive list of potential performance determinants

These two sets of variables will be utilized within a well-defined strategy to estimate the probabilities of success of athletes at different periods of their athletic development.

Identification of Performance Criteria. All attempts at talent detection are fundamentally based upon prediction of the future performance of athletes given their present level of attributes and capacities and the environment in which they evolve. The cornerstone of this process is the precise definition of the actual performance desired within the sport context. As Cronbach (1971) outlined, if a performance in any domain is to be predicted, it must be objectively operationalized, using appropriate performance criteria. These performance criteria are made up of the objectives and sub-objectives that are necessarily carried out in order that the participant successfully complete the sport task (Alain & Salmela, 1980; Russell, 1990). The athletes' performance is thus represented, or measured, by the degree

to which these identified objectives and sub-objectives are realized.

This approach may appear to be straightforward, and in many cases, quite obvious, with certain groups of physical activity or sport. This is indeed the case for certain unidimensional sports. A single terminal objective can be identified that represents the very essence of the activity in question and can be transformed into a single operational definition of the required performance. For example, the terminal objective of a swimmer or a runner is to cover a given distance in the shortest possible time; the objective of a discus thrower is to propel the object as far as possible; and the objective of a pole vaulter is to project himself as high as possible. In these activities, the terminal objective obtained, i.e., the performance criterion, is obvious by its unidimensionality: a time, a distance, or a height. It is this latter characteristic that is important, since it is this criterion that the detection talent instrument is ultimately required to predict. Because the process of talent detection is based upon predicting a numerical value of this criterion measure of performance, it is important that this value is a reliable measure of the abstract concept of "performance."

There are a number of sport specializations in which the performance criteria are neither unidimensional nor immediately obvious. This is most evident in team sports. In such multidimensional sports, it is virtually impossible to identify one single variable that could represent the whole concept of athletic success. Sport performance must then be conceived as the combination of numerous miniperformances or as the realization of a number of sub-objectives. Measures of these miniperformances can then be used as criteria representing the multidimensional performance. The multidimensional performance can be broken down into as many subcomponents, or tasks, as possible to get the best picture of what has to be done by the athlete for him or her to be considered successful. But an effort should be made to integrate these tasks into as few criteria as possible so that the interactive aspect of the performance is not lost. For example, in ice hockey, shooting and skating are important tasks. Instead of selecting one criterion for skating and one for shooting, a single criterion combining the tasks of shooting and skating will be more representative of the real task the player has to perform in game situations.

Task Analysis. The identification of these sub-objectives has to be carried out by means of a systematic analysis of the tasks that the athlete is required to perform. This analysis can be done by means of structured observations in a wide variety of sport settings in order to identify the most dominant behavior patterns (Alain & Salmela, 1980). Again, this can be perceived as a "top-down" approach. The task analysis can also be done in a "bottom-up" approach as described earlier by asking athletes themselves to categorize domain-related problems (Russell, 1990).

From a "top-down" perspective, the task analysis can be carried out at least two different ways. One can take the stance that the task analysis must rely on the way the sport activity is contemporarily practiced. This approach rests upon the assumption that the way in which sport is now practiced is the most appropriate, and that no further task dimensions will come into play which an athlete must overcome in order to succeed. This method has the obvious shortcoming that prospective talents have been detected using qualities that are no longer necessary and, in fact, may prevent the athlete from reaching upper levels of sport performance (Csikszentmihalyi & Robinson, 1986).

A good example of this shift in task requirements occurred when women's gymnastics began to favor "hair-raising" acrobatics rather than graceful artistry, thus favoring small young ectomorphs over graceful, mature mesomorphs. Another good example is found in North American ice hockey. As the teams started to favor a strategy based more on stopping the opponent than on creating an offense (the so-called "anti-hockey"), players' characteristics shifted from small, fast, skillful, and imaginative to large, robust, and unidimensional. This might explain why so many small North American hockey players are exporting their talent to Europe, where larger rinks and a different approach to the game suit their profile better.

The second viewpoint subscribes to the premise that the most efficient means of achieving excellence in sport remains to be discovered and must be determined via hypothetical conceptual models. In team games, for example, these models can be based upon the elaboration of a system of operations based upon principles of attack other than those used conventionally. It may be that the necessary qualities that an athlete must possess will be based upon this new system of operations that is for the moment hypothetical, or temporarily out of style. One might predict a return to artistry in gymnastics and to creativity in North American hockey.

From a "bottom-up" perspective, Russell (1990) found, for example, that highly skilled athletes, when asked to define their sport tasks situations, emphasized metacognitive knowledge and skills rather than focusing on the physical or technical aspects of their sport performance. It is suggested that performers of different skill levels might focus on different aspects of the task. "Novices, for example, may stress the physical demands of training, while middle-level performers might focus on technical skills, and highly skilled athletes emphasize metacognitive task components" (p. 93).

The adoption of one or another of these three perspectives may result in the identification of very different tasks perceived to have to be performed. The underlying assumptions regarding the actual state of knowledge in a given sport discipline must be considered before developing a detection instrument.

In summary, it is important to consider, in the definition of sport performance and the elaboration of the measurement criteria, that for certain sport activities the performance criterion may be directly obtained because of the unidimensional nature of the task to be accomplished. However, for certain complex tasks of either an individual or team nature, it is necessary to break down the performance of the athlete in terms of sub-objectives that must be accomplished. These composite units must be systematically analyzed using an extensive task analysis. Finally, each group of related sub-objectives must be represented by an appropriate integrated measure that will serve as one of the performance criteria.

Identification of Performance Determinants. Once the performance has been appropriately and clearly defined according to the identified sub-objectives, a second task analysis must be carried out. This analysis is aimed at the determination of the underlying factors that are most probably necessary and sufficient for the athlete to attain each of the previously specified objectives. This is based on the assumption that such underlying factors do exist, a popular, although not the only, hypothesis relating individual differences to sport excellence (Kroll, 1970).

These suspected performance determinants are found among the various morphological, organic, perceptual-motor, psychological, and environmental characteristics of an athlete (Bouchard, Brunelle, & Godbout, 1973). This second task analysis is carried out based upon the existing literature within the specific domain and preferably in collaboration with experts within each area, in order that the best multidimensional list of determinants might be compiled. It is from this list of identified variables that the various performance predictors must eventually emerge.

As much as possible, selected predictors must be factors that are "stable," e.g., strongly determined genetically (Bulgakova & Voroncov, 1978; Geron, 1978; Gimbel, 1976; Harre, 1982; Havlicek et al., 1982). Predictions will have more chance to materialize if they are based upon variables with a well-known developmental profile. However, unstable factors should not be excluded completely (Gimbel, 1976; Havlicek et al., 1982). The proposed model allows for a weighting of predictions according to the levels of stability (or instability) of the selected variables. This stability will be measured by a hereditary index as described earlier (Malina, 1986).

A Strategy for Predicting Performance: The Sliding Populations Approach

Accounting for the Dynamic Nature of Performance. Any sound sport talent detection strategy must take into consideration the dynamic nature of sport performance (the criteria) and its underlying elements (the performance determinants). There are two dimensions to this dynamic interaction. First, the relative importance of a particular determinant required to achieve success in a given sport may vary from one stage of learning and development to another (Fleishman, 1972). For example, it was found that while general organic variables such as speed and strength were explaining a large amount of variance in gymnastics performance at age 12, the performance at age 20 depended more upon specific organic factors such as upper body power and by psychological variables such as personality (Régnier & Salmela, 1987).

Second, the performance determinants underlying successful performances and related to the individual (morphological, organic, psychological, and perceptual-motor) may be influenced by growth, development, and training, making one-shot long-term predictions unreliable, especially for athletes during their prepubertal or pubertal periods (Bulgakova & Voroncov, 1978; Geron, 1978; Gimbel, 1976; Harre, 1982; Havlicek et al., 1982).

The use of longitudinal studies is a very reliable way to deal with those two dynamic dimensions (Nesselroade & Baltes, 1979). It allows, through the close follow-up of a group of athletes in a given sport over the period of their athletic development, the identification at different stages of learning and development of a number of key factors that seem to relate to success (Rogosa, 1979). Those key factors make up the detection instrument which then has to be tested on another generation of athletes in order to evaluate its efficiency in detecting top-level performance in the sport (Rogosa, 1979).

Seefeldt (1988), after reviewing the literature on the prediction of the rate of motor skill acquisition, concluded that:

> Virtually all of the investigators (. . .) reported the retrospective prediction of success, often through the use of regression equations that were obtained from cross-sectional studies or computed at the termination of longitudinal studies. None of the investigators attempted to predict the success of individuals in motor performance prior to their involvement in activity programs, nor did they conduct a longitudinal follow-up to determine the accuracy of the original predictions. In no case were the predictive equations applied to other samples as a test of their validity. (pp. 49–50)

Although this approach promoted by Seefeldt is a rigorous one, it also has the important drawback of being very time consuming. The delays involved in producing and testing a detection instrument are so significant that by the time one becomes operational, it might very well be obsolete. This holds especially true for sports characterized by the frequent introduction of new trends, such as judgment sports (gymnastics, figure skating, diving) and some team sports, thus shifting the relative importance of the qualities required to achieve success. This might explain why Seefeldt found no studies reporting a strict application of this procedure for the prediction of motor skill acquisition.

The Sliding Populations. An alternative to the arduous process of longitudinal studies is the "sliding populations" approach (Régnier, 1987), a mixture of the longitudinal and the cross-sectional designs. This is based on the principle that "the reliability of prognosis (. . .) is in inverse proportion to the length of the period for which it is intended to be valid" (Bartmus, Neumann, & de Marées, 1987, p. 416). This process leads to a much faster coverage of the athletes' developmental period while still taking into consideration the dynamic stages of performance. Instead of following the same population of athletes from childhood to maturity, it is suggested that the process be broken down into a num-

ber of smaller steps that can be carried out simultaneously. The developmental continuum should be broken down into different age groups. For every age group or *pool population,* a detection instrument is designed that will allow the estimation of the probability for the athletes from the pool population of reaching the elite level of the following age group, or the *target population.*

For instance, in the example illustrated in Figure 12–2, a detection instrument would be designed to estimate the probabilities of 10-year-old athletes reaching the target population made up of 13-year-old elite athletes. Another instrument would be elaborated to estimate the probabilities of 13-year-old athletes reaching the target population made up of 15-year-old athletes and so on, until a total dynamic developmental profile can be constructed as the comparisons slide across the various populations.

These instruments can all be designed simultaneously by means of a cross-sectional approach. Procedures to follow to elaborate those detection instruments are presented in the next part of this chapter.

During the application stage of the model, each pool population should include a sufficient number of individuals so that potentially good athletes are not left out of the detection process (Csikszentmihalyi & Robinson, 1986, Gimbel, 1976; Montpetit & Cazorla, 1982). Pool-populations for an age group should not be composed of the same individuals used as a target population for the preceding pool-population. In order to prevent late bloomers from escaping detection, pool populations should also include those individuals who barely missed attaining the level of the preceding target population. This is particularly important during the puberty period, when attributes and capacities can improve dramatically over short periods of time due to growth characteristics, turning 14-year-old doubtful prospects into 15-year-old top contenders.

Nevertheless, as time progresses, the population of "successful" athletes becomes smaller and smaller. It also becomes more homogeneous with respect to skill acquisition and psychological factors because of the dropout phenom-

Detection Instrument 1

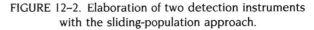

Detection Instrument 2

FIGURE 12–2. Elaboration of two detection instruments with the sliding-population approach.

enon. Csikszentmihalyi and Robinson (1986) describe this phenomenon common to all fields of excellence:

... the youngsters who were not performing at the top in a previous stage are usually no longer in contention for "gifted" status by the time that status and its attendant support change in ways that might benefit them. In highly competitive domains, such as music, math, or sports, the way down is always much broader then the way up; year by year, it becomes more difficult to catch up, and dropping out becomes increasingly easy. (p. 275)

Therefore, even if a "catch-up" phase is built into the detection system, the tools applied for measurement should be more and more sensitive as finer and finer differences must be uncovered across time because of the "dropout" phenomenon.

The Dropouts Among the Talented. In addition to providing alternate reentry routes to limit the number of false negatives (individuals not detected but who eventually become successful), the dropout phenomenon should also be carefully scrutinized for a better understanding of why "successful" candidates leave the development system. A most interesting conceptual framework for studying the dropout phenomenon within a population of talented individuals has been presented by Csikszentmihalyi and Robinson (1986). It looks at the dropout problem of talented youngsters in view of Erikson's map of psychosocial development. The three major crises of identity (adolescence), intimacy (late adolescence), and generativity (young adulthood) are seen as inevitable crossroads where the talented performer might decide to restructure him-or herself around new goals.

Although these conflicts have long been recognized, it has been generally assumed that real genius perseveres despite all the upheavals of the life cycle. "Talent will out" is the common opinion; those who are distracted from its relentless unfolding are obviously the weak and the less gifted. But (...) perhaps it is the most talented people, the ones more sensitive to the possibilities of existence, who drop out of the single-minded pursuit necessary to maintain excellence in a domain of giftedness. (p. 273).

This statement seems to be supported by the results of a study by Jerome, Weese, Plyley, Klavora, and Wiley (1987), who found that gymnasts who were persistent and successful were more obedient, docile, submissive, dependent, and less "socially intelligent" than those who abandoned the sport.

Many other conceptual models designed to discover the underlying factors responsible for dropouts have been developed and could be used as framework for research on dropouts within the particular population of above-average talented individuals in the context of talent detection and development (Ewing, 1981; Gould, 1987; Gould & Petlichkoff, 1988; Roberts, 1984; Smith, 1986).

Variable Contributions of Determinants. The other dynamic dimension of sport performance, the variation for different age groups of the relative importance of performance determinants (Fleishman, 1972), is controlled by the elaboration of a different detection instrument for every pool-population/target-population couple. This approach allows the identification of relevant predictor variables to be adapted to the performance requirements of each group (Csikszentmihalyi & Robinson, 1986).

The sliding populations approach is a dynamic concept for talent detection in sport. It accounts for all the dynamic dimensions of sport performance and for its underlying elements and it speeds up the process of elaborating detection instruments when compared to the longitudinal approach.

Elaboration of the Detection Tool

A specific detection tool has to be designed for every pool-population/target-population couple on the age continuum. First, a performance criterion, or a set of performance criteria relevant for the age group of the target population, must be established (Cronbach, 1971). The second step is to conduct a comprehensive task analysis from which an exhaustive list of potential performance determinants is drawn. The objective of this elaboration phase is to identify from the list of determinants those that represent, as a group, the best set of performance predictors (Kroll, 1970).

A few statistical precautions must be kept in mind. In talent detection research, it has been quite common to use regression analysis techniques on data collected from elite athletes to identify the best performance predictors. It has been suggested that the factors found to predict performance at the elite level can be used as a talent detection tool on populations of younger athletes. It is, of course, statistically incorrect to use a regression equation on a different population from the one for which it has been developed (Nesselroade & Baltes, 1979).

Rulon, Tiedman, Tatsuoka, and Langmuir (1967) proposed an elegant way to bypass this restriction. They suggest the use of discriminant analysis to weight the regression equation with the differences existing a priori between the two populations. In order to do so, the suspected performance determinants of a sample of the pool-population and of a sample of the target-population have to be measured. This is the third step of the elaboration phase. Then, in the fourth step, a discriminant analysis is conducted on those data in order to (1) identify the combination of variables that best discriminate between both populations, and (2) produce the classification equation needed during the application phase of the detection tool to determine the percentage of "similarity" between a member of a new sample of the pool population and the members of the original target population. The performance determinants identified through discriminant analysis can then be viewed as prerequisites for those pool-population members who are to reach the target population.

An important value of the set of variables making up the discriminant function rests in their "developmental stability," or predictability. The more a variable related to performance develops in a predictable fashion over the years, the more valuable it is for talent detection purposes. As already stated above, studies on heredity and sport performance are yielding essential information on the degree of stability of some variables by measuring their heredity coefficient, i.e., what part of their total variance is accounted for by genetics (Malina, 1986). A strong heredity factor means the variable develops in a predictable way and is thus much useful for talent detection.

It is most probable that each variable from the set of discriminating variables will not have the same degree of stability. It is suggested that each one be weighted by its coefficient of heredity. Thus, stable discriminant variables will be attributed more importance in the classification equation. The classification equation is used in the application phase to estimate what probability a member of the pool population has to "make" the target population (Rulon et al., 1967).

Thus a "stability index" will be assigned to each variable included in the discriminant equation. This index is simply calculated by adding 1 to the heredity coefficient. The effect is that variables with a larger heredity coefficient will see their contribution to the classification equation raised substantially, while the influence of the discriminant variables having a low heredity coefficient will be restrained.

The fifth and last step of the elaboration phase is to conduct a regression analysis on a sample of athletes taken from the target population to identify which variables can best predict success among that group of performers (Rulon et al., 1967). That regression analysis must be performed using only the variables included in the discriminant equation found in step four. The performance criterion identified in step one is used as the regression criterion.

The regression analysis is used to (1) determine the variables that best predict performance among the target population, and (2) produce the regression equation that will be used in conjunction with the results from the discriminant analysis to evaluate the probability of success of an athlete taken from a new sample of the pool population (Rulon et al., 1967).

Summary

This model incorporates all the guiding principles underlying sport talent detection into a step-by-step approach to developing talent detection instruments. It emphasizes the importance of having a well-defined and measurable performance concept since the prediction of performance is the ultimate goal of the entire process. It stresses the necessity of relying on a multidisciplinary and a multivariate approach to reflect the complexity of sports performance determinants. This translates into the use of multivariate statistical analysis techniques to account for the numerous interactions between morphological, physiological, psy-

chological, and environmental factors involved in the development of athletic success.

Through the "sliding populations" approach, the model suggests a way to reduce the time and resources needed to develop an exhaustive picture of the talent development process while recognizing the different requirements associated with different career stages. Finally, the model includes stability indexes in order to "hierarchize" the performance determinants according to their level of genetic determination, which should make the predictions more reliable.

It is believed that this model represents a valuable framework for research and professional efforts directed at sport talent detection. Such efforts have been rather timid in certain parts of the world otherwise recognized for their sport science production. The next part of this chapter will look at some of the more practical issues that might explain why the field of sport talent detection has been receiving little attention in many countries.

PRACTICAL ISSUES IN SPORT TALENT DETECTION

A decade ago, while Canadian sport technical directors ranked talent detection by priority just behind coach education and athlete preparation (Gowan, Botterill, & Blimkie, 1979), a survey of Canadian sport scientists ranked talent identification as their last priority of the potential professional tasks related to sports practice. Sport psychologists around the world also gave it a similar low ranking, although researchers from Eastern Europe were less severe in absolute rankings of this area of endeavor (Salmela, 1981, 1984, 1991).

Although the problem has been recognized since then by North American sports administrators (Hoffman, 1982), theoretical and practical work on sport talent detection still comes mostly from Eastern European countries, while there has been a smattering of effort in Canada (Régnier, 1987; Régnier & Salmela, 1983; Régnier, Salmela, & Alain, 1982; Salmela & Régnier, 1983), in France (Montpetit & Cazorla, 1982) and earlier on, in Germany (Bartmus et al., 1987; Gimbel, 1976; Harre, 1982).

In an attempt to discover why talent detection has been neglected in many countries, the following part will first present the most commonly heard reservations about the area of talent identification that come from both scientists and sport practitioners and then attempt to address each point. Special attention will be given to issues related to both athletes and coaches and to the tasks to be performed.

The Athlete

Talent Elimination or Guidance. One of the most common reservations heard when the question of talent detection arises is that the term evokes the loss of choice to participate in a given sport, or the elimination from a particular team. Perhaps it is at this level where the criticisms are most crucial and the whole process has to be reconsidered within a broader, more human framework. It goes without saying that the best interests of the athlete must be maintained as a central focus of the process. It is true that at a young age an athlete does not always possess the attributes and capacities shown to be essential to successful champions in a given sport. A rigid system of talent detection applied mechanically at this point in time might needlessly eliminate someone who through growth, maturation, and training evolves into an individual who could well succeed later.

One of the most predictable things in people is that they change over their lifetimes in the most unpredictable ways. The psychological set that one brings to a given sport has been shown to be particularly sensitive to changes in relationships, finances, success, and the aging process itself. The sport world is full of examples of individuals who did not possess the necessary qualities in their youth but were able to compensate for these deficiencies through diligent training. Naturally, at the recreational or youth sport level, there is no reason for any form of elimination whatsoever, as might occur in the top amateur or professional ranks. There might be a case made, however, for talent guidance rather than talent elimination at the younger ages.

Talent guidance in the sport world is not unlike job counseling within an industrial setting. Athletes belonging to a general sport community or club system might be best served by having their predicted attributes and capacities matched with those activities that are most compatible and then guided to these disciplines. For example, the predicted 1.77-meter adult height of a young female gymnast might be best used as a reason to guide this individual into a sport such as synchronized swimming, diving, or rhythmic gymnastics, where her height would be an asset, not a handicap. It might also be possible to maintain within the program athletes with inappropriate attributes who participate at the recreational level only. Sport "placement" of this nature could occur following the application of talent identification programs in an attempt to increase "job" satisfaction.

Individual or Third-Party Decisions. There has also been some resistance to talent detection programs because these procedures seem to go against the free-choice attitudes toward sport. Sport science, and more particularly, sport psychology evaluation, are looked upon skeptically when there is a talent detection, selection, or guidance decision waiting at the end of the process. There is certainly a justifiable threat of invasion of privacy of individuals if they must be subjected to either physical or psychological testing so that they can either be selected for or cut from a youth sport team. The ethical guidelines presented by such sport psychology bodies as SCAPPS (1984) certainly cover these practices in free-play or recreational-sport situations.

There may, however, be a case made for the use of sport talent detection screening processes when an athlete approaches either a professional team or a national sport federation for a team position, and whose performance outcomes directly affect matters such as profit margins or national sport reputations. This situation parallels that of a job applicant approaching a company for a position when the company requests an application, an interview, reference checks, and a physical or psychological examination prior to engaging this potential talent.

In the latter situation, the company requires third-party evaluation of the candidate in order to carry out the particular goals of its operation. Similarly, high-level or professional athletes should recognize that the specific sport organization needs to gather this talent potential information to realize its often clearly stated goals of winning. The athlete is now in a similar position of the job applicant's freely chosen position. In this sense, talent detection or selection cannot be compared to psychological wire-tapping, unwarranted search, or opening of personal mail (Miner, 1969).

The Coach

At the NCAA gymnastics championships in the 1970s, a top American college coach was asked to deliver a luncheon address to his fellow coaches on his secret for success. This particular individual had achieved remarkable success in a relatively short time period. He quickly got to the point: "Gentlemen, I have for you the secret to success in gymnastics. Salemanship. Get me those horses, and I'll drive them."

As it is in business, top-level North American coaches' success is often based upon attracting to their instruction the candidates who have the best potential. In the case above, the task of predicting success in the future is somewhat easier, since short-term anticipated performances can be better predicted from actual recent past performances than they can by more subtle aptitudes that may be prerequisites to this performance. This passive method of talent identification is often used in North America. The underlying principle is to provide space and equipment for a large number of athletes, let them practice for 10 years, and then skim the cream from the top. This method has serious limitations when the population for a given sport is very small, usually the case when the sport is not intrinsically attractive to the performer. What factors might limit the potential use of talent identification procedures as viewed from the perspective of the coach? The dimensions of economy, scientific expertise, and the validity of sport science predictions immediately come to mind.

Economy of Talent Identification

One of the most frequently heard quotes from coaches and sports administrators in relation to talent identification procedures is, "Just let me see the athlete for a few moments in the gym, and then I'll tell you if the right stuff is there." In many cases, these gifted experts are very apt at spotting gifted athletes by "eyeballing" them. And perhaps it would be worthwhile studying just what pertinent dimensions these experts do detect, and communicating this information to others. As Ulmer states, "As a scientifically based talent search is still problematic, a selection based on success in competition and especially the eye of the coach [is] most important" (Bartmus et al., 1987, p. 417).

However, a recent study in youth baseball carried out in Quebec revealed that a simple but task-specific set of performance variables could differentiate the top players in an elite league from those who could not make the selected all-star team (Régnier, 1987). In fact, the selection based upon this test battery mirrored exactly the choices the coaches had made. One might then say, why use testing procedures when the coaches select the same players? For one reason, it would be more economical, in North America at least, to apply the selected tests over a large population than it would be to have specialized coaches travel from coast to coast.

One other advantage of this form of testing concerns diagnostic purposes. There is an objective measure available, such as a running time in seconds, rather than the simple perception that "He or she is fast!" The athlete can be compared to others in the various parameters of the sport. Testing devices can be used for training since they are in themselves highly motivational. Improvements in certain performance attributes may be seen to improve, even if overall performance does not, and these partial improvements are satisfying to the athlete. Commenting on the possibilities and limitations of talent detection in general and in swimming in particular during a symposium on talent in sports (Bartmus et al., 1987), Germans Ungerechts and Planert summarized this position in stating that "the experience of the coach—an important component of talent finding—should be supplemented by scientific research" (p. 417).

Assuming that willing sport scientists are available to provide support to willing coaches, is it effective to invest time, and perhaps money, in sport science/psychology talent screening or guidance? In certain mass participation sports such as swimming, in which a pool can be filled with hundreds of kids and career length is short, perhaps the answer may be no. In activities in which the coach-athlete ratio is low and top performances result after 7 to 10 years of training, the opposite may be true. Training for such a "first career" in sport can often take longer than specialized medical studies. Wrong decisions are costly in time, energy, and money.

Adoption of early-warning talent identification devices can provide an effective device for "hiring" (selecting) and "placing" (guiding) athletes in satisfying activities that match their personal qualities, rather than just "firing" (cutting) athletes or allowing them to eventually "quit" (retire from) a sport after a long but unsatisfying "career."

CONCLUDING REMARKS

The area of talent detection in sport is a central concern to coaches and researchers in the sport sciences in that the notion of predicting future performance based on present knowledge underlies the competitive process. It is somewhat surprising that such an engaging enterprise has received so little scientific attention from a broad conceptual viewpoint. This theoretical void may be due in part to the reductionist processes of science, which tend to look at increasingly narrow components of human endeavor, thus compartmentalizing inherently complex realities into simpler but often meaningless units of study.

The present chapter has tried to address this overly reductionist approach in two ways. If a conventional "top-down" approach to the study of talent detection is adopted, then this process must include a multidisciplinary, multivariate approach that is extended over a certain minimum duration including at least two stages of the career of an athlete. It thus becomes clear that such a procedure will be costly and time consuming, but potentially profitable.

The other alternative is the "bottom-up" approach, using knowledge acquisition procedures that would center upon existing experts whose knowledge base would be sampled in order to better understand the antecedents of their expertise. This process requires a somewhat different scientific orientation, because of the qualitative nature of the data. Case studies through in-depth interviews of exceptional athletes and biographic data obtained from their relatives, coaches, and friends provide a longitudinal portrait of the development of athletic talent, which, in turn, can be used to detect future outstanding performers. The big picture is intact, but the determination of the appropriate underlying mechanisms is less evident than in the more orthodox approach. The multiplicity of unique combinations of determinants used by athletes to achieve success is also underlined in a more obvious manner with this approach.

Both orientations are fraught with their inherent methodological limitations, and neither provides a simple and economical solution to the process. However, considering the fact that we are attempting to predict inherently variable human behavior in such a complex environment as sport, one would not expect a simple recipe as a solution.

References

Abernethy, B. (1987). Selective attention in fast ball sports II: On expert-novice differences. *Australian Journal of Science and Medicine in Sport, 19,* 7–16.

Ackland, T. R., Bloomfield, J., Elliot, B. C., & Blanksby, B. A. (1990). Talent identification for tennis and swimming. *Journal of Sport Sciences, 8,* 161–162.

Alain, C., & Salmela, J. H. (1980). Analyse des demandes perceptivo-motrices des tâches sportives. *Cahiers de psychologie, 23,* 77–86.

Aronson, R. M. (1981). *Attentional and interpersonal factors as discriminators of elite and non-elite gymnasts.* Unpublished doctoral dissertation, Boston University.

Astrand, P. O., & Rodahl, K. (1986). *Textbook of work physiology.* New York: McGraw-Hill.

Bale, P., Bradbury, D., & Volley, E. (1983). Anthropometric and training variables related to 10 km running performance. *British Journal of Sport Medicine, 17,* 170–173.

Bard, C., Fleury, M., & Goulet, C. (in press). Relationship between strategies and response adequacy in sport situations. *International Journal of Sport Psychology.*

Bar-Or, O. (1975). Predicting athletic performance. *The Physician and Sports Medicine, 3,* 81–85.

Bartmus, U., Neumann, E., & de Marées, H. (1987). The talent problem in sports. *International Journal of Sports Medicine, 8,* 415–416.

Blahüs, P. (1975). (For the prediction of performance capacity in the selection of youth talented for sports). *Téorie a Praxe Telesne Vycshovy, 24,* 471–477.

Bloom, B. S. (1985). *Developing talent in the young.* New York: Ballantine.

Bompa, T. O. (1985). Talent identification. *Science Periodical on Research and Technology in Sport* (February). Ottawa: Coaching Association of Canada.

Boose, J., & Gaines, B. (1988). *Knowledge acquisition tools for expert systems (Vol. 2).* Toronto: Academic Press.

Bouchard, C. (1986). Genetics of aerobic power and capacity. In R. M. Malina & C. Bouchard (Eds.), *Sport and human genetics* (pp. 59–88). Champaign, IL: Human Kinetics.

Bouchard, C., Brunelle, J., & Godbout, P. (1973). *La préparation d'un champion.* Quebec: Pelican.

Bouchard, C., & Lortie, G. (1984). Heredity and endurance training. *Sports Medicine, 1,* 38–64.

Bouchard, C., & Malina, R. M. (1983a). Genetics for the sport scientist: Selected methodological considerations. *Exercise and Sport Sciences Reviews, 11,* 275–305.

Bouchard, C., & Malina, R. M. (1983b). Genetics of physiological fitness and motor performance. *Exercise and Sport Sciences Reviews, 11,* 306–339.

Bouchard, C., & Malina, R. M. (1984). Genetics and Olympic athletes: A discussion of methods and issues. In J. E. L. Carter (Ed.), *Kinanthropometry of Olympic athletes* (pp. 28–38). Basel, Switzerland: Karger.

Bulgakova, N. S., & Voroncov, A. R. (1978). (How to predict talent in swimmers using longitudinal studies). *Teoriza y practika, 7,* 37–40.

Buss, A. H., & Plomin, R. (1975). *A temperament of personality development.* New York: Wiley.

Buss, A. H., & Plomin, R. (1984). *Temperament: Early developing personality traits.* Hillsdale, NJ: Erlbaum.

Calderone, G., Berlutti, G., Leglise, M., Giastella, G., & Mulanori, M. (1987). Caractéristiques morphologiques et biotypie des gymnastes juniors masculins et féminins européens. In B. Pétiot, J. H. Salmela., & B. Hoshizaki (Eds.), *World identification systems for gymnastic talent* (pp. 62–76). Montreal: Sport Psyche Editions.

Callan, V. J., & Gallois, C. (1984). Perceptions of contraceptive methods: A multidimensional scaling analysis. *Journal of Biosocial Science, 18,* 277–286.

Campbell, M. (1975). Predicting running speed from a simple questionnaire. *British Journal of Sport Medicine, 19,* 142–144.

Carron, A. V. (1975). Personality and athletics: A review. In B. S. Rushall (Ed.), *The status of motor learning and sport psychology research* (pp. 5.1–5.12). Dartmouth, Nova Scotia: Sport Science Associates.

Carter, J. E. L. (1970). The somatotypes of athletes: A review. *Human Biology, 42,* 535–539.

Celestino, R., Tapp., J., & Brumet, M. (1979). Locus of control correlates with marathon performance. *Perceptual and Motor Skills, 48,* 1249–1250.

Chase, W. G., & Simon, H. A. (1973a). Perception in chess. *Cognitive Psychology, 4,* 55–81.

Chase, W. G., & Simon, H. A. (1973b). The mind's eye in chess. In W. G. Chase (Ed.), *Visual information processing* (pp. 215–282). New York: Academic Press.

Chi, M. T. H., Glaser, R., & Rees, E. (1982). Expertise in problem solving. Reprinted from R. J. Sternberg (Ed.), *Advances in the psychology of human intelligence* (Vol. 1, pp. 7–75). Hillsdale, NJ: Erlbaum.

Cronbach, L. J. (1971). Test validation. In R. L. Thorndike (Ed.), *Educational measurement,* 2nd ed., pp. 443–507. Washington, DC: American Council on Education.

Csikszentmihalyi, M., & Robinson, R. E. (1986). Culture, time and development of talent. In R. J. Sternberg & J. E. Davidson (Eds.), *Conceptions of giftedness* (pp. 264–284). Cambridge: Cambridge University Press.

De Groot, A. (1966). Perception and memory versus thought: Some old ideas and recent findings. In B. Kleinmuntz (Ed.), *Problem solving* (pp. 19–49). New York: Wiley.

Deshaies, P., Pargman, D., & Thiffault, C. (1979). A psychobiological profile of individual performance in junior hockey players. In G. G. Roberts & K. M. Newell (Eds.), *Psychology of motor behavior and sport—1978* (pp. 36–50). Champaign, IL: Human Kinetics.

Després, J. P., & Bouchard, C. (1984). Monozygotic twin resemblance in fatness and fat cell lypolysis. *Acta Geneticae et Gemellologiae, 33,* 475–480.

Dewey, D., Brawley, L., & Allard, F. (1989). Do the TAIS attentional style scales predict how information is processed? *Journal of Sport and Exercise Psychology, 11,* 171–186.

Dreke, B. (1982, June). (*Experience from a selection of talented children and youth for the training in performance sport.*) Paper presented at the International Conference on Selection and Preparation of Sport Talent. Bratislava, Czechoslovakia.

Erikson, E. H. (1963). *Childhood and society* (2nd ed.). New York: Norton.

Ewing, M. E. (1981). *Achievement orientations and sport behavior of males and females.* Unpublished doctoral dissertation, University of Illinois, Urbana-Champaign.

Feldman, D. H. (1986). Giftedness as a developmentalist sees it. In R. J. Sternbeg & J. E. Davidson (Eds.), *Conceptions of giftedness* (pp. 285–305). Cambridge: Cambridge University Press.

Fenz, W. D., & Epstein, S. (1962). Measurement of approach-avoidance conflict along a stimulus dimension by a thematic aperception test. *Journal of Personality, 30*, 613–632.

Fisher, A. C. (1977). Sport personality assessment: Adversary proceedings. In R. E. Stadulis, C. O. Dotson, V. L. Katch, & J. Schick (Eds.), *Research and practice in physical education* (pp. 174–175). Champaign, IL: Human Kinetics.

Fleishman, E. A. (1972). Structure and measurement of psychomotor abilities. In R. N. Singer (Ed.), *The psychomotor domain* (pp. 78–106). Philadelphia: Lea & Febiger.

Forgas, J. P. (1979a). *Social episodes: The study of interaction routines*. London: Academic Press.

Forgas, J. P. (1979b). Multidimensional scaling: A discovery method in social psychology. In G. P. Ginsburg (Ed.), *Emerging strategies in social psychology* (pp. 253–288). London: Wiley.

Foster, C., & Daniels, J. (1975). Running by the numbers. *Runner's World Magazine, 10*, 14–17.

French, K. E., & Thomas, J. R. (1987). The relation of knowledge development to children's basketball performance. *Journal of Sport Psychology, 9*, 15–32.

Friend, J., & LeUnes, A. (1990), Predicting baseball player performance. *Journal of Sport Behavior, 13*, 73–86.

Gaines, B., & Boose, J. (1988). *Knowledge acquisition tools for expert systems (Vol. 1)*. Toronto: Academic Press.

Geron, E. (1978). Psychological assessment of sport giftedness. In U. Simri (Ed.), *Proceedings of the international symposium on psychological assessment in sport* (pp. 216–231). Netanya, Israel: Wingate Institute.

Gimbel, B. (1976). (Possibilities and problems in sports talent detection research.) *Leistungssport, 6*, 159–167.

Glueck, W. F. (1974). *Personnel: A diagnostic approach*. Dallas: Business Publications.

Gould, D. (1987). Understanding attrition in children's sport. In D. Gould & M. R. Weiss (Eds.), *Advances in pediatric sport sciences—Behavioral Issues* (pp. 61–85). Champaign, IL: Human Kinetics.

Gould, D., & Petlichkoff, L. (1988). Participation motivation and attrition in young athletes. In F. L. Smoll, R. A. Magill, & M. J. Ash (Eds.), *Children in sport* (3rd ed., pp. 161–178). Champaign, IL: Human Kinetics.

Gould, D., Weiss, M., & Weinberg, R. (1981). Psychological characteristics of successful and non-successful Big Ten wrestlers. *Journal of Sport Psychology, 3*, 69–81.

Goulet, C. (1990). *Stratégies perceptives et expertise lors de la préparation au retour de service au tennis*. (Perceptual strategies and expertise during the preparation for a tennis serve return) Unpublished doctoral dissertation, Laval University, Quebec, Canada.

Gowan, G. R., Botterill, C. B., & Blimkie, C. J. R. (1979). Bridging the gap between sport science and sport practice. In P. Klavora, & J. V. Daniels (Eds.), *Coach, athlete and the sport psychologist* (pp. 3–9). Toronto: University of Toronto.

Grabiner, M. D., & McKelvain, R. (1987). Implementation of a profiling/prediction test battery in the screening of elite gymnasts. In B. Petiot, J. H. Salmela, & B. Hoshizaki (Eds.), *World identification systems for gymnastic talent* (pp. 121–125). Montreal: Sport Psyche Editions.

Guilford, J. P. (1956). *Fundamental statistics in psychology and education*. New York: McGraw-Hill.

Harre, D. (1982). *Trainingslehre*. Berlin: Sportverlag.

Havlicek, I., Komadel, L., Komarik, E., & Simkova, N. (1982, June). (*Principles of the selection of youth talented in sport*). Paper presented at the International Conference on the Selection and Preparation of Sport Talent. Bratislava, Czechoslovakia.

Hay, J. G. (1969). Rowing: An analysis of the New Zealand Olympic selection tests. *The Research Quarterly for Exercise and Sport, 40*, 83–90.

Heilbrun, A. B. (1966). Testing for potentialities. In H. A. Otto (Ed.), *Explorations in human potentialities* (pp. 286–298). Springfield, IL: Thomas.

Highlen, P. S., & Bennett, B. B. (1979). Psychological characteristics of successful and unsuccessful elite wrestlers: An exploratory study. *Journal of Sport Psychology, 1*, 123–137.

Hoffman, A. (1982, November). Televised interview of Abigail Hoffman, Director of Sports-Canada, after the 1982 Commonwealth Games.

Hopkins, D. R. U. (1979). Using skill tests to identify successful and unsuccessful basketball performers. *The Research Quarterly, 50*, 381–387.

Hudson, J. L. (1985). Prediction of baseball skill using biomechanical variables. *Research Quarterly for Exercise and Sport, 56*, 115–121.

Jancarik, A., & Salmela, J. H. (1987). Longitudinal changes in physical, organic and perceptual factors in Canadian elite male gymnasts. In B. Petiot, J. H. Salmela, & B. Hoshizaki (Eds.), *World identification systems for gymnastic talent* (pp. 151–159). Montreal: Sport Psyche Editions.

Jerome, W., Weese, R., Plyley, M., Klavora, P., & Howley, T. (1987). The Seneca gymnastics experience. In J. H. Salmela, B. Petiot, & T. B. Hoshizaki (Eds.), *Psychological nurturing and guidance of gymnastic talent* (pp. 90–118). Montreal: Sport Psyche Editions.

Jones, M. B., & Watson, G. G. (1977). Psychological factors in the prediction of athletic performance. In U. Simri (Ed.), *Proceedings of the international symposium on psychological assessment in sport* (pp. 89–102). Netanya, Israel: Wingate Institute.

Kelly, G. A. (1955). *The psychology of personal constructs*. New York: Norton.

Kerr, R., Dainty, D., Booth, M., Gaboriault, G., & McGavern, R. (1979). Talent identification for competitive diving. In P. Klavora & K. A. W. Wipper (Eds.), *Psychological and sociological factors in sport* (pp. 270–276). Toronto: University of Toronto, School of Physical and Health Education.

Kovar, R. (1981). *Human variation in motor abilities and its genetic analysis*. Prague: CSTV, Charles University.

Kroll, W. (1967). Reliability theory and research decision in selection of a criterion score. *The Research Quarterly, 38*, 412–419.

Kroll, W. (1970). Current strategies and problems in personality assessment of athletes. In L. E. Smith (Ed.), *Psychology of motor learning* (pp. 349–367). Chicago: Athletic Institute.

Landers, D. M., Qi, W. M., Daniels, F., & Boutcher, S. (1984). Unraveling some of the mysteries of archery: I. *U.S. Archer, 3*, 260–263.

Landers, D. M., Qi, W. M., Daniels, F., & Boutcher, S. (1984). Unraveling some of the mysteries of archery: II. *U.S. Archer, 4*, 41–43.

Lufi, D., Porat, J. B., & Tenenbaum, G. (1986). Psychological predictors of competitive performance in young gymnasts. *Perceptual and Motor Skills, 63*, 59–64.

Magnussen, D. (1971). An analysis of situational dimensions. *Perceptual and Motor Skills, 32*, 851–867.

Magnussen, D., & Ekehammer, B. (1973). An analysis of situational dimensions: A replication. *Multivariate Behavioral Research, 8*, 331–339.

Mahoney, M. J., & Avener, M. (1977). Psychology of the elite athlete: An exploratory study. *Cognitive therapy and Research, 1,* 135–141.

Malina, R. M. (1986). Genetics of motor development and performance. In R. M. Malina & C. Bouchard (Eds.), *Sport and human genetics* (pp. 23–58). Champaign, IL: Human Kinetics.

Malina, R. M., & Bouchard, C. (1986). *Sport and human genetics.* Champaign, IL: Human Kinetics.

Martens, R. (1975). The paradigmatic crisis of American sport psychology. *Sportwissenschaft, 5,* 9–24.

Martens, R. (1987). Science, knowledge, and sport psychology. *The Sport Psychologist, 1,* 29–55.

Meyers, W. A., Schleser, R., Cooke, C. J., & Cuvillier, C. (1979). Cognitive contributions to the development of gymnastic skills. *Cognitive Therapy and Research, 3,* 75–85.

Miner, J. B. (1969). *Personnel psychology.* London: Macmillan.

Mishel, W. (1973). Toward a cognitive social learning reconceptualization of personality. *Psychological Review, 80,* 252–283.

McDavid, R. F. (1977). Predicting potential in football players. *The Research Quarterly, 48,* 98–104.

McKelvie, S., Valliant, P., & Marjatta, A. (1985). Physical training and personality factors as predictors of marathon time and training injury. *Perceptual and Motor Skills, 60,* 651–655.

Montpetit, R., & Cazorla, G. (1982). La détection du talent en natation. *La Revue de l'Entraîneur, 5,* 26–37.

Morgan, W. P. (1973). Efficacy of psychobiologic inquiry in the exercise and sport science. *Quest, 25,* 39–46.

Morgan, W. P. (1978). Sport personology: The credulous-skeptical argument in perspective. In W. F. Straub (Ed.), *Sport psychology: An analysis of athlete behavior* (pp. 330–339). Ithaca, NY: Mouvement.

Nagle, F. J., Morgan, N. P., Hellickson, R. O., Serfass, R. C., & Alexander, J. F. (1975). Spotting success traits in Olympic contenders. *The Physician and Sports Medicine, 12,* 31–34.

Nesselroade, J. R., & Baltes, P. B. (1979). *Longitudinal research in the study of behavior and development.* New York: Academic Press.

Nideffer, R. M. (1976). *The inner athlete.* New York: Crowell.

Nideffer, R. M. (1990). Use of the Test of Attentional and Interpersonal Style (TAIS) in sport. *The Sport Psychologist, 4,* 285–300.

Nielsen, D., & McGown, C. (1985). Information processing as a predictor of offensive ability in baseball. *Perceptual and Motor Skills, 60,* 775–781.

Ogilvie, B. C., Tutko, T. A., & Young, I. (1965). The psychological profile of champions. In F. Antonelli (Ed.), *Psychologia dello sport* (pp. 201–203). Rome: FMSI.

Orlick, T., & Partington, J. (1988). Mental links to excellence. *The Sport Psychologist, 2,* 105–130.

Partington, J. T. (1970). Dr. Jekill and Mr. High: Multidimensional scaling of alcoholics' self-evaluations. *Journal of Abnormal Psychology, 75,* 131–138.

Patton, M. Q. (1980). *Qualitative evaluation methods.* Beverly Hills, CA: Sage.

Pettenburg, A., Erich, W., Bernink, M., Zonderland, M. & Huisveld, I. (1984). Biological maturation, body composition, and growth of female gymnasts and control groups of schoolgirls and girl swimmers, aged 8 to 14 years: A cross-sectional survey of 1,064 girls. *International Journal of Sports Medicine, 5,* 36–42.

Porat, Y. Lufi, D., & Tenenbaum, G. (1989). Psychological components contribute to select young female gymnasts. *International Journal of Sport Psychology, 20,* 279–286.

Régnier, G. (1987). *Un modèle conceptuel pour la détection du talent sportif.* (A conceptual model for talent detection) Unpublished doctoral dissertation, University of Montreal.

Régnier, G., & Salmela, J. H. (1983). Détection du talent au baseball. (Talent detection in baseball). *Revue de l'entraîneur, 6,* 13–20.

Régnier, G., & Salmela, J. H. (1987). Predictors of success in Canadian male gymnasts. In B. Petiot, J. H. Salmela, & T. B. Hoshizaki (Eds.), *World identification systems for gymnastic talent* (pp. 143–150). Montreal: Sport Psyche Editions.

Régnier, G., Salmela, J. H., & Alain, C. (1982). Strategie für Bestimmung und Entdeckung von Talenten im Sport. *Leistungssport, 12,* 431–440.

Riezebos, M. L., Patterson, D. H., Hall, C. R., & Yushaz, M. S. (1983). Relationship of selected variables to performance in women's basketball. *Canadian Journal of Applied Sport Sciences, 8,* 34–40.

Roberts, G. C. (1984). Achievement motivation in children's sport. *Advances in Motivation and Achievement, 3,* 251–281.

Rogosa, D. (1979). Causal models in longitudinal research: Rationale, formulation and interpretation. In J. R. Nesselroade & P. B. Baltes (Eds.), *Longitudinal research in the study of behaviour and development* (pp. 263–302). New York: Academic Press.

Rulon, P. J., Tiedman, D. V., Tatsuoka, M. M., & Langmuir, C. R. (1967). *Multivariate statistics for personnel classification.* New York: Wiley.

Rumelhart, D. E. (1980). Schemata: The building blocks of cognition. In R. Spiro, B. Bruce, & W. Brewer (Eds.), *Theoretical issues in reading comprehension* (pp. 33–58). Hillsdale, NJ: Erlbaum.

Rumelhart, D. E. (1981). *Understanding understanding.* La Jolla: University of California, Center for Human Information Processing.

Rumelhart, D. E., & Ortony, A. (1977). The representation of knowledge in memory. In R. C. Anderson, R. J. Shapiro, & W. E. Montague (Eds.), *Schooling and the acquisition of knowledge* (pp. 91–135). New York: Erlbaum.

Rushall, B. S. (1970). An evaluation of the relationship between personality and physical performance categories. In G. S. Kenyon (Ed.), *Contemporary psychology of sport* (pp. 157–165). Chicago: Athletic Institute.

Rushall, B. S. (1989). Sport psychology: The key to sporting excellence. *International Journal of Sport Psychology, 20,* 165–190.

Rushall, B. S., & Leet, D. (1979). The prediction of swimming performance in competition from behavioral information. *Canadian Journal of Applied Sport Sciences, 4,* 154–157.

Rushall, B. S., & Jamieson, J. J. (1979). The prediction of swimming performance in competition from behavioral information: A further note. *Canadian Journal of Applied Sport Sciences, 4,* 158–159.

Russell, S. J. (1990). Athletes' knowledge in task perception, definition and classification. *International Journal of Sport Psychology, 21,* 85–101.

Russell, S. J. (1991). *Cognitive factors in the acquisition of high level sport skills.* Unpublished doctoral dissertation, University of Queensland, Australia.

Salmela, J. H. (1981). *The world sport psychology sourcebook.* Ithaca, NY: Mouvement.

Salmela, J. H. (1984). Comparative sport psychology. In J. M. Silva & R. S. Weinberg (Eds.), *Psychological foundations of sport* (pp. 23–34). Champaign, IL: Human Kinetics, 23–34.

Salmela, J. H. (1991). *The world sport psychology sourcebook* (2nd ed.). Champaign, IL: Human Kinetics.

Salmela, J. H., & Régnier, G. (1983, October). A model for sport talent detection. *Science Periodicals on Research and Technology in Sport.* Ottawa: Coaching Association of Canada.

Salmela, J. H., Régnier, G., & Proteau, L. (1987). Analyse bio-behaviorale des déterminants de la performance gymnique. In B. Petiot, J. H. Salmela, & T. B. Hoshizaki (Eds.), *World identification systems for gymnastic talent* (pp. 126–142). Montreal: Sport Psyche Editions.

Salmela, J. H., & Russell, S. J. (1988). The structure of knowledge in developing sport talent. In M. M. Newson (Ed.), *Proceedings of the First I. O.C. World Congress on Sport Sciences* (pp. 370–374). Colorado Springs, CO: USOC.

Scanlan, T. K., Ravizza, K., & Stein, G. L. (1989). An in-depth study of former elite figure skaters: I. Introduction to the project. *Journal of Sport and Exercise Psychology, 11,* 45–64.

Scanlan, T. K., Stein, G. L., & Ravizza, K. (1989). An in-depth study of former elite skaters: II. Sources of enjoyment. *Journal of Sport and Exercise Psychology, 11,* 65–83.

SCAPPS (1984, September). Ethical standards for sport psychology educators, researchers and practitioners. *Science Periodical on Research and Technology in Sport,* Ottawa: Coaching Association of Canada.

Seefeldt, V. (1988). The concept of readiness applied to motor skill acquisition. In F. L. Smoll, R. A. Magill, & M. J. Ash (Eds.), *Children in sport* (3rd ed.), (pp. 45–52). Champaign, IL: Human Kinetics.

Silva, J. M., Shultz, B. B., Haslam, R. W., Martin, T. P., & Murray, D. F. (1985). Discriminating characteristics of contestants at the United States Olympic wrestling trials. *International Journal of Sport Psychology, 16,* 79–102.

Singer, R. N. (1980). *Motor learning and human performance* (3rd ed.). New York: Macmillan.

Singer, R. N. (1988). Psychological testing: What value to coaches and athletes? *International Journal of Sport Psychology, 19,* 87–106.

Smith, R. E. (1986). Toward a cognitive-affective model of athletic burnout. *Journal of Sport Psychology, 8,* 36–50.

Sol, J. B. M. (1987). The Bisdom/Sol aptitude test for female gymnasts. In B. Petiot, J. H. Salmela, & T. B. Hoshizaki (Eds.), *World identification systems for gymnastic talent* (pp. 115–128). Montreal: Sport Psyche Editions.

Spink, K. S. (1990). Psychological characteristics of male gymnasts: Differences between competitive levels. *Journal of Sport Sciences, 8*(2), 149–157.

Starkes, J. L., & Deakin, J. (1984). Perception in sport: A cognitive approach to skilled performance. In W. F. Straub & J. M. Williams (Eds.), *Cognitive sport psychology.* Lansing, NY: Sport Science Associates.

Summers, J. J., & Ford, S. K. (1990). The test of attentional style: An evaluation. *International Journal of Sport Psychology, 21,* 102–111.

Ungerleider, S., Golding, J., & Porter, K. (1989). Mood profiles of masters track and field athletes. *Perceptual and Motor Skills, 68,* 607–617.

Vallerand, R. J. (1983). Attention and decision making: A test of the Test of Attentional and Interpersonal Style (TAIS) in a sport setting. *Journal of Sport Psychology, 5,* 449–459.

Van Schoyck, R. S., & Grasha, A. F. (1981). Attentional variations and athletic ability: The advantages of a sport specific test. *Journal of Sport Psychology, 3,* 149–165.

Vickers, J. N. (1990). *Instructional design for teaching physical activities.* Champaign, IL: Human Kinetics.

Wall, A. E. (1986). A knowledge based approach to motor skill acquisition. In M. G. Wade & H. T. A. Whiting (Eds.), *Motor development in children: Aspects of coordination and control.* Dordrecht, Netherlands: Martinus Nijoff.

Weiss, V. (1976). Der Heritabilitätskoeffizient als prognostischen Wichtung in der Eignungsdiagnose. *Biologische Rundschau, 14,* 376–383.

Williams, L. R. T. (1977). Prediction of high level rowing ability. *Journal of Sport Medicine, 18,* 11–19.

Willimczik, K. (1986). Scientific support in the search of talents in sport. In L. E. Unesthal (Ed.), *Sport psychology theory and practice* (pp. 95–105). Orebro, Sweden: Veje.

·13·

COMPETITIVENESS AND COMPETITIVE ORIENTATION IN SPORT

Diane L. Gill

The study of individual differences is one of the cornerstones of both psychology and sport psychology. Sport psychologists attempt to understand the role of individual differences in sport and exercise behavior in our research, and applied sport psychologists recognize the importance of individualizing approaches to match individual needs and capabilities. Such individual differences are nowhere more apparent than in reactions to competition.

Some eager competitors seek out competition, rise to the challenge, and always give their best performances in the toughest competition. Others are apprehensive, avoid competitive challenges, and tend to "choke" or perform well below expectations. Even at elite levels, when most athletes compete regularly and tend to give their best performances in competition, we see wide variation in individual goals, strategies, and general competitive orientation and behavior. In youth sport, recreational sport, and other sport and exercise settings, we find even greater variation. Clearly some participants are "competitive" whereas others are not at all competitive.

Such individual differences in competitiveness are of interest in themselves, as sport psychologists seek to understand behavior in competitive and noncompetitive sport settings. Individual differences are also of practical concern. Coaches, teachers, and sport psychologists who understand individual differences can individualize instruction and can develop strategies and approaches to accommodate and even take advantage of individual differences. Participants themselves who understand individual variations can adapt and develop strategies and approaches that match their individual needs and capabilities as well as develop interpersonal skills for working with others.

This chapter focuses on these individual differences in *competitiveness,* which can be defined simply as achieve-

ment orientation toward competitive sport, or a sport-specific form of achievement orientation. Martens (1976b, p. 326) more explicitly states:

Competitiveness is defined as a disposition to strive for satisfaction when making comparisons with some standard of excellence in the presence of evaluative others in sport.

As both my simple definition and Martens's definition imply, competitiveness has its roots in the rich theoretical and empirical work on achievement orientation within the psychology literature.

From the early work of Murray (1938) through the achievement motivation work of Atkinson and McClelland (Atkinson, 1964, 1974; McClelland, Atkinson, Clark, & Lowell, 1953), achievement motivation has been widely recognized as a capacity to experience pride in accomplishment or a disposition to strive for success across a wide range of achievement tasks and situations. Murray (1938) first defined achievement motivation as a personality factor when he defined the need to achieve as the desire

To accomplish something difficult. To master, manipulate or organize physical objects, human beings, or ideas. To do this as rapidly and as independently as possible. To overcome obstacles and attain a high standard. To excel one's self. To rival and surpass others. To increase self-regard by the successful exercise of talent. (p. 164)

Both Atkinson and McClelland extended beyond Murray's original work to initiate progressive research programs on achievement motivation and behavior.

Atkinson's model has been particularly influential in sport psychology as well as in psychology. Atkinson conceptualized the personality factor of achievement motivation as

314

two separate motives, the motive to approach success (M_s) and the motive to avoid failure (M_{af}). M_s is similar to Murray's need to achieve, whereas M_{af} is a negative or avoidance motive that reflects anxiety. Indeed, much of the sport psychology work on competitive anxiety adopts constructs and measures similar to those in the achievement literature. Atkinson suggested that the two motives are independent and the combination or resultant must be considered in order to understand achievement behavior. Overall, persons with a high M_s and a low M_{af} are highly motivated to succeed and not very concerned or anxious about failure, so they are likely to be high achievers who rise to challenges and compete successfully.

In contrast, people with a high M_{af} and a low M_s are the ones who become overly anxious, choke, and avoid competitive challenges. Atkinson not only clarified the achievement motivation construct, but he also took an interaction approach in his achievement model. That is, Atkinson proposed that personality and the situation interactively determine achievement behavior. Specifically, the more uncertain the situation, or the closer the competition, the greater the differences among individuals. High achievers particularly like close, uncertain situations and do their best in the closest competition, whereas low achievers try to avoid uncertain situations and become most anxious in the closest competitions.

Atkinson's model could serve as a valuable guide for sport psychology work on competitiveness and competitive achievement. Competitive individuals are the ones who seem to have a high M_s and a low M_{af} as they rise to competitive challenges and seem to give their best in close competition. Those individuals whom we think of as noncompetitive are the ones who avoid competition and the ones who become anxious as they seem overly concerned with avoiding failure. Although the Atkinson model does make sense in that general form, several sport psychologists, most notably Martens, suggested that achievement motivation was too general to be much help in explaining sport achievement and competitive behavior. For example, the individuals who seem to be the high achievers in sport are not necessarily the high achievers in other areas, such as academics, work, or social settings. Likewise, the low achievers or highly anxious competitors are not necessarily highly anxious in other areas.

I will not review all the material on achievement and motivational orientation because those topics are covered in other chapters. In particular, chapters 17 and 18, by Roberts and Duda respectively, cover directly relevant theories and research, and related work may be found in several other chapters. Readers who are interested in more general motivational orientations in sport should refer to an excellent review chapter by Weiss and Chaumeton (1992). Although the present article is limited to competitive sport orientation, many other approaches to motivational orientation (e.g., the task-ego orientation reflected in Duda's [1989] work) represent similar and overlapping views.

CONCEPTUAL FRAMEWORK

Before reviewing work on individual differences in competitive orientation, we should consider the conceptual basis of that work. Generally research on competitiveness, and particularly my work on competitive sport orientation, is influenced by two major sources. First, as already discussed, competitiveness may be defined as a specific form of achievement orientation, and thus, achievement motivation theories provide a conceptual framework for sport psychology work on competitive orientation. Second, one of the most significant trends in sport psychology over the past ten years is the move toward the development and use of sport-specific models, measures, and methodologies. Martens's influential work on competition and competitive anxiety initiated this trend, and this work serves as a major conceptual referent for competitiveness.

Within the achievement orientation literature, the work of Spence and Helmreich (1978, 1983) has been a particularly useful guide for work on competitiveness. Spence and Helmreich (and others) advocate that achievement orientation is best conceptualized and measured as a multidimensional construct, and they specifically identified mastery, work, and competitiveness dimensions (a fourth dimension, personal unconcern, was identified in the original work, but Spence and Helmreich no longer recommend its use). Such a dimensional model implies different styles of achievement. That is, some people take a mastery approach to achievement tasks and strive for excellence; others emphasize hard work; and perhaps most relevant to this chapter, some emphasize social comparison and striving to better others. Individuals vary on achievement dimensions, and might be high on all or low on all, or possess any combination that describes their achievement orientation.

As with other conceptual approaches to achievement orientation, Spence and Helmreich's approach implies that achievement orientation applies across all types of achievement tasks and settings, including sport and exercise activities. However, we might take a different approach to dimensionality and suggest that achievement orientation varies across tasks or domains. An individual's achievement orientation toward sport might be quite different from that individual's orientation toward academics or artistic endeavors. This view represents the move toward sport-specific constructs and measures within sport psychology, which is the second major conceptual basis of the competitiveness research. In particular, my work on competitive orientation stems from Martens's earlier work on competition and particularly his research on competitive anxiety and development of the Sport Competition Anxiety Test (SCAT, Martens, 1977). That initial work and related studies demonstrated the value of sport-specific approaches and provided the impetus for the development of further sport-specific measures such as Vealey's (1986) sport confidence measures and Martens, Vealey, and Burton's (1990) continuing work on competitive anxiety and development of a sport-specific measure of state as well as trait anxiety.

Martens began his work on competition and competitive anxiety by defining competition as a social process and by emphasizing the importance of sport-specific constructs and measures. Specifically, Martens (1976a) offered the following definition:

Competition is a process in which the comparison of an individual's performance is made with some standard in the presence of at least one other person who is aware of the criterion for comparison and can evaluate the comparison process. (p. 14)

We might debate Martens's definition of competition, but it captures most competitive sport activities and will serve our purposes in this chapter. It should be noted, however, that much of the work on sport achievement incorporates both competitive and noncompetitive achievement orientations, and that will become clearer as we progress through the chapter.

Martens's definition of competition as a social process stands in contrast to the traditional psychology work that contrasts competition with cooperation. That work uses what Martens has termed a "reward definition" of competition. Specifically, competition, cooperation, and also individualistic or independent achievement situations are defined by outcomes and how rewards are distributed. In a competitive situation, rewards are distributed unequally; what one wins another necessarily loses. In a cooperative situation rewards are distributed equally; everyone works toward a goal together and the rewards are shared equally by all. Finally, if the situation has an independent reward structure, what one person achieves has no effect on what another achieves or on reward distribution; everyone might be successful or everyone might be unsuccessful.

That reward definition approach to competition and cooperation is reflected in the classic work of Deutsch (1949, 1973), Sherif et al. (1961), the more recent work of Roger and David Johnson (Johnson & Johnson, 1985; Johnson et al., 1981), and in many other studies of competition and cooperation in the psychology and educational literature. That work is important and the competitive or cooperative structure of the situation and the reward system have important implications for sport and for competitive behavior (we will consider some of these implications later).

As Martens emphasized, however, the reward definition with its focus on outcomes does not capture the richness of competition and the dynamic nature of the social process of competition as it occurs in sport. Moreover, Martens's definition of competition as a social process rather than as a set of conditions provides a framework for considering the role of individual differences and the interaction of individual differences with situational factors within a dynamic social process. Martens's model of the competition process, presented in Figure 13–1, starts with a set of defining conditions that represent the *objective competitive situation*. Next, individual differences come into play in the *subjective competitive situation*. Individuals who are highly competitive interpret the situation differently than individuals who are not very competitive.

These subjective perceptions then influence *responses*, which are the actual behaviors in competition including both performance and nonperformance behaviors such as state anxiety or aggressive behavior. Finally, responses have *consequences*, including the obvious immediate consequence of winning or losing, as well as influences on the individual such as changes in skills or attitudes, and influences on the situation.

Scanlan (1978, 1988) used Martens's competition model as a framework in her paper on the antecedents of competitiveness (Scanlan, 1978), which was the first major work attempting to provide a conceptual framework for competitive sport orientation. Scanlan started by taking Martens's approach of defining competition as a subset of achievement. That is, achievement situations involve comparisons to a standard with an evaluation of that comparison as successful or unsuccessful. Competition also involves such comparisons, but competition is restricted to *social* comparisons. That is, someone else must be able to evaluate a comparison. Usually competition involves an opponent who evaluates, but Martens's definition also includes situations that do not involve an opponent (such as a pole vaulter who continues to compete to set a record after all others have dropped out), so long as someone else is present to evaluate. In any case, competition involves *social* comparison, whereas achievement might include nonsocial or internal evaluation as well as social comparisons.

Because sport psychologists had not begun to develop sport-specific constructs and models of competitive orientation, Scanlan relied on achievement theory and research, particularly developmental research, and placed that work within the context of Martens's competition model. Scanlan incorporates White's (1959) work on competence motivation and Veroff's (1969) model of the development of achievement motivation in her framework. White suggests that all individuals start with a basic innate motive to be competent or effective. Veroff's model proceeds from that basic competence motive in a stage model with individuals who successfully master one stage, moving on to the next. First, individuals engage in autonomous achievement activities as they set internal standards and evaluate their success. At about age 4 or 5, children who have exper-

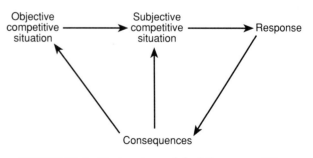

FIGURE 13–1. Martens's model of the competitive process.

From Sport Competition Anxiety Test *by* R. *Martens*, 1977, **Human Kinetics**, *p. 32. Reprinted by permission.*

ienced success at the autonomous stage begin to compare themselves to others in a social comparison stage. Social comparison, then, is competition. According to Veroff, individuals who experience success at this social comparison stage finally advance to an integrated achievement orientation in which they use *either* social or autonomous standards and evaluation processes, depending on the situation.

Taking Veroff's stages, Scanlan suggested that those individuals we identify as "competitive" might be at either the social comparison stage or the integrated stage. Individuals at the autonomous stage would avoid competition, although they might set and strive for achievement goals in noncompetitive ways. Individuals at the social comparison stage would strive for success *only* in competitive settings. We might see these individuals as hypercompetitive types who turn everything into competition. The individual with an integrated achievement orientation would be competitive and strive for success in competition, but that individual would not impose competitive standards inappropriately and might set and strive for internal achievement goals. For example, a golfer might enjoy and perform well in match play competition, but also work hard to meet personal goals and ignore other golfers in practice rounds or in stroke play.

Scanlan followed her initial conceptual efforts with a research program on social processes in children's sport. In particular, her continuing research incorporating varied approaches including recent in-depth interviews and qualitative information has added considerably to our understanding of stress and enjoyment in youth sport. Scanlan did not continue to study individual differences in competitiveness, although her initial work helps provide a framework for further research on competitiveness as a sport-specific achievement construct.

Martens did not follow his discussion of competition by developing competitiveness measures or investigating the role of competitiveness in sport behavior. Instead, he developed a line of research on competitive anxiety, and it serves as a model for the research on competitive orientation discussed in the rest of this chapter. In that competitive anxiety research, Martens (1977) started with the competition model as a framework. He first focused on individual differences that influence the subjective competitive situation. Specifically Martens developed a measure of competitive trait anxiety to assess sport-specific individual differences, demonstrated its validity and reliability through a series of studies, and examined the interactive influences of competitive trait anxiety and situational factors in competition.

Martens and his colleagues (Martens, Vealey & Burton, 1990) proceeded to develop further sport-specific measures and constructs as they focused on state anxiety in competition. Martens's research demonstrated the value of sport-specific measures and the need to consider unique aspects of the sport situation and context in our sport psychology work. The literature on competitiveness discussed next builds on that model.

DEVELOPMENT OF THE SPORT ORIENTATION QUESTIONNAIRE

My work on competitiveness adopts the conceptual framework and sport-specific approach established by Martens, and incorporates the multidimensional view of Spence and Helmreich. At the beginning of this project, achievement orientation seemed a likely candidate for a sport-specific measure. Most sport and exercise activities involve achievement of some sort, and competitive settings dominate. Moreover, given the achievement literature and the observations of those in sport and exercise settings, it seemed quite probable that individuals' sport achievement orientations did not simply reflect general achievement orientation. This project used Martens's competition model and paralleled his SCAT research, but was not aimed specifically at elite athletes in competitive sports.

Instead, I attempted to develop a measure that would tap all aspects of sport achievement orientation and that would be appropriate for individuals in varied competitive and noncompetitive activities. As some of the achievement literature suggests, even participants in highly competitive activities might hold noncompetitive achievement standards and orientations. Indeed, some highly competitive athletes focus on personal standards, and many applied sport psychologists advocate such an approach. In sum, the general achievement research and sport psychology work suggests that competitive sport orientation is multidimensional, but the precise dimensions are elusive. Thus in developing a sport orientation measure, I started by including as many options and items as possible, and adopted an exploratory approach.

The overall research program involves a series of studies with several samples and varied analyses conducted over five years with the assistance of several colleagues. Details on the specific studies may be found in the published reports. This discussion provides an overview of that research, highlights the main findings, and presents general conclusions.

The first step in the actual development of the SOQ was to generate items. Actually this was a continuing process that had been under way informally for some time using information from various sources and class projects, as well as from discussion with colleagues. In particular, before beginning SOQ development, I discussed the competitiveness construct and possible measures with Rainer Martens, and some of his insights contributed to my work and the final SOQ. The first 58-item version was circulated to five raters (all graduate students in a doctoral sport psychology seminar) who rated the items on content and clarity. The 32 items that were rated as definitely clear and representative of sport achievement orientation then formed the first version of the SOQ (called the "Competitiveness Inventory" at that time). Each item is rated on a 5-point scale ranging from "strongly agree" to "strongly disagree" following the same format as the Work and Family Orientation Questionnaire (WOFO), the multidimensional achievement orientation measure developed by Helmreich and Spence (1978). The final 25-item version of the SOQ is included at the end of this chapter for reference and use by readers.

To begin psychometric analyses and refinement of the SOQ, we sampled physical activity classes at the University of Iowa. Activity classes are required of all liberal arts students there, and that includes nearly all undergraduates, so the sample was fairly representative of undergraduate students. At this initial stage, a wider, representative sample was selected rather than an athletic sample to assess competitive orientation across a more diverse group. Also, classes were selected to include both competitive activities (e.g., softball, tennis, volleyball, fencing) and noncompetitive activities (e.g., archery, bowling, jogging, fitness swim) so that those subgroups might be compared. The first study was conducted in 1984, and a second replication study was done in 1985. After some analyses with these samples, we administered the revised and final version of the SOQ to a sample of 266 high school students and a smaller university sample. Finally, within this series of studies, we sampled intercollegiate athletes with the revised SOQ. Table 13–1 provides a summary of sample characteristics.

First, we investigated factor structure to determine if indeed, the SOQ was multidimensional. We used several factor analysis approaches (see Gill & Deeter, 1988, for details), but all extractions, rotations, and analyses pointed to a 3-factor structure. Moreover, the three factors that emerged were logical and interpretable. Table 13–2 presents the factor loadings from a principal components, varimax rotation analysis with the first sample. A nearly identical pattern emerged with oblique rotation and with analyses of the second sample. We labeled the three factors *competitiveness, win,* and *goal* orientation.

Competitiveness, the dominant factor in all analyses, reflects competitiveness as defined earlier in this chapter—that is, competitiveness items reflect an enjoyment of competition and a desire to enter and strive for success in competitive sport achievement settings. The other two factors, each with 6 items, reflect differing orientations to

achievement outcomes. Win orientation suggests a focus on interpersonal comparison and winning in competition, whereas goal orientation suggests a focus on personal performance standards.

The revised 25-item SOQ was administered to the high school sample, and factor analyses with that sample confirmed the initial factor structure. Also, we conducted confirmatory factor analyses with the LISREL program using the results from the first sample to see whether that factor structure applied to the second university sample and the high school sample. These results did indeed "confirm" our 3-factor structure.

After identifying the factors, we considered reliability. Based on the factor analysis results, the items associated with each of the three factors are summed to form three subscales. Internal consistencies were calculated for each scale with each sample, and those alpha coefficients are presented in Table 13-3, along with the overall means and standard deviations for the three samples. We also assessed consistency over time by returning to the activity classes in sample 2 after 4 weeks and readministering the SOQ. Test-retest correlations (.89 for competitiveness, .82 for win, .79 for goal) indicated good reliability over time.

After establishing reliability of the SOQ scores, we turned to the issue of validity—does the SOQ really assess sport achievement orientation, and does it relate to relevant constructs and behaviors? With the first samples, we approached validity be comparing scores of students in competitive and noncompetitive classes. Those students also completed Spence and Helmreich's WOFO, their multidimensional measure of mastery, work, and competitiveness orientation. Gender × Activity Class MANOVAs on the SOQ and WOFO scores revealed both gender and activity class main effects, with no interaction. For WOFO scores, we found gender differences, but no activity class differences. The gender differences replicated Spence and Helmreich's findings that males score much higher on competitiveness and slightly higher on mastery, while females score higher on work.

SOQ scores were of more interest, and we found both gender and activity class differences. Gender differences were evident on all three scores with males higher on competitiveness and win, and females higher on goal orientation. The activity class differences were most pertinent to validity. That multivariate class difference was strong, and follow-up univariate and discriminant analyses suggested that the difference was almost entirely on competitiveness. Students in competitive classes scored much higher on competitiveness ($M = 50.25$) than did students in noncompetitive classes ($M = 44.5$). Results for sample 2 were nearly identical and confirmed these differences (see Gill & Deeter, 1988, for details).

To summarize the group comparisons with the university samples, gender differences on WOFO replicated earlier work, but no activity class differences were found for WOFO. We also found gender differences with the SOQ, and most important, the SOQ discriminated classes suggesting that competitiveness influences choice of activity.

TABLE 13–1. Characteristics of Samples Used in SOQ Development

	Sample 1 (1984) (N = 237)		Sample 2 (1985) (N = 218)	
	Male	Female	Male	Female
Competitive	33	64	77	24
Noncompetitive	40	100	33	84

	High School (N = 266)		University—Summer (N = 86)	
	Male	Female	Male	Female
	126	140	34	52

	University Athletes/Nonathletes (N = 210)	
	Male	Female
Athlete	56	49
Nonathlete	42	63

TABLE 13-2. Factor loadings for SOQ items.

Item	Rotation Factor		
	Competitiveness Var.	Goal Var.	Win Var.
I am a competitive person.	.71	.05	.21
I try my hardest to win.	.75	.10	.21
I am a determined competitor.	.77	.12	.09
I want to be the best every time I compete.	.54	.24	.27
I look forward to competing.	.82	.10	.11
I thrive on competition.	.74	.12	.31
My goal is to be the best athlete possible.	.68	.23	.22
I enjoy competing against others.	.79	.07	.17
I want to be successful in sports.	.71	.17	.18
I work hard to be successful in sports.	.73	.28	.10
The best test of my ability is competing against others.	.69	.06	.23
I look forward to the opportunity to test my skills in competition.	.79	.16	.08
I perform my best when I am competing against an opponent.	.64	.12	.34
Goal Items			
I set goals for myself when I compete.	.35	.58	.04
I am most competitive when I try to achieve personal goals.	.01	.50	.04
I try hardest when I have a specific goal.	.01	.64	.01
Reaching personal performance goals is very important to me.	.08	.77	.04
The best way to determine my ability is to set a goal and try to reach it.	.03	.61	.01
Performing to the best of my ability is very important to me.	.27	.57	.03
Win Items			
Winning is important.	.50	.16	.57
Scoring more points than my opponent is very important to me.	.38	.10	.59
I hate to lose.	.27	.19	.69
The only time I am satisfied is when I win.	.17	.09	.70
Losing upsets me.	.20	.02	.72
I have the most fun when I win.	.44	.06	.47
Percent variance	33.5	10.8	5.3
Cumulative percent variance	33.5	44.3	49.6

This provides good initial validity evidence; the sport-specific SOQ differentiated students in competitive classes from those in noncompetitive classes when a general achievement measure (WOFO) did not.

Given this initial validity evidence, we gathered further data with the high school students and smaller university sample to examine convergent and divergent validity. These samples again completed the SOQ and WOFO, but we also added Martens' (1977) SCAT, the Crowne and Marlowe (1960) social desirability scale, and another sport competitiveness measure, the SCTI developed by Fabian and Ross (1984). Students also answered several questions that were used for classification, specifically, whether or not they participated in competitive sports, in noncompetitive sports, and in nonsport activities (see Gill, Dzewaltowski, & Deeter, 1988, for details).

We conducted two main analyses. First, we examined correlations of the SOQ with other competitiveness measures (presumably high correlation), with other achievement scores (moderate), and with SCAT and social desirability (none at all). Second, multivariate, discriminant analyses

compared participants and nonparticipants in competitive and noncompetitive activities.

All correlations came out as expected (see Table 13-4). All SOQ scores correlated with other competitiveness measures—the SCTI and WOFO competitiveness scores. Also, the SOQ competitiveness and goal scores correlated moderately (about .40) with WOFO mastery and work, but SOQ win did not, suggesting that win orientation may be a unique component of sport achievement. SOQ scores did not correlate with SCAT, indicating that competitive achievement orientation and competitive anxiety are independent and may be examined as independent constructs in future research. Finally, SOQ scores did not correlate with social desirability.

With the multivariate analyses, the most important comparison was between students who indicated they participated in competitive sports and those who did not. As expected, competitive sport participants were higher than nonparticipants on all three SOQ scores, as well as on the other two competitiveness scores (WOFO competitiveness and SCTI). As with the university samples, follow-up

TABLE 13–3. Means, Standard Deviations, and Internal Consistencies for University Samples 1 and 2, and High School Sample 3

	M	SD	Alpha
Competitiveness			
Sample 1	46.9	11.2	.95
Sample 2	48.3	10.9	.94
Sample 3	47.8	11.6	.94
Win orientation			
Sample 1	18.1	5.0	.86
Sample 2	18.8	5.2	.86
Sample 3	19.2	5.6	.85
Goal orientation			
Sample 1	25.5	3.3	.80
Sample 2	25.7	3.4	.79
Sample 3	24.7	4.0	.82

analyses revealed that competitiveness was the major discriminator.

Similar analyses comparing participants and nonparticipants in noncompetitive sports (e.g., jogging or noncompetitive swimming) and in nonsport activities (e.g., debate or band) indicated that competitiveness scores were less important discriminators. For noncompetitive sports, participants had higher scores than nonparticipants in most cases, but not on win orientation. Competitiveness was even less important for nonsport activities. Nonsport participants had lower competitiveness scores than nonpartici-

TABLE 13–4. Correlations Between SOQ Scores and Other Measures

SOQ score	Competitive Measures SCTI		WOFO comp.	
	H.S.	College	H.S.	College
Competitiveness	.79	.70	.65	.71
Win	.53	.51	.70	.70
Goal	.48	.38	.36	.32

	WOFO Achievement Measures					
	Mastery		Work		Personal Unconcern	
	H.S.	College	H.S.	College	H.S.	College
Competitiveness	.44‡	.37‡	.27‡	.09	−.17†	−.12
Win	.18‡	.05‡	.01	−.12	−.17†	−.18
Goal	.48‡	.48‡	.53‡	.40‡	−.10*	.15

	Other Measures		
	SCAT		Social Desirability
	H.S.	College	College
Competitiveness	−.06	−.15	.03
Win	−.02	.03	−.28†
Goal	.17†	−.07	.20

* P < .05; † P < .01; ‡ P < .001.

pants in most cases, and especially so on win orientation. Overall, these correlational and discriminant analyses provided further converging evidence for the SOQ's validity.

GENDER AND COMPETITIVE ORIENTATION

Before moving on to more recent work with athletes, I want to elaborate on gender influences on competitiveness. As noted earlier, we found males scoring higher on competitiveness and win but females scoring higher on goal in the university samples. This same pattern held in the high school sample; males scored higher on SOQ competitiveness and win, the SCTI, and WOFO competitiveness. However, for SOQ goal orientation and general achievement scores, females' scores were just as high or higher than males'. To look further at gender influences on competitiveness, we considered the classification data (see Table 13–5).

Most male high school students were currently participating in competitive sports, but most females were not. With noncompetitive sports, participation rates did not differ for males and females, and for nonsport activities, females were more likely to participate than were males.

All the gender differences and nondifferences suggest the following conclusions (see Gill, 1988, for detailed analyses). Males scored higher than females on competitiveness and competitive sport participation. However, females scored at least as high as males on noncompetitive achievement orientation and were at least as likely to participate in noncompetitive activities, including noncompetitive sport. Thus gender differences in competitiveness are related to competitive experience, but they do not seem to reflect either general achievement orientation or interest in sport and exercise activities per se.

TABLE 13–5. Gender Differences on Classification Data for High School Sample

	Participation in Competitive Sports	
	Yes	No
Males	85 (67.5%)	41 (32.5%)
Females	54 (38.6%)	86 (61.4%)

Chi-square (1, N = 266) = 21.04, P < .001; phi = .29

	Participation in Noncompetitive Sports	
	Yes	No
Males	96 (76.2%)	30 (23.8%)
Females	101 (72.1%)	39 (27.9%)

Chi-square (1, N = 266) = .37, P > .05; phi = .05

	Participation in Nonsport Activities	
	Yes	No
Males	28 (22.2%)	98 (77.8%)
Females	68 (48.6%)	72 (51.4%)

Chi-square (1, N = 266) = 18.84, P < .001; phi = .27

COMPETITIVE ORIENTATIONS AMONG ATHLETES

Results from the studies with the two university samples and the high school sample established sufficient reliability and validity for the SOQ to extend the work to competitive athletes. Specifically, we sampled athletes from four women's teams (softball, swimming, track, and cross-country) and four men's teams (baseball, swimming, gymnastics, and wresting) from a highly competitive intercollegiate program (several teams were ranked in the top 20, and several athletes were competitive at international as well as national levels). We also sampled about the same number of women and men from activity classes as we had in the earlier samples.

These athletes and nonathletes again completed the SOQ and WOFO, and also another measure of competitive orientation, Vealey's (1986, 1988) Competitive Orientation Inventory (COI). Like the SOQ, the COI assesses sport-specific competitive orientation, but its format, assumptions, and scores are quite different. The COI assesses the *relative* importance of winning and performing well in competitive sports. Respondents are presented with a grid containing all combinations of four performances (very good, above average, below average, very poor), and four outcomes (easy win, close win, close loss, big loss), and must then rate how satisfied they would be with each combination on a 0–10 scale. COI scoring is complicated. Sums of squares for rows and columns are calculated to determine the proportion of variance in satisfaction that is due to outcome and the proportion due to performance. For example, someone who is always satisfied with a win and never with a loss, regardless of performance, would have a high outcome score and a low performance score.

An overall Gender × Athlete/Nonathlete MANOVA on SOQ, WOFO, and COI scores revealed gender differences, differences between athletes and nonathletes, and no

interaction. The gender differences replicated earlier work. Males scored higher than females on competitiveness, and especially on win orientation, whereas females scored slightly higher than males on goal orientation. On WOFO, males scored higher on competitiveness, but females scored higher on all other scores. With the COI, males were more outcome-oriented and females were more performance-oriented. Table 13-7 presents the means for male and female athletes and nonathletes on competitive orientation measures.

The athlete/nonathlete comparison addresses the main research question, and Table 13-7 illustrates two important findings. First, the main difference between athletes and nonathletes is on sport-specific competitiveness. Although athletes scored higher than nonathletes on several measures, the univariate and discriminant results clearly indicate that competitiveness is the major discriminator. The second notable finding involves the COI scores. Athletes score much higher than nonathletes on performance orientation and lower on outcome orientation, a finding that seems at odds with much popular thought.

With the athlete sample, we also looked at differences among the 8 teams. These analyses are exploratory, and we cannot draw far-reaching conclusions from a sample with only one team in each sport from a single university. Nevertheless some of the team differences were provocative. One-way analyses of the 8 teams revealed that teams did indeed differ on both SOQ and COI scores. The team differences did not simply reflect gender differences with all men's teams at one end and all women's teams at the other. Generally teams fell along a continuum, although the men wrestlers stood out on some of the scores. For example, the men wrestlers were highest on competitiveness and considerably higher than everyone else on win. For goal, women's cross-country was highest, with wrestling next. With COI scores, outcome and performance scores generally revealed reversed order of teams. Wrestlers were higher on outcome and lower on performance than all other teams.

TABLE 13-6. SOQ and COI Means for Male and Female Athletes and Nonathletes*

	Athletes Males Females	Nonathletes Males Females	Combined Males Females
SOQ			
Competitiveness	59.1 57.1 (58.1)	57.1 43.5 (45.9)	54.9 49.4 (52.0)
Win	24.2 21.5 (22.9)	20.9 17.0 (18.6)	22.7 19.0 (20.7)
Goal	26.4 27.6 (27.0)	24.8 25.5 (25.2)	25.7 26.4 (26.1)
COI			
Outcome	.40 .25 (.33)	.42 .35 (.38)	.41 .30 (.35)
Performance	.49 .67 (.57)	.42 .50 (.47)	.46 .57 (.52)

*Means are indicated in parentheses.

TABLE 13-7. Athlete/Nonathlete Differences on Competitive Orientations

Measure	Athletes		Nonathletes		Univariate F	Discriminant Coefficient
	M	SD	M	SD		
SOQ						
Competitiveness	58.1	6.7	45.9	10.1	98.74*	1.07
Win	22.9	4.7	18.6	5.5	32.56*	.13
Goal	27.0	3.4	25.2	3.6	14.99*	−.16
COI						
Outcome	.33	.26	.38	.24	2.92	.06
Performance	.57	.27	.47	.26	10.05*	.41
WOFO						
Mastery	20.8	3.6	19.1	4.4	10.73*	.18
Work	21.2	2.6	20.6	2.8	3.70	−.03
Competitiveness	15.0	2.8	13.1	3.4	14.56*	−.33
Personal unconcern	9.6	2.5	9.4	2.7	0.70	.13

*$p < .001$

The team differences seemed to reflect the nature of the sport and its competitive structure. In a wrestling match, outcome is the critical measure of success; performance during the match doesn't matter if the wrestler makes an error and gets pinned in the third period. In contrast, swimming and track offer performance scores and personal bests as measures of success. In this study both women's and men's swimming and track scored higher on performance orientation, whereas women's softball and men's baseball scored higher on outcome orientation. Our findings (see Gill & Dzewaltowski, 1988) could reflect characteristics of the particular team, its tradition, the coach, or other unique factors. In any event, athletic teams differ on competitive orientation, and we might probe the sources and consequences of such differences in future work.

The study with athletes ended work on the development and validation of the SOQ. At that point, the SOQ seemed to have good reliability and validity, and seemed to hold promise as a research tool for other work on competitive orientation. The following section describes two subsequent studies that used the SOQ with some relatively unique samples. First, Kang, a former graduate student, administered a translated version of the SOQ to athletes and nonathletes at a major university in Taiwan. Kang, Gill, Acevedo, and Deeter (1990) conducted a Gender × Athlete/Nonathlete analysis paralleling our earlier athlete study and found similar results. Gender differences were nonsignificant, although similar in direction to the U.S. study. As in the U.S., athletes scored higher than nonathletes on all three SOQ scores. Because this university attracts many of Taiwan's international athletes, we also separated the sample into international athletes, university athletes, and nonathletes. International athletes had the highest scores, followed by university athletes, and then nonathletes.

In another study, Acevedo, Gill, and Dzewalowski (1987) used the SOQ as part of a survey with ultramarathon runners participating in the Western States 100 in 1986. The Western States 100 is an ultimate ultramarathon of 100 miles up and down mountains in California with rough

terrain and extreme temperature and altitude changes, so the athlete sample is unique. Within the ultramarathon sample we compared males and females and finishers and nonfinishers (with about equal numbers of each), but neither comparison yielded differences. The lack of gender differences contrasts with our earlier work (indeed, the female ultramarathoners actually scored slightly higher than did males on all SOQ scores), and probably attests to the uniqueness of the sample.

The most interesting finding with the ultramarathoners was simply their overall scores. Their competitiveness scores were slightly higher than our university samples, but lower than the intercollegiate athletes. The ultramarathoners' goal scores were quite high, but their win scores were not only lower than the those of the athletes, but lower than the nonathlete university samples. Data from the ultramarathoners, Taiwanese sample, and our athlete/nonathlete study are combined in Table 13–8 for reference.

Table 13–8 includes the highest and lowest team score and one middle score from the athlete sample for comparison. Generally, all athletes have higher SOQ scores than nonathletes. Competitiveness definitely shows this trend, but we see some exceptions with win and goal orientation. Ultramarathoners are the most notable group as they score quite low on win orientation. Also, a few teams score no higher than nonathletes on win or goal orientation.

To summarize the findings, athletes score higher on both general and sport-specific achievement orientation, but it is sport-specific competitiveness that really separates athletes and nonathletes. Athletes' scores are not uniformly high on win orientation, as the popular media and conventional wisdom might suggest. Instead, athletes are oriented more to performance than to outcome. Finally, although athletes as a group show these orientations, there are wide variations among athletic teams, especially in the relative emphasis on individual performance and win/loss outcomes. Athletes are competitive, but winning is not the only thing.

TABLE 13–8. Athletic Group Comparisons on SOQ Scores

Competitiveness		Win		Goal	
Nonathletes					
Iowa	45.9		18.6		25.2
Taiwan	45.7		20.8		26.5
Athletes, Sports					
Women's Swimming	51.7	Women's Swimming	18.2	Men's Baseball	24.3
Women's Softball	59.1	Men's Swimming	22.4	Women's Swimming	27.1
Men's Wrestling	62.4	Men's Wrestling	27.7	Women's Cross-Country	29.6
Taiwan					
International	54.9		25.3		27.7
University	50.0		22.9		27.3
Ultramarathoners	48.9		15.8		27.6

RELATED WORK AND IMPLICATIONS

All results from the initial studies during the development of the SOQ and subsequent research using the SOQ with athletes provide sufficient data to support the reliability and validity of the SOQ so that it may be used by sport psychologists who want to investigate sport achievement orientations. This multidimensional measure, which separates win and goal orientation from more basic competitiveness, permits insights not possible with a unidimensional measure. Some of the gender differences and the differences among athletic teams illustrate how we can gain a more complete picture with all three scores.

The competitiveness subscale, which is the major component of the SOQ, represents competitiveness as defined in the earlier section. That is, competitiveness is a sport-specific achievement orientation, or the tendency to strive for success and satisfaction in sport competition. This competitiveness subscale follows Martens's competition model and Scanlan's early competitiveness work, and should be useful for investigating competitiveness as defined by them.

The win and goal subscales relate more closely to research on competition as rivalry, and the traditional research on competitive, cooperative, and independent goal structures. Vealey's COI, which assesses the relative importance of performance and outcome goals in competitive sport, reflects similar constructs, although performance and outcome are at opposite ends of a bipolar dimension for Vealey and independent orientations on the SOQ. These win and goal orientations, or the performance-outcome dimension, parallel some of the most prominent achievement research within psychology and education. In particular, the work of Dweck (1986), Ames (1984), and Nicholls (1984), as well as the efforts of Spence and Helmreich (1983), discussed earlier, has had an impact on sport achievement research.

These researchers advocate multidimensional achievement orientations, and all their models suggest that some type of task or performance orientation leads to greater achievement and satisfaction than an ego or outcome orientation, which typically is equated with competition in the educational psychology literature. Within sport psychology, for example, Duda (1989; see also Chapter 18 in this book) has applied Nicholls's task-ego distinction to develop sport-specific measures and has begun to investigate the relationship of task and ego orientation to sport and exercise attitudes and behaviors. Lewthwaite (1990) has proceeded from her work on youth sport with Scanlan to examine the relationship of children's multidimensional goal orientation (particularly mastery and competitive and social orientations) to achievement, satisfaction, and threat or anxiety.

The distinction between task or performance and ego or outcome orientations reflects the traditional research distinction between competition and cooperation or independent achievement. Indeed, examination of the results of studies on competitive, cooperative, and independent goal structures and the newer work on motivational orientation yields similar conclusions and implications. Specifically, despite our popular myths, competition (defined as rivalry or mutually exclusive goals) has detrimental effects on performance, learning, satisfaction and nearly all aspects of achievement and personal development. This is summarized in particularly readable form in Kohn's (1986) appropriately titled book *No Contest: The Case Against Competition*. Kohn lists several commonly held beliefs: (a) competition is part of "human nature" and inevitable, (b) competition motivates us to do our best, (c) competitive contests are the best way to have a good time, and (d) competition builds character (confidence, self-esteem). Kohn then effectively musters considerable evidence to show that all of these are myths and that, indeed, it is no contest.

Detrimental effects of competition on performance and satisfaction were demonstrated in Deutsch's (1949) classic comparisons of competition, cooperation, and independent settings, and many subsequent studies confirm the earlier findings. For example, 25 years after his earliest report, Deutsch (1973) surveyed the many studies in the intervening years and noted consistent confirmation and extension of the early findings. In another study familiar to many in sport psychology, as well as in social psychology, Sherif et al. (1961) demonstrated the detrimental effects of competition on boys in a summer camp setting. In Sherif's Robbers Cave experiment, detrimental effects of competition were overcome only by incorporating superordinate goals, in which all boys had to work together to accomplish the task (essentially a cooperative goal structure). Many studies have been conducted comparing competitive, cooperative, and independent situations other than the widely known studies by Deutsch, Sherif, and their colleagues. Roger and David Johnson are two of the most prominent researchers and advocates of noncompetitive activities in educational settings. Based on a meta-analysis of 122 studies (Johnson, Maruyama, Johnson, Nelson, & Skon, 1981), they concluded that the evidence overwhelmingly indicated that cooperation was superior to competition.

It is important to remember that most of the research just cited defines competition as rivalry in terms of the goal structure. Thus the situation forces an outcome-oriented approach regardless of individual differences. Many of the current advocates of multidimensional achievement approaches, and the sport psychologists who adopt those approaches, support a task or performance orientation and behavior even within sport competition. Moreover, many of the sport psychologists involved in applied work with competitive athletes emphasize performance or goal orientations (e.g., Martens, 1987; Orlick, 1986) to enhance performance and to control anxiety. Burton (1989) demonstrated the value of performance goals over outcome goals in an applied study with swimmers, and pointed out that outcome goals may actually reduce effort and motivation because they are inherently inflexible and uncontrollable.

Unfortunately, it is not easy to focus on performance goals or to develop a performance orientation in sport. As Butt (1987) points out, the competitive social norm is imposed on athletes regardless of individual differences. This imposed structure is of particular concern when we consider children who are just developing their sport orientations. Virtually all the evidence, from anthropology, biology, education, psychology, and everywhere else, indicates that competitiveness is learned and not inevitable. Cross-cultural studies probably provide the strongest evidence. Mead (1937) observed cultural differences in competition and cooperation in her widely known anthropological work.

More recent cross-cultural research has documented cultural differences in competitiveness. As we might expect, Anglo-American children are much more competitive than Mexican or Mexican-American children (Madsen & Shapira, 1970; Nelson & Kagan, 1972), and urban Canadian children are more competitive than Blackfoot Indian children (Miller, 1973). Within sport psychology, Duda (1986) compared Anglo and Navajo children and reported both cultural and gender differences with Anglo males the most

competitive and most concerned with sport achievement. Orlick (1978) and McNally and Orlick (1975) have investigated cooperative sport activities with urban Canadian and Inuit children. Again, both cultural and gender differences were apparent, with Inuit children more receptive to cooperative games than urban children, and girls more receptive than boys.

These cultural differences, as well as the gender differences reported with the SOQ development and in other work, all suggest that competitiveness is learned and heavily influenced by the social context and socialization processes. Eccles and her colleagues (Eccles et al., 1983) have developed a model of achievement that clearly emphasizes socialization and social context in the development of achievement orientation and behaviors, and also illustrates the role of socialization in the development of gender differences in achievement. Eccles and Harold (1991) recently applied the model to sport and demonstrated that the model holds for sport achievement as well as for other areas, that gender differences in children's sport attitudes are strong and emerge at a very early age, and that these gender differences seem to be a consequence of gender socialization rather than "natural" aptitude.

If competitiveness is learned and influenced by social context, then we can encourage cooperative behavior just as we now encourage competitive behavior. Moreover, if we consider competitive sport in the broader sense, rather than assume a competitive goal structure and rivalry orientation as a given, we can encourage task and mastery goal orientations within competitive sport. In his work on cooperative games, Orlick (1978) demonstrated that children could learn cooperative activities, and moreover, that cooperative behaviors carried over into other activities. Certainly those sport psychologists who recognize the value of performance goals should be able to help teachers, coaches, and participants develop a task or performance orientation and deemphasize the structural emphasis on outcomes that leads to undesirable ego involvement.

Perhaps the most important implication for sport psychology research and practice is simply that we should recognize that individual differences exist. Achievement in sport means different things to different people. Even among highly competitive athletes we see wide variations. Although highly competitive sport programs typically equate success with winning or striving to win, many athletes in those programs emphasize personal standards. We may miss some potentially high-achieving sport participants, such as the ultramarathoners, by not offering more noncompetitive, or at least non-win-oriented, activities. Overall, we should present more opportunities for personal goals and challenges within both our competitive and noncompetitive sport and exercise programs. Even beyond that, performance achievement may not be necessary, either. In my idealistic world, we would offer more cooperative, non–achievement-oriented activities for those who are not concerned with either interpersonal or personal performance standards in sport and exercise.

SPORT ORIENTATION QUESTIONNAIRE

The sport orientation questionnaire yields three scores: competitiveness, win orientation, and goal orientation. Each item is scored from 1 to 5 (A = 5, B = 4, C = 3, D = 2, E = 1). To obtain the three scores, total the responses as follows:

Competitiveness—total items 1, 3, 5, 7, 9, 11, 13, 15, 17, 19, 21, 23, and 25.

Win orientation—total items 2, 6, 10, 14, 18, and 22.
Goal orientation—total items 4, 8, 12, 16, 20, and 24.

The following statements describe reactions to sport situations. We want to know how you *usually* feel about sports and competition. Read each statement and circle the letter that indicates how much you agree or disagree with each statement on the scale: A, B, C, D, or E. There are no right or wrong answers; simply answer as you honestly feel. Do not spend too much time on any one statement. Remember, choose the letter that describes how you *usually* feel.

	Strongly agree	Slightly agree	Neither agree nor disagree	Slightly disagree	Strongly disagree
1. I am a determined competitor.	A	B	C	D	E
2. Winning is important.	A	B	C	D	E
3. I am a competitive person.	A	B	C	D	E
4. I set goals for myself when I compete.	A	B	C	D	E
5. I try my hardest to win.	A	B	C	D	E
6. Scoring more points than my opponent is very important to me.	A	B	C	D	E
7. I look forward to competing.	A	B	C	D	E
8. I am most competitive when I try to achieve personal goals.	A	B	C	D	E
9. I enjoy competing against others.	A	B	C	D	E
10. I hate to lose.	A	B	C	D	E
11. I thrive on competition.	A	B	C	D	E
12. I try hardest when I have a specific goal.	A	B	C	D	E
13. My goal is to be the best athlete possible.	A	B	C	D	E
14. The only time I am satisfied is when I win.	A	B	C	D	E
15. I want to be successful in sports.	A	B	C	D	E
16. Performing to the best of my ability is very important to me.	A	B	C	D	E
17. I work hard to be successful in sports.	A	B	C	D	E
18. Losing upsets me.	A	B	C	D	E
19. The best test of my ability is competing against others.	A	B	C	D	E
20. Reaching personal performance goals is very important to me.	A	B	C	D	E
21. I look forward to the opportunity to test my skills in competition.	A	B	C	D	E
22. I have the most fun when I win.	A	B	C	D	E
23. I perform my best when I am competing against an opponent.	A	B	C	D	E
24. The best way to determine my ability is to set a goal and try to reach it.	A	B	C	D	E
25. I want to be the best every time I compete.	A	B	C	D	E

References

Acevedo, E. O., Gill, D. L., & Dzewaltowski, D. A. (1987, Sept.). *Sport-specific psychological characteristics of ultramarathoners.* Paper presented at the Association for the Advancement of Applied Sport Psychology Conference, Newport Beach, CA.

Ames, C. (1984). Competitive, cooperative and individualistic goal structures: A motivational analysis. In R. Ames & C. Ames (Eds.), *Research on motivation in education: Student motivation* (pp. 177–207). New York: Academic Press.

Atkinson, J. W. (1964). *An introduction to motivation.* Princeton, NJ: Van Nostrand.

————. (1974). The mainsprings of achievement-oriented activity. In J. W. Atkinson & J. O. Raynor (Eds.), *Motivation and achievement* (pp. 13–41). New York: Halstead.

Burton, D. (1989). Winning isn't everything: Examining the impact of performance goals on collegiate swimmers' cognitions and performance. *The Sport Psychologist, 3,* 105–132.

Butt, D. S. (1987). *Psychology of sport: The behavior, motivation, personality, and performance of athletes* (2nd ed.). New York: Van Nostrand Reinhold.

Crowne, D. P., & Marlowe, D. (1960). A new scale of social desirability independent of psychopathology. *Journal of Consulting Psychology, 24,* 349–354.

Deutsch, M. (1949). An experimental study of the effects of cooperation and competition upon group processes. *Human relations, 2,* 199–232.

Deutsch, M. (1973). *The resolution of conflict: Constructive and destructive processes.* New Haven: Yale University Press.

Duda, J. L. (1986). A cross-cultural analysis of achievement motivation in sport and the classroom. In L. VanderVelden & J. Humphrey (Eds.), *Current selected research in the psychology and sociology of sport* (pp. 115–134). New York: AMS Press.

———— (1989). Relationship between task and ego orientation and the perceived purpose of sport among high school athletes. *Journal of Sport & Exercise Psychology, 11,* 318–335.

Dweck, C. S. (1986). Motivational processes affecting learning. *American Psychologist, 41,* 1040–1048.

Eccles, J., Adler, T. F., Futterman, C. A., Goff, S. B., Kaczala, C. M., Meece, J. L., & Midgley, C. (1983). Expectations, values, and academic behaviors. In J. T. Spence (Ed.), *Achievement and achievement motivation* (pp. 75–146). San Francisco: W. H. Freeman.

Eccles, J. S., & Harold, R. D. (1991). Gender differences in sport involvement: Applying the Eccles expectancy-value model. *Journal of Applied Sport Psychology, 3,* 7–35.

Fabian, L., & Ross, M. (1984). The development of the Sports Competition Trait Inventory. *Journal of Sport Behavior, 7,* 13–27.

Gill, D. L. (1988). Gender differences in competitive orientation and sport participation. *International Journal of Sport Psychology, 19,* 145–159.

Gill, D. L., & Deeter, T. E. (1988). Development of the Sport Orientation Questionnaire. *Research Quarterly for Exercise and Sport, 59,* 191–202.

Gill, D. L., & Dzewaltowski, D. A. (1988). Competitive orientations among intercollegiate athletes: Is winning the only thing? *The Sport Psychologist, 2,* 212–221.

Gill, D. L., Dzewaltowski, D. A. & Deeter, T. E. (1988). The relationship of competitiveness and achievement orientation to participation in sport and nonsport activities. *Journal of Sport & Exercise Psychology, 10,* 139–150.

Helmreich, R. L., & Spence, J. T. (1978). The Work and Family Orientation Questionnaire: An objective instrument to assess components of achievement motivation and attitudes toward family and career. *Catalog of Selected Documents in Psychology, 8* (2) (Document #1677).

Johnson, D. W., & Johnson, R. T. (1985). Motivational processes in cooperative, competitive, and individualistic learning situations. In C. Ames & R. Ames (Eds.), *Research on motivation in education* (vol. 2) (pp. 249–286). Orlando, FL: Academic Press.

Johnson, D. W., Maruyama, G., Johnson, R., Nelson, D., & Skon, L. (1981). The effects of cooperative, competitive, and individualistic goal structures on achievement: A meta-analysis. *Psychological Bulletin, 89,* 47–62.

Kang, L., Gill, D. L., Acevedo, E. O., & Deeter, T. E. (1990). Competitive orientations among athletes and nonathletes in Taiwan. *International Journal of Sport Psychology, 21,* 146–157.

Kohn, A. (1986). *No contest: The case against competition.* Boston: Houghton Mifflin.

Lewthwaite, R. (1990). Threat perception in competitive trait anxiety: The endangerment of important goals. *Journal of Sport and Exercise Psychology, 12,* 280–300.

Madsen, M. C., & Shapira, A. (1970). Cooperative and competitive behavior of urban Afro-American, Anglo-American, Mexican-American, and Mexican village children. *Developmental Psychology, 3,* 16–20.

Martens, R. (1976a). Competition: In need of a theory. In D. M. Landers (Ed.), *Social problems in athletics* (pp. 9–17). Urbana, IL: University of Illinois Press.

Martens, R. (1976b). Competitiveness in sports. In F. Landry & W. A. R. Orban (Eds.), *Physical activity and human well-being* (pp. 323–343). Miami, FL: Symposia Specialists.

Martens, R. (1977). *Sport Competition Anxiety Test.* Champaign, IL: Human Kinetics.

Martens, R. (1987). *Coaches' guide to sport psychology.* Champaign, IL: Human Kinetics.

Martens, R., Vealey, R. S., & Burton, D. (1990). *Competitive anxiety in sport.* Champaign, IL: Human Kinetics.

McClelland, D. C., Atkinson, J. W., Clark, R. A., & Lowell, E. L. (1953). *The achievement motive.* New York: Appleton-Century-Crofts.

McNally, J. F., & Orlick, T. D. (1975). Cooperative sports structures: A preliminary analysis. *Mouvement, 7,* 267–271.

Mead, M. (1937). *Cooperation and competition among primitive peoples.* New York: McGraw-Hill.

Miller, A. G. (1973). Integration and acculturation of cooperative behavior among Blackfoot Indian and non-Indian Canadian children. *Journal of Cross-Cultural Psychology, 4,* 374–380.

Murray, H. A. (1938). *Explorations in personality.* New York: Oxford University Press.

Nelson, L. L., & Kagan, S. (1972, Sept.). Competition: The star-spangled scramble. *Psychology Today, 5,* 53–56; 90–91.

Nicholls, J. G. (1984). Achievement motivation: Conceptions of ability, subjective experience, task choice, and performance. *Psychological Review, 91,* 328–346.

Orlick, T. (1978). *Winning through cooperation.* Washington, DC: Acropolis Books.

Orlick, T. (1986). *Psyching for sport.* Champaign, IL: Leisure Press.

Scanlan, T. K. (1978). Antecedents of competitiveness. In R. A.

Magill, M. J. Ash, & F. L. Smoll (Eds.), *Children in sport: A contemporary anthology* (pp. 53–75). Champaign, IL: Human Kinetics.

Scanlan, T. K. (1988). Social evaluation and the competition process: A developmental perspective. In F. L. Smoll, R. A. Magill, & M. J. Ash (Eds.), *Children in sport* (3rd. ed.) (pp. 135–148). Champaign, IL: Human Kinetics.

Sherif, M., Harvey, O. J., White, B. J., Hood, R. W., & Sherif, C. W. (1961). *The robbers cave experiment: Intergroup conflict and cooperation.* Norman, OK: University of Oklahoma Press.

Spence, J. T., & Helmreich, R. L. (1978). *Masculinity and femininity: Their psychological dimensions, correlates and antecedents.* Austin: University of Texas Press.

Spence, J. T., & Helmreich, R. L. (1983). Achievement-related motives and behaviors. In J. T. Spence (Ed.), *Achievement and achievement motives* (pp. 7–74). San Francisco: W. H. Freeman.

Vealey, R. S. (1986). Conceptualization of sport-confidence and competitive orientation: Preliminary investigation and instrument development. *Journal of Sport Psychology, 8,* 221–246.

Vealey, R. S. (1988). Sport-confidence and competitive orientation: An addendum on scoring procedures and gender differences. *Journal of Sport & Exercise Psychology, 10,* 471–478.

Veroff, J. (1969). Social comparison and the development of achievement motivation. In C. P. Smith (Ed.), *Achievement-related motives in children* (pp. 46–101). New York: Russell Sage Foundation.

Weiss, M. R., & Chaumeton, N. (1992). Motivational orientations in sport. In T. Horn (Ed.), *Advances in sport psychology.* Champaign, IL: Human Kinetics.

White, R. W. (1959). Motivation reconsidered: The concept of competence. *Psychological review, 66,* 297–333.

·14·

ANXIETY

Dieter Hackfort
Peter Schwenkmezger

TERMINOLOGICAL NETWORK

Everyone knows about it, until he/she is asked to explain it. No one is able to understand it, but everyone has experienced it. Most of us—laypersons as well as researchers—have difficulty describing it. The subject is anxiety and emotion.

Fehr and Russell (1984, p. 464) observed that "Everyone knows what an emotion is, until asked to give a definition. Then, it seems, no one knows." In this perspective, Smith and Lazarus (1989, p. 3) propose that "in any definition we need to distinguish between what can be said about emotion in general, and about specific emotions such as anger, fear, guilt, disgrace, pride, love, etc." Alternatively, research on specific emotions should examine and suggest clarifying characteristics of emotions in general and specifics of single emotions. Anxiety research in general, and research on anxiety in sport in particular, must follow this strategy.

EMOTION AND ANXIETY

From a common-sense perspective as well as from a scientific perspective, anxiety is believed to be an emotion. With respect to theories of differential emotions (see, e.g., Izard, 1977; Plutchik, 1962), it is conceptualized as a fundamental emotion. In cognitive theories on emotions, it is thought of as dependent on special appraisals (see, e.g., Lazarus & Averill, 1972), and in stress research, as a typical stress emotion (see, e.g., Folkins & Sime, 1981). Emotions are regarded as psychological phenomena or functional subsystems similar to motivation and cognition.

Increasingly, the understanding of emotions as processes interacting with cognitive, motivational, volitional, and neurophysiological processes, also regarded as components to or antecedents and consequences of emotions, is

being advanced. These processes have functional meaning in adaptation and action regulation. In reference to this point, emotions have been attributed to serve as synchronizing or disturbing agents. In everyday life we can notice a distinction between so-called "negative" emotions (such as anxiety, anger, and jealousy) and "positive" emotions (such as happiness, pride, and love). The reference for this distinction seems to be predominantly the subjective feelings associated with these emotions and the less specialized functional properties of them. Since Freud emphasized the importance of anxiety as a danger signal, a positive functional meaning of this "negative" emotion has also been recognized.

ANXIETY AND FEAR

The distinction between anxiety and fear can be traced to philosophical reflections. It was identified in psychological theories (Cattell & Scheier, 1961; Freud, 1952), and from phenomenological analyses, leading to the attempt to prove distinguishable physiological patterns among the emotions in psychophysiological experiments (for a summary, see Hackfort & Schwenkmezger, 1985). Despite critical objections, this distinction continues to be discussed in current research literature. The heuristic value of this distinction has recently become obvious, particularly in cognitive theories of anxiety (e.g., Epstein, 1972; Lazarus, 1966) in which the aspect of the control of anxiety is also taken into consideration (see Hackfort, 1987).

The effort to distinguish between anxiety and fear seems justified by the following:

1. A more detailed description of experience and behavior can be achieved.
2. Strategies for coping can be distinguished, and potential

328

therapeutic interventions can be carried out more effectively.

3. Access to the understanding of pathological forms of anxiety, such as phobias or anxiety neuroses, can be improved.

A number of authors have contributed essential and distinctive features and findings to modern anxiety research. For Cattell and Scheier (1961), degree of recognizability is an important factor in the distinction between anxiety and fear. Concrete, easily identifiable stimuli signal a threat and are often associated with fear, while perceptions which only provide *partial* information based on cues or symbols correspond with anxiety. Cattell and Scheier regard uncertainty (as to whether a situation of threat will occur) as the chief characteristic of anxiety. Plutchik (1962) regards fear as an unconditioned reaction with a self-protective function, and anxiety as a product of upbringing and the experience of learning. Fear is stimulus-specific, and anxiety is caused by anticipatory and imaginative processes.

Within the framework of social-psychological investigations, Sarnoff and Zimbardo (1961) refer to differences between anxiety and fear. They base their arguments on Festinger (1954) and Schachter (1959), the former stipulating uncertainty, the latter anxiety, as the cause for affiliation tendencies. Accordingly, social contact can reduce fear (cf. Firestone, Kaplan, & Russel, 1973); anxiety, however, motivates one to avoid a social context. In the investigations of Sarnoff and Zimbardo (1961), anxiety was described as any threat caused by the activation of repressed drives, and fear was operationalized as physical threat produced by electric shock. The conclusion that in fear alone the need to affiliate increased was confirmed in a study by Teichman (1974). Furthermore, this author reports a more distinct affiliative tendency in people with low fear in contrast to highly fearful people.

Lynch, Watts, and Galloway (1973), however, showed proof that it is not the distinction between anxiety and fear that is of importance concerning the need to affiliate, but rather the evaluated appropriateness of these feelings with regard to the given situation of strain. Besides a dependency of the affiliative tendency on certainty or uncertainty regarding one's abilities, opinions, or the emotions themselves (cf. Gerard, 1961), the endeavor to maintain an adequate "personal sphere" seems also to have an effect, "personal sphere" meaning the tendency of a person to keep or to allow neither too large nor too small a distance between others, depending on other personal characteristics such as social apprehension (cf. Hormuth, Martin, & Petermann, 1976; McMahon, 1973; Patterson, 1973). The conclusion seems hardly surprising that a person may tend to seek greater spatial distance and that there is a lower affiliative tendency if the situation of strain through the social component is stress- or anxiety-inducing. This is the case if, for example, personal attractiveness is questioned, and self-concept or role identity is threatened (cf. Dosey & Meisels, 1969). With this, uncertainty about competence and restrictions of the subjective scope of action (see later)

are probably related. Izard (1972, 1981), too, associates fear with a definite danger, and anxiety with ambiguity and uncertainty regarding the risk of danger. Gellhorn (1965), in his neurophysiological approach, describes anxiety as a chronic form of fear.

With some authors, it is important to consider this distinction from an evolutionary perspective. From this viewpoint, fear is seen as a specific reflex-like defense and protection reaction in both animals and humans (e.g., Costello, 1976). In contrast, anxiety is viewed as a complex emotional state that is associated with the development of higher nervous system functions. Fear is regarded as a biological, self-protective, adaptive mechanism, whereas anxiety is associated with learning and socialization processes (cf. Pongratz, 1973). Concerning the point of view espoused in evolution theory, Izard's (1972, 1981) differential theory of emotion must be noted as well. In this view, fear is perceived as a fundamental emotion, whereas anxiety is considered an emotion composed of fear (as a significant component), misery, disgrace, rage, and interest. For Epstein (1977), anxiety is neither identical with fear or activation nor independent of it. He regards anxiety as a state of unoriented activation while one is perceiving danger. Unlike fear, anxiety cannot be channeled into specific behaviors of avoidance. The source of danger in anxiety cannot be determined definitively (a feature of uncertainty, as we will see shortly); therefore no specific activities can be used for coping.

As Seligman (1979) postulates, a need for competence (avoidance of helplessness) and the predictability of events is significant in order to avoid anxiety. Anxiety will not arise if signals of security indicate the absence of situations of danger. After signals indicating danger, fear is experienced, which as a motivating factor triggers efforts of coping or controlling (see Seligman, 1979). If there is contingency between such signals and events, in accordance with the theory, security is engendered due to associated predictability, i.e., the absence of signals as a sign of danger engenders security. The absence of any signals leads to anxiety. If the individual experiences fear-motivated efforts for control as pointless, he/she experiences uncontrollability, which will give rise to depression. Lazarus (1966), according to Freud, also regards anxiety as a signal. In his cognitive-phenomenological approach, he emphasizes that anxiety is not associated with concrete dangers, as is fear, but is conveyed via symbolic elements (see also Lazarus & Averill, 1972; for a summary, see Hackfort & Schwenkmezger, 1985).

In the formulation of his attention-perseverance theory of the differentiation of anxiety (APTAD), Butollo (1979) orients himself toward Lazarus' concept and emphasizes processes of attention, learning by association, and reinforcement. He sees the distinction between anxiety and fear as serving above all for a better differentiation of clearly outlined contents of anxiety (phobias) and anxiety neuroses (freely flowing "groundless" fits of anxiety) (Butollo, 1979). In fear, triggers, contents, and countermeasures are seen as known and describable; in anxiety, this is not regarded as given for the person concerned. The last-named concepts refer to uncertainty regarding the source of danger and the employable techniques of coping in anxiety. As far as fear is concerned, there is certainty regarding these facts, and fear therefore leads to actions of escape. In anxiety, there is an increase in activation that, due to diffuse appraisals of threat and a lack of information, leads to no-intentional, goal-directed behavior for coping.

One can say that anxiety—as opposed to fear—is associated with the development of the higher nervous system and the abilities of abstraction and anticipation. Anxiety seems to be the more recent emotion in terms of evolution and is related to processes of learning and socialization (whereas simple experiments of conditioning are based on the engendering and inducing of fear). Subjective uncertainty with regard to anxiety leads to uncertainty in action and, in the final analysis, to the inability to act. The possibilities for overcoming anxiety individually or therapeutically follow from this transformation into fear, and can be accommodated by specific means of action. Both emotions appear to be closely connected and of importance in sport.

STRESS AND ANXIETY

The physiological stress theory as described by Hans Selye (e.g., 1956) is based on the concept that the human organism can be described as a system following the homeostatic principle ("principle of equilibrium"). If the equilibrium is disturbed, the system is self-regulating ("self-regulations," "adaptation"). These self-regulations can theoretically be conceived as a feedback control system. Regulation of body heat, hormones, intoxicants, and muscular tension are examples from the field of physiology.

According to Selye, the organism responds with a stress reaction when normal adaptations and compensation responses in the regulation process fail. Besides specific responses to specific situations of strain, there is a stereotypically occurring unspecific sequence of responses, the so-called General Adaptation Syndrome (GAS). Three phases can be distinguished: (1) alarm response, (2) stage of resistance, and (3) stage of exhaustion. The first stage, "alarm response," which is further differentiated into an initial shock phase with lower resistance and a countershock phase with defense mechanisms becoming effective (cf. Selye, e.g., 1956), involves a number of physiological concomitants. In the countershock phase, as the phase that characterizes the alarm response in a broader sense, an increase of adrenocortical hormones and a general hyperactivity can be observed.

In the second stage these symptoms recede due to regulation processes in the sense of adaptation. During the third stage, in the case of a long-term stress stimuli, organs may be negatively imparted. Heart, suprarenal gland, liver, skin, stomach, and the intestinal region may be damaged. For more recent results of the physiological stress theory and their connection to psychological approaches, see Taché and Selye (1978).

In the field of psychology, the term *stress* is not applied uniformly, and often no clear distinction is made between stress and anxiety. The following meanings for stress are most frequently reported (cf. Levitt, 1979):

1. A combination of stimuli or a situation which comprises the circumstances a person subjectively experiences as threatening and which can cause anxiety.
2. The process which is triggered if a person is no longer able to cope with the demands of a situation and negative consequences are to be expected in the case of failure.
3. Responses to threatening stimuli.

In spite of differing definitions, it is generally assumed that stress responses are directly connected with the existence of objective features of stimuli. These stimuli are called stressors. They can be either of a physical nature, or of a complex psychological or social nature. According to Janke (1976, p. 38), they may be categorized as follows:

1. External stressors.
   a. changes of the "sensory input" in the sense of overstimulation (noise, light, vibration), or withdrawal of sensory information (sensory deprivation of restriction)
   b. stimuli of pain (electric, thermal, chemical, or mechanical stimulation or lesions)
   c. real or simulated situations of danger (e.g., parachute jumps, accidents, operations, situations of fight).
2. Stimuli leading to deprivation of primary needs.
   a. food
   b. water
   c. sleep
   d. exercise and activity
   e. constant temperature.
3. Stressors of performance.
   a. excessive demands (pressure of time, several jobs, distraction)
   b. too-low demands (monotonous tasks of the same kind)
   c. failure in situations of performance, dissatisfaction with job, examinations.
4. Social stressors.
   a. social isolation
   b. interpersonal conflicts
   c. changes of habits
   d. loss of relatives
   e. isolation from parents.
5. Other stressors.
   a. conflict (decisions between several alternatives)
   b. uncertainty about future events (uncertainty, unpredictability).

Some sport-specific examples include:

1. reactions of spectators
2. acoustic deprivation in diving
3. high-risk sport (climbing, diving, parachuting, motor racing)
4. risk of injury (e.g., in failure of an attempt; in extreme physical exertion; in martial arts)
5. time lag, climatic change, and encountering different food at competitions in other countries/continents
6. conflicts with coach
7. conflicts with members of team
8. conflicts in family/school, etc., due to stress from sport
9. conflicts in decision-making in the course of complex actions in sport (e.g., in team sport; mostly in the context of social situations)

Spielberger (1972) defines stress as closely related to state and trait anxiety. He limits the term exclusively to objective conditions (stimuli) in personal environment. The individual, subjective appraisal of these stimuli as physically or psychologically threatening is characterized by the term "threat." As a consequence of such a threat, the person responds with state-anxiety (a definition follows shortly). High trait anxiety causes a person to have the tendency to perceive many conditions as threatening and to respond with state anxiety. Figure 14–1 shows a schematic representation of the relationship between stress and anxiety.

However, at present, there is no generally accepted way of differentiating between anxiety and stress; i.e., by specific patterns of response on the basis of subjective-psychological, physiological, or behavioral differences. Suggested distinctions are of heuristic importance at a specific point in time.

DEFINITIONS

STATE AND TRAIT ANXIETY

Cattell and Scheier (1961) and Spielberger (1966, 1972, 1983) suggest distinctions between the terms *trait anxiety* and *state anxiety*. Trait anxiety is defined as an acquired behavior disposition, independent of time, causing an individual to perceive a wide range of objectively not very

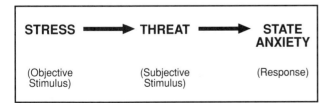

FIGURE 14–1 Schematic representation of the connection between stress and anxiety according to Spielberger (1972).

dangerous circumstances as threatening. It is contrary to objective harmlessness to react with state anxiety.

State anxiety reactions can be described as subjective, consciously perceived feelings of inadequacy and tension accompanied by an increased arousal in the autonomous nervous system. State anxiety varies in intensity and duration depending on (1) the number of stress stimuli operating on the individual and (2) the duration of the subjective threat caused by these stimuli. Endler (1978) has taken this research approach and evidences possibilities of extending it. According to him, neither trait anxiety nor state anxiety present, homogeneous constructs. Trait anxiety can be divided into at least four dimensions: (1) threat to ego in the social field, (2) anxiety due to physical danger, (3) anxiety due to complex, incalculable situations, and (4) anxiety due to everyday situations (Endler & Okada, 1975). State anxiety can be divided into at least two components:

1. A cognitive component, which at a high level of state anxiety leads to persons being rather preoccupied with considerations irrelevant/extraneous to the solution of their task instead of concentrating on the solution of their task. (Example: If a player during a soccer match is preoccupied with considerations about how his or her performance is being judged by the coach or other players, or if he or she thinks of a wasted chance or doubtful decisions made by the referee, this is called irrelevant/extraneous cognition).
2. An emotional component, which includes the experience of subjective excitement when the ego is threatened (e.g., anxiety of injury; fear of failure in performance).

The state-trait approach is first discussed in sport psychology by Martens (1977) and extended by the sport-psychological questions of Endler (1978). We will return to consideration of further empirical investigations in greater detail later in this chapter.

The concept of trait anxiety has been differentiated with respect to such situations as test anxiety (Spielberger, Gonzales, Taylor, Algaze, & Anton, 1978) and speech anxiety (Lamb, 1973). To develop an understanding of sport-related anxiety, Hackfort (see Hackfort, 1987; Hackfort & Nitsch, 1989) proposed a transactional concept of anxiety in the frame of action theory. The fundamentals of that concept are, briefly, (1) the understanding of humans as reflexive beings, interpreting themselves and their circumstances by situational definitions; and (2) the understanding of an objective situation constellation composed of the person, task, and environment, which is transformed by the subjective situational definition in an individual action situation. While trait anxiety is regarded as a personal component, the task-environment constellation is regarded as having anxiety potential.

Anxiety is regarded as a relational construct. State anxiety is dependent on the objective situation constellation (person, task, environment) and the subjective interpretation of that constellation, which is influenced by such personal factors as trait anxiety and resources of stress management or anxiety control. The components of anxiety are not attributed either to the person or the environment but to both components as interacting agents. This transactional concept will be outlined in greater detail later.

TRANSACTIONAL DIFFERENTIATIONS WITH SPECIAL REFERENCE TO SPORT-RELATED ANXIETY

The concept of trait anxiety can be differentiated as a personal concept. If one wants to consider the perception of potentials of anxiety or to appraise environment-task constellations as threatening, this can be described as sensitivity. If a person's readiness to react to certain potentials of anxiety is emphasized, this can be characterized as reactivity. Sensitivity and reactivity vary interindividually and differ intraindividually with regard to various potentials of anxiety. Thus, a ski-jumper, when jumping from a 10-meter diving tower, may well perceive a threat and react with anxiety. The symptoms an athlete reacts with vary from person to person; one individual may show considerable physiological reaction (e.g., "cold sweat"), another may be puzzled (pondering the situation). Which symptoms are displayed also depends on the extent to which this person has developed styles of control that can be described as symptom control and/or to what extent the person tolerates the symptoms (symptom tolerance).

Moreover, tolerance and control must be considered with reference to environment-task factors (tolerance of conditions, control of conditions). Factors that should be mentioned here ensue from the nature and extent of the potential for anxiety. For example, a person may be very sensitive to certain noises, and as a result, cannot simply accept or tolerate them. Such a person may nevertheless be able to control this disturbing influence by means of a corresponding cognitive appraisal ("stimulating", "distracting," etc.). Therefore, if sensitivity and reactivity as personal factors are related to the nature and extent of the potential of anxiety, the susceptibility to anxiety depends on the tolerance and control regarding environment-task factors as conditions on the one hand, and occurring symptoms (e.g., cognitions of concern) on the other.

The following questions underlie the relational or transactional conception of anxiety due to the fact that components of the personal factor, trait anxiety, are related to the components of the constellation environment and task in such a way that state anxiety only arises from the interrelation between them: (1) How does a person-environment-task relation work? and (2) What are the functions of emotions (especially anxiety) in the establishment of relations and in the definition of situations, and, consequently, in the process of acting? (See Hackfort, 1987; Nitsch, 1985; Nitsch & Hackfort, 1981).

The concept of anxiety is illustrated in Figure 14–2. In this model the construct of trait anxiety is divided with the specific aspects established as personal components. In the following, in addition, the value relations brought by the

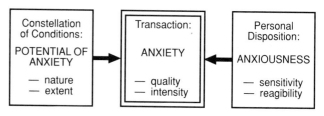

FIGURE 14–2 Anxiety as a relational concept.

person, which, if seen as threatened, lead to anxiety. They shall be differentiated in varied situations (the closer sense potentials of anxiety).

Besides the integration of the personal factor "trait anxiety" in the transactional concept of anxiety and the situation/activity-specific interpretation as, for example, sport-related trait anxiety, a further differentiation is significant. Trait anxiety can be differentiated according to which value relations (e.g., freedom from physical injury, self-realization, social recognition) are experienced as threatening. The different kinds of anxiety resulting from these relations is often referred to as dimensions (anxiety dimensions). Those dimensions are of particular interest in defining the construct of sport-related trait anxiety more precisely.

In general classification attempts which have been mostly carried out by means of factor analyses, most often, anxiety of physical danger/injury has been referred to as a specific dimension (e.g., Becker, 1980). Other factors mentioned are anxiety of failure and anxiety of disgrace (cf. Basowitz, Persky, Korchin, & Grinker, 1955; Hodges & Felling, 1970). When juxtaposing such empirical classification attempts and theoretically founded differentiations, a threat of values can be identified as a relation between them. As a conceptional basis, Maslow's (1954) motivation model can be applied. It is well known that he distinguishes among organism-related, personality-related, social-related, and culture-related motives. If anxiousness (anxiety dimensions) is inferred from this (see Hackfort, 1987), the following dimensions of sport-related trait anxiety can be distinguished also considering further classifications mentioned in the sport-psychological literature (see Hackfort & Schwenkmezger, 1985; Schwenkmezger, 1985a; Vormbrock, 1983): (1) anxiety of physical injury, (2) anxiety of failure, (3) anxiety of competition, (4) anxiety of disgrace, and (5) anxiety of the unknown.

THEORETICAL APPROACHES

PSYCHOANALYTICAL APPROACH

Anxiety is a fundamental concept in psychoanalysis and for the elaboration of psychoanalytic theory. Freud's work included an essential contribution to the understanding of anxiety until modern times. His thoughts on anxiety lead to the first theory of anxiety, which he revised later and replaced with by a second theory of anxiety in "Hemmung, Symptom und Angst" (Gesammelte Werke, 1952).

The first theory of anxiety was framed by Freud as the background of his first topological model. The basis of his idea was that the psyche can be divided into three different partial systems: the subconscious, the preconscious, and the conscious. According to this concept, anxiety is derived from sexual arousal that is constantly produced by the sexually mature organism and leads to tensions that are not eased by sexual reactions. Sexual arousal which is not eased adequately but repressed eventually leads to neurosis or neurotic anxiety. According to Freud, all factors preventing psychological digestion of somatic sexual arousal lead to anxiety neurosis. Symptoms of anxiety neurosis are caused by somatic sexual arousal refused by the psyche; it manifests itself subcortically in reactions that are not at all adequate.

Anxiety neurosis is the central concept of the first theory of anxiety. However, it is not developed comprehensively, but only those components of anxiety are described which, in more recent psychological research, are known as trait anxiety, i.e., the dispositional aspect. The affective state of anxiety, according to Freud, is aroused if the psyche feels incapable of dealing with an impending external task (danger) through an adequate reaction. Freud then relates affective state and anxiety neurosis to each other. Affect and the corresponding neurosis are seen as closely related to each other, the former being the reaction to an exogenous arousal, the latter the reaction to the analogous endogenous arousal. Affect is seen to be a quickly passing state, whereas neurosis is chronic. This results from the exogenous arousal acting as a single force and the endogenous excitement as a constantly effective force.

Freud replaced the first topological model in his work "Das Ich und das Es" (*Gesammelte Werke,* 1952) with the second topological model. The correction and modification of the model were a consequence of Freud's view that the unconscious could not form an instance of its own, but that there also existed unconscious parts in the instance of the ego. These main instances are now known as the id, the ego, and the superego. The id is the unconscious basis from the differentiation of which first the ego, and eventually from the ego, the superego, developed.

This second topological model forms the basis of Freud's second theory of anxiety, which he published in "Hemmung, Symptom und Angst" (*Gesammelte Werke,* 1952). The crucial difference in this concept lies in the dynamic function of anxiety. While in the first theory Freud proceeded from the assumption that anxiety is caused by repression, in the second theory anxiety becomes a prerequisite for repression and all other defense mechanisms. Anxiety is thus no longer to be looked for in the id, but is connected with the ego. Freud presupposes that only the ego can produce anxiety (anxiety is seen as an affective state that can be experienced only by the ego) and that it does so by coming into conflict with its adversaries. Thus, three forms of anxiety can be distinguished:

1. Conflict: ego-superego = anxiety of conscience
2. Conflict: ego-environment = real anxiety
3. Conflict: ego-id = neurotic anxiety

According to Freud (cf., Gesammelte Werke, 1952) anxiety of castration develops into anxiety of conscience and social anxiety. More generally speaking, it is the anger and the punishment of the superego and the loss of its love that the ego identifies as a danger and to which it reacts with the anxiety signal. Real danger is a danger that is known, and real anxiety is anxiety of such a known danger. Neurotic anxiety is anxiety of a danger with which we are not familiar.

Anxiety conceived of in this way can also be described as "signal anxiety," and Freud's second theory of anxiety as "signal theory of anxiety." Anxiety is a signal from the ego in the form of negative emotions (emotions of listlessness) for the id.

The development of anxiety is closely connected with the development of defense mechanisms. In order to reduce anxiety, the ego develops so-called defense mechanisms, such as repression, regression, reaction-formation, denial, intellectualizing, postponing, and so on. In repression, unpleasant memories and ideas are "forgotten." Reaction formation occurs if the impulse-producing anxiety is transformed into the opposite (e.g., hate becomes love). Regression is the return to an earlier stage of development. By postponing, the search for a substitute object is understood, when the choice of the original object of pleasure gratification is blocked by obstacles. Maximum performance in sport in this sense may be seen as a result of processes of postponing, as the original instinctive impulse (possibly a sexual need) could not be gratified.

Fuller (1976) tries to explain the behavior of famous sportsmen and -women psychoanalytically. For example, the childhoods of Muhammad Ali and Francis Chicester are depicted in detail, and each one's performance in sport is derived from considering the events of childhood. By doing so, Fuller attempts to support the hypothesis that Ali's striving for omnipotence should be considered as a defense mechanism in order to demonstrate his being an independent, self-confident man who wishes to dominate the world. The realization of one's own weakness and insignificance and the desire to overcome them therefore present the motivation for a future career in sport. As proof of this hypothesis, Fuller presents medical observations. Accordingly, Ali is supposed to have suffered from emotional disturbances and mortal fear before many of his earlier fights.

Now, how are we to assess the psychoanalytical theory of anxiety and its applicability to sport? As far as empirical results are concerned, the sources of the development of anxiety mentioned by Freud can be confirmed. By means of questionnaire investigations it can be proved that feelings of guilt, strong instinctive demands, and a weak and poorly developed self-confidence represent a characteristic feature that can be interpreted as anxiety (cf. Herrmann, 1969). However, it turns out that for this purpose it is not necessary to adopt categories such as "conscious-unconscious" or "id, ego, or superego," which, moreover, cannot be proved empirically. For similar reasons one has to assume that a major part of Fuller's interpretation attempts will remain pure speculations. Therefore, Ali's anxiety reactions as observed before his fights can be understood as emotional and physiological processes as described within the concept of the prestart state. The unclear concept of defense mechanisms that cannot be defined conclusively is unnecessary.

LEARNING THEORY APPROACH

One of the best investigated theories of the development, maintenance, and removal of anxiety reactions is the theory of two phases, according to Mowrer (1960). Mowrer assumes that anxiety behavior can be acquired and maintained by means of two successive principles of learning: by classic conditioning of the anxiety reaction, and by subsequent instrumental reinforcement of the (motor) reaction of avoidance.

In the first phase, an originally neutral, conditioned stimulus (CS) occurs in temporal closeness to an aversive, unconditioned stimulus (UCS). After one or more performances, a conditioned emotional reaction (CER) arises, namely, the anxiety reaction. It is maintained, even when there is no aversive, unconditioned stimulus. The connections are shown in Figure 14-3.

These connections can be demonstrated particularly clearly in animal experiments. A famous example is represented by Miller (1948): Miller put rats as test animals in the lighter part of a bipartite cage. The light part was fitted with a lattice. Via this lattice aversive stimuli in the form of electric shocks were administered to the test animal. As there was first no way for the animal to escape, the rat reacted with anxiety reactions (trembling, excreting of droppings inter alia). These reactions were retained even if the rat after only a few electric shocks (in the extreme case one shock was sufficient) was put in the light part of the cage where no electric shocks were applied: by the principle of classical conditioning, the rat had learned to react with anxiety to the light part of the cage. In another part of the experiment the test animal was given the chance to escape through a swinging door in the dark part of the cage. The

rat immediately learned to avoid the electric shock by escaping. As a result, anxiety reactions were reduced. This escape behavior is retained for a long time, even if no electric shock is applied. Miller was able to show that rats after far more than 100 trials still avoided the light part of the cage by escaping, even though shocks were no longer applied. This suggests that the rats are capable of acquiring anxiety reactions very quickly (in the extreme case after only one association of CS with UCS) but that escape avoidance behavior is very much resistant to attempts of erasure although the aversive, unconditioned stimulus no longer occurs.

This resistance to attempts to avoid the escape reaction Mowrer explains by the principle of instrumental conditioning. Each reaction avoiding the anxiety-causing, conditioned stimulus (i.e., the light cage in the animal experiment) reduces anxiety (CER). Such a reaction is the avoidance behavior. A reduction of anxiety, however, means a positive reinforcement so that the escape and avoidance reaction are reinforced positively by it, i.e., the probability of their occurrence increases.

The question is whether this result can also be applied to humans. Birbaumer (1977) shows that, given some additional assumptions, corresponding ideas of models can also apply to humans. For example, it can be proved that, as with animals, the motor avoidance reactions of human beings can be retained for a very long time despite the fact that proof of physiological-emotional reactions (CER) cannot be furnished for such a period (cf. Tunner & Birbaumer, 1974). Expectation probably plays an important part here (and the concept may be regarded as a link to cognitive theories). If a person has learned that a conditioned stimulus coincides with an aversive, unconditioned stimulus, he/she will also expect the aversive stimulus (pain, fright, failure) in the future. This expectation, however, can be avoided by not experiencing the original conditioned stimulus as well.

This will be shown clearly in a sport-related example. A student may have acquired a conditioned, emotional reaction (anxiety toward a gymnastic apparatus or an exercise either by having experienced unconditioned stimuli himself/herself (e.g., pain, failure) or by having observed those reactions in others. As he/she also anticipating these aversive stimuli when performing a corresponding exercise, he/she will look for ways of avoiding them. He/she does so either by avoiding an exercise altogether or by modifying it in such a way that, according to his/her own experiences, there will be no more aversive consequences. Only when the aversive expectation is erased will the avoidance behavior be erased as well. Speaking in terms of learning theory, only when a person has learned that the CS (the apparatus or the exercise) will not lead to an aversive stimulus (pain, failure) will the avoidance behavior be erased.

As already briefly mentioned, avoidance behavior will not only manifest itself as the student trying to avoid (if possible) an anxiety-causing exercise. Often the student will simplify or modify the exercise or perform it wrongly or incompletely. Such modes of behavior can be interpreted as

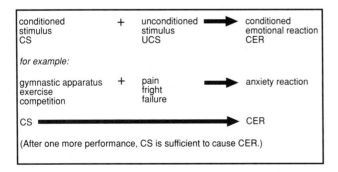

FIGURE 14-3 A model for the classic conditioning of anxiety reactions.

motor strategies of avoidance. According to this learning-theoretical explanation, such behavior can be met most effectively by erasing the expectation of the anxiety-causing stimulus. If the anxiety-causing stimulus in a physical education lesson is a stimulus of pain or fright, this can be achieved if the student is assisted by showing him/her clearly that the perception of risk during an anxiety-causing stimulus can be reduced to a minimum. This also provides a psychological explanation of how conducive to learning such methodical aids are for minimizing the risk of pain or injury during the process of learning. The result, often empirically confirmed, that anxious people, in situations where there is no emphasis on high performance, can perform better in complicated tasks, can also be explained by this theory. This is due to the fact that in situations where there is no emphasis on high performance there is no unconditioned, aversive stimulus (expectation of failure).

COGNITIVE APPROACHES

While in Freud's theory, anxiety is explained as one's attempt to control instinctive energy by means of mechanisms (defense mechanisms), in cognitively oriented theories other ways of controlling anxiety are considered. In these approaches, anxiety is viewed as an emotion triggered by a person's communicative relation with his/her environment. This means that anxiety arises only as a result of expectations (cf. Epstein, 1972, 1976) or appraisals (cf. Lazarus, 1966; Lazarus & Averill, 1972). Presumably, the individual is not subject to passive instinctive energies that he/she has to avert, but rather to cognitive processes that are associated with an active approach to the environment. Anxiety control is based on cognitive processes, i.e., on processes of decision which lead either to direct actions to control the anxiety-inducing situation by escaping or modifying the situation (generally by escape or attack), or to intrapsychological processes appropriate to better comprehension of the situation in a new and subjective way. Intrapsychological processes are the actual cognitive forms of anxiety control.

Following Festinger (1954), Schachter (1959) assumes that persons noticing signs of physiological arousal develop a need for appraising these processes and have a tendency to interpret these physical perceptions. For this purpose, they will turn to situational clue stimuli which can provide an explanation for the arousal level experienced. Because cognition works this way, the quality of the emotion is determined. Whether an unspecific arousal leads to anxiety or joy is therefore dependent on the specific cognition.

Schachter's approach can be characterized by three basic assumptions:

1. A person who cannot account for his/her physiological arousal will look for situational clues for attributing it and the available cognitions will determine the emotion.

2. Previously existing explanations do not cause a need for appraisal.
3. A person with cognitions but with no physiological arousal will not show emotions.

Accordingly, in this approach, independence of arousal and cognition is stressed. Schachter and Singer (1962; cf. also Schachter, 1959, 1964, 1966), in an experiment which became famous, tried to prove the central importance of cognitive processes in the development of emotions. Subsequent to the controversial assumptions of the James-Lange theory (James, 1884, 1890; Lange, 1885) and of the Cannon-Bard theory (Cannon, 1927; 1929, 1931; Bard, 1934; 1950), the question of the reactions persons show in a state of arousal induced by an epinephrine injection was considered. Various experimental groups were exposed to different social situations in order to assess their emotions afterward by means of self-rating scales. The findings confirmed the hypothesis: it is the social context (and not the physiological state of arousal) that accounts for the quality of the emotion.

These assumptions are demonstrable in laboratory experiments and may furnish adequate explanations of these situations rather than for applied sport situations. An athlete, for example, will first eliminate his/her situation in competition and subsequently physiological concomitants of arousal will take place which he/she in turn will associate with the competition (attributions). According to Schachter's (1966) ideas, the athlete in physiological arousal will only choose to exert cognitive processes for interpretation if the arousal (a) preexists and (b) is unaccounted for. In everyday and sport situations it is advisable to proceed from the fact that cognitive processes precede the arousal, which itself, in turn, is evaluated. In more recent theoretical approaches, one even presupposes that cognitions alone are sufficient prerequisites for emotions (cf. Liebhart, 1978; Valins, 1966; Weiner, Russel, & Lerman, 1978). Valins simulated physiological arousal in subjects and was able to show that incorrect feedback information led to the same states of emotion as did feedback information appropriate to reality (the Valins effect). From this he concluded that physiological arousal is involved in the development of emotions (only) as one possible source of information (cf. also Liebhart, 1978).

Within the framework of the theory of causal attribution, Weiner et al. (1978) take the view that arousal is not required for the development of emotions. They hold that cognitions (here, causal attributions) are necessary and sufficient conditions for emotions. Grabitz and Gniech (1978) presume that Schachter's approach is of particular importance due to the present emphasis on attribution theoretical assumptions in research on emotions.

The claim of primacy of cognitive processes is particularly stressed by Lazarus and his group (1966; more recently, Lazarus & Launier, 1978, 1981). They see anxiety as a "side emotion" and a specific pattern of arousal corresponding with this side emotion. Consequently no unspecific arousal as a prerequisite is postulated as by

Schachter, but a specific arousal level is conjectured to be caused by anxiety.

The general, theoretical basis of this theory of anxiety and of coping with anxiety is pointed out by Lazarus and his collaborators in an "approach on a cognitive theory of emotion" (Lazarus, Averill, & Opton, 1970). For Lazarus, anxiety must must be discussed within the framework of the stress and emotion concept (cf. Lazarus & Averill, 1972).

The concept of emotion was described by Lazarus et al. (1970) even though difficulties in integrating it into a psychological theory have caused other scholars to deal with described phenomena in other concepts. Anxiety and fear, for example, are seen as instincts or motivations (as described earlier in this chapter). Duffy (1962) goes so far as to dispute the scientific justification of a theory of emotion, and he opposes it by developing a general "concept of activation" (Duffy, 1962) which as a fundamental concept comprises anxiety, stress, motivation, and emotion. Lazarus and his colleagues argue that emotional concepts include important areas of psychology and thus are crucial for the description and classification of behavior (cf. Lazarus et al., 1970).

The authors distinguish among three aspects of emotions: the biological, the cultural, and the cognitive. These are seen as complementary, and each of the three in its own way leads to similar conclusions (Lazarus et al., 1970).

For Lazarus and his collaborators, the antecedent conditions of anxiety and their interaction can be shown in Figure 14–4. Figure 14–5 elaborates a model of stress development. The function of anxiety is associated with intellectual ability which is characteristic of humans. This ability in turn is responsible for humans' adaptability to constantly changing environmental conditions. Intellectual potency enables one to have the environment at personal disposal by means of symbolic systems. The symbolic systems arrange a person's relation to his/her environment. If the integrity of such a cognitive system is threatened, this results in a state of tension which presents a component of

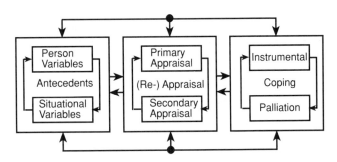

FIGURE 14–5 Transactional model of the development and digestion of stress emotions according to Lazarus and colleagues.

anxiety. If the cognitive system comprises central ideas about a person's personality, i.e., if psychological integrity is at stake, anxiety may become acute. As early as 1966, this aspect was mentioned by Lazarus in connection with the signal function of anxiety. One function of anxiety for him lies in the fact "that the individual may be unaware or dimly aware of the appraisal of threat, and anxiety then may signal to awareness that there is indeed a condition of threat" (Lazarus, 1966). Even though the concept of signal anxiety is seen as possibly misleading, Lazarus and Averill (1972) argue that signal anxiety may well be conceived in terms of feedback in a complex chain of events, for its function as a warning signal may cause the individual to maintain his/her attentiveness or even to increase it in order to realize possible dangers and to be able to face them. However, anxiety must not exceed a certain degree, as this would lead to limited attentiveness, i.e., to selectively as to the focus of attentiveness, and, moreover, it may be directed toward stimuli that are irrelevant to coping with the anxiety (cf. Easterbrook, 1959).

ASSESSMENT OF ANXIETY

METHODOLOGICAL CONSIDERATIONS

During the early years in the advancement of sport psychological research, personality factors in general and especially on anxiety included instruments such as the MMPI (Hathaway & McKinley, 1943), the MAS (Taylor, 1953), and the IPAT Anxiety Scale (Cattell, 1957). These global trait measures did not distinguish between trait anxiety and state anxiety, as operationalized by Spielberger with the State-Trait Anxiety Inventory (STAI) (Spielberger, Gorsuch, & Lushene, 1970). This instrument stimulated research on anxiety in many areas, including sport. Two main observations are:

1. The concept of anxiety (trait anxiety) operationalized in this test seems to refer predominantly to situations in

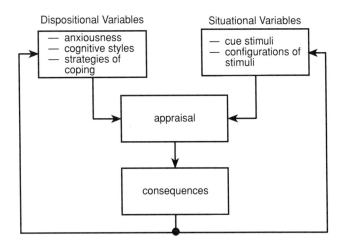

FIGURE 14–4 Antecedents of anxiety and their interaction in the concept of Lazarus.

which self-esteem is threatened, but less to physically harmful situations.

2. While there is substantial evidence for the sensitivity of the STAI-S-Anxiety Scale for changes in anxiety level in sports situations, the trait aspect as a measure in general anxiety proneness seems to be limited in the ability to predict state anxiety in sport-specific situations.

As a consequence of the so-called interactionism debate, situation-specific instruments have been developed (e.g., "Test Anxiety Inventory" by Spielberger et al., 1978; "Speech Anxiety Inventory" by Lamb, 1973) in the hope that better predictions will result for state anxiety in the corresponding situational classes (cf. Mellstrom, Zuckerman, & Cicala, 1978).

Diagnostic methods developed in general anxiety research cannot simply be taken uncritically and used in investigations in sport psychology. Many sport scientists tend to reject methods from general psychology, recommending instead that specific instruments be developed for questions concerning the area of sport psychology (e.g., Nitsch, 1975; Martens, 1977). There are, however, several arguments which speak against such a methodological specificity. The development of adequate psychometric methods is a very long and painstaking undertaking in test construction. The first and most obvious reason for retaining these methods is economy in obtaining results that can be used in education and training as quickly as possible, with a minimum of time-consuming experiments dealing exclusively with methodology. For this reason, it seems necessary to combine methods that have already been developed and validated in general anxiety diagnostics and then to formulate them for applications to sport-specific fields.

Even if one takes the viewpoint that sport psychology is an independent scientific discipline and therefore needs to develop its own specific research instruments, one is faced with new problems. It then follows that measurement methods must be developed for all different kinds of sport. For example, Marten's (1977) sport-anxiety questionnaire cannot be applied to team sports without first undergoing some modifications, since some of the items do not seem to be relevant.

In addition, some psychologists maintain that sport psychology is threatening to break away from its parent discipline and become an applied sport science. The consequences of this would be a loss in quality for the parent discipline and, for both psychology and sport psychology alike, reduced feedback for the research process. As an alternative it is often recommended that sport be regarded as a field of study in which many originally psychological hypotheses can be tested, modified, or rejected (Browne & Mahoney, 1984; Heckhausen, 1979; Nitsch, 1978).

The following discussion summarizes the various possible methods of measuring anxiety and questions about convergence and divergence among the various levels of measurement. This will then be followed by a discussion of more recent approaches and findings in the field of anxiety diagnosis, concluding with sport-specific implications.

MULTILEVEL ASSESSMENT

Before one begins to discuss measurement-theoretical problems of anxiety assessment it is first necessary to draw a distinction between the different approaches for assessing anxiety and anxiety reactions. In general, one distinguishes between assessing anxiety at the cognitive level (self-assessment and assessment by others), records of physiological parameters, and behavioral and nonverbal or expressive indices. At each of these levels there is something different that must be taken into account, which in part prevents a high degree of covariation between parameters of the various measurement levels (for an overview: Hackfort & Schwenkmezger, 1989).

Measuring Anxiety at the Physiological Level

Physiological indicators can be roughly classified as (1) respiratory and cardiovascular, (2) biochemical, and (3) electrophysiological. They can be related to one of three systems in the human organism: the muscular system, the vegetative, autonomic nervous system, and the central nervous system. Parameters frequently studied with regard to anxiety include pulse rate, blood pressure, rate of respiration, biochemical indicators like adrenaline and noradrenaline, and electrophysiological measures such as EEG correlates, muscle potentials, and skin resistance. For a detailed discussion, see Fahrenberg (1977) or Lang (1977).

What advantages do physiological measurements bring to anxiety research? First, they are not tied to verbal statements and are therefore independent of verbal expressive ability. Second, they can be used with almost all kinds of people because the ability of self-observation is not a prerequisite. Third, almost all can be assessed continuously, parallel to behavior; in contrast, with self-observation, the behavior has to be interrupted, particularly in actions which are not yet automatic and in standardized self-ratings.

The disadvantages, however, seem to balance out the advantages. Even analyses which are based on physiological measures are for the most part method-dependent. For example, two different physiological indicators (e.g., heart rate and action potential in an electromyogram), both of which are indices of general arousal or activation, show only slight correlations with each other.

Although it is agreed that physiological side-effects of emotional processes can be measured, until now only a few specific reactions of qualitatively different emotions have been found. This means that an increase in heart rate can occur both in the context of emotion anxiety and in reactions of joy or anger. Which of these emotional reactions occurs is determined by a cognitive evaluation of the stimulus situation. For example, the parallel bars might induce emotion anxiety because of associations with an unhappy previous experience, or emotion joy as a result of victory in a previous competition. Because of the non-stimulus-specific physiological effects of both emotions, however, there will be an increase in heart rate in each situation. In more general terms, specific systems have different functions. Under each condition in mobilizing for a reaction or in concentrating on vegetative functions, certain structures will become active, others will reduce their activity, and still others will remain unaffected (Lang, 1977).

Can physiological indicators of anxiety also be applied in sport-psychological investigations? It is important to note that indicators of the peripheral circulatory system and biochemical indicators cannot legitimately be used when the organism is physically activated in any way. These parameters change much more as a result of physical activity than as a result of stress- or anxiety-inducing situations. In addition, they are very susceptible to artifacts and are method-dependent. There is indeed some evidence to suggest that (1) physical stress is accompanied by increased adrenaline levels and mental stress by increased noradrenaline levels, and (2) the ratio of adrenaline to noradrenaline is a good index of the existence of emotional strain (cf. Frankenhauser, 1969; Lehmann & Keul, 1981). However, obtaining exact measurements of catecholamine in experimental settings—especially in field settings—appears to be a complex technical problem. We shall have to wait and see about the possibility of analyzing catecholamine levels in saliva (cf. Hellhammer, Kirschbaum, & Belkien, 1987).

There are additional hints from investigations considering the psychoneuronal interrelations (see Hellhammer & Ehlert, 1991). It seems that the hippocampus formation is of central importance for the genesis of anxiety. Experiences of ambiguity, unpredictability, and uncontrollability lead to the initiation of anticipatory attempts for control via the hippocampus formation, which activates the corticotropin-releasing hormone (CRH). CRH stimulates the release of ACTH and cortisol and in addition activates further adrenerge systems of the central and autonomous nervous system. On the other hand, the unpleasant quality of the anxiety feeling is connected with different brain-physiological processes that are antagonistic to the CRH effects (e.g., activation of benzodiazepin receptors) by inhibiting the release of ACTH and cortisol. At the same time, feedback processes from cortisol to hippocampus inhibit CRH activity and heighten the sensitivity of the benzodiazepin receptors. Thus the highly complex interrelations lead to a lack in demonstrating biochemical correlates of anxiety in special situations.

So far the only approach remaining for assessing physiological indicators is to record physical activity using structured observational methods. A sport-specific example is provided by Schwenkmezger, Voigt, and Müller (1979). Volleyball players were observed in neutral situations (training games) and stress-inducing ones (examination games). Among other measures, the distance covered in walking and running, the number of actions made during play, and the number of maximal jumps were determined. A comparison of telemetrically recorded heart rates in test and neutral situations was confined to those subjects who had the same number of ball actions, the same number of walking and running steps, the same number of maximal jumps, etc., in both situations over a series of time intervals. Despite an equal amount of physical stress in both situations, heart rate during the test situation was higher than in the neutral situation.

These results were confirmed by self-reports in the state scale of the STAI (Spielberger et al., 1970), recorded before and after each observation segment. Although the method used here represents only a very rough control index of physical stress and it remains unclear whether, for example, increased heart rate might not be a consequence of increased muscle tension during the test situation, the study does point out a possible means of interpreting physiological measures as indicators of emotional processes (e.g., the anxiety reaction). At the same time, this study also illustrates the methodological problems that must be overcome if physiological parameters used as indicators of mental stress are to be considered as being independent of physical stress (Schwenkmezger et al., 1979).

The problems of interpreting physiological data are not confined to assigning quantities to qualities and to methodological difficulties in assessment. There are particular problems related to the principle of autonomic reactions specificity (Lacey, 1950; Lacey & Lacey, 1958). This general principle, which must also be taken into account in sport psychological studies, describes the existence of individual ways of reacting to certain stimuli or stimulus constellations. These were confirmed in studies by Lazarus and Opton (1966), who found different physiological reactions to constant anxiety-inducing situations. There is also some controversy with regard to hormonal processes, which are closely related to the nervous system. Whereas some scholars suggest it may be possible unequivocally to determine the presence of fear and anxiety and to distinguish between them on the basis of catecholamine, adrenaline, and noradrenaline levels (e.g., Schildkraut & Kety, 1967), other scholars believe that catecholamine secretion can be regarded only as an indication of the size of the emotional reaction and not as an indicator of the quality of the emotion (e.g., Frankenhauser, 1969; Levi, 1967). The specificity problem can be subdivided into three subprinciples (Fahrenberg, 1968, 1977): the principle of individual-specific reaction, the principle of stimulus-specific reaction, and the principle of motivation-specific reaction. All three principles influence the general and generalizable interpretation of physiological indicators of anxiety.

Physiological measures assess something that can be termed an indication of physiological excitation. Such measures cannot be related to the construct without resorting to a theory, and the researcher brings the two into contact. Moreover, there are problems in gathering and interpreting physiological data. For example, the influence of the act of collecting physiological data itself is still unclear. Nitsch (1981) points out that we do not know whether one has assessed the reaction to the stressor being studied or the person's specific stress sensitivity toward physiological-medical procedures. In psychophysiological stress and anxiety research, physiological values are registered and interpreted as "indicators" without first having a sufficiently worked out and tested physiological model or even a psychophysiological model available. Correlation-statistical activation research is still superficial, and, although it can help to generate hypotheses, it cannot be used to test them. Moreover, physiological processes can be influenced by climate, general well-being or fitness, different biological rhythms (e.g., daily rhythm), and not least, by the activity itself. For these reasons alone, the low correlations with other data are not surprising (cf. Hackfort & Schwenkmezger, 1985). In some cognitive-psychological contexts it is assumed that physiological excitation only represents one source of information among others for the individual, but cognitions are almost exclusively responsible for the origin of emotions (see Heckhausen, 1977; Liebhart, 1978; Valins, 1966; Weiner et al., 1978).

From this point of view, it is not necessarily a contradiction to view emotions (such as anxiety) as syndromes. However, physiological processes are only of secondary importance: it is not the physiological processes per se that are important, but rather the perception of physiological processes as information for the subjective evaluation of one's own state, the way he/she feels. Lazarus (1966, 1981; Lazarus & Launier, 1978) emphasizes the role of subjective assessment, which influences both emotional reactions and further actions. He assumes that this process of action guidance, which is initiated by mental processes, produces substantial effects on somatic processes (an interaction commonly termed *psychosomatic*) (see Lazarus, 1981).

Measuring Anxiety at the Behavioral Level

The investigation by Epstein and Fenz (1965; Fenz & Epstein, 1967) gives some further hints. In a comparison of the physiological and psychological data of experienced and unexperienced sky divers, correlations seem to be higher for experienced athletes and the level of experience might be a further important variable to explain variance.

What was said earlier about physiological processes with respect to their ambiguity is also true for behavioral data. Although anxiety as a construct is related to certain kinds of behavior (particularly expressive behavior and avoidance behavior), it seems extremely questionable to claim that anxiety can be clearly defined in movement behavior. In scientific theory, anxiety is an abstraction for which behavior may be one empirical indicator, insofar as a particular behavior can be connected theoretically to anxiety. This always has to occur within a hypothetical net, however, since context dependency on the one hand and content ambiguity of a single behavior (Nitsch, 1981) on the other must both be considered.

For example, if one observes a male skier trembling at the beginning of a steep downhill slope, it is not known whether he is trembling because of fear or because of the cold. As one may notice with further observation, if he is seen to begin a run in a cramped, tense, and awkward position, one does not know whether he really is freezing, whether he is not a particularly good skier but a brave one trying this difficult run in spite of his lack of skill, or

whether his posture is a sign of anxiety. The answer becomes clear only when there is additional information—for instance, that it is not cold, or that, although the skier has completed all his lessons, he is not really confident about this run and is doing it only because friends have brought him along and are waiting for him. Observation of behavior for the diagnosis of anxiety is problematic because one cannot distinguish between anxious behavior and coping behavior. This is something that psychologists have been pointing out since Freud's time.

It is true for both expressive and performance behavior that the situation has to transmit an interpretative background so that behavioral data can be adequately evaluated. For this reason the analysis of behavioral data in anxiety research cannot concentrate exclusively on the execution of the movement; it also must consider the person within any specific situation. If one chooses to use movement actions as the subject of analysis and tries to deduce anxiety from movement regulation, then it is essential that the actor's self-statements be recorded. Otherwise, it is impossible for an observer to know whether, for example, inadequate action plans or anxiety has led to disruptions in the action process. Observation of behavior and behavioral data do not seem to be superfluous or inconsequential for an action-theoretical movement analysis, but nor are they sufficient in themselves. Observation methods become useful only in conjunction with procedural data, and observational data only in conjunction with self-statements.

Assessment of anxiety at the behavioral level is usually discussed in the literature for the sake of completeness and far less often for its specific relevance. This is surprising in view of the fact that behavior-diagnostic approaches are available but are only seldom discussed in anxiety diagnosis. One reason for the relatively few references to behavior diagnosis might lie in the not unproblematical realization of data collection methods at this level. For example, one wants to take Birbaumer's (1977) suggestion that, when assessing avoidance-of-flight reactions, expressive behavior, and simple motor sequences like conditioned repression, micro- and macrotremors should be used to measure anxiety at the behavioral level. However, the question of how to ensure objectivity, reliability, and validity arises. In this connection one must bear in mind that, with regard to their function as indicators of a particular process, behavior characteristics can be far removed as explanations from that which they are reflecting (Hackfort, 1983). If classes of anxiety reactions on the behavioral level cited in the literature are ordered according to their casual distance, a distinction should be drawn between expressive behavior, avoidance-and-flight behavior, and achievement behavior.

One cannot consider specific details about methods of assessment here. With regard to expressive behavior, the reader is referred to studies by Ekman and Oster (1979) as well as Hackfort and Nitsch (1989); behavioral indicators are described by Hackfort and Schwenkmezger (1985). Although the assessment of expressive behavior seems obvious as an index of anxiety reactions in sport, it may be appropriate to make a few remarks on several specific flight and avoidance reactions. Avoidance behavior is particularly apparent in the case of encountering a feared opponent. It is relatively easy to identify simulated illnesses and aggravation in such situations as avoidance behavior. In sport, flight and avoidance behavior is often manifested very subtly. Sometimes coaches and teachers are confronted with a flood of doctors' excuses that can be viewed as symptoms of an athlete's or student's dislike for sport. The spectrum of avoidance behavior extends into the lessons themselves and becomes evident when, for example, someone is no longer in the lineup, a sport action (e.g., take-off) is interrupted, or a simple exercise is suddenly substituted for a more complex one. Still another variant of avoidance behavior might occur when a threatened failure or fear of losing leads to a blind, relatively hopeless attack.

Assessment and understanding of flight-and-avoidance behavior is particularly important in sport because trainers, coaches, and teachers with little or no training in psychology tend to rely on their own observations of anxiety symptoms in preference to administering questionnaires or physiological methods.

Measuring Anxiety at the Cognitive Level

One example of classifying anxiety measures at the cognitive level is McReynold's (1968) system, which distinguishes between three major categories:

1. Anxiety scales can attempt to assess either (a) a person's situation-independent, general anxiety level (anxiousness), or (b) his or her anxiety level under situation-specific conditions. Cattell and Scheier (1961) were first to suggest such a distinction and study it systematically. Spielberger (1966, 1975) took this one step further and formulated an interactional theory of anxiety. According to him, a person's anxiety level depends upon the duration and intensity of the threatening stimulus (situation). The number and types of situations that cause any individual person to experience anxiety depend upon his/her personality-specific level of anxiety: the more anxious a person is, the more situations he/she will consider as personally threatening.

2. If anxiety is regarded as a hypothetical construct, then the array of instruments for measuring anxiety can assess either (a) previous conditions or (b) subsequent consequences of anxiety. Previous conditions can include, for example, person-specific factors that either are genetically determined or are acquired during the course of socialization and which reflect stabilized behavioral dispositions. Other previous conditions occur in specific situations, such as when subjectively threatening stimulus constellations generate anxiety. Consequences of anxiety include those reactions that are traditionally characterized as anxiety symptoms. Here, too, one can distinguish between direct and long-term manifestations of anxiety reactions. Direct consequences of threatening situations may include a diminished sense of well-being

or specific physiological reactions; long-term consequences may include expectation of failure following an extended series of failures.

3. A third category, according to McReynolds (1968), is the question of the generality of the measuring instrument. Depending upon one's purpose, he or she can attempt either to (a) obtain a value for a person's general anxiety or (b) assess only specific aspects of anxiety (e.g., fear of physical injury or ego-threat). The majority of instruments introduced for measuring anxiety are very heterogeneous with regard to their methodology. In their theoretical conception and formal design, they take into account different aspects of anxiety measurement. With regard to methodological aspects, one can distinguish among ratings, personality inventories, and questionnaires. For a number of measures one must also take into account the theoretical foundations of the instrument. And, under the aspect of application, the sport-specific relevance of each of the measures should be discussed.

Anxiety questionnaires always include some items related to physiological manifestations as indicators of activation, for example, "I frequently have strong heartbeats" for Wieczerkowski, Nickel, Janowski, Fittkau, and Rauer's (1979) AFS, or the item "I seldom notice my heartbeat and rarely get out of breath" from Spreen's (1961) "Saarbrücker Liste," a German translation of Taylor's (1953) MAS.

A response to this kind of items in sport has a completely different interpretation than, for instance, in everyday cognitive settings, in school, or in a physiological experiment on attention. In sport, high physiological activation is often a prerequisite for optimal performance and is regarded as a positive factor, whereas in the other situations it tends to be disruptive.

This raises the question of whether the questionnaire method is an optimal one for diagnosing sport-related anxiety, both in general and as far as specific groups, particularly children, are concerned.

A major objection to the traditional use of questionnaires to measure fear of anxiety is that they require that the respondent perceive anxiety-related cognitions for himself/herself, to quantify these, and to report them to other people. Sometimes, this occurs in a state of heightened anxiety. Problems of anxiety repression and unwillingness to disclose information cannot be overlooked. Another related problem is that of social desirability, which, according to Nickel (1976), is particularly acute in younger subjects. Response tendencies always come into play when an item is not answered solely on the basis of its content but when other variables distort the measurement intentions. This is particularly true for anxiety questionnaires, where the measurement dimensions and/or intentions can be easily discerned in item formulation. The validity of these instruments depends significantly on such factors as openness, honesty, accurate self-evaluation, and, finally, the self-awareness of the respondent.

An additional problem with children is that they do not understand certain statements, or that they understand them differently from adults. Moreover, the STAI, currently the best-known general instrument, and other measures based on the STAI are symptom-oriented. This does not, however, mean that individual symptom preferences (e.g., in "somaticizers") are taken into account. Nor is there a description of symptoms balanced over all three levels (physiological, psychological, and motoric); with additively registered degrees of anxiety, this sows the seeds of quantification problems which have not yet been discussed.

The personal instructions focus the person's attention on his or her own affective state (current or general). This can result in an intensification of affect processes, something which does not necessarily occur during ordinary dealing with a task and which can cause evaluation problems (cf. Wicklund, 1979, for related statements concerning the theory of self-awareness).

For the reasons previously listed, neither a simple transfer of usual anxiety tests to the field of sport nor the sole use of the questionnaire technique seems very promising.

The question of whether to use general or sport-specific questionnaires will also depend upon the topic being studied. If, for example, one wants to compare the personality structure of athletes to that of a control group or to population norms (Vanek & Hosek, 1977), one will usually choose a questionnaire that is not specific to sport and that also measures the personality trait "anxiousness." Of course, in interpreting the results, it is necessary to bear in mind that top athletes possibly encounter labelizing situations (e.g., extreme training situations or competitions) more often than other groups of people, with the result that they also more frequently experience the labeling symptoms listed in questionnaire items. For this reason alone, they will often have higher anxiety scores. Nitsch (1978) concludes that athletes' higher anxiety scores possibly represent a methodological artifact in that the validating sample is scarcely comparable to the athlete sample.

Taking a general look at questionnaire techniques, one must conclude that their significance is too often misjudged; this is true at both extremes. Whereas some psychologists tend to overrate the validity and value of questionnaires, others reject them out of hand without naming any alternatives. In order to avoid unrealistically high or low expectations, it is recommended that questionnaires be used only in those areas where empirical evidence for their validity has been demonstrated (cf. Guilford, 1964; Häcker & Schwenkmezger, 1984). Information can be obtained which, if other methods had been used, would have been missing or much less precise.

Situation-specific instruments. As a result of the so-called interactionism debate, there is an increased awareness of the importance of taking into account, both conceptually and methodologically, the way in which personality traits appear in different situations. This leads to a demand for situation-specific personality tests. In anxiety research there has been a trend toward situation-specific trait scales, in the hope that better predictions will result for state anxiety in the corresponding situational classes (cf. Mellstrom, Zuckerman, & Cicala, 1978).

Situation- or activity-specific instruments have been developed for measuring trait anxiety, such as test anxiety scales like the Test Anxiety Inventory (Spielberger et al., 1978), or such speech anxiety scales as the Speech Anxiety Inventory by Lamb (1973). In contrast to general anxiety tests (e.g., Taylor's Manifest Anxiety Scale, 1953), in these situation-specific measures, the relationship to a specific situation or to a class of situations is explicitly created by means of the instructions or item formulation (Laux, 1983).

In sport-anxiety research the demand for situation-specific trait scales was welcomed in the hope of improving the prediction of state anxiety in certain sport situations. Based on Spielberger's (1972, 1975) state-trait concept, Martens (1977) developed a questionnaire for measuring trait anxiety in competitive sport situations.

The low correlation with the STAI Trait scale (about $r = .40$) clearly indicates that this sport-specific test accounts for portions of the variance which are not covered by the general measure. Results obtained with the German translation of this scale also indicate, however, that the prediction of state anxiety reactions has not yet been greatly improved (cf. Hackfort & Schwenkmezger, 1985).

Schwenkmezger (1981), for instance, observed that the STAI Trait scale predicts state reactions in sport-related stress situations as well as Martens' (1977; cf. Hackfort & Schwenkmezger, 1985) sport-specific trait-anxiety scale. Similar results have been reported by Singer and Ungerer-Röhrich (1985).

Vormbrock's (1983) sport anxiety questionnaire ("Sportangstfragebogen," SAF) is also based on Spielberger's concept and Endler's (1975, 1978) multidimensional anxiety model. This instrument distinguishes among three dimensions of sport anxiety, each related to different types of sport: 1. "fear of the unknown, injury" items related to gymnastics; (2) "fear of failure in social situations" items related to ball games, and (3) "fear of disgrace" items related to dancing.

Test criteria of the SAF were investigated in a sample of university students, and the instrument was shown to be both valid and reliable. The question remains, however, whether the method of factor analysis used in the SAF for obtaining dimensions of sport anxiety is more appropriate than activity-specific subscale construction.

In the field of test anxiety research, classifications of cognitive relationships into task-relevant and solution-irrelevant cognitions (see Sarason, 1975, 1978, 1980) or into "worry" and "emotionality" aspects (see Liebert & Morris, 1967; Morris & Liebert, 1970) are now generalized into evaluation anxiety. In sport psychology this has been demonstrated by Schwenkmezger (1985a) and Schwenkmezger and Laux (1986). Using an activity-specific scale construction of task-unrelated cognitions in a study of handball players, they found that high-anxious players tend to have more task-unrelated cognitions than low-anxious players. In evaluation situations (selection games with evaluation of personal performance), there was a significant increase in task-unrelated cognitions as compared to training situations; these results support Spielberger's State-Trait Model of Anxiety. In addition, highly significant relationships were found between frequency of task-unrelated cognitions and assessments of individual performance by independent raters.

The multidimensional approach in test anxiety research and the construction of multidimensional trait anxiety measures (e.g., Sarason, 1984) led to the development of the Sport Anxiety Scale (SAS; Smith, Smoll, & Schutz, 1990). SAS has three subscales: somatic anxiety, worry, and concentration disruption. Smith et al. (1990) report adequate reliability, high correlations with the SCAT, and somewhat lower correlations with the STAI trait-scale. The cognitive subscale "concentration disruption" related most strongly to performance in a study with football players. Correlations with test anxiety scales and information about divergent validity were not reported. At present, the researchers claim that SAS would appear to have promise as a research tool (Smith et al., 1990).

Only recently have children and young people been included in research on the development of sport-specific anxiety inventories. Two instruments directed at this age group differ in several ways from the typical questionnaire construction.

Bös and Mechling (1983) developed an instrument (the Sport Anxiety Picture Test, SAPT) for measuring self-concept in anxiety-inducing movements in sport classes. The SAPT is aimed at male and female children between the ages of 9 and 11 and is available in German, English, and Italian. Photographs of school sport situations are combined with answer categories in sentence form.

The SAPT does not distinguish between different dimensions or possible connections with particular activities, and factor analysis results suggest that evaluations of activity-specific abilities are measured.

Based on the situational analysis approach and the assumption that particular sport-specific anxiety dimensions might be effective for different sport activities (e.g., fear of injury and/or fear of disgrace for gymnastics), Hackfort (1983, 1986) distinguished among various types of activity (ballgames, fighting games, gymnastics, swimming/diving, and track and field sports) in developing the "Sportangstdeutungsverfahren" (SAD; or sport anxiety interpretation measure). He also distinguished five dimensions of sport anxiety according to their relationship to central motives, following Maslow's (1954) classification of motives: (1) "fear of disgrace," (2) "fear of competition," (3) "fear of failure," (4) "fear of the unknown," and (5) "fear of injury."

The SAD consists of 22 items in the form of drawings of different situations (picture series). The response categories are also nonverbal (sketches of facial expressions portraying varying degrees of anxiety). The respondent marks an "X" to indicate the extent to which his/her interpretation or definition of the situation is anxiety-thematic. The dimensions that are relevant to the individual are determined by means of a method developed expressly for that purpose, the dimension decision method (DEV). Test-retest reliabilities, important for trait anxiety, lie between $r = .87$ and $r = .94$. Validity was proved in several studies

(see Hackfort & Nitsch, 1989). The test can be used in both group and individual diagnosis.

Although up to now the focus has been primarily on the diagnosis of trait anxiety, it should be pointed out that, along with situational and activity-specific factors, the development of state-anxiety scales is also necessary. Particularly with regard to two-component approaches, the relationships of cognitions to certain activities play an important role in item formulation.

On the bases of a distinction between cognitive and somatic anxiety and self-confidence, Martens, Burton, Riokin, and Simon (1980) developed the Competitive State Anxiety Inventory (CSA). Gould, Petlichkoff, Simons, and Verera (1987), using this instrument, found the (inverted-U-shaped) relationship between somatic state anxiety scores, but no relation between cognitive state anxiety scores and performance in pistol shooting. In a study with swimmers, Burton (1988) found a similar relation between somatic state anxiety and performance but no relationship between cognitive state anxiety and performance. These results seem to support a distinction which is known from test anxiety between worry and emotionality. Further, it seems to be necessary to distinguish sport-related situations, especially regarding the task at hand.

Anxiety diagnosis is left with the methodologically unsatisfactory technique of operationalizing anxiety and styles of anxiety control separately. Another approach that may prove promising is scale combination in the development of specific instruments of diagnosing sport anxiety.

The methods discussed above could certainly provide inspiration for general anxiety research or anxiety research in other fields. The SAPT and SAD are child-appropriate methods in that they take into account the fact that visual perception is very important in this age group (cf. Nickel, 1976) and the manner of item presentation corresponds well with intellectual ability. Questions that arise with other questionnaires for the same age group about how to mark an item like "I have heart palpitations" (since one always has heart palpitations) do not occur here. Another point to remember is that children can have difficulty expressing their feelings and reactions, and this should be considered when constructing, for example, measures of school anxiety. Minimal connections with verbal ability, as found in the SAD, illustrate that there are alternatives to questionnaires, and this is desirable for other reasons as well.

ANXIETY, MOTOR LEARNING, AND PERFORMANCE IN SPORTS

The effect of anxiety on motor performance is discussed on the basis of the following theories: learning and drive-theoretical approaches (Hull/Spence), the inverted-U function, cognitive approaches such as interference theories of anxiety, Spielberger's theory of anxiety and Martens's sport-specific modification, and the distinction between worry and emotionality. Finally, results of meta-analyses of the relationship between anxiety and sport motor performance will be presented.

THE DRIVE THEORY APPROACH

One of the most important theories for the experimental analysis of anxiety and performance in the field of motor performance was developed on the basis of Hull's (1952) behavioristic theory. In brief, the theory states that the strength of a specific behavior (B) is a function of the effective drive state (D) and habit strength *(H): B = f(D × H).* This is specified in the original works by Taylor (1951, 1956) and Spence & Spence (1966).

The drive state is regarded as a hypothetical construct and defined as the sum of all of the energetic components affecting an individual at the time of the behavior. D is connected multiplicatively with habit strength. A habit is a relatively automatic sequence of reactions, mainly motoric. The hypothetical construct "habit strength" represents the intensity of the tendency for a specific reaction to follow a certain stimulus.

In the case of anxiety, this general behavior theory has been supplemented by the assumption that the drive level is dependent upon an emotional reaction that is caused by an aversive stimulus. There are individual differences in the strength of this emotional reaction. For the question of how the intensity of the emotional reaction (in this case, anxiety) should be operationalized, two possibilities are available. (1) Individuals can be classified according to their anxiety level on questionnaires. This method of operationalization is called the *chronic hypothesis,* since it is assumed that situation-independent differences in individuals' anxiety levels are responsible for any performance differences. (2) The second possibility is the induction of different situation-specific anxiety levels by applying stress stimuli, also known as the *situational* or *reactive hypothesis.*

Independent of these hypotheses variants, it follows from drive theory that as a result of low response competition, persons with high drive level will perform better on easier tasks than persons with a lower drive level (see e.g., Krohne, 1980).

In a comprehensive review, Martens (1971, 1974) summarized the results of studies in the field of motorics based on drive-theory postulates. His review included only those studies in which the Manifest Anxiety Scale (MAS) (Taylor, 1953) had been used to operationalize anxiety level. Motor tasks included visual-motor discrimination tasks, tracking, fine-motor sorting, labyrinth tasks, ring throwing, flexibility, balancing, and coordination tasks. Most of the designs permit a twofold evaluation of performance: in terms of the amount and frequency of errors.

According to Martens's conclusions, high-anxious persons do indeed perform better on simple tasks, whereas low-anxious persons have an advantage executing difficult tasks. However, this is true only when the amount of performance per unit of time is used as the dependent variable. If one takes error frequency into account, then only a few studies show results that conform to the hypothesis. If one combines the chronic and situational hypotheses and focus on those studies that distinguish among anxiety levels as well as taking account of the intensity of the aversive stimulus as an additional independent variable, the number of contradictory findings increases.

Hackfort and Schwenkmezger (1985) summarized findings reported in studies of sport motorics. Results concerning the chronic hypothesis, which postulates a connection between chronic forms of anxiety and sport performance level, are questionable methodologically and too inconsistent to allow a clear interpretation. As far as testing of the situative hypothesis is concerned, there are no studies in the sport motorics field that satisfy high methodological standards.

Although comprehensive review articles do not permit any unambiguous conclusions to be drawn, psychophysiological constitution research does provide critical arguments against the chronic hypotheses. Myrtek (1975), for example, investigated relationships between parameters of physical endurance and psychological factors such as emotional lability, physical complaints, and manifest anxiety. Classification analyses revealed four different groups: group 1 describes itself as not very anxious, and displays low endurance ability in the physical area; group 2 also describes itself as low in anxiety, but has a high physical endurance ability; group 3 displays high anxiety levels and high physical stress endurance; and group 4 is characterized by high anxiety levels, coupled with little physical performance ability. The fact that the sizes of the four independent groups identified were almost equal shows that there is no general relationship between physical performance level and anxiety or emotional lability in psychophysiological constitution research. This is confirmed by large correlational studies partly covering the same data, reported by Fahrenberg, Walschburger, Foerster, Myrtek, and Müller (1979).

With process-oriented approaches, the course of the learning process has to be considered as well as the absolute performance level. At the beginning of the learning process, high-anxious persons should perform less well, because for them the task is still difficult. In later stages this task becomes increasingly easier, so that learning progress and level may increase more sharply in anxious individuals. In general psychological tasks in which learning involved verbal material or problem-solving, the hypothesis was confirmed when, in addition to the differentiation according to anxiety level, psychological stress stimuli were used to increase situational anxiety (Krohne, 1980).

The complexity of the relationships involved is illustrated by some of our own studies (Schwenkmezger, 1980, 1981). We were able to show that in learning a gross-motor task (skiing), state anxiety at the beginning of the learning process depends solely upon the trait-anxiety level, probably due to lack of specific experience. With increasing learning progress, however, task-specific cognitions concerning the difficulty of the task or situation-specific judgments of external circumstances of the learning task (steepness of the hill, snow properties, weather, etc.) determine the intensity of the state-anxiety level. At the same time, the influence of trait anxiety decreases. This demonstrates that the interaction between chronic anxiety level, situation-specific stress stimuli, task difficulty, and situation-specific conditions of learning and performance is still, for the most part, largely unexplored, at least in the gross-motor area. These findings also expose extremely difficult methodological problems, because they show that cross-sectional studies always portray only individual time segments, and the results are clear and generalizable only when the exact circumstances at the time of assessing anxiety and motor performance are known. This also holds true for the question of when during the learning process a study takes place. Unless the experimental subjects are carefully chosen, there will probably be great heterogeneity in the sample so that, as in our study, the relationships are obscured as a result.

THE INVERTED-U HYPOTHESIS

When discussing the relationship between anxiety and motor performance, an inverted U-shaped relationship is frequently postulated, as in the Yerkes-Dodson law. Yerkes and Dodson (1908), in fact, studied only the relationship between arousal and performance in animals. In drawing parallels between arousal and performance and between anxiety and performance, in addition to problems associated with generalizing from animal results to humans, at least one additional assumption is required—namely, that anxiety is an indicator of arousal. If one overlooks these difficulties, then, according to Fiske and Maddi (1961), there is good reason to assume that the optimal arousal level required for solving a task is dependent upon the task's complexity. The optimal arousal level is higher for simple tasks than for more complex ones. An arousal level that produces optimal performance with a simple task may lead to impairment in complex tasks.

On the basis of the Yerkes-Dodson law, Martens (1975) was able to demonstrate that different physiological arousal levels are necessary for different sport tasks, if the aim is optimal performance. The differentiation is made according to the proportion of gross- or fine-motor movements. Gross-motor movements require a high level of physiological arousal, whereas fine-motor movements require less.

Landers (1980) accepted a suggestion made by Martens (1974) and attempted to explain the inverted-U relationship between anxiety and performance using Easterbrook's (1959) cue-utilization theory. Easterbrook postulates the following conditions: (1) Level of performance is proportional to the number of cues utilized. (2) The number of cues utilized is inversely proportional to the level of emotional arousal. Under the additional assumption that (a) the simultaneous use of task-relevant and task-irrelevant cues reduces effectiveness and (b) in perception, irrelevant

stimuli are eliminated before relevant stimuli, several conclusions may be drawn. Persons under a low level of arousal have a broad perceptual range, motivational deficits (e.g., lack of effort), or a low selectivity of relevant cues. In this case, performance is low. Perceptual selectivity increases with increasing arousal. Irrelevant cues are eliminated and performance improves. Increases in arousal beyond this optimal level lead to further perceptual narrowing with elimination of task-relevant cues, and performance decreases, in accordance with the inverted-U hypothesis.

Chronic and situational hypotheses can also be formulated for studies on the inverted-U function. For this reason it is important to vary both the person-specific anxiety level and the situation-specific stress level. Such studies have been conducted by Martens and Landers (1970), Weinberg and Ragan (1978), and Sonstroem and Bernado (1982). The results of these studies do not contradict the Yerkes-Dodson law. However, no alternative hypothesis were thoroughly tested in these studies.

Despite the plausibility of the inverted-U function, it must be noted that there are very few empirical results from testing its validity in motor skills. Statements depicting this nonlinear relationship as a well-confirmed scientific principle (e.g., Cratty, 1979) are certainly premature, and more experimental studies are urgently needed.

This holds especially true for clarifying the quality of relationships between anxiety/arousal and performance. Weinberg (1990, pp. 230) stated correctly, "in neither case can arousal be assigned a causal role in producing the performance effects." It is possible that arousal is an effect of perceived poor performance rather than a cause of it, or even more likely, that there is a bidirectional, reciprocal causality between arousal and performance, if any. Neiss (1988), after reviewing the literature, concluded that both the hypothesis of an inverted-U relationship and the construct of arousal should be abandoned and "if cast in psychological terms, the inverted-U hypothesis reveals only that the motivated outperform the apathetic and terrified, and it should be consigned to the true but trivial category" (Neiss, 1988, p. 355).

Anderson (1990), in a critique against Neiss's "reconceptualizing arousal," tried to argue for the pragmatic usefulness of general constructs such as arousal. He cited investigations referring to cognitive performance which seemed to support the inverted-U hypothesis. For further clarification in the motor behavior domain, it seems necessary to explain the reference system of arousal. In sports it is well known that there is no movement and no performance at all if two contrary/antagonistic systems are aroused at the same moment in time (e.g., one synergistic and one antagonistic muscle). The phenomenon of an aroused antagonistic systems is called "tension," and tension refers to anxiety as much as—if not more than—arousal.

The inverted-U hypothesis is characterized as an "optimal arousal theory" (e.g., Kerr, 1989), but this label is also used for Hanin's (1980) concept of an arousal zone of optimal function (ZOF) by Morgan and Ellickson (1989). They elucidate that the ZOF has been neglected or dismissed because it has been erroneously regarded as a reiteration of the inverted-U hypotheses and emphasize correctly that it is quite different: ZOF theory does not argue that a moderate level of arousal is superior to low or high levels but predicts instead that some individuals will perform best when arousal is high, others when it is low, and still others when it is moderate. ZOF represents an intraindividual approach to determine an optimal level of arousal.

This concept was proven by retrospective and prospective simulations using the State-Trait Anxiety Inventory (STAI; Spielberger et al., 1970). Based on this, Hanin (1980) operationalized the ZOF by ranging between plus or minus four points of the athlete's most efficient state anxiety level on the STAI-State scale established by repeated testing of the athlete over a series of competitions. Weinberg (1990) notes that this range represents the standard error of measurement of the STAI. Support for the efficacy of retrospective and prospective assessment of anxiety levels and the concept of ZOF emphasizing an intraindividual approach is shown in studies by Morgan and his colleagues (Morgan & Bradley, 1985; Morgan, O'Connor, Sparling, & Pate, 1987; Raglin & Morgan, 1988) on swimmers and long-distance runners, and by Ebbeck and Weiss (1988), who found that the same level of anxiety was associated with high performance in some athletes and with poor performance in others.

If it is an appropriate conclusion in the frame of ZOF theory that "there is not an optimal level of arousal for a given task" (Morgan & Ellickson, 1989, 168), and characteristics of the task are irrelevant, this would not be in line with results reported in the literature (e.g., Hackfort & Schwenkmezger, 1985). From the perspective of action theory, a sufficient explanation should refer to intraindividual specifics, including (see also Mahoney & Meyers, 1989) the subjective attitude toward anxiety (the person component), task characteristics and their subjective evaluation (the task component), and environmental circumstances and influences, such as social support vs. social inhibition effects (the environment component), for analyzing the person-task-environment constellation as a performance situation.

Future research on ZOF should also include sports-specific instruments and a multidimensional assessment of anxiety. Weinberg (1990, p. 235) asked whether there will be "two separate ZOF's: one for somatic anxiety and one for cognitive anxiety." Perhaps the differentiation between ego-involving and physical harm situations can provide further hints also for distinguishing anxiety provoking situations and symptoms of state anxiety. Hanin (1980) refers to arousal in ZOF theory and states that there is a need to determine the kind of relation between anxiety and arousal that is conceptualized in the frame of ZOF theory.

Kerr (1989) demonstrated, in the context of reversal theory, that it is not sufficient to refer to arousal to explain the relationship between anxiety and performance. He refers to a combination of arousal and hedonic tone as differentiating between anxiety and pleasurable excitement. In addition, Mahoney and Meyers (1989), through interviews with gymnasts, found that personal meanings are important to an understanding of the individual anxiety-performance pattern. Subjective appraisals seem to be as important in analyzing the anxiety-performance relationship as are objective data and level of arousal.

COGNITIVE PERSPECTIVES

The cognitive-psychological analyses of the relationship between anxiety and performance do not reflect a unified group of theories. Distinct from the more mechanistic viewpoint underlying drive theory, cognitive theories emphasize, in addition to person-related variables, the evaluation of the situation, demands of the given task, and the person's own resources (Krohne, 1980). In the following discussion, several important cognitive theories of anxiety will be presented, followed by an analysis of their contributions toward tracing the association between anxiety and motor performance.

As early as Sarason's studies in 1960 and 1978, a cognitive interpretation was suggested for the relationship between anxiety and performance, in the form of the inference theory. Sarason proposed that a distinction should be made between task-irrelevant and task-relevant cognitions in performance situations. Whereas task-irrelevant cognitions (e.g., feelings of inadequacy, fear of failure, a desire to avoid the situation) impair performance, task-related cognitions serve instead to enhance the quality of performance. This can best be illustrated by an experiment carried out by Sarason (1978). Based on their scores of test anxiety on a questionnaire, the participants were divided into groups of high-and low-anxious subjects. Subjects were then assigned to one of five groups, which differed according to the type of instruction received: (1) performance-oriented instruction (the subject was told that his/her own ability would be tested); (2) task-oriented instruction (the subject was told that it was the task itself that was being studied); (3) motivation-oriented instruction (the subject was told that the study concerned determining learning curves in psychological experiments); (4) anxiety-reducing instruction; and (5) neutral instruction (control group).

It was clearly shown that in situations with strong emphasis on performance, subjects high in test anxiety reacted with a significant decrease in performance. Less anxious subjects produced the best performance in this situation. In contrast, subjects with high test anxiety demonstrated a significant increase in performance in situations that were unrelated to performance. This is especially evident when the highly anxious subjects were calmed by instruction or when they were allowed to watch the solving of sample tasks beforehand. In general, it was shown that performance orientation on its own does not always lead to a decrease in performance; this is true only for subjects with high test anxiety. These results, which have been confirmed time and time again in other studies by the Sarason group, also offer clues about the optimal design of a performance situation depending upon the person-specific anxiety level. Even though the instructions given in psychological experiments sometimes seem artificial and not directly generalizable to reality, these results are important confirmation of the need to take into account individual optimal conditions in performance-test situations. Indeed, the requirement of test fairness demands this.

It remains to be shown that these results can be generalized to motor skills, but there is some favorable evidence. Späte and Schwenkmezger (1983), for example, in comparing training games and selection games in handball, observed an anxiety × situation interaction with regard to performance: under selection conditions high-anxious persons were more likely to perform poorly, whereas situational conditions were largely performance-irrelevant for low-anxious persons. The case of the person who is a world champion during training but fails in a competitive situation is supportive evidence for the generalizability of Sarason's results.

Spielberger's Anxiety Theory and Martens's Sport-Specific Modification

Spielberger's (1966, 1972) state-trait anxiety model has been cited very often over the past 15 years. Although it has been modified and expanded in many details, its basic form still holds. Countless researchers interested in a wide assortment of situations have selected this model as the theoretical basis for their work. For this reason, this theory will be dealt with more extensively.

The central feature of the theory is the distinction between trait anxiety and state anxiety. This provides a theoretical framework for the inconsistent distinction between chronic and situational anxiety in drive theory.

State anxiety is defined as a temporary emotional condition of the human organism that varies in intensity and is unstable with regard to time. It is described as consisting of subjective, consciously perceived feelings of tension and anxious expectancy, combined with an increase in activity of the autonomic nervous system. The anxiety-state reaction increases in situations which the individual perceives as threatening, whereby the subjective evaluation of threat does not necessarily correspond to objective danger.

The concept of trait anxiety depicts relatively stable individual differences in susceptibility to anxiety reactions, i.e., in the tendency to perceive a broad spectrum of situations as dangerous or threatening. Trait anxiety also reflects individual differences in the frequency and intensity with which anxiety states have occurred in the past and provides information about the probability that they will occur in the future (cf. Nitsch, 1981, on the intensity or extensity of stress susceptibility).

An anxiety state is induced when, during the evaluation process, an external stimulus is recognized as being threatening. Evaluation is dependent upon trait anxiety, as well as upon inner organismic states and biological needs. Testing of reactions alternatives available to the individual for coping with the threat also plays a part in the evaluation proc-

ess. Thus defense and adaptation processes can reduce the level of state anxiety. When such alternatives are not available, the level of state anxiety has a direct effect on behavior.

High-anxious persons, in contrast to low-anxious persons, tend to respond to threatening situations with a sharper increase in state anxiety. However, just how this abrupt increase works is still an unanswered question (cf. Schwenkmezger, 1985a, for a detailed discussion). In addition, only a very limited range of validity has been demonstrated for the trait-state anxiety model, since it concerns only situations relevant to self-esteem. It provides no predictions for physically threatening situations (Spielberger, 1972).

Schwenkmezger (1985a) analyzed relevant findings in the literature on the validity of the model and presented evidence from his own empirical studies, primarily in sport. He was able to show that the interaction effect, conforming to the model, occurred under an experimentally induced but rather weak or medium form of ego-threat but did not occur under massive threats to self-esteem, as manifested in natural settings (e.g., real examination situations). This was also true for motoric and sport-specific performance tests.

Threats to self-esteem occur because the individual knows the cost of failure (such as a damaged self-image, injured self-esteem, reduced social approval, or material loss resulting from delay in finishing school, university, or professional training), either from previous experience or by watching or hearing from others. Because these consequences are anticipated, such a situation can be characterized as threatening in the sense of Lazarus and Launier's (1978) definition.

Under conditions of a relatively mild ego-threat, the individual has a wider range of interpretations to choose from. The situation is minimally structured, and the subjects often are not able to perceive a threat in a self-esteem-relevant interpretation. In high-anxious persons, such circumstances may lead to mediating processes such as insecurity and disquiet, and allow them to respond with a sharper increase in state anxiety. Low-anxious persons regard the situation as less threatening, since in general, no real consequences occur in laboratory experiments. If, on the one hand, one enters a situation of ego-threat without this wide range of possible interpretations (e.g., actual test situations), then ego-threat becomes evident and subjects react with an increase in state anxiety independent of their trait-anxiety level. The only difference is in the initial level of state anxiety, which is lower for low-anxious persons. The result is parallel increases.

In comparing this version with Spielberger's original model, it is evident that only a partial revision has been made. In the low and medium areas of the threat continuum there are differential increases which are larger for high-anxious persons than for low-anxious persons. Only in the area of extreme self-esteem-threat can parallel increases be observed. This revised model explains why, for relatively mild, experimentally induced threats, interaction effects occur in the sense of a steeper rise in state anxiety with high-anxious persons, whereas under strong actual threat situations more uniform increases are observed.

It is interesting that Eysenck and Matthews (1987), in a completely independent analysis, reached a conclusion similar to the proposed revision of the model. Their comparison of cognitive processes in high- and low-anxious individuals shows that high-anxious persons tend to approach threatening stimuli, whereas low-anxious persons tend to avoid them. These differences were found only under very specific conditions—for example, when threatening and nonthreatening stimuli were simultaneously present or when the threats were mild. According to Eysenck and Matthews there was no difference with massive threats.

Martens (1977) translated Spielberger's theory and tests for use in sport psychology, particularly to the situation of competition. Over the course of their sport-related learning history, individuals can develop a tendency to react with different amounts of anxiety in competitive sport situations. Martens postulates a sport-specific anxiety disposition; the Sport Competition Anxiety Test (SCAT) is an attempt to operationalize this disposition. People with a higher degree of this anxiety tendency are inclined, primarily in competitive situations, to perceive stimuli as threatening and, compared to people with a lower degree of anxiety, react with a significant increase in state anxiety. Consequences of this reaction include impairment of subjective well-being, physiological anxiety reactions, and changes on the behavioral level (e.g., decreased performance). However, several analyses (Hackfort & Schwenkmezger, 1985) and studies by Singer and Ungerer-Röhrich (1985) have demonstrated that Martens's sport-specific anxiety test is no better at predicting state anxiety or motor performance than a more general measure of anxiety such as the STAI (Spielberger et al., 1970). Moreover, conformity to the model was not always demonstrated when this area-specific scale was implemented (cf. Hackfort & Schwenkmezger, 1985, for a summary of findings on this issue).

Distinguishing Emotionality and Worry

Liebert and Morris (1967) showed that state anxiety does not necessarily represent a homogeneous construct, but can be differentiated into two components, emotionality and worry. Worry is described as a cognitive process that takes place prior to, during, and following the execution of a task. Definitional elements include little faith in one's own performance, a high degree of concern, cognitions concerning the comparison of one's own performance with that of others, cognitions concerning the consequences of failure, and worrying about the effects of preparation on the self-esteem-relevant event. Emotionality, on the other hand, consists of affective-physiological symptoms caused by an increased arousal level (nervousness, faster heartbeat, stomach pains, feeling unwell, insecurity, and panic attacks).

Liebert and Morris (1967) treat emotionality and worry as co-components of state anxiety, whereas Wine (1971, 1980, 1982) hypothesizes that there is high intraindividual stability with regard to worry. It follows from this statement that she feels the worry component has the status of a more situation-specific trait. High-anxious persons, therefore, are inclined to worry about their poor performance and be distracted from the task, with the result that the time available for them to solve the task is reduced. In substance, the worry reaction is largely identical to the definition proposed by Liebert and Morris (1967).

With regard to the theoretical foundations for distinguishing between the two components, Morris, Davis, and Hutchings (1981) have suggested several supplements for showing that both components can be defined at the trait level as well as situation-specifically. Thus emotionality can be regarded as a physiological reaction that, when operationalization takes place in the self-descriptive medium, reflects verbal representation patterns of physical reactions. These are induced, on the one hand, by habitual components described as conditioned emotional reactions to test situations and vary individually depending upon the person-related learning history. Conversely, situation-specific stimuli like noxious stimuli, the presence or absence of other persons, etc., also contribute to producing physiological reactions.

The occurrence of the worry reaction, on the other hand, is explained as a complex cognitive process. Person-specific components include learned patterns of thinking about oneself, about one's own personal ability, and about anticipated result expectancies in potentially threatening situations. The concern with oneself, negative self-evaluation, and negative performance expectations are learned by experiencing success and failure, by feedback of evaluations and in comparisons of one's own performance with that of other people. This social learning history determines a habitual worry component, but there are also situational circumstances that evoke worry cognitions, that can be deduced from the current evaluation of the situation. One consequence of these considerations as regards measurement theory is the need to construct trait and state scales for both components.

In several studies of performance tests in school and college, Deffenbacher (1980) showed that there is a moderate correlation between measures of worry components and performance indices; usually negative correlations between $r = -0.30$ and $r = -0.50$ have been found. In these studies, performance parameters did not correlate with measures of emotionality. Similar results were reported by Hodapp, Laux, and Spielberger (1982). Of particular interest in this connection are causal analyses, as published by Hodapp (1982). These confirmed the performance-reducing role of the worry components and also provided indications of possible performance-enhancing effects of the emotionality components.

The fact that some anxiety questionnaires combine worry and emotionality items may be another reason for the nonuniform results reported to date. Future studies should carry out the operationalization of worry and emotionality separately. Hodapp's results also illuminate new ways of approaching this question. Worry may be conceived of as a variable representing cognitive evaluation processes that may be suitable for predicting the performance result. This probably has the form of a linear relationship. Emotionality, on the other hand, could be an indicator of arousal; closer analysis may also reveal curvilinear relationships, e.g., in the form of an inverted-U function.

What Role Does This Theory Play in the Psychomotor Domain?

One of the first analyses of the importance of distinguishing between emotionality and worry in the field of motor abilities was presented by Morris, Smith, Andrews, and Morris (1975). Different performance levels of typing accuracy and typing speed were examined; it was found that, while indicators of emotionality had no relationship whatsoever to performance level, worry components produced negative relationships. These results were consistently independent of performance level.

The usefulness of the differentiation between worry and emotionality in the analyses of sport-related anxiety was demonstrated by Schwenkmezger (1985a). Comprehensive correlational results are presented which reveal that worry cognitions about competence, fears of failure, norms, and comparisons of one's own performance with that of others covary negatively with performance in a performance test in track and field sports, even on the individual-item level. No such relationships were found for emotionality items. Using an activity-specific scale measure of task-unrelated cognitions in a study of handball players, Schwenkmezger and Laux (1986) found that high-anxious players tend to have more task-unrelated cognitions than low-anxious players. In evaluation situations (selection games with evaluation of individual performance) there was a significant increase in task-unrelated cognitions as compared with the number in training situations. These results support Spielberger's state-trait model of anxiety. In addition, highly significant correlations were found between frequency of task-unrelated cognitions and assessments of individual performance by independent raters.

META-ANALYSES

Regardless of theoretical orientation or the question of whether to use indicators of the performance result or the quality of movement, one is of course left with the problem of how to summarize all the empirical results regarding the relationship between anxiety and motor performance. An appropriate methodology to aggregate single effect sizes based on empirical research is the use of meta-analyses. We can discriminate between informal, formal, and formal-statistical meta-analyses.

Informal meta-analyses are qualitative and interpretative summaries on the relationship of anxiety and motor performance regarding the results of many studies in an over-

view, but without any statistical framework. They are often conducted on the basis of a well-formulated psychological theory. Reviews fulfilling this criteria have been published by Landers (1980) on arousal theory, by Eysenck, Nias, and Cox (1982) on theoretical ideas of the biological bases of neuroticism theory, and recently by Neiss (1988) in an integrative overview.

Formal meta-analyses are defined as analyses evaluating empirical research, not only qualitatively but also quantitatively. A widely used method in this sense is, for example, the so-called "vote-counting" strategy. (A far better technique will be described shortly.) Results of each study are counted as either supporting or contradicting a hypothesis.

The first analyses on the topic of anxiety and motor performance conducted in this way are those by Martens (1971), commented on by Spielberger (1971). Some years later, Martens (1974) completed his earlier review. Each review included 43 studies on the basis of drive-theory and about 15 studies on the basis of the inverted-U hypothesis. Unfortunately, the empirical support/nonsupport for drive-theory was equivocal, because approximately an equal number of studies confirmed and rejected the basic hypothesis. Quite similar were the results for the inverted-U hypothesis. Martens (1974) argued that there are many serious difficulties in any attempt to apply drive-theory to the anxiety and motor performance relationship. It is, for example, extremely difficult to classify the habit hierarchy exactly as well as the dominance of correct or incorrect responses. Neiss (1988) came to a quite similar conclusion with the inverted-U hypothesis.

Another problem is that the vote-counting technique can lead to statistically false conclusions. The single studies which founded the basis for such a technique suffer from the fact that they are frequently interpreted by their authors with respect to their theoretical statements, while the pragmatic question about the kind of relationship that exists between anxiety and motor performance remains unanswered.

The major methodological problems are that the studies are based on different samples (number and type of person), using different inferential tests, and without reference to the effect values of interrelations or discrepancies which are of most importance. Hedges and Olkin (1985) demonstrated, in addition, that in case of a true effect in combination with low statistical power, the probability of an inappropriate conclusion increases with the number of studies taken into account.

Frequently, the anxiety measures and the performance indices that have been studied are much too heterogeneous to permit any comparative results whatsoever. Yet another problem lies in the sometimes very specifically constructed anxiety measures. Accordingly, the correlation coefficients must be viewed considering that extremely specific anxiety measures were used, and as a result, a danger of criterion confounding arises, i.e., a close relationship is to be expected because of the similarity between predictor and criterion.

The only promising method for analysis is meta-analysis in a formal-statistical way. This method goes beyond the traditional narrative review by quantifying information from different studies. Effect sizes are integrated on the basis of correlations. However, meta-analysis is not only restricted to correlational studies, since other statistics like F-, t- or p-values can be transformed. The aggregated effect size is defined as the weighted average of all correlation coefficients. The sample size is used as a weight. Supplementary to general analyses, special importance can be given to the question of what other variables can be identified which moderate the relationship.

Kleine (1988, 1990) undertook some very sophisticated meta-analyses on the relationship between anxiety and sport performance. He analyzed results from a total of 37 studies, which included 58 independent samples and 3220 persons. His 1990 study is an extension of the first one, including 77 independent effect sizes drawn from 3589 persons. Altogether, the effect sizes ranged from $r = -.70$ to $r = +.59$. The population effect size was $r_w = -.19$. This global analysis lead to the conclusion that only a small proportion of the variance was explained by such an analysis.

In a next step, Kleine differentiated the studies according to sex, type of anxiety measure, type of sport, and time at which the anxiety measurement was taken. In this way, he analyzed other variables that might be identified as moderating the anxiety-motor performance-relationship. For example, it is stronger in females than in males ($r = -.23$ versus $r = -.12$). The anxiety-performance relationship was stronger in younger groups than in older ones, and it was closer on a lower skill level than in higher skill levels ($r = -.28$ versus $r = -.10$). Differences were identified between contact versus noncontact sports ($r = -.23$ versus $r = -.17$) and in team sports versus individual ones ($r = -.44$ versus $r = -.14$). According to the question of whether sport-specific measures or general anxiety measures are appropriate, it was found that sport-specific measures like the SCAT or the CSAI-1 did not provide better predictions of the anxiety-motor performance relationship than general measures such as the STAI. The relationship was closer in worry than in emotionality measures ($r = -.43$ versus $r = -.11$).

The time at which anxiety was measured is also of influence: longer intervals produce smaller effect sizes, but if anxiety is measured directly before a performance test, the relationship is stronger. The largest effect sizes are observed when anxiety indicators are measured directly following the performance test. In this event, however, the causal relationship is probably reversed, since a failure in performance probably causes an increase in anxiety. Results such as these, in which anxiety is assessed subsequent to performance, are not particularly valuable in explaining the relationship between anxiety and motor performance.

In summary, we can conclude that on the aggregated level not a single effect size was in the positive direction. Although there were differences in the effect size, anxiety and motor performance consistently correlated in the negative direction.

Kleine makes some methodological restrictions in order to qualify his findings. For example, he points out that he has only analyzed publications in which a linear relationship between anxiety and motor performance has been reported. Curvilinear relationships such as those present in the inverted-U function have not yet been examined in meta-analyses. Another reason for this, however, is that in most of the studies he analyzed, no test of linearity relationship was undertaken. A further objection lies in the fact that some of the results he reports involved dependent measures. Nevertheless, such analyses are praiseworthy and the results are interesting, e.g., the negative relationship between anxiety and motor performance has been demonstrated for the first time using meta-analytic statistical procedures based on a statistical rationale.

SPECIAL IMPLICATIONS WITH REFERENCE TO PERFORMANCE AND MOTOR LEARNING

Even though some findings from investigations in the field of sport are interpreted in the perceptive of the inverted-U function, it nevertheless has to be taken into account that:

1. As a rule, sport-nonspecific scales were used (e.g., MAS in Duthie & Roberts, 1970, or STAI in Klavora, 1977), and that for this reason there have been no definite findings and interpretations for sport-specific anxieties, as these trait measures, as mentioned above, refer exclusively to self-esteem-threatening situations (cf. also Spielberger, 1971).
2. After a differentiation of high-anxious persons and low-anxious persons, Klavora (1978) was able to confirm the curvilinear relation for both groups. However, a shift of the curve points indicated that high-anxious persons in prestart anxiety were underactivated, and it therefore seemed as if people with a higher level of anxiety had a higher performance that did low-anxious persons.
3. An inter- and intraindividual level of anxiety, not an absolute level, is related to the curve of performance (see Kauss, 1977).
4. It is the type of task that leads to the shift of the curve. Fiske and Maddi (1961), for example, found that there is a dependence of the optimal level of arousal for the complexity of the task. Walker, Nideffer, and Boomer (1977) confirmed this expectation with divers, Carron (1968) with students, Kauss (1977) with football players, and Griffiths, Steel, and Vaccaro (1979) in a test for diving students.

Oxendine and Temple (1970), on the basis of an overview of investigations on the subject, concluded that:

1. High levels of arousal are a prerequisite for optimal performance in gross-motor activities which require strength, endurance, and speed.
2. High levels of arousal are unfavorable in activities requiring complex skills and fine skills.

3. An arousal slightly above the medium level is more favorable for all motor tasks than a normal or subnormal one.
4. Level of learning has a modifying effect on arousal level (cf. Carron & Morford, 1968; Lazarus, Deese, & Osler, 1952).
5. An orientation exclusively on the performance outcome can offer merely limited evidence. Only an analysis of the performance process, for example, gives a clear idea of the expenditure-effect relation or problematic sequences ("points of trouble") in the course of performance.

Following Krenauer and Schönpflug (1980), it seems advisable not only to pay attention to the phase of performance realization but to include the anticipation phase and the calculation processes (see above) in the analysis. The assumption is well founded that anxiety has not only an effect on the execution of performance but also on the formation of objectives. It is therefore possible to attribute low performance not to disrupted execution of performance but to a lower level of demand. Such a reduction of the level of demand due to anxiety provides a possibility of anxiety control.

6. The process of performance is not only determined by person and task factors but also by environment factors. Geen (1976) has presented an overview on the influence of social environment.

In summary, motor performance depends on three groups of factors. This is illustrated in Figure 14–6.
Also, for motor learning, it can be observed that there is a relationship between task complexity, the anxiety or anxiousness level, and the performance of learning.

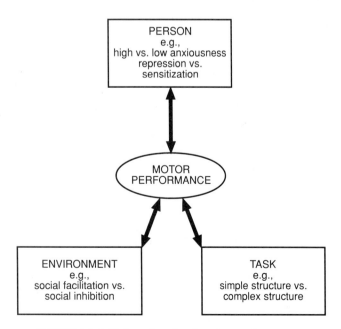

FIGURE 14–6 Determinants of motor performance.

Statements on the effects of anxiety on motor learning include the proposition that anxiety could be termed a "motor" for learning (see Walter, 1977), the statement that with anxiety the process of learning is slower and a lower level of learning is achieved, and the assertion that motor learning with anxiety can be characterized by a high susceptibility to failure (Allmer, 1982). The empirical evidence leads to contrasting considerations (cf. also Hackfort & Schwenkmezger, 1985; Martens, 1971):

1. The concept of anxiety being a motor for learning is derived from results of an investigation by Miller (1948). It was a conditioning experiment with animals. Even though conditioning experiments with humans (e.g., Taylor, 1951) show a quicker conditioning of high-anxious people, this has to be confined to this simple mechanism of learning. Motor learning typically involves a more complex process of learning.
2. Considering the process of learning, support can be found for the observation that high-anxious person at the beginning have more difficulties in learning than low-anxious people, whereas in later stages no differences are found and the results of learning are identical. Karbe (1968) noticed that high-anxious people learned swimming skills more slowly but that the same ultimate level of competence was achieved as with low-anxious people.
3. Pemberton and Cox (1981) disproved the idea that learning under stress is more difficult. Other scholars (see Marteniuk & Wenger, 1970; Sage & Bennett, 1973) were even able to confirm the theory of consolidation (see Walker & Tarte, 1963). Furthermore, the nature of the stressor (anxiety potential) is of importance as is the level of learning (Calvo & Alamo, 1987).

The basis of any conclusions in this area can be described as being not yet sufficient, neither for the theory of consolidation nor for the theory of decrement (see Walker, 1958). In a recent investigation, Calvo, Alamo, and Ramos (1990) demonstrate evidence contrary to the action decrement theory, which argues that high arousal during the acquisition phase is connected with faster learning and facilitates long-term retention due to a more intense activity trace process. They found that "high-trait-anxious subjects had a slower performance under test instruction in high-demanding tasks than did low-trait-anxious subjects, but they were learning similarly" and "anxiety and stress do not impair the quality (accuracy) of learning in high-demanding tasks; but . . . they reduce the speed necessary for such learning" (Calvo, Alamo, & Ramos, 1990, p. 33).
These findings support the distinction between performance effectiveness (quality of performance) and processing efficiency (amount of effort or resources used; see Eysenck & Mathews, 1987) or the already emphasized distinction between result- and process-orientation in analyzing such problems. As to these distinctions, the results by Calvo et al. also offer evidence that anxiety does not

affect learning effectiveness, but instead reduces learning efficiency.

ANXIETY CONTROL IN SPORTS

The topic of anxiety control can be differentiated in two ways: (1) possibilities and techniques of anxiety control used by or for athletes; and (2) possibilities of controlling anxiety by means of sport activities. With respect to both themes, it is necessary to distinguish the aims. Usually the aim of anxiety control for athletes is anxiety reduction. But we also learn from sport situations that coaches try to induce anxiety in athletes "as a motivator" or "as a disturbing agent." Much effort is put into specific exercise programs to reduce anxiety and depression and to investigate the therapeutic potential of such programs. But we also learn from persons who are engaged in sports like rock climbing, parachute jumping, etc., that they like to do such activities "because they get the feeling of anxiety."

It is not possible here to analyze all these considerations. What can be said is that we do not have much empirical research and do not know a lot about the anxiety-inducing strategies to influence motivation and sports performance (see Hackfort, 1979). Little is documented in systematic investigations about the attractiveness of feeling anxiety during some sports. It has still not been clarified if this is only a phenomenological description or a sufficient explanation about what happens when talking about "liking the feeling of anxiety." Perhaps it is not only the feeling of anxiety but also the experience of controlling such a situation, to control one's own feelings and oneself and to touch the limits of self-realization, self-exploration, and growth.

The focus here will be on (1) techniques for reducing anxiety in athletes, and (2) possibilities and evidence for reducing anxiety through experiences in sports and exercise.

INTERVENTION STRATEGIES FOR ANXIETY REDUCTION IN ATHLETES

Scientifically based intervention techniques may be less effective in sports than might be expected or desired because such techniques are not sport-specific enough. Furthermore, athletes (or coaches) may already have developed their own techniques, and this could interfere with scientifically rigorous interventions. Investigations have been carried out referring to so-called "naive" techniques (see Hackfort, 1979; Nitsch & Hackfort, 1979; Hackfort & Schwenkmezger, 1985). These techniques are termed "naive" because they are, contrary to scientifically based techniques, developed by the athlete (or coach) and originate from personal learning experiences; they are applied according to subjective definitions of the situation, and their efficacy is subjectively evaluated, if at all.

To sum up the main results of this research: it could be

stated that most of the persons have their more or less elaborated concepts, beliefs, and convictions about what is appropriate for them in special situations referring to special problems and how to realize them. Sport psychologists should know about this, especially in their practical work, and check the appropriateness of such concepts and techniques.

The whole body of reported techniques can be subdivided by different criteria. With respect to practical aspects, techniques of situation control and techniques of symptom control are differentiated. Techniques of the first group aim at influencing situational conditions; techniques of the second group aim at influencing physiological, cognitive, and/or behavioral symptoms. Referring to cognitive processes, self-suggestions, self-argumentations, and self-instructions can be distinguished. Often behavioral techniques (i.e., motor behavior such as stretching) are combined with cognitive techniques (e.g., the self-instruction, "Relax!"). Sometimes complex programs to overcome anxiety are reported. Before the application of scientifically based techniques the naive ones should be explored by interviewing the athlete and what s/he evaluated.

CONCEPT AND PRACTICE OF DESENSITIZATION STRATEGIES

Desensitization strategies are fundamental for anxiety reduction in sports. Conceptual and procedural orientations and modifications, e.g., the emphasis on cognitive processes, give it classical and actual meaning. Therefore it should be described in more detail here.

Systematic Desensitization (SD) dates back to Wolpe (1958, 1972), who developed this method within the framework of behavioral therapy as a treatment method for reducing neurotic anxieties. It is one among many behavioral-therapeutic methods. Its effectiveness is accounted for by a principle called counterconditioning. Systematic desensitization has now been applied for more than three decades as an effective method for modifying experience and behavior. During this time, with the classic behavioristic and neobehavioristic approaches in behavioral therapy, an emphasis on cognitive processes and the elaboration of a cognitive behavioral therapy followed. The conceptual reorientations involved also concern the theoretical foundation and methodological variations of systematic desensitization (SD).

The term "desensitization" does not mean that a person is intended to be restricted in his/her sensitivity. Rather the attempt is made to reduce undifferentiated perceptions in certain (specifically phobic) situations in favor of a more differentiated reception of information and information processing. This process of modification on the one hand occurs systematically; however, it does not occur "in a stereotyped way."

The application of SD in the clinical area ranges from the most varied specific anxieties (phobias) to social anxieties and frigidity (cf. Paul, 1966). According to Fliegel, Groeger, Künzel, Schulte, and Sorgatz (1981), it has been used for the treatment of virtually all disturbances involving anxiety in some way. When including SD in the spectrum of processes of possible methods of intervention in sport, the following three remarks should be considered:

1. The original reference of SD to psychopathological problems is to be extended, as it is not inherent in the field of application of sport.
2. Methodological principles are regarded as appropriate, and not only in order to be able to reduce anxiety in phobic anxieties.
3. SD emphasizes the role of cognitive processes in managing anxiety (Meichenbaum, 1977, 1979).

Conceptual Bases

If one proceeds from the conviction that anxiety is learned, it is obvious that an athlete can reduce it by "unlearning" it. The unlearning of anxiety in certain situations will take place according to a particular learning process, the conditioning process, which is then used as counterconditioning. In this counterconditioning, the anxiety reaction is inhibited by a reaction incompatible with anxiety (principle of reciprocal inhibition): if it is possible to provoke an anxiety-inhibiting reaction in the presence of anxiety-inducing stimuli, it will weaken the connection between these stimuli and anxiety (Wolpe, 1972).

Such anxiety-inhibiting reactions or reactions incompatible with anxiety present autonomous effects tied to relaxation. If one is, for example, anxious about a competitor (as a result of negative experience), the mere imagining of this opponent may arouse anxiety reactions. If one learns to relax fully and to imagine the anxiety opponent while remaining relaxed, the anxiety reaction is inhibited and the anxiety stimulus (anxiety opponent) loses its effect (anxiety reaction).

Intervention Strategy

SD makes use of the psychoregulatory important interaction between psychological (particularly cognitive), vegetative, and motor processes. Wolpe was able to use the following two ideas and to connect them with each other with respect to their functions (the principle of reciprocal inhibition):

1. Jacobson's (1928) results that deep muscular relaxation can inhibit strong emotional states such as anxiety.
2. Salter's (1949) findings that imagining an anxiety situation offers a way of tackling this anxiety.

The combination of such states of relaxation generated by muscular relaxation with the imagination of anxiety-arousing situations highlights the particular features of SD. In combining the state of relaxation incompatible with anxiety and anxiety-related imaginations (anxiety cognitions), the anxiety reaction is inhibited. This experience makes it possible to "decouple" the connection between (anxiety) situations and (anxiety) reactions and leads to the person changing his/her behavior in this situation.

SD proceeds according to three typical steps.

First, the person learns a relaxation technique. As a rule, it might be the progressive muscular relaxation technique as described by Jacobson (1928), which is practiced in a way that enables the person to put him-/herself in a state of relaxation. Second, an anxiety hierarchy is established. Situations or problems triggering extreme anxiety (top level) and situations merely causing anxiety (bottom level) are ordered hierarchically. Third, anxiety levels ordered hierarchically are coped with seriatim, proceeding from the less severe to the most severe, first in imagination (in-sensu desensitization) and then in reality (in-vivo desensitization) under constant deconditioning.

Confrontation with the real situation can occur at every level. In the process of imaginative dealing with situations, the following phases can be distinguished:

1. The person mentally puts him/herself in the first problematic situation. This leads to a triggering of anxiety with physiological, cognitive, and motor symptoms which the person perceives. He/she signalizes the occurrence of anxiety.
2. Upon this signal the leader instructs the person to stop the imagination and to return into the state of relaxation.

This change is repeated until a successful reconditioning (freedom from anxiety) is achieved.

The application principle is in accordance with concepts of relaxation. In turn, SD has an effect on anxiety arousal and inhibits it (reciprocal inhibition). For the everyday practice of sport, however, it is not possible to receive regular outside help. Accordingly, the athlete has to instruct him/herself as to how to achieve self-control. According to Tunner (1975), there are two prerequisites for a self-controlled desensitization program developed in such a way:

1. Sensitization for one's own anxiety reactions or anxiety symptoms
2. The acknowledgment that relaxation is incompatible with anxiety and that it contributes to overcome anxiety.

After a critical analysis of the research on the application principle of SD, Murray and Jacobson (1971) came to the conclusion that neither physical relaxation nor a hierarchization is of crucial importance for the method's effectiveness. Rather, it is the development of the person's conviction to be able to control the situation that matters. Thus great importance is attached to the cognitive factor "expectation." Among others, Sue (1972) considers relaxation as an encouraging rather than a necessary element of SD. The fact that hierarchizing anxiety situations is unnecessary has been proved by Goldfried and Goldfried (1977). If both components continue to be seen as essential elements of SD, the interaction between them can be considered as a success-determining factor. For the application principle this means negative expectations (negative structures of anticipation, e.g., anxiety, fear of failure) are to be replaced by positive expectations (positive structures of anticipation, e.g., the conviction one can cope, optimism about success). Evidence for this has been furnished by the investigations of Valins and Ray (1967) and Ortlieb (1976).

Procedural Modification

A procedural modification of SD has gained importance, and shall be introduced here briefly as "self-control desensitization" according to Groffmann, Reihl, and Zschintzsch (1980). This method is based on a (cognitive) reinterpretation of SD by Goldfried (1971). The technique is not referred decisively to the effect of (muscular) methods of relaxation and the change in physiological processes to realize the principle of reconditioning. Instead, essentially, cognitive restructuring is developed. This can mean, for example, remembering one's own strong points and considering the opponent's weaknesses. Moreover, the attempt is to make the person more self-reliant, enabling him/her to exert control by imparting universal (not problem-or anxiety-specific) applicable techniques for coping with a wide range of stress situations.

The essential elements are: (1) explanation of the procedure, (2) practice for distinguishing physical anxiety signals, (3) hierarchizing of situations that are difficult to cope with, (4) practice of a method of relaxation, (5) practice of a technique of coping, and (6) testing of this technique in an everyday situation.

With this procedure, not only are processes of conditioning (respectively processes of reconditioning) developed. Learning by verbal action (communicative learning), by imaginative action (learning by internal realization), and by practical action (learning by external realization) are of importance. If one attempts to take these three forms of learning of a method as the basis for systematic coping with problems in sport, the following procedure is advisable:

1. The persons concerned (athletes) and helping persons (coaches) hold discussions in which the kind of problem, the problem development, and possibilities of coping are discussed.
2. The person concerned learns to cope abstractly with the problem.
3. The person concerned learns to cope with the problem in practice.

Relaxation exercises can also be useful, especially in connection with the internal realization process. Even though the proceeding is similar to the model of application of SD, it implies a different orientation as regards the theoretical relation as well as the relation of application. From the learning-theoretical point of view, the principle of conditioning has been given up in favor of the action principle. The relation of application lies in everyday sport-

practical situations, not in the clinical field. Attempts to automize SD (in the technical sense, not in the sense of automatization of movements) are reported by Elwood (1979). Here, the psychologically helping person is replaced, for example, by videotapes, slides, and tape recordings operated by the person concerned or presented to him/her (cf. Lang, 1969, Mann, 1972).

Kowatschew (1973) reports on a method designed specifically for athletes that he calls a "desensitizing method." Even though he describes the method as a "stimulation treatment by stimulating the regulation mechanisms of the nerves by means of a preceding systematic reproduction of the imaginations of the psychologically important moments of the impending competition" (p. 77), he sees the application principle as referring back to SD. The reason for this is that the execution takes place under relaxed conditions (rooms free of disturbances, relaxed body posture) and that the method of preparing oneself for possible problematic experiences (e.g., rude behavior of an audience) by imagination is similar to a component of SD. This method was tested with 15 boxers. Measurements of success showed that effects were achieved with regard to the subjective evaluation of mood, concentration performance, behavior (reaction time), and physiological indices (reduction in pulse rate).

Bauer's (1977) suggestion to use desensitization techniques in dealing with anxiety-arousing situations caused, say, by accidents, seems promising. Successes might possibly be achieved by psychological intervention, for example, if a gymnast after an accident refuses to take part in an exercise because he/she is afraid of further falls. Other authors adhere to steps associated with SD but depart from the original method in such a way that it seems questionable to retain the term. Epuran, Horghidan, and Muresanu (1970), simulated an audience's background noise in order to reduce handball players' anxieties or inhibitions. The method presented by Vanek (1974) of "modelated training" is also often compared to SD. An adaptation of the competitor to general and specific competition conditions is to be achieved by simulation. This method refers to the adaptation with respect to the expected physical, technical-tactical, and psychological stressors. Similar relations are reported to exist between mental preparation and SD.

In none of these methods is the application principle of SD to present anxiety-causing stimuli used; only a prerequisite relaxed state is retained. Besides, such training techniques as a rule include a social situation, as the training partner, coach, and other persons of reference are present. This means that important conditions of relaxation drop out so that there is hardly any similarity with SD remains. Frequently, a relation between the principle of SD and methodological sequences has been established as these are designed according to the didactic principles of "from the easy task to the difficult one" and "from the simple task to the complex one." Although a formal translation is impossible, these principles can nevertheless be connected for the purpose of anxiety reduction.

The use of SD while retaining a phase of relaxation is

also conceivable in sport-specific situations in other ways. Hackfort and Schwenkmezger (1985) have reported case analyses. A modification of this form of therapy for coping with test anxiety was used with university students. This was the case, above all, when anxiety of physical injury was experienced in complicated athletic movements. The following example serves to illustrate this.

A student, master of the hurdle technique, was injured in a training session. As a result, he developed a marked test anxiety which twice prevented successful performance of the act. Thereafter, a practice sequence was developed in which the height of the hurdles was increased by 5 cm after each sequence. The first exercises were designed in such a way that there was no more risk of injury (now the crossbars of hurdles fell down when touched). Before each run (3 hurdles in competition distance), a short supine-position relaxation exercise was carried out. After relaxation, each run was repeated 8 to 10 times without any mistakes before the runner proceeded to the next, more difficult exercise. If the hurdler felt insecure or not sufficiently relaxed, further relaxation phases (with subsequent exercise runs) were interposed. When hurdles were first used, the upper parts were put behind the lower part so that they would fall over more easily upon contact. After four weeks of practice (eight sessions), anxiety was reduced completely and the person was able to execute without any problems.

Problems and Approaches of the New Conceptualization

Meichenbaum (1977, 1979) refers to observational studies on SD which show the importance of cognitive factors in the application of SD. He suggests changing the basic features of SD in the perspective of cognitive behavioral modification in such a way that cognitions can be included more purposively in the method. Following Rachman (1967), he stresses that relaxation is essentially effective as psychic relaxation and he gives hints for encouragement by way of self-instruction. The emphasis of psychic relaxation is particularly important in connection with the sport-practical use of this method insofar as for performance in sport, no full psychic state of relaxation is aimed at, due to the need for an optimal activity-related degree of activation.

But from the perspective of action theory, the cases described above are also referred to as internal representations: a certain situation constellation is mentally reconstructed (internally represented). A wrestler, for example, might imagine him/herself facing his/her anxiety opponent on the mat. He can mentally envision coping successfully with this situation, for example, by mentally performing a version of attack in which he throws the opponent. Such thinking presents an internal realization which is action-directing in the real situation. In this view it is essential for SD to specifically influence cognitions by means of the technique of internal representations. When fully ignoring cognitive processes, the effectiveness of SD would probably be insufficiently explained. When retaining the

above application principles in connection with a consideration of cognitive processes, an effective application of this method can be expected also in the sport-practical situations which are not oriented toward clinical cases.

A problem of SD still unaccounted for lies in the transfer of imaginative coping to real situations. There is evidence of the effectiveness of mental rehearsal (cf. Wieselberg, Dyckman, & Abramowitz, 1979) as well as of the importance of experiences in real situations (methods of confrontation). Preparation for everyday action or actions in sport seem to require a combination of methods. Within the framework of SD, this means the use of pictures in the form of slides and films as well as practical experience in real situations (problem situations).

In addition to the hints mentioned on the applicability of SD or of versions of SD methods in sport, it can be said that the application is particularly promising if the problem refers to specific constellations (e.g., competition, self-depiction in front of audience) or/and specific actions (e.g., a particular part of an exercise or dealing with a so-called anxiety-provoking opponent).

Biofeedback Training (BFT)

Technological developments have led to the development and acceptability of biofeedback techniques. Feedback is a principle of systems control based on the information the system receives about previous performance. When applying this method to living organisms, it is called biofeedback. Psychophysiological biofeedback research is predominantly concerned with the reporting back of physiological parameters of the autonomous and central nervous system; the individual is made aware of these, which are conveyed to him/her by means of apparatuses. An individual can be made aware of, for example, heart rate, blood pressure rates, respiratory frequency, muscle tension, or central-nervous signals (EEG signals) via various sensory systems (e.g., optical or acoustical. Huber, 1977). One is thereby enabled to learn to control and even change one's responses. For example, a person can be instructed to reduce or heart, respiratory, or blood pressure rates by means of relaxation exercises.

Biofeedback and biofeedback training should be differentiated. *Biofeedback (BFB)* refers to the immediate and continuous presentation of one's biosignals (physiological parameters) to him/herself; *biofeedback training* is any attempt to achieve a change in these parameters through such feedback or to maintain them. Such biofeedback training, according to Birbaumer, offers for the first time the possibility to develop directly anxiety-incompatible physiological reactions. The detour of more or less suggestive techniques of relaxation, often wearisome and lengthy, can thereby be avoided. The repeated temporal connection of anxiety-arousing stimuli with a physiological pattern of relaxation leads to a conditioned inhibition of the physiological anxiety reaction (Birbaumer, 1975).

Of particular importance, especially in sport, is EMG-biofeedback training for controlling muscular tension. A very favorable possibility exists in combining BFB-training and SD (cf. Budzynski & Stoyva, 1975; Zaichkowsky, Dorsey, & Mulholland, 1977).

BFB research is still relatively new, and it still raises more questions than there are clear answers on cause-and-effect issues. Problems are seen, for example, in side effects, such as increased attention to the body (hypochondria), untreated misevaluations (misattributions), and high (economical, apparative) expenditure. Criticism is directed toward the theory as it is not yet fully developed and there are insufficient generalizations about both laboratory and everyday situations (cf. Buchkremer, 1979).

The application of BFT in sports has been summarized by Zaichkowsky and Fuchs (1989). They concluded that:

biofeedback training alone or in conjunction with other self-control methods can be an extremely useful way for teaching performers to self-regulate their psychophysiological stress responses and thus to improve performance. (p.241)

But they also mention the lack of empirical evidence, especially with top athletes, and the specific methodological problems associated with this technologically demanding intervention strategy.

Cognitive Strategies

In the last two decades, the focus on cognitions, especially in behavioral therapy, influenced the development of anxiety-control strategies. Some of the numerous procedures for the treatment of anxiety and stress-related disorders are not only useful in the clinical area but also appropriate in sports. A fundamental connection for cognitive strategies in sports is the link between cognition and motion already pointed out by Soviet psychologists such as Wygotsky, Luria, and Galperin, and taken up by Meichenbaum (1977). His central idea refers to the hypothesis that in task solving, language is of special importance.

This holds especially true for motor learning (see Wohl, 1977). Luria (1961) assumed three phases in learning intentional (volitional) motor behavior. In the first phase, motor actions are controlled and accompanied by verbal encouragement by other persons, usually the parents. In the second phase, the child talks to him/herself loudly and thereby regulates the behavior. Later, internal talking takes over the role of self-regulation. Galperin (1969) proceeds from these assumptions in relating internal talking to processes of thinking and interacting with each other, which may occur again loudly and openly once the automatized act of thinking and acting is interrupted. For this reason self-instruction as a specific form of internal talking, according to Meichenbaum, is seen as an important part of the process of thinking. Internal talking helps one to solve problems mentally. In an internal dialogue, the individual interprets feelings and perceptions, regulates and changes evaluations and convictions, and gives him/herself instructions and reinforcement. As such, a central role is attached to language in the development of processes of thinking,

and as thinking is part of actions (cf. Rubinstein, 1973), behavior can be modified by means of specific forms of external and internal talking (cf. Paivio, 1971).

In the context of such techniques and the concept of mental rehearsal, mental training, and imagining (e.g., Paivio, 1971; Richardson, 1967), a strategy of anxiety control by anticipating the sport-specific task has been elaborated and tested (Hackfort & Schwenkmezger, 1985). The basic principle of this method is for the athlete to complement mental exercise with self-instructions to achieve optimal preparation for carrying out motor motions. The method was first constructed within the framework of a sequence in volleyball. In principle, it is transferable to other kinds of sports.

The cognitive preparation for motion consists of a detailed motion description formulated in short sentences in the first person. In the framework of a first analysis, it was drawn up for two skills: "digging" and "setting" in volleyball. The subject is instructed to read the motion description with high concentration and at the same time to imagine the motion mentally. Illustrations (so-called "kinegrams") are intended to help the athlete to imagine the motion. The description of the motion for the selected techniques consist of 13 elements that the person works through once in about 5 minutes. The following effects, which might be anxiety-reducing with respect to situations of performance, are expected.

In the terminology of Meichenbaum, an individual is instructed to deal actively with the situation by talking internally. The subject might realize that he/she is already capable of performing the motion and that as a consequence there is no reason to worry. Possibly this reinforces him/her. This, however, only applies when sufficient provision is made for the athlete to learn the motion. If the form of motion is demanded in tests for a performance assessment, the individual at the same time is given information on the test requirements. As in the description of the motion, all essential elements of the requirements are included. Persons evaluating their performance inadequately through the preparation test are helped and can reevaluate their skill levels.

In a first investigation, the hypothesis considered was that cognitive preparation of motions of examination situations reduces the level of state anxiety immediately before the examination. Moreover, with high-anxious test persons, possibly a greater reduction of anxiety occurs than with low-anxious persons. An experimental group ($N = 47$, including 16 females) of sport students were administered instruction for the cognitive preparation of motion, which was carried out for 20 minutes. The instruction was given one week before a final examination in volleyball as part of the students' B.A. exam. This preparation was repeated twice—on the day before the examination, and about one hour before the examination. Immediately before the examination, the level of state anxiety and other self-evaluations of mood were recorded. A control group (CG) was compared to the experimental group. Figure 14–7 illustrates the findings.

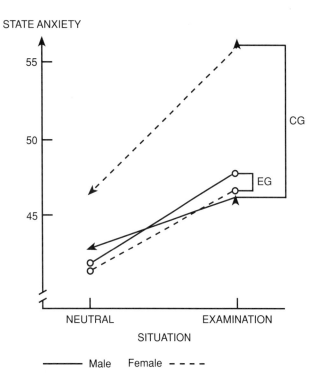

STATE ANXIETY

SITUATION

———— Male   Female - - - -

FIGURE 14–7 State anxiety scores (STAI-S) of male and female test subjects with and without cognitive preparation of motions in a neutral situation and in an examination situation.

The results show clearly that a distinct reduction of state anxiety can be demonstrated with female subjects. With males, however, no effects were found. No differences were observed between high- and low-anxious persons. First analyses, however, lead to the assumption that there is a clear tendency of an increase in performance after cognitive preparation. This seems to be the case above all in long-term cognitive preparation.

How can these effects be accounted for? Various possibilities can be taken into consideration:

1. Due to the fact that female subjects show higher rates of anxiety and stronger state-anxiety reactions, it may be assumed that high levels of anxiety in particular can be reduced by the cognitive preparation of motions. On the other hand, high-anxious male subjects are unable to control state anxiety. As far as female subjects are concerned, high- as well as low-anxious persons profit equally.
2. Furthermore, one may assume that female participants behave more in accordance with the instructions and prepare more intensively.
3. In an earlier analysis (Schwenkmezger et al., 1979) it could be shown that male students tended to overestimate their sport-specific performance, whereas female students showed a more realistic evaluation or had a tendency to underestimate. By the kind of preparation, fe-

male participants noticed how well the learned motion was executed. In the sense of cognitive theory, the result is a realistic evaluation of one's own abilities, a reduction of the threatening feature of the examination, self-reinforcement possibly caused by the reevaluation, and thus control and reduction of anxiety. With male subjects, on the other hand, the effect of the method may have been negative; with some persons, as the preparation of motions revealed, the unrealistic evaluation of their performance and the threatening feature of the examination is maintained.

Further investigations are needed for any confident method of anxiety-reduction techniques to be developed.

Cognitive-affective stress management training. This program "represents an attempt to combine a number of effective clinical techniques into an educational program for self-regulation of emotional responses. These include cognitive restructuring, self-instructional training, somatic and cognitive relaxation skills for arousal control, and the induced affect technique for skill rehearsal under affective arousal" (Smith, 1989, p. 193).

The program may be divided into five phases: (1) pretraining assessment of stress responses, circumstances of occurrence, and how performance is influenced; (2) training rationale emphasizing the conceptualization as an educational program in self-control of emotion and the importance of an athlete's commitment; (3) skill acquisition consisting of the learning of cognitive and somatic relaxation skills, cognitive restructuring, and self-instructional training; (4) skill rehearsal and practice under conditions of induced affect and approximate to real-life situations; and (5) post-training evaluation to assess the effectiveness of inducing performance and self-monitoring. A training manual for this program has been developed by Smith and Rohsenow (1986). Reports about the application in sports have been written by Smith (1984) and Ziegler, Klinzing, and Williamson (1982).

Anxiety control in athletes with special reference to cognitive processes. Summarizing the hints for effective coping and anxiety management, the following steps and elements should be considered in an appropriate strategy for anxiety control:

1. Assessment of anxiety responses, circumstances of occurrence, and preferred coping styles
2. Development of a training concept accepted by the individual athlete
3. Refinement and teaching of basic skills for relaxation (e.g., muscular techniques, respiratory techniques)
4. Refinement and training of cognitive coping techniques (e.g., self-instruction, cognitive restructuring, attentional refocusing) that fit to the techniques normally used by the individual athlete
5. Rehearsal of the skills and techniques under conditions of induced affect and simulated competitive situations

6. Implementation and practice of the trained skills and techniques in real-competitive situations
7. Evaluation of the effectiveness with respect to self-control and performance in order to design the stabilization or modification of the skills and techniques.

The ability to acquire and apply anxiety management techniques will be dependent on the person (individual athlete), the task at hand (motor skill requirements), and the environment (social and ecological circumstances). The eventual goal of such a strategy is the ability of the athlete to use anxiety self-control measures independent of a psychologist (see also, Smith, 1989; Suinn, 1989).

Transcendental Meditation (TM)

In recent years, certain forms of yoga and meditation, especially transcendental meditation (TM), have become popular. Meditation, rooted in the tradition of Indian religion, had already met with great interest in sport in the 1950s owing to the philosopher and archer Eugen Herrigel (1953). Straub (1978, 168) reports that the TM organization, the American Foundation for the Science of Creative Intelligence, has recently formed a separate section for sport. It is hoped that athletes, through training with TM, will feel better, become more relaxed, develop more energy, and learn more quickly. Layman (1978), after examining the literature, has concluded that TM is particularly suitable for soothing athletes and for reducing hyperactivity. Also, Cowger (1974), Marron (1974), and Smith (1975) refer to the anxiety-reducing effects of TM. Experiences with TM in sport, up to now, according to Layman (1978), are said to lead "to translate the preliminary evidence into hypotheses which can be thoroughly tested in the sport situation" (p. 175).

Evidence from sufficient experimental studies with pre- and posttest designs and control groups have not been reported to date. If the effectiveness of the procedure is influenced by the acceptance or rejection of the theoretical/religious background, the data may be in doubt. An investigation carried out by Puryear, Cayce, and Thurston (1976) enforces these concerns. For this purpose, Layman strongly recommends pre- and posttest designs and control group arrangements. For the technique of TM, similar effects as in autogenous training are described. Schilling (1979), too, cites coaches' comments pointing in this direction after an introductory TM course. The same considerations regarding sport-specific suitability can be stated as in the methods mentioned above. This also seems to point to the fact that the effectiveness of the technique remains unimpaired by the rejection or embracing such a concept. An investigation by Puryear et al. (1976) supports this assumption. A method of meditation for the reduction of anxiety first described by Cayce (Puryear & Thurston, 1975) was used. In comparison with a control group, the experimental group after 28 days showed a significant reduction in anxiety (IPAT-Anxiety-Scale).

Muscle Relaxation Techniques

For many years, deep-muscle relaxation has been widely regarded as an effective intervention for the treatment of anxiety and stress-related disorders (Poppen, 1988). The most commonly cited procedure is progressive muscle relaxation as introduced by Jacobson (1928). It is often used as a component in other intervention programs, e.g., systematic desensitization.

Progressive relaxation training (Bernstein & Borkovec, 1973) uses muscle tension-release exercises as a strategy. Careful inspection of the literature reveals inconsistent results for such procedures, and Lehrer (1982) has pointed out that most of the modified versions of Jacobson's method are less effective. Even paradoxical increases in tension and anxiety have been reported in the treatment of patients, according to Lazarus & Mayne (1990). Heide and Borkovec (1984) reported on "relaxation-induced anxiety" (RIA). Nervousness and anxiety may be heightened if the athlete (a) is not able to proceed in relaxation as quickly, as he/she had expected such sensations; or (b) begins to ruminate with progressive relaxation.

It seems necessary also to pay attention to cognitive processes during muscle relaxation and to refer to the focus of concentration of the athlete during such procedures. As an alternative relaxation training procedure, muscle stretching is advocated (e.g., Carlson, Collins, Nitz, Sturgis, & Rogers, 1990). This approach to relaxation differs from the Jacobson method in two aspects: (1) more length-sensitive receptors in the muscle fibers are activated, and (2) this reduces the excitability of the motorneuron pool. In this way it should induce even stronger contrast effects between tension and relaxation and foster learning to discriminate tense muscle groups.

Anxiety Reduction Through Sports and Exercise

In an early investigation of the effects of physical training on mood, Folkins (1976) found that "improvements in physical fitness were accompanied by improvements on two mood measures, anxiety and depression" (p. 387). Although the 36 men participating in this study had been assigned to an exercise and a no-exercise (control) group, they were special because of a high risk of coronary artery disease. This reduces the generalizability of the results.

In a later review on the control and modification of stress emotions through chronic exercise, Folkins and Amsterdam (1977) concluded that "exercise has been associated with an improved sense of well-being and has been correlated with the objective demonstration of reduced psychological and physiological indices of factors such as anxiety, depression, and hostility" (p. 291). Further, in summarizing studies on physical fitness training and mental health, Folkins and Sime (1981) stated, "the research suggests that physical fitness training leads to improved mood, self-concept, and work behavior" (p. 373). But they also stated that most of the studies they referred to had been poorly designed and undertaken predominantly with clinical populations.

These and further problems have been discussed by Schwenkmezger (1985b); they lead to the conclusion that an appropriate answer to the question if exercise does reduce anxiety has to refer to (a) the group of persons and individual characteristics of interest, (b) the exercise program and task characteristics, and (c) the circumstances surrounding the environment. Not only individual characteristics (e.g., kind of anxiety, coping style, expectations, preferred sports), but the kind of exercise, duration, intensity, and frequency, and environmental factors (e.g., social support, ecological influences) have to be considered. Their interrelationships heighten the complexities and difficulties in such investigations.

Nevertheless, recent contributions demonstrate that "acute physical activity of a vigorous nature is associated with a decrement in state anxiety, and this . . . persists for approximately 2-4 hours" (Morgan, 1987). A possible explanation is seen in the distraction from stress-provoking factors, but physiological processes influencing psychological processes have to be considered as well. Several studies by Morgan and his colleagues (e.g., Morgan & Ellickson, 1989) provide evidence that there are possibilities to reduce state anxiety in high-anxious as well as in normalanxious persons engaged in sports and that this effect of exercise lasts longer than meditation or passive interventions.

Based on the assumption of the differential patterning of cognitive and somatic symptoms of anxiety and the assessment with a dual component scale measuring cognitive and somatic trait anxiety Schwartz, Davidson and Goleman (1978) compared the differential effectiveness of meditation and exercise in 77 subjects. A total of 44 subjects regularly (mean = 3.56 one-hour sessions per week) practiced physical exercise, and 33 subjects practiced meditation (at least once daily) over a period of approximately 6 months (median duration). Meditators scored lower on cognitive and higher on somatic anxiety, while exercisers scored lower on somatic and higher on cognitive. The main effect the for group was not significant, indicating that meditators and exercisers did not differ on overall anxiety. Exercisers especially reported significantly higher cognitive versus somatic anxiety. These results suggest differential effects of specific programs to reduce anxiety and support the usage of multidimensional inventories in assessing anxiety and evaluating the effectiveness of exercise as an anxiety-reducing procedure.

With respect to trait anxiety, there are only few studies, with somewhat ambiguous results (see Kerr & Vlaswinkel, 1990). Following Eysenck, Nias, and Cox (1982), it seems that the periods of participating in exercise programs were too brief in most of the studies to influence a personality factor such as trait anxiety. Further research must consider this and therefore should be designed as longitudinal studies with control groups, using general as well as multidimensional measurements to distinguish cognitive and somatic anxiety and anxiety symptoms.

References

Allmer, H. (1982). Angst und Bewegungsverhalten. In B. D. Kirkcaldy (Ed.), Individual differences in sport behavior (pp. 224–241). Cologne: bps.

Anderson, K. J. (1990). Arousal and the inverted-u hypothesis: A critique of Neiss's reconceptualizing arousal. *Psychological Bulletin, 107,* 96–100.

Bard, P. (1934). An emotional expression after decortication with some remarks on certain theoretical views. *Psychological Review, 41,* 424–449.

Bard, P. (1950). Central nervous mechanisms for the expression of anger in animals. In M. L. Reymert (Ed.), *Feelings and emotions: The Mooseheart Symposium* (pp. 211–237). New York: McGraw-Hill.

Basowitz, H., Persky, H., Korchin, S. J., & Grinker, R. R. (1955). *Anxiety and stress.* New York: McGraw-Hill.

Bauer, W. (1977). Psychologische Faktoren der Leistungsbeeinflussung. In K. Carl (Ed.), *Psychologie in Training und Wettkampf* (pp. 85–102). Berlin: Bartels & Wernitz.

Becker, P. (1980). *Studien zur Psychologie der Angst.* Weinheim: Beltz.

Bernstein, D. A., & Borhovec, T. D. (1973). Progressive relaxation training. Champaign, IL: Research Press.

Birbaumer, N. (1975). *Physiologische Psychologie.* Berlin: Springer.

Birbaumer, N. (1977). Angst. In T. Herrmann, P. R. Hofstätter, H. P. Huber & F. E. Weinert (Eds.), *Handbuch psychologischer Grundbegriffe* (pp. 25–38). Munich: Kösel.

Bös, K., & Mechling, H. (1983). *Dimensionen sportmotorischer Leistungen.* Schorndorf: Hofmann.

Browne, M. A., & Mahoney, M. J. (1984). Sport psychology. *Annual Review of Psychology, 35,* 605–625.

Buchkremer, G. (1979). Verhaltenstherapie bei somatischen Erkrankungen. *Mitteilung der DGVT, 11,* 78–113.

Budzynski, T. H., & Stoyva, J. M. (1975). EMG-Biofeedback bei unspezifischen und spezifischen Angstzuständen. In H. Legewie & L. Nusselt (Eds.), *Biofeedback Therapie* (pp. 163–185). Munich: Urban & Schwarzenberg.

Burton, D. (1988). Do anxious swimmers swim slower? Reexamining the exclusive anxiety-performance relationship. *Journal of Sport and Exercise Psychology, 10,* 45–61.

Butollo, W. (1979). *Chronische Angst. Theorie und Praxis der Konfrontationstherapie.* Munich: Urban & Schwarzenberg.

Calvo, M. G., & Alamo, L. (1987). Test anxiety and motor performance: The role of muscular and attentional demands. *International Journal of Psychology, 22,* 165–178.

Calvo, M. G., Alamo, L., & Ramos, P. M. (1990). Test anxiety, motor performance and learning: Attentional and somatic interference. *Personality and Individual Differences, 11,* 29–38.

Cannon, W. B. (1927). The James-Lange theory of emotions: A critical examination and an alternative theory. *American Journal of Psychology, 39,* 106–124.

Cannon, W. B. (1929). *Bodily changes in pain, hunger, fear and rage* (2nd ed.). New York: Appleton-Century-Crofts.

Cannon, W. B. (1931). Against the James-Lange and the thalamic theories of emotions. *Psychological Review, 38,* 281–195.

Carlson, C. R., Collins, F. L., Jr., Nitz, A. J., Sturgis, E. T., & Rogers, J. L. (1990). Muscle stretching as an alternative relaxation training procedure. *Journal of Behavior Therapy & Experimental Psychiatry, 21,* 29–38.

Carron, A. V. (1968). Motor performance under stress. *The Research Quarterly, 39,* 463–469.

Carron, A. V., & Morford, W. R. (1968). Anxiety, stress and motor learning. *Perceptual and Motor Skills, 27,* 507–511.

Cattell, R. B. (1957). *Personality and motivation: Structure and measurement.* New York: World Book.

Cattell, R. B., & Scheier, J. H. (1961). *The meaning and measurement of neuroticism and anxiety.* New York: Ronald.

Costello, C. G. (1976). *Anxiety and depression: The adaptive emotions.* Montreal: McGill Queens University Press.

Cowger, E. L. (1974). The effects of meditation (zazen) upon selected dimensions of personal development. *Dissertation Abstracts, 34/08-A,* 4734.

Cratty, B. J. (1979). *Motorisches Lernen und Bewegungsverhalten.* Bad Homburg: Limpert.

Deffenbacher, J. L. (1980). Worry and emotionality in test anxiety. In I. G. Sarason (Ed.), *Test anxiety* (pp. 111–128). Hillsdale, NJ: Erlbaum.

Dosey, M. A., & Meisels, M. (1969). Personal space and self protection. *Journal of Personal and Social Psychology, 11,* 93–97.

Duffy, E. (1962). *Activation and behavior.* New York: Wiley.

Duthie, J. H., & Roberts, G. C. (1970). Effects of manifest anxiety on learning and performance of a complex motor task. In G. S. Kenyon (Ed.), *Contemporary psychology of sport* (pp. 583–590). Chicago: The Athletic Institute.

Easterbrook, J. A. (1959). The effects of emotion on cue utilization and the organization of behavior. *Psychological Review, 66,* 183–201.

Ebbeck, V., & Weiss, M. R. (1988). The arousal-performance relationship: Task characteristic and performance measures in track and field athletes. *The Sport Psychologist, 2,* 13–27.

Ekman, P., & Oster, H. (1979). Facial expressions of emotion. *Annual Review of Psychology, 30,* 527–554.

Elwood, D. L. (1979). Automatisierungsverfahren. In F. H. Kanfer & A. P. Goldstein (Eds.), *Möglichkeiten der Verhaltensänderung* (pp. 568–609). Munich: Urban & Schwarzenberg.

Endler, N. S. (1975). The case for person-situation interactions. *Canadian Psychological Review, 16,* 12–21.

Endler, N. S. (1978). The interaction model of anxiety: Some possible implications. In R. W. Christina & D. M. Landers (Eds.), *Psychology of motor behavior and sport—1977* (pp. 332–351). Champaign, IL: Human Kinetics.

Endler, N. S., & Okada, M. (1975). A multidimensional measure of trait anxiety: The S-R Inventory of general trait anxiousness. *Journal of Consulting and Clinical Psychology, 43,* 319–329.

Epstein, S. (1972). The nature of anxiety with emphasis upon its relationship to expectancy. In C. D. Spielberger (Ed.), *Anxiety* (Vol. 2, pp. 292–338). London: Academic Press.

Epstein, S. (1976). Anxiety, arousal, and the self-concept. In I. G. Sarason, & C. D. Spielberger (Eds.), *Stress and anxiety* (Vol. 3, pp. 185–224). Washington, DC: Hemisphere.

Epstein, S. (1977). Versuch einer Theorie der Angst. In N. Birbaumer (Ed.), *Psychophysiologie der Angst* (pp. 208–266). Munich: Urban & Schwarzenberg.

Epstein, S., & Fenz, W. D. (1965). Steepness of approach and avoidance gradients in humans as a function of experience: Theory and experiment. *Journal of Experimental Psychology, 70,* 1–12.

Epuran, M., Horghidan, V., & Muresanu, I. (1970). Variations of physical tension during the mental preparation of sportsman for contest. In G. S. Kenyon & T. M. Grogg (Eds.), *Contemporary psychology of sport* (pp. 241–245). Chicago, IL: Athletic Institute.

Eysenck, H. J., Nias, D. K. B., & Cox, D. N. (1982). Sport and personality. *Advances in Behavior Research and Therapy, 4,* 1–56.

Eysenck, M. V., & Mathews, A. (1987). Trait anxiety and cognition. In H. J. Eysenck & I. Martin (Eds.), *Theoretical foundations of behavior therapy* (pp. 197–216). New York: Plenum Press.

Fahrenberg, J. (1968). Aufgaben und Methoden der psychologischen Verlaufsanalyse. In K. J. Groffmann & K. H. Wewetzer (Eds.), *Person als Prozess.* Bern, Switzerland: Huber.

Fahrenberg, J. (1977). Physiological concepts in personality research. In R. B. Cattell & R. M. Dreger (Eds.), *Handbook of modern personality theory* (pp. 585–611). Washington, DC: Hemisphere.

Fahrenberg, J., Walschburger, P., Foerster, F., Myrtek, M., & Müller, W. (1979). Psychologische Aktivierungsforschung. Munich: Minerva.

Fehr, B., & Russell, J. A. (1984). Concept of emotion viewed from a prototype perspective. *Journal or Experimental Psychology: General, 113,* 464–486.

Festinger, L. (1954). A theory of social comparison processes. *Human Relations, 7,* 117–140.

Firestone, I. J., Kaplan, K. J., & Russell, J. C. (1973). Anxiety, fear, and affiliation with similar-state versus dissimilar-state others: Misery sometimes loves nonmiserable company. *Journal of Personality and Social Psychology, 26,* 409–414.

Fiske, D. W., & Maddi, S. R. (1961). *Functions of varied experience.* Homewood, IL: Dorsey Press.

Fliegel, S., Groeger, W. M., Künzel, R., Schulte, D., & Sorgatz, H., (1981). *Verhaltenstherapeutische Standardmethoden.* Munich: Urban & Schwarzenberg.

Folkins, C. H. (1976). Effects of physical training on mood. *Journal of Clinical Psychology, 32,* 385–388.

Folkins, C. H., & Amsterdam, E. A. (1977). Control and modification of stress emotions through chronic exercise. In E. A. Amsterdam, J. H. Wilmore, & A. N. DeMaria (Eds.), *Exercise in cardiovascular health and disease* (pp. 280–294). New York: Yorke Medical Books.

Folkins, C. H., & Sime, W. E. (1981). Physical fitness training and mental health. *American Psychologist, 36,* 373–389.

Frankenhäuser, M. (1969). Biochemische Indikatoren der Aktiviertheit: Die Ausscheidung von Katecholaminen. In W. Schönpflug (Ed.), *Methoden der Aktivierungsforschung* (pp. 195–214). Bern, Switzerland: Huber.

Freud, S. (1952). *Gesammelte Werke.* London: Imago Publishing.

Fuller, R. (1976). *Die Champions: Eine Psychoanalyse des Spitzensportlers.* Frankfurt: Henke.

Galperin, P. J. (1969). Stages in the development of mental arts. In M. Cole & I. Maltzmann (Eds.), *A handbook of contemporary Soviet psychology* (pp. 249–273). New York: Basic Books.

Geen, R. G. (1976). The role of the social environment in the induction and reduction of anxiety. In I. G. Sarason & C. D. Spielberger (Eds.), *Stress and anxiety* (Vol. 3, pp. 105–126). New York: Wiley.

Gellhorn, E. (1965). The neurophysiological basis of anxiety: A hypothesis. *Perspectives in Biology and Medicine, 8,* 488–515.

Gerard, H. B. (1961). Disagreement with others, their credibility and experienced stress. *Journal of Abnormal and Social Psychology, 62,* 554–564.

Goldfried, M. R. (1971). Systematic disensitization as training in self-control. *Journal of Consulting and Clinical Psychology, 37,* 228–234.

Goldfried, M. R., & Goldfried, A. P. (1977). Importance of hierarchy content in the self-control of anxiety. *Journal of Consulting and Clinical Psychology, 1,* 124–134.

Gould, D., Petlichkoff, L., Simons, J., & Vevera, M. (1987). The relationship between Competitive State Anxiety Inventory-2 subscale scores and pistol shooting performance. *Journal of Sport Psychology, 9,* 33–42.

Grabitz, H. J., & Gniech, G. (1978). Die kognitiv-physiologische Theorie der Emotion von Schachter. In D. Frey & M. Irle (Eds.), Theorien der Sozialpsychologie, Vol. 3: *Motivations-und Informationsverarbeitungs-Theorien* (pp. 160–190). Bern, Switzerland: Huber.

Griffiths, T. J., Steel, D. H., & Vaccaro, P. (1979). Relationship between anxiety and performance in scuba diving. *Perceptual and Motor Skills, 48,* 1009–1010.

Groffmann, K. J., Reihl, D., & Zschintzsch, A. (1980). Angst. In W. Wittling (Ed.), *Handbuch der Klinischen Psychologie* (Vol. 5, pp. 220–276). Hamburg: Hoffmann & Campe.

Guilford, J. P. (1964). *Persönlichkeit.* Weinheim: Beltz.

Häcker, H., & Schwenkmezger, P. (1984). Persönlichkeitsfragebogen. In L. R. Schmidt (Ed.), *Lehrbuch der Klinischen Psychologie* (pp. 220–246). Stuttgart: Enke.

Hackfort, D. (1979). *Grundlagen und Techniken der naiven Fremdbeeinflussung im Sport unter besonderer Berücksichtigung der Angstbeeinflussung.* Cologne: bps.

Hackfort, D. (1983). Theoretische und methodische Entwicklungen in der Angstforschung. In E. Apitzsch (Ed.), *Anxiety in sport* (pp. 99–127). Magglingen: Guido Schilling.

Hackfort D. (1986). Theoretical conception and assessment of sport-related anxiety. In C. D. Spielberger & R. Diaz-Guerrero (Eds.), *Cross-cultural anxiety* (Vol. 3, pp. 79–91). Washington, DC: Hemisphere.

Hackfort, D. (1987). *Theorie und Analyse sportbezogener Angstlichkeit.* Schorndorf: Hofmann.

Hackfort, D. (1990). Self and social perception of sport-related trait anxiety. In C. D. Spielberger & R. Diaz-Guerrero (Eds.), *Cross-cultural anxiety* (Vol. 4, pp. 123–131). Washington, DC: Hemisphere.

Hackfort, D., & Nitsch, J. R. (1989). *Das Sportangst-Deutungsverfahren SAD: Grundlagen und Handanweisung.* Schorndorf: Hofmann.

Hackfort, D., & Schwenkmezger, P. (1985). *Angst und Angstkontrolle im Sport.* Cologne: bps.

Hackfort, D., & Schwenkmezger, P. (1989). Measuring anxiety in sports: Perspectives and problems. In D. Hackfort & C. D. Spielberger (Eds.), Anxiety in Sports: An International Perspective (pp. 55–74). Washington, DC: Hemisphere.

Hanin, Y. (1980). A study of anxiety in sports. In W. F. Straub (Ed.), *Sport Psychology: An analysis of athlete behavior* (pp. 236–249). Ithaca, NY: Mouvement Publications.

Hathaway, S. R., & McKinley, J. C. (1943). *Manual for the Minnesota Multiphasic Personality Inventory.* New York: Psychological Corporation.

Heckhausen, H. (1977). Vorkommen und Wirksamkeit aufgabenlösungsfremder Kognitionen während einer Prüfung. In W. Tack (Ed.), *Bericht über den 3. Kongress der Deutschen Gesellschaft für Psychologie in Regensburg* 1976 (pp. 422–423). Göttingen: Hogrefe.

Heckhausen, H. (1979). Sportpsychologie: Auf der Suche nach Identität in einem magischen Dreieck verschiedener Fachwissenschaften. In J. R. Nitsch (Ed.), *Bericht über die 10-*

Jahrestagung der Arbeitsgemeinschaft für Sportpsychologie in Köln 1979 (pp. 43–61). Cologne: bps.

Hedges, L. V., & Olkin, I. (1985). *Statistical methods for metanalysis.* Orlando, FL: Academic Press.

Heide, F. J., & Borkovec, T. D. (1984). Relaxation-induced anxiety: Mechanisms and theoretical implications. *Behavior Research and Therapy, 22,* 1–12.

Hellhammer, D. H., & Ehlert, U. (1991). *Psychoneurobiologie der Angst.* In D. H. Hellhammer & U. Ehlert (Eds.), Verhaltensmedizin: Ergebnisse und Anwendung (pp. 85–96). Bern, Switzerland: Huber.

Hellhammer, D. H., Kirschbaum, C., & Belkien, L. (1987). Measurement of salivary cortisol under psychological stimulation. In J. N. Hingtgen, D. H. Hellhammer, & G. Huppmann (Eds.), *Advanced methods in psychobiology.* Toronto: Hogrefe.

Herrigel, E. (1953). *Zen in the art of archery.* New York: Pantheon Books.

Herrmann, T. (1969). *Lehrbuch der empirischen Persönlichkeitsforschung.* Göttingen: Hogrefe.

Hodapp, V. (1982). Casual inference from nonexperimental research on anxiety and educational achievement. In H. W. Krohne & L. Laux (Eds.), *Achievement, stress, and anxiety* (pp. 355–372). Washington: Hemisphere.

Hodapp, V., Laux, L., & Spielberger, C. D. (1982). Theorie und Messung der emotionalen und kognitiven Komponente der Prüfungsangst. *Zeitschrift für differentielle und diagnostische Psychologie, 3,* 169–184.

Hodges, W. F., & Felling, J. P. (1970). Types of stressful situations and their relation to trait anxiety and sex. *Journal of Consulting and Clinical Psychology, 34,* 333–337.

Hormuth, S., Martin, A., & Petermann, F. (1976). Distanzierungs- und Affiliationseffekte im persönlichen Raum im Zustand der Angst. *Zeitschrift für Sozialpsychologie, 7,* 340–354.

Huber, H. P. (1977). Beobachtung. In T. Herrmann, P. R. Hofstätter, H. P. Huber, & F. E. Weinert (Eds.), *Handbuch psychologischer Grundbegriffe* (pp. 86–91). Munich: Kösel.

Hull, C. L. (1952). *A behavior system.* New Haven: Yale University Press.

Izard, C. E. (1972). Anxiety: A variable combination of interacting fundamental emotions. In C. D. Spielberger (Ed.), *Current trends in theory and research* (Vol. II, pp. 55–106). New York: Academic Press.

Izard, C. E. (1977). *Human emotions.* New York: Plenum.

Izard, C. E. (1981). *Die Emotionen des Menschen* (Human emotions). Weinheim: Beltz.

Jacobson, E. (1928). *Progressive relaxation.* Chicago: University of Chicago Press.

James, W. (1884). What is an emotion? *Mind, 9,* 188–205.

James, W. (1890). *Principles of psychology.* New York: Holt, Rinehart & Winston.

Janke, W. (1976). Psychologische Grundlagen des Verhaltens. In M. von Kerekjarto (Ed.), *Medizinische Psychologie* (pp. 1—101). Berlin: Springer.

Karbe, W. W. (1968). The relationship of general anxiety and specific anxiety concerning the learning of swimming. Dissertation Abstracts, 28/09-A, 3489.

Kauss, D. R. (1977). The effect of anxiety and activation on athletic performance. Dissertation Abstracts International, Vol. 37, 5814-B.

Kerr, J. H. (1989). Anxiety, arousal, and sport performance: An application of reversal theory. In D. Hackfort & C. D. Spielberger (Eds.), *Anxiety in sports* (pp. 137–151). Washington, DC: Hemisphere.

Kerr, J. H., & Vlaswinkel, E. H. (1990). Effects of exercise on anxiety: A review. *Anxiety Research, 2,* 309–321.

Klavora, P. (1978). An attempt to derive inverted-U curves based on the relationship between anxiety and athletic performance. In D. M. Landers & R. W. Christina (Eds.), *Psychology of motor behavior and sport* (Vols. I and II, pp. 369–377). Champaign, IL: Human Kinetics.

Kleine, D. (1988). Angst und sportliche Leistung. In P. Kunath, S. Müller, & H. Schellenberger (Eds.), *Proceedings of the 7th Congress of the European Federation of Sports Psychology* (Vol. 3, pp. 882–890). Leipzig: DHfK.

Kleine, D (1990). Anxiety and sport performance: A meta analysis. *Anxiety Research, 2,* 113–131.

Kowatschew, I. (1973). Die desensibilisierende Methode—Eine neue Form der psychologischen Hilfe. In K. Feige, E. Hahn, H. Rieder, & G. Stabenow (Eds.), *Bericht über den III. Europäischen Kongress für Sportpsychologie* (pp. 77–79). Schorndorf: Hofmann.

Krenauer, M., & Schönpflug, W. (1980). Regulation und Fehlregulation im Verhalten III: Zielsetzung und Ursachenzuschreibung unter Belastung. *Psychologische Beiträge, 22,* 414–431.

Krohne, H. W. (1980). Angsttheorie: Vom mechanistischen zum kognitiven Ansatz. *Psychologische Rundschau, 31,* 12–29.

Lacey, J. I. (1950). Individual differences in somatic response patterns. *Journal of Comparative and Physiological Psychology, 43,* 338–350.

Lacey, J. I., & Lacey, B. C. (1958). Verification and extension of the principle of autonomic response-stereotypy. *American Psychologist, 71,* 51–73.

Lamb, D. H. (1973). The effects of two stressors on state anxiety for students who differ in trait-anxiety. *Journal of Personality and Social Psychology, 7,* 116–126.

Landers, D. M. (1980). The arousal-performance relationship revisited. *Research Quarterly of Exercise and Sport, 51,* 77–90.

Lang, P. J. (1969). The on-line computer in behavior therapy research. *American Psychologist, 24,* 236–239.

Lang, P. J. (1977). *Die Anwendung psychophysiologischer Methoden in Psychotherapie und Verhaltensmodifikation.* Munich: Urban & Schwarzenberg.

Lange, C. G. (1885). *The emotions.* Baltimore: William & Wilkins.

Laux, L. (1983). Neuere Eigenschaftskonzeptionen in der Angst- und Stressforschung. In J. P. Janssen & E. Hahn (Eds.), *Aktivierung, Motivation, Handlung und Coaching im Sport* (pp. 69–76). Schorndorf: Hofmann.

Layman, E. (1978). McCloy: Meditation and sports performance. In W. F. Straub (Ed.), *Sport Psychology. An analysis of athlete behavior* (pp. 169–176). New York: Mouvement Publications.

Lazarus, A. A., & Mayne, T. J. (1990). Relaxation: Some limitations, side effects, and proposed solutions. *Psychotherapy, 27,* 261–266.

Lazarus, R. S. (1966). *Psychological stress and the coping process.* New York: McGraw-Hill.

Lazarus, R. S. (1981). Stress und Stressbewältigung—ein Paradigma. In S. H. Filipp (Ed.), *Kritische Lebensereignisse* (pp. 198–232). Munich: Urban & Schwarzenberg.

Lazarus, R. S., & Averill, J. R. (1972). Emotion and cognition: With special reference to anxiety. In C. D. Spielberger (Ed.), *Anxiety: Current trends in theory and research* (Vol. 2, pp. 242–283). New York: Academic Press.

Lazarus, R. S., & Launier, R. (1978). Stress-related transactions between person and environment. In L. A. Pervin & M. Lewis (Eds.), *Perspectives in interactional psychology* (pp. 287–327). New York: Plenum.

Lazarus, R. S., & Launier, R. (1981). Stressbezogene Transaktionen zwischen Person und Umwelt. In J. R. Nitsch (Ed.), *Stress: Theorien, Untersuchungen, Mussnahmen* (pp. 213–259). Bern, Switzerland: Huber.

Lazarus, R. S., & Opton, E. M. (1966). A study of psychological stress: A summary of theoretical formulations and experimental findings. In C. D. Spielberger (Ed.), *Anxiety and behavior* (pp. 225–262). New York: Academic Press.

Lazarus, R. S., Averill, J. R., & Opton, E. M., Jr. (1970). Toward a cognitive theory of emotion. In M. Arnold (Ed.), *Feelings and emotions* (pp. 207–231). New York: Academic Press.

Lazarus, R. S., Deese, J., & Osler, S. F. (1952). The effects of psychological stress upon performance. *Psychological Bulletin, 49,* 293–317.

Lehmann, M., & Keul, J. (1981). Adrenalin und Nor-Adrenalin-Exkretion bei verschiedenen Belastungen. In P. E. Nowacki & D. Böhmer (Eds.), *Sportmedizin: Aufgaben und Bedeutung für den Menschen in unserer Zeit* (pp. 348–353). Stuttgart: Thieme.

Lehrer, P. M. (1982). How to relax and how not to relax: A reevaluation of the work of Edmund Jacobson—I. *Behavior Research and Therapy, 20,* 417–428.

Levi, L. (1967). Biochemische Indikatoren bei verschiedenen experimentell hervorgerufenen Gefühlszuständen. In P. Kielholz (Ed.), *Angst* (pp. 83–102). Bern, Switzerland: Huber.

Levitt, E. E. (1979). *Die Psychologie der Angst.* Stuttgart: Kohlhammer.

Liebert, R. M., & Morris. L. W. (1967). Cognitive and emotional components of test anxiety: A distinction and some initial data. *Psychological Reports, 20,* 975–978.

Liebhart, E. H. (1978). Wahrgenommene autonome Veränderungen als Determinanten emotionalen Verhaltens. In D. Gorlitz, W. U. Meyer, & B. Weiner (Eds.), *Bielefelder Symposium über Attribution* (pp. 107–138). Stuttgart: Klett.

Luria, A. (1961). *The role of speech in the regulation of normal and abnormal behaviors.* New York: Liveright.

Lynch, S., Watts, W. A., & Galloway, C. (1973). Appropriateness of anxiety and drive for affiliation. *Journal of Research in Personality, 7,* 71–77.

Mahoney, M. J., & Meyers, A. W. (1989). Anxiety and athletic performance: Traditional and cognitive-developmental perspectives. In D. Hackfort & C. D. Spielberger (Eds.), *Anxiety in sports* (pp. 77–94). Washington, DC: Hemisphere.

Mann, J. (1972). Vicarious desensitization of test anxiety through observation of videotaped treatment. *Journal of Counseling Psychology, 19,* 1–7.

Marron, J. P. (1974). Transcendental meditation: A clinical evaluation. Dissertation Abstract International, Vol. 34, (8-B), 4051.

Marteniuk, R. G., & Wenger, H. A. (1970). Facilitation of pursuit rotor learning by induced stress. *Perceptual and Motor Skills, 31,* 471–477.

Martens, R. (1971). Anxiety and motor behavior: A review. *Journal of Motor Behavior, 3,* 151–179.

Martens, R. (1974). Arousal and motor performance. In J. Wilmore (Ed.), *Exercise and sport science review* (pp. 155–188). New York: Wiley.

Martens, R. (1975). *Social psychology and physical activity.* New York: Harper & Row.

Martens, R. (1977). *Sport competition anxiety test.* Champaign, IL: Human Kinetics.

Martens, R., & Landers, D. M. (1970). Motor performance under stress: A test of the inverted-U hypothesis. *Journal of Personality and Social Psychology, 16*, 29–37.

Martens, R., Burton, D., Rivkin, F., & Simon, J. (1980). Reliability and validity of the Competitive State Anxiety Inventory (SCAI). In C. H. Nadeau, W. R. Halliwell, K. M. Newell, & G. C. Roberts (Eds.), *Psychology of motor behavior and sport—1979* (pp. 91–99). Champaign, IL: Human Kinetics.

Maslow, A. H. (1954). *Motivation and personality.* New York: Harper & Row.

McMahon, V. M. (1973). The relationship between locus of control and seating distance in an interview setting. Dissertation Abstracts International, *33*(12B), 6088.

McReynolds, P. (1968). The assessment of anxiety: A survey of available techniques. In P. McReynolds (Ed.), *Advances in psychological assessment* (Vol. 1, pp. 244–264). Palo Alto, CA: Science and Behavior Books.

Meichenbaum, D. (1977). *Cognitive behavior modification. An integrative approach.* New York: Plenum.

Meichenbaum, D. (1979). *Kognitive Verhaltensmodifikation.* Munich: Urban & Schwarzenberg.

Mellstrom, M., Zuckerman, M., & Cicala, G. A. (1978). General versus specific tests in the assessment of anxiety. *Journal of Consulting and Clinical Psychology, 46*, 423–431.

Miller, N. E. (1948). Studies of fear as an acquirable drive. Fear as motivation and fear reduction as reinforcement in the learning of new responses. *Journal of Experimental Psychology, 38*, 89–101.

Morgan, W. P. (1987). Reduction of state anxiety following acute physical activity. In W. P. Morgan & S. E. Golston (Eds.), *Exercise and mental health* (pp. 105–109). Washington: DC: Hemisphere.

Morgan, W. P., & Bradley, P. (1985). *Psychological characteristics of the elite distance runner.* Technical Report. Colorado Springs, CO: United States Olympic Training Center.

Morgan, W. P., & Ellickson, K. A. (1989). Health, anxiety, and physical exercise. In D. Hackfort & C. D. Spielberger (Eds.), *Anxiety in sports* (pp. 165–182). Washington, DC: Hemisphere.

Morgan, W. P., O'Connor, P. J., Sparling, P. G., & Pate, R. R. (1987). Psychologic characterization of the elite female distance runner. *International Journal of Sports Medicine, 8*, 124–131.

Morris, L. W., & Liebert, R. M. (1970). Relationship of cognitive and emotional components of test anxiety to physiological arousal and academic performance. *Journal of Consulting and Clinical Psychology, 35*, 332–337.

Morris, L. W., Davis, M. A., & Hutchings, C. A. (1981). Cognitive and emotional components of anxiety: Literature review and a revised worry-emotionality scale. *Journal for educational Psychology, 73*, 541–555.

Morris, L. W., Smith, L. R., Andrews, E. S., & Morris, N. C. (1975). The relationship of emotionality and worry components of anxiety to motor skills performance. *Journal of Motor Behavior, 7*, 121–130.

Mowrer, O. H. (1960). *Learning theory and behavior.* New York: Wiley.

Murray, E. J., & Jacobson, L. I. (1971). The nature of learning in traditional and behavioral psychotherapy. In A. E. Bergin & S. L. Garfield (Eds.), *Handbook of psychotherapy and behavior change* (p. 709–747). New York: Wiley.

Myrtek, M. (1975). Ergebnisse der psychosomatischen Korrelationsforschung. *Zeitschrift für Klinische Psychologie und Psychotherapie, 23*, 316–330.

Neiss, R. (1988). Reconceptualizing arousal: Psychobiological states in motor performance. *Psychological Bulletin, 103*, 345–366.

Nickel, H. (1976). *Entwicklungspsychologie des Kindes- und Jugendalters,* Vol. II. Bern, Switzerland: Huber.

Nitsch, J. R. (1975). Sportliches Handeln als Handlungsmodell. *Sportwissenschaft, 5*, 39–55.

Nitsch, J. R. (1978). Grundbezüge der Sportpsychologie. In J. R. Nitsch & H. Allmer (Eds.), *Sportpsychologie—eine Standortbestimmung* (pp. 13–25). Cologne: Psychologisches Institut d. Sporthochschule.

Nitsch, J. R. (Ed.). (1981). *Stress:* Theorien, Untersuchungen, Massnahmen. Bern, Switzerland: Huber.

Nitsch, J. R. (1985). Handlungstheoretische Grundannahmen—eine Zwischenbilanz. In G. Hagedorn, H. Karl, & K. Bös (Eds.), *Handeln im Sport* (pp. 26–41). Clausthal-Zellerfeld: dvs.

Nitsch, J. R., & Hackfort, D. (1979). Naive Techniken der Psychoregulation im Sport. In H. Gabler, H. Eberspächer, E. Hahn, J. Kern, & G. Schilling (Eds.), Praxis der Psychologie im Leistungssport (pp. 299–311). Berlin: Bartels & Wernitz.

Nitsch, J. R., & Hackfort, D. (1981). Stress in Schule und Hochschule—eine handlungspsychologische Funktionsanalyse. In J. R. Nitsch (Ed.), *Stress: Theorien, Untersuchungen, Massnahmen* (pp. 263–311). Bern, Switzerland: Huber.

Ortlieb, P. (1976). Sozialpsychologische Aspekte der systematischen Desensibilisierung. *Zeitschrift für Klinische Psychologie, 5*, 53–68.

Oxendine, J. B., & Temple, U. (1970). Emotional arousal and motor performance. *Quest Monograph, 13*, 23–32.

Paivio, A. (1971). *Imagery and verbal processes.* New York: Holt, Rinehart & Winston.

Patterson, M. (1973). Stability of nonverbal immediacy behaviors. *Journal of Experimental Social Psychology, 9*, 97–109.

Paul, G. L. (1966). *Insight vs. desensitization in psychotherapy. An experiment in anxiety reduction.* Stanford: Stanford University Press.

Pemberton, C. L., & Cox, R. H. (1981). Consolidation theory and the effects of stress and anxiety on motor behavior. *International Journal of Sport Psychology, 12*, 131–139.

Plutchik, R. (1962). *The emotions: Facts, theories, and a new model.* New York: Random House.

Pongratz, L. J. (1973). *Lehrbuch der Klinischen Psychologie.* Göttingen: Hogrefe.

Poppen, R. (1988). *Behavioral relaxation training and assessment.* New York: Pergamon.

Puryear, H. B., & Thurston, M. A. (1975). *Meditation and the mind of man.* Virginia Beach, VA: A.R.E. Press.

Puryear, H. B., Cayce, C. T., & Thurston, M. A. (1976). Anxiety reduction associated with meditation: Home study. *Perceptual and Motor Skills, 43*, 527–531.

Rachman, S. (1967). Systematic desensitization. *Psychological Bulletin, 67*, 93–103.

Raglin, J. S., & Morgan, W. P. (1988). Predicted and actual levels of precompetition and anxiety in swimmers. *Journal of Swimming Research, 4*, 5–7.

Richardson, A. (1967). Mental practice: A review and discussion. Parts I and II. *Research Quarterly of Exercise and Sport, 38*, 95–107/263–273.

Rubinstein, S. L. (1973). *Grundlagen der allgemeinen Psychologie.* Berlin: Volk und Wissen.

Sage, G. H., & Bennett, B. (1973). The effects of induced arousal on learning and performance of a pursuit motor skill. *Research Quarterly of Exercise and Sport, 44*, 140–149.

Salter, A. (1949). *Conditional reflex therapy.* New York: Farrar, Straus.

Sarason, I. G. (1975). Anxiety and self-preoccupation. In I. G. Sarason & C. D. Spielberger (Eds.), *Stress and anxiety* (Vol. 2, pp. 27–44). New York: Hemisphere.

Sarason, I. G. (1978). The test anxiety scale: Concept and research. In I. G. Sarason & C. D. Spielberger (Eds.), *Stress and anxiety* (Vol. 6, pp. 193–216). New York: Hemisphere.

Sarason, I. G. (1980). Life stress, self-preoccupation, and social supports. In I. G. Sarason & C. D. Spielberger (Eds.), *Stress and anxiety* (Vol. 7, pp. 73–92). New York: Hemisphere.

Sarason, I. G. (1984). Stress, anxiety, and cognitive interference: Reactions to tests. *Journal of Personality and Social Psychology, 46,* 929–938.

Sarnoff, J., & Zimbardo, P. G. (1961). Anxiety, fear, and social affiliation. *Journal of Abnormal and Social Psychology, 62,* 356–363.

Schachter, S. (1959). *The psychology of affiliation.* Stanford: Stanford University Press.

Schachter, S. (1964). The interaction of cognitive and physiological determinants of emotional state. In L. Berkowitz (Ed.), *Advances in experimental social psychology* (Vol. 1, pp. 49–80). New York: Academic Press.

Schachter, S. (1966). The interaction of cognitive and physiological determinants of emotional state. In C. D. Spielberger (Ed.), *Anxiety and behavior* (pp. 193–224). New York: Academic Press.

Schachter, S., & Singer, J. (1962). Cognitive, social and physiological determinants of emotional state. *Psychological Review, 69,* 379–399.

Schildkraut, J. J., & Kety, S. S. (1967). Biogenic amines and emotion. *Science, 156,* 21–30.

Schilling, G. (1979). Erfahrungsberichte: Psychoregulative Verfahren im Schweizer Sport—mehr als Alibi oder Feuerwehr? In H. Gabler, H. Eberspächer, E. Hahn, J. Kern, & G. Schilling (Eds.), *Praxis der Psychologie im Leistungssport* (pp. 340–348). Berlin: Bartels & Wernitz.

Schwartz, G. E., Davidson, R. J., & Goleman, D. J. (1978). Patterning of cognitive and somatic processes in the self-regulation of anxiety: Effects of meditation versus exercise. *Psychosomatic Medicine, 40,* 321–328.

Schwenkmezger, P. (1980). Untersuchungen zur kognitiven Angsttheorie im sportmotorischen Bereich (state-trait-anxiety). *Zeitschrift für Experimentelle und Angewandte Psychologie, 27,* 607–630.

Schwenkmezger, P. (1981). Eigenschafts- und Zustandsangst als Prädiktoren sportspezifischer Belastung. In FEPSAC (Ed.), *Proceedings of the Vth European Congress of Sport Psychology,* 1979, (Vol. 2, pp. 303–309). Varna: University Press.

Schwenkmezger, P. (1985a). *Modelle der Eigenschafts- und Zustandsangst.* Göttingen: Hogrefe.

Schwenkmezger, P. (1985b). Welche Bedeutung kommt dem Ausdauertraining in der Depressionstherapie zu? *Sportwissenschaft, 15,* 117–135.

Schwenkmezger, P., & Laux, L. (1986). Trait anxiety, worry and emotionality in athletic competition. In C. D. Spielberger & R. Diaz-Guerrero (Eds.), *Cross-cultural anxiety* (Vol. 3, pp. 65–77). Washington, DC: Hemisphere.

Schwenkmezger, P., Voigt, H. F., & Müller, W. (1979). Über die Auswirkung einer Prüfungssituation auf psychologische und physische Belastung und die Spielerleistung im Volleyball. *Sportwissenschaft, 9,* 303–317.

Seligman, M. E. P. (1979). *Erlernte Hilflosigkeit.* Munich: Urban & Schwarzenberg.

Selye, H. (1956). *The stress of life.* New York: McGraw-Hill.

Singer, R., & Ungerer-Röhrich, U. (1985). Zum Vorhersagewert des State-Trait-Angstmodells. Eine empirische Untersuchung an Sportstudent(inn)en, Squash- und Tischtennisspielern. In G. Schilling & K. Herren (Eds.), *Proceedings of the VIth FEPSAC Congress* (Vol 1, pp. 129–138). Magglingen: ETS.

Smith, C. A., & Lazarus, R. S. (1989). Emotion and adaptation. In L.A. Pervin (Ed.), *Handbook of personality: Theory and research.* New York: Guilford.

Smith, J. C. (1975). Meditation as psychotherapy: A review of the literature. *Psychological Bulletin, 82,* 558–564.

Smith, R. E. (1984). Theoretical treatment and approaches to anxiety reduction. In J. M. Silva & R. S. Weinberg (Eds.), *Psychological foundations of sport* (pp. 157–170). Champaign, IL: Human Kinetics.

Smith, R. E. (1989). Athletic stress and burnout: Conceptual models and intervention strategies. In D. Hackfort & C. D. Spielberger (Eds.), *Anxiety in sports* (pp. 183–201). Washington, DC: Hemisphere.

Smith, R. E., & Rohsenow, D. J. (1986). *Cognitive-affective stress management training: A training manual.* Delphi, IN: Center for Induced Affect.

Smith, R. E., Smoll, F. L., & Schutz, R. W. (1990). Measurement and correlates of sport-specific cognitive and somatic trait anxiety: The Sport Anxiety Scale. *Anxiety Research, 2,* 263–280.

Sonstroem, R. J., & Bernardo, P. (1982). Interindividual pregame state anxiety and basketball performance: A reexamination of the inverted U-curve. *Journal of Sport Psychology, 4,* 235–245.

Späte, D., & Schwenkmezger, P. (1983). Leistungsbestimmende psychische Merkmale bei Handballspielern unter besonderer Berücksichtigung von allgemeiner und sportspezifischer Eigenschafts- und Zustandsangst. *Leistungssport, 13,* 11–19.

Spence, J., & Spence, K. W. (1966). The motivational components of manifest anxiety: drive and drive stimuli. In C. D. Spielberger (Ed.), *Anxiety and behavior* (pp. 291–326). New York: Academic Press.

Spielberger, C. D. (1966). Theory and research on anxiety. In C. D. Spielberger (Ed.), *Anxiety and behavior* (pp. 3–20). New York: Academic Press.

Spielberger, C. D. (1971). Trait-state anxiety and motor behavior. *Journal of Motor Behavior, 3,* 265–279.

Spielberger, C. D. (1972). Anxiety as an emotional state. In C. D. Spielberger (Ed.), *Anxiety: Current trends in theory and research* (Vol. I, pp. 23–49). New York: Academic Press.

Spielberger, C. D. (1975). Anxiety: State-trait process. C. D. Spielberger & I. G. Sarason (Eds.), *Stress and anxiety* (Vol. 1, pp. 115–143). Washington: Hemisphere.

Spielberger, C. D. (1983). *Manual for the State-Trait Anxiety Inventory (revised).* Palo Alto, CA: Consulting Psychologists Press.

Spielberger, C. D., Gonzalez, H. P., Taylor, C. J., Algaze, B., & Anton, W. D. (1978). Examination stress and test anxiety. In C. D. Spielberger & I. G. Sarason (Eds.), *Stress and anxiety* (Vol. 5, pp. 167–191). Washington: Hemisphere.

Spielberger, C. D., Gorsuch, R. L., & Lushene, R. E. (1970). *Manual for the State-Trait-Anxiety Inventory (STAI).* Palo Alto, CA: Consulting Psychologists Press.

Spreen, O. (1961). Konstruktion einer Skala zur Messung der manifesten Angst in experimentellen Situationen. *Psychologische Forschung, 26,* 205–223.

Straub, W. F. (1978). Meditation and Sport. In W. F. Straub (Ed.), *Sport psychology. An analysis of athlete behavior* (pp. 168). Ithaca, NY: Mouvement Publications.

Sue, D. (1972). The role of relaxation in systematic desensitization. *Behavior Research Therapy, 2,* 153–158.

Suinn, R. M. (1989). Behavioral intervention for stress management in sports. In D. Hackfort & C. D. Spielberger (Eds.), *Anxiety in sports* (pp. 203–214). Washington, DC: Hemisphere.

Taché, J., & Selye, H. (1978). On stress and coping mechanisms. In C. D. Spielberger & J. G. Sarason (Eds.), *Stress and anxiety,* (Vol. 5, pp. 3–24). New York: Wiley.

Taylor, J. A. (1951). The relationship of anxiety to the conditioned eyelid response. *Journal of Experimental Psychology, 41,* 81–92.

Taylor, J. A. (1953). A personality scale of manifest anxiety. *Journal of Abnormal and Social Psychology, 48,* 285–290.

Taylor, J. A. (1956). Drive theory and manifest anxiety. *Psychological Bulletin, 53,* 303–320.

Teichman, Y. (1974). Predisposition for anxiety and affiliation. *Journal of Personality and Social Psychology, 29,* 405–410.

Tunner, W. (1975). Systematische Desensibilisierung und das Lernen von Strategien zur Bewältigung von Angst. In I. Florin & W. Tunner (Eds.), *Therapie der Angst* (pp. 221–239). Munich: Urban & Schwarzenberg.

Tunner, W., & Birbaumer, N. (1974). Zusammenhang motorischer, autonomer und subjektiver Reaktionen beim Vermeidungslernen. In L. H. Eckensberger & U. S. Eckensberger (Eds.), *Bericht über den 28. Kongress der Deutschen Gesellschaft für Psychologie* (Vol. 3, pp. 162–172). Göttingen: Hogrefe.

Valins, S. (1966). Cognitive effects of false heart-rate feedback. *Journal of Personality and Social Psychology, 4,* 400–408.

Valins, S., & Ray, A. A. (1967). Effects of cognitive desensitization on avoidance behavior. *Journal of Personality and Social Psychology, 7,* 345–350.

Vanek, M. (1974). Zum System der psychologischen Vorbereitung des Sportlers. In E. Rudolph & P. Kunath (Red.), *Studientexte zum Studienkomplex Sportpsychologie* (Kap. 5.5). Leipzig: DHfK.

Vanek, M., & Hosek, V. (1977). *Zur Persönlichkeit des Sportlers.* Schorndorf: Hofmann.

Vormbrock, F. (1983). *Diagnostizierbarkeit von Angst.* Cologne: bps.

Walker, E. L. (1958). Action decrement and its relation to learning. *Psychological Review, 65,* 129–142.

Walker, E. L., & Tarte, R. D. (1963). Memory storage as a function of arousal and time with homogeneous lists. *Journal of Verbal Learning and Verbal Behavior, 2,* 113–119.

Walker, R., Nideffer, R. M., & Boomer, W. (1977). Diving performance as it is correlated with arousal and concentration time. *Swimming Technique, 13,* 117–119/122.

Walter, H. (1977). *Angst bei Schülern.* Munich: Goldmann.

Weinberg, R. S. (1990). Anxiety and motor performance: Where to from here? *Anxiety Research, 2,* 227–242.

Weinberg, R. S., & Ragan, J. (1979). Motor performance under three levels of stress and trait anxiety. *Journal of Motor Behavior, 10,* 169–176.

Weiner, B., Russel, D., & Lerman, D. (1978). Affektive Auswirkungen von Attributionen. In D. Görlitz, W. K. Meyer & B. Weiner (Eds.), *Bielefelder Symposium über Attribution* (pp. 139–174). Stuttgart: Klett.

Wicklund, R. A. (1979). Die Aktualisierung von Selbstkonzepten in Handlungsvollzügen. In S. H Filipp (Ed.), *Selbstkonzeptforschung* (pp. 153–169). Stuttgart: Klett-Cotta.

Wieczerkowski, W., Nickel, H., Janowski, A., Fittkau, B., & Rauer, W. (1979). *Angstfragebogen für Schüler.* Göttingen: Hogrefe.

Wieselberg, H., Dyckman, J. M., & Abramowitz, S. J. (1979). The desensitization derby: In vivo the backstretch, imaginal at the wire? *Journal of Clinical Psychology, 35,* 647–650.

Wine, J. D. (1971). Test anxiety and direction of attention. *Psychological Bulletin, 76,* 92–104.

Wine, J. D. (1980). Cognitive-attentional theory of test anxiety. In I. G. Sarason (Ed.), *Test anxiety: Theory, research, and applications* (pp. 349–385). Hillsdale, NJ: Erlbaum.

Wine, J. D. (1982). Evaluation anxiety: A cognitive-attentional construct. In H. W. Krohne & L. Laux (Eds.), *Achievement, stress, and anxiety* (pp. 207–219). Washington, DC: Hemisphere.

Wohl, A. (1977). *Bewegung und Sprache.* Schorndorf: Hofmann.

Wolpe, J. (1958). *Psychotherapy by reciprocal inhibition.* Stanford, CA: Stanford University Press.

Wolpe, J. (1972). *Praxis der Verhaltenstherapie.* Stuttgart: Huber.

Yerkes, R. M., & Dodson, J. D. (1908). The relationship of strength of stimulus to rapidity of habit formation. *Journal of Comparative Neurology and Psychology, 18,* 459–482.

Zaichkowsky, L. D., & Fuchs, C. Z. (1989). Biofeedback-assisted self-regulation for stress management in sports. In D. Hackfort & C. D. Spielberger (Eds.), *Anxiety in sports* (pp. 235–245). Washington, DC: Hemisphere.

Zaichkowsky, L. D., Dorsey, J., & Mulholland, T. (1977). The effects of biofeedback assisted systematic desensitization in the control of anxiety and performance. In M. Vanek (Ed.), *Bericht über den IV. Weltkongress der ISSP* (pp. 809–812). Prague: o.V.

Ziegler, S. G., Klinzing, J., & Williamson, K. (1982). The effects of two stress management training programs on cardiorespiratory efficiency. *Journal of Sport Psychology, 4,* 280–189.

·15·

AGGRESSION

Joel Thirer

INTRODUCTION

Aggression is one of the most frequently used, often misunderstood terms commonly selected to describe sport situations. On the one hand, it is used to describe performance in a positive, complimentary way, while on the other hand, it is utilized to demean or criticize sport participants and/or fans, or even the nature of sport itself. Seldom does one word have so many contradictory applications and definitions.

In recent years a great deal of interest and an increasing amount of research has been generated in order to ascertain whether participation in, or the passive observation of, athletic contests has any effect on aggressive behavior. The reason for this interest is that controlled aggression is assumed by many to be an inherent, normal aspect of athletic competition. While some forms of competition appear to incite aggressive behavior, constraints in the form of rules and officials stand to block uninhibited aggression. Furthermore, not all forms of athletic competition are overtly aggressive. In many noncontact sports, the only manifestation of aggression may be simply in the more subtle forms of the elements of competition, the meaning being that competitiveness is itself an element of aggression.

Defining Aggression

Perhaps the reason for the confusion that surrounds the usage of the term "aggression" is that the definition is complex, with numerous variables and contingencies affecting its application. One distinction that helps is separating the concept of aggression from the notion of violence. Parens (1987) considers aggression to be the "... attempt to control, act upon, and master ourselves and our environment, including the people within it" (p. 6). Parens sees aggression as having two major forms, the first being "nondestructive aggression," manifested as "assertive, nonhostile,

self-protective, goal-achieving and mastery behaviors." The second form is, he says, "... hostile destructiveness, which we see in angry, nasty, hurtful behaviors: hate, rage, bullying, torturing, vengefulness ...." (p. 7).

Violence, as defined by Siann (1985), involves the "... use of great physical force or intensity, and while it is often impelled by aggressive motivation, [it] may occasionally be used by individuals engaged in a mutual violent interaction which is regarded by both parties as intrinsically rewarding. Aggression involves the intention to hurt or emerge superior to others, does not necessarily involve physical injury (violence), and may or may not be regarded as being underpinned by different kinds of motives" (p. 12). The type of violence that society tends to deplore is what Siann labels "irrational violence." As exemplars of this, she offers child abuse and football (soccer) violence. Siann goes on to point out that even these forms of seemingly irrational violence need to be studied and better understood so that they can ultimately be controlled and replaced by more acceptable behaviors.

When looking for a distinction between aggression and violence, Smith (1983) indicates that "... aggression is generally regarded as the more generic concept. ... [It] is defined as any behavior designed to injure another person, psychologically or physically. Malicious gossip is aggression; so is a punch in the nose. Violence ... refers to the physical side of aggression. Violence is behavior intended to injure another person physically" (p. 2).

A fundamental question that needs to be asked at the outset is whether we should be concerned about aggression and violence relative to sport. With all of the violence and hardship that exist in the world today, are we trivializing the very concepts of aggression and violence when we attempt to make applications to something that some regard as frivolous? The answer, of course, is that we should be very concerned about these unpleasant phenomena. Those with a legitimate, genuine concern for all levels of sport, from early childhood experiences to

365

age group and master's competition, need to be acutely aware of the negative specter of aggression and violence. This applies equally to participant behavior and spectator behavior.

According to Smith (1983), there has been a close parallel between the rise of societal violence in Canada and the United States and violence found in, and associated with, sport. Eitzen and Sage (1989) refer to sport as a microcosm of society; that is to say, whatever behaviors are reflective of a particular culture or society will be exhibited in that society's sport pursuits. Similar notions were expressed earlier by Boucher and Case (1980).

The literature base for aggression and violence in sport is considerable. As of this writing, the SIRLS (Specialized Information Retrieval and Library Services; University of Waterloo) listed 577 citations on the topic of aggression and violence in sport, with the vast majority of these entries coming since 1970.

Instrumental and Goal Reactive Aggression

The purpose of instrumental aggression is to achieve a specific goal. The aggression might take place as a by-product of an athlete's attempt to reach a goal where aggression does not play a specific part. What Husman and Silva (1984) refer to as "proactive assertion" can be differentiated from instrumental aggression in that instrumental aggression may involve injury to an opponent, where proactive assertion usually does not (Anshel, 1990). Pearton (1986) concluded that the increased incidence of participant violence is reflective of the growth of instrumental violence.

Perhaps it is the increased social significance of sport that contributes to an increase in instrumental violence, as Pilz (1982) suggests. He also pointed out that this holds true for females as well as males. Eitzen (1985) noted that there are far too many examples of excessive violence in professional sport. He specifically focuses on examples of illegitimate violence which by intent injures another person. This might more appropriately be categorized as a third level of aggression, goal-reactive aggression.

Whereas proactive assertion would be aggression without the intent to inflict harm and instrumental aggression might be inflicting harm in order to achieve a goal, goal-reactive aggression is done with the intent to injure or harm an opponent. Anshel (1990) states that of the three forms of assertive-aggressive behavior described above, instrumental aggression is clearly the most likely to be exhibited in athletic contests. He dismisses Husman and Silva's (1984) case for proactive assertion being more common in sport than instrumental aggression. Anshel contends that athletes are not likely to hold back so as to avoid injuring other athletes, particularly in the heat of an emotional contest. At the same time, he argues that rarely do episodes arise where even in the heat of a contest one athlete will purposefully inflict injury on an opponent.

Aggression as a Normal, Positive Behavior

If we accept Parens's (1987) definition of nondestructive aggression as assertiveness, goal achieving, nonhostile, and mastery behaviors, we can readily see where this has a place in sport. Indeed, many of the behavioral characteristics that we consider positive manifestations of sport participation involve "aggressive" characteristics. Sliding headfirst into base, diving to make a catch, overpowering one's opponents in football and wrestling, spiking a volleyball, charging the net in tennis, or rebounding a basketball all involve considerable assertive, if not actually aggressive, behavior. Oftentimes athletes act aggressively because they associate a reward with a particular behavior; e.g., garnering a coach's favor, attaining prestige and recognition from teammates, a merit system, or perhaps the cheering of the fans. Social learning theory says that the most important motivation for aggression is the expectation of reward (Bandura, 1973; Michener, DeLamatar, & Schwartz, 1986).

Quite often, the term *aggression* is used interchangeably with *hostility*. This is quite different than the type of aggression that one associates with athletics from a positive standpoint. Freischlag and Schmidke (1980) offer the example that "... a hockey player must be aggressive going after a man with the puck but when he tries to take his head off— knock him out of action after the player has scored a goal— that's (hostile) aggression" (p. 162).

A more appropriate term that could be used as a substitute for "positive" aggression is *assertiveness*. When utilizing legitimate verbal or physical force in order to achieve one's goals in sport, one is not being aggressive, but merely assertive (Silva, 1980). The distinction is that there is intent not to harm the opponent, but merely to establish dominance. Anshel (1990) considers "... blocking in football, checking in ice hockey, maintaining a defensive position for rebounding in basketball, and breaking up a double play in baseball ..." (p. 138) assertive behaviors, as long as they are performed as integral components of the contest and without malice. Anshel characterizes these same actions as aggressive when it is the player's intention to cause injury, or if the behavior is more hostile than necessary to meet the objectives of the performance. According to Cox (1990), assertive behavior in sport has often been misclassified as instrumental aggression. "Assertive behavior in which injury is incidental to the play is not aggression, simply because there is no intent to harm the victim" (p. 270). Cox emphasizes the importance for researchers of distinguishing between assertiveness and instrumental or hostile aggression.

Another consideration is that aggressive behavior in sport may simply be adaptive. LeUnes and Nation (1989) propose that the physical nature of some sports such as basketball, football, and hockey require the adopting of some aggressive characteristics. An athlete is almost required by necessity to establish the fact that he/she will not be pushed around or intimidated.

CLASSICAL THEORIES OF AGGRESSION

Instinct Theory

There is widespread, if perhaps dubious, belief that aggressive behavior is a manifestation of instincts. Freud (1925) proposed that destructive tendencies are an inherent part of the total structure of human beings. Although he indicated that these destructive tendencies are essentially self-directed, he added that they may be other-directed as well. This notion has been advocated by ethologists, who are generally concerned with the biological drives constituting animal behavior. Several researchers are generally associated with the theory that aggression is based on instinct (Ardrey, 1966; Lorenz, 1966; Morris, 1967). Siann (1985) points out that initially, experimental psychologists adopted an energy model to explain aggression. They viewed aggressive behavior as the result of the need to dissipate an aggressive drive. This drive differs from instinct in that it is attributed to particular sets of experiences.

Catharsis Hypothesis

Foremost among the group advocating the instinct theory with direct application to sport psychology is Lorenz (1966), primarily because he made some specific analogies to sport as an acceptable catharsis for violent and aggressive behaviors. Lorenz offered that man suffers from an insufficient discharge of his aggressive drives. He viewed the catharsis hypothesis, which was formalized by Freud (1924), as providing a means for built-up aggressive energy to be eventually discharged. When one acts out aggressive inclinations and drains aggressive energy, there is a corresponding reduction in internal excitation (Hokanson, 1970). If the expression of aggression is prevented or the target is unavailable, Freud (1924) states, either a substitute target must be found or the aggression will become internalized, resulting in either depression or masochism.

Lorenz (1966) actually viewed sport as having more value than simply that of providing an outlet for aggression. He states, "It educates man to a conscious and responsible control of his own fighting behavior" (p. 271). He goes on to say that perhaps the most important aspect of sport as an outlet for aggression is that it provides a healthy "safety valve" for potential militant forms of aggression. He sees sport as directly contributing to countering the dangers of war by promoting personal acquaintances between nations and engendering common enthusiasm. Carroll (1986) supported this idea by indicating that sport might be a civilized substitute for war. This viewpoint is shared by Scott (1970), who contended that sport has a major role to play in the development of peaceful behavior and the control of violence. This is undoubtedly an idealistic perspective, and one wonders how it would be modified while one observed some of the hooliganism that accompanies English soccer games.

This phenomenon is casually explained away by Marsh (1982), who considers the violence accompanying English soccer as relatively harmless and mainly involving ritual display. He goes on to state that perhaps it is this ritualized aggression that is responsible for keeping other, more violent displays of aggression in check. Many would regard this is as an overly simplistic position (Dunning, Murphy, & Williams, 1981).

Another longstanding perception about the catharsis hypothesis as it might be applied to sport is the notion that negative adolescent behaviors can be positively affected by participation in organized athletic activities. Sugden and Yiannakis (1982) raise the question of whether organized sport participation has a deterrent effect on the behavior of juvenile delinquents. Their position is that traditional forms of physical activity do not serve the purpose of mitigating delinquency. Their position supports the earlier notion of Schafer (1969) that conventional sports provides no certainty in diminishing an individual's likelihood to be delinquent.

Sugden and Yiannakis propose the support of alternative types of physical activities such as Outward Bound rather than the use of traditional forms of sport and exercise in dealing with delinquent behavior. Trulson (1986) tested the hypothesis that sport participation can help in the rehabilitation of juvenile delinquents. He found that certain types of sport experiences made a positive contribution to the diminishing of delinquent behaviors—specifically, the type of experience that contained a philosophy of nonviolence (additional social values are inherent in the instruction). In situations where the teaching of these social values was omitted, there was no reduction in delinquent behaviors.

The catharsis hypothesis has far more detractors than supporters. Bandura (1973) indicated that a large body of research involving either direct or vicarious aggressive experiences has demonstrated that aggression will actually be maintained at its original level rather than be reduced. In fact, Bandura notes that it is more likely that the probability of subsequent aggression will be increased, rather than diminished. Feshbach (1970) suggested that three possible effects are present for the direct or vicarious participant in aggression: the reduction of aggressive drive, the reinforcement of aggressive responses, and the potential change in the strength of inhibitions.

More specifically, Ryan (1970) found that there was no simple draining of aggressive tendencies attributable to physical activity. Cheren (1981) considered athletics as a possible control for violence and concluded that exposure to violence is actually a reinforcer, not a catharsis. Similarly, Cataldi (1980) negates the catharsis hypothesis and suggests that athletics provides a better framework for learning than it does for venting aggressive behaviors. This was further supported by Coakley (1981), who stated that both team violence and player violence actually serve as catalysts for spectator violence.

Instinct theory as an explanation for sport violence suffers from four major weaknesses, according to Coakley

(1990). He disputes the notion that there is adequate research available to support the idea that there is a biologically based explanation for aggression in humans. He dismisses most of the biological and ethological research because it has been done almost exclusively with animals. Second, Coakley argues that not all sports provide similar opportunities for the release of aggression. His third point is that there is no available research documenting that catharsis does in fact take place as a result of sport participation. Coakley's final criticism of instinct theory is that it virtually ignores women. He asks, ". . . what are the outlets for their (women's) supposed aggressive instincts?" (p. 144).

The Frustration-Aggression Hypothesis

The initial concept of frustration leading to aggression was put forth by Freud, regarding the suppression of aggression and sexual instincts. This idea gained much more clarity with the publication of the classical book by Dollard, Doob, Miller, Mowrer, and Sears (1939), *Frustration and Aggression*. Originally, they proposed that aggression would always occur as a result of frustration, and similarly, that frustration would always result in aggression. Miller (1941) modified that concept by stating that research has demonstrated that frustration does not always lead to aggression. Sometimes other behaviors result from frustration, such as depression. Rather, Miller postulated that aggression is actually the dominant response to aggression and that it is actually an instigation to aggression.

After many years of research on this subject, the frustration-aggression hypothesis was modified again, this time by Berkowitz (1969, 1978; Berkowitz & Allioto, 1973). In what is referred to as the Berkowitz reformulation, the contention is that learning can coexist along with innate drive. Berkowitz noted that frustration does not always produce aggressive responses. In fact, frustration only heightens one's predisposition toward aggression, rather than directly leading to it. Berkowitz acknowledges that it is possible to derive satisfaction from aggressive behavior. In what he calls the "completion tendency," he describes that a frustrated person derives satisfaction or fulfillment from aggressive behavior if it is acted out to completion after the experience of frustration (Berkowitz, 1964). Berkowitz (1969) adds that other behaviors that are more productive can be learned as responses to frustration.

Finally, as Miller (1941) indicated, frustration can also lead to despair, depression, and even withdrawal. Additionally, aggression can and does often occur without prior frustration. An insult might evoke an aggressive response, even though no goal-directed activity is being blocked. Michener, DeLamater, and Schwartz (1986) point out that aversive events other than frustration can elicit aggression. They cite pain, insults, or physical attack. Aversive events do not directly lead to aggression; instead, a readiness for aggression is created by the arousal of anger. Situational demands will determine whether this anger is translated into aggressive behavior. They note that aggression is more likely when it meets certain criteria such as social approval or target availability, and when the prospect of retaliation is minimal. These notions are consistent with Berkowitz's (1969) belief that there are two prerequisites for frustration to lead to violence: the frustration must lead to anger, and there must be ample opportunity for violence and the presence of appropriate stimulus cues.

The notion that frustration can elicit an aggressive drive in people which contributes to their aggression was defended by Feshbach (1970). He maintained that the infliction of injury is not the ultimate goal of hostile aggression. Instead, by producing pain in the antagonizer, the aggressor can restore his/her self-esteem and gain a sense of power. He advocated that it should be attempted to direct individuals toward the achievement of self-esteem through positive accomplishments as a means of reducing aggression. Mark, Bryant, and Lehman (1983) suggested that diminishing perceived injustices (frustrating agents) such as poor officiating will help to reduce ensuing sports violence.

The fact that the frustration-aggression concept enjoys such widespread acceptance is probably attributable more to its simplicity than to any demonstrable predictive power (Bandura, 1973). Bandura notes that this theory does not hold up well in laboratory studies. He points out that sometimes frustrators act to increase aggression, while at other times they have no effect, or in some cases they actually reduce aggressive responses. Further criticism comes from the fact that some cultures do not include aggression as a typical response to frustration (Bateson, 1941). Buss (1961) added that more typical evokers of an aggressive response are personal insult or threat, rather than the blocking of ongoing behaviors. This notion is supported by Harrell (1980). While studying high school basketball players, Harrell found that the amount of aggression directed toward a player by the opponent was the best predictor for total aggression and personal fouls for that player.

It is the rare individual who can avoid frustration when participating in sport. Everyone from the amateur golfer to the university quarterback can and often does experience frustration with his or her performance. According to Alpert and Crouch (1988), sport experiences often produce frustration, which might then lead to violence. They indicate that ". . . participants who use the sport experience to prove themselves are more likely to experience frustration than those persons who use sport to express themselves" (p. 110). They note that opportunities to use violence are present in some sport situations, and there is a high probability that it will occur given sufficient frustration. Similarly, Benerjee (1982) argued that the poor quality of officiating at international and national soccer matches breeds frustration which contributes to the high rate of violence associated with the sport. This notion is supported by Horn (1985), who indicates that spectators tend to become violent when they believe that a rule is unfair, or that a rule is being applied either unfairly or inaccurately.

The failure rate in athletics is substantially higher than one might realize, according to Thirer, Zackheim, and Summers (1987). One example is that in baseball a good player will get a hit 30% of the time. In other words, the player's failure rate is usually in excess of 70%. Furthermore, the perception of failure is heightened during clutch situations and diminished in noncrucial ones. Repeated failure contributes to a heightened incidence of depression, and it is not inconceivable that in certain situations a heightening of aggressive tendencies is also likely. Anshel (1990) indicates that a frustrated athlete is more likely to attempt to injure an opponent, particularly where the frustration is repetitive.

According to Coakley (1990), sport is sometimes construed as a means of relieving frustration. He notes that the action usually ". . . lends itself to intense involvement and often produces physical exhaustion" (p. 144). This effect does not directly relate to a diminishment of frustration but rather serves as physical and cognitive distraction. Smith (1983) adds that there is also no evidence that observing sporting events will contribute to a diminishment of frustration. In actuality, there is far greater likelihood that sport will actually be more of a frustrator than an agent that acts to diminish frustration. In situations where sport participation causes an apparent decrease in aggressive inclination, it may be attributable to the activity putting time and distance between the agonist and antagonist. Finally, Husman and Silva (1984) offer the notion that ". . . the frustration-aggression hypothesis is of more interest as a historical document than a definitive statement about aggression" (p. 254). They attribute that to the increasingly difficult task of properly defining frustration, particularly in the context of social learning theory.

Social Learning Theory

The foundation of modern social learning theory was originally established by Miller and Dollard (1941). They proposed that imitation is a learned human behavior and that social behavior and learning can be understood by applying principles of general learning. Bandura (1973) broadened the understanding of social learning theory by establishing that social learning can occur via the observation of another person's behavior.

According to social learning theory, psychological functioning is best understood as a continuing interaction between a person's behavior and the prevailing social conditions (Bandura, 1973). Rausch (1965) indicated that a person's response will be best determined by the immediate action that preceded it. New behavior patterns can be developed as a result of either observational or direct experience. Obviously, a reaction following a hostile exchange will probably be quite different from a reaction following a friendly exchange. Social learning theory proposes that an interactive relationship exists between a person and the environment. Actions might not only be regulated by their consequences, but might alter the consequences as well.

In regard to aggression, Bandura (1973) postulated that two forms of social interaction can lead to the development of aggressive behaviors. The foremost means is learning, or the acquiring of new responses as a result of reinforcement. When a behavior is performed and then reinforced via some sort of reward, then that behavior or response is strengthened. Bandura states that conditioning is the most fundamental means of learning. The other means is as a result of modeling, imitation, or vicarious experiences. Simply stated, modeling is the imitation of the observed behaviors of individuals. When exposure to models who are rewarded for aggressive behavior occurs, a reinforcement effect takes place. This is in contrast to a situation where a model is punished for exhibiting aggressive behaviors.

If social learning is primarily achieved as a result of conditioning, and secondarily achieved through imitation, how then do we best explain aggressive, or more specifically, violent behavior in sport? Coakley (1981) attributes the learning of violent behavior in sport to the socialization process. He notes that these types of behavior sometimes receive social approval by people holding significant status in the lives of young athletes. This social approval can come from both peers or coaches. This results in an intensifying of the violent behavior due to the attached social rewards. Vaz (1972), in a study involving teenage Canadian hockey players, noted that physically aggressive play is encouraged by coaches and that techniques of fighting are part of the basic instruction. Bredemeier (1980) supports this notion by suggesting that violence in athletics is positively sanctioned, and that it is a learned behavior. Terry and Jackson (1985) offer the opinion that socialization is the major influence contributing to sport violence, but that additional factors such as situational, moral, and psychological ones also play a role. The evidence of social learning is also supported by Smith (1988), who states that the expression of violence is believed by youthful hockey players to connote strong character and also helps to win hockey games.

Young players tend to chose models who play similar positions, and a high amount of respect was shown for performance and aggressiveness (Russell, 1979). Nideffer (1983) indicates that the professional model, which exhibits substantial aggressive behavior, is inappropriate for youth sport. This notion supports earlier research by Nash and Lerner (1981), who examined the effect of violent role models on how children respond to them and actually play hockey themselves. Their findings demonstrated that in spite of adult supervision which was designed to minimize violence, youngsters were still able to play out their aggressive behaviors.

Another study which surveyed young football players and nonplayers established that a definite relationship exists between the observation of illegal actions and the subsequent adoption of these behaviors by the observers in their own games (Mugno & Feltz, 1985). The effect of coaches cannot be minimized. Luxbacher (1986) stresses the importance of the coach in learning of behavior. His research found that substantially higher levels of reactive aggression were held by players who perceived that winning was very important to their coaches. Finally, on a slightly different note, Moriarty, McCabe, and Prpich (1979) found a strong relationship between prosocial behavior observed on television and their subjects' behavior, and that antisocial television exposure had no effect on their subjects' behavior.

Social Learning Theory: Observation and Audience Effects

Does watching a sports event, either at home on television or as a spectator in a stadium, promote violence and aggression? Coakley (1990) states that there is no clear evidence to support the case for watching sports on television making people more violent. This statement is qualified when he adds that probably only "... a small number of media spectators would be entertained by regularly watching random or blatantly irrational displays of violence in sport" (p. 153). He states that it is difficult to study this phenomenon, because watching television is just a small part of a person's life, and violence makes up just a fraction of most sporting events. Assuming that Coakley disregards the abundance of professional wrestling that is televised (along with demolition derbies, roller derbies, and the like), and limits his remarks to "legitimate" sport, there is still substantial evidence to dispute this viewpoint.

Laboratory studies in which subjects observed aggressive or violent behavior in a film session have been conducted numerous times (Berkowitz & Alioto, 1973; Geen & Berkowitz, 1966; Geen & O'Neal, 1969; Hartmann, 1969). In these cases, viewing an aggressive film led to heightened levels of aggression on the part of the viewer. Berkowitz and Alioto specifically utilized a film that involved boxing in measuring the aggressive responses of the viewers. They suggested that within a laboratory situation the observed violence must be justified in order for aggression to result.

Thirer (1978a) was unable to duplicate these findings. His study exposed female athletes and nonathletes to either a violent film or an instructional one. Pre- and posttest measures of aggression were taken. Thirer utilized a paper-and-pencil measure of aggression, while Berkowitz and Alioto relied on a contrived electric shock performance, which may have been a more accurate measure. Other studies by Leyens, Camino, Parke, and Berkowitz (1975), and Parke, Berkowitz, Leyens, West, and Sebastian (1977) demonstrated that teenage boys who viewed violent films showed increases in their levels of physical aggression. The effects of the viewing were more extreme immediately after the films were seen as compared to periods of later observation. Menzies (1972) found similar results demonstrating that televised violence contributed to an increase in the attitudes toward violence by young prisoners.

Field research is substantially more difficult to control, but it does allow the researcher to observe behavior in more natural settings. Numerous studies of this nature have been conducted over the years, and they generally confirm the hypothesis that there is a strong relationship between media violence and aggressive behavior (Eron, 1963; Eron, Huesmann, Lefkowitz, & Walder, 1972; Singer & Singer, 1981). Longitudinal research by Eron (1980) has demonstrated that there is a relationship between the amount of television children watch and the amount of aggressive behavior they exhibit ten years later. While not indicating that television is the only cause of violence, it shows clearly that there is some relationship, and it is equally clear that the amount of televised violence is substantial. Celozzi, Kazelskis, and Gutsch (1981) found that viewing filmed violence in an ice hockey game served to increase viewers' aggression levels. Clearly the amount of violence in legitimate sport which is televised is minimal when compared with the amount of televised violence in general. However, it does exist, and when taken categorically as a whole, the amount of violence in televised sport is substantial enough to be of some concern where modeling and learned behavior is involved.

Continued exposure to televised violence teaches children to accept such violence as a way of life (Drabman & Thomas, 1975). It contributes toward apathy and serves to inoculate children against the shock of real violence. The conclusion is that in exposing normal children to televised violence, we are increasing their toleration of real-life aggression. Eron (1982) went on to state that how closely a youngster identifies with the aggressive characters seen on television and how realistic the child believes the viewed aggression to be are directly related to how aggressively the child might behave.

In examining the effects of modeling and learning on television viewers, let us focus on some of the behaviors of past and present managers of professional baseball teams. Deaux and Wrightsman (1984) state that observational learning or social modeling is the most frequent method of acquiring aggressive behaviors. Here we can find mature men held up as role models because they are involved in professional sport. Yet some of the on-field behavior of a few of these individuals is notoriously immature—the type of temper tantrum that would be considered unacceptable and bring routine discipline to a five-year-old child. Invading the personal space of an umpire and standing nose to nose, shouting obscenities, kicking dirt on the shoes of the official, and even resorting to physical contact by bumping and pushing the umpires, entertains(?) millions of viewers, both at the ballpark and in front of television at home. In spite of this immaturity, many have been revered by millions of fans. The message some of them deliver is that when you have a problem, you should confront it physically, even settling disputes with your fists!

Perhaps it was the image of the little guy who stood up to the millionaire owner of the team that made so many fans identify with Billy Martin. Whatever the explanation for his popularity, the behaviors he modeled and taught thousands of youngsters and adults are generally deemed inappropriate for sport. No researcher can say with certainty how often a manager's or player's antisocial behavior is modeled on the Little League field. There is good probability that it is not an infrequent occurrence.

A substantial amount of research has been conducted regarding aggression and the observation of athletic events. Horn (1985) indicated that while spectator aggression is not a new phenomenon, it does appear to be growing. He points out that people who watch an aggressive sport tend to become more aggressive in their own behaviors. One of the more frequently cited studies (Goldstein & Arms, 1971) led to the conclusion that watching a football game served to increase spectator hostility without regard to their rooting interest or to which team won. They concluded that viewing an aggressive sport like football actually made spectators more hostile.

A follow-up study by Arms, Russell, and Sandilands (1980) indicated that viewing contact sports such as football and ice hockey serves to heighten aggression scores, while observing a noncontact sport such as a swim meet has no effect on aggression scores. This finding was supported by Russell (1981a), whose research demonstrated that spectators at a violent hockey game showed an increase in their hostility scores by the game's conclusion. Similarly, Arms, Russell, and Sandilands' (1979) research supported the idea that spectators' hostility showed an increase directly attributable to their having observed aggression at both a professional wrestling match and an ice hockey game. Thirer (1978b) suggested that the increase in the popularity of football and hockey over the past two decades may indicate that more exciting and aggressive sports are being sought by people for their vicarious amusement.

Research has demonstrated that even viewing a game like basketball, which is certainly less notorious for violent displays than either football or hockey, increased aggression scores from pre- to post-game (Leuch, Krahenbuhl, & Odenkirk, 1979). Coakley (1981) acknowledged that the structure, commercialization, and organization of both player and team violence actually serves as a catalyst to violence on the part of the spectators.

As noted earlier, the arousal of aggression levels on the part of spectators viewing sport violence seems to be a short-term phenomenon. Russell (1986) studied league attendance records for ice hockey games that contained violent play and the subsequent home game attendance immediately following the violent game. The finding that there was no significant difference in attendance would indicate that there was not necessarily a carryover effect in aggressive arousal from game to game. The study concluded that excessively violent episodes do not enhance the popularity of the sport of hockey. This should not necessarily be taken for a sign that there is only a short-term effect of increased aggression and not a cumulative effect. Remember, the longitudinal research of Eron (1980) demonstrated that a long-term aggression effect does take place for subjects exposed to televised aggression over a period of time.

PATTERNS OF AGGRESSIVE BEHAVIOR ASSOCIATED WITH SPORT

Spectators and Sport Violence

Has there been a reversal in the civilizing process? Have the measures taken by Victorian and Edwardian entrepreneurs become inadequate to control the modern crowd? Are we not in for a new age of spectator violence? It is hard to avoid that impression. American journalists have documented destructive behavior by drunkenly obscene spectators, and British newspapers describe sports-related vandalism in terms reminiscent of the decline and fall of the Roman Empire. (Guttmann, 1986, p. 159)

The literature has firmly established that observation of aggressive or violent behavior clearly contributes to heightened levels of aggression on the part of the observer. This has been demonstrated repeatedly, both in laboratory studies and in field research, in general, as well as in athletic contexts. We can also comfortably conclude that there is no one simple explanation for this effect. Rather, it is a result of a variety of different processes that may or may not be operating in a multiplicity of situations. Guttmann (1986) poses an interesting question in considering whether soccer hooliganism is simply a behavior of lower class youths who have not yet been "civilized." If that is the case, he projects that eventually this type of behavior will cease. However, he cautions that it is possible that spectator aggression is actually indicative of a decline of the civilizing process. If that is the situation, than he sees the riots and vandalism associated with violent fan behavior as a trend that is likely to grow.

In attempting to analyze how best to deal with spectator violence at athletic contests, Coalter (1985) indicated that seating, segregation of rival fans, and a ban on alcohol are effective only when offered in combination rather than individually. Similarly, Cavanaugh and Silva (1980) found that both male and female spectators were alike in that they attributed age, referees, rivalry, alcohol, the nature of the game, crowd density, time remaining, and losing as the major factors contributing to fan misbehavior.

Empirical evidence attests that spectator interest is enhanced by aggressive play or fierce competitiveness, and that this situation is exacerbated by media coverage (Bryant & Zillmann, 1983). Bryant (1988) concluded that the media persistently exploit sport violence. In examining whether or not television viewers actually enjoy observing violence in sport, he found that many actually do! Once again, an assortment of mitigating components contributed to this attitude, such as the observers' propensity for personal aggression, fans' attitudes toward teams and players, moral judgments, and personality factors. Similarly, Dewar (1979) noted after observing 40 professional baseball games that warm weather, cheap seats, lateness of the game, and offensive rallies were factors that might best predict spectator violence.

In attempting to analyze what specifically encourages or

contributes to spectator violence, Gilbert and Twyman (1984) are consistent with the previously cited research. They determined that crowd incitement in order to intimidate opposing teams and officials, availability of alcohol, and overidentification with the teams are contributing factors. Smith (1974) found that 74% of the violent outbreaks by the hockey and soccer spectators he studied were preceded by violent behaviors on the part of the players. In a controlled laboratory study, Lennon and Hatfield (1980) could not correlate the effect of crowding by itself to an increase in aggression levels. However, they did determine that simply viewing a football film had this effect. In isolating crowding in a laboratory setting they did not, or could not, consider the influence of alcohol as a factor. Furthermore, their study did not necessarily explore team affiliation, as a film was used as the mediating stimulus.

Coakley (1990) states that most spectating at sports events is quiet and orderly. Noncontact sports rarely have episodes of spectators acting out-of-sorts, and decorum is generally followed. He indicates that even in the case of contact sports, violent behavior is unusual, with spectators generally being more noisy and emotional than physically aggressive. Coakley's sentiment is consistent with previous notions put forth by Russell (1981b) and Mann (1979), who both noted that serious outbursts by spectators at athletic contests are actually relatively rare. What we must understand here is that it is not absolutely certain that simply watching a football game will lead to violence. Even referring back to Goldstein and Arms' (1971) study, an elevated level of aggression scores on a paper-and-pencil test were found, not violent behavior. An intriguing article by Edwards and Rackages (1977) describes a substantial array of spectator violence. It was interesting to note that a majority of the episodes they recount either directly or indirectly involve alcohol or the hurling of beer cans or whiskey bottles. Certainly we need to consider that while aggression levels may be aroused by certain types of sporting events, this factor alone does not automatically contribute to the onset of spectator violence. It might take any one or a combination of additional factors to be a catalyst once the elevated arousal level is achieved.

An interesting study which examined the effects of abusive spectator behavior on the performance of home and visiting basketball teams was performed by Thirer and Rampey (1979). Throughout a college basketball season precise records were kept regarding the relative timing of fouls, turnovers, and general misplays by both home and visiting teams. Time periods during which the audience had antisocial responses were charted, and the number of infractions, violations, etc., were carefully compared for periods of normal crowd behavior and antisocial behavior. The findings were surprising in that they clearly showed that the home team was more adversely affected by the behavior of the spectators than were the visiting teams. During periods of normal spectator behavior the visiting teams were assessed significantly more penalties than the home team was. However, this statistic reversed itself in the immediate period of time following negative spectator behavior.

The aforementioned study poses as many questions as it answers regarding the effect of crowd behavior on home and visiting teams. Did the behavior of the spectators negatively affect the home team players, or did it perhaps have a negative effect on the officials, who in turn penalized the home team? Both the coaches and players indicated that they believed that the officials were generally fair, and that they did not attribute an increase in negative assessments against the home team to capricious officiating. The researchers concluded that the arousal levels of the home players became too elevated following the negative spectator behavior. This contributed to diminished performance as predicted in the inverted-U hypothesis. This explanation seems reasonable for want of a more precise explanation.

Instigation of Aggression

An interesting component of the aggression literature that has been generally overlooked by sport psychology research is the instigation of aggression. When we consider aggressive behavior in sport, we generally are talking about reactive or provoked situations. These apply to both the athletes on the playing fields as well as to the spectators in the stands or at home watching television. However, aggression research is more complicated than most of the simplistic models that sports scientists have commonly dealt with.

Can a third party interact in a fashion so as to provoke an aggressive response, while not having firsthand involvement in the dynamic behaviors taking place? These patterns of provocation occur in athletics on a regular basis. Coaches exhort their players; relatives and friends urge on those important to them; spectators vociferously encourage a variety of aggressive behaviors (e.g., at a professional wrestling match). Bandura (1973) noted that one element that keeps people from making direct assaults is the likelihood of retaliation. Instead, Bandura suggests that a disguised mode of aggression is often favored by which an indirect series of events takes place that eventually proves injurious to another. The question is, what effect does the encouragement or instigation of others have on the potential for an increased aggressive response?

Milgram (1965) stated that a ". . . situation in which one agent commands another to hurt a third turns up time and again as a significant theme in human relations" (p. 57). This sentiment is echoed by Gaebelein (1973a), who noted that "In our complex society, human physical aggression often tends to involve more than merely one person aggressing against another person. Frequently, an aggressive encounter is instigated or initiated by a third party" (p. 389). Gaebelein found that the more willing the subject was to respond to the instigated aggression, the more aggressive was the instigator in attempting to provoke more aggression. These results were consistent when the sample was comprised of women (Gaebelein, 1973b). Another variation demonstrated that attacked subjects were more likely to provoke more aggression than were nonattacked subjects (Gaebelein & Hay, 1974).

Another explanation for instigative aggression is that the instigator is actually removed from the aggressive act, thereby diminishing his/her personal responsibility (Kilham & Mann, 1974; Tilker, 1970). A diminished sense of responsibility means less guilt on the part of the instigator, and even psychological denial that the provoker is to blame for the consequences of the behavior in question. The implications of the research on instigative aggression for sport, particularly spectator violence and some coaching behaviors, is considerable.

Aggression in Sport and Moral Reasoning

How do athletes or spectators come to terms with the question of moral behavior when they become involved in aggressive or violent conduct? This is an intriguing question, and one which has become the subject of a reasonable amount of research during the 1980s. Bredemeier has been in the forefront in the field of sport psychology regarding research dealing with moral reasoning and athlete behavior. (See Chapter 27.)

Bredemeier and Shields (1984) concluded that moral development is significantly related to athletic aggression. They correlated the moral reasoning levels of male and female basketball players with the coaches' ratings of player aggressiveness and statistical data regarding fouls accumulated throughout the season. Additional research indicated that the stronger the athletes' moral reasoning, the less able they are to accept aggression as legitimate (Bredemeier & Shields, 1985). Specifically, they noted two types of aggression that athletes considered illegitimate: aggression irrelevant to game strategy, and aggression that can cause injury that transcends the scope of the game. Athletes demonstrated two levels of morality: game morality, and everyday morality. The balance between the two is a determinant for either legitimate or illegitimate aggression.

Additional research by Bredemeier and colleagues (Bredemeier, Weiss, Shields, & Cooper, 1986; Bredemeier, Shields, Weiss, & Cooper, 1987) continued to support a distinct link between moral reasoning and aggressive tendencies and behavior. Findings linking aggressive behavior to legitimacy tendencies and a positive correlation between less mature moral reasoning and a greater tendency toward aggression were clearly established.

Before we conclude that the link between moral reasoning and aggressive behavior is absolute, additional research is clearly needed. A study by Case, Greer, and Lacourse (1987) was unable to establish a relationship between moral judgment and attitudes toward unacceptable spectator behavior in sport. They called for additional research in the area, as the variables are highly complex and alternate research models are required for a better understanding. Guttmann (1986) concludes that "Spectators do often behave collectively in ways they shun individually; not many people scream themselves hoarse in their living rooms. Still, most fans are conscious of the canons of civility as they relate to spectatorship. Hooligans are relatively rare, even in England, in comparison to the huge numbers of self-disciplined men and women who attend sports spectacles" (p. 166).

Personality and Aggressive Behavior

Is aggression a personality trait? Lorber and Patterson (1981) define a trait as ". . . an individual's mode of responding which is expressed in a stable fashion across both time and settings" (p. 65). They clearly regard aggression as a personality trait, as do most personologists. The durability of aggression as a behavioral trait has been repeatedly demonstrated in longitudinal personality research (Gersten, Langren, Eisenberg, Semcha-Fagan, & McCarthy, 1976; Patterson, 1980; West & Farrington, 1973). Clearly aggression is a trait, at least according to the components of personality as delineated by standard personality tests commonly used in behavioral research (e.g., Edwards Personal Preference Scale [EPPS]; Cattell Sixteen Personality Factors Test [16PF]; California Personality Inventory [CPI]; Minnesota Multiphasic Personality Inventory [MMPI]).

How accurately traits are measured, and of what value they are to those interested in sport psychology (and in this particular instance, aggressive behavior and sport), remains unclear to some extent. Morgan's (1980) article, "The Trait Psychology Controversy" is a very valuable resource in gaining insight as to many of the issues that still divide sport psychologists on the subject of personality testing.

The sport personality research explicitly includes aggression as a discrete trait. Morgan (1980) indicates that it is inappropriate and inaccurate "to predict state responses from trait measures . . ." (p. 52). Simply stated, this implies that even though an athlete (or spectator) may score high on aggression as a personality trait, it is still difficult to predict how that person may respond to a variety of aggression-provoking stimuli. Cox (1990) indicates that the relationship between the aggression trait and actual acts of aggression is questionable. He doubts that one can predict aggressiveness in a particular situation based simply on a trait measure of aggression. Morgan (1980) advocates a multidimensional model comprising physiological variables and psychological states be used to gain a better understanding of the dynamics of sport-related behavior. This advice is very appropriate where gaining a better understanding of aggression is concerned.

It has been argued that sport is one of the vehicles by which the North American male establishes his sexual identity. He accomplishes this by exaggerated expressions of aggression in terms of his interpersonal style, as well as with other behaviors (Bianchi, 1980). Rainey (1986) supports the notion that aggressive behavior by males is legitimized in sport situations, but his research demonstrated that the sport socialization process also causes females to be less accepting of aggressive behavior.

Kelly and McCarthy (1979) divided college hockey players into high-aggression and low-aggression score groups over a period of seven years. Their analyses revealed that differences did exist in level of play across periods, and that aggression was greater in games at home than away. Colburn (1985) indicated that ice hockey fistfights are reflective of a social ritual, and Dunning (1986) adds that sport serves as a secondary reinforcer of masculine identity. Soccer hooliganism is a product of specific social conditions which lead to an aggressive "masculine" style (Dunning, Maguire, Murphy, & Williams, 1982).

Perception and Aggression

Can aggression sometimes be a by-product of perception? Obviously, the way one reads cues and processes information can have profound effects on determining an appropriate (or inappropriate) response to a stimulus. The signals an opponent sends can often be misunderstood by a receiver, particularly where aggressive play is an element. Frank and Gilovich (1988) explored an interesting theme of aggression and perception. They studied the effect of uniform color on the behavior of athletes. Specifically, they examined whether wearing a predominantly black uniform has any effect on players, opponents, and officials. Their findings showed that the behavior of the player wearing the uniform is definitely affected when that player, or team, switches to black. The switch was accompanied by an immediate increase in the number of penalties assessed. This increase might be attributable to the influence of the color on referees as well as its influence on the players themselves.

In another study of perception, Worrell and Harris (1986) found that players perceived themselves not to be as aggressive as judges observed them to be. They compared scores of self-assessment and judge assessment on the behavior of college ice hockey players. They further found that the play was perceived to be more aggressive at home than away, and in games that were won.

Do players (and coaches) perceive that they need to be more aggressive in order to achieve athletic success in terms of winning? A good deal of evidence suggests otherwise. Ginsberg (1980) noted that the most effective football players whom he studied were those who had the ability to neutralize their aggression. Similarly, Widmeyer and Birch (1979; 1984) were unable to offer support to the notion that aggression will lead to success for either teams or individuals. In a longitudinal study they found no significant relationship between aggression and team performance.

The entire notion of perception is an important one where aggression is concerned. As noted earlier, one justification for aggression is considered to be whether or not a team or player is perceived as having been treated fairly or unfairly. When perceptions are unbalanced there is an increased likelihood that misunderstandings will result in some form of aggressive behavior.

Likely Trends for the '90s

In reviewing the aggression literature for sport and the social sciences, one can easily see that the overwhelming quantity of the research has been conducted during the past thirty years. If one had to identify a narrow window of time to focus on, the period from the early 1960s through the mid '70s seems to be most fruitful in terms of significant publications. Later research has introduced relatively little insight into the problems identified during this period. Rather it has served to verify, replicate, and to a lesser extent, modify what was previously established, or at least hypothesized. Still, some important questions remain unanswered.

It was widely believed in the early 1970s that sport violence had gotten out of hand. Social scientists and the media were overwhelmed with episodic reports of violent behavior associated with athletics by both athletes and spectators. In retrospect, was this a new occurrence? Or did this instead reflect greater media interest and capability in reporting this type of behavior? In truth, it probably was a combination of the two. Sports did not become violent overnight. As the broadcast media became both more sophisticated and more interested in sport, there was a heightened interest in the "sensational" aspects of sport coverage. If that included paying more attention to sports violence, so be it!

On the other hand, there is little question that in Western society, particularly in the United States, there has been a huge escalation in violent behavior since the placid 1950s. This has definitely become a societal problem of major proportion. Sport scientists should not be surprised that there has been an escalation of violence related directly and indirectly to sport, paralleling the general social environment.

Another factor that cannot be overlooked is the influence of television. Even though Coakley (1990) minimizes the effect of television on violent behavior, there are some obvious parallels that cannot be ignored. The 1950s saw the introduction of television into most of the households in the United States. By the 1980s this had spread to most of Western society. For the first time, in the 1960s, we have seen generations of young people weaned on television. Television, and more specifically the broadcast media, serves to bring violence into the household with stark media images and reporting. Of course, this is true for general social behavior, and not just sport. The emotions of fans unable to go to the ballpark were in the past reliant upon radio descriptions of what was going on. Now, the level of excitement has expanded to the point where every play, in slow motion and from a variety of angles, can be viewed from the comfort of your living room.

What lies ahead in the 1990s? For one thing, the rewards associated with professional sport are so extraordinary, that more and more is at stake for professional athletes. This fact by itself can contribute to less tolerance of opponents and a greater sense of urgency attached to success and keeping ones' job. Psychologically the athlete is less likely to feel sorry for an injured player, and rather, is relieved that he or she was spared the same fate.

As far as the fans are concerned, the general state of the economy can be attributable, to some extent, to the way sport is perceived. As more and more athletes become millionaires, the spectators' tolerance and sympathy tends to be reduced. Raised expectations and frustrating performance can interact in insidious ways.

Methods must continue to evolve which limit the likelihood of spectator violence getting out of hand. One obvious method that has been talked about for at least 15 years is eliminating alcohol from athletic arenas. Alcohol is a proven disinhibiter. There are thousands of documented episodes of alcohol contributing to violent behavior at athletic contests. The manufacturers have been relentless in providing the public with the psychological message that having a beer is synonymous with playing and watching sports events. Better controls, and even the total elimination of alcohol from spectator sports, might be called for in order to reduce the likelihood of more violent behavior. The athletic industry needs to take a stand against the temptation of alcohol advertisement dollars and disassociate from it entirely.

Will aggressive and violent behavior at sports events continue to escalate through the 1990s, or have we seen it level off? Unfortunately, the 1980s witnessed the movement of aggressive behavior from sports that were traditionally associated with it (e.g., high-contact sports) to sports that were not at all accustomed to it (e.g., professional tennis). One wonders where the spiral will stop. We have a generation of athletes, both professional and amateur, who have all of the violent role models imaginable. If we accept social learning theory as completely valid, we are probably producing a new generation of athletes and spectators who are less sensitized to violence than ever before. In short, we are dealing with a societal problem of mammoth proportions. Sport scientists can only hope to cope with it as best as possible, and contain violent and aggressive behavior with preventive measures and strict sanctions when it occurs.

Can Sport Psychology Research Contribute Toward Modifying Aggression and Violence in Sport?

The discipline of sport psychology has largely concerned itself with attempting to gain a better understanding of human behavior as it applies to sport. As a discipline, sport psychology is still in its infancy, as compared with other social sciences. Admittedly, some excellent research has emanated from the ranks of contemporary sport psychologists. However, the quantity of research is still just scratching the surface in comparison to that in the larger discipline of psychology. The discipline of sport psychology needs to produce substantially more research than it has over the past two decades.

Quantity should not be confused with quality. Obviously there is a great need for better qualitative research, in addition to the need for a greater quantity of research in sport. So as to not apply a higher standard to sport psychology than to general psychology, a growth in the total amount of research would ideally accompany a proportionate growth in research which is considered qualitative. In the area of aggression, there is great need for high-quality research which will help find better ways for its control.

Sport psychology can make a major contribution to this process, particularly in concert with the other social sciences. A multidisciplinary approach is needed if containment is to be achieved. Carroll (1980) called for a synthesis of explanations in order to better deal with aggressive behavior associated with sports spectators. Similarly, Bredemeier, Lefebvre, and Leith (1980) concluded that there is no single grand design for reducing athletic aggression. Preventive education is a prescription for this societal dilemma. Sport psychology can certainly do its part toward solving the problems of aggression in sport.

References

Alpert, G. P., & Crouch, B. M. (1988). Sports violence: History, overview and suggestions for reduction. *Journal of Applied Research in Coaching and Athletics, 3,* 101–119.

Anshel, M. H. (1990). *Sport psychology: From theory to practice.* Scottsdale, AZ: Gorsuch Scarisbrick.

Ardrey, R. (1966). *The territorial imperative.* New York: Atheneum.

Arms, R. L., Russell, G. W., & Sandilands, M. L. (1979a). Effects on the hostility of spectators of viewing aggressive sports. *Social Psychology Quarterly, 42,* 275–279.

Arms, R. L., Russell, G. W., & Sandilands, M. L. (1979b). Effects of viewing aggressive sports on the hostility of spectators. In R. M. Suinn (Ed.), *Psychology in sports: Methods and applications* (pp. 133–142). Minneapolis: Burgess.

Banerjee, S. S. (1982). Violence in football stadiums must be stamped out. *Olympic Review. 182:* 741–743.

Bandura, A. (1973). *Aggression: A social learning analysis.* Englewood Cliffs, NJ: Prentice-Hall.

Bateson, G. (1941). The frustration-aggression hypothesis and culture. *Psychological Review. 48,* 350–355.

Berkowitz, L. (1964). Aggressive cues in aggressive behavior and hostility catharsis. *Psychological Review. 71,* 104–122.

Berkowitz, L. (1969). *Roots of aggression: A re-examination of the frustration-aggression hypothesis.* New York: Atherton.

Berkowitz, L. (1978). Whatever happened to the frustration-aggression hypothesis? *American Behavioral Scientist, 21,* 691–708.

Berkowitz, L., & Alioto, J. T. (1973). The meaning of an observed event as a determinant of its aggressive consequences. *Journal of Personality and Social Psychology, 28,* 206–217.

Berkowitz, L., & Geen, R. G. (1966). Film violence and the cue properties of available targets. *Journal of Personality and Social Psychology, 3,* 525–530.

Bianchi, E. C. (1980). The superbowl culture of male violence. In D. F. Sabo & R. Runfola (Eds.), *Jock: Sports and male identity* (pp. 117–130). Englewood Cliffs, NJ: Prentice-Hall.

Boucher, R. L., & Case, R. W. (1980). Participant violence in sport: An essay review. *Physical Education Review, 3,* 8–13.

Bredemeier, B. J. (1980). Applications and implications of aggression research. In W. F. Straub (Ed.), *Sport psychology: An analysis of athlete behavior* (pp. 203–213). Ithaca, NY: Mouvement Publications.

Bredemeier, B. J., Lefebvre, L. M., & Leith, L. M. (1980). The modification and control of athletic aggression. In P. Klavora & K. Wipper (Eds.), *Psychological and sociological factors in sport* (pp. 156–161). Toronto: University of Toronto, School of Physical and Health Education.

Bredemeier, B. J., & Shields, D. L. (1984). The utility of moral stage analysis in the investigation of athletic aggression. *Sociology of Sport Journal, 1,* 138–149.

Bredemeier, B. J., & Shields, D. L. (1985). Values and violence in sport today. *Psychology Today, 19,* 23–32.

Bredemeier, B. J., Weiss, M. R., Shields, D. L., & Cooper, A. B. (1986). The relationship of sport involvement with children's moral reasoning and aggression tendencies. *Journal of Sport Psychology, 8,* 304–318.

Bredemeier, B. J., Shields, D. L., Weiss, M. R., & Cooper, A. B. (1987). The relationship between children's legitimacy judgments and their moral reasoning, aggression tendencies, and sport involvement. *Sociology of Sport Journal, 4,* 48–60.

Bryant, J. (1988). *Viewers' Enjoyment of Televised Sports Violence.* Unpublished manuscript. North American Society for the Sociology of Sport. Ninth Annual Meeting. Cincinnati, Ohio.

Bryant, J., & Zillman, D. (1983). Sports violence and the media. In J. H. Goldstein (Ed.), *Sports violence* (pp. 195–211). New York: Springer-Verlag.

Buss, A. H. (1961). *The psychology of aggression.* New York: Wiley.

Carroll, J. (1986). Sport: Virtue and grace. *Theory, Culture and Society, 3,* 91–98.

Carroll, R. (1980). Football hooliganism in England. *International Review of Sport Sociology, 15,* 77–92.

Case, B. W., Greer, H. S., & Lacourse, M. G. (1987). Moral judgement development and perceived legitimacy of spectator behavior in sport. *Journal of Sport Behavior, 10,* 147–156.

Cataldi, P. (1980). Sport and aggression: A safety valve or a pressure cooker? In W. F. Straub (Ed.), *Sport psychology: An analysis of athlete behavior* (pp. 193–202). Ithaca, NY: Mouvement Publications.

Cavanaugh, B. M., & Silva, J. M. (1980). Spectator perceptions of fan misbehavior: An attitudinal inquiry. In C. H. Nadeau, W. R. Halliwell, K. M. Newell, & G. C. Roberts (Eds.), *Psychology of motor behavior and sport—1979* (pp. 189–198). Champaign, IL: Human Kinetics.

Celozzi, M. J., Kazelskis, R., & Gutsch, K. U. (1981). The relationship between viewing televised violence in ice hockey and subsequent levels of personal aggression. *Journal of Sport Behavior, 4,* 157–162.

Cheren, S. (1981). The psychiatric perspective: Psychological aspects of violence in sports. *Arena Review, 5,* 31–36.

Coakley, J. (1981). The sociological perspective: Alternate causations of violence in sport. *Arena Review, 5,* 44–56.

Coakley, J. (1990). *Sport in society.* St. Louis: Times Mirror/Mosby.

Coalter, F. (1985). Crowd behavior at football matches: A study in Scotland. *Leisure Studies, 4,* 111–117.

Colburn, K. (1985). Honor, ritual and violence in ice hockey. *Canadian Journal of Sociology, 10,* 153–170.

Cox, R. H. (1990). *Sport psychology: Concepts and applications.* Dubuque, IA: Brown.

Deaux, K., & Wrightsman, L. S. (1984). *Social psychology in the 80's.* Monterey, CA: Brooks/Cole.

Dewar, C. K. (1979). Spectator fights at professional baseball games. *Review of Sport and Leisure, 4,* 12–25.

Dollard, J., Doob, L., Miller, N., Mowrer, O., & Sears, R. (1939). *Frustration and aggression.* New Haven: Yale University Press.

Drabman, R., & Thomas, M. (1975). Does TV violence breed indifference? *Journal of Communication,* Autumn, 86–89.

Dunning, E. (1986). Sport as a male preserve: Notes on the social sources of masculine identity and its transformation. *Theory Cultures and Society, 3,* 79–90.

Dunning, E., Maguire, J. A., Murphy, P. J., & Williams, J. M. (1982). The social roots of football hooligan violence. *Leisure Studies, 1,* 139–156.

Dunning, E., Murphy, P., & Williams, J. (1981). Ordered segmentation and the socio-genesis of football hooligan violence: A critique of Marsh's ritualized aggression hypothesis and the outline of a sociological alternative. In A. Tomlinson (Ed.), *The sociological study of sport: Configurational and interpretive studies* (pp 36–52). Chelsea, England: Chelsea School of Human Movement, Brighton Polytechnic.

Edwards, H., & Rackages, V. (1977). The dynamics of violence in American sport: Some promising structural and social considerations. *Journal of Sport and Social Issues, 1,* 3–31.

Eitzen, D. S. (1985). Violence in professional sports and public policy. In A. T. Johnson & J. H. Frey (Eds.), *Government and sport: The public policy issues* (pp. 99–114). Totowa, NJ: Rowman & Allanheld.

Eitzen, D. S., & Sage, G. H. (1989). *Sociology of North American sport.* Dubuque, IA: Brown.

Eron, L. D. (1963). Relationship of TV viewing habits and aggressive behavior in children. *Journal of Abnormal and Social Psychology, 67,* 193–196.

Eron, L. D. (1980). Prescription for reduction of aggression. *American Psychologist, 35,* 244–252.

Eron, L. D. (1982). Parent-child interaction, television violence, and aggression in children. *American Psychologist, 37,* 197–211.

Eron, L. D., Huesmann, L. R., Lefkowitz, M. M., & Walder, L. (1972). Does television violence cause aggression? *American Psychologist, 27,* 253–263.

Feshbach, S. (1970). Aggression. In P. H. Mussen (Ed.), *Carmichael's manual of child psychology* (Vol. II, pp. 159–259). New York: Wiley.

Frank, M. G., & Gilovich, T. (1988). The dark side of self and social perception: Black uniforms and aggression in professional sports. *Journal of Personality and Social Psychology, 54,* 74–85.

Freischlag, J., & Schmidke, C. (1980). Violence in sports: Its causes and some solutions. In W. F. Straub (Ed.), *Sport psychology: An analysis of athlete behavior* (pp. 161–165). Ithaca, NY: Mouvement.

Freud, S. (1924). The economic problems in masochism. In J. Strachey (Ed., 1939), *Standard edition of the complete psychological works of Sigmund Freud* (Vol. 19, pp. 155–172). London: Hogarth.

Freud, S. (1925). *Collected papers.* London: Hogarth.

Gaebelein, J. W. (1973a). Third-party instigation of aggression: An experimental approach. *Journal of Personality and Social Psychology, 27,* 389–395.

Gaebelein, J. W. (1973b). Instigative aggression in females. *Psychological Reports, 33,* 619–622.

Gaebelein, J. W. & Hay, W. M. (1974). Third party instigation of aggression as a function of attack and vulnerability. *Journal of Research in Personality, 7,* 324–333.

Geen, R. & O'Neal, E. (1969). Activation of cue-elicited aggression by general arousal. *Journal of Personality and Social Psychology, 11,* 289–292.

Gersten, J. C., Langner, T. S., Eisenberg, J. G., Simcha-Fagan, O., & McCarthy, E. D. (1976). Stability and change in types of behavioral disturbances of children and adolescents. *Journal of Abnormal Child Psychology, 4,* 111–127.

Gilbert, B. & Twyman, L. (1984). Violence: Out of hand in the stands. In D. S. Eitzen (Ed.), *Sport in contemporary society: An anthology* (pp. 112–121). New York: St. Martin's Press.

Ginsberg, G. L. (1980). Aggression and self-mastery in football. *Psychiatric Annals, 10,* 13–22.

Goldstein, J. & Arms, R. (1971). Effects of observing athletic contests on hostility. *Sociometry, 34,* 456–465.

Guttmann, A. (1986). *Sports spectators.* New York: Columbia University Press.

Harrell, W. A. (1980). Aggression by high school basketball players: An observational study of the effects of opponents' aggression and frustration inducing factors. *International Journal of Sport Psychology, 11,* 290–298.

Hartmann, D. (1969). Influence of symbolically modeled instrumental aggression and pain cues on aggressive behavior. *Journal of Personality and Social Psychology, 11,* 280–288.

Hokanson, J. (1970). Psychophysiological evaluation of the catharsis hypothesis. In E. I. Megargee & J. Hokanson (Eds.), *The dynamics of aggression* (pp. 74–86). New York: Harper & Row.

Horn, J. C. (1985). Fan violence: Fighting the injustice of it all. *Psychology Today, 19,* 30–31.

Husman, B. F., & Silva, J. M. (1984). Aggression in sport: Definitional and theoretical considerations. In J. M. Silva & R. S. Weinberg (Eds.), *Psychological foundations of sport* (pp. 246–260). Champaign, IL: Human Kinetics.

Kelly, B. R., & McCarthy, J. F. (1979). Personality dimensions of aggression and its relationship to time and place of action in ice hockey. *Human Relations, 32,* 219–225.

Kilham, W., & Mann, L. (1974). Level of destructive obedience as a function of transmitter and executant roles in the Milgram obedience paradigm. *Journal of Personality and Social Psychology, 29,* 696–702.

Lennon, J. X., & Hatfield, F. C. (1980). The effects of crowding and observation of athletic events on spectator tendency toward aggressive behavior. *Journal of Sport Behavior, 3,* 61–68.

Leuch, M. R., Krahenbuhl, G. S., & Odenkirk, J. E. (1979). Assessment of spectator aggression at intercollegiate basketball contests. *Review of Sport and Leisure, 4,* 40–52.

Leyens, J. P., Camino, L., Parke, R. D., & Berkowitz, L. (1975). Effects of movie violence on aggression in a field setting as a function of group dominance and cohesion. *Journal of Personality and Social Psychology, 32,* 346–360.

Lorber, R., & Patterson, G. R. (1981). The aggressive child: A concomitant of a coercive system. In J. P. Vincent (Ed.), *Advances in family intervention assessment and theory* (Vol. 2, pp. 47–87). New York: JAI Press.

Luxbacher, J. A. (1986). Violence in sports: An examination of the theories of aggression, and how the coach can influence the degree of violence displayed in sport. *Coaching Review, 9,* 14–17.

Mann, L. (1979). Sport crowds viewed from the perspective of collective behavior. In J. H. Goldstein, (Ed.), *Sports, games, and play* (pp. 337–368). London: Erlbaum.

Mark, M. M., Bryant, F. B., & Lehman, D. R. (1983). Perceived injustice and sports violence. In J. H. Goldstein, (Ed.), *Sports violence* (pp. 83–109). New York: Springer-Verlag.

Marsh, P. (1982). Social order on the British soccer terraces. *International Social Science Journal, 34,* 247–256.

Menzies, E. S. (1972). *The effects of repeated exposure to televised violence towards attitudes towards violence among youthful offenders.* (Volume IV). Tallahassee, FL: FCI Research Reports.

Michener, H. A., DeLamater, J. D., & Schwartz, S. H. (1986). *Social psychology.* Orlando, FL: Harcourt Brace Jovanovich.

Milgram, S. (1965). Some conditions of obedience and disobedience to authority. *Human Relations, 18,* 57–65.

Miller, N. E. (1941). The Frustration-Aggression Hypothesis. *Psychological Review, 48,* 337–342.

Miller, N. E., & Dollard, J. (1941). *Social learning and imitation.* New Haven: Yale University Press.

Morgan, W. P. (1980). The trait psychology controversy. *Research Quarterly, 51,* 50–76.

Moriarty, D., McCabe, A., & Prpich, M. (1979). Studies of television and youth sports. *International Journal of Sport Psychology, 10,* 122–129.

Morris, D. (1967). *The naked ape.* New York: McGraw-Hill.

Mugno, D. A., & Feltz, D. L. (1985). The social learning of aggression in youth football in the United States. *Canadian Journal of Applied Sport Sciences, 10,* 26–35.

Nash, J. E., & Lerner, E. (1981). Learning from the pros: Violence in youth hockey. *Youth and Society, 13,* 229–244.

Nideffer, R. M. (1983). Aggression in youth sports. *Coaching Review, 6,* (July/August), 29–31.

Parens, H. (1987). *Aggression in our children.* Northvale, NJ: Jason Aronson.

Parke, R. D., Berkowitz, L., Leyens, J. P., West, S. G., & Sebastian, R. J. (1977). Some effects of violent and nonviolent movies on the behavior of juvenile delinquents. In L. Berkowitz (Ed.), *Advances in experimental social psychology Vol. 10* (pp. 135–172). New York: Academic Press.

Patterson, G. R. (1980). *Coercive family processes.* Eugene, OR: Castalia.

Pearton, R. (1986). Violence in sport and the special case of soccer hooliganism in the United Kingdom. In C. R. Rees & A. W. Miracle (Eds.), *Sport and social theory* (pp. 67–84). Champaign, IL: Human Kinetics.

Pilz, G. A. (1982). Changes of violence in sport. *International Review of Sport Sociology, 17,* 47–71.

Rainey, D. W. (1986). A gender difference in acceptance of sport aggression: A classroom activity. *Teaching of Psychology, 13,* 138–140.

Rausch, H. L. (1965). Interaction sequences. *Journal of Personality and Social Psychology, 2,* 487–499.

Russell, G. W. (1979). Hero selection by Canadian ice hockey players: Skill or aggression? *Canadian Journal of Applied Sport Sciences, 4,* 309–313.

Russell, G. W. (1981a). Spectator moods at an aggressive sports event. *Journal of Sport Psychology, 3,* 217–227.

Russell, G. W. (1981b). Aggression in sport. In P. F. Brain & D. Benton (Eds.), *Multidisciplinary approaches to aggression research* (pp. 431–446). Amsterdam: Elsevier.

Russell, G. W. (1986). Does sports violence increase box office receipts? *International Journal of Sport Psychology, 17,* 173–182.

Ryan, E. (1970). The cathartic effect of vigorous motor activity on aggressive behavior. *Research Quarterly, 41,* 542–555.

Schafer, W. E. (1969). Some sources and consequences of interscholastic athletics: The case of participation and delinquency. *International Review of Sport Sociology, 4,* 63–82.

Scott, J. (1970). Sport and aggression. In G. S. Kenyon (Ed.), *Contemporary psychology of sport* (pp. 11–24). Chicago: Athletic Institute.

Siann, G. (1985). *Accounting for aggression.* Boston: Allen & Unwin.

Silva, J. M., III. (1980). Assertive and aggressive behavior in sport: A definitional clarification. In C. H. Nadeau (Ed.), *Psychology of motor behavior and sport, 1979* (pp. 199–208). Champaign, IL: Human Kinetics.

Singer, J. L., & Singer, D. G. (1981). *Television, imagination, and aggression: A study of preschoolers' play.* Hillsdale, NJ: Erlbaum.

Smith, M. D. (1976). Precipitants of crowd violence. *Sociological Inquiry, 48,* 121–131.

Smith, M. D. (1983). *Violence and sport.* Toronto: Butterworths.

Smith, M. D. (1988). Interpersonal sources of violence in hockey: The influence of parents, coaches, and teammates. In F. L. Smoll, R. A. Magill, & M. J. Ash, (Eds.), *Children in sport* (pp. 301–313). Champaign, IL: Human Kinetics.

Sugden, J., & Yiannakis, A. (1982). Sport and juvenile delinquency: A theoretical base. *Journal of Sport and Social Issues, 6,* 22–30.

Terry, P. C., & Jackson, J. J. (1985). The determinants and control of violence in sport. *Quest, 37,* 27–37.

Thirer, J. (1978a). Change in aggressive attitudes of female athletes and nonathletes after observation of filmed violence. *Journal of Sport Behavior, 1,* 28–36.

Thirer, J. (1978b). Aggression theory applied to sport and physical activity. *Motor Skills: Theory into Practice, 2,* 128–136.

Thirer, J. (1981). The psychological perspective: Analysis of violence in sport. *Arena Review, 5,* 37–43.

Thirer, J., & Rampey, M. S. (1979). Effects of abusive spectators' behavior on performance of home and visiting intercollegiate basketball teams. *Perceptual and Motor Skills, 48,* 1047–1053.

Thirer, J., Zackheim, M. A., & Summers, D. A. (1987). The influence of depression on selected motor performance tasks by college athletes and nonathletes. *Educational and Psychological Research, 7,* 75–89.

Tilker, H. (1970). Socially responsible behavior as a function of observer responsibility and victim feedback. *Journal of Personality and Social Psychology, 14,* 95–100.

Trulson, M. E. (1986). Martial arts training: A novel "cure" for juvenile delinquency. *Human Relations, 39,* 1131–1140.

Vaz, E. (1972). The culture of young hockey players: Some initial observations. In A. W. Taylor (Ed.), *Training-Scientific basis and application* (pp. 222–234). Springfield, IL: Thomas.

West, D. J., & Farrington, D. T. (1973). *Who becomes delinquent?* New York: Crane, Russek & Co.

Widmeyer, W. N., & Birch, J. S. (1979). The relationship between aggression and performance outcome in ice hockey. *Canadian Journal of Applied Sport Sciences, 4,* 91–94.

Widmeyer, W. N., & Birch, J. S. (1984). Aggression in professional ice hockey: A strategy for success or a reaction to failure? *The Journal of Psychology, 117,* 77–84.

Worrell, G. L., & Harris, D. V. (1986). The relationship of perceived and observed aggression of ice hockey players. *International Journal of Sport Psychology, 17,* 34–40.

INDIVIDUAL DIFFERENCES: COGNITIVE AND PERCEPTUAL STYLES

David Pargman

Athletes are exhorted by coaches to "think," to "remember," to "make judgments," and to "learn from mistakes." All of these experiences deal with high-order skills that are dependent upon *cognition* and *perception*. A helpful juxtaposition of these mental activities is provided by Mayer (1983), who describes cognitive processes as involving *sensation* (reception of input stimuli), *perception* (recognition of input stimuli), *learning* (encoding of input information), *memory* (retrieval of input information), and *thinking* (manipulation of perceived, learned, and remembered information). Cognitive processes include reasoning and drawing logical conclusions. These are subsumed within the experience of thinking, which in turn is tantamount to problem solving. A good athlete is a good problem solver, for each stolen base, attempted forward pass, and tennis serve represents a problem that requires resolution.

Although transpiring mentally, thinking may be inferred from overt behavior. When we observe athletes perform, we develop an idea of how they may be solving problems, or at least what the solutions seem to be.

Cognition is undeniably vital to sport skill acquisition and performance. And in order to enhance sport skill acquisition, athletes are today encouraged to employ cognitive techniques such as imagery, mental practice, and cognitive restructuring. Underlying the application of these techniques is the assumption that patterns of cognition (individual style) influence the emotional consequences of that cognition. In other words, cognitive activity bears importantly upon the feelings of athletes and the ways in which they perform. But cognitive activity is assessable and alterable. It is not necessarily alterable because of its assessability, but it is nonetheless alterable. Cognitive therapists such as Beck (1976) and Ellis (1962) have demonstrated this. The implications for sport psychology are, to say the least, substantial. Bandura's programmatic inquiry into the relation between self-efficacy and actual behavior also demonstrates this (Bandura, 1980; Bandura, Adams, Hardy, & Howells, 1980; Bandura, 1981a, 1981b).

Evidence from the epistemological literature indicates that the content of cognitive engagement occurs in keeping with an individual's style: The ways in which different persons interpret the same stimulus thus varies according to their perceptual-cognitive strengths and proclivities. Although the direction and intensity in which cognition proceeds is predicated upon personal variables, it is also likely to be responsive to situational influences. But endowment also accounts for the ways in which persons sense and perceive input stimuli, learn, and think. All of these activities, of course, affect sport behavior.

It is the purpose of this chapter to describe individual variations in cognitive and perceptual styles and to delineate a number of associated training methods that relate to the acquisition and performance of sport skills. Although intervention strategies employed in sport psychology that result in behavioral change need not necessarily involve elaborate cognitive mechanisms, those that are based upon a stimulus-response model do not fall within this category and will not be included here.

The author expresses gratitude to his graduate students Gregg Steinberg and Mark Clementi for their assistance in gathering library materials necessary for the preparation of this chapter.

The first part of this chapter addresses four cognitive styles, the second part, three perceptual styles:

Cognitive Styles	Perceptual Styles
1. Field Dependence-Independence	1. Sensation Seeking
2. Association-Dissociation	2. Extroversion-Introversion
3. Imagery Ability	3. Self-Concept and Body Image
4. Learned Helplessness	

INDIVIDUAL STYLE IN SPORT

Conformity to predetermined biomechanical models is encouraged in many sport contexts. For optimal results the golf and baseball swings should not only be executed in accordance with recognized principles of physics, but also in conformity with the athlete's structural and neuromuscular capabilities. Idiosyncratic movement is acceptable, but its degree varies with factors such as the complexity and grossness of the skill and specific task assignment. For instance, considerable variation exists in the biomechanical form of distance runners. They do not all run alike. An approaching runner may often be easily identified by virtue of his or her running mechanics. Physical or mechanical style is observable and recognizable. Free-throw shooting in basketball represents an individual's mechanical style. Elite players vary in the ways they prepare for and execute their foul shots. Not all pitchers deliver their fastballs in the same way. On the other hand, some sports demand a high degree of adherence to carefully prescribed biomechanical models for performance of inherent skills. Figure skating, gymnastics, and diving do not countenance anything but the most minute departures from well-established paradigms of body-part alignment and movement in narrowly delineated spaces.

Motor skill execution may be modified by training. Increased efficiency, accuracy, and power are a function of enhanced proficiency which accompanies high levels of learning. Errors are reduced as learning increases. Increases in learning accrue from experiences such as trial-by-trial repetitions of a skill and knowledge of results. The coach or teacher strategizes, constructs, and implements the content of such learning experience.

Variability in the cognitive styles of athletes may not be as observable or palpable as that of biomechanical style, but to be sure, it exists. However, it must be determined through psychometric, quantitative, or qualitative procedures. One who observes a runner, foul-shooter, golfer, or diver cannot typically comment with anything more than minimal confidence upon the cognitive style of the performer. "I wish I could know what is going on in his mind," is a common coach's lament in response to an athlete's error-laden performance. Cognitive style is variable and individual.

We now turn to discussion of some examples of different cognitive styles, beginning with field-dependence/independence.

FIELD-DEPENDENCE/INDEPENDENCE

Visual perceptual-cognitive mode is usually a vital factor in sport behavior, where vision itself is probably the most important of all senses. Unless operating within an environment wherein all others are visually disabled, the visually impaired individual participates in sport at substantial disadvantage. Therefore individual visual perceptual-cognitive tendencies are of interest to the sport psychologist. Of special concern is differentiation theory, which addresses ways in which the organism's function is influenced by its understanding of the relationship of physical self to environmental structure. Moreover, such differentiation is manifest in constant or cross-situational behavior. Thus perceptual-cognitive style influences a sizable amount of psychological function.

Although studied often and in considerable depth by others, cognitive style was given a new and creative perspective by Witkin (1973). His designation of two perceptual-cognitive tendencies known as field-dependence and field-independence were subsequently subsumed under the more general heading of psychological differentiation. Witkin viewed them as pervasive psychological differentiation modes that were predicated upon the degree to which an organism uses internal frames of reference as guides for behavior. By this is meant that persons with field-dependent perceptual-cognitive styles tend to rely more on external referents (other persons) than field-independent persons. This field-dependence/independence designation is certainly among the most widely discussed of all cognitive styles.

Assessment Procedures

Witkin employed a number of measurement approaches in order to ascertain degree of field-dependence/independence. Those who studied with him or followed in his footsteps have frequently used assessment approaches: the *Rod-and-Frame Test* (*RFT*) and the *Embedded Figures Test* (*EFT*).

Rod-and-Frame Test (RFT). The RFT requires the subject to be seated in a totally darkened room. Before him or her is a movable luminous square frame containing a luminous slanted rod. The inherent task is to bring the slanted rod within the frame to a vertical position. Some subjects (field-independent) are able to do this despite the slant of the frame. Others can only correctly accomplish the task when the frame is righted (field-dependent).

Embedded Figures Test (EFT). In this test, simple figures must be disembedded from a larger, complex figure. The smaller figure, so to speak, hides within the complex one.

Field-independent persons easily recognize the simple figure. Field-dependent subjects either fail or require a very long period of time to complete the task.

Influence of Field-Dependence/Independence on Social Behavior

Dependence upon internal or external referents for perception of the upright (rod-and-frame test) are also expressed in social behavior.

Those with field-independent styles are more autonomous with reference to the social environment than field-independent persons (Witkin & Goodenough, 1977). They tend to structure circumstances on their own. Those with stronger field-dependent proclivities are more inclined to utilize other persons or external sources as behavioral guides since there is less information available to them from internal sources. This need is heightened when the context in which decision-making occurs is not clearly defined.

Scores on tests that measure degree of field-dependence/independence are continuously distributed, and as such, it is best to consider degrees of tendency, or strength on internal or external dependence. As Witkin suggests, "Certainly, we are not dealing with two distinct categories of people" (1977, p. 17).

It seems that situational ambiguity fosters fuller reliance on others in those with field-dependent proclivities. When a social challenge or situation is structured and unambiguous, field-dependent and field-independent persons demonstrate little or no difference in regard to reliance upon social references. Therefore, the clarity of social structure or its ambiguity is a determinant of the extent to which field-dependent and independent persons integrate views and information deriving from others. Further, with regard to social behavior, field-dependent individuals pay greater attention to, and are more sensitive to, social cues. They tend to seek greater physical and emotional closeness in comparison to field-independent individuals. Field-dependent persons need cues, and they deal with others with more caring and compassion. Thus they require and enjoy more interpersonal relations. The implication here is that athletes with strong dependent tendencies may contribute more to team cohesion (Witkin & Goodenough, 1977).

Another observation of note is that when differences do prevail, they relate only to information-seeking from others. That is, differences have not been observed in other behaviors in social settings such as "... attention seeking, response to extrinsic reinforcement, approval seeking emotional attachment" (Witkin, 1977, p. 19). It is precisely this emphasis upon information-seeking that accounts for the cognitive basis of field-dependence/independence.

Of special interest to the sport psychology scientist is the contrast in tendency to utilize the body to make decisions and to provide structure for ambiguous situations. Field-independence is associated with reliance upon internally derived sources of information for purposes of establishing the upright.

Restructuring the Field

In cognitive terms, "field" refers to the environment. Organizing, reorganizing, or disembedding (e.g., locating a simple figure within a larger geometric figure designed to hide it) the field is a common perceptual challenge for the athlete. Cognitive structuring or making changes in the field based upon incomplete information is a necessity in sport. Examples are anticipating end point locations of athletes on the football field and predicting the slope of a curveball's trajectory when batting in baseball. Passing to a spot in basketball in anticipation of a teammate being there within a second or two is another example. An athlete is frequently engaged in hypothesis formation and testing with regard not only to locomotor problems and animate or inanimate movement in space, but also concepts and ideas. The field-independent athlete is more likely to extrapolate from existing information in predictive attempts, whereas the field-dependent athlete's inclination is to attempt problem resolution by use of only absolute or presently available information. Therefore, for want of a better term, a form of conceptual flexibility may also differentiate dependent from independent athletes. However, field-dependence does not exist in meaningful relationship with a full compliment of cognitive characteristics, but only with those that are emphatically restructural in nature. Generally, field-independent persons are more able in cognitive restructuring tasks than field-dependent persons (Witkin & Goodenough, 1976).

It is important to consider that field-dependence/independence does not necessarily predict athletic success or lack of success. These qualities merely clarify the cognitive approaches taken by persons (athletes) to resolve problems in structural organization. Thus the pathway or process to goal achievement is perhaps explained through cognitive style (field-dependence/independence) rather than goal achievement per se. The appropriateness or correctness of the cognitive style is, of course, task or context specific. Thus cognitive style is believed to be interactive with contextual challenge, despite its enduring properties. Therefore, neither independence nor dependence is generally good or bad. Individuals, however, may gravitate to situations, areas in life, and even sports in keeping with their cognitive styles (Pargman, Schreiber, & Stein, 1974).

Cognitive style demonstrates stability over time and across domains (Witkin, 1977) although specific training interventions have been shown to influence field-dependence. It is best to conclude that although cognitive style is not intractable, it is indeed staunch.

Development of Field-Independence/Dependence

Psychological differentiation (the level at which a person is able to separate the self from the surrounding field) is a developmental concept. Witkin (1962) reported that no further changes in this ability occur between 17 and 24 years of age. Prior to age 17, increases of field-independence occur progressively from a more global or field-dependent mode of perceiving to a more articulated or field-independent mode of perceiving.

Cognitive style might be a function of cortical control, more specifically, of the left and right hemispheres. However, this relationship still exists in hypothesis form only (Goodenough, 1986). Evidence also exists that abilities such as the perceptual-cognitive, visuo-spatial abilities underlying field-dependence/independence may be regulated by genetic factors (Goodenough, et al., 1977) which may underlie the hemispheric lateralization hypothesis.

Another speculation is that cognitive style might be due to a visual driving of the vestibular system (Bischof, 1974). That is, movements of the visual field interact with or stimulate the vestibular system (Dichganus & Brandt, 1974). An additional developmental perspective has emerged from cross-cultural investigation of the field-dependent/independent mode of function.

The Eskimo hunters of the Arctic and the aboriginal hunters of the Australian desert have been observed to be among the most field-independent subjects ever studied. Both of these peoples tend to be more field-independent than samples of subjects who arc farmers. The implication here is that cognitive style of a cultural group may be a function of its economic-cultural environment.

In this view, the cognitive disembedding skills associated with a field-independent cognitive style are more adaptive for the hunter, who is often required to extract information from the surrounding environmental context to locate game and to return home from the hunt. In contrast, the more sedentary existence of the farmer may require less disembedding skill. But the larger and more complexly organized social groups in which the farmer lives, place greater demands on social-interpersonal skill. (Goodenough, 1986, p. 12).

Personality and Field-Dependence/Independence

Personality is related to manner of perceiving the upright in space and is manifest through perception (Witkin et al., 1972). As a personality dimension, field-dependence was viewed by Witkin as an expression of degree of differentiation of the self. Thus field-dependence/independence is a process variable and, in turn, not particularly focused upon goal attainment.

Gender Differences

Sex differences in field-dependence/independence are not as common in non-Western environments as in Western settings. This is likely to be due to the relatively undifferentiated social demands levied on boys and girls in the so-called nomadic non-Western societies characterized by migration. Sedentary groups tend to have within them greater role diversity.

According to Witkin (1973), other psychological entities such as body concept, nature of the self, and controls and defenses used in everyday life correlate well with scores on tests of field-dependence/independence. And the relationship between personality and perceptual abilities has been suggested by the work of Eysenck (1947), Lindauer and Pekauf (1971), Fine (1972), and Collins and Newman (1974).

Field-Dependence/Independence in Athlete Subjects

Although the published literature dealing with field-dependence/independence contain in excess of 3,000 studies, the number concerned predominantly with sport or exercise related variables is quite small. Only about 30 published studies of variable methodological soundness and value are available. Yet the applicability of Witkin's theoretical framework to sport and exercise behavior seems clear and valuable. A number of relevant questions deserve attention, although certainly not dissimilar from queries about variables associated with other psychological constructs:

1. Is field-dependence/independence predictive of sport choice, or the type of sport a person chooses to enter?
2. Do differences in field-dependence/field-independence exist among athletes playing certain positions within the same sport?
3. Can highly skilled athletes be distinguished from athletes of lower skill levels by their field-dependence/field-independence tendencies? Do visuoperceptual differences exist between male and female athletes?
4. Since the essence of field-dependence/field-independence is psychological differentiation, might it be somehow related to physical injury in sport?

Accordingly, hypotheses related to these research questions have been tested in a number of studies. An overview of this small body of literature follows. More work will undoubtedly continue to be conducted and published in the future.

Sport Choice and Level of Performance

Some of the early work in field-dependence sought to differentiate among athletes in various sports according to visual disembedding tendencies. Pargman, Schreiber, and Stein (1974) investigated sport affiliation of 115 male collegiate athletes. Comparisons were made between team and individual sport athletes using the Group Hidden Figures Test (GHFT). Subgroup comparisons were also conducted (baseball, football, hockey, gymnastics, track, swimming, and wrestling). The hypothesis that team sport athletes would be more field-dependent than individual sport athletes was sustained; however, football accounted for most of the difference. Bard (1972) also observed that field-dependent subjects (college female physical educators) performed better in team sport skills and field-independent subjects in individual sport skills.

Bard's (1972) findings somewhat clarify those of Pargman, Schreiber, and Stein (1974) in that they suggest that skill differences may be due to greater frequency of participation. However, the meaningfulness of the Pargman, Schreiber, and Stein (1974) findings is moderate. The significant ANOVA obtained seems to be a result of a difference in scores between the football group and individual sport subgroups with the exception of the hockey group. If the football group were removed from the analysis, no difference in mean GHFT would have been observed.

Krieger (1962) found visual disembedding to be a predictor of tennis-playing ability. And visual disembedding has been found to be among six variables accounting for approximately 65% of the shared variance for predicted football playing ability in college athletes (Pargman, 1976). Nonetheless field-dependence may play a role in sport participation, and further inquiry into this area should be conducted.

On the other hand, Deshaies and Pargman (1976) found no differences between varsity and junior varsity football players in a variety of visual abilities including disembedding, thus suggesting that comparatively more successful players are not characterized by greater visual perceptual attributes. Nor was there any significant relationship between visual disembedding and batting in baseball (Pargman, 1974) and shooting accuracy in basketball (Pargman, Bender, & Deshaies, 1975). Similarly, Williams (1975) found no difference in visual disembedding between classified (higher-level) and unclassified (lower-level) fencers.

It seems that differences in field-dependence may characterize athletes in different sports if the sports are categorized according to the openness or closeness of the preponderance of inherent skills. Swimming and gymnastics (notably closed) were observed to accommodate athletes of greater field-independence than basketball, volleyball, and soccer (preponderance of open skills), wherein participants were more field-dependent (McLeod, 1985). These findings, although predicated upon data collected with the rod-and-frame apparatus, appear to be compatible with those of Pargman, Schreiber, and Stein (1974), whose hypothesis predicted differences in psychological differentiation between team sports in contrast to individual sports. Only collegiate athletes were used as subjects in the Pargman, Schreiber, and Stein study, whereas thirteen 22-year-old athletes were employed in McLeod's study. There is some evidence in support of age-related developmental influence upon visual perceptual cognitive style. Talbot, Godin, Drouin, and Goulet (1984) observed older children (ice hockey players, ages 7 years and 9 months) to be more field-dependent than younger ones (9 years and 6 months).

An interesting line of inquiry was pursued by Pargman and Inomata (1976), who compared the effect of displaced vision (goggles with prisms) upon a motor performance task in field-dependent and field-independent female athletes. In effect, their study examined the relationships among personality, perception, and motor performance. Although a difference was observed between field-dependent and field-independent athletes on a tennis ball-to-target throwing task under two normal vision conditions, during the displaced-vision condition field-independent subjects performed the criterion task with significantly greater accuracy. This finding suggests that the field-dependent subjects relied more heavily upon visual feedback information in order to adapt to the visual distortion and solve the requirements of the task.

Injury

Visual perceptual characteristics may underlie physical trauma in sport. This may be due to discrimination among complex visual stimuli often being critical to discussions about volitional motor behavior (i.e., where and when to run, jump, make body contact with others, etc.) Mean disembedding scores (Group Hidden Figures Test) were compared in groups of "injured, disabled, and noninjured" college football players (Pargman, 1976). Higher scores were associated with the uninjured. "Not disabled" had the next highest, and disabled had the lowest scores. Thus the higher mean disembedding in a static visual field may relate to physical injury in football. Individuals who can extract meaningful cues from their environmental visual field may be less likely to experience injury.

In contrast to this finding are results reported by Pargman, Sachs, and Deshaies (1976). Using the rod-and-frame apparatus they measured the field-dependence/independence of 31 uninjured, 20 injured but not disabled, and 11 disabled (absence from at least 2 consecutive days of practice or competition immediately following injury) football athletes. No significant differences were observed. Data in this study may be suggestive of a low concordance between visual disembedding tested on paper-and-pencil instruments and rod-and-frame performance. Others have also cast doubt on this relationship (Arbuthnot, 1972; Bergman & Engelbrektson, 1973; Raviv & Nabel, 1990). Visual disembedding and field-dependence/independence may share little common variance. Aligning the misplaced vertical rod into an upright position may not tap the same neurological or cognitive resources as may be involved in disembedding tasks, although it appears that some overlap may exist.

Tangentially related to the relationship between sport injury and field dependence are results reported by Morgan and Horstman (1978). They examined the perception of pain in relation to selected psychological states (depression and vigor) and traits (extroversion, anxiety and visual disembedding, which they refer to as a measure of field-dependence/independence). Psychological traits and states accounted for the variance observed in the significant multiple regressions. Since pain is often a concomitant of sport injury, it is included in this discussion. Evidently visual disembedding ability is among those variables that accounts for what Morgan and Horstman refer to as the psychophysical judgment of pain (during a 2-minute exposure to a 3,000-gram force on the periosteum of the second digit of the left forefinger).

An interesting line of inquiry was pursued by Pargman and Ward (1976), who hypothesized a relationship between psychological differentiation and sport skill performance style. In their study, the volleyball service, as performed by 12 female collegiate varsity volleyball athletes, was fragmented through cinematographic techniques into 16 biomechanical variables. These variables were correlated with score on the Group Hidden Figures Test. Results showed a significant relationship between motor performance variables and perceptual cognitive style. Unfortunately, replication of Pargman and Ward's study has not been attempted, nor have additional research efforts been made along these lines. However, their preliminary findings are suggestive of individual sport related biomechanical style being related to visuo-perceptual disembedding.

The question of psychological differentiation (disembedding ability or field-dependence/independence) serving to distinguish between athlete participants of relatively high and low skill levels or between athletes and nonathletes is also of interest. Such distinctions might facilitate identification of successful team applicants or recruits. Indeed, this issue has been addressed; however, findings are equivocal and conclusions are of doubtful meaning. For example, highly skilled tennis players were observed to be significantly more field-dependent than top-class track-and-field athletes and medium-ability tennis players (Barrell & Trippe, 1975). Super-senior tournament tennis players (age 70 years and older) were found to be more field-dependent (rod-and-frame apparatus) than a similarly aged heterogeneral group (Rotella & Bunker, 1978).

On the other hand, Lindquist (1978) found no significant relationship between score on an embedded figures test and figures among ranking in 225 male and female collegiate tennis players. Williams (1975) also observed no difference in scores on a hidden figures test between fencers of comparatively high and low ability, and Raviv and Nabel (1978) reported greater field-dependence in elite male amateur basketball players (Embedded Figures Test) than in lower-status players. But fencers of both ability levels in the Williams study were observed to have better disembedding scores than a normative sample.

However, when the rod-and-frame test was used in a subsequent study (Williams, 1980), skilled fencers were more field-independent than less-skilled fencers. Results from these two studies (Williams, 1975, 1980) are supportive of the low concordance between visual disembedding as assessed by a pencil-and-paper test and rod-and-frame performance, as discussed previously (Arbuthnot, 1972; Bergman & Engelbrektson, 1973; Pargman, 1976; Pargman, Sacks, & Deshaies, 1976). Also, field-dependence/ independence was found to be related to the rate at which a novel motor task was learned. Field-independent subjects learned the task better than field-dependent subjects for the rod-and-frame test (Swinner, 1984) and the Group Embedded Figures Test (MaGillivary, 1980).

Field-Dependence/Independence: Gender Differences in Sport

Female athletes were more field-independent than males (Pargman, 1977) as shown with an embedded figures test, but less field-dependent than male athletes when tested on the rod-and-frame apparatus (McLeod, 1987). The observations of Drouin, Talbot, and Goulet (1986) add to the confusion. They reported no differences by age, gender, level of competition, or sports. However, subjects in the Drouin, Talbot, and Goulet study were French-Canadian university students, in contrast to the American university students studied by Pargman (1977), and Pargman, Schreiber, and Stein (1974). Skill level and the intensity and meaningfulness of the collegiate athletic experience in these two countries vary and could conceivably account for variations in findings. Be that as it may, conclusions about gender differences in athletes seem equivocal, although a considerable amount of reported results has established that females in general (in contemporary Western society) demonstrate greater field-dependence than males (Loader, Edwards, & Henschen, 1982; Swinnen, 1984; Witkin, Goodenough, & Karp, 1967).

The level at which athletes are able to separate the self from the surrounding field may bear upon a number of sport-related variables. Among these are vulnerability to injury, attainment of competitive success, quality of task-specific skill performance, and sport selection itself. A voluminous body of literature focused on psychological differentiation has yielded a variety of general conclusions relative to variables such as gender, age, and vocational/ occupational differences. However, sport and exercise variables have to date been investigated very infrequently. This accounts for the relative "old age" of many of the references cited here. Moreover, some of the studies using athlete subjects have generated findings that are inconsistent with those describing nonathlete populations. It may be that athletes are distinctive, in one way or another, in their modes of disembedding or attempting to solve vertical rod alignment problems. In addition, the examination of hypotheses pertaining to psychological differentiation in which nonvisual sensory systems such as auditory and factual systems, may provide valuable insights into sport-related behavior.

ASSOCIATION/DISSOCIATION

An athlete's preferred or dominant mode of attending to stimuli is his or her *attentional style*. The way in which athletes pay attention, or the extent to which they attend to an infinite number of internal and external physical and psychological stimuli from myriads of social and environmental sources, heavily influences both cognitive and motor responses. The objects of attentional focus and their perceived importance are contingent upon past experiences, needs, and interests. These factors determine which stimuli attract the performer's attention. But the athlete's attentional style appears to be a determinant of the direction, intensity, and perhaps longevity of the focus. In the sport world, the term *concentration* is frequently used in reference to this phenomenon. And it is undoubtedly the exceptional coach who would deny its criticalness in sport skill acquisition and execution. Concentration may also be defined as focusing, but not forcing, attention upon an immediate task. Concentration is an acquired skill that emphasizes not reacting to or not being distracted by irrelevant internal or external stimuli (Schmid & Peper, 1986).

Nideffer's development and application of the concept of attentional style to sport (Nideffer, 1976, 1978, 1981, 1986) is presented in Chapter 24 of this volume. In this chapter, consideration will be given to but one element of attention, not stylistic in the sense of the operational definition of the term style previously offered in this chapter, but involving, nonetheless, an important component, namely *association,* or the tendency to adopt an internal focus of attention (i.e., maintaining awareness of performance factors).

With few exceptions, investigation of association (in contrast to dissociation) within the realm of sport has been limited to subjects who are distance runners, although reference has also been made to long distance swimmers and cyclists (Morgan & Pollock, 1977). In one study, marathon runners were found to be inclined toward dissociation or blocking out sensory feedback (Masters & Lambert, 1989). However, in their earlier study, Morgan and Pollock (1977) identified both association and dissociation among marathon runners. The former focused mostly on the race and on their bodies, but the latter activated various mental strategies to disengage cognitively from the race and the discomfort it typically generated. They paid close attention to sensations in their feet and legs as well as their respiration. Their cognitions were all marathon-related. Elite marathoners, in the Morgan and Pollock study, were associaters. Marathoners of lower than elite status (world class) attempted to dissociate sensory input. Thus the runner is able to ". . . negotiate temporary pain zones and distract from the monotony of the running process. . . ." (Schower, 1986, p. 42).

Morgan and Pollock operationally defined elite marathoners as those who completed the race in times less than 2 hours and 15 minutes, trained 7 days per week, and averaged 100.7 miles per week. Cognitive activity in the dissociators involved images of past events. Morgan and Pollock (1977) referred to anthropological reports of Tibetan monks (Watson, 1973) who allegedly employ dissociative techniques during very long (300-mile) runs over difficult terrain.

While running the monk repeated to himself a secret or sacred phrase (mantra). His reputation was kept in rhythm with the phrase, and his locomotion was put in synchrony with both his reputation and the phrase. The runner fixed his eyes on a distant object, and did not look from side to side, nor did he speak. (p. 111)

An effective analogy between the distance runner and a household furnace has been drawn by Morgan and Pollock (1977) in order to clarify the nature of the two divergent cognitive strategies, association and dissociation. They propose that runners who dissociate represent a faulty furnace thermostat (which they refer to as a *perceptostat*) that regulates all sensory systems. According to this model, dissociation causes the perceptostat to be turned off and remain off until some additional and powerful stimulus causes it to "kick-in" again. Thus the dissociating runner (in whom the thermostat is turned off) proceeds in the face of pain, injury, and the prospect of serious systemic trauma—typically of the skeletal or neuromuscular systems. Whereas switching the perceptostat to an "off" position may enable an athlete to continuing exerting intense competitive effort, this strategy may be responsible for serious injury.

Perhaps the most current and comprehensive attempt to examine association and dissociation strategies in athletes has been made by Houseworth (1990). Impressive is his sample size (99 runners during a 10-mile road race) and his categorization of subjects into three groups: competitive, moderately competitive, and recreational runners. Through a survey instrument developed specifically for this study and administered immediately after the race, Houseworth queried runners as to their association-dissociation experiences. No differences in any of the attentional variables studied were observed among subjects in the three categories. However, all classes of runners used different attentional strategies during different stages of the race according to changing situational demands. During early stages of the run, when perceptions of fatigue and perhaps pain were weak or nonexistent, cognitive strategies were reported to be inconsistent with those called on during the middle or end of the race, at which times emphasis was placed on goals such as passing other competitors or "hanging-in" and finishing. Somewhat similar findings were reported by Silva and Applebaum (1989); however, only two different stages of a marathon race were used in order to determine employed cognitive strategies.

Findings revealed that top finishers used both associative and dissociative techniques. In contrast, lower finishers initiated dissociative strategies earlier in the race and tended to maintain them. It should be noted however, that subjects in the Silva and Appelbaum study were U.S. Olympic marathon trial contestants ($N = 12$) in contrast to the competitive and recreational runners employed as subjects in Houseworth's study.

A very creative approach was shown by Schomer (1987) in order to determine the effect of a mental strategy training program upon physical conditioning and thinking during running endurance training. Subjects, all of whom were marathon runners, used two-way radios that permitted them to communicate with coaches during training runs over a five-week period. Taped transcriptions of the sessions were analyzed for content in order to assess the nature and degree of associative/dissociative thinking and attentional foci. Results revealed an increased proportion of associative thinking in accordance with perceived training effort. The implications here are that cognitive or coping strategies during the distance run vary in accordance with its topographical and longitudinal characteristics, as well as the intensity of perceptions of internal stimuli.

Schomer's (1986) assertion that "Nowhere before has the continuous thought-flow of runners been documented" (p. 43) is correct. His on-the-spot documentation of athletes' cognitions "in the field" is noteworthy. Also of note is his concluding sentence: "Association, when practiced at high effort intensities, is to procure an injury-free and efficient running process" (Schomer, 1986, p. 56).

LEARNED HELPLESSNESS

The primary focus of this section is *cognitive style.* Accordingly, the terms *cognition* and *style* have been clarified, and a number of styles, as well as their relation to sport behavior, addressed. The learned helplessness model as promulgated by Abramson, Seligman, and Teasdale (1978) is actually a theoretical approach to understanding motivation for behavior. However, a considerable amount of related research has demonstrated that in humans it may also be responsible for cognitive as well as emotional deficits. For this reason it is included here and its relevance to sport behavior discussed.

Essentially, learned helplessness occurs when an individual concludes that his or her responses to stimuli are independent of behavioral outcomes and generalizes this understanding to situations in which control is, in fact, possible (Seligman, 1975). In other words, when one believes that his or her behavior will not influence any situational outcome, helplessness ensues. Such tendencies may result in reduced motivation (Dweck & Repucci, 1975), learning deficiencies (Hiroto, 1974), passivity, and depression (Seligman, 1972).

Abramson, Seligman, and Teasdale (1978) constructed a model for learned helplessness based upon an attributional framework. Referred to as the Reformulation Model of Learned Helplessness, it asserts that upon finding themselves helpless, individuals ask, "Why?" and thereby make causal attributions about helplessness. In turn, these attributions influence the generality, chronicity, and type of learned helplessness deficits (Abramson, Seligman, & Teasedale, 1978). For example, if a child explains a noncontingent event (a failure in math class) to his level of skill (an internal and stable cause), learned helpless deficits will be maximized. That is, the child is likely to be weakly motivated to acquire additional skills in another math class. On the other hand, if the child attributes failure in math to effort (an internal, but unstable cause), learned helplessness deficits would be minimal.

Peterson and Seligman (1984) have proposed that individuals possess differing, yet habitual ways for explaining noncontingent events such as failures. This individual difference is called *explanatory style* and can be measured with the Attributional Style Questionnaire (Peterson et al.,

1982). Some people habitually explain failure experiences with internal, stable, and global causes. These individuals possess a "pessimistic" explanatory style and are more likely to display chronic and generalized learned helplessness deficits when confronted with a bad event (Peterson & Seligman, 1984). In comparison, some individuals explain failure with external, unstable, and specific causes. These individuals possess an "optimistic" explanatory style and are less likely to display learned helplessness deficits when confronted with failure (Peterson & Seligman, 1984). Differences in explanatory style have been shown to create both cognitive and behavioral differences in a variety of areas, ranging from health and reported illness (Suls & Miller, 1981), to academic achievement (Peterson & Barrett, 1987), and to work performance (Seligman & Schulman, 1986).

It seems logical that people who provide stable, global, and internal explanations for failures will be less likely to overcome important obstacles to reach a desired goal. This, in turn, will inhibit the attainment of an individual's full potential. On the other hand, those who make unstable, specific, and external explanations for failures should be more likely to reach their full potential. Individuals also have a habitual way of explaining uncontrollable events such as failure experience. This explanatory style influences both behavior and cognitions for future events. In sport, where even the most skilled athletes on occasion encounter failure, tendencies toward helplessness may interact in negative ways with performances that follow failure. Performers who tend to explain failure in a "pessimistic" way are less likely to achieve optimally.

Although it appears to carry implications for learning, performing, and responding cognitively in the sport domain, to date explanatory style has been examined in only a very few studies. These will be discussed in a very brief section that follows. However, a few published studies that investigate learned helplessness in the academic setting merit consideration here in that the variable of academic achievement, particularly in secondary school and at college and university levels, frequently receives attention when interscholastic and intercollegiate sport competition are scrutinized (Adler & Adler, 1987; Eitzen, 1987; Lueptow & Kayser, 1973; Meyer, 1990; Sack, 1987). The academic successes and failures of athletes are perceived by coaches and school administrators as being of great importance. Without satisfying established standards in this area, eligibility to participate is denied. Therefore, explanatory style and its relation to academic achievement deserves attention.

Learned Helplessness in the Academic Setting

Peterson and Barrett (1987) demonstrated that learned helplessness plays a role in determining academic performance among university students. In their experiment, students were given the *Academic Attributional Style Questionnaire,* which was patterned after the *Attributional Style Questionnaire* (ASQ; Peterson et al., 1982), except that it presented the subjects with bad academic events. The study showed that students who explained bad academic events with internal, stable, and global causes received lower grades than students who used external, unstable, and specific explanations for bad academic events. Furthermore, this pattern held up even when their scores on the *Scholastic Aptitude Test* were held constant. This comparison implies that intelligence does not influence explanatory style among students. In addition, students with a pessimistic explanatory style possessed less academic goals and did not seek academic counseling as much as the students who had an optimistic explanatory style. The authors concluded that students who explain bad academic events with internal, stable, and global causes have a greater tendency to feel that their efforts will be futile in changing their academic standing.

Results from Kamen and Seligman's study (cited in Trotter, 1987) revealed that students' explanatory style was a good predictor of academic performance. Students who explained academic failure with unstable, specific, and external causes received better grades than was predicted by their scores on the Scholastic Aptitude Test or their previous grade-point average. The authors concluded that an optimistic explanatory style helps students overcome many academic obstacles which allows them to rise above their predicted potential.

Learned Helplessness in the Athletic Setting

To date, there have been only a few reported studies concerning learned helplessness in the sport setting. One such study conducted by Seligman, Nolen-Hoeksema, Norton, and Norton (1988) investigated the relationship between explanatory style and athletic achievement in swimming. The purpose of this study was twofold: first, to determine if explanatory style is a better predictor of swimming performance than the coach's prediction. A second purpose was to determine if an explanatory style can predict athletic achievement after a defeat.

The first part of this study demonstrated that explanatory style significantly predicted the number of disappointing swims better than the coach's judgment. At the beginning of the season, the coaches rated (from a scale of one to seven) how they thought each swimmer would do after a defeat. Each swimmer also rated his or her performance using the same scale. Results showed that the athletes with a pessimistic explanatory style had a significantly higher number of poor swims than the athletes with an optimistic explanatory style. The coach's judgment did not significantly predict the number of poor swims, but it was in the right direction. Furthermore, the coach's judgment and explanatory style did not correlate. The authors concluded that the coach's prediction of a swimmer's ability and the swimmer's explanatory style are independent of one another.

Another interesting point of this study should be noted. There were significantly more optimistic men swimmers than optimistic women swimmers. The authors suggested that there is more pessimism in women than men even when both sexes have obtained equal status and equally high achievement.

The second part of the study sought to determine how an athlete's explanatory style influences athletic achievement after a negative experience. First, each swimmer was asked by the coach to swim all out in his or her best event and at the end of the swim each was given feedback of a systematically slower time than actually swum. The times chosen were to produce a serious disappointment, but also be small enough to be undetectable. After a five-minute rest, each swimmer was asked to swim the same event.

Results indicated that the swimmers with an optimistic explanatory style swam at least as well after the failure experience as they did in their first swim. However, the swimmers with a pessimistic explanatory style swam significantly slower following the negative feedback. These results have some important implications. First, explanatory style does not seem to be an artifact of athletic talent. This was proved by the fact that a pessimistic explanatory style was equally prevalent in the high-level swimmers as well as in the low-level swimmers. Second, explanatory style can be a useful assessment tool for a coach's judgment about whom to play. This may play an even bigger role after the athlete suffers a defeat. Last, the results suggest that athletes with optimistic explanatory styles should perform better under pressure than athletes with pessimistic explanatory styles. The optimistic athlete should be able to handle the pressure of the many "mini-" failures experienced during a competition better than the pessimistic athlete.

Prapavessis and Carron (1988) also examined maladaptive achievement patterns in young elite tennis players. The purpose was to examine whether athletes have maladaptive patterns associated with learned helplessness and to determine if the presence of these patterns is related to gender and/or skill level.

To determine the achievement pattern, each athlete had to complete two types of questionnaires. In the first, each athlete was asked to recall a recently lost match and determine the causes for the failure from three main categories: *personal factors, match situational factors,* and *mental factors.* Using each factor as a reference point, the athlete determined the stability, globality, and locus of control for each factor. In the second questionnaire, questions involving the cognitive, motivational, and emotional aspects of the failure experience were assessed. Both questionnaires determined the athlete's achievement pattern.

The results of these questionnaires indicated a number of important findings. First, they showed that maladaptive achievement patterns associated with learned helplessness do exist in young elite athletes. Thus maladaptive achievement patterns can develop at early stages of an athletic career. Second, these patterns were as prevalent in the highly skilled players as they were in the lesser skilled athletes. These data are in support of the study done by Seligman et al. (1988) in that maladaptive achievement patterns are not an artifact of skill level. Last, maladaptive achievement patterns were as prevalent in female athletes as they were in male athletes. This conclusion, however, is in opposition to the findings of the study done by Seligman et al. (1988).

PERCEPTUAL STYLES

Differential approaches to integrating environmental stimuli, or the mode commonly employed by individuals to attach meaning to sensations, is considered to be their perceptual style. Whereas cognition involves comparatively higher order processes (e.g., reasoning) that are oriented toward problem solving, perception is more of an interpretive process. Past experiences, associations, and reinforced responses interact with neuroanatomical and structural characteristics to yield meanings attached to incoming stimuli.

With regard to perception, stylistic variations among athletes may very well become manifest in performance differences. In some sports at elite levels of skill, homogeneity is high with regard to variables such as running speed, muscular strength, and endurance, as well as skeletal size. Few quarterbacks in the National Football League are less than 6 feet, 2 inches (approximately 2 meters) in height and few weigh less than 215 pounds (approximately 97.5 kilograms). Similarly, all premier running backs typically complete the critical 40-yard sprint test in less than five seconds. Today, in the National Basketball Association, physical attributes are standardized to the extent that a so-called power forward is at least 6-feet-5 or 6-feet-6 inches tall. Analogous criteria are either implicitly or explicitly promulgated in other sports as well. At high levels of sport achievement, athletes are expected to conform to structural and physical performance criteria. But it may very well be perceptual attributes that actually distinguish between premier and almost premier performers, between champions and runners-up.

In this section we will examine selected perceptual styles chosen because of their pertinence to sport behavior: sensation seeking, extroversion/introversion, and self-concept/body image.

Sensation Seeking

Marvin Zuckerman (1979), whose scholarly efforts have resulted in the delineation of the personality dimension known as sensation-seeking, defines it as "the need for varied, novel, and complex sensations and experiences, and the willingness to take physical and social risks for the sake of experience" (p. 277). According to Zuckerman, high sensation seekers tend to desire activities that are exciting and are inclined to avoid stimuli with little potential for risk taking. High-risk stimuli are not restricted to physically dangerous activities such as skydiving, rock climbing, and white-water kayaking. Any setting perceived as potentially stimulating may be selected. Understandably, sport provides risk and varied opportunities to satisfy the needs of

high sensation seekers (Roland, Franken, & Harrison, 1986). Many situations in sport require behavior that is both emotionally and physically risky behavior not necessarily restricted to athlete participants. Coaches and officials also are obliged to make decisions in high-stimulus environments fraught with physical, emotional, and social risks.

In an early work, Zuckerman and colleagues (Zuckerman, Kilin, Price, & Zoob, 1964) asserted that a level of risk exists for each individual under which he or she prefers to function. They refer to this preference as the *optimal stimulation level.* They also reported a significant negative correlation between anxiety and optimal stimulation level. When functioning at stimulation levels that require uncomfortably high risks, individuals report high levels of anxiety. Those who function at optimal stimulation levels experience relatively low degrees of anxiety. In other words, the athlete with low optimal stimulation requirements who is involved in a high-risk environment or who selects a competitive strategy that is high in physical, emotional, or social risk pursues performance objectives at a deficit.

Obviously, each individual has a unique "ideal" level which falls somewhere on the continuum of all possible stimulation levels. These range from extremely low to extremely high levels of excitement. At the low end of the stimulation continuum, physiological arousal (heart rate, blood pressure, gastrointestinal activity) is very low. In extreme cases at the low end of the scale, there is little arousal, no anxiety, and little cognitive activity, a state many would call disinterest or boredom. At the extreme high end, the individual would, according to Zuckerman (1964), show signs of dangerously high levels of physiological arousal (rapid pulse, perspiration), rapid cognitions, and most likely a substantial amount of anxiety.

The concept of "optimal stimulation level" therefore implies that for each individual in a particular situation there is a condition—somewhere between total absence of arousal and maximum physical and psychological activation—that is appealing; where comfort prevails. The individual is stimulated but not "threatened," physically and emotionally. Accordingly we all require an individual amount of excitement with which we feel and function best. Therefore our interests, pursuits, and preferences are all functions of a personal quest for ideal stimulation conditions. These, in turn, are reflective of particular travel destinations, career and recreation choices, and types of foods and music. Individual decisions regarding sport strategy choice may also reflect the search for optimal stimulation conditions.

Differences in optimal stimulation level between various groups have also been reported. For example, males score significantly higher than females on the *Sensation-Seeking Scale* (Furnham, 1984). Sensation-seeking tendencies were shown to decline significantly with age across both gender populations, most significantly after the age of 40 (Ball, Farnill, & Wangeman, 1984).

Athletes have higher sensation-seeking needs and therefore presumably higher optimal arousal levels than nonathletes. This has been demonstrated across genders and among athletes from a cross-section of both individual and team sports (Gundersheim, 1987).

Assessment of Sensation-Seeking Tendencies: The Sensation-Seeking Scale (SSS)

In 1961, Zuckerman began to construct a questionnaire to measure the need for stimulation or optimal levels of stimulation and arousal in order to predict subject responses to sensory deprivation. Three years later, Zuckerman, Kolin, Price, and Zoob (1964) developed this scale designed to quantify the "Optimal Stimulus Level" construct, and called it Form 1 of the Sensation-Seeking Scale (SSS). Further developments have resulted in the most contemporary instrument known as Form V, which includes the following five scales:

- *The General Scale (GS)*—This factor includes items indicating global feelings concerning lifestyle tendencies.
- *The Thrill- and Adventure-Seeking Scale (TA)*—This scale consists of items which express a desire to participate in outdoor sports and other sports which involve the elements of speed and/or danger.
- *The Experience-Seeking Scale (ES)*—This is sometimes referred to as the "hippie" factor. This subscale's essence is experience for its own sake, and includes items indicating wanderlust, exhibitionism in dress and behavior, the use of marijuana and hallucinatory drugs, association with unusual or unconventional persons, a liking for modern "arousing" music, and the flaunting of "irrational" authority.
- *The Disinhibition Scale (DIS)*—This scale consists of items expressing the hedonistic "playboy philosophy"— heavy drinking, variety in sex partners, "wild parties," and gambling. It is often referred to as the "swinger" subscale.
- *The Boredom Susceptibility Scale (BS)*—This section contains items indicating a dislike of repetition of experience, routine work, predictable, dull, or boring people, and a preference for experiences that change.

The Sensation-Seeking Scale (SSS) is used to measure individual risk-taking tendencies. It has an internal consistency of .85 and a retest reliability of .94 (Zuckerman, 1979). Construct validity of the SSS is reported to be high (Zuckerman & Link, 1968). However, Zuckerman (1979) cautions that conclusive support has not yet been forthcoming. Criterion-related validity has been established through correlation with similar personality instruments (Eysenck & Zuckerman, 1978; Himelstein & Thorne, 1985).

Content validity of the SSS has also been established (Zuckerman, 1979). Form V comprises 40 items, requiring forced-choice responses. The SSS has been demonstrated to correlate with various personality measures, including the Eysenck Personality Questionnaire (Eysenck & Zuckerman, 1978). A significant correlation has also been shown with the SSS and a biographical inventory for mea-

suring risk-taking tendencies (Himelstein & Thorne, 1985). Both male and female populations are fit by the four dimensions within the SSS: Thrill and Adventure, Experience, Disinhibition, and Boredom (Rowland & Franklin, 1986).

Risk

The perception and acceptance of risk is inherently subjective, and these subjective judgments are influenced by cognitive and motivational factors (Jungermann, 1982). Also, individuals tend to be consistent in their interpretations of perceived risk.

A critical variable associated with the perception of risk is the perceived benefit of the risk choice. In most real world situations—gambling casino or basketball court—a high-risk strategy is typically accompanied by a high benefit or "payoff." The gambler who takes a high-risk gamble can expect a large return for his or her money if he or she is successful. Lower-risk gambles do not return as large a profit. Similarly, in basketball, the high-risk strategy of shooting from behind the three-point line is rewarded with three points instead of the usual two, if successful. The benefit is quantifiable and unambiguous in these two examples. However, the perception of the *value* of these benefits remains moot. The low sensation seeker on the basketball court may not consider it worth the high emotional and social risks to attempt a three-point shot. He or she perceives the extra point as a nominal benefit when compared to the risk factor of shooting from a great distance. In this manner the perception of both risk and potential benefit are uniquely individual and subjective.

The sensation-seeking construct adds another motivating factor to this decision-making process. An additional potential benefit of a high-risk choice may be its inherent stimulating quality. To the high sensation seeker, the arousal gained through the use of a high-risk strategy may be benefit enough to make it the choice of preference. Conversely, the low sensation seeker may find that the arousing, and therefore threatening, quality inherent in the risky strategy outweighs any potential quantitative benefit. In this manner, the individual, consciously or unconsciously, weighs the potential benefits and risks of any given strategy choice and makes a decision consistent with his or her subjective interpretations.

The relationship between high sensation-seeking tendencies and preference for high-risk strategies has been demonstrated in both gambling and sport contexts. Across a series of five gambling choices, with monetary reward increasing according to the level of risk, high sensation seekers demonstrated a significant preference for high-risk gambles. Low sensation seekers exhibited a significant preference for low-risk gambles (Kozlowski, 1977). In Kozlowski's study, the greatest difference between the high and low sensation seekers was exhibited for the highest risk gambling option, with high SSs choosing the risky choice far more often than the low sensation-seeking group. This finding may illustrate the relevance of studying high-risk choices in order to clarify differences between high and low stimulus-seeking groups.

Zuckerman (1979b) demonstrated that high sensation seekers have a pronounced tendency to underestimate risk when compared with low sensation seekers. This may suggest that perceptual differences distinguish high and low sensation seekers, which may account for the participation of sensation seekers in activities that are actively avoided by low scorers on the SSS. Stewart and Hemsley (1984) have reported such findings, with high scorers on the SSS viewing situations as less risky than low scorers who were exposed to the same findings.

Sensation Seeking in the Sport Setting

Opportunities abound for "stimulation" in the sport setting. Zuckerman refers to physical and social risks as desirable stimuli to the sensation seeker. It may be argued that both physical and social risks are available in many forms within the realm of sport, enticing the sensation seeker to participate, and repelling the individual who prefers the relative safety of lower stimulation levels. The attractiveness of sports to sensation seekers has been supported by the literature. Rowland, Franken, and Harrison (1986) found that high sensation seekers tend to become involved in more sports, although low SSs tend to remain involved with each sport for longer periods of time. This finding is consistent with the high sensation seeker's purported desire for change and a variety of stimuli. Rowland, Franken, and Harrison also reported the high SS subject's attraction to "high-risk" sporting activities, defined as physically dangerous sports such as skydiving and rock climbing.

Psychological and emotional stimulation are also critical aspects of the sport experience. Social pressures in the form of the evaluative potential of audiences, coaches, and teammates are common to many sports, and critical game situations themselves may be extremely stimulating. The right fielder in baseball, seemingly far from the intensity of the action in the bottom of the ninth inning, never knows if the ball might be hit his way and if the outcome of the game might be decided by his split-second reaction. Such stimulation might provide satisfactory opportunity for some. Others who require higher levels of stimulation may prefer the much more "pressure"-laden role of the closing relief pitcher, who may be the center of attention for thousands of fans with the game's outcome resting primarily on the next pitch. Merely becoming a relief pitcher is to accept high risk levels in the sport setting.

Other positions such as goalie in soccer, lacrosse, water polo, ice hockey, and field hockey involve great psychological risks. Athletes in these positions are vulnerable to social humiliation when and if they permit opponents to score, especially if the score is an easy one. Mistakes may be theirs alone, with no one to share the blame or responsibility. While their teammates who play more "anonymous" positions have other team members with whom to share successes and failures, the goalies and relief pitchers of the world stand exposed and vulnerable to the chastisement of others. It may be postulated, therefore, that high sensation seekers are represented in disproportionate numbers in sport positions of magnified social risk. Surprisingly, this theory has not been tested by researchers in sport psychology.

Sensation seeking in the sport context is often synonymous with physical risk-taking. It would appear that those who engage in sports which offer rough physical contact and risk of injury would qualify as sensation seekers. Similarly, physically dangerous recreational activities such as hang gliding, rock climbing, and skydiving would seem to appeal to the high arousal needs of the sensation seeker. The literature has shown that this is indeed the case.

Robinson (1985) demonstrated that elite rock climbers who had exhibited successful long-term involvement scored significantly higher on the Sensation Seeking Scale than did a control group. Salvage divers who volunteered their services for unusually dangerous rescue and salvage diving scored significantly higher on the SSs than did college students, matched for age and socioeconomic background (Bacon, 1974). Connolly (1981) demonstrated the differences among skiers, ski instructors, and nonskiers on the SSs. These findings support the theory that within a high sensation-seeking group, the highest scorers may take the most risks, as the skiers scored higher than the nonskiers on the SSS and the ski instructors (who spend the most time on skis, therefore inherently take more risks) scored the highest of the three groups.

Personality profiles on motion picture stuntmen (Piet, 1987) also support the link between SSS scores and physical risk, as well as Zuckerman's (1978) hypothesis that sensation-seeking personalities require novel and varied experiences. Stunt actors appear eager for variety of experiences, and show a lack of concern for possible negative consequences of their behaviors. They also exhibit extraordinary ability to concentrate on required tasks in the face of great danger.

Using the SSS to investigate sensation-seeking tendencies of scuba divers, volunteer firemen, and students at the collegiate level, Bacon (1974) found that both the scuba divers and the firemen scored higher than the students, but only the scuba divers scored significantly higher on the Experience- and Thrill-Seeking Subscales. Hymbauch and Garrett (1974) administered the SSS to skydivers ($N = 21$) and non-skydivers ($N = 21$) matched for age, sex, and socioeconomic and occupational variables. The results indicated that the skydivers scored significantly higher than their counterparts on all subscales. These results provide strong support to the discriminant validity of the Zuckerman SSS.

Examination of high risk takers at elite levels of sport competition and of race car drivers by Ogilvie (1967), and Johnsgard and Ogilvie (1967), revealed subjects to be more stable, reserved, self-assured, self-controlled, autonomous, and tough-minded than their less skilled counterparts. Berkowitz (1964) also suggested that the degree of risk one assumes has a relation to the individual's past success in that activity, and therefore a majority of the literature pertaining to high-risk sport participation has been done with skydivers as the population of interest. This is not to suggest that research is limited to skydivers, for hang gliding, scuba diving, and mountain climbing have also been used for sensation seeking studies. An overview of some of these is provided in order to describe the sensation seeker in terms of activity preferences and personality.

Hoover (1978) used skydivers as subjects and attempted to construct a composite personality profile of them. Although he found no significant differences between his control group and the skydivers, Hoover suggested that Freudians would see the divers as struggling with self-destructive urges in the presence of the death instinct. He further theorized that they skydived solely for the psychological experience of combatting gravity, and the experience of exhilaration.

Delk (1973) also studied the personality of skydivers, using only experienced divers (having an average of 531 jumps). He administered a skydiving questionnaire in order to collect personal, sociological, and diving experience data; the Shipley Vocabulary Test; and the Minnesota Multiphasic Personality Inventory (MMPI). Delk (1973) reported results which indicated that high sensation seekers were of superior verbal intelligence, and when compared to adult male MMPI norms, were more free from anxiety, phobia, and depression, and were more likely to be socially deviant and anticonventional; open and lacking from defensiveness; self-confident and positive; impulsive and oriented toward physical action; hedonistic and thrill seeking; extroverted and sociable; and free from health worries.

Arnold (1973) interviewed skydivers and nonjumpers, and found that the nonjumpers viewed jumping mainly in terms of closeness to death. Skydivers with experience, on the other hand, expect the chute to open as a matter of course. Also, nonjumpers viewed a late-opening chute as barely avoiding death, whereas the skydiver saw it as merely opening late (Arnold, 1973).

In profiling skydivers, Arnold (1973) found that the most important factors reported in jumping appeared to be a desire for escape and a desire for community. Participants in skydiving reported feelings of being removed from the world, while experiencing the subjective feeling of floating with the earth appearing as a distant object coming no closer and having no bearing on the skydiver. Arnold reported that skydivers were very dedicated to their sport, and that those who stayed with it manifested a high involvement. Klausner (1970) also found that for experienced skydivers, sky diving tends to be a consuming interest. Also, he suggested that while skydivers are inclined to pursue few other leisure activities, their previous interests centered around activities referred to by Callois and Vertego.

Klausner (1970) attempted to ascertain the relationship between the experience of fear and the experience of enthusiasm, in a classic study of parachutists. The fear variable was assessed through two techniques: a report of fear phenomenologically grasped by the skydivers themselves, and an inference from a projective test concerning the pre-

disposition to fear. Results indicated that the greater the danger to overcome, or the greater the perceived risk, the greater the degree of enthusiasm once the danger has been conquered. Thus it appears that there is an apparent thrill in facing danger, and that fear lessens as participants become more familiar with the challenge. Klausner observed that the ability to control one's own fate was more constant than the perception of possible injury in its influence on the fear of danger and the thrill in overcoming it.

Epstein (1967) also researched the personalities of skydivers with a specific focus on anxiety reaction to jumping. Experienced jumpers approached the sport with a more light-hearted mood than nonexperienced jumpers. This would seem to suggest that having time for mental preparation increases the chance of a more enjoyable experience.

Epstein studied 33 skydivers with an experience level of 100 or more jumps and 33 who had less than 5 jumps. The subjects were instructed to rate their fear and avoidance feelings at 14 points in time before, during, and after the jump. Results of the questionnaire reported the maximum fear was not during the actual period between jumping and the opening of the chute, although this was the point of maximal uncertainty and danger. For the less-experienced divers, the peak avoidance period was at the "ready" signal, prior to the jump. The feeling of fear declined once a commitment was made, according to the jumpers. The experienced jumpers reported later jumps to be more enjoyable and less fear producing, and that enthusiasm tended to be higher during free-fall jumps, and continued to rise during the actual free-fall situation.

Epstein's questionnaire included a picture of a skydiver lying prone on the ground. Subjects were asked to write a story concerning the picture. The stories were scored on both the extent of the perceived harm to the jumper and the attribution of responsibility for the harm. Forty-three percent reported that an accident had occurred but did not specify any harm to the individual; 38% stated that harm was slight; and 29% mentioned serious injury or even death (Epstein, 1967).

Farrell (1967), whose major interest was the motivation behind skydiving, interviewed parachutists to ascertain their reasons for participating in the sport. Most stated they realized that the sport was somewhat unusual, but that there was a "certain something" that encouraged them to continue participation. This motivation appears to be a sudden release of tension, with a surge of exhilaration at the moment of the jump. "Jumping is an unusually intense experience and one with special richness in symbolic meanings. While the act itself is simple, quick, discreet, and demands full commitment, at the same time there must be an urge to jump. That first step is a long one, the men say; but without this one step there cannot be a jump or a jumper" (Farrell, 1967). According to Farrell, the pleasure of jumping and the ability to find gratification in the sport are of great significance, and the thought of making the anxiety less for each succeeding jump may be one reason why jumping is so pleasurable to the participant. For this reason, jumping is only one of an assortment of possible thrills.

High sensation seekers have also been reported to have a greater capacity for vivid imagination than their low sensation seeking counterparts, as they tend to be more sensitized to internal body sensations (Zuckerman, 1979). This suggests that individuals scoring high in sensation seeking would be easier to train in imagery techniques, and would be able to image far more vividly than low sensation seekers. In the sport realm, athletes often use imagery as a medium for improving performance and concentration (Nideffer, 1976), and positive results have been noted in research in this area (Egstrom, 1964; Perry, 1939; Richardson, 1967; Start & Richardson, 1964; Twining, 1949; Vandell, et al., 1943). Unfortunately, at the time of this writing, additional research findings that might further elucidate an alleged relationship between imagery ability and sensation seeking have not been forthcoming.

INTROVERSION AND EXTROVERSION

The terms *introversion* and *extroversion* (I-E) immediately bring to mind the prominent personologist Hans J. Eysenck. Others, such as Freud (1920), Jung (1924), and Guilford (1934), have also incorporated introversion-extroversion in their theoretical frameworks. However, it is Eysenck's system for describing personality that has received a lion's share of attention among sport psychology researchers.

Jung described introversion and extroversion as a turning in and out of the libido (respectively), a primary approach that is essentially compatible with Eysenck's perspective. Both Jung and Eysenck (Eysenck, 1967; Jung, 1924) conceptualized introversion-extroversion as a dimension of arousability, but Eysenck's orientation is more biological, with basic differences lying in the reticular activating system of the brain. Eysenck speaks of nervous system strength with the introvert representing the weak end of the continuum. According to Eysenck, these attributes do not represent two independent types of nervous systems, but rather two endpoints of one continuum. Those with weak systems begin to respond to stimuli at comparatively lower levels of intensity. They are also more highly aroused than extroverts (those with stronger nervous systems) at the same level of physical stimuli. And those with strong nervous systems are better able to withstand extreme intensities of stimulation. Introverts typically seek a reduction in external stimulation since external stimulation increases arousal. Understandably, extroverts are inclined to seek increased stimulation from the environment.

Introverts and extroverts tend to perceive others in the environment differently (Cohen & Scaife, 1973; Cooper & Scalise, 1974; Genthner & Moughan, 1977) and extroverts are more socially responsive to the personality traits of others (Harkins, Becker, & Stonner, 1975). The introversion-extroversion trait is one of the most stable of all personality traits over time.

The introversion-extroversion dimension is further clari-

fied by Eysenck and Eysenck (1963) as comprising two main components: sociability and impulsivity. Subjects who score high on introversion tend to be unsociable and withdrawn. However, Eysenck's structural framework for personality theory includes not only introversion-extroversion, but neuroticism-stability and psychoticism as well. All are measured by the *Eysenck Personality Inventory* (EPI). The EPI was developed as an improvement on its precursor, the *Maudsley Personality Inventory* (MPI), which had previously been Eysenck's instrument for assessing these major personality dimensions. Versions are available for children, adolescents, and adults, and their usefulness, validity, and reliability are well established (Handel, 1976).

Since the scope of this section is limited to perceptual considerations, the neuroticism and psychoticism components will not be included. However, it is helpful at this juncture to note that the three are independent personality dimensions, although some controversy about this exists (Carrigan, 1960).

Etiological Considerations

A number of studies have examined relations between introversion-extroversion and so-called "genetic variables." Some of these may be relevant here in that they may assist coaches and sport psychology consultants in gaining insight into perceptual tendencies in athletes that may be otherwise unobtainable through the formal application of assessment instruments. This inability may be due to temporary unavailability of the instrument or, in the case of some coaches, lack of preparedness to utilize the instrument and interpret resulting scores.

For instance, heredity appears to play an important role in the determination of introversion-extroversion. It emerges as an important descriptor of behavior early in life and remains stable over time. Eysenck (1956) used 13 pairs each of male identical twins, female identical twins, male fraternal twins, and female fraternal twins to demonstrate that identical twins resembled each other significantly more than fraternal twins with regard to introversion-extroversion scores. Also, black college students have been observed to be significantly lower in extroversion than white counterparts (Lowe & Hildman, 1972). These reported relations may serve only explanatory purposes that preclude intervention or attempts to change I-E status. Nonetheless, they partially explain behavior that is perplexing to those who counsel athletes.

Introversion-Extroversion and Sport Behavior

An obviously central question in this section is, "In what ways is the personality trait introversion-extroversion related to sport and exercise–related behavior?" Although a clear and definitive answer has yet to emerge from the literature, there is some evidence that Eysenck's I-E dimension may be viewed as a potentially discriminating factor among athletes of different sports as well as athletes of different skill and experience levels within the same sport.

For example, in a study conducted by Daino (1985), two groups of high school students, competitive tennis players and those who did not participate in sport, were administered the EPI. Significant mean extroversion differences were observed in female subjects ($N = 30$ in each group) but not in male ($N = 36$ in each group) subjects. Female tennis players were significantly more extroverted than nonathletes. When male and female subjects were combined, results indicated significantly higher extroversion scores for the athletes ($N = 66$).

A number of researchers have used runners as subjects. Results of early studies by Morgan (1968, 1974) and Morgan and Costill (1972) have indicated that long-distance runners were more introverted than sprinters as well as other athletes. However, other findings indicate that high level runners are not significantly different from other individual athletes (Morgan & Pollock, 1977). A considerable amount of research suggests that individual sport participation, such as in running, significantly correlates with introversion, and participation in a team sport correlates with extroversion (Wendt & Patterson, 1974). However, results from a study by Hartung and Farge (1977) are of a contradictory nature.

Frazier (1987) has suggested that these discrepant findings may be a consequence of the failure to take into account gender and level of athletic ability. He hypothesized that with these variables accounted for in research designs, no difference in introversion-extroversion would be observed for elite and nonelite marathon runners. In his study the introversion-extroversion scores of 25 female and 73 male marathon runners were examined. The hypothesis was supported: subjects scored much as the normal population did on the EPI. No significant differences were noted between the elite and nonelite athletes; however, a significant interaction of sex with performance reflected higher scores for the elite female runners.

In contrast to Frazier's (1987) results are those of Mikel (1983), who found male and female runners (who ran at least three times a week, for at least 20 minutes each time) to be much more introverted than a college norm group. However, runners were of a wide age range (18 and over) in comparison to those in the normative group. According to Eysenck and Eysenck (1968), extroversion scores decline with age. Female runners were significantly more extroverted than the male runners, which is in disagreement with previous research (Eysenck & Eysenck, 1968). Mikel (1983) suggests that these observed gender differences may vary from sample to sample (different sports, different ages).

These findings are placed in helpful perspective by Kirkaldy (1980), who suggests that if indeed athletes score higher on extroversion, then their general levels of activation would be expected to be lower than those with low scores (nonathletes). Therefore the extroverted athlete would tend to pursue arousing activities throughout the day. This may in part account for their participation in sport.

In addition, a low level of arousal would encourage improvement in performance efficiency since the arousal level in athletes is likely to be higher than in nonathletes due to physical activity. This interpretation may assist in clarifying some observable behavior in sport.

In another study, Kirkaldy (1982) addressed the question of differences in introversion-extroversion scores between *team* and *individual* athletes. Older studies have reported personality differences when comparing such athlete groups (Malumphy, 1968; Rushall, 1967; Warburton & Kane, 1966). In addition to confronting this question, Kirkaldy sought to determine if differences exist in groups of athletes playing different positions in the same sport. Using 199 team and 124 individual sport college athletes, he observed no significant differences in introversion-extroversion. However, when team athletes (mostly field hockey, volleyball, and net ball) were categorized into one of three subgroups (offense, midfield, and defense), males in offensive positions were found to be higher in extroversion. In females, the offensive (attacking) players were comparatively less extroverted.

Kirkaldy (1982) speculates that different levels of "toughness" are expected in defensive male positions in comparison to those in female sports. In order to gain evidence that would conclusively point to introversion-extroversion differences in subgroups of athletes, experimental control over a number of relevant variables would have to be exercised. Among these would be level of skill and degree of prior competitive experience, age, gender, and perhaps degree of risk-taking inherent in the specific position and sport. To date, these variables or even clusters of them have not been incorporated into multivariate experimental approaches.

There is some support for the assertion that athletes generally score higher than nonathletes on extroversion. However, this may not be true for athletes in some sports such as marathon running. Although it is difficult to assert that awareness of such differences can be profitably incorporated into training regimens for athletes, certainly interpersonal and perhaps some skill acquisition strategies employed by coaches may be accordingly enhanced.

SELF-CONCEPT/BODY IMAGE

The concept of self derives essentially from the intricate interaction among three general categories of factors: the real capabilities of an individual, the products of his or her cognitive machinations in which information about the self emanating from social and physical environments is processed, and lastly, the social environment itself, including the information it generates. But other considerations also contribute to perceptions about the self. These include personal values, assessment of personal behavior, and feelings about the compatibility between values and behavior. With reference to this point is the noteworthy work of Harter (1978, 1981a), who has provided a framework for examining the interactions and influence upon self-concept or esteem, of socialization, developmental factors, and individual differences, in children. According to Harter, positive or negative affect directly related to achievement is a consequence of self-perceptions. Perceptions of self-competence are also related to actual achievement (Harter, 1981b; Harter & Connell, 1984). Therefore, the time-honored allegation about believing in oneself in order to realize success has found some support.

Self-concept is expected to fluctuate across situations and is modifiable by a broad array of experiences and strategized interventions (Alpert, 1943). It is obviously an unstable psychological entity that is composed of many dimensions. It is routinely viewed as a critical determinant of well-being and happiness, particularly in children (Horn, 1987; Horn & Hasbrook, 1987; Weiss, 1987; Weiss, Bredemeir, & Shewehuk, 1986; Wylie, 1961). Individuals with strong and positive self-concepts are confident, assured, and assertive in actions with other persons. They also tend to demonstrate comparatively low levels of anxiety (Brustad, 1988; Ornes, 1970).

How are perceptions about various aspects of the self acquired? How do we arrive at evaluations about our physical, social, intellectual, and emotional selves? With reference to the physical self, two modi operandi are available: (1) vision and (2) movement and touch. The first is an obvious pathway to gaining insight into how pretty, tall, dashing, or thin we might be. In other words, we look. We consult the mirror in an effort to answer such questions. We also integrate information derived from tape measures, photographs, and other persons. But movement and touch are also highly valuable sources of data that shape our perceptions about the self. We come to know a great deal about all dimensions of ourselves by moving and physically communicating with the environment. In this context, the implications for sport participation seem very strong.

The Development of Self-Concept

It is generally understood that a well-developed concept of self does not exist at birth (Fitts, 1971). Apparently, ongoing experiences in the child's life continue to influence the development of perceptions about the self. Self-worth emerges and assumes changing direction and strength in keeping with momentary and daily interactions with other persons and events. Motor-skill performance is a vital contributor to this development (Hurlock, 1972), since concepts about the physical self contribute to strong overall self-efficacy and to personality development and functioning in general (White, 1959).

Such factors as child-rearing approaches by parents, interactions with peers and siblings, and confrontation with and responses to multitudes of life crises exert crucial influences upon the developing self-concept (Erikson, 1963). However, since the emphasis in this chapter and volume is focused specifically upon the sport domain, perceptions about such matters as the physical self/body image, physical self-esteem, or confidence, etc.) will be primarily discussed.

Measurement of Physical Self-Concept

Despite the acknowledged criticalness of self-perceptions to healthy human development (Allport, 1955; Erikson, 1963; Piaget, 1952), available measures frequently fail to satisfy essential criteria for test validity (Rentz & White, 1967; Vacchiano & Strauss, 1968; Wylie, 1974). For instance, the well-known measure of self-concept, *The Tennessee Self-Concept Scale* constructed by Fitts (1965), has been indicted as lacking in construct validity (Ryckman, Robbins, Thornton, & Cantrell, 1982). In particular, measures of physical self-concept are often without adequate psychometric properties (Ryckman, Robbins, Thornton, & Cantrell, 1982).

Two instruments that appear to be psychometrically sound and therefore applicable in sport and exercise related research are *The Body Esteem Scale* (BES) developed by Franzoi and Herzog (1986), and the *Physical Self-Efficacy Scale* (PSE) formulated by Ryckman, Robbins, Thornton, and Cantrell (1982). The BES comprises three subscales for females (sexual attractiveness, weight concern, and physical condition) and three subscales for males (physical attractiveness, upper body strength, and physical condition). The BES includes 35 items that are responded to by use of a 5-point Likert scale. The PSE includes 22 six-point Likert items that comprise two subscales: perceived ability, and physical self-presentation confidence. Other body image and movement satisfaction tests are described by Ostrow (1990).

Sport Behavior and Perceptions About the Self

If indeed development of total self-concept is contingent upon perceptions about the physical self, and in view of the changeability of self-perceptions, the assumption that participation in sport and exercise activities is a valuable source of information for the formation of concepts about the self seems plausible. We turn now to selected aspects of the pertinent literature in order to support this assumption, and thereby provide implications for those who conduct research in sport psychology or work in applied settings with coaches and athletes.

Exercise Behavior and Self-Concept

Leonardson (1977) reported a significant positive correlation between perceptions about physical fitness and self-concept score for high school and college subjects. Heaps (1978) provided supportive evidence of Leonardson's findings. Albinson (1974) also showed a positive relationship between self-concept and exercise behavior while comparing physically active and inactive college males. In a study by Albinson (1974), physically active and inactive college males revealed a positive relationship between self-concept and nature of and frequency of exercise behavior. Stoedefalke (1977) and Sonstroem (1978) also reported a positive relationship between self-concept and exercise behavior. They found support for the hypothesis that male college students who participated in a four-week physical conditioning program would experience an increase in self-esteem scores. Also, nonswimmer college men and women who learned to swim as a result of participating in twenty 40-minute swimming lessons were observed to improve significantly on posttest self-concept scores. Finally, Read (1968) found that students who were "constant winners" in college physical education competitive sport programs had a higher degree of self-concept than did "constant losers."

It appears that improved self-concept scores resulting from physical activity interventions of various sorts are observed with a fair degree of consistency in college-aged subjects. However, with young children, this influence appears to be moot. For instance, Brugel (1972) observed no change in self-concept scores for 9-year-old boys who participated in a competition baseball league. Similarly, Bruya (1977) found no change in self-concept scores in school-aged children participating in 2 half-hour physical education sessions per week for 4 weeks. On the other hand, Zaichkowsky, Zaichkowsky, and Martinek (1975) and Martinek, Cheffers, and Zaichkowsky (1978) did find a change.

No significant differences in self-concept were reported by Maul and Thomas (1975) between participants and nonparticipants in a third grade children's gymnastics program. In older children, boys aged 13–16 years, enrolled in a 30-hour fitness program consisting of jogging activities, calisthenic exercises, and swimming pool training, a significant increase in self-concept scores was observed (Collingwood & Willett, 1971). However, since only five subjects were used in this study, generalization of findings to other samples of children is limited. Apparently variables such as length and nature (intensity and specific activities) as well as the degree of positive and/or successful experiences therein influence the changeability of self-concept in young children to a greater extent than in older subjects.

Self-Concept and the Sport Experience

This book is replete with scientific research findings that support the relationship between optimal performance in sport and psychological factors. This relationship is likely to be appreciated and honored even by those who are not routine consumers of the rapidly increasing production of published sport science literature. In this writer's travels and interactions with coaches, athletes, and certainly sport psychology experts, he has rarely encountered any who deny, on an intuitive level, the criticalness of the performance-psychology interaction. As has been established earlier in this chapter, perceptions about the self, and notably perceptions about the physical self, bear meaningfully upon personality development and mental health. In conformity with this tenet as well as the association made in this paragraph, the important question now at hand is, "What is the association between perceptions about the self and sport behavior?"

To begin, the interesting findings reported by Weiss, McAuley, Ebbeck, and Wiese (1990) are helpful. Since attributions about behavioral outcomes have been shown to influence subsequent behavior, Weiss et al. set out to determine the relationship between children's self-esteem and attributions for performance in both physical and achievement domains. Subjects were participants in a seven-week university summer sports program. It was found that subjects ($N = 131$, grades 3–7) high in physical self-esteem, as assessed by the Perceived Competence Scale for Children (Harter, 1982), made causal attributions for perceived success that were more internal, stable, and personally controllable than did low self-esteem children. Similar findings were generated with regard to social self-esteem. In other words, subjects in this study tended to make attributions consistent with the way they viewed their abilities. Since causal attributions have been shown to exert influence over subsequent behaviors, it appears that investment in strategies to change self-esteem would be profitable in terms of improving sport performance.

A well-conceived study purporting to examine the relationship between self-esteem and a dimension of sport-related behavior in youth athletes (wrestlers) was conducted by Lethwaite and Scanlon (1989). Self-esteem was assessed with the Washington Self-Description Questionnaire by Scanlon and Lethwaite (1985). Analysis of questionnaire data revealed that boys with more frequent somatic competitive trait anxiety symptoms had lower self-esteem. If self-esteem is a predictor of somatic anxiety (perceptions of autonomic arousal and affective physiological responses), and if somatic anxiety, in turn, imposes inhibitory effects upon competitive performance, then manipulation of self-esteem would seem to provide opportunity for performance enhancement.

Some interesting work continues to be done in the area of sex role type among females. A high positive correlation between self-esteem and one sex role type in particular—the androgenous type (an ability to display situationally appropriate sex role characteristics)—has been established in the literature (Bem, 1975; Harris, & Jennings, 1977; Heilbrun, 1978; Helmreich & Spence, 1977). Androgenous individuals typically reveal a more positive self-image than either masculine, feminine, or undifferentiated sex role-typed persons. Hall, Durburow, and Progen (1986) were able to ascertain that nonathletes in the feminine sex role type were lower in self-esteem than in all other groups they studied (androgenous, masculine, feminine, and undifferentiated). They concluded that the psychological attributes of sex role seems to provide the strongest frame of reference related to self-esteem. It may be that the so-called "feminine types" participate in sport for motives that relate to beauty, cooperation, and enjoyment (Myers & Lips, 1978) which do not enhance self-esteem to the same extent as motives possibly embraced by androgenous types, such as competition or achievement.

Given the well-established association between sport behavior and psychological factors, it appears appropriate to inquire about the relationship of one such factor, perceptions about the self, and a rather troublesome dimension of sport, namely injury. Along this vein, Young and Cohen (1979) found no difference in self-concept in injured and noninjured female college basketball players. However, interestingly, in a previous study, conducted by the same researchers, using female high school basketball players, results supported the hypothesis that injured athletes possessed higher levels of self-esteem.

Pargman and Lunt (1989) found that college football players with lower self-concept scores and higher tendencies to rely on a more external locus of control, suffered significantly more injuries than did the athletes with higher self-concept who were more internally motivated. Perhaps perceptions about the self, when interacting with other individual psychological factors, bear more forcefully on sport behavioral dependent measures.

And finally, perhaps by way of concluding this section on perceptions about the self in relation to sport behavior, are the results reported by Ibrahim and Morrison (1976). In a straightforward, comparative research design, they set out to determine the self-concept of the typical athlete, either male or female, at both high school and college levels (athletes, $N = 100$; nonathletes, $N = 100$). At the high school level, male athletes were found to have lower scores on the self-concept measure than nonathletes (Fitts, 1965). For high school females, no differences were found between athletes and nonathletes on self-concept. However, at the college level, no significant differences between athletes and nonathletes were found for males or females. In view of the discussion presented at the beginning of this section, these findings are not easy to integrate. They seem to fly in the face of logical assumptions that predict comparatively more positive perceptions about the self in athletes in comparison to nonathletes. Since Ibrahim and Morrison do not attempt to qualify or interpret their findings, it remains appropriate, therefore, to recommend future replicative attempts of their results, with attention to longevity and level of athletic participation as additional variables.

SUMMARY

What has been attempted in this chapter is a description of the very meaningful relationships between cognitive and perceptual factors and sport behavior. In some instances exercise behavior was also alluded to. With this objective in mind, selected individual cognitive and perceptual styles were delineated and critical discussion attempted of pertinent issues and research findings.

First, clarification of the concepts *cognition* and *perception* was offered. *Cognition* was derived as involving higher order (nervous system) experiences than perceptual processes. *Perception* was described as having essentially an integrative function whereby stimuli transmitted to the central nervous system through organs of sensation are sorted and interpreted. Reasoning, thinking, and problem solving were attributed to cognitive processes.

Next, the notion of style was clarified. Its most fundamental character was a tendency to invoke typical patterns of cognition and perception cross-situationally. Among the individual cognitive styles considered were field-dependence/independence, association-dissociation, and trained helplessness. The perceptual styles considered were sensation seeking, self concept, and body image.

From an overview of these styles, their etiological, developmental character, and psychological and behavioral correlates, two broad conclusions are permissible. The first is that few if any of these styles are actually predictive of sport behavior. Whereas in some cases reported correlations are meaningful between a cognitive or perceptual tendency and specific kinds of behavior or proclivities for certain decision-making modes, successful performance in sport is not consequently predictable. These styles explain or describe only preferred cognitive approaches and perceptual directions. What is implied is that in certain kinds of sport, or more specifically, in regard to certain contextual demands, some styles are more supportive of efficient, accurate, or desirable outcomes.

A second conclusion is that not nearly as much published material incorporating these styles in well-conceived sport psychology research is available as one might expected. A need to replicate and expand many of the reported studies is obvious. It is also apparent that since some of these cognitive and perceptual styles have well-defined developmental aspects, properly designed inquiry should be made with regard to the variables of age and gender in sport as well as task-specific contexts.

References

Abramson, L., Seligman, M. E. P., & Teasdale, J. (1978). Learned helplessness in humans: Critique and reformulation. *Journal of Abnormal Psychology, 87,* 49–74.

Adler, P., & Adler, P. A. (1987). Role conflict and identity salience: College athletics and academic role. *The Social Science Journal, 24,* 443–455.

Albinson, J. G. (1974). Life styles of physically active and physically inactive college males. *International Journal of Sport Psychology, 5,* 93–101.

Allport, G. W. (1943). The ego in contemporary psychology. *Psychological Review, 50,* 451.

Allport, G. W. (1955). *Becoming: Basic considerations for a psychology of personality.* New Haven: Yale University Press.

Arbuthnot, J. (1972). Cautionary note on measurement of field independence. *Perceptual and Motor Skills, 35,* 379–488.

Arnold, D. (July 1973). A sociologist's look at sport parachuting. *Parachutist, 47,* 66–68.

Bacon, J. (1974). *Sensation seeking levels for members of high risk volunteer organizations.* Unpublished manuscript, Widener College.

Ball, I. L., Farnill, D., & Wangeman, J. F. (1984). Sex and age differences in sensation seeking: Some national comparisons. *British Journal of Psychology, 75,* 257–265.

Bard, C. (1972). The relation between perceptual style and physical activity. *International Journal of Sport Psychology, 3,* 107–113.

Barrell, G. V., & Frippe, H. R. (1975). Field dependence and physical ability. *Perceptual and Motor Skills, 41,* 216–218.

Beck, A. T. (1976). *Cognitive therapy and emotional disorders.* New York: International Universities Press.

Bem, S. L. (1975). Sex role adaptability: One consequence of psychological androgyny: Further explorations of the expressure domain. *Journal of Personality and Social Psychology, 34,* 1016–1023.

Bergman, H., & Engelbrektson, D. (1973). An examination of factor structure of rod-and-frame test and embedded figures test. *Perceptual and Motor Skills, 37,* 939–947.

Bischof, N. (1974). Optic-vestibular orientation to the vertical. In H. H. Kornhuber (Ed.), *Handbook of sensory physiology: Vestibular system, Part 2* (pp. 155–190). New York: Springer-Verlag.

Brugel, B. A. (1972). *The self-concept of eight- and nine-year-old boys participating in a competitive baseball league.* Unpublished master's thesis, Pennsylvania State University.

Bruya, L. D. (1977). Effect of selected movement skills on positive self-concept. *Perceptual and Motor Skills, 45,* 252–254.

Brustad, R. J. (1988). Affective outcomes in competitive sport: The influence of intrapersonal and socialization factors. *Journal of Sport and Exercise Psychology, 10,* 307–321.

Carrigan, P. M. (1960). Extraversion-introversion as a dimension of personality. A reappraisal. *Psychological Bulletin, 57,* 329–360.

Cohen, L., & Scaife, R. (1973). Self-environmental similarity and satisfaction in a college of education. *Human Relations, 26,* 89–99.

Collingwood, T., & Willett, L. (1971). The effects of physical training upon self concept of body attitude. *Journal of Clinical Psychology, 27,* 411–412.

Collins, J., & Newman, P. (1974). Personality correlates of visual perceptual responses. *Perceptual and Motor Skills, 38,* 1183–1187.

Cooper, J., & Scalise, C. J. (1974). Dissonance produced by devia-
tions from lifestyles: The interaction of Jungian typology and conformity. *Journal of Personality and Social Psychology, 29,* 566–576.

Daino, A. (1985). Personality traits of adolescent tennis players. *International Journal of Sport Psychology, 16,* 120–125.

Delk, J. L. (1973). Some personality characteristics of skydivers. *Life-Threatening Behavior, 3,* 51–57.

Deshaies, P., & Pargman, D. (1976). Selected visual abilities of college football players. *Perceptual and Motor Skills, 43,* 904–906.

Dickgans, J., & Brandt, T. (1974). The psychophysics of visually induced perception of self-motion and tilt. In F. O. Schmitt & F. G. Worden (Eds.), *The neurosciences: Third study program* (pp. 123–129). Cambridge, MA: MIT Press.

Diener, L., & Dweck, C. (1978). An analysis of learned helplessness: Continuous changes in performance strategy and achievement cognitions following failure. *Journal of Personality and Social Psychology, 36,* 451–462.

Drouin, B., Talbot, S., & Goulet, C. (1986). Cognitive styles of French Canadian athletes. *Perceptual and Motor Skills, 63,* 1139–1142.

Dweck, C., & Eliot, R. (1983). Achievement motivation. In E. M. Hetherington (Ed.), *Socialization, personality, and social development.* (643–691). New York: Wiley.

Dweck, C., & Repucci, C. (1973). Learned helplessness and reinforcement responsibility in children. *Journal of Personality and Social Psychology, 25,* 109–116.

Egstrom, G. H. (1964). Effects of an emphasis on conceptualizing techniques during early learning of a gross motor skill. *The Research Quarterly, 35,* 472–481.

Eitzen, D. S. (1987). The educational experiences of intercollegiate student-athletes. *Journal of Sport and Social Issues, 11,* 15–30.

Ellis, A. (1962). *Reasons and emotion in psychotherapy.* Secaucus, NJ: Lyle Stuart.

Epstein, S. (1967). Toward a unified theory of anxiety. *Progress in Experimental Personality Research, 4,* 1–89.

Erikson, E. (1963a). *The challenge of youth.* Garden City, NY: Doubleday.

Erikson, E. (1963b). *Childhood and society* (2nd ed.). New York: Norton.

Eysenck, H. J. (1947). *Dimensions of personality.* London: Routledge and Kegan Paul.

Eysenck, H. J. (1956). The inheritance of extraversion-introversion. *Acta Psychologica, 12,* 95–110.

Eysenck, H. J. (1957). *Manual of the Maudsley Personality Inventory.* London: University of London Press.

Eysenck, H. J. (1967). *The biological basis of personality.* Springfield, IL: Thomas.

Eysenck, H. J., & Eysenck, S. B. G. (1963). *The Eysenck Personality Inventory.* San Diego: Educational and Industrial Testing Service.

Eysenck, H. J., & Eysenck, S. B. G. (1968). *The manual of the Eysenck Personality Inventory.* San Diego: Educational and Industrial Testing Service.

Eysenck, S. B. G., & Eysenck, H. J. (1963). On the dual nature of extraversion. *British Journal of Social and Clinical Psychology, 2,* 46–55.

Eysenck, S., & Zuckerman, M. (1978). The relationship between sensation seeking and Eysenck's dimensions of personality. *British Journal of Psychology, 69,* 483–487.

Farley, F., & Farley, S. V. (1967). Extroversion and stimulus seeking motivation. *Journal of Consulting Psychology, 31,* 215–216.

Farrell, D. (1967). *Sport parachuting: Motivation in play, games and sports.* Springfield, IL: Thomas.

Fine, B. J. (1972). Field-dependent introvert and neuroticism: Eysenck and Witkin united. *Psychological Reports, 31,* 939–956.

Fitts, W. H. (1965). *Tennessee Self-Concept Scale Manual.* Nashville, TN: Counselor Recordings and Tests.

Fitts, W. H. (1971). *The self-concept and self-actualization. Monograph No. 3.* Nashville, TN: The Dede Wallace Center.

Franzoi, S. L., & Herzog, M. E. (1986). The Body Esteem Scale: A convergent and discriminant validity study. *Journal of Personality Assessment, 50,* 24–30.

Frazier, S. E. (1987). Introversion-extraversion measures in elite and nonelite distance runners. *Perceptual and Motor Skills, 64,* 867–872.

Freud, S. (1920). *A general introduction to psycho-analysis.* New York: Liverwright.

Furnham, A. (1984). Extraversion, sensation seeking, stimulus screening and Type "A" behaviour pattern: The relationship between various measures of arousal. *Personality and Individual Differences, 5,* 133–140.

Genthner, R. W., & Moughan, J. (1977). Introverts' and extraverts' response to nonverbal attending behavior. *Journal of Counseling Psychology, 24,* 144–146.

Goodenough, D. R. (1986). History of the field dependence construct. In M. Bertini, D. Pizzamiglio & S. Wagner (Eds.), *Field dependence in psychological theory, research and application* (pp. 5–14). London: Erlbaum.

Goodenough, D. R., Gandini, F., Olkin, L., Pizzamiglio, D., Thayer, D., & Witkin, H. A. (1977). A study of X chromosome linkage with field dependence and spatial visualization. *Behavior Genetics, 7,* 373–387.

Guilford, J. P. (1934). Introversion-extraversion. *Psychological Bulletin, 31,* 331–354.

Gundersheim, J. (1987). Sensation seeking in male and female athletes and nonathletes. *International Journal of Sport Psychology, 18,* 87–99.

Hall, E. G., Durborow, B., & Progen, J. L. (1986). Self-esteem of female athletes and nonathletes relative to sex role type and sport type. *Sex Roles, 15,* 379–390.

Handel, A. (1976). Personality factors among adolescent boys. *Psychological Reports, 39,* 435–445.

Harkins, S., & Green, R. G. (1975). Discriminability and criterion differences between extraverts and introverts during vigilance. *Journal of Research in Personality, 9,* 335–340.

Harkins, S., Becker, L. A., & Stonner, D. (1975). Extraversion-introversion and the effects of favorability and set size on impression formation. *Bulletin of the Psychonomic Society, 5,* 306–307.

Harns, D. V., & Jennings, S. E. (1977). Self-perception of female distance runners. In P. Milvy (Ed.), *The marathon: Physiological, medical, epidemiological and psychological studies.* New York: The New York Academy of Sciences.

Harter, S. (1978). Effectance motivation reconsidered. *Human Development, 21,* 34–64.

Harter, S. (1981a). A model of mastery motivation in children: Individual differences and developmental change. In A. Collins (Ed.), *Minnesota symposium on child psychology* (Vol. 14, pp. 215–255). Hillsdale, NJ: Erlbaum.

Harter, S. (1981b). A new self-report scale of intrinsic versus extrinsic orientation in the classroom. *Developmental Psychology, 17,* 300–312.

Harter, S. (1982). The perceived competence scale for children. *Child Development, 53,* 87–97.

Harter, S., & Connell, J. (1984). A model of children's achievement and related self-perceptions of competence, control and motivational orientation. In J. Nicholls (Ed.), *The development of achievement motivation* (pp. 219–250). Greenwich, CT: JAI Press.

Hartung, G. H., & Farge, E. J. (1977). Personality and physiological traits in middle-aged runners and joggers. *Journal of Gerontology, 32,* 541–548.

Heaps, D. V. (1978). Relating physical and psychological fitness: A psychological point of view. *Journal of Sports Medicine, 18,* 399–400.

Hellison, D. R. (1969). *The effect of physical conditioning on effective attitudes toward the self, the body and physical fitness.* Unpublished doctoral dissertation, Ohio State University, Columbus, OH.

Helmreich, R., & Spence, J. T. (1977). Sex-roles and achievement. In R. W. Christina & D. M. Landers (Eds.), *Psychology of motor behavior and sport* (Vol. 2, pp. 33–44). Champaign, IL: Human Kinetics.

Heilbrun, A. B. (1978). An exploration of antecedents and attributes of androgynous and undifferentiated sex roles. *The Journal of Genetic Psychology, 132,* 97–107.

Hillinger, F. (1970). Introversion and birth order. In H. Eysenck (Ed.), *Readings in extraversion-introversion, Theoretical and methodological issues* (pp. 329–336). London: Staples Press.

Himelstein, P., & Thorne, S. B. (1985). Relationship between the Sensation-Seeking Scale and a biographical inventory designed to predict risk-taking behavior. *Personality and Individual Differences, 6,* 121–122.

Hiroto, D. (1974). Locus of control and learned helplessness. *Journal of Experimental Psychology, 102,* 167–193.

Hoover, T. O. (1978). Skydivers: Speculations of psychodynamics. *Perceptual and Motor Skills, 47,* 629–630.

Horn, T. S. (1987). The influence of teacher-coach behavior on the psychological development of children. In D. Gould & M. R. Weiss (Eds.), *Advances in pediatric sport sciences, Vol. 2, Behavioral issues* (pp. 121–142). Champaign, IL: Human Kinetics.

Horn, T. S., & Hasbrook, C. A. (1987). Psychological characteristics and the criteria children use for self-evaluation. *Journal of Sport Psychology, 9,* 208–221.

Houseworth, S. D. (1990, September). *Field survey of association, dissociation, and meditational attentional strategies used by runners during a 10-mile race.* Presented at the Association for the Advancement of Applied Sport Psychology Annual Conference, San Antonio, TX.

Hurlock, E. (1972). *Child development* (5th ed.). New York: McGraw-Hill.

Hymbaugh, K., & Garrett, J. (1974). Sensation seeking among skydivers. *Perceptual and Motor Skills, 38,* 118.

Ibrahim, H., & Morrison, N. (1976). Self-actualization and self-concept among athletes. *Research Quarterly, 47,* 68–79.

Johnsgard, K., & Ogilvie, B. (1968). The competitive racing driver: A preliminary report. *Journal of Sports Medicine and Physical Fitness, 8,* 87–95.

Jung, C. J. (1924). *Psychological types.* London: Rutledge & Kegan Paul.

Jungermann, H. (1982). The assessment and acceptance of the risks of high technologies. *Psychologische Rundschau, 33,* 217–238.

Kirkaldy, B. D. (1980). An analysis of the relationship between psychophysiological variables connected to human performance and the personality variables extraversion and neuroticism. *International Journal of Sport Psychology, 11,* 276–289.

Kirkaldy, B. D. (1982). Personality and sex differences related to positions in team sports. *International Journal of Sport Psychology, 13,* 141–153.

Klausner, S. Z. (1970). Assertion and obliteration of the self among sport parachutists. In G. Kenyon (Ed.), *Proceedings of the Second International Congress of Sport Psychology* (pp. 375–394). Chicago: The Athletic Institute.

Kozlowski, C. (1977). Demand for stimulation and probability preferences in gambling decisions. *Polish Psychological Bulletin, 8,* 67–73.

Krieger, J. C. (1962). *The Influence of figure ground perception on spatial adjustment in tennis.* Unpublished master's thesis, University of California at Los Angeles.

Lay, N. (1970). *The effect of learning to swim on the self-concept of college men and women.* Unpublished doctoral dissertation, Florida State University.

Leonardson, G. R. (1977). Relationship between self-concept and perceived physical fitness. *Perceptual and Motor Skills, 44,* 62.

Lethwaite, R., & Scanlon, T. K. (1989). Predictors of competitive trait anxiety in male youth sport participants. *Medicine and Science in Sports and Exercise, 21,* 221–229.

Lindauer, M., & Rehkauf, L. (1971). Introversion-extraversion and figure-ground perception. *Journal of Personality and Social Psychology, 19,* 107–113.

Lindquist, L. (1978). Correlation between an embedded figures test and tennis rank order at three levels of skill. *Perceptual and Motor Skills, 47,* 1143–1146.

Loader, E. C., Edwards, S., & Henschen, K. P. (1982). Field-dependent/field-independent characteristics of male and female basketball players. *Perceptual and Motor Skills, 55,* 883–890.

Lowe, J. D., & Hildman, L. K. (1972). EPI scores as a function of race. *British Journal of Personality Assessment, 37,* 165–173.

Lueptow, L. B., & Kayser, B. D. (1973). Athletic involvement, academic achievement and aspiration. *Sociological Focus, 7,* 24–35.

Lynn, R., & Eysenck, J. J. (1961). Tolerance for pain, extraversion, and neuroticism. *Perceptual and Motor Skills, 12,* 161–162.

MacGillivay, W. (1980). Perceptual style, critical viewing time and catching skill. *International Journal of Sport Psychology, 11,* 22–33.

Mahoney, M. (1989). Psychological predictors of elite and nonelite performance in Olympic weightlifting. *International Journal of Sport Psychology, 20,* 1–12.

Malumphy, T. M. (1968). Personality of female athletes in intercollegiate competition. *The Research Quarterly, 39,* 610–620.

Martinek, T. J., Cheffers, J. T. F., & Zaichkowsky, L. S. (1978). Physical activity, motor development, and self-concept: Race and age differences. *Perceptual and Motor Skills, 48,* 147–154.

Masters, K. S., & Lambert, M. J. (1989). The relationship between cognitive coping strategies, reasons for running, injury, and performance of marathon runners. *Journal of Sport and Exercise Psychology, 11,* 161–170.

Maul, T., & Thomas, J. R. (1975). Self concept and participation in children's gymnastics. *Perceptual and Motor Skills, 41,* 701–702.

Mayer, R. E. (1983). *Thinking, problem solving, cognition.* New York: W. H. Freeman.

McLeod, B. (1985). Field dependence as a factor in sports with preponderance of open or closed skills. *Perceptual and Motor Skills, 60,* 369–370.

McLeod, B. (1987). Sex, structured sport activity, and measurement of field dependence. *Perceptual & Motor Skills, 64,* 452–454.

Meyer, B. B. (1990). From idealism to actualization: The academic performance of female collegiate athletes. *Journal of Sport Sociology, 9,* 44–57.

Mikel, K. V. (1983). Extraversion in adult runners. *Perceptual and Motor Skills, 57,* 143–146.

Morgan, W. P. (1968). Personality characteristics of wrestlers participating in the world championships. *Journal of Sports Medicine, 8,* 212–216.

Morgan, W. P. (1974). Selected psychological considerations in sport. *The Research Quarterly, 45,* 374–390.

Morgan, W. P. (1980). Sports personology: The credulous-skeptical argument in perspective. In W. F. Straub (Ed.), *Sport Psychology* (pp. 330–339). Ithaca, NY: Mouvement Publications.

Morgan, W. P., & Costill, D. L. (1972). Psychological characteristics of the marathon runner. *Journal of Sports Medicine, 12,* 42–46.

Morgan, W. P., & Horstman, D. H. (1978). Psychometric correlates of pain perception. *Perceptual and Motor Skills, 47,* 27–39.

Morgan, W. P., & Pollock, M. L. (1977). Psychological characterization of the elite distance runner. In P. Milvey (Ed.), *Annals of the New York Academy of Sciences* (pp. 382–403). New York: New York Academy of Sciences.

Myers, A. M., & Lips, H. M. (1978). Participation in competitive amateur sports as a function of psychological androgyny. *Sex Roles, 4,* 571–588.

Nideffer, R. M. (1976). *The inner athlete: Mind plus muscle or winning.* New York: Crowell.

Nideffer, R. M. (1976). The test of attentional and interpersonal style. *Journal of Personality and Social Psychology, 34,* 394–404.

Nideffer, R. M. (1978). The relationship of attention and anxiety to performance. In W. Straub (Ed.), *Sport psychology: An analysis of athlete behavior* (pp. 231–235). Ithaca, NY: Mouvement Publications.

Nideffer, R. M. (1981). *The ethics and practice of applied sport psychology.* Ithaca, NY: Mouvement Publications.

Nideffer, R. M. (1986). Concentration and attentional training. In J. Williams (Ed.), *Applied sport psychology* (pp. 257–269). Palo Alto, CA: Mayfield.

Ogilvie, B. (1967). What is an athlete? *Journal of Health, Physical Education and Recreation, 38,* 38–50.

Ornes, E. J. (1970). *The relationship between trait anxiety and self-concept.* Unpublished master's thesis, Middle Tennessee State University.

Ostrow, A. C. (1990). *Directory of psychological tests in the sport and exercise sciences.* Morgantown, WV: Fitness Information Technology.

Pargman, D. (1974, December). *Witkin's field dependence-independence theory applied to athletics and athletes.* Paper presented at the meeting of the Florida Association for Health, Physical Education and Recreation, Orlando, FL.

Pargman, D. (1976, October). *Psychophysiological correlates of college football playing ability.* Paper presented at the Southeastern American College of Sports Medicine Annual Fall Meeting, Middle Tennessee State University, Murfreesboro, TN.

Pargman, D. (1976). Visual disembedding and injury in college football players. *Perceptual and Motor Skills, 42,* 762.

Pargman, D. (1977). Perceptual cognitive ability in a function of race, sex and academic achievement in college athletes. *International Journal of Sport Psychology, 8,* 79–91.

Pargman, D., Schreiber, L. E., & Stein, F. (1974). Field dependence of selected athletic sub-groups. *Medicine and Science in Sports, 6,* 283–286.

Pargman, D., Bender, P., & Deshaies, P. (1975). Correlation between visual disembedding and basketball shooting by male and female varsity athletes. *Perceptual and Motor Skills, 41,* 956.

Pargman, D., & Inomata, K. (1976). Field dependence, displaced vision, and motor performance. *Journal of Motor Behavior, 8,* 11–17.

Pargman, D., & Ward, T. (1976). Biomechanical correlates of psychological differentiation in female athletes. *The Research Quarterly, 47,* 750–755.

Pargman, D., Sachs, M., & Deshaies, P. (1976). Field dependence-independence and injury in college football players. *American Corrective Therapy Journal, 30,* 174–175.

Pargman, D., & Lunt, S. (1989). The relationship of self-concept and locus of control to the severity of injury in freshman college football players. *Sports, Training, Medicine and Rehabilitation, 1,* 203–208.

Perry, H. M. (1939). The relative efficiency of actual and imaginary practice in five selected tasks. *Archives of Psychology, 34,* 5–75.

Peterson, C., & Barrett, C. (1987). Explanatory style and academic performance among university freshman. *Journal of Personality and Social Psychology, 53,* 603–607.

Peterson, C., & Seligman, M. (1984). Explanatory style and illness. *Journal of Personality, 55,* 237–265.

Peterson, C., Semmel, A., Von Baeyer, C., Abramson, L., Metalsky, R., & Seligman, M. (1982). The attributional style questionnaire. *Cognitive Therapy and Research, 6,* 287–299.

Piaget, J. (1952). *The origins of intelligence in children* (M. Cook, trans.). New York: International Universities Press.

Praparessis, D., & Carron, L. (1988). Learned helplessness in sport. *The Sport Psychologist, 2,* 189–201.

Ravio, S., & Nabel, N. (1988). Field dependence/independence and concentration as psychological characteristics of basketball players. *Perceptual and Motor Skills, 66,* 831–836.

Ravio, S., & Nabel, N. (1990). Relationship between two different measurements of field-dependence and athletic performance of adolescents. *Perceptual and Motor Skills, 70,* 75–81.

Read, D. A. (1968). *The influence of competitive and noncompetitive programs of physical education on noncompetitive programs of physical education on body image and self concept.* Unpublished doctoral dissertation, Boston University.

Rentz, R. R., & White, W. F. (1967). Congruence of the dimensions of self-as-object and self-as-process. *Journal of Psychology, 67,* 277–285.

Richardson, A. (1967b). Mental practice: A review and discussion (Part 2). *The Research Quarterly, 38,* 263–273.

Rotella, R., & Bunker, L. (1978). Field dependence and reaction time in senior tennis players. *Perceptual and Motor Skills, 46,* 585–586.

Rowland, G. L., & Franken, R. E. (1986). The four dimensions of sensation seeking. *Personality and Individual Differences, 7,* 237–240.

Rowland, G. L., Franken, R. E., & Harrison, K. (1986). Sensation seeking and participation in sporting activities. *Journal of Sport Psychology, 8,* 212–220.

Rushall, B. S. (1967). Personality profiles and a theory of behavior modification for swimmers. *Swimming Techniques, 4,* 66–71.

Ryckman, R. M., Robbins, M. A., Thornton, B., & Cantrell, P. (1982). Development and validation of a physical self-efficacy scale. *Journal of Personality and Social Psychology, 42,* 891–900.

Sack, A. (1987). College sport and the student athlete. *Journal of Sport and Social Issues, 11,* 31–48.

Scanlon, T. K., & Lethwaite, R. (1985). Social psychological aspects of competition for male youth sport participants: III. Determinants of personal performance expectancies. *Journal of Sport Psychology, 7,* 389–399.

Schmid, A., & Peper, E. (1986). Techniques for training concentration. In J. Williams (Ed.), *Applied sport psychology* (pp. 271–284). Mountain View, CA: Mayfield.

Schomer, H. (1986). Mental strategies and the perception of effort of marathon runners. *International Journal of Sport Psychology, 17,* 41–59.

Schomer, H. (1987). Mental strategy training programme for marathon runners. *International Journal of Sport Psychology, 18,* 133–151.

Seligman, M. (1972). Learned helplessness. *Annual Review of Medicine, 23,* 407–412.

Seligman, M., & Schulman, G. (1986). Exploratory style as a predictor of productivity and quitting among life insurance agents. *Journal of Personality and Social Psychology, 50,* 832–838.

Seligman, M., Nolen-Hockseme, R., Norton, M., & Norton, L. (1988). *Athletic achievement and explanatory style.* Unpublished manuscript.

Silva, J. M., & Applebaum, M. S. (1989). Association-dissociation patterns of United States Olympic marathon trial contestants. *Cognition—Therapy and Research, 13,* 185–192.

Smith, R. E. (1981). Development of an integrated coping response through cognitive-affective stress management training. In I. G. Sarason & C. D. Spielbuger (Eds.), *Stress and anxiety* (Vol. 7). Washington, DC: Hemisphere.

Sonstroem, R. J. (1978). Physical estimation and attraction scales: Rationale and research. *Medicine and Science in Sports, 10,* 97–102.

Start, K. B., & Richardson, A. (1964). Imagery and mental practice. *British Journal of Educational Psychology, 34,* 280–284.

Stewart, C. H., & Hemsley, D. R. (1984). Personality factors in the taking of criminal risks. *Personality and Individual Differences, 5,* 119–122.

Stoedefalke, R. G. (1977). Physical fitness programs for adults. In E. A. Amsterdam, J. J. Wilmore, & A. N. Demaria (Eds.), *Exercise in cardiovascular health and disease* (pp. 295–301). New York: Yorke Medical Books.

Suls, J., & Miller, B. (1981). Life events, perceived control and illness: The role of uncertainty in human stress. *Journal of Personality, 7,* 30–34.

Swinnen, S. (1989). Field dependence-independence as a factor in learning complex motor skills and underlying sex differences. *International Journal of Sport Psychology, 15,* 236–249.

Talbot, S., Godin, G., Drouen, D., & Goulet, C. (1984). Cognitive styles of young ice hockey players. *Perceptual and Motor Skills, 59,* 692–694.

Trotter, R. (1987). Stop blaming yourself. *Psychology Today, 21,* 130–139.

Twining, W. H. (1949). Mental practice and physical practice in learning a motor skill. *The Research Quarterly, 20,* 432–435.

Vacchiano, R. B., & Strauss, P. S. (1968). The construct validity of the Tennessee Self Concept Scale. *Journal of Clinical Psychology, 24,* 323–326.

Vandell, R. A., Davis, R. A., & Clugston, H. A. (1943). The function of mental practice in the acquisition of motor skills. *Journal of General Psychology, 29,* 243–250.

Warburton, F. W., & Kane, J. E. (1966). Personality related to sport and physical ability. In J. E. Kane (Ed.), *Readings in physical education*. London: Physical Education Association.

Watson, L. (1973). *Supernature*. Garden City, NY: Doubleday.

Weiss, M. R. (1987). Self-esteem and achievement in children's sport and physical activity. In D. Gould & M. R. Weiss (Eds.), *Advances in pediatric sport sciences, Vol. 2: behavioral issues* (Vol. 2, pp. 87–119). Champaign, IL: Human Kinetics.

Weiss, M. R., Bredemeier, B. J., & Shewchuk, R. M. (1986). The dynamics of perceived competence, perceived control, and motivational orientation in youth sport. In M. Weiss & D. Gould (Eds.), *Sport for children and youths* (pp. 89–102). Champaign, IL: Human Kinetics.

Weiss, M. R., McAuley, E., Ebbeck, V., & Wiese, D. M. (1990). Self-esteem and causal attributions for children's physical and social competence in sport. *Journal of Sport and Exercise Psychology, 12,* 21–36.

Wendt, D. T., & Patterson, T. W. (1974). Personality characteristics of women in intercollegiate competition. *Perceptual and Motor Skills, 38,* 861–862.

White, R. W. (1959). Motivation reconsidered: The concept of competence. *Psychological Review, 66,* 297–333.

Williams, J. M. (1980). Differential figure-general perception in classified and unclassified fencers. *Journal of Sport Psychology, 2,* 74–78.

Williams, J. M. (1980). Perceptual style and fencing skill. *Perceptual and Motor Skills, 40,* 182.

Witkin, H. A. (1973). *Field dependence-independence and psychological differentiation: A bibliography through 1972 with index.* Princeton, NJ: Educational Testing Service.

Witkin, H. A. (1977). *Cognitive styles in personal and cultural adaptation.* Worcester, MA: Clark University Press.

Witkin, H. A., & Goodendough, D. R. (1977). Field dependence and interpersonal behavior. *Psychological Bulletin, 84,* 661–689.

Witkin, H. A., Goodenough, D. R., & Karp, S. A. (1967). Stability of cognitive style from childhood to young adulthood. *Journal of Personality and Social Psychology, 7,* 291–300.

Witkin, H. A., Dyke, R. B., Faterson, H. F., Goodenough, D. R., & Karp, S. A. (1962). *Psychological differentiation.* New York: Wiley.

Witkin, H. A., Lewis, H. B., Hertzman, M., Machover, K., Meissner, P. B., & Wapner, S. (1972). *Personality through perception: An experimental and clinical study.* Westport, CT: Greenwood Press.

Wylie, R. (1961). *The self-concept: A critical survey of pertinent research literature.* Lincoln: University of Nebraska Press.

Wylie, R. C. (1974). *The self-concept* (Vol. 1). Lincoln: University of Nebraska Press.

Young, M. L., & Cohen, D. A. (1979). Self-concept and injuries among female college tournament basketball players. *American Corrective Therapy Journal, 33,* 139–142.

Zaichowsky, L. B., Zaichkowsky, L. D., & Martinek, T. J. (1975). Self concept and attitudinal differences in elementary age school children after participation in a physical activity program. *Movement, 7,* 132–134.

Zuckerman, M. (1979a). *Sensation seeking: Beyond the optimal level of arousal.* Hillsdale, NJ: Erlbaum.

Zuckerman, M. (1979b). Sensation seeking and risk taking. In C. E. Izard (Ed.), *Emotions in personality and psychopathology* (pp. 163–187). New York: Plenum Press.

Zuckerman, M., & Link, K. (1968). Construct validity for the Sensation Seeking Scale. *Journal of Consulting and Clinical Psychology, 32,* 420–426.

Zuckerman, M., Kolin, E., Price, L., & Zoob, I. (1969). Development of a Sensation Seeking Scale. *Journal of Consulting Psychology, 28,* 477–482.

·IV·

SOCIAL-COGNITIVE DIMENSIONS OF MOTIVATION

·17·

MOTIVATION IN SPORT: UNDERSTANDING AND ENHANCING THE MOTIVATION AND ACHIEVEMENT OF CHILDREN

Glyn Roberts

Motivation is one of the central aspects of human affairs. Whether it is a matter of businesspeople disappointed with the effectiveness of the work force, parents discussing the efforts of their children, teachers bemoaning the study habits of pupils, or coaches who complain about the commitment of athletes, all are dealing with motivational concerns. Motivation research has primarily addressed the role of motivation in individual lives. Whether it is the issue of managing the motivation of others, which is the concern of a coach or a teacher, or the issue of managing self-motivation, it is this level of motivation that has primarily consumed the efforts of researchers. This chapter focuses upon that aspect of motivation.

The role of motivation in individual lives is considered an important topic. It is a regrettable fact, however, that motivation is not well understood in the classroom, the auditorium, or on the playing field. For some reason, we in the area of sport psychology have not been very successful in conveying information to coaches and teachers about motivational considerations that are transferable to sport and other physical activity contexts.

Motivation is very misunderstood in the context of sport. One of the most common misunderstandings is the conception that motivation is synonymous with arousal. Coaches assume that pregame locker room inspirational talks and other procedures "motivate" players to enhance performance. That is why coaches sometimes employ such tactics in order to arouse players prior to a game. Despite coaching folklore, arousal and motivation are separate and independent constructs (Roberts, 1992). Arousal can actually undermine performance.

A second misunderstanding revolves around what coaches call "positive thinking." Coaches often extol athletes to imagine themselves winning or achieving success in sporting situations. The argument behind such instructions is that believing that you can win or be successful will enhance your performance to achieve a successful outcome. There is evidence that holding positive expectations can help motivation. However, the expectations have to be realistic or they can undermine motivation (cf. Locke & Latham, 1985). In other words, motivation is not simply positive thinking.

Lastly, many physical education teachers and coaches believe that motivation is genetically endowed. Coaches assume that the inner state of motivation is innate, and if any athlete is judged to be low in motivation, then coaches do not believe that this will or can change. Consequently, they often give up on that particular athlete or student. But motivation is not considered to be innate, it is considered to be a learned attribute on the part of the person (Ames, 1984; Roberts, 1982, 1984). While all of the misperceptions above are grounded on certain beliefs, they are not helpful in understanding the complexity of the process of motivation in sport.

The purpose of this chapter is twofold. First, the chapter will begin with defining motivation, and then the development of our understanding of motivation will be briefly traced under various approaches that have been used in the literature. This segment concludes by describing contemporary research in the social cognitive tradition. Second, the literature will be reviewed that has focused on contemporary social cognitive approaches to understanding the motivation of children in sport. This segment will conclude by emphasizing recent research on enhancing motivation.

MOTIVATION IN SPORT

Typically in the research literature, motivation has referred to those personality factors, social variables, and/or cognitions that are assumed to come into play when a person undertakes a task at which he or she is evaluated, enters into competition with others, or attempts to attain some standard of excellence (Roberts, 1982; 1992). It is assumed that the individual has responsibility for the outcome and that some level of challenge is inherent in the task itself. In such circumstances, the dynamics of the sport context facilitate various motivational dispositions and/or cognitive assessments that influence achievement behaviors. Specifically, under the various conceptual approaches taken in motivation research, it has been hypothesized that the determinants of achievement behavior are approach and/or avoidance motives, expectancies, incentive values of success and failure, and/or cognitive assessments of success and failure (cf. Roberts, 1982, 1984, 1992).

Motivational theories are assumed to explain achievement behaviors. Typically these have been defined as behavioral intensity (trying hard), persistence (continuing to try hard), choice of action possibilities (playing basketball rather than football), and performance (outcomes) (Roberts, 1982). In sport, achievement behaviors are those behaviors witnessed when children try harder, concentrate more, persist longer, pay more attention, perform better, choose to practice longer, join, or drop out of sporting activities. These are the behaviors coaches use to assess the motivation of children in sport. They represent behaviors from which we infer motivation (Maehr & Nicholls, 1980) and define what we refer to when we state that an individual is or is not motivated (Maehr & Braskamp, 1986).

Let us now discuss the theories that have been proposed to explain motivation. In this section the focus will be on the most important general approaches. For more detailed reviews of these approaches, see Dweck and Elliott (1983) and Roberts (1982).

Conceptual Approaches to Understanding Motivation

The history of motivation theory has been the search for the "right" theory. When that theory evolved, it was assumed that a whole range of achievement behaviors would not only be better understood, but intervention opportunities would also be evident. But despite the efforts of many, the search continues. Many theories have been preferred, but no one theory has achieved universal acclaim. Some have advocated a more comprehensive theory of motivation (e.g., Maehr & Braskamp, 1986; Weiner, 1986), but again these have not met with general agreement.

The study of motivation is the investigation of the constructs that energize *and* direct behavior (Roberts, 1992). Theories of motivation must address both aspects. Thus some avenues of research that describe the direction of behavior without specifying why the behavior was energized are not motivational, even though they may help to explain achievement behaviors. An example in sport is the area of goal setting (cf. Weinberg, 1992). Goal setting specifies how achievement behaviors may be mediated, but to date no sufficient psychological explanation of the goal-setting phenomenon has been posited. Motivation theories are predicated on a set of assumptions about individuals and the factors that give impetus to achievement behaviors. Motivation theories ask *why*. When motivation matters, various theoretical models have been proposed as governing motivation and achievement behavior in sport settings.

Motivational theories are viewed as being on a continuum ranging from mechanistic to cognitive (Weiner, 1972). Mechanistic theories view humans as being passive and motivated by psychological drives, while cognitive theories view humans as being active and initiating action through subjective interpretation of the specific achievement contexts in which the individual finds him-or herself. In the early part of this century, mechanistic psychoanalytic drive theories dominated the field of psychology, and terms such as *equilibrium* and *hedonism* were utilized in order to describe motivated behavior. But motivation is more than striving for equilibrium or maximizing hedonism (Weiner, 1986). In addition, theorists gave credence to behaviorism during the 1940s and '50s, but the attraction of trying to understand humans as input-output connectors in terms of motivation waned as the cognitive revolution had its effect on the understanding of motivation (Roberts, 1992).

Among the many alternative approaches advocated, however, four major research traditions may be identified as being particularly significant within the sport context. These research traditions are: (1) need achievement theory; (2) test anxiety theory; (3) expectancy of reinforcement theory; and (4) social cognitive theory (Dweck & Elliott, 1983; Roberts, 1982). A brief overview of each approach follows.

Need Achievement Theory

There is no question that the most influential research tradition in motivation began with Murray (1938) and was further developed by McClelland and Atkinson and their colleagues (e.g., Atkinson, 1957, 1958; McClelland, 1961; McClelland, Atkinson, Clark, & Lowell, 1953). This approach assumed that motive states are the mainsprings of action in sport. These motive states are termed the *motive to achieve success* and the *motive to avoid failure,* and together they form the central constructs of the theory. McClelland believed that the motive interacts with cues from the environment to arouse affective states, typically believed to be pride and shame, which then elicit approach or avoidance behavior in achievement contexts. The approach incorporates a hedonic quality of behavior into an affective-arousal model (for more detailed reviews, see Dweck & Elliott, 1983; Roberts, 1982).

The McClelland-Atkinson tradition is an exemplary

model of psychological theorizing with concomitant empirical research conducted to verify the motive states. The research conducted in sport contexts has generally been similar to research in academic situations (see Carron, 1980; Roberts, 1982). Research has shown that individuals driven by the motive to achieve success select challenging tasks, take intermediate risk, and demonstrate improved performance, but those individuals driven by the motive to avoid failure do not always avoid intermediate risk, or select either easy or extremely challenging tasks, or demonstrate low performance as predicted by the theory (Roberts, 1972). The theory also has been criticized for its ethnocentric bias, the weight it places on elements of personality as the major energizing force of motivated states, and its failure to account for heightened performance of low-achievement-motivation individuals in some situations (Maehr, 1974). Even though much of the original research work by Atkinson (1957) was with children, the approach has not typically utilized children within the sport context. However, the approach has been very important to understanding the process of motivation, and many of the insights into motivation are intact in more contemporary approaches.

The Test Anxiety Approach

Based on the extensive research relating test anxiety to achievement, Sarason and colleagues (Mandler & Sarason, 1952; Sarason, Davidson, Lighthall, Waite, & Ruebrush, 1960) formulated a theory emphasizing the parent-child interaction during the preschool and elementary school years and the evaluative aspects of the school situation on the achievement behavior of children. The motivational variable in this theory is anxiety with evaluation. The research has focused on anxiety-evoking situations such as test taking and performing before peers (such as competition). The line of research has produced a convincing body of evidence indicating that performance on achievement tasks and before peers is influenced by evaluative anxiety. This approach has not been as popular in sport psychology circles, despite a deep interest in anxiety per se. The approach has given us insight into the affect-cognition linkage, however, and into how these linkages affect the ongoing stream of behavior in competitive sport environments. For a more detailed review of the impact of anxiety on behavior in sport, see Martens, Vealey, and Burton (1990).

Expectation of Reinforcement

The third major school of thought in motivation and achievement behavior is based on social learning theory. In particular, Crandall (1963, 1969) was interested in academic and intellectual achievement, particularly in situations where personal skill is important. The major motivational variable in this line of research is the individual's expectancy of reinforcement. These researchers emphasize expectancies rather than motive states, and the approach makes the assumption that achievement behavior is behavior directed toward the attainment of self-approval and the approval of others. The behavior is specifically contingent on criteria of performance competence (Roberts, 1982). The expectancies and values within this approach were precisely measured, and the findings pertaining to specific individual differences such as sex differences in expectancy of success remain among the most robust and important in the literature. Crandall was interested in athletic achievement; however, little work has been completed on the topic. The work that most closely relates to this approach in sport is the coaching effectiveness approach of Smith and Smoll (e.g., Smith, Smoll, & Curtis, 1979) and the self-efficacy approach to motivation (e.g., Feltz, 1988, 1992). However, the self-efficacy approach will be discussed later as a specific approach under the social cognitive rubric.

The Cognitive Approach

The most dramatic way in which the study of motivation has changed in the past 20 years is in the emergence of the cognitive paradigm (Roberts, 1989). The cognitive paradigm is now dominant in the study of motivation. Contemporary motivation research is replete with social cognitive models of motivation. For example, research into perceived competence (e.g., Klint & Weiss, 1987), self-efficacy (e.g., Feltz, 1988), intrinsic motivation (e.g., Vallerand and Reid, 1984), and achievement goals (e.g., Duda, 1992) come under the cognitive approach.

The essential element for a cognitive perspective on motivation is to study the way in which knowledge is acquired, represented, and used by humans. The emphasis is on understanding how cognitions and/or thoughts govern achievement behavior. The attempt is to understand how individuals *think* and how these thoughts govern action. Those scientists who work in the area of motivation and utilize cognitive models believe that behavioral variance in sport is better captured by these models because they incorporate the cognitions and beliefs of individuals. To a cognitive theorist, thought governs action (Weiner, 1972). In other words, the cognitions and beliefs of individuals mediate behavior, and it is up to scientists to describe and explain what constellations of cognitions affect the ongoing stream of achievement behaviors in sport.

When we look at the history of the cognitive revolution that has now taken over psychology, it may be argued that Tolman (1932) was the first psychologist to utilize cognitive constructs. Tolman believed that to understand achievement behavior a more flexible explanatory mechanism than the behavioristic approach was needed. Tolman argued that an individual may have a belief that a particular event will be followed by another event and that courses of action have consequences. Thus it was Tolman who introduced expectancy into the psychological literature, and expectancies have since become important in motivation theories. Choice and decision making began to replace stimulus-response associations in order to explain achievement behavior.

The major resurgence in cognitive constructs being utilized in motivation research can be dated to the late 1950s. It began with a series of unexpected findings that occurred in the laboratory of Harlow and eventually led deCharms (1968) to utilize a cognitive explanation to explain the findings. DeCharms coined the terms *origin* and *pawn* to describe the perception of control that individuals have over their behaviors. These concepts helped explain the unexpected persistence of primates in the Harlow experiments. But it was the work of Heider (1958) and White (1959) that provided the momentum for the present interest in cognitive approaches to motivation. Indeed, Csikszentmihalyi and Nakamura (1989) go so far as to state that the cognitive revolution that overtook psychology in the 1970s and '80s resurrected the study of motivation. This may be debatable, but it certainly gave the study of motivation a conceptual boost and new concepts and variables to study.

It was Bernard Weiner and his colleagues (Weiner, Frieze, Kukla, Reed, Rest, & Rosenbaum, 1971), however, who argued that those individuals who are high or low in achievement motivation, as defined by the need-achievement model, were likely to *think* differently about success and failure. This concept ushered in the beginning of a new era in the study of motivation. Weiner argued that thoughts, and causal attributions in particular, were the important variables to consider in understanding motivation. As Maehr (1989) has stated, Weiner's modest attempt to insert causal attributions into the achievement motivation equation has transformed the energy and focus of motivation research. The situation and its qualitative meaning became more important to understanding motivation, and individual differences and personality aspects became much less important (Maehr, 1989). A brief review of the approach of Weiner in attribution theory now follows. For a more detailed review, see the chapter by Biddle in this *Handbook*.

Attribution Theory

The attribution approach to motivation is reflected in the body of research generated from attribution theory (Weiner, 1979, 1986; Weiner et al., 1971). Attribution theory deals with the rules the average individual uses in attempting to account for the everyday causes of behavior. The researcher assumes the phenomenological outlook of the man in the street, who is attempting to determine the causes of everyday events (Heider, 1958). Attributional theory is concerned with the procedures people use and the naive attributional schema individuals adopt in order to make sense of their lives. This approach regards the human as an active information-processing organism with the inclusion of higher mental processes as determinants of human physical action.

The emphasis of attribution theory has been on expectancy, with affect assuming much more importance of late (Weiner, 1986). Weiner argues that it is the manner in which one attributes the causes of success and failure that affects expectancies of future success and failure and is assumed to affect achievement striving. It has been found that different attributions reflect different expectations of future outcomes. It is this pattern of attributions that has interested researchers the most (see Roberts, 1982).

Most of the research in sport and physical activity settings utilizing attributional theory has been with winning and losing in sport contexts. In the studies investigating how individuals determine the causes of their own and other people's success and failure in sport, winning and losing have been experimentally manipulated, have occurred in natural sport settings, or individuals have been asked to imagine themselves or someone else as winning or losing in a sporting event (cf. Roberts, 1982). The attributions about the outcome are assumed to affect the expectancy for future wins and losses and affect, which in turn affects future achievement behaviors. Research has established, both with populations of children and adults, that individuals utilize information in systematic ways in order to arrive at causal attributions for wins and losses. Individuals analyze sport outcomes in terms of the available information concerning the influence of a given causal factor, and causal attributions are made based on the perceived covariation of cause and effect (see Brawley & Roberts, 1984; Roberts, 1982).

During the 1970s and '80s, attribution work in sport grew in both interest and volume. This corpus of work has been discussed elsewhere by recent reviews (Biddle, this volume; Brawley & Roberts, 1984; McAuley & Duncan, 1990; Rejeski & Brawley, 1983; Roberts, 1982, 1984). Suffice it to say that while research efforts have demonstrated that motivation is very much a product of cognitive processes, the research has not been without criticism. The focus of much attribution work in sport revolves around: (1) the number of causes or attributional elements specified in studies—these elements are more numerous than have been recognized within the sport literature until more recently (e.g., Roberts & Pascuzzi, 1979); (2) the dimensional relevance of particular attributional elements—the dimensional relevance of these elements was often assumed, and researchers simply ignored whether the *meaning* of the attributional element was pertinent to the athletes (e.g., Bukowski & Moore, 1980; Roberts & Pascuzzi, 1979); (3) the meaning of the outcome to the athlete—in sport we often assume that winning and losing are respectively synonymous with success and failure (e.g., Spink & Roberts, 1980); and (4) how and when we should measure attributions (Brawley & Roberts, 1984; McAuley & Duncan, 1990; Roberts, 1982).

Many of these issues have been addressed, and satisfactory resolutions to the criticisms have been advocated (e.g., Brawley & Roberts, 1984; McAuley & Duncan, 1990). But attribution theory has never been able to overcome the criticism that it is less a psychology of motivation and more a social psychology of perception (Roberts, 1982), even though affect has assumed more importance of late (Weiner, 1986).

It is when attribution theory is considered as a means of suggesting interventions that we really note its weakness. Attribution theory is very useful in explaining why things may go wrong and lead to demotivation in the motivational process, but it is not a very effective theory for describing how to put these issues right (Roberts, 1982). While attributional models have been useful in interventions in the classroom (e.g., attribution retraining (Dweck, 1975, 1980)), these attributional models never translated successfully to sport.

Having stated that, however, it must be recognized that the attributional approach has opened up important avenues in the investigation of motivation and is considered to be an important ingredient in any comprehensive theory of motivation utilizing a cognitive perspective. But attribution theory does not constitute a comprehensive theory in and of itself. The theory has never addressed value in the expectancy $\times$ value paradigm in any systematic way, and focuses on why people expect to succeed, not on why they want to succeed (Dweck & Elliott, 1983; Roberts, 1992). But it is a truism to state that every contemporary social cognitive approach to motivation owes its roots to attribution theory. It is to these more recent approaches that we now turn.

Social Cognitive Approaches to Motivation

The social cognitive approach draws on past theories to portray a dynamic process incorporating sets of cognitive, affective, and value-related variables that are assumed to mediate the choice and attainment of achievement goals and achievement behaviors of individuals. In this review, I shall focus on specific formulations, but articulate the general aspects of this social cognitive model. Even though the social cognitive approach utilizes expectancies, competence demonstration, and values within this general formulation, several specific theories have become popular within this framework. These specific theories are often regarded as separate entities. However, there is a great deal of convergence in these models as they utilize very similar constructs (see Roberts, 1992).

The major specific theories most utilized in sport are self-efficacy (Bandura, 1977, 1986), perceived competence (Harter, 1975, 1980), and the various achievement goal perspectives extant (Dweck, 1986; Dweck & Elliott, 1983; Maehr & Braskamp, 1986; Maehr & Nicholls, 1980; Nicholls, 1980, 1984, 1989). Investigations using these theories in sport have increased considerably in the last few years. A brief discussion follows as to how each approach has been used in sport, especially where children are concerned.

Self-Efficacy. The theory of self-efficacy has been one of the most extensively used concepts for investigating motivational issues in sport and exercise. For detailed reviews of this work, see Feltz (1988, 1992), and McAuley (1992). Originally proposed as an explanation of the various intervention procedures utilized in the treatment of anxiety, self-efficacy has been used in sport to explain the mediation of achievement behaviors. Bandura (1977) used the term *self-efficacy* to describe the conviction one has to successfully execute the behavior necessary to produce a certain outcome. Self-efficacy is not concerned with the ability of the person per se, but with the assessment of what the individual can do with his or her competencies (Feltz, 1992; McAuley, 1992). This is why some sport psychologists have utilized self-confidence synonymously with self-efficacy (e.g., Vealey, 1986). The motivational mechanism of self-efficacy theory is the assessment of one's capability to perform at a given level in an achievement context of value to the participant. In short, mastery expectations influence performance (Bandura, 1977).

Research in sport and motor performance has focused on one of two issues in general: (1) the methods used to create self-efficacy; and (2) the relationship of self-efficacy to performance (Feltz, 1988). Both areas of research have used performance measures as dependent measures. The research that has looked at methods of enhancing self-efficacy has established that participant modeling, vicarious experiences, and other antecedents have effected self-efficacy in the predicted directions (Feltz, 1988). However, not all studies show an enhancement of performance. In those studies that have examined the relationship of self-efficacy to sport performance the results do indeed show that a positive performance relationship exists, but the relationship is much more modest than most reviewers confess. Indeed, in some cases the relationship is weak (Feltz, 1982; McAuley, 1985). The general findings suggest that while self-efficacy has shown itself to be a reliable, even if modest, predictor of sport performance, other mechanisms can and do contribute to achievement behaviors (Bandura, 1986; Feltz, 1988).

As an aside, it is a truism that self-efficacy fares better when exercise behavior is considered. Self-efficacy has been shown to affect exercise compliance, reliably predict adherence, and predict cardiac recovery of patients (see McAuley, 1992). The major reason why self-efficacy fares better in predicting exercise achievement behavior is that the dependent measure of importance in exercise can often be defined in terms of persistence. And sport studies that use persistence as a performance measure (e.g., an endurance test) also show stronger and reliable relationships (Feltz, 1988, 1992). It is the studies that use sport performance criteria that appear to have the weaker relationships (see Roberts, 1992). Therefore, there may be some constraints to the usefulness of self-efficacy in sport contexts.

Perceived Competence. Another series of motivational theories revolve around the perception of competence, or ability, on the part of the participant. The work of Harter (1978, 1980) has been used in sport in particular. Based on the seminal work of White (1959), Harter attempted to explain why individuals feel impelled to engage in mastery attempts in achievement contexts. To Harter, perceived competence is a multidimensional motive that directs individuals in the cognitive, social, and physical domains. Success and failure in these domains are evaluated by significant others (parents, teachers, peers), and the perceived competence and intrinsic pleasure gained from these evaluations are seen to increase achievement striving when success is realized. The perception of incompetence and displeasure are assumed to lead to anxiety and a decrease in achievement striving when failure is realized. The appeal of the model is obvious, especially for those researchers who work with children. Further, the model was easily utilized in the sport context. This was due to the fact that Harter had a measurement technology that included perceived competence in the physical domain. Typically studies have looked at the relationship of perceived to actual competence, the antecedents of perceived competence, and the relationship of perceived competence to participation in competitive sports.

A prediction of Harter's (1980) model is that children who perceive themselves competent in sport should be likely to participate in sports. Roberts, Kleiber, and Duda (1981) found that sport participants were higher in perceived competence, as measured by the physical competence scale of Harter, than nonparticipants in sport. The relationship was not strong, and while other research has supported this initial finding, the relationship continues to be weak (e.g., Feltz & Petlickoff, 1983; Ulrich, 1987). Even when Harter's scale was modified to be more sport-specific, the relationships have remained weak (Feltz & Brown, 1984).

It has been suggested that children may participate in sport for many reasons other than the demonstration of competence (Gould, Feltz, Horn, & Weiss, 1982). Klint and Weiss (1987) found that children with high scores of physical competence did engage in sport, but that some participated for affiliation or social reasons. For children, the reasons for being involved in the competitive sport experience may be many (Feltz, 1988). But continued engagement in a context where physical competence is placed at a premium may favor those who wish to demonstrate competence as part of their motivational set.

When researchers have looked at years of playing experience and predicted that those who are higher in perceived competence would remain in competitive sport experience longer, the relationships have remained weak (Feltz & Brown, 1984; Feltz & Petlickoff, 1983; Roberts et al., 1981). Indeed, Roberts and his colleagues suggested that sport participation may have little effect on children's perceptions of competence, rather the domain of sport is attractive to children who already perceive themselves to be high in perceived competence. But this contention is difficult to substantiate. Harter's (1978) model has some other problems within the competitive sport experience. The theory is predicated on a mastery orientation toward achievement striving (see Nicholls, 1989; Roberts, 1992); however, the scale utilized by Harter assumes a more ego-involving conception of ability (Nicholls, 1984). This raises some difficulties when perception of competence is measured within

the competitive sport context (Roberts, 1992). Thus in competitive sport, work utilizing the Harter model must be viewed with some degree of reservation.

Achievement Goal Approaches. Based on the joint and independent theoretical and empirical work of Maehr, Nicholls, and Dweck (e.g., Dweck, 1986; Dweck & Elliott,1983; Maehr & Braskamp, 1986; Maehr & Nicholls, 1980; Nicholls, 1980, 1984, 1989), it is argued that to understand motivation and achievement behavior in all of its forms, the function and meaning of behavior must be taken into account so that the goals of action may be identified. By so doing, multiple goals for behavior are identified, not just one. Variation in behavior may not be the result of high or low motivation, as has been assumed in some theories, but rather the manifestation of different perceptions of what is the appropriate goal within that social context. For example, some children may want to achieve in order to receive social approval from others, but other children may want to achieve in order to demonstrate competence to others. For an individual to invest personal resources such as effort, talent, and time in an activity is dependent on the achievement goal of that individual for that activity (see Maehr & Braskamp, 1986).

The first step to understanding achievement behavior under the achievement goal approach is to recognize that success and failure are psychological states based on the interpretation of the effectiveness of that person's achievement striving (Maehr & Nicholls, 1980; Spink & Roberts, 1981). If the outcome of the achievement striving is seen to reflect desirable attributes to the self, such as high effort or high ability, then the outcome is interpreted as success. For example, if children wish to receive social approval for effort expended, and they actually receive the social approval, then they are satisfied and perceive accomplishment, regardless of the outcome of the effort. Conversely if the outcome is seen to reflect undesirable qualities of the self, such as laziness or poor ability, then the outcome is regarded as a failure. Success, failure, and achievement are only recognized in terms of the goal of behavior for that individual. As is obvious, what is success for one may be failure for another.

Various forms of achievement goals have been identified, but the ones that emerge consistently, across studies in sport, generally reflect the hypotheses of Maehr and Nicholls (1980). Even though Nicholls, Maehr, and Dweck advocate somewhat different approaches today, the original goal orientations are the ones most studied in sport.

The achievement goal approach assumes that two goals in particular function in achievement contexts. These achievement goals have been contrasted as task- versus ego-involved (Duda, 1989; Maehr & Nicholls, 1980; Nicholls, 1984, 1989) as learning- versus performance-oriented (Dweck, 1986; Dweck & Elliott, 1983; Elliott & Dweck, 1988) and as mastery- versus ability-focused (Ames, 1984, 1987, 1992). But the relationship between the task, learning, and mastery goals and between the ego, performance, and ability goals are convergent (Nicholls, 1989; Roberts,

1992). Therefore, these goals can be viewed as synonymous for our purposes in this chapter. For consistency and clarity within the sport contexts, such goals are termed mastery and competitiveness within sport (Roberts, 1992). They are assumed to be orthogonal and relate to how an individual objectively evaluates his or her level of competence within a sport context.

When an individual has a mastery goal perspective, that individual is concerned with demonstrating learning or mastery at the task (Ames, 1984; Dweck, 1986; Maehr & Braskamp, 1986; Nicholls, 1984). The goal drives achievement behavior when learning and mastery are determined to be important to the achiever. The person employs a task-involved perception of ability (Nicholls, 1984, 1989) where perceptions of ability are self-referenced and dependent on learning or improvement at the task.

When one has a competitive goal perspective, he or she is concerned with demonstrating ability compared to others (Ames, 1984; Dweck, 1986; Maehr & Braskamp, 1986; Nicholls, 1984). This goal drives achievement behavior in circumstances where social comparison is extant. The individual employs an ego-involved conception of ability (Nicholls, 1984, 1989) where perceptions of ability are other-referenced and dependent on the subjective assessment of comparing one's ability with that of others. There are considerable data to support the existence and relevance of both of these goals in sport (Duda, 1989, 1992, this volume; Roberts, 1992).

The interesting question under the achievement goal approach is how do individuals develop one goal of action versus another. Nicholls (1984, 1989) argues that the subjective experience of the individual, the social constraints placed on the individual, and the subjective perception of the psychological climate (whether task involvement or ego involvement is extant) of the achievement context will engage one conception of ability versus another. In this way, the individual develops the achievement goal consistent with that conception of ability (Ames, 1992; Ames & Archer, 1987; Nicholls, 1984, 1989; Roberts, 1992). As can be seen, if a task involvement conception of ability is emphasized by teachers, parents, and/or coaches, the child is likely to develop a mastery perspective as an achievement goal. Conversely, if an ego involvement conception of ability is emphasized by significant others, the child is likely to develop a competitive perspective as an achievement goal (Ames, 1992; Nicholls, 1989).

The elements that may engage ego-versus-task-involved conceptions of ability, which lead to the development of the goals of mastery and competitiveness, are tests of valued skills, competition, or other factors that increase self-awareness, such as audiences (Nicholls, 1989; Roberts, 1992). Thus the perceived dynamics of the social context lead to the development of one achievement goal over another (see Ames, 1992; Roberts, 1992). Therefore, it is important at this time to consider the dynamics of the social context of sport in order to appreciate the social dynamics that influence children. What are the social constraints placed on children in sport?

THE DOMAIN OF SPORT

There is no question that organized sports for children have expanded dramatically over the past decade. Estimates of the number of children involved in the United States range up to 30 million in any one year. Estimates of the total number of children involved worldwide range up to 200 million (Roberts, 1992). Competitive sport organizations have directed much attention to developing competitive sport experiences for children across the age span. In one state, for example, there is even competitive wrestling for 4-year-olds. Many attribute this expansion to the impact of televised sports, but the primary reason for the elevation of competitive sports for children is the belief that if we do not introduce skills to children at young ages, the child will never have the potential to become an elite athlete. Therefore, there is a great deal of pressure to develop sport skills in the young, and this pressure comes from sport organizations that believe we need to develop sport skills in children in order to enhance the potential pool of elite athletes in the future.

It is also a truism that as a correlate to this increased emphasis on children's sports, children are more and more likely to participate in childlike versions of recognized adult sport activities in their recreational time (Kleiber & Roberts, 1981). A consequence of the increase in organized sport for children has been a related decrease in the number of children involved in their own recreational game activities (Roberts, 1984). There is a tendency for young children, as they become older, to increase their engagement in organized sport activities.

Although there are conceptual similarities between sport and the games modern children play, they can be distinguished in one important respect—the degree to which participants have control over the design and maintenance of the activity (Kleiber & Roberts, 1983; Roberts, 1984). When children play games, they generally engage in playful competition where the outcome is determined by physical skills, strategy, or chance (Loy, 1969; Roberts & Sutton-Smith, 1962). Sport, on the other hand, is the institutionalization of a game with established rules, national regulations, and a governing administrative superstructure of adults (Loy, 1969). It is true that children may engage in the activity in a playful manner, but the essential feature of sport is in its organizational structure, which provides for the maintenance and direction of the activity through rules interpreted by adults who act as officials. The concern of children within sport is the performance and the outcome rather than with the design and maintenance of the activity, which is more characteristic of recreational games.

Despite the increased number of participants in children's sports, the growing encroachment of sport on children's free time, and the potential impact on the social and moral development of children (Bredemeier & Shields, 1987), little systematic research has been conducted in the domain. One of the hoped-for consequences of this chapter is to increase interest and research on this topic.

However, before addressing the issue of children's motivation in sport, let me set a frame of reference for the context of sport.

The Social Context of Sport

There are many reasons why competitive sport is a context that is appropriate to the study of motivation, especially that of children. Clearly sport competition is a classic achievement-oriented context and conforms to most definitions of achievement-oriented contexts necessary to examine achievement behavior (cf. Roberts, 1984, 1992). The individual or team is striving to achieve a goal or standard of excellence. The individual is responsible for the behaviors leading to the outcome, and the process is evaluative in that the present others can evaluate the performance of the individual in terms of success or failure.

The second reason that sport is an important context for children is that being competent at physical skills is very important to children, boys in particular (Roberts, 1978, 1980, 1984; Scanlan, 1978). It has been suggested that sporting activities may be *the* domain in which young boys utilize social comparison processes in order to determine their standing among their peers and to determine their self-worth (Veroff, 1969). Evans and Roberts (1987) have further suggested that sport contexts are important for children to determine their friendship patterns. Duda (1981) supported this in that with high school boys and girls, she found that boys and girls preferred to be successful in sporting contexts rather than in classroom contexts. Duda further found that boys found failure in sport contexts to be more aversive than failure in academic contexts. In fact, it is almost impossible to underestimate the importance of participating in sport activities for children, boys in particular.

But a paradox exists. Despite viewing sports as a highly desirable context in which to achieve, children apparently lose motivation and drop out of the competitive sport experience at strikingly high rates, especially after age 12. Indeed, by the time they reach 17 years of age, 80% of children have dropped out of the context of sport (Seefeldt, Blievernicht, Bruce, & Gilliam, 1978). This phenomenon is not restricted to North America; Australia and Europe show similar drop-out trends, especially for boys (Roberts, 1984). The question clearly presents itself: Why do children lose motivation and drop out of the sport experience? This question is clearly a motivational issue.

Research into the decrease in motivation of children in sport that leads to dropping out has been disappointing in the past. Most of the evidence has been descriptive in nature, with researchers implicating the structure of the sport experience as the cause of the high drop-out rates (e.g., adults putting too much pressure on children and/or too much emphasis on winning) or concluding that conflict of interest (e.g., "I have other things to do") is a primary reason why children lose motivation and drop out of sport (Orlick & Botterill, 1975; Gould, Feltz, Horn, & Weiss, 1982). It is not surprising, therefore, that sport psycholo-

gists seek more specific causes to explain the issue. Recent research has begun to give insight into this phenomenon. This research has shown that we need to understand how children subjectively perceive the sport situation if we wish to explain the apparent lack of motivation.

UNDERSTANDING THE MOTIVATION OF CHILDREN

As indicated earlier, there are many conceptual approaches to understanding the motivation of children. But it is the more qualitative approach to motivation inherent in the social-cognitive perspective that has given us the most powerful insights into the motivation of children. The approaches of Dweck (e.g., 1986), Nicholls (e.g., 1989), and Ames (e.g., 1984), along with their respective colleagues, have given us the conceptual and empirical insights that have led to greater understanding of children in motivational contexts. Dweck, Nicholls, and Ames all argue that in order to understand the motivation of children, the function and meaning of behavior to the child must be taken into account, and the goal of action considered. These goals of action identified earlier become important in understanding these achievement behaviors. The achievement goal approach assumes that two achievement goals (at least) function in achievement contexts. These achievement goals have been identified as *mastery* and *competitiveness within sport* (Roberts, 1984; 1992). As an aside, these goals are labeled *task* and *ego orientation* by Duda (in this volume) and *mastery* and *performance goals* by Dweck (1986) and Ames (1992). But the goals defined are identical to the mastery and competitiveness goals discussed in this chapter. I simply prefer these latter labels when describing these goals as they are manifested in sport. I prefer the terms *ego* and *task involvement* to refer to the two conceptions of ability that lead to the development of the goals (see Nicholls, 1989; Roberts, 1992). As noted previously, the achievement context of sport is very likely to engage the ego-involved conception of ability, which may direct the child to develop a competitive achievement goal within sport contexts. Thus, when considering achievement behaviors of children in sport, the goal of competitiveness assumes considerable importance.

The literature examining achievement goals has demonstrated that achievement behaviors are related to the achievement goals. If one has the goal of mastery, then the individual is likely to engage in adaptive patterns of behavior. Adaptive patterns of behavior are when a person chooses moderately challenging tasks, focuses on effort within the context, tries hard in the face of difficulty or failure, is interested in the task, and persists in the task over time (Ames, 1984, 1992; Duda, 1989, 1992; Dweck, 1986; Nicholls, 1984, 1989; Roberts, 1984, 1992). The same pattern of adaptive achievement behavior is also assumed to hold for competitive goal-oriented people when their perception of ability is high (Dweck, 1986). That is, when a child is competitive-oriented and has the perception that his or her ability is high, then he or she will also focus on effort, try hard in the face of failure, and persist in the task over time. However, Dweck has argued that adaptive behaviors of individuals who are competitive-oriented is very fragile in the face of failure or difficulty. The perception of ability may weaken, and in such instances maladaptive patterns of behavior will manifest themselves. Maladaptive behaviors are those behaviors when an individual chooses easy or hard tasks in order to avoid challenge, does not exert effort in the achievement context, has deteriorating performance over time, and lacks persistence (Ames, 1984, 1992; Duda, 1989, 1992; Dweck, 1986; Nicholls, 1984, 1989; Roberts, 1984, 1992).

The evidence in support of such manifestations of behaviors consistent with the achievement goal of the individual is now considerable in the academic context. Evidence has shown that learning-oriented (Dweck, 1986), task-involved (Nicholls, 1989), or mastery-oriented (Ames, 1987) children manifest adaptive behaviors in achievement contexts. Further, these same adaptive patterns are present when perception of ability is high. However, when children are performance-oriented (Dweck, 1986), ego-involved (Nicholls, 1989), or ability-focused (Ames, 1987), children manifest maladaptive patterns of behavior in achievement contexts. For extensive reviews, see Ames (1987), Dweck and Leggett (1988), and Nicholls (1989). Although there is evidence to demonstrate that achievement goals do operate in the context of sport, it is less extensive. The evidence to illustrate the approach taken by researchers in sport psychology will be discussed next.

Achievement Goals in Sport

Research in this area has been directed at developing measures of mastery and competitive goals, investigating the behavioral and cognitive correlates of goal perspectives within sport, and investigating the impact of the goal perspectives on the achievement and motivational strategies of children. Let us review the development of measures first.

One of the assumptions made by the achievement goal approach is that different goal perspectives do exist. Therefore, measures to assess each goal have been developed by the different researchers. But unfortunately these measures have been primarily research protocols rather than psychometrically derived measuring instruments. And, as is the case in these situations, each researcher has a different protocol to assess goal strength. However, in sport Duda (1992) as well as Roberts and Balague (1989, 1991) are developing measures of mastery and competitive goals. Roberts and Balague also are developing a scale for children. In essence, the research into developing measures of goal perspectives in sport has been very promising. The goal perspectives of mastery and competitiveness have been orthogonally isolated, and the psychometric properties of the scales are strong (Duda, 1992; Roberts & Balague, 1989, 1991; Roberts, Hall, Jackson, Kimiecik, & Tonymon, 1990).

These measures will be useful for ongoing research into the motivational implications of holding goal perspectives in sport in the future.

The research demonstrating the cognitive correlates of goal perspectives in sport is also somewhat limited. However, the extant evidence shows that the predictions that were supported within the academic domain are supported in the sport domain. That is, holding a mastery-goal perspective shows that individuals hold performance attributions consistent with adaptive achievement behaviors, whereas competitive goal perspective individuals who are low in perception of ability make attributions more consistent with maladaptive achievement striving (see Duda, this volume, for a detailed review). Thus, in sport, the findings are consistent with those in academic settings (Duda, 1992; this volume; Duda & Chi, 1989; Hall, 1990; Jackson & Roberts, 1990; Roberts, Hall, Jackson, Kimiecik, & Tonymon, 1990). For example, Jackson and Roberts (1990) found that competitive goal individuals are less likely than mastery goal individuals to experience positive performance states (such as the experience of peak performance). Further, Hall found that individuals who were low in perceived ability performed better when placed in a mastery-oriented performance climate than when placed in a competitive-oriented performance climate. In summary, the limited available evidence confirms the motivational, behavioral, and cognitive predictions emanating from academic contexts when individuals hold either a mastery or a competitive goal perspective (cf. Duda, 1992; this volume).

It is with more recent data, however, that the predictions of academic contexts have been supported strongly. Nicholls, Patashnick, and Nolen (1985) found that goal perspectives were also related to "world views" of the purposes of education. They observed that a competitive goal was related to the view that education is a means to an end, the end being wealth and status. A mastery goal, on the other hand, was related to the view that one should undergo education so that one's commitment to society and desire to continue learning should be enhanced. Duda (1989) replicated this work in sport and confirmed that competitive goals were related to sport being a means to an end, to extrinsic benefits, and that personal gains should be enhanced. A mastery goal was related to cooperation and personal learning. Roberts, Hall, Jackson, Kimiecik, and Tonymon (1990) extended the research to include achievement strategies in practice and performance. It was found that competitive goals were related to being bored in practice, to focusing upon winning in competition, and to believing that sport should enhance one's status. A mastery goal, on the other hand, was found to be related to satisfaction in sport, to learning and obtaining social approval in practice, and believing that sport should enhance social responsibility. Thus with older subjects, the achievement goal perspectives to understanding achievement behaviors of individuals within sport have had strong support. When we consider children within the sport experience, however, the issue is a little more complex. Let us now turn to that research.

It was Ewing (1981) who provided the first evidence that goal perspectives are important motivational correlates to behavior for children. In her research with 12- to 15-year-old adolescents, Ewing found that the adolescents demonstrated goal perspectives of mastery and competitiveness (along with a social-approval goal perspective). Of equal interest, she found also that individuals who are high in competitiveness were the ones most likely to drop out of sport. That is, competitive goal perspective individuals were most likely to exhibit the maladaptive achievement striving behavior of giving up. Ewing did not measure perception of ability per se, but it might be surmised that it was the competitive goal children who perceived they had low ability that were most likely to drop out. However, further research is needed to verify this hypothesis.

In a follow-up study, Ewing, Roberts, and Pemberton (1985) used factor-analytic procedures to investigate the development of the goals in 9- to 14-year-old children and found developmental differences. Young children (9–11 years of age) showed a clear mastery-goal perspective. The competitive goal perspective did not emerge until the children were approximately 11 to 12 years of age. This confirmed the findings of Nicholls (1978), who discovered that children were unable to distinguish between the concepts of effort and ability until after age 12. For the goal of competitiveness to manifest itself in children, they must be able to assess the relative contribution of effort and ability to success and failure within sport. Children must recognize that ability is capacity and that effort is necessary in order to demonstrate ability. Therefore, young children (under age 11 or 12 years) do not have a competitive goal perspective and are, therefore, unlikely to demonstrate maladaptive behaviors because of an accurate assessment of normative ability. Children may, of course, develop maladaptive behaviors for other reasons. It is only when children are able to differentiate ability and effort that the competitive goal emerges. As Roberts (1984) argued, this is why children do not typically drop out of sport until after the age of 12 years. It is only then that children recognize that ability is capacity, and if they perceive themselves to be low in ability, they exhibit maladaptive achievement striving in order to escape the inevitable assessment of lower capacity than others if they continue to try hard.

More recently, Buchan and Roberts (1991) assessed the perception of success of children at two different ages (9–10 years and 13–14 years) and confirmed this hypothesis. They were interested in determining the achievement goals held by the children at these ages and used both quantitative and interview measurement approaches. Buchan and Roberts noted that the older age children were clearly more competitive-goal-oriented than the younger age group. The younger age group had mixed interpretations pertaining to goal perspectives but predominantly focused on a mastery goal. In addition, Buchan and Roberts found sex differences. Boys are more competitive-goal-oriented than girls. Interestingly no interactions occurred in this data. The interview data supported the above. Children were able to clearly distinguish between mastery and competitive goals when they were in the older age group. For the younger children, however, they tended to focus on mastery. The responses of the younger children clearly showed a focus on effort and improving one's own performance-adaptive achievement striving. Yet by age 13, boys and girls clearly showed a focus on relative ability and recognized that success was primarily geared toward demonstrating greater ability than others.

Watkins and Montgomery (1989) examined the beliefs pertaining to athletic excellence among children and adolescents. They wanted to determine whether beliefs changed over the age span of interest in their study (8–9, 11–12, 14–15, and 17–18 years of age). Watkins and Montgomery found that younger athletes were not able to differentiate athletic excellence as well as the older adolescents. The two younger age groups were similar in their beliefs, whereas the older age groups were able to recognize and label athletic excellence accurately. There was a general rise in the perception that ability was capacity as subjects grew older, which supported other research (Ewing et al., 1985; Nicholls, 1978; Roberts & Buchan, 1991).

In summary, it is quite clear that children do develop the achievement goals of mastery and competitiveness by age 12–13 years of age. By this age, children have clear achievement goals that are consistent with mastery-and/or competitive-goal perspectives.

It should be clear now that the age of the child is important when considering the effect of holding-goal perspectives on achievement behavior. Young children, under age 12, are more likely to be oriented toward a mastery-goal perspective and are also very oriented toward social approval (Ewing, 1981). Because they lack internalized standards of excellence, children look to others for social approval. Thus the cues and feedback given by significant others is critical (Ames, 1989). But it is no less critical for the older age children. Even when children do develop the capacity to differentiate effort and ability (Nicholls, 1978, 1989), it is not inevitable that children all focus on social comparison and develop a competitive goal. However, within the achievement context of sport, we have seen that social comparison and relative ability are important criteria for children to assess their ongoing achievement striving. Thus the social factors and constraints that lead a child to develop one goal versus another become important. Do the situational constraints have an impact on the development of one goal versus another? It is to that aspect we now turn.

The Impact of the Motivational Climate

It is at this point that the research efforts of Ames (1987, in press) become important. Ames argues that parents, teachers, and/or coaches create psychological climates that affect participants in achievement contexts. Ames has looked at how the structure of achievement situations influence the adoption of ego or task conceptions of ability. Children are exposed to goal structures created by adults who govern the achievement context. It is these goal structures that create different processes of self-evaluation and attribution assessments in terms of performance assessment. Coaches, for example, when they talk to athletes about their performances, whether in practice or competition, have choices to make about how to present information to athletes. It is these *choice points* (Ames, 1992) that become critical in determining the motivational climate. By giving certain cues, rewards, and making explicit expectations, the coach structures the motivational climate of the sport context so that task-involved or ego-involved conceptions of ability are the criteria by which performance is evaluated. The coach's goal preferences become manifest, and children perceive the goal structure and act accordingly. In this way the goal structure created by the coach establishes a motivational climate that makes one conception of ability or the other manifest. Children are exposed to the explicit criteria that impinge on their own assessment within the context. The psychological climate created by parents and coaches has the effect of developing one goal perspective over the other.

Coaches have a choice to make of which psychological climate to create. Within sport and exercise settings both competitive and mastery climates can exist. Clearly competitive climates exist in competitive sport when winning is the criterion of success for the coach and the parents. But competitive sport also can have a mastery climate where getting better, or improving from game to game, is the criterion of success of the coaching staff. Similarly practice sessions can be mastery or competitive in orientation, depending on the cues and evaluative feedback given by the coaches and parents. Therefore, it is possible to have either a mastery or a competitive motivational climate in both practice and competitive situations. However, as indicated, the most likely climate to occur in sport is a competitive climate for all of the reasons articulated earlier. The evaluative climate of competition means that coaches have to emphasize mastery criteria if they wish to avoid focusing children on ego involvement conceptions of ability.

The competitive climate forces children to focus on the conception of ability that is ego-involved, and this leads to the development of a competitive goal perspective. This competitive climate leads many children to adopt an ego-involved criterion of ability. This means that children adopt a normative criterion for the assessment of competence. When winning becomes the means of enhancing the competence of children, few win, and this leads many of them to the perception of low ability and to dropping out (cf. Roberts, 1984). For those children who perceive themselves as being able, a normative criterion of assessment is acceptable. These are the children who win, who perceive success, and perceive that they have more ability than children who lose. But something is amiss if some children are systematically encouraged at the expense of others. Yet this inequality of motivation appears inevitable in a competitive system of organized sport for children that focuses on outcomes as the major criterion of success and failure (Roberts, 1984).

There have been some attempts to change the climate in structural terms—modifying the sport itself so that we have smaller playing fields, with fewer children on each team. Where these efforts have been made, such modifications have been reasonably successful. An example is the establishment of the game of mini-rugby in Britain in 1971. This is a game that was devised and adapted to suit the abilities of young players. The exceptionally tough and highly competitive game of rugby as played by adults was considered too complicated for beginners. The range of skills necessary for playing the full game made too many demands on those new to the game. When young players attempted to play the adult, 15-on-a-side game, the result was 30 players hopelessly chasing the ball with little real involvement for most because few players got to actually touch the ball. Consequently mastery of the fundamentals of the game was nearly impossible. Mini-rugby thus is a modified game. In the mini version, fewer players are involved, and the emphasis is on contact with and skillful handling of the ball. The response of the new competitive youth game has been excellent: mini-rugby is now widely played in schools in the British Isles (Williams, 1986). But no systematic research data in the sport realm is currently available to inform us of the motivational impact of such modifications.

While changing the structure of the game can be effective, it is the research that is directed at changing the motivational climate of the classroom or the sports field that is most promising in terms of enhancing the motivational behaviors of children.

The Effect of a Mastery Climate. An important avenue of research has progressed by studying how the structure and demands of creating a mastery, or learning, environment can evoke different goal orientations. As a result, different patterns of achievement behavior are manifested (Ames, 1992; Ames & Ames, 1984; Ames & Archer, 1987, 1990). Ames and colleagues have investigated the effects of such climates on achievement patterns of behavior.

Mastery-related cues are conveyed by many aspects of the learning environment—from how tasks are defined to how children are grouped, to how they are recognized and evaluated by others. The premise of Ames's research is that the nature of children's experiences can influence the degree to which a mastery orientation is salient. Consequently a child will develop adaptive patterns of behavior in mastery climates. Although most of her research has been conducted in classroom settings, Ames's research extends to contexts such as sport, where the information and reward structure is imposed by adults.

The first study (Ames & Archer, 1987) with high school students established a strong relationship between perception of a mastery-goal orientation and motivation. Students who saw their experiences as mastery-oriented were more likely to use effort strategies, prefer challenging tasks, like their class more, and believe that success and effort covaried. In a follow-up study with the same subjects, Ames and Archer (1990) found that for those students who remained with mastery-oriented teachers in subsequent years and had been in a mastery climate the longest had the most marked adaptive achievement behaviors. Children experience new teachers and new settings all the time and are exposed to different motivational climates.

Ames and her colleagues have also investigated the phenomenon with younger children. Powell (1990) found that the extent to which students viewed their learning experiences as mastery-oriented were significantly related to whether they reported using effective strategies for learning math. Ames and Maehr (1989) observed similar patterns for junior high students in science classes. Students who saw their science classes as mastery-oriented were more likely to use effective strategies and show a preference for challenging tasks. Finally Ames (1992) examined these relationships with motivationally "at-risk" children. Children at risk are considered to be physically awkward or cognitively unprepared for learning, lack self-confidence, and are often regarded as learned helpless (Dweck, 1975). These children are typically regarded to be at risk because they are likely to drop out, either mentally or behaviorally.

Ames (1992) taught an experimental group of teachers to create a mastery climate within the classroom. The procedures were complex, but in essence teachers always gave feedback to children anchored to the child's previous performance, never in comparison with other children. The teachers who created a mastery climate, for both the children at risk and normal children, enhanced children's involvement in learning as well as their quality of learning compared to a control group. In other words, mastery climates enhanced adaptive achievement strategies, for all children in the experimental classrooms, especially for the at-risk children. The at-risk children were much less likely to develop the learned helpless syndrome (see Dweck, 1975).

There is no work in sport involving children at the present time that has specifically had adults change the motivational climate of the achievement context. But some indirect evidence exists. Weitzer (1989) found that boys and girls who emphasize mastery goals in sport, regardless of their actual ability, actually participated in physical activities more than competitive-oriented boys and girls, especially so for those children who perceived their ability to be low. Rudisill and colleagues (Rudisill, Meaney, McDermott, & Jibaja-Rusth, 1990) placed children in a mastery or a competitive climate, a self-goal condition, and a control group, where children just performed the motor tasks of study. Children in the mastery-oriented climate persisted longer than those in the other three groups. Other indirect evidence that confirms the motivational impact of changing the climate of the competitive environment is the research that was designed to change the communication behaviors of coaches. Smith, Smoll, and colleagues (Smith, Smoll, Curtis, 1979; Smith, Smoll, & Hunt, 1977) developed a coaching behavior assessment system in order to assess the reinforcement behaviors of coaches. They then intervened so that they had an experimental group of trained coaches who were instructed to increase the frequency of technical instruction, to reinforce appropriate behaviors more frequently, and to reduce punitive coaching behaviors. The

coaches were instructed to be more child-referenced and to engage in less child-controlling behaviors. It may be argued in the present context that these coaches were instructed to create a more mastery-motivational environment than the control group of coaches. The coaches in the trained group were more highly evaluated by the children, the team members were more attracted to each other, and members were higher in self-esteem. Importantly children in the trained coach group were more likely to show persistence in that these children had a greater wish to play the sport the following season.

Horn (1985) also provides some indirect evidence to support the notion that mastery climates enhance adaptive-achievement striving. Horn had "counter-intuitive" findings in her study in that children who received frequent praise for successful performance exhibited lower perceptions of competence, whereas those children who received frequent criticism for performance errors had higher perceptions of competence. It is only when one considers the meaning of the feedback to the children does it make conceptual sense. Children who have low expectations of performance and receive praise for successful performance more frequently than other children, who also manifest the same performance, recognize that the teacher expects less of them than of the other children. Obviously children who receive mistake-contingent feedback frequently recognize that the teacher expects more from them. Therefore, these children have high perceptions of ability. It may be argued that the teacher is creating a mastery climate in the later instance by giving feedback based on the child's own performance, and children are motivated to continue persisting. In the former instance, children recognize that social comparison is extant, and they perceive that their ability is lower than others. Again, Horn provides more indirect evidence that mastery climates have desirable motivational effects.

Thus the evidence is clear. The task or activity can be structured to help children maintain motivation so that they can develop new skills and techniques and help them to set reasonable, short-term goals. Children are recognized for their individual development and progress. Evans and Roberts (1987) have argued that there is an added benefit in that mastery-oriented children are also able to forge stronger social relationships with other children. In other words, they can enhance their peer relationships. Thus it is important to seriously consider creating mastery-motivational climates for children when learning and development are the goals of the coach and/or the teacher.

Although most of the direct research has been conducted in classrooms at the present time, research involving intervention is easily extended to sport settings. Sport stratifies children by ability, normative and social comparisons are unavoidable (see above), and evaluation is clear and unambiguous. Therefore, researchers must work hard to specifically establish mastery goals by emphasizing short-term goals and learning and skill development. Children should be recognized for that individual development. To enhance motivation, children need to be evaluated for their improvement and effort (Ames, 1992; Evans & Roberts, 1987).

FUTURE DIRECTIONS IN MOTIVATION RESEARCH INVOLVING CHILDREN

We have seen in this chapter that holding one achievement goal versus another has a powerful effect on the ongoing stream of achievement behaviors in children. A mastery goal is important if we want children to maintain their achievement striving in contexts of importance to them. But, as we have discussed previously, the context of sport is competitive. It is difficult for children to maintain a mastery goal in the face of continual evaluation with its attendant emphasis on social comparison in competitive contexts. Continual social comparison can only lead to a focus on children's own perception of ability, and this can have negative consequences for achievement behaviors. This is particularly true if such a focus leads the child to utilize ego-involved criteria for ability and performance assessment that may, in turn, develop a stable competitive goal orientation.

The first recommendation for future research, therefore, is to encourage more research aimed at understanding the role of achievement goals in governing the ongoing stream of achievement behaviors of children. But the research enterprise must also be aware of the multivariate complexity of this endeavor (Roberts, 1989). Achievement goals interact with the perception of ability, the structural constraints of the achievement context, as well as the motivational climate perceived by the participant. And we must recognize the subjective interpretation and qualitative nature of much of this motivation process. Accordingly, qualitative research procedures become appropriate in any comprehensive research program into the motivation of children in sport.

Most motivational remediation programs are focused on individual children. If deficient or maladaptive strategies are identified, then motivation training takes on the role of individual remediation. The notion is to make the child or student better equipped "motivationally" to cope with the tasks at hand (Ames, 1992). This makes eminent sense if we are discussing mature students or older children. Individual remediation can take place. But it does not make any sense at all to consider individual remediation for young children's motivational deficits. We must intervene at the level of the teacher, coach, and/or parent.

Roberts (e.g., 1984, 1992) has long argued that adults in charge of children's programs need to create mastery motivational climates if we wish children to maintain motivation and strive to achieve. We must structure the psychological climate of the context so that learning and development, not performance or outcomes, are salient. The learning environment, whether it is the classroom, gymnasium, or playing field, has an important role in shaping and socializing children's motivational patterns. It is the individual student's experiences in these environments and their perceptions and interpretations of these experiences that are critical.

The evidence suggests that if we want students to employ effortful strategies, seek challenging tasks, respond positively to learning situations, we must move toward enhancing the mastery climate of the learning environment, regardless of the context we are considering. When the context conveys a mastery goal orientation, children are more likely to develop adaptive motivational strategies. Restructuring the environment requires identifying those principles and strategies that will make a mastery goal perspective salient to the children. Motivation training involves a comprehensive approach to restructuring and focuses on ways to develop children's experiences within a mastery goal climate. It involves changing the strategies and practices of the teacher, parent, or supervisor.

The second recommendation is to conduct research on intervening at the level of the coach and the parent. Can we create motivational climates such that we minimize the stress and negative normative assessments of ability that children frequently make within the sport experience? In sport, we need to conduct parallel research to that of Carole Ames (e.g., 1992), who is creating mastery motivational climates in the classroom and finding that children, especially children at risk academically, use adaptive achievement strategies and often perform better than their control counterparts in normal classroom environments.

Evans and Roberts (1987) give another reason for encouraging research aimed at creating appropriate intervention protocols. They reported on the relationship between physical competence in activities valued by other children and on social acceptance within the peer group. Indeed, they argued that peer friendship patterns may be strongly related to the competence of children, boys in particular, in physical activity contexts. Evans and Roberts suggested that physical education classes should be used as a means to enhance the physical skills of children who are low in physical competence to determine whether this can improve the social acceptance and status of such children. This research would be critical in determining the relationship of physical competence to important social-acceptance variables.

Finally, future research in motivation must be conceptually informed. Too much research has been merely empirical and descriptive in nature and has generated "random noise" in the literature, against which it is difficult to see the true signal of advancement (Roberts, 1989). Sport psychologists must create and use conceptual models that incorporate multivariate complexity because such models capture the individual and social reality of individuals. Thus more time must be spent creating the appropriate hypotheses that arise out of an understanding of the cognitive complexity of the individual. Scholars need to describe, document, and represent the complex motivational process operating in sport contexts. Only then can we consider the appropriate intervention strategies that may alleviate the cognitive deficits undergirding ineffectual achievement striving (Roberts, 1989).

Let me conclude this chapter with a statement on the

motivational process of children in sport. In this chapter, I have attempted to focus on the variables that impact on the ongoing stream of behavior of children within sport contexts. In common with others before me, I have concluded this chapter by making a plea for more research into the motivational process. But in one respect, "the data are in"! The research is consistent, even if it is incomplete: Creating intense competitive motivational environments for children is demotivating for the vast majority of children. The drop-out rates of children in such contexts are legion (see Brustad, this volume; Roberts, 1984). If there is one aspect we know will work for children, especially those under age 12, it is to be concerned with the motivational climate of the physical context. Creating a mastery motivational climate enhances the motivation and striving for most children in the competitive sport experience.

In sport contexts, success is typically defined by success in competition. And, in this sense, success is clear and unambiguous. But adhering to this belief and placing a major emphasis on outcomes creates a situation where children are given few opportunities to define their experiences as mastery-oriented. If children perceive that they have little chance of developing the necessary skills or of feeling that they are valued players, then children are very likely to drop out and/or employ maladaptive achievement strategies. But sports do not have to be like this, especially sports for children. There is theoretical and empirical support to show that adaptive patterns are associated with a mastery goal orientation. Children can then describe their experiences in relation to mastery concepts. This will enhance the motivation of children and allow them to enjoy the sport experience.

References

Ames, C. (1984). Competitive, cooperative, and individualistic goal structures: A cognitive-motivational analysis. In R. Ames & C. Ames (Eds.), *Research on motivation in education. Vol. 1: Student motivation* (pp. 177–208). New York: Academic Press.

Ames, C. (1987). The enhancement of student motivation. In D.A. Klieber & M. Maehr (Eds.), *Advances in motivation and achievement* (pp. 123–148). Greenwich, CT: JAI Press.

Ames, C. (1992). The relationship of achievement goals to student motivation in classroom settings. In G. C. Roberts (Ed.), *Motivation in sport and exercise*. Champaign, IL: Human Kinetics.

Ames, C., & Ames, R. (1984). Systems of student and teacher motivation: Toward a qualitative definition. *Journal of Educational Psychology, 76,* 536–556.

Ames, C., & Archer, J. (1987). Mothers' beliefs about the role of ability and effort in school learning. *Journal of Educational Psychology. 79,* 409–414.

Ames, C., & Archer, J. (1990). *Longitudinal effects of mastery goal strategies on student learning strategies and motivation.* Unpublished paper. University of Illinois.

Ames, C., & Maehr, M. (1989). *Home and school cooperation in social and motivational development.* Department of Education, OSER Grant No. De-H023T80023.

Atkinson, J. W. (1957). Motivational determinants of risk-taking behavior. *Psychological Review, 64,* 359–372.

Atkinson, J. W. (Ed.). (1958). *Motives in fantasy action and society.* Princeton, NJ: Van Nostrand.

Bandura, A. (1977). Self-efficacy: Toward a unifying theory of behavioral change. *Psychological Review, 84,* 191–215.

Bandura, A. (1986). *Social foundations of thoughts and actions: A social cognitive theory.* Englewood Cliffs, NJ: Prentice-Hall.

Brawley, L., & Roberts, G. C. (1984). Attributions in sport: Research foundations, characteristics, and limitations. In J. M. Silva & R. S. Weinberg (Eds.), *Psychological foundations of sport* (pp. 197–213). Champaign, IL: Human Kinetics.

Bredemier, B. R., & Shields, D. L. (1987). Moral growth through physical activity. In D. R. Gould & M. Weiss (Eds.), *Advances in pediatric sport sciences, Vol. 2: Behavioral issues* (pp. 143–165). Champaign, IL: Human Kinetics.

Buchan, F., & Roberts, G. C. (1991). *Perceptions of success of children in sport.* Unpublished manuscript. University of Illinois.

Bukowski, W. M., & Moore, D. (1980). Winners' and losers' attributions for success and failure in a series of athletic events. *Journal of Sport Psychology, 2,* 195–210.

Carron, A. V. (1980). *Social psychology of sport.* Ithaca, NY: Mouvement Publications.

Crandall, V. C. (1963). Achievement. In H. W. Stevenson (Ed.), *Child Psychology* (pp. 416–459). Chicago, IL: University of Chicago Press.

Crandall, V. C. (1969). Sex differences in expectancy of intellectual and academic reinforcement. In C. P. Smith (Ed.), *Achievement-related motives in children* (pp. 11–45). New York, NY: Academic Press.

Csikszentmihalyi, M., & Nakamura, J. (1989). The dynamics of intrinsic motivation: A study of adolescents. In R. Ames & C. Ames (Eds.), *Research on motivation in education. Vol. 3: Goals and cognitions* (pp. 45–71). New York: Academic Press.

DeCharms, R. (1968). *Personal causation.* New York: Academic Press.

Duda, J. L. (1981). *A cross-cultural analysis of achievement motivation in sport and the classroom.* Unpublished doctoral dissertation. University of Illinois.

Duda, J. L. (1989). Goal perspective and behavior in sport and exercise settings. In C. Ames & M. Maehr (Eds.), *Advances in motivation and achievement: Vol. 6* (pp. 81–115). Greenwich, CT: JAI Press.

Duda, J. L. (1992). Motivation in sport settings: A goal perspective approach. In G. C. Roberts (Ed.), *Motivation in sport and exercise*. Champaign, IL: Human Kinetics.

Duda, J. L., & Chi, L. (1989, September). *The effect of task- and ego-involved conditions on perceived competence and casual attributions in basketball.* Paper presented at the meeting of the Association of Applied Sport Psychology. University of Washington, Seattle, WA.

Dweck, C. S. (1975). The role of expectations and attributions in the alleviation of learned helplessness. *Journal of Personality and Social Psychology, 31,* 674–675.

Dweck, C. S. (1980). Learned helplessness in sport. In C. H. Nadeau, W. R. Halliwell, K. M. Newell, & G. C. Roberts (Eds.), *Psychology of motor behavior and sport, 1979* (pp. 1–11). Champaign, IL: Human Kinetics.

Dweck, C. S. (1986). Motivational processes affecting learning. *American Psychologist, 41,* 1040–1048.

Dweck, C. S., & Leggett, E. L. (1988). A social-cognitive approach to motivation and personality. *Psychological Review, 95,* 265–273.

Dweck, C. S., & Elliott, E. S. (1983). Achievement motivation. E. M. Hetherington (Ed.), *Handbook of child psychology, Vol. 4: Socialization, personality and social development* (pp. 643–691). New York: Wiley.

Elliott, E. S., & Dweck, C. S. (1988). Goals: An approach to motivation and achievement. *Journal of Personality and Social Psychology, 54,* 5–12.

Evans, J., & Roberts, G. C. (1987). Physical competence and the development of children's peer relations. *Quest, 39,* 23–35.

Ewing, M. E. (1981). *Achievement orientations and sports behavior in males and females.* Unpublished doctoral dissertation. University of Illinois.

Ewing, M. E., Roberts, G. C., & Pemberton, C. L. (1985). *A developmental look at children's goals for participation in sport.* Unpublished manuscript, University of Illinois.

Feltz, D. (1982). Path analysis of the causal elements in Bandura's theory of self-efficacy and an anxiety based model of avoidance behavior. *Journal of Personality and Social Psychology, 42,* 764–781.

Feltz, D. (1988). Self-confidence and sports performance. In K. B. Pandoff (Ed.), *Exercise and sport science reviews* (pp. 423–457). New York: Macmillan.

Feltz, D. (in press). Understanding motivation in sport: A self-efficacy perspective. In G. C. Roberts (Ed.), *Motivation in sport and exercise.* Champaign, IL: Human Kinetics.

Feltz, D., & Brown, E. (1984). Perceived competence in soccer skills among young soccer players. *Journal of Sport Psychology, 6,* 385–394.

Feltz, D., & Petlickoff, L. (1983). Perceived competence among interscholastic sport participants and drop-outs. *Canadian Journal of Applied Sport Science, 8,* 231–235.

Gould, D., Feltz, D., Horn, T., & Weiss, M. (1982). Reasons for discontinuing involvement in competitive youth swimming. *Journal of Sport Behavior, 5,* 155–165.

Hall, H. (1990). *A social-cognitive approach to goal-setting: The mediating effects of achievement goals and perceived ability.* Unpublished doctoral dissertation. University of Illinois.

Harter, S. (1975). Developmental differences in the manifestation of mastery motivation on problem-solving tasks. *Child Development, 46,* 370–378.

Harter, S. (1978). Effectance motivation reconsidered: Toward a developmental model. *Human Development, 21,* 34–64.

Harter, S. (1980). The development of competence motivation in the mastery of cognitive and physical skills: Is there still a place for joy? In G. C. Roberts & D. M. Landers (Eds.), *Psychology of motor behavior and sport, 1980* (pp. 3–29). Champaign, IL: Human Kinetics.

Heider, F. (1958). *The psychology of interpersonal relations.* New York: Wiley.

Horn, T. S. (1985). Coaches' feedback and changes in children's perceptions of their physical competence. *Journal of Educational Psychology, 77,* 174–186.

Jackson, S. A., & Roberts, G. C. (in press). Positive performance states of athletes: 1. Toward a conceptual understanding of peak performance. *The Sport Psychologist.*

Klieber, D. A., & Roberts, G. C. (1981). The effects of sport experience in the development of social character: An exploratory investigation. *Journal of Sport Psychology, 3,* 114–122.

Klieber, D. A., & Roberts, G. C. (1983). The relationship between games and sport involvement in later childhood: A preliminary investigation. *Research Quarterly for Exercise and Sport, 54,* 200–204.

Klint, K. A., & Weiss, M. R. (1987). Perceived competence and motives for participating in youth sports: A test of Harter's competence motivation theory. *Journal of Sport Psychology, 9,* 55–65.

Locke, E. A., & Latham, G. P. (1985). The application of goal setting to sports. *Journal of Sport Psychology, 7,* 205–222.

Loy, J. W. (1969). The nature of sport: A definitional effort. *Quest, 10,* 1–15.

Maehr, M. (1974). Culture and achievement motivation. *American Psychologist, 29,* 887–896.

Maehr, M. (1989). Thoughts about motivation. In R. Ames & C. Ames (Eds.), *Research on motivation in education. Vol. 3: Goals and cognitions* (pp. 299–315). New York: Academic Press.

Maehr, M., & Braskamp, L. A. (1986). *The motivational factor. A theory of personal investment.* Lexington, MA: Lexington Books.

Maehr, M., & Nicholls, J. (1980). Culture and achievement motivation: A second look. In N. Warren (Ed.), *Studies in cross-cultural psychology, Vol. 2.* (pp. 53–75). New York: Academic Press.

Mandler, G., & Sarason, S. B. (1952). A study of anxiety and learning. *Journal of Abnormal and Social Psychology, 47,* 166–173.

Martens, R., Vealey, R. S., & Burton, D. (1990). *Competitive anxiety in sport.* Champaign, IL: Human Kinetics.

McAuley, E. (1985). Modeling and self-efficacy: A test of Bandura's model. *Journal of Sport Psychology, 7,* 283–295.

McAuley, E. (1992). Understanding exercise and achievement behavior: A self-efficacy perspective. In G. C. Roberts (Ed.), *Motivation in sport and exercise.* Champaign, IL: Human Kinetics.

McAuley, E., & Duncan, T. (1990). The causal attribution process in sport and physical activity. In S. Graham & V. Folkes (Eds.), *Advances in applied social psychology V: Applications of attribution theory* (pp. 37–52). Hillsdale, NJ: Erlbaum.

McClelland, D. C. (1961). *The achieving society.* New York: Free Press.

McClelland, D. C., Atkinson, J. W., Clark, R. A., & Lowell, E. W. (1953). *The achievement motive.* New York: Appleton-Century-Crofts.

Murray, H. A. (1938). *Explorations in personality.* New York: Oxford University Press.

Nicholls, J. (1978). The development of the concepts of effort and ability, perception of attainment, and the understanding that difficult tasks require more ability. *Child Development, 49,* 800–814.

Nicholls, J. (1980, August). An intentional theory of achievement motivation. In W. U. Meyer & B. Weiner (Chairpersons), *Attributional approaches to human behavior.* Symposium presented at the Center for Interdisciplinary Studies. University of Bielfeld, Germany.

Nicholls, J. (1984). Conceptions of ability and achievement motivation. In R. Ames & C. Ames (Eds.), *Research on motivation in education: Student motivation, Vol. 1* (pp. 39–73). New York: Academic Press.

Nicholls, J. (1989). *The competitive ethos and democratic education.* Cambridge, MA: Harvard University Press.

Nicholls, J., Patashnick, M., & Nolen, S. (1985). Adolescents' theories of education. *Journal of Educational Psychology, 77,* 683–692.

Orlick, T. C., & Botterill, C. (1975). *Every kid can win.* Chicago, IL: Nelson-Hall.

Powell, B. (1990). *Children's perceptions of classroom goal orientation: Relationship to learning strategies and intrinsic motivation.* Unpublished master's thesis. University of Illinois.

Rejeski, W. J., & Brawley L. R. (1983). Attribution theory in sport: Current status and new perspectives. *Journal of Sport Psychology, 5,* 77–99.

Roberts, J. M., & Sutton-Smith, B. (1962). Child training and game involvement. *Ethnology, 1,* 166–185.

Roberts, G. C. (1972). Effect of achievement motivation and social environment on performance of a motor task. *Journal of Motor Behavior, 4,* 37–46.

Roberts, G. C. (1978). Children's assignment of responsibility for winning and losing. In F. Smoll & R. Smith (Eds.), *Psychological perspectives in youth sports* (pp. 145–171). Washington, DC: Hemisphere.

Roberts, G. C. (1982). Achievement motivation in sport. In R. Terjung (Ed.), *Exercise and sport science reviews (Vol. 10)* (pp. 237–269). Philadelphia, PA: Franklin Institute Press.

Roberts, G. C. (1984). Achievement motivation in children's sport. In J. Nicholls (Ed.), *The development of achievement motivation* (pp. 251–281). Greenwich, CT: JAI Press.

Roberts, G. C. (1989). When motivation matters: The need to expand the conceptual model. In J. S. Skinner, C. B. Corbin, D. M. Landers, P. E. Martin, & C. L. Wells (Eds.), *Future directions in exercise/sport research* (pp. 77–84). Champaign, IL: Human Kinetics.

Roberts, G. C. (1992). Motivation in sport and exercise: Conceptual constraints and convergence. In G. C. Roberts (Ed.), *Motivation in sport and exercise.* Champaign, IL: Human Kinetics.

Roberts, G. C., & Pascuzzi, D. (1979). Causal attributions in sport: Some theoretical implications. *Journal of Sport Psychology, 1,* 203–211.

Roberts, G. C., Klieber, D. A., & Duda, J. L. (1981). An analysis of motivation in children's sport: The role of perceived competence in participation. *Journal of Sport Psychology, 3,* 206–216.

Roberts, G. C., & Balague, G. (1989, August). *The development of a social-cognitive scale of motivation.* Paper presented at the Seventh World Congress of Sport Psychology. Singapore.

Roberts, G. C., & Balague, G. (1991, September). *The development and validation of the Perception of Success Questionnaire.* Paper presented at the FEPSAC Congress. Cologne, Germany.

Roberts, G. C., Hall, H., Jackson, S. A., Kimiecik, J., & Tonymon, P. (1990, September). *Goal orientations and perceptions of the sport experience.* Paper presented at the Association for the Advancement of Applied Sport Psychology, San Antonio, TX.

Rudisill, M. E., Meaney, K. S., McDermott, B. A., & Jibaja-Rusth, M. (1990, May). *Influences of various goal-setting orientations on children's persistence and perceived competence in three motor skills.* Paper presented at the annual meeting of the North American Society for the Psychology of Sport and Physical Activity, University of Houston, TX.

Sarason, S. B., Davidson, K., Lightall, F., Waite, F., & Ruebrush, B. (1960). *Anxiety in elementary school children.* New York: Wiley.

Scanlan, T. K. (1978). Children in competition: Examination of state anxiety and social comparison response in the laboratory and in the field. In L. I. Gedvilas & M. E. Kneer (Eds.), *Proceedings of the NCPEAM/NAPECW Conference* (pp. 53–75). Chicago: Office of Publications Services, University of Illinois at Chicago Circle.

Seefeldt, V., Blievernicht, D., Bruce, R., & Gilliam, T. (1978). *Joint legislative study on youth sport programs, phase II: Agency sponsored sports.* State of Michigan.

Smith, R. E., Smoll, F. L., & Hunt, E. (1977). A system for the behavioral assessment of athletic coaches. *Research Quarterly, 48,* 401–407.

Smith, R. E., Smoll, F. L., & Curtis, B. (1979). Coach effectiveness training: A cognitive-behavioral approach to enhancing relationship skills in youth sport coaches. *Journal of Sport Psychology, 1,* 59–75.

Spink, K. S., & Roberts, G. C. (1980). Ambiguity of outcome and causal attributions. *Journal of Sport Psychology, 2,* 237–244.

Tolman, E. C. (1932). *Purposive behavior in animals and men.* New York: Century.

Ulrich, B. D. (1987). Conceptualization of sport competence, and organized sport: Their interrelationships in young children. *Research Quarterly for Exercise and Sport, 58,* 57–67.

Vallerand, R. J., & Reid, G. (1984). On the causal effects of perceived competence on intrinsic motivation: A test of cognitive evaluation theory. *Journal of Sport Psychology, 6,* 94–102.

Vealey, R. S. (1986). Conceptualization of sport confidence and competitive orientation: Preliminary investigation and instrument development. *Journal of Sport Psychology, 8,* 221–246.

Veroff, J. (1969). Social comparison and the development of achievement motivation. In C. P. Smith (Ed.), *Achievement related motives in children* (pp. 46–101). New York: Russell Sage Foundation.

Watkins, B., & Montgomery, A. B. (1989). Conceptions of athletic excellence among children and adolescents. *Child Development, 60,* 1362–1372.

Weinberg, R. (1992). Goal setting and motor performance: A review and critique. In G. C. Roberts (Ed.), *Motivation in sport and exercise.* Champaign, IL: Human Kinetics.

Weiner, B. (1972). *Theories of motivation: From mechanism to cognition.* Chicago, IL: Rand McNally.

Weiner, B. (1979). A theory of motivation for some classroom experiences. *Journal of Educational Psychology, 71,* 3–25.

Weiner, B. (1986). *An attributional theory of motivation and emotion.* New York: Springer-Verlag.

Weiner, B. (1990). History of motivational research in education. *Journal of Educational Psychology, 82,* 616–622.

Weiner, B., Frieze, I., Kukla, A., Reed, L., Rest, S., & Rosenbaum, R. M. (1971). Perceiving the causes of success and failure. In E. E. Jones, D. E. Kanose, H. H. Kelley, R. E. Nisbett, S. Valins, & B. Weiner (Eds.), *Attribution: Perceiving the causes of behavior* (pp. 95–120). Morristown, NJ: General Learning Press.

Weitzer, J. E. (1989). *Childhood socialization into physical activity: Parental roles in perceptions of competence and goal orientation.* Unpublished master's thesis. University of Wisconsin at Milwaukee.

White, R. W. (1959). Motivation reconsidered: The concept of competence. *Psychological Review, 66,* 297–333.

Williams, R. (1986). Mini-Rugby. In G. Gleeson (Ed.), *The growing child in competitive sport* (pp. 80–85). Sevenoaks, U.K.: Hodder and Stoughton.

·18·

GOALS: A SOCIAL-COGNITIVE APPROACH TO THE STUDY OF ACHIEVEMENT MOTIVATION IN SPORT

Joan L. Duda

A preponderance of research in general psychology and sport psychology has focused on the study of motivation. Within this body of literature, the investigation of the antecedents and consequences of *achievement motivation* in particular has spurred considerable interest on the part of researchers.

Since the study of motivation "begins and ends with the study of behavior" (Maehr, 1984, p. 132), a useful theory of achievement motivation should provide an insight into behavioral variation in achievement settings. Drawing from such a theoretical framework, we should be able to predict and understand the psychological mechanisms behind optimal and sustained performance as well as performance debilitation. We would also want to explain and predict why people choose or avoid certain achievement activities that differ in their degree of challenge and focus. A compelling theory of achievement motivation should help us to comprehend vacillations in exerted effort between and within individuals when they are engaged in an achievement enterprise. Moreover, based on such a theoretical model, the reasons behind continued participation as well as discontinued involvement in achievement settings should be readily discerned.

A comprehensive theory of achievement motivation should also do more than forecast and clarify behavioral differences in the context of interest. Variations in the interpretation of and cognitive and affective responses to the achievement activity should be of significance as well. In essence we would want to ascertain how people psychologically and emotionally experience an achievement setting. Further, the theory should provide a conceptual connection between how individuals process an achievement event and their views about the wider function and operation of the activity itself.

In this chapter it is proposed that contemporary social cognitive theories of achievement motivation hold great promise for furthering our understanding of behavioral variability and the social psychological predecessors and effects of achievement-related behaviors in sport. The pertinent frameworks were developed in reference to academic achievement patterns. These theories reinforce the motivational relevance of goals of action, particularly as they interact with perceptions of ability. Stemming from the work of Ames (1984a, 1984b, 1992), Dweck (1986; Dweck & Elliott, 1983), and, especially, Nicholls (1984a, 1984b, 1989, 1992), these goal perspective theories of academic achievement also have implications for comprehending individual differences in the perceived social reality of the athletic context. That is, it is assumed that there is a compatibility between subjectively defined goals in the athletic domain and people's overall values and perceptions of how sport operates.

The major theoretical tenets underlying a goal perspective approach to the study of achievement behavior will be discussed first. The chapter also will include a summary of the academic literature focused on the conceptual and empirical link between goals and the overall meaning of an achievement setting. Sport-specific research will then be reviewed that has tested these formulations. When highlighting this work, it will be pointed out where the sport findings are congruent or inconsistent with previous classroom-based studies. The chapter will conclude with a discussion of future directions in sport research stemming from a goal perspective theory of achievement motivation.

A GOAL PERSPECTIVE APPROACH TO THE STUDY OF ACHIEVEMENT BEHAVIOR: MAJOR THEORETICAL TENETS

Goal perspective theories of achievement motivation assume that there are two predominant goals or bases of subjective success in achievement situations, namely task and ego involvement (Nicholls, 1989). These two goal perspectives relate to the ways in which individuals judge their level of competence. Consistent with other theories of achievement motivation, perceptions of competence are held to the primary focus and determinant of achievement strivings.

When in a state of task involvement, perceptions of ability and the type of events that occasion feelings of success are self-referenced. Skill improvement, task mastery, working hard, and active engagement in the activity itself are fundamental to perceived goal accomplishment when one is task-involved. In ego involvement, emphasis is placed on demonstrating superior competence. Perceived ability is normatively referenced in this case. For someone who is ego-involved, the ultimate source of subjective success would be beating or surpassing others with less effort in a competitive encounter.

Recent social cognitive theories of achievement motivation (Ames, 1984a, 1984b; Dweck, 1983; Nicholls, 1989) maintain that there are important interrelationships between goal perspectives, perceived ability, and behavior. In achievement situations, task involvement is presumed to result in behaviors conducive to long-term accomplishment and investment. Specifically it is argued that the adoption of task-involved goals will lead to a strong work ethic, optimal performance (given the actual capabilities of the individual), and persistence. Task involvement should also correspond to the selection of competitive levels, opponents, and tasks that are conducive to maximal improvement and personal satisfaction—that is, those that are moderately challenging. Importantly, this positive behavioral pattern is predicted when people are task-involved, regardless of their level of perceived competence. Further, due to the concern with personal skill development and the task at hand, task involvement should enhance the probability that individuals feel competent when engaged in achievement activities. In short, it is assumed that a task-involved goal perspective establishes the basis for maximal motivation and adaptive behaviors.

Because comparative judgments concerning one's own demonstrated ability (and exerted effort) to that of others underlies subjective success, maintaining a sense of high competence is much less secure when ego involvement prevails. If an individual is ego-involved and some question about his/her level of competence exists, a low-achievement-oriented behavioral pattern is expected. Such individuals are more likely to reduce their effort, cease trying, or claim a lack of interest when compared to task-involved participants or those who are ego-involved and

confident of their abilities (Jagacinski & Nicholls, 1990). When someone is ego-involved and low in perceived competence, she/he is predicted to choose the extremes in terms of the perceived challenge of the activity (i.e., either an opponent or task that is too difficult or too easy). Performance impairment and dropping out are also assumed to be behavioral consequences of ego involvement when the adequacy of one's ability is in doubt. Although this behavioral pattern is rational if the goal is to "save face" and preserve one's sense of superior competence, such behaviors are obviously maladaptive from an achievement standpoint.

Recent social cognitive theories of achievement motivation hold that situational factors and individual differences affect which goal perspective state predominates. In regard to the former, achievement environments vary in terms of the goal structure emphasized. When environments are marked by interpersonal competition, social evaluation, and normative-based testing and feedback, ego involvement is more likely to result. Situations characterized by an emphasis on learning from one's mistakes, personal skill mastery, the importance of exerting effort, and participation for participation's sake tend to lead to task involvement. In the classroom setting specifically, the work of Ames and her colleagues (Ames, 1984a, 1984b, 1992; Ames & Archer, 1988) clearly indicates how the *motivational climate* or prevailing goal structure can effect the degree to which a student exhibits a task-or ego-involved achievement pattern.

Regardless of the situation at hand, it is also assumed that individuals differ in their tendency to be task-or ego-involved. As suggested in the work of Nicholls (1989), individual differences in dispositional goal orientation are a consequence of socialization experiences within the achievement domain. Interactions with significant others who reinforce a particular goal perspective and continued involvement in environments that manifest a particular motivational climate are believed to result in a proneness for task or ego involvement. In contrast to what is suggested by Dweck and her colleagues (1986; Dweck & Leggett, 1988), empirical work in the academic domain has indicated that these two goal orientations are independent (Nicholls, 1989). That is, orientations to task and ego involvement are not opposite ends of a continuum. People can be strongly task-and ego-oriented, low in both goal orientations, or high in one perspective and low in the other (Duda, 1988).

In general, research in academic settings has supported the major theoretical predictions concerning the interdependence between goals, perceived ability, and achievement behaviors. This work has been both correlational and experimental in design. The classroom-relevant studies conducted to date have typically entailed an examination of the behavioral and psychological correlates/consequences of differences in situational goal structure or dispositional goal orientation. For a thorough discussion of this literature, see reviews by Nicholls (1989, 1992), Ames (1984a, 1984b, 1992), and Dweck (1986; Dweck & Elliott, 1983; Dweck & Leggett, 1988).

BEYOND BEHAVIOR: GOAL PERSPECTIVES AND THE MEANING OF AN ACHIEVEMENT ACTIVITY

Nicholls (1989, 1992) has proposed that the correlates of goal perspectives go far beyond short-and long-term differences in behavior. He has suggested that when individuals favor one goal perspective over another in a specific achievement setting, this difference in motivational focus is consistent with their world views about how that context functions and what is important within and about that context.

For example, factor analytic studies have revealed a convergence between students' academic goal perspective and their beliefs about the causes of success in school (Nicholls, Cheung, Lauer, Patashnick, 1989; Nicholls, Cobb, Wood, Yackel, & Patashnick, 1990; Nicholls, Patashnick, & Nolen, 1985). Task orientation has been found to relate to the beliefs that success in school stems from hard work, trying to understand rather than memorize, and cooperation with one's peers. Ego orientation, in contrast, corresponded to the beliefs that one will be successful in school if she/he has superior ability and tries to outperform others. Thus there appears to be a logical interdependence between goal orientations in a specific achievement context and opinions concerning the nature of the activity or what is required to flourish in this domain.

An individual's predominant goal perspective should also be aligned with her/his philosophy concerning the wider purposes of the achievement activity (Nicholls, 1989). Investigations in school settings have found that ego orientation positively relates to the perception that education should provide one with wealth and social status (Nicholls et al., 1985; Thorkildsen, 1988). On the other hand, the beliefs that school should foster one's commitment to others and society at large, understanding of the world, and interest in learning were linked with task orientation. Drawing from these results, it appears that the perceived function or objective of an achievement activity is theoretically compatible with how individuals subjectively define success within the situation.

It is also reasonable to expect that personal achievement goals would coincide with the perceived appropriateness of diverse means to goal attainment. For instance, Nicholls (1989) has argued that individual differences in goal perspective relate to variability in conceptions of justice and fairness as well as the importance placed on being fair in achievement situations. It is assumed that individuals who tend to be ego-involved are more likely to uphold a sense of justice that is primarily self-serving (Thorkildsen, 1989a, 1989b). Moreover, when the motivational focus is on beating others, it is presumed that people will be more prone to do whatever is necessary to achieve this desired outcome, *regardless of how fair the chosen action might be.*

As described in the previous section, goal perspectives are assumed to relate to achievement behaviors and perceptions of competence. Consequently it seems logical that there should be a link between goals and the degree to which an achievement activity is deemed intrinsically interesting and satisfying. Since task involvement has been found to correspond with an adaptive motivational pattern in the classroom, it would be expected that satisfaction with school would be positively associated with task orientation (Duda & Nicholls, in press; Nicholls et al., 1985, 1989; Thorkildsen, 1988). Further, because the emphasis is on the activity as an end in itself, it is not surprising that a positive relationship between a task-involved goal perspective and intrinsic interest in the classroom has emerged (Ames, 1992; Butler, 1987, 1988).

Thus theorists such as Nicholls advocate that a goal perspective approach to achievement motivation should provide a broader realization of the meaning of an achievement activity to individuals. The implications of differences in goal perspectives go beyond the prediction of behavioral variability. Rather it could be suggested that personal goals are a fundamental element of people's conceptions of reality within specific achievement situations.

GOAL PERSPECTIVES, PERCEIVED COMPETENCE, AND BEHAVIOR IN SPORT

Over the years a variety of theoretical frameworks have guided sport-specific motivation research (see Roberts, 1984, 1992, this volume). Atkinson's (1964) value-expectancy theory of achievement motivation, Weiner's (1979, 1985) attributional theory of achievement motivation, Harter's (1978) theory of competence motivation, Locke's (Locke & Latham, 1984,) theory of goal setting and task performance, and Bandura's (1977, 1986) theory of self-efficacy are notable examples in this regard. Recently a social cognitive perspective, which assumes the preeminence of goals as an important determinant of human action, has provided the conceptual foundation for a considerable number of sport investigations.

Initial goal perspective research specific to the sport domain has been extensively reviewed elsewhere (see Duda, 1989a, 1992; Roberts, 1984). These pristine efforts are briefly discussed in the present work. The focus of this chapter is to review in greater detail more contemporary studies that test and extend a goal perspective theory of achievement motivation in the sport realm.

To date, sport researchers concerned with interrelationships between goal perspectives, perceptions, and behavior in sport have adopted two methodological strategies. One line of investigation has been primarily cross-sectional and/or correlational in scope. In this case individual differences in goal perspective are of interest. Some of these studies have entailed examining the degree of task and ego orientation among subjects differing in their level and/or degree of involvement in the athletic setting (e.g., dropouts versus current participants, organized sport athletes versus recreational sport participants). Other investigations have determined the intercorrelations among dispositional goal perspectives and achievement-related perceptions or attitudes.

A second methodological strategy has been primarily experimental in design. Focusing on the situational factors that influence motivation, these investigations are characterized by a manipulation of the goal structure of the sport (field) or laboratory environment to reflect either a task-or ego-involving motivational climate. This is typically accomplished by informing subjects that the goal of the task is either task-involved (e.g., the focus is on technique improvement or doing one's best) or ego-involved (e.g., the goal is to beat others in competition or surpass performance norms). In other work, different goal structures are created by providing subjects with either self-referenced or normatively referenced feedback.

Behavioral Correlates of Goal Orientation in Sport

Support for contemporary social cognitive theories of achievement motivation in the athletic domain has accrued from studies of the behavioral correlates of goal orientations. For the most part, this work has focused on the relationship of individual differences in goal perspectives to variations in intensity and persistence. Results to date have been consistent with theoretical predictions. To enhance the interpretation of these findings, some words about the measurement and properties of a task and ego goal orientation in sport are in order.

Recent efforts in sport psychology research have been directed toward the assessment of individual differences in orientations to sport achievement (e.g., Ewing, 1981; Gill & Deeter, 1988; Pemberton, Petlichkoff, & Ewing, 1986; Vealey, 1986). At the present time two instruments have been developed to assess dispositional proneness for task and ego involvement in the athletic setting specifically (Balague & Roberts, 1989; Duda, 1989c; Duda & Nicholls, 1991). The Balague and Roberts measure determines the degree to which individuals are focused on mastery and competitive sport goals. These two goal perspectives have been found to be moderately correlated.

The Duda and Nicholls' (1991) instrument (i.e., the Task and Ego Orientation in Sport Questionnaire or TEOSQ) assesses individual differences in the emphasis placed on task-and ego-involved goal perspectives in sport. When completing the questionnaire, subjects are requested to think of when they have personally felt successful in sport and then indicate their agreement with 13 items reflecting task-involved (e.g., "I learn a new skill by trying hard") and ego-involved (e.g., "The others can't do as well as me") criteria. Aligned with Nicholls's (1989) conceptualization of and empirical work on task and ego orientation in the classroom, the two goal orientations assessed in the TEOSQ have been found to be orthogonal.

Psychometric research on the TEOSQ (see Duda, 1992; Duda & Nicholls, 1991) has provided interesting insights into the nature of a task and ego orientation in the athletic environment. First, it has been demonstrated empirically

that regardless of whether a task or ego orientation predominants, a highly task-or ego-oriented individual can be considered *competitive*. Although intrigued with competition, task-versus ego-oriented persons would probably vary in why they approach competitive situations as well as in terms of the objective of the competitive experience. Despite the fact that they are both interested in "winning," it is the relative importance of the competitive outcome in relation to the competitive process *and* the psychological devastation associated with "losing" that seem to discriminate between the two goal orientations. Second, people who tend to emphasize task-versus ego-involved goals are equally goal-directed. What distinguishes these groups are the perceptions and criteria underlying subjective goal attainment. Lastly, whether high in task or ego orientation, such individuals are invested in playing well in sport contests. It is commonly assumed by the practitioner (and some sport researchers) that task-oriented people simply want to "have fun" and have no deep interest in the sport contest (outcome or otherwise). Likewise, it is often assumed that ego-oriented individuals do not care about playing as well as they can and only are concerned about who wins or loses. It is the perceptual basis for concluding whether one played well or not that differs among strongly task-and ego-oriented athletic participants.

Studies examining the behavioral correlates of dispositional goal perspectives have found the emphasis placed on task-involved goals to positively relate to effort exerted and sustained involvement in athletic settings. An ego-involved goal perspective, in contrast, has been linked to a lack of persistence in the sport domain.

The first sport-specific study to examine whether noninvolved individuals, persisters, and dropouts could be distinguished as a function of their goal perspective was conducted by Ewing (1981). Among her sample of young adolescents, those who were highly concerned with demonstrating ability (i.e., focused on ego-involved goals) were more likely to have ceased their involvement in sport.

Duda (1988) assessed the dispositional goal perspective of college students participating in an intramural league. Students who had participated in the activity for a longer period of time were high in task orientation. In a second study (Duda, 1989b), adolescents' preference for task-or ego-involved success and failure was determined. The students were classified in terms of their degree of participation and persistence in sport, i.e., those who have never been involved in sport programs, those who have dropped out, those who participate in recreational sport only, those who participate in interscholastic sport only, and those who are involved in both recreational and interscholastic athletics. Results indicated that the students who were currently involved in sport (recreational and/or interscholastic) placed a greater emphasis on task-involved success than the students who had dropped out or had never been involved in the athletic domain. When contrasted with the other four groups, students who had stopped participating in sport viewed an ego-involved failure (which entails the demonstration of inferior competence) as the least palatable. Similar findings were recently reported by Whitehead (1989) in her work with British sport clubs.

Weitzer (1989) extended this line of research by examining participation in physical activity among children as a function of goal perspective and perceived competence. Including both personal goals and perceptions of ability as potential predictors of behavior results in a more adequate test of contemporary social cognitive theories of achievement motivation. Although this study was not particular to the achievement-related context of organized sport, the findings were aligned with previous research in the athletic context. Weitzer found that children who reported higher levels of involvement in overall physical activity tended to be higher in their orientation to mastery goals. This positive relationship between goals and participation held regardless of the children's level of perceived competence. Children who doubted their physical ability and were primarily ego-involved reported the lowest levels of physical activity. Regular physical activity did correspond to an ego orientation only in the case of children who were confident in their abilities.

In terms of behavioral intensity, the research to date has revealed a positive relationship between task orientation and exerted effort. For example, Duda (1988) found college-level intramural participants who were high in task orientation to indicate that they practice their sport more in their free time than participants who were low in task orientation. Among intercollegiate athletes recovering from injury, a positive association emerged between task orientation and how hard one works while performing prescribed rehabilitation exercises (Duda, Smart, & Tappe, 1989). In studies of students enrolled in college-level individual and team sport skill classes respectively (Duda, Chi, Newton, Walling, & Catley, in press), students who emphasized task-involved goals tended to report that they tried harder in the class.

These investigations do not implicate cause-effect relationships between individual differences in goal perspectives and achievement-related behavior. This work, however, did provide initial evidence suggesting that contemporary social cognitive theories of academic achievement have relevance for the study of behavioral patterns in sport. The stage had been set for more systematic, experimental research in both laboratory and field situations.

The Effect of Situationally Induced Goals in Sport-Related Contexts

In an attempt to experimentally test the predictions embedded in goal perspective theories, the few sport-relevant investigations conducted to date have entailed the creation of either a task-or ego-involving goal structure. The primary focus has been on the prediction of performance and performance-related cognitions such as perceptions of competence, expectations, and causal attributions. Several examples of this type of work are described below.

In the context of intercollegiate swimming, Burton (1989) conducted a quasi-field experiment determining

the effect of a 5-month goal-setting program on perceived ability, perceptions of success, and performance. The goal-setting program was targeted toward teaching the athletes how to set accurate, performance-focused goals and downplay the significance of outcome goals. Performance goals were based on individual mastery and personal improvement with respect to technique and swimming times. In contrast to a control group of intercollegiate swimmers that did not take part in the program, program participants had higher perceived ability and perceived greater post-competition success. Moreover, those trained swimmers who tended to set accurate personal mastery goals exhibited higher performance (as reflected in performance time and race outcome) than swimmers who focused on less accurate goals or members of the control group.

Rudisill (1989) determined the influence of goal-setting orientations on perceived competence, expectations, persistence, performance, and attributions in a laboratory investigation involving college-age students. The subjects were requested to perform a stabilometer-balancing task in one of four goal-setting conditions. In condition one, the students were instructed to set task-mastery goals based on their personal improvement across performance trials on the stabilometer task. In the second condition, normatively based goals were set. Subjects were requested to set their own goals in condition three. A control group was assigned to condition four; students in this condition were not instructed to set performance goals. Perceived competence was measured before and after the four test trials and performance expectations were determined preceding each of these trials. Persistence was assessed in a 3-minute free-time period (following the test trials) during which the students were given the option to practice, sit, or engage in another activity (e.g., reading). Subsequent to the free-time trial, Russell's (1982) Causal Dimension Scale was completed.

Results revealed that students in the normative goal-setting group significantly increased in perceived competence over the test trials and outperformed the other three groups. Students in the task-mastery goal-setting condition, however, also reported a significant increase in perceived competence. The task-mastery group persisted longer and attributed their performance to more controllable factors than students in the other goal-setting conditions. Further, when compared to the other groups, task-mastery subjects had significantly higher performance expectations across trials. In contrast, normative goal students expected to do less well than their counterparts.

Thus, contrary to theoretical predictions, Rudisill (1989) found that the students assigned to the normatively referenced goal group exhibited optimal motivation. This desirable pattern, however, was in respect to their immediate involvement in the task only. Congruent with the tenets of goal perspective theories of achievement motivation, a task-mastery orientation appeared to be consonant with a more long-term, adaptive approach to the task at hand.

In a similar study, Rudisill and her colleagues examined the impact of differential goal setting on perceived competence and the amount of time spent practicing a variety of motor skills among children (Rudisill, Meaney, McDermott, & Jibaja-Rusth, 1990). Analogous to Rudisill's previous investigation (1989), the children were assigned to one of four goal-setting groups. In contrast to the study involving adults, this goal-setting manipulation did not influence perceptions of competence. Children in the task-mastery condition, however, exhibited more persistence in the free-time period than the other three goal-setting groups.

A more stringent test of recent goal perspective theories of achievement motivation necessitates the examination of the predicted interactive effects of goals and levels of perceived ability on behavior and pertinent achievement cognitions. Such experimental work is exemplified in a laboratory investigation by Hall (1989). In particular, Hall determined the effect of task-versus ego-involving goals, perceived competence, and success/failure feedback on motor skill performance and self-and task-related perceptions. Subjects (male college students) were requested to perform a stabilometer task over six trials following a baseline period. If performing in a task-involving situation, only individualized performance feedback was given. For subjects assigned to the ego-involving condition, both personal performance and normative feedback were provided. Perceived competence (high or low) was manipulated via normative feedback following a baseline trial.

Striking differences were revealed between low-perceived-ability subjects in the ego-involving condition and those assigned to the other three groups (i.e., high-perceived-ability subjects in the ego-involving situation and high/low-perceived-ability subjects in the task-involving situation). Specifically, the former group members indicated that they did not try as hard, expected to do less well before, during, and following the performance trials, and felt that they demonstrated less competence throughout the experimental protocol. Not surprisingly, given this maladaptive pattern of task-relevant cognitions, these subjects also performed most poorly.

More experimental investigations like the research of Hall (1989) are clearly needed. Field experiments are also warranted that determine the effect of goals and perceived ability on performance and persistence in real-life sport settings. Sport research is called for that tests recent goal perspective theories in terms of the prediction of other achievement behaviors such as task choice. Furthermore, future work on achievement motivation in sport should examine the behavioral consequences of the interplay between dispositional goal perspectives and situationally induced goals (in concert with varying levels of perceived competence).

How Do Goals Influence Performance and Persistence?

With respect to present and future directions, a useful theory of goal perspectives and athletic achievement should elucidate the mechanisms by which goals affect immediate and sustained performance. One possible mechanism has already been explicated in this chapter. It is proposed that when a state of ego involvement exists, perceptions of ability are much more fragile. Indeed, past work has demonstrated that individuals are less likely to perform up to their potential and maintain their involvement in achievement activities when they do not feel competent (e.g., see Burton & Martens, 1986; Feltz, 1986).

Nicholls (1989) has suggested other ways in which goals might influence performance and persistence. Specifically he suggests that differential states of task and ego involvement may affect how hard one tries, the importance placed on the activity, the stress experienced while performing, and the related capacity to retain one's concentration during task engagement.

Withdrawal of Effort. Research on the relationship between goals and behavioral intensity (or exerted effort) suggests a means by which goal perspectives may influence achievement patterns. Past work in the physical domain has indicated that a strong ego orientation does not seem to coincide with a consistent willingness to try one's best in sport (Duda, 1988; Duda & Chi, 1989; Hall, 1989). Such a finding is most conducive to explanation based on a goal perspective theory of achievement motivation. As pointed out by Jagacinski and Nicholls (1990), one way in which a low-perceived-ability and ego-involved person might survive (and/or protect her/his sense of self) in an achievement activity is to reduce exerted effort. Obviously rescinding effort will not contribute to maximal short- or long-term performance.

Devaluing the Activity. When ego involvement predominates and questions about one's competence exist, another maladaptive strategy would be to downplay the significance of the task or activity at hand (Jagacinski & Nicholls, 1990). A recent study of young male soccer players by Lewthwaite (1990) provides support for this proposed mechanism. She found an inverse relationship between the importance of goals in youth sport and the players' perceptions that these goals might be endangered. It is interesting to point out that the negative intercorrelations emerged in the case of both ego-and task-involved goals.

Based on her findings, Lewthwaite indicated that it was not clear whether young athletes reduce the threat to their self-esteem by devaluing goals that have not or will not be accomplished or "deliberately or unintentionally downplaying negative endangerment experiences associated with important goals" (p. 297). In either case, the devaluing of sport activities does have important motivational consequences. Previous research has indicated that a lack of interest in the athletic context is an important predictor of dropping out of sport (e.g., Burton & Martens, 1986).

Competitive Stress. Another possible mediator of the relationship between goals of action and sport performance/ participation is stress. Preliminary work has suggested that a focus on ego-involved goals tends to relate to higher levels of anxiety in the athletic setting (Duda, Chi, & Newton, 1990; Lewthwaite, 1990; Vealey & Campbell, 1988). Boyd and his colleagues, for example, found a strong ego orientation coupled with low perceived competence to be linked to higher competitive trait anxiety among high school football players (Boyd, Callaghan, & Yin, 1991). Ego orientation also positively related to the players' tendency to "get upset" while playing football (Yin, Boyd, & Callaghan, 1991).

Much more research is needed that explores the possible interdependence between goal orientations and stress responses in sport. Because an abundance of studies have demonstrated that acute and chronic anxiety are hazardous to optimal performance and continued participation in sport respectively, this issue is critical to our understanding of motivation and behavior in the athletic domain.

Concentration and Attention. Given their possible connection to the incidence of stress, sport-specific goal perspectives might also relate to how well individuals keep their concentration while engaged in competition *and* what they focus on while performing. Recently, White and Duda (1991a) determined the degree to which dispositional goal orientation differentially related to the engagement in task-irrelevant and negative self-preoccupying thoughts in elite sport. Intercollegiate skiers completed the Task and Ego Orientation in Sport Questionnaire (Duda, 1989c; Duda & Nicholls, 1991) and the Thoughts Occurrence Questionnaire (TOQ; Sarason, Sarason, Keefe, Hayes, & Shearin, 1986) specific to the sport of skiing. The TOQ contains three subscales and measures the general tendency for experiencing intrusive thoughts (i.e., thoughts concerning social relations/emotions unrelated to the task, thoughts of escape, and task-relevant worries). Task orientation was found to be significantly and negatively correlated with the tendency to have task-relevant worries and thoughts about escaping or withdrawing while skiing.

These findings are consonant with those reported by Newton and Duda (1992a). Following an assessment of the subjects' degree of task and ego orientation in sport, the midgame cognitions of bowlers across three games in a college-level physical education class were examined. The three practice games took place during three consecutive class periods. In general, the results indicated that task orientation positively related to keeping one's concentration and feeling good about the game and negatively correlated to being worried about one's performance. During the first game in particular, there was a positive relationship between ego orientation and reported performance worry.

Use of Learning Strategies. Some evidence exists which implies that goals might impact on achievement-related behaviors by influencing one's employment of effective or ineffective learning strategies. In a recent investigation by

Roberts and his colleagues, college students oriented to mastery goals tended to endorse the importance of practice as a means to enhanced learning and improvement (Roberts, et al., 1990). Vallerand, Gauvin, & Halliwell (1986) observed that children assigned to a "do your best" condition were more likely to try new strategies while performing a motor task than youngsters in a competitive goal condition. In the Newton and Duda study (1992a) a strong task orientation and low ego orientation corresponded to a greater reported use of different strategies among bowlers across three game performances.

Contemporary goal perspective theories of achievement motivation provide a framework for identifying the means by which goals influence action. Such work in the sport domain is clearly in its infancy. Further research efforts on this important topic will require considerable methodological innovation. In essence, adopting more process-oriented as well as longitudinal designs, we will need to unravel how a state of task versus ego involvement affects one's perceptions and responses *while performing a sport activity.* To ascertain the long-term effect of such processes on overall performance and persistence, this will need to be done over time.

GOAL PERSPECTIVES AND THE OVERALL MEANING OF SPORT

There is a constellation of perceptions, attitudes, and beliefs that underlie the subjective meaning or interpretation of athletic achievement (see Figure 18–1). Consistent with predictions stemming from the theoretical contributions of Nicholls (1989) in particular, recent research suggests that the social reality of the sport experience is dependent on the goal orientation of those involved. This work is reviewed below.

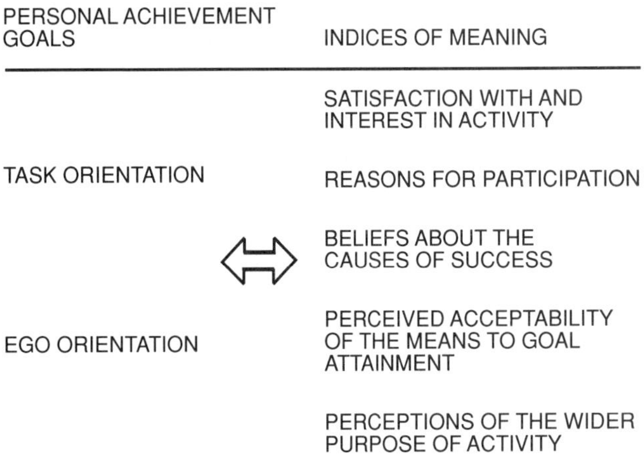

PERSONAL ACHIEVEMENT
GOALS   INDICES OF MEANING

                                         SATISFACTION WITH AND
                                         INTEREST IN ACTIVITY

TASK ORIENTATION   REASONS FOR PARTICIPATION

                          ⟺   BELIEFS ABOUT THE
                                         CAUSES OF SUCCESS

                                         PERCEIVED ACCEPTABILITY
EGO ORIENTATION   OF THE MEANS TO GOAL
                                         ATTAINMENT

                                         PERCEPTIONS OF THE WIDER
                                         PURPOSE OF ACTIVITY

FIGURE 18-1. Goal perspectives and indices of the overall meaning of the athletic domain.

Goals and Beliefs About Sport Success

Previous classroom-based research (Nicholls et al., 1985, 1989, 1990) has revealed that there is a conceptually consistent relationship between the goals that students strive for and the perceived sources of accomplishment in school. In Nicholls's view (1989; Nicholls et al., 1985), personal goals and beliefs about the causes of success in the classroom constitute a student's theory of academic achievement or personal interpretation of "how things work" in that context.

The interdependence between goals and beliefs in the sport domain was first examined by Duda and Nicholls (in press). In this study, high school students completed the Task and Ego Orientation in Sport Questionnaire and were asked "What do you think is most likely to help people do well or succeed in the sport you play most often?" In accord with research in the academic domain, task orientation was found to be positively correlated ($r = .50$) with the belief that sport success stems from working hard, collaborating with others to foster learning, and trying things that one cannot do. Ego orientation, on the other hand, was positively associated ($r = .44$) with the belief that sport achievement is a result of being a better athlete and being better than others at tough competition.

Among a sample of younger sport participants, Hom and his colleagues examined the associations between goals and beliefs about the causes of success (Hom, Duda, & Miller, 1991). The subjects in this investigation were boys and girls ages 8 through 15 years who were involved in a summer basketball camp. The results paralleled the findings of Duda and Nicholls (in press). Task orientation corresponded to the view that success in basketball will come through hard work and sustained motivation. Young athletes who were strongly ego-oriented, in contrast, believed that talent and/or deceptive tactics result in achievement in basketball. Similar findings were reported in studies of young adolescents involved in a summer tennis camp (Newton & Duda, 1992b) and young disabled athletes participating in wheelchair basketball (White & Duda, 1992).

Duda and White (1991) determined whether similar goal-belief dimensions would generalize to a high-level competitive sport situation. Male and female intercollegiate skiers ($N = 143$) indicated their agreement with a variety of reasons why someone would do well in competitive skiing. Factor analysis revealed four perceived beliefs concerning the causes of skiing success, namely effort (e.g., "athletes succeed if they work really hard"), ability (e.g., "athletes succeed if they are better athletes than the others"), external factors (e.g., "athletes succeed if they have the right equipment"), and illegal advantage (e.g., "athletes succeed if they do blood doping").

Elite skiers who were high in ego orientation tended to perceive that taking an illegal advantage, having the ability, and external factors lead to competitive success. Aligned with previous findings in sport (Duda & Nicholls, in press; Hom et al., 1991; Newton & Duda, 1992b; White & Duda, 1992), task orientation positively related to the belief that achievement in skiing is a consequence of hard work and practice. In contrast to classroom-based studies and previous sport research, however, a strong task orientation was also associated with the opinion that possessing high ability results in success.

It seems that at this level of sport involvement, athletes believe that individuals must have high ability to be successful. Ego-oriented athletes, though, tended to perceive that securing achievement required more than talent. In their view, factors outside oneself (like luck or equipment) and the engaging in illicit means were determinants of success in competitive skiing. Moreover, the value of working hard in terms of skiing success was overlooked among high-ego-orientation skiers. Task-oriented elite skiers, on the other hand, deemed ability and hard work as necessary ingredients for achievement.

Thus within the ranks of elite sport competitors, the results of the Duda and White (1991) study suggest that personal goals are compatible with how elite athletes view the causes of successful goal accomplishment. The task-oriented conception of skiing success that emerged should be conducive to maximal motivation and sustained involvement in the sport of skiing. In contrast, the ego-oriented theory of skiing achievement (in which ability and external factors, not effort, are deemed necessary for success) might present motivational problems in the long term for elite athletes. This would especially be true in the case of those intercollegiate skiers who doubt their competence. Further, since the ego-oriented goal-belief dimension reflected the viewpoint that illegal and potentially harmful tactics will lead to success, this motivational orientation should be questioned on the basis of both health-related and ethical concerns.

Goals and Participation Motivation

The reasons why individuals decide to participate in an achievement activity certainly constitute an important component of the subjective meaning of that activity (Maehr & Braskamp, 1986). A useful theory of sport achievement motivation should allow us insight into the variety of participation motives evidenced in athletic contexts. This issue was addressed in recent work by White and Duda (1991b). High school, intercollegiate, and recreational athletes completed the Participation Motivation Questionnaire (Gill, Gross, & Huddleston, 1983) in terms of their present sport involvement. Seven reasons for participation emerged: competition, affiliation, being a member of a team, energy release, skill development, improving one's fitness, and gaining recognition/status. The athletes' degree of task and ego orientation in sport was also assessed.

High-ego-oriented athletes were more likely to participate in sport for the competition and potential for recognition and status and less likely to emphasize team membership and affiliation. Task orientation related positively to the importance placed on fitness and skill development as reasons for athletic involvement. Similar findings were reported by Papaioannou (1990) in his investigation of goal perspectives and reasons for participation in physical education classes. In general, these results suggest that the ways in which sport participants define personal success and judge their level of competence coincide with their overall motives for being there.

Goals and the Perceived Purpose of Sport Involvement

The meaning and meaningfulness of a particular achievement domain should also relate to individuals' beliefs about the function of the enterprise. Stemming from an ecological perspective, personal goals are assumed to be logically consistent with perceptions concerning the purposes of an achievement activity.

In a study of high school athletes, the interdependence between dispositional goal perspectives and perceptions concerning the wider purpose of sport participation was examined (Duda, 1989c). The athletes completed the TEOSQ and then indicated their agreement with a wide array of "things sport should do." In accord with studies specific to the school setting (Nicholls et al., 1985; Thorkildsen, 1988), task orientation positively related to the view that athletic involvement should foster the capacity to cooperate and strive for personal mastery. Athletes high in task orientation were less likely to feel that sport should result in high social status. Conversely, ego orientation was positively associated with the belief that enhancing social status is an important function of sport. Ego-oriented athletes also tended to believe that sport should make people feel important and be more competitive. Ego orientation negatively related to the view that fostering good citizenship was a significant purpose of athletic participation.

Similar findings emerged in a study of college students by Roberts and his associates (Roberts, Hall, Jackson, Kimiecik, & Tonymon, 1990). In particular, they found a mastery goal orientation to be positively correlated with the perceptions that sport should enhance social responsibility and lifetime health. A competitive goal orientation, in contrast, was associated with the belief that sport should increase a participant's status and bring recognition.

Drawing from these results, a task-involved goal perspective is linked to the belief that the intrinsic and prosocial ramifications of sport involvement are what give sport its meaning. To one who is strongly ego-oriented, athletic participation seems to be merely a vehicle to some extrinsic, self-serving end. Interestingly these goal-related differences in perceptions about the wider purposes of sport are also consistent with the patterns of beliefs about the causes of success and participation motives associated with task and ego orientation in sport.

Goals and the Perceived Means to Goal Attainment in Sport

Perceptions of what is deemed an acceptable way to meeting one's goals or participation motives would also comprise an important facet of what sport means to a particular individual. The issue to be addressed in this case relates to whether there is a logical interdependence between personal achievement goals and the perceived legitimacy and desirability of behaviors leading to goal attainment.

Sport-specific research addressing this issue seems to reinforce the contention of Nicholls (1989, p. 133). That is, he suggests that when the emphasis is on winning or beating others (an ego-involved goal) in an achievement setting such as sport, people are more likely to feel that the ends justify the means or "it is worth doing anything to win."

This supposition is supported in the myriad of investigations examining the relationship of competitive level to goal perspectives and attitudes toward fairness and rule-violating behavior in sport. In general, this literature suggests that as the level of competition increases (e.g., from high school to college), athletes tend to report less sportsmanlike attitudes, deemphasize playing fair, and perceive aggression in sport as more acceptable (Allison, 1982; Blair, 1985; Bredemeier, 1985; Kleiber & Roberts, 1981; Silva, 1983). Other research has indicated that a greater emphasis is placed on demonstrating superiority (and, therefore, ego-involved goals) as sport participants "move up the ladder" in terms of their competitive involvement (Chaumeton & Duda, 1988; White & Duda, 1991b).

Recent studies have determined whether it is the adopted goal perspective, in contrast to the level of competition per se, that predicts what an individual might be willing to do to reach his/her goal in sport. Generally speaking, these investigations indicate that ego involvement is linked to less emphasis on fairness and a greater endorsement of aggression in the athletic context.

In a study of high school basketball players, for example, Duda and her colleagues examined the interdependence between dispositional goal perspective and sportsmanship attitudes (Duda, Olson, & Templin, 1991). A second purpose was to ascertain the relationship of task and ego orientation to judgments concerning the legitimacy of intentionally aggressive behaviors. The results indicated that the athletes who were higher in task orientation were less likely to perceive cheating in sport as legitimate. Task orientation was positively associated with the endorsement of sportsmanlike behaviors in the context of interscholastic basketball (e.g., helping an opponent off the floor). In terms of the perceived appropriateness of injurious acts, ego orientation corresponded to higher legitimacy ratings. That is, the higher the ego orientation, the more likely the athlete was to perceive that it was legitimate to engage in intentionally aggressive acts to win a game.

Similar findings concerning the link between goals and legitimacy judgments emerged in a study of high school and college football players (Huston & Duda, 1991). In this investigation, dispositional goal orientation in football was assessed (via the TEOSQ) and the players indicated the degree to which they perceived football-specific acts that increased in their seriousness as acceptable. The results indicated that the endorsement of aggressive behavior in football was primarily a function of individual differences in goal perspective. Competitive level and years of involvement in organized football programs emerged as less potent predictors of attitudes toward aggression.

Goals, Enjoyment, and Intrinsic Interest

Achievement activities that we find satisfying, interesting, and fun are certainly more meaningful in our lives. Contemporary social cognitive theories of achievement motivation assume that goal perspectives differentially relate to the level of satisfaction and intrinsic enjoyment experienced in achievement situations such as sport.

Duda and Nicholls (in press) examined the relationship of goal orientation to reported satisfaction, interest, and boredom in the athletic context among high school students. Aligned with classroom-based work and theoretical predictions (Nicholls, 1989), task orientation was positively related to the perception that sport was satisfying and enjoyable. Task orientation was negatively associated with the degree to which sport was deemed boring.

Similar findings emerged in two studies of college students enrolled in physical education skill classes focused on tennis or the team sports of basketball or volleyball. (Duda, Chi, Newton, Walling & Catley, in press). In both investigations, students were administered the Task and Ego Orientation in Sport Questionnaire and the Intrinsic Motivation Inventory (Ryan, Mims, & Koestner, 1983). Results indicated that a strong task orientation coincides with greater enjoyment of and overall intrinsic interest in the sports of tennis, basketball, or volleyball.

Other work has examined the interdependence between goals and state assessments of enjoyment and satisfaction in sport competition. For example, the relationship of goal orientation and game outcome to postgame affective ratings was determined in a study by Boyd (1990). The subjects in this investigation were Little League baseball players. Regardless of the outcome of the game, players high in ego orientation rated the game as less enjoyable than players low in ego orientation. Among those with a strong ego orientation, game outcome did influence reported postgame satisfaction. High-ego-oriented losers were much less satisfied with the game than high-ego-oriented winners. There were no significant differences in satisfaction ratings among winners and losers who were low in ego orientation.

The meaning of sport to participants and nonparticipants is multidimensional and comprised of a variety of important beliefs and perceptions concerning: (1) the causes of sport success, (2) the reasons for sport participation, (3) the function of sport involvement, (4) the appropriateness and desirability of sportsmanship and aggression in sport, and (5) the degree to which sport is deemed satisfying and enjoyable. The research highlighted in this section strongly suggests that the determination of personal goals provides a greater perspicuity into individual differences in these indices of meaning in the athletic domain.

FURTHER EXTENSIONS OF GOAL PERSPECTIVE WORK IN SPORT

The latest efforts in research on goal orientations in sport reflect important future directions in the study of these critical mediators of achievement-related cognitions, affects, behaviors, and meanings. This work suggests that we should move forward in the investigation of personal achievement goals from both a developmental and cross-cultural perspective. Further, the means by which individuals are socialized into their predominant goal perspective is a critical area of inquiry. Related to this issue are questions concerning how people distinguish social situations in terms of task-and ego-involving characteristics and the implications of this "motivational climate" on their perceptions and achievement behavior. Finally, as the literature on the antecedents and consequences of goal perspectives grows, the time has arrived for intervention-based research that is targeted toward the maximizing of motivation in sport situations.

Developmental Concerns

One of the strengths of contemporary goal perspective theories is their consideration of developmental differences in the social cognitions linked to achievement behavior. Nicholls's contributions to our understanding of the development of achievement motivation are most notable in this regard (Nicholls, 1989; Nicholls & Miller, 1984). Nicholls's work clearly indicates that how children construe their ability and thus subjectively define goal accomplishment is dependent on their stage of cognitive development. This line of research, however, is presently specific to the academic setting. Although sport psychologists have argued for the importance of a developmental perspective to the study of motivation in sport (Duda, 1987; Weiss & Bredemeier, 1983), little work has addressed possible age-related differences in goal orientations and conceptions of ability within the athletic domain (see Buchan & Roberts, 1991; Whitehead & Dalby, 1987). Much more developmentally based research is needed, especially in the context of youth sport.

Cross-Cultural Analysis

The majority of work adopting a goal perspective approach to the study of achievement motivation in sport has been conducted in the United States. Cross-cultural investigations have indicated that diverse social groups differ in the emphasis placed on task-and ego-involved goals and, to some extent, the nature of the goals themselves (Duda,

1985, 1986a, 1986b; Duda & Allison, 1989; Whitehead, 1986; Yamaguchi & Weiss, 1991). Future research should begin to determine the predictive utility of recent social cognitive theories of achievement motivation in terms of the study of sport behavior in a variety of cultures. As pointed out by Duda and Allison (1990), such comparative work should enhance awareness of the social cognitive processes impacting on achievement behaviors. Moreover, cross-cultural research on goals and their correlates will foster understanding of the diverse racial and ethnic groups that participate in sport. Such knowledge is particularly critical to applied sport psychologists who are interested in maximizing motivation among culturally diverse athletic participants and nonparticipants.

Socialization of Goal Orientations

As I have argued elsewhere (Duda, 1992), there is a need to begin to examine the socialization processes that lead to individual differences in goal orientation in sport. One research direction of promise entails the determination of the impact of significant others (such as parents and the coach) on young athletes' proneness to be task- and/or ego-involved. Previous work by Chaumeton and Duda (1988), for example, found that high school coaches positively reinforce and punish their athletes during competition as a function of performance outcome rather than the performance process more than do coaches at a lower level of competitive involvement. The more ego-involving social reinforcement pattern exhibited by the high school coaches paralleled the greater emphasis on ego-involved goals reported by the high school athletes in contrast to the younger groups in this study. The direct relationship between coaches' behaviors and athletes' goal perspective, however, was not examined in the Chaumeton and Duda investigation.

Piparo, Lewthwaite, and Hasbrook (1990) examined young athletes' perceptions of their coaches' behaviors as potential predictors of their goal orientations. The subjects in this study were 200 competitive gymnasts between the ages of 9 and 14 years. Four coach behavior tendencies were considered, namely that the coach: (1) provides encouragement for mastery and enjoyment, (2) demands a task focus, (3) is concerned about social relationships on the team, and (4) has a pressuring style. The results indicated that greater reported coach encouragement for mastery and enjoyment related to a stronger focus on mastery-related goals among the athletes. Athletes who perceived that their coach demanded a task focus tended to emphasis mastery and competitive achievement (or more ego-involving) goals. Greater perceived use by a coach of a pressuring style was a significant and negative predictor of mastery goal orientations.

Unfortunately, Piparo and his colleagues (Piparo et al., 1990) were not able to determine the actual behaviors of the gymnastics coaches. Taking the findings of this study and the work of Chaumeton and Duda (1988) in concert, however, suggests that the coach plays a significant role in shaping the adopted goal orientation of athletes. More systematic research is needed that tests this possibility.

Two recent investigations have focused on the potential role of parents in the socialization of goal orientations. Among a sample of fourth-graders, Weitzer (1989) assessed children's perceptions of parental influence, personal goal orientations, and sources of goal orientations with respect to the physical domain. In the case of boys, parents were not viewed as having a major impact on their perceptions of physical competence or goal orientations. Parents' influence was associated with girls' perceived physical competence. Further, the mothers' influence, in particular, related to the girls' degree of mastery or task orientation.

The interrelationships between parents' goal orientation, parents' perceptions of their child's goal orientation, children's personal goal orientation, and children's perceptions of their parents' goal orientation in sport were the focus of an investigation by Duda and Hom (1991). The subjects in this study were participants in a summer basketball camp and the parent of each child who was most involved with her/his participation. Results indicated that there was little correspondence between parents' degree of task and ego orientation in sport and their children's dispositional goal perspective. Children's personal goals were best predicted by their perceptions of their parents' goal orientation. Parents were strikingly inaccurate in perceiving the emphasis placed on task- and ego-involved goals by their children. Specifically parents tended to believe that their children were more ego-oriented and less task-oriented than what was reported by the children.

One interesting question that stems from the Duda and Hom (1991) study concerns the cues that young athletes use to "pick up" the perceived goal orientation of significant others. In other words, on what basis (if any) do young athletes distinguish task- and ego-involving environments that are created by parents and/or coaches? Further, what are the motivational consequences of these environments on young participants?

Correlates of Perceived Motivational Climate

Education-based work by Ames (Ames, 1992; Ames & Archer, 1988) and Nicholls (1989) clearly demonstrates that students can perceive the goal perspective that predominates in a classroom *and* that this situational goal structure (or motivational climate) is separate from students' personal goal orientation. Importantly, their research also indicates that perceived goal structure predicts students' use of effective learning strategies, enjoyment of school, and beliefs about the causes of academic success.

In a study of high school male basketball players (Seifriz, Duda, & Chi, 1991) an attempt was made to develop a measure of perceived motivational climate in sport and examine the relationship of this construct to perceived ability, intrinsic motivation, and the players' views concerning what leads to basketball success. Also determined was whether the perceived motivational climate varied as a function of a team's record. A third question that was addressed focused on whether the motivational variables of interest could best be predicted by the perceived situational goal structure, dispositional goal orientation, or a combination of both factors.

Midpoint in a competitive season, members ($N = 105$) of nine varsity basketball teams were requested to complete: (1) the Task and Ego Orientation in Sport Questionnaire (Duda, 1989c; Duda & Nicholls, 1991), (2) the Intrinsic Motivation Inventory (Ryan et al., 1986), (3) a 4-item measure of perceived basketball ability, and (4) the Perceived Motivational Climate in Sport Questionnaire. The latter assessment was designed to determine players' perceptions of the degree to which their team's motivational climate was characterized by an emphasis of mastery (task-involving) and performance (ego-involving) goals. When completing this instrument, the players were asked to think of how they felt while playing for their team over the course of the season. To keep the players' focus on the overall team climate rather than on their personal goal orientation, the stem for each item was "On this basketball team. . . ."

Psychometric analyses indicated that the Perceived Motivational Climate in Sport Questionnaire was comprised of two valid and reliable subscales (i.e., a Mastery Goal subscale and a Performance Goal subscale). Items that reflected a team marked by between-player rivalry (e.g., "On this team, outplaying teammates is important"), recognition for a limited number of players (e.g., "On this team, only the top players get noticed by the coach"), and serious repercussions for mistakes (e.g., "On this team, players are punished for mistakes") were included on the Performance Goal subscale. Items reflecting an emphasis on hard work and improvement (e.g., "On this team, trying hard is rewarded"), making mistakes as a part of learning (e.g., "On this team, players are encouraged to work on weaknesses"), and maximal participation of all players in games (e.g., "On this team, all players have an important role") were included on the Mastery Goal subscale.

Results indicated that perceptions of a prevailing mastery-oriented climate related to greater reported enjoyment of and interest in basketball. Basketball players who perceived that their team environment was primarily mastery-oriented also tended to believe that effort leads to success in their sport. Dispositional goal orientation and the two perceived motivational climate subscales were minimally correlated and both significantly predicted players' enjoyment ($R^2 = .25$ and $.23$, respectively). The belief that effort results in basketball success was significantly predicted by individual differences in goal orientation only.

Teams significantly differed in perceived motivational climate—i.e., some teams were viewed as more or less mastery- and performance-oriented than others. When teams were distinguished in relation to season record, teams with a poor winning percentage (less than 25% of their games) perceived their team motivational climate as less mastery-oriented than teams with a higher winning percentage. Teams with the highest winning percentage (greater than 75%) perceived the situational goal structure to be less ego-involving or performance-oriented than teams with a less positive season record.

The findings of the Seifriz et al. study (1991) hold exciting promise for the implementation of theoretically based motivation interventions in sport settings. This work suggests that, similar to the classroom, sport environments can be differentiated with respect to their goal structure and that this aspect of the athletic milieu relates to the quality of athletes' experiences. Moreover, drawing from such research, we have a greater awareness of what aspects of the environment to target (e.g., reducing interteam member competition, increasing the emphasis placed on good effort) if we desire to make a team climate more mastery-oriented and less performance-focused.

A "slice-in-time" design like the one employed in this study, unfortunately, cannot provide us with information on the long-term effects of motivational climate on the socialization of goal orientations. Athletes, at least at the high school level, appear to come into the sport context with their personal goals and ideas about how sport operates, which are not necessarily redundant with the prevailing goal structure. Cross-sectional investigations also do not tell us what influence motivational climate may have on athletes' perceptions, performance, and participation across one or more competitive seasons. Based on the Seifriz et al. (1991) investigation, however, perceived team goal structure in sport can be measured, and this construct appears to be an important piece of the motivational puzzle.

Motivation Interventions from a Goal Perspective Approach

The goal perspective studies conducted to date in the athletic domain have been compelling in their advocacy of a strong task orientation. Achievement-conducive motivational patterns and more adaptive and positive meanings are associated with an emphasis on task-involved goals in sport. In essence, the literature is beginning to call for theoretically and empirically based interventions that foster task involvement among sport participants. The goal-setting study by Burton (1989) just described is one excellent example of this type of work in the context of intercollegiate athletics.

Another illustration is work by Lloyd and Fox (1990). In this field experiment, the teaching mode employed by an instructor of an exercise class was manipulated to reflect either a task- or ego-involving environment (i.e., the focus of the instructor's feedback was on consistent comparisons between students or the self-improvement of individual students). The subjects were adolescent girls who were either high or low in ego orientation. All were participants in a six-week aerobic exercise program. In general, higher motivation was exhibited in the self-referenced exercise class condition. Moreover, the situational goal structure impacted on the prevailing goal perspective among program participants. In particular, the task-involving exercise situation resulted in a decrease in ego orientation among the high-ego-oriented girls. The ego-involving class, on the other hand, produced an increase in the salience of ego-involving girls among the girls who were initially low in ego orientation.

Extrapolating from the results of this investigation and the work of Seifriz et al. (1991) already described, it appears that goal-perspective-based interventions should be sensitive to optimizing the motivational climate as well as addressing individual differences in goal orientation. Not surprisingly, fostering motivation is a complex issue, and we probably will need to be interactionist in our approach to this problem.

CONCLUDING REMARKS

Initial sport research has indicated that personal goals are a crucial organizing principle guiding individuals' interpretation of and psychological and behavioral responses to the domain of athletic achievement. There is reason for optimism at the present time that work emanating from social cognitive theories of goal perspectives and behavior will lead to a deeper grasp of the phenomenology of the sport participant and nonparticipant. This knowledge can provide a firm foundation for programmatic efforts directed toward enhancing motivation in the athletic realm. Much more basic and applied research is warranted before a comprehensive theory of sport achievement is realized.

References

Allison, M. T. (1982). Sportsmanship: Variation based on sex and degree of competitive experience. In A. O. Dunleavy, A. W. Miracle, & C. R. Rees (Eds.), *Studies in the sociology of sport* (pp. 106–118). Fort Worth, TX: Texas Christian University Press.

Ames, C. (1984a). Conceptions of motivation within competitive and noncompetitive goal structures. In R. Schwarzer (Ed.), *Self-related cognitions in anxiety and motivation* (pp. 205–241). Hillsdale, NJ: Erlbaum.

Ames, C. (1984b). Competitive, cooperative, and individualistic goal structures: A motivational analysis. In R. Ames & C. Ames (Eds.), *Research on motivation in education: Student motivation* (pp. 177–207). New York: Academic Press.

Ames, C., (1992). Achievement goals, motivational climate, and motivational process. In G. C. Roberts (Ed.), *Motivation in sport and exercise* (pp. 161–176). Champaign, IL: Human Kinetics.

Ames, C., & Ames, R. (1981). Competitive versus individualistic goal structures: The salience of past performance information for causal attributions and affect. *Journal of Educational Psychology, 73,* 411–418.

Ames, C., & Archer, J. (1988). Achievement goals in the classroom: Students' learning strategies and motivation processes. *Journal of Educational Psychology, 80,* 260–267.

Atkinson, J. W. (1964). *An introduction to motivation.* New York: American Book Company.

Balague, G., & Roberts, G. C. (1989, November). *A social cognitive scale to measure mastery and competitive achievement goals in sport.* Paper presented at the symposium entitled "Motivation in sport and exercise," University of Illinois at Urbana-Champaign.

Bandura, A. (1977). Self-efficacy: Toward a unifying theory of behavioral change. *Psychological Review, 84,* 191–215.

Bandura, A. (1986). *Social foundation of thought and action: A social cognitive theory.* Englewood Cliffs, NJ: Prentice-Hall.

Blair, S. (1985). Professionalization of attitudes toward play in children and adults. *Research Quarterly for Exercise and Sport, 56,* 82–83.

Boyd, M. P. (1990). *The effects of participation orientation and success-failure on post-competitive affect in young athletes.* Unpublished doctoral dissertation, University of Southern California.

Boyd, M., Callaghan, J., & Yin, Z. (1991, June). *Ego-involvement and low competence in sport as a source of competitive trait anxiety.* Paper presented at the North American Society for the Psychology of Sport and Physical Activity, Asilomar, CA.

Bredemeier, B. J. (1985). Moral reasoning and the perceived legitimacy of intentionally injurious sport acts. *Journal of Sport Psychology, 7,* 110–124.

Buchan, F., & Roberts, G. C. (1991, June). *Children's perceptions of success in sport.* Paper presented at the North American Society for the Psychology of Sport and Physical Activity, Asilomar, CA.

Burton, D. (1989). Winning isn't everything: Examining the impact of performance goals on collegiate swimmers' cognitions and performance. *The Sport Psychologist, 2,* 105–132.

Burton, D., & Martens, R. (1986). Pinned by their own goals: An exploratory investigation into why kids drop out of wrestling. *Journal of Sport Psychology, 8,* 183–197.

Butler, R. (1987). Task-involving and ego-involving properties of evaluation: The effects of different feedback conditions on motivational perceptions, interest and performance. *Journal of Educational Psychology, 79,* 474–482.

Butler, R. (1988). Enhancing and undermining intrinsic motivation: The effects of task-involving and ego-involving evaluation on interest and performance. *British Journal of Educational Psychology, 58,* 1–14.

Chaumeton, N., & Duda, J. (1988). Is it how you play the game or whether you win or lose?: The effect of competitive level and situation on coaching behaviors. *Journal of Sport Behavior, 11,* 157–174.

Duda, J. L. (1985). Goals and achievement orientations of Anglo and Mexican-American adolescents in sport and the classroom. *International Journal of Intercultural Relations, 9,* 131–155.

Duda, J. L. (1986a). Perceptions of sport success and failure among white, black, and Hispanic adolescents. In J. Watkins, T. Reilly, & L. Burwitz (Eds.), *Sport science* (pp. 214–222). London: E. & F. N. Spon.

Duda, J. L. (1986b). A cross-cultural analysis of achievement motivation in sport and the classroom. In L. VanderVelden and J. Humphrey (Eds.), *Psychology and sociology in sport: Current selected research* (Vol. I, pp. 115–134). New York: AMS Press.

Duda, J. L. (1987). Toward a developmental theory of achievement motivation in sport. *Journal of Sport Psychology, 9,* 130–145.

Duda, J. L. (1988). The relationship between goal perspectives and persistence and intensity among recreational sport participants. *Leisure Sciences, 10,* 95–106.

Duda, J. L. (1989a). Goal perspectives and behavior in sport and exercise settings. In C. Ames & M. Maehr (Eds.), *Advances in Motivation and Achievement* (Vol. VI., pp. 81–115). Greenwich, CT: JAI Press.

Duda, J. L. (1989b). Goal perspectives, participation and persistence in sport. *International Journal of Sport Psychology, 20,* 42–56.

Duda, J. L. (1989c). The relationship between task and ego orientation and the perceived purpose of sport among male and female high school athletes. *Journal of Sport and Exercise Psychology, 11,* 318–335.

Duda, J. L. (1992). Motivation in sport settings: A goal perspective analysis. In G. Roberts (Ed.), *Motivation in sport and exercise.* (pp. 57–91). Champaign, IL: Human Kinetics.

Duda, J. L., & Allison, M. T. (1989). The attributional theory of achievement motivation: Cross-cultural considerations. *International Journal of Intercultural Relations, 13,* 37–55.

Duda, J. L., & Allison, M. T. (1990). Cross-cultural analysis in exercise and sport psychology: A void in the field. *Journal of Sport and Exercise Psychology, 12,* 114–131.

Duda, J. L., & Chi, L. (1989, September). *The effect of task- and ego-involving conditions on perceived competence and causal attributions in basketball.* Paper presented at the meeting of the Association for the Advancement of Applied Sport Psychology, University of Washington, Seattle, WA.

Duda, J. L., Chi, L., & Newton, M. (1990, May). *Psychometric characteristics of the TEOSQ.* Paper presented at the annual meeting of the North American Society for the Psychology of Sport and Physical Activity, University of Houston, TX.

Duda, J. L., Chi, L., Newton, M., Walling, M., & Catley, D. (in press). Task and ego orientation and intrinsic motivation in sport. *International Journal of Sport Psychology.*

Duda, J. L., & Hom, H. (1991, June). *The interrelationships between children's goal perspectives and parent's goal perspectives in the sport domain.* Paper presented at the meetings of the North American Society for the Psychology of Sport and Physical Activity, Asilomar, CA.

Duda, J. L., Newton, M. & Chi, L. (1990, May). *The relationship of task and ego orientation and expectations to multidimensional state anxiety.* Paper presented at the annual meeting of the North American Society for the Psychology of Sport and Physical Activity, University of Houston, TX.

Duda, J. L., & Nicholls, J. G. (in press). Dimensions of achievement motivation in schoolwork and sport. *Journal of Educational Psychology.*

Duda, J. L., & Nicholls, J. G. (1991) *The Task and Ego Orientation in Sport Questionnaire: Psychometric properties.* Manuscript submitted for publication.

Duda, J. L., Olson, L. K., & Templin, T. (1991). The relationship of task and ego orientation to sportsmanship attitudes and the perceived legitimacy of aggressive acts. *Research Quarterly for Exercise and Sport, 62,* 79–87.

Duda, J. L., Smart, A., & Tappe, M. (1989). Personal investment in the rehabilitation of athletic injuries. *Journal of Sport and Exercise Psychology, 11,* 367–381.

Duda, J. L., & White, S. (1991). *The relationship of goal perspectives to beliefs about the causes of success among elite skiers.* Manuscript under review.

Dweck, C. S. (1986). Motivational processes affecting learning. *American Psychologist, 41,* 1040–1048.

Dweck, C. S., & Elliott, E. (1983). Achievement motivation. In E. M. Hetherington (Ed.), *Handbook of child psychology,* 4th ed., Vol. 4: *Socialization, personality and social development* (pp. 643–691). New York: Wiley.

Dweck, C. S., & Leggett, E. L. (1988). A social cognitive approach to motivation and personality. *Psychological Review, 95,* 1–18.

Eccles, J., Midgley, C., & Adler, T. (1984). Grade-related changes in the school environment: Effects on achievement motivation. In J. Nicholls (Ed.), *The development of achievement motivation* (pp. 283–332). Greenwich, CT: JAI Press.

Elliott, E. S., & Dweck, C. S. (1988). Goals: An approach to motivation and achievement. *Journal of Personality and Social Psychology, 54,* 5–12.

Ewing, M. E. (1981). *Achievement orientations and sport behavior of males and females.* Unpublished doctoral dissertation, University of Illinois at Urbana-Champaign.

Feltz, D., & Petlichkoff, L. (1983). Perceived competence among interscholastic sport participants and dropouts. *Canadian Journal of Applied Sport Sciences, 8,* 231–235.

Gill, D. L., & Deeter, T. E. (1988). Development of the Sport Orientation Questionnaire. *Research Quarterly for Exercise and Sport, 59,* 191–202.

Gould, D., Feltz, D., Horn, T., & Weiss, M. (1982). Reasons for sport attrition in competitive youth swimming. *Journal of Sport Behavior, 5,* 155–165.

Hall, H. K. (1989). *A social-cognitive approach to goal setting: The mediating effects of achievement goals and perceived ability.* Unpublished dissertation, University of Illinois at Urbana-Champaign.

Harter, S. (1978). Effectance motivation reconsidered: toward a developmental model. *Human Development, 21,* 34–64.

Hom, H. L., Duda, J. L., & Miller, A. (1991). *Goals, beliefs, and intrinsic interest among young sport participants.* Paper submitted for publication.

Huston, L., & Duda, J. L. (1991). *The relationship of goal orientation and competitive level to the endorsement of aggressive acts in football.* Paper submitted for publication.

Jagacinski, C. M., & Nicholls, J. G. (1990). Reducing effort to protect perceived ability: "They'd do it but I wouldn't." *Journal of Educational Psychology, 82,* 15–21.

Kleiber, D., & Roberts, G. C. (1981). The effects of sport experience in the development of social character: An exploratory investigation. *Journal of Sport Psychology, 3,* 114–122.

Klint, K., & Weiss, M. R. (1986). Dropping in and dropping out: Participation motives of current and former youth gymnasts. *Canadian Journal of Applied Sport Sciences, 11,* 106–114.

Lewthwaite, R. (1990). Threat perception in competitive trait anxiety: The endangerment of important goals. *Journal of Sport and Exercise Psychology, 12,* 280–300.

Lloyd, L., & Fox, K. R. (1990, September). *The effect of contrasting interventions on the exercise achievement orientation and motivation of adolescent girls.* Paper presented at the meetings of the British Association for the Sport Sciences, Cardiff, Wales.

Locke, E. & Latham, A. (1985). The application of goal setting to sports. *Journal of Sports Psychology, 7,* 205–222.

Maehr, M. L. (1984). Meaning and motivation. In R. Ames & C. Ames (Eds.), *Research on motivation in education* (Vol. I, pp. 38–61). New York: Academic Press.

Maehr, M. L., & Braskamp, L. (1986). *The motivation factor: A theory of personal investment.* Lexington, MA: D. C. Heath.

Maehr, M. L., & Nicholls, J. G., (1980). Culture and achievement motivation: A second look. In N. Warren (Ed.), *Studies in cross-cultural psychology* (pp. 221–267). New York: Academic Press.

Miller, A. (1985). A developmental study of the cognitive basis of performance impairment after failure. *Journal of Personality and Social Psychology, 49,* 529–538.

Newton, M., & Duda, J. L. (1992a). *The relationship of task and ego orientation to mid-activity cognitions and post-performance attributions in a college-level bowling class.* Manuscript under review.

Newton, M., & Duda, J. L. (1992b, April). *The relationship between dispositional goal perspectives and effort, interest, involvement, and trait anxiety in adolescent tennis players.* Paper presented at the American Alliance for Health, Physical Education, Recreation, and Dance, Indianapolis, IN.

Nicholls, J. (1984a). Achievement motivation: Conceptions of ability, subjective experience, task choice, and performance. *Psychological Review, 91,* 328–346.

Nicholls, J. (1984b). Conceptions of ability and achievement motivation. In R. Ames & C. Ames (Eds.), *Research on motivation in education: Student motivation,* Vol. I. (pp. 39–73). New York: Academic Press.

Nicholls, J. G. (1989). *The competitive ethos and democratic education.* Cambridge, MA: Harvard University Press.

Nicholls, J. G. (1992). The general and the specific in the development and expression of achievement motivation. In G. Roberts (Ed.), *Motivation in sport and exercise* (pp. 31–56). Champaign, IL: Human Kinetics.

Nicholls, J. G., Cheung, P. C., Lauer, J., & Patashnick, M. (1989). Individual differences in academic motivation: Perceived ability, goals, beliefs, and values. *Learning and Individual Differences, 1,* 63–84.

Nicholls, J. G., Cobb, P., Wood, T., Yackel, E., & Patashnick, M. (1990). Assessing students' theories of success in mathematics: Individual and classroom differences. *Journal for Research in Mathematics Education, 21,* 109–122.

Nicholls, J., & Miller, A. (1984). Development and its discontents: The differentiation of the concept of ability. In J. Nicholls (Ed.), *Advances in motivation and achievement: The development of achievement motivation* (pp. 185–218). Greenwich, CT: JAI Press.

Nicholls, J. G., Patashnick, M., & Nolen, S. B. (1985). Adolescents' theories of education. *Journal of Educational Psychology, 77,* 683–692.

Papaioannou, A. (1990). *Goal perspectives and motives for participation in P.E. lessons as perceived by 14- and 17-year-old Greek students.* Manuscript submitted for publication.

Pemberton, C., Petlichkoff, L., & Ewing, M. (1986, June). *Psychometric properties of the achievement orientation questionnaire.* Paper presented at the annual meeting of the North American Society for the Psychology of Sport and Physical Activity, Scottsdale, AZ.

Piparo, A. J., Lewthwaite, R., & Hasbrook, C. A. (1990, October). *Social correlates of children's sport goal orientations: Coach behaviors and societal influences.* Paper presented at the annual meeting of the Association for the Advancement of Applied Sport Psychology, San Antonio, TX.

Roberts, G. C. (1984). Achievement motivation in children's sport. In J. Nicholls (Ed.), *The development of achievement motivation* (pp. 251–282). Greenwich, CT: JAI Press.

Roberts, G. C., Hall, H. K., Jackson, S. A., Kimiecik, J., & Tonymon, P. (1990, September). *Goal perspectives and perceptions of the sport experience.* Paper presented at the annual meeting of the Association for the Advancement of Applied Sport Psychology, San Antonio, TX.

Rudisill, M. E. (1989). The influence of various achievement goal orientations on perceived competence and the attributional process. *Journal of Human Movement Studies, 16,* 55–73.

Rudisill, M. E., Meaney, K. S., McDermott, B. A., & Jibaja-Rusth, M. (1990, May). *Influence of various goal-setting orientations on children's persistence and perceived competence in three motor skills.* Paper presented at the annual meeting of the North American Society for the Psychology of Sport and Physical Activity, University of Houston, TX.

Ryan, R. M. (1982). Control and information in the intrapersonal sphere: An extension of cognitive evaluation theory. *Journal of Personality and Social Psychology, 43,* 450–461.

Ryan, R. M., Mims, V., & Koestner, R. (1983). The relationship of reward contingency and interpersonal context to intrinsic motivation: A review and test using cognitive evaluation theory. *Journal of Personality and Social Psychology, 45,* 736–750.

Sarason, I. G., Sarason, B., Keefe, D., Hayes, B., & Shearin, E. (1986). Cognitive interference: Situational determinants and traitlike characteristics. *Journal of Personality and Social Psychology, 51,* 215–226.

Seifriz, J. J., Duda, J. L., & Chi, L. (1991). *The relationship of perceived motivational climate to intrinsic motivation and beliefs about success in basketball.* Manuscript submitted for publication.

Silva, J. (1983). The perceived legitimacy of rule violating behavior in sport. *Journal of Sport Psychology, 5,* 438–448.

Thorkildsen, T. (1988). Theories of education among academically precocious adolescents. *Contemporary Educational Psychology, 13,* 323–330.

Vallerand, R. J., Deci, E. L., & Ryan, R. M. (1988). Intrinsic motivation in sport. In K. Pandolf (Ed.), *Exercise and Sport Sciences Reviews, 16* (pp. 389–425). New York: Macmillan.

Vallerand, R. J., Gauvin, L., & Halliwell, W. R. (1986). Negative effects of competition on children's intrinsic motivation. *Journal of Social Psychology, 126,* 649–657.

Vealey, R. S. (1986). Conceptualization of sport confidence and competitive orientation: Preliminary investigation and instrument development. *Journal of Sport Psychology, 8,* 221–296.

Vealey, R. S., & Campbell, J. L. (1988). Achievement goals of adolescent figure skaters: Impact on self-confidence, anxiety and performance. *Journal of Adolescence Research, 3,* 227–243.

Weiner, B. (1979). A theory of motivation for some classroom experiences. *Journal of Educational Psychology, 71,* 3–25.

Weiner, B. (1985). An attributional theory of achievement motivation and emotion. *Psychological Review, 92,* 548–575.

Weiss, M. R., & Bredemeier, B. J. (1983). Developmental sport psychology: A theoretical perspective for studying children in sport. *Journal of Sport Psychology, 5,* 216–230.

Weitzer, J. E. (1989). *Childhood socialization into physical activity: Parental roles in perceptions of competence and goal orientation.* Unpublished master's thesis, University of Wisconsin at Milwaukee.

White, S. A., & Duda, J. L. (1991a, October). *The interdependence between goal perspectives, psychological skills, and cognitive interference among elite skiers.* Paper presented at the annual meeting of the Association for the Advancement of Applied Sport Psychology, Savannah, GA.

White, S. A. & Duda, J. L. (1991b). *The relationship of gender, level of sport involvement, and participation motivation to goal orientation.* Manuscript submitted for publication.

White, S. A., & Duda, J. L. (1992). *Dimensions of goals—Beliefs about success among disabled athletes.* Manuscript submitted for publication.

Whitehead, J. (1986). A cross-national comparison of attributions underlying achievement orientations in adolescent sport. In J. Watkins, T. Reilly, & L. Burwitz (Eds.), *Sport sciences* (pp. 297–302). London: E. & F. N. Spon.

Whitehead, J. (1989, November). *Achievement motivation and persistence in adolescent sport.* Paper presented at the symposium on "Motivation in Sport and Exercise," University of Illinois at Urbana-Champaign.

Whitehead, J., & Dalby, R. A. (1987, September). *The development of effort and ability attributions in sport.* Paper presented at a conference of the Institute for the Study of Children in Sport, Bedford College of Higher Education, Bedford, U.K.

Yin, Z., Boyd, M., & Callaghan, J. (1991, June). *Patterns between task/ego goal orientations and their cognitive/affective correlates in high school athletes.* Paper presented at the annual meeting of the North American Society for the Psychology of Sport and Physical Activity, Asilomar, CA.

·19·

ATTRIBUTION RESEARCH
AND SPORT PSYCHOLOGY

Stuart Biddle

This chapter will include a review of research on attributions and the attribution process in sport. First it will provide a historical background with a summary of "classical" theories of attribution. Sport attributions will then be discussed in terms of antecedent factors, spontaneous causal thinking, biases, and measurement issues. This will be followed by consideration of individual difference factors and the consequences of making attributions, such as expectancies, emotions, and behavior. The chapter will conclude by looking at areas for future development.

INTRODUCTION

Attributions are perceived causes or reasons that people give for an occurrence related to themselves or others. The term *causal attribution* is often used. However, whether attributions are actually causal is a matter of debate. For example, Buss (1978) has argued that attribution theorists have used a causal framework almost exclusively and have used the terms *cause* and *reason* interchangeably. Buss argues that cause is "that which brings about a change" whereas a reason is "that for which a change is brought about (e.g. goals, purposes, etc.)" (p. 1311). The "correct" use of these terms is advocated by Buss (1978) (see also Hewstone [1989] and Kruglanski [1975]). For the purposes of this paper, the term *causal attribution* will usually be avoided. However, terms associated with thoughts about causes (*causal thought, causal thinking*) are deemed appropriate.

A model of the attribution process is presented in Figure 19–1. This shows a simplified process of the factors affect-

ing the way people arrive at attributions (antecedents), the way attributions may be classified (into elements, such as effort or luck, or dimensions, such as internal/external locus of causality), and the possible consequences of making attributions for motivation, behavior, etc. This model helps to place attributions in the context of a social cognitive process.

HISTORICAL BACKGROUND AND CLASSICAL PERSPECTIVES

Despite the recent upsurge of interest in cognitive and social cognitive paradigms in psychology, attribution theory can be traced back to the work of Heider (1944, 1958). Although later theories have had considerable impact on the field, many of these are based on Heider's theorizing. The perspectives put forward by Jones & Davis (1965), Kelley (1967), and Weiner (1986; Weiner et al., 1972) have been dominant, although the works of Bem (1972), Kruglanski (1975), Schacter and Singer (1962), and Seligman and coworkers (e.g., Abramson, Seligman, & Teasdale, 1978) have all had a significant influence on the theory and application of attributions. Although little use has been made in sport psychology research of some of the perspectives outlined in this section, it is important to make a brief historical sketch in order to understand the attribution processes that have been studied in sport contexts. However, further detail is available elsewhere (e.g., Hewstone, 1989; Weary, Stanley, & Harvey, 1989; Weiner, 1980).

The comments of Dr. Ken Fox (University of Exeter), Dr. Sandy Wolfson (Newcastle Polytechnic), and two anonymous reviewers are acknowledged and appreciated. Thanks are also extended to Trevor Learmouth (University of Exeter Library) for assistance with an on-line computer reference search. This paper was supported by a University of Exeter School of Education Research Grant.

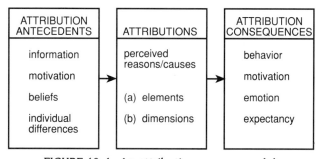

FIGURE 19-1. An attribution process model.
Modified from Kelley & Mischela (1980).

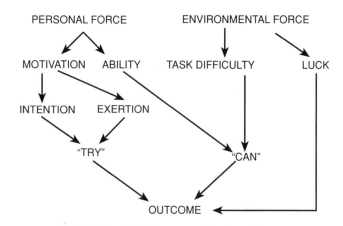

FIGURE 19-2. Heider's model of attribution.

HEIDER'S NAIVE ANALYSIS OF ACTION

Heider has been labeled the founding father of attribution theory, and although his seminal book, *The Psychology of Interpersonal Relations* (Heider, 1958), is often used as the benchmark against which other attribution perspectives are compared, it was some 14 years prior to this that his article in *Psychological Review* was published, which can be cited as the beginning of the contemporary literature on attributions (Heider, 1944). In this paper, Heider suggested that the determination of the locality ("locus") of an attribution was related to the concept of "unit formation." By this he meant that both causes (origins) and effects constituted causal units and that by studying the similarity of closeness between origins and effects, inferences or attributions about the event could be made. Similarly, Heider suggested that "person" attributions were more likely than situational ones because he believed that people were the "prototype of origins." Such suggestions have fuelled a great deal of research into attribution "errors" and "biases," as well as the attribution of responsibility. These issues are discussed in more detail later in this chapter.

Developing these ideas in his book, Heider (1958) began formulating his "naive psychology" or his approach that became known as the "phenomenology of the layperson." Three fundamental propositions stem from this approach. First in order to understand the behavior of individuals, one must first understand how they perceive and describe their social environment. Perceptual processes, therefore, are central to his argument. Second Heider made the assumption that people seek a stable and predictable environment in their effort to control their surroundings and anticipate the behavior of others. Finally Heider suggested that the processes of perceiving objects and people were similar and that in order to understand behavior, people will look toward the dispositional qualities of the individual. This is the same point as the "prototype of origins" idea from his earlier work.

Heider's model of the attribution process is illustrated in Figure 19-2. It should be clear from this diagram that the process of attribution combines personal (internal) and environmental (external) factors. The influence of such an approach cannot be underestimated in subsequent research, including that in sport psychology.

THEORY OF CORRESPONDENT INFERENCES

In 1979, E. E. Jones commented that "getting from acts to dispositions, or more generally, making inferences from behavior about personality, is a ubiquitous activity of paramount significance for all of us" (p. 107). Some 14 years prior to this statement, Jones and Davis had formulated their "theory of correspondent inferences," in which they attempted to explain how people infer dispositions, or personality characteristics, of individuals from their behavior (Jones & Davis, 1965). This approach, therefore, is one of social ("other person") attribution rather than the self-perception more commonly found in the sport psychology literature (Carron, 1980).

The basic process of inferring dispositions from behavior is shown in Figure 19-3. While the actual process of behavior moves from left to right, the process of *inference* is from right to left.

Jones and Davis suggested that dispositional attributions were more clearly identified as a result of processing two types of information about the behavior. First observers of the behavior would learn more about the personality of the individual when the behavior is low in social desirability. In other words, one could assume that Jane is an enthusiastic athlete when she is observed throwing the javelin on her own in the pouring rain. On the other hand, it is less easy to infer her enthusiasm when she is seen at training sessions

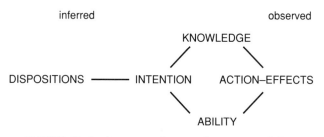

FIGURE 19-3. Correspondence inference model of attributions proposed by Jones & Davis (1965).
Adapted from Hewstone, 1989.

on a sunny day with her boyfriend, who also happens to be a javelin thrower. This is because the attendance at the session could be due either to a keenness to throw the javelin, enthusiasm to be with a close friend, or a liking for sunny weather. In short, the social desirability effect in "correspondence of inference" is operationally defined as the confidence the observer has in making an inference about the behavior in question (Weary et al., 1989).

The second part of this theory states that attributions about the actor are more easily made when the behavior under investigation has unique effects or outcomes. To infer that John has chosen to play squash because he likes to exercise in the company of others is not easy to do when he could also have chosen badminton. Both activities involve being with other people; therefore, little information is revealed about John's preferences or motivations from his choice of sport. However, if the choice were between squash and solo jogging, it would become more likely that, given the choice of squash, we would infer that John enjoys the chosen activity because he is attracted to the social elements of the situation.

The greatest amount of information, therefore, is revealed when there is a correspondence of inference between social desirability (or expectancies) and the commonality of effects. When social desirability is low and the commonality of effects is low, Jones and Davis (1965) suggest that this situation is one of "high correspondence of inference."

The theory of correspondent inference has not been revived in recent research in social psychology, nor has it been used in sport psychology research. The theory does, however, constitute a milestone in the history of attribution theory and is, therefore, important in its own right. It may also provide a useful conceptual framework for understanding attribution processes in sport, such as actor-observer (e.g., athlete-coach) interactions and attribution biases. This possibility will be discussed later.

THE PRINCIPLE OF COVARIATION

Another influential perspective is that of Kelley and his coworkers (Kelley, 1967, 1972; Kelley & Michela, 1980; Kelley & Thibaut, 1978). Kelley's proposition that people interpret everyday events by applying the principle of covariation was considered equally applicable to self and person perception. Kelley suggested that people arrive at a cause for an event by processing information about whether accompanying conditions and circumstances vary or not as the event itself varies. This was considered analogous to experimental methods and in particular the analysis of variance (ANOVA) statistical model in which the event or outcome (the dependent variable) is studied in relation to surrounding conditions (independent variables). As Kelley and Michela (1980) said, "The effect is attributed to the factor with which it covaries" (p. 462).

Essentially the theory proposes that three types of information are used in making an attribution. These are the "in-

dependent variables" in the ANOVA model and refer to (1) consensus information, (2) consistency information, and (3) distinctiveness information. Consensus information refers to the behavior of the individual in question as well as other people. To what extent is the behavior of the person also observed in others? Consistency information refers to the consistency of the behavior over time. To what extent is the observed action consistent with the individual's prior actions? Finally distinctiveness information refers to whether the behavior is distinctive or related to similar behaviors. For example, if Sally enjoys running, does she enjoy running only in the park (high distinctiveness), or does she enjoy running elsewhere too (low distinctiveness)?

Kelley's contribution to attribution theory, like that of Jones and Davis (1965), has been large, and he has provided a significant perspective on both self and person perception processes. However, again the theory has not received much attention in sport psychology, although Peterson (1980) did investigate the covariation hypothesis through an investigation of attributional statements made after American football games. However, only partial support was found for this hypothesis.

Kelley's perspective on attributions has had some explanatory value in areas related to sport, such as education (Jaspars, Hewstone, & Fincham, 1983) and health decision making (King, 1983), and to a lesser extent in exercise behaviors (Biddle & Ashford, 1988).

ACHIEVEMENT ATTRIBUTIONS: THE WORK OF WEINER

Weiner's contribution to the field of attribution theory has been highly significant, nowhere more so than in the area of attribution processes associated with achievement contexts. A full explanation of his approach will not be made in this section, since the majority of sport-related attribution research has used a Weinerian perspective, and as such his theory will underpin a great deal of the rest of this chapter. However, before embarking on a review of sport psychology research based on attribution theories, the background to Weiner's work will be discussed.

Weiner's research started by looking at attributional responses to academic success and failure in the classroom (Weiner, 1979; Weiner et al., 1972), but has since been extended into investigations on links between attributions and emotions (Weiner, Russell, & Lerman, 1978, 1979), behavioral correlates of the attribution-emotion relationship (Weiner, Amirkhan, Folkes, & Verette, 1987; Weiner, Perry, & Magnusson, 1988), and whether people make spontaneous attributions in everyday life (Weiner, 1985a). For a summary of Weiner's research on attributions, particularly his approach to motivation and emotion, see Weiner (1985b, 1986).

Using Heider's analysis as a basis, Weiner and his coworkers extended notions of achievement motivation (Atkinson & Raynor, 1974) and locus of control (Rotter, 1966) to produce a classification model for attributions, and subsequently a more predictive model for the consequences of attributions (Weiner, 1986). These perspectives formed the foundation for sport attribution research and so will be integrated into subsequent sections.

ATTRIBUTION ANTECEDENTS AND ATTRIBUTIONS IN SPORT

Much of the sport psychology research in attribution theory has focused on the antecedent variables of attributions, such as individual differences or expectancies, and the nature of the attributions themselves. This led to early studies that were primarily descriptive.

ATTRIBUTION ELEMENTS AND DIMENSIONS

The approach adopted by Weiner et al. (1972) was also used in early sport psychology attribution research. Using Heider's ideas, Weiner et al. identified four main attributions ("attribution elements") used in achievement contexts. These attributions were (1) personal ability, (2) personal effort, (3) difficulty of the task, and (4) luck. These were not meant to be identified as the *only* attributions in achievement situations, however (Weiner, 1980). Nevertheless two major criticisms can be made. First these four factors were not derived through experimental research, and second many sport psychology researchers adopted only these four factors in early studies. Roberts and Pascuzzi (1979), however, have suggested that a great number of more varied attributions are used in sport, and it is widely accepted that attributions beyond ability, effort, task difficulty, and luck will be used in sport competition. The likely antecedents of these four attribution elements are summarized in Table 19-1.

Weiner also categorized these four elements into clusters or "attribution dimensions." His original model is shown in Figure 19-4, whereby attributions are classified along the dimensions of "locus of causality" (previously referred to as "locus of control"), and "stability." With respect to the locus dimension, attributions associated with the

LOCUS OF CAUSALITY

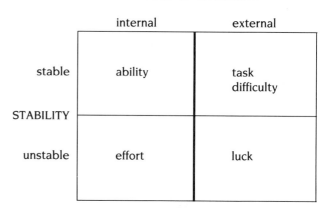

FIGURE 19-4. Weiner's original 2 × 2 model of attribution dimensions and elements.

individual are "internal" (ability and effort), whereas those outside of the individual are "external" (task and luck). Attributions related to enduring features are labeled "stable" (ability and task), whereas factors thought to be more variable are labeled "unstable" (effort and luck). The classification of elements into dimensions is not clear-cut and can lead to errors being made. This is discussed in more detail later.

Weiner (1979) later added a third dimension, that of "controllability." This refinement made it possible to distinguish between elements that are internal but not under a great deal of personal control, such as "natural ability," and internal factors that are more controllable, such as personal effort. The consequences of attributions in terms of their dimensional placement will be discussed later. Weiner's three-dimensional model is shown in Figure 19-5.

TABLE 19-1. Antecedents of the major attribution elements

Attribution	Antecedents
Ability	Percentage, number, and pattern of success; level of difficulty of the task; ego-involved (competitive) goals.
Effort	Relationship between performance and value of the task; perceived physical and mental effort; mastery (task) goals; persistence.
Task Difficulty	Social norms and comparison; characteristics of the task.
Luck	Unique or unusual outcome; independence, and randomness of outcome.

LOCUS OF CAUSALITY

	internal		external	
	stable	unstable	stable	unstable
controllable	stable effort	unstable effort	other's stable effort	other's unstable effort
uncontrollable	ability	mood	task ease	luck

CONTROLLABILITY

FIGURE 19-5. Weiner's reformulated model of attribution dimensions and elements.

Methodological Issues

Attribution Elements. As already suggested, the model in Figure 19–4 is overrestrictive for sport. Roberts and Pascuzzi (1979) administered an open-ended questionnaire to American undergraduate students, who were requested to respond to a variety of sports situations by providing possible attributions to a number of different scenarios. On coding the responses, they found that ability, effort, task difficulty, and luck were used only 45% of the time, suggesting that attribution research in sport relying on these four factors is overrestricted. However, in classifying these elements, the researchers were able to utilize the basic locus × stability model (Figure 19–4) in placing all attributions. However, this study involved hypothetical sports events, and so the extent to which the results can be generalized to real situations has not been determined. The placement of attributions made by Roberts and Pascuzzi (1979) is shown in Figure 19–6.

Attribution Dimensions. The nature of attribution dimensions in sport has not been studied extensively, and most sport psychology studies have accepted uncritically the dimensions of locus, stability, and, more recently, controllability. In attribution theory, there has been some debate about the nature of attribution dimensions. For example, the internal/external distinction has been made and found to have some support, but other dimensions have been supported less consistently (Benson, 1989; de Jong, Koomen, & Melenbergh, 1988; Passer, Kelley, & Michela, 1978; Ronis, Hansen, & O'Leary, 1983). Perhaps the greatest problem is that much of the research has been based on attribution *researchers* determining the dimensional categorization of attributions rather than the subjects themselves. This led Wimer and Kelley (1982) to comment that "for the most part, causal dimensions derive from the minds of attribu-

tion theorists, not laypeople" (p. 1143). This problem needs to be kept in mind when reviewing some studies.

An advance was made, however, with the development of the Causal Dimension Scale (CDS) (Russell, 1982). This scale allowed subjects to make a relatively "spontaneous" or "free response" attribution first, and then to rate the attribution on the three dimensions of locus of causality, stability, and controllability. While the internal consistency of the locus and stability dimensions have been shown to be adequate, the controllability dimension has been problematic (see Biddle, 1988; Biddle & Jamieson, 1988; Mark, Mutrie, Brooks, & Harris, 1984; McAuley, Russell, & Gross, 1983; Vallerand & Richer, 1988).

ATTRIBUTIONS IN SPORT

Given that attributions are responses to specific events, it is not surprising to find that the nature of the event itself will affect the attributions reported. This supports the notion of attribution antecedents, as shown in Table 19–1. Nevertheless, it has been found that certain trends exist in the types of attributions given in sport, although most analyses have been made at the level of dimensions rather than elements.

Self-Serving Bias

Support has been found for the "self-serving bias" in sport attribution research. This "hedonic bias" suggests that strategies operate to protect or enhance self-esteem. Hence attributions may be distorted, such as externalizing the reasons for failure, to protect self-esteem. Alternatively people may actually perceive themselves as being more responsible for successful or positive outcomes than unsuccessful ones. This distortion may be the result of motivational influences and is more likely to occur in situations of importance.

A review by Miller and Ross (1975) found that internal attributions were common under success conditions, but that self-protecting attributions in failure were not so common. The nature and origins of the self-serving bias have been the topic of some debate in psychology (Greenberg, Pyszcznski, & Solomon, 1982; Miller & Ross, 1975; Riess, Rosenfeld, Melburg, & Tedeschi, 1981; Tetlock & Levi, 1982; Zuckerman, 1979). However, Brawley (1984) has suggested that this bias is a function of memory. In a study of tennis, he found evidence for players more frequently and easily remembering their own inputs to team (doubles) efforts (see also Luginbuhl & Bell, 1989; Mark et al., 1984). Others suggest that the bias may not operate at a conscious level at all (Greenberg et al., 1982; Riess et al., 1981). Nevertheless, Whitley & Frieze (1985) conducted a meta-analysis of children's attributions for success and failure and found clear evidence for a self-serving bias. Success was found to elicit attributions to ability and effort more than failure, and it was also found that failure was associated with attributions to task difficulty more than success.

LOCUS OF CAUSALITY

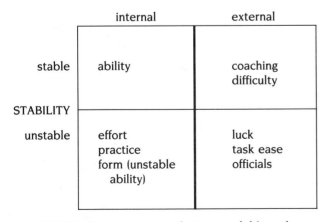

	internal	external
stable	ability	coaching difficulty
unstable	effort practice form (unstable ability)	luck task ease officials

(with STABILITY label on left axis)

FIGURE 19–6. A sport attribution model based on Weiner's classification.
Adapted from Roberts & Pascuzzi, 1979.

Much of the work in sport psychology has investigated the difference in attributions between winners and losers. For example, McAuley and Gross (1983), using the CDS, found that winners of table tennis matches were significantly higher on ratings of internal, unstable, and controllable attributions than losers. Mark et al. (1984), also using the CDS, found that squash tournament winners gave stronger stable attributions than losers, and also slightly more controllable attributions. However, no difference was found for internal attributions. A follow-up study showed that winners again made more stable and controllable attributions than losers (Mark et al., 1984, study 2). Similarly, an analysis of attributional statements in newspaper sports reports showed that successful events were more likely to be attributed to internal, stable, and controllable factors (Watkins, 1986).

Grove, Hanrahan, & McInman (1991) addressed the self-serving issue from the standpoint of player, coach, and spectator. A modified version of the CDS was used to assess attribution dimensions given by males and females in each of the three categories of involvement for both winning and losing games of basketball. No effects were found for gender or involvement category, but a significant effect was found for outcome. This showed that winning situations produced more stable and controllable attributions than were produced by losing situations. No difference was found between winning and losing attributions on the locus of causality dimension.

Mullen & Riordan (1988) have reported a meta-analysis of attributions in sport settings with particular focus on the self-serving bias. Moderate effect sizes (ES) were found for the internal/external dimension (ES = 0.33) and for ability attributions (ES = 0.31), with a smaller effect for effort (ES = 0.20). Little effect was found for task difficulty (ES = 0.09) or luck (ES = 0.10). Mullen & Riordan (1988) concluded that "the data are inconsistent with an intentional motivational explanation and that are more easily reconciled with an unintentional information processing perspective" (pp. 16–17). The reason for such a conclusion is that they found that the magnitude of the self-serving effect for internal/external and ability attributions increased with team size. Attributions to difficulty decreased with group size. Overall, effect sizes were larger for attributions to team performance in team sports and smaller for individual performance in individual sports.

One factor of importance in studying the self-serving bias is that significant group differences often mask the extent of *real* differences. Sometimes winners *and* losers report internal attributions, but winners may have significantly stronger ratings than losers. It may be that the reported internal-external differences are really just showing degrees of internality.

Objective Versus Subjective Outcomes

In addition to investigating attributions for outcome by comparing winners and losers, sport psychologists have also looked at attributions in relation to perceived success and failure. Although winning and losing is an important aspect of sport to investigate, attributions are also likely to be related to other criteria, such as perceptions of personal performance. For example, winners may be dissatisfied with their play, and alternatively losers may be satisfied with their overall play.

A study by Spink and Roberts (1980) is widely cited as an example of this approach. They elicited attributions for winning and losing from players after racquetball matches. Then, based on their assessment of satisfaction with their performance, subjects were classified into one of four categories: satisfied winner ("clear win"), dissatisfied loser ("clear loss"), dissatisfied winner ("ambiguous win"), and satisfied loser ("ambiguous loss").

The results showed that winners made more internal attributions than losers, in accordance with the self-serving bias. However, clear outcome players were shown to have higher internal attributions than those with ambiguous outcomes. Specifically clear outcomes yielded attributions to ability and effort, while ambiguous attributions were related to attributions of task difficulty.

This study by Spink and Roberts (1980) was an important one, since it alerted sport psychologists to the issue of differentiating outcome from performance. However, one problem was that only attributions for outcome (i.e., win/loss) were assessed.

In a study of gymnasts, McAuley (1985) investigated attributions for those scoring high or low in terms of the scores given by judges, and those who perceived their own performance to be successful or unsuccessful. Unfortunately it is not clear whether the gymnasts were required to complete the CDS in response to objective or subjective outcome, or both. The high-scoring gymnasts attributed their "performance" to internal, stable, and controllable factors, and this was also the case for those perceiving their performance to be highly satisfactory. However, McAuley (1985) found that perceived success was a better predictor of attributions than actual performance scores. Leith and Prapavessis (1989), on the other hand, found no difference between open-ended attributions given for objectively evaluated sports when compared to subjectively evaluated ones for "gifted" athletes aged 14 to 16 years.

Group Versus Individual Settings

The studies discussed so far have focused on attributions given for individual performance or outcomes. Many sport situations involve a group outcome and performance, and some studies have addressed this issue. Bukowski and Moore (1980) asked boys (mean age 11.5 years) who had participated in a summer camp team sport program to evaluate the importance of various factors as possible causes of team success and failure. They found that luck and task difficulty were not perceived to be important attributions, and team success was perceived to be related to internal attributions and failure to external attributions.

Bird, Foster, and Maruyama (1980) found that the difference between attributions given for individual performance and those given for team performance were partly a function of team cohesion. There was greater convergence between the two types of attributions for players in cohesive teams. Members from low cohesive teams, however, tended to blame the team for failure but to deny personal responsibility in failure. These findings suggest that studies of attributions within social situations in sport need to account for wider context variables. However, throughout these types of studies there is the problem of subjects confusing attributions for self with those of the team. Indeed, attribution studies in sport have rarely focused on team attributions in comparison with individual attributions.

Spontaneous Causal Thinking: Do We Really Make Attributions in Sport?

The initial studies in sport attribution research relied almost exclusively on having subjects rate attribution statements supplied by the experimenters. Although the results from these studies are reasonably consistent in showing that many attributions are strongly endorsed and that certain attributions are more likely to occur in one situation than in another, they raise the fundamental question of whether people actually engage in causal thought after sports events. Few studies can be located that analyze naturally occurring discourse in sport (see Johnson & Biddle, 1988; Lau & Russell, 1980; Peterson, 1980; Watkins, 1986). Open-ended questionnaires have been used in sport attribution research (e.g., the initial section of the CDS), but these still force subjects into causal thought that might not have otherwise been evident.

The study of naturally occurring attributions, particularly in achievement situations, is not extensive. Weiner (1985a) located 17 published studies that investigated "spontaneous" attributional thought and found clear support for the proposition that attributions do occur as a part of everyday life. However, attributions were found to be more likely when a goal was not attained or when an outcome was unexpected. Assuming that participants in sport have some commitment to winning and playing well, it is likely that those who lose, especially unexpectedly, and/or those who are dissatisfied with their performance, will engage in more attributional thought than others. This does not, however, satisfy the critics who say that attributions are merely post-hoc rationalizations of events, but it does help us to understand the process of how attributions are made and suggests that attributions are made in everyday situations as well as in research contexts.

The methods reported by Weiner (1985a) also provide some possibilities for future sport psychology research. For example, he reports that spontaneous attributions have been researched using available documentary material, for example, newspaper reports (Lau & Russell, 1980; Watkins, 1986), recording of verbal responses (e.g., Diener & Dweck, 1978), as well as using "indirect attributional indi-

ces," such as free recall and the content of sentence completion (Weiner, 1985a).

Johnson and Biddle (1988) investigated the attributional responses of students who had experienced "failure" on a balance board task. Subjects were given feedback that they had failed the task but were then asked to try again and to perform as many trials as they wished. This was taken as the operational definition of "persistence." During these extra trials subjects were asked to verbalize their thoughts and feelings. These were recorded and later coded along similar lines to that adopted by Diener and Dweck (1978). The subjects were split into two groups of "persisters" and "nonpersisters" on the basis of the median score. Free-response attributions were then analyzed for the two groups. The results showed that nonpersisters made proportionately more negative self-statements and attributions than persisters, while the persistent subjects made more strategy-related statements. These findings highlight the need for further research in sport using qualitative methods to establish the nature and extent of spontaneous attributional thought.

Further Methodological Issues in Sport Attributions

A number of important research issues have been discussed in this review, including the use of actual or hypothetical events, objective or subjective outcomes, and the classification of attributions into dimensions. In addition, attribution theory research studies have rarely accounted for key variables prior to the sports contest under investigation. For example, the importance of the event and prior expectations could both contribute to attribution biases. However, few studies have tested these variables prior to assessing attributions.

McAuley and Duncan (1989) investigated the effects on attributions and emotions of outcomes that disconfirmed expectancies (i.e., high expectancy of winning but lost, and high expectancy of losing but won). There were no differences between the two groups on the CDS scales of locus of causality or controllability, but high expectancy losers gave significantly more unstable attributions than other subjects did. Although some studies have investigated the role of the importance of winning in attribution-emotion research (Biddle & Hill, 1988; 1992), prior cognitive states require more extensive testing in sport attribution research.

Summary

Research into attributions in sport has tended to be narrow in its focus. Indeed, Brawley and Roberts (1984) have identified the following characteristics of sport attribution research in laboratory settings: (a) subjects were mainly university students or children; (b) the focus was almost exclusively on self attributions; (c) the experimental tasks were usually novel; (d) the independent variables were usually outcome (i.e., win/loss) or prior wins and losses; (e) some attempts were made to manipulate ego involvement, but rarely was this checked for effectiveness; (f) most subjects were asked to choose attributions from a list provided by the experimenters. These attributions were predominantly ability, effort, task difficulty, and luck.

Although more recent attribution studies in sport psychology have addressed some of these limitations, the diversity of methods has not matched that in some other areas of psychology. Consequently sport attribution research has remained narrow, and much remains to be done to enhance our knowledge in this field.

ATTRIBUTIONS AND INDIVIDUAL DIFFERENCES

The focus so far has been on the types of attributions made by winners or losers, or those satisfied or dissatisfied with their performance in sport. In addition, other individual difference factors, such as gender, age, achievement orientation, and self-esteem may be important antecedents of attributions.

GENDER DIFFERENCES

It is often reported that attributions following sports competition will differ as a function of gender. Specifically it has been suggested that men have higher perceptions of competence and more positive expectations in achievement settings, and therefore tend to attribute success to stable and internal factors more than women (Deaux, 1984). Similarly women, it has been suggested, have lower expectations of success and therefore attribute success to luck or other unstable and external causes, and failure to internal, stable factors such as lack of ability. However, this attributional "modesty" on the part of women is far from clear (Blucker & Hershberger, 1983; Dweck & Goetz, 1978; Lochel, 1983; McHugh, Duquin, & Frieze, 1978).

Deaux (1984) has argued that the difference between men and women in attributions is in terms of the different expectations held by men and women in some situations leading to different attributions, as suggested above. Deaux assumes, therefore, that given equal expectations there should be no difference in attributions between men and women. She goes on to suggest that researchers should look more closely at the nature of the task being attempted and how this influences the expectations held by men and women. These points are similar to those made by Lenney (1977), who has argued that the assumption that women lack self-confidence in achievement contexts, while true in some situations, ignores important and fundamental issues associated with the situational context. She says that women's self-confidence will be dependent on the nature of the task, the availability of clear and unambiguous performance feedback, and the nature of social comparisons being made. In short, situational cues will be important, and since these are likely to affect the attributions made for performance, the assumption that gender differences will exist in

sport achievement contexts is questioned (see Corbin, 1984).

In addition to viewing sex as a subject variable, Deaux (1984) has also suggested that sex should be viewed as a social category—that is to say, "as a cue or type of information on which observers base judgements and individuals choose actions. Here the focus is not on how men and women actually differ, but how people *think* that they differ" (Deaux, 1984, p. 110). The implications of this approach for sport are clear. Many sports are often perceived to be masculine-typed activities, thus leading to particular expectations about the capabilities of men and women in these sports. Subsequent attributions are likely to be affected by these expectations. For example, Deaux and Emswiller (1974) found that people were more likely to attribute the success of a male on a "masculine" task to ability compared to a female having equal success (see Corbin & Nix, 1979). Actor-observer differences are also important in the context of sex/gender as a social category. Deaux (1984) says that the attributions people make for male and female performance will be linked to the expectations that these people hold. Attributions and the attitudes held about men and women are likely to be correlated (Deaux, 1984, 1985).

Maehr and Nicholls (1980) have argued that spurious results have been obtained because the cognitions of women have been viewed in terms of male perspectives. They say that "the situations and tasks used in the study of achievement behavior reflect a masculine definition of achievement more than a feminine definition" (p. 245). In an expansion of this, Maehr and Nicholls (1980) say that males and females hold different achievement goals and therefore define achievement in different ways.

. . . in those situations where it has been studied, achievement behavior has been most often conceived and interpreted in a fashion that is consistent with what we have termed the ability-oriented form of achievement motivation. This turns out to be reasonably appropriate for males, but it fits poorly for females. Female achievement behavior is better described as a combination of ability-oriented motivation and social-approval motivation. (Maehr & Nicholls, 1980, p. 245).

More will be said on achievement goal orientations later in the chapter. However, these comments remind us of the importance of taking a wider perspective on individual differences in attributions.

Although early research suggested that the attributional modesty of women was consistent (see McHugh et al., 1978), subsequent research has reported similar findings for males and females in most cases (Biddle & Hill, 1988; 1992; in press; Croxton, Chiacchia, & Wagner, 1987; Mark et al., 1984; McAuley & Duncan, 1989; Robinson & Howe, 1989; Rudisill, 1988a; Spink & Roberts, 1980; Weiss, McAuley, Ebbeck, & Wiese, 1990), although small gender differences have also been reported on some attribution variables (Riordan, Thomas, & James, 1985; Tenenbaum & Furst, 1985; Zientek & Breakwell, 1988).

Weiner (1986) has suggested that attributional differences of males and females may be the result of different expectations of success, as discussed earlier (see also Deaux, 1984, 1985; Eccles [Parsons], Adler & Meece, 1984). However, the lack of gender differences reported here indicates that expectancies are similar for the two groups in sport. This absence of differences could be the result of sport being predominantly competition within, rather than between, gender groups, which may not be the case in other achievement contexts. It is also possible that males and females, because they have chosen to pursue a similar activity (i.e., sport), may be more similar than different in their psychological profile, including aspects of personality (Eysenck, Nias, & Cox, 1982; Williams, 1978). The assumption, therefore, that males and females attribute success and failure in different ways in sport has not been supported with confidence.

AGE DIFFERENCES

In a review of attribution theory in sport, Rejeski and Brawley (1983) stated that "one glaring omission in the sport attribution research is the absence of developmental studies … most research focuses on a limited age range with little concern for population representativeness. The assumption that similar attributional patterns for achievement outcomes will result across age-groups is erroneous" (p. 94).

This criticism is a valid one and has been echoed by others (Weiss et al., 1990), yet it is surprising that attribution theory research in sport has not adopted a developmental framework, since both attribution theory and the study of children have been popular topics in sport psychology for a number of years. However, not only should a developmental perspective involve the study of children, but it should also consider the attributions made across the lifespan, and therefore include older adults too (see Duda & Tappe, 1988, 1989a, 1989b; Frieze, 1984).

An influential developmental perspective in achievement psychology is that of Nicholls (1984), which has subsequently been discussed in the context of sport (Duda, 1987). Specifically Nicholls and his colleagues suggest that children develop a differentiated set of beliefs concerning achievement, and in particular with respect to effort, ability, and outcome (Nicholls & Miller, 1984). Children aged approximately 5–7 years appear not to be able to differentiate effort, ability, and outcome because their responses indicate that they think people who try hard are successful and those who are successful must have tried hard. Perceptions of ability around the age of 5 or 6 years stem from personal success or failure at a task (i.e., mastery orientation), whereas slightly older children (6–7 years) might start adopting more of a normative perspective by seeing whether others can or cannot do the task. In other words, they will think that tasks that few people can do are "hard" and that success at hard tasks equates with high ability. Children aged 7–9 years tend to think in terms of effort as

the cause of outcomes, and then later (9–10 years) ability and effort start to be differentiated as potential causes of outcomes. It is not until the ages of about 10 or 11 years that this differentiation appears to be complete and children can then see that ability is "capacity" and that this will limit the effect of effort on the outcome of a task (Duda, 1987; Nicholls & Miller, 1984).

Given these developmental "stages," it has been suggested that research into attributions with children must adopt a perspective that accounts for different perceptions of ability, effort, and perceived causes of outcomes. However, in a recent study of children's self-esteem and attributions, Weiss et al. (1990) commented that only a handful of studies had looked at children's attributions, and only one (Bird & Williams, 1980) had attempted to use a developmental approach. Many sport attribution studies have simply investigated attributions for participants of varying ages with little regard to developmental status or age group comparisons (e.g., Carron & Spink, 1980; Scanlan & Passer, 1980; Spink, 1978).

Bird and Williams (1980) investigated the sport-related attributions given by four age groups of boys and girls: 7–9, 10–12, 13–15, and 16–18 years. They were requested to respond to a series of hypothetical sport outcomes. The results showed that children aged 7–9 years explained the sport outcomes for both males and females primarily in terms of effort and luck. Between 10 and 15 years, attributions were similar for the outcomes of males and females. Children of ages 10–12 years perceived a relationship between effort and outcome as well as luck and outcome, whereas the 13–15-year-olds perceived a relationship only between effort and outcome. These trends were independent of the gender of the performer.

Sex-role stereotypes emerged quite strongly in the 16- to 18-year-old group. Specifically male performance was attributed to effort, whereas female performance was seen as more related to luck. Not only does this study reveal interesting findings on age differences in attributions, but it also shows the strength of sex-role stereotyping in attributions (see Deaux, 1984). Unfortunately, the Bird and Williams (1980) study is weakened by the use of only four attributions and by the use of hypothetical rather than real sport situations. Nevertheless it does provide important information on age differences in attributions.

With the increasing emphasis on lifetime sports and exercise involvement (Bouchard, Shephard, Stephens, Sutton, & McPherson, 1990), attribution theory in sport should also investigate attributions among older adults. Age has been discussed as a potentially important variable in attributions (see Banziger & Drevenstedt, 1984; Blank, 1984), but few studies have been conducted from an attributional perspective with older adults in sport psychology (Duda & Tappe, 1988, 1989a, 1989b). The application of attribution principles to different age groups would appear to be a research priority for sport psychology in the 1990s. The expansion of "masters" and "veterans" competitions in various sports gives researchers greater opportunities for studying the attributions of older participants.

ACHIEVEMENT MOTIVATION AND DIFFERENCES IN GOAL ORIENTATION

One of the factors thought to affect achievement attributions is the variable "achievement motivation." This concept has received considerable attention in psychology (e.g., Atkinson & Raynor, 1974; Heckhausen, 1967; Maehr & Nicholls, 1980; Weiner, 1980, 1986), as well as sport psychology (Roberts, 1982; Scanlan & Ragan, 1978; Yukelson, Weinberg, West & Jackson, 1981), despite problems of method and measurement (Fineman, 1977).

The traditional way of defining achievement motivation is to use the Atkinson/McClelland approach (McClelland, 1961; McClelland, Atkinson, Clark, & Lowell, 1953; Atkinson, 1977). Specifically Atkinson (1977) states:

achievement motivation has been referred to as the need for achievement . . . It is an important determinant of aspiration, effort and persistence when an individual expects that performance will be evaluated in relation to some standard of excellence. Such behavior is generally called achievement oriented. (p. 25).

Given the salience of achievement motivation in sport contexts, it has been proposed that constructs associated with achievement motivation are important for sport psychological research and for the study of attributions in particular. For example, Roberts (1978) found that children high in achievement motivation tended to attribute sport success to ability and failure to low effort, whereas children low in achievement motivation attributed their success in sport to luck and ease of the task, and failure to a lack of ability.

This "traditional" approach to achievement motivation, however, may not be the most parsimonious explanation for attributions in sport. For example, Maehr and Nicholls (1980) question this approach by stating that "achievement motivation should be defined in terms of its purpose or meaning for people rather than in terms of overt behavior or the characteristics of situations in which the behavior occurs" (p. 227). In other words, they argue that we need to find out the *meaning* of achievement for different people and should not assume that achievement is universally defined in the same way. This argument is developed further by Joan Duda in this volume, but a brief discussion is appropriate here within the context of achievement-related attributions.

Maehr and Nicholls (1980) suggest that success and failure are not absolute states but subjective appraisals of desirable personal qualities. This means that success and failure will be defined in different ways by various cultures, groups, and individuals. "The analysis of achievement behavior is the analysis of how people infer [the] presence or absence of desirable qualities in themselves and the effects of such inferences on behavior" (Maehr & Nicholls, 1980, p. 236). Rather than define one type of achievement motivation, as has been done traditionally, Maehr and Nicholls define three achievement orientations: ability, task (mastery), and social approval.

The ability orientation refers to behavior characterized by a striving to maintain a favorable perception of one's ability. Individuals who endorse this orientation will want to maximize their chances of attributing success to high ability and will therefore judge their success in terms of beating other people—a social comparison perspective on achievement. The second achievement goal is that of task orientation, sometimes referred to as the mastery-oriented achievement goal. Individuals who adopt this orientation judge their success in terms of the quality of their work; they wish to solve problems for their own sake rather than necessarily to demonstrate high ability.

Some researchers have used this ability/mastery distinction to infer differential attributional thinking after achievement tasks. For example, Dweck and Leggett (1988) suggest that children hold at least two different goals for academic achievement: performance goals (where they are concerned with performing better than others and gaining favorable judgments of their ability), and learning goals (where they are concerned with task mastery and increasing personal competence). Dweck and Leggett propose that children who are primarily oriented toward performance goals, but have a low perception of their ability, will develop "helpless" behavior patterns by avoiding challenge and having low persistence. Attributions for failure will be to low ability. Those who are oriented toward a performance goal but have a high perception of their ability will seek challenges and have high persistence. Similarly children with learning goals, regardless of perceived ability, will adopt a mastery behavior pattern, use attributions for success, and failure to effort and strategy, and will seek challenging situations that enhance learning. Hence the goals will determine the type of attributions used and the behavioral consequences of success and failure.

The third achievement goal identified by Maehr and Nicholls (1980) is that of social approval. This is associated with virtuous intentions and personal commitment, and to gain approval from significant others. Roberts (1984) argues that this focuses the individual on attributions to effort and is more appropriate for young children in sport when they are trying to please the teacher, coach, or their parents.

It is likely that the achievement goals held by an individual, therefore, will influence the attributions made for success and failure, and this has been shown in sport settings (see Duda, 1989). This approach appears to hold more potential than traditional approaches to achievement motivation, which have emphasized a unidimensional trait perspective. However, achievement goals will differ as a function of gender, age, and culture, and hence future attribution studies may need to account for these individual differences (Duda, 1989).

SELF-ESTEEM DIFFERENCES

Self-esteem, and related constructs of perceptions of ability and self-worth, have been studied in a variety of contexts, including sport and physical activity (Fox, 1990; Fox

& Corbin, 1989; Sonstroem, 1984a; Sonstroem & Morgan, 1989). Self-esteem may develop and change as a result of prolonged experiences, yet it may also influence the choice of motivated behaviors.

Earlier in this chapter the self-serving bias was discussed, whereby individuals appear to attribute success more than failure to internal factors. One explanation for this effect is that people are motivated to protect or enhance their self-esteem by making such attributions and will want to appear consistent with their own self-evaluations (see also Greenberg et al., 1982; Riess et al., 1981). Consequently individuals differing in self-esteem or self-perceptions, it has been hypothesized, will make different attributions for success and failure. For example, those high in self-esteem, if the self-consistency view is accepted, will tend to attribute success to internal factors, whereas those low in self-esteem will tend to discount success by using external attributions (Marsh, Cairns, Relich, Barnes, & Debus, 1984).

Few studies have used self-esteem as a variable in attribution studies in sport. However, Weiss et al. (1990) did investigate the relationship between self-esteem and attributions in both sport and social situations with 8 to 13-year-old children. These researchers confirmed earlier research in educational psychology by finding that self-esteem was correlated with attributions for success and failure. Specifically children high in physical self-esteem made attributions that were more internal, stable, and controllable than those of children low in physical self-esteem. Similarly Hanrahan, Grove, and Hattie (1989) found moderate but consistent relationships between a measure of sport attributional style and physical self-esteem. Also, Grove, Hanrahan, and Stewart (1990) found that physical self-esteem and gender predicted attributional dimensions given for recovery from sports injury.

CONSEQUENCES OF ATTRIBUTIONS

Three main areas of attribution consequences will be considered: expectancies, emotions, and behaviors.

ATTRIBUTIONS AND EXPECTATIONS

Weiner (1986) argues that people are guided by anticipations of expected rewards, and this view reflects the shift from mechanistic to cognitive approaches to motivation (Weiner, 1990). Indeed, Heider (1958) suggested that expectations will result from the interaction of personal and environmental factors. For example, he argued that expectations will be high on an easy task, especially for someone high in perceived ability who believes that he/she always tries hard. However, in his analysis of expectations and attributions, Weiner (1986) argues that it is much more difficult to find the determinants of *absolute* expectancy levels, since a number of factors are likely to be influential. Nevertheless, he says that *changes* in expectancy are related to attributions. "For many human endeavours, prediction of just the direction of expectancy shift . . . will facilitate our understanding of motivation and emotion" (Weiner, 1986, p. 81).

In short, Weiner has argued that the stability of the attribution is the most important factor in determining changes in expectancy, and he proposes that current research findings allow the statement of a fundamental psychological "law":

Changes in expectancy of success following an outcome are influenced by the perceived stability of the cause of the event. (p. 114)

This "law" is clarified by the statement of three corollaries:

- If the outcome of an event is ascribed to a stable cause, then that outcome will be anticipated with increased certainty, or with increased expectancy, in the future.
- If the outcome of an event is ascribed to an unstable cause, then the certainty or expectancy of that outcome may be unchanged, or the future will be anticipated to be different from the past.
- Outcomes ascribed to stable causes will be anticipated to be repeated in the future with a greater degree of certainty than outcomes ascribed to unstable causes. (Weiner, 1986, p. 115).

Some sport psychological research has tackled attributions and the consequences these may have for expectations. For example, Singer and McCaughan (1978) found that male high school students showed more positive expectations after success than failure, as expected, but these expectations were enhanced by attributions to stable factors. However, Singer, Grove, Cauraugh, and Rudisill (1985) did not find an effect for expectancy after subjects were given particular types of attributions for poor performance on a balance stabilometer task.

Rudisill (1989), however, did find that expectations, persistence, and performance were enhanced after failure feedback on a balance stabilometer task for subjects high in perceived competence and for those oriented toward attributions competence and for those oriented toward attributions that were internal, controllable, but unstable. After failure it would appear to be more beneficial to feel that future success is possible. This will often require, as shown by Rudisill (1988b, 1989), attributions to controllable factors that, almost by definition, will also be relatively unstable. However, three studies reported by Grove and Pargman (1986) show quite clearly that it was effort rather than ability attributions that related to future expectancies. This suggested that it was the controllability, rather than the stability, of the attribution that was important.

Expectancies, therefore, can be influenced by many factors, including the stability of the attribution. However, the role of future expectancies and confidence has been addressed through other routes, such as self-efficacy, as well as attributions (Bandura, 1986; Schunk, 1984), and self-efficacy has also received considerable attention in sport psychology (Feltz, 1988) as well as in other physical activity settings (see Biddle & Mutrie, 1991). Indeed, Bandura (1990) argues that causal attributions and outcome expectancies are different motivational processes, although both operate through the anticipation of future behavior and performance. Figure 19–7 illustrates Bandura's model by showing that route 1 links outcome expectancies to "anticipatory cognitive motivators" through the process of forward thinking, whereas route 2 shows that attributions link to anticipatory cognitive motivators by retrospective thought. The extent that the two factors are linked is not disputed, however. As Bandura (1990) says, "causal attributions and self-efficacy appraisals involve bidirectional causation. Self-beliefs of efficacy bias causal attribution" (p. 141). Clearly further work is required, going beyond the attribution stability-expectancy link, if we are to understand the mechanisms of self-confidence and expectancy beliefs in sport. Given the general belief that confidence is a crucial ingredient for successful performance and changes in behavior in sport, this should be a research priority.

ATTRIBUTIONS AND EMOTIONAL REACTIONS

The study of attributions and emotions has become more popular in recent years in psychology (Weiner, 1986), including sport psychology (Biddle, 1988; McAuley & Duncan, 1990). However, the link between attributions and emotions was made early in the attribution research literature (Weiner et al., 1972), although the initial proposals were limited in scope. For example, it was suggested that the locus of control (causality) dimension of attributions was related to the feelings of pride and shame. This was derived from achievement motivation theory (Atkinson & Raynor, 1974; Dweck & Elliott, 1983; Weiner, 1980, 1986), since the achievement motive was seen as the ability or capacity for experiencing pride in accomplishment. The pride/shame dimension is clearly a limited view of emotion, and Weiner (1986) has argued for a more diverse range of emotions to be studied. Similarly sport psychological

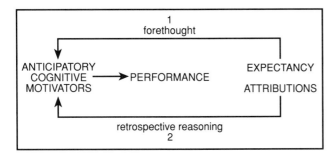

FIGURE 19–7. Attributions and expectations in the promotion of motivation and behavior
Adapted from Bandura, 1990.

research has been overrestrictive in its investigation of emotion, relying on the study of arousal (Landers, 1980) and anxiety (Sonstroem, 1984b), or closely related constructs (Jones & Hardy, 1990), despite pleas for a wider look at emotion in sport (Vallerand, 1983, 1984).

Emotion is a difficult concept to define, although there is general agreement that it consists of at least three components: physiological, behavioral, and subjective experience (Frijda, 1986; Izard, Kagan, & Zajonc, 1984). The literature on emotion and attributions has been restricted to the latter two components, and sport psychology research has almost exclusively reported on attributions and emotions from the perspective of subjective experience.

The basis for the theoretical study of the emotional consequences of attributions was made by Weiner and his colleagues. Specifically Weiner et al. (1978) compiled a list of possible emotional reactions and selected the dominant attributions found in previous achievement attribution studies. Their subjects were then presented with hypothetical situations of academic success and failure, with an appropriate attribution given for the outcome (e.g., a high test score due to high levels of effort). Subjects were then asked to report the type and intensity of emotion that would be experienced in such a situation. In order to overcome some of the weaknesses of using a method involving only hypothetical situations, Weiner et al. conducted another study, this time asking subjects to recall a "critical incident" in their lives when they had experienced academic success and failure (Weiner et al., 1979). Attributions were again supplied, and subjects had to state the type and intensity of emotion felt at the time of this incident.

Despite the methodological problems of these studies, guidelines were established for future studies on attributions and emotions in achievement contexts. First two main types of emotion were identified. "Outcome-dependent" emotion was that which related to the outcome itself (success and failure) rather than to specific attributions. Weiner et al. (1978) referred to these as a "general reaction" to the outcome, such as being pleased or happy. Second they reported "attribution-dependent" emotion—that which related to the stated causes or reasons for the outcome. Weiner and Graham (1984) have stated that as children develop, the use of outcome-dependent emotions decline and attribution-dependent emotions become more prevalent, suggesting a cognitive-developmental influence on the differentiation of emotion.

Subsequent work by Weiner and colleagues has shown that the main attribution dimensions relate to emotions in different ways (Graham, Doubleday, & Guarino, 1984; Weiner, 1986; Weiner, Graham, & Chandler, 1982; Weiner & Handel, 1985; Yirmiya & Weiner, 1986). These studies support the proposition that self-esteem emotions, such as pride, are associated with internal attributions on the locus of causality dimension. Emotions related to expectancy, such as hope, are associated with the stability dimension of attributions, and social emotions, such as pity and guilt, are related to the controllability of the attribution. Social emotions, Weiner (1986) has suggested, can be self-directed,

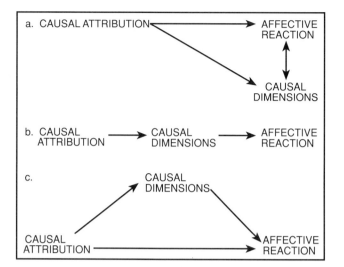

FIGURE 19–8. Attribution-affect models proposed by Russell & McAuley (1986): (a) attribution-affect script model; (b) causal dimension mediation model; (c) attribution dimension additive model.

From Russell, D. & McAuley, E. (1986). Causal attributions, causal dimensions and affective reactions to success and failure. *Journal of Personality and Social Psychology*, 50, 1174–1185. Copyright 1986 by the American Psychological Association. Reprinted with permission of the author.

such as shame and guilt, or "other-directed," such as anger and pity.

Russell and McAuley (1986) put forward three models that could help explain the links between attributions, attribution dimensions, and emotion (see Figure 19–8). They conducted two studies to test these models, one being similar to Weiner et al. (1978) in using a hypothetical academic achievement context, and the second using a real achievement situation. Their results supported an attribution-emotion link, but considerably more so using the hypothetical methodology. The strongest link with emotion was found for the locus of causality dimension, although they concluded that both attribution elements and dimensions were related to emotions, thus supporting their "attribution-dimension additive model" (Figure 19–8c).

Attributions and Emotions in Sport

It is important to understand some of the background to the study of attribution-emotion links, even though the early studies were not in sport. Given that they were conducted in educational achievement contexts, the similarity with sport is quite high. However, despite the obvious role of emotion in sport, and the popularity of attribution research in sport psychology, the study of attribution-emotion links in sport has not been extensive (Weiner, 1981). A summary of attribution-emotion studies in sport is shown in Table 19–2.

One of the first studies in this area in sport psychology was reported by McAuley, Russell, and Gross (1983). They studied attribution-emotion relationships following table-

tennis matches. Assessing attributions with the CDS, they used multiple regression procedures to ascertain the best predictors of emotion from the three attribution dimensions of locus, stability, and control. However, their study provided only weak support for attribution-emotion relationships for winners, and no relationships for losers. One of the weaknesses of their research was that they studied students in a physical education class. Despite the assumption that they "apparently cared about their performances" (p. 284), it is unlikely that this situation would have provided a powerful enough environment to elicit either strong attributions or emotions. At best, the authors should have assessed the strength of task importance and used such ratings in their analyses. Nevertheless McAuley et al. (1983) did provide a useful starting point for this type of research in sport psychology and showed that positive emotions were related to the controllability dimension.

Biddle and Hill (1988) studied students in a competitive one-versus-one cycle ergometer "race" in a laboratory. Subjects were asked to assess their attributions and emotions after winning or losing the race. Results showed that attributions were related to emotions, although this was primarily for internal attributions. In addition, subjects were asked how important it was for them to win the race. This rating was then used to see if the importance of the outcome affected the attribution-emotion relationships. The results showed that it did, but mainly for emotions that could be described as self-esteem–related. For example, attributions of mood, personality, effort, and motivation after winning were related to feelings of pride only when it was considered important to win.

Vallerand (1987) has proposed an "intuitive-reflective appraisal model" of emotion in sport. In this model two types of emotional processing are suggested. First there is the intuitive appraisal, or immediate and relatively automatic appraisal of the event, and second there is the reflective appraisal, where greater thought is given to the outcome, and attributional processing occurs. The intuitive appraisal appears to be similar to Weiner's notion of outcome-dependent, attribution-independent emotion, whereas the reflective appraisal is similar to attribution-dependent, outcome-independent emotion (Weiner, 1986).

In his first study, Vallerand (1987) asked basketball players to rate their intuitive appraisal by giving their general impression of whether they had had a "good or bad game today." Attributions and emotions were also assessed.

For those subjects who perceived their performance as successful, Vallerand (1987) found that the best predictor of emotion was the intuitive appraisal, although this was augmented by attribution ratings. The results were weaker for those subjects perceiving their performance as a failure. In a follow-up study, Vallerand (1987) determined that controllable and stable attribution dimensions were related to self-related emotions under success and failure. In conclusion Vallerand stated that his two studies: (a) support an intuitive-reflective appraisal model of emotion in sport; (b) the intuitive appraisal is an important antecedent of self-related emotion in both success and failure situations;

TABLE 19–2. Summary of attribution-emotion studies in sport

Study	Sample and Task	Measures	Results	Comments
McAuley, Russell, and Gross (1983)	62 male and female American undergraduate students. Table tennis matches in physical education classes.	(a) Russell's (1982) Causal Dimension Scale (CDS) (b) 9 emotion ratings	Gratitude significantly predicted by controllable attributions for winners. No relationship between emotions and attribution dimensions for losers.	
Vallerand (1987): STUDY I	93 male and female Canadian high school basketball players, aged 14–17 years.	(a) subjective appraisal of performance. (b) 8 attributions for performance (c) 6 emotion ratings: 4 "self-related," 2 "general"	For perceived success, self-related and general emotions were predicted by performance appraisal and augmented by internal and external attributions. For perceived failure, self-related emotion was predicted only by performance appraisal, while general emotion was not predicted from either performance appraisal or attributions.	Support for "intuitive-reflective appraisal model"
Vallerand (1987): STUDY II	50 male undergraduate students. Motor and visual coordination task in laboratory.	(a) subjective appraisal of performance (b) importance of performing well (c) CDS (d) 14 emotion ratings; 7 self-related, 7 general	More positive self-related emotion was reported by subjects making more stable and controllable attributions after perceived failure. No effects for locus of causality or importance. General emotions unaffected.	
Robinson & Howe (1987)	17 elite male soccer players in Canada. 3-game period assessed in playoffs (2 wins, 1 loss).	(a) CDS (b) Profile of Mood States (McNair, Lorr & Droppleman, 1977) (c) Subjective appraisal of performance	Emotions (mood) related to controllable attributions for perceived success and uncontrollable attributions for perceived failure. Positive mood related to controllable attributions after winning. Negative mood related to uncontrollable attributions after losing.	Attributions and mood assessed 1 day after matches. Only 7 subjects in perceived success group; 10 subjects in perceived failure group.
Biddle & Hill (1988)	46 male and female British undergraduate students. 1 v 1 30s race on cycle ergometer in laboratory.	(a) 12 attributions (b) 13 positive emotions for winners (c) 16 negative emotions for losers (d) importance of winning	Positive emotion for winners and negative emotion for losers correlated with internal attributions. Pride after winning and unhappiness after losing were dependent on importance of outcome and attributions.	
Robinson & Howe (1989)	746 male and female Canadian school students aged 13–14 years involved in a 6-week team sport program.	(a) subjective appraisal of performance (b) performance attributions (CDS) (c) 10 emotion ratings; 3 general, 4 self-related 3 other-related	Perceived performance was a consistent predictor of all three types of emotion for males and females in perceived success and failure conditions. Attributions added to the prediction of emotions in most cases, and in particular, the locus dimension after success and controllability after failure.	Support for "intuitive-reflective appraisal model."

TABLE 19–2. (Continued)

Study	Sample and Task	Measures	Results	Comments
McAuley & Duncan (1989)	55 male and female American undergraduate students. 1 vs 1 cycle ergometer race manipulated by experimenter to create (a) high expectancy/failure and (b) low expectancy/success groups; hence all subjects operated in an "expectancy disconfirmation" condition	(a) CDS (b) expectancy of success (c) 11 emotion ratings: 6 success, 4 failure, plus "surprise"	For success, no single attribution dimension predicted emotion, although all 3 dimensions in combination did predict feelings of confidence. For failure, depression was related to stability and locus dimensions, and displeasure to locus.	
Biddle & Hill (1992)	58 male and female British undergraduate students in 1 vs 1 simulated competitive fencing task in a laboratory. Outcome manipulated to create clear win and loss.	(a) 12 attributions (b) 28 emotion ratings (c) importance of winning (d) subjective appraisal of performance.	Emotions subjected to factor analysis: 3 factors—"positive self-esteem," "depression-frustration" and "intropunativeness." Positive self-esteem for winners was best predicted performance appraisal, followed by outcome importance and attributions to luck. For losers, positive self-esteem was related only to attributions to mood.	Partial support for "intuitive reflective appraisal model"
Biddle & Hill (in press)	74 male and female squash players in league matches.	(a) 12 attributions for outcome (b) 12 attributions for performance. (c) 16 emotions (d) importance of winning (e) importance of playing well.	Three attribution factors from factor analysis (for both outcome and performance attributions): personal sport ability, unstable, opponent. Three emotion factors: positive self-esteem, relaxation, surprised incompetence. For winners, emotion related more to performance satisfaction rather than attributions. For losers, relaxation related to unstable attributions. For players satisfied with performance self-esteem was predicted by unstable attributions, and for dissatisfied players, opponent attributions predicted emotion alongside perceived importance.	Partial support for "intuitive-reflective appraisal model"

(c) the intuitive appraisal has a greater impact on emotion than the objective outcome; (d) attributional reflective appraisal is also related to emotion but to a lesser extent than the intuitive appraisal.

Support for Vallerand's proposals has been observed in our own research (Biddle & Hill, 1992, in press). Attribution-emotion links were investigated after a series of one-versus-one fencing contests in a laboratory (Biddle & Hill, 1992). The results showed that positive self-esteem emotions for winners were best predicted by performance satisfaction, outcome importance, and internal attributions. Feelings of depression-frustration were related to attributions for winners. For losers, positive self-esteem emotions were associated with attributions to mood. In a follow-up

study (Biddle & Hill, in press), further support was found with squash players. Specifically, for winners, the intuitive appraisal predicted emotion more than attributions, whereas for losers attributions were related to feelings of relaxation. Players satisfied with their performance reported greater positive self-esteem after unstable attributions, and dissatisfied players' emotion was related to opponent attributions.

Robinson and Howe (1989) also investigated the links between attributions and emotions, but this time the subjects were youths aged 13–14 years. These researchers found that perceived personal performance and attribution dimensions predicted emotions for males and females. Contrary to predictions, the controllability dimension was unrelated to emotion in the perceived success condition. However, perceived performance did predict emotion either as the main variable or in addition to attribution dimensions. Perceived performance was the main predictor of emotion under the perceived failure condition. From their study, Robinson and Howe (1989) arrived at three main conclusions: (a) sport emotion is related to perceptions of performance and attributions, but also involves other cognitive antecedents; (b) Weiner's model received only partial support; (c) the effect of the attribution dimensions on emotion was variable. Specifically the locus dimension was found to have an augmenting influence in both success and failure conditions, the stability dimension was only influential under success conditions, and the control dimension only in failure conditions.

The results of Biddle and Hill (1992, in press) and Robinson and Howe (1989) support Vallerand (1987) in showing that a major predictor of sport emotion is the intuitive appraisal (performance satisfaction), but with attributions accounting for significant additional variance.

An interesting expansion to the literature on attributions and emotions has been provided by McAuley and Duncan (1989) in a study of emotions and attributions after disconfirmation of prior expectations. Specifically these researchers manipulated the outcome of a race involving two subjects on cycle ergometers in a laboratory. All subjects involved in the study had their expectation disconfirmed—which is to say that those who had high expectations of performing well lost the contest, and those with low expectations won. The results showed, as predicted, that those whose low expectancies were disconfirmed felt more satisfied and proud, while those whose high expectations were disconfirmed felt more displeased, incompetent, and angry. Results also showed that for subjects whose low expectancies were disconfirmed the only significant relationship was between locus of causality and confidence. For those whose high expectancies were disconfirmed, depression and displeasure were related to external and stable attributions, guilt and shame were related to stable attributions, and surprise and incompetence were related to external attributions.

Such an approach to the attribution-emotion question would appear to be most useful. Prior research has suggested that causal search is more likely when the outcome is unexpected, and that emotional reactions will be intensified under such conditions (Weiner, 1985a, 1986). Further work along these lines appears warranted.

Attributions and Emotions: Summary and Methodological Issues

In attempting a summary of findings in the field of attribution-emotion links in sport, one is hampered by the small number of studies and inconsistent methodologies used. However, initial studies have shown that attributions can have an important role in emotional reactions in sport, yet more recent research (e.g., Biddle & Hill, 1992, in press;

Robinson & Howe, 1989; Vallerand, 1987) has suggested that attributions merely play an augmenting role to the more dominant antecedent of sport emotion, that of perceived performance or "subjective outcome."

FUTURE DIRECTIONS FOR ATTRIBUTION RESEARCH IN SPORT AND PHYSICAL ACTIVITY

A number of researchers have commented on the narrowness of the approach to attribution research in sport (McAuley & Duncan, 1990; Rejeski & Brawley, 1983). New directions in the study of attributions in sport and other physical activity settings, therefore, are considered. Specifically the following issues will be discussed: cultural factors, attributional style, actor-observer differences, learned helplessness, attribution retraining, and health-related exercise.

Culture and Attributions

Aspects of culture, race, and ethnicity in sport psychology have often been ignored. Duda and Allison (1990) analyzed 199 papers published in the *Journal of Sport and Exercise Psychology* between 1979 and 1987 and found that over 96% of the papers did not report the racial or ethnic characteristics of subjects. Duda and Allison (1990) argue for a greater recognition of cultural factors in sport psychology and for more use of cross-cultural methods. The study of attributions, it has been argued, has been dominated by a "Western" perspective (see Bond, 1983; Duda & Allison, 1989; Hewstone, 1989). Future sport attribution studies need to account for cultural perceptions and variability where appropriate.

A number of attribution researchers have addressed this issue in several different contexts, including general achievement motivation (Duda & Allison, 1989), and sport (Duda, 1986; Whitehead, 1986). For a general discussion of societal attributions, see Hewstone (1989), and for a cross-cultural analysis, see Bond (1983).

Two types of attribution research can be identified within a "cultural" perspective. First studies that investigate attributions made across different cultures can be termed "cross-cultural" studies. Second those that investigate the cultural basis of attributions can be referred to as "cultural" studies (Hewstone, 1989). Bond (1983) has posed four fundamental questions for the study of attributions in cross-cultural and cultural contexts. First how frequently do people engage in attributional activity? Although Weiner (1985a) has indicated that attributions are made spontaneously, particularly when a goal has not been met or the outcome is unexpected, this evidence relates to Western culture only. Bond (1983) reports that studies in Nigeria, Hong Kong, India, and Japan have shown that the members of these cultures "can make reliable and functionally meaningful attributions *when asked*" (p. 150). Questions about the use of spontaneous attributions in these cultures remain unanswered.

Bond's (1983) second question was "What causal categories are used?" Maehr and Nicholls (1980) have suggested that success and failure may have different meaning in different cultures, hence attributions for success and failure may also vary as a function of culture. Similarly the categorization of attributions into dimensions, such as the locus of causality and stability dimensions, may be inappropriate for some cultures. These dimensions have been derived from studies that reflect Western culture. Differences have been shown by Duda (1986), even for groups of different cultural backgrounds residing in the same country. Duda investigated the perceptions of success and failure held by white, black, and Hispanic adolescents attending high school in Los Angeles. Using an open-ended format, she asked the subjects to think of a time when they felt successful in their favorite sport activity. They then had to respond to the questions "What was 'success' in this instance? That is, how did you know that you were successful?" (Duda, 1986, p. 217). The same format was used for the recall and rating of an unsuccessful experience.

Duda found that four major criteria formed the foundation of perceptions of success. The four categories identified were task mastery (demonstration of skill; self-improvement), social comparison (competition [winning/losing] against others), social recognition or approval (recognition or approval of performance by others), and group solidarity (affiliation and friendships). The results from Duda's (1986) study showed that perceptions of success and failure in sport differ as a function of both gender and cultural background. In particular, white males tended to value social comparison (competitive) goals. Hispanics favored mastery goals, whereas blacks differed as a function of gender—girls being more oriented toward social comparison, boys toward mastery.

A similar study by Whitehead (1986) investigated the achievement goals and attributions of British school children and compared these with results from the U.S.A. In terms of achievement goals, Whitehead found that the two countries were very similar. Using multiple regression procedures, she predicted goal orientations from attributions given by the children for sport success. She found that no national differences existed on the attributions that predicted the social comparison or task mastery goals. However, British and American children differed considerably on the attributions predicting the social approval goal.

Bond's (1983) third question concerned attributions made in public and private. He suggested that not only will there be differences between attributions made in these situations, but that some cultural differences may also be evident. For example, he reports that research has found that the self-serving bias on attributions for luck is not evident for Hong Kong Chinese, due to their need to appear modest.

Finally Bond (1983) asks, "How does 'culture' exercise its impact?" Having found that attributions may differ between cultures, further analysis is required to ascertain why and how such differences emerge. This question has been largely unanswered in psychology and not even attempted in sport psychology.

In summary, sport attribution studies have all but ignored cultural and cross-cultural issues. Most attribution theorists agree that much of the research into achievement attributions, using perspectives such as Weiner's, is culturally biased, and further work is required that expands into different cultural groups. Duda and Allison (1989) state that "attribution theory may be found to encompass an epistemic content and process particular to the Western world" (p. 50), suggesting that the nature of the attribution process, and the attributions made, is culturally dependent.

ATTRIBUTIONAL STYLE

A tendency to make particular attributions across different situations and time has been termed "attributional style." Despite the attempt to measure this "trait" by Peterson and his colleagues (Peterson & Villanova, 1988; Peterson et al., 1982), it has not been accepted by all researchers as a meaningful or useful construct. For example, Cutrona, Russell, and Jones (1984) found that the Attributional Style Questionnaire (ASQ), developed by Peterson et al. (1982), did not predict attributions for actual negative events very well. Nevertheless, in a meta-analytic review of 104 studies involving about 15,000 subjects, Sweeney, Anderson, and Bailey (1986) concluded that attributions for negative events to internal, stable, and global causes were consistently related to depression, and hence they supported the concept of attributional style.

Little research has been conducted on attributional style in sport. Tenenbaum, Furst, and Weingarten (1984) developed the "Wingate Sport Achievement Responsibility Scale" (WSARS). This scale assesses attributional style, but only along the internal-external dimension. Subjects are asked to respond to success and failure in team and individual sport situations. Psychometric evidence on the scale is provided by Tenenbaum et al. (1984). Tenenbaum and Furst (1985) report its use with individual and team sport athletes. However, no relation was found between WSARS scores and actual attributions made for specific events as assessed by the CDS. Recently, Hanrahan et al. (1989) have reported on the development of the "Sport Attributional Style Scale" (SASS). This instrument asks subjects to read descriptions of positive and negative events in sport and to report their most likely causes along the dimensions of internality, stability, globality, controllability, and intentionality. Preliminary psychometric evidence of its validity and reliability was presented by Hanrahan et al. (1989).

Some support for attributional style in sport has been provided by Prapavessis and Carron (1988). They found that tennis players who displayed maladaptive achievement patterns associated with learned helplessness had an attributional style different from nonhelpless players. Specifically the helpless players made attributions for failure of an internal, stable, and global nature. However, the nature and extent of attributional style in sport has yet to be established with any certainty.

ACTOR-OBSERVER DIFFERENCES IN ATTRIBUTIONS

There has been a bias in sport psychology research toward the study of self-attributions rather than attributions made by observers. Although the literature is extensive on the issue of "other person" attributions, sport psychology has not responded in the same way, despite suggestions that such an approach might prove fruitful in some fields (Biddle, 1986; Rejeski, 1979).

Jones and Nisbett (1972) made a distinction between attributions made by the participant ("actor") and those made by an observer for the behavior of the actor. This "actor-observer" distinction is sometimes referred to as the "divergent perspectives" hypothesis because it is believed that the two individuals process information about the same event in different ways and end up making different types of attributions. Hewstone (1989) suggests that "self" and "other" might be better terms as there will be many cases when people do not "observe" other people's behavior as such. However, "actor" and "observer" are used more frequently in the attribution literature and so will be used here.

Jones and Nisbett (1972) proposed that actors will tend to use situational attributions to explain their behavior, whereas observers will tend to use attributions that center on dispositions or traits of the individual (see Weary et al., 1989). One reason for this tendency is that actors will have information about their own behavior across many situations in the past ("consistency" information; Kelley, 1972), whereas observers may have only the one situation in which to draw inferences about the event. Similarly, some researchers have suggested that perceptual factors account for the difference—which is to say that the actor's perceptual focus will naturally be more external toward the environment, whereas observers will be focused on the actor. However, there are a number of possible explanations and also several qualifying conditions for actor-observer differences, such as whether the observer is an active or inactive participant in the process (see Rejeski, Rae & McCook, 1981; Weary et al., 1989; Wolfsin & Salancik, 1977).

Sport psychology has not used this perspective a great deal, despite the obvious application to such areas as athlete-coach interaction. For example, Rejeski (1979) has suggested that the divergent perspectives approach allows for a greater understanding of attributional conflict between athlete and coach. In situations where the athlete believes her/his failure is due to external factors such as the referee, the coach (the observer) may give attributions that reflect negative aspects of the athlete. Such attributional conflict can be damaging and would require resolution.

Some evidence for the divergence of attributions was reported by Rejeski et al. (1980). They studied track runners and their coaches, and found that the coaches did use more dispositional attributions than the athletes, and, in particu-

lar, that the coaches underestimated the perceived effort reported by athletes. This could be due to the greater perceptual saliency of effort cues for the runner (Rejeski & Lowe, 1980).

The psychology of the sports official is also an underdeveloped area of study in sport psychology but could gain from the use of the actor-observer distinction. In addition, future attribution research in sport might consider the role attributions play in decision making, such as the attributional processes involved in the decision of intent and the subsequent action taken as a result of such inferences.

Similarly actor-observer differences in attributions are clear to see in the relationships between participants and teachers/coaches. Attributional conflict is a potential problem if coaches give their attributions for performance prior to any discussion of how the participant feels about the performance or outcome. However, despite suggestions that attributional conflict may be an issue worthy of further study in sport and exercise (Biddle, 1986; Rejeski, 1979), little research has taken place.

The area of sports spectatorship has received little attention in sport psychological research, although research on the aggressive and violent behaviors of crowds in sport has been conducted (see Mann & Pearce, 1978; Slepicka, 1990). However, given the importance of sport to many spectators, it is surprising that it has remained such an underdeveloped area, and in particular in terms of research that attempts to understand the meaning spectators attach to victory and defeat and the possible consequences of such perceptions. Iso-Ahola (1980) has identified that the attributions spectators give for the performances of both home and visiting teams in American football affect the decision of spectators to attend or not. Specifically Iso-Ahola (1980) presented undergraduate students with information on the performance and attributions for performance of a home team and a visiting team. Subjects then rated their likelihood of attending the match.

Iso-Ahola found that the probability of attending the football games was dependent on the performance of the two teams as well as the attributions given for their performance. In summarizing his results, he stated that:

These causal attributions seem to make a bigger difference when the home team has lost most of its previous games than when it has been successful. People appear to be fairly likely to attend even a game between two losing sides if they have reason to believe that the teams' past failures are due to such external factors as bad luck. . . . The highest probability of attendance was observed in the situation in which both teams had been successful in the past and had succeeded because of their capabilities and hard work. (p. 45).

Clearly this study is just a start in furthering our understanding of why people might or might not choose to attend sports events as a spectator. The weakness is that the situations were hypothetical and could not account for prior team loyalties, local affiliations, and other similar factors. Nevertheless, while many other factors are likely to lead to the decision to attend a game, attributional variables appear to warrant some investigation.

Similarly further research might usefully be applied to the issue of crowd violence from the perspective of attributions, and in particular with respect to actor-observer differences and emotions. One factor that may be an important determinant of aggressive crowd behavior is the attributional response of the group to decisions or incidents on the field of play. The apparent differences made in attributions between actors and observers may be important. For further discussion on attributions and the sports spectator, see Iso-Ahola and Hatfield (1985).

In summary, the divergent perspectives hypothesis has not been studied extensively in sport yet has potential to shed light on a number of important interpersonal issues.

LEARNED HELPLESSNESS IN SPORT

Attributions have been used extensively in an effort to explain deficits in learning and performance after failure. The concept of "learned helplessness" (LH) has received a great deal of attention in psychology (Dweck & Leggett, 1988), and has generated much literature, in clinical psychology in particular (Abramson, Seligman, & Teasdale, 1978; Alloy, Abramson, Metalsky, & Hartlage, 1988; Peterson & Seligman, 1984). Somewhat surprisingly, LH has received little attention in sport psychology (Dweck, 1980; Robinson, 1990).

Learned helplessness was used first by researchers to describe deficits in learning exhibited by animals who had experienced uncontrollable failure. For example, when an animal failed to take advantage of an escape route during the administration of electric shock after previously having been in a situation when escape seemed uncontrollable, an apathetic response ensued. This failure was labeled "learned helplessness" and has been shown in animals and humans (Abramson et al., 1978). Dweck (1980) defined LH as "the perception of independence between one's responses and the occurrence of aversive outcomes . . . that is, the belief that what you do will not affect the course of negative events, that you have no control over negative events" (p. 2). Although the nature of LH remains the subject of much debate (Alloy et al., 1988), one theme to have emerged in recent years is the role that attributions may play in the development, intensity, and persistence of LH deficits. These deficits may be manifested in terms of behavior (e.g., motivational deficits or withdrawal from a situation), cognition (e.g., negative self-statements or difficulties in learning that responses may be related to outcomes), and emotions (e.g., depressed affect or deficits in self-esteem).

The role of attributions in LH was discussed in detail in the seminal paper by Abramson et al. (1978). They said that:

investigators of human helplessness . . . have become increasingly disenchanted with the adequacy of theoretical constructs originating in animal helplessness for understanding helplessness in hu-

mans. And so have we. We now present an attributional framework that resolves several theoretical controversies about the effects of uncontrollability in humans. . . . we argue that when a person finds he is helpless, he asks *why* he is helpless. The causal attribution he makes then determines the generality and chronicity of his helplessness deficits as well as his later self-esteem. (p. 50).

In short, the perception of uncontrollability, or the independence between one's response and the desired outcome, is insufficient to produce LH. Attributions for failure, and attributions for the uncontrollability of the situation, will mediate the perception of response-outcome independence (see Mineka & Henderson, 1985).

Abramson et al. (1978) made several reformulations to the original LH theory. First they made a distinction between "personal helplessness" and "universal helplessness." Personal helplessness is when the event is seen as uncontrollable for oneself but not for others. Universal helplessness, on the other hand, is the belief that control is not possible for all people. It is hypothesized that deficits in self-esteem will be greater under conditions of personal helplessness, since this is predicted to increase the use of internal attributions for failure.

A second reformulation proposed by Abramson et al. (1978) concerned the chronicity of LH. Specifically they suggested that the stability of the attribution for failure will help determine whether the helplessness effects are short-lived (transient) or long-lived (chronic). Similarly their third reformulation stated that the specificity of the attribution would affect the helplessness response. They made a distinction between perceptions of helplessness in a narrow range of situations (specific) and helplessness across a wide range of situations (global). Clearly the prediction is for greater negative cognitive, emotional, and behavioral effects following global attributions than following specific ones.

Abramson et al. (1978), therefore, proposed that LH effects would be greatest when failure was perceived to be uncontrollable and attributions were made to internal, stable, and global factors. No clear test of these proposals has been made in physical activity contexts, although Dweck (1980) and Robinson (1990) have provided useful discussion papers on the potential utility of attributional approaches to failure in sport and physical education contexts.

Johnson and Biddle (1988) conducted an exploratory investigation of helplessness effects using a balance board task in a laboratory. This study was discussed earlier in the context of spontaneous attributional thought. It was found that when results were analyzed for "persisters" and "nonpersisters" on the basis of the median score of the number of trials attempted in the retest phase, the nonpersisters made significantly more negative self-statements and attributions than the persisters. Specifically the attributions made by nonpersisters were mainly to lack of ability (a stable and, perhaps, global factor), and task difficulty (a stable factor). Persisters made more strategy-related statements, indicating a preference for unstable, specific attributions.

Although this study is not a direct test of LH theory, it does show that persistence, itself a characteristic of LH, may be related to attributions and statements of strategy, as suggested by Diener and Dweck (1978). Similarly Prapavessis and Carron (1988), as reported earlier, found support for differences in attributional style between tennis players classified as being helpless and nonhelpless on the basis of questionnaire responses. They found that helpless players attributed failure to internal, stable, and global factors more than nonhelpless players. This study now requires verification using actual sport situations rather than the recall of past events. However, coaches did provide independent ratings of persistence that supported the helplessness hypothesis.

In short, the area of LH in sport is ripe for research, yet may prove a very difficult area to study. If true LH is experienced, by definition many of the subjects will have withdrawn from sport, thus making research with these subjects difficult. However, the adaptive and maladaptive responses to failure in physical education settings may prove a useful area of inquiry (Biddle, 1991; Robinson, 1990).

The perspective on LH provided by Dweck and her colleagues (Dweck & Leggett, 1988; Elliott & Dweck, 1988), and the hypothesized causal pathways to helplessness/hopelessness deficits (Alloy et al., 1988) are important new directions to be considered.

Dweck and Leggett (1988) provide a cogent review on the origins of maladaptive behavior patterns associated with helplessness, and their work was discussed briefly in the section on goal orientations. In particular, they discuss the responses of children to success and failure in the classroom. They suggest that children may not all pursue the same goals in academic achievement and that goals may predict attributions and subsequent adaptive and maladaptive behavior patterns following failure (see also Dweck, 1989; Dweck & Bempechat, 1983; Dweck & Leggett, 1988; Elliott & Dweck, 1988). These goals relate to the seeking of mastery or learning for its own sake ("learning goals"), or to the demonstration of high ability relative to others ("performance goals"). These orientations, in turn, suggest Dweck and Leggett (1988), are related to "implicit theories" of intelligence held by the children. "Specifically, we showed that conceiving of one's intelligence as a fixed entity was associated with adopting the performance goal ... whereas conceiving of intelligence as a malleable quality was associated with the learning goal" (Dweck & Leggett, 1988, p. 256).

Such propositions provide for interesting possibilities in researching the psychology of success and failure in physical education contexts. Are the children who opt out of physical education those who believe that success in physical activities is not possible for them, hold performance goals, and make attributions that predict a helpless orientation? Certainly there is a need for research on the behavioral consequences of LH orientations in sport and physical activity (Robinson, 1990).

Dweck and Leggett (1988) suggest that those holding performance goals, but with a low perception of their own ability, are particularly vulnerable to helplessness deficits. Those pursuing performance goals are more likely to focus on attributions to ability—attributions that have been found to be particularly damaging after failure (Dweck, 1980). Those with learning goals, however, may focus more on attributions to effort and strategy.

Helpless children might be pursuing *performance* goals, in which they seek to establish the adequacy of their ability and avoid giving evidence of its inadequacy ... mastery-oriented individuals ... might be pursuing *learning* goals. They may tend to view achievement situations as opportunities to increase their competence and may pursue, in these situations, the goal of acquiring new skills or extending their mastery. Thus, in challenging achievement situations, helpless children might be pursuing the performance goal of *proving* their ability, whereas the mastery-oriented children might be pursuing the learning goal of *improving* their ability. (Dweck & Leggett, 1988, p. 259).

Such notions are appealing, but research is required in sport and other physical activity settings before applications can be made.

The second development in LH that may have implications for research in sport psychology is that of the linkages between helplessness deficits and their proposed causes. Alloy et al. (1988) put forward their "hopelessness" theory of depression by proposing a causal chain from negative life events to symptoms of "hopelessness depression." This sequence is illustrated in Figure 19–9 and shows distal factors on the left leading to more proximal factors associated with hopelessness on the right. Sport psychological studies on reactions to failure could usefully adopt a similar model. However, little has been done so far in sport psychology on attributional style (see the earlier discussion and Hanrahan et al., 1989), nor on the situational cues outlined in Figure 19–9, such as consensus, consistency, and distinctiveness information.

ATTRIBUTION RETRAINING

When it was found that attributions might play an important role in the reaction of individuals to success and failure, and in particular their recovery from failure, it was logical to attempt to try and change attributions so that subsequent behavior would be more positive. This "therapeutic" approach to attributions has become popular and is used widely in clinical psychology (Brewin, 1988). Similarly attribution change, or "attribution retraining" programs, have been developed (Forsterling, 1988). These seek to alter attributions that are deemed unsuitable and that may lead to cognitive, emotional, or behavioral deficits, and then seek to develop more appropriate attributions that might suggest positive and future-oriented thoughts (Dweck, 1980).

One of the first studies in this area was conducted by Dweck (1975) with 8- to 13-year-old children. She sought to determine whether "altering attributions for failure would enable learned helpless children to deal more effectively

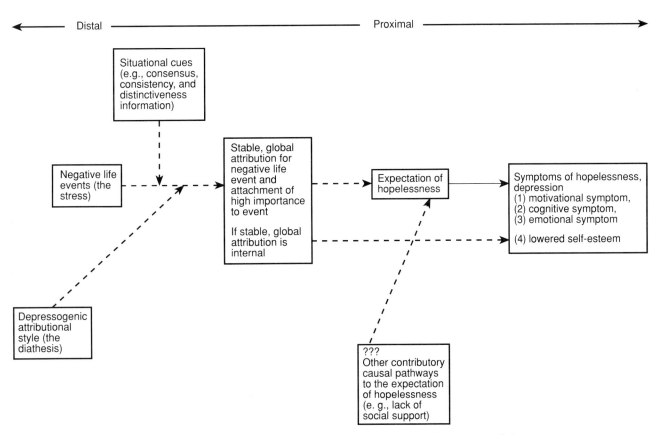

FIGURE 19-9. Distal and proximal factors associated with hopelessness and depression.
From Alloy et al., 1988: *British Journal of Clinical Psychology*, 27, 5–21. Reprinted with permission.

with failure" (p. 674). Dweck studied 12 children who had shown strong reactions to failure on problem-solving tasks and then gave them one of two treatments. One group was provided only with successful experiences, whereas the other was exposed to attribution retraining, such that the children were taught to attribute failure to low effort. The results showed that the success-only group continued to show negative reactions after subsequent failure, whereas the attribution retraining group maintained or improved their performance. Support has also been provided for attribution retraining in a number of other contexts (Forsterling, 1988). Forsterling (1988) suggests at least three different ways of approaching attribution retraining: the attributional model (Weiner, 1986), the learned helplessness model (Abramson et al., 1978), and the self-efficacy model (Bandura, 1986). These are illustrated in Figures 19-10, 19-11, and 19-12.

Weiner's attribution theory suggests that attribution retraining should involve the creation of positive emotional states and expectancies after success and failure by avoiding ability attributions for failure (Figure 19-10). Promoting controllable attributions for failure that suggest positive expectations is favored. However, although lack of effort is usually suggested as the best attribution to give for failure (Dweck, 1975; Forsterling, 1988), there are dangers with this approach. Covington and Omelich (1979) highlight

the importance placed on effort in achievement. If an individual tries hard, but still fails, attributions to low ability are made more likely. This "double-edged sword" of effort attributions means that instead of attributing failure to low

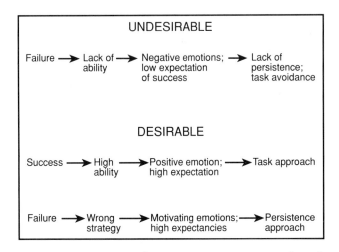

FIGURE 19-10. An attribution retraining sequence based on Weiner's attribution theory.
Adapted from Forsterling, 1988.

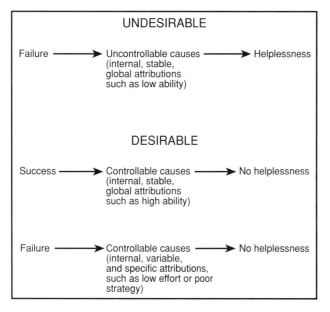

FIGURE 19–11. An attribution retraining sequence based on a learned helplessness model.

Adapted from Forsterling, 1988.

effort, other controllable factors could be used in attribution retraining, such as "strategy."

The LH model of retraining (Figure 19–11) is based on the principles outlined above, namely the avoidance of perceptions of lack of control and the changing of attributions for failure that are internal, stable, and global. Internal attributions can still be used in failure, but it is important that subjects attribute failure to unstable, controllable, and specific factors.

Finally the self-efficacy model of attribution retraining (Figure 19–12) suggests that attributions lead to percep-

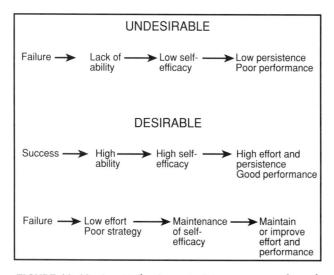

FIGURE 19–12. An attribution retraining sequence based on Bandura's self-efficacy model.

Adapted from Forsterling, 1988.

tions of efficacy for specific behaviors that, in turn, predict persistence and behavior.

Attribution retraining studies have not been conducted in sport. The increasing use of psychological skills training in sport means that such cognitive interventions may prove useful for athletes attempting to reduce the debilitating effects of failure.

ATTRIBUTIONS IN EXERCISE AND HEALTH

The field of exercise and health psychology is becoming increasingly prominent (Biddle & Fox, 1989; Biddle & Mutrie, 1991; Dishman, 1988). The answer to questions pertaining to exercise adoption and maintenance may involve understanding attributional and other interpersonal perception processes. However, to date, relatively little is known about the role of attributions in health-related exercise, although research has been conducted on attributions in other health contexts, including cancer (Gotay, 1985), coronary heart disease rehabilitation (Bar-On & Cristal, 1987), and smoking (see Eiser & van der Pligt, 1988), as well as the covariation principle in the attribution of illness (Magnani & Johnson, 1990).

Our own research efforts in attributions and health-related exercise have been modest, but it appears that little else is available at this time. In a retrospective cross-sectional survey of aerobic exercises and nonexercisers, Biddle and Ashford (1988) found that the two groups differed significantly in terms of attributions for their exercise behavior. In particular, exercisers reported higher scores on internality and controllability, as well as on Kelley's (1967) dimensions of consensus and consistency information. These data suggest that the aerobic exercisers were more likely to have been active in the past (consistency) and were more likely to have modified other health habits (consensus). However, with cross-sectional methods, causality or direction of influence remain unknown.

In an exploratory study of the attributions of adherers and nonadherers to attendance at a commercial health/fitness club, Smith and Biddle (1991) found that clear differences existed between the two groups. Specifically, when asked to what extent effort, ability, difficulty of the task, or luck were factors in their adherence or nonadherence to the exercise program, adherers reported that their attendance was related to their own effort and the relative ease of the task, whereas nonadherers reported that their lack of attendance was mainly due to bad luck, and *not* due to the difficulty of the task or their own lack of ability or effort.

Further examination of attributional processes related to exercise might prove useful as researchers seek answers to important questions concerning the involvement of people in health-related physical activity and exercise (Biddle & Mutrie, 1991). To this end, recent research by McAuley and colleagues (McAuley, 1991; McAuley, Poag, Gleason & Wraith, 1990) is particularly welcomed. Specifically, they have found that exercise involvement of adults is related to attributional thought and to the emotions that are associated with it.

OTHER PERSPECTIVES

It has been stated several times in this chapter that sport attribution research has been narrow. It has focused primarily on the antecedents of self-attributions, with some evidence on the consequences of attributions. In broadening the scope of this research, sport psychologists may wish to investigate other perspectives, such as those associated with intergroup attributions in sport and the possible consequences of attributions in these contexts for understanding intergroup conflict (see Hewstone, 1989). Similarly the explanation of sport behavior given at the level of societal attributions might provide interesting information. Readers are referred to Hewstone (1989) for a thought-provoking and cogent synthesis of this field.

CONCLUSIONS

Attribution theory has been a potent force in social psychology for many years, and sport psychology has followed this lead and devoted much of its journal space to attribution theory and related issues. Given this effort, what are we able to conclude about attributions and sport?

WHAT WE KNOW OR THINK WE KNOW

1. The attribution model developed in educational psychology has provided a useful framework for the study of attributions in sport. However, although the dominant attributions associated with ability, effort, task, and luck have been found in sport, it is thought that sport contexts encourage more diverse attributions to be made than are made in classroom settings. Nevertheless attributions associated with ability and effort appear to be very important in sport.
2. Winners of sports events tend to make attributions to internal and controllable factors more than losers do.
3. The existence of a self-serving bias has been supported in sport research, although the underlying mechanisms have not been clearly identified.
4. Attributions are more likely to be made when the outcome is unexpected or a goal is not reached.
5. Few gender differences have been found in sport research, often in contradiction to research in other contexts.
6. Age differences are thought to exist in the processing of information concerning attributions, and in particular in the differentiation of ability, effort, and outcome.
7. The achievement goal orientations, identified as "mastery" and "ego" orientations, tend to be associated with attributions to effort and ability, respectively.
8. The stability dimension of attributions is associated with the prediction of expectancy change.
9. Both attribution elements and dimensions are associated with emotional feeling, although the exact nature of these relationships is not known.
10. Perceived (subjective) performance is thought to be a more powerful predictor of emotion in sport than the attributions given for either outcome or performance.
11. Attribution research in sport has adopted a narrow perspective and is in need of research investigating wider issues making use of alternative theories and paradigms.

WHAT WE NEED TO KNOW

1. The applicability of alternative theoretical perspectives for sport attribution research.
2. The types of attributions used in real sport settings and the difference between attributions for outcome and those for performance.
3. The dimensional properties of attributions in sport, without sole reliance on one measuring instrument such as the CDS.
4. The role of individual and team attributions within sport team contexts.
5. The nature and content of "spontaneous" attributions in sport.
6. The nature of actor-observer differences in sport attributions.
7. The role of expectancy disconfirmation in sport attributions and emotions.
8. The nature of attributional style in sport and the possible consequences of different styles for emotion and behavior.
9. Developmental trends of attributions for children playing sport.
10. Cultural influences and cross-cultural differences in sport attributions, and the implications for sport behavior.
11. The influence of multidimensional self-esteem, and in particular physical self-worth, on sport attributions and behavior.
12. The nature, type, and predictability of attribution-emotion relationships in sport.
13. The consequences for behavior of links between attributions and emotions.
14. The extent to which learned helplessness exists in sport and the role that attributions may play in its development and/or alleviation.
15. The utility and effectiveness of attribution retraining techniques in sport.
16. The role of attributions in understanding the feelings and behaviors of spectators, officials, and coaches.
17. The nature and content of attributional thought in health-related exercise contexts.

References

Abramson, L. Y., Seligman, M. E. P., & Teasdale, J. D. (1978). Learned helplessness in humans: Critique and reformulation. *Journal of Abnormal Psychology, 87,* 49–74.

Alloy, L. B., Abramson, L. Y., Metalsky, G. I., & Hartlage, S. (1988). The hopelessness theory of depression: Attributional aspects. *British Journal of Clinical Psychology, 27,* 5–21.

Atkinson, J. W. (1977). Motivation for achievement. In T. Blass (Ed.). *Personality variables in social behavior* (pp. 25–108). Hillsdale, NJ: Erlbaum.

Atkinson, J. W., & Raynor, J. O. (1974). *Motivation and achievement.* Washington, DC: Winston.

Bandura, A. (1986). *Social foundations of thought and action: A social cognitive theory.* Englewood Cliffs, NJ: Prentice Hall.

Bandura, A. (1990). Perceived self-efficacy in the exercise of personal agency. *Journal of Applied Sport Psychology, 2,* 128–163.

Banziger, G., & Drevenstedt, J. (1984). Age as a variable in achievement attributions: The Weiner model and beyond. *Basic and Applied Social Psychology, 5,* 97–104.

Bar-On, D., & Cristal, N. (1987). Causal attributions of patients, their spouses and physicians, and the rehabilitation of the patients after their first myocardial infarction. *Journal of Cardiopulmonary Rehabilitation, 7,* 285–298.

Bem, D. J. (1972). Self-perception theory. In L. Berkowitz (Ed.). *Advances in experimental social psychology: Vol. 6* (pp. 1–62). New York: Academic Press.

Benson, M. J. (1989). Attributional measurement techniques: Classification and comparison of approaches for measuring causal dimensions. *The Journal of Social Psychology, 129,* 307–323.

Biddle, S. J. H. (1986). The contribution of attribution theory to exercise behaviour. In J. Watkins, T. Reilly, & L. Burwitz (Eds.), *Sports science* (pp. 285–290). London: E. & F. N. Spon.

Biddle, S. J. H. (1988). Methodological issues in the researching of attribution-emotion links in sport. *International Journal of Sport Psychology, 19,* 264–280.

Biddle, S. J. H. (1991). Motivating achievement in physical education: A psychology of success and failure. In N. Armstrong & A. C. Sparkes (Eds.), *Issues in Physical Education* (pp. 91–108). London: Cassells.

Biddle, S. J. H., & Ashford, B. (1988). Cognitions and perceptions of health and exercise. *British Journal of Sports Medicine, 22,* 135–140.

Biddle, S. J. H., & Fox, K. R. (1989). Exercise and health psychology: Emerging relationships. *British Journal of Medical Psychology, 62,* 205–216.

Biddle, S. J. H., & Hill, A. B. (1988). Causal attributions and emotional reactions to outcome in a sporting contest. *Personality and Individual Differences, 9,* 213–223.

Biddle, S. J. H., & Hill, A. B. (1992). Relationships between attributions and emotions in a laboratory-based sporting contest. *Journal of Sports Sciences, 10,* 65–75.

Biddle, S. J. H., & Hill, A. B. (in press). Attributions for objective outcome and subjective appraisal of performance: Their relationship with emotional reactions in sport. *British Journal of Social Psychology.*

Biddle, S. J. H., & Jamieson, K. I. (1988). Attribution dimensions: Conceptual clarification and moderator variables. *International Journal of Sport Psychology, 19,* 47–59.

Biddle, S. J. H., & Mutrie, N. (1991). *Psychology of physical activity and exercise: A health-related perspective.* London: Springer-Verlag.

Bird, A. M., Foster, C. D., & Maruyama, G. (1980). Convergent and incremental effects of cohesion on attributions for self and team. *Journal of Sport Psychology, 2,* 181–194.

Bird, A. M., & Williams, J. M. (1980). A developmental-attributional analysis of sex role stereotypes for sport performance. *Developmental Psychology, 16,* 319–322.

Blank, T. O. (1984). Meaning and motivation in adult perceptions of causality. *Basic and Applied Social Psychology, 5,* 111–120.

Blucker, J. A., & Hershberger, E. (1983). Causal attribution theory and the female athlete: What conclusions can we draw? *Journal of Sport Psychology, 5,* 353–360.

Bond, M. H. (1983). A proposal for cross-cultural studies of attribution. In M. Hewstone (Ed.), *Attribution theory: Social and functional extensions* (pp. 144–157). Oxford: Blackwell.

Bouchard, C., Shephard, R. J., Stephens, T., Sutton, J. R., & McPherson, B. D. (Eds.) (1990). *Exercise, fitness and health: A consensus of current knowledge.* Champaign, IL: Human Kinetics.

Brawley, L. R. (1984). Unintentional egocentric biases in attributions. *Journal of Sport Psychology, 6,* 264–278.

Brawley, L. R., & Roberts, G. C. (1984). Attributions in sport: Research foundations, characteristics, and limitations. In J. Silva & R. Weinberg (Eds.). *Psychological foundations of sport* (pp. 197–213). Champaign, IL: Human Kinetics.

Brewin, C. R. (1988). Developments in an attributional approach to clinical psychology (Editorial). *British Journal of Clinical Psychology, 27,* 1–3.

Bukowski, W. M., & Moore, D. (1980). Winners' and losers' attributions for success and failure in a series of athletic events. *Journal of Sport Psychology, 2,* 195–210.

Buss, A. R. (1978). Causes and reasons in attribution theory: A conceptual critique. *Journal of Personality and Social Psychology, 36,* 1311–1321.

Carron, A. V. (1980). *Social psychology of sport.* Ithaca, NY: Mouvement.

Carron, A. V., & Spink, K. S. (1980). The stability of causal attributions. *Canadian Journal of Applied Sport Sciences, 5,* 19–24.

Corbin, C. B. (1984). Self-confidence of females in sports and physical activity. *Clinics in Sports Medicine, 3,* 895–908.

Corbin, C. B., & Nix, C. (1979). Sex-typing of physical activities and success predictions of children before and after cross-sex competition. *Journal of Sport Psychology, 1,* 43–52.

Covington, M. V., & Omelich, C. L. (1979). Effort: The double-edged sword in school achievement. *Journal of Educational Psychology, 71,* 169–182.

Croxton, J. S., Chiacchia, D., & Wagner, C. (1987). Gender differences in attitudes toward sports and reactions to competitive situations. *Journal of Sport Behavior, 10,* 137–146.

Cutrona, C. E., Russell, D., & Jones, R. D. (1984). Cross-situational consistency in causal attributions: Does attributional style exist? *Journal of Personality and Social Psychology, 47,* 1043–1058.

Deaux, K. (1984). From individual differences to social categories: Analysis of a decade's research on gender. *American Psychologist, 39,* 105–116.

Deaux, K. (1985). Sex and gender. *Annual Review of Psychology, 36,* 49–81.

Deaux, K., & Emswiller, T. (1974). Explanations for successful performance on sex-linked tasks: What is skill for the male is luck for the female. *Journal of Personality and Social Psychology,* 29, 80–85.

De Jong, P. F., Koomen, W., & Mellenbergh, G. J. (1988). Structure of causes for success and failure: A multidimensional scaling analysis of preference judgments. *Journal of Personality and Social Psychology,* 55, 718–725.

Diener, C. I., & Dweck, C. S. (1978). An analysis of learned helplessness: Continuous changes in performance, strategy and achievement cognitions following failure. *Journal of Personality and Social Psychology,* 36, 451–462.

Dishman, R. K. (Ed.). (1988). *Exercise adherence: Its impact on public health.* Champaign, IL: Human Kinetics.

Duda, J. (1986). Perceptions of sport success and failure among white, black and hispanic adolescents. In J. Watkins, T. Reilly, & L. Burwitz (Eds.), *Sports science* (pp. 214–222). London: E. & F. N. Spon.

Duda, J. (1987). Toward a developmental theory of children's motivation in sport. *Journal of Sport Psychology,* 9, 130–145.

Duda, J. (1989). Goal perspectives and behavior in sport and exercise settings. In C. Ames & M. Maehr (Eds.). *Advances in motivation and achievement: Motivation enhancing environments: Vol. 6* (pp. 81–115). Greenwich, CT: JAI Press.

Duda, J., & Allison, M. T. (1989). The attributional theory of achievement motivation: Cross-cultural considerations. *International Journal of Intercultural Relations,* 13, 37–55.

Duda, J., & Allison, M. T. (1990). Cross-cultural analysis in exercise and sport psychology: A void in the field. *Journal of Sport and Exercise Psychology,* 12, 114–131.

Duda, J., & Tappe, M. K. (1988). Predictors or personal investment in physical activity among middle-aged and older adults. *Perceptual and Motor Skills,* 66, 543–549.

Duda, J., & Tappe, M. K. (1989a). Personal investment in exercise among middle-aged and older adults. In A. Ostrow (Ed.), *Aging and motor behavior* (pp. 219–238). Indianapolis, IN: Benchmark Press.

Duda, J., & Tappe, M. K. (1989b). Personal investment in exercise among adults: The examination of age and gender-related differences in motivational orientation. In A. Ostrow (Ed.), *Aging and motor behavior* (pp. 239–256). Indianapolis, IN: Benchmark Press.

Dweck, C. S. (1975). The role of expectations and attributions in the alleviation of learned helplessness. *Journal of Personality and Social Psychology,* 31, 674–685.

Dweck, C. S. (1980). Learned helplessness in sport. In C. Nadeau, W. Halliwell, K. Newell, & G. Roberts (Eds.), *Psychology of motor behavior and sport: 1979* (pp. 1–11). Champaign, IL: Human Kinetics.

Dweck, C. S. (1989). Motivation. In A. Lesgold & R. Glaser (Eds.), *Foundations for a psychology of education* (pp. 87–136). Hillsdale, NJ: Erlbaum.

Dweck, C. S., & Bempechat, J. (1983). Children's theories of intelligence: Consequences for learning. In S. G. Paris, G. M. Olson & H. W. Stevenson (Eds.), *Learning and motivation in the classroom* (pp. 239–256). Hillsdale, NJ: Erlbaum.

Dweck, C. S., & Elliott, E. S. (1983). Achievement motivation. In E. M. Etherington (Ed.), *Handbook of child psychology: IV. Socialization, personality, and social development* (pp. 643–691). New York: Wiley.

Dweck, C. S., & Goetz, T. E. (1978). Attributions and learned helplessness. In J. H. Harvey, W. Ickes, & R. F. Kidd (Eds.), *New directions in attribution research: Vol II.* (pp. 157–179). Hillsdale, NJ: Erlbaum.

Dweck, C. S., & Leggett, E. L. (1988). A social-cognitive approach to motivation and personality. *Psychological Review,* 95, 256–273.

Eccles (Parsons), J., Adler, T., & Meece, J. L. (1984). Sex differences in achievement: A test of alternative theories. *Journal of Personality and Social Psychology,* 46, 26–43.

Eiser, J. R., & van der Pligt, J. (1988). *Attitudes and decisions.* London: Routledge.

Elliott, E. S., & Dweck, C. S. (1988). Goals: An approach to motivation and achievement. *Journal of Personality and Social Psychology,* 54, 5–12.

Eysenck, H. J., Nias, D. K. B., & Cox, D. N. (1982). Sport and personality. *Advances in Behaviour Research and Therapy,* 4, 1–56.

Feltz, D. L. (1988). Self-confidence and sports performance. *Exercise and Sport Sciences Reviews,* 16, 423–457.

Fineman, S. (1977). The achievement motive construct and its measurement: Where are we now? *British Journal of Psychology,* 68, 1–22.

Forsterling, F. (1988). *Attribution theory in clinical psychology.* Chichester, Sussex: Wiley.

Fox, K. R. (1988). The self-esteem complex and youth fitness. *Quest,* 40, 230–246.

Fox, K. R. (1990). *The Physical Self-Perception Profile manual.* DeKalb, IL: Office of Health Promotion, Northern Illinois University.

Fox, K. R., & Corbin, C. B. (1989). The Physical Self-Perception Profile: Development and preliminary validation. *Journal of Sport and Exercise Psychology,* 11, 408–430.

Frieze, I. H. (1984). Causal attributions for the performances of the elderly: Comments from an attributional theorist. *Basic and Applied Social Psychology,* 5, 127–130.

Frijda, N. (1986). *The emotions.* Cambridge: Cambridge University Press.

Gotay, C. C. (1985). Why me? Attributions and adjustment by cancer patients and their mates at two stages of the disease process. *Social Science and Medicine,* 20, 825–831.

Graham, S., Doubleday, C., & Guarino, P. A. (1984). The development of relations between perceived controllability and the emotions of pity, anger and guilt. *Child Development,* 55, 561–565.

Greenberg, J., Pyszcznski, T., & Solomon, S. (1982). The self-serving attribution bias: Beyond self-presentation. *Journal of Experimental Social Psychology,* 18, 56–67.

Grove, J. R., Hanrahan, S. J., & McInman, A. (1991). Success/failure bias in attributions across involvement categories in sport. *Personality and Social Psychology Bulletin,* 17, 93–97.

Grove, R. J., Hanrahan, S. J., & Stewart, R. M. L. (1990). Attributions for rapid and slow recovery from sports injuries. *Canadian Journal of Sports Science,* 15, 107–114.

Grove, J. R., & Pargman, D. (1986). Relationships among success/failure, attributions, and performance expectancies in competitive settings. In L. Vander Velden & J. H. Humphrey (Eds.), *Psychology and sociology of sport: Current selected research I.* (pp. 85–95). New York: AMS Press.

Hanrahan, S. J., Grove, J. R., & Hattie, J. A. (1989). Development of a questionnaire measure of sport-related attributional style. *International Journal of Sport Psychology,* 20, 114–134.

Heckhausen, H. (1967). *The anatomy of achievement motivation.* New York: Academic Press.

Heider, F. (1944). Social perception and phenomenal causality. *Psychological Review,* 51, 358–374.

Heider, F. (1958). *The psychology of interpersonal relations.* New York: Wiley.

Hewstone, M. (1989). *Causal attribution: From cognitive processes to collective beliefs.* Oxford: Blackwell.

Iso-Ahola, S. E. (1980). Attributional determinants of decisions to attend football games. *Scandinavian Journal of Sports Sciences, 2*(2), 39–46.

Iso-Ahola, S. E., & Hatfield, B. (1985). *Psychology of sports: A social psychological approach.* Dubuque, IA: Brown.

Izard, C. E., Kagan, J., & Zajonc, R. B. (1984). Introduction. In C. E. Izard, J. Kagan & R. B. Zajonc (Eds.), *Emotions, cognition and behavior* (pp. 1–14). New York: Cambridge University Press.

Jaspars, J., Hewstone, M., & Fincham, F. (1983). Attribution theory and research: The state of the art. In J. Jaspars, F. Fincham, & M. Hewstone (Eds.), *Attribution theory and research: Conceptual, developmental and social dimensions* (pp. 3–36). London: Academic Press.

Johnson, L., & Biddle, S. J. H. (1988). Persistence after failure: An exploratory look at "learned helplessness" in motor performance. *British Journal of Physical Education Research Supplement, 5,* 7–10.

Jones, E. E. (1979). The rocky road from acts to dispositions. *American Psychologist, 34,* 107–117.

Jones, E. E., & Davis, K. E. (1965). From acts to dispositions: The attribution process in person perception. In L. Berkowitz (Ed.), *Advances in experimental social psychology: Vol. 2.* (pp. 219–266). London: Academic Press.

Jones, E. E., & Nisbett, R. E. (1972). The actor and the observer: Divergent perceptions of the causes of behavior. In E. E. Jones, D. E. Kanouse, H. H. Kelley, R. E. Nisbett, S. Valins, & B. Weiner (Eds.), *Attribution: Perceiving the causes of behavior* (pp. 79–94). Morristown, NJ: General Learning Press.

Jones, J. G., & Hardy, L. (1990) (Eds.). *Stress and performance in sport.* Chichester: Wiley.

Kelley, H. H. (1967). Attribution theory in social psychology. In D. Levine (Ed.), *Nebraska symposium on motivation: Vol. 15* (pp. 192–240). Lincoln: University of Nebraska Press.

Kelley, H. H. (1972). Attribution in social interaction. In E. E. Jones, D. E. Kanouse, H. H. Kelley, R. E. Nisbett, S. Valins, & B. Weiner (Eds.), *Attribution: Perceiving the causes of behavior* (pp. 1–26). Morristown, NJ: General Learning Press.

Kelley, H. H., & Michela, J. L. (1980). Attribution theory and research. *Annual Review of Psychology, 31,* 457–501.

Kelley, H. H., & Thibaut, J. W. (1978). *Interpersonal relations: A theory of interdependence.* New York: Wiley.

King, J. B. (1983). Attribution theory and the Health Belief Model. In M. Hewstone (Ed.), *Attribution theory: Social and functional extensions.* (pp. 170–186). Oxford: Blackwell.

Kruglanski, A. W. (1975). The endogenous-exogenous partition in attribution theory. *Psychological Review, 82,* 387–406.

Landers, D. M. (1980). The arousal-performance relationship revisited. *Research Quarterly for Exercise and Sport, 51,* 77–90.

Lau, R. R., & Russell, D. (1980). Attributions in the sports pages: A field test of some current hypotheses in attribution research. *Journal of Personality and Social Psychology, 39,* 29–38.

Leith, L. M., & Prapevessis, H. (1989). Attributions of causality and dimensionality associated with sport outcomes in objectively evaluated and subjectively evaluated sports. *International Journal of Sport Psychology, 20,* 224–234.

Lenney, E. (1977). Women's self-confidence in achievement settings. *Psychological Bulletin, 84,* 1–13.

Lochel, E. (1983). Sex differences in achievement motivation. In J. Jaspars, F. D. Fincham, & M. Hewstone (Eds.), *Attribution theory and research: Conceptual, developmental and social dimensions* (pp. 193–220). London: Academic Press.

Luginbuhl, J., & Bell, A. (1989). Causal attributions by athletes: Role of ego involvement. *Journal of Sport and Exercise Psychology, 11,* 399–407.

Maehr, M. L., & Nicholls, J. G. (1980). Culture and achievement motivation: A second look. In N. Warren (Ed.), *Studies in cross-cultural psychology: Vol. II* (pp. 221–267). London: Academic Press.

Magnani, P. S., & Johnson, J. T. (1990). Use of the covariation principle in the attribution of illness. *Basic and Applied Social Psychology, 11,* 283–294.

Mann, L., & Pearce, P. (1978). Social psychology and the sports spectator. In D. J. Glencross (Ed.), *Psychology and sport* (pp. 173–201). Sydney: McGraw-Hill.

Mark, M. M., Mutrie, N., Brooks, D. R., & Harris, D. V. (1984). Causal attributions of winners and losers in individual competitive sports: Toward a reformulation of the self-serving bias. *Journal of Sport Psychology, 6,* 184–196.

Marsh, H. W., Cairns, L., Relich, J., Barnes, J., & Debus, R. L. (1984). The relationship between dimensions of self-attribution and dimensions of self-concept. *Journal of Educational Psychology, 76,* 3–32.

McAuley, E. (1985). Success and causality in sport: The influence of perception. *Journal of Sport Psychology, 7,* 13–22.

McAuley, E. (1991). Efficacy, attributional, and affective responses to exercise participation. *Journal of Sport and Exercise Psychology, 13,* 382–393.

McAuley, E., & Duncan, T. E. (1989). Causal attributions and affective reactions to disconfirming outcomes in motor performance. *Journal of Sport and Exercise Psychology, 11,* 187–200.

McAuley, E., & Duncan, T. E. (1990). The causal attribution process in sport and physical activity. In S. Graham & V. S. Folkes (Eds.), *Attribution theory: Applications to achievement, mental health, and interpersonal conflict* (pp. 37–52). Hillsdale, NJ: Erlbaum.

McAuley, E., & Gross, J. B. (1983). Perceptions of causality in sport: An application of the Causal Dimension Scale. *Journal of Sport Psychology, 5,* 72–76.

McAuley, E., Poag, K., Gleason, A., & Wraith, S. (1990). Attrition from exercise programs: Attributional and affective perspectives. *Journal of Social Behavior and Personality, 5,* 591–602.

McAuley, E., Russell, D., & Gross, J. B. (1983). Affective consequences of winning and losing: An attributional analysis. *Journal of Sport Psychology, 5,* 278–287.

McClelland, D. C. (1961). *The achieving society.* Princeton, NJ: Van Nostrand.

McClelland, D. C., Atkinson, J. W., Clark, R. A., & Lowell, E. L. (1953). *The achievement motive.* New York: Appleton-Century-Crofts.

McHugh, M. C., Duquin, M. E., & Frieze, I. H. (1978). Beliefs about success and failure: Attribution and the female athlete. In C. Oglesby (Ed.), *Women and sport: From myth to reality* (pp. 173–191). Philadelphia: Lea & Febiger.

McNair, D. M., Lott, M., & Droppleman, L. F. (1971). *Profile of mood states manual.* San Diego, CA: Educational and Industrial Testing Service.

Miller, D. T., & Ross, M. (1975). Self-serving biases in the attribution of causality: Fact or fiction? *Psychological Bulletin, 82,* 213–225.

Mineka, S., & Henderson, R. (1985). Controllability and predictability in acquired motivation. *Annual Review of Psychology, 36,* 495–529.

Mullen, B., & Riordan, C. A. (1988). Self-serving attributions for performance in naturalistic settings: A meta-analytic review. *Journal of Applied Social Psychology, 18,* 3–22.

Nicholls, J. G. (1984). Achievement motivation: Conceptions of ability, subjective experience, task choice, and performance. *Psychological Review, 91,* 328–346.

Nicholls, J. G., & Miller, A. T. (1984). Development and its discontents: The differentiation of the concept of ability. In J. G. Nicholls (Ed.), *Advances in motivation and achievement (Vol. 3)* (pp. 185–218). London: JAI Press.

Passer, M. W., Kelley, H. H., & Michela, J. L. (1978). Multidimensional scaling of the causes for negative interpersonal behavior. *Journal of Personality and Social Psychology, 36,* 951–962.

Peterson, C. (1980). Attribution in the sports pages: An archival investigation of the covariation hypothesis. *Social Psychology Quarterly, 43,* 136–141.

Peterson, C., & Seligman, M. E. P. (1984). Causal explanations as a risk factor for depression: Theory and evidence. *Psychological Review, 91,* 347–374.

Peterson, C., Semmel, A., Von Baeyer, C., Abramson, L. Y., Metalsky, G. I., & Seligman, M. E. P. (1982). The Attributional Style Questionnaire. *Cognitive Therapy and Research, 6,* 287–299.

Peterson, C., & Villanova, P. (1988). An expanded attributional style questionnaire. *Journal of Abnormal Psychology, 97,* 87–89.

Prapavessis, H., & Carron, A. V. (1988). Learned helplessness in sport. *The Sport Psychologist, 2,* 189–201.

Rejeski, W. J. (1979). A model of attributional conflict in sport. *Journal of Sport Behavior, 2,* 156–166.

Rejeski, W. J., & Brawley, L. R. (1983). Attribution theory in sport: Current status and new perspectives. *Journal of Sport Psychology, 5,* 77–99.

Rejeski, W. J., & Lowe, C. A. (1980). Nonverbal expression of effort as causally relevant information. *Personality and Social Psychology Bulletin, 6,* 436–440.

Rejeski, W. J., Rae, T., & McCook, W. (1981). Divergent perceptions of athletic outcomes: A field inquiry into the epistemology of active observer. *Perceptual and Motor Skills, 52,* 139–146.

Riess, M., Rosenfeld, P., Melburg, V., & Tedeschi, J. T. (1981). Self-serving attributions: Biased private perceptions and distorted public descriptions. *Journal of Personality and Social Psychology, 41,* 224–231.

Riordan, C. A., Thomas, J. S., & James, M. K. (1985). Attributions in a one-on-one sports competition: Evidence for self-serving biases and gender differences. *Journal of Sport Behavior, 8,* 42–53.

Roberts, G. C. (1978). Children's assignment of responsibility for winning and losing. In F. L. Smoll & R. E. Smith (Eds.), *Psychological perspectives in youth sports* (pp. 145–171). Washington, DC: Hemisphere.

Roberts, G. C. (1982). Achievement motivation and sport behavior. *Exercise and Sport Sciences Reviews, 10,* 236–269.

Roberts, G. C. (1984). Toward a new theory of motivation in sport: The role of perceived ability. In J. Silva & R. S. Weinberg (Eds.), *Psychological foundations of sport* (pp. 214–228). Champaign, IL: Human Kinetics.

Roberts, G. C., & Pascuzzi, D. L. (1979). Causal attributions in sport: Some theoretical implications. *Journal of Sport Psychology, 1,* 203–211.

Robinson, D. W. (1990). An attributional analysis of student demoralisation in physical education settings. *Quest, 42,* 27–39.

Robinson, D. W., & Howe, B. L. (1987). Causal attribution and mood state relationships of soccer players in a sport achievement setting. *Journal of Sport Behavior, 10,* 137–146.

Robinson, D. W., & Howe, B. L. (1989). Appraisal variable/affect relationships in youth sport: A test of Weiner's attributional model. *Journal of Sport and Exercise Psychology, 11,* 431–443.

Ronis, D. L., Hansen, R. D., & O'Leary, V. E. (1983). Understanding the meaning of achievement attributions: A test of derived locus and stability scores. *Journal of Personality and Social Psychology, 44,* 702–711.

Rotter, J. B. (1966). Generalised expectancies for internal versus external control of reinforcement. *Psychological Monographs, 80,* 1–28.

Rudisill, M. E. (1988a). Sex differences in various cognitive and behavioural parameters in a competitive setting. *International Journal of Sport Psychology, 19,* 296–310.

Rudisill, M. E. (1988b). The influence of causal dimension orientations and perceived competence on adults' expectations, persistence, performance, and the selection of causal dimensions. *International Journal of Sport Psychology, 19,* 184–198.

Rudisill, M. E. (1989). Influence of perceived competence and causal dimension orientation on expectations, persistence, and performance during perceived failure. *Research Quarterly for Exercise and Sport, 60,* 166–175.

Russell, D. (1982). The Causal Dimension Scale: A measure of how individuals perceive causes. *Journal of Personality and Social Psychology, 42,* 1137–1145.

Russell, D., & McAuley, E. (1986). Causal attributions, causal dimensions, and affective reactions to success and failure. *Journal of Personality and Social Psychology, 50,* 1174–1185.

Scanlan, T. K., & Passer, M. W. (1980). The attributional responses of young female athletes after winning, tying and losing. *Research Quarterly for Exercise and Sport, 51,* 675–684.

Scanlan, T. K., & Ragan, J. T. (1978). Achievement motivation and competition: Perceptions and responses. *Medicine and Science in Sports, 10,* 276–281.

Schacter, S., & Singer, J. E. (1962). Cognitive, social and physiological determinants of emotional state. *Psychological Review, 69,* 379–399.

Schunk, D. H. (1984). Sequential attributional feedback and children's achievement behaviors. *Journal of Educational Psychology, 76,* 1159–1169.

Singer, R. N., & McCaughan, L. R. (1978). Motivational effects of attributions, expectancy, and achievement motivation during the learning of a novel motor task. *Journal of Motor Behavior, 10,* 245–253.

Singer, R. N., Grove, J. R., Cauraugh, J., & Rudisill, M. (1985). Consequences of attributing failure on a gross motor task to lack of effort or ineffective strategy. *Perceptual and Motor Skills, 61,* 299–306.

Slepicka, P. (1990). Sport spectators from social-psychological aspects. *Acta Universitatis Carolinae Gymnica, 26,* 5–22.

Smith, R. A., & Biddle, S. J. H. (1991). Exercise adherence in the commercial sector. In M. Johnston, M. Herbert, & T. Marteau (Eds.), *Proceedings of the 4th annual conference of the European Health Psychology Society* (pp. 154–155). Leicester: British Psychological Society.

Sonstroem, R. J. (1984a). Exercise and self-esteem. *Exercise and Sport Sciences Reviews, 12,* 123–155.

Sonstroem, R. J. (1984b). An overview of anxiety in sport. In J. Silva & R. Weinberg (Eds.), *Psychological foundations of sport* (pp. 104–117). Champaign, IL: Human Kinetics.

Sonstroem, R. J., & Morgan, W. P. (1989). Exercise and self-esteem: Rationale and model. *Medicine and Science in Sports and Exercise, 21,* 329–337.

Spink, K. S. (1978). Win-loss causal attributions of high school basketball players. *Canadian Journal of Applied Sport Sciences, 3,* 195–201.

Spink, K. S., & Roberts, G. C. (1980). Ambiguity of outcome and causal attributions. *Journal of Sport Psychology, 2,* 237–244.

Sweeney, P. D., Anderson, K., & Bailey, S. (1986). Attributional style in depression: A meta-analytic review. *Journal of Personality and Social Psychology, 50,* 974–991.

Tenenbaum, G., & Furst, D. (1985). The relationship between sport achievement responsibility, attribution and related situational variables. *International Journal of Sport Psychology, 16,* 254–269.

Tenenbaum, G., Furst, D., & Weingarten, G. (1984). Attribution of causality in sport events: Validation of the Wingate Sport Achievement Responsibility Scale. *Journal of Sport Psychology, 6,* 430–439.

Tetlock, P. E., & Levi, A. (1982). Attribution bias: On the inconclusiveness of the cognition-motivation debate. *Journal of Experimental Social Psychology, 18,* 68–88.

Vallerand, R. J. (1983). On emotion in sport: Theoretical and social psychological perspectives. *Journal of Sport Psychology, 5,* 197–215.

Vallerand, R. J. (1984). Emotion in sport: Definitional, historical and social psychological perspectives. In W. Straub & J. Williams (Eds.), *Cognitive sport psychology* (pp. 65–78). Lansing, NY: Sport Science Associates.

Vallerand, R. J. (1987). Antecedents of self-related affects in sport: Preliminary evidence on the intuitive-reflective appraisal model. *Journal of Sport Psychology, 9,* 161–182.

Vallerand, R. J., & Richer, F. (1988). On the use of the Causal Dimension Scale in a field setting: A test with confirmatory factor analysis in success and failure situations. *Journal of Personality and Social Psychology, 54,* 704–712.

Watkins, D. (1986). Attributions in the New Zealand sports pages. *The Journal of Social Psychology, 126,* 817–819.

Weary, G., Stanley, M. A., & Harvey, J. H. (1989). *Attribution.* New York: Springer-Verlag.

Weiner, B. (1979). A theory of motivation for some classroom experiences. *Journal of Educational Psychology, 71,* 3–25.

Weiner, B. (1980). *Human motivation.* New York: Holt, Rinehart & Winston.

Weiner, B. (1981). The role of affect in sport psychology. In G. C. Roberts & D. M. Landers (Eds.), *Psychology of motor behavior and sport: 1980* (pp. 37–48). Champaign, IL: Human Kinetics.

Weiner, B. (1985a). "Spontaneous" causal thinking. *Psychological Bulletin, 97,* 74–84.

Weiner, B. (1985b). An attributional theory of achievement motivation and emotion. *Psychological Review, 92,* 548–573.

Weiner, B. (1986). *An attributional theory of motivation and emotion.* New York: Springer-Verlag.

Weiner, B. (1990). History of motivational research in education. *Journal of Educational Psychology, 82,* 616–622.

Weiner, B., Amirkhan, J., Folkes, V. S., & Verette, J. A. (1987). An attributional analysis of excuse giving: Studies of a naive theory of emotion. *Journal of Personality and Social Psychology, 52,* 316–324.

Weiner, B., Frieze, I. H., Kukla, A., Reed, L., Rest, S., & Rosenbaum, R. M. (1972). Perceiving the causes of success and failure. In E. E. Jones, D. E. Kanouse, H. H. Kelley, R. E. Nisbett, S. Valins & B. Weiner (Eds.), *Attribution: Perceiving the causes of behavior* (pp. 95–120). Morristown, NJ: General Learning Press.

Weiner, B., & Graham, S. (1984). An attributional approach to emotional development. In C. E. Izard, J. Kagan & R. B. Zajonc (Eds.), *Emotions, cognition and behavior* (pp. 167–191). New York: Cambridge University Press.

Weiner, B., Graham, S., & Chandler, C. (1982). Pity, anger and guilt: An attributional analysis. *Personality and Social Psychology Bulletin, 8,* 226–232.

Weiner, B., & Handel, S. J. (1985). A cognition-emotion-action sequence: Anticipated emotional consequences of causal attributions and reported communication strategy. *Developmental Psychology, 21,* 102–107.

Weiner, B., Perry, R. P., & Magnusson, J. (1988). An attributional analysis of reactions to stigmas. *Journal of Personality and Social Psychology, 55,* 738–748.

Weiner, B., Russell, D., & Lerman, D. (1978). Affective consequences of causal ascriptions. In J. H. Harvey, W. Ickes & R. F. Kidd (Eds.). *New directions in attribution research: Vol. 2* (pp. 59–90). Hillsdale, NJ: Erlbaum.

Weiner, B., Russell, D., & Lerman, D. (1979). The cognition-emotion process in achievement-related contexts. *Journal of Personality and Social Psychology, 37,* 1211–1226.

Weiss, M. R., McAuley, E., Ebbeck, V., & Wiese, D. M. (1990). Self-esteem and causal attributions for children's physical and social competence in sport. *Journal of Sport and Exercise Psychology, 12,* 21–36.

Whitehead, J. (1986). A cross-national comparison of attributions underlying achievement orientations in adolescent sport. In J. Watkins, T. Reilly, & L. Burwitz (Eds.), *Sports science* (pp. 297–302). London: E. & F. N. Spon.

Whitley, B. E., & Frieze, I. H. (1985). Children's causal attributions for success and failure in achievement settings: A meta-analysis. *Journal of Educational Psychology, 77,* 608–616.

Williams, J. M. (1978). Personality characteristics of the successful female athlete. In W. F. Straub (Ed.), *Sport psychology: An analysis of athlete behavior* (pp. 249–255). Ithaca, NY: Mouvement.

Wimer, S., & Kelley, H. H. (1982). An investigation of the dimensions of causal attribution. *Journal of Personality and Social Psychology, 43,* 1142–1162.

Wolfsin, M. R., & Salancik, G. R. (1977). Observer orientation and actor-observer differences in attributions for failure. *Journal of Experimental Social Psychology, 13,* 441–451.

Yirmiya, N., & Weiner, B. (1986). Perceptions of controllability and anticipated anger. *Cognitive Development, 1,* 273–280.

Yukelson, D., Weinberg, R. S., West, S., & Jackson, A. (1981). Attributions and performance: An empirical test of Kukla's theory. *Journal of Sport Psychology, 3,* 46–57.

Zientek, C. F. C., & Breakwell, G. M. (1988). Attributions made in ignorance of performance outcome. *International Journal of Sport Psychology, 19,* 38–46.

Zuckerman, M. (1979). Attribution of success and failure revisited, or: The motivational bias is alive and well in attribution theory. *Journal of Personality, 47,* 245–287.

PSYCHOLOGICAL TECHNIQUES FOR INDIVIDUAL PERFORMANCE

·20·

GOAL SETTING IN SPORT

Damon Burton

In sport, both researchers and practitioners commonly believe that goal setting is a relatively simple and straightforward performance enhancement technique. Unfortunately they often quickly learn that it is much easier to set goals than to make them work effectively. Two types of problems are commonly associated with goal-setting programs in sport and exercise. First some athletes find goals to be more stress inducing than motivational. Goals can have a powerful impact on behavior because they become the standards by which success and failure are evaluated, but goals may confirm failure as well as demonstrate success. Consequently individuals with low self-esteem who lose often tend to fixate on the dangers of competitive failure rather than the rewards of success. Such athletes often learn to hate setting goals, particularly short-term ones, because the goals prompt them to worry about failing throughout practices and competitions. Moreover, if these athletes fail to attain even one of their goals, they normally feel like complete failures. Therefore, goals may impair the performance of low-ability performers rather than enhance it.

A second type of competitive goal-setting problem is the failure to develop an ongoing commitment to attain goals. Thus if attaining goals is not directly linked to competitive success, athletes typically do not evaluate goal attainment systematically or reward goal achievement appropriately, prompting minimal commitment to goal-setting programs. For example, if basketball players learn that their level of goal attainment will have little impact on their playing time, they will develop little commitment to goal-setting programs. As commitment to goals diminishes, they lose their performance enhancement capabilities.

Although research and practical experience clearly document that goal setting can be a tremendous performance enhancement tool (Locke & Latham, 1990), how goals are set and individual difference variables among goal setters become extremely important to potential goal effectiveness. Most researchers and practitioners view goal setting as a motivational strategy that enhances performance by focusing attention and promoting increased intensity and per-

sistence. However, without a high degree of commitment to achieving goals, the goal-setting process is undermined and greatly diminishes any performance enhancement effects. Similarly, for some athletes and in some situations goals may promote more stress than positive motivation, thus hurting rather than helping performance.

Surprisingly the goal-setting literature focuses little attention on the negative aspects of improper goal setting. Much of the contemporary research on goal setting comes from industrial and organizational (IO) psychology, where goals are viewed primarily as motivational tools (e.g., Locke, 1968; Locke & Latham, 1985, 1990; Locke, Shaw, Saari, & Latham, 1981; Mento, Steel, & Karren, 1987; Tubbs, 1986; Wood, Mento, & Locke, 1987). The major premise of IO goal-setting research is that a positive linear relationship exists between level of challenge and performance enhancement; the greater the challenge, the better the resulting performance (e.g., Latham & Locke, 1979; Locke & Latham, 1985; Locke et al., 1981; Mento et al., 1987). The notion that goals can be stress producing when set too high has been virtually ignored (see Burton, 1989b). However, contemporary motivation theory suggests that for most individuals motivation is dependent on developing and maintaining high perceived ability through consistent goal attainment (e.g., Elliott & Dweck, 1988; Maehr, 1984; Maehr & Braskamp, 1986; Maehr & Nicholls, 1980; Nicholls, 1984a, 1984b). Unrealistic goals may not only lose their motivational value over time if individuals are not consistently successful, but they also create evaluation stress that impairs performance (e.g., Burton, 1989b). Therefore, a fuller understanding is needed of the goal-setting process so that goals can be adjusted to enhance performance for all types of athletes and in all types of competitive situations.

This chapter has three primary purposes. First the available research and theory on goal setting will be reviewed from the perspective of general IO psychology and sport, and an attempt will be made to explain why goal setting seems to be less effective in sport. Second a model will be presented that focuses on how the individual difference variable of goal-setting style influences the goal-setting process, particularly how and under what circumstances goals can become stress inducing. Finally research surveying the contemporary goal-setting practices of collegiate athletes will be presented to help illuminate the degree of congruence between goal-setting theory and research and the goal-setting implementation strategies commonly used by athletes.

This chapter has been organized into five major sections. In the first section, general goal-setting research and theory will be reviewed, including performance enhancement effects, goal attributes, and moderator variables. Section 2 will review the competitive goal-setting literature, comparing and contrasting it to general goal-setting research. In the third section, explanations for the less consistent and robust goal-setting effects in sport will be identified and evaluated. Section 4 will then present a competitive goal-setting model that outlines and makes specific predictions for how the individual difference measure of goal-setting style influences the goal-setting process. In the final section, preliminary research will be presented surveying the contemporary goal-setting practices of collegiate athletes so that areas of discrepancy between desired and actual goal-setting usage can be better identified and more effective goal-setting programs developed.

REVIEW OF GENERAL GOAL-SETTING RESEARCH

Over the past quarter century, extensive research on goal setting has been conducted, primarily in business and in-

dustry. A number of reviews have been conducted of this goal-setting literature, the most recent review by Edwin Locke and Gary Latham (1990), who have comprehensively reviewed nearly 400 goal-setting research studies. In this first section, some of the major conceptual predictions and key findings in the general goal-setting literature that seem to relate most directly to sport and exercise will be summarized. However, the interested reader is encouraged to consult the Locke and Latham text for a complete review of relevant goal-setting research.

Goal-Setting Theory

Locke and Latham (1990) define goals as "something we consciously want to attain" (p. 7), and they argue that goals have two main attributes: (a) content and (b) intensity. Goal content refers to the object or result being sought (e.g., shooting a score of 71 for a round of golf), whereas goal intensity refers to how much individuals will invest their time and energy to obtain desired results. More importantly Locke and Latham have specified a goal-setting model to describe how the goal-setting process operates and to identify the major variables influencing goal-setting effectiveness (see Figure 20–1).

Locke and Latham's (1990) model specifies that goals influence the direction, intensity, and persistence of behavior as well as stimulate the development of new task-specific strategies that may be necessary to obtain desired levels of performance. The model also identifies five moderator variables that influence the impact that goals have on performance, including: ability, commitment, feedback, task complexity, and situational factors. Finally the model hy-

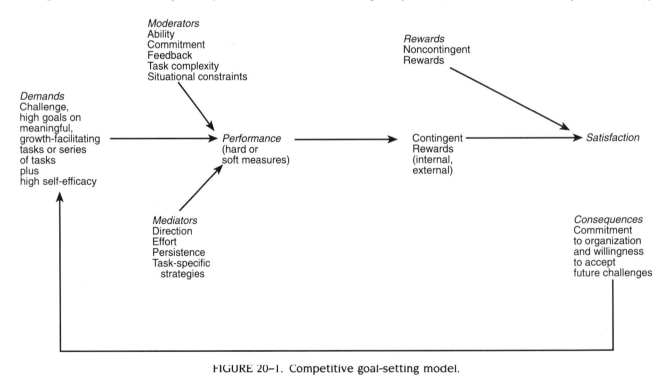

FIGURE 20–1. Competitive goal-setting model.

pothesizes that the combination of goal evaluation and available rewards influence satisfaction and other goal consequences such as organizational commitment and future expectancies. The next three sections will review research findings for (a) the overall effectiveness and generality of goal-setting effects, (b) the impact of goal attributes such as goal difficulty, goal specificity, goal temporality, and goal collectivity on goal effectiveness, and (c) the influence of four moderator variables—commitment, feedback, task complexity, and ability—on the goal-setting–performance relationship.

Do Goals Enhance Performance?

In order to assess the performance enhancement benefits of goals, it is important to evaluate three factors: how consistently goals enhance performance, how large the performance enhancement effects are, and how well goal-setting effects generalize across tasks, populations, and time spans. This section will investigate how well goals meet each of these three performance enhancement criteria.

Overall Goal-Setting Effectiveness. The consensus of available goal-setting research (Chidester & Grigsby, 1984; Hunter & Schmidt, 1983; Locke & Latham, 1990; Locke et al., 1981; Mento et al., 1987; Tubbs, 1986; Wood et al., 1987) confirms that specific-difficult goals prompt higher levels of performance than vague, do-your-best goals, or no goals. Of the 201 studies reviewed by Locke and Latham (1990), goal-setting effects were demonstrated totally or contingently in 183 studies, a 91% success rate. Moreover, 5 meta-analyses of goal-setting research (Chidester & Grigsby, 1984; Hunter & Schmidt, 1983; Mento et al., 1987; Tubbs, 1986; Wood, Mento, & Locke, 1987), each containing from 17 to 53 goal-setting studies and including from 1,278 to 6,635 subjects, demonstrated mean effect sizes ranging from 0.42 to 0.80, representing performance increases of from 8.4% to 16%.

Generalizability of Goal-Setting Effects. A comprehensive review of the goal-setting literature convincingly demonstrates the generalizability of goal-setting findings (Chidester & Grigsby, 1984; Hunter & Schmidt, 1983; Locke & Latham, 1990; Locke et al., 1981; Mento et al., 1987; Tubbs, 1986; Wood et al., 1987). Locke and Latham's (1990) recent review of nearly 400 goal-setting studies confirmed tremendous consistency for the frequency and magnitude of goal-setting effects across different tasks, settings, performance criteria, and types of subjects. Locke and Latham's (1990) review documents goal-setting effects across nearly 90 different tasks, ranging from simple laboratory tasks (e.g., listing nouns, computation) to complex tasks such as prose learning and management simulations and across a great diversity of subject populations that vary in gender, age, race, socioeconomic status, and type of employment (e.g., loggers, factory workers, engi-

neers and scientists, and college professors). Additionally, goal-setting effects have been demonstrated in several other countries besides the United States, using a variety of quantitative and qualitative performance criteria (Bavelas & Lee, 1978; Earley, 1986; Erez & Zidon, 1984; Latham & Marshall, 1982; Matsui, Kakuyama, & Onglatco, 1987; Matsui, Okada, & Mizuguchi, 1981). Finally, goal-setting effects have been documented for time spans as short as 1 minute (Locke, 1982) and as long as 36 months (Ivancevich, 1974). Clearly these data confirm that goal setting is both a highly consistent and effective performance enhancement strategy that works almost universally for most subjects across a variety of tasks and settings. Indeed, these results strongly indicate that goal setting is one of the best performance enhancement techniques available in the behavioral sciences.

Goal Attributes Research

A great deal of goal-setting research has focused on the goal attributes that prompt the greatest increments in performance. This section reviews research for four types of goal attributes: goal difficulty, goal specificity, goal temporality, and goal collectivity.

Goal Difficulty. Locke and Latham's (1990) goal-setting theory postulates a linear relationship between goal difficulty and performance because hard goals prompt greater effort and persistence than do easy goals. Goal-setting theory acknowledges, however, that as individuals reach the limits of their ability at high goal difficulty levels, performance plateaus. Nevertheless the consensus of nearly 200 studies has provided strong support for this "goal difficulty hypothesis." Locke and Latham found that 91% of the 192 goal difficulty studies they reviewed demonstrated positive (140 studies) or contingently positive (35 studies) relationships between hard goals and performance. Moreover, four meta-analyses of goal difficulty research (Chidester & Grigsby, 1984; Mento et al., 1987; Tubbs, 1986; Wood et al., 1987) have been conducted that each reviewed from 12 to 72 goal difficulty studies and included from 1,770 to 7,548 subjects. Results from these meta-analyses demonstrated mean goal difficulty effect sizes ranging from 0.52 to 0.82, representing performance increments of from 10.4% to 16.4%. The consensus of available enumerative and meta-analytic reviews provides strong support for the goal difficulty function.

Goal Specificity. Locke and Latham's (1990) goal-setting theory predicts that goal specificity is a less important goal attribute than goal difficulty, but they argue that making hard goals specific will further enhance performance because specific goals make it more difficult to feel successful with performance levels that are lower than one's goal. They suggest that when goals are vague it is easier for individuals to give themselves the benefit of the doubt in evaluating performance and rate a relatively lower level of performance as acceptable. For example, Kernan and Lord (1989) found that individuals with no specific goals generally evaluated their performance more positively than subjects with specific-hard goals when provided with varying degrees of negative feedback. Additionally Mento and Locke (1989) found that subjects with do-your-best goals anticipated more satisfaction from every level of possible performance than did subjects with specific-hard goals.

Locke and Latham (1990) emphasize that the consensus of available research is that goal specificity does not have a direct performance enhancement effect; rather goal specificity interacts with goal difficulty to influence performance. Thus specific-easy goals may actually be less effective than vague-hard goals (Locke, Chah, Harrison, & Lustgarten, 1989). Research comparing specific-difficult goals with do-your-best goals or no goals was reviewed in the previous section, confirming that specific-hard goals demonstrated consistent (91% of studies) and robust (8–16% productivity gains) performance enhancement effects compared to do-your-best goals or no goals.

Locke and Latham (1990) hypothesize that when goal difficulty is controlled, the major effect of goal specificity is to reduce performance variance. They argue that because goal specificity reduces interpretative leeway in evaluating success, the range of performance variability should be reduced. In support of this prediction, Locke et al. (1989) separated the effects of goal difficulty and goal specificity and found that the more specific the goal, the lower the performance variance. Therefore, goal specificity seems to be an important attribute of effective goals, but its impact is most prominent when combined with goal difficulty in order to maintain more stringent standards for success, thereby reducing performance variability.

Goal Temporality. Locke and Latham's (1990) goal-setting theory makes no predictions about the effectiveness of short-term versus long-term goals, and the existing reviews of goal temporality research (Kirschenbaum, 1985; Locke & Latham, 1990) have revealed equivocal results, suggesting that definite conclusions about the relative effectiveness of short-term versus long-term goals must await future research. Goal temporality theory remains as muddled as its empirical results. Some researchers (e.g., Bandura, 1986) argue that short-term (ST) goals are more effective because they provide more frequent evaluation of success that stimulates development of self-confidence and motivation to strive for even higher levels of performance, thus preventing procrastination and premature discouragement. Burton (1989b) puts it a slightly different way by contending that short-term goals are more flexible and controllable for the athlete. Because ST goals are more flexible, they can more easily be raised and lowered to keep them challenging but realistic. Moreover, because ST goals are more controllable, individuals should more readily take credit for their success as indicative of positive personal attributes such as ability and effort.

Proponents of long-term (LT) goals (e.g., Kirschenbaum, 1985) contend that they may facilitate greater performance improvement than ST goals because they foster "protracted choice." These researchers argue that too frequent goal assessment may prompt excessive evaluation, making it difficult to remain focused on performance because social comparison concerns become more salient (Nicholls, 1984a) and prompting individuals to feel like "pawns" because goals are perceived as controlling rather than informational (e.g., deCharms, 1976; Deci & Ryan, 1985). Thus LT goals allow short-term flexibility that prevents discouragement if individuals should fail to meet daily performance standards. Intuitively some combination of ST and LT goals would seem to be most effective. LT goals would identify the specific objective(s) that individuals are working toward and provide flexibility in improvement rates over time, whereas ST goals would provide the individual steps necessary to accomplish LT goals and stimulate the effort and persistence necessary to improve performance toward that goal.

Locke and Latham's (1990) recent review has suggested that goal temporality has been a relatively unpopular topic of goal-setting research (i.e., only 14 studies), perhaps because of the difficulty of identifying the optimal time span for ST and LT goals. Thus if goals are set too frequently, they become intrusive, distracting, and annoying, and will thus be rejected, whereas if goals are not set often enough, they will be viewed as unreal and not worthy of attention, thus failing to promote increased effort and persistence. Future research must identify the most effective time frames for ST and LT goals, identify how ST and LT goals relate to each other, and then establish their individual and joint impact on performance.

Goal Collectivity. Locke and Latham's (1990) goal-setting theory makes no predictions about the effectiveness of group/team versus individual goals, but available reviews of group goal-setting research (Carroll, 1986; Kondrasuk, 1981; Locke & Latham, 1990; Rodgers & Hunter, 1989) revealed that group goals enhance performance as effectively as individual goals. Locke and Latham's review revealed that 38 out of 41 group goal-setting studies (93%) demonstrated positive or contingently positive performance enhancement effects, virtually the same success rate as for overall goal-setting results. They concluded that group goals, in addition to or instead of individual goals, are necessary or at least facilitative when the task is a group rather than an individual one.

Goal collectivity results were further confirmed in several reviews of the Management by Objectives (MBO) literature (Carroll, 1986; Kondrasuk, 1981; Locke & Latham, 1990; Rodgers & Hunter, 1989). For example, Locke and Latham (1990) reanalyzed Kondrasuk's (1981) review of 185 MBO studies and found that approximately 90% demonstrated positive or contingently positive results. Rodgers and Hunter (1989) recently conducted a meta-analysis of 68 MBO studies and demonstrated that 97% of them showed positive results, and for the 28 studies in which effect size could be computed, the average performance improvement was a whopping 44%.

The issue of goal collectivity is probably not an either/or proposition. Team goals offer direction for establishing appropriate types and levels of individual goals that are then responsible for the specific motivational benefits to individual athletes. The prediction that a combination of team and individual goals will maximize goal effectiveness is also consistent with social loafing research (e.g., Hardy & Latane, 1988; Jackson & Williams, 1985; Latane, 1986; Latane, Williams, & Harkins, 1979). Social loafing is a group performance phenomenon in which individuals working together on a task tend to exert less individual effort than when they perform the same task alone (Jackson & Williams, 1985). Although not extensively studied in sport settings, social loafing has been shown to occur for a variety of physically effortful tasks (e.g., Ingham, Levinger, Graves, & Peckham, 1974; Kerr & Brunn, 1981; Latane et al., 1979).

Interestingly research has confirmed that social loafing is reduced or eliminated when (a) individual efforts are identifiable (Williams, Harkins, & Latane, 1981), and (b) individuals perceive that they have made a unique contribution to group effort or performed difficult tasks (Harkins & Petty, 1982). Thus the implication of social loafing research for goal collectivity is that individuals setting team goals should be prone to loaf unless they also set individual goals that (a) hold each team member responsible for a specific level of performance and (b) these individual goals are perceived indispensible for team success. Regrettably, research testing goal collectivity predictions that a combination of team and individual goals should maximally enhance performance has not been tested adequately enough to allow firm conclusions to be drawn.

Moderators of Goal-Setting Effectiveness

Locke and Latham (1990) have identified four variables that seem to significantly moderate goal-setting effectiveness, including: ability, commitment, feedback, and task complexity. In this section, research assessing the impact of each of these moderator variables on goal-setting effectiveness will be reviewed.

Ability. Locke and Latham (1990) have identified a reciprocal moderating effect between goals and ability. Their review indicates that ability influences goal-setting effectiveness most significantly when goal difficulty exceeds individuals' ability. Thus as individual goal difficulty levels reach the high to impossible range, performance should plateau due to ability limitations. The practical implication of these findings are that goal-setting effects should take longer to appear as individuals approach their performance potential.

Locke and Latham's (1990) review also suggests that high- and low-ability performers should differentially benefit from setting goals, although which group should benefit most from goal setting is still unclear. Locke and Latham argue that goal difficulty effects should be stronger for individuals with high ability than for their low-ability counterparts, primarily at high to impossible levels of difficulty. Their rationale is that low-ability performers may use diffi-

cult goals to enhance their effort and persistence on the task, but if their skills are not well developed, they may actually be automating incorrect skills, thus impairing rather than improving performance. However, two studies (Crawford, White, & Magnusson, 1983; Pritchard, Bigby, Beiting, Coverdale, & Morgan, 1981) found the opposite moderating effect of ability on goal effectiveness, demonstrating that initially low-ability performers improved more after goal setting than did subjects with high ability. However, these studies are somewhat flawed methodologically because ceiling effects may have limited how much goals can help enhance the performance of individuals with high ability. In summary, available research does confirm the moderating effects of ability on goal-setting effectiveness, but specific conclusions about how ability influences the goal-setting process are difficult to discern from existing research.

Commitment. Locke and Latham (1990) have identified an interesting interaction between level of commitment and goal difficulty. They argue that under low goal difficulty, low-commitment individuals probably will perform better than their high-commitment counterparts, whereas under high-goal-difficulty conditions, high-commitment subjects will perform significantly better than their less committed teammates. These predictions suggest that highly committed individuals will attempt to make their performance conform to goals, whether they are high or low, more than will less committed performers, thus supporting the importance of setting difficult goals in order to enhance performance. Research has confirmed that a number of factors can improve commitment, including: the authority of the individual assigning the goals (e.g., Latham, Erez, & Locke, 1988; Latham & Lee, 1986; Latham & Yukl, 1975; Oldham, 1975), peer influences (e.g., Matsui, et al., 1987; Rakestraw & Weiss, 1981), competition (e.g., Locke & Shaw, 1984; Mitchell, Rothman, & Liden, 1985; Shalley, Oldham, & Porac, 1987; public disclosure of goals (e.g., Hayes, Rosenfarb, Wulfert, Munt, Korn, & Zettle, 1985; Hollenbeck, Williams, & Klein, 1989), incentives and rewards (e.g., Huber, 1985; Riedel, Nebeker, & Cooper, 1988; Terborg, 1976), and goal participation (e.g., Earley 1985; Earley & Kanfer, 1985; Erez, 1986; Erez, Earley, & Hulin, 1985). Interestingly, although Locke and Latham's (1990) review of the goal participation literature confirms that participation has a negligible impact on enhancing goal effectiveness through increased commitment, the consensus of four studies (Erez & Arad, 1986; Campbell & Gingrich, 1986; Huber, 1985; Latham & Winters, 1989) was that participation may significantly improve goal effectiveness by allowing greater quantity and quality of input in developing effective task strategies that facilitate performance.

Feedback. Locke and Latham's (1990) goal theory contends that a combination of both goals and feedback are necessary for performance enhancement effects to be demonstrated. In the most comprehensive review of the role of feedback in goal setting to date, Locke and Latham (1990) reviewed 33 studies comparing the effectiveness of goals plus feedback with either goals or feedback individually, finding that 17 out of 18 studies demonstrated that the combination of goals and feedback were significantly better than goals alone, and 21 out of 22 studies revealed that the combination was superior to feedback alone. Moreover, Mento et al. (1987) have demonstrated through their meta-analysis of goal-setting research that when feedback was added to goal setting, productivity increased an additional 17%.

Locke and Latham (1990) suggest that feedback functions in a complex appraisal process to influence goal mechanisms by providing information that either: (a) enhances self-efficacy or perceived ability (e.g., Bandura & Cervone, 1983; Locke, Frederick, Lee, & Bobko, 1984) and/or (b) allows adjustment or improvement of task strategies (e.g., Latham & Baldes, 1975). If feedback indicates a small goal-performance discrepancy, individuals will usually be satisfied and will maintain a similar level of effort. However, if feedback reveals a large goal-performance discrepancy that prompts dissatisfaction with goal progress, the motivational response elicited is predicted to differ, depending on individuals' level of self-efficacy. For high self-efficacy individuals who set high goals, negative feedback should prompt them to substantially increase their effort and persistence levels and the quality of their task strategies, usually enhancing performance. For low self-efficacy individuals who set low goals, negative feedback should impair performance because it prompts reductions in effort and persistence and deterioration in task strategies (Locke & Latham, 1990). Thus the consensus of the general goal-setting literature is that feedback is an important and necessary moderator of goal-setting effects.

Task Complexity. Wood and his colleagues (1989) performed a meta-analysis on 125 goal-setting studies to assess the influence of task complexity as a moderator of goal-setting effects. The tasks used in these studies were independently rated on a 10-point task complexity scale based on Wood's (1986) task complexity criteria. Multiple regression analyses revealed that task complexity predicted 6% of the variance in goal difficulty-performance effects and 9% of the variance in goal difficulty/specificity-performance effects. Moreover, when separate meta-analyses were computed for studies with low, moderate, and high task-complexity ratings, the effect sizes for both goal difficulty and goal difficulty/specificity were larger for simpler as compared to more complex tasks. Thus these results confirm that task complexity does moderate goal-setting effects, although the exact mechanisms for how this happens remain speculative. Locke and Latham (1990) argue that complex tasks often require more than simple motivational effects to enhance performance. Complex tasks require the development of new specific task strategies first and then the motivational effects of attentional focus, effort, and persistence to make new task strategies work. Further research is needed to assess this prediction.

Now that the general goal-setting literature has been briefly reviewed, the next section will summarize findings from the limited goal-setting research in sport, highlighting support for competitive goal-setting effects in general, the impact of goal attributes such as goal difficulty, goal specificity, goal temporality, and goal collectivity on sport performance, and the evidence assessing the role of moderator variables such as ability, commitment, feedback, and task complexity on goal-setting effectiveness in sport and exercise.

REVIEW OF GOAL-SETTING RESEARCH IN SPORT

For whatever reason, sport and exercise have not embraced goal setting as an important research topic. Goal-setting research has only been conducted in the motor domain during the past 15 years, and only slightly more than a dozen studies have been conducted evaluating the impact of goals on sport/exercise performance. Although the reasons for this unpopularity of goal setting as a research topic is not readily apparent, this section will attempt to compare the findings from the limited goal-setting research in sport to those for the general empirical goal-setting literature described in the previous section.

Overall Effectiveness of Goal Setting in Sport

The general goal-setting literature reviewed in the previous section documented that goal setting has been a very popular research topic (i.e., nearly 400 studies), and the magnitude (i.e., 8–16% performance increments) and consistency (i.e., 90% of all studies) of goal-setting effects make it one of the best performance enhancement techniques in the behavioral sciences. Goal-setting research in sport has not yielded as consistent support for the effectiveness of setting goals as the general goal-setting literature. Only two-thirds of the 13 studies identified in sport have demonstrated that athletes setting specific-difficult goals performed significantly better than did performers setting general goals, do-your-best goals, or no goals (Anderson, Crowell, Doman, & Howard, 1988; Barnett & Stanicek, 1979; Burton, 1989a; Burton, 1989b; Burton, Williams-Rice, Phillips, & Daw, 1989; Giannini, Weinberg, & Jackson, 1988; Hall & Byrne, 1988; Hall, Weinberg, & Jackson, 1987; Weinberg, Bruya, Longino, & Jackson, 1988; Yin, Simons, & Callaghan, 1989), whereas the remaining four studies failed to document significant goal-setting effects (Hollingsworth, 1975; Miller & McAuley, 1987; Weinberg, Bruya, & Jackson, 1985; Weinberg, Bruya, Jackson, & Garland, 1986). Thus these results suggest that although goal setting has been an effective performance enhancement strategy in sport, it has not demonstrated the consistency or robustness of performance enhancement effects that have been documented in other domains, primarily business or work settings.

Goal Attributes Research in Sport

Much of the goal-setting research in sport has focused on the impact of selected goal attributes on goal effectiveness. This section will review sport research on the goal attributes of goal difficulty, goal specificity, goal temporality, and goal collectivity.

Goal Difficulty. Previous research has provided strong support for Locke and Latham's goal difficulty hypothesis that the more difficult the goal, the more performance will be enhanced. Goal-setting research in sport has failed to support goal difficulty predictions. Hall, Weinberg, and Jackson (1987) compared hand dynamometer endurance performance of subjects assigned do-your-best, improve-by-40-seconds, and improve-by-70-seconds goals. Although they confirmed that subjects who were assigned the two specific-goal conditions performed better than did do-your-best subjects, they found no goal difficulty effects for the specific goal conditions. Similarly Weinberg, Bruya, Jackson, and Garland (1986) found no goal difficulty effects in their first experiment for subjects assigned to easy, moderate, and extremely hard goal conditions who performed a sit-up task for five weeks.

Two other studies have failed to find differences between difficult and unrealistically hard goals. In Experiment 2, Weinberg, Bruya, Jackson, and Garland (1986) found no goal difficulty effects for subjects randomly assigned to do-your-best, extremely hard, and highly improbable goal conditions for a sit-up task across a 5-week treatment period. Similarly, Burton et al. (1989) compared subjects assigned moderately difficult goals (i.e., 5–15% improvement over previous performance) to those with unrealistically hard goals (i.e., 25–30% improvement) on their performance of 7 basketball skills that varied in task complexity across a 14-week treatment period. Although data trends showed goal difficulty effects, the groups setting moderate versus difficult goals did not differ significantly on their performance for any of the 7 basketball tasks. Overall, goal difficulty results in sport fail to support theoretical predictions.

Goal Specificity. Locke and Latham (1990) argue that when goal difficulty is controlled, the major effect of goal specificity is to reduce performance variance. To date, these predicted effects of goal specificity have not been independently tested in sport.

Goal Temporality. Previous general goal research has revealed equivocal results for goal temporality, with several studies demonstrating that subjects with short-term goals performed better than their counterparts setting long-term goals, whereas other studies have found essentially opposite results. Not surprisingly, goal temporality research in sport has been minimal (i.e., three studies), and results have also been equivocal. Weinberg and his colleagues (Weinberg, Bruya, & Jackson, 1985; Weinberg, Bruya, Longino, & Jackson, 1988) failed to find any goal temporal-

ity effects on an endurance performance task. Subjects who set short-term goals only, long-term goals only, or a combination of short- and long-term goals did not demonstrate significant differences in performance on a 3-minute sit-up task.

However, Hall and Byrne (1988) recently demonstrated that subgoals play an important role in enhancing the effectiveness of long-term goals. Students in five weight-training classes were assigned to one of four experimental treatments: long-term goals, long-term goals plus experimenter-set intermediate goals, long-term goals plus subject-set intermediate goals, and do-your-best goals. Results revealed that both long-term-with-subgoal groups performed significantly better than do-your-best subjects, but the performance of the long-term goal only group approached significance. These findings suggest that long-term goals can facilitate performance most effectively when subgoals are used to mark progress.

Goal Collectivity. General goal collectivity research reviewed in the previous section confirmed that group goals have been as consistently successful at enhancing performance on group tasks (i.e., 93% of studies) as individual goals have been on individual tasks (i.e., 91% of studies), and productivity increases from setting group goals (i.e., 44%) are often much higher than for individual goals (i.e., 8–16%). However, implications from social loafing research argue that setting group/team goals without accompanying individual goals may prompt social loafing. Regrettably, goal collectivity research has not been conducted in sport to date.

Moderator Variables of Competitive Goal-Setting Effectiveness

The previous section reviewed four variables that have been found to significantly moderate goal-setting effectiveness. The first two moderator variables, ability and commitment, have not been researched in sport, but research has assessed the role of feedback and task complexity on competitive goal-setting effectiveness.

Feedback. General goal-setting research reviewed in the previous section documented that feedback is an important moderator of goal-setting effectiveness. Not only does feedback contribute significantly to performance improvement over and above goal-setting effects (i.e., 17%), but goal setting is usually not effective if feedback is absent (Locke & Latham, 1990). Results have been generally positive for the role of feedback in competitive goal-setting effectiveness. Anderson et al. (1988) used a multiple baseline design to assess the effects of goal setting and feedback on the checking performance of a university hockey team over two seasons. The feedback condition was introduced first and the combined group that played both seasons increased checking by 51%, with new players somewhat higher (i.e., 90% increase) and senior players from the first season much lower (i.e., 6% decrease). When goal setting was added to feedback, the combined group improved 20% over checking levels due to feedback alone for the first year and 11% for the second season. Overall, this study confirms the importance of feedback as a moderator of goal-setting effectiveness. However, Hall et al. (1987) attempted to assess whether concurrent or terminal feedback enhanced performance more across goal difficulty conditions. No differences were found between feedback conditions for any of the goal difficulty groups, although these results don't necessarily refute the benefits of feedback because both types of feedback may have facilitated performance.

Task Complexity. Wood and his colleagues (1989) have confirmed that task complexity moderates goal-setting effectiveness. Locke and Latham (1990) suggest that the motivational effects of goals will not enhance performance on complex tasks if individuals are not using appropriate task strategies. Thus task complexity should complicate and lengthen the process by which goals facilitate performance because individuals must first find or develop effective new task strategies and then use the motivational impact of goals (i.e., effort & persistence) to make these new task strategies work. Burton (1989b) has recently assessed the moderating effect of task complexity on students' development of 7 basketball skills. Students assigned moderate difficulty goals performed better on two low- to moderate-complexity basketball skills than did their do-your-best goal classmates, whereas no group differences were apparent on the other five moderate- to high-complexity basketball skills. These results confirm findings from the general goal-setting literature that as task complexity increases, the process of enhancing performance through goal setting lengthens and becomes more complex.

Several generalizations are readily apparent from this review of goal-setting research in sport. First, goal setting has not yet become a popular topic for sport research, a somewhat surprising finding in light of its potentially powerful performance enhancement effects. Second, the limited goal-setting research in sport has not demonstrated nearly the consistency of performance enhancement effects that have been found in the general goal-setting literature. In the next section, several explanations will be offered for why goal-setting results in sport have not been as strong or as consistent as those reported in business and industry settings.

WHY HAVE GOALS BEEN LESS EFFECTIVE IN SPORT?

At least four factors seem plausible to explain why goal-setting effects have been less consistent in sport than in work settings, including: (a) the small sample sizes of studies, (b) athletes operating closer to their performance po-

tential, (c) highly complex skills being performed, and (d) individual differences that influence goal-setting effectiveness. This section will briefly explore each of these explanations for the less consistent and robust competitive goal-setting effects.

Small Sample Size

About one-third of the goal-setting studies in sport have employed small samples of 30 or fewer subjects, and because of the sensitivity of many inferential statistics to sample size, small samples were identified as a possible explanation for the less consistent goal-setting effects in sport. However, careful scrutiny of goal-setting research in sport reveals that the average sample size across the 13 studies was 80 subjects, and most goal conditions had a minimum of 20 subjects. Both sample parameters appear large enough to adequately demonstrate differences in goal-setting effects. Moreover, 4 of the 5 competitive goal-setting studies with sample sizes of 30 or fewer subjects revealed significant goal-setting effects, thus negating sample size as a prime explanation for the less consistent goal-setting effects in sport.

Athletes Operating Closer to Their Performance Potential

The performance limits argument is consistent with Locke and Latham's (1990) predictions for the moderating effects of ability on goal-setting effectiveness. Locke and Latham (1990) present convincing evidence that the goal effectiveness curve flattens out as individuals approach the limits of their ability because ability factors restrict the amount of improvement they can make through goal setting. This explanation seems possible in all four nonsignificant studies in sport, including the sit-up task used by Weinberg and his colleagues (Weinberg et al., 1985; Weinberg et al., 1986), the basketball free-throw task employed by Miller and McAuley (1987), and the juggling task used by Hollingsworth (1975).

Task Complexity

The task complexity argument is consistent with Locke and Latham's (1990) predictions for the moderating effects of task complexity on goal-setting effectiveness. They suggest that complex tasks involve a greater time lag to demonstrate goal-setting effects because new task strategies often have to be developed in order to perform the skill more effectively. Only when individuals have developed effective specific task strategies can the motivational effects of goals stimulate performance increments by prompting greater effort and persistence. This explanation seems plausible for two of the four nonsignificant goal-setting studies in sport. Although this explanation seems unlikely for the relatively simple 3-minute sit-up task used by Weinberg and his colleagues (Weinberg et al., 1985; Weinberg et al., 1986), both juggling (Hollingsworth, 1975) and basketball free-throw shooting (Miller & McAuley, 1987) are complex tasks that may not have had sufficient time during the experimental period (i.e., 12 days and 5 weeks, respectively) to demonstrate goal-setting effects.

Individual Differences

Locke and Latham's (1990) goal-setting theory suggests that individual differences, particularly self-efficacy, should have a significant impact on how individuals respond to goal setting, particularly for complex tasks and goal difficulty levels at the upper ranges of performers' ability. Specifically they predict that when confronted with temporary failure on complex tasks, high self-efficacy performers will increase the quality of their task strategies and put forth elevated levels of effort and persistence to make those strategies work, whereas low self-efficacy competitors will normally display less functional task strategies and reduced effort and persistence. Although self-efficacy has been shown to influence goal effectiveness, individual differences have largely not been assessed or controlled for in sport and nonsport goal-setting research and remain a viable explanation for nonsignificant findings in goal-setting research.

In summary, the somewhat less consistent and robust goal-setting results in sport may be attributable to three factors: performers operating closer to their performance potential, athletes performing highly complex skills that make the demonstration of goal effects a more lengthy and difficult process, and individual differences that prompt specific types of athletes to respond to goal-setting programs in idiosyncratic ways. Although each of these explanations is intriguing in its own right, the role of individual differences in the goal-setting process seems to have been largely neglected by previous goal-setting research and thus appears particularly appropriate for further conceptual and empirical study.

In the next section, a competitive goal-setting (CGS) model will be presented that revolves around a critical individual difference variable termed "goal-setting styles." This model will describe the conceptual framework for goal-setting styles and will make specific predictions about how they influence preferences for particular goal attributes, affect key moderator variables, and impact on performance and consequent variables. Nevertheless it is important to clarify that the purpose of presenting this competitive goal-setting model is not to advance a new goal-setting theory but simply to provide the reader with a heuristic tool for understanding (a) how individual difference variables, particularly goal-setting styles, influence the competitive goal-setting process, and (b) how this more comprehensive model can further aid our understanding and investigation of the goal-setting process in sport (see Figure 20–2).

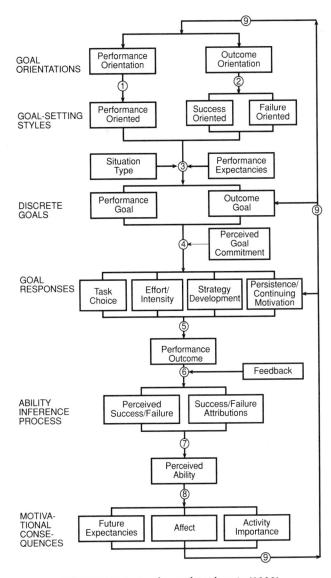

FIGURE 20–2. Locke and Latham's (1990) goal-setting model.

COMPETITIVE GOAL-SETTING MODEL

Consistent with previous motivation research (Elliott & Dweck, 1988; Locke, 1968; Locke & Latham, 1990; Locke et al., 1981; Maehr, 1984; Nicholls, 1984a, 1984b), the CGS model shown in Figure 20–2 predicts that the motivational function of goals is most evident in the top portion of the model between Links 1–5. First, goal orientations interact with perceived ability to prompt the development of three distinct goal-setting styles: performance-oriented (see Link 1 in Figure 20–2), success-oriented, and failure-oriented (see Link 2 in Figure 20–2). These goal-setting styles interact with situation type (i.e., practice versus competition) and performance expectancies to dictate the specific goal set (see Link 3 in Figure 20–2). Next, discrete goals interact with perceived goal commitment to prompt specific goal responses, including task choice, effort/intensity, strategy development, and persistence/continuing motivation (see Link 4 in Figure 20–2) that ultimately dictate how athletes will perform and their competitive outcome (see Link 5 in Figure 20–2).

Based on perceived ability theory and research (e.g., Elliott & Dweck, 1988; Harter, 1981; Nicholls, 1984a, 1984b), the CGS model further predicts that goals also have an important self-evaluation function because they become the standards against which performance and outcome are weighed in order to determine perceived success and failure and to assess specific success/failure attributions (see Link 6 in Figure 20–2), the two primary antecedents of perceived competence or ability (see Link 7 in Figure 20–2). Finally, the CGS model predicts that perceived ability directly influences motivational consequent variables such as future expectancies, affect, and activity importance (see Link 8 in Figure 20–2). Feedback loops then allow motivational consequent variables to subsequently influence goal orientations, specific goals, and goal responses (see Link 9 of Figure 20–2).

Although the CGS model is depicted as a sequential process, this was done as a heuristic tool to facilitate understanding of the separate motivation and self-evaluation functions of goals and to make key model components more explicit. In reality, the model is probably much more complex and feedback loops more extensive. Moreover it is not my intention to venture into the argument about whether cognition precedes affect or vice versa, but rather to suggest that these variables are related, probably in some reciprocal fashion.

The most innovative aspect of the competitive goal-setting model is the prediction that athletes who adopt different goal-setting styles can be expected to set different types of practice and competitive goals that will significantly influence their cognitions and performance. In the next section, the conceptual framework for goal-setting styles will be examined and the specific characteristics of athletes adopting each goal-setting style will be outlined.

Goal-Setting Styles

The notion of an individual difference measure termed "goal-setting styles" is based on contemporary motivation research that combines the concept of goal orientations with personal perceptions of ability (e.g., Ames, 1990; Dweck, 1980; Elliott & Dweck, 1988; Nicholls, 1984a). In examining the genesis of the conception of goal-setting styles, it is important first to review the research on goal orientations. Contemporary conceptions of goal orientations are based on two primary theoretical premises (e.g., Elliot, & Dweck, 1988; Maehr & Nicholls, 1980; Nicholls, 1984a, 1984b). First, perceived competence or ability is conceived as the critical underlying construct responsible for mediating motivational behaviors. Second, individuals' goal orien-

tations are hypothesized to significantly mediate how perceived ability develops and its impact on achievement behavior. Both Nicholls (1984a, 1984b) and Dweck (1975, 1980; Diener & Dweck, 1978; Elliott & Dweck, 1988) have postulated two primary goal orientations in achievement situations. Although these researchers use somewhat different terminology, they define these goal orientations quite similarly. Hereafter, my own terminology will be employed, and these goal orientations will be labeled: (a) performance and (b) outcome.

Athletes adopting a *performance goal orientation* are concerned with increasing perceived ability by mastering new tasks or improving skills. These athletes define success in terms of self-referent standards that focus on learning, skill improvement, and/or task mastery. Performance-oriented competitors assume they have the ability to learn and improve if they put forth sufficient effort; thus even low ability performers adopting this orientation should find sport an enjoyable and rewarding experience if they frequently improve their competence through skill development. Thus athletes adopting a performance orientation focus their attention on the "process" rather than the final "product."

Individuals who adopt an *outcome goal orientation* seek to ". . . maintain positive judgments of their ability and avoid negative judgments by seeking to prove, validate, or document their ability and not discredit it" (Elliott & Dweck, 1988, p. 5). Outcome goal orientations base success/failure on social comparison processes, thus making winning or positive social comparison necessary in order to maintain high perceived ability. For outcome-oriented performers, improvement and task mastery are only important in so far as they provide the means (i.e., process) to the end of achieving positive social comparison (i.e., product).

The CGS model hypothesizes that goal orientation and level of perceived ability interact to create three distinct goal-setting styles: (a) performance-oriented (PO), (b) success-oriented (SO), and (c) failure-oriented (FO). The general focus of each of these goal-setting styles is outlined in column 2 of Table 20–1, and the specific characteristics of each style will be discussed in the following sections.

Performance-Oriented Goal-Setting Style. As noted in columns 2 and 3 of Table 20–1, the primary concern of athletes adopting a PO goal-setting style is learning and improvement, not demonstrating ability to others. PO athletes of all ability levels should view any situation as an opportunity to learn and improve their skills, thus prompting high levels of intrinsic motivation. Consequently, high-and low-skilled PO performers should demonstrate very similar motivational patterns, both in practice and competition. Ability comparison is simply not an issue for PO competitors; they are only interested in raising their own perceived ability through learning and skill development.

Based on learned helplessness and perceived ability research (e.g., Diener & Dweck, 1978; Dweck, 1975, 1980; Elliott & Dweck, 1988; Nicholls, 1984a), the CGS model

TABLE 20–1. Characteristics of Performance-Oriented, Success-Oriented, and Failure-Oriented Goal-Setting Styles.

Goal-Setting Style	General Focus of Goals	Level of Perceived Ability	Success/Failure Attributions	Role of Feedback
Performance Orientation (PO)	Primarily interested in learning, performance improvement, and *increasing* self-referent ability	High or low	*Success*: high effort (ability assumed)	*Positive*: confirms successful learning or performance improvement
			Failure: don't perceive failure	*Negative*: signal to increase effort and/or try new strategies
Success Orientation (SO)	Primarily interested in competitive outcome and positive social comparison as a means of demonstrating high ability	High	*Success*: high ability	*Positive*: confirms successful social comparison
			Failure: internal-unstable-controllable factors such as low effort or poor mental preparation	*Negative*: signal to increase effort and/or try new strategies
Failure Orientation (FO)	Primarily interested in avoiding competition because of fear that negative social comparison will reveal low ability	Low	*Success*: external or uncontrollable factors such as luck or an easy opponent	*Positive*: feedback discounted because success attributed to external and/or uncontrollable factors
			Failure: low ability	*Negative*: confirms unsuccessful social comparisons

predicts that because PO athletes assume the capacity to learn and improve, the amount of improvement made should be a direct function of the effort expended, thus prompting them to attribute success primarily to effort (see column 4 of Table 20–1). Moreover, PO competitors are not predicted to make failure attributions (see column 4 of Table 20–1). Because of their learning focus, lack of success is not threatening to their self-worth and is dealt with by increasing effort or developing new problem-solving strategies.

The CGS model predicts that performers adopting a PO goal-setting style should prefer to set difficult goals, even at the risk of making mistakes, because high goal difficulty will maximize learning and improvement (see the Task Choice section of Table 20–2). PO athletes should also exert high effort in most situations in order to maximize learning and improvement, and high effort is also required to successfully achieve difficult goals (see the Effort/Intensity section of Table 20–2). Moreover, the model also predicts that PO performers should confront failure constructively by remaining focused on the task and maintaining or improving the quality of their problem-solving strategies (see the Strategy Development section of Table 20–2), thus demonstrating high persistence and continuing motivation (see the Persistence/Continuing Motivation section of Table 20–2).

The CGS model predicts that PO athletes should perform consistently better in specific competitions and throughout their competitive careers than either SO and FO performers because they set more challenging goals, give consistently higher effort, use more effective problem-solving strategies, and persist longer in the face of failure (see the Performance section of Table 20–2). Moreover, because of the linear relationship between performance and winning (i.e., the better athletes perform, the better their chances of winning), PO athletes should also win more often than SO and FO competitors of similar ability.

Finally as noted in Table 20–3, the CGS model predicts that PO athletes should experience positive motivational consequences from setting goals. PO competitors have positive future expectancies because their learning focus allows them to remain optimistic about their ability to master skills and improve despite temporary plateaus or setbacks (see the Future Expectancies section of Table 20–3). In fact, when PO athletes have low ability in a valued area, they may be even more motivated to develop these skills (Diener & Dweck, 1978). The model also predicts that PO performers should experience satisfaction and pride from success, and although they should perceive negative affect when unsuccessful, these negative emotions usually motivate PO athletes to improve their performance in the future (see the Affect section of Table 20–3). Finally PO athletes

TABLE 20–2. Goal Response Predictions for Performance-Oriented (PO). Success-Oriented (SO), and Failure-Oriented (FO) Athletes.

Task Choice
PO—choose learning opportunities at the risk of displaying mistakes in order to increase competence.
SO—sacrifice learning opportunities that involve risk of error.
FO—sacrifice learning for moderately easy tasks to avoid displaying low ability or extremely difficult tasks for which they have a built-in excuse for failure.

Effort/Intensity
PO—consistent high effort.
SO—only as high as necessary to still display positive social comparison.
FO—on hard tasks, effort should be low to confuse others about the reason for failure and avoid revealing low ability; on easy tasks, effort should be very high to make sure they don't fail and reveal low ability.

Strategy Development
PO—quality of problem-solving maintained or enhanced under failure.
SO—quality of problem-solving maintained or enhanced under failure.
FO—quality of problem-solving deteriorates sharply under failure.

Persistence/Continuing Motivation
PO—remain high despite extensive failure.
SO—deteriorates only with extensive failure.
FO—deteriorates sharply with minimal failure.

Performance
PO—high performance that eventually will closely approach athletes' performance potential.
SO—perform well enough to win but long-term potential depends on situational factors that necessitate development of full capabilities.
FO—poor performance that should deteriorate over time with continued failure.

TABLE 20–3. Goal Consequences Predictions for Performance-Oriented (PO), Success-Oriented (SO), and Failure-Oriented (FO) Athletes.

Future Expectancies
PO—positive and optimistic because of high self confidence in ability to learn and improve.
SO—positive and optimistic because of high self confidence in talent and ability to win and socially compare well.
FO—negative and pessimistic because of conviction that they lack talent and ability to win and socially compare well.

Affect
PO—consistently high self-confidence, enjoyment, and satisfaction.
SO—consistently high self-confidence, enjoyment, and satisfaction.
FO—anxiety, dissatisfaction, and shame.

Activity Importance
PO—importance of activity should increase over time.
SO—importance of activity should increase over time.
FO—should devalue importance of activity over time.

are predicted to increase their commitment to challenging tasks that help them enhance their perceptions of ability through learning and improvement (see the Activity Importance section of Table 20–3, Burton & Martens, 1986).

Success-Oriented Goal-Setting Style. Competitors with SO goal-setting styles evaluate success based on social comparison and competitive outcome, but they demonstrate high perceived ability because they win consistently and/or socially compare well (see columns 2 and 3 of Table 20–1, Dweck, 1975, 1980; Nicholls, 1984a). As noted in column 2 of Table 20–1, SO performers' primary objective is to maximize positive social comparison in order to demonstrate high perceived ability. Although they view most situations as opportunities to demonstrate competence, SO competitors are optimally motivated, confident, and play their best only when matched against an opponent of similar ability (i.e., moderate goal difficulty, Burton, 1989b). When goal difficulty is too low or high, SO athletes tend to be under- or overconfident, both situations are predicted to lower

motivation and performance (Burton, 1989b). Based on learned helplessness and perceived ability research (e.g., Diener & Dweck, 1978; Dweck, 1975, 1980; Elliott & Dweck, 1988; Nicholls, 1984a), the model predicts that SO athletes normally attribute success to high ability, an internal-stable-controllable factor that creates a positive-optimistic outlook toward competition, whereas failure is typically attributed to internal-controllable-unstable factors such as low effort, poor mental preparation, or the need to develop skills further (see column 4 of Table 20–1). Although SO competitors still worry about failure, they generally respond to failure in a constructive way (e.g., Elliott & Dweck, 1988).

The CGS model hypothesizes that competitors with SO goal-setting styles will avoid challenging goals that involve learning opportunities if they perceive a risk of making public mistakes (see the Task Choice section of Table 20–2). Instead, they are predicted to prefer setting moderately difficult goals on tasks at which they are already reasonably proficient, thus preventing revelation of low ability (e.g., Elliott & Dweck, 1988). SO competitors' effort expenditure is predicted to fluctuate depending on task difficulty (see the Effort/Intensity section of Table 20–2, Nicholls, 1984a). For moderately difficult tasks, SO performers should put forth high effort to reach their goals. However, on easy tasks, SO performers will typically expend as little effort as necessary to win, a strategy that allows them to maximize the demonstration of high ability, whereas on difficult tasks, where the probability of failure is high, SO competitors will normally try hard until they become convinced that successful social comparison is not possible and then concentrate their effort on other tasks at which they are more likely to be successful (e.g., Dweck, 1980; Elliott & Dweck, 1988; Nicholls, 1984a).

The CGS model predicts that SO athletes' positive social comparison history allows them to approach failure in a positive way, maintaining high confidence, remaining task-focused, and developing effective problem-solving strategies (see the Strategy Development section of Table 20–2; Diener & Dweck, 1978; Elliott & Dweck, 1988; Nicholls, 1984a). However, because SO performers need to demonstrate high ability consistently, their continuing motivation should eventually deteriorate following extensive failure (see the Persistence/Continuing Motivation section of Table 20–2; Elliott & Dweck, 1988; Nicholls, 1984a).

The model predicts that SO athletes will generally perform well (see the Performance section of Table 20–2). However, SO athletes are not expected to perform as close to their performance potential as their PO teammates because concerns about positive social comparison reduce SO competitors' performance in two ways (e.g., Dweck, 1980; Elliott & Dweck, 1988; Nicholls, 1984a). First the importance of socially comparing well reduces goal difficulty and limits how long SO athletes will persist in the face of failure. Second the desire to maximize demonstration of ability prompts SO competitors to give low effort against weaker opponents and not look for ways to learn and improve unless pushed to do so in order to win. Thus SO performers' less functional motivational patterns ultimately prevent them from developing to the full extent of their performance potential (e.g., Dweck, 1980; Elliott & Dweck, 1988; Nicholls, 1984a).

As noted in Table 20–3, the CGS model predicts that SO performers should experience positive motivational consequences from the goal-setting process. SO performers typically have optimistic future expectancies because consistent previous success has been attributed to their normatively high "ability," thus forecasting that positive social comparison should continue in future competitions (see the Future Expectancies section of Table 20–3; Dweck, 1980; Nicholls, 1984a). The model also predicts that SO performers should experience satisfaction and pride from success, whereas dissatisfaction over failure coupled with unstable attributional patterns should prompt even higher future motivation (see the Affect section of Table 20–3, Dweck, 1980; Nicholls, 1984a). Finally, SO performers are predicted to increase activity importance for tasks at which they socially compare well in order to further enhance their perceptions of ability (see the Activity Importance section of Table 20–3; Burton & Martens, 1986).

Failure-Oriented Goal-Setting Style. Performers with FO goal-setting styles base success on social comparison, but they have low perceived ability due to a history of poor social comparison (see columns 2 and 3 of Table 20–1, Elliott & Dweck, 1988). As shown in column 2 of Table 20–1, FO competitors' primary objective is to prevent others from finding out they have low ability, thus explaining why they fear competitive situations that offer the risk of publicly revealing their incompetence (e.g., Dweck, 1975, 1980; Elliott & Dweck, 1988). Thus FO performers approach competition with diffidence and anxiety and often perform well below their performance capabilities.

As shown in column 4 of Table 20–1, consistent with learned helplessness and perceived ability research (e.g., Diener & Dweck, 1978; Dweck, 1975, 1980; Elliott & Dweck, 1988; Nicholls, 1984a), the CGS model hypothesizes that FO competitors typically attribute failure to lack of ability, thus reinforcing their negative perceptions of competence. Success, however, is attributed to external and/or uncontrollable factors, such as luck or an easy task, an attributional pattern that prevents FO performers from increasing their feelings of competence (see column 4 of Table 20–1). Regrettably, because FO athletes take all the blame for failure but none of the credit for success, competition will always remain a negative experience for them, reinforcing their negative ability perceptions.

The CGS model hypothesizes that performers with FO goal-setting styles have little interest in learning (see the Task Choice section of Table 20–2). Because they are concerned with concealing their low ability from others, they typically set extreme goals that (a) are moderately easy for tasks at which they are already reasonably proficient, or (b) extremely difficult so they have a built-in excuse for failure (e.g., Dweck, 1980; Elliott & Dweck, 1988; Nicholls, 1984a). The CGS model predicts that FO competitors' effort expenditure should correspond to the level of goal difficulty selected (see the Effort/Intensity section of Table 20–2). If the FO competitor has not completely given up hope of demonstrating high ability, they should set very difficult goals where, despite the high probability of failure, they hope they can "get lucky" and demonstrate their competence, while secure in the knowledge that they have a good excuse for almost certain failure. If FO performers are resigned to having low ability, they should prefer to set easy goals and put forth high effort to ensure that they don't fail. Moderate goal difficulty is predicted to be highly threatening to FO competitors. Thus if they are forced to set moderate goals, they typically will respond by putting forth low effort as an ego-defense mechanism. "Token effort" serves to protect the self-worth of FO competitors by creating confusion about whether failure was due to lack of ability or simply low effort (e.g., Dweck, 1980; Elliott & Dweck, 1988; Nicholls, 1984a).

The CGS model hypothesizes that FO performers should demonstrate a significant deterioration in their problem-solving skills when confronted with failure, probably due to the negative effects of diffidence and anxiety that prompt attentional distraction (see the Strategy Development section of Table 20–2, Dweck, 1980; Elliott & Dweck, 1988; Martens, Burton, Vealey, Bump, & Smith, 1990). Fear of revealing low ability to others should prompt FO performers to respond to failure by developing high levels of anxiety and self-doubt, by focusing internally on their own arousal and self-rumination, and by demonstrating severe deterioration in their problem-solving skills. Finally, FO athletes' persistence and continuing motivation should deteriorate sharply, even with minimal failure (see the Persistence/Continuing Motivation section of Table 2; Elliott & Dweck, 1988; Maehr & Braskamp, 1986; Nicholls, 1984a).

The CGS model predicts that FO athletes should normally perform poorly (see the Performance section of Table

20–2). Fear of failure due to their perceived inability to socially compare well should prompt FO competitors to develop high levels of anxiety that will significantly impair their performance. Moreover, negative competitive cognitions coupled with dysfunctional goal responses, including easy goals, low effort expenditure, poor strategy development (particularly under failure), and low persistence should ensure the continued deterioration of performance over time (e.g., Dweck, 1980; Elliott & Dweck, 1988; Martens et al., 1990).

Finally the model predicts that FO athletes should experience negative motivational consequences from setting goals (see Table 20–3). FO performers are predicted to demonstrate negative future expectancies due to their history of poor social comparison that they attributed to low ability (see the Future Expectancies section of Table 20–3, Dweck, 1980; Nicholls, 1984a). FO competitors are also predicted to experience minimal satisfaction from success that they attribute to external-uncontrollable factors, whereas failure attributed to lack of ability should prompt significant negative affect such as anxiety and shame, which should impair performance and prompt a desire to drop out of sport (see the Affect section of Table 20–3, Nicholls, 1984a). Finally FO competitors are predicted to devalue activities that force them to risk the demonstration of low ability, eventually dropping out of the activity if not constrained to remain (see the Activity Importance section of Table 20–3; Martens & Burton, 1986).

Goal Attribute Preferences

Based on predictions for each goal-setting style reviewed in the previous section, the next section will specify CGS model predictions for the goal attribute preferences of each goal-setting style for: (a) goal specificity, (b) goal difficulty, (c) goal proximity, (d) goal collectivity, and (e) goal valence. These predictions are based on the learned helplessness and perceived ability literatures (e.g., Diener & Dweck, 1978; Dweck, 1975, 1980; Elliott & Dweck, 1988; Maehr & Braskamp, 1986; Nicholls, 1984a), but most of these hypotheses have yet to be empirically tested.

Preferred Goal Attributes of PO Athletes. The CGS model hypothesizes that PO athletes' learning orientation should prompt them to prefer self-referenced goals that are specific, difficult, positive, individual, and a combination of long-term/short-term (see Table 20–4). Performers adopting PO goal-setting styles are predicted to prefer goals with these attributes because they should (a) maximize motivation by either increasing the challenge level or making the performance criteria for attaining success more explicit and (b) provide the maximum information necessary for developing new strategies to facilitate learning and improvement. PO performers are also predicted to set long-term goals and then develop action plans for achieving them that focus on attainment of more specific short-term goals. However, because PO performers are interested in learning as

TABLE 20–4. Goal Attribute Preference Predictions for Performance-Oriented (PO), Success-Oriented (SO), and Failure-Oriented (FO) Athletes.

Performance-Oriented
• self-referenced
• specific
• difficult
• positive
• individual
• long-term/short-term

Success-Oriented
• social-comparative
• specific
• moderately difficult
• positive and negative
• individual
• short-term/long-term

Failure-Oriented
• social-comparative
• general
• moderately easy
• positive
• team
• long-term

a long-term and ongoing process, they should be able to focus more on long-term goals than either SO or FO competitors and delay gratification and accept temporary setbacks as the price that must be paid in order to maximize long-term learning and skill development.

Preferred Goal Attributes of SO Athletes. Because SO competitors define success in terms of positive social comparison, the CGS model predicts that they should prefer goals that are positive/negative, specific, individual/team, moderately difficult, and short-term/long-term (see Table 20–4). SO performers should prefer positively focused goals for new or difficult skills but benefit from more negatively focused goals that emphasize minimizing mistakes for well-learned skills. Model predictions suggest that specific goals should facilitate social comparison, thus allowing SO competitors to demonstrate high ability, whereas moderately difficult goals should maximize the chances of positive social comparison and ensure that SO performers will consistently demonstrate high ability. SO athletes should set both team and individual goals. Individual goals should make the social comparison process more explicit so SO performers can demonstrate high ability. However, rewards are attached most strongly to team goals, and SO performers typically want to win in order to receive those rewards. Moreover, it is often assumed that individuals sacrifice individual accomplishment for team success, so SO performers on winning teams should be assumed to have more ability than individuals on losing teams. This skill of "being a winner" is the most prized sport skill of all. Athletes with SO goal-setting styles should also set a combination of short-and long-term goals (e.g., I want to win the race this week as an important step toward my long-term goal of being an Olympic champion.). However, because of their concern with demonstrating high ability to others, SO performers should place heavier emphasis on short-term than long-term goals, sometimes restricting long-term skill development because it would cause a temporary dropoff in performance that might hurt immediate social comparison.

Preferred Goal Attributes of FO Athletes. Finally the CGS model predicts that FO athletes should dislike competition because of its threat of revealing their low ability, thus prompting them to prefer goals that are general, team-oriented, extremely difficult or moderately easy, long-term, and positively focused (see Table 20–4). General and team-oriented goals make social comparison more difficult, thus lessening its threat. Extremely difficult goals retain a small chance of demonstrating high ability while providing a built-in excuse for failure, whereas moderately easy goals minimize the chances of failure. Long-term goals delay the threatening evaluation process as long as possible. Finally, because FO athletes have a strong fear of failure, they are also predicted to prefer positively focused goals that lessen concern about revealing low ability.

Moderating Variables

Consistent with Locke and Latham's (1990) goal-setting theory, the CGS model predicts that three moderator variables—(a) situation type, (b) perceived goal commitment, and (c) performance feedback—influence goal-setting effectiveness. The next section will outline specific predictions about how these variables moderate the goal-performance relationship for PO, SO, and FO performers.

Situation Type. The CGS model recognizes that goals often have different functions in practice and competition, thus making a particular goal-setting style more salient. Because practices are designed to enhance learning and promote skill development, evaluation pressure is normally low, and the motivational function of goals is therefore more salient, prompting athletes to adopt a PO goal-setting style (e.g., Ames, 1990; Elliott & Dweck, 1988). Conversely competition is designed to facilitate social comparison and outcome evaluation, thus eliciting high evaluation pressure that prompts athletes to adopt SO and FO goal-setting styles (e.g., Ames, 1990; Elliott & Dweck, 1988).

The CGS model is consistent with recent empirical research (e.g., Ames, 1990; Elliott & Dweck, 1988) that suggests situational constraints elicit PO, SO, and FO goal-setting styles that, in turn, influence goal responses (e.g., task choice, strategy development, persistence) and motivational consequences (e.g., affect). Thus the CGS model predicts that practice is more likely to elicit a PO goal-setting style while competition induces SO and FO goal-setting styles among competitors depending on expectations of success and failure. Of course, SO and FO goal-setting styles may be created in practice if the evaluative or social comparison aspects of the situation are highlighted, and a PO goal-setting style can still be elicited in competition if athletes focus on salient learning or performance aspects of the situation.

Goal Commitment. Consistent with Locke and Latham's (1990) goal-setting theory predictions, the CGS model emphasizes that strong goal commitment is necessary for the goal-setting process to function effectively, but the model makes different goal commitment predictions for each goal-setting style. Specifically the model suggests that PO athletes should base their commitment primarily on intrinsic factors, whereas SO and FO performers should weigh extrinsic factors heavily in determining their level of goal commitment (e.g., Ames, 1990; Elliott & Dweck, 1988; Nicholls, 1984a). Thus PO competitors are predicted to demonstrate strong commitment to any goal that helps them to learn or improve their skills.

Similarly the commitment of SO competitors is predicted to be high as long as they perceive the opportunity to demonstrate their competence to others through favorable social comparison (i.e., by winning consistently) and/or desirable extrinsic rewards are available for winning. Finally the model predicts that FO performers will normally have low commitment to any competitive goal because of the threat of publicly revealing low ability. Nevertheless extrinsic factors (e.g., rewards for winning) may still promote reasonably high goal commitment from FO performers, even though the threat of negative public evaluation is still salient (e.g., Ames, 1990; Elliott & Dweck, 1988; Nicholls, 1984a).

Performance and Outcome Feedback. Locke and Latham's (1990) goal-setting theory postulates that feedback may not only facilitate goal-setting effectiveness but actually may be necessary for goals to function. However, the CGS model makes somewhat more complex feedback predictions based on the different role feedback plays for each goal-setting style. Specifically the model predicts that feedback should facilitate goal setting for PO and SO athletes but impair goal-setting effectiveness for FO performers (see column 5 of Table 20–1; Elliott & Dweck, 1988; Nicholls, 1984a). For PO athletes, positive feedback should confirm successful learning and performance improvement, whereas negative feedback should signal the need to increase effort and/or try new strategies to ensure future success.

Similarly, the model hypothesizes that SO athletes utilize positive feedback to confirm successful social comparison and negative feedback as a signal to increase effort or to employ new strategies. Finally the model predicts feedback will impair FO athletes' performance because it makes negative social comparison more explicit. FO athletes are predicted to discount positive feedback because success is attributed to external and uncontrollable factors but readily internalize negative feedback about unsuccessful social comparison as being indicative of low ability (e.g., Dweck, 1980; Elliott & Dweck, 1988; Nicholls, 1984).

Are Goal-Setting Styles Traits or States?

Consistent with much of the history of personality research, goal orientations and their offspring goal-setting styles were originally conceived of as enduring personality predispositions that responded relatively consistently across situations (e.g., Dweck, 1980; Maehr & Braskamp, 1986; Maehr & Nicholls, 1980; Nicholls, 1984a). However, researchers (e.g., Elliott & Dweck, 1988; Hall, 1990) have demonstrated recently that they can experimentally manipulate goal orientations and goal-setting styles. Moreover, when powerful situational constraints prompt individuals to adopt a particular goal-setting style, they tend to respond consistently with model predictions for the goal responses and consequences of that style (e.g., Elliott & Dweck, 1988).

To date, research has not looked at the relative stability of goal-setting styles across situations, and investigators (e.g., Ames, 1990) have only recently begun to investigate what specific situational factors might prompt individuals to change goal-setting styles. However, the state/trait nature of GSS appears to be a promising area of future inquiry because, if GSS shifts do occur, it could explain why athletes who seldom get anxious sometimes choke in important competitions.

Empirical Support for Competitive Goal-Setting Model

A comprehensive review of the empirical support for the CGS model is beyond the scope of this chapter, although the interested reader may wish to consult Burton (1992) for a more complete review of research supporting the model, its components, and its specific predictions. Nevertheless to briefly summarize that review, Burton (1992) found solid initial support for the model, although many specific model predictions have not been empirically tested, particularly in sport. However, three studies that seem particularly supportive of the conception of goal-setting style are reviewed here briefly.

Ames (1990) has convincingly shown that children demonstrate higher academic attainment in performance-oriented classrooms than in outcome-oriented ones. Moreover, Ames's (1990) recent intervention research has demonstrated that students' academic attainment increases as a function of the degree to which their classroom becomes more performance-oriented. Employing Epstein's (1989) "TARGET" concept for helping teachers to make their classrooms more performance-focused by sequentially introducing changes in the task, authority, reward, grouping, evaluation, and time structures of their classrooms, Ames (1990) confirmed that classrooms rated more performance-oriented demonstrated significantly higher academic attainment than did less performance-oriented classrooms. Moreover, as individual classrooms became more performance-oriented over time, academic achievement accelerated.

Burton (1989b) demonstrated similar findings with collegiate swimmers whom he taught to be more performance-oriented through a five-month goal-setting training (GST) program. Burton (1989b) found that GST swimmers became more performance-oriented with training, and by the Big 10 Championships at the end of the season, GST swimmers demonstrated more positive competitive cognitions and greater performance improvement than did non-GST swimmers from another conference school who had not been exposed to any type of goal-setting training.

Finally Pierce and Burton (1991) conducted a seven-week GST program for female junior high school gymnasts. Gymnasts were categorized into goal-setting style groups by both clinical and empirical procedures (i.e., 84% agreement on group assignment between methods), and SO, FO, and PO gymnasts were compared on competitive cognitions and performance across five meets. Consistent with model predictions, not one of the FO gymnasts competed in even one event for all five meets, and most succeeded in avoiding social comparison by refusing to take part in weekly tryouts to win a spot in the competitive lineup. The 3×5 (GSS by Time) ANCOVA results revealed a significant group by time interaction for performance on each athlete's most important event that were consistent with model predictions, whereas similar analyses for competitive cognitions demonstrated trends in the predicted directions, but greater variability in scores prevented them from reaching statistical significance.

As predicted, both high- and low-ability PO gymnasts significantly improved their performance across meets, whereas somewhat surprisingly SO performers experience a slight decrease in their performance scores over the course of the season. Finally MANOVA results also revealed significant differences between GSS groups for their postseason GST program evaluation, with PO gymnasts rating the GST program more favorably than did SO or FO performers.

In the previous section of this chapter, a competitive goal-setting model that was constructed around the individual difference variable goal-setting style was presented, both generally to help further our understanding of goal-setting processes and specifically to account for why empirical goal-setting findings have been less consistent and robust in sport compared to work settings. However, another important concern identified in this review of the competitive goal-setting literature is the relative unpopularity of goal setting as a topic of sport psychology research. One plausible explanation for the limited interest in competitive goal-setting research is that many researchers may believe that goal setting is a straightforward motivational process that is already being used effectively in sport, even though no research has been conducted to confirm or refute this assumption. Just as goal commitment has been demonstrated to be a necessary and essential prerequisite of goal-setting effectiveness, it seems unlikely that goal setting will become a major topic for sport psychology research until researchers become convinced that athletes are not setting goals with the degree of consistency or effectiveness that has been documented in business and industry.

Moreover, little is known about the typical goal-setting patterns of athletes and how closely these practices correspond with contemporary goal-setting theory and research. Although these two rationales suggest that this type of applied research would make both an important and timely contribution to the goal-setting literature, a recent review of the sport and nonsport goal literatures confirmed that such research had been ignored by goal-setting researchers. Thus Burton, Weinberg, and Yukelson recently decided to conduct such a goal-setting practices study (Burton, Weinberg, & Yukelson, 1991). Even though data collection is still ongoing, these results appear to be sufficiently unique and important both to document the need for competitive goal-setting research and to pinpoint those areas where common goal-setting practices are most discrepant with contemporary goal-setting theory and research. Therefore, some preliminary findings from this study will be summarized next.

SURVEY OF GOAL-SETTING PRACTICES AMONG COLLEGIATE ATHLETES

The subsample reported here includes 204 collegiate athletes from eight sports, including: track and field, basketball, tennis, volleyball, swimming, soccer, rowing, and golf. The sample is comprised of 77 males and 127 females who range in age from 17 to 25 years, with a mean age of 19.71 years. Each subject completed the Goal-Setting in Sport Questionnaire, which includes five sections assessing: (a) demographic and background information, (b) frequency of goal-setting strategy usage, (c) effectiveness of goal-setting strategies, (d) goal commitment and effort, and (e) goal-setting preferences and options.

Are Competitive Goal-Setting Practices Optimally Effective?

Although 96% of the sample reported doing some type of goal setting one or more years, descriptive statistics shown in Tables 20–5 and 20–6 reveal that generally athletes set goals only moderately frequently and rated those goals as only moderately effective in helping them develop as athletes. These findings clearly don't appear to be as consistent or robust as results from the IO goal-setting literature and fail to support the assumption that most athletes are already effective goal setters. It is assumed that the reason for less frequent and effective use of goals in collegiate sport are related to specific strategies employed in implementing goal-setting programs. The results of our survey of the specific goal strategies used by collegiate athletes are presented below.

TABLE 20–5. Means and Standard Deviations of Frequency of Goal Setting Strategy Usage by Collegiate Athletes.

Strategy	M	SD
How often have you . . .		
1. set goals to improve sport performance?	6.25	1.88
2. set long-term goals to improve sport performance?	6.11	1.97
3. set short-term goals to improve sport performance?	6.31	1.90
4. set goals for what you want to accomplish in practice?	5.55	2.09
5. set goals for what you want to accomplish in competition?	7.32	1.62
6. set team goals?	6.10	2.26
7. set goals that focus on improving sport skills?	6.50	1.78
8. set goals that focus on improving sport strategies?	5.51	1.99
9. set goals that focus on improving physical conditioning?	6.72	1.94
10. set goals that focus on improving psychological skills?	5.86	2.16
11. set goals that focus on outcome and winning?	6.48	1.90
12. set goals that focus on your overall performance?	6.89	1.68
13. set goals to develop or maintain motivation?	5.92	1.83
14. set goals to develop or maintain self-confidence?	5.52	2.10
15. made outcome goals more important than performance goals?	5.45	2.12
16. set goals for what you want to accomplish outside sports?	6.57	1.92
17. set long-term sport goals that were too easy?	3.78	1.69
18. set long-term sport goals that were too difficult so you became stressed?	5.59	2.13
19. set short-term sport goals that were too easy?	3.84	1.67
20. set short-term sport goals that were too difficult so you became stressed?	5.27	2.11
21. evaluated the effectiveness of your goals?	4.66	2.05
22. found that attractive rewards increased your commitment to achieve your goals?	6.26	2.03
23. written down your goals?	4.90	2.54
24. publicly disclosed your goals?	4.09	2.37
25. developed plans for how to achieve your goals?	5.28	1.97

TABLE 20–6. Means and Standard Deviations of Effectiveness of Goal-Setting Strategies Employed by Collegiate Athletes.

Strategy	M	SD
In your athletic development, how effective has/ have . . .		
1. goal setting been overall?	6.16	1.82
2. your long-term goals been?	6.25	1.85
3. your short-term goals been?	6.18	1.85
4. your practice goals been?	5.84	1.78
5. your competitive goals been?	6.44	1.68
6. your team goals been?	5.73	2.03
7. your skill/technique goals been?	6.25	1.79
8. your strategy goals been?	5.62	1.84
9. your conditioning goals been?	6.77	1.81
10. your psychological skills goals been?	6.16	2.07
11. your outcome goals been in helping you perform well?	5.87	1.98
12. you been setting overall performance goals?	6.03	1.71
13. your goals been in helping you develop and maintain motivation?	5.94	1.86
14. goals been in helping you develop or maintain self-confidence?	5.80	1.94
15. your nonsport goals been in helping you improve the quality of your life?	6.41	1.91
16. easy long-term goals been in helping you perform well?	4.66	1.96
17. difficult long-term goals been in helping you perform well?	5.94	1.96
18. easy short-term goals been in helping you develop as an athlete?	4.44	1.84
19. difficult short-term goals been in helping you develop as an athlete?	5.67	1.87
20. evaluating your goals been?	5.61	1.88
21. rewards been in helping you increase your commitment to achieve your goals?	6.48	1.85
22. writing down your goals been?	5.08	2.48
23. publicly disclosing your goals been?	4.45	2.47
24. developing a plan for how to achieve your goals been?	5.70	2.21

Specific Goal-Setting Strategy Usage Results

Results of the specific goal-setting strategies used by collegiate athletes revealed six major findings of interest. First collegiate athletes reported setting competitive goals more frequently than practice goals, and they reported that competitive goals were more effective than practice goals in promoting their athletic development (see Tables 20–5 and 20–6). Although competitive goals are important in helping athletes perform their best, practice goals should be more important in helping athletes develop their skills to the fullest extent of their potential. The implication of these results is that goal-setting programs may need to do a better job of emphasizing the setting of practice as well as competitive goals.

Second, collegiate athletes reported setting overall performance, outcome, conditioning, and skill development goals more often than strategy or psychological skill development goals, or goals to develop and maintain motivation and self-confidence (see Tables 20–5 and 20–6). Moreover, it can be noted in Tables 20–5 and 20–6 that competitors reported that conditioning, skill development, psychological skills development, and overall performance goals were more effective than strategy, team, nonsport, and outcome goals or goals to develop and maintain motivation and self-confidence. These results suggest that certain types of goals, such as strategy and psychological skill development goals, may be underutilized in sport. Moreover, these results also suggest that athletes don't commonly employ goals directly to develop or maintain either motivation or self-confidence. Evidently, goal-setting programs need to provide performers with better information about how goals can increase psychological variables such as motivation and self-confidence as well as the potential effectiveness of goals for developing strategies, psychological skills, and other less frequently emphasized aspects of performance.

Third, athletes indicated that outcome goals are "sometimes" more important than performance goals (see Table 20–5). This finding supports CGS model predictions that certain situational factors tend to prompt athletes to develop SO and FO rather than PO goal-setting styles. Moreover, these results suggest that future research needs to identify what factors make performance-versus-outcome issues most salient before interventions can successfully help individuals consistently to adopt a PO goal-setting style.

Fourth, performers reported that they seldom set ST and LT goals that were too easy but sometimes set ST and LT goals that are too difficult and that prompt them to become stressed, even though difficult ST and LT goals were rated as more effective than easy ST and LT goals (see Tables 20–5 and 20–6). These findings again are consistent with CGS model predictions that SO and FO athletes may become stressed if goals become too difficult. Therefore, in order to make goals optimally effective, practitioners must make sure that SO and FO competitors keep their goals at a difficulty level that is comfortable for them.

Fifth, although athletes agreed that rewards increased commitment to achieve goals, they reported only "some-

TABLE 20–7. Means, Standard Deviations, and Analysis of Variance Results Assessing the Frequency of Goal-Setting Strategy Usage by Male and Female Collegiate Athletes.

Strategy	Males		Females		
	M	SD	M	SD	F
How often have you set . . .					
1. goals to improve sport performance?	5.95	2.03	6.45	1.76	3.36
2. long-term goals to improve sport performance?	5.92	2.17	6.24	1.82	1.21
3. short-term goals to improve sport performance?	5.82	2.14	6.63	1.65	8.91*
4. goals for what you want to accomplish in practice?	5.30	2.22	5.72	2.00	1.82
5. goals for what you want to accomplish in competition?	6.87	1.90	7.62	1.35	10.22*
6. team goals?	5.32	2.43	6.61	2.00	16.18*
7. goals that focus on improving sport skills?	6.25	2.09	6.67	1.54	2.54
8. goals that focus on improving sport strategies?	5.32	2.19	5.63	1.84	1.17
9. goals that focus on improving physical conditioning?	6.25	2.18	7.02	1.71	7.44*
10. goals that focus on improving psychological skills?	5.47	2.47	6.11	1.90	4.09*
11. goals that focus on outcome and winning?	6.50	1.98	6.47	1.86	.01
12. goals that focus on your overall performance?	6.65	2.07	7.04	1.35	2.62
13. goals to develop or maintain motivation?	5.51	1.98	6.18	1.69	6.26*
14. set goals to develop or maintain self-confidence?	5.25	2.22	5.69	2.02	2.05
15. made outcome goals more important than performance goals?	5.86	2.11	5.19	2.10	4.65*
16. set goals for what you want to accomplish outside sports?	6.62	2.03	6.53	1.85	0.10

TABLE 20–7. (Continued)

Strategy	Males		Females		
	M	SD	M	SD	F
How often have you set . . .					
17. set long-term sport goals that were too easy?	3.53	1.70	3.95	1.66	2.93
18. set long-term sport goals that were too difficult so you became stressed?	5.76	2.21	5.48	2.07	0.83
19. set short-term sport goals that were too easy?	3.92	1.88	3.79	1.53	0.30
20. set short-term sport goals that were too difficult so you became stressed?	5.49	2.26	5.13	2.00	1.34
21. evaluated the effectiveness of your goals?	4.80	2.19	4.56	1.96	0.62
22. found attractive rewards increased your commitment to achieve your goals?	6.22	2.08	6.28	2.00	0.04
23. written down your goals?	4.38	2.41	5.23	2.57	5.28*
24. publicly disclosed your goals?	4.11	2.36	4.08	2.37	0.01
25. developed plans for how to achieve your goals?	5.12	2.26	5.38	1.76	0.79

times" writing down goals, posting them, developing action plans, and evaluating their goals (see Tables 20–5 and 20–6). Interestingly developing action plans and evaluating goals were rated as only moderately effective strategies. Locke and Latham (1990) have demonstrated empirically the importance of action plans and evaluation to goal-setting success. Athletes' failure to use these important goal-setting strategies may partially explain why goals have been only moderately effective in sport.

Finally athletes also rank-ordered their preferred level of goal difficulty and the importance they placed on various types of goals. The goal difficulty preferences generally supported Locke and Latham's (1990) goal difficulty hypothesis. Athletes first preference was moderately difficult goals that are somewhat above the level at which performers thought they could perform, moderate goals equal to their current ability were second choice, very difficult goals that are substantially above the level at which athletes believed they could perform were third, and moderately easy and easy goals were fourth and fifth choices, respectively.

Goal importance preferences were also interesting.

TABLE 20–8. Means, Standard Deviations, and Analysis of Variance Results Assessing the Effectiveness of Goal-Setting Strategies Employed by Male and Female Collegiate Athletes.

Strategy	Males		Females		
	M	SD	M	SD	F
In your athletic development, how effective has/have . . .					
1. goal setting been overall?	5.71	2.01	6.45	1.65	7.76*
2. your long-term goals been?	5.90	2.04	6.47	1.71	4.53*
3. your short-term goals been?	5.55	1.96	6.55	1.67	14.34*
4. your practice goals been?	5.34	2.00	6.14	1.60	9.57*
5. your competitive goals been?	5.91	1.94	6.78	1.43	13.02*
6. your team goals been?	5.16	2.28	6.11	1.82	10.42*
7. your skill/technique goals been?	5.93	2.10	6.44	1.57	3.66*
8. your strategy goals been?	5.58	2.09	5.66	1.68	0.08
9. your conditioning goals been?	6.41	2.03	7.00	1.60	5.14*
10. your psychological skills goals been?	5.83	2.24	6.42	1.89	3.92*
11. your outcome goals been in helping you perform well?	5.71	2.26	5.93	1.81	0.58
12. you been setting overall performance goals?	5.70	1.99	6.27	1.47	5.32*
13. your goals been in helping you develop and maintain motivation?	5.34	1.87	6.34	1.77	14.05*
14. goals been in helping you develop or maintain self-confidence?	5.43	1.96	6.04	1.88	4.70*
15. your nonsport goals been in helping you improve the quality of your life?	6.29	2.06	6.54	1.78	0.80
16. easy long-term goals been in helping you perform well?	4.49	2.03	4.71	1.92	0.62
17. difficult long-term goals been in helping you perform well?	5.79	2.12	5.90	1.84	0.15

TABLE 20–8. (Continued)

Strategy	Males		Females		
	M	SD	M	SD	F
In your athletic development, how effective has/have . . .					
18. easy short-term goals been in helping you develop as an athlete?	4.29	1.88	4.50	1.83	0.63
19. difficult short-term goals been in helping you develop as an athlete?	5.62	1.96	5.67	1.83	0.04
20. evaluating your goals been?	5.34	1.97	5.71	1.87	1.68
21. rewards been in helping you increase your commitment to achieve your goals?	6.03	2.03	6.72	1.73	6.56*
22. writing down your goals been?	4.51	2.45	5.43	2.46	6.45*
23. publicly disclosing your goals been?	4.22	2.37	4.49	2.54	0.53
24. developing a plan for how to achieve your goals been?	5.45	2.44	5.79	2.08	1.10

Overall performance goals were rated as the most important tool by almost all subjects, followed by winning, skill development, and fun in second through fourth position. Conditioning, psychological skill development, strategy development, and social affiliation were the four bottom-rated goals in descending order of importance. It is interesting that although overall performance was rated as the most important goal, winning was rated higher than four specific types of performance goals.

Influence of Gender and Ability on Goal-Setting Strategy Usage

Multivariate analyses of variance were conducted to assess whether athletes of different genders or ability levels would demonstrate differential goal strategy usage.

Gender. Separate MANOVA analyses revealed significant differences in the frequency—$F(25, 167) = 2.80$; $p < 0.001$—and effectiveness—$F(24, 170) = 2.39$; $p < 0.001$—of the goal-setting strategies employed by males and females. Results confirmed that females reported setting goals more frequently than males, and they also reported goal setting was more effective in helping them to

TABLE 20–9. Means, Standard Deviations, and Analysis of Variance Results Assessing the Frequency of Goal-Setting Strategy Usage by High and Low Ability Collegiate Athletes.

Strategy	Low Ability		High Ability		
	M	SD	M	SD	F
How often have you . . .					
1. set goals to improve sport performance?	6.12	1.67	6.29	2.08	0.22
2. set long-term goals to improve sport performance?	6.06	1.95	6.17	2.06	0.09
3. set short-term goals to improve sport performance?	6.36	1.58	6.38	2.03	0.01
4. set goals for what you want to accomplish in practice?	5.94	1.97	5.55	2.18	1.07
5. set goals for what you want to accomplish in competition?	7.18	1.69	7.35	1.72	0.30
6. set team goals?	5.90	2.19	6.10	2.29	0.25
7. set goals that focus on improving sport skills?	6.20	1.62	6.74	1.82	2.90
8. set goals that focus on improving sport strategies?	5.06	1.99	5.87	1.91	5.27*
9. set goals that focus on improving physical conditioning?	6.88	1.75	6.58	2.11	0.68
10. set goals that focus on improving psychological skills?	6.18	1.98	5.68	2.04	1.90
11. set goals that focus on outcome and winning?	6.18	2.05	6.69	1.95	1.98
12. set goals that focus on your overall performance?	7.02	1.53	6.88	1.78	0.20
13. set goals to develop or maintain motivation?	6.00	1.67	5.90	1.80	0.11
14. set goals to develop or maintain self-confidence?	5.32	2.00	5.82	2.06	1.81

TABLE 20–9. (Continued)

Strategy	Low Ability		High Ability		
	M	SD	M	SD	F
15. made outcome goals more important than performance goals?	5.48	2.36	5.51	2.02	0.01
16. set goals for what you want to accomplish outside sports?	6.34	2.23	6.65	1.80	0.74
17. set long-term sport goals that were too easy?	3.36	1.83	3.97	1.69	3.77*
18. set long-term sport goals that were too difficult so you became stressed?	6.40	2.02	5.12	2.01	12.28*
19. set short-term sport goals that were too easy?	3.42	1.64	3.94	1.65	2.97
20. set short-term sport goals that were too difficult so you became stressed?	6.04	2.04	4.82	2.02	10.98*
21. evaluated the effectiveness of your goals?	4.34	2.41	4.95	1.87	2.54
22. found attractive rewards increased your commitment to achieve your goals?	6.06	1.97	6.38	2.11	0.72
23. written down your goals?	4.30	2.65	5.12	2.50	3.08
24. publicly disclosed your goals?	3.64	2.21	4.65	2.42	5.64*
25. developed plans for how to achieve your goals?	4.96	2.02	5.56	1.82	3.01

develop as athletes than did their male counterparts (see Tables 20–7 and 20–8). A comparison of means shown in Table 20–7 reveals that females reported more frequently setting short-term, competitive, team, conditioning, psychological skills development, and written goals than did their male counterparts. They also used goals more frequently to develop and maintain motivation than did male competitors. Males did report making outcome goals more important than performance goals more frequently than did females.

Additionally, as shown in Table 20–8, females rated goal setting as more effective than did males for long-term, short-term, practice, competitive, team, skill development, conditioning, psychological skill development, overall performance, and written goals. Females also found goals more effective for developing and maintaining motivation and self-confidence than did males. The implication of these gender results seems to be that a special effort needs to be made to help males understand and utilize the goal-setting process in sport.

Ability. In order to assess differences in goal-setting strategies for individuals who differ on ability, subjects were rank-ordered on their self-assessment of ability. The upper and lower one-third of the sample were separated and labeled "high" and "low" ability groups. Separate MANOVA analyses then were conducted on the frequency and effectiveness of their goal strategy usage. Results confirmed significant differences in the frequency—$F(25, 101) = 2.04$; $p < 0.01$—but not effectiveness—$F(24, 104) = 1.13$; $p > .33$—of the goal-setting strategies employed by high and low ability collegiate athletes.

Inspection of Table 20–9 reveals that high-ability performers reported setting strategy and long-term goals more frequently than low-ability competitors, and they also publicly disclosed their goals more often than low-ability teammates. Moreover, low-ability performers reported more frequently setting too difficult short-term and long-term goals that prompted them to become stressed than did their high-ability counterparts. These findings are consistent with the CGS model that predicts FO competitors will find goals stressful, thus typically hurting rather than helping performance.

In summary, the findings of this survey of contemporary goal-setting practices among collegiate athletes are consistent with the previous review of goal-setting research in sport that indicated that goal setting is an effective performance enhancement technique, but that it works somewhat less effectively than in work settings. Moreover, these results also suggest that many athletes may not fully understand the goal-setting process and thus fail to use or misuse goal-setting strategies, thus restricting the performance enhancement effects of goals. Therefore, goal setting is an important topic for sport psychology research, and the topics identified in this section seem to be important areas for future research.

SUMMARY

This chapter has first reviewed the general and competitive goal-setting literature and then offered several explanations for why goal setting in sport has not yielded as consistent or robust performance enhancement effects as setting goals in work settings. One of the primary factors identified to account for this discrepancy was the influence of individual difference variables that are predicted to exert an even more powerful impact on goal effectiveness when individuals are performing complex tasks at performance levels that are close to the limits of their ability. The individual difference variable, goal-setting style, was identified and a competitive goal-setting model specified that makes specific predictions for the attributes of each goal-setting style and their impact on goal responses and motivational consequences. A brief review of supporting research was provided, although the reader is urged to consult Burton (in press) for a more comprehensive review of empirical support for the CGS model.

Finally preliminary findings of a survey of contemporary goal-setting practices among collegiate athletes was presented that confirms two important points. First survey results confirm that much remains to be learned about how to maximize goal-setting effectiveness in sport. Second findings suggest that many athletes may not fully understand the goal-setting process and thus fail to employ effective goal-setting strategies or misuse others, limiting the performance enhancement effects of goals. The implication of these results are that greater efforts need to be made to understand the goal-setting process and how goals can be implemented most effectively. This knowledge about how the goal-setting process operates and the specific goal-setting strategies that should maximize performance then need to be passed along to coaches and athletes.

References

Ames, C. (1990, April). *Achievement goals and classroom structure: Developing a learning orientation in students.* Paper presented to the annual meeting of the American Educational Research Association, Boston.

Anderson, D. C., Crowell, C. R., Doman, M., & Howard, G. S. (1988). Performance posting, goal setting, and activity-contingent praise as applied to a university hockey team. *Journal of Applied Psychology, 73,* 87–95.

Bandura, A. (1986). *Social foundations of thought and action: A social-cognitive view.* Englewood Cliffs, NJ: Prentice-Hall.

Bandura, A., & Cervone, D. (1983). Self-evaluative and self-efficacy mechanisms governing the motivational effects of goal systems. *Journal of Personality and Social Psychology, 45,* 1017–1028.

Barnett, M. L., & Stanicek, J. A. (1979). Effects of goal-setting on achievement in archery. *Research Quarterly, 50,* 328–332.

Bavelas, J., & Lee, E. S. (1978). Effect of goal level on performance: A trade-off of quantity and quality. *Canadian Journal of Psychology, 32,* 219–240.

Burton, D. (1989a). The impact of goal specificity and task complexity on basketball skill development. *The Sport Psychologist, 3,* 34–47.

Burton, D. (1989b). Winning isn't everything: Examining the impact of performance goals on collegiate swimmers' cognitions and performance. *The Sport Psychologist, 3,* 105–132.

Burton, D. (1992). The Jekyll/Hyde nature of goals: Reconceptualizing goal setting in sport. In T. Horn (Ed.), *Advances in sport psychology*. Champaign, IL: Human Kinetics.

Burton, D., & Martens, R. (1986). Pinned by their own goals: An exploratory investigation into why young athletes drop out of wrestling. *Journal of Sport Psychology, 8,* 183–197.

Burton, D., Weinberg, R. S., & Yukelson, D. (1991). *Contemporary goal setting practices of collegiate athletes: Gender, sport type, and ability correlates.* Manuscript in preparation.

Burton, D., Williams-Rice, B. T., Phillips, D., & Daw, J. (1989, June). *The impact of goal difficulty and task complexity on basketball skill development.* Paper presented at the annual meeting of the North American Society for the Psychology of Sport and Physical Activity, Kent, OH.

Campbell, D. J., & Gingrich, K. F. (1986). The interactive effects of task complexity and participation on task performance: A field experiment. *Organizational Behavior and Human Decision Processes, 38,* 162–180.

Carroll, S. J. (1986). Management by objectives: Three decades of research and experience. In S. L. Rynes & G. T. Milkovich (Eds.), *Current issues in human resource management.* (pp. 295–312). Plano, TX: Business Publications.

Chidester, T. R., & Grigsby, W. C. (1984). A meta-analysis of the goal setting performance literature. In J. A. Pearce & R. B. Robinson, (Eds.), *Academy of management proceedings,* 202–206. Ada, OH: Academy of Management.

Crawford, K. S., White, M. A., & Magnusson, P. A. (1983). *The impact of goal setting and feedback on the productivity of navy industrial workers.* Navy Personnel Research and Development Center, NPRDC TR 83-4, San Diego.

DeCharms, R. (1976). *Enhancing motivation: Change in the classroom.* New York: Irvington.

Deci, E. L., & Ryan, R. M. (1985). *Intrinsic motivation and self-determination in human behavior.* New York: Plenum.

Diener, C. I., & Dweck, C. S. (1978). An analysis of learned helplessness: Continuous changes in performance, strategy, and achievement cognitions following failure. *Journal of Personality and Social Psychology, 36,* 451–462.

Dweck, C. S. (1975). The role of expectations and attributions in the alleviation of learned helplessness. *Journal of Personality and Social Psychology, 31,* 674–685.

Dweck, C. S. (1980). Learned helplessness in sport. In C. H. Nadeau, W. R. Halliwell, K. M. Newell, & G. C. Roberts (Eds.), *Psychology of motor behavior and sport, 1979* (pp. 139–149). Champaign, IL: Human Kinetics.

Earley, P. C. (1985). Influence of information, choice, and task complexity upon goal acceptance, performance, and personal goals. *Journal of Applied Psychology, 70,* 481–491.

Earley, P. C. (1986). Trust, perceived importance of praise and criticism, and work performance: An examination of feedback in the U.S. and England. *Journal of Management, 12,* 457–473.

Earley, P. C., & Kanfer, R. (1985). The influence of component participation and role models on goal acceptance, goal satisfaction, and performance. *Organizational Behavior and Human Decision Processes, 36,* 378–390.

Elliott, E. S., & Dweck, C. S. (1988). Goals: An approach to motivation and achievement. *Journal of Personality and Social Psychology, 54,* 5–12.

Erez, M. (1986). The congruence of goal setting strategies with socio-cultural values, and its effect on performance. *Journal of Management, 12,* 585–592.

Erez, M., & Arad, R. (1986). Participative goal setting: Social, motivational, and cognitive factors. *Journal of Applied Psychology, 71,* 591–597.

Erez, M., Earley, P. C., & Hulin, C. L. (1985). The impact of participation on goal acceptance and performance: A two-step model. *Academy of Management Journal, 28,* 50–66.

Erez, M., & Zidon, I. (1984). Effect of goal acceptance on the relationship of goal difficulty to performance. *Journal of Applied Psychology, 69,* 69–78.

Giannini, J. M., Weinberg, R. S., & Jackson, A. J. (1988). The effects of mastery, competitive, and cooperative goals on the performance of simple and complex basketball skills. *Journal of Sport and Exercise Psychology, 10,* 408–417.

Hall, H. K. (1990). *A social cognitive approach to goal setting: The mediating effects of achievement goals and perceived ability.* Unpublished doctoral dissertation, University of Illinois, Champaign.

Hall, H. K., & Byrne, A. T. J. (1988). Goal setting in sport: Clarifying recent anomalies. *Journal of Sport and Exercise Psychology, 10,* 184–198.

Hall, H. K., Weinberg, R. S., & Jackson, A. (1987). Effects of goal specificity, goal difficulty, and information feedback on endurance performance. *Journal of Sport Psychology, 9,* 43–54.

Hardy, C. J., & Latane, B. (1988). Social loafing in cheerleaders: Effects of team membership and competition. *Journal of Sport and Exercise Psychology, 10,* 109–114.

Harkins, S. G., & Petty, R. E. (1982). Effects of task difficulty and task uniqueness on social loafing. *Journal of Personality and Social Psychology, 43,* 1214–1229.

Harter, S. (1981). The development of competence motivation in the mastery of cognitive and physical skills: Is there still a place for joy? In G. C. Roberts & D. M. Landers (Eds.), *Psychology of motor behavior and sport, 1980* (pp. 3–29). Champaign, IL: Human Kinetics.

Hayes, S. C., Rosenfarb, I., Wulfert, E., Munt, E. D., Korn, Z., & Zettle, R. D. (1985). Self-reinforcement effects: An artifact of social standard setting? *Journal of Applied Behavior Analysis, 18,* 201–214.

Hollenbeck, J. R., Williams, C. R., & Klein, H. J. (1989). An empirical examination of the antecedents of commitment to difficult goals. *Journal of Applied Psychology, 74,* 18–23.

Hollingsworth, B. (1975). Effects of performance goals and anxiety on learning a gross motor task. *Research Quarterly, 46,* 162–168.

Huber, V. L. (1985). Effects of task difficulty, goal setting and strategy on performance of a heuristic task. *Journal of Applied Psychology, 70,* 492–504.

Hunter, J. E., & Schmidt, F. L. (1983). Quantifying the effects of psychological interventions on employee job performance and work force productivity. *American Psychologist, 38,* 473–478.

Ingham, A., Levinger, G., Graves, J., & Peckham, V. (1974). The Ringelmann effect: Studies of group size and group performance. *Journal of Experimental Social Psychology, 10,* 371–384.

Ivancevich, J. M. (1974). Changes in performance in a management by objectives program. *Administrative Science Quarterly, 19,* 563–574.

Jackson, J. M., & Williams, K. D. (1985). Social loafing on difficult tasks: Working collectively can improve performance. *Journal of Personality and Social Psychology, 49,* 937–942.

Kernan, M. C., & Lord, R. G. (1989). The effects of explicit goals and specific feedback on escalation processes. *Journal of Applied Social Psychology, 19,* 1125–1143.

Kerr, N. L., & Brunn, S. E. (1981). Ringelmann revisited: Alternative explanations for the social loafing effect. *Personality and Social Psychology Bulletin, 7,* 224–231.

Kirschenbaum, D. S. (1985). Proximity and specificity of planning: A position paper. *Cognitive Therapy and Research, 9,* 489–506.

Kondrasuk, J. N. (1981). Studies in MBO effectiveness. *Academy of Management Review, 6,* 419–430.

Latane, B. (1986). Responsibility and effort in organizations. In P. Goodman (Ed.), *Groups and organizations* (pp. 277–303). San Francisco: Jossey-Bass.

Latane, B., Williams, K. D., & Harkins, S. G. (1979). Many hands make light the work: The causes and consequences of social loafing. *Journal of Personality and Social Psychology, 37,* 823–832.

Latham, G. P., & Baldes, J. J. (1975). The "practical significance" of Locke's theory of goal setting. *Journal of Applied Psychology, 60,* 122–124.

Latham, G. P., Erez, M., & Locke, E. A. (1988). Resolving scientific disputes by the joint design of crucial experiments by the antagonists: Application to the Erez-Latham dispute regarding participation in goal setting. *Journal of Applied Psychology (Monograph), 73,* 753–772.

Latham, G. P., & Lee, T. W. (1986). Goal setting. In E. A. Locke (Ed.), *Generalizing from laboratory to field settings* (pp. 101–117). Lexington, MA: Lexington Books.

Latham, G. P., & Locke, E. A. (1979). Goal-setting: A motivational technique that works. *Organizational Dynamics, 8,* 68–80.

Latham, G. P., & Marshall, H. A. (1982). The effects of self-set, participatively set, and assigned goals on the performance of government employees. *Personnel Psychology, 35,* 399–404.

Latham, G. P., & Winters, D. W. (1989). *Separating the cognitive and motivational effects of participation on performance.* Unpublished manuscript, Graduate School of Business, University of Washington.

Latham, G. P., & Yukl, G. A. (1975). Assigned versus participative goal setting with educated and uneducated wood workers. *Journal of Applied Psychology, 60,* 299–302.

Locke, E. A. (1968). Toward a theory of task motivation and incentives. *Organizational Behavior and Human Performance, 3,* 157–189.

Locke, E. A. (1982). Relation of goal level to performance with a short work period and multiple goal levels. *Journal of Applied Psychology, 67,* 512–514.

Locke, E. A., Chah, D. O., Harrison, S., & Lustgarten, N. (1989). Separating the effects of goal specificity from goal level. *Organizational Behavior and Human Decision Processes, 43,* 270–287.

Locke, E. A., Frederick, E., Lee, C., & Bobko, P. (1984). Effect of self-efficacy, goals, and task strategies on task performance. *Journal of Applied Psychology, 69,* 241–251.

Locke, E. A., & Latham, G. P. (1985). The application of goal setting to sports. *Journal of Sport Psychology, 7,* 205–222.

Locke, E. A., & Latham, G. P. (1990). *A theory of goal setting and task performance.* Englewood Cliffs, NJ: Prentice-Hall.

Locke, E. A., & Shaw, K. N. (1984). Atkinson's inverse-U curve and the missing cognitive variables. *Psychological Reports, 55,* 403–412.

Locke, E. A., Shaw, K. N., Saari, L. M., & Latham, G. P. (1981). Goal setting and task performance: 1969–1980. *Psychological Bulletin, 90,* 125–152.

Maehr, M. L. (1984). Meaning and motivation. In R. Ames & C. Ames (Eds.), *Research on motivation in education (Vol. 1)* (115–144). New York: Academic Press.

Maehr, M. L., & Braskamp, L. (1986). *The motivation factor: A theory of personal investment.* Lexington, MA: Heath.

Maehr, M., & Nicholls, J. G. (1980). Culture and achievement motivation: A second look. In N. Warren (Ed.), *Studies in cross-cultural psychology* (pp. 221–267). New York: Academic Press.

Martens, R., Burton, D., Vealey, R. S., Bump, L. A., & Smith, D. E. (1990). Competitive state anxiety inventory–2 (CSAI-2). In R. Martens, R. S. Vealey, & D. Burton, *Competitive anxiety in sport* (pp. 117–190). Champaign, IL: Human Kinetics.

Matsui, T., Kakuyama, T., & Onglatco, M. L. (1987). Effects of goals and feedback on performance in groups. *Journal of Applied Psychology, 72,* 407–415.

Matsui, T., Okada, A., & Mizuguchi, R. (1981). Expectancy theory prediction of the goal theory postulate "the harder the goals, the higher the performance." *Journal of Applied Psychology, 66,* 54–58.

Mento, A. J., & Locke, E. A. (1989). *Studies of the relationship between goals and valences.* Manuscript in preparation.

Mento, A. J., Steel, R. P., & Karren, R. J. (1987). A meta-analytic study of the effects of goal setting on task performance: 1966–1984. *Organizational Behavior and Human Decision Processes, 39,* 52–83.

Miller, J. T., & McAuley, E. (1987). Effects of a goal-setting training program on basketball free-throw self-efficacy and performance. *The Sport Psychologist, 1,* 103–113.

Mitchell, T. R., Rothman, M., & Liden, R. C. (1985). Effects of normative information on task performance. *Journal of Applied Psychology, 70,* 48–55.

Nicholls, J. G. (1984a). Conceptions of ability and achievement motivation. In R. Ames & C. Ames (Eds.), *Research on motivation in education: Student motivation, Vol. 1* (pp. 39–73). New York: Academic Press.

Nicholls, J. G. (1984b). Achievement motivation: Conceptions of ability, subjective experience, task choice, and performance. *Psychological Review, 91,* 328–346.

Oldham, G. R. (1975). The impact of supervisory characteristics on goal acceptance. *Academy of Management Journal, 18,* 461–475.

Pierce, B. E., & Burton, D. (1991). *Effects of goal setting styles on the competitive cognitions and performance of female junior high school gymnasts.* Manuscript submitted for publication.

Pritchard, R. D., Bigby, D. G., Beiting, M., Coverdale, S., & Morgan, C. (1981). *Enhancing productivity through feedback and goal setting.* Air Force Human Resources Laboratory, Brooks Air Force Base, TX. AFHRL-TR-81-7.

Rakestraw, T. L., & Weiss, H. M. (1981). The interaction of social influences and task experience on goals, performance, and performance satisfaction. *Organizational Behavior and Human Performance, 27,* 326–344.

Riedel, J. A., Nebeker, D. M., & Cooper, B. L. (1988). The influence of monetary incentives on goal choice, goal commitment, and task performance. *Organizational Behavior and Human Decision Processes, 42,* 155–180.

Rodgers, R. C., & Hunter, J. E. (1989). *The impact of management by objectives on organizational productivity.* Unpublished manuscript, School of Public Administration, University of Kentucky.

Shalley, C. E., Oldham, G. R., & Porac, J. F. (1987). Effects of goal difficulty, and expected external evaluation on intrinsic motivation: A laboratory study. *Academy of Management Journal, 28,* 628–640.

Terborg, J. R. (1976). The motivational components of goal setting. *Journal of Applied Psychology, 61,* 613–621.

Tubbs, M. E. (1986). Goal Setting: A meta-analytic examination of the empirical evidence. *Journal of Applied Psychology, 71,* 474–483.

Weinberg, R. S., Bruya, L. D., & Jackson, A. (1985). The effects of goal proximity and goal specificity on endurance performance. *Journal of Sport Psychology, 7,* 296–305.

Weinberg, R. S., Bruya, L. D., Jackson, A., & Garland, H. (1986). Goal difficulty and endurance performance: A challenge to the goal attainability assumption. *Journal of Sport Behavior, 10,* 82–92.

Weinberg, R. S., Bruya, L. D., Longino, J., and Jackson, A. (1988). Effect of goal proximity and specificity on endurance performance of primary-grade children. *Journal of Sport and Exercise Psychology, 10,* 81–91.

Williams, K. D., Harkins, S. G., & Latane, B. (1981). Identifiability as a deterrent to social loafing: Two cheering experiments. *Journal of Personality and Social Psychology, 40,* 303–311.

Wood, R. E. (1986). Task complexity: Definition of the construct. *Organizational Behavior and Human Decision Processes, 37,* 60–82.

Wood, R. E., Mento, A. J., & Locke, E. A. (1987). Task complexity as a moderator of goal effects: A meta-analysis. *Journal of Applied Psychology, 72,* 416–425.

Yin, Z., Simons, J., & Callaghan, J. (1989, September). *The application of goal-setting in physical activity: A field study.* Paper presented at the meeting of the Association for the Advancement of Applied Sport Psychology, Seattle, WA.

·21·

IMAGERY

Richard Suinn

INTRODUCTION; GENERAL SPORT PSYCHOLOGY THEORIES

Peak performance enhancement for competitive athletes now has a modern definition. In the past, psychological enhancement techniques for the layperson primarily reflected visions of "psyching up" or "psyching out." "Psyching up" an athlete involved attempts to improve performance via coach-initiated or self-intiated increases in motivational level, or perhaps arousal level. A coach might employ a range of strategies to increase intensity in the athlete, sometimes reminiscent of the old Knute Rockne emotional pep talks to "win one for the Gipper," or through calling attention to derogatory quotations attributed to opponents.

While "psyching up" seems to be a precompetition exercise, "psyching out" is viewed as employed during competition. The athlete seeks to gain advantage over the opponent by use of ploys to overwhelm the opponent's psyche, thereby gaining a psychological edge. Competitors who seek, by their actions, to intimidate their opponents are trying to use "psyching out" strategies. The boxer Muhammed Ali, who predicted the knockout round, or the Austrian Olympic ski racer Franz Klammer who casually permitted rumors to circulate that he was using a specially engineered ski that was unbeatable, or even the weekend golfer who deviously states, "It must be hard for you to hit a decent stroke the way you hold your club," are all practicing psyching-out techniques.

This chapter, however, identifies the modern psychological approaches to performance enhancement, derived from modern psychological theory and techniques. Although self-regulation and arousal/activation goals are still employed, such goals are achieved through skill training with lasting effects, as compared to the transitory influences of the older psyching-up approaches. Sport psychology has also expanded its scope from the narrower emphasis on motivation, personality studies, and work on

emotions, to a broader interest in psychological skills training. Several papers demonstrate these broader approaches to sport performance theory. Suinn (1980) begins with athletic performance itself, and constructs a conceptual model that links performance to psychological training goals (Figure 21–1). The model is equally applicable to novices, recreational athletes of modest performance levels, and competitors of world class levels.

With this model, performance is viewed as the product of aptitude interacting with skill acquisition. Skill acquisition is analyzed into three components: strengthening the correct responses, extinguishing or controlling incorrect responses, and transferring correct responses to game conditions. The three components are in turn divided into subgoals; for instance, correct responses may involve the simple motor response of hitting the ball for a beginner, or the more intricate moves of a new routine for a gymnast, diver, or figure skater. Some of the subgoals are motor, while others might have cognitive foundations. Suinn then discusses the relationship between the types of training that are appropriate for each of the goals or subgoals. For the subgoal of increasing preparatory-arousal responses, autogenic training or biofeedback might be used. For control of incorrect responses such as conditioned emotionality, applied relaxation or anxiety management training are appropriate (Suinn, 1990). Imagery rehearsal techniques, the topic of this chapter, are particularly useful for achieving a variety of goals, including transfer to competitive conditions, enhancement of specific correct responses, and in some cases, elimination of anxiety or negative thoughts.

Another theory has been described by Mahoney (1977). From a cognitive framework, he emphasizes the role of cognitive skills in athletic performance. From his own work and the experiences of others, he identifies four categories of cognitive skills: self-efficacy, arousal regulation, attentional focus, and imagery. Mahoney does not intend to provide a complete coverage of the psychological dimensions in performance, but instead aims at highlighting what he

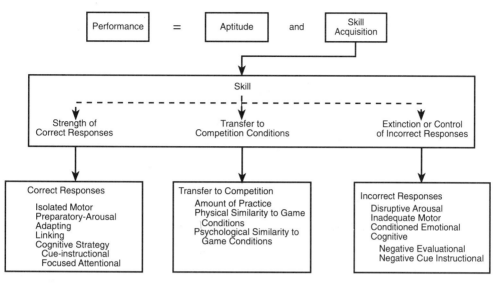

FIGURE 21–1. Factors affecting sports performance.
Source: R. M. Suinn, Psychology and sports performance: Principles and applications. In
R. M. Suinn (Ed.), *Psychology in Sports: Methods and Applications*. New York: Macmillan.

considers to be a much overlooked set of parameters. In common with Suinn, he gives imagery a significant role as one of these parameters. Mahoney suggests that successful use of imagery would include alternating between imagery rehearsal and physical practice, reliance upon proprioceptive and phenomenological or internal imagery perspectives, emphasis on coping imagery, and use of relaxation prior to imagery practice.

Both Mahoney and Suinn have strong foundations in behavioral psychology and often derive their sport psychology conceptualizations and practice from this field. In fact, Suinn has demonstrated that principles of behavior confirmed by research on human clinical problems are also duplicated by research applying the same principles to sport performance (Suinn, 1989). For instance, the greater efficacy of using a coping model for reduction of phobias (Kazdin, 1974) was also replicated for increasing muscle endurance performance at a motor task (Gould & Weiss, 1981). Also, the imagery rehearsal procedure developed by Suinn, *visual-motor behavior rehearsal,* evolved out of his prior modifications of desensitization therapy.

THEORIES OF IMAGERY REHEARSAL MECHANISMS

Theories within sport psychology have also addressed attempts to understand the mechanisms whereby imagery rehearsal enhances motor performance. At least four theoretical formulations have been discussed and studied: (1) the psychoneuromuscular theory or ideo-motor approach (Carpenter, 1894; Jacobson, 1931), (2) the symbolic learning theory or cognitive approach (Morrisett, 1956; Sackett, 1934), (3) the attentional/arousal theory or preparatory set approach (Schmidt, 1982; Vealey, 1987), and (4) the bioinformational theory or information-processing approach (Lang, 1977, 1979, 1985).

Psychoneuromuscular Theory

Briefly, the psychoneuromuscular theory holds that imagery rehearsal duplicates the actual motor pattern being rehearsed, although the neuromuscular innervations with imagery are of a smaller magnitude than in physical practice. Although minute, the neuromuscular activation from imagery is said to be sufficient to enhance the motor schema in the motor cortex or the priming of the corresponding muscle movement nodes (Hale, 1981; MacKay, 1981; Suinn, 1987). This conceptualization and variants have also been referred to as the theory of muscle memory, the muscle potential hypothesis, or the neuromuscular feedback theory (Harris & Robinson, 1986; Mackay, 1981; Vealey, 1987). In the simplest version, the view is that the motor-efferent patterns generated in imagery rehearsal are identical with those achieved for learning or correction or enhancement of performance through physical practice. There do appear to be various forms of evidence for the premise that imagery rehearsal is accompanied by small but measurable neuromuscular activations consistent with the task imagined (Anderson, 1981; Harris & Robinson, 1986; Jacobsen, 1930; Jowdy & Harris, 1990; Shick, 1970; Schramm, 1967; Suinn, 1980).

Jacobson (1930), Schramm (1967), and Suinn (1976) have observed electromyographic (EMG) muscle activity during imagery which appears to mirror the precise motor movements of the task. However, controlled research has been sparse. In a meta-analysis of the literature, Feltz and Landers (1983) repeat the common hypothesis of others that "It is doubtful that mental practice effects are produced by low-gain innervation of muscles that will be used during actual performance" (p. 48). However, their own conclusion is that too few studies are available to test the hypothesis. In their review, "The studies that have examined the psychoneuromuscular theory could not be included in (our) meta-analysis because very few quantitive studies existed and they did not include motor performance measures as a dependent variable" (p. 49).

Since the 1983 meta-analysis of Feltz and Landers, a few new reports have been published. Harris and Robinson (1986) obtained EMG data from the middle deltoid muscles of each arm. Subjects were karate students with different levels of achievement. Imagery rehearsal was developed through audiotaped relaxation and imagery instructions. The imagery task involved each athlete's performing 5 right lateral arm raises, holding each for 10 seconds. Results indicated that

Significantly greater increases in the right deltoid activity were observed during imagery. . . . This finding suggest[s] that muscular innervation during imagery was specific to the muscle [normally] . . . activated in overtly executing the task. Despite the fact that paired muscles were monitored, the one in the limb used in the imaginary arm lift displayed much greater efference. (p. 109)

Jowdy and Harris (1990) were interested in replicating the Harris and Robinson finding that advanced skill subjects showed greater localized muscle innervation during imagery than beginners. Instead of using karate students, they compared members of a juggling club with volunteers who had no prior experience in juggling. Again relaxation and imagery were combined with instructions via audiotape. The task involved visualizing juggling three tennis balls; EMG measures were of the biceps brachii of one arm. Although there were no significant differences across skill levels, results did confirm significant increases in muscle activity during imagery rehearsal. The failure to find a relationship between skill level and muscle innervation led the authors to express some doubt about the validity of the psychoneuromuscular theory. Based on their interpretation of the theory, they expected to obtain higher innervation from the skilled subjects. However, they also noted that the skilled jugglers tended to favor use of wrist flexors over bicep muscles; hence the lack of differences across skill levels might have reflected a research design and measurement deficiency. Moreover, during interviews, the authors discovered differences among the skilled subjects in their ability to develop imagery. And, "Corresponding to their inability or difficulty (in imagery, some skilled) subjects did elicit a lesser amount of muscular activity than those who had reported the ability to feel the movement (of juggling)" (p. 197).

The findings of Harris and Robinson as well as Jowdy and Harris that muscle innervations did occur during imagery are consistent with an earlier report by Hale (1982). Subjects were weightlifters instructed with relaxation and imagery to imagine themselves lifting a 25-pound dumbbell. Imagery rehearsal included both an internal perspective and an external imagery perspective. EMG measurement involved the dominant biceps brachii muscle. Results indicated significant biceps activity compared to baseline for imagery rehearsal using an internal perspective.

Symbolic Learning Theory

The symbolic learning theory hypothesizes that imagery rehearsal gains are more often due to the opportunity to practice the symbolic elements of a motor task, than to muscle activation itself. By this conceptualization, the learning or performance enhancement which occurs relates to cognitive learning. For instance, the cognitive activities might include associating images or subvocal responses that will cue off temporal or spatial elements of a skill, or the individual "can think about what kinds of things might be tried, the consequences of each action can be predicted . . . and the learner can perhaps rule out the inappropriate course of action" (Schmidt, 1982, p. 520). An inference from this theory is that imagery practice would have greater effects in enhancing performance involving high levels of cognitive requirements, such as during spatial tasks, tasks involving strategic planning, or sequential learning tasks.

Prior research appears to offer some support for the greater gains from mental practice on tasks with cognitive components than on tasks that are more purely motor, for instance, on maze-learning tasks versus stabilometer tasks (Minas, 1978; Morrisett, 1956; Ryan & Simons, 1981; Wrisberg & Ragsdale, 1979). Feltz and Landers categorized studies which they reviewed as cognitive or motor, and computed the effects size in their meta-analysis research. They found that both types of tasks showed large effect sizes, although the cognitive tasks effect sizes were somewhat higher (findings for cognitive tasks went as high as 3.31, with motor tasks reaching effect sizes as high as 2.56).

An indirect test of the the symbolic learning theory was conducted by Hall and Erffmeyer (1983) in comparing imagery practice with videotape modeling versus imagery practice without modeling. In behavioral psychology, symbolic learning might be viewed as akin to vicarious learning or observational learning or modeling (Bandura, 1969; Bandura & Jefferies, 1973). Bandura has indicated that "One of the fundamental means by which new modes of behavior are acquired and existing patterns are modified entails modeling and vicarious processes. Indeed, research . . . demonstrates that virtually all learning phenomena resulting from direct experiences can occur on a vicarious basis . . ." (p. 118). In discussing explanations of the mechanisms for observational learning, Bandura identifies cognitive processes: "When a person observes a model's behavior, but otherwise performs no overt responses, he can acquire the modeled responses while they are occurring only in cognitive, representational forms" (p. 133), and further, "[a] major component of modeling phenomena involves the utilization of symbolic representations of modeled patterns in the form of imaginal and verbal contents to guide overt performances" (p. 141).

Hence Bandura accepts the element of symbolic learning in his understanding of observational learning. In testing his theory of observational learning, Bandura has used videotapes as the medium to change behaviors. If we extrapolate from Bandura's theory and research, videotapes can be used as a way of testing the symbolic learning hypothesis of imagery rehearsal. If imagery rehearsal works because it involves symbolic learning or acquisition of cognitive representations, and if videotape modeling also leads to observational learning, then combining the two should produce enhanced effects beyond that achieved by imagery rehearsal alone. Hall and Erffmeyer (1983) showed exactly that. Ten members of a college basketball team were randomly assigned to either a relaxation/imagery group or a relaxation/imagery/videotaped modeling group. In the latter, the subjects observed a videotape of a female basketball player executing 10 consecutive foul shots with perfect form. Subjects then closed their eyes to imagine themselves completing the "perfect" foul shot. Results indicated a significant improvement in foul shooting percentages of the imagery/modeling group compared to the imagery without modeling group. Given the small sample size, and no further analysis of differences in the experience and skill levels of the subjects, these results are interesting, but can only be considered suggestive.

However, support for Hall and Erffmeyer was reported by Gray (1990) with 24 male students in a beginning class in racquetball. As with Hall and Erffmeyer, imagery rehearsal paired with videotape modeling produced more improvements than imagery rehearsal without the modeling. However, the actual level of the improvement was small, although statistically significant. Also, results were significant only for the forehand drive and not for the backhand drive. Gray and Fernandez (in press) also replicated the Hall and Erffmeyer findings with free-throw percentages of varsity basketball players.

The interviews conducted by Jowdy and Harris following their study also offers some indirect support for symbolic elements in imagery rehearsal. They report, "Many subjects did refer to the fact that they created the image of a particular action and then tried to duplicate the imagined action." As one subject said of this phenomenon, "It makes me want to follow the imagery. It's like copying the image so that I maybe can do it without having done the activity" (p. 197). Such a description is certainly congruent with a cognitive learning paradigm for imagery rehearsal.

Arousal or Activation Theory

The arousal or activation theory of imagery rehearsal suggests that the role of imagery rehearsal is in arriving at a preparatory set which enhances learning or performance. More specifically, the imagery establishes a level of arousal or physiological activation that is optimal for the performance in question. Schmidt (1982) observes that the "performer is merely preparing for the action, setting the arousal level, and generally getting prepared for good per-

formance" (p. 520). This approach integrates the notion of optimal arousal levels and self-regulation of activation levels as a primary ingredient for the impact of imagery rehearsal. Feltz and Landers suggest that the arousal serves to "prime" the muscles and that "this type of cognitive rehearsal (imagery) can act to lower the sensory threshold of the performer and facilitate performance . . ." (p. 50). Another perspective on the arousal theory considers the arousal as influencing attention as well. (See Chapter 6 by Abernathy in this *Handbook* for a discussion of attention and arousal.) From this view, the theory is really a theory of attention and arousal. In this elaboration, imagery rehearsal focuses attention on task-relevant thoughts and away from task-irrelevant cues which could disrupt performance. (For more detailed discussion of the role of preparatory-arousal responses, attentional focus responses, and disruptive responses on sport performance, see the chapter by Suinn in Suinn, R. M. (Ed.), *Psychology in sports: Methods and applications* [1980].)

Feltz and Riessinger (1990) compared the influence of "in vivo emotive imagery" plus feedback versus feedback alone on muscle endurance and self-efficacy tasks. The endurance task involved sitting with legs bent and back against the wall, the so-called "skiers' sit" or "phantom-chair task." Subjects were 120 students each competing in endurance with another student who was actually a confederate. Efficacy was controlled through a preliminary "competition" on a Cybex isokinetic test, on which the confederate "lifted" 225 foot-pounds and the subject was told that he/she managed 150 foot-pounds. The emotive imagery involved generating "images that were assumed to elicit feelings of competence and being psyched-up . . . (and) holding out longer than the opponent and being successful" (p. 135). In the feedback condition, subjects were provided with immediate feedback on the duration of their phantom chair performance, for each of two trials. Results indicated that the imagery/feedback group had longer performance times than the feedback-only group on the first trial but not on the second trial. For efficacy, the imagery/feedback group showed higher efficacy than the feedback-only group. The authors concluded that "Our results . . . suggest that in vivo emotive imagery is effective in increasing one's sense of perceived efficacy to endure muscular isometric performance and, to a lesser extent, one's actual performance time" (p. 140). This study can be considered as an indirect test of the attentional/arousal theory of imagery since prior work on emotive imagery suggest that emotive imagery has effects through diverting attention. Further, the content of the imagery was assumed to precipitate emotional elements, such as feelings of competence and success and being psyched up, and hence involved arousal.

Murphy, Woolfolk, and Budney (1988) actually instructed their subjects to develop imagery that evoked emotions, and presumably arousal. Three types of imagery content were used: anger and fear as emotional content, and relaxation as nonemotional content. The motor task involved a hand grip dynamometer; subjects were 24 male volunteers. Subjects were given the dynamometer, instructed to stand and to visualize the images, and then "Upon feeling highly involved, they were to squeeze the dynamometer as hard as they could" (p. 337). Results failed to support the hypothesis that preparatory arousal in imagery content would increase strength performance. Neither anger nor fear conditions led to increasing strength performance above that achieved in the pretest, despite the fact that the imagery did lead to increases in emotional arousal. Interestingly, 75% of the subjects believed that their best performance was associated with anger arousal, when in fact this was true for only 28% of the subjects.

Machlus and O'Brien (1988) conducted a study involving members of six high school track teams. Athletes were randomly assigned to one of six conditions: relaxation, behavioral imagery, relaxation plus behavioral imagery with arousal content, relaxation plus behavioral imagery without arousal content, and attention-placebo. Behavioral imagery content focused on the motor movements, such as "You hear the gun. Your arms move into an alternating back-and-forth motion." Behavioral imagery that included arousal added emotion-toned words, such as "You blast off the blocks as if they were red hot. Your arms move into a vigorous back-and-forth motion." Measures include comparison with baseline times for events. Because of the small sample, given the various numbers of events, the two behavioral imagery groups were combined as were the two arousal imagery groups. Results indicated that the behavioral imagery subjects were the only ones to improve on their competitive times in all of their events.

In contrast, the arousal imagery subjects were able to improve their times in 75% of their events, contrasted with the relaxation group, which improved in 86% of their events. Also, the arousal imagery subjects showed decreases in their performance in 25% of their events, compared with performance decreases by the relaxation group in 14%. This field study appears to suggest that arousal content might not be a useful element in imagery rehearsal training. Both the Murphy et al. and the Machlus and O'Brien studies seem to fail to support the interpretation that imagery rehearsal works best through the mechanism of arousal or activation, since the introduction of arousal in imagery content failed to help performance. On the other hand, another possible interpretation is that both studies created arousal which, when added to the arousal already inherent in imagery rehearsal, increased the activation level beyond an optimal level.

Lee (1990) suggested that the Murphy et al. research relied upon negative emotional states, and hypothesized that positive mood might be more valuable. She also deduced that "If imagery has an effect on performance by inducing a more positive attitude or mood, then the content of the image should not be important. On the other hand, if imagery works through direct imaginal practice of the task to be performed, then the content of the image is critical . . ." (p. 67). She therefore conducted two experiments. In the first, 52 male students were instructed to do as many bent-knee situps as they could in 30 seconds. After a 5-minute recovery, the subjects were then provided with imagery instructions involving becoming "psyched up." One group used imagery relevant to the task, that is, they imagined performing well on the situps. The other group used irrelevant imagery, retrieving memories of any situation in which a positive mood had been experienced. A third group was given instructions involving counting backward, as a control group.

Results indicated that the relevant image group performed significantly better than the other two groups, with the irrelevant image and control group performance equivalent to one another. Lee concluded that the imagery effects operated "to prepare one specifically for a particular task and does not operate simply through a general effect on mood or confidence" (p. 70). In the second study, 142 males faced the same conditions as in the first experiment, except that the Profile of Mood States (POMS) scale was used to directly assess the moods being experienced during the imagery. Results replicated those of the first experiment, with the relevant imagery group showing a 13.9% percent improvement over baseline, compared to 7.7% for the irrelevant imagery group and 3.7% for the control group. Scores from the POMS were entered into a stepwise regression analysis and failed to contribute anything toward predicting situp performance. The author concluded that ". . . it is clear from the results of these two experiments that the content of the image is important and that imagery effects do not occur by affecting mood state" (p. 72).

Bioinformational or Information Processing Theory

The bioinformational or information processing theory approach examines mental imagery in terms of the brain's information processing mechanisms. Lang's (1989) viewpoint presumes that imagery in the brain is organized in precise ways, involving a finite set of propositions about relationships and descriptions of stimulus characteristics, and response characteristics. Imagery involves the activation of a network of such coded propositions stored in long-term memory. Two principles describe stimulus propositions and response propositions. Stimulus propositions contain descriptors about stimuli—for example, the texture and feel of a basketball in one's hand, or the color and weight of a dumbbell being lifted. The response propositions involve assertions about behavior, including verbal aspects, motor aspects, or physiological aspects, such as the experiences of "tensing a muscle."

This information network serves as a prototype for behavior. This prototype can be processed by internally generating prototype-matching information, such as through imagery rehearsal. Processing occurs when a critical number of propositions are accessed. For instance, imagery rehearsal of diving off the starting blocks involves activating the stimulus propositions which would include descriptors of the sounds of the starting gun and the temperature of the water. Response propositions would include muscular changes in the legs pushing off, the arms as they extend, as well as cardiovascular activation. By this theory, for imagery rehearsal to influence athletic performance, response propositions must be activated along with the stimulus propositions. Such response propositions represent the prototype for the overt behavior to be influenced. Once the response prototype is activated, then it can be subjected to revision or alteration, leading to improvements in overt performance.

A related theory by Carroll and Bandura (1982) hypothesizes that motor learning occurs through the symbolic coding and transformation of the information and storage centrally. The subject then attempts to perform the skill, comparing this performance against the internally stored model, making judgments and correcting errors in further replication efforts. This "conception-matching" process is completed at the point that the performance feedback matches the internally coded model. By this explanation, the coding may rely upon either verbal coding or by visual imagery coding (Jeffrey, 1976). Mental practice thereby becomes a method for enhancing coding. Finally, Suinn (1987a) has suggested that imagery rehearsal might involve central nervous system processing with results similar to storage of a computer program, which is later elicited to produce performance.

Mainly working from research on emotions such as anxiety and fear, Lang (1989) has offered a variety of evidence for his theory (Lang, 1989; Levin, Cook, & Lang, 1982; Lang, Levin, Miller, & Kozak, 1983; Lang, Kozak, Miller, Levin, & McLean, 1980). In such studies, psychophysiological anxiety responses are found when the appropriate stimulus or response propositions are evoked, as predicted by the theory. Hecker and Kaczor (1988) applied the same hypothesizing to imagery with athletes as subjects. Women on a college varsity softball team were presented with four imagery scenes: a neutral, relaxed scene; an action scene, of weightlifting with exertion; an athletic anxiety scene, of being under pressure in the batter's box; and a fear scene, of being in a jet plane that is exploding. According to bioinformational theory, the reality-based anxiety scene and action scenes should produce heart rate responses. This is because subjects are able to reproduce the stimulus and response propositions of the familiar events. On the other hand, the fantasy fear scene would not be expected to produce such strong heart rate changes.

Results confirmed a higher heart rate for the reality-based anxiety and action scenes, in comparison with that during fear imagery. The action imagery heart rate was also significantly higher than that during the neutral scene, but no significant differences were found between the anxiety scene heart rate and the neutral scene heart rate (although the difference was in the predicted direction). The authors concluded that they demonstrated some support for the bioinformational theory, since heart rate activation occurred with scenes for which there was familiarity and hence activation was possible of the response prototype. Also, the failure of the fear scene supported the theory that would indicate no activation where the prototype was absent in long-term memory storage. Finally, they indicated that the increase of heart rate during the neutral scene was

inconsistent with the theory, since the scene did not include cardiovascular response propositions.

Hale (1982) sought to test the bioinformational theory by inferring that external imagery should be composed of ocular activity response propositions, while internal imagery should contain predominantly muscular activity response propositions, such as kinesthetic imagery. In the study cited earlier, Hale had subjects use either an internal or an external perspective in their imagery, the former involving imagining actually lifting the dumbbell, the latter involving "seeing yourself" lifting the dumbbell. Although the results were in the predicted direction, the data on ocular activity did not show significant differences across the two approaches. On the other hand, the use of an internal imagery perspective did lead to greater biceps muscle innervation than the external imagery perspective, thereby confirming the hypothesis that the internal perspective would generate more internal muscle response propositions.

The bioinformational approach would also suggest that improving response processing during imagery should facilitate improvement in task performance (Hecker & Kaczor, 1988). Since an internal imagery perspective is more likely to precipitate more elements of the response prototype, then internal imagery might be expected to aid response processing, and in turn promote performance improvement. Some reports on elite athletes suggest greater use of internal imagery. Mahoney and Avener (1977) surveyed Olympic gymnasts and concluded that successful gymnasts often reported reliance upon internal imagery. The "clock test" illustrates the difference between internal versus external imagery perspectives. The athlete is asked to close his/her eyes while the face of a clock is traced on the forehead. The clock hands are traced to read 3 o'clock from the perspective of an external observer. When asked to report the time, the response of "3 o'clock" would represent an external imagery perspective, while a response of "9 o'clock" would suggest an internal imagery perspective.

Doyle and Landers (1980) revised the Mahoney-Avener questionnaire and administered it to 184 rifle and pistol shooters, representing an elite and a subelite group. The elite shooters had participated in the U.S. International Shooting Championships in 1979, while the subelites were state-and junior-level champions who attended a Junior Olympic Shooting Camp at the Olympic Training Center. The authors discovered that the use of mental imagery and level of self-confidence were factors discriminating between the two groups. They also reported that the elite rifle shooters used predominantly internal imagery, whereas the subelite rifle shooters used a mixture of internal and external imagery.

Murphy, Jowdy, and Durtschi (1989) obtained responses to a questionnaire from 87 elite athletes and 34 coaches of such athletes. A little over half (56%) of the athletes indicated that they used internal imagery as they became more skilled in their sport, and 55% indicated that internal imagery was more effective in helping their performance than external imagery (19% disagreed). Additionally, 62% of the coaches believed that the internal imagery perspective was more effective than an external perspective, while 7% suggested that the external perspective was better. Of the athletes, a larger percentage agreed that the use of internal imagery made the imagery clearer (50%), enhanced ability to feel body movements in the imagery (62%), and enhanced ability to become more emotionally involved in the imagery (64%). This contrasted with 31% who felt an external perspective led to clearer imagery, 12% who felt that external perspective improved on one's being able to feel body movements, and 23% who felt that the external perspective enabled one to become more emotionally involved in the imagery. The self-reports that the use of an internal perspective leads to greater performance enhancement can be interpreted by bioinformation theory when placed next to the information that the internal perspective leads to greater clarity, more ability to feel body movements, and better ability to become emotionally involved. By this theory, the internal perspective appears to induce more clear stimulus propositions as well as greater response propositions, with the consequence, therefore, of improved performance.

Suinn and Andrews (1980) surveyed a group of highly proficient competitors, members of a professional Alpine ski team tour. Subjects were members of either the more elite "A" level or the "B" level. The survey was administered by a member of the A circuit, a former president of the skiers' association. Although the questionnaire had different goals from the Mahoney-Avener survey, a few items were similar. No trends were found on internal versus external perspectives used during imagery rehearsal.

Experimental studies of the value of the internal versus the external perspective are not readily found. Harris and Robinson discovered that an internal perspective led to greater EMG activity than the external perspective. Burhans, Richman, and Bergey (1988) reported that external imagery led to improvement in times on a 1.5-mile outdoor track, but there was no comparison with a group using internal imagery. Epstein (1980) compared 30 dart throwers who trained using internal imagery with 30 who trained using external imagery. When compared with the performance of a control group, neither type of training seemed to make a difference in performance. However, the total training time was limited to one hour. Finally, Jowdy and Harris reported that although the internal perspective was adopted by both their skilled and unskilled jugglers, several of the subjects also reported shifting their perspective at times during imagery rehearsal.

According to bioinformation theory, performance effects should be higher where imagery replicates more closely the actual response propositions of the task. Ziegler (1987) distinguished between "active imagery" and "passive imagery." In active imagery, the subjects also go through the actual motions appropriate to the real task. For instance, Ziegler had her subjects stand at a basketball free throw line, imagine themselves completing a free throw, and actually physically complete the motions, but without using the ball. Passive imagery involved the traditional imagery rehearsal without any corollary motions. She compared the

effects with 100 women from a fitness class, using five groups: passive imagery, active imagery, physical practice, passive imagery plus physical practice, and control. Her study can be interpreted as relevant to bioinformational theory, which would predict that the active imagery should be better than the passive imagery. As it turned out, results indicated no significant differences across the three imagery groups. Interestingly, the active imagery group actually improved more than the physical practice group, which showed almost no gains.

MENTAL PRACTICE AND IMAGERY REHEARSAL

Mental practice or *mental rehearsal* are the terms used in early studies of psychological techniques for sport enhancement, and were coined to distinguish such techniques from physical or motor practice. Inasmuch as it was obvious that physically rehearsing a motor skill led to improvements, the question was whether adding mental rehearsal would lend any more to skill acquisition. Early works first appeared around the 1940s, examining the relationship between mental rehearsal and athletic performance (Twinning, 1949; Vandel, Davis, & Clugston, 1943). In 1972, Corbin defined mental practice as the "repetition of a task, without observable movement, with the specific intent of learning" (p. 94). This broad definition considers the term as a generic one, covering a diverse set of activities, which might include closing one's eyes and thinking about a motor movement but without any visual/proprioceptive components, all the way to full-blown imaginal rehearsal with auditory, visual, proprioceptive, and emotional elements.

Possibly because of the broadness of the term, research on mental practice over a 30-year period can best be summarized as not always consistent nor conclusive (Corbin, 1972; Feltz & Landers, 1983; Oxendine, 1968; Richardson, 1967a, 1967b; Suinn, 1982; Weinberg, 1982). Suinn concluded that mental practice frequently has a beneficial effect on either the learning of a new skill or the betterment of performance of an existing skill, although gains were not proved in all research reports. Feltz and Landers similarly stated that "Mental practice effects are not just limited to early learning—they are found in early and later stages of learning and may be task specific" (p. 46). Tentative findings also suggest that experienced athletes profit more from mental practice than novices, and that mental practice can enhance tasks that emphasize either cognitive elements or motor elements.

REVIEW OF RESEARCH ON IMAGERY REHEARSAL

Since there are already available systematic reviews on mental practice in general, this chapter will provide a more focused review of mental practice, specifically on the method known as visual motor behavior rehearsal.

Visual motor behavior rehearsal (VMBR; Suinn, 1976) is a covert activity whereby a person experiences sensory-motor sensations that reintegrate reality experiences, and which include neuromuscular, physiological, and emotional involvement. VMBR involves two steps: relaxation training, followed by imagery rehearsal. Hence unlike many types of mental practice, relaxation is an essential step in VMBR and always precedes the imagery. In contrast to the mental practice instruction "Close your eyes and try to imagine yourself making the free throw," VMBR seeks a full-dimensional reexperiencing of the event: "Be there in the situation again . . . so that you are aware of where you are, what's around you, who's with you . . . you're actually on the basketball court again, the home court . . . score is all tied, the crowd is especially vocal, you have the ball in your hands, breathing a little shallowly . . . you bounce it several times, can feel the firmness . . . take a deep breath to settle down . . . focus on the rim . . ." One useful analogue is to consider VMBR as more similar to dreams than to the intellectual attempts to retrieve an experience through "thinking it over." Dreams appear so realistic that sometimes the dreamer actually is surprised that a dream is not real. On the other hand, VMBR differs from dreams in the amount of control. VMBR is not random in content, but subject to control in terms of what images are produced and what actions occur. Elsewhere I have described VMBR as follows:

The imagery of visuomotor behavior rehearsal apparently is more than sheer imagination. It is a well-controlled copy of experience, a sort of body-thinking similar to the powerful illusion of certain dreams at night. Perhaps the major difference between such dreams and VMBR is that the imagery rehearsal is subject to conscious control. (Suinn, 1976, p. 41)

There are several advantages to VMBR as a mental practice technique. First, VMBR is a standardized training method which is subject to description and therefore replication in both practice and research settings, and indeed, it has prompted research studies. Secondly, the use of VMBR does not seem to demand special skills, such as required, for instance, in the use of imagery through hypnosis. Finally, it has been subjected to research validation with reasonably consistent support for its efficacy.

In the discussions to follow, we will review what is known about imagery in sport performance, limiting ourselves to the literature that relates the use of imagery to enhance performance. The first part consists of case studies on mental practice (VMBR as well as other imagery rehearsal methods), and the second is a group of experimental studies specifically involving VMBR.

CASE REPORTS AND SINGLE CASE DESIGNS: MENTAL PRACTICE AND VMBR

Reports of this type tend to be variable in rigor, ranging from self-reports by well-known athletes to observational reports from consultants on changes following imagery rehearsal. They offer a kind of "grass-roots" background to the value of imagery rehearsal. Testimonials of this type actually do not add much as scientific support, since too many problems surface when the information is examined more carefully. For example, it is possible that the athlete was also engaging in other training activities concurrent with mental training? Might a new weight-training program or a change of technique or even equipment not be the more crucial factor? It is possible that the success is actually the final culmination of several years of effort with the one regime, and that the addition of imagery rehearsal this year was coincidental to the success; e.g., it can take several years for a professional quarterback to learn to read defenses, and the payoff of the cumulative learning may happen to occur in the same year that he tries out imagery rehearsal. It is conceivable that just believing in the value of psychological training, along with the expectation of success, will indirectly alter performance as a form of placebo effect (Mahoney, 1977). Clearly, the anecdotal reports or even reasonable detailed and careful case studies will not provide the answers. However, they do provide an encouraging preliminary introduction that might stimulate needed controlled research and study.

The literature uncovers a number of world famous competitive athletes who attribute their success to imagery rehearsal. A gold medalist in three events, Alpine skier Jean-Claude Killy, reports that the only preparation he had for one race was to mentally ski the course because an injury prevented on-snow practice. He believes that this race turned out to be one of his best performances. Jack Nicklaus (1974), the omnipresent golf champion, writes about an imagery rehearsal method which he uses. In this approach, he first visualizes the ball landing on the green and actually sees the bounce, then he visualizes the arc of the ball in flight, then he visualizes his swing and the ball leaving the ground. His final step is to link these together in proper sequence: visualizing the swing, the ball's trajectory, and its landing and bouncing on the green. He says his shots are 10% swing, 40% setup and stance, and 50% mental picture.

The Olympic high jumper Dwight Stones was identified by his prejump preparation, during which his head was seen to be bobbing in rhythm with his mental image of himself approaching and clearing the bar. Tennis player Chris Evert, known for her consistent high-quality tournament strokes, revealed in a radio interview that she painstakingly rehearsed any forthcoming match. She centered on anticipating her opponent's strategy and style and visualized herself countering with her own attack (Lazarus, 1977). Bill Glass, a defensive end for the Cleveland Browns professional football team in the 1960s, attributes his achieving the honor of becoming an All-Pro in part to imagery. He learned to rehearse the quick-step across the line, throwing off the offensive tackle, and charging the retreating quarterback as if it was all a "motion picture" (Furlong, 1979). Although some athletes, such as Glass, received training in imagery rehearsal from a consultant, many seem to have evolved the approach on their own or after hearing of the preparation from others. After giving a demonstration to members of the U.S. Olympic Cross-Country team, one world-class competitor challenged, "Visualizing is not new to me, I have done this before every race for years on my own . . . my problem is turning the scenes off."

Concurrent with the personal use of imagery by athletes are a number of reports where imagery rehearsal has been systematically prescribed by sports consultants. These case reports differ from the testimonials previously reviewed in that the imagery rehearsal tended to be an intervention aimed at altering poor performance. In two cases, some baseline data was available that permits making pre and post comparisons. Titley (1976) was called in as a consultant to a university football team by its coach. Prior to visual motor behavior rehearsal training, the team's field-goal kicker had missed three field goals from within 35 yards, all of which were crucial in the difference between a win and a loss or tie. VMBR was initiated for stress management and to assure a standardized kicking motion (skill development). In the games following VMBR, this youngster began to improve on his consistency and accuracy from greater distances. He became the leader in the conference in scoring, established 14 school records, and completed an NCAA field goal distance record of 63 yards.

Winning Associates (1978) provides a program including relaxation training, desensitization, mental coping, and imagery rehearsal. Among individual cases, they describe a bowler who averaged scores of 185 before the training and 215 after; a tennis player who won less than 20% of her matches prior to the training and lost only one the remainder of the season; and a college basketball player who improved from shooting 38% from the floor to 50%, and from 61% from the free-throw line to 90%.

Kirchenbaum and Bale (1980) examined the benefits of a broad-based psychological training program which included relaxation and imagery rehearsal, self-monitoring, and the use of positive self-instruction. They called this program Brain Power Golf (BPG). Because of their initial success with one varsity golf team in a prior year, the researchers were given further access to the next year's team as subjects. In fact, the coach had been so impressed by the gains (his golfer went on to win several tournaments) that he used the opportunity for psychological training as inducement during recruitment of new players. Because of the small sample size ($N = 3$), a multiple baseline across subjects research design was relied upon. Subject 1 had a baseline of 18 holes, and was then provided with BPG training and his later performances recorded. Subject 2 was made to wait until three rounds of competition were complete before being offered BPG training; this method provided an extended baseline. Subject 3 was a control subject who did not participate in the training.

By this research design, it was expected that Subject 1 would show an improvement in performance starting from the date of exposure to BPG training (called Period 1), while no changes were expected in Subject 2 or Subject 3 over this same period. During Period 2, the date that Subject 2 was introduced to psychological training, it was ex-

pected that this subject would now also show improvements in performance, while Subject 3 would still be showing no gains, and Subject 1 would continue to retain his prior gains. The results tended to be in the predicted directions. Subject 1 showed no improvement during Period 1 but then reduced his scores by one stroke in Period 2. Subject 3, contrary to expectation, showed a one-stroke improvement during Period 1, but relapsed back to his baseline during Period 2.

Ratings of the relative merits of each part of the BPG training showed imagery rehearsal and self-monitoring to be rated highest, with relaxation next, and positive self-instruction the lowest. It should be noted that the authors observed the level of improvement to be variable over the season with fluctuations. This may have been a function of the insufficient training time since the program was limited to one instructional session, followed later by one to three follow-up meetings (in comparison, see the Kolonay and Weinberg, et al. studies, later in this chapter).

Finally, the authors correctly call attention to the unique problem of assessing improvement in this sport. Is a one-or two-stroke change substantial enough to be considered "improvement"? Kirchenbaum and Bale reply by noting that a "one-stroke differential in . . . 18-hole performance separated Jack Nicklaus from a player who earned $100,000 less than Nicklaus in 1976" (p. 338). This issue of outcome evaluation will remain a difficult one for what is essentially field research with competitive athletic performance as measures. Studies outside the laboratory so far have used well-trained athletes rather than novices. One reason, of course, is that varsity-level competitors have sufficient skill to be able to rehearse the correct responses, instead of inadvertently rehearsing incorrect responses in imagery rehearsal. However, this means that the baseline performance level is already high, and statistically less subject to change. (Consider the improvement possible for a person high jumping six feet two inches prior to training versus the level realistically achievable for a person already jumping seven feet two inches.) Finally, different sports have different scoring systems, and this will affect research (for example, compare the obvious difference between the spread of outcome measures of a marathon race [the New York Marathon ranges from 2 hours to 7 hours] to that of a single gymnastic or diving event [with scores from 1 to 10]).

Similar to Kirchenbaum and Bale, Gough (1989) also studied the effects of imagery using the subjects' own baselines as the control. The procedure involved relaxation (prompted by soft music), followed by imagery rehearsal. Subjects were three members of a baseball varsity team with varying degrees of experience and batting ability. The imagery involved concentrating on hitting the baseball pitch. Outcomes were measured by comparing baseline in daily batting practice with percentage of quality hits in batting practice after training. One of the players improved his hits from a baseline of 12% to 55% after training. Of the three subjects, this one had been the poorest in baseball experience and ability. A second subject, of moderate experience and ability, showed no significant improvement. The third subject, who had the greatest experience and ability, showed an improvement from a baseline of 50% to 70% following training.

Desiderato and Miller (1979) used a combination of VMBR and stress inoculation in a single-subject design with a tennis player. The subject was an experienced tournament competitor on a local and regional club level, but reported persistent anxiety and frequent negative evaluations. Examples of negative cognitions and verbalizations were thoughts or statements such as "You blew it," "Damn dummy," or "Why did you do that?" The VMBR training emphasized playing a crucial point two alternate ways, each ending in winning the point. Stress inoculation (Meichenbaum, 1977) involves the preparation and use of positive self-instructional statements ("Stay cool"), constructive self-statements to cope with errors ("Okay, you double-faulted, concentrate on the next serve"), and self-reinforcing statements ("That's the way to do it, stay in control"). Since the subject appeared to do worse in competitive matches but better in social playing during baseline, data was collected on both competitive and social games. During three baseline weeks, the percentage of deuce games won was in fact higher for noncompetitive games than for competitive matches, 49% versus 29%. After one week of the intervention program, the subject now was winning 55% percent of noncompetitive games and 60% of competitive games. In addition, the subject reported a disappearance of earlier "feelings of disaster" which often preceded matches, and an increase in confidence and an eagerness for competitive challenges.

Schleser, Meyers, and Montgomery (1980) also used a combination of VMBR and cognitive techniques to help correct performances in two women collegiate basketball players. One was a center who needed help with her free-throw shooting, while the other was a forward who wanted help on her field goal shooting. The program used relaxation training and imagery first to practice accurate free throws or field goals. The two subjects were then helped to use imagery rehearsal to visualize an unsuccessful scene, followed by rehearsing stress inoculation and self-instructional statements. Later the athletes used relaxation, imagery rehearsal, and self-instructional statements just prior to physical practice on the basketball court.

Two types of comparative data became available. Since the basketball center wanted help with free throws, and the forward wanted help only on field goals, the imagery rehearsal training for the center was limited to free throws, while it was limited to field goals for the forward. For the center, her free-throw accuracy (the treated behavior) improved from a baseline of 41.3% to 54.8%; in contrast, her field goal accuracy (the untreated behavior) was relatively unchanged, at 48.9% and 47.8%, respectively. For the forward, her field goal accuracy (the treated behavior) improved from 36.7% to 52.2%, in contrast to the free-throw accuracy (the untreated behavior), which was 67.9% and 68.0%, respectively. Another type of comparison was possible because the center discontinued involvement in the intervention program after six weeks but before the season

ended. Hence the authors felt that a multiple baseline with a reversal design was possible, involving a seven-game baseline, a 13-game intervention period, and an 11-game reversal after intervention was discontinued by the athlete.

On free-throw accuracy the three percentage accuracy figures were 41.3%, 54.8%, and 28.6%; this shows the expected improvement during intervention and decline during reversal on the treated behavior. For the untreated behavior of field goal accuracy, the figures were 48.9%, 47.8%, and 54.7%. Although the data did not reach statistical significance, the trends were in the predicted directions and were supported by self-reports from the athletes about the efficacy of the training. Reversal designs generally involve operant reinforcement training, where the reversal comes from the withholding of the reinforcer and where the newly acquired behavior returns to the level prior to training. In this report, a true reversal was not involved since the event was the discontinuation of practice with VMBR and cognitive controls, rather than the removal of reward.

It should be noted that these methods helped in increasing the basketball skills they were meant to correct, and a reversal of skill level would not be expected since the methods do not apply a reinforcement model. Instead, it would appear that the decline represents a motivational change, where the skill level remained the same, but the athlete's desire to perform decreased. This is supported by the decline of percentage accuracy to 28.6%, far below the baseline skill level. In addition, it is interesting to note that the center discontinued the program because she became bored at the repetitiousness of the training. This information implies that compliance with mental training programs is as important as compliance with physical training regimes. Without compliance, improvements are unlikely to occur or to be maintained.

GROUP OR EXPERIMENTAL STUDIES: VMBR

On the whole, carefully controlled studies of imagery rehearsal effects have been difficult to find. For instance, studies on VMBR have been with competitive athletes less subject to laboratory control. A number of practical limitations are involved in such studies of competitors. As will be described later, one problem is obtaining a control group. If athletes are matched on skill level, and if the coaching staff members are not "blind" to the study, then comparable data may be lacking. If the trained (or for that matter the control) athletes start to show improved performances, it will be the rare coach who still stays with the original agreement to enter all competitors in every meet in order to have an equivalent number of subjects in the experimental and control groups to satisfy the researcher's needs. The coach's needs to field the best team or best athletes comes from a pragmatic recognition that the primary goal of the varsity team is to win games or meets, and only secondarily does it aim to provide research data under controlled conditions.

Nevertheless, there have been some reasonably controlled group studies, and some general trends from less rigorous studies. This part of the review will focus solely on the group or experimental studies involving VMBR. In keeping with the conceptual model cited earlier in this chapter, this review will organize the research as those on the use of VMBR to strengthen correct responses or to eliminate incorrect responses. A final discussion will review research on variables influencing the value of VMBR, such as augmentation through use of videomodeling.

Imagery Rehearsal to Strengthen Correct Responses

Kolonay (1977) used VMBR with 72 male basketball players from 8 college basketball teams. The basketball teams were randomly assigned to 4 groups: VMBR training (relaxation followed by imagery rehearsal), relaxation training alone, imagery rehearsal but without relaxation, and no training control. Training was provided through audiotape prior to each of 15 basketball practices, covering a 6-week period. The target behavior involved free-throw shooting.

The results were straightforward: the VMBR athletes increased their foul shooting accuracy by 7%, a significant improvement not only statistically, but also in that the coaches reported that such improvement meant the difference of 8 more winning games in the season (Fensterheim, 1980). The relaxation-only and imagery-rehearsal-only groups showed no changes whatsoever. The selection of the relaxation-only and imagery-only groups derived from consultation between Kolonay and Suinn. It has been Suinn's contention that VMBR, which always begins with relaxation and then proceeds to imagery rehearsal, should be more beneficial than imagery rehearsal alone, since the latter could be simply a version of the more intellective "think about making free throws." The results seem to confirm this hypothesis.

Weinberg, Seabourne, and Jackson (1981) conducted a replication of Kolonay's work but improved it through the addition of a placebo-control group. The subjects were 32 male students enrolled in a karate club. They were assigned to one of four conditions: VMBR (relaxation plus imagery), relaxation alone, imagery alone, or placebo-control. In the control conditions, karate success was described as involving an understanding of the spiritual and cultural philosophy behind karate. Subjects in this condition were then assigned quotations to practice and understand. All training involved meetings twice a week for 6 weeks. The performance task involved karate skills, e.g., front kick; karate skills combinations, e.g., two-step combination punches; and sparring. Judges of these performances were black belt instructors.

Results were significant only for the sparring performances, in which the VMBR group performed better than the relaxation-only, imagery-only, or placebo groups. On the skills combination task, although not reaching statistical significance, the VMBR group achieved the highest

amount of improvement. On the skills task, the VMBR group attained the highest posttest scores, although this might have been a function of the higher pretest scores.

Since improvements in performance might be explained by reductions in disruptive anxiety, the authors examined levels of state anxiety. State anxiety levels for the VMBR and relaxation-only groups were both significantly lower than for the imagery-only or control groups. However, since the improvement in karate performance on sparring occurred only for the VMBR group, the authors concluded that the effects of VMBR go beyond effects due to anxiety reduction alone.

Lane (1978, 1980) initiated studies of basketball and baseball players using VMBR. Working with 16 members of a high school basketball team, Lane divided them into two groups matched on free-throw–percentage accuracy. One group was assigned to VMBR training, while the other received relaxation-only training. The training was in six sessions across three weeks. Comparison of the VMBR with the relaxation-only group showed no statistically significant differences, although the author reported a trend "in favor of the VMBR group" (1978, p. 9). Unfortunately, no statistical comparisons were computed, although a figure in the manuscript suggests an improvement over baseline by both groups. This failure to show differential results between the two groups is inconsistent with the Kolonay and Weinberg, et al. studies. Among the differences between the studies are the differences in sample size and in age: Kolonay's study involved substantially more subjects, and Kolonay and Weinberg, et al. used college-age athletes. Either could explain the inconsistency in results. It is interesting to note that Lane adds that his subjects did not feel that relaxation itself was of much help in improving their free-throw shooting.

In a follow-up, Lane provided VMBR training to three starters, while three other starters on the basketball team refused such training and hence formed a natural control group. VMBR training continued "at various times during the competitive season" (p. 11). Direct comparison between the VMBR and control groups on improvement in free-throw accuracy from the previous season to the current season showed a trend favoring the VMBR group, but the results did not reach statistical significance. However, using chi-square analyses, the VMBR subjects showed significant increase in free throw accuracy ($p = .05$) when their previous year's performances were compared with the current (VMBR) year's effort; similar analyses for the control group did not reach significance. For the VMBR athletes, there was a 12% increase in free throws made; while the control subjects showed a decrease over the same time period. Further analyses showed that the VMBR players demonstrated a greater increase in accuracy on away games than on home games, leading Lane to conclude that "under the most extreme conditions of competition (of away games) . . . the advantages of VMBR training become most clearly evident" (pp. 3, 6).

Noel (1980) recruited male tennis players entered in a tournament ($N = 14$), and formed a VMBR and a control group. In order to determine their baseline performance levels, all subjects played one set of tennis, during which time measures of service accuracy and points played were obtained. Subjects differed in levels of skill, and they were grouped as "high-ability" and "low-ability" for later analyses. The VMBR training involved seven sessions of relaxation and visualizing of tennis serves, lasting approximately 30 minutes per session. In VMBR imagery, the subjects were specifically helped to visualize themselves arriving at the match site, warming up, practicing serves, observing any service errors, and making corrections on the service.

Analysis of covariance showed that high-ability VMBR subjects improved on service accuracy from baseline, while low-ability VMBR subjects worsened. Although the VMBR aimed only at improving service accuracy, data was also obtained on points played. A point was rated as a "winner" if the shot placement was so difficult that the opponent could not position himself for a good return. A point was rated as an "error" if the player was in a position to make a shot but did not. Data were reported in terms of the ratio of winners to errors, and showed a trend for high-ability VMBR subjects to have a higher number of winners to errors in comparison to high-ability control subjects; however, low-ability VMBR subjects tended to show a lower ratio in comparison with low-ability control subjects. These data suggest that imagery rehearsal alone does not guarantee improvement, and is consistent with the earlier mental rehearsal research on the influence of player skill level on performance. It is possible that the higher-ability athlete uses VMBR to overlearn correct behaviors already in the repertoire. On the other hand, without careful guidance, the lower-ability athlete might actually be rehearsing incorrect behaviors, and thus become worse rather than better. Another possibility is that differences in ability to control the imagery might have occurred, such that the subject is unable to visualize the correct behaviors.

An early study by Clark (1960) discovered that not all subjects were able to control their imagery in practicing basketball free throws. In fact, one subject reported that his basketball would not bounce but stuck to the floor in his imagery rehearsal. Clark reported that as subjects reported gains in their ability to visualize and to control their imagery, they experienced gains in self-confidence and in the ability to identify errors in their behaviors.

Nideffer (1971) used VMBR to have A.A.U. competitive divers rehearse the technical aspects of their dives, including body movement, relationship of body position to the position of the water, etc. The VMBR procedure was practiced both at home and at the start of pool practice for about 10 minutes. The VMBR was continued for one month, during which data was obtained on total number of dives executed during practice, number of new dives attempted, and self-report of anxiety. Nideffer reports that there were more dives completed in practice following VMBR, even though some of the time was now taken up by VMBR. There were also increases in the total number of new dives attempted and a decrease in reported anxiety. These data could be in-

terpreted to mean that VMBR practice increased the confidence of the divers in their abilities.

Prediger (personal communication, August 1991) described a procedure that appears similar to VMBR in that relaxation was combined with imagery. Subjects were 120 seventh-grade students assigned to one of three conditions: relaxation plus imagery, relaxation plus imagery plus physical practice, or physical practice alone. The task involved accuracy in field hockey in being able to hit three orange cone targets. Results showed that the physical practice and relaxation plus imagery group improved their accuracy to the same level (70% and 68% gains). In addition, the combination of the physical practice with the imagery/ relaxation practice led to greater gains than the other two groups (gain of 160% in level of accuracy). Further analyses also showed that although only 12 of 40 subjects in the imagery/relaxation group were able to hit any of the targets on pretest, after training, 23 were able to hit the targets, with 2 subjects hitting all three targets. In contrast, none in the physical practice group were able to hit all the targets at posttest.

Imagery Rehearsal to Eliminate Incorrect Responses

A slightly different goal can be reached through imagery rehearsal. Instead of using imagery rehearsal to practice and strengthen the correct behaviors, imagery might be employed to eliminate incorrect responses. One set of incorrect responses are the conditioned emotional reactions (see Figure 21–1), namely, anxiety. Although applied relaxation, desensitization, anxiety management training, and stress inoculation are all direct methods for controlling anxiety, Bennett and Stothart (1978) used VMBR to train athletes in anxiety reduction. Subjects were 44 athletes on teams in four sports: gymnastics, archery, wrestling, and badminton. In addition to relaxation, the treated sample used VMBR to practice cognitive controls over anxiety using competition imagery. The cognitive skills practiced included identifying the presence of anxiety, remembering how to cope, confronting the stress by relaxing, and initiating self-reinforcing statements for progress (Meichenbaum & Cameron, 1974). Control subjects spent an equal time engaged in tasks unrelated to stress control or sports performance, such as card sorting. Anxiety was measured through the Spielberger State-Trait Anxiety Inventory (STAI). Training covered seven sessions.

Analysis of variance reached significance for the comparison of pre-to posttest scores and were not significant across groups, but the interaction was in the predicted direction. In further analysis, the authors discovered that the VMBR group had a higher level of pretest anxiety than the control group; however, since the authors did not report an analysis of covariance, it is not known whether results would have been different if pretest levels were controlled. Through inspection, the authors do conclude that the VMBR group showed "a decline in post-treatment state anxiety scores while the control group did not" (p. 11).

The study also analyzed coaches' ratings of sports performances that were videotaped before and after treatment. Results were not statistically significant. The authors observe that this lack of noticeable improvement could have been due to the subjects' already being at a high enough skill level that improvements in technique would not be noticeable. They also suggest the possibility that the videotape condition was not stressful, and hence any improvements related to stress reduction would not be testable. Two other possibilities also exist. One is that the evidence of gains following stress reduction might be best measured not in technique in practice, but in outcome measures such as consistency or reduction in errors under game conditions. Finally it is possible that the lack of results simply means that the VMBR rehearsal of cognitive anxiety reduction skills either is not useful, or that the cognitive skills are not helpful in anxiety reduction.

Two studies by Weinberg and his associates (Weinberg, Seabourne, & Jackson, 1981, 1982) examined the influence of VMBR on anxiety levels. The studies were of identical designs. Karate students were provided with VMBR training with karate performance being tested. In the 1981 study, subjects were assigned to either a VMBR, a relaxation-only, an imagery-only, or a placebo-control group over 6 weeks. In the 1982 study, subjects were assigned either to a 6-week VMBR group or a 1-day VMBR group. State anxiety was significantly lowered for the VMBR and relaxation-only group, as compared with the imagery-only and placebo-control groups. State anxiety was also significantly reduced for the 6-week VMBR group compared to the 1-day VMBR group. In the 1982 study, when the 1-day VMBR training was conducted at the beginning of karate training, this group showed reductions of state anxiety equivalent to that of the 6-week VMBR group.

Regarding trait anxiety, the VMBR, relaxation-only, imagery-only, and placebo-control groups all showed significant decreases in trait anxiety, and to equivalent levels. Similarly, subjects in both the 6-week VMBR training group and the 1-day VMBR training group showed significant reductions in trait anxiety and to equivalent levels.

Gravel, Lemieux, and Ladouceur (1980) also used VMBR as the mechanism to eliminate incorrect responses. The incorrect responses are the negative evaluational or negative cue-instructional cognitive responses identified by Suinn (1980; also see Figure 21–1), and included feeling inferior to other racers, thinking about pain, and being preoccupied about race conditions. Subjects were trained to use thought-stopping to control these ruminations. VMBR was used to develop competitive scenes where such ruminations would occur, and to rehearse the thought-stopping. Subjects were 12 members of a university cross-country ski team, randomly assigned to the VMBR or the placebo control group. The placebo group watched films of ski racing and were asked to free-associate on words unrelated to racing, then to discuss the results.

Results indicated that the VMBR group showed a statistically significant decrease in the frequencies of interfering ruminations ($p = < .01$), while the placebo group showed no significant changes. Two ancillary findings are important. First, the reported reduction in ruminations occurred mainly between posttest (end of treatment) and follow-up (21 days after treatment ended). The authors suggest that the athletes consolidated their gains during follow-up as a result of *in vivo* competitive experiences in races. Second, the authors discovered that the athletes reported that VMBR helped them to learn to focus on their body state during a race, viewing this as helpful. This is similar to the "associative" running reported by Morgan (1978) as characteristic of the better elite runner. In associative runners, attention is focused on "reading" feedback from muscle groups, respiration, and other physiological signs in order to adopt an appropriate pace. Hence, although the study on cross-country racers began with the objective of removing an interfering cognitive response, it achieved training the athletes as well in acquiring an adaptive response.

A laboratory study by Suinn, Morton, and Brammell (1980) used VMBR to train members of a university cross-country (track) team in "how to run relaxed" during an event. The goal was to eliminate the inefficiency associated with muscle tension during performance. Subjects were 8 VMBR subjects and 8 control subjects. Training began with relaxation training, followed by VMBR with imagery involving identifying muscle signs of tenseness in running, and cues for running in a more relaxed manner. Subjects were encouraged to employ the more relaxed style during *in vivo* training and in between VMBR sessions. Total training in VMBR covered 8 sessions. It was predicted that running "more relaxed" would lead to greater physiological efficiency, since less effort would be employed. Physiological and self-report measures were used.

Subjects were tested on a standard treadmill, providing oxygen consumption (VO_2) and heart rate (HR) data, as well as identifying the anaerobic threshold (AT) of each athlete. The AT served as the baseline for equating the workload at posttesting across athletes; for example, athletes were later tested at a treadmill workload equal to 75% of *their* pretest AT. The self-report measure was the Borg Perceived Exertion Scale, in which the athlete assigns a numerical value to the athlete's estimate of the effort required on the treadmill. Although a control group design was not possible, with the AT design it was possible to compare each trained athlete against his/her own baseline. Subjects ran for 10 minutes to establish a baseline for various workload levels (e.g., 10 minutes at 75% AT), and were then instructed to "run relaxed" for 10 minutes.

Results from the first 10 minutes were then compared against results of the second 10 minutes. Results showed that the three women runners showed a significant mean decrease in HR from the first to the second 10 minutes, at the 65% percent AT workload ($p = .05$). On individual athletes, a trend analysis comparing the slopes of measurements for the first 10 minutes versus the second 10 minutes reached significance for two athletes at the 65% AT, 75% AT, and 85% AT levels of effort, on VO_2 consumption. The trend was for VO_2 consumption to decrease during the second 10 minutes. On the Perceived Effort measure, the VMBR trained subjects rated the second 10 minutes as requiring less effort, while two control subjects in the study rated the second 10 minutes as requiring more effort. It should be kept in mind that the treadmill test was kept at the same workload throughout.

The results of this study were encouraging since there was a more direct assessment of the possible impact of imagery rehearsal on a performance measure other than self-report. The previously reported research on cross-country racers did collect performance data in terms of race results, but the authors did not calculate any statistical analyses because the subjects differed from one another in sex and age level, and hence did not run comparable events. The current study on treadmill performance adds some information on performance, even though the performance is not directly associated with actually running a race. Nevertheless, the change in heart rate and the trend for oxygen consumption to decrease were in keeping with the hypothesis that "running relaxed" should be more efficient, and that VMBR could aid in the acquisition of this style of running. The data do not answer the question of whether race results, such as times, would also show improvement; however, anecdotally, one of the female athletes had the best season she had ever experienced. Also not answered is the difference between the individual athlete's results. Not all athletes improved from the training; there was a tendency for the women to show greater gains than the men.

It is important to note that the results of relaxation on physiological efficiency is consistent with the work of Benson, Dryer, and Hartley (1978). Finally, it is noteworthy that one of the athletes in the current study participated in VMBR with her eyes open. She indicated that she not only could do the visualizing this way, but that it would be more nearly like reality, since she runs a race with her eyes open, and never closed! Observationally, the VMBR trainer (Suinn) did not perceive any obstruction to VMBR in this athlete because she had her eyes open; in fact, she showed reductions in oxygen consumption and in heart rate on posttesting.

One study illustrates the problems of attempting to do controlled research with varsity athletes during a competitive year. Suinn (1972) matched Alpine ski racers on skill levels prior to the race season, assigning one of each matched pair to the VMBR program and the other to a no-treatment control group. However, although the coach had agreed before to race all subjects during the season, he in fact raced only some based upon his observations of their on-snow improvements. It turned out that only one of the control subjects was entered, while all VMBR subjects were entered in the season's meets. What began as a controlled study with race results being the outcome variable from matched samples, ended as a group study without a control comparison. One could consider the coach's decision as data in itself; however, since the coach was not blind to the study, his decision may well have been subject to confounding.

Factors in VMBR Efficacy

A few studies have accepted the conclusion that VMBR does have beneficial effects on performance and have begun to investigate variables which might influence such effects. Weinberg, Seabourne, and Jackson (1982) explored the question of whether the amount of VMBR training made a difference. They compared one group receiving 6 weeks of daily VMBR training with a group receiving only 1 day of VMBR training. Subjects were in two experiments. In the first experiment, 18 karate students were randomly assigned to each of the two conditions; the 1-day VMBR training was offered immediately prior to their final test to qualify for promotion. Experiment 2 involved 14 students assigned to each condition; the 1-day VMBR, however, was offered during the first week instead of the sixth. Both experiments evaluated the effects of VMBR or karate tasks. In experiment 1, the assessment was of karate skills, skill combinations, and sparring, rated by two black belt judges. In experiment 2, the assessments were of sparring and *kata,* i.e., performance of the ritualized set of fighting movements against an imaginary opponent.

Results in experiment 1 did not reach statistical significance on performance measures. However, both groups did show improvements from pretest to posttest on skill combinations and sparring; no improvements were noticeable in the simpler karate skill task. State anxiety significantly decreased for the 6-week VMBR group, while no changes were observable for the 1-day VMBR group.

The authors suspected that the first experiment had a design flaw in having the 1-day VMBR just prior to final testing. This timing could have made the VMBR experience "extremely potent" (p. 214). Hence the research design was changed in experiment 2 to have the 1-day VMBR at the very start. Also, performance of *kata* was included as a more complex task, involving speed, power, form, fluidity, and body control. Results on this study indicated that both VMBR groups showed significantly greater improvement in *kata* from pre-to posttest, but the 6-day VMBR group's improvement was significantly higher than that of the 1-day VMBR group. An identical finding was reported for improvements in sparring. On state anxiety both groups showed equivalent improvements from pre-to posttest.

These findings suggest support for the contention that repeated trials in VMBR are valuable, although there may be some situations in which single exposure has positive effects. Multiple trials have the advantage of ensuring that the participants are involved in sufficient numbers of learning trials to improve on the motor skill in question. Furthermore, additional VMBR trials might also assure that persons with lower initial ability in imagery techniques can have sufficient training in imagery to develop the benefits of imagery rehearsal of their sport. The efficacy of the single-exposure session in experiment one is not readily interpreted since the authors did not obtain further information. Anxiety reduction was not the explanation, since the 1-day VMBR group failed to show any lowering of their state anxiety and anxiety reduction was ruled out in another study by

Weinberg et al. (1981). Possibly the 1-day–exposure group was composed of participants who were already readily skilled in imagery, and hence able to achieve full benefits more quickly.

Hall and Erffmeyer (1983) tested the value which videotape modeling might add to VMBR by having one group of basketball varsity team members view a videotape of foul shooting. A second group were trained with VMBR only. Training covered 30-minute sessions daily for 10 days. Results indicated that the videotape plus VMBR group had significantly higher foul shooting scores than the VMBR group at posttesting. They commented that "the use of imagery requires practice" for effective use, and interpreted their results to show that videotape modeling can facilitate the development of skill in using imagery (p. 346).

Gray and Fernandez (in press) replicated Hall and Erffmeyer's study, with the revision of having both the VMBR and the modeling on the same videotape. Additionally, in order to simulate game conditions, the subjects ran up and down the court between free throws. The subjects were also members of a varsity basketball team. Results supported that of Hall and Erffmeyer in that free-throw shooting performance improved significantly when measured under game conditions following VMBR plus modeling.

Gray (1990) again examined the benefits of videotaped modeling to VMBR but this time with racquetball players and with the videotape covering only racquetball skills— i.e., providing different views of forehand and backhand shots. Subjects were 24 men in a beginners' class, trained either with VMBR plus videotape modeling, or VMBR alone. Results showed significantly greater improvement for the videotape augmented VMBR compared to VMBR alone only for the forehand shots, although both groups did improve across time.

Andre and Means (1986) studied a method similar to VMBR in having relaxation followed by imagery rehearsal. Subjects were 66 volunteers whose task was aiming a Frisbee disk at a basket. Three conditions were used: VMBR, VMBR in slow motion, and a placebo control. The VMBR group involved imagery content emphasizing "visual, kinesthetic, and affective imaginal practice of the . . . throw" (p. 215). The slow motion rehearsal was hypothesized to be beneficial since it "can lead to more vivid and clear-cut experiencing of the imagined motor task . . . (and it is) less likely that mistakes in execution are overlooked, allowing for more adequate correction of the imagined behavior" (p. 124). The placebo control involved viewing promotional films on Frisbee activities and reading instructions about Frisbee unrelated to the experiment's Frisbee task. No statistically significant difference was found across the groups. However, the VMBR group showed an increase of 10.94% in accuracy, compared to 5.62% for slow motion VMBR and 1.57% for the placebo group.

Although it does not directly examine VMBR, a study by Woolfolk, Murphy, and Parrish (1983) offers some relevant information. The Noel study suggested that skilled tennis players profited from VMBR while unskilled players worsened. Woolfolk et al. studied a condition which could explain such deterioration from imagery rehearsal. Thirty college students were matched for golf-putting ability, then randomly assigned to one of three conditions: correct practice imagery, incorrect practice imagery, and no-training control. In the correct practice imagery, subjects rehearsed stroking the golf ball correctly so that the ball falls into the cup. In the incorrect practice imagery, subjects imagined the ball narrowly missing the cup due to incorrect stroking. Results showed that the groups were significantly different from each other in posttest putting accuracy. The correct practice group improved 30.4% from a baseline of 5.2 successful putts in 10 attempts, while the incorrect practice group showed a 21.2% deterioration from their baseline average of 5.2 putts, and the control group showed an increase of 9.9% in accuracy over their initial baseline of 4.6 successful putts. One interpretation suggested by the authors is the increase in self-efficacy or the erosion of self-efficacy resulting from the success of the correct scene or the failure of the incorrect scene. The study seems to demonstrate that imagery rehearsal is a form of practice of a skill, and that the adage "practice makes perfect" should be expanded to include "but imperfect practice makes for imperfection."

IMPLICATIONS FOR RESEARCH

To conclude this chapter, a few final statements are in order. With regard to studies of mental practice, recent reviews continue to uphold the use of imagery rehearsal as an extremely promising technique. Surveys of sport psychologists, coaches, and elite athletes indicate that these individuals have sufficient confidence in mental practice as to rely quite frequently on it as a part of mental training. The research literature, however, is still such that more controlled studies and greater standardization of what is studied are needed. The meta-analysis by Feltz and Landers indicated that mental practice is beneficial, but the specific studies reviewed showed various levels of inconsistencies.

Many of the discrepancies may be real results that reflect the off-and-on benefits of mental practice. Some of the discrepancies are probably attributable to poor research designs. Different studies have involved different mental practice techniques rather than a standard one; hence the diverse results may be due more to the diverse methods. Standardization has also been missing in even the type of instructions given subjects, such as what subjects should be rehearsing in their mental practice (a single movement, a coordinated swing, a visual component, the "muscular feeling," the cognitive elements, the affective/arousal aspects, the total gestalt, etc.). The amount of training in mental imagery has also not been controlled, with assumptions being made that all participants are equally skilled in developing, controlling, and using imagery. There has also been a need for improvement in controls over certain factors under study, such as the level of experience of the subjects, the nature of the task being learned or performed, and the amount and sequence of the practice (Suinn, 1982).

Still unsettled are results where the tasks are mainly cognitive or mainly motor in nature (Feltz and Landers discovered large main effects in their meta-analysis for both types of tasks, though they were seemingly more consistent effects for the cognitive tasks). A further issue is whether the more productive perspective in imagery is internal or external. Although theoretically an internal perspective would seem more beneficial, it can also be argued that the best perspective should be decided more from the standpoint of the goals of the mental practice. An internal perspective might be more valuable during stages of early learning or for a less skilled athlete. An external perspective might be more helpful with a more skilled athlete who is seeking to use mental imagery to assess errors in performance: "Watch yourself and detect what went wrong" (Suinn, 1984). In the survey of elite athletes, coaches, and sports psychologists, Murphy, Jowdy, and Durtschi (1989) discovered that both internal and external perspectives were recommended as solutions for similar problems. However, one view was that internal imagery might be more appropriate for management of "the emotional state (anxiety/arousal), physical state during competition (fatigue, etc.), self-concept, and confidence issues . . . mental skills . . . concentration/ attention . . . and emotional reinforcement of success experience" (p. 27). Similarly, one archer indicated that external imagery was valuable when the problem was ". . . working on my form" (p. 28). The point is that such anecdotal reporting mainly suggests that proper evaluation of the efficacy of internal/external imagery must account for the goals of the training, since there may be some confusion in the field.

Suinn (1984, in press) has identified five goals: technique enhancement, error analysis, error correction, preparation for competition conditions, and confidence enhancement. Perhaps such goals need to be specifically stated in research studies to further tighten the research designs and avoid design problems. For instance, if the subject is a learner, then not only would an internal perspective be more appropriate, but technique enhancement content for the imagery would be more useful than competition conditions imagery. If there is a mismatch between the needs of the subject, the goals, and/or the content of the imagery, then the research outcomes could be negatively affected.

Studies of VMBR appear to be more consistent than studies of other imagery practice methods, with the two strongest documentations coming from the controlled group studies of Kolonay, and those of Weinberg and his colleagues. The main advantage of VMBR for research is the fact that the VMBR technique is standardized, described in the literature; therefore, there is not likely to be any confusion about the nature of the training or the technique under study. Unfortunately, some studies have used very brief sessions of VMBR training, overlooking the basic fact that VMBR might itself be a skill requiring training. Using imagery appropriately is a type of mental skill, and adequate skill development is needed for VMBR to be expected to have maximal effects.

Moreover, VMBR, like any form of mental practice, is a tool. Research on whether the tool is beneficial must take into account the nature of training in using the tool, the characteristics of the user of the tool, and the nature of the "job" demands (see Figure 21–2). Research is needed to further understand how these three variables affect the use of imagery for performance enhancement.

First, we have mentioned the importance of the content of VMBR. However, little is known about what should be rehearsed to reach various goals, that is, what should be the focus or content of the imagery. Conclusions about the use of internal perspective content versus external perspectives are not yet possible, although theory would favor the internal perspective. The addition of arousal in terms of emotional states seems to add little at best and may be disruptive at worst. On the other hand, eliciting emotions in real life without understanding the particular needs of the individual athlete could equally be expected to produce uneven results; some athletes may indeed perform at a higher level when angered, while others lose their self-control under the same circumstances.

To the degree it is sensible to discuss an optimal level of autonomic arousal for sport performance, it also may make sense to consider what level of arousal might be optimal for imagery rehearsal. For VMBR perhaps the term "arousal" would not mean the introduction of emotions into the imagery, but rather the use of stimulus propositions normally associated with optimal sport performance for that individual athlete. Such stimulus conditions might involve, for instance, descriptions of crowd noise and support, environmental conditions, competition scene cues, and the like, as well as response propositions such as attentiveness, a sense of readiness, efficacy, and other factors. As more is known about theories which explain the mechanisms for imagery rehearsal, perhaps more factors will be identified about how to improve on the use of VMBR. The failure of the one study of slow-motion scenes need not be discouraging. It is conceivable that the hypothesis was in the right direction, but that more substantial results might have occurred with a more skilled group of subjects, or with instructions that focused attention on what should be examined in slow motion, or after the subjects had gained more skill in the use of imagery.

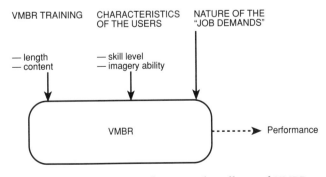

FIGURE 21–2. Factors influencing the effects of VMBR on performance.

Another approach to defining the content of VMBR imagery has already been cited, that is, the relationship between content and the goals of the training. As cited earlier, the goals might change during the course of the season, initially from the goal of learning a new motor movement (such as a new gymnastics routine) to a later goal of preparing for the unique conditions of the upcoming competitive event or preparing for a specific opponent. However, thus far, such program planning has been up to the sport psychologist to decide, based upon on-the-field intuition or experience. What is needed in research are more data on what could constitute the most effective sequence of goals to bring an athlete from the early stages to the final stages of performance.

Figure 21–2 also cites the length of VMBR training as a variable. Some research has suggested that poorer outcomes might be attributable to shorter VMBR training. Certainly theory would support this; we do not anticipate the acquisition of new motor skills after a single trial, so we should not expect an athlete to be highly skilled at using imagery rehearsal after short exposure to this method. However, once the threshold for VMBR is achieved, just how many sessions constitute a sufficient level? A related question involves measurement of this threshold; how can we best determine when an athlete has reached an acceptable level of relaxation and acceptable control of imagery to be ready to profit from VMBR?

A second variable highlighted in Figure 21–2 involves the characteristics of the athlete in determining the value of VMBR. As research appears to suggest, the skill level and imagery ability of the athlete influences outcomes. Those athletes of lower skill level in their sport are less likely to show immediate gains and might even show decrements in their sport performance. This probably reflects the need for more accurate instructions regarding the content of the VMBR imagery rather than any flaw in VMBR. In fact, some VMBR studies such as those of Weinberg and his colleagues were accomplished with novice athletes. More about this factor will be covered later under our discussion of "job demands." Level of imagery ability is also a factor affecting VMBR outcomes. However, a prime issue is whether imagery ability is innate or learnable. Are there some athletes who are incapable of developing and controlling imagery? Is it instead conceivable that anyone can learn to develop and control imagery if sufficient training trials are used, or if the correct training method is used? Since some individuals are known to learn best when the information is processed through their preferred learning modality (some are "visual" learners, some require concrete or hands-on exposure, etc.), is it possible that some athletes will develop better imagery if the emphasis, for example, is on visual sensations or emotional cues?

Finally, the "job demands" in the use of the tool are relevant (the overall level of demands facing the athlete using imagery). A highly proficient athlete of world-class caliber might have basic physical and technique skills so overlearned that the new learning challenge may only be in terms of psychological skills. On the other hand, a novice may be faced with an overwhelming set of demands, including emotional control, lower body technique, upper body technique, balance, coordinated motion, concentration, timing, and retrieval of short-term memory instructions on strategy, as might be the case for a beginning skier or diver. The proper use of imagery might also be a complex issue. For the novice, the job demands might include both skill learning as well as performance "polishing," while performance enhancement might be the primary demand for the expert. Imagery content would therefore be different for athletes at each level. Similarly, the novice may require more detailed instructions and pre-imagery preparation. Can a novice rehearse the correct skiing technique if he/she has never been on skis, and if the "natural" tendency of the body is to adopt the wrong movements?

Pre-imagery preparation might be needed whereby the individual is moved physically through the proper motions and is therefore more able to experience the correct proprioceptive and neuromuscular sensations, to be replicated later in imagery. Imagery instructions might also need to be more detailed, to properly focus the beginner's attention on the proper cues. In contrast, an expert in the sport may need minimal prompting on the fundamentals of the sport, but instead may need instruction on what is needed to smooth out a stroke, snap in place a new routine, or display energy and vigor in a skating routine.

In closing, it is important to reiterate that imagery rehearsal has reached a level of acceptability as to represent a tool in sport psychology training while it is still a research topic demanding further investigation and facts. As a training tool, imagery rehearsal must continue to be carefully applied in accordance with known principles of skill acquisition, skill building, and skill enhancement. Also, imagery rehearsal training should be applied to match the individual level, needs, and characteristics of the athlete as well as the changing needs associated with different times in the competitive season. As a research topic, imagery rehearsal must be studied to further identify the factors that maximize performance results from its application. Imagery rehearsal is not a simple process, as this chapter has demonstrated. However, the potential and promise are there and await the serious researcher, practitioner, and athlete.

References

Anderson, M. P. (1981). Assessment of imaginal processes: Approaches and issues. In T. V. Merluzzi, C. R. Glass, & M. Genest (Eds.), *Cognitive assessment* (pp. 149–187). New York: Guilford Press.

Andre, J. C., & Means, J. R. (1986). Rate of imagery in mental practice: An experimental investigation. *Journal of Sport Psychology, 8,* 124–128.

Bandura, A. (1969). *Principles of behavior modification.* New York: Holt, Rinehart & Winston.

Bandura, A., & Jefferies, R. W. (1973). Role of symbolic coding and rehearsal processes in observational learning. *Journal of Personality and Social Psychology, 26,* 122–130.

Bennett, B. K., & Stothart, C. M. (1978). *The effects of a relaxation-based cognitive technique on sports performances.* Paper presented at the Congress of the Canadian Society for Motor Learning and Sport Psychology, Toronto, Canada.

Benson, H., Dryer, T., & Hartley, L. H. (1978). Decreased VO$_2$ consumption during exercise with elicitation of the relaxation response. *Journal of Human Stress, 4,* 38–42.

Burhans, III, R. S., Richman, C. L., & Bergey, D. B. (1988). Mental imagery training: Effects of running speed performance. *International Journal of Sport Psychology, 19,* 26–37.

Carpenter, W. (1984). *Principles of mental physiology* (4th ed.). New York: Appleton.

Carroll, W., & Bandura, A. (1982). The role of visual monitoring in observational learning of action patterns: Making the unobservable observable. *Journal of Motor Behavior, 14,* 152–167.

Corbin, C. (1972). Mental practice. In W. Morgan (Ed.), *Ergogenic aids and muscular performance* (pp. 688–784). New York: Academic Press.

Desiderato, O., & Miller, I. B. (1979). Improving tennis performance by cognitive behavior modification techniques. *The Behavior Therapist, 2,* 19.

Doyle, L. A., & Landers, D. M. (1980). *Psychological skills in elite and subelite shooters.* Unpublished manuscript.

Epstein, M. L. (1980). The relationship of mental imagery and mental rehearsal to performance of a motor task. *Journal of Sport Psychology, 2,* 211–220.

Feltz, D. L., & Landers, D. M. (1983). The effects of mental practice on motor skill learning and performance: A meta-analysis. *Journal of Sport Psychology, 5,* 25–57.

Feltz, D. L., & Riessinger, C. A. (1990). Effects of in vivo emotive imagery and performance feedback on self-efficacy and muscular endurance. *Journal of Sport & Exercise Psychology, 12,* 132–143.

Fensterheim, H. (1980). A behavioral method for improving sport performance. *Psychiatric Annals, 10,* 54–63.

Furlong, W. (1979). Coping, the power of imagination. *Quest, 30,* 95–96.

Gould, D., & Weiss, M. (1981). The effects of model similarity and model talk on self-efficacy and muscular endurance. *Journal of Sport Psychology, 3,* 17–29.

Gough, D. (1989). Improving batting skills with small-college baseball players through guided visual imagery. *Coaching Clinic, 27,* 1–6.

Gravel, R., Lemieux, G., & Ladouceur, R. (1980). Effectiveness of a cognitive behavioral treatment package for cross-country ski racers. *Cognitive Therapy and Research, 4,* 83–90.

Gray, S. W. (1990). Effect of visuomotor rehearsal with videotaped modeling on racquetball performance of beginning players. *Perceptual and Motor Skills, 70,* 379–385.

Gray, S. W., & Fernandez, S. (in press). Effects of visuo-motor behavior rehearsal with videotaped modeling on basketball shooting performance. *Psychology.*

Hale, B. D. (1982). The effects of internal and external imagery on muscular and ocular concomitants. *Journal of Sport Psychology, 4,* 379–387.

Hall, E. G., & Erffmeyer, E. S. (1983). The effect of visuo-motor behavior rehearsal with videotaped modeling on free throw accuracy of intercollegiate female basketball players. *Journal of Sport Psychology, 5,* 343–346.

Harris, D. V., & Robinson, W. J. (1986). The effects of skill level on EMG activity during internal and external imagery. *Journal of Sport Psychology, 8,* 105–111.

Hecker, J. E., & Kaczor, L. M. (1988). Application of imagery theory to sport psychology: Some preliminary findings. *Journal of Sport & Exercise Psychology, 10,* 363–373.

Jacobsen, E. (1930). Electrical measurement of neuromuscular states during mental activities. *American Journal of Physiology, 94,* 22–34.

Jacobsen, E. (1932). Electrophysiology of mental activities. *American Journal of Psychology, 44,* 677–694.

Jeffrey, R. (1976). The influence of symbolic and motor rehearsal in observational learning. *Journal of Research in Personality, 10,* 116–127.

Jowdy, D. P., & Harris, D. V. (1990). Muscular responses during mental imagery as a function of motor skill level. *Journal of Sport & Exercise Psychology, 12,* 191–201.

Kazdin, A. (1974). Covert modeling, model similarity, and reduction of avoidance behavior. *Behavior Therapy, 5,* 325–340.

Kirchenbaum, D. S., & Bale, R. M. (1980). Cognitive-behavioral skills in golf: Brain power golf. In R. Suinn (Ed.), *Psychology in sports: Methods and applications* (pp. 334–343). Minneapolis, MN: Burgess.

Kolonay, B. J. (1977). *The effects of visuo-motor behavior rehearsal on athletic performance.* Unpublished masters thesis, City University of New York, Hunter College.

Lane, J. F. (1978). *Four studies of visuo-motor behavior rehearsal.* Unpublished manuscript.

Lane, J. F. (1980). Improving athletic performance through visuo-motor behavior rehearsal. In R. Suinn (Ed.), *Psychology in sports: Methods and applications* (pp. 316–320). Minneapolis, MN: Burgess.

Lang, P. J. (1977). Imagery in therapy: An information processing analysis of fear. *Behavior Therapy, 8,* 862–886.

Lang, P. J. (1979). A bio-informational theory of emotional imagery. *Psychophysiology, 16,* 495–512.

Lang, P. J. (1985). The cognitive psychophysiology of emotion: Fear and anxiety. In A. H. Tuma & J. D. Maser (Eds.), *Anxiety and the anxiety disorders* (pp. 131–170). Hillsdale, NJ: Erlbaum.

Lang, P. J., Kozak, M. J., Miller, G. A., Levin, D. N., & McLean, A. (1980). Emotional imagery: Conceptual structure and pattern of somato-visceral response. *Psychophysiology, 17,* 179–192.

Lang, P. J., Levin, D. N., Miller, G. A., & Kozak, J. J. (1983). Fear behavior, fear imagery, and the psychophysiology of emotion: The problem of affective response integration. *Journal of Abnormal Psychology, 92,* 276–306.

Lazarus, L. (1977). *In the mind's eye.* New York: Rawson.

Lee, C. (1990). Psyching up for a muscular endurance task: Effects of image content on performance and mood state. *Journal of Sport & Exercise Psychology, 12,* 66–73.

Levin, D. N., Cook, E. W., & Lang, P. J. (1982). Fear imagery and fear behavior: Psychophysiological analysis of clients receiving treatment for anxiety disorders. *Psychophysiology, 19,* 571–572.

Machlus, S. D., & O'Brien, R. M. (1988, August). *Visuo-motor behavior rehearsal and preparatory arousal in improving athletic speed.* Paper presented to the annual meeting of the American Psychological Association, Atlanta, GA.

MacKay, D. G. (1981). The problem of rehearsal or mental practice. *Journal of Motor Behavior, 13,* 274–285.

Mahoney, M. J. (1977, December). *Cognitive skills and athletics performance.* Paper presented to the 11th Annual Meeting of the Association for Advancement of Behavior Therapy, Atlanta, GA.

Mahoney, M. J., & Avener, M. (1977). Psychology of the elite athlete: An exploratory study. *Cognitive Therapy and Research, 1,* 135–141.

Meichenbaum, D. (1977). *Cognitive behavior modification.* New York: Plenum.

Meichenbaum, D., & Cameron, R. (1974). The clinical potential of modifying what clients say to themselves. In M. Mahoney & C. Thoresen (Eds.), *Self-control: Power to the person* (pp. 263–290). California: Brooks/Cole.

Minas, S. C. (1978). Mental practice of a complex perceptual-motor skill. *Journal of Human Mouvement Studies, 4,* 102–107.

Morgan, W. (1978). The mind of the marathoner. *Psychology Today, 11,* 38–49.

Morrisett, L. N. (1956). *The role of implicit practice in learning.* Unpublished doctoral dissertation, Yale University.

Murphy, S. M., Jowdy, D. P., & Durtschi, S. K. (1989). *Report on the United States Olympic Committee survey on imagery use in sport: 1989.* Colorado Springs, CO: U.S. Olympic Training Center.

Murphy, S. M., Woolfolk, R. L., & Budney, A. J. (1988). The effects of emotive imagery on strength performance. *Journal of Sport & Exercise Psychology, 10,* 334–345.

Nicklaus, J. (1974). *Golf my way.* New York: Simon & Schuster.

Nideffer, R. M. (1971). Deep muscle relaxation: An aid to diving. *Coach and Athlete, 24,* 38.

Noel, R. C. (1980). The effect of visuo-motor behavior rehearsal on tennis performance. *Journal of Sport Psychology, 2,* 220–226.

Oxendine, J. (1968). *Psychology of motor learning.* New York: Meredith.

Richardson, A. (1967a). Mental practice: A review and discussion. Part I. *Research Quarterly, 38,* 95–107.

Richardson, A. (1967b). Mental practice: A review and discussion. Part II. *Research Quarterly, 38,* 263–273.

Ryan, D. E., & Simons, J. (1981). Cognitive demand, imagery, and frequency of mental rehearsal as factors influencing acquisition of motor skills. *Journal of Sport Psychology, 3,* 35–45.

Sackett, R. S. (1934). The influences of symbolic rehearsal upon the retention of a maze habit. *Journal of General Psychology, 10,* 376–395.

Schleser, R., Meyers, A. W., & Montgomery, T. (1980, November). *A cognitive behavioral intervention for improving basketball performance.* Paper presented to the Association for the Advancement of Behavior Therapy, 18th Annual Convention, New York, NY.

Schmidt, R. A. (1982). *Motor control and learning: A behavioral emphasis.* Champaign, IL: Human Kinetics.

Schramm, V. (1967). *An investigation of the electromyographic responses obtained during mental practice.* Unpublished master's thesis, University of Wisconsin, Madison.

Shick, J. (1970). Effects of mental practice in selected volleyball skills for college women. *Research Quarterly, 51,* 88–94.

Suinn, R. M. (1972). Behavior rehearsal training for ski racers. *Behavior Therapy, 3,* 519.

Suinn, R. M. (1980). Psychology and sports performance: Principles and applications. In R. Suinn (Ed.), *Psychology in sports: Methods and applications* (pp. 26–36). Minneapolis, MN: Burgess.

Suinn, R. M. (1982). Imagery and sports. In A. Sheikh (Ed.), *Imagery, current theory, research and application* (pp. 507–534). New York: John Wiley & Sons.

Suinn, R. M. (1984). Visual motor behavior rehearsal: The basic technique. *Scandinavian Journal of Behaviour Therapy, 13,* 131–142.

Suinn, R. M. (1987a). Psychological approaches to performance enhancement. In J. May & M. Asken (Eds.), *Sport psychology: The psychological health of the athlete* (pp. 41–57). New York: PMA Publishing.

Suinn, R. M. (in press). Visualization in sports. In A. Sheikh (Ed.), *Imagery in sports and physical performance.* Amityville, NY: Baywood Publishing.

Suinn, R. M. (1989). Models from behavioral clinical psychology for sport psychology. In J. Skinner, C. Corbin, D. Landers, P. Martin, & C. Wells (Eds.), *Future directions in exercise and sport science research* (pp. 453–473). Champaign, IL: Human Kinetics.

Suinn, R. M. (1990). *Anxiety management training: A behavior therapy.* New York: Plenum Press.

Suinn, R. M., & Andrews, F. A. (1980). *Psychological strategies of professional competitors.* Unpublished manuscript.

Suinn, R. M., Morton, M., & Brammell, H. (1980). *Psychological and mental training to increase efficiency in endurance athletes.* Technical Report to Developmental Subcommittee, U.S. Olympic Women's Athletics.

Titley, R. W. (1976, September). The loneliness of a long-distance kicker. *The Athletic Journal,* 74–80.

Twinning, W. H. (1949). Mental practice and physical practice in learning a motor skill. *Research Quarterly, 20,* 432–435.

Vandell, R. A., Davis, R. A., & Ciugston, H. A. (1943). The function of mental practice in the acquisition of motor skills. *Journal of General Psychology, 29,* 243–250.

Vealey, R. S. (1987, June). *Imagery training for performance enhancement.* Paper presented at the Sports Psychology Institute, Portland, ME.

Weinberg, R. S. (1982). The relationship of mental preparation strategies and performance: A review and critique. *Quest, 33,* 195–213.

Weinberg, R., Seabourne, T., & Jackson, A. (1981). Effects of visuo-motor behavior rehearsal, relaxation, and imagery on karate performance. *Journal of Sport Psychology, 3,* 228–238.

Weinberg, R., Seabourne, T., & Jackson, A. (1982). Effects of visuo-motor behavior rehearsal on state-trait anxiety and performance: Is practice important? *Journal of Sport Behavior, 5,* 209–219.

Winning Associates. (1978). *Athlete's homework manual.* Winning Associates: Morgantown, WV.

Woolfolk, R. L., Murphy, S. M., & Parrish, M. W. (1983, December). *Effects of imagery on motor skill performance.* Presented at World Congress of Behavior Therapy, Washington, DC.

Wrisberg, C. A., & Ragsdale, M. R. (1979). Cognitive demand and practice level: Factors in the mental rehearsal of motor skills. *Journal of Human Mouvement Studies, 5,* 201–208.

Ziegler, S. G. (1987). Comparison of imagery styles and past experience in skills performance. *Perceptual and Motor Skills, 64,* 579–586.

22

OPTIMIZING AROUSAL LEVEL

Leonard Zaichkowsky

Koji Takenaka

Like so many concepts used in the study of psychology, the concept of arousal is complex and as such lacks a universally accepted definition (Venables, 1984). The complexity (or confusion) surrounding the concept is perhaps best illustrated by Sage (1984), who in writing about arousal, provided the following footnote:

Arousal and activation are used interchangeably by most motivation theorists, although there are some who have attempted to make distinctions between the two concepts. In this text, the two words will be considered to be synonymous. "Emotional," "tense," and "anxious" are other adjectives that are frequently used to express the same idea, and in sports, "psyched-up" conveys the same notion. (p. 345)

Sage is quite accurate in his assessment of the use of the arousal concept. Besides the above "synonyms," one could probably add other terms from the English language that convey similar ideas, such as motivation, psychic energy, energy, excitation, vigilance, and mental readiness. The problem of semantics and the fact that anxiety and being "psyched-up" cannot be distinguished from other states such as anger and sexuality has prompted Neiss (1988) to take an extreme position and suggest that the arousal construct has outlived its usefulness for psychology and should be reconceptualized into discrete "psychobiological states." In a follow-up article, Neiss (1990) stated:

By focusing on the elevated physiology and ignoring its psychological context, the construct of arousal lumps together grossly disparate states (e.g., joy, grief, anger) resulting in a breadth that explains nothing. (p. 102)

The focus of this chapter will be to explain the nature of arousal, its effects on athletic performance, and ways in which sport psychologists may help athletes optimize arousal levels. We will first deal with the problem of defining arousal. A discussion of its neurological basis and its measurement will follow. Next, different theoretical views will be presented, followed by a discussion of factors that mediate arousal and performance. We will conclude with a review of the selected ways in which arousal can be regulated for optimal performance.

DEFINING AROUSAL

Because of the proliferation of terms used to describe arousal, it is important to know how scholars, particularly those in the field of motor behavior, have approached the topic. Sage (1984) discusses arousal within the construct of motivation. He sees motivation as having two basic functions. The first is an energizing function, and the second is involved in directing behavior to a specific goal. Magill (1989) likewise views arousal as synonymous with motivation, as he writes, "to motivate an individual is, in effect, to arouse or activate that person in such a way as to prepare himself or herself for the task at hand" (p. 485).

Cox (1990) suggests that "arousal is synonymous with the notion of alertness, as the aroused individual is in a physiological state of readiness" (p. 88). Martens (1987), in expressing his dislike of the term "arousal," chose to use "psychic energy." He felt that arousal, drive, activation, and the like confused psychic energy with physical energy. By using psychic energy to describe the activation of the mind, he felt that coaches would feel comfortable with the concept, since it was closely associated with the sporting terms of "psyching up" and "psyching out." Martens says psychic energy is the "vigor, vitality, and intensity with which the mind functions and is the bedrock of motivation" (p. 92). Brehm and Self (1989) use the term "motivational arousal"

511

to describe intensity of motivation. They go on to describe sympathetic nervous system responses that seemed to be most reflective of motivational arousal.

Ursin (1978) treats activation and arousal synonymously and states:

"activation is . . . the process in the central nervous system that increases the activity in the brain from a lower level to a higher level, and maintains this high level. The activation response is a general energy mobilizing response that provides the conditions for high performance, both physically and psychologically." (p.202)

These writers view arousal as varying on a continuum from extremely low levels, as in sleep, to very high levels of excitement that occur in threatening situations (fight or flight) or perhaps in sexual activity (where considerable research on arousal has been conducted). Early researchers such as Cannon (1929), Hebb (1955), and Malmo (1959) viewed arousal as energy mobilization along a continuum with concomitant psychophysiological responses. Duffy (1934, 1941, 1957), one of the first psychologists to treat the concept of arousal, viewed it as behavior that varied on two dimensions: intensity and direction. The intensity dimension was defined as neural excitation that ranged from coma to extreme excitation.

Because anxiety results in increased central and autonomic nervous system activity, it has unfortunately been confused with arousal (e.g., Klavora, 1979; Sage & Bennett, 1973; Sonstroem & Bernardo, 1982). Essentially, these researchers propose to study arousal but instead measure anxiety and discuss the findings as though arousal was being measured. Although anxiety results in increased physiological activity (like arousal), anxiety refers to states that provide feelings of discomfort and worry (Spielberger, 1966). The two constructs are not the same. Fenz and Epstein (1967), in studying sport parachutists, argued that physiological arousal was distinct from psychological fear. Borkovec (1976) concluded from his work that arousal can be defined by measuring three interacting response components: the physiological, the behavioral, and the cognitive. Ursin (1988) also points out that arousal is not identical to changes in heart rate, galvanic skin response, rise in plasma cortisol or growth hormone, or increases in metabolism. Each of these physiological changes constitutes only a part of the arousal response. He also adds that any of these factors can be altered without affecting the others. It is also true that one cannot make inferences about arousal solely on overt motor behavior. For example, humans or animals "freezing" in fear do not move actively but show all other signs of arousal. It follows then that no one physiological, cognitive, or behavioral measure can be considered a perfect indicator of arousal; rather, each measure provides only partial information about arousal.

According to Neiss (1988), historically, there were two reasons for using the construct of arousal in the psychological literature: (1) its perceived unidimensionality, and (2) its equivalence to fear and anxiety.

Today we know this is not the case. Rather than eliminate the construct from the sport psychology vocabulary, as Neiss (1988) suggests, it would be more appropriate to operationally define it. Based on the current views of arousal, we can say that it is a multidimensional construct that refers to an energizing function of the mind and body. This energy varies along a continuum from low (e.g., sleep) to high (e.g., extreme excitement). It contains a general physiological response in which several systems may be activated simultaneously, including heart rate, sweat gland activity, and electrical activity of the brain. Behavioral responses (e.g., motor performance) and cognitive processes (e.g., appraisal of consequences) are also indicators of arousal.

NEUROPHYSIOLOGY OF AROUSAL

Malmo (1959) and Duffy (1962) made seminal contributions to our understanding of brain mechanisms, autonomic nervous system activity, and other behaviors that accompany changes in arousal. Structures of the central nervous system (CNS) that are closely related to arousal include the cortex of the brain, the reticular formation, the hypothalamus, and the limbic system. Figure 22–1 provides a simplified illustration of how the nervous system is involved in regulating arousal.

Table 22–1 summarizes the nervous system structures as well as their location and function.

According to Ursin (1978), novel stimuli and the perception of threat will induce physiological activity that can be called arousal. In sport, impending competition will result in arousal increases as well. Activity at the level of the reticular formation (RF) or reticular activating system (RAS) is characterized by increased neuronal activity from a vast network of neurons at the level of the brainstem that continues to the cortex. It appears that the RF organizes sensorimotor behavior through its interconnections with the cortex, hypothalamus, and nervous system. The cerebral cortex becomes activated, and this is characterized by rapid, low amplitude, asynchronous patterns known as beta waves. The hypothalamus receives input from higher brain centers in the nervous system as well as from internal organs of the body. As such, it is involved in integrating messages from the cortex and internal organs. The limbic system is also thought to be involved in the regulation of arousal. Although not much is known about this "primitive" brain structure, it is thought to be involved in the development and elaboration of emotions.

The hypothalamus, located at the level of the midbrain, is involved with regulating the sympathetic nervous system and the pituitary gland. It stimulates the adrenal medulla to release adrenaline and noradrenaline. The pituitary gland, also known as the "master gland," is in close proximity to the hypothalamus. It releases adrenocorticotropin hormone (ACTH) into the blood, so that the adrenal cortex is stimulated to release cortisol (Dienstbier, 1989).

The nervous system contains two major divisions, the peripheral nervous system (nerves in the skeletal muscles of

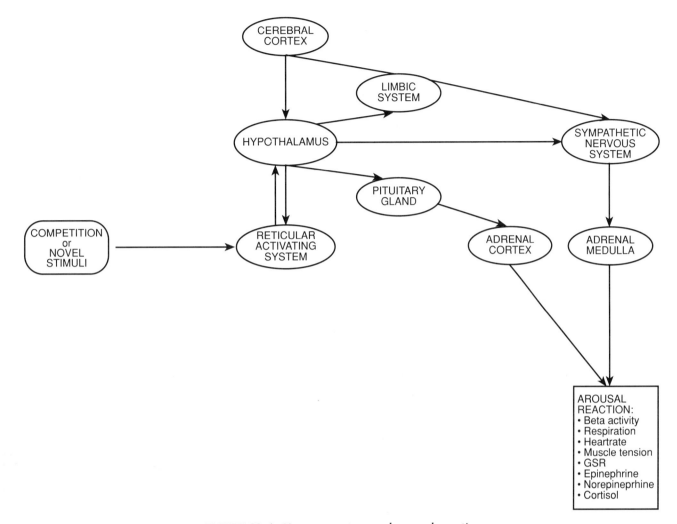

FIGURE 22–1. Nervous system and arousal reaction.

the body), and the autonomic nervous system (ANS) (nerves in the smooth muscles and glands of the body). The ANS is itself divided into two divisions, the sympathetic and parasympathetic. The sympathetic division is primarily responsible for psychophysiological exchanges associated with arousal. These changes include increased heart rate, pupil dilation, increased respiration, release of glucose for the liver, and decreased kidney output. The sympathetic division releases catecholamines known as adrenaline and noradrenaline at the site of the gland or smooth muscles (with the exception of palmar sweat glands). The parasympathetic division of the ANS produces hypoarousal effects and in general a return of bodily function to a state of homeostasis.

THE MEASUREMENT OF AROUSAL

Arousal results in numerous changes in various physiological systems as well as at the biochemical level. These changes are presented in Table 22–2. It is also the case

that researchers attempt to assess levels of arousal by using self-report inventories or questionnaires. These scales were by and large designed to measure anxiety. However, as previously mentioned, the arousal construct is then measured using the same scale because it was presumed the effects, if not identical, were at least similar. The State-Trait Anxiety Inventory (Spielberger, Gorsuch, & Lushene, 1970) is undoubtedly the most widely used scale for this purpose. The Activation Deactivation Adjective Checklist is also a popular research tool (Thayer, 1967). Martens's (1977) Sport Competition Anxiety Test, although a trait measure, has also been used to measure anxiety in sport specific environments.

More recently, researchers have moved toward using multidimensional self-report instruments. They include a scale developed by Schwartz, Davidson, and Goleman (1978) and the Sport Competition Anxiety Inventory—II (Martens, Vealey, & Burton, 1990) These scales attempt to divide anxiety into a somatic component (e.g., "How tense are the muscles in your body?") and a cognitive component (e.g., "Do you worry a lot?").

TABLE 22–1. Nervous system structures involved in arousal.

Structure	Location	Function
Reticular formation	Part of brain stem that continues out of medulla and pons	Involved in sleep, waking, alertness, and optimal brain arousal
Hypothalamus	Between the thalamus and midbrain	Involved in appetitive and sexual behavior, regulation of sympathetic nervous system and pituitary gland
Limbic system	Series of structures, including the hypocampus and amygdala, located near the border between the cerebral hemisphere and the brain stem. The hypothalamus is sometimes considered part of the limbic system.	Primarily concerned with emotional behavior. Amygdala appears to be involved in aggression.
Cerebral cortex	Convoluted outer layer of the human brain	Highest center involved in learning, remembering, planning, and performing motor acts.
Sympathetic nervous system	A branch of the autonomic nervous system (ANS) with nerve fibers originating in thoracic and lumbar regions of the spinal cord	Activates glands and smooth muscles during arousal
Parasympathetic nervous system	A branch of the autonomic nervous system (ANS) with nerve fibers originating in the brain stem and sacral regions of the spinal cord	Maintains appropriate internal states in times of relaxation
Adrenal cortex	Outer layer of two small endocrine glands just above the kidneys	Secretes cortisol that regulates metabolism and stress response
Adrenal medulla (closely related to the ANS, but technically not part of the nervous system)	Inner layer of two small endocrine glands just above the kidneys	Secretes adrenaline (epinephrine) and noradrenaline (norepinephrine), both involved in increased activation of the body
Pituitary gland	Deep inside brain, just below hypothalamus	Releases adrenocorticotropic hormone (ACTH) that stimulates adrenal cortex to release cortisol

As depicted in Table 22–2, a number of physiological indices have been used to measure arousal. Recognizing the complexity of arousal, Cattell (1972) suggested 20 years ago that a minimum of six physiological indices should be taken for the term *arousal* to be used meaningfully. Test batteries have in fact been developed, and they tend to show stability over time (Berman & Johnson, 1985). Measures should include those traditionally used with arousal discriminating properties such as respiration rate, blood pressure, heart rate, electrodermal activity, brain waves, and electromyography from various sites.

Biochemical responses have also served as measures of arousal. According to Dienstbier (1989), sympathetic nervous system arousal features the hypothalmus stimulating the adrenal medulla to release adrenaline and noradrenaline. Pituitary-adrenal-cortical arousal, on the other hand, has the pituitary gland releasing ACTH so that the cortex is stimulated to release cortisol. The work of Ursin et al. (1978) and Vaernes, Ursin, Darragh, & Lamb (1982)

verifies that there are two different arousal responses (catecholomine and cortisol) to stressful situations. To date, researchers in sport psychology have rarely relied on biochemical measures of arousal.

One of the frustrations experienced by researchers is that there are low correlations between self-report scales of arousal and biochemical indicators of arousal as well as low correlations between the various physiological/biological indicators. There are a number of reasons for these low intercorrelations. Lacey and Lacey (1958) suggest that autonomic response stereotypy may be one explanation. That is to say, individuals differ widely in how they reflect arousal. One athlete may demonstrate arousal increase with an elevated heart rate, whereas another may show increases in muscle tension or increased sweat response. Still others may reflect arousal more cognitively. Errors in measurement may also contribute to this problem, and in the case of questionnaires, social desirability may override the scale's ability to discriminate between different arousal levels.

TABLE 22–2. Neurophysiological Indicators of Increased Arousal

Indicator	Response
Electroencephalogram (EEG)—brain waves	Increase from sleep (theta waves) to excitement (beta waves)
Electrocardiogram (EKG)—heart rate (HR)	Generally increases in heart rate with increased arousal
Electromyography (EMG)—muscle tension	Generally increases in muscle tension as arousal increases
Respiration	Generally increases with increased arousal
Blood Pressure	Generally increases with increased arousal
Galvanic Skin Response (GSR)	Increase in arousal results in palmar sweating and a decrease in skin resistance of GSR
Biochemical	Increase in adrenaline and noradrenaline with increases in arousal

THE RELATIONSHIP BETWEEN AROUSAL AND MOTOR PERFORMANCE

Until recently, two main hypotheses regarding the relationship between arousal and motor performance have been advanced and tested: drive theory and the inverted-U hypothesis.

Drive Theory

Drive theory was derived from the learning theory work of Hull (1943) and later modified by Spence and Spence (1966). It predicts that performance (P) is a multiplicative function of drive state (D) and habit strength (H), or P = D × H. Hull saw drive as physiological arousal and habit as the dominance of correct or incorrect responses. Simply stated, drive theory maintains that there is a positive linear relationship between arousal and performance (see Figure 22–2).

After an extensive review of the literature, Martens (1971) concluded that drive theory did not provide an adequate explanation for the relationship between arousal and performance. Today it appears that the perspective of drive theory has faded from prominence for several reasons. First, it is difficult to test in the area of motor performance. For example, it is quite difficult to determine habit hierarchies (i.e., the dominance of correct or incor-rect responses) for complex motor skills. Second, the few studies that have been conducted fail to support the predictions of drive theory (i.e., increased performance with increased arousal). Third, anecdotal reports from athletes and other performers strongly suggest that excessive arousal disrupts performance.

Oxendine (1984), however, argues that linear relationships between arousal and performance do exist for gross motor activities that involve strength, endurance, and speed. These tasks are typically overlearned and do not require extensive information processing and motor control. Examples could include lifting a heavy weight or sprinting. There seems to be some anecdotal support for this position since numerous examples exist showing highly aroused individuals lifting unusually heavy weights or running rapidly for short periods of time. Although these tasks are overlearned and require little information processing, the reports typically come from situations where high performance was necessary because of emergency or life-threatening situations. The rush of epinephrine would be expected to result in superior performance, but it is unlikely to occur in sport. So called "simpler" gross motor tasks such as a bench press still require a great deal of motor control.

Inverted-U Hypothesis

The inverted-U hypothesis, derived from the animal work of Yerkes and Dodson (1908), is also known as the Yerkes-Dodson Law. It posits a curvilinear relationship between arousal and performance. That is, as arousal increases, there is a corresponding increase in performance until an optimal level is reached. Further increases in arousal result in performance decrement. (See Figure 22–2.)

Yerkes and Dodson also demonstrated that, for laboratory animals, optimal arousal varied across different tasks. This was later supported by Broadhurst (1957). Essentially, it was concluded that tasks with higher cognitive demands require lower levels of arousal than tasks with lower cognitive demands. A great number of studies using both laboratory tasks and field measures provide support for the

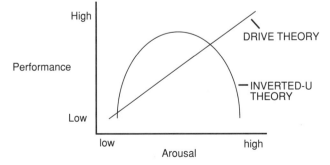

FIGURE 22–2. Drive theory and inverted-U theory.

inverted-U hypothesis. One of the early human studies supporting this hypothesis is that of Stennett (1957). He showed that performance on auditory tasks associated with very high or low levels of physiological function was inferior to tracking performance associated with moderate levels of physiological functioning.

A study by Levitt and Gutin (1971) demonstrated that reaction time performance resembles an inverted-U after subjects were activated through exercise that had varying levels of intensity and duration. The study of Lansing, Schwartz, and Lindsley (1956) on reaction time also supported the notion of the inverted-U. Martens and Landers (1970) assigned high, moderate, and low trait-anxious junior high school boys to three different stress conditions as they performed a steadiness task. Questionnaire data plus heart rate and palmar sweat responses confirmed three distinct levels of arousal. Results indicated that moderate trait-anxious subjects performed significantly better than low and high trait-anxious subjects, thus providing support for the inverted-U hypothesis.

Later, Weinberg and Ragan (1978) manipulated three levels of trait anxiety and stress. Their results demonstrated that high trait-anxious subjects performed a throw for accuracy task best under low stress, and low trait-anxious subjects performed best under high stress, thus confirming inverted-U hypothesis predictions, at least when arousal is operationally defined as anxiety. Because of the possible limited external validity of laboratory tasks for testing the inverted-U hypothesis, a number of researchers have undertaken field studies. The often cited work of Fenz and his colleagues has provided indirect support for the inverted-U hypothesis (Fenz & Epstein, 1967; Fenz & Jones, 1972). These researchers compared heart rate and respiratory rates of experienced and novice parachute jumpers. They noted that technically good jumpers, regardless of experience, had increased levels of arousal prior to jump time, then showed reduced arousal just before executing the jump. Conversely, technically poor jumpers did not show reduced levels of arousal prior to executing jumps.

In an interesting study of 11- and 12-year-old baseball players, Lowe (1971) investigated the inverted-U hypothesis using batting performance and changes in heart rate and subjective behavioral ratings. He also factored in the "criticality" of the situation. He noted that arousal levels increased as "criticality" or importance of the situation increased. It was concluded that when the data were averaged, players hit their best in games of moderate critical situations and less well under low and high criticality. Players varied considerably in optimal levels of arousal, and task difficulty (quality of pitching) influenced the inverted-U relationship.

Klavora (1979) tested the validity of the inverted-U hypothesis by testing 145 Canadian high school basketball players. He had subjects complete the Spielberger state-trait anxiety inventory prior to each game and had coaches evaluate the performance of each player after each game. Results supported the inverted-U hypothesis in showing that the best performances occurred under moderate levels of state anxiety, average performance under conditions of slight under-or overarousal, and poor performance under either very low or high levels of anxiety. Using a paper-and-pencil test of anxiety as a measure of arousal/anxiety, Sonstroem and Bernardo (1982) demonstrated that an inverted-U relationship exists between basketball performance and arousal/anxiety. These researchers assessed the composite performance scores of female university players and plotted these scores against arousal/anxiety scores. They concluded that a moderate level of arousal/anxiety was associated with the highest level of performance.

More recent studies by Gould, Petlichkoff, Simons, and Vevera (1987) and Burton (1988) have demonstrated an inverted-U relationship between somatic arousal/anxiety and performance in the sports of pistol shooting and swimming. Beater and Duda (1985) have also shown that children perform smooth motor patterns under optimal arousal; however, high levels of arousal result in kinematic patterns that are less smooth and efficient.

Not all studies support the inverted-U hypothesis. In investigations where arousal was manipulated by electric shock, performance did not vary as a function of level of arousal. This was demonstrated on a variety of different tasks, such as balancing on a stabilometer (Carron, 1968; Ryan, 1961, 1962), performing simulated guided missile tracking (Bergstrom, 1970), and pursuit rotor tasks (Cox, 1983; Marteniuk & Wenger, 1970; Sage & Bennett, 1973). Several studies have also failed to show an inverted-U relationship between reaction time and various indicators of arousal (Paller & Shapiro, 1983; Stern, 1976; Wankel, 1972). One could argue, however, that reaction time, although important to motor performance, is considerably different from complex motor performance. Giabrone (1973) failed to show a relationship between Big Ten college basketball players' free-throw shooting and levels of arousal. Basler, Fisher, and Munford (1976), Murphy (1966), and Pinneo (1961) also failed to demonstrate the inverted-U hypothesis in their studies.

In his extensive critical review of the arousal construct, Neiss (1988) proposed that we not only abandon the arousal construct but also the proposition of the inverted-U relationship between arousal and human performance. Neiss sees four major problems with the Inverted-U hypothesis. It (1) cannot function as a causal hypothesis, (2) is essentially nonfalsifiable, (3) has trivial value if true, and (4) hinders understanding of individual differences.

Anderson (1990) challenges Neiss's (1989) objections to the inverted-U hypothesis. She presents evidence refuting Neiss's arguments and suggests that arousal as a construct and the inverted-U hypothesis are useful for predicting behaviors in a variety of contexts. Anderson's data, however, come largely from studies on cognitive performance. Although the inverted-U hypothesis does indeed have difficulties, the reasons cited by Neiss do not warrant his radical solution (i.e., abandoning the notion altogether). What is needed is a refinement of the idea much like that proposed by Martens (1987) and Hanin (1989) as well as the utilization of current psychophysiological measurement techniques. Measuring arousal is unquestionably the biggest deterrent to adequate testing of the inverted-U hypothesis.

CONCEPT OF OPTIMAL ZONES

Several writers have expanded on the notion of the inverted-U to include a zone or band width. Hanin first reported on what he called the Zone of Optimal Functioning (ZOF) in the 1970s. Martens (1987) also included a "zone" in his interpretation of the inverted-U. Czikszentmihalyi also used the idea of a zone when he discussed peak performances of high achievers.

Zone of Optimal Functioning (ZOF)

Over the past 20 years, Soviet sport psychologist Hanin collected considerable data on top-flight Soviet athletes to better understand emotional states and optimal performance. His methods included the use of a Russian version of the Spielberger et al. (1970) STAI to determine optimal anxiety levels. According to Hanin (1989), Optimal S-Anxiety (S-Aopt is defined as "the level of performance S-Anxiety that enables a particular athlete to perform at his/her *personal best*" (p. 22). From prestart and retrospective measures of anxiety associated with successful previous performance, Hanin developed what he termed the "zone of optimal functioning" (ZOF). Because of possible errors in athletes' reporting their anxiety, Hanin added and subtracted four points from the athlete's prestart S-anxiety level. Thus each athlete had a bandwidth zone that resulted in maximum performance. Not surprisingly, Hanin discovered large individual differences in optimal anxiety scores which ranged from 26 to 67 on the STAI.

The notion of a zone of optimal functioning is intuitively appealing because it allows for individual differences as well as intra-athlete differences in optimal arousal levels. With the inverted-U, an athlete and coach could determine the band width where the athlete performs best. Unfortunately, Hanin's perspective is limited because he, as well as many other researchers, has conceptualized arousal in terms of anxiety as measured by the STAI. Given our understanding of the multidimensional aspects of arousal, it would have been better to obtain other measure of arousal, particularly physiological indices. Several investigators have, in fact, experimented with this approach to learning more about zones of optimal functioning. Loehr (1991) has reported success in his work with elite tennis players. Essentially, Loehr has tennis players wear a heart rate monitor in order that they may become aware of heart rate values that correspond to optimal performance. Davis (1991), in his work with professional hockey players, has also attempted to help the players become aware of the ZOF using the heart rate monitor. Zaichkowsky (1991) has also collected extensive date on elite and youth sport athletes rep-

resenting a number of different sports in order that they may learn their zones of optimal functioning.

Zone of Optimal Energy

In writing for coaches about arousal or what he called optimal psychic energy, Martens (1987) used the concept of zones much like that of Hanin. Figure 22–3 illustrates Martens's conception of the inverted-U principle. Rather than discussing specific points on the inverted-U, the band width or a zone acknowledges the lack of precision that is associated with the measurement of arousal.

Optimal Arousal States: Flow

A number of writers have provided their own special labels to describe superior performance or intense experience related to arousal. Privette (1983) described flow and peak performance; Maslow (1971) and Ravizza (1977) write about peak experience; Jerome (1980) describes "the sweet spot in time"; and Csikszentmihalyi (1975) discusses flow. Csikszentmihalyi perhaps offered the most insightful view on the concept of flow state. His observations were based on the study of accomplished rock climbers, surgeons, artists, pianists, and athletes. Csikszentmihalyi found a number of qualities common to the flow state:

1. Performers are aware of their actions when performing, but not aware of their awareness. They act and do not have to think about what they are going to do.
2. Performers' attention is focused entirely on what they are doing.
3. Performers lose their self-consciousness or ego, so that there is no evaluation of their doing well or poorly.
4. Performers feel themselves to be in control of their actions.
5. The activity provides performers with clear, unambiguous feedback.
6. Performers require no goals or external rewards since the process itself is intrinsically rewarding.

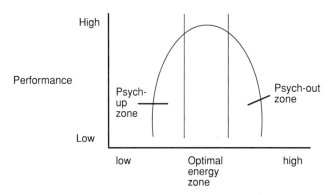

FIGURE 22–3. Zone of optimal energy.

The flow state is achieved when there is an absence of stress, anxiety, and boredom. Pleasant feelings or exhilaration describe optimal arousal. The notion of the flow state or zone is reflected in Figure 22–4.

REVERSAL THEORY

Based on previously mentioned shortcomings of the inverted-U hypothesis, Kerr (1985, 1989) proposed an alternative explanation for the relationship between arousal and performance. He termed this perspective "reversal," which is based upon the theoretical work of Apter (1982, 1984). It attempts to grapple with the complexities of human behavior and offer explanations for inconsistencies associated with human motivation, emotion, and cognition. It uses the terms I like four nouns of *anxiety, excitement, boredom,* and *relaxation* to describe varying levels of arousal. These terms are located on an X-shaped model (see Figure 22–5).

From Figure 22–5 one can determine that high levels of arousal can be interpreted by the individual in two ways which, according to Kerr (1989), can be experienced as feelings of anxiety or feelings of excitement. Similarly, low levels of arousal can be interpreted two different ways and are then experienced by the individual as relaxation or boredom.

Given that high or low levels of arousal can be interpreted in two different ways, Apter (1982) proposes that metamotivational states determine how arousal is interpreted. Metamotivational states are conceptualized as alternative states in which the individual can experience different motives at a given moment. These changes are called "reversals" and provide the origin of the theory's title. The theory is relatively new and as such there is little evidence that would suggest it replace the inverted-U theory. It does, however, deserve attention and research in the field of sport psychology.

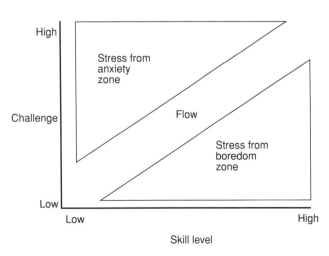

FIGURE 22–4. Optimal energy or flow zone.

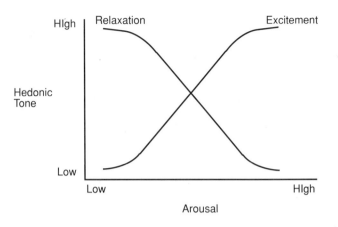

FIGURE 22–5. Reversal theory.

FACTORS THAT MEDIATE AROUSAL AND PERFORMANCE

Although it is not possible to determine the precise level of arousal for optimal performance in sport for a given athlete, some generalizations can be made about factors that influence arousal and performance. Unfortunately the data supporting these generalizations are not voluminous and in some cases are based upon assumptions rather than data.

The Nature of the Task

Yerkes and Dodson (1908) originally proposed that as a task increases in difficulty, peak performance is achieved with less arousal. This proposition was based on their finding that mice made fewer performance errors when an electric shock of medium intensity was applied than when shocks of low or high intensity were used. Testing this hypothesis in the motor domain has been difficult. One problem has been defining "simple" and "complex" tasks. An approach to defining task complexity is offered by Billing (1980), who suggested that task complexity be based on information processing demands and complexity of the motor response. Under this classification, it can be inferred that motor tasks requiring concentration, judgment, discrimination, and fine motor control would be performed best under low or moderate states of arousal. In contrast, motor tasks requiring strength, endurance, speed, or ballistic movements require high levels of arousal.

Using the idea of task complexity, Oxendine (1970) speculated about the level of arousal that is optimal for various sports. He suggested that skills such as the golf putt and the basketball free-throw would require "slight" arousal. Baseball pitchers and football quarterbacks would require slightly more arousal. Moderate arousal would be suitable for gymnasts and boxers. Higher levels of arousal would be needed for swimmers and wrestlers, and extremely high levels of arousal would be needed for football tackling, weight lifting, and sprinting (see Table 22–3).

TABLE 22–3. Hypothesized Optimal Arousal Levels for Selected Sport Skills*

Slight	Slight +	Moderate	High	Extreme
golf putting, basketball	baseball pitching, football quarterbacks	gymnastics, boxing	swimming, wrestling	football tackling, weight lifting, sprinting

*Adapted from Oxendine 1970.

Unfortunately little research has confirmed the importance of the nature of the task and levels of arousal. Levitt and Gutin (1971) used exercise to induce arousal and found that a five-choice reaction time task was performed best at 115 bpm, whereas poorer performance was reported for resting conditions and high heart rates. A later study by Shelton and Mahoney (1978) using weight lifters instructed to "psych up" showed dramatic increases in performance on a simple static strength test (hand dynamometer). Weinberg, Gould, and Jackson (1980) reported that "psyching up" effects were task-specific, facilitating performance on a simple dynamic leg extension test, but having no effect on balancing performance or speed of arm movement.

Skill Level of the Performer

It is also assumed that optimal arousal is dependent upon the skill level of the performer. This view comes largely from observations that generally novice or less-skilled athletes perform poorly under pressure conditions when arousal is high, while experienced or highly skilled athletes tend to excel when pressure in highest. Cox (1990), in discussing skill level and arousal, suggests the application of the following principle:

Highly skilled athletes and athletes performing simple tasks need a moderately high level of arousal for maximum performance. Less skilled athletes and athletes performing a complex task require a relatively low level of arousal for maximum performance. (p. 99)

The limited research on this topic comes under the heading of social facilitation and tests of Zajonc's (1965) general theory of social facilitation. According to Zajonc, the crucial factor that determines whether an audience will improve or inhibit performance is whether the dominant response is correct or incorrect. Correctness of response is determined by the interaction of three factors: (1) task difficulty, (2) skill level, and (3) type of audience.

In general, the presence of spectators will facilitate performance of simple tasks or dominant responses, but audiences hinder performance on complex tasks. (For an elaborate discussion on this topic, see Chapter 28 by Zillman and Pauline in this book.)

Individual Differences

According to Ebbeck and Weiss (1988), for any given task there is no single optimal level of arousal. Individual differences prevail. A plethora of data support this statement. Beside individual differences in skill level, personality differences, and particularly trait anxiety, affect arousal and performance. Data from a multitude of psychophysiological and self-report measures of anxiety show that large individual differences exist in both baseline measures of anxiety/arousal and in individual reactivity to stress and recovery from stress.

Sport psychologist Mahoney (1979) has emphasized the importance of individual differences. "It seems apparent that absolute level of arousal may be only one factor in athletic performance. The person's reactions to that arousal may be a significant determinant of its course and its effect on performance" (p. 436). Neiss (1990) also emphasizes the importance of individual differences in his discussion of arousal. He discusses "clutch players," who excel in pressure situations, and what he refers to as "choke artists," who fail in them. Neiss also notes that in an actual emergency situation, individual differences can be even more striking, with some people freezing in panic and others exhibiting almost superhuman coping resources.

Spielberger (1989), in discussing anxiety, states there are large individual differences in trait anxiety as well as in how people report their state anxiety. In general, people high in state anxiety respond to evaluative situations with greater amounts of arousal than people low in trait anxiety. These different levels of arousal presumably lead to individuals performing differently in similar situations. Individuals high in trait anxiety tend to perform better than individuals with normally low arousal levels on simple tasks. Conversely, high-anxious individuals would tend to do poorly on complex tasks, particularly if novel responses are required. Several studies have shown that high-anxious subjects performed motor tasks best in low-stress situations, while low-anxious subjects performed best under high-stress conditions (Carron, 1968; Weinberg & Hunt, 1976; Weinberg & Ragan, 1978). (Hackfort and Schwenkmezger discuss anxiety in depth in Chapter 14 of this book.)

Hamilton (1986) also found significant differences in performance, favoring low-anxious over high-anxious subjects in cognitive and reaction time tasks; however, these differences did not covary with heart rate and electrodermal activity. Variability in performance and self-reported anxiety could not be explained by differences in physiological arousal. Studies from the test anxiety and performance literature also support the importance of individual differences since high and low test-anxious subjects do not differ on measures of heart rate and electrodermal activity (Holroyd et al., 1978).

Attentional Processes. Although related to the individual differences and skill level, attentional processes deserve special consideration as a factor mediating arousal and performance (see Chapter 6). Several writers have suggested that attention and cue utilization may be the crucial factor in understanding anxiety/arousal and performance. Landers (1978, 1980) hypothesized that as performance anxiety increases, perceptual selectivity also increases. At optimal levels of arousal, better perceptual selectivity should occur through the elimination of task-irrelevant cues. At low levels of arousal, an athlete may fail to eliminate irrelevant stimuli due to an uncritical perceptual focus, while at high levels of arousal, the perceptual range may narrow to the point of eliminating valuable cues. Nideffer (1976, 1989; see also Chapter 24) has offered the most systematic analysis of the role of attention in sport, particularly as it relates to arousal and performance.

Cognitive Appraisal. Cognitive appraisal is another individual differences factor that influences arousal level and performance. How one *interprets* demands of a task, resources, consequences of performance, and perceptions of bodily reactions clearly differs among individuals. Under identical situations, one athlete may appraise the competitive situation as physically and mentally impossible and thus display high anxiety. Another athlete may appraise the situation positively. In this case, optimal physiological arousal will be present but anxiety will be absent.

THE REGULATION OF AROUSAL

Most coaches and athletes would agree that an athlete's mental control is what accounts at least in part for fluctuations in performance. There are occasions when an athlete or a team is excessively aroused and it seems reasonable that strategies should be used to help reduce this arousal. It is also the case that an athlete or team may be underaroused and the arousal level must somehow be increased. This regulation can be manipulated in two ways:

- Self-regulation: The athlete uses strategies to control arousal level.
- External agent regulation: Another person, such as a coach, tries to manipulate arousal.

A variety of strategies for arousal regulation have been utilized by coaches, athletes, and sport psychologists. Many of them can be used either for decreasing *or* increasing arousal, depending upon specific needs. When looking at regulation from the "self" perspective, it is also beneficial to use a categorization proposed by Davidson and Schwartz (1976). These authors classified approaches to stress management as being somatic or cognitive in nature. Somatic techniques would include progressive muscular relaxation and respiration control, whereas cognitive techniques would include imagery and self-talk.

This part of the chapter covers different arousal regulations techniques and analyzes the research (where available) that has investigated the efficacy of these approaches. We will first discuss techniques for decreasing arousal, followed by techniques for increasing arousal. Fundamental to all techniques of arousal regulation is *awareness* on the part of the athlete of his/her level of arousal (before and during competition), as reflected in a number of indices. For example, one must learn to be aware of the amount of anxiety and cognitive load that is present as well as physiological responses such as rate of breathing, muscle tension, heart response, and sweat. Being aware of these states and of optimal performance states enables an athlete to consistently perform at the highest level.

Techniques for Decreasing Arousal

Controlled breathing not only induces relaxation, but it may also facilitate physiological performance by increasing the amount of oxygen available for cardiovascular circulation to active muscles. Proper breathing, therefore, is perhaps the most important arousal regulation technique to be learned. It appears to be the master control system, since it impacts so heavily on the control of other physiological systems. As Harris (1986) accurately points out, many athletes have never learned proper breathing, i.e., deep diaphragmatic breathing. When placed under situational stress, many athletes either hold their breath or breathe rapidly and shallowly from the upper chest. These responses create greater muscular tension and impair performance. Freid (1987a,b) has written extensively on the topic of breathing, and other practitioners such as Peper (1989) have become strong advocates of teaching proper breathing mechanics to athletes. Although proper breathing mechanics are usually taught as part of a "quieting" response, knowledge of respiration techniques and its importance in regulation of arousal can be used for purposes of increasing arousal.

Progressive relaxation is a technique that is used when muscle tension exceeds that which is necessary for optimal performance. The techniques used today are all variations of those developed by Jacobson (1929). He believed that if the relaxation of muscles was induced, it would be impossible for an athlete to be nervous or tense. He also believed that nervousness and tension of "involuntary" muscles and organs could be reduced if associated skeletal muscles were relaxed.

Progressive muscular relaxation (PMR) consists of exercises where an individual tenses a specific muscle group, then, after briefly holding the tension, attempts to induce complete relaxation of the muscle. The individual is instructed to try to be aware of the difference between complete tension and relaxation. All major muscle groups of the body are exercised in this way, usually on a daily basis, for several months. Exercises are usually done while lying down but can also be done in a sitting posture or in a position that simulates competitive form.

As the individual begins to master muscle relaxation, it is common for the exercises to become abbreviated and move from active tensing and relaxing to simple passive relaxation. When acute muscle awareness is mastered, the athlete can simply do what are referred to as *body scans*. This is a quick technique where the athlete merely does a check of tension levels in the involved muscles just prior to competition. Although instructions for inducing progressive relaxation were originally "live" voice, today it is common to use audiotaped suggestions. Scripts for progressive relaxation or modified versions of the technique are available from many sources (Harris, 1986; Martens, 1987).

It is clear that the mastery of Jacobsonian relaxation techniques results in reduced levels of anxiety, muscular tension, and physiological arousal. Research on the efficacy of the specific PMR technique for improving athlete performance, however, is quite sparse. On a logical basis, it appears that if the inverted-U hypothesis is true, then teaching Jacobsonian relaxation to overaroused athletes should result in lowered arousal and an optimal level of performance. Unfortunately, very few researchers have specifically studied progressive muscular relaxation techniques on performance. Usually relaxation techniques that are evaluated involve a combination of techniques, such as breathing techniques, modified progressive relaxation, meditation, and cognitive techniques. Two studies appear to have used "relatively pure" progressive muscular relaxation techniques. One, by Lanning and Hisanaga (1983), investigated the effects of modified progressive relaxation training and breathing on anxiety levels and performance of 24 volleyball players. The data showed that the treated players had lower anxiety and more good serves in play than the controls. Nideffer and Deckner (1970), using a single case design, reported positive results from relaxation training on a shot-putter's performance.

Meditation as an arousal control technique has been used for thousands of years by Eastern cultures but has only recently been introduced into Western culture. An overview of three popularly employed meditational approaches follows: (1) transcendental meditation (TM), (2) relaxation response, and (3) Zen meditation.

Transcendental Meditation (TM). This type of meditation was introduced to the West by Maharishi Mahesh, Yogi of India, and is perhaps the best known technique in North America and Europe. TM teaches the subject to sit in a comfortable position in a quiet environment, focus, and repeat a mantra (simple, rhythmic one-syllable sound), and maintain a passive attitude. Research by Wallace and Benson (1972) has demonstrated unequivocally that TM results in lowered oxygen consumption, heart rate, respiration rate, and increased alpha waves and skin resistance.

Relaxation Response. Benson et al. (1974) later demonstrated that a nearly identical "relaxation response" could be obtained through meditation that did not incorporate the religious and mystical overtones of TM. The Boston cardiologist popularized this meditation technique in his book *The Relaxation Response* (Benson, 1975). Studies by Delmonte (1984) and Michaels, Parra, McCann, and Vander (1979) have also shown that meditation results in lowered physiological functioning.

While it is clear that TM can reduce levels of arousal, it is not clear whether it has a facilitative effect on athletic performance. The data thus far have been primarily anecdotal. In a little-known study, Reddy, Bai, and Rao (1976) showed that subjects trained in TM improved significantly in the 50-meter dash, agility tests, standing broad jump, reaction time, and coordination. In a series of studies, Williams and his colleagues in New Zealand used laboratory tasks and fine motor skills as outcome measures and failed to demonstrate superior learning or performance of meditators over controls (Williams, 1978; Williams & Hebert, 1976; Williams, Lodge, & Reddish, 1977; Williams & Vickerman, 1976). Williams (1978) concluded that lowered arousal and anxiety induced by TM had no effect on learning and performance of novel perceptual fine motor skills such as rotary pursuit or mirror tracing.

Zen Meditation. Zen meditation has been researched and written about extensively in Japan (Hirai, 1975, 1976, 1982; Ikemi & Deshimaru, 1984). The technique consists of three controls:

1. *Control of posture.* Zen meditators assume a legs-folded, erect sitting posture. Well-trained meditators do not sleep during meditation.
2. *Control of respiration.* Zen meditators are taught diaphragmatic breathing, enabling them to inhale larger amounts of air than they might through chest breathing.
3. *Control of the mind.* Studies by Ikemi and Deshimaru (1984) have shown that brain wave changes occur during meditation, and from this, four stages have been documented.

What is interesting about Zen meditation is that the subject meditates with the eyes open. Further, because of the assumed posture, optimal muscle tension is essential. The focus of the mind, rather than being passive, is active and focused, so that there is integration between internal and external states. To date, no studies have been conducted to evaluate the efficacy of Zen meditation on athletic performance.

Imagery is a powerful cognitive technique used in psychology for the treatment of physical and mental illness. Martens (1987) states that there are no less than 35 psychological therapies that use imagery as a component of their treatment programs. The earlier mentioned arousal control techniques incorporate imagery, as do biofeedback, systematic desensitization, hypnosis, and others. Imagery, also referred to as visualization, mental rehearsal, and imagaletics (Cautela & Samdperil, 1989), involves the use of all our senses to create or recreate an experience in the mind. Vealey (1986), in her excellent review of imagery, cited nine uses of imagery techniques in sport, including arousal control:

1. Practicing sport skills
2. Practicing strategy
3. Learning skills
4. Learning strategies
5. Problem solving
6. Practicing psychological skills
7. Increasing perception
8. Aiding recovery from injury
9. Controlling arousal responses.

For purposes of arousal control, imagery can be very effective in re-creating conditions of excitement, flow state, anger, or relaxation. Two theoretical explanations of the imagery phenomenon have been advanced: (1) psychoneuromuscular theory, and (2) Symbolic learning theory

Psychoneuromuscular Theory. This theory postulates that vivid imagined events or behavior should produce neuromuscular responses similar to those of an actual experience. Jacobson (1932) first reported that imagined bending of the arm produced small measurable contraction in the arm flexors. Suinn (1980) later demonstrated that alpine skiers, when imagining a downhill run, could produce EMG patterns that closely approximated those in actual skiing.

Symbolic Learning Theory. This theory, as proposed by Sackett (1934), advocates that imagery works because it helps athletes develop a coding system of movement patterns. Essentially, a motor program is created in the central nervous system. This theory has been supported by Feltz and Landers (1983) and Ryan and Simons (1983). The evidence endorsing the use of imagery is well documented both anecdotally and empirically. Although researchers have not looked specifically at the arousal control function of imagery as it relates to performance, they nevertheless assume that improved performance is at least partly due to the control of arousal. The anecdotal evidence comes from distinguished athletes such as Jack Nicklaus, Greg Lougainas, Jean-Claude Killy, and Canadian Olympians as portrayed in the Canadian Coaching Association videotape "Mind Over Muscle" (1989). The qualitative study reported by Orlick and Partington (1986) also provides strong support for the use of imagery by elite athletes to master optimal levels of arousal control.

The scientific research on imagery in psychology and sport psychology is voluminous. Richardson (1967) first presented a review of the studies in sport, followed by a review by Corbin in 1972. Feltz and Landers (1983) later conducted an extensive meta-analysis of the imagery literature and concluded that the use of imagery was better for enhancing performance than no practice at all.

Autogenic training (AT) was developed by Johannes Schultz in Germany in the early 1930s. Schultz and Luthe (1959) popularized the technique, and now AT is considered to be a prominent modality in relaxation therapy. AT consists of a series of six exercises designed to induce two physical sensations, warmth and heaviness. The stages are:

1. Suggestions of heaviness of limbs
2. Warmth of limbs
3. Calmness of human heart
4. Slow breathing
5. Warmth in the solar plexus
6. Coolness in the forehead.

Like progressive muscular relaxation training, the technique may take anywhere from 2 months to a year to master. Although AT has been practiced extensively in sport psychology, particularly in Eastern Europe, studies specifically testing the efficacy of AT are extremely limited (Spigolon & Annalisa, 1985).

Biofeedback is a powerful technique that facilitates the learning of self-regulation of arousal states. Although primarily used in psychology for inducing hypoarousal states, it can also serve to increase arousal. Biofeedback is a technique that utilizes instrumentation, usually with sensors and transducers, that allows for immediate measurement of biological functions that typically are not under voluntary control. This information is displayed or "fed back" to the individual, thus the term "biofeedback." It is usually the case that a "clinician" also assists the subject in developing strategies for gaining voluntary control over a particular biological function. The major biofeedback modalities that have been used in sport include:

1. Muscle feedback (EMG)
2. Thermal feedback (TEMP)
3. Electrodermal feedback (EDR)
4. Heart rate feedback (HR)
5. Electroencephalographic feedback (EEG).

Biofeedback applications in sport psychology have been documented in several reviews (Zaichkowsky, 1982; Zaichkowsky & Fuchs, 1988, 1989). Although researchers have investigated the efficacy of biofeedback in increasing muscle strength, reducing pain and fatigue, increasing flexibility, regulating heart rate, and the like, the majority of them in sport have investigated biofeedback effects in reducing performance anxiety. To date, the majority of these researchers have used EMG as the modality of choice. In their 1989 review, Zaichkowsky and Fuchs concluded that the majority of studies in which biofeedback was used to control "psychological" stressors demonstrated positive outcomes.

Biofeedback provides tremendous advantages to athletes who are interested in controlling their arousal and maximizing performance. A biofeedback monitor will help an athlete more quickly become aware of how thoughts affect the body and performance. The athlete can quickly see what thoughts affect biological functions, such as heart rate and sweat response, and what cognitive or somatic strategies induce states of hypoarousal, or hyperarousal. Until recently, biofeedback as a technique for teaching arousal control had limited application outside the research laboratory. Many sport psychologists, coaches, and athletes either feel the technique is overly sophisticated for them or that it is too cumbersome to use practically and as such it is underutilized. Without question, improvement in technology as well as education about biofeedback has increased its potential use in sport psychology. Thought Technology of Montreal recently published, in conjunction with the Coaching Association of Canada, a sport psychology training program entitled "Mind Over Muscle: Peak Performance Through Biofeedback." The program creatively incorporates portable electrodermal (GSR) biofeedback with other mental training techniques for teaching performance enhancement.

Another psychophysiological monitoring/biofeedback device that has enormous potential for teaching self-regulation of arousal is a heart rate monitor developed by Polar Electro in Finland but distributed in North America as well. The device telemeters heart rate from a sensor strapped to the chest onto a wristwatch that monitors, displays, and stores heart rate values for later recall. We have effectively used the device to teach heart rate and arousal regulation to a number of recreational, collegiate, Olympic, and professional athletes (Zaichkowsky, 1991). Burrill (1990) conducted a study on junior elite biathlon athletes in which he taught them to raise and lower heart rate in a laboratory. They then practiced regulating heart rate during training using the telemetry watch system. Burrill concluded that heart rate biofeedback training was effective in teaching heart rate awareness and regulation in the early phases of their sport. Davis (1991) used this telemetry heart rate device to monitor heart rate responses of four National Hockey League players during play and while resting between shifts. These data enabled players to become aware of the range of heart rate (where they functioned optimally). Loehr (1991) has also used this monitor to teach tennis players their optimal heart rate zone, both while playing and between points.

It appears that the self-regulation of arousal states will develop as technology in psychophysiology becomes more sophisticated, yet user friendly, and portable for use in sport. Monitors similar to the telemetry heart rate system that record and feed back electrodermal responses, brain waves, and muscle activity will be welcome tools for researchers and practitioners in sport psychology.

Techniques for Increasing Arousal: Energizing

Just as there are occasions when an athlete is overaroused, there will be occasions when an athlete is under-or hypoaroused. In such cases, it will be necessary for the athlete to increase his or her level of arousal (self-regulation) or the coach can structure the environment so that athletes will increase their levels of arousal. This is sometimes referred to as "psyching up" or "energizing."

Awareness. Both self-awareness and awareness on the part of a coach is crucial for determining whether or not arousal needs to be increased. Athletes and coaches should be aware of the signs of hypoarousal and which techniques are most effective for increasing arousal. Coaches must also be sensitive to individual differences in response to energizing techniques.

Several energizing techniques have been used by coaches and athletes and reported elsewhere (Anshel, 1990; Harris, 1986; Martens, 1987). Unfortunately, research on the efficacy of energizing techniques is minimal (Shelton & Mahoney, 1978; Weinberg, Gould, & Jackson, 1980). What is available are anecdotal reports and time-tested coaching techniques that appear to be logical.

Breathing. Being aware of breathing patterns and learning to take slow, deep breaths were discussed earlier as a technique to reduce arousal. By increasing the rhythm of breathing and imagining with each inhalation that energy is being taken in, an athlete can increase physiological *activation* as well as feelings of arousal. They may even use self-talk and the word "energy" or some other energizing word to facilitate increasing arousal.

Stretching and Exercise. The somatic techniques of stretching and exercise not only warm the body up for competition via increasing circulation, they may contribute to energization. Extensive muscle tension interferes with blood circulation and the efficient use of muscles. Stretching and being aware of proper breathing help release this tension.

Precompetitive Workout. This type of workout is related to stretching and exercise. A precompetitive workout occurs anywhere from 4 to 10 hours before the athletic performance. Rather than warming up the muscles, athletes actually simulate important aspects of a game. It is common, for example, for ice-hockey players to have a morning skate so that they may be better prepared for the evening game. Its effectiveness has not been empirically tested. Husak and Hemenway (1986) did, however, test the effects of competition day practice on activation and performance of collegiate swimmers who engaged in brisk workouts four to six hours before competition. Although there were no significant performance effects, the athletes did show a reduction in feelings of tension and anxiety. These workouts can possibly help to reduce anxiety and optimize arousal.

Music and Video. Based on anecdotal reports of coaches and athletes, these two modalities can be powerful energizers. It is important to be aware of the fact that music or videos can produce very different effects on different people. As such, a coach must recognize that not all athletes will find the same music energizing. To date, we are aware of no studies that have evaluated the effectiveness of music in regulating arousal in sport. Rider and Achterberg (1989) have demonstrated that music was effective in enhancing imagery for purposes of decreasing peripheral blood cell counts of lymphocytes and neutrophiles, both of which reflect immune system responses to stress.

Energizing Imagery. This can be a powerful cognitive technique for increasing arousal. Athletes focus on machine images such as a locomotive, a cannon, etc., or on animal images such as a tiger or a greyhound. Perhaps Mohammad Ali's publicized "float like a butterfly, sting like a bee" would be a useful image.

Energizing Verbal Cues. These cues used in conjunction with energizing imagery may effectively increase the athlete's arousal. Energizing words may include *explode, charge, control, blast, power,* or *psych up.* Athletes should also express arousal by showing enthusiasm, emotion, and assertiveness. Awareness of the effectiveness of energizing images and verbal cues is important.

Drawing Energy From the Environment. Some athletes have been known to draw energy from the environment. This may include the crowd, their opponents, their teammates, as well as the venue itself. For others, the sun, the flag, or the national anthem may serve as an important energizing symbol.

Transferring Energy. Athletes can be taught to effectively transfer negative emotions such as anger, fear, disgust, and contempt into emotions that are positive for performance. Rather than committing a foul because of frustration-induced anger, the athletes can redirect, transfer, or channel this energy into positive performance goals. Like all the other skills, an athlete must constantly rehearse the skills for this to be successful.

Distraction. If hypoarousal is caused by fatigue, then it may be appropriate to focus an athlete's attention away from fatigue.

Goal Setting. Hypoarousal, in some cases, may be a result of competing against an opponent where one is knowingly overmatched, or one's team is so far behind in league standings that there is virtually no chance of making the playoffs. One possible solution for energizing arousal is to set realistic but difficult personal performance and team goals. In this way, individual players are challenged by these goals and will likely be more effective. Research on the effectiveness of goal setting in sport is extensive (Hall, Weinberg & Jackson, 1987; O'Brien & Evans, 1984; Weinberg, Bruya, & Jackson, 1985; Weinberg, Bruya, Longino, & Jackson, 1988). Perhaps the best test of the effectiveness of goal setting in sport was described in a dissertation by Burton (1983). He conducted extensive goal-setting training for the University of Illinois swim team and determined that swimmers who were excellent in setting realistic goals were less anxious, concentrated better, were more self-confident, performed better, and felt more satisfied with their participation.

Pep Talks. Coaches, team captains, or other respected team members often attempt to increase arousal levels of athletes through pep talks. Used cogently be effective communicators, the technique can be successful; however, pep talks can just as often be ineffective in increasing arousal. If the same speech is constantly made, then players will filter out the communicator and the message. However, carefully chosen energizing statements involving personal challenges, poems, and statements by great achievers may be effective. Unfortunately research on the effectiveness of pep talks is lacking.

Bulletin Boards. In some cases, coaches use visual messages either to supplement or as a substitute for a pep talk. Here messages are conveyed by well-known performers or someone "anonymous." The messages are usually inspirational or serve to remind the athletes of important tasks they need to accomplish. A common tactic by coaches to increase arousal of their athletes is to show them media reports that are challenging, or inflammatory statements made by opposing coaches or athletes.

SUMMARY

In this chapter, we have attempted to trace the history of the arousal construct and the disagreement that exists with respect to defining arousal. We operationally defined the construct based on prevailing thoughts of the 1980s and 1990s. We then discussed how the nervous system (central and autonomic) functions during different levels of arousal and followed up with a discussion of how arousal is typically measured. Traditional theoretical views of arousal and their relationship to performance (drive theory and inverted-U hypothesis) were presented, as well as variations in thinking on the inverted-U, namely, the concept of zones of optimal functioning. Finally we discussed different ways in which arousal can be increased or decreased using a variety of self-regulation methods or external/environmental methods.

It is clear that the arousal construct is multidimensional, reflecting interacting physiological, cognitive, and affective responses. Measuring these components accurately in a sport context is becoming a reality, particularly for physiological measures. These methodological advances will enable us not only to better understand the relationship between arousal and performance, but also to help teach athletes and coaches about optimal arousal states and how to attain them.

References

Anderson, J. A. (1990). Arousal and the inverted-U hypothesis: A critique of Neiss's "Reconceptualizing arousal." *Psychological Bulletin, 107,* 96–100.

Anshel, M. H. (1990). *Sport psychology: From theory to practice.* Scottsdale, AZ: Gorsuch Scarisbrick.

Apter, M. J. (1982). *The experience of motivation: The theory of psychological reversals.* London: Academic Press.

Apter, M. J. (1984). Reversal theory and personality: A review. *Journal of Research in Personality, 18,* 265–288.

Basler, M. L., Fisher, A. C., & Mumford, N. L. (1976). Arousal and anxiety correlates of gymnastic performance. *The Research Quarterly, 47,* 586–589.

Benson, H. (1975). *The relaxation response.* New York: Morrow.

Benson, H., Breary, J. F., & Carol, M. P. (1974). The relaxation response. *Psychiatry, 37,* 37–46.

Bergstrom, B. (1970). Tracking performance under threat-induced stress. *Scandinavian Journal of Psychology, 11,* 109–114.

Berman, P. S., & Johnson, H. J. (1985). A psychophysiological assessment battery. *Biofeedback and Self-Regulation, 10,* 203–221.

Beuter, A., & Duda, J. L. (1985). Analysis of the arousal/motor performance relationship in children using movement kinematics. *Journal of Sport Psychology, 7,* 229–243.

Billing, J. (1980). An overview of task complexity. *Motor Skills: Theory Into Practice, 4,* 18–23.

Borkovec, T. D. (1976). Physiological and cognitive processes in the regulation of anxiety. In G. E. Schwartz & D. Shapiro (Eds.), *Consciousness and self-regulation: Advances in research* (pp. 188–199). New York: Plenum.

Brehm, J. W., & Self, E. A. (1989). The intensity of motivation. *Annual Review of Psychology, 40,* 109–131.

Broadhurst, P. L. (1957). Emotionality and the Yerkes-Dodson Law. *Journal of Experimental Psychology, 54,* 345–352.

Burton, D. (1988). Evaluation of goalsetting, training on selected cognitions and performance of collegiate swimmers. Unpublished doctoral dissertation, University of Illinois, Urbana-Champaign.

Cannon, W. B. (1928). The mechanism of emotional disturbance of bodily function. *The New England Journal of Medicine, 198,* 877–884.

Carron, A. V. (1968). Motor performance under stress. *The Research Quarterly, 39,* 463–469.

Cattell, R. B. (1972). The nature and genesis of mood states: A theoretical model with experimental measurements concerning anxiety, depression, arousal, and other mood states. In C. D. Spielberger (Ed.), *Anxiety: Current trends in theory and research* (pp. 115–183). New York: Academic Press.

Cautela, J. R., & Samdperil, L. (1989). Imagaletics: The application of covert conditioning to athletic performance. *Journal of Applied Sport Psychology, 1,* 82–97.

Csikszentmihalyi, M. (1975). *Beyond boredom and anxiety.* San Francisco: Jossey Bass.

Cox, R. H. (1983). Consolidation of pursuit rotor learning under conditions of induced arousal. *Research Quarterly for Exercise and Sport, 54,* 223–228.

Cox, R. H. (1990). *Sport psychology: Concepts and applications.* Dubuque, IA: Wm. C. Brown.

Davidson, R. J., & Schwartz, G. E. (1976). The psychobiology of relaxation and related states: A multi-process theory. In D. I. Mostofsky (Ed.), *Behavioral control and modification of physiological activity.* Englewood Cliffs, NJ: Prentice-Hall.

Davis, H. (1991). Passive recovery and optimal arousal in ice hockey. *Perceptual and Motor Skills, 72,* 1–2.

Dienstbier, R. A. (1989). Arousal and physiological toughness: Implications for mental and physical health. *Psychological Review, 96,* 84–100.

Duffy, E. (1934). Emotion: An example of the need for reorientation in psychology. *Psychological Review, 41,* 184–198.

Duffy, E. (1941). The conceptual categories of psychology: A suggestion for revision. *Psychological Review, 48,* 177–203.

Duffy, E. (1957). The psychological significance of the concept of "arousal" or "activation." *Psychological Review, 64,* 265–275.

Duffy, E. (1962). *Activation and behavior.* New York: Wiley.

Ebbeck, V., & Weiss, M. R. (1988). The arousal-performance relationship: Task characteristics and performance measures in track and field athletics. *The Sport Psychologist, 2,* 13–27.

Feltz, D. L., & Landers, D. M. (1983). The effects of mental preparation on motor skill learning and performance: A meta-analysis. *Journal of Sport Psychology, 5,* 25–57.

Fenz, W. D., & Epstein, S. (1967). Gradients of physiological arousal in parachutists as a function of approaching jump. *Psychosomatic Medicine, 29,* 33–51.

Fenz, W. D., & Jones, G. B. (1972). Individual differenced in physiologic arousal and performance in sport parachutists. *Psychosomatic Medicine, 34,* 1–8.

Fried, R. (1987a). Relaxation with biofeedback-assisted guided imagery: The importance of breathing rate as an index of hypoarousal. *Biofeedback and Self-Regulation, 12,* 273–279.

Fried, R. (1987b). *The hyperventilation syndrome—Research and clinical treatment.* Baltimore: Johns Hopkins University Press.

Giabrone, C. P. (1973). Effect of situation criticality on foul shooting. Unpublished master's thesis, University of Illinois, Urbana.

Griffiths, T. J., Steel, D. H., Voccaro, P., & Karpman, M. B. (1981). The effects of relaxation techniques on anxiety and underwater performance. *International Journal of Sport Psychology, 12,* 176–182.

Gould, D., Petlichkoff, L., Simons, J., & Vevera, M. (1987). Relationship between competitive state anxiety inventory—two subscale scores and pistol shooting performance. *Journal of Sport Psychology, 9,* 33–42.

Hall, H. K., Weinberg, R. S., & Jackson, A. (1987). Effects of goal specificity, goal difficulty, and information feedback on endurance performance. *Journal of Sport Psychology, 9,* 43–54.

Hamilton, V. (1986). A cognitive model of anxiety: Implications for theories of personality and motivation. In C. D. Spielberger & I. G. Sarason (Eds.), *Stress and anxiety* (Vol. 10, pp. 229–250). Washington, DC: Hemisphere.

Hanin, Y. L. (1989). Interpersonal and intragroup anxiety in sports. In D. Hackfort & C. Spielberger (Eds.), *Anxiety in sports: An international perspective* (pp. 19–28). New York: Hemisphere.

Harris, D. V. (1986). Relaxation and energizing techniques for regulation of arousal. In J. M. Willimas (Ed.), *Applied sport psychology: Personal growth to peak performance* (pp. 185–207). Palo Alto, CA: Mayfield.

Hirai, T. (1975). *Psychophysiology of Zen.* Tokyo: Igaku-Shoin.

Hirai, T. (1976). *Zen and the mind.* Tokyo: Nichibo.

Hirai, T. (1982). *Science of Zen meditation: The mechanism from EEG.* Tokyo: Kodansha.

Holroyd, K. A., Westbrook, T., Wolf, M., & Badhorn, E. (1978). Performance, cognition, and physiological responding in test anxiety. *Journal of Abnormal Psychology, 87,* 442–451.

Hull, C. L. (1943). *Principles of behavior.* New York: Appleton-Century.

Husak, W. S., & Hemenway, D. P. (1986). The influence of competitive day practice on the activation and performance of collegiate swimmers. *Journal of Sport Behavior, 9,* 95–100.

Ikemi, Y., & Deshimaru, T., (1984). *Self-regulation and Zen.* Tokyo: Nihon Houso Syuppan.

Jacobson, E. (1929). *Progressive relaxation.* Chicago: University of Chicago Press.

Kerr, J. H. (1985). A new perspective for sports psychology. In M. J. Apter, D. Fontana, & S. Murgatroyd (Eds.), *Applications and developments* (pp. 89–102). Cardiff, Wales: University College Cardiff Press.

Kerr, J. H. (1989). Anxiety, arousal, and sport performance. In D. Hackfort & C. Spielberger (Eds.), *Anxiety in sports: An international perspective* (pp. 137–151). New York: Hemisphere.

Klavora, P. (1979). Customary arousal for peak athletic performance. In P. Klavora & J. David (Eds.), *Coach, athlete, and the sport psychologist* (pp. 155–163). Toronto: University of Toronto.

Lacey, J. I., & Lacey, B. (1958). Verification and extension of the principle of autonomic response-stereotypy. *American Journal of Psychology, 71,* 50–73.

Landers, D. M. (1978). Motivation and performance: The role of arousal and attentional factors. In W. F. Straub (Ed.), *Sport psychology: An analysis of athletic behavior* (pp. 75–87). Ithaca, NY: Mouvement Publications.

Landers, D. M. (1980). The arousal-performance relationship revisited. *Research Quarterly for Exercise and Sport, 51,* 77–90.

Lanning, W., & Hisanaga, B. (1983). A study of the relationship between the reduction of competitive anxiety and an increase in athletic performance. *International Journal of Sport Psychology, 14,* 219–227.

Lansing, R. W., Schwartz, E., & Lindsley, D. B. (1956). Reaction time and EEG activation. *American Psychologist, 11,* 433.

Levitt, S. & Gutin, B. (1971). Multiple choice reaction time and movement time during physical exertion. *The Research Quarterly, 42,* 405–410.

Loehr, J. (1991). Personal communication.

Lowe, R. (1971). *Stress, arousal, and task performance of little league baseball players.* Unpublished dissertation. University of Illinois, Urbana–Champaign.

Magill, R. A. (1990). *Motor learning: Concepts and applications.* Dubuque, IA: Brown.

Mahoney, M. J. (1979). Cognitive skills and athletic performance. In P. C. Kendale & S. D. Hollon (Eds.), *Cognitive-behavioral interventions: Theory, research, and procedures* (pp. 423–443). New York: Academic Press.

Malmo, R. B. (1959). Activation: A neurophysiological dimension. *Psychological Review, 66,* 367–386.

Marteniuk, R. G., & Wenger, H. A. (1970). Facilitation of pursuit rotor learning by induced stress. *Perceptual and Motor Skills, 31,* 471–477.

Martens, R. (1971). Anxiety and motor behavior: A review. *Journal of Motor Behavior, 3,* 151–179.

Martens, R. (1977). *Sport competition anxiety test.* Champaign, IL: Human Kinetics.

Martens, R. (1987). *Coaches guide to sport psychology.* Champaign, IL: Human Kinetics.

Martens, R., & Landers, D. M. (1970). Motor performance under stress: A test of the inverted-U hypothesis. *Journal of Personality and Social Psychology, 16,* 29–37.

Martens, R., Vealey, R. S., & Burton, D. (1990). *Competitive anxiety in sport.* Champaign, IL: Human Kinetics.

Murphy, L. E. (1966). Muscular effort, activation level, and reaction time. In E. Mallinoff (Ed.), *Proceedings of the 74th Annual Convention of the American Psychological Association* (pp. 1–2). Washington, DC: American Psychological Association.

Neiss, R. (1988). Reconceptualizing arousal: Psychobiological states in motor performance. *Psychological Bulletin, 103,* 345–366.

Neiss, R. (1990). Ending arousal's reign of error: A reply to Anderson. *Psychological Bulletin, 107,* 101–105.

Nideffer, R. M. (1976). Test of attentional and interpersonal style. *Journal of Personality and Social Psychology, 34,* 394–404.

Nideffer, R. M. (1989). Anxiety, attention, and performance in sports: Theoretical and practical considerations. In D. Hackfort & C. D. Spielberger (Eds.), *Anxiety in sports: An international perspective* (pp. 117–136). New York: Hemisphere.

Nideffer, R. M., & Deckner, C. W. (1970). A case study of improved athletic performance following use of relaxation procedures. *Perceptual and Motor Skills, 30,* 821–822.

Orlick, T., & Partington, J. (1986). *Psyched: Inner views of winning.* Ottawa: Coaching Association of Canada.

O'Brien, F. R., & Evans, F. H. (1984). Goal setting as a motivational technique. In J. M. Silva & R. S. Weinberg (Eds.), *Psychological foundations of sport* (pp. 188–196). Champaign, IL: Human Kinetics.

Oxendine, J. B. (1970). Emotional arousal and motor performance. *Quest, 13,* 23–30.

Oxendine, J. B. (1984). *Psychology of motor learning.* Englewood Cliffs, NJ: Prentice-Hall.

Paller, K., & Shapiro, D. (1983). Systolic blood pressure and a simple reaction time task. *Psychophysiology, 20,* 585–592.

Pinneo, L. R. (1961). The effects of induced muscle tension during tracking on level of activation and on performance. *Journal of Experimental Psychology, 62,* 523–531.

Ravizza, K. (1977). Peak experiences in sport. *Journal of Humanistic Psychology, 17,* 35–40.

Reddy, J. K., Bai, A. J. L., & Rao, V. R. (1976). The effects of the transcendental meditation program on athletic performance. In D. J. Orme-Johnson & I. Farrow (Eds.), *Scientific research on the transcendental meditation program.* (pp. 346–358) Weggis, Switzerland: MERU Press.

Richardson, A. (1967a). Mental practice: A review and discussion (Part I). *The Research Quarterly, 38,* 95–107.

Rider, M. S., & Achterberg, J. (1989). Effect of music-assisted imagery on neutrophils and lymphocytes. *Biofeedback and Self-Regulation, 14,* 247–257.

Ryan, E. D. (1961). Motor performance under stress as a function of the amount of practice. *Perceptual and Motor Skills, 13,* 103–106.

Ryan, E. D. (1962). Effects of stress on motor performance and learning. *The Research Quarterly, 33,* 111–119.

Ryan, E. D., & Simons, J. (1981). Cognitive demand, imagery, and frequency of mental rehearsal as factors influencing acquisition of motor skills. *Journal of Sport Psychology, 3,* 35–45.

Sackett, R. S. (1934). The influence of symbolic rehearsal upon the retention of a maze habit. *Journal of General Psychology, 13,* 113–128.

Sage, G. H. (1984). *Motor learning and control: A neurophysiological approach.* Dubuque, IA: Brown.

Sage, G. H., & Bennett, B. (1973). The effects of induced arousal on learning and performance of a pursuit motor skill. *The Research Quarterly, 44,* 140–149.

Schultz, J. H., & Luthe, W. (1959). *Autogenic training: A psychophysiological approach to psychotherapy.* New York: Grune and Stratton.

Schwartz, G. E., Davidson, R. J., & Goleman, D. (1978). Patterning of cognitive and somatic processes in the self-regulation of anxiety: Effects of meditation versus exercise. *Psychosomatic Medicine, 40,* 321–328.

Shelton, T. O., & Mahoney, M. J. (1978). The content and effect of "psyching-up" strategies in weight lifters. *Cognitive Therapy and Research, 2,* 275–284.

Sonstroem, R. J., & Bernardo, P. (1982). Individual pregame state anxiety and basketball performance: A re-examination of the inverted-U curve. *Journal of Sport Psychology, 4,* 235–245.

Spence, J. T., & Spence, K. W. (1966). The motivational components of manifest anxiety: Drive and drive stimuli. In C. D. Spielberger (Ed.), *Anxiety and behavior* (pp. 291–326). New York: Academic Press.

Spielberger, C. D. (1966). Theory and research on anxiety. In C. D. Spielberger (Ed.), *Anxiety and behavior* (pp. 3–20). New York: Academic Press.

Spielberger, C. D. (1989). Stress and anxiety in sports. In D. Hackfort & C. D. Spielberger (Eds.), *Anxiety in sports: An international perspective* (pp. 3–17). New York: Hemisphere.

Spielberger, C. D., Gorsuch, R. L., & Lushene, R. E. (1970). *STAI manual for the state-trait anxiety inventory.* Palo Alto, CA: Consulting Psychologists Press.

Spigolon, L., & Annalisa, D. (1985). Autogenic training in frogmen. *International Journal of Sport Psychology, 16,* 312–320.

Stennett, R. C. (1957). The relationship of performance level to level of arousal. *Journal of Experimental Psychology, 54,* 54–61.

Stern, R. M. (1976). Reaction time between the get set and go of simulated races. *Psychophysiology, 13,* 149–154.

Suinn, R. M. (1980). Body thinking: Psychology for Olympic champs. In R. M. Suinn (Ed.), *Psychology in sports: Methods and applications* (pp. 141–144). Minneapolis: Burgess.

Thayer, R. E. (1967). Measurement of activation through self-report. *Psychological Reports, 20,* 663–679.

Ursin, H. (1978). Activation, coping, and psychosomatics. In H. Ursin, E. Baade, & S. Levine (Eds.), *Psychobiology of stress: A study of coping men* (pp. 201–228). New York: Academic Press.

Ursin, H. (1988). The instrumental effects of emotional behavior— consequences for the physiological state. In V. Hamilton (Ed.), *Cognitive perspectives on emotion and motivation* (pp. 221–237). Klavor Academic Publisher.

Vaernes, R., Ursin, H., Daragh, A., & Lamb, R. (1982). Endocrine response patterns and psychological correlates. *Journal of Psychosomatic Research, 26,* 123–131.

Venables, P. H. (1984). Arousal: An examination of its status as a concept. In M. G. H. Coles, J. R. Jennings, & J. A. Stern (Eds.), *Psychobiological perspectives: Festschrift for Beatrice and John Lacey* (pp. 134–142). New York: Van Nostrand Reinhold.

Wallace, R. K., & Benson, H. (1972). The physiology of meditation. *Scientific American, 226,* 85–90.

Wankel, L. M. (1972). Competition in motor performance: An experimental analysis of motivational components. *Journal of Experimental Social Psychology, 8,* 427–437.

Weinberg, R. S., Bruya, L. D., & Jackson, A. (1985). The effects of goal proximity on endurance performance. *Journal of Sport Psychology, 1,* 296–305.

Weinberg, R. S., Bruya, L. D., Longini, J. & Jackson, A. (1988). Effects of goal proximity and specificity on endurance performance of primary-grade children. *Journal of Sport and Exercise Psychology, 10,* 81–91.

Weinberg, R. S., Gould, D., & Jackson, A. (1980). Cognition and motor performance effect of psyching-up strategies on three motor tasks. *Cognitive Therapy and Research, 4,* 239–245.

Weinberg, R. S., & Hunt, U. V. (1976). The relationship between anxiety, motor performance, and electromyography. *Journal of Motor Behavior, 8,* 219–224.

Weinberg, R. S., & Jackson, A. (1985). The effects of specific vs. non-specific mental preparation strategies on strength and endurance performance. *International Journal of Sport Psychology, 8,* 175–180.

Weinberg, R. S., & Ragan, J. (1978). Motor performance under three levels of stress and trait anxiety. *Journal of Motor Behavior, 10,* 169–176.

Wilkes, R. L., & Summers, J. J. (1984). Cognition, mediating variables, and strength performance. *Journal of Sport Psychology, 6,* 351–359.

Williams, L. R. T. (1978). Transcendental meditation and mirror-tracing skill. *Perceptual and Motor Skills, 46,* 371–378.

Williams, L. R. T., & Hebert, P. G. (1976). Transcendental meditation and fine perceptual motor skill. *Perceptual and Motor Skills, 43,* 303–309.

Williams, L. R. T., Lodge, B., & Reddish, P. S. (1977). Effects of transcendental meditation on rotary pursuit skill. *The Research Quarterly, 48,* 196–201.

Williams, L. R. T., & Vickerman (1976). Effects of transcendental meditation on fine motor skill. *Perceptual and Motor Skills, 43,* 607–613.

Yerkes, R. M., & Dodson, J. D. (1908). The relation of strength of stimulus to rapidity of habit formation. *Journal of Comparative Neurology and Psychology, 18,* 459–482.

Zaichkowsky, L. D. (1991). Heart rate as an indicator of optimal performance states. Unpublished manuscript, Boston University.

Zaichkowsky, L. D. (1982). Biofeedback for self-regulation of competitive stress. In L. D. Zaichkowsky & W. E. Sime (Eds.), *Stress management for sport* (pp. 55–64). Reston, VA: American Alliance for Health, Physical Education, Recreation, and Dance.

Zaichkowsky, L. D., & Fuchs, C. Z. (1988). Biofeedback applications in exercise and athletic performance. In K. B. Pandolf (Ed.), *Exercise and sport science reviews* (pp. 381–421). New York: Macmillan.

Zaichkowsky, L. D., & Fuchs, C. Z. (1989). Biofeedback-assisted self-regulation for stress management in sports. In D. Hackfort & C. D. Spielberger (Eds.), *Anxiety in sports: An international perspective* (pp. 235–245). New York: Hemisphere.

Zajonc, R. B. (1965). Social facilitation. *Science, 149,* 269–274.

23

RESPONDING TO COMPETITIVE PRESSURE

Robert J. Rotella

J. Dana Lerner

Pressure is inherent to competitive athletics. The challenge of competition is to determine a winner. The more similar the abilities of the competitors and the greater the perceived importance of the event, the more likely that high levels of pressure will be experienced by athletes facing that challenge. They must be able to consistently perform at or near peak levels when exposed to the highest levels of competition. Therefore, athletes need to develop the ability to effectively respond mentally, emotionally, and physically in a competitive environment.

Traditional sport psychology literature examines the effects of pressure on performance in terms of anxiety, arousal, and stress to be managed. The research on anxiety and arousal is discussed in detail in Chapters 14 and 22. There are, however, various concerns to consider regarding this literature due to implications for athletes in competitive situations. Issues surrounding the multidimensional nature of anxiety, the assumed exclusively negative impact of anxiety and subsequent arousal state on performance, the measurement and instrumentation utilized in the research, and the application of these ideas to mental skills training must be considered in order to advance the field of sport psychology.

Whereas only these concerns regarding theories of anxiety and arousal are addressed in this chapter, others associated with cognitive appraisal and the hardy personality style are reviewed. These theories seem to explain the inconsistencies in human behavior as well as account for the individual differences that are so readily apparent in sport performance. By taking advantage of the power of perception and the utility of cognitive appraisal, and by learning the performance skill of trust, athletes can react to competitive situations more productively. The purpose of this chapter is to present a theoretically based and experientially validated approach to teaching athletes how to respond effectively to competitive pressure.

CONCERNS REGARDING THE SPORT PSYCHOLOGY ANXIETY LITERATURE

Various theories, research, and techniques that have evolved from the sport psychology anxiety literature are important to assess.

The Multidimensional Nature of Anxiety

The definitional confusion inherent in the theory of the multidimensional nature of anxiety must be examined as a liability in much of the sport psychology research on performance-stress management. Over the last 20 years, researchers have focused on the multidimensional nature of anxiety (Borkovec, 1976; Davidson & Schwartz, 1976; Landers, 1980; Morris, Davis, & Hutchings, 1981; Schwartz, Davidson, & Goldman, 1978). Cognitive anxiety has been differentiated from somatic anxiety. Cognitive anxiety is conceptualized as worry or the awareness of unpleasant feelings, concerns about performance, and the inability to concentrate (Borkovec, 1976). Somatic anxiety is operationalized as perceptions of physiological arousal such as shakiness, sweating, increased heart rate, rapid respiration, and "butterflies" in the stomach (Davidson & Schwartz, 1976; Kauss, 1980; Martens, Burton, Vealey, Bump, & Smith, 1990; Morris, Davis, & Hutchings, 1981).

One reason for differentiating between these anxiety components is the hypothesis that they are elicited by different antecedents and have differential effects on performance (Davidson & Schwartz, 1978; Gould, Petlichkoff, & Weinberg, 1984; Liebert & Morris, 1967; Martens, Vealey, & Burton, 1990). Somatic anxiety is suggested to be a conditioned response to competitive situations, and cognitive anxiety results from worry and negative expectations.

Multidimensional anxiety theory predicts that cognitive anxiety and somatic anxiety differentially affect sport performance (Burton, 1988; Martens, Vealey, & Burton, 1990).

Investigations based on this concept have shown a negative link between worry and motor task performance (Adam & Van Wieringen, 1988; Lehrer & Woolfolk, 1982; Morris, Smith, Andrews, & Morris, 1975), and worry and actual or expected competitive athletic performance (Barnes, Sime, Dienstbier, & Plaki, 1986; Crocker, 1989; Crocker, Alderman, & Smith, 1988; Furst & Tenenbaum, 1986; Gould, Weiss, & Weinberg, 1981; Mahoney & Avener, 1977). However, the relationship between somatic anxiety and sport performance is more complex. Research indicates that somatic anxiety has no relationship to motor task performance (Adam & Van Wieringen, 1988; Barnes, Sime, Dienstbier, & Plaki, 1986) or has a (perceived and actual) facilitative effect on simple gross motor performance (Helmers, 1991; Taylor, 1987) and fine complex motor tasks (Morris, Smith, Andrews, & Morris, 1975; Murray, 1989; Starkes & Allard, 1983).

The distinction between cognitive and somatic experiences is important in terms of helping athletes to respond effectively to pressure. However, we should not confuse these experiences by labeling arousal as "somatic *anxiety*." Anxiety is a psychological state; arousal is a physiological state (Duffy, 1962; Malmo, 1959; Sage, 1984; see Table 23–1). Although athletes can interpret their experiences differently, their arousal is similar in that it reflects the natural activation of one's physiology. Research as well as experiential evidence reveals that arousal and anxiety have differing effects on performance, and thus must remain as separate constructs.

TABLE 23–1. Indicators of Arousal and Anxiety*

Arousal	Anxiety
• Active stomach "butterflies"	• Lacking sense of confidence
• Unusual feelings of nausea	• Decreased sense of control
• Increased respiration rate	• Disrupted attention
• Increased blood pressure	• Pervading sense of worry, fear, doubt, and dread
• Increased muscle tension	• Worrisome expectation of failure
• Disrupted sleep patterns	• Negative concerns about performance
• Increased perspiration	• Impaired ability to concentrate
• Increased heart rate	• Diminished sense of well-being
• Increased shakiness	• Increased indecision and apprehension
• Elevated levels of epinephrine and norepinephrine	
• Changed brain waves from alpha (8–13 Hz) to beta (14–30 Hz) patterns	
• Increased frequency of urination	

*These characteristics are from Hackfort & Schwenkmezger, 1989; Hemery, 1986; Landers & Boutcher, 1986; Orlick, 1986; and Orlick & Partington, 1986.

The Assumed Negative Impact of Anxiety and Arousal

Numerous investigations have been conducted on the topic of anxiety; the orientation of most of this research has been on the assumed negative impact of anxiety on sport performance (Crocker, 1989; Crocker, Alderman, & Smith, 1989; Endler, 1978; Endler & Hunt, 1966; Feltz, 1982; Fisher & Zwart, 1982; Gruber & Beauchamp, 1979; Hackfort & Spielberger, 1989; Hall & Purvis, 1981; Huddleston & Gill, 1981; Martens, 1977; Martens & Gill, 1976; Martens & Landers, 1970; Martens, Rivkin, & Burton, 1980; Martens & Simon, 1976; McAuley, 1985; Scanlan & Passer, 1977; Silva & Hardy, 1984; Simon & Martens, 1977; Soenstrom & Bernado, 1982; Taylor, 1987).

This focus on the debilitating effects of anxiety on performance has disregarded the significant role of subjective evaluation in influencing affective, physiological, and performance responses to arousing stimuli (Apter, 1976; Bandura, 1977a, 1977b; Beck, 1972; Beck & Rush, 1975; Endler, 1978; Feltz, 1984; Hanin, 1989; Helmers, 1991; Hollandsworth, Glazeski, Kirkland, Jones, & Van Norman, 1979; Kerr, 1989; Lazarus, 1966, 1982, 1984; Lazarus & Averill, 1972; Lazarus & Folkman, 1984; Lazarus & Launier, 1978; Lazarus & Opton, 1966; Lehrer, & Woolfolk, 1982; Mahoney & Meyers, 1989; McAuley, 1985; Murray, 1989; Rotella, Lerner, Allyson, & Bean, 1990; Sarason, 1960, 1975; Silva & Hardy, 1984; Wine, 1971, 1980). The resulting prevalent concept of anxiety in the sport psychology literature is clinically based (Malmo, 1959; Taylor, 1953; Wolpe, 1969) and perhaps has been inappropriately applied to athletes who apparently prefer arousing and competitive situations (Helmers, 1991; Murray, 1989; Rotella, Lerner, Allyson, & Bean, 1990).

Many successful athletes are effective as a result of their tendency to interpret the naturally occurring heightened arousal and nervousness in a positive way (Rotella, Lerner, Allyson, & Bean, 1990). Athletes do not talk about "somatic anxiety." Their jargon includes terms such as "being nervous," "feeling juiced," "being pumped," and "being psyched up," and they typically speak of these reactions in a positive manner (Hemery, 1986; Orlick, 1986; Orlick & Partington, 1986). The emphasis on activation and the universal labeling of such feelings as unpleasant totally discounts the influence of cognitive perceptions and individual differences.

Research on Performance and Anxiety

Many issues surround the research on performance, anxiety, and arousal, as indicated by the nature of the literature. For example, varsity athletes and truly elite athletes in actual athletic competition have not been utilized in past research. Therefore, questions remain about the meaning and implications of these research findings in understanding athletes and competitive sport situations (Dishman, 1983; Greenspan & Feltz, 1989; Owen & Lee, 1987). Also, the long-term effects of various anxiety and arousal regulation strategies on performance are not known due to the lack of longitudinal studies of adherence to such techniques. Based on the compliance literature (Cummings, Becker, Kirscht, & Levin, 1981; Frederickson, Epstein, & Kosevsky, 1975; Kazdin & Bootzin, 1972), questions remain regarding the ability of sport psychologists to motivate athletes to consistently comply to any stress-management technique for more than a few weeks. If athletes are not practicing recommended techniques, can they be effective in performance?

Measurement of Anxiety

There are also concerns with research regarding the measurement of anxiety. The confusion relative to the terms *anxiety, arousal,* and *stress* is evident in many of the anxiety measures selected for research. Most measures that presumably assess anxiety and/or sport competition anxiety seem to measure physiological states of arousal rather than anxiety, a psychological state (Hackfort & Schwenkmezger, 1989). For example, the Sport Competition Anxiety Test, or SCAT (Martens, 1977), has only two items concerning psychological state of mind (worry) prior to and during competition.

SCAT was contrived to measure competitive trait anxiety in sport settings. Although it includes both cognitive and somatic items, it is in actuality a unidimensional measure of anxiety. Athletes scoring high on SCAT (indicating high levels of competitive trait anxiety) are expected to more frequently and more intensely experience high levels of competitive state anxiety, which will result in the deterioration of performance quality. Although it is acknowledged that anxiety has components of both intensity as well as direction (Duffy, 1957; Lazarus, 1966; Malmo, 1957; Sarason, 1960; Spielberger, 1966, 1972), SCAT assesses only the frequency of debilitating anxiety, ignoring the potential for the facilitative effects of anxiety (Martens, 1977).

In an attempt to remedy this situation, a multidimensional anxiety measure, the Competitive State Anxiety Inventory-2 (CSAI-2), has been developed (Martens, Burton, Vealey, Bump, & Smith, 1990). CSAI-2 consists of separate measures of cognitive and somatic anxiety. The research, however, lacks consistent agreement between self-report measures and physiological measures (Martens, Vealey, & Burton, 1990). In response to this lack of congruous research evidence directionally linking somatic factors with cognitive anxiety factors, the authors of the CSAI-2 indicate that "an important area of future inquiry is the relationship between physiological manifestations of anxiety, perceived anxiety, and sport behavior" (Martens, Burton, Vealey, Bump, & Smith, 1990, p. 196). This inquiry should attempt to determine athletes' experiences of anxiety, arousal, and competitive pressure and their respective influence on cognitions and performance rather than attempting to borrow existing theories of anxiety from other disciplines and applying them to the distinctive field of sport psychology.

Another concern regarding measurement issues deals with the assumed interpretations of responses. Arousal is not a psychological state, and high scores on measures of arousal do not indicate negative affect as purported by previous measures. Although SCAT attempts to measure both a somatic factor and a worry factor, high scores on either one are assumed to indicate a negative affect that is detrimental to enjoyment and performance (Martens, 1977). The inventories traditionally used to measure anxiety (i.e., SCAT, CSAI, CSAI-2, SAI) do not ask athletes how they perceive or interpret the items that comprise them. In addition to the anxiety inventories, "all the stress inventories are flawed because they fail to give enough weight to individual differences" (Cherry, 1978, p. 61.). It would appear that no qualitatively different reactions can be identified with these measurement instruments. For example, athletes can score high on SCAT and still perceive the factors it purportedly measures as positive. Such measures wholly deny the role and importance of cognitive appraisal and perception of competitive situations and of the physiological responses that athletes continually experience.

The disadvantages of social desirability and response bias will continue as long as being nervous is viewed by some as a problem requiring some kind of intervention. Response tendencies remain an issue when an item is answered not exclusively on the basis of its content, but on the interpretations and intentions of the respondent answering the question (Williams & Kane, 1989). "The validity of these instruments depends significantly on such factors as openness, honesty, accurate self-evaluation, and, finally, on the self-awareness of the respondent" (Hackfort & Schwenkmezger, 1989, p. 57). This self-evaluation and self-awareness is qualitatively different for different athletes, and the experiences these questionnaires attempt to describe may be interpreted by athletes differently than the answers interpreted by researchers. "In sports, high physiological activation is often a prerequisite for optimal performance and is regarded as a positive factor, whereas in other situations, it tends to be disruptive. This raises the question of whether the questionnaire method is an optimal method for diagnosing sport-related anxiety" (Hackfort & Schwenkmezger, 1989, p. 57).

Mental Skills Training

The flawed philosophy underlying previous research has affected the approach to mental skills training. Numerous stress management and cognitive intervention programs have been designed to enhance competitive athletic performance by regulating anxiety and arousal. The utilization of such programs, however, may be inappropriate due to erroneous generalizations being assumed by practitioners. "Practitioners who utilize results from studies conducted in laboratories, or studies employing contrived settings, tasks, or dependent variables, also rely upon generalizations for which adequate validity has not been established" (Greenspan & Feltz, 1989, p. 219). If to compete effectively, athletes are taught to consistently practice specific techniques such as relaxation exercises, they are, in essence, perceiving their bodies as defective and/or their approaches to sport as seriously tainted.

Another paramount concern regarding the application of research to actual athletic competitions centers around the time frame of the administration of the instruments utilized to assess an athlete's level of anxiety. These measures, which are typically administered before or after competition, do not assess how an athlete feels in actuality *during a contest.* Currently, there is no adequate method to truly evaluate an athlete's subjective experience of anxiety while in the process of competing.

It does not make sense to apply clinically based theories to a field like sport psychology. We seem to overlook many inconsistencies when adapting these theories to sport while exploring simple explanations or ways of predicting behavior and/or performance. There exists a need to investigate a new developmental model of sport performance in competition. Cognitive appraisal, perception, and the hardy personality style theories offer more appropriate interpretations of athletes' responses to athletic contests. They also provide a meaningful impetus for the development of ideas in a direction that fosters personal growth and trust.

COGNITIVE APPRAISAL AND PERCEPTION LITERATURE

Many of the problems raised in the preceding discussion are alleviated upon examination of theories dealing with cognitive appraisal and perception (Allport, 1955; Bem, 1972; Folkman, 1984; Folkman, Lazarus, & DeLongis, 1986; Jones & Hardy, 1989; Kobasa, 1979; Kobasa & Maddi, 1982; Lazarus, 1966, 1981; Lazarus & Folkman, 1984; Lazarus & Launier, 1978; Murray, 1989; Rotella, Lerner, Allyson, & Bean, 1990; Smith, 1980, 1986; Svebak & Stoyva, 1980; and Vallerand, 1987). An understanding of the role of appraisal provides a clearer analysis of individual differences. The perception and cognitive appraisal literature, available but seemingly overlooked and/or underrated in the sport psychology stress management and anxiety literature, has tremendous possibilities for advancing knowledge and proposed techniques. Much of the extant literature is based on traditional approaches. "Diagnostic methods developed in general anxiety research cannot simply be taken over uncritically and used in investigations in the field of sport psychology" (Hackfort & Schwenkmezger, 1989, p. 55).

The field of sport psychology must break away from a medical model and move toward a growth-oriented model emphasizing the positive aspects of being human (Danish & Hale, 1981, 1982; Rotella, 1990). The research on cognitive appraisals (Fish, 1983; Folkman, Lazarus, & DeLongis, 1986; Helmers, 1991; Kobasa, 1979; Kobasa & Maddi, 1981; Lazarus, 1966; Lazarus & Folkman, 1984; Murray, 1989) highlights a healthy humanistic and positive developmental approach. There is a variety of theoretical as well as anecdotal support calling for a fresh look at this literature and how sport psychology consultants can incorporate these concepts into practice so as to more effectively teach athletes how to thrive on pressure. Lazarus's (1966) concept of cognitive appraisal, Kobasa's (1979) hardy personality theory, and some empirical findings on the positive perception of arousal provide theoretical and experimental support for rethinking how to respond to performance stressors.

Cognitive Appraisal

Cognitive appraisal is to be understood as the process of categorizing all facets of a situation (internal or external in origin) with respect to its significance for well-being (Lazarus & Averill, 1972). "It is largely evaluative, focused on meaning or significance, and takes place continuously during waking life" (Lazarus & Folkman, 1984, p. 31). Appraisal-related processes significantly affect the reactions of people—e.g., athletes—to any encounter or sport-related situation. "Thus it appears it is largely the perception of the event and not the event per se that dictates which emotion will be experienced" (Vallerand, 1987, p. 177). The nature and meaning of a situation is associated with threat and challenge appraisals (Lazarus, 1966, 1981; Lazarus & Folkman, 1984). The perception of the demands of a situation as threatening or challenging interacts with the perception of ability or availability of resources required to meet those demands. If athletes perceive that the demands greatly exceed their resources or vice versa, the situation may be perceived as stressful. If athletes perceive a relative balance between their resources and their appraisal of the demands, the stress response may be minimal.

Athletes' continual appraisal of the consequences of any event (such as whether it is critical to self-esteem, one's place on the team, or one's career) also affect the perception of the potential stress of that event. "Whether or not one's cognitive appraisal of potentially stressful situations reflects reality is of little importance in generating a stress response" (Andersen & Williams, 1988, p. 298).

Transactional Models of Stress

Smith's (1980) mediational model of stress reflects the crucial role of cognitive mediators. "Appraisal processes create the psychological reality to which people respond, and the nature and intensity of emotional responses are a function of what individuals tell themselves about the situation and about their ability to cope with it" (Smith, 1980, p. 56).

"The transactional model emphasizes the cognitive interpersonal context of stress" (Meichenbaum, 1985, p. 4). Thus an individual's appraisal processes influence the dynamic relationship or transaction between individual and environment. An athlete's perception of the physiological/emotional responses as well as situational concerns mediate the potential stress of a competitive environment.

"Situations exert their effects on emotions through the intervening influence of thought. Through their own thought processes, people create the psychological reality to which they respond" (Smith, 1986, p. 109).

The literature on perception and appraisal demonstrates that the meaning an individual construes to an event shapes the emotional and behavioral response. Cognitive appraisal describes the evaluative cognitive processes that mediate the potential performance stressors and the athlete's reaction. Sport psychology consultants are in a position to stimulate athletes to make effectively enhancing appraisals of situations, of their available resources, and of their physiological responses to competitive situations.

HARDY PERSONALITY THEORY

Whereas the vast majority of past research has focused on threat appraisals and the negative effects of stress and anxiety, recent research suggests that many people view stress and anxiety as challenging, exciting, and beneficial (Fish, 1983; Folkman, 1984; Folkman & Lazarus, 1986; Helmers, 1991; Jones & Hardy, 1989; Kobasa, 1979; Kobasa & Maddi, 1982; Kobasa, Maddi, & Courington, 1981; Lazarus & Folkman, 1984; Murray, 1989; Svebak & Stoyva, 1980). Kobasa (1979) has studied challenge appraisals and the positive effects of stress and anxiety. The construct of psychological hardiness describes the personalities of people who have the tendency to view stressful situations in a positive way.

People who have hardy personalities are considered to possess three general characteristics: (a) an ability to feel deeply involved in or *committed* to the activities of their lives, (b) the belief that they can *control* or influence the events of their experience, and (c) the anticipation of demands or changes as exciting *challenges* to further development. Viewing stress as challenging, exciting, and beneficial characterizes Kobasa's term *hardiness*, in which one has a sense of control over the situation. These three aspects of this personality style describe how an individual appraises situations as challenging and growth-promoting.

The first orientation, commitment, entails the ability to feel deeply involved in the activities of one's life. It is a belief system that minimizes the perceived threat of any given situation. When an individual has a clear sense of personal values, goals, and capabilities, he or she has a strong commitment to self. Kobasa (1979) describes this as the ability to recognize one's distinctive values, goals, and priorities plus an appreciation of one's capacity to have purpose and make decisions—in other words, as acceptance of the uniqueness of being human. A curiosity about the sense of the meaningfulness of life characterizes this commitment aspect.

The second component outlined in this theory is that of control, which is a belief in one's ability to influence the course of events of one's experience. Three types of control exist in psychological hardiness: decisional control, cogni-

tive control, and coping skill (Kobasa, 1979; Kobasa, Maddi, & Courington, 1981). Decisional control refers to "the capability of autonomously choosing among various courses of action" (Kobasa, 1979, p. 3). This type is inexorably tied with cognitive control or "the ability to interpret, appraise, and incorporate various stressful events into one's ongoing life plan" (Kobasa, 1979, p. 3). Developing coping skills typically follows and implies that this individual has "a greater repertory of suitable responses to stress developed through the motivation to achieve across all situations" (Kobasa, 1979, p. 3). So one believes and acts as if one can influence events taking place around him or her through what one imagines, says, and does. To be psychologically hardy, it is imperative to believe that you can control the events of your experience in terms of what you choose to do and how you choose to respond to various events.

The challenge characteristic is expressed as a tendency to appraise potentially stressful situations as stimulating rather than threatening. Anticipation of demands or changes as exciting challenges will enable one to feel positively about change. Challenge appraisals involve a

focus on the potential for gain or growth inherent in an encounter and they are characterized by pleasurable emotions such as eagerness, excitement, and exhilaration, whereas threat [appraisals] center[s] on the potential harms and are characterized by negative emotions such as fear, anxiety, and anger. (Lazarus & Folkman, 1984, p. 33)

The challenge characteristic entails an expectation that life will change and these changes will stimulate personal development. Therefore, an individual practices responding to the unexpected, knows where to turn for resources to help cope with changes, and responds to the demands of life as challenges that allow for growth. The joy of challenge is to put oneself against the odds.

Therefore, the hardy personality style is a combination of cognition, emotion, and action aimed at survival and the enrichment of life through growth. These beliefs and tendencies are considered useful in facing and responding to potentially stressful events. Through optimistic cognitive appraisals and decisive coping actions, hardy people transform stressful events into less stressful forms (Kobasa, Maddi, Puccetti, & Zola, 1985). Stressful events are held in perspective through optimistic appraisals (Folkman & Lazarus, 1986). Natural changes are perceived as meaningful despite their stress. Having psychological hardiness then allows one to find out more about the changes constituting an event and learn whatever is valuable to incorporate into one's responses. A disposition towards commitment, control, and challenge functions concurrently as well as prospectively as a resistance resource to stress (Kobasa, Maddi, & Courington, 1981).

Thus, hardiness describes the personalities of people who have the tendency to view potentially stressful situations (such as highly competitive contests) in a positive way. Athletes need to know that everyone has the choice to view situations in this manner. This personality style is learned and developed through interactions between people and their interpersonal environment (Kobasa, 1979; Kobasa, Maddi, & Puccetti, 1982). Our perceptions and/or cognitive appraisals of events are strongly influenced by early life experiences and social learning (Bandura, 1977a; Rotter, 1966) and indirect experiences such as modeling (Bandura, 1977a).

Learning a sense of commitment and involvement develops the belief that it is interesting and worthwhile to involve oneself in whatever is going on in one's experience. It is important to invest oneself in one's experiences. Learning a sense of control or influence develops from having to stretch oneself to accomplish something and then succeeding with that achievement. This control and trust enables an individual to think of the self as influential and self-effacing. A sense of challenge is learned through encouragement to construe meaning to various experiences in a variety of ways. Through symbolization, imagination, and judgment one learns to expect change and is prepared to reflect on that change as a stimulus to development.

EMPIRICAL SUPPORT FOR INDIVIDUAL DIFFERENCES IN THE PERCEPTION OF AROUSAL

Research evidence supports some of the basic tenets of traditional anxiety theory which focus on the negative orientation of anxiety (Deshaies, 1981; Gerson & Deshaies, 1978; Gruber & Beauchamp, 1979; Hackfort & Schwenkmezger, 1989; Hall & Purvis, 1981; Klavora, 1978; Landers, 1980; Lazarus & Opton, 1966; Mandler & Sarason, 1952; Mandler & Watson, 1966; Martens, 1977; Martens, Burton, Rivkin, & Simon, 1980; Martens & Landers, 1970; Martens, Rivkin, & Burton, 1980; Martens & Simon, 1976; Sarason, 1960, 1972; Scanlan & Passer, 1977; Simon & Martens, 1977; Sonstroem & Bernado, 1982; Spielberger, 1966; Weinberg, 1977, 1989; Weinberg & Genuchi, 1980; Wine, 1971, 1980). However, the role of cognitive appraisal and the differential perceptions of arousal in affecting athletic performance have been ignored. Other investigations report the positive emotional and performance influence of heightened arousal (Apter, 1976, 1984; Helmers, 1991; Kerr, 1989; Lazarus, Deese, & Osler, 1952; Lazarus & Opton, 1966; Morris, Smith, Andrews, & Morris, 1975; Murray, 1989; Schachter, 1966; Starkes & Allard, 1983; Svebak & Stoyva, 1980). Studies examining high and low trait anxious subjects indirectly demonstrate differing effects of emotion on performance (Hackfort & Schwenkmezger, 1989; Hall & Purvis, 1981; Klavora, 1978; Mandler & Sarason, 1952; Mandler & Watson, 1966; Sarason, 1960, 1975; Weinberg, 1977, 1989; Wine, 1971, 1980). Whereas high trait anxious subjects generally report their experience of anxiety as debilitating, low trait anxious subjects characterize their experiences with arousal and "nerves" as facilitative, even in cases where their actual physiological levels have exceeded those same measures of the high A-trait subjects

(Hollandsworth, Glazeski, Kirkland, Jones, & Van Norman, 1979).

Further support for differential appraisals of the experience of stress and arousal in sport, specifically as positive and enhancing for performance, is found in a recent study by Murray (1989) in which many athletes viewed precompetition arousal as positive. Over 70% of the athletes studied enjoyed the nervousness associated with competition and saw it as helping their performance. Arousal appeared to be a signal that they were energized and ready to compete. Similarly, in an extension of Murray's study, Helmers (1991) found that a majority of athletes perceived cognitive anxiety as debilitating and somatic experiences as either neutral or enhancing to performance. Furthermore, subjects who experienced physiological arousal more often tended to perceive it more positively.

Subsequent investigations have resulted in findings supportive of this view. Researchers have examined how often athletes experienced certain feelings before competition, as measured with the Sport Competition Anxiety Test (SCAT), and how positively or negatively they perceived these precompetitive feelings, as measured with the Competition Anxiety Perception Scale (CAPS). Various categories of athletes, such as individual and team sport athletes, male and female athletes, starters and substitutes, report that precompetitive feelings are helpful or beneficial to their performance (Helmers, 1991; Murray, 1989; Rotella, Lerner, Allyson, & Bean, 1990).

There is a need for more research on the application of these theories and concepts to sport. Although these newer approaches are open to question, as are the older anxiety theories, the ideas and philosophies espoused in the cognitive appraisal, perception, and hardy personality style literature offer consistent explanations for the inconsistencies observed in athletic performance which are attributed to individual differences. Athletes have the option to appraise a competitive situation as well as the arousal and nervousness experienced in those situations either negatively, as debilitating to their performance, or positively, as enhancing to their performance. The theoretical formulations advanced by the appraisal literature encourages sport psychology consultants to teach athletes that they have a choice in deciding how to let their perceptions influence their athletic performance. The choice to trust one's body and to trust one's training, as well as to enjoy the inconsistencies of being human, are theoretically sound ideas, empirically supported and experientially validated.

TOWARD A GROWTH-ORIENTED DEVELOPMENTAL MODEL

Providing athletes with perceptual alternatives for positively viewing arousal, nervousness, and potential stressors has significant implications for helping them to thrive on pressure and enhance their sport performance in the face of competition. The theories of cognitive appraisal, perception, and the hardy personality style view the human mind as having unlimited possibilities. They consider human emotions such as nervousness and anxiety (as elicited by arousal) as natural, wonderful, and a part of a human's uniqueness. It is these naturally occurring responses that need to be trusted, enjoyed, nourished, accepted, and cherished for athletes to become as good as they can be.

This growth-oriented developmental model stands in opposition to the exclusively negative orientation of anxiety as well as to a medical model which considers many of these responses as problems (Danish & Hale, 1981, 1982; Rotella, 1990). It makes sense to examine issues surrounding anxiety, nervousness, and stress in a growth-oriented demeanor since sport psychology is concerned with "supernormal" rather than abnormal populations.

Unfortunately, a common research practice in sport psychology is to borrow theories from the parent discipline and apply them to a sport setting (Martens, 1987). "We have been so eager to test theories of the larger field of psychology in order to confirm our scientific respectability that we have not adequately observed, described, and theorized about our own thing—*sport*" (Martens, 1987, p.51). Sport psychologists should carefully examine their knowledge base. Existing theories serve as important guides for sport psychology, but the information gained from the experiences of sport psychologists interacting with athletes and coaches, though not considered "scientific," should be respected and used appropriately.

A humanistic and developmental philosophy thus emerges, reminding practitioners that applied sport psychology is a field designed to investigate and abet athletes seeking and achieving greatness. Following are some thought-provoking and innovative approaches based on the theoretical and philosophical views previously presented, as well as experiential work with collegiate, professional, and other elite athletes. They should help athletes perform to their highest levels when faced with competitive pressure.

ALTERNATIVE PERCEPTIONS OF AROUSAL

Mahoney and Myers report: "Our review of the arousal and attention research (and the social learning literature in general) suggests that it is not arousal that is central to performance but the athlete's expectations, efficacy beliefs, and strategies for managing and using that arousal" (1989, p. 83). Sport psychology consultants should take a new look at the relationships among anxiety, arousal, potential stressors, and performance.

Everyone has the option to respond to arousal and nervousness either positively or negatively. It is important to remember that this is an *option* arising from one's abilities of appraisal and perception. Arousal, when perceived as a natural and desirable reaction to competition, is positive. Anxiety, which may include worry, fear, doubts, and indecision, is psychological and, at least when experienced before or

during competition, may be negative. When athletes get anxious, their bodies typically, but not always, respond with increased arousal. However, being aroused does not mean the mind will become anxious (Apter, 1976, 1984; Helmers, 1991; Kerr, 1989; Murray, 1989; Rotella, Lerner, Allyson, & Bean, 1990). "Emotion is the result of cognitive appraisal, that is, it is the subjective appraisal of events (including physical events) and not the events per se that produce emotions" (Vallerand, 1987, p. 162).

When the mind does become anxious in response to increased arousal, it may be due to (a) distrusting natural responses, (b) ineffective perceptions due to modeling and indirect social learning (Bandura, 1977a), (c) directly being taught there is something wrong with being aroused, or perhaps (d) early failure experienced while aroused, resulting in poor performance being attributed to the arousal. To be effective, athletes must learn to focus the mind while the body is nervous, excited, and aroused. "Arousal feedback contributes to the ongoing process of appraisal and reappraisal" (Smith, 1986, p. 110). Being highly aroused is indeed unusual, but it is not abnormal. In his Canadian Football League debut, Raghib "Rocket" Ismail (1991) said, "I kept telling myself 'Just relax, just chill, just relax, don't get caught up in everything.' Eventually the mind relaxed, but the body never did." It may be distracting if allowed to be and it may be frightening to some athletes, but it does not need to be, and therefore, being aroused must not be perceived as a problem rather as a natural response that is to be trusted.

". . . There is clearly a great deal of human behavior oriented to the pursuit of high arousal and where high arousal is perceived as positive and pleasurable. . . . In fact much of what we do in our leisure time is directed to the attainment of high arousal" (Svebak & Stoyva, 1980, p. 440). Athletes must understand it is natural to be nervous and accept that being nervous is okay. In fact, many athletes play their sport in order to feel this way! Athletes who enjoy real competition seek out contests where the outcome is uncertain and report enjoying those physiological sensations and cognitive challenges as a major aspect of competition. Dennis Johnson, a guard in the National Basketball Association, enjoys the pressure:

I'm probably the worst shooter of the five players on the court for the [Phoenix] Suns. But when the game is coming down to the final seconds, I want the shot. It's not a point of accuracy; it's poise, confidence and loving the pressure. (Ferguson, 1990, pp. 6–10)

TRUST

It is paramount for the athlete to develop a belief system regarding self-trust when faced with competitive pressure. Sport psychology consultants typically spend much time getting athletes to trust themselves, to believe in themselves, and to strive to continually increase their self-confidence. "The core of this cognitively based analysis (of perception and appraisal) thus concerns the manner in which a person . . . apprehends and interprets any given situation" (Lazarus & Averill, 1972, p. 242). So, before a competition when athletes are going to experience unusual physiological sensations and cognitive nervousness, it is paramount that they continue to trust their bodies and not believe that there is a problem that requires intervention and fixing. A difficult issue for most scientifically trained specialists to understand and appreciate is the simple notion that belief, perception, and trust may not be easily measured but can be experienced and felt by humans.

Most academic sport psychologists have accepted the implied doctrine that the only source of knowledge, true knowledge, is orthodox science. We continually try to make this paradigm work even though we know from our tacit knowledge that it works badly when we want to understand the person. (Martens, 1987, p. 41)

Trust can be defined as letting go of conscious controlling tendencies. As opposed to self-efficacy, which is an expectation (Bandura, 1977b), trust is a cognitive performance skill which is categorical in nature, i.e., one either trusts and releases conscious control, or one does not (Moore & Stevenson, 1991). Trust does not involve some mystical, magical, or psychological technique. Until athletes understand this, they will not trust and they will tend to look to the outside to specific stress management techniques for the answer, rather than looking inside themselves. In this way many athletes can get stuck in a belief system instructing them that the answer is out there somewhere rather than inside—and trust is therefore placed in the technique rather than in themselves.

It must be noted that if everyone looks inside for trust and reasons to trust, they will find it. However, if athletes always look on the outside, in physical or psychological techniques, they will periodically find it the few days when they believe their technique is perfect. This approach will be short lived and inconsistent. But confidence, trust, and composure must always start on the inside and work their way out into the athlete's physical performance. It does not start on the outside and work its way in. Many athletes in a variety of sports with perfect technique have proved this point for years. Martina Navratilova states,

I've gone through lots of denial. I'll say, "I'm fine, I'm not nervous," and [Billie Jean King will] say, "It's O.K., it's natural to be nervous." All my life I've been denying I got nervous when I played [tennis], because that meant I was weak. Billie showed me it wasn't weakness. (Jenkins, 1991, p. 77)

With trust there is also an inner battle every day that must be won, but it is easier when one knows the answer is inside, where there is the ability for control. One approach says that the human machine is broken and it must be fixed; the other approach says that the machine works as long as allowed to do so. This latter view demands complete self-honesty and love of our human machine.

LEARNING SELF-PERCEPTION VERSUS STRESS-MANAGEMENT TECHNIQUES

Without this insight or understanding, the athlete will look on the outside (for techniques), rather than on the inside, where trust, belief, self-acceptance, and the necessary peace of mind are to be found. It is easy to feel a sense of artificial control through the use of stress management techniques. However, accepting the body and surrendering to the efficiency of the human machine is a key step to training the performance skill of trust and learning not to be concerned about being nervous. Based on the theories of appraisal, perception, and the hardy personality style, sport psychologists would teach that athletes must trust what they have trained in practice and that talent and belief and confidence come from inside, not from any techniques.

However, some athletes may not yet be ready to look inside and must therefore utilize various stress-management methods until they understand themselves and are able to trust. Thus such techniques are sometimes taught as a short-term solution, while the ultimate goal is developing and training trust—the most effective solution (i.e., Moore & Stevenson, 1991). By believing that confidence comes from these stress-management techniques, the end result is that instead of fostering trust, athletes learn skills for managing competitive pressure, inherently assuming that this sort of pressure is unnatural or abnormal and that it requires intervention. For example, Tony Meola, goalkeeper for the United States team in the 1990 World Cup soccer tournament, now perceives nervousness as a signal that his body is ready for action.

When I get that feeling, it kind of makes me happy now. Before it was kind of scary. It was kind of like, "What the hell is going on here? I should be okay!" . . . I finally realized that it's just part of life. It's part of the way you should be. . . . It's part of my routine. It's happened game in and game out. Now when it happens, I feel a little more at ease. I'm not scared of it [nervousness and arousal] anymore. I mean, now I think I'm probably more worried about not getting it than getting it. (Newman, 1991, p. 256)

It is completely inconsistent for athletes to learn to trust themselves and then feel they must learn how to manage and/or control their bodies' natural responses to competition. This basic point and an appreciation for the power of perception must be understood and accepted.

GETTING BEYOND SELF-INTIMIDATION

Perhaps the greatest intimidation and "psych-out" of all is to "psych" oneself out by being afraid of oneself, one's own arousal and nervousness—natural responses to competition. Self-intimidation destroys athletic performance because it distracts athletes' attention from the task at hand. Athletes who are intimidated by being nervous are in trouble because they are assured of wasting their attention on their nervousness rather than focusing their mind on the more appropriate task. The result will be poor concentration, diminished performance, and then blaming poor performance on the nervousness.

When athletes view nervousness as adrenaline naturally and marvelously sent to enhance performance in important moments, they see a finely tuned machine deserving of trust. When they view nervousness as unnatural and dangerous, as an enemy that can interfere with effective functioning, athletes see something frightening that needs to be driven away or tamed. In other words, they will get "psyched-out" by their own bodies' responses. They may even begin to believe that competitors win because they do not get nervous. Athletes must get beyond this cycle and realize that many great athletes attribute their exceptional performances to nervousness. In recent years, Jack Nicklaus commented in a personal conversation that he did not know how to play great golf when he was not nervous (Nicklaus, personal communication, March 21, 1989). Curtis Strange, a U.S. Open golf champion, describes in detail the lump in his throat, his shaky hands, and his rapid heartbeat as he came down the final holes to win his second U.S. Open. And these examples are chosen from a sport requiring highly complex movement and fine motor coordination.

By perceiving physiological and emotional responses to the competitive atmosphere as problematic, one creates a problem in need of intervention. Athletes will spend their entire sport career fighting themselves and continually trying to fix the self because these unusual sensations are an integral part of the competitive experience.

THE CHOICE TO MEDIATE PERCEPTION

The continual interchange between the mental appraisal of a situation and of personal abilities and resources and emotional/physiological responses implies that athletes have a choice to mediate cognitions (Lazarus, 1966; Smith, 1980). Sport psychologists should help athletes view themselves as finely tuned machines that work under pressure.

Many athletes have been incorrectly led to believe through the sports media and other sources that great athletes are never nervous prior to, during, and after competition. This is a great intimidation game that, if believed, will cause athletes to believe something is wrong when they feel nervous. This will always hinder, rather than build, self-trust.

For athletes to love competition, they must choose to perceive potentially stressful situations as challenging rather than threatening and love the challenge and uncertainty of good competition (Kobasa, 1979; Lazarus, 1966). They must learn to respond to the feelings resulting from this uncertainty as exciting, beneficial, and welcome. This honest and natural response, which fosters more positive and functional perceptions, will naturally lead to feelings of control, eagerness, and exhilaration rather than fear, threat, anxiety, and/or dread. In a naturalistic research investigation, five of the best hitters in the history of baseball were interviewed regarding their thoughts on the mental aspects of hitting. The topic of stress was discussed only when the interviewer raised the issue. However, when asked about stress,

both [Tony] Oliva and [Stan] Musial said they felt some nerves on Opening Day, but even then they really thought it was more excitement than any form of negative affect. Similarly, [Tony] Oliva said he felt "nervous" before every game and every first at-bat. . . . He did not label it as fear, though, and said it helped his performance: "The more people in the stands, the better you feel like you play. You're more excited." (Hanson, 1991, pp. 249–250)

This approach of encouraging athletes to perceive their responses to competitive pressure as natural, normal, and effective has evolved from the study of the research on appraisal and characteristics of the hardy personality style, as well as from experience interacting with successful athletes. It is the ability of athletes to remain confident and focused on the appropriate task while the body is aroused or nervous that is so essential to athletic success. A wandering mind is a problem. A nervous body is not.

In attempting to help athletes, it is crucial that the sport psychology consultant completely believes that athletes are physiologically and psychologically capable, talented, and healthy until proven otherwise. Any doubts, questions, or preconceived notions about what champions look like or sound like are liable to interfere with performance enhancement effectiveness. Even great athletes can become highly nervous prior to competition and may stay nervous during competition and accept that this is the way it is and always will be. Viewing bodily responses and arousal from this perspective is a must if self-acceptance, self-respect, and self-trust are to be developed.

When sport psychologists place trust in their techniques, they will give credit for great performance to their techniques rather than to the athletes. When the techniques do not work, they will question the athlete who cannot perform. Sport psychologists must remember that their responsibility is to convince the athlete to believe in himself or herself. This is crucial to the development of trust.

The major thrust of sport psychology intervention should be to help athletes build self-trust, self-confidence, concentration, and composure. As a field, sport psychology oftentimes makes the mistake of blindly borrowing from clinically developed approaches for dealing with arousal, stress, and anxiety as cases of pathology. If sport psychology is to borrow from general psychology, perhaps an in-depth examination of the literature on appraisal and perception would be beneficial. (See Allport, 1955; Folkman, 1984; Lazarus, 1966; Kobasa, 1979.) However, these stress-management techniques have been developed for and based on abnormal and/or unhealthy populations and most likely are not designed for people seeking pressure situations and striving for greatness within these situations. "We clearly need to spend more time observing behavior in sport and building our own theories unique to sport" (Martens, 1987, p. 51). It is vital to realize the general cultural tendency for low acceptance of this viewpoint and how that inclination perpetuates the perception that something is wrong with our body and we should therefore not trust it.

PHILOSOPHICAL KEYS

This chapter on responding to competitive pressure is much more of a treatise inviting the adoption of a healthy philosophical attitude rather than promoting some techniques and strategies on which to rely when faced with performance-related pressure. Philosophical keys which are derived from the literature on perception, appraisal, the hardy personality style, tacit knowledge, and experiences working with athletes are integral to interacting with athletes. Sport psychology should stand in opposition to a medical model and move toward a growth-oriented developmental model emphasizing the unique and natural aspects of being human. One must believe that the human system works and responds properly and efficiently in competitive situations.

The literature on cognitive appraisals, self-perception, and hardy personality style, as well as some emerging empirical findings, demonstrate that the meaning an individual attributes to an event (internal or external) shapes emotional, cognitive, and behavioral responses. Providing athletes with perceptual alternatives for positively viewing arousal and potential stressors has significant implications for helping athletes to thrive on pressure and enhance their sport performance in the face of competitive pressure.

To become an effective athlete, it is crucial to build a psychological foundation on the cornerstones of self-acceptance and self-trust. To perform at one's best, self-confidence, self-efficacy and perceived competence are important (Bandura, 1977b; Bem, 1972; Harter, 1982). It will be very difficult to develop these abilities if athletes reject the natural way the mind and body work. This proposed alternative way of appraising the arousal and potential stressors that athletes confront is not a solution for all athletes, but it should be the starting point. Some sport psychologists and coaches only implement the use of unnatural techniques and intervention strategies. Some of these techniques, e.g., progressive relaxation (Jacobson, 1938), the relaxation response (Benson, 1975), biofeedback (Zaichkowsky & Fuchs, 1989), systematic desensitization (Wolpe, 1969), stress inoculation (Meichenbaum, 1977), visuomotor-behavior-rehearsal (Suinn, 1972), hypnosis (Nideffer, 1976), and thought stoppage and cognitive restructuring (Bunker & Williams, 1986) can be effective with some athletes in some situations. Nonetheless they should be used as a last resort, not as the first option. Athletes should be taught to view themselves as finely tuned machines deserving of trust and must learn how to appraise situations they encounter in line with these thoughts. The literature on appraisal as well as experiences with athletes

supports this perspective (i.e. Allport, 1955; Lazarus, 1966, 1981; Lazarus & Folkman, 1984; Lazarus & Launier, 1978).

If athletes must repeat relaxation exercises in order to play games, they would do much better to change their philosophy than to try to change their natural responses to competitive situations. Maintaining a healthy philosophy in a highly competitive society filled with competitive people is a challenge that must be faced daily. However, it is important to fix only that which is broken, and to trust that which works. Athletes must learn to trust that the human machine works beautifully before ever deciding it is broken and therefore must be artificially fixed by strategies that they are not likely to adhere to anyway (Cummings, Becker, Kirscht, & Levin, 1981; Frederickson, Epstein, & Kosevsky, 1975; and Kazdin & Bootzin, 1972).

SUMMARY

Numerous programs have been developed to regulate anxiety and arousal, thereby enhancing athletic performance. Although these programs appear to be generally effective, we question the long-term effectiveness of these programs for most athletes. There are concerns about the impact of these techniques upon self-confidence and self-trust. An alternative way of viewing anxiety and arousal has been presented that focuses on the cognitive appraisal of and the perception of the nervousness and arousal experienced before or during competition. This approach advocates accepting the body's natural response to competition instead of fighting it. Nervousness can be appraised as a normal response to the uncertainty of competition or as something unnatural and dangerous that can interfere with normal functioning. "Because beliefs usually operate at a tacit level to shape a person's perception of his or her relationship to the environment, we are generally unaware of their influence on appraisal" (Lazarus & Folkman, 1984, p. 64).

The implication follows that by altering perceptual appraisals, viewing potentially threatening situations instead as challenging ones, changed beliefs about these situations can be adopted. Because beliefs serve as a perceptual lens, in appraisal, "beliefs determine what is fact, that is, 'how things are' in the environment, and they shape the understanding of its meaning" (Lazarus & Folkman, 1984, p. 63). The power of the mind, the flexibility of perceptions, and the strength available from self-discipline and willpower are human qualities designed to help us function efficiently and effectively. Handling pressure effectively is a matter of perception and getting in the right mind-set. Based on the research dealing with cognitive appraisals, self-perception is the key to trusting a nervous body (Folkman, Lazarus, & DeLongis, 1986; Kobasa, 1979; Kobasa & Maddi, 1981; Lazarus & Folkman, 1984). How sport psychology consultants view anxiety and arousal influences how they help coaches and athletes respond to competitive pressure.

Building trust in the human system and the athlete's skills is an important goal. Sport psychologists must choose wisely when deciding to teach athletes to trust what they have or to appraise situations as threatening and therefore breed dependence on techniques for fixing what has been perceived as a malfunctioning machine. Such techniques are appropriate as a last resort or as an intermediate step, but should never be the first choice nor the ultimate choice in any attempt to enhance performance.

It is vital to emphasize that the greatest cognitive skill of all is to learn to control one's perceptions and appraisals and the way one thinks. This mental discipline is what "willpower" truly means. Training trust, perception, and appraisal are the skills performance enhancement specialists need to be teaching athletes. Competitors must learn the ability to let go and trust during performance what has been trained in practice in order to be free of expectations and fears. Thus, helping athletes to effectively respond to competitive pressure entails teaching them to believe in the human mind and body and reminding them that they have the choice to enjoy and even thrive on the uncertainty of athletic competition.

References

Adam, R. J., & Van Wieringen, P. (1988). Worry and emotionality: Its influence on the performance of a throwing task. *International Journal of Sport Psychology, 19,* 211–225.

Allport, F. H. (1955). *Theories of perception and the concept of structure.* New York: Wiley.

Andersen, Mark B., & Williams, Jean M. (1988). A model of stress and athletic injury: Prediction and prevention. *Journal of Sport and Exercise Psychology, 10,* 294–306.

Apter, M. J. (1976). Some data inconsistent with the optimal arousal theory of motivation. *Perceptual and Motor Skills, 43,* 1209–1210.

Apter, M. J. (1984). Reversal theory and personality: A review. *Journal of Research in Personality, 18,* 265–288.

Bandura, A. (1977a). *Social learning theory.* Englewood Cliffs, NJ: Prentice-Hall.

Bandura, A. (1977b). Self-efficacy: Toward a unifying theory of behavior change. *Psychological Review, 84,* 191–215.

Barnes, M., Sime, W., Dienstbier, R., & Plaki, B. (1986). A test of construct validity of the CSAI-2 questionnaire on male elite swimmers. *International Journal of Sport Psychology, 17,* 364–374.

Beck, A. T. (1972). Cognition, anxiety, and physiological disorders. In C. D. Spielberger (Ed.), *Anxiety: Current trends in theory and research* (Vol. 2, pp. 343–354). New York: Academic Press.

Beck, A. T., & Rush, A. J. (1975). A cognitive model of anxiety formation and anxiety resolution. In I. G. Sarason & C. D. Spielberger (Eds.), *Stress and anxiety* (Vol. 2, pp. 69–80). Washington, DC: Hemisphere.

Bem, D. J. (1972). Self-perception theory. In L. Berkowitz (Ed.), *Advances in experimental social psychology* (Vol. 6, pp. 1–62). New York: Academic Press.

Benson, H. (1975). *The relaxation response.* New York: Morrow.

Borkovec, T. D. (1976). Physiological and cognitive process in the regulation of anxiety. In G. E. Schwartz & D. Shapiro (Eds.), *Consciousness and self-regulation: Advances in research* (Vol. 1, pp. 261–312). New York: Plenum.

Bunker, L. K., & Williams, J. M. (1986). Cognitive techniques for improving performance and building confidence. In J. M. Williams (Ed.), *Applied sport psychology: Personal growth to peak performance* (pp. 235–255). Palo Alto, CA: Mayfield.

Burton, D. (1988). Do anxious swimmers swim slower? Reexamining the elusive anxiety-performance relationship. *Journal of Sport and Exercise Psychology, 10,* 45–61.

Cherry, L. (1978, March). [Interview with Hans Selye, On the real benefits of eustress]. *Psychology Today,* pp. 60–63.

Crocker, P. (1989). A follow-up of cognitive-affective stress management training. *Journal of Sport and Exercise Psychology, 11,* 236–242.

Crocker, P., Alderman, R., & Smith, F. (1988). Cognitive-affective stress management training with high performance youth volleyball players: Effects on affect, cognition, and performance. *Journal of Sport and Exercise Psychology, 10,* 448–460.

Cummings, K. M., Becker, M. H., Kirscht, J. P., & Levin, N. W. (1981). Intervention strategies to improve compliance with medical regimens by ambulatory hemodialysis patients. *Journal of Behavioral Medicine, 4,* 111–127.

Danish, S. J., & Hale, B. D. (1981). Toward an understanding of the practice of sport psychology. *Journal of Sport Psychology, 3,* 90–99.

Danish, S. J., & Hale, B. D. (1982). Let the discussions continue: Further considerations on the practice of sport psychology. *Journal of Sport Psychology, 4,* 10–12.

Davidson, R. J., & Schwartz, G. E. (1976). The psychobiology of relaxation and related states: A multi-process theory. In D. I. Mostofsky (Ed.), *Behavior control and modification of physiological activity* (pp. 399–442). Englewood Cliffs, NJ: Prentice-Hall.

Deshaies, P. (1981). The interactional model of anxiety in a sport competition setting. In G. Roberts & D. Landers (Eds.), *Psychology of motor behavior and sport—1980.* (p. 102). Champaign, IL: Human Kinetics.

Dishman, R. (1983). Identity crises in North American sport psychology: Academics in professional issues. *Journal of Sport Psychology, 5,* 123–134.

Duffy, E. (1957). The psychological significance of the concept of "arousal" or "activation." *Psychological Review, 64,* 265–275.

Duffy, E. (1962). *Activation and behavior.* New York: Wiley.

Endler, N. S. (1978). The interaction model of anxiety: Some possible implications. In D. Landers & R. Christina (Eds.), *Psychology of motor behavior and sport—1977* (pp. 332–351). Champaign, IL: Human Kinetics.

Endler, N. S., Hunt, J. McV., & Rosenstein, A. J. (1962). An S-R inventory of anxiousness. *Psychological Monographs, 76,* 1–33.

Feltz, D. L. (1982). Path analysis of causal elements in Bandura's theory of self-efficacy and an anxiety-based model of avoidance behavior. *Journal of Personality and Social Psychology, 42,* 764–781.

Feltz, D. L. (1984). Self-efficacy as a cognitive mediator of athletic performance. In W. F. Straub & J. M. Williams (Eds.), *Cognitive sport psychology.* (pp. 191–198). Lansing, NY: Sport Science Associates.

Ferguson, Howard E. (1990). *The edge: The guide to fulfilling dreams, maximizing success and enjoying a lifetime of achievement.* Cleveland, Ohio: Getting the Edge Company.

Fish, T. A. (1983). *The relationships among cognitive appraisals and performance in a naturalistic, public speaking situation.* Unpublished dissertation, University of Calgary, Alberta, Canada.

Fisher, A. C., & Zwart, E. F. (1982). Psychological analysis of athletes' anxiety responses. *Journal of Sport Psychology, 4,* 139–158.

Folkman, S. (1984). Personal control and stress and coping processes: A theoretical analysis. *Journal of Personality and Social Psychology, 46,* 839–852.

Folkman, S., Lazarus, R. S., & DeLongis, A. (1986). Appraisal, coping, health status, and psychological symptoms. *Journal of Personality and Social Psychology. 50,* 571–579.

Frederickson, L. W., Epstein, L. H., & Kosevsky, B. P. (1975). Reliability and controlling effects of three procedures for self-monitoring smoking. *Psychological Record, 25,* 255–264.

Furst, D. M., & Tenenbaum, G. (1986). The relationship between worry, emotionality, and sport performance. In D. M. Landers (Ed.), *Sport and elite performers.* (pp. 89–96). Champaign, IL: Human Kinetics.

Gerson, R., & Deshaies, P. (1978). Competitive trait anxiety and performance as predictors of pre-competitive state anxiety. *International Journal of Sport Psychology, 9,* 16–26.

Gould, D., Petlichkoff, L., & Weinberg, R. S. (1984). Antecedents of, temporal changes in, and relationships between CSAI-2 subcomponents. *Journal of Sport Psychology, 6,* 289–304.

Gould, D., Weiss, M. R., & Weinberg, R. S. (1981). Psychological characteristics of successful and nonsuccessful big-ten wrestlers. *Journal of Sport Psychology, 3,* 69–81.

Greenspan, M. J., & Feltz, D. (1989). Psychological interventions with elite athletes in competitive situations: A review. *The Sport Psychologist, 3,* 219–236.

Gruber, J., & Beauchamp, D. (1979). Relevance of the competitive state anxiety inventory in a sport environment. *Research Quarterly, 50,* 207–214.

Hackfort, D., & Schwenkmezger, P. (1989). Measuring anxiety in sports: Perspectives and problems. In D. Hackfort & C. D. Spielberger (Eds.), *Anxiety in sports* (pp. 55–74). New York: Hemisphere.

Hackfort, D., & Spielberger, C. D. (1989). *Anxiety in sports: An international perspective.* New York: Hemisphere.

Hall, E., & Purvis, G. (1981). The relationship of anxiety to competitive bowling. In G. Roberts & D. Landers (Eds.), *Psychology of motor behavior and sport—1980.* (p. 106). Champaign, IL: Human Kinetics.

Hanin, Y. L. (1989). Interpersonal and intragroup anxiety in sports. In D. Hackfort & C. D. Spielberger (Eds.), *Anxiety in sports: An international perspective* (pp. 19–28). New York: Hemisphere.

Hanson, T. (1991). *The mental aspects of hitting.* Unpublished doctoral dissertation, University of Virginia, Charlottesville.

Harter, S. (1982). The perceived competence scale for children. *Child Development, 53,* 87–97.

Helmers, A. M. (1991). *Positive anxiety in sport: Recreational volleyball athletes.* Unpublished master's thesis, University of Virginia, Charlottesville.

Hemery, D. (1986). *Sporting excellence a study of sport's highest achievers.* Champaign, IL: Human Kinetics.

Hollandsworth, Jr., J. G., Glazeski, R. C., Kirkland, K., Jones, G. E., & Van Norman, L. R. (1979). An analysis of the nature and effects of test anxiety: Cognitive, behavioral, and physiological components. *Cognitive Therapy and Research, 3,* 165–180.

Huddleston, S., & Gill, D. L. (1981). State anxiety as a function of skill level and proximity to competition. *Research Quarterly for Exercise and Sport, 52,* 31–34.

Jacobson, E. (1938). *Progressive relaxation.* Chicago: University of Chicago Press.

Jenkins, S. (1991, April). Racket science. *Sports Illustrated,* pp. 66–82.

Jones, J., & Hardy, L. (1989). Stress and cognitive functioning in sport. *Journal of Sports Sciences, 7,* 41–63.

Kauss, D. R. (1980). *Peak performance: Mental game plans for maximizing your athletic potential.* Englewood Cliffs, NJ: Prentice-Hall.

Kazdin, A. E., & Bootzin, R. R. (1972). The token economy: An evaluative review. *Journal of Behavior Therapy and Experimental Psychiatry, 7,* 213–219.

Kerr, J. H. (1989). Anxiety, arousal, and sport performance: An application of reversal theory. In D. Hackfort & C. D. Spielberger (Eds.), *Anxiety in sports: An international perspective* (pp. 137–152). New York: Hemisphere.

Klavora, P. (1978). An attempt to derive inverted-U curves based on the relationship between anxiety and athletic performance. In D. Landers & R. Christina (Eds.), *Psychology of motor behavior and sport—1977* (pp. 369–377). Champaign, IL: Human Kinetics.

Kobasa, S. C. (1979). Stressful life events, personality and health: An inquiry into hardiness. *Journal of Personality and Social Psychology, 37,* 1–11.

Kobasa, S. C., & Maddi, S. R. (1982). Hardiness and health: A prospective study. *Journal of Personality and Social Psychology, 42,* 168–177.

Kobasa, S. C., Maddi, S. R., & Courington, S. (1981). Personality and constitution as mediators in the stress-illness relationship. *Journal of Health and Social Behavior, 22,* 368–378.

Kobasa, S. C., Maddi, S. R., Puccetti, M. C., & Zola, M. A. (1985). Effectiveness of hardiness, exercise and social support as resources against illness. *Journal of Psychosomatic Research, 29,* 525–533.

Landers, D. M. (1980). The arousal-performance relationship revisited. *Research Quarterly for Exercise and Sport, 51,* 77–90.

Lazarus, R. S. (1966). *Psychological stress and the coping process.* New York: McGraw-Hill.

Lazarus, R. S. (1981). The stress and coping paradigm. In C. Eisdorfer (Ed.), *Models for clinical psychopathology* (pp. 177–214). Englewood Cliffs, NJ: Prentice-Hall.

Lazarus, R. S. (1982). Thoughts on the relations between emotions and cognition. *American Psychologist, 37,* 1019–1024.

Lazarus, R. S. (1984). On the primacy of cognition. *American Psychologist, 39,* 124–129.

Lazarus, R. S., & Averill, J. R. (1972). Emotion and cognition: With special reference to anxiety. In C. D. Spielberger (Ed.), *Anxiety: Current trends in theory and research* (Vol. 2, pp. 241–283). New York: Academic Press.

Lazarus, R. S., Deese, J., & Osler, S. F. (1952). The effects of psychological stress upon performance. *Psychological Bulletin, 49,* 293–317.

Lazarus, R. S., & Folkman, S. (1984). *Stress, appraisal, and coping.* New York: Springer.

Lazarus, R. S., & Launier, R. (1978). Stress related transactions between person and environment. In L. A. Pervin & M. Lewis (Eds.), *Perspectives in interactional psychology* (pp. 287–327). New York: Plenum Press.

Lazarus, R. S., & Opton, E. M. (1966). The study of psychological stress: A summary of theoretical formulations and experimental findings. In C. D. Spielberger (Ed.), *Anxiety and behavior* (pp. 225–262). New York: Academic Press.

Lehrer, P. M., & Woolfolk, R. L. (1982). Self-report assessment of anxiety: Physiological, cognitive, and behavioral modalities. *Behavioral Assessment, 4,* 167–177.

Liebert, R. M., & Morris, L. W. (1967). Cognitive and emotional components of test anxiety: A distinction and some initial data. *Psychological Reports, 20,* 975–987.

Mahoney, M. J., & Avener, M. (1977). Psychology of the elite athlete: An exploratory study. *Cognitive Therapy and Research, 1,* 135–141.

Mahoney, M. J., & Meyers, A. W. (1989). Anxiety and athletic performance: Traditional and cognitive-developmental perspectives. In D. Hackfort & C. D. Spielberger (Eds.), *Anxiety in sports* (pp. 77–94). New York: Hemisphere.

Malmo, R. B. (1957). Anxiety and behavioral arousal. *Psychological Review, 64,* 276–287.

Malmo, R. B. (1959). Activation: A neuropsychological dimension. *Psychological Review, 66,* 367–386.

Mandler, G., & Sarason, S. (1952). A study of anxiety and learning. *Journal of Abnormal and Social Psychology, 47,* 166–173.

Mandler, G., & Watson, D. L. (1966). Anxiety and the interruption of behavior. In C. D. Spielberger (Ed.), *Anxiety and behavior* (pp. 263–288). New York: Academic Press.

Martens, R. (1977). *Sport competition anxiety test.* Champaign, IL: Human Kinetics.

Martens, R. (1987). Science, knowledge, and sport psychology. *The Sport Psychologist, 1,* 29–55.

Martens, R., Burton, D., Rivkin, F., & Simon, J. (1980). Reliability and validity of the competitive state anxiety inventory (CSAI). In C. H. Nadeau, W. R. Halliwell, K. M. Newell, & G. C. Roberts (Eds.), *Psychology of motor behavior and sport—1979* (pp. 91–99). Champaign, IL: Human Kinetics.

Martens, R., Burton, D., Vealey, R. S., Bump, L. A., & Smith, D. E. (1990). Development and validation of the competitive state anxiety inventory—2. In R. Martens, R. S. Vealey, & D. Burton (Eds.), *Competitive anxiety in sport* (pp. 117–232). Champaign, IL: Human Kinetics.

Martens, R., & Gill, D. L. (1976). State anxiety among successful and unsuccessful competitors who differ in competitive trait anxiety. *Research Quarterly, 47,* 698–708.

Martens, R., & Landers, D. M. (1970). Motor performance under stress: A test of the inverted-U hypothesis. *Journal of Personality and Social Psychology, 16,* 29–37.

Martens, R., Rivkin, F., & Burton, D. (1980). Who predicts anxiety better: Coaches or athletes? In C. H. Nadeau, W. R. Halliwell, K. M. Newell, & G. C. Roberts (Eds.), *Psychology of motor behavior and sport—1979* (pp. 84–90). Champaign, IL: Human Kinetics.

Martens, R., & Simon, J. A. (1976). Comparison of three predictors of state anxiety in competitive situations. *Research Quarterly, 47,* 381–387.

Martens, R., Vealey, R. S., & Burton, D. (1990). *Competitive anxiety in sport.* Champaign, IL: Human Kinetics.

McAuley, E. (1985). Modeling and self-efficacy: A test of Bandura's model. *Journal of Sport Psychology, 7,* 283–295.

Meichenbaum, D. H. (1977). *Cognitive-behavior modification: An integrative approach.* New York: Plenum.

Meichenbaum, D. H. (1985). *Stress inoculation training.* New York: Pergamon Press.

Moore, W. E., & Stevenson, J. R. (1991). Understanding trust in the performance of complex automatic sport skills. *The Sport Psychologist. 5,* 281–289.

Morris, L., Davis, D., & Hutchings, C. (1981). Cognitive and emotional components of anxiety: Literature review and revised worry-emotionality scale. *Journal of Educational Psychology, 73,* 541–555.

Morris, L., Smith, L., Andrews, E., & Morris, N. (1975). The relationship of emotionality and worry components of anxiety to motor skills performance. *Journal of Motor Behavior, 7,* 121–130.

Murray, J. (1989). *An investigation of competitive anxiety vs. positive affect.* Unpublished master's thesis, University of Virginia, Charlottesville.

Newman, Mark A. (1991). *The psychology of goalkeeping: Perspectives on the mental aspect of goalkeeping in soccer.* Unpublished master's thesis, University of Virginia, Charlottesville.

Nideffer, R. M. (1976). *The inner athlete: Mind plus muscle for winning.* New York: Crowell.

Orlick, T. (1986). *Psyching for sport.* Champaign, IL: Leisure Press.

Orlick, T., & Partington, J. (1986). *Psyched.* Ottawa, Ontario, Canada: Coaching Association of Canada.

Owen, N., & Lee, C. (1987). Current status of sport psychology. *Australian Psychologist, 22,* 62–76.

"Rocket" blasts off in CFL debut. (1991, July 19). *The Daily Progress,* p. B7.

Rotella, R. J. (1990). Providing sport psychology consulting services to professional athletes. *The Sport Psychologist, 4,* 409–417.

Rotella, R. J., Lerner, J. D., Allyson, B., & Bean, J. J. (1990, September). *Arousal as arousing for athletes.* Presentation made at the Fifth Annual Conference of the Association for the Advancement of Applied Sport Psychology, San Antonio, TX.

Rotter, J. B. (1966). *Application of a social learning theory of personality.* New York: Holt, Rinehart & Winston.

Sage, G. H. (1984). *Motor learning and control: a neuropsychological approach.* Dubuque, IA: Brown.

Sarason, I. G. (1960). Empirical findings and theoretical problems in the use of anxiety scales. *Psychological Bulletin, 57,* 403–415.

Sarason, I. G. (1975). Anxiety and self-preoccupation. In I. G. Sarason & C. D. Spielberger (Eds.), *Stress and anxiety* (Vol. 2, pp. 27–44). Washington, DC: Hemisphere.

Scanlan, T., & Passer, M. W. (1977). The effects of competition trait anxiety and game win-loss on perceived threat in a natural competitive setting. In D. M. Landers & R. W. Christina, *Psychology of motor behavior and sport—1976* (Vol. 2, pp. 157–160). Champaign, IL: Human Kinetics.

Schachter, S. (1966). The interaction of cognitive and physiological determinants of emotional state. In C. D. Spielberger (Ed.), *Anxiety and behavior* (pp. 193–224). New York: Academic Press.

Schwartz, G. E., Davidson, R. J., & Goldman, D. (1978). Patterning of cognitive and somatic processes in the self-regulation of anxiety: Effects of meditation versus exercise. *Psychosomatic Exercise, 40,* 321–328.

Silva, J. M., & Hardy, C. J. (1984). Precompetitive affect and athletic performance. In W. F. Straub & J. M. Williams (Eds.), *Cognitive sport psychology* (pp. 79–88). Lansing, NY: Sport Science Associates.

Simon, J. A., & Martens, R. (1977). SCAT as a predictor of A-states in varying competitive situations. In D. M. Landers & R. W. Christina (Eds.), *Psychology of motor behavior and sport—1976* (Vol. 2, pp. 146–155). Champaign, IL: Human Kinetics.

Smith, R. E. (1980). A cognitive-affective approach to stress management training for athletes. In C. H. Nadeau, W. R. Halliwell, K. M. Newell, & G. C. Roberts (Eds.), *Psychology of motor behavior and sport* (pp. 54–72). Champaign, IL: Human Kinetics.

Smith, R. E. (1986). A component analysis of athletic stress. In M. Weiss & D. Gould (Eds.), *Competitive sports for children and youths: Proceedings of the Olympic Scientific Congress (pp. 107–112). Champaign, IL: Human Kinetics.*

Soenstrom, R. J., & Bernado, P. (1982). Intraindividual pregame state anxiety and basketball performance: A re-examination of the inverted-U curve. Journal of Sport Psychology, 4, 235–245.

Spielberger, C. D. (1966). Theory and research on anxiety. In C. D. Spielberger (Ed.), *Anxiety and behavior* (pp. 3–20). New York: Academic Press.

Spielberger, C. D. (1972). *Anxiety: Current trends in theory and research* (Vol. 1), New York: Academic Press.

Starkes, J. L., & Allard, F. (1983). Perception in volleyball: The effects of competitive stress. *Journal of Sport Psychology, 5,* 439–445.

Suinn, R. M. (1972). Removing emotional obstacles to learning and performance by visuomotor behavioral rehearsal. *Behavioral Therapy, 3,* 308–310.

Svebak, S., & Stoyva, J. (1980). High arousal can be pleasant and exciting. The theory of psychological reversals. *Biofeedback and Self-Regulation, 5,* 439–444.

Taylor, J. (1987). Predicting athletic performance with self-confidence and somatic and cognitive anxiety as a function of motor and physiological requirements in six sports. *Journal of Personality, 55,* 139–153.

Taylor, J. A. (1953). A personality scale of manifest anxiety. *Journal of Abnormal and Social Psychology, 48,* 285–290.

Vallerand, R. J. (1987). Antecedents of self-related affects in sport: Preliminary evidence on the intuitive-reflective appraisal model. *Journal of Sport Psychology, 9,* 161–182.

Weinberg, R. S. (1977). Anxiety and motor behavior: A new direction. In D. M. Landers & R. W. Christina, *Psychology of motor behavior and sport—1976* (Vol. 2, pp. 132–139). Champaign, IL: Human Kinetics.

Weinberg, R. S. (1989). Anxiety, arousal, and motor performance: Theory, research, and applications. In D. Hackfort & C. D. Spielberger (Eds.), *Anxiety in sports: An international perspective* (pp. 95–115). New York: Hemisphere.

Weinberg, R. S., & Genuchi, M. (1980). Relationship between competitive trait anxiety, state anxiety, and golf performance: A field study. *Journal of Sport Psychology, 2,* 148–154.

Williams, J. M., & Kane, V. (1989). Response distortion on self-report questionnaire with female collegiate golfers. *The Sport Psychologist, 3,* 212–218.

Wine, J. (1971). Test anxiety and direction of attention. *Psychological Bulletin, 76,* 92–104.

Wine, J. (1980). Cognitive-attentional theory of test anxiety. In I. G. Sarason (Ed.), *Test anxiety: Theory, research and applications.* Hillsdale, NJ: Erlbaum.

Wolpe, J. (1969). *The practice of behavior therapy.* New York: Pergamon.

Zaichkowsky, L. D., & Fuchs, C. Z. (1989). Biofeedback-assisted self-regulation for stress management in sports. In D. Hackfort & C. D. Spielberger (Eds.), *Anxiety in sports: An international perspective* (pp. 235–245). New York: Hemisphere.

·24·

ATTENTION CONTROL TRAINING

Robert N. Nideffer

The book *A.C.T.: Attention Control Training* (Nideffer & Sharpe, 1978) introduced a psychological skills training program based on a set of theoretical constructs linking attentional processes, physiological arousal, and performance. That book, along with *The Inner Athlete* (Nideffer, 1976a), generated much interest on the part of sport psychologists. Over the past 15 years several investigators have developed their own versions of Attention Control Training (ACT) procedures and/or incorporated some form of concentration skills training within what they see as a broader psychological skills training program (Botterill, 1990; Dansereau, 1978; Gordon, 1990; Gould, Petlichkoff, Hodge, & Simons, 1990; Jacobs, 1988; Smith, 1980; Straub, 1989; Suinn, 1987; Unestahl, 1983; Weinberg, Seabourne, & Jackson, 1981; Wristberg & Anshel, 1989).

Although there has been considerable interest in helping athletes and coaches control attentional processes, there has been relatively little consistency with respect to the way the term *attention control training* has been used. In fact, one of the difficulties involved in reviewing the experimental literature on attention control training has to do with the fact that the actual training procedures vary dramatically from one investigation to another. For example, Vealey (1988), in an article reviewing the content of various psychological skills training programs, refers to attention control as a "technique" and to mental rehearsal as a "method," even though ACT programs often have a mental rehearsal component. Another difficulty is that there is a reciprocal relationship between arousal and focus of concentration. Thus, any performance enhancement program, whether it emphasizes controlling concentration or controlling arousal, should affect both.

Attention control training, or ACT, is more (or should be more) than a technique like "centering," breathing, cognitive restructuring, or attentional refocusing. ACT as originally conceived (see Nideffer, 1989a, for a review) is a complex process that involves (1) the assessment of an individual's attentional (concentration) strengths and weaknesses; (2) the assessment of the attentional demands of the particular performance situation; (3) the assessment of particular situational and/or interpersonal characteristics that are likely to affect arousal for an individual, interfering with concentration and negatively affecting performance; (4) the identification of situation-specific performance problems and the differentiation of task-relevant and task-irrelevant cues; and (5) the development of a situation-specific intervention program employing a variety of psychological techniques which may include thought stopping, centering, attentional refocusing (cognitive behavior modification and goal setting), and mental rehearsal or VMBR (visual-motor behavior rehearsal). Any evaluation of ACT should evaluate the theory that underlies the procedures, the validity and utility of the assessment process and/or the assessment tools which guide program development, and the effectiveness of the intervention strategies that are employed.

THE THEORY UNDERLYING ATTENTION CONTROL TRAINING

It is impossible to evaluate attention control training without first evaluating the theoretical constructs that form the foundation for the development of ACT programs (Nideffer, 1989a). Typically, the validity and/or reliability of a theory or a set of procedures is determined on the basis of some type of correlational analysis. When this is the case, a note of caution needs to be introduced regarding the size of correlations we would expect. If the hypothesis is accepted that human attentional characteristics have both state and trait characteristics, then the independent validity of either one of these two characteristics is limited by the other (Selder, Burnett, & Nideffer, 1989). Thus the more trans-situational or traitlike an attentional characteristic (e.g., the more predictive-useful), the less an intervention technique will affect it. By the same logic, the more situation-specific an attentional characteristic (e.g., the more trainable), the less scores on that characteristic can be used to predict behavior across situations.

It is readily apparent that for most people behavior is at least in part situationally determined. At the same time, a great deal of human behavior is predictable (we would not survive if we could not predict the behavior of others with some of accuracy). This means correlations between attentional styles and performance (for groups of individuals) should be moderate if they are reflecting the real world. If they are too low (e.g., not statistically significant) they fail to reflect the trans-situational or trait component of the ability being measured. If they are too high (e.g., accounting for too much of the variance), they are failing to reflect the situational variability (state component) component of behavior. Thus, one priority for researchers should involve identifying those conditions under which attentional behaviors for a group of individuals behave as traits (e.g., through the systematic manipulation of arousal and/or by including level of confidence within the performance setting as an experimental variable). For the practitioner, the priority consists of identifying those situational factors and/or mediating intra-and interpersonal characteristics that will increase the traitlike component of an individual's attentional strengths (Nideffer, 1990).

In the remainder of this chapter, (1) the theoretical assumptions about attentional process which provide the basis for ACT are introduced; (2) empirical and experiential data supporting the attentional constructs is presented; (3) the theoretical link between physiological arousal and the ability to control concentration and motor behavior is described; (4) empirical and experiential evidence for support of the link between arousal, concentration, and performance is delineated; and (5) the process of ACT is described and contrasted with other performance enhancement and/or stress management programs. (Whereas this chapter deals specifically with attentional control training, Abernethy's Chapter 6 in this book is much more comprehensive, covering attention, information processing, and motor performance.)

Attentional Constructs Associated with ACT

ACT is based on four hypotheses about attention as it relates to the process of concentration:

1. *At any point in time an individual's focus of attention will fall into one of four categories.* These categories are determined by the width (broad to narrow) and direction (external or internal) of the individual's focus. Figure 24-1 shows the four types of concentration and describes their use.

2. *Different performance situations require different attentional skills.*
   a. There are differences in the extent to which any of the four types of attention is required. For example,

sport situations involving open skills tend to place greater demands upon the individual to direct attention toward the environment (external), whereas business and education settings place greater demand on the individual to focus attention internally.

   b. There are differences in the frequency and speed with which the individual must be able to shift from one type of attention to another. In a sport like basketball, it seems that the player must shift rapidly from a narrow external focus to a broad external focus. In a sales situation (e.g., at a stock exchange or at an auction), an individual should be able to switch rapidly from a broad internal focus to a narrow external focus. In a sport like golf, shifts can occur much more slowly, as the individual is in control of the speed with which things happen.

3. *Attentional skills, like movement skills, vary from person to person.* Individuals can be described on the basis of their "relative" attentional strengths and/or weaknesses, or "preferred" attentional styles. Individuals like Chris Evert-Mills in tennis and Greg Louganis in diving seemed to have outstanding abilities to narrow and focus their concentration, both in an immediate situation (e.g., to avoid distraction), and over long periods of time (e.g., to maintain a commitment to a program). Athletes like Magic Johnson (basketball) and Wayne Gretzky (hockey) have an exceptional ability to attend to a wide range of external cues, seeing everything that is going on around them. Often, extremely creative individuals are dominated by a broad internal (analytical) focus of attention. The "absent-minded professor" appears to be so much in his/her head that he/she fails to attend to environmental cues.

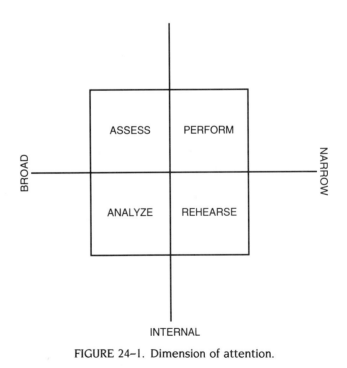

FIGURE 24–1. Dimension of attention.

4. *Attentional characteristics of "normal" individuals are at times traitlike, having some predictive utility across situations (e.g., under high levels of stress). At other times they are statelike, situationally determined, and/or modifiable through training.* As will be shown later, it is the individual's level of arousal that determines whether or not he or she is able and/or willing to shift attention in response to changing performance conditions. When a person's level of arousal is "moderate," he or she is able to shift attention in response to changing environmental demands, in spite of the fact that he or she may have a dominate or preferred attentional style. If arousal drops too low or if it becomes too high, attentional shifting will probably become more difficult and the individual's preferred attentional style will begin to dominate.

VALIDITY OF THE ATTENTIONAL CONSTRUCTS

From a face validity standpoint it is difficult to argue with these four assumptions about attentional characteristics as related to concentration. It is the face validity associated with ACT and the obvious implications that these theoretical (hypothetical) constructs have for real life situations which have excited researchers and practitioners in the field of sport psychology. These attentional constructs provide a bridge between observations made by researchers in the laboratory and performance problems encountered by coaches and managers in sports and business settings. As Meichenbaum (1977) has pointed out, from a practical standpoint the face validity of a theory is often of more importance from a practical and/or motivational standpoint than its statistical validity.

On the practical or applied side, each of us is aware of our attempts to control both the direction and width of our attention. The experience of dreaming provides evidence of the ability to focus attention almost exclusively internally. For example, the ability to mentally subtract 7 from 100 and to then subtract 7 again from 93 provides evidence of the ability to narrow and focus attention internally. Likewise, reacting quickly to changes in the environment in team sports or in discussion groups demonstrates the ability to broaden attention. The challenge is to measure dimensions of attention, and if we can, to train individuals to control these dimensions.

Width and Direction of Attentional Focus

There is a great deal of empirical research that demonstrates the conceptual and practical utility of describing attentional abilities on the basis of both width and direction of attentional focus. The importance of width has been emphasized by Cromwell (1968), Easterbrook (1959), Salmela and Ndoye (1986), and Wachtel (1967). The importance of the direction of attention has been highlighted in the work of Heilbrun (1972), Shakow (1962), and Wrisberg,

Franks, Birdwell, and High (1988). Many studies have been conducted on the orientation of the attentional beam in visual space (see Posner, 1980, for a review).

To a great degree, attempts to assess attentional skills in sport settings have been observational and/or inferred on the basis of performance. For example, an orienting response to a task-irrelevant stimulus in an actual competitive situation provides evidence of a momentary distraction. Likewise, error analyses which show a consistent pattern (e.g., increased percentage of missed volleys in tennis on game points) are often used to infer the presence of task-irrelevant internal and/or external distractors (Fairbank & Nideffer, 1987; Nideffer, 1988a). Experimentally, relative impairment in motor performance, as a function of the presence of auditory and/or visual distractors, has been used to infer attentional distractibility (Broadbent, 1979; Hillyard, Munte, & Neville, 1985; Schneider, Dumais, & Shfiffrin, 1984; Singer, Cauraugh, Murphey, Chen, & Lidor, 1991). Other scholars working in the sport area have studied the effects of auditory or visual distractors on information processing with athletes (Nougier et al., 1991; Starkes & Allard, 1983; Starkes & Deakin, 1984; Zani & Rossi, 1991).

Increasingly, practitioners in the field of sport psychology are attempting to determine the appropriateness of athletes' attentional processes through such techniques as interview and/or mental rehearsal, among others (Orlick & Partington, 1988). Typically, these procedures require subjects to reflect on past performances, identifying differences in their thought content and in their ability to identify and attend to task relevant cues.

The Test of Attentional and Interpersonal Style (TAIS) was developed in 1976 to provide a non-situation-specific, self-report measure of attentional strengths and weaknesses (Nideffer, 1976b). (Although other tests exist for measuring attentional characteristics of performers, the focus of this chapter will be the TAIS). The TAIS provides an indication of a respondent's ability to effectively control both the width (broad to narrow) and direction (external vs. internal) of his/her attention. In addition, the instrument has scales designed to measure external (OET) and internal (OIT) distractibility and the tendency to fail to shift attention from an internal to an external focus in response to changing environmental demands (RED). Several investigators have developed sport-specific measures of the six different TAIS attentional subscales (Albrecht & Feltz, 1987; Burnett, 1989; Vallerand, 1983; Van Schoyck & Grasha, 1981). (Editor's note: It should be pointed out that some scholars have questioned the psychometric properties of the TAIS, and therefore the value of the test; see Chapter 6.)

There are several studies that have demonstrated the validity and reliability of the attentional characteristics measured by the TAIS. Research on anxiety has shown that increasing arousal results in a narrowing of attention (Easterbrook, 1959; Salmela & Ndoye, 1986). From a construct validity standpoint, positive correlations are expected between the tendency to make mistakes because attention has narrowed too much, resulting in a failure to shift (RED), and measures of anxiety. In addition, positive correlations should occur between the tendency to become internally distracted (e.g., by worry and or somatic changes) as measured by the OIT scale on the TAIS and various measures of anxiety. Table 24–1 presents correlations between the TAIS and the measures of anxiety. As may be seen in Table 24-1, correlations support the ability of the TAIS to measure the attentional dimension of width (Nideffer, 1989b).

One of the best sources of evidence for the TAIS's ability to differentiate between a broad external focus of attention (BET) and a broad internal focus of attention (BIT) comes from analyses of differences in attentional abilities as a function of both age and sex (Nideffer & Bond, 1989). There is a large body of research showing that males score higher on measures of analytical thinking than females. Thus, males should have higher scores on the BIT scale on the TAIS than females. In addition, some of the developmental literature suggests that attentional skills and abilities change with age.

Thus, subjects' scores on the BET, BIT, and NAR (narrow focus) scales on the TAIS should increase with age (through adolescence), and individuals are expected to become less distractible as they mature and learn to attend more effectively (e.g., lower scores on OET, OIT, and RED). Table 24–2 represents mean scores on the TAIS, as a function of age, for male and female athletes at the Australian Institute for Sport. A total of 849 males and 516 females were included in the analysis. As may be seen, the data provides construct validity for the TAIS's ability to measure those attentional characteristics it was designed to measure. The underlying of scores in Table 24–2) shows the consistency in the data. Underlined scores indicate that the direction of difference (male relative to female) was consistent across all ages (Bond & Nideffer, 1989).

TABLE 24–1. Relationship Between the TAIS and Anxiety.

| | College | | Police | Intro S. | |
	State	Trait	TMAS	State	Trait
BET	.09	−.17	−.38	−.13	−.21
OET	.03	.48*	.41*	.33*	.31*
BIT	−.49*	−.60*	−.15	−.19	−.29*
OIT	.03	.43*	.58*	.32*	.39*
NAR	.20	−.40*	−.22	−.20	−.26*
RED	.38*	.53*	.35*	.55*	.54*
INFP	−.27	−.31	−.14	−.20	−.28*
BCON	.22	.63*	.41*	.23*	.26*
CON	−.09	−.07	−.01	−.19	−.21
SES	−.41*	−.57*	−.35*	−.46*	−.55*
P/O	−.08	.04	−.05	−.13	−.09
OBS	.22	.41*	.28*	.36*	.28*
EXT	−.30	−.21	−.16	−.31*	−.35*
INT	.29	.24	.38*	.26*	.37*
IEX	−.31	−.26	.07	−.20	−.21
NAE	.21	.37*	.28*	.19	.29*
PAE	−.32	−.30	−.31*	−.27*	−.36*

N = 28, 60, and 83 for college students, police applicants, and introductory psych students, respectively.

TABLE 24–2. Athlete TAIS Scores as a Function of Age and Sex.

| | 13–16 | | 17–18 | | 18–24 | | 25– | |
TAIS Scales	M	F	M	F	M	F	M	F
BET	14.4	14.3	14.9	14.5	14.7	14.4	15.2	14.8
OET	19.6	20.3	18.7	19.5	17.7	19.7*	16.5	17.0
BIT	18.4	18.1	18.8	17.7*	19.0	18.1*	20.3	18.8*
OIT	14.6	14.8	14.8	14.8	14.7	15.0	14.2	14.3
NAR	25.2	24.1	25.4	23.9*	25.7	24.1*	27.0	25.5*
RED	27.1	26.8	27.1	26.3	27.0	26.2	25.8	25.3
INFP	43.9	44.1	44.0	43.6	43.9	43.6	45.6	45.2
BCON	22.6	20.9*	22.0	20.6*	21.7	21.2	19.3	18.6
CON	47.2	45.4*	47.2	45.2*	47.7	45.5*	49.0	45.6
SES	21.6	21.7	21.9	21.2	21.5	19.9	24.9	21.4*
P/O	20.0	19.5	20.1	19.5	20.2	20.0	19.2	19.0
OBS	15.6	15.9	15.8	15.6	15.6	15.9	15.6	15.1
EXT	30.3	31.2	31.1	31.5	28.9	29.2	28.7	29.9
INT	21.1	19.6*	21.7	20.3*	22.2	21.3*	23.0	21.1*
IEX	16.6	16.6	16.5	16.0	16.0	15.1	16.9	16.0*
NAE	15.4	12.6*	14.3	11.9*	14.0	12.9	12.8	12.0
PAE	21.1	21.5	21.4	22.3*	20.4	20.5	20.3	21.5*

*p < .05 (for Tables 24–1 and 24–2)

Looking only at effective vs. ineffective deployment of attention, similar results regarding age and attentional processes have been described by Mahoney, Gabriel, and Perkins (1987). Using the Psychological Skills Inventory for Sport (PSIS), these scholars found that concentration skills increased with age and with level of performance (there was an age by level of performance confounded in the data, however). Additional support for the TAIS's ability to measure direction and width of an individual's attentional focus comes from studies examining subjects' scores as a function of type of sport and/or occupation (DePalma & Nideffer, 1977; Nideffer, 1990; Nideffer & Pratt, 1990).

Different Performance Situations Require Different Attentional Skills

It is intuitively obvious that different performance situations require different attentional skills. The idea that a narrow focus of attention is necessary in closed skill and/or self-paced sports like shooting, diving, and skating has influenced researchers for years (Nideffer, 1976a; Poulton, 1957; Schurr, Ashley, & Joy, 1977; Singer, 1980). Until recently, there has been very little empirical evidence supporting the differential attentional requirements of varying performance settings.

Several researchers have used the TAIS to discriminate between different groups of individuals (DePalma & Nideffer, 1977; Nideffer & Bond, 1989; Selder, Burnett, & Nideffer, 1988). The first study of this kind explored the relationship between the TAIS and psychiatric subclassification (DePalma & Nideffer, 1977). This study provided support for the conceptual independence and practical relevance of the TAIS, BIT, OET, OIT, and NAR scales. These scales were found to differentiate in predictable ways, between business executives, psychiatric patients, college students, and police. As we would expect, psychiatric patients were more overloaded by external and internal stimuli (OET, OIT) and less capable of narrowing their focus of attention (NAR) than college students, police, and business executives. Business executives were more capable of developing an analytical focus of attention (BIT) than the other groups. Looking at psychiatric patients alone, DePalma and Nideffer found that the TAIS discriminated between those patients diagnosed as either good or poor premorbid schizophrenic, neurotic, or character disordered. Differences found were consistent with differences expected on the basis of both psychiatric theory and the behavioral observations of psychiatric subtypes (MacKinnon & Michels, 1971).

As an assessment tool, the TAIS was designed to improve the ability of practitioners to understand, predict, and control behavior across the entire spectrum of human performance. Thus, although it was important to demonstrate that the instrument could discriminate between pathological groups at the lower end of the performance curve, it was just as important to show that the instrument could differentiate between highly effective performers. Evidence demonstrate the TAIS's ability to do this was collected at the Australian Institute for Sport (Nideffer, 1990; Nideffer & Bond, 1989).

Figure 24–2 shows the attentional characteristics of 225 individuals involved in closed skill sports such as diving, 325 individuals involved in open skill sports such as tennis and cycling, and 268 athletes involved in team sports. (Team sports contain open skills as well as closed skills, on occasion.) All athletes included in this analysis were competitive at a national and/or international level. Thus, they were highly effective performers. Research on the TAIS provides support for the belief that closed skill sports in contrast to open skill sports such as tennis and various team sports require a narrow, nondistractible focus of attention. Conversely, sports such as tennis which involve head-to-head competition and reacting to others require athletes to be able to attend to a wide variety of external cues (BET). Data presented in Figure 24–2 provide evidence for the TAIS's ability to differentiate between athletes on the basis of type of sport skill. The data indicate that different sports or performance situations require different attentional demands. The data also demonstrate that different individuals have different attentional strengths and weaknesses. Statistically the differences shown in Figure 24–2 were found to be highly significant (Nideffer & Bond, 1989).

Additional support for the notion that different sport skills require different attentional processes is provided by the research of Mahoney, Gabriel, and Perkins (1987). Their study indicated that athletes involved in closed skill sports reported more frequent concerns or problems related to their confidence, anxiety management, and concentration than did athletes in open skill sports.

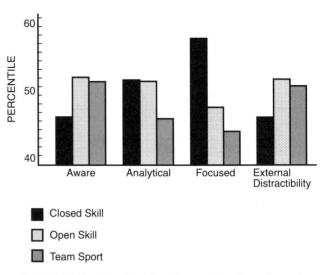

FIGURE 24–2. Attentional style as a function of sport.

Different Individuals Have Different Attentional Strengths and Weaknesses

TAIS data shown in Figure 24–2 provides evidence that different individuals have different attentional strengths and/or weaknesses, and that these differences have implications for performance. To the extent that reliable group differences can be measured like those shown, empirical support is provided for the hypothesis that attentional characteristics have traitlike characteristics. Independent of the absolute amount of variance accounted for, attentional characteristics have some stability across time and across situation. This is not to say, however, that attentional abilities are unaffected by situational factors. It does not mean that everyone has the same level of attentional stability or predictability. Nor does it imply that the traitlike aspects of attentional abilities will account for more of the variance in performance for a given individual or group than situational factors will. In fact, from a practical standpoint, it is important to consider both the state and trait characteristics of a given individual's attentional scores on the TAIS. One of the best ways to do this is by manipulating the subject's response set (Nideffer, 1987, Nideffer, 1989c, Nideffer, 1990).

Data presented in Figure 24–3 are derived from a case study (Nideffer, 1989c). The athlete tested was one of the top ten female tennis players in the world. She agreed to participate in a study examining the effects of menstruation on perception and performance and was asked to take the TAIS under two different instructional sets. For both administrations she was instructed to adopt a more tennis-specific set: "Where possible, please answer the items as you feel they relate to tennis." For the first administration she was to answer as she felt "most of the time." For the second administration she was to respond as she felt "during that phase of her menstrual cycle when she felt most affected by any hormonal changes."

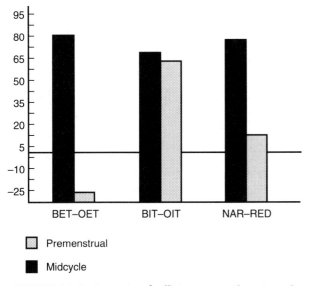

FIGURE 24–3. Attentional efficiency as a function of menstrual cycle in an elite female tennis player.

Figure 24–3 presents "efficiency percentiles." To obtain these, the subject's raw scores on the TAIS were converted to percentile scores. Next, her score on each of the attentionally ineffective scales was subtracted from its effective counterpart (BET-OET, BIT-OIT, NAR-RED). For the average person, we would expect all of the resulting efficiency scores to be plotted at the zero point, or 50th percentile (where the line is in Figure 24–3). If the score on BET is 50 and the score on OET is 50, the remainder after subtracting one from the other is zero.

The mid-cycle date in Figure 24–3 indicate the athlete has described herself as extremely effective (relative to the general population). Any efficiency score greater than zero indicates the person is "above average." A score around the 80th percentile means there was a large positive difference between her ability to attend to a wide range of external cues (as she would have to in doubles) and her tendency to become externally distracted. We would conclude that most of the time, this woman is an extremely effective performer (as her world ranking indicates).

Examine what happens to attention approximately two days prior to the onset of her menstrual cycle. One excellent indicator of the TAIS's ability to discriminate between an internal and external focus of attention comes from the contrast between this woman's efficiency scores in these two different areas as a function of her menstrual cycle. As the data indicate, hormonal changes appear to have little effect on her analytical (internal) efficiency. Changes in the ability to process internal information (BIT) and in the tendency to become internally overloaded (OIT) as a function of menstrual cycle are almost nonexistent. Changes in ability to effectively narrow her focus of concentration (NAR-RED) and in ability to avoid external distractions (BET-OET), however, are quite dramatic.

It is within-subject changes like those just presented that

provide the best evidence that an instrument (in this case the TAIS) differentiates approximately. Within-subject changes provide practitioners with the information needed to help individuals understand, predict, and control their own behavior. Within-subject changes demonstrate the state component of both attentional and interpersonal characteristics and at the same time provide evidence for the individual's ability to alter a performance-relevant behavior or skill.

Implications of Attentional State and Trait Components

The importance of considering the extent to which an individual's scores are reflecting traitlike characteristics as opposed to statelike characteristics should be obvious. The more statelike and/or responsive an individual's attentional skills to environmental demands, the more flexible he/she is, and the more likely he/she will benefit from any training program. On the negative side, the more statelike the athlete's attentional skills, the less useful attention will be for predicting performance.

If we think of human performance as a continuum, then people would be described at the extreme ends of the continuum as behaving in a more consistent, traitlike way. For example, better athletes in sports like tennis and diving appear to have a very narrow focus of attention (e.g., to be at the extreme end of that particular continuum). Their attentional style doesn't seem to be affected by the environment, and their performance across situations is very consistent. As long as the performance arena plays to their dominate attentional style, we would predict they will be successful. At the other end of the continuum, consider children diagnosed as hyperactive and/or as having a learning disability. Children with learning disabilities seem to be unable to narrow their focus of attention. As a result, they are highly distractible even in a relatively sterile environment. Their tendency to become overloaded and distracted is more traitlike than the average person's, because it is more trans-situational.

From a practitioner's perspective, the behaviors of hyperactive children at one extreme and highly successful athletes at the other lead to highly predictable behaviors. At the same time, it is difficult to change these extreme behaviors. Just ask the opponents of great competitors who have tried to "psych them out," and the teachers and parents of hyperactive children. Fortunately, the vast majority of the population's attentional and/or interpersonal skills tend to be more statelike. It is this observation that leads to another critical theoretical assumption that is associated with ACT.

Link Between Attention, Physiological Arousal, and Performance

In contrast to those individuals at the extreme ends of a performance continuum, most people have greater attentional flexibility (adaptability). They are able to make adjustments in their focus of attention in response to changing environmental demands. For this reason, the attentional characteristics of "average" individuals, when considered independently of variables such as task complexity and/or level of arousal, are less predictive of actual behavior than they would be for extreme groups. This conclusion has some implications for research on the relationship between attention and performance.

A few investigators have attempted to determine the predictive utility of the TAIS. One of the major flaws with their research is that they have examined the performance of relatively normal individuals and have not systematically manipulated the level of arousal in their subjects (Nideffer, 1990). Since 1976 it has been emphasized that measurement of attentional styles alone is not enough to predict performance for the average person (Nideffer, 1976a). To use a normal individual's dominant attentional style to predict performance something must be done to increase the trait behavior of that dominant style. The best way to do this is to increase level of arousal. The reason for this can be seen in the relationship between arousal and performance.

Yerkes and Dodson (1908) introduced the "inverted-U" hypothesis in an attempt to describe the relationship between physiological arousal and performance. They suggested that performance drops off on either side of some "optimal" level of arousal. This theory can be contrasted with Hull's drive theory (Hull, 1951). Hull hypothesized a linear relationship between arousal and performance, suggesting that as arousal increases, performance improves. Both theories have been the subject of a great deal of research, and both theories have had direct implications for coaches. Those coaches following Hull's arguments are the ones who insist on psyching up their athletes. Those coaches treating the relationship as an inverted U are more likely to attempt to reduce or raise the arousal level of their athletes, depending on circumstances. Advocates of each position can cite practical examples as well as research to support a particular position.

What appears to be an inconsistency in the laboratory and on the field can be explained if an athlete's attentional style is seen as a mediating variable. If arousal drops below a moderate level or rises above it, it is hypothesized that his or her preferred attentional style will begin to dominate. If that style is broad-internal, then when bored or underaroused in a performance situation, he/she will start to analyze and/or problem-solve. What he/she analyzes, however, may have nothing to do with performance. When this is the case, performance will be less than optimal as predicated by both theories.

As arousal increases within the performance situation to an "optimal" or "moderate" level, a sufficient level of interest is generated to encourage the athlete to attempt to match the attentional demands of the situation. The analytical athlete stops playing irrelevant mental games and simply starts responding to the task. Analytical athletes are those who have a tendency to spend a considerable amount of time thinking about and analyzing their sport and their performances. They want to learn more in order to improve.

They are "students" of the game. The less analytical athlete simply wants to go out and "do it." As the athlete matches the attentional demands of the situation, performance becomes more "optimal." At this point, both drive theory and the inverted-U hypothesis are still making similar predictions about performance.

As arousal increases beyond a "moderate" level, the athlete begins to lose his/her attentional flexibility. The analytical athlete starts to analyze independently of the performance demands. At this point, if the situation is one that plays to the athlete's dominant attentional style, he/she will continue to perform very well. On the other hand, if the situation requires some other attentional focus, performance will deteriorate rapidly. Thus data will sometimes appear to support drive theory, and sometimes will appear to support the inverted-U hypothesis.

The deterioration that we see in performance when arousal is too high is further complicated by a second mediating variable. That variable is the person's level of self-confidence within the performance setting. If the individual is confident and/or not too concerned about failure, he or she may be able to recognize a mistake (e.g., "I'm thinking too much") and redirect attention (at least for a short time) in a task-relevant way. If arousal continues to remain high, we would expect to see a great deal of variability in the athlete's performance over time as he or she continues to battle the tendency to be overly analytical.

If the athlete's level of self-esteem is low, and increasing arousal results in errors because of an inappropriate attentional focus, a different problem (and pattern of errors) develops. The athlete lacking in self-confidence will become hypersensitive to cues, which suggests the possibility of failure (Eysenck, 1989). Thus as he/she makes a mistake because of an inappropriate focus of attention (e.g., becoming too analytical), he/she is unable to redirect attention in a task-relevant way, even for a short time. Mistakes plus a lack of self-confidence lead to an internal preoccupation. The athlete's attention becomes focused on negative thoughts and feelings. Under these conditions we are likely to see the type of behavior that coaches refer to as "choking." It is here that the literature on self-efficacy becomes relevant.

Evidence Supporting the Relationship Between Attentional Processes, Arousal, and Performance

The best evidence for the hypothesized relationship between attentional characteristics arousal and performance comes from actual behavioral observations, interview data, and case histories. A more thorough description of this relationship is described by Nideffer (1988a). In addition to case history data, there is empirical evidence to support the hypothesized relationships between attention, arousal, and performance. One example is the positive correlations between the tendency to make errors of underinclusion (RED) because attentional shifting breaks down, and measures of anxiety as shown in Table 24–1, as well as the positive correlations between anxiety and internal distractibility (OIT), worry, and slow decision making (OBS).

Boney (1982) designed a study to see if TAIS subscales would predict the ability of male and female police trainees to read nonverbal information as measured by the PONS test. This study is important because it represents one of the few attempts to manipulate the stress level of subjects. In his study subjects were randomly placed into a stress or nonstress group. Stress level was manipulated by filming the performance of each member of the stressed group as they took the PONS test, and by telling them the film would be used to evaluate their performance. Table 24–3 presents the results of a regression analysis that was used to analyze each subject's factor scores on the TAIS to predict PONS performance.

There were sex differences in terms of the ability to decode nonverbal information (females were superior to males). These differences are consistent with the general literature. As can be seen in Table 24–3, the TAIS was not a good predictor for males under either the stressed or nonstressed condition. For females, however, results are consistent with predictions given the hypothesized attention, arousal, and performance link. Under stress, TAIS scales indicating performance anxiety (NAR, RED, OBS) and TAIS scales indicating distractibility and impulsivity (OET, OIT, BCON) became significant predictors of female performance. Women who tend to become overloaded and impulsive, and who have performance anxiety, performed more poorly than those who scored low in these areas.

Another source of evidence for the link between attention and arousal can be found in studies where the effects of some type of training program have been examined through pre-and posttesting. Test-retest data on changes in the scores of athletes at the Australian Institute for Sport (AIS) over a 1-year period indicate that positive attentional changes occur along with increases in self-confidence and control (Nideffer & Bond, 1988). At the AIS there was no set mental training program. Instead, training is highly individualized. Athletes are given sport psychology assessments each year, and training programs are developed based on the needs of the individual. Under these conditions, retests indicate that scores on the ineffective attentional scales (OET, OIT, RED) drop by about 8% and scores on the effective scales (BET, BIT, NAR) increase by approximately 8%.

It is not clear what may be accounting for the general improvement in attentional skills as a function of age or maturity, Ripoll (in press) provides perspectives and a study by Goulet, Bard, and Fleury (1989) offers at least one explanation. These investigators examined the effect of experience on the ability of tennis players to make predictions about the type of serve an opponent was hitting. As expected, highly skilled players were able to determine the type of serve (e.g., spin on the ball, position of serve) earlier than less skilled players. Recordings of eye movements indicated that the skilled players attended to different cues. Thus whether experienced athletes have a greater capacity to focus and/or shift attention or not, they are more capable of discriminating between task-relevant and task-irrelevant cues. They have learned what to attend to. A contemporary and comprehensive review on such topics is presented by Ripoll (in press).

Performance Relevant Interpersonal Processes

One of the greatest problems with research on the TAIS and with many ACT programs is that researchers have been so excited by the relevance of attentional processes to performance that they have ignored the fact that certain interpersonal characteristics are important as well. Researchers have designed sport-specific versions of the attentional scales on the TAIS and ignored the interpersonal scales. Unfortunately, unless the attentional scales are examined within a behavioral (situational) context, they are relatively useless. This is due to the mediating effect that arousal and self-confidence can have on attention.

To make predictions about attentional errors and performance problems, it is necessary to look at attentional skills within the context of a person's level of arousal. Interpersonal characteristics like (1) need for control, (2) speed of decision making, (3) self-esteem, (4) willingness to express positive feelings, (5) negative feelings, and (6) thoughts and ideas provide valuable information about the likelihood of arousal increasing within a given performance setting. In addition, these same characteristics are useful for predicting the behavioral response an athlete is likely to engage in as pressure increases (Nideffer, 1989a).

Figures 24–4 and 24–5 show the predictive link between both attentional and interpersonal processes and performance. Figure 24–3 is a plot of the TAIS scales that differentiated between psychiatric subclassifications in the study of Depalma and Nideffer (1977). Figure 24–5 is a plot of the TAIS scales that differentiated between individuals involved in closed skill, open skill, and team sports at the AIS (Bond & Nideffer, 1989). Figures 24–4 and 24–5 indicate

TABLE 24–3. TAIS Factor Scores as Predictors of PONS Scores.

Males—stressed			
TAIS factors			
Extroversion	.259	4.47*	.259
Males—nonstressed			
TAIS factors			
Attentionally effective	.312	6.27*	.312
Females—stressed			
TAIS factors			
Performance anxiety	−.913	66.50†	.623
Overloaded	−.479	18.74†	.813
Impulsive	−.438	16.16†	.912
Females—nonstressed			
TAIS factors			
Impulsive	−.482	8.34*	.481

*$p < .05$ †$p < .01$

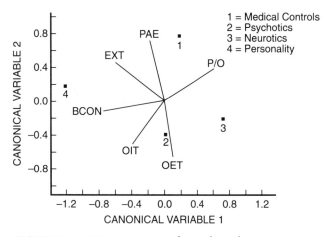

FIGURE 24-4. Discriminant analysis of psychiatric patients.

those TAIS scales that act to significantly differentiate between the various groups. Group "centroids" are plotted against the two predictive equations or functions generated by the analysis. The closer a particular attentional or interpersonal characteristic lies relative to a group centroid, the more descriptive it is of that group. Conversely the farther away the characteristic lies, the less descriptive it is.

An examination of Figure 24-4 shows that hospital controls compared to psychiatric groups tend to be more extroverted (EXT), more expressive of positive affect (PAE), and more physically oriented (P/O). Psychotic patients tend to be distracted by both external (OET) and internal stimuli (OIT), whereas neurotics are more sensitive to external distractions (OET). As we might expect, personality disorders are characterized by their extraversion (EXT) and their behavioral impulsivity (BCON). Given current knowledge, those scales on the TAIS differentiating between psychiatric groups do so in a consistent way. Personality disordered patients are seen as extroverted and impulsive. Their actual behavior provides consensual validation for scores on the TAIS. Likewise, psychotic patients are classified on the basis of hallucinations and/or delusions. These internal distractions make it impossible for them to respond appropriately to the environment (American Psychiatric Association, 1980).

Figure 24-5 provides equally strong support for the construct validity of the TAIS. Closed skill sports like shooting, gymnastics, and diving are sports in which the individual is competing against him-or herself. The athlete is in control of the performance situation. In contrast, individuals involved in open skill sports like tennis, boxing, and fencing are often at the mercy of either their opponents or the environment, having to react quickly to changing conditions or to the unanticipated. Team sports contain open skills that require participants to react quickly to changing conditions. Unlike individual sports, team sports require athletes to work together. Scales on the TAIS discriminating between open skill, closed skill, and team sports are extremely consistent with the different task demands just described.

Figure 24-5 shows that athletes in closed skill sports have a narrower focus of attention (NAR), are less interpersonally competitive (P/O), and are less extroverted (EXT) than athletes in other sports. It should be pointed out that most of the items on the current TAIS P/O scale (it is currently being revised) reflect physical orientation and/or competitiveness. The scale also correlates with the control scale on the TAIS. Individuals who score high in that scale seem to be interpersonally competitive, too. With women over 40 the scale is less predictable of interpersonal competitiveness because women over 40 do not typically have much of an opportunity to compete athletically. Thus their P/O scales are low due to the heavy loading on items related to physical activity.

Individuals in team sports are the most extroverted. External awareness (BET) is closely associated with open skill and team sports. The need to be in control (CON) and self-confidence (SES) as well as physical competitiveness are highest for athletes competing in open skill sports. The fact that these data come from national level and international level athletes is important. Because the data are correlational, a cause-effect relationship cannot be inferred. Nevertheless, we can conclude that success at a high level in each of these sport areas is positively associated with those attentional and interpersonal characteristics that theory, experience, and intuition tell us should make a difference.

Summary

There is considerable evidence supporting the theoretical and practical utility of the attentional constructs that provide the basis for attention control training: (1) attentional processes can be described on the basis of the width and direction of focus, among other factors; (2) different performance situations require different focuses of

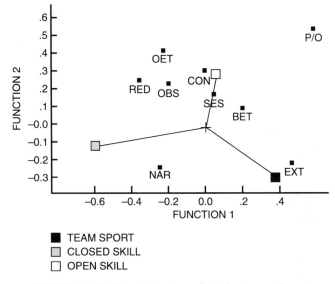

FIGURE 24-5. Discriminant analysis by type of sport (TAIS data).

attention; (3) different individuals have different attentional strengths; (4) attentional abilities have both state and trait characteristics; (5) the TAIS appears to be a valid and reliable measure of task-relevant attentional and interpersonal characteristics; and (6) increases in arousal make dominant attentional characteristics more traitlike. Empirical evidence demonstrating that decreases in arousal will result in preferred attentional styles becoming more dominant remains to be discovered.

In the future, the development of attentional control training programs and research on ACT should be guided by the theoretical assumptions about the relationship between attention, arousal, and performance that have been presented. The attentional demand of tasks must be identified and so must the individual's (or group's) dominant attentional style. Intervention programs seek to find ways to help the individual to retain the attentional flexibility necessary to match task demands. This may require learning arousal control techniques, attentional refocusing, and the identification of task-relevant and irrelevant cues, mental rehearsal techniques, and/or the use of cognitive behavior modification techniques to alter negative self-statements. From a research respective, studies attempting to use attentional variables to predict performance must be designed (e.g., through the manipulation of arousal levels and/or self-control) to force either a match or a mismatch between the attentional demands of the performance setting and the individual's (or group's) attentional style.

ATTENTION CONTROL TRAINING TECHNIQUES AND PROCEDURES

It was mentioned at the beginning of the chapter that ACT is a process, not just a technique. Even so, there is room for a great deal of latitude in the development of ACT programs. For example, there are situations where the assumption can be made that performance enhancement can occur by educating athletes (e.g., making them aware of the discriminate cues). Often, this approach is used to help athletes develop new skills and/or master new tasks. Under these conditions, training is highly situation-specific and may or may not include teaching individuals arousal control techniques. Research in both sport and education has shown that individuals can acquire task-specific attentional skills rapidly (Dansereau, 1985; Derry & Murphy, 1986; Mahoney 1979; Grabe, 1986).

If an assumption is being made or if an assessment is taken of the attentional abilities of the individual and the demands of the performance situation indicating that the effective use of attention is being interfered with, then ACT programs become more complicated. These are situations where the subject has demonstrated the ability to attend and perform effectively, he knows what he should be attending to, and yet he is unable to. For example, if low-esteem and negative self-talk seem to be distracting the individual, some type of cognitive behavior modification is

required before effective concentration can be demonstrated. If the individual's level of arousal is inappropriate, some type of arousal control training is necessary. In these situations, the effectiveness of ACT programs are directly tied to the effectiveness of the various techniques the training programs employ.

In addition to ACT as described by Nideffer and Sharpe (1978), a number of fairly complex performance enhancement and/or stress management programs have been developed that involve forms of attention control training. In contrast to the more situation-specific training associated with ACT, these programs tend to emphasize the development of generalizable skills, or metastrategies. Some of the more familiar programs would include anxiety management training (Suinn & Richardson, 1971), self-instructional training (Meichenbaum, 1974), stress inoculation training (Meichenbaum, 1977), stress management training (Smith, 1980), inner mental training (Unesthal, 1983), and Singer's five-step strategy (Singer, 1988).

All of these stress management, performance enhancement programs have been influenced in one way or another by the ideas and work of the behavioral, cognitive, and social learning theorists such as Beck and Clark (1989), Bandura (1977), Ellis (1962, 1969), and Lazarus (1976). In addition to some shared theoretical influences, these programs tend to have a great deal of overlap in terms of the techniques described. Virtually all of the programs involve some form of relaxation and/or arousal control technique, and they all make use of imagery techniques such as VMBR (Suinn, 1987).

Not only do the programs share theory and technique, but as both Meichenbaum (1977) and Mahoney and Arnkoff (1978) have pointed out, there are also procedural similarities. All of the programs seem to emphasize the following: (1) some form of assessment of the individual and/or the problem; (2) education of the person; (3) training; and (4) practice or rehearsal.

Although there have been relatively few studies designed to examine the effectiveness of the various training programs, those that have been conducted have been generally supportive (Gould, Petlichkoff, Hodge, & Simons, 1990; Gould, Tammen, Murphy, & May, 1989; Greenspan, & Feltz, 1989; Hall & Erffmeyer, 1983; Kendall, Hrycaiko, Martin, & Kendall, 1990; Meyers & Schleser, 1980; Newsham, 1981; Rushall, Hall, Roux, Sasseville, & Rushall, 1989; Singer, Cauraugh, Murphey, Chen, & Lidor, 1991; Singer, DeFrancesco, & Randall, 1989; Straub, 1989; Suinn, 1987; Ziegler, Klinzing, & Williamson, 1982). Research designed to examine the relative effectiveness of different training packages is needed. One reason for this may be the difficulty entailed in attempting to design a research paradigm that responds to the differences that do exist between programs. For example, ACT programs, as defined here, tend to be highly individualized and situation-specific. Inner mental training, on the other hand, is much more general in its approach (Unestahl, 1983).

While well-designed studies of various training programs are lacking, evidence supporting the efficacy of the psychological tools used in these programs is mounting. Relaxation procedures, like progressive relaxation (Jacobson, 1931), centering (Nideffer & Sharpe, 1978), and meditation (Benson, 1985), have been demonstrated to lower heart rate (Deane, 1964), and respiration rate, and to reduce muscle tension (Cox, 1986; Zaichkowsky & Fuchs, 1989).

Mahoney and Arnkoff (1978) concluded that there was a sizable body of literature which demonstrated that the nature of one's "self-talk" could dramatically influence performance. Indeed, considerable research has shown that self-talk can be changed and that those changes can lead to feeling of greater self-efficacy and improved performance (Feltz & Riessinger, 1990; Gould & Weiss, 1981; Wilkes & Summers, 1984). It must be emphasized that such self-talk ultimately results in a redirection of attention to task relevant cues.

Imagery techniques have also been shown to facilitate performance, especially when they have been combined with some form of relaxation, whether this has been an extended relaxation procedure, like progressive relaxation, or a very brief procedure, like centering and/or Benson's relaxation response (Feltz & Landers, 1983; Weinberg, Seabourne & Jackson, 1981; Wrisberg & Anshel, 1989).

There is little doubt that psychological training programs and/or the implementation of psychological techniques can have a beneficial effect on performance when groups of subjects are analyzed. An important question that is beginning to be answered has to do with what can be done to make these procedures even more effective, and/or to better match techniques to the problems of individual athletes. One of the ways to begin to see what can be done to improve training is to examine each of the training program phases within the context of the research literature.

The goal behind assessment is basically twofold. First, it is to identify a problem area and/or treatment focus. Second, it is to gather information that can be used in the education of the client. As Meichenbaum (1977) pointed out, a key to motivation and cooperation in any training involves the presentation of a face valid program to the individual. Without awareness of the program's relevance, and without confidence in the program, positive change cannot take place. That assessment can be useful and is supported by Garfield (1978), who, in an examination of the relationship between client variables and outcome in therapy, found that individuals who were asked to complete psychological tests prior to treatment had a greater tendency to continue in treatment and not drop out.

The importance of a specific treatment focus, education of the subject, and the provision of structure has been shown in a number of research studies. Research by Clark (1960) and by Ryan and Simons (1981, 1983) highlight the fact that mental practice of physical performance is most useful when there is a large cognitive component to the task and subjects are highly skilled. Surveys of the use of imagery indicate that the vast majority of athletes engage in some form of mental rehearsal (Hall, Rodgers, & Barr, 1990; Heishman & Bunker, 1989; Orlick & Partington, 1988;

Ungerleider, Golding, Porter, & Foster, 1989). When imagery is found to be useful, it is usually positive in content and/or leads to a positive coping response (Powell, 1973), and results in a narrowing of attention and a task-relevant focus (Wilkes & Summers, 1984). Unfortunately, it is most likely that relatively few subjects rehearse in any systematic way. Too often, subjects rehearse the wrong things. Woolfolk, Murphy, Gottesfeld, and Aitken (1985) have demonstrated the performance-impairing effects of negative imagery.

Some research seems to be suggesting there are certain subject and/or sport variables that play a role in the type of imagery subjects engage in and/or are responsive to. Hall, Rodgers, and Barr (1990) found that kinesthetic imagery and rehearsal of motor behavior tend to occur more frequently in closed skill sports like skating and diving than in team sports like soccer, football, and squash. A similar finding was reported by Hale (1982). Competitive athletes tend to rehearse winning more than recreational athletes. Preference for simple versus complex tasks has also been found to be associated with performance. Individuals with a stated preference for a simple task tend to perform better in that task than they do in a complex one. In contrast, individuals with a preference for a complex task do not perform better on the complex task than on the simple task (Rejeski & Kenney, 1987). It may be that those individuals with a preference for a simple task are more limited in terms of information-processing capacity.

Finally, recent research on the effects of modeling on performance reinforces earlier findings that model similarity is an important variable (Gould & Weiss, 1981). Psychological techniques involving models, videotaped training, and mental rehearsal are more likely to be effective if the model or the material rehearsed is consistent with the individual's skill level.

CONCLUSIONS

In general, research provides considerable positive support for the use and efficacy of psychological procedures such as progressive relaxation, meditation, centering, self-talk, positive imagery, and visuomotor behavior rehearsal. These procedures have been found useful in helping individuals gain greater control over arousal and in improving performance. Those few studies that have been conducted on more complex training programs, such as ACT, Inner Mental Training, Anxiety Management Training, and Stress Management Training have yielded positive results. Until the present, there have been few studies designed to compare various training programs. Those that have been conducted have failed to report any significant differences.

The failure to find differences should not be surprising for a few reasons. First, given the hypothesized relationship between arousal, attention, and performance, we would expect performance enhancement programs that make adjustments in arousal to affect attention and vice versa. Second, experimental studies have included between-group comparisons on the basis of various training programs. All subjects have been given the same task (e.g., shooting basketballs or throwing darts), and no attempts were made to identify individual differences (e.g., the need to reduce internal distractibility as opposed to external distractibility, or differences in level of self-confidence or level of anxiety) which should affect decisions about the type of procedure that would be most effective and the way the procedure should be introduced. There is typically so much uncontrolled variability (though it is quite controllable if one will complicate the design somewhat and increase the number of subjects) that it is a wonder that anything is significant. The fact that significance is obtained under these conditions suggests that there must be a very strong treatment effect. To see just how strong it is, however, we will have to begin to control factors such as level of arousal, self-confidence, and attentional style.

Where positive effects have been found, variables that seem to be contributing to the general effectiveness of interventions include: (1) assessment, which plays an important role in providing information useful for (a) education of the athlete, (b) provision of structure and a training focus, and (c) increasing adherence to the training program; (2) the mental and physiological rehearsal of positive coping responses; (3) the use of positive self-talk, both to structure the focus of concentration onto task-relevant cues, and to increase the individual's belief in his or her self-efficacy; (4) the use of internal as opposed to external imagery when attempting to affect motor behavior; (5) the rehearsal of tasks that have a large cognitive component (e.g., where decision-making skills are required and/or selective attention is critical); and (6) the use of some form of relaxation to control arousal, reduce distractions, and facilitate imagery. These relaxation techniques may be very brief (e.g., lasting less than 1 minute) or quite long (e.g., lasting 15–20 minutes).

Future Research

Future research attempting to examine the relative effectiveness of mental skills training programs designed to improve attention skills and arousal control should take into consideration any underlying theoretical differences between the programs studied. For example, many of the training programs (at least implicitly) treat the constructs of anxiety, self-concept, and arousal as traits. Not only are these three characteristics treated as traits, but they are often combined as if they are a part of a more global construct. Thus individuals participating in the program are assumed to be anxious, to have low levels of self-esteem, and to have excessively high levels of arousal independent of the performance setting.

A lack of specificity in defining problems leads quite naturally to a lack of specificity of training. Participants are treated as if the only problems they have occur because arousal is too high and/or because of negative, self-destructive thinking. As a result, they are taught general relaxation procedures (e.g., progressive relaxation, meditation), and told that negative thinking (e.g., self-depreciating comments) is universally bad. They are instructed to program themselves with positive self-statements. Somehow, learning to relax and/or to express more positive thoughts independent of the situation is expected to improve performance. All these assumptions lead to the development of research programs which attempt to look at between-group differences.

The theoretical constructs associated with ACT programs emphasize the need for much greater situational specificity and individualization of training programs. Both arousal and self-esteem are seen as mediating variables, affecting the effective deployment of attention within a particular situational context, as well as affecting levels of muscle tension, and distribution of body weight about the athlete's center of mass (Nideffer, 1989d). The evaluation of ACT programs can best be accomplished through the use of single subject studies and/or by increasing sample sizes to the point that individual differences can be accounted for within the experimental design.

Researchers attempting to examine performance impairment as a function of attentional distractibility need to be aware that performance impairment may be triggered by an external distraction (e.g., task irrelevant auditory and/or visual stimulus), but that the time it takes to recover is typically a function of internal distractibility. An examination of performance errors not only requires the recording of the frequency of errors, but the duration of errors as well. In addition, a structure interview could help subjects to identify the presence of internal distractions.

From a practical standpoint, it is important to reduce both frequency and duration of errors. However, emphasis within a training program should depend upon a given individual's performance and the demand of the competitive situation. For example, the frequency of an error becomes a much more critical variable in performance settings such as sprinting, skating, gymnastics, and diving, where one mistake is the difference between winning and losing. In contrast, in sports such as tennis, where the number of unforced errors can be quite high for both contestants, recovery from mistakes (which will also reduce the frequency) becomes more critical.

Future research should accommodate these concerns. As methodology is improved, much more will be known about the potential value of ACT programs and other programs designed to improve attentional functions in various sport settings. Since performance potential is so strongly related to an athlete's ability to direct attentional processes effectively, the value of such research is obvious.

References

Albrecht, R. R., & Feltz, D. (1987). Generality and specificity of attention related to competitive anxiety and sport performance. *Journal of Sport Psychology, 8,* 231–248.

American Psychiatric Association (1980). *Diagnostic and statistical manual of mental disorders:* DSM-III. Washington, DC: American Psychiatric Association.

Bandura, A. (1977). Self-efficacy: Toward a unifying theory of behavior change. *Psychological Review, 84,* 191–215.

Beck, A. T., & Clark, D. A. (1989). Anxiety and depression: An information processing perspective. *Anxiety Research, 1,* 23–36.

Benson, H. (1985). The relaxation response. In A. Monat & R. S. Lazarus (Eds.), *Stress and coping: An anthology* (2nd ed., pp. 315–321). New York: Columbia University Press.

Botterill, C. (1990). Sport psychology and professional hockey. *The Sport Psychologist, 4,* 358–368.

Bond, J., & Nideffer, R. M. (1989). Attentional and interpersonal characteristics of Australian athletes. In R. M. Nideffer (Ed.), *Psychological assessment in sport* (pp. 49–65), San Diego: Enhanced Performance Systems.

Boney, R. (1982). *The role of attentional processes, subject's sex, and stress in the decoding of nonverbal information.* Unpublished doctoral dissertation, California School of Professional Psychology, San Diego.

Burnett, K. (1989). *Attention, arousal, and performance: A test of the predictive utility of Nideffer's theory.* Unpublished master's thesis, San Diego State University.

Carver, C. S., & Scheier, M. F. (1989). A control-process perspective on anxiety. *Anxiety Research, 1,* 17–22.

Clark, I. V. (1960). Effects of mental practice on the development of a certain motor skill. *The Research Quarterly, 31,* 560–569.

Cox. R. H. (1986). *Sport psychology concepts and applications.* Dubuque, IA: Brown.

Cromwell, R. L. (1964). Stimulus redundancy and schizophrenia. *Journal of Nervous and Mental Disease, 146,* 360–375.

Dansereau, D. (1978). The development of a learning strategies curriculum. In H. F. O'Neil (Ed.), *Learning strategies* (pp. 1–30). New York: Academic Press.

Dansereau, D. (1985). Learning strategy research. In J. Segal & R. Glaser (Eds.), *Thinking and learning skills: Relating instruction to basic research* (Vol. 1, pp. 209–240). Hillsdale, NJ: Erlbaum.

Deane, G. (1964). Human heart rate responses during experimentally induced anxiety. A follow-up with controlled respiration. *Journal of Experimental Psychology, 67,* 193–195.

DePalma, D. M., & Nideffer, R. M. (1977). Relationships between the Test of Attentional and Interpersonal Style and psychiatric subclassification. *Journal of Personality Assessment, 41,* 622–631.

Derry, S. J., & Murphy, D. A. (1986). Designing systems that train learning ability: From theory to practice. *Review of Education Research, 56,* 1–39.

Easterbrook, J. A. (1959). The effect of emotion on cue utilization and the organization of behavior. *Psychological Review, 66,* 183–201.

Ellis, A. (1962). *Reason and emotion in psychotherapy.* New York: Lyle Stuart.

Ellis, A. (1969). A cognitive approach to behavior therapy. *International Journal of Psychotherapy, 8,* 896–900.

Eysenck, M. W. (1989). Anxiety and attention. *Anxiety Research, 1,* 9–16.

Fairbank, R. D., & Nideffer, R. M. (1987, April). "Yours! Or how a mental error cost me $100,000.00 and a new car." *Tennis Magazine, 22*(12), 104–106.

Feltz, D. L., & Landers, D. M. (1983). The effects of mental practice on motor skill learning and performance: A meta-analysis. *Journal of Sport Psychology, 5,* 25–57.

Feltz, D. L., & Riessinger, C. A. (1990). Effects of in vivo emotive imagery and performance feedback on self-efficacy and muscular endurance. *Journal of Sport Psychology, 12,* 132–143.

Garfield, S. L. (1978). Research on client variables in psychotherapy. In S. L. Garfield & A. Bergin (Eds.), *Handbook of psychotherapy and behavior change* (pp. 191–232). New York: John Wiley.

Gordon, S. (1990). A mental skills training program for the Western Australian state cricket team. *The Sport Psychologist, 4,* 386–399.

Gould, D., Petlichkoff, L., Hodge, K., & Simons, J. (1990). Evaluating the effectiveness of a psychological skills educational workshop. *The Sport Psychologist, 4,* 249–260.

Gould, D., Tammen, V., Murphy, S., & May, J. (1989). An examination of U.S. Olympic sport psychology consultants and the services they provide. *The Sport Psychologist, 3,* 300–312.

Gould, D., & Weiss, M. (1981). The effects of model similarity and model talk on self-efficacy and muscular endurance. *Journal of Sport Psychology, 3,* 17–29.

Goulet, C., Bard, C., & Fleury, M. (1989). Expertise differences in preparing to return a tennis serve: A visual information processing approach. *Journal of Sport and Exercise Psychology, 11,* 382–398.

Grabe, M. (1986). Attentional processes in education. In G. D. Phye & T. Andre (Eds.), *Cognitive classroom learning* (pp. 49–82). New York: Academic Press.

Greenspan, M. J., & Feltz, D. L. (1989). Psychological interventions with athletes in competitive situations: A Review. *The Sport Psychologist, 3,* 219–236.

Hale, B. D. (1982). The effects of internal and external imagery on muscular and ocular concomitants. *Journal of Sport Psychology, 4,* 379–387.

Hale, B. D. (1986). Internal and external imagery concomitants Revisited: A comment on Harris and Robinson. *Journal of Sport Psychology, 8,* 347–348.

Hall, C. R., Rodgers, W. M., & Barr, K. A. (1990). The use of imagery by athletes in selected sports. *The Sport Psychologist, 4,* 1–10.

Hall, E. G., & Erffmeyer, E. S. (1983). The effects of visuo-motor behavior rehearsal with videotaped modeling on free throw accuracy of intercollegiate female basketball players. *Journal of Sport Psychology, 5,* 343–346.

Heilbrun, A. B. (1972). Style of adaptation to perceived aversive maternal control and internal scanning behavior. *Journal of Consulting and Clinical Psychology, 29,* 15–21.

Heischman, M. F., & Bunker, L. (1989). Use of mental preparation strategies by international elite female lacrosse players from five countries. *The Sport Psychologist, 3,* 14–22.

Hillyard, S. A., Munte, T. F., & Neville, H. J. (1985). Visual-spatial attention, orienting, and brain physiology. In M. Posner & O. S. M. Marin (Eds.), *Attention and performance XI* (pp. 63–84). Hillsdale, NJ: Erlbaum.

Hull, C. L. (1951). *Essentials of behavior.* New Haven, CT: Yale University Press.

Jacobs, A. (1988). *Sport psychology: The winning edge in sport.* (Videotape). Kansas City, MO: The Winning Edge.

Jacobson, E. (1931). Electrical measurements of neuromuscular states during mental activities. *American Journal of Physiology, 96,* 115–121.

Kendall, G., Hrycaiko, D., Martin, G. L., & Kendall, T. (1990). The effects of an imagery rehearsal, relaxation and self-talk package on basketball game performance. *Journal of Sport Psychology, 12,* 157–166.

Lazarus, A. A. (1976). Multi-modal behavior therapy. New York: Springer.

MacKinnon, R. A., & Michels, R. (1971). *The psychiatric interview in clinical practice.* Philadelphia: Saunders.

Mahoney, M. J. (1979). Cognitive skills and athletic performance. In P. C. Kendall & S. D. Hollon (Eds.), Cognitive-behavioral interventions (pp. 423–444). New York: Academic Press.

Mahoney, M. J., & Arnkoff, D. B. (1978). Cognitive and self-control therapies. In S. L. Garfield & A. E. Burgin (Eds.), *Handbook of psychotherapy and behavior change* (pp. 689–722). New York: Wiley.

Mahoney, M. J., Gabriel, T. J., & Perkins, T. S. (1987). Psychological skills and exceptional athletic performance. *The Sport Psychologist, 1,* 181–199.

Meichenbaum, D. (1974). *Cognitive behavior modification.* Morristown, NJ: General Learning Press.

Meichenbaum, D. (1977). *Cognitive behavior modification.* New York: Plenum.

Meyers, A. W., & Schleser, R. (1980). A cognitive behavioral intervention for improving basketball performance. *Journal of Sport Psychology, 2,* 69–73.

Newsham, S. (1981). *Attention Control—An alternative to maximizing performance in running.* Unpublished master's thesis, San Diego State University.

Nideffer, R. M. (1976a). *The inner athlete.* New York: Thomas Crowell.

Nideffer, R. M. (1976b). Test of attentional and interpersonal style. *Journal of Personality and Social Psychology, 34,* 394–404.

Nideffer, R. M. (1986). Concentration and attention control training. In J. Williams (Ed.), *Applied sport psychology,* (pp. 257–269), Palo Alto, CA: Mayfield.

Nideffer, R. M. (1987). Issues in the use of psychological tests in applied settings. *The Sport Psychologist, 1,* 18–28.

Nideffer, R. M. (1988a). Factors contributing to success as an educational sport psychology consultant. In Australian Coaching Council (Eds.), *Overtraining and Recovery, 3* (pp. 19–34). Canberra, Australia: Australian Coaching Council.

Nideffer, R. M. (1989a). Theoretical and practical relationships between attention, anxiety, and performance in sport. In D. Hackfort & C. D. Spielberger (Eds.), *Anxiety in sport: An international perspective* (pp. 117–136). New York: Hemisphere.

Nideffer, R. M. (1989b). *Predicting human behavior: A theory and test of attentional and interpersonal style.* Oakland, CA: Enhanced Performance Services.

Nideffer, R. M. (1989c). The effects of menstrual cycle on athlete performance: A case history. *Sports Medicine Update, 4,* 14–16.

Nideffer, R. M. (1989d). *Attention control training for athletes.* Oakland, CA: Enhanced Performance Services.

Nideffer, R. M. (1990). Use of the Test of Attentional and Interpersonal Style in sport. *The Sport Psychologist, 4,* 285–300.

Nideffer, R. M., & Sharpe, R. (1978). *A.C.T.: Attention control training.* New York: Wyden Books.

Nideffer, R. M., & Bond, J. (1989). Test of attentional and interpersonal style—cultural and sexual differences. *Proceedings of the XXI Banff International Conference on Psychology, Sport and Health Promotion,* Banff, Canada.

Nideffer, R. M., & Pratt, R. W. (1990). *Attention control training for business.* Oakland, CA: Enhanced Performance Services.

Nougier, V., Stein, J. F., & Bonnel, A. M. (in press). Information processing in sport and "orienting of attention." Special issue, H. Ripoll (Ed.), Information processing and decision-making in sport, *International Journal of Sport Psychology.*

Orlick, T., & Partington, J. (1988). Mental links to excellence. *The Sport Psychologist, 2,* 105–130.

Posner, M. I. (1990). Orientating of attention. *Quarterly Journal of Experimental Psychology, 32,* 3–25.

Powell, G. E. (1973). Negative and positive mental imagery in motor skill acquisition. *Perceptual and Motor Skills, 37,* 312.

Poulton, E. C., (1957). On prediction in skilled movements. *Psychological Bulletin, 54,* 467–478.

Rejeski, W. J., & Kenney, E. (1987). Distracting attentional focus from fatigue: Does task complexity make a difference? *Journal of Sport Psychology, 9,* 66–73.

Ripoll, H. (in press). The understanding-acting process in sport. The relationship between the semantic and the sensorimotor visual function. Special issue, H. Ripoll (Ed.), Information processing and decision-making in sport, *International Journal of Sport Psychology.*

Rushall, B. S., Hall, M., Roux, L., Sasseville, J., & Rushall, A. C. (1989). Effects of three types of thought content instructions on skiing performance. *The Sport Psychologist, 2,* 283–297.

Ryan, E. D., & Simons, J. (1981). Imagery and frequency of mental rehearsal as factors influencing acquisition of motor skills. *Journal of Sport Psychology, 3,* 35–45.

Salmela, J. H., & Ndoye, O. D. (1986). Cognitive distortions during progressive exercise. *Perceptual and Motor Skills, 63,* 1067–1072.

Selder, D. J., Burnett, K., & Nideffer, R. M. (1989). Psychological factors associated with the successful completion of Basic Underwater Demolition Seal training. In R. M. Nideffer (Ed.), *Psychological assessment in sport* (pp. 66–76). San Diego: Enhancement Performance Systems.

Shakow, D. (1962). Segmental set. *Archives of General Psychiatry, 6,* 1–17.

Singer, R. N. (1988). Strategies and metastrategies in learning and performing self-paced athletic skills. *The Sport Psychologist, 2,* 49–68.

Singer, R. N., Cauraugh, J. H., Murphey, M., Chen, D., & Lidor, R. (1991). Attentional control, distractors, and motor performance. *Human Performance, 4,* 55–69.

Singer, R. N., DeFrancesco, C., & Randall, L. E. (1989). Effectiveness of global learning strategy practiced in different contexts on primary and transfer self-paced motor tasks. *Journal of Sport & Exercise Psychology, 11,* 290–304.

Smith, R. E. (1980). A cognitive-affective approach to stress management training for athletes. In C. H. Nadeau, W. R. Halliwell, K. M. Newell, & G. C. Roberts, *Psychology of Motor Behavior and Sport*—1979 (pp. 54–72), Champaign, IL: Human Kinetics.

Starkes, J., & Allard, F. (1983). Perception in volleyball: The effects of competitive stress. *Journal of Sport Psychology, 5,* 189–196.

Starkes, J., & Deakin, J. (1984). Perception in sport: A cognitive approach to skilled performance. In W. Straub & J. Williams (Eds.), *Cognitive sport psychology* (pp. 115–128). Lansing, NY: Sport Sciences Associates.

Straub, W. F. (1989). The effect of three different methods of mental training on dart throwing performance. *The Sport Psychologist, 3,* 133–141.

Suinn, R. M. (1987). Behavioral approaches to stress management. In J. R. May & M. J. Asken (Eds.), *Sport psychology: The psycho-*

logical health of the athlete (pp. 41–75). New York: PMA Publishing Corp.

Suinn, R. M., & Richardson, F. (1971). Anxiety management training: A nonspecific behavior therapy program for anxiety control. *Behavior Therapy, 2,* 498–510.

Unestahl, L. E. (1983). *Inner mental training: A systematical self-instructional program for self-hypnosis.* Orebro, Sweden: Veje.

Ungerleider, S., Golding, J., Porter, K., & Foster, J. (1989). An exploratory examination of cognitive strategies used by Masters track and field athletes. *The Sport Psychologist, 3,* 245–253.

Vallerand, R. J. (1983). Attention and decision making: A test of the predictive validity of the test of attentional and interpersonal style (TAIS) in a sport setting. *Journal of Sport Psychology, 5,* 449–459.

Van Schoyck, S. R., & Grasha, A. F. (1981). Attentional style variations and athletic ability: The advantages of a sports-specific test. *Journal of Sport Psychology, 3,* 149–165.

Vealey, R. (1988). Future directions in psychological skills training. *The Sport Psychologist, 2,* 319–336.

Wachtel, P. (1967). Conceptions of broad and narrow attention. *Psychological Bulletin, 68,* 417–429.

Weinberg, R. S., Seabourne, T. G., & Jackson, A. (1981). Effects of visuomotor behavior rehearsal, relaxation, and imagery on karate performance. *Journal of Sport Psychology, 3,* 228–238.

Wilkes, R. L., & Summers, J. J. (1984). Cognitions, mediating variables, and strength performance. *Journal of Sport Psychology, 6,* 351–359.

Woolfolk, R. L., Murphy, S. M., Gottesfeld, D., & Aitken, D. (1985). Effects of mental rehearsal of task motor activity and mental depiction of task outcome on motor skill performance. *Journal of Sport Psychology, 7,* 191–197.

Wrisberg, C. A., & Anshel, M. H. (1989). The effect of cognitive strategies on the free throw shooting performance of young athletes. *The Sport Psychologist, 3,* 95–104.

Wrisberg, C. A., Franks, D. B., Birdwell, M. W., & High, D. M. (1988). Physiological and psychological responses to exercise with an induced attentional focus. *Perceptual and Motor Skills, 66,* 603–116.

Yerkes, R. M., & Dodson, J. D. (1908). The relationship of strength of stimulus to rapidity of habit formation. *Journal of Comparative Neurology and Psychology, 18,* 459–482.

Zaichkowsky, L. D., & Fuchs, C. Z. (1989). Biofeedback-assisted self-regulation for stress management in sports. In D. Hackfort & C. D. Spielberger (Eds.), *Anxiety in sport: An international perspective* (pp. 235–246). New York: Hemisphere.

Zani, A. (1989). Brain evoked responses reflect information processing changes with the menstrual cycle in young female athletes. *Journal of Sport Medicine and Physical Fitness, 29,* 113–121.

Ziegler, S. G., Klinzing, J., & Williamson, K. (1982). The effects of two stress management training programs on cardiorespiratory efficiency. *Journal of Sport Psychology, 4,* 280–289.

·25·

SELF-REGULATION STRATEGIES IN SPORT AND EXERCISE

Debra J. Crews

"Self-regulation" (SR) refers to automatic functioning without the use of external controls. A self-regulated sport or exercise performer would essentially be on "automatic pilot" utilizing self-perceived feedback. SR is an integral part of all interventions (e.g., goal setting, visualization/imagery) used to facilitate performance (Schwartz, 1979). The interventions teach the athlete or exerciser alternative techniques for effective SR. Therefore, two primary questions need to be addressed when considering the effect of SR strategies on performance: (1) Is the participant able to successfully self-regulate the response? (2) Does SR of this response influence performance, either by increasing the likelihood of successful performance or by decreasing the performance decrement?

THEORIES AND MODELS OF SELF-REGULATION

SR theory is encompassed within a general "systems theory" (von Bertalanffy, 1968) approach that originated in engineering technology. Systems theory suggests that the behavior of a system (e.g., athlete, exerciser) is dependent on the dynamic interactions of its parts and that these interactions serve to construct a whole.

Systems theory is actually a "metatheory" approach providing a framework to help explain the contributions and interactions of "subtheories" such as cybernetic SR theory and control theory (Schwartz, 1979). Cybernetic theory presents conceptual mechanisms to explain the process of SR, while control theory offers a behavioral approach to guide SR.

Cybernetic Theory of SR

A subset of general systems theory is cybernetic theory. Cybernetics is the science of human control systems that deals with the comparative study of the various systems in the body (e.g., brain and nervous system). Cybernetic theory addresses "how" a system becomes self-regulatory (Schwartz, 1979). An open loop system of information processing (see Figure 25–1) is inappropriate for cybernetic self-regulatory theory since it does not provide for feedback to the athlete or exerciser about the performance. Cybernetic theory is based on a negative feedback loop in which the behavior (or output) of a system is used to modify the input (see Figure 25–1). "Error" detected at the output is reduced by altering the input.

The negative feedback loop could also be interpreted as a positive feedback loop in which the output is used to increase the likelihood of the correct response occuring repeatedly (Schwartz, 1979). In essence, the negative feedback loop becomes a positive feedback loop in a balanced, automatically functioning system. However, if a change in behavior is desired, internal feedback loops within and between the brain and the body will be altered.

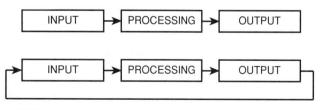

FIGURE 25–1. Open-loop (top) and closed-loop (bottom) feedback systems.

New external and internal feedback connections will eventually return the system to automatic, balanced processing.

If attenuation of the feedback loop, or worse yet, disconnection, occurs, then disregulation occurs (Schwartz, 1979). Disregulation represents an imbalance between the positive and negative feedback loops causing disorder and loss of control (Schwartz, 1977a, 1977b, 1978). Subsequent behaviors lose stability, rhythmicity, and order as disconnection leads to disregulation and ultimately disorder. The automatic functioning of negative feedback mechanisms must be restored to produce smooth, deliberate motor behaviors. This requires coordination of the skeletal muscle, the spinal cord, the cerebellum, and the cortical centers of the brain. This restoration becomes conscious so the system can function correctly. The correctly functioning system then returns to operating at a subconscious level. Disregulation disrupts performance, but more drastically, it can delay recovery time and inhibit the return to SR. An example of this occurs in athletics when a mechanical error needs to be corrected for proper performance execution. The mechanical error may be corrected with the help of a coach or teacher; however, the loss of self-confidence which accompanied the disruption may delay the return to "standard" performance. Patterns of disconnectedness cause disregulation within the feedback loop. Correcting the feedback and reconnecting the appropriate paths within the feedback loop will correct the performance.

Within cybernetic theory, Kanfer and Karoly (1972) have offered a working model of SR. Three phases are presented in the model: (a) self-monitoring, which becomes activated when a change in behavior is desired; (b) self-evaluation, which uses a self-determined standard or criterion as a measure of the behavioral outcome; and (c) self-reinforcement, which is positive if the behavior meets the criterion and negative if it does not comply with the standard (see Figure 25–2). The first step to altering a present behavior is to devise a performance contract in which the performer expresses the behavior change either overtly, by signing a contract, or covertly, as an interaction with another person. At this stage, the performer begins the process of self-monitoring and continues through the model to self-evaluation and self-reinforcement.

Kirschenbaum (1984) has enclosed this three-phase model of SR into a five-stage model to more fully explain the process of SR for the athlete or exerciser (see Figure 25–2). The additional stages attempt to explain the interaction of SR with environmental influences. The model includes problem solving, commitment, execution, environmental management, and generalization. The three-phase model described by Kanfer and Karoly (1972) is included in the execution (i.e., SM, SE, and SR) phase of Kirschenbaum's model (see Figure 25–2). However, the term "self-reinforcement" is perhaps more appropriately labeled "self-consequation" by Kirschenbaum because not all feedback is necessarily reinforcing to the behavior. A contract, which is a necessary precursor for changing behavior in Kanfer and Karoly's (1972) model, may be associated with the commitment phase of Kirschenbaum's (1984) model. The three additional stages of Kirschenbaum's model are explained as: (a) problem solving, which suggests that the athlete or exerciser needs to be able to determine exactly which problem disrupts performance; (b) environmental management, which emphasizes the importance of planning the social and physical environment to maximize energy for focused performance; and (c) generalization, which implies that the changed behavior can be applied in a variety of situations over extended periods of time.

Athletes tend to have difficulty with the first stage of the model, identifying disregulation, or self-regulatory failure, due to the automaticity which develops in highly skilled activities (Kirschenbaum, 1984). If an athlete has taken lessons from a particular coach for many years, it may be difficult to realize that an "inner" problem exists which this coach is not able to detect. Perhaps the athlete has habituated to the attentional cues offered by his/her coach and needs new cues to further enhance performance.

Once this problem is identified, the athlete can commit to making a change either by working with a new coach (if such options exist) or by attempting to find more appropriate cues through self-directed practice. For example, the athlete may overtly sign a contract with a new coach to work with a new approach a minimum of 6 weeks, or she or he may covertly decide to make error detection a primary goal for the next 2 weeks of practice. During these 2 weeks, the athlete will experiment and find appropriate cues to correct the performance. If this goal is not achieved, she or he will then seek assistance from another coach.

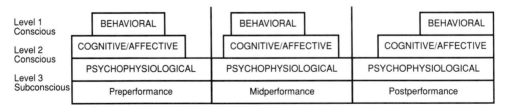

PERFORMANCE

FIGURE 25–2. Combined models of self-regulation. (Note: "Self-reinforcement" [SR] in Kanfer & Karoly [1972] is "self-consequation" in Kirschenbaum [1984].)

It is very difficult to change behavior if the athlete is unaware of the present behavior. Thus, self-monitoring is the first step toward executing the change. Once awareness is present, the athlete compares the performance outcome with a goal or standard. This is the self-evaluation component of execution. Lastly, self-consequation serves to endorse positive outcomes and to alter behavior when negative outcomes exist.

Altering the social and physical environment to maximize energy may include interviewing teachers to decide on the best alternative and on restructuring practice to a time in the day when maximum attention will be devoted to the practice. It will be important to carefully consider all environmental factors which may influence performance and to optimize each one as opportunities present themselves.

New attentional cues which have been acquired through practice need to be applied in competition, and perhaps over an extended period of time (e.g., season). This is the process of generalization, the last stage of Kirschenbaum's model. Learning SR strategies will be of little benefit if they are not transferable to similar situations.

There are many factors which may influence SR and possibly lead to disregulation. Personality characteristics and dispositional styles such as self-motivation and obsessive-compulsive behaviors tend to increase self-regulation (Kirschenbaum, 1984). Familiarity with the task (Kirschenbaum, 1984), sense of mastery (Kirschenbaum, 1984), affect (Kirschenbaum, Tomarken, & Humphrey, 1985), and self-focused attention (Carver & Scheier, 1981) interact with each other and influence the ability to self-regulate. In addition, the five-stage model of SR has the advantage of not only accounting for relationships between behaviors, cognitions, affect, and physiology, but also including environmental variables.

Control Theory

Control theory is another subtheory of systems theory (Glasser, 1981). In contrast to Kirschenbaum's five-stage model of SR, control theory focuses on changing only behaviors and cognitions. It is hypothesized that changing behaviors and cognitions is easier than changing affect and physiology, and that ultimately, affect and physiology will

also be changed. Glasser's (1965) reality therapy concept is based on control theory. Reality therapy assumes that individuals are responsible for their own behavior. The eight steps of reality therapy include: (a) developing a therapeutic relationship, (b) focusing on the current behavior of the client, (c) asking the client to evaluate his or her behavior, (d) developing plans for change, (e) getting a commitment, (f) accepting no excuses, (g) refusing to use punishment, and (h) never giving up on the client. Interestingly, since 1981, Glasser has slightly altered his approach to behavior. He suggests that the brain attempts to control the perception of the external world so that it coincides with the internal world of the individual. Thus, behavior is the control of perceptions; individuals cognitively choose what they want and then behave to bring the real world close to their desired world. Both the cybernetic SR theory offered by Schwartz (1979) and Kirschenbaum's model of SR (1984) encompasses all aspects of the individual (e.g., behavior, cognitions, affect, and physiology) at the conscious and subconscious level. However, control theory addresses only behavior and cognitions at the conscious level to direct one's actions. The typical criticism of reality therapy and control theory is that the individual also receives feedback in the form of affect and physiology, and this feedback is not addressed.

Described in Figure 25–3 is a model which applies the cybernetic SR theory more specifically to sport and exercise performance. All performance is explained in three time phases: pre-, mid-, and postperformance. Preperformance refers to the preparation period for the performance. The preparation period may refer to processes beginning two weeks prior to a competition or to processes occurring within the last second before the movement is initiated. For example, preparation for conference championships in basketball may begin with specific practice strategies the week of the competition and may also include the last second before the release of a free throw.

Midperformance refers to the time period during which the skill is actually being executed. The 2 seconds during a golf swing or the 3 hours of a marathon run are examples of the midperformance time phase.

Postperformance is the time period immediately following the execution of the skill, the completion of the game, or the end of the competition. Athletes may use different SR strategies during each phase of performance. In addition,

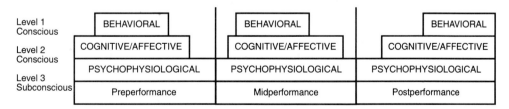

FIGURE 25–3. Self-regulation in sport and exercise: a framework of application.

there are three levels of SR strategies that may be used during the three phases of performance (see Figure 25–3). The first two levels, behavioral and cognitive/affective, are usually at the conscious level of perception, while the third level, psychophysiological, is normally at a subconscious level of awareness.

During performance, athletes incorporate behaviors representing a combination of these three levels into some form of routine. Specific behaviors are executed in a specific order a preset number of times. At some point prior to performance execution, the behaviors will terminate. A cognitive/affective routine coincides with the behavioral routine and may be active for a longer duration of time, but this routine also ends prior to performance. Finally, psychophysiological responses, as they relate to the upcoming performance, persist through the event. An example of how these three levels interact to facilitate performance is evident in the basketball free throw. Behaviorally, the athlete may begin the routine with a deep breath, then place the body in position for the shot, and finally, glance at the target preceding the release. Cognitively, the athlete may be relaxing, lining up the body and ball in relation to the basket, and focusing on the target and feel as the shot is imaged. Last, the athlete switches into an "awareness" mode of automaticity just prior to releasing the ball.

During midperformance, the athlete perceives the correct or incorrect feel, primarily at the subconscious, psychophysiological level, and if necessary, may be able to self-correct the movement. Postperformance the athlete continues the assessment of feel and begins to cognitively interpret the result and to release the emotion associated with the outcome.

While in sport, particularly a closed-skilled sport, it is easy to differentiate the three phases of SR, and the midperformance phase is often the shortest in duration. In contrast to sport, an exercise bout may be composed primarily of the midphase, the exercise bout, with less preperformance and postperformance SR. A typical exercise bout may last from 30 minutes to 1 hour. Thus, the exerciser may include cognitive and behavioral SR strategies in addition to psychophysiological SR. For example, during a 30-minute run, the exerciser may cognitively monitor physiological responses at a conscious level to make decisions about when to push and when to hold back. He or she may also alter body position to effectively run hills. Therefore, the exercise bout requires the constant interaction of all three levels of SR.

Although control theory may offer options for SR pre- and postperformance, it may offer little to midperformance SR since it involves only behavioral and cognitive strategies. Behavioral and cognitive strategies are not incorporated during the midperformance phase in skilled performers, since their performance is more autonomous and less cognitive. The third level of the model, the psychophysiological response, exemplifies a positively self-regulated (autonomous) feedback loop.

Within each phase of the model in Figure 25–3, the athlete/exerciser may incorporate various SR techniques.

Table 25–1 includes examples of options to be used to self-regulate at each level and at each phase of the model. Level 1 provides the behavioral options that athletes and exercisers may incorporate into their training and performance. The preperformance behavioral options for sport and exercise include specific eating and sleeping, which differ for practice, qualifying, and competition. Mid-and postperformance, the participant is primarily modifying routines and assessing routines typical of the execution phase (self-monitoring, self-evaluation, and self-reinforcement/consequation) of Kirschenbaum's model.

Cognitive-affective SR strategies are presented in Level 2 of Table 25–1. Self-monitoring, self-talk, and visualization/imagery are presented for each phase of performance because these options are readily available to the active mind. Goal setting is a technique which is used in both sport and exercise to provide direction to the performer. Attentional focus may be directed internally (self-focused, biofeedback, association) or externally (dissociation) for the three phases of the model.

Level 3, the psychophysiological response, is not normally accessible to the conscious mind and thus the only SR available is a state of heightened awareness of the task. It is at this level of performance that athletes often have a difficult time remembering their performance because it was not at the conscious cognitive/affective level. The SR technique which offers the only possible means of altering the psychophysiological response to subsequent performance is biofeedback (BF) training. Sime (1985) discusses the importance of Level 3 processing for exercisers and labels it "physiological perception." He gives examples of BF training to enhance this perception and subsequent exercise performance.

Various factors (e.g., personality characteristics, task familiarity) have been identified that influence the ability to self-regulate, and these factors also interact with environmental characteristics (Schwartz, 1979). These factors will influence the SR strategies selected by the individual. Thus it is important to understand that the combination of appropriate SR strategies may differ for each individual and may vary in different sport and exercise environments.

Strategies

The remainder of this chapter will provide a review of the sport and exercise research in which the use of SR strategies has been examined. The studies will be discussed separately for sport and exercise and will be divided into the three levels of SR (behavioral, cognitive/affective, and psychophysiological). When possible, the SR strategies will be presented in relation to the three phases of performance. It is not always possible to separate behavioral interventions from cognitive/affective ones or to separate cognitive/affective interventions from psychophysiological ones because the mind is normally active at a conscious level. BF is an example of a SR technique that combines the cognitive/affective level with the psychophysiological

TABLE 25–1. S-R Strategies for Levels 1–3 at Various Stages of Performance.

Preperformance	Midperformance	Postperformance
Behavioral		
1. Contracts: • practice • qualifying	1. Routine modification: • body position	1. Assessment of routines: • maintained attentional focus • maintained emotional control
2. Planning routines: • eating • sleeping • physical practice • mental practice	2. Self-monitoring: • pacing • physiological needs	2. Self-evaluation: • comparison with goals/statistics
3. Self-monitoring: • practice • qualifying • competition		3. Self-reinforcement: • rewarding outcome patterns • rewards
Cognitive-affective		
1. Coal setting • performance • cognitions • affect • physiology	1. Association/dissociation	1. Goal adjustment
2. Self-focused	2. Self-monitoring	2. Self-focused
3. Self-talk	3. Self-talk	3. Self-talk
4. Visualization/imagery	4. Visualization/imagery	4. Visualization/imagery
5. Biofeedback training*		
Psychophysiological		
1. Biofeedback training*	1. Heightened awareness	1. Heightened awareness
2. Heightened awareness		

* "Biofeedback training" is the conscious control of subconscious psychophysiological responses. Therefore, it is listed in cognitive-affective and psychophysiological strategies.

level. Psychophysiological responses which are normally executed at the subconscious level are amplified so the conscious cognitive/affective level can become aware of and alter this response and perhaps correct disregulation.

BEHAVIORAL SR STRATEGIES

Sport

Behavioral SR strategies may include contracts, planning routines, self-monitoring, and self-reinforcement. All these behaviors include a cognitive component because they are of a conscious nature; however, they will be categorized as a *behavioral* strategy for the purpose of this review. Kirschenbaum and Bale's (1984) study of collegiate golfers included most of these overt behavioral strategies in a pre-, mid-, and postperformance mental training program of "Brain Power Golf." The components of the program were deep muscle relaxation, routine planning, imagery, positive self-monitoring, and positive self-statements. The 1977

study included one experimental "starter" and three "non-starters" compared with four control (no mental training program) players. The experimental "starter" markedly improved his game and encouraged three additional players to participate in the 1978 study. Although it was not possible to determine the differential contribution of each aspect of the program, a multiple baseline approach indicated the effectiveness of the total program for all participants.

Self-monitoring has been tested in the sport setting among golfers and bowlers (Johnston-O'Connor & Kirschenbaum, 1986; Kirschenbaum, Ordman, Tomarken, & Holtzbauer, 1982; Kirschenbaum, Wittrock, Smith, & Monstron, 1984). Kirschenbaum et al. (1982) had unskilled and moderately skilled bowlers divided into categories of behavior: (a) instructions on the seven components of effective bowling, (b) positive self-monitoring, (c) instructions plus positive self-monitoring, (d) negative self-monitoring, and (e) no treatment (control). Results indicated that although unskilled bowlers improved, there were no significant differences between treatments.

In an attempt to clarify the unclear results from this

study (Kirschenbaum et al., 1982), Johnston-O'Connor and Kirschenbaum (1986) examined unskilled golfers who had learned the components of the full swing. These players were assigned either to positive self-monitoring, neutral self-monitoring of the swing, or a control (no self-monitoring) condition. The positive self-monitoring instruction group improved in performance and attitude toward golf compared with the other two groups. Although the results of these two studies were somewhat equivocal, it appears that unskilled performers benefit from positive self-monitoring. Additional research is needed using self-monitoring with moderately skilled and highly skilled performers.

Self-reinforcement in the form of monetary reward was studied by Heward (1978). Semiprofessional baseball players received monetary rewards for increasing batting efficiency. Players increased their batting average 22% with monetary reward and showed no change in average during the baseline phase of the study. No other studies have examined the effects of self-reinforcement by itself on sport performance.

Kirschenbaum and Bale (1984) referred to planning in the Brain Power Golf program, as a checklist of factors to consider in the decision-making process, followed by a set pattern of overt behaviors immediately preceding the execution of the shot. A more familiar term used by sport participants is "routine." Routines aid in the SR of performance either by directing attention away from irrelevant information (Nideffer, 1976), by focusing thoughts away from the performance of a well-learned skill (Keele, 1973), and/or by establishing an optimal level of psychological and physiological state for the task (Schmidt, 1988).

Crews and Boutcher (1986a, 1986b) and Boutcher and Crews (1987) examined the effectiveness of specific routines in the game of golf. In the first study (Crews & Boutcher, 1986a), the behaviors of 12 Ladies Professional Golf Association (LPGA) tour players were recorded before each shot. In addition, each routine was timed. Results indicated that the better players were very consistent in their behaviors and in the time frame of the routine, despite the fact that they had significantly longer routines for the full swing and the putt. The authors attributed the increased time frame used to produce these two golf skills to more highly developed mental preparation strategies.

In the 1987 study, Boutcher and Crews pretested 12 collegiate golfers (males, $N = 6$; females, $N = 6$) while putting from 4, 12, and 20 feet from the hole. This was followed by a 6-week training program in which the players learned and practiced an individualized behavioral routine. Players trained for 20 minutes four times each week. Results indicated that experimental females represented the only group to make significantly more putts following training. Interestingly the total time of the routine for all the experimental subjects increased following training without a significant increase in variability.

Lastly, it was of interest to determine whether beginning-level players would benefit from the use of a preshot routine. Thirty beginners were assigned to either a routine or

to a no-routine control group (Crews & Boutcher, 1986b). A full swing seven-iron test suggested that the routine facilitated performance, particularly for players who were slightly above the beginning level of golf performance. It appears that the use of overt behavioral routines aid in SR by reducing variability and ultimately improving performance.

Exercise

The use of *behavioral* strategies to facilitate exercise performance, particularly exercise adherence, is more prevalent than in the sport literature. Several researchers (Dishman, 1988; Kirschenbaum, Johnson, & Stalonas, 1987; Rejeski & Kenney, 1988) endorse the use of a behavioral contract, planning, self-monitoring, and self-reinforcement to maintain motivation to exercise. Numerous techniques are mentioned in these books to facilitate exercise adherence, particularly in the early stages of exercise adoption.

Research is presented to support the use of behavioral contracts and self-monitoring techniques, in various combinations, to enhance exercise adherence (Atkins, Kaplan, Timms, Reinsch, & Lofback, 1984; Epstein, Wing, Koeske, Ossip, & Beck, 1982; Epstein, Wing, Thompson, & Griffin, 1980; Kau & Fischer, 1974). Wysocki, Hall, Iwata, and Riardan (1979) found that exercise behavior increased when combining a behavioral contract with material reinforcement (deposited personal items). However, Oldridge and Jones (1983) combined a written agreement and self-monitoring to increase compliance among cardiac rehabilitation patients and found that the addition of behavioral strategies did not increase attendance. Yet when Keefe and Blumenthal (1980) combined self-monitoring with goal setting, exercise adherence was increased over a two-year period.

Self-reinforcement is another popular behavioral strategy used to enhance exercise behavior. Nelson, Hayes, Spong, Jarrett, and McKnight (1983) found that self-and externally administered reinforcement contributed equally to increasing exercise behavior. Weinberg, Bruya, Garland, and Jackson (1990) examined the effects of goal setting in conjunction with self-reinforcement on exercise performance during a 3-minute sit-up test and a hand dynamometer endurance task. The only difference between the two tasks was that verbal persuasion was individualized for the hand dynamometer task. Positive verbal persuasion did not significantly influence exercise behavior in either condition. In addition, Martin et al. (1984) did not show positive effects on adherence using a lottery as a form of self-reinforcement, while Epstein et al. (1980) found improved adherence using the same technique.

It appears that the findings are equivocal regarding the use of preperformance behavioral strategies to increase the likelihood of exercise behavior. Perhaps the use of behavioral strategies must be individualized to the personality characteristics and past experience of the exerciser. It may be that individualized behavioral strategies are beneficial in the initial stages of an exercise program before exercise itself becomes intrinsically motivating.

COGNITIVE/AFFECTIVE STRATEGIES

Cognitive/affective strategies may include goal setting, self-focused attention, self-talk, visualization/imagery techniques, and the use of planned mental routines. Goal setting, visualization/imagery, and self-focused attention are discussed in other chapters in the handbook and thus will not be the primary focus of this chapter.

Sport

Several studies have been conducted using primarily cognitive strategies to regulate performance (Fenker & Lambiotte, 1987; Hamilton & Fremouw, 1985; Heyman, 1987; Mace, Eastman, & Carrol, 1987; Meyers & Schleser, 1980; Meyers, Schleser, & Okwunabua, 1982). Methodological flaws apparent in several of the studies will be discussed in relation to the findings.

All of the studies incorporated a combination of SR strategies (i.e., relaxation, imagery, cognitive restructuring) and showed performance gains. The combined approach makes it difficult to determine the effectiveness of individual strategies. In addition, other methodological flaws existed in these studies. Only in one study (Fenker & Lambiotte, 1987) was a manipulation check used to determine whether athletes learned the technique, and none of the studies used a control group. A reversal single subject design (Meyers et al., 1982) and a multiple baseline approach (Hamilton & Fremouw, 1985) supported the efficacy of cognitive SR strategies. However, further research using controlled experimental designs is needed.

In contrast, recent studies by Rushall, Hall, Roux, Sasseville, and Rushall (1988) and Wrisberg and Anshel (1989) examined the use of specific cognitive SR strategies within well-controlled experimental designs. Cross-country skiers were given three types of thoughts to be used while skiing: (a) task-relevant statements, to enhance mechanical efficiency, (b) mood words, to increase capacity, and (c) positive self-statements, to improve physiological efficiency. A total of 18 skiers completed each cognitive condition twice, with a control (normal thought) condition between each experimental condition. This multiple baseline approach with a control condition showed that 16 of the skiers improved ski time for the test track in all three cognitive conditions as compared with the normal thought condition.

Wrisberg and Anshel (1989) showed that mental imagery combined with arousal adjustment enhanced free-throw shooting performance among forty 10- to 12-year-old boys. The combined condition (i.e., imagery and arousal adjustment) elicited greater performance improvements than a control condition and an arousal adjustment (only) condition.

Highlen and Bennett (1983) conducted a survey study to assess the psychological factors associated with training and competition of elite divers and wrestlers. Participants answered questions indicating the psychological techniques used in the open (wrestling) and closed (diving) skill activities. The use of imagery and self-talk distinguished qualifying divers from nonqualifying ones, but did not distinguish qualifying and nonqualifying wrestlers. Qualifiers reported using more imagery in training and in competition and reported having better control of their images than nonqualifiers. Qualifiers also reported using self-instructions, while nonqualifiers praised themselves. Qualifying and nonqualifying wrestlers were not differentiated on any of the eight subscales of the 112-item questionnaire.

The use of planned mental routines was discussed in the *behavioral* strategies section of this chapter. Investigations of golfers (Boutcher & Crews, 1987; Kirschenbaum & Bale, 1984) support the use of preshot mental routines to enhance golf performance. These routines are individualized by the athlete and typically include visualization/imagery, self-talk, and specific attentional cues or self-instructions.

Exercise

Both Rejeski and Kenney (1988) and Dishman (1988) cite numerous studies supporting the importance of goal setting. In addition, King and Frederikson (1984) trained subjects to use cognitive restructuring to help reduce the number of missed sessions, while Atkins et al. (1984) used cognitive restructuring to eliminate negative self-talk and improve exercise behavior.

The most popular question regarding cognitive SR strategies examined in research studies has been whether athletes should develop associative (focusing attention on bodily responses) or dissociative (focusing attention away from bodily responses) strategies. It has been found that associative strategies are used more extensively by skilled athletes in their familiar sport (Morgan, Horstman, Cymerman, & Stokes, 1983; Morgan & Pollack, 1977; Schomer, 1986; Spink & Longhurst, 1986), while dissociative strategies enhanced performance in a less familiar activity for both skilled and unskilled athletes (Gill & Strom, 1985; Weinberg, Smith, Jackson, & Gould, 1984). In addition, positive self-talk also led to greater time on a leg muscle endurance task than associative or control strategies (Weinberg et al., 1984).

It is probably too simplistic to categorize all thoughts into two categories such as association or dissociation. For example, self-monitoring of pace, rhythm, and balance during exercise uses both internal and external cues. Sime (1985) has summarized the importance of physiological perception and perceived pacing in exercise performance. He refers to the "perceptostat" that helps the athlete regulate effort and exercise efficiently.

PSYCHOPHYSIOLOGICAL SR STRATEGIES

In Figure 25–3, psychophysiological strategies were presented as "heightened awareness" at a subconscious level. Thus it will be difficult to discuss the nature of this awareness, since it is not at the conscious level. However, the use of biofeedback (BF) offers a technique to amplify psycho-physiological responses and to train the appropriate patterns of response for optimal performance. BF brings these normally involuntary physiological responses into voluntary control at a conscious level through amplification of the signals. It allows athletes and exercisers to find appropriate cues or techniques to SR psychophysiological patterns.

Biofeedback was first introduced to psychology during the 1960s. In 1978, a task force of the Biofeedback Society of America outlined three ways in which BF could be applied to sport and exercise: (a) to reduce anxiety, (b) to rehabilitate injury, and (c) to enhance performance (Zaichkowski & Fuchs, 1988). This chapter focuses on the use of BF to enhance performance as other chapters discuss optimizing arousal levels and injury rehabilitation. For additional reading, Landers (1988) and Lawrence and Johnson (1977) provide a more complete review of BF in motor performance. The task force of 1978 stated that few empirical studies existed which combine BF specifically with sport and exercise. Today, unfortunately, this situation still exists.

Sport

Electromyographic (EMG) BF is the most common BF measure used in sport. It has been assumed that decreased tension in the frontalis muscle or the bicep muscle represents a general decrease in overall body tension and would lead to improved sport performance. Bennett and Hall (1979) assigned high-competitive and low-competitive novice archers to either BF training, a single BF session, or a control (no BF) condition. This unpublished study showed that despite EMG reductions, there was no concommitant improvement in performance. Griffiths (1981), Zaichkowsky, Dorsey, and Mulholland (1979), and Tsukomoto (1979) all showed similar reductions in EMG without changes in performance. DeWitt (1980) conducted a two-part study. In the second experiment, EMG and heart rate (HR) BF improved basketball performance. Goodspeed (1983) also conducted two studies to assess the effects of a combined BF and cognitive/affective mental training program. Study 1 showed decreased anxiety and improved gymnastic performance among advanced level gymnasts following temperature and galvanic skin response BF plus a mental training program. The cognitive/affective training program consisted of relaxation, imagery, and a cognitive technique to reduce anxiety. However, the researchers failed to replicate the results of Study 1 when using beginning and intermediate level gymnasts in Study 2.

Peper and Schmid (1983) combined multiple BF measures (EMG, temperature, HR, and skin conductance) with relaxation and mental training to facilitate the performance of the United States Rhythmic Gymnastics team. Results indicated increased self-report performance associated with increased temperature, decreased EMG, and decreased skin conductance.

Furthermore, two studies (Kappes, Latze, & Travis, 1987; Larkin, Manuck, & Kasprowiczk, 1990) were able to train BF responses but were unable to show concommitant improvements in performance. Kappes et al. (1987) warmed the hands of 51 cross-country skiers during indoor, outdoor, mid-race, and finish checkpoints. Surprisingly, resultant race times were actually slower with hand warming, not faster. Video game performers were given HR BF, control, instruction, and BF plus score feedback (Larkin et al., 1990). All subjects lowered HR and systolic blood pressure, but performance did not improve compared to the control condition. The investigators suggested that HR may not need lowering to improve performance. This is an important observation because many BF measures (e.g., EMG, HR, temperature) are used to produce a relaxation response and it is assumed that performance will improve. However, this may not apply to all athletes. Some athletes may need to increase arousal levels to improve performance.

These studies, some published and some unpublished, pose several methodological concerns. Few of the investigators trained the participants to a criterion level for the BF measure. Therefore, it is difficult to know how effective each athlete was at performing the BF. In addition, two of the studies (Goodspeed, 1983; Peper & Schmid, 1983) combined BF training with other mental training techniques; therefore, it is difficult to know the contribution of individual interventions.

It has only been in the past 5 years that electroencephalographic (EEG) BF has been tested for its potential to enhance performance. Slow potential shift, or a shift in the baseline of the EEG signal, is an indication of readiness to respond. It has been associated with improved golf putting performance (Crews, 1989). Landers et al. (1991) showed that correct slow wave BF in the left hemisphere of the temporal cortex improved performance among elite level archers compared to an incorrect right hemisphere BF condition. In this study, archers were trained to a specific criterion known to indicate the effectiveness of the training (Landers et al., 1991).

Although no empirical studies have been published to date, biomechanical BF also has the potential of improving performance. Atha, Harris, West, and Manley (1985) devised a biodynamic BF device to provide swimmers with auditory velocity and acceleration BF. Morgan (personal communication, March 8, 1991) is presently providing uneconomical runners with auditory and visual stride length BF to possibly improve running economy.

Exercise

EMG BF was used to increase muscle strength among 30 healthy females (Lucca & Rechiuti, 1983). The 19-day program showed that BF produced significant gains compared with an exercise group and a no-exercise control group. Interestingly, strength also increased in the same muscle of the untrained leg, probably due to bilateral transfer. Croce (1986) was also able to show increased maximal force and integrated EMG in a muscle following isokinetic exercise and EMG BF. It appears that muscular strength is increased to a greater extent with BF than with exercise alone.

Lloyd (1972) examined the effectiveness of EMG BF training during isometric exercise and found decreased EMG levels but no significant decrease in pain and no significant increase in endurance time. It is questionable whether reduced EMG activity is a favorable response when endurance time was not increased.

EMG BF has also been used post-exercise to reduce pain or delayed muscle soreness, although results have been equivocal. McGlynn, Laughlin, and Filios (1979) found lower reported pain at 24, 48, and 72 hours post-exercise with the use of EMG BF. Although EMG levels were not different from one another in each time period, they were 50% lower than in the control (no BF) subjects at 48 hours post-exercise. Unfortunately, McGlynn, Laughlin, and Rowe (1979) showed the opposite effect of reduced EMG levels but no reported decrease in pain.

Numerous studies have attempted to control HR during static exercise (Carrol & McGovern, 1983; Clemons & Shattock, 1979; Magnusson, 1976; Moses, Clemens, & Brener, 1986) and during dynamic exercise (Carrol & Ryes-Davies, 1979; Davies, Iber, Keene, MacArthur, & Path, 1986; Fredrikson & Engel, 1985; Goldstein, Ross, & Brady, 1977; Magnusson, 1976; Perski, 1985; Perski & Engel, 1980). Initial experimentation (Moses et al., 1976) showed that HR could be increased during static exercise using HR BF. A later study (Clemons & Shattock, 1979) showed both increased and decreased HR responses during static exercise, with differential effects on performance.

During dynamic exercise, Goldstein et al. (1977) demonstrated changes in HR while subjects exercised on a treadmill. HR decreased as well as systolic blood pressure (SBP) and rate pressure product (HR $\times$ SBP), compared to the same subjects in a control condition, who were simply instructed to decrease HR. Results were maintained during 5 weeks of posttraining. Unexpectedly, in this crossover design, the control subjects who received BF second were unable to learn HR BF control.

Perski and Engel (1980) were able to show crossover effects when subjects received HR BF on a bicycle ergometer. There was an average HR decrease of 20%, but no change in SBP. In a second study (Perski, Tzankoff, & Engel, 1985) experimenters showed decreased HR, oxygen consumption, pulmonary ventilation, and rate pressure product with HR BF on a bicycle ergometer.

Interestingly, Davies et al. (1986) controlled respiration rate and pH levels independent of metabolic rate using respiration BF while subjects completed submaximal incremental work on the bicycle ergometer. Hatfield, Spalding, Mahon, Brody, and Vaccaro (1986) provided respiration BF, control (no BF), and distraction to 10 trained athletes while they exercised on a treadmill just above the anaerobic threshold. Respiration rate was reduced without a decrease in metabolic cost.

Biomechanical BF has also been introduced to the exercise setting. The computerized exercise machine offers the option of variable resistance with visual feedback that varies as a function of force and displacement of the weight. Thus real-time feedback should allow for more efficient strength training and reduced chance of injury. Once the exerciser selects the appropriate pattern of exercise, the machine has the capability of automatically adjusting the force level, speed of movement, and temporal sequence of the pattern. One study (Saar, Ariel, Penny, & Saar, 1982) compared this form of training with traditional weight training equipment and found greater strength gains.

Biofeedback offers a unique and very specific approach to SR. Although it appears that athletes and exercisers can learn to SR almost any response, it is still not certain whether this results in improved performance. Perhaps several methodological considerations need to be addressed to show improved performance. First, the optimal psychophysiological and biomechanical patterns need to be determined. For example, Basmajian and White (1973) found that expert trumpet players had lower tension in the upper lip than that found in the lower lip, but this was not the case with beginning-level performers. A BF study could now be appropriately designed to correct the difference or disregulation of beginners. Too often in sport we offer frontalis EMG BF to everyone, assuming they all need to lower tension in this location to perform well.

Second, it may be necessary to determine appropriate levels of the specific response. For example, HR may need to be at different levels for different athletes, and the optimal pattern (e.g., acceleration, deceleration) may need to be trained at the appropriate level.

Third, it may be important to biofeedback multiple signals to reduce the chance of one response simply accommodating the change in another response. For example, it may be possible to reduce respiration rate at the expense of an increase in HR. Cowings, Billingham, and Toscano (1977) used this approach to train subjects to compensate for motion sickness. They were more successful when using multiple BF responses as opposed to a single response measure.

Finally, it is necessary to train the athlete or exerciser to transfer laboratory BF training to the sport or exercise setting. Encouraging participants to use cues and techniques to alter the physiological response that could also be used during performance will facilitate the transfer of the training effect. It has also been helpful to have the participant position him-or herself in the correct body position for his or her performance while learning the BF (Landers et al., 1991). Future research is needed to replicate the present findings and to determine the long-lasting effects of the BF training technique.

CONCLUSIONS

The use of SR strategies in sport has primarily focused on preperformance techniques. Behavioral, cognitive, and psychophysiological (BF) strategies have been defined and tested. The use of cognitive strategies probably outweighs the use of behavioral or BF techniques. Future research should examine the use of contracts, self-monitoring, and reinforcement as applied to sport. In addition, more highly individualized BF protocols of predetermined patterns using multiple responses and transferable cues will be needed before BF techniques will facilitate sport performance outcomes.

SR strategies for exercise have focused mostly on behavioral factors to encourage exercise participation and somewhat on cognitive factors to facilitate exercise performance. Research has identified strategies to stimulate participation in exercise (contracts, goal setting, self-monitoring, and reinforcements). In addition, if cognitive, psychophysiological, or behavioral stategies could reduce the cost and the discomfort associated with exercise, the participant might be more likely to return to the exercise setting and might progress toward improving fitness at a faster rate.

The models of SR help to understand the feedback loop and intervention strategies designed to reduce disregulatory behaviors. The SR techniques which are most appropriate for the individual athlete or exerciser need further investigation. No research to date has applied control theory—behavioral and cognitive techniques—to sport and exercise. This theory does not include strategies specific to the psychophysiological level, but infers that concomitant changes will occur at this level. This assumption requires confirmation. In addition, comparisons of control theory and SR models would be of interest to clinical and applied sport and exercise psychology application. Further research of SR strategies is critical since SR underlies the effectiveness of every technique used to enhance sport and exercise performance.

References

Atha, J., Harris, D., West, G., & Manley, P. K. (1985). Monitoring performance using a real-time biodynamic feedback device. *International Journal of Sport Biomechanics, 1,* 348–353.

Atkins, C. J., Kaplan, R. M., Timms, R. M., Reinsch, S., & Lofback, K. (1984). Behavioral exercise programs in the management of chronic obstructive pulmonary disease. *Journal of Consulting and Clinical Psychology, 52,* 591–603.

Basmajan, J. V., & White, E. R. (1973). Neuromuscular control of trumpeters' lips. *Nature, 241,* 70.

Bennett, B., & Hall, C. R. (1979, June). *Biofeedback training and archery performance.* Paper presented to the International Congress in Physical Education, Trois Rivières, Quebec.

Boutcher, S. H., & Crews, D. J. (1987). The effect of a preshot attentional routine on a well-learned skill. *International Journal of Sport Psychology, 18,* 30–39.

Carroll, D., & McGovern, M. (1983). Cardiac, respiratory and metabolic changes during static exercise and voluntary heart rate acceleration. *Biological Psychology, 17,* 121–130.

Carroll, D., & Rhys-Davies, L. (1979). Heart rate changes with voluntary exercise rate acceleration. *Biological Psychology, 8,* 241–252.

Carver, C. S., & Scheier, M. F. (1981). *Attention and self-regulation: A control theory approach to human behavior.* New York: Springer-Verlag.

Clemens, W. J., & Shattock, R. J. (1979). Voluntary heart rate control during static muscular effort. *Psychophysiology, 16,* 327–332.

Cowings, P. S., Billingham, J., & Toscano, B. W. (1977). Learned control of multiple autonomic responses to compensate for the debilitating effects of motion sickness. *Therapy in Psychosomatic Medicine, 4,* 318–323.

Crews, D. J. (1989). *The influence of attentive states on golf putting as indicated by cardiac and electrocortical activity.* Unpublished doctoral dissertation, Arizona State University, Tempe, AZ.

Crews, D. J., & Boutcher, S. H. (1986a). An observational behavior analysis of ladies professional golf association tour players. *Journal of Sport Behavior, 9,* 51–58.

Crews, D. J., & Boutcher, S. H. (1986b). Effects of structured preshot behaviors on beginning golf performance. *Perceptual and Motor Skills, 62,* 291–294.

Davies, S. F., Iber, S. A., Keene, C. D., McArthur, C. D., & Path, M. J. (1986). Effect of respiratory alkalosis during exercise on blood lactate. *Journal of Applied Physiology, 61,* 948–952.

DeWitt, D. J. (1980). Cognitive and biofeedback training for stress reduction with university students. *Journal of Sport Psychology, 2,* 288–294.

Dishman, R. K. (Ed.). (1988). *Exercise adherence: Its impact on public health.* Champaign, IL: Human Kinetics.

Epstein, L. H., Wing, R. R., Koeske, R., Ossip, D., & Beck, S. (1982). A comparison of lifestyle change and programmed aerobic exercise on weight and fitness changes in obese children. *Behavior Therapy, 13,* 651–665.

Epstein, L. H., Wing, R. R., Thompson, J. K., & Griffin, W. (1980). Attendance and fitness in aerobics exercise. *Behavior Modification, 4,* 465–479.

Fenker, R., & Lambiotte, J. (1987). A performance enhancement program for a college football team: One incredible season. *The Sport Psychologist, 1,* 224–236.

Frederickson, M., & Engel, B. T. (1985). Learned control of heart rate during exercise in patients with borderline hypertension. *European Journal of Applied Physiology, 54,* 315–320.

Gill, D. L., & Strom, E. H. (1985). The effect of attentional focus on performance of an endurance task. *International Journal of Sport Psychology, 16,* 217–223.

Glasser, W. (1965). *Reality therapy: A new approach to psychiatry.* New York: Harper & Row.

Glasser, W. (1981). *Stations of the mind.* New York: Harper & Row.

Goldstein, D. S., Ross, R. S., & Brady, J. V. (1977). Biofeedback heart rate during exercise. *Biofeedback and Self-Regulation, 2,* 107–125.

Goodspeed, G. A. (1983). *The effects of comprehensive self-regulation training on state anxiety and performance of female gymnasts.* Unpublished doctoral dissertation, Boston University.

Griffiths, J. J., Steele, D. H., Vaccaro, P., & Karpman, M. B. (1981). The effects of relaxation techniques on anxiety and underwater performance. *International Journal of Sport Psychology, 12,* 176–182.

Hamilton, S., & Fremouw, W. (1985). Cognitive-behavioral training for college free-throw performance. *Cognitive Therapy and Research, 9,* 479–483.

Hatfield, B. D., Spalding, T., Mahon, T., Brody, E. B., & Vaccaro, D. (1986). Ventilatory economy as a function of attentional self-focus during treadmill running. *Psychophysiology, 23,* 440–441.

Heward, W. (1978). The effects of reinforcement on the offensive efficiency of a barn-storming baseball team. *Behavior Modification, 2,* 25–29.

Heyman, S. R. (1987). Research and interventions in sport psychology: Issues encountered in working with an amateur boxer. *The Sport Psychologist, 1,* 208–223.

Highlen, P. S., & Bennett, B. B. (1983). Elite divers and wrestlers: A comparison between open-and closed-skill athletes. *Journal of Sport Psychology, 5,* 390–409.

Johnston-O'Connor, E. J., & Kirschenbaum, D. S. (1986). Something succeeds like success: Positive self-monitoring for unskilled golfers. *Cognitive Therapy and Research, 10,* 123–136.

Kanfer, F. H., & Karoly, P. (1972). Self-control: A behavioristic excursion into the lion's den. *Behavior Therapy, 3,* 398–416.

Kappes, B. M., Latze, N. A., & Travis, B. (1987). Infrared hand temperature measurements during the 1986 330K Iditaski cross-country ski race. *Biofeedback and Self-Regulation, 12,* 150.

Kau, M. L., & Fischer, J. (1974). Self-modification of exercise behavior. *Journal of Behavior Therapy and Experimental Psychiatry, 5,* 213–214.

Keefe, F. J., & Blumenthal, J. A. (1980). The life fitness program: A behavioral approach to making exercise a habit. *Journal of Behavior Therapy and Experimental Psychiatry, 11,* 31–34.

Keele, S. W. (1973). *Attention and human performance.* Pacific Palisades: Goodyear.

King, A. C., & Frederickson, L. W. (1984). Low-cost strategies for increasing exercise behavior: Relapse prevention training and social support. *Behavior Modification, 8,* 3–21.

Kirschenbaum, D. S. (1984). Self-regulation and sport psychology: Nurturing an emerging symbiosis. *Journal of Sport Psychology, 6,* 59–183.

Kirschenbaum, D. S., & Bale, R. M. (1984). Cognitive-behavioral skills in golf: Applications to golf and speculations about soccer. In W. F. Straub & J. M. Williams (Eds.), *Cognitive sport psychology* (pp. 275–288). Lansing, NY: Sport Science Associates.

Kirschenbaum, D. S., Johnson, W. G., & Stalonas, P. M. (1987). *Treating childhood and adolescent obesity.* New York: Pergamon Press.

Kirschenbaum, D. S., Ordman, A. M., Tomarken, A. J., & Holtzbauer, R. (1982). Effects of differential self-monitoring and level of mastery on sports performance: Brain power bowling. *Cognitive Therapy and Research, 6,* 335–342.

Kirschenbaum, D. S., Tomarken, A. J., & Humprey, L. L. (1985). Affect and adult self-regulation. *Journal of Personality and Social Psychology, 48,* 509–523.

Kirschenbaum, D. S., Wittrock, D. A., Smith, R. J., & Monstron, W. (1984). Criticism inoculation training: Concept in search of strategy. *Journal of Sport Psychology, 6,* 77–93.

Landers, D. M. (1988). Improving motor skills. In D. Drukman & J. A. Swets (Eds.), *Enhancing Human Performance: Issues, Theories, and Techniques.* Washington, DC: National Academy Press.

Landers, D. M., Petruzzello, S. J., Salazar, W., Crews, D. J., Kubitz, K. A., Gannon, T. L., & Han, M. (1991). The influence of electrocortical biofeedback on performance in pre-elite athletes. *Medicine and Science in Sports and Exercise, 23,* 123–129.

Larkin, K. T., Manuck, S. B., & Kasprowicz, A. L. (1990). The effect of feedback-assisted reduction in heart rate reactivity on video-game performance. *Biofeedback and Self-Regulation, 15,* 285–303.

Lawrence, G. H., & Johnson, L. C. (1977). Biofeedback and performance. In G. E. Schwartz & J. Beatty (Eds.), *Biofeedback theory and research* (pp. 163–179). New York: Academic Press.

Lloyd, A. J. (1972). Auditory EMG feedback during sustained submaximum contraction. *The Research Quarterly, 43,* 39–46.

Lucca, J. A., & Recchuiti, S. J. (1983). Effect of electromyographic biofeedback on an isometric strengthening program. *Physical Therapy, 63,* 200–203.

Mace, R., Eastman, C., & Carroll, D. (1987). The effects of stress-inoculation training on gymnastic performance on the pommelled horse: A case study. *Behavioral Psychotherapy, 15,* 272–279.

Magnusson, E. (1976). The effects of controlled muscle tension on performance and learning of heart rate control. *Biological Psychology, 4,* 81–92.

Martin, J. E., Dubbert, P. M., Katell, A. D., Thompson, J. K., Raczynski, J. R., Lake, M., Smith, P. O., Webster, J. S., Sikora, T., & Cohen, R. E. (1984). Behavioral control of exercise in sedentary adults: Studies 1 through 6. *Journal of Consulting and Clinical Psychology, 52,* 795—811.

McGlynn, G. H., Laughlin, N. T., & Filios, S. P. (1979). The effect of electromyographic feedback on EMG activity and pain in the quadriceps muscle group. *Journal of Sports Medicine and Physical Fitness, 19,* 237–244.

McGlynn, G. H., Laughlin, N. T., & Rowe, V. (1979). Effects of electromyographic feedback and static stretching on artificially induced muscle soreness. *American Journal of Physical Medicine, 58,* 139–148.

Meyers, A., & Schleser, R. (1980). A cognitive behavioral intervention for improving basketball performance. *Journal of Sport Psychology, 2,* 69–73.

Meyers, A., Schleser, R., & Okwumabua, T. (1982). A cognitive behavioral intervention for improving basketball performance. *Research Quarterly for Exercise and Sport, 53,* 344–347.

Morgan, W. P., Horstman, D. H., Cymerman, A., & Stokes, J. (1983). Facilitation of physical performance by means of a cognitive strategy. *Cognitive Therapy and Research, 7,* 251–264.

Morgan, W. P., & Pollack, M. L. (1977). Psychologic characterization of the elite distance runner. *Annals of the New York Academy of Sciences, 301,* 382–403.

Moses, J., Clemens, W. J., & Brener, J. (1986). Bidirectional voluntary heart rate control during static muscular exercise: Metabolic and respiratory correlates. *Psychophysiology, 23,* 510–520.

Nelson, R. O., Haynes, S. C., Spong, R. T., Jarret, R. B., & McKnight, D. L. (1983). Self-reinforcement: Appealing misnomer or effective mechanism? *Behavior Research and Therapy, 21,* 557–566.

Nideffer, R. M. (1976). *The inner athlete.* New York: Thomas Y. Crowell.

Oldridge, N. B., & Jones, N. L. (1983). Improving patient compliance in cardiac rehabilitation: Effects of written agreement and self-monitoring. *Journal of Cardiac Rehabilitation, 3,* 257–262.

Peper, E., & Schmid, A. (1983). The use of electrodermal biofeedback for peak performance training. *Somatics, 4,* 16–18.

Perski, A., & Engel, B. T. (1980). The role of behavioral conditioning in the cardiovascular adjustment of exercise. *Biofeedback and Self-Regulation, 5,* 91–104.

Perski, A., Tzankoff, S. P., & Engel, B. T. (1985). Central control of cardiovascular adjustments to exercise. *Journal of Applied Physiology, 58,* 431–435.

Rejeski, W. J., & Kenney, E. A. (1988). *Fitness motivation: Preventing participant dropout.* Champaign, IL: Life Enhancement Publications.

Rushall, B. S., Hall, M., Roux, L., Sasseville, J., & Rushall, A. C. (1988). Effects of three types of thought content instructions on skiing performance. *The Sport Psychologist, 2,* 283–297.

Saar, D., Ariel, G. B., Penny, M. A., & Saar, I. (1982). Strength study: Comparison between computerized exercise machine and existing modalities of weight training equipment. *Medicine and Science in Sports (Abs.), 14,* 153.

Schmidt, R. A. (1988). *Motor control and learning: A behavioral emphasis* (2nd ed.). Champaign, IL: Human Kinetics.

Schomer, G. (1986). Mental strategies and the perception of effort of marathon runners. *International Journal of Sport Psychology, 17,* 41–59.

Schwartz, G. E. (1977a). Biofeedback and the self-management of disregulation disorders. In R. B. Stuart (Ed.), *Behavioral self-management: Strategies, techniques and outcome* (pp. 49–70). New York: Brunner/Mazel.

Schwartz, G. E. (1977b). Psychosomatic disorders and biofeedback: A psychobiological model of disregulation. In J. D. Maser & M. E. P. Seligman (Eds.), *Psychopathology: Experimental models* (pp. 270–307). San Francisco: Freeman.

Schwartz, G. E. (1978). Psychobiological foundations of psychotherapy and behavior change. In S. L. Garfield & A. E. Bergin (Eds.), *Handbook of psychotherapy and behavior change (2nd ed.,* pp. 63–100). New York: Wiley.

Schwartz, G. E. (1979). Disregulation and systems theory: A biobehavioral framework for biofeedback and behavioral medicine. In N. Birbaumer & H. D. Kimmel (Eds.), *Biofeedback and self-regulation* (pp. 19–48). New York: Erlbaum.

Sime, W. E. (1985). Physiological perception: The key to peak performance in athletic competition. In J. H. Sandweiss & S. L. Wolf (Eds.), *Biofeedback in sport science* (pp. 33–62). New York: Plenum Press.

Spink, K. S., & Longhurst, K. (1986). Cognitive strategies and swimming performances: An exploratory study. *Australian Journal of Science and Medicine in Sport, 18,* 9–13.

Tsukomoto, S. (1979). *The effects of EMG biofeedback assisted relaxation on sport competition anxiety.* Unpublished master's thesis, University of Western Ontario.

Von Bertalanffy, L. (1968). *General systems theory.* New York: Braziller.

Weinberg, R., Bruya, L., Garland, H., & Jackson, A. (1990). Effect of goal difficulty and positive reinforcement on endurance performance. *Journal of Sport and Exercise Psychology, 12,* 144–156.

Weinberg, R. S., Jackson, A., & Gould, D. (1984). Effect of association, dissociation and positive self-talk on endurance performance. *Canadian Journal of Applied Sport Science, 9,* 25–32.

Wrisberg, C. A., & Anshel, M. H. (1989). The effect of cognitive stategies on the free throw shooting performance of young athletes. *The Sport Psychologist, 3,* 95–104.

Wysocki, T., Hall, G., Iwata, B., & Riordan, M. (1979). Behavioral management of exercise: Contracting for aerobic points. *Journal of Applied Behavior Analysis, 12,* 55–64.

Zaichkowski, L. D., & Fuchs, C. Z. (1988). Biofeedback applications in exercise and athletic performance. In K. Pandolf (Ed.), *Exercise and sport science reviews* (pp. 381–422). New York: Macmillan.

Zaichkowski, L. D., Dorsey, J. A., & Mulholland, T. B. (1979). The effects of biofeedback assisted systematic desensitization in the control of anxiety and performance. In M. Vanek (Ed.), *IV svetovy kongress, ISSP* (pp. 809–812). Prague: Olympia.

SOCIAL INFLUENCES

·26·

SOCIALIZATION AND SPORT

Jay Coakley

INTRODUCTION: SOCIALIZATION DEFINED

Definitions of socialization vary by discipline and theoretical framework, but in general, socialization has been conceptualized as a dual process of interaction and development through which human beings learn (1) who they are and how they are connected to the social worlds in which they live, and (2) the orientations used as a basis for individual behavior and group life in those worlds. On the one hand, socialization involves the interaction through which an individual enters a particular social world; on the other hand, it involves the development of an individual's understanding of the structure and dynamics of social life and the orientations used by others as they participate in social life.

Socialization occurs explicitly through relationships and implicitly through observation, inference, modeling, and trial and error (McCall & Simmons, 1982). Since socialization deals with the entire process of becoming human, scholars in each of the behavioral and social sciences have focused on different dimensions of the overall process. Although disciplinary overlap exists in socialization theory and research, there are consistent differences between the work done by psychologists, sociologists, and anthropologists.

DISCIPLINARY APPROACHES TO SOCIALIZATION: A BRIEF OVERVIEW

Throughout most of the twentieth century, especially since the 1920s, "socialization" has attracted the attention of psychologists, sociologists, and anthropologists. Scholars in each of these disciplines have been concerned with the relationship between the individual and society, and with identifying the relative extent to which human development is grounded in biological nature or social relationships and experiences. Conceptual definitions of socialization have varied by discipline, and socialization theory and research has a unique history in each (Clausen, 1968).

In Psychology

Socialization has been a common topic of concern among developmental and social psychologists. Various theories have guided their work (Goldstein, 1980). Freudian theorists have conceptualized socialization in terms of the formation of personality structure and psychosexual development. Learning theorists have conceptualized socialization in terms of classical conditioning, operant conditioning, and the processes of imitation, modeling, and identification. Cognitive theorists have conceptualized socialization in terms of developmental stages tied to a combination of maturation and social experiences. Both learning theories and cognitive theories have generated precise hypotheses testable through controlled experimental research. This research has focused on very specific and limited dimensions of the socialization process and its consequences.

According to Clausen (1968), the author of a widely respected review of socialization research, psychologists "have been especially concerned with establishing the nature of the processes mediating between socialization practices and child rearing, such as identification, the development of conscience, stages or dynamics of cognitive structuring, and the shaping of motivational dispositions" (p. 50). Often, research subjects have been children, and there has been a heavy focus on educational methods and experiences in much of the research. Socialization outcomes among adults have received relatively little attention. Compared to work in other disciplines, the work of psychologists has involved more meticulous efforts to operationalize and validate concepts, replicate studies, and develop systematic theory. Therefore, socialization theory and research in psychology tends to be highly integrated and focused.

Much of the socialization research in psychology has been criticized for being based on rigid and overly mechanistic conceptions of the individual and human development (Baumrind, 1980). This criticism has encouraged longitudinal studies done in naturalistic settings where relationships (such as the family) and the individual, rather than the variable, are used as the units of analysis. These studies are less integrated and focused than has been the case with tightly controlled experimental studies, but they have added considerably to an understanding of the actual behaviors and experiences involved in socialization.

In Sociology

Socialization theory and research in sociology has been less integrated and less focused than in psychology. Methodological approaches including the measurement of concepts and data collection techniques have been more diversified, and the range of research issues has been broader. Sociologists have studied the relationship between socialization and (1) systems of social control, (2) identity and the development of self, (3) role selection and role performance through the life cycle, and (4) social structural factors (such as social class) as they mediate the learning of values and orientations (Clausen, 1968).

Until recently, most of the socialization literature in sociology involved efforts to determine the ways in which human beings were shaped by the influence and constraints of external or systemic forces. Socialization was seen as a process of internalization in which individuals were "shaped" and "molded" by "society" in deterministic ways (Wentworth, 1980). Research tended to focus on the outcomes produced in those people "being socialized," and the effectiveness of socialization was assessed in terms of the extent to which normative conformity and adjustment were associated with taking on and performing social roles in existing sets of relationships and social structures (Inkeles, 1969). Studies frequently involved the selection of a particular socialization outcome as a dependent variable and a selection of two or more independent variables, the effects of which could be relatively and/or jointly assessed. Research subjects in these studies were seen as passive conformists responding to forces in their social environments, and socialization was conceptualized as the social learning that occurred in response to these forces. In other words, research was predicated on a "socialization-as-internalization" model (Wentworth, 1980).

The problem with this socialization-as-internalization approach was that the actual content and dynamics of the interaction between individuals and those through whom the existing social world was presented to the individual were generally excluded from the analysis. This led socialization theory and research to overlook the extent to which socialization involved a process of interaction associated with an individual's entry into a sphere of the social world, and the extent to which that interaction was characterized by tension, misunderstanding, resistance, negotiation,

decision-making, and, occasionally, rejection of the sphere of the social world itself (Wentworth, 1980). The autonomy, creative potential, self-reflective abilities, and identities of individuals as active agents within the social world were seldom considered, nor were the dynamics of control and power relations associated with the process of entering social worlds. In response to this criticism, an increasing number of researchers have used a "socialization-as-interaction" approach grounded in a combination of the following assumptions (Wentworth, 1980):

1. that human beings are active, self-reflective decision-makers whose behaviors are grounded in their definitions of situations,
2. that socialization is a never-ending process through which human beings develop a sense of who they are and how they are connected to the world around them,
3. that social roles and the identities associated with those roles are socially constructed during the socialization process itself,
4. that socialization reflects the self-conceptions, goals, and social resources of *all* those involved,
5. that social groups and societies are created through the relationships human beings form with one another, and that those groups and societies are the sites of control and power relations that in turn influence individual behavior and social relationships.

In summary, socialization theory and research in sociology has varied with assumptions about the extent to which the individual is actively involved in the process of cultural production. Research based on the socialization-as-internalization approach has been least problematic in studies of socialization among infants and young children. This is because infants and young children possess relatively few social resources, and because power mediates an individual's participation in the socialization process; however, there is a growing awareness of reciprocity and resistance even in relationships between young children and adults. Research based on the socialization-as-internalization approach has been very problematic in studies of adolescents and adults, who have social resources and often exert considerable power in the socialization process and in the overall process of cultural production. For this reason, an increasing number of studies done since the early 1960s have been based on the socialization-as-interaction approach (Musgrave, 1987; Wentworth, 1980). These studies have seldom involved hypothesis testing designed to produce statements of "cause and effect" between variables. Instead, they have involved the use of qualitative methods (in-depth interviews and/or observations) designed to (1) uncover the meanings underlying the behaviors and choices made by human beings as they actively enter, participate in, and shape the contexts in which they live their lives, and (2) explicate the dynamics of the control and power relations involved in the process of socialization.

In Anthropology

Among anthropologists, the term "socialization" has generally been used to refer to "the process of transmitting human culture," and the term "enculturation" has been used to refer to "the process of transmitting a particular culture" (Williams, 1983, p. *xiii*). Theory and research in anthropology has usually focused on the latter; major concerns have been with the relationship between culture and personality, child rearing and patterns of cultural conditioning, and gender roles across cultures. Research in each of these areas has contributed to the body of socialization literature across disciplines. Anthropological research has been grounded in a combination of theoretical frameworks used in both psychology and sociology, and it has reflected similar concerns about the nature of the individual-society relationship. Using ethnographic methods, and gathering data in cross-national and cross-cultural settings, anthropologists have qualified and extended theory and research in both psychology and sociology.

SOCIALIZATION AND SPORT

Providing an overview of the literature on socialization and sport is a challenge. Even though most of the research on this topic dates back only to the mid-1960s, studies have focused on numerous questions and issues. Those doing the studies have utilized a wide range of theoretical perspectives and methodological approaches from both sociology and psychology, and they have drawn on a diversified body of work on the relationship between psychosocial development and play, games, and sports. Furthermore, socialization itself has been conceptualized in different ways. The result is a body of literature characterized by considerable diversity and some degree of confusion.

This chapter is certainly not the first comprehensive overview of the literature on socialization and sport. Since socialization has been viewed as a central topic of concern among social scientists who study sport, it has evoked numerous reviews and critiques (Allison, 1982; Coakley, 1986a, 1987; Fishwick & Greendorfer, 1987; Greendorfer, 1978, 1979a, 1983, 1987; Greendorfer & Bruce, 1989; Hasbrook, 1989; Helanko, 1957; Loy & Ingham, 1973; Kenyon, 1970; Kenyon & McPherson, 1973; McCormack & Chalip, 1988; McPherson, 1981, 1986; McPherson & Brown, 1988; McPherson, Curtis, & Loy, 1989; Nixon, 1981, 1990; Sage, 1980a; Snyder, 1970; Snyder & Spreitzer, 1989; *SIRLS*, 1989; Stevenson, 1975, 1985; Theberge, 1984).

The two most influential "early" references on socialization and sport were published in 1973: (1) *Becoming Involved in Physical Activity and Sport,* by Gerald Kenyon and Barry McPherson, and (2) *Play, Games, and Sport in the Psychosocial Development of Children and Youth,* by John Loy and Alan Ingham. In each of these papers there was a general explanation of socialization theory and research, and a presentation of a conceptual/theoretical framework intended to guide subsequent work on (1) so-

cialization *into* sport roles, and (2) socialization *through* play, games, and sport, respectively. Since 1973, most of the work on *socialization into sport* has attempted to identify (1) the characteristics and past experiences of sport participants, and (2) the relative influence of various agents of socialization on those who participate in sports and those who do not. Most of the work on *socialization through sport* has attempted to determine differences in the values and behaviors of those who have participated in particular types of competitive sport programs for some length of time as compared with age peers who have not participated in those programs. Additional research has sought to identify factors leading to and associated with dropping out of competitive sport participation.

Excellent critiques of much of the research on socialization, as well as recommendations for future research, are included in a number of recent papers (Fishwick & Greendorfer, 1987; Greendorfer & Bruce, 1989; Hasbrook, 1989; McPherson, 1986; Nixon, 1990). The overview of socialization and sport presented in this chapter will build on recent critiques provided by others, and focus primarily on the research in which sociological frameworks have been used. There will be a review of research on socialization *into* sport followed by a review of research on socialization *through* sport. Research using psychological frameworks will, for the most part, not be reviewed. Part of the reason for this is that research in sport psychology has seldom focused explicitly and directly on socialization; another reason is that research on skills acquisition, sport performance, and psychological attributes of individual athletes (personality, anxiety, self-esteem, and perceptions of personal competence, motivation, aggressiveness, moral development, and personal adjustment to success and failure, among other things) is extensively reviewed in other chapters in Parts II, III, & IV.

RESEARCH ON SOCIALIZATION INTO SPORT

In their 1973 paper, Kenyon and McPherson outlined a "social role—social system" model to guide analyses of the social learning process associated with entering and performing "sport roles" (including the roles of "elite" and "sub-elite" performers, sport consumers and producers, and sport leaders). The model identified the following sets of factors to be simultaneously included in analyses:

1. the psychological and physical attributes of the person "being socialized";
2. the encouragement and rewards provided by others, especially significant others, and the opportunities for those "being socialized" to "rehearse" various sport roles;
3. the social systems (such as family, peer group, school, and community) in which those "being socialized" were exposed to and influenced by general values, norms, and orientations.

Although Kenyon and McPherson emphasized the dynamic nature of the socialization process when they outlined their model, they never explicitly discussed the ways in which individuals "being socialized" might become active, creative, and even resistent agents within the socialization process, or how the dynamics of socialization were related to individuals' identities or conceptions of self. This oversight has led to recent discussions about whether the social role–social system model is characterized by social determinism which precludes a consideration of individual autonomy in studies of socialization (Theberge, 1984), or whether research based on the model has simply failed to utilize research designs and methodologies that can capture the dynamism implicit in the model (Fishwick Greendorfer, 1987; Greendorfer, 1989; Hasbrook, 1989).

Apart from the discussion of this issue, there is little doubt that the social role–social system model has inspired considerable research on the ways in which the learning of sport roles is related to encouragement and reinforcement coming through relationships with significant others in the social systems of family, peer group, and school. Most of this research has involved the use of surveys in which athletes, primarily young, white, male, athletes in elite, competitive programs, have been asked to recall their histories of participation in sports, the events surrounding their participation, and the influential people in their sport lives. Despite the limitations of this methodology, these studies of socialization into sport led to the following conclusions:

1. Participation in sport roles is positively related to the amount of social support coming from significant others (Furst, 1989; Greendorfcr, 1977; Higginson, 1985; Sage, 1980b; Snyder, & Spreitzer, 1976; Weiss & Knoppers, 1982).
2. The relative influence of various significant others (e.g., father, mother, siblings, teachers, coaches, friends, peers) and the extent and type of encouragement received in particular social systems (e.g., family, peer group, school, and community) vary for "athletes" and "nonathletes" by *gender* (Fagot, 1984; Greendorfer, 1977, 1979a, 1979b; Greendorfer & Lewko, 1978; Lewko & Ewing, 1980; Sage, 1980b; Snyder & Spreitzer, 1973, 1978), *socio-economic status* (Greendorfer, 1978; Hasbrook, 1986a, 1987; Loy, 1972; Watson, 1977), *race* (Greendorfer & Ewing, 1981; Harris & Hunt, 1984; Oliver, 1980), *age* (Butcher, 1985; Rudman, 1989; Snyder, 1972), *place of residence (rural vs. urban)* (Carlson, 1988), *type of sport program (community vs. school sponsored)* (Butcher, 1985), and *culture* (Greendorfer, Blinde, & Pelligrini, 1986; Yamaguchi, 1984).
3. Socialization does involve reciprocity or bi-directional effects in the sense that children's involvement in sport creates responses among adults who sponsor and encourage that involvement (Berlage, 1982; Hasbrook, 1986b; Snyder & Purdy, 1982).

However, apart from these general findings, there is considerable confusion about the relative influence of different

socializing agents during various stages in the life cycle, and for athletes and nonathletes from different backgrounds and with different characteristics. Furthermore, in nearly all these studies, the percent of variance in sport involvement explained by socializing agents is very low (Weiss and Knoppers, 1982), and there is no *detailed* information about the nature of the interaction that occurs in connection with the socialization process.

The existence of this confusion, and the small amount of variance explained, have evoked discussion among those interested in socialization into sport. Some people have attributed the confusion and unexplained variance to methodological factors characteristic in much of the research (Fishwick & Greendorfer, 1987; Greendorfer, 1989; Hasbrook, 1989). For example, samples have been biased and limited; variables such as "significant other influence," "the degree of sport involvement," and "encouragement" have been inconsistently operationalized across studies; and sophisticated multivariate analyses have rarely been used. In light of this critique, there has been a tendency to suggest that confusion will begin to disappear, and the percent of variance explained will begin to increase when (1) research design and data gathering methods become standardized, (2) more variables are included in analyses, and (3) samples are drawn to include nonathletes as well as athletes, athletes at different levels of competition in different sports, and respondents from as many different backgrounds as possible.

Among others, however, confusion and unexplained variance are seen as the inevitable consequences of the use of the social role–social system model; these people have tended to utilize different conceptual approaches in studies of the sport socialization process. Each of these alternative conceptual approaches is based on the general assumptions underlying a "socialization-as-interaction" model. Some people in the sociology of sport have used *interactionist* approaches in which the social construction of identity, the dynamics of participation decisions, and the meanings underlying sport participation are the primary foci of analyses (Curry & Weiss, 1989; Donnelly & Young, 1988; Faulkner, 1974; Scott, 1982; Stevenson, 1982, 1990a, 1990b; White & Coakley, 1986). Others have used *critical theory* and *cultural studies* approaches in which relational issues and the connection between sport practices (including patterns of individual involvement and participation) and processes of subordination and oppression are the primary foci of analyses (Birrell, 1989; Deem, 1986; Foley, 1990; Gruneau, 1975, 1978; Hargreaves, 1986; Messner, 1990a; Robins, 1982; Scraton, 1987; Talbot, 1988b; Whitson, 1990; Willis, 1982).

When "socialization-as-interaction" approaches have been used directly (as is the case for research based on interactionist frameworks), or assumed as an underlying conceptual foundation for research (as is sometimes the case for research based on critical theory or cultural studies), there has been a tendency to emphasize that sport involvement is a process involving various combinations of the following:

1. Participation choices made by individuals
2. The formation of an "athlete identity" within the context of a particular group of sport participants
3. The continued reaffirmation of that identity through social relationships
4. Struggles over the unequal distribution of participation opportunities and the determination of how participation itself will be defined and organized
5. Social-historical processes of dominance and subordination related to race, class, and gender

Socialization research based on interactionist theoretical frameworks has generally used qualitative data collection methods such as observation, participant observation, and in-depth interviews. Findings have been presented in terms of the stages and decision-making that occur throughout the process of sport involvement. In some cases, involvement has been conceptualized as a "career" and studied in terms of the changing orientations, identities, commitments, activities, and relationships of individual participants over time (Faulkner, 1974; Prus, 1984; Scott, 1982; Stevenson, 1982). When sport involvement has been conceptualized as a career, analysis has focused on phases in the involvement process including initial involvement, the continuation of involvement, disinvolvement (rather than "drop-out" or "retirement"), and reinvolvement. Each of these "phases" have been approached through accounts given by the individuals involved. However, all phases have seldom been explored together in any single study of the involvement process.

Research based on interactionist models does not reflect the assumption that human beings "get socialized into sport"; socialization is not viewed in terms of an "instantaneous conversion" model. Instead, it is based on the assumption that human beings become involved in sport through a series of shifting, back-and-forth decisions made within the structural, ideological, and cultural context of their social worlds. Furthermore, interactionists are more apt to be sensitive to events leading up to participation decisions, and interactionists assume that continued involvement is the result of repeated decisions grounded in ever-changing experiences and contexts that either reaffirm or challenge past decisions and patterns of behavior. In other words, sport participation is not a "once and for all" thing to be explained through traditional causal analyses of "participation" and "nonparticipation." This is because sport involvement unfolds on a decision-by-decision basis in the lives of human beings, and decisions about participation cannot be separated from the contexts in which they are made. Therefore, those using interactionist approaches try to uncover and understand the decision-making processes underlying involvement and explain how those decisions are related to the situations in which they were made. The general assumption is that initial participation and continued participation in sport are just as problematic as so-called "nonparticipation" and "dropping out" of sport.

One of the important findings in the studies using interactionist approaches is that identity formation related to sport involvement occurs over time and depends on a number of processes, including acquisition of knowledge about a sport, becoming associated with a sport group, learning the values and perspectives of the sport group, and earning the acceptance of those in the group so that one's identity as a participant is affirmed and reaffirmed over time (Donnelly & Young, 1988). In other words, becoming involved in sport involves a process of identity construction and confirmation; involvement is *not* simply an outcome of exposure to encouragement, reinforcement, and opportunities for "role rehearsal" provided through relationships with significant others operating within social systems characterized by interrelated sets of norms and roles.

Another important finding in research based on an interactionist theoretical framework is that the process of becoming involved in sport among current elite athletes was initiated through a process of recruitment in which first-time participation experiences were sponsored, coerced, or solicited by people who were important in the athletes' lives (Stevenson, 1990a, 1990b). Continued involvement and the selection of a particular sport was then based on a combination of the athletes' assessments of two factors: (1) the potential for success relative to other possible choices, and (2) the people associated with the sport in question. A deepening of involvement or a "commitment" to participation occurred to the extent that the athletes (1) established "entanglements" or ties to a "web of personal relationships" associated with participation, (2) developed a sense of obligation or responsibility to maintain involvement as a member of this "web of relationships," and (3) formed a reputation and identity that was defined as favorable and was consistently confirmed by peers, parents, coaches, or others associated with or seen as important by the athletes. This entire process was driven by the athletes' "conscious, self-reflexive work in developing desirable role-identities and in ensuring their confirmation" (Stevenson, 1990b, p. 250). The point of this study is that involvement is never established in any "final" sense. The social support needed to continually confirm a person's identity as an athlete cannot be taken for granted; and the person is always able to revise decisions about participation or about the commitment of resources to participation. The withdrawal of social support, decisions to cease participation, or shifts in the way resources are allocated may lead to a disengagement from active participation at any point in time.

The problematic nature of decisions to participate in particular sport programs and to maintain that participation over time has been outlined by White and Coakley (1986) in a study of sport participation patterns among adolescents in England. Based on an interactionist approach, in-depth interviews were conducted with 60 young people. The data indicated that decisions to become involved in any sport activity were tied to a complex set of considerations mediated by important social relationships, and constrained by access to resources and by general political, economic, social, and cultural forces. Decisions were often grounded in the young people's considerations of the implications of those decisions for extending control over their lives, for becoming adults, and for developing and displaying personal competence. Gender and socioeconomic status were directly related to the control young people had or perceived they had over their lives. But those young people did not make decisions about sport participation in reaction to any particular factor or set of factors; they did not see sport as a separate sphere of activity in their lives. Instead, they saw it as an activity related in varying degrees to how they conceptualized themselves and what they wanted to do with their lives as they moved from adolescence to adulthood. Identity was a primary factor in their decision-making processes, and simply being an athlete was not an identity that most of the young people perceived as satisfactory or satisfying in light of their overall life goals at this point in their development. Sport participation was seen positively to the extent that it was tied to the process of becoming independent, autonomous, and competent adults within their social worlds.

The White and Coakley (1986) study also calls into question the traditional methodological tactic of dividing research samples into "participants," "nonparticipants," and "dropouts" on the basis of whether respondents are currently involved in a particular sport program. Since sport participation comes in many different forms, and since participation is grounded in a self-reflective decision-making process through which people purposively and intentionally choose to become involved in an activity at varying levels of commitment over time, it is difficult to make clear-cut distinctions between who is a participant and who is not. White & Coakley discovered that young people who had been labeled as nonparticipants and dropouts because they were not currently participating in certain targeted sport programs, or because they had recently ceased participation, were often actively involved in other physical activities and sports on an informal level, or in programs not known to those who had originally labeled them nonparticipants or dropouts. Furthermore, it was found that involvement and commitment to involvement shifted over time depending on new opportunities and changes in young people's lives and self-conceptions.

When sport participation has been approached through critical theory or cultural studies, there has been an emphasis on the extent to which individuals and groups create and negotiate their involvement. Socialization is not the primary focus of this research; instead, it is the struggle associated with determination of what sport will mean in the lives of particular groups or categories of people. Although people using these frameworks focus much of their attention on control and power relations, their work tends to reflect a long tradition of research that has documented and called attention to the unequal distribution of participation opportunities related to gender (Acosta & Carpenter, 1985, 1986, 1990; Boutilier & SanGiovanni, 1983; Coakley, 1990; Greendorfer, 1983; U.S. Commission on Civil Rights, 1980), race and ethnicity (Coakley, 1990; Edwards, 1973; Lapchick, 1984), socioeconomic status (Collins, 1972; Gruneau, 1975; Loy, 1972; Pavia, 1973), age (Curtis & White, 1984; Harootyan, 1982; McPherson, 1984; Rudman, 1989), and

sexual orientation (Lenskyj, 1986; Palzkill, 1990; Pronger, 1990).

In conclusion, research on socialization into sport and sport participation in general is becoming increasingly diversified, the social role-social system approach is being reassessed in light of two decades of studies, and the "socialization-as-interaction" approach (Wentworth, 1980) is becoming more widely utilized in various forms. At this point there will be no attempt to provide an exhaustive set of recommendations for future research. This task has been recently undertaken by McPherson (1986) and others (Hasbrook, 1989; Greendorfer & Bruce, 1989; Nixon, 1990). Their recommendations are comprehensive and, as of this writing, still up to date.

SOCIALIZATION THROUGH SPORT

Between 1950 and 1980 there were many studies of socialization *through* sport. Researchers were eager to explore possible connections between sport participation and participants' general attitudes and behaviors. Studies often tested hypotheses based on popular beliefs about the social developmental consequences of sport participation. It was hoped that science could shed light on questions about whether sport participation actually contributed to the development of positive character traits, turned young people into better students and more successful adults, promoted conformity, reduced delinquency rates, gave rise to conservative social and political attitudes, and provided a basis for strong achievement orientations and moral development. Most of the research on socialization through sport has focused on children and adolescents, although there have been some investigations of collegiate and elite amateur athletes. Adults have seldom been studied, possibly because researchers have assumed that adults are no longer in a "formative" stage of development, or because they have assumed that adult lives are so complex that the effects of sport participation are minimal compared to the socialization effects of other experiences.

Since 1980 the number of studies dealing with the socialization consequences of sport participation has declined. According to Stevenson (1985), this has occurred for two reasons:

1. There was a long record of inconsistent findings, and most studies had found no significant socialization effects of sport participation.
2. Research priorities increasingly became focused on how to promote sport involvement, especially among young people with potential for becoming world-class athletes.

In other words, with some notable exceptions (to be discussed below), many sport sociologists no longer anticipated being able to identify "socialization effects" of sport participation, and they became more concerned with pragmatic questions about the origins of sport participation and the factors related to the development of sport skills, especially top-level sport skills. But despite some inconsistent findings and recent changes in priorities, it is useful to review the research that has been done on socialization through sport, and the critiques of that work.

In 1973, John Loy and Alan Ingham published a comprehensive review of theory and research on the connection between psychosocial development and participation in play, games, and sports. Specifically, they focused on how participation in such activities might be related to the following:

1. The process through which children learn to "fit into" their society by acquiring traits and orientations compatible with dominant social values
2. The development of masculinity and femininity
3. General processes of social mobility, including educational achievement and the development of educational aspirations
4. The dialectical processes underlying the search for self-identity among young people
5. Moral development and attitudes toward fair play and winning

Loy and Ingham closed their review with the following conclusion:

. . . socialization via play, games, and sport is a complex process having both manifest and latent functions, and involving functional and dysfunctional, intended and unintended consequences. (p. 298)

However, before stating this conclusion, they were also careful to point out that as of 1973, neither theory nor data had established the existence of any specific socialization consequences inherently tied to the experience of participation in games or sports. Loy and Ingham were clearly aware of widespread rhetoric heralding the supposed socialization benefits of sport participation, and they intended to encourage their colleagues to move beyond the rhetoric and carefully investigate the conditions under which various types of learning might be associated with particular types of games and game experiences. They also provided a conceptual framework for such investigations. Among other things, their framework emphasized the need for a careful analysis of the structure and interaction that occurs in various types of games and sports.

Correlational Analyses

Much of the research done before and after the Loy-Ingham review has consisted of atheoretical, correlational analyses. These correlational studies have generally presented statistical comparisons of the characteristics of "athletes" and "nonathletes" in specific sport programs (e.g., interscholastic teams or organized community leagues). However, few of these studies have involved pretest—posttest designs, so researchers have found it difficult to make distinctions between the "socialization effects of par-

ticipation" and "selection effects" ("caused" by the special characteristics and qualities possessed by those who self-select into specific programs and/or pass "selection tests" administered by those who control access to participation for particular reasons).

Furthermore, these correlational studies have often been characterized by poor operational definitions of "sport participation," and based on faulty assumptions about sport and sport experiences. For example, the "participation histories" of subjects have seldom been considered. For the most part, duration of participation, commitment to participation, and participation in other sport programs, informal games, or related physical activities have not been taken into account when classifying research subjects as either "athletes" or "nonathletes," nor have they been controlled in statistical analyses. Additionally, most of those doing correlational analyses have grounded their research in two sets of faulty assumptions (McCormack & Chalip, 1988). First, they have assumed that sport participation involves a unique and consistent set of human experiences, that these experiences are similarly shared by everyone in sport, and that these experiences facilitate or cause identifiable changes in the characteristics of sport participants. Second, they have assumed that athletes as a group *passively* internalize specific norms and "moral lessons" through their sport experiences, and that these "character-shaping" experiences are not readily available to people outside of sport. When these assumptions are made, researchers tend to overlook the following:

1. Athletes will have different experiences across different teams, sports, and situations.
2. Athletes will interpret the same experiences in different ways due to differences in their relationships with significant others.
3. Athletes at different stages of development will be influenced in different ways by sport experiences and significant others.
4. Athletes will apply their interpretations of sport experiences in different ways to the decisions they make in the rest of their lives, and they will reinterpret the same experiences and apply them to their lives in different ways as they get older.
5. Those who do not participate in organized sports probably have experiences that overlap with those available in sport.

Those undertaking correlational analyses have generally forgotten that the experience of striving to achieve goals within competitive reward structures is available in most adolescent activities sponsored and organized by adults, and therefore, "competitiveness and societal achievement values are learned regardless of one's participation or lack of participation in organized sport" (McCormack & Chalip, 1988, p. 88). This is true for many other "socialization experiences" in the lives of people of all ages.

Despite these theoretical and methodological weaknesses, correlational analyses have made considerable contributions to the body of literature on "socialization effects." In fact, it is worthwhile to review some of these studies as a means of identifying questions and issues that will inform all types of socialization studies in the future. This overview, however, will focus on the variables that have elicited the most attention by researchers in the sociology of sport.

Sport Participation and Academic Achievement and Aspirations. The relationship between interscholastic sport participation and academic achievement and aspirations has received more attention than any socialization-through-sport topic. This is because it has been easy to add questions on sport participation, grades, and future educational goals in quantitative studies of secondary school students, and this has allowed researchers interested in the socialization consequences of sport participation to tap into externally funded studies of large samples of young people. Underlying this research has been the assumption that sport participation offers young people a special set of learning experiences that are positively correlated to academic achievement and academic aspirations in particular.

These studies have generally found that varsity athletes as a group have higher GPAs and higher educational aspirations than those who do not participate on varsity teams. Taken collectively, the dozens of studies of this relationship have indicated that it is most likely to exist under the following conditions:

1. When athletes are "starters" on their teams for more than one year in "major" (i.e., highly visible and publicized) sports (Schafer & Armer, 1968).
2. When student-athletes perceive they have high status among their peers because of sport participation (Spady, 1970).
3. When the "value climate" of the school emphasizes the importance of athletics and athletic achievement (Spreitzer & Pugh, 1973).
4. When participation occurs on varsity teams in United States schools, as opposed to club teams in Canadian community-based programs (Jerome & Phillips, 1971).
5. When athletes come from families in which there is little or no encouragement of academic achievement (Rehberg & Schafer, 1968).
6. When sport participation is coupled with academic support and encouragement from significant others (Hanks, 1979; McElroy, 1979; Otto & Alwin, 1977).
7. When student athletes are white males (Picou, 1978; Wells & Picou, 1980), or girls participating since the time when Title IX was actively enforced in the United States (Snyder & Spreitzer, 1976, 1978).
8. When sport participation is combined with involvement in academic and other extracurricular activities (Hanks & Eckland, 1976; Rehberg & Cohen, 1975).
9. When coaches provide student-athletes with specific types of academic advice and support (Snyder, 1972).

Unfortunately, most of these findings have not been consistently supported across different studies (Hauser & Lueptow, 1978; Melnick, Vanfossen, & Sabo, 1988; SIRLS, 1986, 1988).

After reviewing numerous studies on this topic, one finds that sport participation is positively associated with academic achievement and aspirations only when it somehow alters important relationships in a young person's life. When participation, for whatever reason, leads parents, friends, coaches, counselors, or teachers to take young people more seriously as human beings *and* as students, and give them more *academic* support and encouragement, participation will be associated with positive academic outcomes. Relationships do not seem to change in academically relevant ways when participation occurs outside school sponsored teams, when athletes participate in "minor" sports or are "low-status" substitutes in "major" sports, when athletes are black (and possibly given athletic encouragement to the exclusion of academic encouragement), when athletes are female (whose participation prior to Title IX was not deemed important by many people), and when athletes are in schools where academics are heavily emphasized and rewarded over and above sport performance (which means athletes already receive considerable academic encouragement through important relationships). It should be noted that these conclusions are based on studies of high school student-athletes. They may apply to intercollegiate athletes at the Division III level, but it is likely that athletes in "big-time revenue-generating" sports at the Division I level seldom get "unique" encouragement to give priority to academic matters to the extent that they would then have better academic records (Messner & Goisser, 1982).

Taken collectively, all these correlational analyses suggest that if a person's important social relationships do not change in academically relevant ways as a result of sport participation, there is no relationship between sport participation and academic achievement or aspirations. Relationships seem to be the vehicles for change; and in some cases, sport participation may cause young people to be noticed by those who can make a positive difference in their academic lives. If and how this happens should be explored in future research focusing on the actual process and meaning of involvement in the lives of people of all ages.

Sport Participation and Social/Occupational Mobility. Occupational mobility has also been a popular topic for those doing socialization-through-sport research. Again, much of this research is grounded in the assumption that sport participation leads to experiences that are somehow related to career patterns. However, correlational analyses have generally shown that former athletes as a group have no more or less career success than others from comparable backgrounds, and they don't appear to have any systematic mobility advantage over their peers in similar jobs (cf. Coakley, 1986b). Former athletes have a wide range of career successes and failures. My interpretation of the research on this topic (Braddock, 1980; Dubois, 1978, 1979; Hanks, 1979; Hanks & Eckland, 1976; Hare, 1971; Howell, Miracle, & Rees,

1984; Howell & Picou, 1983; Loy, 1969; Otto & Alwin, 1977; Picou, McCarter, & Howell, 1985; Sack & Theil, 1979; Semyonov, 1984; *SIRLS,* 1990; Spady, 1970; Stevenson, 1976) leads to the conclusion that future research needs to examine the extent to which participation in highly competitive sports is connected with the following:

1. the completion of academic degrees, the development of job-related skills, and/or the extension of knowledge of how the world outside of sport is organized and how it operates;
2. the provision of consistent social, emotional, and material support for *overall* growth and development from close friends and family members;
3. making friends and developing social contacts with people connected to activities and organizations apart from sport;
4. access to material resources and to opportunities to develop the abilities needed to use those resources to create and nurture career opportunities;
5. the expansion of personal and social experiences leading to the development of nonsport identities and an awareness of personal abilities useful in nonsport situations;
6. serious injuries that permanently affect physical well-being or require expensive long-term medical treatment.

These issues are only some of the research topics suggested by correlational analyses of sport participation and occupational mobility. However, at this time, these topics have not been explored in detail. Although it has been suggested that many of the experiences people commonly have in sport do not lead to the development of the skills needed for social mobility and career success (Thomas & Ermler, 1988), future studies are needed to identify specific dimensions of sport experiences that may be integrated into athletes' lives and then serve as links to a person's work life.

Sport Participation and Deviant Behavior. Those interested in the socialization effects of sport participation have also investigated the possibility that participation may "keep young people off the streets," and out of trouble. Correlational analyses have never found higher rates of deviance among athletes than among so-called "nonathletes," and this finding has held up across sports, across societies, for both males and females, and for those from all racial and social class backgrounds (Buhrmann, 1977; Landers & Landers, 1978; Rankin, 1980; Schafer, 1969; Segrave, 1986; Segrave & Chu, 1978; Segrave & Hastad, 1982; Segrave et al., 1985; *SIRLS,* 1987; Thorlindsson, 1989). However, these analyses provide no information on whether these lower rates of deviance are somehow tied to learning experiences occurring within sport itself.

The idea that sport participation directly discourages deviant behavior has not been directly supported in most of this research. However, one study, utilizing a pretest-posttest design, did find that after a six-month experimen-

tal period juvenile delinquents assigned to a *traditional* Tae Kwon Do training course scored lower on delinquency measures than comparable delinquents assigned to a "modern" Tae Kwon Do course, or to a course in which they jogged and played basketball and football (Trulson, 1986). The traditional course involved the explicit teaching of (1) a philosophy of nonviolence, (2) respect for self and others, (3) the importance of fitness and control over self, (4) confidence in physical skills, (5) and a sense of responsibility. These findings suggest that it is possible for carefully organized sport experiences to discourage deviance. Few sport programs in American communities would contain an explicit emphasis on the 5 points Trulson found to be associated with lower scores on delinquency measures, but future research is needed to explore the dynamics of experiences related to deviant behavior and delinquency.

Sport Participation and Political Orientations. During the 1960s and 1970s some sociologists were concerned that sport participation produced compliant, conforming, and politically conservative people unaware of why others were concerned with issues related to social justice, civil rights, and human rights (Norton, 1971; Petrie, 1973; Rehberg & Cohen, 1971; Schafer, 1971). The possibility that sport participation might serve social control functions by deadening political awareness and encouraging compliance with established authority structures also elicited the attention of social scientists committed to bringing about social change (Edwards, 1973; Scott, 1971).

The data collected during this period generally showed that interscholastic and intercollegiate athletes in the United States measured higher on personal and political conservatism and lower on political awareness than their counterparts not involved in sports (Ogilvie & Tutko, 1971; Norton, 1971; Rehberg & Cohen, 1971; Schafer, 1971), although this pattern was not found in Canadian data (Petrie, 1973). More recent data collected from Canadian university students found that athletes were slightly more conservative on social and economic policy issues than nonathletes, but these differences seemed to have no effect on political behavior (Gelinas, 1988). However, none of the authors of these studies was able to attribute any differences between "athletes" and "nonathletes" to specific dimensions of sport experiences. Since the late 1970s, interest in this topic has waned.

Sport Participation and the Development of Individual Traits and Interpersonal Orientations. Only recently have studies explored the relationship between sport participation and moral reasoning and moral development. This research, summarized by Bredemeier and Shields in Chapter 27, indicates that sport is an ambiguous context that may be negatively associated with moral reasoning (Bredemeier, 1985, 1987, 1988; Bredemeier & Shields, 1986; Bredemeier, Shields, Weiss, & Cooper, 1986). The only exception to this is the finding that sport participation may facilitate moral reasoning among children in cases where sport programs have been carefully and explicitly designed and administered to produce changes in moral reasoning (Bredemeier, Weiss, Shields, & Shewchuk, 1986; Romance, 1984).

Other studies suggest that participation in sport decreases prosocial behaviors such as sharing and helping, and increases antisocial behaviors such as aggression (cf. Barnett & Bryan, 1974; Berkowitz, 1972; Dubois, 1986; Gelfand & Hartman, 1978; Kleiber & Roberts, 1981; McGuire & Thomas, 1975). An experimental field study in which reinforcement strategies were used to increase sportspersonlike behaviors among 12-year-old boys on recreational sport teams found that reinforcement seems to be more effective in reducing antisocial behaviors than in promoting prosocial behaviors, and when prosocial behaviors are learned in a particular sport setting, they do not appear to carry over to other settings, even other sport settings (Giebink & McKenzie, 1985). In a similar study, Kleiber and Roberts (1981) reported data suggesting that to the extent "competition is allowed to dominate the interpersonal relationships in children's sports, their potential for actually facilitating the development of prosocial behavior is entirely lost" (p. 121). Kleiber and Roberts (1981) also suggest that when the display of individual traits such as independence, achievement motivation, courage, and perseverance is emphasized in a sport program, the display of prosocial interpersonal orientations such as cooperation, sharing, helping, empathy, and altruism may be undermined, and vice versa. Although this seems to be consistent with laboratory studies of behaviors in other activities (Bryan, 1977), the connection between such behaviors in sport and the development of personal traits and orientations that guide behavior in other settings has not been explored.

Finally, in a longitudinal study of 8-to 10-year-old boys and girls in competitive and instructional soccer leagues, Dubois (1986, 1990) reported changes in the children's value orientations (related to winning, fitness, sportspersonship, importance of relationships) over the course of a season, but also noted that these changes varied by type of program and by gender. Dubois speculated that differences in the patterns of change may have been due to differences in the ways sport experiences are mediated by past experiences, current relationships with adults, and the overall contexts in which sport participation takes place. However, an absence of data on the actual experiences of the children across different activity spheres, the meanings assigned to those experiences by the children, and the ways those experiences are integrated into the lives of the children makes it difficult to explain the ways in which socialization effects occur in connection with sport participation.

Alternatives to Correlational Analyses

Correlational studies of socialization through sport are often grounded in the assumption that those who participate in sport are passively "shaped" by their sport experiences. This assumption has been rejected by those using interactionist and critical theory (including feminist theory and cultural studies) approaches to the study of sport and

sport experiences. Interactionists have been concerned with the ways in which sport participation is connected to the overall process of identity development, and critical theorists have been concerned with the ways in which sport is connected to the production and reproduction of knowledge, meanings, social practices, and power relations at both personal and structural levels. Both interactionists and critical theorists have used interpretive methods of analysis combined with data collected through in-depth interviews and/or detailed observations; case studies and ethnographies have also been used. Although those using these frameworks do not usually deal directly with socialization issues, it is useful to refer to a few studies that focus on socialization through sport.

Gary Alan Fine's (1987) publication *Little League Baseball and Preadolescent Culture* includes an interactionist theoretical framework and data collected through a combination of participant observation and in-depth interviews done over three seasons with 10 Little League teams. Fine discovered that organized youth baseball consisted of a "world of talk" as well as a world of action, and that talk provided young players with cues as to how they were supposed to view themselves and present themselves to others. The adults who administered these programs defined the children as mature to the extent that they mastered the use and behavioral application of "moral talk." In fact, Fine explained that within the context of youth sport teams "successful socialization" among young boys was defined as "learning when to express the moral verities proclaimed by adults, discerning which ones they 'really' mean, and knowing what moral rhetoric to adopt when caught redhanded" (p. 60). Fine also noted that the young players were usually not so naive as to be taken in completely by the moral messages presented by adults, although the ones who were taken in often experienced severe anxiety and guilt.

Fine observed that coaches were the controllers of the moral order in youth sports and that young players evaluated the moral messages presented by coaches in terms of their perceptions of the coaches' competence and fairness. Within the context of adult control, the children themselves were concerned with their self-presentations and the responses those presentations evoked from their peers. Although parents and coaches seemed to be concerned with the "long-term" implications of the children's behaviors, the children themselves were concerned with immediate peer reactions; the children did not care about how they were going to be when they were 30 years old, or even when they were 14! They wanted to be accepted now. According to Fine, the criteria the boys used to determine acceptance within their peer groups and by their teammates reflected adult concerns, but those concerns were "redefined" and transformed into concerns that fit the boys' immediate lives and had "here-and-now" meanings. The boys also watched carefully to see if adults lived up to their own rhetoric; if they did not, the boys did not respect them or pay much attention to the moral messages they were imparting. The point of Fine's observations was that socialization did occur in connection with involvement on these organized youth sport teams, and the boys on the teams were active participants in the socialization process; they were not passively shaped by their sport experiences. The patterns of socialization found by Fine also tended to reflect the *developmental issues* boys face during preadolescence.

Other studies have used approaches similar to the one used by Fine. Patricia and Peter Adler (1985, 1987, 1991) gathered qualitative data over 10 years in their study of the personal and academic implications of participation on a "big-time" intercollegiate sport team. Their explanations of the dynamics of student-athlete relationships with one another and with "outsiders" outlined the difficulties associated with striking a balance between athletic and academic lives. The Adlers highlighted the decisions made by student-athletes as they moved through each year of their college and intercollegiate experiences. Building on the reported findings of the Adlers, Meyer (1990) interviewed athletes on two women's teams in a Division I sport program and found that their experiences were not the same as the men's; unlike the men, the women became more interested in their academic lives over time, and they encountered fewer problems in balancing their athletic and academic lives.

These studies highlight the fact that sport experiences take on different meanings depending on the contexts and relationships in which they are constructed and mediated. For example, the meanings young women gave to their intercollegiate sport experiences in Division I basketball and volleyball were considerably different than those given to the experiences of young men in a high profile Division I basketball program. Research is now needed to explore the processes through which participation takes on different meanings from one person and group to another, and if those meanings change over time as sport experiences are reinterpreted and applied in new ways in people's lives.

A previously cited study by Donnelly and Young (1988) used observations and in-depth interviews to outline the ways participation in specific sports and sport groups are involved in the overall process of identity development. They found that social relationships occasioned by sport participation play a critical role in the process through which people develop a sense of who they are and how they are connected to the rest of the social world in which they live their lives.

Research using critical and cultural studies frameworks are more concerned with cultural production and reproduction, and they are more apt to use sociohistorical and ethnographic methods. Socialization through sport is seldom directly addressed in this type of research, but study findings often highlight factors having significant socialization implications. For example, Foley's (1990) ethnography about life in a small town in south Texas focused on the local high schools as "sites for popular cultural practices that stage or reproduce social inequality" (p. *xv*). After gathering data intermittently over a period of 14 years, Foley clearly documented that high school sport programs were one of the major popular cultural practices that promoted and reproduced forms of social inequality related to race, ethnicity,

class, and gender within the town. In other words, interscholastic sports were the sites for learning cultural practices affecting social relations across many spheres of life. Similar findings were reported by Eder & Parker (1987), who did an ethnographic study of a racially mixed high school in a medium-sized Midwestern community. The most visible extracurricular activities, interscholastic sports for boys and cheerleading for girls, reproduced social inequities related to gender within the peer culture of the school. Through these activities, young men and women were exposed to values which were then incorporated into student peer groups where they were refined and applied to specific situations in the social lives of the students.

The role of sport as a site for the production and reproduction of gender relations has also been described and analyzed by Messner (1990). Drawing on his in-depth interviews with male former athletes in heavy contact sports, Messner examined "the meanings which athletes themselves construct(ed) around their own participation in violent sports," and the ways in which those meanings were connected to "the larger social construction of masculinities and men's power relations with women" (p. 203). Messner's point was that gender identity is never developed once and for all time, and that sport participation provides a context with powerful implications for the social construction of gender among men, and gender relations as a whole. Similarly, Palzkill's (1990) interviews with women in elite amateur sports led her to conclude that some women reconcile contradictions between their own approaches to the social world and the approaches characteristic in the male domain of sport by developing sexual identities based on a rejection of the traditional polarity of "masculinity" and "femininity." As in Messner's research, Palzkill emphasizes that sport is a site for the social construction of people's sense of who they are and how they are connected to the rest of the world.

In each of these studies sport is not treated as a variable, but as a site for the creation of meanings and the applications of those meanings to oneself and relationships with others. In this way sport becomes linked to an ever-emerging process of social development on both personal and structural levels. The research of the interactionists and those using critical theory and cultural studies approaches has demonstrated that sport participation cannot be analytically approached apart from the overall context of social relations and cultural practices in which social development occurs. Furthermore, it has highlighted the fact that sport participation must be acknowledged as involving experiences that are

1. Diversified
2. Integrated into people's lives in many different ways
3. Given different meanings from one person to the next
4. Given meanings that may change over time and from one situation to the next, even for the same individuals

When research has focused on the general process of "social development," it has been shown that the social relationships occasioned by sport are diversified in terms of how they mediate sport and general life experiences, and in terms of how they are taken into account when people make behavioral decisions. It is likely that future research using these approaches will tell us about how coaches and other adults become important in the lives of young athletes—important as sources of guidelines, as friends providing emotional support, as agents undermining or distorting development, as advocates who intercede in times of need, or as meaningless sources of constraint ignored or systematically demeaned and discredited by athletes. When the focus is on the overall process of "social development," researchers will not be as likely to use a methodology leading all "varsity athletes" to be grouped into a statistical category and compared with everyone else the same age in search of hypothesized "socialization effects" manifested through a preselected set of traits or questionnaire responses. Correlational analyses have provided useful starting points for future research, but it remains for other approaches to produce an understanding of the dynamics of the socialization process as it is related to sport.

CONCLUSION

In the future, fewer studies of socialization into sport will be based on a socialization-as-internalization ap-

proach; the social role–social system model will be used less often to guide research. An increasing emphasis will be put on the use of a socialization-as-interaction approach. In research done by those using interactionist, critical theory, and cultural studies frameworks, there will be more attention paid to how people define themselves and their bodies in connection with sport and physical activities, how they make decisions about participation, how their identities related to sport and physical activities are grounded in social relations and social groups, and how the overall process of involvement in these activities is related to control and power relations and characterized by shifting commitments and opportunities.

In a similar manner, research on socialization through sport will involve fewer correlational analyses and more interpretive approaches utilizing qualitative data. As more studies are grounded in interactionist, critical theory and cultural studies frameworks, sport participation will not be conceptualized as a variable as much as it will be viewed as a site for overall social development and the production and reproduction of cultural practices. As this occurs, the literature on socialization and sport will come to be more closely linked to the general literature on socialization and social relations. This change has already been initiated, and it is hoped it will continue in a way that will revitalize the research on socialization and sport.

References

Acosta, V., & Carpenter, L. (1985). A. Women in athletics: A status report. B. Status of women in athletics: Changes and causes. *JOPERD, 56,* 30–37.

Acosta, V., & Carpenter, L. (1990). *Women in intercollegiate sport: A longitudinal study—Thirteen-year update.* Mimeograph, Brooklyn College, Brooklyn, NY.

Adler, P., & Adler, P. A. (1985). From idealism to pragmatic detachment: The academic performance of college athletes. *Sociology of Education, 58,* 241–250.

Adler, P., & Adler, P. A. (1987). Role conflict and identity salience: College athletics and the academic role. *The Social Science Journal, 24,* 433–455.

Adler, P. A., & Adler, P. (1991). *Backboards and blackboards: College athletes and role engulfment.* New York: Columbia University Press.

Allison, M. T. (1982). Sport, culture and socialization. *International Review of Sport Sociology, 17,* 11–37.

Barnett, M., & Bryan, J. (1974). Effects of competition with outcome feedback on children's helping behavior. *Developmental Psychology, 10,* 838–842.

Baumrind, D. (1980). New directions in socialization research. *American Psychologist, 35,* 639–652.

Best, C. (1981). Differences in social values between athletes and nonathletes. *Research Quarterly for Exercise and Sport, 56,* 366–369.

Berkowitz, L. (1972). Sports, competition, and aggression. In I. Williams & L. Wankel (Eds.), *Fourth Canadian symposium on*

psychology of learning and sport (pp. 321–326). Ottawa: University of Ottawa Press.

Berlage, G. I. (1982). Children's sports and the family. *Arena Review, 6*(1), 43–47.

Birrell, S. (1989). Racial relations theory and sport: Suggestions for a more critical analysis. *Sociology of Sport Journal, 6,* 212–227.

Boutilier, M. A., & SanGiovanni, L. (1983). *The sporting woman.* Champaign, IL: Human Kinetics.

Braddock, J. (1980). Race, sports and social mobility: A critical review. *Sociological Symposium, 30,* 18–38.

Bredemeier, B. J. (1985). Moral reasoning and perceived legitimacy of intentionally injurious acts. *Journal of Sport Psychology, 7,* 110–124.

Bredemeier, B. J. (1987). The relationship between children's legitimacy judgments and their moral reasoning, aggression tendencies, and sport involvement. *Sociology of Sport Journal, 4,* 48–60.

Bredemeier, B. J. (1988). The moral of the youth sport story. In E. W. Brown & C. F. Banta (Eds.), *Competitive sports for children and youth* (pp. 285–296). Champaign IL: Human Kinetics.

Bredemeier, B. J., & Shields, D. L. (1986). Moral growth among athletes and nonathletes: A comparative analysis of females and males. *Journal of Genetic Psychology, 147,* 7–18.

Bredemeier, B. J., Shields, D. L., Weiss, M. R., & Cooper, B. A. B. (1986). The relationship of sport involvement with children's moral reasoning and aggression tendencies. *Journal of Sport Psychology, 8,* 304–318.

Bredemeier, B. J., Weiss, M. R., Shields, D. L., & Shewchuk, R. (1986). Promoting moral growth in a summer sport camp: The implementation of theoretically grounded instructional strategies. *Journal of Moral Education, 15,* 212–220.

Brown, B. A. (1985). Factors influencing the process of withdrawal by female adolescents from the role of competitive age group swimmer. *Sociology of Sport Journal, 2,* 111–129.

Bryan, J. H. (1977). Prosocial behavior. In H. L. Ham & P. A. Robinson (Eds.), *Psychological processes in early education* (pp. 233–259). New York: Academic Press.

Buhrmann, H. G. (1977). Athletics and deviancy: An examination of the relationship between athletic participation and deviant behavior of high school girls. *Review of Sport and Leisure, 7,* 119–128.

Butcher, J. (1985). Longitudinal analysis of adolescent girls' participation in physical activity. *Sociology of Sport Journal, 2,* 130–143.

Carlson, R. (1988). The socialization of elite tennis players in Sweden: An analysis of the players' backgrounds and development. *Sociology of Sport Journal, 5,* 241–256.

Castine, S. C., & Roberts, G. C. (1974). Modeling in the socialization process of the black athlete. *International Review of Sport Sociology, 9,* 59–72.

Clausen, J. A. (1968). A historical and comparative view of socialization theory and research. In J. A. Clausen (Ed.), *Socialization and society* (pp. 18–72). Boston: Little, Brown.

Coakley, J. (1986a). Socialization and youth sports. In C. R. Rees & A. W. Miracle (Eds.), *Sport and social theory* (pp. 135–143). Champaign, IL: Human Kinetics.

Coakley, J. (1986b). *Sport in society: Issues and controversies* (3rd ed.), St. Louis: Times Mirror/Mosby.

Coakley, J. (1987). Children and the sport socialization process. In D. Gould & M. R. Weiss (Eds.), *Advances in pediatric sport sciences,* Vol. 2, behavioral issues (pp. 43–60). Champaign, IL: Human Kinetics.

Coakley, J. (1990). *Sport in society: Issues and controversies.* St. Louis: Times Mirror/Mosby.

Coakley, J., & White, A. (1992). Making decisions: Gender and sport participation among British adolescents. *Sociology of Sport Journal, 9,* 20–35.

Collins, L. J. (1972). Social class and the Olympic athletes. *British Journal of Physical Education, 3,* 25–27.

Curry, T. J., & Weiss, O. (1989). Sport identity and motivation for sport participation: A comparison between American college athletes and Austrian student sport club member. *Sociology of Sport Journal, 6,* 257–268.

Curtis, J., & White, P. (1984). Age and sport participation: Decline in participation with age or increased specialization with age? In N. Theberge & P. Donnelly (Eds.), *Sport and the sociological imagination* (pp. 273–294). Ft. Worth: Texas Christian University Press.

Deem, R. (1986). *All work and no play: The sociology of women and leisure.* Philadelphia: Open University Press.

Donnelly, P., & Young, K. (1988). The construction and confirmation of identity in sport subcultures. *Sociology of Sport Journal, 3,* 223–240.

Dubois, P. E. (1978). Participation in sports and occupational attainment: A comparative study. *Research Quarterly, 49,* 28–37.

Dubois, P. E. (1979). Participation in sport and occupational attainment: An investigation of selected athlete categories. *Journal of Sport Behavior, 2,* 103–114.

Dubois, P. E. (1986). The effects of participation in sport on the value orientations of young athletes. *Sociology of Sport Journal, 3,* 29–42.

Dubois, P. E. (1990). Gender differences in value orientation toward sports: A longitudinal analysis. *Journal of Sport Behavior, 13,* 3–14.

Eder D., & Parker, S. (1987). The cultural production and reproduction of gender: The effect of extracurricular activities on peer-group culture. *Sociology of Education, 60,* 200–213.

Edwards, H. (1973). *Sociology of sport.* Homewood, IL: The Dorsey Press.

Fagot, B. I. (1984). Teacher and peer reactions to boys' and girls' play styles. *Sex Roles, 11,* 691–702.

Faulkner, R. (1974). Coming of age in organizations: A comparative study of career contingencies and adult socialization. *Sociology of Work and Occupations, 1,* 131–173.

Fine, G. A. (1987). *With the boys: Little League baseball and preadolescent culture.* Chicago: University of Chicago Press.

Fishwick, L., & Greendorfer, S. (1987). Socialization revisited: A critique of the sport-related research. *Quest, 39,* 1–9.

Foley, D. E. (1990). *Learning capitalist culture.* Philadelphia: University of Pennsylvania Press.

Furst, D. M. (1989). Sport role socialization: Initial entry into the subculture of officiating. *Journal of Sport Behavior, 12,* 41–52.

Gelfand, D., & Hartman, D. (1978). Some detrimental effects of competitive sports on children's behavior. In R. Magill, M. J. Ash, & F. L. Smoll (Eds.), *Children in sport: A contemporary anthology* (pp. 165–174). Champaign, IL: Human Kinetics.

Gelinas, M. (1988). *The relationship between sport involvement and political attitudes and behaviours.* Unpublished master's thesis, University of Waterloo, Ontario.

Giebink, M. P., & McKenzie, T. L. (1985). Teaching sportsmanship in physical education and recreation: An analysis of interventions and generalization effects. *Journal of Teaching in Physical Education, 4,* 167–177.

Goldstein, J. H. (1980). *Social psychology.* New York: Academic Press.

Greendorfer, S. L. (1977). The role of socializing agents on female sport involvement. *Research Quarterly, 48,* 304–310.

Greendorfer, S. L. (1978). Social class influence on female sport involvement. *Sex Roles, 4,* 619–625.

Greendorfer, S. L. (1979a). Differences in childhood socialization influences on women involved in sport and women not involved in sport. In M. Krotee (Ed.), *The dimensions of sport sociology* (pp. 59–72). New York: Leisure Press.

Greendorfer, S. L. (1979b). Childhood sport socialization influences on male and female track athletes. *Arena Review, 3,* 39–53.

Greendorfer, S. L. (1983). Shaping the female athlete: The impact of the family. In M. A. Boutilier & L. SanGiovanni (Eds.), *The sporting woman* (pp. 135–156). Champaign, IL: Human Kinetics.

Greendorfer, S. L. (1987). Gender bias in theoretical perspectives: The case of female socialization into sport. *Psychology of Women Quarterly, 11,* 327–347.

Greendorfer, S. L., Blinde, E. M., & Pellegrini, A. M. (1986). Differences in Brazilian children's socialization into sport. *International Review for the Sociology of Sport, 21,* 51–64.

Greendorfer, S. L., & Bruce, T. (1989). Rejuvenating sport socialization research. Paper presented at the North American Society for the Sociology of Sport Conference, Washington, DC.

Greendorfer, S. L., & Ewing, M. (1981). Race and gender differences in children's socialization into sport. *Research Quarterly for Exercise and Sport, 52,* 301–310.

Greendorfer, S. L., & Lewko, J. H. (1978). The role of family members in sport socialization of children. *Research Quarterly, 49,* 146–152.

Gruneau, R. S. (1975). Sport, social differentiation and social inequality. In D. W. Ball & J. W. Loy (Eds.), *Sport and social order: Contributions to the sociology of sport* (pp. 117–184). Reading, MA: Addison-Wesley.

Gruneau, R. S. (1978). Elites, class and corporate power in Canadian sport: Some preliminary findings. In F. Landry & W. A. R. Orban (Eds.), *Sociology of sport: Sociological studies and administrative, economic and legal aspects of sport and leisure* (pp. 201–242). Miami, FL: Symposia Specialists.

Hanks, M. (1979). Race, sexual status and athletics in the process of educational achievement. *Social Science Quarterly, 60,* 482–496.

Hanks, M., & Eckland, B. K. (1976). Athletics and social participation in the educational attainment process. *Sociology of Education, 49,* 271–294.

Hare, N. (1971). A study of the black fighter. *Black Scholar, 3,* 2–9.

Hargreaves, J. (1986). *Sport, power and culture.* New York: St. Martin's Press.

Harootyan, R. A. (1982). The participation of older people in sports. In R. M. Pankin (Ed.), *Social approaches to sport* (pp. 122–147). East Brunswick, NJ: Associated University Presses.

Harris, J. (1983). Interpreting youth baseball: Players' understandings of attention, winning, and playing the game. *Research Quarterly for Exercise and Sport, 54,* 330–339.

Harris, J. (1984). Interpreting youth baseball: Players understanding of fun and excitement, danger and boredom. *Research Quarterly for Exercise and Sport, 55,* 379–382.

Harris, O., & Hunt, L. (1984). Race and sports involvement: Some implications of sports for black and white youth. Paper presented at the meetings of the American Alliance for Health, Physical Education, Recreation & Dance, Anaheim, CA.

Hasbrook, C. H. (1986a). The sport participation–social class relationship: Some recent youth sport participation data. *Sociology of Sport Journal, 3,* 154–159.

Hasbrook, C. H. (1986b). Reciprocity and childhood socialization into sport. In L. Vander Velden & J. H. Humphrey (Eds.), *Psychology and sociology of sport: Current selected research* (pp. 135–147). New York: AMS Press.

Hasbrook, C. H. (1987). The sport participation–social class relationship among a selected sample of female adolescents. *Sociology of Sport Journal, 4,* 37–47.

Hasbrook, C. H. (1989). Reconceptualizing socialization. Paper presented at the North American Society for the Sociology of Sport Conference, Washington, DC.

Hauser, W. J., & Lueptow, L. B. (1978). Participation in athletics and academic achievement: A replication and extension. *Sociological Quarterly, 19,* 304–309.

Helanko, R. (1957). Sports and socialization. *Acta Sociologica, 2,* 229–240.

Hewitt, J. P. (1991). *Self and society.* Boston: Allyn and Bacon.

Higginson, D. (1985). The influence of socializing agents in the female sport-socialization process. *Adolescence, 20,* 73–82.

Howell, F. M., Miracle, A. W., & Rees, C. R. (1984). Do high school athletics pay? The effects of varsity participation on socioeconomic attainment. *Sociology of Sport Journal, 1,* 15–25.

Howell, F. M., & Picou, S. (1983). Athletics and income achievements. Paper presented at the meetings of the Southwestern Sociological Association, Houston.

Ingham, A., Dewar, A., & Vealey, R. (1989). Through the eyes of youth: Pee-Wee hockey. Paper presented at the North American Society for the Sociology of Sport Conference, Washington, DC.

Inkeles, A. (1969). Social structure and socialization. In D. A. Goslin (Ed.), *Handbook of Socialization theory and research* (pp. 615–632). Chicago: Rand McNally.

Jerome, W., & Phillips, J. C. (1971). The relationship between academic achievement and interscholastic participation: A comparison of Canadian and American high schools. *Journal of the Canadian Association for Health, Physical Education, and Recreation, 37,* 18–21.

Kenyon, G. (1970). The use of path analysis in sport sociology with reference to involvement socialization. *International Review of Sport Sociology, 5,* 191–203.

Kenyon, G., & McPherson, B. D. (1973). Becoming involved in physical activity and sport: A process of socialization. In G. L. Rarick (Ed.), *Physical activity: Human growth and development* (pp. 303–332). New York: Academic Press.

Kleiber, D., & Roberts, G. (1981). The effects of sport experience in the development of social character: An exploratory investigation. *Journal of Sport Psychology, 3,* 114–122.

Landers, D. M., & Landers, D. M. (1978). Socialization via interscholastic athletics: Its effects on delinquency. *Sociology of Education, 51,* 299–303.

Lapchick, R. (1984). *Broken promises: Racism in American sports.* New York: St. Martin's/Marek.

Lenskyj, H. (1986). *Out of bounds: women, sport and sexuality.* Toronto: Women's Press.

Lewko, J. H., & Ewing, M. E. (1980). Sex differences and parental influence in sport involvement of children. *Journal of Sport Psychology, 2*(1): 63–68.

Loy, J. W. (1969). The study of sport and social mobility. In G. S. Kenyon (Ed.), *Sociology of sport* (pp. 101–119). Chicago: The Athletic Institute.

Loy, J. W. (1972). Social origins and occupational mobility of a selected sample of American athletes. *International Review of Sport Sociology, 7,* 5–23.

Loy, J. W., & Ingham, A. G. (1973). Play, games, and sport in the psychosocial development of children and youth. In G. L. Rarick (Ed.), *Physical activity: Human growth and potential* (pp. 257–302). New York: Academic Press.

McCall, G. J., & Simmons, J. L. (1982). *Social psychology: A sociological approach.* New York: The Free Press.

McCormack, J. B., & Chalip, L. (1988). Sport as socialization: A critique of methodological premises. *The Social Science Journal, 25,* 83–92.

McElroy, M. (1979). Sport participation and educational aspirations: An explicit consideration of academic and sport value climates. *Research Quarterly, 40,* 241–248.

McGuire, J., & Cook, D. L. (1983). The influence of others and the decision to participate in youth sports. *Journal of Sport Behavior, 6,* 9–16.

McGuire, J., & Thomas, M. (1975). Effects of sex, competence and competition on sharing behavior in children. *Journal of Personality and Social Psychology, 32,* 490–494.

McPherson, B. D. (1981). Socialization into and through sport. In G. Luschen & G. H. Sage (Eds.), *Handbook of social science of sport* (pp. 246–273). Champaign, IL: Stipes.

McPherson, B. D. (1984). Sport participation across the life cycle: A review of the literature and suggestions for future research. *Sociology of Sport Journal, 1,* 213–230.

McPherson, B. D. (1986). Socialization theory and research: Toward a "new wave" of scholarly inquiry in a sport context. In C.

R. Rees & A. W. Miracle (Eds.), *Sport and social theory* (pp. 111–134). Champaign, IL: Human Kinetics.

McPherson, B. D., & Brown, B. (1988). The structure, processes, and consequences of sport for children. In F. L. Smoll, R. A. Magill, & M. J. Ash (Eds.), *Children in sport* (pp. 265–286). Champaign, IL: Human Kinetics.

McPherson, B. D., Curtis, J. E., & Loy, J. W. (1989). *The social significance of sport.* Champaign, IL: Human Kinetics.

Melnick, M. J., Vanfossen, B. E., & Sabo, D. F. (1988). Developmental effects of athletic participation among high school girls. *Sociology of Sport Journal, 1,* 22–36.

Messner, M. A. (1990a). When bodies are weapons: Masculinity and violence in sport. *International Review for the Sociology of Sport, 25,* 203–219.

Messner, M. A. (1990b). Mascuinities and athletic careers: Bonding and status differences. In M. A. Messner & D. F. Sabo (Eds.), *Sport, men, and the gender order* (pp. 97–108). Champaign, IL: Human Kinetics.

Messner, M., & Groisser, D. (1982). Intercollegiate athletic participation and academic achievement. In A. O. Dunleavy, A. W. Miracle, & C. R. Rees (Eds.), *Studies in the sociology of sport* (pp. 257–270). Fort Worth, TX: Texas Christian University Press.

Meyer, B. B. (1990). From idealism to actualization: The academic performance of female collegiate athletes. *Sociology of Sport Journal, 7,* 44–57.

Musgrave, P. W. (1987). *Socialising contexts: The subject in society.* Boston: Allen & Unwin.

Nixon, H. L., II. (1981). An exploratory study of the effects of encouragement and pressure on the sports socialization of males and females. In S. L. Greendorfer & A. Yiannakis (Eds.), *Sociology of sport: Diverse perspectives* (pp. 83–94). West Point, NY: Leisure Press.

Nixon, H. L., II. (1990). Rethinking socialization and sport. *Journal of Sport and Social Issues, 14,* 33–47.

Norton, D. J. (1971). *A comparison of political attitudes and political participation of athletes and non-athletes.* Unpublished master's thesis, University of Oregon.

Ogilvie, B. C., & Tutko, T. A. (1971). Sport: If you want to build character, try something else. *Psychology Today, 5,* 60–63.

Oliver, M. (1980). Race, class and the family's orientation to mobility through sport. *Sociological Symposium, 30,* 62–86.

Otto, L. B., & Alwin, D. F. (1977). Athletics, aspirations and attainments. *Sociology of Education, 42,* 102–113.

Palzkill, B. (1990). Between gymshoes and high-heels—the development of a lesbian identity and existence in top class sport. *International Review for the Sociology of Sport, 25,* 221–233.

Pavia, G. R. (1973). An analysis of the social class of the 1972 Australian Olympic team. *Australian Journal of Physical Education, 61,* 14–19.

Petrie, B. M. (1973). The political attitudes of Canadian university students: a comparison between athletes and nonathletes. Paper presented at the American Alliance for Health, Physical Education, and Recreation annual conference, Minneapolis.

Picou, J. S. (1978). Race, athletic achievement and educational aspiration. *Sociological Quarterly, 19,* 429–438.

Picou, J. S., McCarter, V., & Howell, F. M. (1985). Do high school athletics pay? Some further evidence. *Sociology of Sport Journal, 2,* 72–76.

Pronger, B. (1990). *The arena of masculinity.* New York: St. Martin's Press.

Prus, R. (1984). Career contingencies: Examining patterns of involvement. In N. Theberge & P. Donnelly (Eds.), *Sport and the sociological imagination* (pp. 297–317). Fort Worth: Texas Christian University Press.

Raphael, R. (1988). *The men from the boys.* Lincoln, NB: University of Nebraska Press.

Rankin, J. H. (1980). Social factors and delinquency: Interactions by age and sex. *Sociology and Social Research, 64,* 420–434.

Rehberg, R. A., & Cohen, M. (1971). Political attitudes and participation in extra-curricular activities with special emphasis on interscholastic athletics. Paper presented at Sport and Social Deviancy conference, SUNY-Brockport, NY.

Rehberg, R. A., & Cohen, M. (1975). Athletes and scholars: An analysis of the compositional characteristics of these two youth culture categories. *International Review of Sport Sociology, 10,* 91–106.

Rehberg, R. A., & Schafer, W. E. (1968). Participation in interscholastic athletics and college expectations. *American Journal of Sociology, 73,* 732–740.

Roberts, G., Kleiber, D. A., & Duda, J. L. (1981). An analysis of motivation in children's sport: The role of perceived competence in participation. *Journal of Sport Psychology, 3,* 206–216.

Robins, D. (1982). Sport and youth culture. In J. Hargreaves (Ed.), *Sport, culture and ideology* (pp. 136–151). Boston: Routledge & Kegan Paul.

Romance, T. (1984). *A program to promote moral development through elementary school physical education.* Unpublished doctoral dissertation, University of Oregon, Eugene, Oregon.

Rudman, W. J. (1989). Age and involvement in sport and physical activity. *Sociology of Sport Journal, 6,* 228–246.

Rushall, B. (1975). Alternative dependent variables for the study of behavior in sport. In D. M. Landers (Ed.), *Psychology of sport and motor behavior* (pp. 49–59). College Park: The Pennsylvania University.

Sack, A., & Theil, R. (1979). College football and social mobility: A case study of Notre Dame football players. *Sociology of Education, 52,* 60–66.

Sage, G. H. (1980a). Socialization and sport. In G. H. Sage (Ed.), *Sport and American society* (pp. 133–142). Reading, Mass.: Addison-Wesley.

Sage, G. H. (1980b). Parental influence and socialization into sport for male and female intercollegiate athletes. *Journal of Sport and Social Issues, 4,* 1–13.

Schafer, W. E. (1969). Some social sources and consequences of interscholastic athletics: The case of participation and delinquency. In G. Kenyon (Ed.), *Aspects of contemporary sport sociology* (pp. 29–44). Chicago, IL: The Athletic Institute.

Schafer, W. E. (1971). Sport, socialization and the school. Paper presented at the Third Annual Symposium of the Sociology of Sport, Waterloo, Ontario.

Schafer, W. E., & Armer, J. M. (1968). Athletes are not inferior students. *Trans-action, 6*(1), 21–26, 61–62.

Scott, J. (1971). *The athletic revolution.* New York: The Free Press.

Scott, L. (1982). Career contingencies: The social construction of continuing involvements in women's intercollegiate basketball. Paper presented at the North American Society for the Sociology of Sport Conference, Toronto.

Scraton, S. (1987). "Boys muscle in where angels fear to tread"—girls' subcultures and physical activities. In J. Horne, D. Jary, & A. Tomlinson (Eds.), *Sport, leisure and social relations* (pp. 160–186). New York: Routledge & Kegan Paul (Sociological Review Monograph #33).

Segrave, J. (1986). Do organized sports programs deter delinquency? *Journal of Physical Education, Recreation and Dance, 57*(1), 16–17.

Segrave, J., & Chu, D. (1978). Athletics and juvenile delinquency. *Review of Sport and Leisure, 3,* 1–24.

Segrave, J., & Hastad, D. N. (1982). Delinquent behavior and interscholastic athletic participation. *Journal of Sport Behavior, 5,* 96–111.

Segrave, J., Moreau, C., & Hastad, D. N. (1985). An investigation into the relationship between ice hockey participation and delinquency. *Sociology of Sport Journal, 2,* 281–298.

Semyonov, M. (1984). Sport and beyond: Ethnic inequalities in attainment. *Sociology of Sport Journal, 1,* 358–365.

SIRLS Sport & Leisure Database (1986). Annotated bibliography: Sport and academic achievement. *Sociology of Sport Journal, 3,* 87–94.

SIRLS Sport & Leisure Database (1987). Annotated bibliography: Sport and deviance. *Sociology of Sport Journal, 4,* 91–98.

SIRLS Sport & Leisure Database (1988). Annotated bibliography: High school sport. *Sociology of Sport Journal, 5,* 390–398.

SIRLS Sport & Leisure Database (1989). Annotated bibliography: Socialization in sport. *Sociology of Sport Journal, 6,* 294–302.

SIRLS Sport & Leisure Database (1990). Annotated bibliography: Sport and social mobility. *Sociology of Sport Journal, 7,* 95–102.

Snyder, E. E. (1970). Aspects of socialization in sports and physical education. *Quest, 14,* 1–7.

Snyder, E. E. (1972). High school athletes and their coaches: Educational plans and advice. *Sociology of Education, 45,* 313–325.

Snyder, E. E., & Purdy, D. A. (1982). Socialization into sport: Parent and child reverse and reciprocal effects. *Research Quarterly for Exercise and Sport, 53,* 263–266.

Snyder, E. E., & Spreitzer, E. (1973). Family influence and involvement in sports. *Research Quarterly, 44,* 249–255.

Snyder, E. E., & Spreitzer, E. (1976). Correlates of sport participation among adolescent girls. *Research Quarterly, 47,* 804–809.

Snyder, E. E., & Spreitzer, E. (1978). Socialization comparisons of adolescent female athletes and musicians. *Research Quarterly, 49,* 342 350.

Snyder, E. E., & Spreitzer, E. (1989). *Social aspects of sport.* Englewood Cliffs, NJ: Prentice-Hall.

Spady, W. G. (1970). Lament for the letterman: Effects of peer status and extra curricular activities on goals and achievement. *American Journal of Sociology, 75,* 680–702.

Spreitzer, E. E., & Pugh, M. (1973). Interscholastic athletics and educational expectations. *Sociology of Education, 46,* 171–182.

Stevenson, C. L. (1975). Socialization effects of participation in sport: A critical review of the research. *Research Quarterly, 46,* 287–301.

Stevenson, C. L. (1976). Institutionalization and college sport. *Research Quarterly, 47,* 1–8.

Stevenson, C. L. (1982). Career contingencies: Involvement at the national team level. Paper presented at the North American Society for the Sociology of Sport Conference, Toronto.

Stevenson, C. L. (1985). College athletics and "character": The decline and fall of socialization research. In D. Chu, J. O. Segrave, & B. J. Becker (Eds.), *Sport and higher education* (pp. 249–266). Champaign, IL: Human Kinetics.

Stevenson, C. L. (1990a). The athletic career: Some contingencies of sport specialization. *Journal of Sport Behavior, 13,* 103–113.

Stevenson, C. L. (1990b). The early careers of international athletes. *Sociology of Sport Journal, 7,* 238–253.

Talbot, M. (1988a). Understanding the relationship between women and sport: The contributions of British feminist approaches in leisure and cultural studies. *International Review for the Sociology of Sport, 23,* 31–42.

Talbot, M. (1988b). Beating them at our own game? Women's sport involvement. In E. Wimbush & M. Talbot (Eds.), *Relative freedoms: Women and leisure* (pp. 102–114). Philadelphia: Open University Press.

Theberge, N. (1984). On the need for a more adequate theory of sport participation. *Sociology of Sport Journal, 1,* 26–35.

Thomas, C. E., & Ermler, K. L. (1988). Institutional obligations in the athletic retirement process. *Quest, 40,* 137–150.

Thorlindsson, T. (1989). Sport participation, smoking, and drug and alcohol abuse among Icelandic youth. *Sociology of Sport Journal, 6,* 136–143.

Trulson, M. E. (1986). Martial arts training: A novel "cure" for juvenile delinquency. *Human Relations, 39,* 1131–1140.

U.S. Commission on Civil Rights (1980). *More hurdles to clear: Women and girls in competitive athletics.* Washington, DC: U.S. Government Printing Office, Clearinghouse Publication #63.

Watson, G. G. (1977). Games, socialization and parental values: Social class differences in parental evaluation of Little League baseball. *International Review for the Sociology of Sport, 12,* 17–48.

Weiss, M. R., & Knoppers, A. (1982). The influence of socializing agents on female intercollegiate volleyball players. *Journal of Sport Psychology, 4,* 267–279.

Wells, R. H., & Picou, J. S. (1980). Interscholastic athletes and socialization for educational achievement. *Journal of Sport Behavior, 3,* 119–128.

Wentworth, W. M. (1980). *Context and understanding: An inquiry into socialization theory.* New York: Elsevier.

White, A., & Coakley, J. (1986). *Making decisions.* London: Sports Council, Greater London & South East Region.

Whitson, D. (1990). Sport in the social construction of masculinity. In M. A. Messner & D. F. Sabo (Eds.), *Sport, men, and the gender order* (pp. 19–30). Champaign, IL: Human Kinetics.

Williams, T. R. (1983). *Socialization.* Englewood Cliffs, NJ: Prentice-Hall.

Willis, P. (1982). Women in sport in ideology. In J. Hargreaves (Ed.), *Sport, culture and ideology* (pp. 117–135). Boston: Routledge & Kegan Paul.

Yamaguchi, Y. (1987). A cross-national study of socialization into physical activity in corporate settings: The case of Japan and Canada. *Sociology of Sport Journal, 4,* 61–77.

27

MORAL PSYCHOLOGY IN THE CONTEXT OF SPORT

Brenda J. Light Bredemeier

David L. Light Shields

The view that sport is a context for moral education is not new. We can find evidence of this belief throughout history; from the writings of Plato to the contemporary declarations of politicians, educators, and theologians, sport has been portrayed as a builder of character. This claim has found a place in popular folk wisdom and is reflected by the cultural adage "Sport builds character."

Can sport experience really contribute to the development of participant morality? The question has received strikingly little empirical investigation. In this chapter, we will examine one aspect of the concept of character, namely, moral development, as it relates to sport. Moral development is not the totality of what is meant by character, any more than knowledge exhausts what is meant by wisdom, but it is an important part. Moral development refers to the evolving maturity of a person's grasp of the interpersonal rights and responsibilities that characterize social life.

In the first part of the chapter, we briefly review two theoretical approaches to moral development: the social learning and structural developmental perspectives. Since most recent research on sport morality has utilized a structural developmental approach, we elaborate on the two structural developmental theories most frequently used in sport research, those proposed by Lawrence Kohlberg and Norma Haan. In the remainder of the chapter, we present major findings about moral development and sport under three broad categories: (a) a description of the relationship between morality variables and sport involvement, (b) theory building about how sport influences moral reasoning and its development, and (c) practical applications of empirical and theoretical work. We conclude the chapter with some brief suggestions for future research directions.

THEORETICAL APPROACHES TO MORAL DEVELOPMENT

The Social Learning Approach

There are many variants to the social learning approach to moral development. Among the major points of contention are: (1) the primary vehicles through which learning occurs; (2) the most important outcomes or products of learning; and (3) how central innate factors are in producing individual differences (Rushton, 1982). Before briefly illustrating some of these differences, however, let us emphasize the assumptions generally held in common.

First, social learning theorists view moral behavior as nondistinct from other types of behavior. The same learning principles and motivational dynamics that operate in the acquisition, maintenance, and modification of hand-washing behavior control the exhibition of helping, sharing, or acting justly. Second, the degree to which a person acts "morally" is directly related to that person's previous learning history. A person is moral to the degree that he or she has learned to be so. Third, what constitutes "moral" behavior is socially defined. Moral behavior is that behavior which conforms to the prosocial norms of a given society or cultural group. Thus morality is relative. Finally, social learning theorists are methodologically committed to a focus on overt behavior. What happens "in the minds" of people is viewed as fundamentally unknowable; only observable behavior can be subjected to reliable scientific investigation.

Within this broad framework of common assumptions several different moral theories have emerged. Perhaps at

Portions of this text have been adapted from Shields, D., & Bredemeier, B. (1989), Moral reasoning, judgment, and action in sport. In J. Goldstein (Ed.), *Sports, games and play: Social and psychological viewpoints,* 2nd ed. (pp. 59–81). Hillsdale, NJ: Erlbaum.

one end of the spectrum is Eysenck (1977), who emphasizes classical conditioning as the primary learning vehicle, conditioned affect as the focal outcome of learning, and innate differences in the "conditionability" of people's nervous systems as accounting for a large measure of individual differences. An illustrative contrast is Bandura (1977) who emphasizes modeling and reinforcement as the major stimulants for learning, and cognitive constructs as a major learning outcome; little attention is paid to genetic predispositions. In general, the trend in recent years has been toward a modified social learning theory that takes greater account of cognitive factors in the mediation of behavior (Rushton, 1982), though the cognitive factors themselves are said to result from the processes of conditioning, modeling, and reinforcement.

The Structural Developmental Approach

Like social learning theorists, structural developmentalists hold a number of basic assumptions in common while diverging in specific detail. In the next section we will elaborate on the theories of two structural developmental theorists, highlighting their differences. The purpose of the present discussion is to indicate the points of convergence.

One major distinguishing feature of the structural developmental approach is the distinction between two levels of analysis. People's actions or thinking can be analyzed at the level of *content,* or it can be analyzed at the level of *structure.* What people think, how they behave, what answers they give on a questionnaire, how they respond to an experimental manipulation—these are all contents of thought or behavior.

Structural developmental theorists believe that lying beneath or behind these contents is a more or less coherent psychological structure that generates the specific contents. The structure itself is outside of conscious awareness. For example, when we speak, our specific verbal utterances are contents, but lying beneath them is a complex grammatical structure that we use without even being aware of it. Few of us could identify the grammatical rules that we follow, yet our speech is generated from those organizing rules. Similarly, structural developmentalists believe that when people deal with such diverse issues as moral problems, mathematical puzzles, and decisions about social roles, their reasoning is generated from and reflects the organization of identifiable psychological structures. The underlying structures arise from an innate psychological tendency to organize experience into coherent patterns. One of the major theoretical tasks of the structural developmental theorist is to make explicit the implicit structure of these diverse areas of human functioning. Thus in contrast to social learning theorists, structural developmentalists have tended to focus more on moral thought than on moral action.

When structural developmentalists assess moral development, they are not analyzing the correctness of a person's moral beliefs. Two people who are equally mature may hold very different beliefs about moral issues. Moral beliefs reveal something of the content of a person's moral convictions; but structural developmentalists are interested in the relative adequacy of the *structure* that generates these beliefs; they are interested in the pattern of reasoning that a person uses to support his or her beliefs. This brings us to the second major theme held in common by structural developmentalists.

According to structural developmental theory, the structures that underlie a person's reasoning are not static; they change with development. Furthermore, they change in an orderly, progressive way from less adequate to more adequate. As a person's innate tendency to organize experience interacts with his or her actual experience, the underlying structures of reasoning become more differentiated and integrated. By *differentiation* is meant the structural refinement through which both more complex and more subtle aspects of experience can be recognized and responded to appropriately; by *integration* is meant the structural reorganization through which external phenomena are comprehended in a more integrated and parsimonious manner. It is presumed that as psychological structures become more differentiated and integrated, they also become more adequate.

In the following discussion we will review two prominent theories about the developmental course that individuals follow in their march toward moral maturity. With regard to each of these two theories we will ask: What are the basic tenets underlying the theory? What prevents some people in some situations from acting on their most mature moral convictions? And what are the processes of education advocated by those committed to each theory?

Kohlberg's Theory of Moral Development

Kohlberg's work (1981, 1984) is well known and will be only briefly summarized in this chapter. His groundbreaking theory of moral development is rooted in the cognitive developmental approach to psychology most prominently associated with Piaget. Accordingly, the concept of universal stages occupies a central place in Kohlberg's work. Within the Piagetian framework, stage progression is hypothesized to reflect an interactive process between the innate tendency of the developing child to actively organize information and an environment that demands accommodation to its features.

Basic Concepts. The following four key concepts can help us understand Kohlberg's theory of moral development: moral issues, orientations, principles, and stages. Kohlberg believed that certain moral issues or values are universally recognized as important. These include the values of life, property, truthfulness, civil liberties, conscience, rules and laws, affiliation, authority, contract, and trust (Kohlberg, 1976). The content of moral thinking is about these moral values. Sometimes, however, one person's claim on a particular value may come into conflict with claims of others. Kohlberg wrote, "the area of conflicting claims of selves is the area of morality" (Kohlberg, 1984, p. 73). Thus, for example, if a player is asked by a coach to violate a rule, the coach's claim of authority may conflict with the player's claim to obeying rules.

To clarify what is involved in moral thinking, Kohlberg turned to philosophy and isolated four basic types of moral orientations used by various traditions of philosophy (Kohlberg, 1976). A moral orientation is a general approach for dealing with moral conflicts. Each moral orientation focuses on a critical element to help decide right and wrong. The first, the *normative order* orientation, focuses on prescribed rules and roles; decision-making is guided by a consideration of rules. The *consequence* orientation focuses on the impact of various actions on the welfare of others and/or the self; decision-making is guided by beliefs about the outcome of various behavioral options. The *justice* orientation highlights relations of liberty, equality, reciprocity, and contracts between people. In decision-making, this orientation is characterized by a concern for impartiality and fairness. Finally, the *ideal-self* orientation concentrates on an image of the actor as a good self, or as someone with conscience. Those who operate from this orientation seek to maintain personal virtue or integrity and pure motives through their moral decisions.

It is not difficult to see how these basic moral orientations might all come into play in a sport setting. Certainly rules hold a highly prominent place in sport and many, probably most, decisions are based on the rules and prescribed roles. Concern for consequences, particularly the welfare implications for behaviors like aggression, constrain action in certain ways. The structure of the game is designed to ensure fairness and equal opportunity, and some players may rely on this dimension, the "spirit of the game," for their moral guidance. Finally, themes of sportspersonship are often tethered to images of the ideal athlete who exhibits virtues of politeness and good humor in the midst of fierce competition.

Kohlberg's theory is deeply embedded in his conviction that the justice orientation is the most adequate of the four. Only the justice orientation, Kohlberg maintained, can lead to the formulation of a moral principle that can be used to decide fairly among competing moral claims. Rules can conflict with one another. The consequences for one person or group may conflict with those for another; furthermore, consequences often cannot be foreseen with clarity. Conscience, contrary to the popular adage, is too contaminated by cultural baggage to be the best guide. The justice orientation, however, can lead to "a mode of choosing which is universalizable, a rule of choosing which we want all people to adopt always in all situations" (Kohlberg, 1981, p. 39).

To summarize, there are certain universal moral issues that can give rise to moral conflict. Moral conflict can be dealt with through the use of one of four major decision-making strategies, though one of these—the orientation to justice—is the most adequate. Kohlberg's stage theory reflects his investigation into the developmental course by which people come to a mature understanding of justice.

Kohlberg hypothesized an invariant, culturally universal six-stage sequence of moral development. A stage refers to the underlying structure of reasoning. Each moral stage is an integrated, coherent approach to problem-solving that can be applied to whatever content is present in a moral situation.

The details of Kohlberg's six stages are beyond the scope of this chapter, but the general course of development can be noted. In the first two stages, one approaches moral problems through an individualistic or egocentric perspective. Kohlberg calls this the "preconventional" level, since the person does not yet comprehend the way social norms and rules impact on moral responsibility. The next two stages make up the "conventional" level, during which time one approaches problems through the eyes of one's social group or of society as a whole. Finally, at the "postconventional level," one recognizes universal values that are not tied to the particular norms of any given society; ultimately justice is identified as the single moral norm from which all others are derived. (See Bredemeier, 1984, pp. 403–404, for a chart presenting moral stages with sport illustrations.)

Within each stage, Kohlberg also identified type A and type B substages. These were derived from the four moral orientations discussed earlier. In Kohlberg's view, everyone uses all four orientations to some extent, but each person has a clear preference for using either (a) some combination of the normative order and consequence orientations, which Kohlberg called substage A, or (b) some combination of the justice and ideal-self orientations, which he called substage B. Thus, an emphasis on rules or consequences in response to moral problems is indicative of substage A reasoning within any of the stages. In contrast, reasoning at the B substage of each stage is associated with an emphasis on the justice and ideal-self orientations. Kohlberg found the substage theory helpful in explaining why some people at an early stage of development seem to be able to intuit the same moral judgment as is articulately stated by postconventional reasoners. He suggested that those preconventional and conventional reasoners who prefer the B substage dimly perceive the critical moral issues that are finally integrated in a self-conscious way by those at the most mature reasoning level of his model.

From Thought to Action. We do not always behave in the way we think we should. An athlete, for example, may strike an opponent and later regret the action. Why is there a gap between moral thought and action?

The simplest model of the thought-action relationship would suggest that people's ethical behavior could be accurately predicted if their stage of moral reasoning were known. Such a simple model, however, fails to address the complexity of the relationship. As Kohlberg (1984) wrote, "The prediction from stages or principles to action requires that we take account of intermediary judgments that an individual makes" (p. 517). In Kohlberg's view, two critical intermediary judgments come into play: (1) a deontic judgment, or, simply stated, a judgment that a particular act is right or wrong, and (2) a judgment of responsibility, in which one considers the facts of the situation and the needs and motives of self and others in conjunction with one's deontic judgment to determine one's responsibility. For example, Debbie might believe that it would be right to have another player turned in for use of performance-enhancing drugs (deontic judgment), but she may decide against turning the player in because (1) it may be detrimental to the team, (2) she may fear losing a good friend, or (3) she may fear the player would be unfairly treated (responsibility judgment).

While deontic decisions are prescriptive judgments of rightness, responsibility judgments are "an affirmation of the will to act in terms of that [deontic] judgment" (Kohlberg & Candee, 1984, p. 57) given the particulars of the real life context. Blasi (1984, 1989) suggests that the selection of information to be factored in to responsibility judgments is related to how one's self system is organized. Furthermore, the congruence among deontic decisions, responsibility judgments, and moral behavior is encouraged by an individual's tendency toward self-consistency.

Kohlberg (1984) pointed out that moral action often fails to keep pace with mature moral reasoning because people use various "quasi-obligations" or excuses to avoid a judgment of responsibility that parallels their deontic choice. For example, the quasi-obligation of team loyalty may keep the above player from turning in her teammate. Kohlberg also has noted that reasoning reflecting substage B considerations contains fewer excusing complications and fewer quasi-obligations than does reasoning at substage A.

It is not difficult to see why sport action may depart from participants' best moral reasoning. The sport structure itself may encourage the use of substage A reasoning, replete with quasi-obligations. Players' judgments of self-responsibility are further discouraged by the generally accepted practice of concentrating moral authority in the roles of coaches and officials. Players often view their responsibility to opponents as limited to obeying the game rules or informal norms, avoiding officials' negative sanctions, and/or conforming to coaches' orders.

Moral Education. Kohlberg's first approach to moral education was to devise hypothetical moral dilemmas that could be discussed by small groups in educational settings. The teacher's role was that of a Socratic facilitator. This approach built on the work of one of his students, Moshe Blatt, who found that such discussions could promote moral stage growth (Blatt & Kohlberg, 1975). The underlying mechanism responsible for growth was hypothesized to be cognitive conflict or disequilibrium. As students encountered moral reasoning slightly more mature than their own, they were attracted to it. But their own moral reasoning had to change to incorporate the new patterns of reasoning. Change is a slow process whereby an existent pattern of reasoning is disrupted, then reconstructed to meet new challenges.

In Kohlberg's later work (Higgins, Power, & Kohlberg, 1984; Kohlberg & Higgins, 1987), he substantially modified his approach to moral education. He became dissatisfied with the peer dialogue method because it was limited to a discussion of either hypothetical stories or relatively trivial real life ones. Secondly, it was disconnected from moral action; it generated reasoning in a behavioral vacuum.

To correct these difficulties, Kohlberg developed the Just Community approach to moral education. In brief, the Just Community approach involves the formation of a participatory democracy within the school. The Just Community seeks to foster a sense of community identity that becomes the vehicle through which collective moral norms are generated.

This movement into the Just Community approach necessitated a branching beyond Kohlberg's Piagetian roots. Rather than focus specifically on the individual as the focus of concern, Kohlberg began to see group norms as equally important. Groups have moral norms that are *sui generis;* they are not reducible to the sum of the individual's moral perspectives. The shared collective norms help to define the moral atmosphere of a group.

Group norms undergo change along several lines. First, they progress through phases in their acquisition. Norms are initially proposed; then they may be accepted as a group ideal, but with little anticipation of actual behavioral conformity; with further progress, behavioral conformity to collective norms may become expected; finally, the group may come to accept the responsibility of norm enforcement.

Another dimension along which collective norms may be described is their degree of collectiveness. Kohlberg described a fifteen-step sequence in the full empowerment of collective norms. In brief, the sequence moves from norms initially being held only by individuals, with little sense of group identity. Next, people may see the norms as characterizing the group, but only because of authority expectations. Then norms may become "aggregate norms," where they are norms for subgroups but not for the group in its entirety. Finally, norms become truly collective.

Collective moral norms can be characterized by their moral stage. Again, it is important to emphasize that collective norms are *sui generis;* the stage of a collective norm is not equivalent to the average of individuals' moral stages. In general, as group life progresses, improvements in the stage of collective morality will be noted.

We have described progress within the phases, degrees, and stages of collective norms as if they represented clear developmental progressions. In Kohlberg's view, groups may make progress in the indicated direction, but these dimensions of collective norms are not developmental in the way individual moral stages are. Group life is too variable for the use of stringent developmental criteria. Nonetheless, helping groups progress in the development of their collective norms is vital, Kohlberg argued, because the group's moral atmosphere influences both individual moral growth and appropriate moral action by individuals and the group as a whole. We believe the concepts of moral atmosphere and collective norms have significant theoretical, empirical, and practical implications for sport and physical education and have recently developed a checklist to assess the moral atmosphere of physical activity contexts in the upper elementary school (Shields, Getty, & Bredemeier, 1992). We will revisit the issue of moral atmosphere in the conclusion to the chapter.

Haan's Theory of Moral Development

Kohlberg's theory has dominated the landscape of moral development inquiry for the past couple of decades, but a considerable amount of sport research has utilized a related theory of moral development, that of Norma Haan. We will briefly highlight its major features.

Basic Concepts. Haan (1977a, 1978, 1983; Haan, Aerts, & Cooper, 1985) was less concerned than Kohlberg with how people reason about abstract moral issues. Rather, she focused on how people in actual life situations believe moral agreements should be reached and moral disputes negotiated. Haan's basic constructs were derived from an analysis of moral action in the context of simulation games (Haan, 1978). Thus the basic concepts of her theory describe the structure of interpersonal moral action.

There are three major concepts at the heart of Haan's model of moral development: moral balance, moral dialogue, and moral levels. The first concept, moral balance, refers to an interpersonal state when all parties are in basic agreement about respective rights and obligations. When people are in moral balance, an agreement exists—usually informal and unstated—about what should or should not be done and who should do what. For example, in a game of basketball, competitors may be described as in moral balance if they are in basic agreement about the informal norms of play. Similarly, a player and a coach are in moral balance if they have a shared understanding about such issues as the amount of practice required, the type and quality of the coach's input, and the amount of the player's game time.

When two or more people disagree about mutual rights and obligations, they are in a state of moral imbalance. Moral imbalances occur frequently since interpersonal life is characterized by shifting expectations, selective perceptions, and subtle changes in mood and behavior. A moral imbalance can arise between a coach and a player, for example, simply because the coach and player attach different significance to criticisms of their athletic director. Moral life can be described as a process of fluctuation between moral balance and imbalance.

When moral imbalances occur, people use a variety of means to try to reestablish moral balance. Haan collectively called these efforts at restoring moral balance "moral dialogue." The most obvious and clear instance of moral dialogue is open, verbal negotiation. The effort by representatives of a professional athlete and a team to reach a contract through negotiation, for example, is an instance of moral dialogue. But moral dialogue can take many other forms be-

sides explicit dialogue. If a soccer player is tripped in violation of both the rules and informal player norms, then the two players are in moral imbalance. Under such circumstances, the moral dialogue may take the form of the offended player hitting the offending player with extra force during a later play to communicate, "I didn't like what you did to me, and don't do it again." The result may be a restored moral balance; if the communication is unsuccessful at restoring balance, further "dialogue" may continue until balance is achieved or until the relationship ends. In sum, any communication—direct or indirect, verbal or nonverbal —intended to convey information about one's needs or desires in an effort to maintain or restore moral balance is an instance of moral dialogue.

According to Haan (1978), there are five levels in the development of moral maturity. Each level reflects a different understanding of the appropriate structuring of the moral balance. The first two levels make up what can be called the "Assimilation Phase," during which time the person believes that moral balances should be constructed that generally give preference to the needs and concerns of the self. This is not because the person is "selfish," but because the person is unable to comprehend with equal clarity and urgency the felt needs and desires of others. This situation is turned around during the "Accommodation Phase," consisting of levels 3 and 4. People reflecting these levels generally seek to give to the moral exchange more than they receive. Finally, at the "Equilibration Phase," the level 5 person gives equal recognition to all parties' interests.

Haan's model follows the same basic contour of development as Kohlberg's, but the two theorists differ significantly on their depiction of moral maturity. For Haan, no abstract principle of justice is adequate to deal with the intricately nuanced situations of everyday moral life. Instead, she maintained that the morally mature person recognizes that moral dialogue must meet certain procedural criteria for guaranteeing equality if a moral balance is to be considered adequate. Specifically mature moral dialogue allows all parties equal access to relevant information, includes all those who will be affected by decisions reached, seeks to achieve unforced consensus through nondominated discussion, and reflects the particularities of the situation and the parties involved.

From Thought to Action. To help explain the discrepancy that often occurs between thought and action, Haan placed her moral theory within a broader model of psychological functioning (Haan, 1977b). This model highlights both structures, such as the moral structures we have been discussing, and ego processes. Ego processes provide for two types of regulation: (a) they are involved in the intrapsychic integration of outputs from different psychological structures, and (b) they coordinate interchange between the person's ongoing psychological functioning and the environment. A crude analogy would hold that the psychological structures are like the processing chips of a computer and the ego processes are like the circuitry that connects the internal components and coordinates them with input from the keyboard, modem, or other external devices.

The ego processes can be subdivided into two sets: coping ego processes, which reflect accurate and faithful intrapsychic coordinations and interchange with the environment, and defending processes, which reflect a breakdown in accuracy. Coping processes, such as empathy, suppression, concentration, logical analysis, and sublimation, are analogous to properly functioning circuitry, but defensive processes, which include mechanisms like projection, repression, denial, rationalization, and displacement, are like short circuits that distort information.

For action to reflect a person's most mature moral capabilities, the person must remain coping in her or his ego processing. Sometimes, however, accuracy is abandoned for the sake of maintaining a coherent and positive sense of self. Particularly under stress, coping may give way to defending and the quality of moral action may deteriorate. The role of acute stress in eliciting defensive ego processes is of special interest to sport psychologists, since competition often is associated with high levels of stress. It may be, for example, that when excessive emphasis is placed on performance outcome, the resultant stress may encourage temporary moral dysfunctions. This is a relatively unexplored area that is ripe for research.

Moral Education. Haan did not give extensive treatment to moral education. Her focus on moral action rather than moral cognition, however, led her to suggest that it is social disequilibrium, not cognitive disequilibrium, that is the primary vehicle for moral development (1985). As an example of what she meant by social disequilibrium, let us imagine an elementary school child who refuses to share playground equipment. Repeated failure to share the balls and bats will lead, most probably, to robust problems in social relationships. Haan argued that it is these social disruptions, not disequilibrium in abstract cognitive structures, that provide the motivation for reexamining one's way of constructing moral exchange.

The educational implications of Haan's approach have been developed elsewhere (Shields, 1986). In brief, it is important to provide action contexts where dialogue and negotiation among interdependent parties can take place. The group leader can help participants use their coping processes by minimizing unnecessary stress and by monitoring and addressing signs of the use of defending processes. In addition, when participants deviate from the criteria for truth-identifying dialogues, these shortcomings can be discussed by the group.

We have discussed two important theories of moral development and have speculated about some of the ways they may be relevant to the investigation of sport morality; this review has been selective rather than exhaustive. The important works of Jean Piaget (1932) and Carol Gilligan (1982; Gilligan, Lyons, & Hanmer, 1990), for example, have not been reviewed because of a lack of published research by sport psychologists using these frameworks. We now turn to the empirical research that has been done on sport and morality.

EMPIRICAL FINDINGS ABOUT MORALITY AND SPORT

In approaching a new field of investigation, three interrelated categories of questions readily come to mind. The first focuses on *description:* what are the relationships among the variables under investigation? The second set of questions moves from description to *explanation,* with the responses often taking the form of theory building. Finally there are questions about the practical *application* of the research. In this discussion we will present findings from studies on sport and morality as they relate to these three interrelated sets of questions.

Description

Social Learning Studies. A few theorists have used the social learning approach to investigate sport morality. Generally this approach focuses on specific behaviors considered to be prosocial. Such observable behaviors as giving, turn taking, and cooperation have been candidates for investigation.

Kleiber and Roberts (1981) investigated the impact of sport competition on children's cooperation and altruism. Children in the fourth and fifth grades were randomly assigned to either an experimental group or a control group. Those children in the experimental group competed in a kickball tournament for 8 days. Analyses of pre- and posttest results indicated that the experimental children's prosocial behavior declined following their participation in the competitive tournament. Unfortunately generalizations are problematic because (1) the prosocial measure was not validated by observations of actual behavior, (2) the intervention was very short in duration, and (3) the kickball tournament occurred during recess, a context not readily likened to organized competitive sport.

Kleiber and Roberts attempted to replicate existent practices of competitive sport. In contrast, Orlick (1981) used a social learning approach to investigate the possible positive effects of an alternative approach to physical education. Seventy-one 5-year-old children from two schools participated for 18 weeks in either a cooperative games program or a traditional games program. The dependent variable was children's sharing behavior, operationally defined as the amount of candy donated to children in another class. Results were generally in the direction predicted, but were inconsistent. The cooperative games program fostered a significant increase in children's willingness to share in one school, but not in the other. Similarly, the traditional games program resulted in a significant decrease in willingness to share in one school with no significant differences occurring in the other school.

Giebink and McKenzie (1985) used instructions, praise,

modeling, and a contingent reward system in an effort to modify negative social behavior in four boys during physical education and recreation activities. Results generally supported the effectiveness of the intervention with sports-personlike behaviors increasing and antisocial behaviors decreasing. Unfortunately the extremely small sample size and the inability to distinguish which of the interventions was producing what effect limit the study's generalizability.

Structural Developmental Studies. A few investigators have published empirical research using Kohlberg's theory of moral development to assess the maturity of sport participants' moral reasoning. Hall (1981), for example, found that collegiate basketball players' moral reasoning maturity was lower than that of their college peers. Using Rest's "objective measure" of moral development, derived from Kohlberg's model, we replicated Hall's finding in an exploratory study of moral reasoning and behavior among female and male basketball players at the college level (Bredemeier & Shields, 1984). After this inital investigation, we began using Haan's model as our primary measure of moral reasoning maturity in contexts of physical education and sport.

In 1986 we extended the athlete-nonathlete comparisons by testing the reasoning maturity of male and female basketball players and nonathletes at both the high school and college level (Bredemeier & Shields, 1986a). Our moral measure was designed so that respondents reasoned about two hypothetical moral dilemmas set in everyday life contexts and two in sport-specific situations, yielding two distinct scores: one for "life" moral reasoning, and one for "sport" moral reasoning. Among the 50 college students, the nonathletes were again found to have significantly more mature moral reasoning than the basketball players, a finding that held for both sport and life dilemmas. Among the 50 high school students, however, we found no reasoning differences between athletes and nonathletes. The study also revealed gender differences. Both college and high school females reasoned at a more mature level than males in response to sport dilemmas, and high school females also exhibited more mature reasoning in response to the life dilemmas.

In a related study, 20 swimmers were added to the college sample to determine whether the same athlete-nonathlete relationship would hold for college athletes other than basketball players. Swimmers' mean scores for "life" and "sport" moral reasoning were between those of the nonathletes and the basketball players. "Life" reasoning differences only approached significance, but basketball players' "sport" reasoning was less mature than that of both the swimmers and the nonathletes; "sport" reasoning for the latter two groups did not significantly differ.

These studies suggest that it is not experience in sport per se that is associated with less mature moral reasoning. We did not find differences in moral maturity between high school basketball players and nonathletes, nor between college swimmers and nonathletes. A number of questions are suggested by these findings. Does the amount of physical

contact, the length of involvement, the competitive level, or the type of interpersonal interaction in one's sport experience influence the development of one's moral reasoning? Alternately, are people with more mature reasoning less interested in, or purposefully "selected out," of some college athletic programs? The cross-sectional methodology of these studies did not allow such questions to be answered.

Similar issues are raised about the differences between males' and females' sport reasoning. It is not too surprising that, given typical gender socialization and the traditional role of sport in that process, males' moral reasoning may be more influenced by the egocentric aspects of competitive sport, but we have only begun to be explore this area of research (Bredemeier, 1982, 1984).

Moral reasoning maturity is important, but more important is actual behavior. The issues of moral behavior in sport have been investigated primarily with reference to aggression. Preliminary evidence that moral reasoning is related to aggression in sport came from the basketball study (Bredemeier & Shields, 1984) discussed above. In addition to administering a moral maturity measure, we asked the athletes' coaches to rate and rank their players on aggressive behavior on the court. We operationally defined aggression as the initiation of an attack with the intent to injure. Using the coaches' evaluations as a measure of players' aggression, we found significant relationships between stages of moral reasoning and tendencies to aggress. Athletes' preconventional moral reasoning was positively correlated with coaches' evaluations of high aggressiveness, while postconventional moral reasoning was associated with low aggression scores.

We also have begun to explore the relationship between moral thought and sport action among children. Bredemeier (1992a) administered four hypothetical moral dilemmas, together with pencil-and-paper measures designed to assess assertive, aggressive, and submissive action tendencies in both everyday life (Deluty, 1979, 1984) and sport to 106 9- to 13-year-old children. Results indicated that children's moral reasoning scores were predictive of self-reported assertive and aggressive action tendencies in both sport and daily life. Assertion is a conflict resolution strategy that reflects a balancing of one's own needs with those of others, while aggressive responses place personal interests above the needs or rights of others; therefore it was hypothesized that assertion would be associated with more mature moral reasoning and aggression with less mature reasoning. Results confirmed our expectations. Children who were relatively mature in their moral reasoning described themselves as more assertive and less aggressive in response to conflict situations than children with less mature reasoning.

In a related study we examined the relationship of children's sport participation and interest with their moral reasoning maturity and aggression tendencies (Bredemeier, Weiss, Shields, & Cooper, 1986). Girls and boys in the fourth through seventh grades responded to a sport involvement questionnaire as well as moral reasoning and behavioral tendency measures. Analyses revealed that boys' participation and interest in high contact sports and girls' participation in medium contact sports (the highest level of contact sport experience girls reported) were associated with less mature moral reasoning and greater tendencies to aggress. None of the remaining sport involvement-reasoning/behavior associations were significant.

These findings are important for at least two reasons. First, they point to the importance of identifying those factors within sport structures that are key to the relationships among sport involvement and morality variables. Differentiating sports by the amount of physical contact, for example, appears to be one helpful means of categorizing types of sport experience. Second, gender differences in the study highlight the need for an interactive psychological model that considers both environmental influences (e.g., sport structures) and individuals' meaning-construction processes. If the sport structure itself were the only factor mediating the relationship among sport involvement and morality variables, one would anticipate the same general pattern of relationships for females and males.

Several interpretations of the gender differences are possible. One probable explanation is that since females have generally been excluded from high contact sports, their perceptions and attributions about physical contact in medium contact sports may be closer to those of males in high contact sports than to those of males participating in the same medium contact sports.

It is important to remember that from a structuralist perspective, to behave in a particular way (in this case, to aggress or not aggress in a sport context) is neither consistent nor inconsistent with any given level of moral reasoning. Although investigators have found significant correlations between stage or level of moral reasoning and sport aggression, other factors besides reasoning maturity are clearly implicated. One of these factors is an individual's judgment about the legitimacy of a particular behavior, in this case, intentionally injurious sport acts. Two studies were designed to investigate the relationship between sport participants' moral reasoning maturity and their judgment regarding potentially injurious sport behavior.

In one such study, Bredemeier (1985) again used hypothetical sport and life dilemmas with 40 female and male high school and college basketball players. In addition, participants made judgments about the legitimacy of six behaviors with varying implications. In terms of the actor's intention toward an opponent, the six acts, in order of severity, were:

1. nonphysical intimidation
2. physical intimidation
3. making the opponent miss several minutes of play
4. eliminating the opponent from the game due to injury
5. making the opponent miss a season due to injury
6. permanently disabling the opponent

The athletes made judgments under two conditions about the appropriateness of each of the six behaviors in this Continuum of Injurious Acts (CIA): (a) during a mid-week interview session in which hypothetical dilemmas were discussed, and (b) during an interview session immediately following an important late-season game. In the first "hypothetical" condition, the athlete focused on what acts she or he thought would be acceptable for a fictitious football player; in the second "engaged" condition, the athlete made judgments about what would be appropriate in her or his own basketball play.

Results indicated an inverse relationship between players' levels of moral reasoning and the number of intentionally injurious sport acts they judged to be legitimate. Those athletes with more mature moral reasoning accepted fewer acts as legitimate. Also, "sport" moral reasoning was a significantly better predictor than "life" moral reasoning of legitimacy judgments in both the hypothetical and engaged contexts. The relationship was strongest between "sport" moral reasoning and hypothetical judgments, and weakest between "life" moral reasoning and engaged judgments. This pattern suggests that the reasoning-judgment relationship can be most clearly predicted when the contexts are similar and when the judgments, like the moral interviews, pertain to a hypothetical actor.

A second issue examined in this study was differences in legitimacy judgments as a function of sex, school level, and judgment context. Male athletes were found to accept a greater number of CIA acts as legitimate than females, and college athletes a greater number than high school competitors. The gender finding is consistent with a considerable body of literature suggesting that males accept and express more aggression than females (Hyde, 1984). Similarly the school level finding is consistent with the view that an in-sport socialization process tends to encourage the legitimation of aggression (Silva, 1983). Results from the study also indicated that athletes judged significantly more CIA acts as legitimate in the engaged condition than in the hypothetical condition, even though the latter context focused on football, a collision sport structured by rules permitting potentially injurious acts, and the former context focused on basketball, a sport in which relatively limited physical contact is normative. One interpretation of these results is that the stresses of competitive sport experience may erode a person's capacity to make clear judgments consistent with that person's most mature reasoning. A second interpretation is that questions posed in the hypothetical context tended to elicit deontic justice reasoning, while probes in the engaged context encouraged a greater degree of responsibility reasoning. Other interpretations are also possible and future research is needed to disentangle the influence of such factors as (a) the sport involved (football vs. basketball), (b) the timing of the interview (midweek vs. postgame), and (c) the subject of action (hypothetical other vs. self).

A second study of moral reasoning maturity and legitimacy judgments focused on children in the fourth through seventh grades. Bredemeier, Weiss, Shields, and Cooper (1987) showed 78 children slides of potentially injurious sport behaviors and administered moral interviews. The slide series featured male athletes performing the following acts: (1) legal boxing punch, (2) legal football tackle, (3) illegal basketball contact, (4) illegal soccer tackle, (5) legal baseball contact, (6) illegal football tackle, (7) illegal basketball trip, (8) illegal soccer contact, and (9) legal baseball slide. While some of the slides reflected activity within the rules of the sport, all involved action that was judged by the children to carry a high risk of injury. Children were asked to indicate approval or disapproval of the actions depicted. Results paralleled those with college students: children with less mature reasoning judged a significantly greater number of potentially injurious acts to be legitimate than their more mature peers.

Explanation

The second set of research questions moves beyond description and seeks to explain the interrelationships among sport involvement and morality variables. Can models be constructed and tested that enable us to understand how sport involvement interacts with psychosocial dynamics to influence behavior? This question emphasizes interactional mechanisms; answers may reveal how sport experience creates different sets of consequences for different individuals.

Explanatory theories inevitably involve the establishment of cause-effect relations among the variables under study. To date, these studies still lie in the future of sport morality research. However, some of our work may set the stage for theory-building about moral thought and action in sport settings.

To place this research in context, it should be emphasized that most structural developmental theorists have traditionally held that a person's moral reasoning level will remain fairly constant across different types of situations. This is because stages are thought to reflect structured wholes or integrated functional systems; different contents will be acted on in similar ways because of the integrated nature of the underlying thought process. Nonetheless a few highly irregular situations have been shown to alter the person's level of moral reasoning. Research conducted in prisons (Kohlberg, Hickey, & Scharf, 1972), for example, has demonstrated that inmates use lower stages of reasoning in response to prison dilemmas than when they attempt to resolve standard hypothetical dilemmas. Kohlberg has hypothesized that when a group's collective norms reflect a low stage of moral reasoning, then the constraining moral atmosphere may inhibit more advanced moral functioning even among those individuals capable of higher stage thought (see Power, Higgins, & Kohlberg, 1989).

We have suggested that sport might also be one of those unusual contexts where moral reasoning undergoes a change in its underlying structure (Bredemeier & Shields, 1985, 1986c; Shields & Bredemeier, 1984). This hypothesis was generated in light of the "set aside" character of sport activity. Sport is set apart from everyday life both spatially, through marked boundaries, and temporally, by designated playing periods replete with "time-outs." A variety of

symbols—such as whistles, buzzers, flags, uniforms, and special rituals and ceremonies—are used to create and reinforce the "world within a world" character of sport. The separated world of sport is governed by artificial rules and roles, and is oriented toward a goal with no intrinsic meaning or value.

It was noted earlier that in several studies the moral interviews included reasoning about both life and sport dilemmas. To begin to investigate the hypothesis that moral reasoning about issues in sport contexts differs significantly from reasoning about moral issues in most other social contexts, we analyzed reasoning maturity scores to determine whether "sport" scores significantly differed from the "life" scores (Bredemeier & Shields, 1984b). Breaking down a sample of 120 basketball players, swimmers, and nonathletes by school level, sex, and athletic status, we found that "life" reasoning maturity scores were significantly higher than "sport" scores for every subgroup and for the sample as a whole.

Similar analyses were conducted with 110 girls and boys in grades 4 through 7 (Bredemeier, 1990b), revealing that sixth and seventh graders' "sport" reasoning was significantly lower than their "life" reasoning; this life-sport reasoning divergence was significantly greater than for the younger children, who did not demonstrate context-specific reasoning patterns.

Based on these findings, we have proposed a theory of "game reasoning" (Bredemeier & Shields, 1985, 1986b, c; Coakley & Bredemeier, 1988; Shields & Bredemeier, 1984). Still in its early stages of development, the theory holds that the unique context of sport elicits a transformation in moral reasoning such that egocentrism, typically the hallmark of immature morality, becomes a valued and acceptable principle for organizing the moral exchange. In terms of moral reasoning, we have hypothesized that sport offers a context for a "legitimated regression" (Shields, 1986; Shields & Bredemeier, 1984) to a form of moral reasoning that is similar to less mature moral reasoning.

Sport may allow for the temporary suspension of the typical moral obligation to equally consider the interests of all parties in favor of a more egocentric style of moral engagement as an enjoyable and nonserious moral deviation. There may be several reasons why such a moral transformation is culturally sanctioned and viewed as appropriate within the limits of sport. First of all, competition is premised on each party or team seeking self-gain. There is little room in sport for equally considering the desires, goals, and needs of opponents. While competition demands a degree of egocentrism, the unique protective structures of sport function to legitimize it. The carefully planned and rigorously enforced rules protect participants from many of the negative consequences that would typically ensue from egocentric morality. Furthermore, the continual presence of officials and coaches allows for the temporary transference of moral responsibility.

Of course, sport is not a moral free-for-all. Players remain people, and moral responsibility cannot be completely set aside. Just as sport may be a "world within a world," existing within and connected to the real world, so game reasoning does not completely displace or render inoperative basic moral understandings. To remain legitimate, one can only "play" at egocentrism. When the play character of game reasoning is lost, sport can deteriorate into a breeding ground of aggression, cheating, and other moral defaults.

The elaboration and validation of this theory of game reasoning awaits future research, and at this point we can only speculate about potential implications for the theory. If sport does elicit its own special form of moral reasoning, it may help to shed light on some of the earlier findings. Take, for example, the finding that for some college athletes, participation in sport is associated with lower levels of moral reasoning maturity. Perhaps for some college athletes, particularly those for whom sport is a highly salient experience, game reasoning may begin to lose its "set aside" character and have undue influence on moral reasoning beyond the bounds of sport. Several factors may account for why this is more true for participants in some sports than in others. Participation in some elite sports, particularly those for which professional opportunities are available, often includes external rewards contingent on performance; the infusion of "daily life" rewards (e.g., money or educational opportunity) into the sport experience may encourage a blurring of the distinction between sport and everyday life. Also, some sport structures, like basketball, are characterized by a high degree of player interaction, requiring various forms of interpersonal exchange. Other sport structures, like that of swimming, require little or no interpersonal interaction during actual competition; consequently, minimal possibility or necessity for moral exchange and negotiation exists. Experience in more interactive sports may more closely approximate everyday life and thus encourage a blending or confusion between "sport" and "life" moralities.

On an even more speculative level, it might be hypothesized that game reasoning sometimes is used in life contexts other than competitive physical activity. The frequent use of sport images and analogies in contexts such as business and politics may evidence this. Perhaps one reason sport language is so popular in business and political dialogue is precisely due to its power to evoke a game reasoning orientation in which egocentric morality appears legitimized. Without the protective and scrupulously fair structures of sport, however, one wonders whether this nonplayful use of game reasoning is really legitimate.

Application

The final set of research questions is designed to enable teachers and coaches to predict what types of sport and/or physical education experiences will be advantageous to participants. What conditions and strategies facilitate participants' moral growth, and what factors are detrimental to their moral development?

Most of the research in the field of application focuses on physical education rather than sport, and conclusions do not necessarily translate from one to the other. Over the past 20 years, Hellison has been working to develop and field-test a physical education model for teaching self-responsibility to delinquency-prone youth. Hellison and his colleagues (De Busk & Hellison, 1989; Hellison, 1978, 1983, 1985; Hellison, Lifka, & Georgiadis, 1990) report the successful use of physical education instruction with at-risk youth in promoting self-control, respect for the rights of others, and prosocial behavior. Hellison's fieldwork has yielded important insights for those engaged in physical education pedagogy, but more empirical research is needed to test instructional strategies and establish causal relationships.

In a preliminary investigation to determine whether theoretically based instructional strategies can be efficacious in promoting moral growth, we conducted a field experiment designed to explore the effectiveness of a moral development program in a summer sport camp (Bredemeier, Weiss, Shields, & Shewchuk, 1986). Children aged 5 to 7 were matched and randomly assigned to one of three conditions: a control group, a social learning group, and a structural developmental group. During the 6-week intervention program, each group used essentially the same curriculum and the same weekly moral themes (fair play, sharing, verbal and physical aggression, and righting wrongs).

Instructors in the control group employed traditional physical education pedagogy, encouraging conformity to game- or teacher-prescribed rules. Children in the social learning class received reinforcement for prosocial behavior that was also modeled by the instructor and peers. Structural developmental group instructors were trained according to Haan's interactional model to facilitate children's peer-oriented moral dialogue in response to dilemmas that arose in class.

Measures of moral reasoning included a Piagetian intentionality instrument developed for this investigation and a distributive justice scale (Enright, 1981). Analyses revealed significant pre- to posttest gains in the reasoning maturity of children in the social learning and structural developmental groups, but no changes occurred for the control group. Although differences between the experimental and control groups only approached significance, the within-group results were encouraging and seemed to suggest that moral growth can be stimulated by implementing theoretically grounded instructional strategies. Further evidence of the efficaciousness of structural developmental instructional strategies comes from a field experiment by Romance, Weiss, and Bockovan (1986), who implemented an 8-week intervention program through which fifth grade children's moral reasoning was significantly improved.

A second finding from our study (see Shields & Bredemeier, 1989) pertains to the effects of the instructional strategies on the children's coping and defending ego processing. We developed a special exploratory instrument based on the clinical work of Haan (1977b), the Coping and Defending (CAD) measure, and administered it before and after our intervention. Analyses revealed that both posttest coping and defending scores were significantly influenced by instructional strategies.

Children in the structural developmental group improved significantly more in their coping skills than children in either the social learning or control groups, which did not differ from each other. Defending scores for children in both the structural developmental and social learning groups decreased (i.e., improved) significantly more than for children in the control group; defending score improvements among children in the two experimental groups did not differ significantly from each other.

We hypothesized that defensive processing declined in both the structural developmental and social learning groups because both teaching strategies helped to create a low-stress, ego-affirming atmosphere that lessened the necessity for defensiveness. However, only children in the structural developmental group experienced a coping increase in conjunction with a decrease in ego defense. Coping mechanisms are most evidently required when varying viewpoints need to be accurately heard, differentially evaluated, and consistently coordinated. The adult-dominated nature of the social learning pedagogy may be less likely than the interactive, peer-oriented structural developmental approach to foster an improvement in coping mechanisms. These results and interpretations must be viewed with caution, however, because of the nonvalidated nature of the instrument.

In summary, we and our colleagues have found that both structural developmental and social learning strategies can be used to promote moral reasoning maturity through relatively brief interventions. Based on the 1986 summer sport camp study, however, instructional strategies derived from structural developmental theory appear to be superior at improving children's openness to ongoing growth as evidenced by positive changes in both their coping and defending processes. These findings clearly need to be replicated under a variety of circumstances before they can be viewed as conclusive.

FUTURE DIRECTIONS FOR RESEARCH AND APPLICATION

It is clear that there is much work to be done before we have a clear understanding of how sport and physical education experiences relate to the many processes involved in moral thought and action. To date, moral research in the context of sport has focused on only a very few sports and it is difficult to generalize beyond that narrow base. A broader range of both sport and physical education experiences across varying conditions and structures needs to be explored.

The theory of game reasoning that we have tentatively put forward needs to be refined and further tested. Related to this project is the need to consider the role that group moral norms and the moral atmosphere play in sport and physical education settings. It may be, for example, that game reasoning involves an accommodation to the prevailing moral atmosphere of a particular sport context more than a simple internal psychological shift in response to the sport structure itself. In turn, leadership styles may play a significant role in establishing and maintaining group moral norms.

In addition, researchers need to move beyond their tendency to isolate aspects of moral functioning—such as moral reasoning maturity or prosocial behavior—and to incorporate a holistic model of moral social-psychology. Rest (1984), for example, has offered a four-component model of moral action that may provide a useful paradigm in this regard, though it seems to underplay the impact of sociological variables (Weiss & Bredemeier, 1990).

In this chapter, we have offered empirical findings, theoretical suggestions, and practical implications derived from sport morality research. As we have stated, however, research on moral variables in relation to sport and/or physical education is scarce. It is a new area of focus for sport psychologists and it is ripe for additional research. We hope that some of the information and suggestions offered in this chapter will enhance interest in this vital area of sport psychology.

References

Bandura, A. (1977). *Social learning theory.* Englewood Cliffs, NJ: Prentice-Hall.

Blasi, A. (1984). Moral identity: Its role in moral functioning. In W. Kurtines & J. Gewirtz (Eds.), *Morality, moral behavior, and moral development* (pp. 128–39). New York: Wiley.

Blasi, A. (1989). The integration of morality in personality. In I. E. Bilbao (Ed.), *Perspectivas acerca de cambio moral: Posibles intervenciones educativas* (pp. 119–131). San Sebastian: Servicio Editorial Universidad del Pais Vasco.

Blatt, M. M., & Kohlberg, L. (1975). The effects of classroom moral discussion upon children's level of moral judgment. *Journal of Moral Education, 4,* 129–161.

Bredemeier, B. (1982). Gender, justice, and non-violence. *Perspectives, 9,* 106–113.

Bredemeier, B. (1983). Athletic aggression: A moral concern. In

J. Goldstein (Ed.), *Sports violence,* (pp. 46–81). New York: Springer-Verlag.

Bredemeier, B. (1984). Sport, gender and moral growth. In J. Silva & R. Weinberg (Eds.), *Psychological foundations of sport and exercise* (pp. 400–414). Champaign, IL: Human Kinetics.

Bredemeier, B. (1985). Moral reasoning and the perceived legitimacy of intentionally injurious sport acts. *Journal of Sport Psychology, 7,* 110–124.

Bredemeier, B. (1987). The moral of the youth sport story. In E. Brown & C. Branta (Eds.), *Competitive sports for children and youth* (pp. 285–296). Champaign, IL: Human Kinetics.

Bredemeier, B. (1992a). *Children's moral reasoning and their assertive, aggressive, and submissive tendencies in sport and daily life.* Manuscript submitted for publication.

Bredemeier, B. (1992b). *Divergence in children's moral reasoning about issues in daily life and sport specific contexts.* Manuscript submitted for publication.

Bredemeier, B., & Shields, D. (1983). *Body and balance: The development of moral structures through physical education and sport.* Eugene, OR: University of Oregon Publications.

Bredemeier, B., & Shields, D. (1984a). The utility of moral stage analysis in the understanding of athletic aggression. *Sociology of Sport Journal, 1,* 138–149.

Bredemeier, B., & Shields, D. (1984b). Divergence in moral reasoning about sport and life. *Sociology of Sport Journal, 1,* 348–357.

Bredemeier, B., & Shields, D. (1985). Values and violence in sport. *Psychology Today, 19,* 22–32.

Bredemeier, B., & Shields, D. (1986a). Moral growth among athletes and non-athletes: A comparative analysis. *Journal of Genetic Psychology, 147,* 7–18.

Bredemeier, B., & Shields, D. (1986b). Athletic aggression: An issue of contextual morality. *Sociology of Sport Journal, 3,* 15–28.

Bredemeier, B., & Shields, D. (1986c). Game reasoning and interactional morality. *Journal of Genetic Psychology, 147,* 257–275.

Bredemeier, B., & Shields, D. (1987). Moral growth through physical activity: An interactional approach. In D. Gould & M. Weiss (Eds.), *Advances in Pediatric Sport Sciences* (pp. 145–165). Champaign, IL: Human Kinetics.

Bredemeier, B., Weiss, M., Shields, D., & Cooper, B. (1986). The relationship of sport involvement with children's moral reasoning and aggression tendencies, *Journal of Sport Psychology, 8,* 304–318.

Bredemeier, B., Weiss, M., Shields, D., & Cooper, B. (1987). The relationship between children's legitimacy judgments and their moral reasoning, aggression tendencies, and sport involvement. *Sociology of Sport Journal, 4,* 48–60.

Bredemeier, B., Weiss, M., Shields, D., & Shewchuk, R. (1986). Promoting moral growth in a summer sport camp: The implementation of theoretically grounded instructional strategies. *Journal of Moral Education, 15,* 212–220.

Coakley, J., & Bredemeier, B. (1988). *Youth sports: Development of ethical practices.* Unpublished manuscript.

DeBusk, M., & Hellison, D. (1989). Implementing a physical education self-responsibility model for delinquency-prone youth. *Journal of Teaching Physical Education, 8,* 104–112.

Deluty, R. H. (1979). Children's action tendency scale: A self-report measure of aggressiveness, assertiveness, and submissiveness in children. *Journal of Consulting and Clinical Psychology, 47,* 1061–1071.

Deluty, R. H. (1984). Behavioral validation of the children's action tendency scale. *Journal of Behavioral Assessment, 6,* 115–130.

Enright, R. (1981). *A user's manual for the Distributive Justice Scale.* Madison, WI: University of Wisconsin-Madison.

Eysenck, H. J. (1977). *Crime and personality* (3rd ed.). St. Albans, Herts., U.K.: Paladin.

Giebink, M. P., & McKenzie, T. C. (1985). Teaching sportsmanship in physical education and recreation: An analysis of intervention and generalization efforts. *Journal of Teaching Physical Education, 4,* 167–177.

Gilligan, C. (1982). *In a different voice: Psychological theory and women's development.* Cambridge, MA: Harvard University Press.

Gilligan, C., Lyons, N., & Hanmer, T., (Eds.), (1990). *Making connections: The relational worlds of adolescent girls at Emma Willard School.* Cambridge, MA: Harvard University Press.

Haan, N. (1977a). *A manual for interactional morality.* Unpublished manuscript. Berkeley: Institute of Human Development, University of California.

Haan, N. (1977b). *Coping and defending: Processes of self-environment organization.* New York: Academic Press.

Haan, N. (1978). Two moralities in action contexts: Relationship to thought, ego regulation, and development. *Journal of Personality and Social Psychology, 36,* 286–305.

Haan, N. (1983). An interactional morality of everyday life. In N. Haan, R. Bellah, P. Rabinow, & W. Sullivan (Eds.), *Social science as moral inquiry* (pp. 218–250). New York: Columbia University Press.

Haan, N. (1985). Processes of moral development: Cognitive or social disequilibrium. *Developmental Psychology, 21,* 996–1006.

Haan, N., Aerts, E., & Cooper, B. B. (1985). *On moral grounds: The search for a practical morality.* New York: New York University.

Hall, E. (1981). *Moral development of athletes in sport specific and general social situations.* Unpublished doctoral dissertation, Texas Women's University.

Hellison, D. (1978). *Beyond balls and bats: Alienated (and other) youth in the gym.* Washington, DC: AAHPERD.

Hellison, D. (1983). Teaching self-responsibility (and more). *Journal of Physical Education, Recreation, and Dance, 54,* 23ff.

Hellison, D. (1985). *Goals and strategies for teaching physical education.* Champaign, IL: Human Kinetics.

Hellison, D., Lifka, B., & Georgiadis, N. (1990). Physical education for disadvantaged youth: A Chicago story. *Journal of Physical Education, Recreation & Dance, 61,* 36–46.

Higgins, A., Power, C., & Kohlberg, L. (1984). The relationship of moral atmosphere to judgments of responsibility. In W. Kurtines & J. Gewirtz (Eds.), *Morality, moral behavior, and moral development* (pp. 74–106). New York: Wiley.

Hyde, J. S. (1984). How large are gender differences in aggression? A developmental meta-analysis. *Developmental Psychology, 20,* 722–736.

Kleiber, D. A., & Roberts, G. C. (1981). The effects of sports experience in the development of social character: An exploratory investigation. *Journal of Sport Psychology, 3,* 114–122.

Kohlberg, L. (1976). Moral stages and moralization: The cognitive-developmental approach. In T. Lickona (Ed.), *Moral development and behavior: Theory, research and social issues* (pp. 31–53). New York: Holt, Rinehart, and Winston.

Kohlberg, L. (1981). *Essays on moral development: Vol. 1: The philosophy of moral development.* San Francisco: Harper & Row.

Kohlberg, L. (1984). *Essays on moral development: Vol. 2: The psychology of moral development.* San Francisco: Harper & Row.

Kohlberg, L., & Candee, D. (1984). The relationship of moral judgment to moral action. In W. Kurtines & J. Gewirtz (Eds.), *Morality, moral behavior, and moral development* (pp. 52–73). New York: Wiley.

Kohlberg, L., Hickey, J., & Scharf, P. (1972). The justice structure of the prison: A theory and intervention. *The Prison Journal, 51,* 3–14.

Kohlberg, L., & Higgins, A. (1987). School democracy and social interaction. In W. Kurtines & J. Gewirtz (Eds.), *Moral development through social interaction* (pp. 102–128). New York: John Wiley.

Orlick, T. (1981). Positive socialization via cooperative games. *Developmental Psychology, 17,* 126–129.

Piaget, J. (1932). *The moral judgment of the child.* London: Routledge & Kegan Paul.

Power, F. C., Higgins, A., & Kohlberg, L. (1989). *Lawrence*

Kohlberg's approach to moral education. New York: Columbia University Press.

Romance. T., Weiss, M., & Bockovan, J. (1986). A program to promote moral development through elementary school physical education. *Journal of Teachers of Physical Education, 5,* 126–136.

Rushton, J. P. (1982). Social learning theory and the development of prosocial behavior. In N. Eisenberg (Ed.), *The development of prosocial behavior* (pp. 77–105). New York: Academic Press.

Shields, D. (1986). *Growing beyond prejudices.* Mystic, CT: Twenty-Third Publications.

Shields, D., & Bredemeier, B. (1984). Sport and moral growth: A structural developmental perspective. In W. Straub & J. Williams (Eds.), *Cognitive sport psychology* (pp. 89–101). New York: Sport Science Associates.

Shields, D., & Bredemeier, B. (1989). Moral reasoning, judgment, and action in sport. In J. Goldstein (Ed.), *Sports, games, and play: Social and psychological viewpoints,* 2nd ed. (pp. 59–81). Hillsdale, NJ: Erlbaum.

Shields, D., Getty, D., & Bredemeier, B. (1992). *Moral Atmosphere Checklist.* Unpublished manuscript.

Silva, J. (1983). The perceived legitimacy of rule violating behavior in sport. *Journal of Sport Psychology, 5,* 438–448.

Weiss, M., & Bredemeier, B. (1986). Physical education and moral development. In V. Seefeldt (Ed.), *Contributions of physical activity to human well-being* (pp. 373–390). Champaign, IL: Human Kinetics.

Weiss, M., & Bredemeier, B. (1990). Moral development in sport. *Exercise and Sport Science Reviews, 18,* 331–378.

28

SPECTATORS: REACTIONS TO SPORTS EVENTS AND EFFECTS ON ATHLETIC PERFORMANCE

Dolf Zillmann

Paul B. Paulus

This chapter is divided into two distinct sections. First we explore the spectators' reactions to athletic performances and especially to athletic contests. What is it that attracts spectators to the games? What predispositions do they bring? Which are the features of performances and contests that spark euphoria and jubilation? And more generally, which affects and emotions is the mere witnessing of sports events capable of evoking?

After such considerations, we explore the influence of the expressive component of spectators' reactions, along with other signals emitted by spectators or co-acting witnesses, on the focal event: athletic performance. Does the sheer number of spectators, the crowd size, impact on performance? Is the so-called "home-field advantage" the result of supportive crowd behavior that spurs athletes to extraordinary performances? Alternatively, do hostile crowds intimidate athletes and hold performances down? Or is it possible that crowds hostile to particular athletes encourage superior efforts on the part of these athletes and thereby elevate their performance levels? Do different athletes respond differently to crowd support or badgering? And what is it that mediates any such existing influences? These and related issues are addressed by pertinent psychological theory and research findings.

REACTIONS OF SPECTATORS TO SPORTS EVENTS

A Brief History of Spectatorship

It would seem reasonable to assume that spectatorship evolved alongside the active engagement in athletic endeavors. Those who exhibited extraordinary physical skills—lifting weights that others couldn't, hurling objects farther than anybody else, or wrestling all competitors to the ground—should always have found an astounded, if not awed, audience. The symbiosis of athletic performance and spectatorship must have existed since the inception of sports as a social phenomenon. Surprisingly this symbiosis has received little attention, presumably because spectatorship has left fewer traces than active sports participation. Active sports engagements could be traced as far back as 5200 B.C. Hurling implements were found in the coffin of an Egyptian youth (Midwinter, 1986). But such evidence for the emergence of ball sports was without accompanying evidence for spectatorship. Was anybody watching athletic activities in these early days of civilization? In all probability there were witnesses to the events. Whether such witnessing was incidental or constituted an organized social activity can only be speculated upon. But eventually, unquestionable evidence of organized spectatorship came with written records. Moreover, it was carved in stone at ceremonial places and expressed itself in monumental stadium architecture (Schröder, 1927; Smith, 1831).

Greek culture is usually considered the cradle of enlightened sports spectatorship (Harris, 1972; Sansone, 1988). The Greeks have been credited with a reverence for grace, and for graceful physical exercise in particular. In an uncontrived fashion, athletic performances were aligned with poetic and musical expositions. The result was the oldest and most enduring significant sports/spectator institution: the Olympic Games, which ran from 776 B.C. to 393 A.D. The Pythian Games, the Isthmian Games, and the Nemean Games were conducted in a similar spirit. However, the Greeks would not resist adding various forms of wrestling and boxing, as well as chariot racing, to the entertainments at civic and religious ceremonies, thereby paving the way for what was to come in Roman sports (Guttmann, 1986; Harris, 1972).

Any Grecian reverence for athletic grace was soon squelched by a growing appetite for sports spectacles laden with mayhem. Roman urbanization is said to have created and nourished such appetite (Midwinter, 1986). In the interest of controlling social upheaval, extravagant entertainment programs were put in place. The centerpiece of these programs were so-called "blood sports," mainly gladiatorial combat and violent chariot races. Rome's Colosseum accommodated more than 40,000 spectators at gladiatorial events. And Rome's largest racetrack had crowds of approximately 250,000 spectators in attendance for chariot races (Harris, 1972). Such dimensions of spectatorship are unsurpassed in antiquity. Footballing in early China or wrestling in ancient Japan, for instance, drew crowds of comparatively modest size (Midwinter, 1986). And unlike the Roman spectacle, these events were relatively blood free.

The Roman circus not only set attendance records for antiquity, it did so until recent times. However, athletic exhibitions never failed to attract sizable crowds. Evidence for the universal appeal of athletic competition during the pre-industrial period ranges from contests in the Medicis' Italy (Bryson, 1938) to archaic matches in Polynesia (Ellis, 1829). Granted that some blood sports, such as bullfighting in Spain, attracted huge crowds to various stadia and spectatorship must be considered to have been well organized, the organization of sports and, more important here, of spectatorship, climbed to new heights with the industrial revolution. Lending some degree of support to the orthodox Marxist view that spectatorship, as a significant form of recreation, is an outgrowth of the monotony of machine-dictated labor (Ponomarev, 1974; Sansone, 1988), sports events became the weekend love affair for all those whose workday was strictly regulated by production schedules. In England and other industrial nations in Europe, fascination with soccer brought attendance at important matches to 100,000. In 1901, 110,000 spectators paid to see the Soccer Cup final between the Spurs and Sheffield United. Such attendance figures had not been reached since Roman times (Midwinter, 1986). More recently, crowds of such size have become commonplace in the stadia of many cities around the industrial world.

Going to the games is undoubtedly a most significant American pastime, too. Approximately 200 million spectators attend college and professional games each year (U.S. Census Abstracts, 1988). Uncounted fans follow their teams, attending each and every home and on-the-road game. They often spend a good portion of their income in the process (Roberts, 1976; Underwood, 1984; Vamplew, 1988).

"Attending the games" assumed a new meaning, however, with radio and, especially, television coverage of sports events. The new communication technologies raised sports spectatorship more than a thousandfold. If significant contests of the past drew crowds of 100,000, they now attract 100 million and more. So-called "big games" bring such numbers of viewers to the screen with regularity (Eitzen & Sage, 1986). World Cup Soccer matches are seen by over 800 million spectators around the world, and the numbers are growing each year (Michener, 1976). However, not only are the enormous audience sizes imposing, the wealth of sports offerings on television commands respect as well. More than 1,500 hours of network programming per year have been dedicated to sports coverage in recent times. In 1988, sports accounted for over 1,800 hours of network television and for about 5,000 hours of cable television, not counting locally generated sports programs (Eastman & Meyer, 1989). Such programming has placed alternative offerings at the risk of being neglected (Michener, 1976; Snyder & Spreitzer, 1983). Significant sports events have attracted as much as 60% of the viewing audience (Eastman & Meyer, 1989). With continual advancements in communication technology, coverage of sports events is likely to be extended still further. Alternative forms of entertainment are also likely to be dispensed on a larger scale, but interest in athletic competition and sports events may be expected to grow despite it. The simple reason for such a projection is the thrilling uncertainty about the outcome of athletic confrontations and performance comparisons. This uncertainty is inherent in athletic competition. The exhibition of true competition guarantees it—in contrast to the more predictable schemes of alternative entertainment endeavors (Zillmann, Bryant, & Sapolsky, 1989). Sports spectatorship appears headed for a great future. For the coverage of significant athletic events, the world will be a global village indeed.

The Origins of Spectatorship

Much has been written about the origins of sports (Eichel, 1953; Lukas, 1969; Sansone, 1988; Ueberhorst, 1972–1978). Some writers proposed that athletic exhibitions grew out of rituals and cults (Diem, 1960; Guttmann, 1978). Others have emphasized the skill-training function of sports (Lorenz, 1963; Ueberhorst, 1972). Still others have combined ritual elements with skill training in their presumptions about the origins of sport (Gardiner, 1930; Morris, 1981). Whatever the value of these speculations, none sheds much light on the evolution of spectatorship.

There can be little doubt that the athletic exhibitions of ancient times were often closely associated with ceremonies, and with religious ones in particular. Although this linkage may merely reflect that crowds at religious gatherings wanted to be well entertained, it has been alleged that the athletic exhibitions themselves were rituals conveying religious meanings. Athletic actions have been presumed to serve a variety of symbolic functions. For example, in numerous imaginative interpretations of sports events it is asserted, among other things, that catching a ball represents the securement of the sun as the source of life, or that imparting direction onto a projectile with a stick represents efforts at banishing storms and other evil forces (Hye-Kerkdal, 1956; Lukas, 1969). Such symbolism is thought to have survived into contemporary sports. Soccer, for instance, has been considered the ritualized version of the primitive tribal hunt, with tribesmen making their symbolic kill by shooting at the goalmouth (Morris, 1981).

It has been pointed out (Midwinter, 1986) that only the rich fantasy of analysts is capable of drawing such analogies, and that, more important, ignorance about these analogies does not diminish interest in, and fascination with, athletic contests. In view of the fact that athletes and spectators are capable of comprehending and accepting the artificiality and arbitrariness of athletic objectives and conventions without loss of interest and involvement, the proposal that sports originated from vital rituals may have descriptive merit but fails to provide a plausible explanation for competitive athletics and its appeal to spectators. If, for instance, putting a ball through a hoop could symbolize the trapping of the sun, why has the achievement of this objective been made increasingly difficult? And why has it been complicated by defensive opposing parties? The ritual would seem to be best served by easy-to-perform, unfailing actions.

The view that sports derive from, and are an extension of, skill training, especially the practicing of predatory and combative maneuvers, seems more convincing. The relationship between societally relevant fighting skills and sports is well documented (Gardiner, 1930; Poliakoff, 1987). It is easy to imagine that in hunter-and-gatherer societies men practiced throwing spears and tried their luck with bows and arrows in order to develop their hunting skills. Wrestling and stick fighting presumably served to hone defensive skills. On occasion, groups of spectators must have formed as well. Could this have been the birth of spectatorship, tribesmen cheering on their peers, applauding their efforts, and urging them on to better performances?

Not necessarily. If the athletic skill in question would advantage the performer but disadvantage the onlooker, it is difficult to see why the spectator should rejoice in seeing great athletic accomplishments on the part of potential rivals for acceptance and prestige in their community. The likely reaction would be envy and jealousy. If, on the other hand, the athletic skill would benefit performer and onlooker in similar ways, the spectator would have cause, indeed, for celebrating the exhibition of great skill by cohorts.

This line of reasoning makes the consideration of cooperation and rivalry crucial in the projection of spectator reactions. Only if the spectator is able to benefit from the athletic skills displayed, in some tangible and perhaps not-so-tangible ways, will he or she be motivated to applaud them. If these skills are displayed by rivals, possibly by enemies, they can only be threatening and should be deplored. In tribal exemplification, a hunter's display of great agility, strength, and endurance could be applauded by all hunters and nonhunters of the tribe. The same display of skills by a member of a hostile rival group should inspire abomination instead.

It has been proposed (Zillmann, 1990) that athletic competition developed in the context of the division of labor. In ancient times it was practical to determine, by simple performance comparison, the strongest, the fastest, the most agile, or the most enduring persons for appropriate task assignments that would serve the community best. To the extent that these skills benefitted the community as a whole, all onlookers had cause to cheer athletic greatness. The meek could applaud the exhibition of strength by others, and the clumsy could marvel at displays of agility—without interfering envy. In intercommunal skill comparisons, spectators, seeing their communities' athletes outlift, outrun, outjump, outduel, and generally outperform the athletes of neighboring communities, could rejoice in their knowledge that they lived in a community of athletic people capable of securing food and shelter and defending the group against hostile intruders, if need be.

Practical as comparisons of essential motor skills may have been in these early days of civilization, they obviously have lost their significance in modern times. Assisted by machines, the slowest may become the fastest, and the weakest may become the strongest. General agility has grown similarly irrelevant. Why, then, do we still applaud the athletes who can shoot baskets better than others, who can kick or slug balls at goals with greater precision and ferocity than others, or who can hit the ball harder and farther than anybody else? Is it admiration of the ability per se? Or have the social dynamics of ancient times survived in some form, and are they still influencing our reactions to athletic performances?

Contemporary Theory and Research

In this section, we first consider spectator motives: What is it that attracts spectators to the games? What is it that makes them sports fans? Then we examine aspects of athletic competition that have been suspected or shown to produce distinct reactions in spectators: Which are the elements of sports performances that draw the applause of spectators? Which features of play produce euphoria and celebration? And exactly what is it that prompts contempt, dejection, and possibly violence?

Basking in Reflected Glory. Cialdini and his collaborators (Cialdini, Borden, Thorne, Walker, Freeman, & Sloan, 1976; Cialdini & Richardson, 1980) have presented influential theory and research to explain spectators' motives for affiliating themselves with particular athletic performers. They propose, essentially, that "sportsfanship" serves self-presentation or image management. More specifically, these investigators argued that persons in need of enhancing their public image may accomplish this by associating themselves with successful others, and with successful athletes and athletic teams in particular. By declaring themselves fans of winning teams and by displaying their affiliation in public, they should enhance their self-presentation, in accordance with Heider's (1958) balance theory. This should happen despite the fact that benefited persons contributed nothing, at least nothing tangible, to the athletic success from which they may benefit. The judgment that they are "basking in reflected glory" makes that point.

Cialdini et al. (1976) supported their proposal with highly imaginative field research. In a first experiment, apparel of students attending seven major universities was unobtrusively monitored. On each Monday throughout a football season, the number of students in specific classes wearing apparel identifying the university of attendance was recorded. The number of students wearing apparel identifying other universities was also recorded. These numbers were separated for weekends of winning and weekends of losing performances of the home football team. It was found that, as expected, home-team-identifying apparel was more popular after the team's glorious wins than after humbling losses. No parallel difference emerged for alternative apparel. The findings thus demonstrate the students' tendency to bask in unearned, reflected athletic glory.

In a second experiment, Cialdini et al. (1976) tested the proposal that persons whose public image suffered damage would be more strongly motivated to seek glory-by-association through affiliation with successful athletic teams. Students at Notre Dame were approached by phone and asked to take part in an opinion survey concerning university issues. A test of knowledge of campus life was administered, and students were told that they had done either well or poorly on this test. The survey then turned to the nationally ranked football team. Students were asked to describe the outcome of particular games. Half of them described a win over a rival team, the other half a loss. The investigators were interested in and tallied the use of the inclusive "we" and the exclusive "they" in the students' descriptions. The findings revealed a clear tendency for students to talk about their winning team as "us" and their losing team as "them," giving evidence to the basking proposal. Additionally, the data showed that this tendency to bask in reflected glory was particularly strong when a student had suffered a blow to his or her public image. After failing the initial test, students apparently sought to undo the damage by claiming an alliance with successful others—athletes, in this case.

Cialdini and Richardson (1980) extended these findings on image repair to the "blasting" of competing institutions. The greater the degree of inflicted damage, the stronger the subjects' motivation to correct impressions by building up their home institution and by tearing down rival institutions. However, these demonstrations were not specific to athletic programs and the performance of teams within those programs.

Avoiding Reflected Failure. The basking and blasting phenomenon was further examined by Sloan (1982). This investigator used the phone-survey procedures of the second experiment conducted by Cialdini et al. (1976), but additionally created an ingroup-outgroup variation by introducing the survey as one conducted by the "Notre Dame Opinion Survey Center" or the "Midwest Opinion Survey Center," respectively. Students were approached after Notre Dame had either won or lost a basketball game. Descriptions of the games' outcomes were again coded for use of "we" versus "they." The findings actually failed to replicate those of the earlier investigation. No discernible difference emerged in the use of "we" after winning or losing performances when the caller was an outsider. Overall, the usage of "they" was more frequent than the usage of "we." When the caller was an insider (i.e., a member of the Notre Dame university community), however, a significant difference did emerge. Interestingly, this difference does not so much indicate a tendency to bask in reflected glory after a win as it gives evidence of a tendency for subjects to distance themselves from a losing team. After winning performances, usage of "we" and "they" proved to be comparable to that in the descriptions provided to outside callers. After losses, in contrast, the use of "we" dropped sharply when the call came from an insider with greater sensitivity for feelings about the home team's demise.

The Search for Bragging Rights. These findings indicate that both association with winners and dissociation from losers are useful impression-management techniques (Cialdini & Richardson, 1980). It is left unclear, however, to what extent the use of these techniques motivates attendance of games or attention to their media coverage. Sloan (1989) proposed that the techniques in question are part and parcel of "vicarious achievement seeking" and considers the search for bragging rights—along with the protective distancing in case there are none to be had—the main motive for sports spectatorship. Granted that bragging rights are important to sports fans, it is difficult to see their attainment as the major driving force of spectatorship.

First, spectators of athletic contests are not assured of glorious performances on the part of their chosen performers or teams. They have to take chances. If the possibility of a win attracts them to the contest, the possibility of a loss should deter them. Strong attendance motivation is unlikely under these circumstances. Second, if bragging rights are everything, attendance of games is unnecessary. Learning secondhand about the glory of a winning home team entitles everyone around to share in the "We showed 'em!" experience. Third, the focus on benefits that accrue to favorable outcomes of games detracts from what should be considered crucial in the consideration of spectatorship: the spectators' reactions to the athletic event proper. The emotions—the jubilation and the agony—that spectators experience with regularity are left unexplained.

Some research evidence exists, however, that would seem to support the proposal that spectators seek bragging rights. Attendance at games has been shown to be a function of winning performances. Noll (1974) observed that for professional basketball, football, and ice hockey, attendance of home games varied in accordance with the teams' winning ratio. Becker and Suls (1983) similarly observed that attendance at major league baseball games was comparatively high for winning teams and low for losing teams.

But the fact that "people like to see a winner" has any number of alternative explanations. Teams with a winning record are more likely, after all, to exhibit athletic excellence. Moreover, attending the games of an excellent home team minimizes the likelihood of agony and maximizes that of euphoria in response to the play. Hedonistic partiality for this constellation of emotional reactions obviously favors and should motivate attendance of games in which the home team's victory can be considered probable.

Alliance Formation. The work of Cialdini et al. (1976) makes clear that spectators form alliances with athletic groups. In their work, the so-called "unit formation" is unobtrusively assessed through linguistic expression: the self-including "we." Surely not all spectators form alliances with athletes. Spectators may respond to athletic performances in a detached, rather impersonal fashion. No alliance need be formed, and none is to be denied in case of disappointing performances. In such situations, the spectator is just that—namely, a spectator.

Part of the definition of sportsfanship is, however, that fans be "more than mere spectators." The necessary additional characteristic concerns, of course, the formation of alliances: fans must perceive themselves as members of a tacitly existing group to which the objects of their fanship belong. Construing actions as taken by "us" reveals the formation of such imaginary alliances.

Alliance formation is often imposed. In international competition, Americans are bound to adopt the United States team as theirs. Once allied in these terms, American spectators win and lose *with* their American team. In significant sports events, such as the Gold Medal ice hockey game of the 1980 Winter Olympics, all Americans could triumph over a humbled alien nation. Community alliances are similarly automatic. Living in Pittsburgh, for example, places a distinct social disadvantage at declaring oneself a fan of the Houston Oilers. On the other hand, there are numerous tangible benefits to community-team alliances (Zillmann, Bryant, & Sapolsky, 1989). Allying with local institutions, such as high schools or universities, offers similar benefits. The pressures to ally with institutions of this kind are also similar. But some degrees of freedom exist as well. Alliances may be formed with the athletic teams of one's alma mater. They may be continued for life, irrespective of domicile. A USC alumnus, for example, is unlikely to end his alliance after moving to Pennsylvania. Finally, alliances may be formed for highly personal reasons. Someone living in Dallas, for example, may have gone to school with the quarterback of the Green Bay Packers and adopted the Packers as "his" team.

Alliances with athletic teams may also be formed in a less obvious manner. Racial characteristics of the athletes may determine the composition of the allied spectatorship. These suggestions are supported by the findings of an investigation by Sapolsky (1980). Black and white students in Florida were shown an Indiana high school basketball championship game between an all-black team and an all-white one. Respondents did not know these teams, nor the communities they represented. Alliances were nonetheless formed very quickly. Blacks were found to root for the black team and whites for the white team.

On the whole, the conditions that lead to the formation of alliances with athletic teams, including personality characteristics that may predispose spectators to form particularly strong affiliations, have not been subjected to rigorous examination and are poorly understood as a result. What is quite clear from various investigations (Cox, 1985; Nixon, 1975; Sloan, 1989) is that sport generates fanship that is more intense, more obtrusive, and more enduring than it is for other forms of entertaining social activities without direct participation in the spectated events. The fans' commitment and loyalty to the teams of their choice is perhaps best illustrated by the consensual outrage over questionable decisions by referees—decisions that set their team back and that place victory for the team and its following in jeopardy.

All too often, such outrage converts to ugly actions by spectator crowds (Coalter, 1985; Mann, 1989). Involvement with athletic teams apparently can become so intimate that a team's defeat is experienced as a personal humiliation. The formation of such strong bonds between spectators and performers points to the limits of the tactic to avert self-deprecation by blaming poor performances on "them" (Cialdini et al., 1976). It seems to be the rule that sports fans form alliances and then, granted some self-serving distortions in signaling affiliations, suffer through the bad times as much as they enjoy the good times of their athletic heroes.

Disposition Theory of Sports Spectatorship. Disposition theory of sports spectatorship (Zillmann et al., 1989) is largely based on the recognition that spectators tend to form tacit alliances with athletic performers and teams of some renown. The theory focuses on the affective consequences of the indicated alliances for the perception of competitive play and contests that involve the allied performers or teams. It also pertains to game attendance, but treats attendance motivation as secondary: the result of positive affect evoked by past spectating and the anticipation of similarly positive experiences from future spectatorship. On grounds of unit formation (i.e., the "we" experience), the theory projects that seeing an allied athletic party succeed and win will produce more euphoria the stronger the alliance. In parallel fashion, it projects that seeing an allied team fail and lose will produce greater distress the stronger the alliance.

The focus on affective reactions to competitive play led to a more inclusive theory, however. Enjoyment and disappointment in response to sports contests seems determined not only by affective dispositions toward allied teams, but also by dispositions toward competing teams. The theory addresses both aspects of this dispositional constellation. Furthermore, by operationalizing dispositions in terms of the intensity of feelings of liking and disliking for athletic performers, the application of disposition theory is extended from allied performers to all performers who are not met with distinct indifference.

The theory makes the following basic predictions for affective spectator reactions:

1. Enjoyment derived from witnessing the success and victory of athletic competitors (a) increases with positive affective dispositions and (b) decreases with negative affective dispositions toward these competitors.
2. Enjoyment derived from witnessing the failure and defeat of athletic competitors (a) increases with negative affective dispositions and (b) decreases with positive affective dispositions toward these competitors.

The joint application of these proposals leads, of course, to the projection that (a) enjoyment of a contest will be at a maximum when an intensely liked player or team defeats an intensely disliked opponent, and that (b) enjoyment will be at a minimum when the reverse happens. It follows, moreover, that a contest between similarly liked or similarly disliked players or teams will produce intermediate results. If disappointment and acute distress are considered extensions of the absence of enjoyment into "negative enjoyment," the proposals readily extend to negative affect from witnessing athletic contests. For instance, seeing an archrival humiliate the beloved home team should not only result in minimal enjoyment but produce maximal distress. The implications of disposition theory for enjoyment and distress from witnessing athletic competition are summarized in Figure 28–1.

Winning Is Everything. Support for the disposition theory of sports spectatorship comes from various investigations. A first field study was conducted in 1976 on college football (Zillmann et al., 1989). The crowds' vocal reactions were recorded during two matches. The reactions were then coded, play by play, for the amount of expressed enjoyment and disappointment. This was done by coders who were blind to the plays that triggered particular reactions. It was expected, of course, that the crowds should applaud every successful play on the part of the allied home teams, and that they should deplore every failing move on the part of these teams. As can be seen from Figure 28–2, the findings support the expectations. Disposition theory also predicts, however, that success by the rivaling teams should be deplored, and that these teams' failure should be applauded. The findings lend strong support to this prediction. An errant pass by the rival team was nearly as much applauded as a pass completion by the home team. Findings of this kind show that when strong alliances exist, it is not so much the display of athletic excellence as such that is being applauded as it is the allied team's progress toward the ultimate goal: winning.

Studies on televised professional football and on Olympic basketball competition (Zillmann et al., 1989) lead to the same conclusions. In football, effective runs and successfully completed passes were more enjoyed the stronger the affiliation with the team. The same successful plays by a resented team were deplored. The same pattern of responses was found in the enjoyment of Olympic basketball.

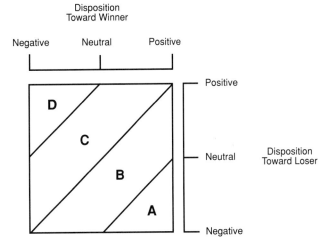

FIGURE 28–1. The dispositional field of athletic competition under win-or-lose conditions. Highly positive dispositions toward the winning performer or team, together with highly negative dispositions toward the losing performer or team, define the subfield of intense enjoyment reactions and euphoria (Region A). Highly negative dispositions toward the winning performer or team, together with highly positive dispositions toward the losing performer or team, define the subfield of distress reactions and dysphoria (Region D). All other dispositional constellations define an area of intermediate enjoyment (Regions B and C). All diagonals from lower left to upper right constitute equivalence lines for enjoyment.

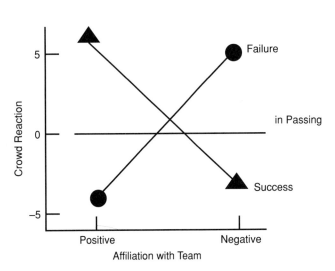

FIGURE 28–2. Enjoyment of, and disappointment with, successful and unsuccessful passing plays in college football as a function of rooting. Vocal crowd reactions served as measures.

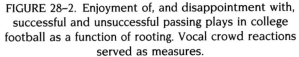

Adapted from Zillmann, Bryant, & Sapolsky, 1989, with permission.

Rooting for the United States team was so strong that even the most impressive scoring plays by our opponents failed to produce appreciable applause.

The aforementioned investigation by Sapolsky (1980) gives further evidence of the overriding importance of dispositional commitment in the enjoyment of sports events. In this investigation, the television coverage of a basketball game had been edited to make an unknown white team defeat an unknown black team and, by parallel scoring and the same margin of victory, to make the black team defeat the white team. Enjoyment of the outcome of the games differed drastically for black and white audiences. Black respondents sided with the black team and enjoyed the black team's victory. White respondents sided with the white team and enjoyed the white team's victory. Because of dispositional commitments, neither the black nor the white spectators could derive much enjoyment from seeing, in an athletic contest, their kind defeated by members of another race.

Effective and Daring Play. Spectators commonly judge athletic maneuvers as great, terrific, gutsy, dull, or stupid. Which kinds of plays within a sport draw such praise or condemnation? And which plays, in accordance with these verdicts, are enjoyed or deplored?

An investigation by Zillmann et al. (1989) sought to answer these questions for football. All conceivable football plays were categorized according to the degree of risk entailed in them, the frequency of employment, and their effectiveness in gaining yardage. These categories were then used to classify the play-by-play enjoyment reactions to a professional football game. Focus was on plays that were successfully executed by a supported, allied team.

The findings, summarized in Figure 28–3, made it very clear that gutsy play, if successful, is greatly enjoyed. Enjoy-ment increased with the perceived riskiness of a play. But enjoyment also increased with the yardage gained by a play, irrespective of riskiness. A long forward pass, for example, is risky because of the possibility of incompletion or interception. If the pass is successfully executed, spectators may enjoy a combination of daring and guts on the part of the athletes of a supported team, the implicit contempt for the opponents, the skill involved in the performance, and, not to be overlooked, a substantial gain of yardage. However, a so-called "broken play" that has none of these characteristics but that ends up in a similar gain of yardage will be enjoyed to a similar degree. The findings show once more that euphoria and applause are primarily evoked by a supported allied team's visible progress toward victory over the opponent.

This conclusion is further supported by findings concerning the commonness of plays. Running the ball, for example, is far more common than, say, the end-around play. The latter maneuver is comparatively original. This originality proves inconsequential for the enjoyment of the play, however. Common and original plays are similarly enjoyed when they produce adequate-to-good yardage, and they are similarly deplored when they do not.

Aggressive and Hateful Play. Much has been said about violence in sports (cf. Goldstein, 1983). The legendary football coach Vince Lombardi branded his sport "violent" and asserted: "That's why the crowds love it!" (cited in Michener, 1976, p. 520). The persisting popularity of combative sports, and of wrestling and boxing in particular, would seem to give sufficient support to the contention that at least a good portion of sports spectators enjoy bruising activities that often lead to the temporary incapacitation, by knockout or injury, of some competitors.

The wealth of suggestions that violence in sports is con-

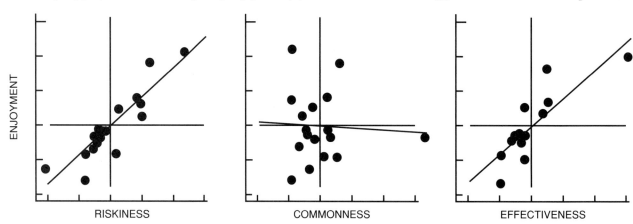

FIGURE 28–3. Enjoyment of successful offensive plays in professional football as a function of riskiness, commonness, and effectiveness of play. Riskiness proved to be the best predictor of enjoyment $(r = 0.90)$. Effectiveness predicted enjoyment almost as well $(r = 0.81)$. In contrast the commonness of play was inconsequential $(r = -0.11)$

Adapted from Zillmann, Bryant, & Sapolsky, 1989, with permission.

ducive to great enjoyment contrasts oddly with the scarcity of research evidence to the point. Only one study exists in which a systematic comparison of the enjoyment of nonaggressive and aggressive play was attempted (Bryant, Comisky, & Zillmann, 1981). In this study, a large number of plays in professional football, drawn from the games of a season, were edited into a random sequence. The level of aggression was ascertained for all plays. Enjoyment reactions were then related to categories of aggressive plays. As can be seen from Figure 28–4, the more permissible violent actions plays entailed, the more male and female respondents enjoyed them. This tendency was particularly strong for men. Male spectators, then, seem to bear out Lombardi's assertion. They apparently derive more pleasure from a bone-jarring tackle than from an ordinary pulldown, and they enjoy an undercut wide-receiver's aerial acrobatics more than an unchallenged reception.

Additional evidence of the enjoyment of rugged play comes from research into the effects of sportscasting (cf. Bryant & Zillmann, 1983). In a study on professional ice hockey (Bryant, Comisky, & Zillmann, 1977), the commentary of the games' television coverage was manipulated. Commentary proved to influence the perception of violence during play. Enjoyment of the game was found to increase with the level of perceived roughness. Specifically, commentary that dwelled on the aggressiveness of actually rather nonaggressive play enhanced the enjoyment of that play by making it appear more violent.

Research on sportscasting has furthermore demonstrated that the spectators' perception of animosity between the competing parties has a strong effect on enjoyment. In an investigation of tennis (Bryant, Brown, Comisky, & Zillmann, 1982), the commentary of a televised match between grand masters (with whom the student respondents were not familiar) was either purely descriptive or embellished by so-called "color men." The embellishment of the play-by-play commentary portrayed the players either as the best of friends in intense competition with one another, or as the worst of enemies who were out to destroy and humiliate each other. Both the perception of competitiveness in the contest and the enjoyment of play were strongly influenced by the color commentary. Specifically focusing on the enmity between the players profoundly increased the perception of competitiveness and, more important, the enjoyment of the match. Adding information about the competitors' friendship, on the other hand, was of no consequence for enjoyment. It merely dampened the perception of the competitiveness of play.

The hype about the animosity between players, teams, coaches, and spectator groups, about heated and hateful long-standing rivalries, that characterizes game promotions and game coverage in many popular sports (Bryant, Comisky, & Zillmann, 1977) thus appears to be based on a valid premise—namely, that spectators cherish hateful competition, if not violent play. There are limits to the "blood thirst," however. Although there are reports that spectators initially applaud crippling injuries to athletes of loathed teams, there is no evidence that spectators respond euphorically to the infliction of permanent injury when they comprehend the gravity of the injury. Undoubtedly, many spectators do enjoy the bruising, stunning, and knocking out that is part of numerous aggressive sports. And quite possibly, they may derive pleasure from witnessing resented athletes getting their just desserts in extracurricular violent activities. It would seem fair, nonetheless, to say that the enjoyment of maiming injuries is aberrant behavior on the part of an insignificant minority of spectators (cf. Bryant & Zillmann, 1983).

The focus on vigor and viciousness in many noncombative sports does not necessarily prove that spectators enjoy violence and are drawn to it. Vigorous, vicious play can be construed as play that gives obtrusive evidence that the competitors play with extraordinary intensity. The dunk in basketball, for example, does no more damage than a lay-up. It is a favorite with spectators, however, presumably because it shows that the dunker "means business." Vigorous, vicious play is basal proof that the competitors "give it their all." This, rather than the casual display of superior motor skills, is what athletic competition should be; and apparently this is what attracts the spectators to the games.

The Beauty of Play. Obviously, not all sports are combative, nor do they entail combative elements. And not all sports take the form of matches in which one party wins at the opponent's expense. Numerous athletic performances have a strong aesthetic component. Diving and skating, for example, are primarily judged by aesthetic criteria. So are all gymnastic performances. Judges score these performances on sets of agreed-upon criteria. Interjudge agreement in the use of these criteria tends to be less than perfect, but it apparently is high enough to sustain such

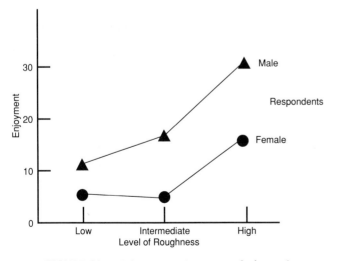

FIGURE 28–4. Viewers' enjoyment of plays of professional football as a function of the degree of violent action involved.

Adapted from Bryant & Zillmann, 1983, with permission.

evaluation systems. Although efforts are made to inform spectators about the criteria in question, applause in response to performances often corresponds very poorly with the judges' appraisals.

The imperfection in the evaluation of aesthetic athletic performances characterizes the research situation as well. Spectators are able to see the beauty in a flawless dive or a great routine on the balance beam, but find it difficult to pinpoint what it was that prompted their aesthetic sensations. Investigators are similarly baffled by the mediation of this type of enjoyment. The stimulus conditions that evoke aesthetic appreciation proved to be highly elusive. Despite much discussion of flow, harmony, and grace in the locomotion of athletes, and despite likening athletic motions to ballet and declaring athletic performances artistic (e.g., Lowe, 1977; Whiting & Masterson, 1974), sports aesthetics is a poorly understood phenomenon, and the contribution of the aesthetic component of athletic performances to enjoyment remains to be determined.

Emotional Afterglow. In contrast, the emotional consequences of attending winning and losing performances on the part of supported, allied teams are quite well understood. For instance, Sloan's (1989) work shows lingering postgame emotions of happiness and depression, respectively, to be predictably linked to the games' outcomes. Hirt and Zillmann (1985) observed increased self-confidence in problem-solving skills after the win of a supported team, and the opposite effect after a loss. Schwarz (1987) found life satisfaction to be enhanced by a great victory in international sports competition; and Schweitzer, Zillmann, Weaver, and Luttrell (1992) observed that, after the humbling defeat of their varsity football team, students' outlook on threatening events was especially gloomy. Because of this chapter's focus on immediate spectator reactions, we bypass these important social consequences of sports spectatorship and turn to the spectators' influence on athletic performance.

EFFECTS OF SPECTATORS ON PERFORMANCE

Introduction

We have analyzed in detail the motivations of spectators and their reactions to sports. Yet how does the presence of the spectators and their reactions affect the performance of athletes? Are athletes sensitive to the presence of spectators, their number, composition, expectations, and overt reactions? Is the presence of spectators a motive for athletic performance? How do the various features of spectatorship affect athletic performance? It is these and other issues that will be the concern of this part of the chapter.

Unfortunately, the gaps in our knowledge on the effects of spectators in sports are much greater than the bits of evidence. While there is considerable literature on the effects of spectators on task performance, most of the research

studies have not involved sports activities. Many of the studies were limited to laboratory investigations and employed tasks that are not likely to be encountered in real-world settings. In these situations, performers have not chosen to perform in front of spectators, and the spectators usually have not chosen to observe a particular activity. The spectators are typically small in number, with experiments often involving only one or two observers. So this situation does not have many of the elements of the sports spectacles that we have highlighted.

One reason that there have been only a limited number of studies of the impact of spectators in sport events is probably that these situations do not lend themselves to careful experimental analysis. It is a difficult, if not impossible, task to manipulate spectator features such as number, composition, and reactions at real-world sport events (assuming the teams involved would even consent to such manipulations). Furthermore, one would have to do so for a series of such events in order to be able to come to meaningful conclusions. Even then, it would be difficult to control the influence of extraneous events such as weather, time of season, record of the opposing team, etc. Given these problems in doing field experiments with actual athletic events, most studies have been limited to correlational analyses of records from sports competitions. These studies have examined the nature of the home advantage, the impact of crowd size, effects of being traded to a new team, etc. Yet these studies have obvious limitations in terms of our ability to make confident inferences. For example, one might find that large crowd sizes are related to greater success of the home team. This result could reflect a positive impact of the number of spectators on home team performance or the fact that success of the home team increases attendance, or both of these factors (cf. Becker & Suls, 1983).

The two most frequently used models for studying spectator effects are the audience and coaction paradigms. In the first, usually one individual is asked to perform a task in front of one or more passive observers. The performance of individuals in this type of condition is then compared with the performance of individuals who do the task while alone in a room. The coaction paradigm involves comparing the performance of individuals who perform their individual task simultaneously in groups of two or more with individuals who perform this task alone. Individuals in the coaction condition thus may serve both as coworkers and spectators. A few studies in naturalistic settings have used somewhat different conditions, ranging from casual spectators to large crowds of spectators. Most of our focus will be on those studies in which the others present are primarily spectators or audience members.

Although each of the various approaches to studying the effects of spectators on athletic performance has its limitations, they all do add some useful pieces to the overall puzzle. We will try to fit these pieces together in a manner that will yield a sensible overall perspective of the influence of spectators on athletic performance. However, many of the conclusions we will derive from our survey will need to be examined in detail with a variety of sport activities before we can have much confidence in their applicability.

Theoretical Models

The experimental study of the effects of spectator presence has a rather long history for an area of study in psychology. In fact, a study by Triplett (1898) on the effects of spectators on the speed of turning fishing reels is often cited as the first experimental social psychology study. Triplett found that children performed with greater speed in a group rather than as individuals. He proposed that this was due to an increased level of energy or dynamogenesis that occurred in group situations. As we shall see, some 70 years later, Zajonc (1965) proposed a similar type of model to account for the complexities he observed in his survey of the literature.

The major theoretical models dealing with the effects of spectators on performers have been developed in the area of social facilitation. Social facilitation is a label for human and animal studies that examine the influence of the presence of other members of the species on task performance. The tradition of using the social facilitation label derives from early studies with animals that focused on the facilitating effects of "other presence" on a variety of instinctive behaviors such as eating, drinking, and sex. Yet it soon became apparent that the presence of others could have both facilitating and inhibiting effects. Zajonc's (1965) review indicated that facilitating effects occurred primarily for instinctive behaviors or tasks that were simple or well learned. Decrements in performance were observed mostly with tasks that were complex or poorly learned. He interpreted this pattern of results in terms of Hull-Spence drive theory (Spence, 1956). He suggested that the presence of others as observers or coactors is a source of drive arousal. This state of heightened drive arousal differentially affects responses that vary in degree of habit strength or dominance. Response tendencies that are quite strong relative to others are termed dominant and are presumed to be facilitated relative to weaker or subordinate responses. For well-learned tasks, the correct responses supposedly have become dominant over the incorrect ones. On poorly learned or complex tasks, incorrect responses may be dominant over correct ones.

Subsequent research has provided a reasonable amount of support for this theoretical model (Geen, 1980; 1989). Some studies have shown that the presence of others can be a source of arousal (e.g., Martens, 1969). There are a number of demonstrations in which dominant responses seem to be facilitated relative to subordinate ones (e.g., Zajonc, 1980; Zajonc & Sales, 1966). Spectators or coactors do generally inhibit performance of complex tasks and facilitate that of simple ones. However, the demonstration of facilitation effects on simple tasks seems to be more difficult than the demonstration of performance decrements (Bond & Titus, 1983). Subsequent analyses proposed that the effects are a bit more complicated than suggested by the Zajonc

model (Paulus, 1983; Seta & Seta, 1983). Furthermore, there has been considerable controversy about "why" the presence of others as spectators and coacters has an impact on behavior or performance. We will briefly outline some of the alternative points of view. However, an extensive discussion of the various theories and their supporting data is beyond the scope of this chapter. A more detailed summary can be found in Geen (1989) and integrative efforts in Geen (1989) and Paulus (1983).

Drive Theories. A number of theoretical models accepted the general notion that spectators can be drive-arousing but varied in their conceptualization of the basis for this arousal. Zajonc (1980) suggested that it was the uncertainty of the performer about the behavior or actions of the spectators that was the basis for the heightened arousal. In a similar vein, Manstead and Semin (1980) and Guerin (1986) argued that it is the need to monitor the audience members that is crucial. For example, an audience that can be easily monitored by the performer may have less impact than one that cannot be easily monitored because they are seated behind the performer instead of in front (Guerin, 1986).

The most extensively investigated alternative to Zajonc's position is that others are a source of drive because of their potential as evaluators (Cottrell, 1972; Paulus & Murdoch, 1971). That is, performers may become anxious in spectator situations because they fear the potential negative social consequences of failure (e.g., negative feedback, loss of face, embarrassment, etc.). Studies that have varied the degree of potential for such negative evaluative outcomes (e.g., expertness of the spectators, the degree to which the performance outcomes can be monitored by the spectators) have generally supported this perspective (Geen, 1989). However, it appears that even spectators who are not able to evaluate performance can have an impact (Bond & Titus, 1983; Schmitt, Gilovich, Goore, & Joseph, 1986). Schmitt et al. (1986) found that having a person with a blindfold and headphones in the same room facilitated the performance of a simple task and hindered the performance of a complex one.

Another view is that it is the distracting qualities of spectators that are critical (Baron, 1986; Sanders, 1981). Spectators may divert one's attention from the task at hand. This may detract from performance directly, and it may lead to arousal because of the conflict experienced between attention to the task and to the observers. Thus the arousal-inducing impact of spectators may derive from their unpredictability, their capacity to be a source of negative evaluative outcomes, and their tendency to distract the individual from task demands.

Self-Theories. A variety of theories propose that self-related processes are important to an understanding of the impact of spectators. Bond (1982) argues that in spectator situations, individuals are motivated by concerns for self-presentation. They want to be judged in favorable terms by the spectators and thus are motivated to work hard when observed. While this should facilitate performance of simple tasks, difficulties encountered on complex tasks lead to embarrassment and consequent further decrements in performance.

Wicklund and Duval (1971) suggest that spectators increase subjective or private self-awareness. When individuals become self-aware, they become aware of discrepancies between ideal or desired performance levels and attained performance. This may increase efforts to do well in spectator situations. However, such efforts may not be translated into performance facilitation when individuals try too hard on tasks involving a high level of skill. Evidence for this type of process comes from research on choking in which it was found that increased self-awareness or self-attention interfered with the performance of skilled tasks (Baumeister, 1984).

Heaton and Sigall (1991) have developed a fairly extensive model of the impact of audience pressure based on self-awareness processes. They propose that individuals who are typically high in self-awareness or self-consciousness are mostly concerned with the extent to which their performance meets certain standards (i.e., success or failure). Audience reactions may be of secondary importance to them. In contrast, low self-conscious individuals may be quite concerned with the reactions of spectators to their performance and may feel pressure when they anticipate not meeting the expectations of their audience. Heaton and Sigall's research supported these predictions.

Motives of Athletes

The different theoretical perspectives we have discussed help us understand the factors underlying the effects of spectators on performance. The theories may also aid us in understanding the motives of athletes who willingly perform in front of spectators. In many cases, the public performance aspect has little to do with the individual athlete's motives. It is simply an inevitable part of the involvement in a particular sport. However, often it is evident that most athletes relish the attention of large crowds of fans. The common lore is that such fan support motivates athletes to higher levels of performance.

In that light, it is interesting that most of the theoretical models emphasize the negative aspects of performing in front of spectators. The spectator situation is viewed as wrought with anxiety or fear. Performers may be concerned that their performance will not measure up and will elicit negative reactions from the audience (Cottrell, 1972; Greer, 1983; Kroll, 1979; Paulus & Murdoch, 1971). There is always an element of uncertainty about the outcomes of such situations, and the consequences of failure are enhanced by the fact that they occurred in public. Failure in public settings could yield a number of negative emotions such as embarrassment, self-criticism, and depression (Bond, 1982). Yet this fear perspective derives primarily from laboratory studies in which individuals are forced to perform certain tasks in front of unfamiliar audiences (Borden, 1980). Situations

in which individuals have chosen to perform certain tasks in front of supportive and enthusiastic spectators may yield quite different reactions. These situations provide an opportunity to demonstrate one's skills in front of a sympathetic and supportive audience. The results of this type of experience can be feelings of satisfaction, pride, and elation.

Thus, while few of us cherish performing unfamiliar tasks in front of unfamiliar or critical spectators, we may enjoy showing off our skills to both friend and foe. Among the motives for such public demonstration of skills could be desire for uniqueness, striving for a sense of competence or efficacy, or attainment of valued social rewards (recognition, praise, adulation). Some people seem to be particularly inclined to seek out public performances. Research by Paivio (1965) using an exhibitionism scale found that children who show such inclinations had received positive evaluations from their parents for their public performances. In contrast, children who were very sensitive to (or fearful of) audiences had been evaluated negatively by their parents and frequently punished for their failures. Degree of training in audience-oriented skills such as singing or dancing was related to low levels of audience sensitivity (Paivio, 1965). Individuals low in self-awareness also appear to be concerned with pleasing their audience (Heaton & Sigall, 1991) and should seek out opportunities to perform in front of audiences if it appears likely that they can satisfy the audience's expectations.

It seems likely that athletes who are engaged in frequent public performances would be low in audience sensitivity and high on exhibitionism. They may have been the recipients of a variety of positive experiences in public performance settings that motivate their continued involvement in spectator sports. For such individuals, larger audiences may be attractive because there are more people present to appreciate their feats. The number of spectators watching an event also can be seen as indicative of the value placed on this event by the community (Edwards & Archambault, 1989). Therefore, athletes who are used to performing in front of large crowds may find it difficult to become motivated in front of small crowds.

Some athletes, such as former baseball star Reggie Jackson, "Mr. October," have developed a reputation for performing at their best in crucial games in which there is a lot of spectator interest. In contrast, athletes who are highly anxious about performance in front of spectators may select sports with less spectator involvement. Alternatively, their anxiety level in spectator situations may prevent them from contributing effectively (Ganzer, 1968; Kroll, 1979) and facilitate a selection process in favor of low audience-sensitive athletes.

Team Characteristics

The impact of spectators on motivation and performance is likely to vary with different types of sports or teams. For example, the role of team cohesion may be an important factor in understanding team success in spectator situations (Edwards & Archambault, 1989; Nixon, 1977). Cohesive teams are those in which there are strong shared positive feelings among team members. Players provide a lot of mutual encouragement and work together in a cooperative way with a minimum of conflict. This type of cooperative spirit is seen as one basis for the phenomenal success of teams from what was formerly the German Democratic Republic (Schellenberger, 1990). The social support provided by a cohesive team may have a calming effect on athletes or teams in otherwise highly stressful spectator situations (Jackson & Latane, 1981; Seta, Paulus, & Schkade, 1976).

Furthermore, it may motivate the athletes to higher levels of performance in order to maintain the valued approval and support of their teammates. This may be particularly true of individuals whose concern for social approval is greater than their fear of social rejection. Sorrentino and Sheppard (1978) compared the performance in 200-yard freestyle competition of approval-oriented swimmers with those whose fear of rejection was greater than their motivation for social approval. Some of the races involved competition between individuals, while others involved competition between groups. Approval-oriented swimmers had faster times in group competition than in individual competition, while rejection-oriented swimmers had faster times in individual competition than in group competition. Apparently, approval-oriented individuals are motivated by the potential social rewards derived from contribution to the success of the group. However, the rejection-oriented individuals' fear of potential rejection in the case of failure lessened their motivation in the group competition situation.

In the case of certain team sports (e.g., football), the impact of personal dispositions may be somewhat limited, since there is some degree of immersion of oneself in the team. Although one's specific actions can still be observed, there may be some division of audience impact because it is shared with one's team members (Latane & Nida, 1980). For example, when the scores of pairs of swimmers are combined, they swim more slowly than individual swimmers (Williams, Nida, Baca, & Latane, 1989). That is, when performers are not individually accountable, they may reduce their efforts or loaf (Latane, Williams, & Harkins, 1979), even in front of spectators. In essence, as the number of spectators increases, social impact is increased. However, as the number of actors or performers increases, the impact of the spectators should be reduced (Jackson & Latane, 1981; Diener, Lusk, DeFour, & Flax, 1980).

Thus spectator impact should be maximal for athletic events that involve individual performances and minimal for those that involve joint activities in which individual contributions cannot be clearly distinguished by observers (e.g., the lineman in football). Of course, in most team sports there is some degree of individual accountability for all players. Yet certain key players (e.g., quarterbacks, pitchers) are more in the focus of spectator attention than others and should demonstrate more sensitivity to variation in spectator variables.

While our analysis suggests that potential spectator impact should be related to player identifiability, it is recognized that spectator interest and reactivity may be greater with team sports than with sports involving individual competition (e.g., track and field, swimming). It may be easier for spectators in a community to relate to a sports team and a team sport than to a sport that focuses on the accomplishments of individual athletes (Edwards & Archambault, 1989).

Characteristics of the Spectators

Spectator events can vary greatly in the number, composition, and characteristics of the spectators. In some of the large sport spectacles, more than 100,000 vocal and emotional spectators may alternatively cheer and ridicule their favorite and opposing teams. Positive reactions are usually reserved for one's own team, but criticism of one's own team and concomitant cheering for the opposing team may occur if one's team is temporarily "in the doghouse" (e.g., after a long losing streak, or being "no-hit" by the opposing pitcher in the ninth inning). How do these reactions of the spectators affect the performance of athletes? Are athletes motivated to perform at higher levels by the adulation of the crowd? Do critical crowd reactions increase determination to overcome adversity or simply reduce the motivation of the athletes to excel? Fortunately, research has provided some answers to these questions.

Spectator Support: The Home Advantage. If supportive audiences are beneficial for athletic performances, one would expect teams to perform best when they are in front of their home crowds. Not only are they on familiar territory when they perform in their own facilities, but the support of the home crowd may enable them to perform at a higher level. Records of various sports do indicate that there is often a home advantage (Edwards & Archambault, 1989; Schwartz & Barsky, 1977). However, this is more evident in certain sports than in others.

The home advantage is fairly small in baseball and football (cf. Paulus, Judd, & Bernstein, 1976), but quite large in basketball and hockey (Altman, 1975; Koppet, 1972; Varca, 1980). Since the latter are played in relatively intimate indoor sites, compared to the more distant open-air stadiums of baseball and football, it may be that proximity of the fans to the action and the noise level they are able to generate in enclosed facilities enhances their impact. With the development of covered stadiums for baseball and football teams, the noise made by the home team may become an important factor in these sports. Boisterous football fans in Seattle and Houston have at times made life fairly miserable for opposing teams.

While the noisy support of home fans may be a critical factor in the strong home advantage effect found in basketball and ice hockey, it is also possible that the continual flow of activity in these sports makes it easier for a crowd to get emotionally involved (Edwards & Archambault, 1989).

This increased level of involvement would be reflected in elevated noise levels and emotional outbursts, such as sustained booing of referee or visiting team actions (Greer, 1983). Unfortunately, thus far no study has provided clear evidence on the role of fan noise per se in the performance of the home team.

Some analyses indicate that offensive aspects of performance are affected more strongly than defensive ones (Edwards & Archambault, 1989). There is also some evidence that the home advantage may be influenced more by decrements in performance of the visiting team than increments in performance of the home team (Silva & Andrew, 1987). However, a precise determination of the degree to which visitor and host performance contribute to the home advantage effect will require assessment of team performance on neutral sites in addition to home and away sites. Of course, in some individualistic sports such as professional tennis and golf, the home advantage factor typically does not come into play, since the athletes involved travel to different sites for each event.

A variety of explanations have been offered for the home advantage effect in sports (Edwards & Archambault, 1989). Among these are the social support of home crowds, familiarity of players with the home environment, feelings of dominance derived from territorial control over one's home "turf," and the positive salience of one's shared team identity with the fans and the community. All of these may play a role, but various analyses suggest that the social support factor may be most important (Greer, 1983; Schwartz & Barsky, 1977).

Spectator Expectations. Is performance always better in front of a familiar or friendly audience? Some studies indicate that performance in front of friends may sometimes be even more anxiety-producing than that in front of strangers (Brown & Garland, 1971). A critical factor may be that one is more concerned with the reactions of one's friends than that of strangers. After all, you may never see the strangers again, while one's friends will carry with them the memory of your performance and may provide future reminders of it. Most of us are more concerned with the image our friends have of us than with our image to strangers who do not play an important role in our lives. The issue of friendly or familiar audiences thus is a double-edged sword. Their supportive nature may be motivating or anxiety-reducing (Wrightsman, 1971; Seta et al., 1976). Yet one may also be concerned about maintaining a positive image with these valued spectators.

This factor of image maintenance is clearly evident in a series of studies that have varied the extent of past success in front of audiences. Seta and Hassan (1980) provided subjects with feedback that they had performed either well or poorly on a task. They were led to expect that their level of success was predictive of their likely performance on a second similar task in front of four spectators. Some subjects were led to believe that the spectators were aware of their past performance, while others believed that the spectators were not so informed. It was found that aware spectators in-

hibited performance in the success condition and facilitated it in the failure condition. The explanation for these results lies in the expectations presumably held by the spectators. If they are aware of one's past success, they should expect continued good performance. However, on an unfamiliar or novel task, one may not be very confident that one will maintain such a good level of performance. The resultant anxiety may inhibit performance on complex or intellective tasks. In contrast, if spectators are aware of one's past poor performance, they should expect similar poor performance in the future. In this case the performer may feel that there is an opportunity to exceed these low expectations, or at least there is little to lose by continued failure and much to gain by possible future success. These individuals may feel little anxiety, but be highly motivated to improve their performance.

Conceptually similar results have been obtained in studies of "choking" by Baumeister and his colleagues (cf., Baumeister & Showers, 1986). For example, in one experiment, subjects performed a task for a baseline period and then were provided a high standard of performance for a subsequent session that was designed to be difficult to attain. The added pressure of the imposed performance standard led to decrements in performance (or choking) relative to other low pressure conditions (Baumeister, 1984). In a subsequent study it was demonstrated that while private expectancies for success were related to high subsequent performance levels, expectations by others that one would be successful were related to decrements in performance—unless one also privately believed that one would be successful (Baumeister, Hamilton, & Tice, 1985).

In both studies it was found that choking effects were most dramatic for people low in typical self-awareness (Fenigstein, Scheier, & Buss, 1975). Baumeister and his colleagues assumed that increased self-focusing or awareness would interfere with skilled performance. Typically, low self-aware people should experience the greatest increase in self-awareness under pressure conditions and hence suffer the greatest decrease in performance. However, the research by Heaton and Sigall (1991) indicates that both low self-aware and high self-aware individuals are prone to choking. Low self-aware individuals tend to choke when they anticipate not being able to please their audience. High self-aware individuals choke when they anticipate themselves or their team doing poorly, regardless of the expectations of the audience.

Baumeister and Steinhilber (1984) related their ideas on choking to the performance of sports teams in a championship series. It was argued that in such a series the home team will have an advantage in the early games, but will lose this advantage in the final game of the series. They propose that as the home team approaches the final game in a series with a supportive home crowd, they will begin thinking of themselves as impending champions. This enhanced self-awareness should inhibit performance. The visiting team should show little inclination for such a self-awareness process, given the hostile environment in which they find themselves.

Consistent with this reasoning, Baumeister and Stein-hilber (1984) found that in baseball World Series which went at least five games (from 1924 to 1982), the home team won 60% of the first two games, but only about 40% of the last games. The home team also made fewer errors than the visitors in the first two games, but made more errors in the seventh game. The home team seems to be particularly at a disadvantage when it can win the championship early in the series (e.g., in game 6 of a 7-game series), compared to when it faces elimination. When the home team *had* to win game 6 to stay in the series, they won about 73% of their games. When they *could* clinch the championship in the 6th game (but didn't have to), they won only 38%. An analysis of NBA championship series led to similar findings (Baumeister & Steinhilber, 1984).

A more detailed analysis of the major league World Series games by Heaton and Sigall (1989) indicates that both fear of failure and a premature focusing on impending success may play a role in the outcome of critical games. The potential role of fear of failure is suggested by the fact that falling behind in the critical seventh game is more likely to lead to a loss and the commitment of fielding errors by the home team than is falling behind in the first 6 games. The fact that a home team also has more difficulty holding a lead in the seventh game than in the prior 6 games (and commits a high number of fielding errors in those seventh games) indicates that premature focusing on impending success may also have detrimental effects.

Unfortunately, other researchers have not been able to find similar results with National Hockey League playoffs (Gayton, Matthews, & Nickles, 1987). It is necessary to be tentative in generalizing the choking and self-awareness concepts to a broad range of sport championships. However, it would seem likely that the psychological processes that play a role in more limited audience settings may also play a role in spectator sports.

A study by Paulus, Shannon, Wilson, and Boone (1972) can be interpreted as consistent with the above line of research (cf. Seta & Hassan, 1980). In this study, student gymnasts performed a gymnastic routine in front of an audience of 17 spectators or alone after both groups had performed this routine alone on a prior day. Those who performed in front of the spectators showed a significant decrement in performance. The decrements in performance were greater for those who demonstrated relatively high levels of skill on the first day than for those who were below average in skill. Although the spectators were not informed about the skill levels of the performers, it is quite possible that the performers assumed the spectators had some knowledge of their prior performance or level of training. Thus the higher skill athletes may have felt pressured to meet higher standards of performance than the lower skill students. Similar results were obtained by Paulus and Cornelius (1974) in a study of gymnasts at another university.

The major conclusion that can be drawn from the above series of studies is that performers may be quite sensitive to the expectations of the spectators. If they feel they can meet or exceed these expectations, performers may do quite well and may even exceed performance levels attained in solitary performance. However, if they do not expect to meet these standards, they may become anxious or frustrated and their performance on complex tasks may deteriorate. This should be especially true with highly valued goals or activities (e.g., in championship series). This line of reasoning has been developed in detail by Seta and his colleagues for a variety of social contexts, including those involving spectators, coactors, and models (cf. Seta, Seta, & Donaldson. 1990; Seta, Seta, & Paulus, 1990). Such a perspective suggests that the most critical feature of spectator situations is not the combined characteristics of the spectators and their overt reactions. Instead, it is the degree of discrepancy between the standards held by the spectators and the expectations of the performers. Positive discrepancies are likely to be exhilarating and motivating. Negative descrepancies should lead to negative emotional reactions and a desire to avoid or escape from such situations.

Although spectator expectations may play an important role in performer reactions, other features and actions on the part of the spectators may also be influential. One feature that has been the focus of much study is the critical or evaluative nature of audiences.

Critical or Evaluative Spectators. It is sometimes claimed that fear of speaking in front of groups is one of the most common fears (Bruskin, 1973; cited in Borden, 1980). Therefore, it is not surprising that the negative element of spectator situations has been emphasized in much of the spectator literature (Cottrell, 1972; Paulus, 1983; Weiss & Miller, 1971). Part of this negativity lies in the potential of spectators to provide critical evaluations of observed performance. This, in turn, could be associated with embarrassment, ridicule, and loss of self-esteem (e.g., Brown & Garland, 1971). These concerns for potential negative outcomes may be inherent in most spectator situations involving performances. However, one would expect that more critical or expert audiences would be even more anxiety-producing. Evidence suggests that this is, in fact, the case (e.g., Henchy & Glass, 1968; Hollingsworth, 1935; Latane & Harkins, 1976; Paivio, 1965).

It would also seem sensible to assume that degree of anxiety produced by an evaluative audience increases with audience size. While this is generally true (cf. Borden, 1980), these effects may reach a ceiling or asymptote at fairly low sizes (Latane & Nida, 1980). In fact, it is often noted that the major effect of variation in audience size in laboratory studies is seen as audience size goes from none to one. Latane (1981) has described this in terms of his theory of social impact and notes that impact of social stimuli is best described by a negatively accelerating function, such that increasing numbers have increasingly smaller impacts.

The increased anxiety, producing impact of larger audiences has been further demonstrated by a series of studies by Seta and his colleagues. Increasing the numbers of audience members increases the degree of reported anxiety (Seta, Crisson, Seta, & Wang, 1989a). Although this suggests an additive function, it appears that some averaging occurs whenever spectators who differ in status or level of expertise are present. For example, two high-status audience members have more impact than an audience consisting of two high-status and two low-status members (Seta, Wang, Crisson, & Seta, 1989b). This type of averaging effect has also been demonstrated with task performance and blood pressure (Seta et al., 1989b; Seta & Seta, 1990). Thus, adding relatively low-status audience members may decrease the overall stressful impact of an audience if the average audience impact is significantly reduced, with only a limited increase in the summative impact. Of course, if enough low-status spectators are added to a group of high-status spectators, an increasing impact will become evident through the summation process (Seta et al., 1989b).

If larger groups of spectators are generally more impactful than smaller groups, one might expect an impact of crowd size on athletic performance. This possibility was examined for the 1973 major league baseball season (Paulus et al., 1976). Crowd size was categorized in terms of less than 10,000, 10,000 to 20,000, 20,000 to 30,000, and greater than 30,000. While no significant effects were observed in the American League, in the National League, larger crowd size was related to decreases in hitting and runs and increases in errors for the home team, and decreases in errors for the away team. This pattern of results for the National League could reflect "choking" due to increased pressure felt by the home team with large crowds. However, crowd size did not affect the overall win/loss record for the home team, indicating that the home teams were able to compensate for their poor play in some areas by better play in others (e.g., pitching, base running).

The fact that similar outcomes were not evident in the American League may reflect that this league had considerably fewer games in the higher attendance categories. That crowd size does not give a strong advantage to the home team may be seen as consistent with the decreasing impact assumption of social impact theory (Latane, 1981). It is also possible that the motivating and inspirational effects of large crowds are counteracted by the increased pressure they place on the performer to do well. With athletic activities that involve complex skills, such as baseball, increased pressure may be counterproductive. In contrast, in athletic activities that involve primarily degree of exertion (e.g., running and swimming), increased pressure due to crowd size or other sources might in fact lead to enhanced performance (cf. Edwards & Archambault, 1989).

Evidence for the above line of reasoning is derived from several studies. Observation of joggers by an attentive observer increases their speed of running (Strube, Miles, & Finch, 1981; Worringham & Messick, 1983). Swimmers whose individual performances are made public swim faster in competitive pairs than alone (Williams et al., 1989). However, when baseball players are under pressure during a period when they are about to be traded, they show a decline in batting average and slugging percentage. Once they are traded and are in a relatively low-pressure adjustment period, their performance in these categories goes back up (Jackson, Buglione, & Glenwick, 1988).

Additional support for the importance of skill level in the impact of spectators has been obtained from studies with basketball and bowling (Paulus, Teng, Camacho, & McDonald, 1991). On the basis of Zajonc's (1966) perspective, one might also expect that highly skilled athletes will show facilitation of their performance in spectator situations, whereas low-skill athletes will show decrements in performance in front of spectators. In one study, male students in college basketball classes were asked to attempt 10 free throws in a casual practice session. On the basis of this performance, students were assigned to an above-or below-average group. In the following class period, these students made 10 attempts either alone or in front of two observers. Relative to solitary performance, performing in front of spectators facilitated the performance of the above-average group and hindered those of the below-average group. A similar study with bowling indicated that competitive instructions enhanced the performance of the above-average students but led to decrements in the performance of below-average students, relative to a no-competition condition. Choking effects were not expected to occur in this study, since the audience members and competitors were not aware of the skill level of the athletes.

Directive Effects of Spectators

An interesting implication of the self-theories we discussed earlier is that spectators may serve as a cue for certain types of behaviors. That is, the individuals being observed may try to gain a favorable impression in the eyes of the spectators by behaving in ways consistent with the expectations or standards of the spectators. These expectations may be implicit from a knowledge of characteristics of the spectators or made explicit by the actions of the spectators.

Cueing Effects of Passive Spectators. One consistent behavioral effect of spectators is that they lead individuals to minimize risky or novel behaviors relative to more normatively common behaviors. On association tasks, individuals give fewer unique or idiosyncratic responses in front of spectators than they do when they are alone (Blank, Staff, & Shaver, 1976; Matlin & Zajonc, 1968). Individuals also exhibit more attitude change in response to persuasive messages when observed than when alone (Borden, Hendrick, & Walker, 1976; Weiss, Miller, Langan, & Cecil, 1971). Other research has found that the presence of spectators may lead to a general inhibition of responding in order to minimize errors or exhibition of socially undesirable behaviors. When being observed, individuals inhibit overt practice of material to be learned (Berger, Carli, Garcia, & Brady, 1982) and withhold responses in order to avoid making errors (Geen, 1985). People are even less likely to look at erotic material in the presence of spectators (Brown, Amoroso, Ware, Pruesse, & Pilkey, 1973), and the imitation of modeled behavior and the occurrence of aggressive responses are inhibited by the presence of spectators (Fouts, 1970; Scheier, Fenigstein, & Buss, 1974).

When there are cues provided as to task-relevant characteristics of the spectators, directive effects become clearly evident (Borden, 1980). Individuals who expected to be tested on a memory task by a female remembered more female items than those who did not have this expectation (Grace, 1951). Individuals also administer higher levels of shock to an opponent in an aggression paradigm when they are observed by a male than when observed by a female (Borden, 1975; Taylor, 1977). Presumably, individuals expect the male observer to be more approving of assertive or aggressive behavior than a female one. When the individual in this situation has information that the observer is either pacifistic or aggressive, they behave more aggressively with the aggressive observer than with the pacifistic one, regardless of the gender of the observer (Borden, 1975).

Active Spectators. Only a few studies have examined the impact of spectators who provide overt behavioral indications of their approval or disapproval of the performer's behavior. One would expect that such reactions would increase both drive arousal and the cue-directive impact of spectators. In fact, overt disapproval leads to increases in heart rate and muscle tension, while overt approval leads to decreases (Boman, 1966; Malmo, Boag, & Smith, 1957). One early study found that "razzing" by an audience hindered the performance of a coordination task (Laird, 1923). This effect could reflect the effects of razzing on arousal, on distraction, or on social inhibition.

With regard to cue effects, when three spectators attempted to persuade the subject in the aggression paradigm to behave aggressively toward a pacifistic opponent, aggressive behavior increased and persisted in subsequent nonspectator sessions (Borden & Taylor, 1973). The presence of three spectators who encourage nonaggressive behavior to an aggressive opponent leads to reduced aggressive behavior. However, this influence does not persist after the spectators leave.

Spectator reactions seem to play an important role in sport events and may be a significant part of the home advantage. The cheering in anticipation of good performance and as a reaction to specific accomplishments can be a strong motivating factor. In contrast, sustained negative reactions (such as booing) to visiting teams and referees may intimidate these groups and provide a further advantage for the home team (Greer, 1983). Greer found that sustained periods of booing in basketball games facilitated the overall performance level of the home team and inhibited the performance of the visiting team during subsequent five-minute periods. Interestingly, the strongest effect involved increased rule violations called on visiting teams, suggesting a possible impact both on the behavior of the visiting teams and on the referees.

In many sports, such as football, basketball, baseball, and hockey, aggressive actions or plays by players often receive favorable reactions from the home crowd. The anticipation of such positive reactions from fans, coaches, and fellow players may increase the frequency of occurrence of these behaviors (Russell & Drewrey, 1976). In this light, it is interesting to note that professional hockey or football teams that wear black uniforms tend to receive more penalties than other teams (Frank & Gilovitch, 1988). The color black appears to have aggressive connotations and may thus elicit aggressive thoughts and actions in both fans and players. Aggressive cues provided by television violence also appear to be sufficient to facilitate aggressive behavior in a game of floor hockey among young boys who typically exhibit high levels of aggressive behavior in other contexts (Josephson, 1987). There is thus a strong basis for expecting a link between aggressive behavior of athletes or teams and the overt encouragement of these behaviors by spectators. Evidence for such an association has been found in college basketball by Thirer and Rampey (1979). Periods of spectator antisocial behavior (e.g., chanting obscenities and throwing objects) were related to increased rule violations by the players from the home team.

A Summary Perspective on Performance Influences

We have provided much evidence that spectators can have dramatic effects on the performance of the activities being observed. Although most research cited was undertaken in laboratory settings, a number of studies done with sports activities have generated results consistent with expectations derived from the laboratory studies. To draw together more clearly the implications of this work, we have provided a summary perspective in Figure 28–5. The model presented is based in part on the cognitive-motivational model of Paulus (1983).

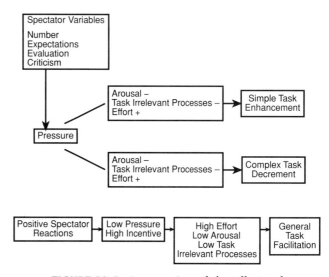

FIGURE 28–5. An overview of the effects of spectators on task performance, based on a cognitive-motivational model.

Paulus, 1983.

The various characteristics of the spectator situation will determine the degree of pressure felt by the performers. In most cases, as the number of spectators, their expectations, and evaluative characteristics or behavior increase, the degree of pressure is increased. This increased pressure can, in turn, affect one or more of three psychological processes—overall level of motivation or effort, level of anxiety or drive arousal, and distracting or task-irrelevant cognitive processes. Increased effort and arousal may serve to increase level of performance on tasks that are simple or require little cognitive capacity (Seta & Seta, 1983). Task-irrelevant factors, such as worries or audience distractions, should not have much impact in this case. When tasks are complex, increased effort may be helpful to some extent, but most complex tasks seem to elicit high levels of effort in themselves (Kahneman, 1973). Thus, the major impact of spectator situations on performance of complex tasks may lie in their arousal and cognitive distracting qualities, leading to decrements in performance.

When spectators are supportive or react positively to the behavior of the performer, pressure should be reduced (Geen, 1980). This should be associated with low levels of arousal and task-irrelevant behavior. However, given that the performer values the positive feedback and support of spectators, levels of effort should be relatively high. As a result, beneficial effects should be observed regardless of type of task (e.g., the home advantage). But positive spectator reactions may not always reduce pressure or facilitate performance. When one is not sure one can maintain one's level of performance, such reactions may increase rather than decrease pressure (Baumeister, 1985). Alternatively, unconditional positive support by spectators (an unlikely situation) could reduce overall level of motivation or effort and produce a low level of performance.

Of course, the exact impact of the spectators on the various processes that we have outlined will depend on the characteristics of the team or sport activity (cohesion, individual versus group activity) and a number of relevant personal characteristics, such as past task success and audience sensitivity. Furthermore, directive features of spectator situations may provide cues for specific behaviors consistent with audience characteristics and expectations (e.g., aggression).

The literature reviewed in this section gives clear evidence that spectators do have an impact on athletic performance. We have provided insight into some critical variables that mediate this influence of audiences. Future studies should enable us to determine more precisely the nature of the processes that underlie such influences—and that also explain more completely spectators' fascination with sports.

References

Altman, I. (1975). *The environment and social behavior: Privacy, personal space, territory, and crowding.* Monterey, CA: Brooks/Cole.

Baron, R. S. (1986). Distraction/conflict theory: Progress and problems. In L. Berkowitz (Ed.), *Advances in experimental social psychology* (Vol. 19, pp. 1–40). New York: Academic Press.

Baumeister, R. F. (1984). Choking under pressure: Self-consciousness and paradoxical effects of incentives on skillful performance. *Journal of Personality and Social Psychology, 46,* 610–620.

Baumeister, R. F., Hamilton, J. C., & Tice, D. M. (1985). Public versus private expectancy of success: Confidence booster or performance pressure? *Journal of Personality and Social Psychology, 48,* 1447–1457.

Baumeister, R. F., & Showers, C. J. (1986). A review of paradoxical performance effects: Chocking under pressure in sports and mental tests. *European Journal of Social Psychology, 16,* 361–383.

Baumeister, R. F., & Steinhilber, A. (1984). Paradoxical effects of supportive audiences on performance under pressure: The home field disadvantage in sports championships. *Journal of Personality and Social Psychology, 47,* 85–93.

Becker, M. A., & Suls, J. (1983). Take me out to the ballgame: The effects of objective, social and temporal performance information on attendance at major league baseball games. *Journal of Sport Psychology, 5,* 302–313.

Berger, S., Carli, L. C., Garcia, R., & Brady, J. J. (1982). Audience effects in anticipatory learning: A comparison of drive and practice-inhibition analyses. *Journal of Personality and Social Psychology, 42,* 478–486.

Blank, T. D., Staff, I., & Shaver P. (1976). Social facilitation of word associations: Further questions. *Journal of Personality and Social Psychology, 34,* 725–733.

Bogeng, G. A. E. (1926). *Geschichte des Sports aller Völker und Zeiten* [History of sports in all peoples and ages] (Vols. 1 & 2). Leipzig: E. U. Seemann.

Boman, T. G. (1966). *An investigation of selected causes and effects of stress in a communication-audience situation.* Unpublished doctoral dissertation, University of Minnesota.

Bond, C. F. (1982). Social facilitation: A self-presentational view. *Journal of Personality and Social Psychology, 42,* 1042–1050.

Bond, C. F., & Titus, L. J. (1983). Social facilitation: A meta-analysis of 241 studies. *Psychological Bulletin, 94,* 264–292.

Borden, R. J. (1975). Witnessed aggression: Influence of an observer's sex and values on aggressive responding. *Journal of Personality and Social Psychology, 31,* 567–573.

Borden, R. J. (1980). Audience influence. In P. B. Paulus (Ed.), *Psychology of group influence* (pp. 99–132). Hillsdale, NJ: Erlbaum.

Borden, R. J., Hendrick, C., & Walker, J. W. (1976). Affective, physiological, and attitudinal consequences of audience presence. *Bulletin of the Psychonomic Society, 7,* 33–36.

Borden, R. J., & Taylor, S. P. (1973). The social instigation and control of physical aggression. *Journal of Applied Social Psychology, 3,* 345–351.

Brown, B. R., & Garland, H. (1971). The effects of incompetency, audience acquaintanceship, and anticipated evaluative feedback on face-saving behavior. *Journal of Experimental Social Psychology, 7,* 490–502.

Brown, M., Amoroso, D. M., Ware, E. E., Pruesse, M., & Pilkey, D. W.

(1973). Factors affecting viewing time of pornography. *Journal of Social Psychology, 90,* 125–135.

Bryant, J., Brown, D., Comisky, P. W., & Zillmann, D. (1982). Sports and spectators: Commentary and appreciation. *Journal of Communication, 32*(1), 109–119.

Bryant, J., Comisky, P., & Zillmann, D. (1977). Drama in sports commentary. *Journal of Communication, 27*(3), 140–149.

Bryant, J., Comisky, P., & Zillmann, D. (1981). The appeal of rough-and-tumble play in televised professional football. *Communication Quarterly, 29,* 256–262.

Bryant, J., & Zillmann, D. (1983). Sports violence and the media. In J. H. Goldstein (Ed.), *Sports violence* (pp. 195–211). New York: Springer-Verlag.

Bryson, F. R. (1938). *The sixteenth-century Italian duel.* Chicago: University of Chicago Press.

Cialdini, R. B., Borden, R. J., Thorne, A., Walker, M. R., Freeman, S., & Sloan, L. R. (1976). Basking in reflected glory: Three (football) field studies. *Journal of Personality and Social Psychology, 34,* 366–375.

Cialdini, R. B., & Richardson, K. D. (1980). Two indirect tactics of image management: Basking and blasting. *Journal of Personality and Social Psychology, 39,* 406–415.

Coalter, F. (1985). Crowd behavior at football matches: A study in Scotland. *Leisure Studies, 4,* 111–117.

Comisky, P., Bryant, J., & Zillmann, D. (1977). Commentary as a substitute for action. *Journal of Communication, 27*(3), 150–153.

Cottrell, N. B. (1972). Social facilitation. In C. G. McClintock (Ed.), *Experimental social psychology* (pp. 185–236). New York: Holt.

Cox, R. H. (1985). *Sport psychology: Concepts and applications.* Dubuque, IA: Brown.

Diem, K. (1960). *Weltgeschichte des Sports und der Leibeserziehung* [World history of sport and physical education]. Stuttgart: Cotta.

Diener, E., Lusk, R., Defour, D., & Flax, R. (1980). Deindividuation: The effects of group size, density, number of observers, and group member similarity on self-consciousness. *Journal of Personality and Social Psychology, 39,* 449–459.

Eastman, S. T., & Meyer, T. P. (1989). Sports programming: Scheduling, costs, and competition. In L. A. Wenner (Ed.), *Media, sports, & society* (pp. 97–119). Newbury Park, CA: Sage Publications.

Edwards, J., & Archambault, D. (1989). The home-field advantage. In J. H. Goldstein (Ed.), *Sports, games, and play* (2nd ed., pp. 333–370). Hillsdale, NJ: Erlbaum.

Eichel, W. (1953). Die Entwicklung der Körperübungen in der Urgemeinschaft [The development of physical exercises in primitive society]. *Theorie und Praxis der Körperkultur, 2,* 14–33.

Eitzen, D. S., & Sage, G. H. (1986). *Sociology of North American sport* (3rd ed.). Dubuque, IA: Brown.

Ellis, E. (1829). *Polynesian researches, No. 1.* London: Fisher, Son, & Jackson.

Fenigstein, A., Scheier, M. F., & Buss, A. H. (1975). Public and private self-consciousness: Assessment and theory. *Journal of Consulting and Clinical Psychology, 43,* 522–527.

Fouts, G. T. (1970). *Imitation of children: The effects of an audience and number of presentations.* Unpublished doctoral dissertation, University of Iowa.

Frank, M. G., & Gilovich, T. (1988). The dark side of self-and social perception: Black uniforms and aggression in professional sports. *Journal of Personality and Social Psychology, 54,* 74–85.

Ganzer, V. J. (1968). The effects of audience presence and test anxiety on learning and retention in a serial learning situation. *Journal of Personality and Social Psychology, 8,* 194–199.

Gardiner, E. N. (1930). *Athletics of the ancient world.* Oxford: Clarendon Press.

Gayton, W. F., Matthews, G. R., & Nickless, C. J. (1987). The home field advantage in sports championships: Does it exist in hockey? *Journal of Sport Psychology, 9,* 183–185.

Geen, R. G. (1980). The effects of being observed on performance. In P. Paulus (Ed.), *Psychology of group influence* (pp. 61–67). Hillsdale, NJ: Erlbaum.

Geen, R. G. (1985). Evaluation apprehension and response withholding in solution of anagrams. *Personality and Individual Differences, 6,* 293–298.

Geen, R. G. (1989). Alternative conceptions of social facilitation. In P. B. Paulus (Ed.), *Psychology of group influence* (pp. 15–51). Hillsdale, NJ: Erlbaum.

Goldstein, J. H. (Ed.). (1983). *Sports violence.* New York: Springer-Verlag.

Grace, H. A. (1951). Effects of different degrees of knowledge about an audience on the contents of communication. *Journal of Social Psychology, 34,* 111–124.

Greer, D. L. (1983). Spectator booing and the home advantage: A study of social influence in the basketball arena. *Social Psychology Quarterly, 46,* 252–261.

Guerin, B. (1986). Mere presence effects in humans: A review. *Journal of Experimental Social Psychology, 22,* 38–77.

Guttmann, A. (1978). *From ritual to record: The nature of modern sport.* New York: Columbia University Press.

Guttmann, A. (1986). *Sports spectators.* New York: Columbia University Press.

Harris, H. A. (1972). *Aspects of Greek and Roman life.* Ithaca, NY: Cornell University Press.

Heaton, A. W., & Sigall, H. (1989). The "championship choke" revisited: The role of acquiring a negative identity. *Journal of Applied Social Psychology, 19,* 1019–1033.

Heaton, A. W., & Sigall, H. (1991). Self-consciousness, self-presentation, and performance under pressure: Who chokes, and when? *Journal of Applied Social Psychology, 21,* 175–188.

Heider, F. (1958). *The psychology of interpersonal relations.* New York: John Wiley.

Henchy, T., & Glass, D. C. (1968). Evaluation apprehension and the social facilitation of dominant and subordinate responses. *Journal of Personality and Social Psychology, 10,* 446–454.

Hirt, E. R., & Zillmann, D. (1985, May). *The effects of team outcome on fan's estimates of their own performance.* Paper presented at the meeting of the Midwestern Psychological Association, Chicago.

Hollingsworth, H. L. (1935). *The psychology of the audience.* New York: American Book.

Hye-Kerkdal, K. (1956). Wettkampfspiel und Dualorganisation bei den Timbira Brasiliens [Contest and dual-organization in Timbira Brazilians]. In J. Haekel, A. Hohenwart-Gerlachstein, & A. Slawik (Eds.), *Die Wiener Schule der Völkerkunde: Festschrift* (pp. 504–533). Wien: Berger.

Jackson, J. M., Buglione, S. A., & Glenwick, D. S. (1988). Major league baseball performance as a function of being traded: A drive theory analysis. *Personality and Social Psychology Bulletin, 14,* 46–56.

Jackson, J. M., & Latane, B. (1981). All alone in front of all of those people: Stage fright as a function of the number and type of co-performers and audience. *Journal of Personality and Social Psychology, 40,* 73–85.

Josephson, W. L. (1987). Television violence and children's aggression: Testing the priming, social script, and disinhibition predictions. *Journal of Personality and Social Psychology, 53,* 882–890.

Kahneman, D. (1973). *Attention and effort.* Englewood Cliffs, NJ: Prentice-Hall.

Koppet, L. (1972, January 9). Home court: The winning edge. *The New York Times,* p. 3.

Kroll, W. (1979). The stress of high performance athletics. In P. Klavora & Y. Daniels (Eds.), *Coach, athlete, and sport psychologist* (pp. 211–219). Champaign, IL: Human Kinetics.

Laird, D. (1923). Changes in motor control and individual variations under the influence of "razzing." *Journal of Experimental Psychology, 6,* 236–246.

Latane, B. (1981). The psychology of social impact. *American Psychologist, 36,* 343–356.

Latane, B., & Harkins, S. (1976). Cross-modality matches suggest anticipated stage fright a multiplicative power function of audience size and status. *Perception and Psychophysics, 20,* 482–488.

Latane, B., & Nida, S. (1980). Social impact theory and group influence: A social engineering perspective. In P. B. Paulus (Ed.). *Psychology of group influence* (pp. 3–34). Hillsdale, NJ: Erlbaum.

Lorenz, K. (1963). *Das sogenannte Böse: Zur Naturgeschichte der Aggression* [The so-called evil: To the natural history of aggression]. Vienna: Borotha-Schoeler.

Lowe, B. (1977). *The beauty of sport: A cross-disciplinary inquiry.* Englewood Cliffs, NJ: Prentice-Hall.

Lukas, G. (1969). *Die Körperkultur in frühen Epochen der Menschheitsentwicklung* [Body culture in the early stages of the development of humankind]. Berlin: Sportverlag.

Malmo, R. B., Boag, T. J., & Smith, A. A. (1957). Physiological study of personal interaction. *Psychosomatic Medicine, 19,* 105–119.

Mann, L. (1989). Sports crowds and the collective behavior perspective. In J. H. Goldstein (Ed.), *Sports, games, and play: Social and psychological viewpoints* (2nd ed., pp. 299–331). Hillsdale, NJ: Erlbaum.

Manstead, A. S. R., & Semin, G. R. (1980). Social facilitation effects: Mere enhancement of dominant responses? *British Journal of Social and Clinical Psychology, 19,* 119–136.

Martens, R. (1969). Palmar sweating and the presence of an audience. *Journal of Experimental and Social Psychology, 5,* 371–374.

Matlin, M. W., & Zajonc, R. D. (1968). Social facilitation of word associations. *Journal of Personality and Social Psychology, 10,* 435–460.

Michener, J. A. (1976). *Sports in America.* New York: Random House.

Midwinter, E. (1986). *Fair game: Myth and reality in sport.* London: Allen & Unwin.

Morris, D. (1981). *The soccer tribe.* London: Cape.

Nixon, H. L. (1975). The axiomatic theory of team success. *Sport Sociology Bulletin, 3,* 1–12.

Nixon, H. L. (1977). Reinforcement effects of sports team success: Cohesiveness related factors. *International Review of Sport Sociology, 12,* 17–38.

Noll, R. G. (1974). Attendance and price setting. In R. G. Noll (Ed.), *Government and the sports business: Studies in the regulation of economic activity* (pp. 115–157). Washington, DC: The Brookings Institution.

Paivio, A. (1965). Personality and audience influence. In B. Maher (Ed.), *Progress in experimental personality research, Vol. 2* (pp. 127–173). New York: Academic Press.

Paulus, P. B. (1983). Group influence on individual task performance. In P. B. Paulus (Ed.), *Basic group processes* (pp. 97–120). New York: Springer-Verlag.

Paulus, P. B., & Cornelius, W. L. (1974). An analysis of gymnastic performance under conditions of practice and spectator observation. *The Research Quarterly, 45,* 56–63.

Paulus, P. B., Judd, B. B., & Bernstein, I. H. (1976). Social facilitation and sports. In *Proceedings of the North American Society for Psychology of Sport and Physical Activity Conference.* Austin, TX.

Paulus, P. B., & Murdoch, P. (1971). Anticipated evaluation and audience presence in the enhancement of dominant responses. *Journal of Experimental Social Psychology, 7,* 280–291.

Paulus, P. B., Shannon, D., Wilson, D., & Boone, T. (1972). The effect of spectator presence on gymnastic performance in a field situation. *Psychonomic Science, 29,* 88–90.

Paulus, P. B., Teng, G., Camacho, L. M., & McDonald, S. (1987). *Audience pressure: When it counts and when it doesn't.* Unpublished manuscript. The University of Texas at Arlington.

Poliakoff, M. B. (1987). *Combat sports in the ancient world: Competition, violence, and culture.* New Haven: Yale University Press.

Ponomarev, N. I. (1974). Some research problems of physical education in the early history of mankind. *History of Physical Education and Sport: Research and Studies, 2,* 27–46.

Roberts, M. (1976). *Fans! How we go crazy over sports.* Washington, DC: New Republic.

Russell, G., & Drewry, B. (1976). Crowd size and competitive aspects of aggression in ice hockey: An archival study. *Human Relations, 29,* 723–735.

Sanders, G. S. (1981). Driven by distraction: An integrative review of social facilitation theory and research. *Journal of Experimental Social Psychology, 17,* 227–251.

Sansone, D. (1988). *Greek athletics and the genesis of sport.* Berkeley: University of California Press.

Sapolsky, B. S. (1980). The effect of spectator disposition and suspense on the enjoyment of sport contests. *International Journal of Sport Psychology, 11,* 1–10.

Scheier, M. F., Fenigstein, A., & Buss, A. H. (1974). Self awareness and physical aggression. *Journal of Experimental Social Psychology, 10,* 264–273.

Schellenberger, H. (1990). *Psychology of team sports.* Toronto: Sport Books.

Schmitt, B. H., Gilovich, T., Goore, N., & Joseph, L. (1986). Mere presence and social facilitation: One more time. *Journal of Experimental Social Psychology, 22,* 242–248.

Schroder, B. (1927). *Der Sport im Altertum* [Sports in antiquity]. Berlin: Hans Schoetz.

Schwartz, B., & Barsky, S. F. (1977). The home advantage. *Social Forces, 55,* 641–661.

Schwartz, N. (1987). *Stimmung als Information: Untersuchungen zum Einfluss von Stimmungen auf die Bewertung des eigenen Lebens* [Mood as information: Investigations of the effect of moods on the evaluation of one's own life]. Berlin: Springer-Verlag.

Schweitzer, K., Zillmann, D., Weaver, J. B., & Luttrell, E. S. (1992). Perception of threatening events in the emotional aftermath of a televised college football game. *Journal of Broadcasting & Electronic Media, 36*(1), 123–131.

Seta, C. E., & Seta, J. J. (1990). *Increments and decrements in performance arousal levels as a function of audience composition.*

Unpublished manuscript. The University of North Carolina at Greensboro.

Seta, J. J., Crisson, J. E., Seta, C. E., & Wang, M. A. (1989). Task performance and perceptions of anxiety: Averaging and summation in an evaluative setting. *Journal of Personality and Social Psychology, 56,* 387–396.

Seta, J. J., & Hassan, R. K. (1980). Awareness of prior success or failure: A critical factor in task performance. *Journal of Personality and Social Psychology, 39,* 70–76.

Seta, J. J., Paulus, P. B., & Schkade, J. K. (1976). The effects of group size and proximity under competitive and cooperative conditions. *Journal of Personality and Social Psychology, 43,* 47–53.

Seta, J. J., & Seta, C. E. (1983). The impact of personal equity processes on performance in a group setting. In P. B. Paulus (Ed.), *Basic group processes* (pp. 121–147). New York: Springer-Verlag.

Seta, J. J., Seta, C. E., & Donaldson, S. (1990). *The impact of comparison processes on coactors' frustration and willingness to expend effort.* Unpublished manuscript. The University of North Carolina at Greensboro.

Seta, J. J., Seta, C. E., & Paulus, P. B. (1990). *Contextual variations in the use of social comparison information: The importance of standards and information.* Unpublished manuscript. The University of North Carolina at Greensboro.

Seta, J. J., Wang, M. A., Crisson, J. E., & Seta, C. E. (1989). Audience composition and felt anxiety: Impact averaging and summation. *Basic and Applied Social Psychology, 10,* 57–72.

Silva, J. M., & Andrew, A. (1987). An analysis of game location and basketball performance in the Atlantic Coast Conference. *International Journal of Sport Psychology, 18,* 288–204.

Sloan, L. R. (1982, November). *The effects of winning and losing on the sports fan: Implications for multifactored theories.* Paper presented at the 3rd annual conference of the North American Society for the Sociology of Sport, Toronto, Ontario.

Sloan, L. R. (1989). The motives of sports fans. In J. H. Goldstein (Ed.), *Sports, games, and play: Social and psychological viewpoints* (2nd ed., pp. 175–240). Hillsdale, NJ: Erlbaum.

Smith, H. (1831). *Festivals, games, and amusements, ancient and modern.* London: Henry Colburn and Richard Bentley.

Snyder, E. E., & Spreitzer, E. A. (1983). *Social aspects of sport* (2nd ed.). Englewood Cliffs, NJ: Prentice-Hall.

Sorrentino, R. M., & Sheppard, B. H. (1978). Effects of affiliation-related motives on swimmers in individual versus group competition: A field experiment. *Journal of Personality and Social Psychology, 36,* 704–714.

Spence, K. W. (1956). *Behavior theory and conditioning.* New Haven: Yale University Press.

Strube, M. J., Miles, M. E., & Finch, W. H. (1981). The social facilitation of simple task: Field tests of alternative explanations. *Personality and Social Psychology Bulletin, 7,* 701–707.

Taylor, S. P. (1977). Third party intervention and control of physical aggression. *International Journal of Group Tensions, 7,* 42–49.

Thirer, J., & Rampey, M. (1979). Effects of abusive spectator behavior on the performance of home and visiting intercollegiate basketball teams. *Perceptual and Motor Skills, 48,* 1047–1053.

Triplett, N. (1898). The dynamogenic factors of pacemaking and competition. *American Journal of Psychology, 9,* 507–533.

Ueberhorst, H. (1972). Ursprungstheorien [Theories of origin]. In H. Ueberhorst (Ed.), *Geschichte der Leibesübungen* (Vol. 1, pp. 11–47). Berlin: Bartels & Wernitz.

Ueberhorst, H. (Ed.). (1972–1978). *Geschichte der Leibesübungen* [History of physical exercise] (Vols. 1-2). Berlin: Bartels & Wernitz.

Ulf, C. (1981). Sport bei den Naturvölkern [Sports in primitive societies]. In I. Weiler, (Ed.) *Der Sport bei den Völkern der alten Welt: Eine Einführung* (pp. 14–52). Darmstadt: Wissenschaftliche Buchgesellschaft.

Underwood, J. (1984). *Spoiled sport: A fan's notes on the troubles of spectator sports.* Boston: Little, Brown.

U.S. Census Abstracts. (1988). *Statistical abstracts of the United States.* Washington, DC: U.S. Government Printing Office.

Vamplew, W. (1988). *Pay up and play the game: Professional sport in Britain, 1875–1914.* Cambridge: Cambridge University Press.

Varca, P. (1980). An analysis of home and away game performance of male college basketball teams. *Journal of Sport Psychology, 2,* 245–257.

Weiler, I. (1981). *Der Sport bei den Völkern der alten Welt: Eine Einführung* [Peoples' sports in the ancient world: An introduction]. Darmstadt: Wissenschaftliche Buchgesellschaft.

Weiss, R. F., & Miller, F. G. (1971). The drive theory of social facilitation. *Psychological Review, 78,* 44–57.

Weiss, R. F., Miller, F. G., Langan, C. J., & Cecil, J. S. (1971). Social facilitation of attitude change. *Psychonomic Science, 55,* 127–142.

Whiting, H. T. A., & Masterson, D. W. (Eds.). (1974). *Readings in the aesthetics of sport.* London: Lepus Books.

Wicklund, R. A., & Duval, S. (1971). Opinion change and performance facilitation as a result of objective self-awareness. *Journal of Experimental Social Psychology, 7,* 319–342.

Williams, K. D., Nida, S. A., Baca, L. D., & Latane, B. (1989). Social loafing and swimming: Effects of identifiability on individual and relay performance of intercollegiate swimmers. *Basic and Applied Social Psychology, 10,* 73–81.

Worringham, C. J., & Messick, D. M. (1983). Social facilitation of running: An unobtrusive study. *Journal of Social Psychology, 121,* 23–29.

Wrightsman, L. S. (1960). Effects of waiting with others on changes in felt level of anxiety. *Journal of Abnormal and Social Psychology, 61,* 216–222.

Zajonc, R. B. (1965). Social facilitation. *Science, 149,* 269–274.

Zajonc, R. B. (1980). Copresence. In P. Paulus (Ed.), *Psychology of group influence* (pp. 35–60). Hillsdale, NJ: Erlbaum.

Zajonc, R. B., & Sales, S. (1966). Social facilitation of dominant and subordinate responses. *Journal of Experimental Social Psychology, 2,* 160–168.

Zillmann, D. (1990). Die Beanblossom-Hypothesen [The Beanblossom hypotheses]. *Semiosis, 15*(1/2), 69–73.

Zillmann, D., Bryant, J., & Sapolsky, B. S. (1989). Enjoyment from sports spectatorship. In J. H. Goldstein (Ed.), *Sports, games, and play: Social and psychological viewpoints* (2nd ed., pp. 241–278). Hillsdale, NJ: Erlbaum.

GROUP DYNAMICS

29

SOCIAL INTERACTIONS

Stephanie Hanrahan

Cindy Gallois

Social psychology has had a great impact on sport psychology. By definition, social psychology is the scientific study of the manner in which the behavior, thoughts, and feelings of one individual influence or are influenced by the behavior and/or characteristics of others. Sport psychology examines the behaviors, thoughts, and feelings of individuals in sport and physical activity contexts. Many of these behaviors are influenced by the behavior and characteristics of others, including coaches, teachers, officials, teammates, exercise leaders, and parents.

Organized sport and physical activity are almost always carried out in the presence of others. The sporting situation inherently involves social interactions. These other people, whether they are spectators, coaches, exercise leaders, or teammates, can affect performance. The most rudimentary form of social interaction within the sport and physical activity context occurs with the mere presence of spectators. Social facilitation and the effects of audiences on athletic performances are discussed by Zillmann and Paulus in Chapter 28 of this *Handbook*. Another major area of research within sport psychology deals with the social interactions of coaches and other leaders with participants, also discussed in the other two chapters (30, 31) in this section of the book.

The present chapter mainly addresses the impact of social interaction on group performance. An initial general discussion of group dynamics based on social psychological research sets the stage for research that is more closely related to sport and physical activities. Research investigating the relationship of individual performance to group performance is presented next. Other factors that may affect group performance, such as group motivation, group coordination, and group size, will be discussed in some detail, along with relevant theory. Research on team cohesion, including many studies that have attempted to determine the influence of team cohesion on performance, will be presented last.

In this chapter we have two main aims. The first is to re-view relevant research on social interaction and to apply it to the sport context. In doing this, we will touch on some areas that sport psychologists have not investigated systematically, as well as some areas in which more research has been conducted. Our second aim is to suggest some useful directions for future research, especially in those areas where little work has been done to date.

SOCIAL LEARNING

Much of the influence exerted by individuals upon each other works through the process of social reinforcement, and many of the major theories guiding research on social factors in sport settings are based on social learning. Social reinforcement involves verbal and nonverbal communication, which influences behavior through social rewards and punishments and takes the form of verbal praise and criticism through the content of messages, tone of voice, facial expressions, or other nonverbal behavior. When sources of information about performance are absent, social reinforcement can have an informational effect on motor performance (Gill, 1986). It can also have a motivational effect when the motor activity is not highly intrinsically motivating to the individual (Wankel, 1975).

An example of the pervasive influence of social reinforcement in sport involves sex-role stereotypes (Reis & Jelsma, 1978). Particular sports have long been assigned as "male" or "female," and members of the "wrong" sex were for many years discouraged from participating in them. Today the effects of these practices linger on in the form of differential coverage, resources, pay to professionals, and so forth, for men and women engaged in the same activity (Hoferek, 1978). At the level of individual players, men and women playing in sports that are stereotyped for the other sex often experience conflict between their self-perceptions as sportspeople and their feelings of masculinity or femininity. This conflict results in less commitment, higher rates of dropout, and less-than-optimal performance (see Sage & Loudermilk, 1979, for a discussion of role conflict among women in sport).

There is yet much room for research into the impact of social learning and reinforcement on sporting performance, particularly with regard to the influence of sex-role stereotypes. We still know relatively little, for example, about the importance of the sporting role, relative to other roles, for women in male-dominated sports, or the relation of role commitment to performance. More experimental field studies of the way increased reporting of a team's performance (e.g., a female basketball team) influences the team's success could also be conducted. If as a society we value equal participation by members of both sexes in sport, it is worth locating the most effective methods of reinforcing it.

A second process in social learning, modeling, involves imitative behavior or learning through observation. A large body of research has demonstrated that models with high social status evoke imitative behavior by others (Bandura, 1973). Within the sporting context, many participants have a very high social status. If esteemed coaches and athletes are observed cheating, or being extremely aggressive, it is not merely a coincidence that others imitate these behaviors.

Indeed, social learning theory (Bandura, 1973) has been argued to provide the best theoretical framework to study aggression (Husman, 1978; see also Bandura & Huston, 1961; Bandura, Ross, & Ross, 1961). Although social learning theorists concentrate on the processes of modeling and social reinforcement, they do not deny that aggression may be grounded in personal attributes. Rather, they contend that patterns of aggressive behavior are acquired and maintained through interaction with significant others and socializing situations (Bredemeier, 1978). For example, Smith (1978), in a study of high school hockey players' perceptions of aggression in professional hockey, concluded that the professional players were serving as high-status models for the amateurs in socializing aggressive behavior and a positive evaluation of aggression on the ice (see also Thirer's chapter [15] on aggression in this book).

Although it has been demonstrated that aggressive behaviors are socially learned, it has also been suggested that moral values and behaviors are socially learned through both modeling and social reinforcement (Shields & Bredemeier, 1984). The sporting environment provides a situation where either moral or immoral standards can be learned (see the chapter in this *Handbook* on moral development). In addition, coaching and teaching both have social reinforcement and modeling as primary components (Gill, 1986). In fact, modeling is of major consideration in the acquisition of many new skills (see chapter on modeling in this book). In addition to acquiring skills through modeling, the attitudes of sport participants are often influenced by the social learning process. Participants' attitudes toward coaches, the activity, and their teammates have been demonstrated to be affected by the social reinforcement behaviors of coaches (Smith, Smoll, & Curtis, 1978).

Many other areas of social psychology emphasize the social learning approach. For example, Rotter's (1966) concept of locus of control is based in social learning theory. Internals believe in the relationship between behavior and rewards and feel that they have some control over their environment, while externals believe that rewards are the result of luck or fate and feel that they have no control over them.

This basic realm in social psychology has been applied to research within sport psychology. In sport, some patterns of attributions have been proposed to be healthier than others. McHugh, Duquin, and Frieze (1978) felt that training athletes to make effort attributions would increase their pride in success and also lead to increased persistence. Similarly Thomas (1977) suggested that by changing the attributional processes of the young athlete so that effort became the causal determinant of success and failure, fewer individuals would drop out because of feelings of little hope for future success.

Social learning theory has also provided the basis for methods in changing athletes' attributions. For example, verbal persuasion as a technique for reattribution training is founded in the idea that attributions can be socially learned, and therefore can be changed (Forsterling, 1985; see Biddle's article, Chapter 19 in this book, on attributions).

SOCIAL EXCHANGE THEORY

In their classic work on social interaction and interpersonal processes, Thibaut and Kelley (1959; see also Kelley & Thibaut, 1978) argued that the social learning process results in aspects of social interactions acquiring differential value for the people involved in them. They proposed that individuals develop a repertoire of social behaviors (or ways of reinforcing others) from which they sample at the beginning of a new social relationship. Depending on the response from others in the social environment, the individual either tends to continue with the interaction patterns he or she has begun, abandons them and tries new behaviors, or leaves the scene and tries again with another person or group. Over time, therefore, people in relationships develop and lock into patterns of interacting that, in principle, maximize the ratio of costs (punishments) to benefits (rewards) for each of them (see Homans, 1950, for another version of this line of reasoning).

The decision about whether a relationship is sufficiently rewarding to stay in it (and perhaps to change behavior to increase the ratio of benefits to costs) or to leave it and try another person or group is determined in large part by the person's relevant social history. Thibaut and Kelley (1959) argued that individuals over the course of their lives develop a *comparison level* for particular relationships that essentially constitutes a kind of average benefit-to-cost ratio for that type of relationship in the person's past. For example, I am more likely to put up with a bullying coach (particularly if the coach produces good results), if my past relationships with coaches have involved bullying or other behaviors that are costly to me than if my past coaches have been kindly and rewarding (as well as effective). The lower my comparison level, the more satisfied I am likely to be with my present relationship. In addition, the decision to stay or to leave is partly based on the alternatives available to the individual at the time, in terms of other relationships or rewarding activities (what Thibaut and Kelley call the *comparison level for alternatives*). The fewer good alternatives I have available to me, the more dependent I am on this relationship, and thus the more power others in the relationship or group have over me.

Social exchange theory has inspired a long tradition of research, much of it laboratory-based, that has demonstrated the success of predictions derived from it in the context of bargaining games. Researchers working within this tradition have been criticized, however, for not examining real-life relationships sufficiently; in more recent years there has been a concerted effort to take the theory into the field, with some success (e.g., see Burgess & Huston, 1979; Kelley & Thibaut, 1978). Carron (1980) reviewed research into coach-athlete interaction that has been conducted from this perspective, and he made some useful suggestions for research and practice. The thinking underlying social exchange theory, meanwhile, has become so basic to research and theory within group dynamics as to be almost unnoticed today. Much of the work reviewed in this chapter implicitly adopts this perspective.

SOCIAL IDENTITY THEORY

The emphasis on learning and reinforcement-based approaches to group dynamics within social psychology generally, and group dynamics in sport psychology in particular, has produced much useful research and theory in the areas of, for example, cohesion, competition, and performance. There has been one side effect of this approach, however, that has been less beneficial—the tendency to characterize all group processes in individual or interpersonal terms (Carron, 1982, and especially Hogg, 1990, presented this issue cogently in the area of group or team cohesion). Interactions in competitive sport have an essentially *intergroup* character, because of the central goal of winning, although there is also an interpersonal side.

Social identity theory (Tajfel, 1978, 1982; Tajfel & Turner, 1979; Turner, 1987; see also Abrams & Hogg, 1990) is an attempt to deal with the group-based or intergroup aspects of group processes, without losing sight of the individual person as the locus of attitudes, norms, decisions, and so forth. Hogg and Abrams (1988) provided a very useful overview of this theory and its application to a number of areas in group dynamics. Tajfel and his colleagues argued that the process

of categorizing people into groups is basic and ubiquitous in social life. In addition this process takes place with respect to the self, so that the resulting categories have the quality of in-groups (categories or groups to which I belong) and out-groups (categories or groups to which I do not belong, but which are relevant to my in-groups for some reason). Indeed, Tajfel et al. (1973) showed that categorization into in-groups and out-groups can take place on entirely arbitrary cues, but that even when this is so, members of in-groups are judged as possessing more desirable characteristics than members of out-groups. Tajfel suggested that social categorization is inevitable, and that once it has occurred, judgments of in-groups and out-groups potentially influence every aspect of social interaction.

Personal and Social Identity

Tajfel and Turner (1979) and Turner (1987) proposed that for the purpose of explicating in-group and out-group relations, the self-concept can usefully be thought of as including two aspects. The first is *personal identity,* made up of my judgments about myself as an individual and my perceptions of my relationships with other individuals (e.g., I might see myself as a fast runner or as more competitive than most of my teammates). These judgments are arrived at by a process of social comparison (Festinger, 1954) with others who are similar in relevant ways—thus mainly with members of in-groups. In making these comparisons, we are motivated to make ourselves distinctive from similar others in positively valued ways. Most naturally occurring social comparisons are downward, with individuals who do not measure up to our own level (see Turner, 1987). Personal identity is likely to be salient when interpersonal attraction is high.

The second aspect of the self-concept in this conceptualization involves *social identity,* made up of an individual's characteristics as a member of various in-groups, and that individual's perceptions of the groups' relations with other relevant out-groups. For example, I might view myself and my team as particularly motivated in a crisis, or as more aggressive than other teams. When social identity is salient, social comparisons are with other groups, rather than with other individuals. Here we are motivated to minimize the differences between members of the in-group (and between members of relevant out-groups), as well as to maximize the differences in appearance, qualities, and behaviors, between the in-group and the out-group (see Turner, 1987). The self and other individuals are depersonalized in the sense that individual qualities are less important than the qualities that define the group. In addition, for me as a group member the most highly valued norms, skills, and personal qualities, instead of being those most central to my own value system, become those that best define and characterize the in-group (that is, those that are most prototypical or normative). Social identity is likely to be salient when the social environment is threatening or when the groups are competing or hostile.

This characterization of the group-in-the-individual (Hogg & Abrams, 1988) has a number of interesting consequences for the analysis of group processes, several of which are of particular interest to this chapter. First the theory postulates that attitudes and values, as well as behavior, change in the direction of group norms under conditions where social identity is salient. Carron (1988) offered a number of examples of changes in team members' values in the service of team performance. Second, decision-making processes are in part determined by the characteristics of relevant out-groups (this has special relevance in the areas of group polarization and groupthink). Next motivation, social facilitation, and social loafing are closely related to the in-group/out-group situation and the normativeness of the task. Finally attraction and cohesion take on a social dimension, which may or may not be correlated with personal attraction (as we will see).

Sport psychologists studying the group dynamics of teams, coach-athlete interactions, motivation, and the like have not paid a great deal of attention to this conceptualization to date. Rather they have attempted to analyze these processes more or less entirely in interpersonal terms. The competitive nature of sport, however, means that team (and individual) processes are mainly intergroup situations; genuinely interpersonal encounters are more the exception than the rule. Social identity theory, therefore, appears to provide a neat theoretical structure for the study of team and interpersonal dynamics in sport settings. We use it here as an added way of integrating some of the findings we review.

Social Identity and Social Exchange

Social exchange theory, as noted earlier, analyzes group interactions in terms of cost-benefit decisions and strategies used by individuals. It is thus essentially an interpersonal approach based on reinforcement and social learning. Thibaut and Kelley's (1959) concepts of comparison level and comparison level for alternatives, however, lead to some interesting extensions into the intergroup domain. First the better the present relationship is relative to the comparison level, the more satisfied the person is with the group, and the more solidarity he or she feels with the group. Individuals who are very satisfied with a group are likely to identify more strongly with it than are those who are not. On the other hand, the *less* favorable the comparison level for alternatives is, the more the individual is dependent on the present group for satisfaction. Individuals with few available alternatives are willing to put up with rather unsatisfactory relationships until something better comes along. For example, in elite sport an athlete on a national team may have a less than satisfactory relationship with other individuals on the team, but this unpleasantness is tolerated as there is only one national team.

Relations between individuals have been described by a number of researchers along two correlated dimensions: intergroup and interpersonal (e.g., Gudykunst, 1986). High intergroup interactions are those where social identity is

very salient (e.g., the interactions between members of two teams in competition). High interpersonal interactions are those where personal identity is salient (for example, those between two friends outside the competition setting). A few social interactions are low on both dimensions (e.g., an interaction with a stranger clerk across a counter) or high on both (e.g., a man and woman who are married), but these are relatively unlikely to occur in sport settings.

The more dependent group members are on a group (i.e., the lower their comparison level for alternatives), the more likely they are to view interactions with out-group members in intergroup terms (see Gallois, Franklyn-Stokes, Giles, & Coupland, 1988; Giles & Johnson, 1987). In these circumstances they are more likely to behave narrowly in terms of the norms defining prototypical behavior for their group and to denigrate behavior that deviates from these norms. On the other hand individuals who are satisfied with their groups (high comparison level), while they may see interactions with out-group members in intergroup terms, are more likely to emphasize the positive characteristics of their groups without necessarily denigrating out-group behavior.

From these propositions one can make some predictions about members of sport teams. First, more satisfied players should perform more flexibly and interact more positively with team members, while low-satisfied individuals should interact more negatively and be more likely to drop out. Volp and Keil (1987) provide some support for this prediction. Second, highly dependent team members should interact more competitively with members of other teams than would less dependent individuals. Third, team members low in both satisfaction and dependence should behave less competitively toward members of other teams. Support for these and related predictions and the impact of these variables on team cohesion and performance awaits future research.

COMMUNICATION IN GROUPS

The communication that takes place during competition and training has been studied surprisingly little, given its importance to performance in sport. Carron (1988) provided a review of some of the research that has been done. Workers in this area can benefit greatly from research in other areas on the dynamics of verbal and nonverbal communication. We will not review that research here (for recent reviews see Argyle, 1988; Burgoon, Buller, & Woodall, 1990; Giles & Robinson, 1990). Instead we will examine briefly some theoretical issues that seem especially relevant.

Dimensions of Communication

There is enormous consensus about the dimensions that characterize interactions between people across a wide variety of situations. From the early work of Osgood, Suci, and Tannenbaum (1957) through more recent research (e.g., Bales, Cohen, & Williamson, 1979; Wish, d'Andrade, &

Goodnow, 1980), interactants have described themselves, their fellow interactants, and their conversations in terms of dominance (or power) (see Brown & Gilman, 1960), affiliation (or solidarity), and interest (or involvement). Occasionally a fourth dimension of task or emotional involvement also appears. It is interesting to note that these dimensions are all affective. It would appear that our first response to an interaction is captured by the feeling it evokes (Forgas, 1986).

Some workers in sport psychology have been swayed by Russell's (1980) circumplex model into minimizing the importance of dominance to the description of communication in sport settings. It should be noted that Russell's research involves asking subjects to imagine environments in which they are alone (e.g., performing a difficult exercise). They then describe these environments using structured adjective scales. In these cases the two dimensions of pleasure and arousal (which are analogous to affiliation and involvement) seem sufficient for the description. When people are interacting, however, dominance comes in as a dimension and in many cases is the most important (e.g., see Carron, 1978). These three dimensions of communication have been found useful in distinguishing among different types of interactions. Wish et al. (1980), for example, used them to describe various aspects of the communications of a family. Researchers might use them to elicit comparisons by athletes of different tasks in their sport. In addition, they might be used to compare successful and less successful performance and indeed to predict performance.

Effective communication in a number of contexts (e.g., work-related communication, marital communication) has been linked to accurate encoding and decoding of verbal and nonverbal messages along these dimensions. Accuracy, in turn, appears to be related not only to skill as a communicator, but also to the quality of the relationship between interactants. Thus an unhappy marriage (Noller, 1984) or ethnic prejudice (Gallois & Callan, 1986) may cause, at least in part, a deficit in the ability to decode the other person or people in a relationship. In some cases people in negative relationships are able to understand the communicative messages of strangers better than those of others in the relationship. This deficit, in its turn, has a number of negative consequences for decision making and other aspects of performance. Noller (1984) describes a negative communication cycle in which negative attitudes toward the other person lead to misunderstandings that in their turn confirm and solidify the negative attitudes, and so on. An extension of this research into team settings should bear fruit in terms of understanding the relationship between effective communication and effective performance. For example, Noller's strategy of asking couples to decode the meaning and emotional tone of each other's nonverbal messages could be used in relationships between coaches and athletes or between teammates. This strategy involves the creation of a number of standard-content messages relevant to the situation, but which can be interpreted in several ways (e.g., "What are you doing?"). One person sends a message with a specific intention (e.g., conveying anger), and the other must decode the intention using nonverbal behavior alone. It is a robust way of distinguishing successful from unsuccessful relationships.

Communication and Intergroup Relations

Some of the findings just described have led to the hypothesis that many aspects of verbal and nonverbal communication serve as markers of social identity. In particular, jargon and slang, accent, gestures, and dress have been studied as markers of membership in specific groups (see Argyle, 1988; Giles & Robinson, 1990). In the case of sport teams, some of this behavior is ritualized, for example, in the wearing of uniforms or the use of specialized team slogans.

Giles and his colleagues (e.g., Giles, Mulac, Bradac, & Johnson, 1987) have proposed that when social identity is activated, group members emphasize those features of their speech, nonverbal behavior, or dress that best distinguish their in-group from out-groups. This process, called *communicative divergence,* is especially likely under conditions of competition or threat. On the other hand, under these conditions members of in-groups are likely to converge in their behavior—that is, to make their behavior as similar to each other (and to members of the group who are considered to be prototypical) as possible. In team settings, the extent of convergence to prototypical in-group behavior and divergence from out-group behavior can serve as an index of the extent to which competitive motives and social identity are active.

The period before a match is one where divergence and strong adherence to team norms are deliberately encouraged by coaches and captains. Often, however, this process carries the risk of underestimating the opposing side, and coaches are acutely aware of the risks of groupthink. An interesting research question involves the optimal amount of divergence from the opposition and convergence to team norms; later sections take up this issue in the contexts of motivation and cohesion.

SOCIAL SITUATIONS: SKILLS, ROLES, AND RULES

Communication among members of sport teams and sporting groups has not been a major research area within sport psychology, with the possible exception of work on leadership and coach-athlete interaction (e.g., see Carron, 1980). Nevertheless it is an area of great and recognized practical importance, especially in terms of the contribution of communication processes to cohesion and team performance. Therefore it seems worth considering some of the theory and research from social psychology and its application to sport situations. Argyle and his colleagues (Argyle, 1988; Argyle & Henderson, 1984; Argyle, Furnham, & Graham, 1981; Furnham, 1983) have proposed a general model of social situations and the roles, rules, and skills that characterize situations.

Social Skills

This model of social situations is derived from Argyle's earlier model of social skills (Argyle, 1969; Trower, Bryant, & Argyle, 1977), in which social skills are viewed as complex motor skills analogous to athletic skills. The earlier model is individually based and looks at social interactions as comprising five main parts: the individual's *goals or motivation* in entering the interaction (which may change as the interaction continues); *perception* of the environment, including stereotypes, attributions, and processing of information; *translation* of information into decisions about how to act, which is related to perceived norms, roles, and rules in the situation; the repertoire of *motor responses* that can be and are used in the situation; and the use of *feedback* from the environment. In each of these areas there are special issues and deficits. Social skills thus can be taught and learned in the same way as any complex motor skill, as long as all five aspects are addressed. Trower et al. (1977), indeed, developed a social skills training system based on this model, intended for teaching basic social skills or specialized skills such as micro-teaching or cross-cultural training. Carron (1980) used the model to integrate some of the research on coach-athlete interaction.

The social skills approach has much to recommend it as a straightforward way of conceptualizing and training social interaction. Since the late 1970s, however, the model has received considerable criticism, largely because of repeated failures to transfer skills from the training setting to real-life situations; Furnham (1983) has called the failure to generalize training the Achilles heel of the social skills-training movement. Thus at the same time that this approach began to be used in sport settings, it was expanded in social psychology to include a much more detailed analysis of social situations.

Argyle et al. (1981) construed situations as containing their own goals, roles, and rules, as well as behaviors and sequences of behavior, language, concepts and beliefs, settings, and difficulties, that set them apart from other situations. This new model thus encapsulates the social skills model in some but not all of the features of situations. To train social skills effectively, in this view, one must also understand roles, rules, and settings. The larger list of features of situations provides a useful starting point for research, most of which to date has focused on goals, roles, and rules. We will review some of the research on team motives (goals) in a later section of this chapter. A brief discussion of the research on roles and rules is presented here.

Social Roles

Social roles are usually considered to comprise sets of behaviors that are associated with a particular social position (Biddle & Thomas, 1966). Roles, like social positions, are defined with respect to other target roles, which are part of the same system. For example, the coach role is defined in terms of the roles for athletes, officials, other coaches, and other figures with whom a coach interacts professionally. Roles thus consist of expectations and the actual behavior attached to a position.

Roles may be institutionally defined, as the roles of coach and team captain are. On the other hand, they may emerge informally through the history of a group or a sport (a possible example of the latter is the role of "policeman" or "enforcer" in hockey; see Carron, 1988; Smith, 1978). A number of researchers have used Bales's (1950; 1966) system of interaction process analysis to categorize team members into informal roles as task or socioemotional specialists. Using a more direct approach, Rees and Segal (1984) asked members of college football teams to name the team members they felt were the best players (the task specialists), as well as those they saw as contributing most to group harmony (the socioemotional specialists). Rees and Segal found that these roles described two distinct groups of players; task specialists were more likely to be first-string players, while socioemotional specialists were more likely to be seniors, and thus more experienced team members. Where there was overlap between the roles, players were both first-string and seniors. A long tradition of research (e.g., see Bales et al., 1979) points to the different expectations for people in these two roles.

Formal roles, too, may acquire expectations that are not strictly part of the original role definition but that involve behaviors related to it. For example, Carron (1978) found that both athletes and coaches expected much higher levels of expressed control (Schutz, 1966) from coaches and more received control from athletes (athletes had a more exaggerated perception of this difference than did coaches). The two roles differed far less in levels of inclusion and affection, although fewer of these behaviors were expected from coaches. These results point once again to the importance of dominance or control in defining roles that differ in status.

An important aspect of roles is the extent to which enacting them causes conflict for the role players. Most role theorists (e.g., Biddle & Thomas, 1966) describe conflict as being situated within a role (intra-role conflict, to do with incompatible expectations for the same role), across two or more roles enacted by the same person (inter-role conflict), and between the personal identity of a role player and the demands or expectations of the role (person-role conflict). To deal in detail with this issue is beyond the scope of this chapter. It is worth pointing out, however, that role conflict, or lack of identification with the sport role, has been described as a predictor of dropouts and lower levels of performance in swimmers (Volp & Keil, 1987), and burnout among coaches (Caccese & Mayerberg, 1984; Capel, Sisley, & Desertrain, 1987), as well as a consequence of sex stereotyping of sports (Sage & Loudermilk, 1979).

Social Rules

Rules, like roles, involve shared expectations about behavior (Argyle et al., 1981). In this case the behavior occurs in particular situations. It need not be attached to particular roles but may instead apply to everyone in the situation. Argyle and colleagues use the rules of games as the archetypes of social rules. They have developed a methodology for studying rules that essentially involves asking people in the situations to describe what people should and should not do. Alternatively they ask subjects to rate the importance of rules articulated by other people (e.g., Argyle & Henderson, 1984). Unlike the formal rules of games, however, many social rules are not easy to articulate; rather they may be most easily understood by observing reactions to their violation. Jones and Gallois (1989) used a methodology for doing this (in the context of rules for managing conflict in marriage) that involved videotaping examples of the situation and then taking participants back through the videotape to find examples of rules being followed or broken. Both these methodologies can readily be applied to sport settings, in order to isolate the important informal rules for conduct during competitive or training interactions.

Argyle et al. (1981) noted that some rules (e.g., be polite, do not make another person feel small) are quite general across social situations, and even across cultures. On the other hand, other rules are quite specific to situations, and may even come into conflict with formal rules or more general rules. For example, Silva (1983) found that male and female collegiate athletes thought it was acceptable to commit fouls on other players in team sports if this resulted in an advantage at a crucial moment in play, a view which certainly conflicts with more general rules about fair play. Such situation-specific rules may define the prototypical behavior (Turner, 1987) for a team member.

Rules vary in importance, but they are always relatively easy to articulate (at least when they are broken) and are relatively stable across time. In this way, they differ from norms, which in many cases define the limits to behaviors and which may change rapidly with situational factors (see Forsyth, 1990). In many respects, however, rules and norms have much in common, and research into rules for interaction in sport settings can usefully tap into the large literature on social norms in general.

This section has considered some general features of social interaction that impinge on performance. In the next section, we take up the issue of performance directly.

INDIVIDUAL AND GROUP PERFORMANCE

Individual ability (general or specific) is significantly related to group effectiveness (Heslin, 1964). Although the abilities of individual members have been demonstrated as having positive and consistent relationships with group performance, the measurement of these abilities, whether objective or subjective, has not always produced good predictors of group performance (McGrath & Altman, 1966). Haythorn (1968) pointed out that the relationship of individual abilities or proficiencies to group effectiveness is in

part dependent on whether the individual tasks are performed in series (e.g., a fast break in basketball), or in parallel (e.g., rowing). Another factor that may influence this relationship is the degree of social interaction required by individual members to produce a successful performance (Napier, 1968).

Laboratory Motor Tasks

Since this book deals with sport psychology, it is necessary to investigate whether the relationship between individual abilities and group performance is maintained when the tasks require physical coordination. In laboratory motor tasks, individual performance scores have a moderately positive relationship with group performance.

In a pegboard assembly task, Comrey (1953) found that less than half the group performance variance (44%) could be predicted from the individual performances. The groups in his study were actually only pairs, so any social interaction or cooperation required for the successful completion of the task was only based on two people. A possible explanation for the poor predictive powers of individual performances in Comrey's study was that the individual and group tasks were slightly different. To test this hypothesis, Comrey and Deskin (1954a, 1954b) repeated the study but changed the design to make the individual and group tasks more comparable. Even with this design change, there was no significant improvement in the prediction of group performance based on individual performances. Only a small proportion of the total variance on the group-performance task was predicted on the basis of how well the group members performed on the same task as individuals.

In comparison, Wiest, Porter, and Ghiselli (1961) found that 72% of the variance in team performance could be accounted for by the individual performances of team members. The task in this study, however, was to solve jigsaw puzzles. An interesting outcome of this study was that team performance was better predicted by the individual proficiency of the better member of the team than it was by the proficiency of the poorer member of the team. Additionally the more similar the individual proficiency of the two members of the team, the more likely they were to form a proficient and effective team.

Using a motor maze task, Gill (1979) found that individual scores predicted 41% of the variance of group performance. Unlike Comrey and his colleagues, however, Gill suggested that this was a major portion of the variance. In an experiment where a control group performed as individuals in both sessions of the motor maze task, Gill found that individual scores predicted 58% of the variance of the individual performances during the second session. She suggested that variability is to be expected in motor and sport performances (Gill, 1984). If individual performances vary from session to session, it is to be expected that individual performance scores will not completely predict the performance of teams.

An additional finding from Gill's (1979) experiments

was that a large discrepancy in ability levels between partners had a negative effect on cooperative performance. This supports Wiest et al.'s (1961) finding that the more similar the abilities of the members of a team, the more likely they were to perform effectively as a team. If this result were found to be true in sporting teams that demand cooperative interaction, it may be more effective for a coach to avoid using a player whose level of ability is much higher than that of others on the team. This, of course, is the opposite of what one would expect. Further research in this area needs to be done.

Team Sports

Although research in laboratories has demonstrated that there is a significant relationship between individual performances and group performance, it needs to be determined if this relationship exists outside the laboratory and on the sporting fields. In 1974, Jones investigated the relationship of team performance and individual or subgroup statistics in the professional sports of tennis, basketball, football, and baseball (Jones, 1974). Since individual performances differ from game to game (Gill, 1979), it is important to note that Jones based all of the performance statistics in his study on a full season of competition. Group effectiveness was positively related to individual effectiveness (tennis and basketball) and subgroup effectiveness (baseball and football).

The conclusion from general social psychology research, laboratory motor task experiments, and field studies in competitive sport is that group performance is more than the addition of individual performances. Although individual or subgroup effectiveness is significantly related to group performance, a team's performance cannot be entirely predicted by the measurement of individual performances. The rest of this chapter discusses social factors that may influence group performance.

MOTIVATION AND GROUP PERFORMANCE

Steiner's (1972) model of group performance indicates that potential group performance is limited by coordination losses between members of the group, as well as motivation losses. Motivation losses in groups has been termed social loafing. The research that investigates social loafing has tended to look at how increases in group size affect individual effort or motivation. Person-oriented and group-oriented motives, however, are separate variables.

Atkinson (1964) described individual motives involved in achievement motivation as the motives to approach success (M_s) and the motives to avoid failure (M_{af}). The corresponding group-oriented motives are the desire for group success (D_{gs}) and the desire to avoid group failure (D_{agf}) (Forward, 1969). In social identity theory terms, these motives are part of personal (M_s and M_{af}) and social (D_{gs} and D_{agf}) identity. Medow and Zander (1965) proposed that just

as an individual with high M_s strives for success, having a desire for group achievement causes individuals to strive for the success of a group in which one is a member. However, because an individual has a strong motive to avoid failure does not necessarily mean that this person also has a strong desire to avoid group failure. Zander and Forward (1968) found that when occupying a central position in a group task, individuals whose M_{af} exceeded their M_s were as concerned about the group's success as individuals whose M_s exceeded their M_{af}. However, when occupying a peripheral role in the group task, these same individuals displayed a strong motive to avoid group failure. These results tentatively support the hypothesis that group and individual achievement tendencies are independent motives.

Another indication that group motives are independent of individual motives is that if individuals are members of strong groups, they have a stronger desire to achieve group success than those who are members of weak groups (Zander & Medow, 1965), regardless of individual motives. Members of weak groups, of course, are likely to be less dependent on their group membership, as they probably have a higher comparison level for alternatives (Thibaut & Kelley, 1959).

Forward (1969) tested the hypothesis that not only are individual and group motives independent, but that they can be additive sources of motivation affecting individuals' resultant tendencies to engage or avoid group achievement activities. To control the relative strengths of D_{gs} and D_{agf}, two group incentive conditions were created. In the D_{gs} condition subjects were informed that their group would win points in proportion to the difficulty of the task if they succeeded, and that they would neither win nor lose points if they failed. In the D_{agf} condition subjects were told that if the group failed they would lose team points inversely proportional to the difficulty of the task, and that if the team succeeded they would neither win nor lose points. Half the members in each group condition had a stronger M_s than M_{af}, whereas the other half of both groups had a stronger M_{af} than M_s. Selection of task difficulty level was used as the measure of the resultant tendency toward engaging in the group task. Choosing a task of intermediate difficulty is indicative of a high tendency to approach success. Individuals in whom M_s was greater than M_{af} selected more intermediate levels of task difficulty than did individuals whose M_{af} was greater than M_s. Similarly subjects in the D_{gs} condition selected tasks of more intermediate difficulty than did those in the D_{agf} condition. Subjects who were higher in M_s than M_{af} felt more comfortable in the D_{gs} condition, whereas subjects higher in M_{af} than M_s felt less tension in the D_{agf} condition. Group achievement tendencies cannot be totally explained on the basis of the personal motives of M_s and M_{af} that individuals bring to group situations.

Desire for Group Success and Group Performance

The desire for group success (D_{gs}) is probably the most studied variable within the area of group motivation. The group motive D_{gs} is a disposition to experience feelings of pride and satisfaction with the group if it successfully accomplishes a challenging group task (Zander, 1971). The relationship between D_{gs} and group performance has been tested in many experiments. A stronger desire for group success tends to result in better group performance in laboratory situations.

In a task that required subjects to count the number of holes in data-processing cards as rapidly and as accurately as possible, members of groups with a greater desire for group success performed better than those with less desire for group success (Zander & Ulberg, 1971). On the other hand, Forward and Zander (1971) found that members of groups that failed developed stronger motives to avoid future group failure. The relationship between D_{gs} and group performance may, therefore, be a reciprocal one—desire for group success may affect performance, but group performance also appears to affect the desire for group success. The task, and how central it is seen to be to the group's identity, may also be an important factor. The influence of group performance on resultant group achievement motives needs further investigation. Most of the studies dealing with the relationship between group motives and performance have focused on the effects of group motives on performance, rather than the other way around.

Zander (1971) reported a few experiments with conflicting results. In the first, D_{gs} was controlled by telling half of the groups that results from a phony questionnaire indicated that they had high D_{gs}, whereas the other half of the groups were told that they had low D_{gs}. Members of the high-D_{gs} group squeezed a grip dynamometer significantly harder than did members of the low-D_{gs} group. In another study there were no significant differences in performances at a group dominoes task between high-and low-D_{gs} groups. Although admitting that the study was informal, Zander suggested that the relationship between D_{gs} and group performance only exists for simple tasks. The dominoes task was more difficult than the grip dynamometer, so there was no significant relationship between D_{gs} and group performance. The control of D_{gs} is suspect, however. A problem with many of these studies investigating D_{gs} and performance is that the desire for group success has not been independently measured. Instead the studies attempt to manipulate D_{gs} and D_{agf}. This weakness may exist because a reliable and valid measure of D_{gs} as it naturally occurs in different individuals has not been used.

Zander and Armstrong (1972) conducted a study in a natural setting, and measured D_{gs} rather than attempting to control it artificially. Since D_{gs} is the disposition to experience feelings of pride and satisfaction with the group if it successfully accomplishes a challenging group task, Zander and Armstrong developed two questions on Likert scales which measured the desire for attaining pride in one's group. In a slipper production line, there was a significant correlation between desire for pride in group and group performance. This relationship between D_{gs} and group performance needs to be demonstrated in sport settings, however, before any assumptions are made by

coaches or athletes that group performance can be improved by increasing individuals' desire for group success or decreasing their desire to avoid group failure.

Similar to Atkinson's model of achievement motivation, Zander's (1971, 1975) model of group success suggests that groups with a high desire for group success are most motivated when there is approximately a 50% chance of group success. Data obtained during the 1963 ascent of Mount Everest suggests that individuals actively attempt to maintain a 50% chance of success (Emerson, 1966). Motivation was maximized through emphasising that the chances of making it to the top were 50–50. If things were going well, members spoke of potential problems. If things were going poorly, members spoke optimistically. Additionally effort appeared to increase when the outcome was uncertain. Although research in achievement motivation has indicated that individuals with high M_s choose intermediate levels of task difficulty (Atkinson, 1964), the findings on Everest not only suggest that this is also true for groups, but that communication between group members will actively attempt to maintain the perception that there is a 50% chance of group success. In their interactions, group members may attempt to maintain a sense of threat or challenge sufficient to preserve a norm of hard work and striving, yet maintain enough satisfaction with the perceived outcome to preserve solidarity and a strong positive sense of social identity. This strategy seems to be used deliberately by coaches and captains before major games or tournaments. Its relation to success in these settings could usefully be investigated further.

SOCIAL IMPACT AND ITS CONSEQUENCES

A major social factor that affects individual performance in groups is group size. One important effect of the number of people working together in a group is that individual effort decreases, compared to when the individual is working alone. This social factor has been termed the *Ringelmann effect,* after the person who first studied this issue. Indeed, the study of this effect, which is now more widely known as social loafing, has been one of the major areas of study within group dynamics for the past decade or so.

Essentially this area examines the factors leading to or preventing performance decrements in groups resulting from individual effort. Its application to sport teams and other settings is obvious. To date, however, sport psychologists have not picked up this line of research to any great extent. In this chapter, therefore, we will treat it in some detail, with a view to presenting possibilities for research.

Group Size and Performance Loss

Ringelmann was a French agricultural engineer working in the 1880s, whose primary interest of study was the relative efficiency of work furnished by animals, machines, and men in various agricultural applications (see Kravitz & Martin, 1986). Individual versus group performance was only a secondary facet of his research. The 28 subjects in Ringelmann's first series of studies were all males who tried to exert maximum force while pulling on a rope. The subjects each pulled alone, as a member of a 7-person group, and as a member of a 14-person group. The mean force per individual was 85.3 kg when they pulled alone, 65.0 kg when they pulled in groups of 7, and 61.4 kg when they pulled in the 14-person group. In another series of studies, subjects pushed at a crossbar that connected the shafts of a two-wheeled cart. Subjects pushed both alone and in pairs. The mean force of the pairs (143.2 kg) was significantly less than the mean sum of the pair members pushing individually (160.8 kg). Ringelmann explained this decrease in performance with increases in group size as being due to lack of simultaneous effort or coordination losses. He supported this explanation by pointing out that similar performance decrements have been observed in draft animals and even in multicylinder combustion engines. Ringelmann also explained that in practical situations people would not place all of their attention into acting simultaneously on command as they did in his experiments. He figured that more work would be lost per individual in a real working situation.

Although there have been some discrepancies in the reporting of Ringelmann's specific results (e.g., Gill, 1986; Ingham, Levinger, Graves, & Peckham, 1974; Kravitz & Martin, 1986; Latane, Williams, & Harkins, 1979), the relative performance for each individual showed a progressive decline with increases in group size; the bigger the group, the bigger the loss of individual performance. Ingham, Levinger, Graves, and Peckham (1974) replicated Ringelmann's results for the rope-pulling task, for groups of up to 3 people. If an individual's efficiency is seen as 100%, pairs showed a decline in efficiency to 91%, and groups of 3 declined to an efficiency of 82%. Further increases in group size, however, did not lead to corresponding linear decreases in group performance. Groups of 6 pulled an average of 78%. Although 78% is very different from the 63% which Ringelmann theoretically proposed for groups of this size, it is extremely close to the 77% he actually found in his 7-person groups.

The studies reported so far all used a within-subjects design—that is, all subjects performed alone as well as in groups of varying sizes. If subjects value success in solitary performances more than in group performances, then they may ration their effort and try harder alone than they do in groups. To account for this possibility, Kerr and Bruun (1981) used a 3 × 2 factorial design, with the first factor being group size (1, 2, or 4) and the second factor being treatment (within subjects or between subjects). The task for this study was pumping a rubber sphygmograph bulb as quickly as possible for 30 seconds. The dependent measure was the volume of air pumped. Performance dropped as group size increased for both the between-subjects and the within-subjects treatments. The Ringelmann effect is therefore not limited to situations in which the subjects sequentially perform in different-sized groups.

Latane, Williams, & Harkins (1979) conducted another experiment that investigated the Ringelmann effect using a different task. Subjects were instructed to clap and shout loudly—alone, in pairs, in groups of four, and in groups of six. In this experiment, whether they were making noise alone or with others, all six subjects were present. The Ringelmann effect was confirmed as the average sound produced per person decreased from the individual performance to 71% in pairs, 51% in fours, and 40% in sixes. After this experiment, however, it was still not known whether the changes in performance were due to individuals decreasing their effort when performing in groups, individuals increasing their effort when performing alone and therefore having the other subjects serve as an audience, or coordination losses such as sound-pressure waves interfering with each other or moment-to-moment individual variations in intensity not being in synchronization with each other.

Faulty Process

Steiner's (1972) model of group performance may help clarify the relationship between individual and group performance in sport. Steiner's model is based on the following equation: Actual Productivity = Potential Productivity − Losses due to Faulty Process. Actual productivity refers to the actual performance of the group. Potential productivity refers to the group's best possible performance if all members of the group performed the task to the best of their ability, and all interactions between members of the group were synchronized in such a manner that no tasks were needlessly duplicated. Potential productivity would happen if the group effectively used all of its available resources in a coordinated manner.

Losses due to faulty process include all individual and interactive actions that cause the actual performance of the group to be less than the potential productivity of the group. According to Steiner (1972) there are two general categories of faulty process—(1) motivation losses and (2) coordination losses. Motivation losses occur when members of the group decrease the amount of effort they put into the group's performance. Motivation losses can often be seen when one or more members of a sporting team appear to slacken their individual effort. Coordination losses occur when timing between group members or strategies used by the group detract from their potential performance. Examples of coordination losses in sport would be rowers getting out of synchronization with each other, or a hockey team unable to make an offensive strategy work because of problems of passing between teammates.

Steiner also differentiated between different types of tasks. One of the many tasks distinctions he made was the difference between divisible and unitary tasks. Divisible tasks require different group members to perform different skills. This is easily demonstrated in many interactive team sports such as football, volleyball, or hockey. In unitary tasks, everyone performs a similar skill, such as running 100 meters in a relay race, rowing, or pulling on a rope in a tug-of-war. For unitary tasks, contest rules can specify how each member's contribution is arranged to influence the group's total performance. In some activities, such as bowling, individual scores are simply added to form the group score. In other activities, individual scores are averaged to arrive at a group score.

Some golf tournaments make the competition a disjunctive task, where the most successful member's score in the group is taken as the measure of the group's performance. Sometimes golfers are paired together, and the best individual score for each hole becomes the team score. One last method of measuring group performance in unitary tasks is making the group score dependent on the least successful member's score. This process would make the task a conjunctive task (Landers, 1974).

Returning to the discussion of the effect of group size on performance, whether a task is conjunctive or disjunctive could logically predict whether or not an increase in group size would result in increases or decreases in group performance. Based on probabilities, it could be argued that as group size increases, the group's performance will decrease for conjunctive tasks, as there would be a greater probability of a new group member performing below the level of the others. For disjunctive tasks, however, increases in group size could lead to increases in group performance, as new members may have greater skills or abilities than existing members (Landers, 1974). A study by Frank and Anderson in 1971 (reported in Landers) demonstrated that increases in group size enhanced group performance for disjunctive tasks, but was detrimental to performance for conjunctive tasks.

Whether a task has conjunctive or disjunctive task demands has also been shown to influence the amount of effort individuals of different ability levels exert (Kerr & Bruun, 1983). In a series of experiments that had subjects either blow as much air as possible or pump air with a rubber bulb, high-ability members worked harder under disjunctive task demands and low-ability members worked harder under conjunctive task demands. These results indicate that the type of task may affect motivational losses in groups differently, depending on the ability levels of group members.

In summary, Steiner's (1972) model of group performance states that a team's actual performance is the result of its potential minus motivation losses and coordination losses. Ringelmann argued that the observed decrements in performance in his studies were due to such coordination losses (Kravitz & Martin, 1986). Latane et al. (1979), however, questioned whether the decreases in performance were due to motivation or coordination losses.

To answer this question, Ingham et al. (1974) separated coordination and motivation losses by eliminating coordination losses. Using the rope-pulling task again, possible coordination losses were avoided by having only one real subject ever pulling on the rope at a time. Blindfolds and confederates who pretended to pull were used to make the subjects believe they were performing in groups of from one to six members. Average performance decreased to 90%

for pairs and to 85% for three-person groups. No further decreases were observed. These results were very similar to those that were obtained when the subjects were not blindfolded and had no confederates pretending to pull (pairs, 91%; threes, 82%). It was concluded that the decrease in performance accompanying increases in group size was due to motivation losses rather than coordination losses.

Latane et al. (1979) did another experiment using shouting, but had both actual groups and pseudo groups. All subjects wore blindfolds and earphones. The background noise played on the earphones while each subject was shouting made it impossible for subjects to determine whether or not others were shouting, how loud others were shouting, and how loud they were shouting themselves. For the actual group conditions, subjects performed in groups of two and six. Coordination losses involving sound cancellation due to interference, directional coordination losses, or temporal coordination losses could still occur in the actual group conditions. In the pseudo-group condition, coordination losses could not occur, because only one subject ever shouted at a time. The average sound produced by the individuals in the actual groups decreased to 66% in pairs and to 36% in sixes. The average sound produced by the individuals in the pseudo groups decreased to 82% in pairs and 74% in sixes. The authors concluded that the decrease in group performance observed in the pseudo groups was due entirely to motivational losses. All subjects knew that other subjects could not see or hear them shout, so that the variation observed in performance could not have been due to enhanced performance when alone as a result of an evaluative audience. Because the decrease in performance was greater for the actual groups than it was for the pseudo groups, the performance decrements observed in the actual groups was concluded as being the result of both coordination and motivation losses. In conclusion, although for some tasks coordination losses may be involved in the decrease in performance as group size increases, the results of Ingham et al. (1974) and Latane et al.'s (1979) studies demonstrate that motivational losses occur in groups.

Social Loafing: Motivation Losses in Groups

Harkins, Latane, and Williams (1980) suggested two possible explanations of the social loafing effect. The first explanation is the allocational strategy, where subjects know that they will be performing in groups as well as alone, so they allocate more energy to the alone condition, where individual performance can be identified. The second possibility is the minimizing strategy, where individuals try to expend as little energy as possible. Working in groups allows people not to work hard without being recognized as lazy.

To test which strategy more correctly reflected the social loafing process, Harkins et al. (1980) had subjects clap while wearing blindfolds and earphones so they could not see or hear others. Subjects were tested in groups of four where they were identified as subject A, B, C, or D. They were told that C would always clap alone, that D would always clap with someone else, and that A and B would sometimes clap alone and sometimes with others. In reality all subjects clapped alone. Subjects who thought they performed both alone and in pairs clapped louder when they thought they were alone. This is the stereotypical social loafing effect, but it does not answer whether the allocational strategy or the minimizing strategy was at work. However, the subjects who felt they were always clapping in groups and therefore had no need to conserve energy for an individual performance produced significantly less sound than subjects who thought they were performing alone. These results suggest that allocational strategies are not in use. A second experiment, which controlled possible extraneous variables such as knowledge that others were performing in different conditions, replicated these findings. Although these results do indicate that allocational strategies are not being used, they do not demonstrate that a minimizing strategy is being used instead.

Latane et al. (1979) proposed that social impact theory can be used to explain social loafing. This theory holds that the impact or effect of any outside social force directed toward a group is divided among its members. Social impact is high under a number of conditions—for example, when the person making the request for the work is of high status or power. The greater the number of people in the group, the less impact from outside social forces there is on each individual. The impact of social forces is diffused. Using this theory to explain social loafing, or motivational losses in groups, the external pressure to work as hard as possible is divided among all group members, so as group size increases each individual feels less pressure to work as hard and as energetically as possible.

If individual performances within a group are identified, then the impact of others' expectations and their potential ability to evaluate the performance of the individual is no longer diffused throughout the group. Williams, Harkins, and Latane (1981) proposed that when the identifiability of individual performances is lost in a group performance, performances decrease because of the diffusion of responsibility. In an experiment to test this proposal, Williams et al. once again used the shouting task. Subjects wore blindfolds and earphones as they did for Latane et al.'s (1979) studies. Each subject shouted alone, in actual groups of two and six, and in pseudo groups of two and six. During this stage of the testing, individual performances in groups were not identified. In the second stage of testing, subjects were led to believe that both individual and group outputs would be monitored, so that each person's contribution to the group output could be determined. To control for coordination losses, the subjects were only tested alone and in pseudo groups at this stage of the study.

As Latane et al. (1979) had found, the results from the first stage demonstrated that solitary performances did not decrease as much for the pseudo groups as it did for the real groups, but there was still evidence for social loafing. In the second stage, when subjects thought that their individual contributions to group performance could be identified,

the results were quite different. Individuals in pseudo groups of two made 98% of the noise they made when tested in the alone condition. Individuals in pseudo groups of six made 92% as much noise as when they were alone. In agreement with social impact theory, the identifiability of individual contributions to group performances virtually eliminated social loafing in groups. An interesting addition to this study by Williams et al. (1981) is that after the experiment, the subjects indicated in response to questions that they felt they shouted just as loudly in groups as they did when they were alone, whether or not their individual performances could be identified. Although the identifiability of individuals eliminated almost all social loafing, it is noteworthy that the participants did not appear to be aware that social loafing had occurred. These results suggest that normative factors also have an impact on social loafing.

This first experiment by Williams et al. (1981) confirmed that high identifiability of individual performances led to consistently high levels of performance across group sizes. In a second experiment, Williams et al. tested the opposite of this, hypothesizing that if people are convinced that their performances are never identifiable, even when performing alone, then there will be a consistently low level of performance across group sizes. The authors randomly assigned subjects to one of three conditions: always identifiable, identifiable only when alone, and never identifiable. As in previous experiments, in the identifiable only when alone condition, subjects exerted less effort in groups than they did when alone. In the always identifiable condition, group size had no effect on performance. Subjects in this condition always produced a large amount of sound pressure. In the never identifiable condition, group size again had no effect on performance, but this time the amount of noise produced was significantly less than in the identifiable conditions. Using a task involving more motor coordination than shouting requires, Kerr and Bruun (1981) also found that when individual contributions to group performance could be identified, no significant social loafing effect occurred. Kerr and Bruun once again had subjects pump a sphygmograph bulb, but this time the volume of air pumped by each subject went into a separate chamber. For the subjects who knew that the experimenter could measure how well each individual performed as part of a group, there was no social loafing effect. Performance did not significantly change as a result of group size.

The identifiability of individual performance definitely appears to influence whether or not social loafing occurs in groups. Shouting or pumping a bulb in a laboratory experiment, however, may be very different from performing a physical task in a sporting situation. Latane, Harkins, and Williams (1980) investigated the hypothesis of identifiability in the sport setting of competitive swimming. When individual lap times were announced (a condition of high identifiability), individuals swam faster in relays than in individual race situations. When lap times were not announced (low identifiability), individuals swam faster in the individual race situation than they did in the relays.

If individuals believe that their individual performances

within a group can be identified, then social loafing does not occur. Thus it would appear that to avoid social loafing in a team, individual performance feedback as well as group performance feedback should be given. In a study investigating the effects of different types of feedback in group situations, Zajonc (1962) had subjects participate in a group reaction time task. The basic procedure was to have each subject react to one of two lights by pressing the appropriate key before a set time interval had elapsed. All subjects first performed alone and then performed in both an easy group task and a difficult group task. In the easy group task, success was achieved when at least one member of the group reacted before the failure time. In the difficult group task, success was only achieved if all group members reacted in time. Half the groups received direct feedback, where all individuals on the team had knowledge of their own performance, the performance of others on the team, and the performance of the team as a group. The other half of the groups were given confounded feedback, where only information about the team's performance as a whole was given. Social loafing did not occur for either feedback situation. Even when individual performance could not be identified (confounded feedback), individuals performed better in the group than when working alone. The improvement in reaction time, however, was significantly greater for the subjects who received direct feedback. Group performance was also significantly better for the groups who received direct feedback than for those who received confounded feedback.

Although these results support the proposal that high identifiability (direct feedback) results in better individual performances within group situations than low identifiability (confounded feedback), these results are unexpected in that the performance of individuals improved when they worked on a group task, regardless of the type of feedback received. One possible explanation for this is that all subjects performed alone before they performed in groups. Although an asymptote was reached and maintained for at least 10 trials during the solitary performance, perhaps subjects still learned to be quicker with more practice. Additionally they may have felt that the solitary trials were just practice at getting to know the equipment, and that when performing in groups they became more motivated as a result of unstated competition or an increase in interest. Nevertheless receiving individual as well as group feedback significantly increased performance.

Agreeing that identifying individual contributions to group performance and having knowledge of previous individual as well as group performance can minimize social loafing effects, Huddleston, Doody, and Ruder (1985) pointed out that these practices are not practical or applicable in all sport situations. Still interested in eliminating social loafing, they proposed that having prior knowledge of the social loafing phenomenon may neutralize its effects. In a study designed to investigate this hypothesis, Huddleston et al. (1985) had female athletes run the 55-meter dash alone and as part of a four-person relay team. Half the teams were told of the social loafing effect on per-

formance and some of the possible causes. They were also told that now that they knew about social loafing they could prevent it from happening when they ran as relay teams. The other teams were not informed about social loafing. The results of the study demonstrated that social loafing occurred for both groups of teams. Whether aware or unaware of the potential for social loafing, subjects ran slower when they were part of the relays than they did when alone. Awareness of social loafing and the possible influences of identifiability and individual feedback did not limit social loafing effects.

Deindividuation

Diener's (1980) theory of deindividuation supports the idea that identifiability is a cause of social loafing. Environmental conditions such as anonymity, high arousal levels, focusing on external events, and close group unity can lead to a reduction in self-awareness. This reduction in self-awareness can then lead to deindividuation. Deindividuation occurs when attention to specific aspects of oneself and an individual conception of oneself as a separate being are prevented. This is very similar to the concept of low identifiability as presented by Williams et al. (1981) and Latane et al. (1980).

Although Diener's (1980) theory suggests a number of consequences of deindividuation, they all focus on the self-regulatory capacities that are lost. Many aspects of these consequences are relevant to social loafing. First, when they are deindividuated, people tend not to monitor their own behavior, and do not perceive the products of their own actions. Because they are not aware of the results of their own behavior, they no longer compare their behavior to personal or social standards. Therefore, deindividuated individuals often have a lessened concern about evaluations by others. The end result of this in a team situation may be social loafing, or decreased motivation by individuals.

Equity of Effort

Disagreeing with Diener's (1980) explanation, Jackson and Harkins (1985) suggested that people working in groups expect their coworkers to loaf, so they reduce their own effort in order to establish equity. They felt that identifiability had nothing to do with the decreased motivation of individuals in group situations. To test their proposal, Jackson and Harkins paired subjects with confederates in a shouting task, using the same procedure as in previous studies where subjects wore blindfolds and earphones. In this study, however, subjects were randomly assigned to one of three conditions. In the first condition the subjects believed that their partners were trying very hard. In the second condition the subjects believed that their partners were not trying to shout very loudly. The third condition was a control condition where the subjects had no expectations about their partners' effort. All subjects performed alone and in pseudo pairs. In the control condition, the typical social loafing response occurred. Subjects shouted significantly louder alone than when they thought they were shouting with their partner. For the other two conditions, all differences between shouting alone and with a pseudo partner were eliminated. In the high-effort condition, the subjects made significantly more noise whether alone or in pseudo pairs than the control group made when alone, while in the low-effort condition, whether alone or in pairs, the subjects' level of noise was significantly below that of the control group in the alone condition. These results support the proposition that social loafing is caused by equity in effort. Subjects matched their partners' level of effort. An interesting finding of this study was that once again subjects appeared to have poor comprehension of their own effort levels. Subjects in all three conditions reported themselves as having displayed the equivalent amount of effort.

Although the equity in effort hypothesis may explain the social loafing phenomenon just as well as identifiability, it is questionable how appropriate these findings are to competitive sport. In most sporting situations, it would probably be assumed by participants that their opponents would be trying very hard to perform well. Similarly in team sports there are few competitive situations where an athlete would think that his or her teammates were not going to try to perform well.

Hardy and Latane (1988) investigated the social loafing effect using cheerleaders as subjects. For cheerleaders, clapping and shouting can be valued and rewarding tasks. So unlike the previous studies that investigated shouting, in this study the participants may have been genuinely interested in the activity. In fact, the decibel level of the shouts of these cheerleaders was far louder than that reported in previous studies. The cheerleaders donned blindfolds and earphones as in previous studies and clapped and shouted alone and in pseudo pairs. Just as with previous results, when cheerleaders thought they were cheering with another person, they only cheered 94% as loud as they had when alone. Once again, social loafing occurred even when the task was meaningful to the subjects.

The suggestion by Jackson and Harkins (1985) that people expect group members to loaf and therefore reduce their own efforts to establish equity was rejected by Hardy and Latane (1988). In their study, the cheerleaders reported that they tried significantly harder in pairs than they did alone. It should be pointed out, however, that the subjects in Jackson and Harkins's study had also stated that they felt that both themselves and their partners had tried harder when in pairs than when alone. Research should be done to investigate which of the two proposals—identifiability or equity of effort—best explains the social loafing phenomenon.

Personal Involvement in the Task

Aside from identifiability and equity of effort, many other factors have been suggested as affecting the magnitude of social loafing. Brickner, Harkins, and Ostrom (1986) suggested that even if individual effort can be identified, people loaf on tasks that are not personally involving, intrinsically important, and/or do not have personal meaning or significant consequences for their lives. Similarly, Brickner et al. felt that if a task was personally involving, then social loafing would not occur.

To test this hypothesis Brickner et al. (1986) created a study with a 2 × 2 design. Subjects' responses were either high or low in identifiability, and the subjects had either high or low involvement in the task: to generate opinions about an issue under consideration by their own or another university. In the low-involvement condition, subjects whose output was identifiable generated significantly more opinions than did subjects whose output was pooled with their partners. In the high-involvement condition, however, there were no significant differences in the number of opinions generated. Brickner et al. used these results as a basis for the suggestion that high personal involvement in a task can override any tendencies toward social loafing.

The results from Hardy and Latane's (1988) study, which were reported previously, do not support this suggestion, however. In this study, social loafing occurred even when the cheerleaders displayed a high degree of personal involvement in the task. A potential explanation for these inconsistencies lies in Brickner et al.'s (1986) methodology. First the identifiability manipulation is questionable. When asked, "How easily will the experimenter be able to identify your thoughts as yours?" or "How easily will the experimenter be able to tell which thoughts you wrote?" there were no significant differences between the high-and low-identifiability groups. Second unlike the other studies, the subjects were not aware that the number of opinions was the variable under scrutiny. It is also questionable whether the number of opinions generated is a valid measure of performance. On the other hand, the context of Hardy and Latane's study, by its artificiality, may have attenuated the personal involvement of the cheerleaders in the task.

Personal Involvement with Others in the Group

At this point, it is not clear whether the degree of personal involvement is a strong predictor of the amount of social loafing experienced in groups. Another factor presented as a mediator of social loafing is how well the individuals in the group know each other. Williams (1981) found that social loafing effects were eliminated when individuals performed with friends rather than with strangers. In Hardy and Latane's (1988) study, however, no significant difference in the degree of social loafing occurred when cheerleaders were paired with someone from their own team, rather than with someone from a different team.

Whereas Williams (1981) suggested that performing in a group made up of strangers may encourage or promote social loafing, Diener's (1980) theory indirectly suggests the opposite. Diener reflected that close group unity may actually encourage deindividuation (low identifiability) because one becomes more immersed in the group and less aware of oneself. It should be noted, however, that in two experiments, Abrams (1984) found that those high school students who were highest in private self-awareness were also those who were most strongly identified with their school and its teams and were most concerned to maintain a positive distinctiveness for their own group. This suggests that intergroup situations (where one is immersed in the group and its goals) may not reduce self-awareness, but may even enhance it. Finally when people perform with friends, the normativeness of the task and its centrality to the group's identity, as well as the extent to which social identity is salient, also become potentially important factors. Future research needs to clarify this area, particularly in actual competitive sport situations.

Task Difficulty and Task Uniqueness

Additional variables that may influence the incidence of social loafing include task difficulty and task uniqueness. Jackson and Williams (1985) proposed that since social loafing is a reduction in the drive to exert effort, any situation in which a reduction in drive is beneficial would result in improved performance in groups. They suggested that high levels of arousal are detrimental to the performance of difficult tasks (see Zajonc, 1965), so working collectively on difficult tasks should improve performance rather than result in social loafing. Subjects completed eight computer mazes, half of which were easy and half of which were difficult. The subjects were put into one of three group conditions: alone, with a coactor (someone working on the same problems completely independently), or collectively with a partner where their scores could not be determined individually. Subjects in the coactor condition (individual-performance identifiable) perceived more pressure than those in the alone condition, and subjects in the collective condition (individual-performance unidentifiable) felt even less pressure than those in the alone condition. This was taken as a demonstration of differences in drive levels. As suggested by Zajonc, subjects in the coactor condition performed more poorly on the difficult mazes but better on the easy mazes than the subjects performing alone. Although there were no significant differences on performance of the easy mazes between those in the coactor situation and the collective situation, those working collectively tended to perform more slowly. People in the collective condition, however, performed better on the difficult task than those in the coactor condition. In practice, it may be advisable to minimize drive and maximize performance by performing difficult tasks in collective groups, the opposite of what most social loafing studies have found.

In a series of experiments, Harkins and Petty (1982) found that when tasks were more challenging or required nonredundant responses social loafing did not occur, even when the subjects' individual responses were unidentifiable. In their first experiment, Harkins and Petty used a brainstorming task where subjects were to list as many uses for a particular object as they could. Difficulty was con-

trolled by the object presented. They were either alone responsible for the list produced, or they shared that responsibility with nine other people. For the easy object, subjects who were alone created significantly more uses for the object than did subjects in groups. For the difficult-object condition, however, the social loafing effect did not occur—subjects made the same number of responses whether they were alone or in a group.

The authors hypothesized that the cause of these results was not simply the difficulty of the task, but rather the subjects' perceptions of whether or not their unique skills were required. For the easy object condition, subjects may have felt that all members of the group could easily come up with uses for the object, whereas in the difficult object group subjects may have felt that since uses of the object where not readily apparent, their own individual skills or talents were required for the group to succeed. To test further the role of task difficulty, Harkins and Petty (1982) undertook a second experiment with a 2 (identifiable performance, unidentifiable performance) × 2 (easy task, difficult task) factorial design. The task for this experiment was pressing a button when a dot was observed on a television screen. Difficulty was controlled by having the contrast on the television either high (easy) or low (difficult). For the easy task, significantly more errors were made by subjects in the unidentifiable condition than by subjects whose individual performances within the group could be identified. For the difficult task, identifiability had no impact on the number of errors made.

To determine whether these results were due to the difficulty of the task or to the feeling that subjects had about having a unique contribution to make to the group score, another experiment was run with the vigilance task. This time, the two factors in the design were identifiability and uniqueness of contribution. Uniqueness was controlled by having all subjects in a group looking at the same quadrant of a television screen, or having each member of the group responsible for a different quadrant of the screen. As predicted, subjects who took part in the same task (non-unique) made significantly more errors in the unidentifiable condition than in the identifiable condition. However, when subjects felt that their contribution to the group was unique (responsible for a particular quadrant of the screen), subjects whose outputs were unidentifiable made no more errors than those whose contributions were identifiable.

In the final experiment of the series, Harkins and Petty (1982) returned to the brainstorming task used in the first experiment. In this study all subjects' outputs were unidentifiable. Uniqueness was controlled by telling half the subjects that all members in the group were thinking of uses of the same object, whereas the others were told that each member in the group had a different object. Subjects who felt they had a unique task within the group made significantly more responses than those who felt they were all working at the same task. Harkins and Petty concluded that social loafing is not entirely dependent on whether or not an individual's contribution to the group performance can be detected. Identifiability is not necessary to reduce social loafing when subjects feel that they can make a unique contribution to the group.

Being able to make a unique contribution to a team performance does not, however, always ensure a high level of effort by the individual. Kerr (1983) found that when subjects performed with a partner who continually failed, the amount of effort exerted by the individual was dependent on the perceived ability of the partner. In his study subjects pumped air using rubber bulbs. If subjects attributed their partners' failures to lack of effort, then the subjects reduced their own efforts, even though group success was dependent on their efforts. If, however, individuals attributed their partners' failures to lack of ability, their own level of effort did not significantly differ from that of subjects performing alone. Therefore the uniqueness of one's contribution to the group only reduces social loafing when that uniqueness is not perceived as being due to other members' laziness.

The fact that almost all proposals suggested to explain or modify social loafing compare their results to those obtained using the degree of individual identifiability as the influencing variable suggests that identifiability is the most acceptable explanation of the social loafing phenomenon. When identifiability of individual performances is lost in a group, performance and/or effort decreases because of the diffusion of responsibility, as suggested by social impact theory (Latane et al., 1979). Although it has not received as much attention in research, the theory of equity of effort (Jackson & Harkins, 1985) should also be considered.

TEAM COHESION

Although group motivation has been investigated in terms of its relationship to group performance, group performance has been studied in greater detail, particularly in sport settings, by looking at team cohesion. As this section will show, the relation between cohesion and task success is complex and problematic. In addition, there have been problems with the measurement of cohesion and with the causal direction of the relationship between cohesion and performance (Carron, 1982, presents a detailed critique of these areas). More recently the interpersonal definition of cohesion has itself been challenged, and a new perspective put forward (see Hogg, 1990).

Traditional Approaches to Cohesion

Cartwright (1968) looked at the determinants and consequences of cohesion. The determinants of cohesion discussed by Cartwright included attractiveness of group members, similarities among members, nature of group goals, type of interdependence among members, activities of the group, style of leadership, the group's atmosphere, and the size of the group. Other researchers have posited proximity and interaction potential (Shaw, 1981), similarity

(Zander, 1982), the homogeneity of group members (Eitzen, 1973), stability in team membership (Essing, 1970; Zaleznik & Moment, 1964), and the size of the team (Davis, 1969; Widmeyer, Brawley, & Carron, 1990) as important factors influencing cohesion. The consequences of cohesion include the ability of the group to retain its members, the power of the group to influence its members, the degree of participation by members, and feelings of security among the members (see Carron, 1982; Cartwright, 1968).

Team cohesion has been empirically shown to be related to a variety of variables. One of these is the satisfaction of team members with the team or its performance. Williams and Hacker (1982), for example, found that satisfaction was a mediating variable between performance and cohesion. Martens and Peterson (1971) also found that seven of their eight cohesion questions discriminated significantly between satisfied and unsatisfied teams (satisfaction was determined by asking all individuals how satisfied they were with playing on their team). Continuing this line of thinking, Martens and Peterson suggested that cohesive teams were more successful, and successful teams had greater satisfaction from participation than did unsuccessful teams. Hacker and Williams (1981) agreed that satisfaction may be a mediating variable in the circular relationship between cohesion and performance. However, not all aspects of this circular relationship stood up to examination by path analysis (Williams & Hacker, 1982). In their study there was no indication that satisfaction led to greater team cohesion or better team performance, and/or that greater cohesion led to better performance. Path analysis results did, however, indicate that success leads to greater satisfaction and increased cohesion, and that increased cohesion leads to greater satisfaction.

In addition to satisfaction, group cohesiveness has also been shown to be related to individual adherence (Carron, Widmeyer, & Brawley, 1988). The measure of cohesion used for these experiments was the Group Environment Questionnaire (Widmeyer, Brawley, & Carron, 1985; see below). Task cohesion, as measured by group integration task and individual attractions to group task, significantly discriminated between adherers and nonadherers on intercollegiate teams. Perceptions of social closeness of the whole team were also significantly related to adherence, for both intercollegiate and recreational teams, as well as to adherence to fitness classes.

Measures of Cohesion

Many of the studies on cohesion have employed the Sport Cohesiveness Questionnaire (Martens, Landers, & Loy, 1972), which has never been fully validated. The Sport Cohesiveness Questionnaire is the name given to the questionnaire first developed in Martens and Peterson's (1971) study. Only those questions asking for an evaluation of the team as a whole in terms of closeness and teamwork were significantly related to performance. The other questions in the questionnaire refer to some form of attraction, either to other individuals or to the team. Thus the Sport Cohesiveness Questionnaire primarily measures the degree to which the members of the team like each other and enjoy each other's company. One dimension of team cohesion that is almost ignored by the Sport Cohesiveness Questionnaire is task cohesion, or the degree to which members of a team work together to achieve a particular task. Lenk's (1969) observation of world-class rowing teams (to be discussed) is a good example of how attraction and task cohesion can operate independently.

Measures of cohesion other than the Sport Cohesiveness Questionnaire have been developed during the past decade. The Team Cohesion Questionnaire (TCQ: Gruber & Gray, 1981, 1982) consists of 13 reliable items that have been demonstrated as measuring 6 different factors of cohesion. In addition to task cohesion and affiliation cohesion, the TCQ also measures team performance satisfaction, self-performance satisfaction, desire for recognition, and value of membership. In addition, the Multidimensional Sport Cohesion Instrument (MSCI) has been developed by Yukelson, Weinberg, and Jackson (1984). These authors demonstrated that the MSCI has construct validity, internal consistency, and factor reliability. They admit, however, that further validation of the instrument is required. Although they began by looking at task-related and social-related aspects of cohesion, the final 41-item questionnaire revealed four common factors: attraction to the group, unity of purpose, quality of teamwork, and valued roles. Further statistical investigation of the MSCI revealed that reducing the questionnaire to 22 items retained the factor structure intact, and inter-item reliability remained strong as well.

The most recent development in team cohesion measurement is the Group Environment Questionnaire (GEQ: Carron, Widmeyer, & Brawley, 1985; Widmeyer, Brawley, & Carron, 1985). Starting with a large item pool, the authors ended up with an 18-item questionnaire with demonstrated content validity, inter-item reliability, and reliability across studies. Factor analyses also revealed some evidence for construct validity. The four scales within the GEQ are group integration task, group integration social, individual attractions to group task, and individual attractions to group social. The process of validating the GEQ was continued by Brawley, Carron, and Widmeyer (1987). A series of three studies demonstrated that the GEQ has concurrent, predictive, and construct validities. The GEQ is the most psychometrically sound measure of team cohesion available to date.

Cohesion and Performance

One variable not directly mentioned by Cartwright (1968), but which is perhaps the most central to the study of cohesion, is group performance. Many studies have investigated the influence of team cohesion on performance. In an early study of high school basketball teams, Fiedler (1954) found no significant correlation between perceived interpersonal similarity and team effectiveness. He also, however, investigated the type of person that most people on the team chose as their best coworker. The results here were the opposite to what was expected. The most preferred teammates in effective teams tended to be somewhat less warm and emotionally less involved with teammates than the most preferred teammates of less effective teams. Further experiments by Fiedler in nonsporting situations suggested that more effective teams tended to be less congenial than relatively ineffective teams. Combined, these results suggest that there is a negative correlation between team cohesion, defined as interpersonal liking, and team performance.

In a study of rifle teams, Myers (1962) investigated the effects of competition and success on team interpersonal relations. As predicted, interpersonal perception of teammates was significantly affected by the level of success enjoyed by the group; successful teams had significantly friendlier interpersonal relations. An unexpected finding, however, was that competition led to better team relations than noncompetition, regardless of the level of success. Unsuccessful competitive teams had better interpersonal relations than unsuccessful noncompetitive teams. Thus both competitive conditions and team success generated better adjustment of individuals within their teams.

Further investigating the relationship between interpersonal relationships and performance, McGrath (1962) studied three-man teams in a rifle marksmanship tournament. Two sets of rifle teams with contrasting patterns of interpersonal relations were created. The positive interpersonal relations group was made up of teams whose members had seen former teammates as warm and supportive. Teams composed of members who had given their former teammates low interpersonal relations scores were designated as the nonpositive interpersonal relations group. Results indicated that an individual's perception of success seems to determine his or her adjustment to a new team situation. Members of teams in the nonpositive interpersonal relations group seemed to define success as effective shooting, and in fact had significantly better marksmanship scores and showed significant improvement over trials. People on the positive interpersonal relations teams seemed to define success as positive interpersonal relations and failed to improve in marksmanship. McGrath concluded that those teams with positive interpersonal relations devoted their efforts to team interaction rather than effective performance at shooting. Similarly Landers and Leuschen (1974) investigated intramural 10-pin bowling teams and found that unsuccessful teams had significantly higher interpersonal attraction ratings than did successful teams. Team cohesion as measured by attraction appears to have a negative relationship with performance.

Lenk (1969) carried this conclusion further in an examination of rowing teams (eights). The German Olympic rowing eight of 1960 consisted of four athletes from each of two clubs. The team split into club cliques, through which conflicts emerged. At times conflict almost led to the destruction of the team. This team, with strong internal conflicts, became the unbeaten Olympic champions. Similarly the world champion eight of 1962, although all from the same club, had strong leadership polarity, with many conflicts and disagreements. This example from elite sport demonstrates that high levels of performance can be attained by groups with high levels of conflict. Team cohesion is not required for good performance.

On the other hand, Klein and Christiansen (1969) found results that disagreed with these conclusions. In their study, basketball teams with high levels of cohesion, as measured by the attractiveness of the group, had more high team performances than low. Teams with low levels of cohesion had more low levels of team performance than high. Their conclusion was that a positive relationship exists between the cohesion of a team and its effectiveness. Bird (1977), studying intercollegiate volleyball teams, supported this conclusion. Using a modified version of the questionnaire developed by Martens and Peterson (1971), they found that cohesion was related to success. No attempt, however, was made to determine whether this relationship was causal and if so, in which direction.

Instead of investigating the relationship between cohesion and performance, Spink (1990) studied whether or not team cohesion was related to collective efficacy, or how well members expected their team to perform. Measuring cohesion using the GEQ, Spink found that for elite volleyball teams there was a significant relationship between team cohesion and collective efficacy. For recreational volleyball teams, however, there was no significant relationship between these two variables. Pease and Miller (1989) similarly found a complex relationship between cohesion and performance in an in-depth study of a single intercollegiate men's basketball team over a season. They noted that there was a positive relationship between cohesion and performance up to a certain point. Beyond this point there appeared to be a ceiling effect on the positive association between these two factors. Later in the season, when social cohesion was very high, team performance appeared to be debilitated as a result of more focus on social interactions than on task performance.

In an intramural basketball league at a nonelite level, Martens and Peterson (1971) measured team cohesiveness and team performance. Cohesiveness was measured by a questionnaire using 9-point Likert-type scales, which eventually became the Sport Cohesiveness Questionnaire (see above). Items on the questionnaire assessed each member's evaluation of every other member, the member's own relationship to the team, and the evaluation of the team as a whole. Only the questions assessing evaluation of the team as a whole, or cohesiveness as a social construct, significantly differentiated between successful and unsuccessful teams. Teams who rated themselves as being closely knit and having a high level of teamwork won significantly more games than did low cohesive teams. These results point out how important measurement of cohesion can be. If ratings of individual members or the value of membership to the team had been the only ones used, no significant relationship between performance and interpersonal relations on the team would have been found (see Carron, 1982).

Using a questionnaire similar to the one they used in 1971, Peterson and Martens (1972) once again investigated intramural basketball teams. This time, however, cohesiveness was measured pre- and postseason. In addition to investigating the effects of success on cohesion, they also investigated the effects of residential affiliation. Although fraternity teams were initially more cohesive than teams from men's residence halls or men's independent associations, there were no differences in postseason cohesiveness as a result of residential affiliation. More in line with the present discussion, however, success increased postseason cohesiveness, regardless of residential affiliation. These findings indicate that for the previous studies, where team cohesion has been positively related to team performance, cohesion may not have been the cause of good performance.

A study by Widmeyer and Martens (1978) further illustrates the importance of the measurement of this complex relationship. They studied the influence of different measures of cohesion on the cohesion-performance relationship, for participants in a three-on-three basketball league. Based on the Sport Cohesiveness Questionnaire, four different approaches were used to assess team cohesion. First each member assessed his friendship with every other member of the team. Second each member rated the contribution that each other member was likely to make to the success and enjoyment of the team. Third each member rated the overall attractiveness of the group for himself. Finally each member gave his direct assessment of the cohesiveness of his team by rating how close-knit the team was and how strong the teamwork was. All responses were obtained after two training sessions and before competition began. When cohesion was assessed by subjects' ratings of their team cohesion or the value of their group membership, cohesion and performance were positively related. When cohesion was measured inferentially, by ratings of individual contributions to friendship, success, and enjoyment, there was no significant relationship between cohesion and performance.

Intramural basketball teams were also studied by Melnick and Chemers (1974). They found no significant relationship between team cohesion and performance. Using questions similar to those used by Martens and Peterson (1971), Melnick and Chemers found that neither teamwork nor team closeness was related to team performance. These authors, however, made several suggestions regarding methodological considerations for future research in this area. First they suggested that only teams that have been together a long time should be used, as they have established a clearly defined, stable social structure. Second the level of competition should be taken into account. It is quite possible that many intramural teams have joined the competition for social reasons. If these teams are not committed to winning, then the performance variables of winning and losing lose their meaning. This point, indeed, highlights the importance of understanding what team members consider to be the central features of their identity, or their reason for being (Turner, 1987; see below). Lastly some objective measure of team ability should be taken as a control variable, if team success is to be accounted for by team cohesion and other group characteristics.

In summary some studies have found a negative relationship between cohesion and performance (Fiedler, 1954; Landers & Leuschen, 1974; Lenk, 1969; McGrath, 1962); a few studies have found that, at least under some circumstances, there is no significant relationship, either positive or negative, between cohesion and performance (Martens & Peterson, 1971; Melnick & Chemers, 1974; Widmeyer & Martens, 1978); and still other studies have noted a positive relationship between cohesion and performance (Bird, 1977; Klein & Christiansen, 1969; Myers, 1962; Peterson & Martens, 1972; Widmeyer & Martens, 1978). There are also inconsistencies in methodology. Some studies have measured cohesiveness preseason and some, postseason. Some have focused on the measurement of friendship or interpersonal attraction, while others have emphasized more social ratings such as closeness to the group.

The relationship between cohesion and performance does seem to depend on the type of sport task. Using task classifications as suggested by Steiner (1972), there appears to be more consistency in results regarding the relationship between team cohesion and performance when the type of task is taken into consideration. For sports involving independence (coordinated action between individuals is not required for performance success), success is not related to cohesion. An example of this would be McGrath's (1962) rifle-shooting study. For sports involving coactive dependence (members performing similar tasks simultaneously), success is not related to cohesion (e.g., Lenk, 1969). For sports involving reactive and proactive dependence (one member of the team initiates the action while another completes the action, like the pitcher and catcher in baseball), although no research has been done on the relationship between cohesion and performance, it is hypothesized that success is not related to cohesion. Lastly, for sports involving interactive dependence, team cohesion and performance are positively related. In these sports, members are mutually dependent on each other, and interaction enhances the opportunity for team success. The bulk of the research within the cohesion area has focused on interactive dependent sports (e.g., Klein & Christiansen, 1969; Peterson & Martens, 1972).

Direction of Causality: Cohesion and Performance

In addition to the wide variation in measurement techniques, relatively few studies have tried to determine whether cohesion leads to success or vice versa. Without knowing whether a relationship is causal, and if so in what direction, the information about a correlational relationship cannot be put to effective use. In a study of aquanauts living underwater for 182 days, Bakeman and Helmreich (1975) investigated the causal direction of the relationship between cohesion and performance. It should be noted that the type of cohesion measured in this study was attrac-

tion, or how much members of groups voluntarily conversed during recreational time. By measuring both cohesion and performance for two different segments of time during the stay underwater, causality could be determined. The correlation between cohesiveness during the first time segment and performance during the second time segment was very low and nonsignificant, suggesting that cohesiveness did not affect performance. However, the correlation between performance during the first time segment and cohesion in the second time segment was large and significant. These results indicate that good performance may be a cause of cohesiveness, rather than being a determinant of performance. In a similar vein, Ruder and Gill (1982) studied both intercollegiate and intramural volleyball teams. Participants completed a version of the Sport Cohesiveness Questionnaire before and after a single match. It was found that for intramural teams, winners increased and losers decreased in cohesion. The same findings were true for intercollegiate players, but only for the more general measures of the cohesion questionnaire.

Carron and Ball's (1977) findings are similar. This time the subjects were teams participating in intercollegiate ice hockey. The questionnaire used to measure cohesiveness was the one used by Martens and Peterson (1971), with the addition of a composite score made up of the average of the seven individual scores. To address the causality question, a cross-lagged correlational design was used. Cohesiveness was measured early, mid-, and postseason. Performance, as measured by win-loss ratio, was measured in mid-and postseason. Performance and subsequent cohesiveness were strongly related, whereas cohesion and subsequent performance were not significantly related.

Landers, Wilkinson, Hatfield, and Barber (1982) also used a cross-lagged correlational design in their study of an intramural basketball league. A modified version of the Sport Cohesiveness Questionnaire was administered early, mid, and late in the season. Performance was also measured at these three times. Unlike previous research (Bakeman & Helmreich, 1975; Carron & Ball, 1977), Landers et al.'s findings showed that performance and cohesion were significantly related, but with no causal predominance of one over the other. One possible explanation for this discrepancy is that the subjects were playing in a league with a more recreational emphasis. In a study of intercollegiate field hockey players, however, Williams and Hacker (1982) also found no causal predominance of either cohesion or performance. This suggested to them that cohesion and performance may have a circular relationship. In further pursuit of this concept, they found that satisfaction may be a mediating variable in the circular relationship between cohesion and performance.

Although the results are not entirely clear, it could safely be argued that performance outcome does affect future team cohesion. It is less clear whether team cohesion also influences future performance. The possible mediating variable of satisfaction needs to be studied further, as does the possible influence of level of competition in sporting environments.

Understanding Cohesion: Individual and Social Levels

As noted above, studies of cohesion have been criticized for lack of clarity in measurement and operationalization of important variables and for lack of specification of the direction of causality between performance and cohesion. In addition, research has been criticized for inadequate attention to type of task and setting, particularly with respect to the competitiveness of the situation. In Argyle et al.'s (1981) terms, team cohesion may be more important to good performance in some sport settings than in others, depending on the prevailing rules and concepts. Finally many studies have been imprecise in their use of the concept of cohesion, failing to distinguish between task and social cohesion, or between cohesion at the interpersonal level and for the group as a whole.

Carron (1982) has blamed many of the problems in the area on the failure of most researchers to follow a clear theoretical model. Instead researchers have tended simply to take up the concept of cohesion and relate it to performance (or to another variable) in a specific sport setting, with little consideration of the relationship of their studies to the field as a whole. Carron (1982) proposed a framework for the study of team cohesion, in which task and social cohesion mediate the relationship of a set of antecedent variables and group and individual outcomes in terms of performance, stability, and satisfaction. Antecedent variables include environmental factors (organizational and contractual), personal factors (personality and initial satisfaction), leadership factors (relationship, style, and behavior), and team factors (ability, stability, norms, desire for group success, and task). Carron's model has advantages in that it allows for predictive path models to be established, but the repetition of variables (measured at different times) at different points in the model captures the cyclic relationship among some of the variables.

Hogg (1992), working in the tradition of social identity theory, goes further. He suggests that an essential problem with the research on cohesion, and perhaps the reason why such research has largely disappeared from mainstream social psychology, is the attempt to reduce a social variable (cohesion) to an individual variable (interpersonal attraction). As is clear from the review above, he is not the first to make this point. Social identity theory, however, may give us a useful way to solve the dilemma created by this incompatibility in levels of explanation—the fact that we must measure cohesion at the individual level, even though it takes place at the group level and is manifestly not merely the sum of the interpersonal attraction between individual team members.

First social identity theory allows the proposition that attraction has both a personal and a social (or group-level) aspect, corresponding to personal and social identity. Interpersonal attraction (liking for other group members as people), in this view, is likely to be largely independent of cohesion, whereas social attraction (that is, the attraction to other group members because they somehow represent the positive characteristics of the team) is likely to be closely related to it. Hogg and Hardie (1991), indeed, found that for members of an Australian rules football team, social attraction for a team member was more closely related than was personal attraction to how prototypical (typical of the team's most important features, or team spirit) the team member was seen to be. Hogg and Hardie also found that team members who identified strongly with the team and its goals rated themselves as more prototypical than did less strongly identified players.

Second, the social-identity perspective leads to the proposition that cohesion is more strongly related to other group variables to the extent that cohesion is central to the group's sense of identity. This proposition is in accord with suggestions by other researchers that some teams see themselves as entirely task-oriented, while others pay more attention to interpersonal concerns. Some settings (for example, formal competitions) are more likely to lead to the first type of team than are others. Some sports may also be more likely to need cohesion as a central characteristic of a team's self-definition than others ("team spirit" and "being a team player" are probably more important in volleyball than in golf; see above). Over and above this, however, some teams may acquire cohesion as a part of their self-definition for accidental or historical reasons. In these cases, cohesion may be a crucial way for members of such a team to distinguish themselves and their fellow team members from rival teams.

Finally this theoretical position allows for a distinction to be made at all points in Carron's (1982) model, between variables affecting personal identity, personal performance, and interpersonal satisfaction on the one hand, and variables affecting group-based attraction, performance, and satisfaction on the other. Empirical tests of these relationships can potentially clear much of the mud from the waters in this area. In any case, this approach provides another useful way to examine the relationship between cohesion and performance.

OVERVIEW

In this chapter we have attempted to survey some important aspects of the relationship between social variables and group performance. We have concentrated on issues relating to the interaction and communication between team members. Special emphasis has been placed on the areas of effort (or lack of effort) and team cohesion, as these are central to the understanding of team performance in sports settings.

In addition to reviewing the major research in these areas, we have tried to present theoretical approaches from social psychology that have to date not received a great deal of research attention in sport psychology. In doing this, our goal has been to open new avenues of research in this important area. For example, much of the general social psychology research on theories of social loafing have emphasized performance. The sporting environment provides the researcher with situations where performances are inherently evaluated. Using this sporting environment to investigate theories of social loafing (e.g., deindividuation, identifiability, and equity of effort) not only provides optimal field situations for the social psychology researcher, but also allows relevant aspects of team performance to be measured and then possibly modified or controlled. Other domains within social psychology that may effectively be applied to sporting situations include the use of communication dimensions to predict performance and the use of social identity theory in team cohesion research.

Obviously many of the facets of social interactions covered in this chapter require the development of more valid and more reliable measures. Problems and concerns with measures of team cohesion have been highlighted. Examples of other psychometric concerns include the effective measurement of desire for group success (D_{gs}) and the level of personal involvement in a particular task.

A key point in studying social interactions within sport and physical activity situations is that both individual and social levels need to be addressed. Since many aspects of individual performance and participation in sport take place within a group environment, the social interactions that take place as well as the effects of these interactions on the individual need to be understood. This can only be done effectively if both individual and social measures are developed. In trying to comprehend this vast area of knowledge within sport psychology, social psychology may offer some valuable theories, ideas, tools, or techniques.

References

Abrams, D. (1984). *Social identity, self-awareness, and intergroup behaviour.* Unpublished doctoral dissertation, University of Kent.

Abrams, D., & Hogg, M. A. (Eds.). (1990). *Social identity theory: Constructive and critical advances.* New York: Harvester.

Argyle, M. (1969). *Social interaction.* New York: Atherton.

Argyle, M. (1988). *Bodily communication* (2nd ed.). London: Methuen.

Argyle, M., Furnham, A., & Graham, J. A. (1981). *Social situations.* Cambridge University Press.

Argyle, M., & Henderson, M. (1984). *The anatomy of relationships.* Harmondsworth, U.K.: Penguin.

Atkinson, J. W. (1964). *An introduction to motivation.* Princeton, NJ: Van Nostrand.

Bakeman, R., & Helmreich, R. (1975). Cohesiveness and performance: Covariation and causality in an undersea environment. *Journal of Experimental Social Psychology, 11,* 478–489.

Bales, R. F. (1950). *Interaction process analysis: A method for the study of small groups.* Reading, MA: Addison-Wesley.

Bales, R. F. (1966). Task roles and social roles in problem solving groups. In B. J. Biddle & E. J. Thomas (Eds.), *Role theory: Concepts and research* (pp. 254–263). New York: Wiley.

Bales, R. F., Cohen, S. P., & Williamson, S. A. (1979). *SYMLOG: A system for the multiple level observation of groups.* New York: Free Press.

Bandura, A. (1973). *Aggression: A social learning analysis.* Englewood Cliffs, NJ: Prentice-Hall.

Bandura, A., & Huston, A. (1961). Identification of a process of incidental learning. *Journal of Abnormal and Social Psychology, 63,* 311–318.

Bandura, A., Ross, D., & Ross, S. (1961). Transmission of aggression through imitation of aggressive models. *Journal of Abnormal and Social Psychology, 63,* 575–582.

Biddle, B. J., & Thomas, E. J. (Eds.) (1966). *Role theory: Concepts and research.* New York: Wiley.

Bird, A. M. (1977). Development of a model for predicting team performance. *Research Quarterly, 48,* 24–32.

Brawley, L. R., Carron, A. V., & Widmeyer, W. N. (1987). Assessing the cohesion of teams: Validity of the Group Environment Questionnaire. *Journal of Sport Psychology, 9,* 275–294.

Bredemeier, B. J. (1978). Applications and implications of aggression research. In W. F. Straub (Ed.), *Sport psychology: An analysis of athlete behavior* (pp. 203–213). Ithaca, NY: Mouvement.

Brickner, M. A., Harkins, S. G., & Ostrom, T. M. (1986). Effects of personal involvement: Thought-provoking implications for social loafing. *Journal of Personality and Social Psychology, 51,* 763–769.

Brown, R., & Gilman, A. (1960). The pronouns of power and solidarity. In T. Sebeok (Ed.), *Style in language* (pp. 253–276). Cambridge, MA: MIT Press.

Burgess, R. L., & Huston, T. L. (Eds.) (1979). *Social exchange in developing relationships.* New York: Academic Press.

Burgoon, J. K., Buller, D., & Woodall, G. (1990). *The unspoken dialogue* (2nd ed.). Englewood Cliffs, NJ: Prentice-Hall.

Caccese, T. M., & Mayerberg, C. K. (1984). Gender differences in perceived burnout of college coaches. *Journal of Sport Psychology, 6,* 279–288.

Capel, S. A., Sisley, B. L., & Desertrain, G. S. (1987). The relationship of role conflict and role ambiguity to burnout in high school basketball coaches. *Journal of Sport Psychology, 9,* 106–117.

Carron, A. V. (1978). Role behavior and coach-athlete interaction. *International Review of Sport Sociology, 13,* 51–65.

Carron, A. V. (1980). *Social psychology of sport.* Ithaca, NY: Mouvement.

Carron, A. V. (1982). Cohesiveness in sport groups: Interpretations and considerations. *Journal of Sport Psychology, 4,* 123–138.

Carron, A. V. (1988). *Group dynamics in sport: Theoretical and practical issues.* London, Ontario: Sportdym.

Carron, A. V., & Ball, J. R. (1977). Cause-effect characteristics of cohesiveness and participation motivation in intercollegiate hockey. *International Review of Sport Sociology, 12,* 49–60.

Carron, A. V., Widmeyer, M. N., & Brawley, L. R. (1985). The development of an instrument to assess cohesion in sport teams: The Group Environment Questionnaire. *Journal of Sport Psychology, 7,* 244–266.

Carron, A. V., Widmeyer, W. N., & Brawley, L. R. (1988). Group cohesion and individual adherence to physical activity. *Journal of Sport and Exercise Psychology, 10,* 127–138.

Cartwright, D. (1968). The nature of group cohesiveness. In D.

Cartwright & A. Zander (Eds.), *Group dynamics: Research and theory* (3rd ed., pp. 91–109). New York: Harper & Row.

Comrey, A. L. (1953). Group performance in a manual dexterity task. *Journal of Applied Psychology, 37,* 207–210.

Comrey, A. L., & Deskin, G. (1954a). Further results on group manual dexterity in men. *Journal of Applied Psychology, 38,* 116–118.

Comrey, A. L., & Deskin, G. (1954b). Group manual dexterity in women. *Journal of Applied Psychology, 38,* 178–180.

Davis, J. H. (1969). *Group performance.* Reading, MA: Addison-Wesley.

Diener, E. (1980). Deindividuation: The absence of self-awareness and self-regulation in group members. In P. B. Paulus (Ed.), *The psychology of group influence* (pp. 209–242). Hillsdale, NJ: Erlbaum.

Eitzen, D. S. (1973). The effect of group structure on the success of athletic teams. *International Review of Sport Sociology, 8,* 7–17.

Emerson, R. (1966). Mount Everest: A case study of communication feedback and sustained goal striving. *Sociometry, 29,* 213–277.

Essing, W. (1970). Team line-up and team achievement in European football. In G. S. Kenyon (Ed.), *Contemporary psychology of sport* (pp. 349–354). Chicago: The Athletic Institute.

Festinger, L. (1954). A theory of social comparison processes. *Human Relations, 7,* 117–140.

Fiedler, F. E. (1954). Assumed similarity measures as predictors of team effectiveness. *Journal of Abnormal and Social Psychology, 49,* 381–388.

Forgas, J. P. (1986). *Interpersonal behaviour: The psychology of social interaction.* Sydney: Pergamon.

Forsterling, F. (1985). Attributional retraining: A review. *Psychological Bulletin, 98,* 495–512.

Forsyth, D. R. (1990). *Group dynamics* (2nd ed.). Pacific Grove, CA: Brooks/Cole.

Forward, J. (1969). Group achievement motivation and individual motives to achieve success and to avoid failure. *Journal of Personality, 37,* 297–309.

Forward, J., & Zander, A. (1971). Choice of unattainable group goals and effects on performance. *Organizational Behavior and Human Performance, 6,* 184–199.

Furnham, A. (1983). Situational determinants of social skill. In R. Ellis & D. Whittington (Eds.), *New directions in social skill research* (pp. 77–114). London: Croom Helm.

Gallois, C. & Callan, V. J. (1986). *Journal of Personality and Social Psychology, 51,* 735–762.

Gallois, C., Franklyn-Stokes, A., Giles, H., & Coupland, N. (1988). Communication accommodation theory and intercultural encounters: Intergroup and interpersonal considerations. In Y. Y. Kim & W. B. Gudykunst (Eds.), *Theories in intercultural communication* (pp. 157–185). Newbury Park, CA: Sage.

Giles, H., & Johnson, P. (1987). Ethnolinguistic identity theory: A social psychological approach to language maintenance. *International Journal of the Sociology of Language, 68,* 256–269.

Giles, H., Mulac, A., Bradac, J. J., & Johnson, P. (1987). Speech accommodation theory: The first decade and beyond. In M. L. McLaughlin (Ed.), *Communication yearbook 10* (pp. 13–48). Beverly Hills, CA: Sage.

Giles, H., & Robinson, W. P. (Eds.). (1990). *Handbook of language and social psychology.* Chichester, U.K.: Wiley.

Gill, D. L. (1979). The prediction of group motor performance from individual member abilities. *Journal of Motor Behavior, 11,* 113–122.

Gill, D. L. (1984). Individual and group performance in sport. In J.

M. Silva & R. S. Weinberg (Eds.), *Psychological foundations of sport* (pp. 315–328). Champaign, IL: Human Kinetics.

Gill, D. L. (1986). *Psychological dynamics of sport.* Champaign, IL: Human Kinetics.

Gruber, J. J., & Gray, G. R. (1981). Factor patterns of variables influencing cohesiveness at various levels of basketball competition. *Research Quarterly for Exercise and Sport, 52,* 19–30.

Gruber, J. J., & Gray, G. R. (1982). Responses to forces influencing cohesion as a function of player status and level of male varsity basketball competition. *Research Quarterly for Exercise and Sport, 53,* 27–36.

Gudykunst, W. B. (1986). Towards a theory of intergroup communication. In W. B. Gudykunst (Ed.), *Intergroup communication* (pp. 152–167). London: Arnold.

Hacker, C. M., & Williams, J. M. (1981). Cohesion, satisfaction, and performance in intercollegiate field hockey. *Psychology of motor behavior and sport—1981: Abstracts.* Monterey, CA: NASPSPA.

Hardy, C. J., & Latane, B. (1988). Social loafing in cheerleaders: Effects of team membership and competition. *Journal of Sport and Exercise Psychology, 10,* 109–114.

Harkins, S. G., Latane, B., & Williams, K. D. (1980). Social loafing: Allocational effort or taking it easy? *Journal of Experimental Social Psychology, 16,* 457–465.

Harkins, S. G., & Petty, R. E. (1982). Effects of task difficulty and task uniqueness on social loafing. *Journal of Personality and Social Psychology, 43,* 1214–1229.

Haythorn, W. W. (1968). The composition of groups: A review of the literature. *Acta Psychologica, 28,* 97–128.

Heslin, R. (1964). Predicting group task effectiveness from member characteristics. *Psychological Bulletin, 62,* 248–256.

Hoferek, M. J. (1978). Toward wider vistas: Societal sex-role models and their relationship to the sports world. In W. F. Straub (Ed.), *Sport psychology: An analysis of athlete behavior* (pp. 293–299). Ithaca, NY: Mouvement.

Hogg, M. A. (1992). *The social psychology of group cohesiveness: From attraction to social identity.* London: Harvester Wheatsheaf.

Hogg, M. A., & Abrams, D. (1988). *Social identifications.* London: Routledge.

Hogg, M. A., & Hardie, E. A. (1991). Social attraction, personal attraction, and self-categorization: A field study. *Personality and Social Psychology Bulletin, 17,* 175–180.

Homans, G. C. (1950). *The human group.* New York: Harcourt, Brace, and World.

Huddleston, S., Doody, S. G., & Ruder, M. K. (1985). The effect of prior knowledge of the social loafing phenomenon on performance in a group. *International Journal of Sport Psychology, 16,* 176–182.

Husman, B. (1978). Aggression: An historical perspective. In W. F. Straub (Ed.), *Sport psychology: An analysis of athlete behavior* (pp. 166–176). Ithaca, NY: Mouvement.

Ingham, A. G., Levinger, G., Graves, J., & Peckham, V. (1974). The Ringelmann effect: Studies of group size and group performance. *Journal of Experimental Social Psychology, 10,* 371–384.

Jackson, J. M., & Harkins, S. G. (1985). Equity in effort: An explanation of the social loafing effect. *Journal of Personality and Social Psychology, 49,* 1199–1206.

Jones, E., & Gallois, C. (1989). Spouses' impressions of rules for communication in private and public marital conflicts. *Journal of Marriage and the Family, 51,* 957–967.

Jones, M. B. (1974). Regressing group on individual effectiveness.

Organizational Behavior and Human Performance, 11, 426–451.

Kelley, H. H., & Thibaut, J. (1978). *Interpersonal relations: A theory of interdependence.* New York: Wiley.

Kerr, N. L. (1983). Motivation losses in small groups: A social dilemma analysis. *Journal of Personality and Social Psychology, 45,* 819–828.

Kerr, N. L., & Bruun, S. E. (1981). Ringelmann revisited: Alternative explanations for the social loafing effect. *Personality and Social Psychology Bulletin, 7,* 224–231.

Kerr, N. L., & Brunn, S. E. (1983). Dispensibility of member effort and group member motivation losses: Free rider effects. *Journal of Personality and Social Psychology, 44,* 78–94.

Klein, M., & Christiansen, G. (1969). Group composition, group structure and group effectiveness of basketball teams. In J. W. Loy & G. S. Kenyon (Eds.), *Sport, culture and society* (pp. 397–408). New York: Macmillan.

Kravitz, D. A., & Martin, B. (1986). Ringelmann rediscovered: The original article. *Journal of Personality and Social Psychology, 50,* 936–941.

Landers, D. M. (1974). Taxonomic considerations in measuring group performances and the analysis of selected group motor performance tasks. In M. G. Wade & R. Martens (Eds.), *Psychology of motor behavior and sport* (pp. 204–221). Champaign, IL: Human Kinetics.

Landers, D. M., & Lueschen, G. (1974). Team performance outcome and the cohesiveness of competitive coacting groups. *International Review of Sport Sociology, 9,* 57–71.

Landers. D. M., Wilkinson, M. O., Hatfield, B. D., & Barber, H. (1982). Causality and the cohesion-performance relationship. *Journal of Sport Psychology, 4,* 170–183.

Latane, B., Harkins, S. G., & Williams, K. D. (1980). *Many hands make light the work: Social loafing as a social disease.* Unpublished manuscript, Ohio State University, Columbus.

Latane, B., Williams, K. D., & Harkins, S. G. (1979). Many hands make light the work: The causes and consequences of social loafing. *Journal of Personality and Social Psychology, 37,* 823–832.

Lenk, H. (1969). Top performance despite internal conflict: An antithesis to a functionalistic proposition. In J. W. Loy & G. S. Kenyon (Eds.), *Sport, culture and society* (pp. 393–397). New York: Macmillan.

Martens, R., Landers, D. M., & Loy, J. W. (1972). *Sport cohesiveness questionnaire.* Champaign: University of Illinois, Department of Physical Education.

Martens, R., & Peterson, J. A. (1971). Group cohesiveness as a determinant of success and member satisfaction in team performance. *International Review of Sport Sociology, 6,* 49–61.

McGrath, J. E. (1962). The influence of positive interpersonal relations on adjustment and effectiveness in rifle teams. *Journal of Abnormal and Social Psychology, 65,* 365–375.

McGrath, J. E., & Altman, I. (1966). *Small group research: A synthesis and critique of the field.* New York: Holt, Rinehart & Winston.

McHugh, M. C., Duquin, M. E., & Frieze, I. H. (1978). Beliefs about success and failure: Attribution and the female athlete. In C. A. Oglesby (Ed.), *Women and sport: From myth to reality* (pp. 173–191). Philadelphia: Lea & Febiger.

Medow, H., & Zander, A. (1965). Aspirations for group chosen by central and peripheral members. *Journal of Personality and Social Psychology, 1,* 224–228.

Melnick, M. J., & Chemers, M. M. (1974). Effects of group structure on the success of basketball teams. *Research Quarterly, 45,* 1–8.

Myers, A. E. (1962). Team competition, success, and adjustment of group members. *Journal of Abnormal and Social Psychology, 65,* 325–332.

Napier, H. S. (1968). Individual vs. group learning on three different tasks. *Journal of Psychology, 69,* 249–257.

Noller, P. (1984). *Nonverbal communication in marital interaction.* New York: Pergamon.

Osgood, C. E., Suci, G. J., & Tannenbaum, P. H. (1957). *The measurement of meaning.* Urbana: University of Illinois Press.

Pease, R., & Miller, M. (1989, August). *Team cohesion and athletic performance: A case study of a basketball team.* Paper presented at the 7th World Congress in Sport Psychology, Singapore.

Peterson, J. A., & Martens, R., (1972). Success and residential affiliation as determinants of team cohesiveness. *Research Quarterly, 43,* 62–76.

Rees, C. R., & Segal, M. W. (1984). Role differentiation in groups: The relationship between instrumental and expressive leadership. *Small group behavior, 15,* 109–123.

Reis, H. T., & Jelsma, B. (1978). A social psychology of sex differences in sport. In W. F. Straub (Ed.), *Sport psychology: An analysis of athlete behavior* (pp. 276–286). Ithaca, NY: Mouvement.

Rotter, J. B. (1966). Generalized expectancies for internal versus external control of reinforcement. *Psychological Monographs, 80* (1, Whole No. 609).

Ruder, M. K., & Gill, D. L. (1982). Immediate effects of win-loss on perceptions of cohesion in intramural volleyball teams. *Journal of Sport Psychology, 4,* 227–234.

Russell, J. A. (1980). A circumplex model of affect. *Journal of Personality and Social Psychology, 39,* 1161–1178.

Sage, G. H., & Loudermilk, S. (1979). The female athlete and role conflict. *Research Quarterly, 50,* 88–103.

Schutz, W. C. (1966). *The interpersonal underworld.* Palo Alto, CA: Science and Behavior.

Shaw, M. E. (1981). *Group dynamics: The psychology of small group behavior (3rd ed.).* New York: McGraw-Hill.

Shields, D. L., & Bredemeier, B. J. (1984). Sport and moral growth: A structural developmental perspective. In W. F. Straub & J. M. Williams (Eds.), *Cognitive sport psychology* (pp. 89–101). Lansing, NY: Sport Science Associates.

Silva, J. M. III (1983). The perceived legitimacy of rule-violating behavior in sport. *Journal of Sport Psychology, 5,* 438–448.

Smith, M. D. (1978). Social learning of violence in minor hockey. In F. L. Smoll and R. E. Smith (Eds.), *Psychological perspectives in youth sports* (pp. 91–106). Washington, DC: Hemisphere.

Smith, R. E., Smoll, F. L., & Curtis, B. (1978). Coaching behaviors in Little League baseball. In F. L. Smoll & R. E. Smith (Eds.), *Psychological perspectives in youth sports* (pp. 173–201). Washington, DC: Hemisphere.

Spink, K. S. (1990). Group cohesion and collective efficacy of volleyball teams. *Journal of Sport and Exercise Psychology, 12,* 301–311.

Steiner, I. D. (1972). *Group process and productivity.* New York: Academic Press.

Tajfel, H. (Ed.). (1978). *Differentiation between social groups: Studies in the social psychology of intergroup relations.* London: Academic.

Tajfel, H. (Ed.). (1982). *Social identity and intergroup relations.* Cambridge University Press.

Tajfel, H., & Turner, J. C. (1979). An integrative theory of intergroup conflict. In S. Worchel & W. G. Austin (Eds.), *The social psychology of intergroup relations.* Monterey, CA: Brooks/Cole.

Thibaut, J., & Kelley, H. H. (1959). *The social psychology of groups*. New York: Wiley.

Thomas, J. R. (1977). Attribution theory and motivation through reward: Practical implications for children's sports. *Motor Skills: Theory into Practice, 1,* 123–129.

Trower, P. Bryant, B., & Argyle, M. (1977). *Social skills and mental health*.

Turner, J. C. (1987). *Rediscovering the social group: A self-categorization theory*. Oxford: Basil Blackwell.

Volp, A., & Keil, U. (1987). The relationship between performance, intention to drop out, and interpersonal conflict in swimmers. *Journal of Sport Psychology, 9,* 358–375.

Wankel, L. M. (1975). The effects of social reinforcement and audience presence on the motor performance of boys with different levels of initial ability. *Journal of Motor Behavior, 7,* 207–216.

Widmeyer, W. N., Brawley, L. R., & Carron, A. V. (1985). *The measurement of cohesion in sport teams: The group environment questionnaire*. London, Ontario: Sports Dynamics.

Widmeyer, W. N., Brawley, L. R., & Carron, A. V. (1990). The effects of group size in sport. *Journal of Sport and Exercise Psychology, 12,* 177–190.

Widmeyer, W. N., & Martens. R. (1978). When cohesion predicts performance outcome in sport. *Research Quarterly, 49,* 372–380.

Wiest, W. M., Porter, L. W., & Ghiselli, E. E. (1961). Relationships between individual proficiency and team performance and efficiency. *Journal of Applied Psychology, 45,* 435–440.

Williams, K. D. (1981). *Social loafing and group cohesion*. Paper presented at a meeting of the Midwestern Psychological Association, Detroit.

Williams, J. M., & Hacker, C. M. (1982). Causal relationships among cohesion, satisfaction, and performance in women's intercollegiate field hockey teams. *Journal of Sport Psychology, 4,* 324–337.

Williams, K., Harkins, S., & Latane, B. (1981). Identifiability and social loafing: Two cheering experiments. *Journal of Personality and Social Psychology, 40,* 303–311.

Wish, M., d'Andrade, A., & Goodnow, J. E. II. (1980). Dimensions of interpersonal communication: Correspondences between structures for speech acts and bipolar scales. *Journal of Personality and Social Psychology, 39,* 848–860.

Yukelson, D., Weinberg, R., & Jackson, A. (1984). A multidimensional sport cohesion instrument for intercollegiate basketball teams. *Journal of Sport Psychology, 6,* 103–117.

Zajonc, R. B. (1962). The effects of feedback and probability of group success on individual and group performance. *Human Relations, 15,* 149–161.

Zajonc, R. B. (1965). Social facilitation. *Science, 149,* 269–274.

Zaleznik, A., & Moment, D. (1964). *The dynamics of interpersonal behavior*. New York: Wiley.

Zander, A. (1971). *Motives and goals in groups*. New York: Academic Press.

Zander, A. (1975). Motivation and performance of sports groups. In D. M. Landers (Ed.), *Psychology of sport and motor behavior II.* (pp. 25–29). University Park, PA: Pennsylvania State University Press.

Zander, A. (1982). *Making groups effective*. San Francisco: Jossey-Bass.

Zander, A., & Armstrong, W. (1972). Working for group pride in a slipper factory. *Journal of Applied Social Psychology, 2,* 193–207.

Zander, A., & Forward, J. (1968). Position in group, achievement motivation, and group aspirations. *Journal of Personality and Social Psychology, 8,* 282–288.

Zander, A., & Medow, H. (1965). Strength of group and desire for attainable group aspirations. *Journal of Personality, 33,* 122–139.

Zander, A., & Ulberg, C. (1971). The group level of aspiration and external social pressures. *Organizational Behavior and Human Performance, 6,* 362–378.

·30·

LEADERSHIP

P. Chelladurai

In recent years the research on sport leadership has taken three different approaches. This chapter reviews the literature on sport leadership in three parts reflecting these three approaches.

The first covers that line of inquiry based on the Multidimensional Model of Leadership (Chelladurai, 1978; Chelladurai & Carron, 1978) and the Leadership Scale for Sports (LSS; Chelladurai, 1978; Chelladurai & Carron, 1981a; Chelladurai & Saleh, 1978, 1980). The second deals with the approach taken by Smith, Smoll, and their associates (e.g., Smith, Smoll, & Curtis, 1978, 1979; Smith, Smoll, & Hunt, 1977a; Smoll, Smith, Curtis, & Hunt, 1978), who proposed a Mediational Model of Leadership and based their research on the Coaching Behavior Assessment System (CBAS). The basic method in this research was to assess relationships between coaches' behaviors and their players' evaluative reactions, train the coaches to improve their behaviors, and evaluate the effects of these changes on a variety of player outcome measures.

The third reviews the literature on the approach initiated by Chelladurai and Haggerty (1978), who, following Vroom and Yetton (1973), proposed a normative model of decision styles in coaching. The research based on this model was focused on the extent of participation in decision making preferred by athletes and/or allowed by coaches in varying situations (Chelladurai & Arnott, 1985; Chelladurai, Haggerty, & Baxter, 1989; Chelladurai & Quek, 1991; Gordon, 1988).

THE MULTIDIMENSIONAL MODEL

The multidimensional model (shown in Figure 30–1 on page 648) is a synthesis and extension of (a) the contingency model of leadership effectiveness (Fiedler, 1967), (b) the path-goal theory of leadership (Evans, 1970; House, 1971; House & Dessler, 1974), (c) the adaptive-reactive theory (Osborn & Hunt, 1975), and (d) the discrepancy model of leadership (Yukl, 1971). These earlier theories focus differentially on the leader, the members, and the situation in which they are placed. The multidimensional model brings all these elements together, and thus places equal emphasis on each one of them.

In the multidimensional model, group performance and member satisfaction are considered to be a function of the congruence among three states of leader behavior—*required, preferred,* and *actual.* The antecedents of these three states of leader behaviors are the characteristics of the situation, the leader, and the members.

Required Leader Behavior

The leader is required to behave in certain ways (Box 4) by the demands and constraints placed by situational characteristics, i.e., the parameters of the organization and its environment (Box 1). For example, the goals and the formal organizational structure of the team and the larger system (e.g., those of professional teams versus those of high school teams), the group task and the associated technology (e.g., team versus individual sports), social norms, cultural values, and government regulations are some of the situational characteristics that impinge on leader behavior.

Leader Behavior Preferred by Members

Members' preferences for specific leader behaviors (Box 6) are largely a function of the individual characteristics (Box 3) of the group members. Personality variables such as need for achievement, need for affiliation, cognitive structure, and competence in the task influence a member's preferences for coaching and guidance, social support, and feedback. In addition, the situational characteristics also affect member preferences. For example, if there is an organizational expectation that a leader will behave in a specific manner, this expectation is held jointly by both leaders and members. Thus both the leaders and members are socia-

ANTECEDENTS   LEADER BEHAVIOR   CONSEQUENCES

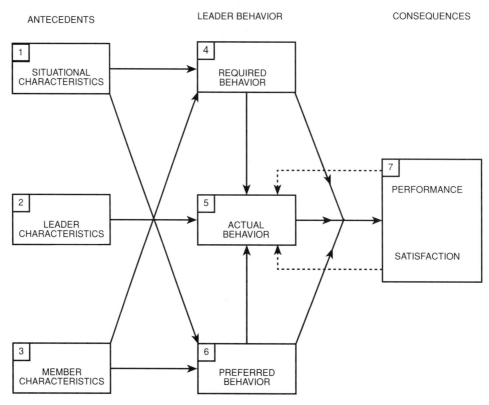

FIGURE 30-1. The multidimensional model of leadership
(Chelladurai, 1991).

lized into the same behavioral expectations and/or preferences in a given context (e.g., group task, the formal authority system, and the primary work group).

Actual Leader Behavior

Some theorists (e.g., Fiedler, 1967) hold that a leader's actual behavior is solely a function of his/her personality, but that view is not widely supported. Instead, it is accepted that leader's personal characteristics including personality, ability, and experience (Box 2) have a strong influence on actual leader behavior. In addition, leaders are considerably influenced by situational requirements (Box 4). For instance, the differing goals of a professional sports team and a high school team would require the respective coaches to exhibit different leadership behaviors. In addition, the athletes in the above two settings would prefer differing leader behaviors (Box 6), and such preferences would influence how a coach actually behaves.

Performance and Satisfaction

Figure 30–1 specifies that performance and satisfaction (Box 7) are a function of the degree of congruence among the three states of leader behavior. In the original schematic description of the model (Chelladurai, 1978; Chelladurai

and Carron, 1978), performance was linked to the congruence between required and actual behaviors, while member satisfaction was linked to the congruence between actual leader behavior and preferred leader behavior. However, Chelladurai and Carron (1978) noted that performance and satisfaction were not independent of each other. "Insofar as the subordinates (athletes) are oriented toward task accomplishment and insofar as the leader (coach) meets these preferences, *both* satisfaction and performance are enhanced. That is, both are direct results of leader behavior" (Chelladurai & Carron, 1978, p. 71). Further, in the absence of empirical support for the notion that performance is a function of the congruence between required and actual behaviors, it is only appropriate to consider performance and satisfaction as being jointly affected by the congruence among all three states of leader behavior as illustrated in Figure 30–1.

Proposed Refinement

Chelladurai (1990) proposed a refinement on the relationship between member characteristics and required leader behavior. In the original model (Chelladurai, 1978), member characteristics were seen to influence leadership only through the construct of preferred leadership because members' preferences were presumed to reflect not only their personal needs and desires, but also their judgments about what was appropriate to their situation. However, in so far as members lack the intelligence, ability, experience, and/or personality dispositions to make those kinds of judgments, the leader would be required to decide for the members. Thus required leader behavior is influenced not only by the contingencies of the situation but also by member characteristics (Chelladurai, 1990). This relationship is illustrated by the line leading from Box 3 to Box 4.

Chelladurai (1990) noted that the linkage between members' individual differences and required leader behavior would be consistent with Hersey and Blanchard's (1977) situational leadership theory, which states that leaders *should* vary their behaviors according to the members' maturity (defined as a combination of members' education, experience, achievement motivation, and willingness to take responsibility). House's path-goal theory (1971) would also subscribe to this position in that it considers subordinate characteristics as one of two classes of situational variables, the other being the environmental demands and pressures.

The Leadership Scale for Sports

The Leadership Scale for Sports (LSS), developed in two stages (Chelladurai & Saleh, 1978; 1980) consists of 40 items representing 5 dimensions of leader behavior described in Table 30-1—*training and instruction, democratic behavior, autocratic behavior, social support,* and *positive feedback (or rewarding behavior).*

TABLE 30-1. Dimensions of leader behavior in sport*

Dimension	Description
Training and instruction	Coaching behavior aimed at improving the athletes' performance by emphasizing and facilitating hard and strenuous training; instructing them in skills, techniques, and tactics of the sport; clarifying the relationship among members; and structuring and coordinating members' activities.
Democratic behavior	Coaching behavior that allows greater participation by athletes in decisions pertaining to group goals, practice methods, and game tactics and strategies.
Autocratic behavior	Coaching behavior which involves independent decision making and stresses personal authority.
Social support	Coaching behavior characterized by a concern for the welfare of individual athletes, positive group atmosphere, and warm interpersonal relations with members.
Positive feedback	Coaching behavior which reinforces an athlete by recognizing and rewarding good performance.

*From: P. Chelladurai (1989).

The five response categories are *always (100% of the time), often (75%), occasionally (50%), seldom (25%),* and *never (0%).* By modifying the items and the stem preceding them, various authors have used the scale to measure (a) athletes' preferences for specific leader behaviors, (b) athletes' perceptions of their coaches' leader behaviors, and/or (c) coaches' perceptions of their own behavior (e.g., Chelladurai, 1984; Chelladurai & Carron, 1983; Chelladurai, Imamura, Yamaguchi, Oinuma, & Miyauchi, 1988; Chelladurai, Malloy, Imamura, & Yamaguchi, 1987; Dwyer & Fischer, 1988b; Garland & Barry, 1988; Gordon, 1986; Horne & Carron, 1985; Liukkonen & Salminen, 1989; Robinson & Carron, 1982; Schliesman, 1987; Summers, 1983; Terry, 1984; Terry & Howe, 1984; Weiss & Friedrichs, 1986).

To the present time, the LSS has been translated into Finnish (Liukkonen & Salminen, 1989; Liukkonen, Salminen, & Telama, 1989a, 1989b), French (Lacoste & Laurencelle, 1989), Greek (Iordanoglou, 1990), Japanese (Chelladurai et al., 1988), Korean (Kim, Lee, & Lee, 1990, Portuguese (Serpa, Lacoste, Pataco, & Santos, 1988), and Swedish (Isberg & Chelladurai, 1990).

Psychometric Properties of the LSS

Reliability. Chelladurai and Saleh (1980) reported that the *test-retest* reliability estimates from the repeat responses of 53 physical education majors after a 4-week interval were .72 for Training Behavior, .82 for Democratic Behavior, .76 for Autocratic Behavior, .71 for Social Support, and .79 for Positive Feedback. These values are adequate and comparable to those reported in the literature for similar scales.

The *internal consistency* estimates reported by several authors are presented in Table 30-2. While the internal consistency estimates are adequate in general, they are relatively higher for the "athletes' perception" version than for the "athletes' preference" version. Further, the internal consistency estimates are rather low for autocratic behavior, particularly in the preference version. These estimates have been generally lower than .60, and some estimates have been lower than even .50. It is known to be significantly associated with various outcomes; however, such results should be viewed with caution.

Validity

Chelladurai and Saleh (1980) claimed *factorial validity* (i.e., construct validity) on the basis of the stability of the 5-factor solution over 3 different data sets (preferences of physical education students, and preferences and perceptions of varsity-level athletes). Kerlinger (1973) had noted that "factor analysis is perhaps the most powerful method of construct validation" (p. 468). In the present context, however, the percentage of variance explained by the 5-factor solutions was 41.2% for physical education students' preferences, 39.3% for athletes' preferences, and 55.8% for ath-

TABLE 30–2. Internal consistency estimates for the LSS dimensions

Source	DIMENSIONS				
	TI	DB	AB	SS	PF
Chelladurai & Saleh (1980):					
Canadian athletes	.83[a]	.75	.45	.70	.82
	.93[b]	.87	.79	.86	.92
Chelladurai (1986):					
Indian athletes	.76[a]	.71	.56	.51	.57
	.87[b]	.78	.49	.70	.61
Chelladurai, et al. (1988):					
Japanese athletes	.81[a]	.72	.55	.72	.73
	.89[b]	.81	.57	.84	.81
Canadian athletes	.77[a]	.67	.55	.78	.77
	.88[b]	.75	.59	.84	.91
Dwyer & Fischer (1988):					
Canadian wrestling coaches	.86[c]	.77	.36	.61	.75
Dwyer & Fischer (1990):					
Canadian wrestlers	.86[b]	.81	.52	.77	.82
Keehner (1988):					
American fitness club members	.99[b]	.97	.93	.97	.98
Isberg & Chelladurai (1990):					
Swedish athletes	.78[a]	.77	.44	.60	.57
	.88[b]	.72	.54	.86	.77
Kim, Lee, & Lee (1990):					
Korean athletes	.81[a]	.74	.61	.76	.66
	.86[b]	.83	.64	.80	.72
Iordanoglou (1990):					
Greek soccer players	.86[b]	.73	.11	.59	.60

[a]Athletes' preferences
[b]Athletes' perceptions
[c]Coaches' perceptions of own behavior

letes' perceptions. This relatively limited amount of explained variance remains a source of concern.

The meaningfulness of the 5-factor solution suggested *content validity*. In addition, the content of the 5 dimensions of leader behavior was consistent with earlier descriptions of leader behavior (e.g., Fleishman, 1957; Halpin & Winer, 1957; House & Dessler, 1974). Chelladurai (1981) further elaborated on the content validity of the LSS by relating leader behaviors to Porter and Lawler's (1968) motivational model (see Figure 30–2). Briefly, training and instruction strengthens the relationship between members' efforts and their performance by enhancing their ability and accurate perception of their role. Positive feedback contributes to members' satisfaction by making rewards equitable and contingent upon performance. Finally, social support makes the effort phase less burdensome by creating a warm and pleasant atmosphere in the work group.

Convergent and discriminant validity were indicated by adequate item-to-total correlations reported in several studies conducted in different contexts. These include: (a) French Canadian hockey players (Lacoste & Laurencelle,

1989); (b) Greek soccer players (Iordanoglou, 1990); (c) Indian athletes (Chelladurai, 1986a); (d) Japanese university athletes (Chelladurai et al., 1988); (e) Korean university athletes (Kim, Lee, & Lee (1990); (f) Swedish athletes (Isberg & Chelladurai, 1990); (g) youth sports (Chelladurai & Carron, 1981a); (h) coaches' perceptions of their own behavior (Dwyer & Fischer, 1988a); and (i) fitness leadership (Keehner, 1988).

Criterion-related validity can be inferred from the empirical support for the theoretical relationships between the 5 dimensions of leader behavior and selected criterion variables. These are (a) athletes' satisfaction (Chelladurai, 1984; Chelladurai et al., 1988; Schliesman, 1987; Weiss & Friedrichs, 1986); (b) performance level of the athletes (Garland & Barry, 1988); (c) performance (Gordon, 1986; Summers, 1983; Weiss & Friedrichs, 1986); (d) dropout behavior in athletics (Robinson & Carron, 1982); and (e) coach-athlete compatibility (Horne & Carron, 1985).

In contrast to the above favorable evaluations, the subscale structure of the LSS was not supported in two studies. Summers (1983) used 3 dimensions of the LSS, training and instruction, social support, and positive feedback, in his study of the influence of perceived ability and perceived team cohesion on coach-player interactions. A lack of support for his hypotheses prompted Summers to evaluate the LSS subscales post hoc. He factor-analyzed the 26 items from the 3 subscales and derived 5 factors. Since there were several overlapping items, he concluded that the coaching behaviors might be highly related to one another. (It should be noted that the orthogonality of the original subscales was lost when Chelladurai and Saleh [1980] selected only the high-loading items to represent the respective factors in the original scale.) Also, when Gordon (1986) conducted a factor analysis of his data there was no support for the subscale structure of the LSS. However, Gordon suggested that his finding could be an artifact of few cases.

The results of Gordon (1986) and Summers (1983) reinforce Nunnally's (1978) admonition that "most measures must be kept under constant surveillance to see if they are behaving as they should" (p. 87). This would be particularly necessary with the LSS, which was not subjected to rigorous conceptual analyses and psychometric procedures during its development. However, the 5-dimensional structure of the LSS cannot be adequately tested by conventional exploratory factor analysis. The purpose of exploratory analysis is to condense the information in a given set of data. Therefore, such an analysis is likely to yield different factor structures with different data sets.

On the other hand, in the analysis of item-to-total correlations, the concern is with the extent to which a given set of data conform to the prespecified subscale structure. This is verified by correlating each item with the sum of the other items from the same subscale and with the sum of the items in each of the other subscales. It would be expected that an item would correlate higher with its own subscale than with other subscales. This was the approach taken in several of the studies cited earlier (Chelladurai & Carron, 1981a; Chelladurai, 1986a; Chelladurai et al., 1986;

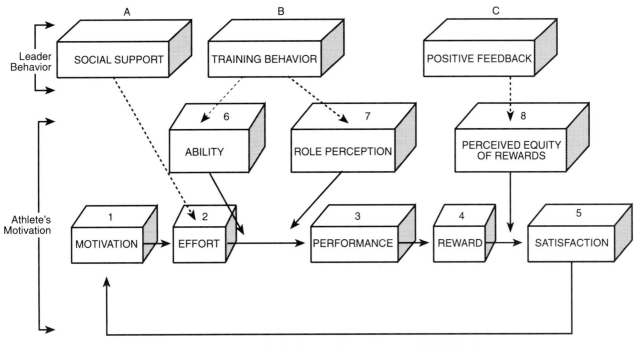

FIGURE 30–2. Leader behavior dimensions and individual
motivation (Chelladurai, 1981).

Chelladurai et al., 1988; Dwyer & Fischer, 1988a; Iordanoglou, 1990; Isberg & Chelladurai, 1990; Keehner, 1988; Kim, Lee, & Lee, 1990; Lacoste & Laurencelle, 1989; Serpa, Lacoste, Pataco, & Santos, 1988).

A more sophisticated and robust approach would be to subject the data to a confirmatory factor analysis that would yield estimates of the extent to which the data fit the hypothesized factor structure. There are several computer programs that perform confirmatory factor analysis. One example is Jöreskog and Sörbom's (1983) program called Linear Structural Relations (LISREL), which constrains the factor analysis to a priori specifications. Since LISREL is now available as part of the Statistical Package for Social Sciences (SPSS), future studies may employ the more rigorous method of confirming the factor structure of the LSS.

RESEARCH ON THE MULTIDIMENSIONAL MODEL OF LEADERSHIP

The studies relating to the multidimensional model are briefly described in the following two discussions: (a) those dealing with the factors affecting the perceived and/or preferred leader behavior, and (b) those dealing with the consequences of leadership.

Antecedents of Leadership

Individual Differences. Gender has been found to be an important determinant of preferred leadership. In their study of 160 physical education students, Chelladurai and Saleh (1978) found that males preferred their coaches to be more autocratic yet more supportive than did female respondents. Similarly, Erle's (1981) study of 335 male and female intramural and intercollegiate hockey players showed that males preferred more training and instruction, more autocratic behavior, more social support, and less democratic behavior from their coaches than did their female counterparts.

With regard to gender and perceived leadership, Serpa, Pataco, and Santos (1991), whose subjects were members of 8 handball teams participating in the World Championships of 1988 (Group C), and Serpa and Antunes (1989), whose subjects were 80 elite female volleyball players belonging to 8 teams participating in the Portuguese National Championship (First Division), reported that the athletes perceived their respective coaches to emphasize training and instruction, and rewarding behavior, which are both task-oriented. They were perceived to place the least emphasis on democratic behavior. In contrast, Liukkonen and Salminen's (1990) study of 399 young Finnish athletes showed that female coaches were perceived to be more democratic and socially supportive than male coaches. Salminen, Liukkonen, and Telama (1990) reported that Finnish female coaches ($n = 37$) perceived themselves to be more instructive, supportive, and rewarding than Finnish male coaches ($n = 60$). These apparently contradictory results can be reconciled if we take into account the levels of competitions. It seems that at the top levels of competition, the coaches of male and female teams tend to be similar in their behaviors.

Personality has been found to be associated with preferred leadership. In the previously cited Erle's (1981) study of leadership preferences of university and intramural hockey players, it was found that those athletes high on *task motivation* preferred more training and instruction, and those high on *affiliation motivation* and *extrinsic motivation* preferred more social support. These results were consistent with theoretical expectations. Chelladurai and Carron (1981b) reported that those athletes high on *cognitive structure* (i.e., the need for more information and structure in one's environment) preferred significantly more training and instruction, and less autocratic behavior, from the coach than those athletes lower on cognitive structure. Also, athletes high on *impulsivity* preferred more social support behavior from the coach than the less impulsive athletes.

Although age, experience, and maturity are not equivalent concepts, the measurements of these concepts in the leadership studies have paralleled each other. Therefore, these studies are reviewed jointly. A comparison between 12- to 15-year-old ($n = 17$) and 17- to 29-year-old ($n = 23$) women basketball players in Portugal showed that the younger players, relative to the older players, preferred more social support and democratic behavior, and less autocratic behavior. There were no significant differences between the two groups in preferred training and instruction, and in rewarding behavior (Serpa, 1990). Within competitive sports, longer experience was found to be associated with higher preference for positive feedback (Erle, 1981) and higher preference for autocratic behavior and social support (Chelladurai & Carron, 1981b).

In an attempt to test Hersey and Blanchard's (1977) Situational Leadership Theory, and their own modification of it, Chelladurai and Carron (1983) administered the preference version of the LSS to high school midget, high school junior, high school senior, and university-level basketball players, a categorization thought to reflect the *maturity* level of the subjects. Trend analysis showed two significant results. First, preference for training and instruction progressively decreased from high school midget through junior to senior levels and increased at the university level. Secondly, the preference for social support progressively increased from the high school midget level to the university level.

Ability of athletes also influences sport leadership. In Liukkonen and Salminen's (1990) study of 399 young Finnish athletes, high-ability athletes perceived their coaches to be more autocratic and less democratic, rewarding, and socially supportive than did the low-ability athletes.

Garland and Barry (1988) grouped their football players into (a) regulars, who started and/or took part in 50% or more of the plays during all games throughout a season; (b) substitutes, who started and/or played in less than 50% of the plays; and (c) survivors, who played only when the outcome was not in question. Garland and Barry considered this grouping to be a continuum of performance (which is a dependent variable in the multidimensional model). However, this grouping of the athletes could also be considered

to be a measure of player ability (which is an antecedent variable in the multidimensional model). Thus the following is a reinterpretation of their results. The more able players, as compared to the less able players, perceived their coaches to emphasize more training and instruction, to be more participative and less autocratic, to be more socially supportive, and to provide more positive feedback. Consistent with the above, Robinson and Carron (1982) found that the dropouts among high school football players perceived their coaches to be more autocratic than either the starters (highly skilled regular members of the team) or survivors (less skilled players who played in 10% or less of the season).

A general conclusion that can be drawn from these limited results is that as athletes gain experience and/or ability, they seem to prefer their coaches to be more autocratic and socially supportive. That leads to the concept of the coach as the benevolent autocrat.

Illustrative of the different perspectives held by coach and athlete, Horne and Carron (1985) found that their Canadian coaches rated themselves higher on training and instruction, democratic behavior, social support, and positive feedback than did their athletes. However, coaches' perceptions of their own autocratic behavior matched the perceptions of the players. Similarly, Salminen, Liukkonen, and Telama (1990) reported that their Finnish coaches ($n = 97$) perceived themselves to be more instructive, socially supportive, and rewarding, and less autocratic, than did their athletes ($n = 399$).

From a different perspective, Gordon (1986) found that coaches' self-reports of own autocratic behavior correlated positively with their expressed behaviors in all other dimensions except democratic behavior. In contrast, athletes' preferences for (and perceptions of) autocratic behavior correlated negatively with their preferences (and perceptions) in all other dimensions of the LSS. In other words, coaches who perceived themselves to be autocratic also perceived themselves to be benevolent, whereas athletes perceived the autocratic coaches to be less benevolent.

Situational variables. The situational variables that have been studied in the context of sport leadership are limited to (a) *organizational goals,* (b) *task type,* and (c) *culture.*

In the previously cited study, Erle (1981) found that the differences in *organizational goals* of intercollegiate hockey teams (pursuit of excellence) and intramural hockey teams (pursuit of pleasure) had a significant effect on preferences for leader behavior. Members of intercollegiate teams preferred greater training and instruction, greater social support, less positive feedback, and less democratic behavior from their coaches.

The task attributes of *dependence* and *variability* were found to have a significant influence in sport leadership (Chelladurai, 1978). More specifically, athletes involved in interdependent tasks (team sports) or variable tasks (open sports such as basketball) preferred more training and instruction than did the athletes in independent tasks (individual sports) or nonvariable tasks (closed sports such as swimming). Athletes in independent tasks and in nonvariable tasks preferred more democratic behavior than their respective counterparts, who preferred more autocratic behavior. Task variability was also significantly and positively correlated with preference for positive feedback (Chelladurai, 1978).

In the Finnish context, team sports coaches were perceived to be more autocratic, and less democratic and socially supportive than coaches of individual sports (Liukkonen & Salminen, 1990). Kim, Lee, and Lee (1990) compared the preferences and perceptions of three groups of Korean athletes involved in individual sports, combative sports, and team sports. They found that these groups differed among themselves in all dimensions except in preferred training and instruction. In general, the combative sports athletes preferred and perceived more autocratic, social support, and positive feedback behaviors from their coaches than did the other groups. Individual sports athletes preferred and perceived more democratic behavior from their coaches than did the other two groups. Serpa (1990) cited a study of 30 judo athletes and 30 middle-and long-distance runners from Portugal. The runners as compared with the judo athletes preferred more of democratic behavior ($M = 3.54$ and 3.25 respectively) and social support ($M = 4.07$ and 3.73 respectively). A general conclusion that can be drawn about the influences of sport type is that as task dependence and/or task variability increase, the need for training and instruction, autocratic behavior, social support, and positive feedback increases.

Terry (1984) was the first to study the effects of *culture* (a situational variable) on sport leadership. He administered the preference version of the LSS to athletes from Canada, Great Britain, the United States, and other nations competing in the 1983 Universiade. In explaining the finding that there were no differences in preferred leadership among different nationalities, Terry noted that "the three viable subject groups (Canada, United States, and Great Britain) all share similar cultural backgrounds and sporting ideologies" (p. 206).

In comparing Japanese physical education students in modern sports (e.g., basketball, volleyball), Japanese in traditional sports (e.g., judo, kendo), and Canadian physical education students in modern sports, Chelladurai et al. (1987) found that the Japanese in modern sports preferred more democratic behavior than the Canadian athletes; the Japanese in traditional sports preferred more autocratic behavior than the other two groups; both groups of Japanese athletes preferred higher levels of social support than the Canadian athletes; and the Canadian athletes preferred more positive feedback than the Japanese in traditional sports. It was concluded that the type of sport moderated the cultural influences.

In a later study, Chelladurai et al. (1988) administered the preferred and perceived versions of the LSS, and a satisfaction scale that assessed member satisfactions with leadership and personal outcome, to Japanese and Canadian university athletes. The results showed that (a) the Japanese athletes preferred more autocratic behavior and social support, while the Canadian athletes preferred significantly more training and instruction; and (b) the Japanese athletes perceived their coaches to be more autocratic, while the Canadian athletes perceived their coaches to provide more training and instruction and to be more democratic and more rewarding.

Consequences of Leadership

To date, three different consequences of leadership have been studied: *satisfaction, performance,* and *coach-athlete compatibility.* In Chelladurai's (1978) study of the leadership preferences and perceptions of 216 university-level male athletes in basketball, track and field, and wrestling, it was found that the congruence between preferred and actual behaviors in the autocratic behavior and positive feedback dimensions affected *satisfaction with the coach* in a curvilinear manner (i.e., members were less satisfied when the actual behavior deviated from preferred behavior in either direction). Also, members were more satisfied with the coach when his or her training and instruction behavior exceeded their preferences.

In a subsequent reanalysis of the data, Chelladurai (1984) treated the individual as the unit of analysis. It was found that the discrepancy between a member's preferences and his individual perceptions of coaching behavior was associated with member satisfaction *with leadership, with team performance,* and *with overall involvement.* Discrepancies in training and instruction and positive feedback (i.e., higher perceptions than preferences) were the most common dimensions of leader behavior affecting the athletes' satisfactions in all three sport groups (basketball, track and field, and wrestling). The effects of the discrepancies were more pronounced on satisfaction with leadership than on the other facets of satisfaction. These findings were corroborated by Horne and Carron (1985), who found that the discrepancies in training and instruction, social support, and positive feedback were significant predictors of *satisfaction with leadership.* The higher the coaches' behaviors in these dimensions relative to preferences, the higher the satisfaction with leadership.

In Schliesman's (1987) study of university track and field athletes, perceived democratic behavior and social support were positively related to general *satisfaction with leadership.* Also, discrepancy scores in training and instruction, social support, and positive feedback were significantly related to satisfaction with the three leader behaviors, respectively. The higher the perception of those behaviors relative to the preferences, the higher the satisfaction. Schliesman noted that the perceived democratic behavior and social support were slightly better predictors of satisfaction with general leadership than the corresponding discrepancy scores.

In examining the relationship of university basketball players' perceptions of their coaches' behavior on the LSS dimensions with various aspects of satisfaction, Weiss and Friedrichs (1986) found that when the teams were the units of analyses (i.e., all variables were averaged over a team), perceived leadership (the five dimensions taken together) was predictive of *team satisfaction*. Positive feedback was the most predictive of team satisfaction. With the individual as the unit of analysis, the leadership variables collectively contributed to *athlete satisfaction*. However, only the unique contributions of perceived democratic behavior and social support were significant. Interestingly perceived social support was most strongly, but negatively, associated with athlete satisfaction.

Dwyer and Fischer (1990) found that their wrestlers were more satisfied with coaches if the coaches were perceived to exhibit higher levels of positive feedback, training, and instruction, and lower levels of autocratic behavior. That is, perceived democratic behavior or social support did not contribute significantly to explained variance in satisfaction with leadership.

In a comparison of Japanese and Canadian university athletes, Chelladurai et al. (1988) found that the Canadian athletes were more satisfied with both leadership and personal outcome than the Japanese athletes. Further, the perceived scores in all 5 dimensions of LSS were significantly correlated with *satisfaction with leadership* in both sets of data. The higher the perceived score (except in autocratic behavior), the higher the satisfaction with leadership. On the other hand, perceived leadership in all dimensions except positive feedback was correlated with *personal outcome* in the Japanese data, while only perceived training and instruction was associated with the same criterion in the Canadian data. In addition to the above, there were also differences in the magnitude of the simple correlations, multiple correlations, and unique variances attributable to the independent variables. Based on these, Chelladurai et al. (1988) concluded that their results "were more supportive of the cultural-influence hypothesis than of the athletic-influence hypothesis" (p. 374).

Summers (1983) administered the items from the 3 scales—training and instruction, social support, and positive feedback—to 128 lacrosse players. Consistent with theoretical expectations, his results showed that *athlete satisfaction* was positively correlated with perceived behavior in all 3 dimensions of leader behavior. Further, as perceived ability increased, (a) the association between social support and players' satisfaction increased, and (b) the relationship between training and instruction and *performance* decreased.

In a study of 131 university-level soccer players, McMillin (1990) found that athletes' perceptions of leader behaviors in all the LSS dimensions were significantly related to their *satisfaction with leadership*. Training and instruction ($R^2 = .44$) and democratic behavior ($R^2 = .12$) contributed the most to the total explained variance ($R^2 = .59$). However, perceived leadership did not have any significant effect on *satisfaction with personal outcome* as measured by Chelladurai et al.'s (1988) Satisfaction Scale for Athletes (SSA).

In general, the foregoing results indicate that athletes are satisfied with leadership to the extent that the coach emphasizes (a) training and instruction that enhance the ability and coordinated effort by members, which in turn contributes to task accomplishment; and (b) positive feedback that recognizes and rewards good performance. These results are consistent with theoretical expectations relating to an achievement-oriented situation such as athletics.

Performance as a consequence of leadership has been inadequately dealt with in the literature. In the previously cited Weiss and Friedrichs's (1986) study of American university basketball players, their perceptions of their coaches' behavior on the LSS dimensions were associated with performance. When the teams were the units of analysis (i.e., all variables were averaged over a team), perceived leadership (the 5 dimensions taken together) was predictive of win/loss percentage. Perceived social support was most strongly, but negatively, associated with win/loss percentage (i.e., higher levels of social support were associated with lower win/loss percentages).

In the Canadian context, Gordon (1986) found that university soccer players from more successful teams perceived more training, autocratic, social support, and positive feedback behaviors in their coaches than players from less successful teams. Also, players' perceptions of both training and positive feedback were closely associated with several measures of coaching effectiveness. In Horne and Carron's (1985) study, the athletes' perceptions of positive feedback were positively correlated with their *perceptions of their own performance*.

From an international perspective, Serpa, Pataco, and Santos (1989) found that members of the best among the 8 handball teams participating in 1988 World Championships (Group C) relative to members of the last-placed team perceived their coach to be emphasizing significantly more autocratic behavior, and significantly less rewarding behavior, social support, and democratic behavior. There was no difference in perceived training and instruction. It is not clear whether the differences in the coaching behaviors led to the performance differential, or whether coaches tend to alter their behaviors according to the performance level of the teams.

As for *coach-athlete compatibility*, Horne and Carron (1985) found that the discrepancy between athletes' perceptions and their preferences for positive feedback and autocratic behavior were the best discriminators of compatible and incompatible dyads. The athletes in compatible dyads perceived their coaches to provide positive feedback equal to or higher than their preferences, and to be autocratic to a lower degree than their preferences. The authors concluded that "it might be best to use the Leadership Scale for Sports in future studies of coach-athlete compatibility" (p. 147).

COMMENTARY

The foregoing review shows that these studies have been piecemeal in that only segments of the multidimensional model have been tested. While such an approach is appropriate in the early stages, it is important that the model's causal linkages be tested in more comprehensive studies employing more sophisticated procedures (e.g., path-analysis, structural equation models).

It is also important that the measurement of the leadership variables of the model be made more reliable and valid. While the acceptance of a 5-factor solution of the original 99 items modified from scales from business and industry was based on an implicit theory (Chelladurai, 1978, 1981; Chelladurai & Saleh, 1980), future research could focus on generating items based on the experiences and insights of both coaches and athletes. Such an exercise might lead to refinements in the existing subscales with new and more meaningful items, and/or the delineation of additional leadership dimensions.

For instance, Serpa (1990) and his associates are presently engaged in developing a scale to measure coaching behaviors that may lead to an anxious mental state among athletes, which, in turn, may affect their performance. After brainstorming and exploratory interviews, they have developed the initial version of a scale called Anxiogenic Behavior Questionnaire (ABQ), with 39 items measuring 8 dimensions of anxiety-producing behaviors. The major implication of their project is that any investigation of coaching behavior must assess not only the high or low levels of positive behaviors exhibited by the coach, but also the extent to which a coach engages in negative behaviors.

Another measurement issue relates to the response categories of the LSS items which refer to the frequencies of leader behaviors and not to the context of such behaviors. For instance, two coaches may be democratic to the same extent in two different sets of circumstances. We must keep in mind that the LSS does not tap these contextual differences. One way to avoid this difficulty would be to append the context to the LSS items. Thus, for example, the statement "I prefer my coach to let athletes share in decision making" is not as informative as "I prefer my coach to let athletes share in decision making regarding practice sessions (or game strategies)."

The operationalization of preferred and actual leader behaviors has been in the tradition of research in industry and business. When the team is the unit of analysis, it is customary to treat the average preferences or perceptions of the team members as the team values for preferred and actual leader behaviors, respectively (e.g., Chelladurai, 1978; Weiss & Friedrichs, 1986). When the individual athlete is the unit of analysis, then the individual preferences and perceptions constitute the preferred and actual leader behaviors (e.g., Chelladurai, 1984). Even when the individual is the unit of analysis, the coach's behavior toward the individual is not fully captured because several of the items in the LSS refer to the behaviors of the coach toward the group as a whole, and not toward the individual per se.

The operationalization of required leader behavior is even more problematic. There has been only one attempt to operationalize required leader behavior (Chelladurai, 1978). The average of the preferences of all subjects from a sport (basketball, in this instance) was used as required leader behavior. Chelladurai argued that since the influences of individual differences on preferred leadership would cancel out when computing the mean score, the average of members' preferences would represent the influences of the macrovariables. Following the same reasoning, an alternate measure of required leader behavior would be the average of the self-reported behaviors of a significant number of successful coaches in a sport.

Finally, while the multidimensional model's notion of congruency (or discrepancy) among the three states of leader behavior is theoretically sound, there has been criticism of the use of discrepancy scores (e.g., Johns, 1981). When both components of the discrepancy score (perceptions and preferences, in our context) are provided by the same subject, "subordinate's [athletes'] perceptions can dominate in those relationships" (White, Crino, & Hatfield, 1985, p. 736). For instance, Chelladurai et al. (1988) found that the perceived leadership scores explained more variance in athletes' satisfactions than the discrepancy scores; therefore, they did not use the discrepancy scores. Schliesman (1986) also found that the perceived democratic behavior and social support were slightly better predictors of satisfaction with general leadership than discrepancy scores. In contrast, Chelladurai (1984) found that the discrepancy scores explained a greater percentage of the variance in athlete satisfaction than either the preferred or perceived leadership scores. Given these equivocal results, researchers would be well advised to be cautious in the use of discrepancy scores.

Instead of requiring the subjects to provide the two independent scores, they could be asked to indicate directly the degree of difference between preferred and perceived leader behaviors (e.g., "much more than I prefer" or "much less than I prefer"). When two individuals (e.g., the coach and the player) provide the component scores, the research question could be reframed to avoid the use of discrepancy scores (Johns, 1981). For instance, the question "Does the athlete's preferred leadership influence athlete satisfaction over and above the coach's expressed leadership?" could be answered through a hierarchical multiple regression analyses without the use of discrepancy terms. Finally, a minimally acceptable approach would be to identify and use that set of scores (preferred, perceived, or discrepancy scores) that account for the greatest amount of variance in the dependent variable(s). At any rate, if difference scores are to be used, it is incumbent on the researcher to report the reliabilities of the discrepancy scores. Further, Johns (1981) suggested that algebraic rather than absolute differences be used.

LEADERSHIP IN YOUTH SPORTS

As noted earlier, another distinct and significant approach to study of leadership is that of Smith and Smoll and their associates (Curtis, Smith, & Smoll, 1979; Smith &

Smoll, 1990; Smith, Smoll, & Curtis, 1978, 1979; Smith, Smoll, & Hunt, 1977a; Smith, Smoll, Hunt, Curtis, & Coppel, 1979; Smith, Zane, Smoll, & Coppel, 1983; Smoll & Smith, 1984, 1989; Smoll, Smith, Curtis, & Hunt, 1978). The distinguishing features of their approach are (a) their mediational model of coaching behaviors, (b) their focus on youth sport, (c) the more elaborate description of leader behaviors, (d) the use of observational measures of leader behaviors in addition to the conventional paper-and-pencil tests, and (e) the emphasis on players' evaluative reactions as the outcome measures.

The Mediational Model

The original and basic model consisted of three elements: *coach behaviors, player perception and recall,* and *player's evaluative reactions.* According to the model, players' attitudes toward their coach and their sport experience are mediated by their perception and recall of the coaches' behaviors. A more elaborate version of this basic model, outlined by Smoll and Smith (1989), is shown in Figure 30–3.

The three fundamental elements of coach behaviors, player perception and recall, and player's evaluative reactions are affected by three sets of factors: *coach individual difference variables, player individual difference variables,* and *situational factors.*

Coach Individual Difference Variables. The individual difference factors include (a) the coach's goals, (b) behavioral intentions (i.e., the antecedents of actual behavior),

(c) instrumentalities (which are a function of the perceived probability of an outcome and the value attached to that outcome), (d) the norms associated with the coaching role, (e) the coach's perceptions of players' motives, (f) self-monitoring (the extent to which the coach analyzes his or her own behavior and its consequences), and (g) the sex of the coach.

Player Individual Difference Variables. The player individual difference variables included in the model are (a) age which has been shown to affect players' perceptions and evaluations of the coaches, (b) the sex of the player, (c) the player's perception of coaching norms, (d) the valence a player attaches to various coaching behaviors, (e) the player's achievement motive in the sporting context, (f) competitive trait anxiety, (g) general self-esteem, defined as one's evaluation of general self-worth, and (h) athletic self-esteem, defined as the individual's evaluation of himself or herself as an athlete.

The Situational Factors. The situational factors affect both coaches' behaviors, and players' perceptions of those behaviors and reactions to them. These factors include (a) the nature of the sport, (b) the level of competition (e.g., competitive versus recreational sport), (c) practice versus game sessions, (d) the previous success/failure record of the team, (e) present game/practice developments (e.g., Is the team losing or winning?), and (f) intrateam attraction.

While several of the variables outlined in the model are yet to be verified and/or measured, the basic variables of (a) the overt behaviors of the coach, (b) player's recall of

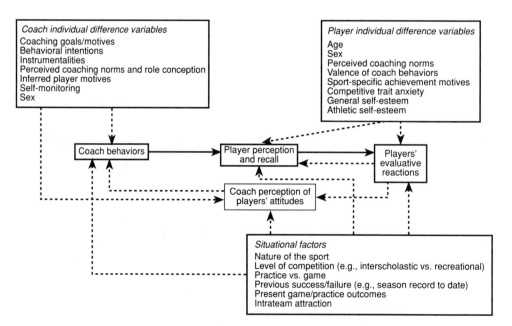

FIGURE 30–3. The mediational model of leadership. From "Leadership behaviors in sport: A theoretical model and research paradigm" by F. L. Smoll and R. E. Smith, 1989, *Journal of Applied Social Psychology,* 19 (18), 1522-1551. Used by permission.

coaching behaviors, and (c) player reactions to coaching and sport experience have been well defined and measured. The methods of measuring the above components are briefly described below.

Measurement of Key Variables

The model emphasizes that the actual leader behaviors as well as the players' perception and recall of those behaviors should be measured. Accordingly, Smith, Smoll, and their associates adopted the observational method to assess the actual leader behavior, and the paper-and-pencil method to assess player perception and recall of that leader behavior. In addition, they also employed the paper-and-pencil method to assess coaches' perceptions of their own behaviors. These three measures are described below.

Observed Leader Behavior. The noteworthy feature of their system is the way actual leadership is measured; they took the approach of observing and coding those behaviors.

The attractiveness of this approach is that it provides a promising methodological alternative to reliance on questionnaires that may well measure the respondent's perceptions and attitudes rather than actual leadership behaviors. Behavioral assessment provides a means of observing and measuring leadership behaviors in naturalistic settings. (Smoll and Smith, 1989, p. 1524)

The Coaching Behavior Assessment System (CBAS) was developed over several years by observing and recording the behaviors of youth soccer basketball and baseball coaches, analyzing these recordings, and categorizing the relevant leader behaviors (Smith, Smoll, & Hunt, 1977a). Subsequent use of the system in coding the behaviors of coaches in basketball, baseball, and football indicated

that the scoring system is sufficiently comprehensive to incorporate the vast majority of coaching behaviors, that individual differences in behavioral patterns can be discerned, and that the coding system can be used easily in field settings. (Smith, Smoll, Hunt, Curtis, & Coppel, 1979, p. 113)

The 12 behavioral dimensions measured by the CBAS (described in Table 30-3) are broadly classified into *reactive* and *spontaneous* behaviors. Reactive behaviors are the coach's responses to (a) desirable performance or effort, (b) mistakes and errors, and (c) misbehaviors. Spontaneous behaviors may be (a) game-related, or (b) game-irrelevant.

Typically, several trained observers record the behaviors of the coaches, noting the situations in which they occurred on portable tape recorders. The training of the observers has been quite extensive. For example, Smith, Zane, Smoll, & Coppel (1983) subjected their observers (7 males and 10 females) to a 4-week training which included:

1. extended study of a training manual, including a programmed learning module (Smith, Smoll, & Hunt, 1977b);

TABLE 30-3. Response categories of the coaching behavior assessment system

Class I: Reactive Behaviors	
Responses to Desirable Performance	
Reinforcement	A positive, rewarding reaction, verbal or nonverbal, to a good play or good effort.
Nonreinforcement	Failure to respond to good performance.
Responses to Mistakes	
Mistake-contingent encouragement	Encouragement given to a player following a mistake.
Mistake-contingent technical instruction	Instructing or demonstrating to a player how to correct a mistake.
Punishment	A negative reaction, verbal or nonverbal, following a mistake.
Punitive technical instruction	Technical instruction given in a punitive or hostile manner following a mistake.
Ignoring mistakes	Failure to respond to a player mistake.
Response to Misbehavior	
Keeping control	Reactions intended to restore or maintain order among team members.
Class II: Spontaneous Behaviors	
Game-Related	
General technical instruction	Spontaneous instruction in the techniques and strategies of the sport (not following a mistake).
General encouragement	Spontaneous encouragement that does not follow a mistake.
Organization	Administrative behavior that sets the stage for play by assigning duties, responsibilities, positions, etc.
Game-Irrelevant	
General communication	Interactions with players unrelated to the game.

From "A system for the behavioral assessment of athletic coaches" by Ronald E. Smith, Frank L. Smoll, & Earl Hunt (1977), *The Research Quarterly*, 48, 401-407. Used by permission.

2. group instruction in use of the coding system, including viewing and discussion of a training videotape (Smith, Smoll, Hunt, & Clarke, 1976);
3. written tests in which trainees were required to define the CBAS categories and score behavioral examples;
4. the scoring of videotaped sequences of a total of 40 randomly ordered coaching behaviors, 4 from each of 10 categories included in that study; and
5. practice and reliability check conducted during basketball games in a program other than the one involved in the main phase of their study.

The scoring by the 17 trainees of the videotaped sequences agreed with those of the experts over 90% of the time. The correlations of the frequencies of leader behaviors observed in a field setting by an observer and an expert across the 10 behavioral dimensions included in the study ranged from .85 to .98, with a median of .96. In this particular study (Smith et al., 1983), two of the categories of the CBAS—Nonreinforcement and Ignoring Mistakes—were omitted because of the difficulty in scoring them in the sport of basketball.

Earlier, Smith, Smoll, and Hunt (1977a) reported that the agreement rate between the coding of 48 randomly ordered videotape sequences of coaching behaviors by 31 trainees and the codings by experts (i.e., two of the authors) was 97.8%. The consistency of coding over time was assessed by asking 24 of the trainees to code the same 48 coaching behavior sequences a second time after one week. The agreement rate between the first and second codings ranged from 87.5% to 100%, with a mean of 96.4%. These authors also reported the results of two other field studies in which the correlation of the coding frequencies of two observers was computed as an index of the inter-rater reliability. In the first study, in which 5 trainees observed the behaviors of a female Little League baseball coach during a 6-inning game, the inter-rater reliability ranged from .77 to .99, with a mean of .88. In the second study, the mean inter-rater reliability among 19 trainees coding the behaviors of a male Little League coach ranged from .50 to .99, with a mean of .88. These high values allow us to place greater confidence in the CBAS.

Players' Perceptions of Coaches' Behaviors. A questionnaire was used to assess players' perception and recall of coaches' behaviors. The players were provided a description and an example of each of the 12 behavioral dimensions of the CBAS. The players were asked to indicate the extent to which their coaches had engaged in each of the behaviors using 7-point scales ranging from *almost never* to *almost always.*

Coaches' Perceptions of Their Own Behaviors. As in the case of the players, coaches were also given a description and example of each of the 12 CBAS categories, and were asked to indicate the extent to which they had engaged in each of those behavior categories on 7-point scales ranging from *almost never* to *almost always.*

Relationships Among Measures of Coach Behavior. As outlined above, coach behaviors have been measured in three different ways: direct observation, coaches' self-perceptions of their own behaviors, and players' perceptions of their coaches' behaviors. Although the target of these measures is the coaches' behaviors, the relationships among them were found to be weak except in the case of observed behaviors and players' recall of those behaviors.

Based on rank-order correlations ($r = .78$) between observed frequencies of coaching behaviors in the 12 categories and players' recall of those behaviors, Smoll, Smith, Curtis, and Hunt (1978) concluded that

aside from keeping control (or maintaining order), which was re-

ported to occur more frequently by the players than it actually did, the relative frequencies of occurrence of behaviors corresponded rather closely with players' perceptions. (p. 534)

However, another set of analyses showed that observed behaviors and players' perceptions were not that closely related. First, the factor structures of the observed behaviors and the player-perceived behaviors were different from each other. In the case of observed behaviors, 4 factors emerged. They were (a) *punitiveness* (positive loadings of punishment, punitive technical instruction, and giving general encouragement versus negative loadings of keeping control and organization), (b) *supportiveness* (positive loadings of reinforcement and mistake-contingent encouragement), (c) *instructiveness* (positive loadings of mistake-contingent technical instruction and general technical instruction and negative loadings of general encouragement and general communication) and (d) *responsiveness* (negative loadings of nonreinforcement and ignoring mistakes).

The factor analysis of the player-perceived behaviors yielded three factors. These were (a) *supportiveness and spontaneity* (positive loadings of reinforcement, keeping control, general technical information, and general encouragement), (b) *punitiveness* (positive loadings of nonreinforcement, punishment, and punitive technical instruction, and (c) *correctiveness* (positive loading of mistake-contingent technical instruction and negative loading of ignoring mistakes). Thus:

Although there are areas of correspondence between observed and perceived behaviors, the factor analytic data indicate that the pattern of overt behaviors is different from the organization of perceived behaviors. (Smoll et al., 1978, p. 538)

The foregoing view is supported by the fact that the factor scores derived from the CBAS observations and player perceptions individually explained 21% and 24%, respectively, of the variance in players' attraction to coach, and they jointly explained 42% of the variance. That is, the contributions of the two sets of measures to player attitudes are unique and distinct. Based on these results, the authors recommended that both behavioral and perceptual data be collected.

In another study, Smith, Smoll, and Curtis (1978) reported that the correlations of coaches' self-reports of their behaviors correlated very minimally with overt CBAS measures. The only significant correlation was between coaches' self-perceptions and CBAS assessment of punishment ($r = .45$). On the other hand, players' perceptions and CBAS measures correlated significantly in several categories—punishment ($r = .54$), punitive technical instruction ($r = .37$), mistake-contingent technical instruction ($r = .31$), and general communication ($r = .26$).

Overall, these results clearly indicate that coaches were not aware of the extent to which they engaged in various categories of behavior. In other words, coaches' self-reports of their behaviors did not bear much resemblance to the assessment made either by observers or by players. Therefore, the use of coaches' self-reports of their behavior should be viewed with extreme caution.

Interestingly, Smith, Smoll, and Curtis (1978) found that coaches perceived themselves to be behaving in ways that would facilitate the attainment of their coaching objectives. In this study, coaches were asked to indicate which of each pair of 8 goals was more important to them. The 8 goals were (a) developing good qualities in youngsters, (b) [developing] interest in the sport, (c) developing a winning team, (d) providing a recreational experience for the children, (e) teaching players to master techniques, (f) working with youngsters, (g) being involved in an enjoyable leisure-time activity, and (h) giving leadership and direction to others. The coaches were also asked to indicate the extent to which each of the 12 CBAS behaviors was instrumental to each of the 8 goals on a 7-point scale ranging from very negative (-3) to very positive ($+3$). The authors derived an instrumentality measure for each of the 12 CBAS measures by multiplying the "coach's importance scores of each of the 8 coaching goals [Value] and the coach's rating of the instrumentality of each behavior in attaining that goal [Expectancy]" (p. 187). Noting that this $E \times V$ instrumentality measure correlated significantly and very highly with coaches' perceptions of their own behaviors (mean $r = .42$), these authors concluded

It thus appears that the perceived instrumentality of behavior as measured in this study is related only to the coaches' cognitive representations of their own behavior. Coaches believe that they are behaving in a way that will be instrumental in achieving their goals,

but this rationality is not reflected in the eyes of other beholders. (p. 187)

Players' Evaluative Reactions. Consistent with the notion that youth sports is largely developmental in nature, Smith, Smoll, and their associates focused on players' attitudes toward their coaches, their teammates, themselves, and their playing experience as the critical outcome. These player evaluative reactions were measured by a 10-item scale shown in Table 30–4. Players were required to respond to each item on a 7-point scale. The anchors for each item are also shown in Table 30–4.

Smoll, Smith, Curtis, and Hunt (1978) reported that all items referring to the attraction of the coach loaded highly on the first of two factors which explained 50.8% of the variance. The second factor accounting for 11.5% variance included "items dealing with attraction toward and cooperation among teammates and, to a lesser extent, liking for the sport" (p. 537).

Research Based on CBAS

The research based on the CBAS is reported under three headings. These include (a) general player attitudes, (b) player self-esteem and coach behavior, and (c) effects of training coaches.

Coach Behavior and Player Attitudes. In the first study based on the CBAS, Smith, Smoll, and Curtis (1978) observed 51 Little League Baseball coaches over 202 games, and coded an average of 1,112 behaviors for each coach. In

TABLE 30–4. Scale measuring players evaluative reactions

	Dislike a lot						Like a lot
How much do you like baseball?	1	2	3	4	5	6	7
How much did you like playing for your coach?	1	2	3	4	5	6	7
How much would you like to have the same coach again next year?	1	2	3	4	5	6	7
How much do you like your coach?	1	2	3	4	5	6	7
How much do your parents like your coach?	1	2	3	4	5	6	7
How much does your coach like you?	1	2	3	4	5	6	7
	Much less						Much more
Do you like baseball more or less than you did at the beginning of the season?	1	2	3	4	5	6	7
	Almost nothing						Almost everything
How much does your coach know about baseball?	1	2	3	4	5	6	7
	Very poorly						Very well
How well did the players on your team get along?	1	2	3	4	5	6	7
	Very poorly						Very well
How well did you like the other players on your team?	1	2	3	4	5	6	7

From "Toward a mediational model of coach-player relationships" by Frank L. Smoll, Ronald E. Smith, Bill Curtis, & Earl Hunt (1978). *The Research Quarterly*, 49, 528–541. Used by permission.

addition to these observed behaviors, the coaches' perceptions of their own behaviors, players' ($N = 542$) perceptions
of coaches' behaviors, and players' postseason attitudes
were also measured through paper-and-pencil tests described above. The results showed that the observed behavioral dimensions of *supportiveness* (high loadings of
reinforcement and mistake-contingent encouragement)
and *instructiveness* (general technical instruction and
mistake-contingent instruction) were significantly and positively related to players' attitudes toward the coach, the
sport, and teammates.

Leader behaviors as perceived by the players were also
associated with the outcome measures. More specifically,
technical instruction and both encouragement categories
were positively related to attitude toward the coach,
whereas punishment and punitive technical instruction had
the opposite effect.

In another study of the consequences of coaching behaviors in basketball, Smith, Zane, Smoll, and Coppel (1983)
found in general that coaching behaviors affected postseason players' liking for basketball, their perceptions of
team solidarity, their evaluation of their coaches, and their
self-esteem. However, coaching behaviors affected the attitudes toward the coach and sport to a greater extent than
they affected perceived team solidarity and players' self-
esteem. Further, general technical instruction was found to
be the more potent behavioral category than the other categories. On the other hand, positive reinforcement, mistake-
contingent encouragement, punitive technical instruction,
organization, and general communication were minimally
related to any of the postseason player variables. The most
surprising result was the minimal effect of positive
reinforcement.

Coach Behavior and Player Self-Esteem. Player self-
esteem has been used both as (a) a moderator of the relationship between coach behavior and player attitudes, and
(b) an outcome measure (Smith, Smoll, & Curtis, 1978).
These authors derived a 14-item measure of general self-
esteem from Coopersmith's (1967) Self-Esteem Inventory.
The response format was a 5-point scale ranging from "Not
at all like me" to "Very much like me." Six of these items
were keyed negatively. This scale's internal consistency
(Cronbach's alpha) and test-retest reliability over 12
months were reported to be .86 and .65, respectively. Another set of 11-point items assessing players' evaluations of
themselves on 10 specific abilities was also used. The particular item measuring "ability in baseball" was the surro-
gate measure of "self-esteem relative to that sport." The
complete scale and the items have not been published
so far.

In the previously cited study by Smith, Smoll, and Curtis
(1978), it was found that a player's self-esteem moderated
the attitudinal responses to coaches. That is,

the low self-esteem child responds most positively to a supportive
or instructive coach-player relationship, or, on the other hand, most
negatively to coaches who are not supportive or instructive. Coach-

ing behaviors had far less impact on high self-esteem children.
(Smoll & Smith, 1989, p. 1531)

In a later study, Smith and Smoll (1990) suggested that
the moderating effects of player self-esteem on the relationship between coach behaviors and player attraction to the
coach can best be understood from the perspective of self-
enhancement theories. Noting that self-enhancement
needs are higher for low self-esteem individuals, they argued that

we might expect, on self-enhancement grounds, that low-self-
esteem people will be especially attracted not only to those who respond to them in a supportive fashion but also to those who try to
help them become more competent. (p. 988)

In reanalyzing the data of Smith, Smoll, and Curtis (1978),
it was found that the above hypothesis was largely supported. Multiple regression analyses clearly showed that
the low-self-esteem subjects who had supportive and instructive coaches expressed the highest levels of attraction
toward the coaches, while the low-self-esteem players who
had less supportive and less instructive coaches expressed
the least amount of attraction to the coaches. Those subjects who were moderate or high on self-esteem were not affected to the same extent by the variations in coaches'
supportiveness or instructiveness.

As for self-esteem as an outcome, Smith, Smoll, and
Curtis (1979) subjected some of the Little League Baseball
coaches (18 from a sample of 31 coaches) to a training program designed to assist them in relating more effectively to
children. Their results showed that the children playing for
the trained coaches exhibited higher levels of self-esteem
than they had a year before. Such increases were not found
among children playing for the nontrained coaches.

Smith, Zane, Smoll, and Coppel (1983) found that only
general technical instruction was negatively related to basketball players' post-season self-esteem. Smith et al. (1983)
offered two explanations for the negative relationship
between general technical instruction and players'
self-esteem.

In the case of self-esteem, teams having players low in self-esteem
may also be low in ability and in need of much technical instruction. On the other hand, high rates of technical instruction may
serve to lower self-esteem by calling attention to the discrepancy
between current play and the desired level of performance. (p.
213)

That low ability (and therefore low self-esteem) members may receive higher levels of instructions is supported
by the findings of Rejeski, Darracott, and Hutslar (1979).
They investigated the "Pygmalion" effects in coaching (i.e.,
whether coaches varied their behaviors according to their
perceptions of players' abilities). Fourteen basketball
coaches of male teams from a community league for children of ages 8 to 15 were observed and coded on the CBAS
behavioral categories for 2 halves of a game and 1 practice

over a period of 3 weeks. At the end of the observational period, the coaches were asked to rank their players on ability. The three top-ranked players and the three bottom-ranked players from each team constituted the two comparison groups (high- and low-expectancy).

The results showed that "low-expectancy children received more general technical information and encountered fewer situations of nonreinforcement than high-expectancy children" (pp. 315–316). Also, although high-expectancy children were reinforced more, they experienced higher levels of nonreinforcement than the low-expectancy children. Based on these results, Rejeski et al. (1979) concluded that coaches, rather than intentionally ignoring low-ability children, simply look for specific correct responses and do not adjust standards for individual abilities. Rejeski et al. continued to advocate that coaches adjust expected criteria based on individual abilities.

In another related study, Horn (1985) investigated the relationship between coaching behaviors (as assessed by the CBAS) on changes in self-perceptions of 72 female junior high school baseball players regarding their competence (cognitive, social, and physical), and their expectations for future athletic success. She also used a measure of a player's ability derived from the estimates of her teammates. A coach's behaviors toward each athlete during games and practices were observed and related to changes in that athlete's self-perceptions of competence, control, and success expectancy. The results showed that the coaching behaviors during games were qualitatively different from the coaching behaviors during practice sessions. That is, the coaches provided more reinforcement and ignored less the successful player performances (i.e., lower frequency of nonreinforcement) during games than in practices. More important, coaching behaviors during practices were significantly associated with changes in players' perceptions of their physical and cognitive competence, and success expectancy. Also, these effects were significant even after controlling for the effects of players' actual ability.

Training Effects on Coach Behavior. The purpose of Smith, Smoll, and Curtis's (1979) research was to train coaches to improve their behaviors, assess their behaviors, and measure the effects of changes in coaching behaviors on players' evaluative reactions. They divided 31 Little League baseball coaches into two random groups, and engaged one group (n = 18) in a preseason training program designed to increase their ability to interact more positively with their players. The three-hour Coach Effectiveness Training program included the presentation of coaching behavior guidelines, and instructed the coaches in behavioral feedback and self-monitoring procedures (see Smoll & Smith, 1980). At the end of the season, 325 players under the charge of the sample of coaches were interviewed. The results showed that the trained group of coaches differed from the control group in observed as well as perceived behaviors. That is, the former group engaged in behaviors consistent with the training program. Further, the players of the trained coaches evaluated

their coaches more positively than the players of untrained coaches. Players of the trained coaches also expressed higher levels of intrateam attraction than the players of the control group of coaches. However, the two groups did not differ in performance as measured by win/loss. The authors concluded that the training programs changed the coaching behaviors both quantitatively and qualitatively, which in turn enhanced players' enjoyment and satisfaction, and their evaluations of their coaches.

Commentary

The distinguishing feature of the Smith and Smoll approach is the manner in which leader behavior is measured—the observational method of the CBAS versus the paper-and-pencil method employed in Chelladurai and Saleh's (1980) Leadership Scale for Sports (LSS). However, a comparison of leadership behavior categories of the two systems shows that they are to a large extent similar in content, although the titles are different. The correspondence between the two systems is shown in Table 30–5.

For example, the reinforcement and nonreinforcement categories in CBAS resemble the LSS dimension of positive feedback; the mistake contingent technical instruction, general technical instruction, and organization are subsumed by the LSS dimension of training and instruction; and general communication is similar to social support in the LSS. In spite of these similarities, the CBAS is distinct in two significant respects. First, the larger number of categories in the CBAS permits a more thorough analysis of leadership in youth sports. This is consistent with the trend in organizational behavior research. For example, Yukl (1981) noted the advantage of describing leadership in terms of more categories in developing his paper-and-pencil *Managerial Behavior Survey (MBS),* which measures 19 dimensions of leader behavior. Apart from this advantage, the CBAS also measures leader behavior in more specific situa-

TABLE 30–5. Approximate Correspondence Between CBAS and LSS Leadership Categories

CBAS Categories	LSS Categories
Reinforcement	Positive feedback
Nonreinforcement	Positive feedback (lack of)
Mistake-contingent encouragement	???
Mistake-contingent technical instruction	Training and instruction
Punishment	???
Punitive technical instruction	Training and instruction
Ignoring mistakes	???
Keeping control	Training and instruction
General technical instruction	Training and instruction
General encouragement	Positive feedback
Organization	Training and instruction
General communication	Social support
???	Democratic behavior
???	Autocratic behavior

tions. For example, although "encouragement" from CBAS is subsumed by the "positive feedback" in the LSS, encouragement is divided into reactive mistake-contingent behavior and spontaneous general encouragement. Thus, the categorization of leader behavior in the CBAS is more elaborate and situation specific. On the other hand, the CBAS does not tap into the extent to which a coach allows his or her athletes to participate in decision making, as is done by the LSS dimensions of democratic and autocratic behaviors.

Smith and Smoll (1990), in outlining the methodological limitations of CBAS, noted that "the CBAS is a broadband coding system that does not presently make distinctions between other potentially important aspects of coaching behaviors, such as verbal and nonverbal responses, magnitude of reinforcement, quality and duration of instruction, and so forth" (p. 991). Also, they suggested that the coding procedures assess the coach's responses to the team as a whole. That is, coach's reactions and behaviors to individual players are not recorded.

Thus our behavioral data are most properly interpreted as assessing differences in the type of general social environment produced by the coaches' behaviors. Studies with finer-grained analyses of the specific interaction patterns created by coaching behaviors are clearly needed. (1990, pp. 991–992)

It must be noted that the foregoing limitations are equally applicable to the LSS dimensions of leader behavior and the paper-and-pencil method of measuring those dimensions.

DECISION STYLES IN COACHING

An important component of leadership is decision making, which is defined as the process of selecting an alternative from among many choices to achieve a desired end. Coaching effectiveness is heavily dependent on the quality of these decisions, and the degree to which these decisions are accepted and executed by the athletes. The quality of a decision is ensured by (a) clearly defining the problem, (b) identifying the opportunities and constraints, (c) setting criteria for selecting an appropriate course of action from among many, (d) generating many alternatives to solve the problem or achieve a goal, (e) evaluating these alternatives on the criteria specified earlier, and (f) selecting the alternative which best fits the criteria. These steps are purported to ensure the rationality of the decisions. They require adequate information, ingenuity, creativity, and innovation on the part of the decision makers. This aspect of decision making is properly called the *cognitive process*.

There is another dimension to decision making which is equally important. It is the *social process* by which the leader allows the members to participate in decision making. The significance of this dimension is highlighted by the fact that it is the members who have to execute the decisions. To the extent that members understand a decision, they will carry it out more effectively. The understanding of the decision is facilitated by member participation in deci-

sion making. Moreover, such participation allows members to feel that it is their decision. Such feelings of ownership lead to greater acceptance of the decision and, therefore, more efficient execution of it.

In addition, in so far as there tends to be more information in a group, participation contributes to the quality of the decision. The availability of more information in the group permits the generation and scrutiny of several alternatives to solve a problem. Also, the divergent orientations of members lead to original and creative solutions to problems. Finally, and more important, an individual's feelings of self-determination arising out of participation in decisions relating the goals and standards of achievement enhance that individual's intrinsic motivation.

While the above advantages point to a participative style, the disadvantages inherent in group decisions may deter a coach from adopting such a style for day-to-day decisions. The first and obvious drawback is that group decisions take time—a scarce commodity. We are all familiar with the inordinate delays due to the discussions and arguments that are an integral part of group decisions. Second, groups cannot adequately handle a complex problem that requires thinking through a number of factors, and a series of steps to link them. For example, the final selection of a soccer team should be based on the talents, skills, and personalities of the players, the compatibility of these individual differences among the players, the suitability of these factors to the strategies and tactics to be employed, and players' acceptance of the coach's leadership and decision-making styles. In this situation, the best individual in the group (presumably the coach) is more likely to make an optimal decision than is the entire group.

Finally, participation in decision making is likely to be effective only if the group is integrated (i.e., the team is characterized by quality interpersonal relations and a lack of conflict). Lack of integration may lead to one of two negative consequences. In a newly formed group, members may "smooth" over different viewpoints in order to establish interaction patterns among themselves. Such a tendency may result in compromise solutions. The other possibility is that the group is characterized by rivalry and internal conflicts. If so, participation by members is not likely to result in optimal decisions. On the other hand, such participation may indeed aggravate the negative climate within the group.

The focus of this section is on the social processes of decision making in coaching. The early writers on this topic noted that traditional coaching practices and values are dehumanizing, and that coaches themselves tend to be insensitive and autocratic (Hendry, 1974; Ogilvie & Tutko, 1966). The purported autocratic orientation was also attributed to personality (Hendry, 1974; Ogilvie & Tutko, 1966; Tutko & Richards, 1971). As a reaction to this view of coaches and their autocratic orientation, scholars like Sage (1973) have advocated a participative approach in coaching. Unfortunately, neither of these viewpoints has taken into account the nature of the problem or the situation in which it occurs. As Maier (1974), Tannenbaum and Schmidt (1973), and Vroom and Yetton (1973) have cogently argued, it is the content and context of the problem that should be the determinant of the particular social process employed. The studies that have been carried out from this perspective are reviewed below.

The Normative Model of Decision Styles in Coaching

Based partly on the works of Vroom and Jago (1974) and Vroom and Yetton (1973) and partly on heuristics, Chelladurai and Haggerty (1978) proposed the normative model of decision styles coaching which is illustrated in Figure 30–4.

Decision styles. The model included the following three decision styles. In the *autocratic decision style,* the final decision is actually made by the coach who may consult one or more members in an attempt to gather information regarding the problem. The *participative decision style* is when the actual decision is made by the group including the coach. The influence of the coach is reduced to that of another member. In the *delegative decision style,* the coach delegates the authority to make the decision to one or more members. The coach's involvement is restricted to announcing or implementing the decision.

Problem Attributes. According to the model, the use of one of the above decision styles in solving a problem is contingent upon the configuration of the attributes of that problem. The attributes incorporated in the model are shown in Table 30–6.

The complete model is conveniently presented in the form of a decision tree or flow chart (see Figure 30–4). To use the model, the decision maker starts on the left-hand side of the flow chart and proceeds to the right based on the "yes" and "no" response to the questions listed on top of the chart. At each terminal point, a feasible decision style(s) is specified by the model as appropriate for each of the 14 situations.

Research on Decision Styles in Coaching

Four studies have been carried out based on Chelladurai and Haggerty's (1978) model. All these studies adopted Vroom and Yetton's (1973) strategy of describing the problem situations in the form of cases and requiring the subjects to choose one of the decision styles in a given situation. The cases represented the presence or absence of the selected problem attributes. A sample case from Chelladurai, Haggerty, and Baxter (1989) is presented in

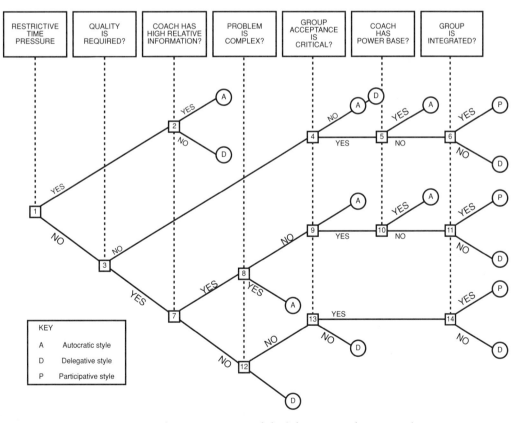

FIGURE 30–4. The normative model of decision styles in coaching.
(Chelladurai & Haggerty, 1978).

TABLE 30–6*. Problem Attributes of the Normative Model of Decision Styles

Attribute	Description
Time pressure	This refers to the availability of time for participative decision making. That is, lack of time would preclude member participation.
Quality requirement	In some cases (e.g., selection of a play-making guard in basketball), the coach has to ensure that an optimal decision is made. In some other cases (e.g., selection of a team manager), the coach may be satisfied with one of several acceptable candidates.
Coach's information	The selection of a particular style of decision making may also be affected by the information and knowledge possessed by the coach relative to the players' information and knowledge. This information may relate to the game, the players, and/or the problem situation.
Problem complexity	Some problems require the decision maker(s) to keep a number of factors in perspective and to think through a series of interlocking steps and procedures that link all the relevant factors (e.g., designing offensive and defensive strategies). According to the model, the coach or the individual wIth the best information is likely to solve complex problems better than the whole group.
Acceptance requirement	In some decision situations (e.g., to play full court press in basketball), the acceptance of the decision as practical and useful is critical for its effective implementation. In other cases (e.g., practicing foul shots), the acceptance may not be so critical, since the execution can easily be monitored and controlled. Accordingly, the greater the need for acceptance, the greater the need for participation.
Coach's power	If the coach has the power to influence the members, then members are likely to accept his or her decisions. Therefore, the need for participation by members is lessened. Coach's power may stem from the control over rewards and punishments, the hierarchical authority, members' love and admiration for the coach, and/or coach's expertise and past performance.

TABLE 30–6*. (Continued)

Attribute	Description
Team integration	The quality of interpersonal relations among the group members (marked by warmth, concern, and respect for each other), and the relative homogeneity of the team in their orientations, tenure, and ability would point to more participation by members. If these conditions are negative (as indicated, e.g., by the presence of internal dissensions and cliques), a participative style will only lead to inferior decisions and disrupt the already fragile solidarity of the team.

*From Chelladurai and Haggerty (1978).

Table 30–7. The selected problem attributes and the choices of decision styles varied from study to study.

Gordon (1986) has been the only researcher to test the model in its entirety. The 14 cases representing the terminal points of Chelladurai and Haggerty's model (see Figure 30–4) were administered to both coaches ($n = 18$) and players ($n = 161$) of university soccer teams in Canada. The decision styles presented to the subjects included the autocratic, participative, and delegative styles described earlier.

TABLE 30–7*. Sample case and descriptive chart

Toward the end of the tryouts, a university coach is concerned about making the final cut. The available players are all newcomers, but the coach has seen them all in action during the previous year at their former high schools. The atmosphere during the tryouts has been very good, and the players get along well with each other. The coach is faced with selecting the final team.

	High	Low
Quality requirement	*	
Coach's information	*	
Problem complexity	*	
Acceptance requirement		*
Team integration	*	

Under the above circumstances, what decision style would you use in selecting the final team? (Circle one response only.)

1. Autocratic I	You solve the problem yourself, using the information available at the time.
2. Autocratic II	You obtain the necessary information from relevant players, then decide yourself.
3. Consultative I	You consult with your players individually, and then make the decision yourself.
4. Consultative II	You consult with your players as a group, then make the decision yourself.
5. Group	You and your players jointly make the decision.

*From Chelladurai, Haggerty, & Baxter (1989)

In addition, the consultive style, in which the coach makes the decision after consulting with one or more players, was also included. The coaches were required to indicate (a) the decision style they would use in any given situation, and (b) their perception of what style other coaches would use in the same situation. The players were asked to indicate (a) their preferred style in each case, and (b) the decision style they expected their coach to use in the same situation. The percentage distribution of the decision style choices over all cases are shown in Table 30–8.

Chelladurai and Arnott (1985) used only four of the problem attributes: quality requirement, coach's information, problem complexity, and team integration (see Table 30–6). Sixteen cases were developed to represent two levels of these four attributes (i.e., their presence or absence) completely crossed with each other. The decision styles included were autocratic, consultive, participative, and delegative styles. The questionnaire was administered to 144 university basketball players (males = 67; females = 77) who were required to indicate the decision style they would *prefer* their coach to use under each situation. These authors carried out both nonparametric (chi square) and parametric (repeated measures ANOVA) analyses in their study. Treating the decision styles as a continuum of coach's influence in decisions and based on the average estimation of 17 experts, they assigned the values of 1 for autocratic style, 3.1 for consultive, 7.2 for participative, and 10 for delegative.

The percentage distribution of the decision style choices over all 16 cases are shown in Table 30–8, along with the results of Gordon (1986). The most notable result in Table 30–8 is the almost total rejection of the delegative style, which was recommended in 7 of the 15 situations outlined in the normative model. Also, autocratic style was the most popular choice. Further, group decision making was chosen less than 20% of the time. As for the rejection of the delegative style, Chelladurai and Arnott (1985) noted that while a coach's influence gradually decreases from 100% in

autocratic style through consultive and participative styles to 0% in delegative style, the players' influence is maximal in participative style and minimal in both the autocratic and the delegative styles. Apparently, if players had to forgo their own influence, they would do so in favor of the coach rather than in favor of another player(s). The contrasting influence patterns of the coach and players are shown in Figure 30–5.

The parametric analyses (in which the few subjects choosing the delegative style were eliminated) showed that the situation had a much larger influence on the decision style choices than did individual differences. Further, female players were influenced much more by the situation (52.3% variance attributable to the situation) than the males (21.3%). Also, female players tended to prefer more participation than male players. Finally, coach's information, and the interaction of quality requirement and problem complexity, had the most influence on subjects' decision style choices. Subjects preferred the autocratic style when both quality requirement and problem complexity were either present or when both were absent. They preferred more participation only when one of these attributes was present. In other words, the players did not want to be involved in serious or trivial problems.

Based on the earlier findings that delegation is not a viable option in team sports, Chelladurai, Haggerty, and Baxter (1989) used the 5 decision styles prescribed by Vroom and Yetton (1973) for group problems. The modified decision styles ranged from purely autocratic style, where the coach solves the problem himself/herself using the available information, to purely participative style, where the coach shares the problem with his/her players and the coach and the players jointly make the decision without any influence on the coach's part. The other three decision styles referred to progressive shifts from autocratic to participative styles when the coach seeks (a) information from one or more athletes, (b) consults with individual players, or (c) consults with the whole group.

Further, only 5 of the problem attributes specified by

TABLE 30–8*. Percentage Distribution of Decision Style Choices by Subgroups

	A	C	G	D
	Decision Styles			
University Soccer (Gordon, 1983)				
Coaches' own choices	46.3%	33.3%	18.5%	1.9%
Coaches' perceptions of other coaches	45.5%	41.2%	12.5%	0.8%
Players' preferences	31.2%	41.9%	12.5%	0.8%
Players' perceptions of coaches' choices	43.0%	39.6%	15.4%	2.0%
University Basketball (Chelladurai & Arnott, 1985)				
Players' preferences				
Females	33.0%	18.1%	46.9%	2.0%
Males	38.9%	25.8%	34.1%	1.2%

A = Autocratic; C = Consultive; G = Group; D = Delegative

*From Chelladurai (1986b)

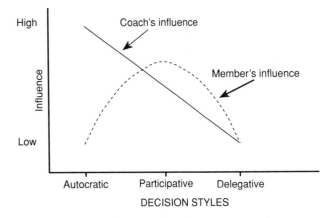

FIGURE 30–5. Coach's and players' relative influence in three decision styles (Chelladurai, 1986b).

Chelladurai & Haggerty (1978)—quality requirement, coach's information, problem complexity, acceptance requirements, and team integration—were included in these two studies. Chelladurai et al. (1989) justified the exclusion of time pressure because its presence automatically led to the autocratic or delegative style based only on coach's information without reference to the other attributes. They also excluded coach's power on the basis that it would likely be similar across comparable institutions (i.e., universities within one province).

Chelladurai et al. (1989) developed 32 cases to incorporate two levels (high or low) of the five problem attributes completely crossed with each other. They administered the questionnaire to 22 coaches (males = 15; females = 7), and 99 players (males = 53; females = 46) of university basketball teams in Ontario, Canada. The coaches indicated their choice of a decision style in each of the 32 situations, while the athletes expressed their preferences of a particular decision style in each of the cases. Following Chelladurai and Arnott (1985), both parametric and nonparametric analyses were carried out. However, the values assigned to the five decision styles were those recommended by Vroom and Yetton (1973)—0 for AI, 0.625 for AII, 5.00 for CI, 8.125 for CII, and 10.00 for G.

The percentage distribution of the total decision style choices over all cases are presented in Table 30–9. The distribution of decision style choices was significantly associated with group membership. Also, within each group, the actual distribution was significantly different from the expected equal distribution across the 5 decision styles. The AI style was chosen more often than any other style by each group. The CII style (consultation with all players on a group basis) was the second most popular choice in all three groups. It must also be noted that the participative style (G) was chosen less than 20% of the time in all three groups. When the AI, AII, and CI style scores are combined (because they all involve minimal influence from the members), the total percentage amounts to 64.8% for coaches, 59.4% for male players, and 57.3% for female players.

The parametric analyses showed that the variance attributable to individual differences (7.4%, 11.3%, and 6.6% in the data of coaches, male, and female players, respectively) was much lower than those attributable to situational differences (30.9, 29.8, and 37.7%). Overall, the 3 groups were similar in preferring a more autocratic style when the

coach's information was high, a more participative style when the acceptance requirement was high, a more autocratic style when both the quality requirement and problem complexity were high than when either or both were low, and lowest levels of participation when quality requirement was high and team integration low. However, coaches' choices were not affected by problem complexity or team integration while these attributes had significant effects on the choices of players of both genders.

The final study was that of Chelladurai and Quek (1991), who were concerned with (a) the decision style choices of high school coaches, (b) the effects of personality on such choices, and (c) the relationship between decision style choices and coaching effectiveness as reflected in win/loss percentage. Their subjects were 51 coaches of high school boys' basketball teams in and around Toronto, Canada. Their questionnaire included (a) the 32 cases of Chelladurai et al. (1989), modified to suit the high school situation, (b) Fiedler and Chemer's (1984) revised Least Preferred Co-worker scale, which is purported to measure one's task versus interpersonal orientation, and (c) Steers and Braunstein's (1976) Manifest Needs Questionnaire, to measure the needs for achievement, affiliation, autonomy, and dominance.

In order to verify the reliability of the instrument containing the 32 cases, Chelladurai and Quek (1991) requested 20 of the coaches to respond to the decision style cases a second time after a lapse of 8 weeks. The test-retest correlations were significant in 21 of the 32 cases ($p < .05$ or less). The magnitude of these significant correlations ranged from .39 to .82, with a mean of .55. The correlations for nine other cases ranged from .20 to .37, with a mean of .30. The values for the remaining two cases were very low (r = .05 and .03). The test-retest correlation of the total participation score (i.e., the average of decision style scores over all 32 cases) was quite high ($r = .83$).

The strategy to assess the internal consistency of the 32 cases was to focus on one of the five attributes at a time, and to divide the cases into 2 subsets based on the high/low rating of the attribute in question. The internal consistency was estimated by computing Cronbach's alpha and Spearman-Brown's equal length split-half reliability coefficient for each subset of cases. This procedure was repeated for each of the 5 attributes. Cronbach's alpha ranged from .69 to .83, with a mean of .77, and Spearman-Brown's coefficients ranged from .68 to .88, with a mean of .79.

The frequency distribution of the total choices is presented in Table 30–9, along with those of Chelladurai et al. (1989). The frequency distribution of the decision style choices was significantly different from the expectations in 28 of the 32 cases. Autocratic style without getting more information (AI) was the most preferred choice (32.5%), and consultation with a few individuals (CI) was the least preferred choice (9.7%).

The parametric analyses showed that the situation and individual differences accounted for 24.1% and 14.9% of the variance in decision style choices, respectively. While the effects of all 5 attributes and their interactions were sig-

TABLE 30–9. Percentage distribution of decision style choices

	Decision Styles				
	AI	AII	CI	CII	G
University basketball (Chelladurai, Haggerty, & Baxter, 1989)					
Coaches	34.8%	20.2%	9.8%	20.2%	15.1%
Male players	28.5%	16.8%	13.9%	21.3%	19.5%
Female players	30.1%	14.0%	13.2%	25.8%	16.3%
High school basketball (Chelladurai & Quek, 1990)					
Coaches	32.5%	15.4%	9.7%	21.3%	21.1%

nificant, coach's information and quality requirement had the most pronounced effects.

The effects of personality variables on decision style choices were mixed. First, Fiedler's LPC scale did not have any effect on decision style choices. As for the other personality variables, it was found that the higher the affiliation need, the higher the preference for more participative styles, and the higher the achievement, autonomy, and dominance needs, the higher the preference for more autocratic styles. These personality variables jointly explained 25% of the variance in the total participation score. Affiliation and domination needs contributed the most to the explained variance (19.6%). However, such effects were evident only when the subjects' global orientation toward participation (i.e., total participation score over all cases) was considered. These effects disappeared when personality variables were considered in the context of individual cases. That is, the effects of personality were superseded by the effects of the problem situation.

The effect of win/loss on coaches' decision style choices was not significant, although winning coaches tended to be more autocratic than losing coaches. Chelladurai and Quek (1991) also compared the frequency distribution of the decision style choices of the high school coaches of their study with that of the university coaches of Chelladurai et al. (1989) and found that the high school coaches were more participative—$X^2 (4, 2336) = 17.2, p < .01$—than the university coaches.

In summary, the problem situation and its attributes influenced the decision style choices to a greater extent than the individual differences among the subjects. Coaches' relative information (leading to more autocratic decisions) and acceptance requirement (leading to more participative decisions) seemed to exert greater influence than other attributes. Also, coaches and players tended to prefer more autocratic styles in dealing with both complex problems requiring high quality decisions and in trivial problems. Despite some minor differences, coaches and players of both sexes tended to be congruent in selecting the same or contiguous decision styles in most cases. AI was the most preferred style, CII was the second most preferred, and CI was the least preferred. They all chose the participative style less than 20% of the time. Further, the sharing of influence with few of the members in the form of either consultation or delegation was not a preferred option among both coaches and players.

Commentary

One of the issues that needs to be addressed is whether the current frameworks and associated research have really tapped all the relevant cues/attributes that impinge on the appropriateness of a decision style in a given situation in coaching. Also, the real life decision situations in coaching could be markedly different than the cases used in the above studies. A useful avenue for research is to ask coaches to describe varying kinds of decision situations they have

encountered, and the decision styles they employed in each situation. From such an inventory of real life decision situations, the relevant attributes of the problem situations can be extracted. With such an inventory of cases and problem attributes, cases may be written for use in subsequent research.

Even with carefully crafted cases, it must be noted that coaches may differ in how they perceive and assess a situation. Insofar as their perceptions may vary, their decision style choices may also vary. In future studies, coaches may be asked to state their perceptions of a situation (i.e., presence or absence of each problem attribute) as well as their decision style choices in each case. Such an approach permits the analysis of the extent to which (a) coaches perceive a situation in similar ways, and (b) their decision style choices are consistent with theoretical expectations, given their own unique perceptions.

From a different perspective, the efficacy of specific decision styles needs to be verified in the context of differing types of sports (e.g., small versus large team complement, open versus closed sports, individual versus team sports). For instance, the delegative style that was rejected by soccer players (Gordon, 1986) and basketball players (Chelladurai & Arnott, 1985) could indeed be a viable decision style in individual sports.

It was alluded to earlier that the delegative style is antithetical to the egalitarian orientations of team sports. But the notion of egalitarianism may not be relevant in sports characterized by a hierarchical substructure which places one or more players in a superior position (e.g., the quarterback in North American football). Further, even in sports without a formal hierarchy, there may exist an informal and socially acceptable pecking order. Such stratified patterns of interactions may permit the delegation of decision making to those leaders.

An overriding consideration in the choice of a decision style by a coach may be his or her inability to successfully engage in participatory procedures (Vroom, 1984). Leading a group in decision making requires the ability to keep the discussions focused, to provide all members an equal opportunity to express their views, and more important, to minimize the effects of the coach's position and status on the interactions in the group. Future research may relate the decision style choices of coaches to their abilities in participative procedures.

Although time pressure was not included as a problem attribute in these cases, its influence in some of the described cases can not be overlooked. For example, a coach deciding on a team strategy during halftime would inevitably face the pressure of time. It would be more profitable to include time pressure as an attribute in future studies and assess its influence.

In conclusion and within the limitations of the studies reviewed, it can be stated that team sports, particularly soccer and basketball, warrant relatively more autocratic decision making. Given the preferences of even the athletes for more autocratic decisions, one should be cautious in criticizing the coaches for their autocratic style of decision making. It should also be noted that the coaches chose more participative styles in specific situations. On a fundamental level, it should be recognized that an autocratic style of decision making is not bad in itself, if such processes are aimed at improving the welfare and performance of the group.

EPILOGUE

Three approaches to the study of leadership in sports have been reviewed and commented upon. This epilogue elaborates upon some of the concerns previously expressed. One of the persistent issues in the study of leadership is that of leader behavior directed at individuals versus group. Graen and Cashman (1975) argued that the leader needs to be heterogenous in his or her behavior toward the members based on the needs and preferences of individual members. In contrast, Cummings (1975) argued that leaders do not behave differently toward their members because of equality considerations and the need to avoid preferential treatment, and time and energy costs associated with differential behaviors. Chelladurai (1978) pointed out that leaders may indeed be homogenous in certain forms of behaviors (i.e., those required by the situation), and heterogenous in some other behaviors (i.e., in their reactions to members' needs and preferences). While such a reconciliation is logical, it is unfortunate that neither the Leadership Scale for Sports nor the Coaching Behavioral Assessment System separates behaviors aimed at the individual from behaviors aimed at the group. It may be profitable to modify both the Leadership Scale for Sports and the Coaching Behavior Assessment System to distinguish and capture the individual-and group-oriented leader behaviors. Obviously, such a procedure entails greater effort, time, and alertness on the part of the investigators.

The foregoing review shows that the leadership dimensions do not predict athlete performance as well as the other outcome measures such as athlete satisfaction and/or player's evaluative reactions. For example, the strength of association between the LSS dimensions and outcome measures progressively decreases from satisfaction with leadership, through satisfaction with team performance, to actual performance. This is not a serious problem in the case of youth sports as studied by Smith, Smoll, and their associates, whose focus has been on the developmental aspects of sport rather than on performance. Insofar as the emphasis is on learning, development, and/or enjoyment (i.e., recreational youth or adult sports), one could be satisfied with the positive evaluations by participants as the desired outcomes.

However, in the case of competitive sports, performance becomes a critical outcome. Therefore, the success of any intervention including leadership should be judged by its relationship to performance enhancement. Unfortunately, the studies reviewed have not substantiated this relationship. Such poor leadership-performance relationships could be attributed to the inadequacy of (a) the leadership scale and/or (b) the performance measures.

Although the LSS, developed 12 years ago, has been widely accepted and used in the sport psychology and sport management scientific community, the behaviors measured by these subscales do not encompass all that a leader does to alter and/or enhance those variables which intervene between leadership and group performance. For example, coaching success is dependent on the extent to which coaches assess the deficiencies in intervening variables such as members' ability, members' effort, members' role perceptions, organization of the work, teamwork and cooperation, and environmental conditions. Following assessment, coaching success is then dependent on the extent to which coaches engage in behaviors which rectify those deficiencies. These aspects of leadership are not considered either in the conceptual model which formed the basis for the LSS or in the operational measure, the scale itself.

The theoretical underpinnings of the LSS are based on House's path-goal theory of leadership, which has as a basis the assumption that a leader influences members by activating their self-interest. This has been referred to as *transactional leadership*. Recently, however, a *transformational* and *charismatic* approach to leadership has been endorsed by numerous scholars (e.g., Bass, 1985; Conger & Kanungo, 1988). An assumption fundamental to this approach is that transformational leadership arouses member's higher-order needs in the service of the group or organization. Charismatic leadership is based on members' belief in the extraordinary qualities of their leader, and their commitment to upholding his or her values. It is important to investigate the extent to which the concepts and elements of transformational and/or charismatic leadership are relevant to the athletic context. The elements that are applicable need to be included in any future revision of the LSS.

As for measurement of performance, Carron (1988) and Courneya and Chelladurai (1991) have noted that conventional measures of performance (e.g., win/loss) are contaminated by several external factors (e.g., random chance, opponent's performance and referee's decisions). Consequently they may not be responsive to psychological interventions including leadership. Thus, it becomes necessary to select those performance, satisfaction, or any other outcome measures that are devoid of such contamination. In the context of baseball, Courneya and Chelladurai (1991) divided the performance measures into three types: (a) *primary* (e.g., batting averages, strikeout/walk ratio, fielding average, stolen bases), (b) *secondary* (e.g., runs batted in, earned-run average, runs allowed), and (c) *tertiary* (e.g., win/loss, run differential, and ratio of final score). They demonstrated through correlational and regression procedures that the primary measures are the closest to skill execution, followed by the secondary and tertiary measures. In other words, the tertiary measures of win/loss, run differential, and ratio of final score are contaminated by such factors as random chance, opponent's outstanding performance, performance strategy, and officials' mistakes. Therefore, they are not likely to reflect any intervention procedures including leadership that are aimed at skill execution. Thus it would be necessary to identify the least contaminated measures of performance in those sports that are of interest in a study.

Although several investigators have included "satisfaction" as a consequence of different factors and/or interventions, there has been no systematic effort to develop a reliable and valid measure of satisfaction in the context of sports. Either single items have been used to measure critical facets of satisfaction (e.g., Chelladurai's [1984] use of single items to measure satisfaction with [a] leadership, [b] individual performance, [c] team performance, and [d] overall involvement), or multiple items have been used to assess limited number of satisfaction facets (e.g., the Chelladurai et al. 1988 scale to measure satisfaction with

leadership and satisfaction with personal outcome). It is important to take a more theoretical approach in defining and describing the different facets of participation over which individuals could be satisfied, and in developing a psychometrically sound scale to measure those facets.

A final point relates to the fundamental notion that leadership is significant only in the context of the group. It has been suggested that members within the group can perform several of the functions of leadership, and thus constitute an effective substitute for the formal group leader (House, 1971; Kerr & Jermier, 1978). Thus future studies of sport leadership may incorporate varying group properties as antecedent, consequent, or moderating variables of leadership.

References

Bass, B. M. (1985). *Leadership and performance beyond expectations.* New York: Free Press.

Carron, A. V. (1988). *Group dynamics in sport.* London, Ontario, Canada: Spodym Publishers.

Chelladurai, P. (1978). *A contingency model of leadership in athletics.* Unpublished doctoral dissertation, University of Waterloo, Canada.

Chelladurai, P. (1981). The coach as motivator and chameleon of leadership styles. *Science Periodical on Research and Technology in Sport.* Ottawa, Canada: Coaching Association of Canada.

Chelladurai, P. (1984). Discrepancy between preferences and perceptions of leadership behavior and satisfaction of athletes in varying sports. *Journal of Sport Psychology, 6,* 27–41.

Chelladurai, P. (1986). Applicability of the Leadership Scale for Sports to the Indian context. *Proceedings of the VIII Commonwealth and International Conference on Sport, Physical Education, Dance, Recreation, and Health,* Sports Science Section (pp. 291–296). Glasgow, Scotland: Management Committee.

Chelladurai, P. (1986). Styles of decision making in coaching. In J. M. Williams (Ed.), *Applied sport psychology: Personal growth to peak performance* (pp. 107–119). Palo Alto, CA: Mayfield.

Chelladurai, P. (1989). *Manual for the Leadership Scale for Sports.* Unpublished manuscript. University of Western Ontario, London, Canada.

Chelladurai, P. (1990). Leadership in sports: A review. *International Journal of Sport Psychology, 21,* 328–354.

Chelladurai, P., & Arnott, M. (1985). Decision styles in coaching: Preferences of basketball players. *Research Quarterly for Exercise and Sport, 56,* 15–24.

Chelladurai, P., & Carron, A. V. (1978). *Leadership.* Ottawa: Sociology of Sport Monograph Series, Canadian Association for Health, Physical Education, and Recreation.

Chelladurai, P., & Carron, A. V. (1981a). Applicability to youth sports of the leadership scale for sports. *Perceptual and Motor Skills, 53,* 361–362.

Chelladurai, P., & Carron, A. V. (1981b). Task characteristics and individual differences, and their relationship to preferred leadership in sports. *Psychology of Motor Behavior and Sport—1982* (p. 87). College Park, MD: North American Society for the Psychology of Sport and Physical Activity.

Chelladurai, P., & Carron, A. V. (1983). Athletic maturity and preferred leadership. *Journal of Sport Psychology, 5,* 371–380.

Chelladurai, P., & Haggerty, T. R. (1978). A normative model of decision styles in coaching. *Athletic Administrator, 13,* 6–9.

Chelladurai, P., Haggerty, T. R., & Baxter, P. R. (1989). Decision style choices of university basketball coaches and players. *Journal of Sport and Exercise Psychology, 11,* 201–215.

Chelladurai, P., Imamura, H., & Yamaguchi, Y. (1986). Subscale structure of the Leadership Scale for Sports in the Japanese context: A preliminary report. *Proceedings of the FISU/CESU Conference, Universiade '85* (pp. 372–377). Kobe, Japan: The International University Sports Federation (FISU).

Chelladurai, P., Imamura, H., Yamaguchi, Y., Oinuma, Y., & Miyauchi, T. (1988). Sport leadership in a cross-national setting: The case of Japanese and Canadian university athletes. *Journal of Sport and Exercise Psychology, 10,* 374–389.

Chelladurai, P., Malloy, D., Imamura, H., & Yamaguchi, Y. (1987). A cross-cultural study of preferred leadership in sports. *Canadian Journal of Sport Sciences, 12,* 106–110.

Chelladurai, P., & Quek, C. B. (1992). Situational and personality effects on the decision style choices of high school basketball coaches. Submitted for publication.

Chelladurai, P., & Saleh, S. D. (1978). Preferred leadership in sports. *Canadian Journal of Applied Sport Sciences, 3,* 85–92.

Chelladurai, P., & Saleh, S. D. (1980). Dimensions of leader behavior in sports: Development of a leadership scale. *Journal of Sport Psychology, 2,* 34–45.

Conger, J. A., & Kanungo, R. N. (1988). *Charismatic leadership: The elusive factor in organizational research.* San Francisco, CA: Jossey-Bass.

Coopersmith, S. (1967). *The antecedents of self-esteem.* San Francisco, CA: Freeman.

Courneya, K. S., & Chelladurai, P. (1991). A model of performance measures in baseball. *Journal of Sport and Exercise Psychology, 13,* 16–25.

Cummings, L. L. (1975). Assessing the Graen/Cashman model and comparing it with other approaches. In J. G. Hunt & L. L. Larson (Eds.), *Leadership frontiers* (pp. 181–185). Kent, OH: Kent State University.

Curtis, B., Smith, R. E., & Smoll, F. L. (1979). Scrutinizing the skipper: A study of leadership behavior in the dugout. *Journal of Applied Psychology, 64,* 391–400.

Dwyer, J. M., & Fischer, D. G. (1988a). Psychometric properties of the coach's version of Leadership Scale for Sports. *Perceptual and Motor Skills, 67,* 795–798.

Dwyer, J. M., & Fischer, D. G. (1988b). Leadership style of wrestling coaches. *Perceptual and Motor Skills, 67,* 706.

Dwyer, J. M., & Fischer, D. G. (1990). Wrestlers' perceptions of coaches' leadership as predictors of satisfaction with leadership. *Perceptual and Motor Skills, 71,* 511–517.

Erle, F. J. (1981). *Leadership in competitive and recreational sport.* Unpublished master's thesis. University of Western Ontario. London, Canada.

Evans, M. G. (1970). The effects of supervisory behavior on the path-goal relationship. *Organizational Behavior and Human Performance, 5,* 277–298.

Fiedler, F. E. (1967). *A theory of leadership effectiveness.* New York: McGraw-Hill.

Fiedler, F. E., & Chemers, M. M. (1984). *Improving leadership effectiveness: The leader match concept* (2nd ed). New York: Wiley.

Fleishman, E. A. (1957). A leader behavior description for industry. In R. M. Stogdill & A. E. Coons (Eds.), *Leader behavior: Its description and measurement* (pp. 103–119). Columbus, OH: The Ohio State University.

Garland, D. J., Barry, J. R. (1988). The effects of personality and perceived leader behavior on performance in collegiate football. *The Psychological Record, 38,* 237–247.

Gordon, A. M. D. (1986). *Behavioral correlates of coaching effectiveness.* Unpublished doctoral dissertation. University of Alberta, Canada.

Gordon, S. (1988). Decision styles and coaching effectiveness in university soccer. *Canadian Journal of Sport Sciences, 13,* 56–65.

Graen, G., & Cashman, J. F. (1975). A role-making model of leadership in formal organizations: A developmental approach. In J. G. Hunt & L. L. Larson (Eds.), *Leadership frontiers* (pp. 181–185). Kent, OH: Kent State University.

Halpin, A. W., & Winer, B. J. (1957). A factorial study of the leader behavior description. In R. M. Stogdill & A. E. Coons (Eds.), *Leader behavior: Its description and measurement* (pp. 39–51). Columbus, OH: The Ohio State University.

Hendry, L. B. (1974). Human factors in sport systems: Suggested models for analyzing athlete-coach interaction. *Human Factors, 16,* 353–362.

Hersey, P., & Blanchard, H. K. (1977). *Management of organizational behavior* (3rd ed). Englewood Cliffs, NJ: Prentice-Hall.

Horn, T. S. (1985). Coaches' feedback and changes in children's perceptions of their physical competence. *Journal of Educational Psychology, 77,* 174–186.

Horne, T., & Carron, A. V. (1985). Compatibility in coach-athlete relationships. *Journal of Sport Psychology, 7,* 137–149.

House, R. J. (1971). A path-goal theory of leader effectiveness. *Administrative Science Quarterly, 16,* 321–338.

House, R. J., & Dessler, G. (1974). A path-goal theory of leadership. In J. G. Hunt & L. L. Larson (Eds.), *Contingency approaches to leadership* (pp. 29–55). Carbondale, IL: Southern Illinois University Press.

Iordanoglou, D. (1990). *Perceived leadership in Greek soccer: A preliminary investigation.* Unpublished manuscript. University of Manchester, Department of Education.

Isberg, L., & Chelladurai, P. (1990). *The Leadership Scale for Sports: Its applicability to the Swedish context.* Unpublished manuscript, University College of Falun/Borlänge, Sweden.

Johns, G. (1981). Difference score measures of organizational behavior variables: A critique. *Organizational Behavior and Human Performance, 27,* 443–463.

Jöreskog, K. G., & Sörbom, D. (1983). *LISREL: Analysis of linear structural relations by the method of maximum likelihood.* Chicago, IL: National Educational Resources.

Keehner, S. L. (1988). *A study of perceived leadership behavior and program adherence.* Unpublished doctoral dissertation, University of Maryland.

Kerlinger, F. N. (1973). *Foundations of behavioral research* (2nd ed.). New York: Holt, Rinehart and Winston.

Kerr, S., & Jermier, J. M. (1978). Substitutes for leadership: Their meaning and measurement. *Organizational Behavior and Human Performance, 22,* 375–403.

Kim, B-H., Lee, H-K., & Lee, J-Y. (1990). *A study on the coaches' leadership behavior in sports.* Unpublished manuscript, Korea Sport Science Institute.

Lacoste, P. L., & Laurencelle, L. (1989). *The French validation of the Leadership Scale for Sports.* Unpublished abstract, Université du Québec à Trois-Rivières, Canada.

Liukkonen, J., & Salminen, S. (1989). *Three coach-athlete relationship scales in relation to coaching climate.* Paper presented at the 6th International Congress on Sport Psychology, Lahti, Finland. February 13–15, 1989.

Liukkonen, J., & Salminen, S. (1990). *The athletes' perception of leader behavior of Finnish coaches.* Paper presented at the World Congress on Sport for All, Tampere, Finland, June 3–7, 1990.

Liukkonen, J., Salminen, S., & Telama, R. (1989a). *The relationship between coach-athlete interaction measured by observation and interaction measured by means of a questionnaire in children's sport.* Paper presented at the AIESEP World Congress, Jyväskylä, Finland. June 17–22, 1989.

Liukkonen, J., Salminen, S., & Telama, R. (1989b). *The psychological climate of training sessions in Finnish youth sports.* Paper presented at the 7th ISSP World Congress in Sport Psychology, Singapore. August 7–12, 1989.

Maier, N. R. F. (1974). *Psychology in industrial organizations.* Boston: Houghton Mifflin.

McMillin, C. J. (1990). *The relationship of athlete self-perceptions and athlete perceptions of leader behaviors to athlete satisfaction.* Unpublished doctoral dissertation, University of Virginia.

Nunnally, J. C. (1978). *Psychometric theory.* New York: McGraw-Hill.

Ogilvie, B. C., & Tutko, T. A. (1966). *Problem athletes and how to handle them.* London: Pelham Books.

Osborn, R. N., & Hunt, J. G. (1975). An adaptive-reactive theory of leadership: The role of macro variables in leadership research. In J. G. Hunt & L. L. Larson (Eds.), *Leadership frontiers* (pp. 27–44). Kent, OH: Kent State University.

Porter, L. W., & Lawler, E. E. (1968). *Managerial attitudes and performance.* Homewood, IL: Richard D. Irwin.

Rejeski, W., Darracott, C., & Hutslar, S. (1979). Pygmalion in youth sport: A field study. *Journal of Sport Psychology, 1,* 311–319.

Robinson, T. T., & Carron, A. V. (1982). Personal and situational factors associated with dropping out versus maintaining participation in competitive sport. *Journal of Sport Psychology, 4,* 364–378.

Sage, G. M. (1973). The coach as management: Organizational leadership in American sport. *Quest, 19,* 35–40.

Salminen, S., Liukkonen, J., & Telama, R. (1990). *The differences in coaches' and athletes' perception of leader behavior of Finnish coaches.* Paper presented at the AIESEP Congress, Lough-borough, England, July, 1990.

Schliesman, E. S. (1987). Relationship between the congruence of preferred and actual leader behavior and subordinate satisfaction with leadership. *Journal of Sport Behavior, 10,* 157–166.

Serpa, S. (1990). *Research work on sport leadership in Portugal.* Unpublished manuscript. Lisbon Technical University.

Serpa, S., & Antunes, I. (1989). *Leadership styles of elite Portuguese women's volleyball coaches.* Paper presented at the 6th International Congress on Sport Psychology. Lahti, Finland.

Serpa, S., Lacoste, P., Pataco, V., & Santos, F. (1988). *Methodology of translation and adaptation of a specific sport test—A Leadership Scale for Sports.* Paper presented at the 2nd National Symposium on Psychology Research. Lisbon, Portugal.

Serpa, S., Pataco, V., & Santos, F. (1991). Leadership patterns in handball international competition. *International Journal of Sport Psychology, 22,* 78–89.

Smith, R. E., & Smoll, F. L. (1990). Self-esteem and children's reactions to youth sport coaching behaviors: A field study of self-enhancement processes. *Developmental Psychology, 26,* 987–993.

Smith, R. E., Smoll, F. L., & Curtis, B. (1978). Coaching behaviors in little league baseball. In F. L. Smoll & R. E. Smith (Eds.), *Psychological perspectives on youth sports* (pp. 173–201). Washington, DC: Hemisphere.

Smith, R. E., Smoll, F. L., & Curtis, B. (1979). Coach effectiveness training: A cognitive-behavioral approach to enhancing relationship skills in youth sport coaches. *Journal of Sport Psychology, 1,* 59–75.

Smith, R. E., Smoll, F. L., & Hunt, E. B. (1977a). A system for the behavioral assessment of athletic coaches. *Research Quarterly, 48,* 401–407.

Smith, R. E., Smoll, F. L., & Hunt, E. B. (1977b). Training manual for the Coaching Behavior Assessment System. *Psychological Documents, 7* (ms. no. 1406).

Smith, R.E., Smoll, F.L., Hunt, E.B., & Clarke, S.J. (1976). *CBAS audiovisual training module.* Seattle: University of Washington (Video).

Smith, R. E., Smoll, F. L., Hunt, E. B., Curtis, B., & Coppel, D. B. (1979). Psychology and the bad news bears. In G. C. Roberts & K. M. Newell (Eds.), *Psychology of motor behavior and sport—1978* (pp. 101–130). Champaign, IL: Human Kinetics.

Smith, R. E., Zane, N. W. S., Smoll, F. L., & Coppel, D. B. (1983). Behavioral assessment in youth sports: Coaching behaviors and children's attitudes. *Medicine and Science in Sport and Exercise, 15,* 208–214.

Smoll, F. L., & Smith, R. E. (1980). Psychologically-oriented coach

training programs: Design, implementation, and assessment. In C. H. Nadeau, W. R. Halliwell, K. M. Newell. & G. C. Roberts (Eds.), *Psychology of motor behavior and sport—1979* (pp. 112–129). Champaign, IL: Human Kinetics.

Smoll, F. L., & Smith, R. E. (1984). Leadership research in youth sports. In J. M. Silva III & R. S. Weinberg (Eds.) *Psychological foundations of sport* (pp. 371–386). Champaign, IL: Human Kinetics.

Smoll, F. L., & Smith, R. E. (1989). Leadership behaviors in sport: A theoretical model and research paradigm. *Journal of Applied Social Psychology, 19,* 1522–1551.

Smoll, F. L., Smith, R. E., Curtis, B., & Hunt, E. (1978). Toward a mediational model of coach-player relationships. *Research Quarterly, 49,* 528–541.

Steers, R. M., & Braunstein, D. N. (1976). A behaviorally based measure of manifest needs in work setting. *Journal of Vocational Behavior, 9,* 251–266.

Summers, R. J. (1983). *A study of leadership in a sport setting.* Unpublished master's thesis. University of Waterloo, Canada.

Tannenbaum, R., & Schmidt, W. H. (1973). How to choose a leadership pattern. *Harvard Business Review, 51,* 162–180.

Terry, P. C. (1984). The coaching preferences of elite athletes competing at Universiade '83. *The Canadian Journal of Applied Sport Sciences, 9,* 201–208.

Terry, P. C., & Howe, B. L. (1984). The coaching preferences of athletes. *The Canadian Journal of Applied Sport Sciences, 9,* 188–193.

Tutko, T. A., & Richards, J. W. (1971). *Psychology of coaching.* Boston: Allyn and Bacon.

Vroom, V. H. (1984). Reflections on leadership and decision-making. *Journal of General Management, 9,* 18–36.

Vroom, V. H., & Jago, A. G. (1978). On the validity of the Vroom-Yetton model. *Journal of Applied Psychology, 63,* 151–162.

Vroom, V. H., & Yetton, R. N. (1973). *Leadership and decision-making.* Pittsburgh: University of Pittsburgh Press.

Weiss, M. R., & Friedrichs, W. D. (1986). The influence of leader behaviors, coach attributes, and institutional variables on performance and satisfaction of collegiate basketball teams. *Journal of Sport Psychology, 8,* 332–346.

White, M. C., Crino, M. D., & Hatfield, J. D. (1985). An empirical examination of the parsimony of perceptual congruence scores. *Academy of Management Journal, 28,* 732–737.

Yukl, G. A. (1971). Toward a behavioral theory of leadership. *Organizational Behavior and Human Performance, 6,* 414–440.

Yukl, G. A. (1981). *Leadership in organizations.* Englewood Cliffs, NJ: Prentice-Hall.

·31·

GROUP COHESION IN SPORT
AND EXERCISE

W. Neil Widmeyer
Albert V. Carron
Lawrence R. Brawley

"United we stand. Divided we fall."

When informed that Aesop first pronounced the above adage in 550 B.C., most individuals are somewhat shocked. No doubt their surprise stems from the fact that an idea which is embraced so widely today was expressed over 2,500 years ago. Before documenting the significance of this unitedness characteristic, it is important to clarify its meaning.

The unitedness quality of groups is usually referred to as cohesiveness. In a recent review article, Mudrack (1989a) noted that even though cohesiveness "seems intuitively easy to understand and describe ... this 'ease of description' has failed to translate into an 'ease of definition'" (p. 39). The definition of cohesiveness that has been most often cited is either the one advanced by Festinger, Schachter, and Back (1950, p. 164), which saw cohesiveness as the "total field of forces that act on members to remain in the group," or Festinger's (1950, p. 244) reformulation, which proposed that it was "the resultant of all forces acting on members to remain in the group." However, after citing these definitions, most researchers have ignored a number of important types of forces (e.g., the normative forces that keep members from leaving a group as well as the forces that pull members to alternate groups). Instead, they have treated cohesiveness as only the attraction of the group for its members (Libo, 1953). Mudrack (1989) pointed out that while such a definition is easy to operationalize, it focuses "exclusively on *individuals* at the expense of the *group* and therefore may not entirely capture the concept of *group* cohesiveness" (p. 42).

Two alternate definitions, which do focus on the group, describe cohesiveness as the degree of unification of the group (Van Bergen & Koekebakker, 1959) and the resistance of the group to disruption (Gross & Martin, 1952). While Mudrack's observation that there is incredible variety and indiscriminate usage of definitions in current cohesiveness research is not disputed, it appears that most definitions reflect the attractiveness of the group for its members while a few incorporate the perception of group unity. The problem of establishing an operational definition of cohesiveness based on a constitutive definition is addressed later in this chapter. At this point, a case is made for the importance of the cohesiveness construct.

In underscoring the significance of cohesiveness, it has been previously noted that military generals, politicians, and corporate presidents constantly employ elaborate means to develop what they refer to as "team spirit" or "morale" among their followers (Widmeyer, Brawley, & Carron, 1985). In fact, very recently (1991), President George Bush quoted Dwight D. Eisenhower when he pronounced that "morale is the greatest single factor in successful war." Although morale and cohesion are not usually considered to be synonymous, the former can be viewed as an immediate outcome of the latter.

Perhaps more compelling evidence of the importance attached to group unitedness is the amount of research that has focused on the topic in a wide variety of settings. For ex-

672

ample, the military's interest in cohesiveness is reflected in the fact that research involving group cohesion has been conducted with airplane crews (e.g., Foushee, 1984), army units (e.g., Manning & Fullerton, 1988), tank crews (e.g., Tziner & Vardi, 1983), antiaircraft batteries (e.g., Palmer & Myers, 1968), and R.O.T.C. rifle teams (e.g., McGrath, 1962). The significance of cohesiveness for the fields of business and industry is seen in the variety of work settings in which cohesiveness has been studied. The groups studied have included shoe factory workers (e.g., Horsefall & Arensberg, 1949), scientists and engineers (Pelz & Andrews, 1966), coal miners (e.g., Trist & Bamforth, 1951), survey crews (Fiedler 1953), and carpenters and bricklayers (e.g., VanZelst, 1952). Cohesiveness has been examined extensively in personal growth groups (e.g., Peteroy, 1983), psychotherapy groups (e.g., Roark & Sharah, 1989) and the staffs of residential treatment groups (e.g., Johnson, 1982). Also, cohesiveness has been studied in university housing developments (e.g., Festinger, Schacter, & Back, 1950), classrooms (e.g., Shaw & Shaw, 1962), fraternities (e.g., Gardner & Thompson, 1956), families (e.g., Smith, 1984) and even children's narratives (e.g., Bennett-Kastor, 1986). Finally, cohesion has been investigated in both sport (e.g., Spink, 1990a) and exercise settings (e.g., Carron, Widmeyer, & Brawley, 1988).

In making a case for the significance of cohesiveness in sport, reviewers have sometimes cited common locker room slogans such as "Players play, but *teams win.*" Additional support for the notion lies in media headlines such as "Togetherness is Broncos' secret formula," and "Morale, lack of unity ails Yankees." It has also been noted that "coaches actively promote group closeness through such practices as establishing athletic dormitories, having players wear clothing that identifies them as members of the team, facilitating teams' social activities, and involving players in team goal setting" (Widmeyer, Brawley, & Carron, 1985, p. 1). However, the importance of cohesiveness for sport could also be demonstrated by identifying the amount of research that has been conducted with a wide variety of sport groups. The nature, findings, conclusions, and problems associated with this research are outlined in the remainder of this chapter.

EARLY COHESION RESEARCH IN SPORT

Although the term *cohesion* was used in 1943 by Whyte in his study of groups in the Boston streets, the first systematic investigation of the construct was undertaken in 1950 by Festinger, Schachter, and Back. These investigators demonstrated that friendships in student housing developments were strongly related to physical proximity. It is noteworthy that this study, which is frequently cited by cohesion researchers and reviewers (e.g., Mudrack, 1989a), only examined one aspect of attractiveness—interpersonal attraction.

Usually there is a considerable time lag between the

point when a construct is first examined by researchers in the parent discipline and its eventual investigation by scientists in the sport subdiscipline (e.g., psychology of sport). However, in the case of cohesiveness, its study in sport came very soon after the seminal research by Festinger and his colleagues (1950). In fact, Fred Fiedler examined "interpersonal warmth" within high school basketball teams as early as 1952. What Fiedler found was that the most preferred member of each team perceived large differences between his most preferred teammate and his least preferred teammate. In referring to the "assumed similarity" measure he used, Fiedler stated that "further research is needed to clarify the meaning of this measure" (p. 387). Nevertheless, Fiedler concluded that "members of effective teams prefer highly task oriented persons as coworkers" (p. 388).

Numerous cohesion researchers and reviewers have taken Fiedler's findings to mean that a negative relationship exists between cohesion and performance in sport. This conclusion, which is contrary to the intuitive notion that closeness helps a group to be successful, was reinforced by the work of McGrath (1962), who found that experimentally formed 3-person ROTC rifle teams manifesting poor interpersonal relations (as determined by the assumed similarity measure) performed better than those in which interpersonal relations were good. Further support for a negative cohesion-performance relationship came from a case study of Olympic rowing teams. An article originally written in German by the team coach Hans Lenk (1966) reported that the German Olympic and World Championship rowing teams ("eights") of 1960, 1962, 1963, and 1964, while being the best in the world, had considerable internal conflict. In fact, these teams were characterized by known cliques and even outward brawling among team members in public bars. Lenk (personal communication, 1972) revealed that he was simply pointing out that he, as a coach, was able to take a group of skilled, task-motivated individuals who did not like each other and mold them into world champions. His teams might have been even more successful had they been cohesive! Nevertheless the three early studies by Fiedler (1952), McGrath (1962), and Lenk (1969) left the impression that team closeness was at best unimportant and possibly even detrimental to team performance. This conclusion was certainly contrary to the notion that had been held by the media, coaches, and the general public that team closeness is important for team success.

Most likely the unexpected results of the early studies contributed greatly to continued research of the relationship between team cohesion and team performance in sport. Four studies that followed closely were those conducted by Stogdill (1963), Smith (1968), Klein and Christiansen (1969), and Vander Velden (1971). In each of these investigations, a positive relationship between team closeness and team performance was found.

Stogdill's (1963) research is unique in that he examined "team integration" on every single play during the six home games of the 1962 Ohio State football team. The idea that cohesion is so unstable that it can change every 30 seconds has not had widespread acceptance. However, both practitioners and reviewers have come to realize that cohesion is not a fixed property within athletic teams—i.e., it can increase or decrease during a season. Another aspect of the study worth noting is that "integration" was assessed by independent observers sitting in the stadium rather than by the team members themselves. To the best of our knowledge, this has been the only attempt taken in sport to assess cohesion (a) by outside observers, and (b) at different points in time during a game.

By relating team cohesiveness to team win-loss records, the cohesion-performance *outcome* relationship, rather than the cohesion-performance relationship, is the focus. The fact that a team's performance outcome is influenced not only by its performance but also by the performance of its opponent reduces the strength of the cohesion-performance outcome relationship. To avoid the confound of the opposing team's performance, Smith (1968) examined the impact of task and social cohesion in a classroom setting on such performance measures as number of basketball shots taken and number of basketball shots made. He found that task cohesive groups shot more basketballs and had a higher scoring percentage than socially cohesive groups. It is surprising that subsequent researchers have not attempted to relate cohesion to performance variables rather than simply examining the more easily measured outcome variables.

Klein and Christiansen's (1969) research was different in that it was conducted with experimentally formed 3-person groups. However, the more significant aspect of their work was that not only did they study cohesion's relationship with performance outcome, but also its relationship to process variables such as communication (i.e., number of passes during a basketball game). Vander Velden (1971) did find that cohesion was positively related to group effectiveness in high school basketball. However, Vander Velden's measure of cohesion was adherence—whether members stayed with their team. No other researcher of cohesion in sport has adopted this all-or-nothing view of cohesion.

The findings of Klein and Christiansen (1969), Smith (1968), Stogdill (1963), and Vander Velden (1971) can each be challenged on the basis of certain methodological flaws. Nevertheless each of these pieces of research contributes something to our understanding of cohesion's role in sport as well as how to better research the construct.

Undoubtedly one of the most significant investigations of cohesion in sport was that undertaken by Martens and Peterson (1971). The importance of this work stems not only from the magnitude of the study (1,200 subjects representing 144 intramural basketball teams), but also from its methodological improvements over previous work. This study was the first to utilize the then recently developed Sports Cohesiveness Questionnaire (Martens, Landers, & Loy, 1972). This 9-item multidimensional instrument assesses (a) members' *feelings* toward and *evaluations of* other individual members, (b) members' *feelings* toward

the team as a whole, and (c) members' *perceptions* of the teamwork and the closeness of the team. The researchers demonstrated that it was the latter two measurement categories that differentiated successful teams from unsuccessful ones. Proof of the importance of the study lies in the great number of examinations that it generated in which the Sport Cohesiveness Questionnaire was used to assess cohesion in sport (e.g., Landers & Crum, 1971; Arnold & Straub, 1973; Nixon, 1976; Bird, 1977; and Cotter, 1979). These studies and others examining the cohesion-performance relationship in sport are discussed later in this chapter.

THE PERFORMANCE COHESION RELATIONSHIP: THEORY AND RESEARCH

Given the overriding interest by coaches, athletes, spectators, and the media in the factors associated with performance outcomes in sport (i.e., winning versus losing), it is hardly surprising that early research on cohesiveness concentrated on this general issue. In order to explore what this research tells us, it is beneficial to use the framework suggested by Zanna and Fazio (1982). They pointed out that research on any issue may be organized within a three-level hierarchy. At the base of the hierarchy is the first and simplest question: "Does a relationship exist?" In the present research, this question is: "Does a relationship exist between cohesion and performance in sport?" One auxiliary question that evolves from this fundamental query is related to the *type* of the relationship—whether it is positive or negative. For example, cohesion, because of its impact on individuals within a group, could be predicted to be positively related to group performance in some instances, and negatively in others. That is, strong feelings of cohesiveness might stimulate individual athletes to work extremely hard in order not to let their teammates down. On the other hand, those same feelings of cohesiveness might lead individual athletes to compete less vigorously in order to avoid intragroup competition and conflict.

Another auxiliary question concerns the *strength* of the relationship. This question is tied in with the importance of cohesiveness to team success. That is, cohesion could be positively or negatively related to performance success in groups, but its relative impact might be minimal. Other factors such as player talent, coaching expertise, an unfavorable schedule, and so on, might be so strongly associated with team success that high or low cohesiveness could be, or could at least seem to be, almost irrelevant.

A third auxiliary question concerns the predominant causal *direction* of any relationship. High cohesion could lead to greater team success. At the same time, successful group performance could lead to increased group cohesiveness. Since both of these relationships seem plausible, an important question is which of the two—cohesion leading to performance success or performance success leading to cohesion—is strongest.

According to Zanna and Fazio (1982), the second level in the hierarchy of research questions focuses on the potential *moderators* of the relationship. When (under what conditions) is cohesion related or more highly related to performance success? Task type has often been assumed to be a moderator variable in the cohesion-performance relationship. The underlying reason for this is that high feelings of cohesiveness might be detrimental in individual sports where individuals must compete against teammates as well as opponents (e.g., cross-country). Conversely, in team sports where high intragroup cooperation is essential (e.g., basketball), cohesiveness might be critical for success. Discovering the moderators of the cohesiveness-performance relationship is important. Once these are better understood, the development of a theoretical framework that includes cohesion-performance relationsips is possible.

The third level in the hierarchy of research questions centers around understanding the *mediators* of relationships. The concern in this regard is with "why" cohesiveness might relate to performance success in some instances but not others. It is also concerned with "what" factors cause the relationship. Thus, for example, if cohesion is positively related to performance success, a question that then arises concerns the mechanisms through which this occurs. One possibility is that cohesion contributes to enhanced interaction and communication, which help to clarify group goals, which in turn leads to better group performance. Some other possible mediators of the cohesion-performance outcome relationship might be role clarity, role acceptance, status consensus, and member conformity. Each of these variables has been thought to be both an outgrowth of cohesion and an antecedent to performance success. Mediators can also be used to explain the reverse causal flow. For example, it might be that team performance success leads to member satisfaction, which then leads to greater group cohesion. Longitudinal research involving at least three temporal measures of the variables is needed to determine the nature of any causal relationship and thus the role of any mediators.

The Presence of a Cohesion-Performance Relationship

Table 31–1 provides an overview of research which has examined the cohesion-performance relationship. Insofar as the first and simplest question in the hierarchy is concerned—Is there a relationship?—it is clear that the answer is yes. The nature of this relationship is also evident from the results summarized in Table 31–1. In approximately 83% of the studies reported, the cohesion-performance relationship has been positive, showing that higher team cohesiveness is associated with greater team success. There were only a minimal number of studies in which a negative relationship has been reported (i.e., higher cohesion associated with reduced team success). Finally, only one study has reported no relationship.

Although these data do provide strong support for the cohesion-performance relationship, scientists must still view them with some caution. These are the results from *published* research only. Rosenthal (1966) has pointed out that there is a strong tendency for research journals to accept and publish the results from those studies in which a significant effect has been observed. When nothing is found—particularly in areas where a relationship has been previously observed and reported—there is a tendency to treat the findings as an anomaly and/or ignore them.

Common sense contributes to the suggestion that team success is the product of a number of factors with cohesion being one of these. Thus, the second auxiliary question posed earlier concerning the strength of the relationship is also important. Cohesion could contribute to success, but its contribution might be so small as to be practically meaningless. The strength of a relationship is usually expressed in statistical terms as the amount of explained variance—the variation in one variable (i.e., high and low scores) that can be explained by the variation in the second variable (comparable high and low scores). When correlational data are used, the percent of explained variance is calculated by squaring the correlation coefficient and multiplying the resulting value by 100.

A series of studies carried out by Carron and Ball (1977), Landers, Wilkinson, Hatfield, and Barber (1982), and Williams and Hacker (1982) provide interesting data to examine the importance of cohesiveness for subsequent team success. Their results are summarized in Table 31–2. Both cohesion and team success were measured at three time periods during the season—in the early, middle, and postseason. A composite score using 7 items from the Sport Cohesiveness Questionnaire (friendship, influence, enjoyment, sense of belonging, value of membership, closeness, and teamwork) was the measure of cohesiveness used (Martens, Landers, & Loy, 1972). As the top portion of Table 31–2 shows, the relationship between an early measure of cohesion and a later measure of performance varied ($r = .566$ and .632). In short, between 32% and 40% of the variation in team success can be accounted for by a team's cohesiveness.

Another series of studies reported by Widmeyer and his colleagues (Gossett & Widmeyer, 1981; Spence, 1980; Widmeyer & Gossett, 1978; Widmeyer & Martens, 1978) examined the relative contributions of cohesion and ability to team success across a variety of sport teams. The results from these studies were remarkably consistent. For female and male teams at both the intramural and intercollegiate levels, ability was over three times more important for team success than cohesiveness. Typically, cohesiveness accounted for 16% to 22% of the explained variance in team success while ability accounted for 54% to 60%. Some might think that the amount of cohesion variance accounted for is relatively small. However, in many sport leagues where parity is attempted through such procedures as drafting players in reverse order of finish, having an advantage of close to 20% appeals to most coaches.

Table 31–2 also provides some evidence to examine the third auxiliary issue within the first-level question in the research hierarchy, namely, the predominant causal direction

TABLE 31–1. An Overview of the Studies Examining the Cohesion-Performance
Relationship in Sport Groups (Adapted from Carron, 1988).

Studies Demonstrating a Positive Cohesion-Performance Relationship

Authors	Sample	Important Cohesion Variables
Arnold & Straub (1972)	College basketball	Teamwork, closeness
Bolger (1983)	High school/college basketball	Task cohesion
Carron & Ball (1976)	College ice hockey	Teamwork, closeness, enjoyment
Carron & Chelladurai (1981)	High school basketball	Sense of belonging, enjoyment, value of membership
Carron & Chelladurai (1981)	High school wrestling	Sense of belonging, enjoyment, value of membership
Dawe & Carron (1990)	High school hockey	Task cohesion, social cohesion
Gossett & Widmeyer (1981)	College basketball	"Direct cohesion" (i.e., teamwork, value of membership, closeness, enjoyment, sense of belonging)
Gossett & Widmeyer (1981)	College hockey	"Direct cohesion" (see above)
Klein & Christiansen (1969)	3-on-3 basketball	Attractiveness of the group
Landers et al. (1982)	Intramural basketball	Friendship
Martens & Peterson (1971)	Intramural basketball	Value of membership, teamwork, being close-knit
Ruder & Gill (1982)	College volleyball	Direct measure of cohesion
Ruder & Gill (1982)	Intramural volleyball	Teamwork, sense of belonging, direct measure of cohesion
Salminen (1987)	Junior ice hockey	Composite index from the Sport Cohesiveness Questionnaire
Shangi & Carron (1987)	High school basketball	ATG-T, ATG-S, GI-T, GI-S
Smith (1986)	Basketball class	Members told they were equally interested in task
Spence (1980)	Intramural basketball	"Direct cohesion" (see above)
Stogdill (1963)	College football	"Team integration" assessed by 6 observers
Vander Velden (1971)	High school basketball	Adherence to team membership
Williams & Hacker (1982)	College field hockey	Teamwork, closeness, sense of belonging, value of membership
Widmeyer & Martens (1978)	3-on-3 basketball	"Direct cohesion" (see above)
Widmeyer, Brawley, & Carron (1990)	3-on-3 basketball	Social cohesion, task cohesion
Widmeyer & Gossett (1978)	Intramural basketball	"Direct cohesion" (see above)
Williams & Widmeyer (1991)	College golf	Members' attraction to their groups' task (ATG-T)

Studies Demonstrating a Negative Cohesion-Performance Relationship

Author(s)	Sample	Important Cohesion Variables
Fiedler (1952)	High school basketball	Assumed similarity
Grace (1954)	High school basketball	Sociometric choice
Landers & Lueschen (1974)	Intramural bowling	Personal attraction
Lenk (1969)	International rowing	Personal attraction
McGrath (1962)	Rifle shooting	Personal attraction

Studies Demonstrating No Cohesion-Performance Relationship

Author(s)	Sample	Important Cohesion Variables
Melnick & Chemers (1974)	Intramural basketball	

TABLE 31–2. Cohesion-Performance Relationships Across Time*

Relationship of Early Cohesion Measures to Later Performance Measures

Authors	Early to Mid-season	Mid to Post-season	Early to Post-season
Carron & Ball (1977)	.225	.391	.072
Landers et al. (1982)	.800	.720	.810
Williams & Hacker (1982)	.720	.720	.620
Average†	.633	.632	.566

Relationships of Early Performance Measures to Later Cohesion Measures

Authors	Early to Mid-season	Mid to Post-season	Early to Post-season
Carron & Ball (1977)	.528	.770	.790
Landers et al. (1982)	.850	.640	.750
Williams & Hacker (1982)	—	.870	.870
Average†	.726	.776	.810

*Cohesion was assessed by a composite index comprising measures of friendship, influence, enjoyment, sense of belonging, value of membership, closeness, and teamwork.

†Z-transformations were used to compute averages.

of the cohesion-performance relationship. It is apparent from the top portion of Table 31–2 that when early cohesiveness was correlated with later measures of team success, the values ranged between .566 and .632. On the other hand, when early team success was correlated with later measures of team cohesiveness (presented in the lower portion of Table 2), the values ranged between .726 and .810. These data support a conclusion that the causal link between performance and cohesion is somewhat stronger than the causal link between cohesion and performance.

A qualifying note on this conclusion was advanced by Carron (1980), however. He pointed out that all items in the Sport Cohesiveness Questionnaire, with the exception of teamwork, assess attraction—"the interpersonal attraction of individuals to other competitors, the attraction of individuals to the group and the general attractiveness of the group itself. It does not reflect a task-oriented cohesiveness, a cohesiveness represented in enhanced coordination within the group" (p. 254). Thus, Carron felt that the above conclusion could be paraphrased to state that there is stronger support for the conclusion that the level of performance success experienced by the team contributes to increased perceptions by the members that the team is more attractive. There is lesser support for the suggestion that high perceptions of team attractiveness contribute to team success.

Finally, it should be noted that regardless of the measure of cohesion in each of these studies, it was not performance that was being assessed, but rather performance outcome. As we pointed out earlier, performance outcome is depen-

dent on not only the team's performance but also the performance of the opposing team. On the other hand, the outcome of a contest can directly influence the cohesion of a team, irrespective of the behavior/performance of the opposing team. Thus the directness of the performance outcome-cohesion link may explain why this relationship is stronger than the cohesion-performance outcome relationship.

Moderators of the Cohesion-Performance Relationship

The question of when (i.e., under what conditions) cohesion and performance are positively related has not received a great deal of attention. Possibly, this results from the fact that the overwhelming majority of studies (i.e., 83%; see Table 31–1) have reported a positive relationship between cohesion and performance outcome. One exception was a study by Landers and Lueschen (1974) with intramural bowling teams; teams lower in cohesiveness were more successful than teams higher in cohesiveness. In an attempt to explain their results, Landers and Lueschen suggested that *task type* might be a moderating variable between cohesion and performance (see Table 31–3). A distinction between what Steiner (1972) referred to as divisible and unitary tasks was used to illustrate their point. With divisible tasks, group performance requires a division of labor; each individual group member must effectively complete a different task for the group to be successful. Football teams are a good example. With a unitary task, however, all group members must perform the same skill; bowling teams are a good example. Landers and Lueschen proposed that in unitary tasks, the lack of interdependence in task performance can contribute to increased competitiveness among members (and reduced cohesiveness) and better individual performance. This same intragroup competitiveness and reduced cohesiveness would be detrimental in divisible tasks where member cooperation is important.

TABLE 31–3. Possible Moderating Variables in the Cohesion-Performance Relationship

Moderator Variable	Level	Relationship
Task Type	Independent	lower cohesion = Improved performance
	Dependent	higher cohesion = Improved performance
Group Drive	High	Positive cohesion = Performance relationship
	Low	Negative cohesion = Performance relationship
Norm for Productivity	High	Positive cohesion = Performance relationship
	Low	Negative cohesion = Performance relationship

Carron and Chelladurai (1979) also supported the importance of task type as a moderator of the cohesion-performance relationship. They pointed out that sports can be differentiated on the basis of (a) the amount of task interdependence present and (b) the methods by which member coordination is achieved. In team sports such as synchronized swimming, bowling, cross-country, swimming, and track relays, team members perform independently. The coordination necessary among team members to carry out the group task can be standardized through a set of fixed rules, schedules, or routines prior to competition. In these sports, there is little or no task cooperation by team members during the competition itself. Thus cohesion is relatively less important for team success. On the other hand, in team sports such as basketball or ice hockey, there is a high level of task interdependence required among team members to complete the group task. Some coordination can be achieved by establishing and practicing various routines and plans-for-action prior to competition. Nonetheless, however, a considerable amount of the coordination necessary for team success is dynamic, requiring mutual adjustments among teammates during competition. In this context, cohesion is relatively more important for team success.

Recently, Williams and Widmeyer (1991) argued that even though cohesion may not be as crucial for success in a coacting sport (i.e., unitary task) as it is in an interacting sport (i.e., divisible task), nevertheless it still can have a positive impact on group performance in activities involving independent member contributions. Their research demonstrated that there was, in fact, a significant positive relationship ($r^2 = 12\%$) between team task cohesion and team performance outcome in the coacting sport of golf. Williams and Widmeyer proposed that cohesion enhances the performance outcome of golf teams by reducing coordination losses prior to competition (i.e., by increasing communication during practices and practice rounds) and by reducing motivation losses during both practice and competition.

It was pointed out earlier that the overwhelming majority of studies in the sport sciences have reported a positive relationship between cohesion and performance. This has not been the case in research in business and industry. In fact, one reviewer, Ralph Stogdill (1972), questioned "how can one continue to believe that productivity and cohesiveness are positively related when the results of competent research indicate that in many cases the opposite is true?" (p. 26). Stogdill proposed that *group drive* (or *task motivation*) is an important moderator variable that helps explain why both negative and positive results have been reported between cohesion and performance in management science research. On the basis of a comprehensive review of the literature, he concluded that variance in group productivity is more closely associated with variance in group motivation than in group cohesiveness. In short, while high cohesiveness is likely to lead to better performance if members' motivation is high, when cohesiveness is high but the group is poorly motivated, the cohesion-performance relationship will be negative.

Widmeyer and Martens (1978) did not find that task motivation moderated the cohesion-performance outcome relationship within 3-on-3 recreational basketball teams. Although neither task nor interaction motivation added to cohesion's prediction of performance outcome, self-motivation increased the amount of variance accounted for by a significant 7%. In addition, it should be noted that neither the gender of the players nor the level of competition moderated the cohesion-performance outcome relationship.

Other authors have suggested that the *norm for productivity*—a variable similar to group drive—serves as a moderator of the cohesion-performance relationship (Berkowitz, 1954; Schachter, Ellertson, McBride, & Gregory, 1951). The norm for productivity is a generalized expectation held by group members concerning the level of productivity considered appropriate. Not surprisingly, highly cohesive groups exert considerable pressure on their members to adhere to group norms; less cohesive groups have less influence. Schachter et al. (1951) varied both the cohesiveness and the pressures for group productivity in task-oriented groups. They observed that when the norm for productivity was high, both high and low cohesive groups showed improved performance. On the other hand, they also found that when the norm for productivity was low, the high cohesive groups were less productive than the low cohesive groups. Group influence plays a strong role in the adherence of individuals to group norms (as any union worker involved in work-to-rule campaigns can testify).

It should be noted that in discussing the moderators of the cohesion-performance outcome relationship, the causal flow has not been indicated. It is possible that variables such as task type and member motivation could be altering the relationship, both when cohesion was influencing performance outcome and when performance outcome was influencing cohesion.

Suspected Mediators of the Cohesion-Performance Relationship

It was pointed out previously that a mediator is an important linking variable in a causal sequence—it is the mechanism (i.e., the why) through which one variable influences another. The designs used in sport science research to examine the cohesion-performance relationship have not been concerned with the role of mediator variables. Consequently, the results from this research do not permit definitive conclusions on *why* or *how* cohesion influences performance outcome and/or performance outcome influences cohesiveness. However, some reasonable hypotheses seem possible.

Team stability would seem to be one mediator variable in the cohesion-performance relationship. Part of the basis for this claim is that research in a large variety of contexts has shown that groups which maintain their membership over longer durations are more effective (e.g., Caplow, 1964; Shelly, 1964; Theberge & Loy, 1976). Theberge and Loy (1976), using data from professional baseball teams for the period 1951 to 1960, found that a higher turnover rate among athletes was associated with a poorer win-loss record ($r = -.540$), league standing ($r = -.550$), and a greater number of games behind first place ($r = .570$). Another basis for this claim is that group cohesion has also been linked with team stability. For example, research has shown that some forms of adherence, such as lack of absenteeism, lateness, and dropout behavior, are better in more cohesive sport groups and exercise classes (Carron, Widmeyer, & Brawley, 1988; Spink, 1990). Also, individuals in more cohesive groups hold a stronger belief in their group's ability to withstand the destructive potential of negative outcomes (Brawley, Carron, & Widmeyer, 1988). Possibly, high levels of cohesiveness cause group members to maintain their involvement with the group. In turn, this stability in membership leads to greater group effectiveness.

Two other potential mediators of the cohesion-performance relationship are role acceptance (the affective component of role involvement in the group which reflects group members' satisfaction with their responsibilities) and role clarity (the cognitive component reflecting group members' understanding of their responsibilities). Dawe and Carron (1990) tested members of high school hockey teams on role clarity and role acceptance and task and social cohesion three times during the course of the season—early, mid-season and post-season. Team success as represented by the ratio of wins to total number of games played was also obtained. Early measures of cohesiveness were found to be moderately correlated with subsequent measures of role clarity and acceptance (average $r = .610$). And early measures of role acceptance and clarity were found to have a low relationship with subsequent performance success (average $r = .315$).

A number of other variables intuitively would seem to be mediators of the cohesion-performance relationship (cf. Carron, 1988). For example, cohesiveness has been shown to be positively related to increased goal acceptance and conformity (Schachter et al., 1951). A link between these two factors and improved performance seems obvious. Similarly, cohesiveness is positively related to interaction and communication (e.g., Lott & Lott, 1961). Again, it seems reasonable to hypothesize that groups where members interact and communicate more frequently will be more successful. Quite some time ago, Klein and Christiansen (1969) demonstrated that cohesive basketball teams passed the ball more often among themselves. In addition, they found that teams which passed the ball more often were more successful. Finally, cohesion has been linked to member satisfaction (e.g., Carron, Ball, & Chelladurai, 1977). On the basis of their research with women's field hockey teams, Williams and Hacker (1982) concluded that the cohesion, satisfaction, and performance relationship was circular in nature—cohesiveness contributes to satisfaction, which contributes to performance success, which in turn contributes to cohesiveness. This conclusion contrasts to

that offered by Martens and Peterson (1971). It was their belief that a team's performance success led to member satisfaction, which in turn led to team cohesion. More research is needed to determine the causal nature of the cohesion-satisfaction and the satisfaction-performance success relationships.

OTHER ANTECEDENTS AND CONSEQUENCES OF COHESION IN SPORT

Recently, a large percentage of sport cohesion research has examined antecedents and consequences other than performance success. For example, Widmeyer and Williams (1991) utilized Carron's (1982) conceptual framework of cohesion to identify possible antecedents of team unity in the coacting sport of golf. They found that member satisfaction was the best predictor of all four aspects of cohesion assessed by the Group Environment Questionnaire. This instrument and the aspects of cohesion it assesses (ATG-T, ATG-S, GI-T, & GI-S) are covered in detail later in this chapter, in a discussion devoted to the measurement of cohesion. Specifically, Widmeyer and Williams assessed members' satisfaction with (a) the recognition they were receiving, (b) the opportunities to develop golf skills, (c) their social interaction with teammates, and (d) the level of competition. In addition, they found that task variables such as task communication (during practice, practice rounds, and tournaments) and prior team performance were more strongly related to the task aspects than to the social aspects of cohesion. On the other hand, prior liking and similarity of playing experience were more closely related to the social aspects. Having a team goal was not as strongly related to cohesion as was member recognition of the importance of the team goal. While coaches' efforts to foster cohesion were moderately related to all cohesion measures, team size was only related to members' attractions to their group's task (ATG-T). Surprisingly, this latter relationship was positive. A "big pond" theory was proposed in which it was argued that if a member's score is used to represent a group, the group is more attractive to the member if it is a large group. The Widmeyer and Williams data did not reflect Carron's (1982) framework in that the cohesion of these coacting teams was more highly related to individual factors such as member satisfaction than it was to environmental, leadership, or team factors. Nevertheless, the study does suggest that team cohesion can be fostered in a coacting sport.

In the Widmeyer and Williams (1991) study, the positive team size–team cohesion relationship may have been due to the fact that only the cohesion of the traveling squad (i.e., the starters) was assessed. The notion that the cohesiveness felt by some members is more important or at least different from that felt by others is not new. In a study of baseball teams conducted some 20 years ago, Landers and Crum (1971) found that the cohesiveness of the infielders was greater than that of the outfielders. Gossett and Widmeyer

(1981) identified "core" basketball players as those individuals who participated in at least one-third of league playing time. These researchers found that although core players were more cohesive and displayed less cohesion variability than noncore players, these differences were not significant. More recently, Granito and Rainey (1988) assessed the cohesiveness of starting and nonstarting football players at high school and university levels. They found that while there was no difference in social cohesion, starters scored higher than nonstarters on the two task measures of cohesion (i.e., members' attractions to their team's task and members' perceptions of the team's task integration). Spink (1989) noted that the teams Granito and Rainey (1988) studied were either not successful or only moderately successful. In his research, Spink found that among successful teams, starters and nonstarters could not be differentiated on any of the four aspects of cohesion measured by the Group Environment Questionnaire. However, among nonsuccessful teams, the starters were more strongly attracted to the group's task (ATG-T) than were the nonstarters.

In another study, Spink (1990a) investigated the relationship between cohesion and collective efficacy in elite and recreational volleyball teams. He found that cohesiveness and collective efficacy were positively related in elite teams but unrelated in recreational teams. More specifically, elite teams whose members were highly attracted to their group's task (ATG-T) and/or those who perceived their group to be very socially close (GI-S) had higher collective efficacy than did teams whose members gave low ratings to these aspects of cohesion. While the task cohesion (ATG)–collective efficacy relationship had been predicted, the social cohesion (GI-S)–collective efficacy link had not. Spink (1990) explained the latter relationship by noting that it had been shown earlier (Carron, Widmeyer, & Brawley, 1988) that GI-S was strongly associated with member adherence in sport teams. Spink then reasoned that the greater team stability resulting from this adherence is likely to promote greater collective efficacy. Although this sounds feasible, the stability–collective efficacy link has not been empirically demonstrated. Nevertheless, based on the levels of research questions advanced earlier in this chapter, it can be concluded that level of competition *moderates* the cohesion-collective efficacy relationship.

The cohesion-adherence research cited by Spink (1990) was conducted by Carron, Widmeyer, and Brawley (1988). In their work, these researchers employed stepwise discriminant function analyses and found that the function which discriminated adherers from nonadherers in elite sport teams used three of the four cohesion measures: members' attractions to their team's task (ATG-T), members' perceptions of their team's task integration (GI-S), and members' perceptions of their team's social integration (GI-S). Within fitness classes, the cohesion variables that discriminated adherers from nonadherers were the two individual attraction measures, ATG-T and ATG-S.

Carron, Widmeyer, and Brawley (1988) examined the relationship between cohesion and another form of adherence, namely the absenteeism and lateness of recreation sport participants. Here, they found that the type of cohesion which best discriminated adherers from nonadherers was members' perceptions of their group's social integration (GI-S). The researchers concluded that the cohesion-adherence relationship varies across different groups. For example, in more individual activities such as fitness classes, individual attraction measures are better predictors, whereas in competitive sport teams, perceptions of group integration are more important. Among recreational sport teams, adherence of members is more dependent on social cohesion (GI-S), while that of elite team members is more task related (GI-T).

Recently, Westre and Weiss (1991) examined the relationship between team cohesion and football players' perceptions of their coaches' leadership style and behaviors. These researchers found that coaches who were seen as providing higher levels of social support, training and instruction, positive feedback, and a democratic style have players who perceive higher levels of task cohesion within their teams. In addition, it was shown that this relationship was moderated by both team and individual success, as well as by starter/nonstarter playing status, but not by either offensive or defensive position. Specifically, it was found that

(a) players with higher perceptions of team success reported higher levels of team cohesion and perceived coaches as exhibiting higher frequencies of democratic style and positive feedback; (b) players with higher perceptions of individual success reported higher levels of attraction toward group cohesion and perceived their coaches as higher in positive feedback; (c) starters reported higher levels of attraction toward group cohesion than did nonstarters. (p. 51)

Although the design of this study did not allow for any casual interpretations, the researchers do suggest how "each of the significant leader behaviors can contribute to higher levels of task cohesion in a variety of ways" (p. 51). In addition, they postulate why cohesion and leadership perceptions might be greater for players and teams who perceive that they were more successful and for players who were in the starting lineups of their teams.

The last research to be presented in this section examines a *mediator* of the cohesion–performance outcome relationship. It can be argued that group cohesion influences group performance outcome by reducing group process losses—losses in intermember coordination and losses in intramember motivation. McNight, Williams, and Widmeyer (1991) found that team cohesion was a significant predictor of social loafing (i.e., a motivation loss) by members of swimming relay teams. Members of teams that were more cohesive were less likely to loaf. The researchers also showed that cohesion was a better predictor of social loafing than was the often reported variable of member identifiability.

In this section, it has been shown that cohesion is related to member satisfaction, intrateam communication, prior liking among members, coaches' efforts to foster cohesion, the importance of the team goal, collective efficacy, perceptions of leadership style and behavior, and social loafing. It was also shown that certain cohesion relationships were *moderated* by the starting status of members, by the perceptions of team and individual success, and by level of competition. Overall, the investigations indicate that researchers are interested in antecedents and consequences of cohesion other than performance outcome.

The foregoing pages offer a substantial amount of research concerning cohesion and its relationship to performance and other outcomes (e.g., adherence), as well as a discussion of the moderators and mediators of these relationships. This research perspective spans a number of years in which the approaches to investigating the relationship varied. A central aspect of these different approaches that may define the nature of future research progress is the conceptual definition of cohesion and the theory about this concept (cf. Mudrack, 1989a, b). Inasmuch as the most recent views of the concept and theory are more concretely elaborated and have serious implications for measurement, the reader may feel previous research should be ignored. Clearly, this is not being recommended in the present chapter. Instead, the reader should be discriminating about what each study offers to the cohesion-performance literature by considering whether the studies, from the earliest to the most recent, remedied or controlled for conceptual and measurement problems.

In order to make clear the importance of this advice, the following discussion begins with the most recent definition and conceptual model of cohesion and the related approach to measurement. In addition, the latter aspect of the chapter considers a selection of important problems and future directions sport science investigators must entertain. Without considering the challenges presented by these issues, it is our opinion that progress in understanding group cohesion, its place in sport group dynamics, and its role relative to group outputs will continue to be slow.

COHESION: CONCEPTUALLY DEFINED

A variety of papers have summarized the pros and cons of various definitions of cohesion from a historical perspective. The interested reader can peruse a series of references as cited in Carron (1988) or in Mudrack's (1989a, b) recent articles on group cohesion. It is not the purpose of this chapter to provide such an account when it has been done well elsewhere. However, Mudrack's recent analysis makes clear that the complexity of the cohesion construct has made it difficult to define precisely or consistently. Further, such difficulty translates to problems of operational definition, measurement, and manipulation in research.

What is interesting about Mudrack's analysis is that in two different social psychology journals he concludes that an appropriate definition/reconceptualization of group cohesiveness may already exist in the sport psychology literature. The definition he draws upon is one by Carron (1982): "a dynamic process which is reflected in the tendency for a

group to stick together and remain united in the pursuit of its goals and objectives" (p. 124). Clearly, this definition avoids the problems of earlier definitions based on either the metaphor of the atom (e.g., Festinger, Schacter, & Back, 1950) or on the unidimensional notion of attraction to the group (e.g., Libo, 1953). The multidimensional nature of cohesion may incorporate both concepts, and this is implicitly recognized in Carron's definition. Colloquially expressed, the "bottom line" is that cohesion investigators must recognize the multidimensionality of cohesion in conceptually defining, theorizing, and measuring the construct in future research. It is to these latter points that attention is now turned.

The reader may question the worth of adopting a new definition of cohesion, but as noted by Mudrack (1989a), most researchers have been "inexcusably sloppy" in defining cohesion. He recommended tying the definition of cohesion to its measurement by making it applicable to settings being investigated. If such a practice was followed in sport science, there would be consistency in the cohesion construct–operational definition link for studies throughout the literature.

The conceptual definition offered by Carron (1982) was advanced in relation to the discussion of groups in sport, although it may be more generic to groups in general. Consistent with this definition and prior to Mudrack's analysis, Carron and his colleagues developed a conceptual model and instrument to measure team cohesion (e.g., Carron et al., 1985; Widmeyer et al., 1985; Brawley et al., 1987; Carron, 1988; Brawley, 1991). To appreciate the development process involved in their new instrument, it is worthwhile considering the measurement approaches which preceded the Carron et al. (1985) instrument.

MEASUREMENT OF COHESION

Generally, the various unidimensional approaches to operationally define and measure cohesion have seen cohesion as interpersonal attraction (e.g., friendship), individual attraction to the group (e.g., personal value of membership), similarity of other group members (e.g., similarity of task interests), and commitment to the group (e.g., resistance to switching groups.) Carron (1988) has critically evaluated these elsewhere, noting that these measurement approaches are borrowed from work and social groups.

As early as 1972, sport researchers realized the problems of measuring cohesion in sport from a unidimensional perspective. Their response to the challenge posed by these problems was to combine ideas about attraction between individuals in a group, between a group member and his or her group, and concepts about the entire group. An instrument called the Sport Cohesiveness Questionnaire (SCQ; Martens, Landers, & Loy, 1972) was developed and was the basis for numerous cohesion studies of sport teams between 1972 and 1987. Many of these studies have been mentioned in the preceding pages and concerned questions of whether cohesion was (a) necessary for group performance, (b) a consequence of team success, (c) dependent on some level of performance, or (d) unrelated to team performance.

For the majority of these sport-related studies, Mudrack's (1989a) criticism of failure to consistently link concept to operational definition applied. The tendency for sport investigators to borrow definitions and measurement procedures from the parent literature without critical evaluation is quite evident. In group dynamics research, conceptual definitions, operational definitions, and measurement links were poorly made with frightening consistency. Mudrack (1989b) reviewed 23 recent studies between the years of 1975 and 1985 and found that no two studies measured cohesion in exactly the same way. This profile of inconsistency in measurement is also characteristic of the sport research during that time (see Table 31–1, for examples). Thus it becomes extremely difficult to determine if all sport studies were measuring the same construct. To a degree, this criticism also applied to the SCQ because the instrument was used in various forms. Furthermore, the measurement veracity of the instrument was never checked. Although the SCQ was of a more multidimensional nature than other sport cohesion measurement tools, it had not been developed by a process allowing for assessment of its psychometric properties.

RECENT MEASUREMENT APPROACHES

Carron (1982) offered a frame of reference to distinguish cohesion from its antecedents and consequences and to aid categorization of prior research. However, he stressed the need for the development of a conceptual model to guide measurement and research. Two groups of investigators independently responded to Carron's (1982) suggestion for the development of new cohesion instruments. The first group used a data-driven approach to develop their instrument, while the second used a theoretical approach.

The Data-Driven Approach

The Multidimensional Sport Cohesion Instrument. The first group, Yukelson, Weinberg, and Jackson (1984), developed the Multidimensional Sport Cohesion Instrument (MSCI). Their approach has been labeled "data driven" because the instrument "emerges" from data-concerning responses to items drawn from other cohesion instruments and group dynamics–related concepts. Their view was that a clear measurement instrument would be revealed if a good post hoc model could be developed from the data obtained. While Yukelson et al. (1984) surveyed the group dynamics literature broadly to develop items for their instrument, the data-driven approach did not offer the cohesion concept to operational definition link noted as a major research problem by Mudrack (1989a). The item pool of the MSCI mixed potential antecedents and consequences of cohesion with items that attempted to measure the concept per se. In one sense, this approach represents an advancement because the authors recognized the multidimensionality of the cohesion concept. Thus they sampled items broadly with the notion that the emerging factor structure of subjects' responses would reveal dimensions of cohesion.

At best, what this strategy would have the potential to offer is a clear factor structure of antecedents-cohesion-consequences factors. However, most of any investigator's efforts at writing an item that represents a construct that is not confounded by other constructs have some degree of error. This becomes all the more difficult when the development of an instrument is not guided by some theoretical/conceptual model, as was the case for the MSCI. Finally, the authors wrote the items specific to the sport of basketball and developed their instrument in that context. Thus there is some question as to how adaptable the instrument would be in a variety of team sport settings. Could cohesion be measured regardless of team type and context? The MSCI represented a step in the right direction in seeking to measure multiple aspects of cohesion, but other questions regarding its use as a viable instrument remain unresolved.

The Theory-Driven Approach

At approximately the same time as the development of the MSCI, the second research group was involved in developing both a new conceptual model of cohesion and a related instrument. Carron, Widmeyer, and Brawley (1985) proceeded from Carron's (1982) definition of cohesion as mentioned earlier. To develop the conceptual model, they reviewed literature about the nature of the group and group cohesion. This review highlighted many of the problems discussed in the review by Mudrack (1989a). Two distinctions made clear by this review were observed to arise consistently. The first distinction is between individual and group aspects of group life, and the second distinction is between the task and social aspects of group involvement (e.g., Carron, 1988; Mikalachki, 1969; Mudrack, 1989b; Van Bergen & Koekebakker, 1959). The review and resulting construct analysis resulted in the development of a conceptual model of cohesion that included these two distinctions as a central aspect of the model. Using this conceptual model as a basis, Carron et al. advanced preliminary hypotheses and initiated the early stages of theory development. Also the conceptual model became the guide for the development of their instrument to measure group cohesion.

The Conceptual Model. The model is based on the assumption that both the individual and group aspects of cohesion are represented, in part, as multiple beliefs and perceptions of individual members of a group. The model proposes that each group member integrates the information from various aspects of the social world that are relevant and meaningful to the group such that a variety of perceptions and beliefs are generated. These beliefs/perceptions are about ways in which the group and its members remain united in the pursuit of group goals and objectives, about how the group sticks together, and they can be classified into two broad categories within the conceptual model.

The first category is Group Integration, which concerns the beliefs and perceptions individual group members hold about the group (team) as a totality. The second category is the Individual's Attractions to the Group, and it concerns each group member's personal beliefs and perceptions about what both initially attracted the person and what continues to attract the person to the group. This initial division corresponds to the first major distinction found in the cohesion literature. Both of these categories are further divided into task and social orientations, corresponding to the second major distinction in aspects of group life and a group's cohesiveness.

The conceptual model, therefore, has four related dimensions concerning the multiple beliefs and perceptions that are a part of the dynamic process characterizing a group's or a team's cohesiveness. These beliefs and perceptions are thought to act *together* in creating a group's and individual group member's sense of cohesiveness. Their integrated totality represents an indicant of the multidimensional construct of cohesion. The four related dimensions are Group Integration—Task and Social (GI-T and GI-S) and Individual Attractions to the Group—Task and Social (ATG-T and ATG-S). From a theoretical perspective, each dimension alone could be sufficient to encourage athletes in a group to "stick with" or remain united with their group. However, given that group cohesiveness is characterized as a dynamic process, it seems more probable that some of each dimension will contribute to a given team's overall level of cohesion.

The relative contribution of each dimension to cohesiveness is hypothesized as varying over time, depending upon the impact of suspected moderator variables. For example, level of group development (e.g., months or years a team has been together; time of season) or nature of the group (e.g., their motivational base having a task or social focus) might influence the degree to which a particular dimension contributes to cohesion. As these moderators are part of what constitutes the social experience of the group, and of the individual member within the group, they are hypothesized to affect the beliefs and perceptions that are indicants of the four dimensions of cohesion. Therefore, for example, a group/team with a *task focus* as its motivational base may have more experiences occurring over time that contribute to stronger and greater numbers of task-related beliefs and perceptions (i.e., GI-T and ATG-T), in comparison to the number and strength of experiences that contribute to social percepts of cohesiveness.

The changing nature of beliefs and perceptions over time is consistent with Carron's (1982) definition of cohesion and with the notion in group dynamics that as the group's characteristics increase or decrease in stability, so will the behavior and beliefs of individual group members. The changes in behavior and beliefs of individual members will correspond to changes that occur in matters of consequence to the whole group (cf. Sherif & Sherif, 1969). While various antecedents to and consequences of group process may influence the development of cohesion in dynamic fashion over time, their influence in the conceptual model is presumed to operate (at least in part) *through* the perceptions and beliefs of individual team members. In terms of Carron's (1982) organizational model of factors related to cohesion, the influence of factors internal and external to the group would operate *through* beliefs and percepts of group members.

Following this reasoning, the influence of such factors is taken into account in the conceptual model offered by Carron et al. (1985) through their effects on beliefs about aspects of cohesiveness. Figure 31–1 schematically illustrates the conceptual model of cohesiveness as it derives from the operation of internal and external factors on beliefs.

In summary, group members perceive and believe that their group can supply them with various task and social provisions that fulfill their needs. Believing in and receiving these provisions is thought to cause athletes to be attracted to their team (i.e., ATG perceptions). The perceptions of and beliefs in a team's united purpose to reach a group goal or objective, as well as the group's unity about being socially supportive for group task or social concerns, are motivations for an athlete to continue as a member of a team (i.e., GI perceptions). The combination of these different beliefs helps to define aspects of cohesiveness on a team. Individual members both observe behavior and confirm beliefs about the multiple aspects of cohesion which, from the individual member's psychological perspective, adds to and reinforces a sense that he or she does wish to remain with the team and that the team is united. The extent to which an individual group member can describe the strength of his or her perception about each of the four aspects of cohesion makes possible the measurement of each.

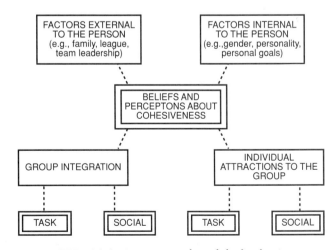

FIGURE 31-1. A conceptual model of cohesion.

It is recognized that the four related dimensions concerning various perceptions of cohesion are likely a product of a complex person-environment interaction occurring as a team progresses through its season. It is assumed that the process of a team becoming cohesive is one that happens through social learning as team athletes interact with their environment. These notions are at the basis of the conceptual model, are related to the way the Carron et al. (1985) instrument was developed, and are associated with the procedures for measuring sport team cohesion. The important concept-operational definition link deemed as necessary by Mudrack (1989a, b) was accomplished by developing the Group Environment Questionnaire.

The Group Environment Questionnaire. The GEQ instrument development process and operational definitions of cohesion are described in detail elsewhere (Carron et al., 1985; Widmeyer et al., 1985; Brawley, Carron, & Widmeyer, 1987, 1988; Carron, Brawley, & Widmeyer, 1988.) However, the process evolved from the conceptual model described above. The link between the concepts and the measure was not only facilitated by the model but also by involving members of teams in the development process. Their phenomenology was examined to ensure a face valid instrument that linked each of the four dimensions of cohesion to their respective measurements. In so doing, the measures were meaningful to team athletes and free of items that would either reflect aspects of investigator bias or ignore the concept-operational definition link. Thus the GEQ may represent one sport cohesion instrument to which Mudrack's criticisms (1989a, b) fail to apply. The development proccss produced an 18-item, 4-scale measure. The subsequent validation process for the GEQ has shown it to be both valid and reliable from several perspectives.

In brief, the GEQ has been used to examine various questions about cohesion in both sport and fitness contexts (Brawley et al., 1987, 1988; Shangi & Carron, 1987; Widmeyer et al., 1985, 1988). Perceptions of Group Integration-Task predicted the membership of athletes to team sports while Individual Attraction to the Group-Task predicted the membership of athletes to coactive teams (e.g., swim teams, wrestling teams). Duration of team membership has also been correctly predicted from an aspect of cohesion assessed by the GEQ. Level of cohesion has been related to each of the following variables: attributions for responsibility for performance outcomes, team performance, increased adherence and reduced absenteeism, and group size. In the last case, cohesion varied as a function of size. The relationships between cohesion and antecedent or consequence variables are also moderated by size (Widmeyer, Brawley, & Carron, 1992). Most recently there have been preliminary indications of a relationship between team cohesion and member satisfaction and intrateam communication (Widmeyer & Williams, 1991), collective efficacy (Spink, 1990), and to some extent, social loafing (McNight, Williams, & Widmeyer, 1991). The specifics of these studies have been discussed earlier in this chapter.

While the studies using the recently developed GEQ have examined previously assessed and unassessed variables, there is a need for both replication and extension of this research. This is also applicable for studies that have used cohesion measures of questionable validity (e.g., see Table 31–1) in which the GEQ could be used to replace such measures and the research questions used in those studies could be reexamined.

The Future

Given the criticisms about cohesion research by Brawley, 1990; Carron, 1988; and Mudrack (1989a, b), it should be clear that there is a need to conduct cohesion research with much greater care. The first steps toward improving research in this area have been taken by addressing the need for a conceptual model and a related cohesion measurement instrument. For the future, however, the quality and quantity of research must be enhanced so that we can make more definitive statements in answering the three levels of research questions posed earlier in this chapter. Without moving in this direction, it seems questionable whether our current level of research either advances our knowledge in some way or contributes to practice. To advance cohesion research, what issues must be considered?

ISSUES OF CONCERN FOR FUTURE RESEARCH

Evaluating the Past

Part of what has already been discussed in this chapter concerns (a) the reevaluation of the conceptual definition of cohesion and its measurement, (b) categorization of previous research using Carron's (1982) organizational framework, and (c) a synopsis of the already completed sport cohesion research, addressing three "generations" of research questions posed about any social phenomena. That is, does the phenomenon occur, under what conditions, and why? Recently there has been heightened awareness in sport science about problems of conceptualizing and measuring cohesion. However, even with all the recent promise shown in cohesion research by using new instruments, there is still more we can learn by evaluating *prior* research.

If we are considering the relationships of antecedent and consequence variables to cohesion, we must also know if these variables and not just cohesion were validly conceptualized and accurately measured. For example, for performance or for satisfaction, how were the measures conceptualized and linked to their operational definitions? In the case of performance, is an accurate measure (conceptual or operational) the win-loss ratio, team improvement, or some other perception of performance? Which is likely to be directly related or indirectly related to the concepts of Group Integration or Attractions to the Group? Concerning satisfaction, sport science researchers have been cavalier in their measurement, often using one item to assess the team's or the individual's satisfaction with either team unity or performance. By contrast, the concept of satisfaction has certainly been given major attention by psychologists in organizational behavior who link it to job performance. O'Reilly (1991) notes that by some estimates, over 4,000 studies have concerned job satisfaction, and that researchers continue to develop and refine measures. Although not identical, surely team performance satisfaction must be given more than the attention of a single item in order to be measured validly and accurately in sport science.

Thus future research into antecedent-cohesion-consequence relationships could benefit by a look at our errors in examining independent or control variables in previous cohesion research. We should avoid exclusive preoccupation with the "main" research solution as being the measurement of cohesion. It is but one important solution. As an example, Widmeyer, Brawley, and Carron (1990) were critical of their own work when operationalizing the independent variable of group size and how it affected perceptions of cohesiveness in a recreational basketball setting. The arbitrary group size divisions the investigators applied in this setting had the potential to lack generality across studies and reflect experimenter bias. Fortunately their realization of the problem led to checks on the ecological validity of group size divisions through the use of group member perceptions. Luckily the members' perceptions of group size confirmed the investigators' arbitrary guesses, but without such a check, explanations for unexpected results in group size-cohesion relations would have been untenable. Preoccupation with the dependent variable of cohesion could have led to a major independent variable oversight and a series of errors for future studies. If we are to advance future cohesion-related research, we must critically evaluate *all* major variables used in previous research questions.

Unsolved Problems

Unit of Analysis. An issue that applies to group dynamics in general and sport science in particular is whether the group or the individual should be the unit of analysis. This is most relevant for the study of cohesion. The unit of analysis partly governs the choice of statistical procedure. To illustrate this point, consider that each team member could provide cohesion responses and the sum of the responses in each dimension of multidimensional cohesion would reflect each group member's perceptions of cohesion. Within a team, then, there would be a distribution of responses based on the number of responding players on the team. Therefore, a team mean and variance based on the number of players is obtained. By contrast, if the unit of analysis is the group, the mean of the team is often the single score used to represent the team's cohesiveness. A number of teams would be required in order to constitute a sample, then a mean and variance for the distribution of team (*vs.*

individual member) cohesion scores would be possible. The drawback, as noted by Gossett and Widmeyer (1981), is that the variability in each team's cohesion is often ignored when the unit average (team mean) is the operational definition for purposes of using groups as units of analysis. Their point was that the variability within a team may be a reflection of the agreement or consensus about the level of cohesiveness measured. A unit score does not reveal this information, and the mean alone is misleading.

Brawley (1991) has suggested the assignment of different relative weights to different aspects of cohesion by taking into account their variability. Thus the relative importance accorded each aspect of cohesion by a team athlete is considered. However, this weighting does not necessarily remedy the group versus individual unit of analysis problem. Even if the group is used as the unit of analysis and has a representative score, the group analysis requires data collection on many teams in order to obtain sufficient statistical power necessary for the study design. This can become a logistics problem because of league size, geography, homogeneity of the sample, and so forth.

Still another solution may be to have the entire group answer the investigators' questions as a unit. However, social pressure to reach a common response might eliminate interesting variability within a team. On the other hand, some investigators may argue that degree of consensus is indeed a reflection of cohesiveness. Still others could claim that the team was offering favorable self-presentations, which would not be a true reflection of the accuracy and variability of responses to the various dimensions of team cohesion.

As yet there is no definitive answer to this problem, and researchers tend to ignore it. The best advice seems to be to choose the unit of analysis based upon the *nature of the research question,* rather than arbitrarily. The advantage to following this advice is that it forces the researcher to a priori consider the research question and its link to both sample and analysis before data is collected.

Cohesion Affecting Performance. Although this issue was addressed earlier, it was emphasized that the research thus far has had limited success at providing a definitive answer to whether cohesion did affect performance. Part of the solution to this unsolved problem may lie in the need to change the way we investigate the question "Does cohesion cause performance?" Perhaps the question that should be asked is "What *processes* build team cohesion *and* simultaneously contribute to group performance?" (Brawley, 1990). How can we understand the cause-effect question without determining the group processes involved? It seems clear that they should be identified and studied more closely. The process may not be identified so easily unless we clarify whether the cause-effect relationship operates directly or happens indirectly, through mediator variables. It is not clear that there is a one-to-one relationship with, for example, the outcome of group task effectiveness and cohesion. Could not a team choose a task strategy, be united in its choice and subsequent carrying out of the strategy, then have it fail because the choice of strategy, but not its execution, was ill conceived? If this is a fairly common situation (e.g., improper scouting of an opponent, thus inappropriate strategy choice), then simply correlating cohesion and performance may sometimes be misleading. For example, an interactive team would have reflected cohesive behavior while carrying out the poor strategy. The resultant failure would be unrelated or inversely related to their positive cohesion. Thus it is important to differentiate the team's cohesive behavior from outcomes. While there may be a strong relationship between the two in some situations, there may not in others. How do we determine what these situations may be?

The answer may lie in how closely the processes that develop cohesion and those that lead to group task effectiveness are interwoven. From the perspective of Carron et al.'s (1985) conceptual model of cohesion, perhaps the cohesion dimension most closely linked to performance outcome is Group Integration-Task. In fact, this hypothesis could be tested experimentally. Consider the following ideas as one means of doing so.

Zander (1982), in his book *Making Groups Effective*, drew upon the group dynamics literature to suggest techniques for team building in business and industry. The majority of recommendations Zander makes involve task-and goal-related processes requiring interactions between group members. Thus the building of a stronger cohesion-task effectiveness link could lead to strong team cohesion centered around the group's task. In a study using an intervention design, the results observed would indicate that the effectiveness intervention encouraged increased cohesion *and* improved performance relative to a no-treatment control group. Of course, this experiment also requires that a meaningful operational definition of performance, or task-effectiveness, or success, is employed. The successful intervention would demonstrate that interactive processes between members cause the team's task performance to improve. While the interaction between members occurs, a sense of Group Integration-Task (cohesion) is promoted. The control group, on the other hand, would have to show less systematic improvement in either variable over time or a change in only one of the two variables. For example, cohesion might improve while performance stayed the same.

In brief, it seems that more progress toward solving this research problem might occur if investigators of cohesion-performance relationships considered the complexities of group process that affect *both* variables. The time for simple correlational studies is past.

Cohesion and Motivated Group Behavior. Although a number of consequences of group cohesion other than performance have already been discussed, only a few research examples have described motivated behavior (e.g., social loafing, adherence, absenteeism/lateness, attributions of responsibility). In the majority of cases, the motivated behavior influenced by cohesion has been that of individual group members. However, it is reasonable to hypothesize that the group variable of cohesiveness should provoke mo-

tivated behavior by the group as a whole. The hypothesized relationship would be stronger between the group-oriented aspects of cohesion (i.e., Group Integration), and the various aspects of total group behavior from which we infer team motivation.

Exceptions to the tendency to study cohesion's effect on individual member motivation have been group motivation studies by Ball and Carron (1976) and Gossett and Widmeyer (1981). In both investigations, it was found that greater effort toward achieving group goals was associated with the presence of group cohesion. Group effort is certainly one set of behaviors from which we can infer team motivation. However, other behaviors are also viable indicants of group motivation and may be made easier or encouraged by team cohesion. Examples of such variables would be (a) a team's persistence, (b) its involvement in problem-solving in the face of obstacles to objectives, (c) following goals without question, (d) group tenacity in the pursuit of goals, (e) and group sanction of either nonconformity or unacceptable individual member behavior. Although the Group Integration aspect of cohesion should encourage the display of such motivated group behavior, sport investigators have characteristically avoided its study. Part of the reason for the scant research on entire group behaviors may be both the problem of operationally defining them and then practically carrying out the measurement and data collection (e.g., unit of analysis problem, observation of total group behavior problem). Nonetheless, until problems are solved or the ambition is gained for such study, the question of whether cohesion influences the degree of consistency in group-motivated behavior will remain unanswered. This will also be the case in determining which aspects of cohesion (i.e., ATG or GI, task or social) most strongly influence specific kinds of group-motivated behavior.

This third unsolved problem certainly needs a solution if we are to build a scientific knowledge base about groups in exercise and sport. From an applied viewpoint, it seems that knowing that cohesion would motivate either sport or exercise group behavior would be useful for team building interventions.

Research Pitfalls

In some ways, the following pitfalls can be considered endemic to more areas in sport science than the study of group cohesion. However, they are so characteristic of much of the past research in cohesion, it is worth pointing out the limitations they impose on the literature so they can be avoided or reduced in the future. The four pitfalls are: (a) failure to use theory or some guiding framework to conduct research, (b) ignoring the dynamic nature of cohesion, (c) an almost exclusive focus on the investigation of sport teams versus other types of sport groups, and (d) a tendency to consider competitions as the focal group event to study, versus other events such as practice. There are other pitfalls that may present themselves in research but are less common to the published literature.

Failure to Use Theory. Brawley (1990), Carron (1988), McGrath (1984), Widmeyer et al. (1985), and Zander (1979) all mention that the area of group dynamics generally, and cohesion specifically, is characterized by fragmented research. There is no cohesion theory to systematically guide the posing of research questions and the collection and interpretation of data. The metaphor of "bricks scattered about the brickyard" is most apt in describing the bulk of cohesion research. Like bricks scattered about, our knowledge about cohesion and its influence on the group and on individual members is both unsystematic and limited.

Efforts toward developing organizational frameworks (cf. Carron, 1988) or theories (cf. McGrath, 1984) may be useful in helping future cohesion researchers avoid this pitfall. It is important to realize the benefits to be gained for cohesion research if theory-oriented approaches are used. Not only can research hypotheses be generated a priori versus post hoc, but seemingly disparate facts can be organized into some kind of meaningful order. In good theories, constructs tend to be well specified and a more concise link between construct, operational definition, and measurement follows. Theory also provides a framework and target that allows investigators to (a) identify unexamined aspects of a psychological puzzle or (b) validate ideas about the cohesion of sport groups. In validation, theory is the foundation through which explanations of cohesiveness can be offered or against which failures to demonstrate predicted cohesion-related behavior can be understood and explained. Thus use of theory, even at its most preliminary level, will offer cohesion some systematic future direction.

Snapshot Research. If Carron's (1982) conceptual definition of cohesion is taken into consideration in future research, more studies must consider the "dynamic process" aspect of this phenomenon. The majority of cohesion research to date has been what might be termed "snapshot." Like a single photograph, only specific points in time have been captured where something is revealed about specific games or seasonal time points. However, many group processes can change over the course of a season or years of belonging to a team, thereby altering the nature of cohesion over time (e.g., increasing or decreasing). To understand these changing and possibly reciprocal relationships between antecedents-cohesion-consequences, studies need to be prospective and longitudinal. Thus, change can be hypothesized a priori and the necessary time can be allowed to observe the nature of predicted changes. This is in direct contrast to the typical one-time snapshot investigation where post hoc speculation is offered about the dynamic nature of cohesion either preceding an event or future events. Post hoc speculation does not always offer stable ground as a foundation for future research. Notable exceptions to this research pitfall have been studies con-

ducted by Carron and Ball on performance (1977) and Williams and Hacker on satisfaction (1982). Both investigated interactive teams (e.g., ice hockey, field hockey) over time.

Finally, it should be noted that what we learn from the more dynamic video of longitudinal studies is not just a larger description. Relative to the three levels of research questions mentioned earlier in the chapter, we may learn about the change in team cohesion that occurs with different levels of development experienced by the team (cf. Carron, 1988). For example, as a group develops and becomes more stable in its characteristics, type and strength of cohesion may vary, length of time to develop different dimensions of cohesion may vary, and performance-cohesion relationships may indeed be reciprocal. The explanation for the variability in these examples may require a search for the influence of moderator (i.e., second research question about conditions affecting) and mediator (i.e., the third research question about why something occurs) variables.

It should be noted that research strategies may also have to change in order for us to conduct longitudinal research. An example of how this might be done is to look to some of the longitudinal studies in the earlier group dynamics literature as guides. Consider Sherif and Sherif's (1969) report of their famous studies of preadolescent boys' outdoor sport camps (e.g., The Robber's Cave Experiment) or Whyte's (1943) book, *Street Corner Society,* about his three-year participant observation of groups in a Boston slum. These famous studies used a *variety* of methodological data collection approaches to provide a qualitatively *and* quantitatively rich longitudinal data set. In both examples, emerging and changing group cohesion was linked with the development of, for example, clearly defined group structure, and to competition.

It is not advocated that the research paradigms of these examples be duplicated in order to avoid the pitfall of snapshot research. What is being emphasized is that across time, samples of many of the team's (group's) behaviors must be collected by a variety of methods that can be used in a convergent fashion. Thus, unobtrusive observation, questionnaires, interviews, and coach feedback might be used over time to confirm the processes that make cohesion dynamic, or to confirm the reciprocal nature of the cohesion-performance relationship.

Only Sport and Competition? The last two pitfalls are quite related. Although it is understandable why sport psychologists examine cohesion research questions relative to both competition and performance, it is often perplexing as to why these are almost the only contexts examined as influencing or being influenced by cohesion. Even if all the cohesion problems mentioned earlier had been remedied, what we know about cohesion would be mainly in relation to the team and competition-related performance. There are many other sport groups and physical activities, yet the pitfall into which most researchers have blundered is the exclusive sport and competition focus. Why is this necessarily bad? Unfortunately, such a focus has made us ignore *other types of physical activity groups* such as fitness classes, cardiac or injury rehabilitation groups, sport governing agencies, master's sport clubs, and recreational sport leagues. The different nature of these groups will likely moderate both the type and degree of cohesiveness developed. If only interactive sport teams are investigated, it will be difficult to determine if conceptual models of cohesion such as the one developed by Carron et al. (1985) have generality. It will also mean that knowledge about cohesiveness in sport and physical activity will be quite limited. Without data on various forms of groups and their respective cohesiveness properties, opportunities to understand multidimensional cohesion will be constrained.

Similar to the pitfall of exclusively studying team sport is the exclusive attention paid to investigating *cohesion-competition* relations. Performance interests have typically pushed sport psychologists in this direction. However, if cohesion is indeed dynamic and develops with time, then a focus on competition alone ignores a great deal of what constitutes the primary interaction time of the team: the practice setting. It would be safe to estimate that as much as 80% of a team's interactions revolve around practice. Surely this time is relevant to the development of cohesion. At a minimum, this time period must be studied just to exclude this possible hypothesis. Brawley (1991) notes that practices, scrimmages, and other team functions make up the bulk of time in which teams interact. It is these interactions, with their high frequency of communication, between-player contact, practicing of team tasks and selection of goals, and sharing of team frustrations, that contribute to the development of team cohesion (Brawley, 1991; Carron, 1988; Zander, 1982). It seems naive to think that cohesion can realistically be studied in teams and the other physical activity groups mentioned if these instances of major group interaction outside competition are continually ignored.

While there are certainly other pitfalls to avoid in conducting research on cohesiveness, these four global pitfalls need to be immediately addressed. Widmeyer, Brawley, and Carron (1992) and their colleagues have attempted to initiate this process in a variety of investigations that systematically test a conceptual model, an instrument (the GEQ), and different types of physical activity groups (e.g., fitness classes, triathletes, recreational sport games), but this work only scratches the surface. Other investigators must take up these challenges.

Systematic Research Efforts

It has recently been emphasized that sport psychologists should increase their efforts in doing more group dynamics research (Widmeyer, Brawley, & Carron, 1992). Much of sport and physical activity occurs in groups. Widmeyer et al. emphasize that it may be difficult to understand team athlete behavior if that behavior is studied in isolation of group influence. Similarly, if cohesion is a dynamic group property, it may have reciprocal relationships with many team and team member behaviors. Thus the study of cohesion may be a key to understanding more about the social psychology of groups and of individual athletes in physical activity. The latter part of the discussion in this chapter has offered considerations for improving our future research investigations of cohesion. Similarly, with the intent of clarifying the review of the cohesion-performance research, the introduction to the present chapter provided a three-level hierarchy of research questions that characterizes description and explanation of a phenomenon. Brawley (1990) combined the content of these suggestions and schematically summarized them to suggest one way research might proceed systematically in future. This summary is offered in Figure 31–2.

The common link to systematic research is the use of theory. Basic necessities are a willingness to test, revise, and modify theory and research, rather than encouraging repetition of single-minded research. As well, seeking answers to each level of research question will ultimately contribute to the goals of gaining more knowledge and will result in the revision of existing theory. If this approach is used, it will change any future review of cohesion research relative to what was reported concerning cohesion-performance relations at the outset of this chapter. The steps in Figure 31–2 both challenge and force investigators to be more systematic in their cohesion research efforts.

Aside from the use of theory, a key necessity in Figure 31–2 is the asking of the three levels of research questions in successive fashion within specific lines of cohesion research. It would be of little use if one group of researchers only described the phenomena (Level 1) while others attempted to exclusively identify moderators (Level 2) and still others, mediators (Level 3) of cohesion-related behavior. The success of investigating these three questions depends upon research that systematically and successively builds on the question previously answered.

The importance of conceptual distinctions between these research questions has been made quite clear elsewhere in an excellent paper on the moderator-mediator variable distinction by Baron and Kenny (1986). This paper is useful for the study of cohesion specifically and for social psychology in general. How these authors recommend using moderators and mediators both separately and collectively offers a means of clarifying, for example, how cohesion may account for divergences in an individual member's or in a sport group's behavior. The conceptual notions, research strategies, and related statistical procedures appropriate to help answer questions of the second and third level of the research hierarchy are described. Cohesion investigators should follow these suggestions in the context of the process suggested in Figure 31–2 to meet the challenges raised in the present chapter. The chapter authors will follow Baron and Kenny's advice in their own sport cohesion research. Hopefully, they will be joined by others.

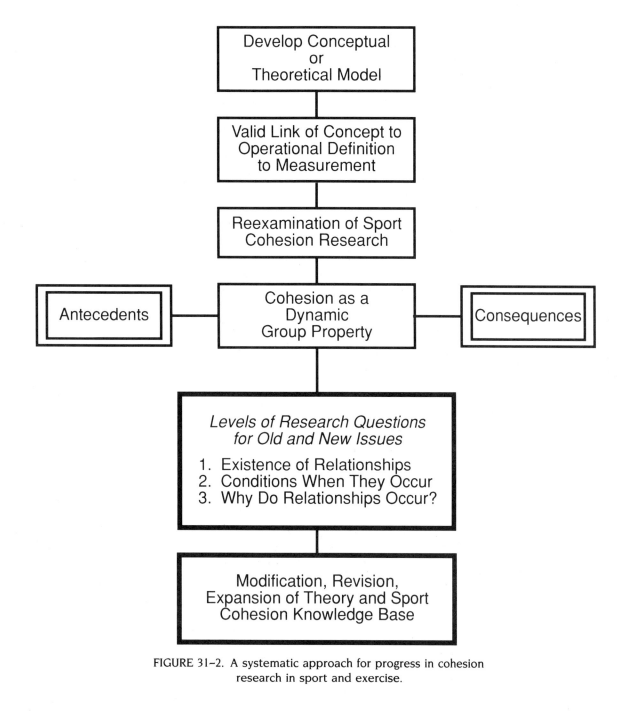

FIGURE 31–2. A systematic approach for progress in cohesion
research in sport and exercise.

References

Arnold, G., & Straub, W. (1973). Personality and group cohesiveness as determinants of success among interscholastic basketball teams. In I. Williams & L. Wankel (Eds.), *Proceedings of the Fourth Canadian Psycho-Motor Learning and Sport Psychology Symposium* (pp. 346–353). Ottawa: Dept. of National Health and Welfare.

Bakeman, R., & Helmreich, R. (1975). Cohesiveness and performance: Covariation and causality in an undersea environment. *Journal of Experimental Social Psychology, 11,* 478–489.

Ball, J. R., & Carron, A. V. (1976). The influence of team cohesion and participation motivation upon performance success in intercollegiate ice hockey, *Canadian Journal of Applied Sport Sciences, 1,* 241 275.

Baron, R. M., & Kenny, D. A. (1986). The moderator-mediator variable distinction in social psychological research: Conceptual, strategic, and statistical considerations. *Journal of Personality and Social Psychology. 51,* 1173–1182.

Bennett-Kastor, T. (1986). Cohesion and prediction in child narrative. *Journal of Child Language, 13,* 353–370.

Berkowitz, L. (1954). Group standards, cohesiveness, and productivity. *Human Relations, 7,* 509–514.

Bird, A. M. (1977). Development of a model for predicting team performance. *Research Quarterly, 48,* 24–32.

Bolger, P. (1983). *The relationship of task and social cohesion to sex, status, participation level, and performance of high school and university basketball teams.* Unpublished master's thesis, University of Western Ontario, London, Ontario.

Brawley, L. R. (1990). Group cohesion: Status, problems and future directions. *International Journal of Sport Psychology, 21,* 355–379.

Brawley, L. R., Carron, A. V., & Widmeyer, W. N. (1987). Assessing the cohesion of teams: Validity of the Group Environment Questionnaire. *Journal of Sport Psychology, 9,* 275–294.

Brawley, L. R., Carron, A. V., & Widmeyer, W. N. (1988). Exploring the relationship between cohesion and group resistance to disruption. *Journal of Sport and Exercise Psychology, 10,* 199–213.

Caplow, T. (1964). *Principles of organization.* New York: Harcourt, Brace & World.

Carron, A. V., & Ball, J. R. (1977). Cause-effect characteristics of cohesiveness and participation motivation in intercollegiate hockey. *International Review of Sport Sociology, 12,* 49–60.

Carron, A. V. (1980). *Social psychology of sport.* Ithaca, NY: Mouvement.

Carron, A. V. (1982). Cohesiveness in sport groups. Interpretations and considerations. *Journal of Sport Psychology, 4,* 123–138.

Carron, A. V. (1988). *Group dynamics in sport.* London, Ontario: Spodym Publishers.

Carron, A. V., Ball, J. R., & Chelladurai, P. (1977). Motivation for participation, success in performance and their relationship to individual and group satisfaction. *Perceptual and Motor Skills, 45,* 835–841.

Carron, A. V., & Chelladurai, P. (1979). Cohesiveness as a factor in sport performance. *International Review of Sport Sociology, 16,* 21–41.

Carron, A. V., Widmeyer, W. N., & Brawley, L. R. (1985). The development of an instrument to assess cohesion in sport teams: The Group Environment Questionnaire. *Journal of Sport Psychology, 7,* 244–266.

Carron, A. V., Widmeyer, W. N., & Brawley, L. R. (1988). Group cohesion and individual adherence to physical activity. *Journal of Sport and Exercise Psychology, 10,* 119–126.

Cotter, L. (1979, April). Group cohesiveness and team success among women's intercollegiate basketball teams. Paper presented at the meeting of the American Alliance for Health, Physical Education, and Recreation. New Orleans.

Dawe, S. W. L., & Carron, A. V. (1990, October). *Interrelationships among role acceptance, role clarity, task cohesion, and social cohesion.* Paper presented at the meeting of the Canadian Society for Psychomotor Learning and Sport Psychology. Windsor, Ontario.

Festinger, L., Schachter, S., & Back, K. (1950). *Social pressures in informal groups: A study of a housing project.* New York: Harper & Bros.

Fiedler, F. E. (1953). Assumed similarity measures as predictors of team effectiveness in surveying. Urbana, IL: Bureau of Research and Service, University of Illinois (Mimeo) (Tech. Rep. No. 6 Contract N6 ori-07135).

Fiedler, F., Hartman, W., & Rudin, S. (1952). *The relationship of interpersonal perception to effectiveness in basketball teams.* Suppl. Tech. Rep. No. 3, Contract N60T1-07135.) Urbana, IL: Bureau of Records and Service, University of Illinois.

Fouslee, H. C. (1984). Dyads and triads at 35,000 feet: Factors affecting group process and aircrew performance. *American Psychologist, 39,* 885–893.

Gardner, E., & Thompson, G. (1956). *Social relations and morale in small groups.* New York, NY: Appleton-Century-Crofts.

Gill, D. L. (1977). Cohesiveness and performance in sport groups. In R. S. Hutton (Ed.), *Exercise and sport science reviews* (Vol. 5, pp. 131–155), Santa Barbara, CA: Journal Publishing Affiliates.

Gossett, D., & Widmeyer, W. N. (1981, May). *Improving cohesion's prediction of performance outcome in sport.* Paper presented at the Annual Meeting of the North American Society for the Psychology of Sport and Physical Activity, Monterey, CA.

Grace, H. (1954). Conformance and performance. *Journal of Social Psychology, 40,* 333–335.

Granito, V., & Rainey, D. (1988). Differences in cohesion between high school and college football teams and starters and nonstarters. *Perceptual and Motor Skills, 66,* 471–477.

Gross, N., & Martin, W. (1952). On group cohesion. *American Journal of Sociology, 57,* 533–546.

Hewitt, J. (1978). Change in liking others as a result of others' performance. *Journal of Social Psychology, 106,* 125–126.

Horsefall, A., & Arensberg, C. (1949). Teamwork and productivity in a shoe factory. *Human Organization, 8,* 13–26.

Johnson, S. (1982). Staff cohesion in residential treatment. *Child Care Quarterly, 11*(3), 204–211.

Klein M. & Kristiansen, C. (1969). Group composition, group structure and group effectiveness in basketball teams. In J. Loy & G. Kenyon (Eds.) *Sport, culture, and society* (pp. 397–408), London: Macmillan.

Landers, D., & Crum, T. (1971). The effects of team success and formal structure on interpersonal relations and cohesiveness of baseball teams. *International Journal of Sport Psychology, 2,* 88–96.

Landers, D. M., & Lueschen, G. (1974). Team performance outcome and cohesiveness of competitive co-acting groups. *International Review of Sport Sociology, 9,* 57–69.

Landers, D. M., Wilkinson, M. O., Hatfield, B. D., & Barber, H. (1982). Causality and the cohesion-performance relationship. *Journal of Sport Psychology, 4,* 170–183.

Lenk, H. (1969). Top performance despite internal conflict. An antithesis to a functionalistic proposition. In J. Loy & G. Kenyon (Eds.) *Sport, culture, and society* (pp. 393–397). London: Macmillan.

Libo, L. (1953). *Measuring group cohesiveness.* Ann Arbor, MI: University of Michigan Press.

Lott, A. J., & Lott, B. E. (1961). Group cohesiveness, communication level, and conformity. *Journal of Abnormal and Social Psychology, 62,* 408–412.

Manning, F. J., & Fullerton, T. D. (1988). Health and well-being in highly cohesive units of the U.S. Army. *Journal of Applied Social Psychology, 18,* 503–519.

Martens, R., Landers, D. M., & Loy, J. W. (1972). *Sport cohesiveness questionnaire.* Washington, DC: AAHPERD Publications.

Martens, R., & Peterson, J. (1976). Group cohesiveness as a determinant of success and member satisfaction in team performance. *International Review of Sport Psychology, 6,* 49–71.

McGrath, J. (1962). The influence of positive interpersonal relations on adjustment and effectiveness in rifle teams. *Journal of Abnormal and Social Psychology, 65,* 365–375.

McGrath, J. (1984). *Groups: Interaction and performance.* Englewood Cliffs, NJ: Prentice-Hall.

McNight, P. E., Williams, J. M., & Widmeyer, W. N. (1991, April). Cohesion and identifiability in reducing social loafing. Paper presented at the meeting of the Arizona Exercise Science Symposium, Tucson, AZ.

Mikalachki, A. (1969). *Group cohesion reconsidered: A study of blue collar work groups.* London, Ontario: University of Western Ontario, School of Business Administration.

Mudrack, P. E. (1989a). Defining group cohesiveness: A legacy of confusion. *Small Group Behavior, 20,* 37–49.

Mudrack, P. E. (1989b) Group cohesiveness and productivity: A closer look. *Human Relations, 42,* 771–785.

O'Reilly, C. A. (1991). Organizational behavior: Where we've been, where we're going. *Annual Review of Psychology. 42,* 427–458.

Palmer, F., & Myers, T. (1968). Sociometric choices and group productivity among radar crews. *Bibliography of Publications,* Washington, DC: Human Resources Research Office.

Pepitone, A., & Kleiner, K. (1957). The effect of threat and frustration on group cohesiveness. *Journal of Abnormal and Social Psychology, 54,* 192–199.

Peteroy, E. T. (1983). Cohesiveness development in an ongoing therapy group: An exploratory study. *Small Group Behavior, 14:* 269–272.

Pelz, D. C., & Andrews, F. M. (1966). *Scientists in organizations.* New York: Wiley.

Roark, A. E., & Sharah, H. S. (1989). Factors related to group cohesiveness. *Small Group Behavior, 20,* 62–69.

Rosenthal, R. (1966). *Experimenter effects in behavioral research.* New York: Appleton-Century-Crofts.

Schachter, S., Ellertson, N., McBride, D., & Gregory, D. (1951). An experimental study of cohesiveness and productivity. *Human Relations, 4,* 229–238.

Shangi, G., & Carron, A. V. (1978). Group cohesion and its relationship with performance and satisfaction among high school basketball players. *Canadian Journal of Sport Sciences, 12,* 20.

Shaw, M. E., & Shaw, L. M. (1962). Some effects of sociometric grouping on learning in a second grade classroom. *Journal of Social Psychology, 57,* 453–458.

Shelley, M. W. (1964). The mathematical representation of the individual in models of organizational problems. In W. W. Cooper, H. J. Leavitt, & M. W. Shelley II (Eds.), *New perspectives in organizational research* (pp. 351–390). New York: Wiley.

Sherif, M. & Sherif, C. W. (1969). *Social psychology.* New York: Harper & Row.

Smith, G. (1968). *Analysis of the concept of group cohesion in a simulated athletic setting.* Unpublished master's thesis, London, Ontario: University of Western Ontario.

Smith, H. (1984). Family cohesion through leisure and recreation. *Journal of Physical Education Recreation and Dance, 55,* 32–62.

Spence, E. (1980). *The relative contributions of ability and cohesion for team performance outcome in intramural basketball.* Unpublished manuscript, University of Waterloo, Waterloo, Ontario.

Spink, K. (1989, October). *Group cohesion and starting status in successful and less successful elite volleyball teams.* Paper presented at the meeting of the Canadian Society for Psychomotor Learning and Sport Psychology. Victoria, British Columbia.

Spink, K. (1990a). Cohesion and collective efficacy of volleyball teams. *Journal of Sport and Exercise Psychology, 12,* 301–311.

Spink, K. S. (1990b, October). *Cohesion and adherence in exercise classes.* Paper presented at the meeting of the Canadian Society for Psychomotor Learning and Sport Psychology. Windsor, Ontario.

Steiner, I. D. (1972). *Group processes and productivity.* New York: Academic Press.

Stogdill, R. M. (1963). *Team achievement under high motivation.* Research Monograph No. 113, Bureau of Business Research. Ohio State University, Columbus, OH.

Stogdill, R. M. (1972). Group productivity, drive, and cohesiveness. *Organizational Behavior and Human Performance, 8,* 26–43.

Theberge, N., & Loy, J. W. (1976). Replacement processes in sport organizations: The case of professional baseball. *International Review of Sport Sociology, 11,* 73–93.

Trist, E., & Bamforth, K. (1951). Some social and psychological consequences of the long-wall method of coal mining. *Human Relations, 4,* 3–38.

Tziner, A., & Vardi, Y. (1983). Ability as a moderator between cohesiveness and tank crews' performance. *Journal of Occupational Behaviour, 4,* 137–143.

Van Bergen, A., & Koekebakker, J. (1959). Group cohesiveness in laboratory experiments. *Acta Psychologica, 16,* 81–98.

Vander Velden, L. (1971). *Relationships among members, team and situational variables and basketball team success: A social-psychological inquiry.* Unpublished doctoral dissertation, University of Wisconsin, Madison, WI.

VanZelst, R. H. (1952). Sociometrically selected work teams increase production. *Personnel Psychology, 3,* 175–185.

Westre, K., & Weiss, M. (1991). The relationship between perceived coaching behaviors and group cohesion in high school football teams. *The Sport Psychologist, 5,* 41–54.

Whyte, W. H., Jr. (1943). *Street corner society.* Chicago: University of Chicago Press.

Widmeyer, W. N., Brawley, L. R., & Carron, A. V. (1985). *The measurement of cohesion in sport teams: The Group Environment Questionnaire.* London, Ontario: Sports Dynamics.

Widmeyer, W. N., Brawley, L. R., & Carron, A. V. (1990). Group size in sport. *Journal of Sport and Exercise Psychology. 12,* 177–190.

Widmeyer, W. N., Brawley, L. R., & Carron, A. V. (1992). Group dynamics in sport. In T. Horne (Ed.), *Advances in sport psychology.* Champaign, IL: Human Kinetics.

Widmeyer, W. N., & Gossett, D. M. (1978, June). *The relative contributions of ability and cohesion to team performance outcome in intramural basketball.* Paper presented at the annual meeting of the North American Society for the Psychology of Sport and Physical Activity, Tallahassee, FL.

Widmeyer, W. N., & Martens, R. (1978). When cohesion predicts performance outcome in sport. *Research Quarterly, 49,* 372–380.

Widmeyer, W. N., & Williams, J. M. (1991). Predicting cohesion in coacting teams. *Small Group Research, 22,* 548–557.

Williams, J. M., & Hacker, C. M. (1982). Causal relationships among cohesion, satisfaction, and performance in women's intercollegiate field hockey teams. *Journal of Sport Psychology, 4,* 324–337.

Williams, J., & Widmeyer, W. N. (1991). The cohesion-performance outcome relationship in a coacting sport. *Journal of Sport & Exercise Psychology, 13,* 364–371.

Yukelson, D., Weinberg, R., & Jackson, A. (1984). A multidimensional group cohesion instrument for intercollegiate basketball teams. *Journal of Sport Psychology, 6,* 103–117

Zander, A. (1982). *Making groups effective.* San Francisco, CA: Jossey-Bass.

Zanna, M. P., & Fazio, R. H. (1982). The attitude-behavior relation: Moving toward a third generation of research. In M. P. Zanna, E. T. Higgins, & C. P. Herman (Eds.), *Consistency in social behavior: The Ontario symposium,* (Vol. 2, pp. 283–301). Hillsdale, NJ: Erlbaum.

LIFE-SPAN DEVELOPMENT

·32·

YOUTH IN SPORT: PSYCHOLOGICAL CONSIDERATIONS

Robert J. Brustad

Tens of millions of children and adolescents around the world currently engage in some form of organized sport competition. The extensive involvement of youngsters in structured sport programs has generated considerable speculation and controversy regarding the psychological consequences of early sport participation. Until recently, these discussions have been fueled largely by opinion rather than research. Only within the past 15 years have sport psychologists devoted systematic research attention to the study of youth sport behavior.

Precise data on the number of youngsters involved in organized sport are difficult to obtain. However, it is evident that for every elite-level adult athlete there are thousands of young athletes engaged in sport at a different level of challenge. In the United States, it has been estimated that 20 million children between the ages of 6 and 18 years currently participate in some form of organized sport program in nonschool settings (Martens, 1986). Participation rates among Australian children have been estimated to be even higher, involving 67% of preadolescent girls and 75% of preadolescent boys (Robertson, 1986). Clearly these data show that organized sport involvement is an integral part of childhood and adolescence for youngsters in industrial societies.

Children's sport involvement can also be fairly intense. Research conducted in the United States by Gould and Martens (1979) indicated that the young athletes in their sample spent an average of 12 hours a week engaged in sport over the course of an 18-week season. Since many youngsters are involved in a number of sport programs throughout the year, it is likely that a large proportion of a youngster's free time may be devoted to sport participation. The psychological impact of this involvement clearly deserves attention.

In this chapter, research that has addressed four major

concerns related to the psychological characteristics of youth sport involvement will be described and critiqued. The first concern pertains to psychological readiness for competition. Essentially, this topic addresses the question "At what age is it appropriate for children to begin to compete?" A second concern relates to children's motives for participating in and dropping out of sport. This topic has engendered a great deal of attention due to concerns that sport attrition may be reflective of an inability of organized sport to meet children's needs. The subsequent discussion examines psychological stress and anxiety in youth sport. A particularly important focus of this research relates to identifying the sources of stress experienced by young athletes so that youth sport practitioners can restructure programs to reduce the incidence of negative affective outcomes for children in sport. The final discussion addresses issues and concerns related to the effects of adult involvement in children's sport programs.

The attempt will be to provide a comprehensive account of research conducted in each of the four identified areas. Due to space limitations, it is not possible to address all topics related to the psychological aspects of children's sport involvement. In Chapter 27, Bredemeier and Shields describe research findings pertaining to the influence of sport involvement upon children's ethical reasoning and behavior. Readers are also referred to Coakley's Chapter 26 on sport socialization, as socialization influences certainly impact the psychological characteristics of the youth sport experience.

It is very important to note that most of the known research on the psychological aspects of youth sport involvement has been conducted in North America, particularly in the United States. Considerable caution is recommended, therefore, before generalizing the findings obtained in this cultural context to youngsters in other cultures. However, knowledge about the evolution of youth sport research in North America should prove to be quite beneficial in assisting the development of pediatric sport psychology research in other nations.

PSYCHOLOGICAL READINESS FOR SPORT COMPETITION

Cultural perceptions about the value of sport participation for youngsters and the continual quest for athletic success have steadily increased levels of sport involvement and specialization during childhood. Reports indicate that involvement in organized sports competition can begin as as early as age 3 in the United States (Martens, 1986), age 4 in Australia (Robertson, 1986), and age 6 in Brazil (Ferreira, 1986) and Canada (Valeriote & Hansen, 1986).

At what age is it appropriate for children to begin competing in sports? This issue can best be addressed with reference to the concept of readiness. Readiness has been described as the level of maturation or experience needed for learning or some other benefit to be realized (Seefeldt, 1988). It has been proposed that readiness exists when there is a match between a child's level of growth, development, and maturation on the one hand and the demands of the task on the other (Malina, 1988). Thus we may consider psychological readiness for sport to occur when a youngster has sufficient psychological maturation and/or experience to derive benefits from his or her sport participation. Full benefit will be achieved only if the child is also physically and emotionally ready to participate.

The psychological readiness of children to compete has rarely been considered in establishing age-related standards for sport participation. For the most part, entry standards take into account only the typical physical (size and maturational) and motor (skill) characteristics of youngsters (Malina, 1988). Unfortunately age-based standards are unable to accommodate the considerable variability in maturity status of children at a given chronological age, nor are they established with a concern for the psychological and emotional consequences for children of premature participation.

What constitutes psychological readiness for competitive sport? Youth sport researchers have contended that the desire to compare skills with others is a primary attraction of sport participation for youngsters (Passer, 1988a; Roberts, 1980; Scanlan, 1988). In a larger context, developmental and social psychologists have long recognized that an important psychological benefit to children of play and games is that these activities enable one to develop a reflected view, or understanding, of oneself in relation to others, and thereby provide a means for developing an appreciation of personal capacities (e.g., Erikson, 1963; Mead, 1934; Sage, 1986). Thus, an important aspect of psychological readiness occurs when children seek out opportunities to compare their skills with others and thereby acquire information about themselves (Passer, 1988a).

A second important aspect of psychological readiness occurs when the child reaches a level of cognitive maturity such that he or she displays a sufficient understanding of the competitive process (Passer, 1988a; Roberts, 1980). Such an understanding entails an appreciation of the social nature of competition, particularly with regard to the cooperative and strategic aspects of sport, and an awareness of the nature of individual roles within a cooperating group. Coakley (1986) argued that children are generally attracted by the excitement of sport before they have developed a mature conception of competition.

With respect to the first component of psychological readiness, children do not generally begin to actively compare their abilities with others until they are at least 5 or 6 years old (Veroff, 1969). Through later childhood and into adolescence, however, the social comparison motive is increasingly evident. The desire to compare physical and motor skills is a major component of these social comparison processes since athletic ability is a highly valued attribute among children and adolescents (Duda, 1981, cited in Roberts, 1984; Scanlan, 1988). The extent to which children are motivated to engage in social comparison processes is also related to sociocultural and situational factors. Research indicates that the competitive behavior of children from various cultures is influenced by the extent to which social comparison information is made salient to them (Toda, Shinotsuka, McClintock, & Stech, 1978).

Although children begin to demonstrate the desire to compare abilities with others during early childhood, the means by which they proceed in making such comparisons lacks sophistication. Until the age of 8 or 9, children tend to rely heavily on objective outcomes, such as winning or losing, and upon adult feedback to provide them with information about personal ability in sport (Horn & Hasbrook, 1986, 1987; Horn & Weiss, 1991). It is not until the age of 10 years that children generally prefer to use information obtained from peers as an informational source in making judgments about personal competence. Furthermore, research indicates that prior to adolescence there is only a very weak correlation between children's perceptions of competence and their actual competence as assessed by teachers or coaches (Horn & Weiss, 1991; Nicholls, 1978; Weiss & Horn, 1990).

In order to effectively compare physical abilities with others, a child must be able to make a mature differentiation among the various elements influencing performance outcomes. In particular, the concept of ability must be distinguished from effort and task difficulty (Duda, 1987; Nicholls, 1978). Research conducted in nonsport contexts indicates that this differentiation is usually not complete until the age of 11 or 12 years (Nicholls, 1978; Nicholls & Miller, 1984). Prior to this time, children are likely to regard effort as the cause of all achievement outcomes (ages 7–9 years), or only to partially differentiate the roles of ability and effort in performance outcomes (ages 9–10 years).

The second component of psychological readiness involves a mature conception of the social nature of competition. Coakley (1986) argued that children cannot fully benefit from competitive situations until they have the capacity to understand their roles in relation to the roles of others within this context. Generally it is not until the age of 8 to 10 years that a child develops the necessary role-taking abilities to allow them to understand another person's point of view (Selman 1971, 1976). This appreciation of other perspectives is essential in order for one to cooperate effectively with others. Since youth sports are primarily team-oriented cooperative activities, a child must have sufficient cognitive development and social experience in order to act in accordance with the strategies and rules of the sport. However, evidence indicates that a fully mature "third-party" perspective, in which the child can distinguish various points of view in a reasonably objective manner, does not normally appear until the age of 10 or 12 years (Selman 1971, 1976).

Premature sport involvement may result in undesirable emotional consequences for children. The limited capacity of children to develop accurate conceptions of ability may result in inappropriate aspirations and achievement goals (Passer, 1988a). When expectations for performance are too high, youngsters are likely to experience frustration, discouragement, and low self-esteem. Roberts (1980) argued that children are not able to develop realistic achievement goals until they can make appropriate attributions for achievement outcomes. A mature attributional capacity will not be present until children can differentiate among ability, task difficulty, and effort in influencing performance outcomes.

The tendency for young athletes to rely upon adult feedback in assessing their competence may also have an emotional impact upon youngsters. If adults do not convey ability-related information in a sensitive and encouraging way, a child may interpret this feedback as an indication of low ability (Roberts, 1980). The limited amount of research conducted on the relationship between coaches' feedback and youngsters' self-perceptions indicates that coaches have considerable influence on young athletes' self-esteem (Smith, Smoll, & Curtis, 1979; Smith, Zane, Smoll, & Coppel, 1983) and ability perceptions (Horn, 1985).

Given the nature of individual variability in maturational processes, it is not possible to identify a specific chronological age at which it can be confidently stated that children are psychologically ready to engage in competitive sport. Various researchers have proposed recommendations based upon certain cognitive-developmental and social characteristics.

Passer (1988a) argued that children should be discouraged from becoming involved in competitive sport prior to age 7 or 8 years because they have not yet attained a level of cognitive development that will allow them to enjoy, and benefit from, the social comparison of abilities. Coakley (1986) similarly contended that organized sport competition should not begin before age 8 because children's understanding of the social relationships involved in competitive sport is not advanced enough to make these activities attractive to them. Roberts (1980) is even more conservative, suggesting that competitive sport involvement should

be encouraged only when children's cognitive reasoning abilities have fully matured at ages 10 to 13. Malina (1986) suggested that children should not compete in sport until their parents are psychologically ready! Parental readiness entails a willingness to encourage the child's participation without constantly intervening on his or her behalf.

If psychological readiness for competition is regarded as a match between the psychological capacities of the child and the demands of the activity, then it would be wise to consider restructuring youth sport programs to make them more compatible with children's cognitive capacities during their years of sport involvement. Such a restructuring would place greater emphasis upon the aspects of fun, excitement, and skill development during the early and middle childhood years while reducing the emphasis upon strategic elements and competitive outcomes. Emphasis upon strategic and competitive elements should be introduced during late childhood and adolescence as children develop the maturity to understand strategies and roles.

Coakley (1986) stated that children should not begin competing before the age of 8 but that "it is never too early to engage in expressive physical activities" (1986, p. 59). As an expressive physical activity, youth sport should be structured so that it meets developmentally appropriate outcomes for its participants. By focusing upon skill development goals during childhood rather than emphasizing competitive strategies, children will be more likely to attain the positive psychological outcomes that they deserve through their sport involvement.

PARTICIPATION MOTIVATION AND ATTRITION

Research related to children's motives for participation in sport, and the factors underlying their decisions to discontinue sport involvement, are two of the most heavily investigated areas in pediatric sport psychology. Understanding the reasons why children terminate their sport participation is a particularly important research topic because of concerns that attrition or dropout behavior is the consequence of undesirable psychological experiences for young athletes. Consequently researchers and practitioners alike have identified the topic of "why young athletes stop participating in sports" as the most important youth sport issue of practical significance that should be addressed by sport psychologists (Gould, 1982).

The study of participation motivation and attrition in youth sport is a complex task. Each must be examined with regard to a variety of social, psychological, and developmental factors operating during childhood and adolescence. Furthermore, both participation motivation and attrition patterns need to be studied within the framework of contemporary motivational theory, since each represents a unique aspect of motivation.

In order to address children's motives for participating in sport and for discontinuing this involvement, it is appropriate first to examine levels of participatory involvement.

Martens (1986) estimated that about 20 million youngsters between the ages of 6 and 18 years are actively involved in some form of nonschool organized sport activity in the United States. This total represents approximately 44% of all the children in this age range. An additional 5 million young people are believed to participate in high school sports.

The most systematic attempts to examine age-related participation patterns in North America were conducted through the Michigan Youth Sport Institute in the late 1970s (State of Michigan, 1976, 1978a, 1978b). These studies revealed that involvement levels in popular and traditional sports such as baseball, softball, swimming, and basketball increased dramatically for both boys and girls from ages 5 through 11 years. However, at age 11 a sharp decline is apparent in involvement levels, and this dropoff continues throughout adolescence. The factors responsible for this decline are the subject of considerable controversy.

Children's Motives for Sport Participation

A substantial amount of research attention has been devoted to the identification of children's motives for sport participation. Most of this research has been descriptive in nature and was conducted during the late 1970s and early 1980s. This research has been helpful in generating an empirical base for the study of children's participatory behaviors in sport from which more theoretically based approaches can proceed (Weiss & Chaumeton, 1991). Due to the limitations of descriptive research, only the major findings of these investigations will be addressed. For more complete reviews of this literature, the reader is directed to Gould and Petlichkoff, 1988, and Weiss (in press).

Sapp and Haubenstricker (1978) assessed the participatory motives of over 1,000 male and female athletes, ages 11 to 18 years, involved in agency-sponsored sport programs in the state of Michigan. They found that "having fun" and "improving skills" were cited by an overwhelming majority as the primary motives for their sport involvement. Gill, Gross, and Huddleston (1985) examined motives for sport involvement in 1,100 young male and female sport camp participants. Their results indicated that children highly value improving skills, having fun, learning new skills, playing for the challenge, and being physically fit as reasons for sport involvement. Gould, Feltz, and Weiss (1985) found that fun, fitness, skill improvement, the social atmosphere of the team, and a desire for challenge were the most highly rated factors by young swimmers. Longhurst and Spink (1987), in their study of Australian children, found that the most frequently cited participatory motives for these youngsters were improving skills, being physically fit, enjoyment of competition, learning new skills, and the desire for challenge.

In their review of the participation motivation literature, Weiss and Petlichkoff (1989) concluded that the most commonly identified motives can be classified into four general categories. These motivational categories include compe-

tence (learning and improving skills), affiliation (being part of a group), fitness, and fun. Furthermore, it should be recognized that most children cite multiple motives underlying their sport participation (Gould & Horn, 1984; Weiss & Petlichkoff, 1989).

Children's Motives for Sport Withdrawal

Research on children's withdrawal from competitive sport differs from the participation motivation research in at least two ways. First, whereas little disagreement exists regarding the nature of children's participatory motives, much less consensus exists about the factors underlying children's decisions to terminate their sport involvement. Second, children's disengagement from sport has more frequently been addressed in light of motivational theories. These theoretical perspectives will be addressed more fully later.

Orlick's (1973, 1974) studies sparked considerable interest and controversy regarding the factors underlying children's sport withdrawal. Orlick interviewed youth sport participants, ranging in age from 7 to 18 years, about their intended future involvement in sport. He found that the majority of youngsters who decided that they would not continue their participation in sport during the following season cited the negative aspects of involvement as being responsible for this decision. These negative aspects included lack of playing time, the competitive emphasis of the program, and an overemphasis on winning. Orlick's findings strongly suggested that the structure of youth sport was inadequate in meeting children's participatory motives, and was responsible for dropout behavior.

Sapp and Haubenstricker's (1978) subsequent research painted a much less gloomy portrait of the youth sport attrition process. Overall, they found that the incidence of sport attrition was higher than had been anticipated, with 37% of youngsters in the 11- to 18-year age group and 24% of the children in the 6- to 10-year age group indicating that they would not continue participating in their sport during the following season. However, the negative experiences so commonly cited in Orlick's studies were infrequently reported by these youngsters. In fact, negative experiences were identified by fewer than 15% of the children as a motive for discontinuing their sport involvement. The more frequently cited reasons were "work" by the older age group and "other reasons" by the younger children.

Gould, Feltz, Horn, and Weiss (1982) examined the motives for attrition of 50 former swimmers, ages 10 to 18 years. The most frequently cited motives were "other things to do," "not enough fun," "wanted to participate in another sport," and "not as good as I wanted to be." Overall, 84% of the swimmers identified factors related to conflict of interest as an important or very important motive in their decision to discontinue swimming involvement.

In their study of former swimmers, Sefton and Fry (1981, cited in Gould, 1987) found that a variety of factors were responsible for the decision to discontinue sport participation. The major reasons for dropping out included too much time spent, dissatisfaction with practices, and the desire to participate in other activities.

Robinson and Carron (1982) analyzed the perceptions of 98 current or former football players with regard to intrapersonal and situational aspects of their participation. According to participatory status, these individuals were classified as football dropouts, starters, or nonstarters. The major findings from the study were that the dropouts, in contrast to the starters and nonstarters, generally did not feel as much social support for their participation on the team, did not have favorable perceptions of their ability, and were more likely to view the coach as an autocrat.

Klint and Weiss (1986) examined the withdrawal motives of 37 former competitive gymnasts. Overall, the former gymnasts indicated that the major reasons they withdrew from the sport was due to the desire to pursue other interests, excessive pressure, not having enough fun, and the extensive time commitment.

In summarizing the research findings on sport attrition, it is clear that the most commonly identified motive for withdrawal involves "having other things to do." It is unclear, however, from this descriptively based research whether youngsters find other activities attractive at least in part because of dissatisfaction with their sport experiences or whether this attraction represents a normal process of sampling different activities during adolescence (Weiss & Petlichkoff, 1989). However, with the exception of Orlick's research, there is limited support for the contention that sport withdrawal is primarily attributable to inherently negative aspects of youth sport involvement.

Critique of Participation Motivation/Attrition Research

The descriptively based research reviewed here has provided an excellent framework from which to study children's participatory behavior in sport. Furthermore, this research will contribute to the generation of more theoretically derived research that addresses children's sport behavior in the broader context of motivational theory. However, certain methodological and conceptual problems within the existing research have made it difficult to develop a clear understanding of the factors influencing children's participatory behavior.

In measuring children's motives for participation and attrition, most researchers have relied upon closed format, self-report questionnaires. These questionnaires typically specify a number of motives and utilize a Likert-type scale on which the youngster is asked to indicate the extent to which each motive reflects his or her reasons for participating in, or disengaging from, a particular sport. It is likely that this type of self-report format will provide only a superficial description of a young athlete's perspective on his or her sport involvement. It is important to recognize that sport participation is very highly valued within the social structure of children and adolescents (Coleman, 1961;

Duda, 1981), and that many youngsters have invested considerable time and energy in their sport involvement. The traditional measurement approach thus limits insight into children's thoughts and feelings about an important aspect of their lives. Additional approaches, including open-ended interviews and questionnaires, are recommended as a means of providing a greater depth of understanding of children's views.

Little attention has been paid to the influence of developmental factors in youngsters' descriptions of their motives. For example, both children and adolescents may report that they participate for "fun," but a child may consider "fun" to be related to the play aspects of sport involvement, whereas the adolescent may view "fun" as the excitement of competition. Only Brodkin and Weiss (1990) have addressed developmental differences in motives for sport participation, and this research revealed age-related differences in participatory motives for competitive swimmers across the lifespan. Future research needs to consider developmental characteristics influencing children's participatory behavior.

Participation motivation and attrition research has also been limited by terminological problems in characterizing children's participatory status. Classifying an individual as a "dropout" may often be inappropriate since research indicates that a high percentage of young athletes who withdraw from one sport reenter the sport, or participate in another sport, at a later date (Gould et al., 1982; Klint & Weiss, 1986). Gould and Petlichkoff (1988) suggest that sport withdrawal should thus be examined across a continuum that ranges from sport-specific (e.g., dropping out of basketball) to domain-specific (dropping out of all sport programs).

An additional shortcoming has been that almost all studies have examined only children's initial motives for engaging in sport, or have assessed these motives at only one point in time (Weiss, in press). This approach implicitly suggests that such motives are stable characteristics when it should be assumed that they are shaped over time by intrapersonal, developmental, and social influences.

Finally, research seeking to identify partipation motives has not been comprehensive in scope. Weiss and Petlichkoff (1989) recently identified a number of intrapersonal and contextual factors that likely contribute to children's participatory decisions. Some of these "missing links" include developmental characteristics, participatory status of the individual, type of sport, type of program, and level of intensity of sport involvement.

Theoretical Perspectives on Sport Participation and Attrition

Research on children's participatory involvement in sport has infrequently been guided by contemporary motivational theories. Consequently, we currently have a poor understanding of relationships among children's initial motives for sport participation, their motivational characteristics while engaged, and the factors underlying children's decisions to disengage from sport.

In his review of research on attrition in youth sport, Gould (1987) identified three theoretical frameworks that might assist our understanding of children's sport involvement and withdrawal. These frameworks included competence motivation theory (Harter, 1978, 1981), achievement orientation theory (Maehr & Nicholls, 1980; Nicholls, 1984), and Smith's (1986) model of sport withdrawal, which includes components from social exchange (Thibaut & Kelly, 1959) and cognitive-affective theories (Smith, 1986). These theories will be reviewed in accordance with both sport participation and attrition patterns.

Harter's competence motivation theory proposes that individuals have an inherent desire to feel and express competence in the social, cognitive, and physical domains of achievement (Harter, 1978). However, the actual expression of this motive toward competence is mediated by underlying self-related cognitions, particularly self-perceptions of competence and control. When children believe that they have adequate ability and situational control within a particular domain of achievement, they will engage in mastery behaviors within that domain. Thus competence motivation theory would predict that sport participants should have higher perceptions of competence and control than nonparticipants and dropouts.

Competence motivation theory has been the most frequently used theoretical framework for the study of participation motivation. In accordance with the predictions of competence motivation theory, Roberts, Kleiber, and Duda (1981) observed that sport participants, in contrast to nonparticipants, had more favorable self-perceptions of physical and cognitive competence. Similarly Feltz and Petlichkoff (1983) found that active sport participants had higher levels of perceived competence than did sport dropouts. However, in contrast to these findings, Klint (1985, cited in Klint and Weiss, 1987) determined that former gymnasts and recreational gymnasts reported higher levels of perceived physical and social competence than did current competitive gymnasts.

A follow-up study by Klint and Weiss (1987) investigated the relationship between competence perceptions and participatory motives in young gymnasts. This study revealed that gymnasts high in perceived physical competence were more motivated by skill development reasons than were their counterparts with lower perceived physical competence. Similarly gymnasts with higher perceived social competence were more motivated by affiliation opportunities than were their counterparts with lower social competence. Klint and Weiss contended that these findings were consistent with the predictions of competence motivation theory since these gymnasts were motivated to demonstrate competence in those areas in which they perceived themselves to possess high ability.

Achievement orientation theory (Maehr & Nicholls, 1980; Nicholls, 1984, 1989) has also been employed as a means of understanding youth sport participatory behavior. Similar to competence motivation theory, achievement ori-

entation theory regards self-perceptions of competence as central influences upon motivated behavior. However, achievement orientation theory also considers individual differences in the subjective meaning of achievement to be additionally important influences upon motivation.

Nicholls (1984) proposed the existence of two distinct perspectives on success operative in achievement situations such as sport. These views on achievement have been termed *task-involved* and *ego-involved* goal perspectives. An individual with a task-involved perspective holds a self-referenced view on achievement, in which success is subjectively defined as personal improvement and task mastery. An individual holding an ego-involved perspective, however, subjectively defines success as performing better than others and thus uses social comparison information to determine success outcomes. In their earlier work, Maehr and Nicholls (1980) had also proposed the existence of a social approval goal perspective, but this orientation is not believed to be operative in most achievement situations, including sport.

With regard to participatory behaviors and motivational patterns in achievement contexts, Nicholls (1984, 1989) has proposed that ability perceptions and goal perspectives interact to influence behavior. He contended that since task-involved individuals define success as personal improvement, they will select appropriately challenging tasks and display effort and persistence while engaged, even if they possess a relatively low perception of competence in a particular area of achievement. Conversely, ego-involved persons are concerned primarily with demonstrating competence relative to others, and thus, if they perceive low personal ability, will avoid activities that highlight the manifestation of this lack of ability. As applied to sport involvement and attrition, achievement orientation theory proposes that task-involved individuals should be motivated to participate, and remain, in sport as long as an appropriate level of personal challenge is present. However, ego-involved individuals are likely to engage in sport only if they perceive that they have more ability than others and are, therefore, prone to terminate their sport involvement when it becomes apparent that they possess less ability than others.

Cognitive-developmental influences upon children's means of appraising competence may also have an effect upon motivational processes in sport, according to achievement motivation theory. Academic research suggests that youngsters become increasingly capable of differentiating the roles of ability and effort in contributing to success and failure outcomes with age (Nicholls, 1978; Nicholls, Jagacinski, & Miller, 1984). If similar changes occur in children's abilities to identify the causes of outcomes in sport, this may have implications for the persistence of youngsters in sport (Duda, 1987; Roberts, 1984).

Roberts (1984) speculated that the high incidence of dropout occurring during late childhood and early adolescence may be partly attributable to children's increasing capacity to accurately appraise personal ability. He suggested that ego-involved youngsters should be particularly disposed to drop out of sport if it becomes apparent that they do not possess as much ability as others. Although many youngsters cite reasons unrelated to ability for dropping out, Roberts suggested that the stated reasons may be superficial and socially desirable explanations that mask underlying perceptions of low ability.

Achievement orientation theory has been employed to predict patterns of youth sport attrition in two instances. Based on Maehr and Nicholls's (1980) conceptualization of ability, task, and social approval orientations, Ewing (1981, cited in Roberts, 1984) examined the relationship between achievement orientations and sport participation patterns. As part of this study, Ewing developed the Achievement Orientation Questionnaire (AOQ) to measure goal perspectives in sport. Ewing found that active youth sport participants were more likely to display a social approval orientation, whereas dropouts were more likely to demonstrate an ability orientation. She conjectured that the structure of organized sports encourages the development of a social approval orientation and that youngsters with this goal perspective are therefore more inclined to remain in sport.

Burton and Martens (1986) contrasted wrestlers and former wrestlers, ages 7 to 17 years, on levels of perceived competence, significant other influence, and additional motivational factors. They found that current wrestlers demonstrated higher levels of perceived ability, more functional attributions, and more positive wrestling expectancies, and valued wrestling success more than did the wrestling dropouts. Although the wrestling dropouts demonstrated lower perceptions of competence than the current wrestlers, they rarely cited ability-related reasons as being responsible for their decision to discontinue wrestling involvement. In general, the dropouts cited reasons such as having other things to do, or not caring much about wrestling. Although the findings of this research were discussed by the authors in light of achievement orientation theory, interpretation of these results is complicated by the fact that the achievement goal orientations of the wrestlers were never directly assessed.

Two additional studies have employed achievement orientation theory to examine sport participation in high school students. Petlichkoff (1988, cited in Weiss, in press) examined the relationship between achievement goal perspectives and participatory behavior in 557 high school athletes during a basketball season. According to the involvement status of these individuals at three points in time during the season, she categorized these young athletes as "starters," "nonstarters," "survivors," "cuttees," and "dropouts." She did not find a relationship to exist between goal perspectives and participatory status but did find that task-involved individuals were more satisfied with their sport experiences than were ego-oriented individuals. Petlichkoff did not assess perceived ability levels of these athletes and former athletes.

Duda (1989) examined the relationship between goal perspectives and sport participation and persistence in 871 high school students. Subjects were categorized as (1) cur-

rent participants in organized and recreational sport; (2) current organized sport participants only; (3) current recreational sport participants only; (4) sport dropouts; or (5) those never involved in sport. Her findings indicated that current organized sport and organized/recreational sport participants demonstrated stronger task-and ego-involved orientations than dropouts and nonparticipants. This research also demonstrated that task and ego orientations are not necessarily dichotomous or mutually exclusive perspectives but may both be present simultaneously.

In concept, achievement orientation theory has considerable appeal as a means of describing youth sport participatory behavior. However, the explanatory value of this theory has been limited for at least two reasons. First a major contention of Nicholls's (1984, 1989) theory has not yet been empirically tested. Nicholls proposed that goal perspectives and competence perceptions act in concert to influence motivated behavior. Specifically Nicholls contended that ego-involved individuals with low perceived competence will desire to avoid those achievement situations in which they believe that their low ability will be manifested. However, high perceived competence, ego-involved individuals, and high- and low-perceived competence task-involved individuals would not be expected to drop out of achievement contexts such as sport. Youth sport research conducted to date has either looked only at achievement orientations, or only at competence perceptions, and thereby has failed to test whether the interactional effect proposed by Nicholls does, in fact, occur.

The second impediment to assessing the usefulness of achievement orientation theory in describing youth sport behavior is related to persistent difficulties in operationalizing achievement goal orientations. Research attempting to measure the goal perspectives of young athletes has been inconsistent with regard to the number and nature of achievement goals operative in the sport setting (e.g., Ewing, 1981 cited in Roberts, 1984; Pemberton, Petlichkoff, & Ewing, 1986; Petlichkoff, 1988 cited in Weiss, in press; Vealey & Campbell, 1988). Recently, Duda and Nicholls (1989) developed the Task and Ego Orientation in Sport Questionnaire (TEOSQ), which has demonstrated high internal consistency and satisfactory test-retest reliability with samples of high school athletes (Duda, 1989). The TEOSQ will need to be tested with a youth sport population to determine if it is a valid and reliable measure of children's achievement orientations in sport. Through the use of this measure, or a developmentally appropriate modification, investigators may be able to confidently employ goal orientation constructs in future youth sport research.

Smith's (1986) conceptual model of sport withdrawal has been identified as a third viable approach to the study of youth sport attrition (Gould, 1987). Integral to his explanation of sport attrition processes is the distinction between sport dropout and sport burnout. Smith contends that sport dropout results largely from a change of interests or a logical cost/benefit analysis by the athlete, whereas sport burnout is withdrawal from sport due to chronic stress. He incorporates two theoretical perspectives into his conceptual model to distinguish between dropout and burnout behavior.

With regard to sport dropout, Smith believes that social exchange theory (Thibaut & Kelly, 1959) best explains the findings of the attrition research conducted to date. Social exchange theory maintains that behavior is motivated by the desire to maximize the probability of positive experiences and to minimize the probability of negative experiences. Also, according to this theory, individuals will continue to engage in a given activity, even when the costs outweigh the benefits, until an appropriate alternative activity becomes available. This explanation of sport dropout is consistent with two patterns of findings in the attrition literature. First, the most frequently cited motive for sport dropout is "having other things to do." Since sport attrition rates are high during adolescence, and since youngsters do have many alternative opportunities available to them at this age, it is logical from this perspective to expect high rates of sport attrition during adolescence as youngsters identify a variety of attractive alternatives to sport participation. Second, since most youngsters cite multiple motives for both sport participation and sport dropout, it seems apparent that youngsters' participatory behavior is not the result of a single factor but is likely to be influenced by a weighing of the costs and benefits of continued participation. To the extent that youngsters engage in a rational cost-benefit analysis regarding their sport participation, social exchange theory may be a viable explanation of sport dropout.

Petlichkoff's (1988) research is the only study to include a cost-benefit analysis of sport dropout behavior. In her study of high school basketball players, she found that starters and nonstarters had higher levels of satisfaction than did survivors, dropouts, or cuttees. However, the survivors had lower levels of satisfaction than did the dropouts, suggesting that these survivors either had fewer alternative opportunities to pursue, or perceived additional "costs" to dropping out. In fact, the survivors reported that they perceived a strong negative stigma to dropping out and this "cost" was a factor in their decisions to remain on the team.

Although Smith believes that social exchange theory best explains sport dropout, he proposed an alternative explanation for sport burnout. Sport burnout is characterized by a lack of interest in continuing sport involvement as a consequence of chronic stress experiences within this domain. In the instance of burnout, the desire to withdraw from participation is not the result of a rational cost/benefit analysis but rather the consequence of the desire to escape chronic stress, and is best explained by cognitive-affective theories of stress (e.g., Lazarus, 1966). Burnout is viewed as a rather infrequent occurrence in young athletes but would most likely happen to those youngsters who are most intensively engaged in sport.

Gould (1987) proposed a model of youth sport withdrawal that addresses the intrapersonal, motivational, and situational influences central to each of the theoretical frameworks he identified as appropriate to the study of sport attrition. Although this model was designed for heuristic purposes only, it may prove beneficial as a guide to future research. With similar intentions, Gould and Petlichkoff (1988) developed an integrative model to guide participation motivation research. Readers are referred to these overviews.

Future Directions in Participation Motivation/Attrition Research

Knowledge about the factors underlying youngsters' decisions to participate and withdraw from organized sport has developed considerably over the past decade. However, in order to further advance this knowledge base, researchers must acknowledge the limitations inherent in traditional approaches and more fully address the complete picture of children's participatory behavior in sport.

A primary limitation of current research paradigms on children's participatory behavior has been the implicit assumption that dropping out of sport is an unfortunate consequence for children. A more rational approach is to assume that children have a variety of interesting activities to pursue of which sport participation is only one (Weiss & Petlichkoff, 1989). Furthermore, fewer sport opportunities are available to older children and adolescents as they move out of nonschool sport activities that emphasize participation to school-sponsored athletic programs that emphasize competition and require high ability.

The terminology used to characterize participatory status is in need of refinement. Participatory status should be viewed along a continuum that reflects level of participatory involvement (Gould, 1987; Weiss, in press; Weiss & Petlichkoff, 1989). Furthermore, involvement classifications need to remain consistent with research that indicates that many youngsters fully intend to sample a variety of sports (Gould et al., 1982; Klint & Weiss, 1986; Weiss, in press). With regard to sport withdrawal, it is particularly essential to refine the terminology used to describe sport dropouts. For example, Klint and Weiss (1986) characterized former competitive gymnasts as fitting into one of three distinct categories. Reluctant dropouts were those who were forced to discontinue participation because of injury or cost of the sport. Voluntary dropouts were identified as those who were interested in sampling other activities but who were not necessarily dissatisfied with their gymnastics experience. Resistant dropouts were characterized as those for whom the costs of continued participation clearly outweighed the benefits of continuing. Klint and Weiss contended that the psychological consequences of withdrawal for each group of athletes is likely to be quite different as a consequence of their underlying motives for withdrawal. In a similar vein, Smith (1986) has identified the importance of distinguishing between sport dropouts and burnouts due to the distinct sets of circumstances contributing to their sport withdrawal.

Weiss and Petlichkoff (1989) have described a number of "missing links" in the literature on participatory behavior in sport. They suggest that researchers need to more closely consider the influence of a variety of intrapersonal and situational variables upon children's participatory decisions. Intrapersonal variables include differences among children in their initial and ongoing participation motives, differences in cognitive and physical developmental levels, differences in the intensity of sport involvement, and differences in children's self-perception characteristics. Contextual variables no doubt also influence these participatory experiences, including the type of program, type of sport, and personal characteristics of coaches and others involved in the sport with the youngster. Weiss and Petlichkoff also suggest that research on children's participatory involvement could greatly benefit from longitudinal, rather than cross-sectional, approaches in which youngsters are followed through various participatory phases. In essence, they argue that children's sport behavior will not be further understood until the various components of the youth sport experience are much more closely examined.

Findings from the participation motivation and attrition research can be helpful in assisting youth sport coaches and administrators to provide more positive sport experiences for youngsters. Recognizing individual difference factors in youngsters with regard to their participatory motives, sport-related goals, and developmental status should certainly be a primary focus of youth sport programs. Second, youth sport practitioners need to be aware of the variety of motives children have for sport involvement and should structure programs to meet these multiple motives. Finally, young athletes should be consulted for their suggestions about how the sport experience could be made more enjoyable. Klint and Weiss (1986), in their study of young competitive gymnasts, found that these athletes had many recommendations for improving their sport experience, such as limiting practice hours, increasing social opportunities, and limiting segregation according to ability.

Understanding children's motives for participating in sport and for discontinuing this involvement is very important from both a research perspective and an applied perspective. In order to advance this knowledge base in the 1990s, it will be essential that investigators expand their research efforts by incorporating comprehensive, theoretically based perspectives that more fully address the variety of factors that shape children's participatory experiences.

PSYCHOLOGICAL STRESS IN CHILDREN'S SPORT

Since the inception of youth sport programs in the United States, there has been concern for the amount of psychological stress that children experience as a consequence of structured sport involvement (Wiggins, 1987). Since the 1930s, various education, medical, and recreational leaders have discouraged sport involvement for chil-

dren because of beliefs that competitive youth sport is too stressful (Berryman, 1988). At the present time, youth sport practitioners and researchers still consider psychological stress in youth sport to be a high priority issue demanding greater attention (Gould, in press).

The topic of psychological stress in youth sport has received attention because of concerns that highly pressurized sport experiences may have aversive short-and long-term emotional and psychological outcomes for some young athletes (Brower, 1978; Smilkstein, 1980). Concern also exists that high levels of stress and anxiety will contribute to children dropping out of sport competition at an early age. Although the participation motivation literature is not strongly supportive of the notion that youngsters discontinue their participation because of aversive psychological experiences, certain studies have found that "too much stress" or "not having enough fun" are reasons cited by at least a fair proportion of youngsters (Orlick, 1973, 1974; Klint & Weiss, 1986).

The topic of competitive stress in youth sports has received considerable research attention in North America. During the initial phases of study from the late 1950s through the mid-1970s, the major question that was posed was "How stressful is competitive sport for children?" However, subsequent research indicated that it is not possible to generalize about levels of stress experienced by young athletes because of the great variability among youngsters in stress responses to organized sport competition (Scanlan & Passer, 1978, 1979; Simon & Martens, 1979). A more refined subsequent question became "What are the factors contributing to psychological stress in young athletes?" Further exploration of this topic suggested that individual differences in cognitions, particularly self-perception and sport appraisal characteristics, helped to explain the largest part of the variance in children's stress responses. At the present time, research continues to focus upon identifying intrapersonal and social contributors to, and correlates of, competitive stress in young athletes. Gould (in press) suggested that future research needs to target chronically high anxious young athletes because these athletes are at greatest risk of experiencing negative psychological outcomes from their sport experiences.

Research on psychological stress in youth sport has almost exclusively focused upon anxiety. Although researchers have frequently used the terms *stress* and *anxiety* interchangeably, they are not synonomous. Stress refers to the presence of physical or psychological imbalance within an organism and is a response to the disruption of homeostasis (Selye, 1974). Stress is also not necessarily a negative characteristic. For example, physiogical conditioning is enhanced through the gradual introduction of, and adaptation to, physical stress. Psychological stress refers to a general class of behaviors which occur as a result of imbalance such as feelings of overload, burnout, and anxiety. Anxiety is thus just one manifestation of psychological stress, and refers specifically to those feelings of apprehension, tension, and physiological arousal that accompany worry about future events (Spielberger, 1966).

Conceptual Overview of Competitive Stress in Youth Sport

Why might youngsters experience psychological stress, particularly anxiety, during their participation in competitive sport? Contemporary research on this issue has been in accordance with current theories of emotion which propose that individual differences in cognitive appraisal processes are primarily responsible for differences in emotional response patterns (e.g., Lazarus & Folkman, 1984; Weiner, 1985). This perspective has stimulated youth sport researchers to examine more closely children's cognitions about their sport behavior.

Current theorists contend that the perception of threat is strongly related to the experience of anxiety (Lazarus & Folkman, 1984). When personally valued goals are threatened, or when individuals perceive that they have inadequate personal resources to achieve these valued goals, anxiety will be heightened (Martens, 1977; McGrath, 1970). A number of influences are likely to increase the perception of threat experienced by young athletes. These influences reflect societal values, social and structural characteristics of youth sport, and family influences.

First, athletic ability is a highly valued personal characteristic, at least within the social structure of North American children and adolescents (Coleman, 1961; Duda, 1981, cited in Roberts, 1984). Given the tremendous importance placed upon the acquisition of sport skills by youngsters, threat may be appraised when individuals perceive that they may not attain the level of athletic proficiency that is desired, or when opportunities to display athletic ability are limited.

Threat may be similarly experienced when the specific participatory motives of the young athlete are incongruent with the goals of the youth sport program or coach. Previously cited participation motivation research indicates that youngsters are attracted to youth sport by a variety of motives. Threat may be experienced when personally valued outcomes appear unattainable. For example, if a youngster is attracted to competitive sport because of the desire for positive social interaction, but his or her coach primarily values winning, the youngster is likely to experience stress regarding his or her involvement. Since it is difficult for organized sport to meet the goals of each of its participants, it is to be expected that some youngsters will experience stress as a consequence of this incongruence (Passer, 1988b).

A third potential source of threat in competitive youth sport pertains to the pervasiveness of social evaluation opportunities within the sport context (Scanlan, 1982, 1988). Since athletic competition takes place in highly visible public settings there is always the possibility of incurring negative evaluation from others as a consequence of poor performance. Furthermore, for the child with low perceived ability, the public nature of sport competition may heighten anxiety.

Fourth, family interactional patterns, expectations, and reinforcement characteristics may dispose certain youngsters to experience chronically high levels of anxiety in achievement situations. Academic research on high test anxious children reveals that certain familial characteristics are related to the child's experience of test anxiety. For example, high test-anxious youngsters typically have parents who provide little emotional support under problem-solving conditions (Hermens, ter Laak, & Maes, 1972), and who positively reinforce objective outcomes such as grades, but not effort (Dusek, 1980). It is likely that parental behaviors contribute to the experience of anxiety for certain young athletes, particularly given the extensive involvement of parents in their children's sport experiences.

The assessment of psychological stress in youth sport has almost exclusively involved the measurement of state and trait anxiety. Spielberger (1966) first discriminated the state and trait anxiety constructs. State anxiety is a temporary condition characterized by feelings of tension, apprehension, and irritability. State anxiety thus has both cognitive (worry) and somatic (physiological) components. Trait anxiety is a more enduring characteristic of the individual and refers to the tendency to perceive certain types of circumstances as threatening to self, and to respond with high levels of state anxiety when confronted with these circumstances. (See Chapter 14.)

Measurement of State Anxiety

State anxiety in competitive sport has been assessed primarily through the use of psychophysiological measures and self-report instruments. Psychophysiological measures have included galvanic skin response (Skubic, 1955), heart rates (Hanson, 1967), and heart rates and respiration (Lowe & McGrath, 1971, cited in Gould, in press) as indexes of state anxiety. The difficulty with using psychophysiological measures to assess state anxiety is that these measures are incapable of distinguishing between elevated physical response as a consequence of physiological activation as opposed to somatic anxiety. For example, Hanson (1967) monitored the heart rates of youth baseball players at various points before, during, and after a game. Results indicated that mean heart rates increased from 95 beats per minute (bpm) prior to the game to 127 bpm in the field and to 167 while batting. However, since most of the players later reported that they did not experience stress while batting, it appears that physiological activation, and not somatic anxiety, was generally responsible for the rise in heart rates.

Self-report measures have been the most frequently utilized means of assessing children's competitive state anxiety. Initial investigations used Spielberger's (1973) State Anxiety Inventory for Children or the Competitive State Anxiety Inventory for Children (CSAI-C) developed by Martens, Burton, Rivkin, and Simon (1980). On each scale an overall state anxiety score is obtained by summing the individual scale items. More recently, the CSAI-C was revised to create the CSAI-2 (Martens, Burton, Vealey, Smith, & Bump, 1983) in order to separate the cognitive (worry) and somatic (physiological arousal) components of state anxiety. The research reported on children's state anxiety responses in sport has utilized one of these three measures.

State Anxiety Levels in Youth Sport

A well-designed study by Simon and Martens (1979) provides considerable insight into levels of state anxiety experienced by youngsters in various sport conditions, and about the relative amounts of anxiety experienced in sport and nonsport achievement circumstances. Simon and Martens administered the CSAI-C inventory to boys ages 9 to 14 years, prior to their involvement in a variety of evaluative conditions. These conditions included taking an academic test, participating in a physical education class competition, performing with the band in a solo role or as a member of a group, practicing with an organized sport team, or competing in any of seven different organized sports (baseball, basketball, tackle football, gymnastics, ice hockey, swimming, and wrestling).

Three major findings emerged from the Simon and Martens study. First, state anxiety levels were higher for these boys during sport competition than they were during practice sessions. However, the rise in state anxiety from practice to competition was only slight to moderate. Second, the highest mean level of state anxiety in any condition was recorded by the band soloists, indicating that involvement in activities other than competitive sport can also provoke anxiety in youngsters. Third, among athletes engaged in organized sports, wrestlers and gymnasts experienced higher levels of state anxiety than did team sport athletes.

An examination of the mean anxiety scores in each of the sport conditions would seem to suggest that competitive sport is not overly anxiety-provoking for youngsters. The mean score for the young wrestlers was 19.52 on the CSAI-C, which has a range of 10 (lowest) to 30 (highest). Simon and Martens concluded that competitive sport does not appear to be overly stressful for youngsters but that circumstances which maximize the opportunity for personal evaluation by others will increase state anxiety.

In their study assessing the state anxiety levels of a group of 13-and 14-year-old wrestlers prior to a competitive tournament match, Bump, Gould, Petlichkoff, Peterson, and Levin (1985, cited in Gould, in press) obtained a mean value on the CSAI-C of 18.9, which was very close to the mean value reported by Simon and Martens. Furthermore, only 9% of these youngsters had scores of 25 or greater, which would be considered extremely high. These researchers also concluded that psychological stress in young athletes is not excessive, as evidenced by these CSAI-C scores.

Some problems exist, however, in inferring from scores on an anxiety questionnaire that few young athletes experience psychological stress. First, raw scores on the CSAI scales may not adequately portray the variability among youngsters in state anxiety levels. The scale scores may, perhaps, be representative of anxiety levels for those in the middle of the range but not for those at the extremes. Second, it is possible that adolescents, particularly males, may tend to underreport their state anxiety levels prior to competition. This could occur for social desirability reasons or due to the desire to retain self-confidence prior to competition. Third, youngsters who find competitive sport to be very stressful may be infrequent sport participants, and thus may not be represented in the sport research. Finally, it must be remembered that anxiety is but just one manifestation of psychological stress. Stress may manifest itself in other forms such as feelings of "burnout" or reduced intrinsic motivation, and these stress responses have been infrequently assessed.

Sources of Precompetition State Anxiety

Identifying the sources of youngsters' sport-related anxiety is an important undertaking because it will allow researchers and practitioners to gain a better appreciation of children's perspectives on their sport involvement. Present-day understanding of the contributors to children's precompetitive state anxiety has resulted largely from a line of research initiated by Tara Scanlan and colleagues (e.g., Scanlan & Lewthwaite, 1984; Scanlan & Passer, 1978, 1979).

In general, the research conducted to date strongly supports the belief that individual differences in children's cognitive appraisal characteristics contribute to observed differences in children's state anxiety levels in sport. At least seven factors have been identified in the literature as sources of children's competitive state anxiety.

Self-esteem appears to be a predictor of precompetition state anxiety levels for young athletes. Low self-esteem boys and girls display higher state anxiety levels than do high self-esteem children (Scanlan & Passer, 1978, 1979). Since self-esteem reflects beliefs about self-worth and personal capacity (Coopersmith, 1967), this finding suggests that low self-esteem children fear that they are unlikely to attain personally valued goals because of insufficient ability.

A second predictor of precompetition state anxiety is competitive trait anxiety (CTA). High-CTA boys and girls are disposed to experience higher precompetitive state anxiety than are low-CTA children (Martens & Gill, 1976; Scanlan & Lewthwaite, 1984; Scanlan & Passer, 1978, 1979). Since high-CTA children generally perceive greater threat in sport than do low-CTA children (Martens, 1977), it is logical to assume that they will generally experience higher state anxiety in specific sport contexts as well. An awareness of children's levels of trait anxiety regarding competition would help youth sport coaches and parents better anticipate the state anxiety reactions of youngsters to competitive circumstances.

A third appraisal characteristic influencing precompetitive state anxiety levels involves expectations about personal and team performance in the upcoming competition. Low personal performance expectancies have been related to high state anxiety in two studies (Scanlan & Lewthwaite, 1984; Scanlan & Passer, 1978), and in a third study this result was also found for boys but not for girls (Scanlan & Passer, 1979). Similarly, players who have low expectations for their team's performance experience greater precompetition state anxiety (Scanlan & Passer, 1978, 1979).

A fourth predictor of precompetition anxiety is worry about performing up to one's ability level. Gould, Horn, & Spreeman (1983b) found that the two major sources of prematch stress in their sample of young wrestlers were worries about performing up to their level of ability and worries about improving upon their most recent performance. Losing ranked only fifth as a source of worry for these young athletes. Feltz and Albrecht (1986) obtained almost identical results in their study on elite young runners, ages 9 to 15 years. The top two worries for these young runners were also about performing up to their level of ability and improving upon their last performance. As a source of stress, losing ranked only seventh. It is important to note that, in general, worry about losing has not been identified as a major cause of anxiety for young athletes.

Some youngsters appear to experience anxiety as a consequence of worry about adult expectations and performance standards. Scanlan and Lewthwaite (1984) found that wrestlers who reported higher levels of parental pressure to participate in the sport experienced higher levels of prematch state anxiety. High state anxiety in these wrestlers was also predicted by the tendency to worry frequently about meeting parental and coach expectations. Weiss, Weise, and Klint (1989) found that the top two precompetition worries for their sample of young male gymnasts were worries about "what my parents will think" and about "letting my parents down." It appears that many adults contribute to the experience of anxiety for young athletes by communicating their own ambitious expectations to youngsters.

State anxiety levels also seem to be related to the type of sport (individual or team) in which the individual participates. Simon and Martens (1979) assessed the precompetitive state anxiety of 468 male youth sport athletes using the CSAI-C. They found that wrestlers and gymnasts reported the highest levels of state anxiety, whereas team sport athletes in football, hockey, and baseball demonstrated lower levels. Griffin (1972; cited in Gould, in press) also found that young females engaged in individual sports experienced higher levels of precompetitive anxiety than did female team sport athletes. Since individual sports maximize opportunities for social comparison and evaluation, it is logical that athletes participating in these sports would also experience greater prematch stress than would team sport athletes (Passer, 1988b).

Game or match importance is also related to precompetition anxiety. Participating in championship competition was identified as a major source of stress by elite young wrestlers (Gould, Horn, & Spreeman, 1983b) and runners (Feltz & Albrecht, 1986). This finding is as expected, since season-long goals are likely to be threatened by poor performance in championship competitions.

While youth sport research has identified common sources of precompetitive anxiety in young athletes in-volved in a variety of sports, it is important to note that no single source of stress has been cited by an overwhelming proportion of athletes within any study (Gould et al., 1983b). This outcome further emphasizes the extent of individual difference factors in the experience of competitive anxiety. Furthermore, it suggests that psychological stress in youth sport cannot be reduced simply by focusing upon a few aspects of the youth sport experience.

Measurement of Competitive Trait Anxiety in Youth Sport

Competitive trait anxiety represents a person's general tendency to appraise competitive situations as threatening (Martens, 1977). Since the high-CTA child is chronically disposed to view competition as threatening, this child may be considered to be most "at risk" of experiencing negative psychological outcomes as a consequence of sport participation, and/or to discontinue sport participation at an early age. Therefore, understanding the etiology of high-CTA is an important task for youth sport researchers.

Competitive trait anxiety in youth sport has been measured almost exclusively by Martens's (1977) Sport Competition Anxiety Test (SCAT). The children's form of SCAT contains 10 questions that ask children to report the frequency with which they experience certain worries about competition. The scale also includes five "dummy" questions that are unrelated to trait anxiety and are not scored. SCAT has established acceptable levels of validity and reliability (see Martens, 1977) and has proven to be a better predictor of anxiety experienced during competition than have general trait anxiety scales or coaches' ratings of players' anxiety (Martens, Rivkin, & Burton, 1980; Martens & Simon, 1976). The research reported in the following discussion utilized SCAT in each instance.

Lewthwaite and Scanlan (1989) suggested that the SCAT contains a predominance of items measuring somatic anxiety and does not effectively identify cognitive aspects of competitive trait anxiety. They suggested that measurement of trait anxiety in sport should remain consistent with theoretical approaches (e.g., Borkovec, 1976; Morris, Davis, & Hutchings, 1981), which posit that the cognitive and somatic components of anxiety operate relatively independently. They encouraged the development of additional measures to identify cognitive (worry) aspects of anxiety in youth sport.

As a means of better distinguishing somatic and cognitive aspects of anxiety in sport, Smith, Smoll, and Schutz (1990) recently developed the Sport Anxiety Scale (SAS). Initial factor analyses indicated that athletes distinguished three aspects of sport-related trait anxiety: somatic anxiety, worry, and concentration disruption. The SAS measures each of these components separately. This new scale has undergone considerable testing with high school and college athletes and has demonstrated respectable levels of validity and reliability (see Smith, et al., 1990). To date, however, no one has attempted to use the SAS with young athletes. It is recommended that researchers test this measure with young athletes, and/or modify the scale as is deemed appropriate.

Sources of Competitive Trait Anxiety

Passer (1983) first examined sources of trait anxiety in young athletes in his sample of male soccer players. His focus was upon differences in self-perception characteristics and sources of worry that might distinguish high- and low-CTA youngsters. High-CTA and low-CTA players were operationally defined as those who scored in the upper and lower quartiles, respectively, of the range of obtained SCAT scores. Passer found that high-CTA players had lower self-esteem and lower expectations for personal performance and worried more frequently about personal performance and incurring negative evaluations from significant others. However, he did not find high-CTA players to be lower in perceived soccer competence, as had been anticipated. Passer's conclusions were that fear of failure and fear of negative evaluation by others are important sources of threat for high-CTA children.

Brustad and Weiss (1987) replicated and extended Passer's research by examining self-perceptions and sources of worry in high-, medium-, and low-CTA male baseball and female softball players. Similar to Passer's findings, the high-CTA boys in this study demonstrated lower self-esteem and had more frequent performance-related worries than did their low-CTA counterparts. However, no significant differences were found on any of the self-perception or worry variables between CTA groups for the girl softball players. In a subsequent study, Brustad (1988) found that high-CTA male and female basketball players had lower self-esteem and more frequent worries about evaluation and performance than did their low-CTA counterparts.

Weiss, Bredemeier, and Brustad (1987) examined correlates of competitive trait anxiety in children, ages 8 to 13 years, participating in a summer sports camp. These researchers directly tested hypotheses from Harter's (1978, 1981) theory of competence motivation. As predicted by Harter's theory, high-CTA children had lower levels of perceived competence and more external perceptions of control than did children at medium-or low-CTA levels. Furthermore, high-CTA girls had lower levels of intrinsic motivation than did their medium-or low-CTA counterparts.

Lewthwaite and Scanlan (1989) desired to distinguish the contributors to somatic and cognitive aspects of CTA. They retained 8 items from SCAT which loaded heavily on the physical symptoms of anxiety as their somatic trait anxiety scale. They included 2 separate scales of cognitive anxiety, which assessed worries about failure and worries about adult expectations and evaluation. For the elite young wrestlers in their study, they found that those wrestlers experiencing greater somatic anxiety had lower self-esteem, reported experiencing greater emotional upset when they performed poorly, and expressed a greater desire to avoid

competing in a tournament match. Wrestlers with more frequent worries about failure placed greater importance on wrestling well and experienced more emotional upset when they performed poorly. Youngsters with more frequent worries about adult expectations also reported greater emotional upset with poor performance and perceived greater parental pressure to wrestle, greater parental upset and coach upset with poor performance, and more negative adult evaluations.

Lewthwaite (1990) examined the role of perceived threat to personally valued goals in the frequency and intensity of competitive trait anxiety experienced by 9- to 15-year-old male soccer players. As predicted, boys who perceived greater threat to personally valued effort/mastery or competitive achievement goals experienced higher levels of trait anxiety. Endangerment of personally valued goals was more strongly related to the intensity than to the frequency of CTA symptoms. Since SCAT measures only the frequency with which children experience symptoms of anxiety, it would be beneficial for researchers to continue to assess the intensity of such symptoms, as Lewthwaite has done.

In the research findings on the correlates of competitive trait anxiety, a relatively clear pattern emerges regarding the self-perception and worry characteristics of high-CTA youngsters. High trait-anxious youngsters seem to have relatively unfavorable views of their own competence, as reflected by low levels of self-esteem (Brustad, 1988; Brustad & Weiss, 1987; Lewthwaite & Scanlan, 1989; Passer, 1983) and frequent worries about personal performance (Brustad, 1988; Brustad & Weiss, 1987; Passer, 1983). Furthermore high-CTA children seem to worry extensively about incurring negative performance evaluations from others (Brustad, 1988; Lewthwaite & Scanlan, 1989; Passer, 1983). Additional correlates of CTA that have been identified in the literature, such as low perceived competence (Weiss et al., 1987), external control perceptions (Weiss et al., 1987), and goal endangerment (Lewthwaite, 1990), provide strong support for the belief that factors which magnify the perception of threat contribute to the experience of anxiety for young athletes.

Developmental Contributors to Anxiety

The manifestation of anxiety in youngsters may reflect developmental influences in addition to the identified social and intrapersonal factors. Research on academic test anxiety in children indicates that children's anxiety levels increase over the elementary school years (Hill, 1972; Hill & Sarason, 1966) and may peak during early adolescence (Manley & Rosmeier, 1972). Norms reported by Martens (1977) and additional cross-sectional data (Gould et al., 1983a; Passer, 1983) indicate that CTA scores also increase from middle childhood through adolescence.

In their review of research on test anxiety in school children, Wigfield and Eccles (1990) contended that cognitive developmental factors affecting children's processing of evaluative feedback contributes strongly to increases in anxiety during the childhood and early adolescent period. Research indicates that children are not very accurate at estimating their abilities relative to others' abilities during the early elementary school years (Nicholls, 1978) and that they tend to be overly optimistic in their expectancies for future performance (Parsons & Ruble, 1977). With age and development, however, children begin to integrate social comparison information into the formation of their self-judgments (Horn & Hasbrook, 1986, 1987; Nicholls, 1978; Ruble, 1983), and by the fourth grade children's self-perceptions of ability begin to show some correlation with actual performance (Nicholls, 1978). Furthermore, children become increasingly reliant upon social comparison sources of information during childhood and adolescence (Horn & Hasbrook, 1986, 1987). Since children initially tend to overestimate their abilities relative to others', the increasing accuracy of their estimates with age tends to reduce the favorability of their perceptions. Children may be likely to experience stress as a consequence of the realization that they are not as talented as others in certain valued achievement domains. In addition, as older children and adolescents increasingly utilize social comparison processes with age, they are also likely to become more sensitive to social evaluation by others, and this may contribute to anxiety in evaluative circumstances such as sport.

Another cognitive-developmental factor that may be related to the tendency for youngsters to demonstrate greater anxiety with age pertains to the increasing capacity of children to differentiate the concepts of ability and effort (Nicholls, 1978, 1984). Younger children (ages 5 to 6 years) tend to equate ability and effort and to think that trying harder will increase ability. Children of ages 7 to 9 are more likely to believe that effort is the cause of outcomes and that equal effort will result in equivalent outcomes for all individuals. Older children realize that effort and ability are distinct contributors to achievement but that possessing low ability limits future success possibilities. This realization may create psychological stress for the youngster who perceives that he or she has low ability but recognizes that putting forth greater effort will not be sufficient to attain personally valued outcomes.

Developmentally based research has implications for our understanding of anxiety in sport. First, it is important to recognize that while levels of anxiety may increase with age in young athletes, this rise is not entirely attributable to sport-related factors. Second, it is important for sport researchers to further delve into developmental factors as they influence psychological stress in youth sport so that these factors may be distinguished from intrapersonal and social contributors.

Sources and Intrapersonal Correlates of Sport Enjoyment

To gain a better perspective on negative affective outcomes for youngsters in sport, it may be helpful to look at the "flip side" of this consequence by examining the intrapersonal and social correlates of positive affective outcomes for young athletes. To date, only a limited amount of research has been devoted to understanding those factors contributing to positive affective outcomes for children in sport. Such research will also assist in our understanding of children's motivational processes in sport, particularly sport persistence.

Wankel and Kreisel (1985a) conducted an exploratory examination of children's sport enjoyment with a paired-comparison format and found that comparing skills with others, game excitement, personal accomplishment, and improving skills were rated as the most important sources of enjoyment for youth sport competitors. Similar information was obtained when young athletes were asked to respond in an open-ended format, although being with friends was also ranked highly by this group of subjects (Wankel & Kreisel, 1985b).

Scanlan and Lewthwaite (1986) examined correlates of season-long enjoyment in male age-group wrestlers ages 9 to 14 years. They found that greater enjoyment for these athletes was predicted by high parental satisfaction with performance, positive adult involvement and interactions, a low frequency of negative maternal interactions, and high perceived ability. These results clearly indicate that parents assume an important role in shaping children's affective experiences in sport. These researchers also found a relatively strong correlation ($r = .70$) between level of sport enjoyment and the extent to which these wrestlers wished to compete in the sport the following season.

Brustad (1988), in his study of young basketball players, found that motivational orientation and perceived parental pressure were predictive of season-long enjoyment levels for both his male and female subjects. Specifically, an intrinsic motivational orientation, as demonstrated by a preference for challenging rather than easy tasks, and low perceived parental pressure were associated with greater enjoyment. An additionally important finding was that team win-loss record and personal ability levels (as assessed by each player's coach) were not related to enjoyment levels.

Scanlan, Stein, and Ravizza (1989) conducted a retrospective study of sources of enjoyment for former elite figure skaters. Using open-ended interview techniques, they found that five characteristics of enjoyment were most commonly reported by these former skaters. The first category was social and life opportunities which reflected the enjoyment experienced by forming affiliations with others and/or having opportunities for unique experiences outside the sport realm (e.g., travel). A second category was identified as perceived competence, which reflected satisfaction with one's level of sport achievement. Social recognition of competence was a third characteristic of enjoyment and referred to the satisfaction resulting from having others recognize competence. A fourth theme was the act of skating, which referred specifically to the enjoyment resulting from the physical sensations and self-expression inherent in skating. The final category was identified as special cases and pertained to both a sense of personal uniqueness and the development of life coping skills that resulted from participation in the sport. Drawing upon the varied sources of enjoyment reported by these skaters, Scanlan and Simons (1992) recently proposed that understanding the unique aspects of enjoyment for young athletes is a research topic in need of much greater attention.

In summary, the limited amount of research conducted on sport enjoyment suggests that similar social and intrapersonal variables influence young athletes' positive and negative affective experiences in sport contexts. More research is clearly needed on this topic, particularly to address the relationship between sport enjoyment and motivational characteristics, such as intrinsic/extrinsic motivational orientation and sport persistence.

Future Directions in Stress and Anxiety Research

Relative to other psychological aspects of youth sport involvement, a considerable amount of research attention has been devoted to understanding children's affective experiences in sport. From both conceptual and measurement standpoints, research has evolved considerably over the past decade. A few suggestions will be made to encourage the further development of research in this area.

First, it is necessary to examine characteristics of the stress response other than anxiety. For example, athletes who engage in sport at high levels of intensity for extended periods of time frequently report "burnout," yet this aspect of psychological stress has not been studied. Smith (1986) has provided a cognitive-affective framework from which burnout can be studied in sport. Second, in accordance with the work of Lewthwaite and Scanlan (1989) and Smith et al. (1990), it is suggested that investigators further explore the unique characteristics of somatic and cognitive forms of anxiety. Assessing these two aspects independently should contribute to a better understanding of the nature of young athletes' anxiety experiences. Third, research has consistently identified parental influences as important contributors to children's affective experiences in sport. Further research is needed to examine the specific means by which parental involvement shapes children's sport-related emotional experiences. Finally since contemporary research focuses heavily upon the cognitive appraisal processes underlying emotion, it is important for youth sport researchers to more closely examine cognitive developmental changes as they impact on appraisal characteristics. From a conceptual standpoint, both Nicholls's (1984, 1989) and Harter's (1978, 1981) theories are appropriate to guide developmentally based research on anxiety in youth sport.

ADULT INVOLVEMENT IN YOUTH SPORT: PSYCHOLOGICAL OUTCOMES FOR CHILDREN

Adult influence in children's sport is pervasive. Youth sport leagues are organized by adults, teams are coached by adults, and competitions are heavily attended by adults,

particularly parents. The extent of adult influence in children's sport has been attacked by some critics who contend that adults focus too heavily on winning, which induces stress and takes the fun out of youth sport for many participants (Brower, 1978; Smilkstein, 1980).

A rather dramatic example of the extent to which parents can become involved in the sport experiences of their children is provided by research on minor hockey in Canada. McPherson and Davidson (1980, cited in Smith, 1988) found that 80% of the players had parents who attended at least three-quarters of their games. An additional finding was that at least 25% of parents attend their children's practices at least two or three times a month. It is apparent even to casual observers that parents become extensively involved in their children's youth sport experiences and that this involvement has psychological effects upon young athletes.

It is unfortunate that concern for the effects of adult involvement is not matched by an equivalent amount of research on this topic. Perhaps because this area of research is both emotionally charged and difficult to study, the knowledge base regarding the effects of adult involvement has lagged behind other areas in pediatric sport psychology. Elsewhere it has been proposed that much more systematic research is needed to understand the specific means by which parental involvement may shape children's motivational and affective experiences in sport (Brustad, 1992).

This section will examine the existing knowledge base on the relationship between adult involvement and sport outcomes for children by addressing three important psychological concerns. First, in accordance with current research emphases in youth sport psychology, the effect of adults upon children's self-perception characteristics will be examined. Second, the relationship between adult behaviors and children's motivational processes will be addressed. Third, the influence of adults upon children's affective experiences in sport will be explored.

Adult Influence Upon Children's Self-Perception Characteristics

Current theories of youth sport behavior regard children's self-perception characteristics as critical mediators of their motivational and affective patterns (Harter, 1978, 1981; Nicholls, 1984, 1989). Research in both sport and academic areas has been supportive of these theoretical contentions. For example, highly competent children who underestimate their abilities tend to work at an inappropriately low level of challenge (Harter, 1983) and display less self-initiative and persistence on achievement tasks (Ames, 1978; Phillips, 1984). Children with higher levels of perceived competence are also more likely to engage in, and persist at, sport (Feltz & Petlichkoff, 1983; Roberts, Kleiber, & Duda, 1981).

During their sport involvement, children's self-perceptions are likely to be heavily influenced by adults for two reasons. First, adults are extensively involved in the youth sport domain and thereby provide a great deal of information to children about their personal capacities. Second, as a consequence of cognitive-developmental characteristics, children prefer to use adult sources of feedback in assessing their abilities in achievement situations (Frieze & Bar-Tal, 1980; Horn & Hasbrook, 1986, 1987). Horn and Hasbrook's research reveals that children of ages 8 to 11 years demonstrate a preference for adult sources of information in judging their sport competence, whereas older children and adolescents (ages 12 to 14 years) rely more heavily upon peer-based social comparison processes. Since youth sport participation levels appear to peak at about 11 years of age (State of Michigan, 1978a), it is evident that adults are important sources of information for youngsters during the years of peak involvement.

Parental feedback is certainly an important source of ability information for young athletes. Harter's (1978, 1981) theory of competence motivation proposes that parents exert the primary influence upon children's developing self-perceptions of competence and control. According to Harter, parents shape children's emerging perceptions of self through the type of evaluative feedback that they provide in response to the child's achievement efforts. If children receive consistent and positive feedback for both the product and the process of their mastery efforts, they will develop favorable perceptions of their personal competence and control over subsequent performance, according to Harter. These favorable self-perceptions, in turn, will contribute to the enhancement of self-esteem and intrinsic motivation, and reduce performance anxiety.

The relationship between parental behaviors and children's self-perception characteristics has been a focus of academic research. Parsons, Adler, and Kaczala (1982) found that children's perceptions of their mathematics ability and their perceptions regarding the difficulty and level of effort required for math were more strongly linked to their parents' beliefs about the child's capacity than to the child's own demonstrated level of ability. Phillips (1984, 1987) also examined the relationship between parental belief systems and the academic self-perceptions of third-and fifth-grade students. Her research focused on highly competent students, ranking in the upper 25% of their grade level on the basis of achievement test scores, but who differed in the favorability of their self-perceptions of academic ability. The children with less favorable self-perceptions of ability believed that their parents shared these low perceptions, and that their parents had low expectations for their future level of achievement. The motivational profile of these low-perceived-competence children conformed to the expectations of competence motivation theory as these children expected schoolwork to be more difficult and to require more effort than did the high-perceived-competence group.

The research findings obtained from academic contexts highlight the influence of parents in shaping children's self-appraisals. This influence is likely to be even greater in sport than in classroom settings since parents have more firsthand opportunities to participate in the sport experiences of their children and to provide immediate and specific feedback to their children in these contexts. Unfortunately, only a limited amount of research has examined parental influence upon children's sport-related self-perceptions. Felson and Reed (1986) found that parental judgments of upper elementary school children's abilities in athletics and academics were strongly related to the child's self-appraisals even when levels of actual ability were statistically controlled. Scanlan and Lewthwaite (1984) found that young wrestlers who perceived greater parental (and coach) satisfaction with their performance demonstrated higher general expectancies for their future wrestling performance. Weitzer (1989) found that fourth-grade girls who reported higher levels of parental involvement in their sport experiences demonstrated more favorable self-perceptions of competence.

Coaches also assume an important role in shaping children's self-perception characteristics and more systematic attention has been devoted to this area of influence than has been focused upon parental influence. In a series of highly regarded studies, Smith, Smoll, and colleagues (Smith, Smoll, & Curtis, 1978, 1979; Smith, Smoll, & Hunt, 1977; Smith, Zane, Smoll, & Coppel, 1983) found that coaching behaviors substantially influence children's self-perception characteristics and psychosocial and affective experiences in sport. Similarly, Horn (1985) found that the verbal feedback provided by coaches to young female athletes was significantly related to differences among players in perceived competence.

In the first phase of their research, Smith et al. (1977) developed a system to categorize coaching behaviors. The Coaching Behavior Assessment System (CBAS) resulted from direct observation of youth sport coaches and yielded 12 behavioral categories that included reactive and spontaneous coaching behaviors to a variety of player behaviors (e.g. desirable performance, mistakes, etc.) At the conclusion of the sport season, players were interviewed in their homes about aspects of their experience. The findings of this study (Smith et al., 1978) indicated that relationships did exist between coaching behaviors and children's psychological and affective outcomes. In particular, it was found that players low in self-esteem appeared to be most affected by behavioral differences among coaches. Players who started the season with low self-esteem appeared to benefit most from playing for coaches who emphasized a "positive approach" in providing feedback to players. The empirical findings of this study led to the development of a set of behavioral recommendations for coaches.

The second phase of their research involved the implementation of an intervention program with coaches of Little League baseball players ages 10 to 15 years (Smith et al., 1979). Eighteen of these coaches received preseason training in a program designed to help them in communicating more effectively with children. The intervention program encouraged the coaches to increase the frequency of technical instruction, to provide a greater frequency of reinforcement, and to reduce the use of punishment. The remaining 13 coaches represented the control group and did not receive this training. Results indicated that the training sessions did enhance the communication effectiveness of the coaches. More important, children who played for the trained coaches exhibited a significant increase in self-esteem over the previous year, evaluated their coaches more favorably, and had a higher level of attraction to team members, even though win-loss records did not differ between teams with trained and untrained coaches. As hypothesized, low self-esteem children benefited the most from playing for trained coaches.

The relationship between coaching behaviors and children's self-perception and attitudinal characteristics was further examined in a study of coaches and athletes in a youth basketball league (Smith et al., 1983). This research indicated that coaching behaviors were significantly, but rather weakly, related to self-esteem and team solidarity. However, differences in coaching behaviors were strongly related to players' postseason attitudes, accounting for over half the variance in players' attitudes toward the coach and sport. More specifically, coaches who provided more mistake-contingent technical instruction, less general (nonspecific) feedback, and less punishment and engaged in fewer "controlling" behaviors had athletes who evaluated them more highly and expressed higher levels of sport enjoyment.

Horn (1985) further explored relationships between coaching behaviors in practice and competitive settings with changes in adolescent female softball players' competence perceptions. Whereas the series of studies conducted by Smith and Smoll focused upon coaches' communications to the team as a whole, Horn examined the effects of different coach feedback patterns to individual team members. Previous research (Rejeski, Darracott, & Hutslar, 1979) indicated that there is considerable intrateam variability in the type of feedback received by young athletes according to differences in coach expectations for performance.

Horn found that while skill improvement was the primary contributor to positive changes in self-perceptions of ability for these athletes, certain behaviors of coaches in practice also contributed significantly to the enhancement of these perceptions. Specifically players who most frequently received verbal feedback from the coach following successful performance manifested lower perceptions of competence than their counterparts. In addition, those players receiving a high frequency of criticism in response to performance errors had higher perceptions of competence than did those players receiving less criticism. Although these findings appeared to be contradictory to "commonsense" expectations about the effects of reinforcement in achievement situations, Horn observed that these findings are consistent with research on the relationship between adult expectational levels and patterns of feedback provided to children (Cooper & Good, 1983; Meyer et al., 1979). Generally, low-expectancy students are likely to receive more frequent, but less specific, feedback from teachers following successes. It is believed that the student who receives this type of feedback is likely to infer low ability because the teacher does not praise others who

have performed at a similar level on the task. Furthermore, since technical feedback conveys the impression that one has the capacity to perform at a higher level of skill, children who receive less technical feedback may be prone to infer low ability.

Adult Influence Upon Children's Motivational Processes

Identifying contributors to, and correlates of, motivation in young athletes is central to understanding youth sport behavior. Levels of sport persistence, achievement goal preferences, and intrinsic/extrinsic motivational orientations are important motivational characteristics of children that are likely to be influenced by parents and coaches. Given the prevalent use of extrinsic rewards in youth sport and the importance attached to sport achievement by adults, it is likely that parents and coaches have considerable influence in shaping children's developing motivational processes. Unfortunately the relationship between adult behaviors and children's motivational processes in sport has received scant research attention.

Harter's (1981) model of competence motivation proposes that the nature of parental response to children's mastery efforts directly impacts on children's perceptions of competence and control and subsequent intrinsic/extrinsic motivational orientation. Research indicates that children's perceptions of parental support are related to self-esteem, positive affect, and intrinsic motivation levels of youngsters in classroom settings (Harter, 1988).

In accordance with competence motivation theory, Brustad and Weigand (1989) examined relationships between parental reinforcement patterns and intrinsic/extrinsic motivational orientations in young male and female soccer players. Factor analytic procedures revealed that these youngsters perceived three distinct characteristics of parental response to their sport involvement. These aspects included parental affective patterns, parental expectation levels, and importance of sport success to parents. The results of the study revealed that youngsters who perceived higher levels of parental affective support for their efforts in sport displayed higher levels of intrinsic motivation, as demonstrated by a greater preference for challenge, than did their counterparts who perceived less parental affective support. Thus these findings were consistent with predictions from competence motivation theory.

Weitzer (1989) examined the relationship between levels of parental involvement and children's sport-related achievement orientations. Sport involvement was operationalized as the extent to which children perceived that their parents encouraged them to engage in sport, as well as the current level of parental participation and instruction in their child's sport experiences. In his sample of fourth-grade children, Weitzer found that for the girls, greater maternal involvement was related to a stronger mastery goal orientation. For the boys, no relationships between parental involvement levels and achievement goal orientations were found.

The influence of coaches upon children's motivational characteristics has not received direct attention. However, Smith et al. (1979) did find that children playing for coaches who had received coaching-effectiveness training demonstrated a stronger desire to play the sport again the following season than did their counterparts who played for untrained coaches. Clearly more research is needed to determine the influence of coaches upon children's sport motivation.

Adult Involvement In Sport: Affective Outcomes for Children

Virtually all research that has examined adult involvement in the sport experiences of children has identified relationships among adult behaviors and children's affective outcomes in sport contexts. Although much of this research was previously reported in the section on stress and anxiety in youth sport, a brief summary will be presented here to characterize the major patterns of influence as they have been identified.

Children's perceptions of "parental pressure" to participate and succeed in sport have been consistently linked to negative affective experiences for children in this domain. Passer (1983) found that children high in competitive trait anxiety are characterized, in part, by the tendency to worry more frequently about incurring negative evaluations from significant others. Scanlan and Lewthwaite (1984) noted that young wrestlers who perceived high levels of parental pressure to wrestle were likely to have high state anxiety regarding wrestling competition. These researchers also observed that greater season-long enjoyment was related to high levels of parental satisfaction with performance, positive adult involvement and interactions, and low frequency of negative maternal interactions. Similarly, Brustad (1988) determined that greater season-long enjoyment in young basketball players was related to a lower perception of parental pressure to participate for both the boys and the girls in his study. Lewthwaite and Scanlan (1989) reported that elite young wrestlers who worried frequently about adult expectations perceived high levels of parental pressure to wrestle.

Overall it seems clear that parental behaviors exert considerable influence upon the nature of children's affective experiences in sport. However, further research is needed to identify the specific characteristics of parent-child interactions and parental sport involvement that result in favorable or unfavorable affective outcomes for young athletes. Furthermore, it would be beneficial to initiate research on the influence of coaches on children's sport-related affective experiences.

Critique of Research on Adult Involvement in Youth Sport

More than any other area of pediatric sport psychology, the study of adult influence upon children's psychosocial development has tremendous room for growth. The limited amount of existing research in the area suggests that adult behaviors exert an important mediating influence upon the quality of children's sport experiences. In addition to the general recommendation that more research needs to be devoted to the study of adult influence in children's sport, three specific recommendations will be made to direct these research efforts.

An initial, general observation is that the bulk of sport science research on adult influence in youth sport comes from a sociological rather than a psychological perspective. For example, research on children's sport socialization processes has yielded a great deal of descriptive information identifying the socializing agents (i.e., father, siblings) that typically influence children to become involved in sport. However, this research also needs to address the psychological consequences of this socialization process, in particular, motivational characteristics (Brustad, 1992). To date, research has tended to address adult influence in only a superficial way. To rectify this situation, it is recommended that psychological theories be employed that are sensitive to socialization influences (e.g., Harter, 1978, 1981).

Second, more research needs to apply process-product and longitudinal approaches to the study of adult influence. Research on coaching behaviors conducted by Smith and Smoll (for a complete review, see Smoll & Smith, 1989) is the prototype for this line of research. By examining the relationship between specific adult behaviors and children's psychological outcomes (Smith et al., 1977), they were able to develop an empirically based framework that permitted the generation of specific hypotheses about how adult behaviors affect children psychologically. Their subsequent intervention program enabled them to determine that the link between certain coaching behaviors and outcomes for children was not purely correlational (Smith et al., 1978, 1979). This research has had a deservedly major impact on the pediatric sport psychology knowledge base. More research needs to examine the influence of specific adult behaviors over time.

With only a few exceptions (Horn, 1985; Smith et al., 1978, 1979, 1983) adult behavior in sport has been assessed only indirectly, primarily through children's perceptions of parental attitudes, values, and expectations. A third recommendation is that researchers study adult behaviors directly. In particular, it would be helpful to explore more fully adult perspectives on the meanings, values, and anticipated outcomes of children's sport involvement. To date, research has yet to examine parental and coach perspectives on the significance of youth sport involvement.

RECOMMENDATIONS FOR FUTURE YOUTH SPORT RESEARCH

The knowledge base regarding the psychological aspects of children's sport involvement has advanced considerably over the past decade. Nevertheless, research on children's sport behavior receives a disproportionately small amount of attention from sport psychologists relative to the tremendous numbers of youngsters involved in sport at this level of participation, and the importance of this participation upon children's psychological development. Four general recommendations will be made here to encourage the continued advancement of the knowledge base in this area.

The first recommendation is to encourage the use of broadly based theoretical approaches to the study of youth sport behavior. Since the sport experiences of youngsters are shaped by an interaction among psychological, social, developmental, and physical influences, it is imperative that our research frameworks recognize and address the influence of these varied contributors (Gould, 1988; Weiss & Bredemeier, 1983). A diversity of research approaches will be needed to understand the youth sport experience. Multivariate approaches can assist in our understanding of the relative contribution of various influences to children's sport experiences. Longitudinal approaches are needed to address change over time in individual psychological characteristics. Qualitative research methodologies may provide a greater depth of understanding regarding children's perspectives on their sport involvement.

The second recommendation addresses the content of youth sport research. At the present time, many important research questions are simply not being asked. For example, research has barely addressed the role of adults, particularly parents, in shaping children's sport experiences. This knowledge gap represents a critical omission in our body of knowledge. Similarly little is known about the long-term psychological effects of youth sport involvement. In sum, a variety of important topics have not been yet been addressed by researchers. Thus the second recommendation is to expand the scope of research within our field to address additional pertinent research questions.

Third it is important for youth sport researchers to pursue research that will have applied benefit for the millions of current participants. It is essential to "conduct youth sport research that counts" (Gould, 1988, p. 321). Gould cites the work of of Smith, Smoll, and colleagues (e.g., Smith et al., 1979, 1983) as a standard for applied research to which researchers might aspire. Their work has made a substantial empirical contribution to the youth sport knowledge base but also has an enduring impact upon the development of training programs for youth sport coaches. Research that counts will continue to have applied relevance to youth sport practitioners and participants.

Finally it is extremely important to broaden the youth sport knowledge base so that an appreciation for the nature of cultural and ethnic diversity is reflected in this body of knowledge. The current knowledge base has largely been derived from a relatively small, homogeneous sample of North American youngsters. The next great advance in pediatric sport psychology will occur as a consequence of expanded research interest outside of North America. Such an effort will contribute both to broadening the knowledge base and to enhancing the quality of the youth sport experience for the millions of participants.

References

Ames, C. (1978). Children's achievement attitudes and self-reinforcement: Effects of self-concept and competitive reward structure. *Journal of Educational Psychology, 70,* 345–355.

Berryman, J. W. (1988). The rise of highly organized sports for preadolescent boys. In F. L. Smoll, R. A. Magill, & M. J. Ash (Eds.), *Children in Sport* (3rd ed., pp. 3–16). Champaign, IL: Human Kinetics.

Borkovec, T. D. (1976). Physiological and cognitive processes in the regulation of anxiety. In G. E. Schwartz & D. Shapiro (Eds.), *Consciousness and self-regulation* (Vol. 1, pp. 261–312). New York: Plenum.

Brodkin, P., & Weiss, M. R. (1990). Developmental differences in motivation for participating in competitive swimming. *Journal of Sport and Exercise Psychology, 12,* 248–263.

Brower, J. J. (1978). Little League baseballism: Adult dominance in a "child's game." In R. Martens (Ed.), *Joy and sadness in children's sports* (pp. 39–49). Champaign, IL: Human Kinetics.

Brustad, R. J. (1988). Affective outcomes in competitive youth sport: The influence of intrapersonal and socialization factors. *Journal of Sport and Exercise Psychology, 10,* 307–321.

Brustad, R. J. (1992). Integrating socialization influences into the study of children's motivation in sport. *Journal of Sport and Exercise Psychology, 14,* 59–77.

Brustad, R. J., & Weigand, D. A. (1989, June). *Relationships of parental attitudes and affective patterns to levels of intrinsic motivation in young male and female athletes.* Paper presented at the annual meeting of the North American Society for the Psychology of Sport and Physical Activity: Kent, OH.

Brustad, R., & Weiss, M. R. (1987). Competence perceptions and sources of worry in high, medium, and low competitive trait-anxious young athletes. *Journal of Sport Psychology, 9,* 97–105.

Bump, L., Gould, D., Petlichkoff, L., Peterson, K., & Levin, R. (1985, May). *The relationship between achievement orientations and state anxiety in youth wrestlers.* Paper presented at the annual meeting of the North American Society for the Psychology of Sport and Physical Activity. Gulfpark, MS.

Burton, D., & Martens, R. (1986). Pinned by their own goals: An exploratory investigation into why kids drop out of wrestling. *Journal of Sport Psychology, 8,* 183–197.

Coakley, J. (1986). When should children begin competing? A sociological perspective. In M. R. Weiss & D. Gould (Eds.), *Sport for children and youths* (pp. 59–63). Champaign, IL: Human Kinetics.

Coleman, J. S. (1961). Athletics in high school. *The Annals of the American Academy of Political and Social Science, 338* (November), 33–43.

Cooper, H., & Good, T. (1983). *Pygmalion grows up: Studies in the expectation communication process.* New York: Longman.

Coopersmith, S. (1967). *The antecedents of self-esteem.* San Francisco: Freeman.

Duda, J. L. (1981). *A cross-cultural analysis of achievement moti-*

vation in sport and the classroom. Unpublished doctoral dissertation. Champaign, IL: University of Illinois.

Duda, J. L. (1987). Toward a developmental theory of children's motivation in sport. *Journal of Sport Psychology, 9,* 130–145.

Duda, J. L. (1989). Goal perspectives, participation and persistence in sport. *International Journal of Sport Psychology, 20,* 42–56.

Duda, J. L., & Nicholls, J. G. (1989). *The task and ego orientation in sport questionnaire: Psychometric properties.* Manuscript submitted for publication.

Dusek, J. B. (1980). The development of test anxiety in children. In I. G. Sarason (Ed.), *Test anxiety: Theory, research, and applications* (pp. 87–110). Hillsdale, NJ: Erlbaum.

Erikson, E. H. (1963). *Childhood and society.* New York: Norton.

Ewing, M. E. (1981). *Achievement orientations and sport behavior of males and females.* Unpublished doctoral dissertation, University of Illinois: Urbana-Champaign.

Felson, R. B., & Reed, M. (1986). The effect of parents on the self-appraisals of children. *Social Psychology Quarterly, 49,* 302–308.

Feltz, D. L., & Albrecht, R. R. (1986). Psychological implications of competitive running. In M. R. Weiss & D. Gould (Eds.), *Sport for children and youth* (pp. 225–230). Champaign, IL: Human Kinetics.

Feltz, D. L., & Petlichkoff, L. M. (1983). Perceived competence among interscholastic sport participants and dropouts. *Canadian Journal of Applied Sport Sciences, 8,* 231–235.

Ferreira, M. B. R. (1986). Youth sport in Brazil. In M. R. Weiss & D. Gould (Eds.), *Sport for children and youths* (pp. 11–15). Champaign, IL: Human Kinetics.

Frieze, I., & Bar-Tal, D. (1980). Developmental trends in cue utilization for attributional judgments. *Journal of Applied Development Psychology, 1,* 83–94.

Gill, D. L., Gross, J. B., & Huddleston, S. (1985). Participation motivation in youth sports. *International Journal of Sport Psychology, 14,* 1–14.

Gould, D. (1982). Sport psychology in the 1980s: Status, direction and challenge in youth sport research. *Journal of Sport Psychology, 4,* 203–218.

Gould, D. (1987). Understanding attrition in youth sport. In D. Gould & M. R. Weiss (Eds.), *Advances in pediatric sport sciences, Vol. 2: Behavioral Issues* (pp. 61–85). Champaign, IL: Human Kinetics.

Gould, D. (1988). Sport psychology: Future directions in youth sport research. In F. L. Smoll, R. A. Magill, & M. J. Ash (Eds.), *Children in sport* (3rd ed., pp. 317–333). Champaign, IL: Human Kinetics.

Gould, D. (In press). Intensive sports participation and the prepubescent athlete: Competitive stress and burnout effects. In B. Cahill (Ed.), *Intensive training and participation in youth sports.* Champaign, IL: Human Kinetics.

Gould, D., Feltz, D., Horn, T., & Weiss, M. (1982). Reasons for attrition in competitive youth swimming. *Journal of Sport Behavior, 5,* 155–165.

Gould, D., Feltz, D., & Weiss, M. (1985). Motives for participating in competitive youth swimmers. *International Journal of Sport Psychology, 16,* 126–140.

Gould, D., & Horn, T. (1984). Participation motivation in young athletes. In J. M. Silva & R. S. Weinberg (Eds.), *Psychological foundations of sport* (pp. 359–370). Champaign, IL: Human Kinetics.

Gould, D., Horn, T., & Spreeman, J. (1983a). Competitive anxiety in junior elite wrestlers. *Journal of Sport Psychology, 5,* 58–71.

Gould, D., Horn, T., & Spreeman, J. (1983b). Sources of stress in junior elite wrestlers. *Journal of Sport Psychology, 5,* 159–171.

Gould, D., & Martens, R. (1979). Attitudes of volunteer coaches toward significant youth sport issues. *The Research Quarterly, 50,* 369–380.

Gould, D., & Petlichkoff, L. (1988). Participation motivation and attrition in young athletes. In F. L. Smoll, R. J. Magill, & M. J. Ash (Eds.), *Children in sport* (3rd ed., pp. 161–178). Champaign, IL: Human Kinetics.

Griffin, M. R. (1972). An analysis of state and trait anxiety experienced in sports competition at different age levels. *Foil* (Spring), 58–64.

Hanson, D. L. (1967). Cardiac response to participation in Little League baseball competition as determined by telemetry. *The Research Quarterly, 38,* 384–388.

Harter, S. (1978). Effectance motivation reconsidered. *Human Development, 21,* 34–64.

Harter, S. (1981). A model of intrinsic mastery motivation in children: Individual differences and developmental change. In W. A. Collins (Ed.), *Minnesota symposium on child psychology* (Vol. 14, pp. 215–255). Hillsdale, NJ: Erlbaum.

Harter, S. (1983). Developmental perspectives on the self-system. In E. M. Hetherington (Ed.), *Handbook of child psychology, socialization, personality, and social development* (pp. 275–385). New York: Wiley.

Harter, S. (1988). Causes, correlates, and the functional role of global self-worth: A life-span perspective. In J. Kolligan & R. Sternberg (Eds.). *Perceptions of competence and incompetence across the life-span* (pp. 67–98). New Haven, CT: Yale University Press.

Hermens, H., ter Laak, J., & Maes, P. (1972). Achievement motivation and fear of failure in family and school. *Developmental Psychology, 6,* 520–528.

Hill, K. T. (1972). Anxiety in the evaluative context. In W. Hartup (Ed.), *The young child* (Vol. 2, pp. 225–263). Washington, DC: National Association for the Education of Young Children.

Hill, K. T., & Sarason, S. B. (1966). *The relation of test anxiety and defensiveness to test and school performance over the elementary school years: A further longitudinal study.* Monographs for the Society for Research in Child Development, *31*(2, Serial No. 104).

Horn, T. S. (1985). Coaches' feedback and changes in children's perceptions of their physical competence. *Journal of Educational Psychology, 77,* 174–186.

Horn, T. S., & Hasbrook, C. A. (1986). Informational components underlying children's perceptions of their physical competence. In M. R. Weiss & D. Gould (Eds.), *Sport for children and youths* (pp. 81–88). Champaign, IL: Human Kinetics.

Horn, T. S., & Hasbrook, C. A. (1987). Psychological characteristics and the criteria children use for self-evaluation. *Journal of Sport Psychology, 9,* 208–221.

Horn, T. S., & Weiss, M. R. (1991). A developmental analysis of children's self-ability judgements in the physical domain. *Pediatric Exercise Science, 3,* 310–326.

Klint, K. A. (1985). *Participation motives and self-perceptions of current and former athletes in youth gymnastics.* Unpublished master's thesis, University of Oregon: Eugene.

Klint, K. A., & Weiss, M. R. (1986). Dropping in and dropping out: Participation motives of current and former youth gymnasts. *Canadian Journal of Applied Sport Sciences, 11,* 106–114.

Klint, K. A., & Weiss, M. R. (1987). Perceived competence and motives for participating in youth sports: A test of Harter's competence motivation theory. *Journal of Sport Psychology, 9,* 55–65.

Lazarus, R. S. (1966). *Psychological stress and the coping process.* New York: McGraw-Hill.

Lazarus, R. S., & Folkman, S. (1984). *Stress, appraisal, and coping.* New York: Springer.

Lewthwaite, R. (1990). Threat perception in competitive trait anxiety: The endangerment of important goals. *Journal of Sport and Exercise Psychology, 12,* 280–300.

Lewthwaite, R., & Scanlan, T. K. (1989). Predictors of competitive trait anxiety in male youth sport participants. *Medicine and Science in Sports and Exercise, 21,* 221–229.

Longhurst, K., & Spink, K. S. (1987). Participation motivation of Australian children involved in organized sport. *Canadian Journal of Applied Sport Sciences, 12,* 24–30.

Lowe, R., & McGrath, J. E. (1971). *Stress, arousal and performance: Some findings calling for a new theory.* Report No. AF1161-67. Washington, DC: Air Force Office of Strategic Research.

Maehr, M. L., & Nicholls, J. G. (1980). Culture and achievement motivation: A second look. In N. Warren (Ed.), *Studies in cross-cultural psychology* (Vol. 3, pp. 221–267). New York: Academic Press.

Malina, R. M. (1986). Readiness for competitive sport. In M. R. Weiss & D. Gould (Eds.), *Sport for children and youths* (pp. 45–50). Champaign, IL: Human Kinetics.

Malina, R. M. (1988). Growth and maturation of young athletes: Biological and social considerations. In F. L. Smoll, R. J. Magill, & M. J. Ash (Eds.), *Children in sport* (3rd ed., pp. 83–101). Champaign, IL: Human Kinetics,

Manley, M. J., & Rosmeier, R. A. (1972). Developmental trends in general and test anxiety among junior and senior high school students. *Journal of Genetic Psychology, 120,* 219–226.

Martens, R. (1977). *Sport competition anxiety test.* Champaign, IL: Human Kinetics.

Martens, R. (1986). Youth sports in the U.S.A. In M. R. Weiss & D. Gould (Eds.), *Sport for children and youths* (pp. 27–31). Champaign, IL: Human Kinetics.

Martens, R., Burton, D., Rivkin, F., Simon, J. (1980). Reliability and validity of the Competitive State Anxiety Inventory (CSAI). In C. H. Nadeau, W. R. Halliwell, K. M. Newell, G. C. Roberts (Eds.), *Psychology of motor behavior and sport—1979* (pp. 91–99). Champaign, IL: Human Kinetics.

Martens, R., Burton, D., Vealey, R., Smith, D., & Bump, L. (1983). *The development of the Competitive State Anxiety Inventory-2 (CSAI-2).* Unpublished manuscript. University of Illinois at Urbana-Champaign.

Martens, R. M., & Gill, D. L. (1976). State anxiety among successful and unsuccessful competitors who differ in competitive trait anxiety. *The Research Quarterly, 47,* 698–708.

Martens, R., Rivkin, F., & Burton, D. (1980). Who predicts anxiety better: Coaches or athletes? In C. H. Nadeau, W. R. Halliwell, K. M. Newell, & G. C. Roberts (Eds.), *Psychology of motor behavior and sport—1979* (pp. 91–99). Champaign, IL: Human Kinetics.

Martens, R., & Simon, J. A. (1976). Comparison of three predictors of state anxiety in competitive situations. *The Research Quarterly, 47,* 381–387.

McGrath, J. E. (1970). A conceptual formulation for research on stress. In J. E. McGrath (Ed.), *Social and psychological factors in stress* (pp. 10–21). New York: Holt, Rinehart & Winston.

McPherson, B. D., & Davidson, L. (1980). *Minor hockey in Ontario: Toward a positive learning environment for children in the 1980s.* Toronto: Ontario Government Book Store.

Mead, G. H. (1934). *Mind, self, and society.* Chicago: University of Chicago Press.

Meyer, W., Bachmann, M., Biermann, U., Hempelmann, M., Ploger, F., & Spiller, H. (1979). The informational value of evaluative behavior: Influences of praise and blame on perceptions of ability. *Journal of Educational Psychology, 71,* 259–268.

Morris, L. W., Davis, M. A., & Hutchings, C. J. (1981). Cognitive and emotional components of anxiety: Literature review and a revised worry-emotionality scale. *Journal of Educational Psychology, 73,* 541–555.

Nicholls, J. G. (1978). The development of the concepts of effort and ability, perception of own attainment, and the understanding that difficult tasks require more ability. *Child Development, 49,* 800–814.

Nicholls, J. G. (1984). Conceptions of ability and achievement motivation. In R. Ames & C. Ames (Eds.), *Research on motivation in education: Student motivation* (Vol. 1, pp. 39–73). New York: Academic Press.

Nicholls, J. G. (1989). *Competence and accomplishment: A psychology of achievement motivation.* Cambridge, MA: Harvard University Press.

Nicholls, J. G., Jagacinski, C. M., & Miller, A. T. (1986). Conceptions of ability in children and adults. In R. Schwarzer (Ed.), *Self-related cognitions in anxiety and motivation* (pp. 265–284). Hillsdale, NJ: Erlbaum.

Nicholls, J. G., & Miller, A. T. (1984). Development and its discontents: The differentiation of the concept of ability. In J. G. Nicholls (Ed.), *Advances in motivation and achievement: The development of achievement motivation* (pp. 185–218). Greenwich, CT: JAI Press.

Orlick, T. D. (1973, January/February). Children's sport: A revolution is coming. *Canadian Association for Health, Physical Education and Recreation Journal, 40,* 12–14.

Orlick, T. D. (1974, November/December). The athletic dropout: A high price of inefficiency. *Canadian Association for Health, Physical Education and Recreation Journal, 41,* 21–27.

Parsons, J. E., Adler, T. F., & Kaczala, C. M. (1982). Socialization of achievement attitudes and beliefs: Parental influences. *Child Development, 53,* 310–321.

Parsons, J. E., & Ruble, D. N. (1977). The development of achievement-related expectancies. *Child Development, 48,* 1075–1079.

Passer, M. W. (1983). Fear of failure, fear of evaluation, perceived competence and self-esteem in competitive trait anxious children. *Journal of Sport Psychology, 5,* 172–188.

Passer, M. W. (1988a). Psychological issues in determining children's age-readiness for competition. In F. L. Smoll, R. A. Magill & M. J. Ash (Eds.), *Children in Sport* (3rd ed., pp. 67–78). Champaign, IL: Human Kinetics.

Passer, M. W. (1988b). Determinants and consequences of children's competitive stress. In F. L. Smoll, R. A. Magill, & M. J. Ash (Eds.). *Children in sport* (3rd ed., pp. 203–227). Champaign, IL: Human Kinetics.

Pemberton, C. L., Petlichkoff, L. M., & Ewing, M. E. (1986, June). *Psychometric properties of the Achievement Orientation Questionnaire.* Paper presented at the annual meeting of the North American Society for the Psychology of Sport and Physical Activity, Scottsdale, AZ.

Petlichkoff, L. M. (1988). *Motivation for sport persistence: An empirical examination of underlying theoretical constructs.* Unpublished doctoral dissertation, University of Illinois at Urbana-Champaign.

Phillips, D. (1984). The illusion of incompetence among academically competent children. *Child Development, 55,* 2000–2016.

Phillips, D. (1987). Socialization of perceived academic competence among highly competent children. *Child Development, 58,* 1308–1320.

Rejeski, W., Darracott, C., & Hutslar, S. (1979). Pygmalion in youth sports: A field study. *Journal of Sport Psychology, 1,* 311–319.

Roberts, G. C. (1980). Children in competition: A theoretical perspective and recommendations for practice. *Motor Skills: Theory Into Practice, 4,* 37–50.

Roberts, G. C. (1984). Toward a new theory of motivation in sport: The role of perceived ability. In J. M. Silva & R. S. Weinberg (Eds.), *Psychological foundations of sport* (pp. 214–228). Champaign, IL: Human Kinetics.

Roberts, G. C., Kleiber, D. A., & Duda, J. L. (1981). An analysis of motivation in children's sport: The role of perceived competence in participation. *Journal of Sport Psychology, 3,* 206–216.

Robertson, I. (1986). Youth sport in Australia. In M. R. Weiss & D. Gould (Eds.), *Sport for children and youths* (pp. 5–10). Champaign, IL: Human Kinetics.

Robinson, T., & Carron, A. (1982). Personal and situational factors associated with dropping out versus maintaining participation in competitive sport. *Journal of Sport Psychology, 4,* 364–378.

Ruble, D. N. (1983). The role of social comparison processes in achievement-related self-socialization. In E. T. Higgins, D. N. Ruble, & W. W. Hartup (Eds.), *Social cognition and social development: A sociocultural perspective* (pp. 134–157). New York: Cambridge University Press.

Sage, G. H. (1986). The effects of physical activity on the social development of children. In G. A. Stull & H. M. Eckert (Eds.), *Effects of physical activity on children* (pp. 22–29). Champaign, IL: Human Kinetics.

Sapp, M., & Haubenstricker, J. (1978, April). *Motivation for joining and reasons for not continuing in youth sport programs in Michigan.* Paper presented at the annual meeting of the American Alliance for Health, Physical Education, Recreation, and Dance, Kansas City, MO.

Scanlan, T. K. (1982). Social evaluation: A key developmental element in the competition process. In F. L. Smoll, R. A. Magill, & M. J. Ash (Eds.), *Children in sport* (1st ed., pp. 138–152). Champaign, IL: Human Kinetics.

Scanlan, T. K. (1988). Social evaluation and the competition process. In R. A. Magill, M. J. Ash, & F. L. Smoll (Eds.), *Children in sport: A contemporary approach* (3rd ed., pp. 135–148). Champaign, IL: Human Kinetics.

Scanlan, T. K., & Lewthwaite, R. (1984). Social psychological aspects of competition for male youth sport participants: I: Predictors of competitive stress. *Journal of Sport Psychology, 6,* 208–226.

Scanlan, T. K., & Lewthwaite, R. (1986). Social psychological aspects of competition for male youth sport participants: IV: Predictors of enjoyment. *Journal of Sport Psychology, 8,* 25–35.

Scanlan, T. K., & Passer, M. W. (1978). Factors related to competitive stress among male youth sport participants. *Medicine and Science in Sports, 10,* 103–108.

Scanlan, T. K., & Passer, M. W. (1979). Sources of competitive stress in young female athletes. *Journal of Sport Psychology, 1,* 151–159.

Scanlan, T. K., & Simons, J.P. (1992). The construct of sport enjoyment. In G. C. Roberts (Ed.), *Motivation in sport and exercise.* Champaign, IL: Human Kinetics (pp. 199–215).

Scanlan, T. K., Stein, G. L., & Ravizza, K. (1989). An in-depth study of former elite figure skaters: II. Sources of enjoyment. *Journal of Sport and Exercise Psychology, 11,* 65–83.

Seefeldt, V. (1988). The concept of readiness applied to motor skill acquisition. In F. L. Smoll, R. A. Magill, & M. J. Ash (Eds.), *Children in sport* (3rd ed., pp. 45–52). Champaign, IL: Human Kinetics.

Sefton, J. M. M., & Fry, D. A. P. (1981). *A report on participation in competitive swimming.* Saskatoon, Canada: Canadian Amateur Swimming Association (Saskatchewan Section).

Selman, R. L. (1971). Taking another's perspective: Role-taking development in early childhood. *Child Development, 42,* 1721–1734.

Selman, R. L. (1976). Social-cognitive understanding: A guide to educational and clinical practice. In T. Lickona (Ed.), *Moral development and behavior* (pp. 299–316). New York: Holt, Rinehart & Winston.

Selye, H. (1974). *Stress without distress.* New York: New American Library.

Simon, J., & Martens, R. (1979). Children's anxiety in sport and nonsport evaluative activities. *Journal of Sport Psychology, 1,* 160–169.

Skubic, E. (1955). Emotional responses of boys to Little League and Middle League competitive baseball. *The Research Quarterly, 26,* 342–352.

Smilkstein, G. (1980). Psychological trauma in children and youth in competitive sport. *The Journal of Family Practice, 10,* 737–739.

Smith, M. D. (1988). Interpersonal sources of violence in hockey: The influence of parents, coaches, and teammates. In F. L. Smoll, R. A. Magill, & M. J. Ash (Eds.), *Children in sport* (3rd ed., pp. 301–313.). Champaign, IL: Human Kinetics.

Smith, R. E. (1986). Toward a cognitive-affective model of athletic burnout. *Journal of Sport Psychology, 8,* 36–50.

Smith, R. E., Smoll, F. L., & Curtis, B. (1978). Coaching behaviors in Little League baseball. In F. L. Smoll & R. E. Smith (Eds.), *Psychological perspectives in youth sports* (pp. 173–201). Washington, DC: Hemisphere.

Smith, R. E., Smoll, F. L., & Curtis, B. (1979). Coach effectiveness training: A cognitive behavioral approach to enhancing relationship skills in youth sport coaches. *Journal of Sport Psychology, 1,* 59–75.

Smith, R. E., Smoll, F. L., & Hunt, B. (1977). A system for the behavioral assessment of athletic coaches. *The Research Quarterly, 48,* 401–407.

Smith, R. E., Smoll, F. L., & Schutz, R. W. (1990). Measurement and correlates of sport-specific cognitive and somatic trait anxiety: The sport anxiety scale. *Anxiety Research, 2,* 263–280.

Smith, R. E., Zane, N. S., Smoll, F. L., & Coppell, D. B. (1983). Behavioral assessment in youth sports: Coaching behaviors and children's attitudes. *Medicine and Science in Sports and Exercise, 15,* 208–214.

Smoll, F. L., & Smith, R. E. (1989). Leadership behaviors in sport: A theoretical model and research paradigm. *Journal of Applied Social Psychology, 19,* 1522–1551.

Spielberger, C. D. (1966). Theory and research on anxiety. In C. D. Spielberger (Ed.), *Anxiety and behavior* (pp. 3–23). New York: Academic Press.

Spielberger, C. D. (1973). *Preliminary test manual for the State-Trait Anxiety Inventory for Children.* Palo Alto, CA: Consulting Psychologists.

State of Michigan. (1976). *Joint legislative study on youth sport programs—Phase I.* East Lansing, MI: Youth Sport Institute.

State of Michigan. (1978a). *Joint legislative study on youth sport programs—Phase II.* East Lansing, MI: Youth Sport Institute.

State of Michigan. (1978b). *Joint legislative study on youth sport programs—Phase III.* East Lansing, MI: Youth Sport Institute.

Thibaut, J. W., & Kelly, H. H. (1959). *The social psychology of groups*. New York: Wiley.

Toda, M., Shinotsuka, H., McClintock, C. G., & Stech, F. J. (1978). Development of competitive behavior as a function of culture, age, and social comparison. *Journal of Personality and Social Psychology, 36,* 825–839.

Valeriote, T. A., & Hansen, L. (1986). Youth sport in Canada. In M. R. Weiss & D. Gould (Eds.), *Sport for children and youths* (pp. 17–20). Champaign, IL: Human Kinetics.

Vealey, R. S., & Campbell, J. L. (1988). Achievement goals of adolescent figure skaters: Impact on self-confidence, anxiety, and performance. *Journal of Adolescent Research, 3,* 227–243.

Veroff, J. (1969). Social comparison and the development of achievement motivation. In C. P. Smith (Ed.), *Achievement related motives in children* (pp. 46–101). New York: Sage Foundation.

Wankel, L. M., & Kreisel, P. S. (1985a). Factors underlying enjoyment of youth sports: Sport and age group comparisons. *Journal of Sport Psychology, 7,* 51–64.

Wankel, L. M., & Kreisel, P. S. (1985b). Methodological considerations in youth sport motivation research: A comparison of open-ended and paired comparison approaches. *Journal of Sport Psychology, 7,* 65–74.

Weiss, M. R. (In press). Psychological effects of intensive sports participation on children and youth: Self-esteem and motivation. In B. Cahill (Ed.), *Intensive training and participation in youth sports*. Champaign, IL: Human Kinetics.

Weiss, M. R., & Bredemeier, B. J. (1983). Developmental sport psychology: A theoretical perspective for studying children in sport. *Journal of Sport Psychology, 5,* 216–230.

Weiss, M. R., Bredemeier, B. J., & Brustad, R. J. (1987, June). *Competitive trait anxiety in children's sport: The relationship to perceived competence, perceived control, and motivational orientation*. Paper presented at the annual meeting of the North American Society for the Psychology of Sport and Physical Activity, Vancouver, British Columbia.

Weiss, M. R., & Chaumeton, N. (1992). Motivational orientations in sport. In T. S. Horn (Ed.), *Advances in sport psychology*. Champaign, IL: Human Kinetics.

Weiss, M. R., & Horn, T. S. (1990). The relation between children's accuracy estimates of their physical competence and achievement-related characteristics. *Research Quarterly for Exercise and Sport, 61,* 250–258.

Weiss, M. R., & Petlichkoff, L. M. (1989). Children's motivation for participation in and withdrawal from sport: Identifying the missing links. *Pediatric Exercise Science, 1,* 195–211.

Weiss, M. R., Weise, D. M., & Klint, K. A. (1989). Head over heels with success: The relationship between self-efficacy and performance in competitive youth gymnastics. *Journal of Sport and Exercise Psychology, 11,* 444–451.

Weitzer, J. E. (1989). *Childhood socialization into physical activity: Parental roles in perceptions of competence and goal orientations*. Unpublished master's thesis. University of Wisconsin–Milwaukee.

Wigfield, A., & Eccles, J. S. (1990). Test anxiety in elementary and secondary school students. *Educational Psychologist, 24,* 159–183.

Wiggins, D. K. (1987). A history of organized play and highly competitive sport for American children. In D. Gould & M. R. Weiss (Eds.) *Advances in pediatric sport sciences (Vol. 2): Behavioral issues* (pp. 1–24). Champaign, IL: Human Kinetics.

33

GENDER AND SPORT

Carole A. Oglesby

Karen L. Hill

Gender/sport relations is a relatively new content area of sport psychology. Its emergence appears to be a product of several forces but most notably the combined effects of the following: (a) an activist/reformist social philosophy that has opened access of the traditional sport domain to masses of women, thus necessitating redefinitional process, and (b) the feminist critique of positivist traditions in psychology and sport science. An attempt to review the relevant literature in this content area reveals that its precursor was "women in sport," and even now, some may see these two labels as synonymous. This unfortunate misconception, and other elements of confusion to be addressed here, combine to make this content area a challenging one for researchers and theorists.

A great majority of the studies that might be brought to bear on questions of gender relations and sport have been comparative studies in which the possibility of male/female differences and similarities in sport performance and/or experience have been examined (Hall, 1990). This same state of affairs exists generally in the psychology literature (Fine & Gordon, 1989; Hare-Mustin & Marecek, 1988).

These two critiques of the psychology research on gender have delineated "alpha" and "beta" biases present in virtually all the research to date, and these biases may be found in sport science as well. The alpha bias occurs when gender differences are exaggerated or maximized, as, for example, when only statistically significant differences are regarded as "worthy" of discussion and publication. Maccobey and Jacklin (1974) thoroughly documented the effects of this particular form of bias, which runs through psychology research. The beta bias occurs when differences are minimized or completely dismissed from examination. The degree of beta bias in the sport psychology literature (past and present) might be assessed by noting the percentage of published studies that featured only one-sex subjects, yet failed to sex-limit the generalizations of the data.

There is benefit in conducting research with a focus on comparisons of men and women. Since women have been so underresearched, there is also great benefit in undertaking research focusing only on them. Additionally little formal descriptive, qualitative research portraying and analyzing women's and men's sporting experiences has been reported, so a real need exists in this area. We propose, however, that data produced simply by utilizing sex or gender as a dichotomous variable among humans and then examining its individual or group effects in the laboratory, on a survey, or through a field/court observation or an interview should *not* be taxonomically organized in the gender/sport relations content area.

The similarities and differences between various groups (age/race/class/sex) on variables such as achievement motivation, emotional control, attention control, moral development, and the like belong in each variable's taxonomic family. Continuing with this line of thought, the expert on anxiety control should, theoretically, know more about sex differences and similarities in anxiety control than the expert in gender/sport relations. Obviously the interaction of the two experts would be informing and enriching. The expertise of the gender/sport relations scholar focuses on what Connell (1987) has called the gender order a "historically constructed pattern of power relations between men and women and definitions of masculinity/femininity" (pp. 98–99). In our formulations throughout this chapter, we focus on the psychosocial relational construct of gender as it creates and is created by sport. Gender is seen as a pervasive and powerful psychosocial mediator influencing sport experiences of participants, male and female, in complex patterns we are only beginning to conceptually untangle. Gender/sport relations concepts build upon gender difference/similarity data, but that is only one potential source of theorizing and analysis.

We define gender/sport relations as a sport psychology content area focusing on the interactive effects of gender identity constructs and sport. Consistent with other applications of constructivism, gender identity is seen as invented, rather than discovered, on a social and individual basis. Rather than passively observing the reality of gender identity, socially and individually we construct its meanings, and these become tools in organizing perceptions and experiences. Person (1980) has suggested that there are three components to one's constructed gender identity: (a) position in the mosaic of sex of assignment; (b) core qualities of gender (traditional variations of masculine/feminine); and (c) behaviors enacted in accord with personal understandings of gendering. In this chapter we explore several questions arising from investigations of the interactive effects of gender identity and sport.

In this introductory segment, we present our definitional frame, which concludes with a statement of the important assumptions underlying this review. The second segment characterizes earlier work in this content area, focusing particularly on positivistic notions of biophysiological sex differences with regard to the appropriateness of sport for women and socialization practices as a singular rationale for the position of women in the world of sport. The third section attempts to reconstruct gender/sport relations as an area of study, concluding with a brief picture of recent developments in gender/sport studies and men. We conclude with remarks about future directions in the content area.

IMPORTANT ASSUMPTIONS AND PRINCIPLES UNDERLYING GENDER/SPORT RELATIONS

Throughout this chapter we build upon and cite the work of scores of theorists and researchers. It seems important additionally to recognize three large-scale frames of reference invaluable to us.

From developmental and neurophysiological psychology (e.g., Hebb, 1949; Piaget, 1952; and Vygotsky, 1962; Carlson, 1991) come suggestions of the following principles:

1. A biogenetic basis for cognitive sets, structural elements that facilitate and influence particular sensory interpretations and actions.
2. Critical developmental periods that facilitate particular cognitive structures and have life-long effects.
3. Organism-environmental interaction as the basis for life-long development.

Principles from the so-called "Third Force" psychologies (existential, humanistic, and/or human potential) and family systems work include:

4. The necessity for, and evolution of, a language for individual transformations.
5. The healing of polarities of thought and the transformation of paradox.
6. Positive views of interpersonal systems change.
   Principles from social psychology and sociology include:
7. Power and authority relations and value hierarchies.
8. Dynamics of oppression.
9. Analysis of large-scale social systems.

EARLIER WORK IN GENDER/SPORT RELATIONS

Although it is possible to identify both alpha and beta bias in past sport psychology work regarding gender, the overwhelming overt influence in the literature has been the focus on difference. To a great degree, the concentration on gender difference has channeled research efforts in all subdisciplines and blinded our view of the similarities in mechanisms of performance for females and males.

This viewpoint is fueled by the tendency of researchers to conceptualize gender as two independent sets (see Figure 33–1), one for males and the other for females. It might more appropriately be viewed as a union of sets (see Figure 33–2), since all humans share, in varying proportions, the same male and female sex hormones, and overlapping distributions exist for virtually all human characteristics, both physical and psychological (Carlson, 1991). This crucial misconception encourages neglect of the common elements found in both sets, among which are the shared feel-

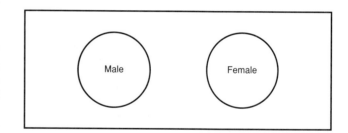

FIGURE 33–1. "Separate sets" conceptualization of gender.

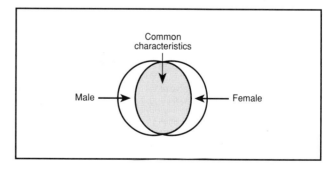

FIGURE 33–2. "Union of sets" conceptualization of gender.

ings, values, aspirations, and actions of human individuals. As a species, humans are the least dimorphic of all primates (Fausto-Sterling, 1985), yet our quest to know and understand ourselves has seemed to be aimed at investigating this tiny percentage of dimorphism and ignoring our many similarities.

The importance of this bias toward independent set conceptualization versus union-of-sets conceptualization lies in the way it has colored past research on gender and sport. Researchers using the frame of reference of independent sets portrayed in Figure 33–1 bring different underlying assumptions regarding gender to their research than investigators approaching the topic from the union-of-sets frame of reference. It is our contention that the union-of-sets conceptualization of gender more accurately reflects the relationship between males and females in every culture. A consequence of the underlying assumptions of the separate sets conceptualization (see Figure 33–2) is that it leads to different conclusions that are biased toward limiting the sporting experience of both males and females than would be the case if the union-of-sets conceptualization were employed.

Complicating the effect of the initial conceptualization phenomena is the problem of defining gender as a separate construct from sex of assignment. Traditionally, gender has been viewed as a psychosocial phenomenon based on one's biological sex. It encompasses the cultural customs, expectations, and roles associated with being male or female in a particular society. By contrast, biological sex has been defined "by chromosomes, gonads, internal and external genitalia, hormones, and secondary sexual characteristics" (Person, 1980, p. 5) as a culturally independent biogenetic given. Sex of assignment has been perceived as a binary biological reality unaffected by environment, circumstances, values, or learning. Recent thought (Butler, 1990) has challenged the notion that the category of sex itself is, in fact, culturally independent. Positing that sex is not a totally objective, value-free binary phenomena but rather that each individual is a mosaic of male and female biological components invites a unique and challenging frame of reference for interpreting experimental data.

There is not space, nor would it be appropriate, to launch into a full discussion of sex of assignment. The reader is invited to explore the notion of the "mosaic" of sex of assignment through either a basic neurophysiological text (Carlson, 1991) or the lengthy research efforts of Money and Erhardt (1972). Suffice it to point out that an understanding of sex of assignment as an "event" that evolves from the presence of an xx or xy chromosome is extremely simplistic. The "gender verification" tests in athletics are conducted in such a way as to be sensitive to the presence of the y chromosome. Female athletes have been disqualified from competition because their cell chromosomal structure was xoy and xxy—variations but hardly performance-altering aberrations (International Relations and Major Games Directorate of Fitness and Amateur Sport, 1991). Also, many confusions of sex of assignment have been noted medically when, through unintended circum-

stances, fetal development has been disrupted due to hormonal "baths" at critical periods by inappropriate hormones. Even that which we have regarded as the ultimate simplicity is complex.

The researcher's frame of reference regarding the role of sex in determining behavior plays a crucial role in the conclusions drawn from studies on gender and sport. Research on sex differences in sport (there is no research on sex similarities [Bleier, 1984]) is historically significant because it has been used, or more correctly, misused, to justify the exclusion and limitation of women in sport.

Earlier Work Continued: Biological Differences on Gender and Sport

Studies in exercise physiology have long shown that sex differences in performance exist. Among American adults, for example, men are 50% stronger in most muscle groups than women. Men also tend to have less body fat, and they exceed women in maximal oxygen consumption by about 20%, on the average (Brooks & Fahey, 1984). Women, on the other hand, tend to excel in flexibility and balance (Hudson, 1978). While we know that these sex-related differences exist, we do not know how many of these differences are due to physiological factors and how many are due to social or cultural factors. For example, it is not possible at this time to discern how much of the 50% difference in strength between the average American male and female is due to innate physiological factors and how much is due to the fact that in many societies girls and women are not encouraged to participate in activities that would develop the potential in their muscles, while men are mandated to lift loads and perform tasks that do develop the potential in their muscles.

Studies comparing men and women on strength measures cannot control for the fact that it is often the case that men's muscles are trained differently than women's because of the activities and roles that the different sexes engage in from birth as part of the socialization process. Douglas and Miller's (1977) survey on research in strength differences between males and females concludes "that the social influences (on strength) are so great that inherent physiological differences in strength cannot yet be estimated" (p. 172).

The fact that expectations influenced by sex role stereotypes contribute to and create differences in physical performance between men and women is a confounding variable in virtually all reported sex-related differences in the literature. Fausto-Sterling (1985) writes, "the question 'What fraction of our behavior is biologically based?' is impossible even in theory to answer, and unanswerable questions drop out of the realm of science altogether, entering instead that of philosophy and morality" (p. 8).

The enculturation process not only confounds studies on sex differences in performance to the extent that we cannot accurately measure them, but it also assigns value to these differences. As quickly as the biologists observe differences between men and women, sociocultural institutions, acting outside the rules of scientific objectivity and logic, seek to assign meaning and value to those differences. Due to the patriarchal bias of these institutions, the result is often the arbitrary assignment of male advantage valued over female advantage (Duquin, 1978).

Although sex differences have been used in the past to exclude girls and women from sport (Hudson, 1978), current research on the benefits and safety of sport for women shows that athletic training offers women the same physiological advantages it provides for men. Physiological adaptations to training which include increased strength, decreased percentage of body fat, increased maximal oxygen consumption, and increased muscle metabolism occur for females as well as males, although not always via the same biological mechanisms or to the same degree. Training produces significant improvements for females as well as males, and improved performances in athletic records for women attest to the fact that many of the differences in performance that were considered "a fact of nature" just a few years ago were actually the result of a lack of physical conditioning (Dyer, 1982).

A conclusion that is overwhelmingly supported by research is that both males and females respond to and benefit from physical training. Furthermore, sport and exercise is safe and healthy for females as well as males, if they are physically conditioned and compete against opponents of similar skill (Wells, 1985).

Earlier Work Continued: Social Role on Gender and Sport

Paralleling the exercise science focus on biogenetic differences was the psychosocial focus on socialization. Socialization is conceptualized as the process by which institutions of culture such as the family, church, school, and state imbued individuals with mores and roles supported by the society (Sears, 1970). The cyclic process of socialization was described as follows. Through the socialization process individuals are taught how to behave and what is expected of them. Sex roles, behaviors, attributes, and tasks associated with being male or female in a culture are imposed on individuals through a socialization process that begins at birth. Sex roles identify certain activities and qualities as being appropriate for males and/or females. Consequently, qualities such as passivity, submissiveness, and meekness become associated with and define the less powerful group, usually females, while qualities such as boldness, vigor, and strength become associated with and define the empowered group, usually males. Role conflict occurs when individuals choose to engage in activities or express qualities that have been reserved for the opposite sex.

In the late 1960s, a few sport theorists suggested that women could experience role conflict when they chose to engage in sport as do men who choose to become accomplished in dance (Duquin, 1978; Felshin, 1974; Harris,

1972). In the realm of sport, role conflict was potentially experienced by girls who demanded a chance to play and by boys who refused to play. To the degree that role conflict becomes a barrier to developing individual talents and skills, it functions as a limiting factor for achieving growth and potential within individuals in society. Rigid gender role socialization can become a form of mind-binding and, like the ancient Chinese practice of foot-binding, it may inhibit growth in order to promote socially mandated power distribution. It shapes the mind by compelling the individual to actualize only role-appropriate behaviors, eliminating the possibilities of other unapproved, but possibly gratifying, actions for both males and females. Rigid binding constrains the mind to visualize only gender appropriate actions, and what the mind cannot visualize it cannot actualize.

Some would attribute principally to socialization the findings in a recent study of 4,000 United States elementary school children. In this study Eccles and Harold (1991) found that although girls actually scored only 2% lower than boys on a battery of motor skills test, they self-rated their skills as 14% lower than the boys. The same study showed that by the end of first grade, girls had lower expectations, investment, and confidence in sport skills than boys.

Evolution of Gender and Sport Research: The Case of Attribution

The evolution of research in gender and sport can be characterized as swinging from investigative studies which identified differences assumed to be the result of socialization to more complex, contextual, and systems analysis approaches. Examination of attribution research demonstrates that initially social role stereotyping provided an underlying rational for male/female differences in attribution. More recent formulations of attribution, however, identify social role stereotyping as only one of many components that interact to explain attributions. We present the evolution of research in this area as an example of the manner in which the reconceptualization of gender relations in sport builds upon earlier work.

Attribution research (described more fully elsewhere in the *Handbook*) investigates the explanations used by athletes and others to account for success or failure in performance. Attribution theory assumes that these causal explanations affect subsequent motivation, affective responses, and future behavior in sport (Weiner, 1974). The theoretical model that became the foundation for most of the studies on attribution done in the 1970s was proposed by Weiner. This model categorizes attribution along two dimensions: an internal and external control dimension, and a stable and unstable dimension. Using these, Weiner classified personal ability as an internal/stable attribution, personal effort as an internal/unstable attribution, task as an external/stable attribution, and luck as an external/unstable attribution. Athletes who attribute their successes to internal, personally controlled attributions and their failures to external attributions are said to have a self-enhancing bias because their attributions assign their success to personal qualities and enhance self-esteem. Athletes who attribute their successes to external attributions such as luck or easy tasks and their failures to internal attributions such as personal ability are said to have a self-depreciating bias.

Studies done in the late 1960s and early 1970s on gender and attribution indicated that males tend to make internal attributions for positive performance outcomes (self-appreciating bias) while females tend to adopt external attributions for success and internal attribution for failure (self-depreciating bias; Bar-Tal & Frieze, 1976; Deaux & Emswiller, 1974; Feather, 1969; McHugh, Duquin, & Frieze, 1978; Simon & Feather, 1973). Explanations for these findings (attributions about the attributions) exploited the impact of social role in contributing to male and female attributions. The explanations suggested that the reason females attributed success in sport to external factors was the internalization of societal norms suggesting that females are unsuited for successful performance in sport and have limited potential in this area (Neal & Tutko, 1975). Therefore, success in a male domain such as sport must be due to luck or some other external force. Furthermore, females socialized to conform to feminine social roles are not expected to be successful in sport and do not need to protect their egos by using a self-enhancing bias when explaining sport performance. Male social roles, on the other hand, require ego investment into sport and achievement-related performance that results in the adoption of a self-enhancing bias.

As research on attribution theory evolved in the 1980s it was characterized by more detail and dynamic complexity than earlier research. Detail complexity evolved as more interacting variables of attribution were discovered, and dynamic complexity evolved as researchers recognized that these components may impact on each other through interacting feedback loops. Earlier research explained male and female attributions as linear cause-and-effect chains with socialization as an underlying causal factor, while recent research has adopted more of a systems and contextual approach to the problem. This generalization is not meant to imply that all early research done on attribution was simplistic and linear, but only that the work done in the 1970s has evolved into a more complex view of attribution in the 1980s.

It was the contradictions and inconsistent findings of the earlier studies that eventually led to the recognition that the different way in which individuals explain performance successes and failures "is not a static outcome of gender, but it depends on the dynamic interaction of varying individuals and perceptions within social settings" (Durkin, 1987, p. 158). While recent research recognizes social role designation of gender-appropriate tasks as a component of attribution (Deaux, 1976, 1984; Lenney, 1977), it has also identified a host of other variables that influence attribution. Thus detail complexity was increased as perceived

ability (Roberts & Duda, 1984), sport confidence and competitive orientation (Vealey, 1988), recent performance, expectations before performance, and the difference between outcome and initial expectation (Valle & Frieze, 1976), social comparison (Darley & Goethals, 1980), gender schematic or aschematic orientation of self (Markus, Crane, Bernstein, & Siladi, 1982), and skill level (Vealey, 1988) were added to the list of components that affect attribution.

New models that include this detail complexity and account for the dynamic interaction of components are the next necessary step in broadening the conceptualization of attribution and gender. As this kind of enhanced understanding proceeds in each taxonomic area, our knowledge of the implications for gender/sport relations may be advanced as well.

RECONSTRUCTED VIEWS OF GENDER/SPORT RELATIONS

Our study of the traditional perceptions and conceptions of sport lead us to a characterization of a massive gender-influenced misunderstanding of the nature of the sport experience. Public perceptions are shaped by ancient patriarchal patterns that work to the detriment of males and females alike. Sport is seen as the masculine embodied; the male being is seen as superior in sport performance. We fail to see that sport is a cultural product, created by humans who project onto any activity into which they enter the deep core of each psyche, which is bigendered, as Freud knew, as Jung knew, as we all know—but we forget. We are required to forget by the "public consciousness," and sport is and has been a principle purveyor of this consciousness. Any discussion of reconstructions of gender and sport requires a brief sketch of the psychohistory of these terms. In this context, let us divide human existence into four very uneven eras (see Tables 33–1 and 33–2). These eras are most closely applicable to Western, European-based cultures. Other authors must be utilized to review this context in Eastern and African cultures.

The period termed "prehistory" is beautifully, though necessarily incompletely, chronicled by Rich (1977). One could postulate that the diminished place of women in later periods of Western civilization was a reaction to the awe and fear of woman, with her mysterious gift of fertility, during prehistory. Investigations of this time are largely closed to us unless and until new finds or new archeological techniques emerge. In the period termed "ancient" here, we see the formal beginning of sport as we know it and this activity was largely a domain of men. As Spears (1978) has pointed out, only the exceptional woman was involved in sport.

It is our contention that during the period when universal schooling was becoming a reality in Western Europe and the United States, a hybrid form of exercise and sport began that was specifically designed for women. Oglesby (Holland & Oglesby, 1977; Oglesby, 1991) has argued that instead of using a generic team "sport," which almost without

TABLE 33–1. Discernable Eras in Sport/Gender Analysis

Prehistory
Goddess worship; Amazon mythology; gender relations little known; sport unknown and improbable

Ancient History
Beginnings of recorded history to acceptance of universal schooling

Men	Women
Sphere of sport: military and/or holy	Sphere of domestic (Existence of "exceptional" women recognized)

Near History
Mid 1800s to the contemporary women's movement

Traditional-Sport	Sport-for-Women*
Activities, variously defined by mass culture and academics, but perceived to be a preparatory vehicle for manhood.	Stylized, trivialized, diminutive version of "true" sport.

Now and Future
Directions for the future are clouded.

*Overt, explicit labels for culturally approved sets of experiences that (a) made some provision for the health and vitality of women and (b) recreated traditional masculinity and femininity as legitimate sex-role attributes.

TABLE 33–2. Descriptors of Traditional Sport and Sport-for-Women

Traditional Sport	Sport-for-Women
Specialized, intense	In balance with other aspects of life; diffuse energy
Exclusive/elite	Inclusive (sport for every girl, every girl in sport)
Profit/win–oriented, public, spectatorial	Educational, developmental, private
Rule-bound, serious	Natural, spontaneous, fun
Risky/adventurous	Safe, medically sound
Aggressive, dominance-oriented opponent is enemy	Friendly, cooperative opponent is cocreator of "the game"
Coached and led by men	Coached and led by women

exception refers to men's sport, we should designate either "traditional sport" or "sport for women" as our point of reference. Use of these distinguishing labels points the way to recognition of the women's world of sport, a world known only to those who played. The "separate spheres" of sport persisted formally in the United States until the sweeping changes of Title IX of the Higher Education Act of 1972. The specific characteristics of these two sporting forms, which appear to be created specifically to conform to and create traditional masculinity and femininity, are shown in Table 33–2. For a more detailed exposition of these concepts, the two previously cited works are helpful.

With the thunderbolts of the contemporary feminist movement came the theoretical end to the separate spheres of sport and then emerged the possibilities of at least four scenarios (see Table 33–3). One possibility, when law or policy dictates that males and females participate together, is that a pretense of some kind is carried out and no substantive changes in sport structures occur. For example, in some physical education classes in the United States where boys and girls are supposed to participate together, two sports are offered to students: gymnastics and wrestling. Roll call is taken, and then, by some strange "coincidence," a female teacher covers gymnastics and it "happens" that all girls (and only girls) "choose" this activity. A male teacher covers wrestling and all boys (and only boys) take that activity. "Gym class" is coed, but nothing really has changed since the last century. Certainly this does not happen everywhere, but we must realize that many people can resist change rather successfully.

If scenario 2 came to pass, all sports persons would participate in sport along the lines of "sport-for-women" of the early to mid 1900s. The people who promote "new" or "cooperative" sport for all come the closest to this model, but it does not seem in danger of taking over the world of sport.

Scenario 3 is the exaggeration of traditional male-dominated sport, although now women will be participating with exactly the same style and manner. The movie *Rollerball,* in which players gave their lives to the game and killed to win, was an exaggeration of this motif. Some in the United States fear that this scenario is coming true, and literature by Bredemeier (1984, 1986) and Duquin (1984, 1990) on moral development and sport addresses this concern. As violence is seen to coexist with sport and as sport is exploited to vindicate social domination, the "*Rollerball* scenario" comes true.

The fourth possibility posits a transformed sport experience. As sport has functioned in the past, transformed sport would both exemplify and create a new gender identity framework. In this framework each individual strives to find

TABLE 33–3. Possible Scenarios for Future Sport

1. Federal government and/or feminists gone mad and, although we pretend to "do sport" differently, nothing really changes.

2. Sport-for-women becomes sport-for-all
   • Cooperative games
   • New games
   • No participation that all can't do together

3. "Traditional sport" subsumes all
   • Escalation of elitism
   • Escalation of violence
   • Escalation of "win justifies anything"
   • Sport approximates war and war becomes sport

4. *Transformed sport*
• Independence	Dependence/interdependence
• Activity	Passivity/quiet
• Ruled, bounded	Chaotic/inventive/improvisation
• Opponent is the challenge	Love/care for the challenger

her/his own internal balance of each pole of the qualities once seen as the dichotomous polarities of traditional sexuality. For example, just as each individual will strive in life to develop an appropriate balance of independence, dependence, and interdependence, a similar balance would be sought in sport. In transformed sport, it would be recognized that the squeeze play and hit-and-run in baseball/softball both require and teach dependence and interdependence. In both of these situations, a runner must break with the pitch to advance to the next base. The runner knows that she/he will surely be "out" unless the batter hits the ball or bunts. With that knowledge, however, she/he must not wait to run until the hit is made. The commitment to run is carried out in trust or the strategy is doomed to fail. Success is based on total dependence. These qualities of dependence and interdependence are valuable "lessons" from the game, as is independence. The traditions of sport and masculinity make this difficult to see. In attempting to make the hidden "feminine" dimension of traditional sport more recognizable, Oglesby (1990, p. 243) has presented the following:

Passive—I will rest; I will wait; as in Aikido, I will let her move me.
Subordinate—My advancement is not as important as our advancement.
Dependent—Without his effort, I will not succeed.
Chaotic—Strategically I will do this now, for no one will expect it.
Nonviolence—I care for my teammates, my opponents, and myself; thus my intent is not to inflict pain but rather,
Nurturance—to show my care. My level of play can only increase as the challenge of my opponent increases. I honor the challenger.

In transformed sport we recognize that the pure form of either type of "separate spheres" sport is toxic. Clearly *Rollerball* sport is toxic. Similarly women sport activists of the seventies and eighties were moved by the realization that recreational low-organized spontaneous sport-for-women left females without the experiences of intensity, discipline, excellence, challenge, and the institutional resources of society.

Research and informed professional *practice* in physical education and sport psychology (i.e., teaching, coaching, administration, sport psychology) must seek to envision a transformed sport and to reduce resistance and barriers to its acceptance in society. We will return to this issue of resistance later.

Relationship and Endeavor

A second area in which reconstructed concepts of gender and sport are called for might be labeled as a shift from "endeavor *or* relationship" to one of "endeavor *and* relationship." If sport psychologists initiated studies that examine motivations associated with her/his significant relationships in the sport setting with an eye to possible impact upon performance (endeavor), then we believe we will find evidence that carries out a theme already discovered in the work of Matina Horner (1970—achievement motivation/fear of success); Sandra Bem (1975—gender identity/androgyny); Irene Frieze (McHugh et al., 1978—attribution theory/self-aggrandizing and self-deprecating biases) and Carol Dweck (1975—learned helplessness). In each instance, a researcher began pursuing a particular issue in anticipation of significant gender-related findings. In each instance, a new subtlety of a basic psychological construct was identified among women, and in each instance, the psychological quality was later found to have predictive value among men as well but in attenuated form or in special populations not before researched (e.g., learned helplessness among white rural males of low socioeconomic status).

In the research conducted on high achievement of women in sport, special note has almost invariably been made of the context of sport as an "achievement arena" or to a "nontraditional context" for women as compared to their "traditional world of relationship." Even in research that may be regarded as avant-garde or cutting-edge, such as that by Bredemeier (to which we shall return), a distinction is made between "everyday life" and "sport," a distinction which seems to presuppose the female athlete's entry into "competition against" and then reentry into the world of "relationship with."

In the course of our perusal of qualitative research data and years of experiential involvement with sportswomen, it has dawned on us that "relationship" infuses every aspect of a female's sporting life. Social norms do not press her into ever higher levels of athletic achievement, so it is usually a "relationship" that motivates and informs her persistence—parents, a caring (or exploitive) coach, friendships at the gym or rink. "I did it for my coach—I owe it all to my dad" . . . in the women's sport world, which, in the past, was essentially devoid of money, recognition, glamor, perhaps even approval, such a comment of dedication suggests that relationship *and* endeavor become fused in ways that could be highly positive or negative.

For example, in sport psychology, there has been some debate about the relative efficacy of "associative cognitive strategies" and "dissociative strategies." Associative strategies ostensibly attune the athlete ever more closely to her/his own bodily function and the awareness of perceptual/sensory feedback interactions in personal space, while dissociative strategies facilitate denial and unawareness of such signals. Dissociative strategies are particularly noted to dominate the thinking of athletes as they consider the moral dilemmas of injury to opponents either accidentally, in the course of play, or strategically, as is said to occur often in traditional sport. We have never seen the question of gender, nor the issue of the differential impact of associative/disassociative strategies under differential relationship conditions, discussed in sport psychology. This seems a critical omission.

There are several areas of life where "relationship and

endeavor" have been acknowledged as intimately intertwined: in parent-child rearing, in the therapeutic model, in concepts of role models and mentoring. If we examine the role of relationship in sport performance for females and males, the implications of the findings may be far reaching.

Moral Development and Gender Commandments

In Maccobey and Jacklin's (1974) classic work assessing the psychology of sex differences, only the data on differences in aggression seemed consistently to stand their tests of rigor. In sport study, research on "aggression" has given way to a larger, more appropriate focus on the moral development and moral choice systems of athletes. The interrelation of gender, sport, and moral development is another area for reconstruction in the years ahead. Let us focus on but one of the many issues one can identify. Why do we find it so difficult to facilitate change in the beliefs both males and females hold about female athleticism, female physicality, and female sport superiority in an individual case over males? Oglesby (1989) has speculated that the timing coincidence of the initial formations of moral decisioning structures and gender identity structures results in a "gender judgment" bias that resists modification throughout life. Such a speculation is undergirded by findings from a review of neurophysiological studies of infants and those of classic developmental psychologists. From the latter, we know that at least by ages 2 to 4, primitive constructs are formed at the core of personal identity: self, gender, self-other relations, and moral precepts of good and bad. We know that these early formulations are of necessity simple, categorical, and either/or in quality. A study (Bornstein, 1966) done on infant eye-tracking and fixing at age 6 months illustrates that infants can react selectively to categories of color and that they apparently related to "prototypes" as best representatives of color categories as well. Another bit of evidence comes into play here as Sacks, in *Seeing Voices* (1989), discusses the ages at which children easily learn American Sign Language as their "native tongue." Sacks talks about the acuity of the 1- to 3-year-old to movement in fingers, hands, face, eyes, and lips before s/he learns "not to attend" to these cues, as children do if they are able to utilize sound instead of visual cuing.

It appears that the very young child, aged perhaps 1 to 3, learns "self," quickly followed by "boy/girl" in a primitive category system in which *athleticism* is the prototypical characteristic for the "boy" category. This "learning/ socializing" system may be communicated in subtleties of posture, expression, holding, lifting, carrying, and time of response which we have not begun to fathom. We hypothesize that an "oughtness" of right/wrong to these categorizations is picked up in the child's early formulations of moral decisioning and is resistant to profound change life-long. The fusion of gender categorizations with the power of good/bad connotations has been called by Oglesby the arrival of the "gender commandments." Children aged 4 to 5

and 8 to 10 were interviewed with the intent to "capture" the children before and after establishment of the "commandments," but the data indicated that age 4 to 5 years is too late.

The children were asked to complete stories about a boy and a girl in regard to two different situations. One was a spontaneous "bike race," which was undertaken when the two, equally equipped and experienced, were on a picnic with friends. The second was a question about responses to the sight of speed bumps in the roadway ahead; would the boy and girl speed up and fly, or slow down and be safe?

For the older children, the ideology was clear. In the absence of specific knowledge of two real people, both boys and girls reported significantly more often that the girl would lose and the girl would slow down. For the 4-to 5-year-olds, both boys and girls were divided on who would win the race, but the count went 7 to 1 that the girl would slow down while the boy would fly over the speed bumps. The ideology of "license" for the boy and "needing permission" for the girl was heavily in the thinking of boys and girls even at this age.

Gender Study and Men

Special mention and recognition should go to a relatively small band of scholar/researchers who insist that the new feminist scholarship on gender include the analysis of men and their special relationships to sport. The recent publication of *Sport, Men and the Gender Order* (Messner & Sabo, 1990) has codified a major portion of this new work.

Messner and Sabo point out first that the perceived isomorphism between traditional sport and traditional masculinity has shielded the necessity to "study" the patterns and practices of men's involvement in sport. Such investigation was relegated to the assumption, to the natural, to the obvious. The development of gender/sport relations (with its initial focus on women) brought forward the need for reconceptualizations, for "when feminist theory focuses almost exclusively on women's experiences, the conceptualization of gender as a relational process is lost" (Messner & Sabo, p. 13).

There are many important themes and analyses brought forward by the "men and gender" scholars. The radical critics of traditional sport speak of the parallels between the hegemonic masculine orientation and various psychosocial ills, including militarism, authoritarianism, and specific violence toward women. These areas beg for more empirical research and continued theorizing. Another wing of this discussion focuses on masculinity and oppression, particularly expressed as racism in the world of sport. The psychology of race, racial relations, oppression, and stigmatization are part of the context of sport worldwide, and men and gender studies puts these variables on the research menu for the sport scholar and professional.

Connell (1987) argues for much more detail and dynamic complexity in our understanding of the "masculinity" construct. He points out that during given periods in given societies, there are many masculinities, from the hegemonic to the marginalized and stigmatized (nondominant males often of color, poor, or gay). Sabo, of note, has emphasized the cost to men of the traditional masculine (even within its gifts of privilege) influencing men to deny their own pain, their own emotions, and their bonds with other men.

A final variation in the gender/sport relations and men research, newly initiated, is that concerned with women coaching boys or men. Staurowsky (1990) reports of her findings in regard to qualitative interviews of women who coach boys team sport groups in the United States. Gender constructions linking sport expertise with masculinity and leadership with male superiority seem to deny the possibility that females coach males. Circumstance/individual interactions create occasions, however, when women coaches have been very successful with boys' teams. Staurowsky's findings point out that patriarchal assumptions potentially weaken sports leadership structure through differentially using gender, as distinct from competence requirements, as a criterion for inclusion.

FUTURE STUDY OF GENDER/SPORT RELATIONS

The recent growth of interest, both in publication and in conferences, on gender and sport seems likely to continue, and the simple additive increase in knowledge about males and females and their patterns of relations in sport is badly needed. Beyond that major requirement, there are three other areas which we view as critical for the advancement of knowledge. One might say we have three wishes for the "genie" of the research lamp.

The influences of the past, the stereotypes of traditional sexuality concepts (the "mind-binding"), could reasonably be seen as disqualifying all past data. We can see how an intelligent person might argue for "throwing out" all past data on psychological differences/similarities between females and males in sport because it is so hopelessly confounded with policies and practices of female exclusion and limitation. Instead, we suggest that the genie of the research lamp should give us the energy and insight to utilize the process of *deconstruction* on all previous research in this content area.

Deconstruction (Hare-Mustin & Maracek, 1988) was developed as a method of literary interpretation but has also been used with therapeutic discourse and scientific texts. Eagleton (1983) states that texts can have a variety of meanings beyond their original intent, and language is not seen as a fixed correspondence between word and object but rather "a sprawling, limitless web where there is constant circulation of elements" (p. 124). Deconstruction readings, focusing on what is *not* said as well as what is said, utilize gaps, inconsistencies, and metaphoric associations in the context of the "common knowledge" of an author's time and place to supply new and alternative meanings to a text.

Thus rather than beginning anew the study of gender and sport, we have the possibility, perhaps even the responsibility, to de-and reconstruct our fund of knowledge on gender and sport and build new knowledge taking into account this fund of knowledge.

A second wish to be made in the area of future directions borrows directly from a tongue-in-cheek creation of Fine and Gordon (1989) in their assessment of feminism's impact on psychology. They obtained "penetration" and "ovulation" indices (PI and OI) for psychology literature and we believe something similar is definitely needed as regards gender/sport relations impact on sport psychology literature. The "penetration index" is the degree to which (in our example) gender/sport articles and studies from "gender" journals and books (e.g., *Sex Roles: A Journal of Research*) are cited in bibliographies of mainstream sport psychology journals. In Fine and Gordon, feminist journal articles showed up in *Developmental Psychology* bibliographies .03% in 1981 and .02% in 1986 (not much PI). We speculate that gender/sport relations work doesn't undergird much of the basic applied research either. The ovulation index (OI) was, for Fine and Gordon, the frequency of articles in mainstream psychology journals on race and gender. Our OI would identify the frequency of articles on gender/sport relations in mainstream sport psychology journals. Data are needed on this, ideally collected on "completed research" publications as well as refereed journal articles.

The third thing we would ask of our genie would be outcome research utilizing balanced sport (or transformed sport, in our terminology) programs as a "treatment" to increase participant health and development. If sport programs were assessed—even graded, if you will—for the emotional/cognitive impact on participants, we could increase accountability for the immense personal and national expenditures on sport.

FINAL COMMENTS

What contributions does the study of gender and sport make to the sport psychologist working with unique individual athletes in an applied setting? There is a challenge here. First, the majority of studies published on gender and sport are quantitative analyses done with the intent of uncovering generalizations which can be applied to a large defined population. The sport psychologist in the field is working to assist a unique individual athlete in exploring individualistic, interpersonal, and intrapersonal phenomena which impact upon performance. It seems that the research goals are far removed from the sport psychologist's basic task. This potential conflict holds for all topics in sport that depend upon quantitative "scientific" research as the "gold standard." We can defend the tradition of quantitative research by positing that the generalizations resulting from this work can be used as "guideposts" by the sport psychologist in the search for specific individual phenomena.

Research findings in gender and sport offer the athlete and sport psychologist checkpoints from which further individualistic journeys may proceed.

Generalizations from gender and sport research, for example, can be used to examine the extent to which gender, as an intervening variable, may be influencing an athlete's motivation, anxiety level, attributions, or aggressive behavior. The sport psychologist can also examine how the athlete's success or failure in sport influences interactions with significant others in his/her life.

The contextual nature of research seen lately has multiplied the number of checkpoints and identified multiple paths that the sport psychologist and athlete can explore. Professional support and encouragement for qualitative research providing different but highly useful types of checkpoints is also necessary.

The literature on flow or peak performance may possibly provide descriptions of a truly genderless state, for individuals (in their bliss) seem to leave such considerations behind. The transcendence of gender is probably one of the rarer occurrences in sporting life, however, so we highly recommend extending and expanding efforts to more fully understand and predict behavior from the vantage point of gender.

References

Alvarado, D. (1990, September 2). In sport, only big difference between sexes is confidence. *Philadelphia Inquirer,* p. 6e.

Bar-Tal, D., & Frieze, I. (1976). Attribution of success and failure for actors and observers. *Journal of Research in Personality, 10,* 256–265.

Bleier, R. (1984). *Science and gender.* New York: Pergamon Press.

Bem, S. (1975). Sex role adaptability: One consequence of psychological androgyny. *Journal of Personality and Social Psychology, 31,* 634–643.

Birrell S., & Richter, D. (1987). Is a diamond forever? Feminist transformations of sport. *Women Studies International Forum, 10,* 395–409.

Bornstein, M. (1966). Two kinds of perceptual organization near the beginning of life. *Minnesota Symposia on Child Psychology.* Minneapolis: University of Minnesota.

Boutilier, M. A., & San Giovanni, L. (1983). *The sporting woman.* Champaign, IL: Human Kinetics.

Bredemeier, B. (1984). Sport, gender, and moral growth. In J. Silva & R. Weinberg (Eds.), *Psychological foundations of sport* (pp. 400–413). Champaign, IL: Human Kinetics.

Bredemeier, B., & Shields, D. (1986). Game reasoning and interactional morality. *Journal of Genetic Psychology, 147,* 257–275.

Brooks, G., & Fahey, T. (1984). *Exercise physiology.* New York: Wiley.

Butler, J. (1990). *Gender trouble: Feminism and the subversion of identity.* New York: Routledge.

Carlson, N. C. (1991). *Physiology of behavior* (4th ed.). Boston: Allyn and Bacon.

Connell, R. (1987). *Gender and power: Society, the person and sexual politics.* Stanford, CA: Stanford University Press.

Crawford, M., & Gentry, M. (1989). *Gender and thought: Psychological perspectives.* New York: Springer-Verlag.

Darley, J., & Goethals, G. (1980). People's analyses of the causes of ability linked performances. *Advances in Experimental Social Psychology, 13,* 2–37.

Deaux, K. (1984). From individual differences to social categories. Analysis of a decade's research on gender. *American Psychologist, 39,* 105–116.

Deaux, K., & Emswiller, T. (1974). Explanation for successful performance on sex-linked tasks: What is skill for the male is luck for the female. *Journal of Personality and Social Psychology, 29,* 80–05.

Douglas, J., & Miller, J. (1977). Record breaking women. *Science News, 112,* 172–174.

Duquin, M. (1978). The androgynous advantage. In C. Oglesby (Ed.), *Women and sport: Myth to reality* (pp. 189–170). Philadelphia: Lea & Febiger.

Duquin, M. (1984). Power and authority: Moral consensus and conformity in sport. *International Review for Sociology of Sport, 19.*

Duquin, M. (1991). *Sport, women and the ethic of care.* Paper presented at Girls' and Women's Sport Symposium, Slippery Rock University, Slippery Rock, PA.

Durkin, K. (1987). Social cognition and social context in the construction of sex differences. In M. Baker (Ed.), *Sex differences in human performance* (pp. 141–170). New York: Wiley.

Dweck, C. (1975). The role of expectations and attributions in the alleviation of learned helplessness. *Journal of Personal Social Psychology, 31,* 674–685.

Dyer, K. (1982). *Challenging the men: The social biology of female sporting achievement.* St. Lucia: University of Queensland Press.

Eagleton, T. (1983). *Literary theory: An introduction.* Minneapolis: University of Minnesota Press.

Eccles, J., & Harold, R. (1991). Gender differences in sport involvement: Applying the Eccles expectancy value model. *Journal of Applied Sport Psychology, 3,* 7–35.

Fausto-Sterling, A. (1985). *Myths of gender.* New York: Basic Books.

Feather, M. (1969). Attribution of responsibility and valence of success and failure in relation to initial confidence and task performance. *Journal of Personality and Social Psychology, 13,* 129–144.

Felshin, J. (1974). The triple option for women in sport. *Quest, 17,* 36–40.

Fine, M., & Gordon, S. (1989). Feminist transformations of/despite psychology. In Crawford & M. Gentry, M. (Eds.), *Gender and thought: Psychological perspectives* (pp. 146–174). New York: Springer-Verlag.

Gerber, E., Felshin, J., Berlin, P., & Wyrick, W. (1974). *The American women in sport.* Reading, MA: Addison-Wesley.

Gregory, J. (1979). Women coaching women. *Coaching Review, 2*(12), 12–13.

Hall, M. (1990). How should we theorize gender in the context of sport? In M. Messner & D. Sabo (Eds.), *Sport, men, and the gender order* (pp. 223–240). Champaign, IL: Human Kinetics.

Hall, M.A. (1985). How should we theorize sport in a capitalist patriarchy? *International Review for Sociology of Sport, 20,* 109–116.

Hall, M. A. (1988). The discourse or gender and sport: From femininity to feminism. *Sociology of Sport Journal, 5,* 330–340.

Hare-Mustin, R., & Marecek, J. (1988). The meaning of difference: Gender theory, post modernism, and psychology. *American Psychologist, 43,* 455–464.

Harris, D. (1972). *Women and sport: A national research conference.* University Park, PA: Pennsylvania State University, College of Health, Physical Education, and Recreation.

Hebb, D. (1949). *The organization of behavior.* New York: Wiley.

Holland, J., & Oglesby, C. (1979). Women in sport: The synthesis begins. *Annals, American Academy of Political and Social Science,* September.

Horner, M. (1970). Femininity and successful achievement: A basic inconsistency. In M. Horner (Ed.), *Feminine personality and conflict* (pp. 45–74). Belmont, Brooks/Cole.

Hudson, J. (1978). Physical parameters used for female exclusion from law enforcement and athletics. In C. Oglesby (Ed.), *Women and sport: From myth to reality.* Philadelphia: Lea & Febiger.

International Relations and Major Games Directorate of Fitness and Amateur Sport (1991). *Internation Relations Background Briefing: Gender Verification.* Government of Canada Fitness and Amateur Sport, Toronto, Canada.

Lenney, E. (1977). Women's self-confidence in achievement settings. *Psychological Bulletin, 84,* 1–13.

Lever, J. (1976). Sex differences in the games children play. *Social Problems, 23,* 478–487.

Maccobey, E., & Jacklin, C. (1974). *The psychology of sex differences.* Standord, CA: Stanford University Press.

Markus, H. Crane, M., Bernstein, S., & Siladi, M. (1982). Self-schemas and gender. *Journal of Personality and Social Psychology, 42,* 38–50.

McHugh, M., Duquin, M., & Frieze, I. (1978). Beliefs about success and failure: Attribution and the female athlete. In C. Oglesby (Ed.), *Women and sport: From myth to reality* (pp. 143-173). Philadelphia: Lea & Febiger.

Messner, M., & Sabo, D. (1990). *Sport, men, and the gender order.* Champaign, IL: Human Kinetics.

Money, J. & Erhardt, A. (1972). *Man and woman/boy and girl.* Baltimore and London: The Johns Hopkins University Press.

Neal, P., & Tutko, T. (1975). *Coaching girls and women: Psychological perspectives.* Boston: Allyn and Bacon.

Oglesby, C. (Ed.). (1978). *Women and sport: From myth to reality.* Philadelphia: Lea & Febiger.

Oglesby, C. (1981). *The paradox of racial stereotyping in physical education and sport: Black is inferior or Black is best?* Amherst: University of Massachusetts, Project TEAM, Women's Educational Equity Act Program.

Oglesby, C. (1984). Interaction between gender identity and sport. In J.M. Silva and R.S. Weinberg (Eds.), *Psychological foundations of sport* (pp. 387–399). Champaign, IL: Human Kinetics.

Oglesby, C. (1989). *Gender commandments.* Unpublished presentation, Association for the Advancement of Applied Sports Psychology, Annual Conference, University of North Carolina, Chapel Hill.

Oglesby, C. (1990). Epilogue. In M. Messner & D. Sabo (Eds.), *Sport, men, and the gender order* (pp. 241–247). Champaign, IL: Human Kinetics.

Oglesby, C. (1991). *Women and sport: A new research agenda.* Unpublished proceedings, Smith College, Northampton, MA.

Parsons, T. & Bales, R. (1955). *Family, socialization, and interaction process.* Glencoe, IL: Free Press.

Person, E. (1980). Sexuality as the mainstay of identity: Psychoanalytic perspectives. In C. Stimpson & E. Person (Eds.), *Women, sex, and sexuality* (1980). Chicago: University of Chicago Press.

Piaget, J. (1952). *The origins of intelligence in children.* New York: W. W. Norton.

Puhl, J., Brown, C. H., & Voy, R. O. (1988). *Sport science perspectives for women,* Champaign, IL: Human Kinetics.

Rich, A. (1977). *Of woman born: Motherhood as experience and institution.* New York: Bantam Books.

Roberts, G. & Duda, J. (1984). Motivation in sport: The mediating role of perceived ability. *Journal of Sport Psychology, 6,* 312–324.

Rosenberg, R. (1982). *Beyond separate spheres.* New Haven: Yale University Press.

Sacks, O. (1989). *Seeing voices.* Berkeley, CA: University of California Press.

Sears, R. (1970). Relation of early socialization experiences to self-concept and gender role in middle childhood. *Child Development, 44,* 267–289.

Simon, J., & Feather, N. (1973). Causal attributions for success and failure at university examinations. *Journal of Educational Psychology, 64,* 46–56.

Sloan-Green, T., Oglesby, C., Alexander, A., & Franke, N. (1981). *Black women in sport.* Reston, VA: American Alliance of Health, Physical Education, Recreation, and Dance.

Spears, B. (1978). Prologue: The myth. In C. Oglesby (Ed.), *Women and sport: From myth to reality* (p. 256). Philadelphia: Lea & Febiger.

Staurowsky, E. (1990). Women coaching male athletes. In M. Messner & D. Sabo (Eds.), *Sport, men, and the gender order* (pp. 163–171). Champaign, IL: Human Kinetics.

Valle, V., & Frieze, I. (1976). The stability of causal attributions as a mediator in changing expectations for success. *Journal of Personality and Social Psychology, 33,* 579.

Vealey, R. (1988). Sport-confidence and competitive orientation: An addendum on scoring procedures and gender differences. *Journal of Sport and Exercise Psychology, 10,* 471–478.

Vygotsky, L. (1962). *Thought and language.* (E. Haufmann & G. Vahar, Ed. and Trans.). Cambridge, MA and New York: MIT Press and Wiley & Sons. (Original work published in Russian, 1934)

Weiner, B. (1974). *Achievement motivation and attribution theory.* Morristown, NJ: General Learning Press.

Wells, C.L. (1985). *Women, sport, and performance: A physiological perspective.* Champaign, IL: Human Kinetics.

Women's Sport Foundation. (1983). *Proceedings: New agenda for women and sport.* 342 Madison Ave., Suite 728, New York, NY 10173.

34

EXERCISE AND THE QUALITY OF LIFE

Bonnie G. Berger

Adrian McInman

This chapter reviews and synthesizes the current research focusing on the complex interrelationships between exercise and the quality of life. We have chosen the term *quality of life* to emphasize the positive contributions of exercise. The often-employed phrase *psychological well-being* denotes primarily the absence of negative affect such as anxiety and depression.

Quality of life reflects the harmonious satisfaction of one's goals and desires (Chekola, 1975); it emphasizes the subjective experience rather than the conditions of life (Campbell, Converse, & Rodgers, 1976). Bradburn (1969) describes life quality or "happiness" as an abundance of positive affect and an absence of negative affect. Quality of life also reflects the perceived degree to which individuals are able to satisfy their psychophysiologic needs (Dalkey, Lewis, & Snyder, 1972). See Diener (1984) for a discussion of the general structure of subjective well-being, measurement considerations, and general influences on subjective well-being. Income and subjective well-being (quality of life) appear to be more highly related within a country than between various countries. The personality characteristics of self-esteem, optimism, and neuroticism may have a universal relationship to happiness (Diener, 1984).

Measures of life quality are as varied as are the definitions, but they help clarify the meaning of the term. Andrews and Withey (1976) measure quality of life by their Delighted-Terrible Scale, which asks a single question: how happy do you feel about how happy you are? In contrast to such single-item scales, quality of life measures often reflect global assessment of subjective well-being in a variety of subdomains (Diener, 1984). Many quality of life scales include specific subdomains that vary from measure to measure. Subdomains common to many measures include the biophysical area (health, comfort, food, shelter, exercise), work, self (self-acceptance, humor, honesty, accomplishment), primary social contacts (close relatives, friends), and secondary social components such as acceptance by others, recognition, and prestige (Campbell et al., 1976; Diener, 1984; Flanagan, 1978; Pflaum, 1973). Exercise directly influences the health, exercise, and self subdomains, and indirectly influences the primary and secondary social components.

Life quality as employed in this chapter refers to a state of subjective well-being, and a preponderance of positive affect (e.g., Bradburn, 1969; Diener, 1984; Morris, Lussier, Vaccaro, & Clarke, 1982). Since exercise has been associated with mood benefits, more positive self-concept and self-esteem, increases in self-efficacy, decreases in psychological and physiological stress indices, and the experiences of joy and fun, it can play a pivotal role in life quality. Selected aspects of the relationship between life quality and exercise explored in this chapter include independent sections on the following: (a) the relationship between psychological well-being and exercise in members of the "normal" population, (b) the influence of exercise on self-concept and self-esteem, (c) exercise as the fountain of youth, (d) peak moments in sport and exercise, and (e) exercise adherence.

RELATIONSHIP BETWEEN PSYCHOLOGICAL WELL-BEING AND EXERCISE, PRIMARILY IN MEMBERS OF THE "NORMAL" POPULATION

The relationship between exercise and psychological well-being, an integral component of life quality, is exceed-

We would like to express our sincere appreciation to Michael L. Sachs, friend and colleague, who wrote a draft of the section on "The Runner's, or Exercise, High."

ingly complex. There are many types and forms of exercise. "Exercise" may refer to (a) group or solitary activities, (b) competitive sport and recreational physical activity, (c) aerobic or anaerobic activity, (d) acute and chronic exercise, and (e) activities performed by individuals who differ greatly in fitness and skill levels. It is likely that the psychological benefits, much like the physical benefits, differ across exercise modalities. Even within a single activity, a multitude of factors vary: the practice characteristics, exercise environment, participants, and instructors. The type and extent of psychological benefits of exercise also may differ for participants who vary in age from preschoolers to the elderly. Further complicating the interrelationships, the term *psychological well-being* includes many facets such as physiological and psychological stress responses, fluctuating mood states, longer lasting mood disorders such as anxiety and depression, and personality characteristics.

Despite such complexities, it is possible to generalize across many types of studies and to conclude that habitual exercise *can be* associated with enhanced psychological well-being. See the review by Boutcher in this book and those by Berger (1984a, 1984b), Crews and Landers (1987), Dunn and Dishman (1991), and North, McCullagh, and Tran (1990) for in depth information about the mental health benefits of exercise. Rather than discuss the following generalizations in detail, we present them as a framework for proposing more tentative hypotheses that can guide future research endeavors:

1. Acute decreases in common stress symptoms such as anxiety, depression, and anger have been associated primarily with single exercise sessions in members of the normal population (e.g., Berger, Friedmann, & Eaton, 1988; Berger & Owen, 1988; Morgan & Goldston, 1987a; Steptoe & Bolton, 1988; Steptoe & Cox, 1988). In comparison to possible long-term changes, the acute changes are more clearly associated with the exercise itself.
2. The long-term decreases in anxiety and depression associated with chronic exercise programs tend to occur in members of psychiatric populations (Bosscher, 1991; Martinsen, Hoffart, & Solberg, 1989; Morgan & Goldston, 1987a). ("Psychiatric populations" include individuals who are hospitalized for psychiatric problems, outpatients of psychiatric hospitals, and other people being treated for psychological problems or concerns.) See the edited works by Morgan and Goldston (1987a) and by Sachs and Buffone (1984). If an individual is clinically anxious or depressed, there is more opportunity for long-term mood improvement.
3. Exercise has been shown to be as effective as more traditional stress reduction approaches in reducing anxiety, tension, depression, and anger (Bahrke & Morgan, 1978; Berger et al., 1988; Long, 1985; Long & Haney, 1988a, 1988b). These effects were particularly impressive becuase the participants in these studies were randomly assigned to treatment. Thus exercise was stress reducing even for individuals who were not self-selected exercis-

ers. The observation that exercise was not superior to the other stress reduction techniques emphasizes the need for realistic claims regarding the benefits of exercise.
4. Aerobic exercise involvement and/or high fitness levels have been associated with attenuated physiological responses following exposure to psychosocial stressors (e.g., Blumenthal et al., 1988; Crews & Landers, 1987; Sinyor, Schwartz, Peronnet, Brisson, & Seraganian, 1983). However, as recently concluded in a symposium on exercise, catecholamines, and behavioral stress, the role of exercise in moderating the stress response needs additional exploration (Sothmann, 1991; Dienstbier, 1991; Cox, 1991).
5. Participation in aerobic and in less intense exercise such as walking may serve as a buffer between negative life events and physical illness (Brown & Siegel, 1988; Roth & Holmes, 1985).

The remainder of this section examines specific exercise parameters that seem to influence the psychological benefits. As emphasized throughout the chapter, the mental health benefits of exercise are not automatic and depend on multiple factors. Extensive research is needed to better understand the interrelationships, and to suggest appropriate exercise guidelines to increase the psychological benefits for exercisers ranging from recreational to athletic participants. We will discuss the somewhat limited research and offer suggestions for future directions.

TYPE OF PHYSICAL ACTIVITY

Many researchers have examined the psychological benefits of aerobic exercise (e.g., Boutcher & Landers, 1988; Long & Haney, 1988a, 1988b). An underlying assumption seems to be that aerobic (in contrast to less intense) exercise is associated with mood alteration and/or stress reduction. Jogging repeatedly has been associated with many aspects of psychological well-being: decreased anxiety and depression, enhanced self-concept, stress tolerance, and the runner's high (e.g., Morgan & Goldston, 1987a; Sachs & Buffone, 1984; Sacks & Sachs, 1981). Further, the psychological benefits of jogging have been shown to be as beneficial as other commonly employed stress reduction activities, such as the relaxation response (Benson, 1975), stress inoculation training (Meichenbaum, 1985), and progressive relaxation (Bernstein & Borkovec, 1973) as indicated in recent studies (e.g., Friedmann & Berger, 1991; Berger, Friedmann, & Eaton, 1988; Long, 1985; Long & Haney, 1988a, 1988b).

Recreational swimming resembles jogging in many ways. Not only are both forms of exercise aerobic, they also are individual, repetitive, and rhythmical physical activities. Provided that these are the salient attributed for making an activity beneficial, it is not surprising that swimming has been associated with the same acute mental health benefits as has jogging. Benefits include decreased tension, anxiety, depression, anger, and confusion, and increased vigor (Berger, Grove, & Prapavessis, 1992; Berger & Owen, 1983; Sharp, 1987).

A taxonomy to identify the essential attributes of physical activities that facilitate the enhanced psychological well-being of participants is needed to avoid investigating the psychological benefits of each type of physical activity individually. Such a taxonomy also might serve as a useful guide to examine some of the underlying factors that facilitate the beneficial effects. A taxonomy would be of particular value to sport psychologists, other mental health professionals, physical educators, and individuals in the general population who wish to use exercise for stress reduction and/or for enhancing the quality of life.

Taxonomy for the Psychological Benefits of Exercise

Although sport and motor skill classification systems have been proposed and developed throughout the last 20 years (e.g., Gentile, 1972; Poulton, 1957; Singer & Gerson, 1981), they have little relationship to the psychological benefits of exercise. Recognizing the need for a taxonomy to predict which types of physical activity would have the greatest psychological benefits from exercise, Berger and her colleagues (Berger, 1983/1984, 1986; Berger & Owen, 1988) have proposed an initial system that still requires considerable testing. Their preliminary taxonomy is described here in considerable detail because it highlights many of the major issues in the relationship between psychological well-being and exercise. Some of the factors are based on replicable research; others are more speculative. As illustrated in Table 34–1, there are three primary components: enjoyment of the activity, type of activity or mode characteristics, and practice requirements (Berger & Owen, 1988).

There is a critical need to examine exercise characteristics and parameters that enhance mental health benefits due to an apparent assumption that the well-established guidelines for physiological functioning (e.g., American College of Sports Medicine, 1991) also apply to the psychological benefits of exercise. Emphasizing the relative lack

TABLE 34–1. Preliminary Taxonomy for Maximizing the Psychological Benefits of Exercise

Major Requirements	Subcomponents
Pleasing and enjoyable activity	
Mode characteristics	"Aerobic," or rhythmical abdominal breathing
	Absence of interpersonal competition
	Closed predictable, or temporally and spatially certain activity
Practice requirements	Intensity: moderate
	Duration: at least 20 to 30 minutes
	Frequency: regularly included in weekly schedule

of exercise guidelines, participants in a "state-of-the-art" conference on exercise and mental health concluded that there was a need to investigate "the optimal *mode, intensity, duration, and frequency* [italics added] of exercise required to provide more effective responses to mental stress" (Morgan & Goldston, 1987b, p. 157).

Pleasing and Enjoyable

This requirement adjusts for individual differences and sport preferences. An activity that is mood enhancing and/or stress reducing for most participants may be stress producing for others. For example, some might enjoy the social atmosphere when running on a treadmill in a health club under the curious, often evaluative eyes of other club members; other individuals might find such an experience to be stress producing. Another example of a need for an enjoyable exercise experience is that unpleasant weather conditions such as extreme heat or cold also may negate expected mood changes associated with exercise. Evidence of this possibility was presented by Berger and Owen (1986), who, by chance, tested swimmers on a day that was unbearably hot (106°) in the pool area with the water temperature unusually hot. Swimmers reported no acute mood changes—either positive or negative.

Enjoyment seems to be an important requirement for maximizing the psychological benefits of exercise. If exercise is unpleasant, it is unlikely that participants will "feel better" after exercising. Thus exercise participants who are seeking the psychological benefits of mood enhancement would be well advised to seek alternate activities if some aspect of an activity is unpleasant (Berger & Owen, 1988). Activity "enjoyment" clearly is an individual phenomenon. Since enjoyment is related to exercise adherence (Scanlan & Simons, in press; Wankel, in press) it affects the long-term success of the use of exercise for elevating psychological well-being (Wankel & Berger, 1990).

Mode Characteristics

"Aerobic" or Rhythmical Abdominal Breathing. Although the need for an aerobic quality has been frequently cited in the literature (e.g., Long & Haney, 1988a, 1988b), there is little research directly investigating this characteristic. Undoubtedly aerobic types of exercise have been associated with improvements in psychological well-being (Berger & Owen, 1983; Gurley, Neuringer, & Masse, 1984; Morgan, 1987). However, the psychological effects of less intense exercise have been investigated primarily as a control condition to contrast with aerobic activities (e.g., Gurley et al., 1984).

New evidence suggests that it may be the rhythmical abdominal breathing (generated by aerobic exercise and other less intense types of exercise) that leads to enhanced psychological well-being. Recent psychological studies of Hatha yoga, walking, and riding a bicycle ergometer at light workloads lend credence to the possibility that exercise-associated changes in breathing patterns, rather than the aerobic quality, are associated with psychological benefits. Walking, Hatha yoga, and bicycling meet the general taxonomy requirements (see Table 34–1) except for the aerobic component. Each activity, however, has been associated with enhanced psychological well-being (Berger & Owen, 1988, 1992; Moses, Steptoe, Mathews, & Edwards, 1989; Steptoe & Cox, 1988; Thayer, 1987). It would seem that the three activities encourage participants to engage in abdominal, rhythmical breathing. Thus it may be this characteristic that is generally incorporated in the aerobic requirement and is conducive to enhanced psychological well-being.

Since the importance of rhythmical abdominal breathing in the mood benefits of exercise is speculative and has generated little or no objective research, there is a strong need for studies to clarify the role of aerobic as well as less intense exercise in enhancing mental health. Kabat-Zinn, director of the Stress Reduction Clinic at the University of Massachusetts Medical Center, emphasizes the importance of mindfully tuning in to one's breathing as a technique for stress reduction and pain control. His description of this basic process in meditation can be an integral part of any exercise session:

The easiest and most effective way to begin practicing mindfulness as a formal meditative practice is to simply focus your attention on your breathing and see what happens as you attempt to keep it there. . . . There are a number of different places in the body where the breath can be observed. Obviously one is the nostrils. . . . the chest as it expands and contracts, and another is the belly, which moves in and out with each breath if it is relaxed.

No matter which location you choose, the idea is to be aware of the sensations that accompany your breathing at that particular place and to hold them in the forefront of your awareness from moment to moment. Doing this, we *feel* the air as it flows in and out past the nostrils; we *feel* the movement of the muscles associated with breathing; we *feel* the belly as it moves in and out.

. . . Similarly when we focus on our breathing down in the belly, we are tuning to a region of our body that is below the agitations of our thinking mind and is intrinsically calmer. This is a valuable way of reestablishing inner calmness and balance in the face of emotional upset or when you "have a lot on your mind." (Kabat-Zinn, 1990, pp. 51–52)

Absence of Interpersonal Competition. Glasser (1976) emphasized the importance of an absence of competition in his discussion of exercise characteristics leading to positive addictions. Positive addictions (PA), in contrast to negative addictions, were theorized to lead to confidence, creativity, happiness, and health. As Glasser emphasized, "Not only must we not compete with others, we must learn not to compete with ourselves if we want to reach the PA state" (p. 57).

Intercollegiate competitive swimmers who consistently participate in high-intensity, long-duration training sessions have reported less positive mood profiles than recreational swimmers (Riddick, 1984). More specifically the competitive swimmers were significantly higher in Fatigue and tended to be higher in Tension than the recreational swimmers and a group of sedentary controls. The recreational swimmers were significantly lower in Depression, Anger, and Confusion than were the varsity athletes and the sedentary controls. These results must be regarded as tentative, because Riddick (1984) tested swimmers whenever they were available: before, during, and after swimming sessions. Whether they were tested before or after swimming has a direct influence on their mood states (Berger & Owen, 1983, 1987).

The absence of interpersonal competition could enhance the psychological benefits of physical activity for many reasons. One of these is that noncompetitive activities enable the participant to avoid the negative psychological effects of losing. When one person competes directly against another, losing occurs in sport approximately 50% of the time. For many individuals, losing detracts from such feelings as joy, self-efficacy, pride, accomplishment, competency, and control that are associated with participation in physical activity and/or sport. Glasser's (1976) ideas still require empirical testing, and the noncompetitive requirement may not apply to all individuals. However, the well-established body of literature on competitive anxiety (e.g., Hackfort & Spielberger, 1989) supports the likelihood that many competitors find sport to be stress producing rather than stress reducing.

Another reason (in addition to losing) why competitive sport may not be associated with enhanced psychological well-being is that *competitive sport athletes tend to overtrain.* Overtraining and the subsequent burnout are associated with decrements in psychological well-being (Morgan, Brown, Raglin, O'Connor, & Ellickson, 1987; Morgan, Costill, Flynn, Raglin, & O'Connor, 1988). As concluded by Morgan and colleagues (1987, p. 109), "Perhaps the most notable feature of this particular study is the apparent paradox observed in connection with the exercise-depression relationship. Whereas vigorous exercise is known to reduce depression in moderately depressed individuals . . . depression also seems to be a product of overtraining." Again, it is not clear in the series of studies reported by Morgan and colleagues *when* in reference to the actual swimming the swimmers were tested.

To test the possibility that physically taxing training aspects of competitive sport are related to mood detriments, Berger, Grove, and Prapavessis (1992) examined the relationship between *training distance and mood alteration* in age-group competitive swimmers. Results indicated a significant interaction between training distance and mood. Shortened, tapered practice sessions (3,500–5,000 meters), which typically were held prior to competition, were associated with acute decreases in Total Mood Disturbance scores. More specifically the competitive swimmers reported less Depression and Confusion. However, during the more typical normal-distance practice sessions (6,000–7,000 meters), Total Mood Disturbance significantly increased. The young swimmers reported increased Fatigue and decreased Vigor. Thus competitive swimming practice was associated with mood benefits only when athletes swam practice distances that were shorter than usual. Most athletes complete training sessions that tax their maximal physical capabilities. It seems unlikely that most competitive practice sessions are mood enhancing (Berger et al., 1992; Morgan et al., 1987, 1988).

Closed, Predictable, or Temporally and Spatially Certain.
Jogging and swimming, the two activities repeatedly associated with psychological benefits, are highly predictable, "closed," or "temporally and spatially certain" activities (Berger, 1972; Gentile, 1972; Poulton, 1957; Singer & Gerson, 1981). Such self-paced activities enable the participants to "tune out" the environment and to engage in free association while they are exercising (Berger, 1980). Rybczynski's (1991) observations about the benefits of solitary reading also apply to closed, spatially certain physical activities. Closed sport activities provide opportunity for solitude, contemplation, reflection, and withdrawal. This withdrawal can be from the world around one and withdrawal into oneself.

Glasser (1976, p. 93) supported the importance of predictability when he observed that activities that do not require great mental effort are likely to become positive addictions. Joggers and swimmers often note their appreciation of the solitude and the creativity of their thoughts when exercising, (Berger & Mackenzie, 1980; Glasser, 1976; Rimer, 1990). Noting the importance of solitude when exercising, George Sheehan, the aging running guru, commented, "Where once I found all my good thoughts on the run, I now find them in *other solitary movement* [italics added]. Given the choice I might walk rather than run—or choose to cycle over either one" (1990, p. 210).

It seems that those individuals who self-select to participate in closed, predictable physical activities enjoy the predictability of the activities. Other individuals clearly do not. Many individuals find closed sport activities boring and enjoy the unpredictability of open sports such as tennis, baseball, and basketball. There is little or no information available concerning the mental health benefits of these other types of activities (e.g., Berger, 1972). Since open physical activities usually involve competition against at least one other person, examination of acute mood effects associated with participating in open sports in both winning and losing situations is greatly needed.

Rhythmical and Repetitive Movements.
Repetitive and rhythmical movements, in addition to those that are "closed," do not require much attention. Thus the participant's mind is free to wander while exercising (Berger, 1980; Berger & Mackenzie, 1980). The repetitive monotony of these movements also might encourage introspective and/or creative thinking during participation. Clearly some exercisers enjoy these characteristics; others do not.

Practice Requirements

Intensity: Moderate.
The intensity requirement is controversial. However, moderate exercise seems most likely to be associated with enhancing mental health. Some researchers have indicated that high-intensity exercise (e.g., 80% VO_2 max) may be stress reducing (Boutcher & Landers, 1988; Dishman, 1986; Morgan & Ellickson, 1989). Others have reported that high-intensity exercise is stress producing and counterproductive to enhancing psychological well-being (Berger & Owen, 1988, in press; Steptoe & Cox, 1988). DeVries (1981) has recommended low-intensity exercise as reflected by 30% to 60% of the difference between resting and maximal heartrate values. Elderly men and women who walked for 15 minutes at a relatively low heart rate of 100 bpm significantly reduced the electrical activity in their muscles (deVries & Adams, 1972).

Results of several recent studies have indicated that moderate rather than high-intensity exercise is more effective in enhancing mood (Berger & Owen, 1988; Murphy, Fleck, Dudley, & Callister, 1990; Steptoe & Bolton, 1988; Steptoe & Cox, 1988; Thayer, 1987). Steptoe and Cox (1988) reported that 8-minute trials of high-intensity exercise (100 watts on a bicycle ergometer) was associated with acute increases in Tension and Fatigue as measured by the Profile of Mood States (McNair, Lorr, & Droppleman, 1971). Low-intensity exercise (25 watts) led to positive mood changes in Vigor and Exhilaration. Until there is additional evidence of the psychological benefits of low intensity exercise in the general population, exercise intensity probably should be in the moderate range.

Duration: At Least 20 to 30 Minutes.
Although Thayer (1987) reported that as little as 5 minutes of walking was mood elevating, it seems that 20 to 30 minutes of exercise is needed to generate some of the psychological benefits (Bahrke & Morgan, 1978; Berger & Owen, 1983, 1988; Berger, Friedmann, & Eaton, 1988; Steptoe & Bolton, 1988). Sixty minutes may result in additional psychological advantages (Carmack & Martens, 1979; Mandell, 1979). Glasser (1976) has suggested 40 to 50 minutes are needed to attain the positive addiction state in which the mind spins free. The following subjective description by Mandell (1979) of the relative benefits of exercising for 30 and 120 minutes describes the duration issue that has yet to be investigated in an experimental study:

The first thirty minutes are tough, old man. Creaks, twinges, pain, and stiffness. A counterpoint of breathless, painful self-deprecation.

Thirty minutes out, and something lifts. Legs and arms become light and rhythmic. . . . The fatigue goes away and feelings of power begin. I think I'll run twenty-five miles today. I'll double the size of the research grant request. I'll have that talk with the dean . . .

Then, sometime into the second hour comes the spooky time. Colors are bright and beautiful, water sparkles, clouds breathe, and my body, swimming, detaches from the earth. A loving contentment invades the basement of my mind, and thoughts bubble up without trails. I find the place I need to live if I'm going to live. The running literature says that if you run six miles a day for two months, you are addicted forever. I understand. A cosmic view and peace are located between six and ten miles of running. (Mandell, 1979, pp. 50–57).

There is a paradoxical relationship between exercise duration/distance and psychological benefits. Up to a certain point, exercise is mood enhancing; beyond this point, increasing exercise duration can be detrimental to psychological well-being. Morgan and colleagues (1988) illustrated the relationship in a study of chronic exercise in which training distance was purposely increased to examine possible mood decrements. Distance swum was increased abruptly from 4,000 to 9,000 meters during a 10-day period. Exercise intensity also was unusually high (approximately 94% of VO$_2$ max). As hypothesized, the highly trained collegiate swimmers reported significant *increases* in Depression, Anger, Fatigue, and Total Mood Disturbance scores. It seems that beyond a certain distance, which may vary according to fitness level, increased exercise duration is associated with negative mood states.

Frequency: Regularly Included in a Weekly Schedule. By exercising regularly, but not so frequently as to incur an overuse injury or boredom, the participant increases the likelihood of enjoyment. As she/he becomes more fit, the discomfort of the conditioning process recedes. Habitual exercisers have learned to interpret various physical sensations, to pace themselves, and to relax while exercising. Examining a possible relationship between general fitness levels and the psychological benefits of exercise. Boutcher and Landers (1988) found that a single, high-intensity (80–85% of max HR) session on a treadmill was associated with an acute reduction in state anxiety and an increase in alpha power only for those who had habitually run 30 miles or more per week for the past 2 years. Novice runners did not report any decreases in anxiety after the high-intensity exercise.

Frequent exercise enables the participant to devote less attention to the movement activities as they become more automatic. Noting the increased effort that he must now spend running, now that he is in his seventies and battling cancer, Sheehan (1990, p. 210) observed, "As I age, running is less automatic. . . . And because running is no longer automatic, it is more difficult to dissociate and get off into my right brain. I am unable to meditate quite as readily and pick up on the ideas carried in the stream of consciousness." It seems that participants need to exercise frequently to maintain a minimal fitness level to reap the psychological benefits. As North and colleagues (1990) reported in their meta-analysis of exercise and depression, as the length of an exercise program increased (in the number of weeks and sessions), the mental health benefits increased.

Another reason to exercise on a regular basis is that the mental health effects tend to last for 2 to 4 hours after exercising in normal populations (Morgan, 1987). Recent evidence suggests that the temporal duration of exercise-induced anxiety reduction and decreases in systolic blood pressure after exercise may last 2 to 3 hours longer than that of simple rest, which was short-lived (Raglin & Morgan, 1987).

CONCLUSIONS

The mood benefits that are associated with exercise are not automatic. They may be reduced, eliminated, or even reversed by choosing inappropriate types of exercise and/or by not following appropriate practice guidelines. Throughout this section, we have emphasized that it is "unlikely that all types, volumes, and settings of exercise will affect all aspects of mental health for all people" (Dishman, 1986, p. 328). The tentative physical activity taxonomy developed by Berger (1983/1984, 1986) and tested by Berger and Owen (1988, in press) still requires considerable development. It is presented here in considerable detail because it includes many key considerations in maximizing the psychological benefits. We stress that the taxonomy is not all-inclusive and does not disprove or discount the importance of other exercise considerations that might affect the mental health benefits of exercise. Readers should regard the following conclusions as somewhat speculative.

An overriding requirement for enhancing the psychological benefits of exercise is that the activity be enjoyable or pleasant. It then seems that the exercise mode should include as many of the following qualities as possible: It should promote rhythmical abdominal breathing, be noncompetitive, be a closed or predictable activity, and be characterized by rhythmical and repetitive movements. Finally the practice conditions can further maximize or detract from the psychological benefits. Based on increasing research evidence, the activity should be of moderate intensity, at least 20 to 30 minutes in duration, and of a regular frequency to promote a minimal fitness level.

INFLUENCE OF EXERCISE ON SELF-CONCEPT

Another mediating influence in the exercise–life quality relationship is self-concept. In fact, Diener (1984) reported that high self esteem is one of the strongest predictors of subjective well-being. Campbell and colleagues (1976) noted that of any variable, satisfaction with oneself showed the highest correlation with life satisfaction.

Self-concept is considered to be a central aspect of one's psyche. For instance, James (1950) argued that it is a fundamental human motive; Lecky (1945) believed self-concept to be the basic axiom of life, and McGuire and Padawer-Singer (1982) described it as the central concept in one's conscious life. Nideffer (1976) has suggested that the reason why self-concept is so important is that "we all have a strong desire to feel good about ourselves" (p. 93). A positive self-concept is a central component in psychological well-being; self-esteem is critically tied to the phenomenologically experienced quality of life.

DEFINING SELF-CONCEPT AND SELF-ESTEEM

A continuing unresolved issue in self-concept research is how best to define the terms, *self-concept* and *self-esteem*. This is a serious problem. If researchers cannot define self-concept with some assurance, they cannot be certain whether they are measuring it accurately, let alone enhancing it. Complicating the definitional problem is a debate surrounding the relationship between self-esteem and self-concept. Several researchers have implied that there are no conceptual or empirical distinctions between self-description and self-evaluation (e.g., Shavelson, Hubner, & Stanton, 1976; Shepard, 1979). Thus the terms can be employed interchangeably. Many researchers, however, continue to support the traditional approach and argue that self-concept is a larger entity that incorporates self-esteem (Coopersmith, 1967; Fleming & Courtney, 1984). The traditional view, which is supported by cross-cultural research (Watkins & Dhawan, 1989), suggests that self-concept "conventionally refers to all aspects of knowledge concerning who one is, and self-esteem refers more specifically to the evaluation of who one is" (Rhodewalt & Agustsdottir, 1986, p. 48).

SELF-CONCEPT: A STATE OR TRAIT CHARACTERISTIC?

A question that continues to receive considerable attention is whether self-concept is a malleable state characteristic or a stable trait characteristic. Many researchers have noted the stable nature of self-concept (e.g., Greenwald, 1980; O'Malley & Bachman, 1983; Swann & Read, 1981). In fact, individuals tend to seek out consistent and stable self-concepts (Swann, 1985; Swann & Hill, 1982; Swann & Read, 1981) and to reject information that is contrary to their self-concept (Greenwald & Pratkanis, 1984; Tesser & Campbell, 1983). This may be because it is important to a person's mental health for his/her self-concept to be moderately stable (Rogers, 1951). Thus it is not surprising to find fairly strong self-concept test-retest reliability correlations such as a correlation of .78 with an interval of two years (e.g., Engel, 1959).

Epstein (1973) suggests that a major reason for the stability of self-concept is that "all people to some extent, shield their significant self-concepts from being invalidated, as all people are motivated to avoid anxiety" (p. 410). Extensive psychological intervention programs have been associated with small if any changes in an individual's self-concept (Marsh, Smith, Barnes, & Butler, 1983; Rogers, 1951).

Contrasting with the view that self-concept is a trait characteristic is the possibility that it is a state characteristic. Several studies suggest that self-concept is easily changed (Gergen, 1971; Savin-Williams & Demo, 1983; Turner, 1968) and is characterized by situational specificity (Higgins & King, 1981; Snyder, 1982). For example, it has been shown that self-concept can change with casual exposure to another person (Morse & Gergen, 1970), with exposure to nationalistic advertisements (Pedic, 1989), and from social comparison processes (Rhodewalt & Comer, 1981). Some researchers suggest that self-concept may be a function of mood (Markus & Nurius, 1986; Williams, 1973). "Each identity or self-conception has a particular affect attached to it" (Markus & Nurius, 1986, p. 958). In addition, Natale and Hantas (1982) have shown that affect-induction techniques can change one's self-concept. Although self-concept is changeable, it is likely that the overall stability of self-concept overpowers significant local malleability (Markus & Kunda, 1986; Markus & Wurf, 1987; Marsh, Smith, Barnes, & Butler, 1983). Self-esteem can be affected by immediate circumstances, but it returns to usual levels when conditions again become normal (Coopersmith, 1967).

Two models can explain both the stable and malleable aspects of self-concept. Markus and her coworkers (Markus & Kunda, 1986; Markus & Nurius, 1986; Markus & Wurf, 1987) do not view self-concept as a monolithic entity, but suggest that it is a space, confederation, or system of self-conceptions. There are two dimensions in self-concept: "working self-concept" and a "core self-concept" (Markus & Kunda, 1986). The core self remains relatively stable, and the working self-concept is malleable. The working self-concept is elicited by the immediate social circumstances and is constantly active in thought and memory. It varies with the shifting of thoughts. The working self-concept is affected by immediate past, present, and future events, along with the corresponding emotions, moods, and thoughts.

A second model also includes two aspects of self: the "barometric self-concept" and the "baseline self-concept" (Rosenberg, 1986b). This model is similar to the one proposed by Markus. The barometric self-concept, which is more immediate, situationally specific, and malleable, is comparable to the working self-concept. The more stable baseline self-concept is similar to the core self. As Rosenberg (1986b) summarized:

> The barometric self-concept refers to whether the individual experiences a rapid shift and fluctuation of self-attitudes from moment to moment.... Baseline stability, in contrast, refers to the self-concept change that may take place slowly and over an extended period of time. It is possible for the barometric self-concept to fluctuate greatly, even if the baseline self-concept shows little change. (Rosenberg, 1986b, p. 126)

Although there is little research concerning the relationships between exercise and barometric (or working) self-concept, it is possible that such a model would explain some of the contradictory results reported in the exercise/self-concept research (McInman & Berger, 1992).

MEASURING SELF-CONCEPT

The use of antiquated and/or poorly validated measures is a critical problem in self-concept research (Demo, 1985;

Markus & Nurius, 1986; Wylie, 1974). The Tennessee Self-Concept Scale (TSCS; Fitts, 1964), the most widely used self-concept inventory, is not highly recommended (Marsh & Richards, 1988; Wylie, 1974). The TSCS is too broad and taps into other psychological constructs (Fleming & Courtney, 1984). The subscales also are highly intercorrelated (Gaber, 1984; McGuire & Tinsley, 1981; Roffe, 1981). Convergent validity is low (Moran, Michael, & Dembo, 1978; Wylie, 1974). Serious questions are raised about the reliability and validity of the scale due to the inconsistency of the results when using this scale (Hoffman, Davis, & Nelson, 1988). Widespread use of the TSCS has limited both the progress and quality of research. Despite its limitations, the TSCS has been used in 33% of all self-concept studies pertaining to aerobic exercise, in 80% of the weight-training studies of self-concept (McInman, 1991), and still is used extensively today.

Two new self-concept inventories with sound psychometric properties are well suited to self-concept research in the areas of exercise and sport: the Physical Self-Perception Profile (PSPP, Fox & Corbin, 1989) and the Self-Description Questionnaire series, SDQ, SDQII, and SDQIII (Marsh, 1990a, 1990b, 1990c).

The Self-Description Questionnaire series of self-concept measures consists of three inventories designed for specific age groups. The SDQ is intended for preadolescents (primary school students), the SDQII for early adolescents (high school students), and the SDQIII for late adolescents, university students, and young adults. The SDQ (Marsh, 1990a) has been carefully developed by factor analytic techniques (Marsh, Smith, & Barnes, 1983). In addition, Marsh, Smith, Barnes, and Butler (1983) have provided support for the convergent and divergent validity of the SDQ's seven dimensions. The SDQII assesses 11 dimensions of self-concept (Marsh, 1990b; Marsh, Parker, & Barnes, 1985). All 11 dimensions have been reported to be reliable and to exhibit low correlations with the other subscales (marsh, 1987; Marsh et al., 1985). The SDQIII contains 13 subscales and a 12-item summary scale (Marsh, 1990c; Marsh & O'Neill, 1984). The subscales have been clearly identified by factor analyses and have solid psychometric properties (Byrne & Shavelson, 1986; Marsh, Barnes, & Hocevar, 1985; Marsh & O'Neill, 1984).

The Physical Self-Perception Profile (PSPP) is a more specific, 30-item inventory designed to assess one's view of his/her physical self (Fox, 1990). It contains five subscales: body, strength, condition, sport, and the more global measure of physical self-worth. Each subscale includes six items. Instead of the usual Likert-type format, the PSPP is a four-choice structured alternative format designed to reduce social desirability biases. Fox and Corbin (1989) have reported acceptable psychometric properties for the PSPP.

Methodological Problems

Methodological problems in self-concept research, as in many of the exercise and mental health studies, include the following: lack of theoretical basis, inappropriate statistical procedures, vague sampling techniques, and an overgeneralization of the results. In many studies of the relationship between self-concept and exercise, the exercise programs have been poorly designed. Some have been insufficient to produce fitness improvements; others have used inappropriate physiological test measures (Sonstroem, 1981). Another methodological flaw is that the exercise instructors often are the psychological testers. This common procedure is likely to artificially heighten retest scores due to social desirability and expectancy effects that can inflate exercisers' scores in comparison to those of nonexercising controls.

Two additional methodological problems in exercise and self-concept research include the difficulty of randomly assigning subjects for treatment, and the need for appropriate placebo-control groups. Both problems are difficult to solve. Encouraging subjects to become part of an exercise study is quite difficult, and encouraging participants to comply with a random assignment procedure often is impossible. One solution has been to use a pool of individuals wishing to be part of a program, i.e., those who are "wait-listed" as controls. Wait-listed controls do not solve the problem of the experimental subjects' expectancy effects.

Use of appropriate control groups is a major concern when investigating the relationship between self-concept and exercise. Studies that do not include a control group cannot attribute an effect, even a statistically significant one, to the exercise. Ironically those researchers who employ a control group face the potential problem that such a group is an "activity in its own right, and therefore differences between the exercise and control may be as much—or more—due the effects of the control as to the exercise itself" (Gurley et al., 1984, p. 65). Control groups are important for all exercise and mental health studies and need to be as similar as possible to the experimental subjects. To eliminate potential Hawthorne effects, control subjects must be given attention equal to that of the experimental subjects (Sonstroem, 1981).

Exercise and Self-Concept Research

Cross-Sectional Studies

Many researchers investigating the relationship between self-concept and exercise have employed cross-sectional designs. Exercisers in comparison to nonexercisers have more positive global self-esteem (e.g., Albinson, 1974; Heinzelmann, & Bagley, 1970; Wheeler, 1982). Individuals who are high in measures of physical fitness tend to have higher self-concepts (Schuele, 1980; Tucker, 1987b; Young, 1985) and higher body concepts (Adame, Johnson, Cole, Matthiasson, & Abbas, 1990) than those who are less fit. Thus more positive self-esteem and higher self-concept and body concept are *associated* with high levels of physical fitness.

To present a balanced picture of the exercise and self-concept research, we emphasize that many studies have concluded that there is little or no relationship between various exercise parameters and self-concept (e.g., Balogun, 1987; Sonstroem, 1976; Teagardin, 1983). Thus it seems that "not all people regard physical fitness as important to their own self-esteem" (Sonstroem, 1981, p. 130).

Physical Strength. Physical strength and percentage of body fat are two physical characteristics that may be related to self-concept. Due to the strong emphasis society places on men being strong, it is not surprising that Tucker (1987b) reported that adolescent males who were relatively weak and lacked physical stamina had lower self-concepts. Balogun (1987) also reported a positive correlation between relative muscular strength (strength/kg of body mass) and self-esteem, although grip strength was not highly related to either body image or self-esteem. In an earlier study, Jackson (1981) found no relationship between strength and self-concept as measured by the subscales of the Tennessee Self-Concept Scale. A promising area for future research is the nature of the relationship between physical strength and self-concept, especially in women.

Percent of Body Fat. Body fat appears to be significantly related to self-concept in children, college students, and adults up to the age of 30 (Balogun, 1987; Guyot, Fairchild, & Hill, 1981; Jackson, 1981). Balogun (1987) reported that percent of body fat was negatively correlated with body image ($r = -0.47$) and global self-esteem ($r = -0.30$). Likewise Jackson (1981) reported that 7 of the 10 Tennessee Self-concept Scale dimensions were related to the percentage of body fat of female college students and that 8 of the 10 were related to the percentage of body fat in the male college students.

Longitudinal Studies

Longitudinal studies of the effects of exercise on participants' self-concepts have reported equivocal results. A recent review revealed that only 12 out of 27 (44%) of such studies produced significant improvements in self-concept (McInman, 1991). More encouraging was the observation that five of six studies assessing body-concept or body-cathexis aspects of self-concept reported significant improvements after exercise. Training program studies clearly showed changes in self-concept. Forty-four percent of the exercise training programs resulted in improved global self-concept. A substantial number of the studies (83%) were associated with enhanced body concept or body cathexis.

Length of Program. Changes in self-concept, body concept, and body cathexis seem to require a considerable amount of time. Brown, Morrow, & Livingston, (1982) suggest that exercise programs designed to improve self-concept should be conducted for at least 6 months. Their argument is that the longer the program, the more likely physiological changes will occur and be perceived, thereby promoting improvements in self-concept. There are studies, however, that contradict this general conclusion (McInman, 1991). For example, Collingwood and Willett's (1971) 3-week jogging, calisthenics, and pool activities program resulted in increased total self-concept; McCrory's (1981) 16-week individualized exercise program produced no changes in total self-concept. Methodological and procedural differences, however, may explain these discrepant results.

Frequency of Exercise. The number of days trained per week in such exercise programs appears to be an important factor in designing exercise programs to enhance self-concept (Bruya, 1977; McGowan, Jarman, & Pedersen, 1974). The reinforcement received by subjects from the experimenters nearly everyday may be a dominant factor in determining whether self-concept changes occur. Not many studies include adult participants and more information is needed concerning older individuals. However, until more data are available, it seems that the age of the subjects is not important in determining whether exercise programs change participants' self-concepts (McInman, 1991).

Type of Activity. The type of physical activity (e.g., dance, outdoor adventure training, physical education classes, and weight training) may influence whether the exercise results in changes in self-concept. Many studies of dance have either shown no change (e.g., Dugan, 1978; Jones, 1985) or a decrease in self-concept (Puretz, 1982). Although Gurley et al. (1984) report that self-concept improves in three different levels of dance instruction, the study has a number of flaws, such as the nonrandom selection of subjects.

The influence of outdoor education on self-concept has generated a considerable number of studies. Outward bound/survival courses appear to produce consistent changes in self-concept (Kinghorn, 1978; Marsh, Richards, & Barnes, 1986a, 1986b; Mathias, 1978). Relatively few studies of survival courses have reported no change in self-concept (Ewert, 1983; Willden, 1974). The lack of benefit reported by Ewert could possibly be explained in that this is one of the few studies to include adults as subjects. The lack of change reported by Willden could result from an overly short 6-day program. Unlike aerobic fitness programs, the length of an outdoor education program appears to influence changes in self-concept (McInman, 1991).

The effectiveness of physical education activities in enhancing self-concept is impressive (Anderson, 1979; Marsh & Peart, 1988; Wescott, 1981). These studies have involved a variety of subjects (e.g., second grade children, tenth grade girls, college women, university students) and activities. The type of activity has been predominantly traditional physical education activities, but some researchers have included combinations of physical education with individual movement exploration activities and boxing.

Weight training has enhanced self-concept (Brone &

Reznikoff, 1989; Brown & Harrison, 1986; Trujillo, 1983; Tucker, 1982, 1983b), body cathexis (Tucker, 1983a, 1983b, 1984, 1987a), and body image (Smith, 1977). This was true for diverse subject groups: university males (Tucker, 1982, 1983a, 1983b, 1984, 1987a), university females (Trujillo, 1983), young adult and mature women (Brown & Harrison, 1986), college football players (Brone & Reznikoff, 1989), and mentally retarded males (Smith, 1977).

One reason for the success with weight training may be the length of the courses. None have been less than 8 weeks. Except for three studies, all were conducted for 16 weeks or longer. Another advantage with these studies was the measurement of physiological parameters before and after the courses. Improvement in at least one fitness parameter was observed. While acknowledging the limitations of such research, weight training appears to be an extremely effective method for a variety of individuals in enhancing body concept and self-concept. Further research is needed to clarify the importance of gender, age, and the length of exercise programs in moderating the influence of exercise on self-concept.

CONCLUSIONS

A conclusive summary of the relationship between exercise and self-concept is premature because of the poor methodology that characterizes many studies. Nevertheless some statements can be made with relative confidence. Cross-sectional studies relating various aspects of physical fitness to self-concept have revealed mixed results. Some studies have shown significant relationships; however, the majority have revealed little or no correlations. Physical strength and percentage of body fat are two fitness dimensions that have meaningful correlations with self-concept. Considering the strong social push for individuals to be lean rather than fat in many Western societies, this is hardly surprising.

Studies examining the relationship between exercise intervention programs and self-concept are more informative than are cross-sectional studies. McInman (1991) reports that of the studies he reviewed, 44 percent of the intervention studies demonstrated improvements in *global self-concept* after participation in aerobic programs. There is an even greater likelihood (83%, or five out of six studies) of changes in *body concept* than in general self-concept. The small number of studies measuring body concept emphasizes the tentativeness of this last assertion. Nevertheless the apparently strong relationship between improved body concept and exercise is an appealing hypothesis and suggests the need for additional cross-sectional research.

Similar to the literature relating exercise to mood enhancement, specific characteristics of the exercise program seem to influence the efficiency of programs designed to improve self-concept. Considerable research still is needed to clarify exercise prescription guidelines for enhancing self-concept. The *frequency* of exercise sessions (e.g., the number of sessions per week) appears to have an important impact on the likelihood of enhancing self-concept. The *length* of the total program (e.g., the number of weeks it is held) does not appear to be an important factor except for survival/outward-bound courses and weight-training programs. The *type* of exercise is an important consideration. Few studies support the influence of aerobic dance on self-concept, but such results may reflect a variety of experimental design problems. Physical education classes, weight training, and outward bound/survival courses appear to be excellent exercise modes. These three exercise considerations for program design certainly are not exhaustive and illustrate the need for continued research using the newer self-concept and physical self-concept measures.

EXERCISE AS THE FOUNTAIN OF YOUTH

The influence of exercise on the aging process directly affects the quality, if not the quantity, of life. The discussion that follows has been adapted from "Exercise, Aging and Psychological Well-Being" (Berger & Hecht, 1989) and from "The Role of Physical Activity in the Life Quality of Older Adults" (Berger, 1989).

Research data from a variety of sources suggests that exercise becomes increasingly important for maintaining and improving the quality of life as one becomes older. Too often the word *aging* in Western society is associated with a host of undesirable images: a slow, progressive diminishing of physical abilities, undesirable physical changes in appearance, increasingly poor health, frailty, forgetfulness, and eventually death. A considerable portion of this physical decline can be reduced and delayed by exercising. The axiom "Use it or lose it" is particularly relevant for older individuals in regard to physical prowess.

The pessimistic view of aging is being replaced, albeit slowly, with a new view. Old age is beginning to be regarded as a time for exciting new freedoms, personal exploration, psychological growth, and the general enjoyment of life. The life quality of the older population is improving! Although the complex factors underlying this change have economic, social, and psychological bases, increased exercise is playing a major role in improving older individuals' physical, mental, and psychological functioning.

A new conceptualization of the aging process is greatly needed in view of the evolving shift in the age structure of the population in many industrialized countries. The absolute length of life may be relatively fixed. However, many individuals are living closer to this apparent limit, and the population is aging (Fries, 1980; Jette & Branch, 1981). In the United States, the average life expectancy in 1900 was 47 years; in 1980, it had jumped to 73 years (Fries, 1980). The elderly population in the United States grows 2% per year, double the rate for the population as a whole (Pear, 1991). In addition, the average age of the elderly is increasing (Kart, Metress, & Metress, 1988, p. 5; Spirduso, 1989). The elimination of premature death, decreases in contagious disease such as smallpox, and the postponement of chronic illness have greatly increased life expectancy. Refer to Figure 34–1 for a visual representation of the survival curve.

Age 65 marks the point at which a person is considered to be old or elderly. However, the age range of individuals over the age of 65 is so large that the elderly are often separated into categories. People between the ages of 65 and 75 years comprise the "young-old." Those older than 75 years of age are the "old-old" (Schaie & Geiwitz, 1982). The large increase in the portion of the population that is old, the changing role models, and the greater visibility of old people have attracted the attention of researchers and the general public, who wish to explore the role of exercise in delaying the "normal" aging process.

Interrelationships between exercise and aging are complex, and it is almost impossible to distinguish between decreases in physical abilities resulting from accumulated years of physical inactivity (hypokinetic disease) and those resulting from the aging process itself (Bortz, 1982; Spirduso, 1986). As noted by Smith (1981), "Some of the current research suggests that *50% of the decline frequently attributed to physiological aging is, in reality, disuse atrophy* [italics added] resulting from inactivity in an industrialized world" (p. 16). People in their fifties, and even in their forties, begin to notice a lack of physical endurance, decreased strength, sagging muscles, and increased body fat. A vicious cycle, which is depicted in Figure 34–2, has begun. As a result of the noticeable physical changes, individuals incorporate a feeling of "being old" in their self-concepts and thus reduce their levels of physical activity for fear of injury, heart attack, or social criticism. The decreased physical activity results in even greater deficiency in physical ability, and the cycle of decreased abilities demonstrated in Figure 34–2 continues.

THE EXERCISE–AGING CYCLE

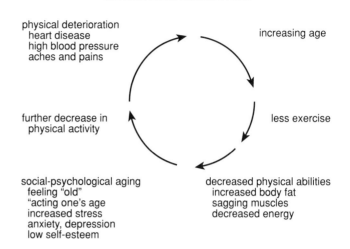

FIGURE 34–2. The exercise-aging cycle.
From Berger & Hecht, 1989. Reprinted by permission.

The importance of exercise in the aging process is highlighted by the results of a recent study of 16,936 Harvard alumni between the ages of 35 and 74 years (Paffenbarger, Hyde, Wing, & Hsieh, 1986). The results (which were adjusted for differences in such factors as cigarette use, body fat, and blood pressure) indicate that men who expend 2,000 or more kcal per week might gain 2 years of added life in comparison to the life expectancy of less active men. As noted by Paffenbarger (1988), the extra years most likely would be "added to the vigorous mainstream of his life experience, not spent confined in a wheelchair or rest home as an aged invalid" (p. 436).

Participation in exercise on a regular basis has major implications for slowing age-related physical deterioration: cardiorespiratory decline (Shephard, 1989), osteoporosis or skeletal decalcification (Smith & Gilligan, 1989), and decreases in muscle fiber size, number, and metabolic rate (Bouchard & Despres, 1989). See Berger and Hecht (1989) and Spirduso and Eckert (1989) for more complete discussion of physiological changes associated with aging. As indicated by the impressive data in Figure 34–3, joggers who are 60 years of age have the same VO_2 max as 20-year-old inactive men. These improvements in physical capacity have major implications for the quality of life. Habitual exercise aids the reversal of the self-perpetuating cycle described in Figure 34–2. Increased physical ability leads to greater physical activity, which in turn increases social interaction, enhances physical and general self-efficacy, and further increases physical capacity.

To break out of the cycle of diminished exercise as described in Figure 34–2, two fallacies must be corrected: (1) a person needs to exercise less as he/she ages and (2) exercise is hazardous to the health of the elderly by either precipitating a heart attack or by exacerbating preexisting medical conditions (Berger & Hecht, 1989). These fallacies

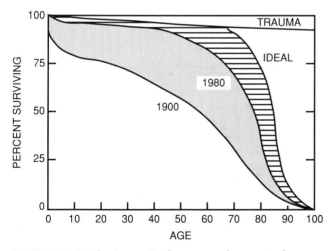

FIGURE 34–1. The increasingly rectangular survival curve. In the United States, approximately 80 percent (stippled area) of the difference between the 1900 curve and the ideal curve was eliminated by 1980. Trauma is now the dominant cause of death in early life.
From Fries, 1980, p. 131. Reprinted by permission.

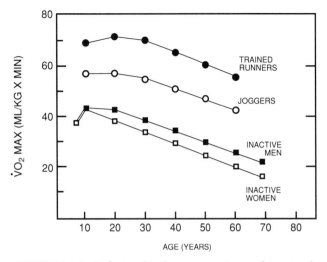

FIGURE 34-3. Relationship between aging and maximal oxygen uptake (VO₂max) in inactive women and men, joggers, and trained runners. These cross-sectional data from Costill (1986, p.173) suggest that after the age of 20, VO₂max declines at a steady rate.

Reprinted by permission.

illustrate the age grading of exercise that is prevalent in persons of all ages (e.g., Ostrow, Keener, & Perry, 1986–1987; Ostrow & Dzewaltowski, 1986) and prevent extensive exercise participation by many of the elderly.

AGE STRATIFICATION: A MAJOR DETRIMENT TO STAYING "YOUNG"

The terms *age stratification, age grading,* and *ageism* refer to prejudicial and discriminatory views about aging that are especially pronounced in the context of exercise. As described by Kart and colleagues (1988),

Age stratification is a conceptual framework for viewing societal processes and changes that affect aging and the state of being old. . . . Members of the age strata differ in the social roles they are expected to play and in the rights and privileges accorded them by society. This is similarly the case for members of different social classes. (p. 71)

Ageism results in diminished self-expectancies as old people follow social scripts and messages to "act one's age." As noted by Ostrow (1983), diminished self-expectancies and the messages that one should be less competitive and expect less from a competitive outcome lead many older individuals to disengage from sport and physical activity. Research on age grading among preschool children (Ostrow et al., 1986-1987), nursing students (Ostrow, Jones, & Spiker, 1981), and older adults themselves (Ostrow & Dzewaltowski, 1986) support the pervasiveness of ageism in reference to exercise. The age grading of exercise by older adults is a major barrier to increasing the number of elderly who exercise. This age grading also

is a detriment to many of the elderly joining their age-group compatriots in testing their limits in masters level competition at community, national, and international levels. The time has come to remove these barriers to enhancing the quality of life.

MAJOR SIGNPOSTS OF PSYCHOLOGICAL HEALTH IN THE ELDERLY

Despite the stereotype that older people become crotchety and cantankerous, psychological well-being does not deteriorate as one ages. Anxiety decreases markedly, and there is evidence that depression is slightly less common in individuals over 50 years of age than in those between the ages of 19 and 49 (Lin, Ensel, & Dean, 1986). Nevertheless depression is still the most common psychiatric complaint (Gatz, Smyer, & Lawton, 1980; Rosenfeld, 1978). Depression in the elderly is difficult to treat because of the substantial reasons for feeling depressed: loss of friends, spouses, and relatives, financial problems, and failing health. Although the causes of depression in the elderly may differ from those in younger populations, there is little relationship between age and the outcome of psychotherapy and/or medication in treating depression (Rosenfeld, 1978). Similar to the results in younger populations, exercise has been an effective treatment mode for older, depressed individuals (Bennett, Carmack, & Gardner, 1982; Martinsen, Medhus, & Sandvik, 1985; Uson & Larrosa, 1982; Valliant & Asu, 1985).

Supporting the importance of psychosocial factors in the aging process, Pelletier (1981) elaborated on characteristics that are common in centenarian communities such as those in the Caucasus Mountains of the Soviet Union and the Ecuadorian Andes. "Physical activity is . . . perhaps the most important factor in the longevity and optimum health exhibited in these centenarian communities" (Pelletier, 1981, p. 299). Specific psychological benefits of exercise for older adults, as reviewed in the following sections, include influences on personality, life satisfaction, self-esteem, and stress indices.

PSYCHOLOGICAL BENEFITS OF EXERCISE FOR OLDER ADULTS

Surprisingly few studies in the exercise and mental health literature have focused on older exercisers, and many of the ones that have been reported are "dated." However, there is evidence that the elderly who exercise report a variety of psychological benefits (e.g., deVries & Adams, 1972; Hogan & Santomier, 1984; Olson, 1975; Sidney & Shephard, 1976). Since methodological problems plague many of the early exercise and mental health studies of the elderly, the results should be interpreted cautiously. Clearly a considerable amount of additional research is needed in this area. Shephard and Sidney (1979) have described some of the experimental concerns that result in "false positive" psychological results: favorable attitudes toward exercise prior to initiation of the study, a desire to please investigators, medical and personal attention received during training, and attitudes reflected by program advertising and exercise leaders. Despite these methodological problems, research on a variety of mental health topics supports a strong relationship between exercise and psychological well-being.

Desirable Personality Characteristics

Older individuals who are intelligent, imaginative, and self-sufficient (common characteristics of self-selected exercisers) may be more able and motivated to include exercise as part of their daily routine than those who are not. Studies agree that older exercisers have more desirable personality characteristics than do nonexercisers (Hartung & Farge, 1977; Young & Ismail, 1977, 1978). However, this probably is due to a selection process. Since personality by definition is stable, it is unlikely to change as a result of exercise.

In a study of adult men (mean age of 43 years), Young and Ismail (1977) compared regular and nonregular exercisers during a 4-year interval. Three groups of participants included those who were: (1) regularly active before and after 1971 (Group 1), (2) inactive before 1971, participated in a semester-long exercise program, and remained active during the subsequent 3 1/2 years (Group 2), and (3) inactive before 1971, participated in the fitness program, and became inactive again (Group 3).

The two active groups improved in physical fitness during the 4-year period. Group 1, the most active group, was significantly more confident and emotionally secure as measured at the beginning of the study than was the most sedentary group. The initial differences remained in evidence at the end of the 4 years. It seems that people who seek exercise may differ in personality from those who do not.

Young and Ismail (1978) also investigated the relationship between fitness and personality in men between the ages of 21 and 61 years. The men initially were separated into high- and low-fitness groups. Then all subjects participated in a 4-month exercise program of jogging, calisthenics, and recreational activities. The high-fitness group was more unconventional, imaginative, adventurous, and trustful than the low-fitness group when measured *at the beginning* and *at the end* of the 4-month program. Again highly fit individuals reported more positive personality characteristics than those in the low-fitness group. It is important to note that the initial differences were not affected by a 4-month exercise program. However, the 16 Personality Factor Questionnaire (16 PF; Cattell, Eber, & Tatsuoka, 1970) may not be an appropriate inventory to measure personality change since it measures personality traits.

Exercise and Life Satisfaction

The correlation between life satisfaction and physical activity is impressively high. Older individuals who are physically active tend to be in better health, report more stamina, report greater ability to cope with stress and tension, and have more positive attitudes toward work (Heinzelmann & Bagley, 1970; Schaie & Geiwitz, 1982). Life satisfaction, in contrast to personality, does seem to change as a result of exercise. Men ($N = 381$) between the ages of 45 and 59 years were randomly assigned to an exercise group that met three times a week for 18 months, or to a control group (Heinzelmann & Bagley, 1970). Compared to the control group, the exercisers reported significantly greater changes in

1. Enhanced personal health, as evidenced by increased stamina, less stress, and more positive feelings about weight reduction.
2. Stronger exercise habits, which included increased walking and stair use and decreased use of the automobile.
3. increased work performance and more positive attitudes toward work.

Happiness. Happiness, the focus of a study by Rosenberg (1986a), would seem to be an important factor in overall life satisfaction. Happiness in older adults ($N = 468$) has been significantly related to the number of memberships in voluntary associations, regardless of type. The correlation between membership specifically in sport groups and happiness, however, was not significant. Older people separated into age groups between 55 and 64 years of age, 65 to 74 years of age, and 75+ years who held memberships in a sports groups were no happier than those with memberships in nonsport organizations. Although it is not clear exactly what sports associations were included, this finding was not surprising. Formal membership in sports organizations, especially at 65 years of age, may be quite different from being physically active.

Avowed happiness in older adults and its relationship to exercise participation, rather than membership in sport groups, is an important area of needed research. Research findings regarding the relationship between life satisfaction and exercise differing in intensity, duration, and frequency are nonexistent at the present time.

Life Quality. A high level of life quality, or state of excellence, has been related to extent of physical activity in masters age-group athletes and in college students (Morris & Husman, 1978; Morris et al., 1982). Women masters competitors who were at least 40 years of age and nationally ranked reported significantly higher life quality as measured by the Pflaum Life Quality Inventory (Pflaum, 1973) than did a normative group of nonrunning adults (Morris et al., 1982). College students who participated in an endurance-conditioning program also reported a significant improvement in life quality (Morris & Husman, 1978). Although there are no data concerning life quality and exercise in the elderly, it seems that life quality in this group would improve as exercisers noted and enjoyed the psychophysiological changes. A study at Brooklyn College is under way at the present time to test this possibility (Berger, Michielli, & Dunbar, in preparation).

Self-Efficacy. Exercise also may be associated with life satisfaction by increasing self-efficacy (Hogan & Santomier, 1984; Oldridge, 1988). Self-efficacy includes two cognitive processes: (1) the belief that one is capable of performing a specific task and (2) the individual's confidence in his/her competence. Individuals who are high in physical self-efficacy feel competent and thus attempt and persist in a wider variety of physical activities than those who are low in self-efficacy. Many older individuals underestimate their physical capabilities because of the widespread ageism in American society (Hogan & Santomier, 1984).

After a 5-week swimming program, adults who were 60 years of age or older ($N = 32$) reported significantly larger changes in swimming self-efficacy than did a nonswimming group of controls ($N = 33$) (Hogan & Santomier, 1984). In addition, 78% of the swimmers reported generalized feelings of self-efficacy and competence. As one swimmer reported, "I am able to do things more easily now—swimming and chores" (Hogan & Santomier, 1984, p. 295).

Self-Concept, Self-Esteem, and Body Image. Exercise also might increase life satisfaction in the elderly by enhancing the participant's body image, self-concept, and self-esteem. (See Berger [1984b], McInman [1991], and Crews's chapter in this book [25] for other discussions of self-concept, self-esteem, and body image and their relationship to physical activity.)

In one of the few studies of body image and exercise in an older population, residents in a nursing home participated in slow stretching, upright exercises, and rhythmic breathing exercises twice a week for 8 weeks (Olson, 1975). Their body image scores significantly improved after the 8-week light exercise program. Improvements in body image also were reported by healthy volunteers (M = 66 years) following an endurance program that met for 1-hour sessions, 4 days a week for 14 weeks (Sidney & Shephard, 1976). Supporting the likelihood that the changes in body image were associated with the exercise program, only those who attended the sessions regularly and exercised at a high intensity (pulse rates of 140 to 150) reported enhanced body image.

Exercise and Decreased Stress

As noted by Berger (1986), psychological stress occurs within an individual and is in response to events that frighten, irritate, excite, or confuse. Stress is a pervasive health problem and results from an individual's negative appraisal of her/his ability to cope. Too much stress is associated with increased illness and mortality (Levy, 1983; Maddi, Bartone, & Puccetti, 1987). Stress also detracts from the quality of life. Since the elderly are as prone to stress as are younger members of the population, it is important that they are familiar with one or more stress reduction activi-

ties. Typical stressors that older individuals encounter include adjusting to retirement, chronic illnesses, death of a spouse and/or friends, inflation and the economic woes of living on a fixed income, and adopting to decreased physical abilities such as visual and auditory acuity.

Exercise can be an ideal stress reduction technique for older adults because of its psychological and physical benefits. As reviewed earlier, exercise is associated with decreased anxiety, tension, depression, anger, fatigue, and confusion, and with enhanced vigor. Regular exercise reduces several physical stress symptoms: elevated heart rate, blood pressure, obesity, and general muscular tension (deVries, 1981; Sharkey, 1990). Although much of the research has focused on young adult populations, there is little reason to assume that the psychological benefits of exercise are age related. If the benefits are *physiologically based* (e.g., decreased systolic blood pressure, increased body temperature, practiced stress response, improved appearance, and increased strength and endurance), the benefits should accrue to the elderly as well as to the young. If the benefits of exercise are *primarily psychological* (e.g., social interaction, feelings of accomplishment, and "time-out" from worries), they also should benefit the old as well as the young. Rather than extrapolate the results of studies employing young people as subjects, however, further research is needed to directly investigate the psychological benefits of exercise for senior citizens.

In comparison to other stress reduction techniques, exercise has specific advantages for older individuals. The side effects of drugs are avoided, and there are a variety of physical benefits: enhanced cardiovascular endurance, increased energy, weight reduction, and an improved appearance. Unlike biofeedback, exercise requires no expensive equipment and can be easily scheduled into one's day. Specific stress symptoms that are reduced with exercise in the elderly include decreases in muscle tension, anxiety, and depression.

Decreased Muscular Tension and Anxiety. DeVries and Adams (1972) investigated the tranquilizing effects of exercise on six men and four women who ranged in age from 52 to 70 years. Since the participants were recruited by advertisements for individuals who had sleep difficulties, they were generally nervous, tense, irritable, restless, and under stress. The 10 participants who scored in the 87th percentile for anxiety on the Taylor Manifest Anxiety Scale (Taylor, 1953) served as their own controls in a double-blind design. They were tested on three occasions in each of the following treatments:

1. 15 minutes of walking at a heart rate of 100 beats per minute
2. 15 minutes of walking at a heart rate of 120 beats per minute
3. 400 mg of meprobamate, a common tranquilizer
4. a placebo condition
5. a control situation in which subjects read (deVries & Adams, 1972)

Stress was measured by electromyographic recordings from the biceps when the participants were at rest and when they performed a "mental stress" task. Results indicated that muscle tension decreased significantly after the subjects walked at the heart rate of 100 beats per minute, but not at the rate of 120 beats. Neither the placebo or control groups reported any changes. The tranquilizer meprobamate did not produce a relaxation effect. However, the 400-mg dosage was very low and may have been ineffective (deVries & Adams, 1972).

In another study of exercise and stress reduction, Long (1983) compared the effectiveness of a walk-jog program with stress inoculation training and a wait-list control group. The male and female volunteers ($N = 73$) ranged in age from 24 to 65 years. Mean age was 40 years. As in the deVries study, the volunteers felt they were unusually stressed and needed help to reduce their stress levels. Participants in the exercise and stress inoculation programs met for 90 minutes in supervised sessions once a week for 10 weeks. They also practiced their specific technique independently twice a week. Since this study is one of the few to focus on exercise and the reduction of psychological stress in an adult sample, the results are particularly interesting. Participants in both the walk-jog and stress inoculation programs reported significantly less tension, state anxiety, and trait anxiety at the end of the 20 weeks (see Figure 34–4). Since fitness improvement was not related to the benefits, Long (1983) concluded that the decrease in psychological stress seemed to be psychologically based.

Decreases in Depression. Several studies of older adults indicate that exercise is associated with decreases in depression (Bennett et al., 1982; Martinsen et al., 1985; Uson & Larrosa, 1982; Valliant & Asu, 1985). These findings are particularly important, because as noted earlier, depression is the major mental health problem of the elderly (Gatz et al., 1980; Rosenfeld, 1978).

A Spanish study examined the effectiveness of exercise in adults between the ages of 60 and 80 (Uson & Larrosa, 1982). Among those who exercised ($n = 30$) for an hour twice a week for 9 months, 70% reported reductions in depression. The exercise program was rather strenuous for the 60–80-year age group. It included warm-up exercises, corrective gymnastic exercises, a 10-minute slow run, and psychomotor activities designed to improve coordination. In contrast to the exercisers, 40% of an age-matched control group ($n = 30$), who belonged to clubs for retired persons, experienced increases in depression. In addition, the exercisers reported fewer visits to the doctor than did the controls during the same 9-month period. Clinically depressed individuals ($N = 38$) who were residents of a nursing home or were participants at a senior community center reported significant decreases in depression after only 8 weeks of exercise (Bennett et al., 1982). The subjects ranged in age from 50 to 98 years and exercised for 45 minutes twice a week. The relatively mild exercise program included only balance and flexibility exercises.

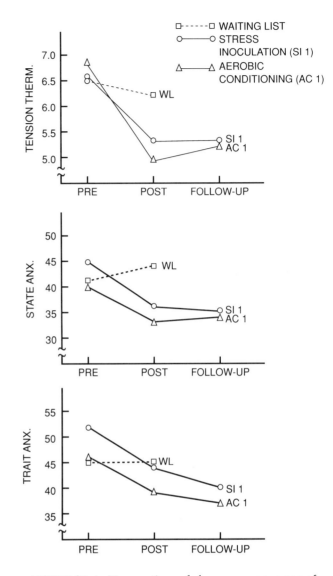

FIGURE 34–4. Mean ratings of change on measures of stress before and after treatment, and at 3-month follow-up.

From Long, 1983, p. 180. Reprinted by permission.

CONCLUSIONS: THE PSYCHOLOGICAL BENEFITS OF EXERCISE FOR OLDER POPULATIONS

The relationship between exercise and quality of life in older individuals has many facets, and all of the contributing factors have not yet been identified. Although the literature involving older populations has major design limitations, existing studies suggest that the psychological benefits of exercise in the elderly are comparable to those in younger populations. As reviewed in this section, exercise has been associated with (a) desirable personality characteristics; (b) enhanced self-efficacy, life-satisfaction, happiness, and life quality; and (c) decreases in tension, anxiety, and depression. As discussed throughout this chapter, not all types of exercise are mood enhancing. In fact, competitive and/or exhausting exercise may be stress producing. Until more data are available, exercisers of all ages should follow the exercise guidelines as suggested in the first part of this chapter.

Kleinman (1989) has expressed a wonderful goal for all of us: that the personal experience of physical activity becomes increasingly qualitative (and less goal-oriented) as we age. "It should provide and enable us to reach a level of maturity, self-knowledge, and enlightenment to which the young can only aspire" (Kleinman, 1989, p. 64).

PEAK MOMENTS IN EXERCISE AND SPORT

Another way that exercise can add to the quality of life is by providing a good opportunity to experience a peak moment. (The discussion of peak moments that follows is adapted from "Peak Moments in Sport: A Literature Review" by A. D. McInman and J. R. Grove, 1991.) Although peak moments cannot be planned or anticipated, Diener (1984) noted in his review of subjective well-being that individuals are happier when they participate in interesting, involving activities. "Whereas telic theories place the locus of happiness in certain-end states, activity theories maintain that happiness is a by-product of human activity. For example, the activity of climbing a mountain might bring greater happiness than reaching the summit" (p. 564).

"Peak moments" include a variety of states or events such as peak experience, flow, peak performance, and the exercise high. Peak moments in exercise and sport are a special bonus of physical activity. Peak moments include "flow," "peak performance," and "peak experiences" and greatly enhance the quality of life (Csikszentmihalyi, 1991). Eventually individuals who exercise regularly are likely to experience some form of a peak moment (Snyder & Spreitzer, 1983). Such an event may be characterized by utter contentment, high elation, outstanding performances, fun, or a variety of other feelings and/or behaviors that add greatly to the quality of life. The fullness and depth of such experiences can be tremendously profound (Park, 1973; Walchuk & Orlick, 1980). This is mirrored in the subjective and introspective statements made by runners who have rich psychological experiences that they achieve by running (Fixx, 1977).

When describing their peak moments in sport and physical activity, individuals report a great deal of similarity in emotional and performance states. This is impressive, considering that peak moments occur in many types of exercise. Of the various emotions and behaviors that are associated with peak moments, six are most prevalent: absorption, detachment, ecstasy, power, altered perceptions of time, and a sense of unity. Not all of the above, however, occur with each peak moment.

Absorption

Peak moments occur most often when the individual is fully immersed in the activity (Csikszentmihalyi, 1975; Murphy, 1977; Ravizza, 1977, 1984; Williams, 1986). The individual is totally channeled into the activity, and his/her existence is for only the present moment (Egger, 1981). It is a matter of being "fully into" what he or she is doing. Such absorption occurs only with intense concentration. Murphy (1977) and Williams (1986) describe this as a "cocoon of concentration." Due to this intense concentration, everything appears vividly clear. What is not clear to researchers, however, is the optimal breadth of attention during such peak moments. Breadth of attention may be activity-specific as there is research support for wide (Maslow, 1968), narrow (Ravizza, 1977), and both wide and narrow attentional styles (Walchuk & Orlick, 1980).

Detachment

During peak moments, individuals tend not to be conscious of their performance (Austin & Pargman, 1981; Egger, 1981; Gallwey, 1982; Murphy & White, 1978; Ravizza, 1984). They act spontaneously with freedom, ease, and a relaxed state of mind. There is awareness, but not awareness of awareness. Participants are usually detached from their surroundings, themselves, and the results of their performance. Often individuals report noticing complete silence, even when they are performing in a noisy arena. Such experiences, however, do not occur if the individual is fearing failure or danger (Ravizza, 1977, 1984). There cannot be critical self-feedback, evaluation, or questioning. Instead there is a sense of control and no concern about the possibility of lack of control.

Ecstasy

A feeling of euphoria often accompanies such moments (Beisser, 1977; Privette, 1983). In fact, this is a major reason why some individuals continue to participate in exercise well into their adult years. Such intrinsic motivation is reinforced by the few rare ecstatic moments when participants lose themselves in something outside of themselves. "I felt like I was radiating in every direction, not with pressure but with joy. I felt a tremendous amount of heat. I was totally filled up with joy like a helium balloon, and it was fantastic" (Ravizza, 1975, p. 399).

Power

Sometimes individuals perceive themselves as having an abnormally high level of power during such moments (Murphy & White, 1978; Privette, 1981b; Ravizza, 1977, 1984). Power can be in the form of physical energy, or in a broader sense, a power of communication between other individuals. Usually, however, it is a feeling that the participants can do no wrong. They may feel that everything they attempt will go well, and that if need be, they could do anything. For instance, such power is expressed forcefully by a woman runner: "I felt very powerful. I guess you could call it in control . . . It feels good . . . I felt as though I could run forever . . . I could jump over the top of buildings" (Berger & Mackenzie, 1980, p. 8).

Altered Perceptions of Time

Due to the intense concentration that individuals have during peak moments, it is not surprising that many people reveal perceptions of altered time. This can be either a quickening, or a slowing of time (Murphy, 1977; Murphy & White, 1978; Ravizza, 1977, 1984). The episode may pass by in what appears to be an unbelievably short period of time. Or, as is more usually the case, a slowing down of time occurs. In such circumstances every detail of the activity is fully absorbed and seen as crystal clear. For instance, some baseball batters have reported that they have seen the seams on the ball when pitched at them at high speed during such moments. Furthermore, motor racing drivers often remark that they sense time slowing down sufficiently for them to be able to execute moves that they would not be able to otherwise (Murphy, 1977). These time changes often are associated with altered spatial perception. For example, bull's eyes on dart boards, ten-pins, and tennis balls often appear larger than usual.

Sense of Unity

Peak moments often are characterized by a feeling of oneness with the environment, as if everything is related. The participant is not separate from the environment, but blends into it, like swimming down a river in a current. Thus there is a common sense of unity (Cerutty, 1967; Furlong, 1976; Park, 1973; Thomas, 1973; Ravizza, 1977). In fact, this integration of the individual with the experience also involves the intertwining of the physical and mental. This harmony of the physical and mental produces a very special feeling of a unified whole; a blending of all.

THEORIES AND MODELS OF PEAK MOMENTS

A number of models have been developed to describe and categorize peak moments in a wide variety of activities. Landsman's (1969) "positive experiences model" is a three-category topology of self, external world, and interpersonal relationships. More recently Panzarella (1980) proposed a "peak experiences model" developed from both content and factor analyses of art-and music-based peak experiences of individuals in art galleries and concert locations. The model includes four major categories: renewal ecstasy, motor-sensory ecstasy, fusion-emotional ecstasy, and withdrawal ecstasy. It also includes three stages: (1) cognitive response and loss of self, (2) climax with motor responses, and (3) a subsiding resulting in an emotional and stimulus-specific response. Thorne's (1963) more detailed model includes both positive and negative experiences. The six-category classification system (sensual, emotional, cognitive, conative, self-actualizing, and climax experiences) has been found to be reliable by a number of other researchers (Allen, Haupt, & Jones, 1964; Ebersole, 1972).

Privette and Bundrick (1987) designed a detailed model that includes peak moments. Their "feeling and performance model" emphasizes the orthogonal continua of feeling and performance that are depicted in Figure 34–5. Peak experiences are situated in the extreme upper right quadrant of the figure. The feeling continuum ranges from an extreme of misery at one end, through worry and boredom, to neutrality, then to enjoyment and joy, and finally to ecstasy at the other extreme. The performance continuum begins at one extreme with total failure, moves through inadequacy and inefficiency to neutrality, effectiveness, and high performance, and then to the other extreme of personal best. The order of these items in the two continua have been validated by Privette (1985a).

The premise underlying Privette's model is that any experience can be classified on the two continua if the participant's feelings and behaviors are known. For example, the top left corner (ecstatic and total failure) is characteristic of a person who is performing very poorly in an extremely important activity, but who is enjoying his/her poor performance. The bottom left corner characterized by total failure and misery would characterize an extremely bad experience in which the individual also felt terrible. The bottom right corner (personal best and miserable) would describe someone who achieved his/her very best, but at the same time felt absolutely miserable about doing so. The center of the figure is neutral and typifies everyday experience. Everyday experiences generally are somewhere between enjoyment and boredom as well as between inefficiency and effectiveness.

The top right quadrant of Figure 34–5 contains peak moments. When performance is in this quadrant, the individual performs well and expresses positive emotion. Peak performance is at the upper extreme end of the performance continuum. From the center of the figure to the upper right hand corner is an area which contains what Csikszentmihalyi (1975) coined as "flow." Flow has fairly equal components of feeling and performance states. The intensity may be minor in what Csikszentmihalyi terms a "micro flow." The extreme end of the feeling continuum is the area of peak experiences. Peak experiences may or may not be accompanied by peak performance.

PEAK MOMENTS: PEAK PERFORMANCE, FLOW, THE RUNNER'S HIGH, AND PEAK EXPERIENCE

Peak Performance

The most obvious characteristic of a peak performance is that the individual exceeds what she/he normally would in this situation. Although it is not the best performance that

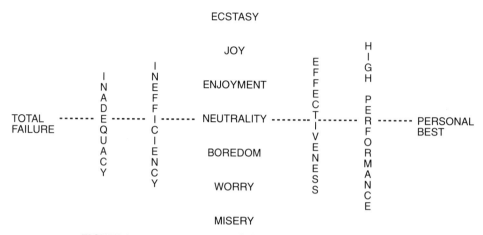

FIGURE 34–5. Experience model of feeling and performance.
From Privette & I. Brundrick, 1987. Reprinted by permission.

anybody has ever achieved, it is rather exceptional behavior by the individual in a specific situation. Privette and Landsman (1983) define peak performance as "behavior that goes beyond the level at which a person normally functions" (p. 195). Thus a peak performance can occur in a wide variety of activities (Privette & Bundrick, 1987). It can occur spontaneously, in response to a placebo, via biofeedback, or as a result of hypnosis (Privette, 1983).

There are five characteristics that describe peak performances: (a) clear focus; (b) high level of performance; (c) initial fascination with the task; (d) spontaneity; and (e) strong sense of self (Privette, 1965, 1981a, 1982a, 1982b, 1983; Privette & Bundrick, 1987; Privette & Landsman, 1983). Additional elements that may characterize peak performances include awareness of power, fulfillment, temporality, and insufficiency of words to describe the moment (Privette, 1982b, 1983; Privette & Bundrick, 1987). Interestingly participation with others may actually hinder the likelihood of a peak performance occurring as they may disrupt the individual's concentration (Privette & Landsman, 1983).

Flow

Flow has an intrinsically enjoyable nature, is fun, and people seek it out (Csikszentmihalyi, 1975, 1991). As recently defined by Csikszentmihalyi (1991), flow is a state of optimal experience, a state "in which people are so involved in an activity that nothing else seems to matter; the experience itself is so enjoyable that people will do it even at great cost, for the sheer sake of doing it" (p. 4). This optimal state of inner experience occurs when skills match the opportunities for action and when "psychic energy—or attention—is invested in realistic goals" (Csikszentmihalyi, 1991, p. 8). Enjoyment is a central element in the flow state. Specific conditions that increase enjoyment, flow, and thus the quality of life include:

1. a challenging activity that requires skill
2. the merging of action and awareness
3. clear goals and feedback
4. concentration on the task at hand
5. the possibility of control
6. loss of self-consciousness
7. the transformation of time (Csikszentmihalyi, 1991, pp. 49–66)

Not all activities are conducive to flow. When questioning university students ($N = 123$) who were between 20 and 50 years of age, Privette and Bundrick (1987) found that sport was the major source of flow experiences. Not one of these subjects mentioned having a flow experience at school, work, in relationships, death, sickness, or in connection with religious events. These results, however, may reflect the particular sample in the study. Csikszentmihalyi (1991) reinforces the likelihood of flow in sport and exercise in his book, *Flow, The Psychology of Optimal Experience: Steps Toward Enhancing the Quality of Life*. However, he also includes separate chapters on the promotion of flow during thought, work, solitude, and interactions with other people.

An essential aspect of flow is a delicate balance between a person's skill level and the task demands (Csikszentmihalyi, 1991). If an individual's abilities exceed the demands of the task, the task is too easy and he/she will be bored. If a person's ability is inadequate to meet the demands of the task, he/she will experience anxiety. The pleasurable experience of flow occurs in a task that demands intense concentration and when there is a matching of personal ability and task demands.

The Runner's High (Exercise High)

The runner's high is a well-known phenomenon that meets many of the characteristics of peak moments. Terms employed to describe this experience include euphoria, unusual strength and power, gracefulness, spirituality, sudden realization of one's potential, glimpsing perfection, moving without effort, and spinning out. (We would like to express our sincere appreciation to Michael L. Sachs, friend and colleague, who wrote a draft of this section on "The Runner's High [Exercise High].") Sachs (1984) has proposed a preliminary definition of the runner's high as "A euphoric sensation experienced during running, usually unexpected, in which the runner feels a heightened sense of well-being, enhanced appreciation of nature, and transcendence of barriers of time and space" (p. 274).

These descriptions of the runner's high are quite similar to those for peak experiences, as discussed in the next portion of this chapter. Thus it is not clear that the runner's or exercise high is a distinct type of peak moment. It may be an often-reported, specialized example of a peak experience. The runner's abilities appear to match the task demands of running, and there is enjoyment, relaxation, feelings of control, and loss of ego. The exercise high usually involves a high level of joy, loss of self, spontaneity, feelings of peak power, and transcendence of time and space. The preceeding lend support to categorizing the runner's high as one type of peak experience.

Dramatically different percentages of runners (from 9% to 78%) report experiencing a runner's high (Sachs, 1984). Despite the huge difference in percentages, however, it is clear that many runners do have such experiences. Among runners who report that they have had a runner's high, the frequency of such an experience varies from rarely (only several times during their running careers) to an average of 29.4% of their runs (Sachs, 1980).

In reviewing descriptions of the exercise high, one is struck by the diversity of these descriptions expressed by the runners and other exercise participants. Some descriptions are congruent with those of peak experiences; others are more characteristic of what one might term "an enhanced sense of well-being." Members of a group of runners may say that they each have experienced the runner's high. However, closer examination of their personal descriptions suggest widely different experiences, ranging from a generalized sense of well-being to peak experiences. When studying the runner's high and similar "highs" experienced by swimmers, cyclists, and other sport participants, one must be aware of both the individual participant's and the researcher's descriptions or interpretations of the phenomenon. The potential difference in definitions may suggest that many individuals who consider themselves as experiencing the exercise high (and this must be acknowledged and hopefully encouraged as a potential motivator to continue exercising) may not be considered as such if a stricter research definition is considered. We suggest that both the runners' and the researchers' interpretations and/or definitions must be considered when working in this area.

Peak Experience

Feelings of bliss, great joy, and/or illumination are some of the stronger emotional characteristics of peak experiences. Such episodes produce a strong sense of self and

freedom from outer restrictions. Maslow (1970) considered peak experiences to be an individual's most exciting, fulfilling, and meaningful moments in life. He also suggested that they are associated with fully functioning individuals (self-actualizers) and that such individuals tend to report more numerous peak experiences than less fully developed individuals.

Peak experiences are very powerful and occur unexpectedly. Not everyone has had one. The percentage of people who have had such an experience is unknown. In one study of university students ($N = 214$), only three students were unaware of having had a peak experience (Allen, Haupt, & Jones, 1964). Thus peak experiences would seem to be a common occurrence. However, Keutzer (1978) reported that 61% of a national sample had not had an experience that "made them feel as though they were very close to a powerful, spiritual force that seemed to lift them out of themselves." Maslow (1970), who developed the concept and has conducted the most research into peak experiences, initially believed that such experiences were very rare. In a sample of 3,000 college students, he found only one self-actualizing person (Maslow, 1970). Maslow later changed his viewpoint and suggested that the number of people reporting peak experiences reflected the type of questions that had been asked (Panzarella, 1980).

Distinguishing Between Peak Performance, Flow, and Peak Experience

Peak Peak experiences are characterized by intense joy. Flow is an intrinsically enjoyable matching of ability and task difficulty, and peak performance is superior functioning (Privette, 1983). As summarized in Table 34–2, peak performance is outstanding behavior with high levels of performance and a clear focus of attention (Privette, 1983). Flow is fun, enjoyable, and results in feelings of control (Csikszentmihalyi, 1991; Privette, 1983). Peak experience involves fulfillment, significance, and/or spirituality, joy, or cosmic and absolute ecstasy (Privette & Bundrick, 1987; Privette & Sherry, 1986).

FACILITATING PEAK PERFORMANCE, FLOW, THE RUNNER'S HIGH, AND PEAK EXPERIENCE

Although little is known, some research suggests three techniques that may facilitate these states: (a) the centering of attention solely on the activity, (b) the use of routines, and (c) the removal of conscious thought (Csikszentmihalyi, 1991; Gallwey, 1982). Of these three techniques, the most important is the centering of attention (Gallwey, 1982). By doing so, extraneous stimuli are prevented from interfering with the important elements of the task.

When centering his/her focus of attention, the individual must not try too hard to concentrate. One should not consciously think about the activity because doing so radically limits the probability of a peak moment (Gallwey,

TABLE 34–2. Major Characteristics of Peak Moments in Sport*

Peak experiences	Flow	Peak performance
High level of joy (ecstasy)	Fun	Superior behavior
Transpersonal & mystical	Enjoyable	High level of performance
Passive	Loss of ego	Clear focus (absorption)
Feeling of unity & fusion	Playful	Strong sense of self
Loss of self	Feeling of control	Fulfillment
Spontaneous	Lost time & space	Not playful
Feeling of peak power	Intrinsic motivation	Intended action but spontaneous performance

*Adapted from Privette (1983) and from McInman & Grove, 1991.

1982). Concentration should not be on eliciting a peak moment. If a person sets out with a focus on a peak moment in mind, it is unlikely to occur. Peak performance, flow, the runner's high, and peak experiences are spontaneous. Thus thinking about them, or planning them, discourages their occurrence. The focus should be on the experience of playing (Nideffer, 1976).

If a person has considerable experience in an activity, then she/he is likely to have formed routines of set behavior. These routines may be so conditioned and/or elaborate that they become automatic. For example, the practice throws, shirt pulling, and ball bouncing that tennis players perform before each serve are excellent examples of such routines. Routines are highly desirable as they allow the individual to focus on the matter at hand and not focus on unnecessary stimuli.

FUTURE RESEARCH NEEDS

Little research into peak moments, especially with regard to exercise, has been undertaken. Peak moments are elusive in nature, difficult to define, and nearly impossible to measure in research studies. Murphy and White (1978) noted the difficulty when they identified over 60 different kinds of sensations. Such definitional problems are exacerbated when researchers change their own definitions over time. For instance, Privette (1965, 1968) initially used the term "transcendent functioning," but later changed it to peak performance (Privette, 1982b, 1983, 1985a, 1985b).

Attempting to remove some of the questioning of the validity of such episodes, researchers have opted more recently for quantitative research methodologies. However, these attempts to improve validity have shifted the emphasis away from what participation in such actually feels like for the participant (Kirk, 1986). Regardless of the methodology employed, the major difficulty lies in determining what questions to ask (McClain & Andrews, 1969; Margoshes & Litt, 1966; Murphy, 1977; Panzarella, 1980). Peak performance, flow, runner's high, and peak experience research is particularly prone to biases due to differences in the education levels of the participants. For instance, Wuthnow (1978) found that 65% of "high peakers" (individuals who experienced a peak experience that had a lasting influence on their life) attended college.

Only 45% of the "nonpeakers" (individuals who had not had a peak experience, or had not had a peak experience that had changed their life) attended college. The percentage of people who have experienced a peak moment is unknown, and the frequency with which peak moments are experienced also is unclear. Some suggest they are a once-in-a-lifetime occurrence (Panzarella, 1980). Others suggest they can be experienced quite regularly (Ravizza, 1984).

Many unanswered questions about peak moments in exercise and sport remain for the enterprising researcher. Some of the more obvious questions are as follows: What are the meanings and consequences of peak moments? Does the likelihood of peak experiences differ across cultures? Do certain personality characteristics increase the occurrence of peak moments? Do older individuals have fewer peak experiences, as Maslow suggests? Do males and females differ in the types and numbers of peak moments? Do flow, the runner's high, peak performance, and peak moments occur more often in various types of sports and exercise?

EXERCISE ADHERENCE

As indicated earlier in this chapter, exercise enhances the quality of life in many ways. Exercise increases psychological well-being throughout the lifespan, enhances self-concept, and provides opportunities for experiencing peak moments. These benefits, however, are realized by a relatively small percentage of the population—those individuals who exercise frequently. Only about 37% of the adult American population follows a regular exercise routine despite the desirable and highly publicized benefits (Harris & Associates, Inc., 1978). A major problem with exercise programs, whether they are designed for the general public, the elderly, psychiatric patients, the obese, or coronary rehabilitation patients is the participant's nonadherence (Bruce, Frederick, Bruce, & Fisher, 1976; Oldridge, 1979; Wanzel, 1978). Regardless of the benefits, exercise is of little value unless people participate on a regular, life-long basis.

Exercise adherence is difficult to define, and researchers differ greatly in their operationalizations of the term (Andrew et al., 1981; O'Connell & Price, 1982; Shaw, 1981).

In addition, the variability in percentage of subjects dropping out of exercise programs is astonishingly large. Martin and Dubbert (1982) reported that *attrition* was between 30% and 70%. Dishman and colleagues (1980) suggested that most *adherence* percentages fall between 40% and 65%. Regardless of the actual dropout rate, virtually all studies show a similar relapse curve, with a rapid decrease in attendance during the initial weeks and then a leveling off of attrition (Blackwall, 1976; Carmody, Senner, Malinov, & Matarazzo, 1980; Dishman, 1982).

Measuring exercise adherence is extremely difficult because of definitional problems. For instance, if an individual had not exercised during 8 consecutive sessions in a 2-week period, he/she would be considered a dropout by Oldridge et al. (1983). Wanzel (1978), however, would not consider the individual a dropout if he/she had been exercising in the preceding weeks, but had simply missed out these 2 weeks. Compounding the measurement dilemma are individuals who drop out of a formal exercise program, but who continue to exercise on their own or enter other exercise programs. Exercise outside the formal program often is not taken into consideration when measuring adherence (Durbeck et al., 1972). One way to circumvent this methodological problem is to use frequency of exercise attendance, rather than exercise adherence, as a dependent measure. Frequency of exercise is simpler to quantify, incurs less definitional debate, but has its own difficulties in regard to measurement.

A variety of factors can increase exercise adherence and discriminate between exercise adherers and nonadherers. Factors reviewed in this section include: (a) situational factors, (b) exercise factors, (c) biological factors, (d) personal factors, (e) social factors, and (f) psychological factors. Interested readers should see the chapter "Methods for Changing Health Behaviors" in the new *Guidelines for Exercise Testing and Prescription* (American College of Sports Medicine, 1991).

SITUATIONAL FACTORS AFFECTING EXERCISE ADHERENCE

Convenience of location is an important influence on exercise adherence (Dishman, 1984). Individuals are not willing to travel far to exercise (Andrew & Parker, 1979; Dishman, 1982; Wankel, 1985) and usually are unaware of adherence problems that large geographical distances from the fitness facility create (Dishman, 1984). The size of the exercise class also affects exercise adherence. Adherence tends to be higher in small than in large groups (Andrew et al., 1981; Massie & Shephard, 1971). However, most individuals usually do not enjoy exercising by themselves. Heinzelmann and Bagley (1970) found that 90% of their 195 male participants preferred to exercise with a group or at least one other person, rather than by themselves.

The social environment also can increase or decrease exercise adherence (Hanson, 1976; Knapp, Gutmann, Squires, & Pollock, 1983; McCready & Long, 1985). Initially participants who maintain their participation in an exercise program do not consider the program's social aspects as important (Knapp et al., 1983; McCready & Long, 1985; Sidney & Shephard, 1976). Health and fitness benefits are the major reasons for entering an exercise program (Heinzelmann & Bagley, 1970; Knapp et al., 1983; Sidney & Shephard, 1976). However, if they remain in a program for some time, exercisers almost invariably state social aspects as a predominant reason for staying in the program (Knapp et al., 1983; Sidney & Shephard, 1976; Wankel, 1985).

Although a high-quality exercise staff does not seem to be a major adherence advantage, a poor quality staff can be a detriment (Andrew et al., 1981; Pratt, Linn, Carmichael, & Webb, 1977). Gettman, Pollock, and Ward (1983) reported no important adherence differences between supervised and unsupervised exercise programs. In another study, poor reception by staff was a major reason cited by postmyocardial infarction patients for dropping out of an exercise program (Andrew et al., 1981). In addition, participants who noted a lack of supervised attention by staff were twice as likely to drop out than those who perceived a high level of attention (Andrew et al., 1981).

EXERCISE TRAINING FACTORS AFFECTING ADHERENCE

There seems to be little relationship between intensity of exercise and adherence—if there are no complications such as medical restrictions, poor motivation, or injuries (Oldridge et al., 1978; Oldridge et al., 1983). However, on a phenomenological level, it seems that many sedentary people do not exercise because they consider exercise to be unpleasant or too much work. Few if any studies have directly examined the exercise intensity-adherence relationship. This would seem to be an important area for future efforts.

Duration of an exercise session does have a significant effect on adherence. The longer the duration, the larger the percentage of dropouts (Andrew et al., 1981; Gillum & Barsky, 1974). Some inactive individuals who start to exercise do so with insufficient caution and tend to overexercise (Lee & Owen, 1985; Pollock et al., 1977; Stalonas, Johnson, & Christ, 1978). As many as 40% of the middle-aged males ($n = 54$) had troublesome complications with a running, strength-training, and ball-training program (Mann et al., 1969). Much of the high injury rate is due to the overexercising of enthusiastic participants. Exercise instructors also can greatly influence the dropout rate due to injury by designing programs appropriate for the participants' current fitness levels. Pollock et al. (1977) reported that injuries increase in direct proportion to the duration of training sessions. That is:

Injury occurred in 22%, 24%, and 54% of the 15, 30, and 45-minute duration groups and in 0%, 12%, and 39% of the 1-, 3-, and 5-day/week groups, respectively. Attrition resulting from injury occurred in 0%, 0%, and 17% and 0%, 4%, and 6% of the same respective groups. (Pollock et al., 1977, p.31)

Some form of injury, or at least minor pain, is likely for previously sedentary individuals who start exercising. Nevertheless much can be done to minimize initial injuries. The overwhelming evidence suggests that the initial 4 to 6 weeks of an exercise program should be relatively short in duration and of light intensity (American College of Sports Medicine, 1991; Stalonas, Johnson, & Christ, 1978) to facilitate adherence. Refer to "Principles of Exercise Prescription" (American College of Sports Medicine, 1991) for additional discussion of exercise mode, duration, intensity, frequency, and progression considerations.

Individualizing exercise programs is extremely important (American College of Sports Medicine, 1991). Nonadherence is associated with a lack of attention to individuals' needs. More than half of an initial group of 36 men and women aged between 44 and 65, dropped out of a 6-month calisthenics program, and only a third of those who completed the program conformed with instructions (Ballantyne et al., 1978). The control group who walked for 20 minutes, however, enjoyed its exercise prescriptions so much that group members performed more than prescribed and consequently destroyed the validity of the group as a true control. An individual's level of aerobic fitness at initiation of an exercise program has little effect on subsequent adherence (Bruce et al., 1976; Dishman & Gettman, 1980; Durbeck et al., 1972). Nevertheless, fitness levels of individuals once they have been participating in a program may be a factor. For example in a 5-year study of 362 male exercisers, Dishman (1981) observed that those who were aerobically more fit were more likely to discontinue. Perhaps the physically fit individuals may feel that they could obtain better fitness gains by spending their time elsewhere.

BIOLOGICAL FACTORS AFFECTING ADHERENCE

Numerous researchers have concluded that there are no age (Andrew et al., 1981; Bernacki, Baun, Williams, & Landgreen, 1983) or gender differences with regard to exercise adherers and dropouts (Andrew et al., 1981; Bernacki et al., 1983; Godin & Shephard, 1986). Some investigators have reported that men who are symptomatic of coronary heart disease are more likely to drop out of exercise programs than are asymptomatic individuals (Dishman & Gettman, 1980; Haynes, Taylor, & Sackett, 1979). However, Dishman (1981) found that coronary heart patients tend to adhere longer. The difference may be one of perception and difficulty of exercise due to symptoms. Individuals who perceive they are at cardiovascular risk and who also find that exercising is not too painful may be likely to adhere longer so as to alleviate coronary heart disease and risk symptoms (Dishman, 1981). Those who do not believe they have a health problem, or those who are having cardiovascular problems due to the exercise, are more likely to drop out. Thus it is not surprising that individuals who know that they have high cholesterol levels are more likely to adhere (Dion, Rogowski, & Oldridge, 1988) than those who have low cholesterol levels.

PERSONAL FACTORS AFFECTING ADHERENCE

A common reason for nonadherence given by dropouts is that they were not satisfied with the program, or that they lost interest in it (Andrew & Parker, 1979; Oldridge & Spencer, 1983; Wankel, 1985). Further supporting the importance of enjoyment, adherers report a greater increase in positive reactions to their program than that reported by dropouts (Raugh & Wall, 1987; Oldridge & Spencer, 1983; Wankel, 1985). In fact, 21% of the variance between dropouts and adherers was explained in Oldridge and Spencer's (1983) study by the perception of direct benefits from exercising.

Lack of time is another major reason individuals cite for dropping out of exercise programs (Andrew et al., 1981; Lee & Owen, 1985; Riddle, 1980). (Lack of time could be considered either a personal or a situational variable.) Many dropouts find it difficult to attend exercise sessions on time and to participate in them to the conclusion of each session. Dropouts report that they find the scheduled class sessions inconvenient, believe that the exercise requires too much time, and perceive that the programs interfere with their work. For some people, these are real concerns. However, for others, these may simply be rationalizations and acceptable excuses (Gettman, 1988; Wanzel, 1978).

Individuals who choose to join an exercise program on their own volition are more likely to adhere than are individuals who have been referred by their doctor (Dishman & Gettman, 1980). A little over one-third of the people referred by their physician dropped out of an exercise program (Oldridge, 1979). Nevertheless, the dropout rate for the physician-referred group was only moderate compared to a group recruited solely via hospital records. Those individuals recruited via hospital records had a nonadherence rate of 52 percent.

Surprisingly there is only one study (Bruce et al., 1976) in which it was reported that individuals dropped out of an exercise program for financial reasons. This may be because programs in many studies have been free to participants, required a minimal payment, or provided payment to the exercisers to participate. Exercise adherence, however, may be related to socioeconomic status. Blue-collar workers are predisposed to dropping out of exercise programs (Oldridge, 1979; Oldridge & Spencer, 1983; Oldridge et al., 1983). The blue-collar workers in Oldridge et al.'s (1983) study were 1.7 times as likely as white-collar workers to drop out of a cardiac rehabilitation program. Oldridge and colleagues (1983) suggested that the blue-collar workers may have had a poorer understanding both of the disease and the rehabilitation process. Education level itself may not influence the likelihood of dropping out of a cardiac rehabilitation program. Instead, Andrew et al. (1981) suggested a more likely reason for the predominance of blue-collar workers dropping out. Individuals whose occupations could be classified as heavy were 1.55 times more likely to drop out than those whose occupations were sedentary. Individuals who have already been physically active at work may be too tired to exercise and predisposed to dropping out of an exercise program (Andrew et al., 1981).

Smoking and obesity are also personal factors that are associated with poor exercise adherence. Smokers consistently drop out of exercise programs more readily than nonsmokers (McCready & Long, 1985; Nye & Poulsen, 1974; Oldridge & Spencer, 1983). The relationship is so strong, in fact, that the smokers in one study were 2.5 times more likely to be dropouts than were the nonsmokers (Oldridge et al., 1983). Dropouts also are more likely than adherers to have higher percentages of body fat (Baun, Bernacki, Riggins, & Landgreen, 1983; Dishman, 1981; Dishman & Gettman, 1980; Dishman, Ickes, & Morgan, 1980; Dishman & Ickes, 1981). Apparently the exercise is difficult and they choose not to continue.

SOCIAL FACTORS AFFECTING ADHERENCE

Adults who have spouse support (Andrew & Parker, 1979; Andrew et al., 1981; McCready & Long, 1985) and/or family support (Andrew & Parker, 1979; Haynes, 1976; Kavanagh et al., 1979) are far more likely to adhere than are those who do not have the support of significant others. The influence of social factors is astonishingly high. Of 143 men who began an exercise program, 80% of those whose wives had positive attitudes toward the program adhered (Heinzelmann & Bagley, 1970). Among the men who dropped out, or who had a poor adherence pattern, only 20% were married to women who had a positive attitude toward the program. It appears that spouse support is more important than family support (Andrew et al., 1981). Family support is important for children's exercise adherence. Children are likely to adhere in exercise or sport regardless of their mothers' current involvement in exercise (Smoll et al., 1979). However, children's intention to exercise has been shown to be related to their mothers' intention to exercise, and their fathers' current physical activity habits (Godin & Shephard, 1986).

PSYCHOLOGICAL FACTORS AFFECTING ADHERENCE

Attitudes toward exercise do not seem to be related to adherence. Individuals with positive attitudes toward exercise are no more likely to adhere to an exercise program than are individuals with a less positive attitude (Dishman & Gettman, 1980; McCready & Long 1985). In addition, attraction to physical activity and perceived values about physical activity are also not related to adherence (Dishman & Gettman, 1980).

Most personality attributes are likewise not related to adherence (Dishman & Gettman, 1980; Howard, Cunningham, & Rechnitzer, 1987; McCready & Long, 1985). However, there is a tendency for individuals with Type A characteristics to drop out of adult coronary rehabilitation programs (Oldridge et al., 1978). Group-dependent individuals are more likely to remain in exercise programs than

are group-independent individuals (Brunner, 1969), and a number of studies have shown a weak relationship between locus of control and exercise adherence (Bonds, 1980; Moore, 1981; O'Connell & Price, 1982). The personality factor of self-motivation does appear to predict attrition from an exercise program with some degree of success (e.g., Burton & Martens, 1986; Dishman, 1984; Dishman & Gettman, 1980; Dishman & Ickes, 1981; Dishman, Ickes, & Morgan, 1980). In Dishman and Ickes's (1981) study, the percentage of adherers with low self-motivation was only 40.6%, compared with 78.1% for highly self-motivated individuals. Throughout the exercise program, self-motivation scores of the dropouts were significantly lower than that of the adherers.

CONCLUSION

Haynes, Taylor, and Sackett (1979) reviewed 853 articles related to compliance in health care and mentioned an additional 568 articles. Their overall conclusion was that the effects of the majority of programs are only temporary because participants do not adhere. Facilitating exercise adherence is critical to encouraging large segments of the world population to reap the demonstrated psychological and physical benefits of exercise. Practical adherence guidelines are: (a) including the exercisers in decision making, (b) adopting flexible exercise standards, (c) setting reasonable and obtainable goals, (d) providing moderate exercise prescriptions, (e) establishing regularity of workouts, (f) deemphasizing competition, (g) providing feedback, (h) including significant others, (i) cultivating personal relationships, (j) using small groups, and (k) ensuring optimal leader qualities.

Future research should examine factors that facilitate long-term exercise participation in specific populations: particular age segments of the general population (e.g., children, teenagers, adults, and the elderly), men and women, psychiatric populations, the overweight and obese, and patients with coronary heart disease. Why are specific groups of individuals exercising, and why do they keep returning for more? Are there similarities and differences across the various groups? At the present time it seems that the most successful exercise adherence interventions are population-specific. Until additional information is available, programs should be organized around specific individuals, rather than the individuals organized around the exercise program.

CONCLUDING OBSERVATIONS

This chapter focused on only five of a multitude of ways that exercise integrally affects the quality of life. Life quality emphasizes a state of excellence and/or an enhanced sense of well-being. Although the study of exercise and health psychology is still in its infancy, the research evidence reviewed in this chapter suggests that habitual exercise is related to mental health. The multiple effects of a myriad of interacting factors challenge researchers to continue the effort to understand the somatopsychic and/or psychosomatic relationship.

Frank, a medical sociologist at the University of Calgary, comments in his recent book *At the Will of the Body* (1991) that serious illness "leaves no aspect of life untouched. . . . Your relationships, your work, your sense of who you are and who you might become, your sense of what life is and ought to be—these all change, and the change is terrifying" (p. 6). The major premise of our chapter is that the same can be said for exercise. Exercise, like illness, directly affects the body and thus the core of who we are. To paraphrase Frank (1991), exercise leaves no aspect of life untouched: relationships, work, sense of who you are and who you might become, and your sense of what life is and ought to be. Although self-attuned exercisers know this on a phenomenological level, researchers need to continue the quest for empirical data to more fully describe, examine, and predict the exercise-body-mind relationships.

In summary the converging research evidence reviewed in this chapter supports the following observations:

1. *Exercise is associated with psychological well-being in members of the "normal" population.* These benefits tend to be associated more with some modes and conditions of exercise than with others. We emphasize that considerable research is needed to investigate exercise guidelines to maximize the changes in anxiety, stress, depression, and anger that have been reported by many exercisers.

2. *Although there is considerable conflicting evidence, habitual exercisers tend to have more positive self-concepts and higher self-esteem and body cathexis than sedentary individuals.* Relatively little is known in this area concerning (a) a possible cause-and-effect relationship and (b) the types of exercise and program characteristics that are most conducive to an enhanced self-concept.

3. *The psychological and physiologic benefits associated with exercise throughout one's lifespan support the increasing importance of exercise as one ages.* Research evidence supports the age-retarding benefits of exercise that facilitate psychological well-being, continued personal development, self-exploration, and enjoyment of a myriad of activities in old age.

4. *Peak moments in exercise greatly enrich the quality and meaning of life.* Such moments, which have been described as "peak experiences," "flow," the "runner's high," and "peak performances," tend to occur often in exercise. Peak moments cannot be planned or predicted at the present time. Thus research on these elusive phenomena continues to challenge the experimenter's resourcefulness.

5. *Exercise is associated with the preceding four sets of benefits only if the individual exercises on a regular basis.* Adherence is a critical consideration when using exercise to enhance life quality. The current research on exercise adherence emphasizes a critical need for additional research on this important psycho-social-physical factor.

References

Adame, D. D., Johnson, T. C., Cole, S. P., Matthiasson, H., & Abbas, M. A. (1990). Physical fitness in relation to amount of physical exercise, body image, and locus of control among college men and women. *Perceptual and Motor Skills, 70,* 1347–1350.

Albinson, J. G. (1974). Life style of physically active and physically inactive college males. *International Journal of Sports Psychology, 5,* 93–101.

Allen, R. M., Haupt, T. D., & Jones, W. (1964). An analysis of peak experiences reported by college students. *Journal of Clinical Psychology, 20,* 207–212.

American College of Sports Medicine. (1991). *Guidelines for exercise testing and prescription* (4th ed.). Philadelphia: Lea & Febiger.

Anderson, J. L. (1979). A comparison of the effects of physical education classes in boxing and gymnastics on the self concepts of college freshman. *Completed Research in Health, Physical Education, Recreation, and Dance, 21,* Abstract No. 109.

Andrew, G. M., Oldridge, N. B., Parker, J. O., Cunningham, D. A., Rechnitzer, P. A., Jones, N. L., Buck, C., Kavanagh, T., Shephard, R. J., Sutton, J. R., & McDonald, W. (1981). Reasons for dropout from exercise programs in post-coronary patients. *Medicine and Science in Sports and Exercise, 13,* 164–168.

Andrew, G. M., & Parker, J. O. (1979). Factors related to dropout of post–myocardial infarction patients from exercise programs. *Medicine and Science in Sports and Exercise, 11,* 376–378.

Andrews, F. M., & Withey, S. B. (1976). *Social indicators of well-being: America's perception of life quality.* New York: Plenum.

Austin, J. S., & Pargman, D. (1981). The inner game approach to performance and skill acquisition. *Motor Skills: Theory into Practice, 5,* 3–12.

Bahrke, M. S., & Morgan, W. P. (1978). Anxiety reduction following exercise and meditation. *Cognitive Therapy and Research, 2,* 323–333.

Ballantyne, D., Clark, A., Dyker, G. S., Gillis, C. R., Hawthorne, V. M., Henry, D. A., Hole, D. S., Murdoch, R. M., Semple, T., & Stewart, G. M. (1978). Prescribing exercise for the healthy assessment of compliance and effects on plasma lipids and lipoproteins. *Health Bulletin,* July, 169–176.

Balogun, J. A. (1987). The interrelationships between measures of physical fitness and self-concept. *Journal of Human Movement Studies, 13,* 255–265.

Baun, W. B., Bernacki, E. J., Riggins, N., & Landgreen, M. L. (1983). Influence of biologic variables on exercise adherence. *Medicine and Science in Sport and Exercise, 15,* 120–121.

Beisser, A. (1977). *The madness in sports.* Bowie, MD: Charles Press.

Bennett, J., Carmack, M. A., & Gardner, V. J. (1982). The effect of a program of physical exercise on depression in older adults. *Physical Educator, 39,* 21–24.

Benson, H. (1975). *The relaxation response.* New York: Avon.

Berger, B. G. (1972). Relationships between the environmental factors of temporal-spatial uncertainty, probability of physical harm, and nature of competition and selected personality characteristics of athletes. *Dissertation Abstracts International, 33,* 1014A. (University Microfilms No. 72-23689, 373).

Berger, B. G. (1980). The meaning of regular jogging: A phenomenological approach. In R. Cox (Ed.), *American Alliance for Health, Physical Education, and Recreation Research Consortium Symposium Papers* (Vol. 2, Book 2). Washington, DC: American Alliance for Health, Physical Education, Recreation, and Dance.

Berger, B. G. (1983/1984). Stress reduction through exercise: The mind-body connection. *Motor Skills: Theory into Practice, 7,* 31–46.

Berger, B. G. (1984a). Running away from anxiety and depression: A female as well as male race. In M. L. Sachs & G. W. Buffone (Eds.), *Running as therapy: An integrated approach* (pp. 138–171). Lincoln, NE: University of Nebraska Press.

Berger, B. G. (1984b). Running toward psychological well-being: Special considerations for the female client. In M. L. Sachs & G. Buffone (Eds.), *Running as therapy: An integrated approach* (pp. 172–197). Lincoln, NE: University of Nebraska Press.

Berger, B. G. (1986). Use of jogging and swimming as stress reduction techniques. In J. H. Humphrey (Ed.), *Current selected research in human stress* (Vol. 1) (pp. 169–190). New York: AMS Press.

Berger, B. G. (1989). The role of physical activity in the life quality of older adults. In W. W. Spirduso & H. M. Eckert (Eds.), *Physical Activity and Aging: American Academy of Physical Education Papers, No. 22* (pp. 42–59). Champaign, IL: Human Kinetics.

Berger, B. G., Friedmann, E., & Eaton, M. (1988). Comparison of jogging, the relaxation response, and group interaction for stress reduction. *Journal of Sport and Exercise Psychology, 10,* 431–447.

Berger, B. G., Grove, J. R., & Prapavessis, H. (1992). *Relationship of training distance and individual characteristics to mood alteration in young competitive swimmers.* Manuscript submitted for publication.

Berger B. G., & Hecht, L. (1989). Exercise, aging, and psychological well-being: The mind-body question. In A. C. Ostrow (Ed.), *Aging and motor behavior* (pp. 117–157). Indianapolis, IN: Benchmark Press.

Berger, B. G., & Mackenzie, M. M. (1980). A case study of a woman jogger: A psychodynamic analysis. *Journal of Sport Behavior, 3,* 3–16.

Berger, B. G., Michielli, D., & Dunbar, C. (in preparation). *Life quality and exercise in the elderly.*

Berger, B. G., & Owen, D. R. (1983). Mood alteration with swimming—swimmers really do "feel better." *Psychosomatic Medicine, 45,* 425–433.

Berger, B. G., & Owen, D. R. (1986). Mood alteration with swimming: A re-evaluation. In L. Vander Velden & J. H. Humphrey (Eds.), *Current selected research in the psychology and sociology of sport* (Vol. 1, pp. 97–114). New York: AMS Press.

Berger, B. G., & Owen, D. R. (1987). Anxiety reduction with swimming: Relationships between exercise and state, trait, and somatic anxiety. *International Journal of Sport Psychology, 18,* 286–302.

Berger, B. G., & Owen, D. R. (1988). Stress reduction and mood enhancement in four exercise modes: Swimming, body conditioning, Hatha yoga, and fencing. *Research Quarterly for Exercise and Sport, 59,* 148–159.

Berger, B. G., & Owen, D. R. (1992). *Mood alteration in yoga and swimming: Aerobic exercise not necessary.* Manuscript submitted for publication.

Berger, B. G., & Owen, D. R. (in press). Preliminary analysis of a causal relationship between swimming and stress reduction: Intense exercise may negate the effects. *International Journal of Sport Psychology.*

Bernacki, E. J., Baun, W. B., Williams, K. S., & Landgreen, M. A. (1983). Effects of age, sex, and time on exercise adherence level changes. *Medicine and Science in Sport and Exercise, 15,* 118.

Bernstein, D. A., & Borkovec, T. D. (1973). *Progressive relaxation training: A manual for the helping professions.* Champaign, IL: Research Press.

Blackwall, B. (1976). Treatment adherence. *British Journal of Psychiatry, 129,* 513–531.

Blumenthal, J. A., Emery, C. F., Walsh, M. A., Cox, D. R., Kuhn, C. M., Williams, R. B., & Williams, R. S. (1988). Exercise training in healthy Type A middle-aged men: Effects on behavioral and cardiovascular responses. *Psychosomatic Medicine, 50,* 418–433.

Bonds, A. G. (1980). The relationship between self-concept and locus of control and patterns of eating, exercise, and social participation in older adults. *Dissertation Abstracts International, 41,* 8021947A.

Bortz, W. M. (1982). Disuse and aging. *Journal of the American Medical Association, 248,* 1203–1208.

Bosscher, R. J. (1991). *Running therapie bij depressie* Unpublished Doctoral dissertation. Amsterdam: Vrije Universiteit, Amsterdam.

Bouchard, C., & Despres, J. P. (1989). Variation in fat distribution with age and health implications. In W. W. Spirduso & H. M. Eckert (Eds.), *Physical activity and aging: American Academy of Physical Education papers, No. 22* (pp. 78–106). Champaign, IL: Human Kinetics Books.

Boutcher, S. H., & Landers, D. M. (1988). The effects of vigorous exercise on anxiety, heart rate, and alpha activity of runners and nonrunners. *Psychophysiology, 25,* 696–702.

Bradburn, N. M. (1969). *The structure of psychological well-being.* Chicago: Aldine.

Brone, R., & Reznikoff, M. (1989). Strength gains, locus of control, and self-description of college football players. *Perceptual and Motor Skills, 69,* 483–493.

Brown, E. Y., Morrow, J. R., Jr., & Livingston, S. M. (1982). Self-concept changes in women as a result of training. *Journal of Sport Psychology, 4,* 354–363.

Brown, J. D., & Siegel, J. M. (1988). Exercise as a buffer of life stress: A prospective study of adolescent health. *Health Psychology, 7,* 341–353.

Brown, R. D., & Harrison, J. M. (1986). The effects of a strength training program on the strength and self-concept of two female age groups. *Research Quarterly for Exercise and Sport, 57,* 315–320.

Bruce, E. H., Frederick, R., Bruce, R. A., & Fisher, L. D. (1976). Comparison of active participants and dropouts in CAPRI cardiopulmonary rehabilitation programs. *American Journal of Cardiology, 37,* 53–60.

Brunner, B. C. (1969). Personality and motivating factors influencing adult participation in vigorous physical activity. *Research Quarterly for Exercise and Sport, 40,* 464–469.

Bruya, L. D. (1977). Effect of selected movement skills on positive self-concept. *Perceptual and Motor Skills, 45,* 252–254.

Burton, D., & Martens, R. (1986). Pinned by their own goals: An exploratory investigation into why kids drop out of wrestling, *Journal of Sport Psychology, 8,* 183–197.

Byrne, B. M., & Shavelson, R. J. (1986). On the structure of adolescent self-concept. *Journal of Educational Psychology, 78,* 474–481.

Campbell, A., Converse, P. E., & Rodgers, W. L. (1976). *The quality of American life: Perceptions, evaluations, and satisfactions.* New York: Russell Sage Foundation.

Carmack, M. A., & Martens, R. (1979). Measuring commitment to running: A survey of runners' attitudes and mental states. *Journal of Sport Psychology, 1,* 25–42.

Carmody, T. P., Senner, J. W., Malinow, M. R., & Matarazzo, J. D. (1980). Physical exercise rehabilitation: Long-term dropout rate in cardiac patients. *Journal of Behavioural Medicine, 3,* 163–169.

Cattell, R. B., Eber, H. W., & Tatsuoka, M. (1970). Handbook for the sixteen personality factor questionnaire. In *Clinical education, industrial and research psychology.* Champaign, IL: Institute for Personality and Ability Testing.

Cerutty, P. W. (1967). *Success in sport and life.* London: Pelham.

Chekola, M. G. (1975). The concept of happiness (Doctoral dissertation, University of Michigan, 1974). *Dissertation Abstracts International, 35,* 4609A. (University Microfilms No. 75-655)

Collingwood, T. R., & Willett, L. (1971). The effects of physical training upon self-concept and body attitude. *Journal of Clinical Psychology, 27,* 411–412.

Coopersmith, S. (1967). *The antecedents of self-esteem.* San Francisco: W. H. Freeman.

Cox, R. H. (1991). Exercise training and response to stress: Insights from an animal model. *Medicine and Science in Sports and Exercise, 23,* 853–859.

Crews, D. J., & Landers, D. M. (1987). A meta-analytic review of aerobic fitness and reactivity to psychosocial stressors. *Medicine and Science in Sports and Exercise, 19*(Suppl.), S114–S120.

Csikszentmihalyi, M. (1975). Play and intrinsic rewards. *Journal of Humanistic Psychology, 15,* 41–63.

Csikszentmihalyi, M. (1991). *Flow: The psychology of optimal experience.* New York: Harper-Collins Perennial.

Csikszentmihalyi, M., & LeFevre, J. (1989). Optimal experience in work and leisure. *Journal of Personality and Social Psychology, 56,* 815–822.

Dalkey, N. C., Lewis, R., & Snyder, D. (1972). *Studies of life quality.* Boston: D. C. Heath.

Demo, D. H. (1985). The measurement of self-esteem: Refining our methods. *Journal of Personality and Social Psychology, 48,* 1490–1502.

deVries, H. A. (1981). Tranquilizer effects of exercise: A critical review. *The Physician and Sportsmedicine, 9*(11), 46–55.

deVries, H. A., & Adams, G. M. (1972). Electromyographic comparison of single doses of exercise and meprobamate as to effects on muscular relaxation. *American Journal of Physical Medicine, 51,* 130–141.

Diener, E. (1984). Subjective well-being. *Psychological Bulletin, 95,* 542–575.

Dienstbier, R. A. (1991). Behavioral correlates of sympathoadrenal reactivity: The toughness model. *Medicine and Science in Sports and Exercise, 23,* 846–852.

Dion, W., Rogowski, B., & Oldridge, N. B. (1988). Age and attendance in patients referred to cardiac rehabilitation. *Medicine and Science in Sports and Exercise,* Supplement, 545.

Dishman, R. K. (1981). Biologic influences on exercise adherence. *Research Quarterly for Exercise and Sport, 52,* 143–159.

Dishman, R. K. (1982). Health psychology and exercise adherence. *Quest, 33,* 166–180.

Dishman, R. K. (1984). Motivation and exercise adherence. In J. M. Silva & R. S. Weinberg, (Eds.), *Psychological foundations of sport,* (pp. 420–434). Champaign, IL: Human Kinetics.

Dishman, R. K. (1986). Mental health. In V. Seefeldt (Ed.), *Physical activity and well-being* (pp. 304–341). Reston, VA: American Alliance for Health, Physical Education, and Dance.

Dishman, R. K., & Gettman, L. R. (1980). Psychobiologic influences on exercise adherence. *Journal of Sport Psychology, 2,* 295–310.

Dishman, R. K., & Ickes, W. (1981). Self-Motivation and adherence to therapeutic exercise. *Journal of Behavioral Medicine, 4,* 421–4.

Dishman, R. K., Ickes, W., & Morgan, W. P. (1980). Self-motivation and adherence to habitual physical activity. *Journal of Applied Social Psychology, 10,* 115–132.

Dugan, M. A. (1978). Effects of a creative approach to dance on the self-concept of mentally retarded adults. *Completed research in health, physical education, recreation, and dance, 20,* Abstract No. 615.

Dunn, A. L., & Dishman, R. K. (1991). Exercise and the neurobiology of depression. In J. O. Holloszy (Ed.), *Exercise and sport sciences reviews* (Vol. 19, pp. 41–98). Baltimore: Williams and Wilkins.

Durbeck, D. C., Heinzelmann, F., Schacter, J., Haskell, W. L., Payne, G. H., Moxley, R. T., Nemiroff, M., Limoncelli, D. D., Arnoldi, L. B., & Fox, S. M. (1972). The National Aeronautics and Space Administration U.S. public health evaluation and enhancement program. *American Journal of Cardiology, 30,* 784–790.

Ebersole, P. (1972). Effects of classification of peak experiences. *Psychological Reports, 30,* 631–635.

Egger, G. (1981). *The sport drug.* Sydney, Australia: George Allen & Unwin.

Epstein, S. (1973). The self-concept revisited: Or a theory of a theory. *American Psychologist, 28,* 404–416.

Ewert, A. W. (1983). A study of the effects of participation in an outward-bound short course upon the reported self-concepts of selected participants. *Completed research in health, physical education, recreation, and dance, 25,* Abstract No. 412.

Fitts, W. H. (1964). *Tennessee Self Concept Scale.* Nashville, TN: Counselor Recordings and Tests.

Fixx, J. F. (1977). *The complete book of running.* New York: Random House.

Flanagan, J. C. (1978). A research approach to improving our quality of life. *American Psychologist, 33,* 138–147.

Fleming, J. S., & Courtney, B. E. (1984). The dimensionality of self-esteem: II. Hierarchical facet model for revised measurement scales. *Journal of Personality and Social Psychology, 46,* 404–421.

Fox, K. R. (1990). *The Physical Self-Perception Profile Manual.* De Kalb, IL: Office for Health Promotion, University of Northern Illinois.

Fox, K. R., & Corbin, C. B. (1989). The Physical Self-Perception Profile: Development and preliminary validation. *Journal of Sport and Exercise Psychology, 11,* 408–430.

Frank, A. W. (1991). *At the will of the body.* Boston: Houghton Mifflin.

Franklin, B. A. (1988). Program factors that influence exercise adherence: Practical adherence skills for the clinical staff. In R. K.

Dishman (Ed.), *Exercise adherence: Its impact on public health*. Champaign, IL: Human Kinetics.

Friedmann, E., & Berger, B. G. (in press). Influence of gender, masculinity and femininity on the effectiveness of three stress reduction techniques: Jogging, relaxation response, and group interaction. *Journal of Applied Sport Psychology, 3,* 61–86.

Fries, J. F. (1980). Aging, natural death, and the compression of morbidity. *The New England Journal of Medicine. 303*(3), 130–135.

Furlong, W. B. (1976, June). The fun in fun. *Psychology Today,* 35–38, 80.

Gaber, L. B. (1984). Structural dimensions in aged self-concept: A Tennessee Self-concept study. *British Journal of Psychology, 75,* 207–212.

Gallwey, W. T. (1982). *The inner game of tennis.* Toronto: Bantam Books.

Gatz, M., Smyer, M. A., & Lawton, M. P. (1980). The mental health system and the older adult. In L. W. Poon (Ed.), *Aging in the 1980s* (pp. 5–18). Washington, DC: American Psychological Association.

Gentile, A. M. (1972). A working model of skill acquisition with application to teaching. *Quest, 17,* 3–23.

Gergen, K. J. (1971). *The concept of self.* New York: Holt, Rinehart and Winston.

Gettman, L. R. (1988). Occupation-related fitness and exercise adherence. In R. K. Dishman (Ed.), *Exercise adherence: Its impact on public health* (pp. 349–367). Champaign, IL: Human Kinetics.

Gettman, L. R., Pollock, M. L., & Ward, A. (1983). Adherence to unsupervised exercise. *The Physician and Sports Medicine, 11,* 56–66.

Gillum, R. F., & Barsky, A. J. (1974). Diagnosis and management of patient noncompliance. *Journal of American Medical Association, 228,* 1563–1567.

Glasser, W. (1976). *Positive addiction.* New York: Harper & Row.

Godin, G., & Shephard, R. J. (1986). Psychosocial factors influencing intentions to exercise of young students from grades 7 to 9. *Research Quarterly for Exercise and Sports, 57,* 41–52.

Greenwald, A. G. (1980). The totalitarian ego: Fabrication and revision of personal history. *American Psychologist, 35,* 603–618.

Greenwald, A. G., & Pratkanis, A. R. (1984). The self. In R. S. Wyer & T. K. Srull (Eds.). *Handbook of social cognition* (Vol. 3, pp. 129–178). Hillsdale, NJ: Erlbaum.

Gurley, V., Neuringer, A., & Massee, J. (1984). Dance and sports compared: Effects on psychological well-being. *Journal of Sports Medicine and Physical Fitness, 24,* 58–68.

Guyot, G. W., Fairchild, L., & Hill, M. (1981). Physical fitness, sport participation, body build, and self-concept of elementary school children. *International Journal of Sport Psychology, 12,* 105–116.

Hackfort, D., & Schwenkmezger, P. (1989). Measuring anxiety in sports: Perspectives and problems. In D. Hackfort & C. D. Spielberger (Eds.), *Anxiety in sports: An international perspective* (pp. 55–74). New York: Hemisphere Publishing.

Hackfort, D., & Spielberger, C. D. (Eds.). (1989). *Anxiety in sports: An international perspective.* New York: Hemisphere Publishing.

Hanson, M. G. (1976). Coronary heart disease, exercise, and motivation in middle-aged males. *Dissertation Abstracts International, 37,* 2755B.

Harris, L., & Associates, Inc. (1978). *Health maintenance survey.* Newport Beach, CA: Pacific Mutual Life Insurance Company.

Hartung, G. H., & Farge, E. J. (1977). Personality and physiological traits in middle-aged runners and joggers. *Journal of Gerontology, 32,* 541–548.

Haynes, B. (1976). A critical review of the "determinants" of patient compliance with therapeutic regimens. In D. L. Sackett and R. B. Haynes (Eds.). *Compliance with therapeutic regimens* (pp. 26–39). Baltimore and London: Johns Hopkins University Press.

Haynes, B., Taylor, D. W., & Sackett, D. L. (Eds.). (1979). *Compliance in health care.* Baltimore: Johns Hopkins University Press.

Heinzelmann, F., & Bagley, R. W. (1970). Response to physical activity programs and their effects on health behavior. *Public Health Report, 85,* 905–911.

Higgins, E. T., & King, G. (1981). Accessibility of social constructs: Information-processing consequences of individual and contextual variability. In N. Cantor & J. F. Kihlstrom (Eds.), *Personality, cognition, and social interaction* (pp. 69–121). Hillsdale, NJ: Erlbaum.

Hoffman, R. G., Davis, G. L., & Nelson, K. S. (1988). Factor analysis of the Tennessee Self-Concept Scale in an adolescent sample. *Educational and Psychological Measurement, 48,* 407–417.

Hogan, P. I., & Santomier, J. P. (1984). Effect of mastering swimming skills on older adults' self-efficacy. *Research Quarterly for Exercise and Sport, 55,* 294–296.

Howard, J. H., Cunningham, D. A., & Rechnitzer, P. A. (1987). Personality and fitness decline in middle-aged men. *International Journal of Sport Psychology, 18,* 100–111.

Jackson, J. M. (1981). The relationship between physical fitness levels and self concept in college males and females. *Completed research in health, physical education, recreation, and dance, 23,* Abstract No. 238.

James, W. (1950). *The principles of psychology.* New York: Dover. (Originally published, 1890.)

Jette, A. M. & Branch, L. G. (1981). The Framingham disability study: II. Physical disability among the aging. *American Journal of Public Health, 71,* 1211–1216.

Jones, A. T. (1985). The effects of jazz dance and aerobic dance on self-concept. *Completed research in health, physical education, recreation, and dance, 27,* Abstract No. 598.

Kabat-Zinn, J. (1990). *Full catastrophe living: Using the wisdom of your body and mind to face stress, pain, and illness.* New York: Delacorte Press.

Kart, C. S., Metress, E. K., & Metress, S. P. (1988). *Aging, health and society.* Boston: Jones and Bartlett.

Kavanagh, T., Shephard, R. J., Chisholm, A. W., Qureshi, S., & Kennedy, J. (1979). Prognostic indexes for patients with ischemic heart disease enrolled in an exercise-centered rehabilitation program. *American Journal of Cardiology, 44,* 1230–1240.

Keutzer, C. S. (1978). Whatever turns you on: Triggers to transcendent experiences. *Journal of Humanistic Psychology, 18*(3), 77–80.

Kinghorn, D. J. (1978). The effect of the BYU Youth Leadership course as a survival experience on the self-acceptance of the participants. *Completed research in health, physical education, recreation, and dance, 20,* Abstract No. 9.

Kirk, D. (1986). The aesthetic experience in sport. *Journal of Human Movement Studies, 12,* 99–111.

Kleinman, S. (1989). Aging and a changing view of the body. In W. W. Spirduso & H. M. Eckert (Eds.), *Physical Activity and Aging: American Academy of Physical Education Papers, No. 22* (pp. 42–59). Champaign, IL: Human Kinetics.

Knapp, D., Gutmann, M., Squires, R. A., & Pollock, M. L. (1983). Exercise adherence among coronary artery bypass surgery (CABS) patients. *Medicine and Science in Sports and Exercise* (Supplement), *15*, S120.

Landsman, T. (1969). The beautiful person. *The Futurist, 3*(3), 41–42.

Lecky, P. (1945). *Self-consistency.* New York: Island Press.

Lee, C., & Owen, N. (1985, Autumn). Reasons for discontinuing regular physical activity subsequent to a fitness course. *The Australian Journal of Health, Physical Education, and Recreation National Journal, 107,* 7–9.

Levy, S. M. (1983). Host differences in neoplastic risk: Behavioral and social contributions to disease. *Health Psychology, 2,* 21–44.

Lin, N., Ensel, W. M., & Dean, A. (1986). The age structure and the stress process. In N. Lin, A. Dean, & W. M. Ensel (Eds.), *Social support, life events, and depression* (pp. 213–231). New York: Academic Press.

Long, B. C. (1983). Aerobic conditioning and stress reduction: Participation or conditioning? *Human Movement Science, 2,* 171–186.

Long, B. C. (1985). Stress-management interventions: A 15-month follow-up of aerobic conditioning and stress inoculation training. *Cognitive Therapy and Research, 9,* 471–478.

Long, B. C., & Haney, C. J. (1988a). Coping strategies for working women: Aerobic exercise and relaxation interventions. *Behavior Therapy, 19,* 75–83.

Long, B. C., & Haney, C. J. (1988b). Long-term follow-up of stressed working women: A comparison of aerobic exercise and progressive relaxation. *Journal of Sport and Exercise Psychology, 10,* 461–470.

McClain, E. W., & Andrews, H. B. (1969). Some personality correlates of peak experiences—A study in self-actualization. *Journal of Clinical Psychology, 25,* 36–38.

McCready, M. L., & Long, B. C. (1985). Locus of control, attitudes towards physical activity, and exercise adherence. *Journal of Sport Psychology, 7,* 346–359.

McCrory, M. (1981). The effects of an exercise program on self-concept and physical fitness of Oklahoma State University commissioned peace officers. *Completed Research in Health, Physical Education, Recreation, and Dance, 23,* Abstract No. 259.

McGowan, R. W., Jarman, B. O., & Pedersen, D. M. (1974). Effects of a competitive endurance training program on self-concept and peer approval. *Journal of Psychology, 86,* 57–60.

McGuire, W. J., & Padawer-Singer, A. (1982). Trait salience in the spontaneous self-concept. *Journal of Personality and Social Psychology, 33,* 743–754.

McGuire, B., & Tinsley, H. E. A. (1981). A contribution to the construct validity of the Tennessee Self-Concept Scale: A confirmatory factor analysis. *Applied Psychological Measurement, 5,* 449–457.

McInman, A. D. (1992). *The effects of weight-training on self-concept.* Unpublished master's thesis, University of Western Australia, Nelands, Western Australia, Australia.

McInman, A. D., & Berger, B. G. (1991). *Self-concept and mood changes associated with aerobic dance.* Manuscript submitted for publication.

McInman, A. D., & Grove, J. R. (1991). Peak moments in sport: A literature review. *Quest, 43,* 333–351.

McNair, D. M., Lorr, M., & Droppleman, L. F. (1971). *Profile of mood states manual.* San Diego: Educational and Industrial Testing Service.

Maddi, S. R., Bartone, P. T., & Puccetti, M. C. (1987). Stressful events are indeed a factor in physical illness: Reply to Schroeder

and Costa (1984). *Journal of Personality and Social Psychology, 52,* 833–843.

Mandell, A. (1979). The second second wind. *Psychiatric Annals, 9,* 57–69.

Mann, G. V., Garrett, H. L., Farhi, A., Murray, H., Billings, F. T., Shute, E., & Schwarten, S. E. (1969). Exercise to prevent coronary heart disease: An experimental study of the effects of training on risk factors for coronary disease in men. *American Journal of Medicine, 46,* 12–27.

Margoshes, A., & Litt, S. (1966). Vivid experiences: Peak and nadir. *Journal of Clinical Psychology, 22,* 175.

Markus, H., & Kunda, Z. (1986). Stability and malleability of the self-concept. *Journal of Personality and Social Psychology, 51,* 858–866.

Markus, H., & Nurius, P. (1986). Possible selves. *American Psychologist, 41,* 954–969.

Markus, H., & Wurf, E. (1987). The dynamic self-concept: A social psychological perspective. *Annual Review of Psychology, 38,* 299–337.

Marsh, H. W. (1987). The factorial invariance of responses by males and females to a multidimensional self-concept instrument: Substantive and methodological issues. *Multivariate Behavioral Research, 22,* 457–480.

Marsh, H. W. (1990a). *The Self Description Questionnaire (SDQ): A theoretical and empirical basis for the measurement of multiple dimensions of late adolescent self-concept: An interim test manual and a research monograph.* San Antonio, TX: The Psychological Corporation.

Marsh, H. W. (1990b). *The Self Description Questionnaire (SDQ) II: A theoretical and empirical basis for the measurement of multiple dimensions of late adolescent self-concept: An interim test manual and a research monograph.* San Antonio, TX: The Psychological Corporation.

Marsh, H. W. (1990c). *The Self Description Questionnaire (SDQ) III: A theoretical and empirical basis for the measurement of multiple dimensions of late adolescent self-concept: An interim test manual and a research monograph.* San Antonio, TX: The Psychological Corporation.

Marsh, H. W., Barnes, J., & Hocevar, D. (1985). Self-other agreement on multidimensional self-concept ratings: Factor analysis and multitrait-multimethod analysis. *Journal of Personality and Social Psychology, 49,* 1360–1377.

Marsh, H. W., & O'Neill, R. (1984). Self Description Questionnaire III: The construct validity of multidimensional self-concept ratings by late adolescents. *Journal of Educational Measurement, 21,* 153–174.

Marsh, H. W., Parker, J., & Barnes, J. (1985). Multidimensional adolescent self-concepts: Their relationship to age, sex, and academic measures. *American Educational Research Journal, 22,* 422–444.

Marsh, H. W., & Peart, N. D. (1988). Competitive and cooperative physical fitness training programs for girls: Effects on physical fitness and multidimensonal self-concepts. *Journal of Sport and Exercise Psychology, 10,* 390–407.

Marsh, H. W., & Richards, G. E. (1988). Tennessee Self Concept Scale: Reliability, internal structure, and construct validity. *Journal of Personality and Social Psychology, 55,* 612–624.

Marsh, H. W., Richards, G. E., & Barnes, J. (1986a). Multidimensional self-concepts: A long-term follow-up of the effect of participation in an outward bound program. *Personality and Social Psychology Bulletin, 12,* 475–492.

Marsh, H. W., Richards, G. E., & Barnes, J. (1986b). Multidimensional self-concepts: The effect of participation in an outward bound program. *Journal of Personality and Social Psychology,* *50,* 195–204.

Marsh, H. W., Smith, I. D., & Barnes, J. (1983). Multitrait-multimethod analyses of the Self-description Questionnaire: Student teacher agreement on multidimensional ratings of student self-concept. *American Educational Research Journal,* *20,* 333–357.

Marsh, H. W., Smith, I. D., Barnes, J., & Butler, S. (1983). Self-concept: Reliability, stability, dimensionality, and the measurement of change. *Journal of Educational Psychology, 75,* 772–790.

Martinsen, E. W., Hoffart, A., & Solberg, O. (1989). Comparing aerobic with nonaerobic forms of exercise in the treatment of clinical depression: A randomized trial. *Comprehensive Psychiatry, 30,* 324–331.

Martinsen, E. W., Medhus, A., & Sandvik, L. (1985). Effects of aerobic exercise on depression: A controlled study. *British Medical Journal, 291,* 109.

Martin, J. E., & Dubbert, P. M. (1982). Exercise applications and promotion in behavioural medicine: Current status and future directions. *Journal of Consulting and Clinical Psychology, 50,* 1004–1017.

Maslow, A. H. (1968). *Toward a psychology of being.* Princeton, NJ: D. Van Nostrand.

Maslow, A. H. (1970). *Motivation and personality* (2nd ed.). New York: Harper & Row.

Massie, J. F., & Shephard, R. J. (1971). Physiological and psychological effects of training: A comparison of individual and gymnasium programs, with a characterization of the exercise "dropout." *Medicine and Science in Sports and Exercise, 3,* 110–117.

Mathias, D. W. (1978). An evaluation of the outward bound solo experience as an agent in enhancing self-concepts. *Completed research in health, physical education, recreation, and dance, 20,* Abstract No. 555.

Mazzeo, R. S. (1991). Catecholamine responses to acute and chronic exercise. *Medicine and Science in Sports and Exercise, 23,* 839–845.

Meichenbaum, D. H. (1985). *Stress inoculation training.* New York: Pergamon.

Moore, S. L. (1981). A study of perceived locus of control in college women athletes in team and individual sports. *Dissertation Abstracts International, 41,* 3479A.

Moran, M., Michael, W. B., & Dembo, M. H. (1978). The factorial validity of three frequently employed self-report measures of self-concept. *Educational and Psychological Measurement, 38,* 547–563.

Morgan, W. P. (1987). Reduction of state anxiety following acute physical activity. In W. P. Morgan & S. E. Goldston (Eds.), *Exercise and mental health* (pp. 105–109). Washington, DC: Hemisphere.

Morgan, W. P., Brown, D. R., Raglin, J. S., O'Connor, P. J., & Ellickson, K. A. (1987). Psychological monitoring of overtraining and staleness. *British Journal of Sports Medicine, 21,* 107–114.

Morgan, W. P., Costill, D. L., Flynn, M. G., Raglin, J. S., & O'Connor, P. J. (1988). Mood disturbance following increased training in swimmers. *Medicine and Science in Sports and Exercise, 20,* 408–414.

Morgan, W. P., & Ellickson, K. A. (1989). Health, anxiety, and physical exercise. In D. Hackfort & C. D. Spielberger (Eds.), *Anxiety in sports: An international perspective* (pp. 165–182). New York: Hemisphere.

Morgan, W. P., & Goldston, S. E. (Eds.). (1987a). *Exercise and mental health.* New York: Hemisphere.

Morgan, W. P., & Goldston, S. E. (1987b). Summary. In W. P. Morgan & S. E. Goldston (Eds.), *Exercise and mental health* (pp. 155–159). New York: Hemisphere.

Morris, A. F., & Husman, B. F. (1978). Life quality changes following an endurance conditioning program. *American Corrective Therapy Journal, 32,* 3–6.

Morris, A. F., Lussier, L., Vaccaro, P., & Clarke, D. H. (1982). Life quality characteristics of national class women masters long distance runners. *Annals of Sports Medicine, 1,* 23–26.

Morse, S., & Gergen, K. J. (1970). Social comparison, self-consistency, and the concept of self. *Journal of Personality and Social Psychology, 16,* 148–156.

Moses, J., Steptoe, A., Mathews, A., & Edwards, S. (1989). The effects of exercise training on mental well-being in the normal population: A controlled trial. *Journal of Psychosomatic Research, 33,* 47–61.

Murphy, M. (1977). Sport as yoga. *Journal of Humanistic Psychology, 17,* 21–33.

Murphy, M., & White, R. A. (1978). *The psychic side of sports.* Reading, MA: Addison-Wesley.

Murphy, S. M., Fleck, S. J., Dudley, G., & Callister, R. (1990). Psychological and performance concomitants of increased volume training in elite athletes. *Journal of Applied Sport Psychology, 2,* 34–50.

Natale, M., & Hantas, M. (1982). Effects of temporary mood states on selective memory about the self. *Journal of Personality and Social Psychology, 42,* 927–934.

Nideffer, R. M. (1976). *The inner athlete.* New York: Crowell.

North, T. C., McCullagh, P., & Tran, Z. V. (1990). Effect of exercise on depression. In K. B. Pandolf & J. O. Holloszy (Eds.), *Exercise and sport sciences reviews* (Vol. 18, pp. 379–415). Baltimore: Williams and Wilkins.

Nye, G. R., & Poulsen, W. T. (1974). An activity programme for coronary patients: A review of morbidity, mortality and adherence after five years. *New Zealand Medical Journal, 79,* 1010–1013.

O'Connell, J. K., & Price, J. H. (1982). Health locus of control of physical-fitness program participants. *Perceptual and Motor Skills, 55,* 925–926.

O'Malley, P., & Bachman, J. (1983). Self-esteem: Change and stability between ages 13 and 23. *Developmental Psychology, 19,* 257–268.

Oldridge, N. B. (1979). Compliance of post myocardial infarction patients to exercise programs. *Medicine and Science in Sports and Exercise, 11,* 373–375.

Oldridge, N. B. (1988). Cardiac rehabilitation: Self-efficacy and quality of life In. N. B. Oldridge, R. C. Rosler, & D. H. Schmidt (Eds.). *Cardiac rehabilitation and clinical exercise programs: Theory and practice* (pp. 213–220). Ann Arbor, MI: McNaughton and Gunn.

Oldridge, N. B., Donner, A. P., Buck, C. W., Jones, N. L., Andrew, G. M., Parker, J. O., Cunningham, D. A., Kavanagh, T., Rechnitzer, P. A., & Sutton, J. R. (1983). Predictors of dropout from cardiac exercise rehabilitation. *American Journal of Cardiology, 51,* 70–74.

Oldridge, N. B., & Spencer, J. (1983). Exercise habits and health perceptions after graduating or dropping out of cardiac rehabilitation. *Medicine and Science in Sport and Exercise, 15,* 120 (Supplement).

Oldridge, N. B., Wicks, J. R., Hanley, C., Sutton, J. R., & Jones, N. L. (1978). Noncompliance in an exercise rehabilitation program for men who have suffered a myocardial infarction. *Canadian Medical Association Journal, 118,* 361–364.

Olson, M. I. (1975). *The effects of physical activity on the body image of nursing home residents.* Unpublished master's thesis, Springfield College, MA.

Ostrow, A. C. (1983). Age-role stereotyping: Implications for physical activity participation. In G. Rowles & R. Ohta (Eds.), *Aging and milieu: Environmental perspectives on growing old* (pp. 153–170). New York: Academic Press.

Ostrow, A. C., & Dzewaltowski, D. A. (1986). Older Adults' perceptions of physical activity participation based on age-role and sex-role appropriateness. *Research Quarterly for Exercise and Sport, 57,* 167–169.

Ostrow, A. C., Jones, D. C., & Spiker, D. D. (1981). Age role expectations and sex role expectations for selected sport activities. *Research Quarterly for Exercise and Sport, 52,* 216–227.

Ostrow, A. C., Keener, R. E., & Perry, S. A. (1986–1987). The age grading of physical activity among children. *International Journal of Aging and Human Development, 24,* 101–111.

Paffenbarger, R. S., Jr. (1988). Contributions of epidemiology to exercise science and cardiovascular health. *Medicine and Science in Sports and Exercise, 20,* 426–438.

Paffenbarger, R. S., Jr., Hyde, R. T., Wing, A. L., & Hsieh, C. (1986). Physical activity, all cause mortality, and longevity of college alumni. *New England Journal of Medicine, 314,* 605–613.

Panzarella, R. (1980). The phenomenology of aesthetic peak experiences. *Journal of Humanistic Psychology, 20*(1), 69–85.

Park, R. J. (1973). Raising the consciousness of sport. *Quest, 26,* 78–82.

Pear, R. (1991, March 10). Medical prognosis: Unwieldy growth fueled by more fees and beneficiaries. *The New York Times,* p. E-4.

Pedic, F. (1989). Effect on social self-esteem of nationalistic appeals in corporate image advertisements. *Australian Journal of Psychology, 41,* 37–47.

Pelletier, K. R. (1981). *Longevity: Fulfilling our biological potential.* New York: Dell.

Pflaum, J. H. (1973). *Development of a life quality inventory.* Unpublished doctoral dissertation, University of Maryland, College Park, MD.

Pollock, M. L., Gettman, L. R., Milesis, C. A., Bah, M. D., Durstine, L., & Johnson, R. B. (1977). Effects of frequency and duration of training on attrition and incidence of injury. *Medicine and Science in Sport and Exercise, 9,* 31–36.

Poulton, E. C. (1957). On prediction in skilled movements. *Psychological Bulletin, 54,* 467–478.

Pratt, T. C., Linn, M. W., Carmichael, J. S., & Webb, N. L. (1977). The alcoholic's perception of the ward as a predictor of aftercare attendance. *Journal of Clinical Psychology, 33,* 915–918.

Privette, G. (1965). Factors associated with functioning which transcends modal behaviour. *Dissertation Abstracts International, 25,* 3406.

Privette, G. (1968). Transcendent functioning. *Teachers College Record, 66,* 733–739.

Privette, G. (1981a). Dynamics of peak performance. *Journal of Humanistic Psychology, 21*(1), 57–67.

Privette, G. (1981b). The phenomenology of peak performance in sports. *International Journal of Sports Psychology, 12,* 51–60.

Privette, G. (1982a). Experiential correlates of peak intellectual performance. *Psychological Reports, 51,* 323–330.

Privette, G. (1982b). Peak performance in sports: A factorial topology. *International Journal of Sport Psychology, 13,* 242–249.

Privette, G. (1983). Peak experience, peak performance, and flow:

A comparative analysis of positive human experiences. *Journal of Personality and Social Psychology, 45,* 1361–1368.

Privette, G. (1985a). Experience as a component of personality theory. *Psychological Reports, 56,* 263–266.

Privette, G. (1985b). Experience as a component of personality theory: Phenomenological support. *Psychological Reports, 57,* 558.

Privette, G., & Bundrick, C. M. (1987). Measurement of experience: Construct and content validity of the experience questionnaire. *Perceptual and Motor Skills, 65,* 315–332.

Privette, G., & Landsman, T. (1983). Factor analysis of peak performance: The full use of potential. *Journal of Personality and Social Psychology, 44,* 195–200.

Privette, G., & Sherry, D. (1986). Reliability and readability of questionaire: Peak performance and peak experience. *Psychological Reports, 58,* 491–494.

Puretz, S. L. (1982). Modern dance's effect on the body image. *International Journal of Sport Psychology, 13,* 176–186.

Raglin, J. S., & Morgan, W. P. (1987). Influence of exercise and quiet rest on state anxiety and blood pressure. *Medicine and Science in Sports and Exercise, 19,* 456–463.

Raugh, D., & Wall, R. (1987). Measuring sports participation motivation. *International Journal of Sports Psychology, 18,* 112–119.

Ravizza, K. (1975). *A subjective study of the athlete's greatest moment in sport.* Proceedings of the 7th Canadian Psychomotor Learning and Sport Psychology Symposium, pp. 399–404.

Ravizza, K. (1977). Peak experiences in sport. *Journal of Humanistic Psychology, 17*(4), 35–40.

Ravizza, K. (1984). Qualities of the peak experience in sport. In J. M. Silva & R. S. Weinberg (Eds.). *Psychological foundations of sport* (pp. 452–461). Champaign, IL: Human Kinetics.

Rhodewalt, F., & Agustsdottir, S. (1986). Effects of self-presentation on the phenomenal self. *Journal of Personality and Social Psychology, 50,* 47–55.

Rhodewalt, F., & Comer, R. (1981). The role of self-attribution differences in the utilization of social comparison information. *Journal of Research in Personality, 15,* 210–220.

Riddick, C. C. (1984). Comparative psychological profiles of three groups of female collegians: Competitive swimmers, recreational swimmers, and inactive swimmers. *Journal of Sport Behavior, 7,* 160–174.

Riddle, P. K. (1980). Attitudes, beliefs, behavioral intentions, and behaviors of women and men toward regular jogging. *Research Quarterly for Exercise and Sport, 51,* 663–674.

Rimer, S. (1990, April 29). Swimming for fitness and solitude. *The New York Times Magazine, Part 2. The Good Health Magazine,* pp. 59–60, 83–84.

Roffe, M. W. (1981). Factorial structure of the Tennessee Self-Concept Scale. *Psychological Reports, 48,* 455–462.

Rogers, C. R. (1951). *Client-centered therapy.* Boston: Houghton Mifflin.

Rosenberg, E. (1986a). Sport voluntary association involvement and happiness among middle-aged and elderly Americans. In B. McPherson (Ed.), *Sport and aging* (pp. 45–52). Champaign, IL: Human Kinetics.

Rosenberg, M. (1986b). Self-concept from middle childhood through adolescence. In J. Suls & A. G. Greenwald (Eds.), *Psychological perspectives on the self* (Vol. 3, pp. 107–136). Hillsdale, NJ: Erlbaum.

Rosenfeld, A. H. (1978). *New views on older lives: A sampler of NIMH-sponsored research and service programs.* (DHEW Publication No. ADM 78-687). Washington, DC: U.S. Government Printing Office.

Roth, D. L., & Holmes, D. S. (1985). Influence of physical fitness in determining the impact of stressful life events on physical and psychologic health. *Psychosomatic Medicine, 47,* 164–173.

Rybczynski, W. (1991). *Waiting for the weekend.* New York: Viking.

Sachs, M. L. (1980). *On the trail of the runner's high: A descriptive and experimental investigation of characteristics of an elusive phenomenon.* Unpublished doctoral dissertation, Florida State University.

Sachs, M. L. (1984). The runner's high. In M. L. Sachs & G. W. Buffone (Eds.), *Running as therapy: An integrated approach* (pp. 273–287). Lincoln, NE: University of Nebraska press.

Sachs, M. L., & Buffone, G. W. (Eds.). (1984). *Running as therapy: An integrated approach.* Lincoln, NE: University of Nebraska Press.

Sacks, M. H., & Sachs, M. L. (Eds.) (1981). *Psychology of running.* Champaign, IL: Human Kinetics.

Sanne, H. M. (1973). Exercise tolerance and physical training of non-selected patients after myocardial infarction. *Acta Medica Scandinavica Supplement, 551,* 1–124.

Savin-Williams, R. C., & Demo, D. H. (1983). Developmental change and stability in adolescent self-concept. *Developmental Psychology, 20,* 1100–1110.

Scanlan, T. K., & Simons, J. P. (in press). The construct of sport enjoyment. In G. C. Roberts (Ed.), *Motivation in sport and exercise.* Champaign, IL: Human Kinetics.

Schaie, K. W., & Geiwitz, J. (1982). *Adult development and aging.* Boston: Little, Brown.

Schuele, M. K. (1980). The relationship of physical fitness in women to self-esteem and locus of control. *Dissertation Abstracts International, 40,* 5380A–5381A.

Sharkey, B. J. (1990). *Physiology of fitness* (3rd ed.). Champaign, IL: Human Kinetics.

Sharp, B. I. (1987). *Swimming and "well-being."* Unpublished doctoral dissertation, Yeshiva University, New York.

Shavelson, R. J., Hubner, J. J., & Stanton, G. C. (1976). Self-concept: Validation of construct interpretations. *Review of Educational Research, 46,* 407–441.

Shaw, L. W. (1981). Effects of a prescribed supervised exercise program on mortality and cardiovascular morbidity in patients after a myocardial infarction. *American Journal of Cardiology, 48,* 39–46.

Sheehan, G. (1990). The ages of the runner. *Annals of Sports Medicine, 5,* 210.

Shepard, L. A. (1979). Self-acceptance: The evaluative component of the self-concept construct. *American Educational Research Journal, 16,* 139–160.

Shephard, R. J. (1989). The aging of cardiovascular function. In W. W. Spirduso & H. M. Ekert (Eds.), *Physical Activity and Aging: American Academy of Physical Education Papers, No. 22* (pp. 175–185). Champaign, IL: Human Kinetics.

Shephard, R. J., & Sidney, K. H. (1979). Exercise and aging. In R. Hutton (Ed.), *Exercise and sport science reviews* (pp. 1–57). Philadelphia: Franklin Press.

Sidney, K. H., & Shephard, R. J. (1976). Attitudes towards health and physical activity in the elderly. Effects of a physical training program. *Medicine and Science in Sports and Exercise, 8,* 246–252.

Singer, R. N., & Gerson, R. F. (1981). Task classification and strategy utilization. in motor skills. *Research Quarterly for Exercise and Sport, 52,* 100–112.

Sinyor, D., Schwartz, S. G., Peronnet, F., Brisson, G., & Seraganian, P. (1983). Aerobic fitness level and reactivity to psychosocial stress: Physiological, biochemical, and subjective measures. *Psychosomatic Medicine, 45,* 205–217.

Smith, E. L. & Gilligan, C. (1986). Exercise, sport, and physical activity for the elderly: Principles and problems of programming. In B. D. McPherson (Ed.), *Sport and aging* (pp. 91–105). Champaign, IL: Human Kinetics.

Smith, E. L., & Gilligan, C. (1989). Osteoporosis, bone mineral, and exercise. In W. W. Spirduso & H. M. Eckert (Eds.), *Physical activity and aging: American Academy of Physical Education papers, No. 22* (pp. 107–119). Champaign, IL: Human Kinetics.

Smith, E. L. (1981). Age: The interaction of nature and nurture. In E. L. Smith & R. C. Serfass (Eds.), *Exercise and aging: The scientific basis* (pp. 11–17). Hillside, NJ: Enslow.

Smith, J. H. (1977). The effects of a weight training program on body image and the development of muscular strength in institutionalized mentally retarded males. *Completed Research in Health, Physical Education, Recreation, and Dance, 19,* Abstract No. 342.

Smoll, F. L., Schutz, R. W., Wood, T. M., & Cunningham, J. K. (1979). Parent-Child relationships regarding physical activity attitudes and behaviors. In G. Roberts & K. Newell (Eds.), *Psychology of motor behavior.* Champaign, IL: Human Kinetics.

Snyder, E. E. & Spreitzer, E. A. (1983). *Social aspects of sport.* Englewood Cliffs, NJ: Prentice-Hall.

Snyder, M. (1982). When believing means doing: Creating links between attitudes and behaviours. In M. P. Zanna, E. T. Higgins, & C. P. Herman (Eds.), *The Ontario Symposium* (Vol. 2, p. 105–130). Hillsdale, NJ: Erlbaum.

Sonstroem, R. J. (1976). The validity of self-perceptions regarding physical and athletic ability. *Medicine and Science in Sport and Exercise, 8,* 126–132.

Sonstroem, R. J. (1981). Exercise and self-esteem: Recommendations for expository research. *Quest, 33,* 124–139.

Sothmann, M. S. (1991). Catecholamines, behavioral stress, and exercise—introduction to the symposium. *Medicine and Science in Sports and Exercise, 23,* 836–838.

Spirduso, W. W. (1986). Physical activity and the prevention of premature aging. In V. Seefeldt (Ed.), *Physical activity and well-being* (pp. 142–160). Reston, VA: American Alliance for Health, Physical Education, Recreation, and Dance.

Spirduso, W. W. (1989). Physical activity and aging: Introduction. In W. W. Spirduso & H. M. Eckert (Eds.), *Physical activity and aging: American Academy of Physical Education papers, No. 22* (pp. 1–5). Champaign, IL: Human Kinetics.

Spirduso, W. W., & Eckert, H. M. (1989). *Physical activity and aging: American Academy of Physical Education papers, No. 22.* Champaign, IL: Human Kinetics.

Stalonas, P. M., Johnson, W. G., & Christ, M. (1978). Behavior modification for obesity: The evaluation of exercise, contingency management, and program adherence. *Journal of Consulting and Clinical Psychology, 46,* 463–469.

Steptoe, A., & Bolton, J. (1988). The short-term influence of high and low intensity physical exercise on mood. *Psychology and Health, 2,* 91–106.

Steptoe, A., & Cox, S. (1988). Acute effects of aerobic exercise on mood. *Health Psychology, 7,* 329–340.

Swann, W. B., Jr. (1985). The self as architect of social reality. In B. R. Schlenker (Ed.), *The self and social life* (pp. 100–126). New York: McGraw-Hill.

Swann, W. B., Jr., & Hill, C. A. (1982). When our identities are mistaken: Reaffirming self-conceptions through social interaction. *Journal of Personality and Social Psychology, 43,* 59–66.

Swann, W. B., Jr., & Read, S. J. (1981). Self-verification processes:

How we sustain our self-conceptions. *Journal of Experimental Social Psychology, 17,* 351–372.

Taylor, J. A. (1953). A personality scale of manifest anxiety. *Journal of Abnormal and Social Psychology, 48,* 285–290.

Teagardin, S. S. (1983). A study of self-concept in relation to physical fitness and motor ability among elementary, middle, and high school girls. *Dissertation Abstracts International, 44,* 1726A.

Tesser, A., & Campbell, J. (1983). Self-definition: The impact of the relative performance and similarity of others. *Social Psychology Quarterly, 43,* 341–347.

Thayer, R. E. (1987). Energy, tiredness, and tension effects of a sugar snack versus moderate exercise. *Journal of Personality and Social Psychology, 52,* 119–125.

Theriault, C. M. (1982). The relationship between personality characteristics and project adventure at Westford Academy. *Completed Research in Health, Physical Education, Recreation, and Dance, 24,* Abstract No. 120.

Thomas, C. E. (1973). The perfect moment: An aesthetic perspective of the sport experience. *Dissertation Abstracts International, 33,* 4162A–4163A.

Thorne, F. C. (1963). The clinical use of nadir experience reports. *Journal of Clinical Psychology, 19,* 248–250.

Trujillo, C. M. (1983). The effect of weight training and running exercise intervention programs on the self-esteem of college women. *International Journal of Sport Psychology, 14,* 162–173.

Tucker, C. J. (1982). Relationship of the self-concept and selected physical fitness variables of adolescent females. *Completed research in health, physical education, recreation, and dance, 24,* Abstract No. 126.

Tucker, L. A. (1983a). Effect of weight training on self-concept: A profile of those influenced most. *Research Quarterly for Exercise and Sport, 54,* 389–397.

Tucker, L. A. (1983b). Muscular strength: A predictor of personality in males. *Journal of Sports Medicine and Physical Fitness, 23,* 213–220.

Tucker, L. A. (1984). Trait psychology and performance: A credulous viewpoint. *Journal of Human Movement Studies, 10,* 53–62.

Tucker, L. A. (1987a). Effect of weight training on body attitudes: Who benefits most? *Journal of Sports Medicine and Physical Fitness, 27,* 70–78.

Tucker, L. A. (1987b). Mental health and physical fitness. *Journal of Human Movement Studies, 13,* 267–273.

Turner, R. H. (1968). The self-conception in social interaction. In C. Gordon & K. Gergen (Eds.), *The self in social interaction* (pp. 93–106). New York: Wiley.

Uson, P. P., & Larrosa, V. R. (1982). Physical activities in retirement age. In J. Partington, T. Orlick, & J. Samela (Eds.), *Sport in perspective* (pp. 149–151), Canada: Coaching Association of Canada.

Valliant, P. M., & Asu, M. E. (1985). Exercise and its effects on cognition and physiology in older adults. *Perceptual and Motor Skills, 61,* 1031–1038.

Walchuk, P., & Orlick, T. (1980). Altered states of consciousness in sport experiences. In P. Klavora & K. A. W. Wipper (Eds.). *Psychological and sociological factors in sport.* Toronto: Publications Division, School of Physical and Health Education, University of Toronto.

Wankel, L. M. (1985). Personal and situational factors affecting exercise involvement: The importance of enjoyment. *Research Quarterly for Exercise and Sports, 56,* 275–282.

Wankel, L. M. (in press). Enjoyment: A key to exercise adherence and psychological benefits. *International Journal of Sport Psychology.*

Wankel, L. M., & Berger, B. G. (1990). The psychological and social benefits of sport and physical activity. *Leisure Research, 21,* 167–182.

Wanzel., R. (1978). Toward preventing dropouts in an industrial and other fitness programs. *Recreation Canada, 36,* 39–42.

Watkins, D., & Dhawan, N. (1989). Do we need to distinguish the constructs of self-concept and self-esteem? *Journal of Social Behavior and Personality, 4,* 555–562.

Wescott, R. (1981). The effect of physical education activity classes on the self concept of college students. *Completed research in health, physical education, recreation, and dance, 23,* Abstract No. 261.

Wheeler, D. (1982). The self-concept of participants in kayaking, skydiving and hand gliding. *Completed research in health, physical education, recreation, and dance, 24,* Abstract No. 33.

Willden, G. D. (1974). An analysis of the self-concept changes occurring in youth participants in the Kearns community school survival adventure program. *Completed research in health, physical education, recreation, and dance, 18,* Abstract No. 660.

Williams, D. D. (1973). Instruction stressing physical fitness compared with instruction stressing skill acquisition upon self-concept in Caucasian and Negro students. *Completed research in health, physical education, recreation, and dance, 17,* Abstract No. 9.

Williams, J. M. (Ed.). (1986). *Applied sport psychology.* Palo Alto, CA: Mayfield.

Wuthnow, R. (1978). Peak experiences: Some empiricial tests. *Journal of Humanistic Psychology, 18,* 59–75.

Wylie, R. C. (1974). *The self-concept: A review of methodological considerations and measuring instruments* (rev. ed., Vol. 1). Lincoln, NE: University of Nebraska Press.

Young, J. R., & Ismail, A. H. (1977). Comparison of selected physiological and personality variables in regular and nonregular adult male exercisers. *Research Quarterly, 48,* 617–622.

Young, J. R., & Ismail, A. H. (1978). Ability of biochemical and personality variables in discriminating between high and low physical fitness levels. *Journal of Psychosomatic Research, 22,* 193–199.

Young, M. L. (1985). Estimation of fitness and physical ability, physical performance, and self-concept among adolescent females. *Journal of Sports Medicine and Physical Fitness, 25,* 144–150.

·35·

CAREER TERMINATION ISSUES AMONG ELITE ATHLETES

Bruce Ogilvie

Jim Taylor

INTRODUCTION

Athletic participation is characterized by glorious peaks and debilitating valleys. Furthermore the range of events and emotions that are experienced through athletic involvement seem to be both numerous and extreme compared to the normal population. Yet of all the powerful experiences encountered by athletes, perhaps the most significant and potentially traumatic is that of career termination. Moreover termination from sports involves a variety of unique experiences that sets it apart from typical retirement concerns.

In response to the apparent significance of this issue, during the past 25 years there has been a small, but steady stream of anecdotal, theoretical, and empirical exploration of career termination among athletes. These considerations have brought attention to the potential difficulties of retirement, have attempted to provide explanations for the process, and have offered evidence of the nature of the termination process.

The issue of career termination has received considerable attention in the popular press. These writings are typically anecdotal in nature and focus on professional athletes (Hoffer, 1990; Putnam, 1991). Moreover the focus of these articles varies from depictions of the difficulties experienced by athletes in their postathletic lives (Alfano, 1982; Bradley, 1976; Elliot, 1982; Jordan, 1975; Kahn, 1972; Morrow, 1978; Plimpton, 1977; Stephens, 1984; Vecsey, 1980) to successful career transitions of athletes (Batten, 1979; White, 1974).

Based on the large proportion of these articles that suggest termination difficulties, it might be concluded that ca-

reer transition trauma is a widespread phenomenon. However, due to the absence of methodological rigor in these investigations, it is impossible to make any conclusive judgments about the prevalence of termination difficulties among athletes. During this period, commensurate interest in career termination began to grow among the professional community. What resulted was a variety of scholarly, though speculative, articles by noted professionals in sport psychology based on their own professional experiences dealing with this issue, available research in the area, and literature from related fields (Broom, 1982; Botterill, 1982; McPherson, 1980; Ogilvie & Howe, 1982; Werthner & Orlick, 1982).

These concerns have raised an important question relative to career termination: What is the incidence of athletes who experience significant distress when leaving their sport? Those individuals who have published their concerns about this issue have mainly been sport psychologists who have provided services to the more elite end of the athletic continuum. Although the question remains as to whether just the tip of the iceberg is being seen, these psychologists are consistent in their concern for what might be the hidden significant number of athletes throughout the sports world who experience difficulties upon career termination (May & Sieb, 1987; Ogilvie, 1982, 1983; Rotella & Heyman, 1986).

The goal of this chapter is to provide an integrative view of career termination among athletes. This objective will be accomplished by considering the following areas: (1) historical and conceptual issues that will assist in the understanding of the growth of career termination as a meaningful avenue of inquiry; (2) theoretical perspectives of career termination; (3) the causes of career termination; (4) evidence of trauma in career termination; (5) factors that contribute to crises of career termination; (6) prevention and treatment of career termination distress; and (7) avenues for future theoretical and empirical investigation into career termination in sports.

The issues that will be considered will focus primarily on the termination crises of athletes who have made sport participation a dominant part of their lives. The term *elite athlete* will be used to distinguish this population from the recreational athlete.

HISTORICAL AND CONCEPTUAL CONCERNS

Career termination received little attention in North America or in most other countries prior to 20 years ago. This may have been due in large part to the fact that elite athletes were more fully integrated into the basic fabric of society than they are now. Specifically, due to limited technology they did not receive a high level of media scrutiny. In addition, their salaries were not significantly higher than the normal population. Also, elite-amateur athletes typically were either students or held full-time jobs away from their sports involvement. As a consequence, their transition to life as an "average" citizen was not as dramatic (Chartland & Lent, 1987).

In contrast, the schism between elite athletes and the general population has grown wider in recent years. The development of cable and satellite television has brought these athletes into the homes of millions of people worldwide, thus placing them "under the microscope." In addition, the current financial rewards of elite athletes, whether professional or "amateur," further separate them from "normal" people (Newman, 1988). These factors then create a lifestyle that is highly discrepant from the one that they might have to adopt following career termination.

The nature of the athlete development system in North America may have also contributed to the lack of concern and study of the postcareer adjustment problems experienced by elite athletes. In particular, largely as a function of the sociopolitical system, athletic development in North America has occurred in a laissez-faire fashion. What this approach emphasizes is the self-responsibility of the athletes in their entrance into the sport, their development during their athletic careers, and, by extension, in their departure from the sport. Additionally, due to the large population of the United States, there was a constant influx of talented athletes that replaced those at the end of their careers, thereby drawing attention away from the career termination of other athletes.

The participation of the sport psychologist at the elite level also inhibits our ability to provide for the career termination needs of elite athletes. Until recently, the team psychologist associated with a national governing body, collegiate team, or professional organization rarely had the opportunity to develop an extended relationship with team members. In fact, even at present, few sport psychologists

have the chance to establish and maintain ongoing relationships with the athletes with whom they work. For example, typical involvement of a sport psychologist consists of two weeks of contact at a training camp or being called upon for some form of performance or crisis intervention (Ogilvie & Howe, 1986). This type of contact rarely presents an opportunity for sport psychologists and athletes to communicate about issues related to career termination. Also, sports organizations often do not want the sport psychologist to address career termination and life after sport, for fear of distracting the athletes from their competitive focus.

In contrast to this approach, which was common in North America, the Eastern European nations were accepting more responsibility for preparing their national athletes for life after sport. This greater awareness would be expected because team psychologists often had long-term relationships with their team members. These professionals frequently established contact with the athletes at the inception of the structure selection process that is common in these countries. Thus relationships were initiated as early as pre-or early teens and often endured until the athlete's middle thirties (Ogilvie & Howe, 1982). Moreover, education and vocational counseling were an integral part of the athletes' developmental process (Chartland & Lent, 1987). It was also true that a significant number of these athletes were studying in areas that were related to their sports participation. Specifically coaching, motor learning, exercise physiology, and physical therapy often became their areas of major interest and, subsequently, their chosen careers following termination of their athletic careers. Because the discrepancy between athletic and postathletic careers was relatively small and the athletes were able to combine their love of sport with a postathletic career, it seems reasonable to suggest that they would be less likely to exhibit problems of adaptation to a life as a noncompetitor (Pawlak, 1984).

Another factor that might attenuate the traumatic effects of career termination on Eastern European athletes is that the average age of their competitors is significantly above that of U.S. elite athletes. This fact may be due in part to the limited pool of talent from which they have to draw. Most of these countries do not have the vast talent pool that emerges from our university and club programs. It might then be expected that these highly select athletes would compete longer, receive more attention throughout the duration of their careers, retire at a later age, and make the transition to noncompetitor more easily.

As a consequence, in clarifying the factors that contribute to difficulties in career termination, it would be valuable to examine alternative systems such as the Eastern Europeans. This knowledge would enable us to consider differences that might explain the divergent responses to career termination as a function of the country that they represent and the nature of the system in which they developed.

It should also be noted that as salaries, prize money, and appearance fees continue to escalate, the ages of the best athletes among nations will tend to be more similar. When marginal professional athletes and world-class amateur competitors are able to earn a living in their sport longer, their incentive to stay in the sport will remain high, thus easing the pressure to terminate their athletic careers prematurely. However, it should be noted that Haerle (1975) reported that professional baseball players who competed longer tended to have more difficulty in finding a second career. As a result, simply being able to stay in a sport longer will not necessarily ease the transition process. Rather, the ability of athletes to make an effective career transition may be related to the length of the career, the reason for staying in the sport, and the level of financial security that results.

Over the past 15 years, there has been an increasing awareness of the need for preretirement planning and counseling outside the sports domain (Kleiber & Thompson, 1980; Manion, 1976; Rowen & Wilks, 1987). Similarly in recent years, there has been a growing concern about career termination on several levels of elite sports. For example, in 1989, the United States Olympic Committee (USOC) developed a manual designed to assist elite athletes in understanding important issues related to career termination and guide them in devising a plan for their postcompetition careers (USOC, 1988). In addition, the USOC implemented career counseling training seminars for interested national athletes that were very well received (Murphy, 1989; Petitpas, Danish, McKelvain, & Murphy, 1990), and many sport psychologists currently working with U.S. Olympic teams provide services related to career termination and planning (Gould, Tammen, Murphy, & May, 1989; May & Brown, 1989).

Professional sports in the U.S. also appear to be responding to this need as well (Dorfman, 1990). Specifically both the National Football League Players Association and the National Basketball Association Players Association have, in recent years, developed similar programs for players whose careers are terminated (Ogilvie & Howe, 1982). Lastly a survey of collegiate athletic advisors indicated that a portion of their responsibilities involved providing vocational counseling (Brooks, Etzel, & Ostrow, 1987). Unfortunately there has been no empirical exploration of the extent to which these services have been used by the elite athletes. It may be that, in contrast to years past when salaries were not highly discrepant from the normal population (Andreano, 1973; Blitz, 1973), with average salaries of over $500,000 per year (Cohen, 1989) and the presence of agents controlling finances (Garvey, 1984), many of these athletes may experience a false sense of security that makes career planning a low priority for them (Hill & Lowe, 1974).

This interest has also spread to the coaching ranks as well. Traditionally, coaches have actively avoided career guidance programs based on the belief that such involvement would act as a distraction to the athletes that would detract from their focus on their performances (Taylor, Ogilvie, Gould, & Gardner, 1990). However, this opposition appears to be softening as coaches at both the professional and elite amateur levels are realizing that providing such opportunities to mature athletes can contribute to the ultimate success of the athletic program (Blann, 1985; Ogilvie & Howe, 1982).

THEORETICAL PERSPECTIVES ON CAREER TERMINATION

Since career termination began to attract attention from the sports scientific community, efforts have been made to conceptualize the process that athletes go through as their careers come to an end. Sports researchers examining this issue have looked outside the sports world as a foundation for developing explanatory models for the athletic population (Hill & Lowe, 1974; Lerch, 1982; Rosenberg, 1981).

Thanatology

Rosenberg (1982) suggests that retirement from sports is akin to social death. This concept, not related to biological death, focuses on how members of a group treat an individual who has recently left the group. Social death is characterized as social isolation and rejection from the former in-group. Ball (1976) suggests that a common reaction to an athlete's release from a team is to ignore the athlete. Furthermore this reaction by former teammates can cause embarrassment and anxiety (Rosenberg, 1982).

This explanation has received support from anecdotal and fictitious accounts of athletes who have experienced similar reactions upon retirement (Bouton, 1970; Deford, 1981; Kahn, 1972). However, the concept of social death has also received considerable criticism. For example, Blinde and Greendorfer (1985) argue that although the depictions of athletic retirement as social death are poignant and dramatic, the thanatological perspective may be an excessively negative characterization of career termination. In addition, Lerch (1982) questions the generality of social death beyond the few dramatic anecdotal cases. He bases this concern on data collected from a large sample of former professional baseball players (Lerch, 1981). The findings of this study indicate that not one of the athletes made reference to death of any sort.

Social Gerontology

This perspective emphasizes aging and considers life satisfaction as being dependent on characteristics of the sports experience. It has been suggested that four social gerontological approaches are most appropriate to the study of retirement from sports (Greendorfer & Blinde, 1985).

Disengagement theory (Cummings et al., 1960) posits that society and the person withdraw for the good of both, enabling younger people to enter the work force and for the retired individuals to enjoy their remaining years. Activity theory (Havighurst & Albrecht, 1953) maintains that lost roles are exchanged for new ones, so that a person's overall activity level is sustained. Continuity theory (Atchley, 1980) suggests that if people have varied roles, the time and energy from the previous role can be reallocated to the remaining roles. Finally social breakdown theory (Kuypers & Bengston, 1973) proposes that retirement becomes associated with negative evaluation, which causes individuals to withdraw from the activity and internalize the negative evaluation. Rosenberg (1981) indicates that each of these theories has value in expanding the understanding of retirement from sports.

Despite the intuitive appeal of the social gerontology perspectives, they have been criticized as inadequate when applied to athletic retirement. Greendorfer and Blinde (1985) indicate that there is no empirical support for the relationship between sport-related factors and adjustment to retirement. Specifically Lerch (1981) tested continuity theory on a sample of professional baseball players and found that continuity factors were not associated with postretirement adjustment. Similar findings were reported by Arviko (1976) and Reynolds (1981) in their studies of professional athletes.

Termination as Transition

Another criticism of both thanatology and social gerontology views is that they consider retirement as a singular, abrupt event (Blinde & Greendorfer, 1985). In contrast, other researchers characterize retirement as a transition or process rather than a discrete event that involves development through life (Carp, 1972; Taylor, 1972). Greendorfer and Blinde (1985) assert that the emphasis from this perspective is on the continuation rather than the cessation of behaviors, the gradual alteration rather than relinquishment of goals and interests, and the emergence of few difficulties in adjustment. Furthermore data collected from former collegiate athletes supports their view of career termination as transition.

The earliest view of athletic retirement as transition was delineated by Hill and Lowe (1974). These researchers briefly applied Sussman's (1971) analytic model of the sociological study of retirement to termination from sport. Sussman, in his multidimensional conceptualization, asserts that perceptions about retirement will be influenced by the following factors: (1) individual (e.g., motives, values, goals, problem solving skills); (2) situational (e.g., circumstances of retirement, preretirement planning, retirement income); (3) structural (e.g., social class, marital status, availability of social systems); (4) social (e.g., family, friends, extended social support); and (5) boundary constraints (e.g., societal definitions, economic cycles, employer attitudes). Schlossberg (1981) offered a similar model that emphasizes athletes' perceptions of the transition, characteristics of the pre-and posttransitional environments, and the attributes of the individual in their roles in the adaptation to the transition.

Hopson and Adams (1977) proposed a seven-step model of transition that is similar to the grieving process: (1) Immobilization (i.e., shock from the event); (2) minimization (i.e., negative emotions associated with a loss are downplayed); (3) self-doubt (in which self-esteem is threatened and depression may ensue); (4) letting go (where the individual works through feelings of loss, anger, and disap-

pointment); (5) testing out (when groundwork for a new direction is laid); (6) searching for meaning (where the individual gains perspective on the difficulties of the earlier stages); and (7) internalization (when this insight is accepted and the transition is complete).

Kübler-Ross's Human Grieving Model.

In a similar fashion, the psychosocial process that athletes experience during career termination may be conceptualized within the framework of the human grieving model proposed by Kübler-Ross (1969). She has defined five distinct sequential stages in the grieving process that she found to be almost universal in her grief-counseling experience: (1) denial against the initial trauma; (2) anger about the perceived injustice and lack of control; (3) bargaining to delay the inevitable; (4) depression over acceptance of the loss; and (5) full acceptance and a reorientation toward the future.

Previous research has demonstrated the value of applying this model to employment issues (Winegardner, Simonetti, & Nykodym, 1984). This grieving model has also proven to be a useful means by which the experiences of the terminated athlete may be understood (Ogilvie & Howe, 1986; Wolff & Lester, 1989).

CAUSES OF CAREER TERMINATION AMONG ATHLETES

The causes of termination of an athletic career are found most frequently to be a function of three factors: chronological age, deselection, and the effects of injury. As these major factors are examined, an attempt will be made to clarify their psychological, social, and physical ramifications in the career termination process. In addition, these factors will be scrutinized in terms of how they interact in the emergence of a crisis in the process of career termination.

Chronological Age

Age is typically considered to be a primary cause of career termination. Anecdotal accounts of former elite athletes underscore the importance of age in career termination (Kahn, 1971; Kramer, 1969). Empirical research has also supported this relationship. For example, in a study of former Yugoslavian professional soccer players, 27% indicated that they were forced to retire because of their age (Mihovilovic, 1968). In addition, a study examining retired boxers reported similar findings (Weinberg & Arond, 1952). Also, Svoboda and Vanek (1982) showed that 13% of Czechoslavian national team athletes terminated their careers because of age. Allison and Meyer (1988) found that 10% of their sample of female tennis professionals retired due to age.

The age of the athletes as contributors to career termination have physiological and psychological implications. Perhaps the most significant is the physiological influence of age. In particular, athletes' ability to compete at the elite level is largely a function of maintaining their physical capabilities at a commensurate level. Relevant physical attributes include strength, endurance, flexibility, coordination, physical composition. Unfortunately a natural part of the maturation process is the slow deterioration of these attributes (Fisher & Conlee, 1979). Some aspects of this process may be slowed through intensive physical conditioning, experience, and motivation (Mihovilovic, 1968; Svoboda & Vanek, 1982). However, others, such as the ability to execute fine motor skills or changes in body composition, are not considered to be remediable.

These changes have implications for both young and old elite athletes. For athletes engaged in sports such as gymnastics and figure skating, the physical changes that accompany puberty, such as height and weight gain, can literally make it impossible for them to execute skills that were previously routine, thus contributing to the premature conclusion of their careers. It should be noted that in response to these changes and their debilitating effects on performance, young athletes are most vulnerable to chemical remedies and eating disorders (Thornton, 1990). Similarly among older athletes loss of muscle mass or agility may contribute to career termination from sports such as football, tennis, and basketball (Fisher & Conlee, 1979).

Age also has psychological components in its influence on career termination. In particular, as suggested by the findings of Werthner and Orlick (1986), as athletes become older, they may lose their motivation to train and compete, and they may conclude that they have reached their competitive goals. In addition, as the athletes mature, their values may change. Svoboda and Vanek (1982) found that the values of Czechoslovakian world-class athletes shifted their priorities away from a self-focus involving winning and traveling toward an other-focus with an emphasis on family and friends.

Deselection

One of the most significant contributors to the incidence of difficulties in the career termination of athletes is the harsh deselection process that occurs at every level of competitive sports (Svoboda & Vanek, 1982). Unlike other areas of life in which people may continue to function regardless of the level of competence, sports rely on the Darwinian philosophy of "survival of the fittest," which places great value on the individuals who survive, but pays little attention to those who are deselected (Ogilvie & Howe, 1982).

Furthermore, this same Darwinian philosophy prevails throughout high school, university, elite-amateur, and professional sport, and the current deselection process is a natural consequence of such a philosophy. The deselection process is clearly illustrated with statistics indicating the re-

ality of attrition factors that operate within the competitive sports world, i.e., the proportion of athletes who successfully ascend succeeding rungs of the competitive ladder. For example, it is estimated that 5% of high school football players received university scholarships and, of these, only 1% have an opportunity to play in the National Football League (Ogilvie & Howe, 1986). Similar statistics are found in basketball (Ogilvie & Howe, 1982). Add to this the fact that the average professional career span of basketball and football players is under 5 years (Ogilvie & Howe, 1986). From this perspective, to represent a career in professional football or basketball as a viable option for any child appears to be the height of deceit. As a result, it is important that the ramifications for those who have been deselected are explored, particularly those who remain committed to participation.

To date, the only study that has specifically looked at the role of deselection among elite-amateur and professional athletes was conducted by Mihovilovic (1968). In his study, 7% of the Yugoslavian professional soccer players polled indicated that they were forced out by younger players. However, as will be discussed later, the theoretical and empirical evidence suggests that career termination difficulties are more likely to occur among these groups of athletes. As a consequence it may be reasonable to assume that deselection is a significant issue for these athletes at the highest rung of the competitive ladder.

Injury

National figures have estimated that in any given year, between 3 to 5 million recreational and competitive athletes experience a sports-related injury (Kraus & Conroy, 1984). Due to the dramatic incidence of injury, there has been a significant increase in psychosocial research directed at gaining greater insight into causal factors associated with injury (Andersen & Williams, 1988). Some of the most important contributions have come from seeking answers to such questions as: Are there injury-prone athletes? What is the relationship between injury and other life crises? What can the study of injuries contribute to our understanding of adherence issues in rehabilitation? Finally, what role does injury play in the career termination of athletes? The quest for answers to these and other important questions is providing an increased understanding of the complexity of the problem of sports injuries (Duda, Smart, & Tappe, 1989; Henschen, 1986; May et al., 1989; Rotella & Heyman, 1986).

Various writers have suggested that injuries may result in serious distress manifested in depression, substance abuse, and suicidal ideation and attempts (Ogilvie & Howe, 1982; Rotella, 1984; Werthner & Orlick, 1982). Furthermore it is believed that career-ending injuries may cause athletes to experience identity crises (Elkin, 1981), social withdrawal (Lewis-Griffith, 1982), and fear, anxiety, and loss of self-esteem (Rotella & Heyman, 1986).

Research has shown that injuries are a significant cause

of career termination. In particular, Mihovilovic (1968) reported that 32% of the Yugoslavian professional soccer players questioned indicated that sport-related injuries were the cause of their career termination. Additionally Werthner and Orlick (1986) found that 14% of a sample of 28 Olympic-caliber Canadian athletes were forced to retire due to injury. Also, Svoboda and Vanek (1982), in their study of Czechoslovakian national team members, indicated that 24% retired because of injury. Similar findings were reported by Weinberg and Arond (1952) and by Hare (1971) in their investigations of former world-class professional boxers. In addition, 15% of the female tennis professionals studied by Allison and Meyer (1988) stated that they were forced to retire due to injury.

Perhaps the most significant factor related to injury to elite athletes that affects career termination is that elite athletes perform at such a high level that even a small reduction in physical capabilities may be sufficient to make them no longer competitive at that level. As a consequence, an injury need not be serious to have dramatic impact on athletes' performances and, in turn, their careers. Moreover, when serious injury does occur, the considerable time and effort required for rehabilitation acts as a contributor to career termination (Feltz, 1986; Heil, 1988; Samples, 1987). This process not only affects the athletes' return to their previous level, but also inhibits the normal improvement that occurs during the course of an athletic career. This event further increases the likelihood that the injury will be career-ending.

Free Choice

An oft-neglected cause of career termination is that of the free choice of the athlete (Blinde & Greendorfer, 1985; Coakley, 1983). The impetus to end a career freely is certainly the most desirable of the causal factors. Reasons why athletes might freely choose to retire may be a function of personal, social, or sport-related issues. On a personal level, athletes might wish to assume a new direction in life (Werthner & Orlick, 1986), seek out new challenges and sources of satisfaction in other areas of life, or have a change in values (Greendorfer & Blinde, 1985; Svoboda & Vanek, 1982). Socially athletes may want to spend more time with family and friends, or immerse themselves in a new social milieu (Svoboda & Vanek, 1982). In terms of the sport itself, athletes might simply find that sports participation no longer provides the enjoyment and fulfillment that it once did (Werthner & Orlick, 1986).

There is some empirical evidence for this particular cause of career termination. In their interviews with Olympic-caliber Canadian athletes, Werthner and Orlick (1986) indicate that 42% of the ex-competitors retired for reasons that were within their control. However, in the Mihovilovic (1968) study, only 4% of the athletes freely chose to end their careers. No researchers have examined this issue among scholastic and collegiate populations.

Other Causes of Career Termination

In addition to the causes discussed above, which have been found to be the predominant reasons for career termination, other factors have been either suggested or reported to also contribute to retirement. These causes include family reasons (Mihovilovic, 1968), problems with coaches or the sports organization (Mihovilovic, 1968; Werthner & Orlick, 1986), and financial difficulties (Werthner & Orlick, 1986).

EVIDENCE OF TRAUMA IN CAREER TERMINATION

Despite the extensive amount of literature on the issue of career termination, there is still considerable debate about the proportion of athletes who experience distress due to retirement and how the distress is manifested. Some early writers such as Sussman (1971) believed professional athletes did not experience difficulties because they knew their sports careers would be short and they prepared appropriately. In addition, he asserted that most professional athletes were assured of second occupations upon retirement. Some more recent researchers, both within and outside of sports, draw similar conclusions. For example, outside of sport, Atchley (1980) and George (1980) suggest that retirement seems to have little influence on personal adjustment and self-identity, and most people possess the necessary coping skills to overcome any problems that arise.

In the sports domain, others make similar arguments (Blinde & Greendorfer, 1985; Coakley, 1983; Greendorfer & Blinde, 1985). These investigators base their judgments predominantly on research at the scholastic and collegiate levels. In fact, substantial research has revealed little evidence of distress due to career termination among these athlete populations. Specifically several studies of high school athletes indicate that, compared to nonathletes, the athletes are more likely to attend college, obtain undergraduate and graduate degrees, achieve greater occupational status, and earn higher incomes (Otto & Alwin, 1977; Phillips & Schafer, 1971). In addition, Sands (1978), in a study of outstanding male scholastic athletes, found that the importance of sports to these athletes declined following high school, and they defined their sports participation as a passing phase of life. Sands concluded that these athletes' departure from scholastic sports was not accompanied by trauma or identity crises.

Less clear findings were reported from research involving collegiate athletes. Snyder and Baber (1979) found that there were no differences between former athletes and nonathletes in terms of life satisfaction or attitudes toward work. Also, the former athletes effectively altered their interests and activities upon graduation. As a result, their results do not support the argument that disengagement from collegiate sports is stressful for former athletes.

Greendorfer and Blinde (1985) also judged that there were few adjustment difficulties among a large sample of male and female ex-college competitors. In support of their position, they indicated that 90% of the respondents looked forward to life after college and about 55% were very or extremely satisfied when their athletic careers ended. However, the authors deemphasize the finding that one-third of their sample indicated that they were very or extremely unhappy with their retirement and that 38% of the males and 50% of the females responded that they very much or extremely missed sport involvement.

Curtis and Ennis (1988) found few indications of distress among a sample of junior-elite Canadian hockey players and a matched sample of nonathletes. Specifically there were no differences in life satisfaction, employment, or marital status. Moreover, though 50% of the athletes indicated that retirement was difficult and 75% experienced a feeling of loss after leaving hockey, these perceptions did not appear to significantly impact the athletes at a practical level including educational, occupational, and family pursuits. Based on these results, the authors conclude that these finding reflect "a brief lament at having to give up hockey, and an occasional longing to relive the competition, camaraderie, and excitement" (p. 102).

Coakley (1983), in a review of relevant literature, states that "the transition out of intercollegiate sport seems to go hand-in-hand with the transition from college to work careers, new friendships, marriage, parenthood, and other roles normally associated with early adulthood" (p. 4). He further argues that the perception that distress is common is based on the biased sampling of male professional athletes participating in spectator sports (Greendorfer & Blinde, 1985) and accounts in the popular media (Coakley, 1983).

At the same time another group of researchers has developed an opposing view. Specifically career termination may cause distress that manifests itself in a wide variety of dysfunctional ways. The majority of those who hold this view have focused on elite-amateur and professional athletes. Anecdotal accounts of athletes with psychological difficulties include financial difficulties and drug abuse (Newman, 1991), attempted suicide (Beisser, 1967; Hare, 1971; Vinnai, 1973), and criminal activity (Hare, 1971; McPherson, 1980).

At a scholarly level it has been asserted that retiring individuals experience a loss of status, identity crisis, and a loss of direction and focus (Ball, 1976; Pollock, 1956; Tuckman & Lorge, 1953). In addition, Ogilvie and Howe (1982) report experiences of working with athletes suffering from alcoholism and acute depression.

There is also some empirical evidence for the occurrence of distress. For example, Mihovilovic (1968) reported that the coaches and management of Yugoslavian professional soccer players believed that retired players drank excessively, resorted to illegal activities, were in a serious psychic state, and had significant fears about the future. In questioning the players themselves, he found that 38% smoked cigarettes more and 16% drank more after their careers ended. Arviko (1976) also found alcoholism to be present in his study of former professional baseball players.

In addition, Hallden (1965) found that 45% of retired Swedish athletes who were interviewed were concerned about their emotional adjustment following the end of their careers. Also, Weinberg and Arond (1952) reported that retired professional boxers experienced severe emotional distress after leaving the boxing world. Unfortunately neither study specified the nature of the emotional difficulties experienced by the athletes.

However, as indicated previously, one criticism of this research is that it is biased toward professional male athletes in team sports. In response to this issue, Allison and Meyer (1988) studied the effects of career termination on a sample of 20 female tennis professionals. Their findings indicate that 50% of the athletes perceived retirement as a relief, an opportunity to re-establish more traditional lifestyles, and felt a sense of satisfaction about their competitive careers. Furthermore it should be noted that 75% remained actively involved in tennis as coaches or in business. The authors conclude that, rather than the social death concept suggested by Rosenberg (1984) and Lerch (1981), retirement may be considered social rebirth (Coakley, 1983). However, the researchers pay little attention to the finding that 30% of the athletes expressed feelings of isolation and loss of identity upon retirement and 10%, who retired unexpectedly due to injury, felt that they had failed to achieve their competitive goals.

FACTORS CONTRIBUTING TO CRISES OF CAREER TERMINATION

In considering the potential for a crisis following career termination, it is important to note that ending a career will not necessarily cause distress (Coakley, 1983; Greendorfer & Blinde, 1985). Rather there are a number of factors that make individuals, including athletes, more vulnerable to difficulties in the transition process (Rosenkoetter, 1985).

Elite athletes, when faced with the end of their careers, are confronted by a wide range of psychological, social, and financial/occupational threats. The extent of these threats will dictate the severity of the crisis they experience as a function of their career termination.

Self-Identity

Most fundamental of the psychological issues that influence adaptation to career termination is the degree to which athletes define their self-worth in terms of their participation and achievement in sports (Greendorfer, 1985; Ogilvie & Howe, 1982; Svoboda & Vanek, 1982). Elite athletes who have been immersed in their sport to the exclusion of other activities will have a self-identity that is composed almost exclusively of their sports involvement (McPherson, 1980). This notion is derived from the early work of the ego psychologists (Ausubel & Kirk, 1977) and the more recent considerations involving self-esteem and self-identity (Wolff & Lester, 1989). Furthermore without the input from their sport, these athletes have little to support their sense of self-worth (Pearson & Petitpas, 1990).

Athletes who are so heavily invested in their sports participation may be characterized as "unidimensional" people because their self-concept does not extend beyond the limits of their sport (Ogilvie & Howe, 1982). Moreover these athletes often have provided themselves with few options for investing their ego in other activities that could bring them similar satisfaction and ego gratification (McPherson, 1980). In support of this position, Erikson (1959) and Marcia (1966) suggest that the search for self-identity requires the examination of many potential alternatives as adulthood approaches. However, the structure of elite sports seldom provides athletes with sufficient time or opportunities for exploring options.

Athletes in this situation typically experience career termination as something very important that is lost and can never be recovered (Werthner & Orlick, 1986). Furthermore the finality of the loss seems impossible to bear and herein lies a significant source of the distress associated with career termination.

Perceptions of Control

Exacerbating this distress is the profound lack of control that athletes have with respect to the end of their careers (McPherson, 1980). Consideration of the three primary causes of career termination discussed above—i.e., age, deselection, and injury—indicates that all are occurrences outside the control of the individual athlete. As a result this absence of control related to an event so intrinsically connected to athletes' self-identities creates a situation that is highly aversive and threatening (Blinde & Greendorfer, 1985; Szinovacz, 1987).

Strong empirical evidence supports the importance of control in career termination. Mihovilovic (1968) reports that 95% of the athletes attributed causes to the end of their careers that were beyond their control and 52% retired suddenly. Additionally 29% of the Olympic-caliber Canadian athletes experienced a decrease in their sense of personal control following retirement (Werthner & Orlick, 1986). Similar results were found by Svoboda and Vanek (1982).

Though this issue has not been addressed extensively in the sports literature, there is considerable research from the areas of clinical, social, and physiological psychology that demonstrates that perceptions of control are related to many areas of human functioning including sense of self-competence (Deci, 1980; White, 1959), the interpretation of self (Kelly, 1967), and other (Jones & Davis, 1965) information. In addition, perceptions of control may influence individuals' feelings of helplessness (Friedlander, 1984–1985), motivation (Wood & Bandura, 1989), physiological changes (Tache & Selye, 1985), and self-confidence (Bandura & Adams, 1977). Also, control has been associated with a variety of pathologies including depression

(Alloy & Abramson, 1982), anxiety (Garfield & Bergin, 1978), substance abuse (Shiffman, 1982), and dissociative disorders (Putnam, 1989).

Social Identity

It has been suggested that retired individuals who experience the most doubt and anxiety are those who feel that they are no longer important to others (Sheldon, 1972). Pollock (1956) and Tuckman and Lorge (1953) also associate retirement with a loss of status and social identity. Certainly due to the high profile of elite athletes today, this issue is a significant concern for them (Gorbett, 1985). McPherson (1980) suggests that athletes define themselves in terms of their popular status. However, this recognition typically lasts only a few years and disappears following retirement. As a result, athletes may question their self-worth and feel the need to regain the lost public esteem.

In addition, athletes whose socialization process occurred primarily in the sports environment may be characterized as "role restricted" (Ogilvie & Howe, 1986). That is, these athletes have only learned to assume certain social roles specific to the athletic setting and are only able to interact with others within the narrow context of sports. As a result, their ability to assume other roles following career termination is severely inhibited (Greendorfer, 1985).

Only one study to date addressed this issue specifically. Arviko (1976) found that former professional baseball players who had a substantial number of social roles during their competitive careers were better adjusted. It is also possible to infer support for this contention from other research. Specifically Haerle (1975) reported that professional baseball players who continued their educations or held meaningful jobs during the off-season had better occupational adjustment following career termination. In addition, Mihovilovic (1968) reported that if the athletes did not plan for another career following termination, the experience could be painful. Similar findings were described by Werthner and Orlick (1986). This educational and occupational preretirement planning may provide other social roles for the athletes. As a result, they possessed roles that they could assume upon career termination.

Social Support

Due to the total psychological and social immersion in the sports world, athletes' primary social support system will often be derived from their athletic involvement (Coakley, 1983; Rosenfeld, Richman, & Hardy, 1989). In other words the vast majority of their friends, acquaintances, and other associations are found in the sports environment and their social activities revolve primarily around their athletic life (Botterill, 1990; Svoboda & Vanek, 1982).

When the athletes' careers end, they are no longer an integral part of the team or organization. As a consequence, the social support that they received previously may no longer be present. Moreover, due to their restricted social identity and the absence of alternative social support systems, they may become isolated, lonely, and unsustained socially, thus leading to significant distress (Greendorfer & Blinde, 1985; McPherson, 1980). In support of this notion, the findings of Remer, Tongate, and Watson (1978) suggest that a support system based entirely in the sports setting will limit athletes' ability to acquire alternative roles and assume a nonsport identity.

The smoothness of the career transition process may also depend on the amount of social support the athletes receive (Coakley, 1983; Svoboda & Vanek, 1982). Werthner and Orlick (1986) report that those Olympic-caliber Canadian athletes who received considerable support from family and friends had an easier transition. In addition the athletes who had the most difficulties indicated that they felt alone as their careers ended and expressed the desire for support during that period.

Mihovilovic (1968) also demonstrated that social support was an important part of the career termination process. Specifically he found that, according to the Yugoslavian soccer players they surveyed, 75% of their friends were from their sports club. Also, 60% of the athletes indicated that these friendships were maintained, but 34% said that the friendships ended after they retired. Moreover, 32% of the respondents stated that their circle of friends diminished following career termination. Additionally Reynolds (1981) reported that, among a sample of retired professional football players, those athletes who received support from close friends and relatives demonstrated the highest level of satisfaction in their current jobs.

Gorbett (1985) also recommends that, in addition to emotional support from family and friends, athletes must receive institutional support. However, in one study (Svoboda & Vanek, 1982), the athletes expressed considerable dissatisfaction over the support they received from their organization during the retirement process. Schlossberg (1981) found that employer support was critical for the transition to retirement outside of sport. Furthermore, Schlossberg (1981) and Manion (1976) suggest that institutional and interpersonal support can best be provided through pre-retirement counselling programs.

Pre-Retirement Planning

A common theme that emerges from the literature on retirement outside of sports is the resistance on the part of individuals to plan for their lives after the end of their careers (Avery & Jablin, 1988; Chartland & Lent, 1987; Rowen & Wilks, 1987; Thorn, 1983). This type of denial may be even more threatening for elite athletes since the immediate rewards are so attractive and the discrepancy between their current lifestyles and that which might occur upon career termination is significant. As a consequence, any acknowledgment or consideration that their athletic careers might end would be a source of significant anxiety, thus warranting avoidance of the issue altogether. Yet it is likely that this denial of the inevitable will have serious, potentially negative, and extended implications for the athletes.

It has been widely asserted that an essential component of effective career transition is sound postathletic career planning (Coakley, 1983; Hill & Lowe, 1974; Pearson & Petitpas, 1990). Substantial research is supportive of this position. Haerle (1975) reported that 75% of the professional baseball players he surveyed did not acknowledge their postcareer lives until the end of their careers. He also found that the level of educational attainment, which may be considered a form of pre-retirement planning, was a significant predictor of postathletic occupational status. Arviko (1976) and Lerch (1981) reported similar findings in their studies of professional baseball and football players, respectively.

Svoboda and Vanek (1982) showed that 41% of the Czechoslovakian national team athletes admitted that they had paid no attention to the reality that their career would end and 31% began to consider the future only immediately before termination. Similar comments were expressed by the Olympic-caliber Canadian athletes interviewed by Werthner and Orlick (1986). In addition, research on former world-class professional boxers has indicated a high incidence of difficulties following retirement (Hare, 1971; Weinberg & Arond, 1952). It was concluded that since the majority of their sample came from lower socioeconomic status environments, they lacked the education and experience to plan for the end of their careers.

Other Contributing Factors

The factors just described have received substantial and consistent attention as potential causes of distress during career termination. In addition, a number of other factors have been suggested to contribute to this process. These variables include socioeconomic status (Hare, 1971; Weinberg & Arond, 1952), financial dependency on the sport (Lerch, 1981; McPherson, 1980; Werthner & Orlick, 1986), minority status (Blinde & Greendorfer, 1985; Hill & Lowe, 1974;), postathletic occupational potential (Hill & Lowe, 1974; Haerle, 1975), health (Gorbett, 1985; Hill & Lowe, 1974), and marital status (Svoboda & Vanek, 1982).

PREVENTION AND TREATMENT OF CRISES OF CAREER TERMINATION

The phenomenon of career termination from sports can best be understood as a complex interaction of stressors. Whether the stressors are physical, psychological, social, or educational/occupational, their effects on athletes may produce some form of distress when athletes are confronted with career termination.

The evidence to date indicates that crises due to career termination occur less often among retiring scholastic and collegiate athletes (Greendorfer & Blinde, 1985; Otto & Alwin, 1977; Phillips & Schafer, 1971; Sands, 1978) and with a greater frequency among elite amateur (Werthner & Orlick, 1986) and professional athletes (Mihovilovic, 1968; Weinberg & Arond, 1952). However, appropriate intervention will decrease the risk that athletes at any level will experience distress following career termination.

The prevention of crises of career termination is a task that is not left to a few people at a particular level of competitive sport. Rather it is the responsibility of individuals involved at all levels and in all areas of sports including parents, educators, coaches, administrators, physicians, and psychologists (Werthner & Orlick, 1986). Moreover, participation of these people in fulfilling their roles in this process can range from the earliest stages of sports participation to the termination process itself (Pearson & Petitpas, 1990).

Early Development

The often single-minded pursuit of excellence that accompanies elite sports participation has potential psychological and social dangers. As discussed above, these risks involve the development of a "unidimensional" person. The personal investment in and the pursuit of elite athletic success, though a worthy goal, may lead to a restricted development. Though there is substantial evidence demonstrating the debilitating effects of deselection upon self-esteem among young athletes (Orlick, 1980; Scanlan, 1985; Smith et al., 1979), little consideration has been given to changing this process in a healthier direction. Most organized youth programs still appear to place the highest priority on winning.

It is important that the indoctrination of a more holistic approach to sports development begins early in the life of the athlete (Pearson & Petitpas, 1990). This perspective relies on a primary prevention model that emphasizes preventing problems prior to their occurrence. Considerable research indicates that primary preventive measures are a useful and efficient means of allocating resources (Conyne, 1987; Cowen, 1983). As a consequence, the first step in the prevention process is to engender in parents and coaches involved in youth sport a belief that long-term personal and social development is more important than short-term athletic success (Ogilvie, 1987). This view is especially relevant because it has been asserted that developing athletes must often face issues that are unique and separate from the normal requirements of development (Remer, Tongate, & Watson, 1978).

It has been further argued that high school and college athletic programs restrict opportunities for personal and social growth (Remer, Tongate, & Watson, 1978; Schafer, 1971). Significant issues in this area include the development of self- and social identities, social roles and behaviors, and social support systems. Moreover examples of this balance not being fostered include the low graduation rates of collegiate basketball and football programs (Sherman, Weber, & Tegano, 1986). Early intervention of these areas will decrease the likelihood that the factors related to crises in career termination such as those mentioned above will

contribute to distress due to career termination later in their lives.

It is also important to emphasize that these two issues—i.e., sports participation and development—are not mutually exclusive. Sports participation may, in fact, become a vehicle through which general "life" skills may be learned (Scanlan, Stein, & Ravizza, 1989). In addition sports may be the foundation upon which children may develop the ability to take psychological and social risks in other areas of their lives. Thus a healthy sports environment may assist athletes to become more fully integrated personally and socially, thereby enabling them to function in a more diverse variety of situations.

Prior to and During Career Termination

In addition to the values, beliefs, and skills that can be instilled in developing athletes, there is much that can be done with the athletes who attain elite status and are currently in the midst of elite athletic careers. As discussed earlier, recognition of the inevitability of career termination and subsequent action in preparation for that eventuality are the best courses of action (Haerle, 1975; Pearson & Petitpas, 1990; Werthner & Orlick, 1986).

Pre-retirement planning that involves reading materials and workshops (Kaminski-da-Rosa, 1985; Manion, 1976; Thorn, 1983; United States Olympic Committee, 1988) are important opportunities for elite athletes to plan for and work toward meaningful lives following career termination. In addition effective money management and long-term financial planning will provide athletes with financial stability following the conclusion of their careers (Hill & Lowe, 1974). It should also be noted that organizational support of this goal is critical to the comfort and commitment experienced by the athletes (Gorbett, 1985; Pearson & Petitpas, 1990; Schlossberg & Leibowitz, 1980).

Therapeutically sport psychologists may assist athletes in clarifying their values, interests, and goals. Also, the athletes could be assisted in working through any emotional distress they may experience during career termination (Kübler-Ross, 1969). Specifically the athletes might be provided with the opportunity to express feelings of doubt, concern, or frustration relative to the end of their careers (Gorbett, 1985). Also, the professional may help the athletes to explore ways of broadening their social identity and role repertoire, thus taking on new, nonsport identities and experiencing feelings of value and self-worth in this new personal conception. Additionally, athletes may be encouraged to expand their social support system to individuals and groups outside of the sports arena (Ogilvie & Howe, 1982).

On a manifest level, the sport psychologist may help the athletes cope with the stress of the termination process (Gorbett, 1985). Traditional therapeutic strategies such as cognitive restructuring (Garfield & Bergin, 1978), stress management (Meichenbaum & Jaremko, 1983), and emotional expression (Yalom, 1980) may be used in this process.

Outside of sport, Brammer and Abrego (1981) offer an interactive model of coping with transition, adapted from Moos and Tsu (1977). This model posits the need to intervene at a variety of levels including the appraisal process, social support systems, internal support systems, emotional and physical distress, and planning and implementing change. In addition, within sport, Wolff and Lester (1989) propose a three-stage therapeutic process comprised of listening/confrontation, cognitive therapy, and vocational guidance to aid athletes in coping with their loss of self-identity and assist them in establishing a new identity. There has been little empirical research examining the significant factors in this process. Outside of sport, Roskin (1982) found that the implementation of a package of cognitive, affective, and social support interventions within didactic and small-group settings significantly reduced depression and anxiety among a high-stress group of individuals composed partly of retirees.

Within sport, Svoboda and Vanek (1982) studied the ability of their sample of Czechoslovakian national team members to cope with the practical and psychological stress of adjustment to their new professions. Their results indicated that 30% were able to meet the new practical demands immediately and 58% were able to adjust within three years. However, psychological adjustment took much longer: 34% adapted immediately, but 17% had not adjusted at all. These researchers also explored the predominant means of coping with career termination. They found that social support was the most important factor. Specifically 37% indicated their family most often, followed by colleagues in their new profession (12%), friends (8%), and their coach (3%).

AVENUES FOR FUTURE RESEARCH

Due to the relative scarcity of systematic investigation into the area of career termination, major contributions can be made to the theoretical and empirical literature. As Landers (1983) has argued, a significant need is apparent in sport psychology for more theory-driven study of important issues. In addition there is a noticeable lack of empirical data to substantiate the positions held by the leading thinkers in the area. As a consequence, a program of empirical research based on a sound working model of the career termination process should be the goal.

Theoretical Development

A major thrust of research development within the area of career termination should be in the theoretical domain. In particular there is a need for a conceptual model specific to sports that incorporate many of the relevant issues that have been discussed in this chapter. Although, as discussed previously, attempts have been made to develop a concep-

tual model of career termination from work done outside of sport (Lerch, 1982; Rosenberg, 1982), these efforts have met with limited success (Blinde & Greendorfer, 1985; Greendorfer & Blinde, 1985).

It is presently suggested that an effective model must fulfill the following criteria: it must (1) identify the causal factors that initiate the career termination process (e.g., age, deselection, injury); (2) specify the factors that differentiate traumatic and healthy responses to career termination (e.g., self-and social identity, perceptions of control, pre-retirement planning); (3) designate the tertiary factors that might mediate this effect (e.g., coping resources, social support); and (4) indicate treatment modalities for distressful reactions to career termination.

Empirical Development

Based on such a conceptual model, a systematic program of research may be implemented that would progressively examine and generate data for each phase of the model. This kind of organized approach would enable researchers to draw meaningful conclusions from sound theory-driven data gathering.

Pertinent empirical questions that should be considered include: (1) does the particular cause of career termination influence the nature of the response from the athletes?; (2) what are the underlying factors relative to these causes that differentiate athletes' responses to career termination?; (3) what are the specific factors that mediate the nature of the response to career termination?; (4) what preventive measures will moderate the distress of career termination?; and (5) what strategies are most effective in the treatment of distress due to career termination?

In addition there are other ancillary concerns that would be worth addressing: (1) what issues in childhood development and early sports participation will influence the career transition process?; (2) what types of changes at the development level may mitigate potential trauma in the career termination process?; (3) are there differences in the type of sport, e.g., individual vs. team, professional vs. amateur, with respect to the athletes' responses to career termination?; and (4) are there gender, age, and cultural differences in athletes' responses to career termination?

CONCLUSIONS

The purpose of this chapter was to provide an overview of relevant issues in the process of career termination among elite athletes. In addition another objective was to discuss the factors that contribute to traumatic reactions to career termination. Lastly a goal was to demonstrate the importance of further understanding of career termination and its influence on athletes.

However, as mentioned earlier, despite its apparent significance some investigators have challenged the seriousness of the matter. For example, Coakley (1983) argues that the transition from high school football is similar to other forms of retirement and, as a result, not worthy of special concern. Moreover, Greensdorfer and Blinde (1985) assert that only 17% of their sample of retired collegiate athletes were unsatisfied with themselves after retirement. Furthermore they question the generalizability of conclusions made about career termination from a sample composed primarily of male professional athletes in spectator sports. As a consequence, they conclude that the magnitude of the problem is overrated. Eitzen and Sage (1982) further question the wisdom of basing concerns about the trauma of career termination on the 2% of the athletic population who are professionals.

However, it is presently suggested that these contentions do not adequately argue against the importance of understanding career termination. Specifically Coakley (1983) and Greendorfer and Blinde (1985) are not selecting a truly elite sample of athletes. Also, as discussed previously, they downplay their findings, which suggest a meaningful number of athletes who indicate that they did experience distress following career termination. Additionally termination from high and collegiate sports is still within the normal developmental process and consequently should not be generalized to older athletes. As a result it would not be expected that these athletes would present considerable trauma upon the termination of their careers. In addition, Greendorfer and Blinde (1985) and Eitzen and Sage (1982) indicate that if only a small portion of the population experience distress, then the issue is not worth considering. To the contrary, fortunately, in our society provision of study and assistance is not based on having a "sufficient" number of people suffering. Moreover, as is often the case, the significant visibility of this select group of elite athletes and the exposure of these issues to the general population may have a positive influence on other individuals faced with similar difficulties.

Based on this review, it is clear that career termination in sport is an important issue worthy of study. However, though there has been considerable discussion about career termination among sport psychology professionals in the field, there has been relatively little systematic exploration of the area. It is hoped that the present integration of current information will act as an impetus for future theoretical and empirical inquiry.

References

Alfano, P. (1982, December 27). When applause ends athletes face financial hurdles. *The Ottawa Citizen*, p. 41.

Allison, M. T., & Meyer, C. (1988). Career problems and retirement among elite athletes: The female tennis professional. *Sociology of Sport Journal, 5,* 212–222.

Alloy, L. B., & Abramson, L. Y. (1982). Learned helplessness, depression, and the illusion of control. *Journal of Personality and Social Psychology, 42,* 1114–1126.

Andersen, M. B., & Williams, J. M. (1988). A model of stress and athletic injury: Prediction and prevention. *Journal of Sport and Exercise Psychology, 10,* 294–306.

Andreano, R. (1973). The affluent baseball player. In J. T. Talamini & C. H. Page (Eds.), *Sport and society* (pp. 308–315). Boston: Little, Brown.

Arviko, I. (1976). *Factors influencing the job and life satisfaction of retired baseball players.* Unpublished master's thesis, University of Waterloo, Ontario.

Atchley, R. C. (1980). *The social forces in later life.* Belmont, CA: Wadsworth.

Ausubel, D., & Kirk, D. (1977). *Ego psychology and mental disease: A developmental approach to psychopathology.* New York: Grune & Stratton.

Avery, C. M. & Jablin, F. M. (1988). Retirement preparation programs and organizational communication. *Communication Education, 37,* 68–80.

Ball, D. W. (1976). Failure in sport. *American Sociological Review, 41,* 726–739.

Bandura, A., & Adams, N. E. (1977). Analysis of self-efficacy theory of behavioral change. *Cognitive Therapy and Research, 1,* 287–308.

Batten, J. (1979, April). After the cheering stops can athletes create new life in the business world? *The Financial Post Magazine,* pp. 14–20.

Beisser, A. (1967). *The madness in sports.* New York: Appleton-Century-Croft.

Blinde, E. M., & Greendorfer, S. L. (1985). A reconceptualization of the process of leaving the role of competitive athlete. *International Review of Sport Sociology, 20,* 87–94.

Blitz, H. (1973, Summer). The drive to win: Careers in professional sports. *Occupational Outlook Quarterly,* pp. 3–16.

Botterill, C. (1982). What "endings" tell us about beginnings. In T. Orlick, J. T. Partington, & J. H. Salmela (Eds.), *Proceedings of the Fifth World Congress of Sport Psychology* (pp. 164–166). Ottawa, Canada: Coaching Association of Canada.

Botterill, C. (1990). Sport psychology and professional hockey. *The Sport Psychologist, 4,* 358–368.

Bouton, J. (1970). *Ball four.* New York: Dell.

Bradley, B. (1976). *Life on the run.* New York: Quadrangle/The New York Times.

Brammer, L. M., & Abrego, P. J. (1981). Intervention strategies for coping with transitions. *The Counseling Psychologist, 9,* 19–35.

Bramwell, S. T., Masuda, M., Wagner, N. N., & Holmes, A. (1975). Psychological factors in athletic injuries: Development and application of the social and athletic readjustment scale (SARRS). *Journal of Human Stress, 2,* 6–20.

Brooks, D. D., Etzel, E. F., & Ostrow, A. C. (1987). Job responsibilities and backgrounds of NCAA Division I athletic advisors and counselors. *The Sport Psychologist, 1,* 200–207.

Broom, E. F. (1982). Detraining and retirement from high level competition: A reaction to "retirement from high level competition": And "career crisis in sport." In T. Orlick, J. T. Partington, & J. H. Salmela (Eds.), *Proceedings of the Fifth World Congress of Sport Psychology* (pp. 183–187). Ottawa, Canada: Coaching Association of Canada.

Carp, F. M. (1972). Retirement as a transitional life stage. In F. M.

Carp (Ed.), *Retirement* (pp. 1–27). New York: Behavioral Publications.

Chartland, J. M., & Lent, R. W. (1987). Sports counseling: Enhancing the development of the student-athlete. *Journal of Counseling and Development, 66,* 164–167.

Coakley, J. J. (1983). Leaving competitive sport: Retirement or rebirth. *Quest, 35,* 1–11.

Cohen, N. (1989, January). The sport 100 salary survey. *Sport,* pp. 75–77.

Conyne, R. (1987). *Primary preventive counseling.* Muncie, IN: Accelerated Development.

Cowen, R. L. (1983). Primary prevention in mental health: Past, present and future. In R. Felnes, I. Jason, J. Moritsuqu, & S. Farber (Eds.), *Preventive psychology: Theory, research, and practice* (pp. 11–25). New York: Pergamon.

Cummings, E., Dean, L. R., Newell, D. S., McCaffrey, I. (1960). Disengagement—A tentative theory of aging. *Sociometry, 13,* 23.

Curtis, J., & Ennis, R. (1988). Negative consequences of leaving competitive sport? Comparative findings for former elite-level hockey players. *Sociology of Sport Journal, 5,* 87–106.

Deford, F. (1981). *Everybody's All-American.* New York: Viking Press.

Dorfman, H. A. (1990). Reflections on providing personal and performance enhancement consulting services in professional baseball. *The Sport Psychologist, 4,* 341–346.

Duda, J. L., Smart, A. E., & Tappe, M. K. (1989). Prediction of adherence in the rehabilitation of athletic injuries. *Journal of Sport & Exercise Psychology, 11,* 318–335.

Eitzen, D. S., & Sage, G. H. (Eds.). (1982). *Sociology of American sport* (2nd ed.). Dubuque, IA: Brown.

Elkin, D. (1981). *The hurried child.* Reading, MA: Addison-Wesley.

Elliott, B. (1982, December 27). Transition into working world can take years in some cases. *The Ottawa Citizen,* pp. 41.

Erikson, E. (1959). *Identity and the life cycle: Selected papers* (Psychological Issues, Monograph 1). New York: Simon and Schuster.

Feldman, L. (1990, February). Fallen angel. *Gentleman's Quarterly,* pp. 218–225.

Feltz, D. L. (1986). The psychology of sports injuries. In E. F. Vinger & P. F. Hoerner (Eds.), *Sports injuries: The unthwarted epidemic* (pp. 336–344). Littleton, MA: PSG.

Fisher, A. G., & Conlee, R. K. (1979). *The complete book of physical fitness* (pp. 119–121). Provo, UT: Brigham Young University Press.

Friedlander, S. (1984–1985). Learned helplessness in children: Perception of control and causal attributions. *Imagination, Cognition, and Personality, 4,* 99–116.

Garfield, S., & Bergin, A. (1978). *Handbook of psychotherapy and behavior change: An empirical analysis* (2nd ed.). New York: Wiley.

George, L. K. (1980). *Role transitions in later life.* Monterey, CA: Brooks/Cole.

Gorbett, F. J. (1985). Psycho-social adjustment of athletes to retirement. In L. K. Bunker, R. J. Rotella, & A. Reilly (Eds.), *Sport psychology: Psychological considerations in maximizing sport performance* (pp. 288–294). Ithaca, NY: Mouvement Publications.

Gould, D., Tammen, V., Murphy, S., & May, J. (1989). An examination of U.S. Olympic sport psychology consultants and the services they provide. *The Sport Psychologist, 3,* 300–312.

Greendorfer, S. L., & Blinde, E. M. (1985). "Retirement" from intercollegiate sport: Theoretical and empirical considerations. *Sociology of Sport Journal, 2,* 101–110.

Greendorfer, S. L., & Blinde, E. M. (1987). Female sport retirement descriptive patterns and research implications. In L. Vander Velden & H. Humphrey (Eds.), *Psychology and sociology of sport* (pp. 167–176). New York: AMS Press.

Haerle, R. K., Jr. (1975). Career patterns and career contingencies of professional baseball players: An occupational analysis. In D. Ball & J. Loy (Eds.), *Sport and social order* (pp. 461–519). Reading, MA: Addison-Wesley.

Hallden, D. (1965). The adjustment of athletes after retiring from sports. In F. Antonelli (Ed.), *Proceedings of the 1st International Congress of Sport Psychology* (pp. 730–733). Rome.

Hare, N. (1971). A study of the black fighter. *The Black Scholar, 3,* 2–9.

Havighurst, R. J., & Albrecht, R. (1953). *Older people.* New York: Longmans, Green.

Heil, J. (1988, October). *Early identification and intervention with injured athletes at risk for failed rehabilitation.* Paper presented at the annual meeting of the Association for the Advancement of Applied Sport Psychology, Nashua, NH.

Henschen, K. P. (1986). Athletic staleness and burnout: Diagnosis, prevention & treatment. In J. M. Williams (Ed.), *Applied sport psychology: Personal growth to peak performance* (pp. 327–342). Palo Alto, CA: Mayfield.

Hill, P., & Lowe, B. (1974). The inevitable metathesis of the retiring athlete. *International Review of Sport Sociology, 4,* 5–29.

Hoffer, R. (1990, December 3). Magic's Kingdom. *Sports Illustrated,* pp. 106–110.

Hopson, B. (1981). Responses to the papers by Schlossberg, Brammer and Abrego. *The Counseling Psychologist, 9,* 36–39.

Hopson, B., & Adams, J. (1977). Toward an understanding of transition: Defining some boundaries of transition. In J. Adams & B Hopson (Eds.), *Transition: Understanding and managing personal change* (pp. 3–25). Montclair, NJ: Allenhald & Osmund.

Jordan, P. (1975). *A false spring.* New York: Bantam.

Kahn, R. (1972). The boys of summer. New York: Harper & Row.

Kaminski-da-Rosa, V. (1985). Planning today for tomorrow's lifestyle. *Training and Development Journal, 39,* 103–104.

Kleiber, D., & Thompson, S. (1980). Leisure behavior and adjustment to retirement: Implications for pre-retirement education. *Therapeutic Recreation Journal, 14,* 5–17.

Kramer, J. (1969). *Farewell to football.* New York: World Books.

Kraus, J. F., & Conroy, C. (1989). Mortality and morbidity from injuries in sport and recreation. *Annual Review of Public Health, 5,* 163–192.

Kübler-Ross, E. (1969). *On death and dying.* New York: Macmillan.

Kuypers, J. A., & Bengston, V. L. (1973). Social breakdown and competence: A model of normal aging. *Human Development, 16,* 181–120.

Landers, D. M. (1983). Whatever happened to theory testing in sport psychology. *Journal of Sport Psychology, 5,* 135–151.

Lerch, S. H. (1981). The adjustment to retirement of professional baseball players. In S. L. Greendorfer & A. Yiannakis (Eds.), *Sociology of sport: Perspectives* (pp. 138–148). West Point, NY: Leisure Press.

Lerch, S. H. (1984). Athletic retirement as social death: An overview. In N. Theberge & P. Donnelly (Eds.), *Sport and the sociological imagination* (pp. 259–272). Fort Worth, TX: Texas Christian University Press.

Lewis-Griffith, L. (1982). Athletic injuries can be a pain in the head. *Women's Sports, 4,* 44.

Manion, U. V. (1976). Preretirement counseling: The need for a new approach, *Personnel and Guidance Journal, 55,* 119–121.

May, J. R., & Brown, L. (1989). Delivery of psychological services to the U.S. Alpine Ski Team prior to and during the Olympics in Calgary. *The Sport Psychologist, 3,* 320–329.

May, J. R., & Sieb, G. E. (1987). Athletic injuries: Psychosocial factors in the onset, sequelae, rehabilitation, and prevention. In J. R. May & M. J. Asken (Eds.), *Sport psychology: The psychological health of the athlete* (pp. 157–186). New York: PMS.

Marcia, J. E. (1966). Development and validation of ego-identity state. *Journal of Personality and Social Psychology, 3,* 551–558.

McPherson, B. P. (1980). Retirement from professional sport: The process and problems of occupational and psychological adjustment. *Sociological Symposium, 30,* 126–143.

Meichenbaum, D., & Juremko, M. (1987). *Stress reduction and prevention.* New York: Plenum.

Mihovilovic, M. (1968). The status of former sportsman. *International Review of Sport Sociology, 3,* 73–96.

Moos, R., & Tsu, V. (1977). The crisis of physical illness: An overview. In R. Moos & V. Tsu (Eds.), *Coping with physical illness* (pp. 9–22). New York: Plenum.

Morrow, L. (1978, February 27). To an athlete getting old. *Time,* p. 45.

Murphy, S. M., Abbot, S., Hillard, N., Petitpas, A., Danish, S., & Holloway, S. (1989, September). *New frontiers in sport psychology: Helping athletes with the career transition process.* Paper presented at the annual meeting of the Association for the Advancement of Applied Sport Psychology, Seattle, WA.

Newman, B. (1989, special issue). Striking the lode. *Sports Illustrated,* pp. 282–285.

Newman, B. (1991, March 11). The last return. *Sports Illustrated,* pp. 38–42.

Ogilvie, B. C. (1982). Career crises in sports. In T. Orlick, J. T. Partington, & J. H. Salmela (Eds.), *Proceedings of the Fifth World Congress of Sport Psychology* (pp. 176–183). Ottawa, Canada: Coaching Association of Canada.

Ogilvie, B. C. (1983). When a dream dies. *Women's Sports Magazine, 5,* 5–7.

Ogilvie, B. C. (1987, October). *Traumatic effects of sports career termination.* Paper presented at the National Conference of Sport Psychology, Washington, DC.

Ogilvie, B. C., & Howe, M. (1982). Career crisis in sport. In T. Orlick, J. T. Partington, & J. H. Salmela (Eds.), *Proceedings of the Fifth World Congress of Sport Psychology* (pp. 176–183). Ottawa, Canada: Coaching Association of Canada.

Ogilvie, B. C., & Howe, M. (1986). The trauma of termination from athletics. In J. M. Williams (Ed.), *Applied sport psychology: Personal growth to peak performance* (pp. 365–382). Palo Alto, CA: Mayfield.

Orlick, T. (1980). *In pursuit of excellence.* Ottawa, Canada: Coaches Association of Canada.

Orlick, T. D., & Botterill, C. (1975). *Every kid can win.* Chicago: Nelson-Hall.

Otto, L. B., & Alwin, D. F. (1977). Athletics, aspirations, and attainments. *Sociology of Education, 42,* 102–113.

Pawlak, A. (1984). The status and style of life of Polish Olympians after completion of their sports careers. *International Review of Sport Sociology, 19,* 169–183.

Pearson, R. E., & Petitpas, A. J. (1990). Transitions of athletes: Developmental and preventive perspectives. *Journal of Counseling & Development, 69,* 7–10.

Peterson, C., Bettes, B. A., & Seligman, M. E. (1985). Depressive symptoms and unprompted causal attributions: Content analysis. *Behavior Research and Therapy, 23,* 379–382.

Petitpas, A., Danish, S., McKelvain, R., & Murphy, S.M. (1990, September). *A career assistance program for elite athletes.* Paper presented at the annual meetings of the Association for the Advancement of Applied Sport Psychology, San Antonio, TX.

Phillips, J. C., & Schafer, W. E. (1971). Consequences of participation in interscholastic sport. *Pacific Sociological Review, 14,* 328–338.

Plimpton, G. (1977, January). The final season. *Harpers,* pp. 63–67.

Pollock, O. (1956). *The social aspects of retirement.* Homewood, IL: Richard D. Irwin.

Putnam, F. W. (1989). Pierre Janet and modern views of dissociation. *Journal of Traumatic Stress, 2,* 413–429.

Putnam, P. (1991, February 18). So long, Sugar. *Sports Illustrated,* pp. 22–25.

Remer, R., Tongate, R. A., & Watson, J. (1978). Athletes: Counseling for the overprivileged minority. *The Personnel and Guidance Journal, 56,* 622–629.

Reynolds, M. J. (1981). The effects of sports retirement on the job satisfaction of the former football player. In S. L. Greendorfer & A. Yiannakis (Eds.), *Sociology of sport: Perspectives* (pp. 127–137). West Point, NY: Leisure Press.

Rosenberg, E. (1981). Gerontological theory and athletic retirement. In S. L. Greendorfer & A. Yiannakis (Eds.), *Sociology of sport: Diverse perspectives* (pp. 119–126). West Point, NY: Leisure Press.

Rosenberg, E. (1984). Athletic retirement as social death: concepts and perspectives. In N. Theberge & P. Donnelly (Eds.), *Sport and the sociological imagination* (pp. 245–258). Fort Worth, TX: Texas Christian University Press.

Rosenfeld, L. B., Richman, J. M., & Hardy, C. J. (1989). Examining social support networks among athletes: Description and relationship to stress. *The Sport Psychologist, 3,* 23–33.

Rosenkoetter, M. M. (1985). Is your older client ready for a role change after retirement? *Journal of Gerontological-Nursing, 11,* 21–24.

Roskin, M. (1982). Coping with life changes: A preventive social work approach. *American Journal of Community Psychology, 10,* 331–340.

Rotella, R. J., & Heyman, S.R. (1986). Stress, injury, and the psychological rehabilitation of athletes. In J. M. Williams (Ed.), *Applied sport psychology: Personal growth to peak performance* (pp. 343–364). Palo Alto, CA: Mayfield.

Rowen, R. B., & Wilks, S. (1987). Pre-retirement planning, a quality of life issue for retirement. *Employee Assistance Quarterly, 2,* 45–56.

Samples, P. (1987). Mind over muscle: Returning the injured athlete to play. *The Physician and Sports Medicine, 15,* 172–180.

Sands, R. (1978). A socio-psychological investigation of the effects of role discontinuity on outstanding high school athletes. *Journal of Sport Behavior, 1,* 174–185.

Scanlan, T. K. (1985). Sources of stress in youth sport athletes. In M. R. Weiss & D. Gould (Eds.), *Sports for children and youth* (pp. 75–89). Champaign, IL: Human Kinetics.

Scanlan, T. K., Stein, G. L., & Ravizza, K. (1989). An in-depth study of former elite figure skaters: II. Sources of enjoyment. *Journal of Sport and Exercise Psychology, 11,* 65–83.

Schafer, W. (1971). *Sport socialization and the school.* Paper presented at the Third International Symposium on the Sociology of Sport, Waterloo, Ontario, Canada.

Schlossberg, N. (1981). A model for analyzing human adaptation to transition. *The Counseling Psychologist, 9,* 2–18.

Sheldon, R. (1977). Self-confidence in preparing for retirement. *The Gerontologist, 17,* 28–38.

Sherman, T. M., Weber, L. J., & Tegano, C. (1986). Conditions for effective academic assistance programs for football student athletes. *Journal of Sport Behavior, 9,* 173–181.

Shiffman, S. (1982). A relapse-prevention hotline. *Bulletin of the Society of Psychologists in Substance Abuse, 1,* 50–54.

Smith, R. E., Smoll, F. L., & Curtis, B. (1979). Coach effectiveness training: A cognitive-behavior approach to enhancing relationships skills in youth sport coaches. *Journal of Sport Psychology, 1,* 59–75.

Snyder, E., & Baber, L. (1979). A profile of former collegiate athletes and non-athletes: Leisure activities, attitudes toward work and aspects of satisfaction with life. *Journal of Sport Behavior, 2,* 211–219.

Stephens, L. (1984, May 11). After cheers fade away, hockey stars find life rough. *The Ottawa Citizen,* p. 43.

Sussman, M.B. (1971). An analytical model for the sociological study of retirement. In F. M. Carp (Ed.), *Retirement* (pp. 29–73). New York: Behavioral Publications.

Svoboda, B., & Vanek, M. (1982). Retirement from high level competition. In T. Orlick, J. T. Partington, & J. H. Salmela (Eds.), *Proceedings of the Fifth World Congress of Sport Psychology* (pp. 166–175). Ottawa, Canada: Coaching Association of Canada.

Szinovacz, M. E. (1987). Preferred retirement satisfaction in women. *International Journal of Aging and Human Development, 24,* 301–317.

Tache, J., & Selye, H. (1985). On stress and coping mechanisms. *Issues in Mental Health Nursing, 7,* 3–24.

Taylor, C. (1972). Developmental conceptions and the retirement process. In F. M. Carp (Ed.), *Retirement* (pp. 77–113). New York: Behavioral Publications.

Thorn, I. (1983). Counseling and career development programs in an organization: Design, implementation, and evaluation. *International Journal for the Advancement of Counseling, 6,* 69–77.

Thornton, J. S. (1990). Feast or famine: Eating disorders in athletes. *The Physician & Sports Medicine, 18,* 116–121.

Tuckman, J. & Lorge, I. (1953). *Retirement and the Industrial Worker.* New York: Macmillan.

United States Olympic Committee. (1988). *Career assessment program for athletes: 1988-89 seminar workbook.* Colorado Springs, CO: USOC.

Vecsey, G. (1980, October 28). Counseling helps many in second career. *New York Times,* pp. A33, 36.

Vinnai, G. (1973). *Footballmania.* London: Orbach & Chambers.

Weinberg, K., & Arond, H. (1952). The occupational culture of the boxer. *American Journal of Sociology, 57,* 460–469.

Werthner, P., & Orlick, T. (1982). Transition from sport: coping with the end. In T. Orlick, J. T. Partington, & J. H. Salmela (Eds.), *Proceedings of the Fifth World Congress of Sport Psychology* (pp. 188–192). Ottawa, Canada: Coaching Association of Canada.

Werthner, P., & Orlick, T. (1986). Retirement experiences of successful Olympic athletes. *International Journal of Sport Psychology, 17,* 337–363.

White, C. (1974). After the last cheers, what do superstars become? *Physician and Sports Medicine, 2,* 75–78.

Winegardner, D., Simonetti, J. L., & Nykodym, N. (1984). Unemployment: The living death? *Journal of Employment-Counseling, 21,* 149–155.

Wolff, R., & Lester, D. (1989). A theoretical basis for counseling the retired professional athlete. *Psychological Reports, 64,* 1043–1046.

Wood, R., & Bandura, A. (1989). Social cognitive theory of organizational management. *Academy of Management Review, 14,* 361–384.

Yalom, I. D. (1980). *Existential psychotherapy.* New York: Harper/Collins.

EXERCISE / HEALTH PSYCHOLOGY

·36·

EXERCISE ADHERENCE

Rod K. Dishman

During the past decade interest by researchers from the fields of sports medicine, public health, and behavioral medicine/health psychology in the determinants of exercise adherence has grown exponentially (Dishman, 1988a). The scientific quality of the research also has begun to mature. Although there has been a small critical mass of researchers in the area who can be viewed as exercise psychologists, the general trends of growth and scientific maturity have been slower and less pronounced in the field of sport psychology (Dishman, 1982b, 1990). Herein, I will restrict the literature reviewed to the English language and to those studies I am familiar with from my personal retrieval system. Studies continue to appear from many countries, but most of the published studies come from North America, Western Europe and Scandinavia, and Australia.

My specific purposes are (1) to provide an overview of the published research on exercise adherence that is consistent with consensus documents previously sanctioned by governmental agencies in the United States (Dishman, Sallis, & Orenstein, 1985), Canada (Bouchard, Shephard, Stephens, Sutton, & McPherson, 1990), and the United Kingdom (Sports Council of Great Britain, 1990), (2) to discuss theoretical models applied to the study of exercise adherence and the strength of the evidence that has accumulated, (3) to summarize key methodology problems that continue to face researchers in this area, and (4) to restate major questions that face future research. To provide a comprehensive overview, I have revised and integrated material from a number of my previous reviews of the topic (Dishman, 1982, 1988b, 1990a, 1990b, 1991; Dishman, Sallis & Orenstein, 1985). Scholars already familiar with these papers will be more interested in the upcoming sequel (Dishman, in press) to our original edited book on exercise adherence (Dishman, 1988a).

BACKGROUND

The Public Health Service of the United States recently designated understanding the determinants of regular participation in physical activity a research priority for the nation (U.S. Department of Health and Human Services, 1991, p. 107). There is now a scientific consensus that moderate leisure time physical activity and occupational activity are associated with decreased premature mortality and increased health (Bouchard, Shephard, Stephens, Sutton, & McPherson, 1990). However, the 1990 participation rate objectives for vigorous and frequent leisure activity (Powell, Spain, Christenson, & Mollenkamp, 1986) were not met (Centers for Disease Control, 1990), and it is now clear that this failure was in part due to the lack of understanding of the determinants that influence free-living physical activity and adherence to supervised exercise programs (Dishman, Sallis, & Orenstein, 1985).

Population estimates (Stephens, Jacobs, & White, 1985) indicate that current participation rates in the U.S. fell far below the 1990 objectives (Centers for Disease Control, 1987; Centers for Disease Control, 1990; Powell, Spain, Christenson, & Mollenkamp, 1986) and below guidelines indicated by epidemiologic evidence (Paffenbarger & Hyde, 1988; Powell, Thompson, Caspersen, & Kendrick, 1987) and consensus among sports medicine experts (American College of Sports Medicine, 1990). The prevalence of vigorous and frequent activity in the U.S. is estimated at 10% of the adult population (Brooks, 1987a, 1987b; Caspersen, Christenson, & Pollard, 1987). This rate is comparable to estimates from Australia (National Heart Foundation of Australia, 1985) and exceeds estimates from the United Kingdom (Sports Council of Great Britain,

Thanks go to Dr. Charles E. Lance for his expertise in developing the path models presented in Figure 36–1 and his discussions about their theoretical interpretation.

1990). It is believed that about 25% of Canadians are highly active (Stephens, Craig, & Ferris, 1986), while Scandinavian estimates also appear to exceed those of the U.S.

I am unaware of estimates from other countries, but it is unlikely that leisure exercise participation rates in other developed and developing nations will exceed those found in North America. Evidence (Stephens, 1987) does suggest that free-living leisure activity has increased in North America and in Western and Eastern Europe during the past 15 years. Although it is not clear that this increase is the result of public health promotion (Dishman, 1990; Godin & Shephard, 1983; Iverson, Fielding, Crow, & Christenson, 1985) and behavioral interventions (Dishman, 1991), this apparent increase is encouraging because it suggests that physical activity patterns can be changed. The magnitude of the increase is not known because the available technology for assessing physical activity in a population has not permitted precise quantification of activity intensity, time spent in activity, or periodicity of activity and inactivity (LaPorte, Montoye, & Caspersen, 1985; Montoye & Taylor, 1984; Slater, Green, Vernor, & Keith, 1987; Washburn & Montoye, 1986).

Despite the increase in physical activity prevalence, estimates of sedentary leisure have remained high and range from 30 to 60% of the North American population, depending on the definition of sedentariness used (Caspersen, Christenson, & Pollard, 1986; Centers for Disease Control, 1987, 1990; Stephens, Craig, & Ferris, 1986). According to the Behavioral Risk Factor Surveillance System coordinated by the U.S. Centers for Disease Control, about 58% of American adults over 18 years of age do not exercise at least 3 days per week for 20 minutes per session (Centers for Disease Control, 1990). The dropout rate from supervised exercise programs reported around the world has remained at roughly 45% during the past 20 years (Dishman, 1988a).

In summary it appears that individuals who in the past have been infrequently active have been encouraged to become more regularly active, but that many sedentary individuals have remained sedentary. If this is the case, it has important implications for the potential effectiveness of interventions designed to increase physical activity. As will be seen later in this chapter, it is possible that some theories and technologies for increasing physical activity may be more or less effective depending on whether they are targeted to individuals with a lifetime history of inactivity, a history of sporadic activity, or to individuals who have a history of sustained activity but have also experienced one or more periods of inactivity. It is becoming increasingly evident that one theory or type of intervention applied in general to all people will not solve the problem of sedentariness. An undergirding objective of this chapter is to move us closer to understanding who will benefit from what type of intervention delivered in what way and when.

To accomplish this objective, the consensus over the determinants of leisure physical activity and adherence to supervised exercise programs will be presented. To complement this empirical evidence, brief descriptions of the most popular theoretical models applied to physical activity and exercise settings follow. It is hoped that the theoretical material will add focus to the empirical studies and that in turn the empirical studies may suggest boundary conditions (i.e., limiting or facilitating circumstances) that clarify the generalizability and usefulness of the theories that have been studied.

KNOWN DETERMINANTS

There is a consensus that known determinants of physical activity can be categorized as past and present personal attributes, past and present environments, and physical activity itself, and it is believed that determinants may differ somewhat for supervised vs. free-living settings and for adoption vs. maintenance of a physical activity pattern (Dishman, 1982a; Dishman, Sallis, & Orenstein, 1985). Results of the relevant literature underlying this consensus are summarized in Table 36–1. The term *determinant* is used to denote a reproducible association or predictive relationship rather than cause-and-effect.

Personal Attributes

Personal attributes have included demographic variables, biomedical status, past and present behaviors, activity history, and psychological traits and states associated with physical activity. Determinants that are descriptive of the individual are important because they can identify personal variables or population segments that may be targets for interventions to increase physical activity or, conversely, describe impediments or people resistive to physical activity interventions.

Demographics

When physical activity is defined by observation, those who do not adopt or adhere to supervised rehabilitative and worksite exercise programs typically have high CHD risk profiles. Smokers and blue-collar workers are likely dropouts from rehabilitative exercise programs for postmyocardial infarction patients (Oldridge, 1982) and are unlikely to utilize worksite exercise facilities (Conrad, 1987; Fielding, 1982; Shephard, 1988). The robustness of these determinants for other supervised settings and the population is less clear. Although blue-collar workers are less likely to be active when total leisure activity is considered (Canada Fitness Survey, 1983; Chubb & Chubb, 1981; Stephens, Jacobs, & White, 1985; Stephens, Craig, & Ferris, 1986), neither smoking nor occupational status appears related to participation in leisure sport (The Miller Lite Report on American Attitudes Toward Sports, 1983; The Perrier Study: Fitness in America, 1979). It appears that smoking is unrelated to physical activity (Norman, 1986), but those who engage in high-intensity, high-frequency fitness regimens may be less likely to be smokers (Blair, Jacobs, & Powell, 1985). Sedentary smokers are likely to complain of exertional fatigue

TABLE 36–1. Summary of variables that may determine the probability of physical activity.

Determinant	Changes in probability	
	Supervised Program	Free-living Activity
Personal Attributes		
Past program participation	++	+ (=)
Past free-living activity	+	+
Contemporary program activity		0
School sports	0	0
Health behaviors	00	+ (=)
Blue-collar occupation	—	--
Smoking	—	0
Overweight (fatness or body mass index)	--	--
*High risk for coronary heart disease	--	--
Type A behavior pattern	--	+
Health, exercise knowledge	0	0
Health Locus of Control	+	+
Attitudes	0	0
Enjoyment of activity	+	+ (=)
Perceived health or fitness	++	-- (=)
Mood disturbance	--	--
*Education (years)	+	++
*Age	00	--
Expect personal health benefit	0	+ (=)
Value exercise outcomes	0	0
Self-efficacy for exercise	+	+
Intention to be active	0	+
Active self-schemata		+
Self-motivation	+	++
Behavioral skills (Goal setting, self-monitoring, self-reinforcement, relapse planning)		+
Environmental Factors and Interventions		
Spouse support	++	+
Perceived lack of time	—	-- (=)
Facilities access or convenience	++	0
Disruptions in routine	--	
Social reinforcement or support (staff, exercise partner)	+	
Past family influences		+ (=)
Peer influence (past or present)		+ (=)
Physician influence		+
School programs	+	+ (=)
Cost	0	0
Medical screening or fitness testing	0	0
*Climate (or geographical region)	--	--
Contracts, agreements, contingencies	++	+ (=)
Stimulus control and reinforcement control	++	
Benefit and cost decision analysis	++	
Relapse prevention training	++	+ (=)
Physical Activity Characteristics		
Activity intensity	--	--
Choice of activity type (perceived)	+	
Perceived effort	— (=)	-- (=)

Key

++ = repeatedly documented increased probability

+ = weak or mixed documentation of increased probability

00 = repeatedly documented that there is no change in probability

0 = weak or mixed documentation of no change in probability

-- = weak or mixed documentation of decreased probability

— = repeatedly documented decreased probability.

Blank spaces indicate no data.

(=) indicates unknown validity of measures employed.

* = likely a selection bias, not a causal determinant.

From *Exercise, Fitness, and Health* (pp. 93) by C. Bouchard, R. J. Shepard, T. Stephens, J. R. Sutton, and B. D. McPherson (Eds.), 1990, Champaign, IL: Human Kinetics. Copyright 1990 by Human Kinetics Publishers, Inc. Reprinted by permission.

regardless of their fitness level (Hughes, Crow, Jacobs, Mittlemark, & Leon, 1984); this might deter their participation.

Participants in a supervised preventive medicine exercise program have been shown to have more formal education than nonparticipants (Oldridge, 1982), and education level is associated with free-living activity in the population (Chubb & Chubb, 1981; Stephens, Jacobs, & White, 1985; Stephens, Craig, & Ferris, 1986). Because concomitant associations seen in the population for low activity with age, fewer years of education, and low income occur in cross-sectional comparisons, the degree to which they represent cause or a selection-bias effect remains unclear. Prospective comparisons of age effects on activity between birth-cohorts and cross-sectional age groups in Harvard alumni (Powell & Paffenbarger, 1985) and users of the Cooper Aerobic Center in Dallas, Texas (Blair, Mulder, & Kohl, 1987) suggest that age is a selection bias, not a cause of inactivity. Results from the 1985 U.S. National Health Interview Survey/Health Promotion Disease Prevention (NHIS-HPDP) Survey show that the proportion of American men who, in the past two weeks, engaged in physical activity equal to or greater than 60% of estimated functional capacity declined from about 10% for ages 18–29 to about 5–7% for ages 65–74, but increased to 17% for men aged 75 years and older. For women, the participation rates decreased from about 9% for ages 18–29 years and plateaued at 5–6% for ages 45 years and older (Caspersen, Pollard, & Pratt, 1987). Age is unrelated to adherence to supervised exercise (Dishman, Sallis, & Orenstein, 1985; Oldridge, 1982).

Biomedical Status

The overweight are less likely to adhere to supervised fitness programs (Dishman, 1981; Epstein, Koeske, & Wing, 1984; Gwinup, 1975; Massie & Shephard, 1971; Mirotznik, Speedling, Stein, & Bronz, 1985; Shephard, 1988; Young & Ismail, 1977). The obese may better respond to alternative routines of moderate activity such as walking than they will to fitness regimens (Epstein, Koeske, & Wing, 1984; Gwinup, 1975), but the obese remain less responsive to public health interventions that include walking and climbing than are individuals of normal weight (Brownell, Stunkard, & Albaum, 1980).

Cardiovascular disease or low metabolic tolerance for physical activity are not reliable predictors of adherence to clinical exercise programs (Bruce, Frederick, Bruce, & Fisher, 1976; Dishman, Sallis, & Orenstein, 1985; Oldridge, 1982). Knowledge of disability, low fitness, or health risk factors alone are insufficient to prompt exercise behavior. Males at risk for coronary heart disease are less likely to enter fitness (Shephard, 1988) or wellness (Conrad, 1987) exercise programs or to adhere after entry (Oldridge, 1982; Shephard & Cox, 1980). In supervised settings, biomedical and demographic entry profiles can predict dropout for some groups, but not with the accuracy required for practical use for individual screening purposes (Dishman, 1981;

Dishman & Ickes, 1981; Oldridge et al., 1983; Ward & Morgan, 1984). Biomedical and demographic factors have low sensitivity for predicting behavior (Gale, Eckhoff, Mogel, & Rodnick, 1984). Also, several factors that are useful for predicting dropout in some patient groups (such as smoking, blue-collar work status, obesity, and angina) are not prevalent in other groups and therefore are not helpful for predicting dropout in those groups.

Past and Present Behaviors

Smoking, occupation, socioeconomic status, and overweightness may represent underlying factors that reinforce sedentary living or create barriers to adopting or maintaining physical activity. Many blue-collar occupations may carry with them the perception of on-job activity adequate for health and fitness despite low actual exertion, and the norms characteristic of low socioeconomic groups may reinforce inactivity. Smoking and being overweight could exert direct barriers for high-intensity activities or signal a generalized pattern of low-frequency health behaviors. Although cross-sectional correlational studies show little association between physical activity and other health-related behaviors (Blair, Jacobs, & Powell, 1985; Norman, 1986; Schoenborn, 1986; Stephens, 1986), many theories of human behavior assume that increasing the occurrence of other behaviors that share common precursors, environments, or outcomes with physical activity will facilitate increases in physical activity.

The degree to which habitual exercise contributes to other risk-behavior changes and the degree to which it is dependent on them has not been directly studied (Blair, Jacobs, & Powell, 1985). However, in a large population-based controlled trial in the U.S., several health-risk behaviors were favorably influenced by an educational-media campaign, while self-reported physical activity remained unchanged across one year (Meyer, Nash, McAlister, Maccoby, & Farquhar, 1980).

Activity History

If demographic or biomedical factors and other behaviors are found to represent selection biases rather than causes of physical activity, the importance of past-activity history assumes great significance for interpreting both past and present determinants, for designing and evaluating plausible interventions, and for predicting future activity.

In supervised programs, past participation in the program is the most reliable predictor of current and future participation (Dishman, Sallis, & Orenstein, 1985) for adult men and women in supervised programs for adult fitness, cardiac rehabilitation, and weight loss. Organized sport experience might contribute knowledge, skills, and predispositions useful for activity in later years, and it is amenable to large-scale public intervention. I am unaware of any prospective study showing a relationship between adherence to cardiac rehabilitation exercise programs or for free-living physical activity with participation in interscholastic or intercollegiate athletics. This illustrates the need for cautious interpretation of the cross-sectional retrospective studies linking youth sport history with contemporary adult physical activity (Powell & Dysinger, 1988). Our recent report (Dishman, 1988b) on Caucasian males was able to control confounding effects by age, fitness, fatness, and cardiovascular health and employed standardized activity measures. No association was seen between a self-report of past participation in school sports and either a cross-sectional sample of free-living physical activity or a prospective sample of supervised exercise. Future studies should quantify activity intensity, use objective measures of both school and community sport participation and subjective and objective measures of the sport experience, and sample females and other races and ethnic groups.

Although childhood sport experience can be an agent in socializing adult roles, it can also be overridden by other personal and environmental influences that exert a more immediate impact in adulthood. There is a growing literature on participation motivation and determinants of dropout in organized youth sport (Feltz & Ewing, 1987) that parallels public health concerns about childhood activity patterns. However, interpretation of this literature is also difficult because studies have typically involved cross-sectional and correlational comparisons of static groups, and the validity of the self-reports used to assess determinants has not been confirmed.

Psychological Traits and States

Psychological constructs can account for variability in behavior within population segments that are demographically homogeneous and across settings that differ in place and time. Some psychological factors (e.g., attitudes, beliefs, values, expectancies, and intentions) are amenable to change. To understand how advancements in psychological theory and methodology may clarify the determinants of physical activity, it is instructive to first examine the results from empirical studies and prominent theoretical models of general behavior.

Our trait measure of self-motivation (Dishman & Ickes, 1981) has been a more consistent correlate of physical activity (Knapp, 1988; Sonstroem, 1988). Evidence (Heiby, Onorato, & Sato, 1987) suggests that self-motivation may reflect self-regulatory skills such as effective goal setting, self-monitoring of progress, and self-reinforcement believed important for maintaining physical activity (Dishman, 1982). Successful endurance athletes have consistently scored high on self-motivation, and self-motivation has discriminated between adherents and dropouts across a wide variety of settings ranging from athletic conditioning, adult fitness, preventive medicine, cardiac rehabilitation, commercial spas, corporate fitness (Knapp, 1988; Sonstroem, 1988), and free-living activity in college students (Dishman & Steinhardt, 1988). The set-

tings studied have varied in length from five weeks to two years and have included men and women of various fitness levels.

Other studies have shown no differences between adherents and dropouts on self-motivation in adult fitness, dance exercise, and interscholastic sport (Knapp, 1988; Sonstroem, 1988; Ward & Morgan, 1984). Our initial classification model (Dishman & Ickes, 1981) was most accurate when self-motivation scores were combined with body weight and composition. Psychological traits probably interact with aspects of the physical activity setting to determine behavior. Programs with strong social support or reinforcement in settings requiring low-frequency, low-intensity activity may negate differences in self-motivation (Wankel, Yardley, & Graham, 1985). The self-motivated individual may also leave a supervised program but continue a personal program of free-living activity.

Although psychological traits do change, they are resistant to change over the narrow ranges of time, exposure, and settings characteristic of medical and public health interventions. Factors related to knowledge, attitudes, values, and beliefs have proven more responsive to population-based education and persuasion campaigns designed to alter health behaviors.

Knowledge, Attitudes, and Beliefs. Knowledge and belief in the health benefits of physical activity may motivate adoption of an exercise program, but their roles for reinforcing adherence are less clear. Personal goal attainment, satisfaction, and enjoyment of activities have been stronger reinforcers of maintenance of participation in worksite (Shephard, 1988) and gerontological (Stones, Kozma, & Stones, 1987) exercise programs. Inactive members of minority and low socioeconomic groups are relatively uninformed about the health benefits of exercise and its appropriate forms or amounts (Canada Fitness Survey, 1983; Caspersen, Christenson, & Pollard, 1986; The Perrier Study: Fitness in America, 1979; Vega, Sallis, Patterson, Rupp, Atkins, & Nader, 1987). In one U.S. population survey, only 5% of the U.S. population accurately identified the optimal intensity, duration, and frequency of physical activity for cardiopulmonary fitness (Caspersen, Christenson, & Pollard, 1986), but 70% knew the recommended duration and intensity. Estimates from several countries indicate that more than half the public is aware of fitness promotion programs, but less than 20% of the active respondents in one survey felt that they were influenced by such programs (McIntosh, 1980).

Education campaigns may more effectively increase physical activity if they dispel misinformation that might impede activity for some groups and if knowledge about effective goal setting and behavioral skills is reinforced by successful experience or peer models who demonstrate the skills and desirable outcomes.

Those who perceive their health as poor are unlikely to enter or adhere to an exercise program (Morgan, Shephard, & Finucane, 1984; Lindsay-Reid & Osborn, 1980), and, if they do, they are likely to participate at low intensity and low frequency (Sidney & Shephard, 1976). Those who believe that exercise has little value for health and fitness do not expect health outcomes from physical activity and also believe health outcomes are out of their personal control and have been found to exercise less frequently and to drop out sooner in fitness-related programs than peers holding opposite views (Dishman & Ickes, 1981). However, because most entrants into supervised programs share similarly positive attitudes and beliefs about expected outcomes from exercise, their self-perceptions of exercise ability, feelings of health responsibility, and attitude toward exercise have not reliably predicted who will adhere to the program (Andrew, 1981; Dishman, 1982; Dishman & Ickes, 1981). Health beliefs, positive attitudes toward activity, subjective norms and beliefs in the instrumental value of physical activity can influence the intention to be active, but intentions have also failed to predict subsequent participation (Godin, Valois, Shephard, & Desharnais, 1987; Godin, Shephard, & Colantonio, 1986).

It is likely that a lack of knowledge about appropriate physical activity and negative or neutral attitudes and beliefs about physical activity outcomes may impede physical activity for some people, but by themselves positive knowledge, attitudes and beliefs about general health outcomes of physical activity appear inadequate to ensure participation in physical activity.

Efficacy and Outcome Expectancies. There are also mixed findings from both supervised and free-living settings about the roles of efficacy and outcome expectancies as determinants of physical activity. Specific efficacy beliefs about the ability to exercise have predicted compliance with an exercise prescription in both heart patients (Ewart, Stewart, & Gillilan, 1986; Ewart, Taylor, Reese, & DeBusk, 1983) and lung patients (Kaplan, Atkins, & Reinsch, 1984) and free-living activity in a population base (Sallis, Haskell, Fortmann, Vranizan, Taylor, & Solomon, 1986). In young healthy adults, however, a belief in personal control over health outcomes predicts free-living activity, but beliefs and values held specifically for exercise outcomes and personal ability to control them appear unrelated to both free-living and supervised physical activity (Dishman & Steinhardt, 1990).

Other expectancy-value beliefs about physical activity outcomes and perceived barriers to participation have been understudied, but newly developed technology makes this possible (Steinhardt & Dishman, 1989).

Environmental Factors

Access to facilities is perceived as an important participation influence (Canada Fitness Survey, 1983), particularly among the elderly (Shephard, 1987). Also, both the perceived and actual convenience of the exercise setting (Andrew et al., 1981; Gettman, Pollock, & Ward, 1983) are consistent discriminators between those who choose to enter or forego involvement and between those who adhere

or drop out, in supervised exercise programs. In one population-based study of Southern California adults, a weak but significant association was found, after controlling for age, education, and income, between self-reported participation in three or more weekly exercise sessions and the density of commercial exercise facilities located within one kilometer of the home address (Sallis, Hovell, Hofstetter, Elder, Hackley, Caspersen, & Powell, 1990). One half of the sample reported exercising at home, and an early Scandinavian study of heart patients showed that home-based exercise can increase exercise compliance (Sanne, 1973).

There is also some evidence that the structure or organization of job responsibilities at the worksite may influence leisure physical activity. In one population-based study from the Swedish Central Bureau of Statistics Survey of Living Conditions (Johansson, Johnson, & Hall, 1991), monotonous job demands and lack of control over work processes were associated with leisure inactivity for male and female workers aged 16 to 65 after controlling age and education level.

Time

A perceived lack of time is the principal and most prevalent reason given for dropping out of supervised clinical and community exercise programs (Dishman, 1982; Dishman, Sallis, & Orenstein, 1985; Martin & Dubbert, 1985; Oldridge, 1982) and for inactive lifestyles (American Health, 1985; Dishman, Sallis, & Orenstein, 1985; The General Mills American Family Report, 1978–1979, 1979; The Perrier Study: Fitness in America, 1979). For many, however, this may reflect a lack of interest or commitment to physical activity. Population surveys indicate that regular exercisers are more likely than the sedentary to view time as an activity barrier (American Health, 1985; Canada Fitness Survey, 1983; The General Mills American Family Report, 1978–1979, 1979; The Perrier Study: Fitness in America, 1979). It is not yet clear whether time represents a true environmental determinant, a perceived determinant, poor behavioral skills such as time management, or whether it is a rationalization of a lack of motivation to be active.

Physical Activity Characteristics

In addition to establishing national or international standards for physical activity participation based on fitness and epidemiologic criteria, it is important to determine if activity characteristics predispose or impede participation in the population or in specific population segments and settings. If large numbers of people are unwilling or unable to participate with the frequency or at the duration or intensity recommended by professional consensus (e.g., American College of Sports Medicine, 1990), it is possible that lowered standards could actually promote an increase in the activity and fitness of a population if they reduced total sedentariness.

Most studies of supervised exercise programs in adults do not show an association between dropout rates and exercise intensity or perceived exertion (Pollock, 1988). Intensity in these studies is relativized according to an individual's metabolic tolerance for exercise, and this minimizes variation in physical strain and its role as a determinant. Injuries from high-intensity running can directly lead to dropout, but this typically should not occur with significant prevalence until durations of 45 minutes and/or frequencies of 5 days per week are approached by previously untrained individuals (Pollock, 1988). Dropout due to injuries is not more prevalent in the elderly when walking is the physical activity (Pollock, Carroll, Graves, Leggett, Braith, Limacher, & Hagberg, 1991).

In free-living settings where the energy cost of standard activities may require varying percentages of metabolic capacity, exertional perceptions and preferences may be a more important influence on participation. In a study of California adults (Sallis et al., 1986), more men (11%) than women (5%) adopted vigorous exercise such as running during a year's time, but a comparatively higher proportion of women (33%) than men (26%) took up such moderate activities as routine walking, stair climbing, and gardening. Both sexes were more likely to adopt regular activities of a moderate intensity than they were to adopt high-intensity fitness activities. Moderate activities showed a dropout rate (25%–35%) roughly one-half of that seen for vigorous exercise (50%) (Sallis et al., 1986).

At rest the sedentary and unfit complain of chronic fatigue (Chen, 1986; Kohl, Moorefield, & Blair, 1987), and sedentary smokers report excessive fatigue during treadmill exercise (Hughes, Crow, Jacobs, Mittlemark, & Leon, 1984), but it is not now known if chronic fatigue creates a barrier to participation or if alleviation of chronic fatigue with increased fitness is an incentive or reinforcer for participation.

The relationships between fitness, physical activity, perceived exertion, and preferred types and levels of exertion have not been systematically studied as determinants of participation, but we are currently investigating whether differences in perceived exertion can explain variation in leisure physical activity among children 9–11 years of age (Darracott, Dishman, Cureton, & Youngstedt, 1992).

BEHAVIOR CHANGE INTERVENTIONS

Although some recent reports suggest that community (Brownell, Stunkard, & Albaum, 1980; Crow, Blackburn, & Jacobs, 1986) and worksite (Blair, Piserchia, Wilbur, & Crowder, 1986) health promotions can increase physical activity, the collective evidence indicates no predictable impact of health education promotions on the fitness or activity of adults (Fielding, 1982; Godin & Shephard, 1983; Godin, Desharnais, Jobin, & Cook, 1987; Meyer, Nash, McAlister, Maccoby, & Farquhar, 1980; Reid & Morgan, 1979); physician or medical office interventions and school and community promotions with children may hold more promise but have received little study (Iverson, Fielding, Crow, & Christenson, 1985).

Health Risk Appraisal and Fitness Testing

Early studies suggested that health risk appraisal might increase physical activity. Lauzon (1977) reported that health risk appraisal had no effect on smoking, blood pressure, or seat-belt use, but that it increased physical activity, particularly in high-risk males. Leppink and DeGrassi (1977) reported that 6 months after health risk appraisal of 144 patients, 37% had increased, 4% had decreased, and 59% showed no change in their exercise habits. After 18 months, 34% reported increased exercise, 11% decreased exercise, and 55% no change. These studies were uncontrolled, however, and the accuracy and validity of the self-reports of activity were not demonstrated. Establishing an objective baseline for expected improvement is particularly important in studies like these, because patients can be motivated to inflate their reports of physically active behavior in order to give the appearance of complying with their physician's advice.

Similar results have been observed for physical fitness testing. Bruce and colleagues (1980) examined the impact of a physician-supervised graded treadmill test on exercise habits one year later. Of 2,892 men sampled, 2,001 responded to a mail questionnaire; results indicated that 50% of the 1,384 initially sedentary men reported that "the exercise test motivated them to increase daily exercise." No objective measure of actual physical activity was obtained, however. A more controlled study by Driggers, Swedberg, & Johnson (1984) subsequently demonstrated that exercise stress testing had no influence on health behavior, attitudes, objective health measures, or self-reported exercise. Likewise, Ewart and associates (1983) examined the effects of exercise testing on physical activity patterns three weeks after uncomplicated myocardial infarction. The patients' confidence was increased when performing activities similar to the treadmill exercise (e.g., walking, stair climbing, and running), but an increased confidence in performing other activities such as lifting and sexual intercourse required an explanation of the test results by a physician or nurse. Self-reported activity was verified in this study both by daily heart rate monitoring and by demonstration of a decreased heart rate response to standard exercise after training. Increased confidence for leg activity was correlated with an increase in self-reported activity, but there was only a weak association between fitness gains and increased physical activity.

Other studies have examined the combined effects on physical activity of health risk appraisal, fitness assessment, and educational interventions. Reid and Morgan (1979) randomly assigned 124 firefighters to three groups: a control group that received a submaximal fitness test, an exercise prescription, and consultation with a physician; a group that also received a 1-hour media and verbal presentation; and a third group that was also taught to monitor exercise habits by pulse palpation and the use of Cooper's aerobic point system. After 3 months, compliance (as determined by self-report of two or more weekly exercise sessions of at least 15 minutes duration and a decreased heart rate during standard exercise testing) was 29% in the control group and 55% in pooled data from the two experimental groups. After 6 months, however, only about 33% of each group was participating in regular physical activity. Similar findings came from the Stanford Community study, which represents one of the few population-based attempts to modify health habits through intensive health education, media campaigns, and individual patient counseling. Although significant reductions in overall risk were observed in experimental subjects, exercise habits were not changed at 1 or 2 years.

Daltroy (1985) reported on the effectiveness of a randomized educational intervention designed to increase compliance in cardiac patients during the initial 3 months of a prescribed exercise program. Telephone counseling for both patient and spouse, with the mailing of an information brochure, increased program attendance by 12% when the groups were statistically equated in terms of entry characteristics, including coronary risk. However, without this adjustment, attendance rates were equivalent between the intervention (64%) and control (62%) groups. Much of the increased attendance occurred in patients with a high school education or less. Although three-fourths of the patients reported that they continued to be active after dropping out of the formal program, only one-third remained active at an intensity that would maintain cardiorespiratory fitness. Because limited access to facilities and inconvenience have been repeatedly cited as reasons for dropping out of supervised cardiac rehabilitation exercise programs, several studies have implemented home-based interventions. Acquista et al. (1988) combined health-risk appraisal with intensive educational and counseling sessions conducted by nurses in the home. Health behavior plans were tailored to individual risk profiles. In telephone and interview follow-up one year later, 61 of 126 persons (48%) who had reported no regular physical activity at the outset of the study indicated that they had increased their habitual activity. However, this study had no control group, and the self-selected participants (476 volunteered from a population of 3,800) could have been motivated to increase their activity patterns regardless of the intervention. Also, the validity of the interview assessment of physical activity is unclear, and the increase of activity was not quantified.

Controlled studies combining health risk appraisal with education or physical fitness assessment have not been successful in increasing physical activity on follow-up. Godin, Desharnais, Jobin, & Cook (1987) examined the effects of the Canadian Home Fitness Test and the Health Hazard Appraisal on intentions to exercise and exercise behavior over a three-month period. Mere administration of the tests was contrasted with personalized knowledge of the test results. Subjects were assigned to one of four groups: (1) control, (2) fitness appraisal only, (3) health-age appraisal only, or (4) appraisal of both fitness and health-age. Knowledge of results was given to half of the subjects in each group. The Health Hazard Appraisal had no impact on either intended or actual leisure time exercise. Although the fitness test and knowledge of results initially increased intentions to exercise, neither intentions to be active nor actual exercise behavior were changed after three months. Similarly Desharnais and colleagues (1987) examined the Canadian Home Fitness Test and EvaluLife (a Canadian version of health risk appraisal) as possible tactics for increasing leisure exercise. As predicted, only subjects with a high health risk maintained an increased intention to exercise over a three-month period. Exercise behavior was not assessed, however, and prospective studies have shown small or moderate relationships between intentions to exercise and subsequent behavior.

Behavior Modification Studies

Both reinforcement control and stimulus control strategies derived from the traditions of behavior modification or cognitive-behavior modification have been successfully implemented with exercise (Knapp, 1988). I recently reviewed 56 published reports of studies employing behavior modification or cognitive behavior modification approaches to increase or maintain exercise and physical activity (Dishman, 1991). Representative approaches included written agreements, behavior contracts and lotteries, stimulus control, and contingencies have been used successfully in case and quasi-experimental studies. Cognitive-behavioral approaches, including self-monitoring, sensory distraction, goal setting, feedback, and decision making, have appeared equally effective when used alone or when combined in intervention packages.

Behavior modification and cognitive-behavior techniques are usually associated with about a 10% to 25% increase in frequency of physical activity when they are compared with a no-treatment control group, but their impact on changes in intensity and duration of activity is less clear. Moreover, a number of preventive medicine exercise programs have reported comparable absolute adherence rates without the addition of behavior change interventions (Dishman, 1988). Uncontrolled case quasi-controlled multiple baseline studies commonly report increases of 50% to 200%. However, the absolute levels of the increased activity often fall below the frequency, duration, and intensity levels required to increase physical fitness (American College of Sports Medicine, 1990) or to decrease risk for disease morbidity or all-cause mortality (Blair et al., 1989).

With few exceptions (Epstein, Koeske, & Wing, 1984), studies have not focused on health outcomes as the dependent variable for determining intervention effectiveness. Likewise, many interventions have lasted less than 12 weeks with undemonstrated fitness or health changes. Reliable fitness changes require substantial increases in exercise intensity for periods of 8 to 20 weeks or for much longer periods of time at low intensities of activity (American College of Sports Medicine, 1990). Also, the measures of fitness and physical activity used in past studies have usually been estimates, not direct measures. Often the effect on fitness reported for the behavioral interventions has not exceeded the measurement error of the fitness estimates employed.

In general, behavior therapy studies have not demonstrated that the outcomes of treatment with physical activity are dependent on adherence or maintenance of physical activity. Only a few studies show maintenance of activity in follow-up assessments. Follow-up studies typically show that increases in physical activity associated with behavior modification are short-lived after the intervention is removed.

Also, minimally effective intervention conditions for control comparisons have been rare. Therefore generalizations are not possible about specific components of the interventions that are effective for specific populations. Many types of interventions have been associated with increased physical activity, but the superiority of these interventions has not been directly compared. For this reason and because researchers using attention, placebo, or minimally effective comparison conditions show similar changes in physical activity when compared to the intervention condition, it is not clear that the components of the interventions employed exert an influence on physical activity beyond that exerted by social support and reinforcement (Stalonas, Johnson, & Christ, 1978).

Thus the literature on the effectiveness of behavior modification and cognitive-behavior modification interventions for increasing physical activity consistently shows statistically or practically significant effects. However, the pre-experimental and quasi-experimental designs (Campbell & Stanley, 1963; Wilson & O'Leary, 1980) used in most studies, coupled with the failure to link increased exercise with treatment outcome, leads to an uncompelling case for the effectiveness of behavioral interventions for promoting physical activity in behavior therapy. A contributor to the uncompelling nature of the existing evidence has been the failure of most exercise studies to base the interventions on a broader theoretical model of behavior change, and this lack of theory has also characterized the companion literature on the determinants of physical activity. The following section describes theoretical models that may advance both surveillance and intervention studies and critiques representative studies that have applied the models to exercise or physical activity settings.

THEORETICAL MODELS OF PSYCHOLOGICAL DETERMINANTS OF EXERCISE AND PHYSICAL ACTIVITY

Psychological theories can guide the effective implementation of intervention technologies. Several theories are prominent and may have implications for public health promotions of physical activity. Psychological models described can be directed at various stages of planning, adopt-

ing, and maintaining physical activity, and they encompass attitudes, beliefs, or expectations about physical activity and health outcomes, personal ability, control, or efficacy, social norms, and behavioral skills for reducing barriers to activity and reinforcing participation.

Although each of the models describes aspects of physical activity participation, it is unknown if any model or combination of models can explain the determinants of physical activity adequately for public health purposes of increasing physical activity. It seems unlikely that psychological models that exclude or minimize considerations about biological aspects of physical activity will be sufficient to explain and predict physical activity.

Health Belief Model

This model proposes that compliance with a recommendation for a health behavior change depends on the person's perception of vulnerability to a disorder, belief that health risk is increased by noncompliance, and belief that the health effectiveness of the behavior outweighs barriers to making the change (Rosenstock, 1974).

Results of Studies. This model has not proven valid for all health behaviors (Janz & Becker, 1984). Results from exercise studies have been mixed (Sonstroem, 1988), but most researchers have not tested the total model (Lindsay-Reid & Osborn, 1980; Morgan, Shephard, & Finucane, 1984). Valid and reliable measures for perceived benefits and barriers have been available only recently (Steinhardt & Dishman, 1989). Physical activity is perceived as requiring more time and effort than are other health behaviors (Turk, Rudy, & Salovey, 1984), and free-living activity is unreliably associated with other health behaviors in the population (Blair, Jacobs, & Powell, 1985; Norman, 1986; Stephens, 1986). Thus physical activity may be relatively unique among health-related behaviors. In a recent study of exercise compliance among male cardiac patients, components of the health belief model added to the prediction of dropping out from supervised exercise once activity history and smoking status were controlled. Cues that prompt exercise were positively related to compliance. However, severity of the disease threat was positively related to dropout (Oldridge & Streiner, 1990).

General Conclusions. The failure of the health belief model to predict physical activity may in part be due to the positive view of health behaviors held by the general public or the wide range in behavioral demands or complexity of physical activity. Active individuals often perceive their health as good and not vulnerable to disease. Time, convenience, and exertion are viewed as barriers but equally so by the already active. The model was designed for risk-avoidance behavior, not health-promotive behavior. Thus its effectiveness may be less for those who view physical activity as a health-promotive behavior more than for those who see it as an illness-reducing behavior.

Locus of Control

This model proposes that beliefs about personal control over the reinforcement outcomes from behavior influences motivation, particularly in novel circumstances where past experiences cannot aid decision making (Rodin, 1986).

Results of Studies. Exercise studies with adults have yielded mixed results. Cross-sectional comparisons show exercisers to have a more internal locus, whereas prospective studies show inconsistent relationships with supervised adherence (Dishman & Ickes, 1981; Dishman & Steinhardt, 1990). Health locus of control has not predicted compliance with supervised exercise in male cardiac patients (Oldridge & Streiner, 1990). The validity and reliability of exercise-specific measures have not been demonstrated according to classical psychometric theory (Dishman & Steinhardt, 1990).

General Conclusions. Because locus of control encompasses but does not clearly distinguish the importance of beliefs about outcomes of behavior and personal control, it lacks precision for predicting specific behaviors in specific contexts (e.g., supervised exercise). Health locus of control shows promise for predicting free-living physical activity in young adults (Dishman & Steinhardt, 1990) and as a moderating variable for other models, such as self-efficacy (Bandura, 1977) and planned behavior (Ajzen, 1985).

Theory of Reasoned Action

This model proposes that attitudes about a specific exercise prescription (i.e., time, place, and type of exercise) can predict behavior through its interaction with social norms. Both influence exercise intention, which is viewed as the direct mediator of behavior (Ajzen & Fishbein, 1977).

Results of Studies. Studies of free-living physical activity show mixed results over the validity of intentions for predicting physical activity (Godin, Valois, Shepard, & Desharnais, 1987; Godin, Colantonio, Davis, Shephard, & Simand, 1986; Godin, Shephard, & Colantonio, 1986). Components of the model can be related to participation when the total model is not. It appears that behaviorally specific attitudes can directly influence self-reported physical activity independently of intention statements (Godin & Shephard, 1990). Spousal influences on exercise appear to be reliable correlates of participation. The model predicts about one-third of exercise intentions; the range has been from 0.07 to 0.66 (Godin & Shephard, 1990; Godin, Valois, Shepard, & Desharnais, 1987; Godin, Colantonio, Davis, Shephard, & Simand, 1986; Godin, Shephard, & Colantonio, 1986; Godin, Cox, & Shephard, 1983; Godin, Desharnais, Jobin & Cook, 1987; Pender & Pender, 1986; Sonstroem, 1988).

General Conclusions. Intentions seem largely necessary but not sufficient to predict physical activity. The extent to which the active plan their exercise routines and the impact of interventions on intentions and subsequent exercise remains unknown, and it appears that past activity history may be a more reliable predictor of physical activity than is a statement of intentions to be active. Intention statements can be redundant with activity history in the previously active, and they often provide false-positive predictions among the sedentary (Godin, Shephard, & Colantonio, 1986).

Self-Efficacy

This model proposes that in order to attempt and persist at a behavior change, one must perceive a personal ability to carry out the behavior when the outcome is known. According to social-cognitive theory, self-efficacy develops by (a) actual mastery, (b) modeling, (c) verbal persuasion, and (d) emotional signs of coping ability (Bandura, 1977).

Results of Studies. Among post-MI patients, beliefs about ability to exercise can increase following fitness testing or training (Ewart, Taylor, Reese, & DeBusk, 1983; Sanne, Elmfeldt, Grimby, Rydin, & Wilhelmsen, 1973). Self-efficacy beliefs distinguish patients who exceed or do not attain their exercise intensity prescriptions (Ewart, Stewart, & Gillilan, 1986). They also have been shown to be better predictors of exercise compliance than are health control beliefs for chronic obstructive-lung patients (Kaplan, Atkins, & Reinsch, 1984). And they have been related to the adoption of vigorous activity in men and adoption and maintenance of moderate activity for men and women in free-living settings (Desharnais, Bouillon, & Godin, 1986).

Other studies have not supported the generalizability of self-efficacy theory to exercise. Dropouts and adherents in a preventive medicine program were equally likely to perceive increased ability for safe exertion as a benefit of exercise (Sanne, Elmfeldt, Grimby, Rydin, & Wilhelmsen, 1973). Low exercise self-efficacy predicted intention to adopt a worksite exercise program (Davis, Jackson, Kronenfeld, & Blair, 1984).

General Conclusions. Feelings of self-efficacy most accurately predict when they are specific to a narrow range of behaviors and times. Self-efficacy is influenced by actual experience and subjective signs of inability. Therefore, past experience and perceived exertional strain must be considered in exercise studies. Also, self-efficacy does not predict persistence of behavior change when incentives are not present. General feelings of physical ability might be a better predictor of overall physical activity patterns across time, settings, and activities than are specific self-efficacy beliefs (McAuley & Jacobson, 1991).

Theory of Planned Behavior

This model expands the theory of reasoned action by considering perceived and actual control over behavior. It recognizes that intentions are often not implemented because of inability, situational barriers, or the instability of intentions (Ajzen, 1985). Few physical activity studies testing the model have been reported (Dzewaltowski, Noble, & Shaw, 1990). The model may help explain the failure of reasoned-action theory to reliably predict physical activity by integrating self-control and self-efficacy variables. Consideration of real and perceived barriers to behavior provides a conceptual link with the health belief model, and consideration of individual difference variables such as willpower provide a conceptual link with our work showing an effect of self-motivation on exercise adherence.

Physical Activity Model

This model posits that attraction to physical activity is reinforced by increased self-esteem and is mediated by perceived increases in physical ability and fitness due to increased activity (Sonstroem, 1988). Studies of adult fitness programs show a weak relationship between the model and sustained participation but suggest an influence on initial adoption (Dishman & Ickes, 1981; Sonstroem, 1988). The model lacks specificity for activity, place, and time, but this may not be a problem for predicting total activity patterns. It is an attractive model because it provides a link between past activity history, fitness self-perceptions, and attitude. It permits an empirical contrast with more complex models of attitude (Ajzen, 1985; Ajzen & Fishbein, 1977), perceived ability (Bandura, 1977), and self-schemata (Kendzierski, 1990). Its similarity with models of perceived competence could integrate the literature on youth sport participation with determinants of physical activity (Feltz & Ewing, 1987).

Expectancy-Value Decision Theories

This family of theoretical models is based on a view of behavior as a function of self-expectations of the outcomes from a behavior and the evaluation of these outcomes in contrast to outcomes of alternative actions (Feather, 1982).

Results of Studies. These models are conceptually capable of predicting intention or interest in adopting free-living physical activity or resuming participation following relapse (Kendzierski & LaMastro, 1988) equally as well as the models previously considered, but it is not as clear that they can predict maintenance of participation in either free-living or supervised activity (Desharnais, Bouillon, & Godin, 1986; Dishman & Ickes, 1981; Dishman & Steinhardt, 1989; Kendzierski & LaMastro, 1988).

General Conclusions. The models provide a useful global framework for understanding the unique aspects of the pre-ceding models. Each of the preceding models has emanated from the broader decision-theory base. Integration of self-efficacy theory (Bandura, 1977), the health belief model and the theory of planned behavior (Ajzen, 1985) within an expectancy-value umbrella may offer a parsimonious model for explaining adoption of physical activity. It is important for exercise studies to determine the redundancy with outcome-expectancy values of other models that include attitudes and beliefs about outcomes and barriers to physical activity. Consideration of behavioral alternatives to physical activity may help reconcile when perceived barriers to activity are independent from low priorities for participation.

Personal Investment Theory

This model proposes that behavior is determined by the personal meaning that situations hold for the individual. It is assumed that personal meaning consists of personal incentives, the sense of self (perceived competence, self-reliance, goal-directedness, and social identity), and perceived options (Maehr & Braskamp, 1986). Most of the development and supporting evidence for the model comes from research on academic performance in schools.

Results of Studies. A few recent studies of exercise with middle-aged and older adults and with youth have purported to test personal investment theory for exercise (Duda & Tappe, 1988; Tappe, Duda, & Menges-Ehrnwald, 1990). These studies report results consistent with past studies showing that outcome-expectancy values (incentives) and perceived barriers to activity are related to participation in physical activity.

Conclusions. To date, it does not appear that the full personal investment model has been tested for exercise. The stepwise multiple regression and discriminant analysis approaches taken in the published studies have not permitted a test of the model. Furthermore, it is not now clear how personal investment theory is unique or builds upon other decision theories such as outcome-expectancy value, planned behavior, and self-efficacy. It also does not appear that the current technology being used to assess the component variables posited by personal investment theory for exercise (Tappe, Duda, & Menges-Ehrnwald, 1990) has demonstrated construct validity when judged against classical psychometric standards.

Theory of Interpersonal Behavior

The theories discussed up to this point have assumed that exercise participation is the result of a rational decision-making process that, contingent on other factors (e.g., behavioral norms, ability to execute the behaviors), is designed to optimize the attainment of available valued outcomes. However, Triandis (1977) has suggested that some behaviors are engaged in more or less automatically, without a thorough analysis of their possible outcomes. The theory of interpersonal behavior proposes that behavior occurs as a function of behavioral intentions, but also habit (past activity history), and certain facilitating or inhibiting conditions. Behavior can be rationally determined when the interaction of intentions with facilitating/inhibiting conditions is large relative to the interaction of habit with facilitating/inhibiting conditions, or behavior is largely automatic when the ratio of these interactions is inverted. Also, the probability of engaging in the behavior can be low to the extent that facilitating conditions are absent and/or inhibiting conditions are present.

The model views intentions as being determined by social factors, affect, and outomes of the behavior. Included among the important social factors are norms and commitments made to other people and an individual's conception of behavior that is consistent with self-concept.

Results of Studies. The model has been used to conceptually clarify results of studies showing that activity history has predicted physical activity when attitudes or intentions have not (see Godin & Shephard, 1990, for a review). However, it does not appear that a complete test of the model for physical activity has been reported.

Conclusions. The model presents a potentially major advance beyond decision theories because it recognizes the importance of past history and affect. The model addresses circumstances where cognitive factors are unlikely to predict or explain physical activity. If subsequent exercise studies confirm the generalizability of the noncognitive components of the model, important directions for improving the effectiveness of cognitive-educational and cognitive-behavioral interventions will be provided.

Self-Regulatory Theory

This model proposes that behavior is controlled much like a servomechanism, in which goal setting, self-monitoring of behavior, and self-reinforcement are necessary skills to implement behavioral intentions and overcome personal and situational barriers to motivation (Kirschenbaum & Tomarken, 1982; Leventhal, Zimmerman, & Gutmann, 1984).

Results of Studies. Some evidence supports the effectiveness of interventions that include goal setting, self-monitoring, and self-reinforcement (Dishman, 1991; Knapp, 1988; Martin & Dubbert, 1985; Martin, et al., 1984). Cross-sectional study suggests that these skills combine with self-motivation to explain variance in free-living activity (Heiby, Onorato, & Sato, 1987). Interventions have been most effective in multiple-component packages, particularly those using principles of relapse prevention (Knapp, 1988; Marlatt & Gordon, 1985).

General Conclusions. This approach appears particularly

important for explaining maintenance and periodicity of physical activity in free-living physical activity. The assumptions of the model seem particularly suited to understanding the process of relapse among previously active individuals.

Summary of Decision-Based Theories

A number of similarities between the exercise participation models discussed so far have been noted. For example, all of the models consider the role of extrinsic/instrumental motivation as expected outcomes of exercise and the values attached to these outcomes. Second, several emphasize the direct effects of extrinsic/instrumental motivation on exercise participation, as well as effects moderated by individuals' perceptions of ability to exercise or remain physically active. Third, some emphasize the role of subjective norms, the mediating role of behavioral intentions, and the moderating role of personal and situational factors (facilitating conditions or inhibiting conditions or factors related to perceived control for determining exercise participation.

On the other hand, each model makes unique theoretical contributions to the explanation of exercise participation. For example, self-efficacy theory is the only one of the models that explicitly proposes that perceptions of ability to exercise have direct influences on exercise participation. Only outcome-expectancy value theories propose a direct influence by intrinsic motivation, although moderated by ability to exercise, on actual exercise behavior. Only the theory of planned behavior considers possible direct influences of factors related to perceived behavioral control on intentions to exercise and exercise behavior. Finally only the theory of interpersonal behavior considers exercise history to be a direct cause of exercise participation.

These similarities and differences among the models discussed so far can be integrated into a unified model of four phases of exercise participation shown in Figure 36–1. The uniqueness or redundancy of these models must be clarified before progress can be made toward understanding their relative importance for understanding physical activity participation and toward clearly specifying targets for interventions designed to increase physical activity. The model in Figure 36–1 is presented to illustrate possible paths that could be tested. Until more integrated and competitive approaches to theory testing are taken in exercise psychology, it is unlikely that the usefulness and relative importance of most theories that appear applicable to exercise and physical activity will be known. Other models appear applicable to understanding the motivation for the maintenance of physical activity and for guiding interventions designed to increase and maintain exercise and physical activity, but they have received little attention by exercise psychologists, who have largely embraced a social psychology approach to the study of exercise. The following models have particular appeal because they can ad-

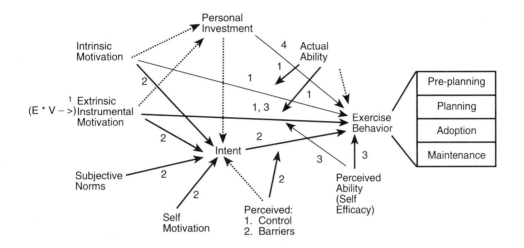

Relationships Proposed by:

1. Expectancy Theory
2. Theory of Planned Behavior
3. Self-Efficacy Theory
4. Personal Investment Theory

FIGURE 36–1. Possible path relationships for competitive tests of components of popular decision theories applied to physical activity. (a) Hypothesized causal connections between components are shown as single-headed arrows leading from explanatory variables to endogenous, or dependent, variables (e.g., arrow connecting Subjective Norms and Intentions), and (b) hypothesized moderator effects are shown as single-headed arrows connecting the moderator and the relationship which is hypothesized to be moderated (e.g., the arrow connecting Ability and the arrow from Intrinsic Motivation to Exercise Behavior). Numbers adjacent to hypothesized effects refer to the exercise participation model which generates them.

vance biological or cognitive-behavioral approaches to the study of exercise behavior.

Opponent-Process Theory

This model proposes that a two-phase process underlies motivated behavior. The primary phase to a stimulus is excitatory, and it initiates a secondary, inhibitory (or opponent) phase that returns arousal to a hedonic neutrality acceptable to the individual. The opponent process grows faster and stronger with stimulus exposure, whereas the initial phase grows weaker and decays more rapidly. Thus an initially pleasurable or aversive response requires increasing stimulus exposure, whereas its absence produces a growing opponent response (Solomon, 1980).

General Conclusions. No physical activity studies have been reported, but the model may help explain maintenance or adherence to habitual physical activity. The theory's biobehavioral nature can account for tangible sen-

sations that may reinforce continued participation. The exclusive reliance of the previous models on cognition has been inadequate for conceptualizing tangible or concrete reinforcing mechanisms for participation among the active (Dishman, 1982).

Relapse Prevention Model

Even among the habitually active, unexpected disruptions in activity routines or settings can interrupt or end a previously continuous exercise program. Relocation, medical events, and travel can impede the continuity of activity reinforcement and create new activity barriers. It is believed, however, that interruptions and life events have less impact as the activity habit becomes more established (Dishman, 1982); their impact may also be diminished if the individual anticipates and plans their occurrence, recognizes them as only temporary impediments, and develops self-regulatory skills for preventing relapses to inactivity.

A popular example of self-regulation is relapse prevention developed by Marlatt and Gordon (1985). The application of relapse prevention to exercise has been described thoroughly by Knapp (1988). The principal components consist of (1) identifying situations that put a person at high risk for relapse, (2) revising plans to avoid or cope with high-risk situations (e.g., time management, relaxation training, confidence building, reducing barriers to activity), (3) correcting positive outcome expectancies so that consequences of not exercising are placed in proper perspective (for example, people tired at the end of the workday may expect to feel refreshed if they rest rather than exercise—they actually may feel guilty, however, while the activity would likely have been invigorating), (4) expecting and planning for lapses, such as scheduling alternative activities while on vacation or after injury, (5) minimizing the abstinence violation effect, whereby a temporary lapse is catastrophized into feelings of total failure, which leads to loss of confidence and complete cessation, (6) correcting a lifestyle imbalance where "shoulds" outweigh "wants" (the focus here is on optimizing the pleasure derived from activity rather than viewing exercise as another obligation), and (7) avoiding urges to relapse by blocking self-dialogues and images of the benefits of not exercising (persons can talk themselves out of exercise in favor of sedentary alternatives).

Knapp (1988) correctly notes that relapse prevention was designed for reducing high-frequency undesired addictive behaviors such as smoking and substance abuse, whereas exercise is a desired but low-frequency behavior for many. Thus the effectiveness of the relapse prevention model for increasing physical activity may require modification. Several exercise intervention studies, however, have reported increased activity rates when components of the total model: identifying high-risk situations, planning for relapse and reducing barriers, and minimizing the abstinence violation effect were combined in broader cognitive behavior modification packages (Belisle, Roskies, & Levesque, 1987; King & Frederiksen, 1984; King & Frederiksen, 1984; Martin et al., 1984).

Perhaps the best tested and most easily implemented cognitive-behavior modification technique relevant for relapse prevention has been the decision balance sheet described by Hoyt and Janis (1975) and replicated by Wankel and colleagues (Wankel, 1984; Wankel, Yardley, & Graham, 1985.) This involves a careful valuation by the patient/client of expected or experienced benefits and costs of activity, in which the caregiver can actively reinforce positive outcomes and diminish negative expectations. Considered are not only activity consequences for the patient but for a spouse, friends, or other family members. Importantly, reinforcement of the decision to begin or resume activity is accompanied by planned strategies for overcoming perceived or real barriers to exercise. In this way the decision balance sheet shares common aspects with the relapse prevention model.

Although behavioral interventions based in part on the principles of relapse prevention report increased exercise frequency, naturalistic studies of free-living exercise are needed to describe the incidence of relapse and the predictive validity of the processes of relapse for exercise behavior.

The Transtheoretical Model

Although a number of early reviews of the exercise adherence literature have acknowledged the appearance of stages of exercise behavior (e.g., Dishman, 1982; Martin & Dubbert, 1985). A clearer view of stages for behavior changes can be found in extensions of the transtheoretical model for behavior change in smoking, weight control, and psychotherapy (Prochaska & DiClemente, 1985) to exercise (Sonstroem, 1988). This model proposes that individuals move sequentially through five major stages of change: precontemplation, contemplation, readiness for action, action, and maintenance while experiencing ten principal processes of change: consciousness raising, self-liberation, dramatic relief, environmental reevaluation, helping relationship, stimulus control, counterconditioning, social liberation, self-reevaluation, and reinforcement management. Cross-sectional studies applying the transtheoretical model to exercise have recently appeared (Marcus & Owen, 1992; Marcus, Selby, Niavra, & Rossi, 1992).

A potential major contribution of the transtheoretical model for increasing and maintaining exercise and physical activity lies in its consideration of the readiness of individuals for change and its capacity to bridge the use of behavior modification and cognitive-behavior modification traditions with population-based approaches to behavior change such as health promotion and education campaigns. Several of the processes of change proposed by the transtheoretical model require consideration of both cognitive (e.g., beliefs and values related to consciousness raising) and behavioral (e.g., stimulus control, reinforcement management, counterconditioning) variables. Also, relapse cannot be understood or controlled without knowledge of the influence of past history on contemporary exercise and physical activity.

LIMITATIONS IN METHODS AND RESEARCH DESIGN

The absence of uniform standards for defining and assessing physical activity and its determinants and the diversity of the variables, population segments, time periods, and settings sampled in published studies make it difficult to interpret and compare results. Often only a few studies have been done in a particular area. Most studies come from supervised settings, and relatively few population studies of determinants have been reported. Available population surveys have used questions with unknown reliability and validity, while generalizability to the population of the more controlled small sample results is also unknown in many instances.

Too few studies are available on children (Dishman & Dunn, 1988), the elderly (Perkins, Rapp, Carlson, & Wallace, 1986; Shephard, 1987; Stones, Kozma, & Stones, 1987), the disabled (Godin, Colantonio, Davis, Shephard, & Simand, 1986; LaPorte et al., 1984), or ethnic and minority groups (Atkins et al., 1987; Schoenborn, 1986; Vega et al., 1987), for example, to permit conclusions about how determinants in these cases may differ from general observations. There are also few comparative animal studies (Hanson, Van Huss, & Strautneik, 1967).

Methodological problems encountered in measuring determinants and assessing physical activity patterns influence the reproducibility and behavioral interpretations of the physical activity determinants that have been investigated. There has been little uniformity of method, theory, subjects, setting, and measurement in past studies of the determinants of physical activity. The number of studies conducted on relatively small numbers of demographically homogeneous subjects in supervised settings and for purposes of adult fitness and preventive medicine has far outnumbered population surveys and community-based studies.

Most studies have been descriptive, relying on correlational data rather than experimental data. There exists a need to standardize exercise programs, and the methods used for assessing physical activity and its correlates, if reproducible and generalizable results are to be obtained. In supervised exercise studies, widely varying definitions of adherent behavior are used. Although the most reliable influence on program adherence appears to be the length of the program period studied, attempts have been made to contrast studies where the period of interest may range from less than 1 month to 36 months. The impact of this on results is best illustrated by the observation that some factors related to adherence early in a program can no longer be related later (Mirotznik, Speedling, Stein, & Bronz, 1985; Ward & Morgan, 1984).

There are also very different types and volumes of activity employed as the exercise stimulus for very different types of subjects. This diversity represents varying behavioral demands on participants and provides differing social support, both of which can likely interact with personal attributes of individuals to influence physical activity participation.

A need also exists to standardize the measures of physical activity. Measurement approaches have included job classification, retrospective self-report, daily self-recording, mechanical, electronic, and physiological surveillance, and observation. There are problems in standardizing results for studies of determinants that cannot use direct observation of physical activity. Although questionnaires validated against biological estimates of activity (e.g., metabolic tolerance) are useful in dichotomizing between high active and sedentary individuals, they are less accurate in distinguishing between levels of activity intensity (Dishman & Steinhardt, 1988). Also, behavior does not ensure that predicted biological change will occur. Importantly, the psychometric properties of self-reported physical activity (i.e., reliability and construct validity) are also largely unknown. The usefulness of activity questionnaires validated from epidemiologic studies for detecting behaviorally significant amounts of activity variance remains unknown for small samples.

Recall assessment of physical activity is a pragmatic approach for large populations where direct observation or objective monitoring cannot be implemented. Validation of recall methods has been limited by the absence of a consensus standard or criterion for comparison (LaPorte, Montoye, & Caspersen, 1985). The lack of uniform assessment methods for physical activity is important for studies of determinants because it makes it difficult to evaluate if determinants of physical activity truly differ across people, settings, and time; if certain determinants, interventions, or theoretical models are associated with unique aspects of the physical activity, or if the various measures simply are each poor estimates of true physical activity. Therefore, for practical and research purposes, it currently seems desirable to evaluate both subjective and objective evidence of exercise behavior when direct observation is not feasible (Dishman, Darracott, & Lambert, 1992).

There is also a need to determine a reliable baseline expectancy for adherence to supervised exercise programs. Uncontrollable inactivity can result from injury (Pollock, 1988). True conflicts in schedule and relocation also occur that are beyond the personal control to influence participation (Oldridge, 1982), but they will not be well explained by most psychological theories.

FUTURE DIRECTIONS

It has been over a decade since I published my first article arguing that it was important for sport psychologists to study the determinants of exercise adherence from the interdisciplinary perspectives of exercise science and health psychology (Dishman, 1982). It is gratifying to see that the topic is included in this important volume, *Handbook on Research in Sport Psychology*. As we embark on the second decade of psychological research on exercise adherence, it will be important to evaluate the progress that has been made so that we can better form questions and strategies that will effectively advance our understanding in ways that can reliably and predictably increase participation in leisure physical activity and exercise around the world.

As part of the implementation plans to attain the U.S. Public Health Service physical fitness and exercise goals for 1990, the Workshop on Epidemiologic and Public Health Aspects of Physical Activity and Exercise was sponsored by the U.S. Department of Health and Human Services and held on September 24–25, 1984, at the Centers for Disease Control in Atlanta, Georgia (Powell & Paffenbarger, 1985). After review and discussion by a panel of experts from the fields of public health and exercise science, recommendations and study questions for the determinants of physical activity were agreed upon as important ones for public health.

Specific recommendations were made under each of the three categories that follow. I recently evaluated the progress and current priority for these recommendations based on newer research and events since the recommendations were made (Dishman, 1988a). An updating of my conclusions follows:

(1) "First, there remains a need to conceptualize and in a general way rank determinants according to priority. Our knowledge will continue to benefit from replication, extension, and direct comparison of factors implicated by previous studies" (Dishman, Sallis, & Orenstein, 1985, p. 168).

Little or no progress has been made in determining how perceived exertion influences activity; precise and valid measures have not been available for population studies. However, it appears that perceived barriers can be validly assessed in the population (Steinhardt & Dishman, 1989) and that they are related to inactivity (Sallis, et al., 1986; Sallis, Hovell, Hofstetter, Elder, Hackley, Caspersen, & Powell, 1990). Whether health risk status and other health habits precede or follow inactivity also remains unknown. Each area remains a high priority for deciding if it is a viable target for intervention.

Little or no progress has been made in identifying and ranking the interactions of personal attributes and environments as they influence physical activity. This remains a priority for advancing theory and for selecting effective interventions for different population segments and physical activity settings, but it cannot occur until available theories are competitively contrasted or remodeled based on path analyses of data from large population-based studies or large sample clinical studies.

Progress has been made in identifying cognitive factors and interventions that influence the planning and adoption of physical activity (Godin & Shephard, 1990) and in clarifying the effectiveness of behavioral and cognitive-behavioral interventions designed to increase and maintain physical activity (Dishman, 1991). The relative importance, additivity, or interaction of population-based promotions of physical activity based on social-cognitive and educational models versus clinically based interventions based on principles of behavior modification or cognitive-behavior modification requires study.

(2) "Second, as our general knowledge grows, it will also be necessary to specify major activity determinants for certain populations and settings" (Dishman et al., 1985, p. 169).

Little or no progress has been made in understanding how determinants differ according to age, race, gender, ethnicity, socioeconomic level or health, disability, and fitness level or who is most likely to benefit from different forms or amounts of physical activity. But research has increased in these areas and they remain priorities.

Progress has been made in clarifying differences and similarities between determinants of moderate leisure physical activity and vigorous exercise related to fitness in supervised and free-living settings (Sallis, et al., 1986).

Progress has also been made toward establishing that sport history (Dishman, 1988b) and age (Blair, Piserchia, Wilbur, & Crowder, 1986; Powell & Paffenbarger, 1985) largely represent selection biases, not true influences on contemporary physical activity. Family and peer influences, socioeconomic status, and education level may be selection bias effects, but they have potential as true determinants. Their study remains a high priority.

Progress has been made in confirming only small cross-sectional associations between physical activity and weight management and possibly smoking abstinence. Physical activity has not correlated consistently with other health behaviors. Although there may be correlations between physical activity and other health behaviors when variability within an individual is considered, it does not appear that variations between individuals in most health behaviors can be explained by variation in physical activity (Norman, 1986). This suggests that generalized health behavior theories or promotions will not be useful for exercise applications when they are focused on a population over a short period of time. Studies of patterns over time in specific demographic groups are needed. Experimental or prospective studies are a high priority for deciding whether general or physical activity-specific theories and interventions are needed for increasing physical activity.

(3) "Third, advancing age and elapsed time after initial adoption of an activity are among the most reliable predictors of inactivity. Thus, it seems likely that past activity environments and experiences are strong influences on present and future participation. Yet, little is now known in these areas" (Dishman, Sallis, & Orenstein, 1985, p. 169).

Little or no progress has been made in understanding how perceptions and preferences for types and intensities are formed and if they influence participation. This remains a high priority for free-living physical activity and for adoption of supervised leisure settings; it may be less important for supervised exercise adherence when activities are varied and intensity is based on initial fitness level.

Little or no progress has been made in understanding if determinants and dispositions for physical activity differ or change at definable ages or life-span stages. It does now appear, however, that inactivity associated with age can be reversed in some groups. This priority has increased in importance due to increases in elderly populations and the apparent ineffectiveness of schools' attempts to increase children's leisure physical activity patterns (Iverson, Fielding, Crow, & Christenson, 1985).

Progress has been made in showing that stages of physical activity include planning, adoption, maintenance, and periodicity and that determinants can differ for the stages. Decision-based theories, promotions, and interventions appear helpful for increasing planning and adoption. In addition, social support, self-motivation, and self-regulatory skills and interventions like relapse prevention seem necessary to maintain or resume a physical activity pattern. The origin and time course for intrinsic reinforcement of physical activity remains unknown, but understanding the process of personal motivation for physical activity remains a high priority for facilitating the success of public health promotion. Biologically oriented theories of reinforcement may be helpful in this regard (Crow & Jacobs, 1986).

In addition, future studies must consider unique cultural and economic-political differences between developed and developing or restructuring nations and between westernized and unwesternized nations. Theoretical models evolving from ideologies that place responsibility on the self to effect behavior change (e.g., most of the decision theories discussed in this chapter) may have less potential to explain or predict physical activity when social and environmental factors do not facilitate personal decision making or direct personal control of behaviors like exercise due to cultural or economic restraints.

References

Acquista, V. W., Watchtel, T. J., Comes, C. I., Salzillo, M., & Stockman, M. (1988). Home-based health risk appraisal and screening program. *Journal of Community Health, 13,* 43–52.

Ajzen, I. (1985). From intentions to actions. A theory of planned behavior. In J. Kuhl & J. Beckman (Eds.). *Action-Control: From Cognition to Behavior* (pp. 11–39). Heidelberg: Springer.

Ajzen, I., & Fishbein, M. (1977). Attitude-behavior relations: A theoretical analysis and review of empirical research. *Psychological Bulletin, 84,* 888–918.

Allen, L. D., & Iwata, B. A. (1980). Reinforcing exercise maintenance using high-rate activities. *Behavior Modification, 4,* 337–354.

American College of Sports Medicine (1978). Position statement on the recommended quantity and quality of exercise for developing and maintaining fitness in healthy adults. *Medicine and Science in Sports and Exercise, 10,* vii–x.

American Health (1985). *Public attitudes and behavior related to exercise.* Princeton, NJ: The Gallup Organization.

Andrew, G. M., Oldridge, N. B., Parker, J. O., Cunningham, D. A., Rechnitzer, P. A., Jones, N. L., Buck, C., Kavanagh, T., Shephard, R. J., Sutton, J. R., & McDonald, W. (1981). Reasons for dropout from exercise programs in post coronary patients. *Medicine and Science in Sports and Exercise, 13,* 164–168.

Atkins, C. J., Patterson, T. L., Roppe, B. E., Kaplan, R. M., Sallis, J. F., & Nadar, P. R. (1987). Recruitment issues, health habits, and the decision to participate in a health promotion program. *American Journal of Preventive Medicine, 3,* 87–94.

Bandura, A. (1977). Self-efficacy: Toward a unifying theory of behavioral change. *Psychological Review, 1984,* 191–215.

Belisle, M., Roskies, E., & Levesque, J. M. (1987). Improving adherence to physical activity. *Health Psychology, 6,* 159–172.

Blair, S. N., Jacobs, Jr., D. R., & Powell, K. E. (1985). Relationships between exercise or physical activity and other health behaviors. *Public Health Reports, 100,* 172–180.

Blair, S. N., Kohl, H. W., Paffenbarger, R. S., Clark, D. G., Cooper, K. H., & Gibbons, L. W. (1989). Physical fitness and all-cause mortality: a prospective study of healthy men and women. *Journal of the American Medical Association, 262:* 2395–2401.

Blair, S. N., Mulder, R. T., & Kohl, H. W. (1987). Reaction to "Secular trends in adult physical activity: Exercise boom or bust?" *Research Quarterly for Exercise and Sport, 58,* 106–110.

Blair, S. N., Piserchia, P. V., Wilbur, C. S., & Crowder, J. H. (1986). A public health intervention model for worksite health promotion: Impact on exercise and physical fitness in a health promotion plan after 24 months. *Journal of the American Medical Association, 255,* 921–926.

Bouchard, C., Shephard, R. J., Stephens, T., Sutton, J. R., & McPherson, B. D. (Eds.). (1990). *Exercise, fitness, and health: a consensus of current knowledge.* Champaign, IL: Human Kinetics Publishers.

Brooks, C. M. (1987). Leisure time physical activity assessment of American adults through an analysis of time diaries collected in 1981. *American Journal of Public Health, 77,* 455–460.

Brownell, K., Stunkard, A. J., & Albaum, J. (1980). Evaluation and modification of exercise patterns in the natural environment. *American Journal of Psychiatry, 137,* 1540–1545.

Bruce, E. H., Frederick, R., Bruce, R. A., & Fisher, L. D. (1976). Comparison of active participants and dropouts in CAPRI cardiopulmonary rehabilitation programs. *American Journal of Cardiology, 37,* 53–60.

Bruce, R. A., DeRoven, T. A., & Hossack, K. F. (1980). Pilot study examining the motivational effects of maximal exercise testing to modify risk factors and health habits. *Cardiology, 11,* 1119.

Canada Fitness Survey (1983). *Fitness and lifestyle in Canada.* Ottawa: Fitness Canada.

Caspersen, C. J., Christenson, G. M., & Pollard, R. A. (1986). Status of the 1990 physical fitness and exercise objectives—evidence from NHIS 1985. *Public Health Reports, 101,* 587–592.

Caspersen, C. J., Pollard, R. A., & Pratt, S. O. (1987). Scoring physical activity data with special consideration for elderly populations. *Proceedings of the 1987 Public Health Conference on Records and Statistics: Data for an Aging Population,* U.S. Department of Health and Human Services, 30–34.

Centers for Disease Control (1987). Sex-, age-, and region-specific prevalence for sedentary lifestyle in selected states in 1985—the Behavioral Risk Factor Surveillance System. *Morbidity and Mortality Weekly Report, 36,* 195–198, 203–204.

Centers for Disease Control (1990). CDC surveillance summaries, June. *Morbidity and Mortality Weekly Report, 39:* (No. 55-2) 8, 1–22.

Chen, M. K. (1986). The epidemiology of self-perceived fatigue among adults. *Preventive Medicine, 15,* 74–81.

Chubb, M., & Chubb, H. R. (1981). *One third of our time? An introduction to recreation behavior and services.* New York: Wiley.

Conrad, P. (1987). Who comes to work-site wellness programs? A preliminary review. *Journal of Occupational Medicine, 29,* 317–320.

Crow, R., & Jacobs, D. (1986). Population strategies to enhance physical activity. *Acta Medica Scandinavica,* Supplement, *711,* 93–112.

Darracott, C. R.; Dishman, R. K.; Cureton, K. (1992). *Are ratings of perceived exertion related to free-living physical activity in children aged 9–11 years?* Manuscript submitted for publication.

Davis, K. E., Jackson, K. L., Kronenfeld, J. J., & Blair, S. N. (1984). Intent to participation in worksite health promotion activities: A model of risk factors and psychosocial variables. *Health Education Quarterly, 11,* 361–377.

Department of Health and Human Services (1980). *Promoting*

health/preventing disease: Objectives for the nation. Fall, Washington, DC: U.S. Government Printing Office.

Department of Health and Human Services (1986). *Midcourse review, 1990 Physical fitness and exercise objectives.* President's Council on Physical Fitness and Sports and Behavioral Epidemiology Branch, Center for Health Promotion, Centers for Disease Control, Washington, DC: U.S. Government Printing Office, Region 3.

DeSharnais, R., Godin, G., & Jobin, J. (1987). Motivational characteristics of EvaluLife and the Canadian Home Fitness Test. *Canadian Journal of Public Health, 78,* 161–164.

Dishman, R. K. (1981). Biologic influences on exercise adherence. *Research Quarterly for Exercise and Sport, 52,* 143–159.

Dishman, R. K. (1982). Compliance/adherence in health-related exercise. *Health Psychology, 1,* 237–267.

Dishman, R. K. (Ed.) (1988a). *Exercise adherence: Its impact on public health.* Champaign, IL: Human Kinetics.

Dishman, R. K. (1988b). Supervised and free-living physical activity: No differences in former athletes and nonathletes. *American Journal of Preventive Medicine, 4,* 153–160.

Dishman, R. K. (1990a). Determinants of participation in physical activity. In C. Bouchard, R. J. Shephard, T. Stephens, J. R. Sutton, & B. D. McPherson (Eds.). Exercise, Fitness, and Health (pp. 75–102). Champaign, IL: Human Kinetics.

Dishman, R. K. (1990b). Physical activity in medical care. In J. S. Torg, R. P. Welsh, & R. J. Shephard (Eds.). Current Therapy in Sports Medicine—2 (pp. 122–129) Philadelphia: B.C. Decker, Inc.

Dishman, R. K. (1991). Increasing and maintaining physical activity and exercise. *Behavior Therapy, 22,* 345–378.

Dishman, R. K. (Ed.) (1993). *Exercise adherence II.* Champaign, IL: Human Kinetics, in press.

Dishman, R. K., Darracott, & Lambert, L. (1992). Failure to generalize determinants of self-reported physical activity to a motion sensor. *Medicine and Science in Sports and Exercise, 24,* in press.

Dishman, R. K., & Dunn, A. L. (1988). Exercise adherence in children and youth: Implications for adulthood. In R. K. Dishman (Ed.). *Exercise adherence: Its impact on public health* (pp. 145–189), Champaign, IL: Human Kinetics.

Dishman, R. K., & Ickes, W. (1981). Self-motivation and adherence to therapeutic exercise. *Journal of Behavioral Medicine, 4,* 421–438.

Dishman, R. K., Sallis, J. F., & Orenstein, D. (1985). The determinants of physical activity and exercise. *Public Health Reports, 100,* 158–171.

Dishman, R. K., & Steinhardt, M. (1990). Health locus of control predicts free-living, but not supervised, physical activity: A test of exercise-specific control and outcome-expectancy hypotheses. *Research Quarterly for Exercise and Sport, 61,* 383–394.

Dishman, R. K., & Steinhardt, M. (1988). Reliability and concurrent validity for a seven-day recall of physical activity in college students. *Medicine and Science in Sports and Exercise, 20,* 14–25.

Driggers, D. A., Swedberg, J., Johnson, R., et al. (1984). The maximum exercise stress test: Is it a behavior modification tool? *Journal of Family Practice, 18,* 715–718.

Duda, J. L., & Tappe, M. K. (1988). Predictors of personal investment in physical activity among middle-aged and older adults. *Perceptual and Motor Skills, 66,* 543–549.

Dzewaltowski, D. A., Noble, J. M., & Shaw, J. M. (1990). Physical activity participation. Social cognitive theory versus the theories of reasoned action and planned behavior. *Journal of Sport and Exercise Psychology, 12,* 388–405.

Epstein, L. H., Koeske, R., & Wing, R. R. (1984). Adherence to exercise in obese children. *Journal of Cardiac Rehabilitation, 4,* 185–195.

Epstein, L. H., Wing, R., Thompson, J. K., & Griffin, R. (1980). Attendance and fitness in aerobics exercise: The effects of contract and lottery procedures. *Behavior Modification, 4,* 465–479.

Ewart, C. K., Stewart, K. J., & Gillilan, R. E. (1986). Usefulness of self-efficacy in predicting overexertion during programmed exercise in coronary artery disease. *American Journal of Cardiology, 57,* 557–561.

Ewart, C. K., Taylor, C. B., Reese, L. B., & DeBusk, R. F. (1983). Effects of early postmyocardial infarction exercise testing on self-perception and subsequent physical activity. *American Journal of Cardiology, 51,* 1076–1080.

Feather, N. T. (1982). *Expectations and actions: Expectancy value models in psychology.* Hillsdale, NJ: Erlbaum.

Feltz, D. L., & Ewing, M. E. (1987). Psychological characteristics of elite young athletes. *Medicine and Science in Sports and Exercise, 19,* S98–S105.

Fielding, J. E. (1982). Effectiveness of employee health improvement programs. *Journal of Occupational Medicine, 24,* 907–916.

Gale, J. B., Eckhoff, W. T., Mogel, S. F., & Rodnick, J. E. (1984). Factors related to adherence to an exercise program for healthy adults. *Medicine and Science in Sports and Exercise, 16,* 544–549.

The General Mills American family report, 1978–1979 (1979). *Family health in an era of stress.* New York: Yankelovich, Skelly, and White.

Gettman, L. R., Pollock, M. L., & Ward, A. (1983). Adherence to unsupervised exercise. *The Physician and Sportsmedicine, 11,* 56–66.

Godin, G., Colantonio, A., Davis, G. M., Shephard, R. J., & Simand, C. (1986). Prediction of leisure time exercise behavior among a group of lower-limb disabled adults. *Journal of Clinical Psychology, 42,* 272–279.

Godin, G., Cox, M., & Shephard, R. J. (1983). The impact of physical fitness education on behavioral intentions towards regular exercise. *Canadian Journal of Applied Sports Science, 8,* 240–245.

Godin, G., Desharnais, R., Jobin, J., & Cook, J. (1987). The impact of physical fitness and health-age appraisal upon exercise intentions and behavior. *Journal of Behavioral Medicine, 10,* 241–250.

Godin, G., Godin, G., & Shephard, R. J. (1983). Physical fitness promotion programmes: Effectiveness in modifying exercise behavior. *Canadian Journal of Applied Sport Sciences, 8,* 104–113.

Godin, G., Shephard, R. J., & Colantonio, A. (1986). The cognitive profile of those who intend to exercise but do not. *Public Health Reports, 101,* 521–526.

Godin, G., Valois, P., Shephard, R. J., & Desharnais, R. (1987). Prediction of leisure-time exercise behavior: A path analysis (LISREL V) model. *Journal of Behavioral Medicine, 10,* 145–158.

Gwinup, G. (1975). Effect of exercise alone on the weight of obese women. *Archives of Internal Medicine, 135,* 676–680.

Hanson, D. L., Van Huss, W., & Strautneik, G. (1967). Effects of forced exercise upon the amount and intensity of the spontaneous activity of young rats. *Research Quarterly for Exercise and Sport, 37,* 221–230.

Heiby, E. M., Onorato, V. A., & Sato, R. A. (1987). Cross-validation of the self-motivation inventory. *Journal of Sport Psychology, 9,* 394–399.

Hoyt, M. F., & Janis, I. L. (1975). Increasing adherence to a stressful decision via a motivational balance-sheet procedure: A field experiment. *Journal of Personal and Social Psychology, 3l,* 833–839.

Hughes, J. R., Crow, R. S., Jacobs, D. R., Mittlemark, M. B., & Leon, A. S. (1984). Physical activity, smoking, and exercise-induced fatigue. *Journal of Behavioral Medicine, 7,* 217–230.

Iverson, D. C., Fielding, J. E., Crow, R. S., & Christenson, G. M. (1985). The promotion of physical activity in the U.S. population: The status of programs in medical, worksite, community, and school settings. *Public Health Reports, 100,* 212–224.

Janz, N. K., & Becker, M. H. (1984). The health belief model: A decade later. *Health Education Quarterly, 11,* 1–47.

Johansson, G., Johnson, J. V., & Hall, E. M. (1991). Smoking and sedentary behavior as related to work organization. *Social Science Medicine, 32,* 837–846.

Kaplan, R. M., Atkins, C. J., & Reinsch, S. (1984). Specific efficacy expectations mediate exercise compliance in patients with COPD. *Health Psychology, 3,* 223–242.

Kau, M. L., & Fisher, J. (1974). Self-modification of exercise behavior. *Journal of Behavior Therapy Exp Psychiatry, 5,* 213–214.

Keefe, F. J., & Blumenthal, J. A. (1980). The life fitness program: A behavioral approach to making exercise a habit. *Journal of Behavior Therapy Exp Psychiatry, 11,* 31–34.

Kendzierski, D. (1990). Self-schemata and exercise. *Basic and Applied Social Psychology, 3,* 231–250.

Kendzierski, D., & LaMastro, V. D. (1988). Reconsidering the role of attitudes in exercise behavior: a decision theoretic approach. *Journal of Applied Social Psychology, 18,* 737–759.

King, A. L., & Frederiksen, L. W. (1984). Low-cost strategies for increasing exercise behavior: Relapse preparation training and support. *Behavior Modification, 3,* 3–21.

Knapp, D. N. (1988). Behavioral management techniques and exercise promotion. In R. K. Dishman (Ed.). *Exercise adherence: Its impact on public health* (pp. 203–236). Champaign, IL: Human Kinetics.

Kohl, H., Moorefield, D. L. & Blair, S. (1987). Is cardiorespiratory fitness associated with general chronic fatigue in apparently healthy men and women? *Medicine and Science in Sports and Exercise* (abstract), *19,* Suppl., S6.

LaPorte, R. E., Adams, L. A., Savage, D. D., Brenes, G., Dearwater, S., & Cook, T. (1984). The spectrum of physical activity, cardiovascular disease and health: An epidemiologic perspective. *American Journal of Epidemiology, 120,* 507–517.

LaPorte, R. E., Montoye, H. J., Caspersen, C. J. (1985). Assessment of physical activity in epidemiologic research: Problems and prospects. *Public Health Reports, 100,* 131–146.

Lauzon, R. R. J. (1977). A randomized controlled trial of the ability of health hazard appraisal to stimulate appropriate risk reduction behavior. In *Proceedings of the 13th Annual Meeting of the Society of Prospective Medicine, Health Education Resources,* 102–103.

Leppink, H. B., & DeGrassi, A. (1977). Changes in risk behavior: A two-year follow-up study. In *Proceedings of the 13th Annual Meeting of the Society of Prospective Medicine, Health Education Resources,* 104–107.

Leventhal, H., Zimmerman, R., & Gutmann, M. (1984). Compliance: A self-regulatory perspective. In D. Gentry (Ed.). *Handbook of behavioral medicine.* New York: Guilford Press.

Lindsay-Reid, E., & Osborn, R. W. (1980). Readiness for exercise adoption. *Social Science Medicine, 14,* 139–146.

Marcus, B. H., & Owen, N. (1992). Motivational readiness, self-efficacy and decision making for exercise. *Journal of Applied Social Psychology, 22,* 3–16.

Marcus, B. H., Selby, V. C., Niavra, R. S., & Rossi, J. S. (1992). Self-efficacy and the stages of exercise behavior change. *Research Quarterly for Exercise and Sport, 63,* 60–66.

Marlatt, G. A., & Gordon, J. R. (Eds.) (1985). *Relapse prevention: Maintenance strategies in the treatment of addictive behaviors.* New York: Guilford Press.

Martin, J. E., & Dubbert, P. M. (1985). Adherence to exercise. *Exercise and Sport Science Reviews, 13,* 137–167.

Martin, J. E., Dubbert, P. M., Katell, A. D., Thompson, J. K., Raczynski, J. R., Lake, M., Smith, P. O., Webster, J. S., Sikova, T., & Cohen, R. E. (1984). The behavioral control of exercise in sedentary adults: Studies 1 through 6. *Journal of Consulting and Clinical Psychology, 52,* 795–811.

Massie, J. F., & Shephard, R. J. (1971). Physiological and psychological effects of training—a comparison of individual and gymnasium programs with a characterization of the exercise "dropout." *Medicine and Science in Sports, 3,* 110–117.

McIntosh, P. (1980). *"Sport for All" programs throughout the world.* Report prepared for UNESCO (Contract No. 207604). New York: UNESCO.

Meyer, A., Nash, J., McAlister, A., Maccoby, N., & Farquhar, J. W. (1980). Skills training in a cardiovascular health education campaign. *Journal of Consulting and Clinical Psychology, 48,* 129–142.

The Miller Lite Report on American Attitudes Toward Sports (1983). Research and Forecasts, Inc.: New York City.

Mirotznik, J., Speedling, E., Stein, R., & Bronz, C. (1985). Cardiovascular fitness program: Factors associated with participation and adherence. *Public Health Reports, 100,* 13–18.

Montoye, H. J., & Taylor, H. L. (1984). Measurement of physical activity in population studies: A review. *Human Biology, 56,* 195–216.

Morgan, P. P., Shephard, R. J., & Finucane, R. (1984). Health beliefs and exercise habits in an employee fitness programme. *Canadian Journal of Applied Sport Science, 9,* 87–93.

National Heart Foundation of Australia (1985). *Risk factor prevalence study: No. 2-1983.* Canberra, Australia: Author.

Norman, R. M. G. (1986). *The nature and correlates of health behavior.* Health Promotion Studies Series No. 2, Health and Welfare, Canada, Ottawa.

Oldridge, N. G. (1982). Compliance and exercise in primary and secondary prevention of coronary heart disease: A review. *Preventive Medicine, 11,* 56–70.

Oldridge, N. G., Donner, A., Buck, C. W., Jones, N. L., Anderson, G. A., Parker, J. O, Cunningham, D. A., Kavanagh, T., Rechnitzer, P. A., & Sutton, J. R. (1983). Predictive indices for dropout: The Ontario Exercise Heart Collaborative Study Experience. *American Journal of Cardiology, 51,* 70–74.

Oldridge, N. B., & Jones, N. L. (1983). Improving patient compliance in cardiac rehabilitation: Effects of written agreement and self-monitoring. *Journal of Cardiac Rehabilitation, 3,* 257–262.

Oldridge, N. B., & Streiner, D. L. (1990). The health belief model: Predicting compliance and dropout in cardiac rehabilitation. *Medicine and Science in Sports and Exercise, 22,* 678–683.

Paffenbarger, R. S., Jr., & Hyde, R. T. (1988). Exercise adherence, coronary heart disease, and longevity. In R. K. Dishman (Ed.), *Exercise adherence: Its impact on public health,* pp. 41–73. Champaign, IL: Human Kinetics.

Perkins, K. A., Rapp, S. R., Carlson, C. R., & Wallace, C. E. (1986). A behavioral intervention to increase exercise among nursing home residents. *Gerontology, 26,* 479–481.

The Perrier study: Fitness in America (1979). New York: Perrier-Great Waters of France, Inc.

Pollock, M. L. (1988). Prescribing exercise for fitness and adherence. In R. K. Dishman (Ed.). *Exercise adherence: Its impact on public health* (pp. 259–277). Champaign, IL: Human Kinetics.

Pollock, J. L., Carroll, J. F., Graves, J. E., Leggett, S. H., Braith, R. W., Limacher, M., & Hagberg, J. M. (1991). Injuries and adherence to walk/jog and resistance training programs in the elderly. *Medicine and Science in Sports and Exercise, 23,* 1194–1200.

Powell, K. E., & Dysinger, W. (1987). Childhood participation in organized school sports as precursors of adult physical activity. *American Journal of Preventive Medicine, 3,* 276–281.

Powell, K. E., & Paffenbarger, Jr., R. S. (1985). Workshop on epidemiologic and public health aspects of physical activity and exercise: A summary. *Public Health Reports, 100,* 118–126.

Powell, K. E., Spain, K. G., Christenson, G. M., & Mollenkamp, M. P. (1986). The status of the 1990 objectives for physical fitness and exercise. *Public Health Reports, 101,* 15–21.

Powell, K. E., Thompson, P. D., Caspersen, C. J., & Kendrick, J. S. (1987). Physical activity and the incidence of coronary heart disease. *Annual Review Public Health, 8,* 253–287.

Prochaska, J. O., & DiClemente, C. C. (1985). Common processes of self-change in smoking, weight control, and psychological distress. In S. Shiffman & T. Willis (Eds.). Coping and Substance use (pp. 345–363). New York: Academic Press.

Reid, E. L., & Morgan, R. W. (1979). Exercise prescription: A clinical trial. *American Journal of Public Health, 69,* 591–595.

Rodin, J. (1986). Aging and health: Effects of the sense of control. *Science, 233,* 1271–1276.

Rosenstock, I. M. (1974). Historical origins of the health belief model. *Health Education Monographs, 2,* 1–9.

Sallis, J. F., Haskell, W. L., Fortmann, S. P., Vranizan, K. M., Taylor, C. B., & Solomon, D. S. (1986). Predictors of adoption and maintenance of physical activity in a community sample. *Preventive Medicine, 15,* 331–341.

Sallis, J. F., Hovell, M. F., Hofstetter, C. R., Elder, J. P., Hackley, M., Caspersen, C. J., & Powell, K. E. (1990). Distance between homes and exercise facilities related to frequency of exercise among San Diego residents. *Public Health Reports, 105,* 179–185.

Sanne, H. M. (1973) Exercise tolerance and physical training of non-selected patients after myocardial infarction. *Acta Medica Scandinavica,* Supplement, *551,* 1–124.

Schoenborn, C. A. (1986). Health habits of U.S. adults, 1985: The "Alameda 7" revisited. *Public Health Reports, 101,* 571–580.

Shephard, R. J. (1987). *Physical activity and aging* (2nd ed.). London: Croom Helm.

Shephard, R. J. (1988). Exercise adherence in corporate settings: Personal traits and program barriers. In R. K. Dishman (Ed.). *Exercise adherence: Its impact on public health* (pp. 305–320). Champaign, IL: Human Kinetics.

Shephard, R. J., & Cox, M. (1980). Some characteristics of participants in an industrial fitness programme. *Canadian Journal of Applied Sport Sciences, 5,* 69–76.

Sidney, K. H., & Shephard, R. J. (1976). Attitude toward health and physical activity in the elderly: Effects of a physical training program. *Medicine and Science in Sports, 8,* 246–252.

Slater, C. H., Green, L. W., Vernor, S. W., & Keith, V. M. (1987). Problems in estimating the prevalence of physical activity from national surveys. *Preventive Medicine, 16,* 107–118.

Solomon, R. L. (1980). The opponent process theory of acquired motivation. *American Psychology, 35,* 691–712.

Sonstroem, R. J. (1988). Psychological models. In R. K. Dishman (Ed.), *Exercise adherence: Its impact on public health* (pp. 125–154). Champaign, IL: Human Kinetics.

Steinhardt, M., & Dishman, R. K. (1989). Reliability and validity of expected outcomes and barriers for habitual physical activity. *Journal of Occupational Medicine, 31,* 536–546.

Stephens, T. (1986). Health practices and health status: Evidence from the Canada Health Survey. *American Journal of Preventive Medicine, 2,* 209–215.

Stephens, T. (1987). Secular trends in adult physical activity: Exercise boom or bust? *Research Quarterly for Exercise and Sport, 58,* 94–105.

Stephens, T., Craig, C. L., & Ferris, B. F. (1986). Adult physical activity in Canada: Findings from the Canada Fitness Survey I. *Canadian Journal of Public Health, 77,* 285–290.

Stephens, T., Jacobs, D. R., Jr., & White, C. C. (1985). A descriptive epidemiology of leisure-time physical activity. *Public Health Reports, 100,* 147–158.

Stones, M. J., Kozma, A., & Stones, L. (1987). Fitness and health evaluations by older exercisers. *Canadian Journal of Public Health, 78,* 18–20.

Tappe, M. K., Duda, J. A., & Menges-Ehrnwald, P. (1990). Personal investment predictors of adolescent motivational orientation toward exercise. *Canadian Journal of Sport Sciences, 15,* 185–192.

U.S. Department of Health and Human Services (1988). *The Behavioral Risk Factor Surveillance System.*

Vega, W. A., Sallis, J. F., Patterson, T., Rupp, J., Atkins, C., & Nader, P. R. (1987). Assessing knowledge of cardiovascular health-related diet and exercise behaviors in Anglo- and Mexican-Americans. *Preventive Medicine, 16,* 696–709.

Wankel, L. M. (1984). Decision-making and social support strategies for increasing exercise involvement. *Journal of Cardiac Rehabilitation, 4,* 124–135.

Wankel, L. M., Yardley, J. K., & Graham, J. (1985). The effects of motivational interventions upon the exercise adherence of high and low self-motivated adults. *Canadian Journal of Applied Sport Sciences, 10,* 147–155.

Ward, A., & Morgan, W. P. (1984). Adherence patterns of healthy men and women enrolled in an adult exercise program. *Journal of Cardiac Rehabilitation, 4,* 143–152.

Washburn, R. A., & Montoye, H. J. (1986). The assessment of physical activity by questionnaire. *American Journal of Epidemiology, 123,* 563–576.

Young, R. J., & Ismail, A. H. (1977). Comparison of selected physiological and personality variables in regular and nonregular adult male exercisers. *Research Quarterly for Exercise and Sport, 48,* 617–622.

EMOTION AND AEROBIC EXERCISE

Steve Boutcher

Emotion is one of the most nebulous, complex concepts in psychology (Strongman, 1987). It touches all aspects of human behavior and has been viewed as adaptation (Plutchik, 1980), conscious experience (Hillman, 1960), and motivation (Leeper, 1970). Some see it as a disruptive process (Duffy, 1962), whereas others believe emotion enhances behavior (Young, 1961). Probably most would agree that it is a multidimensional phenomenon that exerts a number of different influences on human functioning.

More recent theories have attempted to integrate cognitive and physiological dimensions of emotion (Arnold, 1970; Buck, 1985; Leeper, 1970). This is an exciting endeavor because the integration of psychological and physiological processes is seen by many as one of the major future challenges for psychology and related fields. Indeed, several authors have suggested that the study of emotion may be the next major area of examination in psychology (Strongman, 1987; Tomkins, 1981).

From a sport psychology perspective this change of emphasis is timely, as the role of emotion in sport and physical activity has largely been unexplored (Vallerand, 1983). This failure to examine emotion in sport settings is surprising as emotional aspects are indigenous to sport and physical activity. For instance, winning and losing, precompetition state, and loss of play time through injury are typical emotion-generating situations in organized sport. Similarly in physical activity such as running and swimming, emotion also appears to be integral to the exercise experience. For example, the postexercise "feeling better" sensation is one of the major reported psychological reasons for participation in aerobic exercise. The processes and mechanisms responsible for these feelings, however, are poorly understood. The focus of this chapter will be on the influence of aerobic exercise on emotion. An overview of the application of cognitive theories of emotion to organized sport is available in the literature (see Vallerand, 1983).

The major tenet espoused here is that emotion is an integral part of exercise and is influenced by cognitive, physio-

logical, behavioral, and experiential aspects of physical activity. These processes interact and influence emotional states in the exercise situation. For instance, both psychological and physiological processes may generate emotional states during and after actual exercise, whereas cognitions and appraisals may affect both prospective and retrospective emotional assessment of the exercise experience. The view of emotion as a central component of the exercise experience may provide a rich framework to further understand emotion and exercise behavior. The establishment of such a framework would also generate more salient practical implications for increasing the quality of the individual's exercise experience.

The first part of this chapter describes the concept of emotion, after which research examining the exercise/emotion relationship is reviewed. Then a preliminary framework is developed into which extant theories of emotion are integrated to form a more complete model of the exercise/emotion relationship. Finally implications for future research in this area are discussed.

WHAT IS EMOTION?

Emotion has been studied from a number of different perspectives that fall into the general areas of behavior, cognition, and physiology (Buck, 1985). Behavioral researchers have assessed facial expressions as an indicant of emotion and have demonstrated that certain expressions are associated with basic emotional/motivational states (Ekman & Frieson, 1969; Ekman, Hagar, & Frieson, 1981). Other researchers have focused on the influence of cognition on emotion and, by examining how individuals label external and internal stimuli (Schacter & Singer, 1962) and how they appraise situations (Lazarus, 1984), have explained a wide range of emotional phenomena. A third approach emphasizes the physiological basis of emotion and has been directed toward the examination of the central nervous system (Cannon, 1932; Maclean, 1981; Papez, 1937). Theories within each of these areas are so numerous and diverse that they include multiple views of emotion and hundreds of different definitions (see Strongman, 1987). Kleinginna and Kleinginna (1981) have attempted to put all perspectives into one all-embracing definition:

Emotion is a complex set of interactions among subjective and objective factors, mediated by neural/hormonal systems, which can (a) give rise to affective experiences such as feelings of arousal, pleasure/displeasure; (b) generate cognitive processes such as emotionally relevant perceptual effects, appraisals, labeling processes; (c) activate widespread physiological adjustments to the arousing conditions; and (d) lead to behavior that is often, but not always, expressive, goal-directed, and adaptive. (p. 58)

Although the Kleinginnas' view of emotion may be too broad to generate testable research hypotheses, the definition's multifaceted nature captures the complexity of emotion. Thus they support the disparate nature of prior emotional research and suggest that emotion is influenced by a variety of cognitive and physiological factors.

Consequently emotion can be viewed as a complex process that possesses cognitive, physiological, behavioral, and experiential components. Emotion may also involve a number of different components and dimensions. For instance, anger, anticipation, joy, surprise, fear, disgust, and sorrow have all been suggested to be different emotions (Plutchik, 1970). Probably all emotions are involved in exercise, but perhaps the major dimension is hedonic tone or pleasure/displeasure. As an example, a consistent finding is that one of the major reported reasons for running is to obtain the postexercise "feeling better" sensation (Brunner, 1969). Thus feeling good during, after, and toward physical activity may be one of the most important aspects of the exercise process. Consequently this chapter focuses on the pleasure/displeasure dimension of emotion, views affect and mood as being synonymous with emotion, and adopts an integrated view of emotion that involves cognitive, physiological, behavioral, and experiential components.

RESEARCH EXAMINING EMOTION AND AEROBIC EXERCISE

The literature examining emotion and exercise has generally not viewed exercise as a changing, dynamic process, has been descriptive, and has lacked a theoretical framework. The majority of studies have used questionnaire assessment of emotion, although psychophysiological variables have also been utilized. As this literature has been reviewed elsewhere (Brown, 1990), this section will include only a review of those articles that have relevance for the development of a theoretical framework. Other reviews of this area include Folkins and Sime (1981), Hughes (1984), and Morgan and Goldston (1987). For reviews of research examining the influence of exercise on other psychological aspects such as depression and mental

health, see North, McCullough, and Starr (1990) and Morgan and Goldston (1987).

Researchers examining the influence of exercise and emotion are faced with at least two major obstacles. First exercise and aerobic fitness are complex phenomena that are difficult to measure and control adequately (Boutcher, 1990; Boutcher, in press). Second emotion is easily contaminated by a number of factors typically found in testing environments (Kuykendall, Keating, & Wagaman, 1988). Prior research reflects these difficulties as this literature is replete with methodological problems such as a lack of randomization, the failure to use placebo or control groups, and the failure to control for demand characteristics (Brown, 1990; Folkins & Sime, 1981; Hughes, 1984).

In this section an attempt will be made to select certain studies from a number of areas so that a framework to guide future research can be developed. Areas to be discussed will be emotion during exercise, feeling-better states after exercise, the influence of acute and chronic exercise on postexercise anxiety and mood, and psychophysiological responses to exercise (i.e., electroencephalographic and electromyographical activity).

EMOTION DURING EXERCISE

Researchers have attempted to measure emotional states during exercise by using affect scales. In this chapter, affect and emotion are viewed as being synonymous. For instance, the recently developed Feeling Scale (Hardy & Rejeski, 1989) is an 11-point bipolar scale that measures positive and negative affect (emotion). This scale allows affect to be assessed during exercise (e.g., treadmill, ergometer) that may be performed for different lengths of time and at different intensities.

For untrained individuals research has indicated that the affective or emotional response to continuous exercise appears to be load-dependent. That is, as exercise intensity increases affect decreases (Hardy & Rejeski, 1989). Thus positive affect for untrained individuals is greatest at low to moderate levels of exercise, then decreases with work intensity, and is lowest at high work intensity. However, absolute affect and pattern of affect during continuous exercise appear to be influenced by level of fitness. For instance, the absolute affect levels of younger, fitter males (Hardy & Rejeski, 1989) were higher than that of older, unfit males (McAuley & Courneya, 1990) during incremental exercise. The affective response of trained versus untrained subjects, however, has not been reported. It is feasible that because exercise is easier for the trained subject, affect may be higher during hard exercise for the trained compared to that of the untrained.

Interestingly several studies have also indicated that certain psychological variables can influence emotional response during exercise. For example, Rejeski, Best, Griffith, and Kenney (1987) examined the affective response of feminine-typed males on a bicycle ergometer and found that at hard levels of exercise subjects reported significantly lower affect compared to masculine or androgynous males. Also, Boutcher and Trenske (1990) observed the influence of music and deprivation on affect in exercising females. Subjects exercised on a bicycle ergometer at easy, moderate, and heavy loads in either a music, deprived, or control condition. Results indicated that listening to music significantly increased positive affect, even though the exercise load was the same in all three conditions. The authors suggest that music may have distracted individuals from focusing on feelings of discomfiture and also may have elevated the affective state by generating past positive feelings. The ability of music to elevate emotion during exercise may be especially important for those unfit individuals who experience discomfiture during the initial stages of an exercise program. Overall these results indicate that emotion during exercise is reduced by increasing work intensity. This emotional response, however, is influenced by the level of aerobic fitness and psychological influences.

EMOTION AFTER EXERCISE

Other approaches examining emotion in exercise have focused on the postexercise emotional state. Researchers in this area have typically used retrospective recall (i.e., survey research) or have actually involved subjects in some form of aerobic exercise (e.g., treadmill walking or running, bicycle ergometer, swimming) and have then assessed their postexercise emotional response through questionnaires, psychophysiological variables, or a combination of both.

The Feeling-Better Sensation

The feeling-better sensation has largely been addressed by retrospective recall. For instance, a number of surveys have indicated that individuals involved in aerobic exercise, especially running and jogging, have consistently reported that they "feel better" after physical activity. For example, Brunner (1969) analyzed runners' reasons for exercising and found that out of 23 perceived benefits runners listed feeling better physically and mentally as the second most important. Similarly Summers, Machin, and Sargent (1983) surveyed marathon runners and examined the most relevant psychosocial factors associated with running. They found that feeling better and enjoyment was a major perceived benefit of running. Results of numerous other surveys determining perceived benefits of running have produced similar results (e.g., Gondola & Tuckman, 1985). These studies, however, suffer from the typical problems of associative and descriptive research. Thus retrospective recall of an emotional state may be invalid and inaccurate. For instance, committed runners' expectations toward running may be so strong that they perceive that running "should" make them feel better. Morgan (1985) has termed this kind of demand response the "granola effect," whereby the positive view toward aerobic exercise such as running biases subjects' responses so that everything about exercise is seen as healthy and positive.

Nevertheless if the feeling-better sensation is generated by expectation rather than by other psychological and physiological mechanisms, these results in themselves would be important because expectations about exercise are influenced by appraisal and attributional processes and may be a key component in the exercise process (McAuley, in press, a). The role of causal thinking and emotion will be discussed further when Weiner's (1985) model of attribution and emotion is outlined. Overall survey research indicates that exercisers such as runners consistently perceive that one of the major benefits of exercise is the postexercise feeling-better sensation.

Emotional Change After Acute and Chronic Exercise

Researchers studying the effect of acute (after one bout of exercise) and chronic exercise (after a training program) on emotion have attempted to account for some of the methodological problems of survey research but generally have still failed to control for the expectation effect by not randomizing subjects to different treatment conditions. Overall, however, investigators interested in the influence of exercise on anxiety have indicated that vigorous exercise is associated with reduced perceived anxiety levels, whereas light exercise has less effect (for an overview, see Petruzzello, Landers, Hatfield, Kubitz, & Salazar, 1991). This reduction appears to be influenced, however, by the nature of the exercise stimulus and the characteristics of the exerciser.

For instance, Morgan and his associates in a series of studies have examined anxiety states by using the state anxiety scale (Spielberger, Gorsuch, & Lushene, 1970). The rationale for using an anxiety scale to measure emotion is that decreases in state anxiety (A-State) are indicative of positive emotional states. The use of such scales, which do not directly measure emotion and have not been developed specifically for exercise, however, may be questionable. In one of the first studies (Morgan, Roberts, & Feinerman, 1971), subjects were put through a 1-mile treadmill walk and anxiety levels were assessed after the exercise. It was reported that acute exercise did not result in a lowered A-State in comparison to the baseline. However, in a second study (Morgan, 1973) more vigorous exercise did result in significantly lower A-State levels from pre- to postexercise. These results were also replicated in a subsequent study using adults who performed a vigorous 15-minute run.

In a later series of studies (Morgan, 1979; Morgan & Horstman, 1976), A-State anxiety was evaluated during a treadmill walk and a running test of maximal aerobic power. For both conditions A-State increased linearly throughout the first half of exercise and then reached an asymptote for the remainder of the test. After the cessation of exercise, A-State had returned to preexercise levels within 5 minutes. Morgan's studies seem to indicate that after cessation of exercise, vigorous activity decreases A-State below baseline levels, whereas light exercise has little effect. (For a full discussion on anxiety, see Chapter 14 by Hackfort and Schwenkmezger in this book.)

Other researchers have used the Profile of Mood States scale (POMS; McNair, Lorr, & Droppleman, 1971) to assess mood. Generally these studies have produced similar results. For instance, Berger and Owen (1983) studied the relationship between swimming and mood change. The POMS was given to beginning swimmers, intermediate swimmers, and a control group before and after a swimming class. Results indicated that swimmers reported significantly less tension, depression, anger, confusion, and more vigor after exercising than before.

This decrease in anxiety associated with a bout of vigorous activity has also been found after participation in other activities. For instance, Bahrke and Morgan (1978) present evidence to suggest that acute physical activity, noncultic meditation, and reading are equally effective in reducing state anxiety. They also monitored oxygen consumption, HR, and BP as confirmatory variables and found that none of these variables differed significantly following the reading and meditation treatments. They suggested that the underlying cause for this reduction in anxiety may be due to taking a "time-out" from daily activities. Thus Morgan proposed a cognitive explanation for the change in mood, implying that the change in activity acts as a diversion from an otherwise stressful environment. This approach assumes that the acute or chronic physiological changes accompanying aerobic exercise do not play a major role in determining the subsequent mood state.

Boutcher and Landers (1988), however, challenged this view and suggested that the emotional response of trained and untrained individuals may be driven by different mechanisms. As Morgan's subjects appeared to be untrained, these authors suggest that the time-out process may be a possible underlying mechanism for those individuals who have not physiologically adapted to exercise, but for trained individuals the emotional response may be influenced by other mechanisms. To test this notion Boutcher and Landers (1988) had highly trained and untrained subjects complete a vigorous run on a treadmill, whereas in a second session the same subjects sat quietly and read. Anxiety and electroencephalographic (EEG) responses (reported later) did not change after the reading treatment. In contrast, anxiety levels significantly decreased after the run for the trained group but did not decrease for the untrained. Thus in this study quiet reading did not reduce anxiety, either for runners or nonrunners, whereas after exercise the trained compared to the untrained exhibited significantly lower anxiety levels. A recent study by Raglin and Morgan (1987) provides further support for a different emotional response between cognitive strategies (e.g., meditation, reading) and exercise. These authors found that both quiet rest and exercise reduced state anxiety and blood pressure. However, these effects only lasted a couple of minutes after the quiet rest, whereas blood pressure remained lower for up to 3 hours after exercise.

Furthermore a study completed by Schwartz, Davidson, and Golemen (1978) also provides indirect support for the suggestion that trained individuals may differ from untrained ones in emotional response to exercise stimuli. These authors examined trait anxiety profiles of exercisers and meditators and found that global anxiety levels were the same. However, when global anxiety was partitioned into cognitive and somatic components, they found that runners reported higher cognitive and lower somatic levels, whereas meditators scored higher somatic and lower cognitive anxiety. The authors suggest that these results indicate that regular practice of physical exercise may result in less somatic anxiety, whereas regular meditation may result in cognitive relaxation. The retrospective design used in this study, however, does not take into account the effect of dispositional influences.

Thus there is preliminary evidence to indicate that physiological adaptation to exercise may produce a different postexercise emotional response to that of the untrained. Therefore it is possible that experienced and neophyte runners' emotional states may be driven by different processes or mechanisms. Overall results of studies examining the influence of acute exercise on emotion have also indicated that more vigorous as opposed to light exercise is associated with a decrease in postexercise anxiety. Furthermore the duration of anxiety reduction after exercise appears greater than that generated by cognitive strategies such as reading.

The results of studies examining chronic exercise (aerobic exercise training) on emotional state provide some support for these cross-sectional results as some training studies have indicated that aerobic training can result in a decrease in anxiety. These results, however, should be considered preliminary because a number of confounding variables compete with exercise as the mediator of reduced anxiety. Problems have mainly centered on the lack of randomization of subjects to conditions, a failure to measure fitness change, and a failure to control for demand expectations (Boutcher, 1990; Boutcher, in press; Brown, 1990). For instance, in a number of studies, decreased anxiety levels have been found in subjects after aerobic exercise training programs, but in none of these studies was fitness change measured (Berger & Owen, 1983; Bluementhal, Williams, Needels, & Wallace, 1982; Goldwater & Collis, 1985). Folkins (1972) did record lower anxiety levels and an increase in aerobic fitness, but Folkins, Lynch, and Gardner (1972) and McPherson et al. (1965) did not find reduced anxiety levels compared to controls. The equivocality of the results of chronic studies is probably caused by issues concerning the assessment of aerobic fitness and the length of the training program (Boutcher, 1990).

Psychophysiological Changes and Exercise

Although most researchers have administered psychometric instruments to indicate changes in emotion, deVries and his colleagues have conducted a series of studies examining the influence of exercise on electromyographical activity (EMG). For instance, in an initial study EMG activity of the elbow flexor and quadricep muscle groups before, after, and 1 hour after 5 minutes of bench-stepping and a 15-minute rest period was monitored (deVries, 1968). EMG activity in the elbow flexors decreased significantly (58%) by 1 hour postexercise, compared to no change on the control day. In another study, deVries and Adams (1972) compared the effect of walking versus the effect of a relaxant drug (meprobamate) in healthy elderly subjects. Results indicated that walking produced a greater decrease in EMG activity compared to the control and drug conditions. DeVries, Wiswel, Bulbulian, and Moritani (1981) further supported the above results by determining the EMG of high-anxious subjects before and after 10 minutes and 20 minutes of moderate bicycle ergometer exercise and a control condition. EMG activity decreased significantly after exercise in comparison to the values obtained by the exercise group. Overall these studies indicate that aerobic exercise can result in lowered EMG activity. The weaknesses of these studies, however, were that the intensity of the exercise was not well controlled, individual baseline differences were not covaried, and no psychological assessment of emotion or mood was collected (Hatfield & Landers, 1987).

Another psychophysiological variable that has been used in mood research is EEG activity. Researchers exploring the effect of exercise on EEG have mostly measured alpha activity as an indicant of spontaneous EEG. Alpha activity has been used as a general indicant of cortical arousal, with greater levels of alpha activity indicating less cognitive activity. For instance, Pineda and Anderson (1961) put subjects through a maximal exercise test that involved walking on a treadmill for 50 minutes or more, and found that there was a significant increase between rest and maximal exercise in the amount of alpha activity. EEG activity was recorded from the frontal, temporal, and occipital areas. The increase in alpha activity was generally in the 18–23% range and lasted for 5–10 minutes after exercise and then returned to baseline levels. Also, Kamp and Troost (1978) investigated alpha activity of subjects during bicycle ergometry. EEG data were recorded pre- and postexercise after subjects worked to a level that was double their resting HR. The results again showed that normal subjects recorded more alpha activity after exercise. A weakness of these studies was that the researchers did not use control groups.

Wiese, Singh, and Yeudall (1983) also studied the effects of aerobic exercise on alpha power. Ten males and 10 females exercised on an ergometer for 40 minutes and alpha power was recorded before and after that time. With alpha power monitored from the occipital and parietal regions, the exercise group showed a significant increase in alpha power during the postexercise period compared to pre-exercise baseline levels.

Unlike the studies just discussed, Boutcher and Landers (1988) covaried the baseline EEG and found a similar increase in alpha power after the running stimulus for runners and nonrunners but no increase for either group after a reading condition. Thus both groups displayed elevated alpha levels after the run, but only the runners showed a decrease in state anxiety. The authors explained the different anxiety responses by suggesting that the physiological adaptation of the trained runners was responsible for the decreased anxiety. The similar large increase in alpha power for both groups was interpreted to indicate two dissimilar affective states. For the trained runners the increase in alpha power was viewed to indicate a relaxed, energized state, whereas the reduction in cortical activity of the untrained was seen to reflect fatigue. Collectively these results indicate that aerobic exercise consistently results in increases in spontaneous alpha activity.

EMOTION AND OVERTRAINING

Other researchers have analyzed the effect of too much exercise on emotion and psychological state. For instance, in aerobic sports such as swimming debilitating physiological and psychological reactions to heavy training are a constant problem (Boutcher, 1991). Swimming coaches typically use "overreaching" as an essential part of their training programs. Overreaching involves intensive bouts of swimming, usually lasting about 5–10 days at intensities well above the normal training intensity, followed by rest or tapering periods. Swimmers who show decreases in performance during this type of intensive training are usually termed "stale" or "overtrained." From the swimmers' and coaches' standpoint this is a highly undesirable state as the general remedy is immediate stoppage of training or significantly reduced workloads. As estimates for recovery from staleness or overtraining have varied from weeks to 3 months, staleness could have drastic effects on the athlete's career (e.g., missing the Olympic games). Furthermore anecdotal and clinical evidence suggests that intense training may have the potential to increase susceptibility to illness (Boutcher, 1991), which may further prevent sport participation and exacerbate the recovery process. The negative effects of intense training have also been found in competitive and recreational runners (Dressendorfer, Wade, & Scaff, 1985), speed skaters (Gutmann, Pollock, Foster, & Schmidt, 1984), and wrestlers (Morgan, Brown, Raglin, O'Connor, & Ellickson, 1987).

In an overview article, Morgan et al. (1987) have summarized the results of 10 years of research examining mood changes associated with swimming and wrestling. For both groups of athletes it was found that the POMS was sensitive to negative psychological changes brought about by hard exercise. Prior research by Morgan and his colleagues (for an overview, see Morgan et al., 1987) has indicated that elite athletes in a variety of sports exhibit the so-called "iceberg" profile when the six subscores of the POMS (tension, depression, anger, vigor, fatigue, and confusion) are plotted. When suffering from the effects of overtraining, however, their scores reflect an "inverted-iceberg" profile that Morgan suggests is indicative of disturbed mental health.

This profile has been found for both wrestlers and swimmers during chronic overtraining over a season and after acute bouts of hard exercise (Morgan et al., 1987). These studies indicate that excessive exercise can result in both an acute and chronic negative emotional state.

SUMMARY

Research suggests that during exercise positive emotion tends to decrease with work intensity, but this decrease can be affected by psychological variables. Retrospective research in the form of surveys has consistently indicated that aerobic exercisers perceive that they feel better after physical activity. Vigorous exercise results in a significant decrease in state anxiety after the cessation of exercise, whereas light exercise has little effect. Furthermore EMG response after exercise consistently decreases, whereas alpha activity consistently increases. Finally excessive exercise can result in a negative emotional state in activities such as running, wrestling, and swimming.

POSSIBLE PHYSIOLOGICAL AND PSYCHOLOGICAL MECHANISMS INFLUENCING EMOTION DURING AND AFTER EXERCISE

The studies just described are descriptive in nature and have not attempted to reveal the mechanisms underlying emotional change. Thus future research should attempt to isolate mechanisms that may influence emotion and integrate them into a process view of exercise. A process view of exercise would take into account both psychological and physiological changes that may occur through regular participation in an exercise program. Although few researchers have attempted to identify possible mechanisms underlying emotion in exercise, Hatfield (1991) has recently described a number of potential physiological mechanisms. These mechanisms, plus others, are outlined in Table 37–1. These mechanisms are speculative and are only indirectly supported by data, but they may have potential for explaining how exercise can generate positive emotional states after exercise. Further research is needed on this topic.

Briefly the hyperthermic model for explaining the feeling-better sensation concerns the elevation in body temperature accruing from exercise and the resultant ef-

TABLE 37–1. Potential Mechanisms Influencing the Emotional Response to Aerobic Exercise

Physiological	Psychological
Hyperthermic Change	Self-esteem
Visceral Feedback	Mastery
Neurotransmitter Changes	Social Factors
Endorphins	Time-out
Autonomic Rebound	

fects on the brain brought about by the hypothalamus. This notion has been developed from earlier work by Von Euler and Soderberg (1957), who manipulated passive heating in rabbits (see Hatfield, 1991). The basic notion is that the hypothalamus, which is intimately involved in temperature regulation, senses the elevation in core temperature and then inhibits the thalamus, resulting in reduced cortical activation. Hatfield suggests that this reduced cortical activation may induce the relaxed and feeling-better sensations experienced after exercise.

Other indirect evidence to support the hyperthermic model is found in research on the influence of exercise on sleep. For example, aerobic exercise increases slow wave sleep if the exercise is performed in the afternoon (Baekland & Laskey, 1966; Horne & Porter, 1976). This elevation in slow wave sleep does not occur as much if the exercise is performed in the morning and if the exerciser is untrained. Interestingly Horn (1983) found that the increase in slow wave sleep was also influenced by a rise in inner core temperature. When subjects were cooled during a treadmill run, the slow wave sleep did not change. In contrast, uncooled running produced enhanced slow wave sleep. Thus it appears that the raising of inner core temperature is associated with an increase in slow wave sleep. It is feasible that inner core temperature elevation may also elevate emotional state. Because the hypothalamus is involved in both temperature regulation and emotion, it is possible that one of the necessary precursors for a physiologically enhanced emotional state may be an increase in inner core temperature. The influence of increased core temperature on emotion may, however, be a function of fitness and conditioning as thermal adjustment to exercise is affected by training (Davies, 1981).

The visceral afferent feedback model (Hatfield, 1991) focuses on the effects of cardiovascular feedback resulting from exercise. Basically the notion is that continuous rhythmical feedback from exercise may have a dampening effect on certain areas in the brain and may result in relaxed states. This idea is based on work by Bonvallet and Bloch (1961) examining the effect of rhythmical repetitive stimuli on the brainstem area.

Neurotransmitter responses to exercise is another possible mechanism underlying emotional change in exercise. The depletion of biogenic amines (norepinephrine, dopamine, serotonin) has been implicated in a number of different stress states. For instance, norepinephrine depletion has been found to exist in severe depressives (Fawcett, Mass, & Dekirmenjiar, 1972). Treatment for severe depression, such as electroconvulsive therapy and tricyclic antidepressants, increases aminergic transmission (Glowinski & Baldessarini, 1966). Interestingly exercise also increases norepinephrine and dopamine levels in rats (Brown & Van Huss, 1973). Thus it is feasible that the increase in amines through exercise may enhance emotional state. The relationship between amines and psychological state, however, is exceedingly complex, and much further research needs to be conducted to establish the neurotransmitter hypothesis as a legitimate mechanism.

Another biochemical explanation of emotional change concerns the ability of exercise to generate endorphins. Endorphins are naturally occurring chemicals in the brain that may have the ability to offset pain and induce euphoric states (Morgan, 1985). If exercise does increase endorphin level, it is possible that this relationship may be responsible for the generation of positive emotion occurring after exercise. Although a number of researchers have examined the relationship between exercise and endorphins (for an overview, see Sforzo, 1988), results are equivocal (Catlin, Gorelick, Gerner, Aui, & Li, 1980; Farrell, Gates, Morgan, & Pert, 1983). There are several methodological problems in this research that make results uninterpretable at this time. These problems concern the assessment of endorphin in blood plasma, the role of central and peripheral influence, and the failure to assess psychological change (Hatfield, 1991). These problems, however, do not eliminate endorphins as a possible contributor to the increase in positive emotion after exercise.

Autonomic rebound is another physiological mechanism postulated to account for positive emotional state (Boutcher, 1986). The autonomic nervous system consists of the two interacting limbs of the sympathetic and parasympathetic systems. The sympathetic nervous system serves to energize organs such as the heart and vascular system, whereas the parasympathetic nervous branch has an acquiescing effect on the heart. During vigorous exercise the sympathetic nervous system dominates, but at cessation of exercise homeostatic mechanisms restore the heart to parasympathetic influence. This "rebound" to the parasympathetic state could be a training-induced emotional mechanism because parasympathetic states are typically associated with relaxation, low arousal, and restorative functions. Thus conditioned runners may rebound to this parasympathetic state after exercise and may stay in this state for a longer period of time.

Although it is speculative to assert that these mechanisms explain the effects of exercise on emotion, the amount of indirect evidence suggests that physiological drivers of emotion should be considered in future research. Psychological strategies, however, also have the potential to drive emotion. For instance, one of the consistent psychological effects achieved as a result of exercise and physical activity is an increase in self-esteem (Sonstroem, 1984). Individuals in a variety of activities feel better about themselves after physical activity. This increase in reported self-esteem may be due to a number of factors related to the exercise situation (Sonstroem, 1984). Thus self-esteem may be elevated through factors such as improved body image resulting from a loss in body weight or increased muscular tone.

Mastery experiences are another possible generator of emotion. For instance, successfully completing a workout that was previously thought impossible or running a race for the first time may enhance feelings of self-worth and generate positive emotional states. Social factors associated with the exercise setting may also act to generate emotion. For example, a survey of runners (Heitmann, 1986) has indicated that older compared to younger runners place a higher priority on making friends in the exercise situation. Thus developing a coterie of running pals may provide another mechanism for increasing positive emotion.

Another psychological explanation, previously mentioned, is the time-out hypothesis originally suggested by Lazarus and adapted to exercise by Bahrke and Morgan (1978). This hypothesis is a derivation of earlier work on the role of activity in anticipating and confronting stressful situations. Gal and Lazarus (1975) have reviewed this literature and have concluded that by keeping busy and active, while anticipating a threatening event, individuals may reduce their level of anxiety. They further suggest that the process that best explains the stress-reducing effects of motor activities, unrelated to the cause of the stress problem, is a distraction or diversion of attention from the stress cue. Bahrke and Morgan have extended the stress-reducing role of diversion and distraction to activities such as eating, running, swimming, reading, and meditation. They suggest that taking a time-out by engaging in activities of this type creates a diversion from stressful thoughts and induces lower levels of anxiety and enhanced emotional state. The strength of support for the time-out hypothesis in exercise, however, is weakened by the methodological inelegancies of past research and should be more adequately tested in the future. For more in-depth discussion of these mechanisms, see the work of Hatfield (1991).

This brief review indicates that a number of psychological and physiological mechanisms may be involved in the generation of positive emotion through exercise. Furthermore it is also feasible that the influence of these mechanisms may be a function of individual differences, environmental variables, and social factors. For instance, for some exercisers (e.g., highly trained runners) enhanced emotion after participation may only be achieved by vigorous exercise. In contrast, for others environmental factors such as jogging through parks or alongside a lake may be an essential ingredient to generate positive emotion. Thus it is suggested that a framework to view these mechanisms and their interaction with environmental, individual, and social factors should be developed. Such a framework should encapsulate the changing dynamic nature of the exercise/emotion relationship, should allow for psychological and physiological influences on emotion, and should account for individual, environmental, and social influences.

A PRELIMINARY MODEL OF EMOTION AND EXERCISE

The development of such a model would need to be based on the view that exercise is a process that involves ongoing multiple psychological and physiological change. The physiological adaptations to continuous exercise are well documented and provide a starting point for the development of a process model to explain the exercise/emotion relationship. Most individuals involved in continuous aerobic exercise will physiologically adapt to exercise training until the intensity, frequency, and duration of their program is held constant. Continued exercise at a particular level will lead to the individual physiologically adapting to that particular exercise intensity. This process is illustrated in Figure 37–1. As can be seen, the exercise process has been divided into adoption, maintenance, and habituation phases. The adoption phase concerns the neophyte exerciser who has little or no experience in aerobic activity. Individuals at this stage have typically not physiologically adapted to the exercise. The physiological experience could be positive or negative, but for most individuals initial exercise will probably produce physical discomfiture during and after exercise. This may be particularly true if the exercise is too intense and vigorous or the individual is particularly unfit or overweight. However, physiological adaptation to exercise is rapid, and if the exerciser stays with exercise for a number of sessions then the physical discomfiture will tend to dissipate and the individual will now move into the maintenance phase of the exercise process. At this stage the exerciser has physiologically adapted to regular exercise, and for most individuals the initial discomfiture incurred through exercise would have been attenuated. The final stage is habituation and concerns those runners who are physiologically habituated to exercise. At the extreme end of this stage it is possible that negative emotional states could be generated by both too much exercise or by missing an exercise session (Boutcher, 1991).

The implication of this dynamic view of exercise adaptation is that as individuals physiologically adapt to regular exercise, psychological changes may also occur. In particular, emotional states may be influenced by a variety of cognitive and physiological processes at each of the phases of the exercise process. In its present form, however, the model does not integrate the psychological and physiological mechanisms discussed earlier and fails to offer explanations for how multiple factors may influence emotion. Thus extant theories of emotion that have relevance to the exercise process need to be integrated into this framework.

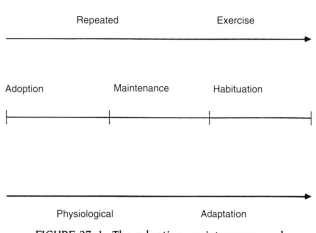

FIGURE 37–1. The adoption, maintenance, and habituation phases occurring as a result of repeated aerobic exercise.

THEORIES OF PERTINENCE FOR EXERCISE/EMOTION RESEARCH

As discussed earlier the major dimension of emotion relevant to exercise is seen to be more general positive and negative emotion as opposed to other specific emotions such as anger, disgust, and so forth. Focusing mainly on the hedonic aspect of emotion reduces the search for pertinent theories from the psychology literature in which over 30 major theories examining many different aspects of emotion have been developed (Strongman, 1987).

To be pertinent to exercise, a theory of emotion must explain how psychological and physiological processes can drive emotion. Unfortunately at the present time no such theory exists. Thus it is necessary to select parts of existing theories and apply them to the exercise process. Theories suitable for this purpose would need to account for cognitive, physiological, and behavioral influences on emotion within the physiological adaptation framework previously described. A possible set of theories that may be suitable for this purpose are attribution theory, social learning theory, social cognitive theory, and opponent-process theory. This section attempts to integrate components of these theories to create a cognitive, behavioral, physiological model of the exercise process. It is beyond the scope of this chapter, however, to describe all of these theories in depth. (At any rate, they are discussed in other chapters.) Instead brief overviews are given and their possible application to the exercise/emotion phenomenon is highlighted.

COGNITIVE APPROACH

Attribution Theory

Attribution theory is concerned with how individuals appraise achievement outcomes in terms of causality (Weiner, 1972). See Chapter 19 by Biddle in this book for a detailed description of this theory. The assumption of the theory is that the individual is capable of controlling thought processes, motivation, and behavior. Early models of attribution have recently been reformulated (Weiner, 1985, 1986) and now include an influential role for emotion in influencing behavior. The major tenet of Weiner's model is that individuals will engage in a causal search to explain outcomes. Originally ability, effort, task difficulty, and luck were identified (Weiner at al., 1971). However, research in sport has indicated that there are numerous other causal ascriptions (Bukowski & Moore, 1980).

Weiner's reformulated model suggests that although causal attributions may influence future behaviors it is more important to examine the causal dimensions underlying these causal ascriptions. Empirical research has indicated that at least three causal dimensions exist. The three most identified are locus of causality, stability, and controllability. Locus of causality concerns whether the individual views the cause of performance to reside internally or externally. The stability dimension refers to the variability of the cause over time, whereas the control dimension determines whether the perceiver views the cause to be controllable or not. The important feature of the theory is that causal attributions are hypothesized to affect future behaviors through the mediation of affect and future expectancies. Thus causal attributions that influence expectancy of success will affect other thoughts and actions. However, Weiner (1986) suggests that future expectancies are not sufficient determinants of actions by themselves. He posits that causal ascriptions can influence a wide range of emotional reactions and that these diverse affective reactions could generate, in turn, a number of different actions. Thus Weiner believes that causal ascriptions influence emotions and that emotional reactions influence motivated behavior.

Consequently Weiner offers an attributional view of the emotion process and proposes that attributional thinking generates specific emotions. He contends that following the outcome of an event there is either a positive or negative emotional reaction based on perceived success or failure of the outcome. If the outcome is successful the emotion is happiness; conversely emotions resulting from failure involve sadness. Weiner labels these emotions as outcome-dependent affects (Weiner et al., 1979). Following outcome appraisals the attributional process will be initiated and causal ascriptions will follow. Depending on the chosen attribution, a different set of emotions may be generated. Weiner suggests that each causal dimension is uniquely related to a specific emotion and labels these later emotional reactions as attribution-dependent.

Weiner suggests that the stability dimension most influences future expectations, whereas the locus of causality and control dimension most influence emotional reactions. He has termed these two dimensions as the attribution-dependent affects. Other researchers, however, have demonstrated that all three causal dimensions are related to emotions (McAuley & Duncan, 1990; Vallerand, 1987). Although the ability of Weiner's model to explain emotion generated by exercise has not been tested, the attribution/ emotion relationship has been recently examined from an exercise adherence perspective. For instance, McAuley, Poag, Gleason, and Wraith (1990) examined dropouts from an exercise program and demonstrated that all three causal dimensions predicted negative emotional reaction.

In acute exercise situations the model would predict that individuals will initially evaluate the outcome of the exercise experience and then emotion will be generated, depending on the positive or negative nature of the evaluation. After this initial evaluation individuals will undergo causal appraisal that could strengthen or modify the prior emotional state. This theory seems to be particularly pertinent to the initial part of the exercise process (the adoption phase). Thus neophyte exercisers' emotional states may be particularly susceptible to attributional thinking. Consequently perceived success at exercising may generate a positive emotional response that in turn may influence future exercise behaviors of the individual.

One of the major weaknesses of the theory in its present form includes the inability of the theory to account for physiological influences on emotion and the requirement of situations that allow time for elaborate causal ascriptions. Arnold (1970) has argued that although reflective appraisals are important influences on emotion, "intuitive appraisal" is the major determinant. Intuitive appraisals are subjective assessments of emotional state that occur automatically and spontaneously. Arnold proposes that spontaneous appraisal is the major determinant of emotional state and that reflective appraisal plays a modifying role. See Vallerand (1983) for an integration of these two approaches to explain emotion in organized sport.

The inclusion of intuitive appraisal in the Weiner model would provide a role for both physiological and cognitive processes occurring during exercise. This is an important point because Weiner focuses primarily on perceived success or failure of outcomes and viewing exercise solely as an outcome situation (e.g., winning or losing) may not be adequate for exercise situations. Thus the process of exercise itself may be instrumental in generating emotion that is initially assessed through intuitive appraisal. This emotion generated as a consequence of exercise may be mediated by one or a combination of the psychological and physiological mechanisms previously described. In summary reflective appraisals and their effect on emotion may provide insight into how emotional states are generated through and after exercise. The inclusion of intuitive appraisal can account for both physiological and cognitive influence on emotional state during exercise as well as that created by exercise outcome. Attributions will be further integrated with self-efficacy in a later part of this article.

COGNITIVE/BEHAVIORAL APPROACH

Classical and Operant Conditioning and Social Learning Theory

Cognitive approaches such as that of Weiner have focused on thinking processes and have largely ignored environmental stimuli. Learning theories, in contrast, focus on the influence of environment on behavior and have ignored thinking processes. Perhaps both are incomplete approaches to understanding human functioning. The most influential learning theories are classical and operant conditioning and social learning theory. Bandura (1986) has recently revised social learning theory to include more cognitive variables and has renamed it social cognitive theory.

Briefly classical conditioning suggests that stimuli occurring in the environment will influence ensuing behaviors. In the exercise situation, physical activity may provide the stimulus and positive emotion may occur as the conditioned response. In contrast, operant conditioning suggests that the consequences of behavior are the major determinants of future behavior. The consequences of behavior are termed reinforcers and can be either positive, negative, or punishing (for an overview, see Bandura, 1977a). In the exercise situation, upon completion of a workout, an individual may be praised by the exercise leader. Over time the exercise and feedback may become positively reinforced. Although the influence of conditioning on the generation of emotion after exercise has not been examined there is a large literature supporting the notion that both classical and operant conditioning are powerful ways of altering behavior.

With regard to conditioning and emotion, the early work of Watson and Rayner (1920) has demonstrated that human emotions, like simple reflexes, can be conditioned. Thus a behavioral explanation of the feeling-better phenomenon would be that individuals learn how to feel better after exercise. Therefore exercisers associate positive emotional feelings with exercise that becomes conditioned with repeated exposure to exercise.

Social Cognitive Theory

Social cognitive theory (Bandura, 1986) uses the same principles as those of operant conditioning but includes an additional role for the ability of the individual to influence the environment. Social cognitive theory is a recent extension of social learning theory and uses self-efficacy as a central concept. Basically self-efficacy suggests that those individuals who are confident in their ability to perform a specific behavior are more likely to perform that behavior compared to those individuals with less confidence. Self-efficacy has been shown to be influential in the choice, effort, and persistence of individuals in a variety of activities (Bandura, 1977b). The four major sources of information that influence an individual's self-efficacy are past performance accomplishment, vicarious experience, social persuasion, and physiological arousal (Bandura, 1977b). Past performance accomplishment is the most influential source of self-efficacy information (for overviews see Feltz, 1988; and McAuley, in press, a). Self-efficacy has also been shown to be an influential factor in physical activity (Feltz, 1984) and exercise adherence (McAuley, 1990).

In regard to acute exercise and emotion, individuals may initially assess their self-efficacy by monitoring sensations of pain and levels of fatigue during and after exercise. Thus self-efficacy may be influenced by the positive and negative emotional states generated by and resulting from physiological mechanisms and attributions caused by exercise. As individuals adapt to exercise and experience more success, the sources driving self-efficacy may then include past performance accomplishment.

McAuley (in press, a) has focused on the relationship between attributions and self-efficacy in the exercise adherence process and has suggested that there are at least two important reciprocal processes involving self-efficacy and attributions. First, causal attributions have the potential to determine self-efficacy (Schunk & Cox, 1986), and second, levels of self-efficacy also may effect subsequent causal thinking (Duncan & McAuley, 1987; McAuley, Duncan, &

McElroy, 1989). It appears that in acute exercise situations the attribution/self-efficacy relationship may be especially relevant.

Thus emotion may be initially generated through actual exercise and then assessed and modified through intuitive and reflective processes. Intuitive appraisal may involve the assessment of hedonic tone (the feeling-better sensation) after exercise, whereas outcome appraisal may involve assessment of goals such as "did I run far enough?" or "did I achieve the time I desired?" Individuals may integrate emotional and informational sources after exercise. The initial primary emotional state may be more likely to be driven by physiological mechanisms during exercise for those individuals who have physiologically adapted to exercise.

In contrast, the emotional states of nonadapted exercisers may be more influenced by cognitive processes during exercise. The initial evaluation of exercise emotional state and exercise outcome for both the trained and untrained may generate casual attributions that in turn may modify an existing emotional state. The information generated by exercising may then provide the basis for the determination of self-efficacy. As self-efficacy is increased or decreased, self-efficacy may then become an important precursor to positive or negative postexercise emotional state.

The reciprocal relationship between emotion, attribution, and self-efficacy is demonstrated in Figure 37–2. As can be seen, the major addition to Weiner's model has been the inclusion of intuitive emotional appraisal as part of the initial emotional process and the addition of self-efficacy as an end product. Clearly, as illustrated in Figure 37–2, once self-efficacy has been established for an exercise situation, it may have an important influence on the initial intuitive and reflective appraisal processes (pre-exercise self-efficacy). There is also potential here to integrate some of the behavioral principles mentioned previously. Thus over time the repeated exposure of the individual to exercise accompanied by positive consequences (increased positive emotion and enhanced self-efficacy) may result in a conditioned emotional response to exercise. This notion is developed further in the next part of this chapter.

BEHAVIORAL/PHYSIOLOGICAL APPROACH

Opponent-Process Theory

The integration of attribution and self-efficacy theories would appear to have special relevance for the early stage of exercise (the adoption phase) where cognitive variables may be more influential than physiological factors for the generation of positive emotion. As previously illustrated, however, physiological mechanisms may also be responsible for the generation of emotional states. So far the model provides a role for cognitive and physiological factors that may underlie the emotional response to exercise. However, in its present form the model does not explain how individ-

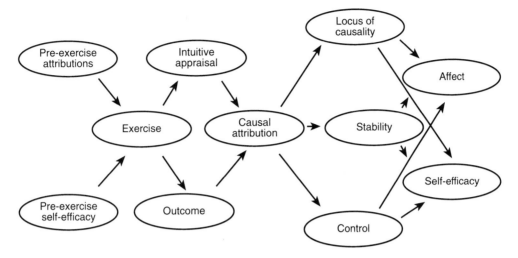

FIGURE 37–2. The integration of intuitive appraisal processes and self-efficacy into Weiner's cognition-emotion process.

uals may become behaviorally conditioned and eventually addicted to exercise.

One theory that does attempt to explain the relationship between physiological and behavioral mechanisms and how these processes change with repeated exposure to a stimulus is the opponent-process theory of acquired motivation (Solomon, 1980; Solomon & Corbitt, 1974). Solomon's theory has been developed from Cannon's work in the late 1920s and '30s, which has been reformulated within a behavioral framework. The opponent-process theory uses the dynamics of drug addiction as a model for the acquisition of a whole range of complex motivations, such as the attraction of sports or the love-attachment relationship in primates. In essence, Solomon's theory suggests that when an unconditioned stimulus or a reinforcer is repeatedly presented to an organism, three major affective phenomena occur (Figure 37–3).

First, when the nervous system is stimulated by an intense affective reaction (e.g., a drug or exercise), there occurs a primary affective reaction (an a-process) that is composed of behavioral, subjective, and physiological components. Once the a-process is activated, the b-process (a secondary affective reaction) is automatically initiated by central mechanisms. The function of the b-process is to bring the organism back to hedonic neutrality. The b-process is seen as being opposite in hedonic quality from the a-process and acts as an opponent-process. As the stimulus eliciting the a-process stops or diminishes, the b-process dominates and dictates that affective state of the organism. The aftereffect (the b-process) has four unique properties: (1) slow rise time relative to the a-process; (2) a relatively long decay time; (3) a tendency to weaken with disuse; and (4) a proneness to strengthen as a function of repeated exposure to the initial stimulus. This relationship between the a- and b-process can be viewed as a type of rebound effect that brings about displeasure after a pleasant experience or pleasure after an unpleasant one.

Second, continual exposure to the stimulus or reinforcer will result in habituation or tolerance. Thus the b-process will get increasingly larger with continual reinforcement until it eventually negates the effects of the a-process during the actual stimulus and becomes the dominant affective state on termination of the stimulus. The habituation process reflects the addictive properties of stimuli and suggests that new affective states can be produced after tolerance is developed. Third, after habituation to the stimulus, a withdrawal syndrome occurs when the stimulus is terminated.

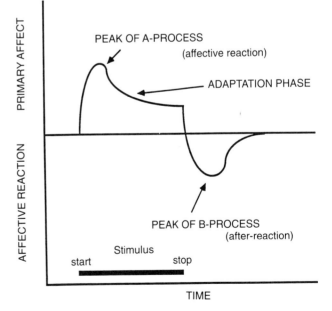

FIGURE 37–3. The standard pattern of emotion dynamics showing the a- and b-processes resulting from a typical stimulus.

The withdrawal syndrome is associated with the b-process, and its affective quality will depend on the nature of the a-process. If the a-process is pleasurable, then the withdrawal will be unpleasant. If the a-process is unpleasant, then the aftereffect will be pleasant.

Support for this theory has come from a number of diverse areas. For instance, data from color vision (Hurvich & Jameson, 1974); ducks and species-specific unconditioned stimuli (Hoffman, Searle, Toffey, & Kozma, 1966; Starr, 1978), adjunctive behaviors (Rosellini, 1985), dogs and unconditioned heart rate changes to electric shock (Church, Lolorado, Overmier, Solomon, & Turner, 1966), parachutists (Fenz & Epstein, 1967), and opiate effects (Wikler, 1966) have been used to provide support for the opponent-process theory.

An example of the affective dynamics of the opponent-process theory may be seen in the typical pattern of opiate use (Figure 37–4). The first doses of an opiate (such as heroin) produce a pleasant, euphoric state followed by a less intense, pleasant state. After the initial "rush," the drug is metabolized and the user goes into a mild state of physiological and psychological discomfiture. Most individuals find this latter state aversive and tend to redose to get rid of these withdrawal symptoms. The first dose produces a pat-tern of affective dynamics similar to that shown in Figure 37–4. The onset of the opiate first produces a peak in State A (the rush) that declines in intensity (the euphoric stage). Then, after the drug wears off, State B, an aversive craving state called the withdrawal syndrome, emerges.

Thus the opponent-process is seen in operation, whereby initial euphoria is followed by an aversive, uncontrollable state. Over time, if the doses are frequently repeated, the rush and the euphoric stage will get smaller with the physiological and psychological aspects of the withdrawal syndrome becoming more and more intense. Thus the motivation of the drug user changes. Initially the opiate was used to experience the pleasant "high" euphoric state. With continued use the motivation changes to avoiding the unpleasant effects of the withdrawal period. In this example concerning opiate use, the reinforcer is positive and the acquired motivational state is aversive. However, other situations exist where the reinforcer can be aversive and the acquired motivational state is positive. Such may be the case with aerobic exercise.

During their first run, for example, most sedentary individuals experience discomfiture in the form of breathing problems, pain in leg muscles, and dizziness. The typical neophyte runner reports unpleasant affect during the run and short-lasting feelings of relief after the session is over. Unless individuals are motivated to participate in a running program because of social pressures, weight loss reasons, or health beliefs, and so forth, the running sessions are not likely to be repeated since their State A is aversive.

However, if the running sessions are continually repeated, two changes may occur. The aversiveness of each session may gradually decline and a withdrawal syndrome (pleasant emotion) may emerge and intensify. Thus the person who sticks to the running program, by repeatedly exposing her/himself to a previously aversive pattern, now has a new source of pleasure. An acquired motivation would have emerged in the form of elevated mood, as predicted by the opponent-process theory. Figure 37–5 demonstrates the possible affective dynamics of the beginning and seasoned runner.

Mechanisms underlying the opponent-process for running could include endorphins, hyperthermia, and the autonomic rebound phenomenon previously discussed. For instance, Solomon (1980) has suggested that when subjects are habituated to stimuli endorphins may be the mechanism whereby the stimulus itself is tolerated. He also suggested that the generation of endorphins during the stimulus may be responsible for inducing the euphoric aftereffects commonly associated with activities such as running.

In summary the opponent-process theory suggests that repeated exposure to powerful stimuli such as aerobic exercise can cause a rebound pattern of emotional response. Thus initial aversive emotional response to a stimulus will gradually become less and less aversive, whereas on cessation of the stimulus, the emotional state will become more and more positive.

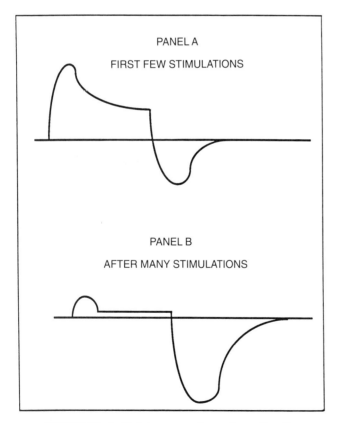

FIGURE 37–4. Opiate use and emotion after the first few stimulations (panel A) and after many stimulations (panel B).

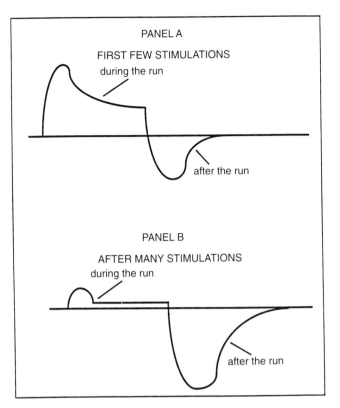

FIGURE 37–5. The pattern of emotion for the nonrunner (panel A) and the runner (panel B).

An Integrated Model

Figure 37–6 illustrates a preliminary framework based on the theories discussed. As can be seen, it is probable that multiple influences are involved in the generation of emotion through exercise. Because the exercise process itself is dynamic, the model attempts to explain how psychological and physiological processes influence emotion and how these processes are affected by physiological change occur-

ring through continued exposure to exercise. The model needs to be viewed as tentative and should be refined by future research.

The key proposals of the model are that cognitive processes in the form of attributions and self-efficacy will be especially important in the generation of emotion in the adoption phase of exercise. Thus the key determinants of emotion for the unfit, neophyte exercise may be expectations, the level of self-efficacy, and the type of attributions and appraisals. This proposition is supported by past research that has indicated that self-efficacy is most influential during the adoption phase of exercise (McAuley, 1990).

A second proposal concerns the influence of behavioral and physiological factors initiated when the individual starts to physiologically adapt to exercise or is exposed to repeated exercise. Here physiological mechanisms developed through adaptation to continual exercise may play a more prominent role in the generation of positive post-exercise emotion. This proposition is supported indirectly by past research that has indicated that trained and untrained subjects can possess different patterns of emotional response to exercise stimuli. It is also feasible, however, that individuals may exercise repeatedly but exercise intensity may not be great enough to bring about significant physiological adaptations. For these individuals repeated exposure to extremely light exercise may bring about little physiological change but may result in behavioral conditioning to the characteristics of the exercise stimulus. For instance, a recreational runners' positive postexercise emotional state may be generated by the conditioning of pleasant cognitions achieved by jogging around an attractive lake.

A third proposal suggests that extreme habitual exercisers may develop excessive exercise behaviors that may be driven by motivation to avoid the unpleasant emotion associated with not exercising. Thus, as suggested by opponent-process theory, an unpleasant emotional state could be caused by both exercise-specific physiological or behavioral processes.

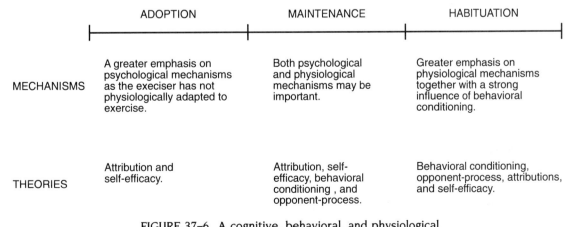

	ADOPTION	MAINTENANCE	HABITUATION
MECHANISMS	A greater emphasis on psychological mechanisms as the exciser has not physiologically adapted to exercise.	Both psychological and physiological mechanisms may be important.	Greater emphasis on physiological mechanisms together with a strong influence of behavioral conditioning.
THEORIES	Attribution and self-efficacy.	Attribution, self-efficacy, behavioral conditioning , and opponent-process.	Behavioral conditioning, opponent-process, attributions, and self-efficacy.

FIGURE 37–6. A cognitive, behavioral, and physiological model of emotional change to exercise.

SUMMARY AND IMPLICATIONS FOR FUTURE RESEARCH

The goal of this chapter has been to develop a tentative model of the exercise/emotion relationship in order to provide a framework for future research. It has been suggested that exercise provides a useful model to explore the cognitive, behavioral, and physiological processes underlying emotion. Research examining emotion during exercise suggests that emotion tends to decrease as work intensity gets harder but that this emotional response can be influenced by variables such as sex type and music. Studies using retrospective recall, state anxiety, EMG, and EEG as indicants of emotional state have demonstrated that vigorous exercise compared to light exercise can result in increases in positive emotion. A number of possible physiological and psychological mechanisms underlying positive emotional state were outlined.

Next a process view of exercise was described. This view suggested that individuals exposed to an aerobic program progress through three stages of physiological adaptation (adoption, maintenance, and habituation). These phases are also accompanied by psychological change with attributions and self-efficacy influences being most significant during the adoption phase of exercise, while behavioral conditioning and opponent-process influences are most influential during the maintenance and habituation phases. All processes, however, are viewed as having input on the emotional state at all levels of the exercise process.

Clearly the complex interplay between psychological and physiological influences on emotion that is modified by physical change to regular exercise has only been globally described. Future research needs to refine this model by exploring in much greater depth and detail the influences of these various cognitive and physiological interacting processes and their interplay with individual, social, and environmental factors.

References

Arnold, M. B. (1970). *Feelings and emotions: The Loyola Symposium.* New York: Academic Press.

Baekland, F., & Laskey, R. (1966). Exercise and sleep patterns in college athletes. *Perceptual and Motor Skills, 23,* 1203–1207.

Bahrke, M. S., & Morgan, W. P. (1978). Anxiety reduction following exercise and meditation. *Cognitive Therapy, 2,* 323–333.

Bandura, A. (1977a). *Social learning theory.* Englewood Cliffs, NJ: Prentice-Hall.

Bandura, A. (1977b). Self-efficacy: Toward a unifying theory of behavioral change. *Psychological Review, 84,* 191–215.

Berger, B. G., & Owen, D. R. (1983). Mood alterations with swimming—Swimmers really do feel better. *Psychosomatic Medicine, 45,* 425–433.

Bluementhal, J. A., Williams, R. S., Needels, T. L., & Wallace, A. (1982). Psychological changes accompany aerobic exercise in healthy middle-aged adults. *Psychosomatic Medicine, 44,* 529–536.

Bonvallet, M., & Bloch, V. (1961). Bulbar control of cortical arousal. *Science, 133,* 119–125.

Boutcher, S. H. (1986). *The effects of running and nicotine on mood states.* Unpublished doctoral dissertation, Arizona State University, Tempe.

Boutcher, S. H. (1990). Aerobic fitness: Measurement and issues. *Journal of Sport and Exercise Psychology, 12,* 235–247.

Boutcher, S. H. (1991). The effects of exercise on immunity and illness. In L. Diamant (Ed.), *Psychology of sports, exercise, and fitness* (pp. 103–118). New York: Harper & Row.

Boutcher, S. H. (in press). Conceptualization and quantification of aerobic fitness and physical activity. In P. Seraganian (Ed.), *Exercise psychology: The influence of physical exercise on psychological processes.* New York: Wiley.

Boutcher, S. H., & Landers, D. M. (1988). The effects of vigorous exercise on anxiety, heart rate, and alpha activity of runners and nonrunners. *Psychophysiology, 25,* 696–702.

Boutcher, S. H., & Trenske, M. (1990). The effects of sensory deprivation and music on rating of perceived exertion and affect during exercise. *Journal of Sport and Exercise Psychology, 12,* 167–176.

Brown, B. S., & Van Huss, W. D. (1973). Exercise and rat brain catecholamines. *Journal of Applied Physiology, 34,* 664–669.

Brown, D. R. (1990). Exercise, fitness, and mental health. In C. Bouchard, R. Shepherd, T. Stephens, J. Sutton, & B. McPhereson (Eds.), *Exercise, fitness, and health,* (pp. 608–620). Champaign, IL: Human Kinetics.

Brunner, B. C. (1969). Personality and motivating factors influencing adult participation in vigorous physical activity. *Research Quarterly, 3,* 464–469.

Buck, R. (1985). Prime theory: An integrated view of motivation and emotion. *Psychological Review, 92,* 389–413.

Bukowski, W. M., & Moore, D. (1980). Winners' and losers' attributions for success and failure in a series of athletic events. *Journal of Sport Psychology, 2,* 195–210.

Cannon, W. B. (1932). *The wisdom of the body.* New York: W. W. Norton.

Catlin, D. H., Gorelick, D. D., Gerner, R. H., Aui, K. K., & Li, C. H. (1980). Clinical effects of β-endorphin infusions. In E. Costa & M. Trabucchi (Eds.), *Neural peptides and neural communication* (pp. 465–472). New York: Raven Press.

Church, R. M., Lolorado, V., Overmier, J. B., Solomon, R. L., & Turner, L. H. (1966). Cardiac responses to shock in curarized dogs: Effects of shock intensity and duration, warning signal, and prior experience with shock. *Journal of Comparative and Physiological Psychology, 62,* 1–7.

Davies, C. T. M. (1981). Effect of acclimatization to heat on the regulation of sweating during moderate and severe exercise. *Journal of Applied Physiology, 50,* 741–749.

DeVries, H. A. (1968). Immediate and long-term effects of exercise upon muscle action potential. *The Journal of Sports Medicine and Physical Fitness, 8,* 1–11.

DeVries, H. A., & Adams, G. M. (1972). Electromyographic comparison of single doses of exercise and meprobamate as to effects on muscular relaxation. *Journal of Sports Medicine and Physical Fitness, 51,* 130–141.

DeVries, H. A., Wiswell, R. A., Bulbulian, R., & Moritani, T. (1981). Tranquilizer effect of exercise. *American Journal of Physical Medicine, 60,* 57–66.

Dressendorfer, R. H., Wade, C. E., & Scaff, J. H. (1985). Increased morning heart rate in runners: A valid sign of overtraining? *The Physician and Sportsmedicine, 13,* 77–86.

Duffy, E. (1962). *Activation and behavior.* New York: John Wiley.

Duncan, T. E., & McAuley, E. (1987). Efficacy expectations and perceptions of causality in motor performance. *Journal of Sport Psychology, 9,* 385–393.

Ekman, P., & Frieson, W. V. (1969). The repertoire of nonverbal behavior: Categories, origins, usage and coding. *Semiotica, 1,* 49–98.

Ekman, P., Hagar, L., & Frieson, W. V. (1981). The symmetry of emotion and deliberate facial action. *Psychophysiology, 18,* 363–369.

Farrell, P. A., Gates, W. K., Morgan, W. P., & Pert, C. B. (1983). Plasma leucine enkephalin-like radioreceptor activity and tension-anxiety before and after competitive running. In H. G. Knuttgen, J. A. Vogel, & J. Poortmans (Eds.), *Biochemistry of exercise* (pp. 637–653). Champaign, IL: Human Kinetics.

Fawcett, J., Mass, J. W., & Dekirmenjiar, H. (1972). Depression and MHPG excretion. *Archives of General Psychiatry, 26,* 246–251.

Feltz, D. L. (1982). Path analysis of the causal elements of Bandura's theory of self-efficacy and an anxiety-based model of avoidance behavior. *Journal of Personality and Social Psychology, 42,* 764–781.

Feltz, D. L. (1988). Self-confidence and sports performance. *Exercise and Sport Sciences Reviews, 16,* 423–458.

Fenz, W. D., & Epstein, S. M. (1967). Gradients of physiological arousal of experienced and novice parachutists as a function of an approaching jump. *Psychosomatic Medicine, 34,* 33–51.

Folkins, C. H. (1972). Effects of physical training on mood. *Journal of Clinical Psychology, 32,* 385–388.

Folkins, C. H., Lynch, S., & Gardner, M. M. (1972). Psychological fitness as a function of physical fitness. *Archives of Physical Medicine and Rehabilitation, 53,* 503–508.

Folkins, C. H., & Sime, W. E. (1981). Physical fitness training and mental health. *American Psychologist, 36,* 373–389.

Gal, R., & Lazarus, R. S. (1975). The role of activity in anticipating and confronting stressful situations. *Journal of Human Stress, 1,* 4–20.

Glowinski, J., & Baldessarini, R. J. (1966). Metabolism of norepinephrine in the central nervous system. *Pharmacological Review, 18,* 1201–1238.

Goldwater, B. C., & Collis, M. L. (1985). Psychologic effects of cardiovascular conditioning: A controlled experiment. *Psychosomatic Medicine, 47,* 174–181.

Gondola, J. C., & Tuckman, B. W. (1985). Psychological mood state in "average" marathon runners. *Perceptual & Motor Skills, 55,* 1295–1300.

Gutmann, M. C., Pollock, M. L., Foster, C., & Schmidt, D. (1984). Training stress in olympic speed skaters: A psychological perspective. *The Physician and Sportsmedicine, 12,* 45–57.

Hardy, C. J., & Rejeski, W. J. (1989). Not what, but how one feels: The measurement of affect during exercise. *Journal of Sport and Exercise Psychology, 11,* 304–317.

Hatfield, D. B. (1991). Exercise and mental health: The mechanism of exercise-induced psychological states. In L. Diamant (Ed.), *Psychology of sports, exercise, and fitness* (pp. 17–49). New York: Harper & Row.

Hatfield, B. D., & Landers, D. M. (1987). Psychophysiological methodology in exercise and sport research. *Exercise and Sport Sciences Reviews, 15,* 351–387.

Heitmann, H. M. (1986). Motives of older adults for participating in physical activity programs. In B. D. McPherson (Ed.), *Sport and aging* (pp. 199–204). Champaign, IL: Human Kinetics.

Hillman, J. (1960). *Emotion.* London: Routledge & Kegan Paul.

Hoffman, H. S., Searle, J. L., Toffey, S., & Kozma, F. (1966). Behavioral control by an imprinted stimulus. *Journal of the Experimental Analysis of Behavior, 9,* 177–189.

Horne, J. A. (1983). Sleep EEG effects with and without additional body cooling. *Electroencephalography and Clinical Neurology, 60,* 33–38.

Horne, J. A., & Porter, J. M. (1976). Time of day effects with standardized exercise upon subsequent sleep. *Journal of Electroencephalography and Clinical Neurology, 40,* 178–184.

Hughes, J. R. (1984). Psychological effects of habitual exercise: A critical review. *Preventive Medicine, 13,* 66–78.

Hurvich, L. M., & Jameson, D. (1974). Opponent process as a model of neural organization. *American Psychologist, 29,* 88–102.

Kamp, A., & Troost, J. (1978). EEG signs of cerebral disorders, using exercise as a provocative method. *EEG Clinical Neurophysiological, 45,* 295–298.

Kleinginna, P. R., & Kleinginna, A. M. (1981). A categorized list of emotional definitions, with suggestions for a consensual definition. *Motivation and Emotion, 5,* 345–379.

Kuykendall, D., Keating, J. P., & Wagaman, J. (1988). Assessing affective states: A methodology for some old problems. *Cognitive Therapy and Research, 12,* 279–294.

Lazarus, R. S. (1984). On the primacy of cognition. *American Psychologist, 37,* 124–129.

Leeper, R. W. (1970). Feelings and emotions. In M. D. Arnold (Ed.), *Feelings and emotions: The Loyola Symposium* (pp. 151–168). New York: Academic Press.

Maclean, P. D. (1981). Role of transhypothalamic pathways in social communication. In P. Morgane & J. Panksepp (Eds.), *Handbook of the hypothalamus: Vol. 3, Part B. Behavioral studies of the hypothalamus* (pp. 259–287). New York: Marcel Dekker.

McAuley, E. (1990, May). *Self-efficacy determinants of exercise behavior in middle-aged adults.* Paper presented at the annual meeting of the North American Society for the Psychology of Sport and Physical Activity, Houston, TX.

McAuley, E. (in press, a). Self-referent thought in sport and physical activity. *Advances in sport psychology.* Champaign, IL: Human Kinetics.

McAuley, E. (in press, b). Understanding exercise behaviors: A self-efficacy perspective. In G. Roberts (Ed.). *Understanding motivation in sport and exercise.* Champaign, IL: Human KInetics.

McAuley, E., & Duncan, T. E. (1989). Causal attributions and affective reactions to disconfirming outcomes in motor performance. *Journal of Sport and Exercise Psychology, 11,* 187–200.

McAuley, E., & Duncan, T. E. (in press). Cognitive appraisal and affective reactions following physical achievement outcomes. *Journal of Sport and Exercise Psychology.*

McAuley, E., Poag, K., Gleason, A., & Wraith, S. (1990). Attrition from exercise programs: Attributional and affective perspectives. *Journal of Social Behavior and Personality, 5,* 591–602.

McNair, D. M., Lorr, M., & Droppleman, L. F. (1971). *Profile of Mood States Manual,* San Diego: Educational and Industrial Testing Service.

McPherson, B. D., Paivio, A., Yuhasz, M., Rechnitzer, P., Pikard, H., & Lefcoe, N. (1965). Psychological effects of an exercise program for postinfarct and normal adult men. *Journal of Sports Medicine and Physical Fitness, 8,* 95–102.

Morgan, W. P. (1973). Influences of acute physical activity on state anxiety. *Proceedings of the National College Physical Education Association for Men,* 76th Annual Meeting, 113–121.

Morgan, W. P. (1979). Anxiety reduction following acute physical activity. *Psychiatric Annals, 9,* 141–147.

Morgan, W. P. (1985). Affective beneficence of vigorous physical activity. *Medicine Science in Sports and Exercise, 17,* 94–100.

Morgan, W. P., Brown, D. R., Raglin, J. S., O'Connor, P. J., & Ellickson, K. A. (1987). Psychological monitoring of overtraining and staleness. *British Journal of Sports Medicine, 21,* 107–114.

Morgan, W. P., & Goldston, S. E. (1987). *Exercise and mental health.* Washington: Hemisphere.

Morgan, W. P., & Horstman, D. H. (1976). Anxiety reduction following acute physical activity. *Medicine and Science in Sports, 8,* 62.

Morgan, W. P., Roberts, G. A., & Feinerman, A. D. (1971). Psychological effects of acute physical activity. *Archives of Physical Medicine and Rehabilitation, 52,* 422–425.

North, T. C., McCullagh, P., & Tran, Z. V. (1990). Effects of exercise on depression. *Exercise and Sport Sciences Reviews, 18,* 379–415.

Papez, J. W. (1937). A proposed mechanism of emotion. *Archives of Neurological Psychiatry, 38,* 725–743.

Petruzzello, S., Landers, D. M., Hatfield, B. D., Kubitz, K. A., & Salazar, W. (1991). A meta-analysis on the anxiety reducing effects of acute and chronic exercise: Outcomes and mechanisms. *Sports Medicine, 11,* 143–182.

Pineda, A., & Anderson, M. A. (1961). Electroencephalographic studies in physical fatigue. *Texas Republic Biological Medicine, 19,* 332–342.

Plutchik, R. (1980). *Emotion: psychoevolutionary synthesis.* New York: Harper & Row.

Raglin, J. S., & Morgan, W. P. (1987). Influence of exercise and quiet rest on state anxiety and blood pressure. *Medicine and Science in Sports and Exercise, 19,* 587–593.

Rejeski, W. J., Best, D., Griffith, P., & Kenney, E. (1987). Sex-role orientation and the responses of men to exercise stress. *Research Quarterly, 58,* 260–264.

Rosellini, R. A. (1985). The opponent-process theory of motivation: VII. Quantitative and qualitative manipulations of food both modulate adjunctive behavior. *Learning and Behavior, 13,* 222–239.

Schacter, S., & Singer, J. (1962). Cognitive, social and physiological determinants of emotional state. *Psychological Review, 69,* 378–399.

Schunk, D. H., & Cox, P. D. (1986). Strategy training feedback with learning disabled students. *Journal of Educational Psychology, 78,* 201–209.

Schwartz, G. E., Davidson, R. J., & Goleman, D. J. (1978). Patterning of cognitive and somatic processes in the self-regulation of anxiety: Effects of meditation versus exercise. *Psychosomatic Medicine, 40,* 321–328.

Sforzo, G. A. (1988). Opiods and exercise: An update. *Sports Medicine, 7,* 109–124.

Solomon, R. L. (1980). The opponent-process theory of acquired motivation. *American Psychologist, 35,* 691–712.

Solomon, R. L., & Corbitt, J. D. (1974). An opponent-process theory of motivation: I. Temporal dynamics of affect. *Psychological Review, 81,* 119–145.

Sonstroem, R. (1984). Exercise and self-esteem. In R. Terjung (Ed.), *Exercise and sport sciences reviews* (pp. 123–154). New York: Macmillan.

Spielberger, C. D., Gorsuch, R. L., & Lushene, R. E. (1970). *Manual for the State-Trait Anxiety Inventory (STAI).* Palo Alto, CA: Consulting Psychologists Press.

Starr, M. D. (1978). An opponent-process theory of motivation: VII. Time and intensity variables in the development of separation-induced distress calling in ducklings. *Journal of Experimental Psychology, 4,* 338–355.

Strongman, K. T. (1987). *The psychology of emotion* (3rd ed.). New York: Wiley.

Summers, J. J., Machin, V. J., & Sargent, G. I. (1983). Psychosocial factors related to marathon running. *Journal of Sport Psychology, 5,* 314–331.

Tomkins, S. S. (1981). The role of facial response in the experience of emotion: A reply to Tourangeau and Ellsworth. *Journal of Personality and Social Psychology, 40,* 355–357.

Vallerand, R. J. (1983). On emotion in sport: Theoretical and social psychological perspectives. *Journal of Sport Psychology, 5,* 197–215.

Vallerand, R. J. (1987). Antecedents of self-related affects in sport: Preliminary evidence of the intuitive-reflective appraisal model. *Journal of Sport Psychology, 9,* 161–182.

Von Euler, C., & Soderberg, U. (1957). The influence of hypothalamic thermoreceptive structures on the electroencephalogram and gamma motor activity. *Electroencephalography and Clinical Neurophysiology, 9,* 391–408.

Watson, J. B., & Rayner, R. (1920). Conditioned emotional reactions. *Journal of Experimental Psychology, 3,* 1–14.

Weiner, B. (1972). *Theories of motivation: From mechanism to cognition.* Chicago: Rand McNally.

Weiner, B. (1985). An attributional theory of achievement, motivation, and emotion. *Psychological Review, 92,* 548–573.

Weiner, B. (1986). *An attributional theory of motivation.* New York: Springer-Verlag.

Wiese, J., Singh, M., & Yeudall, L. (1983). Occipital and parietal alpha power before, during, and after exercise. *Medicine and Science in Sports and Exercise, 15,* 117.

Wikler, A. (1966). *Opiate addiction.* Springfield, IL: Thomas.

Young, P. T. (1961). *Motivation and emotion.* New York: Wiley.

·38·

PSYCHOLOGY OF INJURY AND INJURY REHABILITATION

Jean M. Williams

Nancy Roepke

Epidemiological studies indicate that more than 70,000,000 injuries requiring medical attention or at least a day of restricted activity occur annually in the United States. The incidence of injuries is so serious among children and young adults that injuries have replaced infectious diseases as the leading cause of death and disability (Boyce & Sobolewski, 1989). Conservative estimates indicate that at least 3 to 5 million of these injuries occur within sports and recreation (Kraus & Conroy, 1984). In a study of almost 55,000 school children, Boyce and Sobolewski found that athletic participation accounted for 44% of the injuries to students 14 years and older. Within amateur athletics each year, nearly half of all participants suffer an injury that precludes participation (Garrick & Requa, 1978; Hardy & Crace, 1990) and, according to the Consumer Product Safety Commission, one quarter of these injuries require at least 1 week of nonparticipation (Hardy & Crace, 1990). These injuries take their toll in financial costs, personal tragedy, and limitations on the potential success of an athletic program. The gravity of the athletic injury problem underscores the need for research that delves into both the causes and treatment of injury, including the study of psychological risk factors and treatment protocols.

Over the last two decades, many sports medicine personnel and sport psychology researchers have postulated that a relationship exists between selected psychological variables and athletic injury occurrence and rehabilitation. Fortunately a growing number of researchers are now studying these relationships empirically. Although much remains to be discovered, a sufficient body of knowledge exists to merit including in this book a chapter on psychology and injury and rehabilitation. In the present chapter, research is reviewed on: (1) personality and psychosocial factors that contribute to injury risk; (2) mechanisms whereby such variables might cause injuries; (3) potential interventions for reducing the injuries caused by these factors; and (4) once injury occurs, the psychological aspects of injury rehabilitation. Future research needs and implications for the practitioner also will be discussed.

CAUSES OF INJURY

Although many of the causes for injury are undoubtedly physical in nature (e.g., body build, level of conditioning, equipment failures, playing surface, overtraining), psychological factors also contribute to injury vulnerability and resiliency. The psychological factors that have been researched can be classified as personality or psychosocial variables. The most frequently studied psychosocial variables are life event stress and various personal and environmental variables that might influence the stress–athletic injury relationship. Most of the personality variables that have been studied are fairly stable, enduring qualities within the individual whereas the psychosocial variables concern the individual within a changing social environment.

Personality Factors and Injury Risk

Conjecture from clinical or coaching experience provided the foundation for most of the early discussions of psychological factors and athletic injury risk (e.g., Moore, 1966; Ogilvie & Tutko, 1966; Rosenblum, 1979; Sanderson,

1977). Most of the theorizing concerned personality traits or states. For example, Rosenblum (1979) contended that many injuries are a consequence of depression, guilt, or fear of success. Some of the proposals even had a neo-Freudian aspect to them (e.g., Sanderson, 1977).

Controlled, quantifiable studies on personality and injury proneness also have been conducted, but the results have been inconsistent. Jackson, Jarrett, Bailey, Kausek, Swanson, and Powell (1978) used Cattell's Sixteen Personality Factor Questionnaire (16-PF) to study high school football players. They found tender-minded, dependent players received more injuries than tough-minded, self-reliant players. Valiant (1981) obtained similar results with competitive male distance runners. Irwin (1975) did not find any tender vs. tough-minded differences in high school football players, but he did observe injured players were more reserved (vs. outgoing) than noninjured players. The Jackson et al. athletes who experienced the most severe injuries also were more likely to be reserved compared to the more outgoing personality of athletes with less severe injuries. Brown (1971), on the other hand, found no differences between injured and noninjured football players using the California Psychological Inventory (CPI). Abadie (1976) also found no personality differences when she studied injured and noninjured female athletes in individual and team sports, as measured by the 16-PF. The general (vs. sport-oriented) nature of the 16-PF and CPI, as well as the trait approach underlying the development of the questionnaires (see Fisher, 1984, for a critique of the trait approach), may have contributed to the minimal ability of the tools to identify personality factors related to injury occurrence.

Locus of control and self-concept are two other personality traits that have received some attention in assessing the role of psychological factors in injury vulnerability. Locus of control is a concept dealing with the degree to which individuals view their lives and environment as under their personal control. According to Rotter (1966), who developed the Internal-External Locus of Control Scale most commonly used to measure the construct, an internal orientation is characterized by a belief that one's own actions control personal outcomes in life whereas an external orientation is indicative of an individual who feels himself or herself a victim of chance or circumstances. Early studies yielded mixed support for differences in locus of control influencing athletic injury outcome. Passer and Seese (1983) found no relationship between locus of control and injury occurrence in football players. Dalhauser and Thomas (1979) obtained similar results with football players when locus of control was assessed with Rotter's general tool, but fewer injuries were reported for players with an internal locus of control when assessment was with a specific football scale that they developed.

Self-concept is thought to affect the emotional, physical, social, and cognitive life of the individual (Samuels, 1977). As such, differences in self-concept may play a role in injury vulnerability. Using the Tennessee Self-Concept Scale, Young and Cohen (1981) found injured participants ($n =$

22) in a female high school basketball tournament had a higher overall self-concept prior to the tournament than noninjured ($n = 168$) players. Injured players also viewed themselves more positively concerning what they were (identity), their state of health and physical appearance and skills (physical self), and their personal worth as seen apart from their body or relationships with others (personal self). The authors conjectured that these self-concept characteristics may have led the injured players to take more risks and thus to find themselves in more situations that could result in injury. The preceding results are counterbalanced by an earlier Young and Cohen (1979) study in which self-concept was not found to be related to tournament injuries in female collegiate basketball players. The authors proposed that the smaller number of injured college players compared to injured high school players and the age and education differences may have contributed to the different findings between the two studies.

A more recent study further complicates any definitive conclusions regarding the relationship of self-concept to athletic injury. Lamb (1986) found female college varsity field hockey players with low self-concept scores, as measured by the Tennessee Self-Concept Scale, tended to have more injuries than players with a higher self-concept. Self-concept was measured at the beginning of the season and injury frequency was recorded throughout the season. Of the 127 injuries sustained by the field hockey team, 23% occurred the day before a game. Of the day before injuries, 65%, 28%, and 7% were sustained, respectively, by athletes grouped into the lowest, middle, and top third on self-concept. The author suggested that the injury rates of the athletes with low self-concepts may have reflected a desire on their part not to play in the upcoming competition or to have a built-in excuse for not playing well, thereby protecting their self-esteem. While the conjecture is interesting, the limited number of subjects ($N = 21$) makes questionable any generalization of the results. Clearly any definitive conclusion regarding whether or not self-concept affects injury rates, much less how it might influence injury, remains to be determined. Similar conclusions are appropriate for attempts to identify other personality factors assumed to correlate with the occurrence of athletic injuries.

Life Stress and Athletic Injury Risk

The most extensively researched area in psychology of injury, and the area that perhaps holds the most promise of identifying psychosocial injury risk factors, is the study of life event stress and its relationship to injury occurrence. Interest in this area originally came from the literature indicating that life change events are a contributor to illness and accidents (e.g., Holmes & Rahe, 1967; Sarason, Johnson, & Siegle, 1978; Selzer & Vinokur, 1974; Stuart & Brown, 1981). A major impetus for the health research came from the work of Holmes and Rahe (1967), developers of the Social Readjustment Rating Scale (SRRS), a scale that ranks the magnitude of various life change events for the general population. The scale is based on the assumption that stress is inherently present to varying degrees in response to all environmental stimuli. This stress makes an increased demand upon the body to readjust or adapt, resulting in individuals with high exposure to life-change events, particularly those requiring greater adaptation, being at increased risk for illness. Examples of stressors are events such as the death of a close family member, taking a vacation, and a minor violation of the law. On the SRRS, each life event is given a preset, numerical weighting based on the presumed degree of adaptation required for the typical individual in the general population. Individuals indicate the frequency of each event's occurrence during a specified period of time. A total life-change score is tabulated by adding the weighted scores for the checked items.

Football Injuries. Football players were investigated in the initial five published studies on life-event stress and athletic injuries. Holmes (1970) conducted the first study. Using the SRRS, he gathered data from approximately 100 University of Washington players on their life-change units for the year prior to the football season. Injury statistics from the following football season indicated a 50% injury rate for athletes with high life-change scores compared to only 25% and 9%, respectively, for athletes with medium and low life-change scores. Holmes concluded that life-change stress relates to being at risk for the occurrence of athletic injuries in much the same way as the occurrence of illness.

Since this original study, Bramwell, Masuda, Wagner, and Holmes (1975) modified the SRRS to make it more appropriate for college athletes. Some of the less applicable general adult population stressors were deleted and 20 stressors specific to college students and athletes such as staying eligible, trouble with the coaching staff, and change in playing status were added. The new tool consisted of 57 events and was called the Social Athletic Readjustment Rating Scale (SARRS). Conceptually the SARRS is administered and scored in much the same way as the original tool. Using the new tool, Bramwell et al. studied 82 members of a University of Washington football team. Athletes were divided into low-risk (0–400 score), moderate-risk (400–800 score), and high-risk (greater than 800 score) groups based on their SARRS scores. During the following season, injury rates were 30%, 50%, and 73%, respectively, for the three risk groups. Injured athletes were defined as those players who missed three or more practices or one or more games due to a specific injury. This criterion was chosen because it identified a major time-loss injury and not the minor, nagging injuries commonly suffered by contact sport athletes. The authors concluded that the risk of an injury to a football player increases in direct relationship to the experiencing of challenging life events.

In the third study, Coddington and Troxell (1980) studied high school football players using the Life Event Scale for Adolescents (LESA). Coddington and Troxell did not find a relationship between injury and overall life-change events, but their criterion for injury was stringent (i.e., missing effective participation for more than one week). The authors did find, however, that adolescents suffered injuries during their season if they experienced family instability such as the separation of parents or the death of a parent (referred to as object loss, OL).

Cryan and Alles (1983) replicated Bramwell et al.'s (1975) study, but improved on the design by studying football players from three universities ($N = 151$) and by assessing both the incidence and severity of injuries. An injury occurred whenever an athlete could not participate for one day. Injury severity was determined by the standards of the National Athletic Injury Reporting System (NAIRS). A minor injury permitted returning to play within 7 days. Moderate and major injuries necessitated, respectively, being out between 8 and 21 days or more than 21 days. Cryan and Alles found college football players with high SARRS life-event stress (>500 score) were more likely to be injured (68%) and to sustain multiple injuries compared to the injury rate (39%) for players with lower life-event stress (<500 score). Life-event stress did not affect risk for incurring injuries of varying severity.

In the preceding studies, life-event stress was assessed without tools that distinguished between adaptation required by positive and negative life events. The tools also gave preset weightings to the life events rather than allowing the respondent to indicate the magnitude of effect. Sarason, Johnson, and Siegel (1978), developers of the Life Experience Survey (LES), contend that the effects from adaptation to negative life-change events may be different from those life-change events viewed as positive. They also challenged the ability of preset weightings to adequately reflect the interaction between the environment and the individual's perception of the stressfulness of environmental events. Respondents on the LES are required to indicate whether they perceive a life-change event to be positive or negative and whether the event had no effect (0 score), a little effect (-1 or $+1$ score, depending upon whether the event is rated negative or positive), a moderate effect (-2 or $+2$ score), or a great effect (-3 or $+3$ score). Thus the LES provides an assessment for negative life events, positive life events, and total life events. Sarason et al. (1978) found that positive life change had either no effect or a less detrimental effect on health-related dependent variables compared to the effects of negative life change.

Passer and Seese (1983) were the first to study potential differential effects of negative and positive life change stress on the occurrence of athletic injuries. They modified the LES in much the same way as the SRRS was modified in order to make it more appropriate for an athletic population. The resulting scale included 70 life events and was called the Athletic Life Experiences Survey (ALES). Passer and Seese found that negative life change had a detrimental effect on the injury rates of their Division II football team. The Division I team that they studied had no significant relationship between injury and the life stress measures.

Nonfootball Injuries. From the original 1970 Holmes

study through the 1983 studies, a consistent relationship generally was found between high life stress and the occurrence of athletic injuries in football. The relationship between life stress and athletic injuries somewhat clouds when sports outside of football are examined. Studies of male and female Division I collegiate volleyball players (Williams, Tonymon, & Wadsworth, 1986) and high school and collegiate basketball and cross-country athletes (Williams, Haggert, Tonymon, & Wadsworth, 1986) found no relationship between life stress and athletic injury. To be classified as injured an athlete had to miss 3 or more days of practice. In the study with basketball and cross-country athletes, too small a sample size may have influenced the results, but similar problems did not occur in the volleyball study (N = 179). Williams, Tonymon, and Wadsworth (1986) also attempted to determine whether the SARRS or ALES was the most predictive and valid measure in assessing injury risk. A multiple regression analysis indicated no differences between the two tools in predicting injuries, but the meaningfulness of the results is questionable since neither questionnaire found a relationship between stress and injury. Using the NAIRS classification system, the researchers also found no relation between stress and severity of volleyball injury. The lower overall levels of stress reported by the volleyball players, compared to those reported by the football players, may have affected the stress-injury results.

In two other studies with nonfootball athletes, a significant relationship was found between life stress and injury. High life-stress physical education students participating in a variety of sports (Lysens, Auweele, & Ostyn, 1986) and members of the U.S. alpine ski team (May, Veach, Reed, & Griffey, 1985) were more likely to experience an acute injury (musculoskeletal leg injuries in skiers) than low life-stress physical education students and elite skiers. Lysens et al. (1986) found no significant relationship between life stress and overuse injuries or the severity of an injury. In the May et al. study, the high-stress skiers also experienced more ear, nose, and throat illness problems as well as headaches and sleep disturbance. Lysens et al. assessed life stress with a 74-item Life Event Questionnaire (LEQ). The LEQ was derived from the SARRS by changing specific items in order to make the tool more appropriate for physical education students rather than athletes. Scoring also was greatly modified in that students gave each event experienced an individual score (from a 10-point scale) rather than adaptation demands being determined with a standard score. An injury was defined as any occurring during the sports practice sessions that caused at least 3 days exemption from sports practice. May, Veach, Reed, and Griffey (1985) assessed life stress with the SARRS and the LESA. No criteria were given for injuries other than that athletes were asked to report at the end of the year the frequency and duration of specific illnesses and injuries experienced during the year.

Moderator Variables and Life Stress-Injury Relationships.
The stress-injury relationship was stronger in some football and nonfootball studies than in others, suggesting that differences in measurement tools, injury assessment, and unmeasured variables (e.g., moderator variables) may have affected the results. Baron and Kenny (1986) define a moderator variable as one that somehow affects the direction, or strength, or both of the relation between an independent (predictor) variable and a dependent (criterion) variable. The presence of certain psychological, environmental, or behavioral variables might moderate, or buffer, the potentially detrimental effects of life stress on injury occurrence. On the other hand, the presence or absence of certain variables may increase vulnerability to injury. Research on stress-illness relationships clearly shows a stronger relationship between life events and physical and mental health when differences in the variables that moderate the relationship (e.g., social support) also are considered (e.g., Cohen, 1988; Garrity & Marx, 1985).

Passer and Seese (1983) are to be commended for broadening the scope of research on stressful life events and injury by investigating how certain variables might moderate the life events-injury relationship. They studied trait anxiety, competitive trait anxiety (CTA), and locus of control. Except for CTA, Passer and Seese failed to detect any influence by moderator variables on the occurrence of athletic injuries. A correlation between negative life change and injury occurred for low (r = .37, $p<.05$), but not high (r = −.10, ns) CTA Division II football players.

Williams, Tonymon, and Wadsworth (1986) also studied a potential moderator variable, except that they examined coping resources. Coping resources consisted of a combination of social support and general coping behaviors such as diet and time for self. It was assessed with the Coping Resources Section of the Stress Audit Questionnaire (Miller & Cohen, 1982). Although coping resources failed to moderate the relationship between life-event stress and injury, they did directly influence injury occurrence. Injured volleyball players had lower coping resources than uninjured players, but the mean differences were minimal and coping resources accounted for less than 2% of the variance in injury rates.

MODEL OF STRESS AND ATHLETIC INJURY

By the mid-1980s, the inconsistent results across studies illustrated the need for theory development and refinement in methodology and measurement. Most of the early research on stress and athletic injury was conducted within a narrow scope, minimally considering the complexity of stress and the broad array of psychosocial and behavioral factors that might moderate stress and injury outcome. Further, most of the research was conducted without the benefit of an adequate theoretical framework to explain the relationship between psychosocial factors and injury and the possible mechanisms behind the stress-injury relationships.

A review of the stress-injury and stress-illness literature led Andersen and Williams (Andersen & Williams, 1988; Williams & Andersen, 1986) to propose an interactional theoretical model of injury. The model (see Figure 38–1) identifies various variables that might predict athletic injuries, proposes possible mechanisms underlying the stress-injury relationship, and suggests specific interventions for reducing the risk of athletic injury. According to the model, when athletes are put in a stressful situation such as a demanding practice or a crucial competitive situation, the athlete's history of stressors, personality characteristics, and coping resources contribute interactively to the stress response. It is the severity of the resulting stress response that puts an athlete at increased risk of being injured. The model is predicated on the assumption that two of the basic mechanisms behind the stress-injury relationship are increases in general muscle tension and deficits in attention during stress. The central hypothesis of the model is that individuals with high-stress, personality characteristics that tend to exacerbate the stress response and few coping resources will, when placed in a stressful situation, be more likely to appraise the situation as stressful (i.e., report higher state anxiety) and exhibit greater muscle tension and attentional disruptions. The end result is that these individuals are at greater risk of injury compared to individuals with the opposite profile.

The Stress Response

The central core of the model is the stress response, which is a bidirectional relationship between the person's cognitive appraisal of a potentially stressful external situation and the physiological and attentional aspects of stress. The individual makes some appraisal of the demands of the situation, the adequacy of his or her ability to meet those demands, and the consequences of failure/success in meeting the demands. Whether the cognitive appraisal is accurate or distorted by irrational beliefs or other maladaptive thought patterns is unimportant in the generation of the stress response. If the athlete perceives inadequate resources to meet the demands of the situation and it is important to succeed, the stress response will be activated (higher state anxiety) and manifested physiologically and attentionally.

Of the myriad physiological and attentional changes that occur during the stress response, generalized muscle tension (Nideffer, 1983) and disruptions in attentional focus (Bramwell et al., 1975; Cryan & Alles, 1983; Williams et al., 1986) have been suggested the most frequently as probable mechanisms behind the stress-injury relationship. Unwanted simultaneous contraction of agonist and antagonist muscle groups (often called bracing) is a common response to stressors. This generalized muscle tension can

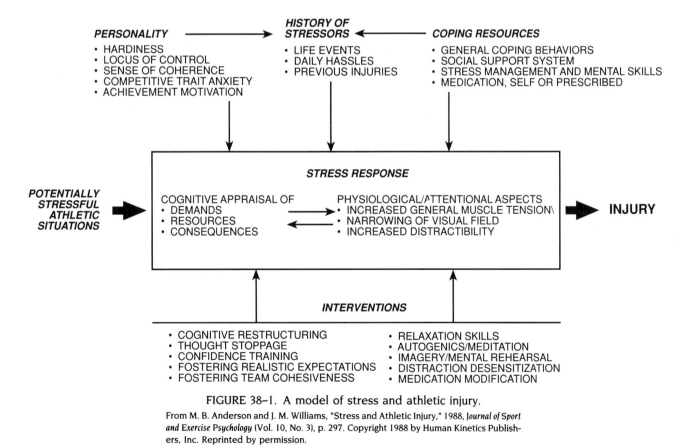

FIGURE 38–1. A model of stress and athletic injury.

From M. B. Anderson and J. M. Williams, "Stress and Athletic Injury," 1988, *Journal of Sport and Exercise Psychology* (Vol. 10, No. 3), p. 297. Copyright 1988 by Human Kinetics Publishers, Inc. Reprinted by permission.

lead to fatigue and reduced flexibility, motor coordination, and muscle efficiency. The end result is a greater risk for incurring injuries such as sprains, strains, and other musculoskeletal injuries.

Correspondingly, with increased stress the attentional field involuntarily narrows and becomes more internally focused (e.g., Hancock, 1984; Landers, 1980; Nideffer & Sharpe, 1978). A narrow internal focus "restricts one's ability to analyze, to deal with a lot of information, to make rational decisions, and even to be aware of what is going on in the environment" (Hardy & Riehl, 1988, p. 117). Attentional disruptions could be produced by preoccupation with stressful events and their possible negative consequences or by a blocking of adaptive responses. If such disruptions lead to a narrowing of peripheral vision, a potential injury could result by not picking up or responding in time to dangerous cues in the periphery, e.g., being blind-sided by an opponent. Attentional disruptions also may result in an athlete failing either to detect or to quickly respond to vital cues in the central field of vision because of attention to task-irrelevant cues. Awareness of the physiological and attentional aspects of the stress response may, in turn, influence the individual's cognitive appraisal of stressful situations.

Above the stress response core of the model are three major areas: personality factors, history of stressors, and coping resources. According to the model, individuals with certain characteristics from these three areas may be more likely to appraise potentially stressful external situations as threatening and, therefore, experience an elevated stress response. Again, it is the elevated stress response that puts these individuals at greater risk for injuries. It is hypothesized that one's stress history contributes directly to the stress response while personality factors and coping resources act on the stress response either directly or through a moderating influence on the effects of the history of stressors. Most of the critiquers of the health literature viewed these moderator variables as merely buffering the effects of life stress. This perspective may be too narrow in that personality factors and coping resources may moderate the stress response regardless of the levels of life stress or other types of stressors. Also, the variables may act singly, or in combination, in directly influencing the stress response and in affecting the magnitude of the relationship between the stressor(s) and injury occurrence and severity.

History of Stressors

A major weakness of earlier stress-injury studies was the measurement of only major stressful events. Stress also may stem from the minor daily problems, irritations, or changes an individual encounters such as heavy traffic, bad weather, daily food preparation, and unchallenging work. In studying illness, a number of researchers found measurement of daily hassles or problems results in better prediction of the effects of stress on psychological symptoms and illness than

the measurement of life events (e.g., Burks & Martin, 1985; Kanner, Coyne, Schaefer, & Lazarus, 1981).

The previous injury history of an individual also may be an important contribution in assessing injury risk. The athlete may return to play before he/she is fully recovered physically or the athlete may be physically but not psychologically prepared to return to sport participation. In either case, fear of reinjury may lead to a considerable stress response and actually may increase the probability of reinjury. A thorough assessment of life events, daily hassles or problems, and previous injuries should give the researcher and practitioner the best estimate of how much at risk of injury (at least from a history-of-stressors standpoint) that individual is and which factors (or combination of factors) within the stress profile are the best predictors of injury.

Personality Factors

Any comprehensive model of the relationship of stress to athletic injury would not be complete without considering personality. The stress-illness literature identifies many personality variables for their role in moderating the stress-illness relationship. Certain personality characteristics may cause some individuals to perceive fewer situations and events as stressful or they may predispose individuals to be less susceptible to the effects of stressors. Most of the personality variables included in the model either moderated the stress-illness relationship or were examined in the stress-athletic injury literature. The list of variables is incomplete and has considerable overlap. The variables in the model provide initial suggestions for future research into identifying how personality predicts individuals most at risk of injury.

The trait of psychological hardiness moderated the stress-illness relationship in several health studies (e.g., Kobasa, Maddi, & Puccetti, 1982). Psychological hardiness is a constellation of characteristics such as curiosity, willingness to commit, seeing change as a challenge and stimulus to development, and having a sense of control over one's life (Kobasa, 1979). Recently the hardiness concept has come under close scrutiny and some refinement is needed (Hull, Van Treuren, & Virnelli, 1987). Locus of control (Rotter, 1966) and Antonovsky's sense of coherence (Antonovsky, 1985) were included in the list of personality factors because of their resemblance to the hardiness concept and because both constructs moderated the relationship between stress and illness. Individuals with high life event stress who scored high in either hardiness or sense of coherence or who were more internal in their locus of control experienced fewer health problems than individuals with high life events and none of these personality characteristics.

Sensation seeking is also hypothesized as moderating the influence of stress on health. Sensation seekers are those individuals who enjoy the strange or unfamiliar and who like to take risks. Sensation avoiders do not care for change, avoid the unfamiliar, and stay away from risky activities. Smith, Johnson, and Sarason (1978), using the Sensation Seeking Scale (Zuckerman, Kolin, Price, & Zoob, 1964), found that subjects with high life-stress/high sensation-seeking scores reported less psychological distress than high life-stress/low sensation-seeking subjects. Within athletics, sensation seekers may experience fewer injuries because they cope better with athletic life events and daily problems or because such events are not perceived to be as stressful as persons low in sensation seeking. On the other hand, individuals who score high on sensation seeking may incur more injuries because of taking greater risks.

Achievement motivation and trait anxiety are included in the model because they are variables that appear to be related to stress. Achievement motivation addresses both the need to succeed and the need to avoid failure. Trait anxiety is described as a general disposition or tendency to perceive situations as threatening and to react with an anxiety response (Spielberger, 1966). Individuals with a high need to avoid failure or with a high trait anxiety may appraise more situations as stressful and consequently experience an elevated stress response compared to individuals with the opposite profile.

Coping Resources

Coping resources comprise a wide variety of behaviors and social networks that aid the individual in dealing with the problems, joys, disappointments, and stresses of life. The resources may be environmentally based, such as social support, or they may be personal resources such as emotional control and good nutrition. The role of coping resources in the stress-illness literature is extensive. Generally researchers have found fewer health problems for high life-stress individuals with high coping resources compared to high life-stress individuals with low coping resources (for a review see Billings & Moos, 1981).

The general coping behaviors category in the coping resources section of the model includes such behaviors as sleep patterns, nutritional habits, and taking time for oneself. Lack of good general coping behaviors may easily lead to higher stress and thus greater risk of injury. A more specific coping resource is the extent and kind of social support system. Agreement on what constitutes social support and the best way to measure it still needs to be determined. Social support typically considers the presence of others whom we know value and care for us and on whom we can rely (Sarason, Levine, Basham, & Sarason, 1983). According to the illness literature, individuals may feel more capable of mastering stress when they believe they are part of a caring network of significant others. Coddington and Troxell (1980), although they did not specifically examine social support, showed more injuries for football players who experienced family instabilities (e.g., separations, divorces, deaths) than those who did not. This could be interpreted as a disruption of the athlete's social support system. The presence of a supportive social network (family, friends,

teachers) may directly inoculate the individual against injury or may attenuate the effects of life events, daily hassles, and personality traits.

The stress management techniques and mental skills (often referred to as psychological skills) an individual has at his or her disposal are another type of coping resource that may influence responses to stress. These psychological techniques are not only coping resources, but also are interventions for dealing with stress and, therefore, will be discussed briefly in the next section. The various coping resources may act singly or in combination. One would expect, however, that the strongest stress-response and stress-injury association occurs among subjects low in all three (general coping behaviors, social support, and psychological coping skills) variables.

The last coping resource listed in the model is medication, self-selected or prescribed. Drug use is common in some societies. Many of these substances influence cognitive perception and physiology and thus could affect the stress response and injury probability. Assessment of drug use is often difficult, if not impossible, because of the frequently clandestine nature of drug use. Identification of substances used and abused by athletes and programs for drug use modification should help not only in injury prevention, but in most all aspects of the individual's life.

The foregoing list of coping variables that may moderate the effects of stressors or that may directly affect the stress response is incomplete and, in some places, redundant. The variables are offered as a springboard for research that should lead to a better understanding of the coping factors involved in injury risk and, therefore, the prevention of injuries.

Interventions

Below the stress response (see Figure 38–1) are two groups of interventions hypothesized to lessen the stress response by addressing either the cognitive appraisal or the physiological/attentional aspects. In addition, these interventions and others may be used to directly influence moderator variables of coping resources and personality factors. Interventions for the cognitive appraisal side of the stress response include techniques to improve confidence and a sense of belonging and techniques to eradicate thinking patterns that create stress and other maladaptive responses. Techniques for improving coach-athlete communication also might be included. If a coach communicates well with his/her athletes by letting them know their capabilities and potential, then the athletes' own appraisals of the demands and resources in athletic situations may be more realistic. Hopefully a lower cognitive response would result from better coach-athlete communication. Interventions for the attentional/physiological aspects of the stress response would be aimed at lowering arousal and enhancing concentration. Bunker and Williams (1986) describe cognitive techniques for both changing dysfunctional thinking and building confidence. Harris (1986) describes several techniques to lower arousal levels (e.g., progressive relaxation, autogenics, meditation, breathing exercises). Schmid and Peper (1986) describe numerous concentration training techniques for decreasing distractibility and helping keep an appropriate attentional focus.

Summary

In summary, past research on injury and stress has been largely atheoretical and too narrow in scope. It has focused on a limited conceptualization of stress and a restricted consideration of the interaction of personal and environmental variables that may either moderate the effects of stressful events or may directly influence the stress response and ultimately injury. The present model provides a broad, theoretical foundation for future investigations into the prediction and prevention of injury and the identification of mechanisms that underlie risk for injury. Any single variable identified in the previous discussion may not be very useful, but, when used in combination with other coping resources and personality and history-of-stressor variables, should identify the athletes most at risk for incurring injuries due to psychological factors.

TESTING THE STRESS-INJURY MODEL

Support for History of Stressors

The best documentation for high life-stress athletes being more vulnerable to athletic injuries is still within the sport of football. This documentation encompasses six studies, the five discussed earlier plus a more recent study by Blackwell and McCullagh (1990). For the most part, attempts also have been successful to extend further the life stress–injury findings to participants in sports other than football. In addition to the findings reported earlier for elite alpine skiers (May, Veach, Reed, & Griffey, 1985) and physical education students (Lysens, Auweele, & Ostyn, 1986), significant life stress–injury relationships have been found with elite gymnasts (Kerr & Minden, 1988), intercollegiate gymnasts (Petrie, 1990); intercollegiate track, baseball, and softball athletes (Hanson, McCullagh, & Tonymon, 1990; Hardy & Riehl, 1988); intercollegiate volleyball, gymnastics, field hockey, soccer, cross-country, track and field, and wrestling athletes (Hardy, Richman, & Rosenfeld, 1991); intercollegiate soccer players (Hardy, O'Connor, & Geisler, 1990); biathletes, race walkers, figure skaters, and basketball players (May, Veach, Southard, & Herring, 1985); and high school wrestlers, basketball players, and gymnasts (Smith, Smoll, & Ptacek, 1990). The Smith, Smoll, & Ptacek (1990) findings occurred only for high life-stress athletes with low social support and psychological skills. Also, Hardy and Riehl (1988) found ALES scores did not predict the risk of injury for tennis players

or injury frequency with female athletes (Hardy et al., 1991).

The equivocal results from studies measuring life stress with the ALES, or a similarly scored tool, prevent a determination of the relative contribution to injury risk for life-change stress from negative (NLE), positive (PLE), and total life events (TLE). For example, NLE stress was the primary injury culprit in the studies by Passer and Seese (1983) and Smith, Smoll, and Ptacek (1990), but Blackwell and McCullagh (1990) found TLE stress contributed the most to injury occurrence and PLE stress the most to the likelihood of being severely injured. Mixed results also were obtained by Hardy and Riehl (1988). Injured athletes, overall, had significantly higher NLE than noninjured athletes, but injured female athletes reported higher scores on TLE compared to uninjured females. Both TLE and NLE significantly predicted injury across sports, but analyses within sports indicated injured softball players reported significantly higher TLE, baseball players higher NLE, and tracksters higher object loss (OL) compared to equivalent uninjured players. Except for track, none of the stress measures predicted injuries in the specific sports. In track, both TLE and OL predicted injuries. These findings led Hardy and Riehl to conclude that the life stress–injury relationship is influenced by both the athlete's sex and the sport. Hardy, O'Connor, & Geisler's (1990) study of Division I soccer players also supported the conclusion that gender affects the relationship between life stress and injury.

The Andersen and Williams (1988) model proposes that stress and, as a result, injury risk may occur from minor daily problems and irritations as well as from major life events. Blackwell and McCullagh (1990) and Smith, Smoll, and Ptacek (1990) have been the only researchers to examine the influence of daily hassles or minor day-to-day problems on injury proneness. Neither group of researchers found a significant relationship between daily problems and athletic injury, but the Blackwell and McCullagh daily hassles means were in the hypothesized direction. Because both studies had methodological limitations, it is premature to conclude that minor daily problems have no effect on athletic injuries. Smith and his colleagues measured minor day-to-day events at the start of the season and Blackwell and McCullagh measured daily hassles at the end of the season. In either case, changes in daily problems should be assessed throughout the season and then subsequent injuries compared to the immediately preceding score for stress from minor daily problems.

Overall, the results of studies examining the history of stressors generally provide evidence for stressful life events influencing injuries in contact and noncontact sports and with male and female athletes in much the same way as life stress affects health. If anything, the relationship of psychosocial variables to injury is much greater than that reported in prospective life stress–health research when health was measured objectively (Rabkin & Streuning, 1976; Schroeder & Costa, 1984).

Generally the risk of being injured increased in direct relationship to the level of life-event stress. The reported strength of the life stress–injury relationship, however, varied considerably across studies. Overall, athletes with high life-event stress were two to five times more likely to be injured than athletes with low life-event stress. The largely positive findings across sports and competitive levels is even more compelling considering the diversity of methods for measuring life stress and defining injury. Eight questionnaires were used to assess life stress, and the criteria for being injured varied from an injury that required seeing an athletic trainer but no modification in activity or reduced practice time (Blackwell & McCullagh, 1990) to missing more than a week of practice (e.g., Coddington & Troxell, 1980). Because of these different operational definitions, it is impossible to determine relative injury risk across sports and competitive levels for athletes with high life-event stress. Diverse operational definitions also contributed to the difficulty in determining the effect of life stress on the severity of injury. Approximately half the studies found a relationship between life stress and injury severity (Blackwell & McCullagh, 1990; Hardy et al., 1990; Hardy & Riehl, 1988; Kerr & Minden, 1988; Petrie, 1990b), and half found no effect (Cryan & Alles, 1983; Hardy et al., 1991; Lysens et al., 1986; Williams et al., 1986).

Support for Personality and Coping Resources Influencing Stress and Injury

According to the Andersen and Williams (1988) model, personality variables and coping resources act directly on the stress response, moderate the effects of the history of stressors, or both. Also, the personality and coping variables may act independently, or in combination, when asserting their influence on injury outcome. Thus simply measuring the history of stressors, even with a comprehensive assessment, fails to best identify subgroups of individuals most at risk for athletic injuries. Unfortunately, personality factors and coping resources have received less attention from researchers than have life events. Consequently knowledge is not as extensive regarding the effect specific personality variables and coping resources have on life stress and injury risk. Even less is known about the potential additive influence of two or more personality and coping variables or the interactions between multiple variables.

Personality Research. To date there has been no personality assessment in athletic injury studies of hardiness, sense of coherence, achievement motivation, and sensation seeking. There are, however, more data on locus of control and trait anxiety than that reported earlier. Kerr and Minden (1988) examined locus of control with a general (Rotter, 1966) rather than sport-specific tool. Their failure to find any relationship between locus of control and injury outcome is consistent with the earlier findings of Passer and Seese (1983), Lysens et al. (1986), and Dalhauser and Thomas (1979), all of whom similarly assessed locus of control. The findings from Dalhauser and Thomas's (1979) specific football locus of control questionnaire continue to

be the only support for the hypothesis that an internal locus of control buffers the effects of stressful events.

Studies by Kerr and Minden (1988) and Lysens et al. (1986) found no support for the hypothesis that high trait-anxious athletes are more injury prone than low trait-anxious athletes. Again the notable exception was when sport-specific competitive trait anxiety (CTA) was assessed rather than general trait anxiety. In addition to the CTA findings of Passer and Seese (1983), Blackwell and McCullagh (1990) found CTA influenced the severity, but not the frequency of injuries. Of the football players who were classified as severely injured (the operational definition for severe injuries was equal to the definition of minor injuries in other studies), 70% were high anxious and 30% were low anxious. Of all players categorized as scoring high or low in CTA, 45% and 21%, respectively, were "severely" injured. The studies of trait anxiety and locus of control suggest that sport-specific tools may be more sensitive in detecting differences in athletic injury vulnerability and resiliency.

Coping Resources Research. Although coping resources have received less attention from researchers over the years than personality factors, the results have been more consistent. Except for Blackwell and McCullagh (1990), all researchers found coping resources either directly affected injury outcome or moderated the influence life stress had on injury vulnerability. Blackwell and McCullagh used the "Vulnerability to Stress" section of the Stress Audit Questionnaire (Miller & Smith, 1982) with football players to examine the combined effects of social support and general coping behaviors such as diet and time for self. These results conflict with Williams, Tonymon, and Wadsworth (1986), who found that the same scale predicted athletic injuries in Division I male and female volleyball players. Very little injury variance, however, was accounted for by coping resources.

Other researchers used instruments that separately examined the influence of different coping resources. Social support directly impacted on athletic injuries in a study by Hardy, Prentice, Kirsanoff, Richman, and Rosenfeld (1987). Athletes with high levels of social support had a lower incidence of injury, regardless of life stress. In a more recent study with female collegiate gymnasts ($N = 103$), social support moderated the life stress–injury relationship (Petrie, 1990b). Social support was measured with the Social Support Questionnaire (SSQ) (Sarason et al., 1983). The SSQ is a 27-item questionnaire that asks questions such as "Whom can you really count on to listen to you when you need to talk?" and "Whom can you really count on to be dependable when you need help?" The SSQ assesses the number of people the subject can count on for support (SSQN) and the second section measures how satisfied the individual is with the overall support received (SSQS). Petrie analyzed only the SSQS data.

With low social support gymnasts (bottom third scores on the SSQS), negative life stress (measured by the Life Events Survey for Collegiate Athletes, LESCA) accounted for 14 to 24% of the variance in minor, severe, and total injuries. No significant relationships between life stress and injury outcome occurred within any of the high social support groups. Data on just negative life stress accounted for only 6 to 12% of the variance in injury outcome. Unfortunately Petrie did not report statistics on whether or not social support directly influenced injury outcome. Petrie proposed that social support, depending on the level, appears to function in two very different ways when athletes experience high negative life stress. High social support seems to protect the athletes from injury, but low social support appears to exacerbate the deleterious effects of life stress such that vulnerability to injury is increased significantly.

Hardy, O'Connor, and Geisler (1990) found social support moderated the relationship between life stress and injury in male ($n = 25$) and female ($n = 20$) collegiate soccer players and also directly influenced injury frequency in males. Males with low social support were more likely to be injured. Social support was measured with the same questionnaire (SSQ) used by Petrie (1990b). For females, social support had both a negative and positive effect on the relationship between life stress and injury. When low in SSQN and SSQS, the life stress measures accounted for 73–92% and 69–85%, respectively, of the variance in injury severity depending on whether TLE, NLE, or OL scores were examined. In contrast, for females with high levels of SSN, TLE scores accounted for 50% of the variance in injury frequency and OL accounted for 55% of the variance. The findings may have been an artifact of the small number of female players ($n = 20$) studied. Replication is needed before generalizing the results to other female soccer players.

Results of a recent study by Hardy et al. (1991) are not consistent with many of the earlier social support findings. With male athletes participating in a variety of intercollegiate sports, Hardy and his colleagues found that high social support, when combined with high object loss and positive life stressors, had a negative rather than positive effect on the well-being of male athletes. In contrast, for male athletes with high negative life events, injury rates decreased when the number of social support providers and the degree of fulfillment for emotional challenge support increased. The researchers concluded that social support was effective with the male athletes only to the degree that there is a match between the stressor and the support type. It should be noted that none of the preceding findings occurred with female athletes. Hardy et al. (1991) also studied female athletes, but found no relationship between social support and injury frequency and severity.

In another recent study, Smith, Smoll, and Ptacek (1990) examined the life event stress (major and minor events), social support, and psychological skills of male and female high school varsity athletes ($N = 451$). The athletes participated in boys and girls basketball, boys wrestling, or girls gymnastics. A modified version of the Adolescent Perceived Events Scale (Compas, Davis, Forsythe, & Wagner, 1987) measured life events. The questionnaire had the subjects classify stressors as positive or negative and as a major event having long-term consequences or a "day-to-day" event that

did not. The social support measure assessed adolescents' subjective appraisals of the individual and group components of their social support network. Items such as assistant coach, trainer, team physician, and athletic religious organizations were added to the questionnaire. The Athletic Coping Skills Inventory (Smith, Smoll, & Schutz, 1988) assessed psychological skills. The scale consists of 42 behavioral self-report items designed to measure a range of coping skills within a sport context. Items included the ability to control arousal and to concentrate and think clearly under stress as well as other coping skills.

Smith, Smoll, and Ptacek (1990) found coping resources moderated the life event–injury relationship, but did not directly affect injury occurrence. Subjects who were low in *both* social support and psychological coping skills exhibited the strongest correlation between major negative life events and subsequent injuries. For high major negative life events subjects who scored in the bottom third on both coping resource tools, 22% of the injury time loss variance was accounted for by major negative life events. The life stress–injury variance increased to more than 30% when more extreme (lower quartile) social support and coping skills subjects were compared. The correlation between negative life events and subsequent injury also was significant for athletes who reported only low levels of psychological coping skills, but accounted for just 6% of the injury variance. All groups having moderate to high levels of social support or psychological coping skills exhibited nonsignificant relations between life stress and injury.

A major methodological advance of the Smith et al. (1990) study was the study of two coping resources and the analysis used to determine how the moderator variables interacted with one another to increase vulnerability or resilience to injury. The authors proposed a distinction between conjunctive moderation, in which multiple moderators must occur in a specific combination or pattern in order to maximize a relation between a predictor (one of the history of stressors) and an outcome variable (some aspect of injury outcome), and disjunctive moderation in which any one of a number of moderators maximizes the predictor-criterion relation. The results with their high stress–low coping resource subjects suggest that social support and psychological coping skills operate in a conjunctive manner (need low scores on both) to increase the injury vulnerability of athletes with high negative life events. In contrast, for athletes with moderate or high scores on social support or psychological coping skills, disjunctive moderation led to nonsignificant relations between life stress and injury. That is, having either of the psychological assets reduced injury vulnerability.

In discussing their results, Smith and his colleagues (1990) indicated that the precise mechanisms by which stressful events lead to injuries is unknown. They proposed that athletes with major negative life events who lack social support and psychological skills may have more vulnerability to the attentional and physiological mechanisms (e.g., Andersen & Williams, 1988) proposed to increase injury risk. Perhaps social support and psychological coping skills affect an athlete's appraisal of demands, resources, and consequences when faced with a potentially stressful practice or competitive situation. High-stress athletes with high coping resources (either social support or psychological coping skills) may appraise such situations as exciting challenges rather than stressors, or they may appraise them as less stressful. If the Andersen and Williams model is valid, the result of such an appraisal would be less physiological and attentional reactivity and, therefore, fewer injuries. Correspondingly high-stress athletes with low levels of social support and psychological coping skills might appraise the same situation as highly threatening because they feel less able to cope with the demands and consequences. The consequence would be an increase in physiological and attentional responses and a resulting higher incidence of injury. We may not know exactly how coping resources affect injury vulnerability, but the preponderance of evidence clearly supports the conclusion that social support either directly affects injury outcome, moderates the life stress–injury relationship, or both. Pending replication of the Smith et al. (1990) study, the same statement might be made for psychological skills. To date, none of the other coping resources proposed in the Andersen and Williams (1988) model have been examined.

Support for Mechanisms Underlying the Stress-Injury Relationship

The Andersen and Williams (1988) model proposes that an elevated stress response, and particularly the accompanying muscle tension and attentional disruptions (narrowing of the visual field and increased distractibility), are what places certain individuals at greater risk for injuries. Andersen (1988) was the only researcher to examine the effect of different levels of life-event stress on generalized muscle tension when performing a stressful task. He found elevated electromyographic responses during the high- versus low-stress condition, but individual differences in life-event stress or moderator variables did not affect increases in muscle tension. Andersen studied the general population, rather than a high-risk subpopulation, and this may have influenced the failure of life-event scores to predict muscle tension.

There is support for attentional disruptions contributing to athletic injuries. Recent studies of elite gymnasts revealed "lack of concentration" or "thinking of other things" as the most commonly given cause of injury (Kerr & Minden, 1988) or the second most commonly given cause of injury (Kerr & Cairns, 1988, as reported in Kerr & Fowler, 1988). In both studies, high life-stress gymnasts experienced greater numbers and severity of injuries compared to low life-stress gymnasts. In fact, Kerr and Fowler (1988) showed that a reanalysis of the Kerr and Minden data indicated gymnasts with the highest life-event scores had four times as many injuries and 4.5 times greater severity of injuries than gymnasts with the lowest life-event scores. Due to the retrospective design of the gymnastic studies, both the

stress-injury relationship and the loss of concentration explanation must be viewed with some caution.

Recent studies offer a more direct testing of at least a portion of the mechanism hypothesis in the stress-injury model. In the first study, Williams, Tonymon, and Andersen (1990) examined whether individuals with high life-event stress, when placed in a stressful performance situation, experience greater state anxiety and peripheral narrowing than individuals with low life-event stress. The authors did not examine the relationship of life-event stress and stress reactivity to injury outcome, but rather examined the prediction of what should occur to state anxiety and peripheral narrowing during a stressful situation for individuals with high and low levels of life-event stress.

Over 300 recreational athletes were screened with the LES and, based on the data, 32 subjects who scored high (>35) or low (<10) on total life-event stress were selected to perform a laboratory task under conditions of low stress (performing only the peripheral vision task) and high stress (the dual task paradigm with distracting noise). ANOVA and regression results offered support for peripheral vision deficits as a potential mechanism in the life stress–injury relationship and very minimal support for the effect of elevated state anxiety. The high life-stress groups experienced at least three to six times greater baseline to stress-condition peripheral narrowing than the respective low-stress groups, but there was great variability in peripheral narrowing. This variability suggests that, for certain subjects, some unmeasured variables may have buffered the adverse impact of high life stress. For example, differences among the athletes in social support and psychological skills for coping with stress may have directly influenced stress reactivity on the laboratory task or may have influenced the impact life-event stress had on the laboratory task.

In a second study, Williams, Tonymon, and Andersen (1991) employed the same design, but also assessed coping resources (social support and general coping behaviors such as diet and time for self) and daily hassles. During the stress condition, high negative life events and total life events led to greater peripheral narrowing and high total life events and daily hassles led to elevated state anxiety. Coping resources did not directly affect stress reactivity, but tended to moderate some of the history-of-stressor effects. As hypothesized, when recreational athletes had high negative life events or daily hassles, high coping resources reduced perceived state anxiety during the stress condition compared to similar recreational athletes with low coping resources.

The design of a third study (Andersen & Williams, 1989) suggested that narrowing during stress might become even greater when speed of responding is assessed rather than simply perception of peripheral targets. The authors proposed that stress may "use up" an individual's resources for processing information and quickly generating appropriate motor patterns. The narrowing found in the preceding studies could easily lead to a failure to pick up or respond in time to vital cues in the periphery and thus avoid an injurious situation (e.g., an unexpected tackle from the side).

The Andersen and Williams model (1988) proposes that the stress reactions found in the studies would put individuals in the hypothesized subpopulations at greater risk for injury, but none of the preceding studies obtained injury data. We also do not know if merely a peripheral narrowing response is a sufficient mechanism for injury risk or if a higher state anxiety response also is needed.

Support for Interventions Reducing Injury Risk

The least researched area in the Andersen and Williams (1988) model is the implementation and assessment of interventions designed to lessen the stress response and reduce injury vulnerability. This is not particularly surprising, considering that a consensus emerged only recently regarding psychosocial injury risk factors and possible mechanisms by which these factors increase vulnerability to injury. The stress-injury model suggests a two-pronged attack to prevent injuries caused by high stress. One set of interventions deals with changing the cognitive appraisals of potentially stressful events, and the second set of interventions deals with modifying the physiological/attentional aspects of stress. Both cognitive and relaxation interventions have been used frequently and successfully to improve performance (Greenspan & Feltz, 1989), but only once was information provided on injury effects. DeWitt (1980) reported basketball and football players detected a noticeable decrease in minor injuries while they participated in a cognitive and physiological (biofeedback) training program. Unfortunately no objective data were kept regarding physical injuries.

Murphy (1988) describes another psychological intervention program in which injuries were not the specific focus, but there may have been some injury benefits from the program. Murphy conducted relaxation sessions with 12 members of a team at the 1987 Olympic Sports Festival, 5 of whom had minor injuries and 2 serious injuries. Relaxation sessions were conducted after every workout until competition, and all 12 athletes were able to compete.

In a recent article, Davis (1991) reported on an archival review of injury data collected by athletic trainers before, during, and after two university teams practiced progressive relaxation and technique/strategy imagery during team workouts. Major findings included a 52% reduction in injuries in the swimming study and a 33% reduction in injuries in the football study. Training sessions lasted 10–15 minutes and were either daily or twice per week. The injury benefits from these two psychosocial programs are even more impressive, considering that both programs targeted general rather than at-risk athletes and neither program included cognitive or concentration training interventions.

Based on their disjunctive moderation findings, Smith et al. (1990) propose that, from an intervention perspective, resiliency to athletic injuries could be increased, either by teaching athletes psychological coping skills or by increasing social support in the athlete's life. The results from other researchers who examined social support also indicate that improving social support should decrease injury frequency and perhaps severity. A number of strategies have been proposed for enhancing social support; some involved the training of coaches (Smith, Smoll, & Curtis, 1979) and others team building (Nideffer, 1981). A recent article by Richman, Hardy, Rosenfeld, and Callanan (1989) is the best source for a variety of strategies coaches and sport psychologists could implement to affect the type and level of social support in student athletes.

FUTURE RESEARCH NEEDS AND DIRECTIONS

Future researchers need to study multiple predictor and moderator variables, and then determine the varying patterns by which the variables interact with one another to affect injury vulnerability and resiliency. The designs employed by Smith, Smoll, and Ptacek (1990), Williams et al. (1991), Petrie (1990b), and Hardy et al. (1991) provide examples of how patterns of relationships might be examined. The Williams et al. study would have been stronger if the additive stress from both life events and hassles also had been examined. The joint influence of social support and psychological coping skills found by Smith and his colleagues particularly appears to be a promising focus for future life event research. Whether or not their disjunctive and conjunctive patterns apply to other sports and age groups (e.g., intercollegiate and professional athletes) remains to be determined. In implementing the preceding suggestions, as well as others, researchers should continue to employ prospective rather than retrospective investigations and gather objective injury data (i.e., monitored and recorded by certified athletic trainers or other qualified personnel). Fortunately fewer than 20% of past stress-injury researchers failed to observe these standards.

One difficulty in studying multiple predictor and moderator variables and, correspondingly, subgroups of individuals that fall in the extreme on the variables is the need for very large sample sizes. Practical necessity may lead to future research projects being composed of investigators from a number of geographical areas. An additional benefit from such an approach is the enhanced generalizability of the results. That is, a subject pool drawn from a multiple sample pool (e.g., many universities) is more likely to be representative of the general population being studied than a sample drawn from a single-sample pool (e.g., one university).

Wherever the sample of subjects is drawn from, at the start of the study, the athletes should be "asymptomatic," that is, free from any time-loss injury or restrictions on the type of participation. If this is not done, these athletes should be isolated to determine what impact their existing injury has on future injuries and the relationship of predictor and moderator variables to injury outcome. As indicated in the Andersen and Williams (1988) model, prior injuries may be one source of stress within an individual's history of stressors that increases injury vulnerability.

Future researchers also need to determine if sport differences, gender, and competitive level differentially affect the relationship between psychosocial factors and injury outcome. Although 18 of the 20 studies reviewed in the life event stress–athletic injury area found some association between high life stress and injury outcome, there was considerable variance across studies in the strength of the relationship. Individual differences in relevant psychosocial variables that were not measured probably contributed to some of these differences, but so too may have differences in gender, sport, and competitive level. For example, studies examining high school athletes (Coddington & Troxell, 1980; Smith, Smoll, & Ptacek, 1990) found the weakest life stress–injury relationship compared to studies with college students. The failure of the high school studies to measure life events with an inventory that contained events specific to athletics also may have caused the weak relationship. When making comparisons across sports, gender, and competitive levels for injury risk due to psychosocial variables, injury data needs to be corrected for differential exposure to possible injury (see Smith, Smoll, & Ptacek, 1990, for a description of how to accomplish this objective). The risk for different types of injuries and the timing of injuries (before, during, or after competition and whether competition resulted in a victory or defeat) also merits investigation when addressing the preceding suggestions.

Another dimension that affects one's ability to accurately make comparisons across studies is the operational definition for life-event stress and injury. As noted earlier, past researchers varied considerably in the tools used to measure life-event stress and the criteria for being injured. Future researchers need to determine the optimal tools for measurement of stressors, personality variables, and coping resources as well as the most meaningful criteria for injury outcome. In terms of life-event stress, tools that measure stress through the respondent's perception of the life event's desirability and impact (e.g., LES, ALES) appear to be superior to those in which a standardized weighting is given (e.g., SRRS, SARRS). Initial data on the newly developed Life Events Survey for Collegiate Athletes (LESCA) suggest that it demonstrates excellent content validity and provides a stable measure of life stress (Petrie, 1990b). It also was found to be a better predictor of athletic injury in collegiate gymnasts than the SARRS. Pending replication in other sports, the LESCA may be the best measure of life-event stress. In making decisions about instrumentation, future researchers also should consider whether the tool in question is general or sports-specific. Sports-specific questionnaires appear to be more effective than general questionnaires in predicting athletic injury. This has been found when measuring life-event stress (e.g., results of Holmes, 1970, compared to Bramwell et al., 1975), trait anxiety (Passer & Seese, 1983), and locus of control (Dalhauser & Thomas, 1979).

New statistical analyses also might advance the effectiveness of future psychology-of-injury research. In assessing the effects of moderator variables, Smith, Smoll, and Ptacek

(1990) made a compelling argument for their correlational approach rather than multiple regression analyses. They noted that a moderated regression analysis (Baron & Kenny, 1986; Cronbach, 1987) is the most frequently recommended approach for assessing moderator influences. Such an analysis examines the main effects of the predictor and moderator variables as well as the interactions between and among the variables. Smith et al. and other researchers (e.g., Dunlap & Kemery, 1987; Hedges, 1987), however, note that this type of analysis often fails to reveal moderator effects, particularly when the significant predictor-criterion relation occurs within only a small subsample. A small at-risk subsample may be the case in athletic injury research (e.g., Smith, Smoll, & Ptacek, 1990). Interestingly athletic injury researchers typically used backwards multiple regression rather than hierarchical regression analyses that examined interaction effects. Future researchers should consider conducting correlational analysis, providing that all assumptions can be met. The analysis entails computing correlations between history-of-stress measures and injuries for groups of subjects who fall within the upper and lower categories of the singular and additive moderator variables. This statistical approach may identify moderator effects that go undetected in multiple regression analyses.

Petrie (1990a) offers another statistical suggestion for future researchers. He recommends that covariance structure modeling (CSM) be used to determine the validity and practical significance of the Andersen and Williams (1988) theoretical model. CSM allows for the simultaneous specification of the measurement and structural components of theoretical models. After obtaining as much data as possible on the stress history, personality, coping resources, and stress responsivity variables within the model, CSM can investigate hypothesized relationships among the variables. The correlations or covariances among the measured variables are used to determine the plausibility of each causal model in the specified population. In addition, Petrie notes that CSM can investigate the psychometric adequacy (in terms of construct validity) of the variables.

Future researchers should assess the heart of the problem, the stress response itself. Athletes varying in stress history, personality, and coping resources should be tested on their stress responsivity. For example, an assessment should be made of how the athlete's state anxiety, peripheral vision, distractibility, and muscle tension changes from baseline to stress conditions. Stress responsivity data, when used in conjunction with paper-and-pencil tests, may provide the clearest picture of injury risk and the best foundation for designing intervention programs to reduce injury risk. Andersen and Williams (in press) note that looking at stress reactivity has occurred for years in medical research. For example, in assessing the risk of cardiac disease, paper-and-pencil tests for Type A behavior and other variables are administered and patients are monitored physiologically during a stress test. It is time for a similar approach to athletic injury research and assessment. See Andersen and Williams (in press) and Williams, Tonymon, and Andersen (1990, 1991) for suggestions of how this might be done.

One of the most exciting avenues for future researchers is the implementation and assessment of prospective injury prevention programs. More specifically, with what types of interventions and subpopulations are injury rates and severity of injuries most likely to be improved? The variable of primary concern is injury rate, but another approach is to monitor the gains athletes make in controlling stress reactivity by retesting them on the psychophysiological and perceptual stress measures previously described. Moreover, does decreasing stress responsivity improve injury resiliency? Once these questions are answered, practitioners will be able to plan the most feasible, cost-effective, and beneficial interventions for reducing injury vulnerability.

Davis (1991) notes that additional pathways by which interventions might reduce injury vulnerability are through performance enhancement and better pain management. Although it has not been not documented, Davis notes that athletic trainers report that athletes are more likely to report injuries following losses and less likely after wins. Regarding the pain management benefits (Kendal & Watson, 1981) of relaxation training, when athletes experience less pain from injuries they may not be as likely to complain of injuries to athletic trainers or they might recover quicker. At minimum, injury intervention researchers should consider monitoring potential performance as well as injury benefits, and performance-enhancement programs should include assessment of possible injury-reduction benefits as well as improvements in performance.

In summary, the research reviewed indicates that determining the psychosocial causes of athletic injuries is a multifaceted problem. Therefore, incorporating a multicomponent assessment process should provide the most fruitful experimental design for identifying psychological processes (e.g., attentional disruptions, lack of coping skills) mediating stress-injury outcomes and subpopulations of athletes most at risk of injuries and for whom interventions need to be targeted. The complex, interactional stress-injury model proposed by Andersen and Williams (Andersen & Williams, 1988; Williams & Andersen, 1986) appears to be a viable theoretical foundation for conducting such research.

IMPLICATIONS FOR THE PRACTITIONER

Injuries, including those contributed to by psychosocial variables, need to be viewed as avoidable rather than unavoidable events. Just as coaches and other sports personnel attempt to reduce injury risk through vehicles such as conditioning programs, teaching proper techniques, and advances in equipment and facilities design, the time has come to reduce injury risk from psychosocial causes. Researchers from early to more recent studies (e.g., Bramwell et al., 1975; Hardy & Riehl, 1988) have argued that clinical use of knowledges regarding psychosocial injury-risk factors is premature. The present authors argue instead that

the monetary, personal, and team/organizational cost of injuries is so serious that no potential means of reducing injuries, even if for only a small percentage of athletes, should be overlooked.

At minimum, sport psychologists should start to educate coaches, athletic trainers, and other sports medicine personnel of psychological variables that may impact on injury. Such knowledge might lead to coaches and other relevant personnel increasing their awareness regarding the nonsport aspects of an athlete's life that might be causing stress. This increased sensitivity might even lead to providing greater social support, and thus potentially buffering some of the harmful effects of stress. Coaches also might want to consider temporarily modifying training by reducing levels of intensity and risk for athletes whom they know are currently experiencing many disruptive stressors without the aid of adequate coping resources. Other subtle, and not so subtle, modifications can be made to reduce unnecessary sources of psychological stress within the practice and competitive environment.

Ultimately coaches and sport psychologists should consider implementing intervention programs for athletes with a high injury-risk profile (e.g., many stressors but few coping skills). Learning techniques for changing faulty thinking patterns and being able to recognize and control indicants of physiological arousal should help athletes cope better with stressful events, thereby increasing injury resiliency. Teaching attentional skills designed to increase the ability to focus attention is another potential strategy for remedial action. Although data to support the injury benefits from such programs are extremely limited, there is a solid theoretical foundation for the recommendations (Andersen & Williams, 1988). The worst consequence of implementing such programs is that the athletes may experience only performance benefits!

A more elaborate approach for identifying at-risk athletes in need of interventions is to include a psychological risk assessment as part of the general physical exam at the start of the athletic season. Life events, social support, and psychological coping skills should be assessed. Until such time that researchers can document a stronger relationship between injury risk and personality and daily hassles, there does not appear to be merit in examining these variables. As new findings emerge, there also may be merit in including an assessment of stress reactivity.

An important caution in any injury risk screening is that the information be used merely to design optimal, cost-effective intervention strategies aimed at reducing risk and not for the purpose of excluding an athlete from sport participation (Andersen & Williams, in press). Practitioners and researchers should never lose sight of the distinction between group versus individual prediction. In all studies there were many athletes with high-risk profiles not being injured and athletes with low-risk profiles being injured. The ultimate value of research into psychological risk factors is the potential for using the knowledge to reduce the tragedy and expense caused by avoidable injuries. It is essential that this knowledge be interpreted properly and not be used in any way that would prove detrimental to the athlete.

PSYCHOLOGICAL ASPECTS OF INJURY REHABILITATION

A great deal of time and energy are invested in obtaining optimal performance in a sport, such that any significant injury is likely to be perceived as a traumatic life event with physical and psychological ramifications. The manner in which individuals deal with an athletic injury may vary greatly, with some athletes adjusting to the stressful event with little difficulty while others are devastated by the experience. It has been suggested that psychological interventions that address the troubling aspects of injury may be a valuable adjunct to the athlete's physical rehabilitation. Roepke and Williams (1990) surveyed injured athletes and athletic trainers regarding the use of psychological techniques and found that both groups highly valued psychological interventions as an integral part of the rehabilitation process. A similar study, by Wiese, Weiss, and Yukelson (1991), but with only athletic trainers, found that using a positive communication style, strategies for setting realistic goals, and methods for encouraging positive self-thoughts were rated as the most important psychological techniques in the rehabilitation process. Support for psychological factors being related to enhanced healing also comes from a recent study by Ievleva and Orlick (1991). They found athletes who healed very rapidly were more likely to use goal setting, positive self-talk, stress control, and healing imagery compared to athletes who healed more slowly. All of this evidence emphasizes the importance of understanding the psychological aspects of injury rehabilitation.

Understanding the Injury

In order to determine which psychological interventions are likely to facilitate the management of an athlete's injury, it is essential to first understand the injury from the athlete's perspective, including the meaning the injury has for the athlete as well as the impact the injury has had on his or her life. In treating an athletic injury from a psychological perspective, one must first establish clear and open communication channels with the injured athlete. To accomplish this, the athlete must feel assured that he or she is interacting in a supportive environment in which any information revealed will be confidential. Members of the treatment team, including sport psychologists, athletic trainers, sports medicine physicians, coaches, and physical therapists, should possess good listening skills and be able to respond to the athlete in an empathic, nonjudgmental, nonthreatening manner. In this type of supportive environment, athletes are more likely to disclose distressing thoughts and feelings related to the injury event.

In learning about the injury, factors that are likely to influence the intensity of the athlete's psychological reaction to the event should be identified. The individual's history of injury, the nature of the injury, type of sport, level of competition, and personality structure of the athlete (Sanderson, 1978) as well as the time of the season and the context in which the injury occurred (Weiss & Troxell, 1986) may all impact on recovery. Moreover the athlete's handling of stress and his or her lifestyle habits, abilities and skills, defensive techniques, motivational factors, and coping skills will all influence the way in which the injury is perceived and handled (Yaffe, 1983).

It is also important to explore the motivation for or meaning the athlete has assigned to his or her involvement in sport (Wiese et al., 1991). Athletic participation may have physical, psychological, and social significance for an individual. A physically fit body that has the ability to engage in vigorous physical activity may provide one with a sense of personal mastery, independence, autonomy, and self-control (Eldridge, 1983), as well as providing one with a sense of personal attractiveness (Sanderson, 1978). Exercise may function to reduce stress and may be emotionally cathartic (Raglin & Morgan, 1987; Robbins & Joseph, 1985). A person's athletic accomplishments may serve a central role as one's source of self-esteem and self-concept. People may be drawn to sport involvement by the fantasy of athletic sexual prowess or may participate because athletic activity allows one to engage in aggressive behavior that is socially sanctioned (Milliner, 1987). Athletics may be one's primary source of social interaction, so that social adequacy and status are derived from active involvement (Eldridge, 1983). Given the multitude of meaning that sport involvement may have for an individual, it follows that the losses associated with the inability to participate may be similarly diverse and widespread. Therefore, losses may be experienced in such areas as occupational self-image, social roles, competition, external rewards, as well as impacting on feelings of control, self-worth, attractiveness, and lovability (Astle, 1986).

While it is not uncommon for an athlete's psychological recovery to lag behind the more rapid physical recovery, an unusually long rehabilitation, a reluctance on the part of the athlete to return to competition, or frequent and vague reporting of pain suggest the need to assess the meaning and function that the injury has for the athlete. Sports injuries may be psychosomatic, may serve as a form of masochism, may represent a sign of masculinity, may be used as a weapon to punish others, or may be the result of counterphobia to aggression (Sanderson, 1977). An athlete who has been performing poorly and is feeling disappointed, rejected, and fearful of future failure and who may be losing personal and social esteem may use accidental injury, intentional injury, or malingering to avoid psychological distress and possibly prevent the loss of an athletic scholarship (Kane, 1984). Therefore, for an athlete who appears resistant to treatment, understanding and exploring the meaning of the injury may help one to uncover whether there are secondary motives or underlying feelings of psychological distress associated with the injury. The athlete's counterproductive thoughts, feelings, and behaviors should be addressed by members of the treatment team, with appropriate referral to a sport psychologist for further intervention.

Injury Management

To elicit an athlete's full participation in rehabilitation, he or she must understand the injury and its impact, and must have the skills needed to deal with the situation. Although individual variability exists, there are common pathways by which athletes will perceive and respond to physical trauma. Specifically athletes generally will experience cognitive, emotional, and behavioral responses to the injury.

Cognitive Responses to Injury. The athlete's cognitive assessment of the injury and the impact this event is likely to have on his or her life will greatly influence emotional reactions as well as behavior. Analyzing athletes who have undergone treatment at a sports medicine clinic, Crossman and Jamieson (1985) found that "Overestimation of the seriousness or disruptive impact of the injury was significantly correlated with reports of more pain, higher state anxiety, and greater feelings of anger, apathy, loneliness, and inadequacy, and was more common among athletes competing at lower levels" (p. 1131). This indicates that those athletes who inaccurately perceive of an injury as more serious than is warranted are increasingly likely to experience affective states known to impair rehabilitation.

In addition to the athlete's cognitive assessment of the injury, his or her attitudes and beliefs can greatly influence the recovery process. As Dunn (1983) notes, if an athlete holds negative attitudes with respect to recovery or the training room, a lowered self-image and decreased motivation are likely to result. Similarly an athlete possessing irrational beliefs is more prone to having elevated daily ratings of depressed mood and anger (Rohsenow & Smith, 1982), emotions likely to interfere with a successful rehabilitation.

The athlete's sense of control, level of commitment, and ability to cope with stress are also likely to increase the probability of certain emotional experiences and actions that may or may not facilitate recovery. In a reciprocal fashion the athlete's affective experiences and behaviors may serve to enhance or alter previously held thoughts and beliefs. Since the athlete's cognitive appraisal of the injury and his or her cognitive approach to rehabilitation may greatly impact on recovery, it follows that interventions designed to facilitate productive thoughts and to channel positive goal-directed behavior would facilitate the successful treatment of the injury.

Emotional Responses to Injury. As noted by Pedersen (1986) and Weiss and Troxell (1986), the irreversible loss incurred by athletic injury is always accompanied by grief. Kübler-Ross (1969) has identified five stages typically experienced during the grief response, which are: (1) denial and isolation, (2) anger, (3) bargaining, (4) depression, and (5) acceptance. While it is unlikely that any two athletes will progress through these stages at the same rate or that there will always be a sequential advancement through these stages, it is valuable for the athlete to be aware that many of the unwelcome feelings and thoughts he or she is experiencing are quite normal and essential to the rehabilitation process.

Those who place a high value on fitness, such as athletes, may be at risk for significant impairment in psychological functioning due to the losses associated with bodily injury. Little (1969) found that of 44 male athletes experiencing neurotic breakdowns, in 72.5% of the cases the precipitant was an illness or injury. Alternatively only 10.5% of the nonathletes experienced neurotic symptoms secondary to a threat to their physical well-being. The seriousness of the injury may also impact on the experiencing of troubling emotional responses. In a study by Smith, Scott, O'Fallon, and Young (1990) involving 72 injured athletes, it was found that frustration, depression, and anger were the most highly rated and frequently endorsed affective symptoms, with the most seriously injured athletes showing the greatest mood disturbance.

In addition to the physical losses, decreases in physical conditioning, and changes in lifestyles experienced as a result of the athlete's inability to participate in sport, there is a sudden deprivation of positive affective experiences acquired through exercise. Vigorous physical activity has been associated with decreases in state anxiety (Raglin & Morgan, 1987) and depression (Mihevic, 1982), and offers athletes the opportunity to experience the optimal state that accompanies a peak performance (Williams, 1986). People who exercise regularly also have better self-concepts and score better on scales of adjustment than those who do not exercise regularly (Kellner, 1985). When individuals who are accustomed to regular vigorous physical exertion are forced to refrain from the activity, numerous negative consequences may result. In a study examining runners who were required to miss a run or series of runs, symptoms experienced as a consequence of this abstinence included irritability, restlessness, frustration, guilt, depression, sleeping problems, digestive tract difficulties, and muscle tension (Robbins & Joseph, 1985). These findings have interesting implications for the injured athlete. It appears that regular physical activity may serve a central role in one's system of psychological well-being. If an athlete is forced to confront the temporary (or permanent) loss of this physical outlet, there is a need to develop alternative methods of dealing with emotions, cognitions, and physical sensations.

Behavioral Responses to Injury. An athlete's cognitions and emotions will influence the behavior he or she will exhibit during recovery. Input from these areas will determine how the athlete will respond to the treatment protocol and how he or she will subsequently reacclimate into the sport environment. A frequent and destructive example of this is the fear of loss or failure that may motivate an athlete to exhibit self-defeating behaviors (Wehlage, 1980). The patient that fears and believes that the return to sport activity will be a negative experience is likely to have that prophecy fulfilled. In catastrophizing, the athlete typically employs negative self-talk and negative imagery, practices that have been demonstrated to impair athletic performance (Woolfolk, Murphy, Gottesfeld, & Aitken, 1985). Further, the negative mood states that are likely to occur during destructive internal dialogues have been shown to impair performance on a physical task (Kavanagh & Hausfeld, 1986).

A second unfortunate behavioral outcome involves the athlete's return to a sport activity before he or she is physically or psychologically prepared. This event may occur because a physician, trainer, or coach verbally or nonverbally encourages the premature return to the sport. Alternatively the athlete may feel that he or she knows his or her body's limitations and capabilities better than others, and may consequently refute sound medical advice and return to the sport unprepared. If the athlete has unrealistically high expectations or is unable to perform at a prior level of functioning, negative cognitions and self-talk, in addition to such feelings as frustration, doubt, anger, and fear are likely to occur. Injured athletes who are psychologically unprepared for a safe and successful return to their sport may face a more lengthy and difficult process of regaining their prior confidence and performance levels than those who are psychologically prepared (Rotella & Campbell, 1983). Moreover, in this state of physical or psychological unpreparedness, the likelihood of reinjury or injury to another body part will increase.

Psychological Skill Development

Since cognitive, affective, and behavioral reactions to injury are interrelated, alterable, and greatly influence an injured athlete's recovery and reintegration into sport, it follows that including psychological interventions in the injury treatment protocol may be advantageous. Therefore, in addition to educating the athlete about the injury, rehabilitation may be facilitated by having the athlete develop skills in the following areas: dealing with emotions, increasing motivation and confidence through goal setting, challenging negative self-talk and changing faulty beliefs, pain management, stress management, and building performance skills. As suggested by Rotella and Heyman (1986), the athlete should be encouraged to perceive of injury as a self-enhancing, learning experience rather than a negative, self-defeating event.

Dealing with Emotions. Athletic patients can be facilitated in progressing through the stages of the grief process identified by Kübler-Ross (1969) that occur in response to loss. During the anger and denial stages in which the athlete is dealing with the shock of the injury, anger may be displaced in the forms of violent outbursts, sarcasm, stubbornness, or "acting out" behaviors, or the anger may be internalized as indicated by the expressions of guilt, self-blame, or preoccupation with physical complaints

(Wehlage, 1980). In addition to displaying anger or denying aspects of the injury, athletes may use the defenses of reaction formation and intellectualization (Astle, 1986). In reaction formation the athlete displays emotions that are exactly the opposite of what he/she is truly experiencing. When intellectualizing, the athlete discusses the loss in terms of ideas, thoughts, and beliefs, but seems disconnected or closed off from his/her emotions. During this early phase, those working with the athlete should discourage the use of defense mechanisms by giving the athlete permission to experience and express distressing emotions appropriately. At this time, and throughout the psychological rehabilitation, the athlete should be given reassurance that the feelings he or she is experiencing are normal and acceptable.

As the athlete enters into the phase of depression and hopelessness, behaviors such as withdrawal, self-reflection, inability to concentrate, and fatigue are common (Pedersen, 1986; Wehlage, 1980). Since it is essential that the patient process these feelings, efforts should not be made to "cheer up" or negate the athlete's feelings or thoughts. Facts should be explained to the athlete, and he or she should be assured of confidentiality to encourage self-disclosure of disturbing feelings.

The acceptance phase is marked by the athlete's resumption of activities (both inclusive and exclusive of athletics). To aid the athlete in reaching this stage, it may be useful to explore the meaning sport involvement holds for the athlete, and to help him or her find other ways of getting those needs met, even temporarily. It may also be valuable to have the injured athlete meet with an athlete who has successfully recovered from a similar injury using the rehabilitation program (DePalma & DePalma, 1989; Ermler & Thomas, 1990). Moreover, it may be beneficial for injured athletes to become involved in support groups in which topics such as concerns and fears, feelings, difficulties, and progress may be shared and discussed (Silva & Hardy, 1991; Wiese & Weiss, 1987).

It is likely that the injured athlete is unable to appropriately process feelings associated with grief and loss if he/she is demonstrating prolonged detachment, lack of spontaneity, and disinterest in activities (Wehlage, 1980). Should this occur, professional counseling or therapy may be warranted.

Increasing Motivation and Confidence Through Goal Setting. After educating the athlete about his or her current condition and the steps involved in the rehabilitation process, the patient should become actively involved in formulating both short-term and long-term goals. It is essential that the athlete be involved in the goal-setting process, so that he or she is afforded an opportunity to make decisions and assume personal responsibility for those choices (O'Block & Evans, 1984). Goal setting not only provides the athlete with a sense of control, but may facilitate motivation, persistence, and commitment. Moreover, goals are more likely to be attained when they are important to the athlete as well as being valued by members of the sports medicine team (Danish, 1986). Goals give the athlete appropriate tasks to attend to and may provide a valuable learning experience as the individual strives to develop new methods to reach those goals. Goals allow the athlete to build confidence incrementally, may be self-esteem-enhancing, and are likely to give the athlete positive expectations for the future. Further, goal setting not only influences performance, but may serve to reduce anxiety (Gould, 1986).

Goals are likely to be most effective when they include both short-and long-term aspirations that are challenging but realistic and that are positive rather than negative (DePalma & DePalma, 1989; Gould, 1986). Goals that are too specific may limit the athlete's progress, while those that are too high may lead to frustration, anxiety, and burnout (O'Block & Evans, 1984). Once goals have been specified, athletes should assist in the establishment of target dates for achievement of the goals. On those selected dates, treatment progress should be assessed, with future goals being evaluated and modified if necessary. By accomplishing these specific, realistic, and challenging short-term and long-term goals, the athlete is given the opportunity to experience sensations such as hard work, sacrifice, reinforcement, pride, and satisfaction (DePalma & DePalma, 1989).

Challenging Negative Self-Talk and Changing Faulty Beliefs. An athlete's self-talk or internal dialogue can influence factors such as concentration, confidence, and persistence. Further, self-talk can create negative emotional states, including fear, anxiety, and depression, which in turn affect behavior. Therefore, the athlete should be taught to recognize and alter his/her self-talk so that it is task relevant, mood appropriate, focused, and positive.

Destructive self-talk may originate from long-standing faulty belief systems. If this is the case, it may be necessary to identify and alter these questionable underlying assumptions or cognitions. As Faris (1985) observed, many injured athletes act on unconscious beliefs that are contrary to sound medical advice (such as the notion that "more is better"). Further, as Rotella and Heyman (1986) note, many athletic trainers and coaches unknowingly encourage these erroneous beliefs.

Building on the work of Ellis's (1962) irrational belief systems and Beck's (1976) faulty thinking styles, a number of cognitive change techniques have been developed. Among these cognitive strategies are cognitive restructuring (Lazarus, 1972), self-instructional training (Meichenbaum, 1974), and cognitive-affective stress management training (Smith, 1980). Central to all of these techniques is the identification, challenge, and elimination of faulty or self-defeating thoughts, followed by the development of problem-solving skills and subsequent coping skills. For injured athletes experiencing disruptive or unproductive thoughts, instruction in the use of cognitive change techniques may enable him/her to prevent negative thoughts and effectively handle difficulties as they arise. Further, the athlete can be encouraged to focus on positive self-talk and positive imagery incorporating the short-term

and long-term goals that he or she is striving toward. Since these skills are easily generalizable, the athlete may benefit from using this knowledge in other areas of his/her life.

Pain Management

Athletes tend to have a higher pain tolerance and threshold for pain than nonathletic populations, perhaps due to reinforcement for insensitivity to pain (Jaremko, Silbert, & Mann, 1981). This higher pain tolerance may lead to decreased incidence of or delays in reporting injuries and underreporting of pain. This situation can be ameliorated by increasing awareness of its possible occurrence and by encouraging open communication. Alternatively, for those athletes experiencing difficulty dealing with the physical pain associated with therapeutic exercises or other aspects of the recovery process, there are several psychological interventions available. Cognitive-behavioral strategies have been shown to be effective in facilitating pain tolerance (for a review of this literature, see Turk, Meichenbaum, & Genest, 1983, Chapter 5). Techniques used to increase pain tolerance often include the use of imagery as a source of distraction or involve the withdrawal of attention from the painful stimulus, skills that may be taught to the athlete.

If an athlete reports pain of a magnitude, intensity, or duration disproportionate to medical indications, it may be necessary to explore the meaning the athlete has assigned to pain and its expression. "Pain behavior" may be used to elicit sympathy, attention, or special favors, or may otherwise serve in a reinforcing capacity. It has been demonstrated that for patients suffering from chronic pain, teaching relevant members of the patients' social support network to ignore "pain behavior" while complimenting and attending to nonpain behavior resulted in a decrease in the incidence of pain reporting and an increase in activity levels (Fordyce et al., 1973). This suggests that for those athletes who use the expression of pain for secondary gains, the utilization of operant-conditioning techniques is likely to diminish the athlete's pain reporting, while increasing recovery-enhancing behaviors. If pain has a much greater significance to the athlete, however, such as constituting the only mechanism by which the athlete may avoid returning to the sport or other activities he/she perceives as aversive, further therapeutic intervention may be warranted.

Stress Management

Stress associated with physical injury may be alleviated by employing relaxation techniques, breathing techniques, imagery, and cognitive interventions. (See Chapter 22 by Zaichkowski and Takenaka and Chapter 23 by Rotella and Lerner in this book for further discussion on this topic.) Training is the process of teaching the body to be free of any excess tension or stress. The physiological untensing of muscles typically leads to a relaxed mental state in which negative feelings may be altered and physical and psychological pain may be alleviated. Since the introduction of progressive relaxation (Jacobson, 1929), Benson's relaxation response (1975), and autogenic training, numerous variations of these approaches have been developed, all of which are designed to diminish unwanted physiological arousal. Many of these modified (abbrieviated) techniques can easily be taught to the injured athlete in a relatively short period of time, and the potential benefits are widespread.

By mastering proper breathing techniques, the injured athlete can learn to induce relaxation or to increase arousal ("energize" the body). Central to many breathing exercises is the slow, deep, diaphragmatic breath. When taking complete breaths, not only is a relaxation response likely to be triggered, but the increased oxygen in the blood produced by this action may also facilitate performance by increasing energy to the muscles (Harris, 1986). While often inherently relaxing in and of itself, deep full breathing can also be accompanied by soothing verbal cues or images to help alleviate stress and anxiety. Alternatively, breathing rhythms can be increased and accompanied by vitalizing words and images to help energize or arouse the athlete. Not only are these techniques advantageous to the injured athlete working in the training room, but these skills can easily and effectively be utilized during practice, competition, or other challenging situations.

Imagery is a mental training technique in which all of the senses (visual, auditory, tactile, olfactory, taste, kinesthetic) are used to create an image in one's mind. Typically used in conjunction with a relaxation technique, this skill can be used to help the injured athlete cope with pain, visualize the healing process, and rehearse effectively handling difficult situations (Thompson, 1986; Wolff & Horland, 1967). Imagery may also be instrumental in helping to prevent the athlete's physical skills from deteriorating. In a meta-analysis of 60 studies examining the effects of mental practice on motor skill learning and performance, Feltz and Landers (1983) determined that mental practice will influence learning and performance, particularly on tasks that have a cognitive component. This suggests that if the injured athlete mentally rehearses the sport activity during the interim in which he/she is unable to physically practice, subsequent performance may be enhanced. Moreover, the continued exposure and familiarity with the activity may help alleviate anxiety and self-doubt.

Although relaxation techniques, breathing techniques, and imagery are useful in alleviating stress, the anxiety that these techniques seek to reduce is involved in a reciprocal relationship with cognition. That is, stress-inducing or anxiety-producing stimuli are thought to elicit interrelated cognitive and physiological responses (Landers, 1980; Smith, 1980). Some people may manifest stress or anxiety cognitively by generating unwelcome or negative internal verbalizations (self-talk) or imagery, some may express overarousal physiologically, and others may experience anxiety in both modalities. Davidson and Schwartz (1976) suggest that for an intervention to be effective it must target the dominant mode in which anxiety is expressed in the individual. Thus for athletes displaying more physiological

reactions, techniques such as progressive relaxation, meditation, imagery, short relaxation inductions, and breathing exercises should be employed. For athletes who manifest anxiety more cognitively, interventions such as those that were described earlier in which negative self-talk and destructive cognitions are altered would be preferable. Ultimately, however, altering the stress and anxiety levels of the injured athlete will require the incorporation of both the cognitive and physiological (emotional) interventions into what Smith (1980) has termed the "integrated coping response" (p. 56).

Building Performance Skills

In addition to teaching athletes techniques that promote physical and psychological recovery, psychological features associated with accomplished performance may be strengthened so that the athlete will possess skills necessary for a successful reintegration into the sport and competition. In a survey of coaches and athletes about traits they considered most important for a "winner," the top responses were self-confidence, positive self-image, good concentration, industriousness, determination, setting goals, mental toughness, aggressiveness, positive self-esteem, self-motivation, positive attitudes, and able communicativeness (Bennett & Pravitz, 1987). Williams (1986) identified a psychological profile that appears to be associated with successful performance, and these psychological characteristics are: appropriate self-regulation of arousal (the athlete is energized and relaxed and is not anxious or fearful), high self-confidence, good concentration with appropriate focus of attention, control, positive preoccupation with sport (imagery and thoughts), and commitment. Therefore, exposing the injured athlete to skills training during injury rehabilitation may facilitate his or her successful reintegration into sport since characteristics such as a positive attitude, positive self-image, high motivation, highly focused attention, and confidence are fostered by psychological interventions.

IMPORTANCE OF CONTINUED SPORT INVOLVEMENT

For some athletes, the emotional losses experienced by injury are exacerbated by restricted opportunities for them to interact with and receive social support from teammates or coaching staff. It has been noted that some coaches function under the false assumption that the best way to encourage an athlete to recover quickly is to limit the athlete's team involvement and minimize interactions with the patient until he or she decides to become uninjured (Rotella, 1988; Rotella & Heyman, 1986). Such actions are likely to lead the athlete to feel guilty for letting the team down, or to feel somehow inadequate for not healing rapidly. Athletes functioning in this type of environment are thus encouraged to ignore injuries and to return to sports activity prematurely, actions that are likely to foster reinjury or more extensive physical damage.

In direct opposition to this philosophical position, it has been suggested that social support from the team is critical to the injured athlete's rehabilitation (Rotella & Heyman, 1986; Silva & Hardy, 1991; Wiese, Weiss, & Yukelson, 1991). An athlete's rehabilitation is typically best facilitated by encouraging the athlete to resume sports-related functions as soon as possible, while refraining from returning to competition too soon. Scheduling rehabilitation during prepractice and practice time when other teammates are present may help the athlete feel connected with the team, and serves to maintain the athlete on a familiar schedule of dedicating certain hours of the day to his/her sport activity (DePalma & DePalma, 1989; Ermler & Thomas, 1990). Although the athlete may be able to engage only minimally in team exercises due to physical limitations, it is important for the athlete to attend practice, team meetings, and competitions as soon as it is feasible. By continuing to attend sports-related functions, the athlete is given the opportunity to maintain involvement with teammates and coaching staff, and these interactions are likely to allow the athlete to feel supported, needed, and valued.

ASSESSING PSYCHOLOGICAL READINESS

There is often a great deal of anxiety surrounding the rehabilitation process and subsequent reintegration into the sport. Anxiety is likely to be destructive to the athlete in terms of both physical and psychological distress, but also due to its ability to impair performance. Arousal, particularly when caused by fear or anxiety, can impair performance by diminishing one's capacity to synthesize relevant information due to attentional narrowing (Landers, 1980), focusing attention internally, or responding to the situation in one's dominant (but inappropriate) attentional mode (Nideffer, 1983). There is also evidence that a high level of arousal is most deleterious to the performance of sports tasks that are complex and/or require fine motor skills coordination (Weinberg & Genuchi, 1980) and decision making (Oxendine, 1980). Anxiety related to fear of reinjury or further injury may lead an athlete to overcompensate for the previously injured body part or may lead to increased muscle tension and an inability to respond to task-relevant cues, resulting in the occurrence of the feared event (Andersen & Williams, 1988; Rotella & Campbell, 1983).

Many athletes fear that the physician has not discovered the full extent of the physical damage incurred (Yaffe, 1983). Others fear that they are not prepared to return to competition because they believe their performance may be impaired or because they fear reinjury. Whether or not it is a direct result of the tension associated with anxiety, there is empirical support demonstrating that these feared events frequently occur. A study examining 138 physical education students to determine predictability of athletic injury found that students with a prior history of injury were at

high risk of recurrence, since 135 of the 499 injuries incurred were reinjuries (Lysens et al., 1984). Reflecting on this study, Lysens and associates echo the fears stated by athletes declaring "This relatively high incidence of reinjuries suggests an underestimation of the severity of the primary injury, an inadequate rehabilitation, and/or a premature return to sports activity" (Lysens et al., 1984, p. 8). These findings indicate the importance of determining both the athlete's physical and psychological preparedness for the return to sport in order to facilitate a safe, successful reintegration into the activity.

It has been suggested that if the athlete has a fear of reinjury or anxiety concerning performance capabilities, techniques such as systematic desensitization, hypnosis, or stress inoculation, may be useful (Feltz, 1986; Rotella & Campbell, 1983). Systematic desensitization involves pairing a relaxation response with a hierarchy of imagined anxiety-producing stimuli, such that, over time, the athlete is able to imagine encountering increasingly fearful situations without experiencing anxiety (Wolpe, 1974). Hypnosis is a technique in which suggestions are offered to the patient while he/she is in a relaxed state, and this intervention may be useful in helping the athlete to increase self-confidence and challenge fears. Stress inoculation involves educating the athlete about stress, providing the athlete with adaptive coping skills to deal with stress, and then exposing the athlete to increasingly difficult situations (real or imagined) to practice effectively dealing with stress (Feltz, 1986).

In summary, the last and vital step needed to ensure a complete psychological recovery following athletic injury is an assessment to determine whether the athlete is ready to return to competition. In addition to an adequate physical recovery, it is essential that the athlete possess certain psychological states. Specifically the athlete must feel confident about his or her recovery and should be encouraged to discuss any fears or thoughts related to the return to sport. Moreover, the opinions and expertise of those members of the treatment team integrally involved in the psychological rehabilitation of the injured athlete should be elicited, and their decisions respected (Wiese & Weiss, 1987). Such precautions would help prevent overly anxious or otherwise psychologically unprepared athletes from returning to competition and risking reinjury while affording the athlete the opportunity to maximize his or her performance skills.

INTEGRATING TREATMENT

One of the most important elements of the treatment protocol is the communication among members of the treatment team. Treatment team members may include the athlete, sport psychologists, sports medicine physicians, athletic trainers, physical therapists, coaches, and in some instances, family members. Frequent reciprocal communication among treatment members will help to ensure that the athlete is receiving consistent information and that all parties involved are working jointly toward the same short-term and long-term treatment goals. It is important for treatment team members to understand the role and function of others working with the athlete, to simplify and coordinate treatment, and to maximize the use of valuable resources. This multidisciplinary approach to athletic rehabilitation may not only facilitate the athlete's recovery, but may provide team members with the opportunity to learn from each other. Further, the athlete may benefit from the role modeling provided by treatment team members who function in an atmosphere of motivation, interest, concern, caring, and mutual respect.

Role of the Sport Psychologist

The role of the sport psychologist in the treatment of the injured athlete is a newly emerging area offering potentially exciting and innovative changes designed to facilitate the rehabilitation process and to enhance the well-being of the athlete. It has been suggested that for the sport psychologist to be most effective, he/she should be a fully integrated member of the sport medicine team and should be involved in all aspects of treatment, including the prevention, assessment, and rehabilitation of the injured athlete (Silva & Hardy, 1991).

One area of involvement for the sport psychologist is that of educator, informing those involved in the athlete's treatment about the psychological impact of injury and how this information may be used to facilitate the athlete's rehabilitation. To this end, Oglesby (1988) and Hardy & Crace (1990) have attempted to offer suggestions to the injured athlete and those involved with him/her about the types of behaviors (e.g., supportiveness; open communication; a realistic positive attitude; patience) that might facilitate the athlete's rapid and successful reintegration into sport.

Sport psychologists may also provide useful information for injury rehabilitation by developing measures designed to assess an athlete's response to injury and his/her available coping mechanisms and supports. This type of assessment is currently under way at the Sports Medicine Program at the Mayo Clinic where injured athletes referred for counseling are interviewed using the Emotional Responses of Athletes to Injury Questionnaire (Smith, Scott, & Wiese, 1990), are given an informal mental status exam, and are administered the Profile of Mood States survey (McNair, Lorr, & Droppleman, 1971) in order to assess the athlete's cur-

rent emotional and psychological functioning, his/her coping resources and the psychosocial impact of the injury.

Similarly, sport psychologists may assist in identifying and intervening with those athletes who are at risk for failed rehabilitation and those who are likely to experience difficulty achieving a successful rehabilitation. Recent efforts in this area include checklists designed to assess the presence or absence of variables thought to place an athlete at risk for rehabilitation difficulties (Heil, 1988; in press). The sport psychologist may also assist the injury rehabilitation process by assessing the athlete's psychological readiness for the return to sport. This might be accomplished by coordinating support groups, so that the athletes are offered an opportunity to share and explore issues related to their injuries.

FUTURE RESEARCH NEEDS

In seeking to understand the psychological aspects of injury rehabilitation, there are a number of areas that merit further exploration. It has been suggested that athletes may not adhere to the stages of grief described by Kübler-Ross (1969) when responding to the losses associated with injury, but may respond quite differently (Smith, Scott, & Wiese, 1990). McDonald and Hardy (1990) examined the affective response patterns of five severely injured university athletes for 4 weeks following injury, and found a high negative correlation between perceived rehabilitation and total mood disturbance. The authors suggested that the athletes' emotional responses seemed to involve a two-stage process, with the first stage including shock, panic, disorganization, and helplessness, and the second stage involving "retreat" into illness or health and acknowledgment of the illness. Clearly, further research is needed to clarify what type of cognitive and emotional responses are characteristically seen in injured athletic populations. It will also be necessary to evaluate the efficacy of psychological interventions. That is, what specific interventions seem to work best under what conditions and with what type of personality characteristics to influence outcomes such as lowering incidences of reinjury or further injury, expediting return to previous level of functioning, and restoring confidence. And finally, it may be useful to explore whether educating those involved with the injured athlete about the psychological aspects of treatment influences their behavior and, if so, whether this change in the support system of the athlete measurably impacts on rehabilitation.

References

Abadie, D. A. (1976). Comparison of the personalities of non-injured and injured female athletes in intercollegiate competition. *Dissertation Abstracts, 15*(2), 82.

Ahadi, S., & Diener, E. (1989). Multiple determinants and effect size. *Journal of Personality and Social Psychology, 56,* 398–406.

Andersen, M. B. (1988). *Psychosocial factors and changes in peripheral vision, muscle tension, and fine motor skills during stress.* Unpublished doctoral dissertation, University of Arizona, Tucson.

Andersen, M. B., & Williams, J. M. (1988). A model of stress and athletic injury: Prediction and prevention. *Journal of Sport and Exercise Physiology, 10,* 294–306.

Andersen, M. B., & Williams, J. M. (in press). Psychological risk factors: Injury prediction and preventative measures. In J. Heil (Ed.), *The sport psychology of injury.* Champaign, IL: Human Kinetics.

Antonovsky, A. (1985). The sense of coherence as a determinant of health. In J. D. Matarazzo, S. M. Weiss, J. A. Herd, & N. E. Miller (Eds.), *Behavioral health: A Handbook of health enhancement and disease prevention* (pp. 37–50). New York: Wiley.

Astle, S. J. (1986). The experience of loss in athletes. *Journal of Sports Medicine, 26,* 279–284.

Baron, R. M., & Kenny, D. A. (1986). The moderator-mediator variable distinction in social psychological research: Conceptual, strategic, and statistical considerations. *Journal of Personality and Social Psychology, 51,* 1173–1182.

Barrera, M., Jr. (1988). Models of social support and life stress: Beyond the buffering hypothesis. In L. H. Cohen (Ed.), *Life events and psychological functioning: Theoretical and methodological issues* (pp. 211–238). Newbury Park, CA: Sage.

Beck, A. (1976). *Cognitive therapy and the emotional disorders.* New York: International Universities Press.

Bennett, J. G., & Pravitz, J. E. (1987). *Profile of a winner: Advanced mental training for athletes.* Ithaca, NY: Sport Sciences International.

Benson, H. (1975). *The relaxation response.* New York: William Morrow.

Billings, A. G., & Moos, R. H. (1981). The role of coping responses and social resources in attenuating the stress of life events. *Journal of Behavioral Medicine, 4,* 139–157.

Blackwell, B., & McCullagh, P. (1990). The relationship of athletic injury to life stress, competitive anxiety and coping resources. *Athletic Training, 25,* 23–27.

Boyce, W. T., & Sobolewski, S. (1989). Recurrent injuries in school children. *American Journal of the Disabled Child, 143,* 338–342.

Bramwell, S. T., Masuda, M., Wagner, N. H., & Holmes, T. H. (1975). Psychological factors in athletic injuries: Development and application of the Social and Athletic Readjustment Rating Scale (SARRS). *Journal of Human Stress, 1,* 6–20.

Brown, R. B. (1971). Personality characteristics related to injuries in football. *The Research Quarterly, 42,* 133–138.

Bunker, L., & Williams, J. M. (1986). Cognitive techniques for improving performance and building confidence. In J. M. Williams (Ed.), *Applied sport psychology: Personal growth to peak performance* (pp. 75–91). Palo Alto, CA: Mayfield.

Burks, N., & Martin, B. (1985). Everyday problems and life change events: On-going versus acute sources of stress. *Journal of Human Stress, 11,* 27–35.

Coddington, R. D., & Troxell, J. R. (1980). The effect of emotional factors on football injury rates: A pilot study. *Journal of Human Stress, 6,* 3–5.

Cohen, L. H. (Ed.) (1988). *Life events and psychological functioning: Theoretical and methodological issues.* Newbury Park, CA: Sage.

Cohen, J., & Cohen, P. (1983). *Applied multiple regression/correlation analysis for the behavioral sciences* (2nd ed.). Hillsdale, NJ: Erlbaum.

Cohen, S., & Willis, T. A. (1985). Stress, social support, and the buffering hypothesis. *Psychological Bulletin, 98,* 310–357.

Compas, B. E., Davis, G. E., Forsythe, C. J., & Wagner, B. M. (1987). Assessment of major and daily stressful events during adolescence: The Adolescent Perceived Events Scale. *Journal of Consulting and Clinical Psychology, 55,* 534–541.

Cronbach, L. J. (1987). Statistical tests for moderator variables: Flaws in analyses recently proposed. *Psychological Bulletin, 102,* 114–117.

Crossman, J., & Jamieson, J. (1985). Differences in perceptions of seriousness and disrupting effects of athletic injury as viewed by athletes and their trainer. *Perceptual and Motor Skills, 61,* 1131–1134.

Cryan, P. O., & Alles, E. F. (1983). The relationship between stress and football injuries. *Journal of Sports Medicine and Physical Fitness, 23,* 52–58.

Dalhauser, M., & Thomas, M. B. (1979). Visual disembedding and locus of control as variables associated with high school football injuries. *Perceptual and Motor Skills, 49,* 254.

Danish, S. J. (1986). Psychological aspects in the care and treatment of athletic injuries. In P. F. Vinger & E. F. Hoerner (Eds.), *Sports injuries: The unthwarted epidemic* (pp. 345–353). Littleton, MA: PSG Publishing.

Davidson, R., & Schwartz, G. (1976). The psychobiology of relaxation and related states: A multi-process theory. In D. Mostofsky (Ed.), *Behavioral control and modification of physiological activity* (pp. 399–442). Englewood Cliffs, NJ: Prentice-Hall.

Davis, J. O. (1991). Sports injuries and stress management: An opportunity for research. *The Sport Psychologist, 5,* 175–182.

DePalma, M. T., & DePalma, B. (1989). The use of instruction and the behavioral approach to facilitate injury rehabilitation. *Athletic Training, 24,* 217–219.

DeWitt, D. J. (1980). Cognitive and biofeedback training for stress reduction with university athletes. *Journal of Sport Psychology, 2,* 288–294.

Dunlap, W. P., & Kemery, E. R. (1987). Failure to detect moderating effects: Is multicollinearity the problem? *Psychological Bulletin, 102,* 418–420.

Dunn, R. (1983). Psychological factors in sports medicine. *Athletic Training, 18,* 34–35.

Eldridge, W. D. (1983). The importance of psychotherapy for athletic-related orthopedic injuries among adults. *Comprehensive Psychiatry, 24,* 271–277.

Ellis, A. (1962). *Reason and emotion in psychotherapy.* New York: Lyle Stewart.

Ermler, K. L., & Thomas, C. E. (1990). Interventions for the alienating effect of injury. *Athletic Training, 25,* 269–271.

Faris, G. J. (1985). Psychological aspects of rehabilitation. *Clinics in Sports Medicine, 4,* 545–551.

Feltz, D. L. (1986). The psychology of sports injuries. In P. F. Vinger & E. F. Hoerner (Eds.), *Sports injuries: The unthwarted epidemic* (pp. 336–344). Littleton, MA: PSG Publishing.

Feltz, D. L., & Landers, D. M. (1983). The effects of mental practice on motor skill learning and performance: A meta-analysis. *Journal of Sport Psychology, 5,* 25–57.

Fischer, A. C. (1984). New directions in sport personality research. In J. M. Silva & R. S. Weinberg (Eds.), *Psychological foundations of sport* (pp. 70–80). Champaign, IL: Human Kinetics.

Fordyce, W., Fowler, R., Lehmann, J., DeLateur, B., Sand, P., & Trieschmann, R. (1973). Operant conditioning in the treatment of chronic pain. *Archives of Physical Medicine and Rehabilitation, 54,* 399–408.

Garrick, J. G., & Requa, R. K. (1978). Injuries in high school sports. *Pediatrics, 61,* 465–473.

Garrity, T. F., & Marx, M. B. (1985). Effects of moderator variables on the response to stress. In S. R. Burchfield (Ed.), *Stress: Psy-*

chological and physiological interactions (pp. 223–240). New York: Hemisphere.

Gould, D. (1986). Goal setting for peak performance. In J. M. Williams (Ed.), *Applied sport psychology: Personal growth to peak performance* (pp. 133–148). Palo Alto, CA: Mayfield.

Greenspan, M. J., & Feltz, D. L. (1989). Psychological interventions with athletes in competitive situations: A review. *The Sport Psychologist, 3,* 219–236.

Hancock, P. A. (1984). Environmental stressors. In J. S. Warm (Ed.), *Sustained attention and human performance* (pp. 103–142). New York: Wiley.

Hanson, S. J., McCullagh, P., & Tonymon, P. (1990). Psychosocial predictors of athletic injury in track and field athletes: A partial test of the Andersen and Williams model. *Proceedings of the Association for the Advancement of Applied Sport Psychology, Fifth Annual Conference (Abstract), 49.*

Hardy, C. J., & Crace, R. K. (May-June 1990). Dealing with injury. *Sport Psychology Training Bulletin, 1,* 1–8.

Hardy, C. J., O'Connor, K. A., & Geisler, P. R. (1990). The role of gender and social support in the life stress injury relationship. *Proceedings of the Association for the Advancement of Applied Sport Psychology, Fifth Annual Conference (Abstract), 51.*

Hardy, C. J., Prentice, W. E., Kirsanoff, M. T., Richman, J. M., & Rosenfeld, L. B. (June 1987). Life stress, social support, and athletic injury: In search of relationships. In J. M. Williams (Chair), *Psychological factors in injury occurrence.* Symposium conducted at the meeting of the North American Society for the Psychology of Sport and Physical Activity, Vancouver, BC, Canada.

Hardy, C. J., Richman, J. M., & Rosenfeld, L. B. (1991). The role of social support in the life stress/injury relationship. *The Sport Psychologist, 5,* 128–139.

Hardy, C. J., & Riehl, M. A. (1988). An examination of the life stress–injury relationship among noncontact sport participants. *Behavioral Medicine, 14,* 113–118.

Harris, D. V. (1986). Relaxation and energizing techniques for regulation of arousal. In J. M. Williams (Ed.), *Applied sport psychology: Personal growth to peak performance* (pp. 185–208). Palo Alto, CA: Mayfield.

Hedges, L. (1987). The meta-analysis of test validity studies: Some new approaches. In H. Braun & H. Wainer (Eds.), *Test validity for the 1990s and beyond* (pp. 191–212). Hillsdale, NJ: Erlbaum.

Heil, J. (1988, October). *Early identification and intervention with injured athletes at risk for failed rehabilitation.* A workshop presented at the Association for the Advancement of Applied Sport Psychology Convention, Nashua, NH.

Heil, J. (in press). Psychological aspects of injury prevention and rehabilitation. In J. Heil (Ed.), *The sport psychology of injury,* Champaign, IL: Human Kinetics.

Holmes, T. H. (1970, February). Psychological screening in *Football injuries: Paper presented at a workshop* (pp. 211–214). Sponsored by Subcommittee on Athletic Injuries, Committee on the Skeletal System, Division of Medical Sciences, National Research Council, 1969. Washington, DC: National Academy of Sciences.

Holmes, T. H., & Rahe, R. H. (1967). The social readjustment scale. *Journal of Psychosomatic Research, 11,* 213–218.

Hull, J. G., Van Treuren, R. R., & Virnelli, S. (1987). Hardiness and health: A critique and alternative approach. *Journal of Personality and Social Psychology, 53,* 518–530.

Ievleva, L., & Orlick, T. Mental links to enhanced healing: An exploratory study. *The Sport Psychologist, 5,* 25–40.

Irvin, R. F. (1975). Relationship between personality and the inci-

dence of injuries to high school football participants. *Dissertation Abstracts International, 36,* 4328-A.

Jackson, D. W., Jarrett, H., Bailey, D., Kausek, J., Swanson, M. J., & Powell, J. W. (1978). Injury prediction in the young athlete: A preliminary report. *The American Journal of Sports Medicine, 6,* 6–12.

Jacobson, E. (1929). *Progressive relaxation: A physiological and clinical investigation of muscular states and their significance in psychology and medical practice.* Chicago: University of Chicago Press.

Jaremko, M. E., Silbert, L., & Mann, T. (1981). The differential ability of athletes and nonathletes to cope with two types of pain: A radical behavioral model. *The Psychological Record, 31,* 265–275.

Kane, B. (1984). Trainer counseling to avoid three face-saving maneuvers. *Athletic Training, 19,* 171–174.

Kanner, A. D., Coyne, J. C., Schaefer, C., & Lazarus, R. S. (1981). Comparison of two modes of stress measurement: Daily hassles and uplifts versus major life events. *Journal of Behavioral Medicine, 4,* 1–39.

Kavanagh, D., & Hausfeld, S. (1986). Physical performance and self-efficacy under happy and sad moods. *Journal of Sport Psychology, 8,* 112–123.

Kellner, R. (1985). Fitness and psychological health. *Annals of Sports Medicine, 2,* 105–110.

Kendal, P. C., & Watson, D. (1981). Psychological preparation for stressful medical procedures. In C. K. Prokap & L. A. Bradley (Eds.), *Medical psychology: Contributions to behavioral medicine* (pp. 197–221). New York: Academic Press.

Kerr, G., & Fowler, B. (1988). The relationship between psychological factors and sports injuries. *Sports Medicine, 6,* 127–134.

Kerr, G., & Minden H. (1988). Psychological factors related to the occurrence of athletic injuries. *Journal of Sport and Exercise Psychology, 10,* 167–173.

Kobasa, S. C. (1979). Stressful life events, personality and health: An inquiry into hardiness. *Journal of Personality and Social Psychology, 37,* 1–11.

Kobasa, S. C., Maddi, S. R., & Puccetti, M. C. (1982). Personality and exercise as buffers in the stress-illness relationship. *Journal of Behavioral Medicine, 5,* 391–404.

Kraus, J. F., & Conroy, C. (1984). Mortality and morbidity from injuries in sports and recreation. *Annual Review of Public Health, 5,* 163–192.

Kübler-Ross, E. (1969). *On death and dying.* New York: Macmillan.

Lamb, M. (1986). Self-concept and injury frequency among female college field hockey players. *Athletic Training, 21,* 220–224.

Landers, D. (1980). The arousal-performance relationship revisited. *Research Quarterly for Exercise and Sport, 51,* 77–90.

Lazarus, A. (1972). *Behavioral therapy and beyond.* New York: McGraw-Hill.

Little, J. C. (1969). The athlete's neurosis—a deprivation crisis. *Acta Psychiatrica, 45,* 187–197.

Lysens, R., Auweele, Y. V., & Ostyn, M. (1986). The relationship between psychosocial factors and sports injuries. *Journal of Sports Medicine and Physical Fitness, 26,* 77–84.

Lysens, R., Steverlynck, A., Auweele, Y. V., Lefevre, J., Renson, L., Claessens, A., & Ostyn, M. (1984). The predictability of sports injuries. *Sports Medicine, 1,* 6–10.

Mahoney, M. J. (1983). *Concentration basic processes* (cassette tape). Psychology Department, Pennsylvania State University.

May, J. R., Veach, T. L., Reed, M. W., & Griffey, M. S. (1985). A psychological study of health, injury and performance in athletes on the U.S. alpine ski team, *Physician and Sports Medicine. 13,* 111–115.

May, J. R., Veach, T. L., Southard, S. W., & Herring (1985). The effects of life change on injuries, illness, and performance. In N. K. Butts, T. G. Gushikin, & B. Zarins (Eds.), *The elite athlete* (pp. 171–179). Jamaica, NY: Spectrum.

McDonald, S. A., & Hardy, C. J. (1990). Affective response patterns of the injured athlete: An exploratory analysis. *The Sport Psychologist, 4,* 261–274.

McNair, D., Lorr, M., & Droppleman, L. F. (1971). *Profile of mood states.* San Diego, CA: Educational and Industrial Testing Services.

Meichenbaum, D. (1974). *Cognitive behavior modification.* Morrison, NJ: General Learning Press.

Mihevic, P. (1982). Anxiety, depression, and exercise. *Quest, 33,* 140–153.

Miller, L. H., & Smith, A. D. (1982, December). Stress audit questionnaire. *Bostonia: In-depth,* pp. 39–54.

Milliner, E. K. (1987). Psychodynamic sport psychiatry. *Annals of Sports Medicine, 3,* 59–64.

Moore, R. A. (1966). *Sport and mental health,* Springfield, IL: Thomas.

Murphy, S. M. (1988). The on-site provision of sport psychology services at the U.S. Olympic Festival. *The Sport Psychologist, 2,* 337–350.

Nideffer, R. M. (1981). *The ethics and practice of applied sport psychology.* Ithaca, NY: Mouvement Publications.

Nideffer, R. M. (1982). The injured athlete: Psychological factors in treatment. *Orthopedic Clinics of North America, 14,* 373–385.

Nuckolls, K. B., Cassell, J., & Kaplan, B. H. (1972). Psychosocial assets, life crisis, and the prognosis of pregnancy. *American Journal of Epidemiology, 95,* 431–441.

O'Block, F., & Evans, F. (1984). Goal setting as a motivational technique. In J. Silva & R. Weinberg (Eds.), *Psychological foundations of sport* (pp. 188–196). Champaign, IL: Human Kinetics.

Ogilvie, B. C., & Tutko, T. (1966). *Problem athletes and how to handle them.* London: Pelham.

Oglesby, C. (1988). Coaches can help the injured cope. *American Coach,* (March-April), 10.

Passer, M. W., & Seese, M. D. (1983). Life stress and athletic injury: Examination of positive versus negative events and three moderator variables. *Journal of Human Stress, 9,* 11–16.

Pedersen, P. (1986). The grief response and injury: A special challenge for athletes and athletic trainers. *Athletic Training, 21,* 312–314.

Petrie, T. A. (1990a). The application of covariance structure modeling to sport psychology research. *Proceedings of the Association for the Advancement of Applied Sport Psychology, Fifth Annual Conference (Abstract),* 92.

Petrie, T. A. (1990b). Life stress, social support, and injury in women collegiate gymnasts. *Proceedings of the 98th Annual Convention of the American Psychological Association (Abstract),* 230.

Rabkin, J. G., & Streuning, E. L. (1976). Life events, stress, and illness. *Science, 194,* 1013–1020.

Raglin, J. S., & Morgan, W. P. (1987). Influence of exercise and quiet rest on state anxiety and blood pressure. *Medicine and Science in Sports and Exercise, 19,* 456–463.

Richman, J. M., Hardy, C. J., Rosenfeld, L. B., & Callahan, A. E. (1989). Strategies for enhancing social support networks in sport: A brainstorming experience. *Journal of Applied Sport Psychology, 1,* 150–159.

Robbins, J. M., & Joseph, P. (1985). Experiencing exercise with-

drawal: Possible consequences of therapeutic and mastery running. *Journal of Sport Psychology, 7,* 23–39.

Roepke, N. J., & Williams, J. M. (1990). *Psychological interventions used in the rehabilitation of the injured athlete.* Unpublished manuscript, University of Arizona, Exercise and Sport Sciences Department, Tucson.

Rohsenow, D. J., & Smith, R. E. (1982). Irrational beliefs as predictors of negative affective states. *Motivation and Emotion, 6,* 299–314.

Rosenblum, S. (1979). Psychological factors in competitive failures in athletes. *American Journal of Sports Medicine, 7,* 198–200.

Rotella, R. J. (1988). Psychological care of the injured athlete. In D. N. Kulund (Ed.), *The injured athlete* (pp. 151–164). Philadelphia: Lippincott.

Rotella, R. J., & Campbell, M. S. (1983). Systematic desensitization: Psychological rehabilitation of injured athletes. *Athletic Training, 18,* 140–142.

Rotella, R. J., & Heyman, S. R. (1986). Stress, injury and the psychological rehabilitation of athletes. In J. M. Williams (Ed.), *Applied sport psychology: personal growth to peak performance* (pp. 343–364). Palo Alto, CA: Mayfield.

Rotter, J. B. (1966). Generalized expectancies for internal versus external control of stress. *Psychological Monographs 80* (Whole).

Samuels, S. C. (1977). *Enhancing self-concept in early childhood.* New York: Human Sciences Press.

Sanderson, F. H. (1978). The psychological implications of injury. *British Journal of Sports Medicine, 12,* 41–43.

Sanderson, R. (1977). Psychology of the injury prone athlete. *British Journal of Sports Medicine, 11,* 56–57.

Sarason, I. G., Levine, H. M., Basham, R. B., & Sarason, B. R. (1983). Assessing social support: The Social Support Questionnaire. *Journal of Personality and Social Psychology, 44,* 127–139.

Sarason, I. G., Johnson, J. H., & Siegel, J. M. (1978). Assessing the impact of life changes: Development of the life experiences survey. *Journal of Consulting and Clinical Psychology, 46,* 932–946.

Schmid, A., & Peper, E. (1986). Techniques for training concentration. In J. M. Williams (Ed.), *Applied sport psychology: Personal growth to peak performance* (pp. 271–284). Palo Alto, CA: Mayfield.

Schroeder, D. H., & Costa, P. H. (1984). Influence of life event stress on physical illness: Substantive effects or methodological flaws? *Journal of Personality and Social Psychology, 46,* 853–863.

Selzer, M. L., & Vinokur, A. (1974). Life events, subjective stress, and traffic accidents. *American Journal of Psychiatry, 131,* 903–906.

Silva, J. M., & Hardy, C. J. (1991). The sport psychologist: Psychological aspects of injury in sport. In F. O. Mueller & A. Ryan (Eds.), *The sports medicine team and athletic injury prevention* (pp. 114–132). Philadelphia: F. A. Davis.

Smith, A. M., Scott, S. G., O'Fallon, W. M., & Young, M. L. (1990). Emotional responses of athletes to injury. *Mayo Clinic Proceedings, 65,* 38–50.

Smith, A. M., Scott, S. G., Wiese, D. M. (1990). The psychological effects of sports injuries. *Sports Medicine, 9,* 352–369.

Smith, R. E. (1980). A cognitive-affective approach to stress management training for athletes. In C. Nadeau, W. Halliwell, K. Newell, & G. Roberts (Eds.), *Psychology and motor behavior and sport* (pp. 54–72). Champaign, IL: Human Kinetics.

Smith, R. E. (1985). A component analysis of athletic stress. In M.

R. Weiss & D. Gould (Eds.), *Sport psychology for children and youth: Proceedings of the 1984 Olympic Scientific Congress* (pp. 107–111). Champaign, IL: Human Kinetics.

Smith, R. E., Johnson, J. H., & Sarason, I. G. (1978). Life change, the sensation-seeking motive, and psychological distress. *Journal of Consulting and Clinical Psychology, 46,* 348–349.

Smith, R. E., & Smoll, F. L. (1988). Technical Report No. 86-1066-86. New York: William T. Grant Foundation.

Smith, R. E., Smoll, F. L., & Curtis, B. (1979). Coach effectiveness training: A cognitive-behavioral approach to enhancing relationship skills in youth sports coaches. *Journal of Sport Psychology, 1,* 59–75.

Smith, R. E., Smoll, F. L., & Ptacek, J. T. (1990). Conjunctive moderator variables in vulnerability and resiliency research: Life stress, social support and coping skills, and adolescent sport injuries. *Journal of Personality and Social Psychology, 58,* 360–369.

Smith, R. E., Smoll, F. L., & Schultz, R. (1988). *The athletic coping skills inventory: Psychometric properties, correlates, and confirmatory factor analysis.* Unpublished manuscript, University of Washington.

Spielberger, C. D. (1966). *Anxiety and behavior.* New York: Academic Press.

Spielberger, C. D., & Associates (1973). *Manual for State-Trait Anxiety Inventory for Children.* Palo Alto, CA: Consulting Psychologist's Press.

Stuart, J. C., & Brown, B. M. (1981). The relationship of stress and coping ability to the incidence of diseases and accidents. *Journal of Psychosomatic Research, 25,* 255–260.

Taylor, S. E. (1990). Health psychology: The science and the field. *American Psychologist, 45,* 40–50.

Thompson, D. L. (1986). *The use of guided imagery to reduce postoperative pain.* Unpublished master's thesis, University of Arizona, Tucson, AZ.

Turk, D., Meichenbaum, D., & Genest, M. (1983). *Pain and behavioral medicine: A cognitive-behavioral perspective.* New York: Guilford Press.

Valliant, P. M. (1981). Personality and injury in competitive runners. *Perceptual and Motor Skills, 53,* 251–253.

Vaux, A., Phillips, J. U., Holly, L., & Thomson, B. (1986). The Social Support Appraisals (SS-A) Scale: Studies of reliability and validity. *American Journal of Community Psychology, 14,* 195–219.

Wehlage, D. F. (1980). Managing the emotional reaction to loss in athletics. *Athletic Training, 15,* 144–146.

Weinberg, R., & Genuchi, M. (1980). Relationship between competitive trait anxiety, state anxiety, and golf performance: A field study. *Journal of Sport Psychology, 2,* 148–154.

Weiss, M. R., & Troxel, R. K. (1986). Psychology of the injured athlete. *Athletic Training, 21,* 104–154.

Wiese, D. M., & Weiss, M. R. (1987). Psychological rehabilitation and physical injury: Implications for the sportsmedicine team. *The Sport Psychologist, 1,* 318–330.

Williams, J. M. (1986). Psychological characteristics of peak performance. In J. M. Williams (Ed.), *Applied sport psychology: Personal growth to peak performance* (pp. 121–132). Palo Alto, CA: Mayfield.

Williams, J. M., & Andersen, M. B. (1986). The relationship between psychological factors and injury occurrence. *Psychology of Motor Behavior and Sport, Abstracts: North American Society for Psychology of Sport and Physical Activity (Abstract),* 15.

Williams, J. M., Haggert, J., Tonymon, P., & Wadsworth, W. A. (1986). Life stress and prediction of athletic injuries in volleyball, basketball, and cross-country running. In L. E. Unestahl (Ed.), *Sport psychology in theory and practice.* Orebro, Sweden: Veje.

Williams, J. M., Tonymon, P., & Andersen, M. B. (1990). Effects of life-event stress on anxiety and peripheral narrowing. *Journal of Behavioral Medicine, 16,* 174–181.

Williams, J. M., Tonymon, P., & Andersen, M. B. (1991). Effects of stressors and coping resources on anxiety and peripheral narrowing in recreational athletes. *Journal of Applied Sport Psychology, 3,* 126–141.

Williams, J. M., Tonymon, P., & Wadsworth, W. A. (1986). Relationship of stress to injury in intercollegiate volleyball. *Journal of Human Stress, 12,* 38–43.

Williams, J. M., & White, K. A. (1983). Adolescent status systems for males and females at three age levels. *Adolescence, 28,* 381–389.

Wolff, B. B., & Horland, A. A. (1967). Effect of suggestion upon experimental pain: A validation study. *Journal of Abnormal Psychology, 72,* 402–407.

Wolpe, J. (1974). *The practice of behavior therapy.* New York: Maxwell House.

Woolfolk, R. L., Murphy, S. M., Gottesfeld, D., & Aitken, D. (1985). Effects of mental rehearsal of task motor activity and mental depiction of task outcome on motor skill performance. *Journal of Sport Psychology, 7,* 191–197.

Yaffe, M. (1983). Sports injuries: Psychological aspects. *British Journal of Hospital Medicine, 29,* 224–228.

Young, M. L., & Cohen, D. A. (1979). Self-concept and injuries among female college tournament basketball players. *American Corrective Therapy Journal, 33,* 139–142.

Young, M. L., & Cohen, D. A. (1981). Self-concept and injuries among female high school basketball players. *Journal of Sports Medicine, 21,* 55–59.

Zuckerman, M., Kolin, E. A., Price, L., & Zoob, I. (1964). Development of a sensation-seeking scale. *Journal of Consulting Psychology, 28,* 477–482.

OVERTRAINING AND STALENESS: PSYCHOMETRIC MONITORING OF ENDURANCE ATHLETES

John S. Raglin

World record performances in sporting events have continually improved since the inception of the modern Olympics. Many factors have played a role in these improvements, including the application of increased knowledge in nutrition, physiology, and biomechanics, as well as advances in equipment design. However, the single most important factor in the improvement is generally regarded to be changes in training practices (Bompa, 1983). For example, when Roger Banister broke the 4-minute mile in 1954, he was training about 30 minutes a day (Bannister, 1989). Since that time, the volume and intensity of training for the mile as well as for many other sporting events has increased dramatically. During the 5 years spanning 1975–1980 alone, it has been estimated that the total number of yearly training hours in various sports has increased by 10 to 22% (Bompa, 1983).

Although intensive physical training, or overtraining, is generally considered to result in improved athletic performance, it also presents the risk of worsened performance to the athlete. With longer competitive seasons and with increasingly extensive training practices, more individuals are placed at risk of experiencing performance problems due to overtraining. The negative consequences of intensive training have been known for many years (Parmenter, 1923) and were referred to as "staleness" in the writings of the early American sport psychologist Coleman Griffith (1926), but it is only recently that researchers have made concerted attempts at more fully understanding and preventing problems resulting from overtraining. The purpose of this chapter is to review selected issues surrounding overtraining. The initial section will outline issues related to the definition of overtraining and staleness. Subsequent sections will present the findings from overtraining research involving both physiological and psychological paradigms. The final part of the chapter will describe the findings from an ongoing longitudinal research effort intended to enhance our understanding of the psychobiological processes underlying overtraining in the sport of swimming.

TRAINING AND OVERTRAINING

The physiological and metabolic adaptations of the healthy individual resulting from training or a consistent program of moderate physical exercise have been well described (Åstrand & Rodahl, 1986), and precise exercise prescriptions for improving and maintaining physical fitness have been established (American College of Sports Medicine, 1990). For example, it is known that 20 minutes of aerobic activity performed at a moderate intensity three to five times a week for a minimum of six weeks will typically result in a 15–20% gain in aerobic fitness in the average individual (American College of Sports Medicine, 1990). This information has served as the basis for the implementation of exercise prescriptions for both healthy and clinical populations. In addition, moderate physical training has consistently been associated with positive changes in mental health, including reduced anxiety and depression (Morgan & Goldston, 1987).

The type of activity previously described differs greatly from the training performed by athletes involved in sports that require a high degree of aerobic fitness. Typically endurance athletes already have acquired the physiologic adaptations that result from moderate physical training, and more intense training is viewed as necessary if continual improvements in performance are to take place. The most commonly utilized example of this process involves periodic cycles of progressively intensified training, often referred to as overtraining, which is undergone in the attempt to maximize performance (Ryan, 1983). Overtraining programs may range in length from days to months, depending on factors such as the type of sport involved, or the importance of the competition the athlete is preparing for (Bompa, 1983). Typically overtraining is initiated by systematically increasing the training (i.e., distance and intensity) above usual levels. This progressively increasing training schedule eventually asymptotes, and further increases in training volume or intensity are not undergone. For the purposes of this chapter, overtraining will be operationalized as a process involving progressively increased training to a high absolute level that is in excess of more routine training undertaken to maintain performance.

Overtraining is an example of the overload principle (Harre, 1982), and it is intended to tax the athlete maximally. The traditional view of overtraining is to stress the athlete to the point where incomplete recovery occurs between training sessions (Harre, 1982). This incomplete recovery is considered necessary for evoking a compensatory "physiological superadaptation" (Bompa, 1983; Harre, 1982). A schedule of overtraining is usually followed by a period of gradually reduced training referred to as a taper. Tapers are periods of recovery undertaken with the goal of eliciting peak performance, and they are initiated several days or weeks prior to important competitions. It has been hypothesized that the improvements in performance that occur following tapers are the result of physiological supercompensations to overtraining (Harre, 1982), but compensatory responses have not been clearly identified (Neufer, 1989). The entire process of systematically increasing and decreasing training has been referred to as periodization (Matveyev, 1981).

The physiological consequences of overtraining have been investigated, but the findings have often been inconclusive or contradictory (Hanne-Paparo, 1983; Kuipers & Keizer, 1988). Performance improvements resulting from overtraining do not appear to involve metabolic or cardiovascular adaptations beyond those that occur with less intense training (Costill, King, Thomas, & Hargreaves, 1985). There is some evidence, however, suggesting that performance improvements comparable to those gained by overtraining can be achieved by a reduced training volume that is performed at a high intensity (Costill, 1985), although these findings have been challenged (Counsilman & Counsilman, 1990). Specifically it has been contended that the external validity of research in support of reducing training volume is limited because of the use of nonelite athletes as test subjects (Counsilman & Counsilman, 1990). Despite the fact that there is only a limited understanding of the physiological changes that occur as a result of overtraining and tapering (Neufer, 1989), research has demonstrated that significant improvements in power and performance occur following tapering (Costill et al., 1985).

It should be emphasized that there is no generally accepted definition of overtraining or staleness, and the literature is fraught with contradictory uses of these and other terms. Unfortunately the situation has not improved since this problem was noted 20 years ago by Wolf (1971), and it remains a source of controversy and confusion that clouds much of the literature. This issue extends beyond one of semantics alone. An analogous debate existed for many years for workers in the area of depression and other mental disorders. However, following the establishment of a generally agreed-upon diagnostic system, many advances were made in both research and practice. The terminology associated with intense physical training and its outcomes will subsequently be reviewed.

MODELS OF OVERTRAINING AND STALENESS

In the case of European researchers, overtraining commonly refers to both the training per se as well as the negative consequences resulting from the training (Harre, 1982; Kereszty, 1971). A narrower view limits the definition of overtraining to the pathological consequences of intense training (Bompa, 1983; Mellerowicz & Barron, 1971). Other terms have been used synonymously with overtraining, including: overwork, overstress, overreaching, overuse, stagnation, staleness, and burnout. Others have attempted to circumvent this lack of consistency by distinguishing between intense training that results in a positive outcome and training where compromised performance or breakdown occurs. In this definition, *overtraining* represents properly prescribed training work that results in improved performance, whereas *overwork* is regarded as either a maladaptive training schedule, or the symptoms that arise as a consequence of such a schedule (Counsilman & Counsilman, 1990). This differentiation, however, is problematic because a categorization of the training as adaptive or maladaptive cannot be accorded until the outcome (i.e., either improved or worsened performance) has been determined. That is, if athletes undergoing increased training do not break down, then the training is considered adaptive (i.e., overtraining), whereas if the same training results in worsened performance it is then defined as excessive (i.e., overwork).

The utility of this definition is further limited by the wide variation in the capability of athletes to undergo overtraining. For example, Counsilman (1971) stated that Mark Spitz, winner of seven gold medals at the 1972 Olympics, never trained more than 10,000 yards per day. However, other members of the same team trained up to 15,000 yards per day, but these individuals never achieved the performance levels of Spitz. This substantial variability in prescribing exercise to athletes must be considered, and it should be recognized that the most talented performers are not necessarily the ones with the greatest capacity to endure periods of overtraining. Furthermore, athletes of equal capability may display heterogenous responses to a given overtraining stimulus. Research has demonstrated that athletes of similar capacity respond differentially to standardized overtraining regimens (Costill et al., 1988; Morgan, Costill, Flynn, Raglin, & O'Connor, 1988) in that some individuals are resistant to the negative effects of intensive training, while others are quite vulnerable. Thus a particular training schedule may improve the performance of one individual, be insufficient for another, and be damaging for a third. The outcome (i.e., either adaptation or maladaptation) may be influenced by the particular psychobiological characteristics of the athlete (i.e., predispositions).

It is possible, of course, to impose training schedules of such an excessive degree that the majority of athletes will experience adverse consequences; however, this normally should not occur. Nevertheless in the case of particularly resistant individuals, such training regimens may be adaptive and necessary for peak performance. An example of this would be the training employed by Vladimir Salnikov, a Soviet Olympic swimming champion. Salnikov completed 2-week overtraining schedules, called "attack mesocycles," and these cycles involved swimming up to 20,000 meters a day (Counsilman & Counsilman, 1990). This distance obviously would be excessive for many elite swimmers, but it appeared to facilitate the performance of Salnikov. In conclusion, it is proposed that a distinction between adaptive and maladaptive training is arbitrary as any such definition is wholly dependent on the eventual outcome of the training. Overtraining can result in either worsened or improved performance, and the result is dependent on the programmatic aspects of the training and the characteristics of the athlete.

In contrast to the previous definitions, Morgan, Brown, Raglin, O'Connor, and Ellickson (1987) describe overtraining as a process. Overtraining is regarded as a stimulus consisting of a systematic schedule of progressively intense physical training of a high absolute and relative intensity. Moreover, overtraining is considered an integral and necessary aspect of endurance training, whereas staleness is regarded as an undesirable response that is a consequence or product of overtraining. It is proposed that viewing overtraining as a process with variable outcomes is preferable to previous approaches. This conceptualization is particularly useful in that it avoids the confounding of *cause* (i.e., overtraining) from *consequence* (i.e., staleness). Moreover, this approach also has the advantage of allowing for evaluations of the dose-response relationship between overtraining and staleness.

THE STALENESS SYNDROME

Staleness represents the complete manifestation of the negative effects of overtraining, and Morgan, Brown, Raglin, O'Connor, and Ellickson (1987) have proposed that staleness warrants syndromic status. The hallmark of the staleness syndrome is a persistent plateau or worsening in performance that is not improved by short-term rest periods or reduced training. Staleness is regarded as a syndrome because it is associated with a host of symptoms and signs, including disturbances in mood and sleep, loss of appetite and weight, reduced libido, as well as muscle soreness and heaviness (Barron, Noakes, Levy, Smith, & Millar, 1985; Kuipers & Keizer, 1988; Morgan, Brown, Raglin, O'Connor, & Ellickson, 1987). Some researchers have further subdivided staleness into sympathetic and parasympathetic types (Kereszty, 1971), but it is unclear if these categories actually represent distinct subtypes of staleness or reflect factors such as: (1) training type and schedule, (2) individual response differences, or (3) different stages in the staleness sequelae.

The staleness syndrome is associated with an array of behavioral symptoms and disturbances, but the primary psychological feature of staleness is depression. Morgan, Brown, Raglin, O'Connor, and Ellickson (1987) have noted that the symptoms associated with the staleness syndrome are identical with those of major depression. Moreover, many of the symptoms commonly ascribed to staleness are similar to the description of melancholia (Kling et al., 1989), a form of depression associated with hypercortisolism.

STALENESS VERSUS BURNOUT

It should be noted that the term *burnout* has often been used as a synonym for staleness in the sport science literature (Henschen, 1990; Mahoney, 1989; Rowland, 1986), but it is suggested here that these should be considered distinct syndromes. Burnout was first used to describe the distress resulting from emotional and mental demands particular to work in the human services fields (Maslach, 1976). More recently it has been proposed that stressors associated with other fields of endeavor, including business (Garden, 1990) and sport (Smith, 1986), can also result in burnout.

Although it is probable that some athletes are in fact negatively affected by the emotional demands of athletics and become "burned out" from sport participation (Smith, 1986), burnout is not analogous to staleness. Stressors due to competition and social factors have been suggested to play a role in the development of staleness (Ryan, 1983), but subsequent research (Morgan et al., 1988) has shown that the physical demands of increased training alone are sufficient to provoke symptoms of distress and staleness. Staleness and burnout do share some common features, including mood disturbances such as depression, but changes in mood disturbances in endurance athletes have been shown to be directly related to training load (Morgan et al., 1987) rather than cognitive factors such as interest or motivation. Loss of interest and motivation are considered central features of burnout, but stale athletes who are unable to perform are often found to be highly motivated

(Raglin, Morgan, & Luchsinger, 1990). Furthermore staleness is associated with physical and perceptual symptoms not found in burnout (Dressendorfer & Wade, 1983; Kuipers & Keizer, 1988).

Staleness is best regarded as a concept particular to sport that has no clear corollaries in nonathletic settings. In fact one of the insidious aspects of staleness is that when a plateau in performance becomes evident, the response of many athletes is to train harder (Counsilman, 1971). This can result in a vicious circle where the athlete exacerbates the condition by continually increasing training in the attempt to overcome a plateau. In this instance the athlete may be regarded as being overmotivated, but not burned out!

Distinguishing staleness from burnout is of more than heuristic interest as it has been proposed (Henschen, 1990) that staleness can be treated by the conventional cognitive tools of applied sport psychology such as imagery or relaxation. But because stale athletes often need both medical and psychological attention (Barron et al., 1985; Morgan, Brown, Raglin, O'Connor, & Ellickson, 1987a), treatment of staleness by means of imagery or other similar techniques is unfounded and may actually place the stale athlete in greater peril by delaying needed psychotherapy or medical treatment. This example illustrates the necessity that interventions in sport psychology take into account the potential for underlying pathology, both physical and mental, prior to the initiation of treatment.

PREVALENCE AND INCIDENCE OF STALENESS

Although staleness is considered to be a problem inherent among endurance activities of all types (Ryan, 1983), information concerning its prevalence in most sports is lacking. However, in the case of elite long-distance runners it has been found that 60% of females (Morgan, O'Connor, Sparling, & Pate, 1987) and 64% of males (Morgan, O'Connor, Ellickson, & Bradley, 1988) have had at least one episode of staleness during their running career. This observation is notable for two reasons. First, staleness is sometimes viewed as a problem largely confined to nonelite or pre-elite athletes, but these research findings demonstrate that elite athletes are at significant risk. Moreover, the 60% prevalence of staleness observed in elite female distance runners is nearly twice as great as that observed in nonelite distance runners (i.e., 33%), a difference attributed to the greater training distance performed by the elite runners (Morgan et al., 1987). Second, it has been proposed that female athletes may be more prone to becoming stale (Ryan, 1983), but the previous findings imply that females are at no greater risk than males and that they should be treated accordingly.

The incidence of staleness during a single monocycle, or training season, across various sports is unknown. However, Morgan, Brown, Raglin, O'Connor, and Ellickson (1987) report an average one-year incidence rate of staleness ranging from 5 to 10% in college swimmers. However, the external validity of these figures is limited, and research is needed to determine the rate of staleness in other sports. Furthermore, the rate of staleness for a given sport can be influenced by training load as well as a given coach's ability in preventing its occurrence.

SUSCEPTIBILITY VERSUS RESISTANCE

There are indications that athletes differ in their susceptibility to staleness. In research involving college swimmers (Raglin & Morgan, 1989), it was found that of those who developed staleness during their freshman season, 91% became stale in one or more subsequent college seasons. In contrast, only 30% of those swimmers who did not become stale as freshmen developed the disorder in a subsequent season, and the difference of 61% between the two groups was statistically significant ($P < 0.05$). This finding suggests that athletes display consistent differences in their propensity toward becoming stale by the age of 18 and indicate that some individuals are at a greater risk of suffering the disorder than others. This observation is consonant with research involving depression, where it has been found that the frequency of affective illnesses increases as a function of the number of previous episodes, with later episodes tending to be more severe (Zis & Goodwin, 1979). Also, some data suggest that the experience of an episode of depression may predispose an individual toward experiencing future episodes (Lewinsohn, Steinmetz, Larson, & Franklin, 1981). The possibility that stale athletes become sensitized to staleness in a similar fashion should be investigated.

It is not known what factors contribute to the risk of staleness, but it seems reasonable to hypothesize that both genetic and developmental variables play a role. Opportunistic factors such as nutritional deficiencies (Costill et al., 1988) and physical illness (Mellerowicz & Barron, 1971) may also place athletes at greater risk of becoming stale. Psychological factors may also be involved. Knapp and colleagues (1984) found that speed skaters with lower levels of self-motivation were more prone to mood disturbance during overtraining than those with higher levels. In contrast, Raglin et al. (1990) found that the same measure of self-motivation did not differ between rowers who displayed excessive mood disturbance during overtraining and those who did not. Further investigation of psychological factors that may predispose athletes toward becoming stale is clearly needed.

TREATMENT OF STALENESS

It has long been recognized (Griffith, 1926; Karpovich, 1941) that staleness can be effectively treated with prolonged rest. In many cases, rest periods of 1 to 2 weeks are sufficient (Bompa, 1983), but it has been observed that even after 6 months of rest, some stale athletes still exhibit disturbed neuroendocrine function (Barron et al., 1985) and have not fully recovered. Alternative or adjunctive forms of treatment, including the use of steroids, sedatives, or vitamins, have been reported (Kereszty, 1971; Mellerowicz & Barron, 1971), but controlled trials involving these or other putative remedies have not been conducted. Staleness can be effectively treated by rest or prevented outright by not training hard, but these obviously are not desirable options for the competitive athlete. Because an episode of staleness can adversely affect performance for a period of months or longer, the development of a reliable means of preventing the disorder in athletes who must overtrain is clearly preferable to treatment.

DISTRESS

In some cases athletes may exhibit several of the symptoms of staleness yet be able to maintain adequate performance. It is proposed that this phenonemon, referred to here as distress, represents an intermediate stage in the development of staleness. This condition is similar to what has been sometimes described as overreaching or overtraining (Kuipers & Keizer, 1988; Ryan, 1983).

Distressed athletes are characterized by training-induced mood disturbances of a greater magnitude than athletes fully capable of tolerating overtraining (Morgan, et al., 1988; Raglin & Morgan, 1989). Although distressed athletes do not necessarily display a plateau or decrement in performance, the perceptual cost of set workloads is greater in distressed athletes as compared to athletes undergoing the same training but who are relatively free from perturbed mood. In other words, the affected athlete is at a stage where he/she can still compete and train at customary levels, but the training is perceived as more effortful than work performed during less intense training cycles. The sensitivity of perceived exertion as a means to assess such overtraining effects has been demonstrated by O'Connor, Morgan and Raglin (1991). These investigators have shown that as swimmers undergo increased training, ratings of perceived exertion by means of the Borg 6-20 scale become significantly elevated following standardized swimming tasks (200-yd swim at 90% $\dot{V}O_{2max}$).

The identification of a distinct intermediate stage of staleness is considered important because distress is viewed as an acute response to overtraining, which may be treated by short-term interventions. Furthermore it has been found that approximately 30% of college varsity female and male swimmers become distressed at some point during the course of a season (Raglin & Morgan, 1989). Coaches who are aware of which athletes are suffering from distress could intervene by reducing training or providing short rest periods, and this would theoretically lead to enhanced performance. If, however, appropriate remedies are not implemented, or if overtraining is extended for too long a period, distress can evolve into the staleness syndrome.

It is clear that an inescapable consideration in the use of overtraining involves the risks inherent with the procedure. Although a cycle of overtraining followed by a training taper is generally believed to improve performance, overtraining can have a counterproductive effect and may result in worsened performance. Furthermore the means by which overtraining results in improved or worsened performance are poorly understood. The challenge for the coach is to schedule overtraining regimens such that each athlete is optimally, but not overly, stressed. This task is made even more difficult by the fact that there are no simple formulae to prescribe overtraining, and because athletes differ greatly, both in their capacity to overtrain as well as in their resistance to its negative effects. Because of these challenges there has been a considerable interest in developing the means to identify athletes who will become stale following overtraining.

PHYSIOLOGICAL MONITORING OF ATHLETES

As there is an obvious advantage in preventing rather than treating staleness, a number of attempts have been made to identify reliable early warning signs of staleness. The majority of efforts in this area involve the investigation of putative physiological markers (Urhausen & Kindermann, 1989). These have included cardiovascular, metabolic, or hormonal measures, but the results of this research have largely been inconclusive (Hanne-Paparo, 1983; Kuipers & Keizer, 1988). For example, an increase in resting morning heart rate has been commonly cited as an indicator that an athlete is training excessively and in danger of becoming stale (Burke, 1990; Dressendorfer, Wade, & Scaff, 1985; Ryan, 1983). However, other investigators have either failed to find changes in resting heart rate for athletes undergoing increased training (Callister, Callister, Fleck, & Dudley, 1990; Kirwan et al., 1988), or have shown decreases in heart rate (Kuipers & Keizer, 1988; Wolf, 1971). This discrepancy is also common among other physiological markers. In reviews of the effects of overtraining, it has been concluded that most physiological variables do not display changes that can consistently be distinguished from the consequences of less intensive training (Hanne-Paparo, 1983; Kuipers & Keizer, 1988).

Some physiological variables behave more predictably during overtraining. Serum creatine kinase (CK), considered to be an indicator of muscle trauma, has consistently been found to be elevated in athletes who are overtraining. For example, Burke, Falsetti, Feld, Patton, and Kennedy (1982) reported that CK values parallel alterations in training distance in swimmers. Although CK has been found to be sensitive to changes in training load, CK values do not appear to differ between athletes who are able to tolerate overtraining and those who show signs of staleness. In a study involving swimmers who underwent 10 days of intensive training (Kirwan et al., 1988), CK was also significantly elevated, but the degree of increase was similar between athletes who could tolerate the training and those who experienced difficulty in completing the training. These findings suggest that CK may be a sensitive marker of alterations in training volume, but that it is not useful in discriminating distressed or stale athletes from those able to tolerate the training.

Investigators have identified several markers that appear to be more specific to staleness. Depletions of muscle glycogen (Costill et al., 1988) and neuroendocrine disturbances, including altered testosterone/cortisol ratios (Adlercreutz et al., 1986), depressed hypothalamic function (Barron et al., 1985), and hypercortisolism (O'Connor, Morgan, Raglin, Barksdale, & Kalin, 1989) have been found in athletes displaying signs of staleness. Furthermore, these factors are either less marked or absent in athletes capable of handling overtraining. Although it has been suggested that each of these mechanisms may contribute toward the development of staleness, it has not been determined if these are causal factors that precede the onset of staleness or, rather, are outcomes of the disorder. Consequently, the value of monitoring these markers in an effort to prevent the onset of staleness is not entirely clear at the present time. In addition, the use of such sophisticated physiological markers in field settings is often precluded because of technological requirements, as well as the expense and time required to perform these assays.

In summary, it appears that although some physiological markers are related to changes in training volume (e.g., Burke et al., 1982), the majority of these markers do not reliably indicate the onset of staleness (Hanne-Paparo, 1983; Kuipers & Keizer, 1988). This may reflect the inadequacy of the variables in question, the lack of consistency among overtraining protocols, or the heterogeneity of the subject groups studied. Some physiological variables, such as muscle glycogen, do appear to be more specific to staleness, but the predictive efficacy of these putative markers remains to be demonstrated. Also, the use of repeated muscle biopsies to monitor athletes would be neither practical nor ethically defensible.

PSYCHOMETRIC MONITORING

Psychological responses to overtraining have been found to be far more consistent than physiological changes. In a summary of a 10-year research project involving the psychometric assessment of college swimmers, Morgan and colleagues (1987) have reported that overtraining is consistently associated with elevations in mood disturbance. Several psychological variables have been evaluated in this research effort, and the most consistent findings have been obtained with the Profile of Mood States (POMS) (McNair, Lorr, & Dropplemann, 1971). The POMS measures the specific mood states of tension, depression, anger, fatigue, and confusion. These factors can also be combined to provide an indication of global or total mood disturbance by adding the negative mood states (tension, depression, anger, fatigue, confusion) and subtracting out the positive factor of vigor. A constant of 100 is usually added to prevent the occurrence of negative scores. The POMS has four instructional sets, and the standard set ("last week including today") was utilized in the majority of this research.

During the initial phases of this research project, mood was assessed at only three points during training: (1) early in the training season when training was minimal, (2) at mid-season during increased training, and (3) late season following a training taper. Figure 39–2 displays representative findings from this work. Early in the season, the swimmers displayed the "Iceberg Profile," a profile indicative of positive mental health that has been found in successful athletes across a variety of sports (Morgan, 1985b).

During overtraining, however, mood disturbance significantly increased, and this is reflected by a flattened mood profile shown in the center panel of Figure 39–1. An important point illustrated by this example is that despite the increase in mood disturbance during increased training, the mood profile of the swimmers at this time did not differ remarkably from that of the population norms (i.e., T50) for the POMS. That is, although these athletes experienced sig-

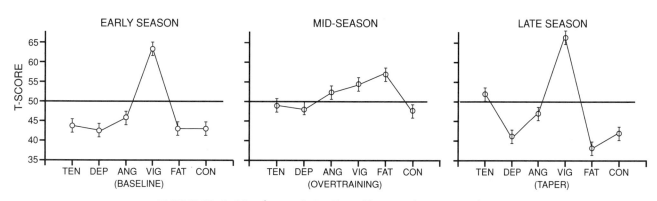

FIGURE 39–1. Mood state (POMS) profiles at select points during competitive training in a group (N = 35) of female and male college varsity swimmers.

nificant elevations in mood disturbance as a consequence of increased training, their profiles do not look abnormal. This finding has implications in the therapeutic process as an athlete complaining of depression or other mood disturbances would appear to be normal when compared to the general population norms for the POMS. However, he/she could be one to even two standard deviations above his/her customary level.

When training is significantly reduced following a taper, the swimmers again exhibit the Iceberg Profile as shown in the panel at the right side of Figure 39–1. Although this posttaper profile does not differ significantly from the early-season values, it has often been found that following a training taper the mood profile is slightly better than the baseline values, suggesting that physiological supercompensation may be paralleled by a corresponding improvement in mood. It should be noted that the previous example reflects the responses of the team as a whole and does not take into account individual differences. It has been found that some swimmers are apparently resistant to intensive training and maintain a positive mood profile throughout the training season, whereas others display extreme negative shifts in mood.

Subsequent stages of this longitudinal research involved administering the POMS more frequently during training, and the findings of this work indicated that a dose-response relationship exists between training volume and mood disturbance. This relationship is illustrated in Figure 39–2; increases in training are paralleled by corresponding elevations in mood disturbance, and mood improves as training is reduced. Additionally female and male swimmers undergoing comparable training schedules consistently display similar mood scores (Morgan, Brown, Raglin, O'Connor, & Ellickson, 1987; O'Connor, et al., 1991; Raglin, Morgan, & O'Connor, 1991.)

The dose-response relationship between training and mood disturbance is not limited to swimmers, and it has also been documented in speed skaters (Guttmann, Pollock, Foster, & Schmidt, 1984), wrestlers (Morgan, Brown, et al., 1987), rowers (Raglin et al., 1990), and run-

ners (Wittig, Houmard, & Costill, 1989). These findings do not support evidence that exercise can serve as a means of both treating or preventing depression and other emotional disturbances (Morgan & Goldston, 1987). Rather they illustrate the fact that different psychological effects can occur, depending on the intensity and duration of the activity (Raglin, 1990a). Not only does overtraining influence mood in a negative and predictable manner, but the neuroendocrine disturbances observed during overtraining are similar to those found in clinically depressed groups. This further supports the proposition that the relationship between overtraining and depression is causal in nature (Raglin, 1990a). In contrast, the research in the area of exercise and mood improvement is generally less compelling, and a causal relationship between exercise and mood improvement has not been as convincingly demonstrated (Morgan, 1985a; Raglin, 1990a).

MOOD DISTURBANCE IN STALENESS AND DISTRESS

Research has shown that mood responses during overtraining are greater in athletes who exhibit performance decrements and other signs of staleness. For example, in a study involving college swimmers who underwent 10 days of intensive training (Costill et al., 1988; Morgan et al., 1988), swimmers who experienced the most difficulty completing the training (i.e., distress) also displayed the largest increase in mood disturbance. Additionally swimmers were accurately classified as healthy or distressed on the basis of either psychometric or physiological data, and the rate of agreement between these classification schemes was 89%. In other words, selected physiological and psychological variables can discriminate between healthy and distressed athletes during overtraining, and a close correspondence exists between these measures.

Raglin et al. (1990) monitored a group of female college rowers undergoing training with the POMS. It was observed that the incidence of significant mood disturbance during heavy training was nearly three times greater in unsuccessful rowers compared to rowers who were later chosen to compete in a regional championship meet. In an investigation involving swimmers undergoing overtraining, O'Connor et al. (1989) found that individuals identified by the coach as exhibiting staleness-related performance problems possessed depression levels that were significantly greater than swimmers free of performance problems. It was also found that swimmers suffering from performance problems had significantly greater elevations in salivary cortisol, a hormone linked to depression, in comparison to swimmers who were performing adequately.

In each of the previous examples, athletes who became distressed or stale during the course of the training displayed the iceberg profile at the outset of training and at the early stages of training could not be distinguished from those who did not become stale from a psychometric stand-

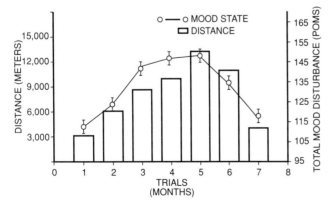

FIGURE 39–2. Changes in mood disturbance (POMS) and training distance across a competitive season in a group of college varsity swimmers.

point. That is, athletes who became stale as a result of overtraining possessed the positive psychological characteristics commonly noted in athletes (Morgan, 1985b) prior to undergoing increased training. It was only following exposure to increased training that differences emerged.

Stale athletes can also be distinguished from those who are simply overtrained by their responses to reductions in training volume. Athletes who show signs of distress or staleness consistently display incomplete improvements in mood disturbance following reduced training. For example, Raglin et al. (1990) found that unsuccessful females on a college rowing team continued to possess elevated mood disturbance following a taper, whereas the better performers responded fully to the taper. Similarly, O'Connor et al. (1989) observed that although stale swimmers displayed a reduction in depression following reduced training, the improvement was significantly smaller in comparison to swimmers judged as healthy. In addition, the levels of depression in the stale athletes remained significantly elevated above baseline values following a taper at the end of the season.

In summary, overtraining has been consistently found to result in mood disturbance, and the magnitude of disturbance has been found to be greater in athletes suffering from the syndrome known as staleness. Evidence indicates that mood disturbances associated with staleness are not fully abated during training tapers, indicating that treatment restricted to reducing training is not adequate. These findings act to reinforce the contention that complete rest is necessary in such cases. In view of evidence showing close correspondence between psychological factors and selected physiological (Morgan et al., 1988) or neuroendocrine changes (O'Connor et al., 1989), staleness is most accurately viewed as a psychobiological phenomenon, and hypothalamic-pituitary-adrenal dysregulation may play a crucial role in the disorder (Barron et al., 1985; O'Connor et al., 1989).

In comparison to most physiological markers, mood changes as measured by the POMS seem reasonably specific and sensitive to staleness. However, it must be noted that the detection of staleness is conducted post hoc. That is, distressed or stale athletes have reliably been characterized psychometrically only after the occurrence of significant performance problems. Presently there is no established means of identifying stale swimmers in the early stages of the disorder through either psychometric or physiological monitoring.

There are additional limitations in the use of psychometric means to monitor and prevent the occurrence of staleness, and these are specifically related to the POMS. Raglin et al. (1991) assessed the changes in specific POMS factors (i.e., tension, depression, anger, vigor, fatigue, confusion) during training in female and male college swimmers. It was found that each of the specific mood factors consistently displayed a dose-response relationship with training distance, with the exception of tension. Tension either remained elevated during training tapers or else continued to increase while training was reduced, and this

nonspecific effect could potentially contribute a source of error in using total mood disturbance as a means to identify athletes thought to be at risk.

It also has been shown that in the case of healthy swimmers (Raglin et al., 1991; Morgan et al., 1987a), the POMS factors of fatigue and vigor consistently display the largest changes in response to overtraining compared to the other mood factors, whereas depression is less affected. Thus the typical mood disturbance profile in response to increased training in athletes who do not become stale primarily involves disturbances in fatigue and vigor, with depression being the least affected of all mood factors. This disturbance profile contrasts greatly with that found in the stale athlete where depression is more pronounced (Morgan et al., 1987a; O'Connor et al., 1989). Thus large increases in POMS total scores may reflect either a "normal" overtraining-induced disturbance that consists primarily of somatically related disturbances (i.e., vigor and fatigue), or a disturbance related to staleness where depression is more pronounced. Additionally it has been found that changes that occur in tension, unlike other POMS factors, sometimes do not reflect alterations in training volume. Each of these problems limit the potential use of the POMS total score as a means to identify distressed or stale athletes.

In an effort to surmount these limitations, research has been initiated to create a psychometric measure of distress that is sensitive to affective changes associated with increased training (Raglin & Morgan, in review). This Training Distress Scale (TDS) is intended to identify athletes who are in the early stages of maladaptation in order that appropriate action can be taken before the condition develops into staleness. The initial validation process utilized POMS data collected during six competitive seasons on 186 members of the University of Wisconsin men's and women's varsity swimming teams. A series of discriminant function analyses were performed to determine which items from the POMS differentiated healthy athletes from those who developed distress or staleness. From these analyses a subset of POMS items was derived that reliably identified distressed or stale swimmers at levels significantly greater than base-rate predictions. Although establishment of the construct validation of the TDS is ongoing, recent pilot work has shown that the TDS is superior in both monitoring and identifying stale athletes in comparison with classifications based on the POMS total (Raglin, 1990b).

The previously described lines of research have culminated in a recent attempt to utilize psychological monitoring of swimmers undergoing overtraining in an applied framework. Morgan and colleagues (Morgan, 1990) monitored 40 college swimmers undergoing a 4-week overtraining period. The psychological responses to overtraining were assessed daily for each swimmer in an attempt to prevent the occurrence of distress or staleness. With the permission of the swimmers and coaches, training distance was titrated (i.e., either decreased or increased) at regular intervals on the basis of POMS and TDS scores. It was found that no swimmers on either the men's or women's team became stale this particular season, and this represented an improvement over previous seasons. It should be emphasized that further research is needed before training load can be routinely titrated on the basis of psychometric responses. Specifically future investigations should incorporate control and placebo comparison groups.

The previously described approach to intervention represents a unique form of psychological intervention that stands in contrast to the majority of paradigms employed in sport psychology. The effectiveness of sport psychology interventions is commonly judged by the extent to which they are accepted and perceived as desirable by the athlete (Gould et al., 1990). However, in the previously described monitoring study, the intervention sometimes involved placing the athlete at somewhat greater distress by increasing training volume. These individuals would experience an elevation in mood disturbance because of the intervention, but in theory should eventually perform better as a consequence of it.

Finally it should be emphasized that the athletes in this investigation agreed to participate with the full knowledge that this type of intervention might occur, and they were aware that the coaches would receive some information concerning their own mood responses. It was also made clear to all of the athletes that they were free to withdraw their participation in the study at any time without penalty. Additionally in this research and each of the previously described monitoring investigations, it is necessary to intervene and provide appropriate support services in cases where the physical or psychological disturbance take on pathological proportions.

SUMMARY

It is a common practice for athletes in endurance sports to periodically undergo periods of intensive training, or overtraining, in the attempt to maximize performance (Ryan, 1983). Although overtraining is generally considered to be necessary for the achievement of optimal performance, it is recognized that this procedure places athletes at risk of developing the syndrome known as staleness. The hallmark of staleness is the experience of a chronic plateau or decay in performance. Stale athletes are also characterized by a host of behavioral and psychological disturbances, particularly depression. Considerable research has been performed in the attempt to provide a greater understanding of staleness, as well as to develop a means of preventing its occurrence. Of this research, the psychological findings appear to be the most consistent. The primary finding from this work is that there is a dose-response relationship between training and mood disturbance (Morgan et al., 1987). As training distance is increased, corresponding elevations in mood disturbance occur, whereas when training is reduced, mood state improves.

Although this dose-response relationship has been observed in groups of athletes participating in a variety of sports, it has also been recognized that there is considerable variability among athletes in their responses to overtraining. Some individuals appear to be resistant to the detrimental effects of overtraining, whereas others are especially sensitive and are at particular risk of becoming stale. During periods of increasing training or overtraining, athletes who eventually become stale have been found to display mood disturbances of a greater magnitude in comparison to healthy athletes undergoing the same training (Morgan et al., 1987a; O'Connor et al., 1989). Moreover, these changes in mood have been found to be related to alterations in neuroendocrine hormones (Barron, et al., 1985; O'Connor et al., 1989) consistent with those observed in depressed patients, and this reinforces the contention that staleness should be considered a psychobiological syndrome. Reductions in training will reverse the negative psychological effects of overtraining for most athletes, but in the case of stale athletes these mood disturbances are only partially abated. Presently the only accepted treatment for staleness is rest, and stale athletes often need medical or psychological care as well.

Although recent findings concerning the psychological and physiological aspects of staleness are promising, further research is needed to determine the cause of staleness and to prevent its occurrence. Furthermore, the possibility that the staleness syndrome may be becoming more prevalent in nonendurance sports should be considered. As competitive seasons become longer and as sports incorporate more extensive training regimens, greater numbers of athletes will be at risk of staleness, indicating a need for the study of overtraining in a greater number of sports. Research paradigms that attempt to integrate psychological and physiological sources of information can potentially provide a more complete understanding of overtraining and staleness, as well as other complex issues in sport (Morgan, 1973).

References

Adlercreutz, H., Harkonen, M., Kuoppasalmi, K., Naveri, H., Huhtaniemi, I., Tikkanen, H., Remes, K., Dessypris, A., & Karvonen, J. (1986). Effect of training on plasma anabolic and catabolic steroid hormones and their response during exercise. *International Journal of Sports Medicine, 7,* 27–28.

American College of Sports Medicine. (1990). The recommended quantity and quality of exercise for developing and maintaining cardiorespiratory and muscular fitness in healthy adults. *Medicine and Science in Sports and Exercise, 22,* 265–274.

Åstrand, P. O., & Rodahl, K. (1986). *Textbook of work physiology.* New York: McGraw-Hill.

Bannister, R. (1989). *The four-minute mile.* New York: Lyons & Burford.

Barron, J. L., Noakes, T. D., Levy, W., Smith, C., & Millar, R. P. (1985). Hypothalamic dysfunction in overtrained athletes. *Journal of Clinical Endocrinology and Metabolism, 60,* 803–806.

Bompa, T. (1983). *Theory and methodology of training: The key to athletic performance.* Dubuque, IA: Kendall/Hunt.

Burke, E. R. (1990, Fall/Winter). Athletes and overtraining: How to sport it, how to avoid it. *American Athletics,* 65–69.

Burke, E. R., Falsetti, H. L., Feld, R. D., Patton, G. S., & Kennedy, C. C. (1982). Creatine kinase levels in competitive swimmers during a season of training. *Scandinavian Journal of Sports Science, 4,* 1–4.

Callister, R., Callister, R. J., Fleck, S. J., & Dudley, G. A. (1990). Physiological and performance responses to overtraining in elite judo athletes. *Medicine and Science in Sports and Exercise, 22,* 816–824.

Costill, D. L. (1985). The 1985 C. H. McCloy research lecture: Practical problems in exercise physiology research. *Research Quarterly for Exercise and Sport, 56,* 378–384.

Costill, D. L., Flynn, M. G., Kirwan, J. P., Houmard, J. A., Mitchell, J. B., Thomas, R., & Park, S. H. (1988). Effects of repeated days of intensified training on muscle glycogen and swimming performance. *Medicine and Science in Sports and Exercise, 20,* 249–254.

Costill, D. L., King, D. S., Thomas, R., & Hargreaves, M. (1985). Effects of reduced training on muscular power in swimmers. *The Physician and Sportsmedicine, 13,* 94–101.

Costill, D. L., Rayfield, F., Kirwan, J., & Thomas, R. (1986). A computer-based system for the measurement of force and power during front swim crawl. *Journal of Swimming Research, 2,* 16–19.

Counsilman, J. (1971). Handling the stress and staleness problems of the hard training athletes. *Proceedings of the International Symposium on the Art and Science of Coaching,* (pp. 15–22). Toronto, Canada.

Counsilman, J. E., & Counsilman, B. E. (1990). No simple answers. *Swimming Technique, 26,* 22–29.

Dressendorfer, R. H., & Wade, C. E. (1983). The muscular overuse syndrome in long-distance runners. *The Physician and Sportsmedicine, 11,* 116–126.

Dressendorfer, R. H., Wade, C. E., & Scaff, J. H., Jr. (1985). Increased morning heart rate in runners: A valid sign of overtraining? *The Physician and Sportsmedicine, 131,* 77–86.

Garden, A. (1990). Burnout: The effect of psychological type on research findings. *Journal of Occupational Psychology, 62,* 223–234.

Gould, D., Petlichkoff, L., Hodge, K., & Simons, J. (1990). Evaluating the effectiveness of a psychological skills education workshop. *The Sport Psychologist, 4,* 249–260.

Griffith, C. R. (1926). *Psychology of coaching.* New York: Charles Scribner.

Guttmann, M. C., Pollock, M. L., Foster, C., & Schmidt, D. (1984). Training stress in Olympic speed skaters: A psychological perspective. *The Physician and Sportsmedicine, 12,* 45–57.

Hanne-Paparo, N. (1983). Overtraining in athletes. *Olympic Review, 194,* 829–832.

Harre, D. (1982). *Principles of sports training.* Berlin, Germany: Sportverlag.

Henschen, K. P. (1990). Prevention and treatment of athletic staleness and burnout. *Science Periodical on Research and Technology in Sport, 10,* 1–8.

Karpovich, P. V. (1941). Fatigue and endurance. *The Research Quarterly, 12,* 416–422.

Kereszty, A. (1971). Overtraining. In L. A. Larson & D. E. Herrmann (Eds.), *Encyclopedia of sport sciences and medicine* (pp. 218–222). New York: Macmillan.

Kirwan, J. P., Costill, D. L., Flynn, M. G., Mitchell, J. B., Fink, W. J., Neufer, D., & Houmard, J. A. (1988). Physiological responses to successive days of intensive training in competitive swimmers. *Medicine and Science in Sports and Exercise, 20,* 255–259.

Kling, M. A., Perini, G. I., Demitrack, M. A., Geracioti, T. D., Linnoila, M., Chrousos, G. P., & Gold, P. W. (1989). Stress-responsive neurohormonal systems and the symptom complex of affective illness. *Psychopharmacology Bulletin, 25,* 312–318.

Knapp, D., Guttmann, M., Foster, C., Pollock, M. (1984). Self-motivation among 1984 Olympic speedskating hopefuls and emotional response and adherence to training. *Medicine and Science in Sports and Exercise, 16,* 114.

Kuipers, H., & Keizer, H. A. (1988). Overtraining in elite athletes: Review and directions for the future. *Sports Medicine, 6,* 79–92.

Lewinsohn, P. M., Steinmetz, J., Larson, D., & Franklin, J. (1981). Depression-related cognitions: Antecedents or consequences? *Journal of Abnormal Psychology, 90,* 213–219.

Mahoney, M. J. (1989). Sport psychology. In I. S. Cohen (Ed.), *The G. Stanley Hall Lectures* (Vol. 9, pp. 101–134). Washington, DC: American Psychological Association.

Maslach, C. (1976). Burned-out. *Human Behavior, 5,* 16–22.

Matveyev, L. (1981). *Fundamentals of sports training.* Moscow: Progress Publishers.

McNair, D. M., Lorr, M., & Dropplemann, L. F. (1971). *Profile of Mood States Manual.* San Diego: Educational and Testing Service.

Mellerowicz, H., & Barron, D. K., (1971). Overtraining. In L. A. Larson & D. E. Herrmann (Eds.), *Encyclopedia of sport sciences and medicine* (pp. 1310–1312). New York: Macmillan.

Morgan, W. P. (1973). Efficacy of psychobiologic inquiry in the exercise and sport sciences. *Quest, 20,* 39–47.

Morgan, W. P. (1985a). Affective beneficence of vigorous physical activity. *Medicine and Science in Sports and Exercise, 17,* 94–100.

Morgan, W. P. (1985b). Selected psychological factors limiting performance: A mental health model. In D. H. Clarke & H. M. Eckert (Eds.), *Limits of human performance* (pp. 70–80). Champaign, IL: Human Kinetics.

Morgan, W. P. (1990, August). Psychological effects of overtraining. In W. P. Morgan (Chair), *Psychobiologic monitoring of overtraining: A prevention model.* Symposium conducted at the National Convention of the American Psychological Association, Boston.

Morgan, W. P., Brown, D. R., Raglin, J. S., O'Connor, P. J., & Ellickson, K. A. (1987). Psychological monitoring of overtraining and staleness. *British Journal of Sports Medicine, 21,* 107–114.

Morgan, W. P., Costill, D. L., Flynn, M. G., Raglin, J. S., & O'Connor, P. J. (1988). Mood disturbance following increased training in swimmers. *Medicine and Science in Sports and Exercise, 20,* 408–414.

Morgan, W. P., & Goldston, S. E. (1987). *Exercise and mental health.* New York: Hemisphere.

Morgan, W. P., O'Connor, P. J., Ellickson, K. A., & Bradley, P. W. (1988). Personality structure, mood states, and performance in elite male distance runners. *International Journal of Sport Psychology, 19,* 247–263.

Morgan W. P., O'Connor P. J., Sparling, P. B., & Pate, R. R. (1987). Psychologic characterization of the elite female distance runner. *International Journal of Sports Medicine, 8,* 124–131.

Neufer, P. D. (1989). The effect of detraining and reduced training volume on the physiological adaptations to aerobic exercise training. *Sports Medicine, 8,* 302–321.

O'Connor, P. J., Morgan, W. P., Raglin, J. S., Barksdale, C. N., & Kalin, N. H. (1989). Mood state and salivary cortisol levels following overtraining in female swimmers. *Psychoneuroendocrinology, 14,* 303–310.

O'Connor, P. J., Morgan, W. P., & Raglin, J. S. (1991). Psychobiologic effects of 3 days of increased training in female and male swimmers. *Medicine and Science in Sports and Exercise, 23,* 1055–1061.

Parmenter, D. C. (1923). Some medical aspects of the training of college athletes. *The Boston Medical and Surgical Journal, 189,* 45–50.

Raglin, J. S. (1990a). Exercise and mental health: Beneficial and detrimental effects. *Sports Medicine, 9,* 323–329.

Raglin, J. S. (1990b, August). Development and validation of an overtraining distress scale. In W. P. Morgan (Chair), *Psychobiologic monitoring of overtraining: A prevention model.* Symposium conducted at the National Convention of the American Psychological Association, Boston.

Raglin, J. S., & Morgan, W. P. (1989). Development of a scale to measure training-induced distress. *Medicine and Science in Sports and Exercise, 21* (Suppl.), s60.

Raglin, J. S., & Morgan, W. P. (1992). *Validation of a distress scale for use in monitoring responses to overtraining.* Manuscript submitted for publication.

Raglin, J. S., Morgan, W. P., & Luchsinger, A. E. (1990). Mood state and self-motivation in successful and unsuccessful women rowers. *Medicine and Science in Sports and Exercise, 22,* 849–853.

Raglin, J. S., Morgan, W. P., & O'Connor, P. J. (1991). Changes in mood states during training in female and male college swimmers. *International Journal of Sports Medicine, 12,* 585–589.

Rowland, T. W. (1986). Exercise fatigue in adolescents: Diagnosis of athlete burnout. *The Physician and Sportsmedicine, 14,* 69–77.

Ryan, A. J. (1983). Overtraining of athletes: A round table. *The Physician and Sportsmedicine, 11,* 93–110.

Smith, R. E. (1986). Toward a cognitive-affective model of athletic burnout. *Journal of Sport Psychology, 8,* 36–50.

Urhausen, A., & Kindermann, W. (1989). Biochemical monitoring of training. In M. Kvist (Ed.), *Paavo Nurmi Congress Book* (pp. 64–67). Turku, Finland: The Finnish Society of Sports Medicine.

Wittig, A. F., Houmard, J. A., & Costill, D. L. (1989). Psychological effects during reduced training in distance runners. *International Journal of Sports Medicine, 10,* 97–100.

Wolf, J. G. (1971). Staleness. In L. A. Larson & D. E. Herrmann (Eds.), *Encyclopedia of sport sciences and medicine* (pp. 1048–1050). New York: Macmillan.

Zis, A. P., & Goodwin, F. K. (1979). Major affective disorders as a recurrent illness: A critical review. *Archives of General Psychiatry, 36,* 385–389.

·40·

PSYCHOLOGY OF DRUG USE

Mark H. Anshel

The use of drugs among sports competitors, particularly anabolic steroids and hallucinogens (the latter also referred to as mind-altering, recreational, or "street" drugs), has received widespread attention in recent years. Considerable anecdotal evidence and, more recently, additional quantitative data have surfaced, indicating that drug abuse among sports competitors is more common than previously recognized. Perhaps no source of information has been more influential toward this perception than the frequent media reports revealing the extent of drug abuse and the positive results of drug tests by high-profiled, elite athletes. Yet despite this evidence, official reaction to them has been inconsistent. Indeed, the absence of assertive and consistent responses to drug abuse among competitors has likely contributed to its proliferation. As Strauss (1987) points out, "Sports officials voice unequivocal disapproval of performance-enhancing drugs and formally ban them. Yet when violations are uncovered, punishment is inconsistent" (p. 13).

Attempts at combating drug abuse in sport must begin with an issue that has received incredibly scant attention by researchers and sports administrators—understanding the *psychological* reasons for using drugs in the first place. If these behaviors can be explained, then cognitive and behavioral strategies can be devised to help prevent and virtually eliminate this problem.

WHAT IS THE PROBLEM?

Ostensibly the reasons for ingesting these substances are to improve sport performance and, less apparently, to improve the athlete's motivation, self-confidence, and other desirable psychological states. Of course, the first problem with such practices is that ingesting these drugs is contrary to the rules of teams and sporting organizations, and in some cases is against the law. Athletes who ingest banned drugs are cheating by gaining an unfair competitive advantage (Strauss, 1987a). This is a problem of *ethics.* From a philosophical perspective, conference presenter Lawrie Woodman (see Anshel, 1990a) reports that "strict control of drug taking in sport begins with establishing equality among participants. If sport is to continue as we know it, then athletes must not have an unfair advantage" (p. 51). Cheating in sport breaks the rules, creates distrust among competitors and officials, and removes the credibility of performance outcomes (Strauss, 1987a). Thus as George Will, respected political columnist from *Newsweek,* writes, "Some athletes probably are nagged by thoughts like: 'My weight-lifting achievement is not mine, it belongs to my medicine cabinet'" (February 4, 1985, p. 85).

Another problem with drug taking is the *addictive properties* of many of these drugs. According to Julien (1981), "A person physically dependent on a drug requires that drug in order to function normally" (p. 24). Apparently the sudden stoppage of stimulants depletes the neurotransmitters, followed by a period of depression, irritability, and increased fatigue. Drugs, including anabolic steroids, are often psychologically and sometimes somatically addictive. In fact, an Australian government inquiry (*Drugs in Sport,* 1990) concluded that dependence on anabolic steroids results in psychobehavioral characteristics that are "strikingly similar" to dependencies seen with other substances (p. 63). For example, the discontinuation of steroid use, not unlike other types of drugs ingested by athletes, has been linked with depression and severe mood disturbance.

Perhaps the most important and dangerous problem with drug use in sport, is the potential *lethal effects* of drugs on the health and well-being of athletes. The literature is replete with research indicating unequivocal evidence on the detrimental medical effects of drug taking (e.g., Chappel, 1987; Donald, 1981; Julien, 1981; Strauss, 1987a). Anecdotal evidence (discussed later) has shown that athletes are literally dying from the use of so-called "performance-enhancing" drugs. So are some nonathletes who are intent on building their musculature or strength beyond the normal route gained by physical training. Apparently steroid abuse is not restricted to athletes. For example, the newspaper *USA Today* (May 3, 1990), reporting on a presentation by Dr. Conrad Andringa, of the Dean Medical Center in Madison, Wisconsin, indicated at the American Academy of Pediatrics conference that steroid use by American teenagers is rising significantly. About one in three steroid users are nonathletes, and although boys outnumber girls four to one, there is growing use among females as a means to cut body fat and increase lean muscle.

The causes of death from sport-related drug abuse are both acute (e.g., dehydration, heat stroke, cardiac arrest) and chronic (e.g., liver cancer, lymphoma, cardiac arrest). Many other physical maladies (e.g., kidney stones, irregular heart beat, sterility, hypertension) and psychological problems (e.g., heightened anxiety, suicidal tendencies, short attention span, depression, aggression, and schizophrenia) have been reported (Corrigan, 1988; Donald, 1981; Lamb, 1984). The potentially fatal effects of certain stimulants and hallucinogens (e.g., cocaine, heroin) are relatively well known. Although examples of these effects are briefly discussed later, the primary purpose of this chapter is to examine the *psychological* reasons for drug taking among athletes, and to suggest the implementation of certain strategies to combat this practice.

WHY DO ATHLETES ABUSE DRUGS?

Initially it would appear irrational that athletes who typically engage in physical and mental training for hundreds of hours in preparing for sport competition, exhibit a high ability for performance success, and possess relatively high self-confidence would feel compelled to engage in any behavior (e.g., drug taking) that would attenuate these feelings or undermine this effort. Therefore, although rarely discussed in the media or studied in academic circles, there must be a psychological rationale for drug taking in sport. Given the extensive pressure on skilled athletes to succeed and "be competitive," a view held and often communicated by their coach, perhaps it is not surprising that performers explore all possible avenues to reach—and go beyond—their performance potential.

Smith (1983) suggests two other, although less salient, reasons for the prevalent use of drugs in sport. The first reason concerns the relatively extensive use of *deterrence strategies* to combat drug taking as opposed to often neglected preventive and curative approaches. Traditionally drug testing and the threat of expulsion from sport have been the primary means of controlling illicit drug ingestion. *Curative techniques* (e.g., personal and group counseling, rehabilitation clinics, continued monitoring of athletes' behaviors) and *preventive measures,* primarily didactics (which can also have a deterrent effect), have also been employed, but with uneven success in the antidrug "arsenal" (Marcello et al., 1989; Tobler, 1986).

The second reason for drug use among competitors is the failure of coaches and sport administrators to enact selected cognitive and behavioral strategies that could predictably inhibit drug use (Anshel, 1991a). The effectiveness of these techniques, discussed in depth later, is directly linked to determining the likely psychological *causes* of drug use in sport. The influence of coaches, peers, and parents, all relatively untapped resources in combating drug abuse, could then be utilized. Preventive strategies would replace reliance on punitive measures to inhibit drug use (e.g., threats, expulsion from the team, using substances to mask the effects of other drugs—cheating). The virtual absence of this information in the extant literature forms the primary purpose of this chapter.

PURPOSES OF THE CHAPTER

This chapter will identify the likely underlying psychological and social causes of drug use in sport, with implications for team and organizational leaders, sport psychology consultants, and parents in the use of selected cognitive and behavioral strategies. Due to the variety of drugs, drug categories (e.g., performance enhancing versus mind altering), the type of sport in which the athletes are involved (e.g., those requiring improved aerobic capacity, strength, or steadiness), and situational factors (e.g., boredom, stress, or the expectations of others such as coaches, fans, parents, sponsors, the media, peers, and teammates), it is likely that different strategies will be compatible with certain situations and individuals more than others. Still, athletes share similar types of experiences and psychological pressures and performance demands so that many of the issues described can be applied to most athletic participants.

The review of selected literature will focus on drugs that have been banned by sport organizations because they are thought to have a facilitative effect on athletic performance. The International Olympic Committee (IOC) refers to the act of ingesting banned drugs as *doping* (Prokop, 1990). *Doping* has been defined as "the administering or use of substances in any form alien to the body or of physiological substances in abnormal amounts and with abnormal methods by healthy persons with the exclusive aim of attaining an artificial and unfair increase of performance in competition. Furthermore various psychological measures to increase performance in sports must be regarded as doping" (Prokop, 1990, p. 5).

The International Olympic Committee has classified five doping categories: stimulants (including hallucinogens such as cocaine that increase central nervous system processes), anabolic steroids, narcotic analgesics (e.g., opium, marijuana, and others that increase euphoria and reduce pain), beta-adrenergic blockers, and diuretics (Chappel, 1987; Park, 1990). Alcohol (and depressants in general), local anaesthetics, and corticosteroids (anti-inflammatory drugs that relieve pain) are not on the IOC list but are tested for in selected international competitions (Chappel, 1987; *Drugs in Sport,* 1990). In addition, two doping methods, blood doping and pharmacological, chemical, and physical manipulation, have also been banned. The effects of these drugs have also been categorized as psychomotor-stimulating substances (stimulants), sympathomimetic substances, and substances stimulating the CNS (e.g., amphetamines, cocaine) or reducing heart rate and blood pressure (e.g., beta blockers). Not included in this review are drugs that are not banned by the IOC and, therefore, are not against the policies of national and international sport organizations, at least for mature-age athletes. Examples include depressants (e.g., alcohol), nicotine, diet regimens (e.g., carbohydrate loading), amino acids, and vitamins.

BRIEF REVIEW OF DRUGS BANNED IN SPORT

The psychological reasons for drug taking can be better understood after reviewing the psychophysiological effects of these banned substances (for complete reviews of these drugs, see Mottram, 1988; Park, 1988; Strauss, 1987; & Williams, 1983).

Anabolic Steroids

Anabolic steroids have been used by athletes in an attempt to increase their strength and power. These steroids increase male hormone (androgen) and decrease female hormone (estrogen) levels. This explains how steroid use results in masculinizing effects such as new facial and body hair, a lower voice, increased muscular bulk and strength, and interference with reproductive function in both sexes. More seriously, prolonged steroid use may cause cancer of the liver and lymphatic system, heightened aggression, premature heart disease, and death (Goldman, 1984).

For example, Lubell (1989) reviewed the literature on the effect of anabolic steroids on aggressive behavior. Despite recognizing the normal limitations of self-reported data, she concluded that "these drugs pose risks not only to consumers of these substances but also to the general public by increasing the odds of violent and antisocial behavior. Apparently several cases in the legal system have associated prolonged steroid use with the insanity plea in recent years, including the case of a skilled pistol shooter who held her sport psychologist hostage at the Australian Institute of Sport. The defendent escaped a jail sentence due to her apparent prolonged abuse of anabolic steroids, which ostensibly produced her violent behavior (*New Idea,* September 8, 1990, pp. 12–13).

Anabolic steroids may also promote cardiovascular disease. Cohen, Noakes, and Benade (1988) measured the effects of anabolic steroid intake on serum total cholesterol (TC) concentrations on male power lifters over eight weeks. Results showed a significant increase in mean TC level, particularly in the low-density lipoprotein (LDL) fraction. LDL, often referred to as "bad" cholesterol, is a known predictor of cardiovascular disease. The authors also found,

however, that mean TC concentration regressed to near baseline levels within two months of total cessation from drug taking.

Another concern about steroids is their addictive properties. Although Smith (1983) contends that steroid "addiction" is a psychological, not a physiological, phenomonen, Brower, Blow, Beresford, and Fuelling (1989) have concluded from a case study of a 24-year-old weight lifter that anabolic steroids, psychoactive compounds, "may even have an addictive potential similar to other drugs of abuse . . ." (p. 31). In addition, "neuronal androgen receptors have been identified in the brain suggesting the neurochemical basis for their psychoactive effects" (p. 32).

There is considerable controversy concerning the benefits of anabolic steroids on athletic performance. Corrigan (1988) asserts that the link between steroid ingestion and improved sport performance is virtually nonexistent. Lamb's (1984) review of related literature not only supports this view, but also reveals that even the desired outcome of gaining strength from steroid use is uncertain. It would appear that any placebo effect notwithstanding (discussed later), steroids *may* improve performance only when strength is a primary component of the sport (e.g., weight lifting, shot-putting). The effect of steroids on performing sport skills that do not rely on strength and power for success is negligible (Anshel, 1990a; Corrigan, 1988).

Stimulants

Stimulant drugs increase the rate and hence the work capacity of the heart, central nervous system, and respiratory system. They are banned in sport due to their neural-stimulating and cardiac-stimulating effects, and they improve athletic performance primarily by inhibiting mental and physical fatigue. Stimulants are divided into three groups: psychomotor (e.g., amphetamines, cocaine, and most diet suppressants), sympathomimetic amines that stimulate the sympathetic and autonomic nervous systems, and miscellaneous central nervous system stimulants (e.g., caffeine and other drugs found in many prescription and over-the-counter cold remedies).

Narcotic Analgesics (Anti-Inflammatories)

Narcotic analgesics have been used by athletes for their pain-killing properties, to slow or stop the inflammation and swelling of tissue, to reduce fever, and to produce feelings of well-being. Examples include codeine, heroin, morphine, and opium. Harmful effects of all analgesics include gastrointestinal disturbances, physical and psychological dependence, and depression of respiration. Nonnarcotic analgesics, which are not habit-forming and do not affect the central nervous system, include aspirin, Tylenol, and others. As pain suppressants, these drugs enable an injured competitor to continue playing despite tissue damage and injury. Anti-inflammatories can actually reduce performance effectiveness in some sports due to their sedative effect. All analgesics are toxic in large doses.

Beta-Adrenergic Blockers

Perhaps best known for the treatment of high blood pressure and some forms of heart disease, beta-blockers are among the few drugs banned by the IOC that do not induce dependence. They have been used to steady and slow the heart rate, which may decrease anxiety and have a steadying effect on natural body tremors. They have been used by rifle and pistol shooters, archers, and bowlers to aid performance.

Diuretics

Diuretics have been used to increase the rate at which water and salts leave the body as urine. The primary purposes for using diuretics are the acute reduction of weight, to overcome fluid retention (often induced by using androgenic steroids), and to modify the excretion rate of urine to alter the urinary concentrations of banned drugs. Athletes, such as jockeys, wrestlers, and boxers, have used diuretics in order to "make weight" for a competition. A rapid depletion of body fluids, in general, and potassium, in particular, can produce heart arrhythmias. Nausea, heat stroke, blood clotting, reduced blood volume, and muscle cramps are other possible outcomes (Russell, 1990).

Two types of drugs that actually inhibit rather than facilitate performance include drugs that alter perceptions (hallucinogens) and drugs that reduce anxiety and tension (depressants).

Hallucinogens

Hallucinogens are often referred to as "recreational," "mind-altering," or "street" drugs (Bell et al., 1987; Julien, 1981). Their primary effect is to alter the perceptions of incoming stimuli. The IOC does not describe these drugs as a separate category of banned drug because it is their effects on the central nervous system that usually places them in the category of stimulant or narcotic analgesic. Because they inhibit response and decision-making time and attentional focus, these drugs inhibit rather than enhance sport performance. Marijuana (a sedative), LSD, PCP, and cocaine (examples of stimulants) are examples. Of course, in addition to being banned by sporting organizations, the use of these drugs is against the federal laws of most countries.

Depressants

Ideally, depressants relieve tension, reduce anxiety, and have a steadying effect on the nervous or fearful athlete. However, the result is often reduced inhibition, which, in turn, reduces judgment and heightens risk taking. In this way, depressants may impair rather than foster sport performance. Because they are addictive, heavy and prolonged use of these drugs may result in severe withdrawal symptoms. Barbiturates, sedative-hypnotics, and alcohol are examples of this form of drug.

Blood Doping

Blood doping involves removing approximately one liter (about two units) of the athlete's blood about one to two months before the competition and then freezing and storing the blood. The athlete's frozen red blood cells are then infused back into the body immediately prior to the competition, producing increased red cell mass and hemoglobin count of up to 15%, improving maximum aerobic capacity. The effect lasts up to two weeks. Ostensibly this technique increases oxygen uptake—the blood's oxygen-carrying capacity—and hence aerobic (endurance) performance. Although having no medical dangers if performed by a physician, the practice is unethical and falls into the IOC's definition of banned drugs because it involves the ingestion of a substance in an abnormal quantity or via an abnormal route of entry into the body to increase performance. Despite the apparent benefits, the results of studies on the effects of blood doping on actual endurance performance have been equivocal.

Why do some athletes ingest these banned substances? As indicated earlier, despite a surprising paucity of research examining the psychological factors that underlie drug use in sport, specific causes and explanations may be identified based on the extant anecdotal and scientific research. First, however, in order to place the validity of this research in perspective, it is necessary to review some of its limitations.

LIMITATIONS IN PAST RELATED RESEARCH

Defining Terms

Research concerned with the prevalence and causes of drug taking among athletes is not unflawed. The first problem concerns agreement on the operational definition of the term *drug* as used within the framework of drug abuse in sport. Athletes ingest different types of drugs for different reasons. Whereas certain investigations have been concerned with the performance-enhancing category (e.g., steroids, stimulants, beta-adrenergic blockers, and so on), while others have focused on hallucinogens (e.g., marijuana, cocaine) or, more commonly, tobacco and alcohol. It is important to differentiate between approved drug usage in medical treatment (e.g., narcotic analgesics such as opium, morphine, and codeine to diminish the perception of pain and therefore reduce suffering from injury or the selected use of steroids to expedite healing from injury) as opposed to drugs that are used to affect motor performance (Chappel, 1987). A competitor who wants to relieve pain from an injury or even prevent the onset of pain, particularly in contact sports, is likely to use—and abuse—any one of several drugs to serve this purpose. The use of drugs to relieve pain may be an end in itself rather than a means to an end (e.g., improving performance or altering perceptions) (Chappel, 1987). In addition, some researchers in nonsport areas include the use of alcohol and tobacco as drug-related behavior, whereas studies involving athletes center more on performance-enhancing and hallucinogenic substances (*Drugs in Sport,* 1990).

An operational definition of drug abuse is also connected to difficulties in generalizing the relative prevalence and causes of drug use in various age groups and among different sports. For instance, it would appear that anabolic steroid use is more prevalent among older, higher skilled competitors than among individuals involved in youth sports. Beta blockers (i.e., drugs that slow selected physiological processes) might be used among pistol and rifle shooters and archers, but not among competitors in contact sports (Bell & Doege, 1987). Thus the various categories and explanations for drug use may not always be mutually exclusive but rather are interactive.

A second problem is determining appropriate from inappropriate drug use, that is, distinguishing between drug use and drug abuse. Julien (1981) contends that the term *drug abuse* is difficult to define because it implies "the use of any drug for other than its assigned purposes" (p. 209), where the concept of "assigned purposes" is vague. Julien prefers the use of the term *drug misuse* to "describe the use of any drug (legal or illegal) for a medical or recreational purpose when other alternatives are available, practical, or warranted, or where drug use endangers either the users or others around them" (p. 210). Thus medically related drug use might include the treatment or prevention of a diagnosed disease or the alleviation of physical or mental discomfort. Recreational drug use, on the other hand, would be to relieve anxiety, achieve a state of disinhibition or euphoria, expand creative abilities, achieve an altered state of consciousness or mood, or escape from uncomfortable or oppressive surroundings.

Research Design

A third limitation in the drug literature is concerned with research design—the lack of random selection in obtaining subjects in related studies. Subjects in most of the drug studies compete at a university in selected areas of a given country. Cross-cultural and ethnic/racial differences in sport and exercise participation have been scant. In their review of related literature, Duda and Allison (1990) concluded that despite evidence of ethnic/racial variability in the areas of psychomotor performance and motor development, "there has been little attempt to consider the ways in which race/ethnicity affects psychological processing and behavior" (p. 117). The authors contend that this limitation "... ignores the general psychology literature reflecting the effect of culture on perceptions and affective responses" (p. 122). In an area of study that has implications for drug abuse in sport, Duda and Allison acknowledged

several cross-cultural studies and gender comparisons on the importance of goal achievement and competitiveness.

For example, their review indicated that American male athletes score significantly higher on these dimensions than male nonathletes, female athletes and nonathletes, and males in other cultures. This may indicate a greater perceived need of American male athletes than others for ingesting performance-enhancing drugs—or the use of mind-altering drugs to escape from sport-related stress and anxiety. Thus generalizing results of drug studies for different areas of a given country and between countries' sexes is tenuous.

Underreporting

Another limitation concerns the underreporting of actual drug use. For example, Pope, Katz, and Champoux (1988) reported that only 17 of 1,010 (1.7%) of the male college student athletes in their sample admitted to ingesting anabolic steroids. The authors admit to the problem of underreporting in comparing their results with other studies in which a far higher percentage of steroid use—as high as 20%—is reported among university competitors (e.g., Dezelsky, Toohey & Shaw, 1985; Heitzinger et al., 1986). In another study, Ljungqvist (1990) reported that "50% of those who [replied to a survey] said that doping was not a problem in their sport." He concluded that "This is an incorrect judgement by those federations" (p. 31). Although the reasons for underreporting are no doubt partially based on ethical and legal considerations, it is also likely that some athletes consume banned substances at the direct or indirect suggestion of their coach. Whether or not athletes would divulge information about the coach's direct (e.g., making an overt request to take drugs) or indirect role (e.g., expectations of extreme and/or rapid weight loss) in fostering the ingestion of banned substances is not known but perhaps unlikely.

Reliance on Anecdotal Evidence

Finally, and perhaps most important, there is the prevalence of anecdotal evidence, usually based on empirical observations, for determining the existence and extent of drug use in sport, in contrast to a more scientific, quantifiable approach. Anecdotal evidence consists of information provided by individuals based on their own experiences or perceptions. Thus a magazine article describing the tribulations of an athlete's addiction to anabolic steroids or the case of someone who died as a result of abusing performance-enhancing drugs is anecdotal. Anecdotal evidence in detailing drug use in sport is widespread and, in fact, forms the primary source of information in this area.

The limitation with this type of information is its inability to provide evidence for the extent of drug use; nor does it provide a cause-and-effect relationship between using steroids and any subsequent effects on health and well-being. As Anshel (1990a) explains, the primary limitations of anecdotal evidence, unlike planned case study or single-subject research, "is often contradictory, difficult to evaluate, and of limited use in assessing the extent to which the phenomenon under study is predictable or valid" (p. 209). To date, much of the related literature concerning drug use in sport has been predicated on individual experiences. Perhaps this avenue has been virtually the only method of acknowledging evidence of the problem. As was indicated earlier, one plausible explanation for this dilemma is the problem of underreporting—the refusal to divulge known information honestly. Still, the limitations of anecdotal evidence must be recognized as a less than reliable method of obtaining valid information, generalizing the results, and drawing conclusions.

Despite these research concerns, anecdotal evidence can still play a vital role in overcoming some of the inherent limitations of self-report data concerned with the illicit activity of drug use. Smith (1983), in opposing reliance on survey research, suggests that a "... more valid source of data would come from a participant observer—a trainer, a team physician, possibly even a player ... who could collect observational data on drug use" (p. 79). In fact, much of the extant literature has relied on precisely the empirical observations of others for obtaining this type of information (e.g., *Drugs in Sport,* 1989, 1990).

It is imperative to recognize the underlying causes of drug taking so that strategies can be devised to reduce, if not eliminate, the problem. Younger athletes are particularly susceptible to the health hazards of ingesting these substances (as is discussed later). Yet despite their apparent widespread use, Murray (1984) asserts that skilled athletes do not like taking steroids. They do so because they are faced with using them or placing themselves at a severe competitive disadvantage. "The pressure to use steroids is like the pressure ... not [to] let the other side gain an advantage; [to] do whatever your opponent does ... or risk being left behind and losing" (p. 196). The fact that athletes continue to ingest anabolic steroids despite mounting evidence of their deleterious effects on health and well-being indicates the extensive pressure to which athletes are exposed to succeed—quite literally at any cost.

LITERATURE REVIEW OF DRUGS IN SPORT

To date, the proliferation of anecdotal evidence concerning drug use in sport has been provided primarily by media reports and government inquiries. Although anecdotal evidence provides a valuable source of information about the existence of a phenomenon, reliance on this form of input without scientific proof may do more harm than good. For example, Shroyer (1990) points out that the prevalent use of individual examples of drug effects has actually contributed to rather than inhibited drug use in sport. She concluded that without long-term studies, little evidence exists that could guide young athletes away from steroids. Many athletes continue to use steroids because they do not

see sufficient evidence that the medical damage is as great as it has been depicted. The result is lost credibility among physicians and educators, who are perceived as overstating the effects of drugs.

Nevertheless it is apparent that anecdotal evidence provided the initial impetus for recognizing the existence of a drug problem in sport—and it continues to do so. Given the difficulty in obtaining valid data from athletes and coaches about behaviors that are undeniably unethical (against the rules) and unhealthy, the paucity of more scientific evidence and relatively heavy reliance on empirical observations is understandable. However, what is of primary importance is to avoid confusing anecdotal reports with the scientific validity and reliability of scientific research.

Anecdotal Evidence

Much of the anecdotal literature, as reported in the print media, has been derived from the empirical observations of athletes themselves. For example, former American Olympic Gold Medal hurdler Edwin Moses (October 10, 1988) asserts that "... at least 50 percent of the athletes in the high-performance sports such as track and field, cycling and rowing would be disqualified if they weren't so adept at beating the tests" (p. 57). Australian Olympic team runner Gael Martin told the (Australian) Senate Standing Committee (*Drugs in Sport,* 1989) that "30 percent of track and field athletes were using steroids" (p. 188), herself included, while training at the Australian Institute of Sport. One likely reason for drug intake is to "stay competitive." According to Martin, "... in track and field, I would say in events below 800 meters and especially for women, ... [not taking drugs] would leave us far behind the rest of the world" (p. 45).

Then there is the case history of selected competitors and the self-reports on their drug experiences. A story in *Sports Illustrated* (October 24, 1988) detailed the effects of prolonged steroid use on Tommy Chaikin, a skilled (American) football lineman with the University of South Carolina. In a self-effacing report on the factors that lead to his "addiction" to anabolic steroids, Chaikin's report provides significant insight into numerous psychological and social pressures that foster drug use in sport: the influences of coaches who encourage steroid use by stating the need to "be competitive," the unspoken but sanctioned use of performance-enhancing drugs by the absence of team rules or of any communication that discouraged drug ingestion. According to Chaikin, "I felt I had the coach's encouragement. . . . he told me, 'Do what you have to do, take what you have to take" (p. 88). Chaikin contends that "... college athletes feel tremendous pressure to succeed," due to the expectations of parents. "Nobody wants to sit on the bench and be a failure" (p. 88). His prolific steroid taking almost took his life. Heightened chronic aggression, severe acne, backache, insomnia, testicular shrinkage, hair loss, depression, poor vision, inability to cope with stress, chronic anxiety, poor concentration, and, even more serious, hypertension, heart murmur, and benign tumors resulted. Only surgery, the immediate cessation of taking steroids, and counseling saved his life. Perhaps not surprisingly, Chaikin says the coaches never called him in the hospital, nor did the university offer to pay any medical expenses. The university claimed his health problems were not related to playing for the team.

Perhaps the most widely known anecdotal evidence for drug use in elite sport was derived from Canadian world-class sprinter Ben Johnson, who strongly asserted to a Canadian government inquiry that his coach knowingly gave him a substance that was banned by international sport organizations (*Time,* June 26, 1989). "Charlie [Francis] was my coach.... If Charlie gave me something to take, I took it" (p. 57). In fact, this coach's testimony at the same inquiry supported Johnson's contention. Francis told Johnson (and other sprinters) "that drugs marked the only route to international success and admitted that he provided such chemicals to his charges" (p. 57). In fact, this coach's testimony at the same inquiry supported Johnson's contention.

The most tragic consequence of drug abuse is death. As reported in the (Sydney, Australia) *Daily Telegraph* (October 26, 1989), a 23-year-old bodybuilder died of cardiac arrest hours before entering the Mr. Australia contest. Police reports indicated that he had ingested 20 tablets of potassium chloride and 11 diuretic tablets within 24 hours. All of the medications were available over the counter. This incident provides ample evidence of the extent to which athletes will go to succeed, literally at all costs.

A more recent and, for Americans, highly publicized example of the fatal consequences of prolonged use of anabolic steroid and growth hormones, is the case of former NFL star defensive player Lyle Alzado. Alzado admitted to taking these drugs over many years at a cost of $20,000–$30,000 per year. Tragically he was diagnosed as having a rare form of brain lymphoma (cancer) in April 1991, at which time he developed the Lyle Alzado National Steroid Education Program to educate young people about the damaging and life-threatening effects of anabolic steroids and human growth hormones ([Durham, NC] *Sun-Herald,* May 15, 1992). Lyle Alzado died of his disease on May 14, 1992. Although doctors could not conclude that steroid use actually caused his cancer, abuse of these drugs has been linked to prostate and liver cancer.

Is it appropriate to link steroid abuse with ingesting mind-altering drugs? Mr. Ron Heitzinger (*Athletic Business,* 1984), director of a consulting firm that specializes in drug education to students and athletes in the United States, claims that the use of steroids and "recreational" drugs often occurs in the same athletes. In fact, he has found that some competitors—almost always forming a subgroup on a team—believe that the recreational use of any drug, from marijuana to steroids, may increase their performance. However, another subgroup on the team abuses drugs because of the so-called "Superman Complex" (discussed later). These players feel that their physical conditioning and current high level of function-

ing will supercede any possible deleterious effect of drugs on their performance. They perceive getting caught as virtually impossible.

Heitzinger asserts that the failure to have specific rules, not providing education (a practice that has been changed in most programs since this interview), not looking at drug abuse as a serious issue, and taking the extreme approach of banning the offending player from the team are the wrong responses. His experiences with athletes confirms widely held perceptions that "serious" sports competitors must deal with the psychological discomfort of dealing with sport in addition to the normal challenges of adolescence. He explains drug use in sport in this way: "There's so much [pressure] put on them to perform, whether it's sports or grades ... that they're trying to minimize that pain. [The players] think they can get rid of the pain by using alcohol and drugs, because it's pleasurable. But ... they're never going to learn to cope [by using drugs]" (p. 54). Heitzinger contends that sport serves as a vehicle to actually reduce dependence on recreational drugs by giving players the ambition to succeed at something. It is the pressures placed on them that accompany their ambitions of success and often initiate drug use, rather than the inherent demands of athletic competition. After all, it has been widely reported that the most common reason young athletes give for participating in sport is to "have fun" (Anshel, 1990c). At some point, sport participation becomes less "fun" and more "work."

Drugs and Weight Lifting/Power Lifting

Perhaps no sport participants have received more recognition for abusing anabolic steroids than those who compete in weight lifting. Weight lifting is a competitive Olympic sport governed by the rules of the International Weightlifting Federation (IWF). The winner lifts the highest total weight on two styles of lift: the snatch and the clean and jerk. Power lifting, on the other hand, is not an Olympic sport. It consists of three lifts: the back squat, the bench press, and the deadlift. Although explaining the movements of each skill is beyond the scope of this chapter, what is important is that the obvious reliance on strength in these sports makes them a high-risk sport for drug abuse. Based on a plethora of anecdotal evidence in the two Australian government inquiries (*Drugs in Sport,* 1989, 1990), the distribution and intake of anabolic steroids in this sport is apparently prolific. What is particularly unique about weight lifting is that virtually all participants, including coaches and medical staff, actually encourage drug use, most often the anabolic steroid testosterone. Examples abound.

Not surprising has been the high number of athletes who have tested positive for steroids (testosterone) after winning medals. According to the Australian government inquiry *Drugs in Sport* (1990), positive drug tests—and disqualifications—were detected in two Canadian weight lifters in the Pan American Games (1983), two weight lifters at the Canadian Weightlifting Federation Competition (1984), eight finalists at the Seoul Olympic Games (1988), and the Gold Medal winner and two other finalists at the 1990 Commonwealth Games. In addition, after a positive drug test was found with the Bulgarian bantamweight Gold Medalist at the 1988 Olympic Games, the entire Bulgarian weight lifting team left for home and refused additional drug tests. The inquiry concluded that drug use in weight lifting is rampant.

More alarming is the support of steroid use by weight lifting coaches. For example, the head weight lifting coach at the Australian Institute of Sport (AIS) (until December 1988) "had supplied and administered anabolic steroids and other banned substances to athletes at the AIS" (*Drugs in Sport,* 1990, p. 148). In addition, "[the coach] admitted he provided the doped urine samples on a number of occasions" to the testing laboratory to circumvent testing procedures (p. 150). Finally, the executive director of the Victorian Weightlifting Association "has, over a long period of time, given to and encouraged the use by his lifters of anabolic steroids" (p. 160).

Allegations of unethical practices were also aimed at the physician who was accountable to the Australian Weightlifting Federation—apparently an example of "the fox guarding the chicken coop." In the inquiry, the physician was accused of forewarning the athletes about the times of impending drug tests and of misinterpreting the test results. No positive drug tests were found among the weight lifters during this physician's tenure as test supervisor. The government committee concluded that this physician committed numerous "indiscretions," despite the doctor's denials of any wrongdoing.

The Australian Powerlifting Federation received allegations of misconduct that virtually mirrored the findings regarding weight lifters. For example, in addition to the multiple incidences of positive drug tests among the athletes, the committee heard testimony that "drug testing in powerlifting became a joke from the very outset because the two appointed drug testing officials were known to be pro-drugs" (*Drugs in Sport,* 1990, p. 242).

Given the plethora of reports in the media concerning drug use, an exhaustive review of the anecdotal literature would be prohibitive. Literally hundreds, perhaps thousands, of articles and other reports, most notably linked to several Olympic Games and other world-class competitions, have confirmed the widespread use of drugs in sport. Providing only cursory evidence in this chapter is intended to reflect the antecedent causes of these self-destructive and unethical behaviors among sport performers (Strauss, 1988). Certainly the causes of drug use in sport varies in accordance with the types of drugs ingested and the level of competition. It should not be surprising, then, that various causes of drug abuse (e.g., boredom versus strength improvement) are based on different personal needs or occur in response to different objectives. It is apparent, however, that the pressures to succeed in elite sport are extraordinarily high. A review of the scientific literature further supports this contention.

Review of Scientific Research

Research on drug use in sport has centered primarily on performance-enhancing drugs, particularly anabolic steroids. How widespread is this behavior? As discussed earlier, underreporting is highly likely in this segment of the literature. For example, Pope, Katz, and Champoux (1988) investigated the prevalence of anabolic steroid use in American college males. Of the 1,010 respondents, only 17 (1.7%) reported using steroids. Four subjects used steroids primarily to improve personal appearance, while the goal of the other respondents, all competitive athletes, was to improve sport performance. Yesalis, Herrick, Buckley, Friedl, Brannon, and Wright (1988) examined anabolic steroid use in American elite body builders. Of the 45 out of 61 competitors who responded to the survey (74%), 15 admitted to having used steroids. Some users also reported having taken diuretics, amphetamines, and human growth hormone.

In their review of related literature, Tricker, Cook, and McGuire (1989) indicate that "between 3 and 20% of [American] college athletes may have used drugs illegally" (p. 155). Anabolic steroid use is pervasive among athletes from male and female high school seniors to contestants in the Mr. America contest (Chappel, 1987). In addition, a survey of 93 National Football League athletes showed that 60% admitted to using amphetamines to improve performance (Cohen, 1979). Drug ingestion by athletes is not unique to the United States. For example, according to an Australian government inquiry (*Drugs in Sport,* 1989), about 70% of Australia's elite swimmers and Olympic track and field squad are thought to have ingested a performance-enhancing aid (p. 62). Bell and Doege (1987) reviewed the literature comparing the use of nonprescribed drugs by athletes and nonathletes. With the exception of the use of anabolic steroids, no significant differences existed between sport competitors and noncompetitors.

Perhaps one reason for continued drug use among athletes is the absence of full agreement among medical personnel about drug abstention. In a recent study of 280 Australian sports trainers who had recently completed a basic or specialty training course and who work in both youth and elite sport, 10% believed there was nothing wrong with young athletes taking performance-enhancing drugs under supervision. While 80% of the sample believed adolescents between ages 12 and 18 were being increasingly exposed to drugs in sport, 6% believed the athletes need the drugs to remain competitive. In addition, fewer than 5% saw it as their role to educate athletes on this topic; they believed this responsibility should belong to the athletes' parents (*The Australian,* May 8, 1991). Bell et al. (1987), on the other hand, suggest that medical personnel, particularly physicians, should be the primary educators of drug use to sport performers.

Although research of a scientific nature has been concerned with the prevalence of drug use in sport, most studies have not focused on its antecedent causes. In a relatively rare study, Anshel (1991b) conducted personal interviews with elite American athletes competing in nine sports. The focus of the study was to ascertain the athletes' feelings about steroid and recreational drug use on his or her team, based on their personal interactions with teammates. The performers were approached over a three-year period (1986 through 1988). The subjects included 94 males and 32 females, ages 18.2 to 23.4 years.

In order to overcome the inherent dangers of under-reporting, a common problem in related literature (Anshel, 1990b; Pope et al., 1988; Williams, 1989), information about the participant's personal use of drugs was not solicited, although respondents were free to include this information. Thus the survey's content was aimed toward the subjects' *perceptions* concerning the likely causes of drug ingestion in sport based on their own experience or firsthand knowledge about incidences of drug taking on their team.

Of the 126 athletes surveyed, 81 (64%) revealed "known" drug use on their team. More specifically, 68 (72%) of the 94 male subjects interviewed and 13 (40%) of the 32 female subjects contended that teammates used a drug acknowledged as illegal or banned from their sport. Forty-three percent (494 of the athletes' 1,156 responses) acknowledged drug use for the purpose of enhancing performance as opposed to recreational use. These are extraordinary report rates, far exceeding the admitted drug use in other surveys (e.g., English, 1987; Pope et al., 1988). This may be due to the personal interview technique used in this study in contrast to the more typical mailed questionnaire. A summary of these results are listed in Table 40–1.

In view of previous research and anecdotal evidence indicating greater use of performance-enhancing and mind-altering (recreational) drugs among sport competitors, the following literature review will focus on these two categories. Physical, psychological/emotional, and social explanations for taking drugs are offered within each of these two categories.

PHYSICAL PERFORMANCE-RELATED DRUG USE

Physical Causes

There are different categories of drugs, one of which has the perceived influence of enhancing sport performance. Two of the most common types of drugs that serve this purpose are psychomotor stimulants and anabolic steroids (Donald, 1983). As indicated earlier, despite evidence to the contrary, one of the most common reasons for drug ingestion is to enhance performance or a component of it such as strength, endurance, aerobic work, or reaction/response time (Lamb, 1984; Williams, 1989). Inversely the intake of substances such as hallucinogens, often referred to as recreational drugs, reduces the speed and efficiency of motor responses.

Pain Reduction. Athletes will take drugs to attenuate pain with no prescription and without the coach's knowledge.

The reasons most often cited for taking drugs for this purpose include to avoid disappointing the coach or losing one's starting status (more typical of the male subjects) (Anshel, 1991b; Donald, 1983). Not all pain-reducing substances are banned in sport. Aspirin and anaesthetic injections (e.g., xylocaine), for instance, are considered legal to reduce or prevent pain. Morphine, however, is banned from sport. According to Donald (1983), "The ban is because of the addictive properties of morphine and other narcotics which have been made illegal. . . ." (p. 34). Nevertheless pain is inherent in most sports. Thus another important reason for banning drugs as a pain reducer, in addition to their addictive properties, is the likelihood of further, more serious injury "under the strain of competition without the controlling effect of pain" (*Drugs in Sport,* 1989, p. 423).

Rehabilitation from Injury. Male and female competitors tend to condone drug taking to expedite recovery from injury (*Drugs in Sport,* 1990; English, 1987; Goldman, 1984). In fact, many athletes do not realize that several medications used for this purpose are banned, at least if taken in certain amounts. Anabolic steroids can be prescribed for medical reasons, including the postoperative recovery of persons undergoing orthopedic surgery (*Drugs in Sport,* 1989; Rotella, 1984). The catabolic (wasting) effects of surgery could be reduced, thus shortening rehabilitation time and recovery. However, additional evidence is needed concerning the benefits of steroids for the treatment of severe overuse injury (Strauss, 1987).

Heightened Energy and Arousal. Anshel (1991b) found that "psyching up" was a reason for drug taking that is apparently far more prevalent for male than female competitors (28.7% and .06%, respectively). This statistic may be at least partially explained by the fact that males tend to engage in traditional contact sports in which heightened aggression is often warranted.

Drug ingestion, particularly anabolic steroids and amphetamines, are two methods of enhancing the athlete's level of excitation and aggression (Donald, 1981; Lombardo, 1987; Strauss, 1987). In particular, two categories of drugs, central nervous system and psychomotor stimulants, serve this purpose.

Relaxation and Lower Arousal. Just two of Anshel's (1991b) subjects (.01%) knew of at least one other participant who used a banned substance to relax or reduce tension. Not surprisingly, drug users in this category tended to be athletes in low-arousal, noncontact sports (e.g., golf) (Chappel, 1987; Donald, 1983).

Medically beta-blockers are used by hypertensive persons who wish to lower high blood pressure, reduce urinary output, and lower stress (Lombardo, 1987). Sometimes athletes want to lower their level of muscular tension and excitation. Beta-blockers, all types of which are banned, are one category of drug that achieves this objective. Golfers, arch-

TABLE 40-1. A Summary of the Number and Percentage of Athletes'
Responses About Their Perceived Causes of Drug Use in Sport as a Function
of Drug Type and Gender.‡

Categories of Drug	Males (n = 94)		Females (n = 32)		Combined (N = 126)	
	Total	Percent*	Total	Percent*	Total	Percent†
Performance-Enhancing	68	72.3	13	40.0	81	64.2
Physical						
Pain Reduction	24	25.5	18	56.2	42	33.3
Injury Rehabilitation	17	18.1	7	22.0	24	19.4
Increase of Energy/Arousal	27	28.7	2	.06	29	23.0
Relaxation	1	.01	1	.03	2	.01
Weight Control	19	20.2	17	53.1	36	28.5
Being Competitive	61	64.8	11	34.3	72	57.1
Psychological/Emotional	27	28.7	14	43.7	41	32.5
Fear of Failure	38	19.8	35	41.1	73	26.4
Self-Confidence	24	25.5	7	21.8	31	24.6
Superman Complex	9	.09	1	.03	10	.08
Social						
Models	21	22.3	11	34.3	32	25.3
Social Support	0	0	4	12.5	4	.03
Recreational	61	64.8	18	56.2	79	62.6
Physical						
Improve Performance	12	12.7	1	.03	13	10.3
Control Pain	8	4.1	4	4.7	12	4.3
Psychological/Emotional						
Reduce Anxiety/Tension	46	48.9	16	50	62	49.2
Boredom	21	22.3	11	34.3	32	25.3
Low Coach Loyalty	5	.05	3	.09	8	.06
Personal Problems	6	.06	10	31.2	16	12.6
Social						
Peer Pressure/Acceptance	4	.04	3	.09	7	.05
Experimentation/Fun	28	29.7	16	50	44	34.9

*Represents the percentage of subjects for each gender.

†Represents the percentage of total number of subjects (N = 126).

‡Used with permission of the *Journal of Sport Behavior*.

ers, bowlers, and pistol and rifle shooters are athletes commonly associated with using this type of substance.

Weight Control. Amphetamines, another category of drug, are often used to control appetite and speed body responses. They quickly reduce weight, allowing the athlete to compete in a lower than "natural" weight group (Donald, 1983). In recent years diuretics have been banned by sport organizations, as they are unsafe when taken continuously or in large doses. This form of drug may be especially common among boxers, wrestlers, and weight lifters where weight is associated with the class at which they compete or may directly influence performance outcome (Goldman, 1984).

The Pressure to Be Competitive. Clearly a primary reason for anabolic steroids in sport is to "be competitive." Drug use for this reason was often in response to the coach's

warning about "superior" opponents or a teammate who was "waiting to take your place."

The pressure to succeed in sport, particularly at the elite level, is extraordinary. The overwhelming acknowledgment of steroid use among these athletes is supported by a plethora of anecdotal evidence. For instance, despite being well aware of the deleterious effects of steroids and the illegality of using them, athletes continue to take drugs because of the prevalent attitude that doping practices are necessary to be competitive (*Drugs in Sport,* 1989).

The sources of this pressure are rarely identified in the fight against the illegal and unethical use of drugs in sport. Coaches (and sponsors) can, and often do, contribute to the competitor's dilemma by reinforcing the need to win "at any cost." The expectations of parents, the media, and peers only fuel the pressure to optimize performance by artificial substance abuse (Chappel, 1987; Lamb, 1984; Williams, 1989). As reported earlier, anecdotal evidence in support of this contention abounds.

Psychological and Emotional Effects

Because athletes' thoughts and emotions often dictate their actions, the fundamental objective of coaches and psychology consultants is to identify the factors that underlie certain feelings (e.g., low self-confidence, stress, and so on), and then plan and implement strategies that favorably influence them. Following are some of the more common psychological and emotional sources of drug use in sport.

Fear of Failure. Extensive social pressure emerges from a "win at all costs" mentality for athletes (Gregg & Rejeski, 1990; Strauss & Curry, 1987). The sources of these pressures include anxiety about certain opponents, intimidation from spectators, preventing or overcoming an injury, and, perhaps most important, not meeting the expectations of coaches, parents, and friends. The resultant fear of failure is tied to a person's strong affiliation between sport success and self-esteem (Chu, 1982). Athletes who derive their self-image directly from success in sport will more likely fear defeat. Given the pervasiveness of the athletes' fear of failure in sport (Anshel, 1990a), the subjects' willingness to admit using drugs to combat this source of stress may have been underreported in this study.

Low Self-Confidence. For many athletes, drug use is used to build self-confidence (Anshel, 1991b). This category reflected the athletes' doubt about their own skills ("They make me feel better about my ability"). On the other hand, the category "to be more competitive" was a function of comparing one's skills with those of other opponents ("I'm sure 'so and so' are taking them") or related to a superior performance outcome ("If I'm going to perform at 'X' speed, I have to take these").

The relationship between self-confidence and sport performance has received increased attention in contemporary sport research (Feltz, 1988; Vealey, 1986). Self-confidence in trait form (SC-trait) represents individuals' perceptions about their ability to be successful in sport, while state self-confidence (SC-state) reflects individuals' perceptions at a particular moment about their ability to be successful in sport. Despite the absence of research in this area, it is tenable that athletes with low self-confidence and who doubt their performance capabilities would more likely ingest performance-enhancing drugs than their high self-confident counterparts.

One side effect of taking anabolic steroids, perhaps related to low self-confidence, is the increase in aggressiveness (see Gregg and Rejeski, 1990, for a review of related literature), particularly the outburst of anger. According to Gregg and Rejeski, steroids increase blood testosterone levels, which in turn is highly correlated with dominance and aggression. In addition, the authors report that "Anabolic steroids create a very rapid increase in body size" (p. 282), another powerful motive for drug abuse, particularly for the physically immature athlete. Perhaps selected competitors are using steroids to foster aggressive behavior and increase body size in an attempt to overcome low self-confidence. In

Anshel's (1991b) sample of athletes, statements such as "I feel better about myself (or about my ability) after using steroids" or "I know guys who take them to feel more aggressive"—one contact sport subject responded, "steroids make me wanna kick some a--"—communicate a sense of heightened self-confidence with steroid use.

The "Superman" Complex. Some athletes feel impervious to any potential negative side effects of drugs (Collins et al., 1984). For example, according to Mr. Don Weiss, executive director of the National (American) Football League, "It is not easy to convince pro football players that they are vulnerable to the negative health effects of steroids. Some of these young men are such great physical specimens with such great athletic ability that they think they'll be like that forever" (in Shroyer, 1990, p. 115). Ironically detached feelings about the harmful effects of drug taking may be more common with mind-altering drugs (also discussed later). In support of this hypothesis, Marcello et al. (1989) found that drug education programs may have contributed to *increased* drug use among college athletes due to experimentation after the subjects discovered the effects of these drugs.

Athletes are among society's healthiest and physically most attractive models. There is likely a tendency toward the self-perception of invincibility. For some competitors, particularly at the elite level, this misunderstood detachment from danger is accompanied by changes in personality and/or behavioral tendencies. As Collins et al. (1984) note, based on their work with the Cleveland Browns (American) football team, "At the professional level, the athlete often undergoes a personality change. He begins to feel that he has 'made it.'. . . Cocaine, with its phenomenal expense, glamorous allure, and severe legal penalties, is an attractive vehicle for demonstrating wealth, status, and power" (p. 487).

This explanation is consistent with Nicholson's (1989) contention that information about negative ramifications from certain actions (e.g., drug ingestion) will not necessarily alter behavior. The tendency to address long-term rather than acute effects of drugs, a common strategy in educational settings, only exacerbates the problem. Athletes who exhibit the "Superman" complex do not feel constrained by the deleterious effects of drugs, even after obtaining valid information about its possible detrimental effects to health.

Perhaps the most cogent explanation of the Superman complex stems from the developmental psychology literature. Elkind (1985) contends that adolescence is accompanied by egocentric thinking—the person is convinced of his or her personal uniqueness—which allows a person to acknowledge risk, but without the understanding that they may be personally at risk. This creates a sense of personal power, invincibility, and indestructibility. Drug taking, then, is reframed from a risk-taking activity to just another experience that the person wishes to engage in.

Perfectionism. Some individuals never appear pleased

with their accomplishments, even with the appropriate recognition and adulation of others. For these people, "good" is never quite good enough. This self-perception is a symptom of perfectionism, a condition regarded by clinical psychologists as "unhealthy." A perfectionist is someone who has trouble discriminating between realistic and idealized standards (Hewitt & Flett, 1991). They bypass attainable excellence in pursuit of unattainable perfection. Perfectionists will set themselves up for failure with extraordinarily high expectations and will engage in self-criticism whether or not they reach their lofty goals. Perfectionists will "pick apart" their performance, looking for the inevitable one defect, even after an admirable performance and a successful outcome. On the other hand, healthy individuals who may also possess high standards do not usually devalue themselves to a similar degree, especially in response to success.

Although the antecedents and treatment of perfectionism go beyond the scope of this chapter, it would appear that the perfectionist athlete is a "ripe" candidate for drug abuse (Hewitt, Mittelstaedt & Flett, 1990). For example, Hewitt et al. (1990) found, in their study of 50 college students, that persons with perfectionist standards who express the need to perform well in most activities may be prone to experience depression. In a sport context, selected athletes may be driven to reach consistent "perfect" performance with anabolic steroids or other drugs to improve performance or, inversely, may attempt to escape the pressures of extraordinarily high goals in competitive sport through ingesting mind-altering drugs. Because the perfectionist is typically unable to self-diagnose this psychological characteristic and, hence, is unable to see that their expectations are unrealistic, coaches and sport psychology consultants can provide these individuals with cognitive and behavioral strategies (discussed later) to be more self-accepting and less self-rejecting (Hewitt et al., 1991). Although perfectionism has not been studied within a sport context to date, it would not be surprising to find that many skilled athletes fit the profile of this unhealthy psychological state.

The Placebo Effect. A placebo is defined as "a substance or procedure that is administered with suggestions that it will modify a symptom or sensation but which, unknown to its recipient, has no specific pharmacological impact on the reaction in question" (Ross & Olson, 1981, p. 408). A placebo effect occurs when administering the placebo alters the recipient's actions or functions consistent with the person's expectations. The placebo effect, studied extensively in a variety of psychophysiological contexts, has been shown to have both positive and negative effects on the subject's actions, attitudes, and emotions.

Research on the placebo effect has direct implications for the causes and *performance outcomes* of drug taking in sport. Put simply, it may be that if athletes merely believe that a drug will have a desirable effect, it likely will. Research evidence on the placebo effect in performing motor tasks, albeit relatively scant, is virtually unequivocal. For example, Pomeranz and Krasner (1969) tested 36 males and

females on a hand dynamometer task. All subjects were told that "the study was concerned with testing the effects of a new drug whose major use is as a reliever of muscular fatigue" (p. 16). The placebo group was further informed that they had been assigned to the "drug" group, a drug that "had already undergone extensive testing and had proved very effective" (p. 16). The results of executing six maximal squeezes on the hand dynamometer, after statistically controlling for initial differences among subjects, revealed significantly superior performance, i.e., longer endurance, by the placebo group. No marked sex differences were found. In other studies of human performance, a placebo effect appeared to explain the runner's high in distance running (Hinton & Taylor, 1986) and has improved muscular strength and endurance (Barber, 1966). Placebos have also effectively attenuated or eliminated chronic and acute pain, and have influenced somatic and cognitive arousal (see Jospe, 1978, Morgan & Brown, 1983, & Ross & Olson, 1981, for reviews of related literature).

For instance, Smith and Bozymowski (1965) examined the influence of attitude toward physical warm-up on enduring a physical task. Female subjects were categorized as having favorable or unfavorable attitudes toward warm-up, then engaged in an obstacle course without warming up and following a 3-minute warm-up session. Subjects who had a favorable attitude toward warm-up performed significantly better in the warm-up condition than those with an unfavorable attitude. Thus the subjects' attitude toward warm-up dictated their performance quality as opposed to any actual physiological benefits of warming up.

According to Ross et al., explanations for the placebo effect, particularly leading to desirable results, include: (1) reduced anxiety about the subjects' symptoms, (2) individuals' accentuating the positive, (3) the recipients' compliance with the demands of the situation, as opposed to a true perception of any change in their condition—an implication that subjects are faking their improvement, (4) a change in somatic responses (e.g., activation of the endorphin system), an explanation especially compatible with the attenuation of pain and explaining the runner's high, and (5) the subjects' attributions, i.e., the interpretations of apparent changes in their manifest state to the effects of the placebo. The authors suggest that attributions may be a particularly powerful placebo agent in drug taking in that withdrawal from a substance may be used to explain the cause of poorer performance. It appears then that although selected drugs significantly influence physiological processes, any favorable effect on sport *performance* may be more dependent on psychological phenomena than previously recognized.

Social Causes

Perhaps there is no greater cause for succumbing to drug ingestion than in response to social—and societal—pressures. Athletes experience significantly more stress as a function of the competitive environment than their nonathlete counterparts. Examples include peer pressure, demands on one's time, expectations from others, and criticisms from coaches and the media.

Models. According to Gill (1986), modeling occurs "any time we learn by demonstration or change our behavior to imitate behaviors we have observed. Modeling can facilitate or inhibit behaviors" (p. 180). Skilled athletes serve as the primary modes of social influence for all sports participants. The development of appropriate (e.g., training and effort) and inappropriate (e.g., cheating, drug taking) behaviors in young athletes is often derived from their older, more experienced counterparts (Chu, 1982). The modeling effect is reinforced by media reports that publicize incidences of drug abuse by professional athletes (Collins et al., 1984). It is highly likely that the media's reporting of drug use by "established" sports stars influences the use of performance-enhancing drugs among intercollegiate athletes, many of whom aspired to compete at higher (i.e., Olympic or professional) levels. Perceptions that elite athletes ingest drugs and that "if it doesn't hurt so and so, it won't hurt me," especially among less skilled athletes who aspire to a higher status in sport, provide an attractive rationale (*Drugs in Sport,* 1989; Nicholson, 1989; Nicholson & Agnew, 1989). Thus for many athletes, drug use is "sanctioned" through observing their elite models.

Modeling has a particularly influential effect during adolescence. Psychologists regard adolescence as a time when young people explore their identity and experiment with drugs, particularly alcohol and tobacco, often developing behavioral patterns that affect the rest of their life (Wragg, 1990). The adolescent is seeking a more mature identity by engaging in behaviors that form the "rites of passage" from childhood to adult status. Erickson (1968) contends that the search for identity is the primary task and crisis of adolescence. Since adult status is the eventual goal of the younger person, then the behavioral characteristics of adulthood become especially attractive. Thus the young athletes' acknowledgment of drug use in their adult sport models signals that such behavior is commensurate with the status of elite competition (Berger, 1988).

Social Support. Athletes may ingest a banned substance due to the lack of social support. This means that steroid use served as a vehicle to gain acceptance and approval among peers and coaches. Athletes may feel that they must "do more" to gain recognition by altering their physique or markedly improving their performance (*Drugs in Sport,* 1989, 1990). Because this reasoning exists at rather subconscious levels and, therefore, is not likely to be articulated, there may have been a degree of underreporting on this factor.

Social support is a primary need of athletes, particularly from teammates and coaches (Rosenfeld, Richman & Hardy, 1989). The authors operationally define social support in a sport context as involving a network of personalities to meet a recipient's needs for venting feelings, providing companionship and reassurance, reducing un-

certainty during stressful times, aiding mental and physical recovery from stress and fatigue, and improving communication skills. Their findings indicated that although competitors rely on coaches and teammates for technical support and appreciation (i.e., skill development and reinforcement of performance), coaches in particular are not providing listening support, emotional support, or shared social support. This is likely due to the coach's need, "first, to maintain the emotional distance necessary to sustain their role as authority and, second, to avoid affecting morale by singling out particular athletes with whom to share a more personal or supportive relationship" (p. 30).

Statements in Anshel's (1991b) study such as "No one ever tells me I'm doing a good job" or "There's no one to turn to when I need to talk to somebody" indicate a lack of social support. Perhaps more than any other rationale for drug use among athletes, the absence of social support can create drug dependency to either enhance performance (i.e., to gain needed recognition from others) or as a means to cope with stress or relieve boredom (i.e., "recreational" purposes).

RECREATIONAL DRUG USE

Hallucinogens, more commonly referred to as recreational drugs, mind-altering drugs, "street" drugs, or "designer" drugs, traditionally serve the purpose of consciousness alteration (Smith, 1983). What is particularly disturbing about the unprescribed intake and nonmedical use of such drugs in sport is their addictive effects. It is important to point out here that addiction to a chemical occurs far less frequently than addiction to a sensation or an experience (Julien, 1981; Smith, 1983). Thus although there are exceptions, ". . . it is not the drug that addicts people, but people who addict themselves" (Smith, 1983, p. 75). This is an important point with respect to the abuse of recreational drugs among athletes because, contrary to media reports, the psychological and emotional factors associated with drug abuse and dependence supercede the pharmacological effects. Addiction then may be far more preventable and controllable than previously thought (suggested strategies are discussed later).

The primary problem with research in this area, discussed earlier, is underreporting. As Smith (1983) surmises, "When you're dealing with an illicit activity like drug use . . . the accuracy of self-report data is highly questionable, and many of the drug users probably wouldn't answer the survey" (p. 79). The literature reviewed here may lend further insight into the causes of ingesting recreational drugs. Nevertheless psychological explanations of using so-called recreational drugs in sport may be hypothesized from media reports and the extant theoretical and scientific literature. These are divided into the same three categories of causes as performance-enhancing drugs discussed previously: physical, psychological/emotional, and social. Anshel's (1991b) found that 79 (62.6%) of the 126 athletes in his survey acknowledged recreational drug use—that is, taking drugs unrelated to improving sport performance. Due to the legal implications of ingesting various types of "recreational" drugs, it is possible that acknowledging their use may have been underreported in this study, a factor shown in other investigations.

Physical Causes

Recreational drugs are used by athletes to have a favorable effect on sport performance or to reduce physical discomfort. For example, the class of drugs called stimulants heightens aggression and inhibits fatigue (Chappel, 1987). Examples of stimulants include cocaine, most diet-suppressant drugs, amphetamines, caffeine, and epinephrine.

Enhance Sport Performance. Most often, athletes who ingest hallucinogens to improve performance reflect a need to increase aggression, especially in contact sports, or to escape potentially dangerous or uncertain situations (e.g., competing against an opponent perceived as superior or highly skilled) (Anshel, 1991b).

Chappel (1987) reports that stimulants reduce recovery time of neuronal activity that, in turn, can increase alertness, speed reaction time, and foster attention and concentration. Chappel's review of related literature reveals that the effect of stimulants on sport performance can be direct (e.g., increased stimulation, which promotes coordination, form, strength, and endurance) or indirect (e.g., reducing fatigue and increasing the tendency toward, and extent of, risk-taking and aggressive behavior). However, hallucinogens can reduce attentional focus and concentration in complex motor tasks. Several athletes in this survey indicated that marijuana or cocaine were taken on game day to have a relaxing or psyching-up effect, respectively. The respondents contended that these responses were desirable and ostensibly improved performance.

Cope with Pain and Injury. Athletes ingest drugs to psychologically cope with physical discomfort (*Drugs in Sport,* 1990). Under such relatively rare circumstances, the athletes felt that medical treatment was not sufficient to eliminate pain and consequently had to turn to less conventional methods to meet this objective.

It is ironic that the category of recreational drugs is used for dual purposes that are antagonistic. On the one hand, they can speed bodily responses (stimulants) and alter internal and external perceptual processes (hallucinogens). Yet, conversely, recreational drugs "can lead to rough play and increased risk of injury" (Chappel, 1987, p. 193). It is this distortion of the athlete's perceptions and internal sensations that can provide a relief from, and reduce, pain.

Psychological/Emotional Causes

By far the most common rationale for using recreational drugs among athletes is psychologically and emotionally founded (Anshel, 1991b; Wragg, 1990). Many of these athletes view taking drugs as a response to overcome reaching or retaining some undesirable emotional state.

Unpleasant Emotions or Feelings. Emotions such as stress, tension, anxiety, and depression may be antecedent causes of ingesting hallucinogens. Recreational drug use may reflect a short-term approach to managing stress and other undesirable emotions. Drug taking may attenuate the stress and tension associated with the pressures to succeed at sport over a prolonged time period—a full season. The lack of opportunities for recreation and academic pursuits also contributed markedly to heightened stress. Mind-altering drugs provided the most convenient mental escape.

Although there is no attempt here to identify the conditions of stress, tension, anxiety, and depression as clinically synonymous—they are not—the conditions were grouped into one category in Anshel's (1991b) study based on the similarity of the athletes' responses and the difficulty in deciphering among their clinical properties within the context of most surveys in this area. Anshel found that the category of reducing unpleasant emotions received by far the most prevalent response in the category of recreational drug use.

Strauss and Curry (1987) contend that "The immediate pressures to win are stronger for many athletes than the admonition not to use drugs. Potential dangers are remote while victory is today's problem" (p. 7). This pressure leads to ingesting substances that, presumably, will foster success or, in the case of "mind altering" drugs, will allow the person to mentally escape from their present situation (Donald, 1983; Egger, 1981). A depressed state can contribute to drug ingestion if its purpose is to reduce stress due to failure or to psychologically "escape" from the pressures associated with competition (Anshel, 1990a). One appropriate strategy in response to this problem is for coaches to promote an atmosphere that alleviates the stress and anxiety associated with winning. Instead, the athlete's energy and emotions should be directed toward realistic, yet challenging, goals (Anshel, 1990a; 1990b).

Anxiety in sport, in both trait and state forms, is thought to be due, at least partly, to low self-confidence, low self-esteem, and the person's appraisal of a given situation as potentially threatening (Spielberger, 1989). Although anxiety, per se, is an inherent component of competition, the ability to cope with these feelings often separates successful from less successful performance (Mahoney & Meyers, 1989). The effects of anxiety on performance are worsened when the competitor anticipates (and fears) failure (Scheier and Carver, 1985).

Not surprisingly one of the athlete's greatest sources of stress, especially in contact sports, is the fear of experiencing an injury (Rotella, 1985). Rather than disclose this feeling candidly, the sentiments of several athletes in Anshel's (1991b) survey were couched in more euphemistic terms. Examples included "I don't have to think about getting hurt" or "Taking [a certain drug] lets me go all-out without getting uptight about injuries. Besides, injuries are just part of the game." A popular approach to masking this fear is to heighten aggression and arousal while lowering inhibitions toward vigorous effort. Certain drugs, mostly stimulants and hallucinogens (e.g., marijuana), serve this purpose (Egger, 1981). As a result, the athlete feels a sense of imperviousness to the dangers of competing, takes more risks, and performs more aggressively and confidently (Donald, 1983). Consequently the fear of any potentially unpleasant outcome of competition such as injury or pain is reduced.

Boredom. For many individuals, experimentation with recreational drugs, often ingested in group (social) situations, can help overcome boredom (Julien, 1981). This may be especially prevalent in sport during periods when team-related activities are unplanned, especially when traveling and on weekends.

Whereas drug use can be a function of low incentive or loyalty, as indicated earlier, competitors can also tire of redundancy in the team's practices or in some other aspect of their participation (Egger, 1981). These athletes do not feel challenged. Athletes normally need excitement and new direction, a concept referred to as sensation seeking (Zuckerman, 1979). Straub (1982) found that athletes in high-risk sports (e.g., hang gliding and automobile racing) on the average scored higher in sensation seeking than athletes in low-risk sport participants (e.g., bowling).

The extent of the athletes' idle time exacerbates the problem of low excitement, especially at the elite level. Collins et al. (1984), who examined drug dependency with the Cleveland Browns' professional (American) football team, explain that "The professional football player works only six months a year. His unstructured lifestyle can be put to productive use . . . but for [a] drug-involved [athlete] idle time is another 'enabling' circumstance. He has little accountability for his time; he can stay up all night and all day 'basing,' then 'crash' for long periods. As long as he shows up for a few meetings, practices, and games, he thinks nothing will be discovered or said" (p. 487). One additional source of boredom is the absence of meaningfulness attached to the athlete's sport involvement.

Reduced Loyalty to Team and Coach. Recreational drug taking is fostered if athletes have feelings such as "My coach won't play me anyway, so it doesn't matter whether I'm ready to play." This may include smoking marijuana even minutes before a game. This finding reflects the high loyalty that most elite athletes have toward their coach and team. Still, the failure of some coaches to identify the team role of each athlete and promote feelings of importance, especially for substitute team members, is a contributory factor toward drug use.

Some athletes are uninspired by an approaching contest

(e.g., not taking an opponent seriously), feel unattached to the team's objectives, or perceive their team role as virtually meaningless to the contest's outcome. Loyalty to the coach may be low or inconsistent. Players with low coach loyalty do not monitor nor take seriously their physical and mental status prior to and during the contest. They are not psyched-up, but rather "psyched-out." Drug intake, usually of a recreational variety, may create the sense of excitement that is missing from their actual participation (Anshel, 1987).

Personal Problems. Drug taking may be a response to difficulty in responding to a personal problem, almost always independent of their sport involvement. The more frequent disclosure of problems by females (31.2%) than males (.06%) in Anshel's (1991b) study may partially reflect the more open personal communication style of female athletes (Officer and Rosenfeld, 1985).

The athlete's personal life can be a potential source of support—or extreme stress. Factors such as family, social life, and a host of issues and events that are experienced away from the sport environment may have a marked impact on the mental preparation and performance of any competitor. The family, in particular, is an essential source of emotional support. Orlick and Partington's (1986) interviews with 16 Canadian Olympic athletes showed that elite athletes need and often receive the love, acceptance, and support of their immediate family. Consequently when this source of comfort is missing, perhaps due to deceased or divorced parents or poor relationships with family members, often the competitor is less capable of coping with sport demands. They are more susceptible to mentally escape or become "psyched up" to participate at optimal levels. Ingesting recreational drugs (e.g., cocaine or marijuana) or stimulants (e.g., amphetamines, cocaine, among others) is more likely.

Social Causes

The athlete's social environment is instrumental in partially dictating his or her actions away from the sport arena (Chu, 1982). Chu reports that the power and influence of the peer group among athletes is similar to that of nonsport populations, and both of which are more influential in predicting behavior than family members, at least in adolescence (also see Chappel, 1987). In Anshel's (1991b) study, the athletes' close association with peers may have underrepresented socially based causes of drug use in sport.

Peer Pressure and Acceptance. Perhaps not surprisingly, pressure from peers or gaining acceptance by a group is a likely underreported cause of drug taking, given the prevalence of peer influence on behavior, especially among adolescents and sport participants (Nicholson, 1989; Wragg, 1990).

Collins, Pippenger, and Janesz (1984), in their report on a drug prevention and rehabilitation program with the

Cleveland Browns (American) football team, contend that the elite athlete "... begins to feel that he has 'made it'; he has achieved his lifelong goal of acceptance in the ranks of the world's top professional athletes. The temptation is overwhelming to play the role as a macho superstar.... Drug abuse fits into this nonconformist behavior pattern" (p. 487).

The power of peer influences was indicated in a study (Martin & Anshel, 1991) in which athletes were asked about a suggested course of action in response to drug use by a teammate. Martin and Anshel found that athletes were significantly more inclined to choose a peer prevention assistance strategy than to ask coaches or parents to deal with a drug problem on the team. Even so, coaches were the preferred source of assistance as compared to parents.

The extensive influence and pressure among peers on attitudes and behavior is well known. According to the social pressures model (Goodstadt & Sheppard, 1982; Nicholson, 1989), potential drug users need to: (a) develop counterarguments to resist environmental and personal influences (i.e., social pressures) that encourage drug use, (b) learn the skills to identify these pressures, and (c) understand the immediate and short-term *social* consequences of drug use. Despite the known influence of peer group pressure and peer acceptance as factors that influence drug use, abusers of foreign substances, including athletes, are unlikely to admit it (Chappel, 1987; Whitlock, 1980). The low number of athletes admitting to recreational drug use supports the contention that succumbing to peer pressure is a rejected, yet subconscious motive for drug use.

From the perspective of psychological maturation and development, the need for social acceptance and pressure to conform makes the adolescent particularly susceptible to peer influence. Wragg (1990) describes the peer group as "... a critical agent of socialization as dependence on the family is reduced and the young person seeks to belong and fit into new relations with peers" (p. 237). Heightened self-consciousness during adolescence magnifies the need to conform to the peer group. Hence in their eagerness to attain social acceptance, adolescents become aware of the types of approval-earning behaviors—the need to please other people—that will facilitate popularity. Wragg (1990) concludes that these developmental characteristics, "... coupled with a setting or context where [drugs] are readily available, clearly implies that adolescence is a time of increased susceptibility to risk from drug use" (p. 238).

Experimentation/Fun. Anshel (1991b) found that 34.9% of his sample surmised that athletes on their team engage in recreational drugs for the purposes of fun or experimentation. The players typically did not perceive the use of such substances as acutely fatal; nor did the athletes recognize evidence of long-term deleterious consequences. Attempts at "just one hit" and denial of any possible addiction to the drug (i.e., feelings of total self-control over one's drug-taking behaviors) contributed to their comfort with drug experimentation.

This finding is consistent with Collins et al. (1984), who attributed this cause of recreational drug use among professional (American) football players. In this way, athletes and their nonathletic peers share similar characteristics. Chappel (1987) reported a survey of 4,941 high school seniors showing that male and female athletes "did not differ from their peers in using alcohol and other drugs. Experimentation and regular use of drugs was widespread" (p. 187). In fact, the use of chewing tobacco (a stimulant) is "much higher among athletes than in the general public" (p. 189). Thus it is apparent that athletes do not differ markedly from their nonathletic counterparts in terms of the social and personal needs and pressure associated with drug taking.

Although many of the reasons offered for drug use were not surprising, of particular interest was the revealing nature of selected causes that may be considered unique to elite sports competitors in contrast to nonelite athletes and nonathletes. For example, it was apparent that the pressures associated with achieving and maintaining sport success or problems unrelated to sport participation (e.g., the reduced time to pursue academic study; attempting to meet the approval of coaches, parents, spectators, the media, and corporate sponsors) are unique to athletes. Yet these factors apparently exacerbate the athletes' susceptibility to drug use for various reasons. On the other hand, the present data do not suggest that athletes are helpless victims in the decision to use foreign substance. It is clear that most athletes are making rational decisions about taking banned substances. As Smith (1983) surmises, "athletes have easy access to drugs, and they have money for the more expensive drugs" (p. 76). Many competitors have the perception that they will not "get caught." According to Collins et al. (1984), "Arrests and convictions for ... drug offenses are few relative to the magnitude of the problem.... If few are arrested, fewer still are convicted and sentenced. Many drug-involved athletes know that prosecution is unlikely...." (p. 487). It is likely then that many performers are taking advantage of their elevated position in sport by feeling impervious to the ramifications of drug violations.

English (1987) explains the likely causes and specific motives of anabolic steroid use among competitors based on Jessor's Problem Behavior Theory (see Jessor, 1982, for a detailed discussion). Briefly Jessor proposes that behavior is a function of changes in a person's social and personal identity. "Problem" behavior does not reflect an act in itself, but rather is defined relative to how certain actions are interpreted given a particular situation, culture, and point in time. Thus drug ingestion may be viewed as desirable—even necessary—to some individuals, given certain situational demands, implications, expectations, roles, or personal needs.

English suggests that taking steroids is due to athletes': (1) blocked or unattainable goals (i.e., their need to overcome limited abilities), (2) expression of solidarity in a group (i.e., gaining peer acceptance), (3) way of coping with anxiety (i.e., with the frustrations and fears associated with failure, and as compensation for poor performance),

(4) confirmation of their identity (i.e., an attempt to overcome psychologically contrived inadequacies), (5) rebellion against adult and societal authority, and (6) psychological transition to the elite category (i.e., developing a "win at all costs" philosophy). According to English, "... the use of steroids may serve as a transitional marker that announces to teammates and other competitors that the athletes are willing to pay a price for success regardless of the cost to their health" (p. 55).

DRUG TAKING AND YOUNG ATHLETES

Most studies related to drugs in sport include mature, adult—usually university—athletes. There has been surprisingly scant research on drug taking among adolescent-aged athletes. In one relatively rare study on this topic, Martin and Anshel (1991) examined the attitudes toward ingesting various drugs, related and unrelated to sport performance, of 94 elite adolescent male and female Australian athletes. The athletes, representing nine sports, were participating in a required drug education program. The questionnaire focused on the athletes' attitudes toward drug use, drug prevention, and their intention to use drugs.

In addition to these definitions, the participants were informed about the effect of each drug on motor performance and, in certain cases, the reasons for using the drugs (e.g., anti-inflammatories for reducing pain). The athletes were asked to indicate their feelings about the appropriateness of using each of the drug types under three scenarios during the training/competition season, away from the training/competition season, and in response to an injury in order to compete. Thus subjects were not requested to indicate their actual past behaviors but rather the degree of support for using different drugs in various circumstances. A similar procedure was followed when investigating drug prevention strategies in which the athletes were asked to indicate the extent to which they agreed with a set course of alternative preventive actions. These actions included encouraging an athlete not to take the drug, encouraging an athlete to seek assistance, asking the coach to help, asking the drug abuser's parents to help, asking their own parents to help, and doing nothing about the drug taking.

The authors found that athletes in this study were inclined to agree with using alcohol and tobacco before and during the competition season, and using anti-inflammatories in response to an injury. In contrast, athletes were inclined to disagree with the use of anabolic steroids at any time. If these athletes were offered a performance-enhancing drug, they were inclined not to take it, but more so if the drug were detectable by drug testing. If the performance-enhancing drug was undetectable, athletes were more likely to use it. When placed in a scenario where they could take a drug (under a contrived name) that had relatively "minor" side effects and was undetectable, athletes were more inclined to condone its use,

even if the drug only marginally improved athletic performance.

A particularly important finding was that the athletes favored using the contrived drug if it was undetectable than if it was detectable with drug testing. This result supports the notion that drug testing would be an effective deterrent to drug use among these athletes, a strategy contrary to the sport-related drug prevention work by Heitzinger and Associates (1986), who found that the use of sanctions and rules was basically ineffective. However, their data collection occurred between 1981 and 1986, a time when drug testing was clearly less effective in contrast to more rigorous standards, punitive measures, and scientific sophistication in contemporary drug testing programs (Tricker, Cook, & McGuire, 1989).

The athletes generally agreed with using anti-inflammatories, both during and away from the competition season and in response to injury. This finding is not surprising, at least in Australia, in that Australian sport allows for free, uninhibited use of anti-inflammatories at any time, including on the field, unlike other countries where more restrictive guidelines are in place. While anti-inflammatories decrease unpleasant symptoms of an injury, they often do not affect the cause of the injury. Athletes who readily accept the use of anti-inflammatories and continue to train and compete with an injury whose symptoms are being suppressed by anti-inflammatories are setting a scenario for long-term disability (Tricker, Cook, and McGuire, 1989).

Although Martin and Anshel's (1991) findings are comforting in that elite adolescent athletes did not condone ingesting anabolic steroids, the performers found nothing wrong with using the other drugs. Pharmacological evidence suggests that the abuse of drugs such as beta-blockers, diuretics, stimulants and analgesics can be similarly as dangerous and/or potentially performance enhancing as anabolic steroids (Donald, 1983). Yet these drugs did not receive the same negative scores as anabolic steroids by the athletes in this study. If, as Kandel (1975) warns, adolescents move in a stepwise fashion from "softer" to "harder" drugs, then interventions that deter athletes from feeling favorable toward using relatively less harmful drugs appear warranted. Interventions with adolescent-aged athletes would seem particularly relevant if, according to Marcello et al. (1989) and Wragg (1990), athletes form their attitudes about the appropriateness of drug use prior to college age. Attitudes of strongly rejecting drug use should be developed early in life, before drug use occurs.

Two issues are becoming increasingly apparent. First, drug use among athletes is preventable. A review of the psychological reasons for drug abuse in sport indicates that cognitive and behavioral techniques should be instituted that, predictably, would be more effective in preventing—or at least controlling—drug use among athletes than reliance on drug testing and other antidoping, reactive efforts. Interestingly the *Proceedings of the International Symposium on Drug Abuse in Sports (Doping)* held at the 1988 Olympic Games in Seoul, South Korea, was devoted to the science and effectiveness of drug testing. Information on other means of combating drug intake to prevent problems from occurring was omitted. Second, the coach should be taking a far greater role in the fight against drugs among athletes than has heretofore been recognized. Sport organizations and leaders, particularly coaches, have significant roles to play in drug prevention than has been previously recognized.

STRATEGIES FOR COMBATING DRUG ABUSE IN SPORT

It is apparent that athletes ingest different types of drugs for various reasons. Consequently the strategies needed to prevent or at least inhibit drug use vary accordingly. For example, taking hallucinogens may occur for experimental or stress-reducing reasons, whereas steroids may be taken to build muscles and gain self-confidence. These explanations suggest the use of different cognitive and behavioral preventive techniques. Research in examining the effects of the more traditional techniques is available. However, only theoretical and empirical documentation exists that supports using each of the more novel approaches.

TRADITIONAL APPROACHES TO PREVENTING DRUG ABUSE

Ellichson and Abbey (1987) suggest that preventive educational programs hold the greatest potential for effective reduction of drug use. However, the effectiveness of these community-based educational programs with athletes is a far less encouraging scenario. These traditional programs are categorized, in accordance with their objectives, as deterrence strategies, educational programs, the skills strategy model, alternative activities, and the peer program.

Deterrence Strategies

One type of drug prevention program that is currently widely used in sport is known as a deterrence strategy (Marcello, Danish & Stolberg, 1989). Professional and amateur sport governing bodies often suggest the use of deterrence strategies, such as drug testing and associated sanctions, as a means of decreasing drug taking (Tricker and Cook, 1989). Deterrence strategies assume that drug use occurs because there is a low degree of risk associated with using drugs (Reilly, 1988). However, Hawkins, Lishner, and Catalano (1985) have concluded that the etiological research does not suggest that adolescent drug use results from a rational cost-benefit analysis of the real physical and psychosocial risks of drug taking. In fact, individuals most likely to abuse drugs are not even concerned with the possibility of detection. Consequently there is a strong likelihood that the logic of a deterrent measure may have little appeal to potential drug takers (Reilly, 1988).

In support of this contention, a survey of high school, college, and professional athletes conducted by Heitzinger and Associates (1986) revealed that sanctions and rules deterred relatively few athletes. The majority of drug users continued their drug use pattern unabated. Similarly, Hawkins et al. (1985) concluded that deterrent strategies only had a limited value with adolescent drug use, unless accompanied by other prevention strategies. There is also considerable doubt whether education has a significant deterrent role in reducing drug intake.

Educational Approaches

The effectiveness of educating athletes about abusive drug intake has been equivocal. What would these peer educators teach to athletes? Quantitative evidence suggests that education is not doing the job of preventing drug abuse among competitors. For example, as reported by Tricker et al. (1989), data was gathered on 9,891 U.S. college athletes by the drug education consulting firm Heitzinger and Associates between 1981 and 1986. Among their findings was that "drug education deterred [only] about 5% of the regular users from experimenting with drugs; drug testing and knowledge of punishment deterred 5% of the social users . . ." (p. 158).

Contrary to this finding, Nicholson and Agnew (1989) suggest that young athletes have a limited and consistently inaccurate knowledge of the health consequences associated with drug use. Thus it would seem that education to increase the person's knowledge about harmful drug effects, particularly in the short term, should be an integral part of the program (Reilly, 1988).

Another apparent need in the drug education arsenal is determining which drugs are more likely to be ingested during the season as opposed to between seasons. For example, the elite adolescent athletes in Martin and Anshel's (1991) study were more inclined toward drug taking during the off-season than during the season, particularly of tobacco and alcohol. Steroids were not viewed favorably at any time. Thus informing athletes about the effects on in-season performance of drug taking between seasons appears warranted. There is no "best" time to take drugs for athletes who are committed to improving their performance. While there may be a break from the rigors of hard training and competition, adequate fitness levels must be maintained, including supplementary strength and aerobic conditioning.

Originally the objectives of drug education programs were to disseminate accurate information—separating fact from fiction—about the negative consequences of drug ingestion, as well as alcohol and tobacco, to influence subsequent attitudes and behaviors of potential users. Ryan (1982) suggests that the "Education of athletes to prevent them from starting drug abuse or to reclaim them from it has probably been successful to some degree. It is impossible to measure the effects exactly, but without drug education the situation would probably be much worse" (p. 50).

Marcello et al. (1989) initiated a drug prevention program for university student athletes in the United States.

Their program consisted of education about performance-enhancing and recreational drugs; skill training in the areas of decision making, risk assessment, stress management, assertiveness training, resisting peer pressure, and a component to maximize the transfer of learned skills to outside settings. The findings indicated that the program was less than successful. Among their results was an overemphasis placed on the amount of time spent in teaching resistance to peer pressure. Apparently "pro-usage attitudes are influenced by parental modeling, media advertising, cultural, ethnic and religious factors, and peer influences prior to their arrival at college," as opposed to the assumption that the school environment fosters drug abuse (p. 208). This result may partially explain the limited success associated with educational programs on drug abuse.

According to Nicholson's (1989) review of related literature, there are several underlying factors that may explain the limited success of education in controlling drug use. First, education is based on the tenet that people use drugs because they have no knowledge of the associated negative effects. Consequently the individual is expected to develop a negative attitude toward drug use that, in turn, will dictate desirable behavior. Apparently the learner's knowledge does increase after educational programs, but rarely is attitude or behavior affected. Second, knowledge of the negative health consequences of drugs does not tend to decrease their use. Third, changes in attitude are not often caused by altering one's knowledge, nor do attitudinal changes necessarily alter behaviors. Finally, the emphasis—and often overexaggeration—of the adverse health effects of drug use is not accepted as realistic; the educators' message loses credibility with their audience. Nicholson concludes that "what is usually referred to as education is, in fact, information dissemination. . . . While distribution of information . . . plays an important consciousness-raising function, it should not be considered as a strategy to reduce the drug use of athletes" (pp. 50–51). Given the continued pervasiveness and extraordinary cost of controlling illegal drug intake in sport, other methods to address the issue appear warranted.

Drug educators have made two mistaken assumptions about the effect of a knowledge-based intervention. One assumption was that if the intervention provided drug users with accurate knowledge about the consequences of drug use, then the users would rationally respond by changing their drug-taking attitudes and behaviors. Again, as was demonstrated with deterrence strategies, the etiological research does not suggest that adolescents analyze the advantages and disadvantages of drug use prior to ingesting drugs (Hawkins, et al., 1985).

The second incorrect assumption was that provoking fear in the individual would inhibit drug use (Reilly, 1988). This assumption was flawed for the same reasons as the first assumption; drug users do not usually make rational judgments based on the advantages and disadvantages of drug use. In fact, often the curiosity aroused by these programs has actually increased initial drug experimentation (Marcello et al., 1989; Stuart, 1974). Evaluations of the knowledge-based approaches have shown no effect on the frequency or extent of drug use (Hanson, 1980; Kinder, Pope, & Walfish, 1980; Stuart, 1974). Therefore, it has become apparent that such programs should form only one of several components toward broader based drug prevention programs (Marcello, et al., 1989; Strauss, 1988).

Finally, Bell et al. (1987) feel that physicians should have a primary role in the drug prevention effort. Suggested strategies include "taking part in educational efforts in schools and among team members and by involving themselves in testing programs" (p. 108). The authors also feel that physicians should refrain from prescribing anabolic steroids, amphetamines, and other potentially harmful substances, should inform colleagues and the public about the problem, and should support the development of programs to reduce the illegal prescription and distribution of drugs. Issues in drug education programs that should be addressed include psychological and physical addiction, changes in mood, increasing the probability of injury through masking pain, reducing the effects of off-season training, and the possible onset of diseases (e.g., cancer, arthritis).

Skills Strategies Model

Another community-based model, currently in use in athlete drug education, is the skill strategies model (Marcello et al., 1989). This model assumes that athletes become involved in drug taking because of poor interpersonal skills (Reilly, 1988). That is, there is an inability on the part of the athlete to recognize and/or make decisions to resist drug use. The skills strategies program aims to equip the individual with the motivation, skills, and knowledge to identify the pressures of drug use and to develop counters to deal with these pressures.

Hawkins et al. (1985) suggest three types of skill-based programs used in community drug prevention: (1) reducing impulsiveness by addressing antisocial behavior, (2) training in proper decision making, and (3) learning to assess risks by recognizing and resisting social influences of drug use. These programs have had positive results in preventing and delaying smoking (Evans, Rozelle, Maxwell-Raines, Dill, Guthrie, Henderson, & Hill, 1981) and in improving decision making and assertiveness communication skills (Botvin, 1982).

Marcello et al. (1989), however, found that the frequency of drug ingestion among university students was relatively unchanged using the skill-based model. The authors surmise that this was likely due to social and environmental factors that promoted pro-usage attitudes and behavioral patterns toward alcohol, "recreational" drugs, and tobacco. Interestingly the use of drugs on campus was significantly linked to attitudes and behaviors developed prior to their arrival at college. They concluded that "Contrary to what is often assumed . . . student athletes don't become prone to substance abuse in college. The pro-usage attitudes are influenced by parental modeling, media advertising, cultural, ethnic, and religious factors, and peer influences prior to their arrival at college" (p. 208). This recommendation fully concurs with Hawkins et al.'s (1985) suggestions that skills strategies are most effective in early adolescent intervention situations.

This model may be particularly effective if drug use among adolescents occurs in an sequential step-wise fashion from "soft" (legal) drugs such as tobacco to "hard" (illegal) drugs such as marijuana, as suggested by Kandel (1978). Consequently the risk assessment strategy, which can reduce the use of legal drugs, may hold promise for delaying and preventing more widespread drug experimentation with illegal substances (Evans et al. 1981; Reilly, 1988).

According to Hawkins et al. (1985), it is not yet clear whether or not life-skill strategies reduce the likelihood of drug abuse because important socializing predictors such as the family, school, or early behavioral problems are not addressed. In addition, the authors contend that the entire life-skills program addresses factors related to initiation and experimentation with drugs rather than "serious" drug abuse. Thus separate athlete-based interventions are needed that consider the unique socialization processes that athletes encounter (e.g., the pressure to be competitive and win, coping with stress, meeting the expectations of others) (Anshel, 1991a).

Alternative Activities Model

The alternative activities model works on the assumption that provision of "positive" activities more appealing than drug use will influence the person's decision to take drugs (Reilly, 1988). Examples of alternative approaches for the adolescent age group include community and leisure activities, academic tutoring, or training in real life skills such as household management, résumé writing, and job interview techniques. Appropriate alternative activities appear to be crucial to the success of any educational program. Swisher and Hu (1983), based on their review of research, support the hypothesis that some alternative activities such as academic pursuits, sports, and involvement in religious activities minimize drug intake. Social and vocational activities, on the other hand, may actually *foster* drug use.

The alternative activities approach appears intuitively appealing for a sport performance-oriented population. The objective of this program is to convince athletes of the credible alternatives to drug use. If athletes are using selected drugs to enhance sport performance, then substance abuse should be reduced or eliminated if physiological, psychological, and behavioral intervention strategies are used instead. However, the efficacy of this approach has heretofore not been tested.

Personal Development Program Model

Whereas educational models of drug prevention predict that knowledge about the deleterious effects of drug use re-

duces consumption, the personal development program assumes that drug ingestion results from psychological deficiencies. Low self-esteem and self-confidence are the two primary personal disorders that ostensibly foster drug use (Tobler, 1986). However, the results of past research have not shown a strong relationship between self-esteem and drug use (Gerslick, Grady, Sexton and Lyons, 1987; Kandel, 1978). Polich, Ellickson, Reuter, and Kahan (1984) found that programs based on overcoming personal deficiencies have yielded inconclusive results. The relationship between completing these programs, particularly in attempts to increase self-esteem, and abusing drugs is relatively low.

The Peer Program

The peer program has received relatively little exposure in the drug education literature. The peer approach consists of peer leaders or older adolescents communicating messages about drug use through planned recreational and/or educational activities and discussions. Murray and Perry (1985) suggested that the peer leader (message sender) must be credible to the receiver about problems associated with drug use. Senders with low credibility include adults, in general, and teachers, in particular, as they tend to be seen as "too far removed" from the subject. Older adolescents or peer leaders appear to be more credible sources of prevention messages (Palmer, 1989). Tobler's (1986) meta-analysis of 143 adolescent drug prevention programs revealed that peer programs showed a definite superiority to other outcome measures, especially in terms of drug use. Yet the peer support program model has rarely been tested in the area of athlete drug education. Martin and Anshel (1991) found that the elite athletes in their survey preferred to consult with peers about drug use rather than approach their coach or parents.

NEW APPROACHES FOR COMBATING DRUG USE

The prevailing view among experts is that most traditional approaches to preventing drug use, particularly when focused on deterrence and curative means, have not performed up to expectations. New strategies appear warranted. Many, if not most, of these new approaches require input from the coach and, to a slightly lesser extent, from sport organizations and parents. The coach's influence on athletes' thoughts and actions has been known for many years (Anshel, 1990c; Gill, 1986). Athletes tend to place considerable value on the coach's words and behaviors. But as Taylor (1985) notes, "Many times the pressures placed on the coach to win cloud his/her otherwise proper judgment" (p. 119). The failure to play a more active role in the efforts to stem drug use is an example of improper judgment. A study conducted by the newspaper *USA Today* (February 1, 1990) illustrates this point. They found that "only 54 percent of coaches said their school has an anti-steroids drug policy" (p. 1B). It would appear that recognizing the existence, or at least the potential, of a drug problem on the team is a necessary component of combating drug use.

Following are selected cognitive and behavioral strategies for combating drug use (also see Anshel, 1986, 1987, 1991a). Cognitive techniques deal with influencing the athlete's behaviors and attitudes intellectually and psychologically through verbal and nonverbal communication. Behavioral techniques, also referred to as contingency management (Martin & Lumsden, 1987; Rushall & Siedentop, 1972), serve to shape the environment to control and influence subsequent behavior.

Cognitive Techniques

Use a Support Group. Perhaps among the first structured attempts at dealing with drug abuse on a sports team, particularly at the elite level, was conducted by the Cleveland Browns (American) football team (Collins et al., 1984). In addition to medical and psychological treatment programs in place, the team ownership hired a psychiatrist to conduct group and individual therapies and establish self-help meetings for players and their wives. The preventative component of the program was "The Inner Circle," which consisted of a group of identified, drug-involved players. As the authors describe the program, "Group discussions typically dealt with who was relapsing and why, and the need for changes in the individual's lifestyle to support staying 'clean'.... Rather than participating in coverups and deceptions, the players saw that relapses were 'contagious,' and that when one member was in trouble, others would soon follow.... The group eventually became responsible for much of its own therapeutic work in keeping its individual members away from drugs.... Relapses, once frequent, eventually became extremely rare" (p. 490).

The key to this program is the use of participation, communication, pressure, and control by the players' peer group (i.e., teammates) rather than from a higher authority, toward whom others might not trust or feel loyal. Palmer (1989) found that high school seniors served as excellent peer educators and role models in drug prevention among high school student athletes and nonathletes.

Show Concern. Coaches must communicate their feelings to team members concerning the potential dangers and poor ethics of drug use. Coaches—intentionally or unintentionally—sanction drug use among their athletes by refusing to acknowledge the importance of abstaining from drugs and informing the athletes of their feelings.

Set Limits on Unacceptable Behavior. Athletes, not unlike others, need to know the boundaries that separate acceptable from unacceptable behavior. This is particularly the case in sport when factors such as competitiveness, winning, and pressures from peers, coaches, parents, fans, even sponsors, foster the tendency to break rules and ignore proper ethics. The players must acknowledge accountability for their actions. In this way, setting limits protects the

athlete against these pressures. It is particularly important that the ramifications of breaking the team's drug policy are realistic and implemented. Unfortunately individuals will test these limits by behaving in a manner that forces a display of authority and sincerity. Children test the authority of their parents, students test the rules of their teachers, and athletes test their coaches (Ginott, 1969).

Develop a Team Policy. The team, indeed, the sporting organization, must have a specific written and expressed policy that strictly forbids drug use and states the consequences for violating this policy. The absence of such a policy may be perceived by team members as actually sanctioning drug use (Anshel, 1986; 1990a; 1991a). The policy should be distributed to each athlete in written and verbal form.

Teach Coping Skills. Orlick (1990) and Orlick and Partington (1986) claim that the ability to cope with stress and maintain self-control are among the most salient required mental skills of successful athletes. It is important to recognize that stress has many different sources, related and unrelated to the contest. For example, opponents and coaches may create severe stress during the game, whereas boredom (e.g., the lack of playing time) or dealing with the termination of a season may be other sources of stress that are independent of sport performance. The athlete's ability to cope successfully with the array of stressors in his or her sport career will likely make a significant contribution toward avoiding the influence of drugs.

The sport psychology literature is replete with suggested cognitive strategies and psychological interventions to manage stress and anxiety, while building self-confidence and attaining optimal arousal. Examples of mental techniques include positive self-talk, mental imagery, self-regulation, attentional control training, self-hypnosis, biofeedback, thought stopping, and others (see Williams, 1986, for a detailed review of these techniques).

Be Aware of the Athlete's Mental Status. As with any other person, athletes may have a troubled life away from the sport arena. Difficulties with academic pursuits, poor family or social relationships, or the lack of a meaningful relationship with their coach may foster drug use.

Allow for Input from Participants. The objective here is to enhance the athlete's perception of having a meaningful team role. Opportunities to make decisions about various issues with which they are directly affected (e.g., team policy or game strategies)—or at least discuss issues with the coach before decisions are made—would promote team loyalty and athlete accountability for their actions. It also indicates that coaches respect their players, a perception that is very important in promoting team cohesion and a supportive team climate (Fisher, Mancini, Hirsch, Proulx, & Staurowsky, 1982).

Behavioral Techniques

Behavioral techniques, in contrast to cognitive approaches, involve: (1) setting up situations that foster certain desirable responses from the athletes, and/or (2) using verbal or nonverbal techniques that reinforce favorable behaviors or performance outcomes (Martin & Lumsden, 1987).

The Role of Peers. The primary source of pressure to use—or the support to discourage using—drugs, in sport and elsewhere, is the peer group. For example, the results of a survey of 8,000 high school athletes by Heitzinger et al. (1986) revealed that 65 percent would talk to a peer before approaching an adult with a drug-related problem. Therefore, it is not surprising, as suggested from the results of this study, that developing peer support skills is the most effective drug use prevention intervention. A peer support program gives athletes the opportunity to relate with teammates about drug use in a manner that promotes the team's integrity and the drug user's self-esteem. Older, more established team members appear to be the peer leaders best suited for this task. A supportive network is established among squad members and, as such, athletes feel less isolated and alone. The result is less likelihood to resort to maladaptive behaviors such as drug taking (Reilly, 1988).

If, as is generally agreed, athletes form attitudes toward drug use during their adolescence, an all-out effort should be undertaken to provide athletes with information about steroid use, particularly from coaches and former or current athletes who are perceived as credible sources of information. Other suggestions should reduce pressure and stress. These include increasing the players' self-confidence, setting challenging but reasonable performance goals, and ensuring skill mastery and improvement.

Drug Testing. The athletes surveyed by Martin and Anshel (1991) would be deterred from using a performance-enhancing drug because of its detectability. Thus future education programs should also emphasize drug testing and sanctioning processes. While drug testing programs have heretofore been relatively infrequent, they have now become a more common reality for elite athletes—probably so much so that emphasizing drug testing programs and sanctions may contribute toward effective drug use prevention. For elite junior athletes, sport is most likely an experience from which the threat of elimination can be a powerful behavioral controller.

One benefit of drug testing and sanctions is that athletes are provided with a genuine counterargument to resist the social pressures that encourage drug taking. According to Anshel (1991b), the athlete can respond to drug-using peers, "Look, if I get caught with drugs, the league says I'll be suspended for the remainder of the season and the whole team will be hurt!" In this way the athlete can maintain his/her integrity while assertively stating his/her opposition to drug use.

Teach Skills. If most athletes take drugs to facilitate their performance, then this same objective can be met—without drugs—by teaching sport skills and strategies. Good coaches are good teachers (Anshel, 1990c). Athletes will more likely perceive their involvement in sport as successful and, consequently, in less need of artificial means to perform at superior levels, if: (1) it is apparent their skills are improving, and (2) the coach positively reinforces this performance change by verbally and nonverbally communicating his or her approval (Martin & Lumsden, 1987).

Use Proper Goal-Setting Techniques. One of the most effective means of monitoring performance improvement in sport is through the effective use of goal setting. A plethora of published evidence is available indicating proper goal-setting techniques (for reviews of related literature, see Anshel, 1990c; & Gill, 1986). One of the benefits of goal setting is to gauge desirable changes in performance quality. Ostensibly then the athlete's interpretation of this positive information feedback is that drug use is unnecessary and contraindicated.

Develop a Plan of Action. If an incidence of drug abuse does occur, it is imperative that the coach and the sport organization know in advance exactly how they intend to respond to it. A physician, lawyer, psychologist, clergy, school administrators, and parents should be accessible on a 24-hour basis. Team leaders should think through an appropriate response (e.g., should parents be contacted at this time or is it better to first speak with the athlete or with legal counsel?), and then should respond assertively and without hesitation.

Structure Some of Their Free Time. The anecdotal literature is replete with examples linking excessive and unstructured free time with drug use (e.g., Collins et al., 1984). Data is available indicating that the person's peer group is the single most important source for determining recreational activities, including drug taking (Rosenfeld et al., 1989; Wragg, 1990). To avoid placing an unfair burden on coaches and to reduce or eliminate athlete resentment of "intruding" on their free time, it is important to make available to players attractive alternatives to experimenting with drugs in overcoming boredom, especially while traveling. Examples include providing entertainment, educational sessions (guest speakers), and opportunities for open discussions.

THE COACH'S ROLE IN COMBATING DRUGS IN SPORT

Researchers and practitioners have virtually ignored the role of coaches in efforts to prevent drug abuse. It has been widely acknowledged for many years that a coach has a far greater influence in regulating athletes' behaviors and attitudes than any other individual. In particular, the coach is arguably the most important agent in preventing drug use, both on and off the team (Anshel, 1986, 1990a; Smith, 1983). Unfortunately this influence is not always directed toward athletes' best interests concerning drug taking. For instance, Australian Olympic runner Gael Martin contends that "there would be very few athletes taking steroids without the knowledge of their coaches..." (*Drugs in Sport*, 1989, p. 189).

To what extent should coaches have a role in regulating the behaviors of their athletes away from the sport arena? Should the coach feel responsible to ascertain, or be held responsible for, an athlete's actions off the field or court? Does the coach have a legal or ethical right to know what the athletes are doing on their own time? Perhaps a "hands off" policy for coaches would be more appropriate if drug use in sport were not so widespread, dangerous, illegal, and unethical. In addition, previous attempts at eliminating drug use—specifically education, counseling, threats, and punitive measures—have been relatively unsuccessful. Coaches have more credibility and loyalty from players than any other source to alter their feelings and actions. This avenue for regulating—even preventing—drug use has gone virtually untapped.

Another important issue concerns the coach's intentional or unintentional role in actually sanctioning drug use. Alarmingly government inquiries in recent months have shown that selected coaches of elite athletes have actually *encouraged* their athletes to take anabolic steroids against the rules of their sport organizations. Intentional and direct encouragement occurs when coaches advise that "taking steroids is the only way to stay competitive." The unintentional or indirect approach is manifested by requiring the participant to reach a certain body weight, obtain a demanding performance goal, making critical statements about the athlete's physical status or performance, or by ignoring drug-taking behavior. All of these actions sanction taking drugs.

One example of *direct* responsibility for drug use is to encourage cheating. For example, the *Sydney* (Australia) *Morning Herald* (June 15, 1989) reported that an Australian world-class female athlete was asked by an assistant track and field coach "... to provide a urine specimen. [The coach] said that the specimen was urgently needed to substitute for the specimen of another athlete ... who had been picked for random drug testing by officials" (p. 48). The athlete complied.

Indirect evidence of the coach's encouragement to take drugs stems from not having a team policy that prohibits drug use—or not adhering to the policy—and by making unreasonable and unhealthy physical demands on the competitor. Clinical psychologists contend that the conditions of anorexia nervosa and bulimia are often a function of such demands, especially among female athletes (Donald, 1983).

Despite the consistent pressure to win, *the coach who allows performance outcome to supercede the concern for the player's health and welfare is as dishonest and unethical in performing his or her job as is the drug-induced ath-*

lete. Winning should not be at the expense of the athlete's health and psychological well-being. It is probably true that athletes, rather than their coaches, must take the primary responsibility for their own actions, particularly when those actions are illegal and unethical. However, competitors need protection and a support network on whom to depend to cope with sport-related pressure and stress. The players need help in meeting the responsibilities of competition because they do not have the psychological resources to cope. They have a distinct psychosocial environment that engenders different attitudes, emotions, and predisposing factors to drug use from those of their nonathletic peers (Anshel, 1991a, 1991b). The consequence of this pressure may lead to drug abuse. If the competitor views drugs as potentially benefiting performance, then attaching one's self-esteem to sport success may heighten the probability of using drugs. Coaches are the primary source of raising or maintaining the performer's positive self-esteem and providing protection from the chronic pressure inherent in sport. The use of cognitive and behavioral strategies, described earlier, is aimed primarily at the person who is in the best position to implement them—the team's coach (Anshel, 1986).

According to Woodman (in Anshel, 1990a), "The root of the problem is people. The misuse of drugs in sport is a people problem; it is not just the system or the rules. The issue is ultimately one of codes or conduct of standards and it is people who set standards. If we fail to recognize and confront the drug problem in sport, the concept of athletic competition will change as we now know it" (p. 51).

CONCLUSION

Hopefully awareness of the current status of drugs in sport has raised a red flag concerning the continued need to approach these problems in a systematic and aggressive manner. Athletes are under tremendous pressure to succeed in an environment that is inherently stressful. It is unrealistic to expect them to eliminate the problem of drug abuse without external support. Educational programs, drug testing, team and league policies, and closer monitoring of the athletes' attitudes and behaviors by coaches and sport administrators—during and after the competition season—are warranted.

One issue that emerges from close scrutiny of the psychological causes of drug taking is that the underlying causes—and remedies—are *multidimensional*. It is clear that, in addition to personal characteristics, situational and environmental issues exacerbate the pressures placed on athletes to achieve success in sport. Examples include the expectations of others, particularly the coach, defining "success" as a function of outcome rather than performance improvement, pressure from teammates to "try it, it can't hurt you" or "everyone else does it, so it must be okay" and the perception of social acceptance, particularly through media reports of high-profiled athletes who take drugs—the modeling effect.

According to White (1959), humans have an intrinsic, even instinctual, need to demonstrate competent behaviors, primarily through interaction with, and mastery of, the environment. Competence motivation becomes achievement motivation when a person sets goals, directs efforts toward, and derives satisfaction from, achieving those goals. Athletes, perhaps more than many others, are driven to achieving the impossible—performing consistent and error-free skilled movement. It is in the athlete's best interests to acknowledge the boundaries of their human capabilities and inherent limitations. Coaches and parents can do more to define realistic boundaries of performance that is desirable and acceptable. As American philosopher and novelist George Santayana asserts, "knowledge of what is possible is the beginning of happiness" (*Little Essays,* 1920, p. 105).

In this way, perhaps athletes are not unlike any other subgroup that derives its self-esteem and primary sense of gratification from tasks in which its members are successful. Given the effects of these drugs on human perform-

ance, perhaps it is understandable that athletes would be tempted to engage in any activity that would help ensure success in sport—even to the possible detriment of their health and future career in sport.

Additional scientific research to ascertain the extent of drug use in contemporary sport is still needed. Information is slowly being generated about the effectiveness of drug education programs and other cognitive and behavioral strategies in reducing, even eliminating, drug use among athletes. It is hoped that the results of existing studies will galvanize researchers to go beyond the limitations of the all-too-often reported anecdotal evidence. Assessments of the relationships between the athlete's knowledge, attitudes, and drug-taking behaviors, particularly in comparing male and female competitors in different sports and age groups, need to be undertaken in a systematic and scientific fashion. Only then can coaches, parents, sport administrators, sport psychology consultants, and athletes work jointly to inhibit the illegal, unethical, and unhealthy use of drugs among those individuals who have traditionally been the healthiest models in our society, sports competitors. Nothing less than the integrity of the game is at stake.

References

Anshel, M. H. (May/June, 1986). The coach's role in preventing drug abuse by athletes. *Coaching Review, 9,* 29–32, 34–35.

Anshel, M. H. (November 15, 1987). *Coaching strategies for managing drug abuse in sport.* A presentation to coaches of the United States Olympic Ski Team, Colorado Springs, CO.

Anshel, M. H. (1990a). Commentary on the national drugs in sport conference—1989. Treating the causes and symptoms. *Australian Journal of Science and Medicine in Sport, 22,* 49–56.

Anshel, M. H. (January, 1990b). *Suggested cognitive and behavioural strategies for reducing/preventing drug abuse in sport.* A paper presented at the 1990 Commonwealth Games Conference, Auckland, New Zealand.

Anshel, M. H. (1990c). *Sport psychology: From theory to practice.* Scottsdale, AZ: Gorsuch Scarisbrick.

Anshel, M. H. (1991a). Cognitive and behavioral strategies for combating drug abuse in sport: Implications for coaches and sport psychology consultants. *The Sport Psychologist, 5,* 152–166.

Anshel, M. H. (1991b). Causes for drug abuse in sport: A survey of intercollegiate athletes. *Journal of Sport Behavior, 14,* 283–307.

Athletic Business (September 1984). *Drugs in sports, Part 2: Unraveling the issues,* pp. 48–54.

Barber, T. X. (1966). The effects of "hypnosis" and motivational suggestions on endurance and strength: A critical review of research studies. *British Journal of Social and Clinical Psychology, 5,* 42–50.

Bell, J. A., & Doege, T. C. (1987). Athletes' use and abuse of drugs. *The Physician and Sportsmedicine, 15,* 99–106, 108.

Berger, K. S. (1988). *The developing person through the life span.* New York: Worth Publishing.

Botvin, G. (1984). *Drug abuse and drug abuse research.* Rockville, MD: First Report to Congress from the Secretary, Department of Health and Human Services, National Institute on Drug Abuse.

Brower, K. J., Blow, F. C., Beresford, T. P., & Fuelling, C. (1989). An-

abolic androgenic steroid dependence. *Journal of Clinical Psychiatry, 50,* 31–32.

Chaikin, T., & Telander, R. (October 24, 1988). The nightmare of steroids. *Sports Illustrated,* pp. 84–93, 97–98, 100–102.

Chappel, J. N. (1987). Drug use and abuse in the athlete. In J. R. May and M. J. Asken (Eds.), *Sport psychology: The psychological health of the athlete* (pp. 187–212). New York: PMA Publishing.

Chu, D. (1982). *Dimensions of sport studies.* New York: John Wiley.

Cohen, J. C., Noakes, T. D., & Benade, A. J. S. (1988). Hypercholesterolemia in male power lifters using anabolic-androgenic steroids. *The Physician and Sportsmedicine, 16,* 49–50; 53–54; 56.

Cohen, S. (1979). Doping: Drugs in sport. *Drug Abuse and Alcoholism Newsletter, 8* (1).

Collins, G. B., Pippenger, C. E., & Janesz, J. W. (1984). Links in the chain: An approach to the treatment of drug abuse on a professional football team. *Cleveland Clinic Quarterly, 51,* 485–492.

Corrigan, B. (Oct.–Dec. 1988). Doping in sport. *Sports Coach, 12,* 11–17.

Donald, K. (1983). *The doping game.* Brisbane, Australia: Boolarang.

Drugs in Sport: An interim report of the Senate standing committee on environment, recreation and the arts. (May 1989). Canberra, ACT: Australian Government Publishing Service.

Drugs in Sport: Second report of the Senate standing committee on environment, recreation and the arts. (May 1990). Canberra, ACT: Australian Government Publishing Service.

Duda, J. L., & Allison, M. T. (1990). Cross-cultural analysis in exercise and sport psychology: A void in the field. *Journal of Sport & Exercise Psychology, 12,* 114–131.

Egger, G. (1981). *The sport drug.* Boston: George, Allen & Unwin.

Elkind, D. (1985). Egocentrism in adolescence. *Child Development, 38,* 1025–1034.

Ellichson, P. L., & Abby, R. D. (1987). *Toward more effective drug prevention programs*. Santa Monica, CA: Rand Corporation.

English, G. (1987). A theoretical explanation of why athletes choose to use steroids, and the role of the coach in influencing behavior. *National Strength and Conditioning Association Journal, 9,* 53–56.

Erikson, E. H. (1968). *Identity: Youth and crisis*. New York: W. W. Norton.

Evans, R., Rozelle, R., Maxwell-Raines, B., Dill, C., Guthrie, R., Henderson, A., & Hill, P. (1981). Social modelling films to deter smoking in adolescents: Results of a three-year field investigation. *Journal of Applied Psychology, 66,* 399–414.

Feltz, D. L. (1988). Self-confidence and sports performance. In K. B. Pandolf (Ed.), *Exercise and sport sciences reviews,* Vol. 16, pp. 423–457. New York: Macmillan.

Fisher, A. C., Mancini, V. H., Hirsch, R. L., Proulx, T. J., & Staurowsky, E. J. (1982). Coach-athlete interactions and team climate. *Journal of Sport Psychology, 4,* 388–404.

Gerslick, K., Grady, K., Sexton, E., & Lyons, M. (1981). Personality and sociodemographic factors in adolescent drug use. In D. J. Lettiers & J. P. Ludford, (Eds.), *Drug abuse and the American adolescent* (pp. 81–16). Rockville, MD: U.S. Department of Health and Human Services, National Institute on Drug Abuse, Research Monograph No. 38, 81–1166.

Gill, D. (1986). *Psychological dynamics of sport*. Champaign, IL: Human Kinetics.

Ginott, H. (1969). *Between parent and teenager*. New York: Avon.

Goldman, B. (1984). *Death in the locker room: Steroids and sports*. South Bend, IN: Icarus Press.

Goodstadt, M. S., & Sheppard, M. A. (Fall 1982). Relationships between drug education and drug use: Carts and horses. *Journal of Drug Issues, 12,* 431–442.

Gregg, E., & Rejeski, W. J. (1990). Social psychobiologic dysfunction associated with anabolic steroid abuse: A review. *The Sport Psychologist, 4,* 275–284.

Griffin, N. S., Keogh, J. F., & Maybee, R. (1984). Performer perceptions of movement confidence. *Journal of Sport Psychology, 6,* 395–407.

Hanson, D. (1980). Drug education, does it work? In F. Scarpitti & S. Datesman (Eds.), *Drugs and youth culture: Annual reviews of drug and alcohol abuse* (Vol. 4, pp. 212–236). Beverly Hills, CA: Sage.

Hanson, T. W., & Gould, D. (1988). Factors affecting the ability of coaches to estimate their athletes' trait and state anxiety levels. *The Sport Psychologist, 2,* 298–313.

Hawkins, J., Lishner, D., & Catalano, R. (1985). Childhood predictors and the prevention of adolescent substance abuse. In C. Jones & Battjes R. (Eds.), *Etiology of drug abuse: Implications for preventions* (pp. 77–125). Rockville, Maryland: U.S. Department of Health and Human Services, National Institute on Drug Abuse Research, Monograph No. 56.

Heitzinger and Associates (1986). *1981–1986 Data collection and analysis: High school, college, professional athletes alcohol/drug survey*. 333 W. Miflin, Madison, WI.

Hewitt, P. L., & Flett, G. L. (1991). Perfectionism in the self and social contexts: Conceptualization, assessment, and association with psychopathology. *Journal of Personality and Social Psychology, 60,* 456–470.

Hewitt, P. L., Mittelstaedt, W., & Flett, G. L. (1990). Self-oriented perfectionism and generalized performance importance in depression. *Individual Psychology Journal of Adlerian Theory, Research and Practice, 46,* 67–73.

Hinton, E. R., & Taylor, S. (1986). Does placebo response mediate runner's high? *Perceptual and Motor Skills, 62,* 789–790.

Horner, M. S. Toward an understanding of achievement-related conflicts in women. *Journal of Social Issues, 28,* 157–175.

Jessor, R. (1982). Problem behavior and developmental transition in adolescence. *The Journal of School Health, 12,* 295–300.

Jospe, M. (1978). *The placebo effect in healing*. Lexington, MA: D. C. Heath.

Julien, R. M. (1981). *A primer of drug action* (3rd ed.). San Francisco: W. H. Freeman.

Kandel, D. B. (1978). *Longitudinal research on drug use: Empirical findings and methodological issues*. Washington, DC: Hemisphere-Wiley.

Kinder, B. N., Pope, N. E., & Walfish, S. (1980). Drug and alcohol education programs: A review of outcome studies. *The International Journal of the Addictions, 15,* 1035–1054.

Lamb, D. R. (1984). Anabolic steroids in athletics: How well do they work and how dangerous are they? *The American Journal of Sports Medicine, 12,* 31–38.

Ljungqvist, A. (1990). The anti-doping efforts of international federation. In J. Park (Ed.), *Proceedings of the international symposium on drug abuse in sports (doping)* (pp. 29–32). Seoul, South Korea: Korea Institute of Science and Technology.

Lombardo, J. A. (1987). Stimulants. In R. H. Strauss (Ed.), *Drugs and performance in sports* (pp. 69–86). Philadelphia: W. B. Saunders.

Lubell, A. (1989). Does steroid abuse cause—or excuse—violence? *The Physician and Sportsmedicine, 17,* 176, 178–180, 185.

Mahoney, M. J., & Meyers, A. W. (1989). Anxiety and athletic performance: Traditional and cognitive-developmental perspectives. In D. Hackfort & C. D. Spielberger (Eds.), *Anxiety in sports: An international perspective* (pp. 77–94). New York: Hemisphere.

Marcello, R. J., Danish, S. J., & Stolberg, A. L. (1989). An evaluation of strategies developed to prevent substance abuse among student-athletes. *The Sport Psychologist, 3,* 196–211.

Martin, G. L., & Lumsden, J. A. (1987). *Coaching: An effective behavioral approach*. St. Louis: Times Mirror/Mosby.

Martin, M. B., & Anshel, M. H. (1991). Attitudes of elite junior athletes on drug-taking behaviors: Implications for drug prevention programs. *Drug Education Journal of Australia, 5,* 223–238.

Morgan, W. P., & Brown, D. R. (1983). Hypnosis. In M. H. Williams (Ed.), *Ergogenic aids* (pp. 223–252). Champaign, IL: Human Kinetics.

Moses, E. (October 10, 1988). An athlete's Rx for the drug problem. *Newsweek,* p. 57.

Mottram, D. R. (Ed.) (1988). *Drugs in sport*. London, England: E. & F. N. Spon Ltd.

Murray, D. & Perry, C. (1985). The prevention of adolescent drug abuse: Implications of etiological development, behavioral and environmental models. In C. Jones & R. Battjes (Eds.), *Prevention* (pp. 77–126). Rockville, Maryland: U.S. Department of Health and Human Services, National Institute and Drug Abuse, Research Monograph No. 56.

Murray, T. H. (1984). Comments from the lay press. *The Physician and Sportsmedicine, 12,* 187–188.

Nicholson, N. (1989). The role of drug education. In S. Haynes & M. Anshel (Eds.), *Proceedings of the 1989 National Drugs in Sport Conference—Treating the Causes and Symptoms* (pp. 48–57). University of Wollongong, Wollongong, NSW, Australia.

Nicholson, N., & Agnew, M. (1989). *Education strategies to reduce drug use in sport.* Canberra, ACT: Australian Sports Drug Agency.

Officer, S. A., & Rosenfeld, L. B. (1985). Self-disclosure to male and female coaches by female high school athletes. *Journal of Sport Psychology, 6,* 360–370.

Orlick, T., & Partington, J. (1986). *Psyched: Inner views of winning.* Ottawa, Canada: Coaching Association of Canada.

Palmer, J. (Fall 1989). High school senior athletes as peer educators and role models: An innovative approach to drug prevention. *Journal of Alcohol and Drug Education, 35,* 23–27.

Park, J. (Ed.) (1991). *Proceedings of the International Symposium on Drug Abuse in Sports (Doping)* (pp. 51–70). Seoul, Korea: Korea Institute of Science and Technology.

Polich, J., Ellickson, P., Reuter, P., & Kahan, P. (1984). *Strategies for controlling adolescent drug use.* Santa Monica, CA: The Rand Corporation.

Pomeranz, D. M., & Krasner, L. (1969). Effect of a placebo on a simple motor response. *Perceptual and Motor Skills, 28,* 15–18.

Pope, H. G., Katz, D. L., & Champoux, R. (July, 1988). Anabolic-androgenic steroid use among 1,010 college men. *The Physician and Sportsmedicine, 16,* 75–77; 80–81.

Prokop, L. (1990). The history of doping. In J. Park (Ed.), *Proceedings of the international symposium on drug abuse in sports (doping)* (pp. 1–9). Seoul, South Korea: Korea Institute of Science and Technology.

Reilly, C. (1988). *An evaluation of the peer support program.* (Report No. A 88/5). Sydney, NSW, Australia: New South Wales Department of Health.

Rosenfeld, L. B., Richman, J. M., & Hardy, C. J. (1989). Examining social support networks among athletes: Description and relationship to stress. *The Sport Psychologist, 3,* 23–33.

Ross, M., & Olson, J. M. (1981). An expectancy-attribution model of the effects of placebos. *Psychological Review, 88,* 408–437.

Rotella, R. J. (1984). Psychological care of the injured athlete. In L. Bunker, R. J. Rotella, & A. S. Reilly (Eds.), *Sport psychology: Psychological considerations in maximizing sport performance* (pp. 151–164). Ithaca, NY: Mouvement.

Rushall, B. S., & Siedentop, D. (1972). *The development and control of behavior in sport and physical education.* Philadelphia: Lea & Febiger.

Russell, D. G. (1990). *Drugs and medicines in sport.* Wellington, New Zealand: Royal Society of New Zealand.

Ryan, A. J. (1982). Advantage, drug-free athletes. *The Physician and Sportsmedicine, 10,* 50.

Scheier, M. F., & Carver, C. S. (1985). Optimism, coping, and health: Assessment and implication of generalized outcome expectancies. *Health Psychology, 4,* 219–247.

Shroyer, J. (1990). Getting tough on anabolic steroids: Can we win the battle? *The Physician and Sportsmedicine, 18,* 106, 108–110, 115, 118.

Silva, J. M. (1982). An evaluation of fear of success in female and male athletes and nonathletes. *Journal of Sport Psychology, 4,* 92–96.

Smith, G. (1983). Recreational drugs in sport. *The Physician and Sportsmedicine, 11,* 75–76, 79, 82.

Smith, J. L., & Bozymowski, M. F. (1965). Effect of attitude toward warm-ups on motor performance. *Research Quarterly, 36,* 78–85.

Spielberger, C. D. (1989). Stress and anxiety in sports. In D. Hackfort & C. D. Spielberger (Eds.), *Anxiety in sports: An international perspective* (pp. 3–18). New York: Plenum.

Stuart, R. (1974). Teaching facts about drugs: Pushing or preventing? *Journal of Educational Psychology, 66,* 189–201.

Straub, W. F. (1982). Sensation seeking among high-and low-risk male athletes. *Journal of Sport Psychology, 4,* 246–253.

Strauss, R. H. (October–December 1988). Drug abuse in sports: A three-pronged response. *Sports Coach, 12,* 23.

Strauss, R. H. (1987a). *Drugs and performance in sports.* Philadelphia: W. B. Saunders.

Strauss, R. H. (1987b). Anabolic steroids. In R. H. Strauss (Ed.), *Drugs and performance in sports* (pp. 59–68). Philadelphia: W. B. Saunders.

Strauss, R. H., & Curry, T. J. (1987). Magic, science, and drugs. In R. H. Strauss (Ed.), *Drugs & performance in sports* (pp. 3–10). Philadelphia: W. B. Saunders.

Swisher, J., & Hu, T. (1986). Alternatives to drug abuse: Some are and some are not. In T. Glynn, C. Leukefeld, & J. Ludford (Eds.), *Preventing adolescent drug abuse: Intervention strategies* (pp. 141–153). Rockville, MD: U.S. Department of Health and Human Services, National Institute on Drug Abuse, Research Monograph, No. 47, 141–153.

Taylor, W. N. (1985). *Hormonal manipulation: A new era of monstrous athletes.* Jefferson, NC: McFarland.

Tobler, N. (1986.) Meta-analysis of 143 adolescent drug prevention programs: Quantitative outcome results of program participants compared to a control or comparison group. *The Journal of Drug Issues, 16,* 537–567.

Tricker, R., & Cook, D. L. (1989). The current status of drug intervention and prevention in college athletic programs. *Journal of Alcohol and Drug Education, 34,* 38–45.

Tricker, R., Cook, D. L., & McGuire, R. (1989). Issues related to drug abuse in college athletics: Athletes at risk. *The Sport Psychologist, 3,* 155–165.

Vealey, R. S. (1986). Conceptualization of sport-confidence and competitive orientation: Preliminary investigation and instrument development. *Journal of Sport Psychology, 8,* 221–246.

White, R. W. (1959). Motivation reconsidered: The concept of competence. *Psychological Review, 66,* 297–333.

Whitlock, F. A. (1980). *Drugs: Drinking and recreational drug use in Australia.* Stanmore, NSW, Australia: Cassell Australia.

Will, G. F. (February 4, 1985). Exploring the racer's edge. *Newsweek,* p. 88.

Williams, J. M. (1986). *Applied sport psychology: Personal growth to peak performance.* Palo Alto, CA: Mayfield.

Williams, M. H. (1989). *Beyond training: How athletes enhance performance legally and illegally.* Champaign, IL: Leisure Press.

Williams, M. H. (1983). *Ergogenic aids in sport.* Champaign, IL: Human Kinetics.

Wragg, J. (1990). The impact of adolescent development: Implications for the timing, evaluation, and development of drug education programs. *Drug Education Journal of Australia, 4,* 233–239.

Wright, J. E. (1980). Anabolic steroids and athletics. *Exercise Sport Science Reviews, 8,* 149–202.

Yesalis, C. E., Herrick, R. T., Buckley, W. E., Friedl, K. E., Brannon, D., & Wright, J. E. (1988). Self-reported use of anabolic-androgenic steroids by elite power-lifters. *The Physician and Sportsmedicine, 16,* 91–94; 96–98.

Zuckerman, M. (1979). *Sensation-seeking: Beyond the optimal level of arousal.* Hillsdale, NJ: Erlbaum.

·41·

PSYCHOLOGICAL/BEHAVIORAL EFFECTS OF ANABOLIC-ANDROGENIC STEROIDS

Michael S. Bahrke

Charles E. Yesalis

Anabolic-androgenic steroids (AAS) are a group of synthetic derivatives of the male hormone testosterone that have been modified to prolong their presence in the bloodstream and, in the case of athletes, to maximize gains in muscular strength and size (anabolic effect) and minimize their masculinizing (androgenic) effects (Kopera, 1985; Winters, 1990). They are often consumed (orally and/or intramuscularly) by users, including athletes, in amounts that exceed recommended therapeutic doses by ten-to a hundredfold (Duchaine, 1989; Pope & Katz, 1988). Users are also known to "cycle" (6–12-week periods of use), "stack" (use several kinds of AAS concurrently), and "pyramid" (increasing and decreasing amounts of) AAS (Duchaine, 1989). The use of AAS is associated with many undesirable, harmful, or even fatal effects, including a variety of hepatic abnormalities, changes in cardiovascular risk factors, endocrinologic alterations, and psychological and behavioral changes (Haupt & Rovere, 1984; Hickson, Ball, & Falduto, 1989; Lamb, 1984). However, the incidence of serious effects thus far reported has been extremely low (Friedl, 1990). Nevertheless for several decades experts in the field have consistently stated that the long-term effects of AAS use are unknown (Yesalis, Wright, & Bahrke, 1989).

AAS's have been used by athletes to enhance performance for many years (Wright, 1978, 1982). The first reports of widespread use appeared in the 1950s among weight lifters and bodybuilders. Since that time AAS use has permeated a myriad of sports (Ljungqvist, 1975; Silvester, 1973). It is now evident that the use of AAS, at least in the United States, is not limited to elite amateur athletes but has trickled down through the colleges to the high school and junior high school levels, including recreational athletes and

nonathletes (Yesalis, Anderson, Buckley, & Wright, 1990). A nationwide study of AAS use found that 6.6% of male high school seniors have used them (Buckley et al., 1988). The use of AAS, has also become a major health concern, resulting in their classification as a controlled substance, where distribution without a prescription is a felony punishable by up to five years imprisonment and up to a $250,000 fine. Possession of AAS in the U.S.A. is a misdemeanor punishable by up to one year imprisonment and a minimum of a $1,000 fine (Congressional Record, Senate, 1990).

The purposes of this chapter are to discuss the: (1) use of androgens for the treatment of mental disorders; (2) psychological/behavioral effects of androgen therapy in androgen-deficient individuals; (3) psychological/behavioral effects of AAS use among athletes, including AAS dependency and prevention and the treatment of AAS abuse; and (4) methodological issues involved in assessing the relationship between androgen levels and mood and behavior.

MENTAL DISORDERS AND ANDROGEN THERAPY

Androgen preparations were rather widely and successfully used in the treatment of involutional psychoses, melancholia, and depression for many years (Altschule & Tillotson, 1948; Ault, Hoctor, & Werner, 1937; Beumont, Bancroft, Beardwood, & Russell, 1972; Burnett, 1963; Danziger & Blank, 1942; Guirdham, 1940; Hamilton, 1937; Heller & Myers, 1944; Itil, 1976; MacMaster & Alamin, 1963; Sansoy, Roy, & Shields, 1971; Tec, 1974; Thomas & Hill,

1940; Vogel, Klaiber, & Broverman, 1985; Werner, 1939, 1943; Werner, Johns, Hoctor, Ault, Kohler, & Weis, 1934; Wynn & Landon, 1961). Recently, however, in contrast to these earlier findings, more focused clinical reports have suggested that affective and psychotic syndromes, some of violent proportions, may be associated with the use of anabolic steroids in particular individuals (Annitto & Layman, 1980; Choi, Parrott, & Cowan, 1989; Conacher & Workman, 1989; Freinhar & Alvarez, 1985; Katz & Pope, 1990; Leckman & Scahill, 1990; Moore, 1988; Pope & Katz, 1987, 1988, 1990).

Several cases have recently been reported wherein presumed psychological and behavioral effects of anabolic steroids are alleged by defendants to have significantly influenced the commission of criminal acts (Conacher & Workman, 1989; *Indianapolis Star,* 1988; Lubell, 1989; *Maryland v. Michael D. Williams,* 1986; Moss, 1988; *Newsweek,* 1988; *Racine Journal-Times,* 1990; *Roanoke Times,* 1988; Fort Lauderdale *Sun-Sentinel,* 1988). This legal strategy has been identified in the popular press as the "dumbbell defense" (*Newsweek,* 1988).

EFFECTS OF ANABOLIC STEROIDS ON THE NERVOUS SYSTEM

Anabolic steroids have been shown to have significant effects on both the development and function of the nervous system. Many years ago, androgens were shown to act directly on the brain (Phoenix, Goy, Gerall, & Young, 1959). These authors suggested that during early development androgens acted to organize neural pathways involved in male behaviors, while during adulthood they acted on differentiated pathways to activate previously organized behaviors. Data from animal studies indicate that both estrogens and androgens act on neural structures that are identical to, or closely associated with, sensory pathways and the ventricular recess organs of the hypothalamus (Stumpf & Sar, 1976). Androgens have been reported to selectively stimulate neurons of the somatomotor system and circuits associated with aggression (Stumpf & Sar, 1976). Androgens have been shown to affect the morphology of mammalian central nervous system neurons in adulthood (DeVoogd, 1987).

Researchers (Itil, Cora, Akpinar, Herrmann, & Patterson, 1974) have demonstrated quantitatively the physiological correlates of certain previously reported behavioral effects of anabolic steroids. These include an increase of mental alertness, mood elevation, improvement of memory and concentration, and reduction of sensations of fatigue, all of which can be partly related to the "stimulatory" effects of anabolic steroids on the central nervous system. Electroencephalographic profiles resulting from varying dosages of anabolic steroids were found to be very similar to those seen with such psychostimulants as dextroamphetamine and the tricyclic antidepressants. Others (Broverman, Klaiber, Kobayashi, & Vogel, 1968; Klaiber, Broverman, &

Kobayashi, 1967; Stenn, Klaiber, Vogel, & Broverman, 1972) have concluded that the adrenergic-like effects of testosterone on brain function are a result of an elevation of the brain's norepinephrine level, which might result from the inhibition of monoamine oxidase activity in the brain.

Further speculation indicates that the "heightened" state of behavioral reactivity that facilitates the automatization of behavior may well be due to an increased level of norepinephrine in the brain.

Inasmuch as improvements in muscle strength and power can, in part, be accounted for by neural factors, including neurotransmitter levels (Hakkinen & Komi, 1983; Moritani & DeVries, 1979), findings that androgens may in some manner modify neural and neuromuscular functions support the concept of a significant role for these mechanisms in the production of ergogenic effects (Alen, Hakkinen, & Komi, 1984; Brooks, 1980; Hakkinen & Alen, 1986; Wilson, 1988).

ANDROGEN DEFICIENCIES AND ANDROGEN THERAPY

Although the primary use of AAS is in replacement therapy for male hypogonadism, other medical uses of AAS include the treatment of osteoporosis, mammary carcinoma, anemias, and hereditary angioneurotic edema, and for growth promotion in various forms of stunted growth. Observation and clinical trials indicate that adjuvant therapy with AAS can be supportive in the treatment of conditions characterized by negative nitrogen balance—e.g., major surgery, cachexia of various origins, burns, traumata, convalescence from illness, injuries and immobilizations, as well as during radiotherapy and therapy with cytotoxic drugs (Kochakian, 1976; Kruskemper, 1968).

Several studies have been conducted over the years examining the effects of androgen therapy in individuals with androgen deficiencies (Davidson, Camargo, & Smith, 1979; Franchi, Luisi, & Kicovic, 1978; Franchimont, Kicovic, Mattei, & Roulier, 1978; Luisi & Franchi, 1980; O'Carroll, Shapiro, & Bancroft, 1985; Salmimies, Kockott, Pirke, Vogt, & Schill, 1982; Skakkebaek, Bancroft, Davidson, & Warner, 1981; Wu, Bancroft, Davidson, & Nicol, 1982). Results from these studies are mixed. Some demonstrate significant positive psychological changes with AAS (Franchi et al., 1978; Franchimont et al., 1978; Luisi & Franchi, 1980; O'Carroll et al., 1985; Skakkebaek et al., 1981), others do not (Davidson et al., 1979; O'Carroll & Bancroft, 1984; Salmimies et al., 1982; Wu et al., 1982). However, no adverse or undesired psychological or behavioral effects were observed in these studies.

Interestingly, five of the six (83%) studies, in which oral androgens were administered (Franchi et al., 1978; Franchimont et al., 1978; Luisi & Franchi, 1980; O'Carroll et al., 1985; Skakkebaek et al., 1981), reported improved mood states following therapy; the results of the two studies using intramuscular injections of various testosterone esters (Davidson et al., 1979; Salmimies et al., 1982) indicated no change in mood states. Finally, in a carefully controlled, double-blind crossover comparison of biweekly injections of testosterone esters or placebo in two groups of men with *normal* testosterone levels, O'Carroll and Bancroft (1984) found no significant change in mood ratings following 12 weeks of treatment. However, it is unknown whether long-term use or the use of pharmocological doses by otherwise healthy individuals, particularly adolescents, might result in similar outcomes.

In addition to the above studies, which have examined the effects of androgen therapy in androgen-deficient males, other studies have been carried out over the past 2 decades to assess the contraceptive efficiency of hormonally induced azoospermia in normal men (Burris, Ewing, & Sherins, 1988; Matsumoto, 1990; Schearer et al., 1978). In an investigation conducted by the World Health Organization Task Force on Methods for the Regulation of Male Fertility (1990), 157 of 271 men became azoospermic following weekly testosterone injections and were followed over a one-year efficacy phase. Although subjects withdrew from the study for several reasons, only three participants reported increased aggressiveness and libido resulting from the injections as the cause for their discontinuation. Problems of increased aggressiveness or libido for men who remained in the study were not reported by the authors.

EFFECTS OF WEIGHT TRAINING AND ANABOLIC-ANDROGENIC STEROIDS ON ATHLETE BEHAVIOR

Very few studies are available on the personality and psychological characteristics of the changes that might be incurred as a result of heavy resistance training in competitive weight lifters and bodybuilders, separate from those using AAS. Three of the four studies discussed here were conducted prior to the systematic use of AAS and provide an opportunity to isolate the effect of resistance training on behavior. In a study examining the personalities of track athletes, student pilots, physical education majors, and students enrolled in weight lifting, Henry (1941) found that weight lifters were significantly more introverted, hypersensitive, hypochondriac, and felt inferior. Thune (1949), in a study of YMCA weight lifters, reported a lack of self-confidence or aggressiveness and a desire "to be more manly" were major factors encouraging men to participate in a weightlifting program. In a comparison of 20 weight lifters and 20 nonweightlifting males, weight lifters were found to have significantly greater feelings of masculine inadequacy, rejection, dependency, and homosexual tendencies, leading Harlow (1951) to conclude that "weight training seems to be an attempted solution for feelings of masculine inadequacy and inferiority." On the other hand, in 1983, Freedson, Mihevic, Loucks, and Girandola found 10 competitive female body builders to be somewhat less

anxious, neurotic, depressed, angry, fatigued, and confused, and more extroverted, vigorous, and self-motivated than the general population, indicating "good mental health." Unfortunately no mention is made by Freedson et al. (1983) as to whether their subjects were AAS users.

Beyond the few studies examining the personality and psychological alterations that may accompany weight lifting, there is little understanding of the extent to which resistance (or other) training may affect and/or facilitate the expression of aggression. Psychological and behavioral changes, such as increased aggressiveness and irritability, have been reported on an anecdotal basis by athletes using anabolic steroids as well as by their families and friends (Goldman, Bush, & Klatz, 1984; Taylor, 1982; Taylor, 1987a, b; Wright, 1978, 1982). It is possible, however, that, as occurs with the use of so many drugs, many of the subjectively perceived psychological and behavioral changes reported by anabolic steroid users are a direct result of expectancy, imitation, or role modeling. Observing the actions of other anabolic steroid users and athletes may greatly influence the expectations and behaviors of those in the initial and early continuation of use. In addition, aggressive or even violent behavior that may be unacceptable outside the athletic environment may not only be fully acceptable but actually encouraged and even required within the weight room or on the playing field.

Ergogenic Effects of Anabolic-Androgenic Steroids

Several researchers (Brooks, 1980; Ryan, 1981; Wilson & Griffin, 1980) have suggested that some, if not most, of the ergogenic benefits of anabolic steroids may derive from their psychological effects. It is possible that anabolic steroid use may elevate arousal (Rejeski, Brubaker, Herb, Kaplan, & Manuck, 1988), increase self-confidence and pain threshold (Holzbauer, 1976), and facilitate expression of the "all-out" physical effort demanded during training and competition in a variety of sports. In the absence of adequate external forces, internal discipline, or social coping skills, these phenomena could lead to expression of aggression at inappropriate times.

Hervey et al, (1976) have reported that one value of taking anabolic steroids, as expressed by some athletes, lay in the reduction of fatigue during the training season, thereby allowing for more training to be done. Freed, Banks, Longson, & Burley (1975) provide anecdotal or self-reported information that athletes using anabolic steroids generally are less easily fatigued, allowing for longer, more frequent, and/or more intense training sessions. This could be related to the fact that anabolic steroids can block and reverse the catabolic effects of glucocorticosteroids that are released during periods of stress including physical exertion (Boone et al., 1990; Kochakian, 1976; Kruskemper, 1968; Williams, 1981). Brooks (1980) has suggested that the increases in aggression and energy that the athlete feels may be the result of the neurological changes previously mentioned. In cases where anabolic steroids do improve physical or physiological capacities or performance, the improvement is likely due, to some extent, to increases in training per se as well as to any pharmacological effect. Despite these suggestions and self-reports, scientific data supporting the notion that psychological changes (enhanced arousal, confidence, aggression, motivation) play a primary role in mediating any ergogenic effects of anabolic steroids is lacking.

PSYCHOLOGICAL/BEHAVIORAL EFFECTS OF ANABOLIC-ANDROGENIC STEROIDS AMONG ATHLETES

Several studies have examined the side effects of anabolic steroids (Annitto & Layman, 1980; Freinhar & Alvarez, 1985; Haupt & Rovere, 1984; Lindstrom, Nilsson, Katzman, Janzon, & Dyming, 1990; Pope & Katz, 1987; Strauss, Ligget, & Lanese, 1985; Strauss, Wright, Finerman, & Catlin, 1983; Tilzey, Heptonstall, & Hamblin, 1981). Currently the most frequently quoted report concerning the psychological and behavioral effects of anabolic steroids is that of Pope and Katz (1988). This report serves as an example of the problems typically encountered in examining the psychological and behavioral effects associated with anabolic steroid use by athletes. Pope and Katz interviewed 41 steroid users with a structured diagnostic interview. Self-reports of various psychiatric syndromes during anabolic steroid use were compared with periods of no anabolic steroid use.

Results indicate that according to DSM-III-R criteria, five subjects (12%) manifested psychotic symptoms, four others (10%) had "subthreshold" or equivocal psychotic symptoms, five subjects (12%) reported a manic episode, and 22% developed a full affective syndrome during anabolic steroid use. It is unclear whether these groups were mutually exclusive. None of the 41 subjects recalled adverse effects of anabolic steroids sufficient to require medical consultation, and apparently none sought treatment for their mental health disturbances. Although Pope and Katz do not elaborate on their recruitment of participants, other than to report that they were volunteers obtained by advertisements at 38 gymnasia in the Boston and Santa Monica areas and paid $25 for a confidential interview, they do state that ". . . despite our considerable efforts at recruitment, only a minority of steroid users were willing to be interviewed." Unfortunately the difficulty Pope and Katz had in obtaining subjects raises questions about the representativeness of their sample relative to the population of anabolic steroid users. Given the vast pool of potential participants, their difficulty in obtaining volunteers could suggest a low incidence of psychiatric problems among anabolic steroid users as well as a basic mistrust of the medical and scientific establishment.

It is conceivable that those anabolic steroid users who elected to participate in the study were individuals with the greatest severity and frequency of mental disturbance. It is also probably safe to assume that individuals willing to take anabolic steroids and other drugs of questionable origin, content, and purity, and with serious legal as well as health effects differ from the population on a wide variety of characteristics, including mental health. Fifteen percent of Pope and Katz's subjects reported past alcohol abuse or dependence and 32% reported other prior substance abuse or dependence, including cannabis (17%) and cocaine (12%).

Interpretation of the reports of these subjects must be tempered by the lack of information regarding the extent to which their use occurred concurrently with anabolic steroids and with psychiatric symptoms and by the absence of knowledge on the interaction of anabolic steroids and such drugs of abuse. Seventeen percent had a first-degree relative with a major affective disorder (somewhat higher than what would be expected (Kaplan & Sadock, 1990) and two subjects reported symptoms of a full affective disorder when not taking steroids. Finally, while it is difficult to establish the extent to which anabolic steroids may have contributed to the psychotic episodes reported by Pope and Katz, and while the media have sensationalized their findings somewhat, it seems likely that, with more widespread use of anabolic steroids and increased efforts to document such reactions, additional cases will be forthcoming.

In a more recent investigation, Perry, Andersen, and Yates (1990) used two self-report instruments, the Personality Disorder Questionnaire and the Symptom Checklist-90, and a verbal interview based on the National Institutes of Mental Health's Diagnostic Interview Schedule to examine mental status changes in 20 competitive and noncompetitive anabolic steroid-using weight lifters. Based on responses to the SCL-90, significant percentages of subjects admitted to increased hostility and aggression (95%), depression (70%), paranoid thoughts (70%), and psychotic features (65%) during steroid use. With respect to the personality disorder findings, the steroid users displayed more personality disturbances overall compared with a control group of 20 weight lifters who did not use anabolic steroids and a sex- and age-matched control group from the local community—85%, 50%, and 35%, respectively.

Although no individual personality disorder or trait differences were significant between steroid users and the weight-lifter controls, both steroid user and nonsteroid user weight-lifter groups exhibited more flamboyant features (histrionic, narcissistic, antisocial, and borderline) when contrasted to the community controls. The DIS was unable to identify any psychiatric diagnoses that were occurring more frequently in either the weight-lifter control or the steroid group. No cases of panic disorder, major depressive episode (recurrent), grief reaction, mania (bipolar), or atypical bipolar disorder were found. Interestingly there were two cases of major depression (single episode) in the controls and one in the steroid users. Alcohol abuse was diagnosed in 65% (13) of the weight-lifter controls while 7 (35%) cases of abuse and 2 (10%) cases of dependence were recognized in the steroid users. Drug abuse was observed in one control and one steroid user, while drug dependence was seen in one of the steroid users. Although this study relied on self-report and interview data only and used a relatively small and local sample, it appears to provide basic knowledge for further research strategies.

As part of an effort to assess physiological and psychological states accompanying anabolic steroid usage, Bahrke, Wright, Strauss, and Catlin (in press, to be published late 1992) examined the psychological characteristics and subjectively perceived behavioral and somatic changes accompanying steroid usage in 12 current anabolic steroid users. The results obtained from the users were compared with results obtained from 14 previous users (no AAS use more recent than 1 month) and 24 nonusers. Although both current and former users reported subjectively perceived changes in enthusiasm, aggression, irritability, insomnia, muscle size, and libido when using anabolic steroids, these changes were not confirmed in comparison across groups using standardized psychological inventories (Buss-Durkee Hostility Inventory and Profile of Mood States Questionnaire).

The presence of subjectively perceived, anabolic steroid-associated behavioral and somatic changes in the absence of significant differences in standard psychological inventory responses illustrates the complexity of these relationships and dictates the need for additional research. The findings of Bahrke et al. (in press, to be published in late 1992) are both compatible with and complementary to anecdotes, case reports, and data from individual psychiatrists. The "negative" findings do not negate the possibility of anabolic steroids precipitating aberrant behavior in some users. The general impression, however, is that irritability is slightly increased in many users and that in a small number of users who are premorbid, anabolic steroid use may well be sufficient to "push them over the edge" and contribute to irrational or violent behavior, particularly where the use of other drugs of abuse is involved (Bahrke, Wright, O'Connor, Strauss, & Catlin, 1990).

In an investigation similar to the Bahrke et al. (1990, 1992) studies, Lefavi, Reeve, and Newland (1990) used the Multi-Dimensional Anger Inventory and the Steroid-Symptom Scale to compare 13 present steroid users with 14 nonusers and 18 former users, and concluded that anabolic steroid use may be associated with more frequent episodes of anger that are of greater intensity and duration and are characterized by a more hostile attitude toward others.

For the most part, individuals use anabolic steroids to significantly improve appearance and/or performance beyond what would be expected from training alone (Catlin & Hatton, 1991). Also, individuals using anabolic steroids appear to believe that higher doses and continued use will result in greater gains (Alen & Hakkinen, 1985; Alen, Hakkinen, & Komi, 1984; Alen, Rahkila, Reinila, Reijo, 1987; Alen, Reinila, & Vihko, 1985; Forbes, 1985; Hakkinen & Alen, 1986; Hervey et al., 1976; Kilshaw, Harkness, Hobson, & Smith, 1975). When individuals discontinue using anabolic steroids, their size and strength diminish, often very dramatically (Alen & Hakkinen, 1985; Alen, Hakkinen, & Komi, 1984; Alen et al., 1984, 1987; Forbes, 1985; Hakkinen & Alen, 1986), and this outcome, as well as

any psychological effects of use that serve to create a new body image, improved self-esteem, heightened libido, and general euphoria, are thought to motivate renewed use of anabolic steroids (Yesalis, Streit, Vicary, Friedl, Brannon, & Buckley, 1989; Yesalis, Vicary, Buckley, Streit, Katz, & Wright, 1990).

Anabolic-Androgenic Steroids and Dependency

As with corticosteroids (Alcena & Alexopoulos, 1985; Alpert & Seigerman, 1986; Amatruda, Hurst, & D'Esopo, 1965; Byyny, 1976; Dixon & Christy, 1980; Judd, Burrows, & Norman, 1983; Kaufmann, Kahaner, Peselow, & Gershon, 1982), increasing attention and discussion is being focused on the withdrawal effects that athletes encounter when they cease use of anabolic steroids, leading many experts to conclude that AAS use may lead to psychological dependence in some users (Brower, 1990; Brower, Blow, Beresford, & Fuelling, 1989; Brower, Blow, Eliopulos, & Beresford, 1989; Brower, Blow, Young, & Hill, 1991; Brower, Eliopulos, Blow, Catlin, & Beresford, 1990; Dimeff & Malone, 1991; Goldman, Bush, & Klatz, 1984; Hays, Littleton, & Stillner, 1990; Kashkin & Kleber, 1989; Pope & Katz, 1988; Tennant, Black, & Voy, 1988; Yesalis, Vicary, Buckley, Streit, Katz, & Wright, 1990).

Interestingly many of the same effects attributed to anabolic steroid use are alleged to occur following anabolic steroid cessation. Purported withdrawal effects include mood swings, violent behavior, rage, and depression, possibly severe enough to lead to thoughts of suicide. However, these findings must be tempered by the fact that individual responses to different anabolic steroids, doses, and lengths of administration likely vary somewhat unpredictably. Further, beyond these initial reports, no threshold dosage that may produce the effects (mood swings, violent behavior, rage, depression) or time course concerning the onset or elimination of these effects once anabolic steroid use has been initiated or terminated have been fully documented. (This may depend, in part, on the length of anabolic steroid use, particular desired as well as undesired effects experienced, dosage, and a host of other factors.)

As Svare (1990) has indicated, several critical variables involved in modulating the behavioral effects of androgens in animals, including sex, dose/duration, route of administration, type of androgen, and genotype, must be addressed when examining human anabolic steroid abuse. Finally, weight training per se may be addictive in the sense of promoting compulsive, stereotypical, and repetitive behavior to include not only the strength training but dieting, drug use, and a host of other lifestyle variables as well.

Prevention and Treatment of Anabolic-Androgenic Steroid Abuse

The use of educational intervention programs for the prevention and treatment of anabolic steroid abuse has been examined in several studies. Hallagen, Hallagen, and

Snyder (1989) and Thompson, Cleary, Folker, Carlson, Carlson, Elliot, and Goldberg (1991) have proposed that education is the most feasible alternative for curbing anabolic steroid use by adolescents. On the other hand, Bents, Young, Bosworth, Boyea, Elliot, and Goldberg (1990) found that an educational program that emphasized alternatives to anabolic steroid use such as nutrition principles and strength-training techniques was more effective in improving attitudes toward potential anabolic steroid use than either an education program in which no alternatives were discussed or no intervention program.

Furthermore, Goldberg, Bents, Bosworth, Trevisan, and Elliot (1991) found that an anabolic steroid education program that emphasized only the negative ("scare tactics") consequences of AAS was ineffective. Yet another report (Frankle & Leffers, 1990) suggests that education alone may not be as effective as clinical assessment and consultation in the care of individuals abusing anabolic steroids. In addition to education and motivation of the individual, the Council on Scientific Affairs of the American Medical Association (1988) has recommended several general solutions to the problem, including regulatory action limiting the production or distribution of drugs, or both, and drug testing of competitors. Medication has also been suggested for amelioration of the symptoms of anabolic steroid withdrawal (Rosse & Deutsch, 1990).

MAJOR METHODOLOGICAL ISSUES

As mentioned previously, any attempt to evaluate and summarize the psychological and behavioral effects associated with the use of anabolic steroids, particularly by athletes, is complicated by the numerous methodological shortcomings of many of the investigations, including inappropriate sampling strategies, lack of adequate control groups, use of several types, doses, and length of administration of anabolic steroids, and a variety of techniques used to assess the psychological and behavioral outcomes.

A significant number of researchers did not control for or report family or previous personal history of mental illness and/or aggressive behavior, thereby resulting in a possible selection bias in the study population. In addition, the selection of physically and/or mentally ill patients, persons, volunteers, etc. as subjects raises the question of the generalizability of the findings to otherwise healthy individuals. As McGraw (1990) has pointed out, there may be a causal link between traumatic events in individuals' lives and their subsequent decisions to use anabolic steroids. Many of the studies reported here were conducted with small sample sizes, thus reducing the statistical power available to detect significant differences. Furthermore, small sample sizes have precluded the examination of steroid effects in additional subgroups such as age, race, gender, educational level, and social class. Small sample size makes it difficult to control for potential confounding variables using multivariate statistical techniques. Sampling of blood and urine was inconsistent among studies, with respect to timing, or was often unreported. Often multiple samples were not obtained.

A number of studies failed to incorporate control groups. Many researchers, for ethical and legal reasons, did not randomly assign subjects to treatment, use comparable reference groups, or take advantage of single-or double-blind designs.

Not all anabolic steroids are the same; significant variation among anabolic steroids regarding acute physical effects has been noted (Herrmann & Beach, 1976; Kruskemper, 1968; Williams, 1981), and there is significant individual variation in response to the same androgen and dose (Bardin, Catterall, & Janne, 1990). Caution must be exercised when attempts are made to generalize the psychological and behavioral effects (findings) from a study using one type of anabolic steroid to a different steroid used in another study. There is also the possibility that adverse reactions may represent toxic responses in some individuals (Kochakian, 1990).

Also, while reporting the average steroid dose used, some studies failed to examine or report any dose/response relationship. In addition, even when the dosage was provided, estimating the bioavailable equivalence between oral and injectable anabolic steroids is difficult. Moreover, in hypogonadal patients it appears that oral anabolic steroids are the only type of anabolic steroids that produce positive mood changes. However, the doses of injectable steroids administered in these studies often tended to be below those required to restore and maintain normal plasma testosterone levels. In other users (athletes) it is the oral anabolic steroids that are associated with the adverse psychological changes. Finally because as much as 50–80 percent or more of the anabolic steroids used by athletes may have been obtained from "black market" sources (Frankle, Cicero, & Payne, 1984; Yesalis, Herrick, Buckley, Friedl, Brannon, & Wright, 1988) case reports of individuals using these drugs must be evaluated accordingly, given the absence of knowledge concerning their actual content.

Defining aggression (see Chapter 15, "Aggression," in this book) and assessing aggressive behavior is itself difficult (Kreuz & Rose, 1972). Since a variety of psychological/behavioral assessment techniques including inventories were used across studies, comparability of findings between studies is difficult. In some cases, nonstandardized and/or unpublished inventories were used. As a result, some of the questionnaires may have been inadequate for detecting behavioral change.

Finally, an overriding concern is the accurate documentation of any change in behavior with anabolic steroid use. No studies of actual behavior while in athletic competition have been reported. Some studies were unclear regarding how changes in behavior associated with anabolic steroid use were determined. It is possible that some of the behavioral differences reported resulted from some investigations relying on self-reports and other self-defined measures of behavioral change, while others used observers and/or interviews to document behavioral changes. Consequently psychological changes that failed to be manifested as abnormal behavior may have either gone unrecognized or been overreported.

SUMMARY

Both prospective and retrospective methods have been used to evaluate the psychological and behavioral effects of anabolic steroids. However, statements regarding this topic must remain tentative due to the diversity of study designs and results. Many of the reported behavioral effects have come primarily from studies using a small number of subjects in which patients were administered anabolic steroids for a variety of clinical conditions. These studies have found positive or unchanged moods and behavior. Extremely small numbers of athletes have been studied, and the findings derived from patient populations can only be generalized to athletes with caution, particularly as athletes are known to use several drugs concurrently (Frankle et al., 1984) and to use "black market" drugs (Buckley, Yesalis, Friedl, Anderson, Streit, & Wright, 1988; Burkett & Falduto, 1984; Frankle et al., 1984; Windsor & Dumitru, 1989), the content of which may be suspect. And lastly the interactive effects of anabolic steroids and environmental factors, stress levels, and often drugs of various types (including analgesics, antiinflammatories, alcohol, and other psychoactive substances) on feelings and behavior remain unresolved in humans.

Future research will undoubtedly need to examine the positive psychological effects of anabolic steroid use as has occurred in the majority of patient samples. There may be significant numbers of individuals whose mental health has been *improved* through anabolic steroid use.

Both medical and legal concerns regarding the psychological and behavioral effects of anabolic steroids have been raised. Unfortunately objective evidence documenting the short-term psychological and behavioral changes accompanying and following anabolic steroid use by athletes is extremely limited and inconclusive. As indicated, many of the studies in this area suffer from methodological inadequacies. As several researchers have pointed out (Cicero & O'Connor, 1990; Yesalis, Wright, & Bahrke, 1989; Yesalis, Wright, & Lombardo, 1989; Yesalis, Anderson, Buckley, & Wright, 1990; Yesalis, Vicary, & Buckley, 1990), extremely little is known about the long-term health impact of anabolic steroids and their interactions with other drugs, including drugs of abuse. Consequently the need for much additional research is strongly indicated.

Although some athletes, coaches, sports physicians, scientists, and the media believe that anabolic steroids exert a positive effect by enhancing performance through altered psychological states, others point out the potential negative effects of violent and aggressive behavior. With present estimates of a million or more anabolic steroid users in the United States, an extremely small percentage of anabolic steroid-using athletes appear to experience mental disturbances that result in their seeking clinical treatment, and of those who do, some may already suffer from existing mental health and/or other substance abuse problems. At this point a cause-effect relationship has yet to be established. Moreover, of the seemingly small population of individuals who do experience significant psychological and behavioral changes, most apparently recover without legal or other problems when the use of androgens is terminated.

References

Alcena, V., & Alexopoulos, G. S. (1985). Ulcerative colitis in association with chronic paranoid schizophrenia: a review of steroid-induced psychiatric disorders. *Journal of Clinical Gastroenterology, 7,* 400–404.

Alen, M., & Hakkinen, K. (1985). Physical health and fitness of an elite bodybuilder during 1 year of self-administration of testosterone and anabolic steroids: a case study. *International Journal of Sports Medicine, 6,* 24–29.

Alen, M., Hakkinen K., & Komi, P. V. (1984). Changes in neuromuscular and muscle fiber characteristics of elite power athletes self-administering androgenic and anabolic steroids. *Acta Physiologica Scandinavica, 122,* 535–544.

Alen, M., Rahkila, P., Reinila, M., & Reijo, V. (1987). Androgenic-anabolic steroid effects on serum thyroid, pituitary and steroid hormones in athletes. *American Journal of Sports Medicine, 15,* 357–361.

Alen, M., Reinila, M., & Vihko, R. (1985). Response of serum hormones to androgen administration in power athletes. *Medicine and Science in Sports and Exercise, 17,* 354–359.

Alpert E., & Seigerman, C. (1986). Steroid withdrawal psychosis in a patient with closed head injury. *Archives of Physical Medicine and Rehabilitation, 67,* 766–769.

Altschule, M. D., & Tillotson, K. J. (1948). The use of testosterone in the treatment of depressions. *New England Journal of Medicine, 239,* 1036–1038.

Amatruda, T. T., Hurst, M. M., & D'Esopo N. D. (1965). Certain endocrine and metabolic facets of the steroid withdrawal syndrome. *Journal of Clinical Endocrinology and Metabolism, 25,* 1207–1217.

Annitto, W. J., & Layman, W. A. (1980). Anabolic steroids and acute schizophrenic episode. *Journal of Clinical Psychiatry, 41,* 143–144.

Ault, C. C., Hoctor, E. F., & Werner, A. A. (1937). Theelin therapy in the psychoses. *Journal of the American Medical Association, 109,* 1786–1788.

Bahrke, M. S., Wright, J. E., O'Connor, J. S., Strauss, R. H., & Catlin, D. H. (1990). Selected psychological characteristics of anabolic-androgenic steroid users. *New England Journal of Medicine, 323,* 834–835.

Bahrke, M. S., Wright, J. E., Strauss, R. H., & Catlin, D. H. (in press). Psychological moods and subjectively perceived behavioral and somatic changes accompanying anabolic-androgenic steroid usage. *American Journal of Sports Medicine.*

Bardin, C. W., Catterall, J. F., & Janne, O. A. (1990). The androgen–

induced phenotype. In G. C. Lin & L. Erinoff (Eds.), *Anabolic steroid abuse*. NIDA Research Monograph. Rockville, MD: National Institute on Drug Abuse.

Bents, R., Young, J., Bosworth, E., Boyea, S., Elliot, D., & Goldberg, L. (1990). An effective educational program alters attitudes toward anabolic steroid use among adolescent athletes. *Medicine and Science in Sports and Exercise, 22,* S64.

Beumont, P. J. V., Bancroft, J. H. J., Beardwood, C. J., & Russell, G. F. (1972). Behavioural changes after treatment with testosterone: case report. *Psychological Medicine, 2,* 70–72.

Boone, J. B., Lambert, C. P., Flynn, M. G., Michaud, T. J., Rodriguez-Zayas, J. A., & Andres, F. F. (1990). Resistance exercise effects on plasma cortisol, testosterone and creatine kinase activity in anabolic-androgenic steroid users. *International Journal of Sports Medicine, 11,* 293–297.

Brooks, R. V. (1980). Anabolic steroids and athletes. *Physician and Sportsmedicine, 8,* 161–163.

Broverman, D. M., Klaiber, E. L., Kobayashi, Y., & Vogel, W. (1968). Roles of activation and inhibition in sex differences in cognitive abilities. *Psychological Reviews, 75,* 23–50.

Brower, K. J. (1990). Rehabilitation for anabolic-androgenic steroid dependence. *Clinical Sports Medicine, 1,* 171–181.

Brower, K. J., Blow, F. C., Beresford, T. P., & Fuelling, C. (1989). Anabolic-androgenic steroid dependence. *Journal of Clinical Psychiatry, 50,* 31–33.

Brower, K. J., Blow, F. C., Eliopulos, G. A., & Beresford, T. P. (1989). Anabolic androgenic steroids and suicide. *American Journal of Psychiatry, 146,* 1075.

Brower, K. J., Blow, F. C., Young, J. P., & Hill, E. M. (1991). Symptoms and correlates of anabolic-androgenic steroid dependence. *British Journal of Addiction, 86,* 759–768.

Brower, K. J., Eliopulos, G. A., Blow, F. C., Catlin, D. H., & Beresford, T. P. (1990). Evidence for physical and psychological dependence on anabolic-androgenic steroids in eight weight lifters. *American Journal of Psychiatry, 147,* 510–512.

Buckley, W. E., Yesalis, C. E., Friedl, K. E., Anderson, W. A., Streit, A. L., & Wright, J. E. (1988). Estimated prevalence of anabolic steroid use among male high school seniors. *Journal of the American Medical Association, 260,* 3441–3445.

Burkett, L. N., & Falduto, M. T. (1984). Steroid use by athletes in a metropolitan area. *Physician and Sportsmedicine, 12,* 69–74.

Burnett, P. C. (1963). A steroidal pyrazole as an anabolic agent in the treatment of geriatric mental patients. *Journal of the American Geriatric Society, 11,* 979–982.

Burris, A. S., Ewing, L. L., & Sherins, R. J. (1988). Initial trial of slow-release testosterone microspheres in hypogonadal men. *Fertility and Sterility, 50,* 493–497.

Byyny, R. L. (1976). Withdrawal from glucocorticoid therapy. *New England Journal of Medicine, 295,* 30–32.

Catlin, D. H., & Hatton, C. K. (1991). Use and abuse of anabolic and other drugs for athletic enhancement. *Advances in Internal Medicine, 36,* 399–424.

Choi, P. Y. L., Parrott, A. C., & Cowan, D. (1989). Adverse behavioural effects of anabolic steroids in athletes: a brief review. *Clinical Sports Medicine, 1,* 183–187.

Cicero, T. J., & O'Connor, L. H. (1990). Abuse liability of anabolic steroids and their possible role in the abuse of alcohol, morphine and other substances. In G. C. Lin & L. Erinoff (Eds.) *Anabolic steroid abuse*. NIDA Research Monograph. Rockville, MD: National Institute on Drug Abuse.

Conacher, G. N., & Workman, D. G. (1989). Violent crime possibly associated with anabolic steroid use. *American Journal of Psychiatry, 146,* 679.

Congressional Record—Senate. November 2, 1990. Title XIX—Anabolic Steroids Control Act of 1990.

Council on Scientific Affairs, American Medical Association. (1988). Drug abuse in athletics. *Journal of the American Medical Association, 259,* 1703–1705.

Danziger, L., & Blank, H. R. (1942). Androgen therapy of agitated depressions in the male. *Medical Annals of the District of Columbia, 11,* 181–183.

Davidson, J. M., Camargo, C. A., & Smith, E. R. (1979). Effects of androgen on sexual behavior in hypogonadal men. *Journal of Clinical Endocrinology and Metabolism, 48,* 955–958.

DeVoogd, T. J. (1987). Androgens can affect the morphology of mammalian CNS neurons in adulthood. *Trends in Neuroscience, 10,* 341–342.

Dimeff, R., & Malone, D. (1991). Psychiatric disorders in weightlifters using anabolic steroids. *Medicine and Science in Sports and Exercise, 23,* S18.

Dixon, R. B., & Christy N. P. (1980). On the various forms of corticosteroid withdrawal syndrome. *American Journal of Medicine, 68,* 224–230.

Duchaine, D. (1989). *Underground steroid handbook II.* Venice, CA: HLR Technical Books.

Forbes, G. B. (1985). The effect of anabolic steroids on lean body mass: the dose response curve. *Metabolism, 34,* 571–573.

Franchi, F., Luisi, M., & Kicovic, P. M. (1978). Long-term study of oral testosterone undecanoate in hypogonadal males. *International Journal of Andrology, 1,* 270–278.

Franchimont, P., Kicovic, P. M., Mattei, A., & Roulier, R. (1978). Effects of oral testosterone undecanoate in hypogonadal male patients. *Clinical Endocrinology, 9,* 313–320.

Frankle, M. A., Cicero, G. J., & Payne, J. (1984). Use of androgenic anabolic steroids by athletes. *Journal of the American Medical Association, 252,* 482.

Frankle, M. A., & Leffers, D. (1990). Hooked on hormones. *Journal of the American Medical Association, 263,* 2049.

Freed, D. L., Banks, A. J., Longson, D., & Burley, D. M. (1975). Anabolic steroids in athletics: Crossover double-blind trial on weightlifters. *British Medical Journal, 2,* 471–473.

Freedson, P. S., Mihevic, P. M., Loucks, A. B., & Girandola, R. N. (1983). Physique, body composition, and psychological characteristics of competitive female body builders. *Physician and Sportsmedicine, 11,* 85–93.

Freinhar, J. P., & Alvarez, W. (1985). Androgen-induced hypomania. *Journal of Clinical Psychiatry, 46,* 354–355.

Friedl, K. (1990). Reappraisal of the health risks associated with the use of oral and injectable androgenic steroids. In G. C. Lin & L. Erinoff (Eds.), *Anabolic steroid abuse*. NIDA Research Monograph. Rockville, MD: National Institute on Drug Abuse.

Goldberg, L., Bents, R., Bosworth, E., Trevisan, L., & Elliot, D. L. (1991). Anabolic steroid education and adolescents: do scare tactics work? *Pediatrics, 87,* 283–286.

Goldman, B., Bush, P., & Klatz, R. (1984). *Death in the locker room: steroids and sports*. South Bend, IN: Icarus Press.

Guirdham, A. (1940). Treatment of mental disorders with male sex hormone. *British Medical Journal, 1,* 10–12.

Hakkinen, K., & Alen, M. (1986). Physiological performance, serum hormones, enzymes and lipids of an elite power athlete during training with and without androgens and during prolonged detraining. *Journal of Sports Medicine, 26,* 92–100.

Hakkinen, K., & Komi, P. V. (1983). Electromyographic changes during strength training and detraining. *Medicine and Science in Sports and Exercise, 15,* 455–460.

Hallagan, J. B., Hallagan, L. F., & Snyder, M. B. (1989). Anabolic-androgenic steroid use by athletes. *New England Journal of Medicine, 321,* 1042–1045.

Hamilton, J. B. (1937). Treatment of sexual underdevelopment with synthetic male hormone substance. *Endocrinolology, 21,* 649–654.

Harlow, R. G. (1951). Masculine inadequacy and compensatory development of physique. *Journal of Personality, 19,* 312–323.

Haupt, H. A., & Rovere, G. D. (1984). Anabolic steroids: a review of the literature. *American Journal of Sports Medicine, 12,* 469–484.

Hays, L. R., Littleton, S., & Stillner, V. (1990). Anabolic steroid dependence. *American Journal of Psychiatry, 147,* 122.

Heller, C. G., & Myers, G. B. (1944). The male climacteric, its symptomatology, diagnosis and treatment. *Journal of the American Medical Association, 126,* 472–477.

Henry, F. (1941). Personality differences in athletes and physical education and aviation students. *Psychological Bulletin, 38,* 745.

Herrmann, W. M., & Beach, R. C. (1976). Psychotropic effects of androgens: a review of clinical observations and new human experimental findings. *Pharmakopsychologie, 9,* 205–219.

Hervey, G. R., Hutchinson, I., Knibbs, A. V., Burkinshaw, L., Jones, P. R. M., Norgan, N. G., & Levell, M. J. (1976). "Anabolic" effects of methandienone in men undergoing athletic training. *Lancet, 2,* 699–702.

Hickson, R. C., Ball, K. L., & Falduto, M. T. (1989). Adverse effects of anabolic steroids. *Medical Toxicology and Adverse Drug Experience, 4,* 254–271.

Holzbauer, M. (1976). Physiological aspects of steroids with anaesthetic properties. *Medical Biology, 54,* 227–242.

Indianapolis Star (Indianapolis, IN). (Sunday, February 14, 1988). Ex-player's odd behavior due to steroids use, doctor says, p. B-4.

Itil, T. M. (1976). The neurophysiological models in the development of psychotropic hormones. In T. M. Itil et al. (Eds.), *Psychotropic Action of Hormones.* New York: Spectrum.

Itil, T. M., Cora, R., Akpinar, S., Herrmann, W. M., & Patterson, C. J. (1974). "Psychotropic" action of sex hormones: computerized EEG in establishing the immediate CNS effects of steroid hormones. *Current Therapeutic Research, 16,* 1147–1170.

Judd, F. K., Burrows, G. D., & Norman, T. R. (1983). Psychosis after withdrawal of steroid therapy. *Medical Journal of Australia, 2,* 350–351.

Kaplan, H. I., & Sadock, B. J. (1990). *Pocket handbook of psychiatry* (6th ed.). Baltimore, MD: Williams & Wilkins.

Kashkin, K. B., & Kleber, H. D. (1989). Hooked on hormones? An anabolic steroid addiction hypothesis. *Journal of the American Medical Association, 262,* 3166–3170.

Katz, D. L., & Pope, H. G. (1990). Anabolic-androgenic steroid-induced mental status changes. In G. C. Lin & L. Erinoff (Eds.), *Anabolic steroid abuse.* NIDA Research Monograph. Rockville, MD: National Institute on Drug Abuse.

Kaufmann, M., Kahaner, K., Peselow, E. D., & Gershon, S. (1982). Steroid psychoses: Case report and brief overview. *Journal of Clinical Psychiatry, 43,* 75–76.

Kilshaw, B. H., Harkness, R. A., Hobson, B. M., & Smith, A. W. M. (1975). The effects of large doses of the anabolic steroid methandienone on an athlete. *Clinical Endocrinology, 4,* 537–541.

Klaiber, E. L., Broverman, D. M., & Kobayashi, Y. (1967). The automatization cognitive style, androgens, and monoamine oxidase. *Psychopharmacologia, 11,* 320–336.

Kochakian, C. D. (Ed.) (1976). *Anabolic-androgenic steroids.* New York: Springer-Verlag.

Kochakian, C. D. (1990). History of anabolic-androgenic steroids. In G. C. Lin & L. Erinoff (Eds.), *Anabolic steroid abuse.* NIDA Research Monograph. Rockville, MD: National Institute on Drug Abuse.

Kopera, H. (1985). The history of anabolic steroids and a review of clinical experience with anabolic steroids. *Acta Endocrinologica, 110* (Suppl. 271), 11–18.

Kreuz, L. E., & Rose, R. M. (1972). Assessment of aggressive behavior and plasma testosterone in a young criminal population. *Psychosomatic Medicine, 34,* 321–332.

Kruskemper, H. (1968). *Anabolic steroids.* New York: Academic Press.

Lamb, D. R. (1984). Anabolic steroids in athletics: how well do they work and how dangerous are they? *American Journal of Sports Medicine, 12,* 31–38.

Leckman, J. F., & Scahill, L. (1990). Possible exacerbation of tics by androgenic steroids. *New England Journal of Medicine, 322,* 1674.

Lefavi, R. G., Reeve, T. G., & Newland, M. C. (1990). Relationship between anabolic steroid use and selected psychological parameters in male bodybuilders. *Journal of Sport Behavior, 13,* 157–166.

Lindstrom, M., Nilsson, A. L., Katzman, P. L., Janzon, L., & Dymling, J. F. (1990). Use of anabolic-androgenic steroids among bodybuilders—frequency and attitudes. *Journal of Internal Medicine, 227,* 407–411.

Ljungqvist, A. (1975). The use of anabolic steroids in top Swedish athletes. *British Journal of Sports Medicine, 9,* 82.

Lubell, A. (1989). Does steroid abuse cause or excuse violence? *Physician and Sportsmedicine, 17,* 176–185.

Luisi, M., & Franchi, F. (1980). Double-blind group comparative study of testosterone undecanoate and mesterolone in hypogonadal male patients. *Journal of Endocrinology Investigations, 3,* 305–308.

MacMaster, D. R., & Alamin, K. (1963). Treatment of severe weight loss with methandrostenolone—a less virilizing anabolic agent. *American Journal of Psychiatry, 120,* 179–180.

Maryland v. Michael David Williams. (April 1986). Circuit Court Record for St. Mary's County, pp. 5630–5635.

Matsumoto, A. M. (1988). Is high-dosage testosterone an effective male contraceptive agent? *Fertility and Sterility, 50,* 324–328.

McGraw, J. M. (1990). The psychology of anabolic steroid use. *Journal of Clinical Psychiatry, 51,* 260.

Moore, W. V. (1988). Anabolic steroid use in adolesence. *Journal of the American Medical Association, 260,* 3484–3486.

Moritani, T., & DeVries, H. A. (1979). Neural factors versus hypertrophy in the time course of muscle strength gain. *American Journal of Physical Medicine, 58,* 115–130.

Moss, D. C. (October 1, 1988). And now the steroid defense? *American Bar Association Journal,* pp. 22–24.

Newsweek. (May 23, 1988). The insanity of steroid abuse, p. 75.

O'Carroll, R., & Bancroft, J. (1984). Testosterone therapy for low sexual interest and erectile dysfunction in men: A controlled study. *British Journal of Psychiatry, 145,* 146–151.

O'Carroll, R., Shapiro, C., & Bancroft, J. (1985). Androgens, behavior and nocturnal erection in hypogonadal men: The effects of varying the replacement dose. *Clinical Endocrinology, 23,* 527–538.

Perry, P. J., Andersen, K. H., & Yates, W. R. (1990). Illicit anabolic steroid use in athletes. *American Journal of Sports Medicine, 18,* 422–428.

Phoenix, C. H., Goy, R. W., Gerall, A. A., & Young, W. C. (1959). Organizing action of prenatally administered testosterone propionate on the tissues mediating mating behavior in the female guinea pig. *Endocrinology, 65,* 369–382.

Pope, H. G., & Katz, D. L. (1987). Bodybuilder's psychosis. *Lancet, 1,* 863.

Pope, H. G., & Katz, D. L. (1988). Affective and psychotic symptoms associated with anabolic steroid use. *American Journal of Psychiatry, 145,* 487–490.

Pope, H. G., & Katz, D. L. (1990). Homicide and near-homicide by anabolic steroid users. *Journal of Clinical Psychiatry, 51,* 28–31.

Racine Journal Times (Racine, WI). (Friday, April 20, 1990). Botsch blames his steroid abuse, p. 1.

Rejeski, W. J., Brubaker, P. H., Herb, R. A., Kaplan, J. R., & Manuck, S. B. (1988). The role of anabolic steroids on baseline and stress heart rate in cynomolgus monkeys. *Health Psychology, 7* (4), 299–307.

Roanoke Times (Roanoke, VA). (Saturday, June 25, 1988). Killing try is blamed on drugs.

Rosse, R. D., & Deutsch, S. I. (1990). Hooked on hormones. *Journal of the American Medical Association, 263,* 2048–2049.

Ryan, A. J. (1981). Anabolic steroids are fool's gold. *Federation Proceedings, 40,* 2682–2688.

Salmimies, P., Kockott, G., Pirke, K. M., Vogt, H. J., & Schill, W. B. Effects of testosterone replacement on sexual behavior in hypogonadal men. *Archives of Sexual Behavior, 11,* 345–353.

Sansoy, O. M., Roy, A. N., & Shields, L. M. (1971). Anabolic action and side effects of oxandrolone in 34 mental patients. *Geriatrics, 26,* 139–143.

Schearer, S. B., Alvarez-Sanchez, F., Anselmo, J., Brenner, P., Coutino, E., Latham-Faundes, A., Frick, J., Heinild, B., & Johansson, E. D. B. (1978). Hormonal contraception for men. *International Journal of Andrology* (Suppl. 2), 680–712.

Silvester, L. J. (1973). Anabolic steroids and the Munich Olympics. *Scholastic Coach, 43,* 90–92.

Skakkebaek, N. E., Bancroft, J., Davidson, W., & Warner, P. (1981). Androgen replacement with oral testosterone undecanoate in hypogonadal men: A double blind controlled study. *Clinical Endocrinology, 14,* 49–61.

Stenn, P. G., Klaiber E. L., Vogel, W., & Broverman, D. M. (1972). Testosterone effects upon photic stimulation of the electroencephalogram (EEG) and mental performance of humans. *Perceptual and Motor Skills, 34,* 371–378.

Strauss, R. H., Ligget, M. T., & Lanese, R. R. (1985). Anabolic steroid use and perceived effects in ten weight-trained women athletes. *Journal of the American Medical Association, 253,* 2871–2873.

Strauss, R. H., Wright, J. E., Finerman, G. A. M., & Catlin, D. H. (1983). Side effects of anabolic steroids in weight-trained men. *Physician and Sportsmedicine, 11,* 87–96.

Stumpf, W. E., & Sar, M. (1976). Steroid hormone target sites in the brain: the differential distribution of estrogen, progestin, androgen and glucocorticosteroid. *Journal of Steroid Biochemistry, 7,* 1163–1170.

Sun-Sentinel (Ft. Lauderdale, FL). (Thursday, June 2, 1988). Doctor: steroid rage led to killing.

Svare, B. B. (1990). Anabolic steroids and behavior: a preclinical research prospectus. In G. C. Lin & L. Erinoff (Eds.), *Anabolic steroid abuse.* NIDA Research Monograph. Rockville, MD: National Institute on Drug Abuse.

Taylor, W. N. (1982). *Anabolic steroids and the athlete.* Jefferson, NC: McFarland.

Taylor, W. N. (1987a). Commentary: synthetic anabolic-androgenic steroids: a plea for controlled substance status. *Physician and Sportsmedicine, 15,* 140–150.

Taylor, W. N. (1987b). Anabolic steroids: A plea for control. *Chiropractic Sports Medicine, 1,* 47–52.

Tec, L. (1974). Nandrolone in anorexia nervosa. *Journal of the American Medical Association, 229,* 1423.

Tennant, F., Black, D. L., & Voy, R. O. (1988). Anabolic steroid dependence with opioid-type features. *New England Journal of Medicine, 319,* 578-c.

Thomas, H. B., & Hill, R. T. (1940). Testosterone propionate and the male climacteric. *Endocrinology, 26,* 953–954.

Thompson, H., Cleary, B., Folker, R., Carlson, H., Carlson, N., Elliot, D., & Goldberg, L. (1991). Adolescent athletes and anabolic steroid abuse: Features that characterize the potential user. *Medicine and Science in Sports and Exercise, 23,* S18.

Thune, J. B. (1949). Personality of weightlifters. *Research Quarterly, 20,* 296–306.

Tilzey, A., Heptonstall, J., & Hamblin, T. (1981). Toxic confusional state and choreiform movements after treatment with anabolic steroids. *British Medical Journal, 283,* 349–350.

Vogel, W., Klaiber, E. L., & Broverman, D. M. (1985). A comparison of the antidepressant effects of a synthetic androgen (mesterolone) and amitriptyline in depressed men. *Journal of Clinical Psychiatry, 46,* 6–8.

Werner, A. A. (1939). The male climacteric. *Journal of the American Medical Association, 112,* 1441–1443.

Werner, A. A. (1943). The male climacteric: Additional observations of thirty-seven patients. *Journal of Urology, 49,* 872–882.

Werner, A. A., Johns, G. A., Hoctor, E. F., Ault, C. C, Kohler, L. H., & Weis, M. W. (1934). Involutional melancholia: a probable etiology and treatment. *Journal of the American Medical Association, 103,* 13–16.

Williams, R. H. (Ed.) (1981). *Textbook of endocrinology* (6th ed.). Philadelphia, PA: W. B. Saunders.

Wilson, J. D. (1988). Androgen abuse by athletes. *Endocrine Reviews, 9,* 181–199.

Wilson, J. D., & Griffin, J. E. (1980). The use and misuse of androgens. *Metabolism, 29,* 1278–1295.

Windsor, R., & Dumitru, D. (1989). Prevalence of anabolic steroid use by male and female adolescents. *Medicine and Science in Sport and Exercise, 21,* 494–497.

Winters, S. J. (1990). Androgens: endocrine physiology and pharmacology. In G. C. Lin & L. Erinoff (Eds.), *Anabolic steroid abuse.* NIDA Research Monograph. Rockville, MD: National Institute on Drug Abuse.

World Health Organization Task Force on Methods for the Regulation of Male Fertility. Contraceptive efficacy of testosterone-induced azoospermia in normal men. *Lancet, 336,* 955–959.

Wright, J. E. (1978). *Anabolic steroids and sports.* Natick, MA: Sports Science Consultants.

Wright, J. E. (1982). *Anabolic steroids and sports,* Vol. II. Natick, MA: Sports Science Consultants.

Wu, F. C. W., Bancroft, J., Davidson, D. W., & Nicol, K. (1982). The behavioural effects of testosterone undecanoate in adult men with Klinefelter's Syndrome: a controlled study. *Clinical Endocrinology, 16,* 489–497.

Wynn, V., & Landon, J. (1961). A study of the androgenic and some related effects of methandienone. *British Medical Journal, 1,* 998–1003.

Yesalis, C. E., Anderson, A., Buckley, W., &. Wright, J. E. (1990). Incidence of the non-medical use of anabolic-androgenic steroids. In G. C. Lin & L. Erinoff (Eds.), *Anabolic Steroid Abuse.* NIDA Research Monograph. Rockville, MD: National Institute on Drug Abuse.

Yesalis, C. E., Herrick, R., Buckley, W., Friedl, K. E., Brannon, D., & Wright, J. E. (1988). Self-reported use of anabolic-androgenic steroids by elite power lifters. *Physician and Sportsmedicine, 16,* 91–100.

Yesalis, C. E., Streit, A. L., Vicary, J. R., Friedl, K. E., Brannon, D., & Buckley, W. (1989). Anabolic steroid use: Indications of habituation among adolescents. *Journal of Drug Education, 19,* 103–116.

Yesalis, C. E., Wright, J. E., & Bahrke, M. S. (1989). Epidemiological and policy issues in the measurement of the long-term health effects of anabolic-androgenic steroids. *Sports Medicine, 8,* 129–138.

Yesalis, C. E., Wright, J. E., & Lombardo, J. A. (1989). Anabolic-androgenic steroids: a synthesis of existing data and recommendations for future research. *Clinical Sports Medicine, 1,* 109–134.

Yesalis, C. E., Vicary, J., Buckley W., Streit, A., Katz, D., & Wright, J. (1990). Indications of psychological dependence among anabolic-androgenic steroid abusers. In G. C. Lin & L. Erinoff (Eds.), *Anabolic steroid abuse.* NIDA Research Monograph. Rockville, MD: National Institute on Drug Abuse.

PSYCHOMETRICS

·42·

SPORT-SPECIFIC AND CULTURALLY ADAPTED MEASURES IN SPORT AND EXERCISE PSYCHOLOGY RESEARCH: ISSUES AND STRATEGIES

Lise Gauvin

Storm J. Russell

Measurement issues have been an ongoing preoccupation in sport and exercise psychology, highlighted by the recent publication of Ostrow's (1990) *Directory of Psychological Tests in the Sport and Exercise Sciences* and Anshel's (1987) article on instrumentation. More recently there have been calls for researchers to remain abreast of measurement issues and to revise the process of establishing psychometric properties for questionnaires to be used in sport and exercise psychology (Ebbeck, Wood, & Horn, 1991). Martens (1979) and Orlick (1974) have argued for better measures of social-psychological variables related to physical activity. Despite the considerable effort that has been directed toward test and scale development and recent attempts to provide instrumentation guidelines (Schutz & Gessaroli, this volume), many researchers are still grappling with the often difficult task of achieving reliable and valid measurement in sport and exercise settings.

Two particular measurement issues present ongoing methodological challenges for sport and exercise psychology researchers. The first has to do with the continuing trend toward the development of specific tests and questionnaires for different sport and exercise settings (Ebbeck, 1991). This trend toward measurement specificity has been accompanied by a corresponding move away from more generalized tests of abilities, beliefs, attitudes, cognitive and affective styles, and personality traits. There appears to be an almost unquestioning acceptance of the value of sport and exercise-specific tests over tests of generalized psychological traits, aptitudes, attitudes, and abilities and an associated assumption that "more specific" is synonymous with "better." There is a need for some critical evaluation, some methodological stock taking, of the measurement decisions that are being made in the name of increased specificity. This is because the trend toward sport/exercise-specific measures in preference to more generalized tests has implications for the development of knowledge in sport and exercise psychology. To this end, some clarification of the reasons and purposes of psychological testing is called for, as well as the development of theoretically sound criteria to aid in methodological decision making in both test construction and application.

The second issue concerns the influence of cultural and subcultural factors in measurement and the challenges associated with adapting and translating test instruments for use with multicultural populations. Cross-cultural measurement issues have not received a great deal of attention

---

Authorship of this paper is considered to be joint. Names are listed in alphabetical order.

in the sport and exercise psychology testing literature (Duda & Allison, 1990). This lack of discussion is somewhat surprising, given that sport and exercise transcend so many geographical and cultural boundaries, and that it is widely acknowledged that such cultural factors can potentially produce major distortions and inaccuracies in test interpretation (Anastasi, 1976; Cronbach & Drenth, 1972). Thus an examination of the issues involved in cross-cultural adaptation of measures is called for.

These two issues, measurement specificity and cross-cultural adaptation, form the focus of this chapter. The specific purposes of this chapter are to discuss the need (or lack of need) to develop and preferentially use sport/exercise-specific tests and scales at the expense of more generalized measures, and to describe procedures and considerations involved in adapting paper-and-pencil tests and scales for cross-cultural testing. The discussion is designed to complement that presented by Schutz and Gessaroli (Chapter 43 in this volume) on different statistical methods for test development, and to recast instrument use, selection, and adaptation in the broader context of the scientific method.

MEASUREMENT IN SPORT AND EXERCISE PSYCHOLOGY RESEARCH

Measurement has been defined as "rules for assigning numbers to objects to represent quantities of attributes" (Nunnally, 1978, p. 2). It is what allows us to render abstract theoretical concepts, which are the end products and tools of scientific inquiry, into data points or empirical facts.

According to Kerlinger (1979), "measures" can include both "tests" and "scales" and are regarded as the "quantitative estimates of the amount of a property or characteristic that individuals or groups possess" (p. 25). A test is "a systematic procedure in which individuals being tested are presented with a set of constructed stimuli, called items, to which they respond in one way or another" (Kerlinger, 1979, p. 25). An example of a test from the field of sport psychology would be the Sport Competition Anxiety Test (SCAT, Martens, Vealey, & Burton, 1990). The SCAT allows the researcher to classify subjects according to their tendency to perceive competitive situations as threatening and to react to those situations with state anxiety. Norms exist for classifying college students as well as children.

A "scale" or "questionnaire," on the other hand, is "like a test although it lacks the competitive flavor; it is an instrument so constructed that different numbers can be assigned to different individuals to indicate different amounts of some property or attribute" (Kerlinger, 1979, p. 26). An example of a test would be a self-efficacy scale designed for a particular study to assess perceived capabilities of performing a specific behavior. A typical self-efficacy scale ranges from 1 to 100 and requires individuals to indicate their confidence in being able to perform a given behavior. Norms

for selected tasks typically do not exist, but the scores obtained by subjects do allow for between-subject as well as within-subject comparisons.

A test differs from a scale or questionnaire in that tests are designed to classify subjects on a given attribute in comparison to a normative group, whereas a scale can distribute subjects along the quantity of an attribute only within the limited sample under investigation (Nunnally, 1978). Tests allow researchers to draw substantive conclusions about the quantity of an attribute a subject possesses, whereas a scale does not allow for such interpretations.

Nunnally (1978) suggested that psychological tests may have three major purposes: (1) the establishment of a functional relationship with respect to a particular variable, (2) the representation of a specific universe of content, and (3) the measurement of psychological characteristics. The researcher attempting to establish a functional relationship with a particular variable predicts a given outcome based on information yielded from the test. Examples of tests concerned primarily with the first purpose are tests of aptitude, such as talent-detection measures developed to predict later high-level performance (e.g., Régnier, Salmela, & Russell, Chapter 12 in this volume), tests of motor ability to predict piloting and sharpshooting success (e.g., Fleishman, 1956; Fleishman & Bartlett, 1969), or academic aptitude tests such as the Graduate Record Examinations (GRE) used to predict the likelihood of success in graduate school.

Tests measuring abilities, aptitudes, or achievement have sometimes been referred to as "knowledge-based" tests (Rust & Golombok, 1989) and are usually concerned with representing a specific universe of content such as the repertoire of psychological skills and coping strategies employed by elite athletes (e.g., Mahoney, Gabriel, & Perkins, 1987) or participants' imagery abilities (e.g., Hall, Pongrac, & Buckholz, 1985).

Tests that aim to measure psychological characteristics have been called person-based tests (Rust & Golombok, 1989). An example of the use of this type of test is the situation in which a researcher wants to measure psychological dimensions or cognitive style characteristics pertinent to sport and exercise performance but which also occur in other domains. The measurement of introversion-extroversion (e.g., Eysenck, 1973), attitudes toward physical activity (e.g., Kenyon, 1968; Schutz, Smoll, & Wood, 1985), or of social physique anxiety (e.g., Hart, Leary, & Rejeski, 1989) are also good examples of attempts to assess underlying psychological characteristics. These characteristics are considered relevant across both sport or nonsport situations.

In contrast to the tests described above, scales or questionnaires are often study-specific and are usually designed to operationalize a given construct or variable of interest. To test the theory of planned behavior (Ajzen & Madden, 1986), for example, a researcher may want to develop study-specific and behavior-specific measures of attitudes, intentions, and other variables in the model. To study various aspects of self-efficacy theory (Bandura, 1986), researchers often formulate task-specific measures of self-confidence or of the subject's self-perceived capacity to perform a particular behavior.

Nonspecific questionnaires or scales could also be used for similar purposes. For example, a researcher examining the effects of different rewards on intrinsic motivation and sentiments of global competence could develop a scale to assess the extent to which the subject feels competent after having received the reward. Alternatively a scale of the perceived importance of performing well on a given task could be used by a researcher investigating ego involvement in a laboratory task.

These examples illustrate that either sport-specific or nonspecific measures can be appropriate, dependent on the focus and the purpose of the study. How then do we strike a balance between specificity and generality, and what criteria should we use in making these kinds of measurement decisions? In order to further clarify the issues involved, and to provide some basic guidelines regarding testing specificity decisions, it is useful to review the basic tenets of the scientific method and the implications these have for testing in sport and exercise psychology.

THE SCIENTIFIC METHOD AND RESEARCH IN SPORT AND EXERCISE PSYCHOLOGY

As defined by Kerlinger (1979), "science is an enterprise concerned with knowledge and understanding of natural phenomena" (p. 3). The purposes of scientific inquiry are to produce and test theories that describe, explain, and predict natural phenomena (Rosenthal & Rosnow, 1984). These goals are achieved through the use of objective and empirical methods. Objectivity refers to both a characteristic and a procedure that allow researchers to agree upon the significance and meaning of what has been done or what has been observed (Kerlinger, 1979).

The empirical quality of scientific research means that evidence or facts are collected in rigorously controlled studies and brought to bear on the understanding of a phenomenon (Kerlinger, 1979). According to this view of science, the solving of practical problems and concerns without reference to theory and a larger body of knowledge is not an objective pursued in research. (That is not to say that practical problems should not be of interest to research. In fact, we espouse the Lewinian ideal of conducting theoretical research on socially relevant problems (Lewin, 1951) and recognize that some major scientific discoveries occurred following the analysis of a "practical" problem. However, the pursuit of knowledge through the scientific method, as opposed to the tenacity, authority, or a priori methods, requires that certain principles be respected, among which objectivity and empirical quality figure prominently [Rosenthal & Rosnow, 1984].) At any rate knowledge gained through scientific research can and

should be used subsequently by practitioners, who have no theoretical interest in the advancement of knowledge, to aid in the resolution of practical dilemmas.

Scientific research in sport and exercise psychology is therefore fundamentally an enterprise concerned with the furthering of knowledge and understanding of social psychological phenomena as they occur in sport and exercise settings. Research in sport and exercise psychology allows for the development of theory about social psychological phenomena occurring in sport and exercise settings. Measurement in sport and exercise psychology is designed to render concrete or to examine empirically those phenomena related to the particular aspect of either sport, exercise, social, or psychological functioning under investigation.

With regard to testing, the applied concerns and endeavors of the sport and exercise psychology practitioner are aided by the knowledge and sometimes the measurement tools developed through research. For example, knowledge of a person's level of trait anxiety as well as the extent to which state anxiety is experienced cognitively or somatically may indicate which of several methods of stress management is best suited to a given individual. Similarly knowledge of the affective consequences of different attributions can provide the sport psychology practitioner with a more accurate understanding of a particular client's frame of mind following a competitive outcome. The results of a test of cognitive coping skills for a given athlete may provide a useful starting point for the development of a mental preparation program. However, these applied concerns should not be misconstrued or confounded with the fundamental essence of scientific research, that of the development of knowledge and testing theory.

An ongoing problem in testing in the field of sport and exercise psychology is that practical utility has sometimes promoted the development and use of increasingly situation- and population-specific measures over more generalized psychological tests. Sport and exercise psychology practitioners have a need for instruments that can be used for very specific purposes, in very narrow settings, and with very limited populations. Thus we have seen a proliferation of context-specific, sport-specific, and even league-specific measures of psychological parameters. While perhaps having practical application in certain narrowly defined areas, overly specific tests and scales may contribute little to the development of sport psychological knowledge. Unless such instruments are developed within a theoretical and methodological framework that has as its fundamental purpose the advancement of knowledge, then their place in a science of sport and exercise psychology is unquestionably limited.

The issue of scientific relevance is not simply a matter of validity. A given test may fulfill certain criteria for validity and reliability but still may have limited import for the advancement of knowledge. Essentially, the conceptual distinction between single-purpose, study-specific questionnaires and psychometrically sound tests and scales needs to be clearly understood and any limitations deriving from an application of the former type of measure addressed in the discussion of results.

In addition to the above concerns, measurement in sport and exercise psychology is further complicated by a certain duality of theoretical perspectives and associated underlying assumptions. On the one hand, sport and physical activity can be viewed as unique social psychological phenomena that require separate research scrutiny. The work on exercise-induced affect (Gauvin & Brawley, in press; Hardy & Rejeski, 1989; Morgan, 1982), rated perceived exertion (Mihevic, 1983; Morgan, 1981, 1982; Rejeski, 1985), competitive trait anxiety (Martens et al., 1990), and talent detection in sport (Régnier, Salmela, & Russell, Chapter 12 in this volume) exemplifies this approach. For example, the Feeling Scale, FS (Hardy & Rejeski, 1989), was designed to tap how one feels during aerobic exercise and, more specifically, to measure exercise-induced affect. The scale has proved useful in describing how people feel when performing exercise at varying intensities (Hardy & Rejeski, 1989) as well as in understanding its relationship to other constructs such as anxiety (Rejeski, Hardy, & Shaw, 1991) and androgyny (Rejeski, Best, Griffith, & Kenney, 1987).

From another perspective, sport and exercise can be regarded simply as other forms of social-psychological interaction that can be investigated under the broader framework of social psychological theory. McAuley and Gross's (1983) study of the applicability of the Causal Dimension Scale in sport illustrates this approach. Specifically the Causal Dimension Scale (Russell, 1982) was developed to assess the extent to which attributions for an event are internal, stable, or controllable, as judged by the person making the attributions. Psychometric data support its validity and reliability (Russell, 1982; Russell, McAuley, & Tarico, 1987). McAuley and Gross (1983) examined the utility of the Causal Dimension Scale by studying the attributions made for success and failure following a table tennis match. They found that winning players made more internal, stable, and controllable attributions than losing players and thereby documented the internal consistency of the scale in a sport setting.

Measurement in sport and exercise psychology can, therefore, be either sport or exercise specific, or alternatively nonspecific. It is the particular conceptual approach adopted that should resolve the question of whether sport-specific or nonspecific measurement is more appropriate. The approach investigating sport and exercise phenomena as unique and as warranting investigation in their own right may be more inclined to the development and use of sport/exercise-specific measures and the study of behavior in more narrowly defined settings. An approach that treats exercise and sport within a broader social-psychological context, may be more likely to use nonspecific measures and focus on identifying underlying dimensions of human behavior that have meaning across a wide range of social-psychological settings.

What then are the major issues that need to be considered in directing instrumentation decisions regarding spe-

cificity? Among the major considerations in this regard is the potential loss in generalizability of results.

SPORT/EXERCISE SPECIFIC VERSUS NONSPECIFIC TESTS: THEORETICAL CONCERNS

The use of sport/exercise-specific tests, especially when they are not utilized within a strong conceptual framework, creates the risk of obtaining findings that pertain only to a very limited part of reality. Many sport/exercise-specific tests, by definition, are limited to operationalizing phenomena relevant to specifically defined sport or exercise settings. Thus knowledge gained through the use of such tests may not necessarily be generalizable to nonsport settings. In employing such sport/exercise-specific tests, therefore, researchers run the risk of explaining "everything about nothing." While the understanding of sport and exercise is important in and of itself, at some point linkages with a broader knowledge structure and theory of human functioning need to be made.

The main determinant of how far-reaching the findings of any given piece of research will be, then, derives from the initial conceptualization and operationalization of the variables of interest. If the sport/exercise-specific measures are made specific in order to conform to the operationalization assumptions inherent in a given theoretical framework, then results can have relevance to all situations to which the theory applies. If the study-specific or sport and exercise measures are developed and applied in the absence of a theoretical framework, however, the findings will likely have no bearing on existing knowledge or understanding because they cannot be related to that knowledge other than in a post hoc fashion.

At the other extreme there is the risk of knowing "nothing about everything," as many researchers, frustrated with either the limitations of the more generalized psychological measures or in some cases with the complete lack of appropriate instrumentation, will agree. It is quite possible that instruments providing information that has relevance for larger sections of the population may contribute little or nothing to our knowledge or understanding of skilled human performance within a particular sport context.

It would be unwise, however, to assume that this is always the case. There are many intrapersonal factors studied by researchers in psychology that also have relevance for the development of knowledge in the field of sport and exercise psychology. For example, Hart et al. (1989) developed the Social Physique Anxiety Scale (SPAS) to assess the degree to which people become anxious when others observe or evaluate their physiques. As suggested by these authors, the scale is useful in examining both the link between general interpersonal concerns and social physique anxiety, as well as the role of social physique anxiety in determining fitness behavior. The concept and scale, therefore, has relevance for both sport/exercise contexts as well as other areas of human activity. Instruments such as the SPAS need not be made sport/exercise specific to allow for the advancement of knowledge. In fact, making them sport/exercise specific may be counterproductive in that factors such as their external validity would be negatively affected.

The proliferation of psychological tests in the sport and exercise sciences, the duality of research foci, the applied concerns of the field of sport and exercise psychology, and the potential loss of generalizability of findings highlight the importance of further critical discussion of the commonly perceived need for sport/exercise-specific measurement.

CONSIDERATIONS IN SELECTING SPORT/EXERCISE SPECIFIC VERSUS NONSPECIFIC TESTS AND QUESTIONNAIRES

In making the final decision as to whether or not a sport/exercise-specific test is indeed required for a particular piece of research, it is argued that a strong theoretical rationale for the existence of sport/exercise-specific content or dimensions needs to be presented. The purposes of scientific inquiry as these relate to the social sciences are essentially to produce general rules and generalizable laws of social-psychological functioning (Kerlinger, 1979; Rosenthal & Rosnow, 1984). From this perspective, the employment of sport/exercise-specific tests and scales must be justified in terms of a given theoretical framework that demands either study-specific or sport/exercise-specific measurement, and the theoretical rationale for either the development or the application of a sport-specific measure within a particular research context needs to be clearly articulated. Unless this is done, such measures cannot be considered psychologically valid instruments in the accepted sense of the word.

To further aid in the decision-making process, it is useful to consider the "big" outcomes and foci of the research. If the primary purpose is to understand some unique aspect of sport and exercise phenomena that bears little or no relation to human behavior more generally, then it is likely that a sport/exercise-specific test or scale will be more appropriate. Alternatively research designed to test generalized psychological phenomena using sport or exercise settings will accordingly require tests that can be generalized beyond the particular setting.

An important question that should be addressed then is whether the psychological variables of interest are uniquely associated with sport, exercise, or movement phenomena. If the answer to this question is yes, as in the case of efficacy cognitions related to a given sport task, or attitudes toward physical activity, then a sport/exercise-specific test or scale will probably be required. Conversely if the constructs are thought to be unrelated to situational factors, as in the case of human information-processing capacities, then a nonspecific test or scale is indicated. As a

general rule of thumb, knowledge-based tests have more chance of being sport and exercise specific, whereas person-based tests may require either specific or nonspecific tests or questionnaires, depending on the particular theoretical context.

Furthermore the practical use of a test or questionnaire should not be the primary motivation for the development of that test. As mentioned previously, the aims of a given research study as they relate to knowledge development should not be confounded with the equally important, but often different, concerns of the practitioner. The skills required for the correct application of the scientific method and those required for effective counselling in an applied sport psychology setting are quite distinct. Both endeavors may require the use of tests and scales and may also, in certain circumstances, be undertaken by the same individual on different occasions. However, the conceptual basis for test construction and the later application of that test in a clinical or performance setting are two very different issues, and problems arise when these are confused.

Finally many researchers prefer to have empirical strategies to confirm the selection of sport/exercise-specific tests and scales over more generalized tests and scales. While no fail-safe empirical strategies exist to disentangle the sport specificity issue, researchers may be tempted to rely on an estimate of the amount of variance explained to gauge the importance of a given test or scale. A common rule of thumb in such an approach is that if a significant portion of the variance is explained, then the test, whether sport/exercise specific or not, is considered useful. While such a strategy has appeal, it should be noted that many methodologists (Glass, McGaw, & Smith, 1980) have suggested that the effect sizes typically recorded in the social sciences are rather small in comparison to those recorded in the biological or physical sciences. Basing decisions about test utility on the amount of variance explained might therefore lead to a rejection of tests and scales that may eventually lead to the advancement of knowledge. The selection of a sport/exercise-specific test over a generalized test should rest on a solid conceptual rationale in addition to a quantitative estimate of the amount of variance explained.

CROSS-CULTURAL CONSIDERATIONS INVOLVED IN TEST USE

Whether a researcher chooses a sport-and exercise-specific or a nonspecific test or questionnaire, careful consideration also needs to be given to how a particular cultural environment affects instrumentation (Brislin, Lonner, & Thorndike, 1973; Cronbach & Drenth, 1972; Duda & Allison, 1990). In addition to the obvious language differences, more subtle cultural differences can affect test results, even when that test has been accurately translated. These differences can have implications for the way in which the test is administered, the style of questioning, as well as the context in which the questions are framed (Anastasi, 1976; Cronbach & Drenth, 1972). For example, the group administration of standardized paper-and-pencil questionnaires that require the subject to rate various intrapersonal characteristics and states is an approach widely used in North America. This "traditional" approach to data collection may be inappropriate in other cultures where testing subjects in a group setting is neither possible nor desirable, where reporting of internal states is viewed as obtrusive, or where the use of rating scales is very uncommon (Cho, 1972). The researcher needs to be sensitive to such cultural issues when developing or adapting tests for use with different cultural or subcultural groups. Concepts, relationships, and test results that are valid in Asia or Africa may not apply in North America or Europe, and vice versa.

Although cultural variations can be perceived as a nuisance by researchers, they do in fact provide excellent opportunities to examine the generalizability of certain psychological constructs across widely disparate populations and to study the covariation between culture and psychological parameters (Berry, 1980; Duda & Allison, 1990; Lonner, 1980). Cross-cultural research may contribute important insights into aspects of basic human functioning not otherwise available. It makes sense that an effect observed across a wide range of cultural groups is more likely to reflect a fundamental aspect of human psychological processes than one that is observed in only a small proportion of a relatively homogeneous group. Conversely the absence of similarities between culturally different groups points to the necessity of searching for new and broader explanations not suspected in unicultural research.

Duda's (1986) work on goal perspectives in Navaho Indians and Anglo-Americans, for example, has revealed that the Navaho Indians described success and failure in terms of behaviors (e.g., doing one's best, moving well) and outcome (e.g., winning, coming in first), while the Anglo-Americans equated success and failure with outcome only. Subsequent research and instrumentation related to the consequences of success and failure perceptions must therefore account for such differences, which in turn must be incorporated into a broader theory of motivation.

Similarly a study by Lambert, Hamers, and Frasure-Smith (1979) revealed that child-rearing practices among English-and French-speaking residents of Montreal differed in significant ways. Generally French-speaking mothers adopted more of an extended family approach in dealing with their offsprings' friends, whereas English-speaking mothers tended to be nurturing only toward their own children. This information may have measurement implications in examining, for example, the development of social support systems in youth sport.

With regard to measurement, the conduct of cross-cultural research involves, at the very least, the translation, the validation, and in some cases the adaptation of paper-and-pencil questionnaires for use in countries where either the same language is spoken by different groups or where two or more languages are spoken. In more complex situations, measurement in cross-cultural sport and exercise psychology research may involve virtually all aspects of test development and application, including modifying administration conditions, style of questioning, or content of measures.

BASIC MEASUREMENT CONSIDERATIONS: IS THE CONSTRUCT BEING MEASURED SUSCEPTIBLE TO CULTURAL INFLUENCE?

An extremely important consideration in cross-cultural research is the identification of both the source and the nature of specific cultural and subcultural influences (Anastasi, 1976; Eckensberger, 1972; Sanday, 1972). The researcher must address whether or not the variables under investigation are likely to be influenced by cultural differences. Factors that are likely to be affected by culture and socialization include values, norms, attitudes, beliefs, child-rearing practices, gender stereotypes, or power relations between teammates and coworkers. However, it has been suggested that even biological data can have relevance in cross-cultural research. In turn, cultural beliefs and more are likely to affect what is considered appropriate and inappropriate behavior in different social situations including the testing situation.

The criteria for membership in a given cultural or subcultural group are also an important concern. Culture or subculture is at least partially a function of place of residence, languages spoken, race, and gender. Factors such as religious practices, family structures, socioeconomic status, and even participation or nonparticipation in sport/exercise probably are also important to consider and may reflect differing degrees of cultural or subcultural influence (Anastasi, 1976). These latter effects may be quite subtle. In some cases, people may share the same language, race, and gender but, because of their particular socialization, may belong to different cultural or subcultural groups. For example, two English-speaking Caucasian females residing in a large North American city might be viewed as being part of the same cultural group. However, knowledge that one was brought up in a second generation of Catholic Italian immigrants in Canada while the second was raised in a third generation of Protestant Scottish immigrants in the United States might lead to classification into different subcultural groups. Thus establishing criteria for membership in a given cultural or subcultural group is an important concern in cross-cultural research.

In sum, if the researcher recognizes that cultural or subcultural factors may indeed influence the constructs of interest, and that there are implications for issues such as the relevance of certain items or for test administration, then these influences need to be identified and strategies developed to deal with them and integrate them into the research process. The first step in this process is a thorough conceptual analysis of the variables of interest and a careful observation of the culture with which the test or instrument is to be used.

TEST ADMINISTRATION AND STYLE OF MEASUREMENT

An important issue is to determine whether the measurement strategies (e.g., writing, personal interviews) are culturally unusual (Cronbach & Drenth, 1972). For example, in the Ivory Coast of Africa, it is viewed as extremely intrusive to question athletes about the use of fetishes or other superstition-related rituals, even though it is believed that their use is widespread as a mental preparation strategy (Dagrou, Gauvin, & Halliwell, 1991). An interviewer who is not sensitive to such issues, or a test that has not been appropriately adapted to account for these differences, will, at best, fail to achieve its purpose and, at worst, yield highly spurious results.

Similarly, many of the paper-and-pencil tests and questionnaires used in sport and exercise psychology research rely heavily on the subject's capacity to read, write, and associate numbers with abstract concepts. Obviously subject literacy is an important concern and may render the use of standardized paper-and-pencil questionnaires impossible or at the very least impractical. Some alternative methods to paper-and-pencil tests and questionnaires may include interviews, observations, the administration of tests that do not require reading, and collecting consensual information about a subject from significant others (Duda & Allison, 1990; Pareek & Venkateswara, 1980). Thus the first step in dealing with culturally diverse groups consists of evaluating the appropriateness of the methods of measurement for the culture.

THE ADAPTATION OF TESTS AND MEASURES: AN EXTENSION TO TEST CONSTRUCTION

If the consideration of cultural differences reveals that the content of a given test or scale must be adapted for a target population, then efforts must be devoted to item development, selection, and analysis (Anastasi, 1976; Irvine & Carroll, 1980). For example, in the study of the personality trait of outgoingness or extraversion, it is customary to have subjects self-rate the typicality of certain behaviors. These behaviors are often presented in some social context. The item "At parties, I walk up to people and start a conversation" illustrates this approach. This item would obviously be inappropriate in some cultures. In certain Middle Eastern cultures, women may not attend social gatherings that are parties in the Western sense of the word. In many cultures, initiating a conversation is viewed as rude and for women as a sexual overture.

It is important then that the bank of test items be examined to detect any cultural biases that may affect results in a given cultural context (Anastasi, 1976). A bank of items that has relevance for the target population but is also conceptually equivalent to the original set of testing items may need to be developed. This new, adapted set of items may then be tested with a pilot sample of subjects and results to assess the degree to which the internal consistency and statistical structure of the original item set has been maintained, if the test is to remain valid. Item adaptation for different cultural groups then is not simply a case of changing certain items. The structure of the adapted set of test items must be evaluated statistically with a culturally appropriate sample.

To use another example, Aylwin (1985), an Irish researcher, has developed a test called the Modes of Thought Questionnaire (MOTQ), which is designed to assess subjects' cognitive style. One section of the test requires subjects to rate the extent to which a series of word pairs automatically comes to mind. Some of the word pairs include words that are commonly used in Ireland but are not frequently used by North Americans. For example, a "hedgehog" in Ireland is referred to as a "porcupine" in North America. Thus the adaptation of questionnaires is not limited to circumstances where language is different, but also includes situations in which the same language is spoken by culturally different populations.

Developing both a conceptual and a statistical rationale for the selection of items, as well as closely following other statistical guidelines for item-analysis procedures, is just as important for test adaptation to different cultural and subcultural populations as in cross-cultural analyses.

THE TRANSLATION OF TESTS AND QUESTIONNAIRES: AN EXTENSION TO TEST CONSTRUCTION

Researchers interested in cross-cultural research often choose to translate and validate previously standardized tests and questionnaires because this process is usually more time efficient and more cost effective than constructing a new test (Brislin, 1980; Brislin et al., 1973). It should be noted that while these procedures are more time and cost effective, the actual economy is only moderate because the time and work involved in validating and producing a reliable version of the original measurement instrument may be similar to that involved in developing a new test. However, given that researchers are often interested in relating data to previous findings, the translation option is very attractive.

Certain procedures need to be followed in translating a psychological measurement instrument. Several authors have suggested a four-step approach (Brislin 1980; Brislin et al., 1973; Vallerand & Halliwell, 1983).

In order to produce a working version of the questionnaire in a target language, the back-translation procedure is often useful. Back translation consists of having a bilingual individual translate the original version into the target language. This translated version is then given to another individual who translates it back into the original language. The original version and back-translated versions are then compared to detect any differences that might contaminate the version in the target language.

Several problems may arise in applying this procedure. First, if differences between the original and back-translated meanings are found, this does not necessarily indicate problems with the version in the target language. The translators could have made erroneous translations. Thus in eliciting the help of bilingual persons to conduct the translations, it is imperative that the individuals have strong language skills. Several authors suggest that only professional translators should be used because they are the only professionals who are highly skilled in packaging meaning in different languages.

However, translators should also be familiar with the constructs being examined. The translator's task is obviously to convey the meaning of the various items on the questionnaire. The questionnaire items may include subtle differences that would only be detected by an individual who has an understanding of the concept being measured. Furthermore, since sport offers numerous examples of domain-specific terms, including a lay-up or a fast break in basketball, such terms could present a problem for a translator unfamiliar with that particular sport. In using the back-translation method then, the researcher must strive to find individuals who have an extensive knowledge of the two languages as well as a good understanding of the concepts being measured.

A second and related issue is the presence of colloquialisms in original versions of questionnaires. It is common to include such "slang" expressions because they cogently express an idea, a thought, a feeling, or an attitude in the words used by a given target group. Such expressions, however, pose a problem for the translation of questionnaires. For example, the expression "to have a lot of drive," which is used in English to suggest that someone demonstrates keenness, liveliness, and determination, does not have a literal translation in the French language. French-speaking people, however, frequently use an expression that communicates the same concept but literally means "to have a lot of heart in your stomach."

Another example is the use of the word "high." In an athlete population, this word refers to postexercise exhilaration or more generally to a feeling of euphoria. The same word in a population of drug users would likely have a completely different meaning. If the word was used with a non–North American population, the word might not have any colloquial meaning at all, but would simply be perceived as a spatial descriptor. The point is that prior to translation, the meaning of the colloquialisms must be extracted and then words to express this same idea must be found in the target language or dialect.

Brislin et al. (1973) have suggested that the translation and/or the evaluation of the version in the target language should be scrutinized by a committee. The role of the committee is to judge the clarity of each item in the target language and the equivalence of the version in the target language with the original version. The clarity refers to the extent to which the phrasing, terminology, and meaning of an item are unambiguous. The equivalence refers to the extent to which two parallel statements evoke an identical meaning. The work of the committee is best performed in frequent but short meetings because the judgments required are often mentally fatiguing. Once the committee feels comfortable with a target version, then the validation process may begin.

Two techniques other than the use of a committee, which have been proposed to examine the viability of a test or questionnaire in a target language, are the random probe and test administration with bilingual individuals (Brislin, 1980; Brislin et al., 1973; Vallerand & Halliwell, 1983).

The random-probe technique consists of administering a preliminary version of a questionnaire to a small sample of people in the target population, requesting that they explain why they answered a random set of items in a given way. This process may be repeated at different time intervals. The purpose of this procedure is to examine whether the test or questionnaire is indeed tapping the construct of interest that would be reflected in the content of the subjects' explanation. Testing at two time periods allows for a verification of the reliability of the explanation. Successful random-probe testing would encourage the researcher to proceed with the validation and development of norms.

A second strategy to evaluate the preliminary version of a test or questionnaire consists of administering it to a subset of bilingual individuals who are familiar with the two target cultures. Comparisons could be made to establish the equivalence or lack of equivalence between different groups. In the best of scenarios, no differences would be obtained among scores obtained from bilingual subjects completing alternative versions of a measure. In many cases, though, differences will appear and their interpretation can be problematic. The differences could be attributed to either true differences between cultures or to a lack of equivalence between measures in two different languages.

Alternatively previous studies demonstrate that bilingual people sometimes adopt a demeanor and manner that is suited to the culture associated with the language they are speaking. Thus differences obtained between bilingual groups filling out the original and target questionnaires could lead to different conclusions about their respective characteristics when in fact they point to influence factors that had been ignored in unicultural research. The central issue is that the researcher must use a multitude of strategies to examine the relation between translated and original versions of measures and to seek converging evidence on their equivalence.

REPLICATION AND EXTENSION OF EXISTING VALIDITY, RELIABILITY, AND NORMATIVE DATA

It is suggested that data supporting the validity and reliability of the test or questionnaire in the target cultural group should be collected prior to using culturally adapted measures in research (Anastasi, 1976; Brislin, 1980; Cronbach, 1984). In the case where no differences are expected in relation to cultural factors and the language of the test or questionnaire is the same, then replication of original validity and reliability data is the most appropriate route. On the other hand, when the cultural factors are expected to influence constructs, hypotheses pertaining to cultural influences should be derived prior to testing.

The overall objective at this stage of the adaptation procedure will be to provide evidence of the validity, especially the construct validity, and reliability of the measure in the target language. The production of normative data is especially important in situations where there are cultural differences, where conclusions are to be drawn for the culture itself, or where cross-cultural comparisons are to be made.

CONSIDERATIONS FOR CULTURALLY APPROPRIATE TESTS AND QUESTIONNAIRES

In sum it is obviously important that researchers give proper consideration to the existence of cultural influences and adapt measurement instruments accordingly. This holds true both when the language spoken in culturally distinct groups is different or when culturally distinct groups share a common language.

The first step for the researcher is to determine conceptually whether cultural factors will have an influence on the constructs under investigation. If the answer is no, then only translating and validating the questionnaire may be required if the language spoken in the target cultural group is different. On the other hand, if the answer is yes, then the formulation of hypotheses about how the construct will change because of cultural influences is appropriate. Alternatively, the extent to which the methods of measurement are unusual for the cultural group and the criteria required for classification of subjects in different cultural and subcultural groups must also be considered. The hypotheses can be tested during the construction and validation phase

of the measure or alternatively may be taken into consideration in adapting the measurement strategy. Finally potential confounding factors related to the actual test administration need to be identified and anticipated.

CONCLUSION

The purposes of this chapter were to focus discussion on two important issues in instrumentation in sport and exercise psychology, namely sport specificity and cross-cultural adaptation.

The selection of sport/exercise-specific tests and scales or nonspecific tests and scales requires a careful conceptual analysis of the constructs under investigation, an examination of the measurement assumptions of the theoretical framework employed, and in some cases, a consideration of the amount of variance explained in the target variables. The necessity of cross-culturally adapting tests and scales also requires a conceptual analysis, the focus of which is to identify cultural factors that might influence test development, administration, and interpretation. Developing alternative styles of questioning, adapting test items, and translating existing paper-and-pencil measures are all useful strategies toward this end.

Kerlinger (1973) stated that measurement is the "Achilles heel" of the social sciences. Measurement in sport and exercise psychology research suffers from the same woes. An ongoing re-evaluation of the type of instrumentation used, of its underlying purposes and assumptions as well as its meaning for the advancement of knowledge, is recommended to overcome the ubiquitous challenge of developing quality instrumentation for sport and exercise psychology research.

References

Ajzen, I., & Madden, T. J. (1986). Prediction of goal-directed behavior: Attitudes, intentions, and perceived behavioral control. *Journal of Experimental Social Psychology, 22,* 453–474.

Anshel, M. H. (1987). Psychological inventories used in sport psychology research. *The Sport Psychologist, 1,* 331–349.

Anastasi, A. (1972). *Psychological testing* (4th ed.). New York: Macmillan.

Aylwin, S. M. (1985). *Structure in thought and feeling.* New York: Methuen.

Bandura, A. (1986). *Social foundation of thought and action: A social cognitive theory.* Englewood Cliffs, NJ: Prentice-Hall.

Berry, J. W. (1980). Introduction to methodology. In H. C. Triandis & J. W. Berry (Eds.), *Handbook of cross-cultural psychology: Vol. 2. Methodology* (pp. 1–28). Boston: Allyn & Bacon.

Brislin, R. W. (1980). Translation and content analysis of oral and written material. In H. C. Triandis & J. W. Berry (Eds.), *Handbook of cross-cultural psychology: Vol. 2. Methodology* (pp. 389–444). Boston: Allyn & Bacon.

Brislin, R. W., Lonner, W. J., & Thorndike, R. M. (1973). *Crosscultural research methods.* New York: Wiley.

Cho, S. (1972). Procedures for group test administration in developing countries. In L. J. Cronbach & P. J. D. Drenth (Eds.), *Mental tests and cultural adaptation* (pp. 135–140). The Hague, Netherlands: Mouton.

Cronbach, L. J. (1984). *Essentials of psychological testing.* New York: Harper & Row.

Cronbach, L. J., & Drenth, P. J. D. (Eds.). (1972). *Mental tests and cultural adaptation.* The Hague, Netherlands: Mouton.

Dagrou, E., Gauvin, L., & Halliwell, W. R. (1991). La préparation mentale chez les athlètes ivoriens. *International Journal of Sport Psychology, 22,* 15–34.

Duda, J. L. (1986). A cross-cultural analysis of achievement motivation in sport and in the classroom. In L. VanderVelden & J. Humphrey (Eds.), *Current selected research in the psychology and sociology of sport* (pp. 115–132). New York: AMS Press.

Duda, J. L., & Allison, M. T. (1990). Cross-cultural analysis in exercise and sport psychology: A void in the field. *Journal of Sport and Exercise Psychology, 12,* 114–131.

Ebbeck, V. (1991, June). The current practice of reporting psychometric properties in sport psychology research. In V. Ebbeck (Chair), *Questionnaire development in sport psychology re-*

search: Rejuvenating the psychometric process. Symposium conducted at the meeting of the North American Society for the Psychology of Sport and Physical Activity, Asilomar, CA.

Ebbeck, V., Wood, T. M., & Horn, T. S. (1991, June). In V. Ebbeck (Chair), *Questionnaire development in sport psychology research: Rejuvenating the psychometric process.* Symposium conducted at the meeting of the North American Society for the Psychology of Sport and Physical Activity, Asilomar, CA.

Eckensberger, H. (1972). The necessity of a theory for applied cross-cultural research. In L. J. Cronbach & P. J. D. Drenth (Eds.), *Mental tests and cultural adaptation* (pp. 99–107). The Hague, Netherlands: Mouton.

Eysenck, H. J. (1973). *The biological basis of personality.* Springfield, IL: Thomas.

Feltz, D. L. (1982). Path analysis of the causal elements in Bandura's theory of self-efficacy and an anxiety-based model of avoidance behavior. *Journal of Personality and Social Psychology, 42,* 764–781.

Fleishman, E. A. (1956). Psychomotor selection tests: Research and application in the United States Air Force. *Personnel Psychology, 9,* 449–467.

Fleishman, E. A., & Bartlett, C. J. (1969). Human abilities. *Annual Review of Psychology, 20,* 349–380.

Gauvin, L., & Brawley, L. R. (In press, 1992). Alternative psychological models and methodologies for the study of exercise and affect. In P. Seraganian (Ed.), *The effects of physical exercise on psychological processes.* New York: Wiley.

Glass, G. V., McGaw, B., & Smith, M. L. (1980). *Meta-analysis in social research.* Beverly Hills, CA: Sage.

Hall, C., Pongrac, J., & Buckholz, E. (1985). The measurement of imagery ability. *Human Movement Science, 4,* 107–118.

Hardy, C. J., & Rejeski, W. J. (1989). Not what but how one feels: The measurement of affect during exercise. *Journal of Sport and Exercise Psychology, 11,* 304–317.

Hart, E. A., Leary, M. R., & Rejeski, W. J. (1989). The measurement of social physique anxiety. *Journal of Sport and Exercise Psychology, 11,* 94–104.

Irvine, S. H., & Carroll, W. K. (1980). Testing and assessment across cultures: Issues in methodology and theory. In H. C. Triandis & J. W. Berry (Eds.), *Handbook of cross-cultural psychology: Vol. 2. Methodology* (pp. 181–245). Boston: Allyn & Bacon.

Kenyon, G. S. (1968). Six scales for assessing attitude toward physical activity. *The Research Quarterly, 39,* 566–574.

Kerlinger, F. N. (1979). *Behavioral research: A conceptual approach.* New York: Holt, Rinehart & Winston.

Kerlinger, F. N. (1973). *Foundations of behavioral research* (2nd ed.). New York: Holt, Rinehart & Winston.

Lambert, W. W., Hamers, J. F., & Frasure-Smith, N. (1979). *Childrearing values.* New York: Praeger.

Lewin, K. (1951). *Field theory in social science: Selected papers on group dynamics.* New York: Harper & Row.

Lonner, W. J. (1980). The search for psychological universals. In H. C. Triandis & W. W. Lambert (Eds.), *Handbook of cross-cultural research: Vol. 1. Perspectives* (pp. 143–204). Boston: Allyn & Bacon.

Mahoney, M. J., Gabriel, T. J., & Perkins, T. S. (1987). Psychological skills and exceptional athletic performance. *The Sport Psychologist, 1,* 181–199.

Martens, R. (1979). About smocks and jocks. *Journal of Sport Psychology, 1,* 94–99.

Martens, R., Vealey, R., & Burton, D. (1990). *Competitive anxiety in sport.* Champaign, IL: Human Kinetics.

McAuley, E., & Gross, J. B. (1983). Perceptions of causality in sport: An application of the causal dimension scale. *Journal of Sport Psychology, 5,* 72–76.

Mihevic, P. (1983). Sensory cues for perceived exertion: A review. *Medicine and Science in Sports, 13,* 150–163.

Morgan, W. P. (1981). Psychophysiology of self-awareness during vigorous physical activity. *Research Quarterly for Exercise and Sport, 52,* 385–427.

Morgan, W. P. (1982). Psychological effects of exercise. *Behavioral Medicine Update, 4,* 25–30.

Nunnally, J. C. (1978). *Psychometric theory* (2nd ed.). New York: McGraw-Hill.

Orlick, T. D. (1974). An interview schedule designed to assess family sports environment. *International Journal of Sport Psychology, 5,* 13–27.

Ostrow, A. C. (Ed.). (1990). *Directory of psychological tests in the sport and exercise sciences.* Morgantown, WV: Fitness Information Technology.

Pareek, U., & Venkateswara, R. (1980). Cross-cultural surveys and interviewing. In H. C. Triandis & J. W. Berry (Eds.), *Handbook of cross-cultural psychology: Vol. 2. Methodology* (pp. 127–180). Boston: Allyn & Bacon.

Price-Williams, D. R. (1985). Cultural psychology. In G. Lindzey & E. Aronson (Eds.), *Handbook of social psychology: Vol. 1. Theory and methods* (pp. 993–1042). New York: Random House.

Rejeski, W. J. (1985). Perceived exertion: An active or passive process? *Journal of Sport Psychology, 7,* 371–378.

Rejeski, W. J., Best, D., Griffith, P., & Kenney, E. (1987). Sex-role orientation and the responses of men to exercise stress. *Research Quarterly for Exercise and Sport, 58,* 260–264.

Rejeski, W. J., Hardy, C. J., & Shaw, J. (1991). Psychometric confounds of assessing state anxiety in conjunction with acute bouts of vigorous exercise. *Journal of Sport and Exercise Psychology, 13,* 65–74.

Rosenthal, R., & Rosnow, R. L. (1984). *Essentials of behavioral research.* New York: McGraw-Hill.

Russell, D. W. (1982). The Causal Dimension Scale: A measure of how individuals perceive causes. *Journal of Personality and Social Psychology, 42,* 1137–1145.

Russell, D. W., McAuley, E., & Tarico, V. (1987). Measuring causal attributions for success and failure: A comparison of methods for assessing causal dimensions. *Journal of Sport and Exercise Psychology, 52,* 1248–1257.

Rust, J., & Golombok, S. (1989). *Modern psychometrics: The science of psychological assessment.* New York: Routledge.

Sanday, P. R. (1972). A model for the analysis of cross-cultural determinants of between-groups variation in intelligence. In L. J. Cronbach & P. J. D. Drenth (Eds.), *Mental tests and cultural adaptation* (pp. 89–98). The Hague, Netherlands: Mouton.

Schutz, R. W., Smoll, F. L., & Wood, T. M. (1985). Inventories and norms for children's attitudes toward physical activity. *Research Quarterly for Exercise and Sport, 56,* 256–265.

Thompson, W. R. (1980). Cross-cultural use of biological data and perspectives. In H. C. Triandis & W. W. Lambert (Eds.), *Handbook of cross-cultural psychology: Vol. 1. Perspectives* (pp. 205–252). Boston: Allyn & Bacon.

Triandis, H. C. & Berry, J. W. (Eds.). (1980). *Handbook of cross-cultural research: Vol. 2. Methodology.* Boston: Allyn & Bacon.

Vallerand, R. J., & Halliwell, W. R. (1983). Vers une méthodologie de la validation trans-culturelle de questionnaires psychologiques: Implications pour la psychologie du sport. *Canadian Journal of Applied Sport Sciences, 8,* 9–18.

·43·

USE, MISUSE, AND DISUSE OF PSYCHOMETRICS IN SPORT PSYCHOLOGY RESEARCH

Robert W. Schutz

Marc E. Gessaroli

Over 25 years ago Jacob Cohen wrote a chapter dealing with the use and misuse of statistics, entitled "Some Statistical Issues in Psychological Research" (Cohen, 1965). His introduction contained the following paragraph (p. 95):

Statistical analysis is a tool, not a ritualistic religion. It is for use, not for reverence, and it should be approached in the spirit that it was made for psychologists rather than vice versa. As one of many tools in the psychologist's kit, it is frequently not relevant and is sometimes of considerable utility. It is certainly not as important as, nor can it even partly replace, good ideas or well-conceived experimental stratagems, although it may be virtually indispensable in testing out an idea or rounding out a good experiment.

The validity of this statement has not declined over the last 27 years, and it is a basic underlying assumption of our chapter. The only revision we suggest is that, given the nature of much of the current research in sport psychology, we would expand Cohen's "experimental stratagems" to include quasi-experiments, surveys, and all other research methodologies for which data analysis is warranted. If the research question is well formulated, the theoretical foundation well developed, the methodology appropriate for the question posed, and the data reliable and valid, then the potential for contribution to knowledge exists. Unfortunately an inappropriate or erroneous data analysis occasionally negates or delays that contribution, but the potential is still there. However, without these factors, no data analysis can salvage the study. We have all read articles in which a complex data-analytic strategy has been employed in an attempt to make much of nothing; however, despite the apparent "success" (i.e., publication), the contribution to knowledge is not realized. Thus the focus of this chapter is on the identification of statistical procedures that will assist the sport psychology researcher in maximizing the interpretation and generalizability of the data.

It is interesting to note what Cohen listed as the four key issues in statistical analyses back in 1965: power and error rates, significance versus effect size, one-tailed versus two-tailed hypotheses, and nonparametric statistics. The latter two are, in general, nonissues today, but the first two can still be considered major concerns. In reviewing the sport psychology literature (details of our procedures are given later), we noted an apparent disconcern about power and type II errors—the majestical and omnipotent significance level continues to be worshiped. It can be shown that the power of a "typical" statistical test to detect a moderate $d = .5$) population effect is only .47, where "typical" refers to a two-tailed t-test (independent means) with 30 subjects per group (Cohen, 1990). Our review indicates that many sport psychology researchers still do not calculate power and the required sample size before initiating a study. Cohen (1977) and Kraemer and Thiemann (1987) provide comprehensive and easy-to-follow guidelines for sample-size determination.

The related issue of interpreting significance level and neglecting effect size is also a criticism that could well be

We wish to thank Antoinette Klawer and Jinsheng Xue for their assistance in identifying and summarizing the articles used as examples in this paper.

901

leveled at the analyses and interpretation of our literature. It is not difficult to find examples where an investigator has shown that a test statistic is significant at say $p < .05$ and then proceeded to discuss the theoretical importance of that finding without any reference to the magnitude of the effect. We all know that correlations of less than .20 are statistically significant for sample sizes of less than 100. We also know that a correlation of .20 represents a communality of only 4%. Regrettably some of us tend to emphasize the significance and try to ignore the magnitude of the effect. It does not matter which effect size one chooses to report (e.g., Cohen's *d,* omega squared, or the correlation ratio), but, as Thomas (1983) has strongly recommended, all authors should be required to qualify and quantify statements of significance with reports of effect size.

Thus some of the statistical issues of the 1960s are still issues. However, they are probably issues because of neglect and oversight, not because of ignorance. It is our contention that the statistical analyses in the sport psychology literature represent a reasonably sophisticated application of current applied statistics. There are examples of state-of-the-art statistical modeling applications, and there exist examples of "let's analyze everything every which-way and hope we get something" attempts. In general, sport psychologists are statistically more sophisticated than their colleagues in exercise physiology, but not as sophisticated as the social psychologists (as represented by publications in the *Journal of Personality and Social Psychology).*

In this chapter we discuss the use and misuse of statistics under three general headings: statistical analyses for comparing means (ANOVA and MANOVA), statistical analyses of relationships (correlation, regression, and structural equation modeling), and the statistical procedures of inventory development and assessment. Mathematically, ANOVA, MANOVA, multiple regression, and discriminant analysis can all be modeled as special cases of the more general canonical variate analysis model (Darlington, Weinberg, & Walberg, 1977). Depending on whether the "independent" or "dependent" set of variables has more than one measure, and whether the variables are continuous or categorical (with dummy coding), each of the above techniques can be viewed as a special case of canonical analysis. However, we have chosen to present ANOVA/MANOVA and correlation/regression as two distinct methodologies, because this appears to be the traditional approach familiar to most sport psychologists.

For each of the above methodologies we attempt to identify procedures and studies that we feel indicate *good use* and studies that suggest *misuse.* We also note *nonuse,* or the uncommon use, of a number of potentially powerful and useful statistical procedures that remain virtually ignored by sport psychologists. Finally we present a number of *issues* involving current debates of the appropriateness of certain statistical procedures and/or the preferred choice of alternative methodologies. Our purpose is not to educate the reader on the theory or application of specific statistical procedures—there are numerous textbooks that do that very well. Rather, our purpose is to point out to the reader

the appropriateness or inappropriateness of certain techniques, and provide an awareness of some of the statistical methodologies that appear to have been neglected by sport psychologists. In all instances we have attempted to provide references that would be practical and understandable to a researcher with a basic statistical background.

Our appraisal and evaluation of the statistical procedures used by researchers in sport psychology is based on a rather limited but thorough examination of published literature. We conducted two independent literature reviews, one for the first two sections (means, relationships) and one for the last section (inventory development). All reports of empirical research (but not reviews, tutorials, etc.) in the broadly defined areas of sport psychology and motor learning were identified and the statistical procedures enumerated and evaluated. No attempt was made to evaluate the research problem, methodology, measures, or substantive interpretation. For the first literature review we examined all articles within each issue for at least one year for each of four journals: *Journal of Sport and Exercise Psychology* (1990, 4 issues), *Research Quarterly for Exercise and Sport* (1988 and 1990, 8 issues), *International Journal of Sport Psychology* (1990, 4 issues), and *The Sport Psychologist* (1990, 3 issues). These 19 periodicals contained 51 research articles that met our criteria for inclusion. The literature reviewed to identify statistical techniques in inventory development consisted of all 1990 issues of: *Journal of Motor Behavior, Journal of Exercise and Sport Psychology, Journal of Human Movement Studies,* and *Research Quarterly for Exercise and Sport.* This review yielded only about 10 studies that included inventory development or assessment as a primary component.

STATISTICAL ANALYSES FOR COMPARING AVERAGES

This is certainly the most common application of the sport psychology papers in the journals we reviewed. The majority of the studies reported in the four journals surveyed had as their major focus the comparison of means—either between-group differences (e.g., male-female, novice-elite, treatment-control), or change over time (e.g., pre-post intervention, feedback-no feedback, trials 1 through 10). Of the 51 papers we examined, 78% ($N = 40$) of them used a *t*-test, ANOVA, or MANOVA, or some combination of the three, as the primary method of analysis. A more specific breakdown of the type of statistical analysis applied is as follows: *t*-test or ANOVA for a randomized groups design (independent means), 12%; *t*-test or ANOVA for a repeated measures or mixed model design (dependent means for at least one factor), 45%; T^2 or MANOVA for a randomized groups design, 15%; and T^2 or MANOVA for a repeated measures or mixed model design, 6%. Thus over 50% of the empirical studies we selected involved the measurement and analysis of change over time. Because the methods of analyses, assumptions, and issues regarding use and misuse are quite different for the randomized groups and repeated measures studies, they are presented and discussed separately in the following sections.

Differences Between Samples (Independent Means)

Possible Analyses. The available analyses for testing differences among means are the familiar *t*-tests, ANOVAs, and MANOVAs summarized in Table 43–1.

General Comments. The motor learning studies, of which there were only a few, dealt almost exclusively with performance change over trials (under various conditions of information given or withheld), and thus the following section deals only with the sport psychology domain. The sport psychology research reports were of two basic types. First, the between-group studies in which samples from two or more discrete populations were compared—for example, sighted and unsighted, a number of age groups, male and female, skilled and less skilled. Second, studies utilizing a true experimental or quasi-experimental design in which subjects were randomly assigned to two or more treatment conditions—for example, long-term and short-term goal setting, feedback and nonfeedback, four levels of goal setting, task-specific imagery, and off-task imagery. Although the following observation falls outside the purpose of this chapter, the statistical analyses of the data, we feel it important to comment on what we perceive to be a methodological weakness in many of these studies. Many of the research reports of the first kind identified above, comparisons of individuals differing in some demographic or organismic variable, appeared theoretically weak. The primary research question seemed to be, "I wonder if these two groups are different on one or more of these variables?" Little or no rationale was provided to support any hypotheses as to why the independent variable might lead to differences on the dependent variable. This is unfortunate, and in sharp contrast to most of the studies of the second kind (experiments and quasi-experiments) in which there was a serious attempt to develop a theoretical rationale, evaluate some testable hypotheses deduced from that theory, and generalize the results to other populations, treatments, or conditions.

In general, the published research suggests that researchers are becoming appropriately sophisticated in the use of analysis-of-variance procedures. The use of multiple *t*-tests is, finally, a relatively infrequent event—but certainly not an obsolete procedure. For example, Boutcher and

TABLE 43–1. Analyses for Testing Differences Between Samples

Independent variables	Number of dependent variables	
	One	Two or more
One: 2 levels	*t*-test	Hotelling's T²
> 2 levels	one-way ANOVA	one-way MANOVA
Two or more	N-way ANOVA	N-way MANOVA

Zinsser (1990) conducted a total of 38 *t*-tests in a study on cardiac deceleration involving elite and beginner golfers ($N = 30$). Given that they generated an additional 14 test statistics (2 three-way ANOVAs, 2 correlations), this far exceeds Schutz's very liberal "Absolute Bottom Line Rule" (ABLR) that the total number of significance tests (*p*-values) in a study must not exceed the total number of subjects. This large number of *t*-tests came about not because of a large number of dependent variables, but because of a possible misuse of the paired *t*-test. They compared baseline heart rate levels (interbeat intervals) with those taken at each of 7 subsequent times during and after execution of a golf putt. Although the research hypothesis is not clearly stated, the question of interest may have been more appropriately answered with a repeated measures ANOVA or some type of curve fitting. If multiple pairwise comparisons were absolutely necessary, then an adjusted probability level should have been used (e.g., Bonferroni, Scheffe).

The majority of studies that applied an ANOVA or MANOVA for a randomized groups design appear to have been well analyzed. There is only one issue that raise here, and that concerns the choice of conducting one multivariate analysis versus performing multiple univariate analyses. Of course the more general issues of sample size, violations of assumptions, and data mining versus theory testing hold here as they do for most of our statistical analyses.

Issue: Multivariate Versus Multiple Univariate Analyses. The concepts of per comparison (PC) and experimentwise (EW) or familywise (FW) type I error rates are well known. We have been taught to minimize our EW error rate as much as possible, but at the same time try to retain a reasonable level of power—that is, do not set our PC alpha level too low. Thus we often use ANOVA and follow up a significant omnibus *F*-statistic with a post hoc multiple comparison procedure that protects us against too high an EW type I error rate. We do this with one of the following tests: Tukey HSD, Newman-Keuls (now often referred to as the Student-Newman-Keuls procedure), or Scheffe (but, hopefully, never the very liberal Duncan Multiple Range Test).

Most of us are also cognizant of the inflation in our EW error rate brought about by conducting a *t*-test or *F*-test (ANOVA) on each one of a large number of *dependent* variables. In the last 20 years the availability of the necessary computer hardware and software have provided all of us with the ability to conduct multivariate tests; Hotelling's T^2 instead of multiple *t*-tests, and MANOVA instead of multiple ANOVAs. These multivariate procedures purport to provide an initial overall test of the equality of the mean vectors at some probability level. If the probability value associated with our multivariate test statistic is sufficiently small (e.g., $< .05$), we reject the null hypothesis of equal group (trials, conditions, etc.) means for the set of dependent variables and proceed with some type of univariate procedures for each one of our dependent variables. Which procedure we use as a follow-up to our multivariate test is a point of some debate, but univariate ANOVAs or *t*-tests, step-down *F*s, simultaneous confidence intervals, and discriminant analysis are some of the choices. Most multivariate statistics texts cover this issue (Tabachnick & Fidell, 1989, is probably the most readable). We have frequently made the case for a need for a greater utilization of multivariate statistical procedures for the purposes of data interpretation and to reduce the problem of "probability pyramiding" inherent in multiple *t*-tests or ANOVAs (e.g., Schutz, 1978; Schutz & Gessaroli, 1987; Schutz, Smoll, & Gessaroli, 1983).

Until recently the choice between multiple univariate tests and one multivariate test was a nonissue for most researchers and applied statisticians. When possible (i.e., when it was theoretically justifiable and there was an adequate sample size) we used the multivariate procedure. However, that philosophy is now being challenged. For some of us, who liked to think that we were up-to-date and statistically sophisticated, the arguments against multivariate tests are difficult to accept—but these arguments are strong and compelling. The essence of the case in support of multiple univariate analyses over a multivariate analysis is well presented by Huberty and Morris (1989). They reviewed the 1986 issues of six psychological journals, five of which were American Psychological Association publications. They identified 222 articles that used multiple ANOVAs and/or MANOVA as the primary analysis. The majority, 59%, used multiple ANOVAs without a preliminary MANOVA, and 40% of the studies applied a preliminary MANOVA before using ANOVAs as a follow-up. Only 1% (*N* = 3) of the articles used MANOVA without follow-up ANOVAs (one MANOVA was nonsignificant and discriminant analysis was used in the other two). Huberty and Morris assert that the "MANOVA-ANOVAs approach is seldom, if ever, appropriate" (p. 302). They support Bird and Hadzi-Pavlovic's (1983) opinion that the type I error rate is not fully controlled by first conducting an overall MANOVA. When control of the EW rate is desirable (and we think it always is), Huberty and Morris suggest using either a simultaneous test procedure or some type of error-splitting protocol (e.g., Bonferroni). In both cases the researcher is faced with a considerable loss of power for each dependent variable test. Their solution to this is the obvious, familiar, and often impractical approach—increase the sample size. They remind us that the multivariate and univariate analyses address different questions, and the choice of which to use must be based on the nature of the research question. It is our view that most of the research questions posed by the authors of the papers we reviewed were of the form, "Do these groups differ on one or more of these dependent variables?" If that is so, then the multiple univariate ANOVA approach is preferred. If, however, the primary research question is of the form, "What combination of these dependent variables distinguishes these groups, and which variables contribute most to the between-group variance?" then a preliminary MANOVA is appropriate. However, the follow-up analyses in this case should be a discriminant analysis, with the *F*-to-remove or the standardized discriminant function weights providing an indication of the relative importance of the dependent variables.

Differences Within Samples (Correlated Means)

Possible Analyses. The statistical procedures given above for the independent means tests can also be used with repeated measures designs (except that we would have a *t*-test for correlated means, etc.). However, the data analyst has a choice of treating the repeated measures as univariate or multivariate. The usual method is to treat them as univariate measures and perform a repeated measures ANOVA when there is only one dependent variable and a repeated measures MANOVA (called a multivariate mixed model, MMM, MANOVA) when two or more dependent variables are analyzed simultaneously. This was the method used in at least 23 of the 26 studies reported here. Another approach is to treat the repeated measures multivariately (and thus avoid some of the restrictive assumptions inherent in a repeated measures ANOVA). In this case the single dependent variable repeated measures design is analyzed using the "MANOVA method," and the multiple dependent variable repeated measures design is analyzed with a procedure referred to as the "doubly multivariate (DM)" MANOVA. Hertzog and Rovine (1985) and Schutz and Gessaroli (1987) provide extensive discussions and examples of these procedures, and Hand and Taylor (1987) provide a very thorough treatment of all aspects of MANOVA for repeated measures. In summary, our choices are as follows:

TABLE 43–2. Analyses for Testing Differences Within Samples

Method of analysis	Number of dependent variables	
	One	Two or more
RM treated as univariate	ANOVA	Multivariate Mixed Model (MMM) MANOVA
RM treated as multivariate	MANOVA method	Doubly Multivariate (DM) MANOVA

General Comments. As noted previously, approximately 50% of the research reports examined were based on studies using a repeated measures design. Twenty-three of the 51 papers reported the results of one of more ANOVAs, which included at least one repeated measures factor, and three of the papers claimed to have performed a repeated measures MANOVA. The appropriate statistical analyses for most experimental designs involving repeated measures are procedures similar to those reported above for the randomized groups designs: *t*-test, Hotelling's T^2, ANOVA, and MANOVA. The basic difference is that the between-subject variability is removed from the error term for all effects involving repeated measures. In general, this results in a more powerful statistical test for a given alpha level, or, alternatively, it provides equal power with fewer subjects. In most of the motor learning/control and sport psychology studies, repeated measures are not used in a conscious attempt to increase power, but rather are necessary to examine the research question, which involves the measurement and evaluation of change.

There are three points that merit discussion with respect to the analysis and interpretation of the repeated measures designs. Two of the issues, testing and adjusting for violations of the assumptions of circularity and sphericity, and follow-up procedures for repeated measures factors, have been clarified for us by psychometricians in the last 10 to 15 years. However, as is usually the case, it seems to take at least 20 years before users of statistics adopt a "new" procedure. Our review of the sport psychology literature indicates that researchers in our field rarely incorporate the appropriate adjustments needed for repeated measures designs. The third issue has been with us for a very long time and on the surface would seem like a rather simple problem. What is the best method of analysis for a simple pretest-posttest design? The statisticians are still arguing over this, and we will attempt to identify the nature of this debate and propose a general rule.

Nonuse: Adjustment for Violations of Assumptions. Assume that we wish to analyze a two-way mixed model design (Groups by Trials) with an ANOVA procedure. Most textbooks published before the mid-1970s (and some since then) stated that a necessary condition for valid F-tests on the Trials main effect and the Group by Trials interaction was that of compound symmetry—that is, equal variances and equal covariances. It has been well documented that violation of this assumption results in an inflation of the F-values for these effects, thus inflating the type I error rate (Davidson, 1972).

In the 1970s it was shown that the assumption of compound symmetry was unnecessarily strict (Huynh & Feldt, 1970, 1976; Rouanet & Lepine, 1970). It is now accepted that the necessary condition for an exact F-test for any within-subject effect is that of *sphericity*. The repeated measures, when transformed by a set of orthonormal weights (e.g., trend analysis), must be uncorrelated with each other and have equal variances. With a mixed model design it is necessary for the pooled (over groups) covariance matrix to exhibit sphericity and the covariance matrices to be equal for all groups. This condition is referred to as multisample sphericity or *circularity*. Fortunately it is now very easy for the data analyst to ascertain the degree to which these assumptions have been violated and make the necessary adjustments. The degree to which the data meet the assumptions can be quantified by the parameter epsilon (e), and this statistic is now printed out in many of the commercial statistics packages (BMDP2V, SPSSx, SYSTAT). An e value of 1.0 indicates that all is well (no violations, perfect sphericity), and a low e value (i.e., below .70, in general) tells us that the assumptions have been violated to the extent that the reported p-values may be serious underestimates of the true values.

These computer programs also provide adjusted p-values for all repeated measures effects, often labeled the H-F (Huynh-Feldt) and G-G (Greenhouse-Geisser) proba-

bilities. One or the other of these values is the probability value that should always be reported. The H-F probability is the appropriate one in most cases as it provides an adjustment relative to the degree of violation. The G-G statistic is overly conservative, being based on a worst-case-possible scenario. One word of caution should be noted: Hertzog and Rovine (1985) suggest that serious consequences could occur when e is less than .75, and that the H-F adjusted p-value may underestimate the true p-value in such cases. The more conservative G-G adjustment is appropriate in such situations.

To what extent is this an issue in research in our field? In motor learning studies it should be a major concern, as most of the learning or performance experiments in this area involve a large number of trials. The greater the number of trials, the greater the likelihood that the sphericity assumption will be violated. Gessaroli and Schutz (1983), in reanalyzing data sets from a number of published studies, found that epsilon was frequently below .50 in studies with 20 repeated measures. Clearly there is a need here to test for possible nonsphericity and, if necessary, to utilize the appropriate adjusted p-value. In sport psychology the situation may not be as severe, as many of the repeated-measures studies are of the pretest-posttest kind. In that case there is only one covariance between trials and $e = 1.0$. A substantial number of studies, however, included three or more repeated conditions—for example, effective responses of athletes measured twice a week for 4 weeks, competitive state anxiety measured pre-, mid-, and postcompetition, and six mood scores (treated as six levels of a repeated-measures factor!) measured pre-and postclass on each of 3 days. A few of the sport psychology papers we reviewed reported an adjusted p-value, and those that did appeared to use the overly conservative G-G approach. These studies did not report e values, so we could not ascertain if a G-G method was appropriate. One study (Berger & Owen, 1988) stated that the H-F adjusted p-values were used (but they reported the unadjusted values) and, to their credit, they also gave a value of e with each F-statistic reported. Although their intention was noble, it appears to be an example of a misuse of the procedure.

The H-F procedure is appropriate, in an orthogonal factorial design with repeated measures, for adjusting an upwardly biased F-statistic caused by small to moderate multisample nonsphericity ($e > .70$) in the variance-covariance matrices. For serious nonsphericity ($e < .60$) the H-F procedure will lead to some inflation in the type I error rates, and if this occurs in a nonorthogonal design (unequal cell sizes), the degree of bias can be extreme. Milligan, Wong, and Thompson (1987) showed empirical rates of type I error as high as .40 for an alpha of .05. The cell sizes for the six groups in the Berger and Owen study varied from 8 to 33, and epsilon values were as low as .47. Under these circumstances the H-F adjusted p-values (and the reported nonadjusted values) may be much lower than they should be. There are many ways in which the analyses reported in this study could be revised, and so it is difficult to provide a recommendation for this particular problem.

However, assuming that the ANOVAs performed were appropriate for the design, three suggestions are: (1) keep cell sample sizes approximately equal (to the extent that the maximum ratio is less than 2:1), (2) do not use an error term based on a pooled variance-covariance matrix (use group-or level-specific matrices), and (3) use the more conservative G-G adjusted p-values when $e < .75$. Kesselman and Kesselman (1990) provide a good review of the issues in analyzing nonorthogonal repeated measures designs and present tables showing the degree of inflation under various conditions.

Misuse: Multiple Comparisons with Repeated Measures.

Researchers in sport psychology appear knowledgeable about the application of post hoc multiple comparison procedures. In the studies we reviewed there were examples of all five common procedures: Duncan's (which we shun because of its extremely liberal EW error rate), Newman-Keuls, Tukey's, Scheffe's, and the Dunn or Bonferroni alpha-splitting procedure. We were disappointed not to see any preplanned contrasts, other than two applications of a trend analysis. One would like to think that our field has advanced its theories to the point where we could, in some instances, be testing for specific differences.

The issue here is the inappropriateness of these common multiple comparison procedures as follow-up tests for repeated-measures factors in a mixed model factorial design. The fact that our researchers are still using Tukey's, Scheffe's, and Newman-Keuls's tests is not surprising, as the empirical work on repeated-measures multiple comparisons is very recent. Kesselman and Kesselman (1988) have shown that under certain sets of conditions the empirical percentage of type I errors could be as high as 70% for the Tukey test and 64% for the Bonferroni procedure. There are many combinations of conditions that lead to such highly inflated error rates, and it would be prudent for all of us to carefully examine this Kesselman and Kesselman paper before applying any post hoc multiple comparison tests to a repeated-measures main effect, or to an interaction that includes a repeated-measures factor.

Very simply, the following combination of conditions leads to extreme levels of inflation: a mixed model with at least 3 groups, 4 or more levels of the repeated-measures factor, unequal cell sizes negatively paired with unequal covariance matrices, and a standard ordinary-least-squares-on-unweighted-means method of analysis. At least two of these conditions will likely be present in your next study! Approximately half of the studies reported in our literature use at least two levels of a between-subject factor, and many of them observe the subjects at least four times. We know from our previous studies that unequal covariance matrices are common, especially in studies comparing divergent groups (e.g., novice-elite, male-female).

Our review of the literature for this chapter indicates that most studies end up with unequal cell-sample sizes, often to the extent of exceeding a 2:1 ratio. We assume that virtually all analyses are conducted using the standard default procedures in most statistical packages—that is, ordinary-least squares with unweighted means. What we do not know is if there is a negative pairing of unequal covariances and unequal cell sizes (the smallest cells have the largest variances and covariances). If a positive pairing exists, then most of the multiple comparison procedures are overly conservative (the Bonferroni produces 0.42% type I errors at $\alpha = .05$, and $e = .40$), and therefore provide very little power. Thus we could be conducting our multiple comparison tests at an empirical alpha level of as high as .70 or as low as .004! A key contributor to the inflation of the type I error rate is the unweighted means analysis. Kesselman and Kesselman (1988) recommend that a weighted means procedure be applied in the presence of unequal cell sizes. Thus at this point our recommendations to those who use post hoc multiple comparison tests are: use a weighted means analysis if you have unequal N, try to obtain near-equal cell sizes, use large-sized samples, and choose the Bonferroni approach over other methods.

Issue: The Pretest-Posttest Design.

Many psychometricians are still debating the merits of a variety of procedures for analyzing the classic two-group pretest-posttest design, although some of us find this state of affairs surprising. This rather simple but very efficient design continues to be the design used in numerous sport psychology studies, and researchers in our field tend to analyze their data using one of three procedures: a t-test for independent means using the pretest-to-posttest change scores as the dependent variable, an ANOVA for a 2 × 2 factorial design, or an ANCOVA on the posttest scores using the pretest as the covariate. The first two procedures yield identical results, the F-statistic for the group by time interaction being equal to the square of the t-statistic on the change scores. Over 15 years ago Huck and McLean (1975) suggested that the repeated-measures ANOVA was an inappropriate analysis for the pretest-posttest design, and we are still being warned against its possible misuse (e.g., Jennings, 1988; Stanek, 1988). However, few behavioral scientists have followed this advice, and the ANOVA method is still the most commonly used procedure for this design in our literature.

Despite the admonitions by Jennings and others, our position is that the repeated measures ANOVA is the most suitable alternative for most data sets (see Schutz, 1989). When the assumptions are violated, then their results may be invalid—as is the case with any statistical technique. Jennings and others base their arguments on that premise—that is, the assumptions are often violated. However, Jennings presents evidence from a case so bizarre that it is not realistic to even consider it as occurring in an empirical study. The pretest-posttest correlations in Jennings's three-group example are approximately −1.0, 1.0, and 0.0. Although it is quite likely that one group will show a decrement in performance and one group an improvement, it is highly improbable that we would observe a strong negative correlation within a group from pretest to posttest. The data in Jennings's example violate the ANCOVA assumptions of equal slopes and the ANOVA assumptions of equal variances and covariances. If our data do exhibit such characteristics (and it would be advisable for us to examine our data for such possibilities), then the suggestions by Jennings and others should be followed and we need to apply a regression model that fits the data characteristics. For most practical situations, the ANOVA procedures as specified in the recent statistical reference texts are appropriate (e.g., Winer, Brown, & Michels, 1991).

Nonuse: Log-Linear Models. Knoke and Burke (1980), in their monograph on log-linear models, state that "during the past decade a revolution in contingency table analysis has swept through the social sciences, casting aside most of the older forms for determining relationships among variables measured at discrete levels" (p. 7). It appears that our sport psychologists did not participate in that revolution, as we found no log-linear applications in the literature we reviewed. It is likely that the primary reason for this is that the collection and analysis of categorical data is not a part of most sport psychology studies.

Our review did identify two studies in which the data were presented in multiway contingency tables and analyzed with a series of chi-squares. In those studies the analysis of choice should have been log-linear analysis. A secondary reason for the absence of log-linear analyses is that sport psychologists often treat their ordinal data as continuous and use traditional ANOVA methods for the analysis. This is acceptable under some circumstances, but when the variables used in the analysis are based on single measures obtained from 3- or 4-point scales, then it is unlikely that the data meet the assumptions required for valid application of ANOVA or MANOVA. In such cases log-linear analysis is recommended. Log-linear models are used to describe data that has been summarized in the form of multidimensional frequency tables.

In contrast to ANOVA, which involves the partitioning of variance, log-linear models are based on the probabilities associated with the various cells in the contingency table. The analyses, using maximum likelihood estimation, allows for model fitting, hypothesis testing, and parameter estimation. The results can be expressed in a format similar to the decomposition of the total sum of squares for ANOVA; thus main effects and interactions among the categorical variables can be identified and tested for significance. If the research question requires a distinction between independent and dependent (explanatory and response) variables, then logit-linear analysis, a special form of log-linear analysis, can be applied.

Sport psychologists should take greater advantage of these relatively new statistical techniques. Kenny's book (1983) provides a comprehensive and quite readable treatment of log-linear analysis, Knoke and Burke's (1980) short monograph gives a good overview, and Baker (1981) presents a clear distinction between log-linear and logit-linear models.

STATISTICS OF RELATIONSHIPS

General Comments

Only 9 of the 51 studies used correlation-regression type techniques as the predominant mode of analysis. Six papers reported multiple regression, two utilized discriminant function analyses, and one employed a cluster analysis. This is somewhat surprising and represents a characteristic of data analyses in this field not shared by many other disciplines in the social and behavioral sciences. It is also possible, and we think likely, that regression procedures are used to a greater degree in European journals than in the North American publications we reviewed. One reason why researchers in other fields of study (in the social and behavioral sciences) may place a greater emphasis in regression is that they do not conduct true or quasi experiments to the same extent as we do, and thus the need for tests of differences between means is not as great. It is also apparent that sport psychologists rarely use multiple regression procedures for the analysis of experiments, whereas the applied linear regression approach is frequently used as a general methodology by researchers in other fields and other countries. The reason for the reliance on ANOVA/MANOVA methods by North American sport psychologists is not clear, but we assume it has its roots in the education and training of most of our researchers. During the 1970s and 1980s, most courses in statistical methodology stressed the Fisherian hypothesis-testing approach, with the ANOVA-based texts by Kirk (1968) and Winer (1971) predominating. More recent graduates, having been exposed to the writings of Cohen and Cohen (1975) and Pedhazur (1982), are more likely to use a regression model to test hypotheses about group status and change. Some of the recent intermediate-level textbooks do an excellent job of presenting both methods of analysis (ANOVA and regression), along with their communalities and unique aspects (e.g., Keppel & Zedeck, 1989). Hopefully our students and these new publications will encourage us to take advantage of the greater flexibility of an applied regression approach.

The use of multiple regression over ANOVA/MANOVA for the analysis of experimental data is not necessarily advocated. In many instances the results would be identical, and the more familiar ANOVA-type presentation of results would provide a clearer representation to most readers. However, in some instances the regression approach does have advantages, and in such cases it is the appropriate technique. For example, in nonorthogonal designs (unequal cell sizes) the interaction and main effects are not independent, leading to ambiguous interpretation of the unique contribution of each. Sequential model testing with multiple regression provides an estimate of the contribution of one effect over and above that of the other.

A second situation in which multiple regression is to be preferred over ANOVA is in the case of continuous independent variables. In a number of the studies identified in our review the independent variable was measured on an interval scale (or at least a many-level ordinal scale) and then dichotomized for analysis. That is, if the independent variable was stress-level, measured by an inventory yielding a stress score with a possible range of 10–50, the researcher would create two or three stress categories (high, medium, low) and use this new 3-level nominal scale in an ANOVA. Cohen (1983) and others have shown that we suffer a considerable loss of information in such a procedure and that it should be avoided at all times. A multiple regression approach can handle the continuous independent variable (and, of course, it can also incorporate nominal and ordinal measures as independent variables). Hopefully, there will be an increase in the use of regression in the analysis of experimental data over the next 10 years.

Nonuse/Misuse: Hierarchical Regression/Stepwise Regression

In general there were some encouraging aspects and some discouraging aspects to the correlation/regression analyses reported in the sport psychology studies we reviewed. It was encouraging to find that three of the six multiple regression studies used a hierarchical multiple linear regression (Dishman & Sternhardt, 1990; Dzewaltowski, Noble, & Show, 1990; McAuley & Duncan, 1990). These researchers are testing theoretical models and not just seeking relationships. Their analyses provided statistical data on the proportion of variance accounted for by each independent variable (or set of variables) above that already accounted for by the independent variables entered previously. The order of forced entry was determined a priori on theoretical grounds. The discouraging aspect was that the remaining 50% of the multiple regression papers based their conclusions solely on the results of stepwise regression (and additionally, in another study, on stepwise discriminant analysis). Stepwise regression is a very powerful heuristic tool that capitalizes on chance to find a particular set of variables to yield the maximum obtainable R^2 for that specific sample. As recommended by Cohen and Cohen (1983), stepwise procedures should only be performed with very large sample sizes (they advocate a subject-to-variable ratio of 40:1, which seems overly strict) and only when the results can be cross-validated on an independent sample. These conditions were not present in the sport psychology studies reported in the literature we reviewed.

Misuse: Simple Correlations

Divergent Groups. A significant number of studies calculated correlation matrices on a pooled sample of divergent (or potentially divergent) groups such as males and females, or athletes and nonathletes. In some cases there was no description provided regarding what preliminary analyses were done to justify this, and the reader is left with the impression that none were done. In one study the authors state that a *t*-test was conducted on one of the variables and,

based on a nonsignificant result, the two groups were pooled for correlational analyses (and subsequent factor analysis). This is better than nothing, but certainly not sufficient. The lack of a between-group difference in means does not imply that the nature and strength of the bivariate relationship is the same within each group. Virtually all statistics textbooks these days include a section describing how correlations can be inflated or depressed by combining two or more data sets that exhibit differences in mean values in one or both of the measures and/or have substantially different within-group correlations. Authors who combine groups for subsequent correlational analyses need to provide evidence to justify their procedures.

Statistical Significance. A second concern we have has to do with the process of determining "significance" for a multitude of zero-order correlations within a study. Fortunately sport psychologists are less prone than exercise physiologists to examine a 20 by 20 correlation matrix, identify the half dozen "significant" correlations, and then make conclusions on the bases of these few chance happenings. Unfortunately it does happen—in 5 of the 51 papers we reviewed. In one paper (Lewthwaite, 1990), the conclusions of an otherwise apparently excellent study are questionable because of the large number of unadjusted significant tests performed on simple correlation coefficients. Lewthwaite used a number of sophisticated multivariate techniques (factor analysis, cluster analysis), but drew many of her conclusions from the significance tests done on 115 correlation coefficients. Using a per comparison alpha of .05, the experimentwise type I error rate for this many significance tests is greater than .99! It may be unfair to identify this particular paper, as other researchers may have done just as many or more such significance tests—but they were not as explicit in stating so. A study with 20 variables could yield 190 zero-order correlations, so it is quite possible that other studies also had type I error rates that approached 1.0.

The appropriate procedure to follow when testing if one or more of a number of correlation coefficients are different from zero is similar to that employed in multiple comparison tests on means. An adjustment must be made, based on the total number of significant tests to be performed, in order to control the EW type I error rate. For correlations, Wallace and Snedecor developed a table of critical *r*'s for testing the significance of all correlations in matrices of order 3 by 3 up to 25 by 25. This valuable table is not included in most statistical texts, but it can be found in Shavelson (1988). As expected, when one is searching a large correlation matrix for significant coefficients, the magnitude required for significance is also large: .674 for the 25-variable situation with df = 50 and a .05 level of significance, two-tailed (in contrast to .273 for the standard unadjusted test). The use of this adjustment appears to have been overlooked by most researchers, reviewers, and editors. Hopefully that will change.

Nonuse: Structural Equation Modeling

The statistical tool of the 1990s, and of the latter half of the 1980s for many disciplines, is structural equation modeling (SEM). Breckler (1990) identified 63 applications of SEM in the *Journal of Personality and Social Psychology* during the period 1977–1987, with the majority of those appearing over the last half of that 10-year span. During that same 10-year period, to our knowledge very few studies published in sport psychology and related journals used SEM. There are some exceptions—for example, Feltz reported a path analysis in 1983, there has been the occasional use of confirmatory factor analysis, a number of workshops and tutorials have been presented at major conferences, and we are aware of a few papers in press that employ a full structural model. In comparison to areas such as social psychology, personality, and sociology, we have been extremely slow to incorporate this flexible and powerful new methodology into our research. Later we speculate on why researchers in our field have been reticent in using SEM to test their theories. First we will provide a very cursory overview of this procedure.

Structural equation modeling incorporates confirmatory factor analysis, multiple regression and path analysis in a single data analytic methodology. Although SEM has been the most common label used to describe this process, a number of other terms are used synonymously: covariance structure modeling, causal modeling, structural equation modeling with latent variables, and the analysis of covariance structures. Essentially it is a mathematical formulation of a conceptual theory and involves the decomposition of the covariances or correlations among a set of observed variables into estimates of the strength of relationships among unobserved constructs. The model is comprised of two basic components: a *measurement model* and a *structural model*. The measurement model employs confirmatory factor analysis and defines the theoretical (*latent*) constructs in terms of the observed (*manifest*) variables. The structural model employs regressionlike procedures and defines the relationships among the latent variables. By combining these two aspects into a unified model, the error and unexplained variance inherent in factor analysis and regression can be included as part of the causal theory being tested. Consequently inferences regarding the latent constructs can be distinguished from the effects of errors in the latent constructs themselves and in the measured variables they represent. This is markedly different from the classical regression analyses, in which all independent variables are modeled without error. Additionally the researcher can include mediator and moderator effects, reciprocal causation, correlated measurement errors, or any of a number of other relationships into the model to be tested.

The parameters of the model are generated using any one of a number of estimation procedures, but the maximum likelihood method is the most common. The parameter estimates of primary interest to the researcher are the factor loadings (*lambdas*), the regression coefficients (*gammas*) reflecting the relationship between the exogenous or independent and endogenous or dependent latent variables, and the coefficients (*betas*) estimating the relationships among the endogenous variables. Most computer programs provide measures of the goodness-of-fit of the data to the hypothesized model and standard errors and *t*-statistics of all parameter estimates. Thus the researcher is able to identify what component of the model may have been misspecified and, if theoretically justifiable, revise the model and retest it. The results of the revised model can be statistically compared to the original model to determine if there is a significantly better fit.

One possible reason for the reluctance of sport psychology researchers to utilize SEM is that the methodology has not been appropriate for the research questions asked and/or the nature of the data collected. We think that is not a valid reason. First, our literature abounds with inventory development and validation studies—for which confirmatory factor analysis should be, in most cases, the methodology of choice. The theoretical basis for much of the empirical work on constructs such as sport anxiety is sufficiently well developed that we should be testing theoretical models, not generating them with data-driven results such as those yielded by exploratory factor analysis. Second, our periodicals contain numerous reports of studies involving a large number of variables in which the underlying purpose centers around questions regarding how well these variables measure some smaller set of unobserved constructs, and how these constructs interrelate. The analysis of such data sets often involves a series of independent (conceptually independent but not empirically independent) statistical procedures; two or three factor analyses and item analyses, correlations, a number of multiple regressions and/or discriminant functions, a canonical correlation or two, and the examination of a very large number of zero-order correlation coefficients. Without knowing the precise purposes and/or hypotheses of these studies, it is impossible to suggest a most appropriate analysis. However, it appears that a SEM approach would have enabled the researcher to perform a comprehensive and unified test of their theory.

A second possible reason for the relative scarcity of SEM applications is that our researchers are overwhelmed by the apparent complexity of this analysis. This may be justifiable, as the underlying mathematical model and computational algorithms require a mathematical background beyond that possessed by most of us. However, in the last 10 years there have been a number of publications that provide comprehensive explanations of SEM in a manner understandable to our researchers. Long's (1983) short and concise treatment provides a good introduction, Hayduk's text (1987) is very helpful for those doing their analysis with the LISREL computer program, and Bollen (1989) provides excellent coverage of the basics as well as of many of the more subtle and complex aspects of SEM. Virtually every behavioral science journal has published at least one introductory article on SEM, and many have devoted complete issues to the topic (e.g., *Child Development, 38,* 1987; *Multivariate Behavioral Research, 25,* 1990). Anderson and

Gerbing's (1988) article provides some excellent recommendations regarding the sequential steps and decision-making procedures involved in conduction SEM analyses. Obviously there now exists a wealth of information on the topic of SEM, and it is time that sport psychologists started to take advantage of it.

Apart from the difficulties in understanding SEM, the practical aspects of actually running an SEM computer program may intimidate some researchers. In general, it is considerably more difficult to set up the control commands, run the program successfully, and interpret the output with SEM than with the traditional "significant-nonsignificant" type of ANOVA and regression analyses. Nevertheless the programs and the manuals are becoming more user-friendly, and with time and patience (or, better yet, with the aid of an experienced user) the analyses can be done by sport psychologists. There are four main programs, all exist in a PC or Mac version, and all have been incorporated into one of the main commercial statistical packages. LISREL (Joreskog & Sorbom, 1989), an add-on to SPSSx, is the best known and probably the most comprehensive in terms of options and output. EQS (Bentler, 1985) has now been included as part of the BMDP system, LISCOMP (Muthen, 1987) is part of SAS, and Steiger's EzPath (1990), the most user-friendly in terms of control command input, has recently been integrated with SYSTAT. Consequently whatever mainframe or personal computer system is used at an institution, there will be a well-developed SEM program available that is compatible with that system.

There is one final reason why some of our scholars may have chosen not to test their theoretical models using SEM procedures. SEM may not be a valid methodology in many situations, perhaps even in most situations. Although we do not subscribe to the latter part of this statement, there are psychometricians who do not support the SEM approach as commonly applied (e.g., Freedman, 1987; Rogosa, 1987). Additionally there are an increasing number of methodologists who are concerned over the misuse of SEM. Breckler (1990), Cohen et al. (1990), and others have expressed concern about the misuse of some or all components of SEM. Thus it is possible that some of our researchers have considered the advantages and disadvantages of SEM and chosen to take a conservative approach and delay adoption of this technique until there exists unanimous acceptance of the procedure. In our view this is unwise as there never will be unanimous acceptance of any "new" procedure. Years ago prominent statisticians were dismissing multivariate statistics, factor analysis, etc.—but these techniques seem to have proven their worth.

As with most statistical procedures, the problems lie not with the methodology, but with the user (or rather, the misuser). Given that the propensity for misuse is directly proportional to the complexity of the method, it is easy to see how SEM can be misused. This is especially true given the early statements regarding the possibilities for inferring causality from correlational data—something we all would like to be able to do! While it is true that "causal models" can be tested with LISREL and similar programs, the tests

can only provide evidence to refute a theoretical causal relationship or support that it is plausible that the data came from a population where such hypothesized relationships existed. Biddle and Marlin (1987) provide a succinct discussion of causality within a SEM framework. It is our recommendation that sport psychology researchers make greater use of SEM techniques, but read extensively on the subject first and seek consultation from a colleague experienced with the application and knowledgeable in the theory.

STATISTICS OF INVENTORY DEVELOPMENT AND ASSESSMENT

One of the most common measurement problems facing researchers in sport psychology is the construction and assessment of an inventory. There are usually several steps in the process, each requiring the researcher to make decisions based on the results of some type of analysis. Once the researcher has developed an initial item pool, very generally the items are selected for inclusion into the inventory if the scale of which the item is a part shows adequate evidence of reliability and validity. Researchers in sport psychology seem to be quite aware of the need to show evidence of reliability and validity for their inventory; however, quite often the statistical methods used are weak. Many of these weaknesses lie in the misapplication, misunderstanding, or misinterpretation of some aspect of factor analysis. Researchers in our field, as well as those in others, are often using techniques that are now outdated or have been shown to be inadequate. Factor analysis can be used in the assessment of the reliability or validity (e.g., in the analyses of multitrait-multimethod matrices) of the inventory as a whole or with subscales contained within the total inventory. Because of its popularity as an analytical tool, some uses, misuses, and disuses of factor analysis will be overviewed in this section. The section ends with discussions of other selected issues that we feel are relevant to measurement in sport psychology research. Included here is a discussion of a commonly misinterpreted concept, internal consistency.

This section deals only with the statistical analysis aspects of inventory development. We acknowledge that there are many other important methodological components to the construction and validation of a psychological instrument, however, in keeping with the topic of this chapter, only the statistical aspects are treated here.

Factor Analysis

General Comments. A prevalent methodology in the sport psychology literature, factor analysis has undergone many significant developments since it became popular with a large number of researchers in the 1960s. These developments to the theory and practice of factor analysis, unfortunately, have not yet found their way into the literature to the extent one would expect. While there are researchers who do make use of the more modern methods, there are still many researchers who are using techniques advocated in the 1960s and that are now out of date. It is our intention to overview some of these misuses of factor analysis as well as to indicate areas where this powerful tool might help researchers in the development and assessment of their inventory.

Misuse: Exploratory Factor Analysis. Basically there are two very general types of factor analysis that are used in varying degrees by sport psychology researchers: Exploratory Factor Analysis (EFA) and Confirmatory Factor Analysis (CFA). The distinction between the two lies primarily in the logic underlying the techniques. Quite generally EFA is data-driven while CFA is theory-driven. That is, in EFA, we hope to discover factors that best explain the correlations among the data. The number of factors that we "retain" is that suggested from our examination of the statistical results from each of a number of solutions (each based on a different number of factors.) Our interpretation of the factors is based on the factor loadings obtained after a somewhat arbitrary choice of rotational techniques is used to transform the factor loadings to make them more interpretable (i.e., simple structure). Each decision regarding the number of factors or the interpretation of the results is solely dependent upon the observed item (variable) intercorrelations based on data from the sample; nowhere is it necessary for any possible theoretical explanation to be taken into account. Of course, at the end of the analysis the researcher may attempt to match the interpretation of the "best" factor solution with some theory. Confirmatory Factor Analysis, on the other hand, is based on the possible theory explaining the item intercorrelations. The researcher is able to specify a priori, among other things, the number of factors, the pattern of factor loadings and the amount of correlation among the factors. The result of the CFA will be a test of the proposed factor structure.

EFA VERSUS CFA IN INVENTORY DEVELOPMENT

Most often the sport psychology researcher developing a multiscale inventory has a pool of items and wishes to determine the factor structure underlying the responses to the items. The need for this usually derives from some desire to assess if the items in the inventory are measuring the same factors as suggested from the theory used as the basis of the questionnaire. Of course, in saying this we are assuming that the development of the specific items was theory-driven. A good example of such an approach in the initial phases of questionnaire development is provided by Carron, Widmeyer, & Brawley (1985) with the Group Environment Questionnaire. Using this theory-driven approach to item development, items are written that reflect high and low levels of observable behaviors that operationally define the construct. The important point to note for our discussion is that, in doing this, there should be a one-to-one correspondence between items and constructs. If items are written for specific constructs, then it is our opinion that

the nature of any analysis that wishes to assess the congruence between the observed data with the theoretical model should be *confirmatory.* That is, one should be able to explicitly test whether the hypothesized relationship between item and construct (dimension) is consistent with the structure underlying the observed data. We acknowledge that in the initial stages of inventory development it may be necessary to use EFA as a preliminary step. In such cases this should be followed by a CFA and cross-validation on an independent sample.

EFA VERSUS PRINCIPAL COMPONENT ANALYSIS

Another common error that one sees is inappropriate equating of EFA and principal component analysis (PCA). This is somewhat understandable, given that both techniques do attempt to obtain factors (or components) that best explain the multivariate information among the variables. It is often unclear in some studies which technique, EFA or PCA, has been used. Contributing to this confusion is the inclusion of PCA as one of the possible options in the Factor Analysis procedure in some canned computer packages (e.g., BMDP, SPSSx). Such a structuring of the control language implies that one is doing a factor analysis using a principal component procedure. Clearly then, in such instances the researcher is not to be blamed for any confusion.

The researcher should be aware, however, that PCA and Factor Analysis are theoretically and conceptually different, although their results may often be quite similar. The goal of EFA is to obtain factors that best explain the *correlations* among the variables while in PCA the objective is to derive components that maximally explain the total *variance* among the variables. By the mathematics defining the procedures, it is quite possible to explain all the correlations (or covariances) among a set of variables with very few factors, but, in PCA, the total variance is always explained by as many components as there are variables (assuming an appropriate covariance or correlation matrix). It is our view that, given the objective to assess the degree of communality among what the items measure, a Factor Analysis is preferred over a Principal Component Analysis in the assessment of the dimensionality underlying a scale.

Misuse: Global Scale Scores. Another issue in the development of an inventory deals with the combining of subscales of an inventory to obtain "global" measures. For example, if the inventory has three scales the researcher sometimes will use the three-scale scores separately as well as combining (or averaging) the three scores to obtain an overall or "global" measure. The researcher, in combining and interpreting the subscales in such a fashion, is implying that the subscales (the first-order factors) that are combined (or averaged) all share something in common—i.e., the "global" trait (the second-order factor). The existence of a "global" trait common to several scales may be, and often is, a reasonable assertion, but it is rarely tested. It would seem necessary before combining subscales to first verify the existence of this common information with a second-order factor analysis.

A second-order factor analysis derives a factor (or factors) that best explains the correlations among the first-order factors. (It should be noted, though, that it is always possible to obtain a second-order factor that perfectly explains the correlations among the first-order factors if there are two first-order factors defining the second-order factor. In these cases, the researcher must examine the magnitude of the correlation between the two first-order factors to determine if the existence of a second-order factor is reasonable.) With this meaning of a "global" measure in mind, it is indeed somewhat puzzling to find some researchers who perform a first-order factor analysis with a varimax rotation yielding uncorrelated factors. Then, having interpreted their factors from such an analysis, they proceed to combine the independent factors (subscales) into one "global" measure. Given that the subscales from the orthogonal solution share nothing in common, it is difficult to conceptualize what this new "global" score does in fact measure.

Those researchers who do perform a second-order factor analysis usually proceed in two steps. First, a first-order factor analysis is carried out, allowing for a nonorthogonal solution so as to estimate the correlations among the first-order factors. Then these interfactor correlations are used for the second-order factor analysis. While these researchers are to be commended for providing evidence of higher-order structure within their inventories, it should be cautioned that this two-step approach is not optimal. Confirmatory techniques allow for second-order factor analyses to be completed within one analysis. Confirmatory second-order factor analyses are available with most of the Structural Equation Modeling programs such as EQS (Bentler, 1985) and LISREL (Joreskog & Sorbom, 1989).

Nonuse: Simultaneous Factor Analysis. Quite often the factorial structure from one sample is wished to be generalized to other samples. Traditionally one would perform separate Exploratory Factor Analyses for each of the groups and attempt to compare the results. Usually this would entail transforming the factor structure from one group to maximize its resemblance, in some sense, to that of the target group. Several methods that have been developed to do this are reviewed by Evans (1971). These methods, however, all have the weakness of being exploratory in nature and do not have associated tests of significance. Another more direct approach, related to CFA, is called Multiple-Group Factor Analysis or Simultaneous Factor Analysis. Multiple-Group Factor Analysis compares two or more groups of individuals on the similarity of their a priori factor structures. For example, if the primary population is known to have a certain factor structure, this same factor structure can be specified for the generalization sample, and the likelihood of this equality can be tested with a significance test. Of course this technique also allows us to test more stringent assumptions across samples such as the equality of factor loadings, factor correlations, etc. Examples of such analyses are provided in the manual for LISREL.

Issues.

CORRELATED VERSUS UNCORRELATED FACTORS

The issue of whether to rotate factor solutions to obtain correlated or uncorrelated factors has been the subject of a considerable amount of debate. One of the objectives in an EFA is to rotate the original factor solution (i.e., transform the factor loadings) to make the final solution more interpretable. Usually this means that a rotation is needed that will yield factor loadings that best approximate "simple structure." There are a number of such rotations available. The rotations can be divided into two main categories—those leading to solutions with uncorrelated (orthogonal) factors and those leading to solutions with correlated (oblique or nonorthogonal) factors. Hakstian (1971) and Hakstian and Abel (1974) have investigated the relative performance of some oblique rotations. According to McDonald (1985), one advantage of interpreting factor solutions with correlated factors is that the factor loadings are more stable across replications with different samples. Solutions with uncorrelated factors have the interpretational advantage of allowing for an unambiguous assessment of the item-factor correlation as indicated by the factor loadings (assuming that both the items and factors have variances set to unity). Of course, the interpretational advantage gained with orthogonal factors may be offset by the lack of external validity. It would seem unreasonable to think that the factors measured by the different scales within an inventory would, in reality, be all uncorrelated.

One possible scenario where it is advantageous to obtain uncorrelated (orthogonal) factors, however, is when the factor scores (preferably, in the form of component scores or unit weighted sums) are to be used in subsequent analyses such as a multiple regression or discriminant analysis. Scores based on uncorrelated factors in these analyses have the desirable effect of eliminating the collinearity problem among the independent variables. The researcher is able to unambiguously interpret the regression or discriminant weights and assess the relative contribution of each variable (factor) to the overall solution. Of course, the utility of this procedure depends on two conditions being met: (1) The variables used in the subsequent analyses are the factor scores that are directly derived from the orthogonal factor solution and are not simply the sum of those items with high factor loadings; and (2) The factors obtained from the orthogonal solution are interpretable and meaningful. The inclusion of variables that have ambiguous interpretations in any analysis is strongly discouraged at any time.

NUMBER OF FACTORS RETAINED

An issue related to both EFA and PCA is the question of how many factors/components to interpret in the analysis. Many different indices or rules of thumb have been proposed to aid the researcher, (the two most common being the number of eigenvalues greater than one and the scree test. In our view, if a CFA is not feasible, then the adequacy of an EFA solution with a particular number of factors should be judged based on how well the solution explains the correlations (covariances) among the variables. A researcher should examine the matrix of residual correlations (this is not always provided as a default in the major canned computer programs) to assess the adequacy of the solution. A rule of thumb, when assessing the magnitude of the residual correlations, is that with moderate to large original correlations among the variables, the residual correlations should not exceed 0.10. A popular index describing the "average" magnitude of the residual correlation matrix is the Root Mean-Square Residual (RMSR). Care should be taken when interpreting the RMSR. It is possible to obtain a seemingly adequate RMSR but still have a small number of variables whose correlations have not been adequately explained, thereby requiring an additional factor.

CATEGORICAL AND ORDINAL DATA

Items used in psychological inventories are almost always scored on an ordinal scale. Most items require an individual to respond on some type of Likert scale (e.g., a scale of 1 to 5, with 1 corresponding to "totally disagree" and 5 to "totally agree"). Other scales have items that simply ask the respondent to decide whether or not the statement in the item reflects the way the respondent feels. Such items are dichotomous (e.g., yes/no). The researcher wanting to perform a factor analysis with these items is faced with a problem, as a basic assumption underlying factor analysis is that the variables (items) be normally distributed. Clearly typical scale items do not satisfy this requirement, and the researcher is left with the question, "What do I do?"

One common approach is to treat the Likert data as being responses on a continuous scale and then perform the factor analysis as usual. This does not seem unreasonable and does not seriously affect the results of the factor analysis if there are at least 5 categories in the Likert scale and if the data are not highly skewed. The researcher should provide some evidence of the distribution of the responses for each item before a "traditional" factor analysis is performed. What if the items are highly skewed or have less than 5 categories? There have been major advances in the past decade with respect to methods for adequately dealing with ordinal or nonnormal data in a factor analysis. Asymptotically Distribution-Free (ADF) estimation procedures have been developed to use when the data are continuous but nonnormal (see Browne, 1984). Muthen (1984) developed the Categorical Variable Methodology (CVM) estimation procedures, which allow for proper factor analyses with ordinal data. Both of these estimation procedures theoretically yield valid tests of significance when used in a confirmatory factor analysis. Again, most of the popular structural equation computer packages have, as options, these estimation procedures.

We recommend the following data analytic strategy for the researcher wishing to analyze either categorical or nonnormal variables in a factor analysis: (a) If the items on a Likert scale have at least 5 categories, then check the distributions of the items. If almost all the items have skewness and kurtosis absolute values within 1.0, then a factor analysis using common estimation procedures (e.g., maximum likelihood) will not seriously affect the results (Muthen & Kaplan, 1985); (b) If the items in the scale have at least 5 categories but are highly skewed, then use either CVM or ADF estimation procedures; (c) If the items have less than 5 categories, then CVM estimation should be used.

Internal Consistency

General Comments. An essential criterion in the development of scales in a psychological inventory is that items that are used to calculate scores for a particular scale should all measure the "same thing." The most common procedure used in assessing the adequacy of items in a scale is to calculate the degree of internal consistency of the scale. Usually an index such as Cronbach's alpha is used if the items are polychotomous, or the Kuder-Richardson formula 20 (KR-20) may be used if the items are dichotomous. The general logic is clearly outlined by Kaplan and Saccuzzo (1989), who, in discussing Cronbach's alpha and the KR-20, state:

All of the measures of internal consistency evaluate the extent to which the different items on a test measure the same ability or trait. They all will give low estimates of reliability if the test is designed to measure several traits. Using the domain sampling model, we define a domain that represents a single trait or characteristic, and each item is an individual sample of this general characteristic. When the items do not measure the same characteristic, the test will not be internally consistent. (p. 103)

Misuse: Internal Consistency as a Measure of Scale Homogeneity. Unfortunately, and somewhat surprisingly to most of us, the above interpretation of internal consistency being synonymous with scale homogeneity is incorrect! Several papers (e.g., Green, Lissitz, & Mulaik, 1977; McDonald, 1985; Novick & Lewis, 1967) have clearly and convincingly indicated that the coefficient alpha is not a measure of homogeneity. Green et al. provide an example showing that a scale consisting of 10 items representing 5 underlying dimensions has a value of Cronbach's alpha equal to .811! Green et al. (p. 831) write, "Certainly high internal consistency as indicated by a high coefficient alpha will result when a general common factor runs through the items of the test. But this does not rule out obtaining high internal consistency as measured by coefficient alpha when there is no general factor running through the test items. . . . In other words, while homogeneity implies high internal consistency, high internal consistency need not imply homogeneity." Of course, these problems with coefficient alpha also lead to questions regarding the validity of correlating the items with the total scale score (i.e., point-biserial) to help determine the adequacy of the item for the scale.

Researchers in sport psychology need not feel singled out for failing to realize this distinction. It appears that many measurement specialists have either ignored or have been unaware of this work, and, as a result, most textbooks still advocate using internal consistency estimates as measures of scale homogeneity. The question then remains: "How can I assess the degree of scale homogeneity?" From the previous discussion it is clear that items on a scale are considered to be homogeneous if there is a common attribute that all the items measure. It would appear that factor analysis should provide us with the answer.

The purpose of factor analysis is to derive latent variables that best explain what the items (or measured variables) have in common. From this perspective, the latent variable can be equated conceptually to the construct that the total score of the scale is supposed to represent. This information leads directly to a solution to the researcher's problems resulting from the realization that internal consistency does not measure scale homogeneity. If the items are homogenous, then one factor should underlie the responses to these items and adequately explain the correlations among the variables. That is, the partial correlations among the variables, after controlling for the first factor, should be quite low (theoretically, they should be zero). In addition, the factor loadings provide us with information regarding the strength of the relationship between the factor and the item. Where a point-biserial correlation measures the correlation between the item and the total score of the scale (an observed score measure of the construct), if the variances of both the items and the factor have been set to unity, the factor loadings are simply the correlations between each of the items and the factor (or construct). Intuitively this seems to be more appealing than the point-biserial correlation as a measure of the relationship between the item and the construct because the construct is a latent variable that does not include the error of measurement found in the total score.

Although a high degree of internal consistency is implied by scale homogeneity, one cannot directly conclude that "perfect" scale homogeneity will yield to "perfect" internal consistency. Factor analysis, it should be remembered, simply determines how many factors can explain the correlations among the items. This does not imply that one needs to have very high correlations among the items to have one factor perfectly explain the correlations among the items. Let us consider two hypothetical examples. (1) We have a 10-item scale where each of the items correlate .10 with each other; (2) we have a 10-item scale where each of the items correlate .80 with each other. A factor analysis of either inter-item correlation matrix will indicate that one factor perfectly explains the correlations among the variables. That is, in both cases, the items have only one factor in common. However, the degree of internal consistency is not the same for both scales. The internal consistency can be directly obtained from the factor loadings using a formula found in McDonald (1985, p. 217). The factor loadings in case (1) would all be equal to .316 and in case (2) would be equal to .894. The corresponding coefficient alphas for the two scales are .526 and .976, respectively. Clearly a researcher should not automatically assume a high internal consistency reliability with a one-factor solution.

In summary the first step for a researcher in the assessment of internal consistency is to perform a factor analysis

and determine if there is a factor common to all the items. This may mean that a one-factor solution (which is optimal) or a multiple-factor solution having one "general" factor is obtained. Under these conditions, the interpretation of coefficient alpha as a measure of internal consistency (in our usual definition) makes sense and should be calculated in the second step.

SOME CONCLUSIONS REGARDING STATUS AND FUTURE

Given the findings and issues raised above, what, if anything, needs to be done with respect to the utilization of statistical methodologies in sport psychology research? Following the tenets of most evaluation procedures, it would be useful to assess the status, determine if change is necessary, and ascertain possible future directions. The answers to the following three questions are our attempts at this evaluation.

Question #1: Current Status

What is the current status of statistical expertise, as evidenced in the published literature, of researchers in sport psychology? The previous part of this chapter has dealt with this question. In general, and in comparison to 20 years ago, researchers are still analyzing experimental data with descriptive statistics, *t*-tests, and ANOVAs, but are becoming more careful in addressing the issues of type I error rates and power. Additionally they are making appropriate use of many, but not all, of the multivariate techniques now available. More significant, however, is the gradual shift away from experimental analysis and toward more complex statistical applications in inventory development, reliability and validity studies, survey analyses, and longitudinal intervention studies.

Question #2: Is Change Needed, and If So, What and How?

The answer to the first part of this question is obvious—at least it is to us. Yes, we have to be continually changing and utilizing the best available tools—and the tools change as our knowledge grows. For example, factor analysis, as most of us know it, is probably an outmoded tool. Our knowledge about many phenomena has progressed to a level of understanding in which the traditional exploratory factor analysis procedures are no longer appropriate. Thurstone himself acknowledged that "Factor analysis has its principal usefulness at the borderline of science . . . where basic and fruitful concepts are essentially lacking and where crucial experiments have been difficult to conceive" (1947, p. 56). Hopefully by now we have developed some "fruitful concepts" and can test them with more appropriate confirmatory factor analysis techniques.

John Tukey, on retiring after 44 years of statistical involvement, suggested a number of ways in which applied statisticians should change (Tukey, 1986). His advice is relevant to sport psychologists as users of statistics:

1. Increase the impact of results on consumers by focusing on meaningful results and using the most effective display techniques. It is 15 years since Tukey (1977) published his revolutionary text, *Exploratory Data Analysis.* His suggestions for data presentation, such as the stem-and-leaf display, have been adopted by researchers in business, economics, agriculture, and even in the life sciences. For some reason, behavioral scientists, especially sport psychologists, have been very slow to take advantage of this simple but effective technique.
2. "Pay more attention to the strategy of dealing with data, as compared with the tactics of carrying out a specified analysis" (p. 72). For those of us who are more interested in method than in content, this is a most valid warning. Perhaps some of us are overly intent on using the latest technique and fall into the "have method (or instrument), need problem" trap. Or if we do use a new technique appropriately, we place undue emphasis on explaining our method at the expense of explaining our results. The data are what lends support to or refutes our theories—the ts, Fs, R^2's, and p's are just tools to assist us in drawing some conclusions about the reliability and generalizability of our findings.
3. Tukey's third suggestion for change is directed at the statistical consultants, but it has relevance for those of us who seek statistical assistance as well as for those of us who provide it. Tukey stated that statistical methodologists must become more humble and helpful, less arrogant and aloof, and could benefit from large doses of "antihubrisines." Similar to the antihistamines taken by those who suffer from excessive histamines, antihubrisines are actions taken to decrease *hubris,* a Greek word meaning extreme pride, the kind that would be punishable by the gods.

Tukey goes on to explain:

To statisticians, hubris should mean the kind of pride that fosters an inflated idea of one's powers and thereby keeps one from being more than marginally helpful to others. Hubris is the greatest danger that accompanies formal data analysis, including formalized statistical analysis. The feeling of "Give me (or more likely even, give my assistant) the data, and I will tell you what the real answer is!" is one we must all fight against again and again, and yet again. (p. 74).

Question #3: What Does the Future Hold for Statistical Analyses?

At the risk of being somewhat presumptuous, we will make some speculations regarding the future role of statistics in sport psychology research. We foresee future researchers traveling down two paths, one quite obvious and traditional, the other bordering on science fiction.

The first path is the one on which we have plodded along for decades. It will continue to be a slow but steady advance along the reductionist path, adhering to the methods and philosophies of traditional positivism in science. As individuals we will gradually learn more and more about less and less. This has been the nature of scientific inquiry for over 300 years, ever since Descartes proposed his reductionist theory. It may not have been the best method of discovering and generating knowledge, but it is the best method known to most of us, and it has served us reasonably well. Some changes will occur, and we will become more willing to adopt alternative methodologies (e.g., qualitative research) and philosophies (e.g., feminist epistemology). Our statistical techniques will continue to develop along lines similar to the structural equation modeling approach, that is, more emphasis on comprehensive model building and less on multiple repeated significance tests. Perhaps we might even finally adopt some Bayesian methods in which we take advantage of a priori knowledge about the probability of an outcome. The fact that we will continue to use these traditional scientific methods is perfectly acceptable—but it must not be our only path as we enter the twenty-first century.

In addition to our reductionist-type systematic attempts to build better mousetraps, we will enter into a new era. Technological advances are going to lead us (perhaps force us) into a completely new way of generating and analyzing problems, maybe even into a new way of thinking. In the last 30 years computers have revolutionized the way in which we can summarize, synthesize, and display numerical information, but we still use them primarily as sophisticated notepads, calculators, and typewriters. However, we are now entering a new era of information technology, namely "interactive hypermedia." James Burke (1989) refers to this as "evolutionary technological complexification," and predicts that our current level of technological and scientific complexification is minuscule in comparison to what lies ahead.

This interactive hypermedia computer system will enable us to examine complex interactions involving facts and theories, past and present, generalities and uniqueness, all within a common framework. As data analysts we might be able to interface a number of major data bases (e.g., large-scale surveys, census tapes, the results of all studies on stress published in *JSEP*) with computer-stored information on psychological and physiological theories of the relationships among lifestyle, personality, activity patterns, health, and longevity. We could then explore and test these relationships, modify theory, and "think" in three and four dimensions. It would be like a gigantic simulation model of life in which the operator would be an interactive component. One could vary any parameter and observe the effect on all other aspects of the model.

Unfortunately, we have not had the education or training to be able even to think about analyses at the level of complexification that will eventually be required. Although our students will probably be doing much the same as we have done, as this new technology may still be 20 years away, our students' students could well experience this methodological revolution. Therefore we must start now. We need to instill in our students the need to look beyond the narrow and restrictive framework within which we have taught them.

We need to accept these new and formidable technological and methodological systems, to be open to learning from our students, and to encourage them to be users of, and not used by, the new technology.

References

Anderson, J. C., & Gerbing, D. W. (1988). Structural equation modeling in practice: A review and recommended two-step approach. *Psychological Bulletin, 103,* 411–423.

Baker, F. B. (1981). Log-linear, logit-linear models: A didactic. *Journal of Educational Statistics, 6,* 75–102.

Bentler, P. M. (1985). *Theory and implementation of EQS: A structural equations program.* Los Angeles: BMDP Statistical Software.

Berger, B. G., & Owen, D. R. (1988). Stress reduction and mood enhancement in four exercise modes: Swimming, body conditioning, Hatha yoga, and fencing. *Research Quarterly for Exercise and Sport, 59,* 148–160.

Biddle, B. J., & Marlin, M. (1987). Causality, confirmation, credulity, and structural equation modeling. *Child Development, 58,* 4–17.

Bird, K. D., & Hadzi-Pavlovic, D. (1983). Simultaneous test procedures and the choice of a test statistic in MANOVA. *Psychological Bulletin, 93,* 167–178.

Bollen, K. A. (1989). *Structural equations with latent variables.* New York: Wiley.

Boutcher, S. H., & Zinsser, N. W. (1990). Cardiac deceleration of elite and beginning golfers during putting. *Journal of Sport and Exercise Psychology, 12,* 37–47.

Breckler, S. J. (1990). Applications of covariance structure modeling in psychology: Cause for concern? *Psychological Bulletin, 107,* 260–273.

Browne, M. W. (1984). Asymptotically distribution-free methods for the analysis of covariance structures. *British Journal of Mathematical and Statistical Psychology, 37,* 62–83.

Burke, J. (1989). *Goodbye Descartes! Information and change.* Public Lecture, Vancouver, B.C.

Carron, A. V., Widmeyer, W. N., & Brawley, L. R. (1985). The development of an instrument to assess cohesion in sport teams: The Group Environment Questionnaire. *Journal of Sport Psychology, 7,* 244–266.

Cohen, J. (1965). Some statistical issues in psychological research. In B. Wolman (Ed.), *Handbook of Clinical Psychology* (pp. 95–121). New York: McGraw-Hill.

Cohen, J. (1977). *Statistical power analysis for the behavioral sciences.* New York: Academic Press.

Cohen, J. (1983). The cost of dichotomization. *Applied Psychological Measurement, 7,* 149–253.

Cohen, J. (1990). Things I have learned (so far). *American Psychologist, 45,* 1304–1312.

Cohen, J., & Cohen, P. (1975). *Applied multiple regression/correlation analysis for the behavioral sciences.* Hillsdale, NJ: Erlbaum.

Cohen, P., Cohen, J., Teresi, J., Marchi, M., & Velez, C. (1990). Problems in the measurement of latent variables in structural equations causal models. *Applied Psychological Measurement, 14,* 183–196.

Darlington, R., Weinberg, S., & Walberg, H. (1973). Canonical variate analysis and related techniques. *Review of Educational Research, 43,* 433–454.

Davidson, M. L. (1972). Univariate versus multivariate tests in repeated-measures experiments. *Psychological Bulletin, 77,* 446–452.

Dishman, R. K., & Steinhardt, M. (1990). Health locus of control predicts free-living, but not supervised, physical activity: A test of exercise-specific control and outcome-expectancy hypotheses. *Research Quarterly for Exercise and Sport, 61,* 383–394.

Dzewaltowski, D. A., Noble, J. M., & Show, J. M. (1990). Physical activity participation: Social cognitive theory versus the theories of reasoned action and planned behavior. *Journal of Sport and Exercise Psychology, 12,* 388–405.

Evans, G. T. (1971). Transformation of factor matrices to achieve congruence. *British Journal of Mathematical and Statistical Psychology, 24,* 22–48.

Feltz, D. L., & Mugno, D. A. (1983). A replication of the path analysis of the causal elements in Bandura's theory of self-efficacy and the influence of autonomic perception. *Journal of Sport Psychology, 5,* 263–277.

Freedman, D. A. (1987). As others see us: A case study in path analysis. *Journal of Educational Statistics, 12,* 101–128.

Gessaroli, M. E., & Schutz, R. W. (1983). Variable error: Variance-covariance heterogeneity, block size and type I error rates. *Journal of Motor Behavior, 15,* 74–95.

Green, S. B., Lissitz, R. W., & Mulaik, S. A. (1977). Limitations of coefficient alpha as an index of test unidimensionality. *Educational and Psychological Measurement, 37,* 827–838.

Hakstian, A. R. (1971). A comparative evaluation of several prominent methods of oblique factor transformation. *Psychometrika, 36,* 175–193.

Hakstian, A. R., & Abel, R. A. (1989). A further comparison of oblique factor transformation methods. *Psychometrika, 39,* 429–444.

Hand, D. J., & Taylor, C. C. (1987). *Multivariate analysis of variance and repeated measures.* New York: Chapman and Hall.

Hayduk, L. A. (1987). *Structural equation modeling with LISREL.* London: The Johns Hopkins Press.

Hertzog, C., & Rovine, M. (1985). Repeated-measures analysis of variance in developmental research: Selected issues. *Child Development, 56,* 787–809.

Huberty, C. J., & Morris, J. D. (1989). Multivariate analysis versus multiple univariate analyses. *Psychological Bulletin, 105,* 302–308.

Huck, S. W., & McLean, R. A. (1975). Using a repeated measures ANOVA to analyze data from a pretest-posttest design: A potentially confusing task. *Psychological Bulletin, 82,* 511–518.

Huynh, H., & Feldt, L. S. (1970). Conditions under which the mean square ratios in repeated measurements designs have exact F-distributions. *Journal of the American Statistical Association, 65,* 1582–1589.

Huynh, H., & Feldt, L. S. (1976). Estimation of the Box correlation for degrees of freedom from sample data in randomized block and split-plot designs. *Journal of Educational Statistics, 1,* 69–82.

Jennings, E. (1988). Models for pretest-posttest data: Repeated measures ANOVA revisited. *Journal of Educational Statistics, 13,* 273–280.

Joreskog, K. G., & Sorbom, D. (1989). *LISREL 7: A Guide to the Program and Applications.* Chicago: SPSS, Inc.

Judd, C. M., Jessor, R., & Donovan, J. E. (1986). Structural equation models and personality research. *Journal of Personality, 54,* 149–198.

Kaplan, R. M., & Saccuzzo, D. P. (1989). *Psychological testing: Principles, applications and issues* (2nd ed.). Belmont, CA: Brooks/Cole.

Kenney, J. J. (1983). *Analyzing quantitative data: Introductory log-linear analysis for behavioral research.* New York: Praeger.

Kesselman, H. J., & Kesselman, J. C. (1988). Repeated measures multiple comparison procedures: Effects of violating multisample sphericity in unbalanced designs. *Journal of Educational Statistics, 13,* 215–226.

Kesselman, J. C., & Kesselman, H. J. (1990). Analyzing unbalanced repeated measures designs. *British Journal of Mathematical and Statistical Psychology, 43,* 265–282.

Kirk, R. E. (1968). *Experimental design: Procedures for the behavioral sciences.* Belmont, CA: Cole.

Knoke, D., & Burke, P. J. (1980). *Log-linear models.* Beverly Hills, CA: Sage.

Kraemer, H., & Thiemann, S. (1987). *How many subjects?* Beverly Hills, CA: Sage.

Lewthwaite, R. (1990). Threat perception in competitive trait anxiety: The endangerment of important goals. *Journal of Sport and Exercise Psychology, 12,* 280–300.

Long, J. S. (1983). *Covariance structure models: An introduction to LISREL.* Beverly Hills, CA: Sage Publications.

McAuley, E., & Duncan, T. E. (1990). Cognitive appraisal and affective reactions following physical achievement outcomes. *Journal of Sport and Exercise Psychology, 12,* 415–426.

McDonald, R. P. (1985). *Factor analysis and related methods.* Hillsdale, NJ: Erlbaum.

Milligan, G. W., Wong, D. S., & Thompson, P. A. (1987). Robustness properties of nonorthogonal analysis of variance. *Psychological Bulletin, 101,* 464–470.

Muthen, B. (1984). A general structural equation model with dichotomous, ordered categorical, and continuous latent variable indicators. *Psychometrika, 49,* 115–132.

Muthen, B. (1987). *LISCOMP: Analysis of Linear Structural Equations with a Comprehensive Measurement Model.* Mooresville, IN: Scientific Software.

Muthen, B., & Kaplan, D. (1985). A comparison of some methodologies for the factor analysis of non-normal Likert variables. *British Journal of Mathematical and Statistical Psychology, 38,* 171–189.

Novick, M. R., & Lewis, C. (1967). Coefficient alpha and the reliability of composite measurements. *Psychometrika, 32,* 1–13.

Pedhazur, E. J. (1982). *Multiple regression in behavioral research.* Fort Worth: Holt, Rinehart & Winston.

Rogosa, D. (1987). Casual models do not support scientific conclusions: A comment in support of Freedman. *Journal of Educational Statistics, 12,* 185–195.

Rouanet, H., & Lepine, D. (1970). Comparison between treatments in a repeated-measurement design: ANOVA and multivariate methods. *The British Journal of Mathematical and Statistical Psychology, 23,* 147–163.

Saville, D. J. (1990). Multiple comparison procedures: The practical solution. *The American Statistician, 44,* 174–180.

Schutz, R. W. (1978). Specific problems in the measurement of change: Longitudinal studies, difference scores, and multivariate analyses. In D. M. Landers & R. W. Christina (Eds.), *Psychology of motor behavior & sport—1977* (pp. 151–175). Champaign, IL: Human Kinetics.

Schutz, R. W. (1989). Analyzing change. In J. Safrit & T. Wood (Eds.), *Measurement concepts in physical education and exercise science* (pp. 206–228). Champaign, IL: Human Kinetics.

Schutz, R. W., & Gessaroli, M. E. (1987). The analysis of repeated measures designs involving multiple dependent variables. *Research Quarterly for Exercise and Sport, 58,* 132–149.

Schutz, R. W., Smoll, F., & Gessaroli, M. (1983). Multivariate statistics: A self-test and guide to their utilization. *Research Quarterly for Exercise and Sport, 53,* 255–263.

Shavelson, R. J. (1988). *Statistical reasoning for the behavioral sciences.* Boston: Allyn & Bacon.

Stanek, E. J. (1988). Choosing a pretest-posttest analysis. *The American Statistician, 42,* 178–183.

Steiger, J. H. (1989). *EZPATH: A supplementary module for SYSTAT and SYGRAPH.* Evanston, IL: SYSTAT.

Tabachnick, B. G., & Fidell, L. S. (1989). *Using multivariate statistics.* New York: Harper & Row.

Thomas, J. (1983). Editor's viewpoint. *Research Quarterly for Exercise and Sport, 54,* ii.

Thurstone, L. L. (1947). *Multiple factor analysis.* Chicago: University of Chicago Press.

Tukey, J. W. (1986). Sunset salvo. *The American Statistician, 40,* 72–76.

Tukey, J. W. (1977). *Exploratory data analysis.* Reading, MA: Addison-Wesley.

Winer, B. J. (1971). *Statistical principles in experimental design.* New York: McGraw-Hill.

Winer, B. J., Brown, D. R., & Michels, K. M. (1991). *Statistical principles in experimental design.* 3rd ed. New York: McGraw-Hill.

PROFESSIONAL ETHICS IN SPORT PSYCHOLOGY

·44·

PROFESSIONAL ETHICS IN SPORT PSYCHOLOGY

Michael L. Sachs

What is sport psychology? This question, often asked, has been addressed in other forums (e.g., Rejeski & Brawley, 1988) and in Chapter 1 in this volume. Professionalization of the field of sport psychology (Silva, 1989) will be a significant issue in the 1990s and beyond. Assuming for the moment, however, an understanding of what sport psychology encompasses, we come to potentially trickier questions of what and who is a sport psychologist, and what ethical principles should guide the work of sport psychologists. These questions move from an intellectual exercise of defining our field to a delineation of criteria with ethical and legal ramifications.

LEGAL ISSUES

All states have licensing laws that restrict use of the terms "psychology," "psychologist," and "psychological." While almost anyone can hang up a shingle and call him or herself a "therapist" or a "counselor" in many states, as soon as one calls oneself a psychologist, one faces legal issues. These issues have been specified through licensing laws designed to restrict the practice of psychology to those who have adequate training in the field. Psychological services, according to the law, should be provided only by those meeting certain standards. These generally include graduation from a doctoral program in psychology (although some states allow for programs that are primarily psychological in nature and do not have to be psychology departments per se), coursework in specified areas of study, and supervised experience.

While the "therapist" or "counselor" may be providing services that are psychological in nature, and therefore be in potential violation of the law, most state licensing boards are more concerned with individuals who illegally call themselves psychologists. Many sport psychologists are licensed psychologists and have every legal right to call themselves sport psychologists. Sport psychologists in academia are also protected by their place of employment, if their work is maintained within the academic setting. However, nonlicensed practitioners who work as sport psychologists in academic settings but leave the halls of academia for the outside world and still call themselves sport psychologists may run afoul of the letter, if not the spirit, of the law.

ETHICAL ISSUES

The ethical issues in this area may, in some ways, get a bit trickier. The key question from an ethical standpoint, however, boils down to one's competence in providing certain services of a psychological nature. The nonlicensed "sport psychologist" (using this term inappropriately from a legal standpoint) who provides psychological services may not only be running afoul of the law but also may be violating ethical standards. However, if the practitioner has developed competencies in educational sport psychology, for example, and is "only" providing these kinds of services, then he/she may be acting ethically from a competency perspective (even if not from a legal one). One could certainly suggest that practicing psychology illegally is unethical, and it would be hard to dispute this point. Similarly, if the practitioner's competencies extend to areas within counseling and clinical psychology, and services are restricted to these areas (i.e., eating disorders, substance abuse), this might also be "acceptable" ethically, though not legally. Unacceptable ethical behavior would, of course, arise if individuals competent in educational sport psychology do work of a

The contributions of a number of individuals in developing this chapter are appreciated, including Kate Hays, Judy van Raalte, Britt Brewer, and an anonymous reviewer. Appreciation is extended to Kate Hays, in particular, for suggestions on presentation of concepts and phrasing in several sections of the chapter that were adopted as recommended.

counseling or clinical nature that is beyond their level of competence.

Similar concerns arise in some cases with licensed psychologists providing services within sport psychology. Just as psychologists trained in marital and family counseling would not ethically note themselves as having expertise in substance abuse counseling (unless, of course, they were trained in this area), psychologists who do not have training in exercise and sport should not be calling themselves "sport psychologists." There are, unfortunately, some individuals who call themselves sport psychologists but do not have the training that many in the field feel is important.

It is important to note, however, that many licensed psychologists are excellent clinicians or counselors—they are very highly skilled in their areas of expertise. However, sport psychology may not be one of those areas, and this clinical or counseling excellence *does not necessarily transfer* to the exercise and sport setting. Some individuals operate under the misconception that there is a simple transfer in skills from clinical or counseling training to exercise and sport settings—this is simply not the case. There is a level of expertise concerning exercise and sport that is needed before practitioners should be working in this area or, certainly, before they should be advertising themselves as "sport psychologists."

There are, therefore, ethical and legal concerns with nonlicensed practitioners who provide psychological services in inappropriate settings, and with licensed psychologists who move beyond their area(s) of expertise and inappropriately provide sport psychology services. One approach to this problem is through some sort of certification process. Attention to this area has been given in the past by a number of groups, such as NASPSPA (the North American Society for the Psychology of Sport and Physical Activity), CSPLSP (the Canadian Society for Psychomotor Learning and Sport Psychology), and the United States Olympic Committee's sports medicine group. More recently, an attempt to address this issue has been made by the Association for the Advancement of Applied Sport Psychology (AAASP). AAASP has developed criteria for certification. These criteria are provided in the Appendix along with an address for further information.

AAASP's Certification Committee, first headed by Daniel Kirschenbaum and more recently by Leonard Zaichkowsky, worked for quite a few years through many legal, ethical, professional and philosophical issues to develop certification criteria. Certification by AAASP as a "Certified Consultant, Association for the Advancement of Applied Sport Psychology" provides the consumer (the potential client) with an indication that the certified individual has met a minimum set of educational and experiential standards. This certified individual may, therefore, be better qualified to work in a consulting capacity involving sport psychological issues than someone without this background and level of training. Much of this expertise is gained through the range of coursework and experiences outlined in the AAASP criteria.

Other sport psychology groups may become involved in

issues related to academic training or even certification in the future. Landers (1991), in the newsletter of Division 47 (Exercise and Sport Psychology) of the American Psychological Association (APA), has noted that "Whether we agree or not with the certification requirements of other sport psychology associations, the issue of academic training necessary to be considered qualified must be addressed" (p. 1).

In summary, therefore, there are ethical and legal concerns with nonlicensed practitioners providing psychological services in inappropriate settings. There are similar concerns when some licensed psychologists overstep their expertise and provide sport psychology services.

ETHICAL ISSUES IN SPORT PSYCHOLOGY

Ethical issues in sport psychology have been acknowledged for more than a decade. Nideffer (1981) published a book entitled *The Ethics and Practice of Applied Sport Psychology,* and various organizations (e.g., NASPSPA and CSPLSP) worked on ethical standards in the early 1980s. Zeigler (1987) has addressed the need for a code of ethics for sport psychologists. Morgan (1989) has suggested that "it is imperative that sport psychologists adhere to" (p. 102) ethical principles and standards developed by the American Psychological Association. A number of areas/issues are prominent in considering ethical perspectives within sport psychology, and these are addressed below.

Ethical Principles of Psychologists

The APA has developed a set of ethical principles that have been in place, with revisions, since 1953. The standards were recently amended and have been published in the *American Psychologist* (American Psychological Association, 1990). Ten principles are addressed: responsibility, competence, moral and legal standards, public statements, confidentiality, welfare of the consumer, professional relationships, assessment techniques, research with human participants, and care and use of animals. The reader is encouraged to become familiar with these principles, as they are the guidelines for ethical practice for psychologists. The APA notes that "These Ethical Principles apply to psychologists, to students of psychology, and to others who do work of a psychological nature under the supervision of a psychologist." Furthermore, the principles "are intended for the guidance of nonmembers of the Association who are engaged in psychological research or practice" (p. 391).

In addition to the ethical principles themselves, extensive sets of cases have been reviewed through the years in the *American Psychologist.* These can aid in understanding the principles and their application in specific situations. A casebook on the ethical principles is available (American Psychological Association, 1987). Additionally, the Ethics Committee of APA reports regularly to the membership on its work (Report of the Ethics Committee, 1991).

Ethical principles and standards are, of course, not solely the province of psychologists. The American College Personnel Association (ACPA), a division of the American Association for Counseling and Development, "is an association whose members are dedicated to enhancing the worth, dignity, potential, and uniqueness of each individual within post-secondary educational institutions" (American College Personnel Association, 1990, p. 11). Given that many sport psychologists are employed at colleges and universities, it may be helpful to know that the ACPA's ethical standards and guidelines (American College Personnel Association, 1990) are also established and, in areas such as professional responsibility and competence, are quite similar to those developed by the APA.

Within APA there has also been attention given to ethical issues in teaching and academic life, a related area to educational and clinical issues within sport psychology and quite relevant to the professional role of many sport psychologists. A Task Force on Ethical Issues in Teaching and Academic Life of Division Two (Teaching of Psychology) of APA has prepared an annotated bibliography covering these issues (Task Force on Ethical Issues in Teaching and Academic Life, 1990).

Specific Issues

Beyond the general applicability of the ethical principles to psychologists, there are specific issues which are of particular importance to sport psychologists and require further elaboration than may be contained in the ethical principles.

Clarification of Sport Psychologist's Role. For whom does the sport psychologist "work"? Issues of role relationships and dual relationships are critical ones within sport psychology (Ogilvie, 1979). On the surface, the question "For whom does the sport psychologist work?" may appear simple to answer: The duty of psychologists is toward their clients first and foremost. However, in some sport settings the "client" is not necessarily an individual. It is one thing to be in private practice and have Jane Athlete present with a problem about performance anxiety or an eating disorder, for example. It is another thing to be employed by the New York Knickerbockers and have Joe Athlete come in and discuss some basketball-related or other concerns. In the latter case, under what conditions does the practitioner have an obligation to share some/all of the information with the coach/management of the team?

There is no simple answer to this question, particularly when working for a team or organization. In one sense, the "simple" answer is that whatever arrangement is entered into must be clearly specified in advance, preferably in writing, and explained and understood by the athletes and team. Ideally, all consultations between athlete and sport psychologist would be privileged, unless both parties agreed that the matter should be brought to the attention of others (coach, athletic director/general manager [AD/

GM]). Since situations are rarely ideal, however, it may be necessary in some employment settings to ensure that it is clear, particularly to the athlete, that in some or all cases information may be shared with the coach or AD/GM, as necessary. Athletes may be wary of bringing issues to the sport psychologist in such cases, but at least everyone is clear about what will be kept confidential and what will be shared. Often this can be specified ahead of time (e.g., in the case of substance abuse issues), but issues that are not anticipated will then need to be discussed by the psychologist and athlete concerning disclosure to others.

Some sport psychologists may feel uncomfortable, of course, sharing information with a coach or AD/GM. These sport psychologists may feel that this would be a violation of the trust established with the athlete, even if sharing information was agreed to before sessions with the athlete began. In such instances the sport psychologist should not work for the team or organization in the first place. It is far easier to avoid getting into these ethical dilemmas (or sharing information, or breaking confidentiality) in the first place than to deal with them later on. In some cases disagreements are unavoidable, but having "everything" in writing at the beginning of employment/working with athletes provides more of a safety net for sport psychologists if they say no or if they decide to resign after undue pressure to divulge information that prior agreements indicated would remain confidential.

In some cases, sport psychologists may have the opportunity to serve as a coach with the team, or one of the team's coaches may have (or get) the training necessary to serve as a sport psychologist with the team. This dual relationship of sport psychologist and coach raises some difficult ethical questions (Ellickson & Brown, 1990). Issues such as responsibility to athlete, client, or team, interpersonal boundaries, power (see below), and confidentiality raise sufficient questions that sport psychologists would be strongly advised to avoid such dual relationships if at all possible. If you are the coach, obtaining the assistance of a colleague to serve as sport psychologist for individual athletes may be the best strategy.

Power. Sport psychologists may find themselves in positions of power, with respect to authority and/or dependence. In particular, sport psychologists need to be careful, as do psychologists in general, about the potential level of dependence clients may develop. The athlete needs to develop strategies (be they psychological skills or strategies for problems such as substance abuse) that can be implemented without the sport psychologist being present. A relationship based on dependency is destined for failure in the long run, if not in the short run. Sport psychologists cannot be present for *all* practices/competitions. Even if they could be, the athletes are the ones performing and using the psychological skills and strategies, and they must be able to do this independently.

Occasionally the sport psychologist may be perceived as having some degree of power (authority) if information is shared with the coach about sessions with the athlete (see the discussion on confidentiality for more on this topic). It should be made clear in advance that the sport psychologist doesn't make decisions about playing time, roles, etc., and that these decisions are made by coach or management. If it appears that the sport psychologist does indeed have some power in this regard, the circumstances should be clarified for all concerned. These are areas in which the sport psychologist clearly should not be playing a role, and ideally the sport psychologist should avoid getting into such situations entirely.

Power issues may also arise in considering sport as a primarily male-identified activity. A sociological analysis of these issues is beyond the scope of this chapter, but issues related to predominantly male institutional structures must be considered within the context of a male-dominant culture. Gould, Tammen, Murphy, and May (1989) found, for example, that 36 (81.8%) of 44 sport psychologists working with sports affiliated with the United States Olympic Committee were male. These issues relating to hierarchy and authority are ones that need to be addressed.

The Role and Management of Intimacy with Clients. The sport arena is, in many respects, an intimate one. One starts with athletes who are healthy, dynamic individuals, competing in revealing outfits, engaging in physical contact, perspiring intensely, etc. Locker rooms provide for intimacy of a visual nature, as teammates or friends are aware of one's physical characteristics. On the playing field or court there are often hugs, pats on the back or behind, high-fives, and other physical contacts. These settings can bring individuals together as teammates and members of a group (including coaches) in ways that other organizational settings can never approach. In general, these gestures of intimacy are seen as supportive of friendship and may serve to cement close relationships that last well beyond membership on the team.

Intimacy takes on a different perspective when individuals in other roles (e.g., coach, athletic trainer, sport psychologist) are involved with athletes. A critical area for psychologists in considering intimacy is that of sexual relationships. The Ethical Principles are explicitly clear in this area (Principle 7d): "Psychologists do not exploit their professional relationships with clients, supervisees, students, employees, or research participants sexually or otherwise" (American Psychological Association, 1990, p. 393).

There is no question that sexual relationships between sport psychologists and clients are unethical. As alluded to above, there may be considerable attraction between a young, attractive athlete in excellent physical shape and a sport psychologist who may also be in superb physical condition (often young as well, particularly in the case of a student doing an internship, or even "aging jock" sport psychologists who may feel vulnerable and wish to "recapture their youth"). This attraction may take place regardless of sexual preference (both heterosexual or homosexual relationships have the potential of developing, depending on the individual's sexual orientation). Whatever attraction may develop, however, must remain unexpressed. The sport

psychologist must resolve his or her own issues, perhaps in consultation with a colleague or with one's supervisor if one is an intern.

Principle 7d goes on to note: "Psychologists do not condone or engage in sexual harassment. Sexual harassment is defined as deliberate or repeated comments, gestures, or physical contacts of a sexual nature that are unwanted by the recipient" (American Psychological Association, 1990, p. 393). This is an area where the boundaries may be less clear, given socialization processes within sport. As noted above, there are many instances in which physical contacts in a sport setting take place—hugs, pats on the back or behind, high-fives, etc. These are generally considered quite normal and not given a second thought. However, particularly when a male sport psychologist is working with female athletes or a female sport psychologist is working with male athletes, a seemingly innocuous gesture may be misinterpreted. The action of a male patting the behind of a female athlete as she comes off the basketball court after playing may well be seen as inappropriate. Similarly, a hug between sport psychologist and athlete may be misinterpreted if too long or too strong.

The safest way to approach this area is to ask permission before engaging in *any* physical contact with the client. It is important to keep in mind individual differences between clients, particularly with regard to different histories of exploitative touch/harassment. Just as in therapy one would (should) ask permission before touching a client (one might, for example, want to give the client a hug during a difficult period), the same rule should apply in the sport setting. While no one might misconstrue high-fives between sport psychologists and clients, hugs could be misinterpreted. It is where that line is crossed, and where misinterpretation can take place by the athlete/client and/or others, that clarification must be made.

If one is the type of person who finds such physical contacts a part of his/her personal and or professional approach, then one should make sure one has permission to engage in these actions before proceeding. Primary concern here is for the client: the risk of traumatizing the client with exploitative touch/harassment is significant. A secondary consideration is that it is better to be clear about these matters than to risk being hit with a complaint or lawsuit about sexual harassment when this was clearly not one's intent.

Competence in Clinical and/or Educational Sport Psychology. Ethical principle 2, competence, emphasizes that

Psychologists recognize the boundaries of their competence and the limitations of their techniques. They only provide services and only use techniques for which they are qualified by training and experience (American Psychological Association, 1990, p. 390).

The area of competence is one of particular concern to sport psychologists. Many individuals who come from a physical education background, in particular, have developed competencies in educational sport psychology. Educational sport psychology encompasses the teaching of psychological skills, generally with athletes interested in performance enhancement. The label of Psychological Skills Training (PST; Vealey, 1988) is usually applied here, although other terms, such as "mental toughness training" or just "mental training," are occasionally used (Ravizza, 1988). PST usually covers skills such as relaxation/stress management, visualization, concentration, positive self-talk, and goal setting. Competency in teaching these skills is often, although not always, also possessed by clinical/counseling psychologists, especially those working within a cognitive, behavioral, or cognitive-behavioral framework.

Much of the demand for sport psychological services is in the PST area. Athletes in particular are looking for that edge, that improvement in their performance that will help them be more successful (i.e., win). The psychological or mental side of things is often the last area considered, but may, of course, be the most important. Occasionally, however, athletes present problems of a clinical nature. These may encompass substance abuse (usually alcohol, cocaine, or steroids), eating disorders, relationship issues with family or friends, etc. These problems may be identical to those experienced by nonathletes. It is important to remember that athletes are people as well, with lives outside the athletic arena. However much athletes' identities may be tied up in their sport, they still have an outside world in which they live, and other people with whom they interact. The problems may not be specific to sport per se. One must acknowledge, though, that the fact that a person is an athlete, and the kind of activity in which he or she participates, are critical elements in the formulation of a treatment plan and for working with the athlete to effect meaningful change.

An additional important point to remember is that the educational sport psychologist is not using PST on an inanimate object, but is in fact working with an entire person, and that the specific PST approach used needs to be understood within a context. A client may or may not present issues that become clearer later on. For example, if one is teaching goal setting, are the client's issues poor capacity to break goals into component parts, underlying conflict over achieving more than one's parent, overuse syndrome, depression, a signal of other current interpersonal problems, and/or other issues?

The clinical issues that arise must be addressed by sport psychologists with training in clinical or counseling psychology. Clinical sport psychology assumes competency in these clinical issues, and persons with training in educational sport psychology but *not* in the clinical side of things must recognize these limitations and refer athletes with clinical problems to a clinical sport psychologist.

As noted above, sport psychologists must be aware of their limitations in areas of expertise and be prepared to refer clients to other sport psychologists with the appropriate expertise. It is helpful initially to have done a personal assessment of one's limitations, and then be prepared with names of colleagues who have the expertise one is lacking. The colleague should obviously be one with the experience needed, and not merely a friend with whom one plays

tennis (for example). In dealing with professional issues, personal considerations must be set aside and referrals made to individuals with the level of expertise needed to help one's clients. These referrals must ensure smooth (and actual) transfer to someone else, and quality continuity of care.

It is also important not to neglect the recreational sport participant who may have motivation or adherence problems, or perhaps exercise addiction (Sachs & Pargman, 1984), at the other end of the spectrum. Here again, training in clinical/counseling psychology, or health psychology, as appropriate, may be needed in order to work with clients with problems of this nature.

Competence in Specialty Areas. As noted above, there are numerous areas within counseling or clinical psychology that may be encountered within the sport setting (Heyman, 1987). These include substance abuse and eating disorders (Black, 1991). Occasionally phobias (such as fear of flying) will present themselves. Most psychologists have had some experience, in the classroom and in internship settings, with a wide variety of psychological problems. However, the level of expertise may not be sufficient for a psychologist to be able to deal as effectively as ethically required with an individual who has a substance abuse problem (for example). In such cases psychologists should, first, be able to recognize their limitations and, second, be able to refer the client to another psychologist who has the level of expertise required. One does greater harm to the client trying to bluff one's way through an area in which one is ill prepared in lieu of referring the individual to another psychologist with the level of expertise to be of real help.

Competence in Working with Diverse Populations. Ethical principle two, Competence, notes that "Psychologists recognize differences among people, such as those that may be associated with age, sex, [and] socioeconomic and ethnic backgrounds. When necessary, they obtain training, experience, or counsel to assure competent service or research relating to such persons" (American Psychological Association, 1990, p. 391). In sport, as in society at large, we encounter individuals with a diverse array of demographic characteristics, including sex (male/female) and race (Caucasian, African-American, Latino, etc.). Smith (1991) notes that only 5–8% of "all physical education teaching, coaching, and sport leadership positions are filled by nonethnic minorities" (p. 39). However, many of the athletes sport psychologists will work with will have a multicultural background. Smith suggests some issues and strategies for working with multicultural athletes. There is also a fairly extensive literature in clinical/counseling psychology concerning working with clients with different cultural and ethnic backgrounds.

In society in general a potential client may have a wide range of options in choosing a psychologist who, on the surface, might appear to be someone with whom a successful therapeutic alliance can be formed. In a sport setting, however, if one is "*the* sport psychologist" assigned to a team, the athlete may seemingly have little choice in coming for help (other than not coming for help at all). The African-American female may feel uncomfortable seeking help from a Caucasian male, or a Caucasian male from a Caucasian female, etc. The permutations are virtually endless.

We are all creatures of our own socialization experiences. A few of us have prejudices we express overtly, although more of us have covert biases. More likely, we have ways of responding to individuals of another gender or race or ethnic background that are at a level we would find difficult even to acknowledge. Patterns of responding may seem so natural that we may lose sight of their potential to result in unequal treatment of others or bias the ways in which we work with other individuals. One example is brought out by Anshel (1990), who interviewed 26 African-American football players at an NCAA (National Collegiate Athletic Association) Division I institution. Anshel found that

the subjects reported a general lack of sensitivity on the part of coaches to individual and sociocultural needs of black players. . . . Blacks unequivocally perceived a sense of unfairness, racism, and a general lack of psychological support by white coaches. (p. 235)

If one interviewed the Caucasian coaches they almost certainly would deny any intent to be unfair, racist, or otherwise discriminatory toward their African-American players. However, the end result may be a failure to interact on a meaningful level with sensitivity and awareness of the needs of other individuals with different backgrounds of a sexual and or racial/ethnic nature.

It behooves the psychologist, from a standpoint of both ethics as well as competence, to be knowledgeable in issues relevant to sex/gender, racial/ethnic considerations, cross-cultural issues (e.g., working with a soccer team composed of athletes from diverse national origins), and sexual preference. While this may not make a difference on the surface (e.g., initially all one may "see" is a Caucasian female sport psychologist), knowledge about and sensitivity to these issues will quickly become apparent in discussions with the client, and rapport may develop and an effective therapeutic alliance ensue. These issues are important whether one is working in an educational context or in a clinical role. The fact that one is knowledgeable and sensitive to this diversity of issues will also become known to other athletes on the team (news travels fast), making it more likely that others will seek assistance if problems exist or if performance enhancement work is desired.

Competence in Working with Participants in Different Sports. There are a myriad of sports in which athletes participate (and millions of recreational participants engaging in a diverse array of physical activities). Within the United States Olympic Committee (USOC) itself, for example, there are 41 different National Governing Bodies (NGBs) in charge of different sports. Almost all of these sports are part of the Olympic Games.

No one individual is going to be knowledgeable about all sports, particularly to the extent of, for example, knowing what playing the game really involves in terms of physical and mental effort. The author's sport background, for example, encompasses tennis and basketball and running. I feel I have a good degree of knowledge about these sports. However, as much as I may know about the game of football, I really have only an intellectual feeling for what it is really like to play the game, in terms of getting hit repeatedly, playing with injuries, playing under adverse weather conditions, etc. I might, therefore, be much less qualified to work with a football team or football players than someone with football experience. This consideration should enter into any decision to work with particular athletes and/or teams.

Sometimes, of course, an opportunity presents itself in which one feels one could be helpful, but one is not particularly knowledgeable about the sport. The best cure is knowledge, of course (Ravizza, 1988). The sport psychologist should learn about the rules of the game and some history of the sport both generally and specifically at a school or conference (if relevant), should watch numerous games (preferably live, but on tape if need be, depending on the time of year), should talk with players and coaches about what practicing and competing involve, and so on. There is no real substitute for actually having played the game, but one can come close by educating oneself about the sport. From an ethical standpoint this is a minimum level of competence/expertise that would be expected for someone working with athletes or teams in particular sports.

A somewhat divergent point of view, however, might suggest a more narrow perspective of PST, with the sport psychologist having expertise in PST but not the sport per se. Although the sport psychologist would have some basic knowledge about the sport, adopting a consultative view would suggest that the *athlete* has the expertise concerning the sport and is coming to the sport psychologist to learn how to handle and integrate the mental aspects of participation/excellence. In some ways this can be a very empowering model for the client. Related to this line of thinking, to the extent that the sport psychologist is knowledgeable about the sport, the risk may be present of blurring role relationships/functions (e.g., sport psychologist/coach noted earlier), potential overidentification with the athlete, and countertransference issues.

It is clear that this area can be viewed from a number of different perspectives and identification of the "best" approach remains to be resolved. An interesting side note to the issue of competence in working with athletes in different sports is the ethical issue potentially involved in working with some sports at all. Concerns about the sport of boxing, for example, have raised some issues (Heyman, 1990). Debate and decisions concerning these issues eventually return to the individual sport psychologist and his or her own choice. Sport psychologists may need to consider their own backgrounds and their degree of comfort in working with athletes in different sports.

Use of Psychological Tests. Psychological tests are used extensively in sport psychology. Although used most often in research, testing is also used in applied sport psychology. A sport psychologist might administer one or more psychological inventories as part of an initial psychological evaluation of an athlete, or as a precursor to working with a team. These might include, for example, personality tests, mood inventories, anxiety measures, psychological skills measures, and attentional measures. It should be noted that many psychological tests are intended for use by psychologists with clinical/counseling training, while other, generally sport-specific, measures are appropriate for use by educational sport psychologists.

Gould, Tammen, Murphy, and May (1989) found, for example, that 28 consultants (62.8%) working with sports affiliated with the United States Olympic Committee used at least one psychological inventory in their work, although 15 (37.2%) "did not use tests or instruments in their applied work" (p. 307). Gould et al. found that the consultants used 26 different instruments, with the following tests/instruments used by at least four consultants: Profile of Mood States, Sport Competition Anxiety Test, Test of Attentional and Interpersonal Style, Competitive State Anxiety Inventory—2, and the Psychological Skills Inventory for Sport. An excellent directory of almost two hundred psychological tests in the sport and exercise sciences is available (Ostrow, 1990).

It should be noted, however, that not all sport psychologists endorse the use of psychological testing, at least initially, citing concerns of lack of relevancy and waste of time (Orlick, 1989). Athletes may also be put off by encountering a battery of inventories early in the process of working with the sport psychologist. In circumstances where use of psychological tests is being considered, a number of points are important to review.

First, the psychometric properties of the test(s) should be known. Using a test with unknown validity and reliability may provide GIGO (Garbage In, Garbage Out). Most tests have manuals with extensive information on the psychometric properties of the instrument, but some (e.g., the Athletic Motivation Inventory) purportedly have this information but make it difficult, if not impossible, to obtain. The sport psychologist should beware of any instrument which is not psychometrically sound.

Second, one must make sure that the test is being used for the purpose and for the population for which it was designed. A test designed to measure personality may tell little, if anything, about a person's psychological skills. An inventory designed for use with adults should not be used with junior high school students. A test designed as a trait measure should not be used as a state measure (of anxiety, for example). These points should go without saying, but there are too many instances in the literature where these points have been forgotten.

Third, one should not use an inventory for selection purposes for a team, either initially or to determine playing time. Many of the inventories in existence today provide useful information for understanding an athlete and perhaps suggest areas in which the athlete can improve. However, the tests are rarely designed to select athletes for

teams or playing time, and have too much error variance to be used in this regard. Although this caveat is usually noted in test manuals, it is easy to forget when the coach remembers, in the "back of his/her mind," that Johnny/Susie scored low on aggressiveness and then decides to put the player on second string. The sport psychologist has to be extremely careful in selecting tests in the first place, and then about the amount and type of information that is shared with athlete and coach. Coaches need to be educated about the appropriate use of tests, reliability/validity issues, state/trait issues (as appropriate), etc. The sport psychologist must also guard against pressures from coaches and administrators to use specific tests if these tests are inappropriate for the purpose envisioned.

Fourth, the sport psychologist can serve a vital role in interpretation of test results. Information should be provided only to individuals who know what to do with the information, or in ways that the individual (particularly the athlete) can understand. If information is shared with the individual who has taken the test, the information must be presented in a way in which the person can clearly understand the meaning of the information and the limitations of the data. Similarly, simply providing another person, such as the coach, with a set of test results without ensuring that this person knows what to do with the results is unethical, and may have serious consequences for the athletes and team if the information is misused. If the coach, for example, has the training in psychology or education to understand what the test results mean, then it may be appropriate to share information with the coach. Otherwise, only individuals (such as sport psychologists) with experience in testing should have access to the results, particularly the raw data, from psychological testing.

An additional important note concerns receiving permission to share test results with individuals other than the person taking the test. Aside from the issue of understanding the nature of the information, the sport psychologist should always get permission in writing, using an appropriate consent form, to release the information. *No* information should be released without this written authorization from the client.

Psychological tests can provide useful information for the sport psychologist. However, use of tests must be carefully considered in the first place, and then appropriate use of the information obtained must be a primary concern. Additional information concerning these issues, including responsibilities and competencies of users of educational and psychological tests, is available (e.g., American Psychological Association, 1985).

Group as Compared with Individual Work. Sport psychologists often work with teams, which may mean dealing with small to comparatively larger groups of individuals. Training in group dynamics, the sociology of groups, and/or group therapy or counseling are strongly recommended for the sport psychologist. The role of the sport psychologist with a team can take many different forms. One often hears, for example, of sport psychologists conducting relaxation/

visualization sessions with groups of athletes. At the beginning of one's interaction with a team or group of athletes, one may indeed find it both appropriate and "economical" to provide introductory lectures and practice sessions on certain psychological skills for these groups of athletes.

At some point, however, a question must be raised about the appropriateness of such an undertaking, from both a quality of practice as well as an ethical perspective. To what degree or at what point do sessions (involving, for example, relaxation and visualization) need to be individualized? Individuals have different levels of skill in relaxation and visualization (as in the other psychological skills), and different or preferred modes within visualization (for example) in using verbal/visual/tactile images, etc. These must be addressed individually, at some level, for the most effective results. One could also make a strong case that psychological skills such as goal setting and positive self-talk should be done individually with each athlete.

The individual approach is ideal. If quality and ethical considerations are addressed initially, and time/cost issues still dictate a group approach, then this may be the best (and maybe the only) way to proceed in providing services for a team/group of athletes.

Confidentiality. Confidentiality is an integral part of the ethical framework of psychologists in general (see Principle 5 of the APA Ethical Principles, American Psychological Association, 1990, pp. 392–393.). Sport psychologists are no exception. A first level of questions in this area relates to our earlier discussion concerning the person/organization for whom one works. The extent of disclosure to management about one's clients depends on the initial agreements between therapist and client and therapist and organization. Confidentiality is designed to ensure privacy and facilitate the development of trust between therapist and client. The privilege of waiver of confidentiality rests with the client. With the agreement of all parties concerned, confidentiality can shift from an absolute framework to a conditional one, with disclosures permitted, depending on what these agreements permit one to share with others.

It should be noted that in some situations, such as with sexual abuse of children, therapists may be under a legal requirement in their state to disclose information to authorities. These issues will generally be covered as part of graduate education and training. However, these types of situations are only rarely encountered in the sport psychological realm.

In cases where confidentiality is understood to be maintained (i.e., information is not shared with others), the sport psychologist needs to consider at what level one can even share information about the identity of one's clients. One may feel comfortable in acknowledging that one is indeed working with Team X, but that may be the extent to which one can ethically go. The ethical bounds of the client's privilege of confidentiality suggest that it is not even ethically acceptable to respond to a question such as "Are you working with Joe Superstar?" Even indicating that a given person is a client compromises confidentiality; mentioning any details about the nature of the counseling completely breaks the bounds.

Similarly, in reporting research with teams, one must be careful to disguise information. One may need to refer to an unnamed team (for example, a "basketball team at a major university" may be as much information as you want to reveal). However, the specific players always remain unidentified or unidentifiable. Talking about Basketball Team X and test scores for the starting point guard, even if he or she remains unnamed, may not be ethical. As the sports talk shows are fond of saying, it wouldn't take a rocket scientist to figure out that the starting point guard for Team X is Joe Superstar, even if Joe hasn't been named specifically. One must be *very* careful in disguising team names, player names, and positions, etc., in order to protect the athletes with whom one works—and oneself, from ethical violations in this area.

Talking about work with Joe or Jane Athlete should be done only with the written permission of the athlete. It is tempting to "name-drop" the names of star athletes with whom one has worked, but unless one has permission to do so, one is committing a serious ethical violation, not to mention adding possible legal complications that can result in one's getting sued by an athlete (anything is possible in our increasingly litigious society). Therapists are subject to those all-too-human tendencies of basking in reflected glory, overidentification, and narcissism. Working with star athletes may feed into these tendencies, but the therapist will need to learn appropriate ways to channel these inclinations. A good place to start may be to explore ways to understand more about oneself and one's own issues through consultation/supervision.

An additional note about confidentiality that is important to consider concerns working with minors (children and adolescents). The ethical/legal issues surrounding consent (and consent forms) and disclosure of information become more complex when parents have legal rights with respect to their children but therapists have ethical responsibilities concerning confidentiality.

Supervision. The learning process for psychologists, including sport psychologists, is an ongoing one. In internships one generally finds structured situations in which students work with an individual or group and meet with their supervisor on a regular basis (often once per week). This supervision is a key element in the learning process for students (as well as supervisors) in developing expertise in dealing with clients with different presenting problems.

It is generally advisable, as well, for more "established" sport psychologists to have a colleague (or several colleagues) with whom one can consult on a regular or occasional basis. These supervisory sessions, of course, serve to maintain confidentiality but provide professional guidance that may be needed. There will always be cases one finds particularly challenging. Discussing such cases with a respected colleague may either help clarify and support one's course of analysis/treatment or suggest more effective alternative approaches.

Third-Party Payments. An additional area in which ethical issues may arise is in third-party insurance payments. Clients will often work with sport psychologists and pay 100% of the fee themselves. Occasionally, however, insurance companies (or third parties) will pay for some or all of the cost of treatment. Third-party payment is usually forthcoming only for mental disorders found in the DSM-III-R (the Diagnostic and Statistical Manual of Mental Disorders, Third Edition, Revised; American Psychiatric Association, 1987a).

The purpose of DSM-III-R is to provide clear descriptions of diagnostic categories in order to enable clinicians and investigators to diagnose, communicate about, study, and treat the various mental disorders (American Psychiatric Association, 1987b, p. vii)

These descriptions enable clinicians to diagnose mental disorders and differentiate among them. The disorders have different numbers (e.g., bulimia nervosa is 307.51, obsessive compulsive disorder is 300.30, etc.). Each disorder has a specific list of criteria that aid in determining if a disorder is present.

Athletes or recreational sport participants with psychological problems may see sport psychologists for counseling that is clearly reimbursable through third-party payment. As noted earlier, in some cases these problems may have little or nothing to do with the fact that the person is an athlete. Often, however, the fact that the individual is an athlete has a bearing on the *type and severity* of the disorder and the *course of development* of the disorder (and subsequent treatment). However, the nature of the problem still falls within a general clinical/counseling framework. The client should be aware of the clinical diagnosis and plans for treatment.

The trickier ethical issue comes in considering PST, and educational sport psychology. Under what conditions, if any, would working with a tennis player who is having problems with concentration on the tennis court fall into one of the diagnostic categories in DSM-III-R? Does this player have a disorder that would be reimbursable by a third-party payer (again assuming the tennis player is not paying for this him/herself)? In many/most instances, the answer would appear to be "no"—a mental disorder of the type (or at least meeting all the criteria) dealt with in DSM-III-R would probably not be present.

However, imagine you are sitting in your office, calmly shooting a nerf ball through the small hoop on your wall into the basket below, imagining you're playing with the Philadelphia 76ers. The phone rings with a call from Joe Tennis Player who wants to see you. Joe is one of the better tennis players in the area and comes in and describes how concentration problems are making it difficult for him to play well, affecting his enjoyment of the game, his success, or his general relationships with his family, etc. The DSM-III-R category of Adjustment Disorder (309.28, for example: Adjustment Disorder with Mixed Emotional Features, "when the predominant manifestation is a combination of depression and anxiety or other emotions"—American Psychiatric Association, 1987b, p. 184) may be appropriate.

Adjustment disorders include the consideration that impairment in functioning may extend to "usual social activities or relationships with others" (p. 183). That certainly seems to be applicable in Joe Tennis Player's case. However, there are also time constraints, which consider that "a reaction to an identifiable psychosocial stressor (or multiple stressors) . . . occurs within three months of the onset of the stressor(s)" (p. 183) and "the maladaptive reaction has persisted for no longer than six months" (p. 183).

From a broader perspective, insurance companies probably did not have improving Joe's tennis game in mind when third party payment considerations were put into effect. From a sport psychological standpoint, however, tennis may be an essential element of Joe's identity and a central factor of his happiness in life, affecting his ability to function effectively in work, at home, and in family settings. Helping Joe improve his tennis-playing ability through PST in the area of concentration may be quite ethically sound and justify reimbursement.

In any case, sport psychologists should become familiar with third-party payment rules and regulations if bills for services go to others beside the client. The ethical considerations and potential legal concerns in billing for third-party payment when such billing is unjustified make it critical for the sport psychologist to consider each case carefully on its own merits and act appropriately. The sport psychologist should also be sensitive to the needs and wishes of the client concerning third-party billing. The parents of an adolescent tennis player with whom I worked did not want any bills sent to a third party (the father's insurer) because of fear that there would be a "record" of their son having seen a psychologist and that this might have effects in the future on applying to colleges, etc. While such fears may appear on the surface to be unjustified, they may be "real" to the client and should be honored. In such cases, the client may pay the entire fee, or some accommodation on adjusting the fee may be necessary.

Marketing the Sport Psychologist. Principle 4 of APA's Ethical Principles of Psychologists (American Psychological Association, 1990) addresses public statements. This principle concerns the information one can furnish about one's background and services provided, parameters of announcing/advertising the availability of products or services, etc. As sport psychology becomes more well known and more psychologists become interested in working in this area, concerns about ethical issues in public statements, as well as competence and others addressed earlier, may arise. DeFrancesco and Cronin (1988) address some practical suggestions for implementing a marketing plan for sport psychologists, but also note a number of ethical concerns. They suggest that "Professional service ethics would prohibit the providing of unneeded services to the client; only real needs should be addressed. In addition, professional service ethics would dictate that only actual problems should be diagnosed and treated" (pp. 36–37).

Interestingly, these are issues that address more of the practice concerns (e.g., competence, responsibility) and less of the marketing issues that may arise in false advertising, breaches of confidentiality (naming famous athletes with whom one has worked without permission to do so), misrepresenting what sport psychology can do for an athlete, and other similar concerns. These are all addressed in Principle 4 of the Ethical Principles of Psychologists, and the sport psychologist should be intimately familiar with the points covered in this principle. Sport psychology may be especially vulnerable at this point in its development to ethical violations in this area. The field is a "hot" (i.e., popular) one, and may be often subject to the glare of inappropriate publicity. Additionally, some of one's clients may be more likely to be "hot" (i.e., visible in the public eye). Finally, some areas within sport psychology, particularly performance enhancement, are still new enough that unsubstantiated claims may be more likely. There will, unfortunately, be violations of this principle in the future, given past experience in other areas of psychology. The profession must be vigilant and address any general issues in this area and specific problems with individual psychologists as they arise.

Additional Training Opportunities in Sport Psychology

Additional training opportunities are beginning to develop. Indeed, some are already in place. Division 47 of APA and the Association for the Advancement of Behavior Therapy, among others, have had workshops in the past dealing with sport psychology. Other organizations, such as the USOC, have sponsored workshops and seminars in this area. AAASP, in particular, is developing continuing education programs as part of a program of service delivery including conference and regional workshops and independent study programs. These will hopefully reach fruition within the next few years.

There are many books and articles available in applied sport psychology. Sachs (1991), for example, noted 48 books in a reading list in applied sport psychology focusing upon PST. Videotapes and audiotapes are available, as are newsletters. Other valuable resources, such as the *Sport Psychology Training Bulletin* (P. O. Box 52234, Durham, NC 27717-2234), edited by Charles Hardy and Kelly Crace, have been developed for athletes, coaches, and parents.

There will be many training opportunities in sport psychology in the coming years. Certainly, ethical issues will be discussed as part of many of the workshops and seminars that will be held. Information concerning these will be available in newsletters and publications of AAASP (such as the newsletter and the *Journal of Applied Sport Psychology*), Division 47 of APA, and journals such as *The Sport Psychologist* and the *Journal of Sport and Exercise Psychology*.

FUTURE DIRECTIONS IN PROFESSIONAL ETHICS

All sport psychologists have at least some exposure to professional ethics in their graduate programs. Some programs do a more effective job than others in training students to integrate the ethical principles discussed above into their personal and professional frames of reference. Our challenge in the future will be to ensure that sport psychologists are successful in integrating these ethical principles into their practice. Education and training will need to be obtained from the field of psychology in general, from workshops and resources such as Pope and Vasquez (1991), and sport psychology in particular.

Continuing education, as noted through the training opportunities mentioned above, will provide an opportunity for current sport psychologists and sport psychologists-to-be to gain knowledge in this area. This knowledge is integral to success as a professional in our field. The formation of ethics committees in our field, such as the one formed by AAASP (chaired by Al Petitpas of Springfield College), will help in educating sport psychologists on ethical issues and potentially reviewing cases/issues as they arise.

Issues encompassing certification, confidentiality, intimacy, and marketing will be raised in our evolving field in the years to come. Unfortunately, while most psychologists strive to be ethical, there are enough "bad apples" (individuals who are unethical to begin with), as well as well-intentioned individuals who make mistakes, that ethical issues will be a subject of discussion as long as there is a field of sport psychology. Continuing attention to these issues will be critical in the future.

APPENDIX: AAASP CERTIFICATION CRITERIA

Necessary levels of preparation in the substantive content areas generally require successful completion of at least three graduate semester hours or their equivalent (e.g., passing suitable exams offered by an accredited doctoral program). However, up to four upper-level undergraduate courses may be substituted for this requirement (unless specifically designated as requiring graduate credit only). It is not always necessary to take one course to satisfy each requirement. However, one course or experience cannot be used to satisfy more than one criterion except for #2.

1. Completion of a doctoral degree.
2. Knowledge of scientific and professional ethics and standards. (Can meet requirement by taking one course on these topics or by taking several courses in which these topics comprise parts of the courses or by completing other comparable experiences.)
3. Knowledge of the sport psychology subdisciplines of intervention/performance enhancement, health/exercise psychology, and social psychology as evidenced by three courses or two courses and one independent

study in sport psychology (two of these courses must be taken at the graduate level).

4. Knowledge of the biomechanical and/or physiological bases of sport (e.g., kinesiology, biomechanics, exercise physiology).

5. Knowledge of the historical, philosophical, social or motor behavior bases of sport (e.g., motor learning/control, motor development, issues in sport/physical education, sociology of sport, history and philosophy of sport/physical education).

6. Knowledge of psychopathology and its assessment (e.g., abnormal psychology, psychopathology).

7. Training designed to foster basic skills in counseling (e.g., coursework on basic intervention techniques in counseling, supervised practica in counseling, clinical, or industrial/organizational psychology) (graduate level only).

8. Supervised experience, with a qualified person (i.e., one who has an appropriate background in applied sport psychology), during which the individual receives training in the use of sport psychology principles and techniques (e.g., supervised practica in applied sport psychology in which the focus of the assessments and interventions are participants in physical activity, exercise, or sport) (graduate level only).

9. Knowledge of skills and techniques within sport or exercise (e.g., skills and techniques classes, clinics, formal coaching experiences, organized participation in sport or exercise).

10. Knowledge and skills in research design, statistics, and psychological assessment (graduate level only).

At least two of the following four criteria must be met through educational experiences that focus on general psychological principles (rather than sport-specific ones).

11. Knowledge of the biological bases of behavior (e.g., biomechanics/kinesiology, comparative psychology, exercise physiology, neuropsychology, physiological psychology, psychopharmacology, sensation).

12. Knowledge of the cognitive-affective bases of behavior (e.g., cognition, emotion, learning, memory, motivation, motor development, motor learning/control, perception, thinking).

13. Knowledge of the social bases of behavior (e.g., cultural, ethnic, and group processes; gender roles in sport; organizational and systems theory; social psychology; sociology of sport).

14. Knowledge of individual behavior (e.g., developmental psychology, exercise behavior, health psychology, individual differences, personality theory).

For further information, please contact Michael L. Sachs, Ph.D., Dept. of Physical Education–048-00, Temple University, Philadelphia, PA 19122.

References

American College Personnel Association. (1990). Statement of ethical principles and standards. *Journal of College Student Development, 31,* 11–16.

American Psychiatric Association. (1987a). *Diagnostic and statistical manual of mental disorders* (3rd ed.). Washington, DC: American Psychiatric Association.

American Psychiatric Association. (1987b). *Quick reference to the diagnostic criteria from DSM-III-R.* Washington, DC: American Psychiatric Association.

American Psychological Association. (1985). *Standards for educational and psychological testing.* Washington, DC: American Psychological Association.

American Psychological Association. (1987). *Casebook on ethical principles of psychologists.* Washington, DC: American Psychological Association.

American Psychological Association. (1990). Ethical principles of psychologists (Amended June 2, 1989). *American Psychologist, 45,* 390–395.

Anshel, M. H. (1990). Perceptions of black intercollegiate football players: Implications for the sport psychology consultant. *The Sport Psychologist, 4,* 235–248.

Black, D. R. (Ed.) (1991). *Eating disorders among athletes: Theory, issues, and research.* Reston, VA: American Alliance for Health, Physical Education, Recreation, and Dance.

DeFrancesco, C., & Cronin, J. J. (1988). Marketing the sport psychologist. *The Sport Psychologist, 2,* 28–38.

Ellickson, K. A., & Brown, D. R. (1990). Ethical considerations in dual relationships: The sport psychologist–coach. *Journal of Applied Sport Psychology, 2,* 186–190.

Gould, D., Tammen, V., Murphy, S., & May, J. (1989). An examination of U. S. Olympic sport psychology consultants and the services they provide. *The Sport Psychologist, 3,* 300–312.

Heyman, S. R. (1987). Counseling and psychotherapy with athletes: Special considerations. In J. R. May & M. J. Asken (Eds.), *Sport psychology: The psychological health of the athlete* (pp. 135–156). New York: PMA Publishing Corp.

Heyman, S. R. (1990). Ethical issues in performance enhancement approaches with amateur boxers. *The Sport Psychologist, 4,* 48–54.

Landers, D. M. (1991, Summer). President's message. *Exercise and Sport Psychology Newsletter, 5,* 1.

Morgan, W. P. (1989). Sport psychology in its own context: A recommendation for the future. In J. S. Skinner, C. B. Corbin, D. M. Landers, P. E. Martin, & C. L. Wells (Eds.), *Future directions in exercise and sport science research* (pp. 97–110). Champaign, IL: Human Kinetics.

Nideffer, R. M. (1981). *The ethics and practice of applied sport psychology.* Ithaca, NY: Mouvement Publications.

Ogilvie, B. C. (1979). The sport psychologist and his professional credibility. In P. Klavora & J. V. Daniel (Eds.), *Coach, athlete, and the sport psychologist* (pp. 44–55). Toronto, Ontario, Canada: University of Toronto.

Orlick, T. (1989). Reflections of sportpsych consulting with individual and team sport athletes at summer and winter Olympic games. *The Sport Psychologist, 3,* 358–365.

Ostrow, A. C. (Ed.) (1990). *Directory of psychological tests in the sport and exercise sciences*. Morgantown, WV: Fitness Information Technology, Inc.

Pope, K. S., & Vasquez, M. J. T. (1991). *Ethics in psychotherapy and counseling: A practical guide for psychologists*. San Francisco, CA: Jossey-Bass.

Ravizza, K. (1988). Gaining entry with athletic personnel for season-long consulting. *The Sport Psychologist, 2,* 243–254.

Rejeski, W. J., & Brawley, L. R. (1988). Defining the boundaries of sport psychology. *The Sport Psychologist, 2,* 231–242.

Report of the Ethics Committee, 1989 and 1990. (1991). *American Psychologist, 46,* 750–757.

Sachs, M. L. (1991). Reading list in applied sport psychology: Psychological skills training. *The Sport Psychologist, 5,* 88–91.

Sachs, M. L., & Pargman, D. (1984). Running addiction. In M. L. Sachs & G. W. Buffone (Eds.), *Running as therapy: An integrated approach* (pp. 231–252). Lincoln, NE: University of Nebraska Press.

Silva, III, J. M. (1989). Toward the professionalization of sport psychology. *The Sport Psychologist, 3,* 265–273.

Smith, Y. R. (1991). Issues and strategies for working with multicultural athletes. *Journal of Physical Education, Recreation, and Dance, 62*(3), 39–44.

Task Force on Ethical Issues in Teaching and Academic Life (1990). *Annotated bibliography: Ethical issues in teaching and academic life*. Washington, DC: Division 2, American Psychological Association.

Vealey, R. S. (1988). Future directions in psychological skills training. *The Sport Psychologist, 2,* 318–336.

Zeigler, E. F. (1987). Rationale and suggested dimensions for a code of ethics for sport psychologists. *The Sport Psychologist, 1,* 138–150.

EPILOGUE

Research is, after all, an intensely personal matter. Professional fame may not be the goal of every investigator, but each of us cherishes his own ideas as if they were his children and is as little likely to be willing to forego recognition of his parentage. Our allegiance to our discipline is stronger than we are prepared to believe. It is painful to see how a cherished principle which may constitute an essential component of one's scientific or professional identity may be utterly ignored or treated as quite inconsequential by a colleague from another field. It is thus that many efforts at collaboration prove abortive, or if carried through, are poorly productive, since each participant feels he has sacrificed an important tenet in the interests of a common goal which is depreciated thereby. (Cohen, 1963, p. ix)

With the above quotation we bring the *Handbook of Research on Sport Psychology* to a close. It is clear that if these words reflect the experience of most researchers, the trend toward collaborative efforts in research across all fields is remarkable. In this *Handbook,* we have attempted to bolster this trend by presenting scholarly activity from around the world that has in many instances been the product of collaborative multiauthored chapter manuscripts. It is hoped that the contents of this book provide the reader with a current perspective with regard to research in sport psychology. Furthermore, as we approach the year 2000, the material contained in this volume will serve as a basis for understanding and continuing research in the very broad and rapidly expanding field of sport psychology.

While every aspect of sport psychology could not have been included in a single volume, much of the recent major research has been overviewed. In many instances, in addition, authors have suggested directions for future study. We planned to have a concluding chapter on future directions in sport psychology, but for various reasons this idea did not materialize. We therefore choose to offer this epilogue, which addresses the issues related to future directions in sport psychology research from the perspectives of the authors themselves.

As we evaluate the current state of sport psychology research, we note that there are still gaping holes in our knowledge base and in the number and type of important issues that might be explored in depth. Simultaneously sport psychologists can take great pride in the great strides that have been made in the past and look forward to accomplishments that will occur during the next decade and beyond.

Many of the major research thrusts in the immediate future are likely to evolve from a number of the topics addressed in this book. A particular focus of current research is those topical themes that were identified by the editors with collaboration from the advisory board. Authors were then asked to write chapters in their area of expertise. In addition, the editors wanted to close this book with a look to the future and to meaningful research directions. Therefore they asked the authors to respond to the question, "What do you believe will be the major research thrust(s) in sport psychology during the next five years?" The suggested response length was a single paragraph of moderate length.

Twenty-two authors chose to respond to this question, with most expressing some misgivings regarding their responses due to the magnitude and extreme diversity of research issues currently being advanced in the professional literature of sport psychology. Nonetheless these authors did respond, and their ideas are presented here with minimal editing. An attempt has been made to arrange the responses in a meaningful sequence, with transitional comments provided by the editors. Finally careful review of the 22 statements reveals that there is no single, clearly defined direction for sport psychology research predicted during the next five years. Rather, several directions are identified in the statements, which include a projected increase in the importance of field research in applied settings and in case study research, an increase in the study of youth sport issues, more interest in the methodology used in conducting sport psychology research, a trend toward cognitive-based research, a need for enhanced sport psychology theory development, the importance of motivation in sport, imagery as a major psychological factor in sport performance enhancement, suggestions relative to increased emphasis on the study of spectator behavior, athlete energy control and manipulation, and moral development and pro-social behavior. After this brief introduction, we present the ideas of the authors concerning the immediate future direction(s) of sport psychology research.

APPLIED SETTINGS AND INTEGRATIVE EFFORTS

Craig Wrisberg's suggestions are perhaps indicative of a representative and salient beginning to this future-oriented *epilogue trieste* in sport psychology research:

Your request for a paragraph containing my view as to the single research topic that will be the most important in the next five years is a difficult one. With the recent political events in Germany and in the former Soviet Union, I anticipate the possibility of *increased collaboration* among sport scientists from a variety of nations on problems/factors associated with elite athletic performance. Research will be more multidimensional in scope as scientists attempt to identify the *constellation* of factors (e.g., physiological, psychological, social, emotional) that should be considered in the selection and training of athletes in different sports. In short, I feel that the trend will be away from narrowly focused laboratory studies and toward more ecologically valid field experiments that are both theoretically based and methodologically sound. With increasing sophistication of instrumentation we should be able to address problems in field settings without sacrificing as much control or precision as we did in the past.

Stephanie Hanrahan, who coauthored the chapter concerning social interactions, reflects several of Wrisberg's ideas and introduces others in her comments:

I find it very difficult to specify a single topic of research that will define the general research direction within sport psychology over the next five years. I would find it almost as difficult to specify a single topic of research that defines the general research direction during the *past* five years. I think that most researchers when responding to this question automatically search their own areas of expertise for the answer. Trying to ignore my own biases of interest and perceived importance, I believe that the current trend of applied field research will continue, but that the emphasis will move away from applied sport psychology for elite athletes to the potential role of sport psychology in the lives of the average sport participant or exerciser. I believe that this move has already started with the expansion of health and exercise psychology.

Both Wrisberg and Hanrahan emphasize a trend in sport psychology toward field study. Further, the issues of international cooperation, increased study of average athletes, and need for increasingly sophisticated methodology and hardware are addressed in their contributions. Wrisberg differs from Hanrahan in his suggestion regarding the study of elite athletes in the rapidly changing international political environment.

Dieter Hackfort addresses the issues surrounding the challenge to surmount the long-standing tendency to categorize research into classical categories with the corresponding mandate toward integration of all components. He suggests a departure from the "semantic difference centered" study to which we have become accustomed, and a corresponding movement toward a holistic research approach. These ideas are revolutionary in content and indicate a positive departure from the more static approaches

often selected for sport psychology study. His emphasis on increased collaboration is reflected in many of the epilogue responses that are included here:

Progress in sport psychology in the next years will not so much depend on concentration on one or another single research topic but on finding a research direction to overcome thinking in classical categories such as cognition, emotion, motivation, volition, etc., and a separation of research in such areas. We have to develop more integrative theories that enable us to focus more on functional links rather than merely on semantic differences. The question is whether classical concepts, terminology, and methodological conventions enable or hinder us to realize this. From my perspective the concept of "sport-related action" may be the integrative frame for analyzing the functional meaning and interrelations of psychological processes regulating our acting in sports. To act is to move, to feel, and to think at the same moment in time. Cognitive and emotional processes are interrelated and reflect motion. When analyzing these functional links, we have to also consider the biological and the social level of different process relations.

I am not convinced that the currently preferred analogies of computer processes are appropriate schema for the explanation or even the description of psychological processes. Perhaps they are merely a new mechanistic and misleading approach. To understand subjects as subjects (and not objects) of our research, we have to consider that they are reflexive, defining situations and organizing situations, that they are acting and not only reacting, thus changing the environment and themselves continuously. Such a perspective entails a lot of consequences, and the main task for sport psychology research is to develop a new style of asking questions, defining problems, and forming methodological strategies enabling us to find answers for an improved application of sport psychological knowledge.

Gershon Tenenbaum and Michael Bar-Eli also indicate that the integrative approach will be a major consideration in future sport psychology research:

It is our belief that scientists in the domain of sport psychology are becoming aware of the fact that human behavior within the context of sport and exercise can never be fully understood, controlled, or predicted by a single variable or pattern of variables. Therefore, future research will adopt a more integrative approach, in which individual (emotional, cognitive, and biological) and social domains will interact. Thus the topic of future research will be: "integrative models and experiments to explore emotions and cognition in sport and exercise.

Leonard Zaichkowsky advocates the increasing use of case study methods and suggests that the issues surrounding ethnic differences will come under increased research scrutiny in the coming years. He also alludes to the need for research concerning the transition of athletes in sport settings:

We need to continue testing the efficacy of interventions using qualitative methodology and quantitative methods that are sensitive to testing psycho-educational intervention (e.g. single-case experiments). Cross-cultural issues in sport are under-researched and rarely written about. This is an expanding concern, particularly in professional sport. For example, major league baseball needs to address acculturation problems of Hispanics, hockey is now receiving a large influx of European players—also with issues surrounding acculturation. Career transition research is minimal. Not much is known about the transition from youth sport to high school, or the elite clubs transition from high school to college, the transition from college to professional sport, or the transition out of sport.

Wrisberg, Hanrahan, Hackfort, Tenenbaum and Bar-Eli, and Zaichkowsky address the desirability of field research and integrative approaches in future sport psychology research. Their comments indicate the greatest degree of commonality among the 22 respondents. Zaichkowsky clearly enunciates a number of the future directions indicated in the comments of the other respondents to the epilogue question, and in this sense his remarks fairly summarize this section of the epilogue.

YOUTH SPORT

The next most frequently identified topical area is that concerning several dimensions of youth sport. Stuart Biddle, who wrote the chapter on attribution research, was specific in his comments regarding the importance of research on this topic with children. He also endorsed the study of motivation for all age groups:

In terms of attributions, I feel that the most important area to develop is the understanding of the relationships between attributions and subsequent behavior, particularly with respect to children developing an active lifestyle through sport and exercise. Related to this, an important direction for sport psychology is to identify the motivational determinants of physical activity across the lifespan.

In a related statement, David Pargman addressed several additional youth sport issues:

In my opinion, the area in sport psychology that is most important in terms of future research is sport-related stress, burnout, and withdrawal in youth. It is necessary to make inquiry in this direction beyond the anecdotal and descriptive approaches often used to date. Children are society's most important resource for a secure and productive future. It is incumbent upon those of us working in the behavioral aspects of sport to attract youth to well-conceived sport programs, to develop and sustain their motivation for continued participation, and to ensure that their experience is profitable, safe, and enjoyable.

Guy Régnier also expresses the opinion that youth and youth sport issues are of paramount present and future importance:

In Chapter 12, talent detection has been described as an ongoing process closely interrelated with the talent development process. There can be no magic tests that will accurately predict success at one point in time. Thus talent detection cannot be conducted as a "one-shot operation." In that aspect of the ongoing process, the most promising research orientation for talent detection in general is trying to understand the expertise of coaches and athletes via the use of qualitative data acquisition and analysis. It is clear that by systematically talking to and learning from experts, we can open the door to teaching about expertise. This was referred to in Chapter 12 as the "bottom-up approach" to talent detection. Still in line with the concept of talent detection as an ongoing process, but more specifically from a psychological point of view, research is very much needed to better understand how psychological skills such as mental toughness, agility, focusing, and planning are acquired and developed by children and teenagers.

METHODOLOGY

The three foregoing statements reflect the expanding interest in youth sport as a vital element in the immediate future for sport psychology research. Allied to both of the foregoing groups of topics addressed as future issues is that of methodological concerns. John S. Raglin and Storm J. Russell view methodological considerations as important in the continued pursuit of excellence in sport psychology research. Raglin notes:

The prevailing methodology by which future research in sport psychology is conducted may be of more consequence than any trend in research topics. The field of sport psychology has been described by Dishman as being in a state of crisis. This crisis appears to be analogous to what Kuhn has described as a field in the throes of a paradigm shift. It is becoming increasingly clear that sport research based on a single strategy—be it psychological or physiological—is insufficient to address the complex issues inherent to the psychobiological world of sport. In my view, for the field to remain healthy it will be necessary to develop a research perspective that incorporates *both* psychological and physiological measures. Nearly 20 years ago Morgan spoke of this need, but his call has been largely unheeded. We have now reached the juncture where we cannot ignore it.

Russell's suggestions reflect Raglin's comments and add specificity in terms of available and emerging methodology. She includes statements concerning the impact of technology on theory:

I believe that some of the most important developments in sport and exercise psychology over the next five years will be methodologically related, which in turn will have profound effects both on theory development and on the essential ways in which research is conducted. The fast growth and widespread availability of increasingly ingenious hardware and software options, along with the corresponding development of increasingly sophisticated multivariate statistical models, now make it possible to address questions that five years ago would not have been considered. These technical developments also allow greater opportunity for theory development and theory testing.

Changes in the way we think about and do research are already occurring. It is no longer uncommon to pick up a sport and exercise psychology journal, for example, and read about the application of such models as LISREL, MANOVA, and ALSCAL to different research contexts, as well as the more usual ANOVAs, t-tests, and simple regressions. Similarly, in the area of qualitative data methods, we now have available an impressive and growing assortment of software packages such as HYPERQUAL and FREETEXT. They enable the systematic, standardized treatment of qualitative data forms like protocols, interview transcripts, and self-reports. The rapid growth in design and analysis options will have particular implications for both the range of topics being examined (for example, the growing interest in athlete and coach knowledge structures), as well as for the ways in which research is conducted in more traditional areas (for example, the use of structural equations to examine multivariate models of exercise adherence). It will also mean a new, increased emphasis on theory testing and development in sport and exercise psychology as new and better methods of evaluating complex, multivariate models of behavior become available.

THEORY DEVELOPMENT

Both Raglin and Russell clearly address methodological developments and their importance. Like several of the authors earlier in this epilogue, Raglin also addressed integrative techniques and the mandate for psychophysiological study in the future. Closely allied to this view of methodological necessity is the need for theory-based research. Qiu Yijun and Bob Rotella allude to cognitive-based research needs in the future and build on Russell's comments concerning theory development.

Qiu Yijun is concerned with theory and clinical practice:

Sport psychology, research on the psychological laws of those involved in physical activities, is an applied sport science. There are two important research areas. One is theoretical research; another is clinical research.

In theoretical research, the importance of using cognitive psychology methods should be emphasized. We should update our conceptual structure using modern psychological knowledge, especially cognitive and social-psychological methods. Clinical services are important in sport psychology. In order to contribute to talent detection, psychological diagnosis and training, and rehabilitation, we need to undertake more clinical research.

Rotella comments on the necessity for "good thinking" among athletes via the use of techniques that we have already at hand. Rotella states that cognition will remain a key element in sport psychology research.

I believe the greatest need in research for the next five years addresses issues related to how to get athletes to consistently *comply* with thinking effectively. Good thinking is simple and basic. We must stop creating new techniques and spend our energy studying how to get athletes to do what we already know is good for them.

Both Richard H. Cox and Joan Duda have provided comments concerning theory and its increasing relevance in developing sport psychology research. Cox discusses theories and models in the following way:

Drive theory and inverted-U theory have provided useful models for sport psychologists to study the relationship between changes in arousal level and athletic performance. Over the next five years, researchers will turn considerable attention to the investigation of models that will more accurately describe this relationship. In this

regard, "Catastrophe Theory" and the concept of a "Zone of Optimal Performance" will be investigated as alternatives or modifications in Yerkes and Dodson's concept of the inverted-U.

Duda is more specific about theoretical directions in her own particular area of research motivation:

In my own research, I became attracted to contemporary goal perspective theories of achievement motivation for several reasons. First, I am intrigued by conceptual models that emphasize the point that people differ in how they process and respond to achievement-related experiences. Second, since I am disappointed with theories of motivation (as well as sport psychologists!) which/who are primarily focused on the prediction of performance, the fact that this theory is also concerned with variability in intensity, persistence, and task choice was appealing. Optimal or limited motivation is surely reflected in all of these behavioral indices. Finally, I have found goal perspective theory to provide a heuristic framework for integrating and further interpreting other theories and research findings in sport psychology.

To date, work testing the validity of the constructs and tenets embedded in goal perspective theory within the sport domain has supported the application of this approach to our field. In terms of future directions stemming from a goal perspective model of motivation, there are several areas of investigation that will further our theoretical and applied knowledge. As individual differences in dispositional goal perspective appear to be a potent predictor of the meaning of sport involvement, more research is needed on the socialization processes by which children form such dispositions. The stability and pliability of dispositional goal perspectives over time also needs to be examined. In so doing, future research should determine the impact of the motivational climate created by coaches, teachers, parents, etc. on sport participants' goal orientations and behavioral/cognitive responses to the athletic setting. Lastly, it would be interesting to ascertain the personal and situational factors that influence the goal perspective *state* athletes hold during a competitive encounter. People fall into states of task and ego involvement while competing . . . what are the precipitating factors and what is different (if anything) in how they move and what they are thinking while in one state or the other?

Duda's comments provide a clear summary of future theory direction in sport psychology. Her concern for research in sport motivation is reinforced by several authors, who propose other directions. Lise Gauvin and Michael Sachs mention exercise adherence among other research topics that they believe will come to the fore in the near future.

Sachs offers these comments:

Research directions are difficult to identify, but this is what I think *should be* the most important research area during the next five years. An area of research that has the greatest potential to significantly affect the lives of many individuals is that of motivation and adherence for sport participation. If we can develop effective strategies that will get people exercising on a regular basis in the first place, and subsequently continue (adhere) with it, we will have gone a long way toward improving the physical and psychological health of the population. Although we know a great deal about how programs should be developed, both theoretically and practically, we have not succeeded in improving adherence rates dramatically enough. The operative word is *effective*—what strategies will get people to continue participating?

Gauvin offers the following comments:

The large number of contributions to the *Handbook* illustrates the diversity that characterizes the field. The identification of the single most important research direction in the next five years thus constitutes a major challenge. However, I believe that exercise psychology issues should develop at an accelerated rate. Indeed, we should be involved in deciphering the nature and magnitude of the exercise and well-being relationship, as well as understanding problems associated with exercise adherence, coping with injuries, dealing with abuse of drugs or ergogenic aids, and the role of exercise in the treatment of various psychological disorders. Such efforts should advance knowledge in these areas. Future intervention strategies that should be used by fitness and allied health professionals with nonexercisers must be identified. Issues related to health and well-being also seem paramount to current societal concerns and should be addressed more substantially. As other authors have mentioned, the field of sport psychology has reached an age of accountability, both from a scientific standpoint and an applied perspective. I think that the study of exercise psychology issues affords researchers the best means of being accountable.

INTERVENTION

Gauvin introduces sport psychology accountability into the epilogue with dramatic effect. Other authors discuss the idea of accountability with imagery, a popular technique used in the mental preparation of the athlete for an event. Denis Glencross and Yves Vanden Auweele feel that imagery will be a major research area in the next few years.

Glencross makes these comments:

Expert systems and knowledge structures, in the development and performance of human skills, will be a major new initiative and will influence coaching and training methodology and techniques. This thrust has implications for our understanding of images (as a form of knowledge) and how mental rehearsal, mental practice, visualization, and so on may be effectively applied and implemented.

Vanden Auweele is more precise.

I believe that imagery should be the most important research direction during the next five years. In my opinion, imagery is one of the most "sport-specific" topics in sport psychology, and research on that topic will provide us with new theoretical insights in the functioning of the athlete as well as workable suggestions for performance enhancement.

AUDIENCE EFFECTS

Dolf Zillmann specifically addresses audience effects and concomitant variables in his future projections concerning research in sport psychology.

Sport psychology has focused on athletic *performance,* and rightly so. However, in efforts to enhance performance, seemingly at any cost, the audience, for whom highly skilled athletes typically perform, has been very much neglected. Professional, semiprofessional, and high-level nonprofessional athletic competition is, after all, a form of entertainment designed to excite, thrill, engage, and inspire the audience that pays for this service. Why, then, has there been next to no systematic research to explore the variables in athletic competition that create excitement and that produce recreation in the best sense of the word? Sport psychology of the future must analyze spectator behavior in greater depth: What is it that gets spectators involved with performers and teams? Exactly what is it that excites and gratifies them? What are the recreational benefits of watching sports? These and related topics should be explored to a point where existing sports can be altered and new sports can be devised in order to best serve the customer: the sports fan who appreciates athletic exhibition.

THE ECLECTIC VIEW

Richard M. Suinn presents a multifaceted picture of the future in the following comments:

The question of the *single* most important research topic during the next five years would be challenging enough were the question the *seven* most important research topics, much less the single topic! Hence I will hedge a bit and refer to a publication in 1989 in which I cited seven promising and needed research topics as clustering under the headings of: refinements of the VMBR method, assessment of and variables involved in motivation, transfer of principles of behavioral psychology to performance enhancement, the integration of brain-physiology-body research, factors involved in consistency and slumps in performance, energy as a concept and a consequence of training methods, and the role of self-efficacy. If I were to select the most fascinating and slippery topic, it would be understanding energy control and manipulation. If I were to select the ones with the most potential for major insights and new breakthroughs in theory and practice, they would be brain/physiology/body research, and understanding consistency, peak performance, and slumps. If you force me into identifying one single area, using any criteria, I would offer the hope that we could identify brain activity associated with training that leads to what we call "flow" or consistency in peak performance.

MORAL PSYCHOLOGY

Brenda Bredemeier and David Shields, who coauthored the chapter on moral psychology in the context of sport, comment as follows:

"Well, here it is . . . I know that you will not be shocked to discover that we believe that moral development is the most important topic for sport psychology research in the next five years."

Moral development and prosocial behavior in sport is a crucial topic for sport psychologists conducting research in the coming five years. This is true for many reasons, and we will highlight three.

First, science responds to the pressing questions of culture, and media coverage of an increasing number of ethical scandals in the world of sport has helped to raise public consciousness and concern. Citizens are questioning moral improprieties in sport at both the institutional and personal level, and sport psychologists are in an ideal position to investigate how sport can facilitate moral development and to identify ways the sport experience may discourage prosocial behavior.

Second, theory and research on moral development recently have undergone dramatic transformations. Moral theorists are on the cutting edge of a movement in the broader discipline of psychology to integrate emphases on individual development, social processes, and personal behavior; also, moral researchers investigating female development have challenged traditional empirical methods and helped to change the nature of social science as we know it and do it. Sport psychology researchers who wish to study morality—even those who choose to investigate other topics in social psychology—will most certainly benefit from the richness and diversity of emerging theoretical perspectives and the innovative developments in the field of moral psychology.

Finally, many moral researchers are developing, testing, and modifying their theories in the context of real-life activity; their insights into the processes of moral education are essential in our training of sport psychology consultants, coaches, and physical educators.

FINAL COMMENTS

The relative place of theoretical, academic, and applied research in the total matrix of the study of sport psychology will become more clearly defined in the near future. The contents of this *Handbook* will certainly help to describe a wide assortment of important sport psychology topics.

The responses included in this epilogue are thought-provoking, and the editors thank those authors who chose to respond. Their insights give us a preview of future directions in sport psychology. In future editions of the *Handbook,* these and other authors may offer differing or divergent views concerning new research directions. We will be interested in reviewing these future-oriented comments when this *Handbook* is revised.

The purpose of this *Handbook* was to describe contemporary themes in sport psychology research. Having done this, the *Handbook* defines what we now know about sport psychology. In this context it may be useful in improving present and future research practices. This ongoing exercise can form the basis for new and innovative approaches in sport psychology during the 1990s and beyond.

References

Cohen, R. A., Preface. In J. E. Birren, R. N. Butler, S. W. Greenhouse, L. Sokoloff, and M. R. Yarrow (Eds.) (1963). *Human aging.* Baltimore, MD: U.S. Department of Health, Education and Welfare.

INTERNATIONAL ADVISORY BOARD

AUTHOR INDEX

Wolpe, J., 350, 352, 529, 537, 834
Wong, D. S., 905
Wood, C. A., 198, 199, 229
Wood, J. M., 228
Wood, R. E., 469, 472, 474
Wood, T. M., 751, 891, 892
Woodrow, H., 129, 131, 136
Woodworth, R. S., 216, 242
Woolacott, M. H., 74
Woolfolk, R. L., 495, 496, 506, 552, 831
Woollacott, M. G., 76
Workman, D. G., 878
Worrell, G. L., 374
Worringham, C. J., 614
Wragg, J., 863, 864, 865, 866, 867, 872
Wraith, S., 458, 807
Wright, D. L., 229
Wright, J. E., 858, 877, 879, 880, 881,
  882, 883
Wrightsman, L. S., 370, 612
Wrisberg, C. A., 12, 61, 67, 151, 494,
  544, 552, 563, 934, 935
Wughalter, E. H., 159, 228
Wulf, G., 229
Wundt, W., 127
Wurf, E., 735
Wuthnow, R., 748
Wylie, R. C., 394, 736
Wynn, V., 878
Wysocki, T., 562

Yaffe, M., 829, 834
Yalom, I. D., 771
Yamaguchi, Y., 649, 650, 651, 653, 654,
  655, 669

Yando, R., 118, 120
Yanowitz, B., 207
Yarbus, A. L., 155
Yardley, J. K., 783, 792
Yates, K. E., 232, 233
Yates, W. R., 880
Yellott, S., 156
Yerkes, R. M., 7, 344, 515, 518, 548
Yesalis, C. E., 858, 877, 881, 882, 883
Yetton, R. N., 647, 663, 665, 666
Yeudall, L., 803
Yiannakis, A., 367
Yijun, Q., 936
Yin, Z., 427
Yirmiya, M., 448
Yoshida, S., 53
Yoshida, T., 54
Yoshimoto, T., 54
Young, D. E., 202, 204
Young, J., 882
Young, J. P., 881
Young, J. R., 741
Young, K., 574, 575, 581
Young, M. L., 396, 736, 816, 830
Young, P. T., 799
Young, R. J., 782
Young, W. C., 878
Yu, A. P., 85
Yuhasz, M. S., 293, 802
Yukelson, D., 121, 483, 639, 682
Yukl, G. A., 647, 661
Yussen, S. R., 122

Zackheim, M. A., 369
Zaichkowsky, L., 934, 935

Zaichkowsky, L. B., 395
Zaichkowsky, L. D., 153, 266, 278, 280,
  355, 395, 511, 517, 522, 523, 537, 552,
  564
Zajonc, R. B., 448, 519, 609, 614, 635, 637
Zakay, D., 172, 184
Zaleznik, A., 638
Zander, A., 630, 631, 638, 686, 687, 688
Zane, N. S., 697, 710, 711, 713
Zane, N. W. S., 656, 657, 658, 660
Zani, A., 544
Zanna, M. P., 674, 675
Zeeman, E. C., 9
Zeigler, E. F., 3, 922
Zelaznik, H. N., 68, 142, 217, 251
Zidon, I., 469
Ziegler, S. G., 280, 356, 498, 551
Ziewaez, L. E., 18
Zigler, E., 118, 120
Zillmann, D., 20, 371, 600, 601, 602,
  604, 605, 606, 607, 608, 937
Zimbardo, P. G., 329
Zimmerman, R., 790
Zimny, S. T., 228
Zinsser, N. W., 132, 135, 903
Zis, A. P., 843
Zoeller, M., 117
Zola, M. A., 532
Zoob, I., 388, 389, 821
Zschintzsch, A., 353
Zubin, J., 144
Zuckerman, J., 112, 113, 115, 120
Zuckerman, M., 130, 388, 389, 390, 392,
  441, 821, 865
Zwart, E. F., 6, 10

SUBJECT INDEX

disorder characterizations of, 550
exercise adherence and, 783–84
extroversion with meta-analysis in research on, 265–68
field-dependence/independence and, 382
French research on, 34–35
hardy, 532–33
injury and, 815–16
Japanese research on, 54
leadership and, 652
meta-analysis on data about, 265–68
multivariate and multidimensional models in research on, 268–72
new directions in research on, 274–75
of older adults, 741
paradigmatic and methodological trends in research on, 258–61
past research on, 260, 285
Profile of Mood States in research on, 262–65
research in sport psychology, 5–7, 260, 285
shifts in emphasis of research on, 275–78
situation-related intra-individual diagnosis, 281–85
situation-specific tests of, 341
sports and, 579–80
stress-injury model and, 820–21, 823–25
Personality Disorder Questionnaire, 880
Personal problems, drug use and, 865
"Personal sphere," 329
Personology. *See also* Sport personology
future research on, 274–75
paradigmatic and methodological trends in academic, 258–60
shifts in emphasis of research on, 275–78
Pertinence-based model of selective attention, 157
Physical activity model of exercise adherence, 789
Physical fitness, 48–49, 85
Physical measures. *See* Physiological measures
Physical practice, 115
Physical Self-Efficacy Scale (PSE), 394
Physical Self-Perception Profile (PSPP), 736
Physical strength, 737
Physiological measures
of alertness, 130–31
of anxiety, 130–31, 337–39
of arousal, 130–31
of attentional capacity, 143–44
of selective attention, 154
in unidisciplinary multivariate studies of performance determinants, 292
Physiological stress theory, 330
Piagetian theory of cognitive development, 19, 74–75
Placebo effect of drugs, 862
Planned behavior theory of exercise adherence, 789
Play, 606–8
Player. *See* Athlete
PLE (positive life events), 822

PMR (progressive muscular relaxation), 520–21
Political orientations, 579
POMS. *See* Profile of Mood States
Pool population, 305
PO (performance-oriented) goal-setting style, 476–78, 480–81, 482
Positive addictions (PA), 732
"Positive experiences model" of peak moments, 745
Positive life events (PLE), 822
Positive thinking, 405
Postperformance, 559–60
Power, 744–45
Practice conditions
alertness and, 135
attentional capacity and, 151–52
automaticity and, 150–51
bilateral transfer and, 234–37
content-specific, 151
contextual interference and, 226–29
distribution of practice and, 219–21
of dual tasks, 148–50
fatigue and, 221–24
historical perspective of, 213–14
instruction design and, 138–39
learning versus performance distinction and, 214
measures of learning and, 214–16
motor learning and, 214
nature of, 213
observations about, 237
part versus whole task practice and, 229–32
psychological refractory period and, 151
psychological well-being and, 733–34
retention/transfer and, 216–17
selective attention and, 160
simulation and, 232–34
skill levels and, 61–62
variability of practice and, 224–26
vigilance and, 138–39
Precompetitive workout, 523
Preparedness. *See* Alertness
Preperformance, 559
Pre-retirement planning, 769
Pressure. *See* Competitive pressure
Pretest-posttest design, 906–7
Preventive measures for drug abuse, 852
Primary-task paradigm, 140, 144–45
Priming, 249
Principal component analysis (PCA), 911, 912
Probabilistic models in sport psychology research, 281
Problem solving, intelligence and, 182
Procedural knowledge, 92
Processing speed, 88–89
Professional ethics in sport psychology
AAASP certification criteria and, 930–31
additional training of sport psychologist and, 930
clarification of sport psychologist and, 923
competence of sport psychologist and, 924–26
confidentiality and, 928
future directions of, 930

group versus individual work and, 927–28
intimacy of sport psychologist with client and, 924
legal issues, 921–22
marketing sport psychologist and, 929–30
power of sport psychologist and, 923–24
psychological tests and, 926–27
supervision of sport psychologist and, 928
third-party payments and, 929
Profile of Mood States (POMS)
development of, 262
in elite performance research, 262–65
Iceberg Profile and, 6, 262–65
mood assessment and, 6, 802
overtraining and, 845, 846, 848
in personality research, 262–65
Progressive muscular relaxation (PMR), 520–21
Progressive relaxation, 520, 832–33
PSE (Physical Self-Efficacy Scale), 394
PSEP (Psychological Skills Education Program), 12
PSIS (Psychological Skills Inventory for Sport), 12–13, 545
PSMT (Pedestal Sight Manipulation Test), 196
PSPP (Physical Self-Perception Profile), 736
PST (psychological skills training) programs, 23
"Psyching out," 492
"Psyching up," 492, 523–24
Psychoanalytical approach to anxiety, 332–34
Psychological diagnosis of athlete, 51
"Psychological performance crisis," 185
Psychological refractory period (PRP), 146, 151
Psychological selection of athlete, 50–51
Psychological Skills Education Program (PSEP), 12
Psychological Skills Inventory for Sport (PSIS), 12–13, 545
Psychological skills training (PST) programs, 23
Psychological tests, 926–27. *See also* specific names of
Psychological variables, 290–91, 292
Psychological well-being
decrements, 732
denotation of, 729
enjoyment of physical activity and, 731
exercise and, 729–30
mode characteristics of physical activity and, 731–33
practice conditions and, 733–34
Psychology, 571–72
Psychometrics
for averages, 902–7
future of, 914–16
of inventory development and assessment, 910–14
issues of, 901–2
Leadership Scale for Sports and, 649–51
overtraining and, 845–46